中华人民共和国进出口税则
（法律文本）

Customs Tariff of Import and Export of the People's Republic of China
（The Legal Texts）

(2014)

（Enforced from January 1，2014）

国务院关税税则委员会办公室
中华人民共和国财政部关税司 编

Compiled by the Office of Customs Tariff Commission of the State Council
Tariff Policy Department of Ministry of Finance P.R.C.

中国财政经济出版社
China Financial & Economic Publishing House

图书在版编目（CIP）数据

中华人民共和国进出口税则：法律文本=Customs tariff of import and export of the People's Republic of China. 2014：汉英对照/国务院关税税则委员会办公室，中华人民共和国财政部关税司编. —北京：中国财政经济出版社，2014.1

ISBN 978-7-5095-5055-7

Ⅰ. ①中… Ⅱ. ①国… ②中… Ⅲ. ①进出口贸易-关税-税则-中国-2014-汉、英 Ⅳ. ①D922.221

中国版本图书馆 CIP 数据核字（2014）第 005654 号

中国财政经济出版社 出版

URL：http://www.cfeph.cn

E-mail：cfeph@cfeph.cn

社址:北京海淀区阜成路甲 28 号 邮政编码：100142

发行处电话：88190406 财经书店电话：64033436

北京富生印刷厂印刷 各地新华书店经销

889×1194 毫米 16 开 89.75 印张 3 033 000 字

2014 年 1 月第 1 版 2014 年 1 月北京第 1 次印刷

印数:1—4 000 定价：280.00 元

ISBN 978-7-5095-5055-7/D · 0288

（图书出现印装问题，本社负责调换）

反盗版举报热线：88190492、88190446

使用说明

《中华人民共和国进出口税则》是《中华人民共和国进出口关税条例》(以下简称"《条例》")的组成部分，主要包括进口税则、出口税则、本国子目注释等。

一、进口税则

进口税则商品分类目录采用《商品名称及编码协调制度》。进口税则税目税率表设置税则号列、货品名称、最惠国税率、协定税率、特惠税率、普通税率等栏目。

（一）最惠国税率

根据《条例》规定，原产于共同适用最惠国待遇条款的世界贸易组织成员的进口货物，原产于与中华人民共和国签订含有相互给予最惠国待遇条款的双边贸易协定的国家或者地区的进口货物，以及原产于中华人民共和国境内的进口货物，适用最惠国税率。

以从价或从量方式计征关税的最惠国税率，在最惠国税率栏中直接列明；以其他方式计征关税的最惠国税率在最惠国税率栏脚注中列明。

非全税目信息技术产品的最惠国税率在最惠国税率栏中列明；其税则号列前标注"ex"，表示适用该税率的应税货物以货品名称栏中的描述为准。

（二）协定税率

根据《条例》规定，原产于与中华人民共和国签订含有关税优惠条款的区域性贸易协定的国家或者地区的进口货物，适用协定税率。

根据《亚太贸易协定》及相关协议，对原产于大韩民国、斯里兰卡民主社会主义共和国、孟加拉人民共和国、印度共和国、老挝人民民主共和国的部分进口货物，实施协定税率。

根据《中华人民共和国与东盟全面经济合作框架协议》及相关协议，对原产于文莱达鲁萨兰国、柬埔寨王国、印度尼西亚共和国、老挝人民民主共和国、马来西亚、缅甸联邦、菲律宾共和国、新加坡共和国、泰王国、越南社会主义共和国的部分进口货物，实施协定税率。

Explanation of Customs Tariff of Import and Export of the People's Republic of China

Customs Tariff of Import and Export of the People's Republic of China, which mainly comprises *Import Tariff*, *Export Tariff*, and Domestic Heading Explanation Notes, is a component part of *Regulations of the People's Republic of China on Import and Export Duties* (hereinafter referred to as " *Regulations*").

I. Import Tariff

The Harmonized Commodity Description and Coding System are introduced into the goods classification of the *Import Tariff*. The columns in the schedule of the *Import Tariff* are composed of tariff line, article description, Most Favored Nation (MFN) tariff rate, Agreement tariff rate, special preferential tariff rate, and general tariff rate.

(i) Most Favored Nation (MFN) Tariff Rates

According to the *Regulations*, the MFN tariff rates shall apply to the import goods originating in the members of the World Trade Organization providing that the MFN treatment is reciprocal between the People's Republic of China and these members, and the import goods originating in the countries and regions with which the People's Republic of China has concluded bilateral agreements that comprises reciprocal tariff preference clauses, and the import goods originating in the customs territory of the People's Republic of China.

Ad valorem and specific rates of the MFN tariffs are described in the column of the MFN tariff rate, the MFN tariff rates which in the form other than ad valorem or specific rates are described in the footnotes.

The MFN tariff rates on Specific Information Technology Products are described in the column of the MFN tariff rate. The tariff lines prefixed by "ex" indicate their MFN tariff rates apply to the import goods that conform to the respective article description.

(ii) Agreement Tariff Rates

According to the *Regulations*, the agreement tariff rates shall apply to the import goods originating in the countries and regions with which the People's Republic of China has concluded a regional trade agreement that comprises preferential tariff clauses.

According to *Asia Pacific Trade Agreement* and relevant agreements, the agreement tariff rates shall apply to certain import goods originating in the Republic of Korea, the Democratic Socialist Republic of Sri Lanka, the People's Republic of Bangladesh, the Republic of India, and the Lao People's Democratic Republic.

According to *Framework Agreement on Comprehensive Economic Co-Operation between China and ASEAN* and relevant agreements, the agreement tariff rates shall apply to certain import goods originating in Negara Brunei Darussalam, the Kingdom of Cambodia, the Republic of Indonesia, the Lao People's Democratic Republic, Malaysia, the Union of Myanmar, the Republic of the Philippines, the Republic of Singapore, the Kingdom of Thailand, and the Socialist Republic of Viet Nam.

根据《中华人民共和国政府与智利共和国政府自由贸易协定》及相关协议，对原产于智利共和国的部分进口货物，实施协定税率。

According to *Free Trade Agreement between the Government of the People's Republic of China and the Government of the Republic of Chile* and relevant agreements, the agreement tariff rates shall apply to certain import goods originating in the Republic of Chile.

根据《中华人民共和国政府与巴基斯坦伊斯兰共和国政府自由贸易协定》及相关协议，对原产于巴基斯坦伊斯兰共和国的部分进口货物，实施协定税率。

According to *Free Trade Agreement between the Government of the People's Republic of China and the Government of the Islamic Republic of Pakistan* and relevant agreements, the agreement tariff rates shall apply to certain import goods originating in the Islamic Republic of Pakistan.

根据《中华人民共和国政府与新西兰政府自由贸易协定》及相关协议，对原产于新西兰的部分进口货物，实施协定税率。

According to *Free Trade Agreement between the Government of the People's Republic of China and the Government of New Zealand* and relevant agreements, the agreement tariff rates shall apply to certain import goods originating in New Zealand.

根据《中华人民共和国政府与新加坡共和国政府自由贸易协定》及相关协议，对原产于新加坡共和国的部分进口货物，实施协定税率。

According to *Free Trade Agreement between the Government of the People's Republic of China and the Government of the Republic of Singapore* and relevant agreements, the agreement tariff rates shall apply to certain import goods originating in the Republic of Singapore.

根据《中华人民共和国政府与秘鲁共和国政府自由贸易协定》及相关协议，对原产于秘鲁共和国的部分进口货物，实施协定税率。

According to *Free Trade Agreement between the Government of the People's Republic of China and the Government of the Republic of Peru* and relevant agreements, the agreement tariff rates shall apply to certain import goods originating in the Republic of Peru.

根据《中华人民共和国政府与哥斯达黎加共和国政府自由贸易协定》及相关协议，对原产于哥斯达黎加共和国的部分进口货物，实施协定税率。

According to *Free Trade Agreement between the Government of the People's Republic of China and the Government of the Republic of Costa Rica* and relevant agreements, the agreement tariff rates shall apply to certain import goods originating in the Republic of Costa Rica.

根据《内地与香港关于建立更紧密经贸关系的安排》、《内地与澳门关于建立更紧密经贸关系的安排》及相关协议，对原产于香港、澳门已完成原产地标准核准的进口货物，实施零关税。

According to *Mainland /Hong Kong Closer Economic Partnership Arrangement* and *Mainland / Macao Closer Economic Partnership Arrangement* and relevant agreements, the zero tariff rates shall apply to the import goods conforming to the approved rules of origin and originating in the Hong Kong Special Administrative Region, China and the Macao Special Administrative Region, China.

根据《海峡两岸经济合作框架协议》，对原产于台湾地区的部分进口货物，实施协定税率。

According to *Cross-Straits Economic Cooperation Framework Agreement*, the agreement tariff rates shall apply to certain import goods originating in Taiwan, China.

协定税率及其适用国别或地区在协定税率栏中标示，其中以从价或从量以外方式计征关税的协定税率见脚注。国别或地区代码表附后。

The agreement tariff rates which in the form of ad valorem and specific rates and their applicable countries and regions are indicated in the column of the Agreement Tariff Rate. The agreement tariff rates which in the form other than ad valorem or specific rates are described in the footnotes. The table of codes of countries and regions is attached.

（三）特惠税率

(iii) Special Preferential Tariff Rates

根据《条例》规定，原产于与中华人民共和国签订含有特殊关税优惠条款的贸易协定的国家或者地区的进口货物，适用特惠税率。

According to the *Regulations*, the special preferential tariff rates shall apply to the import goods originating in countries and regions with which the People's Republic of China has concluded a trade agreement that comprises special preferential tariff clauses.

根据中华人民共和国政府与有关国家政府间换文协议，对原产于老挝人民民主共和国、孟加拉人民共和国、柬埔寨王国、缅甸联邦、埃塞俄比亚联邦民主共和国、安哥拉共和国、贝宁共和国、布隆迪共和国、赤道几内亚共和国、多哥共和国、厄立特里亚国、刚果民主共和国、吉布提共和国、几内亚共和国、几内亚比绍共和国、科

According to the Exchange Letter between the government of the People's Republic of China and the related governments, the special preferential tariff rates shall apply to certain import goods originating in the Lao People's Democratic Republic, the People's Republic of Bangladesh, the Kingdom of Cambodia, the Union of Myanmar, The Federal Democratic Republic of Ethiopia, The Republic of Angola, The Republic of Benin, The Republic of Burundi, The Republic of

摩罗联盟、莱索托王国、利比里亚共和国、卢旺达共和国、马达加斯加共和国、马里共和国、马拉维共和国、毛里塔尼亚伊斯兰共和国、莫桑比克共和国、尼日尔共和国、塞拉利昂共和国、塞内加尔共和国、苏丹共和国、索马里联邦共和国、坦桑尼亚联合共和国、乌干达共和国、赞比亚共和国、乍得共和国、中非共和国、阿富汗伊斯兰共和国、尼泊尔联邦民主共和国、东帝汶民主共和国、萨摩亚独立国、瓦努阿图共和国、也门共和国的部分进口货物，实施特惠税率。

Equatorial Guinea, The Republic of Togo, The State of Eritrea The Democratic Republic of Congo, The Republic of Djibouti, The Republic of Guinea, The Republic of Guinea-Bissau, Union of Comoros, The Kingdom of Lesotho, The Republic Of Liberia, The Republic of Rwanda, The Republic of Madagascar, The Republic of Mali, The Republic of Malawi, The Islamic Republic of Mauritania, The Republic of Mozambique, The Republic of Niger, The Republic of Sierra Leone, The Republic of Senegal, The Republic of the Sudan, The Federal Republic of Somalia, The United Republic of Tanzania, The Republic of Uganda, The Republic of Zambia, The Republic of Chad, The Central African Republic, The Islamic Republic of Afghanistan, The Federal Democratic Republic of Nepal, Democratic Republic of Timor-Leste, The Independent State of Samoa, The Republic of Vanuatu, The Republic of Yemen.

特惠税率及其适用国别或地区在特惠税率栏中标示，其中以从价或从量以外方式计征关税的特惠税率见脚注。国别或地区代码表附后。

The special preferential tariff rates which in the form of ad valorem and specific rates and their applicable countries and regions are indicated in the column of the Special Preferential Tariff Rate. The special preferential tariff rates which in the form other than ad valorem or specific rates are described in the footnotes. The table of codes of countries and regions is attached.

（四）普通税率

(iv) General Tariff Rates

根据《条例》规定，原产于除适用最惠国税率、协定税率、特惠税率国家或地区以外的国家或者地区的进口货物，以及原产地不明的进口货物，适用普通税率。

The general tariff rates shall apply to the import goods with undetermined origins and originating in the countries and regions that are not applicable to the MFN tariff rates, agreement tariff rates, or special preferential tariff rates.

以从价或从量方式计征关税的普通税率，在进口税则普通税率栏中直接列明；以其他方式计征关税的普通税率在普通税率栏脚注中列明。

The general tariff rates which in the form of ad valorem and specific rates are decribed in the column of the General Tariff Rate. The general tariff rates which in the form other than ad valorem or specific rates are described in the footnotes.

（五）配额税率

(v) Tariff Quota Rates

根据《条例》规定，按照国家规定实行关税配额管理的进口货物，关税配额内的，适用关税配额税率。

According to the *Regulations*, Where the quantity of import goods that are subject to tariff quota administration in accordance with the provisions of the State is within the tariff quota, the tariff quota rates shall apply.

根据《中华人民共和国政府与新西兰政府自由贸易协定》，对原产于新西兰的部分产品，适用国别配额税率。

According to *Free Trade Agreement between the Government of the People's Republic of China and the Government of New Zealand*, the country-specific quota rates shall apply to certain import goods originating in New Zealand.

关税配额税率在最惠国税率栏的脚注中列明。

All the tariff quota rates are described in the footnotes other than in the column of the MFN tariff rate.

（六）暂定税率

(vi) Interim Tariff Rates

根据《条例》规定，适用最惠国税率、协定税率、特惠税率、关税配额税率的进口货物在一定期限内可以实行暂定税率。

According to the *Regulations*, the import goods that are applicable to the MFN tariff rates, agreement tariff rates, special preferential tariff rates, and tariff quota rates may apply to the interim tariff rates within a specific time limit.

适用最惠国税率的进口货物有暂定税率的，应当适用暂定税率；适用协定税率、特惠税率的进口货物有暂定税率的，应当从低适用税率；适用关税配额税率的进口货物有暂定税率的，应当适用暂定税率。适用普通税率的进口货物，不适用暂定税率。

Where there are interim tariff rates on import goods to which the MFN tariff rates are applicable, such interim tariff rates shall apply; where there are interim tariff rates on import goods to which the agreement tariff rates or the special tariff rates are applicable, the lower tariff rates shall apply; where there are interim tariff rates on import goods to which the tariff quota rates are applicable, such interim tariff rates shall apply. Interim tariff rates shall not apply to the import goods to which the general tariff rates are applicable.

1．最惠国暂定税率

最惠国暂定税率在最惠国税率栏中以前置“△”标示（如“△8”表示该税目最惠国暂定税率为8%）。以从价或从量以外方式计征关税的最惠国暂定税率见脚注。税则号列前标注“ex”，表示适用该税率的应税进口货物以货品名称栏中的描述为准。

2．关税配额暂定税率

关税配额暂定税率在最惠国税率栏的脚注中列明。

二、出口税则

出口税则的商品分类目录与进口税则相同。出口税则设置税则号列、货品名称、出口税率等栏目。

根据《条例》规定，对出口货物在一定期限内可以实行暂定税率；适用出口税率的出口货物有暂定税率的，应当适用暂定税率。

出口商品暂定税率见出口商品暂定税率表。税则号列前标注“ex”，表示适用该税率的应税出口货物以货品名称栏中的描述为准。

三、关税减免

特定地区、特定企业或者特定用途的进出口货物减征或者免征关税的，以及其他依法减征或者免征关税的，按照国务院的有关规定执行。

四、计量单位

税率计量单位代码如下。

1. MFN Interim Tariff Rates

The MFN Interim Tariff rates are indicated with the fore mark of “△” in the column of the MFN tariff rate (for example, “△8” indicates that the MFN interim tariff rate on the respective tariff line is 8%). The MFN interim tariff rates which in the form other than ad valorem or specific rates are described in the footnotes. The tariff lines prefixed by “ex” indicate their MFN interim tariff rates apply to the import goods that conform to the respective article description.

2. Interim Tariff Quota Rates

The interim tariff quota rates are described in the footnotes other than in the column of the MFN tariff rate.

II. Export Tariff

The goods classification of the *Export Tariff* is consistent with the *Import Tariff*. The columns in the schedule of the *Export Tariff* are composed of tariff line, article description, and export tariff rate.

According to the *Regulations*, interim tariff rates may apply to export goods within a specific time limit. Where there are interim tariff rates on export goods to which the export tariff rates are applicable, such interim tariff rates shall apply.

Interim tariff rates of the export goods refer to the “Table of Interim Tariff Rate on Export Goods”. The tariff lines prefixed by “ex” indicate their export tariff rates apply to the export goods that conform to the respective article description.

III. Tariff Reduction and Exemption

Tariff reduction or exemption granted to import and export goods of special areas, special enterprises or for special uses, as well as other temporary tariff reduction or exemption, shall be governed by the relevant provisions of the State Council.

IV. Abbreviations and Symbols

The abbreviations and symbols used in the *Import Tariff* and the *Export Tariff* are listed in the following table.

计量单位代码	计量单位中文名称	abbreviation or symbol	unit
￥	人民币元	￥	Renminbi
kg	千克	kg	kilogram
ton	公吨	ton	metric ton
L	公升	L	liter
m²	平方米	m²	square meter
set	台、套	set	set
$	美元	$	US Dollar

五、本国子目注释

本国子目注释是国务院关税税则委员会对进口税则、出口税则解释的一部分。

六、文本效力

进出口税则内容以中文文本为准；英文译文仅供参考，不具法律效力。

七、附录

为查阅方便，在附录中收集整理了进口商品从量税、复合税税目税率表，关税配额商品税目税率表和《条例》(中英文文本)等。

V. Domestic Heading Explanation Notes

Domestic heading explanation notes, which explained by Customs Tariff Commission of the State Council, are the component parts of the *Import Tariff* and the *Export Tariff*.

VI. Force of the Text

The Chinese version of the *Import Tariff* and the *Export Tariff* is authentic. The English version is for reference only.

VII. Appendix

The appendix embodies the Table of Specific Rate and Compound Rate on Import Goods, the Table of Tariff Quota Rate on Import Goods, and both Chinese and English versions of the *Regulations* etc.

国别或地区代码表

序号	中文简称	英文代码	国家（组）及地区名称	包括国家或地区
1	亚太	APTA	亚太贸易协定国家	大韩民国、斯里兰卡民主社会主义共和国、孟加拉人民共和国、印度共和国、老挝人民民主共和国
2	文莱	BN	文莱达鲁萨兰国	文莱达鲁萨兰国
3	柬埔寨	KH	柬埔寨王国	柬埔寨王国
4	印尼	ID	印度尼西亚共和国	印度尼西亚共和国
5	老挝	LA	老挝人民民主共和国	老挝人民民主共和国
6	马来西亚	MY	马来西亚	马来西亚
7	缅甸	MM	缅甸联邦	缅甸联邦
8	菲律宾	PH	菲律宾共和国	菲律宾共和国
9	新加坡*	SG*	新加坡共和国（中国—东盟自贸区协议项下）	新加坡共和国（中国—东盟自贸区协议项下）
10	新加坡	SG	新加坡共和国（中国—新加坡自贸区协议项下）	新加坡共和国（中国—新加坡自贸区协议项下）
11	泰国	TH	泰王国	泰王国
12	越南	VT	越南社会主义共和国	越南社会主义共和国
13	东盟	ASEAN	东盟 10 国	文莱达鲁萨兰国、柬埔寨王国、印度尼西亚共和国、老挝人民民主共和国、马来西亚、缅甸联邦、菲律宾共和国、新加坡共和国、泰王国和越南社会主义共和国
14	巴基斯坦	PK	巴基斯坦伊斯兰共和国	巴基斯坦伊斯兰共和国
15	智利	CL	智利共和国	智利共和国
16	新西兰	NZ	新西兰	新西兰
17	秘鲁	PE	秘鲁共和国	秘鲁共和国

18	哥斯达黎加	CR	哥斯达黎加共和国	哥斯达黎加共和国
19	香港	HK	香港特别行政区	香港特别行政区
20	澳门	MO	澳门特别行政区	澳门特别行政区
21	台湾	TW	台湾地区	台湾地区
22	亚太二国	APTA2	亚太 2 国	孟加拉人民共和国、老挝人民民主共和国
23	最不发达三十五国	LDC35	埃塞俄比亚联邦民主共和国等 35 个最不发达国家	埃塞俄比亚联邦民主共和国、安哥拉共和国、贝宁共和国、布隆迪共和国、多哥共和国、厄立特里亚国、刚果民主共和国、吉布提共和国、几内亚共和国、几内亚比绍共和国、科摩罗联盟、莱索托王国、利比里亚共和国、卢旺达共和国、马达加斯加共和国、马里共和国、马拉维共和国、莫桑比克共和国、塞拉利昂共和国、塞内加尔共和国、苏丹共和国、坦桑尼亚联合共和国、乌干达共和国、赞比亚共和国、乍得共和国、中非共和国、尼日尔共和国、阿富汗伊斯兰共和国、尼泊尔联邦民主共和国、东帝汶民主共和国、萨摩亚独立国、瓦努阿图共和国、也门共和国、柬埔寨王国、缅甸联邦共和国
24	最不发达四国	LDC4	孟加拉人民共和国等 4 个最不发达国家	孟加拉人民共和国、赤道几内亚共和国、毛里塔尼亚伊斯兰共和国、索马里联邦共和国

Table of Codes of Countries and Regions

No.	Code	Countries (Group) or Regions	Relevant Countries and Regions
1	APTA	Countries under Asia Pacific Trade Agreement	Republic of Korea, Democratic Socialist Republic of Sri Lanka, People's Republic of Bangladesh, Republic of India, Lao People's Democratic Republic
2	BN	Negara Brunei Darussalam	Negara Brunei Darussalam
3	KH	Kingdom of Cambodia	Kingdom of Cambodia
4	ID	Republic of Indonesia	Republic of Indonesia
5	LA	Lao People's Democratic Republic	Lao People's Democratic Republic
6	MY	Malaysia	Malaysia
7	MM	Union of Myanmar	Union of Myanmar
8	PH	Republic of Philippines	Republic of Philippines
9	SG*	Republic of Singapore under China-ASEAN FTA	Republic of Singapore under China-ASEAN FTA
10	SG	Republic of Singapore under China-Singpore FTA	Republic of Singapore under China-Singpore FTA
11	TH	Kingdom of Thailand	Kingdom of Thailand
12	VT	Socialist Republic of Viet Nam	Socialist Republic of Viet Nam
13	ASEAN	Members of ASEAN	Negara Brunei Darussalam, Kingdom of Cambodia, Republic of Indonesia, Lao People's Democratic Republic, Malaysia, Union of Myanmar, Republic of Philippines, Republic of Singapore, Kingdom of Thailand, Socialist Republic of Viet Nam
14	PK	Islamic Republic of Pakistan	Islamic Republic of Pakistan
15	CL	Republic of Chile	Republic of Chile
16	NZ	New Zealand	New Zealand
17	PE	Republic of Peru	Republic of Peru
18	CR	Republic of Costa Rica	Republic of Costa Rica
19	HK	Hong Kong Special Administrative Region, China	Hong Kong Special Administrative Region, China
20	MO	Macao Special Administrative Region, China	Macao Special Administrative Region, China
21	TW	Taiwan, China	Taiwan, China
22	APTA2	Two countries of APTA	People's Republic of Bangladesh, Lao People's Democratic Republic

续表

No.	Code	Countries (Group) or Regions	Relevant Countries and Regions
23	LDC35	35 Least Developing Countries	The Federal Democratic Republic of Ethiopia, The Republic of Angola, The Republic of Benin, The Republic of Burundi, The Republic of Togo, The State of Eritrea, The Democratic Republic of Congo, The Republic of Djibouti, The Republic of Guinea, The Republic of Guinea-Bissau, Union of Comoros, The Kingdom of Lesotho, The Republic of Liberia, The Republic of Rwanda, The Republic of Madagascar, The Republic of Mali, The Republic of Malawi, The Republic of Mozambique, The Republic of Sierra Leone, The Republic of Senegal, The Republic of the Sudan, The United Republic of Tanzania, The Republic of Uganda, The Republic of Zambia, The Republic of Chad, The Central African Republic, The Republic of Niger，The Islamic Republic of Afghanistan, The Federal Democratic Republic of Nepal, Democratic Republic of Timor-Leste, The Independent State of Samoa, The Republic of Vanuatu, The Republic of Yemen，Kingdom of Cambodia，Union of Myanmar
24	LDC4	4 Least Developing Countries	The People's Republic of Bangladesh, The Republic of Equatorial Guinea, The Islamic Republic of Mauritania, The Federal Republic of Somalia

总 目 录
Contents

中华人民共和国进口税则…………………………………………………………………… (1)
Customs Tariff of Import of the People's Republic of China

中华人民共和国出口税则…………………………………………………………………… (1337)
Customs Tariff of Export of the People's Republic of China

出口商品暂定税率表………………………………………………………………………… (1344)
Interim Duty Rate on Exported Goods

部分本国子目注释…………………………………………………………………………… (1357)
Domestic Heading Explanation Notes

附录
Appendix

附录一　关税配额商品税目税率表……………………………………………………………… (1373)
Tariff Quota Rate on Imported Goods

附录二　进口商品暂定税率表………………………………………………………………… (1375)
Interim Duty Rate on Imported Goods

附录三　进口商品从量税、复合税税目税率表………………………………………………… (1404)
Specific and Compound Duty Rate on Imported Goods

附录四　中华人民共和国进境物品进口税率表………………………………………………… (1408)
Duty Rate on Inward Articles of the People's Republic of China

附录五　中华人民共和国进出口关税条例……………………………………………………… (1409)
Regulations of the People's Republic of China on Import and Export Duties

中华人民共和国进口税则

（2014 年 1 月 1 日起实施）

Customs Tariff of Import of the People's Republic of China

(Enforced from January 1, 2014)

进口税则目录

Index of Import Tariff

归类总规则 ………………………………………………… (11)

第一类 活动物;动物产品

第一章 活动物 ………………………………………… (13)

第二章 肉及食用杂碎 ………………………………… (24)

第三章 鱼、甲壳动物、软体动物及其他水生无脊椎动物 ………………………………………… (37)

第四章 乳品;蛋品;天然蜂蜜;其他食用动物产品 ………………………………………… (83)

第五章 其他动物产品 ………………………………… (90)

第二类 植物产品

第六章 活树及其他活植物;鳞茎、根及类似品;插花及装饰用簇叶 ……………………… (97)

第七章 食用蔬菜、根及块茎 …………………… (103)

第八章 食用水果及坚果;柑桔属水果或甜瓜的果皮 ………………………………………… (120)

第九章 咖啡、茶、马黛茶及调味香料 …………… (132)

第十章 谷物 …………………………………………… (140)

第十一章 制粉工业产品;麦芽;淀粉;菊粉;面筋 ………………………………………… (144)

第十二章 含油子仁及果实;杂项子仁及果实;工业用或药用植物;稻草、秸秆及饲料 …… (149)

第十三章 虫胶;树胶、树脂及其他植物液、汁 …… (167)

第十四章 编结用植物材料;其他植物产品 ……… (171)

第三类 动、植物油、脂及其分解产品;精制的食用油脂;动、植物蜡

第十五章 动、植物油、脂及其分解产品;精制的食用油脂;动、植物蜡 ……………………… (173)

GENERAL RULES FOR THE INTERPRETATION OF THE HARMONIZED SYSTEM …………………… (11)

SECTION Ⅰ LIVE ANIMALS;ANIMAL PRODUCTS

Chapter 1 Live animals ………………………………… (13)

Chapter 2 Meat and edible meat offal ……………… (24)

Chapter 3 Fish and crustaceans, molluscs and other aquatic invertebrates …………………… (37)

Chapter 4 Dairy produce; birds' eggs; natural honey; edible products of animal origin, not elsewhere specified or included …………………… (83)

Chapter 5 Products of animal origin, not elsewhere Specified or included …………………… (90)

SECTION Ⅱ VEGETABLE PRODUCTS

Chapter 6 Live trees and other plants; bulbs, roots and the like; cut flowers and ornamental foliage ……………………………………… (97)

Chapter 7 Edible vegetables and certain roots and tubers ……………………………………… (103)

Chapter 8 Edible fruit and nuts; peel of citrus fruit or melons ……………………………………… (120)

Chapter 9 Coffee, tea, mate and spices …………… (132)

Chapter 10 Cereals ……………………………………… (140)

Chapter 11 Products of the milling industry; malt; starches; inulin; wheat gluten ………… (144)

Chapter 12 Oil seeds and oleaginous fruits; miscellaneous grains, seeds and fruit; industrial or medicinal plants; straw and fodder ……………… (149)

Chapter 13 Lac; gums, resins and other Vegetable saps and extracts ……………………… (167)

Chapter 14 Vegetable plaiting materials; vegetable products not elsewhere specified or included ……………………………………… (171)

SECTION Ⅲ ANIMAL OR VEGETABLE FATS AND OILS AND THEIR CLEAVAGE PRODUCTS; PRE PARED EDIBLE FATS; ANIMAL OR VEGETABLE WAXES

Chapter 15 Animal or vegetable fats and oils and their cleavage products; prepared edible fats; animal or vegetable waxes …………… (173)

第四类 食品;饮料、酒及醋;烟草、烟草及烟草代用品的制品

第十六章 肉、鱼、甲壳动物、软体动物及其他水生无脊椎动物的制品 …………………… (182)
第十七章 糖及糖食 …………………………… (193)
第十八章 可可及可可制品 …………………… (196)
第十九章 谷物、粮食粉、淀粉或乳的制品;糕饼点心 …………………………… (198)
第二十章 蔬菜、水果、坚果或植物其他部分的制品 …………………………… (203)
第二十一章 杂项食品 …………………………… (219)
第二十二章 饮料、酒及醋 ……………………… (224)
第二十三章 食品工业的残渣及废料;配制的动物饲料 …………………………… (229)
第二十四章 烟草及烟草代用品的制品 ………… (235)

第五类 矿产品

第二十五章 盐;硫磺;泥土及石料;石膏料、石灰及水泥 ………………………… (237)
第二十六章 矿砂、矿渣及矿灰 ………………… (253)
第二十七章 矿物燃料、矿物油及其蒸馏产品;沥青物质;矿物蜡 ……………………… (261)

第六类 化学工业及其相关工业的产品

第二十八章 无机化学品;贵金属、稀土金属、放射性元素及其同位素的有机及无机化合物 …………………………… (273)
第二十九章 有机化学品 ………………………… (314)
第三十章 药品 …………………………… (379)
第三十一章 肥料 …………………………… (393)
第三十二章 鞣料浸膏及染料浸膏;鞣酸及其衍生物;染料、颜料及其他着色料;油漆及清漆;油灰及其他类似胶粘剂;墨水、油墨 …………………………… (399)
第三十三章 精油及香膏;芳香料制品及化妆盥洗品 …………………………… (411)

SECTION Ⅳ PREPARED FOODSTUFFS; BEVERAGES, SPIRITS AND VINEGAR; TOBACCO AND MANUFACTURED TOBACCO SUBSTITUTES

Chapter 16 Preparations of meat, of fish or of crustaceans, molluscs or other aquatic invertebrates …… (182)
Chapter 17 Sugars and sugar confectionery ………… (193)
Chapter 18 Cocoa and cocoa preparations ………… (196)
Chapter 19 Preparations of cereals, flour, starch or milk; pastrycook's products ………… (198)
Chapter 20 Preparations of vegetables, fruit, nuts or other parts of plants ………………… (203)
Chapter 21 Miscellaneous edible preparations ……… (219)
Chapter 22 Beverages, spirits and vinegar ………… (224)
Chapter 23 Residues and waste from the food industries; prepared animal fodder ……………… (229)
Chapter 24 Tobacco and manufactured tobacco substitutes ……………………………… (235)

SECTION Ⅴ MINERAL PRODUCTS

Chapter 25 Salt; sulphur; earths and stone; plastering materials, lime and cement ………… (237)
Chapter 26 Ores, slag and ash …………………… (253)
Chapter 27 Mineral fuels, mineral oils and products of their distillation; bituminous Substances; mineral waxes ………………………… (261)

SECTION Ⅵ PRODUCTS OF THE CHEMICAL OR ALLIED INDUSTRIES

Chapter 28 Inorganic chemicals; organic or inorganic compounds of precious metals, of rare-earth metals of radioactive elements or of isotopes ……………………………… (273)
Chapter 29 Organic chemicals …………………… (314)
Chapter 30 Pharmaceutical products …………… (379)
Chapter 31 Fertilizers ……………………………… (393)
Chapter 32 Tanning or dyeing extracts; tannins and their derivatives; dyes, pigments and other colouring matter; paints and varnishes; putty and other mastics; inks ………… (399)
Chapter 33 Essential oils and resinoids; perfumery, cosmetic or toilet preparations ………… (411)

第三十四章　肥皂、有机表面活性剂、洗涤剂、润滑剂、人造蜡、调制蜡、光洁剂、蜡烛及类似品、塑型用膏、“牙科用蜡”及牙科用熟石膏制剂 ······ (418)

第三十五章　蛋白类物质;改性淀粉;胶;酶 ······ (425)

第三十六章　炸药;烟火制品;火柴;引火合金;易燃材料制品 ······ (429)

第三十七章　照相及电影用品 ······ (431)

第三十八章　杂项化学产品 ······ (441)

第七类　塑料及其制品;橡胶及其制品

第三十九章　塑料及其制品 ······ (461)

第四十章　橡胶及其制品 ······ (488)

第八类　生皮、皮革、毛皮及其制品;鞍具及挽具;旅行用品、手提包及类似容器;动物肠线(蚕胶丝除外)制品

第四十一章　生皮(毛皮除外)及皮革 ······ (506)

第四十二章　皮革制品;鞍具及挽具;旅行用品、手提包及类似容器;动物肠线(蚕胶丝除外)制品 ······ (518)

第四十三章　毛皮、人造毛皮及其制品 ······ (524)

第九类　木及木制品;木炭;软木及软木制品;稻草、秸秆、针茅或其他编结材料制品;篮筐及柳条编结品

第四十四章　木及木制品;木炭 ······ (528)

第四十五章　软木及软木制品 ······ (550)

第四十六章　稻草、秸秆、针茅或其他编结材料制品;篮筐及柳条编结品 ······ (552)

Chapter 34　Soap, organic surface-active agents, washing preparations, lubricating preparations, artificial waxes, prepared waxes, polishing or scouring preparations, candles and similar articles, modelling pastes, “dental waxes” and dental preparations with a basis of plaster ······ (418)

Chapter 35　Albuminoidal substances; modified starches; glues; enzymes ······ (425)

Chapter 36　Explosives; pyrotechnic products; matches; pyrophoric alloys; certain combustible preparations ······ (429)

Chapter 37　Photographic or cinematographic goods ······ (431)

Chapter 38　Miscellaneous chemical products ······ (441)

SECTION Ⅶ　PLASTICS AND ARTICLES THEREOF; RUBBER AND ARTICLES THEREOF

Chapter 39　Plastics and articles thereof ······ (461)

Chapter 40　Rubber and articles thereof ······ (488)

SECTION Ⅷ　RAW HIDES AND SKINS, LEATHER, FURSKINS AND ARTICLES THEREOF; SADDLERY AND HARNESS; TRAVEL GOODS, HANDBAGS AND SIMILAR CONTAINERS; ARTICLES OF ANIMAL GUT (OTHER THANSILK-WORM GUT)

Chapter 41　Raw hides and skins (other than furskins) and leather ······ (506)

Chapter 42　Articles of leather; saddlery and harness; travel goods, handbags and similar containers; articles of animal gut (other than silk-worm gut) ······ (518)

Chapter 43　Furskins and artificial fur; manufactures thereof ······ (524)

SECTION Ⅸ　WOOD AND ARTICLES OF WOOD; WOOD CHARCOAL; CORK AND ARTICLES OF CORK; MANUFACTURES OF STRAW, OF ESPARTO OR OF OTHER PLAITING MATERIALS; BASKETWARE AND WICKERWORK

Chapter 44　Wood and articles of wood; wood charcoal ······ (528)

Chapter 45　Cork and articles of cork ······ (550)

Chapter 46　Manufactures of straw, of esparto or of other plaiting materials; basketware and wickerwork ······ (552)

第十类　木浆及其他纤维状纤维素浆；回收（废碎）纸或纸板；纸、纸板及其制品

第四十七章　木浆及其他纤维状纤维素浆；回收（废碎）纸或纸板 ……………………（557）

第四十八章　纸及纸板；纸浆；纸或纸板制品 ………（561）

第四十九章　书籍、报纸、印刷图画及其他印刷品；手稿、打字稿及设计图纸 ……………（578）

第十一类　纺织原料及纺织制品

第五十章　蚕丝 ………………………………（591）

第五十一章　羊毛、动物细毛或粗毛；马毛纱线及其机织物 ………………………………（596）

第五十二章　棉花 ………………………………（604）

第五十三章　其他植物纺织纤维；纸纱线及其机织物 ………………………………（621）

第五十四章　化学纤维长丝 ……………………（628）

第五十五章　化学纤维短纤 ……………………（644）

第五十六章　絮胎、毡呢及无纺织物；特种纱线；线、绳、索、缆及其制品 ……………………（662）

第五十七章　地毯及纺织材料的其他铺地制品 ……（670）

第五十八章　特种机织物；簇绒织物；花边；装饰毯；装饰带；刺绣品 ……………………（674）

第五十九章　浸渍、涂布、包覆或层压的纺织物；工业用纺织制品 ……………………（686）

第六十章　针织物及钩编织物 …………………（696）

第六十一章　针织或钩编的服装及衣着附件 ………（705）

第六十二章　非针织或非钩编的服装及衣着附件 ………………………………（729）

第六十三章　其他纺织制成品；成套物品；旧衣着及旧纺织品；碎织物 ……………………（757）

SECTION X　PULP OF WOOD OR OF OTHER FIBROUS CELLULOSIC MATERIAL; RECOVERED (WASTE AND SCRAP) PAPER OR PAPERBOARD; PAPER AND PAPERBOARD AND ARTICLES THEREOF

Chapter 47　Pulp of wood or of other fibrous cellulosic material; recovered (waste and scrap) paper or paperboard ……………………（557）

Chapter 48　Paper and paperboard; articles of paper pulp, of paper or of paperboard ………………（561）

Chapter 49　Printed books, newspapers, pictures and other products of the printing industry; manuscripts, typescripts and plans ………（578）

SECTION XI　TEXTILES AND TEXTILE ARTICLES

Chapter 50　Silk ………………………………（591）

Chapter 51　Wool, fine or coarse animal hair; horsehair yarn and woven fabric …………………（596）

Chapter 52　Cotton ………………………………（604）

Chapter 53　Other vegetable textile fibres; paper yarn and woven fabrics of paper yarn ………（621）

Chapter 54　Man-made filaments ……………………（628）

Chapter 55　Man-made staple fibres ………………（644）

Chapter 56　Wadding, felt and nonwovens; special yarns; twine, cordage, ropes and cables and articles thereof ……………………（662）

Chapter 57　Carpets and other textile floor coverings ………………………………（670）

Chapter 58　Special woven fabrics; tufted textile fabrics; lace; tapestries; trimmings; embroidery ………………………………（674）

Chapter 59　Impregnated, coated, covered or laminated textile fabrics; textile articles of a kind suitable for industrial use ……………（686）

Chapter 60　Knitted or crocheted fabrics ……………（696）

Chapter 61　Articles of apparel and clothing accessories, knitted or crocheted ……………………（705）

Chapter 62　Articles of apparel and clothing accessories, not knitted or crocheted ……………（729）

Chapter 63　Other made up textile articles; sets; worn clothing and worn textile articles; rags ………………………………（757）

第十二类　鞋、帽、伞、杖、鞭及其零件；已加工的羽毛及其制品；人造花；人发制品

第六十四章　鞋靴、护腿和类似品及其零件 ……… (771)

第六十五章　帽类及其零件 ……… (779)

第六十六章　雨伞、阳伞、手杖、鞭子、马鞭及其零件 ……… (782)

第六十七章　已加工羽毛、羽绒及其制品；人造花；人发制品 ……… (784)

第十三类　石料、石膏、水泥、石棉、云母及类似材料的制品；陶瓷产品；玻璃及其制品

第六十八章　石料、石膏、水泥、石棉、云母及类似材料的制品 ……… (787)

第六十九章　陶瓷产品 ……… (800)

第七十章　玻璃及其制品 ……… (807)

第十四类　天然或养殖珍珠、宝石或半宝石、贵金属、包贵金属及其制品；仿首饰；硬币

第七十一章　天然或养殖珍珠、宝石或半宝石、贵金属、包贵金属及其制品；仿首饰；硬币 ……… (822)

第十五类　贱金属及其制品

第七十二章　钢铁 ……… (842)

第七十三章　钢铁制品 ……… (877)

第七十四章　铜及其制品 ……… (901)

第七十五章　镍及其制品 ……… (916)

第七十六章　铝及其制品 ……… (922)

第七十七章　（保留为税则将来所用）

第七十八章　铅及其制品 ……… (933)

SECTION XII　FOOTWEAR, HEADGEAR, UMBRELLAS, SUN UMBRELLAS, WALKING-STICKS, SEAT-STICKS, WHIPS, RIDING-CROPS AND PARTS THEREOF; PREPARED FEATHERS AND ARTICLES MADE THEREWITH; ARTIFICIAL FLOWERS; ARTICLES OF HUMAN HAIR

Chapter 64　Footwear, gaiters and the like; parts of such articles ……… (771)

Chapter 65　Headgear and parts thereof ……… (779)

Chapter 66　Umbrellas, sun umbrellas, walking-sticks, seat-sticks, whips, riding-crops and parts thereof ……… (782)

Chapter 67　Prepared feathers and down and articles made of feathers or of down; artificial flowers; articles of human hair ……… (784)

SECTION XIII　ARTICLES OF STONE, PLASTER, CEMENT, ASBESTOS, MICA OR SIMILAR MATERIALS; CERAMIC PRODUCTS; GLASS AND GLASSWARE

Chapter 68　Articles of stone, plaster, cement, asbestos, mica or similar materials ……… (787)

Chapter 69　Ceramic products ……… (800)

Chapter 70　Glass and glassware ……… (807)

SECTION XIV　NATURAL OR CULTURED PEARLS, PRECIOUS OR SEMI-PRECIOUS STONES, PRECIOUS METALS, METALS CLAD WITH PRECIOUS METAL, AND ARTICLES THEREOF; IMITATION JEWELLERY; COIN

Chapter 71　Natural or cultured pearls, precious or semiprecious stones, precious metals, metals clad with precious metal, and articles thereof; imitation jewellery; coin ……… (822)

SECTION XV　BASE METALS AND ARTICLES OF BASE METAL

Chapter 72　Iron and steel ……… (842)

Chapter 73　Articles of iron or steel ……… (877)

Chapter 74　Copper and articles thereof ……… (901)

Chapter 75　Nickel and articles thereof ……… (916)

Chapter 76　Aluminium and articles thereof ……… (922)

Chapter 77　(Reserved for possible future use in the Tariff)

Chapter 78　Lead and articles thereof ……… (933)

第七十九章 锌及其制品 …………………………… (937)

第八十章 锡及其制品 …………………………… (941)

第八十一章 其他贱金属、金属陶瓷及其制品 …… (945)

第八十二章 贱金属工具、器具、利口器、餐匙、餐叉及其零件 …………………………… (954)

第八十三章 贱金属杂项制品 …………………… (967)

第十六类 机器、机械器具、电气设备及其零件;录音机及放声机、电视图像、声音的录制和重放设备及其零件、附件

第八十四章 核反应堆、锅炉、机器、机械器具及其零件 …………………………… (975)

第八十五章 电机、电气设备及其零件;录音机及放声机、电视图像、声音的录制和重放设备及其零件、附件 ……………… (1119)

第十七类 车辆、航空器、船舶及有关运输设备

第八十六章 铁道及电车道机车、车辆及其零件;铁道及电车道轨道固定装置及其零件、附件;各种机械(包括电动机械)交通信号设备 ……………………… (1198)

第八十七章 车辆及其零件、附件,但铁道及电车道车辆除外 …………………………… (1206)

第八十八章 航空器、航天器及其零件 ………… (1235)

第八十九章 船舶及浮动结构体 ……………… (1238)

第十八类 光学、照相、电影、计量、检验、医疗或外科用仪器及设备、精密仪器及设备;钟表;乐器;上述物品的零件、附件

第九十章 光学、照相、电影、计量、检验、医疗或外科用仪器及设备、精密仪器及设备;上述物品的零件、附件 ……………… (1243)

Chapter 79 Zinc and articles thereof ……………… (937)

Chapter 80 Tin and articles thereof ……………… (941)

Chapter 81 Other base metals; cermets; articles thereof ……………… (945)

Chapter 82 Tools, implements, cutlery, spoons and forks, of base metal ……………… (954)

Chapter 83 Miscellaneous articles of base metal …… (967)

SECTION XVI MACHINERY AND MECHANICAL APPLIANCES; ELECTRICAL EQUIPMENT; PARTS THEREOF; SOUND RECORDERS AND REPRODUCERS, TELEVISION IMAGE AND SOUND RECORDERS AND REPRODUCERS, AND PARTS AND ACCESSORIES OF SUCH ARTICLES

Chapter 84 Nuclear reactors, boilers, machinery and mechanical appliances; parts thereof … (975)

Chapter 85 Electrical machinery and equipment and parts thereof; sound recorders and reproducers, television image and sound recorders and reproducers, and parts and accessories of such articles ……………… (1119)

SECTION XVII VEHICLES, AIRCRAFT, VESSELS AND ASSOCIATED TRANSPORT EQUIPMENT

Chapter 86 Railway or tramway locomotives, rolling-stock and parts thereof; railway or tramway track fixtures and fittings and parts thereof; mechanical (including electro-mechanical) traffic signal ling equipment of all kinds ……………… (1198)

Chapter 87 Vehicles other than railway or tramway rolling-stock, and parts and accessories thereof ……………… (1206)

Chapter 88 Aircraft, spacecraft and parts thereof …… (1235)

Chapter 89 Ships, boats and floating structures …… (1238)

SECTION XVIII OPTICAL, PHOTOGRAPHIC, CINEMATOGRAPHIC, MEASURING, CHECKING, PRECISION, MEDICAL OR SURGICAL INSTRUMENTS AND APPARATUS; CLOCKS AND WATCHES; MUSICAL INSTRUMENTS; PARTS AND ACCESORIES THEREOF

Chapter 90 Optical, photographic, cinematographic, measuring, checking, precision, medical or surgical instruments and apparatus; parts and accessories thereof ……………… (1243)

第九十一章　钟表及其零件 ………………………… (1285)

第九十二章　乐器及其零件、附件 ………………… (1293)

第十九类　武器、弹药及其零件、附件

第九十三章　武器、弹药及其零件、附件 ………… (1297)

第二十类　杂项制品

第九十四章　家具；寝具、褥垫、弹簧床垫、软座垫及类似的填充制品；未列名灯具及照明装置；发光标志、发光铭牌及类似品；活动房屋 …………………………… (1301)

第九十五章　玩具、游戏品、运动用品及其零件、附件 …………………………………… (1311)

第九十六章　杂项制品 …………………………… (1321)

第二十一类　艺术品、收藏品及古物

第九十七章　艺术品、收藏品及古物 ……………… (1333)

Chapter 91　Clocks and watches and parts thereof …………………………………………… (1285)

Chapter 92　Musical instruments; parts and accessories of such articles ……………………… (1293)

SECTION XIX　ARMS AND AMMUNITION;PARTS AND ACCESSORIES THEREOF

Chapter 93　Arms and ammunition; parts and accessories thereof ……………………… (1297)

SECTION XX　MISCELLANEOUS MANUFACTURED ARTICLES

Chapter 94　Furniture; bedding; mattresses, mattress supports, cushions and similar stuffed furnishings; lamps and lighting fittings, not elsewhere specified or included; illuminated signs, illuminated name-plates and the like; prefabricated buildings …… (1301)

Chapter 95　Toys, games and sports requisites; parts and accessories thereof ……………… (1311)

Chapter 96　Miscellaneous manufactured articles … (1321)

SECTION XXI　WORKS OF ART, COLLECTORS' PIECES AND ANTIQUES

Chapter 97　Works of art, collectors, pieces and antiques ……………………………… (1333)

归类总规则

GENERAL RULES FOR THE INTERPRETATION OF THE HARMONIZED SYSTEM

货品在本税则目录上的归类，应遵循以下原则：

Classification of goods in the Nomenclature shall be governed by the following Rules:

规则一 类、章及分章的标题，仅为查找方便而设；具有法律效力的归类，应按税目条文和有关类注或章注确定，如税目、类注或章注无其他规定，按以下规则确定。

1. The titles of Sections, Chapters and sub-Chapters are provided for ease of reference only; for legal purposes, classification shall be determined according to the terms of the headings and any relative Section or Chapter Notes and provided such headings or Notes do not otherwise require, according to the following provisions.

规则二 （一）税目所列货品，应视为包括该项货品的不完整品或未制成品，只要在进口或出口时该项不完整品或未制成品具有完整品或制成品的基本特征；还应视为包括该项货品的完整品或制成品（或按本款可作为完整品或制成品归类的货品）在进口或出口时的未组装件或拆散件。

2. (a) Any reference in a heading to an article shall be taken to include a reference to that article incomplete or unfinished, provided that, as presented, the incomplete or unfinished article has the essential character of the complete or finished article. It shall also be taken to include a reference to that article complete or finished(or falling to be classified as complete or finished by virtue of this Rule), presented unassembled or disassembled.

（二）税目中所列材料或物质，应视为包括该种材料或物质与其他材料或物质混合或组合的物品。税目所列某种材料或物质构成的货品，应视为包括全部或部分由该种材料或物质构成的货品。由一种以上材料或物质构成的货品，应按规则三归类。

(b) Any reference in a heading to a material or substance shall be taken to include a reference to mixtures or combinations of that material or substance with other materials or substances. Any reference to goods of a given material or substance shall be taken to include a reference to goods consisting wholly or partly of such material or substance. The classification of goods consisting of more than one material or substance shall be according to the principles of Rule 3.

规则三 当货品按规则二（二）或由于其他原因看起来可归入两个或两个以上税目时，应按以下规则归类：

3. When by application of Rule 2(b) or for any other reason, goods are, prima facie, classifiable under two or more headings, classification shall be effected as follows:

（一）列名比较具体的税目，优先于列名一般的税目。但是，如果两个或两个以上税目都仅述及混合或组合货品所含的某部分材料或物质，或零售的成套货品中的某些货品，即使其中某个税目对该货品描述得更为全面、详细，这些货品在有关税目的列名应视为同样具体。

(a) The heading which provides the most specific description shall be preferred to headings providing a more general description. However, when two or more headings each refer to part only of the materials or substances contained in mixed or composite goods or to part only of the items in a set put up for retail sale, those heading are to be regarded as equally specific in relation to those goods, even if one of them gives a more complete or precise description of the goods.

（二）混合物、不同材料构成或不同部件组成的组合物以及零售的成套货品，如果不能按照规则三（一）归类时，在本款可适用的条件下，应按构成货品基本特征的材料或部件归类。

(b) Mixtures, composite goods consisting of different materials or made up of different components, and goods put up in sets for retail sale, which cannot be classified by reference to Rule 3(a), shall be classified as they consisted of the material or component which gives them their essential character, insofar as this criterion is applicable.

（三）货品不能按照规则三（一）或（二）归类时，应按号列顺序归入其可归入的最末一个税目。

(c) When goods cannot be classified by reference to Rule 3(a) or Rule 3(b), they shall be classified under the heading which occurs last in numerical order among those which equally merit consideration.

规则四 根据上述规则无法归类的货品，应归入与其最相类似的货品的税目。

4. Goods which cannot be classified in accordance with the above Rules shall be classified under the heading appropriate to the goods to which they are most akin.

规则五 除上述规则外，本规则适用于下列货品的归类：

（一）制成特殊形状仅适用于盛装某个或某套物品并适合长期使用的照像机套、乐器盒、枪套、绘图仪器盒、项链盒及类似容器，如果与所装物品同时进口或出口，并通常与所装物品一同出售的，应与所装物品一并归类。但本款不适用于本身构成整个货品基本特征的容器。

（二）除规则五（一）规定的以外，与所装货品同时进口或出口的包装材料或包装容器，如果通常是用来包装这类货品的，应与所装货品一并归类。但明显可重复使用的包装材料和包装容器可不受本款限制。

5. In addition to the foregoing Rules, the following Rules shall apply in respect of the goods referred to therein:

(a) Camera cases, musical instrument cases, gun cases, drawing instrument cases, necklace cases and similar containers, specially shaped or fitted to contain a specific article or set of articles, suitable for long term use and presented with the articles for which they are intended, shall be classified with such articles when of a kind normally sold therewith. This Rule does not, however, apply to containers which give the whole its essential character.

(b) Subject to the provisions of Rule 5(a) above, packing materials and packing containers presented with the goods there in shall be classified with the goods if they are of a kind normally used for packing such goods. However, this provision is not binding when such packing materials or packing containers are clearly suitable for repetitive use.

规则六 货品在某一税目项下各子目的法定归类，应按子目条文或有关的子目注释以及以上各条规则来确定，但子目的比较只能在同一数级上进行。除本税则目录条文另有规定的以外，有关的类注、章注也适用于本规则。

6. For legal purposes, the classification of goods in the subheadings of a heading shall be determined according to the terms of those sub-headings and any related Subheading Notes and, mutatis mutandis, to the above Rules, on the understanding that only subheadings at the same level are comparable. For the purposes of this Rule the relative Section and Chapter Notes also apply, unless the context otherwise requires.

第一类

活动物；动物产品

注释：

一、本类所称的各属种动物，除条文另有规定的以外，均包括其幼仔在内。

二、除条文另有规定的以外，本目录所称干的产品，均包括经脱水、蒸发或冷冻干燥的产品。

SECTION Ⅰ

LIVE ANIMALS; ANIMAL PRODUCTS

Notes:

1. Any reference in this Section to a particular genus or species of an animal, except where the context otherwise requires, includes a reference to the young of that genus or species.
2. Except where the context otherwise requires, throughout the Nomenclature any reference to "dried" products also covers products which have been dehydrated, evaporated or freeze-dried.

第一章
活 动 物

注释：

本章包括所有活动物，但下列各项除外：

一、税号 03.01、03.06、03.07 或 03.08 的鱼、甲壳动物、软体动物及其他水生无脊椎动物；

二、税号 30.02 的培养微生物及其他产品；

三、税号 95.08 的动物。

Chapter 1
Live animals

Notes:

This Chapter covers all live animals except:

1.Fish and crustaceans, molluscs and other aquatic invertebrates, of heading No.03.01, 03.06, 03.07 or 03.08;

2.Cultures of micro-organisms and other products of heading No.30.02; and

3.Animals of heading No.95.08.

序号 No.	税则号列 Tariff Line	货品名称	最惠国税率 MFN(%)	协定税率 Agreement(%)		特惠税率 S.P.(%)		普通税率 Gen.(%)	Article Description
	01.01	**马、驴、骡：**							**Live horses, asses, mules and hinnies:**
		-马：							-Horses:
1	0101.2100	--改良种用	0			0	最不发达35国LDC35,最不发达4国LDC4	0	--Pure-bred breeding
2	0101.2900	--其他	10	0 1 5	东盟ASEAN,新西兰NZ,哥斯达黎加CR 智利CL 巴基斯坦PK,秘鲁PE	0	最不发达35国LDC35,最不发达4国LDC4	30	--Other
		-驴：							-Asses:
3	0101.3010	---改良种用	0			0	最不发达35国LDC35,最不发达4国LDC4	0	---Pure-bred breeding
4	0101.3090	---其他	10	0 1 5	东盟ASEAN,新西兰NZ,哥斯达黎加CR 智利CL 巴基斯坦PK,秘鲁PE	0	最不发达35国LDC35,最不发达4国LDC4	30	---Other

序号 No.	税则号列 Tariff Line	货品名称	最惠国税率 MFN(%)	协定税率 Agreement(%)		特惠税率 S.P.(%)		普通税率 Gen.(%)	Article Description
5	0101.9000	-其他	10	0 1 5	东盟ASEAN,新西兰NZ,哥斯达黎加CR 智利CL 巴基斯坦PK,秘鲁PE	0	最不发达35国LDC35,最不发达4国LDC4	30	-Other
	01.02	**牛:**							**Live bovine animals:**
		-家牛:							-Cattle:
6	0102.2100	--改良种用	0			0	最不发达35国LDC35,最不发达4国LDC4	0	--Pure-bred breeding
7	0102.2900	--其他	10	0 1 5	东盟ASEAN,新西兰NZ,哥斯达黎加CR 智利CL 巴基斯坦PK,秘鲁PE	0	最不发达35国LDC35,最不发达4国LDC4,缅甸MM,老挝LA,柬埔寨KH	30	--Other
		-水牛:							-Buffalo:
8	0102.3100	--改良种用	0			0	最不发达35国LDC35,最不发达4国LDC4	0	--Pure-bred breeding
9	0102.3900	--其他	10	0 1 5	东盟ASEAN,新西兰NZ,哥斯达黎加CR 智利CL 巴基斯坦PK,秘鲁PE	0	最不发达35国LDC35,最不发达4国LDC4,缅甸MM,老挝LA,柬埔寨KH	30	--Other
		-其他:							-Other:
10	0102.9010	---改良种用	0			0	最不发达35国LDC35,最不发达4国LDC4	0	---Pure-bred breeding

序号 No.	税则号列 Tariff Line	货品名称	最惠国税率 MFN(%)	协定税率 Agreement(%)	特惠税率 S.P.(%)	普通税率 Gen.(%)	Article Description
11	0102.9090	---其他	10	0 东盟ASEAN,新西兰NZ,哥斯达黎加CR 1 智利CL 5 巴基斯坦PK,秘鲁PE	0 最不发达35国LDC35,最不发达4国LDC4,缅甸MM,老挝LA,柬埔寨KH	30	---Other
	01.03	**猪：**					**Live swine:**
12	0103.1000	-改良种用	0		0 最不发达35国LDC35,最不发达4国LDC4	0	-Pure-bred breeding
		-其他： --重量在50公斤以下：					-Other: --Weighing less than 50kg:
13	0103.9110	---重量在10公斤以下	10	0 东盟ASEAN,智利CL,新西兰NZ,秘鲁PE,哥斯达黎加CR 5 巴基斯坦PK	0 最不发达35国LDC35,最不发达4国LDC4,缅甸MM,柬埔寨KH	50	---Weighing less than 10kg
14	0103.9120	---重量在10公斤及以上，但在50公斤以下	10	0 东盟ASEAN,智利CL,新西兰NZ,秘鲁PE,哥斯达黎加CR 5 巴基斯坦PK	0 最不发达35国LDC35,最不发达4国LDC4,缅甸MM,柬埔寨KH	50	---Weighing 10kg or more, but less than 50kg
15	0103.9200	--重量在50公斤及以上	10	0 东盟ASEAN,智利CL,新西兰NZ,秘鲁PE,哥斯达黎加CR 5 巴基斯坦PK	0 最不发达35国LDC35,最不发达4国LDC4,缅甸MM,老挝LA,柬埔寨KH	50	--Weighing 50kg or more
	01.04	**绵羊、山羊：** -绵羊：					**Live sheep and goats:** -Sheep:

序号 No.	税则号列 Tariff Line	货品名称	最惠国税率 MFN(%)	协定税率 Agreement(%)	特惠税率 S.P.(%)	普通税率 Gen.(%)	Article Description
16	0104.1010	---改良种用	0		0 最不发达35国LDC35,最不发达4国LDC4	0	---Pure-bred breeding
17	0104.1090	---其他	10	0 东盟ASEAN,智利CL,新西兰NZ,秘鲁PE,哥斯达黎加CR 5 巴基斯坦PK	0 最不发达35国LDC35,最不发达4国LDC4	50	---Other
		-山羊：					-Goats:
18	0104.2010	---改良种用	0		0 最不发达35国LDC35,最不发达4国LDC4	0	---Pure-bred breeding
19	0104.2090	---其他	10	0 东盟ASEAN,智利CL,新西兰NZ,秘鲁PE,哥斯达黎加CR 5 巴基斯坦PK	0 最不发达35国LDC35,最不发达4国LDC4	50	---Other
	01.05	**家禽，即鸡、鸭、鹅、火鸡及珍珠鸡：**					**Live poultry, that is to say, fowls of the species Gallus domesticus, ducks, geese, turkeys and guinea fowls:**
		-重量不超过185克：					-Weighing not more than 185g:
		--鸡：					--Fowls of the species Gallus domesticus:
20	0105.1110	---改良种用	0		0 最不发达35国LDC35,最不发达4国LDC4	0	---Pure-bred breeding
21	0105.1190	---其他	10	0 东盟ASEAN,新西兰NZ,哥斯达黎加CR 1 智利CL 5 巴基斯坦PK,秘鲁PE	0 最不发达35国LDC35,最不发达4国LDC4,缅甸MM,老挝LA	50	---Other
		--火鸡：					--Turkeys:
22	0105.1210	---改良种用	0		0 最不发达35国LDC35,最不发达4国LDC4	0	---Pure-bred breeding

序号 No.	税则号列 Tariff Line	货品名称	最惠国税率 MFN(%)	协定税率 Agreement(%)	特惠税率 S.P.(%)	普通税率 Gen.(%)	Article Description
23	0105.1290	---其他	10	0 东盟ASEAN,新西兰NZ,哥斯达黎加CR 1 智利CL 5 巴基斯坦PK,秘鲁PE	0 最不发达35国LDC35,最不发达4国LDC4	50	---Other
		--鸭:					--Ducks:
24	0105.1310	---改良种用	0		0 最不发达35国LDC35,最不发达4国LDC4	0	---Pure-bred breeding
25	0105.1390	---其他	10	0 东盟ASEAN,智利CL,新西兰NZ,秘鲁PE,哥斯达黎加CR 5 巴基斯坦PK	0 最不发达35国LDC35,最不发达4国LDC4,老挝LA	50	---Other
		--鹅:					--Geese:
26	0105.1410	---改良种用	0		0 最不发达35国LDC35,最不发达4国LDC4	0	---Pure-bred breeding
27	0105.1490	---其他	10	0 东盟ASEAN,智利CL,新西兰NZ,秘鲁PE,哥斯达黎加CR 5 巴基斯坦PK	0 最不发达35国LDC35,最不发达4国LDC4,老挝LA	50	---Other
		--珍珠鸡:					--Guinea fowls:
28	0105.1510	---改良种用	0		0 最不发达35国LDC35,最不发达4国LDC4	0	---Pure-bred breeding
29	0105.1590	---其他	10	0 东盟ASEAN,智利CL,新西兰NZ,秘鲁PE,哥斯达黎加CR 5 巴基斯坦PK	0 最不发达35国LDC35,最不发达4国LDC4,老挝LA	50	---Other
		-其他: --鸡:					-Other: --Fowls of the species Gallus domesticus:
30	0105.9410	---改良种用	0		0 最不发达35国LDC35,最不发达4国LDC4	0	---Pure-bred breeding

序号 No.	税则号列 Tariff Line	货品名称	最惠国 税 率 MFN(%)	协定税率 Agreement(%)		特惠税率 S.P.(%)		普通 税率 Gen.(%)	Article Description
31	0105.9490	---其他	10	0 5	东盟ASEAN,智利CL,新西兰NZ,秘鲁PE,哥斯达黎加CR 巴基斯坦PK	0	最不发达35国LDC35,最不发达4国LDC4	50	---Other
		--其他:							--Other:
32	0105.9910	---改良种用	0			0	最不发达35国LDC35,最不发达4国LDC4	0	---Pure-bred breeding
		---其他:							---Other:
33	0105.9991	----鸭	10	0 5	东盟ASEAN,智利CL,新西兰NZ,秘鲁PE,哥斯达黎加CR 巴基斯坦PK	0	最不发达35国LDC35,最不发达4国LDC4	50	----Ducks
34	0105.9992	----鹅	10	0 5	东盟ASEAN,智利CL,新西兰NZ,秘鲁PE,哥斯达黎加CR 巴基斯坦PK	0	最不发达35国LDC35,最不发达4国LDC4	50	----Geese
35	0105.9993	----珍珠鸡	10	0 5	东盟ASEAN,智利CL,新西兰NZ,秘鲁PE,哥斯达黎加CR 巴基斯坦PK	0	最不发达35国LDC35,最不发达4国LDC4	50	----Guinea fowls
36	0105.9994	----火鸡	10	0 5	东盟ASEAN,智利CL,新西兰NZ,秘鲁PE,哥斯达黎加CR 巴基斯坦PK	0	最不发达35国LDC35,最不发达4国LDC4	50	----Turkeys
	01.06	**其他活动物:** -哺乳动物: --灵长目:							**Other live animals:** -Mammals: --Primates:
37	0106.1110	---改良种用	0			0	最不发达35国LDC35,最不发达4国LDC4	0	---Pure-bred breeding
38	0106.1190	---其他	10	0 5	东盟ASEAN,智利CL,新西兰NZ,秘鲁PE,哥斯达黎加CR 巴基斯坦PK	0	最不发达35国LDC35,最不发达4国LDC4	50	---Other

序号 No.	税则号列 Tariff Line	货品名称	最惠国税率 MFN(%)	协定税率 Agreement(%)		特惠税率 S.P.(%)		普通税率 Gen.(%)	Article Description
		--鲸、海豚及鼠海豚(鲸目哺乳动物)；海牛及儒艮(海牛目哺乳动物)；海豹、海狮及海象(鳍足亚目哺乳动物)：							--Whales, dolphins and porpoises (mammals of the order Cetacea); manatees and dugongs (mammals of the order Sirenia); seals, sea lions and walruses (mammals of the suborder Pinnipedia):
		---鲸、海豚及鼠海豚(鲸目哺乳动物)；海牛及儒艮(海牛目哺乳动物)：							---Whales, dolphins and porpoises (mammals of the order Cetacea); manatees and dugongs (mammals of the order Sirenia)
39	0106.1211	----改良种用	10 △0	0 5	东盟ASEAN,智利CL,新西兰NZ,秘鲁PE,哥斯达黎加CR 巴基斯坦PK	0	最不发达35国LDC35,最不发达4国LDC4	50	----Pure-bred breeding
40	0106.1219	----其他	10	0 5	东盟ASEAN,智利CL,新西兰NZ,秘鲁PE,哥斯达黎加CR 巴基斯坦PK	0	最不发达35国LDC35,最不发达4国LDC4	50	----Other
		---海豹、海狮及海象(鳍足亚目哺乳动物)：							---Seals, sea lions and walruses (mammals of the suborder Pinnipedia):
41	0106.1221	----改良种用	0			0	最不发达35国LDC35,最不发达4国LDC4	0	----Pure-bred breeding
42	0106.1229	----其他	10	0 1 5	东盟ASEAN,新西兰NZ,哥斯达黎加CR 智利CL 巴基斯坦PK,秘鲁PE	0	最不发达35国LDC35,最不发达4国LDC4	50	----Other
		--骆驼及其他骆驼科动物：							--Camels and other camelids (Camelidae):
43	0106.1310	---改良种用	0			0	最不发达35国LDC35,最不发达4国LDC4	0	---Pure-bred breeding
44	0106.1390	---其他	10	0 1 5	东盟ASEAN,新西兰NZ,哥斯达黎加CR 智利CL 巴基斯坦PK,秘鲁PE	0	最不发达35国LDC35,最不发达4国LDC4	50	---Other

序号 No.	税则号列 Tariff Line	货品名称	最惠国税率 MFN(%)		协定税率 Agreement(%)		特惠税率 S.P.(%)	普通税率 Gen.(%)	Article Description
		--家兔及野兔:							--Rabbits and hares:
45	0106.1410	---改良种用	0			0	最不发达35国LDC35,最不发达4国LDC4	0	---Pure-bred breeding
46	0106.1490	---其他	10	0 1 5	东盟ASEAN,新西兰NZ,哥斯达黎加CR 智利CL 巴基斯坦PK,秘鲁PE	0	最不发达35国LDC35,最不发达4国LDC4	50	---Other
		--其他:							--Other:
47	0106.1910	---改良种用	0			0	最不发达35国LDC35,最不发达4国LDC4	0	---Pure-bred breeding
48	0106.1990	---其他	10	0 1 5	东盟ASEAN,新西兰NZ,哥斯达黎加CR 智利CL 巴基斯坦PK,秘鲁PE	0	最不发达35国LDC35,最不发达4国LDC4	50	---Other
		-爬行动物(包括蛇及龟鳖):							-Reptiles (including snakes and turtles):
		---改良种用:							---Pure-bred breeding:
49	0106.2011	----鳄鱼苗	0			0	最不发达35国LDC35,最不发达4国LDC4	0	----Crocodiles for cultivation
50	0106.2019	----其他	0			0	最不发达35国LDC35,最不发达4国LDC4	0	----Other
51	0106.2020	---食用	10	0 5	东盟ASEAN,智利CL,新西兰NZ,秘鲁PE,哥斯达黎加CR 巴基斯坦PK	0	最不发达35国LDC35,最不发达4国LDC4,缅甸MM	50	---For human consumption
52	0106.2090	---其他	10	0 5	东盟ASEAN,智利CL,新西兰NZ,秘鲁PE,哥斯达黎加CR 巴基斯坦PK	0	最不发达35国LDC35,最不发达4国LDC4	50	---Other

序号 No.	税则号列 Tariff Line	货品名称	最惠国税率 MFN(%)	协定税率 Agreement(%)		特惠税率 S.P.(%)		普通税率 Gen.(%)	Article Description
		-鸟:							-Birds:
		--猛禽:							--Birds of prey:
53	0106.3110	---改良种用	0			0	最不发达35国LDC35,最不发达4国LDC4	0	---Pure-bred breeding
54	0106.3190	---其他	10	0 5	东盟ASEAN,智利CL,新西兰NZ,秘鲁PE,哥斯达黎加CR 巴基斯坦PK	0	最不发达35国LDC35,最不发达4国LDC4	50	---Other
		--鹦形目(包括普通鹦鹉、长尾鹦鹉、金刚鹦鹉及美冠鹦鹉):							--Psittaciformes (including parrots, parakeets, macaws and cockatoos):
55	0106.3210	---改良种用	0			0	最不发达35国LDC35,最不发达4国LDC4	0	---Pure-bred breeding
56	0106.3290	---其他	10	0 5	东盟ASEAN,智利CL,新西兰NZ,秘鲁PE,哥斯达黎加CR 巴基斯坦PK	0	最不发达35国LDC35,最不发达4国LDC4	50	---Other
		--鸵鸟;鸸鹋:							--Ostriches; emus (Dromaius novaehollandiae):
57	0106.3310	---改良种用	0			0	最不发达35国LDC35,最不发达4国LDC4	0	---Pure-bred breeding
58	0106.3390	---其他	10	0 5	东盟ASEAN,智利CL,新西兰NZ,秘鲁PE,哥斯达黎加CR 巴基斯坦PK	0	最不发达35国LDC35,最不发达4国LDC4	50	---Other
		--其他:							--Other:
59	0106.3910	---改良种用	0			0	最不发达35国LDC35,最不发达4国LDC4	0	---Pure-bred breeding
		---食用:							---For human consumption:

序号 No.	税则号列 Tariff Line	货品名称	最惠国税率 MFN(%)	协定税率 Agreement(%)	特惠税率 S.P.(%)	普通税率 Gen.(%)	Article Description
60	0106.3921	----乳鸽	10	0 东盟ASEAN,智利CL,新西兰NZ,秘鲁PE,哥斯达黎加CR 5 巴基斯坦PK	0 最不发达35国LDC35,最不发达4国LDC4,缅甸MM	50	----Squabs
61	0106.3923	----野鸭	10	0 东盟ASEAN,智利CL,新西兰NZ,秘鲁PE,哥斯达黎加CR 5 巴基斯坦PK	0 最不发达35国LDC35,最不发达4国LDC4,缅甸MM	50	----Teals
62	0106.3929	----其他	10	0 东盟ASEAN,智利CL,新西兰NZ,秘鲁PE,哥斯达黎加CR 5 巴基斯坦PK	0 最不发达35国LDC35,最不发达4国LDC4,缅甸MM	50	----Other
63	0106.3990	---其他	10	0 东盟ASEAN,智利CL,新西兰NZ,秘鲁PE,哥斯达黎加CR 5 巴基斯坦PK	0 最不发达35国LDC35,最不发达4国LDC4	50	---Other
		-昆虫: --蜂:					-Insects: --Bees:
64	0106.4110	---改良种用	0		0 最不发达35国LDC35,最不发达4国LDC4	0	---Pure-bred breeding
65	0106.4190	---其他	10	0 东盟ASEAN,新西兰NZ,哥斯达黎加CR 1 智利CL 5 巴基斯坦PK,秘鲁PE 9 亚太APTA	0 最不发达35国LDC35,最不发达4国LDC4	50	---Other
	ex01064190	赤眼蜂	△0				Live trichogramma
		--其他:					--Other:
66	0106.4910	---改良种用	0		0 最不发达35国LDC35,最不发达4国LDC4	0	---Pure-bred breeding
67	0106.4990	---其他	10	0 东盟ASEAN,新西兰NZ,哥斯达黎加CR 1 智利CL 5 巴基斯坦PK,秘鲁PE 9 亚太APTA	0 最不发达35国LDC35,最不发达4国LDC4	50	---Other
	ex01064990	捕食螨	△0				Live predatory mite

序号 No.	税则号列 Tariff Line	货品名称	最惠国税率 MFN(%)	协定税率 Agreement(%)		特惠税率 S.P.(%)		普通税率 Gen.(%)	Article Description
		-其他： ---改良种用：							-Other: ---Pure-bred breeding:
68	0106.9011	----蛙苗	0			0	最不发达35国LDC35,最不发达4国LDC4	0	----Tadpole and young frogs
69	0106.9019	----其他	0			0	最不发达35国LDC35,最不发达4国LDC4	0	----Other
70	0106.9090	---其他	10	0 1 5 9	东盟ASEAN,新西兰NZ,哥斯达黎加CR 智利CL 巴基斯坦PK,秘鲁PE 亚太APTA	0	最不发达35国LDC35,最不发达4国LDC4	50	---Other

第二章
肉及食用杂碎

注释:

本章不包括:

一、税号 02.01 至 02.08 或 02.10 的不适合供人食用的产品;

二、动物的肠、膀胱、胃(税号 05.04)或动物血(税号 05.11、30.02);

三、税号 02.09 所列产品以外的动物脂肪(第十五章)。

Chapter 2
Meat and edible meat offal

Notes:

This Chapter does not cover:

1.Products of the kinds described in headings No.02.01 to 02.08 or 02.10, unfit or unsuitable for human consumption;

2.Guts, bladders or stomachs of animals (heading No.05.04) or animal blood (heading No.05.11 or 30.02); or

3.Animal fat, other than products of heading No.02.09 (Chapter 15).

序号 No.	税则号列 Tariff Line	货品名称	最惠国税率 MFN(%)	协定税率 Agreement(%)	特惠税率 S.P.(%)	普通税率 Gen.(%)	Article Description
	02.01	**鲜、冷牛肉:**					**Meat of bovine animals, fresh or chilled:**
71	0201.1000	-整头及半头	20	0 东盟ASEAN,智利CL 4.4 新西兰NZ 13.3 秘鲁PE 14.7 哥斯达黎加CR	0 最不发达35国LDC35,最不发达4国LDC4,老挝LA,柬埔寨KH	70	-Carcasses and half-carcasses
72	0201.2000	-带骨肉	12	0 东盟ASEAN 1.2 智利CL 2.7 新西兰NZ 6 巴基斯坦PK 8.5 秘鲁PE 8.8 哥斯达黎加CR	0 最不发达35国LDC35,最不发达4国LDC4,老挝LA,柬埔寨KH	70	-Other cuts with bone in
73	0201.3000	-去骨肉	12	0 东盟ASEAN 1.2 智利CL 2.7 新西兰NZ 6 巴基斯坦PK 8.5 秘鲁PE 8.8 哥斯达黎加CR	0 最不发达35国LDC35,最不发达4国LDC4,柬埔寨KH	70	-Boneless
	02.02	**冻牛肉:**					**Meat of bovine animals, frozen:**
74	0202.1000	-整头及半头	25	0 东盟ASEAN,智利CL 5 哥斯达黎加CR 5.6 新西兰NZ 16.7 秘鲁PE	0 最不发达35国LDC35,最不发达4国LDC4,老挝LA,柬埔寨KH	70	-Carcasses and half-carcasses

序号 No.	税则号列 Tariff Line	货品名称	最惠国税率 MFN(%)	协定税率 Agreement(%)	特惠税率 S.P.(%)	普通税率 Gen.(%)	Article Description
75	0202.2000	-带骨肉	12	0 东盟ASEAN 1.2 智利CL 2.4 哥斯达黎加CR 2.7 新西兰NZ 6 巴基斯坦PK 8.5 秘鲁PE	0 最不发达35国LDC35,最不发达4国LDC4,老挝LA,柬埔寨KH	70	-Other cuts with bone in
76	0202.3000	-去骨肉	12	0 东盟ASEAN 1.2 智利CL 2.4 哥斯达黎加CR 2.7 新西兰NZ 6 巴基斯坦PK 8.5 秘鲁PE	0 最不发达35国LDC35,最不发达4国LDC4,柬埔寨KH	70	-Boneless
	02.03	**鲜、冷、冻猪肉：**					**Meat of swine, fresh, chilled or frozen:**
		-鲜或冷的：					-Fresh or chilled:
		--整头及半头：					--Carcasses and half-carcasses:
77	0203.1110	---乳猪	20	0 东盟ASEAN,智利CL,新西兰NZ 4 哥斯达黎加CR 10 秘鲁PE	0 最不发达35国LDC35,最不发达4国LDC4,老挝LA,柬埔寨KH	70	---Sucking pig
78	0203.1190	---其他	20	0 东盟ASEAN,智利CL,新西兰NZ,秘鲁PE 4 哥斯达黎加CR	0 最不发达35国LDC35,最不发达4国LDC4,老挝LA,柬埔寨KH	70	---Other
79	0203.1200	--带骨的前腿、后腿及其肉块	20	0 东盟ASEAN,新西兰NZ 2 智利CL 4 哥斯达黎加CR 10 秘鲁PE	0 最不发达35国LDC35,最不发达4国LDC4,老挝LA,柬埔寨KH	70	--Hams, shoulders and cuts thereof, with bone in
80	0203.1900	--其他	20	0 东盟ASEAN,智利CL,新西兰NZ,秘鲁PE 4 哥斯达黎加CR	0 最不发达35国LDC35,最不发达4国LDC4,老挝LA,柬埔寨KH	70	--Other
		-冻的：					-Frozen:

序号 No.	税则号列 Tariff Line	货品名称	最惠国税率 MFN(%)	协定税率 Agreement(%)	特惠税率 S.P.(%)	普通税率 Gen.(%)	Article Description
		--整头及半头:					--Carcasses and half-carcasses:
81	0203.2110	---乳猪	12	0 东盟ASEAN,新西兰NZ 1.2 智利CL 2.4 哥斯达黎加CR 6 巴基斯坦PK,秘鲁PE	0 最不发达35国LDC35,最不发达4国LDC4,老挝LA,柬埔寨KH	70	---Sucking pig
82	0203.2190	---其他	12	0 东盟ASEAN,新西兰NZ 1.2 智利CL 2.4 哥斯达黎加CR 6 巴基斯坦PK,秘鲁PE	0 最不发达35国LDC35,最不发达4国LDC4,老挝LA,柬埔寨KH	70	---Other
83	0203.2200	--带骨的前腿、后腿及其肉块	12	0 东盟ASEAN,智利CL,新西兰NZ,秘鲁PE 2.4 哥斯达黎加CR 6 巴基斯坦PK	0 最不发达35国LDC35,最不发达4国LDC4,老挝LA,柬埔寨KH	70	--Hams, shoulders and cuts thereof, with bone in
84	0203.2900	--其他	12	0 东盟ASEAN,智利CL,新西兰NZ 2.4 哥斯达黎加CR 6 巴基斯坦PK 8 秘鲁PE	0 最不发达35国LDC35,最不发达4国LDC4,柬埔寨KH	70	--Other
	02.04	**鲜、冷、冻绵羊肉或山羊肉:**					**Meat of sheep or goats, fresh, chilled or frozen:**
85	0204.1000	-鲜或冷的整头及半头羔羊	15	0 东盟ASEAN,智利CL 3.3 新西兰NZ 10 秘鲁PE 11 哥斯达黎加CR 12 巴基斯坦PK	0 最不发达35国LDC35	70	-Carcasses and half-carcasses of lamb, fresh or chilled
		-其他鲜或冷的绵羊肉:					-Other meat of sheep, fresh or chilled:
86	0204.2100	--整头及半头	23	0 东盟ASEAN,智利CL 5.1 新西兰NZ 15.3 秘鲁PE 16.9 哥斯达黎加CR	0 最不发达35国LDC35	70	--Carcasses and half-carcasses
87	0204.2200	--带骨肉	15	0 东盟ASEAN,智利CL 3.3 新西兰NZ 10 秘鲁PE 11 哥斯达黎加CR 12 巴基斯坦PK	0 最不发达35国LDC35	70	--Other cuts with bone in
88	0204.2300	--去骨肉	15	0 东盟ASEAN,智利CL 3.3 新西兰NZ 8.8 秘鲁PE 11 哥斯达黎加CR 12 巴基斯坦PK	0 最不发达35国LDC35	70	--Boneless

序号 No.	税则号列 Tariff Line	货品名称	最惠国税率 MFN(%)	协定税率 Agreement(%)	特惠税率 S.P.(%)	普通税率 Gen.(%)	Article Description
89	0204.3000	-冻的整头及半头羔羊	15	0 东盟ASEAN 1.5 智利CL 3.3 新西兰NZ 10.6 秘鲁PE 11 哥斯达黎加CR 12 巴基斯坦PK	0 最不发达35国LDC35	70	-Carcasses and half-carcasses of lamb, frozen
		-其他冻的绵羊肉：					-Other meat of sheep, frozen:
90	0204.4100	--整头及半头	23	0 东盟ASEAN 2.3 智利CL 5.1 新西兰NZ 16.2 秘鲁PE 16.9 哥斯达黎加CR	0 最不发达35国LDC35	70	--Carcasses and half-carcasses
91	0204.4200	--带骨肉	12	0 东盟ASEAN 1.2 智利CL 2.7 新西兰NZ 6 巴基斯坦PK 8.5 秘鲁PE 8.8 哥斯达黎加CR	0 最不发达35国LDC35	70	--Other cuts with bone in
92	0204.4300	--去骨肉	15	0 东盟ASEAN 1.5 智利CL 3.3 新西兰NZ 10.6 秘鲁PE 11 哥斯达黎加CR 12 巴基斯坦PK	0 最不发达35国LDC35	70	--Boneless
93	0204.5000	-山羊肉	20	0 东盟ASEAN,智利CL 4.4 新西兰NZ 11.7 秘鲁PE 14.7 哥斯达黎加CR	0 最不发达35国LDC35	70	-Meat of goats
	02.05	**鲜、冷、冻马、驴、骡肉：**					**Meat of horses, asses, mules or hinnies, fresh, chilled or frozen:**
94	0205.0000	鲜、冷、冻马、驴、骡肉	20	0 东盟ASEAN,智利CL,新西兰NZ 4 哥斯达黎加CR 10 秘鲁PE	0 最不发达35国LDC35	70	Meat of horses, asses, mules or hinnies, fresh, chilled or frozen
	02.06	**鲜、冷、冻牛、猪、绵羊、山羊、马、驴、骡的食用杂碎：**					**Edible offal of bovine animals, swine, sheep, goats, horses, asses, mules or hinnies, fresh, chilled or frozen:**
95	0206.1000	-鲜、冷牛杂碎	12	0 东盟ASEAN,智利CL 2.4 哥斯达黎加CR 2.7 新西兰NZ 6 巴基斯坦PK 7 秘鲁PE	0 最不发达35国LDC35,最不发达4国LDC4,老挝LA,柬埔寨KH	70	-Of bovine animals, fresh or chilled
		-冻牛杂碎：					-Of bovine animals, frozen:

序号 No.	税则号列 Tariff Line	货品名称	最惠国税率 MFN(%)	协定税率 Agreement(%)		特惠税率 S.P.(%)		普通税率 Gen.(%)	Article Description
96	0206.2100	--舌	12	0 1.2 2.4 6	东盟ASEAN,新西兰NZ 智利CL 哥斯达黎加CR 巴基斯坦PK,秘鲁PE	0	最不发达35国LDC35,最不发达4国LDC4,老挝LA,柬埔寨KH	70	--Tongues
97	0206.2200	--肝	12	0 2.4 6	东盟ASEAN,智利CL,新西兰NZ,秘鲁PE 哥斯达黎加CR 巴基斯坦PK	0	最不发达35国LDC35,最不发达4国LDC4,老挝LA,柬埔寨KH	70	--Livers
98	0206.2900	--其他	12	0 1.2 2.4 6	东盟ASEAN,新西兰NZ 智利CL 哥斯达黎加CR 巴基斯坦PK,秘鲁PE	0	最不发达35国LDC35,最不发达4国LDC4,老挝LA,柬埔寨KH	70	--Other
99	0206.3000	-鲜、冷猪杂碎	20	0 4 10	东盟ASEAN,智利CL,新西兰NZ 哥斯达黎加CR 秘鲁PE	0	最不发达35国LDC35,最不发达4国LDC4,缅甸MM,老挝LA,柬埔寨KH	70	-Of swine, fresh of chilled
		-冻猪杂碎:							-Of swine, frozen:
100	0206.4100	--肝	20	0 4 10	东盟ASEAN,智利CL,新西兰NZ 哥斯达黎加CR 秘鲁PE	0	最不发达35国LDC35,最不发达4国LDC4,老挝LA,柬埔寨KH	70	--Livers
101	0206.4900	--其他	12	0 1.2 2.4 6	东盟ASEAN,新西兰NZ 智利CL 哥斯达黎加CR 巴基斯坦PK,秘鲁PE	0	最不发达35国LDC35,最不发达4国LDC4,老挝LA,柬埔寨KH	70	--Other

序号 No.	税则号列 Tariff Line	货品名称	最惠国税 率 MFN(%)	协定税率 Agreement(%)	特惠税率 S.P.(%)	普通税率 Gen.(%)	Article Description
102	0206.8000	-其他鲜或冷杂碎	20	0 东盟ASEAN,智利CL 4 哥斯达黎加CR 4.4 新西兰NZ 11.7 秘鲁PE	0 最不发达35国LDC35,最不发达4国LDC4,柬埔寨KH	70	-Other, fresh or chilled
103	0206.9000	-其他冻杂碎	18	0 东盟ASEAN 1.8 智利CL 3.6 哥斯达黎加CR 4 新西兰NZ 12.7 秘鲁PE 14.4 巴基斯坦PK	0 最不发达35国LDC35,最不发达4国LDC4,柬埔寨KH	70	-Other, frozen
	02.07	**税号 01.05 所列家禽的鲜、冷、冻肉及食用杂碎：**					**Meat and edible offal, of the poultry of heading No.01.05, fresh, chilled or frozen:**
		-鸡：					-Of fowls of the species Gallus domesticus:
104	0207.1100	--整只，鲜或冷的	20	0 东盟ASEAN,智利CL,新西兰NZ,秘鲁PE 4 哥斯达黎加CR	0 最不发达35国LDC35,最不发达4国LDC4,缅甸MM,老挝LA,柬埔寨KH	70	--Not cut in pieces, fresh or chilled
105	0207.1200	--整只，冻的	1.3元/千克	0 文莱BN,印尼ID,马来西亚MY,缅甸MM,菲律宾PH,新加坡*SG*,泰国TH,越南VT,新西兰NZ 4 哥斯达黎加CR 10 秘鲁PE 0.13元/千克 智利CL	0 最不发达35国LDC35,最不发达4国LDC4,缅甸MM,老挝LA,柬埔寨KH	5.6元/千克	--Not cut in pieces, frozen
		--块及杂碎，鲜或冷的：					--Cuts and offal, fresh or chilled:
		---块：					---Cuts:
106	0207.1311	----带骨的	20	0 东盟ASEAN,智利CL,新西兰NZ,秘鲁PE 4 哥斯达黎加CR	0 最不发达35国LDC35,最不发达4国LDC4,缅甸MM,老挝LA,柬埔寨KH	70	----With bone

序号 No.	税则号列 Tariff Line	货品名称	最惠国税率 MFN(%)	协定税率 Agreement(%)		特惠税率 S.P.(%)		普通税率 Gen.(%)	Article Description
107	0207.1319	----其他	20	0 4	东盟ASEAN,智利CL,新西兰NZ,秘鲁PE 哥斯达黎加CR	0	最不发达35国LDC35,最不发达4国LDC4,缅甸MM,老挝LA,柬埔寨KH	70	----Other
		---杂碎：							---Offal:
108	0207.1321	----翼（不包括翼尖）	20	0 4	东盟ASEAN,智利CL,新西兰NZ,秘鲁PE 哥斯达黎加CR	0	最不发达35国LDC35,最不发达4国LDC4,缅甸MM,老挝LA,柬埔寨KH	70	----Midjoint wing
109	0207.1329	----其他	20	0 4	东盟ASEAN,智利CL,新西兰NZ,秘鲁PE 哥斯达黎加CR	0	最不发达35国LDC35,最不发达4国LDC4,缅甸MM,老挝LA,柬埔寨KH	70	----Other
		--块及杂碎，冻的：							--Cuts and offal, frozen:
		---块：							---Cuts:
110	0207.1411	----带骨的	0.6元/千克	0 0.3元/千克	文莱BN,印尼ID,老挝LA,马来西亚MY,缅甸MM,菲律宾PH,新加坡*SG*,泰国TH,越南VT,智利CL,新西兰NZ,秘鲁PE,哥斯达黎加CR 巴基斯坦PK	0	最不发达35国LDC35,最不发达4国LDC4,缅甸MM,老挝LA,柬埔寨KH	4.2元/千克	----With bone
111	0207.1419	----其他	0.7元/千克	0 5 0.07元/千克 0.35元/千克	文莱BN,印尼ID,老挝LA,马来西亚MY,缅甸MM,菲律宾PH,新加坡*SG*,泰国TH,越南VT,新西兰NZ,哥斯达黎加CR 秘鲁PE 智利CL 巴基斯坦PK	0	最不发达35国LDC35,最不发达4国LDC4,缅甸MM,老挝LA,柬埔寨KH	9.5元/千克	----Other

序号 No.	税则号列 Tariff Line	货品名称	最惠国税率 MFN(%)	协定税率 Agreement(%)		特惠税率 S.P.(%)		普通税率 Gen.(%)	Article Description
		---杂碎：							---Offal:
112	0207.1421	----翼（不包括翼尖）	0.8 元/千克	0 0.4 元/千克	文莱BN,印尼ID,老挝LA,马来西亚MY,缅甸MM,菲律宾PH,新加坡*SG*,泰国TH,越南VT,智利CL,新西兰NZ,秘鲁PE,哥斯达黎加CR 巴基斯坦PK	0	最不发达35国LDC35,最不发达4国LDC4,缅甸MM,老挝LA,柬埔寨KH	8.1 元/千克	----Midjoint wing
113	0207.1422	----鸡爪	0.5 元/千克	0 5 0.1 元/千克 0.25 元/千克	文莱BN,印尼ID,老挝LA,马来西亚MY,缅甸MM,菲律宾PH,新加坡*SG*,泰国TH,越南VT,新西兰NZ,哥斯达黎加CR 秘鲁PE 智利CL 巴基斯坦PK	0	最不发达35国LDC35,最不发达4国LDC4,缅甸MM,老挝LA,柬埔寨KH	3.2 元/千克	----Chicken claw
114	0207.1429	----其他	0.5 元/千克	0 5 0.05 元/千克 0.25 元/千克	文莱BN,印尼ID,老挝LA,马来西亚MY,缅甸MM,菲律宾PH,新加坡*SG*,泰国TH,越南VT,新西兰NZ,哥斯达黎加CR 秘鲁PE 智利CL 巴基斯坦PK	0	最不发达35国LDC35,最不发达4国LDC4,缅甸MM,老挝LA,柬埔寨KH	3.2 元/千克	----Other
		-火鸡：							-Of turkeys:
115	0207.2400	--整只，鲜或冷的	20	0 4	东盟ASEAN,智利CL,新西兰NZ,秘鲁PE 哥斯达黎加CR	0	最不发达35国LDC35,最不发达4国LDC4,老挝LA	70	--Not cut in pieces, fresh or chilled
116	0207.2500	--整只，冻的	20	0 2 4 10	东盟ASEAN,新西兰NZ 智利CL 哥斯达黎加CR 秘鲁PE	0	最不发达35国LDC35,最不发达4国LDC4,老挝LA	70	--Not cut in pieces, frozen
117	0207.2600	--块及杂碎，鲜或冷的	20	0 4	东盟ASEAN,智利CL,新西兰NZ,秘鲁PE 哥斯达黎加CR	0	最不发达35国LDC35,最不发达4国LDC4,老挝LA	70	--Cuts and offal, fresh or chilled

序号 No.	税则号列 Tariff Line	货品名称	最惠国税率 MFN(%)	协定税率 Agreement(%)		特惠税率 S.P.(%)		普通税率 Gen.(%)	Article Description
118	0207.2700	--块及杂碎，冻的	10	0 1 5	东盟ASEAN,新西兰NZ,哥斯达黎加CR 智利CL 巴基斯坦PK,秘鲁PE	0	最不发达35国LDC35,最不发达4国LDC4,老挝LA	70	--Cuts and offal, frozen
		-鸭：							-Of ducks :
119	0207.4100	--整只，鲜或冷的	20	0 4 10	东盟ASEAN,智利CL,新西兰NZ 哥斯达黎加CR 秘鲁PE	0	最不发达35国LDC35,最不发达4国LDC4,缅甸MM,老挝LA,柬埔寨KH	70	--Not cut in pieces, fresh or chilled
120	0207.4200	--整只，冻的	20	0 4 10	东盟ASEAN,智利CL,新西兰NZ 哥斯达黎加CR 秘鲁PE	0	最不发达35国LDC35,最不发达4国LDC4,缅甸MM,老挝LA,柬埔寨KH	70	--Not cut in pieces, frozen
121	0207.4300	--肥肝，鲜或冷的	20	0 4 10	东盟ASEAN,智利CL,新西兰NZ 哥斯达黎加CR 秘鲁PE	0	最不发达35国LDC35,最不发达4国LDC4,老挝LA,柬埔寨KH	70	--Fatty livers, fresh or chilled
122	0207.4400	--其他，鲜或冷的	20	0 4 10	东盟ASEAN,智利CL,新西兰NZ 哥斯达黎加CR 秘鲁PE	0	最不发达35国LDC35,最不发达4国LDC4,缅甸MM,老挝LA,柬埔寨KH	70	--Other, fresh or chilled
123	0207.4500	--其他，冻的	20	0 4 10	东盟ASEAN,智利CL,新西兰NZ 哥斯达黎加CR 秘鲁PE	0	最不发达35国LDC35,最不发达4国LDC4,缅甸MM,老挝LA,柬埔寨KH	70	--Other, frozen

序号 No.	税则号列 Tariff Line	货品名称	最惠国税率 MFN(%)	协定税率 Agreement(%)		特惠税率 S.P.(%)		普通税率 Gen.(%)	Article Description
		-鹅:							-Of geese :
124	0207.5100	--整只，鲜或冷的	20	0 4 10	东盟ASEAN,智利CL,新西兰NZ 哥斯达黎加CR 秘鲁PE	0	最不发达35国LDC35,最不发达4国LDC4,缅甸MM,老挝LA,柬埔寨KH	70	--Not cut in pieces, fresh or chilled
125	0207.5200	--整只，冻的	20	0 4 10	东盟ASEAN,智利CL,新西兰NZ 哥斯达黎加CR 秘鲁PE	0	最不发达35国LDC35,最不发达4国LDC4,缅甸MM,老挝LA,柬埔寨KH	70	--Not cut in pieces, frozen
126	0207.5300	--肥肝，鲜或冷的	20	0 4 10	东盟ASEAN,智利CL,新西兰NZ 哥斯达黎加CR 秘鲁PE	0	最不发达35国LDC35,最不发达4国LDC4,老挝LA,柬埔寨KH	70	--Fatty livers, fresh or chilled
127	0207.5400	--其他，鲜或冷的	20	0 4 10	东盟ASEAN,智利CL,新西兰NZ 哥斯达黎加CR 秘鲁PE	0	最不发达35国LDC35,最不发达4国LDC4,缅甸MM,老挝LA,柬埔寨KH	70	--Other, fresh or chilled
128	0207.5500	--其他，冻的	20	0 4 10	东盟ASEAN,智利CL,新西兰NZ 哥斯达黎加CR 秘鲁PE	0	最不发达35国LDC35,最不发达4国LDC4,缅甸MM,老挝LA,柬埔寨KH	70	--Other, frozen
129	0207.6000	-珍珠鸡	20	0 4 10	东盟ASEAN,智利CL,新西兰NZ 哥斯达黎加CR 秘鲁PE	0	最不发达35国LDC35,最不发达4国LDC4,老挝LA,柬埔寨KH	70	-Of guinea fowls

序号 No.	税则号列 Tariff Line	货品名称	最惠国税率 MFN(%)	协定税率 Agreement(%)	特惠税率 S.P.(%)	普通税率 Gen.(%)	Article Description
	02.08	**其他鲜、冷、冻肉及食用杂碎:**					**Other meat and edible meat offal, fresh, chilled or frozen:**
		-家兔或野兔的:					-Of rabbits or hares:
130	0208.1010	---鲜、冷兔肉，兔头除外	20	0 东盟ASEAN,新西兰NZ 2 智利CL 4 哥斯达黎加CR 10 秘鲁PE	0 最不发达35国LDC35	70	---Meat of rabbits, fresh or chilled, excluding head
131	0208.1020	---冻兔肉，兔头除外	20	0 东盟ASEAN,新西兰NZ 2 智利CL 4 哥斯达黎加CR 10 秘鲁PE	0 最不发达35国LDC35	70	---Meat of rabbits, frozen, excluding head
132	0208.1090	---其他	20	0 东盟ASEAN,新西兰NZ 2 智利CL 4 哥斯达黎加CR 10 秘鲁PE	0 最不发达35国LDC35	70	---Other
133	0208.3000	-灵长目的	23	0 东盟ASEAN,智利CL,新西兰NZ 4.6 哥斯达黎加CR 11.5 秘鲁PE	0 最不发达35国LDC35	70	-Of primates
134	0208.4000	-鲸、海豚及鼠海豚(鲸目哺乳动物)的;海牛及儒艮(海牛目哺乳动物)的;海豹、海狮及海象(鳍足亚目哺乳动物)的	23	0 东盟ASEAN,智利CL,新西兰NZ 4.6 哥斯达黎加CR 11.5 秘鲁PE	0 最不发达35国LDC35	70	-Of whales, dolphins and porpoises (mammals of the order Cetacea); manatees and dugongs (mammals of the order Sirenia); seals, sea lions and walruses (mammals of the suborder Pinnipedia)
135	0208.5000	-爬行动物(包括蛇及龟鳖)的	23	0 东盟ASEAN,智利CL,新西兰NZ 4.6 哥斯达黎加CR 11.5 秘鲁PE	0 最不发达35国LDC35	70	-Of reptiles (including snakes and turtles)
136	0208.6000	-骆驼及其他骆驼科动物的	23	0 东盟ASEAN,智利CL,新西兰NZ 4.6 哥斯达黎加CR 11.5 秘鲁PE	0 最不发达35国LDC35	70	-Of camels and other camelids (Camelidae)
		-其他:					-Other:
137	0208.9010	---乳鸽的	20	0 东盟ASEAN,新西兰NZ 2 智利CL 4 哥斯达黎加CR 10 秘鲁PE	0 最不发达35国LDC35	70	---Squabs
138	0208.9090	---其他	23	0 东盟ASEAN,智利CL,新西兰NZ 4.6 哥斯达黎加CR 11.5 秘鲁PE	0 最不发达35国LDC35	70	---Other
	02.09	**未炼制或用其他方法提取的不带瘦肉的肥猪肉、猪脂肪及家禽脂肪，鲜、冷、冻、干、熏、盐腌或盐渍的:**					**Pig fat, free of lean meat, and poultry fat, not rendered or otherwise extracted, fresh, chilled, frozen, salted, in brine, dried or smoked:**

序号 No.	税则号列 Tariff Line	货品名称	最惠国税率 MFN(%)	协定税率 Agreement(%)		特惠税率 S.P.(%)		普通税率 Gen.(%)	Article Description
139	0209.1000	-猪的	20	0 2 4 10	东盟ASEAN,新西兰NZ 智利CL 哥斯达黎加CR 秘鲁PE	0	最不发达35国LDC35	70	-Of pigs
140	0209.9000	-其他	20	0 2 4 10	东盟ASEAN,新西兰NZ 智利CL 哥斯达黎加CR 秘鲁PE	0	最不发达35国LDC35	70	-Other
	02.10	**肉及食用杂碎，干、熏、盐腌或盐渍的；可供食用的肉或杂碎的细粉、粗粉：**							**Meat and edible meat offal, salted, in brine, dried or smoked; edible flours and meals of meat or meat offal:**
		-猪肉： --带骨的前腿、后腿及其肉块：							-Meat of swine: --Hams, shoulders and cuts thereof, with bone in:
141	0210.1110	---带骨的腿	25	0 5	东盟ASEAN,智利CL,新西兰NZ,秘鲁PE 哥斯达黎加CR	0	最不发达35国LDC35,最不发达4国LDC4,老挝LA,柬埔寨KH	80	---Hams and shoulders, with bone in
142	0210.1190	---其他	25	0 5	东盟ASEAN,智利CL,新西兰NZ,秘鲁PE 哥斯达黎加CR	0	最不发达35国LDC35,最不发达4国LDC4,老挝LA,柬埔寨KH	80	---Other
143	0210.1200	--腹肉（五花肉）	25	0 5	东盟ASEAN,智利CL,新西兰NZ,秘鲁PE 哥斯达黎加CR	0	最不发达35国LDC35,最不发达4国LDC4,老挝LA,柬埔寨KH	80	--Bellies (streaky) and cuts thereof
144	0210.1900	--其他	25	0 2.5 5 12.5	东盟ASEAN,新西兰NZ 智利CL 哥斯达黎加CR 秘鲁PE	0	最不发达35国LDC35,最不发达4国LDC4,缅甸MM,柬埔寨KH	80	--Other

序号 No.	税则号列 Tariff Line	货品名称	最惠国税率 MFN(%)	协定税率 Agreement(%)		特惠税率 S.P.(%)		普通税率 Gen.(%)	Article Description
145	0210.2000	-牛肉	25	0 5 12.5	东盟ASEAN,智利CL,新西兰NZ 哥斯达黎加CR 秘鲁PE	0	最不发达35国LDC35,最不发达4国LDC4,老挝LA,柬埔寨KH	80	-Meat of bovine animals
		-其他，包括可供食用的肉或杂碎的细粉、粗粉：							-Other, including edible flours and meals of meat or meat offal:
146	0210.9100	--灵长目的	25	0 5 12.5	东盟ASEAN,智利CL,新西兰NZ 哥斯达黎加CR 秘鲁PE	0	最不发达35国LDC35,最不发达4国LDC4,老挝LA,柬埔寨KH	80	--Of primates
147	0210.9200	--鲸、海豚及鼠海豚(鲸目哺乳动物)的；海牛及儒艮(海牛目哺乳动物)的；海豹、海狮及海象(鳍足亚目哺乳动物)的	25	0 5 12.5	东盟ASEAN,智利CL,新西兰NZ 哥斯达黎加CR 秘鲁PE	0	最不发达35国LDC35,最不发达4国LDC4,老挝LA,柬埔寨KH	80	--Of whales, dolphins and porpoises (mammals of the order Cetacea); of manatees and dugongs (mammals of the order Sirenia); of seals, sea lions and walruses (mammals of the suborder Pinnipedia)
148	0210.9300	--爬行动物（包括蛇及龟鳖）的	25	0 5 12.5	东盟ASEAN,智利CL,新西兰NZ 哥斯达黎加CR 秘鲁PE	0	最不发达35国LDC35,最不发达4国LDC4,老挝LA,柬埔寨KH	80	--Of reptiles (including snakes and turtles)
149	0210.9900	--其他	25	0 2.5 5 12.5	东盟ASEAN,新西兰NZ 智利CL 哥斯达黎加CR 秘鲁PE	0	最不发达35国LDC35,最不发达4国LDC4,老挝LA,柬埔寨KH	80	--Other

第三章
鱼、甲壳动物、软体动物及其他水生无脊椎动物

Chapter 3
Fish and crustaceans，molluscs and other aquatic invertebrates

注释:

一、本章不包括:

（一）税目 01.06 的哺乳动物；

（二）税目 01.06 的哺乳动物的肉（税目 02.08 或 02.10）；

（三）因品种或鲜度不适合供人食用的死鱼（包括鱼肝及鱼卵）、死甲壳动物、死软体动物及其他死水生无脊椎动物（第五章）;不适合供人食用的鱼、甲壳动物、软体动物、其他水生无脊椎动物的粉、粒（税号 23.01）；

（四）鲟鱼子酱及用鱼卵制成的鲟鱼子酱代用品（税号 16.04）。

二、本章所称“团粒”，是指直接挤压或加入少量粘合剂制成的粒状产品。

Notes:

1. This Chapter does not cover:

(a) Mammals of heading No.01.06;

(b) Meat of mammals of heading No.01.06 (heading No.02.08 or 02.10);

(c) Fish (including livers and roes thereof) or crustaceans, molluscs or other aquatic invertebrates, dead and unfit or unsuitable for human consumption by reason of either their species or their condition (Chapter 5); flours, meals or pellets of fish or of crustaceans, molluscs or other aquatic invertebrates, unfit for human consumption (heading No.23.01) ;or

(d) Caviar or caviar substitutes prepared from fish eggs (heading No.16.04).

2. In this Chapter the term“pellets”means products which have been agglomerated either directly by compression or by the addition of a small quantity of binder.

序号 No.	税则号列 Tariff Line	货品名称	最惠国税率 MFN(%)	协定税率 Agreement(%)		特惠税率 S.P.(%)		普通税率 Gen.(%)	Article Description
	03.01	**活鱼:**							**Live fish:**
		-观赏鱼:							-Ornamental fish:
150	0301.1100	--淡水鱼	17.5	0 10.5 14	东盟ASEAN,智利CL,新西兰NZ,秘鲁PE,香港HK 哥斯达黎加CR 巴基斯坦PK	0	最不发达 35 国 LDC35,最不发达 4 国 LDC4	80	--Freshwater
151	0301.1900	--其他	17.5	0 10.5 14	东盟ASEAN,智利CL,新西兰NZ,秘鲁PE,香港HK 哥斯达黎加CR 巴基斯坦PK	0	最不发达 35 国 LDC35,最不发达 4 国 LDC4	80	--Other
		-其他活鱼:							-Other live fish:
		--鳟鱼（河鳟、虹鳟、克拉克大麻哈鱼、阿瓜大麻哈鱼、吉雨大麻哈鱼、亚利桑那大麻哈鱼、金腹大麻哈鱼）:							--Trout (Salmo trutta, Oncorhynchus mykiss, Oncorhynchus clarki, Onco-rhynchus aguabonita, Oncorhynchus gilae, Oncorhynchus apache and Oncorhynchus chrysogaster):

序号 No.	税则号列 Tariff Line	货品名称	最惠国税率 MFN(%)	协定税率 Agreement(%)		特惠税率 S.P.(%)		普通税率 Gen.(%)	Article Description
152	0301.9110	---鱼苗	0			0	最不发达35国LDC35,最不发达4国LDC4	0	---Fry
153	0301.9190	---其他	10.5	0 5 6.3 8	东盟ASEAN,智利CL,新西兰NZ,秘鲁PE 巴基斯坦PK 哥斯达黎加CR 亚太APTA	0	最不发达35国LDC35,最不发达4国LDC4	40	---Other
		--鳗鱼（鳗鲡属）:							--Eels (Anguilla spp.):
154	0301.9210	---鱼苗	0			0	最不发达35国LDC35,最不发达4国LDC4	0	---Fry
155	0301.9290	---其他	10	0 5 6 6.7	东盟ASEAN,智利CL,新西兰NZ,秘鲁PE 巴基斯坦PK 哥斯达黎加CR 亚太APTA	0	最不发达35国LDC35,最不发达4国LDC4,缅甸MM,柬埔寨KH	40	---Other
		--鲤科鱼（西鲤、黑鲫、草鱼、鲢属、鲮属、青鱼）:							--Carp (Cyprinus carpio, Carassius carassius, Ctenopharyngodon idellus, Hypophthalmichthys spp., Cirrhinus spp., Mylopharyngodon piceus):
156	0301.9310	---鱼苗	0			0	最不发达35国LDC35,最不发达4国LDC4	0	---Fry
157	0301.9390	---其他	10.5	0 5 6.3 8	东盟ASEAN,智利CL,新西兰NZ,秘鲁PE 巴基斯坦PK 哥斯达黎加CR 亚太APTA	0	最不发达35国LDC35,最不发达4国LDC4,缅甸MM,柬埔寨KH	40	---Other
		--大西洋及太平洋蓝鳍金枪鱼:							--Atlantic and Pacific bluefin tunas (Thunnus thynnus, Thunnus orientalis):

序号 No.	税则号列 Tariff Line	货品名称	最惠国税率 MFN(%)	协定税率 Agreement(%)	特惠税率 S.P.(%)	普通税率 Gen.(%)	Article Description
158	0301.9410	---鱼苗	0		0 最不发达35国LDC35,最不发达4国LDC4	0	---Fry
		---其他:					---Other:
159	0301.9491	----大西洋蓝鳍金枪鱼	10.5	0 东盟ASEAN,新西兰NZ,秘鲁PE,香港HK 1.1 智利CL 5 巴基斯坦PK 6.3 哥斯达黎加CR 8 亚太APTA	0 最不发达35国LDC35,最不发达4国LDC4,缅甸MM,柬埔寨KH	40	----Atlantic bluefin tunas (Thunnus thynnus)
160	0301.9492	----太平洋蓝鳍金枪鱼	10.5	0 东盟ASEAN,新西兰NZ,香港HK,台湾TW 1.1 智利CL 5 巴基斯坦PK 5.3 秘鲁PE 6.3 哥斯达黎加CR 8 亚太APTA	0 最不发达35国LDC35,最不发达4国LDC4,缅甸MM,柬埔寨KH	40	----Pacific bluefin tunas (Thunnus orientalis)
		--南方蓝鳍金枪鱼:					--Southern bluefin tunas (Thunnus maccoyii):
161	0301.9510	---鱼苗	0		0 最不发达35国LDC35,最不发达4国LDC4	0	---Fry
162	0301.9590	---其他	10.5	0 东盟ASEAN,新西兰NZ,秘鲁PE,香港HK 1.1 智利CL 5 巴基斯坦PK 6.3 哥斯达黎加CR 8 亚太APTA	0 最不发达35国LDC35,最不发达4国LDC4,缅甸MM,柬埔寨KH	40	---Other
		--其他:					--Other:
		---鱼苗:					---Fry:
163	0301.9911	----鲈鱼	0		0 最不发达35国LDC35,最不发达4国LDC4	0	----Of perches
164	0301.9912	----鲟鱼	0		0 最不发达35国LDC35,最不发达4国LDC4	0	----Of sturgeon

序号 No.	税则号列 Tariff Line	货品名称	最惠国税率 MFN(%)	协定税率 Agreement(%)		特惠税率 S.P.(%)		普通税率 Gen.(%)	Article Description
165	0301.9919	----其他	0			0	最不发达35国LDC35,最不发达4国LDC4	0	----Other
		---其他:							---Other:
166	0301.9991	----罗非鱼	10.5	0 1.1 5 5.3 6.3	东盟ASEAN,新西兰NZ,香港HK 智利CL 巴基斯坦PK 秘鲁PE 哥斯达黎加CR	0	最不发达35国LDC35,最不发达4国LDC4,缅甸MM,柬埔寨KH	40	----Tilapia
167	0301.9992	----鲀	10.5	0 1.1 5 6.3 8	东盟ASEAN,新西兰NZ,秘鲁PE,香港HK 智利CL 巴基斯坦PK 哥斯达黎加CR 亚太APTA	0	最不发达35国LDC35,最不发达4国LDC4,缅甸MM,柬埔寨KH	40	----Puffer fish
168	0301.9993	----其他鲤科鱼	10.5	0 5 6.3 8	东盟ASEAN,智利CL,新西兰NZ,秘鲁PE 巴基斯坦PK 哥斯达黎加CR 亚太APTA	0	最不发达35国LDC35,最不发达4国LDC4,缅甸MM,柬埔寨KH	40	----Other carp
169	0301.9999	----其他	10.5	0 1.1 5 5.3 6.3 8	东盟ASEAN,新西兰NZ,香港HK,台湾TW 智利CL 巴基斯坦PK 秘鲁PE 哥斯达黎加CR 亚太APTA	0	最不发达35国LDC35,最不发达4国LDC4,缅甸MM,柬埔寨KH	40	----Other
	03.02	**鲜、冷鱼，但税号03.04的鱼片及其他鱼肉除外：**							**Fish, fresh or chilled, excluding fish fillets and other fish meat of heading No.03.04:**
		-鲑科鱼，但鱼肝及鱼卵除外：							-Salmonidae, excluding livers and roes:
170	0302.1100	--鳟鱼（河鳟、虹鳟、克拉克大麻哈鱼、阿瓜大麻哈鱼、吉雨大麻哈鱼、亚利桑那大麻哈鱼、金腹大麻哈鱼）	12	0 1.2 6 7.2	东盟ASEAN,新西兰NZ 智利CL 巴基斯坦PK,秘鲁PE 哥斯达黎加CR	0	最不发达35国LDC35,最不发达4国LDC4	40	--Trout (Salmo trutta, Oncorhynchus my kiss, Oncorhynchus clarki, Oncorhynchus aguabonita, Oncorhynchus gilae, Oncorhynchus apache and Oncorhynchus chrysogaster)

序号 No.	税则号列 Tariff Line	货品名称	最惠国税率 MFN(%)	协定税率 Agreement(%)		特惠税率 S.P.(%)		普通税率 Gen.(%)	Article Description
171	0302.1300	--大麻哈鱼〔红大麻哈鱼、细磷大麻哈鱼、大麻哈鱼（种）、大鳞大麻哈鱼、银大麻哈鱼、马苏大麻哈鱼、玫瑰大麻哈鱼〕	10	0 1 5 6	东盟ASEAN,新西兰NZ 智利CL 巴基斯坦PK,秘鲁PE 哥斯达黎加CR	0	最不发达35国LDC35,最不发达4国LDC4	40	--Pacific salmon (Oncorhynchus nerka, Oncorhynchus gorbuscha, Oncorhynchus keta, Oncorhynchus tschawytscha, Oncorhynchus kisutch, Oncorhynchus masou and Oncorhynchus rhodurus)
		--大西洋鲑鱼及多瑙哲罗鱼：							--Atlantic salmon (Salmo salar) and Danube salmon (Hucho hucho):
172	0302.1410	---大西洋鲑鱼	10	0 1 5 6	东盟ASEAN,新西兰NZ 智利CL 巴基斯坦PK,秘鲁PE 哥斯达黎加CR	0	最不发达35国LDC35,最不发达4国LDC4	40	---Atlantic salmon (Salmo salar)
173	0302.1420	---多瑙哲罗鱼	10	0 1 5 6	东盟ASEAN,新西兰NZ 智利CL 巴基斯坦PK,秘鲁PE 哥斯达黎加CR	0	最不发达35国LDC35,最不发达4国LDC4	40	---Danube salmon (Hucho hucho)
174	0302.1900	--其他	12	0 5 7.2 8	东盟ASEAN,智利CL,新西兰NZ,秘鲁PE 巴基斯坦PK 哥斯达黎加CR 亚太APTA	0	最不发达35国LDC35,最不发达4国LDC4	40	--Other
		-比目鱼，但鱼肝及鱼卵除外：							-Flat fish (Pleuronectidae, Bothidae, Cynoglossidae, soleidae, Scophthalmidae and Citharidae), excluding livers and roes:
175	0302.2100	--庸鲽鱼	12	0 5 7.2 9	东盟ASEAN,智利CL,新西兰NZ,秘鲁PE 巴基斯坦PK 哥斯达黎加CR 亚太APTA	0	最不发达35国LDC35,最不发达4国LDC4	40	--Halibut (Reinhardtius hippoglossoides, Hippoglossus hippoglossus, Hippog-lossus stenolepis)
176	0302.2200	--鲽鱼	12	0 5 7.2 9	东盟ASEAN,智利CL,新西兰NZ,秘鲁PE 巴基斯坦PK 哥斯达黎加CR 亚太APTA	0	最不发达35国LDC35,最不发达4国LDC4	40	--Plaice (Pleuronectes platessa)
177	0302.2300	--鳎鱼	12	0 5 7.2 9	东盟ASEAN,智利CL,新西兰NZ,秘鲁PE 巴基斯坦PK 哥斯达黎加CR 亚太APTA	0	最不发达35国LDC35,最不发达4国LDC4	40	--Sole (Solea spp.)

序号 No.	税则号列 Tariff Line	货品名称	最惠国税率 MFN(%)	协定税率 Agreement(%)		特惠税率 S.P.(%)		普通税率 Gen.(%)	Article Description
178	0302.2400	--大菱鲆(瘤棘鲆)	12	0 1.2 5 6 7.2	东盟ASEAN,新西兰NZ 智利CL 巴基斯坦PK 亚太APTA,秘鲁PE 哥斯达黎加CR	0	最不发达35国LDC35,最不发达4国LDC4,柬埔寨KH	40	--Turbots (Psetta maxima, Scophthalmidae)
179	0302.2900	--其他	12	0 1.2 5 6 7.2	东盟ASEAN,新西兰NZ 智利CL 巴基斯坦PK 亚太APTA,秘鲁PE 哥斯达黎加CR	0	最不发达35国LDC35,最不发达4国LDC4,柬埔寨KH	40	--Other
		-金枪鱼(金枪鱼属)、鲣鱼或狐鲣(鲣),但鱼肝及鱼卵除外:							-Tunas (of the genus Thunnus), skipjack or stripe-bellied bonito (Euthynnus (Katsuwonus) pelamis), excluding livers and roes:
180	0302.3100	--长鳍金枪鱼	12	0 1.2 5 6 7.2 9	东盟ASEAN,新西兰NZ 智利CL 巴基斯坦PK 秘鲁PE 哥斯达黎加CR 亚太APTA	0	最不发达35国LDC35,最不发达4国LDC4,柬埔寨KH	40	--Albacore or longfinned tunas (Thunnus alalunga)
181	0302.3200	--黄鳍金枪鱼	12	0 5 7.2 9	东盟ASEAN,智利CL,新西兰NZ,秘鲁PE,香港HK 巴基斯坦PK 哥斯达黎加CR 亚太APTA	0	最不发达35国LDC35,最不发达4国LDC4	40	--Yellowfin tunas (Thunnus albacares)
182	0302.3300	--鲣鱼或狐鲣	12	0 5 7.2 8	东盟ASEAN,智利CL,新西兰NZ,秘鲁PE 巴基斯坦PK 哥斯达黎加CR 亚太APTA	0	最不发达35国LDC35,最不发达4国LDC4	40	--Skipjack or stripe-bellied bonito
183	0302.3400	--大眼金枪鱼	12	0 6 7.2	东盟ASEAN,智利CL,新西兰NZ,秘鲁PE 巴基斯坦PK 哥斯达黎加CR	0	最不发达35国LDC35,最不发达4国LDC4,缅甸MM,柬埔寨KH	40	--Bigeye tunas (Thunnus obesus)
		--大西洋及太平洋蓝鳍金枪鱼:							--Atlantic and Pacific bluefin tunas (Thunnus thynnus, Thunnus orientalis):

序号 No.	税则号列 Tariff Line	货品名称	最惠国税 率 MFN(%)	协定税率 Agreement(%)		特惠税率 S.P.(%)		普通税率 Gen.(%)	Article Description
184	0302.3510	---大西洋蓝鳍金枪鱼	12	0 6 7.2	东盟ASEAN,智利CL,新西兰NZ,秘鲁PE 巴基斯坦PK 哥斯达黎加CR	0	最不发达35国LDC35,最不发达4国LDC4,缅甸MM,柬埔寨KH	40	---Atlantic bluefin tunas (Thunnus thynnus)
185	0302.3520	---太平洋蓝鳍金枪鱼	12	0 5 7.2 8	东盟ASEAN,智利CL,新西兰NZ,秘鲁PE 巴基斯坦PK 哥斯达黎加CR 亚太APTA	0	最不发达35国LDC35,最不发达4国LDC4,缅甸MM,柬埔寨KH	40	---Pacific bluefin tunas (Thunnus orientalis)
186	0302.3600	--南方蓝鳍金枪鱼	12	0 6 7.2	东盟ASEAN,智利CL,新西兰NZ,秘鲁PE 巴基斯坦PK 哥斯达黎加CR	0	最不发达35国LDC35,最不发达4国LDC4,缅甸MM,柬埔寨KH	40	--Southern bluefin tunas (Thunnus maccoyii)
187	0302.3900	--其他	12	0 5 7.2 8	东盟ASEAN,智利CL,新西兰NZ,秘鲁PE 巴基斯坦PK 哥斯达黎加CR 亚太APTA	0	最不发达35国LDC35,最不发达4国LDC4,缅甸MM,柬埔寨KH	40	--Other
		-鲱鱼(大西洋鲱鱼、太平洋鲱鱼)、鳀鱼(鳀属)、沙丁鱼(沙丁鱼、沙瑙鱼属)、小沙丁鱼属、黍鲱或西鲱、鲭鱼〔大西洋鲭、澳洲鲭(鲐)、日本鲭(鲐)〕、对称竹荚鱼、新西兰竹荚鱼及竹荚鱼(竹荚鱼属)、军曹鱼及剑鱼,但鱼肝及鱼卵除外:							-Herrings (Clupea harengus, Clupea pallasii), anchovies (Engraulis spp.), sardines (Sardina pilchardus, Sardinops spp.), sardinella (Sardinella spp.), brisling or sprats (Sprattus sprattus), mackerel (Scomber scombrus, Scomber australasicus, Scomber japonicus), jack and horse mackerel (Trachurus spp.), cobia (Rachycentron canadum) and swordfish (Xiphias gladius), excluding livers and roes :

序号 No.	税则号列 Tariff Line	货品名称	最惠国税率 MFN(%)	协定税率 Agreement(%)		特惠税率 S.P.(%)		普通税率 Gen.(%)	Article Description
188	0302.4100	--鲱鱼(大西洋鲱鱼、太平洋鲱鱼)	12	0 5 7.2 8	东盟ASEAN,智利CL,新西兰NZ,秘鲁PE 巴基斯坦PK 哥斯达黎加CR 亚太APTA	0	最不发达35国LDC35,最不发达4国LDC4	40	--Herrings (Clupea harengus, Clupea pallasii)
189	0302.4200	--鳀鱼(鳀属)	12	0 1.2 5 7.2 8	东盟ASEAN,新西兰NZ,秘鲁PE,香港HK,台湾TW 智利CL 巴基斯坦PK 哥斯达黎加CR 亚太APTA	0	最不发达35国LDC35,最不发达4国LDC4,缅甸MM,柬埔寨KH	40	--Anchovies (Engraulis spp.)
190	0302.4300	--沙丁鱼(沙丁鱼、沙瑙鱼属)、小沙丁鱼属、黍鲱或西鲱	12	0 5 7.2 8	东盟ASEAN,智利CL,新西兰NZ,秘鲁PE 巴基斯坦PK 哥斯达黎加CR 亚太APTA	0	最不发达35国LDC35,最不发达4国LDC4	40	--Sardines (Sardina pilchardus, Sardinops spp.), sardinella (Sardinella spp.), brisling or sprats (Sprattus sprattus)
191	0302.4400	--鲭鱼〔大西洋鲭、澳洲鲭(鲐)、日本鲭(鲐)〕	12	0 5 7.2 8	东盟ASEAN,智利CL,新西兰NZ,秘鲁PE 巴基斯坦PK 哥斯达黎加CR 亚太APTA	0	最不发达35国LDC35,最不发达4国LDC4	40	--Mackerel (Scomber scombrus, Scomber australasicus, Scomber japonicus)
192	0302.4500	--对称竹荚鱼、新西兰竹荚鱼及竹荚鱼(竹荚鱼属)	12	0 1.2 5 7.2 8	东盟ASEAN,新西兰NZ,秘鲁PE,香港HK,台湾TW 智利CL 巴基斯坦PK 哥斯达黎加CR 亚太APTA	0	最不发达35国LDC35,最不发达4国LDC4,缅甸MM,柬埔寨KH	40	--Jack and horse mackerel (Trachurus spp.)
193	0302.4600	--军曹鱼	12	0 1.2 5 7.2 8	东盟ASEAN,新西兰NZ,秘鲁PE,香港HK,台湾TW 智利CL 巴基斯坦PK 哥斯达黎加CR 亚太APTA	0	最不发达35国LDC35,最不发达4国LDC4,缅甸MM,柬埔寨KH	40	--Cobia (Rachycentron canadum)
194	0302.4700	--剑鱼	12	0 1.2 5 7.2 8	东盟ASEAN,新西兰NZ,秘鲁PE,香港HK 智利CL 巴基斯坦PK 哥斯达黎加CR 亚太APTA	0	最不发达35国LDC35,最不发达4国LDC4	40	--Swordfish (Xiphias gladius)

序号 No.	税则号列 Tariff Line	货品名称	最惠国税率 MFN(%)	协定税率 Agreement(%)	特惠税率 S.P.(%)	普通税率 Gen.(%)	Article Description
		-犀鳕科、多丝真鳕科、鳕科、长尾鳕科、黑鳕科、无须鳕科、深海鳕科及南极鳕科鱼，但鱼肝及鱼卵除外：					-Fish of the families Bregmacerotidae, Euclichthyidae, Gadidae, Macrouridae, Melanonidae, Merlucciidae, Moridae and Muraenolepididae, excluding livers and roes:
195	0302.5100	--鳕鱼(大西洋鳕鱼、格陵兰鳕鱼、太平洋鳕鱼)	12	0 东盟ASEAN,智利CL,新西兰NZ,秘鲁PE 5 巴基斯坦PK 7.2 哥斯达黎加CR 8 亚太APTA	0 最不发达35国LDC35,最不发达4国LDC4	40	--Cod (Gadus morhua, Gadus ogac, Gadus macrocephalus)
196	0302.5200	--黑线鳕鱼(黑线鳕)	12	0 东盟ASEAN,智利CL,新西兰NZ,秘鲁PE 5 巴基斯坦PK 7.2 哥斯达黎加CR 8 亚太APTA	0 最不发达35国LDC35,最不发达4国LDC4	40	--Haddock (Melanogrammus aeglefinus)
197	0302.5300	--绿青鳕鱼	12	0 东盟ASEAN,智利CL,新西兰NZ,秘鲁PE 5 巴基斯坦PK 7.2 哥斯达黎加CR 8 亚太APTA	0 最不发达35国LDC35,最不发达4国LDC4	40	--Coalfish (Pollachius virens)
198	0302.5400	--狗鳕鱼(无须鳕属、长鳍鳕属)	12	0 东盟ASEAN,新西兰NZ,秘鲁PE,香港HK,台湾TW 1.2 智利CL 5 巴基斯坦PK 7.2 哥斯达黎加CR 8 亚太APTA	0 最不发达35国LDC35,最不发达4国LDC4,缅甸MM,柬埔寨KH	40	--Hake (Merluccius spp., Urophycis spp.)
199	0302.5500	--狭鳕鱼	12	0 东盟ASEAN,新西兰NZ,秘鲁PE,香港HK,台湾TW 1.2 智利CL 5 巴基斯坦PK 7.2 哥斯达黎加CR 8 亚太APTA	0 最不发达35国LDC35,最不发达4国LDC4,缅甸MM,柬埔寨KH	40	--Alaska Pollack (Theraga chalcogramma)
200	0302.5600	--蓝鳕鱼(小鳍鳕、南蓝鳕)	12	0 东盟ASEAN,新西兰NZ,秘鲁PE,香港HK,台湾TW 1.2 智利CL 5 巴基斯坦PK 7.2 哥斯达黎加CR 8 亚太APTA	0 最不发达35国LDC35,最不发达4国LDC4,缅甸MM,柬埔寨KH	40	--Blue whitings (Micromesistius poutassou, Micromesistius australis)

序号 No.	税则号列 Tariff Line	货品名称	最惠国税率 MFN(%)	协定税率 Agreement(%)	特惠税率 S.P.(%)	普通税率 Gen.(%)	Article Description
201	0302.5900	--其他	12	0 东盟ASEAN,新西兰NZ,秘鲁PE,香港HK,台湾TW 1.2 智利CL 5 巴基斯坦PK 7.2 哥斯达黎加CR 8 亚太APTA	0 最不发达35国LDC35,最不发达4国LDC4,缅甸MM,柬埔寨KH	40	--Other
		-罗非鱼（口孵非鲫属）、鲶鱼（(鱼芒)鲶属、鲶属、胡鲶属、真鮰属）、鲤科鱼（西鲤、黑鲫、草鱼、鲢属、鲮属、青鱼）、鳗鱼（鳗鲡属）、尼罗河鲈鱼（尼罗尖吻鲈）及黑鱼（鳢属），但鱼肝及鱼卵除外:					-Tilapias (Oreochromis spp.), catfish (Pangasius spp., Silurus spp., Clarias spp., Ictalurus spp.), carp (Cyprinus carpio, Carassius carassius, Ctenopharyngodon idellus, Hypophthalmichthys spp., Cirrhinus spp., Mylopharyngodon piceus), eels (Anguilla spp.), Nile perch (Lates niloticus) and snakeheads (Channa spp.), excluding livers and roes:
202	0302.7100	--罗非鱼（口孵非鲫属）	12	0 东盟ASEAN,新西兰NZ 1.2 智利CL 6 巴基斯坦PK,秘鲁PE 7.2 哥斯达黎加CR	0 最不发达35国LDC35,最不发达4国LDC4,缅甸MM,柬埔寨KH	40	--Tilapias (Oreochromis spp.)
203	0302.7200	--鲶鱼（(鱼芒)鲶属、鲶属、胡鲶属、真鮰属）	12	0 东盟ASEAN,新西兰NZ,秘鲁PE,香港HK,台湾TW 1.2 智利CL 5 巴基斯坦PK 7.2 哥斯达黎加CR 8 亚太APTA	0 最不发达35国LDC35,最不发达4国LDC4,缅甸MM,柬埔寨KH	40	--Catfish (Pangasius spp., Silurus spp., Clarias spp., Ictalurus spp.)
204	0302.7300	--鲤科鱼（西鲤、黑鲫、草鱼、鲢属、鲮属、青鱼）	12	0 东盟ASEAN,新西兰NZ,秘鲁PE,香港HK,台湾TW 1.2 智利CL 5 巴基斯坦PK 7.2 哥斯达黎加CR 8 亚太APTA	0 最不发达35国LDC35,最不发达4国LDC4,缅甸MM,柬埔寨KH	40	--Carp (Cyprinus carpio, Carassius carassius, Ctenopharyngodon idellus, Hypophthalmichthys spp., Cirrhinus spp., Mylopharyngodon piceus)
205	0302.7400	--鳗鱼（鳗鲡属）	12	0 东盟ASEAN,智利CL,新西兰NZ,秘鲁PE,香港HK 5 巴基斯坦PK 7.2 哥斯达黎加CR 8 亚太APTA	0 最不发达35国LDC35,最不发达4国LDC4,缅甸MM	40	--Eels (Anguilla spp.)

序号 No.	税则号列 Tariff Line	货品名称	最惠国 税率 MFN(%)	协定税率 Agreement(%)		特惠税率 S.P.(%)		普通 税率 Gen.(%)	Article Description
206	0302.7900	--其他	12	0 1.2 5 7.2 8	东盟ASEAN,新西兰NZ,秘鲁PE,香港HK,台湾TW 智利CL 巴基斯坦PK 哥斯达黎加CR 亚太APTA	0	最不发达35国LDC35,最不发达4国LDC4,缅甸MM,柬埔寨KH	40	--Other
		-其他鱼,但鱼肝及鱼卵除外:							-Other fish, excluding livers and roes :
207	0302.8100	--角鲨及其他鲨鱼	12	0 1.2 5 6 7.2 9	东盟ASEAN,新西兰NZ,香港HK 智利CL 巴基斯坦PK 秘鲁PE 哥斯达黎加CR 亚太APTA	0	最不发达35国LDC35,最不发达4国LDC4	40	--Dogfish and other sharks
208	0302.8200	--魟鱼及鳐鱼(鳐科)	12	0 1.2 5 7.2 8	东盟ASEAN,新西兰NZ,秘鲁PE,香港HK,台湾TW 智利CL 巴基斯坦PK 哥斯达黎加CR 亚太APTA	0	最不发达35国LDC35,最不发达4国LDC4,缅甸MM,柬埔寨KH	40	--Rays and skates (Rajidae)
209	0302.8300	--南极犬牙鱼(南极犬牙鱼属)	12	0 1.2 5 7.2 8	东盟ASEAN,新西兰NZ,秘鲁PE,香港HK 智利CL 巴基斯坦PK 哥斯达黎加CR 亚太APTA	0	最不发达35国LDC35,最不发达4国LDC4,缅甸MM,柬埔寨KH	40	--Toothfish (Dissostichus spp.)
210	0302.8400	--尖吻鲈鱼(舌齿鲈属)	12	0 1.2 5 7.2 8	东盟ASEAN,新西兰NZ,秘鲁PE,香港HK,台湾TW 智利CL 巴基斯坦PK 哥斯达黎加CR 亚太APTA	0	最不发达35国LDC35,最不发达4国LDC4,缅甸MM,柬埔寨KH	40	--Seabass (Dicentrarchus spp.)
211	0302.8500	--菱羊鲷(鲷科)	12	0 1.2 5 7.2 8	东盟ASEAN,新西兰NZ,秘鲁PE,香港HK,台湾TW 智利CL 巴基斯坦PK 哥斯达黎加CR 亚太APTA	0	最不发达35国LDC35,最不发达4国LDC4,缅甸MM,柬埔寨KH	40	--Seabream (Sparidae)

序号 No.	税则号列 Tariff Line	货品名称	最惠国税率 MFN(%)	协定税率 Agreement(%)		特惠税率 S.P.(%)		普通税率 Gen.(%)	Article Description
		--其他:							--Other:
212	0302.8910	---带鱼	12	0 1.2 6 7.2 8	东盟ASEAN,新西兰NZ,香港HK 智利CL 秘鲁PE 哥斯达黎加CR 亚太APTA,巴基斯坦PK	0	最不发达35国LDC35,最不发达4国LDC4	40	---Scabber fish (Trichurius)
213	0302.8920	---黄鱼	12	0 1.2 5 6 7.2 8	东盟ASEAN,新西兰NZ,香港HK 智利CL 巴基斯坦PK 秘鲁PE 哥斯达黎加CR 亚太APTA	0	最不发达35国LDC35,最不发达4国LDC4	40	---Yellow croaker (Pseudosicaena)
214	0302.8930	---鲳鱼	12	0 1.2 5 6 7.2 8	东盟ASEAN,新西兰NZ,香港HK 智利CL 巴基斯坦PK 秘鲁PE 哥斯达黎加CR 亚太APTA	0	最不发达35国LDC35,最不发达4国LDC4	40	---Butterfish (Pamus)
215	0302.8940	---鲀	12	0 1.2 5 6 7.2 8	东盟ASEAN,新西兰NZ,香港HK 智利CL 巴基斯坦PK 秘鲁PE 哥斯达黎加CR 亚太APTA	0	最不发达35国LDC35,最不发达4国LDC4,缅甸MM,柬埔寨KH	40	---Puffer fish
216	0302.8990	---其他	12	0 1.2 5 7.2 8	东盟ASEAN,新西兰NZ,秘鲁PE,香港HK,台湾TW 智利CL 巴基斯坦PK 哥斯达黎加CR 亚太APTA	0	最不发达35国LDC35,最不发达4国LDC4,缅甸MM,柬埔寨KH	40	---Other
217	0302.9000	-鱼肝及鱼卵	12	0 6 7.2	东盟ASEAN,智利CL,新西兰NZ,秘鲁PE 巴基斯坦PK 哥斯达黎加CR	0	最不发达35国LDC35,最不发达4国LDC4,柬埔寨KH	50	-Livers and roes
	03.03	**冻鱼，但税号03.04的鱼片及其他鱼肉除外:**							**Fish, frozen, excluding fish fillets and other fish meat of heading No.03.04:**
		-鲑科鱼，但鱼肝及鱼卵除外:							-Salmonidae, excluding livers and roes:

序号 No.	税则号列 Tariff Line	货品名称	最惠国税率 MFN(%)	协定税率 Agreement(%)		特惠税率 S.P.(%)		普通税率 Gen.(%)	Article Description
218	0303.1100	--红大麻哈鱼	10	0 1 5 6 6.7	东盟ASEAN,新西兰NZ 智利CL 巴基斯坦PK,秘鲁PE 哥斯达黎加CR 亚太APTA	0	最不发达35国LDC35,最不发达4国LDC4,柬埔寨KH	40	--Sockeye salmon (red salmon) (Oncorhynchus nerka)
219	0303.1200	--其他大麻哈鱼〔细磷大麻哈鱼、大麻哈鱼（种）、大鳞大麻哈鱼、银大麻哈鱼、马苏大麻哈鱼、玫瑰大麻哈鱼〕	10	0 1 5 6 6.7	东盟ASEAN,新西兰NZ 智利CL 巴基斯坦PK,秘鲁PE 哥斯达黎加CR 亚太APTA	0	最不发达35国LDC35,最不发达4国LDC4,柬埔寨KH	40	--Other Pacific salmon (Oncorhynchus gorbuscha, Oncorhynchus keta, Oncorhynchus tschawytscha, Oncorhynchus kisutch, Oncorhynchus masou and Oncorhynchus rhodurus)
220	0303.1300	--大西洋鲑鱼及多瑙哲罗鱼	10	0 1 5 6	东盟ASEAN,新西兰NZ 智利CL 巴基斯坦PK,秘鲁PE 哥斯达黎加CR	0	最不发达35国LDC35,最不发达4国LDC4	40	--Atlantic salmon (Salmo salar) and Danube salmon (Hucho hucho)
221	0303.1400	--鳟鱼(河鳟、虹鳟、克拉克大麻哈鱼、阿瓜大麻哈鱼、吉雨大麻哈鱼、亚利桑那大麻哈鱼、金腹大麻哈鱼)	12	0 1.2 6 7.2	东盟ASEAN,新西兰NZ 智利CL 巴基斯坦PK,秘鲁PE 哥斯达黎加CR	0	最不发达35国LDC35,最不发达4国LDC4	40	--Trout (Salmo trutta, Oncorhynchus mykiss, Oncorhynchus clarki, Oncorhynchus aguabonita, Oncorhynchus gilae, Oncorhynchus apache and Oncorhynchus chrysogaster)
222	0303.1900	--其他	10	0 5 6 6.7	东盟ASEAN,智利CL,新西兰NZ,秘鲁PE 巴基斯坦PK 哥斯达黎加CR 亚太APTA	0	最不发达35国LDC35,最不发达4国LDC4	40	--Other
		-罗非鱼（口孵非鲫属）、鲶鱼（(鱼芒)鲶属、鲶属、胡鲶属、真鮰属）、鲤科鱼（西鲤、黑鲫、草鱼、鲢属、鲮属、青鱼）、鳗鱼（鳗鲡属）、尼罗河鲈鱼（尼罗尖吻鲈）及黑鱼（鳢属），但鱼肝及鱼卵除外:							-Tilapias (Oreochromis spp.), catfish (Pangasius spp., Silurus spp., Clarias spp., Ictalurus spp.), carp (Cyprinus carpio, Carassius carassius, Ctenopharyngodon idellus, Hypophthalmichthys spp., Cirrhinus spp., Mylopharyngodon piceus), eels (Anguilla spp.), Nile perch (Lates niloticus) and snakeheads (Channa spp.), excluding livers and roes:

序号 No.	税则号列 Tariff Line	货品名称	最惠国税率 MFN(%)	协定税率 Agreement(%)		特惠税率 S.P.(%)		普通税率 Gen.(%)	Article Description
223	0303.2300	--罗非鱼(口孵非鲫属)	10	0 1 5 6	东盟ASEAN,新西兰NZ 智利CL 亚太APTA,巴基斯坦PK,秘鲁PE 哥斯达黎加CR	0	最不发达35国LDC35,最不发达4国LDC4,亚太2国APTA2,缅甸MM,柬埔寨KH	40	--Tilapias (Oreochromis spp.)
224	0303.2400	--鲶鱼((鱼芒)鲶属、鲶属、胡鲶属、真鮰属)	10	0 1 3.8 5 6	东盟ASEAN,新西兰NZ,香港HK,台湾TW 智利CL 秘鲁PE 亚太APTA,巴基斯坦PK 哥斯达黎加CR	0	最不发达35国LDC35,最不发达4国LDC4,亚太2国APTA2,缅甸MM,柬埔寨KH	40	--Catfish (Pangasius spp., Silurus spp., Clarias spp., Ictalurus spp.)
225	0303.2500	--鲤科鱼(西鲤、黑鲫、草鱼、鲢属、鲮属、青鱼)	10	0 1 3.8 5 6	东盟ASEAN,新西兰NZ,香港HK,台湾TW 智利CL 秘鲁PE 亚太APTA,巴基斯坦PK 哥斯达黎加CR	0	最不发达35国LDC35,最不发达4国LDC4,亚太2国APTA2,缅甸MM,柬埔寨KH	40	--Carp (Cyprinus carpio, Carassius carassius, Ctenopharyngodon idellus, Hypophthalmichthys spp., Cirrhinus spp., Mylopharyngodon piceus)
226	0303.2600	--鳗鱼(鳗鲡属)	12	0 1.2 6 7.2 8	东盟ASEAN,新西兰NZ,香港HK 智利CL 秘鲁PE 哥斯达黎加CR 亚太APTA,巴基斯坦PK	0	最不发达35国LDC35,最不发达4国LDC4	40	--Eels (Anguilla spp.)
227	0303.2900	--其他	10	0 1 3.8 5 6	东盟ASEAN,新西兰NZ,香港HK,台湾TW 智利CL 秘鲁PE 亚太APTA,巴基斯坦PK 哥斯达黎加CR	0	最不发达35国LDC35,最不发达4国LDC4,亚太2国APTA2,缅甸MM,柬埔寨KH	40	--Other
		-比目鱼(鲽科、鲆科、舌鳎科、鳎科、菱鲆科、刺鲆科),但鱼肝及鱼卵除外:							-Flatfish (Pleuronectidae, Bothidae, Cynoglossidae, soleidae, Scophthalmidae and itharidae), excluding livers and roes:

序号 No.	税则号列 Tariff Line	货品名称	最惠国税率 MFN(%)	协定税率 Agreement(%)	特惠税率 S.P.(%)	普通税率 Gen.(%)	Article Description
		--庸鲽鱼：					--Halibut (Reinhardtius hippoglossoides, Hippoglossus hippoglossus, Hippog-lossus stenolepis):
228	0303.3110	---格陵兰庸鲽鱼	10 △5	0 东盟ASEAN,智利CL,新西兰NZ,秘鲁PE,香港HK 5 巴基斯坦PK 6 哥斯达黎加CR 6.7 亚太APTA	0 最不发达35国LDC35,最不发达4国LDC4	40	---Greenland halibut
229	0303.3190	---其他	10	0 东盟ASEAN,智利CL,新西兰NZ,秘鲁PE,香港HK 5 巴基斯坦PK 6 哥斯达黎加CR 6.7 亚太APTA	0 最不发达35国LDC35,最不发达4国LDC4	40	---Other
230	0303.3200	--鲽鱼	12 △2	0 东盟ASEAN,智利CL,新西兰NZ,秘鲁PE 7.2 哥斯达黎加CR 8 亚太APTA,巴基斯坦PK	0 最不发达35国LDC35,最不发达4国LDC4	40	--Plaice (Pleuronectes platessa)
231	0303.3300	--鳎鱼	12	0 东盟ASEAN,智利CL,新西兰NZ,秘鲁PE 7.2 哥斯达黎加CR 8 亚太APTA,巴基斯坦PK	0 最不发达35国LDC35,最不发达4国LDC4	40	--Sole (Solea spp.)
232	0303.3400	--大菱鲆（瘤棘鲆）	10	0 东盟ASEAN,新西兰NZ 1 智利CL 5 秘鲁PE 6 哥斯达黎加CR 8 亚太APTA,巴基斯坦PK	0 最不发达35国LDC35,最不发达4国LDC4	40	--Turbots (Psetta maxima, Scophthalmidae)
233	0303.3900	--其他	10	0 东盟ASEAN,新西兰NZ 1 智利CL 5 秘鲁PE 6 哥斯达黎加CR 8 亚太APTA,巴基斯坦PK	0 最不发达35国LDC35,最不发达4国LDC4	40	--Other
		-金枪鱼（金枪鱼属）、鲣鱼或狐鲣（鲣），但鱼肝及鱼卵除外：					-Tunas (of the genus Thunnus), skipjack or stripe-bellied bonito (Euthynnus (Katsuwonus) pelamis), excluding livers and roes:
234	0303.4100	--长鳍金枪鱼	12	0 东盟ASEAN,智利CL,新西兰NZ,秘鲁PE 5 巴基斯坦PK 7.2 哥斯达黎加CR 9 亚太APTA	0 最不发达35国LDC35,最不发达4国LDC4	40	--Albacore or longfinned tunas (Thunnus alalunga)

序号 No.	税则号列 Tariff Line	货品名称	最惠国税率 MFN(%)	协定税率 Agreement(%)		特惠税率 S.P.(%)		普通税率 Gen.(%)	Article Description
235	0303.4200	--黄鳍金枪鱼	12	0 5 7.2 9	东盟ASEAN,智利CL,新西兰NZ,秘鲁PE 巴基斯坦PK 哥斯达黎加CR 亚太APTA	0	最不发达35国LDC35,最不发达4国LDC4	40	--Yellowfin tunas (Thunnus albacares)
236	0303.4300	--鲣鱼或狐鲣	12	0 5 7.2 9	东盟ASEAN,智利CL,新西兰NZ,秘鲁PE 巴基斯坦PK 哥斯达黎加CR 亚太APTA	0	最不发达35国LDC35,最不发达4国LDC4	40	--Skipjack or stripe-bellied bonito
237	0303.4400	--大眼金枪鱼	12	0 6 7.2	东盟ASEAN,智利CL,新西兰NZ,秘鲁PE,香港HK 巴基斯坦PK 哥斯达黎加CR	0	最不发达35国LDC35,最不发达4国LDC4,缅甸MM,柬埔寨KH	40	--Bigeye tunas (Thunnus obesus)
		--大西洋及太平洋蓝鳍金枪鱼：							--Atlantic and Pacific bluefin tunas (Thunnus thynnus, Thunnus orientalis):
238	0303.4510	---大西洋蓝鳍金枪鱼	12	0 6 7.2	东盟ASEAN,智利CL,新西兰NZ,秘鲁PE 巴基斯坦PK 哥斯达黎加CR	0	最不发达35国LDC35,最不发达4国LDC4,缅甸MM,柬埔寨KH	40	---Atlantic bluefin tunas (Thunnus thynnus)
239	0303.4520	---太平洋蓝鳍金枪鱼	12	0 1.2 5 7.2 9	东盟ASEAN,新西兰NZ,秘鲁PE 智利CL 巴基斯坦PK 哥斯达黎加CR 亚太APTA	0	最不发达35国LDC35,最不发达4国LDC4,缅甸MM,柬埔寨KH	40	---Pacific bluefin tunas (Thunnus orientalis)
240	0303.4600	--南方蓝鳍金枪鱼	12	0 6 7.2	东盟ASEAN,智利CL,新西兰NZ,秘鲁PE 巴基斯坦PK 哥斯达黎加CR	0	最不发达35国LDC35,最不发达4国LDC4,缅甸MM,柬埔寨KH	40	--Southern bluefin tunas (Thunnus maccoyii)

序号 No.	税则号列 Tariff Line	货品名称	最惠国税率 MFN(%)	协定税率 Agreement(%)	特惠税率 S.P.(%)	普通税率 Gen.(%)	Article Description
241	0303.4900	--其他	12	0 东盟ASEAN,新西兰NZ,秘鲁PE 1.2 智利CL 5 巴基斯坦PK 7.2 哥斯达黎加CR 9 亚太APTA	0 最不发达35国LDC35,最不发达4国LDC4,缅甸MM,柬埔寨KH	40	--Other
		-鲱鱼（大西洋鲱鱼、太平洋鲱鱼）、沙丁鱼（沙丁鱼、沙瑙鱼属）、小沙丁鱼属、黍鲱或西鲱、鲭鱼〔大西洋鲭、澳洲鲭（鲐）、日本鲭（鲐）〕、对称竹荚鱼、新西兰竹荚鱼及竹荚鱼(竹荚鱼属)、军曹鱼及剑鱼，但鱼肝及鱼卵除外:					-Herrings (Clupea harengus, Clupea pallasii), sardines (Sardina pilchardus, Sardinops spp.), sardinella (Sardinella spp.), brisling or sprats (Sprattus sprattus), mackerel (Scomber scombrus, Scomber australasicus, Scomber japonicus), jack and horse mackerel (Trachurus spp.), cobia (Rachycentron canadum) and swordfish (Xiphias gladius), excluding livers and roes:
242	0303.5100	--鲱鱼（大西洋鲱鱼、太平洋鲱鱼）	10 △2	0 东盟ASEAN,智利CL,新西兰NZ,秘鲁PE 5 巴基斯坦PK 6 哥斯达黎加CR 6.7 亚太APTA	0 最不发达35国LDC35,最不发达4国LDC4	40	--Herrings (Clupea harengus, Clupea pallasii)
243	0303.5300	--沙丁鱼(沙丁鱼、沙瑙鱼属)、小沙丁鱼属、黍鲱或西鲱	12	0 东盟ASEAN,新西兰NZ 1.2 智利CL 5 巴基斯坦PK 6 秘鲁PE 7.2 哥斯达黎加CR 8 亚太APTA	0 最不发达35国LDC35,最不发达4国LDC4	40	--Sardines (Sardina pilchardus, Sardinops spp.), sardinella (Sardinella spp.), brisling or sprats (Sprattus sprattus)
244	0303.5400	--鲭鱼〔大西洋鲭、澳洲鲭（鲐）、日本鲭（鲐）〕	10	0 东盟ASEAN,新西兰NZ 1 智利CL 3.8 秘鲁PE 6 哥斯达黎加CR 6.7 亚太APTA,巴基斯坦PK	0 最不发达35国LDC35,最不发达4国LDC4	40	--Mackerel (Scomber scombrus, Scomber australasicus, Scomber japonicus)
245	0303.5500	--对称竹荚鱼、新西兰竹荚鱼及竹荚鱼(竹荚鱼属)	10	0 东盟ASEAN,新西兰NZ,香港HK,台湾TW 1 智利CL 3.8 秘鲁PE 5 亚太APTA,巴基斯坦PK 6 哥斯达黎加CR	0 最不发达35国LDC35,最不发达4国LDC4,亚太2国APTA2,缅甸MM,柬埔寨KH	40	--Jack and horse mackerel (Trachurus spp.)

序号 No.	税则号列 Tariff Line	货品名称	最惠国税率 MFN(%)	协定税率 Agreement(%)		特惠税率 S.P.(%)		普通税率 Gen.(%)	Article Description
246	0303.5600	--军曹鱼	10	0 1 3.8 5 6	东盟ASEAN,新西兰NZ,香港HK,台湾TW 智利CL 秘鲁PE 亚太APTA,巴基斯坦PK 哥斯达黎加CR	0	最不发达35国LDC35,最不发达4国LDC4,亚太2国APTA2,缅甸MM,柬埔寨KH	40	--Cobia (Rachycentron canadum)
247	0303.5700	--剑鱼	10	0 1 5 6	东盟ASEAN,新西兰NZ,秘鲁PE,香港HK 智利CL 亚太APTA,巴基斯坦PK 哥斯达黎加CR	0	最不发达35国LDC35,最不发达4国LDC4,亚太2国APTA2	40	--Swordfish (Xiphias gladius)
		-犀鳕科、多丝真鳕科、鳕科、长尾鳕科、黑鳕科、无须鳕科、深海鳕科及南极鳕科鱼，但鱼肝及鱼卵除外:							-Fish of the families Bregmacerotidae, Euclichthyidae, Gadidae, Macrouridae, Melanonidae, Merlucciidae, Moridae and Muraenolepididae, excluding livers and roes:
248	0303.6300	--鳕鱼（大西洋鳕鱼、格陵兰鳕鱼、太平洋鳕鱼）	10 △2	0 5 6 6.7	东盟ASEAN,智利CL,新西兰NZ,秘鲁PE 巴基斯坦PK 哥斯达黎加CR 亚太APTA	0	最不发达35国LDC35,最不发达4国LDC4	40	--Cod (Gadus morhua, Gadus ogac, Gadus macrocephalus)
249	0303.6400	--黑线鳕鱼（黑线鳕）	12	0 5 7.2 8	东盟ASEAN,智利CL,新西兰NZ,秘鲁PE 巴基斯坦PK 哥斯达黎加CR 亚太APTA	0	最不发达35国LDC35,最不发达4国LDC4	40	--Haddock (Melanogrammus aeglefinus)
250	0303.6500	--绿青鳕鱼	12	0 5 7.2 8	东盟ASEAN,智利CL,新西兰NZ,秘鲁PE 巴基斯坦PK 哥斯达黎加CR 亚太APTA	0	最不发达35国LDC35,最不发达4国LDC4	40	--Coalfish (Pollachius virens)
251	0303.6600	--狗鳕鱼（无须鳕属、长鳍鳕属）	12	0 1.2 6 7.2	东盟ASEAN,新西兰NZ 智利CL 巴基斯坦PK,秘鲁PE 哥斯达黎加CR	0	最不发达35国LDC35,最不发达4国LDC4	40	--Hake (Merluccius spp., Urophycis spp.)

序号 No.	税则号列 Tariff Line	货品名称	最惠国税率 MFN(%)	协定税率 Agreement(%)	特惠税率 S.P.(%)	普通税率 Gen.(%)	Article Description
252	0303.6700	--狭鳕鱼	10	0 东盟ASEAN,新西兰NZ,香港HK,台湾TW 1 智利CL 3.8 秘鲁PE 5 亚太APTA,巴基斯坦PK 6 哥斯达黎加CR	0 最不发达35国LDC35,最不发达4国LDC4,亚太2国APTA2,缅甸MM,柬埔寨KH	40	--Alaska Pollack (Theraga chalcogramma)
253	0303.6800	--蓝鳕鱼（小鳍鳕、南蓝鳕）	10	0 东盟ASEAN,新西兰NZ,香港HK,台湾TW 1 智利CL 3.8 秘鲁PE 5 亚太APTA,巴基斯坦PK 6 哥斯达黎加CR	0 最不发达35国LDC35,最不发达4国LDC4,亚太2国APTA2,缅甸MM,柬埔寨KH	40	--Blue whitings (Micromesistius poutassou, Micromesistius australis)
254	0303.6900	--其他	10	0 东盟ASEAN,新西兰NZ,香港HK,台湾TW 1 智利CL 3.8 秘鲁PE 5 亚太APTA,巴基斯坦PK 6 哥斯达黎加CR	0 最不发达35国LDC35,最不发达4国LDC4,亚太2国APTA2,缅甸MM,柬埔寨KH	40	--Other
		-其他鱼，但鱼肝及鱼卵除外：					-Other fish, excluding livers and roes:
255	0303.8100	--角鲨及其他鲨鱼	12	0 东盟ASEAN,新西兰NZ 1.2 智利CL 6 秘鲁PE 7.2 哥斯达黎加CR 9 亚太APTA,巴基斯坦PK	0 最不发达35国LDC35,最不发达4国LDC4	40	--Dogfish and other sharks
256	0303.8200	--魟鱼及鳐鱼（鳐科）	10	0 东盟ASEAN,新西兰NZ,香港HK,台湾TW 1 智利CL 3.8 秘鲁PE 5 亚太APTA,巴基斯坦PK 6 哥斯达黎加CR	0 最不发达35国LDC35,最不发达4国LDC4,亚太2国APTA2,缅甸MM,柬埔寨KH	40	--Rays and skates (Rajidae)

序号 No.	税则号列 Tariff Line	货品名称	最惠国税率 MFN(%)	协定税率 Agreement(%)		特惠税率 S.P.(%)		普通税率 Gen.(%)	Article Description
257	0303.8300	--南极犬牙鱼（南极犬牙鱼属）	10	0 1 5 6	东盟ASEAN,新西兰NZ,秘鲁PE,香港HK 智利CL 亚太APTA,巴基斯坦PK 哥斯达黎加CR	0	最不发达35国LDC35,最不发达4国LDC4,亚太2国APTA2,缅甸MM,柬埔寨KH	40	--Toothfish (Dissostichus spp.)
258	0303.8400	--尖吻鲈鱼(舌齿鲈属)	12	0 5 7.2 8	东盟ASEAN,智利CL,新西兰NZ,秘鲁PE,香港HK 巴基斯坦PK 哥斯达黎加CR 亚太APTA	0	最不发达35国LDC35,最不发达4国LDC4	40	--Seabass (Dicentrarchus spp.)
		--其他:							--Other:
259	0303.8910	---带鱼	10	0 1 5 6	东盟ASEAN,新西兰NZ,香港HK 智利CL 亚太APTA,巴基斯坦PK,秘鲁PE 哥斯达黎加CR	0	最不发达35国LDC35,最不发达4国LDC4,亚太2国APTA2,缅甸MM,柬埔寨KH	40	---Scabber fish (Trichurius)
260	0303.8920	---黄鱼	10	0 1 5 6	东盟ASEAN,新西兰NZ,香港HK 智利CL 亚太APTA,巴基斯坦PK,秘鲁PE 哥斯达黎加CR	0	最不发达35国LDC35,最不发达4国LDC4,亚太2国APTA2,缅甸MM,柬埔寨KH	40	---Yellow croaker (Pseudosicaena)
261	0303.8930	---鲳鱼	10	0 1 5 6	东盟ASEAN,新西兰NZ,香港HK 智利CL 亚太APTA,巴基斯坦PK,秘鲁PE 哥斯达黎加CR	0	最不发达35国LDC35,最不发达4国LDC4,亚太2国APTA2,缅甸MM,柬埔寨KH	40	---Butterfish (Pamus)

序号 No.	税则号列 Tariff Line	货品名称	最惠国税率 MFN(%)	协定税率 Agreement(%)	特惠税率 S.P.(%)	普通税率 Gen.(%)	Article Description
262	0303.8990	---其他	10	0 东盟ASEAN,新西兰NZ,香港HK,台湾TW 1 智利CL 3.8 秘鲁PE 5 亚太APTA,巴基斯坦PK 6 哥斯达黎加CR	0 最不发达35国LDC35,最不发达4国LDC4,亚太2国APTA2,缅甸MM,柬埔寨KH	40	---Other
263	0303.9000	-鱼肝及鱼卵	10	0 东盟ASEAN,新西兰NZ 1 智利CL 5 巴基斯坦PK 6 哥斯达黎加CR 9 亚太APTA	0 最不发达35国LDC35,最不发达4国LDC4	50	-Livers and roes
	03.04	**鲜、冷、冻鱼片及其他鱼肉（不论是否绞碎）：**					**Fish fillets and other fish meat (whether or not minced), fresh, chilled or frozen:**
		-鲜或冷的罗非鱼（口孵非鲫属）、鲶鱼（(鱼芒)鲶属、鲶属、胡鲶属、真鮰属）、鲤科鱼（西鲤、黑鲫、草鱼、鲢属、鲮属、青鱼）、鳗鱼（鳗鲡属）、尼罗河鲈鱼（尼罗尖吻鲈）及黑鱼（鳢属）的鱼片：					-Fresh or chilled fillets of tilapias (Oreochromis spp.), catfish (Pangasius spp., Silurus spp., Clarias spp., Ictalurus spp.), carp (Cyprinus carpio, Carassius carassius, Ctenopharyngodon idellus, Hypophthalmichthys spp., Cirrhinus spp., Mylopharyngodon piceus), eels (Anguilla spp.), Nile perch (Lates niloticus) and snakeheads (Channa spp.):
264	0304.3100	--罗非鱼（口孵非鲫属）	12	0 东盟ASEAN,新西兰NZ,香港HK 1.2 智利CL 2.4 哥斯达黎加CR 5 巴基斯坦PK 6 秘鲁PE 9 亚太APTA	0 最不发达35国LDC35,最不发达4国LDC4,缅甸MM	70	--Tilapias (Oreochromis spp.)
265	0304.3200	--鲶鱼（(鱼芒)鲶属、鲶属、胡鲶属、真鮰属）	12	0 东盟ASEAN,新西兰NZ,香港HK 1.2 智利CL 2.4 哥斯达黎加CR 5 巴基斯坦PK 6 秘鲁PE 9 亚太APTA	0 最不发达35国LDC35,最不发达4国LDC4,缅甸MM	70	--Catfish (Pangasius spp., Silurus spp., Clarias spp., Ictalurus spp.)

序号 No.	税则号列 Tariff Line	货品名称	最惠国税率 MFN(%)	协定税率 Agreement(%)		特惠税率 S.P.(%)		普通税率 Gen.(%)	Article Description
266	0304.3300	--尼罗河鲈鱼（尼罗尖吻鲈）	12	0 1.2 2.4 5 6 9	东盟ASEAN,新西兰NZ,香港HK 智利CL 哥斯达黎加CR 巴基斯坦PK 秘鲁PE 亚太APTA	0	最不发达35国LDC35,最不发达4国LDC4,缅甸MM	70	--Nile Perch (Lates niloticus)
267	0304.3900	--其他	12	0 1.2 2.4 5 6 9	东盟ASEAN,新西兰NZ,香港HK 智利CL 哥斯达黎加CR 巴基斯坦PK 秘鲁PE 亚太APTA	0	最不发达35国LDC35,最不发达4国LDC4,缅甸MM	70	--Other
		-鲜或冷的其他鱼片:							-Fresh or chilled fillets of other fish:
268	0304.4100	--大麻哈鱼〔红大麻哈鱼、细磷大麻哈鱼、大麻哈鱼(种)、大鳞大麻哈鱼、银大麻哈鱼、马苏大麻哈鱼、玫瑰大麻哈鱼〕、大西洋鲑鱼及多瑙哲罗鱼	12	0 1.2 2.4 5 6 9	东盟ASEAN,新西兰NZ,香港HK 智利CL 哥斯达黎加CR 巴基斯坦PK 秘鲁PE 亚太APTA	0	最不发达35国LDC35,最不发达4国LDC4,缅甸MM	70	--Pacific salmon (Oncorhynchus nerka, Oncorhynchus gorbuscha, Oncorhynchus keta, Oncorhynchus tschawytscha, Oncorhynchus kisutch, Oncorhynchus masou and Oncorhynchus rhodurus), Atlantic salmon (Salmo salar) and Danube salmon (Hucho hucho)
269	0304.4200	--鳟鱼(河鳟、虹鳟、克拉克大麻哈鱼、阿瓜大麻哈鱼、吉雨大麻哈鱼、亚利桑那大麻哈鱼、金腹大麻哈鱼)	12	0 1.2 2.4 5 6 9	东盟ASEAN,新西兰NZ,香港HK 智利CL 哥斯达黎加CR 巴基斯坦PK 秘鲁PE 亚太APTA	0	最不发达35国LDC35,最不发达4国LDC4,缅甸MM	70	--Trout (Salmo trutta, Oncorhynchus mykiss, Oncorhynchus clarki, Oncorhynchus aguabonita, Oncorhynchus gilae, Oncorhynchus apache and Oncorhynchus chrysogaster)
270	0304.4300	--比目鱼（鲽科、鲆科、舌鳎科、鳎科、菱鲆科、刺鲆科）	12	0 1.2 2.4 5 6 9	东盟ASEAN,新西兰NZ,香港HK 智利CL 哥斯达黎加CR 巴基斯坦PK 秘鲁PE 亚太APTA	0	最不发达35国LDC35,最不发达4国LDC4,缅甸MM	70	--Flat fish (Pleuronectidae, Bothidae, Cynoglossidae, Soleidae, Scophthalmidae and Citharidae)
271	0304.4400	--犀鳕科、多丝真鳕科、鳕科、长尾鳕科、黑鳕科、无须鳕科、深海鳕科及南极鳕科鱼	12	0 1.2 2.4 5 6 9	东盟ASEAN,新西兰NZ,香港HK 智利CL 哥斯达黎加CR 巴基斯坦PK 秘鲁PE 亚太APTA	0	最不发达35国LDC35,最不发达4国LDC4,缅甸MM	70	--Fish of the families Bregmacerotidae, Euclichthyidae, Gadidae, Macrouridae, Melanonidae, Merlucciidae, Moridae and Muraenolepididae
272	0304.4500	--剑鱼	12	0 1.2 2.4 5 9	东盟ASEAN,新西兰NZ,秘鲁PE,香港HK 智利CL 哥斯达黎加CR 巴基斯坦PK 亚太APTA	0	最不发达35国LDC35,最不发达4国LDC4,缅甸MM	70	--Swordfish (Xiphias gladius)

序号 No.	税则号列 Tariff Line	货品名称	最惠国税率 MFN(%)	协定税率 Agreement(%)	特惠税率 S.P.(%)	普通税率 Gen.(%)	Article Description
273	0304.4600	--南极犬牙鱼(南极犬牙鱼属)	12	0 东盟ASEAN,新西兰NZ,秘鲁PE,香港HK 1.2 智利CL 2.4 哥斯达黎加CR 5 巴基斯坦PK 9 亚太APTA	0 最不发达35国LDC35,最不发达4国LDC4,缅甸MM	70	--Toothfish (Dissostichus spp.)
274	0304.4900	--其他	12	0 东盟ASEAN,新西兰NZ,香港HK 1.2 智利CL 2.4 哥斯达黎加CR 5 巴基斯坦PK 6 秘鲁PE 9 亚太APTA	0 最不发达35国LDC35,最不发达4国LDC4,缅甸MM	70	--Other
		-其他，鲜或冷的:					-Other, fresh or chilled:
275	0304.5100	--罗非鱼(口孵非鲫属)、鲶鱼((鱼芒)鲶属、鲶属、胡鲶属、真鮰属)、鲤科鱼(西鲤、黑鲫、草鱼、鲢属、鲮属、青鱼)、鳗鱼(鳗鲡属)、尼罗河鲈鱼(尼罗尖吻鲈)及黑鱼（鳢属)	12	0 东盟ASEAN,新西兰NZ,香港HK 1.2 智利CL 2.4 哥斯达黎加CR 5 巴基斯坦PK 6 秘鲁PE 9 亚太APTA	0 最不发达35国LDC35,最不发达4国LDC4,缅甸MM	70	--Tilapias (Oreochromis spp.), catfish (Pangasius spp., Silurus spp., Clarias spp., Ictalurus spp.), carp (Cyprinus carpio, Carassius carassius, Ctenopharyngodon idellus, Hypophthalmichthys spp., Cirrhinus spp., Mylopharyngodon piceus), eels (Anguilla spp.), Nile perch (Lates niloticus) and snakeheads (Channa spp.)
276	0304.5200	--鲑科鱼	12	0 东盟ASEAN,新西兰NZ,香港HK 1.2 智利CL 2.4 哥斯达黎加CR 5 巴基斯坦PK 6 秘鲁PE 9 亚太APTA	0 最不发达35国LDC35,最不发达4国LDC4,缅甸MM	70	--Salmonidae
277	0304.5300	--犀鳕科、多丝真鳕科、鳕科、长尾鳕科、黑鳕科、无须鳕科、深海鳕科及南极鳕科鱼	12	0 东盟ASEAN,新西兰NZ,香港HK 1.2 智利CL 2.4 哥斯达黎加CR 5 巴基斯坦PK 6 秘鲁PE 9 亚太APTA	0 最不发达35国LDC35,最不发达4国LDC4,缅甸MM	70	--Fish of the families Bregmacerotidae, Euclichthyidae, Gadidae, Macrouridae, Melanonidae, Merlucciidae, Moridae and Muraenolepididae
278	0304.5400	--剑鱼	12	0 东盟ASEAN,新西兰NZ,秘鲁PE,香港HK 1.2 智利CL 2.4 哥斯达黎加CR 5 巴基斯坦PK 9 亚太APTA	0 最不发达35国LDC35,最不发达4国LDC4,缅甸MM	70	--Swordfish (Xiphias gladius)

序号 No.	税则号列 Tariff Line	货品名称	最惠国税率 MFN(%)	协定税率 Agreement(%)	特惠税率 S.P.(%)	普通税率 Gen.(%)	Article Description
279	0304.5500	--南极犬牙鱼（南极犬牙鱼属）	12	0 东盟ASEAN,新西兰NZ,秘鲁PE,香港HK 1.2 智利CL 2.4 哥斯达黎加CR 5 巴基斯坦PK 9 亚太APTA	0 最不发达35国LDC35,最不发达4国LDC4,缅甸MM	70	--Toothfish (Dissostichus spp.)
280	0304.5900	--其他	12	0 东盟ASEAN,新西兰NZ,香港HK 1.2 智利CL 2.4 哥斯达黎加CR 5 巴基斯坦PK 6 秘鲁PE 9 亚太APTA	0 最不发达35国LDC35,最不发达4国LDC4,缅甸MM	70	--Other
		-冻的罗非鱼（口孵非鲫属）、鲶鱼（(鱼芒)鲶属、鲶属、胡鲶属、真鮰属）、鲤科鱼（西鲤、黑鲫、草鱼、鲢属、鲮属、青鱼）、鳗鱼（鳗鲡属）、尼罗河鲈鱼（尼罗尖吻鲈）及黑鱼（鳢属）的鱼片：					-Frozen fillets of tilapias (Oreochromis spp.), catfish (Pangasius spp., Silurus spp., Clarias spp., Ictalurus spp.), carp (Cyprinus carpio, Carassius carassius, Ctenopharyngodon idellus, Hypophthalmichthys spp., Cirrhinus spp., Mylopharyngodon piceus), eels (Anguilla spp.), Nile perch (Lates niloticus) and snakeheads (Channa spp.):
281	0304.6100	--罗非鱼（口孵非鲫属）	10	0 东盟ASEAN,新西兰NZ,秘鲁PE,哥斯达黎加CR,香港HK 1 智利CL 5 巴基斯坦PK	0 最不发达35国LDC35,最不发达4国LDC4,缅甸MM,柬埔寨KH	70	--Tilapias (Oreochromis spp.)
		--鲶鱼（(鱼芒)鲶属、鲶属、胡鲶属、真鮰属）：					--Catfish (Pangasius spp., Silurus spp., Clarias spp., Ictalurus spp.):
		---叉尾鮰鱼（真鮰属）：					---Of Ictalurus spp.:
282	0304.6211	----斑点叉尾鮰鱼	10	0 东盟ASEAN,新西兰NZ,秘鲁PE,哥斯达黎加CR,香港HK 1 智利CL 5 巴基斯坦PK	0 最不发达35国LDC35,最不发达4国LDC4	70	----Channel catfish (Ictalurus punctatus)
283	0304.6219	----其他	10	0 东盟ASEAN,新西兰NZ,秘鲁PE,哥斯达黎加CR,香港HK 1 智利CL 5 巴基斯坦PK	0 最不发达35国LDC35,最不发达4国LDC4	70	----Other

序号 No.	税则号列 Tariff Line	货品名称	最惠国税率 MFN(%)	协定税率 Agreement(%)		特惠税率 S.P.(%)		普通税率 Gen.(%)	Article Description
284	0304.6290	---其他	10	0 1 3.8 5	东盟ASEAN,新西兰NZ,哥斯达黎加CR,香港HK,台湾TW 智利CL 秘鲁PE 巴基斯坦PK	0	最不发达35国LDC35,最不发达4国LDC4,缅甸MM,柬埔寨KH	70	---Other
285	0304.6300	--尼罗河鲈鱼（尼罗尖吻鲈）	10	0 1 3.8 5	东盟ASEAN,新西兰NZ,哥斯达黎加CR,香港HK,台湾TW 智利CL 秘鲁PE 巴基斯坦PK	0	最不发达35国LDC35,最不发达4国LDC4,缅甸MM,柬埔寨KH	70	--Nile Perch (Lates niloticus)
286	0304.6900	--其他	10	0 1 3.8 5	东盟ASEAN,新西兰NZ,哥斯达黎加CR,香港HK,台湾TW 智利CL 秘鲁PE 巴基斯坦PK	0	最不发达35国LDC35,最不发达4国LDC4,缅甸MM,柬埔寨KH	70	--Other
		-冻的犀鳕科、多丝真鳕科、鳕科、长尾鳕科、黑鳕科、无须鳕科、深海鳕科及南极鳕科鱼的鱼片：							-Frozen fillets of fish of the families Bregmacerotidae, Euclichthyidae, Gadidae, Macrouridae, Melanonidae, Merlucciidae, Moridae and Muraenolepididae:
287	0304.7100	--鳕鱼（大西洋鳕鱼、格陵兰鳕鱼、太平洋鳕鱼）	10	0 1 3.8 5	东盟ASEAN,新西兰NZ,哥斯达黎加CR,香港HK,台湾TW 智利CL 秘鲁PE 巴基斯坦PK	0	最不发达35国LDC35,最不发达4国LDC4,缅甸MM,柬埔寨KH	70	--Cod (Gadus morhua, Gadus ogac, Gadus macrocephalus)
288	0304.7200	--黑线鳕鱼（黑线鳕）	10	0 1 3.8 5	东盟ASEAN,新西兰NZ,哥斯达黎加CR,香港HK,台湾TW 智利CL 秘鲁PE 巴基斯坦PK	0	最不发达35国LDC35,最不发达4国LDC4,缅甸MM,柬埔寨KH	70	--Haddock (Melanogrammus aeglefinus)

序号 No.	税则号列 Tariff Line	货品名称	最惠国税率 MFN(%)	协定税率 Agreement(%)		特惠税率 S.P.(%)		普通税率 Gen.(%)	Article Description
289	0304.7300	--绿青鳕鱼	10	0 1 3.8 5	东盟ASEAN,新西兰NZ,哥斯达黎加CR,香港HK,台湾TW 智利CL 秘鲁PE 巴基斯坦PK	0	最不发达35国LDC35,最不发达4国LDC4,缅甸MM,柬埔寨KH	70	--Coalfish (Pollachius virens)
290	0304.7400	--狗鳕鱼(无须鳕属、长鳍鳕属)	10	0 1 3.8 5	东盟ASEAN,新西兰NZ,哥斯达黎加CR,香港HK,台湾TW 智利CL 秘鲁PE 巴基斯坦PK	0	最不发达35国LDC35,最不发达4国LDC4,缅甸MM,柬埔寨KH	70	--Hake (Merluccius spp., Urophycis spp.)
291	0304.7500	--狭鳕鱼	10	0 1 3.8 5	东盟ASEAN,新西兰NZ,哥斯达黎加CR,香港HK,台湾TW 智利CL 秘鲁PE 巴基斯坦PK	0	最不发达35国LDC35,最不发达4国LDC4,缅甸MM,柬埔寨KH	70	--Alaska Pollack (Theraga chalcogramma)
292	0304.7900	--其他	10	0 1 3.8 5	东盟ASEAN,新西兰NZ,哥斯达黎加CR,香港HK,台湾TW 智利CL 秘鲁PE 巴基斯坦PK	0	最不发达35国LDC35,最不发达4国LDC4,缅甸MM,柬埔寨KH	70	--Other
		-其他冻鱼片:							-Frozen fillets of other fish:
293	0304.8100	--大麻哈鱼〔红大麻哈鱼、细磷大麻哈鱼、大麻哈鱼(种)、大鳞大麻哈鱼、银大麻哈鱼、马苏大麻哈鱼、玫瑰大麻哈鱼〕、大西洋鲑鱼及多瑙哲罗鱼	10	0 1 3.8 5	东盟ASEAN,新西兰NZ,哥斯达黎加CR,香港HK,台湾TW 智利CL 秘鲁PE 巴基斯坦PK	0	最不发达35国LDC35,最不发达4国LDC4,缅甸MM,柬埔寨KH	70	--Pacific salmon (Oncorhynchus nerka, Oncorhynchus gorbuscha, Oncorhynchus keta, Oncorhynchus tschawytscha, Oncorhynchus kisutch, Oncorhynchus masou and Oncorhynchus rhodurus), Atlantic salmon (Salmo salar) and Danube salmon (Hucho hucho)
294	0304.8200	--鳟鱼(河鳟、虹鳟、克拉克大麻哈鱼、阿瓜大麻哈鱼、吉雨大麻哈鱼、亚利桑那大麻哈鱼、金腹大麻哈鱼)	10	0 1 3.8 5	东盟ASEAN,新西兰NZ,哥斯达黎加CR,香港HK,台湾TW 智利CL 秘鲁PE 巴基斯坦PK	0	最不发达35国LDC35,最不发达4国LDC4,缅甸MM,柬埔寨KH	70	--Trout (Salmo trutta, Oncorhynchus mykiss, Oncorhynchus clarki, Oncorhynchus aguabonita, Oncorhynchus gilae, Oncorhynchus apache and Oncorhynchus chrysogaster)

序号 No.	税则号列 Tariff Line	货品名称	最惠国税率 MFN(%)	协定税率 Agreement(%)	特惠税率 S.P.(%)	普通税率 Gen.(%)	Article Description
295	0304.8300	--比目鱼（鲽科、鲆科、舌鳎科、鳎科、菱鲆科、刺鲆科）	10	0 东盟ASEAN,新西兰NZ,哥斯达黎加CR,香港HK,台湾TW 1 智利CL 3.8 秘鲁PE 5 巴基斯坦PK	0 最不发达35国LDC35,最不发达4国LDC4,缅甸MM,柬埔寨KH	70	--Flat fish (Pleuronectidae, Bothidae, Cynoglossidae, Soleidae, Scophthalmidae and Citharidae)
296	0304.8400	--剑鱼	10	0 东盟ASEAN,新西兰NZ,秘鲁PE,哥斯达黎加CR,香港HK 1 智利CL 5 巴基斯坦PK	0 最不发达35国LDC35,最不发达4国LDC4,缅甸MM,柬埔寨KH	70	--Swordfish (Xiphias gladius)
297	0304.8500	--南极犬牙鱼(南极犬牙鱼属)	10	0 东盟ASEAN,新西兰NZ,秘鲁PE,哥斯达黎加CR,香港HK 1 智利CL 5 巴基斯坦PK	0 最不发达35国LDC35,最不发达4国LDC4,缅甸MM,柬埔寨KH	70	--Toothfish (Dissostichus spp.)
298	0304.8600	--鲱鱼（大西洋鲱鱼、太平洋鲱鱼）	10	0 东盟ASEAN,新西兰NZ,哥斯达黎加CR,香港HK,台湾TW 1 智利CL 3.8 秘鲁PE 5 巴基斯坦PK	0 最不发达35国LDC35,最不发达4国LDC4,缅甸MM,柬埔寨KH	70	--Herrings (Clupea harengus, Clupea pallasii)
299	0304.8700	--金枪鱼(金枪鱼属)、鲣鱼或狐鲣(鲣)	10	0 东盟ASEAN,新西兰NZ,哥斯达黎加CR,香港HK,台湾TW 1 智利CL 3.8 秘鲁PE 5 巴基斯坦PK	0 最不发达35国LDC35,最不发达4国LDC4,缅甸MM,柬埔寨KH	70	--Tunas (of the genus Thunnus), skipjack or stripe-bellied bonito (Euthynnus (Katsuwonus) pelamis)
300	0304.8900	--其他	10	0 东盟ASEAN,新西兰NZ,哥斯达黎加CR,香港HK,台湾TW 1 智利CL 3.8 秘鲁PE 5 巴基斯坦PK	0 最不发达35国LDC35,最不发达4国LDC4,缅甸MM,柬埔寨KH	70	--Other

序号 No.	税则号列 Tariff Line	货品名称	最惠国税率 MFN(%)	协定税率 Agreement(%)		特惠税率 S.P.(%)		普通税率 Gen.(%)	Article Description
		-其他，冻的：							-Other, frozen:
301	0304.9100	--剑鱼	10	0 1 5	东盟ASEAN,新西兰NZ,秘鲁PE,哥斯达黎加CR 智利CL 巴基斯坦PK	0	最不发达35国LDC35,最不发达4国LDC4,亚太2国APTA2,缅甸MM	70	--Swordfish (Xiphias gladius)
302	0304.9200	--南极犬牙鱼(南极犬牙鱼属)	10	0 1 5	东盟ASEAN,新西兰NZ,秘鲁PE,哥斯达黎加CR 智利CL 巴基斯坦PK	0	最不发达35国LDC35,最不发达4国LDC4,亚太2国APTA2,缅甸MM	70	--Toothfish (Dissostichus spp.)
303	0304.9300	--罗非鱼（口孵非鲫属）、鲶鱼（(鱼芒)鲶属、鲶属、胡鲶属、真鮰属）、鲤科鱼（西鲤、黑鲫、草鱼、鲢属、鲮属、青鱼）、鳗鱼（鳗鲡属）、尼罗河鲈鱼（尼罗尖吻鲈）及黑鱼（鳢属）	10	0 1 5	东盟ASEAN,新西兰NZ,秘鲁PE,哥斯达黎加CR 智利CL 巴基斯坦PK	0	最不发达35国LDC35,最不发达4国LDC4,亚太2国APTA2,缅甸MM	70	--Tilapias (Oreochromis spp.), catfish (Pangasius spp., Silurus spp., Clarias spp., ctalurus spp.), carp (Cyprinus carpio, Carassius carassius, Ctenopharyngodon idellus, Hypophthalmichthys spp., Cirrhinus spp., Mylopharyngodon piceus), eels (Anguilla spp.), Nile perch (Lates niloticus) and snakeheads (Channa spp.)
304	0304.9400	--狭鳕鱼	10	0 1 5	东盟ASEAN,新西兰NZ,秘鲁PE,哥斯达黎加CR 智利CL 巴基斯坦PK	0	最不发达35国LDC35,最不发达4国LDC4,亚太2国APTA2,缅甸MM	70	--Alaska Pollack (Theraga chalcogramma)
305	0304.9500	--犀鳕科、多丝真鳕科、鳕科、长尾鳕科、黑鳕科、无须鳕科、深海鳕科及南极鳕科鱼，狭鳕鱼除外	10	0 1 5	东盟ASEAN,新西兰NZ,秘鲁PE,哥斯达黎加CR 智利CL 巴基斯坦PK	0	最不发达35国LDC35,最不发达4国LDC4,亚太2国APTA2,缅甸MM	70	--Fish of the families Bregmacerotidae, Euclichthyidae, Gadidae, Macrouridae, Melanonidae, Merlucciidae, Moridae and Muraenolepididae, other than Alaska Pollack (Theraga halcogramma)

序号 No.	税则号列 Tariff Line	货品名称	最惠国税率 MFN(%)	协定税率 Agreement(%)	特惠税率 S.P.(%)	普通税率 Gen.(%)	Article Description
306	0304.9900	--其他	10	0 东盟ASEAN,新西兰NZ,秘鲁PE,哥斯达黎加CR 1 智利CL 5 巴基斯坦PK	0 最不发达35国LDC35,最不发达4国LDC4,亚太2国APTA2,缅甸MM	70	--Other
	03.05	**干、盐腌或盐渍的鱼；熏鱼，不论在熏制前或熏制过程中是否烹煮；适合供人食用的鱼的细粉、粗粉及团粒：**					**Fish, dried, salted or in brine; smoked fish, whether or not cooked before or during the smoking process; flours, meals and pellets of fish, fit for human consumption:**
307	0305.1000	-适合供人食用的鱼的细粉、粗粉及团粒	10	0 东盟ASEAN,智利CL,新西兰NZ,秘鲁PE,哥斯达黎加CR,澳门MO 5 巴基斯坦PK	0 最不发达35国LDC35,最不发达4国LDC4	80	-Flours, meals and pellets of fish, fit for human consumption
308	0305.2000	-干、熏、盐腌或盐渍的鱼肝及鱼卵	10	0 东盟ASEAN,新西兰NZ 1 智利CL 5 巴基斯坦PK 6 哥斯达黎加CR	0 最不发达35国LDC35,最不发达4国LDC4	80	-Livers and roes, dried, smoked, salted or in brine
		-干、盐腌或盐渍的鱼片，但熏制的除外：					-Fish fillets, dried, salted or in brine, but not smoked:
309	0305.3100	--罗非鱼（口孵非鲫属）、鲶鱼（(鱼芒)鲶属、鲶属、胡鲶属、真鮰属）、鲤科鱼（西鲤、黑鲫、草鱼、鲢属、鲮属、青鱼）、鳗鱼（鳗鲡属）、尼罗河鲈鱼（尼罗尖吻鲈）及黑鱼（鳢属）	10	0 东盟ASEAN,新西兰NZ,哥斯达黎加CR,香港HK,澳门MO 1 智利CL 5 巴基斯坦PK,秘鲁PE 7.8 亚太APTA	0 最不发达35国LDC35,最不发达4国LDC4,亚太2国APTA2,缅甸MM	80	--Tilapias (Oreochromis spp.), catfish (Pangasius spp., Silurus spp., Clarias spp., Ictalurus spp.), carp (Cyprinus carpio, Carassius carassius, Ctenopharyngodon idellus, Hypophthalmichthys spp., Cirrhinus spp., Mylopharyngodon piceus), eels (Anguilla spp.), Nile perch (Lates niloticus) and snakeheads (Channa spp.)
310	0305.3200	--犀鳕科、多丝真鳕科、鳕科、长尾鳕科、黑鳕科、无须鳕科、深海鳕科及南极鳕科鱼	10	0 东盟ASEAN,新西兰NZ,哥斯达黎加CR,香港HK,澳门MO 1 智利CL 5 巴基斯坦PK,秘鲁PE 7.8 亚太APTA	0 最不发达35国LDC35,最不发达4国LDC4,亚太2国APTA2,缅甸MM	80	--Fish of the families Bregmacerotidae, Euclichthyidae, Gadidae, Macrouridae, Melanonidae, Merlucciidae, Moridae and Muraenolepididae

序号 No.	税则号列 Tariff Line	货品名称	最惠国税率 MFN(%)	协定税率 Agreement(%)		特惠税率 S.P.(%)		普通税率 Gen.(%)	Article Description
311	0305.3900	--其他	10	0 1 5 7.8	东盟ASEAN,新西兰NZ,哥斯达黎加CR,香港HK,澳门MO 智利CL 巴基斯坦PK,秘鲁PE 亚太APTA	0	最不发达35国LDC35,最不发达4国LDC4,亚太2国APTA2,缅甸MM	80	--Other
		-熏鱼，包括鱼片，但食用杂碎除外：							-Smoked fish, including fillets, other than edible fish offal:
		--大麻哈鱼〔红大麻哈鱼、细磷大麻哈鱼、大麻哈鱼（种）、大鳞大麻哈鱼、银大麻哈鱼、马苏大麻哈鱼、玫瑰大麻哈鱼〕、大西洋鲑鱼及多瑙哲罗鱼：							--Pacific salmon (Oncorhynchus nerka, Oncorhynchus gorbuscha, Oncorhynchusketa, Oncorhynchus tschawytscha, Oncorhynchus kisutch, Oncorhynchus masou and Oncorhynchus rhodurus), Atlantic salmon (Salmo salar) and Danube salmon (Hucho hucho):
312	0305.4110	---大西洋鲑鱼	14	0 2.8 7	东盟ASEAN,智利CL,新西兰NZ,秘鲁PE,香港HK 哥斯达黎加CR 巴基斯坦PK	0	最不发达35国LDC35	80	---Atlantic salmon
313	0305.4120	---大马哈鱼及多瑙哲罗鱼	14	0 2.8 11.2	东盟ASEAN,智利CL,新西兰NZ,秘鲁PE 哥斯达黎加CR 巴基斯坦PK	0	最不发达35国LDC35	80	---Pacific salmon and Danube salmon
314	0305.4200	--鲱鱼（大西洋鲱鱼、太平洋鲱鱼）	16	0 3.2 12.8	东盟ASEAN,智利CL,新西兰NZ,秘鲁PE 哥斯达黎加CR 巴基斯坦PK	0	最不发达35国LDC35	80	--Herrings (Clupea harengus, Clupea pallasii)
315	0305.4300	--鳟鱼(河鳟、虹鳟、克拉克大麻哈鱼、阿瓜大麻哈鱼、吉雨大麻哈鱼、亚利桑那大麻哈鱼、金腹大麻哈鱼)	14	0 1.4 2.8 7 11.2	东盟ASEAN,新西兰NZ,澳门MO 智利CL 哥斯达黎加CR 秘鲁PE 巴基斯坦PK	0	最不发达35国LDC35,最不发达4国LDC4,亚太2国APTA2,缅甸MM	80	--Trout (Salmo trutta, Oncorhynchus mykiss, Oncorhynchus clarki, Oncorhynchus aguabonita, Oncorhynchus gilae, Oncorhynchus apache and Oncorhynchus chrysogaster)
316	0305.4400	--罗非鱼（口孵非鲫属）、鲶鱼（(鱼芒)鲶属、鲶属、胡鲶属、真鮰属）、鲤科鱼（西鲤、黑鲫、草鱼、鲢属、鲮属、青鱼）、鳗鱼（鳗鲡属）、尼罗河鲈鱼（尼罗尖吻鲈）及黑鱼（鳢属）	14	0 1.4 2.8 7 11.2	东盟ASEAN,新西兰NZ,澳门MO 智利CL 哥斯达黎加CR 秘鲁PE 巴基斯坦PK	0	最不发达35国LDC35,最不发达4国LDC4,亚太2国APTA2,缅甸MM	80	--Tilapias (Oreochromis spp.), catfish (Pangasius spp., Silurus spp., Clarias spp., Ictalurus spp.), carp (Cyprinus carpio, Carassius carassius, Ctenopharyngodon idellus, Hypophthalmichthys spp., Cirrhinus spp., Mylopharyngodon piceus), eels (Anguilla spp.), Nile perch (Lates niloticus) and snakeheads (Channa spp.)

序号 No.	税则号列 Tariff Line	货品名称	最惠国税率 MFN(%)	协定税率 Agreement(%)		特惠税率 S.P.(%)		普通税率 Gen.(%)	Article Description
317	0305.4900	--其他	14	0 1.4 2.8 7 11.2	东盟ASEAN,新西兰NZ,澳门MO 智利CL 哥斯达黎加CR 秘鲁PE 巴基斯坦PK	0	最不发达35国LDC35,最不发达4国LDC4,亚太2国APTA2,缅甸MM	80	--Other
		-干鱼(不包括食用杂碎),不论是否盐腌,但熏制的除外:							-Dried fish, other than edible fish offal, whether or not salted but not smoked:
318	0305.5100	--鳕鱼(大西洋鳕鱼、格陵兰鳕鱼、太平洋鳕鱼)	16	0 3.2 12.8	东盟ASEAN,智利CL,新西兰NZ,秘鲁PE,澳门MO 哥斯达黎加CR 巴基斯坦PK	0	最不发达35国LDC35	80	--Cod (Gadus morhua, Gadus ogac, Gadus macrocephalus)
		--其他:							--Other:
319	0305.5910	---海龙、海马	2	0	东盟ASEAN,智利CL,巴基斯坦PK,新西兰NZ,秘鲁PE,哥斯达黎加CR	0	最不发达35国LDC35,最不发达4国LDC4,亚太2国APTA2,缅甸MM,柬埔寨KH	20	---Pipefish and hippocampi
320	0305.5990	---其他	16	0 1.6 8 9.6	东盟ASEAN,新西兰NZ,香港HK,澳门MO 智利CL 秘鲁PE 哥斯达黎加CR	0	最不发达35国LDC35,最不发达4国LDC4,亚太2国APTA2,缅甸MM	80	---Other
		-盐腌及盐渍的鱼(不包括食用杂碎),但干或熏制的除外:							-Fish, salted but not dried or smoked and fish in brine, other than edible fish offal:
321	0305.6100	--鲱鱼(大西洋鲱鱼、太平洋鲱鱼)	16	0 3.2 8 11.1	东盟ASEAN,智利CL,新西兰NZ,秘鲁PE 哥斯达黎加CR 巴基斯坦PK 亚太APTA	0	最不发达35国LDC35	80	--Herrings (Clupea harengus, Clupea pallasii)
322	0305.6200	--鳕鱼(大西洋鳕鱼、格陵兰鳕鱼、太平洋鳕鱼)	16	0 3.2 8 12	东盟ASEAN,智利CL,新西兰NZ,秘鲁PE 哥斯达黎加CR 巴基斯坦PK 亚太APTA	0	最不发达35国LDC35,最不发达4国LDC4	80	--Cod (Gadus morhua, Gadus ogac, Gadus Macrocephalus)

序号 No.	税则号列 Tariff Line	货品名称	最惠国税率 MFN(%)	协定税率 Agreement(%)	特惠税率 S.P.(%)	普通税率 Gen.(%)	Article Description
323	0305.6300	--鳀鱼	16	0 东盟ASEAN,新西兰NZ 1.6 智利CL 3.2 哥斯达黎加CR 8 巴基斯坦PK,秘鲁PE 12 亚太APTA	0 最不发达35国LDC35	80	--Anchovies (Engraul is spp.)
324	0305.6400	--罗非鱼（口孵非鲫属）、鲶鱼（(鱼芒)鲶属、鲶属、胡鲶属、真鮰属）、鲤科鱼（西鲤、黑鲫、草鱼、鲢属、鲮属、青鱼）、鳗鱼（鳗鲡属）、尼罗河鲈鱼（尼罗尖吻鲈）及黑鱼（鳢属）	16	0 东盟ASEAN,新西兰NZ,香港HK 1.6 智利CL 3.2 哥斯达黎加CR 8 秘鲁PE 12.8 巴基斯坦PK	0 最不发达35国LDC35,最不发达4国LDC4,亚太2国APTA2,缅甸MM	80	--Tilapias (Oreochromis spp.), catfish (Pangasius spp., Silurus spp., Clarias spp., Ictalurus spp.), carp (Cyprinus carpio, Carassius carassius, Ctenopharyngodon idellus, Hypophthalmichthys spp., Cirrhinus spp., Mylopharyngodon piceus), eels (Anguilla spp.), Nile perch (Lates niloticus) and snakeheads (Channa spp.)
		--其他：					--Other:
325	0305.6910	---带鱼	16	0 东盟ASEAN,新西兰NZ,香港HK 1.6 智利CL 3.2 哥斯达黎加CR 8 秘鲁PE 12.8 巴基斯坦PK	0 最不发达35国LDC35,最不发达4国LDC4,亚太2国APTA2,缅甸MM	80	---Scabber fish (Trichuri us)
326	0305.6920	---黄鱼	16	0 东盟ASEAN,新西兰NZ,香港HK 1.6 智利CL 3.2 哥斯达黎加CR 8 秘鲁PE 12.8 巴基斯坦PK	0 最不发达35国LDC35,最不发达4国LDC4,亚太2国APTA2,缅甸MM	80	---Yellow croaker (Pseudosicaena)
327	0305.6930	---鲳鱼	16	0 东盟ASEAN,新西兰NZ,香港HK 1.6 智利CL 3.2 哥斯达黎加CR 8 秘鲁PE 12.8 巴基斯坦PK	0 最不发达35国LDC35,最不发达4国LDC4,亚太2国APTA2,缅甸MM	80	---Butterfish (Pampus)
328	0305.6990	---其他	16	0 东盟ASEAN,新西兰NZ,香港HK 1.6 智利CL 3.2 哥斯达黎加CR 8 秘鲁PE 12.8 巴基斯坦PK	0 最不发达35国LDC35,最不发达4国LDC4,亚太2国APTA2,缅甸MM	80	---Other

序号 No.	税则号列 Tariff Line	货品名称	最惠国税率 MFN(%)	协定税率 Agreement(%)		特惠税率 S.P.(%)		普通税率 Gen.(%)	Article Description
		-鱼鳍、鱼头、鱼尾、鱼鳔及其他可食用杂碎：							-Fish fins, heads, tails, maws and other edible fish offal:
329	0305.7100	--鲨鱼翅	15	0 1.5 7.5 9	东盟ASEAN,新西兰NZ,澳门MO 智利CL 秘鲁PE 哥斯达黎加CR	0	最不发达35国LDC35,最不发达4国LDC4,亚太2国APTA2,缅甸MM,柬埔寨KH	80	--Shark fins
330	0305.7200	--鱼头、鱼尾、鱼鳔	16	0 3.2 12.8	东盟ASEAN,智利CL,新西兰NZ,秘鲁PE 哥斯达黎加CR 巴基斯坦PK	0	最不发达35国LDC35	80	--Fish heads, tails and maws
331	0305.7900	--其他	16	0 3.2 12.8	东盟ASEAN,智利CL,新西兰NZ,秘鲁PE 哥斯达黎加CR 巴基斯坦PK	0	最不发达35国LDC35	80	--Other
	03.06	**带壳或去壳的甲壳动物，活、鲜、冷、冻、干、盐腌或盐渍的；熏制的带壳或去壳甲壳动物，不论在熏制前或熏制过程中是否烹煮；蒸过或用水煮过的带壳甲壳动物，不论是否冷、冻、干、盐腌或盐渍的；适合供人食用的甲壳动物的细粉、粗粉及团粒：**							**Crustaceans, whether in shell or not, live, fresh, chilled, frozen, dried, salted or in brine; smoked crustaceans, whether in shell or not, whether or not cooked before or during the smoking process; crustaceans, in shell, cooked by steaming or by boiling in water, whether or not chilled, frozen, dried, salted or in brine; flours, meals and pellets of crustaceans, fit for human consumption:**
		-冻的：							-Frozen:
332	0306.1100	--岩礁虾和其他龙虾(真龙虾属、龙虾属、岩龙虾属)	10	0 5	东盟ASEAN,智利CL,新西兰NZ,秘鲁PE,哥斯达黎加CR 巴基斯坦PK	0	最不发达35国LDC35,最不发达4国LDC4,缅甸MM,柬埔寨KH	70	--Rock lobster and other sea crawfish (Palinurus spp., Panulirusspp., Jasus spp.)
333	0306.1200	--鳌龙虾(鳌龙虾属)	10	0 5 7.2	东盟ASEAN,智利CL,新西兰NZ,秘鲁PE,哥斯达黎加CR 巴基斯坦PK 亚太APTA	0	最不发达35国LDC35,最不发达4国LDC4,柬埔寨KH	70	--Lobsters (Homarus spp.)

序号 No.	税则号列 Tariff Line	货品名称	最惠国税率 MFN(%)	协定税率 Agreement(%)		特惠税率 S.P.(%)		普通税率 Gen.(%)	Article Description
		--蟹:							--Crabs:
334	0306.1410	---梭子蟹	10	0 1 5	东盟ASEAN,新西兰NZ,哥斯达黎加CR 智利CL 巴基斯坦PK,秘鲁PE	0	最不发达35国LDC35,最不发达4国LDC4,亚太2国APTA2,缅甸MM,柬埔寨KH	70	---Swimming crab
335	0306.1490	---其他	10	0 1 5	东盟ASEAN,新西兰NZ,哥斯达黎加CR 智利CL 巴基斯坦PK,秘鲁PE	0	最不发达35国LDC35,最不发达4国LDC4,亚太2国APTA2,缅甸MM,柬埔寨KH	70	---Other
336	0306.1500	--挪威海螯虾	16	0 1.6 3.2 8 12.8	东盟ASEAN,新西兰NZ 智利CL 哥斯达黎加CR 秘鲁PE 巴基斯坦PK	0	最不发达35国LDC35,最不发达4国LDC4,柬埔寨KH	70	--Norway lobsters (Nephrops norvegicus)
		--冷水小虾及对虾(长额虾属、褐虾):							--Cold-water shrimps and prawns (Pandalus spp., Crangon crangon):
		---冷水小虾:							---Cold-water shrimps:
337	0306.1611	----虾仁	8	0 4	东盟ASEAN,智利CL,巴基斯坦PK,新西兰NZ,秘鲁PE,哥斯达黎加CR,香港HK 亚太APTA	0	最不发达35国LDC35,最不发达4国LDC4,缅甸MM,柬埔寨KH	70	----Shelled
338	0306.1612	----其他,北方长额虾	5	0 2.5	东盟ASEAN,智利CL,巴基斯坦PK,新西兰NZ,秘鲁PE,哥斯达黎加CR,香港HK 亚太APTA	0	最不发达35国LDC35,最不发达4国LDC4,缅甸MM,柬埔寨KH	70	----Other, Northem pandalus (Pandalus)

序号 No.	税则号列 Tariff Line	货品名称	最惠国税率 MFN(%)	协定税率 Agreement(%)		特惠税率 S.P.(%)		普通税率 Gen.(%)	Article Description
339	0306.1619	----其他	5	0 2.5	东盟ASEAN,智利CL,巴基斯坦PK,新西兰NZ,秘鲁PE,哥斯达黎加CR,香港HK 亚太APTA	0	最不发达35国LDC35,最不发达4国LDC4,缅甸MM,柬埔寨KH	70	----Other
		---冷水对虾:							---Cold-water prawns:
340	0306.1621	----虾仁	8	0 4	东盟ASEAN,智利CL,巴基斯坦PK,新西兰NZ,秘鲁PE,哥斯达黎加CR,香港HK 亚太APTA	0	最不发达35国LDC35,最不发达4国LDC4,缅甸MM,柬埔寨KH	70	----Shelled
341	0306.1629	----其他	5	0 2.5	东盟ASEAN,智利CL,巴基斯坦PK,新西兰NZ,秘鲁PE,哥斯达黎加CR,香港HK 亚太APTA	0	最不发达35国LDC35,最不发达4国LDC4,缅甸MM,柬埔寨KH	70	----Other
		--其他小虾及对虾:							--Other shrimps and prawns:
		---小虾:							---Shrimps:
342	0306.1711	----虾仁	8	0 4	东盟ASEAN,智利CL,巴基斯坦PK,新西兰NZ,秘鲁PE,哥斯达黎加CR,香港HK 亚太APTA	0	最不发达35国LDC35,最不发达4国LDC4,缅甸MM,柬埔寨KH	70	----Shelled
343	0306.1719	----其他	5	0 2.5	东盟ASEAN,智利CL,巴基斯坦PK,新西兰NZ,秘鲁PE,哥斯达黎加CR,香港HK 亚太APTA	0	最不发达35国LDC35,最不发达4国LDC4,缅甸MM,柬埔寨KH	70	----Other
		---对虾:							---Prawns:

序号 No.	税则号列 Tariff Line	货品名称	最惠国税率 MFN(%)	协定税率 Agreement(%)		特惠税率 S.P.(%)		普通税率 Gen.(%)	Article Description
344	0306.1721	----虾仁	8	0 4	东盟ASEAN,智利CL,巴基斯坦PK,新西兰NZ,秘鲁PE,哥斯达黎加CR,香港HK 亚太APTA	0	最不发达35国LDC35,最不发达4国LDC4,缅甸MM,柬埔寨KH	70	----Shelled
345	0306.1729	----其他	5	0 2.5	东盟ASEAN,智利CL,巴基斯坦PK,新西兰NZ,秘鲁PE,哥斯达黎加CR,香港HK 亚太APTA	0	最不发达35国LDC35,最不发达4国LDC4,缅甸MM,柬埔寨KH	70	----Other
		--其他，包括适合供人食用的甲壳动物的细粉、粗粉及团粒：							--Other, including flours, meals and pellets of crustaceans, fit for human consumption:
		---淡水小龙虾：							---Freshwater crawfish:
346	0306.1911	----虾仁	16	0 3.2 12.8	东盟ASEAN,智利CL,新西兰NZ,秘鲁PE 哥斯达黎加CR 巴基斯坦PK	0	最不发达35国LDC35,最不发达4国LDC4,柬埔寨KH	70	----Shelled
347	0306.1919	----其他	16	0 3.2 12.8	东盟ASEAN,智利CL,新西兰NZ,秘鲁PE 哥斯达黎加CR 巴基斯坦PK	0	最不发达35国LDC35,最不发达4国LDC4,柬埔寨KH	70	----Other
348	0306.1990	---其他	16	0 1.6 3.2 8 12.8	东盟ASEAN,新西兰NZ 智利CL 哥斯达黎加CR 秘鲁PE 巴基斯坦PK	0	最不发达35国LDC35,最不发达4国LDC4,柬埔寨KH	70	---Other
		-未冻的：							-Not frozen:
		--岩礁虾和其他龙虾(真龙虾属、龙虾属、岩龙虾属)：							--Rock lobster and other sea crawfish (Palinurus spp., Panulirus spp., Jasus spp.):
349	0306.2110	---种苗	0			0	最不发达35国LDC35,最不发达4国LDC4	0	---For cultivation

序号 No.	税则号列 Tariff Line	货品名称	最惠国税率 MFN(%)	协定税率 Agreement(%)	特惠税率 S.P.(%)	普通税率 Gen.(%)	Article Description
350	0306.2190	---其他	15	0 东盟ASEAN,智利CL,新西兰NZ,秘鲁PE,香港HK 3 哥斯达黎加CR	0 最不发达35国LDC35,最不发达4国LDC4,缅甸MM,柬埔寨KH	70	---Other
		--鳌龙虾(鳌龙虾属):					--Lobsters (Homarus spp.):
351	0306.2210	---种苗	0		0 最不发达35国LDC35,最不发达4国LDC4	0	---For cultivation
352	0306.2290	---其他	15	0 东盟ASEAN,智利CL,新西兰NZ,秘鲁PE,香港HK 3 哥斯达黎加CR 12 巴基斯坦PK	0 最不发达35国LDC35,最不发达4国LDC4,缅甸MM,柬埔寨KH	70	---Other
		--蟹:					--Crabs:
353	0306.2410	---种苗	0		0 最不发达35国LDC35,最不发达4国LDC4	0	---For cultivation
		---其他:					---Other:
354	0306.2491	----中华绒螯蟹	14	0 东盟ASEAN,新西兰NZ,秘鲁PE 1.4 智利CL 2.8 哥斯达黎加CR 7 巴基斯坦PK	0 最不发达35国LDC35,最不发达4国LDC4,柬埔寨KH	70	----Freshwater crabs, live
355	0306.2492	----梭子蟹	14	0 东盟ASEAN,新西兰NZ,香港HK 1.4 智利CL 2.8 哥斯达黎加CR 7 秘鲁PE 11.2 巴基斯坦PK	0 最不发达35国LDC35,最不发达4国LDC4,柬埔寨KH	70	----Swimming crab
356	0306.2499	----其他	14	0 东盟ASEAN,新西兰NZ,香港HK 1.4 智利CL 2.8 哥斯达黎加CR 7 秘鲁PE	0 最不发达35国LDC35,最不发达4国LDC4,柬埔寨KH	70	----Other

序号 No.	税则号列 Tariff Line	货品名称	最惠国税率 MFN(%)	协定税率 Agreement(%)		特惠税率 S.P.(%)		普通税率 Gen.(%)	Article Description
		--挪威海螯虾:							--Norway lobsters (Nephrops norvegicus):
357	0306.2510	---种苗	0			0	最不发达35国LDC35,最不发达4国LDC4	0	---For cultivation
358	0306.2590	---其他	14	0 1.4 2.8 11.2	东盟ASEAN,新西兰NZ,秘鲁PE,香港HK 智利CL 哥斯达黎加CR 巴基斯坦PK	0	最不发达35国LDC35,最不发达4国LDC4,缅甸MM,柬埔寨KH	70	---Other
		--冷水小虾及对虾(长额虾属、褐虾):							--Cold-water shrimps and prawns (Pandalus spp., Crangon crangon):
359	0306.2610	---种苗	0			0	最不发达35国LDC35,最不发达4国LDC4	0	---For cultivation
360	0306.2620	---鲜、冷对虾	15	0 3 12	东盟ASEAN,智利CL,新西兰NZ,秘鲁PE,香港HK 哥斯达黎加CR 巴基斯坦PK	0	最不发达35国LDC35,最不发达4国LDC4,缅甸MM,柬埔寨KH	70	---Prawns, fresh or chilled
361	0306.2690	---其他	12	0 2.4 6	东盟ASEAN,智利CL,新西兰NZ,秘鲁PE,香港HK 哥斯达黎加CR 巴基斯坦PK	0	最不发达35国LDC35,最不发达4国LDC4,缅甸MM,柬埔寨KH	70	---Other
		--其他小虾及对虾:							--Other shrimps and prawns:
362	0306.2710	---种苗	0			0	最不发达35国LDC35,最不发达4国LDC4	0	---For cultivation

序号 No.	税则号列 Tariff Line	货品名称	最惠国税 率 MFN(%)	协定税率 Agreement(%)	特惠税率 S.P.(%)	普通税率 Gen.(%)	Article Description
363	0306.2720	---鲜、冷对虾	15	0 东盟ASEAN,智利CL,新西兰NZ,秘鲁PE,香港HK 3 哥斯达黎加CR 12 巴基斯坦PK	0 最不发达 35 国 LDC35,最不发达 4 国 LDC4,缅甸MM,柬埔寨KH	70	---Prawns, fresh or chilled
364	0306.2790	---其他	12	0 东盟ASEAN,智利CL,新西兰NZ,秘鲁PE,香港HK 2.4 哥斯达黎加CR 6 巴基斯坦PK	0 最不发达 35 国 LDC35,最不发达 4 国 LDC4,缅甸MM,柬埔寨KH	70	---Other
		--其他，包括适合供人食用的甲壳动物的细粉、粗粉及团粒：					--Other, including flours, meals and pellets of crustaceans, fit for human consumption:
365	0306.2910	---种苗	0		0 最不发达 35 国 LDC35,最不发达 4 国 LDC4	0	---For cultivation
366	0306.2990	---其他	14	0 东盟ASEAN,新西兰NZ,秘鲁PE,香港HK 1.4 智利CL 2.8 哥斯达黎加CR 11.2 巴基斯坦PK	0 最不发达 35 国 LDC35,最不发达 4 国 LDC4,缅甸MM,柬埔寨KH	70	---Other
	03.07	**带壳或去壳的软体动物，活、鲜、冷、冻、干、盐腌或盐渍的；熏制的带壳或去壳软体动物，不论在熏制前或熏制过程中是否烹煮；适合供人食用的软体动物的细粉、粗粉及团粒：**					**Molluscs, whether in shell or not, live, fresh, chilled, frozen, dried, salted or in brine; smoked molluscs, whether in shell or not, whether or not cooked before or during the smoking process; flours, meals and pellets of molluscs, fit for human consumption:**
		-牡蛎（蚝）：					-Oysters:
		--活、鲜或冷的：					--Live, fresh or chilled:
367	0307.1110	---种苗	0		0 最不发达 35 国 LDC35,最不发达 4 国 LDC4	0	---For cultivation

序号 No.	税则号列 Tariff Line	货品名称	最惠国税率 MFN(%)	协定税率 Agreement(%)		特惠税率 S.P.(%)		普通税率 Gen.(%)	Article Description
368	0307.1190	---其他	14	0 1.4 2.8 7 11.2	东盟ASEAN,新西兰NZ,香港HK 智利CL 哥斯达黎加CR 秘鲁PE 巴基斯坦PK	0	最不发达35国LDC35,最不发达4国LDC4,缅甸MM	70	---Other
369	0307.1900	--其他	14	0 1.4 2.8 7 11.2	东盟ASEAN,新西兰NZ,香港HK 智利CL 哥斯达黎加CR 秘鲁PE 巴基斯坦PK	0	最不发达35国LDC35,最不发达4国LDC4,缅甸MM	70	--Other
		-扇贝，包括海扇:							-Scallops, including queen scallops, of the genera Pecten, Chlamys or Placopecten:
		--活、鲜或冷的:							--Live, fresh or chilled:
370	0307.2110	---种苗	0			0	最不发达35国LDC35,最不发达4国LDC4	0	---For cultivation
371	0307.2190	---其他	14	0 1.4 2.8 7 11.2	东盟ASEAN,新西兰NZ,香港HK 智利CL 哥斯达黎加CR 秘鲁PE 巴基斯坦PK	0	最不发达35国LDC35,最不发达4国LDC4,缅甸MM	70	---Other
372	0307.2900	--其他	14	0 1.4 2.8 5.2 11.2	东盟ASEAN,新西兰NZ 智利CL 哥斯达黎加CR 秘鲁PE 巴基斯坦PK	0	最不发达35国LDC35,最不发达4国LDC4,缅甸MM	80	--Other
		-贻贝:							-Mussels (Mytilus spp., Perna spp.):
		--活、鲜或冷的:							--Live, fresh or chilled:
373	0307.3110	---种苗	0			0	最不发达35国LDC35,最不发达4国LDC4	0	---For cultivation
374	0307.3190	---其他	14	0 2.8 11.2	东盟ASEAN,智利CL,新西兰NZ,秘鲁PE,香港HK 哥斯达黎加CR 巴基斯坦PK	0	最不发达35国LDC35,最不发达4国LDC4,缅甸MM,柬埔寨KH	70	---Other

序号 No.	税则号列 Tariff Line	货品名称	最惠国税率 MFN(%)	协定税率 Agreement(%)		特惠税率 S.P.(%)		普通税率 Gen.(%)	Article Description
375	0307.3900	--其他	14	0 1.4 2.8 7 9.8	东盟ASEAN,新西兰NZ 智利CL 哥斯达黎加CR 巴基斯坦PK,秘鲁PE 亚太APTA	0	最不发达35国LDC35,最不发达4国LDC4,缅甸MM,柬埔寨KH	70	--Other
		-墨鱼及鱿鱼：							-Cuttle fish (Sepia officinalis, Rossia macrosoma, Sepiola spp.) and squid (Ommastrephes spp., Loligo spp., Nototodarus spp., Sepioteuthis spp.):
		--活、鲜或冷的：							--Live, fresh or chilled:
376	0307.4110	---种苗	0			0	最不发达35国LDC35,最不发达4国LDC4	0	---For cultivation
377	0307.4190	---其他	12	0 1.2 2.4 6	东盟ASEAN,新西兰NZ,香港HK 智利CL 哥斯达黎加CR 巴基斯坦PK,秘鲁PE	0	最不发达35国LDC35,最不发达4国LDC4,缅甸MM,柬埔寨KH	70	---Other
378	0307.4900	--其他	12	0 1.2 2.4 6 10	东盟ASEAN,新西兰NZ,香港HK,澳门MO 智利CL 哥斯达黎加CR 秘鲁PE 亚太APTA,巴基斯坦PK	0	最不发达35国LDC35,最不发达4国LDC4,缅甸MM,柬埔寨KH	70	--Other
		-章鱼：							-Octopus (Octopus spp.):
379	0307.5100	--活、鲜或冷的	17	0 1.7 3.4 8.5 13.6	东盟ASEAN,新西兰NZ,香港HK 智利CL 哥斯达黎加CR 秘鲁PE 巴基斯坦PK	0	最不发达35国LDC35	70	--Live, fresh or chilled
380	0307.5900	--其他	17	0 1.7 3.4 8.5 13.6	东盟ASEAN,新西兰NZ,香港HK,澳门MO 智利CL 哥斯达黎加CR 秘鲁PE 巴基斯坦PK	0	最不发达35国LDC35,最不发达4国LDC4	70	--Other

序号 No.	税则号列 Tariff Line	货品名称	最惠国税率 MFN(%)	协定税率 Agreement(%)		特惠税率 S.P.(%)		普通税率 Gen.(%)	Article Description
		-蜗牛及螺，海螺除外：							-Snails, other than sea snails:
381	0307.6010	---种苗	0			0	最不发达35国LDC35,最不发达4国LDC4	0	---For cultivation
382	0307.6090	---其他	14	0 2.8 11.2	东盟ASEAN,智利CL,新西兰NZ,秘鲁PE 哥斯达黎加CR 巴基斯坦PK	0	最不发达35国LDC35,最不发达4国LDC4,柬埔寨KH	70	---Other
		-蛤、鸟蛤及舟贝(蚶科、北极蛤科、鸟蛤科、斧蛤科、缝栖蛤科、蛤蜊科、中带蛤科、海螂科、双带蛤科、截蛏科、竹蛏科、砗磲科、帘蛤科):							-Clams, cockles and ark shells (families Arcidae, Arcticidae, Cardiidae, Donacidae, Hiatellidae, Mactridae, Mesodesmatidae, Myidae, Semelidae, Solecurtidae, Solenidae, Tridacnidae and Veneridae) :
		--活、鲜或冷的：							--Live, fresh or chilled:
383	0307.7110	---种苗	0			0	最不发达35国LDC35,最不发达4国LDC4	0	---For cultivation
		---其他：							---Other:
384	0307.7191	----蛤	14	0 1.4 2.8 11.2	东盟ASEAN,新西兰NZ,秘鲁PE,香港HK 智利CL 哥斯达黎加CR 巴基斯坦PK	0	最不发达35国LDC35	70	----Clams
385	0307.7199	----其他	14	0 1.4 2.8 7 11.2	东盟ASEAN,新西兰NZ,香港HK 智利CL 哥斯达黎加CR 秘鲁PE 巴基斯坦PK	0	最不发达35国LDC35,最不发达4国LDC4,缅甸MM,柬埔寨KH	70	----Other
		--其他：							--Other:
386	0307.7910	---蛤	10	0 1	东盟ASEAN,新西兰NZ,哥斯达黎加CR 智利CL	0	最不发达35国LDC35,最不发达4国LDC4	70	---Clams

序号 No.	税则号列 Tariff Line	货品名称	最惠国税 率 MFN(%)	协定税率 Agreement(%)		特惠税率 S.P.(%)		普通税率 Gen.(%)	Article Description
387	0307.7990	---其他	10	0 1 5	东盟ASEAN,新西兰NZ,哥斯达黎加CR,澳门MO 智利CL 秘鲁PE	0	最不发达35国LDC35,最不发达4国LDC4,缅甸MM,柬埔寨KH	70	---Other
		-鲍鱼（鲍属）: --活、鲜或冷的:							-Abalone (Haliotis spp.): --Live, fresh or chilled:
388	0307.8110	---种苗	0			0	最不发达35国LDC35,最不发达4国LDC4	0	---For cultivation
389	0307.8190	---其他	14	0 1.4 2.8 7 11.2	东盟ASEAN,新西兰NZ,香港HK 智利CL 哥斯达黎加CR 秘鲁PE 巴基斯坦PK	0	最不发达35国LDC35,最不发达4国LDC4,缅甸MM,柬埔寨KH	80	---Other
390	0307.8900	--其他	10	0 1 5	东盟ASEAN,新西兰NZ,哥斯达黎加CR,香港HK,澳门MO 智利CL 巴基斯坦PK	0	最不发达35国LDC35,最不发达4国LDC4,缅甸MM,柬埔寨KH	80	--Other
		-其他,包括适合供人食用的细粉、粗粉及团粒: --活、鲜或冷的:							-Other, including flours, meals and pellets, fit for human consumption: --Live, fresh or chilled:
391	0307.9110	---种苗	0			0	最不发达35国LDC35,最不发达4国LDC4	0	---For cultivation
392	0307.9190	---其他	14	0 1.4 2.8 7 11.2	东盟ASEAN,新西兰NZ,香港HK 智利CL 哥斯达黎加CR 秘鲁PE 巴基斯坦PK	0	最不发达35国LDC35,最不发达4国LDC4,缅甸MM,柬埔寨KH	70	---Other

序号 No.	税则号列 Tariff Line	货品名称	最惠国税率 MFN(%)	协定税率 Agreement(%)		特惠税率 S.P.(%)		普通税率 Gen.(%)	Article Description
393	0307.9900	--其他	10	0 1 5	东盟ASEAN,新西兰NZ,哥斯达黎加CR,澳门MO 智利CL 秘鲁PE	0	最不发达35国LDC35,最不发达4国LDC4,缅甸MM,柬埔寨KH	70	--Other
	03.08	**不属于甲壳动物及软体动物的水生无脊椎动物，活、鲜、冷、冻、干、盐腌或盐渍的；熏制的不属于甲壳动物及软体动物的水生无脊椎动物，不论在熏制前或熏制过程中是否烹煮；适合供人食用的不属于甲壳动物及软体动物的水生无脊椎动物的细粉、粗粉及团粒：**							**Aquatic invertebrates other than crustaceans and molluscs, live, fresh, chilled, frozen, dried, salted or in brine; smoked aquatic invertebrates other than crustaceans and molluscs, whether or not cooked before or during the smoking process; flours, meals and pellets of aquatic invertebrates other than crustaceans and molluscs, fit for human consumption:**
		-海参(仿刺参、海参纲)：							-Sea cucumbers (Stichopus japonicus, Holothurioidea):
		--活、鲜或冷的：							--Live, fresh or chilled:
394	0308.1110	---种苗	0			0	最不发达35国LDC35,最不发达4国LDC4	0	---For cultivation
395	0308.1190	---其他	14	0 1.4 2.8 7 11.2	东盟ASEAN,新西兰NZ,香港HK 智利CL 哥斯达黎加CR 秘鲁PE 巴基斯坦PK	0	最不发达35国LDC35,最不发达4国LDC4,缅甸MM,柬埔寨KH	70	---Other
396	0308.1900	--其他	10	0 1 5	东盟ASEAN,新西兰NZ,哥斯达黎加CR 智利CL 秘鲁PE	0	最不发达35国LDC35,最不发达4国LDC4,缅甸MM,柬埔寨KH	80	--Other

序号 No.	税则号列 Tariff Line	货品名称	最惠国 税　率 MFN(%)	协定税率 Agreement(%)	特惠税率 S.P.(%)	普通 税率 Gen.(%)	Article Description
		-海胆(球海胆属、拟球海胆、智利海胆、食用正海胆):					-Sea urchins (Strongylocentrotus spp., Paracentrotus lividus, Loxechinus albus, Echichinus esculentus):
		--活、鲜或冷的:					--Live, fresh or chilled:
397	0308.2110	---种苗	0		0 最不发达35国LDC35,最不发达4国LDC4	0	---For cultivation
398	0308.2190	---其他	14	0 东盟ASEAN,新西兰NZ,香港HK 1.4 智利CL 2.8 哥斯达黎加CR 7 秘鲁PE 11.2 巴基斯坦PK	0 最不发达35国LDC35,最不发达4国LDC4,缅甸MM,柬埔寨KH	70	---Other
399	0308.2900	--其他	10	0 东盟ASEAN,新西兰NZ,哥斯达黎加CR,澳门MO 1 智利CL 5 秘鲁PE	0 最不发达35国LDC35,最不发达4国LDC4,缅甸MM,柬埔寨KH	70	--Other
		-海蜇(海蜇属):					-Jellyfish (Rhopilema spp.):
		---活、鲜或冷的:					---Live, fresh or chilled:
400	0308.3011	----种苗	0		0 最不发达35国LDC35,最不发达4国LDC4	0	----For cultivation
401	0308.3019	----其他	14	0 东盟ASEAN,新西兰NZ,香港HK 1.4 智利CL 2.8 哥斯达黎加CR 7 秘鲁PE 11.2 巴基斯坦PK	0 最不发达35国LDC35,最不发达4国LDC4,缅甸MM,柬埔寨KH	70	----Other
402	0308.3090	---其他	10	0 东盟ASEAN,新西兰NZ,哥斯达黎加CR,澳门MO 1 智利CL 5 秘鲁PE	0 最不发达35国LDC35,最不发达4国LDC4,缅甸MM,柬埔寨KH	70	---Other

序号 No.	税则号列 Tariff Line	货品名称	最惠国税率 MFN(%)	协定税率 Agreement(%)		特惠税率 S.P.(%)		普通税率 Gen.(%)	Article Description
		-其他：							-Other:
		---活、鲜或冷的：							---Live, fresh or chilled:
403	0308.9011	----种苗	0			0	最不发达35国LDC35,最不发达4国LDC4	0	----For cultivation
404	0308.9012	----其他沙蚕	14	0 1.4 2.8 7 11.2	东盟ASEAN,新西兰NZ,香港HK 智利CL 哥斯达黎加CR 秘鲁PE 巴基斯坦PK	0	最不发达35国LDC35,最不发达4国LDC4,缅甸MM,柬埔寨KH	70	----Clamworm
405	0308.9019	----其他	14	0 1.4 2.8 7 11.2	东盟ASEAN,新西兰NZ,香港HK 智利CL 哥斯达黎加CR 秘鲁PE 巴基斯坦PK	0	最不发达35国LDC35,最不发达4国LDC4,缅甸MM,柬埔寨KH	70	----Other
406	0308.9090	---其他	10	0 1 5	东盟ASEAN,新西兰NZ,哥斯达黎加CR,澳门MO 智利CL 秘鲁PE	0	最不发达35国LDC35,最不发达4国LDC4,缅甸MM,柬埔寨KH	70	---Other

第四章
乳品；蛋品；天然蜂蜜；其他食用动物产品

注释：

一、所称“乳”，是指全脂乳及半脱脂或全脱脂的乳。

二、税号 04.05 所称：

（一）“黄油”，仅指从乳中提取的天然黄油、乳清黄油及调制黄油（新鲜、加盐或酸败的，包括罐装黄油），按重量计乳脂含量在 80%及以上，但不超过 95%，乳的无脂固形物最大含量不超过 2%，以及水的最大含量不超过 16%。黄油中不含添加的乳化剂，但可含有氯化钠、食用色素、中和盐及无害乳酸菌的培养物。

（二）“乳酱”是一种油包水型可涂抹的乳状物，乳脂是该制品所含的唯一脂肪，按重量计其含量在 39%及以上，但小于 80%。

三、乳清经浓缩并加入乳或乳脂制成的产品，若同时具有下列三种特性，则视为乳酪归入税号 04.06：

（一）按干重计乳脂含量在 5%及以上的；

（二）按重量计干质成分至少为 70%，但不超过 85%的；

（三）已成形或可以成形的。

四、本章不包括：

（一）按重量计乳糖含量（以干燥无水乳糖计）超过 95%的乳清制品（税号 17.02）；

（二）白蛋白（包括按重量计干质成分的乳清蛋白含量超过 80%的两种或两种以上的乳清蛋白浓缩物）（税号 35.02）及球蛋白（税号 35.04）。

子目注释：

一、子目号 0404.10 所称“改性乳清”，是指由乳清成分构成的制品，即全部或部分去除乳糖、蛋白或矿物质的乳清、加入天然乳清成分的乳清及由混入天然乳清成分制成的产品。

Chapter 4
Dairy produce; birds' eggs; natural honey; edible products of animal origin, not elsewhere specified or included

Notes:

1. The expression “milk” means full cream milk or partially or completely skimmed milk.

2. For the purposes of heading No.04.05:

(a) The term “butter” means natural butter, whey butter or recombined butter (fresh, salted or rancid, including canned butter) derived exclusively from milk, with a milkfat content of 80% or more but not more than 95% by weight, a maximum milk solids-not-fat content of 2% by weight and a maximum water content of 16% by weight. Butter does not contain added emulsifiers, but may contain sodium chloride, food colours, neutralizing salts and cultures of harmless lactic-acid-producing bacteria.

(b) The expression “dairy spreads” means a spreadable emulsion of the water-in-oil type, containing milkfat as the only fat in the product, with a milkfat content of 39% or more but less than 80% by weight.

3. Products obtained by the concentration of whey and with the addition of milk or milkfat are to be classified as cheese in heading No.04.06 provided that they have the three following characteristics:

(a) A milkfat content, by weight of the dry matter, of 5% or more;

(b) A dry matter content, by weight, of at least 70% but not exceeding 85%; and

(c) They are moulded or capable of being moulded.

4. This Chapter does not cover:

(a) Products obtained from whey, containing by weight more than 95% lactose, expressed as anhydrous lactose calculated on the dry matter (heading No.17.02); or

(b) Albumins (including concentrates of two or more whey proteins, containing by weight more than 80% whey proteins, calculated on the dry matter) (heading No.35.02) or globulins (heading No.35.04).

Subheading Notes:

1. For the purpose of subheading No.0404.10, the expression “modified whey” means products consisting of whey constituents, that is, whey from which all or part of the lactose, proteins or minerals have been removed, whey to which natural whey constituents have been added and products obtained by mixing natural whey constituents.

二、子目号 0405.10 所称“黄油”，不包括脱水黄油及印度酥油（子目号 0405.90）。

2. For the purposes of subheading No.0405.10 the term “butter” does not include dehydrated butter or ghee (subheading No.0405.90).

序号 No.	税则号列 Tariff Line	货品名称	最惠国税率 MFN(%)	协定税率 Agreement(%)		特惠税率 S.P.(%)		普通税率 Gen.(%)	Article Description
	04.01	**未浓缩及未加糖或其他甜物质的乳及奶油：**							**Milk and cream, not concentrated nor containing added sugar or other sweetening matter:**
407	0401.1000	-按重量计脂肪含量不超过 1%	15	0 1.5 7.5 11 12	东盟ASEAN,新西兰NZ,澳门MO 智利CL 秘鲁PE 哥斯达黎加CR 巴基斯坦PK	0	最不发达 35 国 LDC35, 最不发达 4 国 LDC4	40	-Of a fat content, by weight, not exceeding 1%
408	0401.2000	-按重量计脂肪含量超过 1%，但不超过 6%	15	0 1.5 4.5 7.5 11 12	东盟ASEAN,香港HK,澳门MO 智利CL 新西兰NZ 秘鲁PE 哥斯达黎加CR 巴基斯坦PK	0	最不发达 35 国 LDC35, 最不发达 4 国 LDC4	40	-Of a fat content, by weight, exceeding 1% but not exceeding 6%
409	0401.4000	-按重量计脂肪含量超过 6%，但不超过 10%	15	0 1.5 4.5 7.5 11 12	东盟ASEAN,澳门MO 智利CL 新西兰NZ 秘鲁PE 哥斯达黎加CR 巴基斯坦PK	0	最不发达 35 国 LDC35, 最不发达 4 国 LDC4	40	-Of a fat content, by weight, exceeding 6% but not exceeding 10%
410	0401.5000	-按重量计脂肪含量超过 10%	15	0 1.5 4.5 7.5 11 12	东盟ASEAN,澳门MO 智利CL 新西兰NZ 秘鲁PE 哥斯达黎加CR 巴基斯坦PK	0	最不发达 35 国 LDC35, 最不发达 4 国 LDC4	40	-Of a fat content, by weight, exceeding 10%
	04.02	**浓缩、加糖或其他甜物质的乳及奶油：**							**Milk and cream, concentrated or containing added sugar or other sweetening matter:**
411	0402.1000	-粉状、粒状或其他固体形状，按重量计脂肪含量不超过 1.5%	10	0 1 4.2 5 7 7.1 7.3	东盟ASEAN,香港HK,澳门MO 智利CL 新西兰NZ 巴基斯坦PK 亚太APTA 秘鲁PE 哥斯达黎加CR	0	最不发达 35 国 LDC35, 最不发达 4 国 LDC4	40	-In powder, granules or other solid forms, of a fat content, by weight, not exceeding 1.5%
		-粉状、粒状或其他固体形状，按重量计脂肪含量超过 1.5%：							-In powder, granules or other solid forms, of a fat content, by weight, exceeding 1.5%:

序号 No.	税则号列 Tariff Line	货品名称	最惠国税率 MFN(%)	协定税率 Agreement(%)	特惠税率 S.P.(%)	普通税率 Gen.(%)	Article Description
412	0402.2100	--未加糖或其他甜物质	10	0 东盟ASEAN,香港HK,澳门MO 1 智利CL 4.2 新西兰NZ 7 亚太APTA,巴基斯坦PK 7.1 秘鲁PE 7.3 哥斯达黎加CR	0 最不发达35国LDC35,最不发达4国LDC4	40	--Not containing added sugar or other sweetening matter
413	0402.2900	--其他	10	0 东盟ASEAN,香港HK,澳门MO 1 智利CL 4.2 新西兰NZ 5 巴基斯坦PK 7.1 秘鲁PE 7.3 哥斯达黎加CR	0 最不发达35国LDC35,最不发达4国LDC4	40	--Other
		-其他:					-Other:
414	0402.9100	--未加糖或其他甜物质	10	0 东盟ASEAN,香港HK,澳门MO 1 智利CL 4.2 新西兰NZ 5 巴基斯坦PK,秘鲁PE 7.3 哥斯达黎加CR	0 最不发达35国LDC35,最不发达4国LDC4	90	--Not containing added sugar or other sweetening matter
415	0402.9900	--其他	10	0 东盟ASEAN,新西兰NZ 1 智利CL 5 巴基斯坦PK 7.1 秘鲁PE 7.3 哥斯达黎加CR	0 最不发达35国LDC35,最不发达4国LDC4	90	--Other
	04.03	**酪乳、结块的乳及奶油、酸乳、酸乳酒及其他发酵或酸化的乳和奶油，不论是否浓缩、加糖、加其他甜物质、加香料、加水果、加坚果或加可可：**					**Buttermilk, curdled milk and cream, yogurt, kephir and other fermented or acidified milk and cream, whether or not concentrated or containing added sugar or other sweetening matter or flavoured or containing added fruit, nuts or cocoa:**
416	0403.1000	-酸乳	10	0 东盟ASEAN,新西兰NZ,香港HK,澳门MO 1 智利CL 5 巴基斯坦PK,秘鲁PE 7.3 哥斯达黎加CR	0 最不发达35国LDC35,最不发达4国LDC4	90	-Yogurt
417	0403.9000	-其他	20	0 东盟ASEAN,新西兰NZ,香港HK,澳门MO 2 智利CL 10 秘鲁PE 14.7 哥斯达黎加CR	0 最不发达35国LDC35	90	-Other
	04.04	**乳清，不论是否浓缩、加糖或其他甜物质；其他税号未列名的含天然乳的产品，不论是否加糖或其他甜物质：**					**Whey, whether or not concentrated or containing added sugar or other sweetening matter; products consisting of natural milk constituents, whether or not containing added sugar or other sweetening matter, not elsewhere specified or included:**

序号 No.	税则号列 Tariff Line	货品名称	最惠国税率 MFN(%)	协定税率 Agreement(%)	特惠税率 S.P.(%)	普通税率 Gen.(%)	Article Description
418	0404.1000	-乳清及改性乳清，不论是否浓缩、加糖或其他甜物质	6 △2	0 东盟ASEAN,智利CL,新西兰NZ,秘鲁PE 4.4 哥斯达黎加CR 5 巴基斯坦PK	0 最不发达35国LDC35	30	-Whey and modified whey, whether or not concentrated or containing added sugar or other sweetening matter
419	0404.9000	-其他	20	0 东盟ASEAN,智利CL,新西兰NZ 10 秘鲁PE 14.7 哥斯达黎加CR	0 最不发达35国LDC35	90	-Other
	04.05	**黄油及其他从乳中提取的脂和油；乳酱：**					**Butter and other fats and oils derived from milk;dairy spreads:**
420	0405.1000	-黄油	10	0 东盟ASEAN 1 智利CL 3 新西兰NZ 5 巴基斯坦PK,秘鲁PE 7.3 哥斯达黎加CR	0 最不发达35国LDC35,最不发达4国LDC4	90	-Butter
421	0405.2000	-乳酱	10	0 东盟ASEAN,智利CL,新西兰NZ,秘鲁PE,澳门MO 5 巴基斯坦PK 7.3 哥斯达黎加CR 8.1 亚太APTA	0 最不发达35国LDC35,最不发达4国LDC4	90	-Dairy spreads
422	0405.9000	-其他	10	0 东盟ASEAN,智利CL 3 新西兰NZ 5 巴基斯坦PK,秘鲁PE 7.3 哥斯达黎加CR	0 最不发达35国LDC35,最不发达4国LDC4	90	-Other
	04.06	**乳酪及凝乳：**					**Cheese and curd:**
423	0406.1000	-鲜乳酪（未熟化或未固化的），包括乳清乳酪；凝乳	12	0 东盟ASEAN,香港HK,澳门MO 1.2 智利CL 3.6 新西兰NZ 6 巴基斯坦PK,秘鲁PE 8.8 哥斯达黎加CR	0 最不发达35国LDC35,最不发达4国LDC4	90	-Fresh (unripened or uncured) cheese, including whey cheese, and curd
424	0406.2000	-各种磨碎或粉化的乳酪	12	0 东盟ASEAN,智利CL,新西兰NZ,香港HK 6 巴基斯坦PK 8 秘鲁PE 8.8 哥斯达黎加CR		90	-Grated or powdered cheese, of all kinds
425	0406.3000	-经加工的乳酪，但磨碎或粉化的除外	12	0 东盟ASEAN,智利CL 3.6 新西兰NZ 6 巴基斯坦PK 8 秘鲁PE 8.8 哥斯达黎加CR	0 最不发达35国LDC35	90	-Processed cheese, not grated or powdered
426	0406.4000	-蓝纹乳酪和娄地青霉生产的带有纹理的其他乳酪	15	0 东盟ASEAN,智利CL,新西兰NZ 7.5 秘鲁PE 11 哥斯达黎加CR 12 巴基斯坦PK	0 最不发达35国LDC35	90	-Blue-veined cheese and other cheese containing veins produced by Penicillium roqueforti

序号 No.	税则号列 Tariff Line	货品名称	最惠国税率 MFN(%)	协定税率 Agreement(%)		特惠税率 S.P.(%)		普通税率 Gen.(%)	Article Description
427	0406.9000	-其他酪	12	0 3.6 6 8.8	东盟ASEAN,智利CL 新西兰NZ 巴基斯坦PK,秘鲁PE 哥斯达黎加CR	0	最不发达35国LDC35,最不发达4国LDC4	90	-Other cheese
	04.07	**带壳禽蛋，鲜、腌制或煮过的：**							**Birds, eggs, in shell, fresh, preserved or cooked:**
		-孵化用受精禽蛋：							-Fertilised eggs for in-cubation:
428	0407.1100	--鸡的	0			0	最不发达35国LDC35,最不发达4国LDC4	0	--Of fowls of the species Gallus domesticus
429	0407.1900	--其他	0			0	最不发达35国LDC35,最不发达4国LDC4	0	--Other
		-其他鲜蛋：							-Other fresh eggs:
430	0407.2100	--鸡的	20	0 4 10	东盟ASEAN,智利CL,新西兰NZ 哥斯达黎加CR 秘鲁PE	0	最不发达35国LDC35,最不发达4国LDC4,缅甸MM,柬埔寨KH	80	--Of fowls of the species Gallus domesticus
431	0407.2900	--其他	20	0 4 10	东盟ASEAN,智利CL,新西兰NZ 哥斯达黎加CR 秘鲁PE	0	最不发达35国LDC35,最不发达4国LDC4,缅甸MM,柬埔寨KH	80	--Other
		-其他：							-Other:
432	0407.9010	---咸蛋	20	0 4	东盟ASEAN,智利CL,新西兰NZ,秘鲁PE 哥斯达黎加CR	0	最不发达35国LDC35,最不发达4国LDC4,缅甸MM	90	---Salted egg
433	0407.9020	---皮蛋	20	0 4	东盟ASEAN,智利CL,新西兰NZ,秘鲁PE 哥斯达黎加CR	0	最不发达35国LDC35	90	---Lime preserved eggs

序号 No.	税则号列 Tariff Line	货品名称	最惠国税率 MFN(%)	协定税率 Agreement(%)		特惠税率 S.P.(%)		普通税率 Gen.(%)	Article Description
434	0407.9090	---其他	20	0 4	东盟ASEAN,智利CL,新西兰NZ,秘鲁PE 哥斯达黎加CR	0	最不发达35国LDC35	90	---Other
	04.08	**去壳禽蛋及蛋黄,鲜、干、冻、蒸过或水煮、制成型或用其他方法保藏的,不论是否加糖或其他甜物质:**							**Birds, eggs, not in shell, and egg yolks, fresh, dried, cooked by steaming or by boiling in water, moulded, frozen or otherwise preserved, whether or not containing added sugar or other sweetening matter:**
		-蛋黄:							-Egg yolks:
435	0408.1100	--干的	20	0 4 10	东盟ASEAN,智利CL,新西兰NZ 哥斯达黎加CR 秘鲁PE	0	最不发达35国LDC35	90	--Dried
436	0408.1900	--其他	20	0 4 10	东盟ASEAN,智利CL,新西兰NZ 哥斯达黎加CR 秘鲁PE	0	最不发达35国LDC35	90	--Other
		-其他:							-Other:
437	0408.9100	--干的	20	0 2 4 10	东盟ASEAN,新西兰NZ 智利CL 哥斯达黎加CR 秘鲁PE	0	最不发达35国LDC35	90	--Dried
438	0408.9900	--其他	20	0 4 10	东盟ASEAN,智利CL,新西兰NZ,香港HK 哥斯达黎加CR 秘鲁PE	0	最不发达35国LDC35	90	--Other
	04.09	**天然蜂蜜:**							**Natural honey:**
439	0409.0000	天然蜂蜜	15	0 1.5 3 7.5 12	东盟ASEAN,新西兰NZ 智利CL 哥斯达黎加CR 秘鲁PE 巴基斯坦PK	0	最不发达35国LDC35,最不发达4国LDC4,老挝LA,柬埔寨KH	80	Natural honey
	04.10	**其他税号未列名的食用动物产品:**							**Edible products of animal origin, not elsewhere specified or included:**
440	0410.0010	---燕窝	25	0 5 12.5	东盟ASEAN,智利CL,新西兰NZ,香港HK,澳门MO 哥斯达黎加CR 秘鲁PE	0	最不发达35国LDC35,最不发达4国LDC4,缅甸MM,柬埔寨KH	80	---Salanganes nests
		---蜂产品:							---Bee products:

序号 No.	税则号列 Tariff Line	货品名称	最惠国 税 率 MFN(%)	协定税率 Agreement(%)		特惠税率 S.P.(%)		普通 税率 Gen.(%)	Article Description
441	0410.0041	----鲜蜂王浆	15	0 3 7.5 12	东盟ASEAN,智利CL, 新西兰NZ 哥斯达黎加CR 秘鲁PE 巴基斯坦PK	0	最不发达35国LDC35	70	----Pure royal jelley
442	0410.0042	----鲜蜂王浆粉	15	0 3 7.5 12	东盟ASEAN,智利CL, 新西兰NZ 哥斯达黎加CR 秘鲁PE 巴基斯坦PK	0	最不发达35国LDC35	70	----Pure royal jelley, in powder
443	0410.0043	----蜂花粉	20	0 4 10	东盟ASEAN,智利CL, 新西兰NZ 哥斯达黎加CR 秘鲁PE	0	最不发达35国LDC35	70	----Bee pollen
444	0410.0049	----其他	20	0 4 10	东盟ASEAN,智利CL, 新西兰NZ 哥斯达黎加CR 秘鲁PE	0	最不发达35国LDC35	70	----Other
445	0410.0090	---其他	20	0 4 10	东盟ASEAN,智利CL, 新西兰NZ,台湾TW 哥斯达黎加CR 秘鲁PE	0	最不发达35国LDC35,最不发达4国LDC4,缅甸MM	70	---Other

第五章 其他动物产品

Chapter 5 Products of animal origin, not elsewhere specified or included

注释:

一、本章不包括:

（一）食用产品（整个或切块的动物肠、膀胱和胃以及液态或干制的动物血除外）;

（二）生皮或毛皮（第四十一章、第四十三章），但税号 05.05 的货品及税号 05.11 的生皮或毛皮的边角废料仍归入本章;

（三）马毛及废马毛以外的动物纺织原料（第十一类）;

（四）供制帚、制刷用的成束、成簇的材料（税号 96.03）。

二、仅按长度而未按发根和发梢整理的人发，视为未加工品，归入税号 05.01。

三、本目录所称“兽牙”，是指象、河马、海象、一角鲸和野猪的长牙、犀角及其他动物的牙齿。

四、本目录所称“马毛”，是指马科、牛科动物的鬃毛和尾毛。

Notes:

1. This Chapter does not cover:

(a) Edible products (other than guts, bladders and stomachs of animals, whole and pieces thereof, and animal blood, liquid or dried) ;

(b) Hides or skins (including furskins) other than goods of heading No.05.05 and parings and similar waste of raw hides or skins of heading No.05.11 (Chapter 41 or 43) ;

(c) Animal textile materials, other than horsehair and horsehair waste (Section Ⅺ) ;or

(d) Prepared knots or tufts for broom or brush making (heading No.96.03).

2. For the purposes of heading No.05.01, the sorting of human hair by length (provided the root ends and tip ends respectively are not arranged together) shall be deemed not to constitute working.

3. Throughout the Nomenclature, elephant, hippopotamus, walrus, narwhal and wild boar tusks, rhinoceros horns and the teeth of all animals are regarded as “ivory”.

4. Throughout the Nomenclature, the expression “horsehair” means hair of the manes or tails of equine or bovine animals.

序号 No.	税则号列 Tariff Line	货品名称	最惠国税率 MFN(%)	协定税率 Agreement(%)		特惠税率 S.P.(%)		普通税率 Gen.(%)	Article Description
	05.01	**未经加工的人发，不论是否洗涤；废人发:**							**Human hair, unworked, whether or not washed or scoured; waste of human hair:**
446	0501.0000	未经加工的人发，不论是否洗涤；废人发	15	0 3 7.5 12	东盟ASEAN,智利CL,新西兰NZ 哥斯达黎加CR 秘鲁PE 巴基斯坦PK	0	最不发达35国LDC35	90	Human hair, unworked, whether or not washed or scoured; waste of human hair
	05.02	**猪鬃、猪毛；獾毛及其他制刷用兽毛；上述鬃毛的废料:**							**Pigs', hogs', or boars', bristles and hair; badger hair and other brush making hair; waste of such bristles or hair:**

序号 No.	税则号列 Tariff Line	货品名称	最惠国税率 MFN(%)	协定税率 Agreement(%)		特惠税率 S.P.(%)		普通税率 Gen.(%)	Article Description
		-猪鬃、猪毛及其废料：							-Pigs', hogs', or boars', bristles and hair and waste thereof:
447	0502.1010	---猪鬃	20	0 4 10	东盟ASEAN,智利CL,新西兰NZ 哥斯达黎加CR 秘鲁PE	0	最不发达35国LDC35	90	---Bristles
448	0502.1020	---猪毛	20	0 4 10	东盟ASEAN,智利CL,新西兰NZ 哥斯达黎加CR 秘鲁PE	0	最不发达35国LDC35	90	---Hair
449	0502.1030	---废料	20	0 4 10	东盟ASEAN,智利CL,新西兰NZ 哥斯达黎加CR 秘鲁PE	0	最不发达35国LDC35	90	---Waste
		-其他：							-Other:
		---獾毛及其他制刷用兽毛：							---Badger hair and other brush making hair:
450	0502.9011	----山羊毛	20	0 4 10	东盟ASEAN,智利CL,新西兰NZ 哥斯达黎加CR 秘鲁PE	0	最不发达35国LDC35	90	----Goat hair
451	0502.9012	----黄鼠狼尾毛	20	0 4 10	东盟ASEAN,智利CL,新西兰NZ 哥斯达黎加CR 秘鲁PE	0	最不发达35国LDC35	90	----Weasel tail hair
452	0502.9019	----其他	20	0 4 10	东盟ASEAN,智利CL,新西兰NZ 哥斯达黎加CR 秘鲁PE	0	最不发达35国LDC35	90	----Other
453	0502.9020	---废料	20	0 4 10	东盟ASEAN,智利CL,新西兰NZ 哥斯达黎加CR 秘鲁PE	0	最不发达35国LDC35	90	---Waste
	05.04	**整个或切块的动物（鱼除外）的肠、膀胱及胃，鲜、冷、冻、干、熏、盐腌或盐渍的：**							**Guts, bladders and stomachs of animals (other than fish), whole and pieces thereof, fresh, chilled, frozen, salted, in brine, dried or smoked:**
		---肠衣：							---Casings:
454	0504.0011	----盐渍猪肠衣（猪大肠头除外）	20	0 2 4 10	东盟ASEAN,新西兰NZ 智利CL 哥斯达黎加CR 亚太APTA,巴基斯坦PK,秘鲁PE	0	最不发达35国LDC35	90	----Hog casings, salted
455	0504.0012	----盐渍绵羊肠衣	18	0 1.8 3.6 9	东盟ASEAN,新西兰NZ 智利CL 哥斯达黎加CR 亚太APTA,巴基斯坦PK,秘鲁PE	0	最不发达35国LDC35	90	----Sheep casings, salted

序号 No.	税则号列 Tariff Line	货品名称	最惠国税率 MFN(%)	协定税率 Agreement(%)		特惠税率 S.P.(%)		普通税率 Gen.(%)	Article Description
456	0504.0013	----盐渍山羊肠衣	18	0 1.8 3.6 9	东盟ASEAN,新西兰NZ 智利CL 哥斯达黎加CR 亚太APTA,巴基斯坦PK,秘鲁PE	0	最不发达35国LDC35	90	----Goat casings, salted
457	0504.0014	----盐渍猪大肠头	20	0 2 4 10	东盟ASEAN,新西兰NZ 智利CL 哥斯达黎加CR 亚太APTA,巴基斯坦PK,秘鲁PE	0	最不发达35国LDC35	90	----Hog fat-ends, salted
458	0504.0019	----其他	18	0 1.8 3.6 9	东盟ASEAN,新西兰NZ 智利CL 哥斯达黎加CR 亚太APTA,巴基斯坦PK,秘鲁PE	0	最不发达35国LDC35	90	----Other
		---胃：							---Gizzard:
459	0504.0021	----冷、冻的鸡胗	1.3元/千克	0 4 10 0.13元/千克 0.65元/千克	文莱BN,柬埔寨KH,印尼ID,马来西亚MY,缅甸MM,菲律宾PH,新加坡*SG*,泰国TH,越南VT,新西兰NZ 哥斯达黎加CR 秘鲁PE 智利CL 亚太APTA,巴基斯坦PK	0	最不发达35国LDC35	7.7元/千克	----Cold, frozen gizzard
460	0504.0029	----其他	20	0 2 4 10	东盟ASEAN,新西兰NZ 智利CL 哥斯达黎加CR 亚太APTA,巴基斯坦PK,秘鲁PE	0	最不发达35国LDC35,最不发达4国LDC4	90	----Other
461	0504.0090	---其他	20	0 2 4 10	东盟ASEAN,新西兰NZ 智利CL 哥斯达黎加CR 亚太APTA,巴基斯坦PK,秘鲁PE	0	最不发达35国LDC35	80	---Other
	05.05	**带有羽毛或羽绒的鸟皮及鸟体其他部分；羽毛及不完整羽毛（不论是否修边）、羽绒，仅经洗涤、消毒或为了保藏而作过处理，但未经进一步加工；羽毛或不完整羽毛的粉末及废料：**							**Skins and other parts of birds, with their feathers or down; feathers and parts of feathers (Whether or not with trimmed edges) and down, not further worked than cleaned, disinfected or treated for preservation; powder and waste of feathers or parts of feathers:**
462	0505.1000	-填充用羽毛；羽绒	10 △5	0 5 7.5	东盟ASEAN,智利CL,新西兰NZ,秘鲁PE,哥斯达黎加CR 巴基斯坦PK 亚太APTA	0	最不发达35国LDC35,最不发达4国LDC4	100	-Feathers of a kind used for stuffing; down
		-其他：							-Other:

序号 No.	税则号列 Tariff Line	货品名称	最惠国税率 MFN(%)	协定税率 Agreement(%)		特惠税率 S.P.(%)		普通税率 Gen.(%)	Article Description
463	0505.9010	---羽毛或不完整羽毛的粉末及废料	10	0 5	东盟ASEAN,智利CL,新西兰NZ,秘鲁PE,哥斯达黎加CR 巴基斯坦PK	0	最不发达35国LDC35,最不发达4国LDC4	35	---Powder and waste of feathers or parts of feathers
464	0505.9090	---其他	10	0 5	东盟ASEAN,智利CL,新西兰NZ,秘鲁PE,哥斯达黎加CR 巴基斯坦PK	0	最不发达35国LDC35,最不发达4国LDC4	90	---Other
	05.06	**骨及角柱，未经加工或经脱脂、简单整理（但未切割成形）、酸处理或脱胶；上述产品的粉末及废料：**							**Bones and horn-cores, unworked, defatted, simply prepared (but not cut to shape), treated with acid or degelatinized; powder and waste of these products:**
465	0506.1000	-经酸处理的骨胶原及骨	12	0 2.4 6	东盟ASEAN,智利CL,新西兰NZ,秘鲁PE 哥斯达黎加CR 巴基斯坦PK	0	最不发达35国LDC35,最不发达4国LDC4,老挝LA	50	-Ossein and bones treated with acid
		-其他： ---骨粉、骨废料：							-Other: ---Powder and waste of bones:
466	0506.9011	----含牛羊成分的	12	0 1.2 2.4 6	东盟ASEAN,新西兰NZ 智利CL 哥斯达黎加CR 巴基斯坦PK,秘鲁PE	0	最不发达35国LDC35,最不发达4国LDC4,老挝LA	35	----Of bovine and sheep
467	0506.9019	----其他	12	0 1.2 2.4 6	东盟ASEAN,新西兰NZ 智利CL 哥斯达黎加CR 巴基斯坦PK,秘鲁PE	0	最不发达35国LDC35,最不发达4国LDC4,老挝LA	35	----Other
468	0506.9090	---其他	12	0 1.2 6 7.2	东盟ASEAN,新西兰NZ,澳门MO 智利CL 巴基斯坦PK,秘鲁PE 哥斯达黎加CR	0	最不发达35国LDC35,最不发达4国LDC4,老挝LA	50	---Other
	05.07	**兽牙、龟壳、鲸须、鲸须毛、角、鹿角、蹄、甲、爪及喙，未经加工或仅简单整理但未切割成形；上述产品的粉末及废料：**							**Ivory, tortoise-shell, whalebone and whalebone hair, horns, antlers, hooves, nails, claws and beaks, unworked or simply prepared but not cut to shape; powder and waste of these products:**

序号 No.	税则号列 Tariff Line	货品名称	最惠国税率 MFN(%)	协定税率 Agreement(%)		特惠税率 S.P.(%)		普通税率 Gen.(%)	Article Description
469	0507.1000	-兽牙；兽牙粉末及废料：	10	0 5	东盟ASEAN,智利CL,新西兰NZ,秘鲁PE,哥斯达黎加CR 巴基斯坦PK	0	最不发达35国LDC35,最不发达4国LDC4	30	-Ivory; ivory powder and waste
		-其他：							-Other:
470	0507.9010	---羚羊角及其粉末和废料	3	0	东盟ASEAN,智利CL,巴基斯坦PK,新西兰NZ,秘鲁PE,哥斯达黎加CR	0	最不发达35国LDC35,最不发达4国LDC4	14	---Antelope horns and powder or waste thereof
471	0507.9020	---鹿茸及其粉末	11	0 2.2 5	东盟ASEAN,智利CL,新西兰NZ,秘鲁PE 哥斯达黎加CR 巴基斯坦PK	0	最不发达35国LDC35,最不发达4国LDC4	30	---Pilose antlers and powder thereof
472	0507.9090	---其他	10	0 5	东盟ASEAN,智利CL,新西兰NZ,秘鲁PE,哥斯达黎加CR 巴基斯坦PK	0	最不发达35国LDC35,最不发达4国LDC4	50	---Other
	05.08	**珊瑚及类似品，未经加工或仅简单整理但未经进一步加工；软体动物壳、甲壳动物壳、棘皮动物壳、墨鱼骨，未经加工或仅简单整理但未切割成形，上述壳、骨的粉末及废料：**							**Coral and similar materials, unworked or simply prepared but not otherwise worked; shells of molluscs, crustaceans or echinoderms and cuttle-bone, unworked or simply prepared but not cut to shape, powder and waste thereof:**
473	0508.0010	---粉末及废料	12	0 1.2 2.4 6	东盟ASEAN,新西兰NZ,香港HK 智利CL 哥斯达黎加CR 秘鲁PE	0	最不发达35国LDC35,最不发达4国LDC4	35	---Powder and waste
474	0508.0090	---其他	12	0 1.2 2.4 6	东盟ASEAN,新西兰NZ,香港HK 智利CL 哥斯达黎加CR 巴基斯坦PK,秘鲁PE	0	最不发达35国LDC35,最不发达4国LDC4	50	---Other
	05.10	**龙涎香、海狸香、灵猫香及麝香；斑蝥；胆汁，不论是否干制；供配制药用的腺体及其他动物产品，鲜、冷、冻或用其他方法暂时保藏的：**							**Ambergris, castoreum, civet and musk; cantharides; bile, whether of not dried; glands and other animal products used in the preparation of pharmaceutical products, fresh, chilled, frozen or otherwise provisionally preserved:**

序号 No.	税则号列 Tariff Line	货品名称	最惠国 税 率 MFN(%)	协定税率 Agreement(%)		特惠税率 S.P.(%)		普通 税率 Gen.(%)	Article Description
475	0510.0010	---黄药	3	0	东盟ASEAN,智利CL,巴基斯坦PK,新西兰NZ,秘鲁PE,哥斯达黎加CR	0	最不发达35国LDC35,最不发达4国LDC4	14	---Bezoar
476	0510.0020	---龙涎香、海狸香、灵猫香	7	0 5	东盟ASEAN,智利CL,新西兰NZ,秘鲁PE,哥斯达黎加CR 巴基斯坦PK	0	最不发达35国LDC35	50	---Ambergris, castoreum and civet
477	0510.0030	---麝香	7	0 5	东盟ASEAN,智利CL,新西兰NZ,秘鲁PE,哥斯达黎加CR 巴基斯坦PK	0	最不发达35国LDC35	20	---Musk
478	0510.0040	---斑蝥	7	0 5	东盟ASEAN,智利CL,新西兰NZ,秘鲁PE,哥斯达黎加CR 巴基斯坦PK	0	最不发达35国LDC35,最不发达4国LDC4	50	---Cantharides
479	0510.0090	---其他	6	0 5	东盟ASEAN,智利CL,新西兰NZ,秘鲁PE,哥斯达黎加CR 巴基斯坦PK	0	最不发达35国LDC35,最不发达4国LDC4	20	---Other
	05.11	**其他税号未列名的动物产品；不适合供人食用的第一章或第三章的死动物：**							**Animal products not elsewhere specified or included; dead animals of Chapter 1 or 3, unfit for human consumption:**
480	0511.1000	-牛的精液	0			0	最不发达35国LDC35,最不发达4国LDC4	0	-Bovine semen
		-其他： --鱼、甲壳动物、软体动物、其他水生无脊椎动物的产品；第三章的死动物： ---鱼的：							-Other: --Products of fish or crustaceans, molluscs or other aquatic invertebrates; dead animals of Chapter3: ---Fish:
481	0511.9111	----受精鱼卵	12 △0	0 1.2 2.4 6	东盟ASEAN,新西兰NZ,秘鲁PE 智利CL 哥斯达黎加CR 巴基斯坦PK	0	最不发达35国LDC35,最不发达4国LDC4	35	----Fertilized fish eggs
482	0511.9119	----其他	12	0 1.2 2.4 6	东盟ASEAN,新西兰NZ 智利CL 哥斯达黎加CR 秘鲁PE	0	最不发达35国LDC35,最不发达4国LDC4	35	----Other

序号 No.	税则号列 Tariff Line	货品名称	最惠国税率 MFN(%)	协定税率 Agreement(%)		特惠税率 S.P.(%)		普通税率 Gen.(%)	Article Description
483	0511.9190	---其他	12	0 1.2 2.4 6	东盟ASEAN,新西兰NZ 智利CL 哥斯达黎加CR 巴基斯坦PK,秘鲁PE	0	最不发达35国LDC35,最不发达4国LDC4	35	---Other
		--其他:							--Other:
484	0511.9910	---动物精液（牛的精液除外）	0			0	最不发达35国LDC35,最不发达4国LDC4	0	---Animal semen, other than bovine semen
485	0511.9920	---动物胚胎	0			0	最不发达35国LDC35,最不发达4国LDC4	0	---Animal embryo
486	0511.9930	---蚕种	0			0	最不发达35国LDC35,最不发达4国LDC4	0	---Silkworm graine
487	0511.9940	---马毛及废马毛，不论是否制成有或无衬垫的毛片	15	0 3 7.5 12	东盟ASEAN,智利CL,新西兰NZ 哥斯达黎加CR 秘鲁PE 巴基斯坦PK	0	最不发达35国LDC35	90	---Horsehair and horsehair waste, whether or not put up as a layer with or without supporting material
488	0511.9990	---其他	12	0 2.4 6	东盟ASEAN,智利CL,新西兰NZ 哥斯达黎加CR 巴基斯坦PK,秘鲁PE	0	最不发达35国LDC35,最不发达4国LDC4	35	---Other

第二类

植 物 产 品

注释：

本类所称"团粒"，是指直接挤压或加入按重量计比例不超过3%的粘合剂制成的粒状产品。

SECTION Ⅱ

VEGETABLE PRODUCTS

Note:

In this Section the term "pellets" means products which have been agglomerated either directly by compression or by the addition of a binder in a proportion not exceeding 3% by weight.

第六章
活树及其他活植物；
鳞茎、根及类似品；
插花及装饰用簇叶

注释：

一、除税号06.01的菊苣植物及其根以外，本章包括通常由苗圃或花店供应为种植或装饰用的活树及其他货品（包括植物秧苗）；但不包括马铃薯、洋葱、青葱、大蒜及其他第七章的产品。

二、税号06.03、06.04的各种货品，包括全部或部分用这些货品制成的花束、花篮、花圈及类似品，不论是否有其他材料制成的附件。但这些货品不包括税号97.01的拼贴画或类似的装饰板。

Chapter 6
Live trees and other plants;
bulbs, roots and the like;
cut flowers and ornamental foliage

Notes:

1. Subject to the second part of heading No.06.01, this Chapter covers only live trees and goods (including seedling vegetables) of a kind commonly supplied by nursery gardeners or florists for planting or for ornamental use; nevertheless it does not include potatoes, onions, shallots, garlic or other products of Chapter 7.
2. Any reference in heading No.06.03 or 06.04 to goods of any kind shall be construed as including a reference to bouquets, floral baskets, wreaths and similar articles made wholly or partly of goods of that kind, account not being taken of accessories of other materials. However, these headings do not include collages or similar decorative plaques of heading No.97.01.

序号 No.	税则号列 Tariff Line	货品名称	最惠国税率 MFN(%)	协定税率 Agreement(%)	特惠税率 S.P.(%)	普通税率 Gen.(%)	Article Description
	06.01	**鳞茎、块茎、块根、球茎、根颈及根茎，休眠、生长或开花的；菊苣植物及其根，但税号12.12的根除外：**					**Bulbs, tubers, tuberous roots, corms, crowns and rhizomes, dormant, in growth or in flower; chicory plants and roots other than roots of heading No.12.12:**
		-休眠的鳞茎、块茎、块根、球茎、根颈及根茎：					-Bulbs, tubers, tuberous roots, corms, crowns and rhizomes, dormant:

序号 No.	税则号列 Tariff Line	货品名称	最惠国 税　率 MFN(%)	协定税率 Agreement(%)	特惠税率 S.P.(%)	普通 税率 Gen.(%)	Article Description
489	0601.1010	---番红花球茎	4	0 东盟ASEAN,智利CL,巴基斯坦PK,新西兰NZ,秘鲁PE,哥斯达黎加CR 2 亚太APTA	0 最不发达35国LDC35,最不发达4国LDC4,老挝LA	14	---Stigma croci corms
		---百合球茎:					---Lily corms:
490	0601.1021	----种用	0		0 最不发达35国LDC35,最不发达4国LDC4	0	----Seed
491	0601.1029	----其他	5	0 东盟ASEAN,智利CL,巴基斯坦PK,新西兰NZ,秘鲁PE,哥斯达黎加CR 2.5 亚太APTA	0 最不发达35国LDC35,最不发达4国LDC4,老挝LA	40	----Other
		---其他:					---Other:
492	0601.1091	----种用	0		0 最不发达35国LDC35,最不发达4国LDC4	0	----Seed
493	0601.1099	----其他	5	0 东盟ASEAN,智利CL,巴基斯坦PK,新西兰NZ,秘鲁PE,哥斯达黎加CR 2.5 亚太APTA	0 最不发达35国LDC35,最不发达4国LDC4,老挝LA	40	----Others
494	0601.2000	-生长或开花的鳞茎、块茎、块根、球茎、根颈及根茎;菊苣植物及其根	15	0 东盟ASEAN,新西兰NZ 1.5 智利CL 3 哥斯达黎加CR 7.5 亚太APTA,巴基斯坦PK,秘鲁PE	0 最不发达35国LDC35	80	-Bulbs, tubers, tuberous roots, corms, crowns and rhizomes, in growth or in flower; chicory plants and roots
	06.02	**其他活植物(包括其根)、插枝及接穗;蘑菇菌丝:**					**Other live plants (including their roots) cuttings and ships; mushroom spawn:**
495	0602.1000	-无根插枝及接穗	0		0 最不发达35国LDC35,最不发达4国LDC4	0	-Unrooted cuttings and slips
		-食用水果或食用坚果的树、灌木,不论是否嫁接:					-Trees, shrubs and bushes, grafted or not, of kinds which bear edible fruit or nuts:

序号 No.	税则号列 Tariff Line	货品名称	最惠国税率 MFN(%)	协定税率 Agreement(%)	特惠税率 S.P.(%)	普通税率 Gen.(%)	Article Description
496	0602.2010	---种用苗木	0		0 最不发达35国LDC35,最不发达4国LDC4	0	---Seedlings
497	0602.2090	---其他	10	0 东盟ASEAN,新西兰NZ,哥斯达黎加CR 1 智利CL 5 亚太APTA,巴基斯坦PK,秘鲁PE	0 最不发达35国LDC35,最不发达4国LDC4	80	---Other
		-杜鹃，不论是否嫁接：					-Rhododendrons and azaleas, grafted or not:
498	0602.3010	---种用	0		0 最不发达35国LDC35,最不发达4国LDC4	0	---Seedlings
499	0602.3090	---其他	15	0 东盟ASEAN,智利CL,新西兰NZ 3 哥斯达黎加CR 7.5 秘鲁PE 12 巴基斯坦PK	0 最不发达35国LDC35	80	---Other
		-玫瑰，不论是否嫁接：					-Roses, grafted or not:
500	0602.4010	---种用	0		0 最不发达35国LDC35,最不发达4国LDC4	0	---Seedlings
501	0602.4090	---其他	15	0 东盟ASEAN,智利CL,新西兰NZ 3 哥斯达黎加CR 7.5 秘鲁PE 12 巴基斯坦PK	0 最不发达35国LDC35	80	---Other
		-其他：					-Other:
502	0602.9010	---蘑菇菌丝	0		0 最不发达35国LDC35,最不发达4国LDC4	0	---Mushroom spawn
		---其他：					---Other:
503	0602.9091	----种用苗木	0		0 最不发达35国LDC35,最不发达4国LDC4	0	----Seedlings

序号 No.	税则号列 Tariff Line	货品名称	最惠国税率 MFN(%)	协定税率 Agreement(%)		特惠税率 S.P.(%)		普通税率 Gen.(%)	Article Description
504	0602.9092	----兰花	10	0 1 5	东盟ASEAN,新西兰NZ,哥斯达黎加CR 智利CL 巴基斯坦PK,秘鲁PE	0	最不发达35国LDC35,最不发达4国LDC4	80	----Orchid
505	0602.9093	----菊花	10	0 1 5	东盟ASEAN,新西兰NZ,哥斯达黎加CR 智利CL 巴基斯坦PK,秘鲁PE	0	最不发达35国LDC35,最不发达4国LDC4	80	----Chrysathemum
506	0602.9094	----百合	10	0 1 5	东盟ASEAN,新西兰NZ,哥斯达黎加CR 智利CL 巴基斯坦PK,秘鲁PE	0	最不发达35国LDC35,最不发达4国LDC4	80	----Lily
507	0602.9095	----康乃馨	10	0 1 5	东盟ASEAN,新西兰NZ,哥斯达黎加CR 智利CL 巴基斯坦PK,秘鲁PE	0	最不发达35国LDC35,最不发达4国LDC4	80	----Carnation
508	0602.9099	----其他	10	0 1 5	东盟ASEAN,新西兰NZ,哥斯达黎加CR 智利CL 亚太APTA,巴基斯坦PK,秘鲁PE	0	最不发达35国LDC35,最不发达4国LDC4	80	----Other
	06.03	**制花束或装饰用的插花及花蕾,鲜、干、染色、漂白、浸渍或用其他方法处理的:**							**Cut flowers and flower buds of a kind suitable for bouquets or for ornamental purposes, fresh, dried, dyed, bleached, impregnated or otherwise prepared:**
		-鲜的:							-Fresh:
509	0603.1100	--玫瑰	10	0 1 5	东盟ASEAN,新西兰NZ,秘鲁PE,哥斯达黎加CR 智利CL 亚太APTA,巴基斯坦PK	0	最不发达35国LDC35,最不发达4国LDC4,老挝LA	100	--Roses
510	0603.1200	--康乃馨	10	0 1 5	东盟ASEAN,新西兰NZ,秘鲁PE,哥斯达黎加CR 智利CL 亚太APTA,巴基斯坦PK	0	最不发达35国LDC35,最不发达4国LDC4,老挝LA	100	--Carnations

序号 No.	税则号列 Tariff Line	货品名称	最惠国税 率 MFN(%)	协定税率 Agreement(%)		特惠税率 S.P.(%)		普通税率 Gen.(%)	Article Description
511	0603.1300	--兰花	10	0 1 5	东盟ASEAN,新西兰NZ,秘鲁PE,哥斯达黎加CR,台湾TW 智利CL 亚太APTA,巴基斯坦PK	0	最不发达35国LDC35,最不发达4国LDC4,老挝LA	100	--Orchids
512	0603.1400	--菊花	10	0 1 5	东盟ASEAN,新西兰NZ,秘鲁PE,哥斯达黎加CR 智利CL 亚太APTA,巴基斯坦PK	0	最不发达35国LDC35,最不发达4国LDC4,老挝LA	100	--Chrysanthemums
513	0603.1500	--百合花（百合属）	10	0 1 5	东盟ASEAN,新西兰NZ,秘鲁PE,哥斯达黎加CR 智利CL 亚太APTA,巴基斯坦PK	0	最不发达35国LDC35,最不发达4国LDC4,老挝LA	100	--Lilies (Lilium spp.)
514	0603.1900	--其他	10	0 1 5	东盟ASEAN,新西兰NZ,秘鲁PE,哥斯达黎加CR 智利CL 亚太APTA,巴基斯坦PK	0	最不发达35国LDC35,最不发达4国LDC4,老挝LA	100	--Other
515	0603.9000	-其他	23	0 4.6 11.5	东盟ASEAN,智利CL,新西兰NZ,香港HK 哥斯达黎加CR 亚太APTA,巴基斯坦PK,秘鲁PE	0	最不发达35国LDC35,最不发达4国LDC4,老挝LA	100	-Other
	06.04	**制花束或装饰用的不带花及花蕾的植物枝、叶或其他部分、草、苔藓及地衣，鲜、干、染色、漂白、浸渍或用其他方法处理的：**							**Foliage, branches and other parts of plants, without flowers or flowerbuds, and grasses, mosses and lichens, being goods of a kind suitable for bouquets or for ornamental purposes, fresh, dried, dyed, bleached, impregnated or otherwise prepared:**
		-鲜的：							-Fresh:
516	0604.2010	---苔藓及地衣	23	0 2.3 4.6 11.5	东盟ASEAN,新西兰NZ 智利CL 哥斯达黎加CR 秘鲁PE	0	最不发达35国LDC35	100	---Mosses and lichens

序号 No.	税则号列 Tariff Line	货品名称	最惠国税率 MFN(%)	协定税率 Agreement(%)		特惠税率 S.P.(%)		普通税率 Gen.(%)	Article Description
517	0604.2090	---其他	10	0 1 5	东盟ASEAN,新西兰NZ,哥斯达黎加CR 智利CL 巴基斯坦PK,秘鲁PE	0	最不发达35国LDC35,最不发达4国LDC4	100	---Other
		-其他:							-Other:
518	0604.9010	---苔藓及地衣	23	0 2.3 4.6 11.5	东盟ASEAN,新西兰NZ 智利CL 哥斯达黎加CR 秘鲁PE	0	最不发达35国LDC35	100	---Mosses and lichens
519	0604.9090	---其他	10	0 5	东盟ASEAN,智利CL,新西兰NZ,秘鲁PE,哥斯达黎加CR,香港HK 巴基斯坦PK	0	最不发达35国LDC35,最不发达4国LDC4	100	---Other

第七章
食用蔬菜、根及块茎

注释：

一、本章不包括税号 12.14 的草料。

二、税号 07.09、07.10、07.11 及 07.12 所称"蔬菜"，包括食用的蘑菇、块菌、油橄榄、刺山柑、菜葫芦、南瓜、茄子、甜玉米、辣椒、茴香菜、欧芹、细叶芹、龙蒿、水芹、甜茉乔栾那。

三、税号 07.12 包括干制的归入税号 07.01 至 07.11 的各种蔬菜，但下列各项除外：

（一）作蔬菜用的脱荚干豆（税号 07.13）；

（二）税号 11.02 至 11.04 所列形状的甜玉米；

（三）马铃薯细粉、粗粉、粉末、粉片、颗粒及团粒（税号 11.05）；

（四）用税号 07.13 的干豆制成的细粉、粗粉及粉末（税号 11.06）。

四、本章不包括辣椒干及辣椒粉（税号 09.04）。

Chapter 7
Edible vegetables and certain roots and tubers

Notes:

1.This Chapter does not cover forage products of heading No.12.14.

2. In headings No.07.09, 07.10, 07.11 and 07.12 the word "vegetables" includes edible mushrooms, truffles, olives, capers, marrows, pumpkins, aubergines, sweet corn (*Zea may svar.saccharata*), fruits of the genus *Capsicum* or of the genus *Pimenta*, fennel, parsley, chervil, tarragon, cress and sweet marjoram (*Majorana hortensis or Origanum majorana*).

3. Heading No.07.12 covers all dried vegetables of the kinds falling in headings No.07.01 to 07.11, other than:

(a) dried leguminous vegetables, shelled (heading No.07.13);

(b) sweet corn in the forms specified in headings No.11.02 to 11.04;

(c) flour, meal, powder, flakes, granules and pellets of potatoes (heading No.11.05);

(d) flour, meal and powder of the dried leguminous vegetables of heading No.07.13 (heading No.11.06).

4. However, dried or crushed or ground fruits of the genus *Capsicum* or of the genus *Pimenta* are excluded from this Chapter (heading No.09.04).

序号 No.	税则号列 Tariff Line	货品名称	最惠国税率 MFN(%)	协定税率 Agreement(%)	特惠税率 S.P.(%)	普通税率 Gen.(%)	Article Description
	07.01	**鲜或冷藏的马铃薯：**					**Potatoes, fresh or chilled:**
520	0701.1000	-种用	13	0 东盟ASEAN,智利CL,新西兰NZ,秘鲁PE 2.6 哥斯达黎加CR 6.5 巴基斯坦PK	0 最不发达35国LDC35,最不发达4国LDC4	70	-Seed
521	0701.9000	-其他	13	0 东盟ASEAN,智利CL,新西兰NZ,秘鲁PE 2.6 哥斯达黎加CR 5 巴基斯坦PK 9 亚太APTA	0 最不发达35国LDC35,最不发达4国LDC4,柬埔寨KH	70	-Other
	07.02	**鲜或冷藏的番茄：**					**Tomatoes, fresh or chilled:**

序号 No.	税则号列 Tariff Line	货品名称	最惠国税率 MFN(%)	协定税率 Agreement(%)		特惠税率 S.P.(%)		普通税率 Gen.(%)	Article Description
522	0702.0000	鲜或冷藏的番茄	13	0 2.6 6.5	东盟ASEAN,智利CL,新西兰NZ,秘鲁PE 哥斯达黎加CR 巴基斯坦PK	0	最不发达35国LDC35,最不发达4国LDC4	70	Tomatoes, fresh or chilled
	07.03	**鲜或冷藏的洋葱、青葱、大蒜、韭葱及其他葱属蔬菜：**							**Onions, shallots, garlic, leeks and other alliaceous vegetables, fresh or chilled:**
		-洋葱及青葱：							-Onions and shallots:
523	0703.1010	---洋葱	13	0 2.6 5 6.5	东盟ASEAN,智利CL,新西兰NZ,秘鲁PE 哥斯达黎加CR 巴基斯坦PK 亚太APTA	0	最不发达35国LDC35,最不发达4国LDC4,缅甸MM,柬埔寨KH	70	---Onions
524	0703.1020	---青葱	13	0 2.6 5 6.5	东盟ASEAN,智利CL,新西兰NZ,秘鲁PE 哥斯达黎加CR 巴基斯坦PK 亚太APTA	0	最不发达35国LDC35,最不发达4国LDC4,缅甸MM,柬埔寨KH	70	---Shallots
		-大蒜：							-Garlic:
525	0703.2010	---蒜头	13	0 2.6 6.5	东盟ASEAN,智利CL,巴基斯坦PK,新西兰NZ,秘鲁PE 哥斯达黎加CR 亚太APTA	0	最不发达35国LDC35	70	---Garlic bulbs
526	0703.2020	---蒜苔及蒜苗（青蒜）	13	0 2.6 6.5	东盟ASEAN,智利CL,巴基斯坦PK,新西兰NZ,秘鲁PE 哥斯达黎加CR 亚太APTA	0	最不发达35国LDC35	70	---Garlic stems, garlic seedlings
527	0703.2090	---其他	13	0 2.6 6.5	东盟ASEAN,智利CL,巴基斯坦PK,新西兰NZ,秘鲁PE 哥斯达黎加CR 亚太APTA	0	最不发达35国LDC35	70	---Other
		-韭葱及其他葱属蔬菜：							-Leeks and other alliaceous vegetables:
528	0703.9010	---韭葱	13	0 2.6 6.5	东盟ASEAN,智利CL,新西兰NZ,秘鲁PE 哥斯达黎加CR 巴基斯坦PK	0	最不发达35国LDC35,最不发达4国LDC4,柬埔寨KH	70	---Leeks

序号 No.	税则号列 Tariff Line	货品名称	最惠国税率 MFN(%)	协定税率 Agreement(%)	特惠税率 S.P.(%)	普通税率 Gen.(%)	Article Description
529	0703.9020	---大葱	13	0 东盟ASEAN,智利CL,新西兰NZ,秘鲁PE 2.6 哥斯达黎加CR 6.5 巴基斯坦PK	0 最不发达35国LDC35,最不发达4国LDC4,柬埔寨KH	70	---Scallion
530	0703.9090	---其他	13	0 东盟ASEAN,智利CL,新西兰NZ,秘鲁PE 2.6 哥斯达黎加CR 6.5 巴基斯坦PK	0 最不发达35国LDC35,最不发达4国LDC4,柬埔寨KH	70	---Other
	07.04	**鲜或冷藏的卷心菜、菜花、球茎甘蓝、羽衣甘蓝及类似的食用芥菜类蔬菜：**					**Cabbages, cauliflowers, kohlrabi, kale and similar edible brassicas, fresh or chilled:**
531	0704.1000	-菜花及硬花甘蓝	10	0 东盟ASEAN,智利CL,新西兰NZ,秘鲁PE,哥斯达黎加CR 5 巴基斯坦PK	0 最不发达35国LDC35,最不发达4国LDC4	70	-Cauliflowers and headed broccoli
532	0704.2000	-抱子甘蓝	13	0 东盟ASEAN,智利CL,新西兰NZ,秘鲁PE 2.6 哥斯达黎加CR 6.5 巴基斯坦PK	0 最不发达35国LDC35	70	-Brussels sprouts
		-其他：					-Other:
533	0704.9010	---卷心菜	13	0 东盟ASEAN,智利CL,新西兰NZ,秘鲁PE 2.6 哥斯达黎加CR 6.5 巴基斯坦PK	0 最不发达35国LDC35,最不发达4国LDC4,老挝LA	70	---Cabbage (Brassica oleracea var. capitata)
534	0704.9020	---西兰花	13	0 东盟ASEAN,智利CL,新西兰NZ,秘鲁PE 2.6 哥斯达黎加CR 6.5 巴基斯坦PK	0 最不发达35国LDC35,最不发达4国LDC4,老挝LA	70	---Cabbage (Brassica oleracea var. italica)
535	0704.9090	---其他	13	0 东盟ASEAN,智利CL,新西兰NZ,秘鲁PE 2.6 哥斯达黎加CR 6.5 巴基斯坦PK	0 最不发达35国LDC35,最不发达4国LDC4,老挝LA	70	---Other
	07.05	**鲜或冷藏的莴苣及菊苣：**					**Lettuce (lactuca sativa) and chicory (Cichorium spp.), fresh or chilled:**
		-莴苣：					-Lettuce:

序号 No.	税则号列 Tariff Line	货品名称	最惠国税率 MFN(%)		协定税率 Agreement(%)		特惠税率 S.P.(%)	普通税率 Gen.(%)	Article Description
536	0705.1100	--结球莴苣（包心生菜）	10	0	东盟ASEAN,智利CL,巴基斯坦PK,新西兰NZ,秘鲁PE,哥斯达黎加CR	0	最不发达35国LDC35,最不发达4国LDC4	70	--Cabbage lettuce (head lettuce)
537	0705.1900	--其他	10	0	东盟ASEAN,智利CL,巴基斯坦PK,新西兰NZ,秘鲁PE,哥斯达黎加CR	0	最不发达35国LDC35,最不发达4国LDC4	70	--Other
		-菊苣:							-Chicory:
538	0705.2100	--维特罗夫菊苣	13	0	东盟ASEAN,智利CL,巴基斯坦PK,新西兰NZ,秘鲁PE	0	最不发达35国LDC35	70	--Witloof chicory (Cichoriym intybus var.foliosum)
				2.6	哥斯达黎加CR				
539	0705.2900	--其他	13	0	东盟ASEAN,智利CL,巴基斯坦PK,新西兰NZ,秘鲁PE	0	最不发达35国LDC35	70	--Other
				2.6	哥斯达黎加CR				
	07.06	**鲜或冷藏的胡萝卜、萝卜、色拉甜菜根、婆罗门参、块根芹、小萝卜及类似的食用根茎:**							**Carrots, turnips, salad beetroot, salsify, celeriac, radishes and similar edible roots, fresh or chilled:**
540	0706.1000	-胡萝卜及萝卜	13	0	东盟ASEAN,智利CL,新西兰NZ,秘鲁PE	0	最不发达35国LDC35	70	-Carrots and turnips
				2.6	哥斯达黎加CR				
				6.5	巴基斯坦PK				
541	0706.9000	-其他	13	0	东盟ASEAN,智利CL,新西兰NZ,秘鲁PE	0	最不发达35国LDC35	70	-Other
				2.6	哥斯达黎加CR				
				6.5	巴基斯坦PK				
	07.07	**鲜或冷藏的黄瓜及小黄瓜:**							**Cucumbers and gherkins, fresh or chilled:**
542	0707.0000	鲜或冷藏的黄瓜及小黄瓜	13	0	东盟ASEAN,智利CL,新西兰NZ,秘鲁PE	0	最不发达35国LDC35,最不发达4国LDC4,柬埔寨KH	70	Cucumbers and gherkins, fresh or chilled
				2.6	哥斯达黎加CR				
				5	巴基斯坦PK				
				6.5	亚太APTA				
	07.08	**鲜或冷藏的豆类蔬菜，不论是否脱荚:**							**Leguminous vegetables, shelled or unshelled, fresh or chilled:**
543	0708.1000	-豌豆	13	0	东盟ASEAN,智利CL,巴基斯坦PK,新西兰NZ,秘鲁PE	0	最不发达35国LDC35,最不发达4国LDC4,柬埔寨KH	70	-Peas (Pisum sativum)
				2.6	哥斯达黎加CR				
				6.5	亚太APTA				

序号 No.	税则号列 Tariff Line	货品名称	最惠国税率 MFN(%)	协定税率 Agreement(%)		特惠税率 S.P.(%)		普通税率 Gen.(%)	Article Description
544	0708.2000	-豇豆及菜豆	13	0 2.6 6.5	东盟ASEAN,智利CL,巴基斯坦PK,新西兰NZ,秘鲁PE 哥斯达黎加CR 亚太APTA	0	最不发达35国LDC35,最不发达4国LDC4,老挝LA,柬埔寨KH	70	-Beans (Vigna spp., Phaseolus spp.)
545	0708.9000	-其他豆类蔬菜	13	0 2.6 6.5	东盟ASEAN,智利CL,巴基斯坦PK,新西兰NZ,秘鲁PE 哥斯达黎加CR 亚太APTA	0	最不发达35国LDC35,最不发达4国LDC4,柬埔寨KH	70	-Other leguminous vegetables
	07.09	**鲜或冷藏的其他蔬菜:**							**Other vegetables, fresh or chilled:**
546	0709.2000	-芦笋	13	0 2.6 6.5	东盟ASEAN,智利CL,巴基斯坦PK,新西兰NZ,秘鲁PE 哥斯达黎加CR 亚太APTA	0	最不发达35国LDC35,最不发达4国LDC4	70	-Asparagus
547	0709.3000	-茄子	13	0 2.6 6.5	东盟ASEAN,智利CL,巴基斯坦PK,新西兰NZ,秘鲁PE 哥斯达黎加CR 亚太APTA	0	最不发达35国LDC35,最不发达4国LDC4	70	-Aubergines (egg-plants)
548	0709.4000	-芹菜,但块根芹除外	10	0	东盟ASEAN,智利CL,巴基斯坦PK,新西兰NZ,秘鲁PE,哥斯达黎加CR	0	最不发达35国LDC35,最不发达4国LDC4	70	-Celery other than celeriac
		-蘑菇及块菌:							-Mushrooms and truffles:
549	0709.5100	--伞菌属蘑菇	13	0 2.6	东盟ASEAN,智利CL,巴基斯坦PK,新西兰NZ,秘鲁PE 哥斯达黎加CR	0	最不发达35国LDC35,最不发达4国LDC4,柬埔寨KH	90	--Mushrooms of the genus Agaricus
		--其他:							--Other:
550	0709.5910	---松茸	13	0 2.6	东盟ASEAN,智利CL,巴基斯坦PK,新西兰NZ,秘鲁PE 哥斯达黎加CR	0	最不发达35国LDC35,最不发达4国LDC4,柬埔寨KH	90	---Sungmo

序号 No.	税则号列 Tariff Line	货品名称	最惠国税率 MFN(%)	协定税率 Agreement(%)		特惠税率 S.P.(%)		普通税率 Gen.(%)	Article Description
551	0709.5920	---香菇	13	0 2.6	东盟ASEAN,智利CL,巴基斯坦PK,新西兰NZ,秘鲁PE 哥斯达黎加CR	0	最不发达35国LDC35,最不发达4国LDC4,柬埔寨KH	90	---Shiitake
552	0709.5930	---金针菇	13	0 2.6	东盟ASEAN,智利CL,巴基斯坦PK,新西兰NZ,秘鲁PE,台湾TW 哥斯达黎加CR	0	最不发达35国LDC35,最不发达4国LDC4,柬埔寨KH	90	---Winter mushroom
553	0709.5940	---草菇	13	0 2.6	东盟ASEAN,智利CL,巴基斯坦PK,新西兰NZ,秘鲁PE 哥斯达黎加CR	0	最不发达35国LDC35,最不发达4国LDC4,柬埔寨KH	90	---Paddy Straw mushroom
554	0709.5950	---口蘑	13	0 2.6	东盟ASEAN,智利CL,巴基斯坦PK,新西兰NZ,秘鲁PE 哥斯达黎加CR	0	最不发达35国LDC35,最不发达4国LDC4,柬埔寨KH	90	---Tricholoma mongolicum Imai
555	0709.5960	---块菌	13	0 2.6	东盟ASEAN,智利CL,巴基斯坦PK,新西兰NZ,秘鲁PE 哥斯达黎加CR	0	最不发达35国LDC35	90	---Truffle
556	0709.5990	---其他	13	0 2.6	东盟ASEAN,智利CL,巴基斯坦PK,新西兰NZ,秘鲁PE 哥斯达黎加CR	0	最不发达35国LDC35,最不发达4国LDC4,柬埔寨KH	90	---Other
557	0709.6000	-辣椒，包括甜椒	13	0 2.6 6.5	东盟ASEAN,智利CL,巴基斯坦PK,新西兰NZ,秘鲁PE 哥斯达黎加CR 亚太APTA	0	最不发达35国LDC35,最不发达4国LDC4,柬埔寨KH	70	-Fruits of the genus Capsicum or of the genus Pimenta
558	0709.7000	-菠菜	13	0 2.6	东盟ASEAN,智利CL,巴基斯坦PK,新西兰NZ,秘鲁PE,香港HK 哥斯达黎加CR	0	最不发达35国LDC35,最不发达4国LDC4	70	-Spinach, New Zealand spinach and orache spinach (garden spinach)
		-其他：							-Other:

序号 No.	税则号列 Tariff Line	货品名称	最惠国税 率 MFN(%)	协定税率 Agreement(%)		特惠税率 S.P.(%)		普通税率 Gen.(%)	Article Description
559	0709.9100	--洋蓟	13	0 2.6	东盟ASEAN,智利CL,巴基斯坦PK,新西兰NZ,秘鲁PE,香港HK 哥斯达黎加CR	0	最不发达35国LDC35,最不发达4国LDC4,柬埔寨KH	70	--Globe artichokes
560	0709.9200	--油橄榄	13	0 2.6	东盟ASEAN,智利CL,巴基斯坦PK,新西兰NZ,秘鲁PE,香港HK 哥斯达黎加CR	0	最不发达35国LDC35,最不发达4国LDC4,柬埔寨KH	70	--Olives
561	0709.9300	--南瓜、笋瓜及瓠瓜（南瓜属）	13	0 2.6	东盟ASEAN,智利CL,巴基斯坦PK,新西兰NZ,秘鲁PE,香港HK 哥斯达黎加CR	0	最不发达35国LDC35,最不发达4国LDC4,柬埔寨KH	70	--Pumpkins, squash and gourds (Cucurbita spp.)
		--其他：							--Other:
562	0709.9910	---竹笋	13	0 2.6	东盟ASEAN,智利CL,巴基斯坦PK,新西兰NZ,秘鲁PE 哥斯达黎加CR	0	最不发达35国LDC35,最不发达4国LDC4,老挝LA,柬埔寨KH	70	---Bamboo shoots
563	0709.9990	---其他	13	0 2.6	东盟ASEAN,智利CL,巴基斯坦PK,新西兰NZ,秘鲁PE,香港HK 哥斯达黎加CR	0	最不发达35国LDC35,最不发达4国LDC4,柬埔寨KH	70	---Other
	07.10	**冷冻蔬菜（不论是否蒸煮）：**							**Vegetables (uncooked or cooked by steaming or boiling in water), frozen:**
564	0710.1000	-马铃薯	13	0 2.6 6.5	东盟ASEAN,智利CL,新西兰NZ,秘鲁PE 哥斯达黎加CR 巴基斯坦PK	0	最不发达35国LDC35	70	-Potatoes
		-豆类蔬菜，不论是否脱荚：							-Leguminous vegetables, shelled or unshelled:
565	0710.2100	--豌豆	13	0 2.6 6.5	东盟ASEAN,智利CL,新西兰NZ,秘鲁PE 哥斯达黎加CR 巴基斯坦PK	0	最不发达35国LDC35	70	--Peas (Pisum sativum)
		--豇豆及菜豆：							--Beans (Vigna spp., Phaseolus spp.):

序号 No.	税则号列 Tariff Line	货品名称	最惠国税率 MFN(%)	协定税率 Agreement(%)		特惠税率 S.P.(%)		普通税率 Gen.(%)	Article Description
566	0710.2210	---红小豆（赤豆）	13	0 2.6 6.5	东盟ASEAN,智利CL,新西兰NZ,秘鲁PE 哥斯达黎加CR 巴基斯坦PK	0	最不发达35国LDC35,最不发达4国LDC4,柬埔寨KH	70	---Adzuki beans
567	0710.2290	---其他	13	0 2.6 6.5	东盟ASEAN,智利CL,新西兰NZ,秘鲁PE 哥斯达黎加CR 巴基斯坦PK	0	最不发达35国LDC35,最不发达4国LDC4,柬埔寨KH	70	---Other
568	0710.2900	--其他	13	0 2.6 6.5	东盟ASEAN,智利CL,新西兰NZ,秘鲁PE 哥斯达黎加CR 巴基斯坦PK	0	最不发达35国LDC35,最不发达4国LDC4,柬埔寨KH	70	--Other
569	0710.3000	-菠菜	13	0 2.6 6.5	东盟ASEAN,智利CL,新西兰NZ,秘鲁PE 哥斯达黎加CR 巴基斯坦PK	0	最不发达35国LDC35	70	-Spinach, New Zealand spinach and orache spinach (garden spinach)
570	0710.4000	-甜玉米	10	0 5	东盟ASEAN,智利CL,新西兰NZ,秘鲁PE,哥斯达黎加CR 巴基斯坦PK	0	最不发达35国LDC35,最不发达4国LDC4	70	-Sweet corn
		-其他蔬菜：							-Other vegetables:
571	0710.8010	---松茸	13	0 2.6 6.5	东盟ASEAN,智利CL,新西兰NZ,秘鲁PE 哥斯达黎加CR 巴基斯坦PK	0	最不发达35国LDC35,最不发达4国LDC4,柬埔寨KH	70	---Sungmo
572	0710.8020	---蒜苔及蒜苗（青蒜）	13	0 2.6 6.5	东盟ASEAN,智利CL,新西兰NZ,秘鲁PE 哥斯达黎加CR 巴基斯坦PK	0	最不发达35国LDC35,最不发达4国LDC4,柬埔寨KH	70	---Garlic stems, garlic seedlings
573	0710.8030	---蒜头	13	0 2.6 6.5	东盟ASEAN,智利CL,新西兰NZ,秘鲁PE 哥斯达黎加CR 巴基斯坦PK	0	最不发达35国LDC35,最不发达4国LDC4,柬埔寨KH	70	---Garlic bulbs

序号 No.	税则号列 Tariff Line	货品名称	最惠国税率 MFN(%)	协定税率 Agreement(%)		特惠税率 S.P.(%)		普通税率 Gen.(%)	Article Description
574	0710.8040	---牛肝菌	13	0 2.6 6.5	东盟ASEAN,智利CL,新西兰NZ,秘鲁PE 哥斯达黎加CR 巴基斯坦PK	0	最不发达35国LDC35,最不发达4国LDC4,柬埔寨KH	70	---Boletus (Porcini)
575	0710.8090	---其他	13	0 2.6 6.5	东盟ASEAN,智利CL,新西兰NZ,秘鲁PE 哥斯达黎加CR 巴基斯坦PK	0	最不发达35国LDC35,最不发达4国LDC4,柬埔寨KH	70	---Other
576	0710.9000	-什锦蔬菜	10	0 5	东盟ASEAN,智利CL,新西兰NZ,秘鲁PE,哥斯达黎加CR 巴基斯坦PK	0	最不发达35国LDC35,最不发达4国LDC4,柬埔寨KH	70	-Mixtures of vegetables
	07.11	**暂时保藏（例如，使用二氧化硫气体、盐水、亚硫酸水或其他防腐液）的蔬菜，但不适于直接食用的：**							**Vegetables provisionally preserved (for example, by sulphur dioxide gas, in brine, in suphur water or in other preservative solutions), but unsuitable in that state for immediate consumption:**
577	0711.2000	-油橄榄	13	0 2.6	东盟ASEAN,智利CL,巴基斯坦PK,新西兰NZ,秘鲁PE 哥斯达黎加CR	0	最不发达35国LDC35	70	-Olives
578	0711.4000	-黄瓜及小黄瓜	13	0 2.6	东盟ASEAN,智利CL,巴基斯坦PK,新西兰NZ,秘鲁PE 哥斯达黎加CR	0	最不发达35国LDC35	70	-Cucumbers and gherkins
		-蘑菇及块菌： --伞菌属蘑菇： ---盐水的：							-Mushrooms and truffles: --Mushrooms of the genus Agaricus: ---In brine:
579	0711.5112	----白蘑菇	13	0 2.6	东盟ASEAN,智利CL,巴基斯坦PK,新西兰NZ,秘鲁PE 哥斯达黎加CR	0	最不发达35国LDC35	90	----White mushroom
580	0711.5119	----其他	13	0 2.6	东盟ASEAN,智利CL,巴基斯坦PK,新西兰NZ,秘鲁PE 哥斯达黎加CR	0	最不发达35国LDC35	90	----Other
581	0711.5190	---其他	13	0 2.6	东盟ASEAN,智利CL,巴基斯坦PK,新西兰NZ,秘鲁PE 哥斯达黎加CR	0	最不发达35国LDC35	90	---Other
		--其他：							--Other:

序号 No.	税则号列 Tariff Line	货品名称	最惠国税率 MFN(%)	协定税率 Agreement(%)		特惠税率 S.P.(%)		普通税率 Gen.(%)	Article Description
		---盐水的:							---In brine:
582	0711.5911	----松茸	13	0 2.6	东盟ASEAN,智利CL,巴基斯坦PK,新西兰NZ,秘鲁PE 哥斯达黎加CR	0	最不发达35国LDC35	90	----Sungmo
583	0711.5919	----其他	13	0 2.6	东盟ASEAN,智利CL,巴基斯坦PK,新西兰NZ,秘鲁PE 哥斯达黎加CR	0	最不发达35国LDC35	90	----Other
584	0711.5990	---其他	13	0 2.6	东盟ASEAN,智利CL,巴基斯坦PK,新西兰NZ,秘鲁PE 哥斯达黎加CR	0	最不发达35国LDC35	90	---Other
		-其他蔬菜；什锦蔬菜:							-Other:
		---盐水的:							---In brine:
585	0711.9031	----竹笋	13	0 2.6 6.5	东盟ASEAN,智利CL,巴基斯坦PK,新西兰NZ,秘鲁PE 哥斯达黎加CR 亚太APTA	0	最不发达35国LDC35	70	----Bamboo shoots
586	0711.9034	----大蒜	13	0 2.6 6.5	东盟ASEAN,智利CL,巴基斯坦PK,新西兰NZ,秘鲁PE 哥斯达黎加CR 亚太APTA	0	最不发达35国LDC35	70	----Garlic
587	0711.9039	----其他	13	0 2.6 6.5	东盟ASEAN,智利CL,巴基斯坦PK,新西兰NZ,秘鲁PE 哥斯达黎加CR 亚太APTA	0	最不发达35国LDC35	70	----Other
588	0711.9090	---其他	13	0 2.6 6.5	东盟ASEAN,智利CL,巴基斯坦PK,新西兰NZ,秘鲁PE 哥斯达黎加CR 亚太APTA	0	最不发达35国LDC35	90	---Other
	07.12	**干蔬菜，整个、切块、切片、破碎或制成粉状，但未经进一步加工的:**							**Dried vegetables, whole, cut, sliced, broken or in powder, but not further prepared:**
589	0712.2000	-洋葱	13	0 2.6 6.5	东盟ASEAN,智利CL,新西兰NZ,秘鲁PE 哥斯达黎加CR 巴基斯坦PK	0	最不发达35国LDC35,最不发达4国LDC4	80	-Onions
		-蘑菇、木耳、银耳及块菌:							-Mushrooms, wood ears (Auricularia spp.), jelly fungi (Tremella spp.)and truffles:
590	0712.3100	--伞菌属蘑菇	13	0 2.6 5 9	东盟ASEAN,智利CL,新西兰NZ,秘鲁PE 哥斯达黎加CR 巴基斯坦PK 亚太APTA	0	最不发达35国LDC35,最不发达4国LDC4	80	--Mushrooms of the genus Agaricus

序号 No.	税则号列 Tariff Line	货品名称	最惠国税率 MFN(%)	协定税率 Agreement(%)		特惠税率 S.P.(%)		普通税率 Gen.(%)	Article Description
591	0712.3200	--木耳	13	0 2.6 6.5	东盟ASEAN,智利CL,新西兰NZ,秘鲁PE 哥斯达黎加CR 巴基斯坦PK	0	最不发达35国LDC35	100	--Wood ears (Auricularia spp.)
592	0712.3300	--银耳	13	0 2.6 6.5	东盟ASEAN,智利CL,新西兰NZ,秘鲁PE 哥斯达黎加CR 巴基斯坦PK	0	最不发达35国LDC35	90	--Jelly fungi (Tremella spp.)
		--其他：							--Other:
593	0712.3910	---香菇	13	0 2.6 5 9	东盟ASEAN,智利CL,新西兰NZ,秘鲁PE 哥斯达黎加CR 巴基斯坦PK 亚太APTA	0	最不发达35国LDC35	100	---Shiitake
594	0712.3920	---金针菇	13	0 2.6 5 9	东盟ASEAN,智利CL,新西兰NZ,秘鲁PE 哥斯达黎加CR 巴基斯坦PK 亚太APTA	0	最不发达35国LDC35	100	---Winter mushroom
595	0712.3930	---草菇	13	0 2.6 5 9	东盟ASEAN,智利CL,新西兰NZ,秘鲁PE 哥斯达黎加CR 巴基斯坦PK 亚太APTA	0	最不发达35国LDC35	100	---Paddy straw mushroom
596	0712.3940	---口蘑	13	0 2.6 5 9	东盟ASEAN,智利CL,新西兰NZ,秘鲁PE 哥斯达黎加CR 巴基斯坦PK 亚太APTA	0	最不发达35国LDC35	100	---Tricholoma mongolicum Imai
597	0712.3950	---牛肝菌	13	0 2.6 5 9	东盟ASEAN,智利CL,新西兰NZ,秘鲁PE 哥斯达黎加CR 巴基斯坦PK 亚太APTA	0	最不发达35国LDC35	100	---Boletus; Porcini
598	0712.3990	---其他	13	0 2.6 9	东盟ASEAN,智利CL,新西兰NZ,秘鲁PE 哥斯达黎加CR 亚太APTA,巴基斯坦PK	0	最不发达35国LDC35	100	---Other
		-其他蔬菜；什锦蔬菜：							-Other vegetables; mixtures of vegetables:
599	0712.9010	---笋干丝	13	0 2.6 6.5	东盟ASEAN,智利CL,新西兰NZ,秘鲁PE 哥斯达黎加CR 巴基斯坦PK	0	最不发达35国LDC35,最不发达4国LDC4	80	---Bamboo shoots
600	0712.9020	---紫萁（薇菜干）	13	0 2.6 6.5	东盟ASEAN,智利CL,新西兰NZ,秘鲁PE 哥斯达黎加CR 巴基斯坦PK	0	最不发达35国LDC35	80	---Osmund
601	0712.9030	---金针菜（黄花菜）	13	0 2.6 6.5	东盟ASEAN,智利CL,新西兰NZ,秘鲁PE 哥斯达黎加CR 巴基斯坦PK	0	最不发达35国LDC35	80	---Day lily flowers

序号 No.	税则号列 Tariff Line	货品名称	最惠国税率 MFN(%)	协定税率 Agreement(%)	特惠税率 S.P.(%)	普通税率 Gen.(%)	Article Description
602	0712.9040	---蕨菜	13	0 东盟ASEAN,智利CL,新西兰NZ,秘鲁PE 2.6 哥斯达黎加CR 6.5 巴基斯坦PK	0 最不发达35国LDC35	80	---Wild brake
603	0712.9050	---大蒜	13	0 东盟ASEAN,智利CL,新西兰NZ,秘鲁PE 2.6 哥斯达黎加CR 6.5 巴基斯坦PK	0 最不发达35国LDC35	80	---Garlic
604	0712.9060	---甜椒	13	0 东盟ASEAN,智利CL,新西兰NZ,秘鲁PE 2.6 哥斯达黎加CR 6.5 巴基斯坦PK	0 最不发达35国LDC35	80	---Capsicum annuum Var.grossum
		---其他:					---Other:
605	0712.9091	----辣根	13	0 东盟ASEAN,智利CL,新西兰NZ,秘鲁PE 2.6 哥斯达黎加CR 6.5 巴基斯坦PK	0 最不发达35国LDC35,最不发达4国LDC4	80	----Horseradish
606	0712.9099	----其他	13	0 东盟ASEAN,智利CL,新西兰NZ,秘鲁PE 2.6 哥斯达黎加CR 6.5 巴基斯坦PK	0 最不发达35国LDC35,最不发达4国LDC4	80	----Other
	07.13	**脱荚的干豆，不论是否去皮或分瓣：**					**Dried leguminous vegetables, shelled, whether or not skinned or split:**
		-豌豆：					-Peas (Pisum sativum):
607	0713.1010	---种用	0		0 最不发达35国LDC35,最不发达4国LDC4	0	---Seed
608	0713.1090	---其他	5	0 东盟ASEAN,智利CL,巴基斯坦PK,新西兰NZ,秘鲁PE,哥斯达黎加CR	0 最不发达35国LDC35,最不发达4国LDC4	20	---Other
		-鹰嘴豆：					-Chickpeas (garbanzos):
609	0713.2010	---种用	0		0 最不发达35国LDC35,最不发达4国LDC4	0	---Seed
610	0713.2090	---其他	7	0 东盟ASEAN,智利CL,新西兰NZ,秘鲁PE,哥斯达黎加CR 5 巴基斯坦PK	0 最不发达35国LDC35,最不发达4国LDC4	20	---Other

序号 No.	税则号列 Tariff Line	货品名称	最惠国税率 MFN(%)	协定税率 Agreement(%)		特惠税率 S.P.(%)		普通税率 Gen.(%)	Article Description
		-豇豆属及菜豆属：							-Beans (Vigna spp., Phaseolus spp.):
		--绿豆：							--Beans of the species Vigna mungo (L.) Hepper or Vigna radiata (L.) Wilczek:
611	0713.3110	---种用	0			0	最不发达35国LDC35,最不发达4国LDC4	0	---Seed
612	0713.3190	---其他	3	0 1.5	东盟ASEAN,智利CL,巴基斯坦PK,新西兰NZ,秘鲁PE,哥斯达黎加CR 亚太APTA	0	最不发达35国LDC35,最不发达4国LDC4,缅甸MM,柬埔寨KH	11	---Other
		--红小豆（赤豆）：							--Adzuki beans:
613	0713.3210	---种用	0			0	最不发达35国LDC35,最不发达4国LDC4	0	---Seed
614	0713.3290	---其他	3	0	东盟ASEAN,智利CL,巴基斯坦PK,新西兰NZ,秘鲁PE,哥斯达黎加CR	0	最不发达35国LDC35,最不发达4国LDC4,柬埔寨KH	14	---Other
		--芸豆：							--Kidney beans, including white pea beans (Phaseolus vulgaris):
615	0713.3310	---种用	0			0	最不发达35国LDC35,最不发达4国LDC4	0	---Seed
616	0713.3390	---其他	7.5	0 5	东盟ASEAN,智利CL,新西兰NZ,秘鲁PE,哥斯达黎加CR 巴基斯坦PK	0	最不发达35国LDC35,最不发达4国LDC4,柬埔寨KH	20	---Other

序号 No.	税则号列 Tariff Line	货品名称	最惠国税率 MFN(%)	协定税率 Agreement(%)		特惠税率 S.P.(%)		普通税率 Gen.(%)	Article Description
617	0713.3400	--巴姆巴拉豆	7	0 3.5	东盟ASEAN,智利CL,巴基斯坦PK,新西兰NZ,秘鲁PE,哥斯达黎加CR 亚太APTA	0	最不发达35国LDC35,最不发达4国LDC4,柬埔寨KH	20	--Bambara beans (Vigna subterranea or Voandzeia subterranea)
618	0713.3500	--牛豆(豇豆)	7	0 3.5	东盟ASEAN,智利CL,巴基斯坦PK,新西兰NZ,秘鲁PE,哥斯达黎加CR 亚太APTA	0	最不发达35国LDC35,最不发达4国LDC4,柬埔寨KH	20	--Cow peas (Vigna unguiculata)
619	0713.3900	--其他	7	0 3.5	东盟ASEAN,智利CL,巴基斯坦PK,新西兰NZ,秘鲁PE,哥斯达黎加CR 亚太APTA	0	最不发达35国LDC35,最不发达4国LDC4,柬埔寨KH	20	--Other
		-扁豆:							-Lentils:
620	0713.4010	---种用	0			0	最不发达35国LDC35,最不发达4国LDC4	0	---Seed
621	0713.4090	---其他	7	0 5	东盟ASEAN,智利CL,新西兰NZ,秘鲁PE,哥斯达黎加CR 巴基斯坦PK	0	最不发达35国LDC35,最不发达4国LDC4	20	---Other
		-蚕豆:							-Broad beans (Vicia faba var.Major) and horse beans (Vicia faba var.equina, Vicia faba var.minor):
622	0713.5010	---种用	0			0	最不发达35国LDC35,最不发达4国LDC4	0	---Seed
623	0713.5090	---其他	7	0 5	东盟ASEAN,智利CL,新西兰NZ,秘鲁PE,哥斯达黎加CR 巴基斯坦PK	0	最不发达35国LDC35,最不发达4国LDC4	20	---Other
		-木豆（木豆属）:							-Pigeon peas (Cajanus cajan):

序号 No.	税则号列 Tariff Line	货品名称	最惠国税率 MFN(%)	协定税率 Agreement(%)		特惠税率 S.P.(%)		普通税率 Gen.(%)	Article Description
624	0713.6010	---种用	0			0	最不发达35国LDC35,最不发达4国LDC4	0	---Seed
625	0713.6090	---其他	7	0 5	东盟ASEAN,智利CL,新西兰NZ,秘鲁PE,哥斯达黎加CR 巴基斯坦PK	0	最不发达35国LDC35,最不发达4国LDC4	20	---Other
		-其他:							-Other:
626	0713.9010	---种用干豆	0			0	最不发达35国LDC35,最不发达4国LDC4	0	---Seed
627	0713.9090	---其他	7	0 5	东盟ASEAN,智利CL,新西兰NZ,秘鲁PE,哥斯达黎加CR 巴基斯坦PK	0	最不发达35国LDC35,最不发达4国LDC4	20	---Other
	07.14	**鲜、冷、冻或干的木薯、竹芋、兰科植物块茎、菊芋、甘薯及含有高淀粉或菊粉的类似根茎,不论是否切片或制成团粒;西谷茎髓:**							**Manioc, arrowroot, salep, Jerusalem artichokes, sweet potatoes and similar roots and tubers with high starch or inulin content, fresh, chilled, frozen or dried, whether or not sliced or in the form of pellets; sago pith:**
		-木薯:							-Manioc (cassava):
628	0714.1010	---鲜的	10	0 5	东盟ASEAN,智利CL,新西兰NZ,秘鲁PE,哥斯达黎加CR 巴基斯坦PK	0	最不发达35国LDC35,最不发达4国LDC4,老挝LA,柬埔寨KH	30	---Fresh
629	0714.1020	---干的	5	0	东盟ASEAN,智利CL,巴基斯坦PK,新西兰NZ,秘鲁PE,哥斯达黎加CR	0	最不发达35国LDC35,最不发达4国LDC4,老挝LA,柬埔寨KH	30	---Dried

序号 No.	税则号列 Tariff Line	货品名称	最惠国税率 MFN(%)	协定税率 Agreement(%)		特惠税率 S.P.(%)		普通税率 Gen.(%)	Article Description
630	0714.1030	---冷或冻的	10	0 5	东盟ASEAN,智利CL,新西兰NZ,秘鲁PE,哥斯达黎加CR 巴基斯坦PK	0	最不发达35国LDC35,最不发达4国LDC4,老挝LA,柬埔寨KH	80	---Chilled or frozen
		-甘薯: ---鲜的:							-Sweet potatoes: ---Fresh:
631	0714.2011	----种用	0			0	最不发达35国LDC35,最不发达4国LDC4	50	----For cultivation
632	0714.2019	----其他	13	0 2.6 5 6.5	东盟ASEAN,智利CL,新西兰NZ,秘鲁PE 哥斯达黎加CR 巴基斯坦PK 亚太APTA	0	最不发达35国LDC35,最不发达4国LDC4,老挝LA,柬埔寨KH	50	----Other
633	0714.2020	---干的	13	0 2.6 5 6.5	东盟ASEAN,智利CL,新西兰NZ,秘鲁PE 哥斯达黎加CR 巴基斯坦PK 亚太APTA	0	最不发达35国LDC35,最不发达4国LDC4,老挝LA,柬埔寨KH	50	---Dried
634	0714.2030	---冷或冻的	13	0 2.6 5 6.5	东盟ASEAN,智利CL,新西兰NZ,秘鲁PE 哥斯达黎加CR 巴基斯坦PK 亚太APTA	0	最不发达35国LDC35,最不发达4国LDC4,老挝LA,柬埔寨KH	80	---Chilled or frozen
635	0714.3000	-山药	13	0 2.6 5 6.5	东盟ASEAN,智利CL,新西兰NZ,秘鲁PE 哥斯达黎加CR 巴基斯坦PK 亚太APTA	0	最不发达35国LDC35,最不发达4国LDC4,老挝LA,柬埔寨KH	50	-Yams (Dioscorea spp.)
636	0714.4000	-芋头(芋属)	13	0 2.6 5 6.5	东盟ASEAN,智利CL,新西兰NZ,秘鲁PE 哥斯达黎加CR 巴基斯坦PK 亚太APTA	0	最不发达35国LDC35	50	-Taro (Colocasia spp.)

序号 No.	税则号列 Tariff Line	货品名称	最惠国税率 MFN(%)	协定税率 Agreement(%)	特惠税率 S.P.(%)	普通税率 Gen.(%)	Article Description
637	0714.5000	-箭叶黄体芋(黄肉芋属)	13	0 东盟ASEAN,智利CL,新西兰NZ,秘鲁PE 2.6 哥斯达黎加CR 5 巴基斯坦PK 6.5 亚太APTA	0 最不发达35国LDC35,最不发达4国LDC4,老挝LA,柬埔寨KH	50	-Yautia (Xanthosoma spp.)
		-其他:					-Other:
638	0714.9010	---荸荠	13	0 东盟ASEAN,智利CL,新西兰NZ,秘鲁PE 2.6 哥斯达黎加CR 5 巴基斯坦PK 6.5 亚太APTA	0 最不发达35国LDC35,最不发达4国LDC4,老挝LA,柬埔寨KH	50	---Water chestnut
		---藕:					---Lotus (Nelumbo nucifera) rootstock:
639	0714.9021	----种用	0		0 最不发达35国LDC35,最不发达4国LDC4	0	----For cultivation
640	0714.9029	----其他	13	0 东盟ASEAN,智利CL,新西兰NZ,秘鲁PE 2.6 哥斯达黎加CR 5 巴基斯坦PK 6.5 亚太APTA	0 最不发达35国LDC35,最不发达4国LDC4,老挝LA,柬埔寨KH	50	----Other
641	0714.9090	---其他	13	0 东盟ASEAN,智利CL,新西兰NZ,秘鲁PE 2.6 哥斯达黎加CR 5 巴基斯坦PK 6.5 亚太APTA	0 最不发达35国LDC35,最不发达4国LDC4,老挝LA,柬埔寨KH	50	---Other

第八章
食用水果及坚果；
柑橘属水果或甜瓜的果皮

Chapter 8
Edible fruit and nuts;
peel of citrus fruit or melons

注释：

一、本章不包括非供食用的坚果或水果。

二、冷藏的水果和坚果应按相应的鲜果税号归类。

三、本章的干果可以部分复水或为下列目的进行其他处理：

（一） 为保藏或保持其稳定性（例如，经适度热处理或硫化处理、添加山梨酸或山梨酸钾）；

（二） 为改进或保持其外观（例如，添加植物油或少量葡萄糖浆）。

但必须保持干果的特征。

Notes:

1. This Chapter does not cover inedible nuts or fruits.
2. Chilled fruits and nuts are to be classified in the same headings as the corresponding fresh fruits and nuts.
3. Dried fruit or dried nuts of this Chapter may be partially rehydrated, or treated for the following purposes:

(a) For additional preservation or stabilization (for example, by moderate heat treatment, sulphuring, the addition of sorbic acid or potassium sorbate);

(b) To improve or maintain their appearance (for example, by the addition of vegetable oil or small quantities of glucose syrup);

provided that they retain the character of dried fruit or dried nuts.

序号 No.	税则号列 Tariff Line	货品名称	最惠国税率 MFN(%)	协定税率 Agreement(%)		特惠税率 S.P.(%)		普通税率 Gen.(%)	Article Description
	08.01	**鲜或干的椰子、巴西果及腰果，不论是否去壳或去皮：**							**Coconuts, Brazil nuts and cashewnuts, fresh or dried, whether or not shelled or peeled:**
		-椰子：							-Coconuts:
642	0801.1100	--干的	12	0 5 6 8.8	东盟ASEAN,智利CL,新西兰NZ,秘鲁PE,澳门MO 巴基斯坦PK 亚太APTA 哥斯达黎加CR	0	最不发达35国LDC35,最不发达4国LDC4,柬埔寨KH	80	--Desiccated
643	0801.1200	--未去内壳（内果皮）	12	0 5 6 8.8	东盟ASEAN,智利CL,新西兰NZ,秘鲁PE 巴基斯坦PK 亚太APTA 哥斯达黎加CR	0	最不发达35国LDC35,最不发达4国LDC4,柬埔寨KH	80	--In the inner shell (endocarp)
		--其他：							--Other:
644	0801.1910	---种用	0			0	最不发达35国LDC35,最不发达4国LDC4	0	---Seedlings

序号 No.	税则号列 Tariff Line	货品名称	最惠国税率 MFN(%)	协定税率 Agreement(%)		特惠税率 S.P.(%)		普通税率 Gen.(%)	Article Description
645	0801.1990	---其他	12	0 5 6 8.8	东盟ASEAN,智利CL,新西兰NZ,秘鲁PE 巴基斯坦PK 亚太APTA 哥斯达黎加CR	0	最不发达35国LDC35,最不发达4国LDC4,柬埔寨KH	80	---Other
		-巴西果:							-Brazil nuts:
646	0801.2100	--未去壳	10	0 5 7.3	东盟ASEAN,智利CL,新西兰NZ,秘鲁PE,澳门MO 巴基斯坦PK 哥斯达黎加CR	0	最不发达35国LDC35,最不发达4国LDC4	80	--In shell
647	0801.2200	--去壳	10	0 5 7.3	东盟ASEAN,智利CL,新西兰NZ,秘鲁PE,澳门MO 巴基斯坦PK 哥斯达黎加CR	0	最不发达35国LDC35,最不发达4国LDC4	80	--Shelled
		-腰果:							-Cashew nuts:
648	0801.3100	--未去壳	20 △10	0 10 14.7	东盟ASEAN,智利CL,新西兰NZ,澳门MO 秘鲁PE 哥斯达黎加CR	0	最不发达35国LDC35,最不发达4国LDC4,柬埔寨KH	70	--In shell
649	0801.3200	--去壳	10	0 5 7.3	东盟ASEAN,智利CL,新西兰NZ,秘鲁PE,澳门MO 巴基斯坦PK 哥斯达黎加CR	0	最不发达35国LDC35,最不发达4国LDC4,缅甸MM,柬埔寨KH	70	--Shelled
	08.02	**鲜或干的其他坚果，不论是否去壳或去皮：**							**Other nuts, fresh or dried, whether or not shelled or peeled:**
		-扁桃仁:							-Almonds:
650	0802.1100	--未去壳	24 △10	0 2.4 12 17.6	东盟ASEAN,新西兰NZ,澳门MO 智利CL 秘鲁PE 哥斯达黎加CR	0	最不发达35国LDC35	70	--In shell
651	0802.1200	--去壳	10	0 1 5 7.3	东盟ASEAN,新西兰NZ,澳门MO 智利CL 巴基斯坦PK,秘鲁PE 哥斯达黎加CR	0	最不发达35国LDC35,最不发达4国LDC4	70	--Shelled
		-榛子:							-Hazelnuts or filberts (Corylus spp):

序号 No.	税则号列 Tariff Line	货品名称	最惠国税率 MFN(%)	协定税率 Agreement(%)		特惠税率 S.P.(%)		普通税率 Gen.(%)	Article Description
652	0802.2100	--未去壳	25	0 2.5 12.5 18.3	东盟ASEAN,新西兰NZ,澳门MO 智利CL 秘鲁PE 哥斯达黎加CR	0	最不发达35国LDC35	70	--In shell
653	0802.2200	--去壳	10	0 5 7.3	东盟ASEAN,智利CL,新西兰NZ,秘鲁PE,澳门MO 巴基斯坦PK 哥斯达黎加CR	0	最不发达35国LDC35,最不发达4国LDC4	70	--Shelled
		-核桃:							-Walnuts:
654	0802.3100	--未去壳	25	0 2.5 12.5 18.3	东盟ASEAN,新西兰NZ,澳门MO 智利CL 秘鲁PE 哥斯达黎加CR	0	最不发达35国LDC35	70	--In shell
655	0802.3200	--去壳	20	0 2 10 14.7	东盟ASEAN,新西兰NZ,澳门MO 智利CL 秘鲁PE 哥斯达黎加CR	0	最不发达35国LDC35	70	--Shelled
		-栗子:							-Chestnuts (Castanea spp.):
		--未去壳:							--In shell:
656	0802.4110	---板栗	25	0 2.5 12.5 18.3	东盟ASEAN,新西兰NZ,澳门MO 智利CL 秘鲁PE 哥斯达黎加CR	0	最不发达35国LDC35	70	---Chestnuts (Castanea spp.)
657	0802.4190	---其他	25 △20	0 2.5 12.5 18.3	东盟ASEAN,新西兰NZ,澳门MO 智利CL 秘鲁PE 哥斯达黎加CR	0	最不发达35国LDC35	70	---Other
		--去壳:							--Shelled:
658	0802.4210	---板栗	25	0 2.5 12.5 18.3	东盟ASEAN,新西兰NZ,澳门MO 智利CL 秘鲁PE 哥斯达黎加CR	0	最不发达35国LDC35	70	---Chestnuts (Castanea spp.)
659	0802.4290	---其他	25 △20	0 2.5 12.5 18.3	东盟ASEAN,新西兰NZ,澳门MO 智利CL 秘鲁PE 哥斯达黎加CR	0	最不发达35国LDC35	70	---Other
		-阿月浑子果(开心果):							-Pistachios:
660	0802.5100	--未去壳	10 △5	0 5 7.3	东盟ASEAN,智利CL,新西兰NZ,秘鲁PE,澳门MO 巴基斯坦PK 哥斯达黎加CR	0	最不发达35国LDC35	70	--In shell

序号 No.	税则号列 Tariff Line	货品名称	最惠国税率 MFN(%)	协定税率 Agreement(%)		特惠税率 S.P.(%)		普通税率 Gen.(%)	Article Description
661	0802.5200	--去壳	10 △5	0 5 7.3	东盟ASEAN,智利CL,新西兰NZ,秘鲁PE,澳门MO 巴基斯坦PK 哥斯达黎加CR	0	最不发达35国LDC35	70	--Shelled
		-马卡达姆坚果(夏威夷果):							-Macadamia nuts :
		--未去壳:							--In shell:
662	0802.6110	---种用	0			0	最不发达35国LDC35,最不发达4国LDC4	70	---For cultivation
663	0802.6190	---其他	24	0 12 17.6	东盟ASEAN,智利CL,新西兰NZ,澳门MO 秘鲁PE 哥斯达黎加CR	0	最不发达35国LDC35	70	---Other
664	0802.6200	--去壳	24	0 12 17.6	东盟ASEAN,智利CL,新西兰NZ,澳门MO 秘鲁PE 哥斯达黎加CR	0	最不发达35国LDC35	70	--Shelled
665	0802.7000	-可乐果(可乐果属)	24	0 12 17.6	东盟ASEAN,智利CL,新西兰NZ,澳门MO 秘鲁PE 哥斯达黎加CR	0	最不发达35国LDC35	70	-Kola nuts (Cola spp.)
666	0802.8000	-槟榔果	10	0 5 7.3	东盟ASEAN,智利CL,新西兰NZ,秘鲁PE,澳门MO 亚太APTA,巴基斯坦PK 哥斯达黎加CR	0	最不发达35国LDC35,最不发达4国LDC4	30	-Areca nuts
		-其他:							-Other:
667	0802.9020	---白果	25 △20	0 12.5 18.3	东盟ASEAN,智利CL,新西兰NZ,澳门MO 秘鲁PE 哥斯达黎加CR	0	最不发达35国LDC35	70	---Gingko nuts
668	0802.9030	---松子仁	25	0 12.5 18.3	东盟ASEAN,智利CL,新西兰NZ,澳门MO 秘鲁PE 哥斯达黎加CR	0	最不发达35国LDC35	70	---Pine-nuts, shelled
669	0802.9090	---其他	24	0 12 17.6	东盟ASEAN,智利CL,新西兰NZ,澳门MO 秘鲁PE 哥斯达黎加CR	0	最不发达35国LDC35	70	---Other
	08.03	**鲜或干的香蕉，包括芭蕉:**							**Bananas, including plantains, fresh or dried:**
670	0803.1000	-芭蕉	10	0 1 5 6.9 7.3	东盟ASEAN,新西兰NZ,澳门MO,台湾TW 智利CL 巴基斯坦PK,秘鲁PE 亚太APTA 哥斯达黎加CR	0	最不发达35国LDC35,最不发达4国LDC4,老挝LA,柬埔寨KH	40	-Plantains

序号 No.	税则号列 Tariff Line	货品名称	最惠国税率 MFN(%)	协定税率 Agreement(%)		特惠税率 S.P.(%)		普通税率 Gen.(%)	Article Description
671	0803.9000	-其他	10	0 1 5 6.9 7.3	东盟ASEAN,新西兰NZ,澳门MO,台湾TW 智利CL 巴基斯坦PK,秘鲁PE 亚太APTA 哥斯达黎加CR	0	最不发达35国LDC35,最不发达4国LDC4,老挝LA,柬埔寨KH	40	-Other
	08.04	**鲜或干的椰枣、无花果、菠萝、鳄梨、番石榴、芒果及山竹果:**							**Dates, figs, pineapples, avocados, guavas, mangoes and man gosteens, fresh or dried:**
672	0804.1000	-椰枣	15	0 7.5 11	东盟ASEAN,智利CL,巴基斯坦PK,新西兰NZ,澳门MO 秘鲁PE 哥斯达黎加CR	0	最不发达35国LDC35	40	-Dates
673	0804.2000	-无花果	30	0 3 15 22	东盟ASEAN,巴基斯坦PK,新西兰NZ,澳门MO 智利CL 秘鲁PE 哥斯达黎加CR	0	最不发达35国LDC35	70	-Figs
674	0804.3000	-菠萝	12	0 7.9 8.8	东盟ASEAN,智利CL,巴基斯坦PK,新西兰NZ,秘鲁PE,香港HK,澳门MO 亚太APTA 哥斯达黎加CR	0	最不发达35国LDC35,最不发达4国LDC4,柬埔寨KH	80	-Pineapples
675	0804.4000	-鳄梨	25	0 2.5 12.5 18.3	东盟ASEAN,巴基斯坦PK,新西兰NZ,秘鲁PE,澳门MO 智利CL 亚太APTA 哥斯达黎加CR	0	最不发达35国LDC35,最不发达4国LDC4,柬埔寨KH	80	-Avocados
		-番石榴、芒果及山竹果:							-Guavas, mangoes and mangosteens:
676	0804.5010	---番石榴	15	0 7.5 11	东盟ASEAN,智利CL,巴基斯坦PK,新西兰NZ,澳门MO 亚太APTA,秘鲁PE 哥斯达黎加CR	0	最不发达35国LDC35	80	---Guavas
677	0804.5020	---芒果	15	0 10.6 11	东盟ASEAN,智利CL,巴基斯坦PK,新西兰NZ,秘鲁PE,澳门MO 亚太APTA 哥斯达黎加CR	0	最不发达35国LDC35,最不发达4国LDC4	80	---Mangoes
678	0804.5030	---山竹果	15	0 7.5 11	东盟ASEAN,智利CL,巴基斯坦PK,新西兰NZ,秘鲁PE,澳门MO 亚太APTA 哥斯达黎加CR	0	最不发达35国LDC35	80	---Mangosteens

序号 No.	税则号列 Tariff Line	货品名称	最惠国 税 率 MFN(%)	协定税率 Agreement(%)	特惠税率 S.P.(%)	普通 税率 Gen.(%)	Article Description
	08.05	**鲜或干的柑橘属水果：**					**Citrus fruit, fresh or dried:**
679	0805.1000	-橙	11	0 东盟ASEAN,巴基斯坦PK,澳门MO,台湾TW 1.1 智利CL 2.4 新西兰NZ 4.1 秘鲁PE 8.1 哥斯达黎加CR	0 最不发达35国LDC35,最不发达4国LDC4	100	-Oranges
		-柑橘；杂交柑橘：					-Mandarins (including tangerines and satsumas); clementines, wilkings and similar citrus hybrids:
680	0805.2010	---蕉柑	12	0 东盟ASEAN,巴基斯坦PK,澳门MO 1.2 智利CL 2.7 新西兰NZ 6 秘鲁PE 8.8 哥斯达黎加CR	0 最不发达35国LDC35	100	---Chiao-Kan
681	0805.2020	---阔叶柑橘	12	0 东盟ASEAN,巴基斯坦PK,澳门MO 1.2 智利CL 2.7 新西兰NZ 6 秘鲁PE 8.8 哥斯达黎加CR	0 最不发达35国LDC35	100	---Latifolia Citrus
682	0805.2090	---其他	12	0 东盟ASEAN,巴基斯坦PK,澳门MO 1.2 智利CL 2.7 新西兰NZ 4.5 秘鲁PE 8.8 哥斯达黎加CR	0 最不发达35国LDC35	100	---Other
683	0805.4000	-葡萄柚，包括柚	12	0 东盟ASEAN,巴基斯坦PK,新西兰NZ,香港HK,澳门MO 1.2 智利CL 6 秘鲁PE 8.8 哥斯达黎加CR	0 最不发达35国LDC35,最不发达4国LDC4	100	-Grapefruit, including pomelos
684	0805.5000	-柠檬及酸橙	11	0 东盟ASEAN,巴基斯坦PK,澳门MO,台湾TW 1.1 智利CL 2.4 新西兰NZ 4.1 秘鲁PE 5.5 亚太APTA 8.1 哥斯达黎加CR	0 最不发达35国LDC35,最不发达4国LDC4	100	-Lemons (*Citrus limon, Citrus limonum*) and limes (*Citrus aurantifolia*)
685	0805.9000	-其他	30	0 东盟ASEAN,智利CL,巴基斯坦PK,新西兰NZ,秘鲁PE,澳门MO 15 亚太APTA 22 哥斯达黎加CR	0 最不发达35国LDC35	100	-Other
	08.06	**鲜或干的葡萄：**					**Grapes, fresh or dried:**
686	0806.1000	-鲜的	13	0 东盟ASEAN,新西兰NZ 1.3 智利CL,秘鲁PE 2.6 哥斯达黎加CR 6.5 巴基斯坦PK	0 最不发达35国LDC35	80	-Fresh

序号 No.	税则号列 Tariff Line	货品名称	最惠国税率 MFN(%)	协定税率 Agreement(%)		特惠税率 S.P.(%)		普通税率 Gen.(%)	Article Description
687	0806.2000	-干的	10	0 1 5	东盟ASEAN,新西兰NZ,哥斯达黎加CR,澳门MO 智利CL 巴基斯坦PK,秘鲁PE	0	最不发达35国LDC35	80	-Dried
	08.07	**鲜的甜瓜（包括西瓜）及木瓜：**							**Melons (including watermelons) and papaws (papayas), fresh:**
		-甜瓜，包括西瓜：							-Melons (including watermelons):
688	0807.1100	--西瓜	25	0 5 12.5	东盟ASEAN,智利CL,新西兰NZ 哥斯达黎加CR 亚太APTA,巴基斯坦PK,秘鲁PE			70	--Watermelons
		--其他：							--Other:
689	0807.1910	---哈蜜瓜	12	0 2.4 5 6	东盟ASEAN,智利CL,新西兰NZ,秘鲁PE,台湾TW 哥斯达黎加CR 巴基斯坦PK 亚太APTA	0	最不发达35国LDC35,最不发达4国LDC4	70	---Hami melons
690	0807.1920	---罗马甜瓜及加勒比甜瓜	12	0 1.2 2.4 5 6	东盟ASEAN,新西兰NZ 智利CL 哥斯达黎加CR 巴基斯坦PK 亚太APTA,秘鲁PE	0	最不发达35国LDC35,最不发达4国LDC4	70	---Cantaloupe and Galia melons
691	0807.1990	---其他	12	0 1.2 5 6 7.2	东盟ASEAN,新西兰NZ 智利CL 巴基斯坦PK 亚太APTA,秘鲁PE 哥斯达黎加CR	0	最不发达35国LDC35,最不发达4国LDC4	70	---Other
692	0807.2000	-木瓜	25	0 5 12.5	东盟ASEAN,智利CL,新西兰NZ 哥斯达黎加CR 秘鲁PE	0	最不发达35国LDC35,最不发达4国LDC4,柬埔寨KH	70	-Papaws(papayas)
	08.08	**鲜的苹果、梨及榅桲：**							**Apples, pears and quinces, fresh:**
693	0808.1000	-苹果	10	0 1 5	东盟ASEAN,新西兰NZ,哥斯达黎加CR 智利CL 巴基斯坦PK,秘鲁PE	0	最不发达35国LDC35,最不发达4国LDC4	100	-Apples
		-梨：							-Pears:
694	0808.3010	---鸭梨及雪梨	12	0 1.2 2.4 5 6 10	东盟ASEAN,新西兰NZ 智利CL 哥斯达黎加CR 巴基斯坦PK 秘鲁PE 亚太APTA	0	最不发达35国LDC35	100	---Ya pears, Hsueh pears

序号 No.	税则号列 Tariff Line	货品名称	最惠国税率 MFN(%)	协定税率 Agreement(%)		特惠税率 S.P.(%)		普通税率 Gen.(%)	Article Description
695	0808.3020	---香梨	12	0 1.2 2.4 5 6 10	东盟ASEAN,新西兰NZ 智利CL 哥斯达黎加CR 巴基斯坦PK 秘鲁PE 亚太APTA	0	最不发达35国LDC35	100	---Xiang pears
696	0808.3090	---其他	10	0 1 5	东盟ASEAN,新西兰NZ,哥斯达黎加CR 智利CL 巴基斯坦PK,秘鲁PE	0	最不发达35国LDC35	100	---Other
697	0808.4000	-榅桲	16	0 1.6 3.2 8 12.8	东盟ASEAN,新西兰NZ 智利CL 哥斯达黎加CR 秘鲁PE 巴基斯坦PK	0	最不发达35国LDC35	100	-Quinces
	08.09	**鲜的杏、樱桃、桃(包括油桃)、梅及李:**							**Apricots, cherries, peaches (including nectarines), plums and sloes, fresh:**
698	0809.1000	-杏	25	0 2.5 5 12.5	东盟ASEAN,新西兰NZ 智利CL 哥斯达黎加CR 秘鲁PE	0	最不发达35国LDC35	70	-Apricots
		-樱桃:							-Cherries:
699	0809.2100	--欧洲酸樱桃	10	0 5	东盟ASEAN,智利CL,新西兰NZ,哥斯达黎加CR 巴基斯坦PK,秘鲁PE	0	最不发达35国LDC35,最不发达4国LDC4	70	--Sour cherries (*Prunus cerasus*)
700	0809.2900	--其他	10	0 5	东盟ASEAN,智利CL,新西兰NZ,哥斯达黎加CR 巴基斯坦PK,秘鲁PE	0	最不发达35国LDC35,最不发达4国LDC4	70	--Other
701	0809.3000	-桃,包括油桃	10	0 5	东盟ASEAN,智利CL,新西兰NZ,哥斯达黎加CR 巴基斯坦PK,秘鲁PE	0	最不发达35国LDC35,最不发达4国LDC4	70	-Peaches, including nectarines
702	0809.4000	-梅及李	10	0 5	东盟ASEAN,智利CL,新西兰NZ,哥斯达黎加CR 巴基斯坦PK,秘鲁PE	0	最不发达35国LDC35	70	-Plums and sloes
	08.10	**其他鲜果:**							**Other fruit, fresh:**
703	0810.1000	-草莓	14	0 1.4 3.1	东盟ASEAN,新西兰NZ,秘鲁PE 智利CL 哥斯达黎加CR	0	最不发达35国LDC35,最不发达4国LDC4	80	-Strawberries

序号 No.	税则号列 Tariff Line	货品名称	最惠国税率 MFN(%)	协定税率 Agreement(%)	特惠税率 S.P.(%)	普通税率 Gen.(%)	Article Description
704	0810.2000	-木莓、黑莓、桑椹及罗甘莓	25	0 东盟ASEAN,新西兰NZ 2.5 智利CL 5 哥斯达黎加CR 12.5 秘鲁PE	0 最不发达35国LDC35	80	-Raspberries, blackberries, mulberries and loganberries
705	0810.3000	-黑、白或红的穗醋栗（加仑子）及醋栗	25	0 东盟ASEAN,新西兰NZ 2.5 智利CL 5 哥斯达黎加CR 12.5 秘鲁PE	0 最不发达35国LDC35	80	-Black, white or red currants and gooseberries
706	0810.4000	-蔓越桔及越桔	30	0 东盟ASEAN,新西兰NZ,秘鲁PE 3 智利CL 6 哥斯达黎加CR		80	-Cranberries, bilberries and other fruits of the genus *Vaccinium*
707	0810.5000	-猕猴桃	20	0 东盟ASEAN 2 智利CL 4 哥斯达黎加CR 4.4 新西兰NZ 10 秘鲁PE 16 巴基斯坦PK 16.5 亚太APTA	0 最不发达35国LDC35	80	-Kiwifruit
708	0810.6000	-榴莲	20	0 东盟ASEAN,智利CL,新西兰NZ 4 哥斯达黎加CR 10 秘鲁PE	0 最不发达35国LDC35,最不发达4国LDC4,柬埔寨KH	80	-Durian
709	0810.7000	-柿子	20	0 东盟ASEAN,新西兰NZ,秘鲁PE,香港HK 2 智利CL 4 哥斯达黎加CR 16 巴基斯坦PK 16.4 亚太APTA	0 最不发达35国LDC35	80	-Persimmons
		-其他：					-Other:
710	0810.9010	---荔枝	30	0 东盟ASEAN,智利CL,新西兰NZ 6 哥斯达黎加CR 15 秘鲁PE 20 亚太APTA,巴基斯坦PK	0 最不发达35国LDC35	80	---Lychee
711	0810.9030	---龙眼	12	0 东盟ASEAN,智利CL,新西兰NZ,秘鲁PE 2.4 哥斯达黎加CR 6 巴基斯坦PK	0 最不发达35国LDC35,最不发达4国LDC4,柬埔寨KH	80	---Longan
712	0810.9040	---红毛丹	20	0 东盟ASEAN,智利CL,新西兰NZ 4 哥斯达黎加CR 10 秘鲁PE	0 最不发达35国LDC35	80	---Rambutan
713	0810.9050	---番荔枝	20	0 东盟ASEAN,智利CL,新西兰NZ,秘鲁PE 4 哥斯达黎加CR	0 最不发达35国LDC35	80	---Sugar apple

序号 No.	税则号列 Tariff Line	货品名称	最惠国税率 MFN(%)	协定税率 Agreement(%)		特惠税率 S.P.(%)		普通税率 Gen.(%)	Article Description
714	0810.9060	---杨桃	20	0 4	东盟ASEAN,智利CL,新西兰NZ,秘鲁PE 哥斯达黎加CR	0	最不发达35国LDC35	80	---Carambola
715	0810.9070	---莲雾	20	0 4 10 16 16.4	东盟ASEAN,智利CL,新西兰NZ 哥斯达黎加CR 秘鲁PE 巴基斯坦PK 亚太APTA	0	最不发达35国LDC35	80	---Wax apple
716	0810.9080	---火龙果	20	0 4 10 16 16.4	东盟ASEAN,智利CL,新西兰NZ,台湾TW 哥斯达黎加CR 秘鲁PE 巴基斯坦PK 亚太APTA	0	最不发达35国LDC35	80	---Dragon fruit
717	0810.9090	---其他	20	0 2 4 16 16.4	东盟ASEAN,新西兰NZ,秘鲁PE,香港HK 智利CL 哥斯达黎加CR 巴基斯坦PK 亚太APTA	0	最不发达35国LDC35	80	---Other
	08.11	**冷冻水果及坚果，不论是否蒸煮、加糖或其他甜物质：**							**Fruit and nuts, uncooked or cooked by steaming or boiling in water, frozen, whether or not containing added sugar or other sweetening matter:**
718	0811.1000	-草莓	30	0 3 6 15	东盟ASEAN,新西兰NZ 智利CL 哥斯达黎加CR 秘鲁PE	0	最不发达35国LDC35	80	-Strawberries
719	0811.2000	-木莓、黑莓、桑椹、罗甘莓、黑、白或红的穗醋栗（加仑子）及醋栗	30	0 3 6 15	东盟ASEAN,新西兰NZ 智利CL 哥斯达黎加CR 秘鲁PE	0	最不发达35国LDC35	80	-Raspberries, blackberries, mulberries, loganberries, black, white or red cur-rants and gooseberries
		-其他：							-Other:
720	0811.9010	---栗子，未去壳	30	0 6 15	东盟ASEAN,智利CL,新西兰NZ 哥斯达黎加CR 秘鲁PE	0	最不发达35国LDC35	80	---Chestnuts, in shell
721	0811.9090	---其他	30	0 3 6 15	东盟ASEAN,新西兰NZ 智利CL 哥斯达黎加CR 秘鲁PE			80	---Other
	08.12	**暂时保藏（例如，使用二氧化硫气体、盐水、亚硫酸水或其他防腐液）的水果及坚果，但不适于直接食用的：**							**Fruit and nuts, provisionally preserved (for example, bysulphur dioxide gas, in brine, in sulphur water or in other preservative solutions), but unsuitable in that state for immediate consum-ption:**

序号 No.	税则号列 Tariff Line	货品名称	最惠国税率 MFN(%)	协定税率 Agreement(%)		特惠税率 S.P.(%)		普通税率 Gen.(%)	Article Description
722	0812.1000	-樱桃	30	0 3 6 15	东盟ASEAN,新西兰NZ 智利CL 哥斯达黎加CR 秘鲁PE			80	-Cherries
723	0812.9000	-其他	25	0 2.5 5 12.5	东盟ASEAN,新西兰NZ 智利CL 哥斯达黎加CR 秘鲁PE	0	最不发达35国LDC35	80	-Other
	08.13	**税号08.01至08.06以外的干果;本章的什锦坚果或干果:**							**Fruit, dried, other than that of headings No.08.01 to 08.06; mixtures of nuts or dried fruits of this Chapter:**
724	0813.1000	-杏	25	0 5 12.5	东盟ASEAN,智利CL,新西兰NZ,澳门MO 哥斯达黎加CR 秘鲁PE	0	最不发达35国LDC35	70	-Apricots
725	0813.2000	-梅及李	25	0 2.5 5 12.5	东盟ASEAN,新西兰NZ,澳门MO 智利CL 哥斯达黎加CR 秘鲁PE	0	最不发达35国LDC35	70	-Prunes
726	0813.3000	-苹果	25	0 2.5 5 12.5	东盟ASEAN,新西兰NZ,澳门MO 智利CL 哥斯达黎加CR 秘鲁PE	0	最不发达35国LDC35	70	-Apples
		-其他干果:							-Other fruit:
727	0813.4010	---龙眼干、肉	20	0 4 10	东盟ASEAN,智利CL,新西兰NZ,澳门MO 哥斯达黎加CR 秘鲁PE	0	最不发达35国LDC35,最不发达4国LDC4,柬埔寨KH	70	---Longans and longan pulps
728	0813.4020	---柿饼	25	0 5 12.5	东盟ASEAN,智利CL,新西兰NZ,澳门MO 哥斯达黎加CR 秘鲁PE	0	最不发达35国LDC35,最不发达4国LDC4,柬埔寨KH	70	---Persimmons
729	0813.4030	---红枣	25	0 5 12.5	东盟ASEAN,智利CL,新西兰NZ,澳门MO 哥斯达黎加CR 秘鲁PE	0	最不发达35国LDC35,最不发达4国LDC4,柬埔寨KH	70	---Red jujubes
730	0813.4040	---荔枝干	25	0 5 12.5	东盟ASEAN,智利CL,新西兰NZ,澳门MO 哥斯达黎加CR 秘鲁PE	0	最不发达35国LDC35,最不发达4国LDC4,柬埔寨KH	70	---Preserved litchi

序号 No.	税则号列 Tariff Line	货品名称	最惠国税率 MFN(%)	协定税率 Agreement(%)	特惠税率 S.P.(%)	普通税率 Gen.(%)	Article Description
731	0813.4090	---其他	25	0 东盟ASEAN,新西兰NZ,澳门MO 2.5 智利CL 5 哥斯达黎加CR 12.5 秘鲁PE	0 最不发达35国LDC35,最不发达4国LDC4,柬埔寨KH	70	---Other
732	0813.5000	-本章的什锦坚果或干果	18	0 东盟ASEAN,智利CL,新西兰NZ,澳门MO 3.6 哥斯达黎加CR 9 秘鲁PE 14.4 巴基斯坦PK	0 最不发达35国LDC35	70	-Mixtures of nuts or dried fruits of this Chapter
	08.14	**柑橘属水果或甜瓜（包括西瓜）的果皮，鲜、冻、干或用盐水、亚硫酸水或其他防腐液暂时保藏的：**					**Peel of citrus fruitor melons (includeing watermelons), fresh, frozen, dried or provisionally preserved in brine, insulphur water or in other preservative solutions:**
733	0814.0000	柑橘属水果或甜瓜（包括西瓜）的果皮，鲜、冻、干或用盐水、亚硫酸水或其他防腐液暂时保藏的	25	0 东盟ASEAN,新西兰NZ,澳门MO 2.5 智利CL 5 哥斯达黎加CR 12.5 秘鲁PE	0 最不发达35国LDC35	70	Peel of citrus fruit or melons(including watermelons), fresh, frozen, dried or provisionally preserved in brine, in sulphur water or in other preservative solutions

第九章
咖啡、茶、马黛茶及调味香料

Chapter 9
Coffee, tea, maté and spices

注释：

一、税号 09.04 至 09.10 所列产品的混合物，应按下列规定归类：

（一）同一税号的两种或两种以上产品的混合物仍应归入该税号；

（二）不同税号的两种或两种以上产品的混合物应归入税号 09.10。

税号 09.04 至 09.10 的产品（或上述（一）或（二）项的混合物）如添加了其他物质，只要所得的混合物保持了原产品的基本特性，其归类应不受影响。基本特性已经改变的，则不应归入本章；构成混合调味品的，应归入税号 21.03。

二、本章不包括荜澄茄椒或税号 12.11 的其他产品。

Notes:

1. Mixtures of the products of headings No.09.04to09.10are to be classified as follows:

(a) Mixtures of two or more of the products of the same heading are to be classified in that heading;

(b) Mixtures of two or more of the products of different headings are to beclassified in heading No.09.10.

The addition of other substances to the products of headings No.09.04to09.10 (or to the mixtures referred to in paragraph (a) or (b) above) shall not affect their classification provided the resulting mixtures retain the essential character of the goods of those headings. Otherwise such mixtures are not classifiedin this Chapter; those constituting mixed condiments or mixed seasonings are classified in heading No.21.03.

2. This Chapter does not cover Cubeb pepper (Piper cubeba) or other products of heading No.12.11.

序号 No.	税则号列 Tariff Line	货品名称	最惠国税率 MFN(%)	协定税率 Agreement(%)		特惠税率 S.P.(%)		普通税率 Gen.(%)	Article Description
	09.01	**咖啡，不论是否焙炒或浸除咖啡碱；咖啡豆荚及咖啡豆皮；含咖啡的咖啡代用品：**							**Coffee, whether or not roasted or decaffeinated; coffee husks and skins; coffee substitutes containing coffee in any proportion:**
		-未焙炒的咖啡：							-Coffee, not roasted:
734	0901.1100	--未浸除咖啡碱	8	0 4.8	智利CL,新西兰NZ 哥斯达黎加CR	0	最不发达35国LDC35,最不发达4国LDC4,老挝LA,柬埔寨KH	50	--Not decaffeinated
735	0901.1200	--已浸除咖啡碱	8	0	智利CL,新西兰NZ	0	最不发达35国LDC35,最不发达4国LDC4,老挝LA,柬埔寨KH	50	--Decaffeinated
		-已焙炒的咖啡：							-Coffee, roasted:

序号 No.	税则号列 Tariff Line	货品名称	最惠国税率 MFN(%)	协定税率 Agreement(%)		特惠税率 S.P.(%)		普通税率 Gen.(%)	Article Description
736	0901.2100	--未浸除咖啡碱	15	0 1.5 9	新西兰NZ,香港HK,澳门MO 智利CL 哥斯达黎加CR	0	最不发达35国LDC35,最不发达4国LDC4,老挝LA,柬埔寨KH	80	--Not decaffeinated
737	0901.2200	--已浸除咖啡碱	15	0 1.5 12	东盟ASEAN,新西兰NZ,澳门MO 智利CL 巴基斯坦PK	0	最不发达35国LDC35,最不发达4国LDC4,老挝LA,柬埔寨KH	80	--Decaffeinated
		-其他:							-Other:
738	0901.9010	---咖啡豆荚及咖啡豆皮	10	0 5	东盟ASEAN,智利CL,新加坡SG,新西兰NZ,秘鲁PE,哥斯达黎加CR 巴基斯坦PK	0	最不发达35国LDC35,最不发达4国LDC4,老挝LA,柬埔寨KH	30	---Coffee husks and skins
739	0901.9020	---含咖啡的咖啡代用品	30	0	东盟ASEAN,智利CL,新加坡SG,新西兰NZ,澳门MO	0	最不发达35国LDC35,最不发达4国LDC4,老挝LA,柬埔寨KH	80	---Coffee substitutes containing coffee
	09.02	**茶,不论是否加香料:** -绿茶(未发酵),内包装每件净重不超过3公斤:							**Tea, whether or not flavoured:** -Green tea (not fermented) in immediate packings of a content not exceeding 3kg:
740	0902.1010	---花茶	15	0 3 7.5	东盟ASEAN,智利CL,新加坡SG,新西兰NZ,澳门MO 哥斯达黎加CR 亚太APTA,巴基斯坦PK,秘鲁PE	0	最不发达35国LDC35	100	---Flavoured
741	0902.1090	---其他	15	0 3 7.5	东盟ASEAN,智利CL,新加坡SG,新西兰NZ,澳门MO,台湾TW 哥斯达黎加CR 亚太APTA,巴基斯坦PK,秘鲁PE	0	最不发达35国LDC35,最不发达4国LDC4	100	---Other
		-其他绿茶(未发酵):							-Other green tea (not fermented):

序号 No.	税则号列 Tariff Line	货品名称	最惠国税率 MFN(%)	协定税率 Agreement(%)		特惠税率 S.P.(%)		普通税率 Gen.(%)	Article Description
742	0902.2010	---花茶	15	0 3 7.5	东盟ASEAN,智利CL,新加坡SG,新西兰NZ,澳门MO 哥斯达黎加CR 亚太APTA,巴基斯坦PK,秘鲁PE	0	最不发达35国LDC35	100	---Flavoured
743	0902.2090	---其他	15	0 3 7.5	东盟ASEAN,智利CL,新加坡SG,新西兰NZ,澳门MO,台湾TW 哥斯达黎加CR 亚太APTA,巴基斯坦PK,秘鲁PE	0	最不发达35国LDC35,最不发达4国LDC4	100	---Other
		-红茶（已发酵）及半发酵茶，内包装每件净重不超过3公斤：							-Black tea (fermented) and partly fermented tea, in immediate packings of a content not exceeding 3kg:
744	0902.3010	---乌龙茶	15	0 3 7.5	东盟ASEAN,智利CL,新加坡SG,新西兰NZ,香港HK,澳门MO,台湾TW 哥斯达黎加CR 亚太APTA,巴基斯坦PK,秘鲁PE	0	最不发达35国LDC35	100	---Oolong tea
745	0902.3020	---普洱茶	15	0 3 7.5	东盟ASEAN,智利CL,新加坡SG,新西兰NZ,香港HK,澳门MO 哥斯达黎加CR 亚太APTA,巴基斯坦PK,秘鲁PE	0	最不发达35国LDC35	100	---Pu-er tea
746	0902.3090	---其他	15	0 3 7.5	东盟ASEAN,智利CL,新加坡SG,新西兰NZ,香港HK,澳门MO,台湾TW 哥斯达黎加CR 亚太APTA,巴基斯坦PK,秘鲁PE	0	最不发达35国LDC35,最不发达4国LDC4	100	---Other
		-其他红茶（已发酵）及半发酵茶：							-Other black tea (fermented) and other partly fermented tea:
747	0902.4010	---乌龙茶	15	0 3 7.5	东盟ASEAN,智利CL,新加坡SG,新西兰NZ,香港HK,澳门MO,台湾TW 哥斯达黎加CR 亚太APTA,巴基斯坦PK,秘鲁PE	0	最不发达35国LDC35,最不发达4国LDC4,缅甸MM,老挝LA,柬埔寨KH	100	---Oolong tea

序号 No.	税则号列 Tariff Line	货品名称	最惠国税率 MFN(%)	协定税率 Agreement(%)		特惠税率 S.P.(%)		普通税率 Gen.(%)	Article Description
748	0902.4020	---普洱茶	15	0 3 7.5	东盟ASEAN,智利CL,新加坡SG,新西兰NZ,香港HK,澳门MO 哥斯达黎加CR 亚太APTA,巴基斯坦PK,秘鲁PE	0	最不发达35国LDC35,最不发达4国LDC4,缅甸MM,老挝LA,柬埔寨KH	100	---Pu-er tea
749	0902.4090	---其他	15	0 3 7.5	东盟ASEAN,智利CL,新加坡SG,新西兰NZ,香港HK,澳门MO,台湾TW 哥斯达黎加CR 亚太APTA,巴基斯坦PK,秘鲁PE	0	最不发达35国LDC35,最不发达4国LDC4,缅甸MM,老挝LA,柬埔寨KH	100	---Other
	09.03	**马黛茶：**							**Mate:**
750	0903.0000	马黛茶	10	0 5	东盟ASEAN,智利CL,新加坡SG,新西兰NZ,秘鲁PE,哥斯达黎加CR 巴基斯坦PK	0	最不发达35国LDC35,最不发达4国LDC4	100	Mate
	09.04	**胡椒；辣椒干及辣椒粉：**							**Pepper of the genus Piper; dried or crushed or ground fruits of the genus Capsicum or of the genus Pimenta:**
		-胡椒：							-Pepper:
751	0904.1100	--未磨	20	0 4 10	智利CL,新西兰NZ 哥斯达黎加CR 秘鲁PE	0	最不发达35国LDC35	70	--Neither crushed nor ground
752	0904.1200	--已磨	20	0 4 10	智利CL,新西兰NZ,香港HK 哥斯达黎加CR 亚太APTA,巴基斯坦PK,秘鲁PE	0	最不发达35国LDC35	70	--Crushed or ground
		-辣椒：							-Fruits of the genus Capsicum or of the genus Pimenta:
753	0904.2100	--干，未磨	20	0 4 10	东盟ASEAN,智利CL,新加坡SG,新西兰NZ,秘鲁PE,香港HK 哥斯达黎加CR 亚太APTA,巴基斯坦PK	0	最不发达35国LDC35	70	--Dried, neither crushed nor ground
754	0904.2200	--已磨	20	0 4 10	东盟ASEAN,智利CL,新加坡SG,新西兰NZ,秘鲁PE,香港HK 哥斯达黎加CR 亚太APTA,巴基斯坦PK	0	最不发达35国LDC35	70	--Crushed or ground

序号 No.	税则号列 Tariff Line	货品名称	最惠国税率 MFN(%)	协定税率 Agreement(%)		特惠税率 S.P.(%)		普通税率 Gen.(%)	Article Description
	09.05	**香子兰豆：**							**Vanilla:**
755	0905.1000	-未磨	15	0 3 7.5 12	东盟ASEAN,智利CL,新加坡SG,新西兰NZ 哥斯达黎加CR 秘鲁PE 巴基斯坦PK	0	最不发达35国LDC35,最不发达4国LDC4	50	-Neither crushed nor ground
756	0905.2000	-已磨	15	0 3 7.5 12	东盟ASEAN,智利CL,新加坡SG,新西兰NZ 哥斯达黎加CR 秘鲁PE 巴基斯坦PK	0	最不发达35国LDC35,最不发达4国LDC4	50	-Crushed or ground
	09.06	**肉桂及肉桂花：**							**Cinnamon and cinnamon tree flowers:**
		-未磨：							-Neither crushed nor ground:
757	0906.1100	--锡兰肉桂	5	0	东盟ASEAN,智利CL,巴基斯坦PK,新西兰NZ,秘鲁PE,哥斯达黎加CR	0	最不发达35国LDC35,最不发达4国LDC4	50	--Cinnamon (Cinnamomum zeylanicum blume)
758	0906.1900	--其他	5	0	东盟ASEAN,智利CL,巴基斯坦PK,新西兰NZ,秘鲁PE,哥斯达黎加CR	0	最不发达35国LDC35,最不发达4国LDC4	50	--Other
759	0906.2000	-已磨	15	0 3 7.5 12	东盟ASEAN,智利CL,新加坡SG,新西兰NZ,香港HK 哥斯达黎加CR 秘鲁PE 巴基斯坦PK	0	最不发达35国LDC35	50	-Crushed or ground
	09.07	**丁香（母丁香、公丁香及丁香梗）：**							**Cloves (whole fruit, cloves and stems):**
760	0907.1000	-未磨	3	0	东盟ASEAN,智利CL,巴基斯坦PK,新西兰NZ,秘鲁PE,哥斯达黎加CR	0	最不发达35国LDC35,最不发达4国LDC4,柬埔寨KH	14	-Neither crushed nor ground
761	0907.2000	-已磨	3	0	东盟ASEAN,智利CL,巴基斯坦PK,新西兰NZ,秘鲁PE,哥斯达黎加CR	0	最不发达35国LDC35,最不发达4国LDC4,柬埔寨KH	14	-Crushed or ground
	09.08	**肉豆蔻、肉豆蔻衣及豆蔻：**							**Nutmeg, mace and cardamoms:**
		-肉豆蔻：							- Nutmeg:

序号 No.	税则号列 Tariff Line	货品名称	最惠国税率 MFN(%)	协定税率 Agreement(%)		特惠税率 S.P.(%)		普通税率 Gen.(%)	Article Description
762	0908.1100	--未磨	8	0 5	东盟ASEAN,智利CL,新西兰NZ,秘鲁PE,哥斯达黎加CR 巴基斯坦PK	0	最不发达35国LDC35,最不发达4国LDC4,老挝LA,柬埔寨KH	30	--Neither crushed nor ground
763	0908.1200	--已磨	8	0 5	东盟ASEAN,智利CL,新西兰NZ,秘鲁PE,哥斯达黎加CR 巴基斯坦PK	0	最不发达35国LDC35,最不发达4国LDC4,老挝LA,柬埔寨KH	30	--Crushed or ground
		-肉豆蔻衣:							-Mace:
764	0908.2100	--未磨	8	0 5	东盟ASEAN,智利CL,新西兰NZ,秘鲁PE,哥斯达黎加CR 巴基斯坦PK	0	最不发达35国LDC35,最不发达4国LDC4,老挝LA,柬埔寨KH	30	--Neither crushed nor ground
765	0908.2200	--已磨	8	0 5	东盟ASEAN,智利CL,新西兰NZ,秘鲁PE,哥斯达黎加CR 巴基斯坦PK	0	最不发达35国LDC35,最不发达4国LDC4,老挝LA,柬埔寨KH	30	--Crushed or ground
		-豆蔻:							-Cardamoms :
766	0908.3100	--未磨	3	0	东盟ASEAN,智利CL,巴基斯坦PK,新西兰NZ,秘鲁PE,哥斯达黎加CR	0	最不发达35国LDC35,最不发达4国LDC4,老挝LA,柬埔寨KH	14	--Neither crushed nor ground
767	0908.3200	--已磨	3	0	东盟ASEAN,智利CL,巴基斯坦PK,新西兰NZ,秘鲁PE,哥斯达黎加CR	0	最不发达35国LDC35,最不发达4国LDC4,老挝LA,柬埔寨KH	14	--Crushed or ground
	09.09	**茴芹子、八角茴香、小茴香子、芫荽子、枯茗子及黄蒿子;杜松果:**							**Seeds of anise, badian, fennel, coriander, cumin or caraway; juniper berries:**

序号 No.	税则号列 Tariff Line	货品名称	最惠国税率 MFN(%)	协定税率 Agreement(%)		特惠税率 S.P.(%)		普通税率 Gen.(%)	Article Description
		-芫荽子：							-Seeds of coriander:
768	0909.2100	--未磨	15	0 3 7.5 12	东盟ASEAN,智利CL,新加坡SG,新西兰NZ 哥斯达黎加CR 秘鲁PE 巴基斯坦PK	0	最不发达35国LDC35	50	--Neither crushed nor ground
769	0909.2200	--已磨	15	0 3 7.5 12	东盟ASEAN,智利CL,新加坡SG,新西兰NZ 哥斯达黎加CR 秘鲁PE 巴基斯坦PK	0	最不发达35国LDC35	50	--Crushed or ground
		-枯茗子：							-Seeds of cumin:
770	0909.3100	--未磨	15	0 3 7.5	东盟ASEAN,智利CL,新加坡SG,新西兰NZ 哥斯达黎加CR 亚太APTA,巴基斯坦PK,秘鲁PE	0	最不发达35国LDC35	50	--Neither crushed nor ground
771	0909.3200	--已磨	15	0 3 7.5	东盟ASEAN,智利CL,新加坡SG,新西兰NZ 哥斯达黎加CR 亚太APTA,巴基斯坦PK,秘鲁PE	0	最不发达35国LDC35	50	--Crushed or ground
		-茴芹子或八角茴香、蒿子或小茴香子；杜松果： --未磨：							-Seeds of anise, badian, caraway or fennel; juniper berries: --Neither crushed nor ground:
772	0909.6110	---八角茴香	20	0 4 10	东盟ASEAN,智利CL,新加坡SG,新西兰NZ 哥斯达黎加CR 秘鲁PE	0	最不发达35国LDC35	90	---Star aniseed
773	0909.6190	---其他	15	0 3 7.5 12	东盟ASEAN,智利CL,新加坡SG,新西兰NZ 哥斯达黎加CR 秘鲁PE 巴基斯坦PK	0	最不发达35国LDC35	50	---Other
		--已磨：							--Crushed or ground:
774	0909.6210	---八角茴香	20	0 4 10	东盟ASEAN,智利CL,新加坡SG,新西兰NZ 哥斯达黎加CR 秘鲁PE	0	最不发达35国LDC35	90	---Star aniseed
775	0909.6290	---其他	15	0 3 7.5 12	东盟ASEAN,智利CL,新加坡SG,新西兰NZ 哥斯达黎加CR 秘鲁PE 巴基斯坦PK	0	最不发达35国LDC35	50	---Other
	09.10	**姜、番红花、姜黄、麝香草、月桂叶、咖喱及其他调味香料：**							**Ginger, saffron, turmeric (curcuma), thyme, bay leaves, curry and other spices:**
		-姜：							-Ginger :

序号 No.	税则号列 Tariff Line	货品名称	最惠国税率 MFN(%)	协定税率 Agreement(%)		特惠税率 S.P.(%)		普通税率 Gen.(%)	Article Description
776	0910.1100	--未磨	15	0 3 7.5	东盟ASEAN,智利CL,新加坡SG,新西兰NZ 哥斯达黎加CR 亚太APTA,巴基斯坦PK,秘鲁PE	0	最不发达35国LDC35,最不发达4国LDC4,老挝LA,柬埔寨KH	50	--Neither crushed nor ground
777	0910.1200	--已磨	15	0 3 7.5	东盟ASEAN,智利CL,新加坡SG,新西兰NZ 哥斯达黎加CR 亚太APTA,巴基斯坦PK,秘鲁PE	0	最不发达35国LDC35,最不发达4国LDC4,老挝LA,柬埔寨KH	50	--Crushed or ground
778	0910.2000	-番红花	2	0	东盟ASEAN,智利CL,巴基斯坦PK,新西兰NZ,秘鲁PE,哥斯达黎加CR	0	最不发达35国LDC35,最不发达4国LDC4	14	-Saffron
779	0910.3000	-姜黄	15	0 3 7.5	东盟ASEAN,智利CL,新加坡SG,新西兰NZ,香港HK 哥斯达黎加CR 亚太APTA,巴基斯坦PK,秘鲁PE	0	最不发达35国LDC35,最不发达4国LDC4,柬埔寨KH	50	-Turmeric (curcuma)
		-其他调味香料:							-Other spices:
780	0910.9100	--本章注释一（二）所述的混合物	15	0 3 7.5	东盟ASEAN,智利CL,新加坡SG,新西兰NZ,香港HK,澳门MO 哥斯达黎加CR 亚太APTA,巴基斯坦PK,秘鲁PE	0	最不发达35国LDC35,最不发达4国LDC4	50	--Mixtures referred to in Note 1 (b) to this Chapter
781	0910.9900	--其他	15	0 3 7.5 12	东盟ASEAN,智利CL,新加坡SG,新西兰NZ,香港HK 哥斯达黎加CR 秘鲁PE 巴基斯坦PK	0	最不发达35国LDC35,最不发达4国LDC4	50	--Other

第十章 谷物

Chapter 10 Cereals

注释：

一、

（一）本章各税号所列产品必须带有谷粒，不论是否成穗或带杆。

（二）本章不包括已去壳或经其他加工的谷物。但去壳、碾磨、磨光、上光、半熟或破碎的稻米仍应归入税号10.06。

二、税号10.05不包括甜玉米（第七章）。

子目注释：

所称“硬粒小麦”，是指硬粒小麦属的小麦及以该属具有相同染色体数目（28）的小麦种间杂交所得的小麦。

Notes:

1.

(a) The products specified in the headings of this Chapter are tobe classified in those headings only if grains are present, whether or not in the ear or on the stalk.

(b) This Chapter does not cover grains which have been hulled or otherwise worked. However, rice, husked, milled, polished, glazed, parboiled or broken remains classified in heading No.10.06.

2. Heading No.10.05 does not cover sweet corn (Chapter 7).

Subheading Note:

The term “durum wheat” means wheat of the *Triticum durum* species and the hybrids derived from the inter-specific crossing of *Triticum durum* which have the same number (28) of chromosomes as that species.

序号 No.	税则号列 Tariff Line	货品名称	最惠国税率 MFN(%)	协定税率 Agreement(%)		特惠税率 S.P.(%)		普通税率 Gen.(%)	Article Description
	10.01	**小麦及混合麦：**							**Wheat and maslin:**
		-硬粒小麦：							-Durum wheat:
782	1001.1100	--种用	65[①]	20	东盟ASEAN			180	--Seed
783	1001.1900	--其他	65[②]	20	东盟ASEAN			180	--Other
		-其他：							-Other:
784	1001.9100	--种用	65[③]	20	东盟ASEAN			180	--Seed
785	1001.9900	--其他	65[④]	20	东盟ASEAN			180	--Other
	10.02	**黑麦：**							**Rye:**
786	1002.1000	-种用	0			0	最不发达35国LDC35,最不发达4国LDC4	0	-Seed
787	1002.9000	-其他	3	0	东盟ASEAN,智利CL,巴基斯坦PK,新西兰NZ,秘鲁PE,哥斯达黎加CR	0	最不发达35国LDC35,最不发达4国LDC4	8	-Other

① 配额税率（In-quota rate）：1%。
② 配额税率（In-quota rate）：1%。
③ 配额税率（In-quota rate）：1%。
④ 配额税率（In-quota rate）：1%。

序号 No.	税则号列 Tariff Line	货品名称	最惠国税率 MFN(%)	协定税率 Agreement(%)		特惠税率 S.P.(%)		普通税率 Gen.(%)	Article Description
	10.03	**大麦：**							**Barley:**
788	1003.1000	-种用	0			0	最不发达35国LDC35,最不发达4国LDC4	160	-Seed
789	1003.9000	-其他	3	0	东盟ASEAN,亚太APTA,智利CL,巴基斯坦PK,新西兰NZ,秘鲁PE,哥斯达黎加CR	0	最不发达35国LDC35,最不发达4国LDC4	160	-Other
	10.04	**燕麦：**							**Oats:**
790	1004.1000	-种用	0			0	最不发达35国LDC35,最不发达4国LDC4	0	-Seed
791	1004.9000	-其他	2	0	东盟ASEAN,智利CL,巴基斯坦PK,新西兰NZ,秘鲁PE,哥斯达黎加CR	0	最不发达35国LDC35,最不发达4国LDC4	8	-Other
	10.05	**玉米：**							**Maize(corn):**
792	1005.1000	-种用	20[①]					180	-Seed
793	1005.9000	-其他	65[②]					180	-Other
	10.06	**稻谷、大米：**							**Rice:**
		-稻谷：							-Rice in husk(paddy or rough):
		---种用：							---Seed:
794	1006.1011	----籼米	65[③]					180	----Long grain
795	1006.1019	----其他	65[④]	20	东盟ASEAN			180	----Other
		---其他：							---Other:
796	1006.1091	----籼米	65[⑤]					180	----Long grain
797	1006.1099	----其他	65[⑥]	20	东盟ASEAN			180	----Other
		-糙米：							-Husked(brown)rice:
798	1006.2010	---籼米	65[⑦]					180	---Long grain
799	1006.2090	---其他	65[⑧]	20	东盟ASEAN			180	---Other
		-精米，不论是否磨光或上光：							-Semi-milled or wholly milled rice, whether or not polished or glazed:
800	1006.3010	---籼米	65[⑨]					180	---Long grain

① 配额税率（In-quota rate）：1%。
② 配额税率（In-quota rate）：1%。
③ 配额税率（In-quota rate）：1%。
④ 配额税率（In-quota rate）：1%。
⑤ 配额税率（In-quota rate）：1%。
⑥ 配额税率（In-quota rate）：1%。
⑦ 配额税率（In-quota rate）：1%。
⑧ 配额税率（In-quota rate）：1%。
⑨ 配额税率（In-quota rate）：1%。

序号 No.	税则号列 Tariff Line	货品名称	最惠国税率 MFN(%)	协定税率 Agreement(%)		特惠税率 S.P.(%)		普通税率 Gen.(%)	Article Description
801	1006.3090	---其他	65①	20	东盟ASEAN			180	---Other
		-碎米：							-Broken rice:
802	1006.4010	---籼米	65②	20	东盟ASEAN			180	---Long grain
803	1006.4090	---其他	65③	20	东盟ASEAN			180	---Other
	10.07	**食用高粱：**							**Grain sorghum:**
804	1007.1000	-种用	0			0	最不发达35国LDC35,最不发达4国LDC4	0	-Seed
805	1007.9000	-其他	2	0	东盟ASEAN,智利CL,巴基斯坦PK,新西兰NZ,秘鲁PE,哥斯达黎加CR	0	最不发达35国LDC35	8	-Other
	10.08	**荞麦、谷子及加那利草子；其他谷物：**							**Buckwheat, millet and canary seed; other cereals:**
806	1008.1000	-荞麦	2	0	东盟ASEAN,智利CL,巴基斯坦PK,新西兰NZ,秘鲁PE,哥斯达黎加CR	0	最不发达35国LDC35,最不发达4国LDC4	8	-Buckwheat
		-谷子：							-Millet:
807	1008.2100	--种用	2	0	东盟ASEAN,智利CL,巴基斯坦PK,新西兰NZ,秘鲁PE,哥斯达黎加CR	0	最不发达35国LDC35,最不发达4国LDC4,老挝LA	8	--Seed
808	1008.2900	--其他	2	0	东盟ASEAN,智利CL,巴基斯坦PK,新西兰NZ,秘鲁PE,哥斯达黎加CR	0	最不发达35国LDC35,最不发达4国LDC4,老挝LA	8	--Other
809	1008.3000	-加那利草子	2	0	东盟ASEAN,智利CL,巴基斯坦PK,新西兰NZ,秘鲁PE,哥斯达黎加CR	0	最不发达35国LDC35,最不发达4国LDC4,老挝LA	8	-Canary seeds
		-直长马唐（马唐属）：							-Fonio (Digitaria spp.):
810	1008.4010	---种用	0			0	最不发达35国LDC35,最不发达4国LDC4	0	---Seed

① 配额税率（In-quota rate）：1%。
② 配额税率（In-quota rate）：1%。
③ 配额税率（In-quota rate）：1%。

序号 No.	税则号列 Tariff Line	货品名称	最惠国税率 MFN(%)	协定税率 Agreement(%)		特惠税率 S.P.(%)		普通税率 Gen.(%)	Article Description
811	1008.4090	---其他	3	0	东盟ASEAN,智利CL,巴基斯坦PK,新西兰NZ,秘鲁PE,哥斯达黎加CR	0	最不发达35国LDC35,最不发达4国LDC4,老挝LA	8	---Other
		-昆诺阿藜:							-Quinoa (Chenopodium quinoa):
812	1008.5010	---种用	0			0	最不发达35国LDC35,最不发达4国LDC4	0	---Seed
813	1008.5090	---其他	3	0	东盟ASEAN,智利CL,巴基斯坦PK,新西兰NZ,秘鲁PE,哥斯达黎加CR	0	最不发达35国LDC35,最不发达4国LDC4,老挝LA	8	---Other
		-黑小麦:							-Triticale:
814	1008.6010	---种用	0			0	最不发达35国LDC35,最不发达4国LDC4	0	---Seed
815	1008.6090	---其他	3	0	东盟ASEAN,智利CL,巴基斯坦PK,新西兰NZ,秘鲁PE,哥斯达黎加CR	0	最不发达35国LDC35,最不发达4国LDC4,老挝LA	8	---Other
		-其他谷物:							-Other cereals:
816	1008.9010	---种用	0			0	最不发达35国LDC35,最不发达4国LDC4	0	---Seed
817	1008.9090	---其他	3	0	东盟ASEAN,智利CL,巴基斯坦PK,新西兰NZ,秘鲁PE,哥斯达黎加CR	0	最不发达35国LDC35,最不发达4国LDC4,老挝LA	8	---Other

第十一章
制粉工业产品；麦芽；淀粉；菊粉；面筋

注释：

一、本章不包括：

（一）作为咖啡代用品的焙制麦芽（税号 09.01 或 21.01）；

（二）税号 19.01 的经制作的细粉、粗粒、粗粉或淀粉；

（三）税号 19.04 的玉米片及其他产品；

（四）税号 20.01、20.04 或 20.05 的经制作或保藏的蔬菜；

（五）药品（第三十章）；

（六）具有芳香料制品或化妆盥洗品性质的淀粉（第三十三章）。

二、

（一）下表所列谷物碾磨产品按干制品重量计如果同时符合以下两个条件，应归入本章；但是，整粒、滚压、制片或磨碎的谷物胚芽均应归入税目 11.04：

1. 淀粉含量（按修订的尤艾斯旋光法测定）超过表列第（2）栏的比例；

2. 灰分含量（除去任何添加的矿物质）不超过表列第（3）栏的比例。

否则，应归入税号 23.02。

（二）符合上述规定归入本章的产品，如果用表列第（4）或第（5）栏规定孔径的金属丝网筛过筛，其通过率按重量计不低于表列比例的，应归入税号 11.01 或 11.02。

否则，应归入税号 11.03 或 11.04。

三、税号 11.03 所称“粗粒”及“粗粉”，是指谷物经碾碎所得的下列产品：

（一）玉米产品，用 2 毫米孔径的金属丝网筛过筛，通过率按重量计不低于 95%的；

（二）其他谷物产品，用 1.25 毫米孔径的金属丝网筛过筛，通过率按重量计不低于 95%的。

Chapter 11
Products of the milling industry; malt; starches; inulin; wheat gluten

Notes:

1.This Chapter does not cover:

(a) Roasted malt put up as coffee substitutes (heading No.09.01 or 21.01);

(b) Prepared flours, groats, meals or starches of heading No.19.01;

(c) Corn flakes or other products of heading No.19.04;

(d) Vegetables, prepared or preserved,of heading No.20.01, 20.04 or 20.05;

(e) Pharmaceutical products (Chapter 30); or

(f) Starches having the character of perfumery,cosmetic or toilet preparations (Chapter 33).

2.

(A) Products from the milling of the cereals listed in the table below fall in this Chapter if they have, by weight on the dry product (However, germ of cereals, whole, rolled, flaked or ground is always classified in heading No.11.04):

(a) a starch content (determined by the modified Ewers polarimetric method) exceeding that indicated in Column (2); and

(b) an ash content (after deduction of any added minerals) not exceeding that indicated in Column (3).

Otherwise, they fall in heading No.23.02.

(B) Products falling in this Chapter under the above provisions shall be classified in heading No.11.01 or 11.02 if the percentage passing through a woven metal wire cloth sieve with the aperture indicated in Column (4) or (5) is not less, by weight, than that shown against the cereal concerned.

Otherwise, they fall in heading No.11.03 or 11.04.

3. For the purposes of heading No.11.03, the terms“groats” and“meal”mean products obtained by the fragmentation of cereal grains, of which:

(a) in the case of maize (corn) products,at least 95% by weight passes through a woven metal wire cloth sieve with an aperture of 2mm;

(b) in the case of other cereal products, at least 95% by weight passes through a woven metal wire cloth sieve with an aperture of 1.25mm.

序号 No.	税则号列 Tariff Line	货品名称	最惠国税 率 MFN(%)	协定税率 Agreement(%)		特惠税率 S.P.(%)		普通税率 Gen.(%)	Article Description
	11.01	**小麦或混合麦的细粉：**							**Wheat or maslin flour:**
818	1101.0000	小麦或混合麦的细粉	65[1]					130	Wheat or maslin flour
	11.02	**其他谷物细粉，但小麦或混合麦的细粉除外：**							**Cereal flours other than of wheat or maslin:**
819	1102.2000	-玉米细粉	40[2]					130	-Maize (corn) flour
		-其他：							-Other:
		---大米细粉：							---Rice flour:
820	1102.9011	----籼米的	40[3]					130	----Of long grain
821	1102.9019	----其他	40[4]	20	东盟ASEAN			130	----Other
822	1102.9090	---其他	5	0	东盟ASEAN,智利CL,巴基斯坦PK,新西兰NZ,秘鲁PE,哥斯达黎加CR	0	最不发达 35 国LDC35,最不发达 4 国LDC4,柬埔寨KH	14	---Other
	11.03	**谷物的粗粒、粗粉及团粒：**							**Cereal groats, meal and pellets:**
		-粗粒及粗粉：							-Groats and meal:
823	1103.1100	--小麦的	65[5]					130	--Of wheat
824	1103.1300	--玉米的	65[6]					130	--Of maize (corn)
		--其他：							--Other:
825	1103.1910	---燕麦的	5	0	东盟ASEAN,智利CL,巴基斯坦PK,新西兰NZ,秘鲁PE,哥斯达黎加CR	0	最不发达 35 国LDC35,最不发达 4 国LDC4	14	---Of oats
		---大米的：							---Of rice:
826	1103.1921	----籼米的	10[7]					70	----Of long grain
827	1103.1929	----其他	10[8]					70	----Other
828	1103.1990	---其他	5	0	东盟ASEAN,智利CL,巴基斯坦PK,新西兰NZ,秘鲁PE,哥斯达黎加CR	0	最不发达 35 国LDC35,最不发达 4 国LDC4,柬埔寨KH	14	---Other
		-团粒：							-Pellets:
829	1103.2010	---小麦的	65[9]					180	---Of wheat

[1] 配额税率（In-quota rate）：6%。
[2] 配额税率（In-quota rate）：9%。
[3] 配额税率（In-quota rate）：9%。
[4] 配额税率（In-quota rate）：9%。
[5] 配额税率（In-quota rate）：9%。
[6] 配额税率（In-quota rate）：9%。
[7] 配额税率（In-quota rate）：9%。
[8] 配额税率（In-quota rate）：9%。
[9] 配额税率（In-quota rate）：10%。

序号 No.	税则号列 Tariff Line	货品名称	最惠国税率 MFN(%)	协定税率 Agreement(%)		特惠税率 S.P.(%)		普通税率 Gen.(%)	Article Description
830	1103.2090	---其他	20	0 4 10	东盟ASEAN,智利CL,新加坡SG,新西兰NZ 哥斯达黎加CR 秘鲁PE	0	最不发达35国LDC35	50	--Of other cereals
	11.04	**经其他加工的谷物（例如，去壳、滚压、制片、制成粒状、切片或粗磨），但税号10.06的稻谷、大米除外；谷物胚芽，整粒、滚压、制片或磨碎的：**							**Cereal grains otherwise worked (for example, hulled, rolled, flaked, pearled, sliced or kibbled), except rice of heading No.10.06;germ of cereals, whole, rolled, flaked or ground:**
		-滚压或制片的谷物：							-Rolled or flaked grains:
831	1104.1200	--燕麦的	20	0 2 4 10	东盟ASEAN,新加坡SG,新西兰NZ 智利CL 哥斯达黎加CR 秘鲁PE	0	最不发达35国LDC35	50	--Of oats
		--其他：							--Other:
832	1104.1910	---大麦的	20	0 4 10	东盟ASEAN,智利CL,新加坡SG,新西兰NZ 哥斯达黎加CR 秘鲁PE	0	最不发达35国LDC35	50	---Of barley
833	1104.1990	---其他	20	0 4 10	东盟ASEAN,智利CL,新加坡SG,新西兰NZ 哥斯达黎加CR 秘鲁PE	0	最不发达35国LDC35	50	---Other
		-经其他加工的谷物（例如，去壳、制成粒状、切片或粗磨）：							-Other worked grains (for example, hulled, pearled, sliced or kibbled):
834	1104.2200	--燕麦的	20	0 2 4 10	东盟ASEAN,新加坡SG,新西兰NZ 智利CL 哥斯达黎加CR 秘鲁PE	0	最不发达35国LDC35	50	--Of oats
835	1104.2300	--玉米的	65[①]					180	--Of maize (corn)
		--其他：							--Other:
836	1104.2910	---大麦的	65	0 13 32.5	东盟ASEAN,智利CL,新加坡SG,新西兰NZ 哥斯达黎加CR 秘鲁PE	0	最不发达35国LDC35	114	---Of barley
837	1104.2990	---其他	20	0 4 10	东盟ASEAN,智利CL,新加坡SG,新西兰NZ 哥斯达黎加CR 秘鲁PE	0	最不发达35国LDC35	50	---Other
838	1104.3000	-谷物胚芽，整粒、滚压、制片或磨碎的	20	0 4 10	东盟ASEAN,智利CL,新加坡SG,新西兰NZ 哥斯达黎加CR 秘鲁PE	0	最不发达35国LDC35	50	-Germ of cereals, whole, rolled, flaked or ground

① 配额税率（In-quota rate）：10%。

序号 No.	税则号列 Tariff Line	货品名称	最惠国税率 MFN(%)	协定税率 Agreement(%)		特惠税率 S.P.(%)		普通税率 Gen.(%)	Article Description
	11.05	**马铃薯的细粉、粗粉、粉末、粉片、颗粒及团粒：**							**Flour, meal, powder, flakes, granules and pellets of potatoes:**
839	1105.1000	-细粉、粗粉及粉末	15	0 3 12	东盟ASEAN,智利CL,新加坡SG,新西兰NZ,秘鲁PE 哥斯达黎加CR 巴基斯坦PK	0	最不发达35国LDC35	50	-Flour, meal and powder
840	1105.2000	-粉片、颗粒及团粒	15	0 1.5 3 7.5 12	东盟ASEAN,新加坡SG,新西兰NZ 智利CL 哥斯达黎加CR 秘鲁PE 巴基斯坦PK	0	最不发达35国LDC35	50	-Flakes, granules and pellets
	11.06	**用税号07.13的干豆或税号07.14的西谷茎髓及植物根茎、块茎制成的细粉、粗粉及粉末；用第八章的产品制成的细粉、粗粉及粉末：**							**Flour, meal and powder of the dried leguminous vegetables of heading No.07.13, of sago or of roots or tubers of heading No.07.14; or of the products of Chapter 8:**
841	1106.1000	-用税号07.13的干豆制成的	10	0	东盟ASEAN,智利CL,新加坡SG,新西兰NZ,秘鲁PE,哥斯达黎加CR	0	最不发达35国LDC35,最不发达4国LDC4,柬埔寨KH	30	-Of the dried leguminous vegetables of heading No.07.13
842	1106.2000	-用税号07.14的西谷茎髓及植物根茎、块茎制成的	20	0 4	东盟ASEAN,智利CL,新加坡SG,新西兰NZ,秘鲁PE 哥斯达黎加CR	0	最不发达35国LDC35,最不发达4国LDC4,缅甸MM,老挝LA,柬埔寨KH	50	-Of sago or of roots or tubers of heading No.07.14
843	1106.3000	-用第八章的产品制成的	20	0 2 4 10	东盟ASEAN,新加坡SG,新西兰NZ 智利CL 哥斯达黎加CR 亚太APTA,巴基斯坦PK,秘鲁PE	0	最不发达35国LDC35	80	-Of the products of Chapter 8
	11.07	**麦芽，不论是否焙制：**							**Malt, whether or not roasted:**
844	1107.1000	-未焙制	10	0 1 5	东盟ASEAN,新加坡SG,新西兰NZ,哥斯达黎加CR 智利CL 巴基斯坦PK,秘鲁PE	0	最不发达35国LDC35	50	-Not roasted

序号 No.	税则号列 Tariff Line	货品名称	最惠国税率 MFN(%)	协定税率 Agreement(%)		特惠税率 S.P.(%)		普通税率 Gen.(%)	Article Description
845	1107.2000	-已焙制	10	0	东盟ASEAN,新加坡SG,新西兰NZ,哥斯达黎加CR	0	最不发达35国LDC35	50	-Roasted
				1	智利CL				
				5	巴基斯坦PK,秘鲁PE				
	11.08	**淀粉；菊粉：**							**Starches; inulin:**
		-淀粉：							-Starches:
846	1108.1100	--小麦淀粉	20	0	东盟ASEAN,智利CL,新加坡SG,新西兰NZ	0	最不发达35国LDC35	50	--Wheat starch
				4	哥斯达黎加CR				
				10	秘鲁PE				
847	1108.1200	--玉米淀粉	20	0	东盟ASEAN,智利CL,新加坡SG,新西兰NZ,秘鲁PE	0	最不发达35国LDC35	50	--Maize (corn) starch
				4	哥斯达黎加CR				
848	1108.1300	--马铃薯淀粉	15	0	东盟ASEAN,智利CL,新加坡SG,新西兰NZ	0	最不发达35国LDC35	50	--Potato starch
				3	哥斯达黎加CR				
				7.5	秘鲁PE				
				12	巴基斯坦PK				
849	1108.1400	--木薯淀粉	10	0	东盟ASEAN,智利CL,新加坡SG,新西兰NZ,秘鲁PE,哥斯达黎加CR	0	最不发达35国LDC35,最不发达4国LDC4	50	--Manioc (cassava) starch
				5	巴基斯坦PK				
850	1108.1900	--其他	20	0	东盟ASEAN,智利CL,新加坡SG,新西兰NZ	0	最不发达35国LDC35	50	--Other starches
				4	哥斯达黎加CR				
				10	秘鲁PE				
851	1108.2000	-菊粉	20	0	东盟ASEAN,智利CL,新加坡SG,新西兰NZ	0	最不发达35国LDC35	50	-Inulin
				4	哥斯达黎加CR				
				10	秘鲁PE				
	11.09	**面筋，不论是否干制：**							**Wheat gluten, whether or not dried:**
852	1109.0000	面筋，不论是否干制	18	0	东盟ASEAN,智利CL,新加坡SG,新西兰NZ	0	最不发达35国LDC35	80	Wheat gluten, whether or not dried
				3.6	哥斯达黎加CR				
				9	秘鲁PE				
				14.4	巴基斯坦PK				

第十二章
含油子仁及果实；杂项子仁及果实；工业用或药用植物；稻草、秸秆及饲料

注释：

一、税号 12.07 主要包括棕榈果及棕榈仁、棉子、蓖麻子、芝麻、芥子、红花子、罂粟子、牛油树果。但不包括税号 08.01 或 08.02 的产品及油橄榄（第七章或第二十章）。

二、税号 12.08 不仅包括未脱脂的细粉和粗粉，而且包括部分或全部脱脂以及用其本身的油料全部或部分复脂的细粉和粗粉。但不包括税号 23.04 至 23.06 的残渣。

三、甜菜子、草子及其他草本植物种子、观赏用花的种子、蔬菜种子、林木种子、果树种子、巢菜子（蚕豆除外）、羽扇豆属植物种子，可一律视为种植用种子，归入税号 12.09。

但下列各项即使作种子用，也不归入税号 12.09：

（一）豆类蔬菜或甜玉米（第七章）；
（二）第九章的调味香料及其他产品；
（三）谷物（第十章）；
（四）税号 12.01 至 12.07 或 12.11 的产品。

四、税号 12.11 主要包括下列植物或这些植物的某部分：罗勒、琉璃苣、人参、海索草、甘草、薄荷、迷迭香、芸香、鼠尾草及苦艾。但税号 12.11 不包括：

（一）第三十章的药品；
（二）第三十三章的芳香料制品及化妆盥洗品；
（三）税号 38.08 的杀虫剂、杀菌剂、除草剂、消毒剂及类似产品。

五、税号 12.12 的“海草及其他藻类”不包括：

Chapter 12
Oil seeds and oleaginous fruits; miscellaneous grains, seeds and fruit; industrial or medicinal plants; straw and fodder

Notes:

1. Heading No.12.07 applies, *inter alia*, to palm nuts and kernels, cotton seeds, castor oil seeds, sesamum seeds, mustard seeds, safflower seeds, poppy seeds and shea nuts (karite nuts). It does not apply to products of heading No.08.01 or 08.02 or to olives (Chapter 7 or Chapter 20).

2. Heading No.12.08 applies not only to non-defatted flours and meals but also to flours and meals which have been defatted or partially defatted and wholly or partially re-fatted with their original oils. It does not, however, apply to residues of headings No.23.04 to 23.06.

3. For the purposes of heading No.12.09 , beet seeds, grass and other herbage seeds, seeds of ornamental flowers, vegetable seeds, seeds of forest trees, seeds of fruit trees, seeds of vetches(other than those of the species Vicia faba) or of lupines are to be regarded as “seeds of a kind used for sowing”.

Heading No.12.09 does not, however, apply to the following even if for sowing:

(a) Laguminous vegetables or sweet corn (Chapter 7);
(b) Spices or other products of Chapter 9;
(c) Cereals (Chapter 10); or
(d) Products of headings No.12.01 to 12.07 or 12.11.

4. Heading No.12.11 applies, inter alia, to the following plants or parts thereof: Basil, borage, ginseng, hyssop, liquorice, all species of mint, rosemary, rue, sage and wormwood. Heading No.12.11does not, however , apply to:

(a)Medicaments of Chapter 30;
(b)Perfumery, cosmetic or toilet preparations of Chapter 33; or
(c)Insecticides, fungicides, herbicides, disinfectants or similar products of heading No.38.08.

5. For the purposes of heading No.12.12, the term “seaweeds and other algae” does not include:

（一） 税号 21.02 的已死的单细胞微生物；

（二） 税号 30.02 的培养微生物；

（三） 税号 31.01 或 31.05 的肥料。

(a)Dead singlecell micro-organisms of heading No.21.02;

(b)Cultures of micro-organisms of heading No.30.02; or

(c)Fertillizers of heading No.31.01 or 31.05.

子目注释：

子目 1205.10 所称“低芥子酸油菜子”，是指所获取的固定油中芥子酸含量按重量计低于 2%，以及所得的固体成分每克葡萄糖苷酸（酯）含量低于 30 微摩尔的油菜子。

Subheading Note:

For the purposes of subheading No.1205.10, the expression “low erucic acid rape or colza seeds” means rape of colza seeds yielding a fixed oil which has an erucic acid content of less than 2% by weight and yielding a solid component which contains less than 30 micromoles of glucosinolates per gram.

序号 No.	税则号列 Tariff Line	货品名称	最惠国税率 MFN(%)	协定税率 Agreement(%)		特惠税率 S.P.(%)		普通税率 Gen.(%)	Article Description
	12.01	大豆，不论是否破碎：							Soya beans, whether or not broken:
853	1201.1000	-种用	0			0	最不发达35国LDC35,最不发达4国LDC4	180	-Seed
		-其他：							-Other:
854	1201.9010	---黄大豆	3	0 0.3	东盟ASEAN,亚太APTA,巴基斯坦PK,新西兰NZ,秘鲁PE,哥斯达黎加CR 智利CL	0	最不发达35国LDC35,最不发达4国LDC4,老挝LA,柬埔寨KH	180	---Yellow soya beans
855	1201.9020	---黑大豆	3	0	东盟ASEAN,亚太APTA,智利CL,巴基斯坦PK,新西兰NZ,秘鲁PE,哥斯达黎加CR	0	最不发达35国LDC35,最不发达4国LDC4,老挝LA,柬埔寨KH	180	---Black soya beans
856	1201.9030	---青大豆	3	0	东盟ASEAN,亚太APTA,智利CL,巴基斯坦PK,新西兰NZ,秘鲁PE,哥斯达黎加CR	0	最不发达35国LDC35,最不发达4国LDC4,老挝LA,柬埔寨KH	180	---Green soya beans
857	1201.9090	---其他	3	0	东盟ASEAN,亚太APTA,智利CL,巴基斯坦PK,新西兰NZ,秘鲁PE,哥斯达黎加CR	0	最不发达35国LDC35,最不发达4国LDC4	180	---Other

序号 No.	税则号列 Tariff Line	货品名称	最惠国税率 MFN(%)	协定税率 Agreement(%)		特惠税率 S.P.(%)		普通税率 Gen.(%)	Article Description
	12.02	**未焙炒或未烹煮的花生，不论是否去壳或破碎：**							**Ground-nuts, not roasted or otherwise cooked, whether or not shelled or broken:**
858	1202.3000	-种用	0			0	最不发达35国LDC35,最不发达4国LDC4	0	-Seed
		-其他：							-Other:
859	1202.4100	--未去壳	15	0 3 7.5 12	东盟ASEAN,智利CL,新加坡SG,新西兰NZ 哥斯达黎加CR 秘鲁PE 巴基斯坦PK	0	最不发达35国LDC35,最不发达4国LDC4,老挝LA	70	--In shell
860	1202.4200	--去壳，不论是否破碎	15	0 3 7.5 12	东盟ASEAN,智利CL,新加坡SG,新西兰NZ 哥斯达黎加CR 秘鲁PE 巴基斯坦PK	0	最不发达35国LDC35,最不发达4国LDC4,老挝LA	70	--Shelled, whether or not broken
	12.03	**干椰子肉：**							**Copra:**
861	1203.0000	干椰子肉	15	0 3 7.5	东盟ASEAN,智利CL,新加坡SG,新西兰NZ 哥斯达黎加CR 亚太APTA,巴基斯坦PK,秘鲁PE	0	最不发达35国LDC35,最不发达4国LDC4,柬埔寨KH	30	Copra
	12.04	**亚麻子，不论是否破碎：**							**Linseed, whether or not broken:**
862	1204.0000	亚麻子，不论是否破碎	15	0 3 7.5 12	东盟ASEAN,智利CL,新加坡SG,新西兰NZ 哥斯达黎加CR 秘鲁PE 巴基斯坦PK	0	最不发达35国LDC35	70	Linseed, whether or not broken
	12.05	**油菜子，不论是否破碎：**							**Rape or colza seeds, whether or not broken:**
		-低芥子酸油菜籽：							-Low erucic acid rape or colza seeds:
863	1205.1010	---种用	0			0	最不发达35国LDC35,最不发达4国LDC4	80	---Seed
864	1205.1090	---其他	9	0 0.9	东盟ASEAN,亚太APTA,巴基斯坦PK,新西兰NZ,秘鲁PE,哥斯达黎加CR 智利CL	0	最不发达35国LDC35	80	---Other

序号 No.	税则号列 Tariff Line	货品名称	最惠国税率 MFN(%)	协定税率 Agreement(%)		特惠税率 S.P.(%)		普通税率 Gen.(%)	Article Description
		-其他：							-Other:
865	1205.9010	---种用	0			0	最不发达35国LDC35,最不发达4国LDC4	80	---Seed
866	1205.9090	---其他	9	0 0.9	东盟ASEAN,亚太APTA,巴基斯坦PK,新西兰NZ,秘鲁PE,哥斯达黎加CR 智利CL	0	最不发达35国LDC35	80	---Other
	12.06	**葵花子，不论是否破碎：**							**Sunflower seeds, whether or not broken:**
867	1206.0010	---种用	0			0	最不发达35国LDC35,最不发达4国LDC4	0	---Seed
868	1206.0090	---其他	15	0 1.5 3 7.5 12	东盟ASEAN,新加坡SG,新西兰NZ 智利CL 哥斯达黎加CR 秘鲁PE 巴基斯坦PK	0	最不发达35国LDC35	70	---Other
	12.07	**其他含油子仁及果实，不论是否破碎：**							**Other oil seeds and oleaginous fruits, whether or not broken:**
		-棕榈果及棕榈仁：							-Palm nuts and kernels:
869	1207.1010	---种用	0			0	最不发达35国LDC35,最不发达4国LDC4	0	---Seed
870	1207.1090	---其他	10	0 5	东盟ASEAN,智利CL,新加坡SG,新西兰NZ,秘鲁PE,哥斯达黎加CR 巴基斯坦PK	0	最不发达35国LDC35,最不发达4国LDC4,柬埔寨KH	70	---Other
		-棉子：							-Cotton seeds:
871	1207.2100	---种用	0			0	最不发达35国LDC35,最不发达4国LDC4	0	---Seed
872	1207.2900	---其他	15	0 3 7.5 12	东盟ASEAN,智利CL,新加坡SG,新西兰NZ 哥斯达黎加CR 秘鲁PE 巴基斯坦PK	0	最不发达35国LDC35	70	---Other

序号 No.	税则号列 Tariff Line	货品名称	最惠国税率 MFN(%)	协定税率 Agreement(%)		特惠税率 S.P.(%)		普通税率 Gen.(%)	Article Description
		-蓖麻子:							-Castor oil seeds:
873	1207.3010	---种用	0			0	最不发达35国LDC35,最不发达4国LDC4	0	---Seed
874	1207.3090	---其他	15	0 3 7.5	东盟ASEAN,智利CL,新加坡SG,新西兰NZ 哥斯达黎加CR 秘鲁PE	0	最不发达35国LDC35,最不发达4国LDC4,缅甸MM,老挝LA,柬埔寨KH	70	---Other
		-芝麻:							-Sesamum seeds:
875	1207.4010	---种用	0			0	最不发达35国LDC35,最不发达4国LDC4	0	---Seed
876	1207.4090	---其他	10	0 9	东盟ASEAN,智利CL,新加坡SG,新西兰NZ,秘鲁PE,哥斯达黎加CR 亚太APTA,巴基斯坦PK	0	最不发达35国LDC35,最不发达4国LDC4,缅甸MM,老挝LA,柬埔寨KH	70	---Other
		-芥子:							-Mustard seeds:
877	1207.5010	---种用	0			0	最不发达35国LDC35,最不发达4国LDC4	0	---Seed
878	1207.5090	---其他	15	0 3 7.5 12	东盟ASEAN,智利CL,新加坡SG,新西兰NZ 哥斯达黎加CR 秘鲁PE 巴基斯坦PK	0	最不发达35国LDC35	70	---Other
		-红花子:							-Safflower (*Carthamus tinctorius*) seeds:
879	1207.6010	---种用	0			0	最不发达35国LDC35,最不发达4国LDC4	0	---Seed

序号 No.	税则号列 Tariff Line	货品名称	最惠国税率 MFN(%)	协定税率 Agreement(%)		特惠税率 S.P.(%)		普通税率 Gen.(%)	Article Description
880	1207.6090	---其他	20	0 4 10	东盟ASEAN,智利CL,新加坡SG,新西兰NZ 哥斯达黎加CR 秘鲁PE	0	最不发达35国LDC35	70	---Other
		-甜瓜的子:							-Melon seeds:
881	1207.7010	---种用	0			0	最不发达35国LDC35,最不发达4国LDC4	0	---Seed
		---其他:							---Other:
882	1207.7091	----黑瓜子	20	0 4 10	东盟ASEAN,智利CL,新加坡SG,新西兰NZ 哥斯达黎加CR 秘鲁PE	0	最不发达35国LDC35	80	----Black watermelon seeds
883	1207.7092	----红瓜子	20	0 4 10	东盟ASEAN,智利CL,新加坡SG,新西兰NZ 哥斯达黎加CR 秘鲁PE	0	最不发达35国LDC35	80	----Red watermelon seeds
884	1207.7099	----其他	30	0 6 15	东盟ASEAN,智利CL,新西兰NZ 哥斯达黎加CR 秘鲁PE	0	最不发达35国LDC35,最不发达4国LDC4	70	----Other
		-其他:							-Other:
885	1207.9100	--罂粟子	20	0 4 10	东盟ASEAN,智利CL,新加坡SG,新西兰NZ 哥斯达黎加CR 秘鲁PE	0	最不发达35国LDC35	70	--Poppy seeds
		--其他:							--Other:
886	1207.9910	---种用	0			0	最不发达35国LDC35,最不发达4国LDC4	0	---Seed
		---其他:							---Other:
887	1207.9991	----牛油树果	20	0 2 4 10	东盟ASEAN,新加坡SG,新西兰NZ 智利CL 哥斯达黎加CR 秘鲁PE	0	最不发达35国LDC35,最不发达4国LDC4,缅甸MM	70	----Shea nuts (karite nuts)
888	1207.9999	----其他	10	0 1 5	东盟ASEAN,新加坡SG,新西兰NZ,哥斯达黎加CR 智利CL 巴基斯坦PK,秘鲁PE	0	最不发达35国LDC35,最不发达4国LDC4,缅甸MM,老挝LA,柬埔寨KH	70	----Other

序号 No.	税则号列 Tariff Line	货品名称	最惠国税率 MFN(%)	协定税率 Agreement(%)	特惠税率 S.P.(%)	普通税率 Gen.(%)	Article Description
	12.08	**含油子仁或果实的细粉及粗粉，但芥子粉除外：**					**Flours and meals of oil seeds or oleaginous fruits, other than those of mustard:**
889	1208.1000	-大豆粉	9	0 东盟ASEAN,智利CL,新西兰NZ,秘鲁PE,哥斯达黎加CR 5 巴基斯坦PK	0 最不发达35国LDC35,最不发达4国LDC4,柬埔寨KH	70	-Of soya beans
890	1208.9000	-其他	15	0 东盟ASEAN,智利CL,新加坡SG,新西兰NZ,香港HK 3 哥斯达黎加CR 7.5 秘鲁PE 12 巴基斯坦PK	0 最不发达35国LDC35,最不发达4国LDC4,柬埔寨KH	80	-Other
	12.09	**种植用的种子、果实及孢子：**					**Seeds, fruit and spores, of a kind used for sowing:**
891	1209.1000	-糖甜菜子	0		0 最不发达35国LDC35,最不发达4国LDC4	0	-Sugar beet seeds
		-饲料植物种子：					-Seeds of forage plants:
892	1209.2100	--紫苜蓿子	0		0 最不发达35国LDC35,最不发达4国LDC4	0	--Lucerne (alfalfa) seeds
893	1209.2200	--三叶草子	0		0 最不发达35国LDC35,最不发达4国LDC4	0	--Clover (*Trifolium spp.*) seeds
894	1209.2300	--羊茅子	0		0 最不发达35国LDC35,最不发达4国LDC4	0	--Fescue seeds
895	1209.2400	--草地早熟禾子	0		0 最不发达35国LDC35,最不发达4国LDC4	0	--Kentucky blue grass (*Poa pratensis L.*) seeds

序号 No.	税则号列 Tariff Line	货品名称	最惠国税率 MFN(%)	协定税率 Agreement(%)		特惠税率 S.P.(%)		普通税率 Gen.(%)	Article Description
896	1209.2500	--黑麦草种子	0			0	最不发达35国LDC35,最不发达4国LDC4	0	--Rye grass (*Lolium multiflorum Lam., Lolium perenne L.*) seeds
		--其他：							--Other:
897	1209.2910	---甜菜籽，糖甜菜籽除外	0			0	最不发达35国LDC35,最不发达4国LDC4	0	---Sugar beet seed
898	1209.2990	---其他	0			0	最不发达35国LDC35,最不发达4国LDC4	0	---Other
899	1209.3000	-草本花卉植物种子	0			0	最不发达35国LDC35,最不发达4国LDC4	0	-Seeds of herbaceous plants cultivated principally for their flowers
		-其他：							-Other:
900	1209.9100	--蔬菜种子	0			0	最不发达35国LDC35,最不发达4国LDC4	0	--Vegetable seeds
901	1209.9900	--其他	0			0	最不发达35国LDC35,最不发达4国LDC4	0	--Other
	12.10	**鲜或干的啤酒花，不论是否研磨或制成团粒；蛇麻腺：**							**Hop cones, fresh or dried, whethr or not ground, powdered or in the form of pellets;lupulin:**
902	1210.1000	-啤酒花，未经研磨也未制成团粒	20	0 4 10	东盟ASEAN,智利CL,新加坡SG,新西兰NZ 哥斯达黎加CR 秘鲁PE	0	最不发达35国LDC35	50	-Hop cones, neither ground nor powdered nor in the form of pellets
903	1210.2000	-啤酒花，经研磨或制成团粒；蛇麻腺	10	0 5	东盟ASEAN,智利CL,新加坡SG,新西兰NZ,秘鲁PE,哥斯达黎加CR 巴基斯坦PK	0	最不发达35国LDC35,最不发达4国LDC4	50	-Hop cones, ground, powdered or in the form of pellets; lupulin

序号 No.	税则号列 Tariff Line	货品名称	最惠国税率 MFN(%)	协定税率 Agreement(%)		特惠税率 S.P.(%)		普通税率 Gen.(%)	Article Description
	12.11	**主要用作香料、药料、杀虫、杀菌或类似用途的植物或这些植物的某部分（包括子仁及果实），鲜或干的，不论是否切割、压碎或研磨成粉：**							**Plants and parts of plants (including seeds and fruits), of a kind used primarily in perfumery, in pharmacy or for insecticidal, fungicidal or similar purposes, fresh or dried, whether or not cut, crushed or powdered:**
		-人参：							-Ginseng roots:
904	1211.2010	---西洋参	7.5	0 5	东盟ASEAN,智利CL,新加坡SG,新西兰NZ,秘鲁PE,哥斯达黎加CR,香港HK,澳门MO 巴基斯坦PK	0	最不发达35国LDC35,最不发达4国LDC4	70	---American ginseng
905	1211.2020	---野山参（西洋参除外）	20	0 4 10 16 16.4	东盟ASEAN,智利CL,新加坡SG,新西兰NZ 哥斯达黎加CR 秘鲁PE 巴基斯坦PK 亚太APTA	0	最不发达35国LDC35	90	---Wild ginseng (other than American ginseng)
		---其他：							---Other:
906	1211.2091	----鲜的	20	0 4 10	东盟ASEAN,智利CL,新加坡SG,新西兰NZ,香港HK 哥斯达黎加CR 秘鲁PE	0	最不发达35国LDC35	50	----fresh
907	1211.2099	----其他	20	0 4 10	东盟ASEAN,智利CL,新加坡SG,新西兰NZ,香港HK 哥斯达黎加CR 秘鲁PE	0	最不发达35国LDC35	50	----Other
908	1211.3000	-古柯叶	9	0 5	东盟ASEAN,智利CL,新西兰NZ,秘鲁PE,哥斯达黎加CR 巴基斯坦PK	0	最不发达35国LDC35,最不发达4国LDC4,柬埔寨KH	50	-Coca leaf
909	1211.4000	-罂粟杆	9	0 5	东盟ASEAN,智利CL,新西兰NZ,秘鲁PE,哥斯达黎加CR 巴基斯坦PK	0	最不发达35国LDC35,最不发达4国LDC4,柬埔寨KH	50	-Poppy straw
		-其他：							-Other:
		---主要用作药料的植物及其某部分：							---Of a kind used primarily in pharmacy:

序号 No.	税则号列 Tariff Line	货品名称	最惠国税率 MFN(%)	协定税率 Agreement(%)		特惠税率 S.P.(%)		普通税率 Gen.(%)	Article Description
910	1211.9011	----当归	6	0 3	东盟ASEAN,智利CL,巴基斯坦PK,新西兰NZ,秘鲁PE,哥斯达黎加CR 亚太APTA	0	最不发达35国LDC35,最不发达4国LDC4,柬埔寨KH	30	----Radix angelicae sinensis
911	1211.9012	----三七（田七）	6	0 3	东盟ASEAN,智利CL,巴基斯坦PK,新西兰NZ,秘鲁PE,哥斯达黎加CR 亚太APTA	0	最不发达35国LDC35,最不发达4国LDC4,柬埔寨KH	20	----Radix pseudoginseng
912	1211.9013	----党参	6	0 3	东盟ASEAN,智利CL,巴基斯坦PK,新西兰NZ,秘鲁PE,哥斯达黎加CR 亚太APTA	0	最不发达35国LDC35,最不发达4国LDC4	20	----Radix codonopsitis
913	1211.9014	----黄连	6	0 3	东盟ASEAN,智利CL,巴基斯坦PK,新西兰NZ,秘鲁PE,哥斯达黎加CR 亚太APTA	0	最不发达35国LDC35,最不发达4国LDC4	20	----Rhizoma coptidis
914	1211.9015	----菊花	6	0 3	东盟ASEAN,智利CL,巴基斯坦PK,新西兰NZ,秘鲁PE,哥斯达黎加CR 亚太APTA	0	最不发达35国LDC35,最不发达4国LDC4,柬埔寨KH	20	----Flos chrysanthemi
915	1211.9016	----冬虫夏草	6	0 3	东盟ASEAN,智利CL,巴基斯坦PK,新西兰NZ,秘鲁PE,哥斯达黎加CR,澳门MO 亚太APTA	0	最不发达35国LDC35,最不发达4国LDC4,柬埔寨KH	20	----Cordyceps sinensis
916	1211.9017	----贝母	6	0 3	东盟ASEAN,智利CL,巴基斯坦PK,新西兰NZ,秘鲁PE,哥斯达黎加CR 亚太APTA	0	最不发达35国LDC35,最不发达4国LDC4,柬埔寨KH	20	----Bulbs fritillariae thunbergii
917	1211.9018	----川芎	6	0 3	东盟ASEAN,智利CL,巴基斯坦PK,新西兰NZ,秘鲁PE,哥斯达黎加CR 亚太APTA	0	最不发达35国LDC35,最不发达4国LDC4,柬埔寨KH	20	----Rhizoma ligustici

序号 No.	税则号列 Tariff Line	货品名称	最惠国税率 MFN(%)	协定税率 Agreement(%)	特惠税率 S.P.(%)	普通税率 Gen.(%)	Article Description
918	1211.9019	----半夏	6	0 东盟ASEAN,智利CL,巴基斯坦PK,新西兰NZ,秘鲁PE,哥斯达黎加CR 3 亚太APTA	0 最不发达35国LDC35,最不发达4国LDC4,柬埔寨KH	20	----Rhizoma pinelliae
919	1211.9021	----白芍	6	0 东盟ASEAN,智利CL,巴基斯坦PK,新西兰NZ,秘鲁PE,哥斯达黎加CR 3 亚太APTA	0 最不发达35国LDC35,最不发达4国LDC4,柬埔寨KH	20	----Radix paeoniae lactiflorae
920	1211.9022	----天麻	6	0 东盟ASEAN,智利CL,巴基斯坦PK,新西兰NZ,秘鲁PE,哥斯达黎加CR 3 亚太APTA	0 最不发达35国LDC35,最不发达4国LDC4,柬埔寨KH	20	----Rhizoma gastrodiae
921	1211.9023	----黄芪	6	0 东盟ASEAN,智利CL,巴基斯坦PK,新西兰NZ,秘鲁PE,哥斯达黎加CR 3 亚太APTA	0 最不发达35国LDC35,最不发达4国LDC4,柬埔寨KH	30	----Radix astragali
922	1211.9024	----大黄、籽黄	6	0 东盟ASEAN,智利CL,巴基斯坦PK,新西兰NZ,秘鲁PE,哥斯达黎加CR 3 亚太APTA	0 最不发达35国LDC35,最不发达4国LDC4,柬埔寨KH	20	----Rhubarb
923	1211.9025	----白术	6	0 东盟ASEAN,智利CL,巴基斯坦PK,新西兰NZ,秘鲁PE,哥斯达黎加CR 3 亚太APTA	0 最不发达35国LDC35,最不发达4国LDC4,柬埔寨KH	20	----Rhizoma atractylodis macrocephalae
924	1211.9026	----地黄	6	0 东盟ASEAN,智利CL,巴基斯坦PK,新西兰NZ,秘鲁PE,哥斯达黎加CR 3 亚太APTA	0 最不发达35国LDC35,最不发达4国LDC4,柬埔寨KH	20	----Radix rehmanniae
925	1211.9027	----槐米	6	0 东盟ASEAN,智利CL,巴基斯坦PK,新西兰NZ,秘鲁PE,哥斯达黎加CR 3 亚太APTA	0 最不发达35国LDC35,最不发达4国LDC4,柬埔寨KH	20	----Flos sophorae

序号 No.	税则号列 Tariff Line	货品名称	最惠国税率 MFN(%)	协定税率 Agreement(%)		特惠税率 S.P.(%)		普通税率 Gen.(%)	Article Description
926	1211.9028	----杜仲	6	0 3	东盟ASEAN,智利CL,巴基斯坦PK,新西兰NZ,秘鲁PE,哥斯达黎加CR 亚太APTA	0	最不发达35国LDC35,最不发达4国LDC4,柬埔寨KH	20	----Cortex eucommiae
927	1211.9029	----茯苓	6	0 3	东盟ASEAN,智利CL,巴基斯坦PK,新西兰NZ,秘鲁PE,哥斯达黎加CR 亚太APTA	0	最不发达35国LDC35,最不发达4国LDC4,缅甸MM,老挝LA,柬埔寨KH	20	----Poria
928	1211.9031	----枸杞	6	0 3	东盟ASEAN,智利CL,巴基斯坦PK,新西兰NZ,秘鲁PE,哥斯达黎加CR 亚太APTA	0	最不发达35国LDC35,最不发达4国LDC4,柬埔寨KH	30	----Fructus lycii
929	1211.9032	----大海子	6	0 3	东盟ASEAN,智利CL,巴基斯坦PK,新西兰NZ,秘鲁PE,哥斯达黎加CR 亚太APTA	0	最不发达35国LDC35,最不发达4国LDC4,柬埔寨KH	20	----Bantaroi seeds
930	1211.9033	----沉香	3	0 1.5	东盟ASEAN,智利CL,巴基斯坦PK,新西兰NZ,秘鲁PE,哥斯达黎加CR 亚太APTA	0	最不发达35国LDC35,最不发达4国LDC4,柬埔寨KH	20	----Aloes wood
931	1211.9034	----沙参	6	0 3	东盟ASEAN,智利CL,巴基斯坦PK,新西兰NZ,秘鲁PE,哥斯达黎加CR 亚太APTA	0	最不发达35国LDC35,最不发达4国LDC4,柬埔寨KH	20	----Adenophora axilliflora
932	1211.9035	----青蒿	6	0 5	东盟ASEAN,智利CL,新西兰NZ,秘鲁PE,哥斯达黎加CR 巴基斯坦PK	0	最不发达35国LDC35,最不发达4国LDC4,柬埔寨KH	20	----Southernwood

序号 No.	税则号列 Tariff Line	货品名称	最惠国税率 MFN(%)	协定税率 Agreement(%)		特惠税率 S.P.(%)		普通税率 Gen.(%)	Article Description
933	1211.9036	----甘草	6 △0	0 5	东盟ASEAN,智利CL,新西兰NZ,秘鲁PE,哥斯达黎加CR 巴基斯坦PK	0	最不发达35国LDC35,最不发达4国LDC4	30	----Liquorice roots
934	1211.9037	----黄芩	6	0 3	东盟ASEAN,智利CL,巴基斯坦PK,新西兰NZ,秘鲁PE,哥斯达黎加CR 亚太APTA	0	最不发达35国LDC35,最不发达4国LDC4,缅甸MM,老挝LA,柬埔寨KH	20	----Radix scutellariae
935	1211.9038	----椴树(欧椴)花及叶	6	0 3	东盟ASEAN,智利CL,巴基斯坦PK,新西兰NZ,秘鲁PE,哥斯达黎加CR 亚太APTA	0	最不发达35国LDC35,最不发达4国LDC4,缅甸MM,老挝LA,柬埔寨KH	20	----Flowers and leaves of Linden (*tilia europaea*)
936	1211.9039	----其他	6	0 3	东盟ASEAN,智利CL,巴基斯坦PK,新西兰NZ,秘鲁PE,哥斯达黎加CR 亚太APTA	0	最不发达35国LDC35,最不发达4国LDC4,缅甸MM,老挝LA,柬埔寨KH	20	----Other
937	1211.9050	---主要用作香料的植物及其某部分	8	0 4	东盟ASEAN,智利CL,巴基斯坦PK,新西兰NZ,秘鲁PE,哥斯达黎加CR 亚太APTA	0	最不发达35国LDC35,最不发达4国LDC4,柬埔寨KH	50	---Of a kind used primarily in perfumery
		---其他：							---Other:
938	1211.9091	----鱼藤根、除虫菊	3	0 1.5	东盟ASEAN,智利CL,巴基斯坦PK,新西兰NZ,秘鲁PE,哥斯达黎加CR 亚太APTA	0	最不发达35国LDC35,最不发达4国LDC4,柬埔寨KH	11	----Derris roots and pyrethrum

序号 No.	税则号列 Tariff Line	货品名称	最惠国税率 MFN(%)	协定税率 Agreement(%)	特惠税率 S.P.(%)	普通税率 Gen.(%)	Article Description
939	1211.9099	----其他	9	0 东盟ASEAN,智利CL,新西兰NZ,秘鲁PE,哥斯达黎加CR 4.5 亚太APTA,巴基斯坦PK	0 最不发达35国LDC35,最不发达4国LDC4,柬埔寨KH	30	----Other
	12.12	**鲜、冷、冻或干的刺槐豆、海草及其他藻类、甜菜及甘蔗，不论是否碾磨；主要供人食用的其他税号未列名的果核、果仁及植物产品（包括未焙制的菊苣根）：**					**Locust beans, seaweeds and other algae, sugar beet and sugar cane, fresh, chilled, frozen or dried, whether or not ground; fruit stones and kernels and other vegetable products (including unroasted chicory roots of the variety *Cichorium intybus sativum*) of a kind used primarily for human consumption, not elsewhere specified or included:**
		-海草及其他藻类：					-Seaweeds and other algae:
		--适合供人食用的:					--Fit for human consumption:
940	1212.2110	---海带	20	0 东盟ASEAN,新加坡SG,新西兰NZ 2 智利CL 4 哥斯达黎加CR 10 亚太APTA,巴基斯坦PK,秘鲁PE	0 最不发达35国LDC35	70	---Sea tangle
941	1212.2120	---发菜	20	0 东盟ASEAN,新加坡SG,新西兰NZ 2 智利CL 4 哥斯达黎加CR 10 亚太APTA,巴基斯坦PK,秘鲁PE	0 最不发达35国LDC35	70	---Blackmoss
		---裙带菜:					---Pinnatifida:
942	1212.2131	----干的	15	0 东盟ASEAN,新加坡SG,新西兰NZ 1.5 智利CL 3 哥斯达黎加CR 7.5 亚太APTA,巴基斯坦PK 8.8 秘鲁PE	0 最不发达35国LDC35	70	----Dried
943	1212.2132	----鲜的	15	0 东盟ASEAN,新加坡SG,新西兰NZ 1.5 智利CL 3 哥斯达黎加CR 7.5 亚太APTA,巴基斯坦PK 8.8 秘鲁PE	0 最不发达35国LDC35	70	----Fresh

序号 No.	税则号列 Tariff Line	货品名称	最惠国税率 MFN(%)	协定税率 Agreement(%)	特惠税率 S.P.(%)	普通税率 Gen.(%)	Article Description
944	1212.2139	----其他	15	0 东盟ASEAN,新加坡SG,新西兰NZ 1.5 智利CL 3 哥斯达黎加CR 7.5 亚太APTA,巴基斯坦PK 8.8 秘鲁PE	0 最不发达35国LDC35	70	----Other
		---紫菜:					---Laver:
945	1212.2141	----干的	15	0 东盟ASEAN,新加坡SG,新西兰NZ 1.5 智利CL 3 哥斯达黎加CR 7.5 亚太APTA,巴基斯坦PK 8.8 秘鲁PE	0 最不发达35国LDC35	70	----Dried
946	1212.2142	----鲜的	15	0 东盟ASEAN,新加坡SG,新西兰NZ 1.5 智利CL 3 哥斯达黎加CR 7.5 亚太APTA,巴基斯坦PK 8.8 秘鲁PE	0 最不发达35国LDC35	70	----Fresh
947	1212.2149	----其他	15	0 东盟ASEAN,新加坡SG,新西兰NZ 1.5 智利CL 3 哥斯达黎加CR 7.5 亚太APTA,巴基斯坦PK 8.8 秘鲁PE	0 最不发达35国LDC35	70	----Other
		---麒麟菜:					---Eucheuma:
948	1212.2161	----干的	15	0 东盟ASEAN,新西兰NZ 1.5 智利CL 3 哥斯达黎加CR 7.5 亚太APTA,巴基斯坦PK 8.8 秘鲁PE	0 最不发达35国LDC35,最不发达4国LDC4	70	----Dried
949	1212.2169	----其他	15	0 东盟ASEAN,新西兰NZ 1.5 智利CL 3 哥斯达黎加CR 7.5 亚太APTA,巴基斯坦PK 8.8 秘鲁PE	0 最不发达35国LDC35	70	----Other
		---江蓠:					---Gracilaria:
950	1212.2171	----干的	15	0 东盟ASEAN,新西兰NZ 1.5 智利CL 3 哥斯达黎加CR 7.5 亚太APTA,巴基斯坦PK 8.8 秘鲁PE	0 最不发达35国LDC35	70	----Dried
951	1212.2179	----其他	15	0 东盟ASEAN,新西兰NZ 1.5 智利CL 3 哥斯达黎加CR 7.5 亚太APTA,巴基斯坦PK 8.8 秘鲁PE	0 最不发达35国LDC35	70	----Other
952	1212.2190	---其他	15 △2	0 东盟ASEAN,新加坡SG,新西兰NZ 1.5 智利CL 3 哥斯达黎加CR 7.5 亚太APTA,巴基斯坦PK 8.8 秘鲁PE	0 最不发达35国LDC35,最不发达4国LDC4	70	---Other

序号 No.	税则号列 Tariff Line	货品名称	最惠国税率 MFN(%)	协定税率 Agreement(%)	特惠税率 S.P.(%)	普通税率 Gen.(%)	Article Description
953	1212.2900	--其他	15 △2	0 东盟ASEAN,新加坡SG,新西兰NZ 1.5 智利CL 3 哥斯达黎加CR 7.5 亚太APTA,巴基斯坦PK 8.8 秘鲁PE	0 最不发达35国LDC35,最不发达4国LDC4	70	--Other
		-其他:					-Other:
954	1212.9100	--甜菜	20	0 东盟ASEAN,智利CL,新加坡SG,新西兰NZ 4 哥斯达黎加CR 10 秘鲁PE	0 最不发达35国LDC35	70	--Sugar beet
955	1212.9200	--刺槐豆	20	0 东盟ASEAN,智利CL,新加坡SG,新西兰NZ 4 哥斯达黎加CR 10 亚太APTA,巴基斯坦PK,秘鲁PE	0 最不发达35国LDC35	70	--Locust beans (carob)
956	1212.9300	--甘蔗	20	0 东盟ASEAN,智利CL,新西兰NZ 4 哥斯达黎加CR 10 秘鲁PE	0 最不发达35国LDC35,最不发达4国LDC4,缅甸MM,老挝LA,柬埔寨KH	70	--Sugar cane
957	1212.9400	--菊苣根	20	0 东盟ASEAN,智利CL,新西兰NZ 6 哥斯达黎加CR 15 秘鲁PE	0 最不发达35国LDC35,最不发达4国LDC4	70	--Chicory roots
		--其他:					--Other:
		---杏、桃（包括油桃）、梅或李的核及核仁:					---Apricot, peach (including nectarine) or plum stones and kernels:
958	1212.9911	----苦杏仁	20	0 东盟ASEAN,新加坡SG,新西兰NZ 2 智利CL 4 哥斯达黎加CR 10 秘鲁PE	0 最不发达35国LDC35	80	----Bitter
959	1212.9912	----甜杏仁	20	0 东盟ASEAN,新加坡SG,新西兰NZ,香港HK 2 智利CL 4 哥斯达黎加CR 10 秘鲁PE	0 最不发达35国LDC35	80	----Sweet
960	1212.9919	----其他	20	0 东盟ASEAN,新加坡SG,新西兰NZ 2 智利CL 4 哥斯达黎加CR 10 秘鲁PE	0 最不发达35国LDC35	80	----Other
		---其他:					---Other:

序号 No.	税则号列 Tariff Line	货品名称	最惠国税率 MFN(%)	协定税率 Agreement(%)		特惠税率 S.P.(%)		普通税率 Gen.(%)	Article Description
961	1212.9993	----白瓜子	20	0 4 10	东盟ASEAN,智利CL,新加坡SG,新西兰NZ 哥斯达黎加CR 秘鲁PE	0	最不发达35国LDC35	80	----Pumpkin seeds
962	1212.9994	----莲子	20	0 4 10	东盟ASEAN,智利CL,新加坡SG,新西兰NZ 哥斯达黎加CR 秘鲁PE	0	最不发达35国LDC35	80	----Lotus seeds (Semen Nelumbinis)
963	1212.9996	----甜叶菊叶	30	0 6 15	东盟ASEAN,智利CL,新加坡SG,新西兰NZ 哥斯达黎加CR 秘鲁PE	0	最不发达35国LDC35,最不发达4国LDC4	70	----Leaves of stevia
964	1212.9999	----其他	30	0 6 15	东盟ASEAN,智利CL,新加坡SG,新西兰NZ 哥斯达黎加CR 秘鲁PE	0	最不发达35国LDC35,最不发达4国LDC4	70	----Other
	12.13	**未经处理的谷类植物的茎、秆及谷壳，不论是否碎、碾磨、挤压或制成团粒：**							**Cereal straw and husks, unprepared, whether or not chopped, ground, pressed or in the form of pellets:**
		未经处理的谷类植物的茎、秆及谷壳，不论是否切碎、碾磨、挤压或制成团粒：							Cereal straw and husks, unprepared, whether or not chopped, ground, pressedor in the form of pellets:
965	1213.0010	---未经处理的稻草的茎、杆	12	0 2.4 6	东盟ASEAN,智利CL,新加坡SG,新西兰NZ,秘鲁PE 哥斯达黎加CR 巴基斯坦PK	0	最不发达35国LDC35,最不发达4国LDC4,柬埔寨KH	35	---Cereal straw, unprepared
966	1213.0090	---其他	12	0 2.4 6	东盟ASEAN,智利CL,新加坡SG,新西兰NZ,秘鲁PE 哥斯达黎加CR 巴基斯坦PK	0	最不发达35国LDC35,最不发达4国LDC4,柬埔寨KH	35	---Other
	12.14	**芜菁甘蓝、饲料甜菜、饲料用根、干草、紫苜蓿、三叶草、驴喜豆、饲料羽衣甘蓝、羽扇豆、巢菜及类似饲料，不论是否制成团粒：**							**Swedes, mangolds, fodder roots, hay, lucerne (alfalfa), clover, sainfoin, for age kale, lupines, vetches and similar forage products, whether or not in the form of pellets:**

序号 No.	税则号列 Tariff Line	货品名称	最惠国税率 MFN(%)	协定税率 Agreement(%)		特惠税率 S.P.(%)		普通税率 Gen.(%)	Article Description
967	1214.1000	-紫苜蓿粗粉及团粒	5	0	东盟ASEAN,智利CL,巴基斯坦PK,新西兰NZ,秘鲁PE,哥斯达黎加CR	0	最不发达35国LDC35,最不发达4国LDC4,柬埔寨KH	35	-Lucerne (alfalfa) meal and pellets
968	1214.9000	-其他	9	0 5	东盟ASEAN,智利CL,新西兰NZ,秘鲁PE,哥斯达黎加CR 巴基斯坦PK	0	最不发达35国LDC35,最不发达4国LDC4,柬埔寨KH	35	-Other
	ex12149000	其他紫苜蓿（粗粉及团粒除外）	△7						Other lucerne (alfalfa), excluding meal and pellets
	ex12149000	以除紫苜蓿外的禾本科和豆科为主的多种混合天然饲草	△4						Mixed non-artificial forage grass majorly composed of poaceae and fabaceae other than lucerne

第十三章
虫胶；树胶、树脂及其他植物液、汁

注释:

税号 13.02 主要包括甘草、除虫菊、啤酒花、芦荟的浸膏及鸦片，但不包括:

一、按重量计蔗糖含量在 10%以上或制成糖食的甘草浸膏（税号 17.04）;

二、麦芽膏（税号 19.01）;

三、咖啡精、茶精、马黛茶精（税号 21.01）;

四、构成含酒精饮料的植物汁、液（第二十二章）;

五、樟脑、甘草甜及税号 29.14 或 29.38 的其他产品;

六、罂粟杆浓缩物，按重量计生物碱含量不低于 50%（税目 29.39）;

七、税号 30.03 或 30.04 的药品及税号 30.06 的血型试剂;

八、鞣料或染料的浸膏（税号 32.01 或 32.03）;

九、精油、浸膏、净油、香膏、提取的油树脂或精油的水馏液及水溶液;饮料制造业用的以芳香物质为基料的制剂（第三十三章）;

十、天然橡胶、巴拉塔胶、古塔波胶、银胶菊胶、糖胶树胶或类似的天然树胶（税号 40.01）。

本国注释:

子目号 1302.1100 的鸦片，我国禁止进口。

Chapter 13
Lac; gums, resins and other vegetable saps and extracts

Notes:

Heading No.13.02 applies, inter alia, to liquorice extract and extract of pyrethrum, extract of hops, extract of aloes and opium. The heading does not apply to:

1. Liquorice extract containing more than 10% by weight of sucrose or put up as confectionery (heading No.17.04);
2. Malt extract (heading No.19.01);
3. Extracts of coffee, tea or mate (heading No.21.01);
4. Vegetable saps or extracts constituting alcoholic beverages (Chapter 22);
5. Camphor, glycyrrhizin or other products of heading No.29.14 or 29.38;
6. Concentrates of poppy straw containing not less than 50% by weight of alkaloids (heading 29.39);.
7. Medicaments of heading No.30.03 or 30.04 or blood-grouping reagents (heading No.30.06);
8. Tanning or dyeing extracts (heading No.32.01 or 32.03);
9. Essential oils, concretes, absolutes, resinoids, extracted oleoresins, aqueous distillates or aqueous solutions of essential oils or preparations based on odoriferous substances of a kind used for the manufacture of beverages (Chapter 33);or
10. Natural rubber, balata, guttapercha, guayule, chicle or similar natural gums (heading No.40.01).

National note:

Opium of Subheading No.1302.1100 is subject to import ban.

序号 No.	税则号列 Tariff Line	货品名称	最惠国税率 MFN(%)	协定税率 Agreement(%)	特惠税率 S.P.(%)	普通税率 Gen.(%)	Article Description
	13.01	**虫胶；天然树胶、树脂、树胶脂及油树脂（例如，香树脂）:**					**Lac; natural gums, resins, gumresins and oleoresins (for example, balsams):**
969	1301.2000	-阿拉伯胶	15	0 东盟ASEAN,智利CL,巴基斯坦PK,新加坡SG,新西兰NZ,秘鲁PE 3 哥斯达黎加CR	0 最不发达35国LDC35,最不发达4国LDC4	40	-Gum Arabic
		-其他:					-Other:

序号 No.	税则号列 Tariff Line	货品名称	最惠国税率 MFN(%)	协定税率 Agreement(%)		特惠税率 S.P.(%)		普通税率 Gen.(%)	Article Description
970	1301.9010	---胶黄耆树胶（卡喇杆胶）	15	0 3	东盟ASEAN,智利CL,巴基斯坦PK,新加坡SG,新西兰NZ,秘鲁PE 哥斯达黎加CR	0	最不发达35国LDC35	40	---Gum tragacanth
971	1301.9020	---乳香、没药及血竭	3	0	东盟ASEAN,智利CL,巴基斯坦PK,新西兰NZ,秘鲁PE,哥斯达黎加CR	0	最不发达35国LDC35,最不发达4国LDC4	17	---Olibanum, myrrh and dragon's blood
972	1301.9030	---阿魏	3	0	东盟ASEAN,智利CL,巴基斯坦PK,新西兰NZ,秘鲁PE,哥斯达黎加CR	0	最不发达35国LDC35,最不发达4国LDC4	17	---Asafoetida
973	1301.9040	---松脂	15	0 3	东盟ASEAN,智利CL,巴基斯坦PK,新加坡SG,新西兰NZ,秘鲁PE 哥斯达黎加CR	0	最不发达35国LDC35,最不发达4国LDC4	45	---Pine-resin
974	1301.9090	---其他	15	0 3	东盟ASEAN,智利CL,巴基斯坦PK,新加坡SG,新西兰NZ,秘鲁PE 哥斯达黎加CR	0	最不发达35国LDC35,最不发达4国LDC4	45	---Other
	13.02	**植物液汁及浸膏；果胶、果胶酸盐及果胶酸酯；从植物产品制得的琼脂、其他胶液及增稠剂，不论是否改性：**							**Vegetable saps and extracts; pectic substances, pectinates and pectates; agar-agar and other mucilages and thickeners, whether or not modified, derived from vegetable products:**
		-植物液汁及浸膏：							-Vegetable saps and extracts:
975	1302.1100	--鸦片	0			0	最不发达35国LDC35,最不发达4国LDC4	0	--Opium
976	1302.1200	--甘草的	6△0	0 5	东盟ASEAN,智利CL,新西兰NZ,秘鲁PE,哥斯达黎加CR 巴基斯坦PK	0	最不发达35国LDC35,最不发达4国LDC4	20	--Of liquorice
977	1302.1300	--啤酒花的	10	0 5	东盟ASEAN,智利CL,新加坡SG,新西兰NZ,秘鲁PE,哥斯达黎加CR 巴基斯坦PK	0	最不发达35国LDC35,最不发达4国LDC4	80	--Of hops

序号 No.	税则号列 Tariff Line	货品名称	最惠国 税 率 MFN(%)	协定税率 Agreement(%)		特惠税率 S.P.(%)		普通 税率 Gen.(%)	Article Description
		--其他:							--Other:
978	1302.1910	---生漆	20	0	东盟ASEAN,新加坡SG,新西兰NZ	0	最不发达35国LDC35	90	---Crude lacquer
				2	智利CL				
				4	哥斯达黎加CR				
				10	秘鲁PE				
979	1302.1920	---印楝素	3	0	东盟ASEAN,智利CL,巴基斯坦PK,新西兰NZ,秘鲁PE,哥斯达黎加CR	0	最不发达35国LDC35,最不发达4国LDC4	11	---Azadirachtin
980	1302.1930	---除虫菊的或含鱼藤酮植物根茎的	3	0	东盟ASEAN,智利CL,巴基斯坦PK,新西兰NZ,秘鲁PE,哥斯达黎加CR	0	最不发达35国LDC35,最不发达4国LDC4	11	---Of pyrethrum or of the roots of plants containing rotenone
981	1302.1940	---银杏的	20	0	东盟ASEAN,新加坡SG,新西兰NZ	0	最不发达35国LDC35	80	---Ginkgo biloba
				2	智利CL				
				4	哥斯达黎加CR				
				10	秘鲁PE				
				15	亚太APTA,巴基斯坦PK				
982	1302.1990	---其他	20	0	东盟ASEAN,新加坡SG,新西兰NZ	0	最不发达35国LDC35	80	---Other
				2	智利CL				
				4	哥斯达黎加CR				
				10	秘鲁PE				
				15	亚太APTA,巴基斯坦PK				
	ex13021990	苦参碱	△3						Matrine
983	1302.2000	-果胶、果胶酸盐及果胶酸酯	20	0	东盟ASEAN,智利CL,新加坡SG,新西兰NZ	0	最不发达35国LDC35	80	-Pectic substances, pectinates and pectates
				4	哥斯达黎加CR				
				10	秘鲁PE				
		-从植物产品制得的胶液及增稠剂，不论是否改性:							-Mucilages and thickeners, whether or not modified, derived from vegetable products:
984	1302.3100	--琼脂	10	0	东盟ASEAN,新加坡SG,新西兰NZ,哥斯达黎加CR	0	最不发达35国LDC35,最不发达4国LDC4	80	--Agar-agar
				1	智利CL				
				5	巴基斯坦PK,秘鲁PE				
985	1302.3200	--从刺槐豆、刺槐豆子或瓜尔豆制得的胶液及增稠剂，不论是否改性	15	0	东盟ASEAN,巴基斯坦PK,新加坡SG,新西兰NZ	0	最不发达35国LDC35	80	--Mucilages and thickeners, whether or not modified, derived from locust beans locust bean seeds or guar seeds
				1.5	智利CL				
				3	哥斯达黎加CR				
				7.5	秘鲁PE				
				10	亚太APTA				
		--其他:							--Other:

序号 No.	税则号列 Tariff Line	货品名称	最惠国税率 MFN(%)	协定税率 Agreement(%)		特惠税率 S.P.(%)		普通税率 Gen.(%)	Article Description
		---海草及其他藻类制品：							--Mucilages and thickeners, whether or not modified, derived from seaweeds and other algae:
986	1302.3911	----卡拉胶	15	0 1.5 3 7.5 12	东盟ASEAN,新加坡SG,新西兰NZ 智利CL 哥斯达黎加CR 秘鲁PE 巴基斯坦PK	0	最不发达35国LDC35	80	----Carrageenan
987	1302.3912	----褐藻胶	15	0 1.5 3 7.5 12	东盟ASEAN,新加坡SG,新西兰NZ 智利CL 哥斯达黎加CR 秘鲁PE 巴基斯坦PK	0	最不发达35国LDC35	80	----Algin
988	1302.3919	----其他	15	0 1.5 3 10.6 12	东盟ASEAN,新加坡SG,新西兰NZ 智利CL 哥斯达黎加CR 秘鲁PE 巴基斯坦PK	0	最不发达35国LDC35	80	----Other
989	1302.3990	---其他	15	0 1.5 3 8.8 12	东盟ASEAN,新加坡SG,新西兰NZ 智利CL 哥斯达黎加CR 秘鲁PE 巴基斯坦PK	0	最不发达35国LDC35	80	---Other

第十四章
编结用植物材料；
其他植物产品

Chapter 14
Vegetable plaiting materials; vegetable products not elsewhere specified or included

注释：

一、本章不包括归入第十一类的下列产品：

主要供纺织用的植物材料或植物纤维，不论其加工程度如何；或经过处理使其只能作为纺织原料用的其他植物材料。

二、税号 14.01 主要包括竹（不论是否劈开、纵锯、切段、圆端、漂白、磨光、染色或进行不燃处理）、劈开的柳条、芦苇及类似品和藤心、藤丝、藤片。但不包括木片条（税号 44.04）。

三、税号 14.04 不包括木丝（税号 44.05）及供制帚、制刷用成束、成簇的材料（税号 96.03）。

Notes:

1.This Chapter does not cover the following products which are to be classified in Section XI:

Vegetable materials or fibres of vegetable materials of a kind used primarily in the manufacture of textiles, however prepared, or other vegetable materials which have undergone treatment so as to render them suitable for use only as textile materials.

2. Heading No.14.01 applies, inter alia, to bamboos (whether or not split, sawn lengthwise, cut to length, rounded at the ends, bleached, rendered non-in-flammable, polished or dyed), split osier, reeds and the like, to rattan cores and to drawn or split rattans.The heading does not apply to chipwood (heading No.44.04).

3. Heading No.14.04 does not apply to wood wool (heading No.44.05) and prepared knots or tufts for broom or brush making (heading No.96.03).

序号 No.	税则号列 Tariff Line	货品名称	最惠国税率 MFN(%)	协定税率 Agreement(%)	特惠税率 S.P.(%)	普通税率 Gen.(%)	Article Description
	14.01	**主要作编结用的植物材料（例如，竹、藤、芦苇、灯芯草、柳条、酒椰叶，已净、漂白或染色的谷类植物的茎秆，椴树皮）：**					**Vegetable materials of a kind used primarily for plaiting (for example, bamboos, rattans, reeds, rushes, osier, raffia, cleaned, bleached or dyed cereal straw, and lime bark):**
990	1401.1000	-竹	10	0 东盟ASEAN,智利CL,新加坡SG,新西兰NZ,秘鲁PE,哥斯达黎加CR 5 巴基斯坦PK	0 最不发达35国LDC35,最不发达4国LDC4,老挝LA,柬埔寨KH	70	-Bamboos
991	1401.2000	-藤	10	0 东盟ASEAN,智利CL,新加坡SG,新西兰NZ,秘鲁PE,哥斯达黎加CR 5 巴基斯坦PK	0 最不发达35国LDC35,最不发达4国LDC4,老挝LA,柬埔寨KH	35	-Rattans
		-其他：					-Other:

序号 No.	税则号列 Tariff Line	货品名称	最惠国税率 MFN(%)	协定税率 Agreement(%)		特惠税率 S.P.(%)		普通税率 Gen.(%)	Article Description
992	1401.9010	---谷类植物的茎秆（麦秸除外）	10	0 1 5	东盟ASEAN,新加坡SG,新西兰NZ,哥斯达黎加CR 智利CL 巴基斯坦PK,秘鲁PE	0	最不发达35国LDC35,最不发达4国LDC4,柬埔寨KH	70	---Cereal straw (other than wheat straw)
993	1401.9020	---芦苇	10	0 5	东盟ASEAN,智利CL,新加坡SG,新西兰NZ,秘鲁PE,哥斯达黎加CR 巴基斯坦PK	0	最不发达35国LDC35,最不发达4国LDC4,柬埔寨KH	70	---Reeds
		---灯芯草属：							---Rushes:
994	1401.9031	----蔺草	10	0 5	东盟ASEAN,智利CL,新加坡SG,新西兰NZ,秘鲁PE,哥斯达黎加CR 巴基斯坦PK	0	最不发达35国LDC35,最不发达4国LDC4,柬埔寨KH	70	----Juncaceae
995	1401.9039	----其他	10	0 5	东盟ASEAN,智利CL,新加坡SG,新西兰NZ,秘鲁PE,哥斯达黎加CR 巴基斯坦PK	0	最不发达35国LDC35,最不发达4国LDC4,柬埔寨KH	70	----Other
996	1401.9090	---其他	10	0 1 5	东盟ASEAN,新加坡SG,新西兰NZ,哥斯达黎加CR 智利CL 巴基斯坦PK,秘鲁PE	0	最不发达35国LDC35,最不发达4国LDC4,柬埔寨KH	70	---Other
	14.04	**其他税号未列名的植物产品：**							**Vegetable products not elsewhere specified or included:**
997	1404.2000	-棉短绒	4	0	东盟ASEAN,智利CL,巴基斯坦PK,新西兰NZ,秘鲁PE,哥斯达黎加CR	0	最不发达35国LDC35,最不发达4国LDC4	30	-Cotton linters
		-其他：							-Other:
998	1404.9010	---主要供染料、鞣料用的植物原料	5	0 2.9 4.3	东盟ASEAN,智利CL,巴基斯坦PK,新西兰NZ,哥斯达黎加CR 秘鲁PE 亚太APTA	0	最不发达35国LDC35,最不发达4国LDC4	45	---Raw vegetable materials of a kind used primarily in dyeing or tanning
999	1404.9090	---其他	15	0 3	东盟ASEAN,智利CL,新加坡SG,新西兰NZ,秘鲁PE 哥斯达黎加CR	0	最不发达35国LDC35,最不发达4国LDC4	70	---Other

第 三 类

动、植物油、脂及其分解产品；精制的食用油脂；动、植物蜡

第十五章

动、植物油、脂及其分解产品；精制的食用油脂；动、植物蜡

注释：

一、本章不包括：

（一）税号 02.09 的猪脂肪及家禽脂肪；

（二）可可脂、可可油（税号 18.04）；

（三）按重量计税号 04.05 所列产品的含量超过 15% 的食品（通常归入第二十一章）；

（四）税号 23.01 的油渣或税号 23.04 至 23.06 的残渣；

（五）第六类的脂肪酸、精制蜡、药品、油漆、清漆、肥皂、芳香料制品、化妆盥洗品、磺化油及其他货品；

（六）从油类提取的油膏（税号 40.02）。

二、税号 15.09 不包括用溶剂提取的橄榄油（税号 15.10）。

三、税号 15.18 不包括变性的油、脂及其分离品，这些货品应归入其相应的未变性油、脂及其分离品的税号。

四、皂料、油脚、硬脂沥青、甘油沥青及羊毛脂残渣，归入税号 15.22。

子目注释：

子目 1514.11 及 1514.19 所称“低芥子酸菜子油”，是指按重量计芥子酸含量低于 2%的固定油。

SECTION Ⅲ

ANIMAL OR VEGETABLE FATS AND OILS AND THEIR CLEAVAGE PRODUCTS; PREPARED EDIBLE FATS;ANIMAL OR VEGETABLE WAXES

Chapter 15

Animal or vegetable fats and oils and their cleavage products; prepared edible fats; animal or vegetable waxes

Notes:

1. This Chapter does not cover:

(a) Pig fat or poultry fat of heading No.02.09;

(b) Cocoa butter, fat or oil (heading No.18.04);

(c) Edible preparations containing by weight more than 15% of the products of heading No.04.05 (generally Chapter 21);

(d) Greaves (heading No.23.01) or residues of headings No.23.04 to 23.06;

(e) Fatty acids, prepared waxes, medicaments, paints, varnishes, soap, perfumery, cosmetic or toilet preparations, sulphonated oils or other goods of SectionⅥ;or

(f) Factice derived from oils (heading No.40.02).

2. Heading No.15.09 does not apply to oils obtained from olives by solvent extraction (heading No.15.10).

3. Heading No.15.18 does not cover fats or oils or their fractions, merely denatured, which are to be classified in the heading appropriate to the corresponding undenatured fats and oils and their fractions.

4. Soap-stocks, oil foots and dregs, stearin pitch, glycerol pitch and wool grease residues fall in heading No.15.22.

Subheading Note:

For the purposes of subheadings 1514.11 and 1514.19, the expression “low erucic acid rape of colza oil” means the fixed oil which has an erucic acid content of less than 2% by weight.

序号 No.	税则号列 Tariff Line	货品名称	最惠国税率 MFN(%)	协定税率 Agreement(%)	特惠税率 S.P.(%)	普通税率 Gen.(%)	Article Description
	15.01	**猪脂肪（包括已炼制的猪油）及家禽脂肪，但税号 02.09 及 15.03 的货品除外：**					**Pig fat (including lard) and poultry fat, other than that of heading No.02.09 or 15.03:**

序号 No.	税则号列 Tariff Line	货品名称	最惠国税率 MFN(%)	协定税率 Agreement(%)		特惠税率 S.P.(%)		普通税率 Gen.(%)	Article Description
1000	1501.1000	-猪油	10	0	东盟ASEAN,智利CL,新加坡SG,新西兰NZ,秘鲁PE,哥斯达黎加CR,香港HK,澳门MO	0	最不发达35国LDC35,最不发达4国LDC4	35	-Lard
1001	1501.2000	-其他猪脂肪	10	0	东盟ASEAN,智利CL,新加坡SG,新西兰NZ,秘鲁PE,哥斯达黎加CR,香港HK,澳门MO	0	最不发达35国LDC35,最不发达4国LDC4	35	-Other pig fat
1002	1501.9000	-其他	10	0	东盟ASEAN,智利CL,新加坡SG,新西兰NZ,秘鲁PE,哥斯达黎加CR,香港HK,澳门MO	0	最不发达35国LDC35,最不发达4国LDC4	35	-Other
	15.02	**牛、羊脂肪，但税号15.03的货品除外：**							**Fats of bovine animals, sheep or goats, other than those of heading No.15.03:**
1003	1502.1000	-牛、羊油脂	8 △4	0	东盟ASEAN,亚太APTA,智利CL,巴基斯坦PK,新西兰NZ,秘鲁PE,哥斯达黎加CR,澳门MO	0	最不发达35国LDC35,最不发达4国LDC4	30	-Tallow
1004	1502.9000	-其他	8 △4	0	东盟ASEAN,亚太APTA,智利CL,巴基斯坦PK,新西兰NZ,秘鲁PE,哥斯达黎加CR,澳门MO	0	最不发达35国LDC35,最不发达4国LDC4	70	-Other
	15.03	**猪油硬脂、液体猪油、油硬脂、食用或非食用脂油，未经乳化、混合或其他方法制作：**							**Lard stearin, lard oil, oleostearin, oleooil and tallow oil, not emulsified or mixed or otherwise prepared:**
1005	1503.0000	猪油硬脂、液体猪油、油硬脂、食用或非食用脂油，未经乳化、混合或其他方法制作	10	0	东盟ASEAN,智利CL,新加坡SG,新西兰NZ,秘鲁PE,哥斯达黎加CR,澳门MO	0	最不发达35国LDC35,最不发达4国LDC4	30	Lard stearin, lard oil, oleostearin, oleooil and tallow oil, not emulsified or mixed or otherwise prepared
	15.04	**鱼或海生哺乳动物的油、脂及其分离品，不论是否精制，但未经化学改性：**							**Fats and oils and their fractions, of fish or marine mammals, whether or not refined, but not chemically modified:**
1006	1504.1000	-鱼肝油及其分离品	12	0 2.4	东盟ASEAN,智利CL,新加坡SG,新西兰NZ,秘鲁PE,澳门MO 哥斯达黎加CR	0	最不发达35国LDC35	30	-Fish-liver oils and their fractions

序号 No.	税则号列 Tariff Line	货品名称	最惠国税率 MFN(%)	协定税率 Agreement(%)		特惠税率 S.P.(%)		普通税率 Gen.(%)	Article Description
1007	1504.2000	-除鱼肝油以外的鱼油、脂及其分离品	12	0 1.2 2.4 4.5	东盟ASEAN,新加坡SG,新西兰NZ,澳门MO 智利CL 哥斯达黎加CR 秘鲁PE	0	最不发达35国LDC35	50	-Fats and oils and their fractions, of fish, other than liver oils
1008	1504.3000	-海生哺乳动物的油、脂及其分离品	14.4	0 2.9	东盟ASEAN,智利CL,新加坡SG,新西兰NZ,秘鲁PE,澳门MO 哥斯达黎加CR	0	最不发达35国LDC35	50	-Fats and oils and their fractions of marine mammals
	15.05	**羊毛脂及从羊毛脂制得的脂肪物质(包括纯净的羊毛脂):**							**Wool grease and fatty substances derived therefrom (including lanolin):**
1009	1505.0000	羊毛脂及从羊毛脂制得的脂肪物质(包括纯净的羊毛脂):	20	0 2 4 10	东盟ASEAN,新加坡SG,新西兰NZ 智利CL 哥斯达黎加CR 秘鲁PE	0	最不发达35国LDC35	70	Wool grease and fatty substances derived therefrom(including lanolin):
	15.06	**其他动物油、脂及其分离品，不论是否精制，但未经化学改性:**							**Other animal fats and oils and their fractions, whether or not refined, but not chemically modified:**
1010	1506.0000	其他动物油、脂及其分离品，不论是否精制，但未经化学改性	20	0 4 10	东盟ASEAN,智利CL,新加坡SG,新西兰NZ,澳门MO 哥斯达黎加CR 秘鲁PE	0	最不发达35国LDC35	70	Other animal fats and oils and their fractions, whether or not refined, but not chemically modified
	15.07	**豆油及其分离品，不论是否精制，但未经化学改性:**							**Soya-bean oil and its fractions, whether or not refined, but not chemically modified:**
1011	1507.1000	-初榨的,不论是否脱胶	9					190	-Crude oil whether or not degummed
1012	1507.9000	-其他	9					190	-Other
	15.08	**花生油及其分离品，不论是否精制，但未经化学改性:**							**Ground-nut oil and its fractions, whether or not refined, but not chemically modified:**
1013	1508.1000	-初榨的	10	0	东盟ASEAN,新加坡SG			100	-Crude oil
1014	1508.9000	-其他	10	0	东盟ASEAN,新加坡SG			100	-Other
	15.09	**油橄榄油及其分离品，不论是否精制，但未经化学改性:**							**Olive oil and its fractions, whether or not refined, but not chemically modified:**
1015	1509.1000	-初榨的	10	0 1 5	东盟ASEAN,新加坡SG,新西兰NZ,哥斯达黎加CR,澳门MO 智利CL 秘鲁PE	0	最不发达35国LDC35	30	-Virgin
1016	1509.9000	-其他	10	0	东盟ASEAN,新加坡SG,新西兰NZ,秘鲁PE,哥斯达黎加CR,香港HK,澳门MO	0	最不发达35国LDC35	30	-Other

序号 No.	税则号列 Tariff Line	货品名称	最惠国税率 MFN(%)	协定税率 Agreement(%)		特惠税率 S.P.(%)		普通税率 Gen.(%)	Article Description
				1	智利CL				
	15.10	**其他橄榄油及其分离品，不论是否精制，但未经化学改性，包括掺有税号15.09的油或分离品的混合物：**							**Other oils and their fractions, obtained solely from olives, whether or not refined, but not chemically modified, including blends of these oils or fractions with oils or fractions of heading No.15.09:**
1017	1510.0000	其他橄榄油及其分离品，不论是否精制，但未经化学改性，包括掺有税号15.09的油或分离品的混合物	10	0 1	东盟ASEAN,新加坡SG,新西兰NZ,秘鲁PE,哥斯达黎加CR,澳门MO 智利CL	0	最不发达35国LDC35	30	Other oils and their fractions, obtained solely from olives, whether or not refined, but not chemically modified, including blends of these oils or fractions with oils or fractions of heading No.15.09
	15.11	**棕榈油及其分离品，不论是否精制，但未经化学改性：**							**Palm oil and its fractions, whether or not refined, but not chemically modified:**
1018	1511.1000	-初榨的	9					60	-Crude oil
		-其他：							-Other:
1019	1511.9010	---棕榈液油（熔点19～24°C）	9					60	---Palm olein
1020	1511.9020	---棕榈硬脂（熔点44～56°C）	8					60	---Palm stearin
	ex15119020	固态棕榈硬脂（50°C≤熔点≤56°C）	△2						Solid palm stearin (melting point no less than 50 centigrade and no more than 56 centigrade)
1021	1511.9090	---其他	9					60	---Other
	15.12	**葵花油、红花油或棉子油及其分离品，不论是否精制，但未经化学改性：**							**Sunflower-seed, safflower or cotton-seed oil and fractions thereof, whether or not refined, but not chemically modified:**
		-葵花油或红花油及其分离品：							-Sunflower-seed or safflower oil and fractions thereof:
1022	1512.1100	--初榨的	9	0	东盟ASEAN,澳门MO			160	--Crude oil
1023	1512.1900	--其他	9	0	东盟ASEAN,澳门MO			160	--Other
		-棉子油及其分离品：							-Cotton-seed oil and its fractions:
1024	1512.2100	--初榨的，不论是否去除棉子酚	10	0	东盟ASEAN,新加坡SG,澳门MO			70	--Crude oil, whether or not gossypol has been removed
1025	1512.2900	--其他	10	0	东盟ASEAN,新加坡SG,澳门MO			70	--Other

序号 No.	税则号列 Tariff Line	货品名称	最惠国税率 MFN(%)	协定税率 Agreement(%)		特惠税率 S.P.(%)		普通税率 Gen.(%)	Article Description
	15.13	**椰子油、棕榈仁油或巴巴苏棕榈果油及其分离品，不论是否精制，但未经化学改性：**							**Coconut(copra)palm kernel or babassu oil and fractions thereof, whether or not refined, but not chemically modified:**
		-椰子油及其分离品：							-Coconut(copra)oil and its fractions:
1026	1513.1100	--初榨的	9	0 4.5	东盟ASEAN,智利CL,新西兰NZ,秘鲁PE,哥斯达黎加CR,澳门MO 亚太APTA,巴基斯坦PK	0	最不发达35国LDC35	40	--Crude oil
1027	1513.1900	--其他	9	0 4.5	东盟ASEAN,智利CL,新西兰NZ,秘鲁PE,哥斯达黎加CR,澳门MO 亚太APTA,巴基斯坦PK	0	最不发达35国LDC35,最不发达4国LDC4	40	--Other
		-棕榈仁油或巴巴苏棕榈果油及其分离品：							-Palm kernel or babassu oil and fractions thereof:
1028	1513.2100	--初榨的	9	0	东盟ASEAN,智利CL,新西兰NZ,秘鲁PE,哥斯达黎加CR,澳门MO	0	最不发达35国LDC35	40	--Crude oil
1029	1513.2900	--其他	9	0	东盟ASEAN,智利CL,新西兰NZ,秘鲁PE,哥斯达黎加CR,澳门MO	0	最不发达35国LDC35	40	--Other
	15.14	**菜子油或芥子油及其分离品，不论是否精制，但未经化学改性：**							**Rape, colza or mustard oil and fractions thereof, whether or not refined, but not chemically modified:**
		-低芥子酸菜子油及其分离品：							-Low erucic acid rape of colza oil and its fractions:
1030	1514.1100	--初榨的	9					170	--Crude oil
1031	1514.1900	--其他	9					170	--Other
		-其他：							-Other:
		--初榨的：							--Crude oil:
1032	1514.9110	---菜子油	9					170	---Rape oil
1033	1514.9190	---芥子油	9					170	---Mustard oil
1034	1514.9900	--其他	9					170	--Other
	15.15	**其他固定植物油、脂（包括希蒙得木油）及其分离品，不论是否精制，但未经化学改性：**							**Other fixed vegetable fats and oils (including jojoba oil) and fractions thereof, whether or not refined, but not chemically modified:**
		-亚麻子油及其分离品：							-Linseed oil and its fractions:
1035	1515.1100	--初榨的	15	0 3 7.5	东盟ASEAN,智利CL,新加坡SG,新西兰NZ,澳门MO 哥斯达黎加CR 秘鲁PE	0	最不发达35国LDC35	30	--Crude oil

序号 No.	税则号列 Tariff Line	货品名称	最惠国税率 MFN(%)	协定税率 Agreement(%)		特惠税率 S.P.(%)		普通税率 Gen.(%)	Article Description
1036	1515.1900	--其他	15	0 3 7.5	东盟ASEAN,智利CL,新加坡SG,新西兰NZ,澳门MO 哥斯达黎加CR 秘鲁PE	0	最不发达35国LDC35	30	--Other
		-玉米油及其分离品:							-Maize(corn)oil and its fractions:
1037	1515.2100	--初榨的	10	0	东盟ASEAN,新加坡SG,澳门MO	0	最不发达35国LDC35,最不发达4国LDC4,老挝LA,柬埔寨KH	160	--Crude oil
1038	1515.2900	--其他	10	0	东盟ASEAN,新加坡SG,澳门MO	0	最不发达35国LDC35,最不发达4国LDC4,老挝LA,柬埔寨KH	160	--Other
1039	1515.3000	-蓖麻油及其分离品	10	0	东盟ASEAN,智利CL,新加坡SG,新西兰NZ,秘鲁PE,哥斯达黎加CR,澳门MO	0	最不发达35国LDC35,最不发达4国LDC4,老挝LA,柬埔寨KH	70	-Castor oil and its fractions
1040	1515.5000	-芝麻油及其分离品	12	0 2.4	东盟ASEAN,智利CL,新加坡SG,新西兰NZ,秘鲁PE,澳门MO 哥斯达黎加CR	0	最不发达35国LDC35,最不发达4国LDC4,老挝LA,柬埔寨KH	20	-Sesame oil and its fractions
		-其他:							-Other:
1041	1515.9010	---希蒙得木油及其分离品	20	0 2 4	东盟ASEAN,新加坡SG,新西兰NZ,澳门MO 智利CL 哥斯达黎加CR	0	最不发达35国LDC35,最不发达4国LDC4,柬埔寨KH	70	---Jojoba oil and its fractions
1042	1515.9020	---印楝油及其分离品	20	0 2 4	东盟ASEAN,新加坡SG,新西兰NZ,澳门MO 智利CL 哥斯达黎加CR	0	最不发达35国LDC35	70	---Neem oil and its fractions

序号 No.	税则号列 Tariff Line	货品名称	最惠国税率 MFN(%)	协定税率 Agreement(%)		特惠税率 S.P.(%)		普通税率 Gen.(%)	Article Description
1043	1515.9030	---桐油及其分离品	20	0 4	东盟ASEAN,智利CL,新加坡SG,新西兰NZ,澳门MO 哥斯达黎加CR	0	最不发达35国LDC35,最不发达4国LDC4,柬埔寨KH	70	---Tung oil and its fractions
1044	1515.9090	---其他	20	0 2 4	东盟ASEAN,新加坡SG,新西兰NZ,澳门MO 智利CL 哥斯达黎加CR	0	最不发达35国LDC35,最不发达4国LDC4,缅甸MM,老挝LA,柬埔寨KH	70	---Other
	15.16	**动、植物油、脂及其分离品，全部或部分氢化、相互酯化、再酯化或反油酸化，不论是否精制，但未经进一步加工：**							**Animal or vegetable fats and oil and fractions thereof, partly or wholly hydrogenated, inter-esterified, re-esterified or elaidinized, whether or not refined, but not further prepared:**
1045	1516.1000	-动物油、脂及其分离品	5	0	文莱BN,印尼ID,马来西亚MY,缅甸MM,菲律宾PH,新加坡*SG*,泰国TH,越南VT,智利CL,新西兰NZ,秘鲁PE,哥斯达黎加CR,澳门MO	0	最不发达35国LDC35,最不发达4国LDC4	70	-Animal fats and oils and fractions thereof
1046	1516.2000	-植物油、脂及其分离品	25	0 2.5 5 12.5	东盟ASEAN,新西兰NZ,澳门MO 智利CL 哥斯达黎加CR 秘鲁PE	0	最不发达35国LDC35	70	-Vegetable fats and oils and fractions thereof
	15.17	**人造黄油；本章各种动、植物油、脂及其分离品混合制成的食用油、脂或制品，但税号15.16的食用油、脂及其分离品除外：**							**Margarine; edible mixtures or preparations of animal or vegetable fats or oils or of fractions of different fats or oils of this Chapter, other than edible fats or oils or their fractions of heading No.15.16:**
1047	1517.1000	-人造黄油，但不包括液态的	30	0 3 6	东盟ASEAN,新加坡SG,新西兰NZ,澳门MO 智利CL 哥斯达黎加CR			80	-Margarine, excluding liquid margarine
		-其他:							-Other:

序号 No.	税则号列 Tariff Line	货品名称	最惠国税率 MFN(%)	协定税率 Agreement(%)		特惠税率 S.P.(%)		普通税率 Gen.(%)	Article Description
1048	1517.9010	---起酥油	25	0 5 12.5	东盟ASEAN,智利CL,新西兰NZ,香港HK,澳门MO 哥斯达黎加CR 秘鲁PE	0	最不发达35国LDC35	70	---Shortening
1049	1517.9090	---其他	25	0 5 12.5	东盟ASEAN,智利CL,新西兰NZ,香港HK,澳门MO 哥斯达黎加CR 秘鲁PE	0	最不发达35国LDC35	70	---Other
	15.18	**动、植物油、脂及其分离品，经过熟炼、氧化、脱水、硫化、吹制或在真空、惰性气体中加热聚合及用其他化学方法改性的，但税号15.16的产品除外；本章各种油、脂及其分离品混合制成的其他税号未列名的非食用油、脂或制品：**							**Animal or vegetable fats and oils and fractions thereof, boiled, oxidized, dehydrated, sulphurized, blown, polymerized by heat in vacuum or in inert gas or otherwise chemically modified, excluding those of heading No.15.16; inedible mixtures or prepa-rations of animal or vegetable fats or oils or of fractions of different fats or oils of this Chapter, not elsewhere specified or included:**
1050	1518.0000	动、植物油、脂及其分离品，经过熟炼、氧化、脱水、硫化、吹制或在真空、惰性气体中加热聚合及用其他化学方法改性的，但税号15.16的产品除外；本章各种油、脂及其分离品混合制成的其他税号未列名的非食用油、脂或制品	10	0 1 5	东盟ASEAN,新加坡SG,新西兰NZ,哥斯达黎加CR,澳门MO 智利CL 秘鲁PE	0	最不发达35国LDC35,最不发达4国LDC4	70	Animal or vegetable fats and oils and fractions thereof, boiled, oxidized, dehydrated, sulphurized, blown, polymerized by heat in vacuum or in inert gas or otherwise chemically modified, excluding those of heading No.15.16; inedible mixtures or preparations of animal or vegetable fats or oils or of fractions of different fats or oils of this Chapter, not elsewhere specified or included
	15.20	**粗甘油；甘油水及甘油碱液：**							**Glycerol, crude; glycerol waters and glycerol lyes:**
1051	1520.0000	粗甘油；甘油水及甘油碱液	20 △6	0 4 10	东盟ASEAN,智利CL,新加坡SG,新西兰NZ,香港HK,澳门MO 哥斯达黎加CR 秘鲁PE	0	最不发达35国LDC35	50	Glycerol, crude; glycerol waters and glycerol lyes

序号 No.	税则号列 Tariff Line	货品名称	最惠国税率 MFN(%)	协定税率 Agreement(%)		特惠税率 S.P.(%)		普通税率 Gen.(%)	Article Description
	15.21	**植物蜡（甘油三酯除外）、蜂蜡、其他虫蜡及鲸蜡，不论是否精制或着色：**							**Vegetable waxes other than triglyce-rides), beeswax, other insect waxes and spermaceti, whether or not refined or coloured:**
1052	1521.1000	-植物蜡	20	0 4 10	东盟ASEAN,智利CL,新加坡SG,新西兰NZ 哥斯达黎加CR 秘鲁PE	0	最不发达35国LDC35	80	-Vegetable waxes
		-其他：							-Other:
1053	1521.9010	---蜂蜡	20	0 4 10	东盟ASEAN,智利CL,新加坡SG,新西兰NZ 哥斯达黎加CR 秘鲁PE	0	最不发达35国LDC35	80	---Beeswax
1054	1521.9090	---其他	20	0 4 10	东盟ASEAN,智利CL,新加坡SG,新西兰NZ 哥斯达黎加CR 秘鲁PE	0	最不发达35国LDC35	80	---Other
	15.22	**油鞣回收脂；加工处理油脂物质及动、植物蜡所剩的残渣：**							**Degras; residues resulting from the treatment of fatty substances of animal or vegetable waxes:**
1055	1522.0000	油鞣回收脂；加工处理油脂物质及动、植物蜡所剩的残渣	20	0 4 10	东盟ASEAN,智利CL,新加坡SG,新西兰NZ 哥斯达黎加CR 秘鲁PE	0	最不发达35国LDC35	50	Degras; residues resulting from the treatment of fatty substances of animal or vegetable waxes

第四类
食品；饮料、酒及醋；烟草、烟草及烟草代用品的制品

注释：

本类所称“团粒”，是指直接挤压或加入按重量计比例不超过3%的粘合剂制成的粒状产品。

SECTION IV
PREPARED FOODSTUFFS; BEVERAGES, SPIRITS AND VINEGAR; TOBACCO AND MANUFACTURED TOBACCO SUBSTITUTES

Note:

In this Section the term “pellets” means products which have been agglomerated either directly by compression or by the addition of a binder in a proportion not exceeding 3% by weight.

第十六章
肉、鱼、甲壳动物、软体动物及其他水生无脊椎动物的制品

注释：

一、本章不包括用第二章、第三章及税号05.04所列方法制作或保藏的肉、食用杂碎、鱼、甲壳动物、软体动物或其他水生无脊椎动物。

二、本章的食品按重量计必须含有20%以上的香肠、肉、食用杂碎、动物血、鱼、甲壳动物、软体动物或其他水生无脊椎动物及其混合物。对于含有两种或两种以上前述产品的食品，则应按其中重量最大的产品归入第十六章的相应税号。但本条规定不适用于税号19.02的包馅食品和税号21.03及21.04的食品。

子目注释：

一、子目号1602.10的“均化食品”，是指用肉、食用杂碎或动物血经精细均化制成供婴幼儿食用或营养用的零售包装食品（每件净重不超过250克）。为了调味、保藏或其他目的，均化食品中可以加入少量其他配料，还可以含有少量可见的肉粒或食用杂碎粒。归类时该子目优先于税号16.02的其他子目。

二、税号16.04或16.05项下各子目所列的是鱼、甲壳动物、软体动物及其他水生无脊椎动物的俗名，它们与第三章中相同名称的鱼、甲壳动物、软体动物及其他水生无脊椎动物种类范围相同。

Chapter 16
Preparations of meat, of fish or of crustaceans, molluscs or other aquatic invertebrates

Notes:

1. This Chapter does not cover meat, meat offal, fish, crustaceans, molluscs or other aquatic invertebrates, prepared or preserved by the processes specified in Chapter 2 or 3 or heading No.05.04.
2. Food preparations fall in this Chapter provided that they contain more than 20% by weight of sausage, meat, meat offal, blood, fish or crustaceans, molluscs or other aquatic invertebrates, or any combination thereof. In cases where the preparation contains two or more of the products mentioned above, it is classified in the heading of Chapter 16 corresponding to the component or components which predominate by weight. These provisions do not apply to the stuffed products of heading No.19.02 or to the preparations of heading No.21.03 or 21.04.

Subheading Notes:

1. For the purposes of subheading No.1602.10, the expression “homogenized preparations” means preparations of meat, meat offal or blood, finely homogenized, put up for retail sale as infant food or for dietetic purposes, in containers of a net weight content not exceeding 250g. For the application of this definition no account is to be taken of small quantities of any ingredients which may have been added to the preparation for seasoning, preservation or other purposes. These preparations may contain a small quantity of visible pieces of meat or meat offal. This subheading takes precedence over all other subheadings of heading No.16.02.
2. The fish, crustaceans, mollusks and other aquatic invertebrates specified in the subheahings of heading No.16.04 or 16.05 under their common names only, are of the same species as those mentioned in Chapter 3 under the same name.

序号 No.	税则号列 Tariff Line	货品名称	最惠国税率 MFN(%)	协定税率 Agreement(%)		特惠税率 S.P.(%)		普通税率 Gen.(%)	Article Description
	16.01	**肉、食用杂碎或动物血制成的香肠及类似产品；用香肠制成的食品：**							**Sausages and similar products, of meat, meat offal or blood; food preparations based on these products:**
		肉、食用杂碎或动物血制成的香肠及类似产品；用香肠制成的食品：							Sausages and similar products, of meat, meat offal or blood; food preparations based on these products:
1056	1601.0010	---用天然肠衣做外包装的香肠及类似产品	15	0 1.5 3 7.5 12	东盟ASEAN,新加坡SG,新西兰NZ,香港HK,澳门MO 智利CL 哥斯达黎加CR 秘鲁PE 巴基斯坦PK	0	最不发达35国LDC35	90	---Sausages and similar products coated with natural casings
1057	1601.0020	---其他香肠及类似产品	15	0 1.5 3 7.5 12	东盟ASEAN,新加坡SG,新西兰NZ,香港HK,澳门MO 智利CL 哥斯达黎加CR 秘鲁PE 巴基斯坦PK	0	最不发达35国LDC35	90	---Other sausages and similar products
1058	1601.0030	---用香肠制成的食品	15	0 1.5 3 7.5 12	东盟ASEAN,新加坡SG,新西兰NZ,澳门MO 智利CL 哥斯达黎加CR 秘鲁PE 巴基斯坦PK	0	最不发达35国LDC35	90	---Sausage based food products
	16.02	**其他方法制作或保藏的肉、食用杂碎或动物血：**							**Other Prepared or preserved meat, meat offal or blood:**
1059	1602.1000	-均化食品	15	0 3 7.5 12	东盟ASEAN,智利CL,新加坡SG,新西兰NZ 哥斯达黎加CR 秘鲁PE 巴基斯坦PK	0	最不发达35国LDC35	90	-Homogenized preparations
1060	1602.2000	-动物肝	15	0 3 7.5 12	东盟ASEAN,智利CL,新加坡SG,新西兰NZ,香港HK 哥斯达黎加CR 秘鲁PE 巴基斯坦PK	0	最不发达35国LDC35	90	-Of liver of any animal
		-税号01.05的家禽的：							-Of poultry of heading No.01.05:
1061	1602.3100	--火鸡的	15	0 3 7.5 12	东盟ASEAN,智利CL,新加坡SG,新西兰NZ 哥斯达黎加CR 秘鲁PE 巴基斯坦PK	0	最不发达35国LDC35	90	--Of turkeys
		--鸡的：							--Of fowls of the species *Gallus domesticus:*

序号 No.	税则号列 Tariff Line	货品名称	最惠国税率 MFN(%)	协定税率 Agreement(%)		特惠税率 S.P.(%)		普通税率 Gen.(%)	Article Description
1062	1602.3210	---罐头	15	0	东盟ASEAN,新加坡SG,新西兰NZ,澳门MO	0	最不发达35国LDC35	90	---In airtight containers
				1.5	智利CL				
				3	哥斯达黎加CR				
				7.5	秘鲁PE				
				12	巴基斯坦PK				
		---其他:							---Other:
1063	1602.3291	----鸡胸肉	15	0	东盟ASEAN,智利CL,新加坡SG,新西兰NZ,香港HK	0	最不发达35国LDC35	90	----Chicken breast filets
				3	哥斯达黎加CR				
				7.5	秘鲁PE				
				12	巴基斯坦PK				
1064	1602.3292	----鸡腿肉	15	0	东盟ASEAN,新加坡SG,新西兰NZ,香港HK	0	最不发达35国LDC35	90	----Chicken leg meat
				1.5	智利CL				
				3	哥斯达黎加CR				
				7.5	秘鲁PE				
				12	巴基斯坦PK				
1065	1602.3299	----其他	15	0	东盟ASEAN,新加坡SG,新西兰NZ,香港HK,澳门MO	0	最不发达35国LDC35	90	----Other
				1.5	智利CL				
				3	哥斯达黎加CR				
				7.5	秘鲁PE				
				12	巴基斯坦PK				
		--其他:							--Other:
1066	1602.3910	---罐头	15	0	东盟ASEAN,智利CL,新加坡SG,新西兰NZ,澳门MO	0	最不发达35国LDC35	90	---In airtight containers
				3	哥斯达黎加CR				
				7.5	秘鲁PE				
				12	巴基斯坦PK				
		---其他:							---Other:
1067	1602.3991	----鸭的	15	0	东盟ASEAN,智利CL,新加坡SG,新西兰NZ,香港HK	0	最不发达35国LDC35	90	----Of duck
				3	哥斯达黎加CR				
				7.5	秘鲁PE				
				12	巴基斯坦PK				
1068	1602.3999	----其他	15	0	东盟ASEAN,智利CL,新加坡SG,新西兰NZ,澳门MO	0	最不发达35国LDC35	90	----Other
				3	哥斯达黎加CR				
				7.5	秘鲁PE				
				12	巴基斯坦PK				
		-猪的:							-Of swine:
1069	1602.4100	--后腿及其肉块	15	0	东盟ASEAN,智利CL,新加坡SG,新西兰NZ,澳门MO	0	最不发达35国LDC35	90	--Hams and cuts thereof
				3	哥斯达黎加CR				
				7.5	秘鲁PE				
				12	巴基斯坦PK				

序号 No.	税则号列 Tariff Line	货品名称	最惠国税率 MFN(%)	协定税率 Agreement(%)		特惠税率 S.P.(%)		普通税率 Gen.(%)	Article Description
1070	1602.4200	--前腿及其肉块	15	0	东盟ASEAN,智利CL,新加坡SG,新西兰NZ,澳门MO	0	最不发达35国LDC35	90	--Shoulders and cuts thereof
				3	哥斯达黎加CR				
				7.5	秘鲁PE				
				12	巴基斯坦PK				
		--其他，包括混合的肉：							--Other, including mixtures:
1071	1602.4910	---罐头	15	0	东盟ASEAN,新加坡SG,新西兰NZ,澳门MO	0	最不发达35国LDC35	90	---In airtight containers
				1.5	智利CL				
				3	哥斯达黎加CR				
				7.5	秘鲁PE				
				12	巴基斯坦PK				
1072	1602.4990	---其他	15	0	东盟ASEAN,新加坡SG,新西兰NZ,香港HK,澳门MO	0	最不发达35国LDC35	90	---Other
				1.5	智利CL				
				3	哥斯达黎加CR				
				7.5	秘鲁PE				
				12	巴基斯坦PK				
		-牛的：							-Of bovine animals:
1073	1602.5010	---罐头	12	0	东盟ASEAN,新加坡SG,新西兰NZ,澳门MO	0	最不发达35国LDC35	90	---In airtight containers
				1.2	智利CL				
				2.4	哥斯达黎加CR				
				6	巴基斯坦PK,秘鲁PE				
1074	1602.5090	---其他	12	0	东盟ASEAN,新加坡SG,新西兰NZ,香港HK,澳门MO	0	最不发达35国LDC35	90	---Other
				1.2	智利CL				
				2.4	哥斯达黎加CR				
				6	巴基斯坦PK,秘鲁PE				
		-其他，包括动物血的食品：							-Other, including preparations of blood of any animal:
1075	1602.9010	---罐头	15	0	东盟ASEAN,智利CL,新加坡SG,新西兰NZ,澳门MO	0	最不发达35国LDC35	90	---In airtight containers
				3	哥斯达黎加CR				
				7.5	秘鲁PE				
				12	巴基斯坦PK				
1076	1602.9090	---其他	15	0	东盟ASEAN,智利CL,新加坡SG,新西兰NZ,澳门MO	0	最不发达35国LDC35	90	---Other
				3	哥斯达黎加CR				
				7.5	秘鲁PE				
				12	巴基斯坦PK				
	16.03	**肉、鱼、甲壳动物、软体动物或其他水生无脊椎动物的精及汁：**							**Extracts and juices of meat, fish or crustaceans, molluscs or other aquatic invertebrates:**

序号 No.	税则号列 Tariff Line	货品名称	最惠国税率 MFN(%)	协定税率 Agreement(%)		特惠税率 S.P.(%)		普通税率 Gen.(%)	Article Description
1077	1603.0000	肉、鱼、甲壳动物、软体动物或其他水生无脊椎动物的精及汁	23	0 4.6 11.5	东盟ASEAN,智利CL,新加坡SG,新西兰NZ,香港HK 哥斯达黎加CR 秘鲁PE	0	最不发达35国LDC35	90	Extracts and juices of meat, fish or crustaceans, molluscs or other aquatic invertebrates
	16.04	**制作或保藏的鱼；鲟鱼子酱及鱼卵制的鲟鱼子酱代用品：**							**Prepared or preserved fish; caviar and caviar substitutes prepared from fish eggs:**
		-鱼，整条或切块，但未绞碎：							-Fish, whole or in pieces, but not minced:
		--鲑鱼：							--Salmon:
1078	1604.1110	---大西洋鲑鱼	12	0 1.2 2.4 6	东盟ASEAN,新加坡SG,新西兰NZ,香港HK 智利CL 哥斯达黎加CR 巴基斯坦PK	0	最不发达35国LDC35	90	---Atalantic salmon
1079	1604.1190	---其他	12	0 1.2 2.4 6	东盟ASEAN,新加坡SG,新西兰NZ 智利CL 哥斯达黎加CR 巴基斯坦PK	0	最不发达35国LDC35	90	---Other
1080	1604.1200	--鲱鱼	12	0 2.4 6	东盟ASEAN,智利CL,新加坡SG,新西兰NZ,秘鲁PE 哥斯达黎加CR 巴基斯坦PK	0	最不发达35国LDC35	90	--Herrings
1081	1604.1300	--沙丁鱼、小沙丁鱼属、黍鲱或西鲱	5	0 0.5 1.9	东盟ASEAN,巴基斯坦PK,新西兰NZ,哥斯达黎加CR,澳门MO 智利CL 秘鲁PE	0	最不发达35国LDC35,最不发达4国LDC4,柬埔寨KH	90	--Sardines, sardinella and brisling or sprats
1082	1604.1400	--金枪鱼、鲣鱼及狐鲣（狐鲣属）	5	0 0.5	东盟ASEAN,巴基斯坦PK,新西兰NZ,秘鲁PE,哥斯达黎加CR,香港HK 智利CL	0	最不发达35国LDC35,最不发达4国LDC4,柬埔寨KH	90	--Tunas, skipjack and bonito (*Sarda spp.*)
1083	1604.1500	--鲭鱼	12	0 1.2 2.4 4.5 6	东盟ASEAN,新加坡SG,新西兰NZ 智利CL 哥斯达黎加CR 秘鲁PE 巴基斯坦PK	0	最不发达35国LDC35	90	--Mackerel
1084	1604.1600	--鳀鱼	12	0 1.2 2.4 4.5 6	东盟ASEAN,新加坡SG,新西兰NZ 智利CL 哥斯达黎加CR 秘鲁PE 巴基斯坦PK	0	最不发达35国LDC35	90	--Anchovies

序号 No.	税则号列 Tariff Line	货品名称	最惠国税率 MFN(%)	协定税率 Agreement(%)	特惠税率 S.P.(%)	普通税率 Gen.(%)	Article Description
1085	1604.1700	--鳗鱼	12	0 东盟ASEAN,新加坡SG,新西兰NZ,香港HK 1.2 智利CL 2.4 哥斯达黎加CR 5 巴基斯坦PK 9.9 亚太APTA	0 最不发达35国LDC35,最不发达4国LDC4	90	--Eels
		--其他:					--Other:
1086	1604.1920	---罗非鱼	12	0 东盟ASEAN,新加坡SG,新西兰NZ,香港HK 1.2 智利CL 2.4 哥斯达黎加CR 6 巴基斯坦PK	0 最不发达35国LDC35	90	---Tilapia
		---叉尾鮰鱼:					---Of Ictalurus:
1087	1604.1931	----斑点叉尾鮰鱼	12	0 东盟ASEAN,新加坡SG,新西兰NZ,香港HK 1.2 智利CL 2.4 哥斯达黎加CR 5 巴基斯坦PK 9.9 亚太APTA	0 最不发达35国LDC35,最不发达4国LDC4	90	----Channel catfish (*Ictalurus punctatus*)
1088	1604.1939	----其他	12	0 东盟ASEAN,新加坡SG,新西兰NZ,香港HK 1.2 智利CL 2.4 哥斯达黎加CR 5 巴基斯坦PK 9.9 亚太APTA	0 最不发达35国LDC35,最不发达4国LDC4	90	----Other
1089	1604.1990	---其他	12	0 东盟ASEAN,新加坡SG,新西兰NZ,香港HK,澳门MO 1.2 智利CL 2.4 哥斯达黎加CR 5 巴基斯坦PK 9.9 亚太APTA	0 最不发达35国LDC35,最不发达4国LDC4	90	---Other
		-其他制作或保藏的鱼:					-Other prepared or preserved fish:
		---罐头:					---In airtight containers:
1090	1604.2011	----鱼翅	12	0 东盟ASEAN,新加坡SG,新西兰NZ,香港HK,澳门MO 1.2 智利CL 2.4 哥斯达黎加CR 5 巴基斯坦PK 6 秘鲁PE 9.9 亚太APTA	0 最不发达35国LDC35	90	----Shark fin
1091	1604.2019	----其他	12	0 东盟ASEAN,新加坡SG,新西兰NZ,香港HK,澳门MO 1.2 智利CL 2.4 哥斯达黎加CR 5 巴基斯坦PK 6 秘鲁PE 9.9 亚太APTA	0 最不发达35国LDC35	90	----Other
		---其他:					---Other:

序号 No.	税则号列 Tariff Line	货品名称	最惠国税率 MFN(%)	协定税率 Agreement(%)		特惠税率 S.P.(%)		普通税率 Gen.(%)	Article Description
1092	1604.2091	----鱼翅	12	0	东盟ASEAN,新加坡SG,新西兰NZ,香港HK,澳门MO	0	最不发达35国LDC35	90	----Shark fin
				1.2	智利CL				
				2.4	哥斯达黎加CR				
				5	巴基斯坦PK				
				6	秘鲁PE				
				9.9	亚太APTA				
1093	1604.2099	----其他:	12	0	东盟ASEAN,新加坡SG,新西兰NZ,香港HK,澳门MO	0	最不发达35国LDC35	90	----Other
				1.2	智利CL				
				2.4	哥斯达黎加CR				
				5	巴基斯坦PK				
				6	秘鲁PE				
				9.9	亚太APTA				
		-鲟鱼子酱及鲟鱼子酱代用品:							-Caviar and caviar substitutes :
1094	1604.3100	--鲟鱼子酱	12	0	东盟ASEAN,智利CL,新加坡SG,新西兰NZ,秘鲁PE	0	最不发达35国LDC35	90	--Caviar
				2.4	哥斯达黎加CR				
				6	巴基斯坦PK				
1095	1604.3200	--鲟鱼子酱代用品	12	0	东盟ASEAN,智利CL,新加坡SG,新西兰NZ,秘鲁PE	0	最不发达35国LDC35	90	--Caviar substitutes
				2.4	哥斯达黎加CR				
				6	巴基斯坦PK				
	16.05	**制作或保藏的甲壳动物、软体动物及其他水生无脊椎动物:**							**Crustaceans, molluscs and other aquatic invertebrates, pprepard or preserved:**
1096	1605.1000	-蟹	5	0	文莱BN,印尼ID,马来西亚MY,缅甸MM,菲律宾PH,新加坡*SG*,泰国TH,越南VT,巴基斯坦PK,新西兰NZ,秘鲁PE,哥斯达黎加CR,香港HK	0	最不发达35国LDC35,最不发达4国LDC4	90	-Crab
				0.5	智利CL				
		-小虾及对虾:							-Shrimps and prawns :
1097	1605.2100	--非密封包装	5	0	东盟ASEAN,巴基斯坦PK,新西兰NZ,秘鲁PE,哥斯达黎加CR,香港HK	0	最不发达35国LDC35,最不发达4国LDC4,柬埔寨KH	90	--Not in airtight container
				0.5	智利CL				
1098	1605.2900	--其他	5	0	东盟ASEAN,巴基斯坦PK,新西兰NZ,秘鲁PE,哥斯达黎加CR,香港HK	0	最不发达35国LDC35,最不发达4国LDC4,柬埔寨KH	90	--Other
				0.5	智利CL				

序号 No.	税则号列 Tariff Line	货品名称	最惠国税率 MFN(%)	协定税率 Agreement(%)		特惠税率 S.P.(%)		普通税率 Gen.(%)	Article Description
1099	1605.3000	-龙虾	5	0	文莱BN,印尼ID,马来西亚MY,缅甸MM,菲律宾PH,新加坡*SG*,泰国TH,越南VT,智利CL,巴基斯坦PK,新西兰NZ,秘鲁PE,哥斯达黎加CR,香港HK	0	最不发达35国LDC35,最不发达4国LDC4,柬埔寨KH	90	-Lobster
		-其他甲壳动物:							-Other crustaceans:
		---淡水小龙虾:							---Freshwater crawfish:
1100	1605.4011	----虾仁	5	0	文莱BN,印尼ID,马来西亚MY,缅甸MM,菲律宾PH,新加坡*SG*,泰国TH,越南VT,智利CL,巴基斯坦PK,新西兰NZ,秘鲁PE,哥斯达黎加CR	0	最不发达35国LDC35,最不发达4国LDC4,柬埔寨KH	90	----Shelled
1101	1605.4019	----其他	5	0	文莱BN,印尼ID,马来西亚MY,缅甸MM,菲律宾PH,新加坡*SG*,泰国TH,越南VT,智利CL,巴基斯坦PK,新西兰NZ,秘鲁PE,哥斯达黎加CR	0	最不发达35国LDC35,最不发达4国LDC4,柬埔寨KH	90	----Other
1102	1605.4090	---其他	5	0	文莱BN,印尼ID,马来西亚MY,缅甸MM,菲律宾PH,新加坡*SG*,泰国TH,越南VT,智利CL,巴基斯坦PK,新西兰NZ,秘鲁PE,哥斯达黎加CR,澳门MO	0	最不发达35国LDC35,最不发达4国LDC4,柬埔寨KH	90	---Other
		-软体动物:							-Molluscs:
1103	1605.5100	--牡蛎（蚝）	5	0	文莱BN,印尼ID,马来西亚MY,缅甸MM,菲律宾PH,新加坡*SG*,泰国TH,越南VT,巴基斯坦PK,新西兰NZ,哥斯达黎加CR,香港HK,澳门MO	0	最不发达35国LDC35,最不发达4国LDC4	90	--Oysters
				0.5	智利CL				
				1.9	秘鲁PE				
				3.9	亚太APTA				
1104	1605.5200	--扇贝，包括海扇	5	0	文莱BN,印尼ID,马来西亚MY,缅甸MM,菲律宾PH,新加坡*SG*,泰国TH,越南VT,巴基斯坦PK,新西兰NZ,哥斯达黎加CR,香港HK,澳门MO	0	最不发达35国LDC35,最不发达4国LDC4	90	--Scallops, including queen scallops
				0.5	智利CL				
				1.9	秘鲁PE				
				3.9	亚太APTA				

序号 No.	税则号列 Tariff Line	货品名称	最惠国税率 MFN(%)	协定税率 Agreement(%)		特惠税率 S.P.(%)		普通税率 Gen.(%)	Article Description
1105	1605.5300	--贻贝	5	0	文莱BN,印尼ID,马来西亚MY,缅甸MM,菲律宾PH,新加坡*SG*,泰国TH,越南VT,巴基斯坦PK,新西兰NZ,哥斯达黎加CR,香港HK,澳门MO	0	最不发达35国LDC35,最不发达4国LDC4	90	--Mussels
				0.5	智利CL				
				1.9	秘鲁PE				
				3.9	亚太APTA				
1106	1605.5400	--墨鱼及鱿鱼	5	0	文莱BN,印尼ID,马来西亚MY,缅甸MM,菲律宾PH,新加坡*SG*,泰国TH,越南VT,巴基斯坦PK,新西兰NZ,哥斯达黎加CR,香港HK,澳门MO	0	最不发达35国LDC35,最不发达4国LDC4	90	--Cuttle fish and squid
				0.5	智利CL				
				1.9	秘鲁PE				
				3.9	亚太APTA				
1107	1605.5500	--章鱼	5	0	文莱BN,印尼ID,马来西亚MY,缅甸MM,菲律宾PH,新加坡*SG*,泰国TH,越南VT,巴基斯坦PK,新西兰NZ,哥斯达黎加CR,香港HK,澳门MO	0	最不发达35国LDC35,最不发达4国LDC4	90	--Octopus
				0.5	智利CL				
				1.9	秘鲁PE				
				3.9	亚太APTA				
		--蛤、鸟蛤及舟贝:							--Clams, cockles and arkshells:
1108	1605.5610	---蛤	5	0	文莱BN,印尼ID,马来西亚MY,缅甸MM,菲律宾PH,新加坡*SG*,泰国TH,越南VT,巴基斯坦PK,新西兰NZ,哥斯达黎加CR,香港HK	0	最不发达35国LDC35,最不发达4国LDC4	90	---Clams
				0.5	智利CL				
				3.9	亚太APTA				
1109	1605.5620	---鸟蛤及舟贝	5	0	文莱BN,印尼ID,马来西亚MY,缅甸MM,菲律宾PH,新加坡*SG*,泰国TH,越南VT,巴基斯坦PK,新西兰NZ,哥斯达黎加CR,香港HK,澳门MO	0	最不发达35国LDC35,最不发达4国LDC4	90	---Cockles and arkshells
				0.5	智利CL				
				1.9	秘鲁PE				
				3.9	亚太APTA				

序号 No.	税则号列 Tariff Line	货品名称	最惠国税率 MFN(%)	协定税率 Agreement(%)		特惠税率 S.P.(%)		普通税率 Gen.(%)	Article Description
1110	1605.5700	--鲍鱼	5	0	文莱BN,印尼ID,马来西亚MY,缅甸MM,菲律宾PH,新加坡*SG*,泰国TH,越南VT,巴基斯坦PK,新西兰NZ,哥斯达黎加CR,香港HK,澳门MO	0	最不发达35国LDC35,最不发达4国LDC4	90	--Abalone
				0.5	智利CL				
				1.9	秘鲁PE				
				3.9	亚太APTA				
1111	1605.5800	--蜗牛及螺，海螺除外	5	0	文莱BN,印尼ID,马来西亚MY,缅甸MM,菲律宾PH,新加坡*SG*,泰国TH,越南VT,巴基斯坦PK,新西兰NZ,哥斯达黎加CR,香港HK,澳门MO	0	最不发达35国LDC35,最不发达4国LDC4	90	--Snails, other than sea snails
				0.5	智利CL				
				1.9	秘鲁PE				
				3.9	亚太APTA				
1112	1605.5900	--其他	5	0	文莱BN,印尼ID,马来西亚MY,缅甸MM,菲律宾PH,新加坡*SG*,泰国TH,越南VT,巴基斯坦PK,新西兰NZ,哥斯达黎加CR,香港HK,澳门MO	0	最不发达35国LDC35,最不发达4国LDC4	90	--Other
				0.5	智利CL				
				1.9	秘鲁PE				
				3.9	亚太APTA				
		-其他水生无脊椎动物：							-Other aquatic invertebrates:
1113	1605.6100	--海参	5	0	文莱BN,印尼ID,马来西亚MY,缅甸MM,菲律宾PH,新加坡*SG*,泰国TH,越南VT,巴基斯坦PK,新西兰NZ,哥斯达黎加CR,香港HK,澳门MO	0	最不发达35国LDC35,最不发达4国LDC4	90	--Sea cucumbers
				0.5	智利CL				
				1.9	秘鲁PE				
				3.9	亚太APTA				
1114	1605.6200	--海胆	5	0	文莱BN,印尼ID,马来西亚MY,缅甸MM,菲律宾PH,新加坡*SG*,泰国TH,越南VT,巴基斯坦PK,新西兰NZ,哥斯达黎加CR,香港HK,澳门MO	0	最不发达35国LDC35,最不发达4国LDC4	90	--Sea urchins
				0.5	智利CL				
				1.9	秘鲁PE				
				3.9	亚太APTA				

序号 No.	税则号列 Tariff Line	货品名称	最惠国税率 MFN(%)	协定税率 Agreement(%)		特惠税率 S.P.(%)		普通税率 Gen.(%)	Article Description
1115	1605.6300	--海蜇	15	0	东盟ASEAN,新加坡SG,新西兰NZ,香港HK	0	最不发达35国LDC35,最不发达4国LDC4	90	--Jellyfish
				1.5	智利CL				
				3	哥斯达黎加CR				
				12	巴基斯坦PK				
1116	1605.6900	--其他	5	0	文莱BN,印尼ID,马来西亚MY,缅甸MM,菲律宾PH,新加坡*SG*,泰国TH,越南VT,巴基斯坦PK,新西兰NZ,哥斯达黎加CR,香港HK,澳门MO	0	最不发达35国LDC35,最不发达4国LDC4	90	--Other
				0.5	智利CL				
				1.9	秘鲁PE				
				3.9	亚太APTA				

第十七章
糖及糖食

Chapter 17
Sugars and sugar confectionery

注释：

本章不包括：

一、含有可可的糖食（税号18.06）；

二、税号29.40的化学纯糖（蔗糖、乳糖、麦芽糖、葡萄糖及果糖除外）及其他产品；

三、第三十章的药品及其他产品。

子目注释：

一、子目号1701.12、1701.13及1701.14所称"原糖"，是指按重量计干燥状态的蔗糖含量对应的旋光读数低于99.5°的糖。

二、子目1701.13仅包括非离心甘蔗糖，其按重量计干燥状态的蔗糖含量对应的旋光读数不低于69°但低于93°。该产品仅含肉眼不可见的不规则形状天然他形微晶，外被糖蜜残余及其他甘蔗成分。

Notes:

This Chapter does not cover:

1. Sugar confectionery containing cocoa (heading No.18.06);
2. Chemically pure sugars (other than sucrose, lactose, maltose, glucose and fructose) or other products of heading No.29.40; or
3. Medicaments or other products of Chapter 30.

Subheading Notes:

1. For the purposes of subheadings No.1701.12, 1701.13 and 1701.14, "raw sugar" means sugar whose content of sucrose by weight, in the dry state, corresponds to a polarimeter reading of less than 99.5°.
2. Subheading 1701.13 covers only cane sugar obtained without centrifugation, whose content of sucrose by weight, in the dry state, corresponds to a polarimeter reading of 69° or more but less than 93°. The product contains only natural anhedral microcrystals, of irregular shape, not visible to the naked eye, which are surrounded by residues of molasses and other constituents of sugar cane.

序号 No.	税则号列 Tariff Line	货品名称	最惠国税率 MFN(%)	协定税率 Agreement(%)	特惠税率 S.P.(%)	普通税率 Gen.(%)	Article Description
	17.01	**固体甘蔗糖、甜菜糖及化学纯蔗糖：**					**Cane or beet sugar and chemically pure sucrose, in solid form:**
		-未加香料或着色剂的原糖：					-Raw sugar not containing added flavouring or colouring matter:
1117	1701.1200	--甜菜糖	50①			125	--Beet sugar
1118	1701.1300	--本章子目注释二所述的甘蔗糖	50②			125	--Cane sugar specified in Subheading Note 2 to this Chapter
1119	1701.1400	--其他甘蔗糖	50③			125	--Other cane sugar
		-其他：					-Other:
1120	1701.9100	--加有香料或着色剂	50④			125	--Containing added flavouring or colouring matter
		--其他：					--Other:
1121	1701.9910	---砂糖	50⑤			125	---Granulated sugar

① 配额税率（In-quota rate）：15%。
② 配额税率（In-quota rate）：15%。
③ 配额税率（In-quota rate）：15%。
④ 配额税率（In-quota rate）：15%。
⑤ 配额税率（In-quota rate）：15%。

序号 No.	税则号列 Tariff Line	货品名称	最惠国税率 MFN(%)	协定税率 Agreement(%)	特惠税率 S.P.(%)	普通税率 Gen.(%)	Article Description
1122	1701.9920	---绵白糖	50[1]			125	---Superfine sugar
1123	1701.9990	---其他	50[2]			125	---Other
	17.02	**其他固体糖，包括化学纯乳糖、麦芽糖、葡萄糖及果糖；未加香料或着色剂的糖浆；人造蜜，不论是否掺有天然蜂蜜；焦糖：**					**Other sugars, including chemically pure lactose, maltose, glucose and fructose, in solid form; sugar syrups not containing added flavouring or colouring matter; artificial honey, whether or not mixed with natural honey; caramel:**
		-乳糖及乳糖浆：					-Lactose and lactose syrup:
1124	1702.1100	--按重量计干燥无水乳糖含量在99%及以上	10	0 东盟ASEAN,智利CL,新加坡SG,新西兰NZ,秘鲁PE,哥斯达黎加CR,澳门MO 5 巴基斯坦PK	0 最不发达35国LDC35,最不发达4国LDC4	80	--Containing by weight 99% or more lactose, expressed as anhydrous lactose, calculated on the dry matter
1125	1702.1900	--其他	10	0 东盟ASEAN,智利CL,新加坡SG,新西兰NZ,秘鲁PE,哥斯达黎加CR,澳门MO 5 巴基斯坦PK	0 最不发达35国LDC35,最不发达4国LDC4	80	--Other
1126	1702.2000	-槭糖及槭糖浆	30	0 东盟ASEAN,智利CL,新加坡SG,新西兰NZ,澳门MO 6 哥斯达黎加CR 15 秘鲁PE		80	-Maple sugar and maple syrup
1127	1702.3000	-葡萄糖及葡萄糖浆，不含果糖或按重量计干燥状态的果糖含量在20%以下	30	0 东盟ASEAN,智利CL,新加坡SG,新西兰NZ,澳门MO 6 哥斯达黎加CR 15 秘鲁PE		80	-Glucose and glucose syrup, not containing fructose or containing in the dry state less than 20% by weight of fructose
1128	1702.4000	-葡萄糖及葡萄糖浆，按重量计干燥状态的果糖含量在20%及以上，但在50%以下	30	0 东盟ASEAN,智利CL,新加坡SG,新西兰NZ,澳门MO 6 哥斯达黎加CR 15 秘鲁PE		80	-Glucose and glucose syrup, containing in the dry state at least 20% but less than 50% by weight of fructose
1129	1702.5000	-化学纯果糖	30	0 东盟ASEAN,智利CL,新加坡SG,新西兰NZ,澳门MO 6 哥斯达黎加CR 15 秘鲁PE		80	-Chemically pure fructose
1130	1702.6000	-其他果糖及果糖浆，按重量计干燥状态的果糖含量在50%以上	30	0 东盟ASEAN,智利CL,新加坡SG,新西兰NZ,澳门MO 6 哥斯达黎加CR 15 秘鲁PE		80	-Other fructose and fructose syrup, containing in the dry state more than 50% by weight of fructose

[1] 配额税率（In-quota rate）：15%。

[2] 配额税率（In-quota rate）：15%。

序号 No.	税则号列 Tariff Line	货品名称	最惠国税率 MFN(%)	协定税率 Agreement(%)		特惠税率 S.P.(%)		普通税率 Gen.(%)	Article Description
1131	1702.9000	-其他，包括转化糖	30	0 3 6 21.2	东盟ASEAN,新加坡SG,新西兰NZ,香港HK,澳门MO 智利CL 哥斯达黎加CR 秘鲁PE	0	最不发达35国LDC35,最不发达4国LDC4	80	-Other, including invert sugar
	17.03	**制糖后所剩的糖蜜：**							**Molasses resulting from the extraction or refining or sugar:**
1132	1703.1000	-甘蔗糖蜜	8	0 5	东盟ASEAN,智利CL,新西兰NZ,秘鲁PE,哥斯达黎加CR 巴基斯坦PK	0	最不发达35国LDC35,最不发达4国LDC4	50	-Cane molasses
1133	1703.9000	-其他	8	0 5	东盟ASEAN,智利CL,新西兰NZ,秘鲁PE,哥斯达黎加CR 巴基斯坦PK	0	最不发达35国LDC35,最不发达4国LDC4	50	-Other
	17.04	**不含可可的糖食（包括白巧克力）：**							**Sugar confectionery (including white chocolate), not containing cocoa:**
1134	1704.1000	-口香糖，不论是否裹糖	12	0 1.2 2.4 5 8.5 9.5	东盟ASEAN,新加坡SG,新西兰NZ,香港HK 智利CL 哥斯达黎加CR 巴基斯坦PK 秘鲁PE 亚太APTA	0	最不发达35国LDC35,最不发达4国LDC4	50	-Chewing gum, whether or not sugarcoated
1135	1704.9000	-其他	10	0 1 5 8.2	东盟ASEAN,新加坡SG,新西兰NZ,哥斯达黎加CR,香港HK,澳门MO 智利CL 秘鲁PE 亚太APTA,巴基斯坦PK	0	最不发达35国LDC35,最不发达4国LDC4	50	-Other

第十八章
可可及可可制品

注释：

一、本章不包括税号 04.03、19.01、19.04、19.05、21.05、22.02、22.08、30.03、30.04 的制品。

二、税号 18.06 包括含有可可的糖食及注释一以外的其他含可可的食品。

Chapter 18
Cocoa and cocoa preparations

Notes:

1. This Chapter does not cover the preparations of heading No.04.03, 19.01, 19.04, 19.05, 21.05, 22.02, 22.08, 30.03, or 30.04.
2. Heading No.18.06 includes sugar confectionery containing cocoa and, subject to Note 1 to this Chapter, other food preparations containing cocoa.

序号 No.	税则号列 Tariff Line	货品名称	最惠国税率 MFN(%)	协定税率 Agreement(%)		特惠税率 S.P.(%)		普通税率 Gen.(%)	Article Description
	18.01	**整颗或破碎的可可豆，生的或焙炒的：**							**Cocoa beans, whole or broken, raw or roasted:**
1136	1801.0000	整颗或破碎的可可豆，生的或焙炒的	8 △2	0 5	东盟ASEAN,智利CL,新西兰NZ,秘鲁PE,哥斯达黎加CR 巴基斯坦PK	0	最不发达35国LDC35,最不发达4国LDC4	30	Cocoa beans, whole or broken, raw or roasted
	18.02	**可可荚、壳、皮及废料：**							**Cocoa shells, husks, skins and other cocoa waste:**
1137	1802.0000	可可荚、壳、皮及废料	10	0 5	东盟ASEAN,智利CL,新加坡SG,新西兰NZ,秘鲁PE,哥斯达黎加CR 巴基斯坦PK	0	最不发达35国LDC35,最不发达4国LDC4	30	Cocoa shells, husks, skins and other cocoa waste
	18.03	**可可膏，不论是否脱脂：**							**Cocoa paste, whether or not defatted:**
1138	1803.1000	-未脱脂	10	0 5	东盟ASEAN,智利CL,新西兰NZ,秘鲁PE,哥斯达黎加CR 巴基斯坦PK	0	最不发达35国LDC35	30	-Not defatted
1139	1803.2000	-全脱脂或部分脱脂	10	0 5	东盟ASEAN,智利CL,新西兰NZ,秘鲁PE,哥斯达黎加CR 巴基斯坦PK	0	最不发达35国LDC35	30	-Wholly or partly defatted
	18.04	**可可脂、可可油：**							**Cocoa butter, fat and oil:**
1140	1804.0000	可可脂、可可油	22	0 4.4 11	东盟ASEAN,智利CL,新西兰NZ 哥斯达黎加CR 秘鲁PE	0	最不发达35国LDC35,最不发达4国LDC4	70	Cocoa butter, fat and oil
	18.05	**未加糖或其他甜物质的可可粉：**							**Cocoa powder, not containing added sugar or other sweetening matter:**

序号 No.	税则号列 Tariff Line	货品名称	最惠国税率 MFN(%)	协定税率 Agreement(%)		特惠税率 S.P.(%)		普通税率 Gen.(%)	Article Description
1141	1805.0000	未加糖或其他甜物质的可可粉	15	0 3 7.5 12	东盟ASEAN,智利CL,新西兰NZ 哥斯达黎加CR 秘鲁PE 巴基斯坦PK	0	最不发达35国LDC35	40	Cocoa powder, not containing added sugar or other sweetening matter
	18.06	**巧克力及其他含可可的食品：**							**Chocolate and other food preparations containing cocoa:**
1142	1806.1000	-加糖或其他甜物质的可可粉	10	0 1 5	东盟ASEAN,新西兰NZ,哥斯达黎加CR 智利CL 巴基斯坦PK,秘鲁PE	0	最不发达35国LDC35	50	-Cocoa powder, containing added sugar or other sweetening matter
1143	1806.2000	-其他重量超过2公斤的块状或条状含可可食品，或液状、膏状、粉状、粒状或其他散装形状的含可可食品，容器包装或内包装每件净重超过2公斤的	10	0 1 5 7.7	东盟ASEAN,新加坡SG,新西兰NZ,哥斯达黎加CR,香港HK,澳门MO 智利CL 巴基斯坦PK,秘鲁PE 亚太APTA	0	最不发达35国LDC35	50	-Other preparations in blocks, slabs or bars weighing more than 2kg or in liquid, paste, powder, granular or other bulk form in containers or immediate packings, of a content exceeding 2kg
		-其他块状或条状的含可可食品：							-Other, in blocks, slabs or bars:
1144	1806.3100	--夹心	8	0 5 6.4	东盟ASEAN,智利CL,新西兰NZ,秘鲁PE,哥斯达黎加CR,香港HK,澳门MO 巴基斯坦PK 亚太APTA	0	最不发达35国LDC35,最不发达4国LDC4	50	--Filled
1145	1806.3200	--不夹心	10	0 1 5 7.7	东盟ASEAN,新加坡SG,新西兰NZ,哥斯达黎加CR,香港HK,澳门MO 智利CL 巴基斯坦PK,秘鲁PE 亚太APTA	0	最不发达35国LDC35	50	--Not filled
1146	1806.9000	-其他	8	0 5 6.4	东盟ASEAN,智利CL,新西兰NZ,秘鲁PE,哥斯达黎加CR,香港HK,澳门MO 巴基斯坦PK 亚太APTA	0	最不发达35国LDC35,最不发达4国LDC4	50	-Other

第十九章
谷物、粮食粉、淀粉或乳的制品；糕饼点心

注释：

一、本章不包括：

（一）按重量计含香肠、肉、食用杂碎、动物血、鱼、甲壳动物，软体动物、其他水生无脊椎动物及其混合物超过20%的食品（第十六章），但税号19.02的包馅食品除外；

（二）用粮食粉或淀粉制的专作动物饲料用的饼干及其他制品（税号23.09）；

（三）第三十章的药品及其他产品。

二、税目19.01所称：

（一）"粗粒"是指第十一章谷物的粗粒；

（二）"细粉"及"粗粉"，是指：

1. 第十一章谷物的细粉及粗粉；
2. 其他章植物的细粉、粗粉及粉末，但不包括干蔬菜、马铃薯和干豆类的细粉、粗粉及粉末（应分别归入税目07.12、11.05和11.06）。

三、税号19.04不包括按重量计全脱脂可可含量超过6%或用巧克力完全包裹的食品以及税号18.06的其他含可可食品（税号18.06）。

四、税号19.04所称"其他方法制作的"，是指制作或加工程度超过第十章或第十一章各税号或注释所规定范围的。

Chapter 19
Preparations of cereals, flour, starch or milk; pastrycook's products

Notes:

1. This Chapter does not cover:

(a) Except in the case of stuffed products of heading No.19.02, food preparations containing more than 20% by weight of sausage, meat, meat offal, blood, fish or crustaceans, molluscs or other aquatic inverte-brates, or any combination thereof (Chapter 16) ;

(b) Biscuits or other articles made from flour or from starch, specially prepared for use in animal feeding (heading No.23.09) ; or

(c) Medicaments or other products of Chapter 30.

2. For the purposes of heading No.19.01:

(a) The term "groats" means cereal groats of Chapter 11;

(b) The terms "flour" and "meal" mean:

(1) Cereal flour and meal of Chapter 11; and

(2) Flour,meal and powder of vegetable origin of any Chapter, other than flour, meal or powder of dried vegetables (heading No.07.12), of potatoes (heading No.11.05) or of dried leguminous vegetables (heading No.11.06).

3. Heading No.19.04 does not cover preparations containing more than 6% by weight of cocoa calculated on a totally defatted basis or completely coated with chocolate or other food preparations containing cocoa (heading No.18.06) .

4.For the purposes of heading No.19.04, the expression "otherwise prepared" means prepared or processed to an extent beyond that provided for in the headings of or Notes to Chapter 10 or Chapter 11.

序号 No.	税则号列 Tariff Line	货品名称	最惠国税率 MFN(%)	协定税率 Agreement(%)		特惠税率 S.P.(%)		普通税率 Gen.(%)	Article Description
	19.01	**麦精；细粉、粗粒、粗粉、淀粉或麦精制的其他税目未列名的食品，不含可可或按重量计全脱脂可可含量低于40%；税目04.01至04.04所列货品制的其他税目未列名的食品，不含可可或按重量计全脱脂可可含量低于5%：**							**Malt extract; food preparations of flour, groats, meal, starch or malt extract, not containing cocoa or containing less than 40% by weight of cocoa calculated on a totally defatted basis, not elsewhere specified or included; food preparations of goods of headings No.04.01 to 04.04, not containing cocoa or containing less than 5% by weight of cocoa calculated on a totally defatted basis, not elsewhere specified or included:**
		-供婴幼儿食用的零售包装食品:							-Preparations for infant use, put up for retail sale:
1147	1901.1010	---配方奶粉	15 △5	0 1.5 3 7.5 12	东盟ASEAN,新加坡SG,新西兰NZ,澳门MO 智利CL 哥斯达黎加CR 秘鲁PE 巴基斯坦PK	0	最不发达35国 LDC35	40	---Formula milk powder
1148	1901.1090	---其他	15 △5	0 1.5 3 7.5 12	东盟ASEAN,新加坡SG,新西兰NZ,澳门MO 智利CL 哥斯达黎加CR 秘鲁PE 巴基斯坦PK	0	最不发达35国 LDC35	40	---Other
1149	1901.2000	-供烘焙税号19.05所列面包糕饼用的调制品及面团	25	0 2.5 5 12.5	东盟ASEAN,新加坡SG,新西兰NZ,香港HK,澳门MO 智利CL 哥斯达黎加CR 秘鲁PE	0	最不发达35国 LDC35	80	-Mixes and doughs for the preparation of bakers' wares of heading No.19.05
1150	1901.9000	-其他	10 △5	0 1 5	东盟ASEAN,新加坡SG,新西兰NZ,哥斯达黎加CR,香港HK,澳门MO 智利CL 巴基斯坦PK,秘鲁PE	0	最不发达35国 LDC35	80	-Other
	19.02	**面食，不论是否煮熟、包馅（肉馅或其他馅）或其他方法制作，例如，通心粉、面条、汤团、馄饨、饺子、奶油面卷；古斯古斯面食，不论是否制作：**							**Pasta, whether or not cooked or stuffed (with meat or other substances) or otherwise prepared, such as spaghetti, macaroni, noodles, lasagne, gnocchi, ravioli cannelloni; couscous, whether or not prepared:**

序号 No.	税则号列 Tariff Line	货品名称	最惠国税率 MFN(%)	协定税率 Agreement(%)		特惠税率 S.P.(%)		普通税率 Gen.(%)	Article Description
		-生的面食,未包馅或未经其他方法制作:							-Uncooked pasta, not stuffed or otherwise prepared:
1151	1902.1100	--含蛋	15	0 1.5 3 7.5 12	东盟ASEAN,新加坡SG,新西兰NZ,香港HK,澳门MO 智利CL 哥斯达黎加CR 秘鲁PE 巴基斯坦PK	0	最不发达35国LDC35,最不发达4国LDC4	80	--Containing eggs
1152	1902.1900	--其他	15	0 1.5 3 7.5 12	东盟ASEAN,新加坡SG,新西兰NZ,香港HK,澳门MO 智利CL 哥斯达黎加CR 秘鲁PE 巴基斯坦PK	0	最不发达35国LDC35,最不发达4国LDC4	80	--Other
1153	1902.2000	-包馅面食,不论是否烹煮或经其他方法制作	15	0 1.5 3 7.5 12	东盟ASEAN,新加坡SG,新西兰NZ,香港HK,澳门MO 智利CL 哥斯达黎加CR 秘鲁PE 巴基斯坦PK	0	最不发达35国LDC35,最不发达4国LDC4	80	-Stuffed pasta, whether or not cooked or otherwise prepared
		-其他面食:							-Other pasta:
1154	1902.3010	---米粉干	15	0 3 7.5 12	东盟ASEAN,智利CL,新加坡SG,新西兰NZ,澳门MO 哥斯达黎加CR 秘鲁PE 巴基斯坦PK	0	最不发达35国LDC35	80	---Rice vermicelli, cooked
1155	1902.3020	---粉丝	15	0 3 7.5 12	东盟ASEAN,智利CL,新加坡SG,新西兰NZ,澳门MO 哥斯达黎加CR 秘鲁PE 巴基斯坦PK	0	最不发达35国LDC35	80	---Bean vermicelli, cooked
1156	1902.3030	---即食或快熟面条	15	0 3 7.5 13.1	东盟ASEAN,智利CL,新加坡SG,新西兰NZ,香港HK,澳门MO 哥斯达黎加CR 巴基斯坦PK,秘鲁PE 亚太APTA	0	最不发达35国LDC35,最不发达4国LDC4	80	---Instant noodle
1157	1902.3090	---其他	15	0 1.5 3 7.5 13.1	东盟ASEAN,新加坡SG,新西兰NZ,香港HK,澳门MO 智利CL 哥斯达黎加CR 巴基斯坦PK,秘鲁PE 亚太APTA	0	最不发达35国LDC35	80	---Other
1158	1902.4000	-古斯古斯面食	25	0 5 12.5	东盟ASEAN,智利CL,新加坡SG,新西兰NZ,澳门MO 哥斯达黎加CR 秘鲁PE	0	最不发达35国LDC35	80	-Couscous

序号 No.	税则号列 Tariff Line	货品名称	最惠国税率 MFN(%)	协定税率 Agreement(%)	特惠税率 S.P.(%)	普通税率 Gen.(%)	Article Description
	19.03	**珍粉及淀粉制成的珍粉代用品，片、粒、珠、粉或类似形状的：**					**Tapioca and substitutes therefor prepared from starch, in the form of flakes, grains, pearls, siftings or in similar forms:**
1159	1903.0000	珍粉及淀粉制成的珍粉代用品，片、粒、珠、粉或类似形状的	15	0 东盟ASEAN,智利CL,新加坡SG,新西兰NZ,澳门MO 3 哥斯达黎加CR 7.5 秘鲁PE 12 巴基斯坦PK	0 最不发达35国LDC35,最不发达4国LDC4	80	Tapioca and substitutes therefor prepared from starch, in the form of flakes, grains, pearls, siftings or in similar forms
	19.04	**谷物或谷物产品经膨化或烘炒制成的食品（例如，玉米片）；其他税号未列名的预煮或经其他方法制作的谷粒（玉米除外）、谷物片或经其他加工的谷粒（细粉及粗粉除外）：**					**Prepared foods obtained by the swelling or roasting of cereals or cereal products (for example, corn flakes); cereals (other than maize (corn)) in grain form or in the form of flakes or other worked grains (except flour, groats and meal), pre-cooked or otherwise prepared, not elsewhere specified or included:**
1160	1904.1000	-谷物或谷物产品经膨化或烘炒制成的食品	25	0 东盟ASEAN,新加坡SG,新西兰NZ,澳门MO 2.5 智利CL 5 哥斯达黎加CR 12.5 秘鲁PE	0 最不发达35国LDC35	80	-Prepared foods obtained by the swelling or roasting of cereals or cereal products
1161	1904.2000	-未烘炒谷物片制成的食品及未烘炒的谷物片与烘炒的谷物片或膨化的谷物混合制成的食品	30	0 东盟ASEAN,智利CL,新加坡SG,新西兰NZ 6 哥斯达黎加CR 20 秘鲁PE		80	-Prepared foods obtained from unroasted cereal flakes or from mixtures of unroasted cereal flakes and roasted cereal flakes or swelled cereals
1162	1904.3000	-碾碎的干小麦	30	0 东盟ASEAN,智利CL,新加坡SG,新西兰NZ,澳门MO 6 哥斯达黎加CR 20 秘鲁PE		80	-Bulgur wheat
1163	1904.9000	-其他	30	0 东盟ASEAN,智利CL,新加坡SG,新西兰NZ,香港HK,澳门MO 6 哥斯达黎加CR 17.5 秘鲁PE		80	-Other
	19.05	**面包、糕点、饼干及其他烘焙糕饼，不论是否含可可；圣餐饼、装药空囊、封缄、糯米纸及类似制品：**					**Bread, pastry, cakes, biscuits and other bakers'wares, whether or not containing cocoa; communion wafers, empty cachets of a kind suitable for pharmaceutical use, sealing wafers, rice paper and similar products:**

序号 No.	税则号列 Tariff Line	货品名称	最惠国税率 MFN(%)	协定税率 Agreement(%)		特惠税率 S.P.(%)		普通税率 Gen.(%)	Article Description
1164	1905.1000	-黑麦脆面包片	20	0	东盟ASEAN,智利CL,新加坡SG,新西兰NZ,澳门MO	0	最不发达35国LDC35	80	-Crispbread
				4	哥斯达黎加CR				
				10	秘鲁PE				
1165	1905.2000	-姜饼及类似品	20	0	东盟ASEAN,智利CL,新加坡SG,新西兰NZ,澳门MO	0	最不发达35国LDC35	80	-Gingerbread and the like
				4	哥斯达黎加CR				
				10	秘鲁PE				
		-甜饼干;华夫饼干及圣餐饼:							-Sweet biscuits; waffles and wafers:
1166	1905.3100	--甜饼干	15	0	东盟ASEAN,新加坡SG,新西兰NZ,香港HK,澳门MO	0	最不发达35国LDC35,最不发达4国LDC4	80	--Sweet biscuits
				1.5	智利CL	7.5	亚太2国APTA2		
				3	哥斯达黎加CR				
				7.5	秘鲁PE				
				12.4	亚太APTA,巴基斯坦PK				
1167	1905.3200	--华夫饼干及圣餐饼	15	0	东盟ASEAN,新加坡SG,新西兰NZ,香港HK,澳门MO	0	最不发达35国LDC35,最不发达4国LDC4	80	--Waffles and wafers
				1.5	智利CL	7.5	亚太2国APTA2		
				3	哥斯达黎加CR				
				7.5	巴基斯坦PK,秘鲁PE				
				12.4	亚太APTA				
1168	1905.4000	-面包干、吐司及类似的烤面包	20	0	东盟ASEAN,智利CL,新加坡SG,新西兰NZ,澳门MO	0	最不发达35国LDC35	80	-Rusks, toasted bread and similar toasted products
				4	哥斯达黎加CR				
				10	秘鲁PE				
1169	1905.9000	-其他	20	0	东盟ASEAN,新加坡SG,新西兰NZ,香港HK,澳门MO	0	最不发达35国LDC35	80	-Other
						10	亚太2国APTA2		
				2	智利CL				
				4	哥斯达黎加CR				
				10	秘鲁PE				
				16	巴基斯坦PK				
				17.1	亚太APTA				

第二十章
蔬菜、水果、坚果或植物其他部分的制品

注释：

一、本章不包括：

（一）用第七章、第八章或第十一章所列方法制作或保藏的蔬菜、水果或坚果；

（二）按重量计含香肠、肉、食用杂碎、动物血、鱼、甲壳动物、软体动物、其他水生无脊椎动物及其混合物超过20%的食品（第十六章）；

（三）税号19.05的烘焙糕饼及其他制品；

（四）税号21.04的均化混合食品。

二、税号20.07及20.08不包括制成糖食的果冻、果膏、糖衣杏仁或类似品（税号17.04）及巧克力糖食（税号18.06）。

三、税号20.01、20.04及20.05仅酌情包括用本章注释一（一）以外的方法制作或保藏的第七章或税号11.05、11.06的产品（第八章产品的细粉、粗粉除外）。

四、干重量在7%及以上的番茄汁归入税号20.02。

五、税目20.07所称"烹煮的"是指，在常压或减压下，通过减少水分或其他方法增加产品粘稠度的热处理。

六、税号20.09所称"未发酵及未加酒精的水果汁"，是指按容量计酒精浓度（标准见第二十二章注释二）不超过0.5%的水果汁。

子目注释：

一、子目号2005.10所称"均化蔬菜"，是指蔬菜经精细均化制成供婴幼儿食用或营养用的零售包装食品（每件净重不超过250克）。为了调味、保藏或其他目的，均化蔬菜中可以加入少量其他配料，还可以含有少量可见的蔬菜粒。归类时，子目号2005.10优先于税号20.05的其他子目。

Chapter 20
Preparations of vegetables, fruit, nuts or other parts of plants

Notes:

1. This Chapter does not cover:

(a) Vegetables, fruit or nuts, prepared or preserved by the processes specified in Chapter 7, 8 or 11;

(b) Food preparations containing more than 20% by weight of sausage, meat, meat offal, blood, fish or crustaceans, molluscs or other aquatic invertebrates, or any combination there of (Chapter 16); or

(c) Bakers' wares and other products of heading 19.05; or

(d) Homogenized composite food preparations of heading No.21.04.

2. Headings No.20.07 and 20.08 do not apply to fruit jellies, fruit pastes, sugar-coated almonds or the like in the form of sugar confectionery (heading No.17.04) or chocolate confectionery (heading No.18.06) .

3. Headings No.20.01, 20.04 and 20.05 cover, as the case may be, only those products of Chapter 7 or of heading No.11.05 or 11.06 (other than flour, meal and powder of the products of Chapter 8) which have been prepared or preserved by processes other than those referred to in Note 1(a).

4. Tomato juice, the dry weight content of which is 7% or more, is to be classified in heading No.20.02.

5. For the purposes of heading No.20.07, the expression "obtained by cooking" means obtained by heat treatment at atmospheric pressure or under reduced pressure to increase the viscosity of a product through reduction of water content or other means.

6. For the purposes of heading No.20.09, the expression "juices, unfermented and not containing added spirit" means juices of an alcoholic strength by volume (see Note 2 to Chapter 22) not exceeding 0.5% vol.

Subheading Notes:

1. For the purposes of subheading No.2005.10, the expression "homogenized vegetables" means preparations of vegetables, finely homogenized, put up for retail sale as infant food or for dietetic purposes, in containers of a net weight content not exceeding 250g. For the application of this definition no account is to be taken of small quantities of any ingredients which may have been added to the preparation for seasoning, preparation or other purposes. These preparations may contain a small quantity of visible pieces of vegetables. Subheading No.2005.10 takes precedence over all other subheadings of heading No.20.05.

二、子目号 2007.10 所称“均化食品”，是指果实经精细均化制成供婴幼儿食用或营养用的零售包装食品（每件净重不超过 250 克）。为了调味、保藏或其他目的，均化食品中可以加入少量其他配料，还可以含有少量可见的果粒。归类时，子目号 2007.10 优先于税号 20.07 的其他子目。

三、子目 2009.12、2009.21、2009.31、2009.41、2009.61 及 2009.71 所称“白利糖度值”，是指直接从白利糖度计读取的度数或在 20℃时从折射计读取的以蔗糖百分比含量计的折射率，在其他温度下读取的数值应折算为 20℃时的折射率。

2. For the purposes of subheading No.2007.10, the expression “homogenized preparations” means preparations of fruit, finely homogenized, put up for retail sale as infant food or for dietetic purposes, in containers of a net weight content not exceeding 250g. For the application of this definition no account is to be taken of small quantities of any ingredients which may have been added to the preparation for seasoning, preservation or other purposes. These preparations may contain a small quantity of visible pieces of fruit. Subheading No.2007.10 takes precedence over all other subheadings of heading No.20.07.

3. For the purposes of subheadings No.2009.12, 2009.21, 2009.31, 2009.41, 2009.61 and 2009.71, the expression “Brix value” means the direct reading of degrees Brix obtained from a Brix hydrometer of refractive index expressed in terms of percentage sucrose content obtained from a refractometer, at a temperature of 20℃ or corrected for 20℃ if the reading is made at a different temperature.

序号 No.	税则号列 Tariff Line	货品名称	最惠国税率 MFN(%)	协定税率 Agreement(%)	特惠税率 S.P.(%)	普通税率 Gen.(%)	Article Description
	20.01	**蔬菜、水果、坚果及植物的其他食用部分，用醋或醋酸制作或保藏的：**					**Vegetables, fruit, nuts and other edible parts of plants, prepared or preserved by vinegar or acetic acid:**
1170	2001.1000	-黄瓜及小黄瓜	25	0 东盟ASEAN,智利CL,新加坡SG,新西兰NZ 5 哥斯达黎加CR 12.5 秘鲁PE	0 最不发达35国LDC35	70	-Cucumbers and gherkins
		-其他：					-Other:
1171	2001.9010	---大蒜	25	0 东盟ASEAN,智利CL,新加坡SG,新西兰NZ 5 哥斯达黎加CR 12.5 秘鲁PE	0 最不发达35国LDC35 12.5 亚太2国APTA2	70	---Garlic
1172	2001.9090	---其他	25	0 东盟ASEAN,新加坡SG,新西兰NZ,澳门MO 2.5 智利CL 5 哥斯达黎加CR 12.5 秘鲁PE	0 最不发达35国LDC35 12.5 亚太2国APTA2	70	---Other
	20.02	**番茄，用醋或醋酸以外的其他方法制作或保藏的：**					**Tomatoes prepared or preserved otherwise than by vinegar or acetic acid:**
		-番茄，整个或切片：					-Tomatoes, whole or in pieces:

序号 No.	税则号列 Tariff Line	货品名称	最惠国税率 MFN(%)	协定税率 Agreement(%)		特惠税率 S.P.(%)		普通税率 Gen.(%)	Article Description
1173	2002.1010	---罐头	19	0 1.9 3.8 9.5	东盟ASEAN,新加坡SG,新西兰NZ,澳门MO 智利CL 哥斯达黎加CR 秘鲁PE	0	最不发达35国LDC35	80	---In airtight containers
1174	2002.1090	---其他	25	0 2.5 5 12.5	东盟ASEAN,新加坡SG,新西兰NZ 智利CL 哥斯达黎加CR 秘鲁PE	0	最不发达35国LDC35	70	---Other
		-其他: ---番茄酱罐头:							-Other: ---Tomato paste, in airtight containers:
1175	2002.9011	----重量不超过5kg的番茄酱罐头	20	0 4	东盟ASEAN,智利CL,新加坡SG,新西兰NZ,秘鲁PE,澳门MO 哥斯达黎加CR	0	最不发达35国LDC35	80	----Tomato paste, in airtight containers, weighing not more than 5kg
1176	2002.9019	----重量大于5kg的番茄酱罐头	20	0 4	东盟ASEAN,智利CL,新加坡SG,新西兰NZ,秘鲁PE,澳门MO 哥斯达黎加CR	0	最不发达35国LDC35	80	----Tomato paste, in airtight containers, weighing more than 5kg
1177	2002.9090	---其他	18	0 3.6 14.4	东盟ASEAN,智利CL,新加坡SG,新西兰NZ,秘鲁PE,澳门MO 哥斯达黎加CR 巴基斯坦PK	0	最不发达35国LDC35	70	---Other
	20.03	**蘑菇及块菌，用醋或醋酸以外的其他方法制作或保藏的：**							**Mushrooms and truffles, prepared or preserved otherwise than by vinegar or acetic acid:**
		-伞菌属蘑菇: ---罐头:							-Mushrooms: ---In airtight containers:
1178	2003.1011	----小白蘑菇	25	0 2.5 5 12.5	东盟ASEAN,新加坡SG,新西兰NZ,澳门MO 智利CL 哥斯达黎加CR 秘鲁PE	0	最不发达35国LDC35	90	----Small white agaric
1179	2003.1019	----其他	25	0 2.5 5 12.5	东盟ASEAN,新加坡SG,新西兰NZ,澳门MO 智利CL 哥斯达黎加CR 秘鲁PE	0	最不发达35国LDC35	90	----Other
1180	2003.1090	---其他	25	0 2.5 5 12.5	东盟ASEAN,新加坡SG,新西兰NZ,澳门MO 智利CL 哥斯达黎加CR 秘鲁PE	0	最不发达35国LDC35	90	---Other
		-其他:							-Other:
1181	2003.9010	---罐头	25	0 5 12.5	东盟ASEAN,智利CL,新加坡SG,新西兰NZ,澳门MO 哥斯达黎加CR 秘鲁PE	0	最不发达35国LDC35	90	---In airtight containers

序号 No.	税则号列 Tariff Line	货品名称	最惠国税率 MFN(%)	协定税率 Agreement(%)		特惠税率 S.P.(%)		普通税率 Gen.(%)	Article Description
1182	2003.9090	---其他	25	0 5 12.5	东盟ASEAN,智利CL,新加坡SG,新西兰NZ,澳门MO 哥斯达黎加CR 秘鲁PE	0	最不发达35国LDC35	90	---Other
	20.04	**其他冷冻蔬菜，用醋或醋酸以外的其他方法制作或保藏的，但税号20.06的产品除外：**							**Other vegetables prepared or preserved otherwise than by vinegar or acetic acid, other than products of heading No.20.06:**
1183	2004.1000	-马铃薯	13	0 1.3 2.6 6.5	东盟ASEAN,新加坡SG,新西兰NZ 智利CL 哥斯达黎加CR 巴基斯坦PK,秘鲁PE	0	最不发达35国LDC35,最不发达4国LDC4	70	-Potatoes
1184	2004.9000	-其他蔬菜及什锦蔬菜	25	0 2.5 5 12.5	东盟ASEAN,新加坡SG,新西兰NZ 智利CL 哥斯达黎加CR 秘鲁PE	0	最不发达35国LDC35	70	-Other vegetables and mixtures of vegetables
	20.05	**其他未冷冻蔬菜，用醋或醋酸以外的其他方法制作或保藏的，但税号20.06的产品除外：**							**Other vegetables prepared or preserved otherwise than by vinegar or acetic acid, not frozen, other than products of heading No.20.06:**
1185	2005.1000	-均化蔬菜	25	0 5 12.5	东盟ASEAN,智利CL,新加坡SG,新西兰NZ 哥斯达黎加CR 秘鲁PE	0	最不发达35国LDC35	70	-Homogenized vegetables
1186	2005.2000	-马铃薯	15	0 1.5 3 7.5 12	东盟ASEAN,新加坡SG,新西兰NZ,香港HK 智利CL 哥斯达黎加CR 秘鲁PE 巴基斯坦PK	0	最不发达35国LDC35	70	-Potatoes
1187	2005.4000	-豌豆	25	0 5 12.5	东盟ASEAN,智利CL,新加坡SG,新西兰NZ 哥斯达黎加CR 秘鲁PE	0	最不发达35国LDC35	70	-Peas (Pisum sativum)
		-豇豆及菜豆：							-Beans (Vigna spp., phaseolus spp.):
		--脱荚的：							--Beans, shelled:
		---罐头:							---In airtight containers:
1188	2005.5111	----赤豆馅	25	0 5 12.5	东盟ASEAN,智利CL,新加坡SG,新西兰NZ,香港HK,澳门MO 哥斯达黎加CR 秘鲁PE	0	最不发达35国LDC35	80	----Red bean paste

序号 No.	税则号列 Tariff Line	货品名称	最惠国税率 MFN(%)	协定税率 Agreement(%)		特惠税率 S.P.(%)		普通税率 Gen.(%)	Article Description
1189	2005.5119	----其他	25	0 5 12.5	东盟ASEAN,智利CL,新加坡SG,新西兰NZ,香港HK,澳门MO 哥斯达黎加CR 秘鲁PE	0	最不发达35国LDC35	80	----Other
		---其他:							---Other:
1190	2005.5191	----赤豆馅	25	0 5 12.5	东盟ASEAN,智利CL,新加坡SG,新西兰NZ 哥斯达黎加CR 秘鲁PE	0	最不发达35国LDC35	70	----Red bean paste
1191	2005.5199	----其他	25	0 5 12.5	东盟ASEAN,智利CL,新加坡SG,新西兰NZ,香港HK 哥斯达黎加CR 秘鲁PE	0	最不发达35国LDC35	70	----Other
		--其他:							--Other:
1192	2005.5910	---罐头	25	0 5 12.5	东盟ASEAN,智利CL,新加坡SG,新西兰NZ,澳门MO 哥斯达黎加CR 秘鲁PE	0	最不发达35国LDC35	80	---In airtight containers
1193	2005.5990	---其他	25	0 5 12.5	东盟ASEAN,智利CL,新加坡SG,新西兰NZ 哥斯达黎加CR 秘鲁PE	0	最不发达35国LDC35	70	---Other
		-芦笋:							-Asparagus:
1194	2005.6010	---罐头	25	0 5 12.5	东盟ASEAN,智利CL,新加坡SG,新西兰NZ,澳门MO 哥斯达黎加CR 秘鲁PE	0	最不发达35国LDC35	80	---In airtight containers
1195	2005.6090	---其他	25	0 5 12.5	东盟ASEAN,智利CL,新加坡SG,新西兰NZ 哥斯达黎加CR 秘鲁PE	0	最不发达35国LDC35	70	---Other
1196	2005.7000	-油橄榄	10	0 1 5	东盟ASEAN,新加坡SG,新西兰NZ,哥斯达黎加CR 智利CL 巴基斯坦PK,秘鲁PE	0	最不发达35国LDC35	70	-Olives
1197	2005.8000	-甜玉米	10	0 5	东盟ASEAN,智利CL,新加坡SG,新西兰NZ,秘鲁PE,哥斯达黎加CR 巴基斯坦PK	0	最不发达35国LDC35	80	-Sweet corn (Zea mays var.saccharata)
		-其他蔬菜及什锦蔬菜:							-Other vegetables and mixtures of vegetables:
		--竹笋:							--Bamboo shoots:
1198	2005.9110	---竹笋罐头	25	0 2.5 5 12.5	东盟ASEAN,新加坡SG,新西兰NZ,澳门MO 智利CL 哥斯达黎加CR 秘鲁PE	0	最不发达35国LDC35	80	---In airtight containers

序号 No.	税则号列 Tariff Line	货品名称	最惠国税率 MFN(%)	协定税率 Agreement(%)		特惠税率 S.P.(%)		普通税率 Gen.(%)	Article Description
1199	2005.9190	---其他	25	0 2.5 5 12.5	东盟ASEAN,新加坡SG,新西兰NZ 智利CL 哥斯达黎加CR 秘鲁PE	0	最不发达35国LDC35	70	---Other
		--其他:							--Other:
1200	2005.9920	---蚕豆罐头	25	0 2.5 5 12.5	东盟ASEAN,新加坡SG,新西兰NZ,澳门MO 智利CL 哥斯达黎加CR 秘鲁PE	0	最不发达35国LDC35	80	---Broad beans, in airtight containers
1201	2005.9940	---榨菜	25	0 5 12.5	东盟ASEAN,智利CL,新加坡SG,新西兰NZ 哥斯达黎加CR 秘鲁PE	0	最不发达35国LDC35	70	---Hot pickled mustard tubers
1202	2005.9950	---咸蕨菜	25	0 5 12.5	东盟ASEAN,智利CL,新加坡SG,新西兰NZ 哥斯达黎加CR 秘鲁PE	0	最不发达35国LDC35	70	---Chueh tsai (fiddle-head), salted
1203	2005.9960	---咸藠头	25	0 5 12.5	东盟ASEAN,智利CL,新加坡SG,新西兰NZ 哥斯达黎加CR 秘鲁PE	0	最不发达35国LDC35	70	---Scallion, salted
		---其他:							---Other:
1204	2005.9991	----罐头	25	0 2.5 5	东盟ASEAN,新加坡SG,新西兰NZ,秘鲁PE,澳门MO 智利CL 哥斯达黎加CR	0	最不发达35国LDC35	70	----In airtight containers
1205	2005.9999	----其他	25	0 2.5 5	东盟ASEAN,新加坡SG,新西兰NZ,秘鲁PE 智利CL 哥斯达黎加CR	0	最不发达35国LDC35	70	----Other
	20.06	**糖渍蔬菜、水果、坚果、果皮及植物的其他部分（沥干、糖渍或裹糖的）：**							**Vegetables, fruit, nuts, fruit-peel and other parts of plants, preserved by sugar (drained, glac or crystallized):**
1206	2006.0010	---蜜枣	30	0 6 15	东盟ASEAN,智利CL,新加坡SG,新西兰NZ,香港HK 哥斯达黎加CR 秘鲁PE	0	最不发达35国LDC35,最不发达4国LDC4,缅甸MM	90	---Preserved jujubes
1207	2006.0020	---橄榄	30	0 3 6 21.2	东盟ASEAN,新加坡SG,新西兰NZ,香港HK 智利CL 哥斯达黎加CR 秘鲁PE	0	最不发达35国LDC35,最不发达4国LDC4,缅甸MM	90	---Preserved olives

序号 No.	税则号列 Tariff Line	货品名称	最惠国税率 MFN(%)	协定税率 Agreement(%)		特惠税率 S.P.(%)		普通税率 Gen.(%)	Article Description
1208	2006.0090	---其他	30	0 3 6 21.2	东盟ASEAN,新加坡SG,新西兰NZ,香港HK,澳门MO 智利CL 哥斯达黎加CR 秘鲁PE	0	最不发达35国LDC35,最不发达4国LDC4,缅甸MM	90	---Other
	20.07	**烹煮的果酱、果冻、柑橘酱、果泥及果膏，不论是否加糖或其他甜物质：**							**Jams, fruit jellies, marmalades, fruit or nut pur e and fruit or nut pastes, being cooked preparations, whether or not containing added sugar or other sweetening matter:**
1209	2007.1000	-均化食品	30	0 3 6 21.2	东盟ASEAN,新加坡SG,新西兰NZ 智利CL 哥斯达黎加CR 秘鲁PE			80	-Homogenized preparations
		-其他：							-Other:
1210	2007.9100	--柑橘属水果的	30	0 6 15	东盟ASEAN,智利CL,新加坡SG,新西兰NZ,澳门MO 哥斯达黎加CR 秘鲁PE	0	最不发达35国LDC35,最不发达4国LDC4,缅甸MM	80	--Citrus fruit
		--其他：							--Other:
1211	2007.9910	---罐头	5	0 0.5 1 2.5	东盟ASEAN,巴基斯坦PK,新西兰NZ,澳门MO 智利CL 哥斯达黎加CR 秘鲁PE	0 2.5	最不发达35国LDC35,最不发达4国LDC4 亚太2国APTA2	80	---In airtight containers
1212	2007.9990	---其他	5	0 0.5 2.5 3.7	东盟ASEAN,巴基斯坦PK,新西兰NZ,澳门MO 智利CL 秘鲁PE 哥斯达黎加CR	0 2.5	最不发达35国LDC35,最不发达4国LDC4 亚太2国APTA2	80	---Other
	20.08	**用其他方法制作或保藏的其他税号未列名水果、坚果及植物的其他食用部分，不论是否加酒、加糖或其他甜物质：**							**Fruit, nuts and other edible parts of plants, otherwise prepared, or preserved, whether or not containing added sugar or other sweetening matter or spirit, not elsewhere specified or included:**

序号 No.	税则号列 Tariff Line	货品名称	最惠国税率 MFN(%)		协定税率 Agreement(%)		特惠税率 S.P.(%)	普通税率 Gen.(%)	Article Description
		-坚果、花生及其他子仁，不论是否混合：							-Nuts, groundnuts and other seeds, whether or not mixed together:
		--花生：							--Ground-nuts:
1213	2008.1110	---花生米罐头	30	0 6	东盟ASEAN,智利CL,新加坡SG,新西兰NZ,香港HK,澳门MO 哥斯达黎加CR			90	---Ground-nut kernels, in airtight containers
1214	2008.1120	---烘焙花生	30	0 6	东盟ASEAN,智利CL,新加坡SG,新西兰NZ,香港HK,澳门MO 哥斯达黎加CR	0	最不发达35国LDC35,最不发达4国LDC4,柬埔寨KH	80	---Roasted ground-nuts
1215	2008.1130	---花生酱	30	0 6	东盟ASEAN,智利CL,新加坡SG,新西兰NZ 哥斯达黎加CR			90	---Ground-nut butter
1216	2008.1190	---其他	30	0 6	东盟ASEAN,智利CL,新加坡SG,新西兰NZ,香港HK,澳门MO 哥斯达黎加CR			80	---Other
		--其他，包括什锦坚果及其他子仁：							--Other, including mixtures:
1217	2008.1910	---核桃仁罐头	20	0 2 4 10	东盟ASEAN,新加坡SG,新西兰NZ,香港HK,澳门MO 智利CL 哥斯达黎加CR 亚太APTA,巴基斯坦PK,秘鲁PE	0	最不发达35国LDC35,最不发达4国LDC4,老挝LA,柬埔寨KH	90	---Walnut meats, in airtight containers
1218	2008.1920	---其他果仁罐头	13	0 1.3 2.6 5 6.5	东盟ASEAN,新加坡SG,新西兰NZ,香港HK,澳门MO 智利CL 哥斯达黎加CR 巴基斯坦PK 亚太APTA,秘鲁PE	0	最不发达35国LDC35,最不发达4国LDC4,老挝LA,柬埔寨KH	90	---Other nuts, in airtight containers
		---其他：							---Other:
1219	2008.1991	----栗仁	10	0 1 5	东盟ASEAN,新加坡SG,新西兰NZ,哥斯达黎加CR,香港HK,澳门MO 智利CL 亚太APTA,巴基斯坦PK,秘鲁PE	0	最不发达35国LDC35,最不发达4国LDC4,老挝LA,柬埔寨KH	80	----Chestnut seed
1220	2008.1992	----芝麻	10	0 1 5	东盟ASEAN,新加坡SG,新西兰NZ,秘鲁PE,哥斯达黎加CR,香港HK,澳门MO 智利CL 亚太APTA,巴基斯坦PK	0	最不发达35国LDC35	80	----Sesames

序号 No.	税则号列 Tariff Line	货品名称	最惠国税率 MFN(%)	协定税率 Agreement(%)		特惠税率 S.P.(%)		普通税率 Gen.(%)	Article Description
1221	2008.1999	----其他	10	0 1 5	东盟ASEAN,新加坡SG,新西兰NZ,哥斯达黎加CR,香港HK,澳门MO 智利CL 亚太APTA,巴基斯坦PK,秘鲁PE	0	最不发达35国LDC35,最不发达4国LDC4,老挝LA,柬埔寨KH	80	----Other
		-菠萝:							-Pineapples:
1222	2008.2010	---罐头	15	0 7.5 11	智利CL,新西兰NZ,澳门MO 秘鲁PE 哥斯达黎加CR	0	最不发达35国LDC35,最不发达4国LDC4,老挝LA	90	---In airtight containers
1223	2008.2090	---其他	15	0 7.5 11	智利CL,新西兰NZ 秘鲁PE 哥斯达黎加CR	0	最不发达35国LDC35,最不发达4国LDC4,老挝LA	80	---Other
		-柑橘属水果:							-Citrus fruit:
1224	2008.3010	---罐头	20	0 14.7	东盟ASEAN,智利CL,新加坡SG,新西兰NZ,秘鲁PE,澳门MO 哥斯达黎加CR	0	最不发达35国LDC35,最不发达4国LDC4,老挝LA	90	---In airtight containers
1225	2008.3090	---其他	20	0	东盟ASEAN,智利CL,新加坡SG,新西兰NZ,秘鲁PE,哥斯达黎加CR,香港HK	0	最不发达35国LDC35,最不发达4国LDC4,老挝LA	80	---Other
		-梨:							-Pears:
1226	2008.4010	---罐头	20	0 2 4 10	东盟ASEAN,新加坡SG,新西兰NZ,澳门MO 智利CL 哥斯达黎加CR 秘鲁PE	0	最不发达35国LDC35,最不发达4国LDC4,老挝LA	90	---In airtight containers
1227	2008.4090	---其他	20	0 2 4 10	东盟ASEAN,新加坡SG,新西兰NZ 智利CL 哥斯达黎加CR 秘鲁PE	0	最不发达35国LDC35,最不发达4国LDC4,老挝LA	80	---Other

序号 No.	税则号列 Tariff Line	货品名称	最惠国税率 MFN(%)	协定税率 Agreement(%)		特惠税率 S.P.(%)		普通税率 Gen.(%)	Article Description
1228	2008.5000	-杏	20	0 2 4 10	东盟ASEAN,新加坡SG,新西兰NZ 智利CL 哥斯达黎加CR 秘鲁PE	0	最不发达35国LDC35	90	-Apricots
		-樱桃:							-Cherries:
1229	2008.6010	---罐头	20	0 2 4 10	东盟ASEAN,新加坡SG,新西兰NZ 智利CL 哥斯达黎加CR 秘鲁PE	0	最不发达35国LDC35	90	---In airtight containers
1230	2008.6090	---其他	20	0 2 4 10	东盟ASEAN,新加坡SG,新西兰NZ 智利CL 哥斯达黎加CR 秘鲁PE	0	最不发达35国LDC35	90	---Other
		-桃:							-Peaches:
1231	2008.7010	---罐头	10	0 5	东盟ASEAN,智利CL,新加坡SG,新西兰NZ,哥斯达黎加CR,澳门MO 巴基斯坦PK,秘鲁PE	0	最不发达35国LDC35,最不发达4国LDC4,老挝LA	90	---In airtight containers
1232	2008.7090	---其他	20	0 2 4 10	东盟ASEAN,新加坡SG,新西兰NZ,香港HK 智利CL 哥斯达黎加CR 秘鲁PE	0	最不发达35国LDC35,最不发达4国LDC4,老挝LA	80	---Other
1233	2008.8000	-草莓	15	0 1.5 3 7.5 12	东盟ASEAN,新加坡SG,新西兰NZ 智利CL 哥斯达黎加CR 秘鲁PE 巴基斯坦PK	0	最不发达35国LDC35	90	-Strawberries
		-其他，包括子目号2008.19以外的什锦果实:							-Other, including mixtures other than those of subheading No.2008.19:
1234	2008.9100	--棕榈芯	5	0	东盟ASEAN,智利CL,巴基斯坦PK,新西兰NZ,秘鲁PE,哥斯达黎加CR	0	最不发达35国LDC35,最不发达4国LDC4,柬埔寨KH	80	--Palm hearts
1235	2008.9300	--蔓越橘(大果蔓越橘、小果蔓越橘、越橘)	15	0 1.5 3 7.5 12	东盟ASEAN,新加坡SG,新西兰NZ,香港HK,澳门MO 智利CL 哥斯达黎加CR 秘鲁PE 巴基斯坦PK	0	最不发达35国LDC35,最不发达4国LDC4,柬埔寨KH	80	--Cranberries (Vaccinium macrocarpon, Vaccinium oxycoccos, Vaccinium vitis-idaea)

序号 No.	税则号列 Tariff Line	货品名称	最惠国税率 MFN(%)	协定税率 Agreement(%)		特惠税率 S.P.(%)		普通税率 Gen.(%)	Article Description
1236	2008.9700	--什锦果实	10	0 1 5	东盟ASEAN,新加坡SG,新西兰NZ,哥斯达黎加CR,澳门MO 智利CL 巴基斯坦PK,秘鲁PE	0	最不发达35国LDC35,最不发达4国LDC4,柬埔寨KH	80	--Mixtures
		--其他:							--Other:
1237	2008.9910	---荔枝罐头	20	0 4 10	东盟ASEAN,智利CL,新加坡SG,新西兰NZ,香港HK,澳门MO 哥斯达黎加CR 秘鲁PE	0	最不发达35国LDC35	90	---Lychee can
1238	2008.9920	---龙眼罐头	15	0 3 7.5	智利CL,新西兰NZ,香港HK,澳门MO 哥斯达黎加CR 秘鲁PE	0	最不发达35国LDC35,最不发达4国LDC4,柬埔寨KH	80	---Longan can
		---海草及其他藻类制品:							---Seaweed and otheralga product:
1239	2008.9931	----调味紫菜	15	0 3 7.5	东盟ASEAN,智利CL,新加坡SG,新西兰NZ,香港HK,澳门MO 哥斯达黎加CR 秘鲁PE	0	最不发达35国LDC35,最不发达4国LDC4,柬埔寨KH	90	----Seasoned laver
1240	2008.9932	----盐腌海带	15	0 1.5 3 7.5 12	东盟ASEAN,新西兰NZ,香港HK,澳门MO 智利CL 哥斯达黎加CR 秘鲁PE 巴基斯坦PK	0	最不发达35国LDC35,最不发达4国LDC4,柬埔寨KH	80	----Salted sea tangle
1241	2008.9933	----盐腌裙带菜	15	0 1.5 3 7.5 12	东盟ASEAN,新西兰NZ,香港HK,澳门MO 智利CL 哥斯达黎加CR 秘鲁PE 巴基斯坦PK	0	最不发达35国LDC35,最不发达4国LDC4,柬埔寨KH	80	----Salted undaria pinnatifida
1242	2008.9939	----其他	15	0 1.5 3 7.5 12	东盟ASEAN,新西兰NZ,香港HK,澳门MO 智利CL 哥斯达黎加CR 秘鲁PE 巴基斯坦PK	0	最不发达35国LDC35,最不发达4国LDC4,柬埔寨KH	80	----Other
1243	2008.9940	---清水荸荠（马蹄）罐头	25	0 2.5 5 12.5	东盟ASEAN,新加坡SG,新西兰NZ,澳门MO 智利CL 哥斯达黎加CR 秘鲁PE	0	最不发达35国LDC35	80	---Water chestnut (Eleocharis dulcis), in airtight containers

序号 No.	税则号列 Tariff Line	货品名称	最惠国税率 MFN(%)	协定税率 Agreement(%)		特惠税率 S.P.(%)		普通税率 Gen.(%)	Article Description
1244	2008.9990	---其他	15	0 1.5 3 7.5 12	东盟ASEAN,新加坡SG,新西兰NZ,香港HK,澳门MO 智利CL 哥斯达黎加CR 秘鲁PE 巴基斯坦PK	0	最不发达35国LDC35,最不发达4国LDC4,柬埔寨KH	80	---Other
	20.09	**未发酵及未加酒精的水果汁（包括酿酒葡萄汁）、蔬菜汁，不论是否加糖或其他甜物质：**							**Fruit juices (including grape must) and vegetable juices, unfermented and not containing added spirit, whether or not containing added sugar or other sweetening matter:**
		-橙汁：							-Orange juice:
1245	2009.1100	--冷冻的	7.5	0 1.7 3.8 5	东盟ASEAN,智利CL,哥斯达黎加CR,香港HK,澳门MO 新西兰NZ 秘鲁PE 巴基斯坦PK	0	最不发达35国LDC35,最不发达4国LDC4,老挝LA,柬埔寨KH	90	--Frozen
1246	2009.1200	--非冷冻的，白利糖度值不超过20	30	0 3 6.7 15	东盟ASEAN,新加坡SG,香港HK,澳门MO 智利CL 新西兰NZ 秘鲁PE	0	最不发达35国LDC35,最不发达4国LDC4,老挝LA,柬埔寨KH	90	--Not frozen, of a Brix value not exceeding 20
1247	2009.1900	--其他	30	0 6.7 15	东盟ASEAN,智利CL,新加坡SG,澳门MO 新西兰NZ 秘鲁PE	0	最不发达35国LDC35,最不发达4国LDC4,老挝LA,柬埔寨KH	90	--Other
		-葡萄柚(包括柚)汁：							-Grapefruit (including pomelo) juice:
1248	2009.2100	--白利糖度值不超过20的	15	0 3 12	东盟ASEAN,智利CL,新加坡SG,新西兰NZ,秘鲁PE,香港HK,澳门MO 哥斯达黎加CR 巴基斯坦PK	0	最不发达35国LDC35,最不发达4国LDC4,老挝LA	90	--Of a Brix value not exceeding 20
1249	2009.2900	--其他	15	0 3 12	东盟ASEAN,智利CL,新加坡SG,新西兰NZ,秘鲁PE,澳门MO 哥斯达黎加CR 巴基斯坦PK	0	最不发达35国LDC35,最不发达4国LDC4,老挝LA	90	--Other

序号 No.	税则号列 Tariff Line	货品名称	最惠国税率 MFN(%)	协定税率 Agreement(%)		特惠税率 S.P.(%)		普通税率 Gen.(%)	Article Description
		-其他未混合的柑橘属水果汁： --白利糖度值不超过20的：							-Juice of any other single citrus fruit: --Of a Brix value not exceeding 20:
1250	2009.3110	---柠檬汁	18	0 1.8 3.6 9 14.4 16.8	东盟ASEAN,新加坡SG,新西兰NZ,香港HK,澳门MO 智利CL 哥斯达黎加CR 秘鲁PE 巴基斯坦PK 亚太APTA	0 9	最不发达35国LDC35,最不发达4国LDC4,柬埔寨KH 亚太2国APTA2	90	---Lemon juice
1251	2009.3190	---其他	18	0 1.8 3.6 9 14.4 16.8	东盟ASEAN,新加坡SG,新西兰NZ,香港HK,澳门MO 智利CL 哥斯达黎加CR 秘鲁PE 巴基斯坦PK 亚太APTA	0 9	最不发达35国LDC35,最不发达4国LDC4,柬埔寨KH 亚太2国APTA2	90	---Other
		--其他：							--Other:
1252	2009.3910	---柠檬汁	18	0 3.6 14.4 16.8	东盟ASEAN,智利CL,新加坡SG,新西兰NZ,秘鲁PE,澳门MO 哥斯达黎加CR 巴基斯坦PK 亚太APTA	0 9	最不发达35国LDC35,最不发达4国LDC4,柬埔寨KH 亚太2国APTA2	90	---Lemon juice
1253	2009.3990	---其他	18	0 3.6 14.4 16.8	东盟ASEAN,智利CL,新加坡SG,新西兰NZ,秘鲁PE,澳门MO 哥斯达黎加CR 巴基斯坦PK 亚太APTA	0 9	最不发达35国LDC35,最不发达4国LDC4,柬埔寨KH 亚太2国APTA2	90	---Other
		-菠萝汁：							-Pineapple juice:
1254	2009.4100	--白利糖度值不超过20	10	0 2	智利CL,新西兰NZ,秘鲁PE,香港HK,澳门MO 哥斯达黎加CR	0	最不发达35国LDC35,最不发达4国LDC4,老挝LA,柬埔寨KH	90	--Of a Brix value not exceeding 20

序号 No.	税则号列 Tariff Line	货品名称	最惠国税率 MFN(%)	协定税率 Agreement(%)		特惠税率 S.P.(%)		普通税率 Gen.(%)	Article Description
1255	2009.4900	--其他	10	0	智利CL,新西兰NZ,秘鲁PE,澳门MO	0	最不发达35国LDC35,最不发达4国LDC4,老挝LA,柬埔寨KH	90	--Other
				2	哥斯达黎加CR				
1256	2009.5000	-番茄汁	30	0	东盟ASEAN,智利CL,新加坡SG,新西兰NZ,澳门MO	0	最不发达35国LDC35,最不发达4国LDC4,老挝LA	80	-Tomato juice
				6	哥斯达黎加CR	15	亚太2国APTA2		
				15	秘鲁PE				
		-葡萄汁,包括酿酒葡萄汁:							-Grape juice (including grape must):
1257	2009.6100	--白利糖度值不超过30的	20	0	东盟ASEAN,新加坡SG,新西兰NZ,香港HK,澳门MO	0	最不发达35国LDC35	90	--Of a Brix value not exceeding 30
				2	智利CL				
				4	哥斯达黎加CR				
				11.7	秘鲁PE				
1258	2009.6900	--其他	20	0	东盟ASEAN,新加坡SG,新西兰NZ,澳门MO	0	最不发达35国LDC35	90	--Other
				2	智利CL				
				4	哥斯达黎加CR				
				11.7	秘鲁PE				
		-苹果汁:							-Apple juice:
1259	2009.7100	--白利糖度值不超过20的	20	0	东盟ASEAN,智利CL,新加坡SG,新西兰NZ,秘鲁PE,香港HK,澳门MO	0	最不发达35国LDC35	90	--Of a Brix value not exceeding 20
				4	哥斯达黎加CR				
1260	2009.7900	--其他	20	0	东盟ASEAN,新加坡SG,新西兰NZ,澳门MO	0	最不发达35国LDC35	90	--Other
				2	智利CL				
				4	哥斯达黎加CR				
				10	秘鲁PE				
		-其他未混合的水果汁或蔬菜汁:							-Juice of any other single fruit or vegetable:
1261	2009.8100	--蔓越橘汁(大果蔓越橘、小果蔓越橘、越橘)	20	0	东盟ASEAN,新加坡SG,新西兰NZ,香港HK,澳门MO	0	最不发达35国LDC35,最不发达4国LDC4,缅甸MM,老挝LA	90	--Cranberry (Vaccinium macrocarpon, Vaccinium oxycoccos, Vaccinium vitis-idaea) juice
				2	智利CL				
				4	哥斯达黎加CR				
				10	亚太APTA,巴基斯坦PK,秘鲁PE				

序号 No.	税则号列 Tariff Line	货品名称	最惠国税率 MFN(%)	协定税率 Agreement(%)		特惠税率 S.P.(%)		普通税率 Gen.(%)	Article Description
		--其他:							--Other:
		---水果汁:							---Fruit juice:
1262	2009.8912	----芒果汁	20	0	东盟ASEAN,新加坡SG,新西兰NZ,香港HK,澳门MO	0	最不发达35国LDC35,最不发达4国LDC4,缅甸MM,老挝LA	90	----Mango juice
				2	智利CL				
				4	哥斯达黎加CR				
				10	秘鲁PE				
				16	巴基斯坦PK				
				17.4	亚太APTA				
1263	2009.8913	----西番莲果汁	20	0	东盟ASEAN,新加坡SG,新西兰NZ,香港HK,澳门MO	0	最不发达35国LDC35,最不发达4国LDC4,缅甸MM,老挝LA	90	----Passion-fruit juice
				2	智利CL				
				4	哥斯达黎加CR				
				10	秘鲁PE				
				16	巴基斯坦PK				
				17.4	亚太APTA				
1264	2009.8914	----番石榴果汁	20	0	东盟ASEAN,新加坡SG,新西兰NZ,香港HK,澳门MO	0	最不发达35国LDC35,最不发达4国LDC4,缅甸MM,老挝LA	90	----Guva juice
				2	智利CL				
				4	哥斯达黎加CR				
				10	秘鲁PE				
				16	巴基斯坦PK				
				17.4	亚太APTA				
1265	2009.8915	----梨汁	20	0	东盟ASEAN,新加坡SG,新西兰NZ,香港HK,澳门MO	0	最不发达35国LDC35,最不发达4国LDC4,缅甸MM,老挝LA	90	----Pear juice
				2	智利CL				
				4	哥斯达黎加CR				
				10	亚太APTA,巴基斯坦PK,秘鲁PE				
1266	2009.8919	----其他	20	0	东盟ASEAN,新加坡SG,新西兰NZ,香港HK,澳门MO	0	最不发达35国LDC35,最不发达4国LDC4,缅甸MM,老挝LA	90	----Other
				2	智利CL				
				4	哥斯达黎加CR				
				10	亚太APTA,巴基斯坦PK,秘鲁PE				
1267	2009.8920	---蔬菜汁	20	0	东盟ASEAN,新加坡SG,新西兰NZ,香港HK,澳门MO	0	最不发达35国LDC35,最不发达4国LDC4,缅甸MM	80	---Vegetable juice
				2	智利CL				
				4	哥斯达黎加CR				
				10	亚太APTA,巴基斯坦PK,秘鲁PE				
		-混合汁:							-Mixtures of juices:

序号 No.	税则号列 Tariff Line	货品名称	最惠国 税　率 MFN(%)	协定税率 Agreement(%)		特惠税率 S.P.(%)		普通 税率 Gen.(%)	Article Description
1268	2009.9010	---水果汁	20	0 4 16 17.4	东盟ASEAN,智利CL,新加坡SG,新西兰NZ,秘鲁PE,香港HK,澳门MO 哥斯达黎加CR 巴基斯坦PK 亚太APTA	0 10	最不发达35国LDC35,最不发达4国LDC4,老挝LA,柬埔寨KH 亚太2国APTA2	90	---Of fruit juices
1269	2009.9090	---其他	20	0 4	东盟ASEAN,智利CL,新加坡SG,新西兰NZ,秘鲁PE,香港HK,澳门MO 哥斯达黎加CR	0 10	最不发达35国LDC35,最不发达4国LDC4,老挝LA,柬埔寨KH 亚太2国APTA2	80	---Other

第二十一章 杂 项 食 品

Chapter 21 Miscellaneous edible preparations

注释:

一、本章不包括:

（一）税号 07.12 的什锦蔬菜;

（二）含咖啡的焙炒咖啡代用品（税号 09.01）;

（三）加香料的茶（税号 09.02）;

（四） 税号 09.04 至 09.10 的调味香料或其他产品;

（五）按重量计含香肠、肉、食用杂碎、动物血、鱼、甲壳动物、软体动物、其他水生无脊椎动物及其混合物超过 20%的食品（第十六章），但税号 21.03 或 21.04 的产品除外;

（六）税号 30.03 或 30.04 的药用酵母及其他产品;

（七）税号 35.07 的酶制品。

二、上述注释一（二）所述咖啡代用品的精汁归入税号 21.01。

三、税号 21.04 所称“均化混合食品”，是指两种或两种以上的基本配料，例如，肉、鱼、蔬菜或果实等，经精细均化制成供婴幼儿食用或营养用的零售包装食品（每件净重不超过 250 克）。为了调味、保藏或其他目的，可以加入少量其他配料，还可以含有少量可见的小块配料。

Notes:

1. This Chapter does not cover:

(a) Mixed vegetables of heading No.07.12;

(b) Roasted coffee substitutes containing coffee in any proportion (heading No.09.01) ;

(c) Flavoured tea (heading No.09.02) ;

(d) Spices or other products of headings No.09.04 to 09.10;

(e) Food preparations, other than the products described in heading No.21.03 or 21.04, containing more than 20% by weight of sausage, meat, meat offal, blood, fish or crustaceans, molluscs or other aquatic invertebrates, or any combination thereof (Chapter16) ;

(f) Yeast put up as a medicament or other products of heading No.30.03 or 30.04; or

(g) Prepared enzymes of heading No.35.07.

2. Extracts of the substitutes referred to in Note 1(b) above are to be classified in heading No.21.01.

3. For the purposes of heading No.21.04, the expression “ homogenized composite food preparations ” means preparations consisting of a finely homogenized mixture of two or more basic ingredients such as meat, fish, vegetables, fruit or nuts, put up for retail sale as infant food or for dietetic purposes, in containers of a net weight content not exceeding 250g. For the application of this definition, no account is to be taken of small quantities of any ingredients which may be added to the mixture for seasoning, preservation or other purposes.Such preparations may contain a small quantity of visible pieces of ingredients.

序号 No.	税则号列 Tariff Line	货品名称	最惠国税 率 MFN(%)	协定税率 Agreement(%)	特惠税率 S.P.(%)	普通税率 Gen.(%)	Article Description
	21.01	**咖啡、茶、马黛茶的浓缩精汁及以其为基本成分或以咖啡、茶、马黛茶为基本成分的制品；烘焙菊苣和其他烘焙咖啡代用品及其浓缩精汁：**					**Extracts, essences and concentrates, of coffee, tea or mat and preparations with a basis of these products or with a basis of coffee, tea or mat ;roasted chicory and other roasted coffee substitutes, and extracts, essences and concentrates thereof:**

序号 No.	税则号列 Tariff Line	货品名称	最惠国税率 MFN(%)	协定税率 Agreement(%)		特惠税率 S.P.(%)		普通税率 Gen.(%)	Article Description
		-咖啡浓缩精汁及以其为基本成分或以咖啡为基本成分的制品：							-Extracts, essences and concentrates of coffee, and preparations with a basis of these extracts, essences or concentrates or with a basis of coffee:
1270	2101.1100	--浓缩精汁	17	0 1.7 3.4 13.6	东盟ASEAN,新加坡SG,新西兰NZ,香港HK,澳门MO 智利CL 哥斯达黎加CR 巴基斯坦PK	0	最不发达35国LDC35,最不发达4国LDC4	130	--Extracts, essences and concentrates
1271	2101.1200	--以浓缩精汁或咖啡为基本成分的制品	30	0 3 6	东盟ASEAN,新加坡SG,新西兰NZ,香港HK 智利CL 哥斯达黎加CR			130	--Preparations with a basis of extracts, essences or concentrates or with a basis of coffee
1272	2101.2000	-茶、马黛茶浓缩精汁及以其为基本成分或以茶、马黛茶为基本成分的制品	32	0 3.2 6.4 16	东盟ASEAN,新加坡SG,新西兰NZ,香港HK,澳门MO 智利CL 哥斯达黎加CR 亚太APTA,巴基斯坦PK,秘鲁PE	0	最不发达35国LDC35	130	-Extracts, essences and concentrates, of tea or maté, and preparations with a basis of these extracts, essences or concentrates or with a basis of tea or mate
1273	2101.3000	-烘焙菊苣和其他烘焙咖啡代用品及其浓缩精汁	32	0 3.2 6.4	东盟ASEAN,新加坡SG,新西兰NZ 智利CL 哥斯达黎加CR	0	最不发达35国LDC35	130	-Roasted chicory and other roasted coffee substitutes, and extracts, essences and concentrates thereof
	21.02	**酵母（活性或非活性）；已死的其他单细胞微生物（不包括税号30.02的疫苗）；发酵粉：**							**Yeasts (active or inactive); other singlecell micro-organisms, dead (but not including vaccines of heading No.30.02); prepared baking powders:**
1274	2102.1000	-活性酵母	25	0 2.5 5 12.5	东盟ASEAN,新加坡SG,新西兰NZ,香港HK,澳门MO 智利CL 哥斯达黎加CR 秘鲁PE	0	最不发达35国LDC35	80	-Active yeasts
1275	2102.2000	-非活性酵母；已死的其他单细胞微生物	25	0 2.5 5 12.5	东盟ASEAN,新加坡SG,新西兰NZ,澳门MO 智利CL 哥斯达黎加CR 秘鲁PE	0	最不发达35国LDC35	70	-Inactive yeasts; other single-cell micro-rganisms, dead
1276	2102.3000	-发酵粉	25	0 5 12.5	东盟ASEAN,智利CL,新加坡SG,新西兰NZ,澳门MO 哥斯达黎加CR 秘鲁PE	0	最不发达35国LDC35	70	-Prepared baking powders

序号 No.	税则号列 Tariff Line	货品名称	最惠国税率 MFN(%)	协定税率 Agreement(%)		特惠税率 S.P.(%)		普通税率 Gen.(%)	Article Description
	21.03	**调味汁及其制品；混合调味品；芥子粉及其调制品：**							**Sauces and preparations there for; mixed condiments and mixes seasonings; mustard flour and meal and prepared mustard:**
1277	2103.1000	-酱油	28 △15	0 5.6 14	东盟ASEAN,智利CL,新加坡SG,新西兰NZ,香港HK,澳门MO 哥斯达黎加CR 秘鲁PE	0	最不发达35国LDC35,最不发达4国LDC4,柬埔寨KH	90	-Soya sauce
1278	2103.2000	-番茄沙司及其他番茄调味汁	15	0 1.5 3 7.5 12	东盟ASEAN,新加坡SG,新西兰NZ,香港HK,澳门MO 智利CL 哥斯达黎加CR 秘鲁PE 巴基斯坦PK	0	最不发达35国LDC35,最不发达4国LDC4,柬埔寨KH	90	-Tomato ketchup and other tomato sauces
1279	2103.3000	-芥子粉及其调制品	15	0 3 7.5 12	东盟ASEAN,智利CL,新加坡SG,新西兰NZ,澳门MO 哥斯达黎加CR 秘鲁PE 巴基斯坦PK	0	最不发达35国LDC35,最不发达4国LDC4,柬埔寨KH	70	-Mustard flour and meal and prepared mustard
		-其他：							-Other:
1280	2103.9010	---味精	21	0 4.2 10.5 18.2	东盟ASEAN,智利CL,新加坡SG,新西兰NZ,香港HK,澳门MO 哥斯达黎加CR 秘鲁PE 亚太APTA,巴基斯坦PK	0	最不发达35国LDC35	130	---Gourmet powder
1281	2103.9020	---别特酒(Aromaticbitters),按体积计酒精含量44.2%～49.2%,按重量计含1.5%～6%的香料、各种配料以及4%～10%的糖	21	0 2.1 4.2 14.8	东盟ASEAN,新加坡SG,新西兰NZ,香港HK,澳门MO 智利CL 哥斯达黎加CR 秘鲁PE	0	最不发达35国LDC35	90	---Aromatic bitters, 44.2%~49.2% of which is alcoholic strength by volume, 1.5%~6% of which is spiles and various ingredients by weight and 4%~10% of which is sugar by weight
1282	2103.9090	---其他	21	0 2.1 4.2 12.3 18.4	东盟ASEAN,新加坡SG,新西兰NZ,香港HK,澳门MO 智利CL 哥斯达黎加CR 秘鲁PE 亚太APTA,巴基斯坦PK	0	最不发达35国LDC35,最不发达4国LDC4	90	---Other
	21.04	**汤料及其制品；均化混合食品：**							**Soups and broths and preparations therefor; homogenized composite food preparations:**

序号 No.	税则号列 Tariff Line	货品名称	最惠国税率 MFN(%)	协定税率 Agreement(%)		特惠税率 S.P.(%)		普通税率 Gen.(%)	Article Description
1283	2104.1000	-汤料及其制品	15	0	东盟ASEAN,新加坡SG,新西兰NZ,香港HK,澳门MO	0	最不发达35国LDC35	90	-Soups and broths and preparations therefor
				1.5	智利CL				
				3	哥斯达黎加CR				
				7.5	秘鲁PE				
				12	巴基斯坦PK				
1284	2104.2000	-均化混合食品	32	0	东盟ASEAN,新加坡SG,新西兰NZ,澳门MO	0	最不发达35国LDC35	90	-Homogenized composite food preparations
				3.2	智利CL				
				6.4	哥斯达黎加CR				
				16	秘鲁PE				
	21.05	**冰淇淋及其他冰制食品，不论是否含可可:**							**Ice cream and other edible ice, whether or not containing cocoa:**
1285	2105.0000	冰淇淋及其他冰制食品，不论是否含可可	19	0	东盟ASEAN,新加坡SG,新西兰NZ,香港HK,澳门MO	0	最不发达35国LDC35	90	Ice cream and other edible ice, whether or not containing cocoa
				1.9	智利CL				
				3.8	哥斯达黎加CR				
				9.5	秘鲁PE				
	21.06	**其他税号未列名的食品:**							**Food preparations not elsewhere specified or included:**
1286	2106.1000	-浓缩蛋白质及人造蛋白物质	10	0	东盟ASEAN,新加坡SG,新西兰NZ,哥斯达黎加CR,澳门MO	0	最不发达35国LDC35	90	-Protein concentrates and textured protein substances
				1	智利CL				
				5	巴基斯坦PK,秘鲁PE				
		-其他:							-Other:
1287	2106.9010	---制造碳酸饮料的浓缩物	35	0	东盟ASEAN,新加坡SG,新西兰NZ,香港HK,澳门MO	0	最不发达35国LDC35	100	---Beverage bases
				3.5	智利CL				
				7	哥斯达黎加CR				
				17.5	秘鲁PE				
1288	2106.9020	---制造饮料用的复合酒精制品	20	0	东盟ASEAN,新加坡SG,新西兰NZ,香港HK,澳门MO	0	最不发达35国LDC35	180	---Compound alcoholic preparations of a kind used for the manufacture of beverages
				2	智利CL				
				4	哥斯达黎加CR				
				10	秘鲁PE				
1289	2106.9030	---蜂王浆制剂	3	0	东盟ASEAN,智利CL,巴基斯坦PK,新西兰NZ,秘鲁PE,哥斯达黎加CR,香港HK,澳门MO	0	最不发达35国LDC35,最不发达4国LDC4,老挝LA	80	---Royal jelly, put up as tonic essences
1290	2106.9040	---椰子汁	10	0	缅甸MM,新西兰NZ,哥斯达黎加CR,香港HK,澳门MO	0	最不发达35国LDC35,最不发达4国LDC4,缅甸MM,老挝LA	90	---Coconut juice
				1	智利CL				
				5	秘鲁PE				
				9	亚太APTA,巴基斯坦PK				

序号 No.	税则号列 Tariff Line	货品名称	最惠国税率 MFN(%)	协定税率 Agreement(%)		特惠税率 S.P.(%)		普通税率 Gen.(%)	Article Description
1291	2106.9050	---海豹油胶囊	20	0	东盟ASEAN,新加坡SG,新西兰NZ,香港HK,澳门MO	0	最不发达35国LDC35	90	---Seal-oil capsule
				2	智利CL				
				4	哥斯达黎加CR				
				10	秘鲁PE				
				18.4	亚太APTA,巴基斯坦PK				
1292	2106.9090	---其他	20	0	东盟ASEAN,新加坡SG,新西兰NZ,香港HK,澳门MO	0	最不发达35国LDC35	90	---Other
				2	智利CL				
				4	哥斯达黎加CR				
				10	秘鲁PE				
				18.4	亚太APTA,巴基斯坦PK				
	ex21069090	乳蛋白部分水解配方、乳蛋白深度水解配方、氨基酸配方、无乳糖配方特殊婴幼儿奶粉	△5						Partial hydrolyzed, extensively hydrolyzed milk protein, amino acid based and lactose-free infant formula milk powder

第二十二章 饮料、酒及醋

Chapter 22 Beverages, spirits and vinegar

注释：

一、本章不包括：

（一）本章的产品（税号22.09的货品除外）经配制后，用于烹饪而不适于作为饮料的制品（通常归入税号21.03）；

（二）海水（税号25.01）；

（三）蒸馏水、导电水及类似的纯净水（税号28.53）；

（四）按重量计浓度超过10%的醋酸（税号29.15）；

（五）税号30.03或30.04的药品；

（六）芳香料制品及盥洗品（第三十三章）。

二、本章及第二十章和第二十一章所称“按容量计酒精浓度”，应是温度在20℃时测得的浓度。

三、税号22.02所称“无酒精饮料”，是指按容量计酒精浓度不超过0.5%的饮料。含酒精饮料应分别归入税号22.03至22.06或税号22.08。

子目注释：

子目号2204.10所称“汽酒”，是指温度在20℃时装在密封容器中超过大气压力3巴及以上的酒。

Notes:

1. This Chapter does not cover:

(a) Products of this Chapter (other than those of heading No.22.09) prepared for culinary purposes and thereby rendered unsuitable for consumption as beverages (generally heading No.21.03) ;

(b) Sea water (heading No.25.01) ;

(c) Distilled or conductivity water or water of similar purity (heading No. 28.53) ;

(d) Acetic acid of a concentration exceeding 10% by weight of acetic acid (heading No.29.15) ;

(e) Medicaments of heading No.30.03 or 30.04;or

(f) Perfumery or toilet preparations (Chapter 33) .

2. For the purposes of this Chapter and of Chapter 20 and 21, the “alcoholic strength by volume” shall be determined at a temperature of 20℃.

3. For the purposes of heading No.22.02, the term “non-alcoholic beverages” means beverages of an alcoholic strength by volume not exceeding 0.5% vol. Alcoholic beverages are classified in headings No.22.03 to 22.06 or heading No.22.08 as appropriate.

Subheading Note:

For the purposes of subheading No.2204.10, the expression “sparkling wine” means wine which, when kept at a temperature of 20℃ in closed containers, has an excess pressure of not less than 3 bars.

序号 No.	税则号列 Tariff Line	货品名称	最惠国税率 MFN(%)	协定税率 Agreement(%)		特惠税率 S.P.(%)		普通税率 Gen.(%)	Article Description
	22.01	**未加糖或其他甜物质及未加味的水，包括天然或人造矿泉水及汽水；冰及雪：**							**Waters, including natural or artificial mineral waters and aerated waters, not containing added sugar or other sweetening matter or flavoured; ice and snow:**
		-矿泉水及汽水：							-Mineral waters and aerated waters:
1293	2201.1010	---矿泉水	20	0 4 10	东盟ASEAN,智利CL,新加坡SG,新西兰NZ,香港HK,澳门MO 哥斯达黎加CR 秘鲁PE	0	最不发达35国LDC35,最不发达4国LDC4	90	---Mineral waters

序号 No.	税则号列 Tariff Line	货品名称	最惠国税 率 MFN(%)	协定税率 Agreement(%)		特惠税率 S.P.(%)		普通税率 Gen.(%)	Article Description
1294	2201.1020	---汽水	20	0 4 10	东盟ASEAN,智利CL,新加坡SG,新西兰NZ,澳门MO 哥斯达黎加CR 秘鲁PE	0	最不发达35国LDC35,最不发达4国LDC4	90	---Aerated waters
		-其他:							-Other:
1295	2201.9010	---天然水	10	0 5	东盟ASEAN,智利CL,新加坡SG,新西兰NZ,秘鲁PE,哥斯达黎加CR,香港HK,澳门MO 巴基斯坦PK	0	最不发达35国LDC35	30	---Natural waters
1296	2201.9090	---其他	10	0 5	东盟ASEAN,智利CL,新加坡SG,新西兰NZ,秘鲁PE,哥斯达黎加CR,香港HK 巴基斯坦PK	0	最不发达35国LDC35	30	---Other
	22.02	**加味、加糖或其他甜物质的水，包括矿泉水及汽水，其他无酒精饮料，但不包括税号20.09的水果汁或蔬菜汁：**							**Waters, including mineral waters and aerated waters, containing added sugar or other sweetening matter or flavoured, and other non-alcoholic beverages, not including fruit or vegetable juices of heading No.20.09:**
1297	2202.1000	-加味、加糖或其他甜物质的水，包括矿泉水及汽水	20	0 2 4 10	东盟ASEAN,新加坡SG,新西兰NZ,香港HK,澳门MO 智利CL 哥斯达黎加CR 秘鲁PE	0	最不发达35国LDC35	100	-Waters, including mineral waters and aerated waters, containing added sugar or other sweetening matter or flavoured
1298	2202.9000	-其他	35	0 3.5 7 17.5 29.5	东盟ASEAN,新加坡SG,新西兰NZ,香港HK,澳门MO 智利CL 哥斯达黎加CR 秘鲁PE 亚太APTA,巴基斯坦PK	0	最不发达35国LDC35,最不发达4国LDC4	100	-Other
	22.03	**麦芽酿造的啤酒：**							**Beer made from malt:**
1299	2203.0000	麦芽酿造的啤酒	0			0	最不发达35国LDC35,最不发达4国LDC4	7.5元/升	Beer made from malt
	22.04	**鲜葡萄酿造的酒，包括加酒精的；税号20.09以外的酿酒葡萄汁：**							**Wine of fresh grapes, including fortified wines; grape must other than that of heading No.20.09:**

序号 No.	税则号列 Tariff Line	货品名称	最惠国税率 MFN(%)	协定税率 Agreement(%)		特惠税率 S.P.(%)		普通税率 Gen.(%)	Article Description
1300	2204.1000	-汽酒	14	0 1.4 2.8 7 11.2	东盟ASEAN,新加坡SG,新西兰NZ 智利CL 哥斯达黎加CR 秘鲁PE 巴基斯坦PK	0	最不发达35国LDC35	180	-Sparkling wine
		-其他酒；加酒精抑制发酵的酿酒葡萄汁：							-Other wine; grape must with fermentation prevented or arrested by the addition of alcohol:
1301	2204.2100	--装入2升及以下容器的	14	0 1.4 2.8 9.3 11.2	东盟ASEAN,新加坡SG,新西兰NZ,香港HK 智利CL 哥斯达黎加CR 秘鲁PE 巴基斯坦PK	0	最不发达35国LDC35	180	--In containers holding 2L or less
1302	2204.2900	--其他	20	0 2 4 13.3	东盟ASEAN,新加坡SG,新西兰NZ 智利CL 哥斯达黎加CR 秘鲁PE	0	最不发达35国LDC35	180	--Other
1303	2204.3000	-其他酿酒葡萄汁	30	0 3 6 17.5	东盟ASEAN,新加坡SG,新西兰NZ 智利CL 哥斯达黎加CR 秘鲁PE			90	-Other grape must
	22.05	**味美思酒及其他加植物或香料的用鲜葡萄酿造的酒：**							**Vermouth and other wine of fresh grapes flavoured with plants or aromatic substances:**
1304	2205.1000	-装入2升及以下容器的	65	0 6.5 13 37.9	东盟ASEAN,新加坡SG,新西兰NZ 智利CL 哥斯达黎加CR 秘鲁PE			180	-In containers holding 2L or less
1305	2205.9000	-其他	65	0 13 37.9	东盟ASEAN,智利CL,新加坡SG,新西兰NZ 哥斯达黎加CR 秘鲁PE			180	-Other
	22.06	**其他发酵饮料（例如，苹果酒、梨酒、蜂蜜酒）；其他税号未列名的发酵饮料的混合物及发酵饮料与无酒精饮料的混合物：**							**Other fermented beverages (for example, cider, perry, mead); mixtures of fermented beverages and mixtures of fermented beverages and non-alcoholic beverages, not elsewhere specified or included:**
		其他发酵饮料（例如，苹果酒、梨酒、蜂蜜酒）；其他税号未列名的发酵饮料的混合物及发酵饮料与无酒精饮料的混合物:							Other fermented beverages (for example, cider, perry, mead); mixtures of fermented beverages and mixtures of fermented beverages and non-alcoholic beverages, not elsewhere specified or included:

序号 No.	税则号列 Tariff Line	货品名称	最惠国税率 MFN(%)	协定税率 Agreement(%)		特惠税率 S.P.(%)		普通税率 Gen.(%)	Article Description
1306	2206.0010	---黄酒	40	0 8 22.2	东盟ASEAN,智利CL,新加坡SG,新西兰NZ,香港HK,澳门MO 哥斯达黎加CR 秘鲁PE	0	最不发达35国LDC35	180	---Chinese rice wine
1307	2206.0090	---其他	40	0 8 22.2	东盟ASEAN,智利CL,新加坡SG,新西兰NZ,香港HK,澳门MO 哥斯达黎加CR 秘鲁PE	0	最不发达35国LDC35	180	---Other
	22.07	**未改性乙醇，按容量计酒精浓度在80%及以上；任何浓度的改性乙醇及其他酒精：**							**Undenatured ethyl alcohol of an alcoholic strength by volume of 80% vol or higher; ethyl alcohol and other spirits, denatured, of any strength:**
1308	2207.1000	-未改性乙醇，按容量计酒精浓度在80%及以上	40	0 8 20	东盟ASEAN,智利CL,巴基斯坦PK,新加坡SG,新西兰NZ,澳门MO 哥斯达黎加CR 秘鲁PE	0	最不发达35国LDC35	100	-Undenatured ethyl alcohol of an alcoholic strength by volume of 80% vol or higher
1309	2207.2000	-任何浓度的改性乙醇及其他酒精	30 △5	0 3 6	东盟ASEAN,巴基斯坦PK,新加坡SG,新西兰NZ,秘鲁PE 智利CL 哥斯达黎加CR	0	最不发达35国LDC35	80	-Ethyl alcohol and other spirits, denatured, of any strength
	22.08	**未改性乙醇，按容量计酒精浓度在80%以下；蒸馏酒、利口酒及其他酒精饮料：**							**Undenaturated ethyl alcohol of an alcoholic strength by volume of less than 80% vol; spirits, liqueurs and other spirituous beverages:**
1310	2208.2000	-蒸馏葡萄酒制得的烈性酒	10	0 1 5	东盟ASEAN,新加坡SG,新西兰NZ,哥斯达黎加CR 智利CL 巴基斯坦PK,秘鲁PE	0	最不发达35国LDC35,最不发达4国LDC4	180	-Spirits obtained by distilling grape wine or grape marc
1311	2208.3000	-威士忌酒	10	0 1 5	东盟ASEAN,新加坡SG,新西兰NZ,哥斯达黎加CR 智利CL 巴基斯坦PK,秘鲁PE	0	最不发达35国LDC35,最不发达4国LDC4	180	-Whiskies
1312	2208.4000	-朗姆酒及蒸馏已发酵甘蔗产品制得的其他烈性酒	10	0 5	东盟ASEAN,智利CL,新加坡SG,新西兰NZ,秘鲁PE,哥斯达黎加CR 巴基斯坦PK	0	最不发达35国LDC35,最不发达4国LDC4	180	-Rum and other spirit obtained by distilling fermented sugarcane products

序号 No.	税则号列 Tariff Line	货品名称	最惠国税率 MFN(%)	协定税率 Agreement(%)		特惠税率 S.P.(%)		普通税率 Gen.(%)	Article Description
1313	2208.5000	-杜松子酒	10	0 5	东盟ASEAN,智利CL,新加坡SG,新西兰NZ,秘鲁PE,哥斯达黎加CR 巴基斯坦PK	0	最不发达35国LDC35,最不发达4国LDC4	180	-Gin and geneva
1314	2208.6000	-伏特加酒	10	0 5 8.8	东盟ASEAN,智利CL,新加坡SG,新西兰NZ,秘鲁PE,哥斯达黎加CR 巴基斯坦PK 亚太APTA	0	最不发达35国LDC35,最不发达4国LDC4	180	-Vodka
1315	2208.7000	-利口酒及柯迪尔酒	10	0 1 5 8.8	东盟ASEAN,新加坡SG,新西兰NZ,哥斯达黎加CR 智利CL 巴基斯坦PK,秘鲁PE 亚太APTA	0	最不发达35国LDC35,最不发达4国LDC4	180	-Liqueurs and cordials
		-其他:							-Other:
1316	2208.9010	---龙舌兰酒	10	0 5 8.8	东盟ASEAN,智利CL,新加坡SG,新西兰NZ,秘鲁PE,哥斯达黎加CR 巴基斯坦PK 亚太APTA	0	最不发达35国LDC35	180	---Tequila, Mezcal
1317	2208.9020	---白酒	10	0 1 5 8.8	东盟ASEAN,新加坡SG,新西兰NZ,哥斯达黎加CR,澳门MO 智利CL 巴基斯坦PK,秘鲁PE 亚太APTA	0	最不发达35国LDC35,最不发达4国LDC4	180	---Chinese spirits
1318	2208.9090	---其他	10	0 1 5 8.8	东盟ASEAN,新加坡SG,新西兰NZ,哥斯达黎加CR,澳门MO 智利CL 巴基斯坦PK,秘鲁PE 亚太APTA	0	最不发达35国LDC35,最不发达4国LDC4	180	---Other
	22.09	**醋及用醋酸制得的醋代用品:**							**Vinegar and substitutes for vinegar obtained from acetic acid:**
1319	2209.0000	醋及用醋酸制得的醋代用品	20 △15	0 2 4 10	东盟ASEAN,新加坡SG,新西兰NZ,香港HK,澳门MO 智利CL 哥斯达黎加CR 秘鲁PE	0	最不发达35国LDC35	70	Vinegar and substitutes for vinegar obtained from acetic acid

第二十三章
食品工业的残渣及废料；配制的动物饲料

注释：

税号 23.09 包括其他税号未列号的配制动物饲料，这些饲料是由动、植物原料加工而成的，并且已改变了原料的基本特性，但加工过程中的植物废料、植物残渣及副产品除外。

子目注释：

子目 2306.41 所称“低芥子酸油菜子”，是指第十二章子目注释一所定义的油菜子。

Chapter 23
Residues and waste from the food industries; prepared animal fodder

Notes:

Heading No.23.09 includes products of a kind used in animal feeding, not elsewhere specified or included, obtained by processing vegetable or animal materials to such an extent that they have lost the essential characteristics of the original material, other than vegetable waste, vegetable residues and by-products of such processing.

Subheading Note:

For the purposes of subheading No.2306.41, the expression “low erucic acid rape or colza seeds” means seeds as defined in Subheading Note 1 to Chapter 12.

序号 No.	税则号列 Tariff Line	货品名称	最惠国税率 MFN(%)	协定税率 Agreement(%)		特惠税率 S.P.(%)		普通税率 Gen.(%)	Article Description
	23.01	**不适于供人食用的肉、杂碎、鱼、甲壳动物、软体动物或其他水生无脊椎动物的渣粉及团粒；油渣：**							**Flours, meals and pellets, of meat or meat offal, of fish or of crustaceans, molluscs or other aquatic invertebrates, unfit, for human consumption; greaves:**
		-肉、杂碎的渣粉及团粒；油渣：							-Flours, meals and pellets, of meat or meat offal; greaves:
		---肉骨粉：							---Flours and meals, of meat bones:
1320	2301.1011	----含牛羊成分的	2	0	东盟ASEAN,智利CL,巴基斯坦PK,新西兰NZ,秘鲁PE,哥斯达黎加CR	0	最不发达35国LDC35,最不发达4国LDC4	11	----Of bovine and sheep
1321	2301.1019	----其他	2	0	东盟ASEAN,智利CL,巴基斯坦PK,新西兰NZ,秘鲁PE,哥斯达黎加CR	0	最不发达35国LDC35,最不发达4国LDC4	11	----Other
1322	2301.1020	---油渣	5	0	东盟ASEAN,智利CL,巴基斯坦PK,新西兰NZ,秘鲁PE,哥斯达黎加CR,香港HK	0	最不发达35国LDC35,最不发达4国LDC4	50	---Greaves

序号 No.	税则号列 Tariff Line	货品名称	最惠国税率 MFN(%)	协定税率 Agreement(%)		特惠税率 S.P.(%)		普通税率 Gen.(%)	Article Description
1323	2301.1090	---其他	5	0	东盟ASEAN,智利CL,巴基斯坦PK,新西兰NZ,秘鲁PE,哥斯达黎加CR	0	最不发达35国LDC35,最不发达4国LDC4	30	---Other
		-鱼、甲壳动物、软体动物或其他水生无脊椎动物的渣粉及团粒:							-Flours, meals and pellets, of fish or of crustaceans, molluscs or other aquatic invertebrates:
1324	2301.2010	---饲料用鱼粉	2	0 0.2 1.2	东盟ASEAN,亚太APTA,巴基斯坦PK,新西兰NZ,香港HK 智利CL,秘鲁PE 哥斯达黎加CR	0	最不发达35国LDC35,最不发达4国LDC4	11	---Flours and meals of fish, of a kind used in animal feeding
1325	2301.2090	---其他	5	0 0.5 1.9	东盟ASEAN,亚太APTA,巴基斯坦PK,新西兰NZ,哥斯达黎加CR,香港HK 智利CL 秘鲁PE	0	最不发达35国LDC35,最不发达4国LDC4	30	---Other
	23.02	**谷物或豆类植物在筛、碾或其他加工过程中所产生的糠、麸及其他残渣，不论是否制成团粒:**							**Bran, sharps and other residues, whether or not in the form of pellets, derived from the sifting, milling or other working of cereals or of leguminous plants:**
1326	2302.1000	-玉米的	5	0	东盟ASEAN,智利CL,巴基斯坦PK,新西兰NZ,秘鲁PE,哥斯达黎加CR	0	最不发达35国LDC35,最不发达4国LDC4	30	-Of maize (corn)
1327	2302.3000	-小麦的	3	0	东盟ASEAN,智利CL,巴基斯坦PK,新西兰NZ,秘鲁PE,哥斯达黎加CR	0	最不发达35国LDC35,最不发达4国LDC4	30	-Of wheat
1328	2302.4000	-其他谷物的	5	0	东盟ASEAN,智利CL,巴基斯坦PK,新西兰NZ,秘鲁PE,哥斯达黎加CR	0	最不发达35国LDC35,最不发达4国LDC4	30	-Of other cereals
1329	2302.5000	-豆类植物的	5	0	东盟ASEAN,智利CL,巴基斯坦PK,新西兰NZ,秘鲁PE,哥斯达黎加CR,香港HK	0	最不发达35国LDC35,最不发达4国LDC4	30	-Of leguminous plants

序号 No.	税则号列 Tariff Line	货品名称	最惠国税率 MFN(%)	协定税率 Agreement(%)		特惠税率 S.P.(%)		普通税率 Gen.(%)	Article Description
	23.03	**制造淀粉过程中的残渣及类似的残渣，甜菜渣、甘蔗渣及制糖过程中的其他残渣，酿造及蒸馏过程中的糟粕及残渣，不论是否制成团粒：**							**Residues of starch manufacture and similar residues, beet-pulp, bagasses and other waste of sugar manufacture, brewing or distilling dregs and waste, whether or not in the form of pellets:**
1330	2303.1000	-制造淀粉过程中的残渣及类似的残渣	5	0	东盟ASEAN,智利CL,巴基斯坦PK,新西兰NZ,秘鲁PE,哥斯达黎加CR	0	最不发达35国LDC35,最不发达4国LDC4	30	-Residues of starch manufacture and similar residues
1331	2303.2000	-甜菜渣、甘蔗渣及制糖过程中的其他残渣	5	0	东盟ASEAN,智利CL,巴基斯坦PK,新西兰NZ,秘鲁PE,哥斯达黎加CR	0	最不发达35国LDC35,最不发达4国LDC4	30	-Beet-pulp, bagasses and other waste of sugar manufacture
1332	2303.3000	-酿造及蒸馏过程中的糟粕及残渣	5	0	东盟ASEAN,智利CL,巴基斯坦PK,新西兰NZ,秘鲁PE,哥斯达黎加CR	0	最不发达35国LDC35,最不发达4国LDC4	30	-Brewing or distilling dregs and waste
	23.04	**提炼豆油所得的油渣饼及其他固体残渣，不论是否碾磨或制成团粒：**							**Oil-cake and other solid residues, whether or not ground or in the form ofpellets, resulting from the extraction of soyabean oil:**
1333	2304.0010	---油渣饼	5	0 0.5	东盟ASEAN,亚太APTA,巴基斯坦PK,新西兰NZ,秘鲁PE,哥斯达黎加CR 智利CL	0	最不发达35国LDC35,最不发达4国LDC4	30	---Oil-cake
1334	2304.0090	---其他	5	0	东盟ASEAN,亚太APTA,智利CL,巴基斯坦PK,新西兰NZ,秘鲁PE,哥斯达黎加CR	0	最不发达35国LDC35,最不发达4国LDC4	30	---Other
	23.05	**提炼花生油所得的油渣饼及其他固体残渣，不论是否碾磨或制成团粒：**							**Oil-cake and other solid residues, whether or not ground or in the form of pellets, resulting from the extraction of ground-nut oil:**

序号 No.	税则号列 Tariff Line	货品名称	最惠国税率 MFN(%)	协定税率 Agreement(%)		特惠税率 S.P.(%)		普通税率 Gen.(%)	Article Description
1335	2305.0000	提炼花生油所得的油渣饼及其他固体残渣，不论是否碾磨或制成团粒	5	0	东盟ASEAN,智利CL,巴基斯坦PK,新西兰NZ,秘鲁PE,哥斯达黎加CR	0	最不发达35国LDC35,最不发达4国LDC4	30	Oil-cake and other solid residues, whether or not ground or in the form of pellets, resulting from the extraction of ground-nut oil
	23.06	**税号23.04或23.05以外的提炼植物油脂所得的油渣饼及其他固体残渣，不论是否碾磨或制成团粒：**							**Oil-Cake and other solid residues, whether or not ground or in the form of pellets, resulting from the extraction of vegetable fats or oils, other than those of heading No.23.04 or 23.05:**
1336	2306.1000	-棉子的	5	0	东盟ASEAN,智利CL,巴基斯坦PK,新西兰NZ,秘鲁PE,哥斯达黎加CR	0	最不发达35国LDC35,最不发达4国LDC4	30	-Of cotton seeds
1337	2306.2000	-亚麻子的	5	0	东盟ASEAN,智利CL,巴基斯坦PK,新西兰NZ,秘鲁PE,哥斯达黎加CR	0	最不发达35国LDC35,最不发达4国LDC4,老挝LA	30	-Of linseed
1338	2306.3000	-葵花子的	5	0	东盟ASEAN,智利CL,巴基斯坦PK,新西兰NZ,秘鲁PE,哥斯达黎加CR	0	最不发达35国LDC35,最不发达4国LDC4	30	-Of sunflower seeds
		-油菜子的：							-Of rape or colza seeds:
1339	2306.4100	--低芥子酸的	5	0	东盟ASEAN,智利CL,巴基斯坦PK,新西兰NZ,秘鲁PE,哥斯达黎加CR	0	最不发达35国LDC35	30	--Of low erucic acid rape or colza seeds
1340	2306.4900	--其他	5	0	东盟ASEAN,智利CL,巴基斯坦PK,新西兰NZ,秘鲁PE,哥斯达黎加CR	0	最不发达35国LDC35	30	--Other
1341	2306.5000	-椰子或干椰肉的	5	0 2.5	东盟ASEAN,智利CL,巴基斯坦PK,新西兰NZ,秘鲁PE,哥斯达黎加CR 亚太APTA	0	最不发达35国LDC35,最不发达4国LDC4,柬埔寨KH	30	-Of coconut or copra

序号 No.	税则号列 Tariff Line	货品名称	最惠国税率 MFN(%)	协定税率 Agreement(%)	特惠税率 S.P.(%)	普通税率 Gen.(%)	Article Description
1342	2306.6000	-棕榈果或棕榈仁的	5	0 东盟ASEAN,智利CL,巴基斯坦PK,新西兰NZ,秘鲁PE,哥斯达黎加CR	0 最不发达35国LDC35,最不发达4国LDC4,柬埔寨KH	30	-Of palm nuts or kernels
1343	2306.9000	-其他	5	0 东盟ASEAN,智利CL,巴基斯坦PK,新西兰NZ,秘鲁PE,哥斯达黎加CR	0 最不发达35国LDC35,最不发达4国LDC4,老挝LA	30	-Other
	23.07	**葡萄酒渣；粗酒石：**					**Wine lees; argol:**
1344	2307.0000	葡萄酒渣；粗酒石	5	0 东盟ASEAN,智利CL,巴基斯坦PK,新西兰NZ,秘鲁PE,哥斯达黎加CR	0 最不发达35国LDC35,最不发达4国LDC4	30	Wine lees; argol
	23.08	**动物饲料用的其他税号未列名的植物原料、废料、残渣及副产品，不论是否制成团粒：**					**Vegetable materials and vegetable waste, vegetable residues and by-products, whether or not in the form of pellets, of a kind used in animal feeding, not elsewhere specified or included:**
1345	2308.0000	动物饲料用的其他税号未列名的植物原料、废料、残渣及副产品，不论是否制成团粒	5	0 东盟ASEAN,智利CL,巴基斯坦PK,新西兰NZ,秘鲁PE,哥斯达黎加CR	0 最不发达35国LDC35	35	Vegetable materials and vegetable waste, vegetable residues and by-products, whether or not in the form of pellets, of a kind used in animal feeding, not elsewhere specified or included
	23.09	**配制的动物饲料：**					**Preparations of a kind used in animal feeding:**
		-零售包装的狗食或猫食：					-Dog or cat food, put up for retail sale:
1346	2309.1010	---罐头	15	0 东盟ASEAN,新加坡SG,新西兰NZ,香港HK,澳门MO 1.5 智利CL 3 哥斯达黎加CR 7.5 秘鲁PE 12 巴基斯坦PK	0 最不发达35国LDC35	90	---In airtight containers
1347	2309.1090	---其他	15	0 东盟ASEAN,新加坡SG,新西兰NZ,香港HK,澳门MO 1.5 智利CL 3 哥斯达黎加CR 7.5 秘鲁PE 12 巴基斯坦PK	0 最不发达35国LDC35	90	---Other

序号 No.	税则号列 Tariff Line	货品名称	最惠国税率 MFN(%)	协定税率 Agreement(%)		特惠税率 S.P.(%)		普通税率 Gen.(%)	Article Description
		-其他:							-Other:
1348	2309.9010	---制成的饲料添加剂	5	0 0.5 2.5	东盟ASEAN,巴基斯坦PK,新西兰NZ,哥斯达黎加CR,香港HK 智利CL 亚太APTA,秘鲁PE	0	最不发达35国LDC35,最不发达4国LDC4	14	---Preparations for use in making the complete feeds or supplementary feeds
1349	2309.9090	---其他	6.5 △4	0 0.7 3.2 3.3	东盟ASEAN,巴基斯坦PK,新西兰NZ,哥斯达黎加CR,香港HK,澳门MO 智利CL 秘鲁PE 亚太APTA	0	最不发达35国LDC35,最不发达4国LDC4	14	---Other

第二十四章
烟草及烟草
代用品的制品

Chapter 24
Tobacco and manufactured tobacco substitutes

注释:

本章不包括药用卷烟（第三十章）。

子目注释:

子目 2403.11 所称“水烟料”，是指由烟草和甘油混合而成用水烟筒吸用的烟草，不论是否含有芳香油及提取物、糖蜜或糖，也不论是否用水果调味，但供在水烟筒中吸用的非烟草产品不归入该子目。

Notes:

This Chapter does not cover medicinal cigarettes (Chapter 30).

Subheading note:

For the purposes of subheading 2403.11, the expression “water pipe tobacco” means tobacco intended for smoking in a water pipe and which consists of a mixture of tobacco and glycerol, whether or not containing aromatic oils and extracts, molasses or sugar, and whether or not flavoured with fruit. However, tobacco-free products intended for smoking in a water pipe are excluded from this subheading.

序号 No.	税则号列 Tariff Line	货品名称	最惠国税率 MFN(%)	协定税率 Agreement(%)	特惠税率 S.P.(%)	普通税率 Gen.(%)	Article Description
	24.01	**烟草；烟草废料：**					**Unmanufactured tobacco; tobacco refuse:**
		-未去梗的烟草：					-Tobacco, not stemmed/ stripped:
1350	2401.1010	---烤烟	10	0 新西兰NZ 1 智利CL 9.4 亚太APTA,巴基斯坦PK		70	---Flue-cured
1351	2401.1090	---其他	10	0 新西兰NZ 1 智利CL		70	---Other
		-部分或全部去梗的烟草：					-Tobacco, partly or wholly stemmed/ stripped:
1352	2401.2010	---烤烟	10	0 新西兰NZ 1 智利CL		70	---Flue-cured
1353	2401.2090	---其他	10	0 新西兰NZ 1 智利CL		70	---Other
1354	2401.3000	-烟草废料	10	0 新西兰NZ 1 智利CL 5 秘鲁PE	0 最不发达35国LDC35,最不发达4国LDC4	70	-Tobacco refuse
	24.02	**烟草或烟草代用品制成的雪茄烟及卷烟：**					**Cigars, cheroots, cigarillos and cigarettes, of tobacco or of tobacco substitutes:**
1355	2402.1000	-烟草制的雪茄烟	25	0 新西兰NZ 2.5 智利CL		180	-Cigars, cheroots and cigarillos, containing tobacco
1356	2402.2000	-烟草制的卷烟	25	0 新西兰NZ 2.5 智利CL		180	-Cigarettes containing tobacco
1357	2402.9000	-其他	25	0 新西兰NZ 2.5 智利CL		180	-Other

序号 No.	税则号列 Tariff Line	货品名称	最惠国 税 率 MFN(%)	协定税率 Agreement(%)	特惠税率 S.P.(%)	普通 税率 Gen.(%)	Article Description
	24.03	**其他烟草及烟草代用品的制品；“均化”或“再造”烟草；烟草精汁：**					**Other manufactured tobacco and manufactured tobacco substitutes; “homogenized” or “reconstituted” tobacco; tobacco extracts and essences:**
		-供吸用的烟草，不论是否含有任何比例的烟草代用品：					-Smoking tobacco, whether or not containing tobacco substitutes in any proportion:
1358	2403.1100	--本章子目注释所述的水烟料	57	0 新西兰NZ 5.7 智利CL 50 亚太APTA,巴基斯坦PK		180	--Water pipe tobacco specified in Subheading note to this Chapter
1359	2403.1900	--其他	57	0 新西兰NZ 5.7 智利CL 50 亚太APTA,巴基斯坦PK		180	--Other
		-其他：					-Other:
1360	2403.9100	--“均化”或“再造”烟草	57	0 新西兰NZ 5.7 智利CL		180	--“Homogenized” or “reconstituted” tobacco
	ex24039100	再造烟草	△40				Reconstituted tobacco
1361	2403.9900	--其他	57	0 新西兰NZ 5.7 智利CL		180	--Other

第五类
矿　产　品

第二十五章
盐；硫磺；泥土及石料；石膏料、石灰及水泥

注释：

一、除条文及注释四另有规定的以外，本章各税号只包括原产状态的矿产品，或只经过洗涤（包括用化学物质清除杂质而未改变产品结构的）、破碎、磨碎、研粉、淘洗、筛分以及用浮选、磁选和其他机械物理方法（不包括结晶法）精选过的货品，但不得经过焙烧、煅烧、混合或超过税目所列的加工范围。

本章产品可含有添加的抗尘剂，但所加剂料并不使原产品改变其一般用途而适合于某些特殊用途。

二、本章不包括：

（一）升华硫磺、沉淀硫磺及胶态硫磺（税号 28.02）；

（二）土色料，按重量计三氧化二铁含量在 70%及以上（税号 28.21）；

（三）第三十章的药品及其他产品；

（四）芳香料制品及化妆盥洗品（第三十三章）；

（五）长方砌石、路缘石、扁平石（税号 68.01）、镶嵌石或类似石料（税号 68.02）及铺屋顶、饰墙面或防潮用的板岩（税号 68.03）；

（六）宝石或半宝石（税号 71.02 或 71.03）；

（七）每颗重量不低于 2.5 克的氯化钠或氧化镁培养晶体（光学元件除外）（税号 38.24）；氯化钠或氧化镁制的光学元件（税号 90.01）；

（八）台球用粉块（税号 95.04）；

（九）书写或绘画用粉笔及裁缝划粉（税号 96.09）。

三、既可归入税号 25.17 又可归入本章其他税号的产品，应归入税号 25.17。

四、税号 25.30 主要包括：未膨胀的蛭石、珍珠岩及绿

SECTION V
MINERAL PRODUCTS

Chapter 25
Salt; sulphur; earths and stone; plastering materials, lime and cement

Notes:

1. Except where their context or Note 4 to this Chapter otherwise requires, the headings of this Chapter cover only products which are in the crude state or which have been washed (even with chemical substances eliminating the impurities without changing the structure of the product), crushed, ground, powdered, levigated, sifted, screened, concentrated by flotation, magnetic separation or other mechanical or physical processes (except crystallization), but not products which have been roasted, calcined, obtained by mixing or subjected to processing be yond that mentioned in each heading.

   The products of this Chapter may contain an added antidusting agent, provided that such addition does not render the product particularly suitable for specific use rather than for general use.

2. This Chapter does not cover:

   (a) Sublimed sulphur, precipitated sulphur or colloidal sulphur (heading No.28.02);

   (b) Earth colours containing 70% or more by weight of combined iron evaluated as Fe_2O_3 (heading No.28.21);

   (c) Medicaments or other products of Chapter 30;

   (d) Perfumery, cosmetic or toilet preparations (Chapter 33);

   (e) Setts, curbstones or flagstones (heading No.68.01); mosaic cubes or the like (heading No.68.02); roofing, facing or damp course slates (heading No.68.03);

   (f) Precious or semi-precious stones (heading No.71.02 or 71.03);

   (g) Cultured crystals (other than optical elements) weighing not less than 2.5g each, of sodium chloride or of magnesium oxide, of heading No.38.24;optical elements of sodium chloride or of magnesium oxide (heading No.90.01);

   (h) Billiard chalks (heading No.95.04); or

   (i) Writing or drawing chalks or tailors' chalks (heading No, 96.09).

3. Any products classifiable in heading No.25.17 and any other heading of this Chapter are to be classified in heading No.25.17.

4. Heading No.25.30 applies, *inter alia*, to: vermiculite,

泥石；不论是否煅烧或混合的土色料；天然云母氧化铁；海泡石（不论是否磨光成块）；琥珀；模制后未经进一步加工的片、条、杆或类似形状的粘聚海泡石及粘聚琥珀；黑玉；菱锶矿（不论是否煅烧），但不包括氧化锶；破碎陶器；砖或混凝土的碎块。

perlite and chlorites, unexpanded; earth colours, whether or not calcined or mixed together; natural micaceous iron oxides; meerschaum (whether or not in polished pieces); amber; agglomerated meerschaum and agglomerated amber, in plates, rods, sticks or similar forms, not worked after moulding; jet; strontianite (whether or not calcined), other than strontium oxide; broken pieces of pottery, brick or concrete.

序号 No.	税则号列 Tariff Line	货品名称	最惠国税率 MFN(%)	协定税率 Agreement(%)		特惠税率 S.P.(%)		普通税率 Gen.(%)	Article Description
	25.01	**盐（包括精制盐及变性盐）及纯氯化钠，不论是否为水溶液，也不论是否添加抗结块剂或松散剂；海水：**							**Salt (including table salt and denatured salt) and pure sodium chloride, whether or not in aqueous solution or containing added anticaking or free-flowing agents; sea water:**
		---盐：							---Salt:
1362	2501.0011	----食用盐	0			0	最不发达35国LDC35,最不发达4国LDC4	0	----Edible salt
1363	2501.0019	----其他	0			0	最不发达35国LDC35,最不发达4国LDC4	0	----Other
1364	2501.0020	---纯氯化钠	3	0	东盟ASEAN,智利CL,巴基斯坦PK,新西兰NZ,秘鲁PE,哥斯达黎加CR	0	最不发达35国LDC35,最不发达4国LDC4,老挝LA	35	---Pure sodium chloride
1365	2501.0030	---海水	0			0	最不发达35国LDC35,最不发达4国LDC4	0	---Sea water
	25.02	**未焙烧的黄铁矿：**							**Unroasted iron pyrites:**
1366	2502.0000	未焙烧的黄铁矿	3 △1	0	东盟ASEAN,智利CL,巴基斯坦PK,新西兰NZ,秘鲁PE,哥斯达黎加CR	0	最不发达35国LDC35,最不发达4国LDC4	20	Unroasted iron pyrite

序号 No.	税则号列 Tariff Line	货品名称	最惠国税率 MFN(%)	协定税率 Agreement(%)		特惠税率 S.P.(%)		普通税率 Gen.(%)	Article Description
	25.03	**各种硫磺，但升华硫磺、沉淀硫磺及胶态硫磺除外：**							**Sulphur of all kinds, other than sublimed sulphur, precipitated sulphur and colloidal sulphur:**
1367	2503.0000	各种硫磺，但升华硫磺、沉淀硫磺及胶态硫磺除外	3 △1	0	东盟ASEAN,智利CL,巴基斯坦PK,新西兰NZ,秘鲁PE,哥斯达黎加CR	0	最不发达35国LDC35	17	Sulphur of all kinds, other than sublimed sulphur, precipitated sulphur and colloidal sulphur
	25.04	**天然石墨：**							**Natural graphite:**
		-粉末或粉片：							-In powder or in flakes:
1368	2504.1010	---磷片	3 △1	0	东盟ASEAN,智利CL,巴基斯坦PK,新西兰NZ,秘鲁PE,哥斯达黎加CR	0	最不发达35国LDC35,最不发达4国LDC4	30	---In flakes
		---其他:							---Other:
1369	2504.1091	----球化石墨	3	0	东盟ASEAN,智利CL,巴基斯坦PK,新西兰NZ,秘鲁PE,哥斯达黎加CR	0	最不发达35国LDC35,最不发达4国LDC4	30	----Spherical Graphite
1370	2504.1099	----其他	3	0	东盟ASEAN,智利CL,巴基斯坦PK,新西兰NZ,秘鲁PE,哥斯达黎加CR	0	最不发达35国LDC35,最不发达4国LDC4	30	----Other
1371	2504.9000	-其他	3	0	东盟ASEAN,智利CL,巴基斯坦PK,新西兰NZ,秘鲁PE,哥斯达黎加CR	0	最不发达35国LDC35,最不发达4国LDC4	30	-Other
	25.05	**各种天然砂，不论是否着色，但第二十六章的含金属矿砂除外：**							**Natural sands of all kinds, whether or not coloured, other than metal-bearing sands of Chapter26:**
1372	2505.1000	-硅砂及石英砂	3 △1	0	东盟ASEAN,智利CL,巴基斯坦PK,新西兰NZ,秘鲁PE,哥斯达黎加CR	0	最不发达35国LDC35,最不发达4国LDC4	40	-Silica sands and quartz sands
1373	2505.9000	-其他	3 △1	0	东盟ASEAN,智利CL,巴基斯坦PK,新西兰NZ,秘鲁PE,哥斯达黎加CR	0	最不发达35国LDC35,最不发达4国LDC4	40	-Other

序号 No.	税则号列 Tariff Line	货品名称	最惠国税率 MFN(%)	协定税率 Agreement(%)		特惠税率 S.P.(%)		普通税率 Gen.(%)	Article Description
	25.06	**石英（天然砂除外）；石英岩，不论是否粗加修整或仅用锯或其他方法切割成矩形（包括正方形）的板、块：**							**Quartz (other than natural sands); quartzite, whether or not roughly trimmed or merely cut, by sawing or otherwise, into blocks or slabs of a rectangular (including square) shape:**
1374	2506.1000	-石英	3 △1	0	东盟ASEAN,智利CL,巴基斯坦PK,新西兰NZ,秘鲁PE,哥斯达黎加CR	0	最不发达35国LDC35,最不发达4国LDC4	40	-Quartz
1375	2506.2000	-石英岩	3 △1	0	东盟ASEAN,智利CL,巴基斯坦PK,新西兰NZ,秘鲁PE,哥斯达黎加CR	0	最不发达35国LDC35,最不发达4国LDC4	40	-Quartzite
	25.07	**高岭土及类似土，不论是否煅烧：**							**Kaolin and other kaolinic clays, whether or not calcined:**
		高岭土及类似土，不论是否煅烧:							Kaolin and other kaolinic clays, whether or not calcined:
1376	2507.0010	---高岭土	3 △1	0	东盟ASEAN,智利CL,巴基斯坦PK,新西兰NZ,秘鲁PE,哥斯达黎加CR	0	最不发达35国LDC35,最不发达4国LDC4	50	---Kaolin
1377	2507.0090	---其他	3 △1	0	东盟ASEAN,智利CL,巴基斯坦PK,新西兰NZ,秘鲁PE,哥斯达黎加CR	0	最不发达35国LDC35,最不发达4国LDC4	50	---Other
	25.08	**其他粘土（不包括税号68.06的膨胀粘土）、红柱石、蓝晶石及硅线石，不论是否煅烧；富铝红柱石；火泥及第纳斯土：**							**Other clays (not including expanded clays of heading No.68.06), andalusite, kyanite and sillimanite, whether or not calcined; mullite; chamotte or dinas earths:**
1378	2508.1000	-膨润土	3	0	东盟ASEAN,智利CL,巴基斯坦PK,新西兰NZ,秘鲁PE,哥斯达黎加CR	0	最不发达35国LDC35,最不发达4国LDC4	50	-Bentonite

序号 No.	税则号列 Tariff Line	货品名称	最惠国税率 MFN(%)	协定税率 Agreement(%)		特惠税率 S.P.(%)		普通税率 Gen.(%)	Article Description
1379	2508.3000	-耐火粘土	3 △1	0	东盟ASEAN,智利CL,巴基斯坦PK,新西兰NZ,秘鲁PE,哥斯达黎加CR	0	最不发达35国LDC35,最不发达4国LDC4	20	-Fire-clay
1380	2508.4000	-其他粘土	3	0	东盟ASEAN,智利CL,巴基斯坦PK,新西兰NZ,秘鲁PE,哥斯达黎加CR	0	最不发达35国LDC35,最不发达4国LDC4	50	-Other clays
1381	2508.5000	-红柱石、蓝晶石及硅线石	3	0	东盟ASEAN,智利CL,巴基斯坦PK,新西兰NZ,秘鲁PE,哥斯达黎加CR	0	最不发达35国LDC35,最不发达4国LDC4	40	-Andalusite, kyanite and sillimanite
1382	2508.6000	-富铝红柱石	3	0	东盟ASEAN,智利CL,巴基斯坦PK,新西兰NZ,秘鲁PE,哥斯达黎加CR	0	最不发达35国LDC35,最不发达4国LDC4	40	-Mullite
1383	2508.7000	-火泥及第纳斯土	3	0	东盟ASEAN,智利CL,巴基斯坦PK,新西兰NZ,秘鲁PE,哥斯达黎加CR	0	最不发达35国LDC35,最不发达4国LDC4	20	-Chamotte or dinas earths
	25.09	**白垩:**							**Chalk:**
1384	2509.0000	白垩	3	0	东盟ASEAN,智利CL,巴基斯坦PK,新西兰NZ,秘鲁PE,哥斯达黎加CR	0	最不发达35国LDC35,最不发达4国LDC4	45	Chalk
	25.10	**天然磷酸钙、天然磷酸铝钙及磷酸盐白垩:**							**Natural calcium phosphates, natural aluminium calcium phosphates and phosphatic chalk:**
		-未碾磨:							-Unground:
1385	2510.1010	---磷灰石	3 △0	0	东盟ASEAN,智利CL,巴基斯坦PK,新西兰NZ,秘鲁PE,哥斯达黎加CR	0	最不发达35国LDC35,最不发达4国LDC4	11	---Apatite
1386	2510.1090	---其他	3	0	东盟ASEAN,智利CL,巴基斯坦PK,新西兰NZ,秘鲁PE,哥斯达黎加CR	0	最不发达35国LDC35,最不发达4国LDC4	20	---Other
		-已碾磨:							-Ground:

序号 No.	税则号列 Tariff Line	货品名称	最惠国税率 MFN(%)		协定税率 Agreement(%)		特惠税率 S.P.(%)	普通税率 Gen.(%)	Article Description
1387	2510.2010	---磷灰石	3 △0	0	东盟ASEAN,智利CL,巴基斯坦PK,新西兰NZ,秘鲁PE,哥斯达黎加CR	0	最不发达35国LDC35,最不发达4国LDC4	11	---Apatite
1388	2510.2090	---其他	3	0	东盟ASEAN,智利CL,巴基斯坦PK,新西兰NZ,秘鲁PE,哥斯达黎加CR	0	最不发达35国LDC35,最不发达4国LDC4	20	---Other
	25.11	**天然硫酸钡（重晶石）;天然碳酸钡（毒重石），不论是否煅烧，但税号28.16的氧化钡除外:**							**Natural barium sulphate (barytes);natural barium carbonate (witherite), whether or not calcined, other than barium oxide of heading No.28.16:**
1389	2511.1000	-天然硫酸钡（重晶石）	3 △1	0	东盟ASEAN,智利CL,巴基斯坦PK,新西兰NZ,秘鲁PE,哥斯达黎加CR	0	最不发达35国LDC35	45	-Natural barium sulphate (barytes)
1390	2511.2000	-天然碳酸钡（毒重石）	3	0	东盟ASEAN,智利CL,巴基斯坦PK,新西兰NZ,秘鲁PE,哥斯达黎加CR	0	最不发达35国LDC35	45	-Natural barium carbonate (witherite)
	25.12	**硅质化石粗粉（例如各种硅藻土）及类似的硅质土，不论是否煅烧，其表观比重不超过1:**							**Siliceous fossil meals (for example, kieselguhr, tripolite and diatomite) and similar siliceous earths, whether or not calcined, of an apparent specific gravity of 1 or less:**
		硅质化石粗粉（例如各种硅藻土）及类似的硅质土，不论是否煅烧，其表观比重不超过1:							Siliceous fossil meals (for example, kieselguhr, tripolite and diatomite) and similar siliceous earths, whether or not calcined, of an apparent specific gravity of 1or less:
1391	2512.0010	---硅藻土	3	0	东盟ASEAN,智利CL,巴基斯坦PK,新西兰NZ,秘鲁PE,哥斯达黎加CR	0	最不发达35国LDC35,最不发达4国LDC4	40	---Kieselguhr
1392	2512.0090	---其他	3	0	东盟ASEAN,智利CL,巴基斯坦PK,新西兰NZ,秘鲁PE,哥斯达黎加CR	0	最不发达35国LDC35,最不发达4国LDC4	40	---Other

序号 No.	税则号列 Tariff Line	货品名称	最惠国税率 MFN(%)	协定税率 Agreement(%)		特惠税率 S.P.(%)		普通税率 Gen.(%)	Article Description
	25.13	**浮石;刚玉岩;天然刚玉砂;天然石榴石及其他天然磨料,不论是否热处理:**							**Pumice stone; emery; natural corundum, natural garnet and other natural abrasives, whether or not heat-treated:**
1393	2513.1000	-浮石	3	0	东盟ASEAN,智利CL,巴基斯坦PK,新西兰NZ,秘鲁PE,哥斯达黎加CR	0	最不发达35国LDC35,最不发达4国LDC4	35	-Pumice stone
1394	2513.2000	-刚玉岩、天然刚玉砂、天然石榴石及其他天然磨料	3	0	东盟ASEAN,智利CL,巴基斯坦PK,新西兰NZ,秘鲁PE,哥斯达黎加CR	0	最不发达35国LDC35,最不发达4国LDC4	17	-Emery, natural corundum, natural garnet and other natural abrasives
	25.14	**板岩,不论是否粗加修整或仅用锯或其他方法切割成矩形(包括正方形)的板、块:**							**Slate, whether or not roughly trimmed or merely cut, by sawing or otherwise, into blocks or slabs of a rectangular (including square) shape:**
1395	2514.0000	板岩,不论是否粗加修整或仅用锯或其他方法切割成矩形(包括正方形)的板、块	3	0	东盟ASEAN,智利CL,巴基斯坦PK,新西兰NZ,秘鲁PE,哥斯达黎加CR	0	最不发达35国LDC35,最不发达4国LDC4	50	Slate, whether or not roughly trimmed or merely cut, by sawing or otherwise, into blocks or slabs of a rectangular (including square) shape
	25.15	**大理石、石灰华及其他石灰质碑用或建筑用石,表观比重为2.5及以上,蜡石,不论是否粗加修整或仅用锯或其他方法切割成矩形(包括正方形)的板、块:**							**Marble, travertine, ecaussine and other calcareous monumental or building stone of an apparent specific gravity of 2.5 or more, and alabaster, whether or not roughly trimmed or merely cut, by sawing or otherwise, into blocks or slabs of a rectangular (including square) shape:**
		-大理石及石灰华:							-Marble and travertine:
1396	2515.1100	--原状或粗加修整	4 △0	0	东盟ASEAN,智利CL,巴基斯坦PK,新西兰NZ,秘鲁PE,哥斯达黎加CR	0	最不发达35国LDC35,最不发达4国LDC4	80	--Crude or roughly trimmed

序号 No.	税则号列 Tariff Line	货品名称	最惠国税率 MFN(%)	协定税率 Agreement(%)		特惠税率 S.P.(%)		普通税率 Gen.(%)	Article Description
1397	2515.1200	--用锯或其他方法切割成矩形，包括正方形	4 △0	0	东盟ASEAN,智利CL,巴基斯坦PK,新西兰NZ,秘鲁PE,哥斯达黎加CR	0	最不发达35国LDC35,最不发达4国LDC4	80	--Merely cut, by sawing or otherwise, into blocks or slabs of a rectangular (including square) shape
1398	2515.2000	-其他石灰质碑用或建筑用石蜡石	3 △0	0	东盟ASEAN,智利CL,巴基斯坦PK,新西兰NZ,秘鲁PE,哥斯达黎加CR	0	最不发达35国LDC35,最不发达4国LDC4	50	-Ecaussine and other calcareous monumental or building stone; alabaster
	25.16	**花岗岩、斑岩、玄武岩、砂岩以及其他碑用或建筑用石，不论是否粗加修整或仅用锯或其他方法切割成矩形（包括正方形）的板、块:**							**Granite, porphyry, basalt, sandstone and other monumental or building stone, whether or not roughly trimmed or merely cut, by sawing or otherwise, into blocks or slabs of a rectangular (including square) shape:**
		-花岗岩:							-Granite:
1399	2516.1100	--原状或粗加修整	4 △0	0 2	东盟ASEAN,智利CL,巴基斯坦PK,新西兰NZ,秘鲁PE,哥斯达黎加CR 亚太APTA	0	最不发达35国LDC35,最不发达4国LDC4	50	--Crude or roughly trimmed
1400	2516.1200	--仅用锯或其他方法切割成矩形，包括正方形	4 △0	0 2	东盟ASEAN,智利CL,巴基斯坦PK,新西兰NZ,秘鲁PE,哥斯达黎加CR 亚太APTA	0	最不发达35国LDC35,最不发达4国LDC4	50	--Merely cut, by sawing or otherwise, into blocks or slabs of a rectangular (including square) shape
1401	2516.2000	-砂岩	3 △0	0 2.1	东盟ASEAN,智利CL,巴基斯坦PK,新西兰NZ,秘鲁PE,哥斯达黎加CR 亚太APTA	0	最不发达35国LDC35,最不发达4国LDC4	50	-Sandstone
1402	2516.9000	-其他碑用或建筑用石	3 △0	0 2.1	东盟ASEAN,智利CL,巴基斯坦PK,新西兰NZ,秘鲁PE,哥斯达黎加CR 亚太APTA	0	最不发达35国LDC35,最不发达4国LDC4	50	-Other monumental or building stone

序号 No.	税则号列 Tariff Line	货品名称	最惠国税率 MFN(%)	协定税率 Agreement(%)		特惠税率 S.P.(%)		普通税率 Gen.(%)	Article Description
	25.17	**通常作混凝土粒料、铺路、铁道路基或其他路基用的卵石、砾石及碎石，圆石子及燧石，不论是否热处理;矿渣、浮渣及类似的工业残渣，不论是否混有本税号第一部分所列的材料;沥青碎石;税号25.15、25.16所列各种石料的碎粒、碎屑及粉末，不论是否热处理:**							**Pebbles, gravel, broken or crushed stone, of a kind commonly used for concrete aggregates, for road metalling or for railway or other ballast, shingle and flint, whether or not heat-treated; macadam of slag, dross or similar industrial waste, whether or not incorporating the materials cited in the first part of the heading; tarred macadam; granules, chippings and powder, of stones of heading No.25.15 or 25.16, whether or not heat-treated:**
1403	2517.1000	-通常作混凝土粒料、铺路、铁道路基或其他路基用的卵石、砾石及碎石，圆石子及燧石，不论是否热处理	4	0	东盟ASEAN,智利CL,巴基斯坦PK,新西兰NZ,秘鲁PE,哥斯达黎加CR	0	最不发达35国LDC35,最不发达4国LDC4	50	-Pebbles, gravel, broken or crushed stone, of a kind commonly used for concrete aggregates, for road metalling or for railway or other ballast, shingle and flint, whether or not bead-treated
1404	2517.2000	-矿渣、浮渣及类似的工业残渣，不论是否混有子目号2517.10所列的材料	3	0	东盟ASEAN,智利CL,巴基斯坦PK,新西兰NZ,秘鲁PE,哥斯达黎加CR	0	最不发达35国LDC35,最不发达4国LDC4	50	-Macadam of slag, dross or similar industrial waste, whether or not incorporating the materials cited in subheading No.2517.10
1405	2517.3000	-沥青碎石	3	0	东盟ASEAN,智利CL,巴基斯坦PK,新西兰NZ,秘鲁PE,哥斯达黎加CR	0	最不发达35国LDC35,最不发达4国LDC4	50	-Tarred macadam
		-税号25.15及25.16所列各种石料的碎粒、碎屑及粉末，不论是否热处理:							-Granules, chippings and powder, of stones of heading No.25.15 or 25.16, whether or not heat-treated:
1406	2517.4100	--大理石的	3	0	东盟ASEAN,智利CL,巴基斯坦PK,新西兰NZ,秘鲁PE,哥斯达黎加CR	0	最不发达35国LDC35,最不发达4国LDC4	50	--Of marble

序号 No.	税则号列 Tariff Line	货品名称	最惠国税率 MFN(%)	协定税率 Agreement(%)		特惠税率 S.P.(%)		普通税率 Gen.(%)	Article Description
1407	2517.4900	--其他	3	0	东盟ASEAN,智利CL,巴基斯坦PK,新西兰NZ,秘鲁PE,哥斯达黎加CR	0	最不发达35国LDC35,最不发达4国LDC4	50	--Other
	25.18	**白云石，不论是否煅烧或烧结、粗加修整或仅用锯或其他方法切割成矩形（包括正方形）的板、块；夯混白云石：**							**Dolomite, whether or not calcined; including dolomite roughly trimmed or merely cut, by sawing or otherwise, into blocks or slabs of a rectangular (including square) shape; dolomite ramming mix:**
1408	2518.1000	-未煅烧或烧结的白云石	3 △1	0	东盟ASEAN,智利CL,巴基斯坦PK,新西兰NZ,秘鲁PE,哥斯达黎加CR	0	最不发达35国LDC35,最不发达4国LDC4	40	-Dolomite, not calcinecd or sintered
1409	2518.2000	-已煅烧或烧结的白云石	3 △1	0	东盟ASEAN,智利CL,巴基斯坦PK,新西兰NZ,秘鲁PE,哥斯达黎加CR	0	最不发达35国LDC35,最不发达4国LDC4	40	-Calcined or sintered dolomite
1410	2518.3000	-夯混白云石	3 △1	0	东盟ASEAN,智利CL,巴基斯坦PK,新西兰NZ,秘鲁PE,哥斯达黎加CR	0	最不发达35国LDC35,最不发达4国LDC4	40	-Dolomite ramming mix
	25.19	**天然碳酸镁（菱镁矿）;熔凝镁氧矿;烧结镁氧矿，不论烧结前是否加入少量其他氧化物;其他氧化镁，不论是否纯净:**							**Natural magnesium carbonate (magnesite); fused magnesia; dead-burned (sintered) magnesia, whether or not containing small quantities of other oxides added before sintering; other magnesium oxide, whether or not pure:**
1411	2519.1000	-天然碳酸镁（菱镁矿）	3 △1	0	东盟ASEAN,智利CL,巴基斯坦PK,新西兰NZ,秘鲁PE,哥斯达黎加CR	0	最不发达35国LDC35,最不发达4国LDC4	40	-Natural magnesium carbonate (magnesite)
		-其他:							-Other:

序号 No.	税则号列 Tariff Line	货品名称	最惠国 税率 MFN(%)	协定税率 Agreement(%)		特惠税率 S.P.(%)		普通 税率 Gen.(%)	Article Description
1412	2519.9010	---熔凝镁氧矿	3 △1	0	东盟ASEAN,智利CL,巴基斯坦PK,新西兰NZ,秘鲁PE,哥斯达黎加CR	0	最不发达35国LDC35,最不发达4国LDC4	40	---Fused magnesia
1413	2519.9020	---烧结镁氧矿（重烧镁）	3 △1	0	东盟ASEAN,智利CL,巴基斯坦PK,新西兰NZ,秘鲁PE,哥斯达黎加CR	0	最不发达35国LDC35,最不发达4国LDC4	40	---Dead-burned (sintered) magnesia
1414	2519.9030	---碱烧镁（轻烧镁）	3 △1	0	东盟ASEAN,智利CL,巴基斯坦PK,新西兰NZ,秘鲁PE,哥斯达黎加CR	0	最不发达35国LDC35,最不发达4国LDC4	40	---Light-burned magnesia
		---其他:							---Other:
1415	2519.9091	----化学纯氧化镁	3	0	东盟ASEAN,智利CL,巴基斯坦PK,新西兰NZ,秘鲁PE,哥斯达黎加CR	0	最不发达35国LDC35,最不发达4国LDC4	35	----Magnesium oxide, chemically pure
1416	2519.9099	----其他	3	0	东盟ASEAN,智利CL,巴基斯坦PK,新西兰NZ,秘鲁PE,哥斯达黎加CR	0	最不发达35国LDC35,最不发达4国LDC4	40	----Other
	ex25199099	其他氧化镁含量在70%（含70%）以上的矿产品	△1						Other mineral substances,containing MgO 70% or more
	25.20	**生石膏;硬石膏;熟石膏（由煅烧的生石膏或硫酸钙构成），不论是否着色，也不论是否带有少量促凝剂或缓凝剂:**							**Gypsum; anhydrite; plasters (consisting of calcined gypsum or calcium sulphate) whether or not coloured, with or without small quantities of accelerators or retarders:**
1417	2520.1000	-生石膏;硬石膏	5	0	东盟ASEAN,智利CL,巴基斯坦PK,新西兰NZ,秘鲁PE,哥斯达黎加CR,香港HK	0	最不发达35国LDC35,最不发达4国LDC4,老挝LA	80	-Gypsum; anhydrite
		-熟石膏:							-Plasters:
1418	2520.2010	---牙科用	5	0 0.5	东盟ASEAN,巴基斯坦PK,新西兰NZ,秘鲁PE,哥斯达黎加CR 智利CL	0	最不发达35国LDC35,最不发达4国LDC4,老挝LA	40	---For dental use

序号 No.	税则号列 Tariff Line	货品名称	最惠国税率 MFN(%)	协定税率 Agreement(%)		特惠税率 S.P.(%)		普通税率 Gen.(%)	Article Description
1419	2520.2090	---其他	5	0 0.5	东盟ASEAN,巴基斯坦PK,新西兰NZ,秘鲁PE,哥斯达黎加CR 智利CL	0	最不发达35国LDC35,最不发达4国LDC4,老挝LA	80	---Other
	25.21	**石灰石助熔剂;通常用于制造石灰或水泥的石灰石及其他钙质石:**							**Limestone flux; limestone and other calcareous stone, of a kind used for the manufacture of lime or cement:**
1420	2521.0000	石灰石助熔剂;通常用于制造石灰或水泥的石灰石及其他钙质石	5	0	东盟ASEAN,智利CL,巴基斯坦PK,新西兰NZ,秘鲁PE,哥斯达黎加CR,香港HK	0	最不发达35国LDC35,最不发达4国LDC4	50	Limestone flux; limestone and other calcareous stone, of a kind used for the manufacture of lime or cement
	25.22	**生石灰、熟石灰及水硬石灰，但税号28.25的氧化钙及氢氧化钙除外:**							**Quicklime, slaked lime and hydraulic lime, other than calcium oxide and hydroxide of heading No.28.25:**
1421	2522.1000	-生石灰	5	0 0.5	东盟ASEAN,巴基斯坦PK,新西兰NZ,秘鲁PE,哥斯达黎加CR 智利CL	0	最不发达35国LDC35,最不发达4国LDC4	80	-Quicklime
1422	2522.2000	-熟石灰	5	0	东盟ASEAN,智利CL,巴基斯坦PK,新西兰NZ,秘鲁PE,哥斯达黎加CR	0	最不发达35国LDC35,最不发达4国LDC4	80	-Slaked lime
1423	2522.3000	-水硬石灰	5	0	东盟ASEAN,智利CL,巴基斯坦PK,新西兰NZ,秘鲁PE,哥斯达黎加CR	0	最不发达35国LDC35,最不发达4国LDC4	80	-Hydraulic lime
	25.23	**硅酸盐水泥、矾土水泥、矿渣水泥、富硫酸盐水泥及类似的水凝水泥，不论是否着色，包括水泥熟料:**							**Portland cement, aluminous cement, slag cement, supersulphate cement and similar hydraulic cements, whether or not coloured or in the form of clinkers:**
1424	2523.1000	-水泥熟料	8	0 5	东盟ASEAN,智利CL,新西兰NZ,秘鲁PE,哥斯达黎加CR,香港HK,台湾TW 巴基斯坦PK	0	最不发达35国LDC35,最不发达4国LDC4	30	-Cement clinkers

序号 No.	税则号列 Tariff Line	货品名称	最惠国税率 MFN(%)	协定税率 Agreement(%)		特惠税率 S.P.(%)		普通税率 Gen.(%)	Article Description
		-硅酸盐水泥:							-Portland cement:
1425	2523.2100	--白水泥，不论是否人工着色	6	0 4.5	东盟ASEAN,智利CL,巴基斯坦PK,新西兰NZ,秘鲁PE,哥斯达黎加CR,台湾TW 亚太APTA	0	最不发达35国LDC35,最不发达4国LDC4	30	--White cement, whether or not artificially coloured
1426	2523.2900	--其他	8	0 5 6	东盟ASEAN,智利CL,新西兰NZ,秘鲁PE,哥斯达黎加CR,香港HK,澳门MO,台湾TW 巴基斯坦PK 亚太APTA	0	最不发达35国LDC35,最不发达4国LDC4	30	--Other
1427	2523.3000	-矾土水泥	6	0 5	东盟ASEAN,智利CL,新西兰NZ,秘鲁PE,哥斯达黎加CR 巴基斯坦PK	0	最不发达35国LDC35,最不发达4国LDC4	30	-Aluminous cement
1428	2523.9000	-其他水凝水泥	8	0 5	东盟ASEAN,智利CL,新西兰NZ,秘鲁PE,哥斯达黎加CR 巴基斯坦PK	0	最不发达35国LDC35,最不发达4国LDC4	30	-Other hydraulic cements
	25.24	**石棉:**							**Asbestos:**
1429	2524.1000	-青石棉	5	0	东盟ASEAN,智利CL,巴基斯坦PK,新西兰NZ,秘鲁PE,哥斯达黎加CR	0	最不发达35国LDC35	30	-Crocidlite
		-其他:							-Other:
1430	2524.9010	---长纤维石棉	5	0	东盟ASEAN,智利CL,巴基斯坦PK,新西兰NZ,秘鲁PE,哥斯达黎加CR	0	最不发达35国LDC35	30	---of long staple
1431	2524.9090	---其他	5	0	东盟ASEAN,智利CL,巴基斯坦PK,新西兰NZ,秘鲁PE,哥斯达黎加CR	0	最不发达35国LDC35	35	---Other
	25.25	**云母，包括云母片；云母废料:**							**Mica, including splittings; mica waste:**
1432	2525.1000	-原状云母及劈开的云母片	5 △1	0	东盟ASEAN,智利CL,巴基斯坦PK,新西兰NZ,秘鲁PE,哥斯达黎加CR	0	最不发达35国LDC35,最不发达4国LDC4	30	-Crude mica and mica rifted into sheets or splittings
1433	2525.2000	-云母粉	5	0	东盟ASEAN,智利CL,巴基斯坦PK,新西兰NZ,秘鲁PE,哥斯达黎加CR	0	最不发达35国LDC35,最不发达4国LDC4	30	-Mica powder

序号 No.	税则号列 Tariff Line	货品名称	最惠国税率 MFN(%)	协定税率 Agreement(%)		特惠税率 S.P.(%)		普通税率 Gen.(%)	Article Description
1434	2525.3000	-云母废料	5	0	东盟ASEAN,智利CL,巴基斯坦PK,新西兰NZ,秘鲁PE,哥斯达黎加CR	0	最不发达35国LDC35,最不发达4国LDC4	30	-Mica waste
	25.26	**天然冻石，不论是否粗加修整或仅用锯或其他方法切割成矩形（包括正方形）的板、块;滑石:**							**Natural steatite, whether or not roughly trimmed or merely cut, by sawing or otherwise, into blocks or slabs or a rectangular (including square) shape; talc:**
		-未破碎及未研粉:							-Not crushed, not powdered:
1435	2526.1010	---冻石	3	0	东盟ASEAN,智利CL,巴基斯坦PK,新西兰NZ,秘鲁PE,哥斯达黎加CR	0	最不发达35国LDC35,最不发达4国LDC4	50	---Natural steatite
1436	2526.1020	---滑石	3 △1	0	东盟ASEAN,智利CL,巴基斯坦PK,新西兰NZ,秘鲁PE,哥斯达黎加CR	0	最不发达35国LDC35,最不发达4国LDC4	50	---Talc
		-已破碎或已研粉:							-Crushed or powdered:
1437	2526.2010	---冻石	3	0	东盟ASEAN,智利CL,巴基斯坦PK,新西兰NZ,秘鲁PE,哥斯达黎加CR	0	最不发达35国LDC35,最不发达4国LDC4	50	---Natural steatite
1438	2526.2020	---滑石	3 △1	0	东盟ASEAN,智利CL,巴基斯坦PK,新西兰NZ,秘鲁PE,哥斯达黎加CR	0	最不发达35国LDC35,最不发达4国LDC4	50	---Talc
	25.28	**天然硼酸盐及其精矿（不论是否煅烧），但不包括从天然盐水析离的硼酸盐；天然粗硼酸，含硼酸干重不超过85%:**							**Natural borates and concentrates thereof (whether or not calcined), but not including borates separated from natural brine; natural boric acid containing not more than 85% of H_3BO_3 calculated on the dry weight:**

序号 No.	税则号列 Tariff Line	货品名称	最惠国税率 MFN(%)	协定税率 Agreement(%)	特惠税率 S.P.(%)	普通税率 Gen.(%)	Article Description
1439	2528.0010	--天然硼砂及其精矿（不论是否煅烧）	3 △0	0 东盟ASEAN,智利CL,巴基斯坦PK,新西兰NZ,秘鲁PE,哥斯达黎加CR	0 最不发达35国LDC35,最不发达4国LDC4	30	--Natural sodium borates and concentrates thereof (whether or not calcined)
1440	2528.0090	--其他	5 △0	0 东盟ASEAN,巴基斯坦PK,新西兰NZ,哥斯达黎加CR 0.5 智利CL 2.5 秘鲁PE	0 最不发达35国LDC35,最不发达4国LDC4	30	--Other
	25.29	**长石;白榴石;霞石及霞石正长岩;萤石（氟石）:**					**Feldspar; leucite; nepheline and nepheline syenite; fluorspar:**
1441	2529.1000	-长石	3 △1	0· 东盟ASEAN,智利CL,巴基斯坦PK,新西兰NZ,秘鲁PE,哥斯达黎加CR	0 最不发达35国LDC35,最不发达4国LDC4	50	-Feldspar
		-萤石:					-Fluorspar:
1442	2529.2100	--按重量计氟化钙含量在97%及以下	3	0 东盟ASEAN,智利CL,巴基斯坦PK,新西兰NZ,秘鲁PE,哥斯达黎加CR	0 最不发达35国LDC35,最不发达4国LDC4	50	--Containing by weight 97% or less of calcium fluoride
1443	2529.2200	--按重量计氟化钙含量在97%以上	3	0 东盟ASEAN,智利CL,巴基斯坦PK,新西兰NZ,秘鲁PE,哥斯达黎加CR	0 最不发达35国LDC35,最不发达4国LDC4	50	--Containing by weight more than 97% of calcium fluoride
1444	2529.3000	-白榴石;霞石及霞石正长岩	5	0 东盟ASEAN,智利CL,巴基斯坦PK,新西兰NZ,秘鲁PE,哥斯达黎加CR	0 最不发达35国LDC35,最不发达4国LDC4	50	-Leucite; nepheline and nepheline syenite
	25.30	**其他税号未列名的矿产品:**					**Mineral substances not elsewhere specified or included:**
		-未膨胀的蛭石、珍珠岩及绿泥石:					-Vermiculite, perlite and chlorites, unexpanded:
1445	2530.1010	---绿泥石	5	0 东盟ASEAN,智利CL,巴基斯坦PK,新西兰NZ,秘鲁PE,哥斯达黎加CR	0 最不发达35国LDC35,最不发达4国LDC4	30	---Chlorites

序号 No.	税则号列 Tariff Line	货品名称	最惠国税率 MFN(%)	协定税率 Agreement(%)		特惠税率 S.P.(%)		普通税率 Gen.(%)	Article Description
1446	2530.1020	---未膨胀的蛭石和珍珠岩	5	0	东盟ASEAN,智利CL,巴基斯坦PK,新西兰NZ,秘鲁PE,哥斯达黎加CR	0	最不发达35国LDC35,最不发达4国LDC4	30	---Vermiculite, perlite unexpanded
1447	2530.2000	-硫镁矾矿及泻盐矿（天然硫酸镁）	3	0	东盟ASEAN,智利CL,巴基斯坦PK,新西兰NZ,秘鲁PE,哥斯达黎加CR	0	最不发达35国LDC35,最不发达4国LDC4	30	-Kieserite, epsomite (natural magnesium sulphates)
		-其他:							-Other:
1448	2530.9010	---矿物性药材	3	0	东盟ASEAN,智利CL,巴基斯坦PK,新西兰NZ,秘鲁PE,哥斯达黎加CR	0	最不发达35国LDC35,最不发达4国LDC4	30	---Mineral medicinal substances
1449	2530.9020	---稀土金属矿	0			0	最不发达35国LDC35,最不发达4国LDC4	0	---Ores of rare earth metals
		---其他:							---Other:
1450	2530.9091	----硅灰石	3	0	东盟ASEAN,智利CL,巴基斯坦PK,新西兰NZ,秘鲁PE,哥斯达黎加CR	0	最不发达35国LDC35,最不发达4国LDC4	50	----Wollastonite
1451	2530.9099	----其他	3	0	东盟ASEAN,智利CL,巴基斯坦PK,新西兰NZ,秘鲁PE,哥斯达黎加CR	0	最不发达35国LDC35,最不发达4国LDC4	50	----Other
	ex25309099	天青石	△1						Celesite
	ex25309099	锂辉石矿	△0						Spodumene
	ex25309099	废镁砖	△1						Waste magnesia brick
	ex25309099	未煅烧的水镁石	△1						Brucite

第二十六章
矿砂、矿渣及矿灰

注释：

一、本章不包括：

（一）铺路用的矿渣及类似的工业废渣（税号 25.17）；

（二）天然碳酸镁（菱镁矿），不论是否煅烧（税号 25.19）；

（三）储油罐的淤渣，主要成分为税号 27.10 项下的油品；

（四）第三十一章的碱性熔渣；

（五）矿物棉（税号 68.06）；

（六）贵金属或包贵金属的废碎料；主要用于回收贵金属的含贵金属或贵金属化合物的其他废碎料（税号 71.12）；

（七）通过熔炼所产生的铜锍、镍锍或钴锍（第十五类）。

二、税号 26.01 至 26.17 所称"矿砂"，是指冶金工业中提炼汞、税号 28.44 的金属以及第十四类、第十五类金属的矿物，即使这些矿物不用于冶金工业，也包括在内。但税号 26.01 至 26.17 不包括不是以冶金工业正常加工方法处理的各种矿物。

三、税号 26.20 只适用于：（一）在工业上提炼金属或作为生产金属化合物基本原料的矿渣、矿灰及残渣，但焚化城市垃圾所产生的灰、渣除外（税目 26.21）；（二）含有砷的矿渣、矿灰及残渣，不论其是否含有金属，用于提取或生产砷、金属及其化合物。

子目注释：

一、子目 2620.21 所称"含铅汽油的淤渣及含铅抗震化合物的淤渣"，是指取自含铅汽油及含铅抗震化合物（例如，四乙铅）储罐的淤渣，主要含有铅、铅化合物以及铁的氧化物。

Chapter 26
Ores, slag and ash

Notes:

1. This Chapter does not cover：

(a) Slag or similar industrial waste prepared as macadam (heading No.25.17) ;

(b) Natural magnesium carbonate (magnesite) , whether or not calcined (heading No.25.19) ;

(c) Sludges from the storage tanks of petroleum oils, consisting mainly of such oils(heading 27.10) ;

(d) Basic slag of Chapter 31;

(e) Slag wool, rock wool or similar mineral wools (heading No.68.06) ;

(f) Waste or scrap of precious metal or of metal clad with precious metal; other waste or scrap containing precious metal or precious metal compounds, of a kind used principally for the recovery of precious metal (heading No.71.12) ; or

(g) Copper, nickel or cobalt mattes produced by any process of smelting (Section XV) .

2. For the purposes of headings Nos.26.01 to 26.17, the term "ores" means minerals of mineralogical species actually used in the metallurgical industry for the extraction of mercury, of the metals of heading No.28.44 or of the metals of Section XIV or XV, even if they are intended for non-metallurgical purposes. Headings Nos.26.01 to 26.17do not, however, include minerals which have been submitted to processes not normal to the metallurgical industry.

3. Heading No.26.20 applies only to: (a) Slag, ash and residues of a kind used in industry either for the extraction of metals or as a basis for the manufacture of chemical compounds of metals, excluding ash and residues from the incineration of municipul waste (hending 26.21); and (b) Slag, ash and residues containing arsenic, whether or not containing metals, of a kind used either for the extraction of arsenic or metals or for the manufacture of their chemical compounds.

Subheading Notes:

1. For the purposes of subheading 2620.21, "leaded gasoline sludges and leaded anti-knock compound sludges" mean sludges obtained from storage tanks of leaded gasoline and leaded anti-knock compounds (for example, tetraethyl lead), and consisting essentially of lead, lead compounds and iron oxide.

二、含有砷、汞、铊及其混合物的矿渣、矿灰及残渣，用于提取或生产砷、汞、铊及其化合物，归入子目 2620.60。

2. Slag, ash and residues containing arsenic, mercury, thallium or their mixtures, of a kind used for the extraction of arsenic or those metals classified in subheading 2620.60.

序号 No.	税则号列 Tariff Line	货品名称	最惠国税率 MFN(%)	协定税率 Agreement(%)	特惠税率 S.P.(%)	普通税率 Gen.(%)	Article Description
	26.01	**铁矿砂及其精矿，包括焙烧黄铁矿：**					**Iron ores and concentrates, including roasted iron pyrites:**
		-铁矿砂及其精矿，但焙烧黄铁矿除外：					-Iron ores and concentrates, other than roasted iron pyrites:
		--未烧结：					--Non-agglomerated:
1452	2601.1110	---平均粒度小于 0.8 毫米的	0		0 最不发达 35 国 LDC35, 最不发达 4 国 LDC4	0	---Of a granularity less than 0.8mm
1453	2601.1120	---平均粒度不小于 0.8 毫米，但不大于 6.3 毫米的	0		0 最不发达 35 国 LDC35, 最不发达 4 国 LDC4	0	---Of a granularity of 0.8mm or more, but not exceeding 6.3mm
1454	2601.1190	---其他	0		0 最不发达 35 国 LDC35, 最不发达 4 国 LDC4	0	---Other
1455	2601.1200	--已烧结	0		0 最不发达 35 国 LDC35, 最不发达 4 国 LDC4	0	--Agglomerated
1456	2601.2000	-焙烧黄铁矿	0		0 最不发达 35 国 LDC35, 最不发达 4 国 LDC4	0	-Roasted iron pyrites
	26.02	**锰矿砂及其精矿，包括以干重计含锰量在 20%及以上的锰铁矿及其精矿：**					**Manganese ores and concentrates, including ferruginous manganese ores and concentrates with a manganese content of 20% or more, calculated on the dry weight:**

序号 No.	税则号列 Tariff Line	货品名称	最惠国税率 MFN(%)	协定税率 Agreement(%)	特惠税率 S.P.(%)	普通税率 Gen.(%)	Article Description
1457	2602.0000	锰矿砂及其精矿，包括以干重计含锰量在20%及以上的锰铁矿及其精矿	0		0 最不发达35国LDC35，最不发达4国LDC4	0	Manganese ores and concentrates, including ferruginous manganese ores and concentrates with a manganese content of 20% or more, calculated on the dry weight
	26.03	**铜矿砂及其精矿：**					**Copper ores and concentrates:**
1458	2603.0000	铜矿砂及其精矿	0		0 最不发达35国LDC35，最不发达4国LDC4	0	Copper ores and concentrates
	26.04	**镍矿砂及其精矿：**					**Nickel ores and concentrates:**
1459	2604.0000	镍矿砂及其精矿	0		0 最不发达35国LDC35，最不发达4国LDC4	0	Nickel ores and concentrates
	26.05	**钴矿砂及其精矿：**					**Cobalt ores and concentrates:**
1460	2605.0000	钴矿砂及其精矿	0		0 最不发达35国LDC35，最不发达4国LDC4	0	Cobalt ores and concentrates
	26.06	**铝矿砂及其精矿：**					**Aluminium ores and concentrate:**
1461	2606.0000	铝矿砂及其精矿	0		0 最不发达35国LDC35，最不发达4国LDC4	0	Aluminium ores and concentrate
	26.07	**铅矿砂及其精矿：**					**Lead ores and concentrates:**
1462	2607.0000	铅矿砂及其精矿	0		0 最不发达35国LDC35，最不发达4国LDC4	0	Lead ores and concentrates
	26.08	**锌矿砂及其精矿：**					**Zinc ores and concentrates:**
1463	2608.0000	锌矿砂及其精矿	0		0 最不发达35国LDC35，最不发达4国LDC4	0	Zinc ores and concentrates

序号 No.	税则号列 Tariff Line	货品名称	最惠国税率 MFN(%)	协定税率 Agreement(%)	特惠税率 S.P.(%)	普通税率 Gen.(%)	Article Description
	26.09	**锡矿砂及其精矿:**					**Tin ores and concentrates:**
1464	2609.0000	锡矿砂及其精矿	0		0 最不发达35国LDC35, 最不发达4国LDC4	0	Tin ores and concentrates
	26.10	**铬矿砂及其精矿:**					**Chromium ores and concentrates:**
1465	2610.0000	铬矿砂及其精矿	0		0 最不发达35国LDC35, 最不发达4国LDC4	0	Chromium ores and concentrates
	26.11	**钨矿砂及其精矿:**					**Tungsten ores and concentrates:**
1466	2611.0000	钨矿砂及其精矿	0		0 最不发达35国LDC35, 最不发达4国LDC4	0	Tungsten ores and concentrates
	26.12	**铀或钍矿砂及其精矿:**					**Uranium or thorium ores and concentrates:**
1467	2612.1000	-铀矿砂及其精矿	0		0 最不发达35国LDC35, 最不发达4国LDC4	0	-Uranium ores and concentrates
1468	2612.2000	-钍矿砂及其精矿	0		0 最不发达35国LDC35, 最不发达4国LDC4	0	-Thorium ores and concentrates
	26.13	**钼矿砂及其精矿:**					**Molybdenum ores and concentrates:**
1469	2613.1000	-已焙烧	0		0 最不发达35国LDC35, 最不发达4国LDC4	0	-Roasted
1470	2613.9000	-其他	0		0 最不发达35国LDC35, 最不发达4国LDC4	0	-Other

序号 No.	税则号列 Tariff Line	货品名称	最惠国税率 MFN(%)	协定税率 Agreement(%)	特惠税率 S.P.(%)	普通税率 Gen.(%)	Article Description
	26.14	**钛矿砂及其精矿:**					**Titanium ores and concentrates:**
1471	2614.0000	钛矿砂及其精矿	0		0 最不发达35国LDC35, 最不发达4国LDC4	0	Titanium ores and concentrates
	26.15	**铌、钽、钒或锆矿砂及其精矿:**					**Niobium, tantalum, vanadium or zirconium ores and concentrates:**
1472	2615.1000	-锆矿砂及其精矿	0		0 最不发达35国LDC35, 最不发达4国LDC4	0	-Zirconium ores and concentrates
		-其他:					-Other:
1473	2615.9010	---水合钽铌原料（钽铌矿富集物）	0		0 最不发达35国LDC35, 最不发达4国LDC4	0	---Hydrated Tantalum/ Niobium materials or enriched materials from Tantalum/ Niobium Ore
1474	2615.9090	---其他	0		0 最不发达35国LDC35, 最不发达4国LDC4	0	---Other
	26.16	**贵金属矿砂及其精矿:**					**Precious metal ores and concentrates:**
1475	2616.1000	-银矿砂及其精矿	0		0 最不发达35国LDC35, 最不发达4国LDC4	0	-Silver ores and concentrates
1476	2616.9000	-其他	0		0 最不发达35国LDC35, 最不发达4国LDC4	0	-Other
	26.17	**其他矿砂及其精矿:**					**Other ores and concentrates:**
		-锑矿砂及其精矿:					-Antimony ores and concentrates:
1477	2617.1010	---生锑（锑精矿，选矿产品）	0		0 最不发达35国LDC35, 最不发达4国LDC4	0	---Crude antimony (Antimony concentrates which are mineral products)

序号 No.	税则号列 Tariff Line	货品名称	最惠国税率 MFN(%)	协定税率 Agreement(%)		特惠税率 S.P.(%)		普通税率 Gen.(%)	Article Description
1478	2617.1090	---其他	0			0	最不发达35国LDC35,最不发达4国LDC4	0	---Other
		-其他:							-Other:
1479	2617.9010	---朱砂（辰砂）	3	0	东盟ASEAN,智利CL,巴基斯坦PK,新西兰NZ,秘鲁PE,哥斯达黎加CR	0	最不发达35国LDC35,最不发达4国LDC4	14	---Cinnabar
1480	2617.9090	---其他	0			0	最不发达35国LDC35,最不发达4国LDC4	0	---Other
	26.18	**冶炼钢铁所产生的粒状熔渣（熔渣砂）:**							**Granulated slag (slag sand) from the manufacture of iron or steel:**
1481	2618.0010	---主要含锰	4	0 0.4	东盟ASEAN,巴基斯坦PK,新西兰NZ,秘鲁PE,哥斯达黎加CR 智利CL	0	最不发达35国LDC35	35	---Containing mainly Manganese
	ex26180010	冶炼钢铁产生的锰渣，含锰量大于25%	△1						Granulated slag from the manufacture of iron or steel,containing manganese more than 25%
1482	2618.0090	---其他	4	0 0.4	东盟ASEAN,巴基斯坦PK,新西兰NZ,秘鲁PE,哥斯达黎加CR 智利CL	0	最不发达35国LDC35	35	---Other
	26.19	**冶炼钢铁所产生的熔渣、浮渣（粒状熔渣除外）、氧化皮及其他废料:**							**Slag, dross (other than granulated slag), scalings and other waste from the manufacture of iron or steel:**
1483	2619.0000	冶炼钢铁所产生的熔渣、浮渣（粒状熔渣除外）、氧化皮及其他废料	4	0 0.4	东盟ASEAN,巴基斯坦PK,新西兰NZ,秘鲁PE,哥斯达黎加CR 智利CL	0	最不发达35国LDC35	35	Slag, dross (other than granulated slag), scalings and other waste from the manufacture of iron or steel
	ex26190000	冶炼钢铁产生的熔渣、浮渣、氧化皮及其他废料，五氧化二钒含量大于20%	△1						Slag, dross scalings and other from manufacture of iron or steel, containing V_2O_5>20%
	26.20	**含有金属、砷及其化合物的矿渣、矿灰及残渣（冶炼钢铁所产生的灰、渣除外）:**							**Slag, ash and residues (other than from the manufacture of iron or steel) containing metals, arsenic or their compounds:**

序号 No.	税则号列 Tariff Line	货品名称	最惠国税率 MFN(%)	协定税率 Agreement(%)		特惠税率 S.P.(%)		普通税率 Gen.(%)	Article Description
		-主要含锌:							-Containing mainly zinc:
1484	2620.1100	--含硬锌	4	0 0.4	东盟ASEAN,巴基斯坦PK,新西兰NZ,秘鲁PE,哥斯达黎加CR 智利CL	0	最不发达35国LDC35,最不发达4国LDC4	35	--Hard zinc spelter
1485	2620.1900	--其他	4	0 0.4	东盟ASEAN,巴基斯坦PK,新西兰NZ,秘鲁PE,哥斯达黎加CR 智利CL	0	最不发达35国LDC35,最不发达4国LDC4	35	--Other
		-主要含铅:							-Containing mainly lead:
1486	2620.2100	--含铅汽油的淤渣及含铅抗震化合物的淤渣	4	0	东盟ASEAN,智利CL,巴基斯坦PK,新西兰NZ,秘鲁PE,哥斯达黎加CR	0	最不发达35国LDC35,最不发达4国LDC4	35	--Leaded gasoline sludges and leaded anti-knock compound sludges
1487	2620.2900	--其他	4	0	东盟ASEAN,智利CL,巴基斯坦PK,新西兰NZ,秘鲁PE,哥斯达黎加CR	0	最不发达35国LDC35,最不发达4国LDC4	35	--Other
1488	2620.3000	-主要含铜	4	0 0.4	东盟ASEAN,巴基斯坦PK,新西兰NZ,秘鲁PE,哥斯达黎加CR 智利CL	0	最不发达35国LDC35,最不发达4国LDC4	35	-Containing mainly copper
1489	2620.4000	-主要含铝	4	0	东盟ASEAN,智利CL,巴基斯坦PK,新西兰NZ,秘鲁PE,哥斯达黎加CR	0	最不发达35国LDC35,最不发达4国LDC4	35	-Containing mainly aluminium
1490	2620.6000	-含砷、汞、铊及其混合物，用于提取或生产砷、汞、铊及其化合物	4	0	东盟ASEAN,智利CL,巴基斯坦PK,新西兰NZ,秘鲁PE,哥斯达黎加CR	0	最不发达35国LDC35,最不发达4国LDC4	35	-Containing arsenic, mercury, thallium or their mixtures, of a kind used for the extraction of arsenic or those metals or for the manufacture of their chemical compounds.
		-其他:							-Other:
1491	2620.9100	--含锑、铍、镉、铬及其混合物	4	0	东盟ASEAN,智利CL,巴基斯坦PK,新西兰NZ,秘鲁PE,哥斯达黎加CR	0	最不发达35国LDC35,最不发达4国LDC4	35	--Containing antimony, beryllium, cadmium, chromium or their mixtures
		--其他:							--Other:

序号 No.	税则号列 Tariff Line	货品名称	最惠国 税率 MFN(%)	协定税率 Agreement(%)		特惠税率 S.P.(%)		普通 税率 Gen.(%)	Article Description
1492	2620.9910	---主要含钨	4	0 0.4	东盟ASEAN,巴基斯坦PK,新西兰NZ,秘鲁PE,哥斯达黎加CR 智利CL	0	最不发达35国LDC35,最不发达4国LDC4	35	---Containing mainly tungsten
1493	2620.9990	---其他	4	0 0.4	东盟ASEAN,巴基斯坦PK,新西兰NZ,秘鲁PE,哥斯达黎加CR 智利CL	0	最不发达35国LDC35,最不发达4国LDC4	35	---Other
	ex26209990	含其他金属及化合物的矿灰及残渣，五氧化二钒含量大于20％	△1						Ash and residues containing V_2O_5>20%
	26.21	**其他矿渣及矿灰，包括海藻灰（海草灰）；焚化城市垃圾所产生的灰、渣:**							**Other slag and ash, including seaweed ash (kelp); ash and residues from the incineration of municipal waste:**
1494	2621.1000	-焚化城市垃圾所产生的灰、渣	4	0	东盟ASEAN,智利CL,巴基斯坦PK,新西兰NZ,秘鲁PE,哥斯达黎加CR	0	最不发达35国LDC35,最不发达4国LDC4	35	-Ash and residues from the incineration of municipal waste
1495	2621.9000	-其他	4	0 0.4	东盟ASEAN,巴基斯坦PK,新西兰NZ,秘鲁PE,哥斯达黎加CR,香港HK 智利CL	0	最不发达35国LDC35,最不发达4国LDC4	35	-Other

第二十七章
矿物燃料、矿物油及其蒸馏产品；沥青物质；矿物蜡

注释：

一、本章不包括：

（一）单独的已有化学定义的有机化合物，但纯甲烷及纯丙烷应归入税号 27.11；

（二）税号 30.03 及 30.04 的药品；

（三）税号 33.01、33.02 及 38.05 的不饱和烃混合物。

二、税号 27.10 所称“石油及从沥青矿物提取的油类”，不仅包括石油、从沥青矿物提取的油及类似油，还包括那些用任何方法提取的主要含有不饱和烃混合物的油，但其非芳族成分的重量必须超过芳族成分。然而，它不包括温度在 300℃时，压力转为 1013 毫巴后减压蒸馏出的液体合成聚烯烃以体积计小于 60%的货品（第三十九章）。

三、税目 27.10 所称“废油”，是指主要含石油及从沥青矿物提取的油类（参见本章注释二）的废油，不论其是否与水混合。它们包括：

（一）不再适于作为原产品使用的废油（例如，用过的润滑油、液压油及变压器油）；

（二）石油储罐的淤渣油，主要含有石油及高浓度的在生产原产品时使用的添加剂（例如，化学品）；

（三）水乳浊液状或与水混合的废油，例如，浮油、清洗油罐所得的油或机械加工中已用过的切削油。

子目注释：

一、子目号 2701.11 所称“无烟煤”，是指含挥发物（以干燥、无矿物质计）不超过 14%的煤。

Chapter 27
Mineral fuels, mineral oils and products of their distillation; bituminous substances; mineral waxes

Notes:

1. This Chapter does not cover:
   (a) Separate chemically defined organic compounds, other than pure methane and propane which are to be classified in heading No.27.11;
   (b) Medicaments of heading No.30.03 or 30.04; or
   (c) Mixed unsaturated hydrocarbons of heading No.33.01, 33.02 or 38.05.

2. References in heading No.27.10 to “petroleum oils and oils obtained from bituminous minerals” include not only petroleum oils and oils obtained from bituminous minerals but also similar oils, as well as those consisting mainly of mixed unsaturated hydrocarbons, obtained by any process, provided that the weight of the non-aromatic constituents exceeds that of the aromatic constituents. However, the references do not include liquid synthetic polyolefins of which less than 60% by volume distils at 300℃, after conversion to 1,013 millibars when a reduced-pressure distillation method is used (Chapter 39).

3. For the purposes of heading 27.10, “waste oils” means waste containing mainly petroleum oils and oils obtained from bituminous minerals(as described in Note 2 to this Chapter) , whether or not mixed with water. These include:
   (a) Such oils no longer fit for use as primary products (for example, used lubricating oils, used hydraulic oils and used transformer oils) ;
   (b) Sludge oils from the storage tanks of petroleum oils, mainly containing such oils and a high concentration of additives (for example, chemicals) used in the manufacture of the primary products; and
   (c) Such oils in the form of emulsions in water or mixtures with water, such as those resulting from oil spills, storage tank washings, or from the use of cutting oils for machining operations.

Subheading Notes:

1. For the purposes of subheading No.2701.11, “anthracite” means coal having a volatile matter limit (on a dry, mineral-matter-free basis) not exceeding 14%.

二、子目号2701.12所称“烟煤”，是指含挥发物（以干燥、无矿物质计）超过14%，并且热值（以潮湿、无矿物质计）等于或大于5833大卡/公斤的煤。

2. For the purposes of subheading No.2701.12, “bituminous coal” means coal having a volatile matter limit (on a dry, mineral-matter-free basis) exceeding 14% and a calorific value limit(on a moist, mineral-matter-free basis) equal to or greater than 5,833 kcal/kg.

三、子目号2707.10、2707.20、2707.30及2707.40所称“粗苯”、“粗甲苯”、“粗二甲苯”、“萘”，是分别指按重量计苯、甲苯、二甲苯、萘的含量在50%以上的产品。

3. For the purposes of subheadings 2707.10, 2707.20, 2707.30 and 2707.40, the terms “benzole (benzene)” , “toluole (toluene)” , “xylole (xylenes)” , “naphthalene” and “phenols” apply to products which contain more than 50% by weight of benzene, toluene, xylene or naphthalene, respectively.

四、子目2710.12所称“轻油及其制品”，是指温度在210℃时以体积计馏出量（包括损耗）在90%及以上的产品（以美国标准试验法D86为准）。

4. For the purposes of subheading 2710.12, “light oils and preparations” are those of which 90% or more by volume (including losses) distil at 210℃ (ASTMD 86 method) .

五、税目27.10所称“生物柴油”，是指从动植物油脂（不论是否使用过）得到的用作燃料的脂肪酸单烷基酯。

5. For the purposes of the subheadings of heading 27.10, the term “biodiesel” means mono-alkyl esters of fatty acids of a kind used as a fuel, derived from animal or vegetable fats and oils whether or not used.

序号 No.	税则号列 Tariff Line	货品名称	最惠国税率 MFN(%)	协定税率 Agreement(%)		特惠税率 S.P.(%)		普通税率 Gen.(%)	Article Description
	27.01	**煤;煤砖、煤球及用煤制成的类似固体燃料:**							**Coal; briquettes, ovoids and similar solid fuels manufactured from coal:**
		-煤，不论是否粉化，但未制成型:							-Coal, whether or not pulverized, but not agglomerated:
1496	2701.1100	--无烟煤	3 △0	0	东盟ASEAN,智利CL,巴基斯坦PK,新西兰NZ,秘鲁PE,哥斯达黎加CR	0	最不发达35国LDC35,最不发达4国LDC4,老挝LA	20	--Anthracite
		--烟煤:							--Bituminous coal:
1497	2701.1210	---炼焦煤	3 △0	0	东盟ASEAN,智利CL,巴基斯坦PK,新西兰NZ,秘鲁PE,哥斯达黎加CR	0	最不发达35国LDC35,最不发达4国LDC4,老挝LA	20	---Coking coal

序号 No.	税则号列 Tariff Line	货品名称	最惠国税率 MFN(%)	协定税率 Agreement(%)		特惠税率 S.P.(%)		普通税率 Gen.(%)	Article Description
1498	2701.1290	---其他	6 △0	0 5	东盟ASEAN,智利CL,新西兰NZ,秘鲁PE,哥斯达黎加CR 巴基斯坦PK	0	最不发达35国LDC35,最不发达4国LDC4,老挝LA	20	---Other
1499	2701.1900	--其他煤	5 △0	0 3.5	东盟ASEAN,智利CL,巴基斯坦PK,新西兰NZ,秘鲁PE,哥斯达黎加CR 亚太APTA	0	最不发达35国LDC35,最不发达4国LDC4,老挝LA	20	--Other coal
1500	2701.2000	-煤砖、煤球及用煤制成的类似固体燃料	5 △0	0	东盟ASEAN,智利CL,巴基斯坦PK,新西兰NZ,秘鲁PE,哥斯达黎加CR	0	最不发达35国LDC35,最不发达4国LDC4,老挝LA	50	-Briquettes, ovoids and similar solid fuels manufactured from coal
	27.02	**褐煤，不论是否制成型，但不包括黑玉:**							**Lignite, whether or not agglomerated, excluding jet:**
1501	2702.1000	-褐煤，不论是否粉化,但未制成型	3	0	东盟ASEAN,智利CL,巴基斯坦PK,新西兰NZ,秘鲁PE,哥斯达黎加CR	0	最不发达35国LDC35,最不发达4国LDC4	20	-Lignite, whether or not pulverized, but not agglomerated
1502	2702.2000	-制成型的褐煤	3	0	东盟ASEAN,智利CL,巴基斯坦PK,新西兰NZ,秘鲁PE,哥斯达黎加CR	0	最不发达35国LDC35,最不发达4国LDC4	20	-Agglomerated ignite
	27.03	**泥煤（包括肥料用泥煤），不论是否制成型:**							**Peat (including peat litter), whether or not agglomerated:**
1503	2703.0000	泥煤（包括肥料用泥煤），不论是否制成型	5	0	东盟ASEAN,智利CL,巴基斯坦PK,新西兰NZ,秘鲁PE,哥斯达黎加CR	0	最不发达35国LDC35	20	Peat (including peat litter), whether or not agglomerated
	27.04	**煤、褐煤或泥煤制成的焦炭及半焦炭，不论是否制成型;甑炭:**							**Coke and semi-coke of coal, of lignite or of peat, whether or not agglomerated; retort carbon:**
1504	2704.0010	---焦炭及半焦炭	5 △0	0 0.5 2.5	东盟ASEAN,巴基斯坦PK,新西兰NZ,秘鲁PE,哥斯达黎加CR 智利CL 亚太APTA	0	最不发达35国LDC35	11	---Coke and semi-coke

序号 No.	税则号列 Tariff Line	货品名称	最惠国税率 MFN(%)	协定税率 Agreement(%)		特惠税率 S.P.(%)		普通税率 Gen.(%)	Article Description
1505	2704.0090	---其他	5 △0	0 0.5 2.5	东盟ASEAN,巴基斯坦PK,新西兰NZ,秘鲁PE,哥斯达黎加CR 智利CL 亚太APTA	0	最不发达35国LDC35	11	---Other
	27.05	**煤气、水煤气、炉煤气及类似气体，但石油气及其他烃类气除外:**							**Coal gas, water gas, producer gas and similar gases, other than petroleum gases and other gaseous hydrocarbons:**
1506	2705.0000	煤气、水煤气、炉煤气及类似气体，但石油气及其他烃类气除外	5 △1	0	东盟ASEAN,智利CL,巴基斯坦PK,新西兰NZ,秘鲁PE,哥斯达黎加CR	0	最不发达35国LDC35	20	Coal gas, water gas, producer gas and similar gases, other than petroleum gases and other gaseous hydrocarbons
	27.06	**从煤、褐煤或泥煤蒸馏所得的焦油及其他矿物焦油，不论是否脱水或部分蒸馏，包括再造焦油:**							**Tar distilled from coal, from lignite or from peat, and other mineral tars, whether or not dehydrated or partially distilled, including reconstituted tare:**
1507	2706.0000	从煤、褐煤或泥煤蒸馏所得的焦油及其他矿物焦油，不论是否脱水或部分蒸馏，包括再造焦油	6 △1	0 5	东盟ASEAN,智利CL,新西兰NZ,秘鲁PE,哥斯达黎加CR 巴基斯坦PK	0	最不发达35国LDC35	30	Tar distilled from coal, from lignite or from peat, and other mineral tars, whether or not dehydrated or partially distilled, including reconstituted tars
	27.07	**蒸馏高温煤焦油所得的油类及其他产品;芳族成分重量超过非芳族成分的类似产品:**							**Oils and other products of the distill-ation of high temperature coal tar; similar products in which the weight of the aromatic constituents exceeds that of the non-aromatic constituents:**
1508	2707.1000	-粗苯	6	0 5	东盟ASEAN,智利CL,新西兰NZ,秘鲁PE,哥斯达黎加CR 巴基斯坦PK	0	最不发达35国LDC35,最不发达4国LDC4	20	-Benzole
1509	2707.2000	-粗甲苯	6	0 5	东盟ASEAN,智利CL,新西兰NZ,秘鲁PE,哥斯达黎加CR 巴基斯坦PK	0	最不发达35国LDC35,最不发达4国LDC4	30	-Toluole

序号 No.	税则号列 Tariff Line	货品名称	最惠国税率 MFN(%)	协定税率 Agreement(%)		特惠税率 S.P.(%)		普通税率 Gen.(%)	Article Description
1510	2707.3000	-粗二甲苯	6 △2	0 5	东盟ASEAN,智利CL,新西兰NZ,秘鲁PE,哥斯达黎加CR 巴基斯坦PK	0	最不发达35国LDC35,最不发达4国LDC4	20	-Xylole
1511	2707.4000	-萘	7	0 5 6	东盟ASEAN,智利CL,新西兰NZ,秘鲁PE,哥斯达黎加CR 巴基斯坦PK 亚太APTA	0	最不发达35国LDC35,最不发达4国LDC4	30	-Naphthalene
1512	2707.5000	-其他芳烃混合物，温度在250℃时馏出物以体积计（包括损耗）在65%及以上（以美国标准试验法D86为准）	7 △3	0 5	东盟ASEAN,智利CL,新西兰NZ,秘鲁PE,哥斯达黎加CR 巴基斯坦PK	0	最不发达35国LDC35,最不发达4国LDC4	30	-Other aromatic hydrocarbon mixtures of which 65% or more by volume (including losses) distils at 250℃by the ASTM D86 method
		-其他:							-Other:
1513	2707.9100	--杂酚油	7	0 5	东盟ASEAN,智利CL,新西兰NZ,秘鲁PE,哥斯达黎加CR 巴基斯坦PK	0	最不发达35国LDC35,最不发达4国LDC4	30	--Creosote oils
		--其他:							--Other:
1514	2707.9910	---酚	7	0 5	东盟ASEAN,智利CL,新西兰NZ,秘鲁PE,哥斯达黎加CR 巴基斯坦PK	0	最不发达35国LDC35,最不发达4国LDC4	30	---Phenols
1515	2707.9990	---其他	7	0 5	东盟ASEAN,智利CL,新西兰NZ,秘鲁PE,哥斯达黎加CR 巴基斯坦PK	0	最不发达35国LDC35,最不发达4国LDC4	30	---Other
	27.08	**从煤焦油或其他矿物焦油所得的沥青及沥青焦:**							**Pitch and pitch coke, obtained from coal tar or from other mineral tars:**
1516	2708.1000	-沥青	7	0 0.7 5	东盟ASEAN,新西兰NZ,秘鲁PE,哥斯达黎加CR 智利CL 巴基斯坦PK	0	最不发达35国LDC35	35	-Pitch
1517	2708.2000	-沥青焦	6	0 5	东盟ASEAN,智利CL,新西兰NZ,秘鲁PE,哥斯达黎加CR 巴基斯坦PK	0	最不发达35国LDC35	11	-Pitch coke
	ex27082000	针状沥青焦	△3						Xylole

序号 No.	税则号列 Tariff Line	货品名称	最惠国税率 MFN(%)	协定税率 Agreement(%)	特惠税率 S.P.(%)	普通税率 Gen.(%)	Article Description
	27.09	**石油原油及从沥青矿物提取的原油:**					**Petroleum oils and oils obtained from bituminous minerals, crude:**
1518	2709.0000	石油原油及从沥青矿物提取的原油	0		0 最不发达35国LDC35, 最不发达4国LDC4	85元/吨	Petroleum oils and oils obtained from bituminous minerals, crude
	27.10	**石油及从沥青矿物提取的油类，但原油除外;以上述油为基本成分（按重量计不低于70%）的其他税号未列名制品;废油:**					**Petroleum oils and oils obtained from bituminous minerals, other than crude; preparations not elsewhere specified or included, containing by weight 70% or more of petroleum oils or of oils obtained from bituminous minerals, these oils being the basic constituents of the preparations; waste oils:**
		-石油及从沥青矿物提取的油类（但原油除外）以及以上述油为基本成分(按重量计不低于70%)的其他税目未列名制品，不含有生物柴油，但废油除外:					-Petroleum oils and oils obtained from bituminous minerals (otherthan crude) and preparations not elsewhere specified or included,containing by weight 70% or more of petroleum oils or of oils obtained from bituminous minerals, these oils being the basic constituents of the preparations, other than those containing biodiesel and other than waste oils:
		--轻油及其制品:					--Light oils and preparations:
1519	2710.1210	---车用汽油及航空汽油	5 △1	0 东盟ASEAN,巴基斯坦PK,新加坡SG,新西兰NZ,哥斯达黎加CR 0.5 智利CL	0 最不发达35国LDC35	14	---Motor gasoline, aviation gasoline
1520	2710.1220	---石脑油	6 △0	0 东盟ASEAN,巴基斯坦PK,新加坡SG,新西兰NZ,哥斯达黎加CR 0.6 智利CL 5.4 亚太APTA	0 最不发达35国LDC35	20	---Naphtha
1521	2710.1230	---橡胶溶剂油，油漆溶剂油、抽提溶剂油	6	0 新西兰NZ,哥斯达黎加CR 0.6 智利CL		30	---Rubber solvent, paint solvent, extractive solvent
		---其他:					---Other:

序号 No.	税则号列 Tariff Line	货品名称	最惠国税率 MFN(%)	协定税率 Agreement(%)		特惠税率 S.P.(%)		普通税率 Gen.(%)	Article Description
1522	2710.1291	----壬烯	9	0 0.9	新西兰NZ,哥斯达黎加CR 智利CL			20	----Nonene
	ex27101291	壬烯(碳九混合异构体含量高于90%)	△4						Motor gasoline & aviation gasoline
1523	2710.1299	----其他	9	0 0.9	新西兰NZ,哥斯达黎加CR 智利CL			20	----Other
	ex27101299	异戊烯同分异构体混合物	△5						ISOpentene
		--其他:							--Other:
		---煤油馏分:							---Kerosene distillages:
1524	2710.1911	----航空煤油	9 △0	0 0.9 5	东盟ASEAN,新加坡SG,新西兰NZ,秘鲁PE,哥斯达黎加CR,台湾TW 智利CL 巴基斯坦PK	0	最不发达35国LDC35	14	----Aviation kerosene
1525	2710.1912	----灯用煤油	9	0 0.9 4.5	新西兰NZ,哥斯达黎加CR 智利CL 秘鲁PE			14	----Lamp-kerosene
1526	2710.1919	----其他	6	0 0.6 5	东盟ASEAN,新加坡SG,新西兰NZ,秘鲁PE,哥斯达黎加CR,台湾TW 智利CL 巴基斯坦PK	0	最不发达35国LDC35	20	----Other
	ex27101919	正构烷烃(C9～C13)	△2						n-Alkanes（C9～C13）
		---柴油及其他燃料油:							---Diesel oils and other fuel oils:
1527	2710.1922	----5～7号燃料油	6 △1	0 0.6 5	东盟ASEAN,新加坡SG,新西兰NZ,秘鲁PE,哥斯达黎加CR 智利CL 巴基斯坦PK	0	最不发达35国LDC35	20	----Fuel oils No.5～No.7
1528	2710.1923	----柴油	6 △1	0 0.6 3	新西兰NZ,哥斯达黎加CR 智利CL 秘鲁PE			11	----Diesel oil
1529	2710.1929	----其他	6	0 0.6 3 5	东盟ASEAN,新加坡SG,新西兰NZ,哥斯达黎加CR,澳门MO 智利CL 秘鲁PE 巴基斯坦PK			20	----Other
	ex27101929	350度以下馏出物体积百分比小于20%，550度以下馏出物体积百分比大于80%的蜡油	△0						Paraffin oils:350°C distillage<20%, 550°C distillage>80%
		---润滑油、润滑脂及其他重油:							---Lubricating oils, lubricating greases and other heavy oils:

序号 No.	税则号列 Tariff Line	货品名称	最惠国税率 MFN(%)	协定税率 Agreement(%)		特惠税率 S.P.(%)		普通税率 Gen.(%)	Article Description
1530	2710.1991	----润滑油	6	0 0.6 5.4	东盟ASEAN,巴基斯坦PK,新西兰NZ,秘鲁PE,哥斯达黎加CR,香港HK,澳门MO 智利CL 亚太APTA	0	最不发达35国LDC35,最不发达4国LDC4	17	----Lubricating grease
1531	2710.1992	----润滑脂	6	0 0.6 5.4	东盟ASEAN,巴基斯坦PK,新西兰NZ,秘鲁PE,哥斯达黎加CR 智利CL 亚太APTA	0	最不发达35国LDC35	17	----Lubricating oils
1532	2710.1993	----润滑油基础油	6	0 0.6 5	东盟ASEAN,新西兰NZ,秘鲁PE,哥斯达黎加CR,台湾TW 智利CL 巴基斯坦PK	0	最不发达35国LDC35	17	----Basic oils for lubricating oils
1533	2710.1994	----液体石蜡和重质液体石蜡	6	0 0.6 5.4	东盟ASEAN,巴基斯坦PK,新西兰NZ,秘鲁PE,哥斯达黎加CR,台湾TW 智利CL 亚太APTA	0	最不发达35国LDC35	20	----Liquid paraffin and heavy liquid paraffin
1534	2710.1999	----其他	6	0 0.6 5	东盟ASEAN,新西兰NZ,秘鲁PE,哥斯达黎加CR,香港HK 智利CL 巴基斯坦PK	0	最不发达35国LDC35	20	----Other
1535	2710.2000	-石油及从沥青矿物提取的油类（但原油除外）以及以上述油为基本成分（按重量计不低于70%）的其他税目未列名制品，含有生物柴油，但废油除外	6	0 0.6	东盟ASEAN,巴基斯坦PK,新加坡SG,新西兰NZ,哥斯达黎加CR,台湾TW 智利CL	0	最不发达35国LDC35	20	-Petroleum oils and oils obtained from bituminous minerals (other than crude) and preparations not elsewhere specified or included, containing by weight 70% or more of petroleum oils or of oils obtained from bituminous minerals, these oils being the basic constituents of the preparations, containing biodiesel, other than waste oils
		-废油:							-Waste oils:
1536	2710.9100	--含多氯联苯(PCBs)、多氯三联(PCTs)或多溴联苯(PBBs)的	6	0 1.2 5	东盟ASEAN,智利CL,新西兰NZ,秘鲁PE 哥斯达黎加CR 巴基斯坦PK	0	最不发达35国LDC35	20	--Containing polychlorinated biphenyls (PCBs), polychlorinated terphenyls (PCTs) or polybrominated biphenyls (PBBs)
1537	2710.9900	--其他	6	0 1.2 5	东盟ASEAN,智利CL,新西兰NZ,秘鲁PE 哥斯达黎加CR 巴基斯坦PK	0	最不发达35国LDC35	20	--Other

序号 No.	税则号列 Tariff Line	货品名称	最惠国税率 MFN(%)	协定税率 Agreement(%)		特惠税率 S.P.(%)		普通税率 Gen.(%)	Article Description
	27.11	**石油气及其他烃类气:**							**Petroleum gases and other gaseous hydrocarbons:**
		-液化的:							-Liquefied:
1538	2711.1100	--天然气	0			0	最不发达35国LDC35,最不发达4国LDC4	20	--Natural gas
1539	2711.1200	--丙烷	5 △1	0 0.5 3.5	东盟ASEAN,巴基斯坦PK,新西兰NZ,秘鲁PE,哥斯达黎加CR 智利CL 亚太APTA	0	最不发达35国LDC35	20	--Propane
		--丁烷:							--Butanes:
1540	2711.1310	---直接灌注香烟打火机及类似打火器用，其包装容器的容积超过300立方厘米	11	0 1.1 2.2 5	东盟ASEAN,新加坡SG,新西兰NZ,秘鲁PE 智利CL 哥斯达黎加CR 巴基斯坦PK	0	最不发达35国LDC35	80	---Liquid or liquefied-gas fuels in containers of a kind used for filling or refilling cigarette or similar lighters and of a capacity exceeding 300cm³
1541	2711.1390	---其他	5 △1	0 0.5 2.5	东盟ASEAN,巴基斯坦PK,新西兰NZ,哥斯达黎加CR 智利CL 秘鲁PE			20	---Other
1542	2711.1400	--乙烯、丙烯、丁烯及丁二烯	5	0	东盟ASEAN,智利CL,巴基斯坦PK,新西兰NZ,秘鲁PE,哥斯达黎加CR	0	最不发达35国LDC35	20	--Ethylene, propylene, butylene and butadiene
		--其他:							--Other:
1543	2711.1910	---直接灌注香烟打火机及类似打火器用的燃料，其包装容器的容积超过300立方厘米	10	0 1 5 7	东盟ASEAN,新西兰NZ,秘鲁PE,哥斯达黎加CR 智利CL 巴基斯坦PK 亚太APTA	0	最不发达35国LDC35	80	---Liquid or liquefied-gas fuels in containers of a kind used for filling or refilling cigarette or similar lighters and of a capacity exceeding 300cm³
1544	2711.1990	---其他	3	0 1.5 2.1	东盟ASEAN,智利CL,巴基斯坦PK,新西兰NZ,哥斯达黎加CR 秘鲁PE 亚太APTA			20	---Other
		-气态的:							-In gaseous state:
1545	2711.2100	--天然气	0			0	最不发达35国LDC35,最不发达4国LDC4	20	--Natural gas

序号 No.	税则号列 Tariff Line	货品名称	最惠国税率 MFN(%)	协定税率 Agreement(%)		特惠税率 S.P.(%)		普通税率 Gen.(%)	Article Description
1546	2711.2900	--其他	6	0 5	东盟ASEAN,智利CL,新西兰NZ,秘鲁PE,哥斯达黎加CR 巴基斯坦PK	0	最不发达35国LDC35	20	--Other
	27.12	**凡士林;石蜡、微晶石蜡、疏松石蜡、地蜡、褐煤蜡、泥煤蜡、其他矿物蜡及用合成或其他方法制得的类似产品,不论是否着色:**							**Petroleum jelly; paraffin wax, microcrystalline petroleum wax, slack wax, ozokerite, lignite wax, peat wax, other mineral waxes, and similar products obtained by synthesis or by other processes, whether or not coloured:**
1547	2712.1000	-凡士林	8	0 0.8 5	东盟ASEAN,新西兰NZ,秘鲁PE,哥斯达黎加CR 智利CL 巴基斯坦PK	0	最不发达35国LDC35,最不发达4国LDC4	45	-Petroleum jelly
1548	2712.2000	-石蜡,按重量计含油量小于0.75%	8	0 5	东盟ASEAN,智利CL,新西兰NZ,秘鲁PE,哥斯达黎加CR 巴基斯坦PK	0	最不发达35国LDC35,最不发达4国LDC4	45	-Paraffin wax containing by weight less than 0.75% of oil
		-其他:							-Other:
1549	2712.9010	---微晶石蜡	8	0 5	东盟ASEAN,智利CL,新西兰NZ,秘鲁PE,哥斯达黎加CR 巴基斯坦PK	0	最不发达35国LDC35,最不发达4国LDC4	45	---Microcrystalline petroleum wax
1550	2712.9090	---其他	8	0 5	东盟ASEAN,智利CL,新西兰NZ,秘鲁PE,哥斯达黎加CR 巴基斯坦PK	0	最不发达35国LDC35,最不发达4国LDC4	45	---Other
	27.13	**石油焦、石油沥青及其他石油或从沥青矿物提取的油类的残渣:**							**Petroleum coke, Petroleum bitumen and other residues of petroleum oils or of oils obtained from bituminous minerals:**
		-石油焦:							-Petroleum coke:
		--未煅烧:							--Not calcined:
1551	2713.1110	---硫的重量百分比小于3%的	3	0	东盟ASEAN,智利CL,巴基斯坦PK,新西兰NZ,秘鲁PE,哥斯达黎加CR	0	最不发达35国LDC35,最不发达4国LDC4	11	---Containing by weight less than 3% of Sulphur

序号 No.	税则号列 Tariff Line	货品名称	最惠国税率 MFN(%)	协定税率 Agreement(%)		特惠税率 S.P.(%)		普通税率 Gen.(%)	Article Description
1552	2713.1190	---其他	3	0	东盟ASEAN,智利CL,巴基斯坦PK,新西兰NZ,秘鲁PE,哥斯达黎加CR	0	最不发达35国LDC35,最不发达4国LDC4	11	---Other
		--已煅烧:							--Calcined:
1553	2713.1210	---硫的重量百分比小于0.8%的	3	0	东盟ASEAN,智利CL,巴基斯坦PK,新西兰NZ,秘鲁PE,哥斯达黎加CR	0	最不发达35国LDC35,最不发达4国LDC4	11	---Containing by weight less than 0.8% of Sulphur
1554	2713.1290	---其他	3	0	东盟ASEAN,智利CL,巴基斯坦PK,新西兰NZ,秘鲁PE,哥斯达黎加CR	0	最不发达35国LDC35,最不发达4国LDC4	11	---Other
1555	2713.2000	-石油沥青	8	0 5 5.6	东盟ASEAN,智利CL,新西兰NZ,秘鲁PE,哥斯达黎加CR 巴基斯坦PK 亚太APTA	0	最不发达35国LDC35,最不发达4国LDC4	35	-Petroleum bitumen
1556	2713.9000	-其他石油或从沥青矿物提取的油类的残渣	6	0 5	东盟ASEAN,智利CL,新西兰NZ,秘鲁PE,哥斯达黎加CR 巴基斯坦PK	0	最不发达35国LDC35,最不发达4国LDC4	35	-Other residues of petroleum oils or of oils obtained from bituminous minerals
	27.14	**天然沥青(地沥青)、沥青页岩、油页岩及焦油砂;沥青岩:**							**Bitumen and asphalt, natural; bituminous or oil shale and tar sands; asphaltites and asphaltic rocks:**
1557	2714.1000	-沥青页岩、油页岩及焦油砂	6	0 5	东盟ASEAN,智利CL,新西兰NZ,秘鲁PE,哥斯达黎加CR 巴基斯坦PK	0	最不发达35国LDC35,最不发达4国LDC4	20	-Bituminous or oil shale and tar sands
		-其他:							-Other:
1558	2714.9010	---天然沥青(地沥青)	8 △4	0 5	东盟ASEAN,智利CL,新西兰NZ,秘鲁PE,哥斯达黎加CR 巴基斯坦PK	0	最不发达35国LDC35,最不发达4国LDC4	35	---Natural bitumen and asphalt
1559	2714.9020	---乳化沥青	0			0	最不发达35国LDC35,最不发达4国LDC4	20	---Emulsified bitumen and asphalt

序号 No.	税则号列 Tariff Line	货品名称	最惠国 税率 MFN(%)	协定税率 Agreement(%)		特惠税率 S.P.(%)		普通 税率 Gen.(%)	Article Description
1560	2714.9090	---其他	3	0	东盟ASEAN,智利CL,巴基斯坦PK,新西兰NZ,秘鲁PE,哥斯达黎加CR	0	最不发达35国LDC35,最不发达4国LDC4	20	---Other
	27.15	**以天然沥青（地沥青）、石油沥青、矿物焦油或矿物焦油沥青为基本成分的沥青混合物（例如，沥青胶粘剂、稀释沥青）：**							**Bituminous mixtures based on natural asphalt, on natural bitumen, on petroleum bitumen, on mineral tar or on mineral tar pitch (for example, bituminous mastics, cut-backs):**
1561	2715.0000	以天然沥青（地沥青）、石油沥青、矿物焦油或矿物焦油沥青为基本成分的沥青混合物（例如，沥青胶粘剂、稀释沥青）	8	0 0.8 5	东盟ASEAN,新西兰NZ,秘鲁PE,哥斯达黎加CR,澳门MO 智利CL 巴基斯坦PK	0	最不发达35国LDC35,最不发达4国LDC4	35	Bituminous mixtures based on natural asphalt, on natural bitumen, on petroleum bitumen, on mineral tar or on mineral tar pitch (for example, bituminous mastics, cut-backs)
	27.16	**电力:**							**Electrical energy:**
1562	2716.0000	电力	0			0	最不发达35国LDC35,最不发达4国LDC4	8	Electrical energy

第六类

化学工业及其相关工业的产品

注释:

一、

（一）凡符合税号28.44或28.45规定的货品（放射性矿砂除外），应分别归入以上税号而不归入本目录的其他税号；

（二）除上述（一）款另有规定的以外，凡符合税号28.43、28.46或28.52规定的货品，应分别归入这两个税号而不归入本类的其他税号。

二、除上述注释一另有规定的以外，凡由于按一定剂量或作为零售包装而可归入税号30.04、30.05、30.06、32.12、33.03、33.04、33.05、33.06、33.07、35.06、37.07或38.08的货品，应分别归入以上税号，而不归入本目录的其他税号。

三、由两种或两种以上单独成分配套的货品，其部分或全部成分属于本类范围以内，混合后则构成第六类或第七类的货品，应按混合后产品归入相应的税号，但其组成成分必须同时符合下列条件:

（一）其包装形式足以表明这些成分不需经过改装就可一起使用的;

（二）一起进口或出口的;

（三）这些成分的属性及相互比例足以表明是相互配用的。

SECTION Ⅵ

PRODUCTS OF THE CHEMICAL OR ALLIED INDUSTRIES

Notes:

1. (a) Goods (other than radioactive ores) answering to a description in heading No.28.44 or 28.45 are to be classified in those headings and in no other heading of the Nomenclature;

(b) Subject to paragraph (A) above, goods answering to a description in heading No.28.43 , 28.46 or 28.52 are to be classified in those headings and in no other heading of this Section.

2. Subject to Note 1 above, goods classifiable in heading No.30.04, 30.05, 30.06, 32.12, 33.03, 33.04, 33.05, 33.06, 33.07, 35.06, 37.07, or 38.08 by reason of being put up in measured doses or for retail sale are to be classified in those headings and in no other headings of the Nomenclature.

3. Goods put up in sets consisting of two or more separate constituents, some or all of which fall in this Section and are intended to be mixed together to obtain a product of Section Ⅵ or Ⅶ, are to be classified in the heading appropriate to that product, provided that the constituents are:

(a) having regard to the manner in which they are put up, clearly identifiable as being intended to be used together without first being repacked;

(b) presented together; and

(c) identifiable, whether by their nature or by the relative proportions in which they are present, as being complementary one to another.

第二十八章

无机化学品；贵金属、稀土金属、放射性元素及其同位素的有机及无机化合物

注释:

一、除条文另有规定的以外，本章各税号只适用于:

（一）单独的化学元素及单独的已有化学定义的化合物，不论是否含有杂质;

（二）上述（一）款产品的水溶液;

Chapter 28

Inorganic chemicals; organic or inorganic compounds of precious metals, of rare-earth metals of radioactive elements or of isotopes

Notes:

1. Except where the context otherwise requires, the headings of this Chapter apply only to:

(a) Separate chemical elements and separate chemically defined compounds, whether or not containing impurities;

(b) The products mentioned in (a) above dissolved in water;

（三）溶于其他溶剂的上述（一）款产品，但该产品处于溶液状态只是为了安全或运输所采取的正常必要方法，其所用溶剂并不使该产品改变其一般用途而适合于某些特殊用途；

（四）为了保存或运输需要，加入稳定剂（包括抗结块剂）的上述（一）、（二）、（三）款产品；

（五）为了便于识别或安全起见，加入抗尘剂或着色剂的上述（一）、（二）、（三）、（四）款产品，但所加剂料并不使原产品改变其一般用途而适合于某些特殊用途。

二、除以有机物质稳定的连二亚硫酸盐及次硫酸盐（税号 28.31），无机碱的碳酸盐及过碳酸盐（税号 28.36），无机碱的氰化物、氧氰化物及氰络合物（税号 28.37），无机碱的雷酸盐、氰酸盐及硫氰酸盐（税号 28.42），税号 28.43 至 28.46 及 28.52 的有机产品，以及碳化物（税号 28.49）之外，本章仅包括下列碳化合物：

（一）碳的氧化物，氰化氢及雷酸、异氰酸、硫氰酸及其他简单或络合氰酸（税号 28.11）；

（二）碳的卤氧化物（税号 28.12）；

（三）二硫化碳（税号28.13）；

（四）硫代碳酸盐、硒代碳酸盐、碲代碳酸盐、硒代氰酸盐、碲代氰酸盐、四氰硫基二氨基络酸盐及其他无机碱络合氰酸盐（税号28.42）；

（五）用尿素固化的过氧化氢（税号28.47）、氧硫化碳、硫代羰基卤化物、氰、卤化氰、氨基氰及其金属衍生物（税号28.53），不论是否纯净，但氰氨化钙除外（第三十一章）。

三、除第六类注释一另有规定的以外，本章不包括：

（一）氯化钠或氧化镁（不论是否纯净）及第五类的其他产品；

(c) The products mentioned in (a) above dissolved in other solvents, provided that the solution constitutes a normal and necessary method of putting up these products adopted solely for reasons of safety or for transport, and that the solvent does not render the product particularly suitable for specific use rather than for general use;

(d) The products mentioned in (a), (b) or (c) above with an added stabilizer(including an anti-caking agent necessary for their preservation or transport;

(e) The products mentioned in (a), (b), (c) or (d) above with an added antidusting agent or a colouring substance added to facilitate their identification or for safety reasons, provided that the additions do not render the product particularly suitable for specific use rather than for general use.

2. In addition to dithionites and sulphoxylates, stabilized with organic substances (heading No.28.31), carbonates and peroxocarbonates of inorganic bases (heading No.28.36), cyanides, cyanide oxides and complex cyanides of inorganic bases (heading No.28.37), fulminates, cyanates and thiocyanates, of inorganic bases (heading No.28.42), organic products included in headings No.28.43 to 28.46 and 28.52 and carbides (heading No.28.49), only the following compounds of carbon are to the classified in this Chapter:

(a) Oxides of carbon, hydrogen cyanide and fulminic, isocyanic, thiocyanic and other simple or complex cyanogen acids (heading No.28.11) ;

(b) Halide oxides of carbon (heading No.28.12) ;

(c) Carbon disulphide (heading No.28.13) ;

(d) Thiocarbonates, selenocarbonates, tellurocarbonates, selenocyanates, tellurocyanates, tetrathiocyanato diamminochromates (reineckates) and other complex cyanates, of inorganic bases (heading No.28.42) ;

(e) Hydrogen peroxide, soildified with urea (heading No. 28.47), carbon oxysulphide, thiocarbonyl halides, cyanogen, cyanogen halides and cyanamide and its metal derivatives (heading No.28.53) other than calcium cyanamide, whether or not pure (Chapter 31) .

3. Subject to the provisions of Note 1 to SectionⅥ, this Chapter does not cover:

(a) Sodium chloride or magnesium oxide, whether or not pure, or other products of SectionⅤ;

（二）上述注释二所述以外的有机——无机化合物；

（三）第三十一章注释二、三、四或五所述的产品；

（四）税号32.06的用作发光剂的无机产品；税目32.07的搪瓷玻璃料及其他玻璃，呈粉、粒或粉片状的；

（五）人造石墨（税号38.01）；税号38.13的灭火器的装配药及已装药的灭火弹；税号38.24的零售包装的除墨剂；税号38.24的每颗重量不少于2.5克的碱金属或碱土金属卤化物的培养晶体（光学元件除外）；

（六）宝石或半宝石（天然、合成或再造）及这些宝石、半宝石的粉末（税号71.02至71.05），第七十一章的贵金属及贵金属合金；

（七）第十五类的金属（不论是否纯净）、金属合金或金属陶瓷，包括硬质合金（与金属烧结的金属碳化物）；

（八）光学元件，例如用碱金属或碱土金属卤化物制成的（税号90.01）。

四、由本章第二分章的非金属酸和第四分章的金属酸所构成的已有化学定义的络酸，应归入税号28.11。

五、税号28.26至28.42只适用于金属盐、铵盐及过氧酸盐。除条文另有规定的以外，复盐及络盐应归入税号28.42。

六、税号28.44只适用于：

（一）锝（原子序数43）、钷（原子序数61）、钋（原子序数84）及原子序数大于84的所有化学元素；

（二）天然或人造放射性同位素（包括第十四类及第十五类的贵金属和贱金属的放射性同位素），不论是否混合；

（三）上述元素或同位素的无机或有机化合物，不论是否已有化学定义或是否混合；

（四）含有上述元素或同位素及其无机或有机化合物并且具有某种放射性强度超过 74 贝克勒尔/克（0.002 微居里/克）的合金、分散体（包括金属陶瓷）、陶瓷产品及混合物；

(b) Organo-inorganic compounds other than those mentioned in Note 2 above;

(c) Products mentioned in Note 2, 3, 4 or 5 to Chapter 31;

(d) Inorganic products of a kind used as luminophores, of heading No.32.06; glass frit and other glass in the form of powder, granules or flakes, of heading 32.07;

(e) Artificial graphite (heading No.38.01) ; products put up as charges for fire-extinguishers or put up in fire-extinguishing grenades, of heading No.38.13; ink removers put up in packings for retail sale, of heading No.38.24, cultured crystals (other than optical elements) weighing not less than 2.5g each, of the halides of the alkali or alkaline-earth metals, of heading No.38.24;

(f) Precious or semi-precious stones (natural, synthetic or reconstructed) or dust or powder of such stones (headings Nos.71.02 to 71.05) , or precious metals or precious metal alloys of Chapter 71;

(g) The metals, whether or not pure, metal alloys or cermets, including sintered metal carbides (metal carbides sintered with a metal) , of Section XV; or

(h) Optical elements, for example, of the halides of the alkali or alkaline-earth metals (heading No.90.01) .

4. Chemically defined complex acids consisting of a nonmetalacid of sub-Chapter II and a metal acid of sub-Chapter IVare to be lassified in heading No.28.11.

5. Headings Nos.28.26 to 28.42 apply only to metal or ammonium salts or peroxysalts. Except where the context otherwise requires, double or complex salts are to be classified in heading No.28.42.

6. Heading No.28.44 applies only to:

(a) Technetium (atomic No.43), promethium (atomic No.61), polonium (atomic No.84) and all elements with an atomic number greater than 84;

(b) Natural or artificial radioactive isotopes (including those of the precious metals or of the base metals of Sections XIV and XV), whether or not mixed together;

(c) Compounds, inorganic or organic, of these elements or isotopes, whether or not chemically defined, whether or not mixed together;

(d) Alloys, dispersions (including cermets) , ceramic products and mixtures containing these elements or istopes or inorganic or organic compounds thereof and having a specific radioactivity exceeding 74 Bq/g (0.002 μCi/g) ;

（五）核反应堆已耗尽（已辐照）的燃料元件（释热元件）；

（六）放射性的残渣，不论是否有用。

税号 28.44、28.45 及本注释所称“同位素”，是指：

1. 单独的核素，但不包括自然界中以单一同位素状态存在的核素；

2. 同一元素的同位素混合物，其中一种或几种同位素已被浓缩，即人工地改变了该元素同位素的自然构成。

七、税号 28.48 包括按重量计含磷量超过 15%的磷化铜（磷铜）。

八、经掺杂用于电子工业的化学元素（例如，硅、硒），如果拉制后未经加工或呈圆筒形、棒形，应归入本章；如果已切成圆片、薄片或类似形状，则归入税号 38.18。

(e) Spent (irradiated) fuel elements (cartridges) of nuclear reactors;

(f) Radioactive residues whether or not usable. The term “isotopes”, for the purposes of this Note and of the wording of headings Nos.28.44 and 28.45, refers to:

-individual nuclides, excluding, however, those existing in nature in the monoisotopic state;

-mixtures of isotopes of one and the same element, enriched in one or several of the said isotopes, that is, elements of which the natural isotopic composition has been artificially modified.

7. Heading No.28.48 includes copper phosphide (phosphor copper) containing more than 15% by weight of phosphorus.

8. Chemical elements (for example, silicon and selenium) doped for use in electronics are to be classified in this Chapter, provided that they are in forms unworked as drawn, or in the form of cylinders or rods. When cut in the form of discs, wafers or similar forms, they fall in heading No.38.18.

子目注释：

子目 2852.10 所称“已有化学定义”是指符合第二十八章注释一(一)至（五）或第二十九章注释一（一）至（八）规定的汞的无机或有机化合物。

Subheading Notes:

For the purposes of subheading 2852.10, the expression “chemically defined” means all organic or inorganic compounds of mercury meeting the requirements of paragraphs (a) to (e) of Note 1 to Chapter 28 or paragraphs (a) to (h) of Note 1 to Chapter 29.

序号 No.	税则号列 Tariff Line	货品名称	最惠国税率 MFN(%)	协定税率 Agreement(%)		特惠税率 S.P.(%)		普通税率 Gen.(%)	Article Description
		第一分章 化学元素							Ⅰ.CHEMICAL ELEMENTS
	28.01	**氟、氯、溴及碘:**							**Fluorine, chlorine, bromine and iodine:**
1563	2801.1000	-氯	5.5	0 0.6 5	东盟ASEAN,新西兰NZ,秘鲁PE,哥斯达黎加CR 智利CL 巴基斯坦PK	0	最不发达35国LDC35	80	-Chlorine
1564	2801.2000	-碘	5.5	0 5	东盟ASEAN,新西兰NZ,哥斯达黎加CR 巴基斯坦PK	0	最不发达35国LDC35	30	-Iodine
		-氟;溴:							-Fluorine; bromine:
1565	2801.3010	---氟	5.5	0	东盟ASEAN,智利CL,巴基斯坦PK,新西兰NZ,秘鲁PE,哥斯达黎加CR	0	最不发达35国LDC35	30	---Fluorine

序号 No.	税则号列 Tariff Line	货品名称	最惠国税率 MFN(%)	协定税率 Agreement(%)		特惠税率 S.P.(%)		普通税率 Gen.(%)	Article Description
1566	2801.3020	---溴	5.5 △1	0	东盟ASEAN,智利CL,巴基斯坦PK,新西兰NZ,秘鲁PE,哥斯达黎加CR	0	最不发达35国LDC35	30	---Bromine
	28.02	**升华硫磺、沉淀硫磺;胶态硫磺:**							**Sulphur, sublimed or precipitated; colloidal sulphur:**
1567	2802.0000	升华硫磺、沉淀硫磺;胶态硫磺	5.5 △1	0	东盟ASEAN,智利CL,巴基斯坦PK,新西兰NZ,秘鲁PE,哥斯达黎加CR	0	最不发达35国LDC35	17	Sulphur, sublimed or precipitated; colloidal sulphur
	28.03	**碳(碳黑及其他税号未列名的其他形态的碳):**							**Carbon (carbon blacks and other forms of carbon not elsewhere specified or included):**
1568	2803.0000	碳(碳黑及其他税号未列名的其他形态的碳)	5.5	0 4.4	东盟ASEAN,智利CL,巴基斯坦PK,新西兰NZ,秘鲁PE,哥斯达黎加CR,香港HK,台湾TW 亚太APTA	0	最不发达35国LDC35,最不发达4国LDC4	35	Carbon (carbon blacks and other forms of carbon not elsewhere specified or included)
	28.04	**氢、稀有气体及其他非金属:**							**Hydrogen, rare gases and other nonmetals:**
1569	2804.1000	-氢	5.5	0	东盟ASEAN,智利CL,巴基斯坦PK,新西兰NZ,秘鲁PE,哥斯达黎加CR,香港HK	0	最不发达35国LDC35,最不发达4国LDC4	30	-Hydrogen
		-稀有气体:							-Rare gases:
1570	2804.2100	--氩	5.5	0 0.6 5	东盟ASEAN,新西兰NZ,秘鲁PE,哥斯达黎加CR,香港HK 智利CL 巴基斯坦PK	0	最不发达35国LDC35,最不发达4国LDC4	30	--Argon
1571	2804.2900	--其他	5.5	0 5	东盟ASEAN,智利CL,新西兰NZ,秘鲁PE,哥斯达黎加CR,香港HK 巴基斯坦PK	0	最不发达35国LDC35,最不发达4国LDC4	30	--Other
1572	2804.3000	-氮	5.5	0 5	东盟ASEAN,智利CL,新西兰NZ,秘鲁PE,哥斯达黎加CR,香港HK 巴基斯坦PK	0	最不发达35国LDC35,最不发达4国LDC4	30	-Nitrogen
1573	2804.4000	-氧	5.5	0 0.6 5	东盟ASEAN,新西兰NZ,秘鲁PE,哥斯达黎加CR,香港HK 智利CL 巴基斯坦PK	0	最不发达35国LDC35,最不发达4国LDC4	80	-Oxygen

序号 No.	税则号列 Tariff Line	货品名称	最惠国税率 MFN(%)	协定税率 Agreement(%)	特惠税率 S.P.(%)	普通税率 Gen.(%)	Article Description
1574	2804.5000	-硼；碲	5.5	0 东盟ASEAN,智利CL,巴基斯坦PK,新西兰NZ,秘鲁PE,哥斯达黎加CR	0 最不发达35国LDC35,最不发达4国LDC4	17	-Boron; tellurium
	ex28045000	碲	△0				Polysilicon
		-硅:					-Silicon;
		--按重量计含硅量不少于99.99%:					--Containing by weight not less than 99.99% of silicon:
		---经掺杂用于电子工业的直径在7.5厘米及以上的单晶硅棒:					---Monocrystals doped for use in electronics, in the form of cylinders or rods, 7.5cm or more in diameter:
1575	2804.6117	----直径在30厘米及以上的	4	0 东盟ASEAN,智利CL,巴基斯坦PK,新西兰NZ,秘鲁PE,哥斯达黎加CR	0 最不发达35国LDC35,最不发达4国LDC4	11	----30cm or more in diameter
1576	2804.6119	----其他	4	0 东盟ASEAN,智利CL,巴基斯坦PK,新西兰NZ,秘鲁PE,哥斯达黎加CR	0 最不发达35国LDC35,最不发达4国LDC4	11	----Other
1577	2804.6120	---经掺杂用于电子工业的其他单晶硅棒	4	0 东盟ASEAN,智利CL,巴基斯坦PK,新西兰NZ,秘鲁PE,哥斯达黎加CR	0 最不发达35国LDC35,最不发达4国LDC4	17	---Other monocrystals doped for use in electronics, in the form of cylinders or rods
1578	2804.6190	---其他	4	0 东盟ASEAN,智利CL,巴基斯坦PK,新西兰NZ,秘鲁PE,哥斯达黎加CR	0 最不发达35国LDC35,最不发达4国LDC4	30	---Other
	ex28046190	多晶硅（纯度高于99.9999999%）	△1				Polycrystalline silicon (containing Si>99.9999999%)
1579	2804.6900	--其他	4	0 东盟ASEAN,智利CL,巴基斯坦PK,新西兰NZ,秘鲁PE,哥斯达黎加CR	0 最不发达35国LDC35,最不发达4国LDC4	30	--Other
		-磷:					-Phosphorus:
1580	2804.7010	---黄磷（白磷）	5.5	0 东盟ASEAN,智利CL,巴基斯坦PK,新西兰NZ,秘鲁PE,哥斯达黎加CR	0 最不发达35国LDC35,最不发达4国LDC4	30	---Yellow phosphorus (white phosphorus)

序号 No.	税则号列 Tariff Line	货品名称	最惠国税率 MFN(%)	协定税率 Agreement(%)		特惠税率 S.P.(%)		普通税率 Gen.(%)	Article Description
1581	2804.7090	---其他	5.5	0	东盟ASEAN,智利CL,巴基斯坦PK,新西兰NZ,秘鲁PE,哥斯达黎加CR	0	最不发达35国LDC35,最不发达4国LDC4	30	---Other
1582	2804.8000	-砷	5.5	0	东盟ASEAN,智利CL,巴基斯坦PK,新西兰NZ,秘鲁PE,哥斯达黎加CR	0	最不发达35国LDC35,最不发达4国LDC4	30	-Arsenic
		-硒:							-Selenium:
1583	2804.9010	---经掺杂用于电子工业的晶体棒	4	0 0.4 2	东盟ASEAN,巴基斯坦PK,新西兰NZ,哥斯达黎加CR 智利CL 秘鲁PE	0	最不发达35国LDC35,最不发达4国LDC4	17	---Crystals doped for use in electronics, in the form of cylinders or rods
1584	2804.9090	---其他	5.5 △0	0 0.6 4.1	东盟ASEAN,巴基斯坦PK,新西兰NZ,哥斯达黎加CR 智利CL 秘鲁PE	0	最不发达35国LDC35	30	---Other
	28.05	**碱金属、碱土金属;稀土金属、钪及钇,不论是否相互混合或相互熔合;汞:**							**Alkali or alkaline-earth metals; rare-earth metals, scandium and yttrium, whether or not intermixed or interalloyed; mercury:**
		-碱金属及碱土金属:							-Alkali metals or alkaline-earth metals:
1585	2805.1100	--钠	5.5 △1	0	东盟ASEAN,智利CL,巴基斯坦PK,新西兰NZ,秘鲁PE,哥斯达黎加CR	0	最不发达35国LDC35	30	--Sodium
1586	2805.1200	--钙	5.5 △1	0	东盟ASEAN,智利CL,巴基斯坦PK,新西兰NZ,秘鲁PE,哥斯达黎加CR	0	最不发达35国LDC35	30	--Calcium
1587	2805.1900	--其他	5.5 △1	0	东盟ASEAN,智利CL,巴基斯坦PK,新西兰NZ,秘鲁PE,哥斯达黎加CR	0	最不发达35国LDC35	30	--Other
		-稀土金属、钪及钇,不论是否相互混合或相互熔合:							-Rare-earth metals, scandium and yttrium, whether or not intermixed or interalloyed:
		---稀土金属、钪及钇,未相互混合或相互熔合:							---Not intermixed or interalloyed:
1588	2805.3011	----钕	5.5 △0	0	东盟ASEAN,智利CL,巴基斯坦PK,新西兰NZ,秘鲁PE,哥斯达黎加CR	0	最不发达35国LDC35	30	----Neodymium

序号 No.	税则号列 Tariff Line	货品名称	最惠国税率 MFN(%)	协定税率 Agreement(%)		特惠税率 S.P.(%)		普通税率 Gen.(%)	Article Description
1589	2805.3012	----镝	5.5 △0	0	东盟ASEAN,智利CL,巴基斯坦PK,新西兰NZ,秘鲁PE,哥斯达黎加CR	0	最不发达35国LDC35	30	----Dysprosium
1590	2805.3013	----铽	5.5 △0	0	东盟ASEAN,智利CL,巴基斯坦PK,新西兰NZ,秘鲁PE,哥斯达黎加CR	0	最不发达35国LDC35	30	----Terbium
1591	2805.3014	----镧	5.5 △0	0	东盟ASEAN,智利CL,巴基斯坦PK,新西兰NZ,秘鲁PE,哥斯达黎加CR	0	最不发达35国LDC35	30	----Lanthanum
1592	2805.3015	----铈	5.5 △0	0	东盟ASEAN,智利CL,巴基斯坦PK,新西兰NZ,秘鲁PE,哥斯达黎加CR	0	最不发达35国LDC35	30	----Cerium
1593	2805.3016	----镨	5.5 △0	0	东盟ASEAN,智利CL,巴基斯坦PK,新西兰NZ,秘鲁PE,哥斯达黎加CR	0	最不发达35国LDC35	30	----Praseodymium
1594	2805.3017	----钇	5.5 △0	0	东盟ASEAN,智利CL,巴基斯坦PK,新西兰NZ,秘鲁PE,哥斯达黎加CR	0	最不发达35国LDC35	30	----Yttrium
1595	2805.3019	----其他	5.5 △0	0	东盟ASEAN,智利CL,巴基斯坦PK,新西兰NZ,秘鲁PE,哥斯达黎加CR	0	最不发达35国LDC35	30	----Other
		---稀土金属、钪及钇，相互混合或相互熔合:							---Intermixed or interalloyed:
1596	2805.3021	----电池级	5.5 △0	0	东盟ASEAN,智利CL,巴基斯坦PK,新西兰NZ,秘鲁PE,哥斯达黎加CR	0	最不发达35国LDC35	30	----Battery grade
1597	2805.3029	---其他	5.5 △0	0	东盟ASEAN,智利CL,巴基斯坦PK,新西兰NZ,秘鲁PE,哥斯达黎加CR	0	最不发达35国LDC35	30	----Other
1598	2805.4000	-汞	5.5	0 0.6	东盟ASEAN,巴基斯坦PK,新西兰NZ,秘鲁PE,哥斯达黎加CR 智利CL	0	最不发达35国LDC35	17	-Mercury
		第二分章 无机酸及非金属无机氧化物							Ⅱ. INORGANIC ACIDS AND INOR-GANIC OXYGEN COMPOUNDS OF NON-METALS
	28.06	**氯化氢（盐酸）;氯磺酸:**							**Hydrogen chloride (hydrochloric acid); chorosulphuric acid:**
1599	2806.1000	-氯化氢（盐酸）	5.5	0 0.6 5	东盟ASEAN,新西兰NZ,秘鲁PE,哥斯达黎加CR 智利CL 巴基斯坦PK	0	最不发达35国LDC35	80	-Hydrogen chloride (hydrochloric acid)

序号 No.	税则号列 Tariff Line	货品名称	最惠国 税 率 MFN(%)	协定税率 Agreement(%)		特惠税率 S.P.(%)		普通 税率 Gen.(%)	Article Description
1600	2806.2000	-氯磺酸	5.5	0	东盟ASEAN,智利CL,巴基斯坦PK,新西兰NZ,秘鲁PE,哥斯达黎加CR	0	最不发达35国LDC35	40	-Chlorosulphuric acid
	28.07	**硫酸;发烟硫酸:**							**Sulphuric acid; oleum:**
1601	2807.0000	硫酸;发烟硫酸	5.5 △1	0 0.6 5	东盟ASEAN,新西兰NZ,秘鲁PE,哥斯达黎加CR 智利CL 巴基斯坦PK	0	最不发达35国LDC35	35	Sulphuric acid; oleum
	28.08	**硝酸;磺硝酸:**							**Nitric acid; sulphonitric acids:**
1602	2808.0000	硝酸;磺硝酸	5.5	0 0.6 5	东盟ASEAN,新西兰NZ,秘鲁PE,哥斯达黎加CR 智利CL 巴基斯坦PK	0	最不发达35国LDC35	40	Nitric acid; sulphonitric acids
	28.09	**五氧化二磷;磷酸;多磷酸，不论是否已有化学定义:**							**Diphosphorus pentaoxide; phosphoric acid; polyphosphoric acids, whether or not chemically defined:**
1603	2809.1000	-五氧化二磷	1	0	东盟ASEAN,智利CL,巴基斯坦PK,新西兰NZ,秘鲁PE,哥斯达黎加CR	0	最不发达35国LDC35	8	-Diphosphorus pentaoxide
		-磷酸及多磷酸:							-Phosphoric acid and polyphosphoric acids:
		---磷酸及偏磷酸、焦磷酸:							---Phosphoric acid, metaphosphoric acid and pyrophosphoric acid:
1604	2809.2011	----食品级磷酸	1	0	东盟ASEAN,智利CL,巴基斯坦PK,新西兰NZ,秘鲁PE,哥斯达黎加CR	0	最不发达35国LDC35	8	----Phosphoric acid, food grade
1605	2809.2019	----其他	1	0	东盟ASEAN,智利CL,巴基斯坦PK,新西兰NZ,秘鲁PE,哥斯达黎加CR	0	最不发达35国LDC35	8	----Other
1606	2809.2090	---其他	5.5	0 5	东盟ASEAN,智利CL,新西兰NZ,秘鲁PE,哥斯达黎加CR 巴基斯坦PK	0	最不发达35国LDC35	35	---Other
	28.10	**硼的氧化物;硼酸:**							**Oxides of boron; boric acids:**
1607	2810.0010	---硼的氧化物	5.5	0 0.6 2.8	东盟ASEAN,巴基斯坦PK,新西兰NZ,哥斯达黎加CR 智利CL 秘鲁PE	0	最不发达35国LDC35	30	---Oxides of boron
1608	2810.0020	---硼酸	5.5	0 0.6 2.8	东盟ASEAN,巴基斯坦PK,新西兰NZ,哥斯达黎加CR 智利CL 秘鲁PE	0	最不发达35国LDC35	30	---Boric acids

序号 No.	税则号列 Tariff Line	货品名称	最惠国税率 MFN(%)	协定税率 Agreement(%)		特惠税率 S.P.(%)		普通税率 Gen.(%)	Article Description
	28.11	**其他无机酸及非金属无机氧化物:**							**Other inorganic acids and other inorganic oxygen compounds of non-metals:**
		-其他无机酸:							-Other inorganic acids:
1609	2811.1100	--氟化氢（氢氟酸）	5.5	0	东盟ASEAN,智利CL,巴基斯坦PK,新西兰NZ,秘鲁PE,哥斯达黎加CR	0	最不发达35国LDC35,最不发达4国LDC4	35	--Hydrofluoric acid
		--其他:							--Other:
1610	2811.1910	---氢氰酸	5.5	0 0.6	东盟ASEAN,巴基斯坦PK,新西兰NZ,秘鲁PE,哥斯达黎加CR 智利CL	0	最不发达35国LDC35,最不发达4国LDC4	35	---Hydrocyanic acid
1611	2811.1920	---硒化氢	5.5	0 0.6 5	东盟ASEAN,新西兰NZ,秘鲁PE,哥斯达黎加CR 智利CL 巴基斯坦PK	0	最不发达35国LDC35,最不发达4国LDC4	35	---Hydrogen selenide
1612	2811.1990	---其他	5.5	0 0.6 5	东盟ASEAN,新西兰NZ,秘鲁PE,哥斯达黎加CR 智利CL 巴基斯坦PK	0	最不发达35国LDC35,最不发达4国LDC4	35	---Other
		-其他非金属无机氧化物:							-Other inorganic oxygen compounds of nonmetals:
1613	2811.2100	--二氧化碳	5.5	0 5	东盟ASEAN,智利CL,新西兰NZ,秘鲁PE,哥斯达黎加CR,香港HK 巴基斯坦PK	0	最不发达35国LDC35,最不发达4国LDC4	30	--Carbon dioxide
		--二氧化硅:							--Silicon dioxide:
1614	2811.2210	---硅胶	5.5	0 5	东盟ASEAN,智利CL,新西兰NZ,秘鲁PE,哥斯达黎加CR,澳门MO 巴基斯坦PK	0	最不发达35国LDC35,最不发达4国LDC4	30	---Silica gel
1615	2811.2290	---其他	5.5	0 5	东盟ASEAN,智利CL,新西兰NZ,秘鲁PE,哥斯达黎加CR,澳门MO 巴基斯坦PK	0	最不发达35国LDC35,最不发达4国LDC4	30	---Other

序号 No.	税则号列 Tariff Line	货品名称	最惠国税率 MFN(%)	协定税率 Agreement(%)		特惠税率 S.P.(%)		普通税率 Gen.(%)	Article Description
1616	2811.2900	--其他	5.5	0 0.6 5	东盟ASEAN,新西兰NZ,秘鲁PE,哥斯达黎加CR,香港HK 智利CL 巴基斯坦PK	0	最不发达35国LDC35,最不发达4国LDC4	30	--Other
		第三分章 非金属卤化物及硫化物							III. HALOGEN OR SULPHUR COMPOUNDS OF NON-METALS
	28.12	**非金属卤化物及卤氧化物:**							**Halides and halide oxides of non-metals:**
		-氯化物及氯氧化物:							-Chlorides and chloride oxides:
1617	2812.1010	---氯化亚砜	5.5 △2	0 0.6 5	东盟ASEAN,新西兰NZ,秘鲁PE,哥斯达黎加CR 智利CL 巴基斯坦PK	0	最不发达35国LDC35	30	---Sulphoxide chloride
1618	2812.1020	---氧氯化磷(磷酰氯;三氯氧磷)	5.5	0 0.6 5	东盟ASEAN,新西兰NZ,秘鲁PE,哥斯达黎加CR 智利CL 巴基斯坦PK	0	最不发达35国LDC35	30	---Phosphorus oxychloride (phosphoryl monochloride, phosphorus oxytrichloride)
1619	2812.1030	---碳酰二氯(光气)	5.5	0 0.6	东盟ASEAN,巴基斯坦PK,新西兰NZ,秘鲁PE,哥斯达黎加CR 智利CL	0	最不发达35国LDC35	30	---Carbonyl dichloride (phosgene)
		---非金属氯化物:							---Other chlorides of non-metals:
1620	2812.1041	----一氯化硫(氯化硫)	5.5	0 0.6	东盟ASEAN,巴基斯坦PK,新西兰NZ,秘鲁PE,哥斯达黎加CR 智利CL	0	最不发达35国LDC35	30	----Sulfur monochloride
1621	2812.1042	----二氯化硫	5.5	0 0.6	东盟ASEAN,巴基斯坦PK,新西兰NZ,秘鲁PE,哥斯达黎加CR 智利CL	0	最不发达35国LDC35	30	----Sulfur dichloride
1622	2812.1043	----三氯化磷	5.5	0 0.6	东盟ASEAN,巴基斯坦PK,新西兰NZ,秘鲁PE,哥斯达黎加CR 智利CL	0	最不发达35国LDC35	30	----Phosphorus trichloride
1623	2812.1044	----三氯化砷	5.5	0 0.6	东盟ASEAN,巴基斯坦PK,新西兰NZ,秘鲁PE,哥斯达黎加CR 智利CL	0	最不发达35国LDC35	30	----Arsenic trichloride
1624	2812.1045	----五氯化磷	5.5	0 0.6	东盟ASEAN,巴基斯坦PK,新西兰NZ,秘鲁PE,哥斯达黎加CR 智利CL	0	最不发达35国LDC35	30	----Phosphorus pentachloride
1625	2812.1049	---其他	5.5	0 0.6 5	东盟ASEAN,新西兰NZ,秘鲁PE,哥斯达黎加CR 智利CL 巴基斯坦PK	0	最不发达35国LDC35	30	----Other

序号 No.	税则号列 Tariff Line	货品名称	最惠国 税率 MFN(%)	协定税率 Agreement(%)		特惠税率 S.P.(%)		普通 税率 Gen.(%)	Article Description
1626	2812.1090	---其他	5.5	0 0.6	东盟ASEAN,巴基斯坦PK,新西兰NZ,秘鲁PE,哥斯达黎加CR 智利CL	0	最不发达35国LDC35	30	---Other
		-其他: ---氟化物及氟氧化物:							-Other: ---Fluorid and oxy-fluoride:
1627	2812.9011	----三氟化氮	5.5	0	东盟ASEAN,智利CL,巴基斯坦PK,新西兰NZ,秘鲁PE,哥斯达黎加CR	0	最不发达35国LDC35	30	----Nitrogen trifluoride
1628	2812.9019	----其他	5.5	0	东盟ASEAN,智利CL,巴基斯坦PK,新西兰NZ,秘鲁PE,哥斯达黎加CR	0	最不发达35国LDC35	30	----Other
1629	2812.9090	---其他	5.5	0	东盟ASEAN,智利CL,巴基斯坦PK,新西兰NZ,秘鲁PE,哥斯达黎加CR	0	最不发达35国LDC35	30	---Other
	28.13	**非金属硫化物;商品三硫化二磷:**							**Sulphides of nonmetals; commercial phosphorus trisulphides:**
1630	2813.1000	-二硫化碳	5.5	0	东盟ASEAN,智利CL,巴基斯坦PK,新西兰NZ,秘鲁PE,哥斯达黎加CR,香港HK	0	最不发达35国LDC35	30	-Carbon disulphide
1631	2813.9000	-其他	5.5	0	东盟ASEAN,智利CL,巴基斯坦PK,新西兰NZ,秘鲁PE,哥斯达黎加CR	0	最不发达35国LDC35	30	-Other
		第四分章 无机碱和金属氧化物、氢氧化物及过氧化物							Ⅳ. INORGANIC BASES AND OXIDES, HYDROXIDES AND PEROXIDES OF METALS
	28.14	**氨及氨水:**							**Ammonia, anhydrous or in aqueous solution:**
1632	2814.1000	-氨	5.5 △0	0 0.6	东盟ASEAN,巴基斯坦PK,新西兰NZ,秘鲁PE,哥斯达黎加CR 智利CL	0	最不发达35国LDC35,最不发达4国LDC4	35	-Anhydrous ammonia
1633	2814.2000	-氨水	5.5 △0	0	东盟ASEAN,智利CL,巴基斯坦PK,新西兰NZ,秘鲁PE,哥斯达黎加CR	0	最不发达35国LDC35,最不发达4国LDC4	35	-Ammonia in aqueous solution
	28.15	**氢氧化钠(烧碱);氢氧化钾(苛性钾);过氧化钠及过氧化钾:**							**Sodium hydroxide (caustic soda); potassium hydroxide (caustic potash); peroxides or sodium or potassium:**

序号 No.	税则号列 Tariff Line	货品名称	最惠国税率 MFN(%)	协定税率 Agreement(%)		特惠税率 S.P.(%)		普通税率 Gen.(%)	Article Description
		-氢氧化钠（烧碱）:							-Sodium hydroxide (caustic soda):
1634	2815.1100	--固体	10	0 7	智利CL,新西兰NZ,秘鲁PE,哥斯达黎加CR 亚太APTA,巴基斯坦PK	0	最不发达35国LDC35,最不发达4国LDC4	35	--Solid
1635	2815.1200	--水溶液（氢氧化钠浓溶液及液体烧碱）	8	0 5.6	智利CL,新西兰NZ,秘鲁PE,哥斯达黎加CR 亚太APTA,巴基斯坦PK	0	最不发达35国LDC35,最不发达4国LDC4	35	--In aqueous solution (soda lye or liquid soda)
1636	2815.2000	-氢氧化钾（苛性钾）	5.5	0 5	东盟ASEAN,智利CL,新西兰NZ,秘鲁PE,哥斯达黎加CR 巴基斯坦PK	0	最不发达35国LDC35,最不发达4国LDC4	30	-Potassium hydroxide (caustic potash)
1637	2815.3000	-过氧化钠及过氧化钾	5.5	0	东盟ASEAN,智利CL,巴基斯坦PK,新西兰NZ,秘鲁PE,哥斯达黎加CR	0	最不发达35国LDC35,最不发达4国LDC4	30	-Peroxides of sodium or potassium
	28.16	**氢氧化镁及过氧化镁;锶或钡的氧化物、氢氧化物及过氧化物:**							**Hydroxide and peroxide of magnesium; oxides, hydroxides and peroxides, of strontium or barium:**
1638	2816.1000	-氢氧化镁及过氧化镁	5.5	0 5	东盟ASEAN,智利CL,新西兰NZ,秘鲁PE,哥斯达黎加CR 巴基斯坦PK	0	最不发达35国LDC35	30	-Hydroxide and peroxide of magnesium
1639	2816.4000	-锶或钡的氧化物、氢氧化物及过氧化物	5.5 △2	0 5	东盟ASEAN,智利CL,新西兰NZ,秘鲁PE,哥斯达黎加CR 巴基斯坦PK	0	最不发达35国LDC35	30	-Oxides, hydroxides and peroxides, of strontium or barium
	28.17	**氧化锌及过氧化锌:**							**Zinc oxide; Zinc peroxide:**
1640	2817.0010	---氧化锌	5.5	0 2.1	东盟ASEAN,智利CL,巴基斯坦PK,新西兰NZ,哥斯达黎加CR 秘鲁PE	0	最不发达35国LDC35,最不发达4国LDC4	40	---Zinc oxide
1641	2817.0090	---过氧化锌	5.5	0 2.8	东盟ASEAN,智利CL,巴基斯坦PK,新西兰NZ,哥斯达黎加CR 秘鲁PE	0	最不发达35国LDC35,最不发达4国LDC4	30	---Zinc peroxide

序号 No.	税则号列 Tariff Line	货品名称	最惠国税率 MFN(%)	协定税率 Agreement(%)		特惠税率 S.P.(%)		普通税率 Gen.(%)	Article Description
	28.18	**人造刚玉，不论是否已有化学定义;氧化铝;氢氧化铝:**							**Artificial corundum, whether or not chemically defined; aluminium oxide; aluminium hydroxide:**
		-人造刚玉，不论是否已有化学定义:							-Artificial corundum, whether or not chemically defined:
1642	2818.1010	---棕刚玉	5.5	0	东盟ASEAN,智利CL,巴基斯坦PK,新西兰NZ,秘鲁PE,哥斯达黎加CR	0	最不发达35国LDC35,最不发达4国LDC4	20	---Brown corundum
1643	2818.1090	---其他	5.5	0	东盟ASEAN,智利CL,巴基斯坦PK,新西兰NZ,秘鲁PE,哥斯达黎加CR	0	最不发达35国LDC35,最不发达4国LDC4	20	---Other
1644	2818.2000	-氧化铝，但人造刚玉除外	8 △0	0 5	东盟ASEAN,智利CL,新加坡SG,新西兰NZ,秘鲁PE,哥斯达黎加CR 巴基斯坦PK	0	最不发达35国LDC35,最不发达4国LDC4	30	-Aluminium oxide, other than artificial corundum
1645	2818.3000	-氢氧化铝	5.5	0	东盟ASEAN,智利CL,巴基斯坦PK,新西兰NZ,秘鲁PE,哥斯达黎加CR	0	最不发达35国LDC35,最不发达4国LDC4	30	-Aluminium hydroxide
	28.19	**铬的氧化物及氢氧化物:**							**Chromium oxides and hydroxides:**
1646	2819.1000	-三氧化铬	5.5	0	东盟ASEAN,智利CL,巴基斯坦PK,新西兰NZ,秘鲁PE,哥斯达黎加CR	0	最不发达35国LDC35,最不发达4国LDC4	20	-Chromium trioxide
1647	2819.9000	-其他	5.5	0	东盟ASEAN,智利CL,巴基斯坦PK,新西兰NZ,秘鲁PE,哥斯达黎加CR	0	最不发达35国LDC35,最不发达4国LDC4	30	-Other
	28.20	**锰的氧化物:**							**Manganese oxide:**
1648	2820.1000	-二氧化锰	5.5	0	东盟ASEAN,智利CL,巴基斯坦PK,新西兰NZ,秘鲁PE,哥斯达黎加CR	0	最不发达35国LDC35,最不发达4国LDC4	40	-Manganese dioxide

序号 No.	税则号列 Tariff Line	货品名称	最惠国税率 MFN(%)	协定税率 Agreement(%)		特惠税率 S.P.(%)		普通税率 Gen.(%)	Article Description
1649	2820.9000	-其他	5.5	0	东盟ASEAN,智利CL,巴基斯坦PK,新西兰NZ,秘鲁PE,哥斯达黎加CR	0	最不发达35国LDC35,最不发达4国LDC4	30	-Other
	28.21	**铁的氧化物及氢氧化物;土色料,按重量计三氧化二铁含量在70%及以上:**							**Iron oxides and hydroxides; earth colours containing 70% or more by weight of combined iron evaluated as Fe_2O_3:**
1650	2821.1000	-铁的氧化物及氢氧化物	5.5	0	东盟ASEAN,智利CL,巴基斯坦PK,新西兰NZ,秘鲁PE,哥斯达黎加CR	0	最不发达35国LDC35,最不发达4国LDC4	30	-Iron oxides and hydroxides
1651	2821.2000	-土色料	5.5	0	东盟ASEAN,智利CL,巴基斯坦PK,新西兰NZ,秘鲁PE,哥斯达黎加CR	0	最不发达35国LDC35,最不发达4国LDC4	45	-Earth colours
	28.22	**钴的氧化物及氢氧化物;商品氧化钴:**							**Cobalt oxides and hydroxides; commercial cobalt oxides:**
		钴的氧化物及氢氧化物;商品氧化钴:							Cobalt oxides and hydroxides; commercial cobalt oxides:
1652	2822.0010	---四氧化三钴	5.5 △2	0	东盟ASEAN,智利CL,巴基斯坦PK,新西兰NZ,秘鲁PE,哥斯达黎加CR	0	最不发达35国LDC35	30	---Cobalt tetroxide
1653	2822.0090	---其他	5.5 △2	0	东盟ASEAN,智利CL,巴基斯坦PK,新西兰NZ,秘鲁PE,哥斯达黎加CR	0	最不发达35国LDC35	30	---Other
	28.23	**钛的氧化物:**							**Titanium oxides:**
1654	2823.0000	钛的氧化物	5.5	0	东盟ASEAN,智利CL,巴基斯坦PK,新西兰NZ,秘鲁PE,哥斯达黎加CR	0	最不发达35国LDC35	30	Titanium oxides
	28.24	**铅的氧化物;铅丹及铅橙:**							**Lead oxides; red lead and orange lead:**
1655	2824.1000	-一氧化铅(铅黄、黄丹)	5.5	0 0.6	东盟ASEAN,巴基斯坦PK,新西兰NZ,秘鲁PE,哥斯达黎加CR 智利CL	0	最不发达35国LDC35	30	-Lead monoxide (litharge, massicot)
		-其他:							-Other:
1656	2824.9010	---铅丹及铅橙	5.5	0 0.6	东盟ASEAN,巴基斯坦PK,新西兰NZ,秘鲁PE,哥斯达黎加CR 智利CL	0	最不发达35国LDC35	45	---Red lead and orange lead

序号 No.	税则号列 Tariff Line	货品名称	最惠国税率 MFN(%)	协定税率 Agreement(%)		特惠税率 S.P.(%)		普通税率 Gen.(%)	Article Description
1657	2824.9090	---其他	5.5	0	东盟ASEAN,智利CL,巴基斯坦PK,新西兰NZ,秘鲁PE,哥斯达黎加CR	0	最不发达35国LDC35	30	---Other
	28.25	**肼（联氨）、胲（羟胺）及其无机盐;其他无机碱;其他金属氧化物、氢氧化物及过氧化物:**							**Hydrazine and hydroxylamine and their inorganic salts; other inorganic bases; other metal oxides, hydroxides and peroxides:**
		-肼（联氨）、胲（羟胺）及其无机盐:							-Hydrazine and hydroxylamine and their inorganic salts:
1658	2825.1010	---水合肼	5.5	0	东盟ASEAN,智利CL,巴基斯坦PK,新西兰NZ,秘鲁PE,哥斯达黎加CR	0	最不发达35国LDC35,最不发达4国LDC4	30	---Hydrazine hydrate
1659	2825.1020	---硫酸羟胺	5.5	0 5	东盟ASEAN,智利CL,新西兰NZ,秘鲁PE,哥斯达黎加CR 巴基斯坦PK	0	最不发达35国LDC35,最不发达4国LDC4	30	---Hydroxyamine sulfate
1660	2825.1090	---其他	5.5	0 5	东盟ASEAN,智利CL,新西兰NZ,秘鲁PE,哥斯达黎加CR 巴基斯坦PK	0	最不发达35国LDC35,最不发达4国LDC4	30	---Other
		-锂的氧化物及氢氧化物:							-Lithium oxide and hydroxide:
1661	2825.2010	---氢氧化锂	5.5	0	东盟ASEAN,智利CL,巴基斯坦PK,新西兰NZ,秘鲁PE,哥斯达黎加CR	0	最不发达35国LDC35,最不发达4国LDC4	30	---Lithium hydroxide
1662	2825.2090	---其他	5.5	0	东盟ASEAN,智利CL,巴基斯坦PK,新西兰NZ,秘鲁PE,哥斯达黎加CR	0	最不发达35国LDC35,最不发达4国LDC4	30	---Other
		-钒的氧化物及氢氧化物:							-Vanadium oxides and hydroxides:
1663	2825.3010	---五氧化二钒	5.5	0	东盟ASEAN,智利CL,巴基斯坦PK,新西兰NZ,秘鲁PE,哥斯达黎加CR	0	最不发达35国LDC35,最不发达4国LDC4	30	---Divanadium pentaoxide

序号 No.	税则号列 Tariff Line	货品名称	最惠国税率 MFN(%)	协定税率 Agreement(%)		特惠税率 S.P.(%)		普通税率 Gen.(%)	Article Description
1664	2825.3090	---其他	5.5	0	东盟ASEAN,智利CL,巴基斯坦PK,新西兰NZ,秘鲁PE,哥斯达黎加CR	0	最不发达35国LDC35,最不发达4国LDC4	30	---Other
1665	2825.4000	-镍的氧化物及氢氧化物	5.5 △2	0	东盟ASEAN,智利CL,巴基斯坦PK,新西兰NZ,秘鲁PE,哥斯达黎加CR	0	最不发达35国LDC35,最不发达4国LDC4	30	-Nickel oxides and hydroxides
1666	2825.5000	-铜的氧化物及氢氧化物	5.5	0 0.6	东盟ASEAN,巴基斯坦PK,新西兰NZ,秘鲁PE,哥斯达黎加CR 智利CL	0	最不发达35国LDC35,最不发达4国LDC4	30	-Copper oxides and hydroxides
1667	2825.6000	-锗的氧化物及二氧化锆	5.5	0	东盟ASEAN,智利CL,巴基斯坦PK,新西兰NZ,秘鲁PE,哥斯达黎加CR	0	最不发达35国LDC35,最不发达4国LDC4	30	-Germanium oxides and zirconium dioxide
1668	2825.7000	-钼的氧化物及氢氧化物	5.5	0 0.6	东盟ASEAN,巴基斯坦PK,新西兰NZ,哥斯达黎加CR 智利CL	0	最不发达35国LDC35,最不发达4国LDC4	30	-Molybdenum oxides and hydroxides
1669	2825.8000	-锑的氧化物	5.5	0	东盟ASEAN,智利CL,巴基斯坦PK,新西兰NZ,秘鲁PE,哥斯达黎加CR	0	最不发达35国LDC35,最不发达4国LDC4	30	-Antimony oxides
		-其他: ---钨的氧化物及氢氧化物:							-Other: ---Tungsten oxides and hydroxides:
1670	2825.9011	----钨酸	5.5	0	东盟ASEAN,智利CL,巴基斯坦PK,新西兰NZ,秘鲁PE,哥斯达黎加CR	0	最不发达35国LDC35,最不发达4国LDC4	30	----Tungstic acid
1671	2825.9012	----三氧化钨	5.5	0	东盟ASEAN,智利CL,巴基斯坦PK,新西兰NZ,秘鲁PE,哥斯达黎加CR	0	最不发达35国LDC35,最不发达4国LDC4	30	----Tungstic oxide

序号 No.	税则号列 Tariff Line	货品名称	最惠国税率 MFN(%)	协定税率 Agreement(%)		特惠税率 S.P.(%)		普通税率 Gen.(%)	Article Description
1672	2825.9019	----其他	5.5	0	东盟ASEAN,智利CL,巴基斯坦PK,新西兰NZ,秘鲁PE,哥斯达黎加CR	0	最不发达35国LDC35,最不发达4国LDC4	30	----Other
		---铋的氧化物及氢氧化物:							---Bismuth oxides and hydroxides:
1673	2825.9021	----三氧化二铋	5.5	0	东盟ASEAN,智利CL,巴基斯坦PK,新西兰NZ,秘鲁PE,哥斯达黎加CR	0	最不发达35国LDC35,最不发达4国LDC4	30	----Bismuth trioxide
1674	2825.9029	----其他	5.5	0	东盟ASEAN,智利CL,巴基斯坦PK,新西兰NZ,秘鲁PE,哥斯达黎加CR	0	最不发达35国LDC35,最不发达4国LDC4	30	----Other
		---锡的氧化物及氢氧化物:							---Tin oxides and hydroxides:
1675	2825.9031	----二氧化锡	5.5	0	东盟ASEAN,智利CL,巴基斯坦PK,新西兰NZ,秘鲁PE,哥斯达黎加CR	0	最不发达35国LDC35,最不发达4国LDC4	30	----Tin dioxide
1676	2825.9039	----其他	5.5	0	东盟ASEAN,智利CL,巴基斯坦PK,新西兰NZ,秘鲁PE,哥斯达黎加CR	0	最不发达35国LDC35,最不发达4国LDC4	30	----Other
		---铌的氧化物及氢氧化物:							---Niobium oxide and hydroxide:
1677	2825.9041	----一氧化铌	5.5	0	东盟ASEAN,智利CL,巴基斯坦PK,新西兰NZ,秘鲁PE,哥斯达黎加CR	0	最不发达35国LDC35,最不发达4国LDC4	30	----Columbium monoxide
1678	2825.9049	----其他	5.5	0	东盟ASEAN,智利CL,巴基斯坦PK,新西兰NZ,秘鲁PE,哥斯达黎加CR	0	最不发达35国LDC35,最不发达4国LDC4	30	----Other
1679	2825.9090	---其他	5.5	0	东盟ASEAN,智利CL,巴基斯坦PK,新西兰NZ,秘鲁PE,哥斯达黎加CR	0	最不发达35国LDC35,最不发达4国LDC4	30	---Other

序号 No.	税则号列 Tariff Line	货品名称	最惠国税率 MFN(%)	协定税率 Agreement(%)		特惠税率 S.P.(%)		普通税率 Gen.(%)	Article Description
		第五分章 无机酸盐、无机过氧酸盐及金属酸盐、金属过氧酸盐							Ⅴ. SALTS AND PEROXYSALTS, OFINORGANIC ACIDS AND METALS
	28.26	**氟化物;氟硅酸盐、氟铝酸盐及其他氟络盐:**							**Fluorides; fluorosilicates, fluoroaluminates and other complex fluorine salts:**
		-氟化物:							-Fluorides:
		--氟化铝:							--Of aluminium:
1680	2826.1210	---无水氟化铝	5.5	0	东盟ASEAN,智利CL,巴基斯坦PK,新西兰NZ,秘鲁PE,哥斯达黎加CR	0	最不发达35国LDC35,最不发达4国LDC4	30	---Anhydrous fluorides of aluminium
1681	2826.1290	---其他	5.5	0	东盟ASEAN,智利CL,巴基斯坦PK,新西兰NZ,秘鲁PE,哥斯达黎加CR	0	最不发达35国LDC35,最不发达4国LDC4	30	---Other
		--其他:							--Other:
1682	2826.1910	---铵的氟化物	5.5	0	东盟ASEAN,智利CL,巴基斯坦PK,新西兰NZ,秘鲁PE,哥斯达黎加CR	0	最不发达35国LDC35,最不发达4国LDC4	30	---Of ammonium
1683	2826.1920	---钠的氟化物	5.5	0	东盟ASEAN,智利CL,巴基斯坦PK,新西兰NZ,秘鲁PE,哥斯达黎加CR	0	最不发达35国LDC35,最不发达4国LDC4	30	---Of sodium
1684	2826.1990	---其他	5.5	0 5	东盟ASEAN,智利CL,新西兰NZ,秘鲁PE,哥斯达黎加CR 巴基斯坦PK	0	最不发达35国LDC35,最不发达4国LDC4	30	---Other
1685	2826.3000	-六氟铝酸钠(人造冰晶石)	5.5	0	东盟ASEAN,智利CL,巴基斯坦PK,新西兰NZ,秘鲁PE,哥斯达黎加CR	0	最不发达35国LDC35,最不发达4国LDC4	30	-Sodium hexafluoroaluminate (synthetic cryolite)
		-其他:							-Other:
1686	2826.9010	---氟硅酸盐	5.5	0 5	东盟ASEAN,智利CL,新西兰NZ,秘鲁PE,哥斯达黎加CR,香港HK 巴基斯坦PK	0	最不发达35国LDC35,最不发达4国LDC4	30	---fluorosilicates

序号 No.	税则号列 Tariff Line	货品名称	最惠国税率 MFN(%)	协定税率 Agreement(%)		特惠税率 S.P.(%)		普通税率 Gen.(%)	Article Description
1687	2826.9090	---其他	5.5	0 5	东盟ASEAN,智利CL,新西兰NZ,秘鲁PE,哥斯达黎加CR 巴基斯坦PK	0	最不发达35国LDC35,最不发达4国LDC4	30	---other
	28.27	**氯化物、氯氧化物及氢氧基氯化物;溴化物及溴氧化物;碘化物及碘氧化物:**							**Chlorides, chloride oxides and chloride hydroxides; bromides and bromide oxides; iodides and iodide oxides:**
		-氯化铵:							-Ammonium chloride:
1688	2827.1010	---肥料用	4	0	东盟ASEAN,智利CL,巴基斯坦PK,新西兰NZ,秘鲁PE,哥斯达黎加CR	0	最不发达35国LDC35,最不发达4国LDC4	11	---For use as fertilizer
1689	2827.1090	---其他	5.5	0 5	东盟ASEAN,智利CL,新西兰NZ,秘鲁PE,哥斯达黎加CR 巴基斯坦PK	0	最不发达35国LDC35,最不发达4国LDC4	30	---Other
1690	2827.2000	-氯化钙	5.5	0 5	东盟ASEAN,智利CL,新西兰NZ,秘鲁PE,哥斯达黎加CR 巴基斯坦PK	0	最不发达35国LDC35,最不发达4国LDC4	50	-Calcium chloride
		-其他氯化物:							-Other chlorides:
1691	2827.3100	--氯化镁	5.5	0 5	东盟ASEAN,智利CL,新西兰NZ,秘鲁PE,哥斯达黎加CR 巴基斯坦PK	0	最不发达35国LDC35,最不发达4国LDC4	30	--Of magnesium
1692	2827.3200	--氯化铝	5.5	0 5	东盟ASEAN,智利CL,新西兰NZ,秘鲁PE,哥斯达黎加CR 巴基斯坦PK	0	最不发达35国LDC35,最不发达4国LDC4	30	--Of aluminium
1693	2827.3500	--氯化镍	5.5	0 5	东盟ASEAN,智利CL,新西兰NZ,秘鲁PE,哥斯达黎加CR 巴基斯坦PK	0	最不发达35国LDC35,最不发达4国LDC4	30	--Of nickel
		--其他:							--Other:

序号 No.	税则号列 Tariff Line	货品名称	最惠国税率 MFN(%)	协定税率 Agreement(%)		特惠税率 S.P.(%)		普通税率 Gen.(%)	Article Description
1694	2827.3910	---氯化锂	5.5	0 0.6 4.4	东盟ASEAN,巴基斯坦PK,新西兰NZ,哥斯达黎加CR 智利CL 亚太APTA	0	最不发达35国LDC35,最不发达4国LDC4	30	---Lithium chloride
1695	2827.3920	---氯化钡	5.5	0 0.6 4.4	东盟ASEAN,巴基斯坦PK,新西兰NZ,哥斯达黎加CR 智利CL 亚太APTA	0	最不发达35国LDC35,最不发达4国LDC4	30	---Barium chleride
1696	2827.3930	---氯化钴	5.5	0 0.6 4.4	东盟ASEAN,巴基斯坦PK,新西兰NZ,秘鲁PE,哥斯达黎加CR 智利CL 亚太APTA	0	最不发达35国LDC35,最不发达4国LDC4	30	---Cobalt chleride
1697	2827.3990	---其他	5.5	0 0.6 4.4	东盟ASEAN,巴基斯坦PK,新西兰NZ,哥斯达黎加CR 智利CL 亚太APTA	0	最不发达35国LDC35,最不发达4国LDC4	30	---Other
		-氯氧化物及氢氧基氯化物:							-Chloride oxides and chloride hydroxides:
1698	2827.4100	--铜的氯氧化物及氢氧基氯化物	5.5	0 0.6 2.8	东盟ASEAN,巴基斯坦PK,新西兰NZ,哥斯达黎加CR 智利CL 秘鲁PE	0	最不发达35国LDC35,最不发达4国LDC4	30	--Of copper
		--其他:							--Other:
1699	2827.4910	---锆的氯氧化物及氢氧基氯化物	5.5	0 5	东盟ASEAN,智利CL,新西兰NZ,秘鲁PE,哥斯达黎加CR 巴基斯坦PK	0	最不发达35国LDC35,最不发达4国LDC4	30	---Of Zirconium
1700	2827.4990	---其他	5.5	0 5	东盟ASEAN,智利CL,新西兰NZ,秘鲁PE,哥斯达黎加CR 巴基斯坦PK	0	最不发达35国LDC35,最不发达4国LDC4	30	---Other
		-溴化物及溴氧化物:							-Bromides and bromide oxides:
1701	2827.5100	--溴化钠及溴化钾	5.5	0	东盟ASEAN,智利CL,巴基斯坦PK,新西兰NZ,秘鲁PE,哥斯达黎加CR	0	最不发达35国LDC35,最不发达4国LDC4	30	--Bromides of sodium or of potassium

序号 No.	税则号列 Tariff Line	货品名称	最惠国税率 MFN(%)	协定税率 Agreement(%)		特惠税率 S.P.(%)		普通税率 Gen.(%)	Article Description
1702	2827.5900	--其他	5.5	0	东盟ASEAN,智利CL,新西兰NZ,秘鲁PE,哥斯达黎加CR	0	最不发达35国LDC35,最不发达4国LDC4	30	--Other
				5	巴基斯坦PK				
1703	2827.6000	-碘化物及碘氧化物	5.5	0	东盟ASEAN,新西兰NZ,哥斯达黎加CR	0	最不发达35国LDC35,最不发达4国LDC4	30	-Iodides and iodide oxides
				0.6	智利CL				
				5	巴基斯坦PK				
	28.28	**次氯酸盐;商品次氯酸钙;亚氯酸盐;次溴酸盐:**							**Hypochlorites; commercial calcium hypochlorite; chlorites; hypobromites:**
1704	2828.1000	-商品次氯酸钙及其他钙的次氯酸盐	12	0	东盟ASEAN,智利CL,新加坡SG,新西兰NZ,秘鲁PE	0	最不发达35国LDC35	80	-Commercial calcium hypochlorite and other calcium hypochlorites
				2.4	哥斯达黎加CR				
				5	巴基斯坦PK				
				8.4	亚太APTA				
1705	2828.9000	-其他	5.5	0	东盟ASEAN,智利CL,新西兰NZ,秘鲁PE,哥斯达黎加CR	0	最不发达35国LDC35	30	-Other
				5	巴基斯坦PK				
	28.29	**氯酸盐及高氯酸盐;溴酸盐及过溴酸盐;碘酸盐及高碘酸盐:**							**Chlorates and perchlorates; bromates and perbromates; iodates and periodates:**
		-氯酸盐:							-Chlorates:
1706	2829.1100	--氯酸钠	12	0	东盟ASEAN,智利CL,新加坡SG,新西兰NZ,秘鲁PE	0	最不发达35国LDC35	30	--Of sodium
				2.4	哥斯达黎加CR				
				6	巴基斯坦PK				
		--其他:							--Other:
1707	2829.1910	---氯酸钾（洋硝）	5.5	0	东盟ASEAN,智利CL,巴基斯坦PK,新西兰NZ,秘鲁PE,哥斯达黎加CR	0	最不发达35国LDC35	20	---Potassium chlorate
1708	2829.1990	---其他	5.5	0	东盟ASEAN,智利CL,巴基斯坦PK,新西兰NZ,秘鲁PE,哥斯达黎加CR	0	最不发达35国LDC35	30	---Other
1709	2829.9000	-其他	5.5	0	东盟ASEAN,新西兰NZ,秘鲁PE,哥斯达黎加CR	0	最不发达35国LDC35	30	-Other
				0.6	智利CL				
				5	巴基斯坦PK				
	28.30	**硫化物;多硫化物,无论是否已有化学定义:**							**Sulphides; polysulphides, whether or not chemically defined:**
		-钠的硫化物:							-Sodium sulphides:

序号 No.	税则号列 Tariff Line	货品名称	最惠国税率 MFN(%)	协定税率 Agreement(%)		特惠税率 S.P.(%)		普通税率 Gen.(%)	Article Description
1710	2830.1010	---硫化钠	5.5	0 0.6 5	东盟ASEAN,新西兰NZ,秘鲁PE,哥斯达黎加CR 智利CL 巴基斯坦PK	0	最不发达35国LDC35,最不发达4国LDC4	40	---Sodium sulphide
1711	2830.1090	---其他	5.5	0 0.6	东盟ASEAN,巴基斯坦PK,新西兰NZ,秘鲁PE,哥斯达黎加CR 智利CL	0	最不发达35国LDC35,最不发达4国LDC4	30	---Other
		-其他:							-Other:
1712	2830.9020	---硫化锑	5.5	0	东盟ASEAN,智利CL,巴基斯坦PK,新西兰NZ,秘鲁PE,哥斯达黎加CR	0	最不发达35国LDC35,最不发达4国LDC4	45	---Antimony sulphide
1713	2830.9030	---硫化钴	5.5	0	东盟ASEAN,智利CL,巴基斯坦PK,新西兰NZ,秘鲁PE,哥斯达黎加CR	0	最不发达35国LDC35,最不发达4国LDC4	30	---Cobalt sulphide
1714	2830.9090	---其他	5.5	0 5	东盟ASEAN,智利CL,新西兰NZ,秘鲁PE,哥斯达黎加CR 巴基斯坦PK	0	最不发达35国LDC35,最不发达4国LDC4	30	---Other
	28.31	**连二亚硫酸盐及次硫酸盐:**							**Dithionites and sulphoxylates:**
		-钠的连二亚硫酸盐及次硫酸盐:							-Of sodium:
1715	2831.1010	---钠的连亚二硫酸盐	5.5	0 5	东盟ASEAN,智利CL,新西兰NZ,秘鲁PE,哥斯达黎加CR 巴基斯坦PK	0	最不发达35国LDC35	30	---Dithionites
1716	2831.1020	---钠的次硫酸盐	5.5	0 5	东盟ASEAN,智利CL,新西兰NZ,秘鲁PE,哥斯达黎加CR 巴基斯坦PK	0	最不发达35国LDC35	30	---Sulphoxylates
1717	2831.9000	-其他	5.5	0 5	东盟ASEAN,智利CL,新西兰NZ,秘鲁PE,哥斯达黎加CR 巴基斯坦PK	0	最不发达35国LDC35	30	-Other
	28.32	**亚硫酸盐;硫代硫酸盐:**							**Sulphites; thiosulphates:**
1718	2832.1000	-钠的亚硫酸盐	5.5	0 0.6 5	东盟ASEAN,新西兰NZ,秘鲁PE,哥斯达黎加CR 智利CL 巴基斯坦PK	0	最不发达35国LDC35	30	-Sodium sulphites

序号 No.	税则号列 Tariff Line	货品名称	最惠国税率 MFN(%)	协定税率 Agreement(%)		特惠税率 S.P.(%)		普通税率 Gen.(%)	Article Description
1719	2832.2000	-其他亚硫酸盐	5.5	0	东盟ASEAN,智利CL,巴基斯坦PK,新西兰NZ,秘鲁PE,哥斯达黎加CR	0	最不发达35国LDC35	30	-Other sulphites
1720	2832.3000	-硫代硫酸盐	5.5	0 5	东盟ASEAN,智利CL,新西兰NZ,秘鲁PE,哥斯达黎加CR 巴基斯坦PK	0	最不发达35国LDC35	30	-Thiosulphates
	28.33	**硫酸盐;矾;过硫酸盐:**							**Sulphates; alums; peroxosulphates (persulphates):**
		-钠的硫酸盐:							-Sodium sulphates:
1721	2833.1100	--硫酸钠	5.5	0 0.6 5	东盟ASEAN,新西兰NZ,秘鲁PE,哥斯达黎加CR 智利CL 巴基斯坦PK	0	最不发达35国LDC35	40	--Disodium sulphate
1722	2833.1900	--其他	5.5	0 5	东盟ASEAN,智利CL,新西兰NZ,秘鲁PE,哥斯达黎加CR 巴基斯坦PK	0	最不发达35国LDC35	30	--Other
		-其他硫酸盐:							-Other sulphates:
1723	2833.2100	--硫酸镁	5.5	0 0.6 5	东盟ASEAN,新西兰NZ,秘鲁PE,哥斯达黎加CR 智利CL 巴基斯坦PK	0	最不发达35国LDC35,最不发达4国LDC4	30	--Of magnesium
1724	2833.2200	--硫酸铝	5.5	0 0.6 5	东盟ASEAN,新西兰NZ,秘鲁PE,哥斯达黎加CR 智利CL 巴基斯坦PK	0	最不发达35国LDC35,最不发达4国LDC4	30	--Of aluminium
1725	2833.2400	--镍的硫酸盐	5.5	0 5	东盟ASEAN,智利CL,新西兰NZ,秘鲁PE,哥斯达黎加CR 巴基斯坦PK	0	最不发达35国LDC35,最不发达4国LDC4	30	--Of nickel
1726	2833.2500	--铜的硫酸盐	5.5	0 0.6 5	东盟ASEAN,新西兰NZ,秘鲁PE,哥斯达黎加CR 智利CL 巴基斯坦PK	0	最不发达35国LDC35,最不发达4国LDC4	30	--Of copper
1727	2833.2700	--硫酸钡	5.5	0 5	东盟ASEAN,智利CL,新西兰NZ,秘鲁PE,哥斯达黎加CR 巴基斯坦PK	0	最不发达35国LDC35,最不发达4国LDC4	30	--Of barium
		--其他:							--Other:

序号 No.	税则号列 Tariff Line	货品名称	最惠国税率 MFN(%)	协定税率 Agreement(%)	特惠税率 S.P.(%)	普通税率 Gen.(%)	Article Description
1728	2833.2910	---硫酸亚铁	5.5	0 东盟ASEAN,智利CL,新西兰NZ,秘鲁PE,哥斯达黎加CR 5 巴基斯坦PK	0 最不发达35国LDC35,最不发达4国LDC4	45	---Ferrous sulphate
1729	2833.2920	---铬的硫酸盐	5.5	0 东盟ASEAN,智利CL,巴基斯坦PK,新西兰NZ,秘鲁PE,哥斯达黎加CR	0 最不发达35国LDC35,最不发达4国LDC4	30	---Of chromium
1730	2833.2930	---硫酸锌	5.5	0 东盟ASEAN,智利CL,新西兰NZ,秘鲁PE,哥斯达黎加CR 5 巴基斯坦PK	0 最不发达35国LDC35,最不发达4国LDC4	30	---Of zinc
1731	2833.2990	---其他	5.5	0 东盟ASEAN,智利CL,新西兰NZ,秘鲁PE,哥斯达黎加CR 5 巴基斯坦PK	0 最不发达35国LDC35,最不发达4国LDC4	30	---Other
		-矾:					-Alums:
1732	2833.3010	---钾铝矾	5.5	0 东盟ASEAN,智利CL,巴基斯坦PK,新西兰NZ,秘鲁PE,哥斯达黎加CR	0 最不发达35国LDC35,最不发达4国LDC4	45	---Potassium aluminum sulfate
1733	2833.3090	---其他	5.5	0 东盟ASEAN,智利CL,巴基斯坦PK,新西兰NZ,秘鲁PE,哥斯达黎加CR	0 最不发达35国LDC35,最不发达4国LDC4	30	---Other
1734	2833.4000	-过硫酸盐	5.5	0 东盟ASEAN,智利CL,新西兰NZ,秘鲁PE,哥斯达黎加CR 5 巴基斯坦PK	0 最不发达35国LDC35,最不发达4国LDC4	30	-Peroxosulphates (persulphates)
	28.34	**亚硝酸盐;硝酸盐:**					**Nitrites; nitrates:**
1735	2834.1000	-亚硝酸盐	5.5	0 东盟ASEAN,智利CL,新西兰NZ,秘鲁PE,哥斯达黎加CR 5 巴基斯坦PK	0 最不发达35国LDC35,最不发达4国LDC4	30	-Nitrites
		-硝酸盐:					-Nitrates:
		--硝酸钾:					--Of potassium:

序号 No.	税则号列 Tariff Line	货品名称	最惠国税率 MFN(%)	协定税率 Agreement(%)		特惠税率 S.P.(%)		普通税率 Gen.(%)	Article Description
1736	2834.2110	---肥料用	4 △1	0 0.4	东盟ASEAN,巴基斯坦PK,新西兰NZ,秘鲁PE,哥斯达黎加CR 智利CL	0	最不发达35国LDC35,最不发达4国LDC4	11	---For use as fertilizer
1737	2834.2190	---其他	5.5	0 0.6 5	东盟ASEAN,新西兰NZ,秘鲁PE,哥斯达黎加CR 智利CL 巴基斯坦PK	0	最不发达35国LDC35,最不发达4国LDC4	30	---Other
		--其他:							--Other:
1738	2834.2910	---硝酸钴	5.5	0	东盟ASEAN,智利CL,巴基斯坦PK,新西兰NZ,秘鲁PE,哥斯达黎加CR	0	最不发达35国LDC35,最不发达4国LDC4	30	---Of cobalt
1739	2834.2990	---其他	5.5	0 5	东盟ASEAN,智利CL,新西兰NZ,秘鲁PE,哥斯达黎加CR 巴基斯坦PK	0	最不发达35国LDC35,最不发达4国LDC4	30	---Other
	ex28342990	硝酸钡	△2						Barium nitrate
	28.35	**次磷酸盐、亚磷酸盐、磷酸盐及多磷酸盐，无论是否已有化学定义:**							**Phosphinates (hypophosphites), phosphonates (phosphites), phosphates and polyphosphates, whether or not chemically defined:**
1740	2835.1000	-次磷酸盐及亚磷酸盐	5.5	0 5	东盟ASEAN,智利CL,新西兰NZ,秘鲁PE,哥斯达黎加CR 巴基斯坦PK	0	最不发达35国LDC35,最不发达4国LDC4	20	-Phosphinates(hypophosphites)and phosphonates(phosphites)
		-磷酸盐:							-Phosphates:
1741	2835.2200	--磷酸一钠及磷酸二钠	5.5	0 5	东盟ASEAN,智利CL,新西兰NZ,秘鲁PE,哥斯达黎加CR 巴基斯坦PK	0	最不发达35国LDC35,最不发达4国LDC4	20	--Of mono-or disodium
1742	2835.2400	--钾的磷酸盐	5.5	0 5	东盟ASEAN,智利CL,新西兰NZ,秘鲁PE,哥斯达黎加CR 巴基斯坦PK	0	最不发达35国LDC35,最不发达4国LDC4	20	--Of potassium
		--正磷酸氢钙（磷酸二钙）:							--Calcium hydrogenorthophosphate(dicalcium phosphate):

序号 No.	税则号列 Tariff Line	货品名称	最惠国税率 MFN(%)	协定税率 Agreement(%)		特惠税率 S.P.(%)		普通税率 Gen.(%)	Article Description
1743	2835.2510	---饲料级的	5.5	0 5	东盟ASEAN,智利CL,新西兰NZ,秘鲁PE,哥斯达黎加CR 巴基斯坦PK	0	最不发达35国LDC35,最不发达4国LDC4	20	---Feed Grade
1744	2835.2520	---食品级的	5.5	0 5	东盟ASEAN,智利CL,新西兰NZ,秘鲁PE,哥斯达黎加CR 巴基斯坦PK	0	最不发达35国LDC35,最不发达4国LDC4	20	---Food Grade
1745	2835.2590	---其他	5.5	0 5	东盟ASEAN,智利CL,新西兰NZ,秘鲁PE,哥斯达黎加CR 巴基斯坦PK	0	最不发达35国LDC35,最不发达4国LDC4	20	---Other
1746	2835.2600	--其他磷酸钙	5.5	0 5	东盟ASEAN,智利CL,新西兰NZ,秘鲁PE,哥斯达黎加CR 巴基斯坦PK	0	最不发达35国LDC35,最不发达4国LDC4	20	--Other phosphates of calcium
		--其他:							--Other:
1747	2835.2910	---磷酸三钠	5.5	0 5	东盟ASEAN,智利CL,新西兰NZ,秘鲁PE,哥斯达黎加CR 巴基斯坦PK	0	最不发达35国LDC35,最不发达4国LDC4	20	---Of trisodium
1748	2835.2990	---其他	5.5	0 5	东盟ASEAN,智利CL,新西兰NZ,秘鲁PE,哥斯达黎加CR 巴基斯坦PK	0	最不发达35国LDC35,最不发达4国LDC4	20	---Other
		-多磷酸盐:							-Polyphosphates:
		--三磷酸钠（三聚磷酸钠）:							--Sodium triphosphate (sodium tripoly-phosphate):
1749	2835.3110	---食品级的	5.5	0 5	东盟ASEAN,智利CL,新西兰NZ,秘鲁PE,哥斯达黎加CR 巴基斯坦PK	0	最不发达35国LDC35,最不发达4国LDC4	20	---Food Grade
1750	2835.3190	---其他	5.5	0 5	东盟ASEAN,智利CL,新西兰NZ,秘鲁PE,哥斯达黎加CR 巴基斯坦PK	0	最不发达35国LDC35,最不发达4国LDC4	20	---Other
		--其他:							--Other:

序号 No.	税则号列 Tariff Line	货品名称	最惠国税率 MFN(%)	协定税率 Agreement(%)		特惠税率 S.P.(%)		普通税率 Gen.(%)	Article Description
		---六偏磷酸钠:							---Sodium Hexametaphosphate:
1751	2835.3911	----食品级的	5.5	0 5	东盟ASEAN,智利CL,新西兰NZ,秘鲁PE,哥斯达黎加CR 巴基斯坦PK	0	最不发达35国LDC35,最不发达4国LDC4	20	----Food Grade
1752	2835.3919	----其他	5.5	0 5	东盟ASEAN,智利CL,新西兰NZ,秘鲁PE,哥斯达黎加CR 巴基斯坦PK	0	最不发达35国LDC35,最不发达4国LDC4	20	----Other
1753	2835.3990	---其他	5.5	0 5	东盟ASEAN,智利CL,新西兰NZ,秘鲁PE,哥斯达黎加CR 巴基斯坦PK	0	最不发达35国LDC35,最不发达4国LDC4	20	---Other
	28.36	**碳酸盐;过碳酸盐;含氨基甲酸铵的商品碳酸铵:**							**Carbonates; peroxocarbonates (per-carbonates); commercial ammonium carbonate containing ammonium carbamate:**
1754	2836.2000	-碳酸钠（纯碱）	5.5	0 5	东盟ASEAN,智利CL,新西兰NZ,秘鲁PE,哥斯达黎加CR 巴基斯坦PK	0	最不发达35国LDC35,最不发达4国LDC4	35	-Disodium carbonate
1755	2836.3000	-碳酸氢钠（小苏打）	5.5	0 5	东盟ASEAN,智利CL,新西兰NZ,秘鲁PE,哥斯达黎加CR 巴基斯坦PK	0	最不发达35国LDC35,最不发达4国LDC4	45	-Sodium hydrogencarbonate (sodium bicar bonate)
1756	2836.4000	-钾的碳酸盐	5.5	0 5	东盟ASEAN,智利CL,新西兰NZ,秘鲁PE,哥斯达黎加CR 巴基斯坦PK	0	最不发达35国LDC35,最不发达4国LDC4	30	-Potassium carbonates
1757	2836.5000	-碳酸钙	5.5	0 5	东盟ASEAN,智利CL,新西兰NZ,秘鲁PE,哥斯达黎加CR 巴基斯坦PK	0	最不发达35国LDC35,最不发达4国LDC4	45	-Calcium carbonate
1758	2836.6000	-碳酸钡	5.5 △1	0 5	东盟ASEAN,智利CL,新西兰NZ,秘鲁PE,哥斯达黎加CR 巴基斯坦PK	0	最不发达35国LDC35,最不发达4国LDC4	40	-Barium carbonate

序号 No.	税则号列 Tariff Line	货品名称	最惠国税率 MFN(%)	协定税率 Agreement(%)		特惠税率 S.P.(%)		普通税率 Gen.(%)	Article Description
		-其他:							-Other:
1759	2836.9100	--锂的碳酸盐	5.5 △2	0 0.6 5	东盟ASEAN,新西兰NZ,哥斯达黎加CR 智利CL 巴基斯坦PK	0	最不发达35国LDC35,最不发达4国LDC4	30	--Lithium carbonates
1760	2836.9200	--锶的碳酸盐	5.5 △2	0 5	东盟ASEAN,智利CL,新西兰NZ,秘鲁PE,哥斯达黎加CR 巴基斯坦PK	0	最不发达35国LDC35,最不发达4国LDC4	30	--Strontium carbonate
		--其他:							--Other:
1761	2836.9910	---碳酸镁	5.5	0 0.6 5	东盟ASEAN,新西兰NZ,秘鲁PE,哥斯达黎加CR 智利CL 巴基斯坦PK	0	最不发达35国LDC35,最不发达4国LDC4	45	---Magnesium carbonate
1762	2836.9930	---碳酸钴	5.5 △2	0 0.6 5	东盟ASEAN,新西兰NZ,秘鲁PE,哥斯达黎加CR 智利CL 巴基斯坦PK	0	最不发达35国LDC35,最不发达4国LDC4	30	---Cobalt carbonate
1763	2836.9940	---商品碳酸铵及其他铵的碳酸盐	5.5	0	东盟ASEAN,智利CL,巴基斯坦PK,新西兰NZ,秘鲁PE,哥斯达黎加CR	0	最不发达35国LDC35,最不发达4国LDC4	30	---Commercial ammonium carbonate and other ammonium carbonates
1764	2836.9950	---碳酸锆	5.5	0 5	东盟ASEAN,智利CL,新西兰NZ,秘鲁PE,哥斯达黎加CR 巴基斯坦PK	0	最不发达35国LDC35,最不发达4国LDC4	30	---Zirconium carbonates
1765	2836.9990	---其他	5.5	0 5	东盟ASEAN,智利CL,新西兰NZ,秘鲁PE,哥斯达黎加CR,澳门MO 巴基斯坦PK	0	最不发达35国LDC35,最不发达4国LDC4	30	---Other
	28.37	**氰化物、氧氰化物及氰络合物:**							**Cyanides, cyanide oxides and complex cyanides:**
		-氰化物及氧氰化物:							-Cyanides and cyanide oxides:
		--氰化钠及氧氰化钠:							--Of sodium:
1766	2837.1110	---氰化钠	5.5	0 0.6	东盟ASEAN,巴基斯坦PK,新西兰NZ,秘鲁PE,哥斯达黎加CR 智利CL	0	最不发达35国LDC35	20	---Sodium cyanide

序号 No.	税则号列 Tariff Line	货品名称	最惠国税率 MFN(%)	协定税率 Agreement(%)		特惠税率 S.P.(%)		普通税率 Gen.(%)	Article Description
1767	2837.1120	---氧氰化钠	5.5	0	东盟ASEAN,巴基斯坦PK,新西兰NZ,秘鲁PE,哥斯达黎加CR	0	最不发达35国LDC35	30	---Sodium cyanide oxide
				0.6	智利CL				
				5	亚太APTA				
		--其他:							--Other:
1768	2837.1910	---氰化钾	5.5	0	东盟ASEAN,智利CL,巴基斯坦PK,新西兰NZ,秘鲁PE,哥斯达黎加CR	0	最不发达35国LDC35	20	---Potassium cyanide
1769	2837.1990	---其他	5.5	0	东盟ASEAN,智利CL,巴基斯坦PK,新西兰NZ,秘鲁PE,哥斯达黎加CR	0	最不发达35国LDC35	30	---Other
1770	2837.2000	-氰络合物	5.5	0	东盟ASEAN,智利CL,巴基斯坦PK,新西兰NZ,秘鲁PE,哥斯达黎加CR	0	最不发达35国LDC35	30	-Complex cyanides
	28.39	**硅酸盐;商品碱金属硅酸盐:**							**Silicates; commercial alkali metal silicates:**
		-钠盐:							-Of sodium:
1771	2839.1100	--偏硅酸钠	5.5	0	东盟ASEAN,智利CL,新西兰NZ,秘鲁PE,哥斯达黎加CR	0	最不发达35国LDC35	40	--Sodium metasilicates
				5	巴基斯坦PK				
		--其他:							--Other:
1772	2839.1910	---硅酸钠	5.5	0	东盟ASEAN,智利CL,新西兰NZ,秘鲁PE,哥斯达黎加CR	0	最不发达35国LDC35	30	---Sodium silicate
				5	巴基斯坦PK				
1773	2839.1990	---其他	5.5	0	东盟ASEAN,智利CL,新西兰NZ,秘鲁PE,哥斯达黎加CR	0	最不发达35国LDC35	30	---Other
				5	巴基斯坦PK				
1774	2839.9000	-其他	5.5	0	东盟ASEAN,智利CL,新西兰NZ,秘鲁PE,哥斯达黎加CR	0	最不发达35国LDC35	30	-Other
				5	巴基斯坦PK				
	ex28399000	锆的硅酸盐	△2						Ziconium silicate
	28.40	**硼酸盐及过硼酸盐:**							**Borates; peroxoborates (perborates):**
		-四硼酸钠（精炼硼砂）:							-Disodium tetraborate (refined borax):
1775	2840.1100	--无水四硼酸钠	5.5 △2	0	东盟ASEAN,智利CL,巴基斯坦PK,新西兰NZ,秘鲁PE,哥斯达黎加CR	0	最不发达35国LDC35	20	--Anhydrous
1776	2840.1900	--其他	5.5 △2	0	东盟ASEAN,巴基斯坦PK,新西兰NZ,秘鲁PE,哥斯达黎加CR	0	最不发达35国LDC35	20	--Other
				0.6	智利CL				
1777	2840.2000	-其他硼酸盐	5.5	0	东盟ASEAN,智利CL,巴基斯坦PK,新西兰NZ,秘鲁PE,哥斯达黎加CR	0	最不发达35国LDC35	30	-Other borates

序号 No.	税则号列 Tariff Line	货品名称	最惠国税率 MFN(%)	协定税率 Agreement(%)		特惠税率 S.P.(%)		普通税率 Gen.(%)	Article Description
1778	2840.3000	-过硼酸盐	5.5	0	东盟ASEAN,智利CL,巴基斯坦PK,新西兰NZ,秘鲁PE,哥斯达黎加CR	0	最不发达35国LDC35	30	-Peroxoborates (perborates)
	28.41	**金属酸盐及过金属酸盐:**							**Salts of oxometallic or peroxometallic acids:**
1779	2841.3000	-重铬酸钠	5.5	0	东盟ASEAN,智利CL,巴基斯坦PK,新西兰NZ,秘鲁PE,哥斯达黎加CR	0	最不发达35国LDC35,最不发达4国LDC4	20	-Sodium dichromate
1780	2841.5000	-其他铬酸盐及重铬酸盐;过铬酸盐	5.5	0 5	东盟ASEAN,智利CL,新西兰NZ,秘鲁PE,哥斯达黎加CR 巴基斯坦PK	0	最不发达35国LDC35,最不发达4国LDC4	30	-Other chromates and dichromates; peroxochromates
		-亚锰酸盐、锰酸盐及高锰酸盐:							-Manganites, manganates and perman ganates:
1781	2841.6100	--高锰酸钾	5.5	0 5	东盟ASEAN,智利CL,新西兰NZ,秘鲁PE,哥斯达黎加CR 巴基斯坦PK	0	最不发达35国LDC35,最不发达4国LDC4	30	--Potassium permanganate
		--其他:							--Other:
1782	2841.6910	---锰酸锂	5.5	0	东盟ASEAN,智利CL,巴基斯坦PK,新西兰NZ,秘鲁PE,哥斯达黎加CR	0	最不发达35国LDC35,最不发达4国LDC4	30	---Lithium manganate
1783	2841.6990	---其他	5.5	0	东盟ASEAN,智利CL,巴基斯坦PK,新西兰NZ,秘鲁PE,哥斯达黎加CR	0	最不发达35国LDC35,最不发达4国LDC4	30	---Other
		-钼酸盐:							-Molybdates:
1784	2841.7010	---钼酸铵	5.5	0 0.6 5	东盟ASEAN,新西兰NZ,秘鲁PE,哥斯达黎加CR 智利CL 巴基斯坦PK	0	最不发达35国LDC35,最不发达4国LDC4	30	---Ammonium molybdates
1785	2841.7090	---其他	5.5	0 0.6 5	东盟ASEAN,新西兰NZ,秘鲁PE,哥斯达黎加CR 智利CL 巴基斯坦PK	0	最不发达35国LDC35,最不发达4国LDC4	30	---Other
		-钨酸盐:							-Tungstates (wolframates):

序号 No.	税则号列 Tariff Line	货品名称	最惠国税率 MFN(%)		协定税率 Agreement(%)		特惠税率 S.P.(%)	普通税率 Gen.(%)	Article Description
1786	2841.8010	---仲钨酸铵	5.5	0	东盟ASEAN,智利CL,巴基斯坦PK,新西兰NZ,秘鲁PE,哥斯达黎加CR	0	最不发达35国LDC35,最不发达4国LDC4	30	---Ammonium paratungstate
1787	2841.8020	---钨酸钠	5.5	0	东盟ASEAN,智利CL,巴基斯坦PK,新西兰NZ,秘鲁PE,哥斯达黎加CR	0	最不发达35国LDC35,最不发达4国LDC4	30	---Sodium tungstate
1788	2841.8030	---钨酸钙	5.5	0	东盟ASEAN,智利CL,巴基斯坦PK,新西兰NZ,秘鲁PE,哥斯达黎加CR	0	最不发达35国LDC35,最不发达4国LDC4	30	---Calcium wolframate
1789	2841.8040	---偏钨酸铵	5.5	0	东盟ASEAN,智利CL,巴基斯坦PK,新西兰NZ,秘鲁PE,哥斯达黎加CR	0	最不发达35国LDC35,最不发达4国LDC4	30	---Ammonium metatungstate
1790	2841.8090	---其他	5.5	0	东盟ASEAN,智利CL,巴基斯坦PK,新西兰NZ,秘鲁PE,哥斯达黎加CR	0	最不发达35国LDC35,最不发达4国LDC4	30	---Other
1791	2841.9000	-其他	5.5	0 5	东盟ASEAN,智利CL,新西兰NZ,秘鲁PE,哥斯达黎加CR 巴基斯坦PK	0	最不发达35国LDC35,最不发达4国LDC4	30	-Other
	ex28419000	钴酸锂	△2						Lithium cobaltate
	28.42	**其他无机酸盐及过氧酸盐（包括不论是否已有化学定义的硅铝酸盐），但迭氮化物除外:**							**Other Salts of inorganic acids or peroxoacids (including aluminosilicates whether or not chemically defined), other than azides:**
1792	2842.1000	-硅酸复盐及硅酸络盐，（包括不论是否已有化学定义的硅铝酸盐）	5.5	0 5	东盟ASEAN,智利CL,新西兰NZ,秘鲁PE,哥斯达黎加CR,香港HK 巴基斯坦PK	0	最不发达35国LDC35	30	-Double or complex silicates, including aluminosilicates whether or not chemically defined
		-其他:							-Other:
		---雷酸盐、氰酸盐及硫氰酸盐:							---Fulminates, cyanates and thiocyanates:
1793	2842.9011	----硫氰酸钠	5.5	0 5	东盟ASEAN,智利CL,新西兰NZ,秘鲁PE,哥斯达黎加CR 巴基斯坦PK	0	最不发达35国LDC35	30	----Sodium sulfocyanate

序号 No.	税则号列 Tariff Line	货品名称	最惠国税率 MFN(%)	协定税率 Agreement(%)		特惠税率 S.P.(%)		普通税率 Gen.(%)	Article Description
1794	2842.9019	----其他	5.5	0 5	东盟ASEAN,智利CL,新西兰NZ,秘鲁PE,哥斯达黎加CR 巴基斯坦PK	0	最不发达35国LDC35	30	----Other
1795	2842.9020	---碲化镉	5.5	0 5	东盟ASEAN,智利CL,新西兰NZ,秘鲁PE,哥斯达黎加CR 巴基斯坦PK	0	最不发达35国LDC35	30	---Cadmium telluride
1796	2842.9030	---锂镍钴锰氧化物	5.5	0 5	东盟ASEAN,智利CL,新西兰NZ,秘鲁PE,哥斯达黎加CR 巴基斯坦PK	0	最不发达35国LDC35	30	---Lithium nickel cobalt manganese oxide
1797	2842.9040	---磷酸铁锂	5.5	0 5	东盟ASEAN,智利CL,新西兰NZ,秘鲁PE,哥斯达黎加CR 巴基斯坦PK	0	最不发达35国LDC35	30	---Lithium iron phosphate
1798	2842.9050	---硒酸盐及亚硒酸盐	5.5	0 5	东盟ASEAN,智利CL,新西兰NZ,秘鲁PE,哥斯达黎加CR 巴基斯坦PK	0	最不发达35国LDC35	30	---Selenate and selenite
1799	2842.9090	---其他	5.5	0 5	东盟ASEAN,智利CL,新西兰NZ,秘鲁PE,哥斯达黎加CR 巴基斯坦PK	0	最不发达35国LDC35	30	---Other
		第六分章 杂项产品							Ⅳ. MISCELLANEOUS
	28.43	**胶态贵金属;贵金属的无机或有机化合物,不论是否已有化学定义;贵金属汞齐:**							**Colloidal precious metals; inorganic or organic compounds of precious metals, whether or not chemically defined; amalgams of precious metals:**
1800	2843.1000	-胶态贵金属	5.5	0	东盟ASEAN,智利CL,巴基斯坦PK,新西兰NZ,秘鲁PE,哥斯达黎加CR	0	最不发达35国LDC35	30	-Colloidal precious metals
		-银化合物:							-Silver compounds:
1801	2843.2100	--硝酸银	5.5	0	东盟ASEAN,智利CL,巴基斯坦PK,新西兰NZ,秘鲁PE,哥斯达黎加CR,香港HK	0	最不发达35国LDC35	30	--Silver nitrate
1802	2843.2900	--其他	5.5	0	东盟ASEAN,智利CL,巴基斯坦PK,新西兰NZ,秘鲁PE,哥斯达黎加CR,香港HK	0	最不发达35国LDC35	30	--Other
1803	2843.3000	-金化合物	5.5	0	东盟ASEAN,智利CL,巴基斯坦PK,新西兰NZ,秘鲁PE,哥斯达黎加CR,香港HK	0	最不发达35国LDC35	30	-Gold compounds
1804	2843.9000	-其他贵金属化合物;贵金属汞齐	5.5	0 0.6 5	东盟ASEAN,新西兰NZ,秘鲁PE,哥斯达黎加CR,香港HK 智利CL 巴基斯坦PK	0	最不发达35国LDC35	30	-Other compounds; amalgams

序号 No.	税则号列 Tariff Line	货品名称	最惠国税率 MFN(%)	协定税率 Agreement(%)		特惠税率 S.P.(%)		普通税率 Gen.(%)	Article Description
	28.44	**放射性化学元素及放射性同位素（包括可裂变或可转换的化学元素及同位素）及其化合物；含上述产品的混合物及残渣：**							**Radioactive chemical elements and radioactive isotopes (including the fissile or fertile chemical elements and isotopes) and their compounds; mixtures and residues containing these products:**
1805	2844.1000	-天然铀及其化合物；含天然铀或天然铀化合物的合金、分散体（包括金属陶瓷）、陶瓷产品及混合物	5.5	0	东盟ASEAN,智利CL,巴基斯坦PK,新西兰NZ,秘鲁PE,哥斯达黎加CR	0	最不发达35国LDC35,最不发达4国LDC4	30	-Natural uranium and its compounds; aloys, dispersions (including cermets), ceramic products and mixtures containing natural uranium or natural uranium compounds
1806	2844.2000	-U_{235}浓缩铀及其化合物；钚及其化合物；含U_{235}浓缩铀、钚或它们的化合物的合金、分散体（包括金属陶瓷）、陶瓷产品及混合物	5.5	0	东盟ASEAN,智利CL,巴基斯坦PK,新西兰NZ,秘鲁PE,哥斯达黎加CR	0	最不发达35国LDC35,最不发达4国LDC4	30	-Uranium enriched in U_{235} and its compounds; plutonium and its compounds;alloys dispersion (including cermets), ceramic products and mixtures containing uranium enriched in U_{235}, plutonium or compounds of these products
1807	2844.3000	-U_{235}贫化铀及其化合物；钍及其化合物；含U_{235}贫化铀、钍或它们的化合物的合金、分散体（包括金属陶瓷）、陶瓷产品及混合物	5.5	0	东盟ASEAN,智利CL,巴基斯坦PK,新西兰NZ,秘鲁PE,哥斯达黎加CR	0	最不发达35国LDC35,最不发达4国LDC4	30	-Uranium depleted in U_{235} and its compounds; thorium and its compounds; alloys, dispersions (including cermets), ceramic products and mixtures containing uranium depleted in U_{235}, thorium or compounds of these products
		-除子目号2844.10、2844.20及2844.30以外的放射性元素、同位素及其化合物；含这些元素、同位素及其化合物的合金、分散体（包括金属陶瓷）、陶瓷产品及混合物：							-Radioactive elements and isotopes and compounds other than those of subheading No.2844.10, 2844.20 or 2844.30; alloys, dispersions (including cermets), ceramic products and mixtures containing these elements, isotopes or compounds; radioactive residues:
1808	2844.4010	---镭及镭盐	4	0	东盟ASEAN,智利CL,巴基斯坦PK,新西兰NZ,秘鲁PE,哥斯达黎加CR	0	最不发达35国LDC35,最不发达4国LDC4	14	---Radium and its salts

序号 No.	税则号列 Tariff Line	货品名称	最惠国税率 MFN(%)	协定税率 Agreement(%)		特惠税率 S.P.(%)		普通税率 Gen.(%)	Article Description
1809	2844.4020	---钴及钴盐	4	0	东盟ASEAN,智利CL,巴基斯坦PK,新西兰NZ,秘鲁PE,哥斯达黎加CR	0	最不发达35国LDC35,最不发达4国LDC4	14	---Cobalt and its salts
1810	2844.4090	---其他	5.5	0	东盟ASEAN,智利CL,巴基斯坦PK,新西兰NZ,秘鲁PE,哥斯达黎加CR	0	最不发达35国LDC35,最不发达4国LDC4	30	---Other
1811	2844.5000	-核反应堆已耗尽(已辐照)的燃料元件(释热元件)	5.5	0	东盟ASEAN,智利CL,巴基斯坦PK,新西兰NZ,秘鲁PE,哥斯达黎加CR	0	最不发达35国LDC35	30	-Spent (irradiated) fuel elements (cartridges) of nuclear reactors
	28.45	**税号28.44以外的同位素;这些同位素的无机或有机化合物,不论是否已有化学定义:**							**Isotopes other than those of heading No.28.44; compounds, inorganic or organic, of such isotopes, whether or not chemically defined:**
1812	2845.1000	-重水(氧化氘)	5.5	0	东盟ASEAN,智利CL,巴基斯坦PK,新西兰NZ,秘鲁PE,哥斯达黎加CR	0	最不发达35国LDC35	30	-Heavy water (deuterium oxide)
1813	2845.9000	-其他	5.5	0	东盟ASEAN,智利CL,巴基斯坦PK,新西兰NZ,秘鲁PE,哥斯达黎加CR	0	最不发达35国LDC35	30	-Other
	28.46	**稀土金属、钇、钪及其混合物的无机或有机化合物:**							**Compounds, inorganic or organic, of rareearth metals, of yttrium or of scandium or of mixtures of these metals:**
		-铈的化合物:							-Ceric compounds:
1814	2846.1010	---氧化铈	5.5 △0	0 3.9	东盟ASEAN,智利CL,巴基斯坦PK,新西兰NZ,秘鲁PE,哥斯达黎加CR 亚太APTA	0	最不发达35国LDC35	30	---Cerium oxide
1815	2846.1020	---氢氧化铈	5.5 △0	0 3.9	东盟ASEAN,智利CL,巴基斯坦PK,新西兰NZ,秘鲁PE,哥斯达黎加CR 亚太APTA	0	最不发达35国LDC35	30	---Cerium hydroxide
1816	2846.1030	---碳酸铈	5.5 △0	0 3.9	东盟ASEAN,智利CL,巴基斯坦PK,新西兰NZ,秘鲁PE,哥斯达黎加CR 亚太APTA	0	最不发达35国LDC35	30	---Cerium carbonate

序号 No.	税则号列 Tariff Line	货品名称	最惠国税率 MFN(%)	协定税率 Agreement(%)		特惠税率 S.P.(%)		普通税率 Gen.(%)	Article Description
1817	2846.1090	---其他	5.5 △0	0	东盟ASEAN,智利CL,巴基斯坦PK,新西兰NZ,秘鲁PE,哥斯达黎加CR	0	最不发达35国LDC35	30	---Other
				3.9	亚太APTA				
		-其他:							-Other:
		---氧化稀土（氧化铈除外）:							---Rare-earth oxides (other than cerium oxide):
1818	2846.9011	----氧化钇	5.5 △0	0	东盟ASEAN,智利CL,巴基斯坦PK,新西兰NZ,秘鲁PE,哥斯达黎加CR	0	最不发达35国LDC35	30	----Yttrium oxide
1819	2846.9012	----氧化镧	5.5 △0	0	东盟ASEAN,智利CL,巴基斯坦PK,新西兰NZ,秘鲁PE,哥斯达黎加CR	0	最不发达35国LDC35	30	----Lanthanum oxide
1820	2846.9013	----氧化钕	5.5 △0	0	东盟ASEAN,智利CL,巴基斯坦PK,新西兰NZ,秘鲁PE,哥斯达黎加CR	0	最不发达35国LDC35	30	----Neodymium oxide
1821	2846.9014	----氧化铕	5.5 △0	0	东盟ASEAN,智利CL,巴基斯坦PK,新西兰NZ,秘鲁PE,哥斯达黎加CR	0	最不发达35国LDC35	30	----Europium oxide
1822	2846.9015	----氧化镝	5.5 △0	0	东盟ASEAN,智利CL,巴基斯坦PK,新西兰NZ,秘鲁PE,哥斯达黎加CR	0	最不发达35国LDC35	30	----Dysprosium oxide
1823	2846.9016	----氧化铽	5.5 △0	0	东盟ASEAN,智利CL,巴基斯坦PK,新西兰NZ,秘鲁PE,哥斯达黎加CR	0	最不发达35国LDC35	30	----Terbium oxide
1824	2846.9017	----氧化镨	5.5 △0	0	东盟ASEAN,智利CL,巴基斯坦PK,新西兰NZ,秘鲁PE,哥斯达黎加CR	0	最不发达35国LDC35	30	----Praseodymium oxide
1825	2846.9019	----其他	5.5 △0	0	东盟ASEAN,智利CL,巴基斯坦PK,新西兰NZ,秘鲁PE,哥斯达黎加CR	0	最不发达35国LDC35	30	----Other
		---氯化稀土:							---Rare-earth chlorides:
1826	2846.9021	----氯化铽	5.5 △0	0	东盟ASEAN,智利CL,巴基斯坦PK,新西兰NZ,秘鲁PE,哥斯达黎加CR	0	最不发达35国LDC35	30	----Terbium chlorinates
1827	2846.9022	----氯化镝	5.5 △0	0	东盟ASEAN,智利CL,巴基斯坦PK,新西兰NZ,秘鲁PE,哥斯达黎加CR	0	最不发达35国LDC35	30	----Dysprosium chlorinates
1828	2846.9023	----氯化镧	5.5 △0	0	东盟ASEAN,智利CL,巴基斯坦PK,新西兰NZ,秘鲁PE,哥斯达黎加CR	0	最不发达35国LDC35	30	----Lanthanum chlorinates

序号 No.	税则号列 Tariff Line	货品名称	最惠国税率 MFN(%)	协定税率 Agreement(%)		特惠税率 S.P.(%)		普通税率 Gen.(%)	Article Description
1829	2846.9024	----氯化钕	5.5 △0	0	东盟ASEAN,智利CL,巴基斯坦PK,新西兰NZ,秘鲁PE,哥斯达黎加CR	0	最不发达35国LDC35	30	----Neodymium chlorinates
1830	2846.9025	----氯化镨	5.5 △0	0	东盟ASEAN,智利CL,巴基斯坦PK,新西兰NZ,秘鲁PE,哥斯达黎加CR	0	最不发达35国LDC35	30	----Praseodymium chlorinates
1831	2846.9026	----氯化钇	5.5 △0	0	东盟ASEAN,智利CL,巴基斯坦PK,新西兰NZ,秘鲁PE,哥斯达黎加CR	0	最不发达35国LDC35	30	----Yttrium chlorinates
1832	2846.9028	----混合氯化稀土	5.5 △0	0	东盟ASEAN,智利CL,巴基斯坦PK,新西兰NZ,秘鲁PE,哥斯达黎加CR	0	最不发达35国LDC35	30	----Mixture of rareearth chlorides
1833	2846.9029	----其他	5.5 △0	0	东盟ASEAN,智利CL,巴基斯坦PK,新西兰NZ,秘鲁PE,哥斯达黎加CR	0	最不发达35国LDC35	30	----Other
		---氟化稀土:							---Rare-earth fluorides:
1834	2846.9031	----氟化铽	5.5 △0	0	东盟ASEAN,智利CL,巴基斯坦PK,新西兰NZ,秘鲁PE,哥斯达黎加CR	0	最不发达35国LDC35	30	----Terbium fluorides
1835	2846.9032	----氟化镝	5.5 △0	0	东盟ASEAN,智利CL,巴基斯坦PK,新西兰NZ,秘鲁PE,哥斯达黎加CR	0	最不发达35国LDC35	30	----Dysprosium fluorides
1836	2846.9033	----氟化镧	5.5 △0	0	东盟ASEAN,智利CL,巴基斯坦PK,新西兰NZ,秘鲁PE,哥斯达黎加CR	0	最不发达35国LDC35	30	----Lanthanum fluorides
1837	2846.9034	----氟化钕	5.5 △0	0	东盟ASEAN,智利CL,巴基斯坦PK,新西兰NZ,秘鲁PE,哥斯达黎加CR	0	最不发达35国LDC35	30	----Neodymium fluorides
1838	2846.9035	----氟化镨	5.5 △0	0	东盟ASEAN,智利CL,巴基斯坦PK,新西兰NZ,秘鲁PE,哥斯达黎加CR	0	最不发达35国LDC35	30	----Praseodymium fluorides
1839	2846.9036	----氟化钇	5.5 △0	0	东盟ASEAN,智利CL,巴基斯坦PK,新西兰NZ,秘鲁PE,哥斯达黎加CR	0	最不发达35国LDC35	30	----Yttrium fluorides
1840	2846.9039	----其他	5.5 △0	0	东盟ASEAN,智利CL,巴基斯坦PK,新西兰NZ,秘鲁PE,哥斯达黎加CR	0	最不发达35国LDC35	30	----Other
		---碳酸稀土:							---Rare-earth carbonate:

序号 No.	税则号列 Tariff Line	货品名称	最惠国税率 MFN(%)	协定税率 Agreement(%)		特惠税率 S.P.(%)		普通税率 Gen.(%)	Article Description
1841	2846.9041	----碳酸镧	5.5 △0	0	东盟ASEAN,智利CL,巴基斯坦PK,新西兰NZ,秘鲁PE,哥斯达黎加CR	0	最不发达35国LDC35	30	----Lanthanum carbonates
1842	2846.9042	----碳酸铽	5.5 △0	0	东盟ASEAN,智利CL,巴基斯坦PK,新西兰NZ,秘鲁PE,哥斯达黎加CR	0	最不发达35国LDC35	30	----Terbium carbonates
1843	2846.9043	----碳酸镝	5.5 △0	0	东盟ASEAN,智利CL,巴基斯坦PK,新西兰NZ,秘鲁PE,哥斯达黎加CR	0	最不发达35国LDC35	30	----Dysprosium carbonates
1844	2846.9044	----碳酸钕	5.5 △0	0	东盟ASEAN,智利CL,巴基斯坦PK,新西兰NZ,秘鲁PE,哥斯达黎加CR	0	最不发达35国LDC35	30	----Neodymium carbonates
1845	2846.9045	----碳酸镨	5.5 △0	0	东盟ASEAN,智利CL,巴基斯坦PK,新西兰NZ,秘鲁PE,哥斯达黎加CR	0	最不发达35国LDC35	30	----Praseodymium carbonates
1846	2846.9046	----碳酸钇	5.5 △0	0	东盟ASEAN,智利CL,巴基斯坦PK,新西兰NZ,秘鲁PE,哥斯达黎加CR	0	最不发达35国LDC35	30	----Yttrium carbonates
1847	2846.9048	----混合碳酸稀土	5.5 △0	0	东盟ASEAN,智利CL,巴基斯坦PK,新西兰NZ,秘鲁PE,哥斯达黎加CR	0	最不发达35国LDC35	30	----Mixture of rare-earth carbonate
1848	2846.9049	----其他	5.5 △0	0	东盟ASEAN,智利CL,巴基斯坦PK,新西兰NZ,秘鲁PE,哥斯达黎加CR	0	最不发达35国LDC35	30	----Other
		---其他:							---Other:
1849	2846.9091	----镧的其他化合物	5.5 △0	0	东盟ASEAN,智利CL,巴基斯坦PK,新西兰NZ,秘鲁PE,哥斯达黎加CR	0	最不发达35国LDC35	30	----Of Lanthanum
1850	2846.9092	----钕的其他化合物	5.5 △0	0	东盟ASEAN,智利CL,巴基斯坦PK,新西兰NZ,秘鲁PE,哥斯达黎加CR	0	最不发达35国LDC35	30	----Of Neodymium
1851	2846.9093	----铽的其他化合物	5.5 △0	0	东盟ASEAN,智利CL,巴基斯坦PK,新西兰NZ,秘鲁PE,哥斯达黎加CR	0	最不发达35国LDC35	30	----Of Terbium
1851	2846.9094	----镝的其他化合物	5.5 △0	0	东盟ASEAN,智利CL,巴基斯坦PK,新西兰NZ,秘鲁PE,哥斯达黎加CR	0	最不发达35国LDC35	30	----Of Dysprosium
1853	2846.9095	----镨的其他化合物	5.5 △0	0	东盟ASEAN,智利CL,巴基斯坦PK,新西兰NZ,秘鲁PE,哥斯达黎加CR	0	最不发达35国LDC35	30	----Of Praseodymium

序号 No.	税则号列 Tariff Line	货品名称	最惠国税率 MFN(%)	协定税率 Agreement(%)		特惠税率 S.P.(%)		普通税率 Gen.(%)	Article Description
1854	2846.9096	----钇的其他化合物	5.5 △0	0	东盟ASEAN,智利CL,巴基斯坦PK,新西兰NZ,秘鲁PE,哥斯达黎加CR	0	最不发达35国LDC35	30	----Of Yttrium
1855	2846.9099	----其他	5.5 △0	0	东盟ASEAN,智利CL,巴基斯坦PK,新西兰NZ,秘鲁PE,哥斯达黎加CR	0	最不发达35国LDC35	30	----Other
	28.47	**过氧化氢，不论是否用尿素固化:**							**Hydrogen peroxide, whether or not solidified with urea:**
1856	2847.0000	过氧化氢，不论是否用尿素固化	5.5	0 5	东盟ASEAN,智利CL,新西兰NZ,秘鲁PE,哥斯达黎加CR 巴基斯坦PK	0	最不发达35国LDC35	30	Hydrogen peroxide, whether or not solidified with urea
	28.48	**磷化物，不论是否已有化学定义，但不包括磷铁:**							**Phosphides, whether or not chemically defined, excluding ferrophosphorus:**
1857	2848.0000	磷化物，不论是否已有化学定义，但不包括磷铁	5.5	0 0.6	东盟ASEAN,巴基斯坦PK,新西兰NZ,秘鲁PE,哥斯达黎加CR 智利CL	0	最不发达35国LDC35	20	Phosphides, whether or not chemically defined, excluding ferrophosphorus
	28.49	**碳化物，不论是否已有化学定义:**							**Carbides, whether or not chemically defined:**
1858	2849.1000	-碳化钙	5.5	0	东盟ASEAN,智利CL,巴基斯坦PK,新西兰NZ,秘鲁PE,哥斯达黎加CR	0	最不发达35国LDC35	45	-Of calcium
1859	2849.2000	-碳化硅	5.5	0 5	东盟ASEAN,智利CL,新西兰NZ,秘鲁PE,哥斯达黎加CR 巴基斯坦PK	0	最不发达35国LDC35	30	-Of silicon
		-其他:							-Other:
1860	2849.9010	---碳化硼	5.5	0	东盟ASEAN,智利CL,巴基斯坦PK,新西兰NZ,秘鲁PE,哥斯达黎加CR	0	最不发达35国LDC35	30	---Of boron
1861	2849.9020	---碳化钨	5.5	0	东盟ASEAN,智利CL,巴基斯坦PK,新西兰NZ,秘鲁PE,哥斯达黎加CR	0	最不发达35国LDC35	30	---Of tungsten
1862	2849.9090	---其他	5.5	0	东盟ASEAN,智利CL,巴基斯坦PK,新西兰NZ,秘鲁PE,哥斯达黎加CR	0	最不发达35国LDC35	30	---Other
	28.50	**氢化物、氮化物、迭氮化物、硅化物及硼化物，不论是否已有化学定义，但可归入税号28.49的碳化物除外:**							**Hydrides, nitrides, azides, silicides and borides, whether or not chemically defined, other than compounds which are also carbides of heading No.28. 49:**

序号 No.	税则号列 Tariff Line	货品名称	最惠国税率 MFN(%)	协定税率 Agreement(%)		特惠税率 S.P.(%)		普通税率 Gen.(%)	Article Description
		氢化物、氮化物、迭氮化物、硅化物及硼化物，不论是否已有化学定义，但可归入税号 28.49 的碳化物除外							Hydrides, nitrides, azides, silicides and borides, whether or not chemically defined, other than compounds which are also carbides of heading No.28.49
		---氮化物:							---Nitrides:
1863	2850.0011	----氮化锰	5.5	0 3.9	东盟ASEAN,智利CL,巴基斯坦PK,新西兰NZ,秘鲁PE,哥斯达黎加CR,香港HK 亚太APTA	0	最不发达 35 国 LDC35	30	----Manganese nitride
1864	2850.0019	----其他	5.5	0 3.9	东盟ASEAN,智利CL,巴基斯坦PK,新西兰NZ,秘鲁PE,哥斯达黎加CR,香港HK 亚太APTA	0	最不发达 35 国 LDC35	30	----Other
1865	2850.0090	---其他	5.5	0 3.9	东盟ASEAN,智利CL,巴基斯坦PK,新西兰NZ,秘鲁PE,哥斯达黎加CR,香港HK 亚太APTA	0	最不发达 35 国 LDC35	30	---Other
	28.52	**汞的无机或有机化合物，不论是否已有化学定义，汞齐除外:**							**Inorganic or organic compounds of mercury, whether or not chemically defined, excluding amalgams:**
1866	2852.1000	-已有化学定义的	5.5	0	东盟ASEAN,智利CL,巴基斯坦PK,新西兰NZ,秘鲁PE,哥斯达黎加CR,香港HK	0	最不发达 35 国 LDC35	30	- Chemically defined
1867	2852.9000	-其他	5.5	0 5	东盟ASEAN,智利CL,新西兰NZ,秘鲁PE,哥斯达黎加CR 巴基斯坦PK	0	最不发达 35 国 LDC35,最不发达 4 国 LDC4	30	- Other
	28.53	**其他无机化合物（包括蒸馏水、导电水及类似的纯净水）;液态空气（不论是否除去稀有气体）;压缩空气;汞齐，但贵金属汞齐除外:**							**Other inorganic compounds (including distilled or conductivity water and water of similar purity); liquid air (whether or not rare gases have been removed); compressed air; amalgams, other than amalgams of precious metals:**
1868	2853.0010	---饮用蒸馏水	5.5	0 0.6	东盟ASEAN,巴基斯坦PK,新西兰NZ,秘鲁PE,哥斯达黎加CR,香港HK,澳门MO 智利CL	0	最不发达 35 国 LDC35	70	---Distilled water for human consumption

序号 No.	税则号列 Tariff Line	货品名称	最惠国税率 MFN(%)	协定税率 Agreement(%)		特惠税率 S.P.(%)		普通税率 Gen.(%)	Article Description
1869	2853.0020	---氯化氰	5.5	0	东盟ASEAN,巴基斯坦PK,新西兰NZ,秘鲁PE,哥斯达黎加CR	0	最不发达35国LDC35	30	---Chlorocyanogen, cyanogen chloride
				0.6	智利CL				
1870	2853.0030	---镍钴锰氢氧化物	6.5	0	东盟ASEAN,新西兰NZ,秘鲁PE,哥斯达黎加CR,香港HK,澳门MO	0	最不发达35国LDC35	30	---Nickel cobalt manganese composite hydrogenoxide
				0.7	智利CL				
				5	巴基斯坦PK				
1871	2853.0090	---其他	5.5	0	东盟ASEAN,新西兰NZ,秘鲁PE,哥斯达黎加CR,香港HK,澳门MO	0	最不发达35国LDC35	30	---Other
				0.6	智利CL				
				5	巴基斯坦PK				

第二十九章 有机化学品

Chapter 29 Organic chemicals

注释:

一、除条文另有规定的以外，本章各税号只适用于:

（一）单独的已有化学定义的有机化合物，不论是否含有杂质;

（二）同一有机化合物的两种或两种以上异构体的混合物（不论是否含有杂质），但无环烃异构体的混合物（立体异构体除外），不论是否饱和，应归入第二十七章;

（三）税号 29.36 至 29.39 的产品，税号 29.40 的糖醚、糖缩醛、糖酯及其盐类和税号 29.41 的产品，不论是否已有化学定义;

（四）上述（一）、（二）、（三）款产品的水溶液;

（五）溶于其他溶剂的上述（一）、（二）、（三）款的产品，但该产品处于溶液状态只是为了安全或运输所采取的正常必要方法，其所用溶剂并不使该产品改变其一般用途而适合于某些特殊用途;

（六）为了保存或运输的需要，加入稳定剂（包括抗结块剂）的上述（一）、（二）、（三）、（四）、（五）各款产品;

（七）为了便于识别或安全起见，加入抗尘剂、着色剂或气味剂的上述（一）、（二）、（三）、（四）、（五）、（六）各款产品，但所加剂料并不使原产品改变其一般用途而适合于某些特殊用途;

（八）为生产偶氮染料而稀释至标准浓度的下列产品: 重氮盐，用于重氮盐、可重氮化的胺及其盐类的偶合剂。

二、本章不包括:

（一）税号 15.04 的货品及税号 15.20 的粗甘油;

Notes:

1. Except where the context otherwise requires, the headings of this Chapter apply only to:

(a) Separate chemically defined organic compounds, whether or not containing impurities;

(b) Mixtures of two or more isomers of the same organic compound (whether or not containing impurities) , except mixtures of acyclic hydrocarbon isomers (other than stereoisomers) , whether or not saturated (Chapter 27) ;

(c) The products of headings 29.36 to 29.39 or the sugar ethers, sugar acetals and sugar esters, and their salts, of heading 29.40, or the products of heading 29.41, whether or not chemically defined;

(d) The products mentioned in (a), (b) or (c) above dissolved in water;

(e) The products mentioned in (a), (b) or (c) above dissolved in other slovents provided that the solution constitutes a normal and necessary method of putting up these products adopted solely for reasons of safety or for transport and that the solvent does not render the product particularly suitable for specific use rather than for general use;

(f) The products mentioned in (a), (b), (c), (d) or (e) above with an added stabilizer (including an anticaking agent) necessary for their preservation or transport;

(g) The products mentioned in (a), (b), (c), (d), (e) or (f) above with an added anti-dusting agent or a colouring or odoriferous substance added to facilitate their identification or for safety reasons, provided that the additions do not render the product particularly suitable for specific use rather than for general use;

(h) The following products, diluted to standard strengths, for the production of azo dyes:diazonium salts, couplers used for these salts and diazotisable amines and their salts.

2. This Chapter does not cover:

(a) Goods of heading No.15.04 or crude glycerol of heading No.15.20;

（二）乙醇（税号 22.07 或 22.08）；

（三）甲烷及丙烷（税号 27.11）；

（四）第二十八章注释二所述的碳化合物；

（五）税目 30.02 的免疫制品

（六）尿素（税号 31.02 或 31.05）；

（七）植物性或动物性着色料（税号 32.03）、合成有机着色料、用作荧光增白剂或发光体的合成有机产品（税号 32.04）及零售包装的染料或其他着色料（税号 32.12）；

（八）酶（税号 35.07）；

（九）聚乙醛、六亚甲基四胺（乌洛托品）及类似物质，制成片、条或类似形状作为燃料用的，以及包装容器的容积不超过 300 立方厘米的直接灌注香烟打火机及类似打火器用的液体燃料或液化气体燃料（税号 36.06）；

（十）灭火器的装配药及已装药的灭火弹（税号 38.13）；零售包装的除墨剂（税号 38.24）；

（十一）光学元件，例如用酒石酸乙二胺制成的（税号 90.01）。

三、可以归入本章两个或两个以上税号的货品，应归入有关税号中的最后一个税号。

四、税号 29.04 至 29.06、29.08 至 29.11 及 29.13 至 29.20 的卤化、磺化、硝化或亚硝化衍生物均包括复合衍生物，例如，卤磺化、卤硝化、磺硝化及卤磺硝化衍生物。

硝基及亚硝基不作为税号29.29的含氮基官能团。

税号 29.11、29.12、29.14、29.18 及 29.22 所称“含氧基”，仅限于税号 29.05 至 29.20 的各种含氧基(其特征为有机含氧基）。

五、

（一）本章第一分章至第七分章的酸基有机化合物与这些分章的有机化合物构成的酯应归入有

(b) Ethyl alcohol (heading No.22.07 or 22.08) ;

(c) Methane or propane (heading No.27.11) ;

(d) The compounds of carbon mentioned in Note 2 to Chapter 28;

(e) Immunological products of heading 30.02;

(f) Urea (heading No.31.02 or 31.05) ;

(g) Colouring matter of vegetable or animal origin (heading No.32.03) , synthetic organic colouring matter, synthetic organic products of a kind used as fluores cent brightening agents or as luminophores (heading No.32.04) or dyes or other colouring matter put up in forms or packings for retail sale (heading No.32.12) ;

(h) Enzymes (heading No.35.07) ;

(i) Metaldehyde, hexamethylenetetramine or similar substances, put up in forms (for example, tablets, sticks or similar forms) for use as fuels, or liquid or liquefied_gas fuels in containers of a kind used for filling or refilling cigarette or similar lighters and of a capacity not exceeding 300cm^3 (heading No.36.06) ;

(j) Products put up as charges for fire-extinguishers or put up in fire-extinguishing grenades, of heading No.38.13; ink removers put up in packings for retail sale, of heading No.38.24;or

(k) Optical elements, for example, of ethylenediamine tartrate (heading No.90.01).

3. Goods which could be included in two or more of the headings of this Chapter are to be classified in that one of those headings which occurs last in numerical order.

4. In headings Nos.29.04 to 29.06, 29.08 to 29.11 and 29.13 to 29.20, any reference to halogenated, sulphonated, nitrated or nitrosated derivatives includes a reference to compound derivatives, such as sulphohalogenated, nitrohalogenated, nitrosulphonated or nitrosulphohalogenated derivatives.

Nitro or nitroso groups are not to be taken as “nitrogenfunctions” for the purpose of heading No.29.29.

For the purposes of headings Nos.29.11, 29.12, 29.14, 29.18 and 29.22, “oxygen-function” is to be restricted to the functions (the characteristic organic oxygen-containing groups) referred to in headings Nos.29.05 to 29.20.

5.

(a) The esters of acid-function organic compounds of sub-Chapters Ⅰ to Ⅶ with organic compounds of

关税号中的最后一个税号；

（二）乙醇与本章第一分章至第七分章的酸基有机化合物所构成的酯，应按有关酸基化合物归类。

（三）除第六类注释一及第二十八章注释二另有规定的以外：

1. 第一分章至第十分章及税号 29.42 的有机化合物的无机盐，例如，含酸基、酚基或烯醇基的化合物及有机碱的无机盐，应归入相应的有机化合物的税号；

2. 第一分章至第十分章及税号 29.42 的有机化合物之间生成的盐，应按生成该盐的碱或酸（包括酚基或烯醇基化合物）归入本章有关税号中的最后一个税号；

3. 除第十一分章或税目 29.41 的产品外，配位化合物应按该化合物所有金属键（金属-碳键除外）“断开”所形成的片段归入第二十九章有关税目中的最后一个税目。

（四）除乙醇外，金属醇化物应按相应的醇归类（税号 29.05）。

（五）羧酸酰卤化物应按相应的酸归类。

六、税号 29.30 及 29.31 的化合物是指有机化合物，其分子中除含氢、氧或氮原子外，还含有与碳原子直接连接的其他非金属或金属原子（例如，硫、砷或铅）。

税号 29.30（有机硫化合物）及税号 29.31（其他有机—无机化合物）不包括某些磺化或卤化衍生物（含复合衍生物）。这些衍生物分子中除氢、氧、氮之外，只有具有磺化或卤化衍生物（或复合衍生物）性质的硫原子或卤素原子与碳原子直接连接。

these sub- Chapters are to be classified with that compound which is classified in the heading which occurs last in numerical order in these sub-Chapters.

(b) Esters of ethyl alcohol with acid-function organic compounds of sub-Chapters Ⅰ to Ⅶ are to be classified in the same heading as the corresponding acid-function compounds.

(c) Subject to Note 1 to Section Ⅵ and Note 2 to Chapter28:

(1) Inorganic salts of organic compounds such as acid, phenol or enol-function compounds or organic bases, of sub-Chapters Ⅰ to Ⅹ or heading No.29.42, are to be classified in the heading appropriate to the organic compound;

(2) Salts formed between organic compounds of sub-Chapters Ⅰ to Ⅹ or heading No.29.42 are to be classified in the heading appropriate to the base or to the acid (including phenol or enol-function compounds) from which they are formed, whichever occurs last in numerical order in the Chapter; and

(3) Co-ordination compounds, other than products classifiable in sub-Chapter XI or heading 29.41, are to be classified in the heading which occurs last in numerical order in Chapter 29, among those appropriate to the fragments formed by “cleaving” of all metal bonds, other than metal carbon bonds.

(d) Metal alcoholates are to be classified in the same heading as the corresponding alcohols except in the case of ethanol (heading No.29.05) .

(e) Halides of carboxylic acids are to be classified in the same heading as the corresponding acids.

6. The compounds of headings Nos.29.30 and 29.31 are organic compounds the molecules of which contain, in addition to atoms of hydrogen, oxygen or nitrogen, atoms of other non-metals of or metals (such as sulphur, arsenic or lead) directly linked to carbon atoms.

Heading No.29.30 (organo-sulphur compounds) and heading No.29.31 (other organo-inorganic compounds) do not include sulphonated or halogenated derivatives (in cluding compound derivatives) which, apart from hydrogen, oxygen and nitrogen, only have directly linked to carbon the atoms of sulphur or of a halogen which give them their nature of sulphonated or halogenated derivatives (or compound derivatives) .

七、税号 29.32、29.33 及 29.34 不包括三节环环氧化物、过氧化酮、醛或硫醛的环聚合物、多元羧酸酐、多元醇或酚与多元酸构成的环酯及多元酸酰亚胺。

7. Headings Nos.29.32, 29.33 and 29.34do not include epoxides with a three-membered ring, ketone peroxides, cyclic polymers of aldehydes or of thioaldehydes, anhydrides of polybasic carboxylic acids, cyclic esters of polyhydric alcohols or phenols with polybasic acids, and imides of polybasic acids.

本条规定只适用于由本条所列环化功能形成环内杂原子的化合物。

These provisions apply only when the ring-position heteroatoms are those resulting solely form the cyclising function or functions here listed.

八、税目 29.37 所称:

（一）"激素"包括激素释放因子、激素刺激和释放因子、激素抑制剂以及激素抗体;

（二）"主要起激素作用"，不仅适用于激素衍生物以及主要起激素作用的结构类似物，也适用于在本税目所列产品合成过程中主要用作中间体的激素衍生物以及结构类似物。

8. For the purposes of heading 29.37:

(a) the term"hormones"includes hormone-releasing or hormone-stimulating factors, hormone inhibitors and hormone antagonists (anti-hormones) ;

(b) the expression"used primarily as hormones"applies not only to hormone derivatives and structural analogues used primarily for their hormonal effect, but also to those derivatives and structural analogues used primarily as intermediates in the synthesis of products of this heading.

子目注释:

一、属于本章任一税号项下的一种（组）化合物的衍生物，如果该税号其他子目未明确将其包括在内，而且有关的子目中又无列名为"其他"的子目，则应与该种（组）化合物归入同一子目。

二、第二十九章注释三不适用于本章的子目。

Subheading Notes:

1. Within any one heading of this Chapter, derivatives of a chemical compound (or group of chemical compounds) are to be clas sified in the same subheading as that compound (or group of compounds) provided that they are not more specifically covered by any other subheading and that there is no residual subheading named "other" in the series of subheadings concerned.

2. Note 3 to Chapter 29 does not apply to the subheadings of this Chapter.

序号 No.	税则号列 Tariff Line	货品名称	最惠国税率 MFN(%)	协定税率 Agreement(%)		特惠税率 S.P.(%)		普通税率 Gen.(%)	Article Description
		第一分章 烃类及其卤化、磺化、硝化或亚硝化衍生物							Ⅰ. HYDROCARBONS AND THEIR HALOGENATED, SULPHONATED, NITRATED OR NITROSATED DERIVATIVES
	29.01	**无环烃:**							**Acyclic hydrocarbons:**
1872	2901.1000	-饱和	2	0	东盟ASEAN,智利CL,巴基斯坦PK,新西兰NZ,秘鲁PE,哥斯达黎加CR,香港HK	0	最不发达 35 国 LDC35	30	-Saturated
		-不饱和:							-Unsaturated:

序号 No.	税则号列 Tariff Line	货品名称	最惠国税率 MFN(%)	协定税率 Agreement(%)		特惠税率 S.P.(%)		普通税率 Gen.(%)	Article Description
1873	2901.2100	--乙烯	2	0	东盟ASEAN,智利CL,巴基斯坦PK,新西兰NZ,秘鲁PE,哥斯达黎加CR	0	最不发达35国LDC35	20	--Ethylene
1874	2901.2200	--丙烯	2 △1	0	东盟ASEAN,智利CL,巴基斯坦PK,新西兰NZ,秘鲁PE,哥斯达黎加CR,台湾TW	0	最不发达35国LDC35	20	--Propene (propylene)
		--丁烯及其异构体:							--Butene (butylene) and isomers thereof:
1875	2901.2310	---1-丁烯	2	0	东盟ASEAN,智利CL,巴基斯坦PK,新西兰NZ,秘鲁PE,哥斯达黎加CR	0	最不发达35国LDC35	20	---1-butene
1876	2901.2320	---2-丁烯	2	0	东盟ASEAN,智利CL,巴基斯坦PK,新西兰NZ,秘鲁PE,哥斯达黎加CR	0	最不发达35国LDC35	20	---2-butene
1877	2901.2330	---2-甲基丙稀	2	0	东盟ASEAN,智利CL,巴基斯坦PK,新西兰NZ,秘鲁PE,哥斯达黎加CR	0	最不发达35国LDC35	20	---2-methyl-propene
		--1，3-丁二烯及异戊二烯:							--Buta-1, 3-diene and isoprene:
1878	2901.2410	---1,3-丁二烯	2	0	东盟ASEAN,智利CL,巴基斯坦PK,新西兰NZ,秘鲁PE,哥斯达黎加CR,台湾TW	0	最不发达35国LDC35	20	---Buta-1,3-diene
1879	2901.2420	---异戊二烯	2	0	东盟ASEAN,智利CL,巴基斯坦PK,新西兰NZ,秘鲁PE,哥斯达黎加CR,台湾TW	0	最不发达35国LDC35	20	---isoprene
		--其他:							--Other:
1880	2901.2910	---异戊烯	2	0	东盟ASEAN,智利CL,巴基斯坦PK,新西兰NZ,秘鲁PE,哥斯达黎加CR	0	最不发达35国LDC35	30	---Isopentene
1881	2901.2920	---乙炔	2	0	东盟ASEAN,智利CL,巴基斯坦PK,新西兰NZ,秘鲁PE,哥斯达黎加CR	0	最不发达35国LDC35	45	---Acetylene
1882	2901.2990	---其他	2	0	东盟ASEAN,智利CL,巴基斯坦PK,新西兰NZ,秘鲁PE,哥斯达黎加CR	0	最不发达35国LDC35	30	---Other
	29.02	**环烃:**							**Cyclic hydrocarbons:**
		-环烷烃、环烯及环萜烯:							-Cyclanes, cyclenes and cycloterpenes:
1883	2902.1100	--环己烷	2	0	东盟ASEAN,智利CL,巴基斯坦PK,新西兰NZ,秘鲁PE,哥斯达黎加CR	0	最不发达35国LDC35	30	--Cyclohexane
		--其他:							--Other:

序号 No.	税则号列 Tariff Line	货品名称	最惠国税率 MFN(%)	协定税率 Agreement(%)		特惠税率 S.P.(%)		普通税率 Gen.(%)	Article Description
1884	2902.1910	---蒎烯	2	0	东盟ASEAN,智利CL,巴基斯坦PK,新西兰NZ,秘鲁PE,哥斯达黎加CR	0	最不发达35国LDC35	30	---Pinene
1885	2902.1920	---4-烷基-4'-烷基双环己烷	2	0	东盟ASEAN,智利CL,巴基斯坦PK,新西兰NZ,秘鲁PE,哥斯达黎加CR	0	最不发达35国LDC35	30	---4-alkyl-4'-alkyl-bicyclohexyl
1886	2902.1990	---其他	2	0	东盟ASEAN,智利CL,巴基斯坦PK,新西兰NZ,秘鲁PE,哥斯达黎加CR	0	最不发达35国LDC35	30	---Other
1887	2902.2000	-苯	2	0	东盟ASEAN,智利CL,巴基斯坦PK,新西兰NZ,秘鲁PE,哥斯达黎加CR	0	最不发达35国LDC35	20	-Benzene
1888	2902.3000	-甲苯	2	0	东盟ASEAN,智利CL,巴基斯坦PK,新西兰NZ,秘鲁PE,哥斯达黎加CR	0	最不发达35国LDC35	30	-Toluene
		-二甲苯:							-Xylenes:
1889	2902.4100	--邻二甲苯	2	0	东盟ASEAN,智利CL,巴基斯坦PK,新西兰NZ,秘鲁PE,哥斯达黎加CR,台湾TW	0	最不发达35国LDC35	20	--o-Xylene
1890	2902.4200	--间二甲苯	2	0	东盟ASEAN,智利CL,巴基斯坦PK,新西兰NZ,秘鲁PE,哥斯达黎加CR,台湾TW	0	最不发达35国LDC35	20	--m-Xylene
1891	2902.4300	--对二甲苯	2	0	东盟ASEAN,智利CL,巴基斯坦PK,新西兰NZ,秘鲁PE,哥斯达黎加CR,台湾TW	0	最不发达35国LDC35	20	--p-Xylene
1892	2902.4400	--混合二甲苯异构体	2	0	东盟ASEAN,智利CL,巴基斯坦PK,新西兰NZ,秘鲁PE,哥斯达黎加CR,台湾TW	0	最不发达35国LDC35	20	--Mixed xylene isomers
1893	2902.5000	-苯乙烯	2	0 1.4	智利CL,巴基斯坦PK,新西兰NZ,秘鲁PE,哥斯达黎加CR 亚太APTA			30	-Styrene
1894	2902.6000	-乙苯	2	0	东盟ASEAN,智利CL,巴基斯坦PK,新西兰NZ,秘鲁PE,哥斯达黎加CR	0	最不发达35国LDC35	30	-Ethylbenzene
1895	2902.7000	-异丙基苯	2	0	东盟ASEAN,智利CL,巴基斯坦PK,新西兰NZ,秘鲁PE,哥斯达黎加CR	0	最不发达35国LDC35	30	-Cumene
		-其他:							-Other:
1896	2902.9010	---四氢萘	2	0	东盟ASEAN,智利CL,巴基斯坦PK,新西兰NZ,秘鲁PE,哥斯达黎加CR	0	最不发达35国LDC35	11	---Tetrahydronaphthalene (tetralin)

序号 No.	税则号列 Tariff Line	货品名称	最惠国税率 MFN(%)	协定税率 Agreement(%)		特惠税率 S.P.(%)		普通税率 Gen.(%)	Article Description
1897	2902.9020	---精萘	2	0	东盟ASEAN,智利CL,巴基斯坦PK,新西兰NZ,秘鲁PE,哥斯达黎加CR	0	最不发达35国LDC35	35	---Naphthalene
1898	2902.9030	---十二烷基苯	2	0	东盟ASEAN,智利CL,巴基斯坦PK,新西兰NZ,秘鲁PE,哥斯达黎加CR,台湾TW	0	最不发达35国LDC35	30	---Dodecylbenzene
1899	2902.9040	--- 4-(4'-烷基环己基)环己基乙烯	2	0	东盟ASEAN,智利CL,巴基斯坦PK,新西兰NZ,秘鲁PE,哥斯达黎加CR	0	最不发达35国LDC35	30	---4-(4'-alkylcyclohexyl) cyclohexylethene
1900	2902.9090	---其他	2	0	东盟ASEAN,智利CL,巴基斯坦PK,新西兰NZ,秘鲁PE,哥斯达黎加CR	0	最不发达35国LDC35	30	---Other
	29.03	**烃的卤化衍生物:**							**Halogenated derivatives of hydrocarbons:**
		-无环烃的饱和氯化衍生物:							-Saturated chlorinated derivatives of acyclic hydrocarbons:
1901	2903.1100	--一氯甲烷及氯乙烷	5.5	0	东盟ASEAN,智利CL,巴基斯坦PK,新西兰NZ,秘鲁PE,哥斯达黎加CR	0	最不发达35国LDC35	30	--Chloromethane (methyl chloride) and chloroethane (ethyl chloride)
1902	2903.1200	--二氯甲烷	8	0	东盟ASEAN,智利CL,新西兰NZ,秘鲁PE,哥斯达黎加CR,香港HK	0	最不发达35国LDC35	30	--Dichloromethane (methylene chloride)
				5	巴基斯坦PK				
1903	2903.1300	--氯仿（三氯甲烷）	10	0	东盟ASEAN,智利CL,新西兰NZ,秘鲁PE,哥斯达黎加CR,台湾TW	0	最不发达35国LDC35	30	--Chloroform (trichloromethane)
				5	巴基斯坦PK				
				9	亚太APTA				
1904	2903.1400	--四氯化碳	8	0	东盟ASEAN,智利CL,新西兰NZ,秘鲁PE,哥斯达黎加CR	0	最不发达35国LDC35	30	--Carbon tetrachloride
				5	巴基斯坦PK				
1905	2903.1500	--1，2-二氯乙烷（ISO）	5.5 △1	0	智利CL,新西兰NZ,哥斯达黎加CR			30	--1, 2-Dichloroethane (ISO) (ethylene dichloride)
		--其他:							--Other:
1906	2903.1910	---1，1，1-三氯乙烷（甲基氯仿）	8	0	东盟ASEAN,智利CL,新西兰NZ,秘鲁PE,哥斯达黎加CR	0	最不发达35国LDC35	30	---1, 1, 1-Trichloroethane (methylchloro form)
				5	巴基斯坦PK				
1907	2903.1990	---其他	5.5	0	东盟ASEAN,智利CL,新西兰NZ,秘鲁PE,哥斯达黎加CR	0	最不发达35国LDC35	30	---Other
				5	巴基斯坦PK				
		-无环烃的不饱和氯化衍生物:							-Unsaturated chlorinated derivatives of acyclic hydrocarbons:

序号 No.	税则号列 Tariff Line	货品名称	最惠国税率 MFN(%)	协定税率 Agreement(%)		特惠税率 S.P.(%)		普通税率 Gen.(%)	Article Description
1908	2903.2100	--氯乙烯	5.5 △1	0 3.9	东盟ASEAN,智利CL,巴基斯坦PK,新西兰NZ,秘鲁PE,哥斯达黎加CR,台湾TW 亚太APTA	0	最不发达35国LDC35	30	--Vinyl chloride (chloroethylene)
1909	2903.2200	--三氯乙烯	8	0 5	东盟ASEAN,智利CL,新西兰NZ,秘鲁PE,哥斯达黎加CR 巴基斯坦PK	0	最不发达35国LDC35	30	--Trichloroethylene
1910	2903.2300	--四氯乙烯（全氯乙烯）	5.5	0	东盟ASEAN,智利CL,巴基斯坦PK,新西兰NZ,秘鲁PE,哥斯达黎加CR	0	最不发达35国LDC35	30	--Tetrachloroethylene (perchloroethylene)
		--其他:							--Other:
1911	2903.2910	---3-氯-1-丙烯（氯丙烯）	5.5	0	东盟ASEAN,智利CL,巴基斯坦PK,新西兰NZ,秘鲁PE,哥斯达黎加CR	0	最不发达35国LDC35	30	---3-Chloropropene
1912	2903.2990	---其他	5.5	0	东盟ASEAN,智利CL,巴基斯坦PK,新西兰NZ,秘鲁PE,哥斯达黎加CR	0	最不发达35国LDC35	30	---Other
		-无环烃的氟化、溴化或碘化衍生物:							-Fluorinated, brominated or iodinated derivatives of acyclic hydrocarbons:
1913	2903.3100	--1，2-二溴乙烷（ISO）	5.5	0 5	东盟ASEAN,智利CL,新西兰NZ,秘鲁PE,哥斯达黎加CR,香港HK 巴基斯坦PK	0	最不发达35国LDC35	30	--Ethylene dibromide (ISO)
		--其他:							--Other:
1914	2903.3910	---1，1，3，3，3-五氟-2-三氟甲基-1-丙烯（全氟异丁烯;八氟异丁烯）	5.5	0	东盟ASEAN,智利CL,巴基斯坦PK,新西兰NZ,秘鲁PE,哥斯达黎加CR	0	最不发达35国LDC35	30	---1, 1, 3, 3, 3-Pentafluro–2-trifluromethyl-1-propene (Perfluor-olisobutylene, isobutylene octafluoride)
1915	2903.3990	---其他	5.5	0 5	东盟ASEAN,智利CL,新西兰NZ,秘鲁PE,哥斯达黎加CR,香港HK 巴基斯坦PK	0	最不发达35国LDC35	30	---Other
		-含有两种或两种以上不同卤素的无环烃卤化衍生物:							-Halogenated derivatives of acyclic hydrocarbons containing two or more different halogens:
1916	2903.7100	--一氯二氟甲烷	5.5	0 5	东盟ASEAN,智利CL,新西兰NZ,秘鲁PE,哥斯达黎加CR 巴基斯坦PK	0	最不发达35国LDC35	30	--Chlorodifluoromethane
1917	2903.7200	--二氯三氟乙烷	5.5	0 5	东盟ASEAN,智利CL,新西兰NZ,秘鲁PE,哥斯达黎加CR 巴基斯坦PK	0	最不发达35国LDC35	30	--Dichlorotrifluoroethanes

序号 No.	税则号列 Tariff Line	货品名称	最惠国税率 MFN(%)	协定税率 Agreement(%)		特惠税率 S.P.(%)		普通税率 Gen.(%)	Article Description
1918	2903.7300	--二氯一氟乙烷	5.5	0	东盟ASEAN,智利CL,新西兰NZ,秘鲁PE,哥斯达黎加CR	0	最不发达35国LDC35	30	--Dichlorofluoroethanes
				5	巴基斯坦PK				
1919	2903.7400	--一氯二氟乙烷	5.5	0	东盟ASEAN,智利CL,新西兰NZ,秘鲁PE,哥斯达黎加CR	0	最不发达35国LDC35	30	--Chlorodifluoroethanes
				5	巴基斯坦PK				
1920	2903.7500	--二氯五氟丙烷	5.5	0	东盟ASEAN,智利CL,新西兰NZ,秘鲁PE,哥斯达黎加CR	0	最不发达35国LDC35	30	--Dichloropentafluoro-propanes
				5	巴基斯坦PK				
1921	2903.7600	--溴氯二氟甲烷、溴三氟甲烷及二溴四氟乙烷	5.5	0	东盟ASEAN,智利CL,巴基斯坦PK,新西兰NZ,秘鲁PE,哥斯达黎加CR	0	最不发达35国LDC35	30	--Bromochlorodi-fluoromethane, bromo-trifluoromethane and dibromotetrafluoro-ethanes
		--其他，仅含氟和氯的全卤化物：							--Other, perhalogenated only with fluorine and chlorine:
1922	2903.7710	---三氯氟甲烷	5.5	0	东盟ASEAN,智利CL,新西兰NZ,秘鲁PE,哥斯达黎加CR	0	最不发达35国LDC35	30	---Trichlorofluoromethane
				5	巴基斯坦PK				
1923	2903.7720	---其他仅含氟和氯的甲烷、乙烷及丙烷的全卤化物	5.5	0	东盟ASEAN,智利CL,巴基斯坦PK,新西兰NZ,秘鲁PE,哥斯达黎加CR	0	最不发达35国LDC35	30	---Other methane, ethane and propane perhalo-genated derivatives only with fluorine and chlorinederivatives
1924	2903.7790	---其他	5.5	0	东盟ASEAN,智利CL,新西兰NZ,秘鲁PE,哥斯达黎加CR	0	最不发达35国LDC35	30	---Other
				5	巴基斯坦PK				
1925	2903.7800	--其他全卤化衍生物	5.5	0	东盟ASEAN,智利CL,巴基斯坦PK,新西兰NZ,秘鲁PE,哥斯达黎加CR	0	最不发达35国LDC35	30	--Other perhalogenated derivatives
		--其他：							--Other:
1926	2903.7910	---其他仅含氟和氯的甲烷、乙烷及丙烷的卤化衍生物	5.5	0	东盟ASEAN,智利CL,新西兰NZ,秘鲁PE,哥斯达黎加CR	0	最不发达35国LDC35	30	---Other methane, ethane and propane halo-genated derivatives only with fluorine and chlorine
				5	巴基斯坦PK				
1927	2903.7990	---其他	5.5	0	东盟ASEAN,智利CL,巴基斯坦PK,新西兰NZ,秘鲁PE,哥斯达黎加CR	0	最不发达35国LDC35	30	---Other
		-环烷烃、环烯烃或环萜烯烃的卤化衍生物：							-Halogenated derivatives of cyclanic, cyclenic or cycloterpenic hydrocar-bons :

序号 No.	税则号列 Tariff Line	货品名称	最惠国税率 MFN(%)	协定税率 Agreement(%)		特惠税率 S.P.(%)		普通税率 Gen.(%)	Article Description
1928	2903.8100	--1,2,3,4,5,6-六氯环己烷〔六六六（ISO)〕，包括林丹（ISO，INN）	5.5	0	东盟ASEAN,智利CL,巴基斯坦PK,新西兰NZ,秘鲁PE,哥斯达黎加CR	0	最不发达35国LDC35	30	--1,2,3,4,5,6-Hexachlorocyclohexane (HCH (ISO)), including lindane (ISO, INN)
1929	2903.8200	--艾氏剂（ISO)、氯丹（ISO）及七氯（ISO）	5.5	0	东盟ASEAN,智利CL,巴基斯坦PK,新西兰NZ,秘鲁PE,哥斯达黎加CR	0	最不发达35国LDC35	30	--Aldrin (ISO), chlordane (ISO) and heptachlor (ISO)
1930	2903.8900	--其他	5.5	0	东盟ASEAN,智利CL,巴基斯坦PK,新西兰NZ,秘鲁PE,哥斯达黎加CR	0	最不发达35国LDC35	30	--Other
		-芳烃卤化衍生物:							-Halogenated derivatives of aromatic hydrocarbons :
		--氯苯、邻二氯苯及对二氯苯:							--Chlorobenzene, o-dichlorobenzene and p-dichlorobenzene:
1931	2903.9110	---邻二氯苯	5.5	0	东盟ASEAN,智利CL,巴基斯坦PK,新西兰NZ,秘鲁PE,哥斯达黎加CR	0	最不发达35国LDC35	30	---o-Dichlorobenzene
1932	2903.9190	---其他	5.5	0 5	东盟ASEAN,智利CL,新西兰NZ,秘鲁PE,哥斯达黎加CR 巴基斯坦PK	0	最不发达35国LDC35	30	---Other
1933	2903.9200	--六氯苯（ISO）及滴滴涕（ISO，INN）〔1,1,1-三氯-2,2-双（4-氯苯基）乙烷〕	5.5	0	东盟ASEAN,智利CL,巴基斯坦PK,新西兰NZ,秘鲁PE,哥斯达黎加CR	0	最不发达35国LDC35	30	--Hexachlorobenzene (ISO) and DDT (ISO) (clofenotane (INN), 1,1,1-trichloro-2, 2-bis (p-chlorophenyl) ethane)
		--其他:							--Other:
1934	2903.9910	---对氯甲苯	5.5	0	东盟ASEAN,智利CL,巴基斯坦PK,新西兰NZ,秘鲁PE,哥斯达黎加CR	0	最不发达35国LDC35	30	---p-Chlorotoluene
1935	2903.9920	---3,4-二氯三氟甲苯	5.5	0	东盟ASEAN,智利CL,巴基斯坦PK,新西兰NZ,秘鲁PE,哥斯达黎加CR	0	最不发达35国LDC35	30	---3, 4-Dichlorotrifluoride toluene
1936	2903.9930	---4-(4-烷基苯基)-1-(4-烷基苯基)-2-氟苯	5.5	0 5	东盟ASEAN,智利CL,新西兰NZ,秘鲁PE,哥斯达黎加CR 巴基斯坦PK	0	最不发达35国LDC35	30	---4-(4-alkylphenyl)-1-(4-alkylphenyl)-2-fluorobenzene
1937	2903.9990	---其他	5.5	0 5	东盟ASEAN,智利CL,新西兰NZ,秘鲁PE,哥斯达黎加CR 巴基斯坦PK	0	最不发达35国LDC35	30	---Other
	29.04	**烃的磺化、硝化或亚硝化衍生物，不论是否卤化:**							**Sulphonated, nitrated or nitrosated derivatives of hydrocarbons, whether or not halogenated:**

序号 No.	税则号列 Tariff Line	货品名称	最惠国税率 MFN(%)	协定税率 Agreement(%)		特惠税率 S.P.(%)		普通税率 Gen.(%)	Article Description
1938	2904.1000	-仅含磺基的衍生物及其盐和乙酯	5.5	0 5	东盟ASEAN,智利CL,新西兰NZ,秘鲁PE,哥斯达黎加CR,香港HK 巴基斯坦PK	0	最不发达35国LDC35	30	-Derivatives containing only sulpho groups, their salts and ethyl esters
		-仅含硝基或亚硝基的衍生物:							-Derivatives containing only nitro or only nitroso groups:
1939	2904.2010	---硝基苯	5.5	0 0.6	东盟ASEAN,巴基斯坦PK,新西兰NZ,秘鲁PE,哥斯达黎加CR 智利CL	0	最不发达35国LDC35	20	---Nitrobenzene
1940	2904.2020	---硝基甲苯	5.5	0 0.6	东盟ASEAN,巴基斯坦PK,新西兰NZ,秘鲁PE,哥斯达黎加CR 智利CL	0	最不发达35国LDC35	30	---Nitrotoluene and nitrochlorobenzene
1941	2904.2030	---二硝基甲苯	5.5	0 0.6	东盟ASEAN,巴基斯坦PK,新西兰NZ,秘鲁PE,哥斯达黎加CR 智利CL	0	最不发达35国LDC35	20	---Dinitrotoluene and dinitrochlorobenzene
1942	2904.2040	---三硝基甲苯（TNT）	5.5	0 0.6	东盟ASEAN,巴基斯坦PK,新西兰NZ,秘鲁PE,哥斯达黎加CR 智利CL	0	最不发达35国LDC35	40	---Trinitrotoluene
1943	2904.2090	---其他	5.5	0 0.6 5	东盟ASEAN,新西兰NZ,秘鲁PE,哥斯达黎加CR 智利CL 巴基斯坦PK	0	最不发达35国LDC35	30	---Other
		-其他:							-Other:
		---硝基氯化苯:							---Nitrochlorobenzene:
1944	2904.9011	----邻硝基氯化苯	5.5	0	东盟ASEAN,智利CL,巴基斯坦PK,新西兰NZ,秘鲁PE,哥斯达黎加CR	0	最不发达35国LDC35	30	----o-nitrochlorobenzene
1945	2904.9012	----间硝基氯化苯	5.5	0	东盟ASEAN,智利CL,巴基斯坦PK,新西兰NZ,秘鲁PE,哥斯达黎加CR	0	最不发达35国LDC35	30	----m-nitrochlorobenzene
1946	2904.9013	----对硝基氯化苯	5.5	0	东盟ASEAN,智利CL,巴基斯坦PK,新西兰NZ,秘鲁PE,哥斯达黎加CR	0	最不发达35国LDC35	30	----p-nitrochlorobenzene
1947	2904.9020	---二硝基氯化苯	5.5	0	东盟ASEAN,智利CL,巴基斯坦PK,新西兰NZ,秘鲁PE,哥斯达黎加CR	0	最不发达35国LDC35	20	---Dinitrochlorobenzene
1948	2904.9030	---三氯硝基甲烷（氯化苦;硝基氯仿）	5.5	0	东盟ASEAN,智利CL,巴基斯坦PK,新西兰NZ,秘鲁PE,哥斯达黎加CR	0	最不发达35国LDC35	30	---Trichloronitromethane (chloropicrin, nitrochloroform)
1949	2904.9090	---其他	5.5	0 5	东盟ASEAN,智利CL,新西兰NZ,秘鲁PE,哥斯达黎加CR 巴基斯坦PK	0	最不发达35国LDC35	30	---Other

序号 No.	税则号列 Tariff Line	货品名称	最惠国税率 MFN(%)	协定税率 Agreement(%)		特惠税率 S.P.(%)		普通税率 Gen.(%)	Article Description
		第二分章 醇类及其卤化、磺化、硝化或亚硝化衍生物							II. ALCOHOLS AND THEIR HALOGENATED, SULPHONATED, NITRATED OR NITROSATED DERIVATIVES
	29.05	**无环醇及其卤化、磺化、硝化或亚硝化衍生物:**							**Acyclic alcohols and their halogenated, sulphonated, nitrated or nitrosated derivatives:**
		-饱和一元醇:							-Saturated monohydric alcohols:
1950	2905.1100	--甲醇	5.5	0 0.6	东盟ASEAN,巴基斯坦PK,新西兰NZ,哥斯达黎加CR,香港HK 智利CL			30	--Methanol (methyl alcohol)
		--丙醇及异丙醇:							--Propan-1-ol (propyl alcohol) and propan-2-ol (isopropyl alcohol):
1951	2905.1210	---丙醇	5.5 △3	0 0.6	东盟ASEAN,巴基斯坦PK,新西兰NZ,秘鲁PE,哥斯达黎加CR 智利CL	0	最不发达35国LDC35	30	---Propan-1-ol (propyl alcohol)
1952	2905.1220	---异丙醇	5.5	0 0.6	东盟ASEAN,巴基斯坦PK,新西兰NZ,秘鲁PE,哥斯达黎加CR,台湾TW 智利CL	0	最不发达35国LDC35	30	---Propan-2-ol (isopropyl alcohol)
1953	2905.1300	--正丁醇	5.5	0	东盟ASEAN,智利CL,巴基斯坦PK,新西兰NZ,秘鲁PE,哥斯达黎加CR,台湾TW	0	最不发达35国LDC35	30	--Butan-1-ol (n-butyl alcohol)
		--其他丁醇:							--Other butanols:
1954	2905.1410	---异丁醇	5.5	0	东盟ASEAN,智利CL,巴基斯坦PK,新西兰NZ,秘鲁PE,哥斯达黎加CR,台湾TW	0	最不发达35国LDC35	30	---iso-butyl alcohol
1955	2905.1420	---仲丁醇	5.5	0	东盟ASEAN,智利CL,巴基斯坦PK,新西兰NZ,秘鲁PE,哥斯达黎加CR	0	最不发达35国LDC35	30	---sec-butyl alcohol
1956	2905.1430	---叔丁醇	5.5	0	东盟ASEAN,智利CL,巴基斯坦PK,新西兰NZ,秘鲁PE,哥斯达黎加CR	0	最不发达35国LDC35	30	---tert-butgl alcohol
		--辛醇及其异构体:							--Octanol (octyl alcohol) and isomers thereof:
1957	2905.1610	---正辛醇	5.5	0 5	东盟ASEAN,智利CL,新西兰NZ,哥斯达黎加CR 巴基斯坦PK			30	---n-octyl alchol
1958	2905.1690	---其他	5.5	0 5	东盟ASEAN,智利CL,新西兰NZ,哥斯达黎加CR 巴基斯坦PK			30	---Other

序号 No.	税则号列 Tariff Line	货品名称	最惠国税率 MFN(%)	协定税率 Agreement(%)		特惠税率 S.P.(%)		普通税率 Gen.(%)	Article Description
1959	2905.1700	--十二醇、十六醇及十八醇	7	0 5	东盟ASEAN,智利CL,新西兰NZ,秘鲁PE,哥斯达黎加CR 巴基斯坦PK	0	最不发达35国LDC35	30	--Dodecan-1-ol (lauryl alcohol), hexade can-1-ol (cetyl alcohol)and octadecan-1-ol (stearyl alcohol)
		--其他:							--Other:
1960	2905.1910	---3，3-二甲基丁-2-醇（频哪基醇）	5.5	0 0.6	东盟ASEAN,巴基斯坦PK,新西兰NZ,秘鲁PE,哥斯达黎加CR 智利CL	0	最不发达35国LDC35	30	---3, 3-Dimethyl-2-butanol (pinacolyl alcohol)
1961	2905.1990	---其他	5.5	0 5	东盟ASEAN,智利CL,新西兰NZ,秘鲁PE,哥斯达黎加CR 巴基斯坦PK	0	最不发达35国LDC35	30	---Other
		-不饱和一元醇:							-Unsaturated monohydric alcohols:
		--无环萜烯醇:							--Acyclic terpene alcohols:
1962	2905.2210	---香叶醇、橙花醇（3，7-二甲基-2，6-辛二烯-1-醇）	5.5	0	东盟ASEAN,智利CL,巴基斯坦PK,新西兰NZ,秘鲁PE,哥斯达黎加CR	0	最不发达35国LDC35	30	---Geraniol, nerol (cis-3, 7-Dimethyl-2, 6-octadien-1-ol)
1963	2905.2220	---香茅醇（3，7-二甲基-6-辛烯-1-醇）	5.5	0 5	东盟ASEAN,智利CL,新西兰NZ,秘鲁PE,哥斯达黎加CR 巴基斯坦PK	0	最不发达35国LDC35	30	---Citronellol (3,7-Dimethyl-6-octen -1-ol)
1964	2905.2230	---芳樟醇	5.5	0 5	东盟ASEAN,智利CL,新西兰NZ,秘鲁PE,哥斯达黎加CR 巴基斯坦PK	0	最不发达35国LDC35	30	---Linalool
1965	2905.2290	---其他	5.5	0 5	东盟ASEAN,智利CL,新西兰NZ,秘鲁PE,哥斯达黎加CR 巴基斯坦PK	0	最不发达35国LDC35	30	---Other
1966	2905.2900	--其他	5.5	0 5	东盟ASEAN,智利CL,新西兰NZ,秘鲁PE,哥斯达黎加CR 巴基斯坦PK	0	最不发达35国LDC35	30	--Other
		-二元醇:							-Diols:
1967	2905.3100	--1，2_乙二醇	5.5	0	智利CL,新西兰NZ,哥斯达黎加CR			30	--Ethylene glycol (ethanediol)
1968	2905.3200	--1，2-丙二醇	5.5 △3	0 5	东盟ASEAN,智利CL,新西兰NZ,秘鲁PE,哥斯达黎加CR 巴基斯坦PK	0	最不发达35国LDC35	30	--Propylene glycol (propane-1, 2-diol)
		--其他:							--Other:
1969	2905.3910	---2，5-二甲基已二醇	4	0	东盟ASEAN,智利CL,巴基斯坦PK,新西兰NZ,秘鲁PE,哥斯达黎加CR	0	最不发达35国LDC35	11	---2, 5-dimethyl hexandiol
1970	2905.3990	---其他	5.5	0 5	东盟ASEAN,智利CL,新西兰NZ,秘鲁PE,哥斯达黎加CR 巴基斯坦PK	0	最不发达35国LDC35	30	---Other

序号 No.	税则号列 Tariff Line	货品名称	最惠国税率 MFN(%)	协定税率 Agreement(%)		特惠税率 S.P.(%)		普通税率 Gen.(%)	Article Description
	ex29053990	1，3－丙二醇	△3						1,3-dihydroxypropare
		-其他多元醇:							-Other polyhydric alcohols:
1971	2905.4100	--2-乙基-2-（羟甲基）丙烷-1，3-二醇（三羟甲基丙烷）	5.5	0	东盟ASEAN,智利CL,巴基斯坦PK,新西兰NZ,秘鲁PE,哥斯达黎加CR	0	最不发达35国LDC35	30	--2-Ethyl-2-(hydroxymethyl) propane-1, 3-diol (trimethylolpropane)
1972	2905.4200	--季戊四醇	5.5	0	东盟ASEAN,新西兰NZ,秘鲁PE,哥斯达黎加CR	0	最不发达35国LDC35	30	--Pentaerythritol
				0.6	智利CL				
				5	巴基斯坦PK				
1973	2905.4300	--甘露糖醇	8	0	东盟ASEAN,智利CL,新西兰NZ,秘鲁PE,哥斯达黎加CR	0	最不发达35国LDC35,最不发达4国LDC4	30	--Mannitol
				5	巴基斯坦PK				
1974	2905.4400	--山梨醇	14	0	东盟ASEAN,智利CL,新加坡SG,新西兰NZ,秘鲁PE	0	最不发达35国LDC35	40	--D-glucitol (sorbitol)
				2.8	哥斯达黎加CR				
				11.2	巴基斯坦PK				
1975	2905.4500	--丙三醇（甘油）	14 △3	0	东盟ASEAN,智利CL,新加坡SG,新西兰NZ,秘鲁PE,澳门MO	0	最不发达35国LDC35	50	--Glycerol
				2.8	哥斯达黎加CR				
				7	巴基斯坦PK				
				11.2	亚太APTA				
		--其他:							--Other:
1976	2905.4910	---木糖醇	5.5	0	东盟ASEAN,智利CL,新西兰NZ,秘鲁PE,哥斯达黎加CR	0	最不发达35国LDC35	30	---xylitol
				5	巴基斯坦PK				
1977	2905.4990	---其他	5.5	0	东盟ASEAN,智利CL,新西兰NZ,秘鲁PE,哥斯达黎加CR	0	最不发达35国LDC35	30	--Other
				5	巴基斯坦PK				
		-无环醇的卤化、磺化、硝化或亚硝化衍生物:							-Halogenated, sulphonated, nitrated or nitrosated derivatives of acyclic alcohols:
1978	2905.5100	--乙氯维诺（INN）	5.5	0	东盟ASEAN,智利CL,巴基斯坦PK,新西兰NZ,秘鲁PE,哥斯达黎加CR	0	最不发达35国LDC35	30	--Ethchlorvynol (INN)
1979	2905.5900	--其他	5.5	0	东盟ASEAN,智利CL,新西兰NZ,秘鲁PE,哥斯达黎加CR	0	最不发达35国LDC35	30	--Other
				5	巴基斯坦PK				
	29.06	**环醇及其卤化、磺化、硝化或亚硝化衍生物:**							**Cyclic alcohols and their haloge-nated, sulphonated, nitrated or nitrosated derivatives:**

序号 No.	税则号列 Tariff Line	货品名称	最惠国税率 MFN(%)	协定税率 Agreement(%)		特惠税率 S.P.(%)		普通税率 Gen.(%)	Article Description
		-环烷醇、环烯醇及环萜烯醇:							-Cyclanic, cyclenic or cycloterpenic:
1980	2906.1100	--薄荷醇	5	0	东盟ASEAN,智利CL,巴基斯坦PK,新西兰NZ,秘鲁PE,哥斯达黎加CR	0	最不发达35国LDC35	70	--Menthol
1981	2906.1200	--环己醇、甲基环己醇及二甲基环己醇	5.5	0	东盟ASEAN,智利CL,新西兰NZ,秘鲁PE,哥斯达黎加CR	0	最不发达35国LDC35	30	--Cyclohexanol, methylcyclohexanols and dimethylcyclohexanols
				5	巴基斯坦PK				
		--固醇及肌醇:							--Sterols and inositols:
1982	2906.1310	---固醇	5.5 △3	0	东盟ASEAN,智利CL,巴基斯坦PK,新西兰NZ,秘鲁PE,哥斯达黎加CR	0	最不发达35国LDC35	30	---Sterol
1983	2906.1320	---肌醇	5.5	0	东盟ASEAN,智利CL,新西兰NZ,秘鲁PE,哥斯达黎加CR	0	最不发达35国LDC35	30	---Inositol
				5	巴基斯坦PK				
		--其他:							--Other:
1984	2906.1910	---萜品醇	5.5	0	东盟ASEAN,新西兰NZ,秘鲁PE,哥斯达黎加CR	0	最不发达35国LDC35	30	---Terpineols
				0.6	智利CL				
				5	巴基斯坦PK				
1985	2906.1990	---其他	5.5	0	东盟ASEAN,智利CL,新西兰NZ,秘鲁PE,哥斯达黎加CR	0	最不发达35国LDC35	30	---Other
				5	巴基斯坦PK				
		-芳香醇:							-Aromatic:
1986	2906.2100	--苄醇	5	0	东盟ASEAN,智利CL,巴基斯坦PK,新西兰NZ,秘鲁PE,哥斯达黎加CR	0	最不发达35国LDC35	30	--Benzyl alcohol
		--其他:							--Other:
1987	2906.2910	---2-苯基乙醇	5.5	0	东盟ASEAN,智利CL,新西兰NZ,秘鲁PE,哥斯达黎加CR	0	最不发达35国LDC35	30	---2-Phenyl ethyl alcohol
				5	巴基斯坦PK				
1988	2906.2990	---其他	5.5	0	东盟ASEAN,智利CL,新西兰NZ,秘鲁PE,哥斯达黎加CR	0	最不发达35国LDC35	30	---Other
				5	巴基斯坦PK				
		第三分章 酚、酚醇及其卤化、磺化、硝化或亚硝化衍生物							III.PHENOLS, PHENOL-ALCOHOLS, AND THEIR HALOGENATED, SULPHONATED, NITRATED OR NITROSATED DERIVATIVES
	29.07	**酚;酚醇:**							**Phenols; phenol-alcohols:**
		-一元酚:							-Monophenols:

序号 No.	税则号列 Tariff Line	货品名称	最惠国税率 MFN(%)	协定税率 Agreement(%)		特惠税率 S.P.(%)		普通税率 Gen.(%)	Article Description
		--苯酚及其盐:							--Phenol (hydroxybenzene) and its salts:
1989	2907.1110	---苯酚	5.5	0	东盟ASEAN,智利CL,巴基斯坦PK,新西兰NZ,秘鲁PE,哥斯达黎加CR	0	最不发达35国LDC35,最不发达4国LDC4	30	---Phenol
1990	2907.1190	---其他	5.5	0	东盟ASEAN,智利CL,巴基斯坦PK,新西兰NZ,秘鲁PE,哥斯达黎加CR	0	最不发达35国LDC35,最不发达4国LDC4	30	---Other
		--甲酚及其盐:							--Cresol and its salts:
		---甲酚:							---Cresol:
1991	2907.1211	----间甲酚	5.5 △3	0	东盟ASEAN,智利CL,巴基斯坦PK,新西兰NZ,秘鲁PE,哥斯达黎加CR	0	最不发达35国LDC35,最不发达4国LDC4	30	----m-Cresol
1992	2907.1212	----邻甲酚	5.5 △3	0	东盟ASEAN,智利CL,巴基斯坦PK,新西兰NZ,秘鲁PE,哥斯达黎加CR	0	最不发达35国LDC35,最不发达4国LDC4	30	----o-Cresol
1993	2907.1219	----其他	5.5	0 5	东盟ASEAN,智利CL,新西兰NZ,秘鲁PE,哥斯达黎加CR 巴基斯坦PK	0	最不发达35国LDC35,最不发达4国LDC4	30	----Other
1994	2907.1290	---其他	5.5	0	东盟ASEAN,智利CL,巴基斯坦PK,新西兰NZ,秘鲁PE,哥斯达黎加CR	0	最不发达35国LDC35,最不发达4国LDC4	30	---Other
		--辛基酚、壬基酚及其异构体以及它们的盐:							--Octylphenol, nonylphenol and their isomers;salts thereof:
1995	2907.1310	---壬基酚	5.5	0	东盟ASEAN,智利CL,巴基斯坦PK,新西兰NZ,秘鲁PE,哥斯达黎加CR	0	最不发达35国LDC35,最不发达4国LDC4	30	---Nonylphenol
1996	2907.1390	---其他	5.5	0	东盟ASEAN,智利CL,巴基斯坦PK,新西兰NZ,秘鲁PE,哥斯达黎加CR	0	最不发达35国LDC35,最不发达4国LDC4	30	---Other

序号 No.	税则号列 Tariff Line	货品名称	最惠国税率 MFN(%)	协定税率 Agreement(%)		特惠税率 S.P.(%)		普通税率 Gen.(%)	Article Description
		--萘酚及其盐:							--Naphthols and their salts:
1997	2907.1510	---2-萘酚（β-萘酚）	5.5	0	东盟ASEAN,智利CL,巴基斯坦PK,新西兰NZ,秘鲁PE,哥斯达黎加CR	0	最不发达35国LDC35,最不发达4国LDC4	30	---2-Naphthols (β-naphthol)
1998	2907.1590	---其他	5.5	0 5	东盟ASEAN,智利CL,新西兰NZ,秘鲁PE,哥斯达黎加CR 巴基斯坦PK	0	最不发达35国LDC35,最不发达4国LDC4	30	---Other
		--其他:							--Other:
1999	2907.1910	---邻仲丁基酚、邻异丙基酚	4 △2	0	东盟ASEAN,智利CL,巴基斯坦PK,新西兰NZ,秘鲁PE,哥斯达黎加CR	0	最不发达35国LDC35,最不发达4国LDC4	11	---o-Sec-butyl phenol, o-isopropyl phenol
2000	2907.1990	---其他	5.5	0 5	东盟ASEAN,智利CL,新西兰NZ,秘鲁PE,哥斯达黎加CR 巴基斯坦PK	0	最不发达35国LDC35,最不发达4国LDC4	30	---Other
		-多元酚;酚醇:							-Polyphenols;phenol-alcohols:
2001	2907.2100	--间苯二酚及其盐	5.5	0 5	东盟ASEAN,智利CL,新西兰NZ,秘鲁PE,哥斯达黎加CR 巴基斯坦PK	0	最不发达35国LDC35,最不发达4国LDC4	30	--m-Dihydroxybenzene (resorcinol) and its salts
		--对苯二酚及其盐:							--p-Dihydroxybenzene (hydroquinone) and its salts:
2002	2907.2210	---对苯二酚	5.5	0 5	东盟ASEAN,智利CL,新西兰NZ,秘鲁PE,哥斯达黎加CR 巴基斯坦PK	0	最不发达35国LDC35,最不发达4国LDC4	30	---Hydroquinone
2003	2907.2290	---其他	5.5	0	东盟ASEAN,智利CL,巴基斯坦PK,新西兰NZ,秘鲁PE,哥斯达黎加CR	0	最不发达35国LDC35,最不发达4国LDC4	30	---Other
2004	2907.2300	--4，4′-异亚丙基联苯酚（双酚A，二苯基酚丙烷）及其盐	5.5	0 5	东盟ASEAN,智利CL,新西兰NZ,秘鲁PE,哥斯达黎加CR 巴基斯坦PK	0	最不发达35国LDC35,最不发达4国LDC4	30	--4,4′-Isopropylidenediphenol (bisph-enol A, di-phenylolpropane) and its salts

序号 No.	税则号列 Tariff Line	货品名称	最惠国税率 MFN(%)	协定税率 Agreement(%)		特惠税率 S.P.(%)		普通税率 Gen.(%)	Article Description
		--其他:							--Other:
2005	2907.2910	---邻苯二酚	4	0	东盟ASEAN,智利CL,巴基斯坦PK,新西兰NZ,秘鲁PE,哥斯达黎加CR	0	最不发达35国LDC35,最不发达4国LDC4	11	---o-Dihydroxybenzene (catechol, pyrocatechol)
2006	2907.2990	---其他	5.5	0 5	东盟ASEAN,智利CL,新西兰NZ,秘鲁PE,哥斯达黎加CR 巴基斯坦PK	0	最不发达35国LDC35,最不发达4国LDC4	30	---Other
	29.08	**酚及酚醇的卤化、磺化、硝化或亚硝化衍生物:**							**Halogenated, sulphonated, nitrated or nitrosated derivatives of phenols or phenolalcohols:**
		-仅含卤素取代基的衍生物及其盐:							-Derivatives containing only halogen substituents and their salts:
2007	2908.1100	--五氯苯酚(ISO)	5.5	0 5	东盟ASEAN,智利CL,新西兰NZ,秘鲁PE,哥斯达黎加CR 巴基斯坦PK	0	最不发达35国LDC35	30	--Pentachlorophenol (ISO)
		--其他:							--Other:
2008	2908.1910	---对氯苯酚	4	0	东盟ASEAN,智利CL,巴基斯坦PK,新西兰NZ,秘鲁PE,哥斯达黎加CR	0	最不发达35国LDC35	11	---p-Chlorophenol
2009	2908.1990	---其他	5.5	0 5	东盟ASEAN,智利CL,新西兰NZ,秘鲁PE,哥斯达黎加CR 巴基斯坦PK	0	最不发达35国LDC35	30	---Other
		-其他:							-Other:
2010	2908.9100	--地乐酚(ISO)及其盐	5.5	0 5	东盟ASEAN,智利CL,新西兰NZ,秘鲁PE,哥斯达黎加CR 巴基斯坦PK	0	最不发达35国LDC35	30	--Dinoseb (ISO) and its salts
2011	2908.9200	--4,6-二硝基邻甲酚〔二硝酚(ISO)〕及其盐	5.5	0 5	东盟ASEAN,智利CL,新西兰NZ,秘鲁PE,哥斯达黎加CR 巴基斯坦PK	0	最不发达35国LDC35	30	--4,6-Dinitro-o-cresol (DNOC (ISO)) and its salts
		--其他:							--Other
2012	2908.9910	---对硝基酚、对硝基酚钠	5.5	0	东盟ASEAN,智利CL,巴基斯坦PK,新西兰NZ,秘鲁PE,哥斯达黎加CR	0	最不发达35国LDC35	30	---p-Nitrophenol, sodium p-nitro-phenolate
2013	2908.9990	---其他	5.5	0 5	东盟ASEAN,智利CL,新西兰NZ,秘鲁PE,哥斯达黎加CR 巴基斯坦PK	0	最不发达35国LDC35	30	---Other

序号 No.	税则号列 Tariff Line	货品名称	最惠国税率 MFN(%)	协定税率 Agreement(%)		特惠税率 S.P.(%)		普通税率 Gen.(%)	Article Description
		第四分章 醚、过氧化醇、过氧化醚、过氧化酮、三节环环氧化物、缩醛及半缩醛及其卤化、磺化、硝化或亚硝化衍生物							Ⅳ. ETHERS, ALCOHOL PEROXIDES, ETHER PEROXIDES, KETONE PEROXIDES, EPOXIDES WITH A THREE-MEMBERED RING, ACETALS AND HEMIACETALS, AND THEIR HALOGEN-ATED, SULPHONATED, NITRATED OR NITROSATED DERIVATIVES
	29.09	**醚、醚醇、醚酚、醚醇酚、过氧化醇、过氧化醚、过氧化酮（不论是否已有化学定义）及其卤化、磺化、硝化或亚硝化衍生物:**							**Ethers, ether-alcohols, ether-phenols, ether-alcohol-phenols, alcohol pero-xides, ether per-oxides, ketone perox-ides (whether or not chemically defined), and their halogenated, sul-phonated, nitrated or nitrosated derivatives:**
		-无环醚及其卤化、磺化、硝化或亚硝化衍生物:							-Acyclic ethers and their haloge-nated, sulpho-nated, nitrated or ni-trosated derivatives:
2014	2909.1100	--乙醚	5.5	0	东盟ASEAN,智利CL,巴基斯坦PK,新西兰NZ,秘鲁PE,哥斯达黎加CR	0	最不发达35国LDC35,最不发达4国LDC4	30	--Diethyl ether
		--其他:							--Other:
2015	2909.1910	---甲醚	5.5	0 5	东盟ASEAN,智利CL,新西兰NZ,哥斯达黎加CR 巴基斯坦PK			30	---Methyl ether
2016	2909.1990	---其他	5.5	0 5	东盟ASEAN,智利CL,新西兰NZ,哥斯达黎加CR 巴基斯坦PK			30	---Other
2017	2909.2000	-环烷醚、环烯醚或环萜烯醚及其卤化、磺化、硝化或亚硝化衍生物	5.5	0	东盟ASEAN,智利CL,巴基斯坦PK,新西兰NZ,秘鲁PE,哥斯达黎加CR	0	最不发达35国LDC35,最不发达4国LDC4	30	-Cyclanic, cyclenic or cycloterpenic ethers and their halogenated, sul-phonated, nitrated or nitrosated derivatives
		-芳香醚及其卤化、磺化、硝化或亚硝化衍生物:							-Aromatic ethers and their halogenated, sul-phonated, nitrated or nitro-sated derivatives:

序号 No.	税则号列 Tariff Line	货品名称	最惠国税率 MFN(%)	协定税率 Agreement(%)		特惠税率 S.P.(%)		普通税率 Gen.(%)	Article Description
2018	2909.3010	---1-烷氧基-4-（4-乙烯基环己基）-2，3-二氟苯	5.5	0 5	东盟ASEAN,智利CL,新西兰NZ,秘鲁PE,哥斯达黎加CR 巴基斯坦PK	0	最不发达35国LDC35,最不发达4国LDC4	30	---1-alkoxy-4-(4-vinylcyclohexyl)-2,3-difluoro benzene
2019	2909.3090	---其他	5.5	0 5	东盟ASEAN,智利CL,新西兰NZ,秘鲁PE,哥斯达黎加CR 巴基斯坦PK	0	最不发达35国LDC35,最不发达4国LDC4	30	---Other
		-醚醇及其卤化、磺化、硝化或亚硝化衍生物:							-Ether-alcohols and their haloge-nated, sulphonated, nitrated or nitrosated derivatives:
2020	2909.4100	--2，2′-氧联二乙醇（二甘醇）	5.5 △3	0	东盟ASEAN,智利CL,巴基斯坦PK,新西兰NZ,哥斯达黎加CR,台湾TW			30	--2, 2′-Oxydiethanol (diethylene glycol, digol)
2021	2909.4300	--乙二醇或二甘醇的单丁醚	5.5	0 5	东盟ASEAN,智利CL,新西兰NZ,秘鲁PE,哥斯达黎加CR,澳门MO,台湾TW 巴基斯坦PK	0	最不发达35国LDC35,最不发达4国LDC4	30	--Monobutyl ethers of ethylene glycol or of diethylene glycol
2022	2909.4400	--乙二醇或二丁醇的其他单烷基醚	5.5	0 5	东盟ASEAN,智利CL,新西兰NZ,秘鲁PE,哥斯达黎加CR 巴基斯坦PK	0	最不发达35国LDC35,最不发达4国LDC4	30	--Other monoalkylethers of ethylene glycol or of diethylene glycol
		--其他:							--Other:
2023	2909.4910	---间苯氧基苄醇	4	0 0.4	东盟ASEAN,巴基斯坦PK,新西兰NZ,秘鲁PE,哥斯达黎加CR 智利CL	0	最不发达35国LDC35,最不发达4国LDC4	11	---m-Phenoxy benzalcohol
2024	2909.4990	---其他	5.5	0 0.6 5	东盟ASEAN,新西兰NZ,秘鲁PE,哥斯达黎加CR 智利CL 巴基斯坦PK	0	最不发达35国LDC35,最不发达4国LDC4	30	---Other
2025	2909.5000	-醚酚、醚醇酚及其卤化、磺化、硝化或亚硝化衍生物	5.5	0 5	东盟ASEAN,智利CL,新西兰NZ,秘鲁PE,哥斯达黎加CR 巴基斯坦PK	0	最不发达35国LDC35,最不发达4国LDC4	30	-Ether-phenols, ether-alcohol-phenols and their halogenated, sulphonated, nitrated or nitrosated derivatives

序号 No.	税则号列 Tariff Line	货品名称	最惠国税率 MFN(%)	协定税率 Agreement(%)		特惠税率 S.P.(%)		普通税率 Gen.(%)	Article Description
2026	2909.6000	-过氧化醇、过氧化醚、过氧化酮及其卤化、磺化、硝化或亚硝化衍生物	5.5	0 0.6 5	东盟ASEAN,新西兰NZ,秘鲁PE,哥斯达黎加CR 智利CL 巴基斯坦PK	0	最不发达35国LDC35,最不发达4国LDC4	30	-Alcohol peroxides, ether peroxides, ketone peroxides and their halogenated, sulphonated, nitrated or nitrosated derivatives
	29.10	**三节环环氧化物、环氧醇、环氧酚、环氧醚及其卤化、磺化、硝化或亚硝化衍生物:**							**Epoxides, epoxyalcohols, epoxyphenols and epoxyethers, with a three-membered ring, and their halogenated, sulphonated, nitrated or nitrosated derivatives:**
2027	2910.1000	-环氧乙烷（氧化乙烯）	5.5	0	东盟ASEAN,智利CL,巴基斯坦PK,新西兰NZ,秘鲁PE,哥斯达黎加CR	0	最不发达35国LDC35	30	-Oxirane (ethylene oxide)
2028	2910.2000	-甲基环氧乙烷(氧化丙烯）	5.5	0	东盟ASEAN,智利CL,巴基斯坦PK,新西兰NZ,秘鲁PE,哥斯达黎加CR	0	最不发达35国LDC35	30	-Methyloxirane (propylene oxide)
2029	2910.3000	-1-氯-2，3-环氧丙烷（表氯醇）	5.5	0 5	东盟ASEAN,智利CL,新西兰NZ,秘鲁PE,哥斯达黎加CR,台湾TW 巴基斯坦PK	0	最不发达35国LDC35	30	-1-Chloro-2, 3-epoxypropane (epichlorohydrin)
2030	2910.4000	-狄氏剂（ISO，INN）	5.5	0 5	东盟ASEAN,智利CL,新西兰NZ,秘鲁PE,哥斯达黎加CR 巴基斯坦PK	0	最不发达35国LDC35	30	-Dieldrin (ISO, INN)
2031	2910.9000	-其他	5.5	0 5	东盟ASEAN,智利CL,新西兰NZ,秘鲁PE,哥斯达黎加CR,澳门MO 巴基斯坦PK	0	最不发达35国LDC35	30	-Other
	29.11	**缩醛及半缩醛，不论是否含有其他含氧基，及其卤化、磺化、硝化或亚硝化衍生物:**							**Acetals and hemiacetals, whether or not with other oxygen function, and their halogenated, sulphonated, nitrated or nitrosated derivatives:**
2032	2911.0000	缩醛及半缩醛，不论是否含有其他含氧基，及其卤化、磺化、硝化或亚硝化衍生物	5.5	0 5	东盟ASEAN,智利CL,新西兰NZ,秘鲁PE,哥斯达黎加CR 巴基斯坦PK	0	最不发达35国LDC35	30	Acetals and hemiacetals, whether or not with other oxygen function, and their halogenated, sulphonated, nitrated or nitrosated derivatives
		第五分章 醛基化合物							Ⅴ.ALDEHYDE-FUNCTION COMPOUNDS
	29.12	**醛，不论是否含有其他含氧基;环聚醛;多聚甲醛:**							**Aldehydes, whether or not with other oxygen function; cyclic polymers of aldehydes; paraformaldehyde:**

序号 No.	税则号列 Tariff Line	货品名称	最惠国税率 MFN(%)	协定税率 Agreement(%)		特惠税率 S.P.(%)		普通税率 Gen.(%)	Article Description
		-不含其他含氧基的无环醛:							-Acyclic aldehydes without other oxygen function:
2033	2912.1100	--甲醛	5.5	0	东盟ASEAN,巴基斯坦PK,新西兰NZ,秘鲁PE,哥斯达黎加CR	0	最不发达35国LDC35	30	--Methanal (formaldehyde)
				0.6	智利CL				
2034	2912.1200	--乙醛	5.5	0	东盟ASEAN,智利CL,巴基斯坦PK,新西兰NZ,秘鲁PE,哥斯达黎加CR	0	最不发达35国LDC35	30	--Ethanal (acetaldehyde)
2035	2912.1900	--其他	5.5	0	东盟ASEAN,智利CL,新西兰NZ,秘鲁PE,哥斯达黎加CR	0	最不发达35国LDC35	30	--Other
				5	巴基斯坦PK				
	ex29121900	乙二醛	△3						Glyoxal (Ethanedial)
		-不含其他含氧基的环醛:							-Cyclic aldehydes without other oxygen function:
2036	2912.2100	--苯甲醛	5.5	0	东盟ASEAN,智利CL,新西兰NZ,秘鲁PE,哥斯达黎加CR	0	最不发达35国LDC35	30	--Benzaldehyde
				5	巴基斯坦PK				
		--其他:							--Other:
2037	2912.2910	---铃兰醛（对叔丁基-α-甲基-氧化肉桂醛）	5.5	0	东盟ASEAN,智利CL,新西兰NZ,秘鲁PE,哥斯达黎加CR	0	最不发达35国LDC35	30	---Lilial (p-tert-butyl-α-methyl-oxocinn amaldehyde)
				5	巴基斯坦PK				
2038	2912.2990	---其他	5.5	0	东盟ASEAN,智利CL,新西兰NZ,秘鲁PE,哥斯达黎加CR	0	最不发达35国LDC35	30	---Other
				5	巴基斯坦PK				
		-醛醇、醛醚、醛酚及含其他含氧基的醛:							-Aldehyde-alcohols, aldehyde-ethers, aldehyde-phenols and aldehydes with other oxygen function:
2039	2912.4100	--香草醛（3-甲氧基-4-羟基苯甲醛）	5.5	0	东盟ASEAN,智利CL,新西兰NZ,秘鲁PE,哥斯达黎加CR	0	最不发达35国LDC35	30	--Vanillin (4-hydroxy-3-metho-xybenzaldehyde)
				5	巴基斯坦PK				
2040	2912.4200	--乙基香草醛（3-乙氧基-4-羟基苯甲醛）	5.5	0	东盟ASEAN,智利CL,新西兰NZ,秘鲁PE,哥斯达黎加CR	0	最不发达35国LDC35	30	--Ethylvanillin (3-ethoxy-4-hydrox-yben-zaldehyde)
				5	巴基斯坦PK				
		--其他:							--Other:
2041	2912.4910	---醛醇	5.5	0	东盟ASEAN,智利CL,新西兰NZ,秘鲁PE,哥斯达黎加CR	0	最不发达35国LDC35	30	---Aldehyde-alcohols
				5	巴基斯坦PK				
2042	2912.4990	---其他	5.5	0	东盟ASEAN,智利CL,新西兰NZ,秘鲁PE,哥斯达黎加CR	0	最不发达35国LDC35	30	---Other
				5	巴基斯坦PK				

序号 No.	税则号列 Tariff Line	货品名称	最惠国税率 MFN(%)	协定税率 Agreement(%)		特惠税率 S.P.(%)		普通税率 Gen.(%)	Article Description
2043	2912.5000	-环聚醛	5.5	0	东盟ASEAN,智利CL,巴基斯坦PK,新西兰NZ,秘鲁PE,哥斯达黎加CR	0	最不发达35国LDC35	30	-Cyclic-polymers of aldehydes
2044	2912.6000	-多聚甲醛	5.5	0 5	东盟ASEAN,智利CL,新西兰NZ,秘鲁PE,哥斯达黎加CR 巴基斯坦PK	0	最不发达35国LDC35	30	-Paraformaldehyde
	29.13	**税号 29.12 所列产品的卤化、磺化、硝化或亚硝化衍生物:**							**Halogenated, sulphonated, nitrated or nitrosated derivatives of prod-ucts of heading No.29.12:**
2045	2913.0000	税号 29.12 所列产品的卤化、磺化、硝化或亚硝化衍生物	5.5	0 5	东盟ASEAN,智利CL,新西兰NZ,秘鲁PE,哥斯达黎加CR 巴基斯坦PK	0	最不发达35国LDC35	30	Halogenated, sulphonated, nitrated or nitrosated derivatives of products of heading No.29.12
		第六分章 酮基化合物及醌基化合物							Ⅵ.KETONE-FUNCTION COMPOUNDS AND QUINONE-FUNCTION COMPOUNDS
	29.14	**酮及醌，不论是否含有其他含氧基，及其卤化、磺化、硝化或亚硝化衍生物:**							**Ketones and quinones, whether or not with other oxygen function, and their halogenated, sulphonated, nitrated or nitrosated derivatives:**
		-不含其他含氧基的无环酮:							-Acyclic ketones without other oxy-gen function:
2046	2914.1100	--丙酮	5.5	0	东盟ASEAN,智利CL,巴基斯坦PK,新西兰NZ,秘鲁PE,哥斯达黎加CR	0	最不发达35国LDC35	20	--Acetone
2047	2914.1200	--丁酮［甲基乙基（甲）酮］	5.5	0 0.6	东盟ASEAN,巴基斯坦PK,新西兰NZ,秘鲁PE,哥斯达黎加CR,澳门MO 智利CL	0	最不发达35国LDC35	30	--Butanone (methyl ethyl ketone)
2048	2914.1300	--4-甲基-2-戊酮［甲基异丁基（甲）酮］	5.5	0	东盟ASEAN,智利CL,巴基斯坦PK,新西兰NZ,秘鲁PE,哥斯达黎加CR	0	最不发达35国LDC35	30	--4-Methyl-2-pentanone (isobutyl methyl ketone)
2049	2914.1900	--其他	5.5	0 5	东盟ASEAN,智利CL,新西兰NZ,秘鲁PE,哥斯达黎加CR 巴基斯坦PK	0	最不发达35国LDC35	30	--Other
		-不含其他含氧基的环烷酮、环烯酮或环萜烯酮:							-Cyclanic, cyclenic or cycloterpenic ketones without other oxygen function:

序号 No.	税则号列 Tariff Line	货品名称	最惠国税率 MFN(%)	协定税率 Agreement(%)		特惠税率 S.P.(%)		普通税率 Gen.(%)	Article Description
2050	2914.2200	--环己酮及甲基环己酮	5.5	0	东盟ASEAN,智利CL,巴基斯坦PK,新西兰NZ,秘鲁PE,哥斯达黎加CR	0	最不发达35国LDC35	30	--Cyclohexanone and methylcyclo-hexanone
2051	2914.2300	--芷香酮及甲基芷香酮	5.5	0	东盟ASEAN,智利CL,巴基斯坦PK,新西兰NZ,秘鲁PE,哥斯达黎加CR	0	最不发达35国LDC35	30	--Ionones and methylio-nones
		--其他:							--Other:
2052	2914.2910	---樟脑	5.5	0	东盟ASEAN,智利CL,新西兰NZ,秘鲁PE,哥斯达黎加CR	0	最不发达35国LDC35	40	---Camphor
				5	巴基斯坦PK				
2053	2914.2990	---其他	5.5	0	东盟ASEAN,智利CL,新西兰NZ,秘鲁PE,哥斯达黎加CR	0	最不发达35国LDC35	30	---Other
				5	巴基斯坦PK				
		-不含其他含氧基的芳香酮:							-Aromatic ketones with-out other oxygen func-tion:
2054	2914.3100	--苯丙酮（苯基丙-2-酮）	5.5	0	东盟ASEAN,智利CL,巴基斯坦PK,新西兰NZ,秘鲁PE,哥斯达黎加CR	0	最不发达35国LDC35	30	--Propiophenone (phenyl-propan-2-one)
		--其他:							--Other:
2055	2914.3910	---苯乙酮	4	0	东盟ASEAN,智利CL,巴基斯坦PK,新西兰NZ,秘鲁PE,哥斯达黎加CR	0	最不发达35国LDC35	11	---Acetophenone
2056	2914.3990	---其他	5.5	0	东盟ASEAN,智利CL,新西兰NZ,秘鲁PE,哥斯达黎加CR	0	最不发达35国LDC35	30	---Other
				5	巴基斯坦PK				
2057	2914.4000	-酮醇及酮醛	5.5	0	东盟ASEAN,智利CL,新西兰NZ,秘鲁PE,哥斯达黎加CR	0	最不发达35国LDC35	30	-Ketone-alcohols and ketonealde-hydes
				5	巴基斯坦PK				
		-酮酚及含有其他含氧基的酮:							-Ketone-phenols and ketones with other oxy-gen function:
		---酮酚:							---Ketene-alcohols:
2058	2914.5011	----覆盆子酮	5.5	0	东盟ASEAN,智利CL,巴基斯坦PK,新西兰NZ,秘鲁PE,哥斯达黎加CR	0	最不发达35国LDC35	30	----Raspberry ketone
2059	2914.5019	----其他	5.5	0	东盟ASEAN,智利CL,新西兰NZ,秘鲁PE,哥斯达黎加CR	0	最不发达35国LDC35	30	----Other
				5	巴基斯坦PK				
2060	2914.5020	---2-羟基-4-甲氧基二苯甲酮	5.5	0	东盟ASEAN,智利CL,新西兰NZ,秘鲁PE,哥斯达黎加CR	0	最不发达35国LDC35	30	---2-hydroxy-4-methoxy benzophenone
				5	巴基斯坦PK				

序号 No.	税则号列 Tariff Line	货品名称	最惠国税率 MFN(%)	协定税率 Agreement(%)		特惠税率 S.P.(%)		普通税率 Gen.(%)	Article Description
2061	2914.5090	---其他	5.5	0 5	东盟ASEAN,智利CL,新西兰NZ,秘鲁PE,哥斯达黎加CR 巴基斯坦PK	0	最不发达35国LDC35	30	---Other
		-醌:							-Quinones:
2062	2914.6100	--蒽醌	5.5	0 5	东盟ASEAN,智利CL,新西兰NZ,秘鲁PE,哥斯达黎加CR 巴基斯坦PK	0	最不发达35国LDC35	30	--Anthraquinone
		--其他:							--Other:
2063	2914.6910	---辅酶Q10	5.5	0	东盟ASEAN,智利CL,巴基斯坦PK,新西兰NZ,秘鲁PE,哥斯达黎加CR	0	最不发达35国LDC35	30	---Coenzyme Q
2064	2914.6990	---其他	5.5	0	东盟ASEAN,智利CL,巴基斯坦PK,新西兰NZ,秘鲁PE,哥斯达黎加CR	0	最不发达35国LDC35	30	---Other
2065	2914.7000	-卤化、磺化、硝化或亚硝化衍生物	5.5	0 5	东盟ASEAN,智利CL,新西兰NZ,秘鲁PE,哥斯达黎加CR 巴基斯坦PK	0	最不发达35国LDC35	30	-Halogenated, sulphonated, nitrated or nitrosated derivatives
		第七分章 羧酸及其酸酐、酰卤化物、过氧化物和过氧酸以及它们的卤化、磺化、硝化或亚硝化衍生物							Ⅶ.CARBOXYLIC ACIDS AND THEIR ANHYDRIDES, HALIDES, PER-OXIDES AND PEROXYACIDS AND THEIR HALOGENATED, SULPHONATED, NITRATED OR NITROSATED DERIVATIVES
	29.15	**饱和无环一元羧酸及其酸酐、酰卤化物、过氧化物和过氧酸以及它们的卤化、磺化、硝化或亚硝化衍生物:**							**Saturated acyclic monocarboxylic acids and their-anhydrides, halides, peroxides and peroxyacids;their halogenated, sulphonated, nitrated or nitrosated derivatives:**
		-甲酸及其盐和酯:							-Formic acid, its salts and esters:
2066	2915.1100	--甲酸	5.5	0 5	东盟ASEAN,智利CL,新西兰NZ,秘鲁PE,哥斯达黎加CR 巴基斯坦PK	0	最不发达35国LDC35,最不发达4国LDC4	40	--Formic acid
2067	2915.1200	--甲酸盐	5.5	0 0.6 5	东盟ASEAN,新西兰NZ,秘鲁PE,哥斯达黎加CR 智利CL 巴基斯坦PK	0	最不发达35国LDC35,最不发达4国LDC4	30	--Salts of formic acid

序号 No.	税则号列 Tariff Line	货品名称	最惠国税率 MFN(%)	协定税率 Agreement(%)		特惠税率 S.P.(%)		普通税率 Gen.(%)	Article Description
2068	2915.1300	--甲酸酯	5.5	0 5	东盟ASEAN,智利CL,新西兰NZ,秘鲁PE,哥斯达黎加CR 巴基斯坦PK	0	最不发达35国LDC35,最不发达4国LDC4	30	--Esters of formic acid
		-乙酸及其盐;乙酸酐:							-Acetic acid and its salts; acetic anhydride:
		--乙酸:							--Acetic acid:
		---冰乙酸:							---Acetic acid, glacial:
2069	2915.2111	----食品级的	5.5	0 5	东盟ASEAN,智利CL,新西兰NZ,秘鲁PE,哥斯达黎加CR,台湾TW 巴基斯坦PK	0	最不发达35国LDC35,最不发达4国LDC4	30	----Food grade
2070	2915.2119	----其他	5.5	0 5	东盟ASEAN,智利CL,新西兰NZ,秘鲁PE,哥斯达黎加CR,台湾TW 巴基斯坦PK	0	最不发达35国LDC35,最不发达4国LDC4	30	----Other
2071	2915.2190	---其他	5.5	0 5	东盟ASEAN,智利CL,新西兰NZ,秘鲁PE,哥斯达黎加CR 巴基斯坦PK	0	最不发达35国LDC35,最不发达4国LDC4	50	---Other
2072	2915.2400	--乙酸酐	5.5	0	东盟ASEAN,智利CL,巴基斯坦PK,新西兰NZ,秘鲁PE,哥斯达黎加CR	0	最不发达35国LDC35,最不发达4国LDC4	50	--Acetic anhydride
		--其他							--Other
2073	2915.2910	---乙酸钠	5.5	0 5	东盟ASEAN,智利CL,新西兰NZ,秘鲁PE,哥斯达黎加CR 巴基斯坦PK	0	最不发达35国LDC35,最不发达4国LDC4	50	---Sodium acetate
2074	2915.2990	---其他	5.5	0 5	东盟ASEAN,智利CL,新西兰NZ,秘鲁PE,哥斯达黎加CR 巴基斯坦PK	0	最不发达35国LDC35,最不发达4国LDC4	50	---Other
		-乙酸酯:							-Esters of acetic acid:
2075	2915.3100	--乙酸乙酯	5.5	0 5	东盟ASEAN,智利CL,新西兰NZ,秘鲁PE,哥斯达黎加CR 巴基斯坦PK	0	最不发达35国LDC35,最不发达4国LDC4	30	--Ethyl acetate

序号 No.	税则号列 Tariff Line	货品名称	最惠国税率 MFN(%)	协定税率 Agreement(%)		特惠税率 S.P.(%)		普通税率 Gen.(%)	Article Description
2076	2915.3200	--乙酸乙烯酯	5.5	0 5	东盟ASEAN,智利CL,新西兰NZ,秘鲁PE,哥斯达黎加CR,台湾TW 巴基斯坦PK	0	最不发达35国LDC35,最不发达4国LDC4	30	--Vinyl acetate
2077	2915.3300	--乙酸（正）丁酯	5.5	0	东盟ASEAN,智利CL,巴基斯坦PK,新西兰NZ,秘鲁PE,哥斯达黎加CR	0	最不发达35国LDC35,最不发达4国LDC4	30	--n-Butyl acetate
2078	2915.3600	--地乐酚（ISO）乙酸酯	5.5	0 0.6 5	东盟ASEAN,新西兰NZ,秘鲁PE,哥斯达黎加CR 智利CL 巴基斯坦PK	0	最不发达35国LDC35,最不发达4国LDC4	30	--Dinoseb (ISO) acetate
2079	2915.3900	--其他	5.5	0 5	东盟ASEAN,智利CL,新西兰NZ,秘鲁PE,哥斯达黎加CR 巴基斯坦PK	0	最不发达35国LDC35,最不发达4国LDC4	30	--Other
2080	2915.4000	-一氯代乙酸、二氯乙酸或三氯乙酸及其盐和酯	5.5	0 5	东盟ASEAN,智利CL,新西兰NZ,秘鲁PE,哥斯达黎加CR 巴基斯坦PK	0	最不发达35国LDC35,最不发达4国LDC4	30	-Mono-, di-or tri-chloroacetic acids, their salts and esters
		-丙酸及其盐和酯:							-Propionic acid, its salts and esters:
2081	2915.5010	---丙酸	5.5 △3	0 5	东盟ASEAN,智利CL,新西兰NZ,秘鲁PE,哥斯达黎加CR 巴基斯坦PK	0	最不发达35国LDC35,最不发达4国LDC4	30	---Propionic acid
2082	2915.5090	---其他	5.5	0 5	东盟ASEAN,智利CL,新西兰NZ,秘鲁PE,哥斯达黎加CR 巴基斯坦PK	0	最不发达35国LDC35,最不发达4国LDC4	30	---Other
2083	2915.6000	-丁酸、戊酸及其盐和酯	5.5	0 5	东盟ASEAN,智利CL,新西兰NZ,秘鲁PE,哥斯达黎加CR 巴基斯坦PK	0	最不发达35国LDC35,最不发达4国LDC4	30	-Butanoic acids, pentanoic acids, their salts and esters
		-棕榈酸、硬脂酸及其盐和酯:							-Palmitic acid, stearic acid, their salts and esters:

序号 No.	税则号列 Tariff Line	货品名称	最惠国税率 MFN(%)	协定税率 Agreement(%)		特惠税率 S.P.(%)		普通税率 Gen.(%)	Article Description
2084	2915.7010	---硬脂酸	7	0 0.7 5	东盟ASEAN,新西兰NZ,秘鲁PE,哥斯达黎加CR 智利CL 巴基斯坦PK	0	最不发达35国LDC35,最不发达4国LDC4	50	---Stearic acid
2085	2915.7090	---其他	5.5	0 0.6 5	东盟ASEAN,新西兰NZ,秘鲁PE,哥斯达黎加CR 智利CL 巴基斯坦PK	0	最不发达35国LDC35,最不发达4国LDC4	30	---Other
2086	2915.9000	-其他	5.5	0 5	东盟ASEAN,智利CL,新西兰NZ,秘鲁PE,哥斯达黎加CR,澳门MO 巴基斯坦PK	0	最不发达35国LDC35,最不发达4国LDC4	30	-Other
	29.16	**不饱和无环一元羧酸、环一元羧酸及其酸酐、酰卤化物、过氧化物和过氧酸以及它们的卤化、磺化、硝化或亚硝化衍生物:**							**Unsaturated acyclic monocarboxylic acids, cyclic monocarboxylic acids, their anhydrides, halides, peroxides and peroxyacids;their halogenated, sulphonated, nitrated or nitrosated derivatives:**
		-不饱和无环一元羧酸及其酸酐、酰卤化物、过氧化物和过氧酸以及它们的衍生物:							-Unsaturated acyclic monocarboxylic acids, their anhydrides, halides, peroxides, peroxyacids and their derivatives:
2087	2916.1100	--丙烯酸及其盐	6.5	0	东盟ASEAN,智利CL,新西兰NZ,秘鲁PE,哥斯达黎加CR	0	最不发达35国LDC35	30	--Acrylic acid and its salts
		--丙烯酸酯:							--Esters of acrylic acid:
2088	2916.1210	---丙烯酸甲酯	6.5	0 5	东盟ASEAN,智利CL,新加坡SG,新西兰NZ,秘鲁PE,哥斯达黎加CR 巴基斯坦PK	0	最不发达35国LDC35	30	---Methacylate
2089	2916.1220	---丙烯酸乙酯	6.5	0 5	东盟ASEAN,智利CL,新加坡SG,新西兰NZ,秘鲁PE,哥斯达黎加CR 巴基斯坦PK	0	最不发达35国LDC35	30	---Ethyl Acrylate
2090	2916.1230	---丙烯酸丁酯	6.5	0 5	东盟ASEAN,智利CL,新加坡SG,新西兰NZ,秘鲁PE,哥斯达黎加CR 巴基斯坦PK	0	最不发达35国LDC35	30	---N-Butyl Acrylate
2091	2916.1240	---丙烯酸异辛酯	6.5	0 5	东盟ASEAN,智利CL,新加坡SG,新西兰NZ,秘鲁PE,哥斯达黎加CR 巴基斯坦PK	0	最不发达35国LDC35	30	---2-Ethylhexyl acrylate

序号 No.	税则号列 Tariff Line	货品名称	最惠国税率 MFN(%)	协定税率 Agreement(%)		特惠税率 S.P.(%)		普通税率 Gen.(%)	Article Description
2092	2916.1290	---其他	6.5	0	东盟ASEAN,智利CL,新加坡SG,新西兰NZ,秘鲁PE,哥斯达黎加CR	0	最不发达35国LDC35	30	---Other
				5	巴基斯坦PK				
2093	2916.1300	--甲基丙烯酸及其盐	6.5	0	东盟ASEAN,智利CL,新西兰NZ,秘鲁PE,哥斯达黎加CR,台湾TW	0	最不发达35国LDC35	80	--Methacrylic acid and its salts
				5	巴基斯坦PK				
2094	2916.1400	--甲基丙烯酸酯	6.5	0	东盟ASEAN,智利CL,新西兰NZ,秘鲁PE,哥斯达黎加CR,台湾TW	0	最不发达35国LDC35	80	--Esters of methacrylic acid
				5	巴基斯坦PK				
2095	2916.1500	--油酸、亚油酸或亚麻酸及其盐和酯	6.5	0	东盟ASEAN,智利CL,新西兰NZ,秘鲁PE,哥斯达黎加CR,香港HK	0	最不发达35国LDC35	30	--Oleic, linoleic or linolenic acids, their salts and esters
				5	巴基斯坦PK				
2096	2916.1600	--乐杀螨（ISO）	6.5	0	东盟ASEAN,智利CL,新西兰NZ,秘鲁PE,哥斯达黎加CR	0	最不发达35国LDC35	30	-- Binapacryl (ISO)
				5	巴基斯坦PK				
2097	2916.1900	--其他	6.5	0	东盟ASEAN,智利CL,新西兰NZ,秘鲁PE,哥斯达黎加CR	0	最不发达35国LDC35	30	--Other
				5	巴基斯坦PK				
		-环烷一元羧酸、环烯一元羧酸或环萜烯一元羧酸及其酸酐、酰卤化物、过氧化物和过氧酸以及它们的衍生物:							-Cyclanic, cyclenic or cycloterpenic monocarboxylic acids, their anhy-drides, halides, peroxides, peroxy-acids and their derivatives:
2098	2916.2010	---二溴菊酸、DV菊酸甲酯	4	0	东盟ASEAN,智利CL,巴基斯坦PK,新西兰NZ,秘鲁PE,哥斯达黎加CR	0	最不发达35国LDC35	11	---Dibromochrysanthemicacid, DV chrysanthemimono carboxylate
2099	2916.2090	---其他	6.5	0	东盟ASEAN,智利CL,新西兰NZ,秘鲁PE,哥斯达黎加CR	0	最不发达35国LDC35	30	---Other
				5	巴基斯坦PK				
		-芳香一元羧酸及其酸酐、酰卤化物、过氧化物和过氧酸以及它们的衍生物:							-Aromatic monocarboxylic acids, their anhydrides, halides, peroxides, peroxyacids and their derivatives:
2100	2916.3100	--苯甲酸及其盐和酯	6.5	0	东盟ASEAN,智利CL,新西兰NZ,秘鲁PE,哥斯达黎加CR	0	最不发达35国LDC35	30	--Benzoic acid, its salts and esters
				5	巴基斯坦PK				
2101	2916.3200	--过氧化苯甲酰及苯甲酰氯	6.5	0	东盟ASEAN,智利CL,新西兰NZ,秘鲁PE,哥斯达黎加CR	0	最不发达35国LDC35	30	--Benzoyl peroxide and benzoyl chloride
				5	巴基斯坦PK				
2102	2916.3400	--苯乙酸及其盐	6.5	0	东盟ASEAN,智利CL,新西兰NZ,秘鲁PE,哥斯达黎加CR	0	最不发达35国LDC35	30	--Phenylacetic acid and its salts
				5	巴基斯坦PK				

序号 No.	税则号列 Tariff Line	货品名称	最惠国税率 MFN(%)	协定税率 Agreement(%)		特惠税率 S.P.(%)		普通税率 Gen.(%)	Article Description
		--其他:							--Other:
2103	2916.3910	---邻甲基苯甲酸	6.5	0 5	东盟ASEAN,智利CL,新西兰NZ,秘鲁PE,哥斯达黎加CR 巴基斯坦PK	0	最不发达35国LDC35	30	---m-Methylbenzoic acid
2104	2916.3920	---布洛芬	6.5	0 5	东盟ASEAN,智利CL,新西兰NZ,秘鲁PE,哥斯达黎加CR 巴基斯坦PK	0	最不发达35国LDC35	30	---Brufen (Ibuprofen)
2105	2916.3990	---其他	6.5	0 5	东盟ASEAN,智利CL,新西兰NZ,秘鲁PE,哥斯达黎加CR 巴基斯坦PK	0	最不发达35国LDC35	30	---Other
	29.17	**多元羧酸及其酸酐、酰卤化物、过氧化物和过氧酸以及它们的卤化、磺化、硝化或亚硝化衍生物:**							**Polycarboxylic acids, their anhy-drides, hal-ides, peroxides and peroxyacids; their halo-genated, sulphonated, nitrated or nitrosated derivatives:**
		-无环多元羧酸及其酸酐、酰卤化物、过氧化物和过氧酸以及它们的衍生物:							-Acyclic-polycarboxylic acids, their anhydrides, halides, peroxides, per-oxyacids and their de-rivatives:
		--草酸及其盐和酯:							--Oxalic acid, its salts and esters:
2106	2917.1110	---草酸	6.5	0 5	东盟ASEAN,智利CL,新西兰NZ,秘鲁PE,哥斯达黎加CR 巴基斯坦PK	0	最不发达35国LDC35	40	---Oxalic acid
2107	2917.1120	---草酸钴	9	0 5	东盟ASEAN,智利CL,新西兰NZ,秘鲁PE,哥斯达黎加CR 巴基斯坦PK	0	最不发达35国LDC35	30	---Cobalt oxalate
2108	2917.1190	---其他	6.5	0 5	东盟ASEAN,智利CL,新西兰NZ,秘鲁PE,哥斯达黎加CR 巴基斯坦PK	0	最不发达35国LDC35	30	---Other
2109	2917.1200	--己二酸及其盐和酯	6.5	0 5	东盟ASEAN,智利CL,新西兰NZ,秘鲁PE,哥斯达黎加CR 巴基斯坦PK	0	最不发达35国LDC35	30	--Adipic acid, its salts and esters
		--壬二酸、癸二酸及其盐和酯:							--Azelaic acid, sebacic acid, their salts and es-ters:
2110	2917.1310	---癸二酸及其盐和酯	6.5	0 5	东盟ASEAN,智利CL,新西兰NZ,秘鲁PE,哥斯达黎加CR 巴基斯坦PK	0	最不发达35国LDC35	30	---Sebacic acid, its salts and esters
2111	2917.1390	---其他	6.5	0 5	东盟ASEAN,智利CL,新西兰NZ,秘鲁PE,哥斯达黎加CR 巴基斯坦PK	0	最不发达35国LDC35	30	---Other

序号 No.	税则号列 Tariff Line	货品名称	最惠国税率 MFN(%)	协定税率 Agreement(%)		特惠税率 S.P.(%)		普通税率 Gen.(%)	Article Description
2112	2917.1400	--马来酐	6.5	0 5	东盟ASEAN,智利CL,新西兰NZ,秘鲁PE,哥斯达黎加CR 巴基斯坦PK	0	最不发达35国LDC35	30	--Maleic anhydride
2113	2917.1900	--其他	6.5	0 5	东盟ASEAN,智利CL,新西兰NZ,秘鲁PE,哥斯达黎加CR,澳门MO 巴基斯坦PK	0	最不发达35国LDC35	30	--Other
		-环烷多元羧酸、环烯多元羧酸、环萜烯多元羧酸及其酸酐、酰卤化物、过氧化物和过氧酸以及它们的衍生物:							-Cyclanic, cyclenic or cycloterpenic polycarboxylic acids, their anhydrides, halides, peroxides, peroxyacids and their derivatives:
2114	2917.2010	---四氢苯酐	4	0	东盟ASEAN,智利CL,巴基斯坦PK,新西兰NZ,秘鲁PE,哥斯达黎加CR	0	最不发达35国LDC35	11	---Tetrahydro benzoic anhydride
2115	2917.2090	---其他	6.5	0 5	东盟ASEAN,智利CL,新西兰NZ,秘鲁PE,哥斯达黎加CR 巴基斯坦PK	0	最不发达35国LDC35	30	---Other
		-芳香多元羧酸及其酸酐、酰卤化物、过氧化物和过氧酸以及它们的衍生物:							-Aromatic polycarboxylic acids, their anhydrides, halides, peroxides, peroxyacids and their derivatives:
2116	2917.3200	--邻苯二甲酸二辛酯	6.5	0 0.7 5	东盟ASEAN,新西兰NZ,秘鲁PE,哥斯达黎加CR,台湾TW 智利CL 巴基斯坦PK	0	最不发达35国LDC35	30	--Dioctyl orthophthalates
2117	2917.3300	--邻苯二甲酸二壬酯及邻苯二甲酸二癸酯	6.5	0 0.7 5	东盟ASEAN,新西兰NZ,秘鲁PE,哥斯达黎加CR,台湾TW 智利CL 巴基斯坦PK	0	最不发达35国LDC35	30	--Dinonyl or didecyl orthophthalates
		--其他邻苯二甲酸酯:							--Other esters of orthophthalic acid:
2118	2917.3410	---邻苯二甲酸二丁酯	6.5	0 0.7 5	东盟ASEAN,新西兰NZ,秘鲁PE,哥斯达黎加CR 智利CL 巴基斯坦PK	0	最不发达35国LDC35	30	---Dibutyl orthophthalates
2119	2917.3490	---其他	6.5	0 0.7 5	东盟ASEAN,新西兰NZ,秘鲁PE,哥斯达黎加CR,台湾TW 智利CL 巴基斯坦PK	0	最不发达35国LDC35	30	---Other
2120	2917.3500	--邻苯二甲酸酐	6.5	0 0.7 5	东盟ASEAN,新西兰NZ,秘鲁PE,哥斯达黎加CR 智利CL 巴基斯坦PK	0	最不发达35国LDC35	30	--Phthalic anhydride

序号 No.	税则号列 Tariff Line	货品名称	最惠国税率 MFN(%)	协定税率 Agreement(%)		特惠税率 S.P.(%)		普通税率 Gen.(%)	Article Description
		--对苯二甲酸及其盐:							--Terephthalic acid and its salts:
		---对苯二甲酸:							---Terephthalic acid:
2121	2917.3611	----精对苯二甲酸	6.5	0 6	东盟ASEAN,智利CL,新加坡SG,新西兰NZ,哥斯达黎加CR 亚太APTA,巴基斯坦PK	0	最不发达35国LDC35	30	----Pure terephthalic acid
2122	2917.3619	----其他	6.5	0 6	东盟ASEAN,智利CL,新加坡SG,新西兰NZ,秘鲁PE,哥斯达黎加CR 亚太APTA,巴基斯坦PK	0	最不发达35国LDC35	30	----Other
2123	2917.3690	---其他	6.5	0 5	东盟ASEAN,智利CL,新西兰NZ,秘鲁PE,哥斯达黎加CR 巴基斯坦PK	0	最不发达35国LDC35	30	---Other
2124	2917.3700	--对苯二甲酸二甲酯	6.5	0 5	东盟ASEAN,智利CL,新西兰NZ,秘鲁PE,哥斯达黎加CR 巴基斯坦PK	0	最不发达35国LDC35	30	--Dimethyl terephthalate
		--其他:							--Other:
2125	2917.3910	---间苯二甲酸	6.5	0 0.7 5	东盟ASEAN,新西兰NZ,秘鲁PE,哥斯达黎加CR 智利CL 巴基斯坦PK	0	最不发达35国LDC35	30	---Isophthalic acid
2126	2917.3990	---其他	6.5	0 0.7 5	东盟ASEAN,新西兰NZ,秘鲁PE,哥斯达黎加CR 智利CL 巴基斯坦PK	0	最不发达35国LDC35	30	---Other
	29.18	**含附加含氧基的羧酸及其酸酐、酰卤化物、过氧化物和过氧酸以及它们的卤化、磺化、硝化或亚硝化衍生物:**							**Carboxylic acids with additional oxygen function and their anhy-drides, halides, peroxides and peroxyacids;their halogenated, sulphonated, nitrated or nitrosated derivatives:**
		-含醇基但不含其他含氧基的羧酸及其酸酐、酰卤化物、过氧化物和过氧酸以及它们的衍生物:							-Carboxylic acids with alcohol function but without other oxygen function, their anhydrides, halides, peroxides, peroxyacids and their derivatives:
2127	2918.1100	--乳酸及其盐和酯	6.5	0 5	东盟ASEAN,智利CL,新西兰NZ,秘鲁PE,哥斯达黎加CR 巴基斯坦PK	0	最不发达35国LDC35	30	--Lactic acid, its salts and esters
2128	2918.1200	--酒石酸	6.5	0 0.7 5	东盟ASEAN,新西兰NZ,秘鲁PE,哥斯达黎加CR 智利CL 巴基斯坦PK	0	最不发达35国LDC35	35	--Tartaric acid

序号 No.	税则号列 Tariff Line	货品名称	最惠国税率 MFN(%)	协定税率 Agreement(%)		特惠税率 S.P.(%)		普通税率 Gen.(%)	Article Description
2129	2918.1300	--酒石酸盐及酒石酸酯	6.5	0 0.7 5	东盟ASEAN,新西兰NZ,秘鲁PE,哥斯达黎加CR 智利CL 巴基斯坦PK	0	最不发达35国LDC35	30	--Salts and esters of tartaric acid
2130	2918.1400	--柠檬酸	6.5	0 0.7 5	东盟ASEAN,新西兰NZ,秘鲁PE,哥斯达黎加CR 智利CL 巴基斯坦PK	0	最不发达35国LDC35	35	--Citric acid
2131	2918.1500	--柠檬酸盐及柠檬酸酯	6.5	0 5	东盟ASEAN,智利CL,新西兰NZ,秘鲁PE,哥斯达黎加CR 巴基斯坦PK	0	最不发达35国LDC35	30	--Salts and esters of citric acid
2132	2918.1600	--葡糖酸及其盐和酯	6.5	0 5	东盟ASEAN,智利CL,新西兰NZ,秘鲁PE,哥斯达黎加CR 巴基斯坦PK	0	最不发达35国LDC35	30	--Gluconic acid, its salts and esters
2133	2918.1800	--乙酯杀螨醇（ISO）	6.5	0 5	东盟ASEAN,智利CL,新西兰NZ,秘鲁PE,哥斯达黎加CR 巴基斯坦PK	0	最不发达35国LDC35	30	--Chlorobenzilate (ISO)
		--其他:							--Other:
2134	2918.1910	---2，2-二苯基-2-羟基乙酸（二苯羟乙酸;二苯乙醇酸）	6.5	0 5	东盟ASEAN,智利CL,新西兰NZ,秘鲁PE,哥斯达黎加CR 巴基斯坦PK	0	最不发达35国LDC35	30	---2, 2-Diphenyl-2-hydroxyacetic acid (ahydroxydiphenylacetic acid, benzilic acid)
2135	2918.1990	---其他	6.5	0 5	东盟ASEAN,智利CL,新西兰NZ,秘鲁PE,哥斯达黎加CR 巴基斯坦PK	0	最不发达35国LDC35	30	---Other
		-含酚基但不含其他含氧基的羧酸及其酸酐、酰卤化物、过氧化物和过氧酸以及它们的衍生物:							-Carboxylic acids with phenol fun-ction but without other oxygen function, their anhydrides, halides, peroxides, peroxyacids and their derivatives:
		--水杨酸及其盐:							--Salicylic acid and its salts:
2136	2918.2110	---水杨酸、水杨酸钠	6.5	0 5	东盟ASEAN,智利CL,新西兰NZ,秘鲁PE,哥斯达黎加CR 巴基斯坦PK	0	最不发达35国LDC35	20	---Salicylic acid and sodium salicylate
2137	2918.2190	---其他	6.5	0 5	东盟ASEAN,智利CL,新西兰NZ,秘鲁PE,哥斯达黎加CR 巴基斯坦PK	0	最不发达35国LDC35	30	---Other
		--邻乙酰水杨酸及其盐和酯:							--o-Acetylsalicylic acid, its salts and esters:
2138	2918.2210	---邻乙酰水杨酸（阿斯匹林）	6	0 5	东盟ASEAN,智利CL,新西兰NZ,秘鲁PE,哥斯达黎加CR 巴基斯坦PK	0	最不发达35国LDC35	20	---Acetylsalicylic acid

序号 No.	税则号列 Tariff Line	货品名称	最惠国税率 MFN(%)	协定税率 Agreement(%)		特惠税率 S.P.(%)		普通税率 Gen.(%)	Article Description
2139	2918.2290	---其他	6.5	0 5	东盟ASEAN,智利CL,新西兰NZ,秘鲁PE,哥斯达黎加CR 巴基斯坦PK	0	最不发达35国LDC35	30	---Other
2140	2918.2300	--水杨酸的其他酯及其盐	6.5	0 5	东盟ASEAN,智利CL,新西兰NZ,秘鲁PE,哥斯达黎加CR 巴基斯坦PK	0	最不发达35国LDC35	30	--Other esters of salicylic acid and their salts
2141	2918.2900	--其他	6.5	0 0.7 5	东盟ASEAN,新西兰NZ,秘鲁PE,哥斯达黎加CR,澳门MO 智利CL 巴基斯坦PK	0	最不发达35国LDC35	30	--Other
2142	2918.3000	-含醛基或酮基但不含其他含氧基的羧酸及其酸酐、酰卤化物、过氧化物和过氧酸以及它们的衍生物	6.5	0 5	东盟ASEAN,智利CL,新西兰NZ,秘鲁PE,哥斯达黎加CR 巴基斯坦PK	0	最不发达35国LDC35	30	-Carboxylic acids with aldehyde or ketone function but without other oxygen function, their anhydrides, halides, peroxides, peroxyacids and their derivatives
		-其他:							-Other:
2143	2918.9100	--2，4，5-涕（ISO）（2，4，5-三氯苯氧基乙酸）及其盐或酯	6.5	0 5	东盟ASEAN,智利CL,新西兰NZ,秘鲁PE,哥斯达黎加CR 巴基斯坦PK	0	最不发达35国LDC35	30	--2, 4, 5-T (ISO) (2, 4, 5-trichlorophenoxyacetic acid), its salts and esters
2144	2918.9900	--其他	6.5	0 5	东盟ASEAN,智利CL,新西兰NZ,秘鲁PE,哥斯达黎加CR 巴基斯坦PK	0	最不发达35国LDC35	30	--Other
		第八分章 非金属无机酸酯及其盐以及它们的卤化、磺化、硝化或亚硝化衍生物							Ⅷ. ESTERS OF INORGANIC ACIDS OF NON-METALS AND THEIR SALTS, AND THEIR HALOGENATED, SULPHONATED, NITRATED OR NITROSATED DERIVATIVES
	29.19	**磷酸酯及其盐，包括乳磷酸盐，以及它们的卤化、磺化、硝化或亚硝化衍生物:**							**Phosphoric esters and their salts, including lactophosphates; their halogenated, sulphonated, nitrated or nitrosated derivatives:**
2145	2919.1000	-三（2，3-二溴丙基）磷酸酯	6.5	0 5	东盟ASEAN,智利CL,新西兰NZ,秘鲁PE,哥斯达黎加CR 巴基斯坦PK	0	最不发达35国LDC35	30	-Tris (2, 3-dibromopropyl) phosphate
2146	2919.9000	-其他	6.5	0 5	东盟ASEAN,智利CL,新西兰NZ,秘鲁PE,哥斯达黎加CR 巴基斯坦PK	0	最不发达35国LDC35	30	-Other

序号 No.	税则号列 Tariff Line	货品名称	最惠国税率 MFN(%)	协定税率 Agreement(%)		特惠税率 S.P.(%)		普通税率 Gen.(%)	Article Description
	29.20	**其他非金属无机酸酯（不包括卤化氢的酯）及其盐以及它们的卤化、磺化、硝化或亚硝化衍生物:**							**Esters of other inorganic acids of non-metals (excluding esters of hydrogen halides) and their salts; their halogenated, sulphonated, nitrated or nitrosated derivatives:**
		-硫代磷酸酯及其盐以及它们的卤化、磺化、硝化或亚硝化衍生物:							-Thiophosphoric esters (phosphorothioates) and their salts; their halogenated, sulphonated, nitrated or nitrosated derivatives:
2147	2920.1100	--对硫磷（ISO）及甲基对硫磷（ISO）	6.5	0 5	东盟ASEAN,智利CL,新西兰NZ,秘鲁PE,哥斯达黎加CR 巴基斯坦PK	0	最不发达35国LDC35	30	--Parathion (ISO) and parathion-methyl (ISO) (methyl-parathion)
2148	2920.1900	--其他	6.5	0 5	东盟ASEAN,智利CL,新西兰NZ,秘鲁PE,哥斯达黎加CR 巴基斯坦PK	0	最不发达35国LDC35	30	--Other
		-其他:							-Other:
		---亚磷酸酯:							---Phosphites:
2149	2920.9011	----亚磷酸三甲酯	6.5	0 0.7 5	东盟ASEAN,新西兰NZ,秘鲁PE,哥斯达黎加CR 智利CL 巴基斯坦PK	0	最不发达35国LDC35	30	----Trimethyl phosphite
2150	2920.9012	----亚磷酸三乙酯	6.5	0 0.7 5	东盟ASEAN,新西兰NZ,秘鲁PE,哥斯达黎加CR 智利CL 巴基斯坦PK	0	最不发达35国LDC35	30	----Trimethyl phosphite
2151	2920.9013	----亚磷酸二甲酯	6.5	0 0.7 5	东盟ASEAN,新西兰NZ,秘鲁PE,哥斯达黎加CR 智利CL 巴基斯坦PK	0	最不发达35国LDC35	30	----Dimethyl phosphite
2152	2920.9014	----亚磷酸二乙酯	6.5	0 0.7 5	东盟ASEAN,新西兰NZ,秘鲁PE,哥斯达黎加CR 智利CL 巴基斯坦PK	0	最不发达35国LDC35	30	----Diethyl phosphite
2153	2920.9019	----其他	6.5	0 0.7 5	东盟ASEAN,新西兰NZ,秘鲁PE,哥斯达黎加CR 智利CL 巴基斯坦PK	0	最不发达35国LDC35	30	----Other
2154	2920.9090	---其他	6.5	0 0.7 5	东盟ASEAN,新西兰NZ,秘鲁PE,哥斯达黎加CR 智利CL 巴基斯坦PK	0	最不发达35国LDC35	30	---Other

序号 No.	税则号列 Tariff Line	货品名称	最惠国税率 MFN(%)	协定税率 Agreement(%)		特惠税率 S.P.(%)		普通税率 Gen.(%)	Article Description
	ex29209090	碳酸二苯酯	△2						Diphenyl carbonate
		第九分章 含氮基化合物							Ⅸ. NITROGEN-FUNCTION COMPOUNDS
	29.21	**氨基化合物:**							**Amine-function compounds:**
		-无环单胺及其衍生物以及它们的盐:							-Acyclic monoamines and their derivatives; salts thereof:
2155	2921.1100	--甲胺、二甲胺或三甲胺及其盐	6.5	0 5	东盟ASEAN,智利CL,新西兰NZ,秘鲁PE,哥斯达黎加CR 巴基斯坦PK	0	最不发达35国LDC35	30	--Methylamine, di-or trimethylamine and their salts
		--其他:							--Other:
2156	2921.1910	---二正丙胺	4	0	东盟ASEAN,智利CL,巴基斯坦PK,新西兰NZ,秘鲁PE,哥斯达黎加CR	0	最不发达35国LDC35	11	---Di-n-propylamine
2157	2921.1920	---异丙胺	6.5 △2	0 5	东盟ASEAN,智利CL,新西兰NZ,秘鲁PE,哥斯达黎加CR 巴基斯坦PK	0	最不发达35国LDC35	30	---Isopropyl amine
2158	2921.1930	---N，N—二（2-氯乙基）乙胺	6.5	0 5	东盟ASEAN,智利CL,新西兰NZ,秘鲁PE,哥斯达黎加CR 巴基斯坦PK	0	最不发达35国LDC35	30	---N, N-Bis (2-chloroethyl) ethylamine
2159	2921.1940	---N，N—二（2-氯乙基）甲胺	6.5	0 5	东盟ASEAN,智利CL,新西兰NZ,秘鲁PE,哥斯达黎加CR 巴基斯坦PK	0	最不发达35国LDC35	30	---N, N-Bis (2-chloroethyl) methylamine
2160	2921.1950	---三（2-氯乙基）胺	6.5	0 5	东盟ASEAN,智利CL,新西兰NZ,秘鲁PE,哥斯达黎加CR 巴基斯坦PK	0	最不发达35国LDC35	30	---Tri- (2-chloroethyl) amine
2161	2921.1960	---二烷（甲、乙、正丙或异丙）氨基乙基-2-氯及其质子化盐	6.5	0 5	东盟ASEAN,智利CL,新西兰NZ,秘鲁PE,哥斯达黎加CR 巴基斯坦PK	0	最不发达35国LDC35	30	---N, N-Dialkyl (Me, Et, n-Pr or i-Pr) amino-ethyl-2-chlorides and corresponking protonated salts
2162	2921.1990	---其他	6.5	0 5	东盟ASEAN,智利CL,新西兰NZ,秘鲁PE,哥斯达黎加CR 巴基斯坦PK	0	最不发达35国LDC35	30	---Other
		-无环多胺及其衍生物以及它们的盐:							-Acyclic polyamines and their derivatives;salts thereof:
		--乙二胺及其盐:							--Ethylenediamine and its salts:
2163	2921.2110	---乙二胺	6.5	0 5	东盟ASEAN,智利CL,新西兰NZ,秘鲁PE,哥斯达黎加CR 巴基斯坦PK	0	最不发达35国LDC35	30	---Ethylenediamine

序号 No.	税则号列 Tariff Line	货品名称	最惠国税率 MFN(%)	协定税率 Agreement(%)		特惠税率 S.P.(%)		普通税率 Gen.(%)	Article Description
2164	2921.2190	---其他	6.5	0 5	东盟ASEAN,智利CL,新西兰NZ,秘鲁PE,哥斯达黎加CR 巴基斯坦PK	0	最不发达35国LDC35	30	---Other
		--六亚甲基二胺及其盐:							--Hexamethylenediamine and its salts:
2165	2921.2210	---己二酸己二胺盐（尼龙66盐）	6.5	0 5	东盟ASEAN,智利CL,新西兰NZ,秘鲁PE,哥斯达黎加CR 巴基斯坦PK	0	最不发达35国LDC35	20	---Nylon-66salt
2166	2921.2290	---其他	6.5	0 5	东盟ASEAN,智利CL,新西兰NZ,秘鲁PE,哥斯达黎加CR 巴基斯坦PK	0	最不发达35国LDC35	30	---Other
2167	2921.2900	--其他	6.5	0 5	东盟ASEAN,智利CL,新西兰NZ,秘鲁PE,哥斯达黎加CR 巴基斯坦PK	0	最不发达35国LDC35	30	--Other
2168	2921.3000	-环烷单胺或多胺、环烯单胺或多胺、环萜烯单胺或多胺及其衍生物以及它们的盐	6.5	0 5	东盟ASEAN,智利CL,新西兰NZ,秘鲁PE,哥斯达黎加CR 巴基斯坦PK	0	最不发达35国LDC35	30	-Cyclanic, cyclenic or cycloterpenic monoor polyamines, and their derivatives; salts thereof
		-芳香单胺及其衍生物以及它们的盐:							-Aromatic monoamines and their derivatives; salts thereof:
		--苯胺及其盐:							--Aniline and its salts:
2169	2921.4110	---苯胺	6.5	0 5	东盟ASEAN,智利CL,新西兰NZ,秘鲁PE,哥斯达黎加CR 巴基斯坦PK	0	最不发达35国LDC35	20	---Aniline
2170	2921.4190	---其他	6.5	0 5	东盟ASEAN,智利CL,新西兰NZ,秘鲁PE,哥斯达黎加CR 巴基斯坦PK	0	最不发达35国LDC35	30	---Other
2171	2921.4200	--苯胺衍生物及其盐	6.5	0 5	东盟ASEAN,智利CL,新西兰NZ,秘鲁PE,哥斯达黎加CR 巴基斯坦PK	0	最不发达35国LDC35	30	--Aniline derivatives and their salts
2172	2921.4300	--甲苯胺及其衍生物以及它们的盐	6.5	0 5	东盟ASEAN,智利CL,新西兰NZ,秘鲁PE,哥斯达黎加CR 巴基斯坦PK	0	最不发达35国LDC35	30	--Toluidines and their derivatives; salts thereof
2173	2921.4400	--二苯胺及其衍生物以及它们的盐	6.5	0 5	东盟ASEAN,智利CL,新西兰NZ,秘鲁PE,哥斯达黎加CR 巴基斯坦PK	0	最不发达35国LDC35	30	--Diphenylamine and its derivatives; salts thereof
2174	2921.4500	--1-萘胺（α-萘胺）、2-萘胺（β-萘胺）及其衍生物以及它们的盐	6.5	0 5	东盟ASEAN,智利CL,新西兰NZ,秘鲁PE,哥斯达黎加CR 巴基斯坦PK	0	最不发达35国LDC35	30	--1-Naphthylamine (α-naphthy-lamine), 2-naphthylamine (β-na-phthylamine) and their derivatives; salts thereof

序号 No.	税则号列 Tariff Line	货品名称	最惠国税率 MFN(%)	协定税率 Agreement(%)		特惠税率 S.P.(%)		普通税率 Gen.(%)	Article Description
2175	2921.4600	--安非他明（INN）、苄非他明（INN）、右苯丙胺（INN）、乙非他明、芬坎法明（INN）、利非他明、左苯丙胺（INN）、美芬雷司（INN）、苯丁胺（INN）以及它们的盐	6.5	0 5	东盟ASEAN,智利CL,新西兰NZ,秘鲁PE,哥斯达黎加CR 巴基斯坦PK	0	最不发达35国LDC35	30	--Amfetamine (INN), benzfetamine (INN), dexamfetamine (INN), etilamfetamine (INN), fencamfamin (INN), lefetamine (INN), levamfetamine (INN), mefenorex (INN) and phentermine (INN); salts thereof
		--其他:							--Other:
2176	2921.4910	---对异丙基苯胺	4	0	东盟ASEAN,智利CL,巴基斯坦PK,新西兰NZ,秘鲁PE,哥斯达黎加CR	0	最不发达35国LDC35	11	---p-Isopropyl-aniline
2177	2921.4920	---二甲基苯胺	6.5	0 5	东盟ASEAN,智利CL,新西兰NZ,秘鲁PE,哥斯达黎加CR 巴基斯坦PK	0	最不发达35国LDC35	20	---Dimethylanilines
2178	2921.4930	---2，6-甲基乙基苯胺	4	0	东盟ASEAN,智利CL,巴基斯坦PK,新西兰NZ,秘鲁PE,哥斯达黎加CR	0	最不发达35国LDC35	11	---2, 6-Methyl ethyl aniline
2179	2921.4940	---2，6-二乙基苯胺	6.5	0 5	东盟ASEAN,智利CL,新西兰NZ,秘鲁PE,哥斯达黎加CR 巴基斯坦PK	0	最不发达35国LDC35	20	---2, 6-Diethylaniline
2180	2921.4990	---其他	6.5	0 5	东盟ASEAN,智利CL,新西兰NZ,秘鲁PE,哥斯达黎加CR 巴基斯坦PK	0	最不发达35国LDC35	30	---Other
		-芳香多胺及其衍生物以及它们的盐:							-Aromatic polyamines and their derivatives; salts thereof:
		--邻-、间-、对-苯二胺、二氨基甲苯及其衍生物以及它们的盐:							--o-,m-,p-Phenylenediamine, diaminotoluenes, and their derivatives; salts thereof:
2181	2921.5110	---邻苯二胺	4	0	东盟ASEAN,智利CL,巴基斯坦PK,新西兰NZ,秘鲁PE,哥斯达黎加CR	0	最不发达35国LDC35	11	---o-Phenylenediamine
2182	2921.5190	---其他	6.5	0 5	东盟ASEAN,智利CL,新西兰NZ,秘鲁PE,哥斯达黎加CR 巴基斯坦PK	0	最不发达35国LDC35	30	---Other
2183	2921.5900	--其他	6.5	0 5	东盟ASEAN,智利CL,新西兰NZ,秘鲁PE,哥斯达黎加CR 巴基斯坦PK	0	最不发达35国LDC35	30	--Other
	29.22	**含氧基氨基化合物:**							**Oxygen-function amino-compounds:**

序号 No.	税则号列 Tariff Line	货品名称	最惠国税率 MFN(%)	协定税率 Agreement(%)		特惠税率 S.P.(%)		普通税率 Gen.(%)	Article Description
		-氨基醇（但含有一种以上含氧基的除外）及其醚和酯，以及它们的盐:							-Amino-alcohols, other than those containing more than one kind of oxygen function, their ethers and esters;salts thereof:
2184	2922.1100	--单乙醇胺及其盐:	6.5	0 5	东盟ASEAN,智利CL,新西兰NZ,秘鲁PE,哥斯达黎加CR 巴基斯坦PK	0	最不发达35国LDC35	30	--Monoethanolamine and its salts:
2185	2922.1200	--二乙醇胺及其盐	6.5	0 5	东盟ASEAN,智利CL,新西兰NZ,秘鲁PE,哥斯达黎加CR 巴基斯坦PK	0	最不发达35国LDC35	30	--Diethanolamine and its salts
		--三乙醇胺及其盐:							--Triethanolamine and its salts:
2186	2922.1310	---三乙醇胺	6.5	0 5	东盟ASEAN,智利CL,新西兰NZ,秘鲁PE,哥斯达黎加CR 巴基斯坦PK	0	最不发达35国LDC35	30	---Triethanolamine
2187	2922.1320	---三乙醇胺盐	6.5	0 5	东盟ASEAN,智利CL,新西兰NZ,秘鲁PE,哥斯达黎加CR 巴基斯坦PK	0	最不发达35国LDC35	30	---Salts of triethanolamine
2188	2922.1400	--右丙氧吩（INN）及其盐	6.5	0 5	东盟ASEAN,智利CL,新西兰NZ,秘鲁PE,哥斯达黎加CR 巴基斯坦PK	0	最不发达35国LDC35	30	--Dextropropoxyphene (INN) and its saltsZ
		--其他:							--Other:
2189	2922.1910	---乙胺丁醇	6.5	0 5	东盟ASEAN,智利CL,新西兰NZ,秘鲁PE,哥斯达黎加CR 巴基斯坦PK	0	最不发达35国LDC35	30	---Ethylamino butanol (Ethambutol)
		---二烷（甲、乙、正丙或异丙）氨基乙-2-醇及其质子化盐:							---N, N-Dialkyl-(Me, Et, n-Pr or i-Pr) amino-ethane-2-ols and cor-nesponding protonated salts:
2190	2922.1921	----二甲氨基乙醇及其质子化盐	6.5	0 5	东盟ASEAN,智利CL,新西兰NZ,秘鲁PE,哥斯达黎加CR 巴基斯坦PK	0	最不发达35国LDC35	30	----N, N-Dimethylami-noethanol and corre-sponding protonated salts
2191	2922.1922	----二乙氨基乙醇及其质子化盐	6.5	0 5	东盟ASEAN,智利CL,新西兰NZ,秘鲁PE,哥斯达黎加CR 巴基斯坦PK	0	最不发达35国LDC35	30	----N, N-Diethylamino-ethanol and corre-sponding protonated salts
2192	2922.1929	----其他	6.5	0 5	东盟ASEAN,智利CL,新西兰NZ,秘鲁PE,哥斯达黎加CR 巴基斯坦PK	0	最不发达35国LDC35	30	----Other
2193	2922.1930	---乙基二乙醇胺	6.5	0 5	东盟ASEAN,智利CL,新西兰NZ,秘鲁PE,哥斯达黎加CR 巴基斯坦PK	0	最不发达35国LDC35	30	---Ethyldiethanolamine

序号 No.	税则号列 Tariff Line	货品名称	最惠国税率 MFN(%)	协定税率 Agreement(%)		特惠税率 S.P.(%)		普通税率 Gen.(%)	Article Description
2194	2922.1940	---甲基二乙醇胺	6.5	0	东盟ASEAN,智利CL,新西兰NZ,秘鲁PE,哥斯达黎加CR	0	最不发达35国LDC35	30	---Methyldiethanolamine
				5	巴基斯坦PK				
2195	2922.1950	---本芴醇	6.5	0	东盟ASEAN,智利CL,新西兰NZ,秘鲁PE,哥斯达黎加CR	0	最不发达35国LDC35	30	---Iumefantrine
				5	巴基斯坦PK				
2196	2922.1990	---其他	6.5	0	东盟ASEAN,智利CL,新西兰NZ,秘鲁PE,哥斯达黎加CR	0	最不发达35国LDC35	30	---Other
				5	巴基斯坦PK				
		-氨基萘酚和其他氨基酚（但含有一种以上含氧基的除外）及其醚和酯，以及它们的盐:							-Amino-naphthols and amino-phenols, other than those containing more than one kind of oxygen function, their ethers and esters;salts thereof:
2197	2922.2100	--氨基羟基萘磺酸及其盐	6.5	0	东盟ASEAN,智利CL,新西兰NZ,秘鲁PE,哥斯达黎加CR	0	最不发达35国LDC35	30	--Aminohydroxynaphthalenesulphonic acid and their salts
				5	巴基斯坦PK				
		--其他:							--Other:
2198	2922.2910	---茴香胺、二茴香胺、氨基苯乙醚及其盐	6.5	0	东盟ASEAN,智利CL,新西兰NZ,秘鲁PE,哥斯达黎加CR	0	最不发达35国LDC35	30	---Anisidine, dianisidine, phenetidine and their salts
				5	巴基斯坦PK				
2199	2922.2990	---其他	6.5	0	东盟ASEAN,智利CL,新西兰NZ,秘鲁PE,哥斯达黎加CR	0	最不发达35国LDC35	30	---Other
				5	巴基斯坦PK				
		-氨基醛、氨基酮和氨基醌，但含有一种以上含氧基的除外，以及它们的盐:							-Amino-aldehydes, amino-ketones and amino-quinones, other than those containing more than one kind of oxygen function; salts thereof:
2200	2922.3100	--安非拉酮、美沙酮和去甲美沙酮以及它们的盐	6.5	0	东盟ASEAN,智利CL,新西兰NZ,秘鲁PE,哥斯达黎加CR	0	最不发达35国LDC35	30	--Amfepramone (INN), methadone (INN) and normethadone (INN); salts thereof
				5	巴基斯坦PK				
		--其他:							--Other:
2201	2922.3910	---4-甲基甲卡西酮	6.5	0	东盟ASEAN,智利CL,新西兰NZ,秘鲁PE,哥斯达黎加CR	0	最不发达35国LDC35	30	---4-methyl-methcathinone
				5	巴基斯坦PK				
2202	2922.3990	---其他	6.5	0	东盟ASEAN,智利CL,新西兰NZ,秘鲁PE,哥斯达黎加CR	0	最不发达35国LDC35	30	---Other
				5	巴基斯坦PK				

序号 No.	税则号列 Tariff Line	货品名称	最惠国税率 MFN(%)	协定税率 Agreement(%)		特惠税率 S.P.(%)		普通税率 Gen.(%)	Article Description
		-氨基酸及其酯,但含有一种以上含氧基的除外,以及它们的盐:							-Amino-acids, other than those containing more than one kind of oxygen function, and their esters;salts thereof:
		--赖氨酸及其酯以及它们的盐:							--Lysine and its esters;salts thereof:
2203	2922.4110	---赖氨酸	5	0	东盟ASEAN,智利CL,巴基斯坦PK,新西兰NZ,秘鲁PE,哥斯达黎加CR	0	最不发达35国LDC35	20	---Lysine
2204	2922.4190	---其他	6	0 5	东盟ASEAN,智利CL,新西兰NZ,秘鲁PE,哥斯达黎加CR 巴基斯坦PK	0	最不发达35国LDC35	30	---Other
		--谷氨酸及其盐:							--Glutamic acid and its salts:
2205	2922.4210	---谷氨酸	10 △5	0 5 8.6	东盟ASEAN,智利CL,新加坡SG,新西兰NZ,秘鲁PE,哥斯达黎加CR 巴基斯坦PK 亚太APTA	0	最不发达35国LDC35	90	---Glutamic acid
2206	2922.4220	---谷氨酸钠	10	0 5	东盟ASEAN,智利CL,新加坡SG,新西兰NZ,秘鲁PE,哥斯达黎加CR,香港HK 巴基斯坦PK	0	最不发达35国LDC35	130	---Sodium glutamate
2207	2922.4290	---其他	6.5	0 5	东盟ASEAN,智利CL,新西兰NZ,秘鲁PE,哥斯达黎加CR 巴基斯坦PK	0	最不发达35国LDC35	30	---Other
		--氨基酸(但含有一种以上含氧基的除外)及其酯,以及它们的盐:							--Anthranilic acid and its salts:
2208	2922.4310	---邻氨基苯甲酸(氨茴酸)	6.5	0 5	东盟ASEAN,智利CL,新西兰NZ,秘鲁PE,哥斯达黎加CR 巴基斯坦PK	0	最不发达35国LDC35	20	---Anthranilic acid
2209	2922.4390	---其他	6.5	0 5	东盟ASEAN,智利CL,新西兰NZ,秘鲁PE,哥斯达黎加CR 巴基斯坦PK	0	最不发达35国LDC35	30	---Other
2210	2922.4400	--替利定(INN)及其盐	6.5	0 5	东盟ASEAN,智利CL,新西兰NZ,秘鲁PE,哥斯达黎加CR 巴基斯坦PK	0	最不发达35国LDC35	30	--Tilidine (INN) and its salts
		--其他:							--Other:
		---其他氨基酸:							---Amino acids:
2211	2922.4911	----氨甲环酸	6.5	0 5	东盟ASEAN,智利CL,新西兰NZ,秘鲁PE,哥斯达黎加CR 巴基斯坦PK	0	最不发达35国LDC35	20	----Tranexamic acid

序号 No.	税则号列 Tariff Line	货品名称	最惠国税率 MFN(%)	协定税率 Agreement(%)		特惠税率 S.P.(%)		普通税率 Gen.(%)	Article Description
2212	2922.4919	----其他	6.5	0 5	东盟ASEAN,智利CL,新西兰NZ,秘鲁PE,哥斯达黎加CR 巴基斯坦PK	0	最不发达35国LDC35	20	----Other
		---其他:							---Other:
2213	2922.4991	----普鲁卡因	6	0 5	东盟ASEAN,智利CL,新西兰NZ,秘鲁PE,哥斯达黎加CR 巴基斯坦PK	0	最不发达35国LDC35	20	----Procaine
2214	2922.4999	----其他	6.5	0 5	东盟ASEAN,智利CL,新西兰NZ,秘鲁PE,哥斯达黎加CR 巴基斯坦PK	0	最不发达35国LDC35	30	----Other
		-氨基醇酚、氨基酸酚及其他含氧基氨基化合物:							-Amino-alcohol-phenols, amino-acid-phenols and other amino-compounds with oxygen function:
2215	2922.5010	---对羟基苯甘氨酸及其邓钾盐	6.5	0 5	东盟ASEAN,智利CL,新西兰NZ,秘鲁PE,哥斯达黎加CR 巴基斯坦PK	0	最不发达35国LDC35	30	---Potassium-((3-ethoxy-1-methyl-3-oxoprop-1-enyl)amino) (4-hydroxy-phenyl) acetate
2216	2922.5020	---莱克多巴胺和盐酸莱克多巴胺	6.5	0 5	东盟ASEAN,智利CL,新西兰NZ,秘鲁PE,哥斯达黎加CR 巴基斯坦PK	0	最不发达35国LDC35	30	---Ractopamine; Ractopamine hydrochloride
2217	2922.5090	---其他	6.5	0 5	东盟ASEAN,智利CL,新西兰NZ,秘鲁PE,哥斯达黎加CR 巴基斯坦PK	0	最不发达35国LDC35	30	---Other
	29.23	**季铵盐及季铵碱;卵磷脂及其他磷氨基类脂,无论是否已有化学定义:**							**Quaternary ammonium salts and hydroxides; lecithins and other phosphoaminolipids, whether or not chemically defined:**
2218	2923.1000	-胆碱及其盐	6.5	0 5	东盟ASEAN,智利CL,新西兰NZ,秘鲁PE,哥斯达黎加CR 巴基斯坦PK	0	最不发达35国LDC35	30	-Choline and its salts
2219	2923.2000	-卵磷脂及其他磷氨基类脂	6.5	0 5	东盟ASEAN,智利CL,新西兰NZ,秘鲁PE,哥斯达黎加CR 巴基斯坦PK	0	最不发达35国LDC35	30	-Lecithins and other phosphoamin-olipids
2220	2923.9000	-其他	6.5	0 5	东盟ASEAN,智利CL,新西兰NZ,秘鲁PE,哥斯达黎加CR 巴基斯坦PK	0	最不发达35国LDC35	30	-Other
	29.24	**羧基酰胺基化合物;碳酸酰胺基化合物:**							**Carboxyamide-function compounds; amide-function compounds of carbonic acid:**
		-无环酰胺(包括无环氨基甲酸酯)及其衍生物以及它们的盐:							-Acyclic amides (including acyclic carbamates) and their derivatives; salts thereof:

序号 No.	税则号列 Tariff Line	货品名称	最惠国税率 MFN(%)	协定税率 Agreement(%)		特惠税率 S.P.(%)		普通税率 Gen.(%)	Article Description
2221	2924.1100	--甲丙氨酯（INN）	6.5	0	东盟ASEAN,智利CL,新西兰NZ,秘鲁PE,哥斯达黎加CR	0	最不发达35国LDC35	30	--Meprobamate (INN)
				5	巴基斯坦PK				
2222	2924.1200	--氯乙酰胺（ISO）、久效磷（ISO）及磷胺（ISO）	6.5	0	东盟ASEAN,新西兰NZ,秘鲁PE,哥斯达黎加CR	0	最不发达35国LDC35	30	--Fluoroacetamide (ISO), monocrotophos (ISO) and phosphamidon (ISO)
				0.7	智利CL				
				5	巴基斯坦PK				
		--其他（INN）:							--Other:
2223	2924.1910	---二甲基甲酰胺	6.5	0	东盟ASEAN,新西兰NZ,秘鲁PE,哥斯达黎加CR,香港HK,台湾TW	0	最不发达35国LDC35	30	---N, N-dimethylformamide
				0.7	智利CL				
				5	巴基斯坦PK				
2224	2924.1990	---其他	6.5	0	东盟ASEAN,新西兰NZ,秘鲁PE,哥斯达黎加CR	0	最不发达35国LDC35	30	---Other
				0.7	智利CL				
				5	巴基斯坦PK				
		-环酰胺(包括环氨基甲酸酯）及其衍生物以及它们的盐:							-Cyclic amides (including cyclic carbamates) and their derivatives; salts thereof:
2225	2924.2100	--酰脲及其衍生物以及它们的盐	6.5	0	东盟ASEAN,智利CL,新西兰NZ,秘鲁PE,哥斯达黎加CR	0	最不发达35国LDC35	30	--Ureides and their derivatives; salts thereof
				5	巴基斯坦PK				
2226	2924.2300	--2-乙酰氨基苯甲酸（N-乙酰邻氨基苯甲酸）及其盐	6.5	0	东盟ASEAN,智利CL,新西兰NZ,秘鲁PE,哥斯达黎加CR	0	最不发达35国LDC35	30	--2-Acetamidobenzoic acid (N-acety-lanthranilic acid) and its salts
				5	巴基斯坦PK				
2227	2924.2400	--炔己蚁胺（INN）	6.5	0	东盟ASEAN,智利CL,新西兰NZ,秘鲁PE,哥斯达黎加CR	0	最不发达35国LDC35	30	--Ethinamate (INN)
				5	巴基斯坦PK				
		--其他:							--Other:
2228	2924.2910	---对乙酰氨基苯乙醚（非那西丁）	6	0	东盟ASEAN,新西兰NZ,秘鲁PE,哥斯达黎加CR	0	最不发达35国LDC35	30	---Phenacetin
				0.6	智利CL				
				5	巴基斯坦PK				
2229	2924.2920	---对乙酰氨基酚（扑热息痛）	6	0	东盟ASEAN,新西兰NZ,秘鲁PE,哥斯达黎加CR	0	最不发达35国LDC35	30	---p-Acetaminophenol (paracetanol)
				0.6	智利CL				
				5	巴基斯坦PK				
2230	2924.2930	---阿斯巴甜	6.5	0	东盟ASEAN,新西兰NZ,秘鲁PE,哥斯达黎加CR,澳门MO	0	最不发达35国LDC35	30	---Aspartame
				0.7	智利CL				
				5	巴基斯坦PK				

序号 No.	税则号列 Tariff Line	货品名称	最惠国税率 MFN(%)	协定税率 Agreement(%)		特惠税率 S.P.(%)		普通税率 Gen.(%)	Article Description
2231	2924.2990	---其他	6.5	0 0.7 5	东盟ASEAN,新西兰NZ,秘鲁PE,哥斯达黎加CR,澳门MO 智利CL 巴基斯坦PK	0	最不发达35国LDC35	30	---Other
	29.25	**羧基酰亚胺化合物（包括糖精及其盐）及亚胺基化合物:**							**Carboxyimide-function compounds (including saccharin and its salts) and imine-function compounds:**
		-酰亚胺及其衍生物以及它们的盐:							-Imides and their derivatives; salts thereof:
2232	2925.1100	--糖精及其盐	9	0 0.9 5	东盟ASEAN,新西兰NZ,秘鲁PE,哥斯达黎加CR 智利CL 巴基斯坦PK	0	最不发达35国LDC35	90	--Saccharin and its salts
2233	2925.1200	--格鲁米特（INN）	6.5	0 5	东盟ASEAN,智利CL,新西兰NZ,秘鲁PE,哥斯达黎加CR 巴基斯坦PK	0	最不发达35国LDC35	30	--Glutethimide (INN)
2234	2925.1900	--其他	6.5	0 5	东盟ASEAN,智利CL,新西兰NZ,秘鲁PE,哥斯达黎加CR 巴基斯坦PK	0	最不发达35国LDC35	30	--Other
		-亚胺及其衍生物以及它们的盐:							-Imines and their derivatives; salts thereof:
2235	2925.2100	--杀虫脒（ISO）	6.5	0 5	东盟ASEAN,智利CL,新西兰NZ,秘鲁PE,哥斯达黎加CR 巴基斯坦PK	0	最不发达35国LDC35	30	--Chlordimeform (ISO)
2236	2925.2900	--其他	6.5	0 5	东盟ASEAN,智利CL,新西兰NZ,秘鲁PE,哥斯达黎加CR 巴基斯坦PK	0	最不发达35国LDC35	30	--Other
	29.26	**腈基化合物:**							**Nitrile-function compounds:**
2237	2926.1000	-丙烯腈	6.5 △3	0	智利CL,新西兰NZ,秘鲁PE,哥斯达黎加CR	0	最不发达35国LDC35	30	-Acrylonitrile
2238	2926.2000	-1-氰基胍（双氰胺）	6.5	0 5	东盟ASEAN,智利CL,新西兰NZ,秘鲁PE,哥斯达黎加CR 巴基斯坦PK	0	最不发达35国LDC35	30	-1-cyanoguanidine (dicyandiamide)
2239	2926.3000	-芬普雷司（INN）及其盐;美沙酮中间体（4-氰基-2-二甲氨基-4，4-二苯基丁烷）	6.5	0 5	东盟ASEAN,智利CL,新西兰NZ,秘鲁PE,哥斯达黎加CR 巴基斯坦PK	0	最不发达35国LDC35	30	-Fenproporex (INN) and its salts; methadone (INN) intermediate (4-cyano-2-dimethylamino-4, 4-diphenylbutane)
		-其他:							-Other:
2240	2926.9010	---对氯氰苄	4	0 0.4	东盟ASEAN,巴基斯坦PK,新西兰NZ,秘鲁PE,哥斯达黎加CR 智利CL	0	最不发达35国LDC35	11	---p-Chlorobenzyl cyanide

序号 No.	税则号列 Tariff Line	货品名称	最惠国税率 MFN(%)	协定税率 Agreement(%)		特惠税率 S.P.(%)		普通税率 Gen.(%)	Article Description
2241	2926.9020	---间苯二甲腈	6.5	0	东盟ASEAN,新西兰NZ,秘鲁PE,哥斯达黎加CR	0	最不发达35国LDC35	30	---m-Phthalonitrile
				0.7	智利CL				
				5	巴基斯坦PK				
2242	2926.9090	---其他	6.5	0	东盟ASEAN,新西兰NZ,秘鲁PE,哥斯达黎加CR,香港HK	0	最不发达35国LDC35	30	---Other
				0.7	智利CL				
				5	巴基斯坦PK				
	ex29269090	己二腈	△1						Hexanedinitrile
	29.27	**重氮化合物、偶氮化合物及氧化偶氮化合物:**							**Diazo-, azo-, or azoxy-compounds:**
2243	2927.0000	重氮化合物、偶氮化合物及氧化偶氮化合物	6.5	0	东盟ASEAN,智利CL,新西兰NZ,秘鲁PE,哥斯达黎加CR,澳门MO	0	最不发达35国LDC35	30	Diazo-, azo-.or azoxy-compounds
				5	巴基斯坦PK				
	29.28	**肼（联氨）及胲（羟胺）的有机衍生物:**							**Organic derivatives of hydrazine or of hydro-xylamine:**
2244	2928.0000	肼（联氨）及胲（羟胺）的有机衍生物	6.5	0	东盟ASEAN,智利CL,新西兰NZ,秘鲁PE,哥斯达黎加CR	0	最不发达35国LDC35	20	Organic derivatives of hydrazine or of hydro-xylamine
				5	巴基斯坦PK				
	29.29	**其他含氮基化合物:**							**Compounds with other nitrogen function:**
2245	2929.1010	---2，4-和2，6-甲苯二异氰酸酯混合物（甲苯二异氰酸酯TDI）	6.5	0	东盟ASEAN,智利CL,新西兰NZ,秘鲁PE,哥斯达黎加CR,台湾TW	0	最不发达35国LDC35	30	---Toluene diisocyanate
				5	巴基斯坦PK				
2246	2929.1020	---二甲苯二异氰酸酯（TODI）	6.5	0	东盟ASEAN,智利CL,新西兰NZ,秘鲁PE,哥斯达黎加CR	0	最不发达35国LDC35	30	---o-Xylene diisocyanate
				5	巴基斯坦PK				
2247	2929.1030	---二苯基甲烷二异氰酸酯（纯MDI）	6.5	0	东盟ASEAN,智利CL,新西兰NZ,秘鲁PE,哥斯达黎加CR	0	最不发达35国LDC35	30	---Diphenylmethane diisocyanate
				5	巴基斯坦PK				
2248	2929.1040	---六亚甲基二异氰酸酯	6.5	0	东盟ASEAN,智利CL,新西兰NZ,秘鲁PE,哥斯达黎加CR	0	最不发达35国LDC35	30	---Hexamethelene diiso-cyanate
				5	巴基斯坦PK				
2249	2929.1090	---其他	6.5	0	东盟ASEAN,智利CL,新西兰NZ,秘鲁PE,哥斯达黎加CR	0	最不发达35国LDC35	30	---Other
				5	巴基斯坦PK				
		-其他:							-Other:
2250	2929.9010	---环已基氨基磺酸钠（甜蜜素）	9	0	东盟ASEAN,智利CL,新西兰NZ,秘鲁PE,哥斯达黎加CR	0	最不发达35国LDC35	90	---Sodium cyclamate
				5	巴基斯坦PK				

序号 No.	税则号列 Tariff Line	货品名称	最惠国税率 MFN(%)	协定税率 Agreement(%)		特惠税率 S.P.(%)		普通税率 Gen.(%)	Article Description
2251	2929.9020	---二烷（甲、乙、正丙或异丙）氨基膦酰二卤	6.5	0 5	东盟ASEAN,智利CL,新西兰NZ,秘鲁PE,哥斯达黎加CR 巴基斯坦PK	0	最不发达35国LDC35	30	---N, N-Dialkyl (Me, Et, n-Pr or i-Pr) phosphoramidic dihalides
2252	2929.9030	---二烷（甲、乙、正丙或异丙）氨基膦酸二烷（甲、乙、正丙或异丙）酯	6.5	0 5	东盟ASEAN,智利CL,新西兰NZ,秘鲁PE,哥斯达黎加CR 巴基斯坦PK	0	最不发达35国LDC35	30	---Dialkyl (Me, Et, n-Pr or i-Pr) N, Ndialkyl (Me, Et, n-Pr or i-Pr) -phosphoramidates
2253	2929.9040	---乙酰甲胺磷	6.5	0 5	东盟ASEAN,智利CL,新西兰NZ,秘鲁PE,哥斯达黎加CR 巴基斯坦PK	0	最不发达35国LDC35	30	---Acephate
2254	2929.9090	---其他	6.5	0 5	东盟ASEAN,智利CL,新西兰NZ,秘鲁PE,哥斯达黎加CR 巴基斯坦PK	0	最不发达35国LDC35	30	---Other
		第十分章 有机—无机化合物、杂环化合物、核酸及其盐以及磺（酰）胺							X.ORGANO-INORGANIC COMPOUNDS, HETEROCYCLIC COMPOUNDS, NUCLEIC ACIDS AND THEIR SALTS, AND SULPHONAMIDES
	29.30	**有机硫化合物:**							**Organo-sulphur compounds:**
2255	2930.2000	-硫代氨基甲酸盐(或酯）及二硫代氨基甲酸盐	6.5	0 0.7 5	东盟ASEAN,新西兰NZ,秘鲁PE,哥斯达黎加CR 智利CL 巴基斯坦PK	0	最不发达35国LDC35	30	-Thiocarbamates and dithiocarba-mates
2256	2930.3000	-一硫化二烃氨基硫羰、二硫化二烃氨基硫羰及四硫化二烃氨基硫羰	6.5	0 5	东盟ASEAN,智利CL,新西兰NZ,秘鲁PE,哥斯达黎加CR 巴基斯坦PK	0	最不发达35国LDC35	30	-Thiuram mono-, di or tetrasulphide
2257	2930.4000	-甲硫氨酸（蛋氨酸）	6.5	0 5	东盟ASEAN,智利CL,新西兰NZ,秘鲁PE,哥斯达黎加CR 巴基斯坦PK	0	最不发达35国LDC35	30	-Methionine
2258	2930.5000	-敌菌丹（ISO）及甲胺磷（ISO）	6.5	0 0.7 5	东盟ASEAN,新西兰NZ,秘鲁PE,哥斯达黎加CR 智利CL 巴基斯坦PK	0	最不发达35国LDC35	30	-Captafol (ISO) and methamidophos (ISO)
		-其他:							-Other:
2259	2930.9010	---双巯丙氨酸（胱氨酸）	6.5	0 0.7 5	东盟ASEAN,新西兰NZ,秘鲁PE,哥斯达黎加CR 智利CL 巴基斯坦PK	0	最不发达35国LDC35	30	---Cystine
2260	2930.9020	---二硫代碳酸酯（或盐）[黄原酸酯（或盐）]	6.5	0 0.7 5	东盟ASEAN,新西兰NZ,秘鲁PE,哥斯达黎加CR 智利CL 巴基斯坦PK	0	最不发达35国LDC35	30	---Dithiocarbonates (xanthates)

序号 No.	税则号列 Tariff Line	货品名称	最惠国税率 MFN(%)	协定税率 Agreement(%)		特惠税率 S.P.(%)		普通税率 Gen.(%)	Article Description
2261	2930.9090	---其他	6.5	0 0.7 5	东盟ASEAN,新西兰NZ,秘鲁PE,哥斯达黎加CR,香港HK 智利CL 巴基斯坦PK	0	最不发达35国LDC35	30	---Other
	ex29309090	DL-羟基蛋氨酸	△5						DL-hydroxy-methionine
	29.31	**其他有机-无机化合物:**							**Other organo-inorganic compounds:**
2262	2931.1000	-四甲基铅及四乙基铅	6.5	0 0.7 5	东盟ASEAN,新西兰NZ,秘鲁PE,哥斯达黎加CR 智利CL 巴基斯坦PK	0	最不发达35国LDC35	30	-Tetramethyl lead and tetraethyl lead
2263	2931.2000	-三丁基锡化合物	6.5	0 0.7 5	东盟ASEAN,新西兰NZ,秘鲁PE,哥斯达黎加CR 智利CL 巴基斯坦PK	0	最不发达35国LDC35	30	-Tributyltin compounds
		-其他: ---含有磷原子的:							-Other: ---Containning phosphorus:
2264	2931.9011	----双甘膦	6.5	0 0.7 5	东盟ASEAN,新西兰NZ,秘鲁PE,哥斯达黎加CR 智利CL 巴基斯坦PK	0	最不发达35国LDC35	30	----N-(Phosphonomethyl) iminodiaceticacid
2265	2931.9019	----其他	6.5	0 0.7 5	东盟ASEAN,新西兰NZ,秘鲁PE,哥斯达黎加CR 智利CL 巴基斯坦PK	0	最不发达35国LDC35	30	----Other
2266	2931.9090	---其他	6.5	0 0.7 5	东盟ASEAN,新西兰NZ,秘鲁PE,哥斯达黎加CR 智利CL 巴基斯坦PK	0	最不发达35国LDC35	30	---Other
	29.32	**仅含有氧杂原子的杂环化合物:**							**Heterocyclic compounds with oxygen hetero-atom(s) only:**
		-结构上含有一个非稠合呋喃环（不论是否氢化）的化合物:							-Compounds containing an unfused furan ring (whether or not hydrogenated) in the structure:
2267	2932.1100	--四氢呋喃	6	0 5	东盟ASEAN,智利CL,新西兰NZ,秘鲁PE,哥斯达黎加CR,香港HK,台湾TW 巴基斯坦PK	0	最不发达35国LDC35	20	--Tetrahydrofuran
2268	2932.1200	--2-糠醛	6	0 5	东盟ASEAN,智利CL,新西兰NZ,秘鲁PE,哥斯达黎加CR 巴基斯坦PK	0	最不发达35国LDC35	20	--2-Furaldehyde (furfuraldehyde)

序号 No.	税则号列 Tariff Line	货品名称	最惠国税率 MFN(%)	协定税率 Agreement(%)		特惠税率 S.P.(%)		普通税率 Gen.(%)	Article Description
2269	2932.1300	--糠醇及四氢糠醇	6	0 5	东盟ASEAN,智利CL,新西兰NZ,秘鲁PE,哥斯达黎加CR 巴基斯坦PK	0	最不发达35国LDC35	20	--Furfuryl alcohol and tetrahydrofur-furyl alco-hol
2270	2932.1900	--其他	6.5	0 5	东盟ASEAN,智利CL,新西兰NZ,秘鲁PE,哥斯达黎加CR 巴基斯坦PK	0	最不发达35国LDC35	20	--Other
		-内酯:							-Lactones:
2271	2932.2010	---香豆素、甲基香豆素及乙基香豆素	6.5	0 5	东盟ASEAN,智利CL,新西兰NZ,秘鲁PE,哥斯达黎加CR 巴基斯坦PK	0	最不发达35国LDC35	20	---Coumarin, methyl-coumarins and ethyl-coumarins
2272	2932.2090	---其他内酯	6.5	0 5	东盟ASEAN,智利CL,新西兰NZ,秘鲁PE,哥斯达黎加CR 巴基斯坦PK	0	最不发达35国LDC35	20	---Other lactones
		-其他:							-Other:
2273	2932.9100	--4-丙烯基-1，2-亚甲二氧基苯（异黄樟脑）	6.5	0 5	东盟ASEAN,智利CL,新西兰NZ,秘鲁PE,哥斯达黎加CR 巴基斯坦PK	0	最不发达35国LDC35	20	--Isosafrole
2274	2932.9200	--1-（1，3-苯并二口恶茂-5-基）丙烷-2-酮	6.5	0 5	东盟ASEAN,智利CL,新西兰NZ,秘鲁PE,哥斯达黎加CR 巴基斯坦PK	0	最不发达35国LDC35	20	--1-(1, 3-Benzodioxol-5-yl) propan-2-one
2275	2932.9300	--3，4-亚甲二氧基苯甲醛（胡椒醛）	6.5	0 5	东盟ASEAN,智利CL,新西兰NZ,秘鲁PE,哥斯达黎加CR 巴基斯坦PK	0	最不发达35国LDC35	20	--Piperonal
2276	2932.9400	--4-烯丙基-1，2-亚甲二氧基苯（黄樟脑）	6.5	0 5	东盟ASEAN,智利CL,新西兰NZ,秘鲁PE,哥斯达黎加CR 巴基斯坦PK	0	最不发达35国LDC35	20	--Safrole
2277	2932.9500	--四氢大麻酚（所有的异构体）	6.5	0 5	东盟ASEAN,智利CL,新西兰NZ,秘鲁PE,哥斯达黎加CR 巴基斯坦PK	0	最不发达35国LDC35	20	--Tetrahydrocannabinols (all is omers)
		--其他:							--Other:
2278	2932.9910	---7-羟基苯并呋喃（呋喃酚）	4	0	东盟ASEAN,智利CL,巴基斯坦PK,新西兰NZ,秘鲁PE,哥斯达黎加CR	0	最不发达35国LDC35	11	---Furan phenol
2279	2932.9920	---2，2′-双甲氧羰基-4，4′-双甲氧基-5，6，5′，6′-双亚甲二氧基联苯（联苯双酯）	6.5	0 5	东盟ASEAN,智利CL,新西兰NZ,秘鲁PE,哥斯达黎加CR 巴基斯坦PK	0	最不发达35国LDC35	20	---Bifendate
2280	2932.9930	---蒿甲醚	6.5	0 5	东盟ASEAN,智利CL,新西兰NZ,秘鲁PE,哥斯达黎加CR 巴基斯坦PK	0	最不发达35国LDC35	20	---Artemether

序号 No.	税则号列 Tariff Line	货品名称	最惠国 税率 MFN(%)	协定税率 Agreement(%)		特惠税率 S.P.(%)		普通 税率 Gen.(%)	Article Description
2281	2932.9990	---其他	6.5	0 5	东盟ASEAN,智利CL,新西兰NZ,秘鲁PE,哥斯达黎加CR 巴基斯坦PK	0	最不发达35国LDC35	20	---Other
	29.33	**仅含有氮杂原子的杂环化合物:**							**Heterocyclic compounds with nitrogen heteroatom (s) only:**
		-结构上含有一个非稠合吡唑环(不论是否氢化)的化合物:							-Compounds containing an unfused pyrazole ring (whether or not hydrogenated) in the structure:
2282	2933.1100	--二甲基苯基吡唑酮(安替比林)及其衍生物	6.5	0 5 6	东盟ASEAN,智利CL,新西兰NZ,秘鲁PE,哥斯达黎加CR 巴基斯坦PK 亚太APTA	0	最不发达35国LDC35	20	--Phenazone (antipyrin) and its derivatives
		--其他:							--Other:
2283	2933.1920	---安乃近	6	0 5	东盟ASEAN,智利CL,新西兰NZ,秘鲁PE,哥斯达黎加CR 巴基斯坦PK	0	最不发达35国LDC35	20	---Analgin
2284	2933.1990	---其他	6.5	0 5	东盟ASEAN,智利CL,新西兰NZ,秘鲁PE,哥斯达黎加CR 巴基斯坦PK	0	最不发达35国LDC35	20	---Other
		-结构上含有一个非稠合咪唑环(不论是否氢化)的化合物:							-Compounds containing an unfused imidazole ring (whether or not hydrogenated) in the structure:
2285	2933.2100	--乙内酰脲及其衍生物	6.5	0 5	东盟ASEAN,智利CL,新西兰NZ,秘鲁PE,哥斯达黎加CR 巴基斯坦PK	0	最不发达35国LDC35	30	--Hydantoin and its derivatives
2286	2933.2900	--其他	6.5	0 5	东盟ASEAN,智利CL,新西兰NZ,秘鲁PE,哥斯达黎加CR 巴基斯坦PK	0	最不发达35国LDC35	20	--Other
		-结构上含有一个非稠合吡啶环(不论是否氢化)的化合物:							-Compounds containing an unfused pyridine ring (whether or not hydrogenated) in the structure:
2287	2933.3100	--吡啶及其盐	6	0 5	东盟ASEAN,智利CL,新西兰NZ,秘鲁PE,哥斯达黎加CR,台湾TW 巴基斯坦PK	0	最不发达35国LDC35	20	--Pyridine and its salts
		--六氢吡啶(哌啶)及其盐:							--Piperidine and its salts:
2288	2933.3210	---六氢吡啶(哌啶)	4	0	东盟ASEAN,智利CL,巴基斯坦PK,新西兰NZ,秘鲁PE,哥斯达黎加CR	0	最不发达35国LDC35	11	---Hexahydropyridine (piperidine)

序号 No.	税则号列 Tariff Line	货品名称	最惠国税率 MFN(%)	协定税率 Agreement(%)		特惠税率 S.P.(%)		普通税率 Gen.(%)	Article Description
2289	2933.3220	---六氢吡啶（哌啶）盐	6.5	0 5	东盟ASEAN,智利CL,新西兰NZ,秘鲁PE,哥斯达黎加CR 巴基斯坦PK	0	最不发达35国LDC35	20	---Isoniazidum
2290	2933.3300	--阿芬太尼（INN），阿尼利定（INN），苯氰米特（INN），溴西泮（INN），地芬诺新（INN），地芬诺酯（INN），地匹哌酮（INN），芬太尼（INN），凯托米酮（INN），哌醋甲酯（INN），喷他左辛（INN），哌替啶（INN），哌替啶中间体A（INN），苯环利定（INN），苯哌利定（INN），哌苯甲醇（INN），哌氰米特（INN），哌丙吡胺（INN）和三甲利定（INN）以及它们的盐	6.5	0 5	东盟ASEAN,智利CL,新西兰NZ,秘鲁PE,哥斯达黎加CR 巴基斯坦PK	0	最不发达35国LDC35	20	--Alfentanil (INN), anil-eridine (INN), be-zitra-mide (INN), bro-maze-pam (INN), difenoxin (INN), di-phenoxylate (INN), dipipanone (INN), fen-tanyl (INN), keto-bemidone (INN), methylpheni-date (INN), pentazo-cine (INN), pethidine (INN), inter-mediate A (INN), phencyclidine (INN) (PCP), phenop-eridine (INN), piprad-rol (INN), pipradrol (INN), piritramide (INN), pro-piram (INN) and trimeperidine (INN), salts thereof
		--其他:							--Other:
2291	2933.3910	---二苯乙醇酸-3-奎宁环脂	6.5	0 5	东盟ASEAN,智利CL,新西兰NZ,秘鲁PE,哥斯达黎加CR 巴基斯坦PK	0	最不发达35国LDC35	20	---Benzilic acid-3-quinuclidinate
2292	2933.3920	---奎宁环-3-醇	6.5	0 5	东盟ASEAN,智利CL,新西兰NZ,秘鲁PE,哥斯达黎加CR 巴基斯坦PK	0	最不发达35国LDC35	20	---Quinuclidine-3-ol
2293	2933.3990	---其他	6.5	0 5	东盟ASEAN,智利CL,新西兰NZ,秘鲁PE,哥斯达黎加CR 巴基斯坦PK	0	最不发达35国LDC35	20	---Other
		-结构上含有一个喹啉或异喹啉环系（不论是否氢化）的化合物，但未经进一步稠合的:							-Compounds containing a quinoline or isoquino-line ringsystem (whether or not hydrogenated), not further fused:
2294	2933.4100	--左非诺（INN）及其盐	6.5	0 5	东盟ASEAN,智利CL,新西兰NZ,秘鲁PE,哥斯达黎加CR 巴基斯坦PK	0	最不发达35国LDC35	20	--Levorphanol (INN) and its salts
		--其他:							--Other:
2295	2933.4910	---环丙氟哌酸	6.5	0 5 6	东盟ASEAN,智利CL,新西兰NZ,秘鲁PE,哥斯达黎加CR 巴基斯坦PK 亚太APTA	0	最不发达35国LDC35	20	---Ciprofloxacin
2296	2933.4990	---其他	6.5	0 5	东盟ASEAN,智利CL,新西兰NZ,秘鲁PE,哥斯达黎加CR 巴基斯坦PK	0	最不发达35国LDC35	20	---Other

序号 No.	税则号列 Tariff Line	货品名称	最惠国税率 MFN(%)	协定税率 Agreement(%)		特惠税率 S.P.(%)		普通税率 Gen.(%)	Article Description
		-结构上含有一个嘧啶环（不论是否氢化）或哌嗪环的化合物:							-Compounds containing a pyrimidine ring (whether or not hydrogenated) or piperazine ring in the structure:
2297	2933.5200	--丙二酰脲（巴比土酸）及其盐	6.5	0 5	东盟ASEAN,智利CL,新西兰NZ,秘鲁PE,哥斯达黎加CR 巴基斯坦PK	0	最不发达35国LDC35	20	--Malonylurea (barbituric acid) and its salts
2298	2933.5300	--阿洛巴比妥（INN），异戊巴比妥（INN），巴比妥（INN），布他比妥（INN），正丁巴比妥（INN），环己巴比妥（INN），甲苯巴比妥（INN），戊巴比妥（INN），苯巴比妥（INN），仲丁巴比妥（INN），司可巴比妥（INN），和乙烯比妥（INN）以及它们的盐	6.5	0 5	东盟ASEAN,智利CL,新西兰NZ,秘鲁PE,哥斯达黎加CR 巴基斯坦PK	0	最不发达35国LDC35	20	--Allobarbital (INN), amobarbital (INN), barbital (INN), butalbital (INN), butobarbital, cyclobarbital (INN), methylphenobarbital (INN), pentobarbital (INN), phenobarbital (INN), secbutabarbital (INN), seco-barbital (INN) and vinylbital (INN); salts thereof
2299	2933.5400	--其他丙二酰脲（巴比土酸）的衍生物以及它们的盐	6.5	0 5	东盟ASEAN,智利CL,新西兰NZ,秘鲁PE,哥斯达黎加CR 巴基斯坦PK	0	最不发达35国LDC35	20	--Other derivatives of malonylurea (barbituric acid); salts thereof
2300	2933.5500	--氯普唑仑（INN），甲氯喹酮（INN），甲喹酮（INN）和齐培丙醇（INN）以及它们的盐	6.5	0 5	东盟ASEAN,智利CL,新西兰NZ,秘鲁PE,哥斯达黎加CR 巴基斯坦PK	0	最不发达35国LDC35	20	--Loprazolam (INN), mecloqualone (INN), methaqualone (INN) and zipeprol (INN); salts thereof
		--其他:							--Other:
2301	2933.5910	---胞嘧啶	6.5	0 4.6	东盟ASEAN,智利CL,巴基斯坦PK,新西兰NZ,秘鲁PE,哥斯达黎加CR 亚太APTA	0	最不发达35国LDC35	20	---Cytosine
2302	2933.5990	---其他	6.5	0 4.6	东盟ASEAN,智利CL,巴基斯坦PK,新西兰NZ,秘鲁PE,哥斯达黎加CR 亚太APTA	0	最不发达35国LDC35	20	---Other
		-结构上含有一个非稠合三嗪环（不论是否氢化）的化合物:							-Compounds-containing an unfused triazine ring (whether or not hydrogenated) in the structure:
2303	2933.6100	--三聚氰胺（蜜胺）	6.5	0 5	东盟ASEAN,智利CL,新西兰NZ,秘鲁PE,哥斯达黎加CR 巴基斯坦PK	0	最不发达35国LDC35	20	--Melamine
		--其他:							--Other:
2304	2933.6910	---三聚氰氯	6	0 5	东盟ASEAN,智利CL,新西兰NZ,秘鲁PE,哥斯达黎加CR,澳门MO 巴基斯坦PK	0	最不发达35国LDC35	20	---Cyanuric chloride

序号 No.	税则号列 Tariff Line	货品名称	最惠国税率 MFN(%)	协定税率 Agreement(%)		特惠税率 S.P.(%)		普通税率 Gen.(%)	Article Description
		---异氰脲酸氯化衍生物:							---Chloroisocyanurate:
2305	2933.6921	----二氯异氰脲酸	6.5	0 5	东盟ASEAN,智利CL,新西兰NZ,秘鲁PE,哥斯达黎加CR,澳门MO 巴基斯坦PK	0	最不发达35国LDC35	20	----Dichloroisooyanurate acid
2306	2933.6922	----三氯异氰脲酸	6.5	0 5	东盟ASEAN,智利CL,新西兰NZ,秘鲁PE,哥斯达黎加CR,澳门MO 巴基斯坦PK	0	最不发达35国LDC35	20	----Trichloroisocyanurate acid
2307	2933.6929	----其他	6.5	0 5	东盟ASEAN,智利CL,新西兰NZ,秘鲁PE,哥斯达黎加CR,澳门MO 巴基斯坦PK	0	最不发达35国LDC35	20	----Other
2308	2933.6990	---其他	6.5	0 5	东盟ASEAN,智利CL,新西兰NZ,秘鲁PE,哥斯达黎加CR,澳门MO 巴基斯坦PK	0	最不发达35国LDC35	20	---Other
		-内酰胺:							-Lactams:
2309	2933.7100	--6-己内酰胺	9	0	智利CL,新西兰NZ,哥斯达黎加CR			35	--6-Hexanolactam (epsilon-caprola-ctam)
2310	2933.7200	--氯巴占（INN）和甲乙哌酮（INN）	9	0 5	东盟ASEAN,智利CL,新西兰NZ,秘鲁PE,哥斯达黎加CR 巴基斯坦PK	0	最不发达35国LDC35	15	--Clobazam (INN) and methyprylon (INN)
2311	2933.7900	--其他内酰胺	9	0 5	东盟ASEAN,智利CL,新西兰NZ,秘鲁PE,哥斯达黎加CR 巴基斯坦PK	0	最不发达35国LDC35	20	--Other lactams
2312	2933.9100	--阿普唑仑（INN），卡马西泮（INN），氯氮卓（INN），氯硝西泮（INN），氯拉卓酸，地洛西泮（INN），地西泮（INN），艾司唑仑（INN），氯氟卓乙酯（INN），氟地西泮（INN），氟硝西泮（INN），氟西泮（INN），哈拉西泮（INN），劳拉西泮（INN），氯甲西泮（INN），马吲哚（INN），美达西泮（INN），咪达唑仑（INN），硝甲西泮（INN），去甲西泮（INN），奥沙西泮（INN），匹那西泮（INN），普拉西泮（INN），吡咯戊酮（INN），替马西泮（INN），四氢西泮（INN）和三唑仑（INN）以及它们的盐	6.5	0 5	东盟ASEAN,智利CL,新西兰NZ,秘鲁PE,哥斯达黎加CR 巴基斯坦PK	0	最不发达35国LDC35	20	--Alprazolam (INN), camazepam (INN), chlor-diazepoxide (INN), clonazepam (INN), clorazepate, delorazepam (INN), diazepam (INN), estazolam (INN), ethyl loflazepate (INN), fludi-azepam (INN), fluni-trazepam (INN), fluraze-pam (INN), halazepam (INN), lorazepam (INN), lormetazepam (INN), mazindol (INN), madazepam (INN), mi-dazolam (INN), ni-metazepam (INN), ni-trazepam (INN) nordaze-pam (INN), oxazepam (INN), pinazepam (INN), prazepam (INN), py-rovalerone (INN), te-mazepam (INN), tetraze-pam (INN), and triazdam (INN); salts thereof

序号 No.	税则号列 Tariff Line	货品名称	最惠国税率 MFN(%)	协定税率 Agreement(%)		特惠税率 S.P.(%)		普通税率 Gen.(%)	Article Description
2313	2933.9900	--其他	6.5	0 0.7 5	东盟ASEAN,新西兰NZ,秘鲁PE,哥斯达黎加CR 智利CL 巴基斯坦PK	0	最不发达35国LDC35	20	--Other
	29.34	**核酸及其盐;无论是否已有化学定义;其他杂环化合物:**							**Nucleic acids and their salts;whether or not chemically defined; Other heterocy-clic compounds:**
2314	2934.1000	-结构上含有一个非稠合噻唑环（不论是否氢化）的化合物	6.5	0 5	东盟ASEAN,智利CL,新西兰NZ,秘鲁PE,哥斯达黎加CR 巴基斯坦PK	0	最不发达35国LDC35	20	-Compounds containing an unfused thiazole ring (whether or not hydro-genated) in the structure
2315	2934.2000	-结构上含有一个苯并噻唑环系（不论是否氢化）的化合物，但未经进一步稠合的	6.5	0 5	东盟ASEAN,智利CL,新西兰NZ,秘鲁PE,哥斯达黎加CR 巴基斯坦PK	0	最不发达35国LDC35	20	-Compounds containing in the structure a ben-zothiazole ringsystem (whether or not hydro-genated), not further fused
2316	2934.3000	-结构上含有一个吩噻嗪环系（不论是否氢化）的化合物，但未经进一步稠合的	6.5	0 5	东盟ASEAN,智利CL,新西兰NZ,秘鲁PE,哥斯达黎加CR 巴基斯坦PK	0	最不发达35国LDC35	20	-Compounds containing in the struct-ure a phe-nothiazine ring-system (whether or not hydro-genated), not further fused
		-其他:							-Other:
2317	2934.9100	--阿米雷司（INN），溴替唑仑（INN），氯噻西泮（INN），氯恶唑仑（INN），右吗拉胺（INN），卤恶唑仑（INN），凯他唑仑（INN），美索卡（INN），恶唑仑（INN），匹莫林（INN），苯巴曲嗪（INN），芬美曲嗪（INN）和舒芬太尼（INN）及它们的盐	6.5	0 5	东盟ASEAN,智利CL,新西兰NZ,秘鲁PE,哥斯达黎加CR 巴基斯坦PK	0	最不发达35国LDC35	20	--Aminorex (INN), brotizolam (INN), clotiazepam (INN), cloxazolam (INN), dex-tromoramide (INN), haloxazolam (INN), ketazolam (INN), mesocarb (INN), oxa-zolam (INN), pemoline (INN), phendimetrazine (INN), phenmetrazine (INN) and sufentanil (INN); salts thereof
		--其他:							--Other:
2318	2934.9910	---磺内酯及磺内酰胺	6.5	0 0.7 5	东盟ASEAN,新西兰NZ,秘鲁PE,哥斯达黎加CR 智利CL 巴基斯坦PK	0	最不发达35国LDC35	30	---Sultones and sultams
2319	2934.9920	---呋喃唑酮	6	0 0.6 5	东盟ASEAN,新西兰NZ,秘鲁PE,哥斯达黎加CR 智利CL 巴基斯坦PK	0	最不发达35国LDC35	20	---Furazolidone
2320	2934.9930	---核酸及其盐	6.5	0 0.7 5	东盟ASEAN,新西兰NZ,秘鲁PE,哥斯达黎加CR 智利CL 巴基斯坦PK	0	最不发达35国LDC35	35	---Nucleic acids and their salts

序号 No.	税则号列 Tariff Line	货品名称	最惠国税率 MFN(%)	协定税率 Agreement(%)		特惠税率 S.P.(%)		普通税率 Gen.(%)	Article Description
2321	2934.9940	---奈韦拉平、依发韦仑、利托那韦及它们的盐	6.5	0 0.7 5	东盟ASEAN,新西兰NZ,秘鲁PE,哥斯达黎加CR 智利CL 巴基斯坦PK	0	最不发达35国LDC35	20	---Nevirapine, Efavirenz, Ritonavir and their salts
2322	2934.9950	---克拉维酸及其盐	6.5	0 0.7 5	东盟ASEAN,新西兰NZ,秘鲁PE,哥斯达黎加CR 智利CL 巴基斯坦PK	0	最不发达35国LDC35	20	---Clavulante acid and its salt
2323	2934.9960	---7-苯乙酰氨基-3-氯甲基-4-头孢烷酸对甲氧基苄酯、7-氨基头孢烷酸、7-氨基脱乙酰氧基头孢烷酸	6	0 0.6 5	东盟ASEAN,巴基斯坦PK,新西兰NZ,秘鲁PE,哥斯达黎加CR 智利CL 亚太APTA	0	最不发达35国LDC35	20	---7-Phenylacetamido-3-(chloromethyl) -3-cephem-4-carboxylic acid p-methoxybenzyl ester, 7-aminocephalo-sporianic acid, 7-amino-deacetoxycefanoic acid
2324	2934.9990	---其他	6.5	0 0.7 5	东盟ASEAN,新西兰NZ,秘鲁PE,哥斯达黎加CR 智利CL 巴基斯坦PK	0	最不发达35国LDC35	20	---Other
	29.35	**磺（酰）胺:**							**Sulphonamides:**
2325	2935.0010	---磺胺嘧啶	6.5	0 5	东盟ASEAN,智利CL,新西兰NZ,秘鲁PE,哥斯达黎加CR 巴基斯坦PK	0	最不发达35国LDC35	35	---Sulphadiazine
2326	2935.0020	---磺胺双甲基嘧啶	6.5	0 5	东盟ASEAN,智利CL,新西兰NZ,秘鲁PE,哥斯达黎加CR 巴基斯坦PK	0	最不发达35国LDC35	35	---Sulfadimidine
2327	2935.0030	---磺胺甲噁唑	6.5	0 5	东盟ASEAN,智利CL,新西兰NZ,秘鲁PE,哥斯达黎加CR 巴基斯坦PK	0	最不发达35国LDC35	35	---Sulfamethoxazole
2328	2935.0090	---其他	6.5	0 5	东盟ASEAN,智利CL,新西兰NZ,秘鲁PE,哥斯达黎加CR 巴基斯坦PK	0	最不发达35国LDC35	35	---Other
		第十一分章 维生素原、维生素及激素							XI.PROVITAMINS, VITAMINS AND HORMONES
	29.36	**天然或合成再制的维生素原和维生素（包括天然浓缩物）及其主要用作维生素的衍生物，上述产品的混合物，不论是否溶于溶剂:**							**Provitamins and vitamins, natural or reproduced by synthesis (including natural concentrates), derivatives thereof used primarily as vitamins, and intermixtures of the foregoing, whether or not in any solvent:**

序号 No.	税则号列 Tariff Line	货品名称	最惠国税率 MFN(%)	协定税率 Agreement(%)		特惠税率 S.P.(%)		普通税率 Gen.(%)	Article Description
		-未混合的维生素及其衍生物:							-Vitamins and their derivatives, unmixed:
2329	2936.2100	--维生素A及其衍生物	4	0	东盟ASEAN,智利CL,巴基斯坦PK,新西兰NZ,秘鲁PE,哥斯达黎加CR,澳门MO	0	最不发达35国LDC35,最不发达4国LDC4	20	--Vitamins A and their derivatives
2330	2936.2200	--维生素B_1及其衍生物	4	0	东盟ASEAN,智利CL,巴基斯坦PK,新西兰NZ,秘鲁PE,哥斯达黎加CR,澳门MO	0	最不发达35国LDC35,最不发达4国LDC4	20	--Vitamin B_1 and its derivatives
2331	2936.2300	--维生素B_2及其衍生物	4	0	东盟ASEAN,智利CL,巴基斯坦PK,新西兰NZ,秘鲁PE,哥斯达黎加CR,澳门MO	0	最不发达35国LDC35,最不发达4国LDC4	20	--Vitamin B_2 and its derivatives
2332	2936.2400	--D或DL-泛酸（维生素B_3或维生素B_5）及其衍生物	4	0	东盟ASEAN,智利CL,巴基斯坦PK,新西兰NZ,秘鲁PE,哥斯达黎加CR,澳门MO	0	最不发达35国LDC35,最不发达4国LDC4	20	--D-or DL-Pantothenic acid (Vitamin B_3 or Vitamin B_5) and its derivatives
2333	2936.2500	--维生素B_6及其衍生物	4	0	东盟ASEAN,智利CL,巴基斯坦PK,新西兰NZ,秘鲁PE,哥斯达黎加CR,澳门MO	0	最不发达35国LDC35,最不发达4国LDC4	20	--Vitamin B_6 and its derivatives
2334	2936.2600	--维生素B_{12}及其衍生物	4	0	东盟ASEAN,智利CL,巴基斯坦PK,新西兰NZ,秘鲁PE,哥斯达黎加CR,澳门MO	0	最不发达35国LDC35,最不发达4国LDC4	20	--Vitamin B_{12} and its derivatives
2335	2936.2700	--维生素C及其衍生物	4	0 0.4	东盟ASEAN,巴基斯坦PK,新西兰NZ,秘鲁PE,哥斯达黎加CR,澳门MO 智利CL	0	最不发达35国LDC35,最不发达4国LDC4	20	--Vitamin C and its derivatives
2336	2936.2800	--维生素E及其衍生物	4	0	东盟ASEAN,智利CL,巴基斯坦PK,新西兰NZ,秘鲁PE,哥斯达黎加CR,澳门MO	0	最不发达35国LDC35,最不发达4国LDC4	20	--Vitamin E and its derivatives
2337	2936.2900	--其他维生素及其衍生物	4	0	东盟ASEAN,智利CL,巴基斯坦PK,新西兰NZ,秘鲁PE,哥斯达黎加CR,澳门MO	0	最不发达35国LDC35,最不发达4国LDC4	20	--Other vitamins and their deriv-atives

序号 No.	税则号列 Tariff Line	货品名称	最惠国税率 MFN(%)	协定税率 Agreement(%)		特惠税率 S.P.(%)		普通税率 Gen.(%)	Article Description
2338	2936.9000	-其他，包括天然浓缩物	4	0 0.4	东盟ASEAN,巴基斯坦PK,新西兰NZ,秘鲁PE,哥斯达黎加CR,澳门MO 智利CL	0	最不发达35国LDC35,最不发达4国LDC4	20	-Other, including natural concent-rates
	29.37	**天然或合成再制的激素、前列腺素、血栓烷、血细胞三烯及其衍生物和结构类似物，包括主要用作激素的改性链多肽:**							**Hormones, prostagland-ins, thro-mboxanes and leukotrienes, natu-ral or reproduced by syn-thesis; derivatives and structural anal-ogues thereof, including chain modified polypeptides, used primarily as hor-mones:**
		-多肽激素、蛋白激素、糖蛋白激素及其衍生物和结构类似物:							-Polypeptide hormones, protein hor-mones and glycoprotein hormones, their derivatives and structural analogues:
2339	2937.1100	--生长激素及其衍生物和结构类似物	4	0	东盟ASEAN,智利CL,巴基斯坦PK,新西兰NZ,秘鲁PE,哥斯达黎加CR	0	最不发达35国LDC35	20	--Somatotropin, its de-rivatives and structural analogues
		--胰岛素及其盐:							--Insulin and its salts:
2340	2937.1210	---重组人胰岛素及其盐	4	0	东盟ASEAN,智利CL,巴基斯坦PK,新西兰NZ,秘鲁PE,哥斯达黎加CR	0	最不发达35国LDC35	20	---Recombinant human insulin and its salts
2341	2937.1290	---其他	4	0	东盟ASEAN,智利CL,巴基斯坦PK,新西兰NZ,秘鲁PE,哥斯达黎加CR	0	最不发达35国LDC35	20	---Other
2342	2937.1900	--其他	4	0	东盟ASEAN,智利CL,巴基斯坦PK,新西兰NZ,秘鲁PE,哥斯达黎加CR	0	最不发达35国LDC35	20	--Other
		-甾族激素及其衍生物和结构类似物:							-Steroidal hormones, their derivativ-es and structural analogues:
2343	2937.2100	--可的松、氢化可的松、脱氢可的松及脱氢皮质醇	4	0	东盟ASEAN,智利CL,巴基斯坦PK,新西兰NZ,秘鲁PE,哥斯达黎加CR	0	最不发达35国LDC35	20	--Cortisone, hydrocorti-sone, prednisone (de-hydrocortisone) and prednisolone (dehy-drocortisone)
		--皮质甾类激素的卤化衍生物:							--Halogenated derivatives of corticost-eroidal hor-mones:
2344	2937.2210	---地塞米松	4	0	东盟ASEAN,智利CL,巴基斯坦PK,新西兰NZ,秘鲁PE,哥斯达黎加CR	0	最不发达35国LDC35	30	---Dexamethasone

序号 No.	税则号列 Tariff Line	货品名称	最惠国税率 MFN(%)	协定税率 Agreement(%)		特惠税率 S.P.(%)		普通税率 Gen.(%)	Article Description
2345	2937.2290	---其他	4	0	东盟ASEAN,智利CL,巴基斯坦PK,新西兰NZ,秘鲁PE,哥斯达黎加CR	0	最不发达35国LDC35	30	---Other
		--雌(甾)激素和孕激素:							--Oestrogens and progestogens:
		---动物源的:							---Of animals:
2346	2937.2311	----孕马结合雌激素	4	0	东盟ASEAN,智利CL,巴基斯坦PK,新西兰NZ,秘鲁PE,哥斯达黎加CR	0	最不发达35国LDC35	30	----Pregnant mare congugated estrogens
2347	2937.2319	----其他	4	0	东盟ASEAN,智利CL,巴基斯坦PK,新西兰NZ,秘鲁PE,哥斯达黎加CR	0	最不发达35国LDC35	30	----Other
2348	2937.2390	---其他	4	0	东盟ASEAN,智利CL,巴基斯坦PK,新西兰NZ,秘鲁PE,哥斯达黎加CR	0	最不发达35国LDC35	30	---Other
2349	2937.2900	--其他	4	0	东盟ASEAN,智利CL,巴基斯坦PK,新西兰NZ,秘鲁PE,哥斯达黎加CR	0	最不发达35国LDC35	30	--Other
2350	2937.5000	-前列腺素、血栓烷和白细胞三烯及其衍生物和结构类似物	4	0	东盟ASEAN,智利CL,巴基斯坦PK,新西兰NZ,秘鲁PE,哥斯达黎加CR	0	最不发达35国LDC35	30	-Prostaglandins, thromboxanes and leukotrienes, their derivatives and structural analogues
2351	2937.9000	-其他	4	0	东盟ASEAN,智利CL,巴基斯坦PK,新西兰NZ,秘鲁PE,哥斯达黎加CR	0	最不发达35国LDC35	30	-Other
		第十二分章 天然或合成再制的苷(配糖物)、植物碱及其盐、醚、酯和其他衍生物							Ⅻ. GLYCOSIDES AND VEGETABLE ALKALOIDS, NATURAL OR REPRODUCED BY SYNTHESIS, AND THEIR SALTS, ETHERS, ESTERS AND OTHER DERIVATIVES
	29.38	**天然或合成再制的苷(配糖物)及其盐、醚、酯和其他衍生物:**							**Glycosides, natural or reproduced by synthesis, and their salts, ethers, esters and other deriv-atives:**
2352	2938.1000	-芸香苷(芦丁)及其衍生物	6.5	0 5	东盟ASEAN,智利CL,新西兰NZ,秘鲁PE,哥斯达黎加CR 巴基斯坦PK	0	最不发达35国LDC35	20	-Rutoside (rutin) and its derivatives
		-其他:							-Other:
2353	2938.9010	---齐多夫定、拉米夫定、司他夫定、地达诺新及它们的盐	6.5	0 5	东盟ASEAN,智利CL,新西兰NZ,秘鲁PE,哥斯达黎加CR 巴基斯坦PK	0	最不发达35国LDC35	20	---Zidovudine, Lamivudine, Stavudine, Didanosine and their salts

序号 No.	税则号列 Tariff Line	货品名称	最惠国税率 MFN(%)	协定税率 Agreement(%)		特惠税率 S.P.(%)		普通税率 Gen.(%)	Article Description
2354	2938.9090	---其他	6.5	0 5	东盟ASEAN,智利CL,新西兰NZ,秘鲁PE,哥斯达黎加CR 巴基斯坦PK	0	最不发达35国LDC35	20	---Other
	29.39	**天然或合成再制的生物碱及其盐、醚、酯和其他衍生物:**							**Vegetable alkaloids, natural or reproduced by synthesis, and their salts, ethers, esters and other derivatives:**
		-鸦片碱及其衍生物以及它们的盐:							-Alkaloids of opium and their derivatives;salts thereof:
2355	2939.1100	--罂粟杆浓缩物、丁丙诺啡（INN）、可待因、双氢可待因（INN）、乙基吗啡、埃托啡（INN）、海洛因、氢可酮（INN）、氢吗啡酮（INN）、吗啡、尼可吗啡（INN）、羟考酮（INN）、羟吗啡酮（INN）、福尔可定（INN）、醋氢可酮（INN）和蒂巴因，以及它们的盐	4	0	东盟ASEAN,智利CL,巴基斯坦PK,新西兰NZ,秘鲁PE,哥斯达黎加CR	0	最不发达35国LDC35,最不发达4国LDC4	50	--Concentrates of poppy straw;buprenorphine (INN), codeine, dihydrocodeine (INN), ethylmorphine, etorphine (INN), heroin, hydrocodone (INN), hydromorphone (INN), morphine, nicomorphine (INN), oxycodone (INN), oxymorphone (INN), pholcodine (INN), thebacon (INN) and thebaine;salts thereof
2356	2939.1900	--其他	4	0	东盟ASEAN,智利CL,巴基斯坦PK,新西兰NZ,秘鲁PE,哥斯达黎加CR	0	最不发达35国LDC35,最不发达4国LDC4	50	--Other
2357	2939.2000	-金鸡纳生物碱及其衍生物以及它们的盐	4	0	东盟ASEAN,智利CL,巴基斯坦PK,新西兰NZ,秘鲁PE,哥斯达黎加CR	0	最不发达35国LDC35,最不发达4国LDC4	20	-Alkaloids of cinchona and their derivatives;salts thereof
2358	2939.3000	-咖啡因及其盐	4	0	东盟ASEAN,智利CL,巴基斯坦PK,新西兰NZ,秘鲁PE,哥斯达黎加CR	0	最不发达35国LDC35,最不发达4国LDC4	20	-Caffeine and its salts
		-麻黄碱类及其盐:							-Ephedrines and their salts:
2359	2939.4100	--麻黄碱及其盐	4	0	东盟ASEAN,智利CL,巴基斯坦PK,新西兰NZ,秘鲁PE,哥斯达黎加CR	0	最不发达35国LDC35,最不发达4国LDC4	20	--Ephedrine and its salts

序号 No.	税则号列 Tariff Line	货品名称	最惠国税率 MFN(%)	协定税率 Agreement(%)		特惠税率 S.P.(%)		普通税率 Gen.(%)	Article Description
2360	2939.4200	--假麻黄碱及其盐	4	0	东盟ASEAN,智利CL,巴基斯坦PK,新西兰NZ,秘鲁PE,哥斯达黎加CR	0	最不发达35国LDC35,最不发达4国LDC4	20	--Pseudoephedrine (INN) and its salts
2361	2939.4300	--d-去甲假麻黄碱（INN）及其盐	4	0	东盟ASEAN,智利CL,巴基斯坦PK,新西兰NZ,秘鲁PE,哥斯达黎加CR	0	最不发达35国LDC35,最不发达4国LDC4	20	--d-Norpseudoephedrine and its salts
2362	2939.4400	--去甲麻黄碱及其盐	4	0	东盟ASEAN,智利CL,巴基斯坦PK,新西兰NZ,秘鲁PE,哥斯达黎加CR	0	最不发达35国LDC35,最不发达4国LDC4	20	-- Norephedrine and its salts
2363	2939.4900	--其他	4	0	东盟ASEAN,智利CL,巴基斯坦PK,新西兰NZ,秘鲁PE,哥斯达黎加CR	0	最不发达35国LDC35,最不发达4国LDC4	20	--Other
		-茶碱和氨茶碱及其衍生物以及它们的盐:							-Theophylline and aminophylline (theophylline-ethylenediamine) and their derivatives; salts thereof:
2364	2939.5100	--芬乙茶碱（INN）及其盐	4	0	东盟ASEAN,智利CL,巴基斯坦PK,新西兰NZ,秘鲁PE,哥斯达黎加CR	0	最不发达35国LDC35,最不发达4国LDC4	20	--Fenetylline (INN) and its salts
2365	2939.5900	--其他	4	0	东盟ASEAN,智利CL,巴基斯坦PK,新西兰NZ,秘鲁PE,哥斯达黎加CR	0	最不发达35国LDC35,最不发达4国LDC4	20	--Other
		-麦角生物碱及其衍生物以及它们的盐:							-Alkaloids of rye ergot and their derivatives; salts thereof:
2366	2939.6100	--麦角新碱及其盐	4	0	东盟ASEAN,智利CL,巴基斯坦PK,新西兰NZ,秘鲁PE,哥斯达黎加CR	0	最不发达35国LDC35,最不发达4国LDC4	20	--Ergometrine (INN) and its salts
2367	2939.6200	--麦角胺及其盐	4	0	东盟ASEAN,智利CL,巴基斯坦PK,新西兰NZ,秘鲁PE,哥斯达黎加CR	0	最不发达35国LDC35,最不发达4国LDC4	20	--Ergotamine (INN) and its salts

序号 No.	税则号列 Tariff Line	货品名称	最惠国税率 MFN(%)	协定税率 Agreement(%)		特惠税率 S.P.(%)		普通税率 Gen.(%)	Article Description
2368	2939.6300	--麦角酸及其盐	4	0	东盟ASEAN,智利CL,巴基斯坦PK,新西兰NZ,秘鲁PE,哥斯达黎加CR	0	最不发达35国LDC35,最不发达4国LDC4	20	--Lysergic acid and its salts
2369	2939.6900	--其他	4	0	东盟ASEAN,智利CL,巴基斯坦PK,新西兰NZ,秘鲁PE,哥斯达黎加CR	0	最不发达35国LDC35,最不发达4国LDC4	20	--Other
		--可卡因，芽子碱、左甲苯丙胺、去氧麻黄碱（INN），去氧麻黄碱外消旋体，它们的盐、酯及其他衍生物:							--Cocaine, ecgonine, levometam-fetamine, metamfetamine (INN), metamfetamine race-mate; salts, esters and other derivatives thereof:
2370	2939.9110	---可卡因及其盐	4	0	东盟ASEAN,智利CL,巴基斯坦PK,新西兰NZ,秘鲁PE,哥斯达黎加CR	0	最不发达35国LDC35,最不发达4国LDC4	20	---Cocaine and its salts
2371	2939.9190	---其他	4	0	东盟ASEAN,智利CL,巴基斯坦PK,新西兰NZ,秘鲁PE,哥斯达黎加CR	0	最不发达35国LDC35,最不发达4国LDC4	20	---Other
		-其他:							-Other:
2372	2939.9910	---烟碱及其盐	4	0	东盟ASEAN,智利CL,巴基斯坦PK,新西兰NZ,秘鲁PE,哥斯达黎加CR	0	最不发达35国LDC35,最不发达4国LDC4	20	---Nicotine and its salts
2373	2939.9920	---番木鳖碱（士的年）及其盐	4	0	东盟ASEAN,智利CL,巴基斯坦PK,新西兰NZ,秘鲁PE,哥斯达黎加CR	0	最不发达35国LDC35,最不发达4国LDC4	17	---Strychnine and its salts
2374	2939.9990	---其他	4	0	东盟ASEAN,智利CL,巴基斯坦PK,新西兰NZ,秘鲁PE,哥斯达黎加CR	0	最不发达35国LDC35,最不发达4国LDC4	20	---Other

序号 No.	税则号列 Tariff Line	货品名称	最惠国税率 MFN(%)	协定税率 Agreement(%)		特惠税率 S.P.(%)		普通税率 Gen.(%)	Article Description
		第十三分章 其他有机化合物							Ⅻ. OTHER ORGANIC COMPOUNDS
	29.40	**化学纯糖，但蔗糖、乳糖、麦芽糖、葡萄糖及果糖除外;糖醚、糖缩醛、糖酯及其盐，但不包括税号29.37、29.38 及 29.39 的产品:**							**Sugars, chemically pure, other than sucrose, lactose, maltose, glucose and fructose;sugar ethers, sugar acetals and sugar esters, and their salts, other than products of heading No.29.37, 29.38 or 29.39:**
2375	2940.0000	化学纯糖，但蔗糖、乳糖、麦芽糖、葡萄糖及果糖除外;糖醚、糖缩醛、糖酯及其盐，但不包括税号29.37、29.38 及 29.39 的产品	6	0 5	东盟ASEAN,智利CL,新西兰NZ,秘鲁PE,哥斯达黎加CR 巴基斯坦PK	0	最不发达 35 国 LDC35,最不发达 4 国 LDC4	30	Sugars, chemically pure, other than sucrose, lactose, maltose, glucose and fructose;sugar ethers and sugar esters, and their salts, other than products of heading No.29.37, 29.38 or 29.39
	29.41	**抗菌素:**							**Antibiotics:**
		-青霉素和具有青霉烷酸结构的青霉素衍生物及其盐:							-Penicillins and their derivatives with a penicillanic acid structure; salts thereof:
		---氨苄青霉素及其盐:							---Ampicillin and its salts:
2376	2941.1011	----氨苄青霉素	6	0 5	东盟ASEAN,智利CL,巴基斯坦PK,新西兰NZ,秘鲁PE,哥斯达黎加CR 亚太APTA	0	最不发达 35 国 LDC35,最不发达 4 国 LDC4	20	----Ampicillin
2377	2941.1012	----氨苄青霉素三水酸	6	0 5	东盟ASEAN,智利CL,巴基斯坦PK,新西兰NZ,秘鲁PE,哥斯达黎加CR 亚太APTA	0	最不发达 35 国 LDC35,最不发达 4 国 LDC4	20	----Ampicillin trihydrate
2378	2941.1019	----其他	6	0 5	东盟ASEAN,智利CL,巴基斯坦PK,新西兰NZ,秘鲁PE,哥斯达黎加CR 亚太APTA	0	最不发达 35 国 LDC35,最不发达 4 国 LDC4	20	----Other
		---其他:							---Other:
2379	2941.1091	----羟氨苄青霉素	4	0	东盟ASEAN,智利CL,巴基斯坦PK,新西兰NZ,秘鲁PE,哥斯达黎加CR	0	最不发达 35 国 LDC35,最不发达 4 国 LDC4	20	----Amoxycillin

序号 No.	税则号列 Tariff Line	货品名称	最惠国税率 MFN(%)	协定税率 Agreement(%)		特惠税率 S.P.(%)		普通税率 Gen.(%)	Article Description
2380	2941.1092	----羟氨苄青霉素三水酸	4	0	东盟ASEAN,智利CL,巴基斯坦PK,新西兰NZ,秘鲁PE,哥斯达黎加CR	0	最不发达35国LDC35,最不发达4国LDC4	20	----Amoxycillin tri-hydrate
2381	2941.1093	----6-氨基青霉烷酸（6APA）	4	0	东盟ASEAN,智利CL,巴基斯坦PK,新西兰NZ,秘鲁PE,哥斯达黎加CR	0	最不发达35国LDC35,最不发达4国LDC4	20	----6-Aminopenicillanic acid
2382	2941.1094	----青霉素V	4	0	东盟ASEAN,智利CL,巴基斯坦PK,新西兰NZ,秘鲁PE,哥斯达黎加CR	0	最不发达35国LDC35,最不发达4国LDC4	20	----Penicillin V
2383	2941.1095	----磺苄青霉素	4	0	东盟ASEAN,智利CL,巴基斯坦PK,新西兰NZ,秘鲁PE,哥斯达黎加CR	0	最不发达35国LDC35,最不发达4国LDC4	20	----Sulfobenzylpenicillin
2384	2941.1096	----邻氯青霉素	4	0	东盟ASEAN,智利CL,巴基斯坦PK,新西兰NZ,秘鲁PE,哥斯达黎加CR	0	最不发达35国LDC35,最不发达4国LDC4	20	----Cloxacillin
2385	2941.1099	----其他	4	0	东盟ASEAN,智利CL,巴基斯坦PK,新西兰NZ,秘鲁PE,哥斯达黎加CR	0	最不发达35国LDC35,最不发达4国LDC4	20	----Other
2386	2941.2000	-链霉素及其衍生物以及它们的盐	4	0	东盟ASEAN,智利CL,巴基斯坦PK,新西兰NZ,秘鲁PE,哥斯达黎加CR	0	最不发达35国LDC35,最不发达4国LDC4	20	-Streptomycins and their derivatives; salts thereof
		-四环素及其衍生物以及它们的盐:							-Tetracyclines and their derivatives; salts thereof:
		---四环素及其盐:							---Tetracyclines and their salts:
2387	2941.3011	----四环素	4	0	东盟ASEAN,智利CL,巴基斯坦PK,新西兰NZ,秘鲁PE,哥斯达黎加CR,澳门MO	0	最不发达35国LDC35,最不发达4国LDC4	20	----Tetracyclines

序号 No.	税则号列 Tariff Line	货品名称	最惠国税率 MFN(%)	协定税率 Agreement(%)		特惠税率 S.P.(%)		普通税率 Gen.(%)	Article Description
2388	2941.3012	----四环素盐	4	0	东盟ASEAN,智利CL,巴基斯坦PK,新西兰NZ,秘鲁PE,哥斯达黎加CR,澳门MO	0	最不发达35国LDC35,最不发达4国LDC4	20	----Salts of tetracyclines
2389	2941.3020	---四环素衍生物及其盐	4	0	东盟ASEAN,智利CL,巴基斯坦PK,新西兰NZ,秘鲁PE,哥斯达黎加CR,澳门MO	0	最不发达35国LDC35,最不发达4国LDC4	20	---Tetracyclines derivatives and their salts
2390	2941.4000	-氯霉素及其衍生物以及它们的盐	4	0	东盟ASEAN,智利CL,巴基斯坦PK,新西兰NZ,秘鲁PE,哥斯达黎加CR	0	最不发达35国LDC35,最不发达4国LDC4	20	-Chloramphenicol and its derivative-s; salts thereof
2391	2941.5000	-红霉素及其衍生物以及它们的盐	4	0	东盟ASEAN,智利CL,巴基斯坦PK,新西兰NZ,秘鲁PE,哥斯达黎加CR,澳门MO	0	最不发达35国LDC35,最不发达4国LDC4	20	-Erythromycin and its derivatives; salts thereof
		-其他:							-Other:
2392	2941.9010	---庆大霉素及其衍生物以及它们的盐	4	0 0.4	东盟ASEAN,巴基斯坦PK,新西兰NZ,秘鲁PE,哥斯达黎加CR 智利CL	0	最不发达35国LDC35,最不发达4国LDC4	20	---Gentamycin and its derivatives; salts thereof
2393	2941.9020	---卡那霉素及其衍生物以及它们的盐	4	0 0.4	东盟ASEAN,巴基斯坦PK,新西兰NZ,秘鲁PE,哥斯达黎加CR 智利CL	0	最不发达35国LDC35,最不发达4国LDC4	20	---Kanamycin and its derivatives; salts thereof
2394	2941.9030	---利福平及其衍生物以及它们的盐	4	0 0.4	东盟ASEAN,巴基斯坦PK,新西兰NZ,秘鲁PE,哥斯达黎加CR 智利CL	0	最不发达35国LDC35,最不发达4国LDC4	20	---Rifampicin (RFP); salts thereof
2395	2941.9040	---林可霉素及其衍生物以及它们的盐	4	0 0.4	东盟ASEAN,巴基斯坦PK,新西兰NZ,秘鲁PE,哥斯达黎加CR 智利CL	0	最不发达35国LDC35,最不发达4国LDC4	20	---Lincomycin and its derivatives; salts thereof
		---头孢菌素及其衍生物以及它们的盐:							---Cephamycin and its derivatives; salts thereof:

序号 No.	税则号列 Tariff Line	货品名称	最惠国税率 MFN(%)	协定税率 Agreement(%)		特惠税率 S.P.(%)		普通税率 Gen.(%)	Article Description
2396	2941.9052	----头孢氨苄及其盐	6	0 0.6 5	东盟ASEAN,巴基斯坦PK,新西兰NZ,秘鲁PE,哥斯达黎加CR 智利CL 亚太APTA	0	最不发达35国LDC35,最不发达4国LDC4	20	----Cefalexin and its salts
2397	2941.9053	----头孢唑啉及其盐	6	0 0.6 5	东盟ASEAN,巴基斯坦PK,新西兰NZ,秘鲁PE,哥斯达黎加CR 智利CL 亚太APTA	0	最不发达35国LDC35,最不发达4国LDC4	20	----Cefazolin and its salts
2398	2941.9054	----头孢拉啶及其盐	6	0 0.6 5	东盟ASEAN,巴基斯坦PK,新西兰NZ,秘鲁PE,哥斯达黎加CR 智利CL 亚太APTA	0	最不发达35国LDC35,最不发达4国LDC4	20	----Cefradine and its salts
2399	2941.9055	----头孢三嗪(头孢曲松)及其盐	6	0 0.6 5	东盟ASEAN,巴基斯坦PK,新西兰NZ,秘鲁PE,哥斯达黎加CR 智利CL 亚太APTA	0	最不发达35国LDC35,最不发达4国LDC4	20	----Ceftriaxone and its salts
2400	2941.9056	----头孢哌酮及其盐	6	0 0.6 5	东盟ASEAN,巴基斯坦PK,新西兰NZ,秘鲁PE,哥斯达黎加CR 智利CL 亚太APTA	0	最不发达35国LDC35,最不发达4国LDC4	20	----Cefoperazone and its salts
2401	2941.9057	----头孢噻肟及其盐	6	0 0.6 5	东盟ASEAN,巴基斯坦PK,新西兰NZ,秘鲁PE,哥斯达黎加CR 智利CL 亚太APTA	0	最不发达35国LDC35,最不发达4国LDC4	20	----Cefotaxime and its salts
2402	2941.9058	----头孢克罗及其盐	6	0 0.6 5	东盟ASEAN,巴基斯坦PK,新西兰NZ,秘鲁PE,哥斯达黎加CR 智利CL 亚太APTA	0	最不发达35国LDC35,最不发达4国LDC4	20	----Cefaclor and its salts
2403	2941.9059	----其他	6	0 0.6 5	东盟ASEAN,巴基斯坦PK,新西兰NZ,秘鲁PE,哥斯达黎加CR 智利CL 亚太APTA	0	最不发达35国LDC35,最不发达4国LDC4	20	----Other
2404	2941.9060	---麦迪霉素及其衍生物以及它们的盐	6	0 0.6 4.2	东盟ASEAN,巴基斯坦PK,新西兰NZ,秘鲁PE,哥斯达黎加CR 智利CL 亚太APTA	0	最不发达35国LDC35,最不发达4国LDC4	20	---Midecamycin and its derivatives; salts thereof

序号 No.	税则号列 Tariff Line	货品名称	最惠国税率 MFN(%)	协定税率 Agreement(%)		特惠税率 S.P.(%)		普通税率 Gen.(%)	Article Description
2405	2941.9070	---乙酰螺旋霉素及其衍生物以及它们的盐	4	0 0.4	东盟ASEAN,巴基斯坦PK,新西兰NZ,秘鲁PE,哥斯达黎加CR 智利CL	0	最不发达35国LDC35,最不发达4国LDC4	20	---Acetyl-spiramycin and its derivatives; salts thereof
2406	2941.9090	---其他	6	0 0.6 5	东盟ASEAN,巴基斯坦PK,新西兰NZ,秘鲁PE,哥斯达黎加CR 智利CL 亚太APTA	0	最不发达35国LDC35,最不发达4国LDC4	20	---Other
	29.42	**其他有机化合物:**							**Other organic compounds:**
2407	2942.0000	其他有机化合物	6.5	0 5	东盟ASEAN,智利CL,新西兰NZ,秘鲁PE,哥斯达黎加CR 巴基斯坦PK	0	最不发达35国LDC35,最不发达4国LDC4	30	Other organic compounds

第三十章
药　品

注释:

一、本章不包括:

（一）食品及饮料（例如，营养品、糖尿病食品、强化食品、保健食品、滋补饮料及矿泉水）（第四类），但不包括供静脉摄入用的滋养品;

（二）用于帮助吸烟者戒烟的制剂，例如片剂、咀嚼胶或透皮贴片（税目21.06或38.24）;

（二）经特殊煅烧或精细研磨的牙科用熟石膏（税号25.20）;

（三）适合医药用的精油水馏液及水溶液（税号33.01）;

（四）税号 33.03 至 33.07 的制品，不论是否具有治疗及预防疾病的作用;

（五）加有药料的肥皂及税号34.01的其他产品;

（六）以熟石膏为基本成分的牙科用制品（税号34.07）;

（七）不作治疗及预防疾病用的血清蛋白（税号35.02）。

二、税目 30.02 所称的“免疫制品”是指直接参与免疫过程调节的多肽及蛋白质（税目 29.37 的货品除外），例如单克隆抗体（MAB）、抗体片段、抗体偶联物及抗体片段偶联物、白介素、干扰素（IFN）、趋化因子及特定的肿瘤坏死因子（TNF）、生长因子（GF）、促红细胞生成素及集落刺激因子（CSF）。

三、税号30.03及30.04以及本章注释四（四）所述的非混合产品及混合产品，按下列规定处理:

（一）非混合产品:

1. 溶于水的非混合产品;
2. 第二十八章及第二十九章的所有货品;
3. 税号13.02的单一植物浸膏，只经标定或溶于溶剂的。

（二）混合产品:

1. 胶体溶液及悬浮液（胶态硫磺除外）;
2. 从植物性混合物加工所得的植物浸膏;

Chapter 30
Pharmaceutical products

Notes:

1.This Chapter does not cover:

(a) Foods or beverages(such as dietetic，diabetic or fortified foods，food supplements，tonic beverages and mineral waters) other than nutritional preparations for intraverwas administration (SectionⅣ) ;

(b) Preparations, such as tablets, chewing gum or patches (transdermal systems), intended to assist smokers to stop smoking (heading 21.06 or 38.24);

(c) Plasters specially calcined or finely ground for use in dentistry (heading No.25.20) ;

(d) Aqueous distillates or aqueous solutions of essential oils，suitable for medicinal uses (heading No.33.01) ;

(e) Preparations of headings Nos.33.03 to 33.07，even if they have therapeutic or prophylactic properties;

(f) Soap or other products of heading No.34.01 containing added medicaments;

(g) Preparations with a basis of plaster for use in dentistry (heading No.34.07) ; or

(h) Blood albumin not prepared for therapeutic or prophylactic uses (heading No.35.02) .

2. For the purposes of heading 30.02, the expression “immunological products” applies to peptides and proteins (other than goods of heading 29.37) which are directly involved in the regulation of immunological processes, such as monoclonal antibodies (MAB), antibody fragments, antibody conjugates and antibody fragment conjugates, interleukins, interferons (IFN), chemokines and certain tumor necrosis factors (TNF), growth factors (GF), hematopoietins and colony stimulating factors (CSF).

3. For the purposes of headings Nos.30.03 and 30.04 and of Note4 (d) to this Chapter，the following are to be treated:

(a) As unmixed products:

(1) Unmixed products dissolved in water;

(2) All goods of Chapter 28 or 29;and

(3) Simple vegetable extracts of heading No.13.02，merely standardised or dissolved in any solvent;

(b) As products which have been mixed:

(1) Colloidal solutions and suspensions (other than colloidal sulphur) ;

(2) Vegetable extracts obtained by the treatment of mixtures of vegetable materials; and

3. 蒸发天然矿质水所得的盐及浓缩物。

四、 税号30.06仅适用于下列物品（这些物品只能归入税号30.06而不得归入本目录其他税号）：

（一）无菌外科肠线、类似的无菌缝合材料（包括外科或牙科用无菌可吸收缝线）及外伤创口闭合用的无菌粘合胶布；

（二）无菌昆布及无菌昆布塞条；

（三）外科或牙科用无菌吸收性止血材料；外科或牙科用无菌抗粘连阻隔材料，不论是否可吸收；

（四）用于病人的X光检查造影剂及其他诊断试剂，这些药剂是由单一产品配定剂量或由两种以上成分混合而成的；

（五）血型试剂；

（六）牙科粘固剂及其他牙科填料；骨骼粘固剂；

（七）急救药箱、药包；

（八）以激素、税目29.37的其他产品或杀精子剂为基本成分的化学避孕药物；

（九）专用于人类或作兽药用的凝胶制品，作为外科手术或体检时躯体部位的润滑剂，或者作为躯体和医疗器械之间的偶合剂；

（十）废药物即那些因超过有效保存期等原因而不适于作原用途的药品；

（十一）可确定用于造口术的用具，即裁切成型的结肠造口术、回肠造口术、尿道造口术用袋及其具有粘性的片或底盘。

(3) Salts and concentrates obtained by evaporating natural mineral waters.

4. Heading No.30.06 applies only to the following, which are to be classified in that heading and in no other heading of the nomenclature:

(a)Sterile surgical catgut, similar sterile suture materials (including sterile absorbable surgical or dental yarns) and sterile tissue adhesives for surgical wound closure;

(b)Sterile laminaria and sterile laminaria tents;

(c)Sterile absorbable surgical or dental haemostatics; sterile surgical or dental adhesion barriers, whether or not absorbable;

(d)Opacifying preparations for X-ray examinations and diagnostic reagents designed to be administered to the patient, being unmixed products put up in measured doses or products consisting of two or more ingredients which have been mixed together for such uses;

(e) Blood-grouping reagents;

(f) Dental cements and other dental fillings; bone reconstruction cements;

(g) First-aid boxes and kits;

(h) Chemical contraceptive preparations based on hormones, on other products or heading 29.37 or on spermicides.

(i) Gel preparations designed to be used in human or veterinary medicine as a lubricant for parts of the body for surgical operations or physical examinations or as a coupling agent between the body and medical instruments;

(j) Waste pharmaceuticals, that is, pharmaceutical products which are unfit for their original intended purpose due to, for example, expiry of shelf life; and

(k) Appliances identifiable for ostomy use, that is, colostomy, ileostomy and urostomy pouches cut to shape and their adhesive wafers or faceplates.

序号 No.	税则号列 Tariff Line	货品名称	最惠国税率 MFN(%)	协定税率 Agreement(%)		特惠税率 S.P.(%)		普通税率 Gen.(%)	Article Description
	30.01	**已干燥的器官疗法用腺体及其他器官，不论是否制成粉末；器官疗法用腺体、其他器官及其分泌物的提取物;肝素及其盐;其他供治疗或预防疾病用的其他税号未列名的人体或动物制品:**							**Glands and other organs for organotherapeutic uses, dried, whether or not powdered; extracts of glands or other organs or of their secretions for organotherapeutic uses; heparin and its salts; other human or animal substances prepared for therapeutic or prophylactic uses, not elsewhere specified or included:**
2408	3001.2000	-腺体、其他器官及其分泌物的提取物	3	0	东盟ASEAN,智利CL,巴基斯坦PK,新西兰NZ,秘鲁PE,哥斯达黎加CR	0	最不发达35国LDC35	30	-Extracts of glands or other organs or of their secretions
		-其他:							-Other:
2409	3001.9010	---肝素及其盐	3	0	东盟ASEAN,智利CL,巴基斯坦PK,新西兰NZ,秘鲁PE,哥斯达黎加CR	0	最不发达35国LDC35	30	---Heparin and its salts
2410	3001.9090	---其他	3	0	东盟ASEAN,智利CL,巴基斯坦PK,新西兰NZ,秘鲁PE,哥斯达黎加CR	0	最不发达35国LDC35	30	---Other
	30.02	**人血；治病、防病或诊断用的动物血制品；抗血清、其他血份及免疫制品，不论是否修饰或通过生物工艺加工制得；疫苗、毒素、培养微生物（不包括酵母）及类似产品:**							**Human blood; animal blood prepared for therapeutic, prophylactic or diagnostic uses; antisera, other blood fractions and immunological products, whether or not modified or obtained by means of biotechnological processes; vaccines, toxins, cultures of micro-organisms (excluding yeasts) and similar products:**
2411	3002.1000	-抗血清、其他血份及免疫制品，不论是否修饰或通过生物工艺加工制得	3 △0	0	东盟ASEAN,智利CL,巴基斯坦PK,新西兰NZ,秘鲁PE,哥斯达黎加CR	0	最不发达35国LDC35,最不发达4国LDC4	20	-Antisera, other blood fractions and immunological products, whether or not modified or obtained by means of biotechnological processes
2412	3002.2000	-人用疫苗	3 △0	0	东盟ASEAN,智利CL,巴基斯坦PK,新西兰NZ,秘鲁PE,哥斯达黎加CR	0	最不发达35国LDC35,最不发达4国LDC4	20	-Vaccines for human medicine

序号 No.	税则号列 Tariff Line	货品名称	最惠国税率 MFN(%)	协定税率 Agreement(%)		特惠税率 S.P.(%)		普通税率 Gen.(%)	Article Description
2413	3002.3000	-兽用疫苗	3	0	东盟ASEAN,智利CL,巴基斯坦PK,新西兰NZ,秘鲁PE,哥斯达黎加CR	0	最不发达35国LDC35,最不发达4国LDC4	20	-Vaccines for veterinary medicine
		-其他:							-Other:
2414	3002.9010	---石房蛤毒素	3	0	东盟ASEAN,智利CL,巴基斯坦PK,新西兰NZ,秘鲁PE,哥斯达黎加CR	0	最不发达35国LDC35,最不发达4国LDC4	20	---Saxitoxin
2415	3002.9020	---蓖麻毒素	3	0	东盟ASEAN,智利CL,巴基斯坦PK,新西兰NZ,秘鲁PE,哥斯达黎加CR	0	最不发达35国LDC35,最不发达4国LDC4	20	---Ricitoxin
2416	3002.9030	---细菌及病毒	3	0	东盟ASEAN,智利CL,巴基斯坦PK,新西兰NZ,秘鲁PE,哥斯达黎加CR	0	最不发达35国LDC35,最不发达4国LDC4	20	---Bacteria and Virus
2417	3002.9040	---遗传物质和基因修饰生物体	3 △0	0	东盟ASEAN,智利CL,巴基斯坦PK,新西兰NZ,秘鲁PE,哥斯达黎加CR	0	最不发达35国LDC35,最不发达4国LDC4	20	---Genetics material and Gene modified Organism
2418	3002.9090	---其他	3 △0	0	东盟ASEAN,智利CL,巴基斯坦PK,新西兰NZ,秘鲁PE,哥斯达黎加CR,香港HK	0	最不发达35国LDC35,最不发达4国LDC4	20	---Other
	30.03	**两种或两种以上成分混合而成的治病或防病用药品(不包括税号30.02、0.05或30.06的货品),未配定剂量或制成零售包装:**							**Medicaments (excluding goods of heading 30.02, 30.05 or 30.06) consisting of two or more constituents which have been mixed together for therapeutic or prophylactic uses, not put up in measured doses or in forms or packings for retail sale:**
		-含有青霉素及具有青霉烷酸结构的青霉素衍生物或链霉素及其衍生物:							-Containing penicillins or derivatives thereof, with a penicillanic acid structure, or streptomycins or their derivatives:
		---青霉素:							---Containing penicillins:

序号 No.	税则号列 Tariff Line	货品名称	最惠国 税　率 MFN(%)	协定税率 Agreement(%)		特惠税率 S.P.(%)		普通 税率 Gen.(%)	Article Description
2419	3003.1011	----氨苄青霉素	6	0 4.5	东盟ASEAN,智利CL,巴基斯坦PK,新西兰NZ,秘鲁PE,哥斯达黎加CR 亚太APTA	0	最不发达35国LDC35,最不发达4国LDC4	30	----Ampicillin
2420	3003.1012	----羟氨苄青霉素	6	0 4.5	东盟ASEAN,智利CL,巴基斯坦PK,新西兰NZ,秘鲁PE,哥斯达黎加CR 亚太APTA	0	最不发达35国LDC35,最不发达4国LDC4	30	----Amoxycillin
2421	3003.1013	----青霉素V	6	0 4.5	东盟ASEAN,智利CL,巴基斯坦PK,新西兰NZ,秘鲁PE,哥斯达黎加CR 亚太APTA	0	最不发达35国LDC35,最不发达4国LDC4	30	----Penicillin V
2422	3003.1019	----其他	6	0 4.5	东盟ASEAN,智利CL,巴基斯坦PK,新西兰NZ,秘鲁PE,哥斯达黎加CR 亚太APTA	0	最不发达35国LDC35,最不发达4国LDC4	30	----Other
2423	3003.1090	---其他	6	0 4.5	东盟ASEAN,智利CL,巴基斯坦PK,新西兰NZ,秘鲁PE,哥斯达黎加CR 亚太APTA	0	最不发达35国LDC35,最不发达4国LDC4	30	---Other
		-含有其他抗菌素:							-Containing other antibiotics:
		---头孢菌素:							---Containing cephamycins:
2424	3003.2011	----头孢噻肟	6	0 5.4	东盟ASEAN,智利CL,巴基斯坦PK,新西兰NZ,秘鲁PE,哥斯达黎加CR 亚太APTA	0	最不发达35国LDC35,最不发达4国LDC4	30	----Cefotaxime
2425	3003.2012	----头孢他啶	6	0 5.4	东盟ASEAN,智利CL,巴基斯坦PK,新西兰NZ,秘鲁PE,哥斯达黎加CR 亚太APTA	0	最不发达35国LDC35,最不发达4国LDC4	30	----Ceftazidime
2426	3003.2013	----头孢西丁	6	0 5.4	东盟ASEAN,智利CL,巴基斯坦PK,新西兰NZ,秘鲁PE,哥斯达黎加CR 亚太APTA	0	最不发达35国LDC35,最不发达4国LDC4	30	----Cefoxitin

序号 No.	税则号列 Tariff Line	货品名称	最惠国税率 MFN(%)	协定税率 Agreement(%)		特惠税率 S.P.(%)		普通税率 Gen.(%)	Article Description
2427	3003.2014	----头孢替唑	6	0 5.4	东盟ASEAN,智利CL,巴基斯坦PK,新西兰NZ,秘鲁PE,哥斯达黎加CR 亚太APTA	0	最不发达35国LDC35,最不发达4国LDC4	30	----Ceftezole
2428	3003.2015	----头孢克罗	6	0 5.4	东盟ASEAN,智利CL,巴基斯坦PK,新西兰NZ,秘鲁PE,哥斯达黎加CR 亚太APTA	0	最不发达35国LDC35,最不发达4国LDC4	30	----Cefaclor
2429	3003.2016	----头孢呋辛	6	0 5.4	东盟ASEAN,智利CL,巴基斯坦PK,新西兰NZ,秘鲁PE,哥斯达黎加CR 亚太APTA	0	最不发达35国LDC35,最不发达4国LDC4	30	----Cefuroxime
2430	3003.2017	----头孢三嗪(头孢曲松)	6	0 5.4	东盟ASEAN,智利CL,巴基斯坦PK,新西兰NZ,秘鲁PE,哥斯达黎加CR 亚太APTA	0	最不发达35国LDC35,最不发达4国LDC4	30	----Ceftriaxone
2431	3003.2018	----头孢哌酮	6	0 5.4	东盟ASEAN,智利CL,巴基斯坦PK,新西兰NZ,秘鲁PE,哥斯达黎加CR 亚太APTA	0	最不发达35国LDC35,最不发达4国LDC4	30	----Cefoperazone
2432	3003.2019	----其他	6	0 5.4	东盟ASEAN,智利CL,巴基斯坦PK,新西兰NZ,秘鲁PE,哥斯达黎加CR 亚太APTA	0	最不发达35国LDC35,最不发达4国LDC4	30	----Other
2433	3003.2090	---其他	6	0 4.2	东盟ASEAN,智利CL,巴基斯坦PK,新西兰NZ,秘鲁PE,哥斯达黎加CR 亚太APTA	0	最不发达35国LDC35,最不发达4国LDC4	30	---Other
		-含有激素或税号29.37的其他产品,但不含抗菌素:							-Containing hormones or other products of heading 29.37 but not containing antibiotics:
2434	3003.3100	--含有胰岛素	5	0 3.5	东盟ASEAN,智利CL,巴基斯坦PK,新西兰NZ,秘鲁PE,哥斯达黎加CR 亚太APTA	0	最不发达35国LDC35,最不发达4国LDC4	30	--Containing insulin

序号 No.	税则号列 Tariff Line	货品名称	最惠国税率 MFN(%)	协定税率 Agreement(%)		特惠税率 S.P.(%)		普通税率 Gen.(%)	Article Description
2435	3003.3900	--其他	6	0 4.2	东盟ASEAN,智利CL,巴基斯坦PK,新西兰NZ,秘鲁PE,哥斯达黎加CR 亚太APTA	0	最不发达35国LDC35,最不发达4国LDC4	30	--Other
		-含有生物碱及其衍生物，但不含抗菌素及税号29.37的激素或其他产品:							-Containing alkaloids or derivatives thereof but not containing hormones or other products of heading 29.37 or antibiotics:
2436	3003.4010	---含有奎宁或其盐	5	0	东盟ASEAN,智利CL,巴基斯坦PK,新西兰NZ,秘鲁PE,哥斯达黎加CR	0	最不发达35国LDC35,最不发达4国LDC4	35	---Containing quinine or its salts
2437	3003.4090	---其他	5	0	东盟ASEAN,智利CL,巴基斯坦PK,新西兰NZ,秘鲁PE,哥斯达黎加CR	0	最不发达35国LDC35,最不发达4国LDC4	30	---Other
		-其他:							-Other:
2438	3003.9010	---含有磺胺类	6	0 0.6 4.2	东盟ASEAN,巴基斯坦PK,新西兰NZ,秘鲁PE,哥斯达黎加CR,澳门MO 智利CL 亚太APTA	0	最不发达35国LDC35,最不发达4国LDC4	40	---Containing sulfa drugs
2439	3003.9020	---含有青蒿素及其衍生物	5	0 0.5	东盟ASEAN,巴基斯坦PK,新西兰NZ,秘鲁PE,哥斯达黎加CR,澳门MO 智利CL	0	最不发达35国LDC35,最不发达4国LDC4	30	---Containing artemisinins and their derivatives
2440	3003.9090	---其他	5	0 0.5	东盟ASEAN,巴基斯坦PK,新西兰NZ,秘鲁PE,哥斯达黎加CR,澳门MO 智利CL	0	最不发达35国LDC35,最不发达4国LDC4	30	---Other
	30.04	**由混合或非混合产品构成的治病或防病用药品（不包括税目30.02、30.05或30.06的货品），已配定剂量或（包括制成皮肤摄入形式的）制成零售包装:**							**Medicaments (excluding goods of heading 30.02, 30.05 or 30.06) consisting of mixed or unmixed products for therapeutic or rophylactic uses, put up in measured doses (including those in the form of transdermal administration systems) or in forms of packings for retail sale:**

序号 No.	税则号列 Tariff Line	货品名称	最惠国税 率 MFN(%)	协定税率 Agreement(%)		特惠税率 S.P.(%)		普通税率 Gen.(%)	Article Description
		-含有青霉素及具有青霉烷酸结构的青霉素衍生物或链霉素及其衍生物:							-Containing penicillins or derivatives thereof, with a penicillanic acid structure, or streptomycins or their derivatives:
		---青霉素:							---Containing penicillins:
2441	3004.1011	----氨苄青霉素制剂	6	0 0.6 4.5	东盟ASEAN,巴基斯坦PK,新西兰NZ,秘鲁PE,哥斯达黎加CR,香港HK,澳门MO 智利CL 亚太APTA	0	最不发达35国LDC35,最不发达4国LDC4	30	----Ampicillin
2442	3004.1012	----羟氨苄青霉素制剂	6	0 0.6 4.5	东盟ASEAN,巴基斯坦PK,新西兰NZ,秘鲁PE,哥斯达黎加CR,香港HK,澳门MO 智利CL 亚太APTA	0	最不发达35国LDC35,最不发达4国LDC4	30	----Amoxycillin
2443	3004.1013	----青霉素V制剂	6	0 0.6 4.5	东盟ASEAN,巴基斯坦PK,新西兰NZ,秘鲁PE,哥斯达黎加CR,香港HK,澳门MO 智利CL 亚太APTA	0	最不发达35国LDC35,最不发达4国LDC4	30	----Penicillin V
2444	3004.1019	----其他	6	0 0.6 4.5	东盟ASEAN,巴基斯坦PK,新西兰NZ,秘鲁PE,哥斯达黎加CR,香港HK,澳门MO 智利CL 亚太APTA	0	最不发达35国LDC35,最不发达4国LDC4	30	----Other
2445	3004.1090	---其他	6	0 0.6 4.5	东盟ASEAN,巴基斯坦PK,新西兰NZ,秘鲁PE,哥斯达黎加CR,香港HK,澳门MO 智利CL 亚太APTA	0	最不发达35国LDC35,最不发达4国LDC4	30	---Other
		-含有其他抗菌素:							-Containing other antibiotics:
		---头孢菌素:							---Containing cephamycins:
2446	3004.2011	----头孢噻肟制剂	6	0 0.6 5	东盟ASEAN,巴基斯坦PK,新西兰NZ,秘鲁PE,哥斯达黎加CR,香港HK 智利CL 亚太APTA	0	最不发达35国LDC35,最不发达4国LDC4	30	----Cefotaxime
2447	3004.2012	----头孢他啶制剂	6	0 0.6 5	东盟ASEAN,巴基斯坦PK,新西兰NZ,秘鲁PE,哥斯达黎加CR,香港HK 智利CL 亚太APTA	0	最不发达35国LDC35,最不发达4国LDC4	30	----Ceftazidime

序号 No.	税则号列 Tariff Line	货品名称	最惠国税率 MFN(%)	协定税率 Agreement(%)		特惠税率 S.P.(%)		普通税率 Gen.(%)	Article Description
2448	3004.2013	----头孢西丁制剂	6	0 0.6 5	东盟ASEAN,巴基斯坦PK,新西兰NZ,秘鲁PE,哥斯达黎加CR,香港HK 智利CL 亚太APTA	0	最不发达35国LDC35,最不发达4国LDC4	30	----Cefoxitin
2449	3004.2014	----头孢替唑制剂	6	0 0.6 5	东盟ASEAN,巴基斯坦PK,新西兰NZ,秘鲁PE,哥斯达黎加CR,香港HK 智利CL 亚太APTA	0	最不发达35国LDC35,最不发达4国LDC4	30	----Ceftezole
2450	3004.2015	----头孢克罗制剂	6	0 0.6 5	东盟ASEAN,巴基斯坦PK,新西兰NZ,秘鲁PE,哥斯达黎加CR,香港HK 智利CL 亚太APTA	0	最不发达35国LDC35,最不发达4国LDC4	30	----Cefaclor
2451	3004.2016	----头孢呋辛制剂	6	0 0.6 5	东盟ASEAN,巴基斯坦PK,新西兰NZ,秘鲁PE,哥斯达黎加CR,香港HK 智利CL 亚太APTA	0	最不发达35国LDC35,最不发达4国LDC4	30	----Cefuroxime
2452	3004.2017	----头孢三嗪(头孢曲松)制剂	6	0 0.6 5	东盟ASEAN,巴基斯坦PK,新西兰NZ,秘鲁PE,哥斯达黎加CR,香港HK 智利CL 亚太APTA	0	最不发达35国LDC35,最不发达4国LDC4	30	----Ceftriaxone
2453	3004.2018	----头孢哌酮制剂	6	0 0.6 5	东盟ASEAN,巴基斯坦PK,新西兰NZ,秘鲁PE,哥斯达黎加CR,香港HK 智利CL 亚太APTA	0	最不发达35国LDC35,最不发达4国LDC4	30	----Cefoperazone
2454	3004.2019	----其他	6	0 0.6 5	东盟ASEAN,巴基斯坦PK,新西兰NZ,秘鲁PE,哥斯达黎加CR,香港HK 智利CL 亚太APTA	0	最不发达35国LDC35,最不发达4国LDC4	30	----Other
2455	3004.2090	---其他	6	0 0.6 4.2	东盟ASEAN,巴基斯坦PK,新西兰NZ,秘鲁PE,哥斯达黎加CR,香港HK,澳门MO 智利CL 亚太APTA	0	最不发达35国LDC35,最不发达4国LDC4	30	---Other
		-含有激素或税号29.37的其他产品，但不含抗菌素:							-Containing hormones or other prod-ucts of heading No.29.37 but not containing antibiotics:
		--含有胰岛素:							--Containing insulin:

序号 No.	税则号列 Tariff Line	货品名称	最惠国税率 MFN(%)	协定税率 Agreement(%)		特惠税率 S.P.(%)		普通税率 Gen.(%)	Article Description
2456	3004.3110	---含有重组人胰岛素的	5	0 0.5 3.5	东盟ASEAN,巴基斯坦PK,新西兰NZ,秘鲁PE,哥斯达黎加CR 智利CL 亚太APTA	0	最不发达35国LDC35,最不发达4国LDC4	30	---Containing Recombinant human insulin
2457	3004.3190	---其他	5	0 0.5 3.5	东盟ASEAN,巴基斯坦PK,新西兰NZ,秘鲁PE,哥斯达黎加CR 智利CL 亚太APTA	0	最不发达35国LDC35,最不发达4国LDC4	30	---Other
2458	3004.3200	--含有皮质甾类激素及其衍生物或结构类似物	5	0 0.5 3.5	东盟ASEAN,巴基斯坦PK,新西兰NZ,秘鲁PE,哥斯达黎加CR,香港HK 智利CL 亚太APTA	0	最不发达35国LDC35,最不发达4国LDC4	30	--Containing corticosteroid hormones, their derivatives or structural analogues
2459	3004.3900	--其他	5	0 0.5 3.5	东盟ASEAN,巴基斯坦PK,新西兰NZ,秘鲁PE,哥斯达黎加CR,香港HK 智利CL 亚太APTA	0	最不发达35国LDC35,最不发达4国LDC4	30	--Other
		-含有生物碱及其衍生物，但不含抗菌素及税号29.37的激素或其他产品:							-Containing alkaloids or derivatives thereof but not containing hormones, other products of heading No.29.37 or antibiotics:
2460	3004.4010	---含有奎宁或其盐	5	0 0.5 4	东盟ASEAN,巴基斯坦PK,新西兰NZ,秘鲁PE,哥斯达黎加CR,香港HK 智利CL 亚太APTA	0	最不发达35国LDC35,最不发达4国LDC4	35	---Containing quinine or its salts
2461	3004.4090	---其他	5	0 0.5	东盟ASEAN,巴基斯坦PK,新西兰NZ,秘鲁PE,哥斯达黎加CR,香港HK 智利CL	0	最不发达35国LDC35,最不发达4国LDC4	30	---Other
2462	3004.5000	-含有维生素或税号29.36所列产品的其他药品	6	0 0.6 5	东盟ASEAN,巴基斯坦PK,新西兰NZ,秘鲁PE,哥斯达黎加CR,澳门MO 智利CL 亚太APTA	0	最不发达35国LDC35,最不发达4国LDC4	40	-Other medicaments containing vitamins or other products of heading No.29.36
		-其他:							-Other:
2463	3004.9010	---含有磺胺类	6	0 0.6 4.2	东盟ASEAN,巴基斯坦PK,新西兰NZ,秘鲁PE,哥斯达黎加CR,香港HK,澳门MO 智利CL 亚太APTA	0	最不发达35国LDC35,最不发达4国LDC4	40	---Containing sulfa drugs

序号 No.	税则号列 Tariff Line	货品名称	最惠国税率 MFN(%)	协定税率 Agreement(%)		特惠税率 S.P.(%)		普通税率 Gen.(%)	Article Description
2464	3004.9020	---含有联苯双酯	4	0 0.4 2.8	东盟ASEAN,巴基斯坦PK,新西兰NZ,秘鲁PE,哥斯达黎加CR,澳门MO 智利CL 亚太APTA	0	最不发达35国LDC35,最不发达4国LDC4	30	---Containing biphenyl dicarbxybte
		---中式成药:							---Medicaments of Chinese type:
2465	3004.9051	----中药酒	3	0 2	东盟ASEAN,智利CL,巴基斯坦PK,新西兰NZ,秘鲁PE,哥斯达黎加CR,香港HK,澳门MO 亚太APTA	0	最不发达35国LDC35,最不发达4国LDC4	30	----Medicated liquors or wines
2466	3004.9052	----片仔癀	3	0 2	东盟ASEAN,智利CL,巴基斯坦PK,新西兰NZ,秘鲁PE,哥斯达黎加CR,香港HK,澳门MO 亚太APTA	0	最不发达35国LDC35,最不发达4国LDC4	30	----Pien Tzu Huang
2467	3004.9053	----白药	3	0 2	东盟ASEAN,智利CL,巴基斯坦PK,新西兰NZ,秘鲁PE,哥斯达黎加CR,香港HK,澳门MO 亚太APTA	0	最不发达35国LDC35,最不发达4国LDC4	30	----Bai Yao
2468	3004.9054	----清凉油	3	0 2	东盟ASEAN,智利CL,巴基斯坦PK,新西兰NZ,秘鲁PE,哥斯达黎加CR,香港HK,澳门MO 亚太APTA	0	最不发达35国LDC35,最不发达4国LDC4	30	----Essential balm
2469	3004.9055	----安宫牛黄丸	3	0 2	东盟ASEAN,智利CL,巴基斯坦PK,新西兰NZ,秘鲁PE,哥斯达黎加CR,香港HK,澳门MO 亚太APTA	0	最不发达35国LDC35,最不发达4国LDC4	30	----Angong niuhuang wan
2470	3004.9059	----其他	3	0 2	东盟ASEAN,智利CL,巴基斯坦PK,新西兰NZ,秘鲁PE,哥斯达黎加CR,香港HK,澳门MO 亚太APTA	0	最不发达35国LDC35,最不发达4国LDC4	30	----Other
2471	3004.9060	---含有青蒿素及其衍生物	4	0 0.4	东盟ASEAN,巴基斯坦PK,新西兰NZ,秘鲁PE,哥斯达黎加CR,香港HK,澳门MO 智利CL	0	最不发达35国LDC35,最不发达4国LDC4	30	---Containing artemisinins and their derivatives
2472	3004.9090	---其他	4	0 0.4 2.8	东盟ASEAN,巴基斯坦PK,新西兰NZ,秘鲁PE,哥斯达黎加CR,香港HK,澳门MO 智利CL 亚太APTA	0	最不发达35国LDC35	30	---Other

序号 No.	税则号列 Tariff Line	货品名称	最惠国税率 MFN(%)	协定税率 Agreement(%)		特惠税率 S.P.(%)		普通税率 Gen.(%)	Article Description
	30.05	**软填料、纱布、绷带及类似物品（例如，敷料、橡皮膏、泥罨剂），经过药物浸涂或制成零售包装供医疗、外科、牙科或兽医用：**							**Wadding, gauze, bandages and similar articles (for example, dressings, adhesive plasters, poultices), impregnated or coated with pharmaceutical sub-stances or put up in forms or packings for retail sale for medical, surgical, dental or veterinary purposes:**
		-胶粘敷料及有胶粘涂层的其他物品:							-Adhesive dressings and other articles having an adhesive layer:
2473	3005.1010	---橡皮膏	5	0 0.5	东盟ASEAN,巴基斯坦PK,新西兰NZ,秘鲁PE,哥斯达黎加CR,澳门MO 智利CL	0	最不发达35国LDC35,最不发达4国LDC4	70	---Adhesive plasters
2474	3005.1090	---其他	5	0 0.5	东盟ASEAN,巴基斯坦PK,新西兰NZ,秘鲁PE,哥斯达黎加CR,澳门MO 智利CL	0	最不发达35国LDC35,最不发达4国LDC4	35	---Other
		-其他:							-Other:
2475	3005.9010	---药棉、纱布、绷带	5	0 0.5 3	东盟ASEAN,巴基斯坦PK,新西兰NZ,秘鲁PE,哥斯达黎加CR,香港HK 智利CL 亚太APTA	0	最不发达35国LDC35,最不发达4国LDC4	70	---Absorbent cotton, gauze, bandages
2476	3005.9090	---其他	5	0 0.5	东盟ASEAN,巴基斯坦PK,新西兰NZ,秘鲁PE,哥斯达黎加CR,香港HK,澳门MO 智利CL	0	最不发达35国LDC35,最不发达4国LDC4	35	---Other
	30.06	**本章注释四所规定的医药用品:**							**Pharmaceutical goods specified in Note4to this Chapter:**
2477	3006.1000	-无菌外科肠线、类似的无菌缝合材料（包括外科或牙科用无菌可吸收缝线）及外伤创口闭合用的无菌粘合胶布;无菌昆布及无菌昆布塞条;外科或牙科用无菌吸收性止血材料；外科或牙科用无菌抗粘连阻隔材料，不论是否可吸收	5	0	东盟ASEAN,智利CL,巴基斯坦PK,新西兰NZ,秘鲁PE,哥斯达黎加CR,香港HK,澳门MO	0	最不发达35国LDC35,最不发达4国LDC4	30	-Sterile surgical catgut, similar sterile suture materials (including sterile absorbable surgical or dental yarns) and sterile tissue adhesives for surgical wound closure; sterile laminaria and sterile laminaria tents; sterile absorbable surgical or dental haemostatics; sterile surgical or dental adhesion barriers, whether or not absorbable

序号 No.	税则号列 Tariff Line	货品名称	最惠国税率 MFN(%)	协定税率 Agreement(%)		特惠税率 S.P.(%)		普通税率 Gen.(%)	Article Description
2478	3006.2000	-血型试剂	3	0	东盟ASEAN,智利CL,巴基斯坦PK,新西兰NZ,秘鲁PE,哥斯达黎加CR	0	最不发达35国LDC35,最不发达4国LDC4	20	-Blood-grouping reagents
2479	3006.3000	-X光检查造影剂;用于病人的诊断试剂	4	0	东盟ASEAN,智利CL,巴基斯坦PK,新西兰NZ,秘鲁PE,哥斯达黎加CR	0	最不发达35国LDC35,最不发达4国LDC4	30	-Opacifying preparations for X-ray examinations; diagnostic reagents designed to be administered to the patient
2480	3006.4000	-牙科粘固剂及其他牙科填料;骨骼粘固剂	5	0	东盟ASEAN,智利CL,巴基斯坦PK,新西兰NZ,秘鲁PE,哥斯达黎加CR	0	最不发达35国LDC35,最不发达4国LDC4	30	-Dental cements and other dental fillings; bone reconstruction cements
2481	3006.5000	-急救药箱、药包	5	0	东盟ASEAN,智利CL,巴基斯坦PK,新西兰NZ,秘鲁PE,哥斯达黎加CR	0	最不发达35国LDC35,最不发达4国LDC4	30	-First-aid boxes and kits
		-以激素、税目29.37的其他产品或杀精子剂为基本成分的化学避孕药物:							-Chemical contraceptive preparations based on hormones, on other products of heading 29.37 or on spermicides:
2482	3006.6010	---以激素为基本成分的避孕药	0			0	最不发达35国LDC35,最不发达4国LDC4	0	---Contraceptive preparations based on hormones
2483	3006.6090	---其他	0			0	最不发达35国LDC35,最不发达4国LDC4	0	---Other
2484	3006.7000	-专用于人类或作兽药用的凝胶制品，作为外科手术或体检时躯体部位的润滑剂，或者作为躯体和医疗器械之间的偶合剂	6.5	0 5	东盟ASEAN,智利CL,新西兰NZ,秘鲁PE,哥斯达黎加CR,香港HK 巴基斯坦PK	0	最不发达35国LDC35,最不发达4国LDC4	30	-Gel preparations designed to be used in human or veterinary medicine as a lubricant for parts of the body for surgical operations or physical examinations or as a coupling agent between the body and medical instruments
		-其他:							-Other:

序号 No.	税则号列 Tariff Line	货品名称	最惠国税率 MFN(%)	协定税率 Agreement(%)		特惠税率 S.P.(%)		普通税率 Gen.(%)	Article Description
2485	3006.9100	--可确定用于造口术的用具	10	0	东盟ASEAN,新加坡SG,新西兰NZ,秘鲁PE,哥斯达黎加CR,香港HK,澳门MO	0	最不发达35国LDC35,最不发达4国LDC4	80	--Appliances identifiable for ostomy use
				1	智利CL				
				9.2	亚太APTA,巴基斯坦PK				
2486	3006.9200	--废药物	5	0	东盟ASEAN,智利CL,巴基斯坦PK,新西兰NZ,秘鲁PE,哥斯达黎加CR	0	最不发达35国LDC35,最不发达4国LDC4	30	--Waste pharmaceuticals

第三十一章
肥　料

注释:

一、本章不包括:

（一）税号05.11的动物血;

（二）单独的已有化学定义的化合物（符合下列注释二（一）、三（一）、四（一）或五所规定的化合物除外）;

（三）税号38.24的每颗重量不低于2.5克的氯化钾培养晶体（光学元件除外）;氯化钾光学元件（税号90.01）。

二、税号31.02只适用于下列货品，但未制成税号31.05所述形状或包装:

（一）符合下列任何一条规定的货品:

1.硝酸钠，不论是否纯净;

2.硝酸铵，不论是否纯净;

3.硫酸铵及硝酸铵的复盐，不论是否纯净;

4.硫酸铵，不论是否纯净;

5.硝酸钙及硝酸铵的复盐（不论是否纯净）或硝酸钙及硝酸铵的混合物;

6.硝酸钙及硝酸镁的复盐（不论是否纯净）或硝酸钙及硝酸镁的混合物;

7.氰氨化钙，不论是否纯净或用油处理;

8.尿素，不论是否纯净。

（二）由上述（一）款任何货品相互混合的肥料。

（三）由氯化铵或上述（一）或（二）款任何货品与白垩、石膏或其他无肥效无机物混合而成的肥料。

（四）由上述（一）2或8项的货品或其混合物溶于水或液氨的液体肥料。

三、税号31.03只适用于下列货品，但未制成税号31.05所述形状或包装:

（一）符合下列任何一条规定的货品:

1.碱性熔渣;

2.税号25.10的天然磷酸盐，已焙烧或经过超出清除杂质范围的热处理;

Chapter 31
Fertilizers

Notes:

1. This Chapter does not cover:

(a) Animal blood of heading No.05.11;

(b) Separate chemically defined compounds (other than those answering to the descriptions in Note 2(a), 3(a), 4(a) or 5 below); or

(c) Cultured potassium chloride crystals (other than optical elements) weighing not less than 2.5g each, of heading No.38.24; optical elements of potassium chloride (heading No.90.01) .

2. Heading No.31.02 applies only to the following goods, provided that they are not put up in the forms or packages described in heading No.31.05:

(a) Goods which answer to one or other of the descriptions given below:

(1) Sodium nitrate, whether or not pure;

(2) Ammonium nitrate, whether or not pure;

(3) Double salts, whether or not pure, of ammonium sulphate and ammonium nitrate;

(4) Ammonium sulphate, whether or not pure;

(5) Double salts (whether or not pure) or mixtures of calcium nitrate and ammonium nitrate;

(6) Double salts (whether or not pure) or mixtures of calcium nitrate and magnesium nitrate;

(7) Calcium cyanamide, whether or not pure or treated with oil;

(8) Urea, whether or not pure.

(b) Fertilizers consisting of any of the goods described in (a) above mixed together.

(c) Fertilizers consisting of ammonium chloride or of any of the goods described in (a) or (b) above mixed with chalk, gypsum or other inorganic nonfertilizing substances.

(d) Liquid fertilizers consisting of the goods of subparagraph (a) (2) or (8) above, or of mixtures of those goods, in an aqueous or ammoniacal solution.

3. Heading No.31.03 applies only to the following goods, provided that they are not put up in the forms or packages described in heading No.31.05:

(a) Goods which answer to one or other of the descriptions given below:

(1) Basic slag;

(2) Natural phosphates of heading No.25.10, calcined or further heat-treated than for the removal of impurities;

3. 过磷酸钙（一过磷酸钙、二过磷酸钙或三过磷酸钙）；

4. 磷酸氢钙，按干燥无水产品重量计含氟量不低于0.2%。

（二）由上述（一）款的任何货品相互混合的肥料，不论含氟量多少。

（三）由上述（一）或（二）款的任何货品与白垩、石膏或其他无肥效无机物混合而成的肥料，不论含氟量多少。

四、税号31.04只适用于下列货品，但未制成税号31.05所述形状或包装：

（一）符合下列任何一条规定的货品：

1. 天然粗钾盐（例如，光卤石、钾盐镁矾及钾盐）；

2. 氯化钾，不论是否纯净，但上述注释一（三）所述的产品除外；

3. 硫酸钾，不论是否纯净；

4. 硫酸镁钾，不论是否纯净。

（二）由上述（一）款任何货品相互混合的肥料。

五、磷酸二氢铵及磷酸氢二铵（不论是否纯净）及其相互之间的混合物应归入税号31.05。

六、税号31.05所称“其他肥料”，仅适用于其基本成分至少含有氮、磷、钾中一种肥效元素的肥料用产品。

(3) Superphosphates (single, double or triple);

(4) Calcium hydrogenorthophosphate containing not less than 0.2% by weight of flourine calculated on the dry anhydrous product.

(b) Fertilizers consisting of any of the goods described in (a) above mixed together, but with no account being taken of the fluorine content limit.

(c) Fertilizers consisting of any of the goods described in (a) or (b) above, but with no account being taken of the fluorine content limit, mixed with chalk, gypsum or other inorganic non-fertilizing substances.

4. Heading No.31.04 applies only to the following goods, provided that they are not put up in the forms or packages described in heading No.31.05:

(a) Goods which answer to one or other of the descriptions given below:

(1) Crude natural potassium salts (for example, car-nallite, kainite and sylvite);

(2) Potassium chloride, whether or not pure, except as provided in Note1 (c) above;

(3) Potassium sulphate, whether or not pure;

(4) Magnesium potassium sulphate, whether or not pure.

(b) Fertilizers consisting of any of the goods described in (a) above mixed together.

5. Ammonium dihydrogenorthophosphate (monoammonium phosphate) and diammonium hydrogenorthophosphate (di-ammonium phosphate), whether or not pure, and intermixtures thereof, are to be classified in heading No.31.05.

6. For the purposes of heading No.31.05, the term“other fer-tilizers”applies only to products of a kind used as fertilizers and containing, as an essential constituent, at least one of the fertilizing elements nitrogen, phosphorus or potassium.

序号 No.	税则号列 Tariff Line	货品名称	最惠国税率 MFN(%)	协定税率 Agreement(%)	特惠税率 S.P.(%)	普通税率 Gen.(%)	Article Description
	31.01	**动物或植物肥料，不论是否相互混合或经化学处理；动植物产品经混合或化学处理制成的肥料：**					**Animal or vegetable fertilizers, whether or not mixed together or chemically treated; fertilizers produced by the mixing or chemical treatment of animal or vegetable products:**
		---未经化学处理:					---Not chemically treated:

序号 No.	税则号列 Tariff Line	货品名称	最惠国税率 MFN(%)	协定税率 Agreement(%)		特惠税率 S.P.(%)		普通税率 Gen.(%)	Article Description
2487	3101.0011	----鸟粪	3	0	东盟ASEAN,智利CL,巴基斯坦PK,新西兰NZ,秘鲁PE,哥斯达黎加CR	0	最不发达35国LDC35,最不发达4国LDC4	11	----Guano
2488	3101.0019	----其他	6.5	0 0.7 5	东盟ASEAN,新西兰NZ,秘鲁PE,哥斯达黎加CR,澳门MO 智利CL 巴基斯坦PK	0	最不发达35国LDC35,最不发达4国LDC4	30	----Other
2489	3101.0090	---其他	4	0 0.4	东盟ASEAN,巴基斯坦PK,新西兰NZ,秘鲁PE,哥斯达黎加CR 智利CL	0	最不发达35国LDC35,最不发达4国LDC4	11	---Other
	31.02	**矿物氮肥及化学氮肥:**							**Mineral or chemical fertilizers, nitrogenous:**
2490	3102.1000	-尿素,不论是否水溶液	50①	0 40	香港HK 亚太APTA,巴基斯坦PK			150	-Urea, whether or not in aqueous solution
		-硫酸铵;硫酸铵和硝酸铵的复盐及混合物:							-Ammonium sulphate; double salts and mixtures of ammonium sulphate and ammonium nitrate:
2491	3102.2100	--硫酸铵	4	0	东盟ASEAN,智利CL,巴基斯坦PK,新西兰NZ,秘鲁PE,哥斯达黎加CR	0	最不发达35国LDC35	11	--Ammonium sulphate
2492	3102.2900	--其他	4	0	东盟ASEAN,智利CL,巴基斯坦PK,新西兰NZ,秘鲁PE,哥斯达黎加CR	0	最不发达35国LDC35	11	--Other
2493	3102.3000	-硝酸铵,不论是否水溶液	4	0 0.4	东盟ASEAN,巴基斯坦PK,新西兰NZ,秘鲁PE,哥斯达黎加CR 智利CL	0	最不发达35国LDC35	11	-Ammonium nitrate, whether or not in aqueous solution
2494	3102.4000	-硝酸铵与碳酸钙或其他无肥效无机物的混合物	4	0	东盟ASEAN,智利CL,巴基斯坦PK,新西兰NZ,秘鲁PE,哥斯达黎加CR	0	最不发达35国LDC35	11	-Mixtures of ammonium nitrate with calcium carbonate or other inorganic nonfertilizing substances
2495	3102.5000	-硝酸钠	4	0 0.4	东盟ASEAN,巴基斯坦PK,新西兰NZ,秘鲁PE,哥斯达黎加CR 智利CL	0	最不发达35国LDC35	11	-Sodium nitrate

① 配额税率（In-quota rate）：4%；配额暂定税率为：1%。

序号 No.	税则号列 Tariff Line	货品名称	最惠国税率 MFN(%)	协定税率 Agreement(%)		特惠税率 S.P.(%)		普通税率 Gen.(%)	Article Description
2496	3102.6000	-硝酸钙和硝酸铵的复盐及混合物	4	0	东盟ASEAN,巴基斯坦PK,新西兰NZ,秘鲁PE,哥斯达黎加CR	0	最不发达35国LDC35	11	-Double salts and mixtures of calcium nitrate and ammonium nitrate
				0.4	智利CL				
2497	3102.8000	-尿素及硝酸铵混合物的水溶液或氨水溶液	4	0	东盟ASEAN,智利CL,巴基斯坦PK,新西兰NZ,秘鲁PE,哥斯达黎加CR	0	最不发达35国LDC35	11	-Mixtures of urea and ammonium ni-trate in aqueous or ammoniacal solution
		-其他,包括上述子目未列名的混合物:							-Other, including mixtures not specified in the foregoing subheadings:
2498	3102.9010	---氰氨化钙	4	0	东盟ASEAN,智利CL,巴基斯坦PK,新西兰NZ,秘鲁PE,哥斯达黎加CR	0	最不发达35国LDC35	11	---Calcium cyanamide
2499	3102.9090	---其他	4	0	东盟ASEAN,巴基斯坦PK,新西兰NZ,秘鲁PE,哥斯达黎加CR	0	最不发达35国LDC35	11	---Other
				0.4	智利CL				
	31.03	**矿物磷肥及化学磷肥:**							**Mineral or chemical fertilizers, phosphatic:**
		-过磷酸钙:							-Superphosphates:
2500	3103.1010	---重过磷酸钙	4 △1	0	东盟ASEAN,智利CL,巴基斯坦PK,新西兰NZ,秘鲁PE,哥斯达黎加CR	0	最不发达35国LDC35	11	---Triple superphosphates
2501	3103.1090	---其他	4 △1	0	东盟ASEAN,智利CL,巴基斯坦PK,新西兰NZ,秘鲁PE,哥斯达黎加CR	0	最不发达35国LDC35	11	---Other
2502	3103.9000	-其他	4 △1	0	东盟ASEAN,智利CL,巴基斯坦PK,新西兰NZ,秘鲁PE,哥斯达黎加CR	0	最不发达35国LDC35	11	-Other
	31.04	**矿物钾肥及化学钾肥:**							**Mineral or chemical fertilizers, potassic:**
		-氯化钾:							-Potassium chloride:
2503	3104.2020	---纯氯化钾	3	0	东盟ASEAN,智利CL,巴基斯坦PK,新西兰NZ,秘鲁PE,哥斯达黎加CR	0	最不发达35国LDC35	11	---Pure
2504	3104.2090	---其他	3 △1	0	东盟ASEAN,智利CL,巴基斯坦PK,新西兰NZ,秘鲁PE,哥斯达黎加CR	0	最不发达35国LDC35	11	---Other
2505	3104.3000	-硫酸钾	3 △1	0	东盟ASEAN,智利CL,巴基斯坦PK,新西兰NZ,秘鲁PE,哥斯达黎加CR	0	最不发达35国LDC35	11	-Potassium sulphate
		-其他:							-Other:

序号 No.	税则号列 Tariff Line	货品名称	最惠国 税　率 MFN(%)	协定税率 Agreement(%)		特惠税率 S.P.(%)		普通 税率 Gen.(%)	Article Description
2506	3104.9010	---光卤石、钾盐及其他天然粗钾盐	3 △1	0	东盟ASEAN,智利CL,巴基斯坦PK,新西兰NZ,秘鲁PE,哥斯达黎加CR	0	最不发达35国LDC35	11	---Carnallite, sylvite and other crude natural potassium salts
2507	3104.9090	---其他	3 △1	0	东盟ASEAN,智利CL,巴基斯坦PK,新西兰NZ,秘鲁PE,哥斯达黎加CR	0	最不发达35国LDC35	11	---Other
	31.05	**含氮、磷、钾中两种或三种肥效元素的矿物肥料或化学肥料;其他肥料;制成片及类似形状或每包毛重不超过10公斤的本章各项货品:**							**Mineral or chemical fertilizers containing two or three of the fertilizing elements nitrogen, phosphorus and potassium; other fertilizers; goods of this Chapter in tablets or similar forms or in packages of a gross weight not exceeding 10kg:**
2508	3105.1000	-制成片及类似形状或每包毛重不超过10公斤的本章各项货品	4 △1	0 0.4	东盟ASEAN,巴基斯坦PK,新西兰NZ,秘鲁PE,哥斯达黎加CR,香港HK 智利CL	0	最不发达35国LDC35	11	-Goods of this Chapter in tablets or similar forms or in packages of a gross weight not exceeding 10kg
2509	3105.2000	-含氮、磷、钾三种肥效元素的矿物肥料或化学肥料	50[①]					150	-Mineral or chemical fertilizers containing the three fertilizing elements nitrogen, phosphorus and potassium
2510	3105.3000	-磷酸氢二铵	50[②]					150	-Diammonium hy drogenorthophosphate (diammonium phosphate)
2511	3105.4000	-磷酸二氢铵及磷酸二氨铵与磷酸氢二铵的混合物	4 △1	0	东盟ASEAN,智利CL,巴基斯坦PK,新西兰NZ,秘鲁PE,哥斯达黎加CR	0	最不发达35国LDC35	11	-Ammonium dihydrogenorthophosphate (monoammonium phosphate) and mixtures thereof with diammonium hydrogenorthophosphate (diammonium phosphate)
		-其他含氮、磷两种肥效元素的矿物肥料或化学肥料:							-Other mineral or chemical fertilizers containing the two fertilizing elements nitrogen and phosphorus:

① 配额税率（In-quota rate）：4%；配额暂定税率为：1%。
② 配额税率（In-quota rate）：4%；配额暂定税率为：1%。

序号 No.	税则号列 Tariff Line	货品名称	最惠国税率 MFN(%)	协定税率 Agreement(%)		特惠税率 S.P.(%)		普通税率 Gen.(%)	Article Description
2512	3105.5100	--含有硝酸盐及磷酸盐	4 △1	0 0.4	东盟ASEAN,巴基斯坦PK,新西兰NZ,秘鲁PE,哥斯达黎加CR 智利CL	0	最不发达35国LDC35	11	--Containing nitrates and phosphates
2513	3105.5900	--其他	4 △1	0	东盟ASEAN,智利CL,巴基斯坦PK,新西兰NZ,秘鲁PE,哥斯达黎加CR	0	最不发达35国LDC35	11	--Other
2514	3105.6000	-含磷、钾两种肥效元素的矿物肥料或化学肥料	4 △1	0	东盟ASEAN,智利CL,巴基斯坦PK,新西兰NZ,秘鲁PE,哥斯达黎加CR	0	最不发达35国LDC35	11	-Mineral or chemical fertilizers containing the two fertilizing elements phosphorus and potassium
2515	3105.9000	-其他	4 △1	0 0.4	东盟ASEAN,巴基斯坦PK,新西兰NZ,秘鲁PE,哥斯达黎加CR,香港HK 智利CL	0	最不发达35国LDC35	11	-Other

第三十二章

鞣料浸膏及染料浸膏；鞣酸及其衍生物；染料、颜料及其他着色料；油漆及清漆；油灰及其他类似胶粘剂；墨水、油墨

注释:

一、本章不包括:

（一）单独的已有化学定义的化学元素及化合物（税号32.03及32.04的货品、税号32.06的用作发光体的无机产品、税号32.07所述形状的熔融石英或其他熔融硅石制成的玻璃及税号32.12的零售形状或零售包装的染料及其他着色料除外）；

（二）税号29.36至29.39、29.41及35.01至35.04的鞣酸盐及其他鞣酸衍生物；

（三）沥青胶粘剂（税号27.15）。

二、税号 32.04 包括生产偶氮染料用的稳定重氮盐与偶合物的混合物。

三、税号32.03、32.04、32.05及32.06也包括以着色料为基本成分的制品（例如，税号32.06包括以税号25.30或第二十八章的颜料，金属粉片及金属粉末为基本成分的制品）。该制品是用作原材料着色剂的拼料。但以上税号不包括分散在非水介质中呈液状或浆状的制漆用颜料，例如，税号32.12的瓷漆及税号32.07、32.08、32.09、32.10、32.12、32.13及32.15的其他制品。

四、税号32.08包括由税号39.01至39.13所列产品溶于挥发性有机溶剂的溶液（胶棉除外），但溶剂重量必须超过溶液重量的50%。

五、本章所称“着色料”，不包括作为油漆填料的产品，不

Chapter 32

Tanning or dyeing extracts; tannins and their derivatives; dyes, pigments and other colouring matter; paints and varnishes; putty and other mastics; inks

Notes:

1.This Chapter does not cover:

(a) Separate chemically defined elements or compounds (except those of heading No.32.03 or 32.04, inorganic products of a kind used as luminophores (heading No.32.06), glass obtained from fused quartz or other fused silica in the forms provided for in heading No.32.07, and also dyes and other colouring matter put up in forms or packings for retail sale, of heading No.32.12);

(b) Tannates or other tannin derivatives of products of headings Nos.29.36 to 29.39, 29.41 or 35.01 to 35.04; or

(c) Mastics of asphalt or other bituminous mastics (heading No.27.15).

2.Heading No.32.04 includes mixtures of stabilized diazonium salts and couplers for the production of azo dyes.

3.Headings Nos.32.03, 32.04, 32.05 and 32.06 apply also to preparations based on colouring matter (including, in the case of heading No.32.06, colouring pigments of heading No.25.30 or Chapter 28, metal flakes and metal powders), of a kind used for colouring any material or used as ingredients in the manufacture of colouring preparations.The headings do not apply, however, to pigments dispersed in nonaqueous media, in liquid or paste form, of a kind used in the manufacture of paints, including enamels (heading No.32.12), or to other preparations of heading No.32.07, 32.08, 32.09, 32.10, 32.12, 32.13 or 32.15.

4.Heading No.32.08 includes solutions (other than collodions) consisting of any of the products specified in headings Nos.39.01 to 39.13in volatile organic solvents when the weight of the solvent exceeds 50% of the weight of the solution.

5.The expression “colouring matter” in this Chapter does

论这些产品能否用于水浆涂料的着色。

not include products of a kind used as extenders in oil paints, whether or not they are also suitable for colouring distem pers.

六、税号32.12所称“压印箔”，只包括用以压印诸如书本封面或帽带之类的薄片，这些薄片由以下材料构成：

（一）金属粉（包括贵金属粉）或颜料经胶水、明胶及其他粘合剂凝结而成的；

（二）金属（包括贵金属）或颜料沉积于任何材料衬片上的。

6.The expression “stamping foils” in heading No.32.12 aplies only to thin sheets of a kind used for printing, for example, book covers or hat bands, and consisting of:

(a)Metallic powder(including powder of precious metal) or pigment, agglomerated with glue, gelatin or other binder; or

(b)Metal (including precious metal) or pigment, deposited on a supporting sheet of any material.

序号 No.	税则号列 Tariff Line	货品名称	最惠国税率 MFN(%)	协定税率 Agreement(%)		特惠税率 S.P.(%)		普通税率 Gen.(%)	Article Description
	32.01	**植物鞣料浸膏;鞣酸及其盐、醚、酯和其他衍生物:**							**Tanning extracts of vegetable origin; tannins and their salts, ethers, esters and other derivatives:**
2516	3201.1000	-坚木浸膏	5	0	东盟ASEAN,智利CL,巴基斯坦PK,新西兰NZ,秘鲁PE,哥斯达黎加CR	0	最不发达35国LDC35	35	-Quebracho extract
2517	3201.2000	-荆树皮浸膏	6.5	0	东盟ASEAN,智利CL,新西兰NZ,秘鲁PE,哥斯达黎加CR	0	最不发达35国LDC35	35	-Wattle extract
				5	巴基斯坦PK				
		-其他:							-Other:
2518	3201.9010	---其他鞣料浸膏	6.5	0	东盟ASEAN,智利CL,新西兰NZ,秘鲁PE,哥斯达黎加CR	0	最不发达35国LDC35	40	---Other tanning extracts
				5	巴基斯坦PK				
2519	3201.9090	---其他	6.5	0	东盟ASEAN,智利CL,新西兰NZ,秘鲁PE,哥斯达黎加CR	0	最不发达35国LDC35	35	---Other
				5	巴基斯坦PK				
	32.02	**有机合成鞣料;无机鞣料;鞣料制剂，不论是否含有天然鞣料;预鞣用酶制剂:**							**Synthetic organic tanning substances; inorganic tanning substances; tanning preparations, whether or not containing natural tanning substances; enzymatic preparations for pretanning:**
2520	3202.1000	-有机合成鞣料	6.5	0	东盟ASEAN,智利CL,新西兰NZ,秘鲁PE,哥斯达黎加CR,香港HK	0	最不发达35国LDC35	35	-Synthetic organic tanning substances
				5	巴基斯坦PK				

序号 No.	税则号列 Tariff Line	货品名称	最惠国税率 MFN(%)	协定税率 Agreement(%)		特惠税率 S.P.(%)		普通税率 Gen.(%)	Article Description
2521	3202.9000	-其他	6.5	0 5	东盟ASEAN,智利CL,新西兰NZ,秘鲁PE,哥斯达黎加CR,香港HK,澳门MO 巴基斯坦PK	0	最不发达35国LDC35	35	-Other
	32.03	**动植物质着色料（包括染料浸膏，但动物炭黑除外），不论是否已有化学定义;本章注释三所述的以动植物质着色料为基本成分的制品:**							**Colouring matter of vegetable or ani-mal origin (including dyeing extracts but excluding animal black), whether or not chemically efined; preparations as speci-fied in Note 3 to this Chapter based on col-ouring matter of vege-table or animal origin:**
		---植物质着色料及以其为基本成分的制品:							---Colouring matter of vegetable origin and preparations based thereon:
2522	3203.0011	----天然靛蓝及以其为基本成分的制品	6.5	0 0.7 4.9 5	东盟ASEAN,新西兰NZ,哥斯达黎加CR 智利CL 秘鲁PE 巴基斯坦PK	0	最不发达35国LDC35,最不发达4国LDC4	80	----Natural indigo and preparations based thereon
2523	3203.0019	----其他	6.5	0 0.7 4.9 5	东盟ASEAN,新西兰NZ,哥斯达黎加CR,澳门MO 智利CL 秘鲁PE 巴基斯坦PK	0	最不发达35国LDC35,最不发达4国LDC4	45	----Other
2524	3203.0020	---动物质着色料及以其为基本成分的制品	6.5	0 0.7 4.9 5	东盟ASEAN,新西兰NZ,哥斯达黎加CR 智利CL 秘鲁PE 巴基斯坦PK	0	最不发达35国LDC35,最不发达4国LDC4	50	---Colouring matter of animal origin and preparations based thereon
	32.04	**有机合成着色料，不论是否已有化学定义;本章注释三所述的以有机合成着色料为基本成分的制品;用作荧光增白剂或发光体的有机合成产品，不论是否已有化学定义:**							**Synthetic organic col-ouring matter, whether or not chemically de-fined; preparations as specified in Note 3 to this Chapter based on synthetic or -ganic col-ouring matter; syn-thetic organic products of a kind used as fluores-cent brightening agents or -as luminophores, whether or not chemi-cally defined:**

序号 No.	税则号列 Tariff Line	货品名称	最惠国税率 MFN(%)	协定税率 Agreement(%)		特惠税率 S.P.(%)		普通税率 Gen.(%)	Article Description
		-有机合成着色料及本章注释三所述的以有机合成着色料为基本成分的制品:							-Synthetic organic colouring matter and preparations based thereon as specified in Note 3 to this Chapter:
2525	3204.1100	--分散染料及以其为基本成分的制品	6.5	0 5.8	东盟ASEAN,智利CL,巴基斯坦PK,新西兰NZ,秘鲁PE,哥斯达黎加CR 亚太APTA	0	最不发达35国LDC35,最不发达4国LDC4	35	--Disperse dyes and preparations based thereon
2526	3204.1200	--酸性染料（不论是否预金属络合）及以其为基本成分的制品;媒染染料及以其为基本成分的制品	6.5	0 5.8	东盟ASEAN,智利CL,巴基斯坦PK,新西兰NZ,秘鲁PE,哥斯达黎加CR,香港HK,台湾TW 亚太APTA	0	最不发达35国LDC35,最不发达4国LDC4	35	--Acid dyes, whether or not premetallized, and preparations based there-on; mordant dyes and preparations based thereon
2527	3204.1300	--碱性染料及以其为基本成分的制品	6.5	0 6	东盟ASEAN,智利CL,巴基斯坦PK,新西兰NZ,秘鲁PE,哥斯达黎加CR 亚太APTA	0	最不发达35国LDC35,最不发达4国LDC4	35	--Basic dyes and preparations based thereon
2528	3204.1400	--直接染料及以其为基本成分的制品	6.5	0 6	东盟ASEAN,智利CL,巴基斯坦PK,新西兰NZ,秘鲁PE,哥斯达黎加CR,台湾TW 亚太APTA	0	最不发达35国LDC35,最不发达4国LDC4	35	--Direct dyes and preparations based thereon
		--瓮染料（包括颜料用的）及以其为基本成分的制品:							--Vat dyes (including those usable in that state as pigments) and preparations based thereon:
2529	3204.1510	---合成靛蓝（还原靛蓝）	6.5	0 6	东盟ASEAN,智利CL,巴基斯坦PK,新西兰NZ,秘鲁PE,哥斯达黎加CR 亚太APTA	0	最不发达35国LDC35,最不发达4国LDC4	35	---Synthetic indigo (reductive indigo)
2530	3204.1590	---其他	6.5	0 6	东盟ASEAN,智利CL,巴基斯坦PK,新西兰NZ,秘鲁PE,哥斯达黎加CR 亚太APTA	0	最不发达35国LDC35,最不发达4国LDC4	35	---Other
2531	3204.1600	--活性染料及以其为基本成分的制品	6.5	0 5.8	东盟ASEAN,智利CL,巴基斯坦PK,新西兰NZ,秘鲁PE,哥斯达黎加CR,香港HK,台湾TW 亚太APTA	0	最不发达35国LDC35,最不发达4国LDC4	35	--Reactive dyes and preparations based thereon

序号 No.	税则号列 Tariff Line	货品名称	最惠国税率 MFN(%)	协定税率 Agreement(%)		特惠税率 S.P.(%)		普通税率 Gen.(%)	Article Description
2532	3204.1700	--颜料及以其为基本成分的制品	6.5	0 0.7 4.6	东盟ASEAN,巴基斯坦PK,新西兰NZ,秘鲁PE,哥斯达黎加CR,香港HK,台湾TW 智利CL 亚太APTA	0	最不发达35国LDC35,最不发达4国LDC4	35	--Pigments and preparations based thereon
		--其他，包括由子目号3204.11至3204.19中两个或多个子目所列着色料组成的混合物:							--Other, including mixtures of colouring matter of two or more of the subheadings Nos.3204.11 to 3204.19:
		---硫化染料及以其为基本成分的制品:							---Sulphur dyes and preparations based thereon:
2533	3204.1911	----硫化黑（硫化青）及以其为基本成分的制品	6.5	0 6	东盟ASEAN,智利CL,巴基斯坦PK,新西兰NZ,秘鲁PE,哥斯达黎加CR 亚太APTA	0	最不发达35国LDC35,最不发达4国LDC4	35	----Sulphur black and preparations based thereon
2534	3204.1919	----其他	6.5	0 6	东盟ASEAN,智利CL,巴基斯坦PK,新西兰NZ,秘鲁PE,哥斯达黎加CR 亚太APTA	0	最不发达35国LDC35,最不发达4国LDC4	35	----Other
2535	3204.1990	---其他	6.5	0 6	东盟ASEAN,智利CL,巴基斯坦PK,新西兰NZ,秘鲁PE,哥斯达黎加CR,台湾TW 亚太APTA	0	最不发达35国LDC35,最不发达4国LDC4	35	---Other
2536	3204.2000	-用作荧光增白剂的有机合成产品	6.5	0 6	东盟ASEAN,智利CL,巴基斯坦PK,新西兰NZ,秘鲁PE,哥斯达黎加CR,香港HK,台湾TW 亚太APTA	0	最不发达35国LDC35,最不发达4国LDC4	40	-Synthetic organic products of a kind used as flourescent brightening agents
		-其他:							-Other:
2537	3204.9010	---生物染色剂及染料指示剂	6.5	0 6	东盟ASEAN,智利CL,巴基斯坦PK,新西兰NZ,秘鲁PE,哥斯达黎加CR 亚太APTA	0	最不发达35国LDC35,最不发达4国LDC4	20	---Biological stains and dye indicators
2538	3204.9090	---其他	6.5	0 6	东盟ASEAN,智利CL,巴基斯坦PK,新西兰NZ,秘鲁PE,哥斯达黎加CR 亚太APTA	0	最不发达35国LDC35,最不发达4国LDC4	40	---Other

序号 No.	税则号列 Tariff Line	货品名称	最惠国税率 MFN(%)	协定税率 Agreement(%)		特惠税率 S.P.(%)		普通税率 Gen.(%)	Article Description
	32.05	**色淀;本章注释三所述的以色淀为基本成分的制品:**							**Colour lakes; preparations as specified in Note 3 to this Chapter based on colour lakes:**
2539	3205.0000	色淀;本章注释三所述的以色淀为基本成分的制品	6.5	0 5	东盟ASEAN,智利CL,新西兰NZ,秘鲁PE,哥斯达黎加CR 巴基斯坦PK	0	最不发达35国LDC35,最不发达4国LDC4	35	Colour lakes; preparations as specified in Note 3 to this Chapter based on colour lakes
	32.06	**其他着色料;本章注释三所述的制品,但税号32.03、32.04及32.05的货品除外;用作发光体的无机产品,不论是否已有化学定义:**							**Other colouring matter; preparations as specified in Note 3 to this Chapter, other than those of heading No.32.03, 32.04 or 32.05; inorganic products of a kind used as luminophores, whether or not chemically defined:**
		-以二氧化钛为基本成分的颜料及制品:							-Pigments and preparations based on titanium dioxide:
		--以干物质计二氧化钛含量在80%及以上的:							--Containing 80% or more by weight of titanium dioxide calculated on the dry matter:
2540	3206.1110	---钛白粉	6.5	0 5	东盟ASEAN,智利CL,新西兰NZ,秘鲁PE,哥斯达黎加CR,台湾TW 巴基斯坦PK	0	最不发达35国LDC35,最不发达4国LDC4	30	---Titanium White
2541	3206.1190	---其他	6.5	0 5	东盟ASEAN,智利CL,新西兰NZ,秘鲁PE,哥斯达黎加CR 巴基斯坦PK	0	最不发达35国LDC35,最不发达4国LDC4	30	---Other
2542	3206.1900	--其他	10	0 5	东盟ASEAN,智利CL,新加坡SG,新西兰NZ,秘鲁PE,哥斯达黎加CR,香港HK,台湾TW 巴基斯坦PK	0	最不发达35国LDC35,最不发达4国LDC4	30	--Other
2543	3206.2000	-以铬化合物为基本成分的颜料及制品	6.5	0 5	东盟ASEAN,智利CL,新西兰NZ,秘鲁PE,哥斯达黎加CR 巴基斯坦PK	0	最不发达35国LDC35,最不发达4国LDC4	35	-Pigments and preparations based on chromium compounds

序号 No.	税则号列 Tariff Line	货品名称	最惠国税率 MFN(%)	协定税率 Agreement(%)		特惠税率 S.P.(%)		普通税率 Gen.(%)	Article Description
		-其他着色料及其他制品:							-Other colouring matter and other preparations:
2544	3206.4100	--群青及以其为基本成分的制品	6.5	0 5	东盟ASEAN,智利CL,新西兰NZ,秘鲁PE,哥斯达黎加CR 巴基斯坦PK	0	最不发达35国LDC35,最不发达4国LDC4	35	--Ultramarine and preparations based thereon
		--锌钡白及以硫化锌为基本成分的其他颜料和制品:							--Lithopone and other pigments and preparations based on zinc sulphide:
2545	3206.4210	---锌钡白	6.5	0 5	东盟ASEAN,智利CL,新西兰NZ,秘鲁PE,哥斯达黎加CR 巴基斯坦PK	0	最不发达35国LDC35,最不发达4国LDC4	30	---Lithopone
2546	3206.4290	---其他	6.5	0 5	东盟ASEAN,智利CL,新西兰NZ,秘鲁PE,哥斯达黎加CR 巴基斯坦PK	0	最不发达35国LDC35,最不发达4国LDC4	30	---Other
		--其他: ---以铋化合物为基本成分的颜料及制品:							--Other: ---Pigments and preparations based on Bismuth compounds:
2547	3206.4911	----以钒酸铋为基本成分的颜料及制品	6.5	0 3.3	东盟ASEAN,智利CL,巴基斯坦PK,新西兰NZ,秘鲁PE,哥斯达黎加CR,香港HK,台湾TW 亚太APTA	0	最不发达35国LDC35,最不发达4国LDC4	35	----Pigments and preparations based on Bismuth vanadium tetraoxide
2548	3206.4919	----其他	6.5	0 3.3	东盟ASEAN,智利CL,巴基斯坦PK,新西兰NZ,秘鲁PE,哥斯达黎加CR,香港HK,台湾TW 亚太APTA	0	最不发达35国LDC35,最不发达4国LDC4	35	----Other
2549	3206.4990	---其他	6.5	0 3.3	东盟ASEAN,智利CL,巴基斯坦PK,新西兰NZ,秘鲁PE,哥斯达黎加CR,香港HK,台湾TW 亚太APTA	0	最不发达35国LDC35,最不发达4国LDC4	35	---Other
2550	3206.5000	-用作发光体的无机产品	6.5	0 5 5.9	东盟ASEAN,智利CL,新西兰NZ,秘鲁PE,哥斯达黎加CR 巴基斯坦PK 亚太APTA	0	最不发达35国LDC35,最不发达4国LDC4	35	-Inorganic products of a kind used as luminophores

序号 No.	税则号列 Tariff Line	货品名称	最惠国税率 MFN(%)	协定税率 Agreement(%)		特惠税率 S.P.(%)		普通税率 Gen.(%)	Article Description
	32.07	**陶瓷、搪瓷及玻璃工业用的调制颜料、遮光剂、着色剂、珐琅和釉料、釉底料（泥釉）、光瓷釉以及类似产品;搪瓷玻璃料及其他玻璃，呈粉、粒或粉片状的:**							**Prepared pigments, prepared opacifiers and prepared colours, vitrifiable enamels and glazes, engobes (slips), liquid lustres and similar preparations, of a kind used in the ceramic, enamelling or glass industry;glass frit and other glass, in the form of powder, granules or flakes:**
2551	3207.1000	-调制颜料、遮光剂、着色剂及类似制品	5	0 0.5	东盟ASEAN,巴基斯坦PK,新西兰NZ,秘鲁PE,哥斯达黎加CR 智利CL	0	最不发达35国LDC35,最不发达4国LDC4	50	-Prepared pigments, prepared opacifiers, prepared colours and similar preparations
2552	3207.2000	-珐琅和釉料、釉底料（泥釉）及类似制品	5	0 0.5	东盟ASEAN,巴基斯坦PK,新西兰NZ,秘鲁PE,哥斯达黎加CR 智利CL	0	最不发达35国LDC35,最不发达4国LDC4	50	-Vitrifiable enamels and glazes, engobes (slips) and similar preparations
2553	3207.3000	-光瓷釉及类似制品	5	0	东盟ASEAN,智利CL,巴基斯坦PK,新西兰NZ,秘鲁PE,哥斯达黎加CR	0	最不发达35国LDC35,最不发达4国LDC4	50	-Liquid lustres and similar preparations
2554	3207.4000	-搪瓷玻璃料及其他玻璃，呈粉、粒或粉片状的	5	0 0.5	东盟ASEAN,巴基斯坦PK,新西兰NZ,秘鲁PE,哥斯达黎加CR 智利CL	0	最不发达35国LDC35,最不发达4国LDC4	50	-Glass frit and other glass, in the form of powder, granules or flakes
	32.08	**以合成聚合物或化学改性天然聚合物为基本成分的油漆及清漆（包括瓷漆及大漆），分散于或溶于非水介质的;本章注释四所述的溶液:**							**Paints and varnishes (including enamels and lacquers) based on synthetic polymers or chemically modified natural polymers, dispersed or dissolved in a nonaqueous medium; solutions as defined in Note 4 to this Chapter:**
2555	3208.1000	-以聚酯为基本成分	10	0 1 5 9	东盟ASEAN,新加坡SG,新西兰NZ,哥斯达黎加CR,香港HK,澳门MO,台湾TW 智利CL 巴基斯坦PK,秘鲁PE 亚太APTA	0	最不发达35国LDC35,最不发达4国LDC4	50	-Based on polyesters

序号 No.	税则号列 Tariff Line	货品名称	最惠国税率 MFN(%)	协定税率 Agreement(%)		特惠税率 S.P.(%)		普通税率 Gen.(%)	Article Description
		-以丙烯酸聚合物或乙烯聚合物为基本成分:							-Based on acrylic or vinyl polymers:
2556	3208.2010	---以丙烯酸聚合物为基本成分	10	0 1 5 9	东盟ASEAN,新加坡SG,新西兰NZ,哥斯达黎加CR,台湾TW 智利CL 巴基斯坦PK,秘鲁PE 亚太APTA	0	最不发达35国LDC35	50	---Based on acrylic polymers
	ex32082010	分散于或溶于非水介质的光导纤维用涂料(主要成分为聚胺酯丙烯酸酯类化合物)	△6						Paint for optial fibers (based on polyaminate acrylate resin polymers), dispersed or dissolved in a nonaqueous medium
2557	3208.2020	---以乙烯聚合物为基本成分	10	0 1 5 9	东盟ASEAN,新西兰NZ,哥斯达黎加CR 智利CL 巴基斯坦PK,秘鲁PE 亚太APTA	0	最不发达35国LDC35	50	---Based on vinyl polymers
		-其他:							-Other:
2558	3208.9010	---以聚胺酯类化合物为基本成分	10	0 1 5 9	东盟ASEAN,新加坡SG,新西兰NZ,哥斯达黎加CR 智利CL 巴基斯坦PK,秘鲁PE 亚太APTA	0	最不发达35国LDC35	50	---Based on polyurethane polymers
	ex32089010	光导纤维用涂料(主要成分为聚胺酯丙烯酸酯类化合物)	△6						Paint for optial fibers (based on polyaminate acrylate resin polymers)
2559	3208.9090	---其他	10	0 1 5 9	东盟ASEAN,新加坡SG,新西兰NZ,哥斯达黎加CR,香港HK,澳门MO,台湾TW 智利CL 巴基斯坦PK,秘鲁PE 亚太APTA	0	最不发达35国LDC35	50	---Other
	32.09	**以合成聚合物或化学改性天然聚合物为基本成分的油漆及清漆(包括瓷漆及大漆),分散于或溶于水介质的:**							**Paints and varnishes (including enamels and lacquers) based on synthetic polymers or chemically modified nat-ural polymers, dispersed or dissolved in an aqueous medium:**
2560	3209.1000	-以丙烯酸聚合物或乙烯聚合物为基本成分	10	0 1 5 9	东盟ASEAN,新加坡SG,新西兰NZ,哥斯达黎加CR,澳门MO 智利CL 巴基斯坦PK,秘鲁PE 亚太APTA	0	最不发达35国LDC35,最不发达4国LDC4	50	-Based on acrylic or vinyl polymers
		-其他:							-Other:
2561	3209.9010	---以环氧树脂为基本成分	10	0 1 5	东盟ASEAN,新加坡SG,新西兰NZ,秘鲁PE,哥斯达黎加CR,台湾TW 智利CL 巴基斯坦PK	0	最不发达35国LDC35	50	---Based on epoxy resin

序号 No.	税则号列 Tariff Line	货品名称	最惠国税率 MFN(%)	协定税率 Agreement(%)		特惠税率 S.P.(%)		普通税率 Gen.(%)	Article Description
2562	3209.9020	---以氟树脂为基本成分	10	0 1 5	东盟ASEAN,新加坡SG,新西兰NZ,秘鲁PE,哥斯达黎加CR 智利CL 巴基斯坦PK	0	最不发达35国LDC35	50	---Based on fluororesin
2563	3209.9090	---其他	10	0 1 5	东盟ASEAN,新加坡SG,新西兰NZ,秘鲁PE,哥斯达黎加CR,香港HK,台湾TW 智利CL 巴基斯坦PK	0	最不发达35国LDC35	50	---Other
	32.10	**其他油漆及清漆(包括瓷漆、大漆及水浆涂料);加工皮革用的水性颜料:**							**Other paints and varnishes (including enamels, lacquers and distempers); prepared water pigments of a kind used for finishing leather:**
2564	3210.0000	其他油漆及清漆(包括瓷漆、大漆及水浆涂料);加工皮革用的水性颜料	10	0 1 5 9	东盟ASEAN,新加坡SG,新西兰NZ,哥斯达黎加CR,香港HK,澳门MO,台湾TW 智利CL 巴基斯坦PK,秘鲁PE 亚太APTA	0	最不发达35国LDC35,最不发达4国LDC4	50	Other paints and varnishes (including enamels, lacquers and distempers); prepared water pigments of a kind used for finishing leather
	ex32100000	光导纤维用涂料	△6						Paint for optical fibers
	32.11	**配制的催干剂:**							**Prepared driers:**
2565	3211.0000	配制的催干剂	10	0 5	东盟ASEAN,智利CL,新加坡SG,新西兰NZ,秘鲁PE,哥斯达黎加CR 巴基斯坦PK	0	最不发达35国LDC35	50	Prepared driers
	32.12	**制造油漆(含瓷漆)用的颜料(包括金属粉末或金属粉片),分散于非水介质中呈液状或浆状的;压印箔;零售形状及零售包装的染料或其他着色料:**							**Pigments (including metallic powders and flakes) dispersed in non-aqueous media, in liquid or paste form, of a kind used in the manufacture of paints (including enamels); stamping foils; dyes and other colouring matter put up in forms or packings for retail sale:**
2566	3212.1000	-压印箔	15	0 1.5 3 7.5 12	东盟ASEAN,新加坡SG,新西兰NZ 智利CL 哥斯达黎加CR 秘鲁PE 巴基斯坦PK	0	最不发达35国LDC35	80	-Stamping foils
2567	3212.9000	-其他	10	0 5	东盟ASEAN,智利CL,新加坡SG,新西兰NZ,秘鲁PE,哥斯达黎加CR 巴基斯坦PK	0	最不发达35国LDC35	50	-Other

序号 No.	税则号列 Tariff Line	货品名称	最惠国税率 MFN(%)	协定税率 Agreement(%)		特惠税率 S.P.(%)		普通税率 Gen.(%)	Article Description
	32.13	**艺术家、学生和广告美工用的颜料、调色料、文娱颜料及类似品，片状、管装、罐装、瓶装、扁盒装以及类似形状或包装的:**							**Artists', students' or signboard painters' colours, modifying tints, amusement colours and the like, in tablets, tubes, jars, bottles, pans or in similar forms or packings:**
2568	3213.1000	-成套的颜料	10	0 1 5	东盟ASEAN,新西兰NZ,哥斯达黎加CR 智利CL 巴基斯坦PK,秘鲁PE	0	最不发达35国LDC35	70	-Colours in sets
2569	3213.9000	-其他	10	0 5 9	东盟ASEAN,智利CL,新西兰NZ,秘鲁PE,哥斯达黎加CR 巴基斯坦PK 亚太APTA	0	最不发达35国LDC35,最不发达4国LDC4	70	-Other
	32.14	**安装玻璃用油灰、接缝用油灰、树脂胶泥、嵌缝胶及其他类似胶粘剂;漆工用填料;非耐火涂面制剂，涂门面、内墙、地板、天花板等用:**							**Glaziers' putty, graftig putty, resin cements, caulking compounds and other mastics; painters' fillings; non-refractory surfacing preparations for facades, indoor walls, floors, ceilings or the like:**
		-安装玻璃用油灰、接缝用油灰、树脂胶泥、嵌缝胶及其他类似胶粘剂;漆工用填料:							-Glaziers putty, grafting putty, resin ce-ments, caulking compounds and other mastics; painters fillings:
2570	3214.1010	---半导体器件封装材料	9	0 0.9 5	东盟ASEAN,新西兰NZ,秘鲁PE,哥斯达黎加CR 智利CL 巴基斯坦PK	0	最不发达35国LDC35,最不发达4国LDC4	70	---Encapsulation materials for semiconductor device
2571	3214.1090	---其他	9	0 0.9 5	东盟ASEAN,新西兰NZ,秘鲁PE,哥斯达黎加CR 智利CL 巴基斯坦PK	0	最不发达35国LDC35,最不发达4国LDC4	70	---Other
2572	3214.9000	-其他	9	0 0.9 5	东盟ASEAN,新西兰NZ,秘鲁PE,哥斯达黎加CR,香港HK 智利CL 巴基斯坦PK	0	最不发达35国LDC35,最不发达4国LDC4	70	-Other

序号 No.	税则号列 Tariff Line	货品名称	最惠国税率 MFN(%)	协定税率 Agreement(%)		特惠税率 S.P.(%)		普通税率 Gen.(%)	Article Description
	32.15	**印刷油墨、书写或绘图墨水及其他墨类，不论是否固体或浓缩:**							**Printing ink, writing or drawing ink and other inks, whether or not concentrated or solid:**
		-印刷油墨:							-Printing ink:
2573	3215.1100	--黑色	6.5	0 0.7 4.6	东盟ASEAN,巴基斯坦PK,新西兰NZ,秘鲁PE,哥斯达黎加CR,香港HK,澳门MO 智利CL 亚太APTA	0	最不发达35国LDC35,最不发达4国LDC4	45	--Black
2574	3215.1900	--其他	6.5	0 0.7 4.6	东盟ASEAN,巴基斯坦PK,新西兰NZ,秘鲁PE,哥斯达黎加CR,香港HK,澳门MO,台湾TW 智利CL 亚太APTA	0	最不发达35国LDC35,最不发达4国LDC4	45	--Other
		-其他:							-Other:
2575	3215.9010	---书写墨水	6.5	0 5	东盟ASEAN,智利CL,新西兰NZ,秘鲁PE,哥斯达黎加CR,香港HK,澳门MO 巴基斯坦PK	0	最不发达35国LDC35,最不发达4国LDC4	70	---Writing or drawing inks
2576	3215.9020	---水性喷墨墨水	10	0 5	东盟ASEAN,智利CL,新加坡SG,新西兰NZ,秘鲁PE,哥斯达黎加CR,香港HK,澳门MO 巴基斯坦PK	0	最不发达35国LDC35,最不发达4国LDC4	70	---Water based inkjet ink
2577	3215.9090	---其他	10	0 5	东盟ASEAN,智利CL,新加坡SG,新西兰NZ,秘鲁PE,哥斯达黎加CR,香港HK,澳门MO 巴基斯坦PK	0	最不发达35国LDC35,最不发达4国LDC4	70	---Other

第三十三章
精油及香膏；芳香料制品
及化妆盥洗品

注释：

一、本章不包括：

(一)税号13.01及13.02的天然油树脂及植物浸膏；

(二)税号34.01的肥皂及其他产品；

(三)税号38.05的脂松节油、木松节油和硫酸盐松节油及其他产品。

二、税号33.02所称"香料"，仅指税号33.01所列的物质、从这些物质离析出来的香料组分以及合成芳香剂。

三、税号33.03至33.07主要包括适合作这些税号所列用途的零售包装产品，不论其是否混合（精油水馏液及水溶液除外）。

四、税号33.07所称"芳香料制品及化妆盥洗品"，主要适用于下列产品：香袋；通过燃烧散发香气的制品；香纸及用化妆品浸渍或涂布的纸；隐形眼镜片或假眼用的溶液；用香水或化妆品浸渍、涂布、包覆的絮胎、毡呢及无纺织物；动物用盥洗品。

Chapter 33
Essential oils and resinoids; perfumery, cosmetic or toilet preparations

Notes:

1.This Chapter does not cover:

(a) Natural oleoresins or vegetable extracts of heading No.13.01 or 13.02;

(b) Soap or other products of heading No.34.01;or

(c) Gum, wood or sulphate turpentine or other products of heading No.38.05.

2.The expression "odoriferous substances" in heading No.33.02 refers only to the substances of heading No.33.01, to odoriferous constituents isolated from those substances or to synthetic aromatics.

3.Headings Nos.33.03 to 33.07 apply, *inter alia*, to products, whether or not mixed (other than aqueous distillates and aqueous solutions of essential oils), suitable for use as goods of these headings and put up in packings of a kind sold by retail for such use.

4.The expression "perfumery, cosmetic or toilet preparations" in heading No.33.07 applies, *inter alia*, to the following products:scented sachets; odoriferous preparations which operate by burning; perfumed papers and papers impregnated or coated with cosmetics; contact lens or artificial eye solutions;wadding, felt and nonwovens, impregnated, coated or covered with perfume or cosmetics; animal toilet preparations.

序号 No.	税则号列 Tariff Line	货品名称	最惠国税 率 MFN(%)	协定税率 Agreement(%)	特惠税率 S.P.(%)	普通税率 Gen.(%)	Article Description
	33.01	**精油（无萜或含萜），包括浸膏及净油;香膏;提取的油树脂;用花香吸取法或浸渍法制成的含浓缩精油的脂肪、固定油、蜡及类似品;精油脱萜时所得的萜烯副产品;精油水馏液及水溶液:**					**Essential oils (terpeneless or not), including concretes and absolutes; resinoids; extracted oleoresins; concentrates of essential oils in fats, in fixed oils, in waxes or the like, obtained by enfleurage or maceration; terpenic byproducts of the deterpenation of essential oils; aqueous distillates and aqueous solutions of essential oils:**
		-柑桔属果实的精油:					-Essential oils of citrus fruit:

序号 No.	税则号列 Tariff Line	货品名称	最惠国 税 率 MFN(%)	协定税率 Agreement(%)		特惠税率 S.P.(%)		普通 税率 Gen.(%)	Article Description
2578	3301.1200	--橙油	20	0 4 10	东盟ASEAN,智利CL,新加坡SG,新西兰NZ,澳门MO 哥斯达黎加CR 秘鲁PE	0	最不发达35国LDC35	80	--Of orange
2579	3301.1300	--柠檬油	20	0 4	东盟ASEAN,智利CL,新加坡SG,新西兰NZ,秘鲁PE,澳门MO 哥斯达黎加CR	0	最不发达35国LDC35,最不发达4国LDC4	80	--Of lemon
		--其他:							--Other:
2580	3301.1910	---白柠檬油（酸橙油）	20	0 4	东盟ASEAN,智利CL,新加坡SG,新西兰NZ,秘鲁PE,澳门MO 哥斯达黎加CR	0	最不发达35国LDC35	80	---Of lime
2581	3301.1990	---其他	20	0 4	东盟ASEAN,智利CL,新加坡SG,新西兰NZ,秘鲁PE,澳门MO 哥斯达黎加CR	0	最不发达35国LDC35	80	---Other
		-非柑桔属果实的精油:							-Essential oils other than those of citrus fruit:
2582	3301.2400	--胡椒薄荷油	20	0 4 10	东盟ASEAN,智利CL,新加坡SG,新西兰NZ,澳门MO 哥斯达黎加CR 秘鲁PE	0	最不发达35国LDC35	90	--Of peppermint (Mentha piperita)
2583	3301.2500	--其他薄荷油	15 △5	0 3 7.5 12 14	东盟ASEAN,智利CL,新加坡SG,新西兰NZ,澳门MO 哥斯达黎加CR 秘鲁PE 巴基斯坦PK 亚太APTA	0	最不发达35国LDC35,最不发达4国LDC4	90	--Of other mints
		--其他:							--Other:
2584	3301.2910	---樟脑油	20	0 4 10	东盟ASEAN,智利CL,新加坡SG,新西兰NZ,澳门MO 哥斯达黎加CR 秘鲁PE	0	最不发达35国LDC35	90	---Of camphor
2585	3301.2920	---香茅油	15	0 3 7.5 12	东盟ASEAN,智利CL,新加坡SG,新西兰NZ,澳门MO 哥斯达黎加CR 秘鲁PE 巴基斯坦PK	0	最不发达35国LDC35,最不发达4国LDC4	70	---Of citronella
2586	3301.2930	---茴香油	20	0 4 10	东盟ASEAN,智利CL,新加坡SG,新西兰NZ,澳门MO 哥斯达黎加CR 秘鲁PE	0	最不发达35国LDC35	80	---Of aniseed
2587	3301.2940	---桂油	20	0 4 10	东盟ASEAN,智利CL,新加坡SG,新西兰NZ,澳门MO 哥斯达黎加CR 秘鲁PE	0	最不发达35国LDC35	80	---Of cassia

序号 No.	税则号列 Tariff Line	货品名称	最惠国税率 MFN(%)	协定税率 Agreement(%)		特惠税率 S.P.(%)		普通税率 Gen.(%)	Article Description
2588	3301.2950	---山苍子油	20	0	东盟ASEAN,智利CL,新加坡SG,新西兰NZ,澳门MO	0	最不发达35国LDC35	80	---Of litsea cubeba
				4	哥斯达黎加CR				
				10	秘鲁PE				
2589	3301.2960	---桉叶油	20	0	东盟ASEAN,智利CL,新加坡SG,新西兰NZ,澳门MO	0	最不发达35国LDC35	80	---Of eucalyptus
				4	哥斯达黎加CR				
				10	秘鲁PE				
		---其他:							---Other:
2590	3301.2991	----老鹳草油（香叶油）	20	0	东盟ASEAN,智利CL,新加坡SG,新西兰NZ,澳门MO	0	最不发达35国LDC35	80	----Of geranium
				4	哥斯达黎加CR				
				10	秘鲁PE				
2591	3301.2999	----其他	15	0	东盟ASEAN,智利CL,新加坡SG,新西兰NZ,秘鲁PE,澳门MO	0	最不发达35国LDC35,最不发达4国LDC4	80	----Other
				3	哥斯达黎加CR				
				12	巴基斯坦PK				
	ex33012999	黄樟油	△7						Sassafras oil
		-香膏:							-Resinoids:
2592	3301.3010	---鸢尾凝脂	20 △10	0	东盟ASEAN,智利CL,新加坡SG,新西兰NZ,澳门MO	0	最不发达35国LDC35	80	---Balsam of irises
				4	哥斯达黎加CR				
				10	秘鲁PE				
2593	3301.3090	---其他	20	0	东盟ASEAN,智利CL,新加坡SG,新西兰NZ,澳门MO	0	最不发达35国LDC35	80	---Other
				4	哥斯达黎加CR				
				10	秘鲁PE				
		-其他:							-Other:
2594	3301.9010	---提取的油树脂	20	0	东盟ASEAN,智利CL,新加坡SG,新西兰NZ,秘鲁PE,澳门MO	0	最不发达35国LDC35	80	---Extracted oleoresins
				4	哥斯达黎加CR				
				18	亚太APTA,巴基斯坦PK				
2595	3301.9020	---柑桔属果实的精油脱萜的萜烯副产品	20	0	东盟ASEAN,智利CL,新加坡SG,新西兰NZ,秘鲁PE,澳门MO	0	最不发达35国LDC35	80	---Terpenic byproducts of the deterpenation of essential oils of citrus fruit
				4	哥斯达黎加CR				
				18	亚太APTA,巴基斯坦PK				
2596	3301.9090	---其他	20	0	东盟ASEAN,智利CL,新加坡SG,新西兰NZ,秘鲁PE,澳门MO	0	最不发达35国LDC35,最不发达4国LDC4	80	---Other
				4	哥斯达黎加CR				
				18	亚太APTA,巴基斯坦PK				

序号 No.	税则号列 Tariff Line	货品名称	最惠国税率 MFN(%)	协定税率 Agreement(%)		特惠税率 S.P.(%)		普通税率 Gen.(%)	Article Description
	33.02	**工业原料用的混合香料以及以一种或多种香料为基本成分的混合物(包括酒精溶液);生产饮料用的以香料为基本成分的其他制品:**							**Mixtures of odoriferous substances and mixtures (including alcoholic solutions) with a basis of one or more of these substances, of a kind used as raw materials in industry; other reparations based on odoriferoussubstances, of a kind used for the manufacture of beverages:**
		-食品或饮料工业用:							-Of a kind used in the food or drink industry:
2597	3302.1010	---生产饮料用的以香料为基本成分的制品，按容量计酒精浓度不超过0.5%的	15	0 1.5 3 7.5 12.8	东盟ASEAN,新加坡SG,新西兰NZ,澳门MO 智利CL 哥斯达黎加CR 巴基斯坦PK,秘鲁PE 亚太APTA	0	最不发达35国LDC35	90	---Preparations based on odoriferous substances, of a kind used for the manufacture of beverages, alcoholic strength by volume not exceeding 0.5% vol.
2598	3302.1090	---其他	15	0 1.5 3 7.5 12	东盟ASEAN,新加坡SG,新西兰NZ,澳门MO 智利CL 哥斯达黎加CR 秘鲁PE 巴基斯坦PK	0	最不发达35国LDC35,最不发达4国LDC4	130	---Other
2599	3302.9000	-其他	10	0 1 5	东盟ASEAN,新加坡SG,新西兰NZ,哥斯达黎加CR,香港HK,澳门MO 智利CL 巴基斯坦PK,秘鲁PE	0	最不发达35国LDC35,最不发达4国LDC4	130	-Other
	33.03	**香水及花露水:**							**Perfumes and toilet waters:**
2600	3303.0000	香水及花露水	10	0 1 5 8.2	东盟ASEAN,新加坡SG,新西兰NZ,秘鲁PE,哥斯达黎加CR,香港HK,澳门MO 智利CL 巴基斯坦PK 亚太APTA	0	最不发达35国LDC35,最不发达4国LDC4	150	Perfumes and toilet waters:
	33.04	**美容品或化妆品及护肤品(药品除外),包括防晒油或晒黑油;指(趾)甲化妆品:**							**Beauty or make-up preparations and preparations for the care of the skin (other than medicaments), including sunscreen or sun tan preparations; manicure or pedicure preparations:**

序号 No.	税则号列 Tariff Line	货品名称	最惠国税率 MFN(%)	协定税率 Agreement(%)		特惠税率 S.P.(%)		普通税率 Gen.(%)	Article Description
2601	3304.1000	-唇用化妆品	10	0	东盟ASEAN,新加坡SG,新西兰NZ,秘鲁PE,哥斯达黎加CR,香港HK,澳门MO	0	最不发达35国LDC35	150	-Lip make-up preparations
				1	智利CL				
				5	巴基斯坦PK				
2602	3304.2000	-眼用化妆品	10	0	东盟ASEAN,新加坡SG,新西兰NZ,秘鲁PE,哥斯达黎加CR,香港HK,澳门MO	0	最不发达35国LDC35	150	-Eye make-up preparations
				1	智利CL				
				5	巴基斯坦PK				
2603	3304.3000	-指（趾）甲化妆品	15 △10	0	东盟ASEAN,新加坡SG,新西兰NZ,香港HK,澳门MO	0	最不发达35国LDC35	150	-Manicure or pedicure preparations
				1.5	智利CL				
				3	哥斯达黎加CR				
				7.5	秘鲁PE				
				12	巴基斯坦PK				
		-其他:							-Other:
2604	3304.9100	--粉,不论是否压紧	10	0	东盟ASEAN,新加坡SG,新西兰NZ,秘鲁PE,哥斯达黎加CR,澳门MO	0	最不发达35国LDC35	150	--Powdrs, whether or not compressed
				1	智利CL				
				5	巴基斯坦PK				
2605	3304.9900	--其他	6.5	0	东盟ASEAN,新加坡SG,新西兰NZ,秘鲁PE,哥斯达黎加CR,香港HK,澳门MO	0	最不发达35国LDC35	150	--Other
				0.7	智利CL				
				5.2	巴基斯坦PK				
	ex33049900	护肤品	△5						Skin care products
	33.05	**护发品:**							**Preparations for use on the hair:**
2606	3305.1000	-洗发剂（香波）	6.5	0	东盟ASEAN,新加坡SG,新西兰NZ,秘鲁PE,哥斯达黎加CR,香港HK,澳门MO	0	最不发达35国LDC35,最不发达4国LDC4	150	-Shampoos
				0.7	智利CL				
				5	巴基斯坦PK				
				5.4	亚太APTA				
2607	3305.2000	-烫发剂	15 △10	0	东盟ASEAN,智利CL,新加坡SG,新西兰NZ,澳门MO	0	最不发达35国LDC35	150	-Preparations for permanent waving or straightening
				3	哥斯达黎加CR				
				7.5	秘鲁PE				
				12	巴基斯坦PK				
2608	3305.3000	-定型剂	15 △10	0	东盟ASEAN,新加坡SG,新西兰NZ,澳门MO	0	最不发达35国LDC35	150	-Hair lacquers
				1.5	智利CL				
				3	哥斯达黎加CR				
				7.5	秘鲁PE				
				12	巴基斯坦PK				

序号 No.	税则号列 Tariff Line	货品名称	最惠国税率 MFN(%)	协定税率 Agreement(%)		特惠税率 S.P.(%)		普通税率 Gen.(%)	Article Description
2609	3305.9000	-其他	10	0 1 5 8.5	东盟ASEAN,新加坡SG,新西兰NZ,秘鲁PE,哥斯达黎加CR,香港HK,澳门MO 智利CL 巴基斯坦PK 亚太APTA	0	最不发达35国LDC35,最不发达4国LDC4	150	-Other
	33.06	**口腔及牙齿清洁剂，包括假牙模膏及粉；清洁牙缝用的纱线（牙线），单独零售包装的:**							**Preparations for oral or dental hygiene, including denture fixative pastes and powders; yarn used to clean between the teeth (dental floss), in individual retail package:**
		-洁齿品:							-Dentifrices:
2610	3306.1010	---牙膏	10	0 1 5 7	东盟ASEAN,新加坡SG,新西兰NZ,秘鲁PE,哥斯达黎加CR,香港HK,澳门MO 智利CL 巴基斯坦PK 亚太APTA	0	最不发达35国LDC35,最不发达4国LDC4	150	---Toothpastes
2611	3306.1090	---其他	10	0 1 5 7	东盟ASEAN,新加坡SG,新西兰NZ,秘鲁PE,哥斯达黎加CR 智利CL 巴基斯坦PK 亚太APTA	0	最不发达35国LDC35	150	---Other
2612	3306.2000	-清洁牙缝用的纱线（牙线）	10	0 1 5 9.2	东盟ASEAN,新西兰NZ,秘鲁PE,哥斯达黎加CR 智利CL 巴基斯坦PK 亚太APTA	0	最不发达35国LDC35	70	-Yarn used to clean between the teeth (dental floss)
2613	3306.9000	-其他	10	0 1 5	东盟ASEAN,新加坡SG,新西兰NZ,秘鲁PE,哥斯达黎加CR,香港HK,澳门MO 智利CL 巴基斯坦PK	0	最不发达35国LDC35	70	-Other
	33.07	**剃须用制剂、人体除臭剂、沐浴用制剂、脱毛剂和其他税号未列名的芳香料制品及化妆盥洗品;室内除臭剂，不论是否加香水或消毒剂:**							**Pre-shave, shaving or after-shave preparations, personal deodorants, bath preparations, depilatories and other perfumery, cosmetic or toilet preparations, not elsewhere specified or included; prepared room deodorizers, whether or not perfumed or having disinfectant properties:**

序号 No.	税则号列 Tariff Line	货品名称	最惠国税率 MFN(%)	协定税率 Agreement(%)		特惠税率 S.P.(%)		普通税率 Gen.(%)	Article Description
2614	3307.1000	-剃须用制剂	10	0 1 5 7	东盟ASEAN,新加坡SG,新西兰NZ,秘鲁PE,哥斯达黎加CR 智利CL 巴基斯坦PK 亚太APTA	0	最不发达35国LDC35	150	-Pre-shave, shaving or after-shave preparations
2615	3307.2000	-人体除臭剂及止汗剂	10	0 1 5 7	东盟ASEAN,新加坡SG,新西兰NZ,秘鲁PE,哥斯达黎加CR,澳门MO 智利CL 巴基斯坦PK 亚太APTA	0	最不发达35国LDC35	150	-Personal deodorants and antiperspirants
2616	3307.3000	-香浴盐及其他沐浴用制剂	10	0 1 5 8.5	东盟ASEAN,新加坡SG,新西兰NZ,秘鲁PE,哥斯达黎加CR,香港HK,澳门MO 智利CL 巴基斯坦PK 亚太APTA	0	最不发达35国LDC35	150	-Perfumed bath salts and other bath preparations
		-室内散香或除臭制品，包括宗教仪式用的香:							-Preparations for perfuming or deodorizing rooms, including odoriferous preparations used during religious rites:
2617	3307.4100	--神香及其他通过燃烧散发香气的制品	10	0 5	东盟ASEAN,智利CL,新加坡SG,新西兰NZ,秘鲁PE,哥斯达黎加CR,香港HK 巴基斯坦PK	0	最不发达35国LDC35,最不发达4国LDC4	150	--Agarbatti and other odoriferous preparations which operate by burning
2618	3307.4900	--其他	10	0 1 5	东盟ASEAN,新加坡SG,新西兰NZ,秘鲁PE,哥斯达黎加CR,香港HK 智利CL 巴基斯坦PK	0	最不发达35国LDC35,最不发达4国LDC4	150	--Other
2619	3307.9000	-其他	9	0 5 6.3	东盟ASEAN,智利CL,新西兰NZ,秘鲁PE,哥斯达黎加CR,澳门MO 巴基斯坦PK 亚太APTA	0	最不发达35国LDC35,最不发达4国LDC4	150	-Other

第三十四章
肥皂、有机表面活性剂、洗涤剂、润滑剂、人造蜡、调制蜡、光洁剂、蜡烛及类似品、塑型用膏、“牙科用蜡”及牙科用熟石膏制剂

注释：

一、本章不包括：

（一）用作脱模剂的食用动植物油、脂混合物或制品（税号15.17）；

（二）单独的已有化学定义的化合物；

（三）含肥皂或其他有机表面活性剂的洗发剂、洁齿品、剃须膏及沐浴用制剂（税号33.05、33.06及33.07）。

二、税号34.01所称“肥皂”，只适用于水溶性肥皂。税号34.01的肥皂及其他产品可以含有添加料（例如，消毒剂、磨料粉、填料或药料）。含磨料粉的产品，只有条状、块状或模制形状可以归入税号34.01。其他形状的应作为“去污粉及类似品”归入税号34.05。

三、税号34.02所称“有机表面活性剂”，是指温度在20℃时与水混合配成0.5%浓度的水溶液，并在同样温度下搁置一小时后与下列规定相符的产品：

（一）成为透明或半透明的液体或稳定的乳浊液而未离析出不溶解物质；

（二）将水的表面张力减低到每厘米45达因及以下。

四、税号34.03所称“石油及从沥青矿物提取的油类”，适用于第二十七章注释二所规定的产品。

五、税号34.04所称“人造蜡及调制蜡”，仅适用于：

（一）用化学方法生产的具有蜡质特性的有机产品，不论是否为水溶性的；

（二）各种蜡混合制成的产品；

Chapter 34
Soap, organic surface-active agents, washing preparations, lubricating preparations, artificial waxes, prepared waxes, polishing or scouring preparations, candles and similar articles, modelling pastes, “dental waxes” and dental preparations with a basis of plaster

Notes:

1.This Chapter does not cover:

(a) Edible mixtures or preparations of animal or vegetable fats or oils of a kind used as mould release preparations (heading No.15.17) ;

(b) Separate chemically defined compounds; or

(c) Shampoos, dentifrices, shaving creams and foams, or bath preparations, containing soap or other organic surface-active agents (heading No.33.05, 33.06 or 33.07) .

2.For the purposes of heading No.34.01, the expression“soap”applies only to soap soluble in water.Soap and the other products of heading No.34.01may contain added sub-stances (for example, disinfectants, abrasive powders, fillers or medicaments). Products containing abrasive powders remain classified in heading No.34.01only if in the form of bars, cakes or moulded pieces or shapes.In other forms they are to be classified in heading No.34.05 as “scouring powders and similar preparations”.

3.For the purposes of heading No.34.02, “organic surface active agents” are products which when mixed with water at a concentration of 0.5% at 20℃and left to stand for one hour at the same temperature:

(a) give a transparent or translucent liquid or stable emulsion without separation of insoluble matter; and

(b) reduce the surface tension of water to 4.5×10^{-2}N/m (45dyen/cm) or less.

4.In heading No.34.03 the expression “petroleum oils and oils obtained from bituminous minerals” applies to the products defined in Note 2 to Chapter 27.

5.In heading No.34.04, subject to the exclusions provided below, the expression “artificial waxes and prepared waxes” applies only to:

(a) Chemically produced organic products of a waxy character, whether or not water-soluble;

(b) Products obtained by mixing different waxes;

（三）以一种或几种蜡为基本原料并含有油脂、树脂、矿物质或其他原料的具有蜡质特性的产品。

本税号不包括：

（一）税号15.16、34.02或38.23的产品，不论是否具有蜡质特性；

（二）税号15.21的未混合的动物蜡或未混合的植物蜡，不论是否精制或着色；

（三）税号27.12的矿物蜡或类似产品，不论是否相互混合或仅经着色；

（四）混合、分散或溶解于液体溶剂的蜡（税号34.05、38.09等）。

(c) Products of a waxy character with a basis of one or morewaxes and containing fats, resins, mineral substances or other materials.

The heading does not apply to:

(a) Products of heading No.15.16, 34.02 or 38.23, even if having a waxy character;

(b) Unmixed animal waxes or unmixed vegetable waxes, whether or not refined or coloured, of heading No.15.21;

(c) Mineral waxes or similar products of heading No.27.12, whether or not intermixed or merely coloured;or

(d) Waxes mixed with, dispersed in or dissolved in a liquid medium (headings Nos.34.05, 38.09, etc.) .

序号 No.	税则号列 Tariff Line	货品名称	最惠国税率 MFN(%)	协定税率 Agreement(%)	特惠税率 S.P.(%)	普通税率 Gen.(%)	Article Description
	34.01	**肥皂;作肥皂用的有机表面活性产品及制品，条状、块状或模制形状的，不论是否含有肥皂;洁肤用的有机表面活性产品及制品，液状或膏状并制成零售包装的，不论是否含有肥皂;用肥皂或洗涤剂浸渍、涂面或包覆的纸、絮胎、毡呢及无纺织物:**					**Soap; organic surface-active products and preparations for use as soap, in the form of bars, cakes, moulded pieces or shapes, whether or not containing soap; organic surfaceactive products and preparations for washing the skin, in the form of liguid or cream and put up for retail sale, whether or not containing soap; paper, wadding, felt and nonwovens, impregnated, coated or covered with soap or detergent:**
		-肥皂及有机表面活性产品及制品，条状、块状或模制形状的，以及用肥皂或洗涤剂浸渍、涂面或包覆的纸、絮胎、毡呢及无纺织物:					-Soap and organic surface-active products and prepar ations, in the form of bars, cakes, moulded pieces or shapes, and paper, wadding, felt and nonwovens, impregnated, coated or covered with soap or detergent:

序号 No.	税则号列 Tariff Line	货品名称	最惠国税率 MFN(%)	协定税率 Agreement(%)		特惠税率 S.P.(%)		普通税率 Gen.(%)	Article Description
2620	3401.1100	--盥洗用（包括含有药物的产品）	10	0 1 8.3	东盟ASEAN,新加坡SG,新西兰NZ,秘鲁PE,哥斯达黎加CR,香港HK,澳门MO 智利CL 亚太APTA,巴基斯坦PK	0	最不发达35国LDC35,最不发达4国LDC4,亚太2国APTA2	130	--For toilet use (including medicated products)
		--其他:							--Other:
2621	3401.1910	---洗衣皂	10	0 5	东盟ASEAN,智利CL,新加坡SG,新西兰NZ,秘鲁PE,哥斯达黎加CR,澳门MO 巴基斯坦PK	0	最不发达35国LDC35,最不发达4国LDC4	80	---Laundry soap
2622	3401.1990	---其他	15 △10	0 3 7.5 12	东盟ASEAN,智利CL,新西兰NZ 哥斯达黎加CR 秘鲁PE 巴基斯坦PK	0	最不发达35国LDC35	130	---Other
2623	3401.2000	-其他形状的肥皂	15 △10	0 1.5 3 7.5 12.4	东盟ASEAN,新西兰NZ,香港HK,澳门MO 智利CL 哥斯达黎加CR 巴基斯坦PK,秘鲁PE 亚太APTA	0	最不发达35国LDC35,最不发达4国LDC4,亚太2国APTA2	130	-Soap in other forms
2624	3401.3000	-洁肤用的有机表面活性产品及制品，液状或膏状并制成零售包装的，不论是否含有肥皂	10	0 1 5	东盟ASEAN,新加坡SG,新西兰NZ,秘鲁PE,哥斯达黎加CR,澳门MO 智利CL 巴基斯坦PK	0	最不发达35国LDC35,最不发达4国LDC4	130	-Organic surface-active products and preparations for washing the skin, in the form of liquid or cream and put up for retail sale, whether or not containing soap
	34.02	**有机表面活性剂（肥皂除外）;表面活性剂制品、洗涤剂（包括助洗剂）及清洁剂，不论是否含有肥皂，但税号34.01的产品除外:**							**Organic surface-active agents (other than soap); surface-active preparations, washing preparations (including auxiliary washing preparations) and cleaning preparations, whether or not containing soap, other than those of heading No.34.01:**
		-有机表面活性剂，不论是否零售包装:							-Organic surface-active agents, whether or not put up for retail sale:

序号 No.	税则号列 Tariff Line	货品名称	最惠国税率 MFN(%)	协定税率 Agreement(%)		特惠税率 S.P.(%)		普通税率 Gen.(%)	Article Description
2625	3402.1100	--阴离子型	6.5	0	东盟ASEAN,新西兰NZ,秘鲁PE,哥斯达黎加CR,香港HK,澳门MO	0	最不发达35国LDC35,最不发达4国LDC4	30	--Anionic
				0.7	智利CL				
				5	巴基斯坦PK				
				6	亚太APTA				
2626	3402.1200	--阳离子型	6.5	0	东盟ASEAN,智利CL,新西兰NZ,秘鲁PE,哥斯达黎加CR,香港HK,澳门MO	0	最不发达35国LDC35,最不发达4国LDC4	30	--Cationic
				5	巴基斯坦PK				
				6	亚太APTA				
2627	3402.1300	--非离子型	6.5	0	东盟ASEAN,新西兰NZ,秘鲁PE,哥斯达黎加CR,香港HK,澳门MO,台湾TW	0	最不发达35国LDC35,最不发达4国LDC4	30	--Non-ionic
				0.7	智利CL				
				5	巴基斯坦PK				
				5.9	亚太APTA				
2628	3402.1900	--其他	6.5	0	东盟ASEAN,新西兰NZ,秘鲁PE,哥斯达黎加CR,澳门MO	0	最不发达35国LDC35,最不发达4国LDC4	30	--Other
				0.7	智利CL				
				5	巴基斯坦PK				
				6	亚太APTA				
		-零售包装的制品:							-Preparations put up for retail sale:
2629	3402.2010	---合成洗涤粉	10	0	东盟ASEAN,新加坡SG,新西兰NZ,秘鲁PE,哥斯达黎加CR,澳门MO	0	最不发达35国LDC35	80	---Synthetic detergents in powder form
				1	智利CL				
				5	巴基斯坦PK				
				8.5	亚太APTA				
2630	3402.2090	---其他	10	0	东盟ASEAN,新加坡SG,新西兰NZ,秘鲁PE,哥斯达黎加CR,香港HK,澳门MO	0	最不发达35国LDC35	80	---Other
				1	智利CL				
				5	巴基斯坦PK				
				8.5	亚太APTA				
2631	3402.9000	-其他	9	0	东盟ASEAN,新加坡SG,新西兰NZ,秘鲁PE,香港HK,澳门MO	0	最不发达35国LDC35,最不发达4国LDC4	80	-Other
				0.9	智利CL				
				1.8	哥斯达黎加CR				
				5	巴基斯坦PK				
				7.8	亚太APTA				
	ex34029000	十二烷基苯磺酸钙甲醇溶液（十二烷基苯磺酸钙含量应高于70%）	△7						Calcium dodecyl benzosulfonate methanol solution (Calcium dodecyl benzosulfonate content >70%)

序号 No.	税则号列 Tariff Line	货品名称	最惠国税率 MFN(%)	协定税率 Agreement(%)		特惠税率 S.P.(%)		普通税率 Gen.(%)	Article Description
	34.03	**润滑剂（包括以润滑剂为基本成分的切削油制剂、螺栓或螺母松开剂、防锈或防腐蚀制剂及脱模剂）及用于纺织材料、皮革、毛皮或其他材料油脂处理的制剂，但不包括以石油或从沥青矿物提取的油类为基本成分（按重量计不低于 70%）的制剂:**							**Lubricating preparations (including cutting-oil preparations, bolt or nut release preparations, anti-rust or anticorrosion preparations and mould release preparations, based on lubricants) and preparations of a kind used for the oil or grease treatment of textile materials, leather, furskins or other materials, but excluding preparations containing, as basic constituents, 70% or more by weight of petroleum oils or of oils obtained from bituminous minerals:**
		-含有石油或从沥青矿物提取的油类:							-Containing petroleum oils or oils obtained from bituminous minerals:
2632	3403.1100	--处理纺织材料、皮革、毛皮或其他材料的制剂	10 △8	0 5 9.5	东盟ASEAN,智利CL,新加坡SG,新西兰NZ,秘鲁PE,哥斯达黎加CR,香港HK 巴基斯坦PK 亚太APTA	0	最不发达 35 国 LDC35	50	--Preparations for the treatment of textile materials, leather, furskins or other materials
2633	3403.1900	--其他	10 △8	0 1 5	东盟ASEAN,新加坡SG,新西兰NZ,秘鲁PE,哥斯达黎加CR,香港HK 智利CL 巴基斯坦PK	0	最不发达 35 国 LDC35,最不发达 4 国 LDC4	50	--Other
		-其他:							-Other:
2634	3403.9100	--处理纺织材料、皮革、毛皮或其他材料的制剂	10 △8	0 1 5	东盟ASEAN,新加坡SG,新西兰NZ,哥斯达黎加CR,香港HK 智利CL 巴基斯坦PK,秘鲁PE	0	最不发达 35 国 LDC35	50	--Preparations for the treatment of textile materials, leather, furskins or other materials
2635	3403.9900	--其他	10	0 1 5	东盟ASEAN,新加坡SG,新西兰NZ,哥斯达黎加CR,澳门MO 智利CL 巴基斯坦PK,秘鲁PE	0	最不发达 35 国 LDC35	50	--Other
	34.04	**人造蜡及调制蜡:**							**Artificial waxes and prepared waxes:**
2636	3404.2000	-聚氧乙烯（聚乙二醇）蜡	10	0 5	东盟ASEAN,智利CL,新西兰NZ,秘鲁PE,哥斯达黎加CR 巴基斯坦PK	0	最不发达 35 国 LDC35	70	-Of poly (oxyethylene) (polyethylene glycol)

序号 No.	税则号列 Tariff Line	货品名称	最惠国税率 MFN(%)	协定税率 Agreement(%)		特惠税率 S.P.(%)		普通税率 Gen.(%)	Article Description
2637	3404.9000	-其他	10	0 5	东盟ASEAN,智利CL,新西兰NZ,哥斯达黎加CR 巴基斯坦PK,秘鲁PE	0	最不发达35国LDC35,最不发达4国LDC4	70	-Other
	34.05	**鞋靴、家具、地板、车身、玻璃或金属用的光洁剂、擦洗膏、去污粉及类似制品（包括用这类制剂浸渍、涂面或包覆的纸、絮胎、毡呢、无纺织物、泡沫塑料或海绵橡胶），但不包括税号34.04的蜡:**							**Polishes and creams, for footwear, furniture, floors, coachwork, glass or metal, scouring pastes and powders and similar preparations (whether or not in the form of paper, wadding, felt, nonwovens, cellular plastics or cellular rubber, impregnated, coated or covered with such preparations), excluding waxes of heading No.34.04:**
2638	3405.1000	-鞋靴或皮革用的上光剂及类似制品	10	0 1 5	东盟ASEAN,新加坡SG,新西兰NZ,哥斯达黎加CR,香港HK 智利CL 巴基斯坦PK,秘鲁PE	0	最不发达35国LDC35	80	-Polishes, creams and similar preparations for footwear or leather
2639	3405.2000	-保养木制家具、地板或其他木制品用的上光剂及类似制品	10	0 1 5	东盟ASEAN,新加坡SG,新西兰NZ,哥斯达黎加CR,香港HK 智利CL 巴基斯坦PK,秘鲁PE	0	最不发达35国LDC35	80	-Polishes, creams and similar preparations for the maintenance of wooden furniture, floors or other woodwork
2640	3405.3000	-车身用的上光剂及类似制品，但金属用的光洁剂除外	10	0 1 5	东盟ASEAN,新加坡SG,新西兰NZ,哥斯达黎加CR 智利CL 巴基斯坦PK,秘鲁PE	0	最不发达35国LDC35	80	-Polishes and similar preparations for coachwork, other than metal polishes
2641	3405.4000	-擦洗膏、去污粉及类似制品	10	0 5	东盟ASEAN,智利CL,新西兰NZ,秘鲁PE,哥斯达黎加CR 巴基斯坦PK	0	最不发达35国LDC35	80	-Scouring pastes and powders and other scouring preparations
2642	3405.9000	-其他	10	0 1 5 8.5	东盟ASEAN,新加坡SG,新西兰NZ,哥斯达黎加CR,香港HK 智利CL 巴基斯坦PK,秘鲁PE 亚太APTA	0	最不发达35国LDC35	80	-Other
	34.06	**各种蜡烛及类似品:**							**Candles, tapers and the like:**
2643	3406.0000	各种蜡烛及类似品	10	0 1 5	东盟ASEAN,新加坡SG,新西兰NZ,秘鲁PE,哥斯达黎加CR,澳门MO 智利CL 巴基斯坦PK	0	最不发达35国LDC35	130	Candles, tapers and the like

序号 No.	税则号列 Tariff Line	货品名称	最惠国税率 MFN(%)	协定税率 Agreement(%)		特惠税率 S.P.(%)		普通税率 Gen.(%)	Article Description
	34.07	**塑型用膏，包括供儿童娱乐用的在内;通称为“牙科用蜡”或“牙科造形膏”的制品，成套、零售包装或制成片状、马蹄形、条状及类似形状的;以熟石膏（煅烧石膏或硫酸钙）为基本成分的牙科用其他制品:**							**Modeling pastes, including those put up for childrens'amusement; preparations known as “dental wax” or as “dental impression compounds”, put up in sets, in packings for retail sale or in plates, horseshoe shapes, sticks or similar forms; other preparations for use in dentistry, with a basis of plaster (of calcined gypsum or calcium sulphate):**
2644	3407.0010	---牙科用蜡及造型膏	6.5	0 5	东盟ASEAN,智利CL,新西兰NZ,秘鲁PE,哥斯达黎加CR 巴基斯坦PK	0	最不发达35国LDC35,最不发达4国LDC4	30	---Preparations of a kind known as “dental wax” or as “dental impression compounds”
2645	3407.0020	---以熟石膏为基本成分的牙科用其他制品	6.5	0 5	东盟ASEAN,智利CL,新西兰NZ,秘鲁PE,哥斯达黎加CR 巴基斯坦PK	0	最不发达35国LDC35,最不发达4国LDC4	40	---Other preparations for use in dentistry, with a basis of plaster
2646	3407.0090	---其他	10	0 5	东盟ASEAN,智利CL,新西兰NZ,秘鲁PE,哥斯达黎加CR 巴基斯坦PK	0	最不发达35国LDC35	100	---Other

第三十五章
蛋白类物质；改性淀粉；胶；酶

Chapter 35
Albuminoidal substances; modified starches; glues; enzymes

注释:

一、本章不包括:

（一）酵母（税号21.02）;

（二）第三十章的血份（非治病、防病用的血清白蛋白除外）、药品及其他产品;

（三）预鞣用酶制剂（税号32.02）;

（四）第三十四章的加酶的浸透剂、洗涤剂及其他产品;

（五）硬化蛋白（税号39.13）;

（六）印刷工业用的明胶产品（第四十九章）。

二、税号35.05所称"糊精"，是指淀粉的降解产品，其还原糖含量以右旋糖的干重量计不超过10%。

如果还原糖含量超过10%，应归入税号17.02。

Notes:

1.This Chapter does not cover:

(a) Yeasts (heading No.21.02);

(b) Blood fractions (other than blood albumin not prepared for therapeutic or prophylactic uses)，medicaments or other products of Chapter 30;

(c) Enzymatic preparations for pre-tanning (heading No.32.02)；

(d) Enzymatic soaking or washing preparations or other products of Chapter 34;

(e) Hardened proteins (heading No.39.13); or

(f) Gelatin products of the printing industry (Chapter49).

2.For the purposes of heading No.35.05，the term "dextrins" means starch degradation products with a reducing sugar content，expressed as dextrose on the dry substance，not exceeding 10%.

Such products with a reducing sugar content exceeding 10% fall in heading No.17.02.

序号 No.	税则号列 Tariff Line	货品名称	最惠国税率 MFN(%)	协定税率 Agreement(%)		特惠税率 S.P.(%)		普通税率 Gen.(%)	Article Description
	35.01	**酪蛋白、酪蛋白酸盐及其他酪蛋白衍生物;酪蛋白胶:**							**Casein, caseinates and other casein derivatives; casein glues:**
2647	3501.1000	-酪蛋白	10	0 5	东盟ASEAN,智利CL,新加坡SG,新西兰NZ,秘鲁PE,哥斯达黎加CR 巴基斯坦PK	0	最不发达35国LDC35	35	-Casein
2648	3501.9000	-其他	10	0 1 5	东盟ASEAN,新西兰NZ,哥斯达黎加CR 智利CL 巴基斯坦PK,秘鲁PE	0	最不发达35国LDC35	35	-Other
	35.02	**白蛋白（包括按重量计干质成分的乳清蛋白含量超过80%的两种或两种以上的乳清蛋白浓缩物）、白蛋白盐及其他白蛋白衍生物:**							**Albumins (including concentrates of two or more whey proteins, containing by weight more than 80% whey proteins, calculated on the dry matter), albuminates and other albumin derivatives:**
		-卵清蛋白:							-Egg albumin:
2649	3502.1100	--干的	10	0 5	东盟ASEAN,智利CL,新西兰NZ,秘鲁PE,哥斯达黎加CR 巴基斯坦PK	0	最不发达35国LDC35	80	--Dried

序号 No.	税则号列 Tariff Line	货品名称	最惠国税率 MFN(%)	协定税率 Agreement(%)		特惠税率 S.P.(%)		普通税率 Gen.(%)	Article Description
2650	3502.1900	--其他	10	0	东盟ASEAN,智利CL,新西兰NZ,秘鲁PE,哥斯达黎加CR	0	最不发达35国LDC35	80	--Other
				5	巴基斯坦PK				
2651	3502.2000	-乳白蛋白,包括两种或两种以上的乳清蛋白浓缩物	10	0	东盟ASEAN,智利CL,新西兰NZ,秘鲁PE,哥斯达黎加CR	0	最不发达35国LDC35	35	-Milk albumin, including concentrates of two or more whey proteins
				5	巴基斯坦PK				
2652	3502.9000	-其他	10	0	东盟ASEAN,新西兰NZ,哥斯达黎加CR,香港HK	0	最不发达35国LDC35	35	-Other
				1	智利CL				
				5	巴基斯坦PK,秘鲁PE				
	35.03	**明胶（包括长方形、正方形明胶薄片，不论是否表面加工或着色）及其衍生物；鱼鳔胶;其他动物胶，但不包括税号35.01的酪蛋白胶:**							**Gelatin (including gelatin in rectangular (including square) sheets, whether or not surface-worked or coloured) and gelatin derivatives; isinglass; other glues of animal origin, excluding casein glues of heading No.35.01:**
2653	3503.0010	---明胶及其衍生物	12	0	东盟ASEAN,智利CL,新加坡SG,新西兰NZ,秘鲁PE	0	最不发达35国LDC35	35	---Gelatin and gelatin derivatives
				2.4	哥斯达黎加CR				
				6	巴基斯坦PK				
	ex35030010	明胶	△5						Gelatin
2654	3503.0090	---其他	12	0	东盟ASEAN,智利CL,新加坡SG,新西兰NZ,秘鲁PE	0	最不发达35国LDC35	50	---Other
				2.4	哥斯达黎加CR				
				6	巴基斯坦PK				
	35.04	**蛋白胨及其衍生物；其他税号未列名的蛋白质及其衍生物；皮粉，不论是否加入铬矾:**							**Peptones and their derivatives; other protein substances and their derivatives, not elsewhere specified or included; hide powder, whether or not chromed:**
2655	3504.0010	---蛋白胨	3	0	东盟ASEAN,智利CL,巴基斯坦PK,新西兰NZ,秘鲁PE,哥斯达黎加CR,澳门MO	0	最不发达35国LDC35,最不发达4国LDC4	11	---Peptones
2656	3504.0090	---其他	8	0	东盟ASEAN,智利CL,新西兰NZ,秘鲁PE,哥斯达黎加CR,澳门MO	0	最不发达35国LDC35,最不发达4国LDC4	35	---Other
				5	巴基斯坦PK				

序号 No.	税则号列 Tariff Line	货品名称	最惠国 税 率 MFN(%)	协定税率 Agreement(%)		特惠税率 S.P.(%)		普通 税率 Gen.(%)	Article Description
	35.05	**糊精及其他改性淀粉（例如，预凝化淀粉或酯化淀粉）;以淀粉、糊精或其他改性淀粉为基本成分的胶:**							**Dextrins and other modified starches (for example, pregelatinized or esterified starches); glues based on starches, or on dextrins or other modified starches:**
2657	3505.1000	-糊精及其他改性淀粉	12 △6	0 1.2 2.4 6	东盟ASEAN,新加坡SG,新西兰NZ,香港HK,澳门MO 智利CL 哥斯达黎加CR 巴基斯坦PK,秘鲁PE	0	最不发达35国LDC35	50	-Dextrins and other modified starches
2658	3505.2000	-胶	20	0 4 10	东盟ASEAN,智利CL,新加坡SG,新西兰NZ 哥斯达黎加CR 秘鲁PE	0	最不发达35国LDC35	50	-Glues
	35.06	**其他税号未列名的调制胶及其他调制粘合剂;适于作胶或粘合剂用的产品，零售包装每件净重不超过1公斤:**							**Prepared glues and other prepared adhesives, not elsewhere specified or included; products suitable for use as glues or adhesives, put up for retail sale as glues or adhesives, not exceeding a net weight of 1kg:**
2659	3506.1000	-适于作胶或粘合剂用的产品，零售包装每件净重不超过1公斤	10	0 1 5 9.2	东盟ASEAN,新加坡SG,新西兰NZ,哥斯达黎加CR,香港HK,台湾TW 智利CL 巴基斯坦PK,秘鲁PE 亚太APTA	0	最不发达35国LDC35,最不发达4国LDC4	90	-Products suitable for use as glues or adhesives, put up for retail sale as glues or adhesives, not exceeding a net weight, of 1kg
		-其他:							-Other:
		--以橡胶或税目39.01至39.13的聚合物为基本成分的粘合剂:							--Adhesives based on polymers of headings 39.01 to 39.13or on rubber:
2660	3506.9110	---以聚酰胺为基本成分的	10	0 1 5 7	东盟ASEAN,新加坡SG,新西兰NZ,哥斯达黎加CR,香港HK,澳门MO,台湾TW 智利CL 巴基斯坦PK,秘鲁PE 亚太APTA	0	最不发达35国LDC35,最不发达4国LDC4	90	---Based on polyamide
2661	3506.9120	---以环氧树脂为基本成分的	10	0 1 5 7	东盟ASEAN,新加坡SG,新西兰NZ,哥斯达黎加CR,香港HK,澳门MO,台湾TW 智利CL 巴基斯坦PK,秘鲁PE 亚太APTA	0	最不发达35国LDC35,最不发达4国LDC4	90	---Based on epoxy resin

序号 No.	税则号列 Tariff Line	货品名称	最惠国税率 MFN(%)	协定税率 Agreement(%)		特惠税率 S.P.(%)		普通税率 Gen.(%)	Article Description
2662	3506.9190	---其他	10	0 1 5 7	东盟ASEAN,新加坡SG,新西兰NZ,哥斯达黎加CR,香港HK,澳门MO,台湾TW 智利CL 巴基斯坦PK,秘鲁PE 亚太APTA	0	最不发达35国LDC35,最不发达4国LDC4	90	---Other
2663	3506.9900	--其他	10	0 1 5 8.6	东盟ASEAN,新加坡SG,新西兰NZ,哥斯达黎加CR,香港HK,澳门MO,台湾TW 智利CL 巴基斯坦PK,秘鲁PE 亚太APTA	0	最不发达35国LDC35,最不发达4国LDC4	90	--Other
	35.07	**酶;其他税号未列名的酶制品:**							**Enzymes; prepared enzymes not else-where specified or included:**
2664	3507.1000	-粗制凝乳酶及其浓缩物	6	0 5	东盟ASEAN,智利CL,新西兰NZ,秘鲁PE,哥斯达黎加CR 巴基斯坦PK	0	最不发达35国LDC35,最不发达4国LDC4	30	-Rennet and concentrates thereof
		-其他:							-Other:
2665	3507.9010	---碱性蛋白酶	6	0 0.6 5	东盟ASEAN,新西兰NZ,秘鲁PE,哥斯达黎加CR 智利CL 巴基斯坦PK	0	最不发达35国LDC35,最不发达4国LDC4	30	---Basic proteinase
2666	3507.9020	---碱性脂肪酶	6	0 0.6 5	东盟ASEAN,新西兰NZ,秘鲁PE,哥斯达黎加CR 智利CL 巴基斯坦PK	0	最不发达35国LDC35,最不发达4国LDC4	30	---Basic lipase
2667	3507.9090	---其他	6	0 0.6 5	东盟ASEAN,新西兰NZ,秘鲁PE,哥斯达黎加CR,澳门MO 智利CL 巴基斯坦PK	0	最不发达35国LDC35,最不发达4国LDC4	30	---Other

第三十六章
炸药；烟火制品；火柴；引火合金；易燃材料制品

Chapter 36
Explosives; pyrotechnic products; matches; pyrophoric alloys; certain combustible preparations

注释:

一、本章不包括单独的已有化学定义的化合物，但下列注释二（一）、（二）所述物品除外。

二、税号36.06所称“易燃材料制品”，只适用于:

（一）聚乙醛、六甲撑四胺及类似物质，已制成片、棒或类似形状作燃料用的；以酒精为基本成分的固体或半固体燃料及类似的配制燃料；

（二）直接灌注香烟打火机及类似打火器用的液体燃料或液化气体燃料，其包装容器的容积不超过300立方厘米；

（三）树脂火炬、引火物及类似品。

Notes:

1. This Chapter does not cover separate chemically defined compounds other than those described in Note 2 (a) or (b) below.
2. The expression “articles of combustible materials” in heading No.36.06 applies only to:

(a) Metaldehyde, hexamethylenetetramine and similar substances, put up in forms (for example，tablets, sticks or similar forms) for use as fuels; fuels with as basis of alcohol, and similar prepared fuels, in solid or semi-solid form;

(b) Liquid or liquefied-gas fuels in containers of a kind used for filling or refilling cigarette or similar lighters and of a capacity not exceeding 300 cm^3, and

(c) Resin torches，firelighters and the like.

序号 No.	税则号列 Tariff Line	货品名称	最惠国税率 MFN(%)	协定税率 Agreement(%)		特惠税率 S.P.(%)		普通税率 Gen.(%)	Article Description
	36.01	**发射药:**							**Propellent powders:**
2668	3601.0000	发射药	9	0	东盟ASEAN,智利CL,新西兰NZ,秘鲁PE,哥斯达黎加CR	0	最不发达35国LDC35	50	Propellent powders
				5	巴基斯坦PK				
	36.02	**配制炸药，但发射药除外:**							**Prepared explosives, other than propellent powders:**
2669	3602.0010	---硝铵炸药	9	0	东盟ASEAN,新西兰NZ,秘鲁PE,哥斯达黎加CR	0	最不发达35国LDC35	50	---Based on ammonals nitrate
				0.9	智利CL				
				5	巴基斯坦PK				
2670	3602.0090	---其他	9	0	东盟ASEAN,新西兰NZ,秘鲁PE,哥斯达黎加CR	0	最不发达35国LDC35	50	---Other
				0.9	智利CL				
				5	巴基斯坦PK				
	36.03	**安全导火索;导爆索;火帽或雷管;引爆器;电雷管:**							**Safety fuses; detonating fuses; percussion or detonating caps; igniters; electric detonators:**
2671	3603.0000	安全导火索;导爆索;火帽或雷管;引爆器;电雷管	9	0	东盟ASEAN,新西兰NZ,秘鲁PE,哥斯达黎加CR	0	最不发达35国LDC35,最不发达4国LDC4	50	Safety fuses; detonating fuses; percussion or detonating caps; igniters; electric detonators
				0.9	智利CL				
				5	巴基斯坦PK				

序号 No.	税则号列 Tariff Line	货品名称	最惠国税率 MFN(%)	协定税率 Agreement(%)		特惠税率 S.P.(%)		普通税率 Gen.(%)	Article Description
	36.04	**烟花、爆竹、信号弹、降雨火箭、浓雾信号弹及其他烟火制品:**							**Fireworks, signalling flares, rain rockets, fog signals and other pyrotechnic articles:**
2672	3604.1000	-烟花、爆竹	6	0 5	东盟ASEAN,智利CL,新西兰NZ,秘鲁PE,哥斯达黎加CR 巴基斯坦PK	0	最不发达35国LDC35	130	-Fireworks
2673	3604.9000	-其他	6	0 5	东盟ASEAN,智利CL,新西兰NZ,秘鲁PE,哥斯达黎加CR 巴基斯坦PK	0	最不发达35国LDC35	100	-Other
	36.05	**火柴，但税号36.04的烟火制品除外:**							**Matches, other than pyrotechnic articles of heading No.36.04:**
2674	3605.0000	火柴，但税号36.04的烟火制品除外	6	0 0.6 5	东盟ASEAN,新西兰NZ,秘鲁PE,哥斯达黎加CR 智利CL 巴基斯坦PK	0	最不发达35国LDC35,最不发达4国LDC4	100	Matches, other than pyrotechnic articles of heading No.36.04
	36.06	**各种形状的铈铁及其他引火合金;本章注释二所述的易燃材料制品:**							**Ferro-cerium and other pyrophoric alloys in all forms; articles of combustible materials as specified in Note2 to this Chapter:**
2675	3606.1000	-直接灌注香烟打火机及类似打火器用的液体燃料或液化气体燃料，其包装容器的容积不超过300立方厘米	10	0 5	东盟ASEAN,智利CL,新西兰NZ,秘鲁PE,哥斯达黎加CR,香港HK 巴基斯坦PK	0	最不发达35国LDC35	80	-Liquid or liquefied-gas fuels in containers of a kind used for filling or refilling cigarette or similar lighters and of a capacity not exceeding 300cm³
		--其他:							--Other:
		---铈铁及其他引火合金:							---Ferro-cerium and other pyrophoric alloys:
2676	3606.9011	----已切成形可直接使用	9	0 5	东盟ASEAN,智利CL,新西兰NZ,秘鲁PE,哥斯达黎加CR 巴基斯坦PK	0	最不发达35国LDC35,最不发达4国LDC4	80	----Cut to shape, for immediate use
2677	3606.9019	----其他	9	0 5	东盟ASEAN,智利CL,新西兰NZ,秘鲁PE,哥斯达黎加CR 巴基斯坦PK	0	最不发达35国LDC35,最不发达4国LDC4	50	----Other
2678	3606.9090	---其他	9	0 5	东盟ASEAN,智利CL,新西兰NZ,秘鲁PE,哥斯达黎加CR 巴基斯坦PK	0	最不发达35国LDC35,最不发达4国LDC4	80	---Other

第三十七章
照相及电影用品

Chapter 37
Photographic or cinematographic goods

注释:

一、本章不包括废碎料。

二、本章所称"摄影"，是指光或其他射线作用于感光面上直接或间接形成可见影像的过程。

Notes:

1. This Chapter does not cover waste or scrap.

2. In this Chapter the word "photographic" relates to the process by which visible images are formed, directly or indirectly, by the action of light or other forms of radiation on photosensitive surfaces.

序号 No.	税则号列 Tariff Line	货品名称	最惠国税率 MFN(%)	协定税率 Agreement(%)		特惠税率 S.P.(%)		普通税率 Gen.(%)	Article Description
	37.01	**未曝光的摄影感光硬片及平面软片，用纸、纸板及纺织物以外任何材料制成;未曝光的一次成像感光平片，不论是否分装:**							**Photographic plates and film in the flat, sensitized, unexposed, of any material other than paper, paperboard or textiles; instant print film in the flat, sensitized, unexposed, whether or not in packs:**
2679	3701.1000	-X光用	20 △10	0 2 4 10	新西兰NZ 智利CL 哥斯达黎加CR 秘鲁PE	0	最不发达35国LDC35	40	-For X-ray
2680	3701.2000	-一次成像平片	5	0	东盟ASEAN,智利CL,巴基斯坦PK,新西兰NZ,秘鲁PE,哥斯达黎加CR	0	最不发达35国LDC35,最不发达4国LDC4	40	-Instant print film
		-其他硬片及软片，任何一边超过255毫米:							-Other plates and film, with any side exceeding 255mm:
		---照相制版用:							---For preparing printing plates or cylinders:
2681	3701.3021	----激光照排片	10	0	智利CL,新西兰NZ,秘鲁PE,哥斯达黎加CR,澳门MO	0	最不发达35国LDC35	50	----Laser phototypesetting film
2682	3701.3022	----PS版	10	0	智利CL,新西兰NZ,秘鲁PE,哥斯达黎加CR,澳门MO	0	最不发达35国LDC35	50	----Precoated sensitized plate
2683	3701.3024	----CTP版	10	0 5	文莱BN,印尼ID,马来西亚MY,缅甸MM,菲律宾PH,新加坡*SG*,泰国TH,越南VT,智利CL,新西兰NZ,秘鲁PE,哥斯达黎加CR,澳门MO 巴基斯坦PK	0	最不发达35国LDC35	50	----CTP plate
2684	3701.3025	----柔性印刷版	10	0	智利CL,新西兰NZ,秘鲁PE,哥斯达黎加CR,澳门MO	0	最不发达35国LDC35	50	----flexographic plate

序号 No.	税则号列 Tariff Line	货品名称	最惠国税率 MFN(%)	协定税率 Agreement(%)		特惠税率 S.P.(%)		普通税率 Gen.(%)	Article Description
2685	3701.3029	----其他	10	0	智利CL,新西兰NZ,秘鲁PE,哥斯达黎加CR,澳门MO	0	最不发达35国LDC35	50	----Other
2686	3701.3090	---其他	20	0 4 10	东盟ASEAN,智利CL,新加坡SG,新西兰NZ 哥斯达黎加CR 秘鲁PE	0	最不发达35国LDC35	70	---Other
		-其他:							-Other:
2687	3701.9100	--彩色摄影用	22	0 4.4 11	东盟ASEAN,智利CL,新加坡SG,新西兰NZ 哥斯达黎加CR 秘鲁PE	0	最不发达35国LDC35	70	--For colour photography (polychrome)
		--其他:							--Other:
2688	3701.9920	---照相制版用	10	0 1 5	东盟ASEAN,新西兰NZ,哥斯达黎加CR 智利CL 巴基斯坦PK,秘鲁PE	0	最不发达35国LDC35	40	---For preparing printing plates or cylinders
	ex37019920	石英玻璃基质的未曝光感光硬片	△5						Photographic plates and film, unexposed,quartz based
2689	3701.9990	---其他	25	0 2.5 5 12.5	东盟ASEAN,新加坡SG,新西兰NZ 智利CL 哥斯达黎加CR 秘鲁PE	0	最不发达35国LDC35	70	---Other
	37.02	**成卷的未曝光摄影感光胶片，用纸、纸板及纺织物以外任何材料制成;未曝光的一次成像感光卷片:**							**Photographic film in rolls, sensitized, unexposed, of any material other than paper, paperboard or textiles; instant print film in rolls, sensitized, unexposed:**
2690	3702.1000	-X光用	10	0	智利CL,新西兰NZ,秘鲁PE,哥斯达黎加CR	0	最不发达35国LDC35	40	-For X-ray
		-无齿孔的其他胶片，宽度不超过105毫米:							-Other film, without perforations, of a width not exceeding105mm:
		--彩色摄影用:							--For colour photography (polychrome):
2691	3702.3110	---一次成像卷片	5	0	东盟ASEAN,智利CL,巴基斯坦PK,新西兰NZ,秘鲁PE,哥斯达黎加CR	0	最不发达35国LDC35,最不发达4国LDC4	40	---Instant print film
2692	3702.3190	---其他	40	0 8 20	东盟ASEAN,智利CL,新加坡SG,新西兰NZ 哥斯达黎加CR 秘鲁PE	0	最不发达35国LDC35	433元/平方米	---Other
		--其他涂卤化银乳液的:							--Other, with silver halide emulsion:

序号 No.	税则号列 Tariff Line	货品名称	最惠国税率 MFN(%)	协定税率 Agreement(%)		特惠税率 S.P.(%)		普通税率 Gen.(%)	Article Description
2693	3702.3210	---一次成像卷片	5	0	东盟ASEAN,智利CL,巴基斯坦PK,新西兰NZ,秘鲁PE,哥斯达黎加CR	0	最不发达35国LDC35,最不发达4国LDC4	40	---Instant print film
2694	3702.3220	---照相制版用	10	0	文莱BN,印尼ID,马来西亚MY,缅甸MM,菲律宾PH,新加坡*SG*,泰国TH,越南VT,智利CL,新西兰NZ,秘鲁PE,哥斯达黎加CR	0	最不发达35国LDC35	104元/平方米	---For preparing printing plates or cylinders
				2.25元/平方米	巴基斯坦PK				
2695	3702.3290	---其他	22	0	文莱BN,印尼ID,马来西亚MY,缅甸MM,菲律宾PH,新加坡*SG*,泰国TH,越南VT,智利CL,新加坡SG,新西兰NZ	0	最不发达35国LDC35	202元/平方米	---Other
				4.4	哥斯达黎加CR				
				11	秘鲁PE				
		--其他:							--Other:
2696	3702.3920	---照相制版用	10	0	文莱BN,印尼ID,马来西亚MY,缅甸MM,菲律宾PH,新加坡*SG*,泰国TH,越南VT,智利CL,新西兰NZ,秘鲁PE,哥斯达黎加CR	0	最不发达35国LDC35	104元/平方米	---For preparing printing plates or cylinders
				6元/平方米	巴基斯坦PK				
2697	3702.3990	---其他	22	0	文莱BN,印尼ID,马来西亚MY,缅甸MM,菲律宾PH,新加坡*SG*,泰国TH,越南VT,智利CL,新加坡SG,新西兰NZ	0	最不发达35国LDC35	202元/平方米	---Other
				4.4	哥斯达黎加CR				
				11	秘鲁PE				
		-无齿孔的其他胶片，宽度超过105毫米:							-Other film, without perforations, of a width exceeding 105mm:
2698	3702.4100	--彩色摄影用，宽度超过610毫米，长度超过200米	16	0	智利CL,新西兰NZ	0	最不发达35国LDC35	202元/平方米	--Of a width exceeding 610mm and of a length exceeding 200m, for colour photography (polychrome):
				3.2	哥斯达黎加CR				
				8	秘鲁PE				
		--非彩色摄影用，宽度超过610毫米，长度超过200米:							--Of a width exceeding 610mm and of a length exceeding 200m, other than for colour photography:
		---照相制版用:							---For preparing printing plates or cylinders:

序号 No.	税则号列 Tariff Line	货品名称	最惠国税率 MFN(%)	协定税率 Agreement(%)		特惠税率 S.P.(%)		普通税率 Gen.(%)	Article Description
2699	3702.4221	----印刷电路板制造用光致抗蚀干膜	10	0	文莱BN,印尼ID,马来西亚MY,缅甸MM,菲律宾PH,新加坡*SG*,泰国TH,越南VT,智利CL,新加坡SG,新西兰NZ,秘鲁PE,哥斯达黎加CR	0	最不发达35国LDC35	110元/平方米	----Wide anticorrosive photographic plate for printed circuit processing
				0.3元/平方米	巴基斯坦PK				
2700	3702.4229	----其他	10	0	文莱BN,印尼ID,马来西亚MY,缅甸MM,菲律宾PH,新加坡*SG*,泰国TH,越南VT,智利CL,新西兰NZ,秘鲁PE,哥斯达黎加CR	0	最不发达35国LDC35	110元/平方米	----Other
				0.8元/平方米	巴基斯坦PK				
		---其他:							---Other:
2701	3702.4292	----红色或红外激光胶片	16	0	文莱BN,印尼ID,马来西亚MY,缅甸MM,菲律宾PH,新加坡*SG*,泰国TH,越南VT,智利CL,新加坡SG,新西兰NZ	0	最不发达35国LDC35	213元/平方米	----Red or infra-red laser film
				3.2	哥斯达黎加CR				
				8	秘鲁PE				
	ex37024292	红色或红外激光胶片，宽度>80cm，长度大于1000m	△1.05元/平方米						Red or infra-red laser film width>80cm, length >1000m
2702	3702.4299	----其他	16	0	文莱BN,印尼ID,马来西亚MY,缅甸MM,菲律宾PH,新加坡*SG*,泰国TH,越南VT,智利CL,新加坡SG,新西兰NZ	0	最不发达35国LDC35	213元/平方米	----Other
				3.2	哥斯达黎加CR				
				8	秘鲁PE				
		--宽度超过610毫米，长度不超过200米:							--Of a width exceeding 610mm and of a length not exceeding 200m:
		---照相制版用:							---For preparing printing plates or cylinders:
2703	3702.4321	----激光照排片	10	0	文莱BN,印尼ID,马来西亚MY,缅甸MM,菲律宾PH,新加坡*SG*,泰国TH,越南VT,智利CL,新西兰NZ,秘鲁PE,哥斯达黎加CR	0	最不发达35国LDC35	104元/平方米	----Laser phototypesetting film
				0.9元/平方米	巴基斯坦PK				
2704	3702.4329	----其他	10	0	文莱BN,印尼ID,马来西亚MY,缅甸MM,菲律宾PH,新加坡*SG*,泰国TH,越南VT,智利CL,新西兰NZ,秘鲁PE,哥斯达黎加CR	0	最不发达35国LDC35	104元/平方米	----Other
				1.85元/平方米	巴基斯坦PK				

序号 No.	税则号列 Tariff Line	货品名称	最惠国税率 MFN(%)	协定税率 Agreement(%)		特惠税率 S.P.(%)		普通税率 Gen.(%)	Article Description
2705	3702.4390	---其他	20	0	文莱BN,印尼ID,马来西亚MY,缅甸MM,菲律宾PH,新加坡*SG*,泰国TH,越南VT,智利CL,新加坡SG,新西兰NZ	0	最不发达35国LDC35	202元/平方米	---Other
				4	哥斯达黎加CR				
				10	秘鲁PE				
		--宽度超过105毫米，但不超过610毫米:							--Of a width exceeding 105mm but not exceeding 610mm:
		---照相制版用:							---For preparing printing plates or cylinders:
2706	3702.4421	----激光照排片	10	0	文莱BN,印尼ID,马来西亚MY,缅甸MM,菲律宾PH,新加坡*SG*,泰国TH,越南VT,智利CL,新西兰NZ,秘鲁PE,哥斯达黎加CR	0	最不发达35国LDC35	115元/平方米	----Laser phototypesetting film
				1.0元/平方米	巴基斯坦PK				
2707	3702.4422	----印刷电路板制造用光致抗蚀干膜	10	0	文莱BN,印尼ID,马来西亚MY,缅甸MM,菲律宾PH,新加坡*SG*,泰国TH,越南VT,智利CL,新西兰NZ,秘鲁PE,哥斯达黎加CR	0	最不发达35国LDC35	115元/平方米	----Narrow anticorrosive photographic plate for printed circuit processing
				0.45元/平方米	巴基斯坦PK				
2708	3702.4429	----其他	10	0	文莱BN,印尼ID,马来西亚MY,缅甸MM,菲律宾PH,新加坡*SG*,泰国TH,越南VT,智利CL,新西兰NZ,秘鲁PE,哥斯达黎加CR	0	最不发达35国LDC35	115元/平方米	----Other
				1.45元/平方米	巴基斯坦PK				
2709	3702.4490	---其他	20	0	文莱BN,印尼ID,马来西亚MY,缅甸MM,菲律宾PH,新加坡*SG*,泰国TH,越南VT,智利CL,新加坡SG,新西兰NZ	0	最不发达35国LDC35	202元/平方米	---Other
				4	哥斯达黎加CR				
				10	秘鲁PE				
		-彩色摄影用的其他胶片:							-Other film, for colour photography (polychrome):
2710	3702.5200	--宽度不超过16毫米	47	0	文莱BN,印尼ID,马来西亚MY,缅甸MM,菲律宾PH,新加坡*SG*,泰国TH,越南VT,智利CL,新加坡SG,新西兰NZ	0	最不发达35国LDC35	433元/平方米	--Of a width not exceeding 16 mm
				9.4	哥斯达黎加CR				
				23.5	秘鲁PE				

序号 No.	税则号列 Tariff Line	货品名称	最惠国税率 MFN(%)	协定税率 Agreement(%)		特惠税率 S.P.(%)		普通税率 Gen.(%)	Article Description
2711	3702.5300	--幻灯片用，宽度超过16毫米，但不超过35毫米，长度不超过30米	47	0	文莱BN,印尼ID,马来西亚MY,缅甸MM,菲律宾PH,新加坡*SG*,泰国TH,越南VT,智利CL,新加坡SG,新西兰NZ,香港HK	0	最不发达35国LDC35	433元/平方米	--Of a width exceeding 16mm but not exceeding 35mm and of a length not exceeding 30m, for slides
				9.4	哥斯达黎加CR				
				23.5	秘鲁PE				
		--非幻灯片用，宽度超过16毫米，但不超过35毫米，长度不超过30米:							--Of a width exceeding 16mm but not exceeding 35mm and of a length not exceeding 30m, other than for slides:
2712	3702.5410	---宽度为35毫米，长度不超过2米	18	0	智利CL,新西兰NZ,香港HK	0	最不发达35国LDC35	433元/平方米	---Of a width 35mm and of a length not exceeding 2m
				3.6	哥斯达黎加CR				
				9	秘鲁PE				
2713	3702.5490	---其他	18	0	智利CL,新西兰NZ,香港HK	0	最不发达35国LDC35	433元/平方米	---Other
				3.6	哥斯达黎加CR				
				9	秘鲁PE				
		--宽度超过16毫米，但不超过35毫米，长度超过30米:							--Of a width exceeding 16mm but not exceeding 35mm and of a length exceeding 30m:
2714	3702.5520	---电影胶片	26 △6元/平方米	0	新西兰NZ	0	最不发达35国LDC35	232元/平方米	---Cinematographic film
				5.2	哥斯达黎加CR				
				13	秘鲁PE				
				6.92元/平方米	东盟ASEAN				
				0.9元/平方米	智利CL				
2715	3702.5590	---其他	40	0	新西兰NZ			433元/平方米	---Other
				8	哥斯达黎加CR				
				13.5元/平方米	东盟ASEAN				
				2.7元/平方米	智利CL				
		--宽度超过35毫米:							--Of a width exceeding 35mm:
2716	3702.5620	---电影胶片	24	0	文莱BN,印尼ID,马来西亚MY,缅甸MM,菲律宾PH,新加坡*SG*,泰国TH,越南VT,智利CL,新加坡SG,新西兰NZ	0	最不发达35国LDC35	232元/平方米	---Cinematographic film
				4.8	哥斯达黎加CR				
				12	秘鲁PE				
2717	3702.5690	---其他	40	0	东盟ASEAN,智利CL,新加坡SG,新西兰NZ	0	最不发达35国LDC35	433元/平方米	---Other
				8	哥斯达黎加CR				
				20	秘鲁PE				

序号 No.	税则号列 Tariff Line	货品名称	最惠国税率 MFN(%)	协定税率 Agreement(%)		特惠税率 S.P.(%)		普通税率 Gen.(%)	Article Description
		-其他:							-Other:
2718	3702.9600	--宽度不超过35毫米，长度不超过30米	20	0	智利CL,新西兰NZ	0	最不发达35国LDC35	210元/平方米	--Of a width not exceeding 35 mm and of a length not exceeding 30 m
				4	哥斯达黎加CR				
				10	秘鲁PE				
2719	3702.9700	--宽度不超过35毫米，长度超过30米	18	0	新西兰NZ	0	最不发达35国LDC35	210元/平方米	--Of a width not exceeding 35 mm and of a length exceeding 30 m
				3.6	哥斯达黎加CR				
				9	秘鲁PE				
				0.9元/平方米	智利CL				
				9元/平方米	巴基斯坦PK				
2720	3702.9800	--宽度超过35毫米	18	0	文莱BN,印尼ID,马来西亚MY,缅甸MM,菲律宾PH,新加坡*SG*,泰国TH,越南VT,智利CL,新加坡SG,新西兰NZ	0	最不发达35国LDC35	210元/平方米	--Of a width exceeding 35 mm
				3.6	哥斯达黎加CR				
				9	秘鲁PE				
				8元/平方米	巴基斯坦PK				
	37.03	**未曝光的摄影感光纸、纸板及纺织物:**							**Photographic paper, paperboard and textiles, sensitized, unexposed:**
		-成卷，宽度超过610毫米:							-In rolls of a width exceeding 610mm:
2721	3703.1010	---感光纸及纸板	18	0	新西兰NZ	0	最不发达35国LDC35	100	---Photographic paper and paperboard
				1.8	智利CL				
				3.6	哥斯达黎加CR				
				9	秘鲁PE				
2722	3703.1090	---其他	18	0	新西兰NZ	0	最不发达35国LDC35	70	---Other
				1.8	智利CL				
				3.6	哥斯达黎加CR				
				9	秘鲁PE				
		-其他，彩色摄影用:							-Other, for colour photography (poly-chrome):
2723	3703.2010	---感光纸及纸板	35	0	智利CL,新西兰NZ,香港HK			100	---Photographic paper and paperboard
				7	哥斯达黎加CR				
				20	东盟ASEAN				
2724	3703.2090	---其他	18	0	智利CL,新西兰NZ,香港HK	0	最不发达35国LDC35	70	---Other
				3.6	哥斯达黎加CR				
				9	秘鲁PE				
		-其他:							-Other:
2725	3703.9010	---感光纸及纸板	35	0	新西兰NZ			100	---Photographic paper and paperboard
				3.5	智利CL				
				7	哥斯达黎加CR				
				20	东盟ASEAN				
2726	3703.9090	---其他	18	0	新西兰NZ	0	最不发达35国LDC35	70	---Other
				1.8	智利CL				
				3.6	哥斯达黎加CR				
				9	秘鲁PE				

序号 No.	税则号列 Tariff Line	货品名称	最惠国税率 MFN(%)	协定税率 Agreement(%)		特惠税率 S.P.(%)		普通税率 Gen.(%)	Article Description
	37.04	**已曝光未冲洗的摄影硬片、软片、纸、纸板及纺织物:**							**Photographic plates, film, paper, paperboard and textiles, exposed but not developed:**
2727	3704.0010	---电影胶片	6.5	0 5	东盟ASEAN,智利CL,新西兰NZ,秘鲁PE,哥斯达黎加CR 巴基斯坦PK	0	最不发达35国LDC35	30	---Cinematographic film
2728	3704.0090	---其他	18	0 3.6 9 14.4	东盟ASEAN,智利CL,新加坡SG,新西兰NZ 哥斯达黎加CR 秘鲁PE 巴基斯坦PK	0	最不发达35国LDC35	70	---Other
	37.05	**已曝光已冲洗的摄影硬片及软片，但电影胶片除外:**							**Photographic plates and film, exposed and developed, other than cinematographic film:**
2729	3705.1000	-供复制胶版用	18	0 1.8 3.6 9 14.4	东盟ASEAN,新加坡SG,新西兰NZ 智利CL 哥斯达黎加CR 秘鲁PE 巴基斯坦PK	0	最不发达35国LDC35	70	-For offset reproduction
		-其他:							-Other:
2730	3705.9010	---教学专用幻灯片	0			0	最不发达35国LDC35,最不发达4国LDC4	0	---Lantern slides, for educational use only
		---缩微胶片:							---Microfilms:
2731	3705.9021	----书籍、报刊的	0			0	最不发达35国LDC35,最不发达4国LDC4	0	----For printed books and newspapers
2732	3705.9029	----其他	4	0	东盟ASEAN,智利CL,巴基斯坦PK,新西兰NZ,秘鲁PE,哥斯达黎加CR	0	最不发达35国LDC35	14	----Other
2733	3705.9090	---其他	18	0 3.6 9 14.4	东盟ASEAN,智利CL,新加坡SG,新西兰NZ 哥斯达黎加CR 秘鲁PE 巴基斯坦PK	0	最不发达35国LDC35	70	---Other
	37.06	**已曝光已冲洗的电影胶片，不论是否配有声道或仅有声道:**							**Cinematographic film, exposed and developed, whether or not incorporating sound track or consisting only of sound track:**

序号 No.	税则号列 Tariff Line	货品名称	最惠国税率 MFN(%)	协定税率 Agreement(%)		特惠税率 S.P.(%)		普通税率 Gen.(%)	Article Description
		-宽度在35毫米及以上:							-Of a width of 35mm or more:
2734	3706.1010	---教学专用	0			0	最不发达35国LDC35,最不发达4国LDC4	0	---For educational use only
2735	3706.1090	---其他	5	0 0.5	东盟ASEAN,巴基斯坦PK,新西兰NZ,秘鲁PE,哥斯达黎加CR,香港HK 智利CL	0	最不发达35国LDC35,最不发达4国LDC4	14	---Other
		-其他:							-Other:
2736	3706.9010	---教学专用	0			0	最不发达35国LDC35,最不发达4国LDC4	0	---For educational use only
2737	3706.9090	---其他	4	0	东盟ASEAN,智利CL,巴基斯坦PK,新西兰NZ,秘鲁PE,哥斯达黎加CR,香港HK	0	最不发达35国LDC35,最不发达4国LDC4	14	---Other
	37.07	**摄影用化学制剂(不包括上光漆、胶水、粘合剂及类似制剂);摄影用未混合产品;定量包装或零售包装可立即使用的:**							**Chemical preparations for photogra phic uses (other than varnishes, glues, adhesives and similar preparations); unmixed products for photographic uses, put up in measured portions or put up for retail sale in a form ready for use:**
2738	3707.1000	-感光乳液	8	0 5	东盟ASEAN,智利CL,新西兰NZ,秘鲁PE,哥斯达黎加CR,澳门MO 巴基斯坦PK	0	最不发达35国LDC35,最不发达4国LDC4	35	-Sensitizing emulsions
	ex37071000	感光乳剂(不含银的)	△4						Sensitizing emulsions (without silver component)
		-其他:							-Other:
2739	3707.9010	---冲洗照相胶卷及相片用	16	0 1.6 3.2 8 12.8	东盟ASEAN,新加坡SG,新西兰NZ,香港HK 智利CL 哥斯达黎加CR 秘鲁PE 巴基斯坦PK	0	最不发达35国LDC35	100	---For use in developing photographic film and photographs

序号 No.	税则号列 Tariff Line	货品名称	最惠国 税　率 MFN(%)	协定税率 Agreement(%)		特惠税率 S.P.(%)		普通 税率 Gen.(%)	Article Description
2740	3707.9020	---复印机用	10 △8	0 1 5	东盟ASEAN,新加坡SG,新西兰NZ,哥斯达黎加CR,香港HK,澳门MO 智利CL 巴基斯坦PK,秘鲁PE	0	最不发达35国LDC35,最不发达4国LDC4	45	---For use in photo-copying apparatus
2741	3707.9090	---其他	8	0 0.8 5	东盟ASEAN,新西兰NZ,秘鲁PE,哥斯达黎加CR,香港HK,澳门MO 智利CL 巴基斯坦PK	0	最不发达35国LDC35,最不发达4国LDC4	35	---Other

第三十八章
杂项化学产品

注释:

一、本章不包括:

（一）单独的已有化学定义的元素及化合物，但下列各项除外:

1. 人造石墨（税号38.01）；

2. 制成税号38.08所述的形状或包装的杀虫剂、杀鼠剂、杀菌剂、除草剂、抗萌剂、植物生长调节剂、消毒剂及类似产品;

3. 灭火器的装配药及已装药的灭火弹（税号38.13）；

4. 下列注释二所规定的检定参照物;

5. 下列注释三（一）及三（三）所规定的产品。

（二）配制食品用的与食物或其他营养物质混合的化学品（一般归入税号21.06）；

（三）符合第二十六章注释三（一）或三（二）的规定，含有金属，砷及其混合物的矿渣、矿灰及残渣（包括淤渣，但下水道淤泥除外）（税目26.20）；

（四）药品（税号30.03及30.04）；

（五）用于提取贱金属或生产贱金属化合物的废催化剂（税号26.20），主要用于回收贵金属的废催化剂（税号71.12），或某种形状（例如，精细粉末或纱网状）的金属或金属合金催化剂（第十四类或第十五类）。

二、

（一）税目38.22所称的“检定参照物”，是指附有证书的参照物，该证书标明了参照物属性的指标、确定这些指标的方法以及与每一指标相关的确定度，这些参照物适用于分析、校准和比较。

（二）除第二十八章和二十九章的产品外，检定参照物在本目录中应优先归入税目38.22。

Chapter 38
Miscellaneous chemical products

Notes:

1. This Chapter does not cover:

(a) Separate chemically defined elements or compounds with the exception of the following:

(1) Artificial graphite (heading No.38.01) ;

(2) Insecticides, rodenticides, fungicides, herbicides, anti-sprouting products and plant-growth regulators, disinfectants and similar products, put up as described in heading No.38.08;

(3) Products put up as charges for fire-extinguishers or put up in fire-extinguishing grenades (heading No.38.13) ;

(4) Certified reference materials specified in Note 2 below;

(5) Products specified in Note 3(a) or 3(c) below;

(b) Mixtures of chemicals with foodstuffs or other substances with nutritive value, of a kind used in the preparations of human foodstuffs (generally heading No.21.06) ;

(c) Slag, ash and residues (including sludges, other than sewage sludge), containing metals, arsenic or their mixtures and meeting the requirements of Note 3(a) or 3 (b) to Chapter 26 (heading 26.20) ;

(d) Medicaments (heading No.30.03 or 30.04) ;

(e) Spent catalysts of a kind used for the extraction of base metals or for the manufacture of chemical compounds of base metals (heading No.26.20), spent catalysts of a kind used princi pally for the recovery of precious metal (heading No.71.12) or catalysts consisting or metals of metal alloys in the form of, for example, finely divided powder or woven gauze (Section XIV or XV) .

2.

(a) For the purpose of heading 38.22, the expression “certified reference materials” means reference materials which are accompanied by a certificate which indicates the values of the certified properties, the methods used to determine these values and the degree of certainty associated with each value and which are suitable for analytical, calibrating or referenc ing purboses.

(b) With the exception of the products of Chapter 28 or 29, for the classification of certified reference materials, heading 38.22 shall take precedence over any other heading in the Nomenclature."

三、税号38.24包括不归入本目录其他税号的下列货品:

（一）每颗重量不小于2.5克的氧化镁、碱金属或碱土金属卤化物制成的培养晶体(光学元件除外);

（二）杂醇油;骨焦油;

（三）零售包装的除墨剂;

（四）零售包装的蜡纸改正液，其他改正液及改正带（税目96.12的产品除外）；以及

（五）可熔性陶瓷测温器（例如，塞格测温锥）。

3. Heading No.38.24 includes the following goods which are not to be classified in any other heading of the Nomenclature:

(a) Cultured crystals (other than optical elements) weighing not less than 2.5g each，of magnesium oxide or of the halides of the alkali or alkaline-earth metals;

(b) Fusel oil; Dippel s oil;

(c) Ink removers put up in packings for retail sale;

(d) Stencil correctors, other correcting fluids and correction tapes (other than those of heading 96.12), put up in packings for retail sale; and

(e) Ceramic firing testers, fusible (for example, Seger- cones).

四、本目录所称"城市垃圾"是指一种从家庭、宾馆、餐馆、医院、商店、办公室等收集来的废物、马路和人行道的垃圾以及建筑垃圾或废墟废物。城市垃圾通常含有大量各种各样的材料，例如，塑料、橡胶、木材、纸张、纺织品、玻璃、金属、食物、破碎家具和其他已损坏或被丢弃的物品，但不包括:

（一）已从垃圾中分拣出来的单独的材料或物品，例如，塑料、橡胶、木材、纸张、纺织品、玻璃、金属及电池的废品，这些材料或物品应归入本目录中适当税目;

（二）工业废物;

（三）在第三十章注释四（十）所规定的废药物;

（四）本章注释六（一）所规定的医疗废物。

4. Throughout the Nomenclature, "municipal waste" means waste of a kind collected from households, hotels, restaurants, hospitals, shops, offices, etc., road and pave-ment sweepings, as well as construction and demolition waste. Municipal waste generally contains a large variety of materials such as plastics, rubber, wood, paper, textiles, glass, metals, food materials, broken furniture and other damaged or discarded articles.The term "municipal waste", however, does not cover:

(a) Individual materials or articles segregated from the waste, such as wastes of plastics, rubber, wood, paper, textiles, glass or metals and spent batteries which fall in their appropriate head ings of the Nomenclature;

(b) Industrial waste;

(c) Waste pharmaceuticals, as defined in Note 4(k) to Chapter 30; or

(d) Clinical waste, as defined in Note6(a) below.

五、税目38.25所称"下水道淤泥"，是指城市污水处理厂产生的淤渣，包括预处理的废物、洗涤污垢和性质不稳定的淤泥。但适合作为肥料用的性质稳定的淤泥除外（第三十一章）。

5. For the purposes of heading 38.25, "sewage sludge" means sludge arising from urban effluent treatment plant and includes pretrea-tment waste, scourings and unstabilised sludge. Stabilised sludge when suitable for use as fertiliser is excluded (Chapter 31) .

六、税目38.25所称"其他废物"适用于:

（一）医疗废物，即医学研究、诊断、治疗以及其他内科、外科、牙科或兽医治疗所产生的被污染的废物，通常含有病菌和药物，需作专门的处理(例如，脏的敷料、用过的手套和注射器);

（二）废有机溶剂;

6. For the purposes of heading 38.25, the expression"other wastes" applies to:

(a) Clinical waste, that is, contaminated waste arising from medical research, diagnosis, treatment or other medical, surgical, dental or veterinary procedures, which often contain pathogens and pharmaceutical substances and require special disposal procedures (for example, soiled dressings, used gloves and used syringes) ;

(b) Waste organic solvents;

（三）废的金属酸洗液、液压油、制动油和防冻液；

（四）其他化学工业及相关工业的废物。

但不包括主要含有石油及从沥青矿物提取的油类的废油（税目27.10）。

七、税目38.26所称的“生物柴油”，是指从动植物油脂（不论是否使用过）得到的用作燃料的脂肪酸单烷基酯。

子目注释：

一、子目3808.50仅包括税目38.08的货品，含有一种或多种下列物质：艾氏剂（ISO）；乐杀螨（ISO）；毒杀芬（ISO）；敌菌丹（ISO）；氯丹（ISO）；杀虫脒（ISO）；乙酯杀螨醇（ISO）；滴滴涕（ISO，INN）〔1,1,1-三氯-2,2-双（4-氯苯基）乙烷〕；狄氏剂（ISO，INN）；4,6-二硝基邻甲酚（二硝酚（ISO））及其盐；地乐酚（ISO）及其盐或酯；1,2-二溴乙烷（ISO）；1,2-二氯乙烷（ISO）；氟乙酰胺（ISO）；七氯（ISO）；六氯苯（ISO）；1,2,3,4,5,6-六氯环己烷〔六六六（ISO）〕，包括林丹（ISO，INN）；汞化合物；甲胺磷（ISO）；久效磷（ISO）；环氧乙烷（氧化乙烯）；对硫磷（ISO）；甲基对硫磷（ISO）；五氯苯酚（ISO）及其盐或酯；磷胺（ISO）；2,4,5-涕（ISO）（2,4,5-三氯苯氧基乙酸）及其盐或酯；三丁基锡化合物。

子目3808.50还包括含有苯菌灵（ISO）、克百威（ISO）及福美双（ISO）混合物的粉状制剂。

二、子目3825.41和3825.49所称“废有机溶剂”，是指主要含有有机溶剂的废物，不适合再作原产品使用，不论其是否用于回收溶剂。

(c) Wastes of metal pickling liquors, hydraulic fluids, brake fluids and antifreezing fluids; and

(d) Other wastes from chemical or allied industries.

The expression “other wastes” does not, however, cover wastes which contain mainly petroleum oils or oils obtained from bituminous minerals (heading27.10) .

7. For the purposes of heading 38.26, the term “biodiesel” means mono-alkyl esters of fatty acids of a kind used as a fuel, derived from animal or vegetable fats and oils whether or not used.

Subheading Notes:

1. Subheading 3808.50 covers only goods of heading 38.08, containing one or more of the following substances : aldrin (ISO); binapacryl (ISO); camphechlor (ISO) (toxaphene); captafol (ISO); chlordane (ISO); chlordimeform (ISO); chlorobenzilate (ISO); DDT (ISO) (clofenotane (INN), 1,1,1-trichloro-2,2-bis (p-chlorophenyl) ethane); dieldrin (ISO, INN); 4,6- dinitro-o-cresol (DNOC (ISO)) or its salts; dinoseb (ISO), its salts or its esters; ethylene dibromide (ISO) (1,2-dibromoethane); ethylene dichloride (ISO) (1,2-dichloroethane); fluoroacetamide (ISO); heptachlor (ISO); hexachlorobenzene (ISO); 1,2,3,4,5,6-hexachlorocyclohexane (HCH (ISO)), including lindane (ISO, INN); mercury compounds; methamidophos (ISO); monocrotophos (ISO); oxirane (ethylene oxide); parathion (ISO); parathion-methyl (ISO) (methyl-parathion); pentachlorophenol (ISO), its salts or its esters; phosphamidon (ISO); 2,4,5-T (ISO) (2,4,5-trichlorophenoxyacetic acid), its salts or its esters; tributyltin compounds.

Subheading 3808.50 also covers dustable powder formulations containing a mixture of benomyl (ISO), carbofuran (ISO) and thiram (ISO).

2. For the purposes of subheadings 3825.41 and 3825.49, “waste organic solvents”are wastes containing mainly organic solvents, not fit for further use as presented as primary products, whether or not intended for recovery of the solvents.

序号 No.	税则号列 Tariff Line	货品名称	最惠国税率 MFN(%)	协定税率 Agreement(%)		特惠税率 S.P.(%)		普通税率 Gen.(%)	Article Description
	38.01	**人造石墨;胶态或半胶态石墨;以石墨或其他碳为基本成分的糊状、块状、板状制品或其他半制品:**							**Artificial graphite; colloidal or semi colloidal graphite; preparations based on graphite or other carbon in the form of pastes, blocks, plates or other semi-manufactures:**
2742	3801.1000	-人造石墨	6.5 △3	0 5	东盟ASEAN,智利CL,新西兰NZ,秘鲁PE,哥斯达黎加CR,香港HK 巴基斯坦PK	0	最不发达35国LDC35,最不发达4国LDC4	30	-Artificial graphite
2743	3801.2000	-胶态或半胶态石墨	6.5	0 5	东盟ASEAN,智利CL,新西兰NZ,秘鲁PE,哥斯达黎加CR 巴基斯坦PK	0	最不发达35国LDC35,最不发达4国LDC4	30	-Colloidal or semi-colloidal graphite
2744	3801.3000	-电极用碳糊及炉衬用的类似糊	6.5	0 5	东盟ASEAN,智利CL,新西兰NZ,秘鲁PE,哥斯达黎加CR 巴基斯坦PK	0	最不发达35国LDC35,最不发达4国LDC4	35	-Carbonaceous pastes for electrodes and similar pastes for furnace linings
		-其他:							-Other:
2745	3801.9010	---表面处理的球化石墨	6.5	0 5	东盟ASEAN,智利CL,新西兰NZ,秘鲁PE,哥斯达黎加CR 巴基斯坦PK	0	最不发达35国LDC35,最不发达4国LDC4	35	---Surface modified spherical graphite
2746	3801.9090	---其他	6.5	0 5	东盟ASEAN,智利CL,新西兰NZ,秘鲁PE,哥斯达黎加CR 巴基斯坦PK	0	最不发达35国LDC35,最不发达4国LDC4	35	---Other
	38.02	**活性碳;活性天然矿产品;动物炭黑,包括废动物炭黑:**							**Activated carbon; activated natural mineral products; animal black, including spent animal black:**
		-活性碳:							-activated carbon:
2747	3802.1010	---木质的	6.5	0 5 5.5	东盟ASEAN,智利CL,新西兰NZ,秘鲁PE,哥斯达黎加CR 巴基斯坦PK 亚太APTA	0	最不发达35国LDC35	20	---Of wood
2748	3802.1090	---其他	6.5	0 5 5.5	东盟ASEAN,智利CL,新西兰NZ,秘鲁PE,哥斯达黎加CR 巴基斯坦PK 亚太APTA	0	最不发达35国LDC35	20	---Other

序号 No.	税则号列 Tariff Line	货品名称	最惠国税率 MFN(%)	协定税率 Agreement(%)		特惠税率 S.P.(%)		普通税率 Gen.(%)	Article Description
2749	3802.9000	-其他	10	0 1 5	东盟ASEAN,新加坡SG,新西兰NZ,哥斯达黎加CR 智利CL 巴基斯坦PK,秘鲁PE	0	最不发达35国LDC35	45	-Other
	38.03	**妥尔油，不论是否精炼:**							**Tall oil, whether or not refined:**
2750	3803.0000	妥尔油，不论是否精炼	6.5	0 5	东盟ASEAN,智利CL,新西兰NZ,秘鲁PE,哥斯达黎加CR 巴基斯坦PK	0	最不发达35国LDC35,最不发达4国LDC4	35	Tall oil, whether or not refined
	38.04	**木浆残余碱液，不论是否浓缩、脱糖或经化学处理，包括木素磺酸盐，但不包括税号38.03的妥尔油:**							**Residual lyes from the manufacture of wood pulp, whether or not concentrated, desugared or chemically treated, including lignin sulphonates, but excluding tall oil of heading No.38.03:**
2751	3804.0000	木浆残余碱液，不论是否浓缩、脱糖或经化学处理，包括木素磺酸盐，但不包括税号38.03的妥尔油	6.5	0 5	东盟ASEAN,智利CL,新西兰NZ,秘鲁PE,哥斯达黎加CR 巴基斯坦PK	0	最不发达35国LDC35	35	Residual lyes from the manufacture of wood pulp, whether or not concentrated, desugared or chemically treated, including lignin sulphonates, but excluding tall oil of heading No.38.03
	38.05	**脂松节油、木松节油和硫酸盐松节油及其他萜烯油，用蒸馏或其他方法从针叶木制得;粗制二聚戊烯;亚硫酸盐松节油及其他粗制对异丙基苯甲烷;以a萜品醇为基本成分的松油:**							**Gum, wood or sulphate turpentine and other terpenic oils produced by the distillation or other treatment of coniferous woods; crude dipentene; sulphite turpentine and other crude-paracymene; pine oil containing alpha-terpineol as the main constituent:**
2752	3805.1000	-脂松节油、木松节油和硫酸盐松节油	6.5	0 5	东盟ASEAN,智利CL,新西兰NZ,秘鲁PE,哥斯达黎加CR 巴基斯坦PK	0	最不发达35国LDC35,最不发达4国LDC4	50	-Gum, wood or sulphate turpentine oils
		-其他:							-Other:
2753	3805.9010	---松油	6.5	0 0.7 5	东盟ASEAN,新西兰NZ,秘鲁PE,哥斯达黎加CR 智利CL 巴基斯坦PK	0	最不发达35国LDC35,最不发达4国LDC4	50	---Pine oil

序号 No.	税则号列 Tariff Line	货品名称	最惠国税率 MFN(%)	协定税率 Agreement(%)		特惠税率 S.P.(%)		普通税率 Gen.(%)	Article Description
2754	3805.9090	---其他	6.5	0 5	东盟ASEAN,智利CL,新西兰NZ,秘鲁PE,哥斯达黎加CR 巴基斯坦PK	0	最不发达35国LDC35,最不发达4国LDC4	50	---Other
	38.06	**松香和树脂酸及其衍生物;松香精及松香油;再熔胶:**							**Rosin and resin acids, and derivatives thereof; rosin spirit and rosin oils; run gums:**
		-松香及树脂酸:							-Rosin and resin acids:
2755	3806.1010	---松香	10	0 5	东盟ASEAN,智利CL,新加坡SG,新西兰NZ,秘鲁PE,哥斯达黎加CR,澳门MO 巴基斯坦PK	0	最不发达35国LDC35	70	---Rosin
2756	3806.1020	---树脂酸	10	0 5	东盟ASEAN,智利CL,新西兰NZ,秘鲁PE,哥斯达黎加CR,澳门MO 巴基斯坦PK	0	最不发达35国LDC35	70	---Resin acides
		-松香盐、树脂酸盐及松香或树脂酸衍生物的盐，但松香加合物的盐除外:							-Salts of rosin, of resin acids or of deri-vatives of rosin or resin acids, other than salts of rosin adducts:
2757	3806.2010	---松香盐及树脂酸盐	6.5	0 5	东盟ASEAN,智利CL,新西兰NZ,秘鲁PE,哥斯达黎加CR,澳门MO 巴基斯坦PK	0	最不发达35国LDC35	40	---Salts of rosin, of resin acids
2758	3806.2090	---其他	6.5	0 5	东盟ASEAN,智利CL,新西兰NZ,秘鲁PE,哥斯达黎加CR,澳门MO 巴基斯坦PK	0	最不发达35国LDC35	40	---Other
2759	3806.3000	-酯胶	6.5	0 5	东盟ASEAN,智利CL,新西兰NZ,秘鲁PE,哥斯达黎加CR,澳门MO 巴基斯坦PK	0	最不发达35国LDC35	50	-Ester gums
2760	3806.9000	-其他	6.5	0 5	东盟ASEAN,智利CL,新西兰NZ,秘鲁PE,哥斯达黎加CR,澳门MO 巴基斯坦PK	0	最不发达35国LDC35	40	-Other
	38.07	**木焦油;精制木焦油;木杂酚油;粗木精;植物沥青;以松香、树脂酸或植物沥青为基本成分的啤酒桶沥青及类似制品:**							**Wood tar; wood tar oils; wood creosote; wood naphtha; vegetable pitch; brewers pitch and similar preparations based on rosin, resin acids or on vegetable pitch:**
2761	3807.0000	木焦油;精制木焦油;木杂酚油;粗木精;植物沥青;以松香、树脂酸或植物沥青为基本成分的啤酒桶沥青及类似制品	6.5	0 5	东盟ASEAN,智利CL,新西兰NZ,秘鲁PE,哥斯达黎加CR 巴基斯坦PK	0	最不发达35国LDC35	35	Wood tar; wood tar oils; wood creosote; wood naphtha; vegetable pitch; brewers' pitch and similar preparations based on rosin, resin acids or on vegetable pitch

序号 No.	税则号列 Tariff Line	货品名称	最惠国税率 MFN(%)	协定税率 Agreement(%)	特惠税率 S.P.(%)	普通税率 Gen.(%)	Article Description
	38.08	**杀虫剂、杀鼠剂、杀菌剂、除草剂、抗萌剂、植物生长调节剂、消毒剂及类似产品，零售形状、零售包装或制成制剂及成品（例如，经硫磺处理的带子、杀虫灯芯、蜡烛及捕蝇纸）:**					**Insecticides, rodenticides, fungicides, herbicides, anti-sprouting products and plant-growth regulators, disinfectants and similar products, put up in forms or packings for retail sale or as preparations or articles(for example, sulphur-treated bands, wicks and candles, and fly-papers):**
		-本章子目注释一所规定的货品:					-Goods specified in subheading Note 1 to this chapter:
2762	3808.5010	---零售包装	9	0 东盟ASEAN,新西兰NZ,秘鲁PE,哥斯达黎加CR,香港HK 0.9 智利CL 5 巴基斯坦PK	0 最不发达35国LDC35,最不发达4国LDC4	35	---Put up for retail sale
2763	3808.5090	---其他	5	0 东盟ASEAN,新西兰NZ,秘鲁PE,哥斯达黎加CR,香港HK 0.5 智利CL	0 最不发达35国LDC35,最不发达4国LDC4	11	---Other
		-其他:					-Other:
		--杀虫剂:					--Insecticides:
		---零售包装:					---Put up for retail sale:
2764	3808.9111	----蚊香	10	0 东盟ASEAN,亚太APTA,巴基斯坦PK,新西兰NZ,秘鲁PE,哥斯达黎加CR,澳门MO 1 智利CL	0 最不发达35国LDC35,最不发达4国LDC4	80	----Mosquito smudges
2765	3808.9112	----生物杀虫剂	10	0 东盟ASEAN,新西兰NZ,秘鲁PE,哥斯达黎加CR,香港HK,澳门MO 1 智利CL 5 巴基斯坦PK 7 亚太APTA	0 最不发达35国LDC35,最不发达4国LDC4	35	----Biological products
2766	3808.9119	----其他	10	0 东盟ASEAN,新西兰NZ,秘鲁PE,哥斯达黎加CR,香港HK,澳门MO 1 智利CL 5 巴基斯坦PK 7 亚太APTA	0 最不发达35国LDC35,最不发达4国LDC4	35	----Other

序号 No.	税则号列 Tariff Line	货品名称	最惠国税率 MFN(%)	协定税率 Agreement(%)		特惠税率 S.P.(%)		普通税率 Gen.(%)	Article Description
2767	3808.9190	---其他	6	0 0.6 4.2	东盟ASEAN,巴基斯坦PK,新西兰NZ,秘鲁PE,哥斯达黎加CR,香港HK,澳门MO 智利CL 亚太APTA	0	最不发达35国LDC35,最不发达4国LDC4	11	---Other
		-杀菌剂:							-Fungicides:
2768	3808.9210	---零售包装	9	0 0.9 5	东盟ASEAN,新西兰NZ,秘鲁PE,哥斯达黎加CR,香港HK 智利CL 巴基斯坦PK	0	最不发达35国LDC35,最不发达4国LDC4	35	---Put up for retail sale
2769	3808.9290	---其他	6	0 0.6 5	东盟ASEAN,新西兰NZ,秘鲁PE,哥斯达黎加CR 智利CL 巴基斯坦PK	0	最不发达35国LDC35,最不发达4国LDC4	11	---Other
		-除草剂、抗萌剂及植物生长调节剂:							-Herbicides, anti-sprouting products and plant-growth regulators:
		---除草剂:							---Herbicides:
2770	3808.9311	----零售包装	9	0 0.9 5	东盟ASEAN,新西兰NZ,秘鲁PE,哥斯达黎加CR 智利CL 巴基斯坦PK	0	最不发达35国LDC35,最不发达4国LDC4	35	----Put up for retai sale
2771	3808.9319	----其他	5	0 0.5 4.5	东盟ASEAN,巴基斯坦PK,新西兰NZ,秘鲁PE,哥斯达黎加CR 智利CL 亚太APTA	0	最不发达35国LDC35,最不发达4国LDC4	11	----Other
		---其他:							---Other:
2772	3808.9391	----零售包装	9	0 0.9 5 8.3	东盟ASEAN,新西兰NZ,秘鲁PE,哥斯达黎加CR 智利CL 巴基斯坦PK 亚太APTA	0	最不发达35国LDC35,最不发达4国LDC4	35	----Put up for retail sale
2773	3808.9399	----其他	6	0 0.6 5 5.5	东盟ASEAN,新西兰NZ,秘鲁PE,哥斯达黎加CR 智利CL 巴基斯坦PK 亚太APTA	0	最不发达35国LDC35,最不发达4国LDC4	14	----Other
2774	3808.9400	--消毒剂	9	0 0.9 5	东盟ASEAN,新西兰NZ,秘鲁PE,哥斯达黎加CR,香港HK 智利CL 巴基斯坦PK	0	最不发达35国LDC35,最不发达4国LDC4	35	--Disinfectants

序号 No.	税则号列 Tariff Line	货品名称	最惠国 税率 MFN(%)	协定税率 Agreement(%)		特惠税率 S.P.(%)		普通 税率 Gen.(%)	Article Description
		-其他:							-Other:
2775	3808.9910	---零售包装	9	0 0.9 5	东盟ASEAN,新西兰NZ,秘鲁PE,哥斯达黎加CR,香港HK 智利CL 巴基斯坦PK	0	最不发达35国LDC35,最不发达4国LDC4	35	---Put up for retail sale
2776	3808.9990	---其他	9	0 0.9 5	东盟ASEAN,新西兰NZ,秘鲁PE,哥斯达黎加CR,澳门MO 智利CL 巴基斯坦PK	0	最不发达35国LDC35,最不发达4国LDC4	14	---Other
	38.09	**纺织、造纸、制革及类似工业用的其他税号未列名的整理剂、染料加速着色或固色助剂及其他产品和制剂（例如，修整剂及媒染剂）：**							**Finishing agents, dye carriers to accelerate the dyeing or fixing of dye-stuffs and other products and preparations (for example, dressings and mordants), of a kind used in the textile, paper, leather or like industries, not elsewhere specified or included:**
2777	3809.1000	-以淀粉物质为基本成分	10	0	东盟ASEAN,智利CL,巴基斯坦PK,新加坡SG,新西兰NZ,秘鲁PE,哥斯达黎加CR	0	最不发达35国LDC35,最不发达4国LDC4	35	-With a basis of amylaceous substances
		-其他:							-Other:
2778	3809.9100	--纺织工业及类似工业用	6.5	0 6	东盟ASEAN,智利CL,巴基斯坦PK,新西兰NZ,秘鲁PE,哥斯达黎加CR,香港HK 亚太APTA	0	最不发达35国LDC35,最不发达4国LDC4	35	--Of a kind used in the textile or like industries
2779	3809.9200	--造纸工业及类似工业用	6.5	0 0.7	东盟ASEAN,巴基斯坦PK,新西兰NZ,秘鲁PE,哥斯达黎加CR,香港HK 智利CL	0	最不发达35国LDC35,最不发达4国LDC4	35	--Of a kind used in the paper or like industries
2780	3809.9300	--制革工业及类似工业用	6.5	0 0.7	东盟ASEAN,巴基斯坦PK,新西兰NZ,秘鲁PE,哥斯达黎加CR,香港HK 智利CL	0	最不发达35国LDC35,最不发达4国LDC4	35	--Of a kind used in the leather or like industries

序号 No.	税则号列 Tariff Line	货品名称	最惠国税率 MFN(%)	协定税率 Agreement(%)		特惠税率 S.P.(%)		普通税率 Gen.(%)	Article Description
	38.10	**金属表面酸洗剂;焊接用的焊剂及其他辅助剂;金属及其他材料制成的焊粉或焊膏;作焊条芯子或焊条涂料用的制品:**							**Pickling preparations for metal surfaces; fluxes and other auxiliary preparations for soldering, brazing or welding; soldering, brazing or welding powders and pastes consisting of metal and other materials; preparations of a kind used as cores or coatings for welding electrodes or rods:**
2781	3810.1000	-金属表面酸洗剂;金属及其他材料制成的焊粉或焊膏	6.5	0 0.7 5 6	东盟ASEAN,新西兰NZ,秘鲁PE,哥斯达黎加CR,香港HK,澳门MO 智利CL 巴基斯坦PK 亚太APTA	0	最不发达35国LDC35,最不发达4国LDC4	35	-Pickling preparations for metal surfaces; soldering, brazing or welding powders and pastes consisting of metal and other materials
2782	3810.9000	-其他	6.5	0 5	东盟ASEAN,智利CL,新西兰NZ,秘鲁PE,哥斯达黎加CR 巴基斯坦PK	0	最不发达35国LDC35,最不发达4国LDC4	35	-Other
	38.11	**抗震剂、抗氧剂、防胶剂、粘度改良剂、防腐蚀制剂及其他配制添加剂，用于矿物油（包括汽油）或与矿物油同样用途的其他液体:**							**Anti-knock preparations, oxidation inhibitors, gum inhibitors, viscosity improvers, anti-corrosive preparations and other prepared additives, for mineral oils (including gasoling) or for other liquids used for the same purposes as mineral oils:**
		-抗震剂:							-Anti-knock preparations:
2783	3811.1100	--以铅化合物为基本成分	6.5	0 5	东盟ASEAN,智利CL,新西兰NZ,秘鲁PE,哥斯达黎加CR 巴基斯坦PK	0	最不发达35国LDC35	35	--Based on lead compounds
2784	3811.1900	--其他	6.5	0 5	东盟ASEAN,智利CL,新西兰NZ,秘鲁PE,哥斯达黎加CR 巴基斯坦PK	0	最不发达35国LDC35	35	--Other
		-润滑油添加剂:							-Additives for lubricating oils:
2785	3811.2100	--含有石油或从沥青矿物提取的油类	6.5	0 0.7 5	东盟ASEAN,新西兰NZ,秘鲁PE,哥斯达黎加CR 智利CL 巴基斯坦PK	0	最不发达35国LDC35	35	--Containing petroleum oils or oils obtained from bituminous minerals

序号 No.	税则号列 Tariff Line	货品名称	最惠国税率 MFN(%)	协定税率 Agreement(%)		特惠税率 S.P.(%)		普通税率 Gen.(%)	Article Description
2786	3811.2900	--其他	6.5	0 5 5.5	东盟ASEAN,智利CL,新西兰NZ,秘鲁PE,哥斯达黎加CR,澳门MO 巴基斯坦PK 亚太APTA	0	最不发达35国LDC35	35	--Other
2787	3811.9000	-其他	6.5	0 5	东盟ASEAN,智利CL,新西兰NZ,秘鲁PE,哥斯达黎加CR,香港HK,澳门MO 巴基斯坦PK	0	最不发达35国LDC35	35	-Other
	38.12	**配制的橡胶促进剂;其他税号未列名的橡胶或塑料用复合增塑剂;橡胶或塑料用抗氧制剂及其他复合稳定剂:**							**Prepared rubber accelerators; compounds plasticizers for rubber or plastics, not elsewhere specified or included; anti-oxidizing preparations and other compound stabilizers for rubber or plastics:**
2788	3812.1000	-配制的橡胶促进剂	6	0 5	东盟ASEAN,智利CL,新西兰NZ,秘鲁PE,哥斯达黎加CR 巴基斯坦PK	0	最不发达35国LDC35,最不发达4国LDC4	20	-Prepared rubber accelerators
2789	3812.2000	-橡胶或塑料用复合增塑剂	6.5	0 0.7 5	东盟ASEAN,新西兰NZ,秘鲁PE,哥斯达黎加CR 智利CL 巴基斯坦PK	0	最不发达35国LDC35,最不发达4国LDC4	35	-Compound plasticizers for rubber or plastics
		-橡胶或塑料用抗氧制剂及其他复合稳定剂:							-Anti-oxidizing preparations and other compound stabilizers for rubber or plastics:
2790	3812.3010	---橡胶防老剂	6	0 0.6 5	东盟ASEAN,新西兰NZ,秘鲁PE,哥斯达黎加CR,香港HK 智利CL 巴基斯坦PK	0	最不发达35国LDC35,最不发达4国LDC4	20	---Rubber antioxidants
2791	3812.3090	---其他	6.5	0 0.7 4.6	东盟ASEAN,巴基斯坦PK,新西兰NZ,秘鲁PE,哥斯达黎加CR,香港HK 智利CL 亚太APTA	0	最不发达35国LDC35,最不发达4国LDC4	35	---Other
	38.13	**灭火器的装配药;已装药的灭火弹:**							**Preparations and charges for fire-extinguishers; charged re-extinguishing grenades:**

序号 No.	税则号列 Tariff Line	货品名称	最惠国税率 MFN(%)	协定税率 Agreement(%)		特惠税率 S.P.(%)		普通税率 Gen.(%)	Article Description
2792	3813.0010	---灭火器的装配药	6.5	0 5	东盟ASEAN,智利CL,新西兰NZ,秘鲁PE,哥斯达黎加CR 巴基斯坦PK	0	最不发达35国LDC35,最不发达4国LDC4	35	---Preparations and charges for ire-extinguishers
2793	3813.0020	---已装药的灭火弹	10	0 5	东盟ASEAN,智利CL,新西兰NZ,秘鲁PE,哥斯达黎加CR 巴基斯坦PK	0	最不发达35国LDC35,最不发达4国LDC4	70	---Charged fire-extinguishing grenades
	38.14	**其他税号未列名的有机复合溶剂及稀释剂;除漆剂:**							**Organic composite solvents and thinners, not elsewhere specified or included; prepared paint or varnish removers:**
2794	3814.0000	其他税号未列名的有机复合溶剂及稀释剂;除漆剂	10	0 1 5 9	东盟ASEAN,新加坡SG,新西兰NZ,哥斯达黎加CR,香港HK,澳门MO 智利CL 巴基斯坦PK,秘鲁PE 亚太APTA	0	最不发达35国LDC35,最不发达4国LDC4	50	Organic composite solvents and thinners, not elsewhere specified or included; prepared paint or varnish removers
	38.15	**其他税号未列名的反应引发剂、反应促进剂、催化剂:**							**Reaction initiators, reaction accelerators and catalytic preparations, not elsewhere specified or included:**
		-载体催化剂:							-Supported catalysts:
2795	3815.1100	--以镍及其化合物为活性物的	6.5	0 0.7 5	东盟ASEAN,新西兰NZ,秘鲁PE,哥斯达黎加CR 智利CL 巴基斯坦PK	0	最不发达35国LDC35,最不发达4国LDC4	35	--With nickel or nickel compounds as the active substance
2796	3815.1200	--以贵金属及其化合物为活性物的	6.5 △4	0 5	东盟ASEAN,智利CL,新西兰NZ,秘鲁PE,哥斯达黎加CR,香港HK 巴基斯坦PK	0	最不发达35国LDC35,最不发达4国LDC4	35	--With precious metal or precious metal compounds as the active substance
2797	3815.1900	--其他	6.5	0 0.7 4.6	东盟ASEAN,巴基斯坦PK,新西兰NZ,秘鲁PE,哥斯达黎加CR 智利CL 亚太APTA	0	最不发达35国LDC35,最不发达4国LDC4	35	--Other
2798	3815.9000	-其他	6.5	0 0.7 5 6	东盟ASEAN,新西兰NZ,秘鲁PE,哥斯达黎加CR,澳门MO 智利CL 巴基斯坦PK 亚太APTA	0	最不发达35国LDC35,最不发达4国LDC4	35	-Other

序号 No.	税则号列 Tariff Line	货品名称	最惠国税率 MFN(%)	协定税率 Agreement(%)		特惠税率 S.P.(%)		普通税率 Gen.(%)	Article Description
	38.16	**耐火的水泥、灰泥、混凝土及类似耐火混合制品，但税号38.01的产品除外：**							**Refractory cements, mortars, concretes and similarcompositions, other than products of heading No.38.01:**
2799	3816.0000	耐火的水泥、灰泥、混凝土及类似耐火混合制品，但税号38.01的产品除外	6.5	0 0.7 5	东盟ASEAN,新西兰NZ,秘鲁PE,哥斯达黎加CR 智利CL 巴基斯坦PK	0	最不发达35国LDC35	35	Refractory cements, mortars, concretes and similar compositions, other than products of heading No.38.01
	38.17	**混合烷基苯及混合烷基萘，但税号27.07及29.02的货品除外：**							**Mixed alkylbenzenes and mixed alkylnaphthalenes, other than those of heading No.27.07 or 29.02:**
2800	3817.0000	混合烷基苯及混合烷基萘	6.5	0 5	东盟ASEAN,智利CL,新西兰NZ,秘鲁PE,哥斯达黎加CR,台湾TW 巴基斯坦PK	0	最不发达35国LDC35,最不发达4国LDC4	35	Mixed alkylbenzenes and alkylnaphthalenes38.18
	38.18	**经掺杂用于电子工业的化学元素，已切成圆片、薄片或类似形状;经掺杂用于电子工业的化合物：**							**Chemical elements doped for use in electronics, in the form of discs, wafers or similar forms; chemical compouds doped for use in electronics:**
		---直径在7.5厘米及以上的单晶硅切片：							---Monocrystalline silli-con, in the form of discs, wafers or similar form, 7.5cm or more in diameter:
2801	3818.0011	----直径在15.24厘米及以下的	0			0	最不发达35国LDC35,最不发达4国LDC4	11	----Diameter not exceeding 15.24cm
2802	3818.0019	----其他	0			0	最不发达35国LDC35,最不发达4国LDC4	11	----Other
2803	3818.0090	---其他	0			0	最不发达35国LDC35,最不发达4国LDC4	17	---Other

序号 No.	税则号列 Tariff Line	货品名称	最惠国税率 MFN(%)		协定税率 Agreement(%)		特惠税率 S.P.(%)	普通税率 Gen.(%)	Article Description
	38.19	**闸用液压油及其他液压传动用液体，不含石油或从沥青矿物提取的油类，或者按重量计石油或从沥青矿物提取的油类含量低于 70%:**							**Hydraulic brake fluids and other prepared liquids for hydraulic transmission, not containing or containing less than 70% by weight of petroleum oils or oils obtained from bituminous minerals:**
2804	3819.0000	闸用液压油及其他液压传动用液体，不含石油或从沥青矿物提取的油类，或者按重量计石油或从沥青矿物提取的油类含量低于 70%	6.5	0 5	东盟ASEAN,智利CL,新西兰NZ,秘鲁PE,哥斯达黎加CR,澳门MO 巴基斯坦PK	0	最不发达 35 国 LDC35	35	Hydraulic brake fluids and other prepared liquids for hydraulic transmission, not containing or containing less than 70% by weight of petroleum oils or oils obtained from bituminous minerals
	38.20	**防冻剂及解冻剂:**							**Anti-freezing preparations and prepared de-icing fluids:**
2805	3820.0000	防冻剂及解冻剂	10	0 5	东盟ASEAN,智利CL,新加坡SG,新西兰NZ,秘鲁PE,哥斯达黎加CR,澳门MO 巴基斯坦PK	0	最不发达 35 国 LDC35,最不发达 4 国 LDC4	35	Anti-freezing preparations and prepared de-icing fluids
	38.21	**制成的供微生物（包括病毒及类似品）或植物、人体、动物细胞生长或维持用的培养基:**							**Prepared culture media for the development or maintenance of micro-organisms (including viruses and the like) or of plant, human or animal cells:**
2806	3821.0000	制成的供微生物（包括病毒及类似品）或植物、人体、动物细胞生长或维持用的培养基	3	0	东盟ASEAN,智利CL,巴基斯坦PK,新西兰NZ,秘鲁PE,哥斯达黎加CR,香港HK	0	最不发达 35 国 LDC35	11	Prepared culture media for the development or maintenance of micro-organisms (including viruses and the like) or of plant, human or animal cells
	38.22	**附于衬背上的诊断或实验用试剂及不论是否附于衬背上的诊断或实验用配制试剂，但税号 30.02 及 30.06 的货品除外;检定参照物:**							**Diagnostic or laboratory reagents on a backing and prepared diagnostic or laboratory reagents whether or not on a backing, other than those of heading No.30.02 or 30.06; certified reference materials:**

序号 No.	税则号列 Tariff Line	货品名称	最惠国税率 MFN(%)	协定税率 Agreement(%)	特惠税率 S.P.(%)	普通税率 Gen.(%)	Article Description
2807	3822.0010	---附于衬背上的	4	0 东盟ASEAN,巴基斯坦PK,新西兰NZ,秘鲁PE,哥斯达黎加CR,香港HK 0.4 智利CL	0 最不发达35国LDC35,最不发达4国LDC4	35	---On a backing
2808	3822.0090	---其他	5	0 东盟ASEAN,巴基斯坦PK,新西兰NZ,秘鲁PE,哥斯达黎加CR,香港HK 0.5 智利CL	0 最不发达35国LDC35,最不发达4国LDC4	35	---Other
	38.23	**工业用单羧脂肪酸;精炼所得的酸性油;工业用脂肪醇:**					**Industrial monocarboxylic fatty acids; acidoils from refining; industrial fatty alcohols:**
		-工业用单羧脂肪酸;精炼所得的酸性油:					-Industrial monocarboxylic fatty acids; acid oils from refining:
2809	3823.1100	--硬脂酸	16	0 东盟ASEAN,新西兰NZ 1.6 智利CL 3.2 哥斯达黎加CR 8 秘鲁PE 12.8 巴基斯坦PK	0 最不发达35国LDC35	50	--Stearic acid
2810	3823.1200	--油酸	16 △8	0 东盟ASEAN,智利CL,新加坡SG,新西兰NZ,香港HK 3.2 哥斯达黎加CR 8 秘鲁PE 12.8 巴基斯坦PK	0 最不发达35国LDC35	50	--Oleic acid
2811	3823.1300	--妥尔油脂肪酸	16	0 东盟ASEAN,智利CL,新加坡SG,新西兰NZ 3.2 哥斯达黎加CR 8 秘鲁PE 12.8 巴基斯坦PK	0 最不发达35国LDC35	50	--Tall oil fatty acids
2812	3823.1900	--其他	16	0 东盟ASEAN,智利CL,新加坡SG,新西兰NZ,香港HK,澳门MO 3.2 哥斯达黎加CR 8 秘鲁PE 12.8 巴基斯坦PK	0 最不发达35国LDC35	50	--Other
	ex38231900	植物酸性油	△5				Botanic acid oil
2813	3823.7000	-工业用脂肪醇	13 △9	0 东盟ASEAN,智利CL,新加坡SG,新西兰NZ,秘鲁PE 2.6 哥斯达黎加CR 6.5 巴基斯坦PK	0 最不发达35国LDC35	50	-Industrial fatty alcohols
	38.24	**铸模及铸芯用粘合剂;其他税号未列名的化学工业及其相关工业的化学产品及配制品（包括由天然产品混合组成的）:**					**Prepared binders for foundry moulds or cores; chemical products and prepa-rations of the chemical or allied industries (including those consisting of mixtures of natural products), not elsewhere spelified or included:**

序号 No.	税则号列 Tariff Line	货品名称	最惠国税率 MFN(%)	协定税率 Agreement(%)		特惠税率 S.P.(%)		普通税率 Gen.(%)	Article Description
2814	3824.1000	-铸模及铸芯用粘合剂	6.5	0 5	东盟ASEAN,智利CL,新西兰NZ,秘鲁PE,哥斯达黎加CR 巴基斯坦PK	0	最不发达35国LDC35,最不发达4国LDC4	35	-Prepared binders for foundry moulds or cores
2815	3824.3000	-自身混合或与金属粘合剂混合的未烧结金属碳化物	6.5	0 5	东盟ASEAN,智利CL,新西兰NZ,秘鲁PE,哥斯达黎加CR 巴基斯坦PK	0	最不发达35国LDC35,最不发达4国LDC4	35	-Non-agglomerated metal carbides mixed together or with metallic binders
		-水泥、灰泥及混凝土用添加剂:							-Prepared additives for cements, mortars or concretes:
2816	3824.4010	---高效减水剂	6.5	0 0.7 5	东盟ASEAN,新西兰NZ,秘鲁PE,哥斯达黎加CR,香港HK 智利CL 巴基斯坦PK	0	最不发达35国LDC35,最不发达4国LDC4	35	---High efficiency water reducing admixture
2817	3824.4090	---其他	6.5	0 0.7 5	东盟ASEAN,新西兰NZ,秘鲁PE,哥斯达黎加CR,香港HK 智利CL 巴基斯坦PK	0	最不发达35国LDC35,最不发达4国LDC4	35	---Other
2818	3824.5000	-非耐火的灰泥及混凝土	6.5	0 0.7 5	东盟ASEAN,新西兰NZ,秘鲁PE,哥斯达黎加CR,香港HK,澳门MO 智利CL 巴基斯坦PK	0	最不发达35国LDC35,最不发达4国LDC4	35	-Non-refractory mortars and concretes
2819	3824.6000	-子目号2905.44以外的山梨醇	14	0 2.8 11.2	东盟ASEAN,智利CL,新加坡SG,新西兰NZ,秘鲁PE 哥斯达黎加CR 巴基斯坦PK	0	最不发达35国LDC35	40	-Sorbitol other than that of subheading No.2905.44
		-含有甲烷、乙烷或丙烷的卤化衍生物的混合物::							-Mixtures containing halogenated derivatives of methane, ethane or propane:
2820	3824.7100	--含全氯氟烃(CFCs)的，不论是否含氢氯氟烃(HCFCs)、全氟烃(PFCs)或氢氟烃(HFCs)	6.5	0 5	东盟ASEAN,智利CL,新西兰NZ,秘鲁PE,哥斯达黎加CR,香港HK,澳门MO 巴基斯坦PK	0	最不发达35国LDC35,最不发达4国LDC4	35	--Containing chlorofluorocarbons (CFCs), whether or not containing hydrochlorofluorocarbons (HCFCs), perfluorocarbons (PFCs) orhydrofluorocarbons (HFCs)
2821	3824.7200	--含溴氯二氟甲烷、溴三氟甲烷或二溴四氟乙烷的	6.5	0 5	东盟ASEAN,智利CL,新西兰NZ,秘鲁PE,哥斯达黎加CR 巴基斯坦PK	0	最不发达35国LDC35,最不发达4国LDC4	35	--Containing bromochlorodifluoromethane, bromotrifluoromethane or dibromotetrafluoroethanes

序号 No.	税则号列 Tariff Line	货品名称	最惠国税率 MFN(%)	协定税率 Agreement(%)		特惠税率 S.P.(%)		普通税率 Gen.(%)	Article Description
2822	3824.7300	--含氢溴氟烃(HBFCs)的	6.5	0 5	东盟ASEAN,智利CL,新西兰NZ,秘鲁PE,哥斯达黎加CR,香港HK,澳门MO 巴基斯坦PK	0	最不发达35国LDC35,最不发达4国LDC4	35	--Containing hydrobromofluorocarbons (HBFCs)
2823	3824.7400	--含氢氯氟烃(HCFCs)的，不论是否含全氟烃(PFCs)或氢氟烃(HFCs)	6.5	0 5	东盟ASEAN,智利CL,新西兰NZ,秘鲁PE,哥斯达黎加CR,香港HK,澳门MO 巴基斯坦PK	0	最不发达35国LDC35,最不发达4国LDC4	35	--Containing hydrochlorofluorocarbons (HCFCs), whether or not containing perfluorocarbons (PFCs) or hydrofluorocarbons (HFCs), but not containing chlorofluorocarbons (CFCs)
2824	3824.7500	--含四氯化碳的	6.5	0 0.7 5 6	东盟ASEAN,新西兰NZ,秘鲁PE,哥斯达黎加CR,香港HK,澳门MO 智利CL 巴基斯坦PK 亚太APTA	0	最不发达35国LDC35,最不发达4国LDC4	35	--Containing carbon tetrachloride
2825	3824.7600	--含1，1，1-三氯乙烷（甲基氯仿）的	6.5	0 0.7 5 6	东盟ASEAN,新西兰NZ,秘鲁PE,哥斯达黎加CR,香港HK,澳门MO 智利CL 巴基斯坦PK 亚太APTA	0	最不发达35国LDC35,最不发达4国LDC4	35	--Containing 1, 1, 1-trichloroethane (methyl chloroform)
2826	3824.7700	--含溴化甲烷（甲基溴）或溴氯甲烷的	6.5	0 5	东盟ASEAN,智利CL,新西兰NZ,秘鲁PE,哥斯达黎加CR,香港HK,澳门MO 巴基斯坦PK	0	最不发达35国LDC35,最不发达4国LDC4	35	--Containing bromomethane (methyl bromide) or bromochloromethane
2827	3824.7800	--含全氟烃(PFCs)或氢氟烃(HFCs)的，但不含全氯氟烃(CFCs)或氢氯氟烃(HCFCs)的	6.5	0 0.7 5 6	东盟ASEAN,新西兰NZ,秘鲁PE,哥斯达黎加CR,香港HK,澳门MO 智利CL 巴基斯坦PK 亚太APTA	0	最不发达35国LDC35,最不发达4国LDC4	35	--Containing perfluorocarbons (PFCs) or hydrofluorocarbons (HFCs), but not containing chlorofluorocarbons (CFCs) or hydrochlorofluorocarbons (HCFCs)
2828	3824.7900	--其他	6.5	0 5	东盟ASEAN,智利CL,新西兰NZ,秘鲁PE,哥斯达黎加CR,香港HK,澳门MO 巴基斯坦PK	0	最不发达35国LDC35,最不发达4国LDC4	35	--Other
		-含环氧乙烷(氧化乙烯)、多溴联苯(PBBs)、多氯联苯(PCBs)、多氯三联苯(PCTs)或三（2，3-二溴丙基）磷酸酯的混合物及制品:							-Mixtures and preparations containing oxirane (ethylene oxide), polybrominated biphenyls (PBBs), polychlorinated biphenyls (PCBs), polychlorinated terphenyls (PCTs) or tris (2, 3-dibromopropyl)phosphate :

序号 No.	税则号列 Tariff Line	货品名称	最惠国税率 MFN(%)	协定税率 Agreement(%)		特惠税率 S.P.(%)		普通税率 Gen.(%)	Article Description
2829	3824.8100	--含环氧乙烷（氧化乙烯）的	6.5	0 0.7 5 6	东盟ASEAN,新西兰NZ,秘鲁PE,哥斯达黎加CR,香港HK,澳门MO 智利CL 巴基斯坦PK 亚太APTA	0	最不发达35国LDC35,最不发达4国LDC4	35	--Containing oxirane (ethylene oxide)
2830	3824.8200	--含多氯联苯(PCBs)、多氯三联苯（PCTs）或多溴联苯（PBBs）的	6.5	0 0.7 5 6	东盟ASEAN,新西兰NZ,秘鲁PE,哥斯达黎加CR,香港HK,澳门MO 智利CL 巴基斯坦PK 亚太APTA	0	最不发达35国LDC35,最不发达4国LDC4	35	--Containing polychlorinated biphenyls (PCBs), polychlorinated terphenyls (PCTs) or polybrominated biphenyls (PBBs)
2831	3824.8300	--含三（2，3-二溴丙基）磷酸酯的	6.5	0 0.7 5 6	东盟ASEAN,新西兰NZ,秘鲁PE,哥斯达黎加CR,香港HK,澳门MO 智利CL 巴基斯坦PK 亚太APTA	0	最不发达35国LDC35,最不发达4国LDC4	35	--Containing tris (2, 3-dibromopropyl) phosphate
		-其他:							-Other:
2832	3824.9010	---杂醇油	6.5	0 0.7 5 5.5	东盟ASEAN,新西兰NZ,秘鲁PE,哥斯达黎加CR 智利CL 巴基斯坦PK 亚太APTA	0	最不发达35国LDC35,最不发达4国LDC4	40	---Fusel oil
2833	3824.9020	---除墨剂、蜡纸改正液及类似品	9	0 0.9 5 8.3	东盟ASEAN,新加坡SG,新西兰NZ,秘鲁PE,哥斯达黎加CR 智利CL 巴基斯坦PK 亚太APTA	0	最不发达35国LDC35,最不发达4国LDC4	80	---Ink-removers, stencil correctors and the like
2834	3824.9030	---增炭剂	6.5	0 0.7 5	东盟ASEAN,新西兰NZ,秘鲁PE,哥斯达黎加CR 智利CL 巴基斯坦PK	0	最不发达35国LDC35,最不发达4国LDC4	35	---Carburetant
		---其他:							---Other:
2835	3824.9091	----按重量计含滑石50%以上的混合物	6.5	0 5 6	东盟ASEAN,智利CL,新西兰NZ,秘鲁PE,哥斯达黎加CR,香港HK,澳门MO 巴基斯坦PK 亚太APTA	0	最不发达35国LDC35,最不发达4国LDC4	35	----Mixture containing more than 50% Talc by weight
2836	3824.9092	----按重量计含氧化镁70%以上的混合物	6.5	0 5 6	东盟ASEAN,智利CL,新西兰NZ,秘鲁PE,哥斯达黎加CR,香港HK,澳门MO 巴基斯坦PK 亚太APTA	0	最不发达35国LDC35,最不发达4国LDC4	35	----Mixture containing more than 70% Magnesium Oxide by weight
2837	3824.9093	----表层包覆钴化合物的氢氧化镍（掺杂碳）	6.5	0 5 6	东盟ASEAN,智利CL,新西兰NZ,秘鲁PE,哥斯达黎加CR,香港HK,澳门MO 巴基斯坦PK 亚太APTA	0	最不发达35国LDC35,最不发达4国LDC4	35	----Cobalt compound coated nickel hydroxide (mixed carbon)

序号 No.	税则号列 Tariff Line	货品名称	最惠国税率 MFN(%)	协定税率 Agreement(%)	特惠税率 S.P.(%)	普通税率 Gen.(%)	Article Description
2838	3824.9099	----其他	6.5	0 东盟ASEAN,智利CL,新西兰NZ,秘鲁PE,哥斯达黎加CR,香港HK,澳门MO 5 巴基斯坦PK 6 亚太APTA	0 最不发达35国LDC35,最不发达4国LDC4	35	----Other
	ex38249099	高钛渣（二氧化钛质量百分含量大于70%的）	△0				The Ag electrode paste, dieletric paste, barrier ribs paste phosphor paste used for the plasma display panel production
	ex38249099	按重量计氧化锌含量在50%及以上的混合物	△3				Mixture containing ZnO 50% or more
	38.25	**其他税目未列名的化学工业及其相关工业的副产品;城市垃圾;下水道淤泥;本章注释六所规定的其他废物:**					**Residual products of the chemical or allied industries, not elsewhere spec-ified or included; municipal waste; sewage sludge; other wastes specified in Note 6 to this Chapter:**
2839	3825.1000	-城市垃圾	6.5	0 东盟ASEAN,智利CL,新西兰NZ,秘鲁PE,哥斯达黎加CR 5 巴基斯坦PK	0 最不发达35国LDC35	35	-Municipal waste
2840	3825.2000	-下水道淤泥	6.5	0 东盟ASEAN,智利CL,新西兰NZ,秘鲁PE,哥斯达黎加CR 5 巴基斯坦PK	0 最不发达35国LDC35	35	-Sewage sludge
2841	3825.3000	-医疗废物	6.5	0 东盟ASEAN,智利CL,新西兰NZ,秘鲁PE,哥斯达黎加CR 5 巴基斯坦PK	0 最不发达35国LDC35	35	-Clinical waste
		-废有机溶剂:					-Waste organic solvents:
2842	3825.4100	--卤化物的	6.5	0 东盟ASEAN,智利CL,新西兰NZ,秘鲁PE,哥斯达黎加CR 5 巴基斯坦PK	0 最不发达35国LDC35	35	--Halogenated
2843	3825.4900	--其他	6.5	0 东盟ASEAN,智利CL,新西兰NZ,秘鲁PE,哥斯达黎加CR 5 巴基斯坦PK	0 最不发达35国LDC35	35	--Other
2844	3825.5000	-废的金属酸液、液压油、制动油及防冻液	6.5	0 东盟ASEAN,智利CL,新加坡SG,新西兰NZ,秘鲁PE,哥斯达黎加CR 5 巴基斯坦PK	0 最不发达35国LDC35	35	-Wastes of metal pickling liguors, hyd-raulic fluids, brake fluids and anti freeze fluids
		-其他化学工业及相关工业的废物:					-Other wastes from chemical or allied industries:

序号 No.	税则号列 Tariff Line	货品名称	最惠国税率 MFN(%)	协定税率 Agreement(%)		特惠税率 S.P.(%)		普通税率 Gen.(%)	Article Description
2845	3825.6100	--主要含有有机成分的	6.5	0 0.7 5	东盟ASEAN,新西兰NZ,秘鲁PE,哥斯达黎加CR 智利CL 巴基斯坦PK	0	最不发达35国LDC35	35	--Mainly containing organic constituents
2846	3825.6900	--其他	6.5	0 5	东盟ASEAN,智利CL,新西兰NZ,秘鲁PE,哥斯达黎加CR 巴基斯坦PK	0	最不发达35国LDC35	35	--Other
2847	3825.9000	-其他	6.5	0 5	东盟ASEAN,智利CL,新西兰NZ,秘鲁PE,哥斯达黎加CR,香港HK 巴基斯坦PK	0	最不发达35国LDC35	35	-Other
	38.26	**生物柴油及其混合物，不含或含有按重量计低于70%的石油或从沥青矿物提取的油类：**							**Biodiesel and mixtures thereof, not containing or containing less than 70% by weight of petroleum oils or oils obtained from bituminous minerals:**
2848	3826.0000	生物柴油及其混合物，不含或含有按重量计低于70%的石油或从沥青矿物提取的油类	6.5	0 5 6	东盟ASEAN,智利CL,新西兰NZ,秘鲁PE,哥斯达黎加CR,香港HK,澳门MO 巴基斯坦PK 亚太APTA	0	最不发达35国LDC35,最不发达4国LDC4	35	Biodiesel and mixtures thereof, not containing or containing less than 70% by weight of petroleum oils or oils obtained from bituminous minerals

第七类
塑料及其制品；
橡胶及其制品

注释：

一、由两种或两种以上单独成分配套的货品，其部分或全部成分属于本类范围以内，混合后则构成第六类或第七类的货品，应按混合后产品归入相应的税号，但其组成成分必须同时符合下列条件：

（一）其包装形式足以表明这些成分不需经过改装就可以一起使用的；

（二）一起进口或出口的；

（三）这些成分的属性及相互比例足以表明是相互配用的。

二、除税号 39.18 或 39.19 的货品外，印有花纹、文字、图画的塑料、橡胶及其制品，如果所印花纹、字画作为其主要用途，应归入第四十九章。

第三十九章
塑料及其制品

注释：

一、本目录所称“塑料”，是指税号 39.01 至 39.14 的材料，这些材料能够在聚合时或聚合后在外力（一般是热力和压力，必要时加入溶剂或增塑剂）作用下通过模制、浇铸、挤压、滚轧或其他工序制成一定的形状，成形后除去外力，其形状仍保持不变。

本目录所称“塑料”，还应包括钢纸，但不包括第十一类的纺织材料。

二、本章不包括：

（一）税目 27.10 或 34.03 的润滑油；

（二）税号 27.12 或 34.04 的蜡；

（三）单独的已有化学定义的有机化合物（第二十九章）；

（四）肝素及其盐（税号 30.01）；

SECTION Ⅶ
PLASTICS AND ARTICLES THEREOF; RUBBER AND ARTICLES THEREOF

Notes:

1. Goods put up in sets consisting of two or more separate constituents, some or all of which fall in this Section and are intended to be mixed together to obtain a product of SectionⅥ or Ⅶ, are to be classified in the heading appropriate to that product, provided that the constituents are:

(a) having regard to the manner in which they are put up, clearly identifiable as being intended to be used together without first being repacked;

(b) presented together; and

(c) identifiable, whether by their nature or by the relative proportions inwhich they are present, as being complementary one to another.

2. Except for the goods of heading No.39.18 or 39.19, plastics, rubber, and articles thereof, printed with motifs, characters or pictorial representations, which are not merely incidental to the primary use of the goods, fall in Chapter 49.

Chapter 39
Plastics and articles thereof

Notes:

1. Throughout the Nomenclature the expression "plastics" means those materials of headings Nos.39.01 to 39.14 which are or have been capable, either at the moment of polymerization or at some subsequent stage, of being formed under external influence (usually heat and pressure, if necessary with a solvent or plasticizer) by moulding, casting, extruding, rolling or other process into shapes which are retained on the removal of the external influence.

Throughout the Nomenclature any reference to "plastics" also includes vulcanized fibre. The expression, however, does not apply to materials regarded as textile materials of SectionⅪ.

2. This Chapter does not cover:

(a) Lubricating preparations of heading 27.10 or 34.03;

(b) Waxes of heading No.27.12 or 34.04;

(c) Separate chemically defined organic compounds (Chapter 29) ;

(d) Heparin or its salts (heading No.30.01) ;

（五）税号 39.01 至 39.13 所列的任何产品溶于挥发性有机溶剂的溶液（胶棉除外），但溶剂的重量必须超过溶液重量的 50%（税号 32.08）；税号 32.12 的压印箔；

（六）有机表面活性剂或税号 34.02 的制剂；

（七）再熔胶及酯胶（税号 38.06）；

（八）配制的添加剂，用于矿物油（包括汽油）或与矿物油同样用途的其他液体(税目 38.11)；

（九）以第三十九章的聚乙二醇、聚硅氧烷或其他聚合物为基本成分的液压用液体(税目 38.19)；

（十）附于塑料衬背上的诊断或实验用试剂（税号 38.22）；

（十一）第四十章规定的合成橡胶及其制品；

（十二）鞍具及挽具（税号 42.01）；税号 42.02 的衣箱、提箱、手提包及其他容器；

（十三）第四十六章的缏条、编结品及其他制品；

（十四）税号 48.14 的壁纸；

（十五）第十一类的货品（纺织原料及纺织制品）；

（十六）第十二类的物品（例如，鞋靴、帽类、雨伞、阳伞、手杖、鞭子、马鞭及其零件）；

（十七）税号 71.17 的仿首饰；

（十八）第十六类的物品（机器、机械器具或电气器具）；

（十九）第十七类的航空器零件及车辆零件；

（二十）第九十章的物品（例如，光学元件、眼镜架及绘图仪器）；

（二十一）第九十一章的物品（例如，钟壳及表壳）；

（二十二）第九十二章的物品（例如，乐器及其零件）；

（二十三）第九十四章的物品（例如，家具、灯具、照明装置、灯箱及活动房屋）；

（二十四）第九十五章的物品（例如，玩具、游戏品及运动用品）；

（二十五）第九十六章的物品（例如，刷子、钮扣、拉链、梳子、烟斗的嘴及柄、香烟嘴及类似品、保温瓶的零件及类似品、钢笔、活动铅笔）。

(e) Solutions (other than collodions) consisting of any of the products specified in headings Nos.39.01 to 39.13 in volatile organic solvents when the weight of the solvent exceeds 50% of the weight of the solution (heading No.32.08); stamping foils of heading No.32.12;

(f) Organic surface-active agents or preparations of heading No.34.02;

(g) Run gums or ester gums (heading No.38.06) ;

(h) Prepared additives for mineral oils (including gasoline) or for other liquids used for the same purposes as mineral oils (heading 38.11);

(ij) Prepared hydraulic fluids based on polyglycols, silicones or other polymers of Chapter 39 (heading 38.19);

(k) Diagnostic or laboratory reagents on a backing of plastics (heading No.38.22) ;

(l) Synthetic rubber, as defined for the purposes of Chapter 40, or articles thereof;

(m) Sadlery or harness (heading No.42.01) or trunks, suitcases, handbags or other containers of heading No.42.02;

(n) Plaits, wickerwork or other articles of Chapter 46;

(o) Wall coverings of heading No.48.14;

(p) Goods of SectionⅪ (textiles and textile articles) ;

(q) Articles of Section Ⅻ (for example, footwear, headgear, umbrellas, sun umbrellas, walking • sticks, whips, riding-crops or parts thereof) ;

(r) Imitation jewellery of heading No.71.17;

(s) Articles of Section XVI (machines and mechanical or electrical appliances) ;

(t) Parts of aircraft or vehicles of Section XVII;

(u) Articles of Chapter 90 (for example, optical elements, spectacle frames, drawing instruments) ;

(v) Articles of Chapter 91 (for example, clock or watch cases);

(w) Articles of Chapter 92 (for example, musical instruments or parts thereof) ;

(x) Articles of Chapter 94 (for example, furniture, lamps and lighting fittings. illuminated signs, prefabricated buildings);

(y) Articles of Chapter 95 (for example, toys, games, sports requisites) ;or

(z) Articles of Chapter 96 (for example, brushes, buttons, slide fasteners, combs, mouthpieces or stems for smoking pipes, cigaretteholders or the like, parts of vacuum flasks or the like, pens, propelling pencils).

三、税号 39.01 至 39.11 仅适用于化学合成的下列货品：

（一）温度在 300℃时，压力转为 1013 毫巴后减压蒸馏出的液体合成聚烯烃以体积计小于 60% 的货品（税号 39.01 及 39.02）；

（二）非高度聚合的苯并呋喃—茚树脂（税号 39.11）；

（三）平均至少有五个单体单元的其他合成聚合物；

（四）聚硅氧烷（税号 39.10）；

（五）甲阶酚醛树脂（税号 39.09）及其他预聚物。

四、所称"共聚物"，包括在整个聚合物中按重量计没有一种单体单元的含量在 95%及以上的各种聚合物。

在本章中，除条文另有规定的以外，共聚物（包括共缩聚物、共加聚物、嵌段共聚物及接枝共聚物）及聚合物混合体应按聚合物中重量最大的那种共聚单体单元所构成的聚合物归入相应税号。在本注释中，归入同一税号的聚合物的共聚单体单元应作为一种单体单元对待。

如果没有任何一种共聚单体单元重量为最大，共聚物或聚合物混合体应按号列顺序归入其可归入的最末一个税号。

五、化学改性聚合物，即聚合物主链上的支链通过化学反应发生了变化的聚合物，应按未改性的聚合物的相应税号归类。本规定不适用于接枝共聚物。

六、税号 39.01 至 39.14 所称"初级形状"，只限于下列各种形状：

（一）液状及糊状，包括分散体（乳浊液及悬浮液）及溶液；

（二）不规则形状的块，团、粉（包括压型粉）、颗粒、粉片及类似的散装形状。

七、税号 39.15 不适用于已制成初级形状的单一的热塑材料废碎料及下脚料（税号 39.01 至 39.14）。

3. Headings Nos.39.01 to 39.11apply only to goods of a kind produced by chemical synthesis, falling in the following categories:

(a) Liquid synthetic polyolefins of which less than 60% by volume distils at 300℃, after conversion to 1013 millibars when a reduced-pressure distillation method is used (headings Nos. 39.01 and 39.02);

(b) Resins, not highly polymerized, of the coumarone - indene type (heading No.39.11);

(c) Other synthetic polymers with an average of at least 5 monomer units;

(d) Silicones (heading No.39.10);

(e) Resols (heading No.39.09) and other prepolymers.

4. The expression "copolymers" covers all polymers in which no single monomer unit contributes 95% or more by weight to the total polymer content.

For the purposes of this Chapter, except where the context otherwise requires, copolymers (including copolycondensates, co polyaddition products, block copolymers and graft copolymers) and polymer blends are to be classified in the heading covering polymers of that comonomet unit which predominates by weight over every other single comonomer unit. For the purposes of this Note, constituent comonomer units of polymers falling in the same heading shall be taken together.

If no single comonomer unit predominates, copolymens or polymer blends, as the case may be, are to be classified in the heading which occurs last in numerical order among those which equally merit consideration.

5. Chemically modified polymers, that is those in which only appendages to the main polymer chain have been changed by chemical reaction, are to be classified in the heading appropriate to the unmodified polymer. This provision does not apply to graft copolymers.

6. In headings Nos.39.01 to 39.04, the expression "primary forms" applies only to the following forms:

(a) Liquids and pastes, including dispersions (emulsions and suspensions) and solutions;

(b) Blocks of irregular shape, lumps, powders (including moulding powders), granules, flakes and similar bulk forms.

7. Heading No.39.15 does not apply to waste, parings and scrap of a single thermoplastic material, transformed into primary forms (headings Nos.39.01 to 39.14) .

八、税号 39.17 所称“管子”，是指通常用于输送或供给气体或液体的空心制品或半制品（例如，肋纹浇花软管、多孔管），还包括香肠用肠衣及其他扁平管。除肠衣及扁平管外，内截面如果不呈圆形、椭圆形、矩形（其长度不超过宽度的 1.5 倍）或正几何形，则不能视为管子，而应作为异型材。

8. For the purposes of heading No.39.17, the expression "tubes, pipes and hoses" means hollow products, whether semi-manufactures or finished products, of a kind generally used for conveying, conducting or distributing gases or liquids (for example, ribbed garden hose, perforated tubes). This expression also includes sausage casings and other layflat tubing.However, except for the last-mentioned, those having an internal cross-section other than round, oval, rectangular (in which the length does not exceed 1.5 times the width) or in the shape of a regular polygon are not to be regarded as tubes, pipes and hoses but as profile shapes.

九、税号 39.18 所称“塑料糊墙品”，适用于墙壁或天花板装饰用的宽度不小于 45 厘米的成卷产品，这类产品是将塑料牢固地附着在除纸张以外任何材料的衬背上，并且在塑料面起纹、压花、着色、印制图案或用其他方法装饰。

9. For the purposes of heading No.39.18, the expression "wall or ceiling coverings of plastics" applies to products in rolls, of a width not less than 45 cm, suitable for wall or ceiling decoration, consisting of plastics fixed permanently on a backing of any material other than paper, the layer of plastics (on the face side) being grained, embossed, coloured, design-printed or otherwise decorated.

十、税号 39.20 及 39.21 所称“板、片、膜、箔、扁条”，只适用于未切割或仅切割成矩形（包括正方形）(含切割后即可供使用的);但未经进一步加工的板、片、膜、箔、扁条（第五十四章的物品除外）及正几何形块，不论是否经过印制或其他表面加工。

10. In headings Nos. 39.20 and 39.21, the expression "plates, sheets, film, foil and strip" applies only to plates, sheets, film, foil and strip (other than those of Chapter 54) and to blocks of regular geometric shape, whether or not printed or otherwise surface-woked, uncut or cut into rectangles (including squares) but not further worked (even if when so cut they become articles ready for use) .

十一、税号 39.25 只适用于第二分章以前各税号未包括的下列物品：

（一）容积超过 300 升的囤、柜（包括化粪池）、罐、桶及类似容器；

（二）用于地板、墙壁、隔墙、天花板或屋顶等方面的结构件；

（三）槽管及其附件；

（四）门、窗及其框架和门槛；

（五）阳台、栏杆、栅栏、栅门及类似品；

（六）窗板、百叶窗（包括威尼斯式百叶窗）或类似品及其零件、附件；

（七）商店、工棚、仓库等用的拼装式固定大型货架；

（八）建筑用的特色（例如，凹槽、圆顶及鸽棚式）装饰件；

11. Heading No.39.25 applies only to the following articles, not being products covered by any of the earlier headings of sub-Chapter II :

(a) Reservoirs, tanks (including septic tanks) , vats and similar containers, of a capacity exceeding 300L;

(b) Structural elements used, for example, in floors, walls or partitions, ceilings or roofs;

(c) Gutters and fittings therefor;

(d) Doors, windows and their frames and thresholds for doors;

(e) Balconies, balustrades, fencing, gates and similar barriers;

(f) Shutters, blinds (including Venetian blinds) and similar articles and parts and fittings thereof;

(g) Large-scale shelving for assembly and permanent installation, for example, in shops, workshops, warehouses;

(h) Ornamental architectural features, for example, flutings, cupolas, dovecotes; and

（九）固定装于门窗、楼梯、墙壁或建筑物其他部位的附件及架座，例如，球形把手、拉手、挂钩、托架、毛巾架、开关板及其他护板。

子目注释:

属于本章任一税号项下的聚合物（包括共聚物）及化学改性聚合物应按下列规则归类:

一、在同级子目中有一个“其他”子目的:

（一）子目所列聚合物名称冠有“聚（多）”的（例如，聚乙烯及聚酰胺-6，6），是指列名的该种聚合物单体单元含量在整个聚合物中按重量计必须占95%及以上。

（二）子目号3901.30、3903.20、3903.30及3904.30所列的共聚物，如果该种共聚单体单元含量在整个聚合物中按重量计占95%及以上，即应归入上述子目。

（三）化学改性聚合物如未在其他子目具体列名，应归入列明为“其他”的子目内。

（四）不符合上述（一）、（二）、（三）款规定的聚合物，应按聚合物中重量最大的那种单体单元（与其他各种单一的共聚单体单元相比）所构成的聚合物归入该级其他相应子目。为此，归入同一子目的聚合物单体单元应作为一种单体单元对待。只有在同级子目中的聚合物共聚单体单元才可以进行比较。

二、在同级子目中没有“其他”子目的:

（一）聚合物应按聚合物中重量最大的那种单体单元（与其他各种单一的共聚单体单元相比）所构成的聚合物归入该级相应子目。为此，归入同一子目的聚合物单体单元应作为一种单体单元对待。只有在同级子目中的聚合物共聚单体单元才可以进行比较。

(i) Fittings and mountings intended for permanent installation in or on doors, windows, staircases, walls or other parts of buildings, for example, knobs, handles, hooks, brackets, towel rails, switch-plates and other protective plates.

Subheading Notes:

1. Within any one heading of this Chapter, polymers (including copolymers) and chemically modified polymers are to be classified according to the following provisions:

(a) Where there is a subheading named “Other” in the same series:

(1) The designation in a subheading of a polymer by the prefix “poly” (for example, polyethylene and polyamide-6, 6) means that the constituent monomer unit or monomer units of the named polymer taken together must contribute 95% or more by weight of the total polymer content.

(2) The copolymers named in subheadings Nos.3901.30, 3903.20, 3903.30 and 3904.30 are to be classified in those subheadings, provided that the comonomer units of the named copolymers contribute 95% or more by weight of the total polymer content.

(3) Chemically modified polymers are to be classified in the subheading named “Other”, provided that the chemically modified polymers are not more specifically covered by another subheading.

(4) Polymers not meeting (1), (2) or (3) above, are to be classified in the subheading, among the remaining subheadings in the series, covering polymers of that monomer unit which predominates by weight over every other single comonomer unit. For this purpose, constituent monomer units of polymers falling in the same subheading shall be taken together. Only the constituent comonomer units of the polymers in the series of subheadings under consideration are to be compared.

2. Where there is no subheading named “Other” in the same series:

(a) Polymers are to be classified in the subheading covering polymers of that monomer unit which predominates by weight over every other single comonomer unit. For this purpose, constituent monomer units of polymers falling in the same subheading shall be taken together. Only the constituent comonomer units of the polymers in the series under consideration are to be compared.

（二）化学改性聚合物应按相应的未改性聚合物的子目归类。聚合物混合体应按单体单元比例相等、种类相同的聚合物归入相应子目。

(b) Chemically modified polymers are to be classified in the subheading appropriate to the unmodified polymer. Polymer blends are to be classified in the same subheading as polymers of the same monomer units in the same proportions.

三、子目 3920.43 所称“增塑剂”，包括“次级增塑剂”。

3. For the purposes of subheading 3920.43, the term “plasticisers” includes “secondary plasticisers”.

序号 No.	税则号列 Tariff Line	货品名称	最惠国税率 MFN(%)	协定税率 Agreement(%)		特惠税率 S.P.(%)		普通税率 Gen.(%)	Article Description
		第一分章 初级形状							Ⅰ.PRIMARY FORMS
	39.01	**初级形状的乙烯聚合物:**							**Polymers of ethylene, in primary forms:**
2849	3901.1000	-聚乙烯，比重小于 0.94	6.5	0	新西兰NZ,哥斯达黎加CR,香港HK,澳门MO			45	-Polyethylene having a specific gravity of less than 0.94
				0.7	智利CL				
				6	亚太APTA,巴基斯坦PK				
	ex39011000	比重小于 0.94 的聚乙烯（进口CIF价高于 3800 美元/吨）	△3						Polyethylene, gravity <0.94, (import CIF ≥3800usd/t)
2850	3901.2000	-聚乙烯，比重在 0.94 及以上	6.5	0	新西兰NZ,哥斯达黎加CR,香港HK,澳门MO			45	-Polyethylene having a specific gravity of 0.94 or more
				0.7	智利CL				
				6	亚太APTA,巴基斯坦PK				
	ex39012000	比重在 0.94 及以上的聚乙烯（进口CIF价高于 3800 美元/吨）	△3						Polyethylene, gravity≥0.94, (import CIF ≥3800usd/t)
2851	3901.3000	-乙烯—乙酸乙烯酯共聚物	6.5	0	东盟ASEAN,新西兰NZ,秘鲁PE,哥斯达黎加CR,香港HK	0	最不发达 35 国 LDC35	45	-Ethylene-vinyl acetate copolymers
				0.7	智利CL				
				5	巴基斯坦PK				
				6	亚太APTA				
		-其他:							-Other:
2852	3901.9010	---乙烯—丙烯共聚物（乙丙橡胶）	6.5	0	东盟ASEAN,智利CL,新加坡SG,新西兰NZ,秘鲁PE,哥斯达黎加CR	0	最不发达 35 国 LDC35	45	---Ethylene-propylene copolymers
				5	巴基斯坦PK				
2853	3901.9020	---线型低密度聚乙烯	6.5	0	东盟ASEAN,智利CL,新加坡SG,新西兰NZ,哥斯达黎加CR	0	最不发达 35 国 LDC35,最不发达 4 国 LDC4	45	---Linearity low density polyethylene
				5	巴基斯坦PK				
2854	3901.9090	---其他	6.5	0	东盟ASEAN,智利CL,新加坡SG,新西兰NZ,秘鲁PE,哥斯达黎加CR,香港HK,澳门MO	0	最不发达 35 国 LDC35	45	---Other
				5	巴基斯坦PK				
				6.3	亚太APTA				

序号 No.	税则号列 Tariff Line	货品名称	最惠国税率 MFN(%)	协定税率 Agreement(%)		特惠税率 S.P.(%)		普通税率 Gen.(%)	Article Description
	39.02	**初级形状的丙烯或其他烯烃聚合物:**							**Polymers of propylene or of other olefins, in primary forms:**
2855	3902.1000	-聚丙烯	6.5	0 0.7 5	东盟ASEAN,新加坡SG,新西兰NZ,哥斯达黎加CR,香港HK,澳门MO 智利CL 巴基斯坦PK			45	-Polypropylene
	ex39021000	电工级初级形状聚丙烯树脂(灰分含量不大于 30ppm)	△3						Electrotechonical polypropylene resin in primary forms (Ash content not more than 30ppm)
2856	3902.2000	-聚异丁烯	6.5	0 5	东盟ASEAN,智利CL,新西兰NZ,秘鲁PE,哥斯达黎加CR 巴基斯坦PK	0	最不发达 35 国 LDC35,最不发达 4 国 LDC4	45	-Polyisobutylene
		-丙烯共聚物:							-Propylene copolymers:
2857	3902.3010	---乙烯—丙烯共聚物（乙丙橡胶）	6.5	0 0.7 5 6	东盟ASEAN,新加坡SG,新西兰NZ,秘鲁PE,哥斯达黎加CR,香港HK,台湾TW 智利CL 巴基斯坦PK 亚太APTA	0	最不发达 35 国 LDC35,最不发达 4 国 LDC4	45	---Ethylene-propylene copolymers
2858	3902.3090	---其他	6.5	0 0.7 5 6	东盟ASEAN,新加坡SG,新西兰NZ,秘鲁PE,哥斯达黎加CR,香港HK 智利CL 巴基斯坦PK 亚太APTA	0	最不发达 35 国 LDC35,最不发达 4 国 LDC4	45	---Other
2859	3902.9000	-其他	6.5	0 5	东盟ASEAN,智利CL,新加坡SG,新西兰NZ,秘鲁PE,哥斯达黎加CR,台湾TW 巴基斯坦PK	0	最不发达 35 国 LDC35,最不发达 4 国 LDC4	45	-Other
	39.03	**初级形状的苯乙烯聚合物:**							**Polymers of styrene, in primary forms:**
		-聚苯乙烯:							-Polystyrene:
2860	3903.1100	--可发性的	6.5	0 0.7 5 6	东盟ASEAN,新加坡SG,新西兰NZ,秘鲁PE,哥斯达黎加CR 智利CL 巴基斯坦PK 亚太APTA	0	最不发达 35 国 LDC35,最不发达 4 国 LDC4	45	--Expansible
		--其他:							--Other:
2861	3903.1910	---改性的	6.5	0 5 6	东盟ASEAN,智利CL,新加坡SG,新西兰NZ,秘鲁PE,哥斯达黎加CR,香港HK 巴基斯坦PK 亚太APTA	0	最不发达 35 国 LDC35,最不发达 4 国 LDC4	45	---Modified

序号 No.	税则号列 Tariff Line	货品名称	最惠国税率 MFN(%)	协定税率 Agreement(%)		特惠税率 S.P.(%)		普通税率 Gen.(%)	Article Description
2862	3903.1990	---其他	6.5	0 5 6	东盟ASEAN,智利CL,新加坡SG,新西兰NZ,秘鲁PE,哥斯达黎加CR,香港HK 巴基斯坦PK 亚太APTA	0	最不发达35国LDC35,最不发达4国LDC4	45	---Other
2863	3903.2000	-苯乙烯—丙烯腈（SAN）共聚物	12	0 2.4 6	东盟ASEAN,智利CL,新加坡SG,新西兰NZ,秘鲁PE,台湾TW 哥斯达黎加CR 巴基斯坦PK	0	最不发达35国LDC35	45	-Styrene-acrylonitrile (SAN) copoly-mers
		-丙烯腈—丁二烯—苯乙烯（ABS）共聚物:							-Acrylonitrile-butadiene-styrene (ABS) copoly-mers:
2864	3903.3010	---改性的	6.5	0 5 6	东盟ASEAN,智利CL,新加坡SG,新西兰NZ,秘鲁PE,哥斯达黎加CR,香港HK,澳门MO 巴基斯坦PK 亚太APTA	0	最不发达35国LDC35,最不发达4国LDC4	45	---Modified
2865	3903.3090	---其他	6.5	0 5 6	东盟ASEAN,智利CL,新加坡SG,新西兰NZ,秘鲁PE,哥斯达黎加CR,香港HK,澳门MO 巴基斯坦PK 亚太APTA	0	最不发达35国LDC35,最不发达4国LDC4	45	---Other
2866	3903.9000	-其他	6.5	0 0.7 5 6	东盟ASEAN,新加坡SG,新西兰NZ,秘鲁PE,哥斯达黎加CR,香港HK,台湾TW 智利CL 巴基斯坦PK 亚太APTA	0	最不发达35国LDC35,最不发达4国LDC4	45	-Other
	39.04	**初级形状的氯乙烯或其他卤化烯烃聚合物:**							**Polymers of vinyl chloride or of other halogenated olefins, in primary forms:**
		-聚氯乙烯,未掺其他物质:							-Poly (vinyl chloride), not mixed with any other substances:
2867	3904.1010	---糊树脂	6.5	0 0.7 6	东盟ASEAN,新加坡SG,新西兰NZ,秘鲁PE,哥斯达黎加CR 智利CL 亚太APTA,巴基斯坦PK	0	最不发达35国LDC35,最不发达4国LDC4	45	---paste Poly (vinyl chloride)
2868	3904.1090	---其他	6.5	0 0.7 6	东盟ASEAN,新加坡SG,新西兰NZ,秘鲁PE,哥斯达黎加CR 智利CL 亚太APTA,巴基斯坦PK	0	最不发达35国LDC35,最不发达4国LDC4	45	---Other
		-其他聚氯乙烯:							-Other poly (vinyl chloride):

序号 No.	税则号列 Tariff Line	货品名称	最惠国税率 MFN(%)	协定税率 Agreement(%)		特惠税率 S.P.(%)		普通税率 Gen.(%)	Article Description
2869	3904.2100	--未塑化	6.5	0	东盟ASEAN,智利CL,新加坡SG,新西兰NZ,秘鲁PE,哥斯达黎加CR,香港HK	0	最不发达35国LDC35,最不发达4国LDC4	45	--Non-plasticized
				5	巴基斯坦PK				
2870	3904.2200	--已塑化	6.5	0	东盟ASEAN,新加坡SG,新西兰NZ,秘鲁PE,哥斯达黎加CR,香港HK	0	最不发达35国LDC35,最不发达4国LDC4	45	--Plasticized
				0.7	智利CL				
2871	3904.3000	-氯乙烯—乙酸乙烯酯共聚物	9	0	东盟ASEAN,智利CL,新西兰NZ,秘鲁PE,哥斯达黎加CR	0	最不发达35国LDC35,最不发达4国LDC4	45	-Vinyl chloride-vinyl acetate copolymers
				5	巴基斯坦PK				
				8.6	亚太APTA				
2872	3904.4000	-其他氯乙烯共聚物	12	0	东盟ASEAN,智利CL,新加坡SG,新西兰NZ	0	最不发达35国LDC35	45	-Other vinyl chloride copolymers
				2.4	哥斯达黎加CR				
				6	巴基斯坦PK,秘鲁PE				
				11.4	亚太APTA				
2873	3904.5000	-偏二氯乙烯聚合物	6.5	0	东盟ASEAN,智利CL,新西兰NZ,秘鲁PE,哥斯达黎加CR	0	最不发达35国LDC35,最不发达4国LDC4	45	-Vinylidene chloride polymers
				5	巴基斯坦PK				
		-氟聚合物:							-Fluoro-polymers:
2874	3904.6100	--聚四氟乙烯	10	0	东盟ASEAN,智利CL,新加坡SG,新西兰NZ,秘鲁PE,哥斯达黎加CR	0	最不发达35国LDC35,最不发达4国LDC4	45	--Polytetrafl uoroethyl-ene
				5	巴基斯坦PK				
2875	3904.6900	--其他	6.5	0	东盟ASEAN,智利CL,新西兰NZ,秘鲁PE,哥斯达黎加CR	0	最不发达35国LDC35,最不发达4国LDC4	45	--Other
				5	巴基斯坦PK				
2876	3904.9000	-其他	10	0	东盟ASEAN,智利CL,新西兰NZ,秘鲁PE,哥斯达黎加CR	0	最不发达35国LDC35,最不发达4国LDC4	45	-Other
				5	巴基斯坦PK				
	39.05	**初级形状的乙酸乙烯酯或其他乙烯酯聚合物;初级形状的其他乙烯基聚合物:**							**Polymers of vinyl acetate or of other vinyl esters, in primary forms; other vinyl polymers in primary forms:**
		-聚乙酸乙烯酯:							-Poly(vinyl acetate):

序号 No.	税则号列 Tariff Line	货品名称	最惠国税率 MFN(%)	协定税率 Agreement(%)		特惠税率 S.P.(%)		普通税率 Gen.(%)	Article Description
2877	3905.1200	--水分散体	10	0 1 5	东盟ASEAN,新加坡SG,新西兰NZ,哥斯达黎加CR 智利CL 秘鲁PE	0	最不发达35国LDC35	45	--In aqueous dispersion
2878	3905.1900	--其他	10	0 5	东盟ASEAN,智利CL,新西兰NZ,秘鲁PE,哥斯达黎加CR 巴基斯坦PK	0	最不发达35国LDC35	45	--Other
		-乙酸乙烯酯共聚物:							-Vinyl acetate copolymers:
2879	3905.2100	--水分散体	10	0 5	东盟ASEAN,智利CL,新加坡SG,新西兰NZ,秘鲁PE,哥斯达黎加CR,台湾TW 巴基斯坦PK	0	最不发达35国LDC35	45	--In aqueous dispersion
2880	3905.2900	--其他	10	0 5	东盟ASEAN,智利CL,新加坡SG,新西兰NZ,秘鲁PE,哥斯达黎加CR 巴基斯坦PK	0	最不发达35国LDC35	45	--Other
2881	3905.3000	-聚乙烯醇,不论是否含有未水解的乙酸酯基	14	0 2.8 11.2	东盟ASEAN,智利CL,新加坡SG,新西兰NZ,秘鲁PE,台湾TW 哥斯达黎加CR 巴基斯坦PK	0	最不发达35国LDC35	45	-Poly (vinyl alcohol), whether or not containing unhydrolyzed acetate groups
		-其他:							-Other:
2882	3905.9100	--共聚物	10	0 5	东盟ASEAN,智利CL,新西兰NZ,秘鲁PE,哥斯达黎加CR 巴基斯坦PK	0	最不发达35国LDC35	45	--Copolymers
2883	3905.9900	--其他	10	0 1 5	东盟ASEAN,新西兰NZ,哥斯达黎加CR,香港HK 智利CL 秘鲁PE	0	最不发达35国LDC35	45	--Other
	39.06	**初级形状的丙烯酸聚合物:**							**Acrylic polymers in primary forms:**
2884	3906.1000	-聚甲基丙烯酸甲酯	6.5	0 5 6	东盟ASEAN,智利CL,新西兰NZ,秘鲁PE,哥斯达黎加CR,台湾TW 巴基斯坦PK 亚太APTA	0	最不发达35国LDC35,最不发达4国LDC4	45	-Poly (methyl methacrylate)
		-其他:							-Other:
2885	3906.9010	---聚丙烯酰胺	6.5	0 0.7 5 6	东盟ASEAN,新西兰NZ,秘鲁PE,哥斯达黎加CR,香港HK,台湾TW 智利CL 巴基斯坦PK 亚太APTA	0	最不发达35国LDC35,最不发达4国LDC4	45	---Polyacrylamide
2886	3906.9090	---其他	6.5	0 0.7 5 6	东盟ASEAN,新西兰NZ,秘鲁PE,哥斯达黎加CR,香港HK,台湾TW 智利CL 巴基斯坦PK 亚太APTA	0	最不发达35国LDC35,最不发达4国LDC4	45	---Other

序号 No.	税则号列 Tariff Line	货品名称	最惠国税率 MFN(%)	协定税率 Agreement(%)		特惠税率 S.P.(%)		普通税率 Gen.(%)	Article Description
	ex39069090	聚丙烯酸钠	△3						Sodium polyacrylate
	39.07	**初级形状的聚缩醛、其他聚醚及环氧树脂;初级形状的聚碳酸酯、醇酸树脂、聚烯丙基酯及其他聚酯:**							**Polyacetals, other polyethers and epoxide resins, in primary forms; polycarbonates, alkyd resins, polyallyl esters and other polyesters, in primary forms:**
		-聚缩醛:							-Polyacetals:
2887	3907.1010	---聚甲醛	6.5	0 5 6	东盟ASEAN,智利CL,新加坡SG,新西兰NZ,秘鲁PE,哥斯达黎加CR,香港HK,台湾TW 巴基斯坦PK 亚太APTA	0	最不发达35国LDC35,最不发达4国LDC4	45	---Polyoxymethylene (POM)
2888	3907.1090	---其他	6.5	0 5 6	东盟ASEAN,智利CL,新加坡SG,新西兰NZ,秘鲁PE,哥斯达黎加CR,香港HK 巴基斯坦PK 亚太APTA	0	最不发达35国LDC35,最不发达4国LDC4	45	---Other
		-其他聚醚:							-Other polyethers:
2889	3907.2010	---聚四亚甲基醚二醇	6.5 △3	0 5 6	东盟ASEAN,智利CL,新加坡SG,新西兰NZ,秘鲁PE,哥斯达黎加CR,台湾TW 巴基斯坦PK 亚太APTA	0	最不发达35国LDC35,最不发达4国LDC4	45	---Polvtetramethylene Ether Glycol
2890	3907.2090	---其他	6.5	0 5 6	东盟ASEAN,智利CL,新加坡SG,新西兰NZ,秘鲁PE,哥斯达黎加CR 巴基斯坦PK 亚太APTA	0	最不发达35国LDC35,最不发达4国LDC4	45	---Other
2891	3907.3000	-环氧树脂	6.5	0 0.7 5 6	东盟ASEAN,新加坡SG,新西兰NZ,秘鲁PE,哥斯达黎加CR,香港HK,台湾TW 智利CL 巴基斯坦PK 亚太APTA	0	最不发达35国LDC35,最不发达4国LDC4	45	-Epoxide resins
	ex39073000	溴的质量百分含量在18%及以上或进口CIF价格高于3800美元/吨的环氧树脂(如溶于溶剂,以纯环氧树脂折算溴的百分含量)	△4						Epoxyresins containing by weight more than 18% Bromine) or import CIF>3800usd/t (base on pure epoxyresins if dissolved in solvent)
2892	3907.4000	-聚碳酸酯	6.5 △3	0 5 6.1	东盟ASEAN,智利CL,新西兰NZ,秘鲁PE,哥斯达黎加CR,香港HK,台湾TW 巴基斯坦PK 亚太APTA	0	最不发达35国LDC35,最不发达4国LDC4	45	-Polycarbonates

序号 No.	税则号列 Tariff Line	货品名称	最惠国税率 MFN(%)	协定税率 Agreement(%)		特惠税率 S.P.(%)		普通税率 Gen.(%)	Article Description
2893	3907.5000	-醇酸树脂	10	0 1 5 9.5	东盟ASEAN,新加坡SG,新西兰NZ,哥斯达黎加CR,台湾TW 智利CL 巴基斯坦PK,秘鲁PE 亚太APTA	0	最不发达35国LDC35,最不发达4国LDC4	45	-Alkyd resins
		-聚对苯二甲酸乙二酯: ---切片:							-Poly (ethylene terephthalate): ---In the form of slices or chips:
2894	3907.6011	----高粘度	6.5	0	智利CL,新西兰NZ,秘鲁PE,哥斯达黎加CR	0	最不发达35国LDC35,最不发达4国LDC4	45	----High viscosity
2895	3907.6019	----其他	6.5	0	智利CL,新西兰NZ,秘鲁PE,哥斯达黎加CR,澳门MO	0	最不发达35国LDC35,最不发达4国LDC4	45	----Other
2896	3907.6090	---其他	6.5	0	东盟ASEAN,智利CL,新西兰NZ,秘鲁PE,哥斯达黎加CR,澳门MO	0	最不发达35国LDC35,最不发达4国LDC4	45	---Other
2897	3907.7000	-聚乳酸	6.5 △3	0 0.7 5 6.2	东盟ASEAN,新西兰NZ,秘鲁PE,哥斯达黎加CR,香港HK,澳门MO 智利CL 巴基斯坦PK 亚太APTA	0	最不发达35国LDC35,最不发达4国LDC4	45	-Poly (lactic acid)
		-其他聚酯:							-Other polyesters:
2898	3907.9100	--不饱和	6.5	0 0.7 5	东盟ASEAN,新加坡SG,新西兰NZ,秘鲁PE,哥斯达黎加CR,台湾TW 智利CL 巴基斯坦PK	0	最不发达35国LDC35,最不发达4国LDC4	45	--Unsaturated
		--其他:							--Other:
2899	3907.9910	---聚对苯二甲酸丁二酯	6.5	0 0.7 5 6.2	东盟ASEAN,新西兰NZ,秘鲁PE,哥斯达黎加CR,香港HK,澳门MO 智利CL 巴基斯坦PK 亚太APTA	0	最不发达35国LDC35,最不发达4国LDC4	45	---Polybutylene terephthalate
		---其他:							---Other:
2900	3907.9991	----聚对苯二甲酸—己二醇—丁二醇酯	6.5	0 0.7 5 6.2	东盟ASEAN,新西兰NZ,秘鲁PE,哥斯达黎加CR,香港HK,澳门MO,台湾TW 智利CL 巴基斯坦PK 亚太APTA	0	最不发达35国LDC35,最不发达4国LDC4	45	----Poly (butylene adipata-co-terephthalate)

序号 No.	税则号列 Tariff Line	货品名称	最惠国税率 MFN(%)	协定税率 Agreement(%)		特惠税率 S.P.(%)		普通税率 Gen.(%)	Article Description
2901	3907.9999	----其他	6.5	0 0.7 5 6.2	东盟ASEAN,新西兰NZ,秘鲁PE,哥斯达黎加CR,香港HK,澳门MO,台湾TW 智利CL 巴基斯坦PK 亚太APTA	0	最不发达35国LDC35,最不发达4国LDC4	45	----Other
	39.08	**初级形状的聚酰胺:**							**Polyamides in primary forms:**
		-聚酰胺-6、-11、-12、-6，6、-6，9、-6，10或-6，12:							-Polyamide-6, -11, -12, -6, 6, -6, 9, -6, 10 or -6, 12:
		---切片:							---In the form of slices or chips:
2902	3908.1011	----聚酰胺-6，6切片	6.5	0 5	东盟ASEAN,智利CL,新加坡SG,新西兰NZ,秘鲁PE,哥斯达黎加CR,香港HK 巴基斯坦PK	0	最不发达35国LDC35,最不发达4国LDC4	45	----Of polyamide-6, 6
2903	3908.1012	----聚酰胺-6切片	6.5	0 5	东盟ASEAN,智利CL,新加坡SG,新西兰NZ,秘鲁PE,哥斯达黎加CR,香港HK 巴基斯坦PK	0	最不发达35国LDC35,最不发达4国LDC4	45	----Of polyamide-6
2904	3908.1019	----其他	6.5	0 5	东盟ASEAN,智利CL,新加坡SG,新西兰NZ,秘鲁PE,哥斯达黎加CR,香港HK 巴基斯坦PK	0	最不发达35国LDC35,最不发达4国LDC4	45	----Other
2905	3908.1090	---其他	6.5	0 5	东盟ASEAN,智利CL,新西兰NZ,秘鲁PE,哥斯达黎加CR,香港HK 巴基斯坦PK	0	最不发达35国LDC35,最不发达4国LDC4	45	---Other
2906	3908.9000	-其他	10	0 5	东盟ASEAN,智利CL,新加坡SG,新西兰NZ,秘鲁PE,哥斯达黎加CR 巴基斯坦PK	0	最不发达35国LDC35,最不发达4国LDC4	45	-Other
	39.09	**初级形状的氨基树脂、酚醛树脂及聚氨酯类:**							**Amino-resins, phenolic resins and polyurethanes, in primary forms:**
2907	3909.1000	-尿素树脂;硫尿树脂	6.5	0 0.7 5 6.1	东盟ASEAN,新西兰NZ,秘鲁PE,哥斯达黎加CR,台湾TW 智利CL 巴基斯坦PK 亚太APTA	0	最不发达35国LDC35,最不发达4国LDC4	45	-Urea resins; thiourea resins

序号 No.	税则号列 Tariff Line	货品名称	最惠国税率 MFN(%)	协定税率 Agreement(%)		特惠税率 S.P.(%)		普通税率 Gen.(%)	Article Description
2908	3909.2000	-蜜胺树脂	6.5	0 5 6.1	东盟ASEAN,智利CL,新西兰NZ,秘鲁PE,哥斯达黎加CR,台湾TW 巴基斯坦PK 亚太APTA	0	最不发达35国LDC35,最不发达4国LDC4	45	-Melamine resins
		-其他氨基树脂:							-Other amino-resins:
2909	3909.3010	---聚(亚甲基苯基异氰酸酯)(聚合MDI或粗MDI)	6.5	0 0.7 5 6	东盟ASEAN,新加坡SG,新西兰NZ,秘鲁PE,哥斯达黎加CR,香港HK 智利CL 巴基斯坦PK 亚太APTA	0	最不发达35国LDC35,最不发达4国LDC4	35	---Poly (methylene phenyl isocyanate)
2910	3909.3090	---其他	6.5	0 0.7 5	东盟ASEAN,新加坡SG,新西兰NZ,秘鲁PE,哥斯达黎加CR,台湾TW 智利CL 巴基斯坦PK	0	最不发达35国LDC35,最不发达4国LDC4	45	---Other
2911	3909.4000	-酚醛树脂	6.5	0 0.7 5 6.1	东盟ASEAN,新西兰NZ,秘鲁PE,哥斯达黎加CR,台湾TW 智利CL 巴基斯坦PK 亚太APTA	0	最不发达35国LDC35,最不发达4国LDC4	45	-Phenolic resins
2912	3909.5000	-聚氨基甲酸酯	6.5	0 0.7 5 6	东盟ASEAN,新加坡SG,新西兰NZ,秘鲁PE,哥斯达黎加CR,香港HK,澳门MO,台湾TW 智利CL 巴基斯坦PK 亚太APTA	0	最不发达35国LDC35,最不发达4国LDC4	45	-Polyurethanes
	39.10	**初级形状的聚硅氧烷:**							**Silicones in primary forms:**
2913	3910.0000	初级形状的聚硅氧烷	6.5	0 5 6.1	东盟ASEAN,智利CL,新西兰NZ,秘鲁PE,哥斯达黎加CR,香港HK,台湾TW 巴基斯坦PK 亚太APTA	0	最不发达35国LDC35,最不发达4国LDC4	45	Silicones in primary forms
	39.11	**初级形状的石油树脂、苯并呋喃—茚树脂、多萜树脂、多硫化物、聚砜及本章注释三所规定的其他税号未列名产品:**							**Petroleum resins, coumarone-indene resins, polyterpenes, polysulphides, polysulphones and other products specified in Note 3 to this Chapter, not elsewhere specified or included, in primary forms:**
2914	3911.1000	-石油树脂、苯并呋喃树脂、茚树脂、苯并呋喃茚树脂及多萜树脂	6.5	0 5 6.1	东盟ASEAN,智利CL,新西兰NZ,秘鲁PE,哥斯达黎加CR,台湾TW 巴基斯坦PK 亚太APTA	0	最不发达35国LDC35,最不发达4国LDC4	45	-Petroleum resins, coumarone, indene or coumarone-indene resins and polyterpenes

序号 No.	税则号列 Tariff Line	货品名称	最惠国税率 MFN(%)	协定税率 Agreement(%)		特惠税率 S.P.(%)		普通税率 Gen.(%)	Article Description
2915	3911.9000	-其他	6.5	0 5	东盟ASEAN,智利CL,新西兰NZ,秘鲁PE,哥斯达黎加CR 巴基斯坦PK	0	最不发达35国LDC35,最不发达4国LDC4	45	-Other
	ex39119000	偏苯三酸酐和异氰酸预缩聚物	△3						Precondensed polymer of modified trihydroxy acetate
	ex39119000	芳基酸与芳基胺预缩聚物	△3						Precondensed polymer of modified trihydroxy acetate
	ex39119000	改性三羟乙基脲酸酯类预缩聚物	△3						Precondensed polymer of modified trihydroxy acetate
	39.12	**初级形状的其他税号未列名的纤维素及其化学衍生物:**							**Cellulose and its chemical derivatives, not elsewhere specified or included, in primary forms:**
		-乙酸纤维素:							-Cellulose acetates:
2916	3912.1100	--未塑化	6.5	0 5	东盟ASEAN,智利CL,新西兰NZ,秘鲁PE,哥斯达黎加CR 巴基斯坦PK	0	最不发达35国LDC35	40	--Non-plasticized
2917	3912.1200	--已塑化	6.5	0 5	东盟ASEAN,智利CL,新西兰NZ,秘鲁PE,哥斯达黎加CR 巴基斯坦PK	0	最不发达35国LDC35	40	--Plasticized
2918	3912.2000	-硝酸纤维素(包括胶棉)	6.5	0 5	东盟ASEAN,智利CL,新西兰NZ,秘鲁PE,哥斯达黎加CR 巴基斯坦PK	0	最不发达35国LDC35	45	-Cellulose nitrates (including collodions)
		-纤维素醚:							-Cellulose ethers:
2919	3912.3100	--羧甲基纤维素及其盐	6.5	0 5	东盟ASEAN,智利CL,新西兰NZ,秘鲁PE,哥斯达黎加CR 巴基斯坦PK	0	最不发达35国LDC35	45	--Carboxymethylcellulose and its salts
2920	3912.3900	--其他	6.5	0 0.7 5	东盟ASEAN,新西兰NZ,秘鲁PE,哥斯达黎加CR 智利CL 巴基斯坦PK	0	最不发达35国LDC35	45	--Other
2921	3912.9000	-其他	6.5	0 5	东盟ASEAN,智利CL,新西兰NZ,秘鲁PE,哥斯达黎加CR,香港HK 巴基斯坦PK	0	最不发达35国LDC35	45	-Other
	39.13	**初级形状的其他税号未列名的天然聚合物(例如藻酸)及改性天然聚合物(例如,硬化蛋白、天然橡胶的化学衍生物):**							**Natural polymers (for example, alginic acid) and modified natural polymers (for example, hardened proteins, chemical derivatives of natural rubber), not elsewhere specified or included, in primary forms:**

序号 No.	税则号列 Tariff Line	货品名称	最惠国税率 MFN(%)	协定税率 Agreement(%)		特惠税率 S.P.(%)		普通税率 Gen.(%)	Article Description
2922	3913.1000	-藻酸及其盐和酯	10	0 1 5	东盟ASEAN,新加坡SG,新西兰NZ,哥斯达黎加CR 智利CL 巴基斯坦PK	0	最不发达35国LDC35,最不发达4国LDC4	45	-Alginic acid, its salts and esters
2923	3913.9000	-其他	6.5	0 5	东盟ASEAN,智利CL,新西兰NZ,秘鲁PE,哥斯达黎加CR 巴基斯坦PK	0	最不发达35国LDC35,最不发达4国LDC4	50	-Other
	39.14	**初级形状的离子交换剂，以税号39.01至39.13的聚合物为基本成分的:**							**Ion-exchangers based on polymers of headings Nos.39.01 to 39.13, in primary forms:**
2924	3914.0000	初级形状的离子交换剂，以税号39.01至39.13的聚合物为基本成分的	6.5	0 5	东盟ASEAN,智利CL,新西兰NZ,秘鲁PE,哥斯达黎加CR 巴基斯坦PK	0	最不发达35国LDC35,最不发达4国LDC4	45	Ion-exchangers based on polymers of headings Nos.39.01 to 39.13, in primary forms
		第二分章 废碎料及下脚料;半制品;制成品							Ⅱ.WASTE, PARINGS AND SCRAP; SEMI MANUFACTURES;ARTICLES
	39.15	**塑料的废碎料及下脚料:**							**Waste, parings and scrap, of plastics:**
2925	3915.1000	-乙烯聚合物的	6.5	0 0.7 5	东盟ASEAN,新加坡SG,新西兰NZ,秘鲁PE,哥斯达黎加CR,香港HK,澳门MO 智利CL 巴基斯坦PK	0	最不发达35国LDC35,最不发达4国LDC4	50	-Of polymers of ethylene
2926	3915.2000	-苯乙烯聚合物的	6.5	0 0.7 5	东盟ASEAN,新加坡SG,新西兰NZ,秘鲁PE,哥斯达黎加CR,香港HK,澳门MO 智利CL 巴基斯坦PK	0	最不发达35国LDC35,最不发达4国LDC4	50	-Of polymers of styrene
2927	3915.3000	-氯乙烯聚合物的	6.5	0 5	东盟ASEAN,智利CL,新加坡SG,新西兰NZ,秘鲁PE,哥斯达黎加CR,香港HK,澳门MO 巴基斯坦PK	0	最不发达35国LDC35,最不发达4国LDC4	50	-Of polymers of vinyl chloride
		-其他塑料的:							-Of other plastics:
2928	3915.9010	---聚对苯二甲酸乙二酯的	6.5	0 0.7 1.3 5	东盟ASEAN,新加坡SG,新西兰NZ,秘鲁PE,香港HK,澳门MO 智利CL 哥斯达黎加CR 巴基斯坦PK	0	最不发达35国LDC35,最不发达4国LDC4	50	---Of pdyethylene glycol tevephthalate

序号 No.	税则号列 Tariff Line	货品名称	最惠国税率 MFN(%)	协定税率 Agreement(%)	特惠税率 S.P.(%)	普通税率 Gen.(%)	Article Description
2929	3915.9090	---其他	6.5	0 东盟ASEAN,新加坡SG,新西兰NZ,秘鲁PE,香港HK,澳门MO 0.7 智利CL 1.3 哥斯达黎加CR 5 巴基斯坦PK	0 最不发达35国LDC35,最不发达4国LDC4	50	---Other
	39.16	**塑料制的单丝（截面直径超过1毫米）、条、杆、型材及异型材，不论是否经表面加工，但未经其他加工：**					**Monofilament of which any cross sectional dimension exceeds 1mm, rods, sticks and profile shapes, whether or not surfaceworked but not otherwise worked, of plastics:**
2930	3916.1000	-乙烯聚合物制	10	0 东盟ASEAN,新加坡SG,新西兰NZ,哥斯达黎加CR 1 智利CL 5 巴基斯坦PK,秘鲁PE	0 最不发达35国LDC35	45	-Of polymers of ethylene
		-氯乙烯聚合物制:					-Of polymers of vinyl chloride:
2931	3916.2010	---异型材	10	0 东盟ASEAN,新西兰NZ,秘鲁PE,哥斯达黎加CR 1 智利CL 5 巴基斯坦PK 7 亚太APTA	0 最不发达35国LDC35	45	---Profile shapes
2932	3916.2090	---其他	10	0 东盟ASEAN,新西兰NZ,秘鲁PE,哥斯达黎加CR 1 智利CL 5 巴基斯坦PK 7 亚太APTA	0 最不发达35国LDC35	45	---Other
		-其他塑料制:					-Of other plastics:
2933	3916.9010	---聚酰胺制	10	0 东盟ASEAN,智利CL,新加坡SG,新西兰NZ,秘鲁PE,哥斯达黎加CR,香港HK 5 巴基斯坦PK	0 最不发达35国LDC35	45	---Of polyamides
2934	3916.9090	---其他	10	0 东盟ASEAN,智利CL,新加坡SG,新西兰NZ,秘鲁PE,哥斯达黎加CR 5 巴基斯坦PK	0 最不发达35国LDC35	45	---Other
	39.17	**塑料制的管子及其附件（例如，接头、肘管、法兰）：**					**Tubes, pipes and hoses, and fittings therefor (for example, joints, elbows, flanges), of plastics:**
2935	3917.1000	-硬化蛋白或纤维素材料制的人造肠衣（香肠用肠衣）	10	0 东盟ASEAN,新西兰NZ,秘鲁PE,哥斯达黎加CR 1 智利CL 5 巴基斯坦PK	0 最不发达35国LDC35	50	-Artificial guts (sausage casings) of hardened protein or of cellulosic materials
		-硬管:					-Tubes, pipes and hoses, rigid:

序号 No.	税则号列 Tariff Line	货品名称	最惠国税率 MFN(%)	协定税率 Agreement(%)		特惠税率 S.P.(%)		普通税率 Gen.(%)	Article Description
2936	3917.2100	--乙烯聚合物制	10	0 1 5	东盟ASEAN,新加坡SG,新西兰NZ,哥斯达黎加CR 智利CL 巴基斯坦PK,秘鲁PE	0	最不发达35国LDC35,最不发达4国LDC4	45	--Of polymers of ethylene
2937	3917.2200	--丙烯聚合物制	10	0 5	东盟ASEAN,智利CL,新西兰NZ,秘鲁PE,哥斯达黎加CR 巴基斯坦PK	0	最不发达35国LDC35,最不发达4国LDC4	45	--Of polymers of propylene
2938	3917.2300	--氯乙烯聚合物制	10	0 1 5	东盟ASEAN,新加坡SG,新西兰NZ,哥斯达黎加CR,香港HK 智利CL 巴基斯坦PK,秘鲁PE	0	最不发达35国LDC35,最不发达4国LDC4	45	--Of polymers of vinyl chloride
2939	3917.2900	--其他塑料制	10	0 5	东盟ASEAN,智利CL,新加坡SG,新西兰NZ,秘鲁PE,哥斯达黎加CR 巴基斯坦PK	0	最不发达35国LDC35,最不发达4国LDC4	45	--Of other plastics
		-其他管:							-Other tubes, pipes and hoses:
2940	3917.3100	--软管，最小爆破压力为27.6兆帕斯卡	10	0 1 5 7	东盟ASEAN,新加坡SG,新西兰NZ,秘鲁PE,哥斯达黎加CR,香港HK 智利CL 巴基斯坦PK 亚太APTA	0	最不发达35国LDC35,最不发达4国LDC4	45	--Flexible tubes, pipes and hoses, having a minimum burst pressure of 27.6Mpa
2941	3917.3200	--其他未装有附件的管子，未经加强也未与其他材料合制	6.5	0 0.7 4.6	东盟ASEAN,巴基斯坦PK,新西兰NZ,秘鲁PE,哥斯达黎加CR 智利CL 亚太APTA	0	最不发达35国LDC35,最不发达4国LDC4	45	--Other, not reinforced or otherwise combined with other materials, without fittings
2942	3917.3300	--其他装有附件的管子，未经加强也未与其他材料合制	6.5	0 0.7 4.6	东盟ASEAN,巴基斯坦PK,新西兰NZ,秘鲁PE,哥斯达黎加CR 智利CL 亚太APTA	0	最不发达35国LDC35,最不发达4国LDC4	45	--Other, not reinforced or otherwise combined with other materials, with fittings
2943	3917.3900	--其他	6.5	0 0.7 4.5	东盟ASEAN,新加坡SG,新西兰NZ,秘鲁PE,哥斯达黎加CR 智利CL 亚太APTA,巴基斯坦PK	0	最不发达35国LDC35,最不发达4国LDC4	45	--Other
2944	3917.4000	-管子附件	10	0 1 5 7	东盟ASEAN,新加坡SG,新西兰NZ,哥斯达黎加CR 智利CL 巴基斯坦PK,秘鲁PE 亚太APTA	0	最不发达35国LDC35,最不发达4国LDC4	45	-Fittings

序号 No.	税则号列 Tariff Line	货品名称	最惠国税率 MFN(%)	协定税率 Agreement(%)		特惠税率 S.P.(%)		普通税率 Gen.(%)	Article Description
	39.18	**块状或成卷的塑料铺地制品，不论是否胶粘;本章注释九所规定的塑料糊墙品:**							**Floor coverings of plastics, whether or not self-adhesive, in rolls or in the form of tiles; wall or ceiling coverings of plastics, as defined in Note 9 to this Chapter:**
		-氯乙烯聚合物制:							-Of polymers of vinyl chloride:
2945	3918.1010	---糊墙品	10	0 1 5	东盟ASEAN,新西兰NZ,哥斯达黎加CR 智利CL 巴基斯坦PK,秘鲁PE	0	最不发达35国LDC35	45	---Wall or ceiling coverings
2946	3918.1090	---其他	10	0 1 5	东盟ASEAN,新西兰NZ,哥斯达黎加CR 智利CL 巴基斯坦PK,秘鲁PE	0	最不发达35国LDC35	45	---Other
		-其他塑料制:							-Of other plastics:
2947	3918.9010	---糊墙品	10	0 5	东盟ASEAN,智利CL,新西兰NZ,秘鲁PE,哥斯达黎加CR,香港HK 巴基斯坦PK	0	最不发达35国LDC35	45	---Wall or ceiling coverings
2948	3918.9090	---其他	10	0 5	东盟ASEAN,智利CL,新西兰NZ,秘鲁PE,哥斯达黎加CR,香港HK 巴基斯坦PK	0	最不发达35国LDC35	45	---Other
	39.19	**自粘的塑料板、片、膜、箔、带、扁条及其他扁平形状材料，不论是否成卷:**							**Self-adhesive plates, sheets, film, foil, tape, strip and other flat shapes, of plastics, whether or not in rolls:**
		-成卷，宽度不超过20厘米:							-In rolls of a width not exceeding 20cm:
2949	3919.1010	---丙烯酸树脂类为基本成分	6.5	0 0.7 5	东盟ASEAN,新西兰NZ,秘鲁PE,哥斯达黎加CR 智利CL 巴基斯坦PK	0	最不发达35国LDC35,最不发达4国LDC4	45	---Based on acrylic resin
		---其他:							---Other:
2950	3919.1091	----胶囊型反光膜	6.5	0 0.7 5	东盟ASEAN,新西兰NZ,秘鲁PE,哥斯达黎加CR 智利CL 巴基斯坦PK	0	最不发达35国LDC35,最不发达4国LDC4	45	----Encapsulant reflective film
2951	3919.1099	----其他	6.5	0 0.7 5	东盟ASEAN,新西兰NZ,秘鲁PE,哥斯达黎加CR,台湾TW 智利CL 巴基斯坦PK	0	最不发达35国LDC35,最不发达4国LDC4	45	----Other
		-其他:							-Other:

序号 No.	税则号列 Tariff Line	货品名称	最惠国税率 MFN(%)		协定税率 Agreement(%)		特惠税率 S.P.(%)	普通税率 Gen.(%)	Article Description
2952	3919.9010	---胶囊型反光膜	6.5	0 0.7 4.6	东盟ASEAN,巴基斯坦PK,新西兰NZ,秘鲁PE,哥斯达黎加CR,香港HK 智利CL 亚太APTA	0	最不发达35国LDC35,最不发达4国LDC4	45	---Encapsulant reflective film
2953	3919.9090	---其他	6.5	0 0.7 4.6	东盟ASEAN,巴基斯坦PK,新西兰NZ,秘鲁PE,哥斯达黎加CR,香港HK,台湾TW 智利CL 亚太APTA	0	最不发达35国LDC35,最不发达4国LDC4	45	---Other
	39.20	**其他非泡沫塑料的板、片、膜、箔及扁条，未用其他材料强化、层压、支撑或用类似方法合制:**							**Other plates, sheets, film, foil and strip, of plastics, non-cellular and not reinforced, laminated, supported or similarly combined with other materials:**
		-乙烯聚合物制:							-Of polymers of ethylene:
2954	3920.1010	---乙烯聚合物制电池隔膜	6.5 △3	0 0.7 4.6	东盟ASEAN,巴基斯坦PK,新西兰NZ,秘鲁PE,哥斯达黎加CR,香港HK 智利CL 亚太APTA	0	最不发达35国LDC35,最不发达4国LDC4	45	---Battery separator, of polymers of ethylene
2955	3920.1090	---其他	6.5	0 0.7 4.6	东盟ASEAN,巴基斯坦PK,新西兰NZ,秘鲁PE,哥斯达黎加CR,香港HK,澳门MO,台湾TW 智利CL 亚太APTA	0	最不发达35国LDC35,最不发达4国LDC4	45	---Other
		-丙烯聚合物制:							-Of polymers of propylene:
2956	3920.2010	---丙烯聚合物制电池隔膜	6.5	0 0.7 5	东盟ASEAN,新西兰NZ,秘鲁PE,哥斯达黎加CR,香港HK 智利CL 巴基斯坦PK	0	最不发达35国LDC35,最不发达4国LDC4	45	---Battery separator, of polymers of propylene
2957	3920.2090	---其他	6.5	0 0.7 5	东盟ASEAN,新西兰NZ,秘鲁PE,哥斯达黎加CR,香港HK,澳门MO,台湾TW 智利CL 巴基斯坦PK	0	最不发达35国LDC35,最不发达4国LDC4	45	---Other
2958	3920.3000	-苯乙烯聚合物制	6.5	0 0.7 4.6	东盟ASEAN,巴基斯坦PK,新西兰NZ,秘鲁PE,哥斯达黎加CR,香港HK,台湾TW 智利CL 亚太APTA	0	最不发达35国LDC35,最不发达4国LDC4	45	-Of polymers of styrene

序号 No.	税则号列 Tariff Line	货品名称	最惠国税率 MFN(%)	协定税率 Agreement(%)		特惠税率 S.P.(%)		普通税率 Gen.(%)	Article Description
		-氯乙烯聚合物制:							-Of polymers of vinyl chloride:
2959	3920.4300	--按重量计增塑剂含量不小于6%	6.5	0 4.5	东盟ASEAN,智利CL,新加坡SG,新西兰NZ,秘鲁PE,哥斯达黎加CR,香港HK,台湾TW 亚太APTA,巴基斯坦PK	0	最不发达35国LDC35,最不发达4国LDC4	45	--Containing by weight not less than 6% of pleasticisers
2960	3920.4900	--其他	6.5	0 0.7 4.5	东盟ASEAN,新西兰NZ,秘鲁PE,哥斯达黎加CR,香港HK,澳门MO,台湾TW 智利CL 亚太APTA,巴基斯坦PK	0	最不发达35国LDC35,最不发达4国LDC4	45	--Other
		-丙烯酸聚合物制:							-Of acrylic polymers:
2961	3920.5100	--聚甲基丙烯酸甲酯制	6.5	0 4.6	东盟ASEAN,智利CL,巴基斯坦PK,新西兰NZ,秘鲁PE,哥斯达黎加CR,台湾TW 亚太APTA	0	最不发达35国LDC35,最不发达4国LDC4	45	--Of poly (methyl methacrylate)
2962	3920.5900	--其他	6.5	0 5	东盟ASEAN,智利CL,新西兰NZ,秘鲁PE,哥斯达黎加CR 巴基斯坦PK	0	最不发达35国LDC35,最不发达4国LDC4	45	--Other
		-聚碳酸酯、醇酸树脂、聚烯丙酯或其他聚酯制:							-Of polycarbonates, alkyd resins, polyallyl esters or other polyesters:
2963	3920.6100	--聚碳酸酯制	6.5	0 0.7 4.6	东盟ASEAN,巴基斯坦PK,新西兰NZ,秘鲁PE,哥斯达黎加CR,台湾TW 智利CL 亚太APTA	0	最不发达35国LDC35,最不发达4国LDC4	45	--Of polycarbonates
2964	3920.6200	--聚对苯二甲酸乙二酯制	6.5	0 4.6	东盟ASEAN,智利CL,巴基斯坦PK,新西兰NZ,秘鲁PE,哥斯达黎加CR,香港HK,澳门MO,台湾TW 亚太APTA	0	最不发达35国LDC35,最不发达4国LDC4	45	--Of poly (ethylene terephthalate)
2965	3920.6300	--不饱和聚酯制	10	0 5	东盟ASEAN,智利CL,新西兰NZ,秘鲁PE,哥斯达黎加CR 巴基斯坦PK	0	最不发达35国LDC35,最不发达4国LDC4	45	--Of unsaturated polyesters
2966	3920.6900	--其他聚酯制	10	0 1 5 9	东盟ASEAN,新加坡SG,新西兰NZ,哥斯达黎加CR,台湾TW 智利CL 巴基斯坦PK,秘鲁PE 亚太APTA	0	最不发达35国LDC35,最不发达4国LDC4	45	--Of other polyesters

序号 No.	税则号列 Tariff Line	货品名称	最惠国税率 MFN(%)	协定税率 Agreement(%)		特惠税率 S.P.(%)		普通税率 Gen.(%)	Article Description
		-纤维素及其化学衍生物制:							-Of cellulose or its chemical derivatives:
2967	3920.7100	--再生纤维素制	6.5	0 5	东盟ASEAN,智利CL,新西兰NZ,秘鲁PE,哥斯达黎加CR 巴基斯坦PK	0	最不发达35国LDC35,最不发达4国LDC4	45	--Of regenerated cellulose
2968	3920.7300	--乙酸纤维素制	6.5	0 5	东盟ASEAN,智利CL,新西兰NZ,秘鲁PE,哥斯达黎加CR,香港HK 巴基斯坦PK	0	最不发达35国LDC35,最不发达4国LDC4	45	--Of cellulose acetate
2969	3920.7900	--其他纤维素衍生物制	10	0 5	东盟ASEAN,智利CL,新西兰NZ,秘鲁PE,哥斯达黎加CR 巴基斯坦PK	0	最不发达35国LDC35,最不发达4国LDC4	45	--Of other cellulose derivatives
		-其他塑料制:							-Of other plastics:
2970	3920.9100	--聚乙烯醇缩丁醛制	6.5	0 5	东盟ASEAN,智利CL,新西兰NZ,秘鲁PE,哥斯达黎加CR 巴基斯坦PK	0	最不发达35国LDC35,最不发达4国LDC4	45	--Of poly (vinyl butyral)
	ex39209100	聚乙烯醇缩丁醛膜（厚度不超过3毫米）	△3						Polyvinyl butyral membrane (Thickness≤3mm)
2971	3920.9200	--聚酰胺制	10	0 5	东盟ASEAN,智利CL,新加坡SG,新西兰NZ,秘鲁PE,哥斯达黎加CR 巴基斯坦PK	0	最不发达35国LDC35,最不发达4国LDC4	45	--Of polyamides
2972	3920.9300	--氨基树脂制	6.5	0 5	东盟ASEAN,智利CL,新西兰NZ,秘鲁PE,哥斯达黎加CR 巴基斯坦PK	0	最不发达35国LDC35,最不发达4国LDC4	45	--Of amino-resins
2973	3920.9400	--酚醛树脂制	10	0 5 7	东盟ASEAN,智利CL,新加坡SG,新西兰NZ,秘鲁PE,哥斯达黎加CR 巴基斯坦PK 亚太APTA	0	最不发达35国LDC35,最不发达4国LDC4	45	--Of phenolic resins
		--其他塑料制:							--Of other plastics:
2974	3920.9910	---聚四氟乙烯制	6.5	0 5	东盟ASEAN,智利CL,新西兰NZ,秘鲁PE,哥斯达黎加CR 巴基斯坦PK	0	最不发达35国LDC35,最不发达4国LDC4	45	---Of polytetrafluoroethylene

序号 No.	税则号列 Tariff Line	货品名称	最惠国税率 MFN(%)	协定税率 Agreement(%)	特惠税率 S.P.(%)	普通税率 Gen.(%)	Article Description
2975	3920.9990	---其他塑料制	6.5	0 东盟ASEAN,智利CL,新西兰NZ,秘鲁PE,哥斯达黎加CR,香港HK,台湾TW 5 巴基斯坦PK	0 最不发达35国LDC35,最不发达4国LDC4	45	---Of other plastics
	ex39209990	聚酰亚胺膜（厚度不超过0.03毫米）	△3				Membrane of polyimide (thickness≤0.03mm)
	39.21	**其他塑料板、片、膜、箔、扁条:**					**Other plates, sheets, film, foil and strip, of plastics:**
		-泡沫塑料的:					-Cellular:
2976	3921.1100	--苯乙烯聚合物制	10	0 东盟ASEAN,智利CL,新西兰NZ,秘鲁PE,哥斯达黎加CR 5 巴基斯坦PK 9 亚太APTA	0 最不发达35国LDC35,最不发达4国LDC4	45	--Of polymers of styrene
		--氯乙烯聚合物制:					--Of polymers of vinyl chloride:
2977	3921.1210	---人造革及合成革	9	0 东盟ASEAN,新加坡SG,新西兰NZ,秘鲁PE,哥斯达黎加CR,香港HK,台湾TW 0.9 智利CL 5 巴基斯坦PK	0 最不发达35国LDC35,最不发达4国LDC4	70	---Combined with textile fabrics
2978	3921.1290	---其他	6.5	0 东盟ASEAN,新西兰NZ,秘鲁PE,哥斯达黎加CR,香港HK 0.7 智利CL 5 巴基斯坦PK	0 最不发达35国LDC35,最不发达4国LDC4	45	---Other
		--氨酯聚合物制:					--Of polyurethanes:
2979	3921.1310	---人造革及合成革	9	0 东盟ASEAN,新加坡SG,新西兰NZ,秘鲁PE,哥斯达黎加CR,香港HK,台湾TW 0.9 智利CL 5 巴基斯坦PK 6.3 亚太APTA	0 最不发达35国LDC35,最不发达4国LDC4	70	---Combined with textile fabrics
2980	3921.1390	---其他	6.5	0 东盟ASEAN,巴基斯坦PK,新西兰NZ,秘鲁PE,哥斯达黎加CR,香港HK 0.7 智利CL 4.6 亚太APTA	0 最不发达35国LDC35,最不发达4国LDC4	45	---Other
2981	3921.1400	--再生纤维素制	10	0 东盟ASEAN,智利CL,新西兰NZ,秘鲁PE,哥斯达黎加CR 5 巴基斯坦PK	0 最不发达35国LDC35,最不发达4国LDC4	45	--Of regenerated cellulose
		--其他塑料制:					--Of other plastics:

序号 No.	税则号列 Tariff Line	货品名称	最惠国税率 MFN(%)	协定税率 Agreement(%)		特惠税率 S.P.(%)		普通税率 Gen.(%)	Article Description
2982	3921.1910	---人造革及合成革	9	0 5 6.3	东盟ASEAN,智利CL,新西兰NZ,秘鲁PE,哥斯达黎加CR 巴基斯坦PK 亚太APTA	0	最不发达35国LDC35,最不发达4国LDC4	45	---Combined with textile fabrics
2983	3921.1990	---其他	6.5	0 4.6	东盟ASEAN,智利CL,巴基斯坦PK,新西兰NZ,秘鲁PE,哥斯达黎加CR,台湾TW 亚太APTA	0	最不发达35国LDC35,最不发达4国LDC4	45	---Other
		-其他:							-Other:
2984	3921.9020	---聚乙烯嵌有玻璃纤维的板、片	6.5	0 0.7 4.6	东盟ASEAN,巴基斯坦PK,新西兰NZ,秘鲁PE,哥斯达黎加CR,香港HK 智利CL 亚太APTA	0	最不发达35国LDC35,最不发达4国LDC4	45	---Plates, sheets of polyethylene with glass fibres
2985	3921.9030	---聚异丁烯为基本成分的附有人造毛毡的板、片、卷材	6.5	0 0.7 4.6	东盟ASEAN,巴基斯坦PK,新西兰NZ,秘鲁PE,哥斯达黎加CR,香港HK 智利CL 亚太APTA	0	最不发达35国LDC35,最不发达4国LDC4	45	---Plates, sheets, coils of polyisobutylene with man-made felt
2986	3921.9090	---其他	6.5	0 0.7 4.6	东盟ASEAN,巴基斯坦PK,新西兰NZ,秘鲁PE,哥斯达黎加CR,香港HK,台湾TW 智利CL 亚太APTA	0	最不发达35国LDC35,最不发达4国LDC4	45	---Other
	ex39219090	离子交换膜	△5						Ion exchange membrane
	39.22	**塑料浴缸、淋浴盘、洗涤槽、盥洗盆、坐浴盆、便盆、马桶座圈及盖、抽水箱及类似卫生洁具:**							**Baths, shower-baths, sinks, washbasins, bidets, lavatory pans, seats and covers, flushing cisterns and similar sanitary ware, of plastics:**
2987	3922.1000	-浴缸、淋浴盘、洗涤槽及盥洗盆	10	0 5	东盟ASEAN,智利CL,新西兰NZ,秘鲁PE,哥斯达黎加CR,澳门MO 巴基斯坦PK	0	最不发达35国LDC35,最不发达4国LDC4,老挝LA	80	-Baths, shower-baths, sinks and washbasins
2988	3922.2000	-马桶座圈及盖	10	0 1 5	东盟ASEAN,新西兰NZ,哥斯达黎加CR,澳门MO 智利CL 巴基斯坦PK,秘鲁PE	0	最不发达35国LDC35,最不发达4国LDC4,老挝LA	80	-Lavatory seats and covers

序号 No.	税则号列 Tariff Line	货品名称	最惠国税率 MFN(%)	协定税率 Agreement(%)		特惠税率 S.P.(%)		普通税率 Gen.(%)	Article Description
2989	3922.9000	-其他	10	0 1 5	东盟ASEAN,新西兰NZ,秘鲁PE,哥斯达黎加CR 智利CL 巴基斯坦PK	0	最不发达35国LDC35,最不发达4国LDC4	80	-Other
	39.23	**供运输或包装货物用的塑料制品;塑料制的塞子、盖子及类似品:**							**Articles for the conveyance or packing of goods, of plastics; stoppers, lids, caps and other closures, of plastics:**
2990	3923.1000	-盒、箱(包括板条箱)及类似品	10	0 1 5 7	东盟ASEAN,新加坡SG,新西兰NZ,哥斯达黎加CR,香港HK,澳门MO,台湾TW 智利CL 巴基斯坦PK,秘鲁PE 亚太APTA	0	最不发达35国LDC35,最不发达4国LDC4	80	-Boxes, cases, crates and similar articles
		-袋及包(包括锥形的):							-Sacks and bags (including cones):
2991	3923.2100	--乙烯聚合物制	10	0 1 5	东盟ASEAN,新加坡SG,新西兰NZ,哥斯达黎加CR,香港HK,澳门MO 智利CL 巴基斯坦PK,秘鲁PE	0	最不发达35国LDC35	80	--Of polymers of ethylene
2992	3923.2900	--其他塑料制	10	0 1 5	东盟ASEAN,新加坡SG,新西兰NZ,哥斯达黎加CR,香港HK,澳门MO 智利CL 巴基斯坦PK,秘鲁PE	0	最不发达35国LDC35,最不发达4国LDC4	80	--Of other plastics
2993	3923.3000	-坛、瓶及类似品	6.5	0 0.7 5	东盟ASEAN,新加坡SG,新西兰NZ,哥斯达黎加CR,香港HK 智利CL 巴基斯坦PK	0	最不发达35国LDC35,最不发达4国LDC4	80	-Carboys, bottles, flasks and similar articles
2994	3923.4000	-卷轴、纡子、筒管及类似品	10	0 5 7	东盟ASEAN,智利CL,新加坡SG,新西兰NZ,秘鲁PE,哥斯达黎加CR 巴基斯坦PK 亚太APTA	0	最不发达35国LDC35	35	-Spools, cops, bobbins and similar supports
2995	3923.5000	-塞子、盖子及类似品	10	0 1 5	东盟ASEAN,新加坡SG,新西兰NZ,哥斯达黎加CR,香港HK,台湾TW 智利CL 巴基斯坦PK,秘鲁PE	0	最不发达35国LDC35,最不发达4国LDC4	80	-Stoppers, lids, caps and other closures
2996	3923.9000	-其他	10	0 1 5 7	东盟ASEAN,新加坡SG,新西兰NZ,哥斯达黎加CR,香港HK,澳门MO,台湾TW 智利CL 巴基斯坦PK,秘鲁PE 亚太APTA	0	最不发达35国LDC35	80	-Other

序号 No.	税则号列 Tariff Line	货品名称	最惠国税率 MFN(%)	协定税率 Agreement(%)		特惠税率 S.P.(%)		普通税率 Gen.(%)	Article Description
	39.24	**塑料制的餐具、厨房用具、其他家庭用具及卫生或盥洗用具:**							**Tableware, kitchenware, other household articles and hygienic or toilet articles, of plastics:**
2997	3924.1000	-餐具及厨房用具	10	0 1 5	东盟ASEAN,新加坡SG,新西兰NZ,哥斯达黎加CR,香港HK,澳门MO 智利CL 巴基斯坦PK,秘鲁PE	0	最不发达35国LDC35,最不发达4国LDC4,亚太2国APTA2	80	-Tableware and kitchenware
2998	3924.9000	-其他	10	0 1 5	东盟ASEAN,新加坡SG,新西兰NZ,哥斯达黎加CR,香港HK,澳门MO 智利CL 巴基斯坦PK,秘鲁PE	0	最不发达35国LDC35,最不发达4国LDC4	80	-Other
	39.25	**其他税号未列名的建筑用塑料制品:**							**Builders, ware of plastics, not elsewhere specified or included:**
2999	3925.1000	-囤、柜、罐、桶及类似容器，容积超过300升	10	0 1 5	东盟ASEAN,新西兰NZ,哥斯达黎加CR 智利CL 巴基斯坦PK,秘鲁PE	0	最不发达35国LDC35,最不发达4国LDC4	80	-Reservoirs, tanks, vats and similar containers, of a capacity exceeding 300L
3000	3925.2000	-门、窗及其框架、门槛	10	0 1 5 7	东盟ASEAN,新西兰NZ,哥斯达黎加CR 智利CL 巴基斯坦PK,秘鲁PE 亚太APTA	0	最不发达35国LDC35	80	-Doors, windows and their frames and thresholds for doors
3001	3925.3000	-窗板、百叶窗（包括威尼斯式百叶窗）或类似制品及其零件	10	0 5	东盟ASEAN,智利CL,新西兰NZ,秘鲁PE,哥斯达黎加CR 巴基斯坦PK	0	最不发达35国LDC35	80	-Shutters, blinds (including Venetian blinds) and similar articles and parts thereof
3002	3925.9000	-其他	10	0 1 5	东盟ASEAN,新西兰NZ,哥斯达黎加CR,香港HK 智利CL 巴基斯坦PK,秘鲁PE	0	最不发达35国LDC35	80	-Other
	39.26	**其他塑料制品及税号39.01至39.14所列其他材料的制品:**							**Other articles of plastics and articles of other materials of headings Nos.39.01 to 39.14:**
3003	3926.1000	-办公室或学校用品	10	0 1 5	东盟ASEAN,新加坡SG,新西兰NZ,秘鲁PE,哥斯达黎加CR 智利CL 巴基斯坦PK	0	最不发达35国LDC35,最不发达4国LDC4	80	-Office or school supplies

序号 No.	税则号列 Tariff Line	货品名称	最惠国税率 MFN(%)	协定税率 Agreement(%)		特惠税率 S.P.(%)		普通税率 Gen.(%)	Article Description
		-衣服及衣着附件(包括分指手套、连指手套及露指手套): ---手套(包括分指手套、连指手套及露指手套):							-Articles of apparel and clothing accessories (including gloves, mittens and mitts): ---Gloves, mittens and mitts:
3004	3926.2011	----聚氯乙稀制	10	0 1	东盟ASEAN,新加坡SG,新西兰NZ,秘鲁PE,哥斯达黎加CR,香港HK 智利CL	0	最不发达35国LDC35	90	----of Poly (vinyl chloride)
3005	3926.2019	----其他	10	0 1	东盟ASEAN,新加坡SG,新西兰NZ,秘鲁PE,哥斯达黎加CR,香港HK 智利CL	0	最不发达35国LDC35	90	----Other
3006	3926.2090	---其他	10	0 1	东盟ASEAN,新加坡SG,新西兰NZ,秘鲁PE,哥斯达黎加CR,香港HK 智利CL	0	最不发达35国LDC35,最不发达4国LDC4	90	---Other
3007	3926.3000	-家具、车厢或类似品的附件	10	0 1 5	东盟ASEAN,新加坡SG,新西兰NZ,哥斯达黎加CR 智利CL 巴基斯坦PK,秘鲁PE	0	最不发达35国LDC35,最不发达4国LDC4	80	-Fittings for furniture, coachwork or the like
3008	3926.4000	-小雕塑品及其他装饰品	10	0 5 8.3	东盟ASEAN,智利CL,新西兰NZ,秘鲁PE,哥斯达黎加CR 巴基斯坦PK 亚太APTA	0	最不发达35国LDC35,最不发达4国LDC4	100	-Statuettes and other ornamental articles
		-其他:							-Other:
3009	3926.9010	---机器及仪器用零件	10	0 1 5 9	东盟ASEAN,新加坡SG,新西兰NZ,哥斯达黎加CR,香港HK,澳门MO,台湾TW 智利CL 巴基斯坦PK,秘鲁PE 亚太APTA	0	最不发达35国LDC35,最不发达4国LDC4	35	---Of a kind for used in machines or instruments
3010	3926.9090	---其他	10	0 1 5 9.2	东盟ASEAN,新加坡SG,新西兰NZ,哥斯达黎加CR,香港HK,澳门MO,台湾TW 智利CL 秘鲁PE 亚太APTA,巴基斯坦PK	0	最不发达35国LDC35,最不发达4国LDC4	80	---Other

第四十章
橡胶及其制品

注释:

一、除条文另有规定的以外，本目录所称“橡胶”，是指不论是否硫化或硬化的下列产品：天然橡胶、巴拉塔胶、古塔波胶、银胶菊胶、糖胶树胶及类似的天然树胶、合成橡胶、从油类中提取的油膏以及上述物品的再生品。

二、本章不包括：

（一）第十一类的货品（纺织原料及纺织制品）；

（二）第六十四章的鞋靴及其零件；

（三）第六十五章的帽类及其零件（包括游泳帽）；

（四）第十六类的硬质橡胶制的机械器具、电气器具及其零件（包括各种电气用品）；

（五）第九十章、第九十二章、第九十四章或第九十六章的物品；

（六）第九十五章的物品（运动用分指手套、连指手套、露指手套及税号 40.11 至 40.13 的制品除外）。

三、税号 40.01 至 40.03 及 40.05 所称“初级形状”，只限于下列形状：

（一）液状及糊状，包括胶乳（不论是否预硫化）及其他分散体和溶液；

（二）不规则形状的块、团、包、粉、粒、碎屑及类似的散装形状。

四、本章注释一和税号40.02所称“合成橡胶”，适用于：

（一）不饱和合成物质，即用硫磺硫化能使其不可逆地变为非热塑物质，这种物质能在温度18℃至29℃之间被拉长到其原长度的三倍而不致断裂，拉长到原长度的两倍时，在五分钟内能回复到不超过原长度的一倍半。为了进行上述试验，可以加入交联所需的硫化活化剂或促进剂；也允许含有注释五（二）2及 3 所述的物质。但不能加入非交联所需的物质，例如，增量剂、增塑剂及填料；

Chapter 40
Rubber and articles thereof

Notes:

1. Except where the context otherwise requires, throughout the Nomenclature the expression “rubber” means the following products, whether or not vulcanized or hard: natural rubber, balata, gutta-percha, guayule, chicle and similar natural gums, synthetic rubber, factice derived from oils, and such substances reclaimed.

2. This Chapter does not cover:

(a) Goods of Section Ⅺ (texitils and textile articles) ;

(b) Footwear or parts thereof of Chapter 64;

(c) Headgear or parts thereof (including bathing caps) of Chapter 65 ;

(d) Mechanical or electrical appliances or parts thereof of Section ⅩⅥ (including electrical goods of all kinds) , of hard rubber;

(e) Articles of Chapter 90, 92, 94 or 96; or

(f) Articles of Chapter 95 (other than sports gloves, mittens and mitts and articles of headings Nos.40.11 to 40.13) .

3. In headings Nos.40.01 to 40.03 and 40.05, the expression “primary forms” applies only to the following forms:

(a) Liquids and pastes (including latex, whether or not pre-vulcanized, and other dispersions and solutions) ;

(b) Blocks of irregular shape, lumps, bales, powders, granules, crumbs and similar bulk forms.

4. In Note 1 to this Chapter and in heading No. 40.02, the expression “synthetic rubber” applies to:

(a) Unsaturated synthetic substances which can be irreversibly transformed by vulcanization with sulphur into non-thermoplastic substances which, at a temperature between 18℃ and 29℃, will not break on being extended to three times their original length and will return, after being extended to twice their original length, within a period of five minutes, to a length not greater than one and a half times their original length. For the purposes of this test, substances necessary for the cross-linking, such as vulcanizing activators or accelerators, may be added; the presence of substances as provided for by Note 5 (b) (2) and (3) is also permitted. However, the presence of any substances not necessary for the cross-linking, such as extenders, plasticizers and fillers, is not permitted;

（二）聚硫橡胶（TM）；

（三）与塑料接枝共聚或混合而改性的天然橡胶、解聚天然橡胶以及不饱和合成物质与饱和合成高聚物的混合物，但这些产品必须符合以上（一）款关于硫化、延伸及回复的要求。

(b) Thioplasts (TM); and

(c) Natural rubber modified by grafting or mixing with plastics, depolymerized natural rubber, mixtures of unsaturated synthetic substances with saturated synthetic high polymers provided that all the above-mentioned products comply with the requirements concerning vulcanization, elongation and recovery in(a) above.

五、

（一）税号 40.01 及 40.02 不适用于任何凝结前或凝结后与下列物质相混合的橡胶或橡胶混合物：

1. 硫化剂、促进剂、防焦剂或活性剂（为制造预硫胶乳所加入的除外）；

2. 颜料或其他着色料，但仅为易于识别而加入的除外；

3. 增塑剂或增量剂（用油增量的橡胶中所加的矿物油除外）、填料、增强剂、有机溶剂或其他物质，但以下（二）款所述的除外。

（二）含有下列物质的橡胶或橡胶混合物，只要仍具有原料的基本特性，应归入税号40.01或40.02：

1. 乳化剂或防粘剂；

2. 少量的乳化剂分解产品；

3. 微量的下列物质：热敏剂（一般为制造热敏胶乳用）、阳离子表面活性剂（一般为制造阳性胶乳用）、抗氧剂、凝固剂、碎裂剂、抗冻剂、胶溶剂、保存剂、稳定剂、粘度控制剂或类似的特殊用途添加剂。

5.

(a) Headings Nos. 40.01 and 40.02 do not apply to any rubber or mixture of rubbers which has been compounded, before or after coagulation, with:

(1) vulcanizing agents, accelerators, retarders or activators (other than those added for the preparation of pre-vulcanized rubber latex) ;

(2) pigments or other colouring matter, other than those added solely for the purpose of identification;

(3) plasticizers or extenders (except mineral oil in the case of oil-extended rubber), fillers, reinforcing agents, organic solvents or any other substances, except those permitted under (b).

(b) The presence of the following substances in any rubber or mixture of rubbers shall not affect its classification in heading No.40.01 or 40.02, as the case may be, provided that such rubber or mixture of rubbers retains its essential character as a raw material:

(1) emulsifiers or anti-tack agents;

(2) small amounts of breakdown products of emulsifiers;

(3) very small amounts of the following: heat-sensitive agents (generally for obtaining thermosensitive rubber latexes), cationic surface-active agents (generally for obtaining electro-positive rubber latexes), antioxidants, coagulants, crumbling agents, freeze-resisting agents, peptizers, preservatives, stabilizers, viscosity-control agents , or similar special-purpose additives.

六、税号40.04所称“废碎料及下脚料”，是指在橡胶或橡胶制品生产或加工过程中由于切割、磨损或其他原因所造成没有使用价值的废橡胶及下脚料。

6. For the purposes of heading No.40.04, the expression “waste, parings and scrap” means rubber waste, parings and scrap from the manufacture or working of rubber and rubber goods definitely not usable as such because of cuttingup, wear or other reasons.

七、全部用硫化橡胶制成的线，其任一截面的尺寸超过 5 毫米的，应作为带、杆或型材及异型材归入税号 40.08。

八、税号 40.10 包括用橡胶浸渍、涂布、包覆或层压的织物制成的或用橡胶浸渍、涂布、包覆或套裹的纱线或绳制成的传动带、输送带。

九、税号40.01、40.02、40.03、40.05 及 40.08所称“板”、“片”、“带”，仅指未切割或只简单切割成矩形（包括正方形）的板、片、带及正几何形块，不论是否具有成品的特征，也不论是否经过印制或其他表面加工，但未切割成其他形状或进一步加工。

税号40.08所称“杆”或“型材及异型材”，仅指不论是否切割成一定长度或表面加工，但未经进一步加工的该类产品。

7. Thread wholly of vulcanized rubber，of which any cross-sectional dimension exceeds 5mm，is to be classified as strip，rods or profile shapes，of heading No.40.08.

8. Heading No. 40.10 includes conveyor or transmission belts or belting of textile fabric impregnated，coated，covered or laminated with rubber or made from textile yarn or cord impregnated，coated，covered or sheathed with rubber.

9. In headings Nos.40.01，40.02，40.03，40.05，and 40.08，the expressions “plates”，“sheets” and “strip” apply only to plates，sheets and strip and to blocks of regular geometric shape，uncut or simply cut to rectangular (including square) shape，whether or not having the character of articles and whether or not printed or otherwise surface-worked，but not otherwise cut to shape or further worked.

In heading No.40.08 the expressions “rods” and “profile shapes” apply only to such products，whether or not cut to length or surface-worked but not otherwise worked.

序号 No.	税则号列 Tariff Line	货品名称	最惠国税率 MFN(%)	协定税率 Agreement(%)		特惠税率 S.P.(%)	普通税率 Gen.(%)	Article Description
	40.01	**天然橡胶、巴拉塔胶、古塔波胶、银胶菊胶、糖胶树胶及类似的天然树胶，初级形状或板、片、带:**						**Natural rubber, balata, gutta-percha, guayule, chicle and similar natural gums, in primary forms or in plates, sheets or strip:**
3011	4001.1000	-天然胶乳，不论是否预硫化	20 △10%或720 元/吨，两者从低	0 4	智利CL,新西兰NZ 哥斯达黎加CR		40	-Natural rubber latex, whether or not prevulcanized
		-其他形状的天然橡胶:						-Natural rubber in other forms:
3012	4001.2100	--烟胶片	20 △20%或1200 元/吨，两者从低	0 4 17	智利CL,新西兰NZ 哥斯达黎加CR 亚太APTA,巴基斯坦PK		40	--Smoked sheets
3013	4001.2200	--技术分类天然橡胶（TSNR）	20 △20%或1200 元/吨，两者从低	0 4	智利CL,新西兰NZ 哥斯达黎加CR		40	--Technically specified natural rubber (TSNR)
3014	4001.2900	--其他	20	0 4 17	智利CL,新西兰NZ 哥斯达黎加CR 亚太APTA,巴基斯坦PK		40	--Other

序号 No.	税则号列 Tariff Line	货品名称	最惠国税率 MFN(%)	协定税率 Agreement(%)	特惠税率 S.P.(%)	普通税率 Gen.(%)	Article Description
3015	4001.3000	-巴拉塔胶、古塔波胶、银胶菊胶、糖胶树胶及类似的天然树胶	20	0 东盟ASEAN,智利CL,新加坡SG,新西兰NZ 4 哥斯达黎加CR 10 秘鲁PE	0 最不发达35国LDC35	40	-Balata, gutta-percha, guayule, chicle and similar natural gums
	40.02	**合成橡胶及从油类提取的油膏，初级形状或板、片、带;税号 40.01 所列产品与本税号所列产品的混合物，初级形状或板、片、带:**					**Synthetic rubber and factice derived from oils, in primary forms or in plates, sheets or strip; mixtures of any products of heading No.40.01 with any product of this heading, in primary forms or in plates, sheets or strip:**
		-丁苯橡胶（SBR）；羧基丁苯橡胶（XSBR）:					-Styrene-butadiene rubber (SBR); carboxylated styrene-butadiene rubber (XSBR):
		--胶乳:					--Latex:
3016	4002.1110	---羧基丁苯橡胶	7.5	0 东盟ASEAN,智利CL,新西兰NZ,秘鲁PE,哥斯达黎加CR,香港HK 5 巴基斯坦PK	0 最不发达35国LDC35,最不发达4国LDC4	14	---Carboxylated styrene-butadiene rubber (XSBR)
3017	4002.1190	---其他	7.5	0 东盟ASEAN,智利CL,新西兰NZ,秘鲁PE,哥斯达黎加CR,香港HK 5 巴基斯坦PK	0 最不发达35国LDC35,最不发达4国LDC4	14	---Other
		--其他:					--Other:
		---初级形状的:					---In primary forms:
3018	4002.1911	----未经任何加工的丁苯橡胶	7.5	0 东盟ASEAN,智利CL,新西兰NZ,秘鲁PE,哥斯达黎加CR,香港HK 5 巴基斯坦PK	0 最不发达35国LDC35,最不发达4国LDC4	14	----SBR, not worked
3019	4002.1912	----充油丁苯橡胶	7.5	0 东盟ASEAN,智利CL,新西兰NZ,秘鲁PE,哥斯达黎加CR,香港HK 5 巴基斯坦PK	0 最不发达35国LDC35,最不发达4国LDC4	14	----SBR, oil-filled
3020	4002.1913	----热塑丁苯橡胶	7.5	0 东盟ASEAN,智利CL,新西兰NZ,秘鲁PE,哥斯达黎加CR,香港HK 5 巴基斯坦PK	0 最不发达35国LDC35,最不发达4国LDC4	14	----SBR, thermo-plasticated

序号 No.	税则号列 Tariff Line	货品名称	最惠国税率 MFN(%)	协定税率 Agreement(%)		特惠税率 S.P.(%)		普通税率 Gen.(%)	Article Description
3021	4002.1914	----充油热塑丁苯橡胶	7.5	0 5	东盟ASEAN,智利CL,新西兰NZ,秘鲁PE,哥斯达黎加CR,香港HK 巴基斯坦PK	0	最不发达35国LDC35,最不发达4国LDC4	14	----SBR, oil-filled and thermo-plasticated
3022	4002.1919	----其他	7.5	0	智利CL,新西兰NZ,秘鲁PE,哥斯达黎加CR,香港HK	0	最不发达35国LDC35,最不发达4国LDC4	14	----Other
3023	4002.1990	---其他	7.5	0 5 7.1	东盟ASEAN,智利CL,新西兰NZ,秘鲁PE,哥斯达黎加CR,香港HK 巴基斯坦PK 亚太APTA	0	最不发达35国LDC35,最不发达4国LDC4	35	---Other
		-丁二烯橡胶（BR）:							-Butadiene rubber (BR):
3024	4002.2010	---初级形状的	7.5	0 5	东盟ASEAN,智利CL,新西兰NZ,秘鲁PE,哥斯达黎加CR 巴基斯坦PK	0	最不发达35国LDC35,最不发达4国LDC4	14	---In primary forms
3025	4002.2090	---其他	7.5	0 5 7	东盟ASEAN,智利CL,新西兰NZ,秘鲁PE,哥斯达黎加CR 巴基斯坦PK 亚太APTA	0	最不发达35国LDC35,最不发达4国LDC4	35	---Other
		-异丁烯-异戊二烯（丁基）橡胶(IIR);卤代丁基橡胶（CIIR或BIIR）:							-Isobutene-isoprene (butyl) rubber (IIR); halo-isobutene-isoprene rubber (CIIR or BIIR):
		--异丁烯-异戊二烯（丁基）橡胶（IIR）:							--Isobutene-isoprene (butyl) rubber (IIR):
3026	4002.3110	---初级形状的	6	0 5 5.6	东盟ASEAN,智利CL,新西兰NZ,秘鲁PE,哥斯达黎加CR 巴基斯坦PK 亚太APTA	0	最不发达35国LDC35,最不发达4国LDC4	14	---In primary forms
3027	4002.3190	---其他	7.5	0 5 7.1	东盟ASEAN,智利CL,新西兰NZ,秘鲁PE,哥斯达黎加CR 巴基斯坦PK 亚太APTA	0	最不发达35国LDC35,最不发达4国LDC4	35	---Other
		--其他:							--Other:
3028	4002.3910	---初级形状的	7.5	0 5	东盟ASEAN,智利CL,新西兰NZ,秘鲁PE,哥斯达黎加CR 巴基斯坦PK	0	最不发达35国LDC35,最不发达4国LDC4	14	---In pimary forms

序号 No.	税则号列 Tariff Line	货品名称	最惠国税率 MFN(%)	协定税率 Agreement(%)	特惠税率 S.P.(%)	普通税率 Gen.(%)	Article Description
3029	4002.3990	---其他	7.5	0 东盟ASEAN,智利CL,新西兰NZ,秘鲁PE,哥斯达黎加CR 5 巴基斯坦PK 7.1 亚太APTA	0 最不发达35国LDC35,最不发达4国LDC4	35	---Other
		-氯丁二烯（氯丁）橡胶（CR）:					-Chloroprene (chlorobutadiene) rubber (CR):
3030	4002.4100	--胶乳	7.5	0 东盟ASEAN,智利CL,新西兰NZ,秘鲁PE,哥斯达黎加CR 5 巴基斯坦PK 7.1 亚太APTA	0 最不发达35国LDC35,最不发达4国LDC4	14	--Latex
		--其他:					--Other:
3031	4002.4910	---初级形状的	7.5	0 东盟ASEAN,智利CL,新西兰NZ,秘鲁PE,哥斯达黎加CR 5 巴基斯坦PK	0 最不发达35国LDC35,最不发达4国LDC4	14	---In primary forms
3032	4002.4990	---其他	7.5	0 东盟ASEAN,智利CL,新西兰NZ,秘鲁PE,哥斯达黎加CR 5 巴基斯坦PK 7.1 亚太APTA	0 最不发达35国LDC35,最不发达4国LDC4	35	---Other
		-丁腈橡胶（NBR）:					-Acrylonitrile-butadient rubber (NBR):
3033	4002.5100	--胶乳	7.5	0 东盟ASEAN,智利CL,新西兰NZ,秘鲁PE,哥斯达黎加CR 5 巴基斯坦PK 7.1 亚太APTA	0 最不发达35国LDC35,最不发达4国LDC4	14	--Latex
		--其他:					--Other:
3034	4002.5910	---初级形状的	7.5	0 东盟ASEAN,智利CL,新西兰NZ,秘鲁PE,哥斯达黎加CR 5 巴基斯坦PK	0 最不发达35国LDC35,最不发达4国LDC4	14	---In primary forms
3035	4002.5990	---其他	7.5	0 东盟ASEAN,智利CL,新西兰NZ,秘鲁PE,哥斯达黎加CR 5 巴基斯坦PK	0 最不发达35国LDC35,最不发达4国LDC4	35	---Other
		-异戊二烯橡胶(IR):					-Isoprene rubber (IR):
3036	4002.6010	---初级形状的	3	0 东盟ASEAN,智利CL,巴基斯坦PK,新西兰NZ,秘鲁PE,哥斯达黎加CR	0 最不发达35国LDC35,最不发达4国LDC4	14	---In primary forms

序号 No.	税则号列 Tariff Line	货品名称	最惠国税 率 MFN(%)	协定税率 Agreement(%)		特惠税率 S.P.(%)		普通税率 Gen.(%)	Article Description
3037	4002.6090	---其他	5	0 4.5	东盟ASEAN,智利CL,巴基斯坦PK,新西兰NZ,秘鲁PE,哥斯达黎加CR 亚太APTA	0	最不发达35国LDC35,最不发达4国LDC4	35	---Other
		-乙丙非共轭二烯橡胶（EPDM）:							-Ethylene-propylenenon-conjugated diene rubber (EPDM):
3038	4002.7010	---初级形状的	7.5	0 5	东盟ASEAN,智利CL,新西兰NZ,秘鲁PE,哥斯达黎加CR 巴基斯坦PK	0	最不发达35国LDC35,最不发达4国LDC4	14	---In primary forms
3039	4002.7090	---其他	7.5	0 5 7.1	东盟ASEAN,智利CL,新西兰NZ,秘鲁PE,哥斯达黎加CR 巴基斯坦PK 亚太APTA	0	最不发达35国LDC35,最不发达4国LDC4	35	---Other
3040	4002.8000	-税号40.01所列产品与本税号所列产品的混合物	7.5	0 5	东盟ASEAN,智利CL,新西兰NZ,秘鲁PE,哥斯达黎加CR 巴基斯坦PK	0	最不发达35国LDC35,最不发达4国LDC4	35	-Mixtures of any product of heading No. 40.01 with any product of this heading
		-其他:							-Other:
3041	4002.9100	--胶乳	7.5	0 5	东盟ASEAN,智利CL,新西兰NZ,秘鲁PE,哥斯达黎加CR 巴基斯坦PK	0	最不发达35国LDC35,最不发达4国LDC4	14	--Latex
		--其他: ---其他合成橡胶:							--Other: ---Other synthetic rubber:
3042	4002.9911	----初级形状的	7.5	0 5	东盟ASEAN,智利CL,新西兰NZ,秘鲁PE,哥斯达黎加CR,香港HK,台湾TW 巴基斯坦PK	0	最不发达35国LDC35,最不发达4国LDC4	14	----In primary forms
3043	4002.9919	----其他	7.5	0 5	东盟ASEAN,智利CL,新西兰NZ,秘鲁PE,哥斯达黎加CR,香港HK 巴基斯坦PK	0	最不发达35国LDC35,最不发达4国LDC4	35	----Other
3044	4002.9990	---其他	4	0	东盟ASEAN,智利CL,巴基斯坦PK,新西兰NZ,秘鲁PE,哥斯达黎加CR	0	最不发达35国LDC35,最不发达4国LDC4	14	---Other

序号 No.	税则号列 Tariff Line	货品名称	最惠国税率 MFN(%)	协定税率 Agreement(%)	特惠税率 S.P.(%)	普通税率 Gen.(%)	Article Description
	40.03	**再生橡胶，初级形状或板、片、带:**					**Reclaimed rubber in primary forms or in plates, sheets or strip:**
3045	4003.0000	再生橡胶，初级形状或板、片、带	8	0 东盟ASEAN,智利CL,新西兰NZ,秘鲁PE,哥斯达黎加CR,香港HK 5 巴基斯坦PK	0 最不发达35国LDC35,最不发达4国LDC4	30	Reclaimed rubber in primary forms or in plates, sheets or strip
	40.04	**橡胶（硬质橡胶的除外）的废碎料、下脚料及其粉、粒:**					**Waste, parings and scrap of rubber (other than hard rubber) and powders and granules obtained therefrom:**
3046	4004.0000	橡胶（硬质橡胶的除外）的废碎料、下脚料及其粉、粒	8	0 东盟ASEAN,智利CL,新西兰NZ,秘鲁PE,哥斯达黎加CR 5 巴基斯坦PK 7.6 亚太APTA	0 最不发达35国LDC35	30	Waste, parings and scrap of rubber (other than hard rubber) and powders and granules obtained there-from
	40.05	**未硫化的复合橡胶，初级形状或板、片、带:**					**Compounded rubber, unvulcanized, in pri-mary forms or in plates, sheets or strip:**
3047	4005.1000	-与碳黑或硅石混合	8	0 东盟ASEAN,智利CL,新西兰NZ,秘鲁PE,哥斯达黎加CR,澳门MO 5 巴基斯坦PK	0 最不发达35国LDC35,最不发达4国LDC4	35	-Compounded with car-bon black or silica
3048	4005.2000	-溶液；子目号4005.10以外的分散体	8	0 东盟ASEAN,智利CL,新西兰NZ,秘鲁PE,哥斯达黎加CR 5 巴基斯坦PK	0 最不发达35国LDC35,最不发达4国LDC4	35	-Solutions; dispersions other than those of sub-heading No.4005.10
		-其他:					-Other:
3049	4005.9100	--板、片、带	8	0 东盟ASEAN,智利CL,新西兰NZ,秘鲁PE,哥斯达黎加CR 5 巴基斯坦PK	0 最不发达35国LDC35,最不发达4国LDC4	35	--Plates, sheets and strip
3050	4005.9900	--其他	8	0 东盟ASEAN,智利CL,新西兰NZ,秘鲁PE,哥斯达黎加CR,香港HK 5 巴基斯坦PK	0 最不发达35国LDC35,最不发达4国LDC4	35	--Other
	40.06	**其他形状（例如，杆、管或型材及异型材）的未硫化橡胶及未硫化橡胶制品（例如，盘、环）:**					**Other forms (for exam-ple, rods, tubes and profile shapes) and articles (for example, discs and rings), or unvul-canized rubber:**

序号 No.	税则号列 Tariff Line	货品名称	最惠国税率 MFN(%)	协定税率 Agreement(%)		特惠税率 S.P.(%)		普通税率 Gen.(%)	Article Description
3051	4006.1000	-轮胎翻新用胎面补料胎条	8	0 5	东盟ASEAN,智利CL,新西兰NZ,秘鲁PE,哥斯达黎加CR 巴基斯坦PK	0	最不发达35国LDC35,最不发达4国LDC4	35	-Camel-back strips for retreading rubber tyres
		-其他:							-Other:
3052	4006.9010	---其他形状的未硫化橡胶	8	0 5	东盟ASEAN,智利CL,新西兰NZ,秘鲁PE,哥斯达黎加CR 巴基斯坦PK	0	最不发达35国LDC35,最不发达4国LDC4	35	---Other forms of unvulcanized rubber
3053	4006.9020	---未硫化橡胶制品	14	0 2.8 11.2	东盟ASEAN,智利CL,新加坡SG,新西兰NZ,秘鲁PE 哥斯达黎加CR 巴基斯坦PK	0	最不发达35国LDC35	80	---Articles of unvulcanized rubber
	40.07	**硫化橡胶线及绳:**							**Vulcanized rubber thread and cord:**
3054	4007.0000	硫化橡胶线及绳	14	0 2.8 11.2	东盟ASEAN,智利CL,新加坡SG,新西兰NZ,秘鲁PE,香港HK 哥斯达黎加CR 巴基斯坦PK	0	最不发达35国LDC35	80	Vulcanized rubber thread and cord
	40.08	**硫化橡胶（硬质橡胶除外）制的板、片、带、杆或型材及异型材:**							**Plates, sheets, strip, rods and profile shapes, of vulcanized rubber other than hard rubber:**
		-海绵橡胶制:							-Of cellular rubber:
3055	4008.1100	--板、片、带	8	0 5	东盟ASEAN,智利CL,新西兰NZ,秘鲁PE,哥斯达黎加CR 巴基斯坦PK	0	最不发达35国LDC35,最不发达4国LDC4	35	--Plates, sheets and strip
3056	4008.1900	--其他	8	0 5	东盟ASEAN,智利CL,新西兰NZ,秘鲁PE,哥斯达黎加CR 巴基斯坦PK	0	最不发达35国LDC35,最不发达4国LDC4	35	--Other
		-非海绵橡胶制:							-Of non-cellular rubber:
3057	4008.2100	--板、片、带	8	0 5	东盟ASEAN,智利CL,新西兰NZ,秘鲁PE,哥斯达黎加CR 巴基斯坦PK	0	最不发达35国LDC35,最不发达4国LDC4	35	--Plates, sheets and strip
3058	4008.2900	--其他	8	0 5	东盟ASEAN,智利CL,新西兰NZ,秘鲁PE,哥斯达黎加CR 巴基斯坦PK	0	最不发达35国LDC35,最不发达4国LDC4	35	--Other

序号 No.	税则号列 Tariff Line	货品名称	最惠国税率 MFN(%)	协定税率 Agreement(%)		特惠税率 S.P.(%)		普通税率 Gen.(%)	Article Description
	40.09	**硫化橡胶（硬质橡胶除外）制的管子，不论是否装有附件（例如，接头、肘管、法兰）：**							**Tubes, pipes and hoses, of vulcanized rubber other than hard rubber, with or without their fittings (for example, joints, elbows, flanges):**
		-未经加强或未与其他材料合制:							-Not reinforced or otherwise combined with other materials:
3059	4009.1100	--未装有附件	10.5	0 2.1 5	东盟ASEAN,智利CL,新加坡SG,新西兰NZ,秘鲁PE 哥斯达黎加CR 巴基斯坦PK	0	最不发达35国LDC35	40	--Without fittings
3060	4009.1200	--装有附件	10	0 5	东盟ASEAN,智利CL,新西兰NZ,秘鲁PE,哥斯达黎加CR 巴基斯坦PK	0	最不发达35国LDC35	40	--With fittings
		-用金属加强或只与金属合制:							-Reinforced or otherwise combined only with metal:
3061	4009.2100	--未装有附件	10.5	0 1.1 2.1 5 5.3	东盟ASEAN,新加坡SG,新西兰NZ 智利CL 哥斯达黎加CR 巴基斯坦PK 秘鲁PE	0	最不发达35国LDC35	40	--Without fittings
3062	4009.2200	--装有附件	10	0 5	东盟ASEAN,智利CL,新加坡SG,新西兰NZ,秘鲁PE,哥斯达黎加CR 巴基斯坦PK	0	最不发达35国LDC35	40	--With fittings
		-用纺织材料加强或只与纺织材料合制:							-Reinforced or otherwise combined only with textile materials:
3063	4009.3100	--未装有附件	10.5	0 1.1 2.1 5 5.3	东盟ASEAN,新加坡SG,新西兰NZ 智利CL 哥斯达黎加CR 巴基斯坦PK 秘鲁PE	0	最不发达35国LDC35	40	--Without fittings
3064	4009.3200	--装有附件	10	0 5	东盟ASEAN,智利CL,新西兰NZ,秘鲁PE,哥斯达黎加CR 巴基斯坦PK	0	最不发达35国LDC35	40	--With fittings
		-用其他材料加强或与其他材料合制:							-Reinforced or otherwise combined with other materials:
3065	4009.4100	--未装有附件	10.5	0 1.1 2.1 5 5.3	东盟ASEAN,新加坡SG,新西兰NZ 智利CL 哥斯达黎加CR 巴基斯坦PK 秘鲁PE	0	最不发达35国LDC35	40	--Without fittings

序号 No.	税则号列 Tariff Line	货品名称	最惠国税率 MFN(%)	协定税率 Agreement(%)		特惠税率 S.P.(%)		普通税率 Gen.(%)	Article Description
3066	4009.4200	--装有附件	10	0 1 5	东盟ASEAN,新加坡SG,新西兰NZ,哥斯达黎加CR 智利CL 巴基斯坦PK,秘鲁PE	0	最不发达35国LDC35	40	--With fittings
	40.10	**硫化橡胶制的传动带或输送带及带料:**							**Conveyor or transmission belts or belting, of vulcanized rubber:**
		-输送带及带料:							-Conveyor belts or belting:
3067	4010.1100	--仅用金属加强的	10	0 1 5	东盟ASEAN,新西兰NZ,哥斯达黎加CR 智利CL 巴基斯坦PK,秘鲁PE	0	最不发达35国LDC35	35	--Reinforced only with metal
3068	4010.1200	--仅用纺织材料加强的	10	0 1 5	东盟ASEAN,新西兰NZ,哥斯达黎加CR 智利CL 巴基斯坦PK,秘鲁PE	0	最不发达35国LDC35	35	--Reinforced only with textile materials
3069	4010.1900	--其他	10	0 5	东盟ASEAN,智利CL,新西兰NZ,哥斯达黎加CR 巴基斯坦PK,秘鲁PE	0	最不发达35国LDC35	35	--Other
		-传动带及带料:							-Transmission belts or belting:
3070	4010.3100	--梯形截面的环形传动带（三角带），V形肋状的，外周长超过60厘米，但不超过180厘米	8	0 5	东盟ASEAN,智利CL,新西兰NZ,秘鲁PE,哥斯达黎加CR 巴基斯坦PK	0	最不发达35国LDC35,最不发达4国LDC4	35	--Endless transmission belts of trapezoidal cross-section (V-belts), V-ribbed, of a circumference exceeding 60cm but not exceeding 180cm
3071	4010.3200	--梯形截面的环形传动带（三角带），外周长超过60厘米，但不超过180厘米，V形肋状的除外	8	0 5	东盟ASEAN,智利CL,新西兰NZ,秘鲁PE,哥斯达黎加CR 巴基斯坦PK	0	最不发达35国LDC35,最不发达4国LDC4	35	--Endless transmission belts of trapezoidal cross-section (V-belts), other than V-ribbed, of an outside circumference exceeding 60cm but not exceeding 180cm
3072	4010.3300	--梯形截面的环形传动带（三角带），V形肋状的，外周长超过180厘米，但不超过240厘米	8	0 5	东盟ASEAN,智利CL,新西兰NZ,秘鲁PE,哥斯达黎加CR 巴基斯坦PK	0	最不发达35国LDC35,最不发达4国LDC4	35	--Endless transmission belts of trapezoidal cross-section (V-belts), V-ribbed, of an outside circumference exceeding 180cm but not exceeding 240cm
3073	4010.3400	--梯形截面的环形传动带（三角带），外周长超过180厘米，但不超过240厘米，V形肋状的除外	8	0 5	东盟ASEAN,智利CL,新西兰NZ,秘鲁PE,哥斯达黎加CR 巴基斯坦PK	0	最不发达35国LDC35,最不发达4国LDC4	35	--Endless transmission belts of trapezoidal cross-section (V-belts), Vribbed, of an outside circumference exceeding 180cm but not exceeding 240cm

序号 No.	税则号列 Tariff Line	货品名称	最惠国税率 MFN(%)	协定税率 Agreement(%)		特惠税率 S.P.(%)		普通税率 Gen.(%)	Article Description
3074	4010.3500	--环形同步带，外周长超过60厘米，但不超过150厘米	10	0 5	东盟ASEAN,智利CL,新加坡SG,新西兰NZ,秘鲁PE,哥斯达黎加CR 巴基斯坦PK	0	最不发达35国LDC35	35	--Endless transmission belts of trapezoidal cross-section (V-belts), other than Vribbed, of an outside circumference exceeding 60cm but not exceeding 150cm
3075	4010.3600	--环形同步带，外周长超过150厘米，但不超过198厘米	10	0 5	东盟ASEAN,智利CL,新西兰NZ,秘鲁PE,哥斯达黎加CR 巴基斯坦PK	0	最不发达35国LDC35	35	--Endless synchronous belts, of an outside circumference exceeding 150cm but not exceeding 198cm
3076	4010.3900	--其他	8	0 5 7.6	东盟ASEAN,智利CL,新西兰NZ,秘鲁PE,哥斯达黎加CR 巴基斯坦PK 亚太APTA	0	最不发达35国LDC35,最不发达4国LDC4	35	--Other
	40.11	**新的充气橡胶轮胎:**							**New pneumatic tyres, of rubber:**
3077	4011.1000	-机动小客车(包括旅行小客车及赛车)用	10	0 1 5 9.4	东盟ASEAN,新加坡SG,新西兰NZ,哥斯达黎加CR,台湾TW 智利CL 巴基斯坦PK 亚太APTA	0	最不发达35国LDC35,最不发达4国LDC4	50	-Of a kind used on motor cars (including station wagons and racing cars)
3078	4011.2000	-客运机动车辆或货运机动车辆用	10	0 1 5 9.4	东盟ASEAN,新加坡SG,新西兰NZ,哥斯达黎加CR,台湾TW 智利CL 巴基斯坦PK,秘鲁PE 亚太APTA	0	最不发达35国LDC35	50	-Of a kind used on buses or lorries
	ex40112000	断面宽度30英寸及以上的轮胎	△3						Tyres, having a fracture surface of a width of 30 inches or more
3079	4011.3000	-航空器用	1	0	东盟ASEAN,智利CL,巴基斯坦PK,新西兰NZ,秘鲁PE,哥斯达黎加CR	0	最不发达35国LDC35,最不发达4国LDC4	11	-Of a kind used on aircraft
3080	4011.4000	-摩托车用	15	0 3 7.5 12	东盟ASEAN,智利CL,新加坡SG,新西兰NZ,台湾TW 哥斯达黎加CR 秘鲁PE 巴基斯坦PK	0	最不发达35国LDC35	80	-Of a kind used on motorcycles
3081	4011.5000	-自行车用	20	0 4 10	东盟ASEAN,智利CL,新加坡SG,新西兰NZ,台湾TW 哥斯达黎加CR 秘鲁PE	0	最不发达35国LDC35	80	-Of a kind used on bicycles

序号 No.	税则号列 Tariff Line	货品名称	最惠国税率 MFN(%)	协定税率 Agreement(%)		特惠税率 S.P.(%)		普通税率 Gen.(%)	Article Description
		-其他，人字形胎面或类似胎面的:							-Other, Having a "herring-bone" or similar tread:
3082	4011.6100	--农业或林业车辆及机器用	17.5	0 3.5 8.8 14	东盟ASEAN,智利CL,新加坡SG,新西兰NZ,台湾TW 哥斯达黎加CR 秘鲁PE 巴基斯坦PK	0	最不发达35国LDC35	50	--Of a kind used on agricultural or forestry vehicles and machines
	ex40116100	断面宽度24英寸及以上的轮胎	△6						Tyres,having a fracture surface of a width of 24 inches or more
3083	4011.6200	--建筑业或工业搬运车辆及机器用，辋圈尺寸不超过61厘米	17.5	0 1.8 3.5 8.8 14	东盟ASEAN,新加坡SG,新西兰NZ 智利CL 哥斯达黎加CR 秘鲁PE 巴基斯坦PK	0	最不发达35国LDC35	50	--Of a kind used on construction or industrial handling vehicles and machines and having a rim size not exceeding 61cm
3084	4011.6300	--建筑业或工业搬运车辆及机器用，辋圈尺寸超过61厘米	17.5	0 1.8 3.5 8.8 14	东盟ASEAN,新加坡SG,新西兰NZ 智利CL 哥斯达黎加CR 秘鲁PE 巴基斯坦PK	0	最不发达35国LDC35	50	--Of a kind used on construction or industrial handling vehicles and machines and having a rim size exceeding 61cm
	ex40116300	断面宽度24英寸及以上的轮胎	△8						Tyres,having a fracture surface of a width of 24 inches or more
3085	4011.6900	--其他	17.5	0 1.8 3.5 8.8 14	东盟ASEAN,新加坡SG,新西兰NZ,台湾TW 智利CL 哥斯达黎加CR 秘鲁PE 巴基斯坦PK	0	最不发达35国LDC35	50	--Other
	ex40116900	断面宽度30英寸及以上的轮胎	△6						Tyres, having a fracture surface of a width of 30 inches or more
		-其他:							-Other:
3086	4011.9200	--农业或林业车辆及机器用	25	0 5	东盟ASEAN,智利CL,新加坡SG,新西兰NZ,台湾TW 哥斯达黎加CR	0	最不发达35国LDC35,最不发达4国LDC4	50	--Of a kind used on agricultural or forestry vehicles and machines
	ex40119200	断面宽度24英寸及以上的轮胎	△6						Tyres,having a fracture surface of a width of 24 inches or more
3087	4011.9300	--建筑业或工业搬运车辆及机器用，辋圈尺寸不超过61厘米	25	0 5	东盟ASEAN,智利CL,新加坡SG,新西兰NZ 哥斯达黎加CR			50	--Of a kind used on construction or industrial handling vehicles and machines and having a rim size not exceeding 61cm

序号 No.	税则号列 Tariff Line	货品名称	最惠国税率 MFN(%)	协定税率 Agreement(%)	特惠税率 S.P.(%)	普通税率 Gen.(%)	Article Description
3088	4011.9400	--建筑业或工业搬运车辆及机器用，辋圈尺寸超过61厘米	25	0 东盟ASEAN,新加坡SG,新西兰NZ 2.5 智利CL 5 哥斯达黎加CR		50	--Of a kind used on construction or industrial handling vehicles and machines and having a rim size exceeding 61cm
	ex40119400	断面宽度24英寸及以上的轮胎	△8				Tyres,having a fracture surface of a width of 24 inches or more
3089	4011.9900	--其他	25	0 东盟ASEAN,新加坡SG,新西兰NZ 2.5 智利CL 5 哥斯达黎加CR		50	--other
	ex40119900	断面宽度30英寸及以上的轮胎	△5				Tyres, having a fracture surface of a width of 30 inches or more
	40.12	**翻新的或旧的充气橡胶轮胎;实心或半实心橡胶轮胎、橡胶胎面及橡胶轮胎衬带:**					**Retreaded or used pneumatic tyres of rubber; solid or cushion tyres, tyre treads and tyre flaps, of rubber:**
		-翻新轮胎:					-Retreaded tyres:
3090	4012.1100	--机动小客车（包括旅行小客车及赛车）用	20	0 东盟ASEAN,智利CL,新加坡SG,新西兰NZ 4 哥斯达黎加CR 10 秘鲁PE	0 最不发达35国LDC35	50	--Of a kind used on motor cars, (including station wagons and racing cars)
3091	4012.1200	--机动大客车或货运机动车辆用	20	0 东盟ASEAN,智利CL,新加坡SG,新西兰NZ,香港HK 4 哥斯达黎加CR 10 秘鲁PE	0 最不发达35国LDC35	50	--Of a kind used on buses or corries
3092	4012.1300	--航空器用	20 △8	0 东盟ASEAN,智利CL,新加坡SG,新西兰NZ,香港HK 4 哥斯达黎加CR 10 秘鲁PE	0 最不发达35国LDC35	50	--Of a kind used on aircratr
3093	4012.1900	--其他	20	0 东盟ASEAN,智利CL,新加坡SG,新西兰NZ 4 哥斯达黎加CR 10 秘鲁PE	0 最不发达35国LDC35	50	--Other
		-旧的充气轮胎:					-Used pneumatic tyres:
3094	4012.2010	---汽车用	25	0 东盟ASEAN,智利CL,新加坡SG,新西兰NZ,香港HK 5 哥斯达黎加CR		50	---Of a kind used on motor cars, buses or lorries
3095	4012.2090	---其他	25	0 东盟ASEAN,智利CL,新加坡SG,新西兰NZ,香港HK 5 哥斯达黎加CR		80	---Other
		-其他:					-Other:
3096	4012.9010	---航空器用	3 △1	0 东盟ASEAN,智利CL,巴基斯坦PK,新西兰NZ,秘鲁PE,哥斯达黎加CR	0 最不发达35国LDC35	11	---Of a kind used on aircraft

序号 No.	税则号列 Tariff Line	货品名称	最惠国税率 MFN(%)	协定税率 Agreement(%)		特惠税率 S.P.(%)		普通税率 Gen.(%)	Article Description
3097	4012.9020	---汽车用	22	0	东盟ASEAN,智利CL,新加坡SG,新西兰NZ	0	最不发达35国LDC35	50	---Of a kind used on motor cars, buses or lorries
				4.4	哥斯达黎加CR				
				11	秘鲁PE				
3098	4012.9090	---其他	22	0	东盟ASEAN,智利CL,新加坡SG,新西兰NZ	0	最不发达35国LDC35	50	---Other
				4.4	哥斯达黎加CR				
				11	秘鲁PE				
	40.13	**橡胶内胎:**							**Inner tubes, of rubber:**
3099	4013.1000	-机动小客车(包括旅行小客车及赛车)、客运机动车辆或货运机动车辆用	15	0	东盟ASEAN,智利CL,新加坡SG,新西兰NZ	0	最不发达35国LDC35	50	-Of a kind used on motor cars (including station wagons and racing cars), buses or lorries
				3	哥斯达黎加CR				
				7.5	巴基斯坦PK,秘鲁PE				
				13	亚太APTA				
3100	4013.2000	-自行车用	15	0	东盟ASEAN,智利CL,新加坡SG,新西兰NZ	0	最不发达35国LDC35	80	-Of a kind used on bicycles
				3	哥斯达黎加CR				
				7.5	秘鲁PE				
				12	巴基斯坦PK				
		-其他:							-Other:
3101	4013.9010	---航空器用	3 △1	0	东盟ASEAN,智利CL,巴基斯坦PK,新西兰NZ,秘鲁PE,哥斯达黎加CR	0	最不发达35国LDC35,最不发达4国LDC4	11	---Of a kind used on aircraft
3102	4013.9090	---其他	15	0	东盟ASEAN,智利CL,新加坡SG,新西兰NZ	0	最不发达35国LDC35	50	---Other
				3	哥斯达黎加CR				
				7.5	秘鲁PE				
				12	巴基斯坦PK				
	40.14	**硫化橡胶(硬质橡胶除外)制的卫生及医疗用品(包括奶嘴),不论是否装有硬质橡胶制的附件:**							**Hygienic or pharmaceutical articles (including teats), of vulcanized rubber other than hard rubber, with or without fittings of hard rubber:**
3103	4014.1000	-避孕套	0			0	最不发达35国LDC35,最不发达4国LDC4	0	-Sheath contraceptives
3104	4014.9000	-其他	17.5	0	东盟ASEAN,智利CL,新加坡SG,新西兰NZ,澳门MO	0	最不发达35国LDC35	50	-Other
				3.5	哥斯达黎加CR				
				8.8	秘鲁PE				
				14	巴基斯坦PK				

序号 No.	税则号列 Tariff Line	货品名称	最惠国税率 MFN(%)	协定税率 Agreement(%)		特惠税率 S.P.(%)		普通税率 Gen.(%)	Article Description
	40.15	**硫化橡胶（硬质橡胶除外）制的衣着用品及附件（包括手套）：**							**Articles of apparel and clothing accessories (including gloves), for all purposes, of vulcanized rubber other than hard rubber:**
		-手套:							-Gloves:
3105	4015.1100	--外科用	8	0 5	东盟ASEAN,智利CL,新西兰NZ,秘鲁PE,哥斯达黎加CR 巴基斯坦PK	0	最不发达35国LDC35,最不发达4国LDC4	30	--Surgical
3106	4015.1900	--其他	18	0 3.6 9	东盟ASEAN,智利CL,新加坡SG,新西兰NZ 哥斯达黎加CR 秘鲁PE	0	最不发达35国LDC35,最不发达4国LDC4	80	--Other
		-其他:							-Other:
3107	4015.9010	---医疗用	8	0 5	东盟ASEAN,智利CL,新西兰NZ,秘鲁PE,哥斯达黎加CR 巴基斯坦PK	0	最不发达35国LDC35,最不发达4国LDC4	30	---For medical purpose
3108	4015.9090	---其他	15	0 3 7.5	东盟ASEAN,智利CL,新加坡SG,新西兰NZ 哥斯达黎加CR 秘鲁PE	0	最不发达35国LDC35	90	---Other
	40.16	**硫化橡胶（硬质橡胶除外）的其他制品：**							**Other articles of vulcanized rubber other than hard rubber:**
		-海绵橡胶制:							-Of cellular rubber:
3109	4016.1010	---机器及仪器用零件	8	0 5	东盟ASEAN,智利CL,新西兰NZ,秘鲁PE,哥斯达黎加CR 巴基斯坦PK	0	最不发达35国LDC35,最不发达4国LDC4	30	---Of a kind used in machines or instruments
3110	4016.1090	---其他	15	0 3 7.5 12	东盟ASEAN,智利CL,新加坡SG,新西兰NZ 哥斯达黎加CR 秘鲁PE 巴基斯坦PK	0	最不发达35国LDC35	80	---Other
		-其他:							-Other:
3111	4016.9100	--铺地制品及门垫	18	0 1.8 3.6 9	东盟ASEAN,新加坡SG,新西兰NZ,香港HK 智利CL 哥斯达黎加CR 秘鲁PE	0	最不发达35国LDC35	80	--Floor coverings and mats

序号 No.	税则号列 Tariff Line	货品名称	最惠国税率 MFN(%)	协定税率 Agreement(%)		特惠税率 S.P.(%)		普通税率 Gen.(%)	Article Description
3112	4016.9200	--橡皮擦	18	0 3.6 9	东盟ASEAN,智利CL,新西兰NZ 哥斯达黎加CR 秘鲁PE	0	最不发达35国LDC35	80	--Erasers
		--垫片、垫圈及其他密封垫:							--Gaskets, washers and other seals:
3113	4016.9310	---机器及仪器用	8	0 5	东盟ASEAN,智利CL,新西兰NZ,秘鲁PE,哥斯达黎加CR,香港HK 巴基斯坦PK	0	最不发达35国LDC35,最不发达4国LDC4	30	---Of a kind used in machines or instruments
3114	4016.9390	---其他	15	0 3 7.5	东盟ASEAN,智利CL,新加坡SG,新西兰NZ,香港HK 哥斯达黎加CR 秘鲁PE	0	最不发达35国LDC35,最不发达4国LDC4	80	---Other
3115	4016.9400	--船舶或码头的碰垫，不论是否可充气	18	0 3.6 9	东盟ASEAN,智利CL,新加坡SG,新西兰NZ 哥斯达黎加CR 秘鲁PE	0	最不发达35国LDC35	80	--Boat or dock fenders, whether or not inflatable
3116	4016.9500	--其他可充气制品	18	0 3.6 9	东盟ASEAN,智利CL,新加坡SG,新西兰NZ,澳门MO 哥斯达黎加CR 秘鲁PE	0	最不发达35国LDC35	80	--Other inflatable articles
	ex40169500	液压隔离式蓄能器用胶囊	△9						Hydraulic pressure-insulation type accumulator bladder
		--其他:							--Other:
3117	4016.9910	---机器及仪器用零件	8	0 5 7.6	东盟ASEAN,智利CL,新西兰NZ,秘鲁PE,哥斯达黎加CR,澳门MO 巴基斯坦PK 亚太APTA	0	最不发达35国LDC35,最不发达4国LDC4	30	---Of a kind used in machines or instruments
	ex40169910	奶衬	△4						Liner
3118	4016.9990	---其他	10	0 1 5 9.5	东盟ASEAN,新加坡SG,新西兰NZ,哥斯达黎加CR,澳门MO 智利CL 巴基斯坦PK,秘鲁PE 亚太APTA	0	最不发达35国LDC35,最不发达4国LDC4	80	---Other
	ex40169990	动车组用胶囊、外风挡板	△5						Locomotive fording intercar barrier ,gangway bellows
	40.17	**各种形状的硬质橡胶（例如纯硬质胶），包括废碎料;硬质橡胶制品:**							**Hard rubber (for example, ebonite) in all forms, including waste and scrap; articles of hard rubber:**

序号 No.	税则号列 Tariff Line	货品名称	最惠国税率 MFN(%)	协定税率 Agreement(%)		特惠税率 S.P.(%)		普通税率 Gen.(%)	Article Description
3119	4017.0010	---各种形状的硬质橡胶，包括废碎料	8	0	东盟ASEAN,智利CL,新西兰NZ,秘鲁PE,哥斯达黎加CR,澳门MO	0	最不发达35国LDC35	35	---Hard rubber in all forms, including waste and scrap
				5	巴基斯坦PK				
3120	4017.0020	---硬质橡胶制品	15	0	东盟ASEAN,智利CL,新加坡SG,新西兰NZ,澳门MO	0	最不发达35国LDC35	90	---Articles of hard rubber
				3	哥斯达黎加CR				
				7.5	秘鲁PE				
				12	巴基斯坦PK				

第八类
生皮、皮革、毛皮及其制品；鞍具及挽具；旅行用品、手提包及类似容器；动物肠线（蚕胶丝除外）制品

第四十一章
生皮（毛皮除外）及皮革

注释：

一、本章不包括：

（一）生皮的边角废料（税号 05.11）；

（二）税号 05.05 或 67.01 的带羽毛或羽绒的整张或部分鸟皮；

（三）带毛生皮或已鞣的带毛皮张（第四十三章）：但下列动物的带毛生皮应归入第四十一章、牛（包括水牛）、马、绵羊及羔羊（不包括阿斯特拉罕、喀拉科尔、波斯羔羊或类似羔羊、印度、中国或蒙古羔羊）、山羊或小山羊（不包括也门或蒙古山羊及小山羊）、猪（包括西貒）、小羚羊、瞪羚、骆驼（包括单峰骆驼）、驯鹿、麋、鹿、狍或狗。

二、

（一）税目 41.04 至 41.06 不包括经退鞣（包括预鞣）加工的皮（酌情归入税目 41.01 至 41.03）；

（二）税目 41.04 至 41.06 所称“坯革”包括在干燥前经复鞣、染色或加油（加脂）的皮。

三、本目录所称“再生皮革”，仅指税号 41.15 的皮革。

SECTION Ⅷ
RAW HIDES AND SKINS，LEATHER，FURSKINS AND ARTICLES THEREOF; SADDLERY AND HARNESS; TRAVEL GOODS，HANDBAGS AND SIMILAR CONTAINERS; ARTICLES OF ANIMAL GUT（OTHER THAN SILK-WORM GUT）

Chapter 41
Raw hides and skins（other than furskins）and leather

Notes:

1. This Chapter does not cover:

(a) Parings or similar waste，of raw hides or skins (heading No.05.11);

(b) Birdskins or parts of birdskins，with their feathers or down，of heading No.05.05 or 67.01; or

(c) Hides or skins，with the hair or wool on，raw，tanned or dressed (Chapter43); the following are，however，to be classified in Chapter41，namely，raw hides and skins with the hair or wool on，of bovine animals (including buffalo)，of equine animals，of sheep or lambs (except Astrakhan，Broadtail，Caracul，Persian or similar lambs，Indian，Chinese，Mongolian or Tibetan lambs)，of goats or kids (except Yemen，Mongolian or Tibetan goats and kids)，of swine (including peccary)，of chamois，of gazelle，of camels (including dromedaries), of reindeer，of elk，of deer，of roebucks or of dogs.

2.

(a) Headings 41.04 to 41.06 do not cover hides and skins which have undergone a tanning (including pre-tanning) process which is reversible (headings 41.01 to 41.03，as the case may be);

(b) For the purposes of headings 41.04 to 41.06，the term “crust” includes hides and skins that have been retanned，coloured or fat-liquored (stuffed) prior to drying.

3. Throughout the Nomenclature the expression “composition leather” means only substances of the kind referred to in heading No.41.15.

序号 No.	税则号列 Tariff Line	货品名称	最惠国税率 MFN(%)	协定税率 Agreement(%)	特惠税率 S.P.(%)	普通税率 Gen.(%)	Article Description
	41.01	**生牛皮（包括水牛皮）、生马皮（鲜的、盐腌的、干的、石灰浸渍的、浸酸的或以其他方法保藏，但未鞣制、未经羊皮纸化处理或进一步加工的），不论是否去毛或剖层：**					**Raw hides and skins of bovine(including buffalo)or equine animals (fresh, or salted, dried, limed, pickled or otherwise preserved, but not tanned, parchment dressed or further prepared), whether or not dehaired or split:**
		-未剖层的整张皮，完全干燥的每张重量不超过 8 千克，干盐腌的不超过 10 千克，鲜的、湿盐腌的或以其他方法保藏的不超过 16 千克:					-Whole hides and skins, unsplit, of a weight per skin not exceeding 8kg when simply dried, 10kg when dry-salted, or 16kg when fresh, wet-salted or other wise preserved:
		---牛皮:					---Of bovine animals:
3121	4101.2011	----经退鞣处理的	8	0 东盟ASEAN,智利CL,新西兰NZ,秘鲁PE,哥斯达黎加CR,香港HK 5 巴基斯坦PK 6 亚太APTA	0 最不发达 35 国 LDC35,最不发达 4 国 LDC4	17	----Have undergone a reversible tanning process
3122	4101.2019	----其他	5	0 东盟ASEAN,智利CL,巴基斯坦PK,新西兰NZ,秘鲁PE,哥斯达黎加CR,香港HK	0 最不发达 35 国 LDC35,最不发达 4 国 LDC4,老挝LA,柬埔寨KH	17	----Other
3123	4101.2020	---马皮	5	0 东盟ASEAN,智利CL,巴基斯坦PK,新西兰NZ,秘鲁PE,香港HK 3 哥斯达黎加CR	0 最不发达 35 国 LDC35,最不发达 4 国 LDC4,老挝LA,柬埔寨KH	30	---Of equine animals
		-整张皮，重量超过 16 千克:					-Whole hides and skins, of a weight exceeding 16kg:
		---牛皮:					---Of bovine animals:
3124	4101.5011	----经退鞣处理的	8.4	0 东盟ASEAN,智利CL,新西兰NZ,秘鲁PE,哥斯达黎加CR 5 巴基斯坦PK 7 亚太APTA	0 最不发达 35 国 LDC35,最不发达 4 国 LDC4	17	----Have undergone a reversible tanning process

序号 No.	税则号列 Tariff Line	货品名称	最惠国税率 MFN(%)	协定税率 Agreement(%)		特惠税率 S.P.(%)		普通税率 Gen.(%)	Article Description
3125	4101.5019	----其他	5	0	东盟ASEAN,智利CL,巴基斯坦PK,新西兰NZ,秘鲁PE,哥斯达黎加CR	0	最不发达35国LDC35,最不发达4国LDC4,老挝LA,柬埔寨KH	17	----Other
3126	4101.5020	---马皮	5	0 3	东盟ASEAN,智利CL,巴基斯坦PK,新西兰NZ,秘鲁PE 哥斯达黎加CR	0	最不发达35国LDC35,最不发达4国LDC4,老挝LA,柬埔寨KH	30	---Of equine animals
		-其他,包括整张或半张的背皮及腹皮: ---牛皮:							-Other, including butts, bends and bellies: ---Of bovine animals:
3127	4101.9011	----经退鞣处理的	8.4	0 5 7	东盟ASEAN,智利CL,新西兰NZ,秘鲁PE,哥斯达黎加CR 巴基斯坦PK 亚太APTA	0	最不发达35国LDC35,最不发达4国LDC4	17	----Have undergone a reversible tanning process
3128	4101.9019	----其他	5	0	东盟ASEAN,智利CL,巴基斯坦PK,新西兰NZ,秘鲁PE,哥斯达黎加CR	0	最不发达35国LDC35,最不发达4国LDC4,老挝LA,柬埔寨KH	17	----Other
3129	4101.9020	---马皮	5	0 3	东盟ASEAN,智利CL,巴基斯坦PK,新西兰NZ,秘鲁PE 哥斯达黎加CR	0	最不发达35国LDC35,最不发达4国LDC4,老挝LA,柬埔寨KH	30	---Of equine animals
	41.02	**绵羊或羔羊生皮(鲜的、盐腌的、干的、石灰浸渍的、浸酸的或经其他方法保藏,但未鞣制、未经羊皮纸化处理或进一步加工的),不论是否带毛或剖层,但本章注释一(三)所述不包括的生皮除外:**							**Raw skins of sheep or lambs (fresh, or salted, dried, limed, pickled or otherwise preseved, but not tanned, parch-ment-dressed or further prepared), whether or not with wool on or split, other than those excluded by Note 1© to this chapter:**

序号 No.	税则号列 Tariff Line	货品名称	最惠国税率 MFN(%)	协定税率 Agreement(%)	特惠税率 S.P.(%)	普通税率 Gen.(%)	Article Description
3130	4102.1000	-带毛	7	0 东盟ASEAN,新西兰NZ 0.7 智利CL 4.2 哥斯达黎加CR 5 巴基斯坦PK	0 最不发达35国LDC35,最不发达4国LDC4	30	-With wool on
		-不带毛:					-Without wool on:
		--浸酸的:					--Pickled:
3131	4102.2110	---经退鞣处理的	14	0 东盟ASEAN,智利CL,新加坡SG 3.1 新西兰NZ 8.4 哥斯达黎加CR 11.2 巴基斯坦PK	0 最不发达35国LDC35	30	---Have undergone a reversible tanning process
3132	4102.2190	---其他	9	0 东盟ASEAN,智利CL,新西兰NZ,秘鲁PE 5 巴基斯坦PK 5.4 哥斯达黎加CR 8 亚太APTA	0 最不发达35国LDC35,最不发达4国LDC4	30	---Other
		--其他:					--Other:
3133	4102.2910	---经退鞣处理的	14	0 东盟ASEAN,智利CL,新加坡SG,新西兰NZ,秘鲁PE 7 巴基斯坦PK 8.4 哥斯达黎加CR	0 最不发达35国LDC35	30	---Have undergone a reversible tanning process
3134	4102.2990	---其他	7	0 东盟ASEAN,智利CL,新西兰NZ,秘鲁PE 4.2 哥斯达黎加CR 5 巴基斯坦PK 6 亚太APTA	0 最不发达35国LDC35,最不发达4国LDC4	30	---Other
	41.03	**其他生皮(鲜的、盐腌的、干的、石灰浸渍的、浸酸的或以其他方法保藏,但未鞣制、未经羊皮纸化处理或进一步加工的),不论是否去毛或剖层,但本章注释一(二)或(三)所述不包括的生皮除外:**					**Other raw hides and skins (fresh, or salted, dried, limed, pickled or otherwise preserved, but not tanned, parchment dressed or further prepared), whether or not dehaired or split, other than those excluded by Note1(b) or 1(c)to this Chapter:**
3135	4103.2000	-爬行动物皮	9	0 东盟ASEAN,智利CL,新西兰NZ,秘鲁PE 5 巴基斯坦PK 5.4 哥斯达黎加CR	0 最不发达35国LDC35,最不发达4国LDC4	30	-Of reptiles
3136	4103.3000	-猪皮	9	0 东盟ASEAN,智利CL,新西兰NZ,秘鲁PE 5 巴基斯坦PK 5.4 哥斯达黎加CR	0 最不发达35国LDC35,最不发达4国LDC4,缅甸MM	30	-Of swine

序号 No.	税则号列 Tariff Line	货品名称	最惠国税率 MFN(%)	协定税率 Agreement(%)		特惠税率 S.P.(%)		普通税率 Gen.(%)	Article Description
		-其他: ---山羊板皮:							-Other: ---Dried hides and skins of goats:
3137	4103.9011	----经退鞣处理的	14	0 7 8.4	东盟ASEAN,智利CL,新加坡SG,新西兰NZ,秘鲁PE 巴基斯坦PK 哥斯达黎加CR	0	最不发达35国LDC35	35	----Have undergone a reversible tanning process
3138	4103.9019	----其他	9	0 5 5.4	东盟ASEAN,智利CL,新西兰NZ,秘鲁PE 巴基斯坦PK 哥斯达黎加CR	0	最不发达35国LDC35,最不发达4国LDC4	35	----Other
		---其他山羊或小山羊皮:							---Other hides and skins of goats or of kids:
3139	4103.9021	----经退鞣处理的	14	0 7 8.4	东盟ASEAN,智利CL,新加坡SG,新西兰NZ,秘鲁PE 巴基斯坦PK 哥斯达黎加CR	0	最不发达35国LDC35	30	----Have undergone a reversible tanning process
3140	4103.9029	----其他	9	0 5 5.4	东盟ASEAN,智利CL,新西兰NZ,秘鲁PE 巴基斯坦PK 哥斯达黎加CR	0	最不发达35国LDC35,最不发达4国LDC4	30	----Other
3141	4103.9090	---其他	9	0 5 5.4	东盟ASEAN,智利CL,新西兰NZ,秘鲁PE,香港HK 巴基斯坦PK 哥斯达黎加CR	0	最不发达35国LDC35,最不发达4国LDC4,缅甸MM	30	---Other
	41.04	**经鞣制的不带毛牛皮（包括水牛皮）、马皮及其坯革，不论是否剖层，但未经进一步加工:**							**Tanned or crust hides and skins of bovine (including buffalo) or equine animals, without hair on, whether or not split, but not further prepared:**
		-湿革（包括蓝湿皮）:							-In the wet state (including wet-blue):
		--全粒面未剖层革;粒面剖层革:							--Full grains, unsplit; grain splits:
		---牛皮:							---Of bovine animals:
3142	4104.1111	----蓝湿的	7 △3	0 3.5 4.2	东盟ASEAN,智利CL,巴基斯坦PK,新西兰NZ,秘鲁PE 亚太APTA 哥斯达黎加CR	0 1.4	最不发达35国LDC35,最不发达4国LDC4 亚太2国APTA2	17	----Wet-blue

序号 No.	税则号列 Tariff Line	货品名称	最惠国税率 MFN(%)	协定税率 Agreement(%)		特惠税率 S.P.(%)		普通税率 Gen.(%)	Article Description
3143	4104.1119	----其他	8	0 4 4.8	东盟ASEAN,智利CL,巴基斯坦PK,新西兰NZ,秘鲁PE,香港HK 亚太APTA 哥斯达黎加CR	0 2	最不发达35国LDC35,最不发达4国LDC4 亚太2国APTA2	35	----Other
3144	4104.1120	---马皮	5	0 2.5 3	东盟ASEAN,智利CL,巴基斯坦PK,新西兰NZ,秘鲁PE,香港HK 亚太APTA 哥斯达黎加CR	0 2	最不发达35国LDC35,最不发达4国LDC4 亚太2国APTA2	35	---Of equine animals
		--其他:							--Other:
		---牛皮:							---Of bovine animals:
3145	4104.1911	----蓝湿的	6 △3	0 3 4.2	东盟ASEAN,智利CL,新西兰NZ,秘鲁PE 亚太APTA,巴基斯坦PK 哥斯达黎加CR	0 1.4	最不发达35国LDC35,最不发达4国LDC4 亚太2国APTA2	17	----Wet-blue
3146	4104.1919	----其他	7	0 3.5 4.2	东盟ASEAN,智利CL,巴基斯坦PK,新西兰NZ,秘鲁PE,香港HK 亚太APTA 哥斯达黎加CR	0 1.8	最不发达35国LDC35,最不发达4国LDC4 亚太2国APTA2	35	----Other
3147	4104.1920	---马皮	7 △5	0 3.5 4.2	东盟ASEAN,智利CL,巴基斯坦PK,新西兰NZ,秘鲁PE,香港HK 亚太APTA 哥斯达黎加CR	0 2.1	最不发达35国LDC35,最不发达4国LDC4 亚太2国APTA2	35	---Of equine animals
		-干革（坯革）:							-In the dry state (crust):
3148	4104.4100	--全粒面未剖层革粒面剖层革的	5 △3	0 3 3.5	东盟ASEAN,智利CL,巴基斯坦PK,新西兰NZ,秘鲁PE,香港HK 哥斯达黎加CR 亚太APTA	0 2	最不发达35国LDC35,最不发达4国LDC4 亚太2国APTA2	35	--Full grain, unsplit; grain splits
		--其他:							--Other:

序号 No.	税则号列 Tariff Line	货品名称	最惠国税率 MFN(%)	协定税率 Agreement(%)		特惠税率 S.P.(%)		普通税率 Gen.(%)	Article Description
3149	4104.4910	---机器带用牛、马皮革	5	0	东盟ASEAN,智利CL,巴基斯坦PK,新西兰NZ,秘鲁PE	0	最不发达35国LDC35,最不发达4国LDC4,亚太2国APTA2	20	---For machinery belting
				3	哥斯达黎加CR				
				3.5	亚太APTA				
3150	4104.4990	---其他	7	0	东盟ASEAN,智利CL,新西兰NZ,秘鲁PE,香港HK	0	最不发达35国LDC35,最不发达4国LDC4	35	---Other
				4.2	哥斯达黎加CR	2.1	亚太2国APTA2		
				4.9	亚太APTA,巴基斯坦PK				
	41.05	**经鞣制的不带毛绵羊或者羔羊皮及其坯革，不论是否剖层，但未经进一步加工:**							**Tanned or crust skins of sheep or lambs, without wool on, whether or not split, but not further prepared:**
		-湿革(包括蓝湿皮):							-In the wet state (including wet-blue):
3151	4105.1010	---蓝湿的	14 △10	0	东盟ASEAN,智利CL,新加坡SG	0	最不发达35国LDC35,最不发达4国LDC4	50	---Wet-blue
				3.1	新西兰NZ	2.1	亚太2国APTA2		
				5	巴基斯坦PK				
				7	亚太APTA				
				8.4	哥斯达黎加CR				
3152	4105.1090	---其他	10	0	东盟ASEAN,智利CL,新西兰NZ,秘鲁PE	0	最不发达35国LDC35,最不发达4国LDC4	50	---Other
				5	亚太APTA,巴基斯坦PK	2	亚太2国APTA2		
				6	哥斯达黎加CR				
3153	4105.3000	-干革（坯革）	8	0	东盟ASEAN,智利CL,新西兰NZ,秘鲁PE	0	最不发达35国LDC35,最不发达4国LDC4	50	-In the dry state (crust)
				4.8	哥斯达黎加CR	4.8	亚太2国APTA2		
				5.6	亚太APTA,巴基斯坦PK				

序号 No.	税则号列 Tariff Line	货品名称	最惠国税率 MFN(%)	协定税率 Agreement(%)		特惠税率 S.P.(%)		普通税率 Gen.(%)	Article Description
	41.06	**经鞣制的其他不带毛动物皮及其坯革，不论是否剖层，但未经进一步加工：**							**Tanned or crust hides and skins of other animals, without wool or hair on, whether or not split, but not further prepared:**
		-山羊或小山羊的:							-Of goats or kids:
3154	4106.2100	--湿革（包括蓝湿皮）	14	0	东盟ASEAN,智利CL,新加坡SG,新西兰NZ,秘鲁PE	0	最不发达35国LDC35,最不发达4国LDC4	50	--In the wet state (including wet-blue)
				8.4	哥斯达黎加CR	2.1	亚太2国APTA2		
				12	亚太APTA,巴基斯坦PK				
	ex41062100	蓝湿山羊皮	△10						Goat skin leather, in the wet-blue state, without hair on, but not further prepared, whether or not split
3155	4106.2200	--干革（坯革）	14	0	东盟ASEAN,智利CL,新加坡SG	0	最不发达35国LDC35,最不发达4国LDC4	50	--In the dry state (crust)
				3.1	新西兰NZ	8.4	亚太2国APTA2		
				8.4	哥斯达黎加CR				
				9.8	亚太APTA,巴基斯坦PK				
		-猪的:							-Of swine:
		--湿革（包括蓝湿皮）:							--In the wet state (including wet-blue):
3156	4106.3110	---蓝湿的	14 △10	0	东盟ASEAN,智利CL,新加坡SG,新西兰NZ,秘鲁PE	0	最不发达35国LDC35	50	---Wet-blue
				8.4	哥斯达黎加CR	4.2	亚太2国APTA2		
				11.2	巴基斯坦PK				
3157	4106.3190	---其他	14	0	东盟ASEAN,智利CL,新加坡SG,新西兰NZ,秘鲁PE	0	最不发达35国LDC35	50	---Other
				7	巴基斯坦PK	4.2	亚太2国APTA2		
				8.4	哥斯达黎加CR				
3158	4106.3200	--干革（坯革）	14	0	东盟ASEAN,智利CL,新加坡SG,新西兰NZ,秘鲁PE	0	最不发达35国LDC35	50	--In the dry state (crust)
				8.4	哥斯达黎加CR	4.2	亚太2国APTA2		
				11.2	巴基斯坦PK				
3159	4106.4000	-爬行动物的	14	0	东盟ASEAN,智利CL,新加坡SG,新西兰NZ,秘鲁PE	0	最不发达35国LDC35,最不发达4国LDC4,亚太2国APTA2	50	-Of reptiles
				7	巴基斯坦PK				
				8.4	哥斯达黎加CR				

序号 No.	税则号列 Tariff Line	货品名称	最惠国 税率 MFN(%)		协定税率 Agreement(%)		特惠税率 S.P.(%)	普通 税率 Gen.(%)	Article Description
		-其他:							-Other:
3160	4106.9100	--湿革（包括蓝湿皮）	14	0 8.4 11.2	东盟ASEAN,智利CL,新加坡SG,新西兰NZ,秘鲁PE 哥斯达黎加CR 巴基斯坦PK	0	最不发达35国LDC35,最不发达4国LDC4,亚太2国APTA2	50	--In the wet state (including wet-blue)
3161	4106.9200	--干革（坯革）	14	0 8.4 11.2	东盟ASEAN,智利CL,新加坡SG,新西兰NZ,秘鲁PE 哥斯达黎加CR 巴基斯坦PK	0	最不发达35国LDC35,最不发达4国LDC4,亚太2国APTA2	50	--In the dry state (crust)
	41.07	**经鞣制或半硝处理后进一步加工的不带毛的牛皮革（包括水牛皮革）及马皮革，包括羊皮纸化处理的皮革，不论是否剖层，但税目41.14皮革除外:**							**Leather further prepared after tanning or crusting, including parchment-dressed leather, of bovine (including buffalo) or equine animals, without hair on, whether or not split, other than leather of heading 41.14**
		-整张的:							-Whole hides and skins:
		--全粒面未剖层革:							--Full grains, unsplit:
3162	4107.1110	---牛皮	8	0 4.8	东盟ASEAN,智利CL,新西兰NZ,香港HK 哥斯达黎加CR			50	---Of bovine animals
3163	4107.1120	---马皮	5	0 3	东盟ASEAN,智利CL,巴基斯坦PK,新西兰NZ,秘鲁PE,香港HK 哥斯达黎加CR	0	最不发达35国LDC35,最不发达4国LDC4	50	---Of equine animals
		--粒面剖层革:							--Grain splits:
3164	4107.1210	---牛皮	8 △6	0 4.8	东盟ASEAN,智利CL,新西兰NZ,香港HK 哥斯达黎加CR			50	---Of bovine animals
3165	4107.1220	---马皮	5	0 3	东盟ASEAN,智利CL,巴基斯坦PK,新西兰NZ,秘鲁PE,香港HK 哥斯达黎加CR	0	最不发达35国LDC35,最不发达4国LDC4	50	---Of equine animals
		--其他:							--Other:
3166	4107.1910	---机器带用	5	0 3	东盟ASEAN,智利CL,巴基斯坦PK,新西兰NZ,秘鲁PE 哥斯达黎加CR	0	最不发达35国LDC35,最不发达4国LDC4	50	---For machinery belting

序号 No.	税则号列 Tariff Line	货品名称	最惠国税率 MFN(%)	协定税率 Agreement(%)		特惠税率 S.P.(%)		普通税率 Gen.(%)	Article Description
3167	4107.1990	---其他	7	0 4.2	东盟ASEAN,智利CL,新西兰NZ,香港HK 哥斯达黎加CR			50	---Other
		-其他，包括半张的:							-Other, including sides:
3168	4107.9100	--全粒面未剖层革	5	0 3	东盟ASEAN,智利CL,巴基斯坦PK,新西兰NZ,秘鲁PE 哥斯达黎加CR	0	最不发达35国LDC35,最不发达4国LDC4	50	--Full grains, un split
3169	4107.9200	--粒面剖层革	5	0 3	东盟ASEAN,智利CL,新西兰NZ,秘鲁PE 哥斯达黎加CR	0	最不发达35国LDC35,最不发达4国LDC4	50	--Grain splits
		--其他:							--Other:
3170	4107.9910	---机器带用	5	0 3	东盟ASEAN,智利CL,巴基斯坦PK,新西兰NZ,秘鲁PE 哥斯达黎加CR	0	最不发达35国LDC35,最不发达4国LDC4	50	---For machinery belting
3171	4107.9990	---其他	7	0 4.2	东盟ASEAN,智利CL,新西兰NZ,秘鲁PE,香港HK 哥斯达黎加CR	0	最不发达35国LDC35,最不发达4国LDC4	50	---Other
	41.12	**经鞣制或半硝处理后进一步加工的不带毛的绵羊或羔羊皮革，包括羊皮纸化处理的，不论是否剖层，但税目41.14的皮革除外:**							**Leather further prepared after tanning or crusting, including parchment dressed leather, of sheep or lamb, without wool on, whether or not split, other than leather of heading 41.14:**
3172	4112.0000	经鞣制或半硝处理后进一步加工的不带毛的绵羊或羔羊皮革，包括羊皮纸化处理的，不论是否剖层，但税目41.14的皮革除外	8	0 4.8 5.6	东盟ASEAN,智利CL,新西兰NZ,秘鲁PE,香港HK 哥斯达黎加CR 亚太APTA,巴基斯坦PK	0	最不发达35国LDC35,最不发达4国LDC4	50	Leather further prepared after tanning or crusting, including parchment dressed leather, of sheep or lamb, without wool on, whether or not split, other than leather of heading 41.14
	41.13	**经鞣制或半硝处理后进一步加工的不带毛的其他动物皮革，包括羊皮纸化处理的，不论是否剖层，但税目的41.14的皮革除外:**							**Leather further prepared after tanning or crusting, including parchment dressed leather, of other animals, without wool or hair on, whether or not split, other than leather of heading 41.14:**

序号 No.	税则号列 Tariff Line	货品名称	最惠国税率 MFN(%)	协定税率 Agreement(%)		特惠税率 S.P.(%)		普通税率 Gen.(%)	Article Description
3173	4113.1000	-山羊或小山羊皮的	14	0 3.1 8.4 9.8	东盟ASEAN,智利CL,新加坡SG,香港HK 新西兰NZ 哥斯达黎加CR 亚太APTA,巴基斯坦PK	0	最不发达35国LDC35,最不发达4国LDC4	50	-Of goats or kids
3174	4113.2000	-猪皮的	14	0 8.4	东盟ASEAN,智利CL,新加坡SG,新西兰NZ,秘鲁PE,香港HK 哥斯达黎加CR	0	最不发达35国LDC35	50	-Of swine
3175	4113.3000	-爬行动物皮的	14	0 8.4 11.2	东盟ASEAN,智利CL,新加坡SG,新西兰NZ,秘鲁PE 哥斯达黎加CR 巴基斯坦PK	0	最不发达35国LDC35,最不发达4国LDC4	50	-Of reptiles
3176	4113.9000	-其他	14	0 8.4	东盟ASEAN,智利CL,新加坡SG,新西兰NZ,秘鲁PE 哥斯达黎加CR	0	最不发达35国LDC35,最不发达4国LDC4	50	-Other
	41.14	**油鞣皮革（包括结合鞣制的油鞣皮革）;漆皮及层压漆皮;镀金属皮革:**							**Chamois (including combination chamois) leather; patent leather and patent laminated leather; metallised leather:**
3177	4114.1000	-油鞣皮革（包括结合鞣制的油鞣皮革）	14	0 1.4 7 8.4	东盟ASEAN,新加坡SG,新西兰NZ 智利CL 秘鲁PE 哥斯达黎加CR	0	最不发达35国LDC35	50	-Chamois (including combination chamois) leather
3178	4114.2000	-漆皮及层压漆皮;镀金属皮革	10	0 1 6 9	东盟ASEAN,新加坡SG,新西兰NZ 智利CL 哥斯达黎加CR 亚太APTA,巴基斯坦PK			50	-Patent leather and patent laminated leather; metallised leather
	41.15	**以皮革或皮革纤维为基本成分的再生皮革，成块、成张或成条的，不论是否成卷;皮革或再生皮革的边角废料;不适宜作皮革制品用;皮革粉末:**							**Composition leather with a basis of leather or leather fibre, in slabs, sheets or strip, whether or not in rolls; parings and other waste of leather or of composition leather, not suitable for the manufacture of leather articles; leather dust, powder and flour:**

序号 No.	税则号列 Tariff Line	货品名称	最惠国税率 MFN(%)	协定税率 Agreement(%)		特惠税率 S.P.(%)		普通税率 Gen.(%)	Article Description
3179	4115.1000	-以皮革或皮革纤维为基本成分的再生皮革，成块、成张或成条，不论是否成卷	14	0 8.4	东盟ASEAN,智利CL,新加坡SG,新西兰NZ 哥斯达黎加CR			50	-Composition leather with a basis of leather or leather fibre, in slabs, sheets or strip, whether or not in rolls
3180	4115.2000	-皮革或再生皮革的边角废料，不适宜作皮革制品用;皮革粉末	14	0 8.4	东盟ASEAN,智利CL,新加坡SG,新西兰NZ,秘鲁PE 哥斯达黎加CR	0 4.2	最不发达35国LDC35 亚太2国APTA2	50	-Parings and other waste of leather or of composition leather, not suitable for the manufacture of leather articles;leather dust, powder and flour

第四十二章
皮革制品；鞍具及挽具；旅行用品、手提包及类似容器；动物肠线（蚕胶丝除外）制品

注释：

一、本章所称的“皮革”包括油鞣皮革（包括结合鞣制的油鞣皮革）、漆皮、层压漆皮和镀金属皮革。

二、本章不包括：

（一）外科用无菌肠线或类似的无菌缝合材料（税号30.06）；

（二）以毛皮或人造毛皮衬里或作面（仅饰边的除外）的衣服及衣着附件（分指手套、连指手套及露指手套除外）（税目43.03或43.04）；

（三）网线袋及类似品（税号56.08）；

（四）第六十四章的物品；

（五）第六十五章的帽类及其零件；

（六）税号66.02的鞭子、马鞭或其他物品；

（七）袖扣、手镯或其他仿首饰（税号71.17）；

（八）单独进口或出口的挽具附件或装饰物，例如，马镫、马嚼子、马铃铛及类似品、带扣（一般归入第十五类）；

（九）弦线、鼓面皮或类似品及其他乐器零件（税号92.09）；

（十）第九十四章的物品（例如，家具、灯具及照明装置）；

（十一）第九十五章的物品（例如，玩具、游戏品及运动用品）；

（十二）税号96.06的钮扣、揿扣、钮扣芯或这些物品的其他零件、钮扣坯。

三、（一）除上述注释一所规定的以外，税号42.02也不包括：

1.非供长期使用的带把手塑料薄膜袋，不论是否印制（税号39.23）；

2.编结材料制品（税号46.02）。

（二）税号42.02及42.03的制品，如果装有用贵金属、包贵金属、天然或养殖珍珠、宝石或半宝石（天然、合成或再造）制的零件，即使这些零件不是仅作为小配件或小饰物的，只要其未构成物品的基本特征，仍应归入上

Chapter 42
Articles of leather; saddlery and harness; travel goods, handbags and similar containers; articles of animal gut (other than silk-worm gut)

Notes:

1. For the purposes of this Chapter, the term “leather” includes chamois (including combination chamois) leather, patent leather, patent laminated leather and metallised leather.

2. This Chapter does not cover:

(a) Sterile surgical catgut or similar sterile suture materials (heading No. 30.06);

(b) Articles of apparel or clothing accessories (except gloves, mittens and mitts), lined with furskin or artificial fur or to which furskin or artificial fur is attached on the outside except as mere trimming (heading No. 43.03 or 43.04);

(c) Made up articles of netting (heading No.56.08);

(d) Articles of Chapter 64;

(e) Headgear or parts thereof of Chapter 65;

(f) Whips, riding-crops or other articles of heading No.66.02;

(g) Cuff-links, bracelets or other imitation jewellery (heading No.71.17);

(h) Fittings or trimmings for harness, such as stirrups, bits, horse brasses and buckles, separately presented (generally Section XV);

(i) Strings, skins for drums or the like, or other parts of musical instruments (heading No.92.09);

(j) Articles of Chapter 94 (for example, furniture, lamps and lighting fittings);

(k) Articles of Chapter 95 (for example, toys, games, sports requisites); or

(l) Buttons, press-fasteners, snap-fasteners, press-studs, button moulds or other parts of these articles, button blanks, of heading No. 96.06.

3. (a) In addition to the provisions of Note 1 above, heading No.42.02 does not cover:

(1) Bags made of sheeting of plastics, whether or not printed, with handles, not designed for prolonged use (heading No.39.23);

(2) Articles of plaiting materials (heading No.46.02).

(b) Articles of headings Nos. 42.02 and 42.03 which have parts of precious metal or metal clad with precious metal, of natural or cultured pearls, of precious or semi-precious stones (natural, synthetic or reconstructed) remain classified in those headings even if

述税号。但如果这些零件已构成物品的基本特征，则应归入第七十一章。

such parts constitute more than minor fittings or minor ornamentation, provided that these parts do not give the articles their essential character. If, on the other hand, the parts give the articles their essential character, the articles are to be classified in Chapter 71.

四、税号 42.03 所称“衣服及衣着附件”，主要包括分指手套、连指手套及露指手套（包括运动及防护手套）、围裙及其他防护用衣着、裤吊带、腰带、子弹带及腕带，但不包括表带（税目 91.13）。

4. For the purpose of heading No. 42.03, the expression “articles of apparel and clothing accessories” applies, *inter alia*, to gloves, mittens and mitts (including those for sport or for protection) , aprons and other protective clothing, braces, belts, bandoliers and wrist straps, but excluding watch straps (heading No. 91.13) .

序号 No.	税则号列 Tariff Line	货品名称	最惠国税率 MFN(%)	协定税率 Agreement(%)		特惠税率 S.P.(%)		普通税率 Gen.(%)	Article Description
	42.01	**各种材料制成的鞍具及挽具（包括缰绳、挽绳、护膝垫、口套、鞍褥、马褡裢、狗外套及类似品），适合各种动物用：**							**Saddlery and harness for any animal (including traces, leads, knee pads, muzzles, saddle cloths, saddle bags, dog coats and the like), of any material:**
3181	4201.0000	各种材料制成的鞍具及挽具（包括缰绳、挽绳、护膝垫、口套、鞍褥、马褡裢、狗外套及类似品），适合各种动物用	20	0 4 10 12	东盟ASEAN,智利CL,新加坡SG,新西兰NZ,澳门MO 哥斯达黎加CR 巴基斯坦PK,秘鲁PE 亚太APTA	0 8	最不发达 35 国 LDC35,最不发达 4 国 LDC4 亚太 2 国 APTA2	100	Saddlery and harness for any animal (including traces, leads, knee pads, muzzles, saddle cloths, saddle bags, dog coats and the like), of any material
	42.02	**衣箱、提箱、小手袋、公文箱、公文包、书包、眼镜盒、望远镜盒、照相机套、乐器盒、枪套及类似容器;旅行包、食品或饮料保温包、化妆包、帆布包、手提包、购物袋、钱夹、钱包、地图盒、烟盒、烟袋、工具包、运动包、瓶盒、首饰盒、粉盒、刀叉餐具盒及类似容器，用皮革或再生皮革、塑料片、纺织材料、钢纸或纸板制成，或者全部或主要用上述材料或纸包覆制成：**							**Trunks, suit-cases, vanity-cases, executive-cases, brief-cases, school satchels, spectacle cases, binocular cases, camera cases, musical instrument cases, gun cases, holsters and similar containers; travelling-bags, insulated food or beverages bags, toilet bags, rucksacks, handbags, shopping-bags, wallets, purses, map-cases, cigarett-cases, tobacco-pouches, tool bags, sports bags, bottle-cases, jewellery boxes, powder-boxes, cutlery cases and similar containers, of leather or of composition leather, of sheeting of plastics, of textile materials, of vulcanized fibre or of paperboard, or wholly or mainly covered with such materials or with paper:**

序号 No.	税则号列 Tariff Line	货品名称	最惠国税率 MFN(%)	协定税率 Agreement(%)		特惠税率 S.P.(%)		普通税率 Gen.(%)	Article Description
		-衣箱、提箱、小手袋、公文箱、公文包、书包及类似容器:							-Trunks, suit-cases, vanity-cases, executive-cases, brief-cases, school satchels and similar containers:
		--以皮革或再生皮革作面:							--With outer surface of leather or composition leather:
3182	4202.1110	---衣箱	15	0	东盟ASEAN,智利CL,新加坡SG,新西兰NZ	0	最不发达35国LDC35	100	---Trunks and suit-cases
				3	哥斯达黎加CR	8.3	亚太2国APTA2		
				7.5	秘鲁PE				
				12	巴基斯坦PK				
3183	4202.1190	---其他	10	0	东盟ASEAN,智利CL,新西兰NZ,秘鲁PE,哥斯达黎加CR	0	最不发达35国LDC35,最不发达4国LDC4	100	---Other
				5	巴基斯坦PK	8	亚太2国APTA2		
		--以塑料或纺织材料作面:							--With outer surface of plastics or of textile materials:
3184	4202.1210	---衣箱	20	0	东盟ASEAN,智利CL,新加坡SG,新西兰NZ,台湾TW	0	最不发达35国LDC35	100	---Trunks and suit-cases
				4	哥斯达黎加CR				
				10	秘鲁PE				
				16	巴基斯坦PK				
				17	亚太APTA				
3185	4202.1290	---其他	20	0	东盟ASEAN,智利CL,新加坡SG,新西兰NZ,澳门MO,台湾TW	0	最不发达35国LDC35,最不发达4国LDC4	100	---Other
				4	哥斯达黎加CR				
				10	秘鲁PE				
				16	巴基斯坦PK				
				17	亚太APTA				
3186	4202.1900	--其他	20	0	东盟ASEAN,智利CL,新加坡SG,新西兰NZ,台湾TW	0	最不发达35国LDC35,最不发达4国LDC4	100	--Other
				4	哥斯达黎加CR	8	亚太2国APTA2		
				10	秘鲁PE				
		-手提包,不论是否有背带,包括无把手的:							-Handbags, whether or not with shoulder strap, including those without handle:
3187	4202.2100	--以皮革或再生皮革作面	10	0	东盟ASEAN,新西兰NZ,哥斯达黎加CR,香港HK,澳门MO	0	最不发达35国LDC35,最不发达4国LDC4	100	--With outer surface of leather or composition leather
				1	智利CL				
				5	巴基斯坦PK,秘鲁PE				
				6.9	亚太APTA				

序号 No.	税则号列 Tariff Line	货品名称	最惠国税率 MFN(%)	协定税率 Agreement(%)		特惠税率 S.P.(%)		普通税率 Gen.(%)	Article Description
3188	4202.2200	--以塑料片或纺织材料作面	10	0 1 5 8.2	东盟ASEAN,新加坡SG,新西兰NZ,哥斯达黎加CR,澳门MO,台湾TW 智利CL 巴基斯坦PK,秘鲁PE 亚太APTA	0	最不发达35国LDC35,最不发达4国LDC4	100	--With outer surface of plastic sheeting or of textile materials
3189	4202.2900	--其他	20	0 4 10 14	东盟ASEAN,智利CL,新加坡SG,新西兰NZ,澳门MO 哥斯达黎加CR 秘鲁PE 亚太APTA,巴基斯坦PK	0 8	最不发达35国LDC35 亚太2国APTA2	100	--Other
		-通常置于口袋或手提包内的物品:							-Articles of a kind normally carried in the pocket or in the handbag:
3190	4202.3100	--以皮革或再生皮革作面	10	0 5 6.9	东盟ASEAN,智利CL,新西兰NZ,秘鲁PE,哥斯达黎加CR,澳门MO 巴基斯坦PK 亚太APTA	0	最不发达35国LDC35,最不发达4国LDC4	100	--With outer surface of leather or composition leather
3191	4202.3200	--以塑料片或纺织材料作面	20	0 4 10 14	东盟ASEAN,智利CL,新加坡SG,新西兰NZ,澳门MO 哥斯达黎加CR 秘鲁PE 亚太APTA,巴基斯坦PK	0	最不发达35国LDC35,最不发达4国LDC4	100	--With outer surface of plastic sheeting or of textile materials
3192	4202.3900	--其他	20	0 4 10 14	东盟ASEAN,智利CL,新加坡SG,新西兰NZ 哥斯达黎加CR 秘鲁PE 亚太APTA,巴基斯坦PK	0 8	最不发达35国LDC35 亚太2国APTA2	100	--Other
		-其他:							-Other:
3193	4202.9100	--以皮革或再生皮革作面	10	0 5 8.5	东盟ASEAN,智利CL,新西兰NZ,秘鲁PE,哥斯达黎加CR,澳门MO 巴基斯坦PK 亚太APTA	0	最不发达35国LDC35,最不发达4国LDC4	100	--With outer surface of leather or composition leather
3194	4202.9200	--以塑料片或纺织材料作面	10	0 1 5 8.5	东盟ASEAN,新加坡SG,新西兰NZ,哥斯达黎加CR,澳门MO 智利CL 巴基斯坦PK,秘鲁PE 亚太APTA	0	最不发达35国LDC35,最不发达4国LDC4	100	--With outer surface of plastic sheeting or of textile materials
3195	4202.9900	--其他	20	0 4 10	东盟ASEAN,智利CL,新加坡SG,新西兰NZ,澳门MO 哥斯达黎加CR 秘鲁PE	0	最不发达35国LDC35	100	--Other

序号 No.	税则号列 Tariff Line	货品名称	最惠国税率 MFN(%)	协定税率 Agreement(%)		特惠税率 S.P.(%)		普通税率 Gen.(%)	Article Description
	42.03	**皮革或再生皮革制的衣服及衣着附件:**							**Articles of apparel and clothing accessories, of leather or of composition leather:**
3196	4203.1000	-衣服	10	0 1 5	东盟ASEAN,巴基斯坦PK,新西兰NZ,哥斯达黎加CR,香港HK,澳门MO 智利CL 秘鲁PE	0 8	最不发达35国LDC35,最不发达4国LDC4 亚太2国APTA2	100	-Articles of apparel
		-手套,包括连指或露指的:							-Gloves, mittens and mitts:
3197	4203.2100	--专供运动用	20	0 4 10 14	东盟ASEAN,智利CL,巴基斯坦PK,新加坡SG,新西兰NZ,香港HK,澳门MO 哥斯达黎加CR 秘鲁PE 亚太APTA	0	最不发达35国LDC35	100	--Specially designed for use in sports
		--其他:							--Other:
3198	4203.2910	---劳保手套	20	0 2 4 10	东盟ASEAN,巴基斯坦PK,新加坡SG,新西兰NZ,香港HK,澳门MO 智利CL 哥斯达黎加CR 秘鲁PE	0 8	最不发达35国LDC35 亚太2国APTA2	100	---Working gloves
3199	4203.2990	---其他	20	0 2 4 10	东盟ASEAN,巴基斯坦PK,新加坡SG,新西兰NZ,香港HK,澳门MO 智利CL 哥斯达黎加CR 秘鲁PE	0 8	最不发达35国LDC35 亚太2国APTA2	100	---Other
		-腰带及子弹带:							-Belts and bandoliers:
3200	4203.3010	---腰带	10	0 1 5	东盟ASEAN,巴基斯坦PK,新西兰NZ,哥斯达黎加CR,香港HK,澳门MO 智利CL 秘鲁PE	0 8	最不发达35国LDC35,最不发达4国LDC4 亚太2国APTA2	100	---Belts
3201	4203.3020	---子弹带	10	0 1 5	东盟ASEAN,巴基斯坦PK,新西兰NZ,哥斯达黎加CR,香港HK 智利CL 秘鲁PE	0 8	最不发达35国LDC35,最不发达4国LDC4 亚太2国APTA2	100	---bandoliers

序号 No.	税则号列 Tariff Line	货品名称	最惠国税率 MFN(%)	协定税率 Agreement(%)		特惠税率 S.P.(%)		普通税率 Gen.(%)	Article Description
3202	4203.4000	-其他衣着附件	20	0	东盟ASEAN,智利CL,巴基斯坦PK,新加坡SG,新西兰NZ,香港HK,澳门MO	0	最不发达35国LDC35	100	-Other clothing accessories
				4	哥斯达黎加CR	8	亚太2国APTA2		
				10	秘鲁PE				
	42.05	**皮革或再生皮革的其他制品:**							**Other articles of leather or of composition leather:**
		-皮革或再生皮革的其他制品							-Other articles of leather or of composition leather:
3203	4205.0010	---座套	12	0	东盟ASEAN,智利CL,新加坡SG,新西兰NZ,秘鲁PE,香港HK	0	最不发达35国LDC35,最不发达4国LDC4	100	---Cover of seat
				2.4	哥斯达黎加CR	7.8	亚太2国APTA2		
				6	巴基斯坦PK				
3204	4205.0020	---机器、机械器具或其他专门技术用途的	8	0	东盟ASEAN,智利CL,新西兰NZ,秘鲁PE,哥斯达黎加CR	0	最不发达35国LDC35,最不发达4国LDC4	35	---Of a kind used in machinery or mechanical appliances or for other technical uses
				5	巴基斯坦PK				
3205	4205.0090	---其他	12	0	东盟ASEAN,智利CL,新加坡SG,新西兰NZ,香港HK	0	最不发达35国LDC35,最不发达4国LDC4	100	---Other
				2.4	哥斯达黎加CR	7.8	亚太2国APTA2		
				6	巴基斯坦PK,秘鲁PE				
	42.06	**肠线（蚕胶丝除外）、肠膜、膀胱或筋腱制品:**							**Articles of gut (other than silk-worm gut), of goldbeater's skin, of bladders or of tendons:**
3206	4206.0000	肠线（蚕胶丝除外）、肠膜、膀胱或筋腱制品	20	0	东盟ASEAN,智利CL,新加坡SG,新西兰NZ	0	最不发达35国LDC35	90	Articles of gut (other than silk-worm gut), of goldbeater's skin, of bladders or of tendons
				4	哥斯达黎加CR				
				10	秘鲁PE				

第四十三章
毛皮、人造毛皮及其制品

注释：

一、本目录所称“毛皮”，是指已鞣的各种动物的带毛毛皮，但不包括税号43.01的生毛皮。

二、本章不包括：

（一）带羽毛或羽绒的整张或部分鸟皮（税号05.05或67.01）；

（二）第四十一章的带毛生皮 该章注释一（三）；

（三）用皮革与毛皮或用皮革与人造毛皮制成的分指手套、连指手套及露指手套（税目42.03）；

（四）第六十四章的物品；

（五）第六十五章的帽类及其零件；

（六）第九十五章的物品（例如，玩具、游戏品及运动用品）。

三、税号43.03包括加有其他材料缝合的毛皮和毛皮部分品，以及缝合成衣服、衣服部分品、衣着附件或其他制品的毛皮和毛皮部分品。

四、以毛皮或人造毛皮衬里或作面（仅饰边的除外）的衣服及衣着附件（不包括注释二所述的货品），应分别归入税号43.03或43.04，但毛皮或人造毛皮仅作为装饰的除外。

五、本目录所称“人造毛皮”，是指以毛、发或其他纤维粘附或缝合于皮革、织物或其他材料之上而构成的仿毛皮，但不包括以机织或针织方法制得的仿毛皮（一般应归入税号58.01或60.01）。

Chapter 43
Furskins and artificial fur; manufactures thereof

Notes:

1. Throughout the Nomenclature references to “furskins”, other than to raw furskins of heading No. 43.01, apply to hides or skins of all animals which have been tanned or dressed with the hair or wool on.

2. This Chapter does not cover:

(a) Birdskins or parts of birdskins, with their feathers or down (heading No. 05.05 or 67.01);

(b) Raw hides or skins, with the hair or wool on, of Chapter41 (see Note 1 (c) to that Chapter);

(c) Gloves, mittens and mitts consisting of leather and furskin or of leather and artificial fur (heading No. 42.03);

(d) Articles of Chapter 64;

(e) Headgear or parts thereof of Chapter 65; or

(f) Articles of Chapter 95 (for example, toys, games, sports requisites).

3. Heading No.43.03 includes furskins and parts thereof, assembled with the addition of other materials, and furskins and parts thereof, sewn together in the form of garments or parts or accessories of garments or in the form of other articles.

4. Articles of apparel and clothing accessories (except those excluded by Note 2) lined with furskin or artificial fur or to which furskin or artificial fur is attached on the outside except as mere trimming are to be classified in heading No.43.03 or 43.04 as the case may be.

5. Throughout the Nomenclature the expression “artificial fur” means any imitation of furskin consisting of wool, hair or other fibres gummed or sewn on to leather, woven fabric or other materials, but does not include imitation furskins obtained by weaving or knitting (generally, heading No. 58.01 or 60.01) .

序号 No.	税则号列 Tariff Line	货品名称	最惠国税率 MFN(%)	协定税率 Agreement(%)		特惠税率 S.P.(%)		普通税率 Gen.(%)	Article Description
	43.01	**生毛皮（包括适合加工皮货用的头、尾、爪及其他块、片），但税号 41.01、41.02 或 41.03 的生皮除外:**							**Raw furskins (including heads, tails, paws and other pieces or cuttings, suitable for furrier's use), other than raw hides and skins of heading No. 41.01, 41.02 or 41.03:**
3207	4301.1000	-整张水貂皮，不论是否带头、尾或爪	15 △10	0 3 7.5 12	东盟ASEAN,智利CL,新加坡SG,新西兰NZ,香港HK 哥斯达黎加CR 秘鲁PE 巴基斯坦PK	0	最不发达35国LDC35	100	-Of mink, whole, with or without head, tail or paws
3208	4301.3000	-下列羔羊的整张毛皮，不论是否带头、尾或爪:阿斯特拉罕、喀拉科尔、波斯羔羊及类似羔羊、印度、中国或蒙古羔羊	20	0 4 10	东盟ASEAN,智利CL,新加坡SG,新西兰NZ,香港HK 哥斯达黎加CR 秘鲁PE	0	最不发达35国LDC35	90	-Of lamb, the following: Astrakhan, Broadtail, Caracul, Persian and similar lamb, Indian, Chinese, Mongolian or Tibetan lamb, whole, with or without head, tail or paws
3209	4301.6000	-整张狐皮，不论是否带头、尾或爪	20 △15	0 4 10	东盟ASEAN,智利CL,新加坡SG,新西兰NZ,香港HK 哥斯达黎加CR 秘鲁PE	0	最不发达35国LDC35	100	-Of fox, whole, with or without head, tail or paws
		-整张的其他毛皮，不论是否带头、尾或爪:							-Other furskins, whole, with or without head, tail or paws:
3210	4301.8010	---整张兔皮，不论是否带头、尾或爪	20	0 4 10	东盟ASEAN,智利CL,新加坡SG,新西兰NZ,香港HK 哥斯达黎加CR 秘鲁PE	0	最不发达35国LDC35	90	---Of rabbit or hare, whole, with or without head, tail or paws
3211	4301.8090	---其他	20	0 4 10	东盟ASEAN,智利CL,新加坡SG,新西兰NZ,香港HK 哥斯达黎加CR 秘鲁PE	0	最不发达35国LDC35	90	---Other
		-适合加工皮货用的头、尾、爪及其他块、片:							-Heads, tails, paws and other pieces or cuttings, suitable for furriers use:
3212	4301.9010	---黄鼠狼尾	20	0 4 10	东盟ASEAN,智利CL,新加坡SG,新西兰NZ,香港HK 哥斯达黎加CR 秘鲁PE	0	最不发达35国LDC35	50	---Weasel tails
3213	4301.9090	---其他	20	0 4 10	东盟ASEAN,智利CL,新加坡SG,新西兰NZ,香港HK 哥斯达黎加CR 秘鲁PE	0	最不发达35国LDC35	90	---Other

序号 No.	税则号列 Tariff Line	货品名称	最惠国税率 MFN(%)	协定税率 Agreement(%)		特惠税率 S.P.(%)		普通税率 Gen.(%)	Article Description
	43.02	**未缝制或已缝制（不加其他材料）的已鞣毛皮（包括头、尾、爪及其他块、片），但税号 43.03 的货品除外:**							**Tanned or dressed furskins (including heads, tails, paws and other pieces or cuttings), unassembled, or assembled (without the addition of other materials) other than those of heading No.43.03:**
		-未缝制的整张毛皮，不论是否带头、尾或爪:							-Whole skins, with or without head, tail or paws, not assembled:
3214	4302.1100	--水貂皮	12	0 2.4 6	东盟ASEAN,智利CL,新加坡SG,新西兰NZ,秘鲁PE,香港HK 哥斯达黎加CR 巴基斯坦PK	0	最不发达 35 国 LDC35	130	--Of mink
		--其他:							--Other:
3215	4302.1910	---灰鼠皮、白鼬皮、其他貂皮、狐皮、水獭皮、旱獭皮及猞猁皮	10	0 5	东盟ASEAN,智利CL,新西兰NZ,秘鲁PE,哥斯达黎加CR,香港HK 巴基斯坦PK	0	最不发达 35 国 LDC35	130	---Of gray squirrel, ermine, other marten, fox, otter, marmot and lynx
3216	4302.1920	---兔皮	10	0 5	东盟ASEAN,智利CL,新西兰NZ,秘鲁PE,哥斯达黎加CR,香港HK 巴基斯坦PK	0	最不发达 35 国 LDC35,最不发达 4 国 LDC4	100	---Of rabbit or hare
3217	4302.1930	---下列羔羊皮：阿斯特拉罕、喀拉科尔、波斯羔羊及类似羔羊、印度、中国或蒙古羔羊	20	0 4 10	东盟ASEAN,智利CL,新加坡SG,新西兰NZ,香港HK 哥斯达黎加CR 秘鲁PE	0	最不发达 35 国 LDC35,最不发达 4 国 LDC4	100	---Of lamb, the following: Astrakhan, Broadtail, Caracul, Persian and similar lamb, Indian, Chinese (including Tibetan) or Mongolian lamb
3218	4302.1990	---其他	10	0	东盟ASEAN,智利CL,新西兰NZ,秘鲁PE,哥斯达黎加CR,香港HK	0	最不发达 35 国 LDC35,最不发达 4 国 LDC4	100	---Other
3219	4302.2000	-未缝制的头、尾、爪及其他块、片	20	0 4 10	东盟ASEAN,智利CL,新加坡SG,新西兰NZ,香港HK 哥斯达黎加CR 秘鲁PE	0	最不发达 35 国 LDC35	100	-Heads, tails, paws and other pieces or cuttings, not assembled
		-已缝制的整张毛皮及其块、片:							-Whole skins and pieces or cuttings thereof, assembled:
3220	4302.3010	---灰鼠、白鼬、貂、狐、水獭、旱獭及猞猁的整张毛皮及其块、片	20	0 4 10	东盟ASEAN,智利CL,新加坡SG,新西兰NZ,香港HK 哥斯达黎加CR 秘鲁PE	0	最不发达 35 国 LDC35	130	---Of grey squirrel, ermine, other marten, fox, otter, marmot and lynx

序号 No.	税则号列 Tariff Line	货品名称	最惠国税率 MFN(%)	协定税率 Agreement(%)		特惠税率 S.P.(%)		普通税率 Gen.(%)	Article Description
3221	4302.3090	---其他	20	0	东盟ASEAN,智利CL,新加坡SG,新西兰NZ,香港HK	0	最不发达35国LDC35	100	---Other
				4	哥斯达黎加CR				
				10	秘鲁PE				
	43.03	**毛皮制的衣服、衣着附件及其他物品:**							**Articles of apparel, clothing accessories and other articles of furskin:**
		-衣服及衣着附件:							-Articles of apparel and clothing access-ories:
3222	4303.1010	---毛皮衣服	23	0	东盟ASEAN,新加坡SG,新西兰NZ,香港HK	0	最不发达35国LDC35	150	---Articles of appare
				2.3	智利CL	10.4	亚太2国APTA2		
				4.6	哥斯达黎加CR				
				11.5	秘鲁PE				
3223	4303.1020	---毛皮衣着附件	18	0	东盟ASEAN,新加坡SG,新西兰NZ,香港HK	0	最不发达35国LDC35	150	---Clothing accessories
				1.8	智利CL	9.9	亚太2国APTA2		
				3.6	哥斯达黎加CR				
				9	秘鲁PE				
3224	4303.9000	-其他	18	0	东盟ASEAN,智利CL,新加坡SG,新西兰NZ,秘鲁PE,香港HK	0	最不发达35国LDC35	150	-Other
				3.6	哥斯达黎加CR	9.9	亚太2国APTA2		
				14.4	巴基斯坦PK				
	43.04	**人造毛皮及其制品:**							**Artificial fur and articles thereof:**
3225	4304.0010	---人造毛皮	18	0	东盟ASEAN,智利CL,新加坡SG,新西兰NZ,香港HK	0	最不发达35国LDC35	130	---Artificial fur
				3.6	哥斯达黎加CR	10.8	亚太2国APTA2		
				9	秘鲁PE				
3226	4304.0020	---人造毛皮制品	18	0	东盟ASEAN,智利CL,新加坡SG,新西兰NZ,香港HK	0	最不发达35国LDC35	150	---Articles of artificial fur
						10.8	亚太2国APTA2		
				3.6	哥斯达黎加CR				
				9	秘鲁PE				
				14.4	巴基斯坦PK				

第九类
木及木制品；木炭；软木及软木制品；稻草、秸秆、针茅或其他编结材料制品；篮筐及柳条编结品

SECTION Ⅸ
WOOD AND ARTICLES OF WOOD; WOOD CHARCOAL; CORK AND ARTICLES OF CORK; MANUFACTURES OF STRAW, OF ESPARTO OR OF OTHER PLAITING MATERIALS; BASKETWARE AND WICKERWORK

第四十四章
木及木制品；木炭

Chapter 44
Wood and articles of wood; wood charcoal

注释：

一、本章不包括：

（一）主要作香料、药料、杀虫、杀菌或类似用途的木片、刨花、碎木、木粒或木粉（税号12.11）；

（二）竹或主要作编结用的其他木质材料，未经加工、劈开、纵锯或切段（税号14.01）；

（三）主要作染料或鞣料用的木片、刨花、木粒或木粉（税号14.04）；

（四）活性炭（税号38.02）；

（五）税号42.02的物品；

（六）第四十六章的货品；

（七）第六十四章的鞋靴及其零件；

（八）第六十六章的货品（例如，伞、手杖及其零件）；

（九）税号68.08的货品；

（十）税号71.17的仿首饰；

（十一）第十六类或第十七类的货品（例如，机器零件，机器及器具的箱、罩、壳，车辆部件）；

（十二）第十八类的货品（例如，钟壳、乐器及其零件）；

（十三）火器的零件（税号93.05）；

（十四）第九十四章的物品（例如，家具、灯具及照明器具、活动房屋）；

（十五）第九十五章的物品（例如，玩具、游戏品及运动用品）；

（十六）第九十六章的物品（例如，烟斗及其零件、钮扣、铅笔），但税号96.03所列物品的木身及木柄除外；

（十七）第九十七章的物品（例如艺术品）。

二、本章所称“强化木”，是指经过化学或物理方法处理（对于多层粘合木材，其处理应超出一般粘合需要），从而增加了密度或硬度并改善了机械强度、抗化学或抗电性能的木材。

Notes:

1. This Chapter does not cover:

(a) Wood, in chips, in shavings, crushed, ground or powdered, of a kind used primarily in perfumery, in pharmacy, or for insecticidal, fungicidal or similar purposes (heading No.12.11);

(b) Bamboos or other materials of a woody nature of a kind used primarily for plaiting, in the rough, whether or not split, sawn lengthwise or cut to length (heading No.14.01);

(c) Wood, in chips, in shavings, ground or powdered, of a kind used primarily in dyeing or in tanning (heading No.14.04);

(d) Activated charcoal (heading No.38.02);

(e) Articles of heading No.42.02;

(f) Goods of Chapter 46;

(g) Footwear or parts thereof of Chapter 64;

(h) Goods of Chapter 66 (for example, umbrellas and walking-sticks and parts thereof);

(i) Goods of heading No.68.08;

(j) Imitation jewellery of heading No.71.17;

(k) Goods of Section ⅩⅥ or Section ⅩⅦ (for example, machine parts, cases, covers, cabinets for machines and apparatus and wheel wrights' wares);

(l) Goods of Section ⅩⅧ (for example, clock cases and musical instruments and parts thereof)；

(m) Parts of firearms (heading No.93.05);

(n) Articles of Chapter 94 (for example, furniture, lamps and lighting fittings, prefabricated buildings);

(o) Articles of Chapter 95 (for example, toys, games, sports requisites);

(p) Articles of Chapter 96 (for example, smoking pipes and parts thereof, buttons, pencils) excluding bodies and handles, of wood, for articles of heading No.96.03;

(q) Articles, of Chapter 97 (for example, works of art).

2. In this Chapter, the expression “densified wood” means wood which has been subjected to chemical or physical treatment (being, in the case of layers bonded together, treatment in excess of that needed to ensure a good bond), and which has thereby acquired increased density or hardness together with improved mechanical strength or resistance to chemical or electrical agencies.

三、税号 44.14 至44.21适用于木质碎料板或类似木质材料板、纤维板、层压板或强化木的制品。

四、税号 44.10、44.11 或 44.12 的产品，可以加工成税号 44.09 所述的各种形状，也可以加工成弯曲、瓦楞、多孔或其他形状（正方形或矩形除外），以及经其他任何加工，但未具有其他税号所列制品的特性。

五、税号 44.17 不包括装有第八十二章注释一所述材料制成的刀片、工作刃、工作面或其他工作部件的工具。

六、除上述注释一及其他条文另有规定的以外，本章税目中所称“木”，也包括竹及其他木质材料。

3. Headings No. 44.14 to 44.21 apply to articles of the respective descriptions of particle board or similar board, fibreboard, laminated wood or densified wood as they apply to such articles of wood.

4. Products of heading No.44.10, 44.11 or 44.12 may be worked to form the shapes provided for in respect of the goods of heading No.44.09, curved, corrugated, perforated, cut or formed to shapes other than square or rectangular or submitted to any other operation provided it does not give them the character of articles of other headings.

5. Heading No.44.17 does not apply to tools in which the blade, working edge, working surface or other working part is formed by any of the materials specified in Note 1 to Chapter 82.

6. Subject to Note1above and except where the context otherwise requires, any reference to “wood” in a heading of this Chapter applies also to bamboos and other materials of a woody nature.

子目注释:

一、子目 4401.31 所称“木屑棒”是指由木材加工业、家具制造业及其他木材加工活动中产生的副产品（例如刨花、锯末及碎木片）直接压制而成或加入按重量计不超过 3%的粘合剂后粘聚而成的产品。此类产品呈圆柱状，其直径不超过 25mm，长度不超过 100mm。

二、子目号 4403.41 至 4403.49、4407.21 至 4407.29、4408.31 至 4408.39 及 4412.31 所称“热带木”，是指下列木材：

大叶帽柱木、非洲桃花心木、西非红豆木、箭毒木、阿兰木、圭亚那苦油楝木、非洲甘比山榄木、杜楝木、非洲栎柞木、婆罗双木、美洲轻木、白驼峰楝木、黑驼峰楝木、卡蒂沃木、雪松木、西非褐红椴木、深红色红柳桉木、非洲核桃楝木、阿夫苏木、象牙海岸榄仁木、破布木、吉贝木、丝棉木、乔状黄牛木、安哥拉丛花木、巴西胡桃木、皮蚁木、伊罗科木、拟爱神木、夹竹桃木、巴西红木、绒根木、龙脑香木、开姆帕斯木、羯布罗香木、康多非洲楝木、象牙海岸褐红椴木、象牙海岸翼梧桐木、浅红色红柳桉木、非洲榄仁木、南美樟木、圭亚那铁线子木、西印度桃花心木、猴子果木、肖氏夸利亚木、曼孙梧桐木、马来蝴蝶木、巴栲红柳桉木、粗轴坡垒木、印茄木、斯温漆木、异翅香木、非洲梨木、非洲银叶木、胶木、非洲白梧桐木、加蓬榄木、蓖麻木、爱里古夷苏木、奥文科尔木、中非蜡烛木、紫檀木、人面子木、危地马拉黑黄檀木、印度黑黄檀木、巴西黑黄檀木、巴西柚、巴西花梨木、白坚木、鸡骨常山木、印马四出香木、大沃契希亚木、东西亚棱柱木、萨撇列木、萌生木棉木、苏帕楠木、西波木、苏古皮拉木、红椿木、圭亚那考拉玉蕊木、柚木、安哥拉香桃花心木、非洲阿勃木、南美肉豆蔻木、白柳桉木、白色红柳桉木、白色柳桉木、黄色红柳桉木。

Subheading Notes:

1.For the purposes of subheading 4401.31, the expression “wood pellets” means by-products such as cutter shavings, sawdust or chips, of the mechanical wood processing industry, furniture-making industry or other wood transformation activities, which have been agglomerated either directly by compression or by the addition of a binder in a proportion not exceeding 3% by weight. Such pellets are cylindrical, with a diameter not exceeding 25 mm and a length not exceeding 100 mm.

2.For the purposes of subheadings No.4403.41to4403.49, 4407.21 to 4407.29, 4408.31 to 4408.39 and 4412.31, the expression “tropical wood” means one of the following types of wood:

Abura, Acajou d’Afrique, Afrormosia, Ako, Alan, Andiroba, Aningré, Avodiré, Azobé, Balau, Balsa, Bossé clair, Bossé foncé, Cativo, Cedro, Dabema, Dark Red Meranti, Dib é tou, Douss i é, Framir é, Freijo, Fromager, Fuma, Geronggang, Ilomba, Imb uia, Ipé, Iroko, Jaboty, Jelutong, Jequitiba, Jongkong, Kapur, Kempas, Keruing, Kosipo, Kotib, KotoLight Red Meranti, Limba, Louroé, Macaranduba, Mahogany, Makor, Mandioqueira, Mansonia, Mengkulang, Meranti Bakau, Merawan, Merbau, Merpauh, Mersawa, Moabi, Niangon, Nyatoh, Obeche, Okoum, Onzabili, Orey, Ovengkol, Ozigo, Padauk, Paldao, Palissandre dc Guatemala, Palissandre de Para, Palissandre de Rio, Palissandre de Rose, Pau Amarelo, Pau Marfim, Pulai, Punah, Quaruba, Ramin, Sapelli, Saqui-Saqui, Sepetir, Sipo, Sucupira, Suren, Tauari, Teak, Tiama, Tola, Virola, White Lauan, White Meranti, White Seraya, Yellow Meranti.

序号 No.	税则号列 Tariff Line	货品名称	最惠国税率 MFN(%)	协定税率 Agreement(%)		特惠税率 S.P.(%)		普通税率 Gen.(%)	Article Description
	44.01	**薪柴（圆木段、块、枝、成捆或类似形状）;木片或木粒;锯末、木废料及碎片，不论是否粘结成圆木段、块、片或类似形状:**							**Fuel wood, in logs, in billets, in twigs, in faggots or in similar forms; wood in chips or particles; sawdust and wood waste and scrap, whether or not agglomerated in logs, briquettes, pellets or similar forms:**
3227	4401.1000	-薪柴（圆木段、块、枝、成捆或类似形状）	0			0	最不发达35国LDC35,最不发达4国LDC4	70	-Fuel wood, in logs, in billets, in twigs, in faggots or in similar forms
		-木片或木粒:							-Wood in chips or particles:
3228	4401.2100	--针叶木	0			0	最不发达35国LDC35,最不发达4国LDC4	8	--Coniferous
3229	4401.2200	--非针叶木	0			0	最不发达35国LDC35,最不发达4国LDC4	8	--Non-coniferous
		-锯末、木废料及碎片，不论是否粘结成圆木段、块、片或类似形状:							-Sawdust and wood waste and scrap, whether or not agglomerated in logs, briquettes, pellets or similar forms:
3230	4401.3100	--木屑棒	0			0	最不发达35国LDC35,最不发达4国LDC4	8	--Wood pellets
3231	4401.3900	--其他	0			0	最不发达35国LDC35,最不发达4国LDC4	8	--Other
	44.02	**木炭（包括果壳炭及果核炭），不论是否结块:**							**Wood charcoal (including shell or nut charcoal), whether or not agglomerated:**
3232	4402.1000	-竹的	10.5	0	东盟ASEAN,智利CL,新加坡SG,新西兰NZ,秘鲁PE	0	最不发达35国LDC35	70	-Of bamboo
				2.1	哥斯达黎加CR				
				5	巴基斯坦PK				

序号 No.	税则号列 Tariff Line	货品名称	最惠国税率 MFN(%)	协定税率 Agreement(%)	特惠税率 S.P.(%)	普通税率 Gen.(%)	Article Description
3233	4402.9000	-其他	10.5	0 东盟ASEAN,智利CL,新加坡SG,新西兰NZ,秘鲁PE 2.1 哥斯达黎加CR 5 巴基斯坦PK	0 最不发达35国LDC35	70	-Other
	44.03	**原木，不论是否去皮、去边材或粗锯成方：**					**Wood in the rough, whether or not stripped of bark or sapwood, or roughly squared:**
3234	4403.1000	-用油漆、着色剂、杂酚油或其他防腐剂处理	0		0 最不发达35国LDC35,最不发达4国LDC4	8	-Treated with paint, stains, creosote or other preservatives
		-其他针叶木:					-Other, coniferous:
3235	4403.2010	---红松和樟子松	0		0 最不发达35国LDC35,最不发达4国LDC4	8	---Korean pine and Mongolian scotch pine
3236	4403.2020	---白松（云杉和冷杉）	0		0 最不发达35国LDC35,最不发达4国LDC4	8	---White pine (*spruce and fir*)
3237	4403.2030	---辐射松	0		0 最不发达35国LDC35,最不发达4国LDC4	8	---Radiata pine
3238	4403.2040	---落叶松	0		0 最不发达35国LDC35,最不发达4国LDC4	8	---Larch
3239	4403.2050	---花旗松	0		0 最不发达35国LDC35,最不发达4国LDC4	8	---Douglas fir
3240	4403.2090	---其他	0		0 最不发达35国LDC35,最不发达4国LDC4	8	---Other
		-其他本章子目注释二所列的热带木:					-Other, of tropical wood specified in Subheading Note 2 to this Chapter:

序号 No.	税则号列 Tariff Line	货品名称	最惠国税率 MFN(%)	协定税率 Agreement(%)	特惠税率 S.P.(%)	普通税率 Gen.(%)	Article Description
3241	4403.4100	--深红色红柳安木、浅红色红柳安木及巴栲红柳安木	0		0 最不发达35国 LDC35, 最不发达4国 LDC4	8	--Dark Red Meranti, Light Red Meranti and Meranti Bakau
		--其他（本章子目注释所列热带非针叶木）：					--Other (of tropical non-coniferous wood specified in subheading note 1 to this chapter):
3242	4403.4910	---柚木	0		0 最不发达35国 LDC35, 最不发达4国 LDC4	35	---Teak
3243	4403.4920	---奥克曼（奥克榄）	0		0 最不发达35国 LDC35, 最不发达4国 LDC4	35	---Okoume (*Aukoumed Klaineana*)
3244	4403.4930	---龙脑香木（克隆）	0		0 最不发达35国 LDC35, 最不发达4国 LDC4	35	---Dipterocarpus spp. Keruing
3245	4403.4940	---山樟（香木）	0		0 最不发达35国 LDC35, 最不发达4国 LDC4	35	---Kapur (*Dryobalanops spp.*)
3246	4403.4950	---印加木（波罗格）	0		0 最不发达35国 LDC35, 最不发达4国 LDC4	35	---Intsia spp. (*Mengaris*)
3247	4403.4960	---大干巴豆（门格里斯或康派斯	0		0 最不发达35国 LDC35, 最不发达4国 LDC4	35	---Koompassia spp. (*Mengaris or Kempas*)
3248	4403.4970	---异翅香木	0		0 最不发达35国 LDC35, 最不发达4国 LDC4	35	---Anisopter spp.

序号 No.	税则号列 Tariff Line	货品名称	最惠国税率 MFN(%)	协定税率 Agreement(%)	特惠税率 S.P.(%)	普通税率 Gen.(%)	Article Description
3249	4403.4990	---其他	0		0 最不发达35国LDC35,最不发达4国LDC4	8	---Other
		-其他:					-Other:
3250	4403.9100	--栎木（橡木）	0		0 最不发达35国LDC35,最不发达4国LDC4	8	--Of oak (*Quercus spp.*)
3251	4403.9200	--山毛榉木	0		0 最不发达35国LDC35,最不发达4国LDC4	8	--Of beech (*Fagus spp.*)
		--其他:					--Other:
3252	4403.9910	---楠木	0		0 最不发达35国LDC35,最不发达4国LDC4	35	---Of nan mu (*Phoebe*)
3253	4403.9920	---樟木	0		0 最不发达35国LDC35,最不发达4国LDC4	35	---Of camphor wood
3254	4403.9930	---红木	0		0 最不发达35国LDC35,最不发达4国LDC4	35	---Of rosewood
3255	4403.9940	---泡桐木	0		0 最不发达35国LDC35,最不发达4国LDC4	8	---Of Kiri (*Paulownia*)
3256	4403.9950	---水曲柳	0		0 最不发达35国LDC35,最不发达4国LDC4	8	---Ash
3257	4403.9960	---北美硬阔叶木（包括樱桃木、黑胡桃木、枫木）	0		0 最不发达35国LDC35,最不发达4国LDC4	8	---North American hard wood (including cherry, walnut, and maple)

序号 No.	税则号列 Tariff Line	货品名称	最惠国税率 MFN(%)	协定税率 Agreement(%)		特惠税率 S.P.(%)		普通税率 Gen.(%)	Article Description
3258	4403.9980	---其他未列名的温带非针叶木	0			0	最不发达35国LDC35,最不发达4国LDC4	8	---Other temperate non-coniferous not specified
3259	4403.9990	---其他	0			0	最不发达35国LDC35,最不发达4国LDC4	8	---Other
	44.04	**箍木;木劈条;已削尖但未经纵锯的木桩;粗加修整但未经车圆、弯曲或其他方式加工的木棒,适合制手杖、伞柄、工具把柄及类似品;木片条及类似品:**							**Hoopwood; split poles; piles, pickets and stakes of wood, pointed but not sawn lengthwise; wooden sticks, roughly trimmed but not turned, bent or otherwise worked, suitable for the manufacture of walking-sticks, umbrellas, tool handles or the like; chipwood and the like:**
3260	4404.1000	-针叶木的	8	0 0.8 5	东盟ASEAN,新加坡SG,新西兰NZ,秘鲁PE,哥斯达黎加CR 智利CL 巴基斯坦PK	0	最不发达35国LDC35	50	-Coniferous
3261	4404.2000	-非针叶木的	8	0 0.8 5	东盟ASEAN,新加坡SG,新西兰NZ,秘鲁PE,哥斯达黎加CR 智利CL 巴基斯坦PK	0	最不发达35国LDC35	50	-Non-coniferous
	44.05	**木丝;木粉:**							**Wood wool; wood flour:**
3262	4405.0000	木丝;木粉	8	0 0.8 5	东盟ASEAN,新加坡SG,新西兰NZ,秘鲁PE,哥斯达黎加CR 智利CL 巴基斯坦PK	0	最不发达35国LDC35,最不发达4国LDC4	40	Wood wool; wood flour
	44.06	**铁道及电车道枕木:**							**Railway or tramway sleepers (cross-ties) of wood:**
3263	4406.1000	-未浸渍	0			0	最不发达35国LDC35,最不发达4国LDC4	14	-Not impregnated

序号 No.	税则号列 Tariff Line	货品名称	最惠国税率 MFN(%)	协定税率 Agreement(%)	特惠税率 S.P.(%)	普通税率 Gen.(%)	Article Description
3264	4406.9000	-其他	0		0 最不发达35国 LDC35, 最不发达4国 LDC4	14	-Other
	44.07	**经纵锯、纵切、刨切或旋切的木材，不论是否刨平、砂光或指榫接合，厚度超过6毫米:**					**Wood sawn or chipped lengthwise, sliced or peeled, whether or not planed, sanded or finger-jointed, of a thickness exceeding 6 mm:**
		-针叶木:					-Coniferous:
3265	4407.1010	---红松和樟子松	0		0 最不发达35国 LDC35, 最不发达4国 LDC4	14	---Korean pine and Mongolian scotch pine
3266	4407.1020	---白松（云杉和冷杉）	0		0 最不发达35国 LDC35, 最不发达4国 LDC4	14	---White pine (*spruce and fir*)
3267	4407.1030	---辐射松	0		0 最不发达35国 LDC35, 最不发达4国 LDC4	14	---Rediata pine
3268	4407.1040	---花旗松	0		0 最不发达35国 LDC35, 最不发达4国 LDC4	14	---Douglas fir
3269	4407.1090	---其他	0		0 最不发达35国 LDC35, 最不发达4国 LDC4	14	---Other
		-本章子目注释二所列的热带木:					-Of tropical wood specified in Subheading Note 2 to this Chapter:
3270	4407.2100	--美洲桃花心木	0		0 最不发达35国 LDC35, 最不发达4国 LDC4	14	--Mahogany (Swietenia spp.)

序号 No.	税则号列 Tariff Line	货品名称	最惠国税率 MFN(%)	协定税率 Agreement(%)	特惠税率 S.P.(%)		普通税率 Gen.(%)	Article Description
3271	4407.2200	--苏里南肉豆蔻木、美洲桃花心木、巴西胡桃木及美洲轻木	0		0	最不发达35国 LDC35, 最不发达4国 LDC4	14	--Virola, Imbuia and Balsa
3272	4407.2500	--深红色红柳安木、浅红色红柳安木及巴栲红柳安木	0		0	最不发达35国 LDC35, 最不发达4国 LDC4	14	--Dark Red Meranti, Light Red Meranti and Meranti Bakau
3273	4407.2600	--白柳安木、白色红柳安木、白色柳安木、黄色红柳安木及阿兰木	0		0	最不发达35国 LDC35, 最不发达4国 LDC4	14	--White Lauan, White Meranti, White Seraya, Yellow Meranti and Alan
3274	4407.2700	--沙比利	0		0	最不发达35国 LDC35, 最不发达4国 LDC4	40	--Sapelli
3275	4407.2800	--伊罗科木	0		0	最不发达35国 LDC35, 最不发达4国 LDC4	14	--Iroko
		--其他:						--Other:
3276	4407.2910	---柚木	0		0	最不发达35国 LDC35, 最不发达4国 LDC4	40	---Teak
3277	4407.2920	---非洲桃花心木	0		0	最不发达35国 LDC35, 最不发达4国 LDC4	40	---Acajou
3278	4407.2930	---波罗格	0		0	最不发达35国 LDC35, 最不发达4国 LDC4	40	---Merban
3279	4407.2990	---其他	0		0	最不发达35国 LDC35, 最不发达4国 LDC4	14	---Other

序号 No.	税则号列 Tariff Line	货品名称	最惠国税率 MFN(%)	协定税率 Agreement(%)	特惠税率 S.P.(%)	普通税率 Gen.(%)	Article Description
		-其他:					-Other:
3280	4407.9100	--栎木（橡木）	0		0 最不发达35国LDC35, 最不发达4国LDC4	14	--Of oak (*Quercus spp.*)
3281	4407.9200	--山毛榉木	0		0 最不发达35国LDC35, 最不发达4国LDC4	14	--Of beech (*Fagus spp.*)
3282	4407.9300	--枫木	0		0 最不发达35国LDC35, 最不发达4国LDC4	14	--Of maple (*Acer spp.*)
3283	4407.9400	--樱桃木	0		0 最不发达35国LDC35, 最不发达4国LDC4	14	--Of cherry (*Prunus spp.*)
3284	4407.9500	--白蜡木	0		0 最不发达35国LDC35, 最不发达4国LDC4	14	--Of ash (*Fraxinus spp.*)
		--其他:					--Other:
3285	4407.9910	---樟木、楠木、红木	0		0 最不发达35国LDC35, 最不发达4国LDC4	40	---Of camphor-wood, nanmu or rosewood
3286	4407.9920	---泡桐木	0		0 最不发达35国LDC35, 最不发达4国LDC4	14	---Of Paulownia
3287	4407.9930	---北美硬阔叶材（含黑胡桃木）	0		0 最不发达35国LDC35, 最不发达4国LDC4	14	---North American hard wood (including walnut)
3288	4407.9980	---其他温带非针叶木厚板材	0		0 最不发达35国LDC35, 最不发达4国LDC4	14	---Other temperate non-coniferous wood

序号 No.	税则号列 Tariff Line	货品名称	最惠国税率 MFN(%)	协定税率 Agreement(%)		特惠税率 S.P.(%)		普通税率 Gen.(%)	Article Description
3289	4407.9990	---其他	0			0	最不发达35国LDC35,最不发达4国LDC4	14	---Other
	44.08	**饰面用单板（包括刨切积层木获得的单板）、制胶合板或似多层板用单板以及其他经纵锯、刨切或旋切的木材，不论是否刨平、砂光、拼接或端部接合，厚度不超过6毫米:**							**Sheets for veneering (including those obtained by slicing laminated wood), for plywood or for other similar laminated wood and other wood, sawn lengthwise, sliced or peeled, whether or not planed, sanded, spliced or end-jointed, of a thickness not exceeding 6mm:**
		-针叶木的:							-Coniferous:
		---饰面用单板:							---Veneer sheets:
3290	4408.1011	----用胶合板等多层板制的	8	0	智利CL,新西兰NZ,秘鲁PE,哥斯达黎加CR			40	----Of laminated plywood
3291	4408.1019	----其他	4	0	东盟ASEAN,巴基斯坦PK,新加坡SG,新西兰NZ,秘鲁PE,哥斯达黎加CR	0	最不发达35国LDC35	40	----Other
				0.4	智利CL				
3292	4408.1020	---制胶合板用单板	4	0	东盟ASEAN,巴基斯坦PK,新加坡SG,新西兰NZ,秘鲁PE,哥斯达黎加CR	0	最不发达35国LDC35	17	---Sheets for plywood
				0.4	智利CL				
3293	4408.1090	---其他	4	0	东盟ASEAN,巴基斯坦PK,新加坡SG,新西兰NZ,秘鲁PE,哥斯达黎加CR	0	最不发达35国LDC35	30	---Other
				0.4	智利CL				
		-本章子目注释二所列的热带木:							-Of tropical wood specified in Subheading Note 2 to this Chapter:
		--深红色红柳安木、浅红色红柳安木及巴栲红柳安木:							--Dark Red Meranti, Light Red Meranti and Meranti Bakau:
		---饰面用单板:							---Veneer sheets:
3294	4408.3111	----用胶合板等多层板制的	10	0	智利CL,新西兰NZ,秘鲁PE,哥斯达黎加CR			40	----Of laminated plywood
3295	4408.3119	----其他	4	0	东盟ASEAN,智利CL,巴基斯坦PK,新加坡SG,新西兰NZ,秘鲁PE,哥斯达黎加CR	0	最不发达35国LDC35	40	----Other

序号 No.	税则号列 Tariff Line	货品名称	最惠国税率 MFN(%)	协定税率 Agreement(%)		特惠税率 S.P.(%)		普通税率 Gen.(%)	Article Description
3296	4408.3120	---制胶合板用单板	4	0	东盟ASEAN,智利CL,巴基斯坦PK,新加坡SG,新西兰NZ,秘鲁PE,哥斯达黎加CR	0	最不发达35国LDC35	17	---Sheets for plywood
3297	4408.3190	---其他	4	0	东盟ASEAN,智利CL,巴基斯坦PK,新加坡SG,新西兰NZ,秘鲁PE,哥斯达黎加CR	0	最不发达35国LDC35	30	---Other
		--其他:							--Other:
		---饰面用单板:							---Veneer sheets:
3298	4408.3911	----用胶合板等多层板制的	10	0	智利CL,新西兰NZ,秘鲁PE,哥斯达黎加CR			40	----Of laminated plywood
3299	4408.3919	----其他	4	0	东盟ASEAN,智利CL,巴基斯坦PK,新加坡SG,新西兰NZ,秘鲁PE,哥斯达黎加CR	0	最不发达35国LDC35	40	----Other
3300	4408.3920	---制胶合板用单板	4	0	东盟ASEAN,智利CL,巴基斯坦PK,新加坡SG,新西兰NZ,秘鲁PE,哥斯达黎加CR	0	最不发达35国LDC35	17	---Sheets for plywood
3301	4408.3990	---其他	4	0	东盟ASEAN,智利CL,巴基斯坦PK,新加坡SG,新西兰NZ,秘鲁PE,哥斯达黎加CR	0	最不发达35国LDC35	30	---Other
		-其他:							-Other:
		---饰面用单板:							---Veneer sheets:
3302	4408.9011	----用胶合板等多层板制的	4	0 0.4	新西兰NZ,秘鲁PE,哥斯达黎加CR 智利CL			40	----Of laminated plywood
3303	4408.9012	----温带非针叶木制	3 △1	0	东盟ASEAN,智利CL,巴基斯坦PK,新加坡SG,新西兰NZ,秘鲁PE,哥斯达黎加CR	0	最不发达35国LDC35	40	----Of temperate non-coniferous wood
3304	4408.9013	----竹制	4	0 0.4	新西兰NZ,秘鲁PE,哥斯达黎加CR 智利CL			40	----of bamboo
3305	4408.9019	----其他	3	0	东盟ASEAN,智利CL,巴基斯坦PK,新加坡SG,新西兰NZ,秘鲁PE,哥斯达黎加CR	0	最不发达35国LDC35	40	----Other
	ex44089019	家具饰面单板	△1						Veneer sheets for furniture
		---胶合板用单板:							---Sheets for plywood:
3306	4408.9021	----温带非针叶木制	3	0	东盟ASEAN,智利CL,巴基斯坦PK,新加坡SG,新西兰NZ,秘鲁PE,哥斯达黎加CR	0	最不发达35国LDC35	17	----Of temperate non-coniferous wood
3307	4408.9029	----其他	3	0	东盟ASEAN,智利CL,巴基斯坦PK,新加坡SG,新西兰NZ,秘鲁PE,哥斯达黎加CR	0	最不发达35国LDC35	17	----Other
	ex44089029	胶合板用旋切单板	△1						Peeled sheets for plywood
		---其他:							---Other:

序号 No.	税则号列 Tariff Line	货品名称	最惠国税率 MFN(%)	协定税率 Agreement(%)		特惠税率 S.P.(%)		普通税率 Gen.(%)	Article Description
3308	4408.9091	----温带非针叶木制	3	0	东盟ASEAN,智利CL,巴基斯坦PK,新加坡SG,新西兰NZ,秘鲁PE,哥斯达黎加CR	0	最不发达35国LDC35	30	----Of temperate non-coniferous wood
3309	4408.9099	----其他	3	0	东盟ASEAN,智利CL,巴基斯坦PK,新加坡SG,新西兰NZ,秘鲁PE,哥斯达黎加CR	0	最不发达35国LDC35	30	----Other
	44.09	**任何一边端或面制成连续形状（舌榫、槽榫、半槽榫、斜角、V形接头、珠榫、缘饰、刨圆及类似形状）的木材（包括未装拼的拼花地板用板条及缘板），不论是否刨平、砂光或端部接合:**							**Wood (including strips and friezes for parquet flooring, not assembled) continuously shaped (tongues, grooved, rebated, chamfered, v-jointed, beaded, moulded, rounded or the like) along any of its"edges, ends or faces, whether or not planed, sanded or end-jointed":**
		-针叶木:							-Coniferous:
3310	4409.1010	---地板条（块）	7.5	0 0.8 5	东盟ASEAN,新加坡SG,新西兰NZ,秘鲁PE,哥斯达黎加CR 智利CL 巴基斯坦PK	0	最不发达35国LDC35,最不发达4国LDC4	50	---Floor board strips
3311	4409.1090	---其他	7.5	0 0.8 5	东盟ASEAN,新加坡SG,新西兰NZ,秘鲁PE,哥斯达黎加CR 智利CL 巴基斯坦PK	0	最不发达35国LDC35,最不发达4国LDC4	50	---Other
		-非针叶木:							-Non-coniferous:
		--竹的:							--Of bamboo:
3312	4409.2110	---地板条（块）	4	0 0.4	东盟ASEAN,巴基斯坦PK,新加坡SG,新西兰NZ,秘鲁PE,哥斯达黎加CR 智利CL	0	最不发达35国LDC35,最不发达4国LDC4	50	---Floor board strips
3313	4409.2190	---其他	4	0 0.4	东盟ASEAN,巴基斯坦PK,新加坡SG,新西兰NZ,秘鲁PE,哥斯达黎加CR 智利CL	0	最不发达35国LDC35,最不发达4国LDC4	50	---Other
		--其他:							--Other:
3314	4409.2910	---地板条（块）	4	0 0.4	东盟ASEAN,巴基斯坦PK,新加坡SG,新西兰NZ,秘鲁PE,哥斯达黎加CR 智利CL	0	最不发达35国LDC35,最不发达4国LDC4	50	---Floor board strips

序号 No.	税则号列 Tariff Line	货品名称	最惠国税率 MFN(%)	协定税率 Agreement(%)		特惠税率 S.P.(%)		普通税率 Gen.(%)	Article Description
3315	4409.2990	---其他	4	0 0.4	东盟ASEAN,巴基斯坦PK,新加坡SG,新西兰NZ,秘鲁PE,哥斯达黎加CR 智利CL	0	最不发达35国LDC35	50	---Other
	44.10	**木质碎料板及其他类似木质材料板,(例如,定向板及华夫板),不论是否用树脂或其他有机粘合剂粘合:**							**Particle board and similar board of wood or other ligneous materials (for example, oriented strand board and waferboabd), whether or not agglomerated with resins or other organic binding substances:**
		-木制:							-Of wood:
3316	4410.1100	--碎料板	4					40	--Particle board
3317	4410.1200	--定向刨花板	4					40	--Oriented standard board (OSB)
3318	4410.1900	--其他	4					40	--Other
		-其他:							-Other:
		---碎料板:							---Particle board :
3319	4410.9011	----麦稻秸秆制	7.5					40	----Particle board of wheat/rice straw
3320	4410.9019	----其他	7.5					40	----Other
3321	4410.9090	---其他	7.5					40	---Other
	44.11	**木纤维板或其他木质材料纤维板,不论是否用树脂或其他有机粘合剂粘合:**							**Fibreboard of wood or other ligneous materials, whether or not bonded with resins or other organic substances:**
		-中密度纤维板:							-Medium density fibreboard (MDF):
		--厚度不超过5毫米:							--Of a thickness not exceeding 5mm:
		---密度超过每立方厘米0.8克:							---Of a density exceeding 0.8 g/cm³:
3322	4411.1211	----未经机械加工或盖面的	4					40	----Not mechanically worked or surface covered
3323	4411.1219	----其他	7.5					40	----Other
		---密度超过每立方厘米0.5克,但未超过每立方厘米0.8克:							---Of a density exceeding 0.5 g/cm³ but not exceeding 0.8 g/cm³:
3324	4411.1221	----辐射松制的	4	0	新西兰NZ			40	----Of radiata pine
3325	4411.1229	----其他	4					40	----Other
		---其他:							---Other:
3326	4411.1291	----未经机械加工或盖面的	7.5					40	----Not mechanically worked or surface covered
3327	4411.1299	----其他	4					40	----Other

序号 No.	税则号列 Tariff Line	货品名称	最惠国税率 MFN(%)	协定税率 Agreement(%)		特惠税率 S.P.(%)	普通税率 Gen.(%)	Article Description
		--厚度超过5毫米但未超过9毫米:						--Of a thickness exceeding 5mm but not exceeding 9mm:
		---密度超过每立方厘米0.8克:						---Of a density exceeding 0.8g/cm³:
3328	4411.1311	----未经机械加工或盖面的	4				40	----Not mechanically worked or surface covered
3329	4411.1319	----其他	7.5				40	----Other
		---密度超过每立方厘米0.5克，但未超过每立方厘米0.8克:						---Of a density exceeding 0.5g/cm³ but not exceeding 0.8g/cm³:
3330	4411.1321	----辐射松制的	4	0	新西兰NZ		40	----Of radiata pine
3331	4411.1329	----其他	4				40	----Other
		---其他:						---Other:
3332	4411.1391	----未经机械加工或盖面的	7.5				40	----Not mechanically worked or surface covered
3333	4411.1399	----其他	4				40	----Other
		--厚度超过9毫米:						--Of a thickness exceeding 9mm:
		---密度超过每立方厘米0.8克:						---Of a density exceeding 0.8g/cm³:
3334	4411.1411	----未经机械加工或盖面的	4				40	----Not mechanically worked or surface covered
3335	4411.1419	----其他	7.5				40	----Other
		---密度超过每立方厘米0.5克，但未超过每立方厘米0.8克:						---Of a density exceeding 0.5g/cm³ but not exceeding 0.8g/cm³:
3336	4411.1421	----辐射松制的	4	0	新西兰NZ		40	----Of radiata pine
3337	4411.1429	----其他	4				40	----Other
		---其他:						---Other:
3338	4411.1491	----未经机械加工或盖面的	7.5				40	----Not mechanically worked or surface covered
3339	4411.1499	----其他	4				40	----Other
		-其他:						-Other:
		--密度超过每立方厘米0.8克:						--Of a density exceeding 0.8g/cm³:
3340	4411.9210	---未经机械加工或盖面的	4				40	---Not mechanically worked or surface covered
3341	4411.9290	---其他	7.5				40	---Other
		--密度超过每立方厘米0.5克，但未超过每立方厘米0.8克:						--Of a density exceeding 0.5g/cm³ but not exceeding 0.8g/cm³:
3342	4411.9310	---辐射松制的	4	0	新西兰NZ		40	---Of radiata pine
3343	4411.9390	---其他	4				40	---Other
		--密度未超过每立方厘米0.5克:						--Of a density not exceeding 0.5g/cm³:

序号 No.	税则号列 Tariff Line	货品名称	最惠国税率 MFN(%)	协定税率 Agreement(%)		特惠税率 S.P.(%)		普通税率 Gen.(%)	Article Description
3344	4411.9410	---密度超过每立方厘米0.35克，但未超过每立方厘米0.5克	7.5					40	---Of a density exceeding 0.35g/cm³ but not exceeding 0.5g/cm³
		---密度未超过每立方厘米0.35克:							---Of a density not exceeding 0.35g/cm³:
3345	4411.9421	----未经机械加工或盖面的	7.5					40	----Not mechanically worked or surface covered
3346	4411.9429	----其他	4					40	----Other
	44.12	**胶合板、单板饰面板及类似的多层板:**							**Plywood, veneered panels and similar laminated wood:**
		-竹制的:							-Of bamboo:
		---仅由薄板制的胶合板，每层厚度不超过6毫米:							---Plywood consisting solely of sheets, each ply not exceeding 6mm:
3347	4412.1011	----至少有一表层是本章子目注释二所列的热带木	12	0 2.4	智利CL,新西兰NZ,秘鲁PE 哥斯达黎加CR			30	----With at least one outer ply of tropical wood specified in Subheading Note 2 to this Chapter
3348	4412.1019	----其他	4					30	----Other
3349	4412.1020	---其他，至少有一表层是非针叶木	10	0 5	新西兰NZ,秘鲁PE,哥斯达黎加CR 巴基斯坦PK			30	---Other, with at least one outer ply of non-coniferous wood
		---其他:							---Other:
3350	4412.1091	----至少有一层是本章子目注释二所列的热带木	8					30	----With at least one ply of tropical wood specified in Subheading Note 2 to this Chapter
3351	4412.1092	----其他，至少含有一层木碎料板	10					30	----Other, containing at least one layer of particle board
3352	4412.1099	----其他	4	0	东盟ASEAN,智利CL,巴基斯坦PK,新加坡SG,新西兰NZ,秘鲁PE,哥斯达黎加CR	0	最不发达35国LDC35,最不发达4国LDC4	30	----Other
		-其他仅由薄木板制的胶合板（竹制除外），每层厚度不超过6毫米:							-Other plywood, consisting solely of sheets of wood (other than bamboo), each ply not exceeding 6mm thickness:
3353	4412.3100	--至少有一表层是本章子目注释二所列的热带木	12	0	智利CL,新西兰NZ,秘鲁PE,哥斯达黎加CR			30	--With at least one outer ply of tropical wood specified in Subheading Note 2 to this Chapter

序号 No.	税则号列 Tariff Line	货品名称	最惠国税率 MFN(%)	协定税率 Agreement(%)		特惠税率 S.P.(%)		普通税率 Gen.(%)	Article Description
		--其他，至少有一表层是非针叶木:							--Other, with at least one outer ply of nonconiferous wood:
3354	4412.3210	---至少有一表层是温带非针叶木	4					30	---Other, with at least one outer ply of temperate nonconiferous wood
3355	4412.3290	---其他	4					30	---Other
3356	4412.3900	--其他	4	0 0.4	东盟ASEAN,巴基斯坦PK,新加坡SG,新西兰NZ,秘鲁PE,哥斯达黎加CR 智利CL	0	最不发达35国LDC35,最不发达4国LDC4	30	--Other
		-其他:							-Other:
		--木块芯胶合板，侧板条芯胶合板及板条芯胶合板:							--Blockboard, laminboard and battenboard:
3357	4412.9410	---至少有一表层是非针叶木	10	5	巴基斯坦PK			30	---With at least one outer ply of nonconiferous wood
		---其他:							---Other:
3358	4412.9491	----至少有一层是本章子目注释二所列的热带木	8					30	----With at least one ply of tropical wood specified in Subheading Note 2 to this Chapter
3359	4412.9492	----其他,至少含有一层木碎料板	10					30	----Other, containing at least one layer of particle board
3360	4412.9499	----其他	4	0	东盟ASEAN,智利CL,巴基斯坦PK,新加坡SG,新西兰NZ,秘鲁PE,哥斯达黎加CR	0	最不发达35国LDC35,最不发达4国LDC4	30	----Other
		--其他:							--Other:
3361	4412.9910	---至少有一表层是非针叶木	10	5	巴基斯坦PK			30	---With at least one outer ply of nonconiferous wood
		---其他:							---Other:
3362	4412.9991	----至少有一层是本章子目注释二所列的热带木	8					30	----With at least one ply of tropical wood specified in Subheading Note 2 to this Chapter
3363	4412.9992	----其他,至少含有一层木碎料板	10					30	----Other, containing at least one layer of particle board
3364	4412.9999	----其他	4	0	东盟ASEAN,智利CL,巴基斯坦PK,新加坡SG,新西兰NZ,秘鲁PE,哥斯达黎加CR	0	最不发达35国LDC35	30	----Other

序号 No.	税则号列 Tariff Line	货品名称	最惠国税率 MFN(%)	协定税率 Agreement(%)		特惠税率 S.P.(%)		普通税率 Gen.(%)	Article Description
	44.13	**强化木，成块、板、条或异型的:**							**Densified wood, in blocks, plates, strips or profile shapes:**
3365	4413.0000	强化木，成块、板、条或异型的	6	0 0.6 5	东盟ASEAN,新加坡SG,新西兰NZ,秘鲁PE,哥斯达黎加CR 智利CL 巴基斯坦PK	0	最不发达35国LDC35,最不发达4国LDC4	20	Densified wood, in blocks, plates, strips or profile shapes
	44.14	**木制的画框、相框、镜框及类似品:**							**Wooden frames for paintings, photographs, mirrors or similar objects:**
		木制的画框、相框、镜框及类似品:							Wooden frames for paintings, photographs, mirrors or similar objects:
3366	4414.0010	---辐射松制的	20	0	新西兰NZ			100	---Of radiata pine
3367	4414.0090	---其他	20					100	---Other
	44.15	**包装木箱、木盒、板条箱、圆桶及类似的包装容器;木制电缆卷筒;木托板、箱形托盘及其他装载用木板;木制的托盘护框:**							**Packing cases, boxes, crates, drums and similar packings, of wood; cable-drums of wood; pallets, box pallets and other load boards, of wood; pallet collars of wood:**
3368	4415.1000	-箱、盒、板条箱、圆桶及类似的包装容器;电缆卷筒	7.5	0 0.8 5	东盟ASEAN,新加坡SG,新西兰NZ,秘鲁PE,哥斯达黎加CR 智利CL 巴基斯坦PK	0	最不发达35国LDC35,最不发达4国LDC4	80	-Cases, boxes, crates, drums and similar packing; cable-drums
		-木托板、箱形托盘及其他装载用木板;木制的托盘护框:							-Pallets, box pallets and other load boards; pallet collars:
3369	4415.2010	---辐射松制的	7.5	0	新西兰NZ			80	---Of radiata pine
3370	4415.2090	---其他	7.5					80	---Other
	44.16	**木制大桶、琵琶桶、盆和其他木制箍桶及其零件，包括桶板:**							**Casks, barrels, vats, tubs and other coopers' products and parts thereof, of wood, including staves:**
		木制大桶、琵琶桶、盆和其他木制箍桶及其零件，包括桶板:							Casks, barrels, vats, tubs and other coopers' products and parts thereof, of wood, including staves:
3371	4416.0010	---辐射松制的	16	0	新西兰NZ			80	---Of radiata pine
3372	4416.0090	---其他	16					80	---Other
	44.17	**木制的工具、工具支架、工具柄、扫帚及刷子的身及柄;木制鞋靴楦及楦头:**							**Tools, tool bodies, tool handles, broom or brush bodies and handles, of wood; boot or shoe lasts and trees, of wood:**

序号 No.	税则号列 Tariff Line	货品名称	最惠国税率 MFN(%)	协定税率 Agreement(%)		特惠税率 S.P.(%)		普通税率 Gen.(%)	Article Description
		木制的工具、工具支架、工具柄、扫帚及刷子的身及柄;木制鞋靴楦及楦头:							Tools, tool bodies, tool handles, broom or brush bodies and handles, of wood; boot or shoe lasts and trees, of wood:
3373	4417.0010	---辐射松制的	16	0	新西兰NZ			80	---Of radiata pine
3374	4417.0090	---其他	16					80	---Other
	44.18	**建筑用木工制品，包括蜂窝结构木镶板、已装拼的拼花地板、木瓦及盖屋板:**							**Builders' joinery and carpentry of wood, including cellular wood panels, assembled parquet panels, shingles and shakes:**
		-窗、法兰西式(落地)窗及其框架:							-Windows, French-windows and their frames:
3375	4418.1010	---辐射松制的	4	0	新西兰NZ			70	---Of radiata pine
3376	4418.1090	---其他	4	0	澳门MO			70	---Other
3377	4418.2000	-门及其框架和门槛	4	0 0.4	东盟ASEAN,巴基斯坦PK,新加坡SG,新西兰NZ,秘鲁PE,哥斯达黎加CR,澳门MO 智利CL	0	最不发达35国LDC35,最不发达4国LDC4	70	-Doors and their frames and thresholds
3378	4418.4000	-水泥构件的模板	4	0	东盟ASEAN,智利CL,巴基斯坦PK,新西兰NZ,秘鲁PE,哥斯达黎加CR	0	最不发达35国LDC35,最不发达4国LDC4	70	-Shuttering for concrete constructional work
3379	4418.5000	-木瓦及盖屋板	7.5	0 5	东盟ASEAN,智利CL,新西兰NZ,秘鲁PE,哥斯达黎加CR 巴基斯坦PK	0	最不发达35国LDC35,最不发达4国LDC4	70	-Shingles and shakes
3380	4418.6000	-柱和梁	4	0 0.4	东盟ASEAN,巴基斯坦PK,新加坡SG,新西兰NZ,秘鲁PE,哥斯达黎加CR 智利CL	0	最不发达35国LDC35,最不发达4国LDC4	70	-Posts and beams
		-已装拼的地板:							-Assembled flooring panels:
3381	4418.7100	--马赛克地板用	4	0 0.4	东盟ASEAN,巴基斯坦PK,新加坡SG,新西兰NZ,秘鲁PE,哥斯达黎加CR 智利CL	0	最不发达35国LDC35,最不发达4国LDC4	70	--For mosaic floors
		--其他，多层的:							--Other, multilayer:
3382	4418.7210	---竹制	4	0 0.4	东盟ASEAN,巴基斯坦PK,新加坡SG,新西兰NZ,秘鲁PE,哥斯达黎加CR 智利CL	0	最不发达35国LDC35	70	---Of Bamboos

序号 No.	税则号列 Tariff Line	货品名称	最惠国税率 MFN(%)	协定税率 Agreement(%)		特惠税率 S.P.(%)		普通税率 Gen.(%)	Article Description
3383	4418.7290	---其他	4	0 0.4	东盟ASEAN,巴基斯坦PK,新加坡SG,新西兰NZ,秘鲁PE,哥斯达黎加CR 智利CL	0	最不发达35国LDC35	70	---Other
		--其他:							--Other:
3384	4418.7910	---竹制	4	0 0.4	东盟ASEAN,巴基斯坦PK,新加坡SG,新西兰NZ,秘鲁PE,哥斯达黎加CR 智利CL	0	最不发达35国LDC35	70	---Of Bamboos
3385	4418.7990	---其他	4	0 0.4	东盟ASEAN,巴基斯坦PK,新加坡SG,新西兰NZ,秘鲁PE,哥斯达黎加CR 智利CL	0	最不发达35国LDC35	70	---Other
		-其他:							-Other:
3386	4418.9010	---竹制	4	0 0.4	东盟ASEAN,巴基斯坦PK,新加坡SG,新西兰NZ,秘鲁PE,哥斯达黎加CR 智利CL	0	最不发达35国LDC35,最不发达4国LDC4	70	---Of bamboo
3387	4418.9090	---其他	4	0 0.4	东盟ASEAN,巴基斯坦PK,新加坡SG,新西兰NZ,秘鲁PE,哥斯达黎加CR 智利CL	0	最不发达35国LDC35,最不发达4国LDC4	70	---Other
	44.19	**木制餐具及厨房用具:**							**Tableware and kitchenware, of wood:**
		木制餐具及厨房用具:							Tableware and kitchenware, of wood:
		---一次性筷子:							---One-time chopsticks:
3388	4419.0031	----木制	0			0	最不发达35国LDC35,最不发达4国LDC4	100	----of wood
3389	4419.0032	----竹制	0			0	最不发达35国LDC35,最不发达4国LDC4	100	----of bamboos
		---其他:							---Other:
3390	4419.0091	----竹制	0			0	最不发达35国LDC35,最不发达4国LDC4	100	----Of Bamboos

序号 No.	税则号列 Tariff Line	货品名称	最惠国税率 MFN(%)	协定税率 Agreement(%)	特惠税率 S.P.(%)	普通税率 Gen.(%)	Article Description
3391	4419.0099	----其他	0		0 最不发达35国 LDC35, 最不发达4国 LDC4	100	----Other
	44.20	**镶嵌木（包括细工镶嵌木）；装珠宝或刀具用的木制盒子和小匣子及类似品；木制小雕像及其他装饰品；第九十四章以外的木制家具：**					**Wood marquetry and inlaid wood; caskets and cases for jewellery or cutlery, and similar articles, of wood; statuettes and other ornaments, of wood; wooden articles or furniture not falling in Chapter 94:**
		-木制小雕像及其他装饰品:					-Statuettes and other ornaments, of wood:
		---木刻及竹刻:					---Wood or bamboo carvings:
3392	4420.1011	----木刻	0		0 最不发达35国 LDC35, 最不发达4国 LDC4	100	----Wood carvings
3393	4420.1012	----竹刻	0		0 最不发达35国 LDC35, 最不发达4国 LDC4	100	----Bamboo carvings
3394	4420.1020	---木扇	0		0 最不发达35国 LDC35, 最不发达4国 LDC4	100	---Wooden fans
3395	4420.1090	---其他	0		0 最不发达35国 LDC35, 最不发达4国 LDC4	100	---Other
		-其他:					-Other:
3396	4420.9010	---镶嵌木	0		0 最不发达35国 LDC35, 最不发达4国 LDC4	45	---Wood marquetry and inlaid wood

序号 No.	税则号列 Tariff Line	货品名称	最惠国税率 MFN(%)	协定税率 Agreement(%)	特惠税率 S.P.(%)	普通税率 Gen.(%)	Article Description
3397	4420.9090	---其他	0		0 最不发达35国LDC35,最不发达4国LDC4	100	---Other
	44.21	**其他木制品:**					**Other articles of wood:**
3398	4421.1000	-衣架	0		0 最不发达35国LDC35,最不发达4国LDC4	90	-Clothes hangers
		-其他:					-Other:
3399	4421.9010	---卷轴、纡子、筒管、缝纫用线轴及类似品	0		0 最不发达35国LDC35,最不发达4国LDC4	35	---Spools, cops, bobbins, sewing thread reels and the like
		---圆签、圆棒、冰果棒、压舌片及类似一次性制品:					---Round picks and sticks, sticks for ice-sucker, spatulas and similar one time articles:
3400	4421.9021	----木制	0		0 最不发达35国LDC35,最不发达4国LDC4	35	----Of wood
3401	4421.9022	----竹制	0		0 最不发达35国LDC35,最不发达4国LDC4	35	----Of bamboos
3402	4421.9090	---其他	0		0 最不发达35国LDC35,最不发达4国LDC4	90	---Other

第四十五章
软木及软木制品

Chapter 45
Cork and articles of cork

注释:

本章不包括:

一、第六十四章的鞋靴及其零件;

二、第六十五章的帽类及其零件;

三、第九十五章的物品(例如,玩具、游戏品及运动用品)。

Notes:

This Chapter does not cover:

(a) Footwear or parts of footwear of Chapter 64;

(b) Headgear or parts of headgear of Chapter 65; or

(c) Articles of Chapter 95 (or example, toys, games, sports requisites).

序号 No.	税则号列 Tariff Line	货品名称	最惠国 税 率 MFN(%)	协定税率 Agreement(%)	特惠税率 S.P.(%)	普通 税率 Gen.(%)	Article Description
	45.01	**未加工或简单加工的天然软木;软木废料;碎的、粒状的或粉状的软木:**					**Natural cork, raw or simply prepared; waste cork; crushed, granulated or ground cork:**
3403	4501.1000	-未加工或简单加工的天然软木	6 △1	0 东盟ASEAN,智利CL,新西兰NZ,秘鲁PE,哥斯达黎加CR 5 巴基斯坦PK	0 最不发达35国LDC35	17	-Natural cork, raw or simply prepared
		-其他:					-Other:
3404	4501.9010	---软木废料	0		0 最不发达35国LDC35,最不发达4国LDC4	17	---waste cork
3405	4501.9020	---碎的、粉粒状的或粉状的软木(软木碎、软木粒或软木粉)	0		0 最不发达35国LDC35,最不发达4国LDC4	17	---Crushed, granulated or ground cork
	45.02	**天然软木,除去表皮或粗切成方形,或成长方块、正方块、板、片或条状(包括作塞子用的方块坯料):**					**Natural cork, debarked or roughly squared, or in rectangular (including square) blocks, plates, sheets or strip (including sharp-edged blanks for corks or stoppers):**
3406	4502.0000	天然软木,除去表皮或粗切成方形,或成长方块、正方块、板、片或条状(包括作塞子用的方块坯料)	8	0 东盟ASEAN,智利CL,新西兰NZ,秘鲁PE,哥斯达黎加CR 5 巴基斯坦PK	0 最不发达35国LDC35,最不发达4国LDC4	30	Natural cork, debarked or roughly squared, or in rectangular (including square) blocks, plates, sheets or strip (including sharp-edged blanks for corks or stoppers)
	45.03	**天然软木制品:**					**Articles of natural cork:**

序号 No.	税则号列 Tariff Line	货品名称	最惠国税率 MFN(%)	协定税率 Agreement(%)		特惠税率 S.P.(%)		普通税率 Gen.(%)	Article Description
3407	4503.1000	-塞子	8	0 0.8 5	东盟ASEAN,新西兰NZ,秘鲁PE,哥斯达黎加CR 智利CL 巴基斯坦PK	0	最不发达35国LDC35,最不发达4国LDC4	50	-Corks and stoppers
3408	4503.9000	-其他	10.5	0 2.1 5	东盟ASEAN,智利CL,新加坡SG,新西兰NZ,秘鲁PE 哥斯达黎加CR 巴基斯坦PK	0	最不发达35国LDC35,最不发达4国LDC4	50	-Other
	45.04	**压制软木（不论是否使用粘合剂压成）及其制品:**							**Agglomerated cork (with or without a binding substance) and articles of agglomerated cork:**
3409	4504.1000	-块、板、片及条;任何形状的砖、瓦;实心圆柱体，包括圆片	8.4	0 5	东盟ASEAN,智利CL,新西兰NZ,秘鲁PE,哥斯达黎加CR 巴基斯坦PK	0	最不发达35国LDC35,最不发达4国LDC4	30	-Blocks, plates, sheets and strip; tiles of any shape; solid cylinders, including discs
3410	4504.9000	-其他	0			0	最不发达35国LDC35,最不发达4国LDC4	50	-Other

第四十六章
稻草、秸秆、针茅或其他编结材料制品；篮筐及柳条编结品

Chapter 46
Manufactures of straw，of esparto or of other plaiting materials; basketware and wickerwork

注释:

一、本章所称"编结材料"，是指其状态或形状适于编结、交织或类似加工的材料，包括稻草、秸秆、柳条、竹、藤、灯芯草、芦苇、木片条、其他植物材料扁条（例如，树皮条、狭叶、酒椰叶纤维或其他从阔叶获取的条）、未纺的天然纺织纤维、塑料单丝及扁条、纸带，但不包括皮革、再生皮革、毡呢或无纺织物的扁条、人发、马毛、纺织粗纱或纱线以及第五十四章的单丝和扁条。

二、本章不包括:

（一）税号48.14的壁纸;

（二）不论是否编结而成的线、绳、索、缆（税号56.07）;

（三）第六十四章和第六十五章的鞋靴、帽类及其零件;

（四）编结而成的车辆或车身（第八十七章）;

（五）第九十四章的物品（例如，家具、灯具及照明装置）。

三、税号46.01所称"平行连结的成片编结材料、缏条或类似的编结材料产品"，是指编结材料、缏条及类似的编结材料产品平行排列连结成片的制品，其连结材料不论是否为纺制的纺织材料。

Notes:

1. In this Chapter the expression "plaiting materials" means materials in a state or form suitable for plaiting, interlacing or similar processes; it includes straw，osier or willow，bamboos，rattans，rushes，reeds，strips of wood，strips of other vegetable material (for example，strips of bark，narrow leaves and raffia or other strips obtained from broad leaves)，unspun natural textile fibres，monofilament and strip and the like of plastics and strips of paper，but not strips of leather or composition leather or of felt or nonwovens，human hair，horsehair，textile rovings or yarns，or monofilament and strip and the like of Chapter 54.

2.This Chapter does not cover:

(a) Wall coverings of heading No.48.14;

(b) Twine，cordage，ropes or cables，plaited or not (heading No.56.07);

(c) Footwear or headgear or parts thereof of Chapter 64 or 65;

(d)Vehicles or bodies for vehicles of basketware (Chapter 87); or

(e) Articles of Chapter 94 (for example，furniture，lamps and lighting fittings).

3. For the purposes of heading No.46.01，the expression "plaiting materials，plaits and similar products of plaiting materials，bound together in parallel strands" means plaiting materials，plaits and similar products of plaiting materials，placed side by side and bound together，in the form of sheets，whether or not the binding materials are to spun textile materials.

序号 No.	税则号列 Tariff Line	货品名称	最惠国税率 MFN(%)	协定税率 Agreement(%)		特惠税率 S.P.(%)		普通税率 Gen.(%)	Article Description
	46.01	**用编结材料编成的缏条及类似产品，不论是否缝合成宽条；平行连结或编结的成片材料、缏条或类似的编结材料产品，不论是否制成品（例如，席子、席料、帘子）：**							**Plaits and similar products of plaiting materials, whether or not assembled into strips; plaiting materials, plaits and similar products of plaiting materials, bound together in parallel strands or woven, in sheet form, whether or not being finished articles (for example, mats, matting, screens):**
		-植物材料制的席子、席料及帘子:							-Mats, matting and screens of vegetable materials:
3411	4601.2100	--竹制的	9	0 5	东盟ASEAN,智利CL,新西兰NZ,秘鲁PE,哥斯达黎加CR,澳门MO 巴基斯坦PK	0	最不发达35国LDC35,最不发达4国LDC4,老挝LA	90	--Of bamboo
3412	4601.2200	--藤制的	9	0 5	东盟ASEAN,智利CL,新西兰NZ,秘鲁PE,哥斯达黎加CR,澳门MO 巴基斯坦PK	0	最不发达35国LDC35,最不发达4国LDC4,老挝LA	100	--Of rattan
		--其他:							--Other:
		---草制的:							---Of grass or straw:
3413	4601.2911	----灯心草属材料制的	9	0 5	东盟ASEAN,智利CL,新西兰NZ,秘鲁PE,哥斯达黎加CR,澳门MO 巴基斯坦PK	0	最不发达35国LDC35,最不发达4国LDC4,老挝LA	90	----Of rush
3414	4601.2919	----其他	9	0 5	东盟ASEAN,智利CL,新西兰NZ,秘鲁PE,哥斯达黎加CR 巴基斯坦PK	0	最不发达35国LDC35,最不发达4国LDC4,老挝LA	90	----Other
		---芦苇制的:							---Of reed:
3415	4601.2921	----苇帘	9	0 5	东盟ASEAN,智利CL,新西兰NZ,秘鲁PE,哥斯达黎加CR 巴基斯坦PK	0	最不发达35国LDC35,最不发达4国LDC4,老挝LA	90	----Screens of reed

序号 No.	税则号列 Tariff Line	货品名称	最惠国税率 MFN(%)	协定税率 Agreement(%)		特惠税率 S.P.(%)		普通税率 Gen.(%)	Article Description
3416	4601.2929	----其他	9	0 5	东盟ASEAN,智利CL,新西兰NZ,秘鲁PE,哥斯达黎加CR 巴基斯坦PK	0	最不发达35国LDC35,最不发达4国LDC4,老挝LA	90	----Other
3417	4601.2990	---其他	9	0 5	东盟ASEAN,智利CL,新西兰NZ,秘鲁PE,哥斯达黎加CR 巴基斯坦PK	0	最不发达35国LDC35,最不发达4国LDC4,老挝LA	90	---Other
		-其他: --竹制的:							-Other: --Of bamboo:
3418	4601.9210	---鞭条及类似产品，不论是否缝合成宽条	9	0 5	东盟ASEAN,智利CL,新西兰NZ,秘鲁PE,哥斯达黎加CR,澳门MO 巴基斯坦PK	0	最不发达35国LDC35,最不发达4国LDC4,老挝LA	100	---Plaits and similar products of plaiting materials, whether or not assembled into strips
3419	4601.9290	---其他	9	0 5	东盟ASEAN,智利CL,新西兰NZ,秘鲁PE,哥斯达黎加CR,澳门MO 巴基斯坦PK	0	最不发达35国LDC35,最不发达4国LDC4	90	---Other
		--藤制的:							--Of rattan:
3420	4601.9310	---鞭条及类似产品，不论是否缝合成宽条	9	0 5	东盟ASEAN,智利CL,新西兰NZ,秘鲁PE,哥斯达黎加CR,澳门MO 巴基斯坦PK	0	最不发达35国LDC35,最不发达4国LDC4,老挝LA	100	---Plaits and similar products of plaiting materials, whether or not assembled into strips
3421	4601.9390	---其他	9	0 5	东盟ASEAN,智利CL,新西兰NZ,哥斯达黎加CR,澳门MO 巴基斯坦PK			90	---Other
		--其他植物材料制:							--Of other vegetable materials:
		---稻草制的:							---Of straw:
3422	4601.9411	----缏条（绳）	10	0 5	东盟ASEAN,智利CL,新西兰NZ,秘鲁PE,哥斯达黎加CR 巴基斯坦PK	0	最不发达35国LDC35	90	----Plaits
3423	4601.9419	----其他	10	0 5	东盟ASEAN,智利CL,新西兰NZ,秘鲁PE,哥斯达黎加CR 巴基斯坦PK	0	最不发达35国LDC35	90	----Other
		---其他:							---Other:

序号 No.	税则号列 Tariff Line	货品名称	最惠国税率 MFN(%)	协定税率 Agreement(%)		特惠税率 S.P.(%)		普通税率 Gen.(%)	Article Description
3424	4601.9491	----鞭条及类似产品，不论是否缝合成宽条	9	0 5	东盟ASEAN,智利CL,新西兰NZ,秘鲁PE,哥斯达黎加CR 巴基斯坦PK	0	最不发达35国LDC35,最不发达4国LDC4,老挝LA	100	----Plaits and similar products of plaiting materials, whether or not assembled into strips
3425	4601.9499	----其他	9	0 5	东盟ASEAN,智利CL,新西兰NZ,秘鲁PE,哥斯达黎加CR 巴基斯坦PK	0	最不发达35国LDC35,最不发达4国LDC4	90	----Other
		--其他:							--Other:
3426	4601.9910	---鞭条及类似产品，不论是否缝合成宽条	9	0 5	东盟ASEAN,智利CL,新西兰NZ,秘鲁PE,哥斯达黎加CR 巴基斯坦PK	0	最不发达35国LDC35,最不发达4国LDC4,老挝LA	90	---Plaits and similar products of plaiting materials, whether or not assembled into strips
3427	4601.9990	---其他	9	0 5	东盟ASEAN,智利CL,新西兰NZ,秘鲁PE,哥斯达黎加CR 巴基斯坦PK	0	最不发达35国LDC35	90	---Other
	46.02	**用编结材料直接编成或用税号46.01所列货品制成的篮筐、柳条编结品及其他制品;丝瓜络制品:**							**Basketwork, wicker-work and other articles, made directly to shape from plaiting materials or made up from goods of heading No.46.01; articles of loofah:**
		-植物材料制:							-Of vegetable materials:
3428	4602.1100	--竹制的	9	0 5	东盟ASEAN,智利CL,新西兰NZ,秘鲁PE,哥斯达黎加CR 巴基斯坦PK	0	最不发达35国LDC35,最不发达4国LDC4,柬埔寨KH	100	--Of bamboo
3429	4602.1200	--藤制的	9	0 5	东盟ASEAN,智利CL,新西兰NZ,哥斯达黎加CR 巴基斯坦PK	0	最不发达35国LDC35,最不发达4国LDC4,柬埔寨KH	100	--Of rattan
		--其他:							--Other:
3430	4602.1910	---草制的	9	0 5	东盟ASEAN,智利CL,新西兰NZ,秘鲁PE,哥斯达黎加CR 巴基斯坦PK	0	最不发达35国LDC35,最不发达4国LDC4,柬埔寨KH	100	---Of grass or straw

序号 No.	税则号列 Tariff Line	货品名称	最惠国税率 MFN(%)	协定税率 Agreement(%)		特惠税率 S.P.(%)		普通税率 Gen.(%)	Article Description
3431	4602.1920	---玉米皮制的	9	0 5	东盟ASEAN,智利CL,新西兰NZ,秘鲁PE,哥斯达黎加CR 巴基斯坦PK	0	最不发达35国LDC35,最不发达4国LDC4,柬埔寨KH	100	---Of maize-shuck
3432	4602.1930	---柳条制的	9	0 5	东盟ASEAN,智利CL,新西兰NZ,秘鲁PE,哥斯达黎加CR 巴基斯坦PK	0	最不发达35国LDC35,最不发达4国LDC4,柬埔寨KH	100	---Of osier
3433	4602.1990	---其他	9	0 5	东盟ASEAN,智利CL,新西兰NZ,哥斯达黎加CR 巴基斯坦PK	0	最不发达35国LDC35,最不发达4国LDC4,柬埔寨KH	100	---Other
3434	4602.9000	-其他	9	0 5 8	东盟ASEAN,智利CL,新西兰NZ,秘鲁PE,哥斯达黎加CR,澳门MO 巴基斯坦PK 亚太APTA	0	最不发达35国LDC35,最不发达4国LDC4,柬埔寨KH	100	-Other

第十类

SECTION X

木浆及其他纤维状纤维素浆、回收（废碎）纸或纸板；纸、纸板及其制品

PULP OF WOOD OR OF OTHER FIBROUS CELLULOSIC MATERIAL; ERCOVERED（WASTE AND SCRAP）PAPER OR PAPERBOARD; PAPER AND PAPERBOARD AND ARTICLES THEREOF

第四十七章
木浆及其他纤维状纤维素浆；回收（废碎）纸或纸板

Chapter 47
Pulp of wood or of other fibrous cellulosic material; recovered (waste and scrap) paper or paperboard

注释：

税号47.02所称"化学木浆，溶解级"，是指温度在20℃时浸入含18%氢氧化钠的苛性碱溶液内，一小时后，按重量计含有92%及以上的不溶级分的碱木浆或硫酸盐木浆，或者含有88%及以上的不溶级分的亚硫酸盐木浆。对于亚硫酸盐木浆，按重量计灰分含量不得超过0.15%。

Notes:

For the purposes of heading No. 47.02, the expression "chemical wood pulp, dissolving grades" means chemical wood pulp having by weight an insoluble fraction of 92% or more for soda or sulphate wood pulp of 88% or more for sulphite wood pulp after one hour in a caustic soda solution containing 18% sodium bydroxide (NaOH) at 20℃, and for sulphite wood pulp an ash content that does not exceed 0.15% by weight.

序号 No.	税则号列 Tariff Line	货品名称	最惠国税率 MFN(%)	协定税率 Agreement(%)	特惠税率 S.P.(%)	普通税率 Gen.(%)	Article Description
	47.01	**机械木浆:**					**Mechanical wood pulp:**
3435	4701.0000	机械木浆	0		0 最不发达35国 LDC35, 最不发达4国 LDC4	8	Mechanical wood pulp
	47.02	**化学木浆，溶解级:**					**Chemical wood pulp, dissolving grades:**
3436	4702.0000	化学木浆，溶解级	0		0 最不发达35国 LDC35, 最不发达4国 LDC4	8	Chemical wood pulp, dissolving grades
	47.03	**碱木浆或硫酸盐木浆，但溶解级的除外:**					**Chemical wood pulp, soda or sulphate, other than dissolving grades:**
		-未漂白:					-Unbleached:
3437	4703.1100	--针叶木的	0		0 最不发达35国 LDC35, 最不发达4国 LDC4	8	--Coniferous

序号 No.	税则号列 Tariff Line	货品名称	最惠国税率 MFN(%)	协定税率 Agreement(%)	特惠税率 S.P.(%)	普通税率 Gen.(%)	Article Description
3438	4703.1900	--非针叶木的	0		0 最不发达35国LDC35, 最不发达4国LDC4	8	--Non-coniferous
		-半漂白或漂白:					-Semi-bleached or bleached:
3439	4703.2100	--针叶木的	0		0 最不发达35国LDC35, 最不发达4国LDC4	8	--Coniferous
3440	4703.2900	--非针叶木的	0		0 最不发达35国LDC35, 最不发达4国LDC4	8	--Non-coniferous
	47.04	**亚硫酸盐木浆，但溶解级的除外:**					**Chemical wood pulp, sulphite, other than dissolving grades:**
		-未漂白:					-Unbleached:
3441	4704.1100	--针叶木的	0		0 最不发达35国LDC35, 最不发达4国LDC4	8	--Coniferous
3442	4704.1900	--非针叶木的	0		0 最不发达35国LDC35, 最不发达4国LDC4	8	--Non-coniferous
		-半漂白或漂白:					-Semi-bleached or bleached:
3443	4704.2100	--针叶木的	0		0 最不发达35国LDC35, 最不发达4国LDC4	8	--Coniferous
3444	4704.2900	--非针叶木的	0		0 最不发达35国LDC35, 最不发达4国LDC4	8	--Non-coniferous
	47.05	**用机械与化学联合制浆法制得的木浆:**					**Wood pulp obtained by a combination of mechanical and chemical pulping processes:**

序号 No.	税则号列 Tariff Line	货品名称	最惠国税率 MFN(%)	协定税率 Agreement(%)	特惠税率 S.P.(%)	普通税率 Gen.(%)	Article Description
3445	4705.0000	用机械与化学联合制浆法制得的木浆	0		0 最不发达35国LDC35,最不发达4国LDC4	8	Wood pulp obtained by a combination of mechanical and chemical pulping processes
	47.06	**从回收（废碎）纸或纸板提取的纤维浆或其他纤维状纤维素浆:**					**Pulps of fibres derived from recovered (waste and scrap) paper or paper-board or of other fibrous cellulosic material:**
3446	4706.1000	-棉短绒纸浆	0		0 最不发达35国LDC35,最不发达4国LDC4	8	-Cotton linters pulp
3447	4706.2000	-从回收（废碎）纸或纸板提取的纤维浆	0		0 最不发达35国LDC35,最不发达4国LDC4	8	-Pulps of fibres derived from recovered (waste and scrap) paper or paperboard
3448	4706.3000	-其他，竹浆	0		0 最不发达35国LDC35,最不发达4国LDC4	8	-Other, of bamboo
		-其他:					-Other:
3449	4706.9100	--机械浆	0		0 最不发达35国LDC35,最不发达4国LDC4	8	--Mechanical
3450	4706.9200	--化学浆	0		0 最不发达35国LDC35,最不发达4国LDC4	8	--Chemical
3451	4706.9300	--用机械和化学联合法制得的浆	0		0 最不发达35国LDC35,最不发达4国LDC4	8	--Obtained by a combination of mechanical and chemical processes
	47.07	**回收（废碎）纸或纸板:**					**Recovered (waste and scrap) paper or paper-board:**

序号 No.	税则号列 Tariff Line	货品名称	最惠国税率 MFN(%)	协定税率 Agreement(%)	特惠税率 S.P.(%)	普通税率 Gen.(%)	Article Description
3452	4707.1000	-未漂白的牛皮纸或纸板及瓦楞纸或纸板	0		0 最不发达35国LDC35,最不发达4国LDC4	8	-Unbleached kraft paper or paperboard or of corrugated paper or paperboard
3453	4707.2000	-主要由漂白化学木浆制成未经本体染色的其他纸和纸板	0		0 最不发达35国LDC35,最不发达4国LDC4	8	-Other paper or paperboard made mainly of bleached chemical pulp, not coloured in the mass
3454	4707.3000	-主要由机械浆制成的纸或纸板（例如，报纸、杂志及类似印刷品）	0		0 最不发达35国LDC35,最不发达4国LDC4	8	-Paper or paperboard made mainly of mechanical pulp (for example, news-papers, journals and similar printed matter)
3455	4707.9000	-其他，包括未分选的废碎品	0		0 最不发达35国LDC35,最不发达4国LDC4	8	-Other, including unsorted waste and scrap

第四十八章
纸及纸板；纸浆、纸或纸板制品

注释:

一、除条文另有规定的以外，本章所称“纸”包括“纸板”（不论其厚度或每平方米重量如何）。

二、本章不包括:

（一）第三十章的物品;

（二）税号32.12的压印箔;

（三）香纸及用化妆品浸渍或涂布的纸（第三十三章）;

（四）用肥皂或洗涤剂浸渍、覆盖或涂布的纸或纤维素絮纸（税号34.01）和用光洁剂、擦光膏及类似制剂浸渍、覆盖或涂布的纸或纤维素絮纸（税号34.05）;

（五）税号37.01至37.04的感光纸或感光纸板;

（六）用诊断或实验用试剂浸渍的纸（税号38.22）;

（七）第三十九章的用纸强化的层压塑料板，用塑料覆盖或涂布的单层纸或纸板（塑料部分占总厚度的一半以上），以及上述材料的制品，但税号48.14的壁纸除外;

（八）税号42.02的物品（例如旅行用品）;

（九）第四十六章的物品（编结材料制品）;

（十）纸纱线或纸纱线纺织物（第十一类）;

（十一）第六十四章或第六十五章的物品;

（十二）税号68.05的砂纸或税号68.14的用纸或纸板衬底的云母（但涂布云母粉的纸及纸板归入本章）;

（十三）用纸或纸板衬底的金属箔（通常为第十四类或第十五类）;

（十四）税号92.09的制品;

（十五）第九十五章的物品（例如，玩具、游戏品及运动用品）；或

（十六）第九十六章的物品（例如，钮扣，卫生巾（护垫）及止血塞、婴儿尿布及尿

Chapter 48
Paper and paperboard; articles of paper pulp, of paper or of paperboard

Notes:

1. For the purposes of this Chapter, except where the context Otherwise requires, a reference to “paper” includes references to paperboard (irrespective of thickness or weight per m^2).

2. This Chapter does not cover:

(a) Articles of Chapter 30;

(b) Stamping foils of heading No. 32.12;

(c) Perfumed papers or papers impregnated or coated with cosmetics (Chapter 33);

(d) Paper or cellulose wadding impregnated, coated or covered with soap or detergent (heading No.34.01), or with polishes, creams or similar preparations (heading No.34.05);

(e) Sensitized paper or paperboard of headings Nos.37.01 to 37.04;

(f) Paper impregnated with diagnostic or laboratory reagents (heading No.38.22);

(g) Paper-reinforced stratified sheeting of plastics, or one layer of paper or paperboard coated or covered with a layer of plastics, the latter constituting more than half the total thickness, or articles of such materials, other than wall coverings of heading No.48.14 (Chapter 39);

(h) Articles of heading No.42.02 (for example, travel goods);

(i) Articles of Chapter 46 (manufactures of plaiting material);

(j) Paper yarn or textile articles of paper yarn (Section XI);

(k) Articles of Chapter 64 or Chapter 65;

(l) Abrasive paper or paperboard (heading No. 68.05) or paper-or paperboard-backed mica (heading No.68.14) (paper and paperboard coated with mica powder are, however, to be classified in this Chapter);

(m) Metal foil backed with paper or paperboard (generally Section XIV on XV);

(n) Articles of heading No.92.09;

(o) Articles of Chapter 95 (for example, toys, games, sports requisites) ; or

(p) Articles of Chapter 96 (for example, buttons, sanitary towels (pads) and tampons, napkins (diapers) and napkin

布衬里）。

liners for babies).

三、除注释七另有规定的以外，税号48.01至48.05包括经研光、高度研光、釉光或类似处理、仿水印、表面施胶的纸及纸板；同时还包括用各种方法本体着色或染成斑纹的纸、纸板、纤维素絮纸及纤维素纤维网纸。除税号48.03另有规定的以外，上述税号不适用于经过其他方法加工的纸、纸板、纤维素絮纸或纤维素纤维网纸。

3. Subject to the provisions of Note 7, headings Nos. 48.01 to 48.05 include paper and paperboard which have been subjected to calendering, super-calendering, glazing or similar finishing, false watermarking or surface sizing, and also paper, paperboard, cellulose wadding and webs of cellulose fibres, coloured or marbled throughout the mass by any method. Except where heading No. 48.03 otherwise requires, these headings do not apply to paper, paperboard, cellulose wadding or webs of cellulose fibres which have been otherwise processed.

四、本章所称“新闻纸”，是指所含用机械或化学—机械方法制得的木纤维不少于全部纤维重量的50%的未经涂布的报刊用纸，未施胶或微施胶，每面的粗糙度[帕克印刷面粗糙度（1兆帕）]超过2.5微米，每平方米重量不小于40克，但不超过65克。

4. In this Chapter the expression “newsprint” means uncoated paper of a kind used for the printing of newspapers, of which not less than 50% by weight of the total fibre content consists of wood fibres obtained by a mechanical or chemi-mechanical process, unsized or very lightly sized, having a surface roughness Parker Print Surf (1 Mpa) on each side exceeding 2.5 micrometres (microns), weighing not less than $40g/m^2$ and not more than $65g/m^2$.

五、税目48.02所称“书写、印刷或类似用途的纸及纸板”及“未打孔的穿孔卡片纸及穿孔纸带纸”，是指主要用漂白纸浆或用机械或化学—机械方法制得的纸浆制成的纸及纸板，并且符合下列任一标准：

5. For the purposes of heading 48.02, the expressions “paper and paperboard, of a kind used for writing, printing or other graphic purposes” and “non perforated punch-cards and punch tape paper” mean paper and paperboard made mainly from bleached pulp or from pulp obtained by a mechanical or chemi-mechanical process and satisfying any of the following criteria:

每平方米重量不超过150克的纸或纸板：

（一）用机械或化学—机械方法制得的纤维含量在10%及以上，并且
1. 每平方米重量不超过80克；或
2. 本体着色；

（二）灰分含量在8%以上，并且
1. 每平方米重量不超过80克；或
2. 本体着色；

（三）灰分含量在3%以上，亮度在60%及以上；

（四）灰分含量在3%以上，但不超过8%，亮度低于60%，耐破指数等于或小于2.5千帕斯卡·平方米/克；

（五）灰分含量在3%及以下，亮度在60%及以上，耐破指数等于或小于2.5千帕斯卡·平方米/克。

For paper or paperboard weighing not more than $150g/m^2$:

(a) containing 10% or more of fibres obtained by a mechanical or chemi-mechanical process, and
(1) weighing not more than $80g/m^2$, or
(2) coloured throughout the mass; or

(b) containing more than 8% ash, and
(1) weighing not more than $80g/m^2$, or
(2) coloured throughout the mass; or

(c) containing more than 3% ash and having a brightness of 60% or more; or

(d) containing more than 3% but not more than 8% ash, having a brightness less than 60%, and a burst index equal to or less than $2.5kPa/m^2/g$; or

(e) containing 3% ash or less, having a brightness of 60% or more and a burst index equal to or less than $2.5kPa \cdot m^2/g$.

每平方米重量超过150克的纸或纸板：

For paper or paperboard weighing more than $150g/m^2$:

（一）本体着色；或

（二）亮度在60%及以上，并且

1. 厚度在225微米及以下；或

2. 厚度在225微米以上，但不超过508微米，灰分含量在3%以上；

（三）亮度低于60%，厚度不超过254微米，灰分含量在8%以上。

税目48.02不包括滤纸及纸板（含茶袋纸）或毡纸及纸板。

(a) coloured throughout the mass; or

(b) having a brightness of 60% or more, and

①a caliper of 225 micrometres (microns) or less, or

②a caliper more than 225 micrometres (microns) but not more than 508 micrometres (microns) and an ash content more than 3%; or

(c) having a brightness of less than 60% a caliper of 254 micrometres (microns) or less and an ash content more than 8%.

Heading No. 48.02 does not, however, cover filter paper and paperboard (including tea-bag paper) or felt paper or paperboard.

六、本章所称"牛皮纸及纸板"，是指所含用硫酸盐法或烧碱法制得的纤维不少于全部纤维重量的80%的纸及纸板。

6. In this Chapter "kraft paper and paperboard" means paper and paperhoard of which not less than 80% by weight of the total fibre content consists of fibres obtained by the chemical sulphate or soda processes.

七、除税目条文另有规定的以外，符合税目48.01至48.11中两个或两个以上税号所规定的纸、纸板、纤维素絮纸及纤维素纤维网纸，应按号列顺序归入有关税号中的最末一个税号。

7. Except where the terms of the headings otherwise require, paper, paperboard, cellulose wadding and webs of cellulose fibres answering to a description in two or more of the headings Nos. 48.01 to 48.11 are to be classified under that one of such headings which occurs last in numerical order in the Nomenclature.

八、税号48.01及48.03至48.09仅适用于下列规格的纸、纸板、纤维素絮纸及纤维素纤维网纸：

（一）成条或成卷，宽度超过36厘米；

（二）成张矩形（包括正方形），一边超过36厘米，另一边超过15厘米（以未折叠计）。

8. Headings Nos. 48.01 and 48.03 to 48.09 apply only to paper, paperboard, cellulose wadding and webs of cellulose fibres:

(a) in strips or rolls of width exceeding 36cm; or

(b) in rectangular (including square) sheets with one side exceeding 36cm and the other side exceeding 15cm in the unfolded state.

九、税号48.14所称"壁纸及类似品"，仅限于：

（一）适合作墙壁或天花板装饰用的成卷纸张，宽度不小于45厘米，但不超过160厘米：

1. 起纹、压花、染面、印有图案或经其他装饰的（例如起绒），不论是否用透明的防护塑料涂布或覆盖；

2. 表面饰有木粒或草粒而凹凸不平的；

3. 表面用塑料涂布或覆盖并起纹、压花、染面、印有图案或经其他装饰的；

4. 表面用不论是否平行连结或编织的编结材料覆盖的。

9. For the purposes of heading No.48.14, the expression "wallpaper and similar wall coverings" applies only to:

(a) Paper in rolls, of a width of not less than 45cm and not more than 160cm, suitable for wall or ceiling decoration:

(1) Grained, embossed, surface-coloured, design-printed or otherwise surface-decorated (e.g., with textile flock), whether or not coated or covered with transparent protective plastics;

(2) With an uneven surface resulting from the incorporation of particles of wood, straw, etc.;

(3) Coated or covered on the face side with plastics, the layer of plastics being grained, embossed, coloured, design-printed or otherwise decorated; or

(4) Covered on the face side with plaiting material, whether or not bound together in parallel strands or woven.

（二）适于装饰墙壁或天花板用的经上述加工的纸边及纸条，不论是否成卷。

（三）由几幅拼成的壁纸，成卷或成张，贴到墙上可组成印刷的风景或图案。

既可作铺地制品，也可作壁纸的以纸或纸板为底的产品，应归入税号48.23。

十、税号48.20不包括切成一定尺寸的活页纸张或卡片，不论是否印制、压花、打孔。

十一、税号48.23主要适用于提花机或类似机器用的穿孔纸或卡片，以及纸花边。

十二、除税号48.14及48.21的货品外，印有图案、文字或图画的纸、纸板、纤维素絮纸及其制品，如果所印图案、文字或图画作为其主要用途，应归入第四十九章。

子目注释：

一、子目号4804.11及4804.19所称"牛皮挂面纸"，是指所含用硫酸盐法或烧碱法制得的木纤维不少于全部纤维重量的80%的成卷机器上光或研光纸及纸板，每平方米重量超过115克，并且最低缪伦耐破度符合下表所示（其他重量的耐破度可参照下表换算）：

重 量 （克/平方米）	最低耐破度 （千帕斯卡）
115	393
125	417
200	637
300	824
400	961

二、子目号4804.21及4804.29所称"袋用牛皮纸"，是指所含用硫酸盐法或烧碱法制得的木纤维不少于全部纤维重量的 80%的成卷机器上光纸，每平方米重量不小于 60克，但不超过 115克，并且符合下列一种规格：

(b) Borders and friezes, of paper, treated as above, whether or not in rolls, suitable for wall or ceiling decoration.

(c) Wall coverings of paper made up of several panels, in rolls or sheets, printed so as to make up a scene, design or motif when applied to a wall.

Products on a base of paper or paperboard, suitable for use both as floor coverings and as wall coverings, are to be classified in heading No. 48.23.

10. Heading No. 48.20 does not cover loose sheets or cards, cut to size, whether or not printed, embossed or perforated.

11. Heading No. 48.23 applies, *inter alia*, to perforated paper or paperboard cards for Jacquard or similar machines and paper lace.

12. Except for the goods of heading No. 48.14 or 48.21, paper, paperboard, cellulose wadding and articles thereof, printed with motifs, characters or pictorial representations, which are not merely incidental to the primary use of the goods, fall in Chapter 49.

Subheading Notes:

1. For the purposes of subheadings Nos. 4804.11 and 4804.19. "kraftliner" means machine-finished or machine-glazed paper and paperboard, of which not less than 80% by weight of the total fibre content consists of wood fibres obtained by the chemical sulphate or soda processes, in rolls, weighing more than 115g/m^2 and having a minimum Mullen bursting strength as indicated in the following table or the linearly interpolated or extrapolated equi-valent for any other weight:

Weight **(g /m^2)**	**Minimum Mullen bursting strength** **(kPa)**
115	393
125	417
200	637
300	824
400	961

2. For the purposes of subheadings Nos. 4804.21 and 4804.29, "sack kraft paper" means machine-finished paper, of which not less than 80% by weight of the total fibre content consists of fibres obtained by the chemical sulphate or soda processes, in rolls, weighing not less than 60g/m^2 but not more than 115g/m^2 and meeting one of the following sets of specifications:

（一）缪伦耐破指数不小于3.7千帕斯卡·平方米/克，并且横向伸长率大于4.5%，纵向伸长率大于2%。

（二）至少能达到下表所示的最小撕裂度和抗张强度（其他重量的可参照下表换算）：

重量 克/平方米	最小撕裂度 毫牛顿		最小抗张强度千 牛顿/米	
	纵向	纵向加横向	横向	纵向加横向
60	700	1510	1.9	6
70	830	1790	2.3	7.2
80	965	2070	2.8	8.3
100	1230	2635	3.7	10.6
115	1425	3060	4.4	12.3

三、子目号 4805.11 所称“半化学的瓦楞纸”，是指所含用机械和化学联合法制得的未漂白硬木纤维不少于全部纤维重量的 65%的成卷纸张，并且在温度为 23℃和相对湿度为 50%时，经过 30 分钟的瓦楞芯纸平压强度测定（CMT30），抗压强度超过 1.8 牛顿/克/平方米。

四、子目4805.12包括主要用机械和化学联合法制得的草浆制成的成卷纸张，每平方米重量在130克及以上，并且在温度为23℃和相对湿度为50%时，经过30分钟瓦楞芯纸平压强度测定（CMT30），抗压强度超过1.4牛顿/克/平方米。

五、子目4805.24及4805.25包括全部或主要用回收（废碎）纸及纸板制得的纸浆制成的纸及纸板，强韧箱纸板也可以有一面用染色纸或由漂白或未漂白的非再生浆制得的纸做表层，这些产品缪伦耐破指数不小于2千帕斯卡·平方米/克。

六、子目号4805.30所称“亚硫酸盐包装纸”，是指所含用亚硫酸盐法制得的木纤维超过全部纤维重量的40%的机器砑光纸，灰分含量不超过8%，并且缪伦耐破指数不小于1.47千帕斯卡·平方米/克。

(a) Having a Mullen burst index of not less than 3.7kPa • m^2/g and a stretch factor of more than 4.5% in the cross direction and of more than 2% in the machine direction.

(b) Having minima for tear and tensile as indicated in the following table or the linearly interpolated equivalent for any other eight:

Weight g/m^2	Minimum tear mN		Minimum tensile kN/m	
	Machine direction	Machine direction plus cross direction	Cross direction	Machine direction plus cross direction
60	700	1510	1.9	6
70	830	1790	2.3	7.2
80	965	2070	2.8	8.3
100	1230	2635	3.7	10.6
115	1425	3060	4.4	12.3

3. For the purposes of subheading No. 4805.11, “semichemical fluting paper” means paper, in rolls, of which not less than 65% by weight of the total fibre content consists of unbleached hardwood fibres obtained by a combination of mechanical and chemical pulping processes, and having a CMT 30 (Corrugated Medium Test with 30 minutes of conditioning) crush resistance exceeding 1.8 newtons/g/m^2 at 50% relative humidity, at 23℃.

4. Subheading 4805.12 covers paper, in rolls, made mainly of straw pulp obtained by a combination of mechanical and chemical processes, weighing 130g/m^2 or more, and having a CMT30 (Corrugated Medium Test with 30 minutes of conditioning) crush resistance exceeding 1.4 newtons/g/m^2 at 50% relative humidity, at 23℃.

5. Subheadings 4805.24 and 4805.25 cover paper and paperboard made wholly or mainly of pulp of recovered (waste and scrap) paper or paperboard. Testliner may also have a surface layer of dyed paper or of paper made of bleached or unbleached non-recovered pulp. These products have a Mullen burst index of not less than 2kPa • m^2 /g.

6. For the purposes of subheading No.4805.30, “sulphite wrapping paper” means machine-glazed paper, of which more than 40% by weight of the total fibre content consists of wood fibres obtained by the chemical sulpohite process, having an ash content not exceeding 8% and having a Mullen burst index of not less than 1.47kPa • m^2 /g.

七、子目号4810.22所称“轻质涂布纸”，是指双面涂布纸，其每平方米总重量不超过72克，每面每平方米的涂层重量不超过15克，原纸中所含用机械方法制得的木纤维不少于全部纤维重量的50%。

7. For the purposes of subheading No.4810.22, “lightweight coated paper” means paper, coated on both sides, of a total weight not exceeding $72g/m^2$, with a coating weight not exceeding $15g/m^2$ per side, on a base of which not less than 50% by weight of the total fibre content consists of wood fibres obtained by a mechanical process.

序号 No.	税则号列 Tariff Line	货品名称	最惠国税率 MFN(%)	协定税率 Agreement(%)		特惠税率 S.P.(%)	普通税率 Gen.(%)	Article Description
	48.01	**成卷或成张的新闻纸:**						**Newsprint, in rolls or sheets:**
3456	4801.0000	成卷或成张的新闻纸	5				30	Newsprint, in rolls or sheets
	48.02	**书写、印刷或类似用途的未经涂布的纸及纸板、未打孔的穿孔卡片纸及穿孔纸带纸、成卷或成张矩形（包括正方形），任何尺寸，但税目48.01或48.03的纸除外;手工制纸及纸板:**						**Uncoated paper and paperboard, of a kind used for writing, printing or other graphic purposes, and non perforated punch-cards and punch tape paper, in rolls or rectangular (including square) sheets, of any size, other than paper of heading No.48.01 or 48.03; hand-made paper and paperboard:**
		-手工制纸及纸板:						-Hand-made paper and paperboard:
3457	4802.1010	---宣纸	7.5				70	---Xuan paper
3458	4802.1090	---其他	7.5				70	---Other
		-光敏、热敏、电敏纸及纸板的原纸和原纸板:						-Paper and paperboard of a kind used as a base for photo-sensitive, heat sensitive or electro-sensitive paper or paperboard:
3459	4802.2010	---照相原纸	7.5 △5	0	香港HK		40	---photo poper bese
3460	4802.2090	---其他	7.5	0	香港HK		40	---Other
3461	4802.4000	-壁纸原纸	7.5	0	香港HK		40	-Wallpaper base
		-其他纸及纸板，不含用机械或化学—机械方法制得的纤维或所含前述纤维不超过全部纤维重量的10%:						-Other paper and paperboard, not containing fibres obtained by a mechanical or chemi-mechanical process or of which not more than 10% by weight of the total fibre content consists of such fibres:

序号 No.	税则号列 Tariff Line	货品名称	最惠国税率 MFN(%)	协定税率 Agreement(%)		特惠税率 S.P.(%)	普通税率 Gen.(%)	Article Description
3462	4802.5400	--每平方米重量小于40克	7.5	0	香港HK		30	--Weighing less than $40g/m^2$
3463	4802.5500	--每平方米重量在40克及以上，但不超过150克，成卷	5	0	香港HK		30	--Weighing $40g/m^2$ or more but not more than $150g/m^2$, in rolls
3464	4802.5600	--每平方米重量在40克及以上，但不超过150克，一边不越过435毫米，另一边不超过297毫米（以未折叠计）成张的	5	0	香港HK		30	--Weighing $40g/m^2$ or more but not more than $150g/m^2$, in sheets with one side not exceeding 435mm and the other side not exceeding 297mm in the unfolded state
3465	4802.5700	--其他，每平方米重量在40克及以上，但不超过150克	5	0	香港HK		30	--Other, weighing $40g/m^2$ or more but not more than $150g/m^2$
3466	4802.5800	--每平方米重量超过150克	5	0	香港HK		30	--Weighing more than $150g/m^2$
		-其他纸及纸板，所含用机械或化学—机械方法制得的纤维超过全部纤维重量的10%:						-Other paper and paper-board, of which more than 10% by weight of the total fibre content consists of fibres obtained by a mechanical or chemi-mechanical process:
		--成卷的:						--In rolls:
3467	4802.6110	---新闻纸	7.5				30	---Newsprint
3468	4802.6190	---其他	5	0	香港HK		30	---Other
3469	4802.6200	--成张的，一边不超过435毫米，另一边不超过297毫米（以未折叠计）	5	0	香港HK		30	--In sheets with one side not exceeding 435mm and the other side not exceeding 297mm in the unfolded state
		--其他:						--Other:
3470	4802.6910	---新闻纸	7.5				30	---Newsprint
3471	4802.6990	---其他	5	0	香港HK		30	---Other
	48.03	**卫生纸、面巾纸、餐巾纸以及家庭或卫生用的类似纸、纤维素絮纸和纤维素纤维网纸，不论是否起纹、压花、打孔、染面、饰面或印花，成卷或成张的:**						**Toilet or facial tissue stock, towel or napkin stock and similar paper of a kind used for household or sanitary purposes, cellulose wadding and webs of cellulose fibres, whether or not creped, crinkled, embossed, perforated, surface-coloured, surface-decorated or printed, in rolls or sheets:**

序号 No.	税则号列 Tariff Line	货品名称	最惠国税率 MFN(%)	协定税率 Agreement(%)	特惠税率 S.P.(%)	普通税率 Gen.(%)	Article Description
3472	4803.0000	卫生纸、面巾纸、餐巾纸以及家庭或卫生用的类似纸、纤维素絮纸和纤维素纤维网纸，不论是否起纹、压花、打孔、染面、饰面或印花，成卷或成张的	7.5			40	Toilet or facial tissue stock, towel or napkin stock and similar paper of a kind used for household or sanitary purposes, cellulose wadding and webs of cellulose fibres, whether or not creped, crinkled, embossed, perforated, surface-coloured, surface-decorated or printed, in rolls or sheets
	48.04	**成卷或成张的未经涂布的牛皮纸及纸板，但不包括税号 48.02 或 48.03 的货品:**					**Uncoated kraft paper and paperboard, in rolls or sheets, other than that of heading No.48.02 or 48.03:**
		-牛皮挂面纸:					-Kraftliner:
3473	4804.1100	--未漂白	5			30	--Unbleached
3474	4804.1900	--其他	5			30	--Other
		-袋用牛皮纸:					-Sack kraft paper:
3475	4804.2100	--未漂白	5			30	--Unbleached
3476	4804.2900	--其他	5			30	--Other
		-其他牛皮纸及纸板，每平方米重量不超过 150 克:					-Other kraft paper and paperboard weighing $150g/m^2$ or less:
3477	4804.3100	--未漂白	2			30	--Unbleached
3478	4804.3900	--其他	2			30	--Other
		-其他牛皮纸及纸板，每平方米重量超过 150 克，但小于 225 克:					-Other kraft paper and paperboard weighing more than $150g/m^2$ but less than $225g/m^2$:
3479	4804.4100	--未漂白	2			30	--Unbleached
3480	4804.4200	--本体均匀漂白，所含用化学方法制得的木纤维超过全部纤维重量的 95%	5			30	--Bleached uniformly throughout the mass and of which more than 95% by weight of the total fibre content consists of wood fibres obtained by a chemical process
3481	4804.4900	--其他	2			30	--Other
		-其他牛皮纸及纸板，每平方米重量在 225 克及以上:					-Other kraft paper and paperboard weighing $225g/m^2$ or more:
3482	4804.5100	--未漂白	2			30	--Unbleached
3483	4804.5200	--本体均匀漂白，所含用化学方法制得的木纤维超过全部纤维重量的 95%	5			30	--Bleached uniformly throughout the mass and of which more than 95% by weight of the total fibre content consists of wood fibres obtained by a chemical process

序号 No.	税则号列 Tariff Line	货品名称	最惠国税率 MFN(%)	协定税率 Agreement(%)		特惠税率 S.P.(%)	普通税率 Gen.(%)	Article Description
3484	4804.5900	--其他	2				30	--Other
	48.05	**成卷或成张的其他未经涂布的纸及纸板，加工程度不超过本章注释三所列范围:**						**Other uncoated paper and paperboard, in rolls or sheets, not further worked or processed than as specified in Note 3 to this Chapter:**
		-瓦楞原纸:						-fluting paper:
3485	4805.1100	--半化学的瓦楞原纸	7.5	0	香港HK		30	--Semi-chemical fluting paper
3486	4805.1200	--草浆瓦楞原纸	7.5	0	香港HK		30	--Straw fluting paper
3487	4805.1900	--其他	7.5	0	香港HK		30	--Other
		-强韧箱纸板（再生挂面纸板）:						-Testliner (recycled liner board):
3488	4805.2400	--每平方米重量在150克及以下	7.5	0	香港HK		30	--Weighing 150g/m^2 or less
3489	4805.2500	--每平方米重量超过150克	7.5	0	香港HK		30	--Weighing more than 150g/m^2
3490	4805.3000	-亚硫酸盐包装纸	7.5				30	-Sulphite wrapping paper
3491	4805.4000	-滤纸及纸板	7.5				30	-Filter paper and paper-board
3492	4805.5000	-毡纸及纸板	7.5				30	-Felt paper and paper-board
		-其他:						-Other:
		--每平方米重量在150克及以下:						--Weighing 150g/m^2 or less:
3493	4805.9110	---电解电容器原纸	7.5	0	香港HK		30	---Paper for electrolytic capacitor
3494	4805.9190	---其他	7.5	0	香港HK		30	---Other
3495	4805.9200	--每平方米重量超过150克，但小于225克	7.5				30	--Weighing more than 150g/m^2 but less than 225g/m^2
3496	4805.9300	--每平方米重量在225克及以上	7.5	0	香港HK		30	--Weighing 225g/m^2 or more.
	48.06	**成卷或成张的植物羊皮纸、防油纸、描图纸、半透明纸及其他高光泽透明或半透明纸:**						**Vegetable parchment, greaseproof papers, tracing papers and glassine and other glazed transparent or translucent papers, in rolls or sheets:**
3497	4806.1000	-植物羊皮纸	7.5				40	-Vegetable parchment
3498	4806.2000	-防油纸	7.5				40	-Greaseproof papers
3499	4806.3000	-描图纸	7.5				30	-Tracing papers
3500	4806.4000	-高光泽透明或半透明纸	7.5 △5				40	-Glassine and other glazed transparent or translucent papers
	48.07	**成卷或成张的复合纸及纸板（用粘合剂粘合各层纸或纸板制成），未经表面涂布或未浸渍，不论内层是否有加强材料:**						**Composite paper and paperboard (made by sticking flat layers of paper or paperboard together with an adhesive), not surface-coated or impregnated, whether or not internally reinforced, in rolls or sheets:**

序号 No.	税则号列 Tariff Line	货品名称	最惠国税率 MFN(%)	协定税率 Agreement(%)	特惠税率 S.P.(%)	普通税率 Gen.(%)	Article Description
3501	4807.0000	成卷或成张的复合纸及纸板（用粘合剂粘合各层纸或纸板制成），未经表面涂布或未浸渍，不论内层是否有加强材料	7.5 △5			40	Composite paper and paperboard (made by sticking flat layers of paper or paperboard together with an adhesive), not surface-coated or impregnated, whether or not internally reinforced, in rolls or sheets
	48.08	**成卷或成张的瓦楞纸及纸板（不论是否与平面纸胶合）、皱纹纸及纸板、压纹纸及纸板、穿孔纸及纸板，但税号 48.03 的纸除外：**					**Paper and paperboard, corrugated (with or without glued flat surface sheets), creped, crinkled, embossed or perforated, in rolls or sheets, other than paper of the kind described in heading No.48.03:**
3502	4808.1000	-瓦楞纸及纸板，不论是否穿孔	7.5			30	-Corrugated paper and paperboard, whether or not perforated
3503	4808.4000	-皱纹牛皮纸，不论是否压花或穿孔	7.5			40	-Kraft paper, creped or crinkled, whether or not embossed or perforated
3504	4808.9000	-其他	7.5			40	-Other
	48.09	**复写纸、自印复写纸及其他拷贝或转印纸（包括涂布或浸渍的油印蜡纸或胶印版纸），不论是否印制，成卷或成张的：**					**Carbon paper, self-copy paper and other copying or transfer papers (including coated or impregnated paper for duplicator stencils or offset plates), whether or not printed, in rolls or sheets:**
3505	4809.2000	-自印复写纸	7.5			40	-Self-copy paper
3506	4809.9000	-其他	7.5			40	-Other
	48.10	**成卷或成张矩形（包括正方形）的任何尺寸的单面或双面涂布高岭土或其他无机物质（不论是否加粘合剂）的纸及纸板，未涂布其他涂料，不论是否染面、饰面或印花：**					**Paper and paperboard, coated on one or both sides with kaolin (China clay) or other inorganic substances, with or without a binder, and with no other coating, whether or not surface-coloured, surface-decorated or printed, in rolls or rectangular (including square) sheets, of any size:**

序号 No.	税则号列 Tariff Line	货品名称	最惠国税率 MFN(%)	协定税率 Agreement(%)		特惠税率 S.P.(%)	普通税率 Gen.(%)	Article Description
		-书写、印刷或类似用途的纸及纸板，不含用机械或化学—机械方法制得的纤维或所含前述纤维不超过全部纤维重量的10%:						-Paper and paperboard of a kind used for writing, printing or other graphic purposes, not containing fibres obtained by a mechanical or chemi-mechanical process or of which not more than 10% by weight of the total fibre content consists of such fibres:
3507	4810.1300	--成卷的	5	0	香港HK		40	--In rolls
3508	4810.1400	--成张的，一边不超过435毫米，另一边不超过297毫米（以未折叠计）	5	0	香港HK		40	--In sheets with one side not exceeding 435mm and the other side not exceeding 297mm in the unfolded state
3509	4810.1900	--其他	5	0	香港HK		40	--Other
		-书写、印刷或类似用途的纸及纸板，所含用机械或化学—机械方法制得的纤维超过全部纤维重量的10%:						-Paper and paperboard of a kind used for writing, printing or other graphic purposes, of which more than 10% by weight of the total fibre content consists of fibres obtained by a mechanical or chemi-mechanical process:
3510	4810.2200	--轻质涂布纸	5				40	--Light-weight coated paper
3511	4810.2900	--其他	5	0	香港HK		40	--Other
		-牛皮纸及纸板，但书写、印刷或类似用途的除外:						-Kraft paper and paperboard, other than that of a kind used for writing, printing or other graphic purposes:
3512	4810.3100	--本体均匀漂白，所含用化学方法制得的木纤维超过全部纤维重量的95%，每平方米重量不超过150克	5	0	香港HK,澳门MO		40	--Bleached uniformly throughout the mass and of which more than 95% by weight of the total fibre content consists of wood fibres obtained by a chemical process, and weighing $150g/m^2$ or less
3513	4810.3200	--本体均匀漂白，所含用化学方法制得的木纤维超过全部纤维重量的95%，每平方米重量超过150克	5	0	香港HK,澳门MO		40	--Bleached uniformly throughout the mass and of which more than 95% by weight of the total fibre content consists of wood fibres obtained by a chemical process, and weighing more than $150g/m^2$

序号 No.	税则号列 Tariff Line	货品名称	最惠国税率 MFN(%)	协定税率 Agreement(%)	特惠税率 S.P.(%)	普通税率 Gen.(%)	Article Description
3514	4810.3900	--其他	5	0 香港HK,澳门MO		40	--Other
		-其他纸及纸板:					-Other paper and paper-board:
3515	4810.9200	--多层的	5	0 香港HK,澳门MO		40	--Multi-ply
3516	4810.9900	--其他	7.5	0 香港HK,澳门MO		40	--Other
	48.11	**成卷或成张矩形（包括正方形）的任何尺寸的经涂布、浸渍、覆盖、染面、饰面或印花的纸、纸板、纤维素絮纸及纤维素纤维网纸，但税目48.03、48.09或48.10的货品除外:**					**Paper, paperboard, cellulose wadding and webs of cellulose fibres, coated, impregnated, covered, surface-coloured, surface-decorated or printed, in rolls or rectangular (including square) sheets, of any size, other than goods of the kind described in heading No. 48.03, 48.09 or 48.10:**
3517	4811.1000	-焦油纸及纸板、沥青纸及纸板	7.5	0 香港HK,澳门MO		40	-Tarred, bituminised or asphalted paper and paperboard
		-胶粘纸及纸板:					-Gummed or adhesive paper and paper-board:
3518	4811.4100	--自粘的	7.5	0 香港HK,澳门MO		40	--Self-adhesive
3519	4811.4900	--其他	7.5	0 香港HK,澳门MO		40	--Other
		-用塑料（不包括粘合剂）涂布、浸渍或覆盖的纸及纸板:					-Paper and paperboard coated, impregnated or covered with plastics (excluding adhesives):
		--漂白的，每平方米重量超过150克:					--Bleached, weighing more than 150g/m^2:
3520	4811.5110	---彩色相纸用双面涂塑纸	7.5 △1	0 香港HK,澳门MO		40	---Paper coated on both sides with plastics for colour photography
3521	4811.5190	---其他	7.5	0 香港HK,澳门MO		40	---Other
		--其他:					--Other:
3522	4811.5910	---绝缘纸及纸板	7.5	0 香港HK,澳门MO		30	---Insulating paper and paperboard
		---其他:					---Other:
3523	4811.5991	----镀铝的	7.5	0 香港HK,澳门MO		40	----Aluminized
3524	4811.5999	----其他	7.5	0 香港HK,澳门MO		40	----Other
		-用蜡、石蜡、硬脂精、油或甘油涂布、浸渍、覆盖的纸及纸板:					-Paper and paperboard, coated, impregnated or covered with wax, paraffin wax, stearin, oil or glyecrol:
3525	4811.6010	---绝缘纸及纸板	7.5	0 香港HK,澳门MO		30	---Insulating paper and paperboard
3526	4811.6090	---其他	7.5	0 香港HK,澳门MO		40	---Other
3527	4811.9000	-其他纸、纸板、纤维素絮纸及纤维素纤维网纸	7.5	0 香港HK,澳门MO		40	-Other paper, paperboard, cellulose wadding and webs of cellulose fibres

序号 No.	税则号列 Tariff Line	货品名称	最惠国税 率 MFN(%)	协定税率 Agreement(%)	特惠税率 S.P.(%)	普通税率 Gen.(%)	Article Description
	48.12	**纸浆制的滤块、滤板及滤片:**					**Filter blocks, slabs and plates, of paper pulp:**
3528	4812.0000	纸浆制的滤块、滤板及滤片	7.5			40	Filter blocks, slabs and plates, of paper pulp
	48.13	**烟卷纸，不论是否切成一定尺寸、成小本或管状:**					**Cigarette paper, whether or not cut to size or in the form of booklets or tubes:**
3529	4813.1000	-成小本或管状	7.5			100	-In the form of booklets or tubes
3530	4813.2000	-宽度不超过 5 厘米成卷的	7.5			100	-In rolls of a width not exceeding 5cm
3531	4813.9000	-其他	7.5			100	-Other
	48.14	**壁纸及类似品;窗用透明纸:**					**Wallpaper and similar wall coverings; window transparencies of paper:**
3532	4814.2000	-用塑料涂面或盖面的壁纸及类似品，起纹、压花、着色、印刷图案或经其他装饰	7.5			50	-Wallpaper and similar wall coverings, consisting of paper coated or covered, on the face side, with a grained, embossed, coloured, design-printed or otherwise decorated layer of plastics
3533	4814.9000	-其他	7.5			50	-Other
	48.16	**复写纸、自印复写纸及其他拷贝或转印纸（不包括税号 48.09 的纸）、油印蜡纸或胶印版纸，不论是否盒装:**					**Carbon paper, self-copy paper and other copying or transfer papers (other than those of heading No.48.09), duplicator stencils and offset plates, of paper, whether or not put up in boxes:**
3534	4816.2000	-自印复写纸	7.5			70	-Self-copy paper
		-其他:					-Other:
3535	4816.9010	---热敏转印纸	7.5			40	---Heat transfer paper
3536	4816.9090	---其他	7.5			70	---Other
	48.17	**纸或纸板制的信封、封缄信片、素色明信片及通信卡片;纸或纸板制的盒子、袋子及夹子，内装各种纸制文具:**					**Envelopes, letter cards, plain postcards and correspondence cards, of paper or paperboard; boxes, pouches, wallets and writing compendiums, of paper or paperboard, containing an assortment of paper stationery:**
3537	4817.1000	-信封	7.5			80	-Envelopes
3538	4817.2000	-封缄信片、素色明信片及通信卡片	7.5			80	-Letter cards, plain postcards and correspondence cards

序号 No.	税则号列 Tariff Line	货品名称	最惠国税率 MFN(%)	协定税率 Agreement(%)		特惠税率 S.P.(%)		普通税率 Gen.(%)	Article Description
3539	4817.3000	-纸或纸板制的盒子、袋子及夹子，内装各种纸制文具	7.5					80	-Boxes, pouches, wallets and writing compendiums, of paper or paperboard, containing an assortment of paper stationery
	48.18	**卫生纸及类似纸，家庭或卫生用纤维素絮纸及纤维素纤维网纸，成卷宽度不超过36厘米或切成一定尺寸或形状的;纸浆、纸、纤维素絮纸或纤维素纤维网纸制的手帕、面巾、台布、餐巾、床单及类似的家庭、卫生或医院用品、衣服及衣着附件:**							**Toilet paper and similar paper, cellulose wadding or webs of cellulose fibres, of a kind used for household or sanitary purposes, in rolls of a width not exceeding 36cm, or cut to size or shape; handkerchiefs, cleansing tissues, towels, tablecloths, serviettes, bed sheets and similar household, sanitary or hospital articles, articles of apparel and clothing accessories, of paper pulp, paper, cellulose wadding or webs of cellulose fibres:**
3540	4818.1000	-卫生纸	7.5					80	-Toilet paper
3541	4818.2000	-纸手帕及纸面巾	7.5					90	-Handkerchiefs, cleansing or facial tissues and towels
3542	4818.3000	-纸台布及纸餐巾	7.5					90	-Tablecloths and serviettes
3543	4818.5000	-衣服及衣着附件	7.5	0 5	东盟ASEAN,智利CL,新西兰NZ,秘鲁PE,哥斯达黎加CR 巴基斯坦PK	0	最不发达35国LDC35,最不发达4国LDC4	90	-Articles of apparel and clothing accessories
3544	4818.9000	-其他	7.5					90	-Other
	48.19	**纸、纸板、纤维素絮纸或纤维素纤维网纸制的箱、盒、匣、袋及其他包装容器;纸或纸板制的卷宗盒、信件盘及类似品，供办公室、商店及类似场所使用的:**							**Cartons, boxes, cases, bags and other packing containers, of paper, paper-board, cellulose wadding or webs of cellulose fibres; box files, letter trays and similar articles, of paper or paper-board of a kind used in offices, shops or the like:**
3545	4819.1000	-瓦楞纸或纸板制的箱、盒、匣	5	0	香港HK,澳门MO			80	-Cartons, boxes and cases, of corrugated paper or paperboard

序号 No.	税则号列 Tariff Line	货品名称	最惠国税率 MFN(%)	协定税率 Agreement(%)		特惠税率 S.P.(%)		普通税率 Gen.(%)	Article Description
3546	4819.2000	-非瓦楞纸或纸板制的可折叠箱、盒、匣	5	0	香港HK,澳门MO			80	-Folding cartons, boxes and cases, of non-corrugated paper or paperboard
3547	4819.3000	-底宽 40 厘米及以上的纸袋	7.5	0 0.8 5	东盟ASEAN,新加坡SG,新西兰NZ,秘鲁PE,哥斯达黎加CR 智利CL 巴基斯坦PK	0	最不发达 35 国 LDC35,最不发达 4 国 LDC4	80	-Sacks and bags, having a base of a width of 40cm or more
3548	4819.4000	-其他纸袋,包括锥形袋	7.5					80	-Other sacks and bags, including cones
3549	4819.5000	-其他包装容器,包括唱片套	7.5					80	-Other packing containers, including record sleeves
3550	4819.6000	-办公室、商店及类似场所使用的卷宗盒、信件盘、存储盒及类似品	7.5					80	-Box files, letter trays, storage boxes and similar articles, of a kind used in offices, shops or the like
	48.20	**纸或纸板制的登记本、账本、笔记本、定货本、收据本、信笺本、记事本、日记本及类似品、练习本、吸墨纸本、活动封面(活页及非活页)、文件夹、卷宗皮、多联商业表格纸、页间夹有复写纸的本及其他文具用品;纸或纸板制的样品簿、粘贴簿书籍封面:**							**Registers, account books, note books, order books, receipt books, letter pads, memorandum pads, diaries and similar articles, exercise books, blotting-pads, binders (loose-leaf or other), folders, file covers, manifold business forms, interleaved carbon sets and other articles of stationery, of paper or paperboard; albums for samples or for collections and book covers, of paper or paperboard:**
3551	4820.1000	-登记本、账本、笔记本、定货本、收据本、信笺本、记事本、日记本及类似品	7.5					80	-Registers, account books, note nooks, order books, receipt books, letter pads, memorandum pads, diaries and similar articles
3552	4820.2000	-练习本	7.5					80	-Exercise books
3553	4820.3000	-活动封面(书籍封面除外)、文件夹及卷宗皮	7.5					80	-Binders (other than book covers), folders and file covers
3554	4820.4000	-多联商业表格纸、页间夹有复写纸的本	7.5	0 5	东盟ASEAN,智利CL,新西兰NZ,秘鲁PE,哥斯达黎加CR 巴基斯坦PK	0	最不发达 35 国 LDC35,最不发达 4 国 LDC4	80	-Manifold business forms and interleaved carbon sets

序号 No.	税则号列 Tariff Line	货品名称	最惠国 税　率 MFN(%)	协定税率 Agreement(%)		特惠税率 S.P.(%)		普通 税率 Gen.(%)	Article Description
3555	4820.5000	-样品簿及粘贴簿	7.5					80	-Albums for samples or for collections
3556	4820.9000	-其他	7.5					80	-Other
	48.21	**纸或纸板制的各种标签，不论是否印制:**							**Paper or paperboard labels of all kinds, whether or not printed:**
3557	4821.1000	-印制	7.5	0	香港HK,澳门MO			50	-Printed
3558	4821.9000	-其他	7.5					50	-Other
	48.22	**纸浆、纸或纸板（不论是否穿孔或硬化）制的筒管、卷轴、纡子及类似品:**							**Bobbins, spools, cops and similar supports of paper pulp, paper or paperboard (whether or not perforated or hardened):**
3559	4822.1000	-纺织纱线用	7.5					35	-Of a kind used for winding textile yarn
3560	4822.9000	-其他	7.5					70	-Other
	48.23	**切成一定尺寸或形状的其他纸、纸板、纤维素絮纸及纤维素纤维网纸;纸浆、纸、纸板、纤维素絮纸及纤维素纤维网纸制的其他物品:**							**Other paper, paperboard, cellulose wadding and webs of cellulose fibres, cut to size or shape; other articles of paper pulp, paper, paperboard, cellulose wadding or webs of cellulose fibres:**
3561	4823.2000	-滤纸及纸板	7.5					30	-Filter paper and paperboard
3562	4823.4000	-已印制的自动记录器用打印纸卷、纸张及纸盘	7.5					30	-Rolls, sheets and dials, printed for self-recording apparatus
		-纸或纸板制的盘、碟、盆、杯及类似品:							-Trays, dishes, plates, cups and the like, of paper or paperboard:
3563	4823.6100	--竹浆纸制	7.5	0 0.8 5	东盟ASEAN,新西兰NZ,秘鲁PE,哥斯达黎加CR 智利CL 巴基斯坦PK	0	最不发达35国LDC35,最不发达4国LDC4	90	--Of bamboo
		--其他:							--Other:
3564	4823.6910	---非木植物浆制	7.5	0 0.8 5	东盟ASEAN,新西兰NZ,秘鲁PE,哥斯达黎加CR 智利CL 巴基斯坦PK	0	最不发达35国LDC35,最不发达4国LDC4	90	---Other than those of wood
3565	4823.6990	---其他	7.5	0 0.8 5	东盟ASEAN,新西兰NZ,秘鲁PE,哥斯达黎加CR 智利CL 巴基斯坦PK	0	最不发达35国LDC35,最不发达4国LDC4	90	---Other

序号 No.	税则号列 Tariff Line	货品名称	最惠国税率 MFN(%)	协定税率 Agreement(%)		特惠税率 S.P.(%)		普通税率 Gen.(%)	Article Description
3566	4823.7000	-压制或模制纸浆制品	7.5					90	-Moulded or pressed articles of paper pulp
		-其他:							-Other:
3567	4823.9010	---以纸或纸板为底制成的铺地制品	7.5					90	---Floor coverings on a base of paper or of paperboard
3568	4823.9020	---神纸及类似用品	7.5	0 0.8 5	东盟ASEAN,新西兰NZ,秘鲁PE,哥斯达黎加CR 智利CL 巴基斯坦PK	0	最不发达35国LDC35,最不发达4国LDC4	180	---Joss paper and the like
3569	4823.9030	---纸扇	7.5	0 0.8 5	东盟ASEAN,新西兰NZ,秘鲁PE,哥斯达黎加CR 智利CL 巴基斯坦PK	0	最不发达35国LDC35,最不发达4国LDC4	90	---Paper fans
3570	4823.9090	---其他	7.5	0	香港HK,澳门MO			90	---Other

第四十九章
书籍、报纸、印刷图画及其他印刷品；手稿、打字稿及设计图纸

注释:

一、本章不包括:

（一）透明基的照相负片或正片（第三十七章）;

（二）立体地图、设计图表或地球仪、天体仪，不论是否印刷（税号 90.23）;

（三）第九十五章的扑克牌或其他物品;

（四）雕版画、印刷画、石印画的原本（税号 97.02），税号 97.04 的邮票、印花税票、纪念封、首日封、邮政信笺及类似品，以及第九十七章的超过一百年的古物或其他物品。

二、第四十九章所称“印刷”，也包括用胶版复印机、油印机印制，在自动数据处理设备控制下打印绘制，压印、冲印、感光复印、热敏复印或打字。

三、用纸以外材料装订成册的报纸、杂志和期刊，以及一期以上装订在同一封面里的成套报纸、杂志和期刊，应归入税号 49.01，不论是否有广告材料。

四、税号 49.01 还包括:

（一）附有说明文字，每页编有号数以便装订成一册或几册的整集印刷复制品，例如，美术作品、绘画;

（二）随同成册书籍的图画附刊;

（三）供装订书籍或小册子用的散页、集页或书帖形式的印刷品，已构成一部作品的全部或部分。

但没有说明文字的印刷图画或图解，不论是否散页或书帖形式，应归入税号 49.11。

五、除本章注释三另有规定的以外，税号 49.01 不包括主要作广告用的出版物（例如，小册子，散页印刷品、商业目录、同业公会出版的年鉴、旅游宣传品），这类出版物应归入税号 49.11。

Chapter 49
Printed books, newspapers, pictures and other products of the printing industry; manuscripts, typescripts and plans

Notes:

1. This Chapter does not cover:

(a) Photographic negatives or positives on transparent bases (Chapter 37);

(b) Maps, plans or globes, in relief, whether or not printed (heading No. 90.23);

(c) Playing cards or other goods of Chapter 95; or

(d) Original engravings, prints or lithographs (heading No. 97.02), postage or revenue stamps, stamp-postmarks, first-day covers, postal stationery or the like of heading No. 97.04, antiques of an age exceeding one hundred years or other articles of Chapter 97.

2. For the purposes of Chapter 49, the term “printed” also means reproduced by means of a duplicating machine, produced under the control of an automatic data processing machine, embossed, photographed, photocopied, thermo-copied or typewritten.

3. Newspapers, journals and periodicals which are bound otherwise than in paper, and sets of newspapers, journals or periodicals comprising more than one number under a single cover are to be classified in heading No. 49.01, whether or not containing advertising material.

4. Heading No. 49.01 also covers:

(a) A collection of printed reproductions of, for example, works of art or drawings, with a relative text, put up with numbered pages in a form suitable for binding into one or more volumes;

(b) A pictorial supplement accompanying, and subsidiary to, a bound volume; and

(c) Printed parts of books or booklets, in the form of assembled or separate sheets or signatures, constituting the whole or a part of a complete work and designed for binding.

However, printed pictures or illustrations not bearing a text, whether in the form of signatures or separate sheets, fall in heading No. 49.11.

5. Subject to Note 3 to this Chapter, heading No. 49.01 does not cover publications which are essentially devoted to advertising (for example, brochures, pamphlets, leaflets, trade catalogues, year books published by trade associa-

tions, tourist propaganda). Such publications are to be classified in heading No.49.11.

六、税号 49.03 所称"儿童图画书"，是指以图画为主、文字为辅，供儿童阅览的书籍。

6. For the purposes of heading No. 49.03, the expression "children' s picture books" means books for children in which the pictures form the principal interest and the text is subsidiary.

序号 No.	税则号列 Tariff Line	货品名称	最惠国税 率 MFN(%)	协定税率 Agreement(%)	特惠税率 S.P.(%)	普通税率 Gen.(%)	Article Description
	49.01	**书籍、小册子、散页印刷品及类似印刷品，不论是否单张:**					**Printed books, brochures, leaflets and similar printed matter, whether or not in single sheets:**
3571	4901.1000	-单张的，不论是否折叠	0		0 最不发达35国 LDC35, 最不发达4国 LDC4	0	-In single sheets, whether or not folded
		-其他:					-Other:
3572	4901.9100	--字典或百科全书及其连续出版的分册	0		0 最不发达35国 LDC35, 最不发达4国 LDC4	0	--Dictionaries and encyclopaedias, and serial instalments thereof
3573	4901.9900	--其他	0		0 最不发达35国 LDC35, 最不发达4国 LDC4	0	--Other
	49.02	**报纸、杂志及期刊，不论有无插图或广告材料:**					**Newspapers, journals and periodicals, whether or not illustrated or containing advertising material:**
3574	4902.1000	-每周至少出版四次	0		0 最不发达35国 LDC35, 最不发达4国 LDC4	0	-Appearing at least four times a week
3575	4902.9000	-其他	0		0 最不发达35国 LDC35, 最不发达4国 LDC4	0	-Other
	49.03	**儿童图画书、绘画或涂色书:**					**Children's picture, drawing or colouring books:**

序号 No.	税则号列 Tariff Line	货品名称	最惠国税率 MFN(%)	协定税率 Agreement(%)	特惠税率 S.P.(%)		普通税率 Gen.(%)	Article Description
3576	4903.0000	儿童图画书、绘画或涂色书	0		0	最不发达35国 LDC35,最不发达4国 LDC4	0	Children's picture, drawing or colouring books
	49.04	**乐谱原稿或印本，不论是否装订或印有插图:**						**Music, printed or in manuscript, whether or not bound or illustrated:**
3577	4904.0000	乐谱原稿或印本，不论是否装订或印有插图	0		0	最不发达35国 LDC35,最不发达4国 LDC4	0	Music, printed or in manuscript, whether or not bound or illustrated
	49.05	**各种印刷的地图、水道图及类似图表，包括地图册、挂图、地形图及地球仪、天体仪:**						**Maps and hydrographic or similar charts of all kinds, including atlases, wall maps, topographical plans and globes, printed:**
3578	4905.1000	-地球仪、天体仪	0		0	最不发达35国 LDC35,最不发达4国 LDC4	0	-Globes
		-其他:						-Other:
3579	4905.9100	--成册的	0		0	最不发达35国 LDC35,最不发达4国 LDC4	0	--In book form
3580	4905.9900	--其他	0		0	最不发达35国 LDC35,最不发达4国 LDC4	0	--Other
	49.06	**手绘的建筑、工程、工业、商业、地形或类似用途的设计图纸原稿;手稿;用感兴纸照相复印或用复写纸眷写的上述物品复制件:**						**Plans and drawings for architectural, engineering, industrial, commercial, topographical or similar purposes, being originals drawn by hand; hand -written text; photographic reproductions on sensitized paper and carbon copies of the foregoing:**

序号 No.	税则号列 Tariff Line	货品名称	最惠国税率 MFN(%)	协定税率 Agreement(%)	特惠税率 S.P.(%)	普通税率 Gen.(%)	Article Description
3581	4906.0000	手绘的建筑、工程、工业、商业、地形或类似用途的设计图纸原稿;手稿;用感兴纸照相复印或用复写纸眷写的上述物品复制件	0		0 最不发达35国LDC35,最不发达4国LDC4	0	Plans and drawings for architectural, engineering, industrial, commercial topographical or similar purposes, being originals drawn by hand; hand-written text; photographic reproductions on sensitized paper and carbon copies of the foregoing
	49.07	**在承认或将承认其面值的国家流通或新发行并且未经使用的邮票、印花税票及类似票证;印有邮票或印花税票的纸品;钞票;空白支票;股票、债券及类似所有权凭证:**					**Unused postage, revenue or similar stamps of current or new issue in the country in which they have, or will have, a recognised face value; stamp impressed paper; banknotes; cheque forms; stock, share or bond certificates and similar documents of title:**
3582	4907.0010	---邮票	7.5		0 最不发达35国LDC35	50	---Postage
3583	4907.0020	---钞票	0		0 最不发达35国LDC35,最不发达4国LDC4	50	---Banknotes
3584	4907.0030	---证券凭证	0		0 最不发达35国LDC35,最不发达4国LDC4	50	---Documents of title
3585	4907.0090	---其他	7.5		0 最不发达35国LDC35	50	---Other
	ex49070090	特许权使用凭证(包括软件升级许可证、软件用户许可证等。但游戏软件升级许可证、游戏软件用户许可证除外)	△0				Certificate of Franchise license inculding software upgrade license、software user license, etc.excl.game software upgrade license、software user license
	49.08	**转印贴花纸(移画印花法用图案纸):**					**Transfers (decalcomanias):**
3586	4908.1000	-釉转印贴花纸(移画印花法用图案纸)	7.5		0 最不发达35国LDC35	50	-Transfers (decalcomanias), vitrifiable

序号 No.	税则号列 Tariff Line	货品名称	最惠国税率 MFN(%)	协定税率 Agreement(%)		特惠税率 S.P.(%)		普通税率 Gen.(%)	Article Description
3587	4908.9000	-其他	7.5			0	最不发达35国 LDC35	50	-Other
	49.09	**印刷或有图画的明信片；印有个人问候、祝贺、通告的卡片，不论是否有图画、带信封或饰边：**							**Printed or illustrated postcards; printed cards bearing personal greetings, messages or announcements, whether or not illustrated, with or without envelopes or trimmings:**
3588	4909.0010	---印刷或有图画的明信片	7.5			0	最不发达35国 LDC35	50	---Printed or illustrated postcards
3589	4909.0090	---其他	7.5			0	最不发达35国 LDC35	50	---Other
	49.10	**印刷的各种日历，包括日历芯：**							**Calendars of any kind, printed, including calendar blocks:**
3590	4910.0000	印刷的各种日历，包括日历芯	7.5			0	最不发达35国 LDC35, 最不发达4国 LDC4	50	Calendars of any kind, printed, including calendar blocks
	49.11	**其他印刷品，包括印刷的图片及照片：**							**Other printed matter, including printed pictures and photographs:**
		-商业广告品、商品目录及类似印刷品:							-Trade advertising material, commercial catalogues and the like:
3591	4911.1010	---无商业价值的	0			0	最不发达35国 LDC35, 最不发达4国 LDC4	0	---No commercial value
3592	4911.1090	---其他	7.5	0	香港HK	0	最不发达35国 LDC35	50	---Other
		-其他:							-Other:
3593	4911.9100	--图片、设计图样及照片	7.5			0	最不发达35国 LDC35	50	--Pictures, designs and photographs
		--其他:							--Other:
3594	4911.9910	---纸质的	7.5	0	香港HK	0	最不发达35国 LDC35	50	---Papery
	ex49119910	印有自动数据处理设备用程序的纸张	△0						Paper printed with process for automatic data handling devices
3595	4911.9990	---其他	7.5	0	香港HK	0	最不发达35国 LDC35	50	---Other

第十一类
纺织原料及纺织制品

注释:

一、本类不包括:

（一）制刷用的动物鬃、毛（税号 05.02）；马毛及废马毛（税号 05.11）；

（二）人发及人发制品（税号 05.01、67.03 或 67.04），但通常用于榨油机或类似机器的滤布除外（税号 59.11）；

（三）第十四章的棉短绒或其他植物材料；

（四）税号 25.24 的石棉、税号 68.12 或 68.13 的石棉制品或其他产品；

（五）税号 30.05 或 30.06 的物品；税号 33.06 的用于清洁牙缝的纱线（牙线），单独零售包装的；

（六）税号 37.01 至 37.04 的感光布；

（七）截面尺寸超过 1 毫米的塑料单丝和表面宽度超过 5 毫米的塑料扁条及类似品（例如人造草）（第三十九章），以及上述单丝或扁条的缏条、织物、篮筐或柳条编结品（第四十六章）；

（八）第三十九章的用塑料浸渍、涂布、包覆或层压的机织物、针织物或钩编织物、毡呢或无纺织物及其制品；

（九）第四十章的用橡胶浸渍、涂布、包覆或层压的机织物、针织物或钩编织物、毡呢或无纺织物及其制品；

（十）带毛皮张（第四十一章或第四十三章）、税号 43.03 或 43.04 的毛皮制品、人造毛皮及其制品；

（十一）税号 42.01 或 42.02 的用纺织材料制成的物品；

（十二）第四十八章的产品或物品（例如纤维素絮纸）；

（十三）第六十四章的鞋靴及其零件、护腿、裹腿及类似品；

（十四）第六十五章的发网、其他帽类及其零件；

（十五）第六十七章的货品；

（十六）涂有研磨料的纺织材料（税号 68.05）以及税号 68.15 的碳纤维及其制品；

（十七）玻璃纤维及其制品，但可见底布的玻璃线刺

SECTION XI
TEXTILES AND TEXTILE ARTICLES

Notes:

1. This Section does not cover:

(a) Animal brush-making bristles or hair (heading No. 05.02); horsehair or horsehair waste (heading No. 05.11) ;

(b) Human hair or articles of human hair (heading No. 05.01, 67.03 or 67.04) , except straining cloth of a kind commonly used in oil presses or the like (heading No. 59.11) ;

(c) Cotton linters or other vegetable materials of Chapter 14;

(d) Asbestos of heading No. 25.24 or articles of asbestos or other products of heading No. 68.12 or 68.13;

(e) Articles of heading No.30.05 or 30.06; yarn used to clean between the teeth (dental floss), in individual retail packages, of heading No.33.06;

(f) Sensitized textiles of headings No.37.01 to 37.04;

(g) Monofilament of which any cross-sectional dimension exceeds 1mm or strip or the like (for example, artificial straw) of an apparent width exceeding 5mm, of plastics (Chapter 39) , or plaits or fabrics or other basketware or wickerwork of such monofilament or strip (Chapter 46) ;

(h) Woven, knitted or crocheted fabrics, felt or nonwovens, impregnated, coated, covered or laminated with plastics, or articles thereof, of Chapter 39;

(i) Woven, knitted or crocheted fabrics, felt or nonwovens, impregnated, coated, covered or laminated with rubber, or articles thereof, of Chapter 40;

(j) Hides or skins with their hair or wool on (Chapter41 or 43) or artcles of furskin, artificial fur or articles thereof, of heading No.43.03 or 43.04;

(k) Articles of textile materials of heading No. 42.01 or 42.02;

(l) Products or articles of Chapter 48 (for example, cellulose wadding) ;

(m) Footwear or parts of footwear, gaiters or leggings or similar articles of Chapter 64;

(n) Hair-nets or other headgear or parts thereof of Chapter 65;

(o) Goods of Chapter 67;

(p) Abrasive-coated textile material (Heading No. 68.05) and also carbon fibres or articles of carbon fibres of heading No.68.15;

(q) Glass fibres or articles of glass fibres, other than

绣品除外(第七十章);

(十八)第九十四章的物品(例如,家具、寝具、灯具及照明装置);

(十九)第九十五章的物品(例如,玩具、游戏品、运动用品及网具);

(二十)第九十六章的物品(例如,刷子、旅行用成套缝纫用具、拉链、打字机色带、卫生巾(护垫)及止血塞、婴儿尿布及尿布衬里);或

(二十一)第九十七章的物品。

二、

(一)可归入第五十章至第五十五章及税号 58.09 或 59.02 的由两种或两种以上纺织材料混合制成的货品,应按其中重量最大的那种纺织材料归类。

当没有一种纺织材料重量较大时,应按可归入的有关税号中最后一个税号所列的纺织材料归类。

(二)应用上述规定时:

1. 马毛粗松螺旋花线(税号 51.10)和含金属纱线(税号 56.05)均应作为一种单一的纺织材料,其重量应为它们在纱线中的合计重量;在机织物的归类中,金属线应作为一种纺织材料;

2. 在选择合适的税号时,应首先确定章,然后再确定该章的有关税号,至于不归入该章的其他材料可不予考虑;

3. 当归入第五十四章及第五十五章的货品与其他章的货品进行比较时,应将这两章作为一个单一的章对待;

4. 同一章或同一税号所列各种不同的纺织材料应作为单一的纺织材料对待。

(三)上述(一)、(二)两款规定亦适用于以下注释三、四、五或六所述纱线。

embroi-dery with glass thread on a visible ground of fabric (Chapter 70) ;

(r) Articles of Chapter 94 (for example, furniture, bedding, lamps and lighting fittings) ;

(s) Articles of Chapter 95 (for example, toys games, sports requisites and nets) ;

(t) Articles of Chapter 96 (for example, brushes, travel sets for sewing, slide fasteners, typewriter ribbons, sanitary towels (pads) and tampons, napkins (diapers) and napkin liners for babies) ; or

(u) Articles of Chapter 97.

2.

(a) Goods classifiable in Chapters50 to 55or in heading No. 58.09 or 59.02 and of a mixture of two or more textile materials are to be classified as if consisting wholly of that one textile material which predominates by weight over any other single textile material.

When no one textile material predominates by weight, the goods are to be classified as if consisting wholly of that one textile material which is covered by the heading which occurs last in numerical order among those which equally merit consideration.

(b) For the purposes of the above rule:

(1) Gimped horsehair yarn (heading No. 51.10) and metallized yarn (heading No. 56.05) are to be treated as a single textile material the weight of which is to be taken as the aggregate of the weights of its components; for the classification of woven fabrics, metal thread is to be regarded as a textile material;

(2) The choice of appropriate heading shall be effected by determining first the Chapter and then the applicable heading within that Chapter, disregarding any materials not classified in that Chapter;

(3) When both Chapters 54 and 55 are involved with any other Chapter, Chapters 54 and 55 are to be treated as a single Chapter;

(4) Where a Chapter or a heading refers to goods of different textile materials, such materials are to be treated as a single textile material.

(c) The provisions of paragraphs (A) and (B) above apply also to the yarns referred to in Notes 3, 4, 5 or 6 below.

三、

（一）本类的纱线（单纱、多股纱线或缆线）除下列（二）款另有规定的以外，凡符合以下规格的应作为“线、绳、索、缆”：

1. 丝或绢丝纱线，细度在20000分特以上；

2. 化学纤维纱线（包括第五十四章的用两根及以上单丝纺成的纱线），细度在10000分特以上；

3. 大麻或亚麻纱线：

（1）加光或上光的，细度在1429分特及以上；

（2）未加光或上光的，细度在20000分特以上；

4. 三股或三股以上的椰壳纤维纱线；

5. 其他植物纤维纱线，细度在20000分特以上；

6. 用金属线加强的纱线。

（二）下列各项不按上述（一）款规定办理：

1. 羊毛或其他动物毛纱线及纸纱线，但用金属线加强的纱线除外；

2. 第五十五章的化学纤维长丝丝束以及第五十四章的未加捻或捻度每米少于5转的复丝纱线；

3. 税号50.06的蚕胶丝及第五十四章的单丝；

4. 税号56.05的含金属纱线；但用金属线加强的纱线按上述（一）款6项规定办理；

5. 税号56.06的绳绒线、粗松螺旋花线及纵行起圈纱线。

四、

（一）除下列（二）款另有规定的以外，第五十章、第五十一章、第五十二章、第五十四章和第五十五章所称“供零售用”纱线，是指以下列方式包装的纱线（单纱、股纱线或揽线）：

1. 绕于纸板、线轴、纱管或类似芯子上，其重量（含线芯）符合下列规定：

（1）丝、绢丝或化学纤维长丝纱线，不超过85克；

3.

(A) For the purposes of this Section, and subject to the exceptions in paragraph (B) below, yarns (single, multiple (folded) or cabled) of the following descriptions are to be treated as “twine, cordage, ropes and cables”:

(a) Of silk or waste silk, measuring more than 20000 decitex;

(b) Of man-made fibres (including yarn of two or more monofilaments of Chapter 54), measuring more than10000 decitex;

(c) Of true hemp or flax:

(i) Polished or glazed, measuring 1429 decitex or more; or

(ii) Not polished or glzed, measuring more than 20000 decitex;

(d) Of coir, consisting of three or more plies;

(e) Of other vegetable fibres, measuring more than 20000 decitex, or

(f) Reinforced with metal thread.

(B) Exceptions:

(a) Yarn of wool or other animal hair and paper yarn, other than yarn, rein forced with metal thread;

(b) Man-made filament tow of Chapter 55 and multifilament yarn without twist or with a twist of less than 5 turns per metre of Chapter 54;

(c) Silk worm gut of heading No.50.06, and monofilaments of Chapter 54;

(d) Metallized yarn of Heading No.56.05; yarn reinforced with metal thread is subject to paragraph (A) (f) above; and

(e) Chenille, yarn, gimped yarn and loop wale-yarn of heading No.56.06.

4.

(A) For the purposes of Chapters 50, 51, 52, 54 and 55, the expression “put up for retail sale” in relation to yarn means, subject to the exceptions in paragraph (B) below, yarn (single, multiple (folded) or cabled) put up:

(a) On cards, reels, tubes or similar supports, of a weight (including support) not exceeding:

(i) 85g in the case of silk, waste silk or manmade filament yarn; or

（2）其他纱线，不超过125克。

2. 绕成团、绞或束，其重量符合下列规定：

（1）细度在3000分特以下的化学纤维长丝纱线，丝或绢丝纱线，不超过85克；

（2）细度在2000分特以下的任何其他纱线，不超过125克；

（3）其他纱线，不超过500克。

3. 绕成绞或束，每绞或每束中有若干用线分开的小绞或小束，每小绞或小束的重量相等，并且符合下列规定：

（1）丝、绢丝或化学纤维长丝纱线，不超过85克；

（2）其他纱线，不超过125克。

（二）下列各项不按上述（一）款规定办理：

1. 各种纺织材料制的单纱，但下列两种除外：

（1）未漂白的羊毛或动物细毛单纱；

（2）漂白、染色或印色的羊毛或动物细毛单纱，细度在5000分特以上。

2. 未漂白的多股纱线或缆线：

（1）丝或绢丝制的，不论何种包装；

（2）除羊毛或动物细毛外其他纺织材料制，成绞或成束的。

3. 漂白、染色或印色丝或绢丝制的多股纱线或缆线，细度在133分特及以下；

4. 任何纺织材料制的单纱、多股纱线或缆线：

（1）交叉绕成绞或束的；

（2）绕于纱芯上或以其他方式卷绕，明显用于纺织工业的（例如，绕于纱管、加捻管、纬纱管、锥形筒管或锭子上的或者绕成蚕茧状以供绣花机使用的纱线）。

五、税号52.04、54.01及55.08所称“缝纫线”，是指下列多股纱线或缆线：

（一）绕于芯子（例如，线轴、纱管）上，重量（包括纱芯）不超过1000克；

（二）作为缝纫线上过浆的；

（三）终捻为反手（Z）捻的。

(ii) 125g in other cases;

(b) In balls, hanks or skeins of a weight not exceeding:

(i) 85g in the case of man-made filament yarn of less than 3000 decitex, silk or silk waste;

(ii) 125g in the case of all other yarns of less than 2000 decitex; or

(iii) 500g in other cases.

(c) In hanks or skeins comprising several smaller hanks or skeins separated by dividing threads which render them independent one of the other, each of uniform weight not exceeding:

(i) 85g in the case of silk, waste silk or manmade filament yarn; or

(ii) 125g in other cases.

(B) Exceptions:

(a) Single yarn of any textile material, except:

(i) Single yarn of wool or fine animal hair, unbleached; and;

(ii) Single yarn of wool or fine animal hair, bleached, dyed or printed, measuring more than 5000 decitex;

(b) Multiple (folded) or cabled yarn, unbleached:

(i) Of silk or waste silk, however put up; or

(ii) Of other textile material except wool or fine animal hair, in hanks or skeins;

(c) Multiple (folded) or cabled yarn of silk or waste silk, bleached, dyed or printed, measuring 133 decitex or less; and

(d) Single, multiple (folded) or cabled yarn of any textile material:

(i) In cross-reeled hanks or skeins;or

(ii) Put up on supports or in some other manner indicating its use in the textile industry (for example, on cops, twisting mill tubes, pirns, conical bobbins or spindles, or reeled in the form of cocoons for embroidery looms) .

5. For the purposes of headings Nos.52.04, 54.01 and 55.08 the expression “sewing thread” means multiple (folded) or cabled yarn:

(a) Put up on supports (for example, reels, tubes) of a weight (including support) not exceeding 1000g;

(b) Dressed for use as sewing thread; and

(c) With a final “Z” twist.

六、本类所称“高强力纱”，是指断裂强度大于下列标准的纱线：

尼龙、其他聚酰胺或聚酯制的单纱——60 厘牛顿/特克斯；
尼龙、其他聚酰胺或聚酯制的多股纱线或缆线——53 厘牛顿/特克斯；
粘胶纤维制的单纱、多股纱线或缆线——27 厘牛顿/特克斯。

七、本类所称“制成的”，是指：

（一）裁剪成除正方形或长方形以外的其他形状的；
（二）呈制成状态，无需缝纫或其他进一步加工（或仅需剪断分隔联线）即可使用的（例如，某些抹布、毛巾、台布、方披巾、毯子）；
（三）裁剪成一定尺寸，至少有一边为带有可见的锥形或压平形的热封边，其余各边经本注释其他各项所述加工，但不包括为防止剪边脱纱而用热切法或其他简单方法处理的织物；
（四）已缝边或滚边，或者在任一边带有结制的流苏，但不包括为防止剪边脱纱而锁边或用其他简单方法处理的织物；
（五）裁剪成一定尺寸并经抽纱加工的；
（六）缝合、胶合或用其他方法拼合而成的（将两段或两段以上同样料子的织物首尾连接而成的匹头，以及由两层或两层以上的织物，不论中间有无胎料，层迭而成的匹头除外）；
（七）针织或钩编成一定形状，不论进口或出口时是单件还是以若干件相连成幅的。

八、对于第五十章至第六十章：

（一）第五十章至第五十五章和第六十章，以及除条文另有规定以外的第五十六章至第五十九章，不适用于上述注释七所规定的制成货品；
（二）第五十章至第五十五章及第六十章不包括第五十六章至第五十九章的货品。

6. For the purposes of this Section, the expression “high tenacity yarn” means yarn having a tenacity, expressed in cN/tex (centinewtons per tex), greater than the following:

Single yarn of nylon or other polyamides, or of polyesters 60c N/tex;
Multiple (folded) or cabled yarn of nylon or other polyamides, or of polyesters 53c N/tex;
Single, multiple (folded) or cabled yarn of viscose rayon 27c N/tex.

7. For the purposes of this Section, the expression “made up” means:

(a) Cut otherwise than into squares or rectangles;
(b) Produced in the finished state, ready for use (or merely needing separation by cutting dividing threads) without sewing or other working (for example, certain dusters, towels, table cloths, scarf squares, blankets);
(c) Cut to size and with at least one heat-sealed edge with a visibly tapered or compressed border and the other edges treated as described in any other subparagraph of this Note, but excluding fabrics the cut edges of which have been prevented from unravelling by hot cutting or by other simple means;
(d) Hemmed or with rolled edges, or with a knotted fringe at any of the edges, but excluding fabrics the cut deges of which have been prevented from unravelling by whipping or by other simple means;
(e) Cut to size and having undergone a process of drawn thread work;
(f) Assembled by sewing, gumming or otherwise (other than piece goods consisting of two or more lengths of identical material joined end to end and piece goods composed of two or more textiles assembled in layers, whether or not padded);
(g) Knitted or crocheted to shape, whether presented as separate items or in the form of a number of items in the length.

8. For the purposes of Chapters 50 to 60:

(a) Chapters 50 to 55 and 60 and, except where the context otherwise requires, Chapters 56 to 59 do not apply to goods made up within the meaning of Note 7 above; and;
(b) Chapters 50 to55 and 60 do not apply to goods of Chapters 56 to 59.

九、第五十章至第五十五章的机织物包括由若干层平行纱线以锐角或直角相互层迭，在纱线交叉点用粘合剂或以热粘合法粘合而成的织物。

十、用纺织材料和橡胶线制成的弹性产品归入本类。

十一、本类所称“浸渍”，包括“浸泡”。

十二、本类所称“聚酰胺”，包括“芳族聚酰胺”。

十三、本类及本目录所称“弹性纱线”是指合成纤维纺织材料制成的长丝纱线（包括单丝，变形纱线除外）。这些纱线可拉伸至原长的三倍而不断裂，并可在拉伸至原长两倍后五分钟内回复到不超过原长度的一倍半。

十四、除条文另有规定的以外，各种服装即使成套包装供零售用，也应按各自税号分别归类。本注释所称“纺织服装”，是指税号 61.01 至 61.14 及税号 62.01 至 62.11 所列的各种服装。

子目注释：

一、本类及本目录所用有关名词解释如下：

（一）未漂白纱线：

1. 带有纤维自然色泽并且未经漂染（不论是否整体染色）或印色的纱线；

2. 从回收纤维制得，色泽未定的纱线（本色纱）。

这种纱线可用无色浆料或易褪色染料（可轻易地用肥皂洗去）处理，如果是化学纤维纱线，则整体用消光剂（例如二氧化钛）进行处理。

（二）漂白纱线：

9. The woven fabrics of Chapters 50 to 55 include fabrics consisting of layers of parallel textile yarns superimposed on each other at acute or right angles.These layers are bonded at the intersections of the yarns by an adhesive or by thermal bonding;

10. Elastic products consisting of textile materials combined with rubber threads are classified in this Section.

11. For the purposes of this Section, the expression “impregnated” includes “dipped”.

12. For the purposes of this Section, the expression “polyamides” includes “aramides”.

13. For the purposes of this Section and, where applicable, throughout the nomenclature, the expression “elastomeric yarn” means filament yarn, including monofilament, of synthetic textile material, other than textured yarn, which does not break on being extended to three times its original length and which returns, after being extended to twice its original length, within a period of five minutes, to a length not greater than one and a half times its original length.

14. Unless the context otherwise requires, textile garments of different headings are to be classified in their own headings even if put up in sets for retail sale. For the purposes of this Note, the expression “textile garments” means garments of headings Nos.61.01 to 61.14 and heading Nos.62.01 to 62.11.

Subheading Notes:

1. In the Section , where applicable, throughout the Nomenclature, the following expressions have the meanings hereby assigned to them:

(a) Unbleached yarn

Yarn which:

(1) has the natural colour of its constituent fibres and has not been bleached, dyed (whether or not in the mass) or printed; or

(2) is of indeterminate colour (“grey yarn”) , manufactured from garnetted stock.

Such yarn may have been treated with a colourless dressing or fugitive dye (which disappears after simple washing with soap) and, in the case of man-made fibres, treated in the mass with delustring agent (for example, titanium dioxide) .

(b) Bleached yarn

Yarn which:

1. 经漂白加工、用漂白纤维制得或经染白（除条文另有规定的以外）（不论是否整体染色）及用白浆料处理的纱线；

2. 用未漂白纤维和漂白纤维混纺制得的纱线；

3. 用未漂白纱和漂白纱纺成多股纱线或缆线。

（三）着色（染色或印色）纱线：

1. 染成彩色（不论是否整体染色，但白色或易褪色除外）或印色的纱线，以及用染色或印色纤维纺制的纱线；

2. 用各色染色纤维混合纺制或用未漂白或漂白纤维与着色纤维混合制得的纱线（夹色纱或混色纱），以及用一种或几种颜色间隔印色而获得点纹印迹的纱线；

3. 用已经印色的纱条或粗纱纺制的纱线；

4. 用未漂白纱和漂白纱与着色纱纺成的多股纱线或缆线。

上述定义作相应调整后适用于第五十四章的单丝、扁条或类似产品。

（四）未漂白机织物：

用未漂白纱线织成后未经漂白、染色或印花的机织物。这类织物可用无色浆料或易褪色染料处理。

（五）漂白机织物：

1. 经漂白、染白或用白浆料处理（除条文另有规定的以外）的成匹机织物；

2. 用漂白纱线织成的机织物；

3. 用未漂白纱线和漂白纱线织成的机织物；

（六）染色机织物：

1. 除条文另有规定的以外，染成白色以外的其他单一颜色或用白色以外的其他有色整理剂处理的成匹机织物；

2. 用单一颜色的着色纱线织成的机织物。

(1) has undergone a bleaching process, is made of bleached fibres or, unless the context otherwise requires, has been dyed white (whether or not in the mass) or treated with a white dressing;

(2) consists of a mixture of unbleached and bleached fibres; or

(3) is multiple (folded) or cabled and consists of unbleached and bleached yarns.

(c) Coloured (dyed or printed) yarn

Yarn which:

(1) is dyed (whether or not in the mass) other than white or in a fugitive colour, or printed, or made from dyed or printed fibres;

(2) consists of a mixture of dyed fibres of different colours or of a mixture of unbleached or bleached fibres with coloured fibres (marl or mixture yarns) , or is printed in one or more colours at intervals to give the impression of dots;

(3) is obtained from slivers or rovings which have been printed; or

(4) is multiple (folded) or cabled and consists of unbleached or bleached yarn and coloured yarn.

The above definitions also apply, *mutatis mutandis*, to monofilament and to strip or the like of Chapter 54.

(d) Unbleached woven fabric:

Woven fabric made from unbleached yarn and which has not been bleached, dyed or printed. Such fabric may have treated with a colourless dressing or a fugitive dye.

(e) Bleached woven fabric

Woven fabric which:

(1) has been bleached or, unless the context otherwise requires, dyed white or treated with a white dressing, in the piece;

(2) consists of bleached yarn; or

(3) consists of unbleached and bleached yarn.

(f) Dyed woven fabric

Woven fabric which:

(1) is dyed a single uniform colour other than white (unless the context otherwise requires) or has been treated with a coloured finish other than white (unless the context otherwise requires), in the piece; or

(2) consists of coloured yarn of a single uniform col-

our.

（七）色织机织物：

除印花机织物以外的下列机织物：

1. 用各种不同颜色纱线或同一颜色不同深浅（纤维的自然色彩除外）纱线织成的机织物；

2. 用未漂白或漂白与着色纱线织成的机织物；

3. 用夹色纱线或混色纱线织成的机织物。

不论何种情况，布边或布头的纱线均可忽略不计。

（八）印花机织物：

成匹印花的机织物，不论是否用各色纱线织成。用刷子或喷枪，经转印纸转印、植绒或蜡防印花等方法印成花纹图案的机织物亦可视为印花机织物。

上述各类纱线或织物如经丝光工艺处理并不影响其归类。

上述（四）至（八）的定义在作必要修改后适用于针织或钩编织物。

（九）平纹组织：

每根纬纱在并排的经纱间上下交错而过，而每根经纱也在并排的纬纱间上下交错而过的织物组织。

二、

（一）含有两种或两种以上纺织材料的第五十六章至第六十三章的产品，应根据本类注释二对第五十章至第五十五章或税目 58.09 的此类纺织材料产品归类的规定来确定归类。

（二）运用本条规定时：

1. 应酌情考虑按归类总规则第三条来确定归类；

2. 对由底布和绒面或毛圈面构成的纺织品，在归类时可不考虑底布的属性；

3. 对税号 58.10 的刺绣品及其制品，归类时应

(g) Woven fabric of yarns of different colours:

Woven fabric (other than printed woven fabric) which:

(1) consists of yarns of different colours or yarns of different shades of the same colour (other than the natural colour of the constituent fibres) ;

(2) consists of unbleached or bleached yarn and coloured yarn; or

(3) consists of marl or mixture yarns.

(In all cases, the yarn used in selvedges and piece ends is not taken into consideration.)

(h) Printed woven fabric:

Woven fabric which has been printed in the piece, whether or not made from yarns of differenent colours.

(The following are also regarded as printed woven fabrics:woven fabrics bearing designs made, for example, with a brush or spray gun, by means of transfer paper, by flocking or by the batik process.)

The process of mercerization does not affect the classification of yarns or fabrics within the above categories.

The definitions at (d) to (h) above apply, *mutatis mutandis*, or to knitted crocheted fabrics.

(i) Plain weave:

A fabric construction in which each yarn of the weft passes alternately over and under successive yarns of the warp and each yarn of the warp passes alternately over and under successive yarns of the weft.

2.

(a) Products of Chapters 56 to 63 containing two or more textile materials are to be regarded as consisting wholly of that textile material which would be selected under Note 2 to this Section for the classification of the productof Chapters 50 to 55 or of heading 58.09 consisting of the same textile materials.

(b) For the application of this rule:

(1) where appropriate, only the part which determines the classification under interpretative Rule 3 shall be taken into account;

(2) in the case of textile products consisting of a ground fabric and a pile or looped surface, no account shall be taken of the ground fabric;

(3) in the case of embroidery of heading No.58.10 and

只考虑底布的属性，但不见底布的刺绣品及其制品应根据绣线的属性确定归类。

goods thereof, only the ground fabric shall be taken into account. However, embroidery without visible ground, and goods thereof, shall be classified with reference to the embroidering threads alone.

第五十章 蚕丝

Chapter 50 SILK

序号 No.	税则号列 Tariff Line	货品名称	最惠国税率 MFN(%)	协定税率 Agreement(%)		特惠税率 S.P.(%)		普通税率 Gen.(%)	Article Description
	50.01	**适于缫丝的蚕茧:**							**Silk-worm cocoons suitable for reeling:**
3596	5001.0010	---适于缫丝的桑蚕茧	6	0 5	东盟ASEAN,智利CL,新西兰NZ,秘鲁PE,哥斯达黎加CR 巴基斯坦PK	0	最不发达35国LDC35,最不发达4国LDC4	70	---Bombyx mori cocoons (Mulberry feeding silk-worm cocoons)
3597	5001.0090	---其他	6	0 5	东盟ASEAN,智利CL,新西兰NZ,秘鲁PE,哥斯达黎加CR 巴基斯坦PK	0	最不发达35国LDC35,最不发达4国LDC4	70	---Other
	50.02	**生丝（未加捻）:**							**Raw silk (not thrown):**
		---桑蚕丝:							---Steam filature silk:
3598	5002.0011	----厂丝	9	0 5	东盟ASEAN,智利CL,新西兰NZ,秘鲁PE,哥斯达黎加CR 巴基斯坦PK	0	最不发达35国LDC35,最不发达4国LDC4	80	----Plant reeled (filature silk)
3599	5002.0012	----土丝	9	0 5	东盟ASEAN,智利CL,新西兰NZ,秘鲁PE,哥斯达黎加CR 巴基斯坦PK	0	最不发达35国LDC35,最不发达4国LDC4	80	----Home reeled
3600	5002.0013	----双宫丝	9	0 5	东盟ASEAN,智利CL,新西兰NZ,秘鲁PE,哥斯达黎加CR 巴基斯坦PK	0	最不发达35国LDC35,最不发达4国LDC4	80	----Doupion
3601	5002.0019	----其他	9	0 5	东盟ASEAN,智利CL,新西兰NZ,秘鲁PE,哥斯达黎加CR 巴基斯坦PK	0	最不发达35国LDC35,最不发达4国LDC4	80	----Other

序号 No.	税则号列 Tariff Line	货品名称	最惠国税率 MFN(%)	协定税率 Agreement(%)		特惠税率 S.P.(%)		普通税率 Gen.(%)	Article Description
3602	5002.0020	---柞蚕丝	9	0 5	东盟ASEAN,智利CL,新西兰NZ,秘鲁PE,哥斯达黎加CR 巴基斯坦PK	0	最不发达35国LDC35,最不发达4国LDC4	80	---Tussah silk
3603	5002.0090	---其他	9	0 5	东盟ASEAN,智利CL,新西兰NZ,秘鲁PE,哥斯达黎加CR 巴基斯坦PK	0	最不发达35国LDC35,最不发达4国LDC4	80	---Other
	50.03	**废丝（包括不适于缫丝的蚕茧、废纱及回收纤维）：**							**Silk waste (including cocoons unsuitable for reeling, yarn waste and garnetted stock):**
		---未梳:							---Not carded or combed:
3604	5003.0011	----下茧、茧衣、长吐、滞头	9	0 5	东盟ASEAN,智利CL,新西兰NZ,秘鲁PE,哥斯达黎加CR 巴基斯坦PK	0	最不发达35国LDC35,最不发达4国LDC4	70	----Inferior cocoon (cocoon unsuitable for reeling), blaze, frison and frigon (knub from reeling)
3605	5003.0012	----回收纤维	9	0 5	东盟ASEAN,智利CL,新西兰NZ,秘鲁PE,哥斯达黎加CR 巴基斯坦PK	0	最不发达35国LDC35,最不发达4国LDC4	70	----Garnetted stock
3606	5003.0019	----其他	9	0 5	东盟ASEAN,智利CL,新西兰NZ,秘鲁PE,哥斯达黎加CR 巴基斯坦PK	0	最不发达35国LDC35,最不发达4国LDC4	70	----Other
		---其他:							---Other:
3607	5003.0091	----绵球	9	0 5	东盟ASEAN,智利CL,新西兰NZ,秘鲁PE,哥斯达黎加CR 巴基斯坦PK	0	最不发达35国LDC35,最不发达4国LDC4	70	----Silk tops
3608	5003.0099	----其他	9	0 5	东盟ASEAN,智利CL,新西兰NZ,秘鲁PE,哥斯达黎加CR 巴基斯坦PK	0	最不发达35国LDC35,最不发达4国LDC4	70	----Other
	50.04	**丝纱线（绢纺纱线除外），非供零售用：**							**Silk yarn (other than yarn spun from silk waste) not put up for retail sale:**

序号 No.	税则号列 Tariff Line	货品名称	最惠国税率 MFN(%)	协定税率 Agreement(%)		特惠税率 S.P.(%)		普通税率 Gen.(%)	Article Description
3609	5004.0000	丝纱线（绢纺纱线除外），非供零售用	6	0 5	东盟ASEAN,智利CL,新西兰NZ,秘鲁PE,哥斯达黎加CR,澳门MO 巴基斯坦PK	0	最不发达35国LDC35,最不发达4国LDC4	90	Silk yarn (other than yarn spun from silk waste) not put up for retail sale
	50.05	**绢纺纱线，非供零售用:**							**Yarn spun from silk waste, not put up for retail sale:**
3610	5005.0010	---细丝纱线	6	0 5	东盟ASEAN,智利CL,新西兰NZ,秘鲁PE,哥斯达黎加CR,澳门MO 巴基斯坦PK	0	最不发达35国LDC35,最不发达4国LDC4	90	---Spun from noil
3611	5005.0090	---其他	6	0 5	东盟ASEAN,智利CL,新西兰NZ,秘鲁PE,哥斯达黎加CR,澳门MO 巴基斯坦PK	0	最不发达35国LDC35,最不发达4国LDC4	90	---Other
	50.06	**丝纱线及绢纺纱线，供零售用;蚕胶丝:**							**Silk yarn and yarn spun from silk waste, put up for retail sale; silkworm gut:**
3612	5006.0000	丝纱线及绢纺纱线，供零售用;蚕胶丝	6	0 5	东盟ASEAN,智利CL,新西兰NZ,秘鲁PE,哥斯达黎加CR,澳门MO 巴基斯坦PK	0	最不发达35国LDC35,最不发达4国LDC4	100	Silk yarn and yarn spun from silk waste, put up for retail sale;silk-worm gut
	50.07	**丝或绢丝机织物:**							**Woven fabrics of silk or of silk waste:**
		-细丝机织物:							-Fabrics of noil silk:
3613	5007.1010	---未漂白（包括未练白或练白）或漂白	10	0 5	东盟ASEAN,智利CL,新西兰NZ,秘鲁PE,哥斯达黎加CR 巴基斯坦PK	0	最不发达35国LDC35,最不发达4国LDC4,老挝LA	130	---Unbleaded (unscoured or scoured) or bleached
3614	5007.1090	---其他	10	0 5	东盟ASEAN,智利CL,新西兰NZ,秘鲁PE,哥斯达黎加CR 巴基斯坦PK	0	最不发达35国LDC35,最不发达4国LDC4,老挝LA	130	---Other
		-其他机织物，按重量计丝或绢丝（细丝除外）含量在85%及以上:							-Other fabrics, containing 85% or more by weight of silk or of silk waste other than noil silk:
		---桑蚕丝机织物:							---Of Bombyx mori silk:

序号 No.	税则号列 Tariff Line	货品名称	最惠国税率 MFN(%)	协定税率 Agreement(%)		特惠税率 S.P.(%)		普通税率 Gen.(%)	Article Description
3615	5007.2011	----未漂白(包括未练白或练白)或漂白	10	0 5 9	东盟ASEAN,智利CL,新西兰NZ,秘鲁PE,哥斯达黎加CR 巴基斯坦PK 亚太APTA	0	最不发达35国LDC35,最不发达4国LDC4,老挝LA	130	----Unbleached (unscoured or scoured) or bleached
3616	5007.2019	----其他	10	0 5 9	东盟ASEAN,智利CL,新西兰NZ,秘鲁PE,哥斯达黎加CR,香港HK 巴基斯坦PK 亚太APTA	0	最不发达35国LDC35,最不发达4国LDC4,老挝LA	130	----Other
		---柞蚕丝机织物:							---Of tussah silk:
3617	5007.2021	----未漂白(包括未练白或练白)或漂白	10	0 5 9	东盟ASEAN,智利CL,新西兰NZ,秘鲁PE,哥斯达黎加CR 巴基斯坦PK 亚太APTA	0	最不发达35国LDC35,最不发达4国LDC4,老挝LA	130	----Unbleached (unscoured or scoured) or bleached
3618	5007.2029	----其他	10	0 5 9	东盟ASEAN,智利CL,新西兰NZ,秘鲁PE,哥斯达黎加CR 巴基斯坦PK 亚太APTA	0	最不发达35国LDC35,最不发达4国LDC4,老挝LA	130	----Other
		---绢丝机织物:							---Of silk waste other than noil silk:
3619	5007.2031	----未漂白(包括未练白或练白)或漂白	10	0 5 9	东盟ASEAN,智利CL,新西兰NZ,秘鲁PE,哥斯达黎加CR 巴基斯坦PK 亚太APTA	0	最不发达35国LDC35,最不发达4国LDC4,老挝LA	130	----Unbleached (unscoured or scoured) or bleached
3620	5007.2039	----其他	10	0 5 9	东盟ASEAN,智利CL,新西兰NZ,秘鲁PE,哥斯达黎加CR 巴基斯坦PK 亚太APTA	0	最不发达35国LDC35,最不发达4国LDC4,老挝LA	130	----Other
3621	5007.2090	---其他	10	0 5 9	东盟ASEAN,智利CL,新西兰NZ,秘鲁PE,哥斯达黎加CR 巴基斯坦PK 亚太APTA	0	最不发达35国LDC35,最不发达4国LDC4,老挝LA	130	---Other
		-其他机织物:							-Other fabrics:

序号 No.	税则号列 Tariff Line	货品名称	最惠国税率 MFN(%)	协定税率 Agreement(%)		特惠税率 S.P.(%)		普通税率 Gen.(%)	Article Description
3622	5007.9010	---未漂白（包括未练白或练白）或漂白	10	0 5 8.5	东盟ASEAN,智利CL,新西兰NZ,秘鲁PE,哥斯达黎加CR 巴基斯坦PK 亚太APTA	0	最不发达35国LDC35,最不发达4国LDC4,老挝LA	130	---Unbleached (unscoured or scoured) or bleached
3623	5007.9090	---其他	10	0 5 8.5	东盟ASEAN,智利CL,新西兰NZ,哥斯达黎加CR 巴基斯坦PK,秘鲁PE 亚太APTA	0	最不发达35国LDC35,最不发达4国LDC4,老挝LA	130	---Other

第五十一章
羊毛、动物细毛或粗毛；马毛纱线及其机织物

注释：

本目录所称：

一、"羊毛"，是指绵羊或羔羊身上长的天然纤维；

二、"动物细毛"，是指下列动物的毛:羊驼、美洲驼、驼马、骆驼（包括单峰骆驼）、牦牛、安哥拉山羊、西藏山羊、喀什米尔山羊及类似山羊(普通山羊除外)、家兔(包括安哥拉兔)、野兔、海狸、河狸鼠或麝鼠；

三、"动物粗毛"，是指以上未提及的其他动物的毛，但不包括制刷用鬃、毛（税目 05.02）以及马毛（税目 05.11）。

Chapter 51
Wool, fine or coarse animal hair; horsehair yarn and woven fabric

Note:

Throughout the Nomenclature:

1. "Wool" means the natural fibre grown by sheep or lambs;
2. "Fine animal hair" means the hair of alpaca, llama, vicuna, camel (including dromedary), yak, Angora, Tibetan, Kashmir or similar goats (but not common goats) , rabbit (including Angora rabbit), hare, beaver, nutria or muskrat;
3. "Coarse animal hair" means the hair of animals not mentioned above, excluding brush-making hair and bristles (heading No.05.02) and horsehair (heading No.05.11).

序号 No.	税则号列 Tariff Line	货品名称	最惠国税率 MFN(%)	协定税率 Agreement(%)		特惠税率 S.P.(%)		普通税率 Gen.(%)	Article Description
	51.01	**未梳的羊毛:**							**Wool, not carded or combed:**
		-含脂羊毛，包括剪前水洗毛:							-Greasy, including fleece-washed wool:
3624	5101.1100	--剪羊毛	38[①]	20	东盟ASEAN			50	--Shorn wool
3625	5101.1900	--其他	38[②]	20	东盟ASEAN			50	--Other
		-脱脂羊毛，未碳化:							-Degreased, not carbonized:
3626	5101.2100	--剪羊毛	38[③]	20	东盟ASEAN			50	--Shorn wool
3627	5101.2900	--其他	38[④]	20	东盟ASEAN			50	--Other
3628	5101.3000	-碳化羊毛	38[⑤]	0	澳门MO			50	-Carbonized
				20	东盟ASEAN				
	51.02	**未梳的动物细毛或粗毛:**							**Fine or coarse animal hair, not carded or combed:**
		-细毛:							-Fine animal hair:
3629	5102.1100	--喀什米尔山羊的	9	0	东盟ASEAN,智利CL,新西兰NZ,秘鲁PE,哥斯达黎加CR	0	最不发达35国LDC35,最不发达4国LDC4	45	--Of kashmir (cashmere) goats
				5	巴基斯坦PK				
		--其他:							--Other:

① 配额税率（In-quota rate）：1%；新西兰国别关税配额税率：0%。
② 配额税率（In-quota rate）：1%；新西兰国别关税配额税率：0%。
③ 配额税率（In-quota rate）：1%；新西兰国别关税配额税率：0%。
④ 配额税率（In-quota rate）：1%；新西兰国别关税配额税率：0%。
⑤ 配额税率（In-quota rate）：1%；新西兰国别关税配额税率：0%。

序号 No.	税则号列 Tariff Line	货品名称	最惠国税率 MFN(%)	协定税率 Agreement(%)		特惠税率 S.P.(%)		普通税率 Gen.(%)	Article Description
3630	5102.1910	---兔毛	9	0	东盟ASEAN,智利CL,新西兰NZ,秘鲁PE,哥斯达黎加CR	0	最不发达35国LDC35,最不发达4国LDC4	50	---Of rabbit and hare
				5	巴基斯坦PK				
3631	5102.1920	---其他山羊绒	9	0	东盟ASEAN,智利CL,新西兰NZ,秘鲁PE,哥斯达黎加CR	0	最不发达35国LDC35,最不发达4国LDC4	45	---Of other goats
				5	巴基斯坦PK				
3632	5102.1930	---骆驼毛、骆驼绒	9	0	东盟ASEAN,智利CL,新西兰NZ,秘鲁PE,哥斯达黎加CR	0	最不发达35国LDC35,最不发达4国LDC4	45	---Of camel
				5	巴基斯坦PK				
3633	5102.1990	---其他	9	0	东盟ASEAN,智利CL,新西兰NZ,秘鲁PE,哥斯达黎加CR	0	最不发达35国LDC35	45	---Other
				5	巴基斯坦PK				
3634	5102.2000	-粗毛	9	0	东盟ASEAN,智利CL,新西兰NZ,秘鲁PE,哥斯达黎加CR	0	最不发达35国LDC35,最不发达4国LDC4	50	-Coarse animal hair
				5	巴基斯坦PK				
	51.03	**羊毛或动物细毛或粗毛的废料，包括废纱线，但不包括回收纤维:**							**Waste of wool or of fine or coarse animal hair, including yarn waste but excluding garnetted stock:**
		-羊毛或动物细毛的落毛:							-Noils of wool or of fine animal hair:
3635	5103.1010	---羊毛落毛	38[①]	20	东盟ASEAN			50	---Of wool
3636	5103.1090	---其他	9	0	东盟ASEAN,智利CL,新西兰NZ,秘鲁PE,哥斯达黎加CR	0	最不发达35国LDC35,最不发达4国LDC4	50	---Other
				5	巴基斯坦PK				
		-羊毛或动物细毛的其他废料:							-Other waste of wool or of fine animal hair:
3637	5103.2010	---羊毛废料	13.5	0	东盟ASEAN,新加坡SG,新西兰NZ	0	最不发达35国LDC35	20	---Of wool
				1.4	智利CL				
				2.7	哥斯达黎加CR				
				6.8	巴基斯坦PK,秘鲁PE				
3638	5103.2090	---其他	9	0	东盟ASEAN,智利CL,新西兰NZ,秘鲁PE,哥斯达黎加CR	0	最不发达35国LDC35	50	---Other
				5	巴基斯坦PK				

① 配额税率（In-quota rate）：1%；新西兰国别关税配额税率：0%。

序号 No.	税则号列 Tariff Line	货品名称	最惠国税率 MFN(%)	协定税率 Agreement(%)		特惠税率 S.P.(%)		普通税率 Gen.(%)	Article Description
3639	5103.3000	-动物粗毛废料	9	0 5	东盟ASEAN,智利CL,新西兰NZ,秘鲁PE,哥斯达黎加CR 巴基斯坦PK	0	最不发达35国LDC35,最不发达4国LDC4	50	-Waste of coarse animal hair
	51.04	**羊毛或动物细毛或粗毛的回收纤维:**							**Garnetted stock of wool or of fine or coarse animal hair:**
3640	5104.0010	---羊毛的回收纤维	15	0 3 7.5 12	东盟ASEAN,智利CL,新加坡SG,新西兰NZ 哥斯达黎加CR 秘鲁PE 巴基斯坦PK	0	最不发达35国LDC35	20	---Of wool
3641	5104.0090	---其他	5	0	东盟ASEAN,智利CL,巴基斯坦PK,新西兰NZ,秘鲁PE,哥斯达黎加CR	0	最不发达35国LDC35,最不发达4国LDC4	50	---Other
	51.05	**已梳的羊毛及动物细毛或粗毛(包括精梳片毛):**							**Wool and fine or coarse animal hair, carded or combed (including combed wool in fragments):**
3642	5105.1000	-粗梳羊毛	38①					50	-Carded wool
		-羊毛条及其他精梳羊毛:							-Wool tops and other combed wool:
3643	5105.2100	--精梳片毛	38②					50	--Combed wool in fragments
3644	5105.2900	--其他	38③					50	--Other
		-已梳动物细毛:							-Fine animal hair, carded or combed:
3645	5105.3100	--喀什米尔山羊的	5	0	东盟ASEAN,智利CL,巴基斯坦PK,新西兰NZ,秘鲁PE,哥斯达黎加CR	0	最不发达35国LDC35,最不发达4国LDC4	50	--Of kashmir (cashmere) goats
		--其他:							--Other:
3646	5105.3910	---兔毛	5	0	东盟ASEAN,智利CL,巴基斯坦PK,新西兰NZ,哥斯达黎加CR	0	最不发达35国LDC35,最不发达4国LDC4	70	---Of rabbit or hare
		---其他山羊绒:							---Of other goats:

① 配额税率（In-quota rate）：3%；新西兰国别关税配额税率：0%。
② 配额税率（In-quota rate）：3%；新西兰国别关税配额税率：0%。
③ 配额税率（In-quota rate）：3%；新西兰国别关税配额税率：0%。

序号 No.	税则号列 Tariff Line	货品名称	最惠国税率 MFN(%)	协定税率 Agreement(%)		特惠税率 S.P.(%)		普通税率 Gen.(%)	Article Description
3647	5105.3921	----无毛山羊绒	5	0	东盟ASEAN,智利CL,巴基斯坦PK,新西兰NZ,哥斯达黎加CR	0	最不发达35国LDC35,最不发达4国LDC4	50	----Dehaired goats wool
3648	5105.3929	----其他	5	0	东盟ASEAN,智利CL,巴基斯坦PK,新西兰NZ,哥斯达黎加CR	0	最不发达35国LDC35,最不发达4国LDC4	50	----Other
3649	5105.3990	---其他	5	0	东盟ASEAN,智利CL,巴基斯坦PK,新西兰NZ,哥斯达黎加CR	0	最不发达35国LDC35	50	---Other
3650	5105.4000	-已梳动物粗毛	5	0	东盟ASEAN,智利CL,巴基斯坦PK,新西兰NZ,哥斯达黎加CR	0	最不发达35国LDC35,最不发达4国LDC4	50	-Coarse animal hair, carded or combed
	51.06	**粗梳羊毛纱线，非供零售用:**							**Yarn of carded wool, not put up for retail-sale:**
3651	5106.1000	-按重量计羊毛含量在85%及以上	5	0	东盟ASEAN,智利CL,巴基斯坦PK,新西兰NZ,秘鲁PE,哥斯达黎加CR,香港HK,澳门MO	0	最不发达35国LDC35,最不发达4国LDC4	70	-Containing 85% or more by weight of wool
3652	5106.2000	-按重量计羊毛含量在85%以下	5	0	东盟ASEAN,智利CL,巴基斯坦PK,新西兰NZ,秘鲁PE,哥斯达黎加CR,香港HK,澳门MO	0	最不发达35国LDC35,最不发达4国LDC4	70	-Containing less than 85% by weight of wool
	51.07	**精梳羊毛纱线，非供零售用:**							**Yarn of combed wool, not put up for retail sale:**
3653	5107.1000	-按重量计羊毛含量在85%及以上	5	0 2.5	东盟ASEAN,智利CL,巴基斯坦PK,新西兰NZ,秘鲁PE,哥斯达黎加CR,香港HK,澳门MO 亚太APTA	0	最不发达35国LDC35,最不发达4国LDC4	70	-Containing 85% or more by weight of wool
3654	5107.2000	-按重量计羊毛含量在85%以下	5	0	东盟ASEAN,智利CL,巴基斯坦PK,新西兰NZ,秘鲁PE,哥斯达黎加CR,澳门MO	0	最不发达35国LDC35,最不发达4国LDC4	70	-Containing less than 85% by weight of wool

序号 No.	税则号列 Tariff Line	货品名称	最惠国税率 MFN(%)	协定税率 Agreement(%)		特惠税率 S.P.(%)		普通税率 Gen.(%)	Article Description
	51.08	**动物细毛（粗梳或精梳）纱线，非供零售用:**							**Yarn of fine animal hair (carded or combed), not put up for retail sale:**
		-粗梳: ---按重量计动物细毛含量在85%及以上的:							-Carded: ---Containing 85% or more by weight of fine animal hair:
3655	5108.1011	----山羊绒的	5	0 4.3	东盟ASEAN,智利CL,巴基斯坦PK,新西兰NZ,秘鲁PE,哥斯达黎加CR,澳门MO 亚太APTA	0	最不发达35国LDC35,最不发达4国LDC4	70	----Of cashmere
3656	5108.1019	----其他	5	0 4.3	东盟ASEAN,智利CL,巴基斯坦PK,新西兰NZ,秘鲁PE,哥斯达黎加CR,澳门MO 亚太APTA	0	最不发达35国LDC35,最不发达4国LDC4	70	----Other
3657	5108.1090	---其他	5	0 4.3	东盟ASEAN,智利CL,巴基斯坦PK,新西兰NZ,秘鲁PE,哥斯达黎加CR,澳门MO 亚太APTA	0	最不发达35国LDC35,最不发达4国LDC4	70	---Other
		-精梳: ---按重量计动物细毛含量在85%及以上的:							-Combed: ---Containing 85% or more by weight of fine animal hair:
3658	5108.2011	----山羊绒的	5	0	东盟ASEAN,智利CL,巴基斯坦PK,新西兰NZ,哥斯达黎加CR,澳门MO	0	最不发达35国LDC35,最不发达4国LDC4	70	----Of cashmere
3659	5108.2019	----其他	5	0	东盟ASEAN,智利CL,巴基斯坦PK,新西兰NZ,哥斯达黎加CR,澳门MO	0	最不发达35国LDC35,最不发达4国LDC4	70	----Other
3660	5108.2090	---其他	5	0	东盟ASEAN,智利CL,巴基斯坦PK,新西兰NZ,哥斯达黎加CR,澳门MO	0	最不发达35国LDC35,最不发达4国LDC4	70	---Other
	51.09	**羊毛或动物细毛的纱线，供零售用:**							**Yarn of wool or of fine animal hair, put up for retail sale:**
		-按重量计羊毛或动物细毛含量在85%及以上:							-Containing 85% or more by weight of wool or of fine animal hair:

序号 No.	税则号列 Tariff Line	货品名称	最惠国税率 MFN(%)	协定税率 Agreement(%)		特惠税率 S.P.(%)		普通税率 Gen.(%)	Article Description
		---动物细毛的:							---Of fine animal hair:
3661	5109.1011	----山羊绒的	6	0 5	东盟ASEAN,智利CL,新西兰NZ,秘鲁PE,哥斯达黎加CR 巴基斯坦PK	0	最不发达35国LDC35,最不发达4国LDC4	80	----Of cashmere
3662	5109.1019	----其他	6	0 5	东盟ASEAN,智利CL,新西兰NZ,秘鲁PE,哥斯达黎加CR,澳门MO 巴基斯坦PK	0	最不发达35国LDC35,最不发达4国LDC4	80	----Other
3663	5109.1090	---其他	6	0 5	东盟ASEAN,智利CL,新西兰NZ,秘鲁PE,哥斯达黎加CR,澳门MO 巴基斯坦PK	0	最不发达35国LDC35,最不发达4国LDC4	80	---Other
		-其他: ---动物细毛的:							-Other: ---Of fine animal hair:
3664	5109.9011	----山羊绒的	6	0 5	东盟ASEAN,智利CL,新西兰NZ,哥斯达黎加CR,澳门MO 巴基斯坦PK	0	最不发达35国LDC35,最不发达4国LDC4	80	----Of cashmere
3665	5109.9019	----其他	6	0 5	东盟ASEAN,智利CL,新西兰NZ,哥斯达黎加CR,澳门MO 巴基斯坦PK	0	最不发达35国LDC35,最不发达4国LDC4	80	----Other
3666	5109.9090	---其他	6	0 5	东盟ASEAN,智利CL,新西兰NZ,哥斯达黎加CR,澳门MO 巴基斯坦PK	0	最不发达35国LDC35,最不发达4国LDC4	80	---Other
	51.10	**动物粗毛或马毛的纱线(包括马毛粗松螺旋花线),不论是否供零售用:**							**Yarn of coarse animal hair or of horsehair (including gimped horsehair yarn), whether or not put up for retail sale:**
3667	5110.0000	动物粗毛或马毛的纱线(包括马毛粗松螺旋花线),不论是否供零售用	6	0 5	东盟ASEAN,智利CL,新西兰NZ,秘鲁PE,哥斯达黎加CR,澳门MO 巴基斯坦PK	0	最不发达35国LDC35,最不发达4国LDC4	70	Yarn of coarse animal hair or of horsehair (including gimped horsehair yarn), whether or not put up for retail sale
	51.11	**粗梳羊毛或粗梳动物细毛的机织物:**							**Woven fabrics of carded wool or of carded fine animal hair:**

序号 No.	税则号列 Tariff Line	货品名称	最惠国税率 MFN(%)	协定税率 Agreement(%)		特惠税率 S.P.(%)		普通税率 Gen.(%)	Article Description
		-按重量计羊毛或动物细毛含量在85%及以上:							-Containing 85% or more by weight of wool or of fine animal hair:
		--每平方米重量不超过300克:							--Of a weight not exceeding 300g/m^2:
		---动物细毛的:							---Of fine animal hair:
3668	5111.1111	----山羊绒的	10	0 5 8.5	东盟ASEAN,智利CL,新加坡SG,新西兰NZ,秘鲁PE,哥斯达黎加CR 巴基斯坦PK 亚太APTA	0	最不发达35国LDC35	130	----Of cashmere
3669	5111.1119	----其他	10	0 5 8.5	东盟ASEAN,智利CL,新加坡SG,新西兰NZ,秘鲁PE,哥斯达黎加CR 巴基斯坦PK 亚太APTA	0	最不发达35国LDC35	130	----Other
3670	5111.1190	---其他	10	0 5 8.5	东盟ASEAN,智利CL,新加坡SG,新西兰NZ,哥斯达黎加CR,澳门MO 巴基斯坦PK,秘鲁PE 亚太APTA	0	最不发达35国LDC35	130	---Other
		--其他:							--Other:
		---动物细毛的:							---Of fine animal hair:
3671	5111.1911	----山羊绒的	10	0 5 8.5	东盟ASEAN,智利CL,新加坡SG,新西兰NZ,秘鲁PE,哥斯达黎加CR 巴基斯坦PK 亚太APTA	0	最不发达35国LDC35	130	----Of cashmere
3672	5111.1919	----其他	10	0 5 8.5	东盟ASEAN,智利CL,新加坡SG,新西兰NZ,秘鲁PE,哥斯达黎加CR 巴基斯坦PK 亚太APTA	0	最不发达35国LDC35	130	----Other
3673	5111.1990	---其他	10	0 5 8.5	东盟ASEAN,智利CL,新加坡SG,新西兰NZ,哥斯达黎加CR 巴基斯坦PK,秘鲁PE 亚太APTA	0	最不发达35国LDC35	130	---Other
3674	5111.2000	-其他,主要或仅与化学纤维长丝混纺	10	0 5	东盟ASEAN,智利CL,新加坡SG,新西兰NZ,秘鲁PE,哥斯达黎加CR 巴基斯坦PK	0	最不发达35国LDC35	130	-Other, mixed mainly or solely with manmade filaments
3675	5111.3000	-其他,主要或仅与化学纤维短纤混纺	10	0 5 8.5	东盟ASEAN,智利CL,新加坡SG,新西兰NZ,秘鲁PE,哥斯达黎加CR 巴基斯坦PK 亚太APTA	0	最不发达35国LDC35	130	-Other, mixed mainly or solely with manmade staple fibres
3676	5111.9000	-其他	10	0 5	东盟ASEAN,智利CL,新加坡SG,新西兰NZ,秘鲁PE,哥斯达黎加CR 巴基斯坦PK	0	最不发达35国LDC35	130	-Other
	51.12	**精梳羊毛或精梳动物细毛的机织物:**							**Woven fabrics of combed wool or of combed fine animal hair:**

序号 No.	税则号列 Tariff Line	货品名称	最惠国税率 MFN(%)	协定税率 Agreement(%)		特惠税率 S.P.(%)		普通税率 Gen.(%)	Article Description
		-按重量计羊毛或动物细毛含量在85%及以上:							-Containing 85% or more by weight of wool or of fine animal hair:
3677	5112.1100	--每平方米重量不超过200克	10	0 5	东盟ASEAN,智利CL,新加坡SG,新西兰NZ,哥斯达黎加CR,香港HK,澳门MO 亚太APTA,巴基斯坦PK,秘鲁PE	0	最不发达35国LDC35,最不发达4国LDC4	130	--Of a weight not exceeding $200g/m^2$
3678	5112.1900	--其他	10	0 5	东盟ASEAN,智利CL,新加坡SG,新西兰NZ,哥斯达黎加CR,香港HK,澳门MO 亚太APTA,巴基斯坦PK,秘鲁PE	0	最不发达35国LDC35,最不发达4国LDC4,缅甸MM,老挝LA,柬埔寨KH	130	--Other
3679	5112.2000	-其他,主要或仅与化学纤维长丝混纺	10	0 5	东盟ASEAN,智利CL,新加坡SG,新西兰NZ,秘鲁PE,哥斯达黎加CR,澳门MO 巴基斯坦PK	0	最不发达35国LDC35,最不发达4国LDC4	130	-Other, mixed mainly or solely with manmade filaments
3680	5112.3000	-其他,主要或仅与化学纤维短纤混纺	10	0 5	东盟ASEAN,智利CL,新加坡SG,新西兰NZ,秘鲁PE,哥斯达黎加CR,澳门MO 巴基斯坦PK	0	最不发达35国LDC35,最不发达4国LDC4	130	-Other, mixed mainly or solely with manmade staple fibres
3681	5112.9000	-其他	10	0 5	东盟ASEAN,智利CL,新加坡SG,新西兰NZ,哥斯达黎加CR,澳门MO 巴基斯坦PK,秘鲁PE	0	最不发达35国LDC35,最不发达4国LDC4	130	-Other
	51.13	**动物粗毛或马毛的机织物:**							**Woven fabrics of coarse animal hair or of horsehair:**
3682	5113.0000	动物粗毛或马毛的机织物	10	0 5	东盟ASEAN,智利CL,新加坡SG,新西兰NZ,秘鲁PE,哥斯达黎加CR,澳门MO 巴基斯坦PK	0	最不发达35国LDC35,最不发达4国LDC4	130	Woven fabrics of coarse animal hair or of horsehair

第五十二章
棉 花

Chapter 52
Cotton

子目注释：

子目号 5209.42 及 5211.42 所称“粗斜纹布（劳动布）”，是指用不同颜色的纱线织成的三线或四线斜纹织物，包括破斜纹组织的织物，这种织物以经纱为面，经纱染成一种相同的颜色，纬纱未漂白或经漂白、染成灰色或比经纱稍浅的颜色。

Subheading Note:

For the purposes of subheadings Nos.5209.42 and 5211.42, the expression “denim” means fabrics of yarns of different colours, of 3-thread or 4-thread twill, including broken twill, warp faced, the warp yarns of which are of one and the same colour and the weft yarns of which are unbleached, bleached, dyed grey or coloured a lighter shade of the colour of the warp yarns.

序号 No.	税则号列 Tariff Line	货品名称	最惠国税率 MFN(%)	协定税率 Agreement(%)		特惠税率 S.P.(%)		普通税率 Gen.(%)	Article Description
	52.01	**未梳的棉花：**							**Cotton, not carded or combed:**
3683	5201.0000	未梳的棉花	40[1]	20	东盟ASEAN			125	Cotton, not carded or combed
	52.02	**废棉（包括废棉纱线及回收纤维）：**							**Cotton waste (including yarn waste and garnetted stock):**
3684	5202.1000	-废棉纱线（包括废棉线）	10	0	东盟ASEAN,智利CL,新加坡SG,新西兰NZ,哥斯达黎加CR	0	最不发达35国LDC35	30	-Yarn waste (including thread waste)
				5	秘鲁PE				
		-其他:							-Other:
3685	5202.9100	--回收纤维	10	0	东盟ASEAN,智利CL,新加坡SG,新西兰NZ,秘鲁PE,哥斯达黎加CR,香港HK	0	最不发达35国LDC35,最不发达4国LDC4	30	--Garnetted stock
3686	5202.9900	--其他	10	0	东盟ASEAN,智利CL,新加坡SG,新西兰NZ,哥斯达黎加CR			30	--Other
	52.03	**已梳的棉花：**							**Cotton, carded or combed:**
3687	5203.0000	已梳的棉花	40[2]					125	Cotton, carded or combed
	52.04	**棉制缝纫线，不论是否供零售用：**							**Cotton sewing thread, whether or not put up for retail sale:**
		-非供零售用:							-Not put up for retail sale:

[1] 配额税率（In-quota rate）：1%。对配额外进口的一定数量棉花，适用滑准税形式暂定关税，具体方式式如下：
(1) 当进口棉花完税价格高于或等于 15.000 元/千克时，按 0.570 元/千克计征从量税；
(2) 当进口棉花完税价格低于 15.000 元/千克时，暂定从价税率按下式计算：
$Ri=9.337/Pi+2.77\%\times Pi-1$
对上式计算结果四舍五入保留 3 位小数。其中 Ri 为暂定从价税率，当按上式计算值高于 40%时，Ri 取值 40%；Pi 为关税完税价格，单位为元/千克。

[2] 配额税率（In-quota rate）：1%。

序号 No.	税则号列 Tariff Line	货品名称	最惠国税率 MFN(%)	协定税率 Agreement(%)		特惠税率 S.P.(%)		普通税率 Gen.(%)	Article Description
3688	5204.1100	--按重量计含棉量在85%及以上	5	0	东盟ASEAN,智利CL,新西兰NZ,秘鲁PE,哥斯达黎加CR,澳门MO	0	最不发达35国LDC35,最不发达4国LDC4,老挝LA	40	--Containing 85% or more by weight of cotton
3689	5204.1900	--其他	5	0	东盟ASEAN,智利CL,新西兰NZ,秘鲁PE,哥斯达黎加CR,澳门MO	0	最不发达35国LDC35,最不发达4国LDC4	40	--Other
3690	5204.2000	-供零售用	5	0	东盟ASEAN,智利CL,新西兰NZ,秘鲁PE,哥斯达黎加CR,澳门MO	0	最不发达35国LDC35,最不发达4国LDC4,老挝LA	50	-Put up for retail sale
	52.05	**棉纱线（缝纫线除外），按重量计含棉量在85%及以上，非供零售用：**							**Cotton yarn (other than sewing thread), containing 85% or more by weight of cotton, not put up for retail sale:**
		-未精梳纤维纺制的单纱：							-Single yarn, of uncombed fibres:
3691	5205.1100	--细度在714.29分特及以上（不超过14公支）	5	0 3.5	东盟ASEAN,智利CL,新西兰NZ,秘鲁PE,哥斯达黎加CR,香港HK,澳门MO,台湾TW 亚太APTA,巴基斯坦PK	0	最不发达35国LDC35,最不发达4国LDC4,缅甸MM,老挝LA,柬埔寨KH	40	--Measuring 714.29 decitex or more (not exceeding 14 metric number)
3692	5205.1200	--细度在714.29分特以下，但不细于232.56分特（超过14公支，但不超过43公支）	5	0 3.5	东盟ASEAN,智利CL,新西兰NZ,秘鲁PE,哥斯达黎加CR,香港HK,台湾TW 亚太APTA,巴基斯坦PK	0	最不发达35国LDC35,最不发达4国LDC4,缅甸MM,老挝LA,柬埔寨KH	40	--Measuring less than 714.29 decitex but not less than 232.56 decitex (exceeding 14 metric number but not exceeding 43 metric number)
3693	5205.1300	--细度在232.56分特以下，但不细于192.31分特（超过43公支，但不超过52公支）	5	0 3.5	东盟ASEAN,智利CL,新西兰NZ,秘鲁PE,哥斯达黎加CR,香港HK 亚太APTA,巴基斯坦PK	0	最不发达35国LDC35,最不发达4国LDC4	40	--Measuring less than 232.56 decitex but not less than 192.31 decitex (exceeding 43 metric number but not exceeding 52 metric number)

序号 No.	税则号列 Tariff Line	货品名称	最惠国税率 MFN(%)	协定税率 Agreement(%)		特惠税率 S.P.(%)		普通税率 Gen.(%)	Article Description
3694	5205.1400	--细度在192.31分特以下,但不细于125分特（超过52公支,但不超过80公支）	5	0 3.5	东盟ASEAN,智利CL,新西兰NZ,秘鲁PE,哥斯达黎加CR,香港HK 亚太APTA,巴基斯坦PK	0	最不发达35国LDC35,最不发达4国LDC4,缅甸MM,老挝LA	40	--Measuring less than 192.31 decitex but not less than 125 decitex (exceeding 52 metric number but not exceeding 80 metric number)
3695	5205.1500	--细度在125分特以下（超过80公支）	5	0 3.5	东盟ASEAN,智利CL,新西兰NZ,秘鲁PE,哥斯达黎加CR 亚太APTA,巴基斯坦PK	0	最不发达35国LDC35,最不发达4国LDC4	40	--Measuring less than 125 decitex (exceeding 80 metric number)
		-精梳纤维纺制的单纱:							-Single yarn, of combed fibres:
3696	5205.2100	--细度在714.29分特及以上（不超过14公支）	5	0 3.5	东盟ASEAN,智利CL,新西兰NZ,秘鲁PE,哥斯达黎加CR,香港HK 亚太APTA,巴基斯坦PK	0	最不发达35国LDC35,最不发达4国LDC4,缅甸MM	40	--Measuring 714.29 decitex or more (not exceeding 14 metric number)
3697	5205.2200	--细度在714.29分特以下，但不细于232.56分特（超过14公支，但不超过43公支）	5	0 3.5	东盟ASEAN,智利CL,新西兰NZ,秘鲁PE,哥斯达黎加CR,香港HK 亚太APTA,巴基斯坦PK	0	最不发达35国LDC35,最不发达4国LDC4	40	--Measuring less than 714.29 decitex but not less than 232.56 decitex (exceeding 14 metric number but not exceeding 43 metric number)
3698	5205.2300	--细度在232.56分特以下，但不细于192.31分特（超过43公支，但不超过52公支）	5	0 3.5	东盟ASEAN,智利CL,新西兰NZ,秘鲁PE,哥斯达黎加CR,香港HK 亚太APTA,巴基斯坦PK	0	最不发达35国LDC35,最不发达4国LDC4	40	--Measuring less than 232.56 decitex but not less than 192.31 decitex (exceeding 43 metric number but not exceeding 52 metric number)
3699	5205.2400	--细度在192.31分特以下,但不细于125分特（超过52公支,但不超过80公支）	5	0 3.5	东盟ASEAN,智利CL,新西兰NZ,秘鲁PE,哥斯达黎加CR,香港HK 亚太APTA,巴基斯坦PK	0	最不发达35国LDC35,最不发达4国LDC4,缅甸MM,老挝LA	40	--Measuring less than 192.31 decitex but not less than 125 decitex (exceeding 52 metric number but not exceeding 80 metric number)
3700	5205.2600	--细度在125分特以下,但不细于106.38分特（超过80公支,但不超过94公支）	5	0	东盟ASEAN,智利CL,新西兰NZ,秘鲁PE,哥斯达黎加CR,香港HK	0	最不发达35国LDC35,最不发达4国LDC4	40	--Measuring less than 125 decitex but not less than 106.38 decitex (exceeding 80 metric number but not exceeding 94 metric number)
3701	5205.2700	--细度在106.38分特以下，但不细于83.33分特（超过94公支，但不超过120公支）	5	0	东盟ASEAN,智利CL,新西兰NZ,秘鲁PE,哥斯达黎加CR,香港HK	0	最不发达35国LDC35,最不发达4国LDC4	40	--Measuring less than 106.38 decitex but not less than 83.33 decitex (exceeding 94 metric number but not exceeding 120 metric number)

序号 No.	税则号列 Tariff Line	货品名称	最惠国税率 MFN(%)	协定税率 Agreement(%)	特惠税率 S.P.(%)	普通税率 Gen.(%)	Article Description
3702	5205.2800	--细度在 83.33 分特以下（超过 120 公支）	5	0 东盟ASEAN,智利CL,新西兰NZ,秘鲁PE,哥斯达黎加CR,香港HK	0 最不发达35国LDC35,最不发达4国LDC4	40	--Measuring less than 83.33 decitex (exceeding 120 metric number)
		-未精梳纤维纺制的多股纱线或缆线:					-Multiple (folded) or cabled yarn, of uncombed fibres:
3703	5205.3100	--每根单纱细度在714.29分特及以上（每根单纱不超过 14 公支）	5	0 东盟ASEAN,智利CL,新西兰NZ,哥斯达黎加CR,香港HK,澳门MO 4.5 亚太APTA,巴基斯坦PK		40	--Measuring per single yarn 714.29 decitex or more (not exceeding 14 metric number per single yarn)
3704	5205.3200	--每根单纱细度在714.29 分特以下，但不细于 232.56 分特（每根单纱超过 14 公支，但不超过 43 公支）	5	0 东盟ASEAN,智利CL,新西兰NZ,秘鲁PE,哥斯达黎加CR,香港HK,澳门MO 3.5 亚太APTA,巴基斯坦PK	0 最不发达35国LDC35,最不发达4国LDC4	40	--Measuring per single yarn less than 714.29 decitex but not less than 232.56 decitex (exceeding 14 metric number but not exceeding 43 metric number per single yarn)
3705	5205.3300	--每根单纱细度在232.56 分特以下，但不细于 192.31 分特（每根单纱超过 43 公支，但不超过 52 公支）	5	0 东盟ASEAN,智利CL,新西兰NZ,秘鲁PE,哥斯达黎加CR,香港HK,澳门MO	0 最不发达35国LDC35,最不发达4国LDC4	40	--Measuring per single yarn less than 232.56 decitex but not less than 192.31 decitex (exceeding 43 metric number but not exceeding 52 metric number per single yarn)
3706	5205.3400	--每根单纱细度在192.31 分特以下，但不细于 125 分特（每根单纱超过 52 公支，但不超过 80 公支）	5	0 东盟ASEAN,智利CL,新西兰NZ,秘鲁PE,哥斯达黎加CR,香港HK,澳门MO	0 最不发达35国LDC35,最不发达4国LDC4	40	--Measuring per single yarn less than 192.31 decitex but not less than 125 decitex (exceeding 52 metric number but not exceeding 80 metric number per single yarn)
3707	5205.3500	--每根单纱细度在125 分特以下（每根单纱超过 80 公支）	5	0 东盟ASEAN,智利CL,新西兰NZ,秘鲁PE,哥斯达黎加CR,澳门MO	0 最不发达35国LDC35,最不发达4国LDC4	40	--Measuring per single yarn less than 125 decitex (exceeding 80 metric number per single yarn)
		-精梳纤维纺制的多股纱线或缆线:					-Multiple (folded) or cabled yarn, of combed fibres:
3708	5205.4100	--每根单纱细度在714.29分特及以上（每根单纱不超过 14 公支）	5	0 东盟ASEAN,智利CL,新西兰NZ,哥斯达黎加CR,香港HK,澳门MO 4.5 亚太APTA,巴基斯坦PK	0 最不发达35国LDC35	40	--Measuring per single yarn 714.29 decitex or more (not exceeding 14 metric number per single yarn)

序号 No.	税则号列 Tariff Line	货品名称	最惠国税率 MFN(%)	协定税率 Agreement(%)		特惠税率 S.P.(%)		普通税率 Gen.(%)	Article Description
3709	5205.4200	--每根单纱细度在714.29分特以下，但不细于232.56分特（每根单纱超过14公支，但不超过43公支）	5	0 3.5	智利CL,新西兰NZ,秘鲁PE,哥斯达黎加CR,香港HK,澳门MO 亚太APTA,巴基斯坦PK	0	最不发达35国LDC35,最不发达4国LDC4	40	--Measuring per single yarn less than 714.29 decitex but not less than 232.56 decitex (exceeding 14 metric number but not exceeding 43 metric number per single yarn)
3710	5205.4300	--每根单纱细度在232.56分特以下，但不细于192.31分特（每根单纱超过43公支，但不超过52公支）	5	0	东盟ASEAN,智利CL,新西兰NZ,哥斯达黎加CR,香港HK,澳门MO	0	最不发达35国LDC35,最不发达4国LDC4	40	--Measuring per singleyarn less than 232.56 decitex but not less than 192.31 decitex (exceeding 43 metric number but not exceeding 52 metric number per single yarn)
3711	5205.4400	--每根单纱细度在192.31分特以下，但不细于125分特（每根单纱超过52公支，但不超过80公支）	5	0	东盟ASEAN,智利CL,新西兰NZ,秘鲁PE,哥斯达黎加CR,香港HK,澳门MO	0	最不发达35国LDC35,最不发达4国LDC4	40	--Measuring per single yarn less than 192.31 decitex but not less than 125 decitex (exceeding 52 metric number but not exceeding 80 metric number per single yarn)
3712	5205.4600	--每根单纱细度在125分特以下，但不细于106.38分特（每根单纱超过80公支，但不超过94公支）	5	0 4.5	东盟ASEAN,智利CL,新西兰NZ,秘鲁PE,哥斯达黎加CR,香港HK,澳门MO 亚太APTA,巴基斯坦PK	0	最不发达35国LDC35,最不发达4国LDC4	40	--Measuring per single yarn less than 125 decitex but not less than 106.38 decitex (exceeding 80 metric number but not exceeding 94 metric number per single yarn)
3713	5205.4700	--每根单纱细度在106.38分特以下，但不细于83.33分特（每根单纱超过94公支，但不超过120公支）	5	0 4.5	东盟ASEAN,智利CL,新西兰NZ,秘鲁PE,哥斯达黎加CR,香港HK,澳门MO 亚太APTA,巴基斯坦PK	0	最不发达35国LDC35,最不发达4国LDC4	40	--Measuring per single yarn less than 106.38 decitex but not less than 83.33 decitex (exceeding 94 metric number but not exceeding 120 metric number per single yarn)
3714	5205.4800	--每根单纱细度在83.33分特以下（每根单纱超过120公支）	5	0 4.5	东盟ASEAN,智利CL,新西兰NZ,秘鲁PE,哥斯达黎加CR,香港HK,澳门MO 亚太APTA,巴基斯坦PK	0	最不发达35国LDC35,最不发达4国LDC4	40	--Measuring per single yarn less than 83.33 decitex (exceeding 120 metric number per single yarn)
	52.06	**棉纱线（缝纫线除外），按重量计含棉量在85%以下，非供零售用：**							**Cotton yarn (other than sewing thread), containing less than 85% by weight of cotton, not put up for retail sale:**
		-未精梳纤维纺制的单纱:							-Single yarn, of uncombed fibres:

序号 No.	税则号列 Tariff Line	货品名称	最惠国税率 MFN(%)	协定税率 Agreement(%)		特惠税率 S.P.(%)		普通税率 Gen.(%)	Article Description
3715	5206.1100	--细度在714.29分特及以上(不超过14公支)	5	0 3.5	东盟ASEAN,智利CL,新西兰NZ,哥斯达黎加CR,香港HK,澳门MO 亚太APTA,巴基斯坦PK			40	--Measuring 714.29 decitex or more (not exceeding 14 metric number)
3716	5206.1200	--细度在714.29分特以下,但不细于232.56分特(超过14公支,但不超过43公支)	5	0 3.5	东盟ASEAN,智利CL,新西兰NZ,秘鲁PE,哥斯达黎加CR,香港HK,澳门MO,台湾TW 亚太APTA,巴基斯坦PK	0	最不发达35国LDC35	40	--Measuring less than 714.29 decitex but not less than 232.56 decitex (exceeding 14 metric number but not exceeding 43 metric number)
3717	5206.1300	--细度在232.56分特以下,但不细于192.31分特(超过43公支,但不超过52公支)	5	0	东盟ASEAN,智利CL,新西兰NZ,秘鲁PE,哥斯达黎加CR,香港HK,澳门MO	0	最不发达35国LDC35,最不发达4国LDC4	40	--Measuring less than 232.56 decitex but not less than 192.31 decitex (exceeding 43 metric number but not exceeding 52 metric number)
3718	5206.1400	--细度在192.31分特以下,但不细于125分特(超过52公支,但不超过80公支)	5	0	东盟ASEAN,智利CL,新西兰NZ,秘鲁PE,哥斯达黎加CR,香港HK,澳门MO	0	最不发达35国LDC35,最不发达4国LDC4	40	--Measuring less than 192.31 decitex but not less than 125 decitex (exceeding 52 metric number but not exceeding 80 metric number)
3719	5206.1500	--细度在125分特以下(超过80公支)	5	0 3.5	东盟ASEAN,智利CL,新西兰NZ,秘鲁PE,哥斯达黎加CR,香港HK,澳门MO 亚太APTA,巴基斯坦PK	0	最不发达35国LDC35,最不发达4国LDC4	40	--Measuring less than 125 decitex (exceeding 80 metric number)
		-精梳纤维纺制的单纱:							-Single yarn, of combed fibres:
3720	5206.2100	--细度在714.29分特及以上(不超过14公支)	5	0 4.5	东盟ASEAN,智利CL,新西兰NZ,秘鲁PE,哥斯达黎加CR,香港HK,澳门MO 亚太APTA,巴基斯坦PK	0	最不发达35国LDC35	40	--Measuring 714.29 decitex or more (not exceeding 14 metric number)
3721	5206.2200	--细度在714.29分特以下,但不细于232.56分特(超过14公支,但不超过43公支)	5	0	东盟ASEAN,智利CL,新西兰NZ,秘鲁PE,哥斯达黎加CR,香港HK,澳门MO,台湾TW	0	最不发达35国LDC35	40	--Measuring less than 714.29 decitex but not less than 232.56 decitex (exceeding 14 metric number but not exceeding 43 metric number)
3722	5206.2300	--细度在232.56分特以下,但不细于192.31分特(超过43公支,但不超过52公支)	5	0	东盟ASEAN,智利CL,新西兰NZ,秘鲁PE,哥斯达黎加CR,香港HK,澳门MO	0	最不发达35国LDC35,最不发达4国LDC4	40	--Measuring less than 232.56 decitex but not less than 192.31 decite (exceeding 43 metric number but not exceeding 52 metric number)

序号 No.	税则号列 Tariff Line	货品名称	最惠国税率 MFN(%)	协定税率 Agreement(%)		特惠税率 S.P.(%)		普通税率 Gen.(%)	Article Description
3723	5206.2400	--细度在192.31分特以下，但不细于125分特（超过52公支，但不超过80公支）	5	0	东盟ASEAN,智利CL,新西兰NZ,秘鲁PE,哥斯达黎加CR,香港HK,澳门MO,台湾TW	0	最不发达35国LDC35,最不发达4国LDC4	40	--Measuring less than 192.31 decitex but not less than 125 decitex (exceeding 52 metric number but not exceeding 80 metric number)
3724	5206.2500	--细度在125分特以下（超过80公支）	5	0	东盟ASEAN,智利CL,新西兰NZ,秘鲁PE,哥斯达黎加CR,香港HK,澳门MO	0	最不发达35国LDC35,最不发达4国LDC4	40	--Measuring less than 125 decitex (exceeding 80 metric number)
		-未精梳纤维纺制的多股纱线或缆线:							-Multiple (folded) or cabled yarn, of uncombed fibres:
3725	5206.3100	--每根单纱细度在714.29分特及以上（每根单纱不超过14公支）	5	0	东盟ASEAN,智利CL,新西兰NZ,秘鲁PE,哥斯达黎加CR,香港HK,澳门MO	0	最不发达35国LDC35	40	--Measuring per single yarn 714.29 decitex or more (not exceeding 14 metric number per single yarn)
3726	5206.3200	--每根单纱细度在714.29分特以下，但不细于232.56分特（每根单纱超过14公支，但不超过43公支）	5	0	东盟ASEAN,智利CL,新西兰NZ,秘鲁PE,哥斯达黎加CR,香港HK,澳门MO	0	最不发达35国LDC35	40	--Measuring per single yarn less than 714.29 decitex but not less than 232.56 decitex (exceeding 14 metric number but not exceeding 43 metric number per single yarn)
3727	5206.3300	--每根单纱细度在232.56分特以下，但不细于192.31分特（每根单纱超过43公支，但不超过52公支）	5	0	东盟ASEAN,智利CL,新西兰NZ,秘鲁PE,哥斯达黎加CR,香港HK,澳门MO	0	最不发达35国LDC35,最不发达4国LDC4	40	--Measuring per single yarn less than 232.56 decitex but not less than 192.31 decitex (exceeding 43 metric number but not exceeding 52 metric number per single yarn)
3728	5206.3400	--每根单纱细度在192.31分特以下，但不细于125分特（每根单纱超过52公支，但不超过80公支）	5	0	东盟ASEAN,智利CL,新西兰NZ,秘鲁PE,哥斯达黎加CR,香港HK,澳门MO	0	最不发达35国LDC35,最不发达4国LDC4	40	--Measuring per single yarn less than 192.31 decitex but not less than 125 decitex (exceeding 52 metric number but not exceeding 80 metric number per single yarn)
3729	5206.3500	--每根单纱细度在125分特以下（每根单纱超过80公支）	5	0	东盟ASEAN,智利CL,新西兰NZ,秘鲁PE,哥斯达黎加CR,香港HK,澳门MO	0	最不发达35国LDC35,最不发达4国LDC4	40	--Measuring per single yarn less than 125 decitex (exceeding 80 metric number per single yarn)
		-精梳纤维纺制的多股纱线或缆线:							-Multiple (folded) or cabled yarn, of combed fibres:

序号 No.	税则号列 Tariff Line	货品名称	最惠国税率 MFN(%)	协定税率 Agreement(%)		特惠税率 S.P.(%)		普通税率 Gen.(%)	Article Description
3730	5206.4100	--每根单纱细度在714.29分特及以上（每根单纱不超过14公支）	5	0	东盟ASEAN,智利CL,新西兰NZ,秘鲁PE,哥斯达黎加CR,香港HK,澳门MO	0	最不发达35国LDC35	40	--Measuring per single yarn 714.29 decitex or more (not exceeding 14 metric number per single yarn)
3731	5206.4200	--每根单纱细度在714.29分特以下，但不细于232.56分特（每根单纱超过14公支，但不超过43公支）	5	0	东盟ASEAN,智利CL,新西兰NZ,秘鲁PE,哥斯达黎加CR,香港HK,澳门MO	0	最不发达35国LDC35	40	--Measuring per single yarn less than 714.29 decitex but not less than 232.56 decitex (exceeding 14 metric number but not exceeding 43 metric number per single yarn)
3732	5206.4300	--每根单纱细度在232.56分特以下，但不细于192.31分特（每根单纱超过43公支，但不超过52公支）	5	0	东盟ASEAN,智利CL,新西兰NZ,秘鲁PE,哥斯达黎加CR,香港HK,澳门MO	0	最不发达35国LDC35,最不发达4国LDC4	40	--Measuring per single yarn less than 232.56 decitex but not less then 192.31 decitex (exceeding 43 metric number but not exceeding 52 metric number per single yarn)
3733	5206.4400	--每根单纱细度在192.31分特以下，但不细于125分特（每根单纱超过52公支，但不超过80公支）	5	0	东盟ASEAN,智利CL,新西兰NZ,秘鲁PE,哥斯达黎加CR,香港HK,澳门MO	0	最不发达35国LDC35,最不发达4国LDC4	40	--Measuring per single yarn less than 192.31 decitex but not less than 125 decitex (exceeding 52 metric number but not exceeding 80 metric number per single yarn)
3734	5206.4500	--每根单纱细度在125分特以下（每根单纱超过80公支）	5	0	东盟ASEAN,智利CL,新西兰NZ,秘鲁PE,哥斯达黎加CR,香港HK,澳门MO	0	最不发达35国LDC35,最不发达4国LDC4	40	--Measuring per single yarn less than 125 decitex (exceeding 80 metric number per single yarn)
	52.07	**棉纱线（缝纫线除外），供零售用:**							**Cotton yarn (other than sewing thread) put up for retail sale:**
3735	5207.1000	-按重量计含棉量在85%及以上	6	0 5	东盟ASEAN,智利CL,新西兰NZ,秘鲁PE,哥斯达黎加CR,澳门MO 亚太APTA,巴基斯坦PK	0	最不发达35国LDC35	50	-Containing 85% or more by weight of cotton
3736	5207.9000	-其他	6	0 5	东盟ASEAN,智利CL,新西兰NZ,秘鲁PE,哥斯达黎加CR,澳门MO 巴基斯坦PK	0	最不发达35国LDC35,最不发达4国LDC4	50	-Other
	52.08	**棉机织物，按重量计含棉量在85%及以上，每平方米重量不超过200克:**							**Woven fabrics of cotton, containing 85% or more by weight of cotton, weighing not more than 200g/m^2:**
		-未漂白:							-Unbleached:

序号 No.	税则号列 Tariff Line	货品名称	最惠国税率 MFN(%)	协定税率 Agreement(%)		特惠税率 S.P.(%)		普通税率 Gen.(%)	Article Description
3737	5208.1100	--平纹机织物，每平方米重量不超过100克	10	0	东盟ASEAN,智利CL,巴基斯坦PK,新西兰NZ,秘鲁PE,哥斯达黎加CR,香港HK	0	最不发达35国LDC35	70	--Plain weave, weighing not more than 100g/m^2
3738	5208.1200	--平纹机织物，每平方米重量超过100克	10	0	东盟ASEAN,智利CL,巴基斯坦PK,新加坡SG,新西兰NZ,秘鲁PE,哥斯达黎加CR,香港HK	0	最不发达35国LDC35	70	--Plain weave, weighing more than 100g/m^2
3739	5208.1300	--三线或四线斜纹机织物，包括双面斜纹机织物	10	0	东盟ASEAN,智利CL,巴基斯坦PK,新西兰NZ,秘鲁PE,哥斯达黎加CR,香港HK	0	最不发达35国LDC35	70	--3-thread or 4-thread twill, including cross twill
				8.5	亚太APTA				
3740	5208.1900	--其他机织物	10	0	东盟ASEAN,智利CL,巴基斯坦PK,新加坡SG,新西兰NZ,秘鲁PE,哥斯达黎加CR,香港HK	0	最不发达35国LDC35	70	--Other fabrics
		-漂白:							-Bleached:
3741	5208.2100	--平纹机织物，每平方米重量不超过100克	10	0	东盟ASEAN,智利CL,巴基斯坦PK,新西兰NZ,秘鲁PE,哥斯达黎加CR,香港HK	0	最不发达35国LDC35	70	--Plain weave, weighing not more than 100g/m^2
3742	5208.2200	--平纹机织物，每平方米重量超过100克	10	0	东盟ASEAN,智利CL,巴基斯坦PK,新加坡SG,新西兰NZ,秘鲁PE,哥斯达黎加CR,香港HK	0	最不发达35国LDC35,最不发达4国LDC4,缅甸MM,老挝LA,柬埔寨KH	70	--Plain weave, weighing more than 100g/m^2
3743	5208.2300	--三线或四线斜纹机织物，包括双面斜纹机织物	12	0	东盟ASEAN,智利CL,巴基斯坦PK,新加坡SG,新西兰NZ,秘鲁PE,香港HK	0	最不发达35国LDC35	70	--3-thread or 4-thread twill, icluding cross twill
				2.4	哥斯达黎加CR				
3744	5208.2900	--其他机织物	10	0	东盟ASEAN,智利CL,巴基斯坦PK,新西兰NZ,秘鲁PE,哥斯达黎加CR,香港HK	0	最不发达35国LDC35	70	--Other fabrics
		-染色:							-Dyed:
3745	5208.3100	--平纹机织物，每平方米重量不超过100克	10	0	东盟ASEAN,智利CL,巴基斯坦PK,新西兰NZ,秘鲁PE,哥斯达黎加CR,香港HK,台湾TW	0	最不发达35国LDC35,最不发达4国LDC4	70	--Plain weave, weighing not more than 100g/m^2
3746	5208.3200	--平纹机织物，每平方米重量超过100克	10	0	东盟ASEAN,智利CL,巴基斯坦PK,新加坡SG,新西兰NZ,秘鲁PE,哥斯达黎加CR,香港HK,台湾TW	0	最不发达35国LDC35,最不发达4国LDC4	70	--Plain weave, weighing more than 100g/m^2
				8.5	亚太APTA				

序号 No.	税则号列 Tariff Line	货品名称	最惠国税率 MFN(%)	协定税率 Agreement(%)		特惠税率 S.P.(%)		普通税率 Gen.(%)	Article Description
3747	5208.3300	--三线或四线斜纹机织物，包括双面斜纹机织物	10	0 8.5	东盟ASEAN,智利CL,巴基斯坦PK,新西兰NZ,秘鲁PE,哥斯达黎加CR,香港HK 亚太APTA	0	最不发达35国LDC35,最不发达4国LDC4,缅甸MM,老挝LA,柬埔寨KH	70	--3-thread or 4-thread twill, including cross twill
3748	5208.3900	--其他机织物	10	0 8.5	东盟ASEAN,智利CL,巴基斯坦PK,新加坡SG,新西兰NZ,秘鲁PE,哥斯达黎加CR,香港HK,台湾TW 亚太APTA	0	最不发达35国LDC35,最不发达4国LDC4	70	--Other fabrics
		-色织:							-Of yarns of different colours:
3749	5208.4100	--平纹机织物，每平方米重量不超过100克	10	0	东盟ASEAN,智利CL,巴基斯坦PK,新加坡SG,新西兰NZ,秘鲁PE,哥斯达黎加CR,香港HK	0	最不发达35国LDC35	70	--Plain weave, weighing not more than 100g/m^2
3750	5208.4200	--平纹机织物，每平方米重量超过100克	10	0 7	东盟ASEAN,智利CL,巴基斯坦PK,新加坡SG,新西兰NZ,秘鲁PE,哥斯达黎加CR,香港HK,台湾TW 亚太APTA	0	最不发达35国LDC35,最不发达4国LDC4	70	--Plain weave, weighing more than 100g/m^2
3751	5208.4300	--三线或四线斜纹机织物，包括双面斜纹机织物	10	0	东盟ASEAN,智利CL,巴基斯坦PK,新西兰NZ,秘鲁PE,哥斯达黎加CR,香港HK	0	最不发达35国LDC35	70	--3-thread or 4-thread twill, including cross twill
3752	5208.4900	--其他机织物	10	0 9	东盟ASEAN,智利CL,巴基斯坦PK,新加坡SG,新西兰NZ,秘鲁PE,哥斯达黎加CR,香港HK 亚太APTA	0	最不发达35国LDC35,最不发达4国LDC4,缅甸MM,老挝LA,柬埔寨KH	70	--Other fabrics
		-印花:							-Printed.
3753	5208.5100	--平纹机织物，每平方米重量不超过100克	10	0	东盟ASEAN,智利CL,巴基斯坦PK,新西兰NZ,秘鲁PE,哥斯达黎加CR,香港HK	0	最不发达35国LDC35,最不发达4国LDC4	70	--Plain weave, weighing not more than 100g/m^2
3754	5208.5200	--平纹机织物，每平方米重量超过100克	10	0 8.5	东盟ASEAN,智利CL,巴基斯坦PK,新加坡SG,新西兰NZ,秘鲁PE,哥斯达黎加CR,香港HK 亚太APTA	0	最不发达35国LDC35,最不发达4国LDC4	70	--Plain weave, weighing more than 100g/m^2

序号 No.	税则号列 Tariff Line	货品名称	最惠国税率 MFN(%)	协定税率 Agreement(%)		特惠税率 S.P.(%)		普通税率 Gen.(%)	Article Description
		--其他机织物:							--Other fabrics:
3755	5208.5910	---三线或四线斜纹机织物，包括双面斜纹机织物	10	0	东盟ASEAN,智利CL,巴基斯坦PK,新西兰NZ,秘鲁PE,哥斯达黎加CR,香港HK	0	最不发达35国LDC35	70	---3-thread or 4-thread twill, including cross twill
3756	5208.5990	---其他	10	0 8.5	东盟ASEAN,智利CL,巴基斯坦PK,新西兰NZ,秘鲁PE,哥斯达黎加CR,台湾TW 亚太APTA	0	最不发达35国LDC35	70	---Other
	52.09	**棉机织物，按重量计含棉量在85%及以上，每平方米重量超过200克:**							**Woven fabrics of cotton, containing 85% or more by weight of cotton, weighing more than 200g/m^2:**
		-未漂白							-Unbleached:
3757	5209.1100	--平纹机织物	10	0	智利CL,巴基斯坦PK,新西兰NZ,哥斯达黎加CR,香港HK	0	最不发达35国LDC35,最不发达4国LDC4	70	--Plain weave
3758	5209.1200	--三线或四线斜纹机织物，包括双面斜纹机织物	10	0 7	东盟ASEAN,智利CL,巴基斯坦PK,新加坡SG,新西兰NZ,秘鲁PE,哥斯达黎加CR,香港HK 亚太APTA	0	最不发达35国LDC35	70	--3-thread or 4-thread twill, including cross twill
3759	5209.1900	--其他机织物	10	0	东盟ASEAN,智利CL,巴基斯坦PK,新加坡SG,新西兰NZ,秘鲁PE,哥斯达黎加CR,香港HK	0	最不发达35国LDC35,最不发达4国LDC4	70	--Other fabrics
		-漂白:							-Bleached:
3760	5209.2100	--平纹机织物	12	0 2.4	东盟ASEAN,智利CL,巴基斯坦PK,新加坡SG,新西兰NZ,秘鲁PE,香港HK 哥斯达黎加CR	0	最不发达35国LDC35,最不发达4国LDC4	70	--Plain weave
3761	5209.2200	--三线或四线斜纹机织物，包括双面斜纹机织物	12	0 2.4	东盟ASEAN,智利CL,巴基斯坦PK,新加坡SG,新西兰NZ,秘鲁PE,香港HK 哥斯达黎加CR	0	最不发达35国LDC35	70	--3-thread or 4-thread twill, including cross twill
3762	5209.2900	--其他机织物	12	0 2.4	东盟ASEAN,智利CL,巴基斯坦PK,新加坡SG,新西兰NZ,秘鲁PE,香港HK 哥斯达黎加CR	0	最不发达35国LDC35	70	--Other fabrics
		-染色:							-Dyed:

序号 No.	税则号列 Tariff Line	货品名称	最惠国税率 MFN(%)	协定税率 Agreement(%)		特惠税率 S.P.(%)		普通税率 Gen.(%)	Article Description
3763	5209.3100	--平纹机织物	10	0 8.5	东盟ASEAN,智利CL,巴基斯坦PK,新加坡SG,新西兰NZ,秘鲁PE,哥斯达黎加CR,香港HK,台湾TW 亚太APTA	0	最不发达35国LDC35,最不发达4国LDC4,缅甸MM,老挝LA,柬埔寨KH	70	--Plain weave
3764	5209.3200	--三线或四线斜纹机织物，包括双面斜纹机织物	10	0 8.5	东盟ASEAN,智利CL,巴基斯坦PK,新加坡SG,新西兰NZ,秘鲁PE,哥斯达黎加CR,香港HK,台湾TW 亚太APTA	0	最不发达35国LDC35,最不发达4国LDC4,缅甸MM,老挝LA,柬埔寨KH	70	--3-thread or 4-thread twill, including cross twill
3765	5209.3900	--其他机织物	10	0 8.5	东盟ASEAN,智利CL,巴基斯坦PK,新加坡SG,新西兰NZ,秘鲁PE,哥斯达黎加CR,香港HK,台湾TW 亚太APTA	0	最不发达35国LDC35,最不发达4国LDC4,缅甸MM,老挝LA,柬埔寨KH	70	--Other fabrics
		-色织:							-Of yarns of different colours:
3766	5209.4100	--平纹机织物	10	0	东盟ASEAN,智利CL,巴基斯坦PK,新加坡SG,新西兰NZ,秘鲁PE,哥斯达黎加CR,香港HK,台湾TW	0	最不发达35国LDC35	70	--Plain weave
3767	5209.4200	--粗斜纹布（劳动布）	10	0 8.5	东盟ASEAN,智利CL,巴基斯坦PK,新加坡SG,新西兰NZ,秘鲁PE,哥斯达黎加CR,香港HK,澳门MO,台湾TW 亚太APTA	0	最不发达35国LDC35,最不发达4国LDC4,缅甸MM,老挝LA,柬埔寨KH	70	--Denim
3768	5209.4300	--其他三线或四线斜纹机织物，包括双面斜纹机织物	10	0 9.3	东盟ASEAN,智利CL,巴基斯坦PK,新西兰NZ,秘鲁PE,哥斯达黎加CR,香港HK 亚太APTA	0	最不发达35国LDC35	70	--Other coloured 3 or 4-thread twill, with≥85% cotton, >200g/m^2

序号 No.	税则号列 Tariff Line	货品名称	最惠国税率 MFN(%)	协定税率 Agreement(%)		特惠税率 S.P.(%)		普通税率 Gen.(%)	Article Description
3769	5209.4900	--其他机织物	10	0	东盟ASEAN,智利CL,巴基斯坦PK,新加坡SG,新西兰NZ,秘鲁PE,哥斯达黎加CR,香港HK	0	最不发达35国LDC35	70	--Other fabrics
		-印花:							-Printed:
3770	5209.5100	--平纹机织物	10	0 9.3	东盟ASEAN,智利CL,巴基斯坦PK,新加坡SG,新西兰NZ,秘鲁PE,哥斯达黎加CR,香港HK 亚太APTA	0	最不发达35国LDC35,最不发达4国LDC4	70	--Plain weave
3771	5209.5200	--三线或四线斜纹机织物，包括双面斜纹机织物	10	0	东盟ASEAN,智利CL,巴基斯坦PK,新西兰NZ,秘鲁PE,哥斯达黎加CR,香港HK	0	最不发达35国LDC35	70	--3-thread or 4-thread twill, including cross twill
3772	5209.5900	--其他机织物	10	0 8.5	东盟ASEAN,智利CL,巴基斯坦PK,新西兰NZ,秘鲁PE,哥斯达黎加CR,香港HK 亚太APTA	0	最不发达35国LDC35,最不发达4国LDC4	70	--Other fabrics
	52.10	**棉机织物，按重量计含棉量在85%以下，主要或仅与化学纤维混纺，每平方米重量不超过200克:**							**Woven fabrics of cotton, containing less than 85% by weight of cotton, mixed mainly or solely with man-made fibres, weighing not more than 200g/m^2:**
		-未漂白:							-Unbleached:
3773	5210.1100	--平纹机织物	12 △6	0 2.4 10.2	东盟ASEAN,智利CL,巴基斯坦PK,新加坡SG,新西兰NZ,秘鲁PE,香港HK 哥斯达黎加CR 亚太APTA	0	最不发达35国LDC35,最不发达4国LDC4	90	--Plain weave
		--其他机织物:							--Other fabrics:
3774	5210.1910	---三线或四线斜纹机织物，包括双面斜纹机织物	12 △6	0 2.4	东盟ASEAN,智利CL,巴基斯坦PK,新加坡SG,新西兰NZ,秘鲁PE,香港HK 哥斯达黎加CR	0	最不发达35国LDC35	90	---3-thread or 4-thread twill, including cross twill
3775	5210.1990	---其他	12 △6	0 2.4	东盟ASEAN,智利CL,巴基斯坦PK,新加坡SG,新西兰NZ,秘鲁PE,香港HK 哥斯达黎加CR	0	最不发达35国LDC35,最不发达4国LDC4	90	---Other
		-漂白:							-Bleached:
3776	5210.2100	--平纹机织物	14	0 2.8	东盟ASEAN,智利CL,巴基斯坦PK,新加坡SG,新西兰NZ,秘鲁PE,香港HK 哥斯达黎加CR	0	最不发达35国LDC35,最不发达4国LDC4	90	--Plain weave

序号 No.	税则号列 Tariff Line	货品名称	最惠国税率 MFN(%)	协定税率 Agreement(%)		特惠税率 S.P.(%)		普通税率 Gen.(%)	Article Description
		--其他机织物:							--Other fabrics:
3777	5210.2910	---三线或四线斜纹机织物，包括双面斜纹机织物	14	0	东盟ASEAN,智利CL,巴基斯坦PK,新加坡SG,新西兰NZ,秘鲁PE,香港HK	0	最不发达35国LDC35	90	---3-thread or 4-thread twill, including cross twill
				2.8	哥斯达黎加CR				
3778	5210.2990	---其他	14	0	东盟ASEAN,智利CL,巴基斯坦PK,新加坡SG,新西兰NZ,秘鲁PE	0	最不发达35国LDC35	90	---Other
				2.8	哥斯达黎加CR				
		-染色:							-Dyed:
3779	5210.3100	--平纹机织物	10	0	东盟ASEAN,智利CL,巴基斯坦PK,新加坡SG,新西兰NZ,秘鲁PE,哥斯达黎加CR,香港HK,台湾TW	0	最不发达35国LDC35,最不发达4国LDC4	90	--Plain weave
				8.5	亚太APTA				
3780	5210.3200	--三线或四线斜纹机织物，包括双面斜纹机织物	10	0	东盟ASEAN,智利CL,巴基斯坦PK,新加坡SG,新西兰NZ,秘鲁PE,哥斯达黎加CR,香港HK	0	最不发达35国LDC35	90	--3-thread or 4-thread twill, including cross twill
				8.5	亚太APTA				
3781	5210.3900	--其他机织物	10	0	东盟ASEAN,智利CL,巴基斯坦PK,新加坡SG,新西兰NZ,哥斯达黎加CR,香港HK,台湾TW	0	最不发达35国LDC35	90	--Other fabrics
				5	秘鲁PE				
				8.5	亚太APTA				
		-色织:							-Of yarns of different colours:
3782	5210.4100	--平纹机织物	10	0	东盟ASEAN,智利CL,巴基斯坦PK,新加坡SG,新西兰NZ,秘鲁PE,哥斯达黎加CR,香港HK,台湾TW	0	最不发达35国LDC35	90	--Plain weave
		--其他机织物:							--Other fabrics:
3783	5210.4910	---三线或四线斜纹机织物，包括双面斜纹机织物	10	0	东盟ASEAN,智利CL,巴基斯坦PK,新加坡SG,新西兰NZ,秘鲁PE,哥斯达黎加CR,香港HK	0	最不发达35国LDC35	90	---3-thread or 4-thread twill, including cross twill
3784	5210.4990	---其他	10	0	东盟ASEAN,智利CL,巴基斯坦PK,新加坡SG,新西兰NZ,秘鲁PE,哥斯达黎加CR,香港HK,台湾TW	0	最不发达35国LDC35,最不发达4国LDC4	90	---Other
		-印花:							-Printed:
3785	5210.5100	--平纹机织物	10	0	东盟ASEAN,智利CL,巴基斯坦PK,新西兰NZ,秘鲁PE,哥斯达黎加CR	0	最不发达35国LDC35,最不发达4国LDC4	90	--Plain weave
		--其他机织物:							--Other fabrics:

序号 No.	税则号列 Tariff Line	货品名称	最惠国税率 MFN(%)	协定税率 Agreement(%)		特惠税率 S.P.(%)		普通税率 Gen.(%)	Article Description
3786	5210.5910	---三线或四线斜纹机织物，包括双面斜纹机织物	10	0	东盟ASEAN,智利CL,巴基斯坦PK,新西兰NZ,秘鲁PE,哥斯达黎加CR	0	最不发达35国LDC35	90	---3-thread or 4-thread twill, including cross twill
3787	5210.5990	---其他机织物	10	0	东盟ASEAN,智利CL,巴基斯坦PK,新西兰NZ,秘鲁PE,哥斯达黎加CR	0	最不发达35国LDC35,最不发达4国LDC4	90	---Other fabrics
	52.11	**棉机织物，按重量计含棉量在85%以下，主要或仅与化学纤维混纺，每平方米重量超过200克:**							**Woven fabrics of cotton, containing less than 85% by weight of cotton, mixed mainly or solely with man-made fibres, weighing more than 200g/m²:**
		-未漂白:							-Unbleached:
3788	5211.1100	--平纹机织物	12 △6	0 2.4	东盟ASEAN,智利CL,巴基斯坦PK,新加坡SG,新西兰NZ,秘鲁PE,香港HK 哥斯达黎加CR	0	最不发达35国LDC35,最不发达4国LDC4	90	--Plain weave
3789	5211.1200	--三线或四线斜纹机织物，包括双面斜纹机织物	12 △6	0 2.4	东盟ASEAN,智利CL,巴基斯坦PK,新加坡SG,新西兰NZ,秘鲁PE,香港HK 哥斯达黎加CR	0	最不发达35国LDC35,最不发达4国LDC4	90	--3-thread or 4-thread twill, including cross twill
3790	5211.1900	--其他机织物	12 △6	0 2.4	东盟ASEAN,智利CL,巴基斯坦PK,新加坡SG,新西兰NZ,秘鲁PE,香港HK 哥斯达黎加CR	0	最不发达35国LDC35,最不发达4国LDC4	90	--Other fabrics
3791	5211.2000	-漂白	14	0 2.8	东盟ASEAN,智利CL,巴基斯坦PK,新加坡SG,新西兰NZ,秘鲁PE,香港HK 哥斯达黎加CR	0	最不发达35国LDC35	90	-Bleached
		-染色:							-Dyed:
3792	5211.3100	--平纹机织物	10	0 8.5	东盟ASEAN,智利CL,巴基斯坦PK,新加坡SG,新西兰NZ,秘鲁PE,哥斯达黎加CR,香港HK 亚太APTA	0	最不发达35国LDC35,最不发达4国LDC4	90	--Plain weave
3793	5211.3200	--三线或四线斜纹机织物，包括双面斜纹机织物	10	0 8.5	东盟ASEAN,智利CL,巴基斯坦PK,新加坡SG,新西兰NZ,秘鲁PE,哥斯达黎加CR,香港HK 亚太APTA	0	最不发达35国LDC35	90	--3-thread or 4-thread twill, including cross twill

序号 No.	税则号列 Tariff Line	货品名称	最惠国税率 MFN(%)	协定税率 Agreement(%)		特惠税率 S.P.(%)		普通税率 Gen.(%)	Article Description
3794	5211.3900	--其他机织物	10	0	东盟ASEAN,智利CL,巴基斯坦PK,新加坡SG,新西兰NZ,哥斯达黎加CR,香港HK,台湾TW	0	最不发达35国LDC35,最不发达4国LDC4	90	--Other fabrics
				5	秘鲁PE				
				8.5	亚太APTA				
		-色织:							-Of yarns of different colours:
3795	5211.4100	--平纹机织物	10	0	东盟ASEAN,智利CL,巴基斯坦PK,新西兰NZ,秘鲁PE,哥斯达黎加CR,香港HK	0	最不发达35国LDC35	90	--Plain weave
3796	5211.4200	--粗斜纹布(劳动布)	10	0	东盟ASEAN,智利CL,巴基斯坦PK,新加坡SG,新西兰NZ,秘鲁PE,哥斯达黎加CR,香港HK	0	最不发达35国LDC35	90	--Denim
3797	5211.4300	--其他三线或四线斜纹机织物,包括双面斜纹机织物	10	0	东盟ASEAN,智利CL,巴基斯坦PK,新西兰NZ,秘鲁PE,哥斯达黎加CR,香港HK	0	最不发达35国LDC35	90	--Other coloured 3 or 4-thread twill, <85% cotton, >200g/m^2
3798	5211.4900	--其他机织物	10	0	东盟ASEAN,智利CL,巴基斯坦PK,新加坡SG,新西兰NZ,秘鲁PE,哥斯达黎加CR	0	最不发达35国LDC35	90	--Other fabrics
		-印花:							-Printed:
3799	5211.5100	--平纹机织物	10	0	东盟ASEAN,智利CL,巴基斯坦PK,新西兰NZ,秘鲁PE,哥斯达黎加CR	0	最不发达35国LDC35	90	--Plain weave
3800	5211.5200	--三线或四线斜纹机织物,包括双面斜纹机织物	10	0	东盟ASEAN,智利CL,巴基斯坦PK,新西兰NZ,秘鲁PE,哥斯达黎加CR	0	最不发达35国LDC35	90	--3-thread or 4-thread twill, including cross twill
3801	5211.5900	--其他机织物	10	0	东盟ASEAN,智利CL,巴基斯坦PK,新西兰NZ,秘鲁PE,哥斯达黎加CR	0	最不发达35国LDC35	90	--Other fabrics
				8.5	亚太APTA				
	52.12	**其他棉机织物:**							**Other woven fabrics of cotton:**
		-每平方米重量不超过200克:							-Weighing not more than 200g/m²:
3802	5212.1100	--未漂白	12 △6	0	东盟ASEAN,智利CL,巴基斯坦PK,新加坡SG,新西兰NZ,秘鲁PE,香港HK	0	最不发达35国LDC35,最不发达4国LDC4	80	--Unbleached
				2.4	哥斯达黎加CR				
3803	5212.1200	--漂白	14	0	东盟ASEAN,智利CL,巴基斯坦PK,新加坡SG,新西兰NZ,秘鲁PE,香港HK	0	最不发达35国LDC35	80	--Bleached
				2.8	哥斯达黎加CR				

序号 No.	税则号列 Tariff Line	货品名称	最惠国税率 MFN(%)	协定税率 Agreement(%)		特惠税率 S.P.(%)		普通税率 Gen.(%)	Article Description
3804	5212.1300	--染色	10	0	东盟ASEAN,智利CL,巴基斯坦PK,新西兰NZ,秘鲁PE,哥斯达黎加CR,香港HK	0	最不发达35国LDC35	80	--Dyed
3805	5212.1400	--色织	10	0	东盟ASEAN,智利CL,巴基斯坦PK,新西兰NZ,秘鲁PE,哥斯达黎加CR	0	最不发达35国LDC35	80	--Of yarns of different colours
3806	5212.1500	--印花	10	0	东盟ASEAN,智利CL,巴基斯坦PK,新西兰NZ,秘鲁PE,哥斯达黎加CR	0	最不发达35国LDC35	80	--Printed
		-每平方米重量超过200克:							-Weighing more than 200g/m^2:
3807	5212.2100	--未漂白	12 △6	0 2.4	东盟ASEAN,智利CL,巴基斯坦PK,新加坡SG,新西兰NZ,秘鲁PE,香港HK 哥斯达黎加CR	0	最不发达35国LDC35,最不发达4国LDC4	80	--Unbleached
3808	5212.2200	--漂白	14	0 2.8	东盟ASEAN,智利CL,巴基斯坦PK,新加坡SG,新西兰NZ,秘鲁PE,香港HK 哥斯达黎加CR	0	最不发达35国LDC35	80	--Bleached
3809	5212.2300	--染色	10	0	东盟ASEAN,智利CL,巴基斯坦PK,新西兰NZ,秘鲁PE,哥斯达黎加CR,香港HK	0	最不发达35国LDC35	80	--Dyed
3810	5212.2400	--色织	10	0	东盟ASEAN,智利CL,巴基斯坦PK,新西兰NZ,秘鲁PE,哥斯达黎加CR	0	最不发达35国LDC35	80	--Of yarns of different colours
3811	5212.2500	--印花	10	0	东盟ASEAN,智利CL,巴基斯坦PK,新西兰NZ,秘鲁PE,哥斯达黎加CR	0	最不发达35国LDC35,最不发达4国LDC4	80	--Printed

第五十三章
其他植物纺织纤维；
纸纱线及其机织物

Chapter 53
Other vegetable textile fibres;
paper yarn and woven fabrics of paper yarn

序号 No.	税则号列 Tariff Line	货品名称	最惠国税 率 MFN(%)	协定税率 Agreement(%)		特惠税率 S.P.(%)		普通税率 Gen.(%)	Article Description
	53.01	**亚麻，生的或经加工但未纺制的;亚麻短纤及废麻（包括废麻纱线及回收纤维）:**							**Flax, raw or processed but not spun; flax tow and waste (including yarn waste and garnetted stock):**
3812	5301.1000	-生的或经沤制的亚麻	6	0 5	东盟ASEAN,智利CL,新西兰NZ,秘鲁PE,哥斯达黎加CR 巴基斯坦PK	0	最不发达35国LDC35,最不发达4国LDC4	30	-Flax, raw or retted
		-破开、打成、栉梳或经其他加工但未纺制的亚麻:							-Flax, broken, scutched, hackled or otherwise processed, but not spun:
3813	5301.2100	--破开的或打成的	6 △1	0 5	东盟ASEAN,智利CL,新西兰NZ,秘鲁PE,哥斯达黎加CR 巴基斯坦PK	0	最不发达35国LDC35,最不发达4国LDC4	30	--Broken or scutched
3814	5301.2900	--其他	6	0 5	东盟ASEAN,智利CL,新西兰NZ,秘鲁PE,哥斯达黎加CR 巴基斯坦PK	0	最不发达35国LDC35,最不发达4国LDC4	30	--Other
3815	5301.3000	-亚麻短纤及废麻	6 △1	0 5	东盟ASEAN,智利CL,新西兰NZ,秘鲁PE,哥斯达黎加CR 巴基斯坦PK	0	最不发达35国LDC35,最不发达4国LDC4	30	-Flax tow and waste
	53.02	**大麻，生的或经加工但未纺制的;大麻短纤及废麻（包括废麻纱线及回收纤维）:**							**True hemp (Cannabis sativa L), raw or processed but not spun;tow and waste of true hemp (including yarn waste and garnetted stock):**
3816	5302.1000	-生的或经沤制的大麻	6	0 5	东盟ASEAN,智利CL,新西兰NZ,秘鲁PE,哥斯达黎加CR 巴基斯坦PK	0	最不发达35国LDC35,最不发达4国LDC4	30	-True hemp, raw or retted
3817	5302.9000	-其他	6	0 5	东盟ASEAN,智利CL,新西兰NZ,秘鲁PE,哥斯达黎加CR 巴基斯坦PK	0	最不发达35国LDC35,最不发达4国LDC4	30	-Other

序号 No.	税则号列 Tariff Line	货品名称	最惠国税率 MFN(%)	协定税率 Agreement(%)		特惠税率 S.P.(%)		普通税率 Gen.(%)	Article Description
	53.03	**黄麻及其他纺织用韧皮纤维（不包括亚麻、大麻及苎麻），生的或经加工但未纺制的;上述纤维的短纤及废麻（包括废纱线及回收纤维）：**							**Jute and other textile bast fibres (excluding flax, true hemp and ramie), raw or processed but not spun; tow and waste of these fibres (including yarn waste and garnetted stock):**
3818	5303.1000	-生的或经沤制的黄麻及其他纺织用韧皮纤维	5	0	东盟ASEAN,智利CL,巴基斯坦PK,新西兰NZ,秘鲁PE,哥斯达黎加CR	0	最不发达35国LDC35,最不发达4国LDC4,亚太2国APTA2,缅甸MM,老挝LA,柬埔寨KH	20	-Jute and other textile bast fibres, raw or retted
3819	5303.9000	-其他	5	0	东盟ASEAN,智利CL,巴基斯坦PK,新西兰NZ,秘鲁PE,哥斯达黎加CR	0	最不发达35国LDC35,最不发达4国LDC4,缅甸MM,老挝LA,柬埔寨KH	30	-Other
	53.05	**椰壳纤维、蕉麻（马尼拉麻）、苎麻及其他税号未列名的纺织用植物纤维，生的或经加工但未纺制的;上述纤维的短纤、落麻及废料（包括废纱线及回收纤维）：**							**Coconut, abaca (Manila hemp or Musatextilis Nee), ramie and other vegetable textile fabrics, not elsewhere specified or included, raw or processed but not spun;tow, noils and waste of these fibres (including yarn waste and garnetted stock):**
		---苎麻:							---Ramie:
3820	5305.0011	----生的	5	0	东盟ASEAN,智利CL,巴基斯坦PK,新西兰NZ,秘鲁PE,哥斯达黎加CR	0	最不发达35国LDC35,最不发达4国LDC4	30	----Raw
3821	5305.0012	----经加工但未纺制的	5	0	东盟ASEAN,智利CL,巴基斯坦PK,新西兰NZ,秘鲁PE,哥斯达黎加CR	0	最不发达35国LDC35,最不发达4国LDC4	30	----processed but not spun

序号 No.	税则号列 Tariff Line	货品名称	最惠国税率 MFN(%)	协定税率 Agreement(%)		特惠税率 S.P.(%)		普通税率 Gen.(%)	Article Description
3822	5305.0013	----短纤及废料	5	0	东盟ASEAN,智利CL,巴基斯坦PK,新西兰NZ,秘鲁PE,哥斯达黎加CR	0	最不发达35国LDC35,最不发达4国LDC4	30	----Fibres and weste
3823	5305.0019	----其他	5	0	东盟ASEAN,智利CL,巴基斯坦PK,新西兰NZ,秘鲁PE,哥斯达黎加CR	0	最不发达35国LDC35,最不发达4国LDC4	20	----Other
3824	5305.0020	---蕉麻	3	0	东盟ASEAN,智利CL,巴基斯坦PK,新西兰NZ,秘鲁PE,哥斯达黎加CR	0	最不发达35国LDC35,最不发达4国LDC4	20	---abaca
3825	5305.0091	---其他: ----西沙尔麻及其他纺织用龙舌兰类纤维	5	0	东盟ASEAN,智利CL,巴基斯坦PK,新西兰NZ,秘鲁PE,哥斯达黎加CR	0	最不发达35国LDC35,最不发达4国LDC4	30	---Other: ----Sisal and other textile fabrics of the genus Agave
3826	5305.0092	----椰壳纤维	5	0 4	东盟ASEAN,智利CL,巴基斯坦PK,新西兰NZ,秘鲁PE,哥斯达黎加CR 亚太APTA	0	最不发达35国LDC35,最不发达4国LDC4,缅甸MM,老挝LA,柬埔寨KH	30	----Coconut fabrics
3827	5305.0099	----其他	5	0	东盟ASEAN,智利CL,巴基斯坦PK,新西兰NZ,秘鲁PE,哥斯达黎加CR	0	最不发达35国LDC35,最不发达4国LDC4	30	----Other
3828	**53.06** 5306.1000	**亚麻纱线:** -单纱	6	0 5	东盟ASEAN,智利CL,新西兰NZ,秘鲁PE,哥斯达黎加CR,香港HK,澳门MO 巴基斯坦PK	0	最不发达35国LDC35,最不发达4国LDC4	50	**Flax yarn:** -Single
3829	5306.2000	-多股纱线或缆线	10 △5	0 5	东盟ASEAN,智利CL,新西兰NZ,秘鲁PE,哥斯达黎加CR,香港HK,澳门MO 巴基斯坦PK	0	最不发达35国LDC35,最不发达4国LDC4	50	-Multiple (folded) or cabled

序号 No.	税则号列 Tariff Line	货品名称	最惠国税率 MFN(%)	协定税率 Agreement(%)		特惠税率 S.P.(%)		普通税率 Gen.(%)	Article Description
	53.07	**黄麻纱线或税号53.03的其他纺织用韧皮纤维纱线:**							**Yarn of jute or of other textile bast fibres of heading No.53.03:**
3830	5307.1000	-单纱	6	0 5	东盟ASEAN,智利CL,新西兰NZ,秘鲁PE,哥斯达黎加CR,澳门MO 巴基斯坦PK	0 3	最不发达35国LDC35,最不发达4国LDC4,柬埔寨KH 亚太2国APTA2	35	-Single
3831	5307.2000	-多股纱线或缆线	6	0 5	东盟ASEAN,智利CL,新西兰NZ,秘鲁PE,哥斯达黎加CR,澳门MO 巴基斯坦PK	0 3	最不发达35国LDC35,最不发达4国LDC4,柬埔寨KH 亚太2国APTA2	35	-Multiple(folded)or cabled
	53.08	**其他植物纺织纤维纱线;纸纱线:**							**Yarn of other vegetable textile fibres; paper yarn:**
3832	5308.1000	-椰壳纤维纱线	6	0 5	东盟ASEAN,智利CL,新西兰NZ,秘鲁PE,哥斯达黎加CR,澳门MO 巴基斯坦PK	0	最不发达35国LDC35,最不发达4国LDC4	45	-Coir yarn
3833	5308.2000	-大麻纱线	6	0 5	东盟ASEAN,智利CL,新西兰NZ,秘鲁PE,哥斯达黎加CR,澳门MO 巴基斯坦PK	0	最不发达35国LDC35,最不发达4国LDC4	45	-True hemp yarn
		-其他: ---苎麻纱线:							-Other: ---Ramie yarn:
3834	5308.9011	----按重量计苎麻含量在85%及以上的未漂白或漂白纱线	6	0 5	东盟ASEAN,智利CL,新西兰NZ,秘鲁PE,哥斯达黎加CR,澳门MO 巴基斯坦PK	0	最不发达35国LDC35,最不发达4国LDC4	50	----Containing 85% or more by weight of ramie, unbleached or bleached yarn
3835	5308.9012	----按重量计苎麻含量在85%及以上的色纱线	6	0 5	东盟ASEAN,智利CL,新西兰NZ,秘鲁PE,哥斯达黎加CR,澳门MO 巴基斯坦PK	0	最不发达35国LDC35,最不发达4国LDC4	50	----Containing 85% or more by weight of ramie, coloured yarn
3836	5308.9013	----按重量计苎麻含量在85%以下的未漂白或漂白纱线	6	0 5	东盟ASEAN,智利CL,新西兰NZ,秘鲁PE,哥斯达黎加CR,澳门MO 巴基斯坦PK	0	最不发达35国LDC35,最不发达4国LDC4	50	----Containing less than 85% by weight of ramie, unbleached or bleached yarn

序号 No.	税则号列 Tariff Line	货品名称	最惠国税率 MFN(%)	协定税率 Agreement(%)		特惠税率 S.P.(%)		普通税率 Gen.(%)	Article Description
3837	5308.9014	----按重量计苎麻含量在85%以下的色纱线	6	0 5	东盟ASEAN,智利CL,新西兰NZ,秘鲁PE,哥斯达黎加CR,澳门MO 巴基斯坦PK	0	最不发达35国LDC35,最不发达4国LDC4	50	----Containing less than 85% by weight of ramie, coloured yarn
		---其他:							---Other:
3838	5308.9091	----纸纱线	6	0 5	东盟ASEAN,智利CL,新西兰NZ,秘鲁PE,哥斯达黎加CR,澳门MO 巴基斯坦PK	0	最不发达35国LDC35,最不发达4国LDC4	70	----Paper yarn
3839	5308.9099	----其他	6	0 5	东盟ASEAN,智利CL,新西兰NZ,秘鲁PE,哥斯达黎加CR,澳门MO 巴基斯坦PK	0	最不发达35国LDC35,最不发达4国LDC4	45	----Other
	53.09	**亚麻机织物:** -按重量计亚麻含量在85%及以上: --未漂白或漂白:							**Woven fabrics of flax:** -Containing 85% or more by weight of flax: --Unbleached or bleached:
3840	5309.1110	---未漂白	10	0	东盟ASEAN,智利CL,巴基斯坦PK,新西兰NZ,秘鲁PE,哥斯达黎加CR	0	最不发达35国LDC35,最不发达4国LDC4	80	---Unbleached
3841	5309.1120	---漂白	10	0	东盟ASEAN,智利CL,巴基斯坦PK,新西兰NZ,秘鲁PE,哥斯达黎加CR	0	最不发达35国LDC35,最不发达4国LDC4	80	---Bleached
3842	5309.1900	--其他	10	0 9.3	东盟ASEAN,智利CL,巴基斯坦PK,新西兰NZ,秘鲁PE,哥斯达黎加CR,香港HK 亚太APTA	0	最不发达35国LDC35,最不发达4国LDC4	80	--Other
		-按重量计亚麻含量在85%以下: --未漂白或漂白:							-Containing less than 85% by weight of flax: --Unbleached or bleached:
3843	5309.2110	---未漂白	10	0	东盟ASEAN,智利CL,巴基斯坦PK,新西兰NZ,秘鲁PE,哥斯达黎加CR,澳门MO	0	最不发达35国LDC35,最不发达4国LDC4	80	---Unbleached

序号 No.	税则号列 Tariff Line	货品名称	最惠国税率 MFN(%)	协定税率 Agreement(%)		特惠税率 S.P.(%)		普通税率 Gen.(%)	Article Description
3844	5309.2120	---漂白	10	0	东盟ASEAN,智利CL,巴基斯坦PK,新西兰NZ,秘鲁PE,哥斯达黎加CR,澳门MO	0	最不发达35国LDC35,最不发达4国LDC4	80	---Bleached
3845	5309.2900	--其他	10	0	东盟ASEAN,智利CL,巴基斯坦PK,新西兰NZ,秘鲁PE,哥斯达黎加CR,香港HK,澳门MO	0	最不发达35国LDC35,最不发达4国LDC4	80	--Other
				8.5	亚太APTA				
	53.10	**黄麻或税号53.03的其他纺织用韧皮纤维机织物:**							**Woven fabrics of jute or of other textilebast fibres of heading No.53.03:**
3846	5310.1000	-未漂白	10	0	东盟ASEAN,智利CL,新西兰NZ,秘鲁PE,哥斯达黎加CR	0	最不发达35国LDC35,最不发达4国LDC4,柬埔寨KH	40	-Unbleached
				5	巴基斯坦PK	5	亚太2国APTA2		
3847	5310.9000	-其他	10	0	东盟ASEAN,智利CL,新西兰NZ,秘鲁PE,哥斯达黎加CR	0	最不发达35国LDC35,最不发达4国LDC4,柬埔寨KH	40	-Other
				5	巴基斯坦PK	5	亚太2国APTA2		
	53.11	**其他纺织用植物纤维机织物;纸纱线机织物:**							**Woven fabrics of other vegetable textile fibres; woven fabrics of paper yarn:**
		---苎麻的:							---Of ramie:
3848	5311.0012	----按重量计苎麻含量在85%及以上的未漂白机织物	10	0	东盟ASEAN,智利CL,新西兰NZ,秘鲁PE,哥斯达黎加CR,澳门MO	0	最不发达35国LDC35,最不发达4国LDC4	80	----Containing 85% or more by weight of ramie, unbleached woven fabrics
				5	巴基斯坦PK				
3849	5311.0013	----按重量计苎麻含量在85%及以上的其他机织物	12	0	东盟ASEAN,智利CL,新加坡SG,新西兰NZ,秘鲁PE,澳门MO	0	最不发达35国LDC35,最不发达4国LDC4	80	----Containing 85% or more by weight of ramie, other woven fabrics
				2.4	哥斯达黎加CR				
				6	巴基斯坦PK				

序号 No.	税则号列 Tariff Line	货品名称	最惠国税率 MFN(%)	协定税率 Agreement(%)		特惠税率 S.P.(%)		普通税率 Gen.(%)	Article Description
3850	5311.0014	----按重量计苎麻含量在85%以下的未漂白机织物	10	0 5	东盟ASEAN,智利CL,新西兰NZ,秘鲁PE,哥斯达黎加CR 巴基斯坦PK	0	最不发达35国LDC35,最不发达4国LDC4	80	----Containing less than 85% by weight of ramie, unbleached woven fabrics
3851	5311.0015	----按重量计苎麻含量在85%以下的其他机织物	12	0 2.4 6	东盟ASEAN,智利CL,新加坡SG,新西兰NZ,秘鲁PE,澳门MO 哥斯达黎加CR 巴基斯坦PK	0	最不发达35国LDC35	80	----Containing less than 85% by weight of ramie, other woven fabrics
3852	5311.0020	---纸纱线的	10	0 5	东盟ASEAN,智利CL,新西兰NZ,秘鲁PE,哥斯达黎加CR 巴基斯坦PK	0	最不发达35国LDC35,最不发达4国LDC4	90	---Of paper yarn
3853	5311.0030	---大麻的	10	0 5 9.3	东盟ASEAN,智利CL,新西兰NZ,秘鲁PE,哥斯达黎加CR 巴基斯坦PK 亚太APTA	0	最不发达35国LDC35,最不发达4国LDC4	50	---Of true hemp
3854	5311.0090	---其他	10	0 5 9.3	东盟ASEAN,智利CL,新西兰NZ,秘鲁PE,哥斯达黎加CR 巴基斯坦PK 亚太APTA	0	最不发达35国LDC35,最不发达4国LDC4	50	---Other

第五十四章
化学纤维长丝

注释:

一、本目录所称“化学纤维”，是指通过下列任一方法加工制得的有机聚合物的短纤或长丝:

（一）将有机单体物质加以聚合而制成聚合物，例如，聚酰胺、聚酯、聚烯烃、聚氨基甲酸酯；或通过上述加工将聚合物经化学改性制得（例如，聚乙酸乙烯酯水解得的聚乙烯醇）；或

（二）将天然有机聚合物（例如，纤维素）溶解或经化学处理制成聚合物，例如，铜铵纤维或粘胶纤维；或将天然有机聚合物（例如，纤维素、酪蛋白及其他蛋白质、或藻酸）经化学改性制成聚合物，例如醋酸纤维素纤维或藻酸盐纤维。

对于化学纤维，所称“合成”，是指（一）款所述的纤维;所称“人造”，是指（二）款所述的纤维。税目54.04 或 54.05 的扁条及类似品不视作化学纤维。

对于纺织材料，所称“化学纤维”、“合成纤维”及“人造纤维”，其含义应与上述解释相同。

二、税号 54.02 及 54.03 不适用于第五十五章的合成纤维或人造纤维的长丝丝束。

Chapter 54
Man-made filaments; strip and the like of man made textile materials

Notes:

1. Throughout the Nomenclature，the term “man-made fibres” means staple fibres and filaments of organic polymers produced by manufacturing processes，either:

(a) By polymerisation of organic monomers to produce polymers such as polyamides, polyesters, polyolefins or polyurethanes, or by chemical modification of polymers produced by this process (for example, poly (vinyl alcohol) prepared by the hydrolysis of poly (vinyl acetate); or

(b) By dissolution or chemical treatment of natural organic polymers (for example, cellulose) to produce polymers such as cuprammonium rayon (cupro) or viscose rayon, or by chemical modification of natural organic polymers (for example, cellulose, casein and other proteins, or alginic acid), to produce polymers such as cellulose acetate or alginates.

The terms “synthetic” and “artificial”, used in relation to fibres，mean: synthetic: fibres as defined at（a）; artificial: fibres as defined at（b）. Strip and the like of heading 54.04 or 54.05 are not considered to be man made fibres.

The terms “man-made”，“synthetic” and “artificial” shall have the same meanings when used in relation to“textile materials”.

2. Headings Nos.54.02 and 54.03 do not apply to synthetic or artificial filament tow of Chapter 55.

序号 No.	税则号列 Tariff Line	货品名称	最惠国税率 MFN(%)	协定税率 Agreement(%)		特惠税率 S.P.(%)		普通税率 Gen.(%)	Article Description
	54.01	**化学纤维长丝纺制的缝纫线，不论是否供零售用:**							**Sewing thread of man-made filaments, whether or not put up for retail sale:**
		-合成纤维长丝纺制:							-Of synthetic filaments:
3855	5401.1010	---非供零售用	5	0	东盟ASEAN,智利CL,巴基斯坦PK,新西兰NZ,秘鲁PE,哥斯达黎加CR,香港HK,澳门MO,台湾TW	0	最不发达 35 国 LDC35,最不发达 4 国 LDC4	70	---Not put up for retail sale

序号 No.	税则号列 Tariff Line	货品名称	最惠国税率 MFN(%)	协定税率 Agreement(%)		特惠税率 S.P.(%)		普通税率 Gen.(%)	Article Description
3856	5401.1020	---供零售用	5	0	东盟ASEAN,智利CL,巴基斯坦PK,新西兰NZ,秘鲁PE,哥斯达黎加CR	0	最不发达35国LDC35,最不发达4国LDC4	90	---Put up for retail sale
		-人造纤维长丝纺制:							-Of artificial filaments:
3857	5401.2010	---非供零售用	5	0	东盟ASEAN,智利CL,巴基斯坦PK,新西兰NZ,秘鲁PE,哥斯达黎加CR	0	最不发达35国LDC35,最不发达4国LDC4	35	---Not put up for retail sale
3858	5401.2020	---供零售用	5	0	东盟ASEAN,智利CL,巴基斯坦PK,新西兰NZ,秘鲁PE,哥斯达黎加CR	0	最不发达35国LDC35,最不发达4国LDC4	90	---Put up for retail sale
	54.02	**合成纤维长丝纱线（缝纫线除外），非供零售用，包括细度在67分特以下的合成纤维单丝:**							**Synthetic filament yarn (other than sewing thread), not put up for retail sale, including synthetic monofilament of less than 67 decitex:**
		-尼龙或其他聚酰胺纺制的高强力纱:							-High tenacity yarn of nylon or other polyamides:
		--芳香族聚酰胺纺制:							--Of aramids:
3859	5402.1110	---聚间苯二甲酰间苯二胺纺制	5	0	东盟ASEAN,智利CL,巴基斯坦PK,新西兰NZ,秘鲁PE,哥斯达黎加CR,澳门MO	0	最不发达35国LDC35,最不发达4国LDC4	70	---Of polyisophthaloyl metaphenylene diamine
3860	5402.1120	---聚对苯二甲酰对苯二胺纺制	5	0	东盟ASEAN,智利CL,巴基斯坦PK,新西兰NZ,秘鲁PE,哥斯达黎加CR,澳门MO	0	最不发达35国LDC35,最不发达4国LDC4	70	---Of polyisophthaloyl paraphenylene diamine
3861	5402.1190	---其他	5	0	东盟ASEAN,智利CL,巴基斯坦PK,新西兰NZ,秘鲁PE,哥斯达黎加CR,澳门MO	0	最不发达35国LDC35,最不发达4国LDC4	70	---Other
		--其他:							--Other:
3862	5402.1910	---聚酰胺-6（尼龙-6）纺制	5	0	东盟ASEAN,智利CL,巴基斯坦PK,新西兰NZ,秘鲁PE,哥斯达黎加CR,澳门MO	0	最不发达35国LDC35,最不发达4国LDC4	70	---Of nylon-6

序号 No.	税则号列 Tariff Line	货品名称	最惠国税率 MFN(%)	协定税率 Agreement(%)		特惠税率 S.P.(%)		普通税率 Gen.(%)	Article Description
3863	5402.1920	---聚酰胺-6，6（尼龙-6，6）纺制	5	0	东盟ASEAN,智利CL,巴基斯坦PK,新西兰NZ,秘鲁PE,哥斯达黎加CR,澳门MO	0	最不发达35国LDC35,最不发达4国LDC4	70	---Of nylon-6, 6
3864	5402.1990	---其他	5	0	东盟ASEAN,智利CL,巴基斯坦PK,新西兰NZ,秘鲁PE,哥斯达黎加CR,澳门MO	0	最不发达35国LDC35,最不发达4国LDC4	70	---Other
3865	5402.2000	-聚酯高强力纱	5	0	东盟ASEAN,智利CL,巴基斯坦PK,新西兰NZ,秘鲁PE,哥斯达黎加CR,澳门MO,台湾TW	0	最不发达35国LDC35,最不发达4国LDC4	70	-High tenacity yarn of polyesters
		-变形纱线:							-Textured yarn:
		--尼龙或其他聚酰胺纺制，每根单纱细度不超过50特:							--Of nylon or other polyamides, measuring per single yarn not more than 50 tex:
		---弹力丝:							---Elastic filament:
3866	5402.3111	----聚酰胺-6（尼龙-6）纺制	5	0	东盟ASEAN,智利CL,巴基斯坦PK,新西兰NZ,秘鲁PE,哥斯达黎加CR,香港HK,澳门MO	0	最不发达35国LDC35,最不发达4国LDC4	80	----Of nylon-6
3867	5402.3112	----聚酰胺-6，6（尼龙-6，6）纺制	5	0	东盟ASEAN,智利CL,巴基斯坦PK,新西兰NZ,秘鲁PE,哥斯达黎加CR,香港HK,澳门MO	0	最不发达35国LDC35,最不发达4国LDC4	80	----Of nylon-6, 6
3868	5402.3113	----芳香族聚酰胺纺制	5	0	东盟ASEAN,智利CL,巴基斯坦PK,新西兰NZ,秘鲁PE,哥斯达黎加CR,香港HK,澳门MO	0	最不发达35国LDC35,最不发达4国LDC4	80	----Of aramides
3869	5402.3119	----其他	5	0	东盟ASEAN,智利CL,巴基斯坦PK,新西兰NZ,秘鲁PE,哥斯达黎加CR,香港HK,澳门MO	0	最不发达35国LDC35,最不发达4国LDC4	80	----Other
3870	5402.3190	---其他	5	0	东盟ASEAN,智利CL,巴基斯坦PK,新西兰NZ,秘鲁PE,哥斯达黎加CR,香港HK,澳门MO	0	最不发达35国LDC35,最不发达4国LDC4	70	---Other

序号 No.	税则号列 Tariff Line	货品名称	最惠国税率 MFN(%)	协定税率 Agreement(%)		特惠税率 S.P.(%)		普通税率 Gen.(%)	Article Description
		--尼龙或其他聚酰胺纺制，每根单纱细度超过50特:							--Of nylon or other polyamides, measuring per single yarn more than 50 tex:
		---弹力丝:							---Elastic filament:
3871	5402.3211	----聚酰胺-6（尼龙-6）纺制	5	0	东盟ASEAN,智利CL,巴基斯坦PK,新西兰NZ,秘鲁PE,哥斯达黎加CR,香港HK,澳门MO	0	最不发达35国LDC35,最不发达4国LDC4	80	----Of nylon-6
3872	5402.3212	----聚酰胺-6，6（尼龙-6，6）纺制	5	0	东盟ASEAN,智利CL,巴基斯坦PK,新西兰NZ,秘鲁PE,哥斯达黎加CR,香港HK,澳门MO	0	最不发达35国LDC35,最不发达4国LDC4	80	----Of nylon-6, 6
3873	5402.3213	----芳香族聚酰胺纺制	5	0	东盟ASEAN,智利CL,巴基斯坦PK,新西兰NZ,秘鲁PE,哥斯达黎加CR,香港HK,澳门MO	0	最不发达35国LDC35,最不发达4国LDC4	80	----Of aramids
3874	5402.3219	----其他	5	0	东盟ASEAN,智利CL,巴基斯坦PK,新西兰NZ,秘鲁PE,哥斯达黎加CR,香港HK,澳门MO	0	最不发达35国LDC35,最不发达4国LDC4	80	----Other
3875	5402.3290	---其他	5	0 4.5	东盟ASEAN,智利CL,巴基斯坦PK,新西兰NZ,秘鲁PE,哥斯达黎加CR,香港HK,澳门MO 亚太APTA	0	最不发达35国LDC35,最不发达4国LDC4	70	---Other
		--聚酯纺制:							--Of polyesters:
3876	5402.3310	---弹力丝	5	0	文莱BN,印尼ID,马来西亚MY,缅甸MM,菲律宾PH,新加坡*SG*,泰国TH,越南VT,智利CL,巴基斯坦PK,新西兰NZ,秘鲁PE,哥斯达黎加CR,澳门MO,台湾TW	0	最不发达35国LDC35,最不发达4国LDC4	90	---Elastic filament
3877	5402.3390	---其他	5	0	智利CL,巴基斯坦PK,新西兰NZ,秘鲁PE,哥斯达黎加CR,澳门MO	0	最不发达35国LDC35,最不发达4国LDC4	70	---Other
3878	5402.3400	--聚丙烯纱线	5	0	东盟ASEAN,智利CL,巴基斯坦PK,新西兰NZ,秘鲁PE,哥斯达黎加CR,澳门MO	0	最不发达35国LDC35,最不发达4国LDC4	70	--Of polypropylene

序号 No.	税则号列 Tariff Line	货品名称	最惠国税率 MFN(%)	协定税率 Agreement(%)		特惠税率 S.P.(%)		普通税率 Gen.(%)	Article Description
3879	5402.3900	--其他	5	0	东盟ASEAN,智利CL,巴基斯坦PK,新西兰NZ,秘鲁PE,哥斯达黎加CR,澳门MO	0	最不发达35国LDC35,最不发达4国LDC4	70	--Other
		-其他单纱,未加捻或捻度每米不超过50转:							-Other yarn, single, untwisted or with a twist not exceeding 50 turns per metre:
		--弹性纱线:							--Elastomeric:
3880	5402.4410	---氨纶纱线	5	0	东盟ASEAN,智利CL,巴基斯坦PK,新西兰NZ,秘鲁PE,哥斯达黎加CR,澳门MO	0	最不发达35国LDC35,最不发达4国LDC4	70	---Of polyurethane
3881	5402.4490	---其他	5	0 4.7	东盟ASEAN,智利CL,巴基斯坦PK,新西兰NZ,秘鲁PE,哥斯达黎加CR,香港HK,澳门MO 亚太APTA	0	最不发达35国LDC35,最不发达4国LDC4	70	---Other
		--其他，尼龙或其他聚酰胺纱线:							--Of other nylon or other polyamides:
3882	5402.4510	---聚酰胺-6（尼龙-6）制	5	0 4.7	东盟ASEAN,智利CL,巴基斯坦PK,新西兰NZ,秘鲁PE,哥斯达黎加CR,澳门MO 亚太APTA	0	最不发达35国LDC35,最不发达4国LDC4	70	---Of nylon-6
3883	5402.4520	---聚酰胺-6，6（尼龙-6，6）制	5	0 4.7	东盟ASEAN,智利CL,巴基斯坦PK,新西兰NZ,秘鲁PE,哥斯达黎加CR,澳门MO 亚太APTA	0	最不发达35国LDC35,最不发达4国LDC4	70	---Of nylon-6, 6
3884	5402.4530	---芳香族聚酰胺制	5	0 4.7	东盟ASEAN,智利CL,巴基斯坦PK,新西兰NZ,秘鲁PE,哥斯达黎加CR,澳门MO 亚太APTA	0	最不发达35国LDC35,最不发达4国LDC4	70	---Of aramids
3885	5402.4590	---其他	5	0 4.7	东盟ASEAN,智利CL,巴基斯坦PK,新西兰NZ,秘鲁PE,哥斯达黎加CR,澳门MO 亚太APTA	0	最不发达35国LDC35,最不发达4国LDC4	70	---Other
3886	5402.4600	--其他，部分定向聚酯纱线	5	0	智利CL,巴基斯坦PK,新西兰NZ,秘鲁PE,哥斯达黎加CR,澳门MO	0	最不发达35国LDC35,最不发达4国LDC4	70	--Other, of polyesters, partially oriented

序号 No.	税则号列 Tariff Line	货品名称	最惠国税 率 MFN(%)	协定税率 Agreement(%)		特惠税率 S.P.(%)		普通税率 Gen.(%)	Article Description
3887	5402.4700	--其他，聚酯纱线	5	0 4.7	智利CL,巴基斯坦PK,新西兰NZ,秘鲁PE,哥斯达黎加CR,澳门MO 亚太APTA	0	最不发达35国LDC35,最不发达4国LDC4	70	--Other, of polyesters
3888	5402.4800	--其他，聚丙烯纱线	5	0	东盟ASEAN,智利CL,巴基斯坦PK,新西兰NZ,秘鲁PE,哥斯达黎加CR,澳门MO	0	最不发达35国LDC35,最不发达4国LDC4	70	--Other, of polypropylene
		--其他:							--Other:
3889	5402.4910	---断裂强度大于等于22cN/dtex,且初始模量大于等于750cN/dtex的聚乙烯纱线	5	0	东盟ASEAN,智利CL,巴基斯坦PK,新西兰NZ,秘鲁PE,哥斯达黎加CR,澳门MO	0	最不发达35国LDC35,最不发达4国LDC4	70	---of polyethylene, breaking strengths with not less than 22cN/dtex, initial modulus with not less than 750cN/dtex
3890	5402.4990	---其他	5	0	东盟ASEAN,智利CL,巴基斯坦PK,新西兰NZ,秘鲁PE,哥斯达黎加CR,澳门MO	0	最不发达35国LDC35,最不发达4国LDC4	70	---Other
		-其他单纱,捻度每米超过50转:							-Other, yarn, single, with a twist exceeding 50 turns per metre:
		--尼龙或其他聚酰胺纱线:							--Of nylon or other polyamides:
3891	5402.5110	---聚酰胺-6（尼龙-6）制	5	0	智利CL,巴基斯坦PK,新西兰NZ,秘鲁PE,哥斯达黎加CR,澳门MO	0	最不发达35国LDC35,最不发达4国LDC4	70	---Of nylon-6
3892	5402.5120	---聚酰胺-6，6（尼龙-6，6）制	5	0	东盟ASEAN,智利CL,巴基斯坦PK,新西兰NZ,秘鲁PE,哥斯达黎加CR,澳门MO	0	最不发达35国LDC35,最不发达4国LDC4	70	---Of nylon-6, 6
3893	5402.5130	---芳香族聚酰胺制	5	0	东盟ASEAN,智利CL,巴基斯坦PK,新西兰NZ,秘鲁PE,哥斯达黎加CR,澳门MO	0	最不发达35国LDC35,最不发达4国LDC4	70	---Of aramides
3894	5402.5190	---其他	5	0	东盟ASEAN,智利CL,巴基斯坦PK,新西兰NZ,秘鲁PE,哥斯达黎加CR,澳门MO	0	最不发达35国LDC35,最不发达4国LDC4	70	---Other

序号 No.	税则号列 Tariff Line	货品名称	最惠国税率 MFN(%)	协定税率 Agreement(%)		特惠税率 S.P.(%)		普通税率 Gen.(%)	Article Description
3895	5402.5200	--聚酯纱线	5	0 4.3	智利CL,巴基斯坦PK,新西兰NZ,秘鲁PE,哥斯达黎加CR,澳门MO 亚太APTA	0	最不发达35国LDC35,最不发达4国LDC4	70	--Of polyesters
		--其他:							--Other:
3896	5402.5910	---聚丙烯纱线	5	0	东盟ASEAN,智利CL,巴基斯坦PK,新西兰NZ,秘鲁PE,哥斯达黎加CR,澳门MO	0	最不发达35国LDC35,最不发达4国LDC4	70	---Of polypropylene
3897	5402.5920	---断裂强度大于等于22cN/dtex,且初始模量大于等于750cN/dtex的聚乙烯纱线	5	0	东盟ASEAN,智利CL,巴基斯坦PK,新西兰NZ,秘鲁PE,哥斯达黎加CR,澳门MO	0	最不发达35国LDC35,最不发达4国LDC4	70	---of polyethylene, breaking strengths with not less than 22cN/dtex, initial modulus with not less than 750cN/dtex
3898	5402.5990	---其他	5	0	东盟ASEAN,智利CL,巴基斯坦PK,新西兰NZ,秘鲁PE,哥斯达黎加CR,澳门MO	0	最不发达35国LDC35,最不发达4国LDC4	70	---Other
		-其他纱线(多股纱线或缆线):							-Other yarn, multiple (folded) or cabled:
		--尼龙或其他聚酰胺纺制:							--Of nylon or other polyamides:
3899	5402.6110	---聚酰胺-6(尼龙-6)制	5	0	东盟ASEAN,智利CL,巴基斯坦PK,新西兰NZ,秘鲁PE,哥斯达黎加CR,澳门MO	0	最不发达35国LDC35,最不发达4国LDC4	70	---Of nylon-6
3900	5402.6120	---聚酰胺-6,6(尼龙-6,6)制	5	0	东盟ASEAN,智利CL,巴基斯坦PK,新西兰NZ,秘鲁PE,哥斯达黎加CR,澳门MO	0	最不发达35国LDC35,最不发达4国LDC4	70	---Of nylon-6, 6
3901	5402.6130	---芳香族聚酰胺制	5	0	东盟ASEAN,智利CL,巴基斯坦PK,新西兰NZ,秘鲁PE,哥斯达黎加CR,澳门MO	0	最不发达35国LDC35,最不发达4国LDC4	70	---Of aramides
3902	5402.6190	---其他	5	0	东盟ASEAN,智利CL,巴基斯坦PK,新西兰NZ,秘鲁PE,哥斯达黎加CR,澳门MO	0	最不发达35国LDC35,最不发达4国LDC4	70	---Other

序号 No.	税则号列 Tariff Line	货品名称	最惠国税率 MFN(%)	协定税率 Agreement(%)		特惠税率 S.P.(%)		普通税率 Gen.(%)	Article Description
3903	5402.6200	--聚酯纺制	5	0	东盟ASEAN,智利CL,巴基斯坦PK,新西兰NZ,秘鲁PE,哥斯达黎加CR,澳门MO,台湾TW	0	最不发达35国LDC35,最不发达4国LDC4	70	--Of polyesters
		--其他:							--Other:
3904	5402.6910	---聚丙烯纱线	5	0	东盟ASEAN,智利CL,巴基斯坦PK,新西兰NZ,秘鲁PE,哥斯达黎加CR,澳门MO	0	最不发达35国LDC35,最不发达4国LDC4	70	---Of polypropylene
3905	5402.6920	---氨纶纱线	5	0	东盟ASEAN,智利CL,巴基斯坦PK,新西兰NZ,秘鲁PE,哥斯达黎加CR,澳门MO	0	最不发达35国LDC35,最不发达4国LDC4	70	---Of polyurethane
3906	5402.6990	---其他	5	0	东盟ASEAN,智利CL,巴基斯坦PK,新西兰NZ,秘鲁PE,哥斯达黎加CR,澳门MO	0	最不发达35国LDC35,最不发达4国LDC4	70	---Other
	54.03	**人造纤维长丝纱线（缝纫线除外），非供零售用，包括细度在67分特以下的人造纤维单丝:**							**Artificial filament yarn (other than sewing thread), not put up for retail sale, including artificial monofilament of less than 67 decitex:**
3907	5403.1000	-粘胶纤维纺制的高强力纱	5	0	东盟ASEAN,智利CL,巴基斯坦PK,新西兰NZ,秘鲁PE,哥斯达黎加CR,澳门MO	0	最不发达35国LDC35,最不发达4国LDC4	35	-High tenacity yarn of viscose rayon
		-其他单纱:							-Other yarn, single:
		--粘胶纤维纺制，未加捻或捻度每米不超过120转:							--Of viscose rayon, untwisted or with a twist not exceeding 120 turns per metre:
3908	5403.3110	---竹制	5	0	东盟ASEAN,智利CL,巴基斯坦PK,新西兰NZ,秘鲁PE,哥斯达黎加CR,澳门MO	0	最不发达35国LDC35,最不发达4国LDC4	35	---Of bamboo
3909	5403.3190	---其他	5	0	东盟ASEAN,智利CL,巴基斯坦PK,新西兰NZ,秘鲁PE,哥斯达黎加CR,澳门MO	0	最不发达35国LDC35,最不发达4国LDC4	35	---Other

序号 No.	税则号列 Tariff Line	货品名称	最惠国税率 MFN(%)	协定税率 Agreement(%)		特惠税率 S.P.(%)		普通税率 Gen.(%)	Article Description
		--粘胶纤维纺制，捻度每米超过120转:							--Of viscose rayon, with a twist exceeding 120 turns per metre:
3910	5403.3210	---竹制	5	0	东盟ASEAN,智利CL,巴基斯坦PK,新西兰NZ,秘鲁PE,哥斯达黎加CR,澳门MO	0	最不发达35国LDC35,最不发达4国LDC4	35	---Of bamboo
3911	5403.3290	---其他	5	0	东盟ASEAN,智利CL,巴基斯坦PK,新西兰NZ,秘鲁PE,哥斯达黎加CR,澳门MO	0	最不发达35国LDC35,最不发达4国LDC4	35	---Other
		--醋酸纤维纺制:							--Of cellulose acetate:
3912	5403.3310	---二醋酸纤维纺制	5	0	东盟ASEAN,智利CL,巴基斯坦PK,新西兰NZ,秘鲁PE,哥斯达黎加CR,澳门MO	0	最不发达35国LDC35,最不发达4国LDC4	40	---Of cellulose diacetate
3913	5403.3390	---其他	5	0	东盟ASEAN,智利CL,巴基斯坦PK,新西兰NZ,秘鲁PE,哥斯达黎加CR,澳门MO	0	最不发达35国LDC35,最不发达4国LDC4	35	---Other
3914	5403.3900	--其他	5	0	东盟ASEAN,智利CL,巴基斯坦PK,新西兰NZ,秘鲁PE,哥斯达黎加CR,澳门MO	0	最不发达35国LDC35,最不发达4国LDC4	35	--Other
		-其他纱线(多股纱线或缆线）:							-Other, yarn, multiple (folded) or cabled:
3915	5403.4100	--粘胶纤维纺制	5	0	东盟ASEAN,智利CL,巴基斯坦PK,新西兰NZ,秘鲁PE,哥斯达黎加CR,澳门MO	0	最不发达35国LDC35,最不发达4国LDC4	35	--Of viscose rayon
3916	5403.4200	--醋酸纤维纺制	5	0	东盟ASEAN,智利CL,巴基斯坦PK,新西兰NZ,秘鲁PE,哥斯达黎加CR,澳门MO	0	最不发达35国LDC35,最不发达4国LDC4	35	--Of cellulose acetate
3917	5403.4900	--其他	5	0	东盟ASEAN,智利CL,巴基斯坦PK,新西兰NZ,秘鲁PE,哥斯达黎加CR,澳门MO	0	最不发达35国LDC35,最不发达4国LDC4	35	--Other

序号 No.	税则号列 Tariff Line	货品名称	最惠国税率 MFN(%)	协定税率 Agreement(%)		特惠税率 S.P.(%)		普通税率 Gen.(%)	Article Description
	54.04	**截面尺寸不超过1毫米，细度在67分特及以上的合成纤维单丝;表观宽度不超过5毫米的合成纤维纺织材料制扁条及类似品（例如人造草）:**							**Synthetic monofilament of 67 decitex or more and of which no cross-sectional dimension exceeds 1mm; strip and the like (for example, artificial straw) of synthetic textile materials of an apparent width not exceeing 5mm:**
		-单丝:							-Monofilament
3918	5404.1100	--弹性	5	0	文莱BN,印尼ID,马来西亚MY,缅甸MM,菲律宾PH,新加坡*SG*,泰国TH,越南VT,智利CL,巴基斯坦PK,新西兰NZ,秘鲁PE,哥斯达黎加CR,香港HK	0	最不发达35国LDC35,最不发达4国LDC4	80	--Elastomeric
3919	5404.1200	--其他，聚丙烯制	5	0	文莱BN,印尼ID,马来西亚MY,缅甸MM,菲律宾PH,新加坡*SG*,泰国TH,越南VT,智利CL,巴基斯坦PK,新西兰NZ,秘鲁PE,哥斯达黎加CR,香港HK	0	最不发达35国LDC35,最不发达4国LDC4	80	--Other, of polypropylene
3920	5404.1900	--其他	5	0	文莱BN,印尼ID,马来西亚MY,缅甸MM,菲律宾PH,新加坡*SG*,泰国TH,越南VT,智利CL,巴基斯坦PK,新西兰NZ,秘鲁PE,哥斯达黎加CR,香港HK	0	最不发达35国LDC35,最不发达4国LDC4	80	--Other
3921	5404.9000	-其他	5	0	文莱BN,印尼ID,马来西亚MY,缅甸MM,菲律宾PH,新加坡*SG*,泰国TH,越南VT,智利CL,巴基斯坦PK,新西兰NZ,秘鲁PE,哥斯达黎加CR,澳门MO	0	最不发达35国LDC35,最不发达4国LDC4	80	-Other
	54.05	**截面尺寸不超过1毫米，细度在67分特及以上的人造纤维单丝;表观宽度不超过5毫米的人造纤维纺织材料制扁条及类似品（例如人造草）:**							**Artificial monofilament of 67 decitex or more and of which no cross-sectional dimension exceeds 1mm; strip and the like (for example, artificial straw) of artificial textile materials of an apparent width not exceeding 5mm:**

序号 No.	税则号列 Tariff Line	货品名称	最惠国税率 MFN(%)	协定税率 Agreement(%)		特惠税率 S.P.(%)		普通税率 Gen.(%)	Article Description
3922	5405.0000	截面尺寸不超过1毫米，细度在67分特及以上的人造纤维单丝;表观宽度不超过5毫米的人造纤维纺织材料制扁条及类似品（例如人造草）	5	0	东盟ASEAN,智利CL,巴基斯坦PK,新西兰NZ,秘鲁PE,哥斯达黎加CR,澳门MO	0	最不发达35国LDC35,最不发达4国LDC4	80	Artificial monofilament of 67 decitex or more and of which no cross-sectional dimension exceeds 1mm; strip and the like (for example, artificial straw) of artificial textile materials of an apparent width not exceeding 5mm
	54.06	**化学纤维长丝纱线（缝纫线除外），供零售用:**							**Man-made filament yarn (other than sewing thread), put up for retail sale:**
3923	5406.0010	---合成纤维长丝纱线	5	0	东盟ASEAN,智利CL,巴基斯坦PK,新西兰NZ,秘鲁PE,哥斯达黎加CR,澳门MO	0	最不发达35国LDC35,最不发达4国LDC4	90	---Synthetic filament yarn
3924	5406.0020	---人造纤维长丝纱线	5	0	东盟ASEAN,智利CL,巴基斯坦PK,新西兰NZ,秘鲁PE,哥斯达黎加CR,澳门MO	0	最不发达35国LDC35,最不发达4国LDC4	90	---Artificial filament yarn
	54.07	**合成纤维长丝纱线的机织物，包括税号54.04所列材料的机织物:**							**Woven fabrics of synthetic filament yarn, including woven fabrics obtained from materials of heading No.54.04:**
		-尼龙或其他聚酰胺高强力纱、聚酯高强力纱纺制的机织物:							-Woven fabrics obtained from high tenacity yarn of nylon or other polyamides or of polyesters:
3925	5407.1010	---尼龙或其他聚酰胺高强力纱纺制	10	0	东盟ASEAN,智利CL,巴基斯坦PK,新加坡SG,新西兰NZ,秘鲁PE,哥斯达黎加CR,香港HK,台湾TW	0	最不发达35国LDC35	130	---Of nylon or other polyamides
3926	5407.1020	---聚酯高强力纱纺制	10	0	东盟ASEAN,智利CL,巴基斯坦PK,新加坡SG,新西兰NZ,秘鲁PE,哥斯达黎加CR,台湾TW	0	最不发达35国LDC35	130	---Of polyesters
3927	5407.2000	-扁条及类似品的机织物	10	0	东盟ASEAN,智利CL,巴基斯坦PK,新加坡SG,新西兰NZ,秘鲁PE,哥斯达黎加CR	0	最不发达35国LDC35	130	-Woven fabrics obtained from strip or the like
3928	5407.3000	-第十一类注释九所列的机织物	10	0	东盟ASEAN,智利CL,巴基斯坦PK,新加坡SG,新西兰NZ,秘鲁PE,哥斯达黎加CR	0	最不发达35国LDC35	130	-Fabrics specified in Note 9 to Section XI

序号 No.	税则号列 Tariff Line	货品名称	最惠国税率 MFN(%)	协定税率 Agreement(%)		特惠税率 S.P.(%)		普通税率 Gen.(%)	Article Description
		-其他机织物，按重量计尼龙或其他聚酰胺长丝含量在 85%及以上:							-Other woven fabrics, containing 85% or more by weight of filaments of nylon or other polyamides:
3929	5407.4100	--未漂白或漂白	10	0	东盟ASEAN,智利CL,巴基斯坦PK,新加坡SG,新西兰NZ,秘鲁PE,哥斯达黎加CR,香港HK,台湾TW	0	最不发达 35 国 LDC35	130	--Unbleached or bleached
3930	5407.4200	--染色	10	0 9.5	东盟ASEAN,智利CL,巴基斯坦PK,新加坡SG,新西兰NZ,秘鲁PE,哥斯达黎加CR,香港HK,澳门MO,台湾TW 亚太APTA	0	最不发达 35 国 LDC35,最不发达 4 国 LDC4,缅甸MM,老挝LA,柬埔寨KH	130	--Dyed
3931	5407.4300	--色织	10	0 7	东盟ASEAN,智利CL,巴基斯坦PK,新加坡SG,新西兰NZ,秘鲁PE,哥斯达黎加CR,香港HK,台湾TW 亚太APTA	0	最不发达 35 国 LDC35	130	--Of yarns of different colours
3932	5407.4400	--印花	10	0	东盟ASEAN,智利CL,巴基斯坦PK,新加坡SG,新西兰NZ,秘鲁PE,哥斯达黎加CR	0	最不发达 35 国 LDC35	130	--Printed
		-其他机织物，按重量计聚酯变形长丝含量在 85%及以上:							-Other woven fabrics, containing 85% or more by weight of textured polyester filaments:
3933	5407.5100	--未漂白或漂白	10	0 7	东盟ASEAN,智利CL,巴基斯坦PK,新加坡SG,新西兰NZ,秘鲁PE,哥斯达黎加CR,台湾TW 亚太APTA	0	最不发达 35 国 LDC35	130	--Unbleached or bleached
3934	5407.5200	--染色	10	0 9.5	东盟ASEAN,智利CL,巴基斯坦PK,新加坡SG,新西兰NZ,秘鲁PE,哥斯达黎加CR,香港HK,台湾TW 亚太APTA	0	最不发达 35 国 LDC35,最不发达 4 国 LDC4,缅甸MM,老挝LA,柬埔寨KH	130	--Dyed
3935	5407.5300	--色织	10	0	东盟ASEAN,智利CL,巴基斯坦PK,新加坡SG,新西兰NZ,秘鲁PE,哥斯达黎加CR,台湾TW	0	最不发达 35 国 LDC35	130	--Of yarns of different colours

序号 No.	税则号列 Tariff Line	货品名称	最惠国税率 MFN(%)	协定税率 Agreement(%)		特惠税率 S.P.(%)		普通税率 Gen.(%)	Article Description
3936	5407.5400	--印花	10	0	东盟ASEAN,智利CL,巴基斯坦PK,新加坡SG,新西兰NZ,秘鲁PE,哥斯达黎加CR,台湾TW	0	最不发达35国LDC35	130	--Printed
		-其他机织物,按重量计聚酯长丝含量在85%及以上:							-Other woven fabrics, containing 85% or more by weight of polyester filaments:
3937	5407.6100	--按重量计聚酯非变形长丝含量在85%及以上	10	0 9.5	东盟ASEAN,智利CL,巴基斯坦PK,新加坡SG,新西兰NZ,秘鲁PE,哥斯达黎加CR,香港HK,澳门MO,台湾TW 亚太APTA	0	最不发达35国LDC35,最不发达4国LDC4	130	--Containing 85% or more by weight of nontextured polyester filaments
3938	5407.6900	--其他	10	0 9.5	东盟ASEAN,智利CL,巴基斯坦PK,新加坡SG,新西兰NZ,秘鲁PE,哥斯达黎加CR,台湾TW 亚太APTA	0	最不发达35国LDC35,最不发达4国LDC4	130	--Other
		-其他机织物,按重量计其他合成纤维长丝含量在85%及以上:							-Other woven fabrics, containing 85% or more by weight of synthetic filaments:
3939	5407.7100	--未漂白或漂白	10	0 8.8	东盟ASEAN,智利CL,巴基斯坦PK,新加坡SG,新西兰NZ,秘鲁PE,哥斯达黎加CR,香港HK,台湾TW 亚太APTA	0	最不发达35国LDC35	130	--Unbleached or bleached
3940	5407.7200	--染色	10	0 9.5	东盟ASEAN,智利CL,巴基斯坦PK,新加坡SG,新西兰NZ,秘鲁PE,哥斯达黎加CR,香港HK,台湾TW 亚太APTA	0	最不发达35国LDC35,最不发达4国LDC4,缅甸MM,老挝LA,柬埔寨KH	130	--Dyed
3941	5407.7300	--色织	10	0	东盟ASEAN,智利CL,巴基斯坦PK,新加坡SG,新西兰NZ,秘鲁PE,哥斯达黎加CR	0	最不发达35国LDC35	130	--Of yarns of different colours
3942	5407.7400	--印花	10	0 9.5	东盟ASEAN,智利CL,巴基斯坦PK,新加坡SG,新西兰NZ,秘鲁PE,哥斯达黎加CR 亚太APTA	0	最不发达35国LDC35	130	--Printed
		-其他机织物,按重量计其他合成纤维长丝含量在85%以下,主要或仅与棉混纺:							-Other woven fabrics, containing less than 85% by weight of synthetic filaments, mixed mainly or solely with cotton:

序号 No.	税则号列 Tariff Line	货品名称	最惠国税率 MFN(%)	协定税率 Agreement(%)		特惠税率 S.P.(%)		普通税率 Gen.(%)	Article Description
3943	5407.8100	--未漂白或漂白	10	0	东盟ASEAN,智利CL,巴基斯坦PK,新加坡SG,新西兰NZ,秘鲁PE,哥斯达黎加CR,香港HK	0	最不发达35国LDC35	130	--Unbleached or bleached
3944	5407.8200	--染色	10	0	东盟ASEAN,智利CL,巴基斯坦PK,新加坡SG,新西兰NZ,秘鲁PE,哥斯达黎加CR,香港HK,台湾TW	0	最不发达35国LDC35,最不发达4国LDC4	130	--Dyed
3945	5407.8300	--色织	10	0	东盟ASEAN,智利CL,巴基斯坦PK,新加坡SG,新西兰NZ,秘鲁PE,哥斯达黎加CR,台湾TW	0	最不发达35国LDC35	130	--Of yarns of different colours
3946	5407.8400	--印花	10	0	东盟ASEAN,智利CL,巴基斯坦PK,新加坡SG,新西兰NZ,秘鲁PE,哥斯达黎加CR	0	最不发达35国LDC35	130	--Printed
		-其他机织物:							-Other woven fabrics:
3947	5407.9100	--未漂白或漂白	10	0	东盟ASEAN,智利CL,巴基斯坦PK,新加坡SG,新西兰NZ,秘鲁PE,哥斯达黎加CR,香港HK	0	最不发达35国LDC35	130	--Unbleached or bleached
3948	5407.9200	--染色	10	0	东盟ASEAN,智利CL,巴基斯坦PK,新加坡SG,新西兰NZ,秘鲁PE,哥斯达黎加CR,香港HK,台湾TW	0	最不发达35国LDC35,最不发达4国LDC4,缅甸MM,老挝LA,柬埔寨KH	130	--Dyed
3949	5407.9300	--色织	10	0	东盟ASEAN,智利CL,巴基斯坦PK,新加坡SG,新西兰NZ,秘鲁PE,哥斯达黎加CR,台湾TW	0	最不发达35国LDC35	130	--Of yarns of different colours
3950	5407.9400	--印花	10	0	东盟ASEAN,智利CL,巴基斯坦PK,新加坡SG,新西兰NZ,秘鲁PE,哥斯达黎加CR	0	最不发达35国LDC35	130	--Printed
	54.08	**人造纤维长丝纱线的机织物，包括税号54.05所列材料的机织物:**							**Woven fabrics of artificial filament yarn, including woven fabrics obtained from materials of heading No.54.05:**
3951	5408.1000	-粘胶纤维高强力纱的机织物	10	0	东盟ASEAN,智利CL,巴基斯坦PK,新加坡SG,新西兰NZ,秘鲁PE,哥斯达黎加CR	0	最不发达35国LDC35	130	-Woven fabrics obtained from high tenacity yarn of viscose rayon
		-其他机织物，按重量计人造纤维长丝、扁条或类似品含量在85%及以上:							-Other woven fabrics, containing 85% or more by weight of artificial filament or strip or the like:

序号 No.	税则号列 Tariff Line	货品名称	最惠国税率 MFN(%)	协定税率 Agreement(%)		特惠税率 S.P.(%)		普通税率 Gen.(%)	Article Description
		--未漂白或漂白:							--Unbleached or bleached:
3952	5408.2110	---粘胶纤维制	12	0 2.4	东盟ASEAN,智利CL,巴基斯坦PK,新加坡SG,新西兰NZ,秘鲁PE 哥斯达黎加CR	0	最不发达35国LDC35	130	---Of yarns of viscose rayon
3953	5408.2120	---醋纤纤维制	12	0 2.4	东盟ASEAN,智利CL,巴基斯坦PK,新加坡SG,新西兰NZ,秘鲁PE 哥斯达黎加CR	0	最不发达35国LDC35	130	---Of yarns of cellulose acetate
3954	5408.2190	---其他	12	0 2.4	东盟ASEAN,智利CL,巴基斯坦PK,新加坡SG,新西兰NZ,秘鲁PE 哥斯达黎加CR	0	最不发达35国LDC35	130	---Other
		--染色:							--Dyed:
3955	5408.2210	---粘胶纤维制	10	0	东盟ASEAN,智利CL,巴基斯坦PK,新加坡SG,新西兰NZ,秘鲁PE,哥斯达黎加CR,香港HK	0	最不发达35国LDC35	130	---Of yarns of viscose rayon
3956	5408.2220	---醋纤纤维制	10	0	东盟ASEAN,智利CL,巴基斯坦PK,新加坡SG,新西兰NZ,秘鲁PE,哥斯达黎加CR,香港HK,台湾TW	0	最不发达35国LDC35	130	---Of yarns of cellulose acetate
3957	5408.2290	---其他	10	0	东盟ASEAN,智利CL,巴基斯坦PK,新加坡SG,新西兰NZ,秘鲁PE,哥斯达黎加CR,香港HK,台湾TW	0	最不发达35国LDC35	130	---Other
		--色织:							--Of yarns of different colours:
3958	5408.2310	---粘胶纤维制	10	0	东盟ASEAN,智利CL,巴基斯坦PK,新加坡SG,新西兰NZ,秘鲁PE,哥斯达黎加CR	0	最不发达35国LDC35	130	---Of yarns of viscose rayon
3959	5408.2320	---醋纤纤维制	10	0	东盟ASEAN,智利CL,巴基斯坦PK,新加坡SG,新西兰NZ,秘鲁PE,哥斯达黎加CR	0	最不发达35国LDC35	130	---Of yarns of cellulose acetate
3960	5408.2390	---其他	10	0	东盟ASEAN,智利CL,巴基斯坦PK,新加坡SG,新西兰NZ,秘鲁PE,哥斯达黎加CR,台湾TW	0	最不发达35国LDC35	130	---Other
		--印花:							--Printed:
3961	5408.2410	---粘胶纤维制	10	0	东盟ASEAN,智利CL,巴基斯坦PK,新加坡SG,新西兰NZ,秘鲁PE,哥斯达黎加CR,香港HK	0	最不发达35国LDC35	130	---Of yarns of viscose rayon
3962	5408.2420	---醋纤纤维制	10	0	东盟ASEAN,智利CL,巴基斯坦PK,新加坡SG,新西兰NZ,秘鲁PE,哥斯达黎加CR,香港HK	0	最不发达35国LDC35	130	---Of yarns of cellulose acetate
3963	5408.2490	---其他	10	0	东盟ASEAN,智利CL,巴基斯坦PK,新加坡SG,新西兰NZ,秘鲁PE,哥斯达黎加CR,香港HK	0	最不发达35国LDC35	130	---Other

序号 No.	税则号列 Tariff Line	货品名称	最惠国 税 率 MFN(%)	协定税率 Agreement(%)		特惠税率 S.P.(%)		普通 税率 Gen.(%)	Article Description
		-其他机织物:							-Other woven fabrics:
3964	5408.3100	--未漂白或漂白	10	0	东盟ASEAN,智利CL,巴基斯坦PK,新加坡SG,新西兰NZ,秘鲁PE,哥斯达黎加CR	0	最不发达35国LDC35	130	--Unbleached or bleached
3965	5408.3200	--染色	10	0 9.5	东盟ASEAN,智利CL,巴基斯坦PK,新加坡SG,新西兰NZ,秘鲁PE,哥斯达黎加CR,台湾TW 亚太APTA	0	最不发达35国LDC35,最不发达4国LDC4	130	--Dyed
3966	5408.3300	--色织	10	0	东盟ASEAN,智利CL,巴基斯坦PK,新加坡SG,新西兰NZ,秘鲁PE,哥斯达黎加CR	0	最不发达35国LDC35	130	--Of yarns of different colours
3967	5408.3400	--印花	10	0	东盟ASEAN,智利CL,巴基斯坦PK,新加坡SG,新西兰NZ,秘鲁PE,哥斯达黎加CR	0	最不发达35国LDC35	130	--Printed

第五十五章 化学纤维短纤

Chapter 55 Man-made staple fibres

注释:

税号 55.01 和 55.02 仅适用于每根与丝束长度相等的平行化学纤维长丝丝束。前述丝束应同时符合下列规格:

一、丝束长度超过 2 米;

二、捻度每米少于 5 转;

三、每根长丝细度在 67 分特以下;

四、合成纤维长丝丝束,须经拉伸处理,即本身不能被拉伸至超过本身长度的一倍;

五、丝束总细度大于 20000 分特。

丝束长度不超过 2 米的归入税号 55.03 或 55.04。

Notes:

Headings Nos.55.01 and 55.02 apply only to man-made filament tow, consisting of parallel filaments of a uniform length equal to the length of the tow, meeting the following specifications:

1. Length of tow exceeding 2m;
2. Twist less than 5 turns per metre;
3. Measuring per filament less than 67 decitex;
4. Synthetic filament tow only:the tow must be drawn, that is to say, be incapable of being stretched by more than 100% of its length;
5. Total measurement of tow more than 20000 decitex.

Tow of a length not exceeding 2m is to be classified in heading No.55.03 or 55.04.

序号 No.	税则号列 Tariff Line	货品名称	最惠国税率 MFN(%)	协定税率 Agreement(%)		特惠税率 S.P.(%)		普通税率 Gen.(%)	Article Description
	55.01	**合成纤维长丝丝束:**							**Synthetic filament tow:**
3968	5501.1000	-尼龙或其他聚酰胺制	5	0	东盟ASEAN,智利CL,巴基斯坦PK,新西兰NZ,秘鲁PE,哥斯达黎加CR	0	最不发达35国LDC35,最不发达4国LDC4	70	-Of nylon or other polyamides
3969	5501.2000	-聚酯制	5	0	智利CL,巴基斯坦PK,新西兰NZ,秘鲁PE,哥斯达黎加CR	0	最不发达35国LDC35,最不发达4国LDC4	70	-Of polyesters
3970	5501.3000	-聚丙烯腈或变性聚丙烯腈制	5	0 4.5	智利CL,巴基斯坦PK,新西兰NZ,哥斯达黎加CR 亚太APTA	0	最不发达35国LDC35,最不发达4国LDC4	35	-Acrylic or modacrylic
3971	5501.4000	-聚丙烯制	5	0	东盟ASEAN,智利CL,巴基斯坦PK,新西兰NZ,秘鲁PE,哥斯达黎加CR,香港HK	0	最不发达35国LDC35,最不发达4国LDC4	70	-Of polypropylene
3972	5501.9000	-其他	5	0	东盟ASEAN,智利CL,巴基斯坦PK,新西兰NZ,秘鲁PE,哥斯达黎加CR,香港HK	0	最不发达35国LDC35,最不发达4国LDC4	70	-Other

序号 No.	税则号列 Tariff Line	货品名称	最惠国税率 MFN(%)	协定税率 Agreement(%)		特惠税率 S.P.(%)		普通税率 Gen.(%)	Article Description
	55.02	**人造纤维长丝丝束:**							**Artificial filament tow:**
3973	5502.0010	---二醋酸纤维丝束	3	0 2.1	东盟ASEAN,智利CL,巴基斯坦PK,新西兰NZ,秘鲁PE,哥斯达黎加CR 亚太APTA	0	最不发达35国LDC35,最不发达4国LDC4	40	---Cellulose diacetate filament tow
3974	5502.0090	---其他	5	0 3.5	东盟ASEAN,智利CL,巴基斯坦PK,新西兰NZ,秘鲁PE,哥斯达黎加CR 亚太APTA	0	最不发达35国LDC35,最不发达4国LDC4	35	---Other
	55.03	**合成纤维短纤，未梳或未经其他纺前加工:**							**Synthetic staple fibres, not carded, combed or otherwise processed for spinning:**
		-尼龙或其他聚酰胺制:							-Of nylon or other polyamides:
		--芳族聚酰胺纺制:							--Of aramids:
3975	5503.1110	---聚间苯二甲酰间苯二胺纺制	5	0	东盟ASEAN,智利CL,巴基斯坦PK,新西兰NZ,秘鲁PE,哥斯达黎加CR	0	最不发达35国LDC35,最不发达4国LDC4	70	---Of polyisophthaloyl metaphenylene diamine
3976	5503.1120	---聚对苯二甲酰对苯二胺纺制	5	0	东盟ASEAN,智利CL,巴基斯坦PK,新西兰NZ,秘鲁PE,哥斯达黎加CR	0	最不发达35国LDC35,最不发达4国LDC4	70	---Of polyisophthaloyl paraphenylene diamine
3977	5503.1190	---其他	5	0	东盟ASEAN,智利CL,巴基斯坦PK,新西兰NZ,秘鲁PE,哥斯达黎加CR	0	最不发达35国LDC35,最不发达4国LDC4	70	---Other
3978	5503.1900	--其他	5	0	东盟ASEAN,智利CL,巴基斯坦PK,新西兰NZ,秘鲁PE,哥斯达黎加CR	0	最不发达35国LDC35,最不发达4国LDC4	70	--Other
3979	5503.2000	-聚酯制	5	0 4.5	智利CL,巴基斯坦PK,新西兰NZ,秘鲁PE,哥斯达黎加CR 亚太APTA	0	最不发达35国LDC35,最不发达4国LDC4	70	-Of polyesters
3980	5503.3000	-聚丙烯腈或变性聚丙烯腈制	5	0 4.5	智利CL,巴基斯坦PK,新西兰NZ,秘鲁PE,哥斯达黎加CR 亚太APTA	0	最不发达35国LDC35,最不发达4国LDC4	35	-Acrylic or modacrylic

序号 No.	税则号列 Tariff Line	货品名称	最惠国税率 MFN(%)	协定税率 Agreement(%)		特惠税率 S.P.(%)		普通税率 Gen.(%)	Article Description
3981	5503.4000	-聚丙烯制	5	0	东盟ASEAN,智利CL,巴基斯坦PK,新西兰NZ,秘鲁PE,哥斯达黎加CR	0	最不发达35国LDC35,最不发达4国LDC4	70	-Of polypropylene
		-其他:							-Other:
3982	5503.9010	---聚苯硫醚制	5	0	东盟ASEAN,智利CL,巴基斯坦PK,新西兰NZ,秘鲁PE,哥斯达黎加CR,台湾TW	0	最不发达35国LDC35,最不发达4国LDC4	70	---Of polyphenylene sulfide
3983	5503.9090	---其他	5	0	东盟ASEAN,智利CL,巴基斯坦PK,新西兰NZ,秘鲁PE,哥斯达黎加CR,台湾TW	0	最不发达35国LDC35,最不发达4国LDC4	70	---Other
	55.04	**人造纤维短纤，未梳或未经其他纺前加工:**							**Artificial staple fibres, not carded, combed or otherwise processed for spinning:**
		-粘胶纤维制:							-Of viscose rayon:
3984	5504.1010	---竹制	5	0	东盟ASEAN,智利CL,巴基斯坦PK,新西兰NZ,秘鲁PE,哥斯达黎加CR	0	最不发达35国LDC35,最不发达4国LDC4	35	---Of bamboo
		---木制:							---Of wood:
3985	5504.1021	----阻燃的	5	0	东盟ASEAN,智利CL,巴基斯坦PK,新西兰NZ,秘鲁PE,哥斯达黎加CR	0	最不发达35国LDC35,最不发达4国LDC4	35	----Flame retardant
3986	5504.1029	----其他	5	0	东盟ASEAN,智利CL,巴基斯坦PK,新西兰NZ,秘鲁PE,哥斯达黎加CR	0	最不发达35国LDC35,最不发达4国LDC4	35	----Other
	ex55041029	高湿模量粘胶纤维（湿强≥2.0cn/dtex,干强≥3.0cn/dtex,干伸＞14%，湿伸＞18%，纤度0.89~2.67dtex）	△2						High wet modulus rayon fiber (wet strength≥2.0cn/dtex,dry strength≥3.0cn/dtex,dry elongation＞14%，wet elongation＞18%，titre: 0.89~2.67dtex)
3987	5504.1090	---其他	5	0	东盟ASEAN,智利CL,巴基斯坦PK,新西兰NZ,秘鲁PE,哥斯达黎加CR	0	最不发达35国LDC35,最不发达4国LDC4	35	---Other

序号 No.	税则号列 Tariff Line	货品名称	最惠国税率 MFN(%)	协定税率 Agreement(%)		特惠税率 S.P.(%)		普通税率 Gen.(%)	Article Description
3988	5504.9000	-其他	5	0	东盟ASEAN,智利CL,巴基斯坦PK,新西兰NZ,秘鲁PE,哥斯达黎加CR,台湾TW	0	最不发达35国LDC35,最不发达4国LDC4	35	-Other
	55.05	**化学纤维废料（包括落绵、废纱及回收纤维）：**							**Waste (including noils, yarn waste and garnetted stock) of man-made fibres:**
3989	5505.1000	-合成纤维的	5	0	东盟ASEAN,智利CL,巴基斯坦PK,新西兰NZ,秘鲁PE,哥斯达黎加CR	0	最不发达35国LDC35,最不发达4国LDC4	70	-Of synthetic fibres
3990	5505.2000	-人造纤维的	5	0	东盟ASEAN,智利CL,巴基斯坦PK,新西兰NZ,秘鲁PE,哥斯达黎加CR,香港HK	0	最不发达35国LDC35,最不发达4国LDC4	70	-Of artificial fibres
	55.06	**合成纤维短纤，已梳或经其他纺前加工：**							**Synthetic staple fibres, carded, combed or otherwise processed for spinning:**
		-尼龙或其他聚酰胺制:							-Of nylon or other polyamides:
		---芳族聚酰胺纺制:							---Of aramids:
3991	5506.1011	----聚间苯二甲酰间苯二胺纺制	5	0	东盟ASEAN,智利CL,巴基斯坦PK,新西兰NZ,秘鲁PE,哥斯达黎加CR	0	最不发达35国LDC35,最不发达4国LDC4	70	----Of polyisophthaloyl metaphenylene diamine
3992	5506.1012	----聚对苯二甲酰对苯二胺纺制	5	0	东盟ASEAN,智利CL,巴基斯坦PK,新西兰NZ,秘鲁PE,哥斯达黎加CR	0	最不发达35国LDC35,最不发达4国LDC4	70	----Of polyisophthaloyl paraphenylene diamine
3993	5506.1019	----其他	5	0	东盟ASEAN,智利CL,巴基斯坦PK,新西兰NZ,秘鲁PE,哥斯达黎加CR	0	最不发达35国LDC35,最不发达4国LDC4	70	----Other
3994	5506.1090	---其他	5	0	东盟ASEAN,智利CL,巴基斯坦PK,新西兰NZ,秘鲁PE,哥斯达黎加CR	0	最不发达35国LDC35,最不发达4国LDC4	70	---Other

序号 No.	税则号列 Tariff Line	货品名称	最惠国税率 MFN(%)	协定税率 Agreement(%)		特惠税率 S.P.(%)		普通税率 Gen.(%)	Article Description
3995	5506.2000	-聚酯制	5	0 4.5	智利CL,新西兰NZ,秘鲁PE,哥斯达黎加CR 亚太APTA,巴基斯坦PK	0	最不发达35国LDC35,最不发达4国LDC4	70	-Of polyesters
3996	5506.3000	-聚丙烯腈或变性聚丙烯腈制	5	0 4.5	智利CL,新西兰NZ,秘鲁PE,哥斯达黎加CR 亚太APTA,巴基斯坦PK	0	最不发达35国LDC35,最不发达4国LDC4	35	-Acrylic or modacrylic
		-其他:							-Other:
3997	5506.9010	---聚苯硫醚制	5	0	东盟ASEAN,智利CL,巴基斯坦PK,新西兰NZ,秘鲁PE,哥斯达黎加CR	0	最不发达35国LDC35,最不发达4国LDC4	70	---Of polyphenylene sulfide
3998	5506.9090	---其他	5	0	东盟ASEAN,智利CL,巴基斯坦PK,新西兰NZ,秘鲁PE,哥斯达黎加CR	0	最不发达35国LDC35,最不发达4国LDC4	70	---Other
	55.07	**人造纤维短纤，已梳或经其他纺前加工:**							**Artificial staple fibres, carded, combed or otherwise processed for spinning:**
3999	5507.0000	人造纤维短纤，已梳或经其他纺前加工	5	0	东盟ASEAN,智利CL,巴基斯坦PK,新西兰NZ,秘鲁PE,哥斯达黎加CR	0	最不发达35国LDC35,最不发达4国LDC4	35	Artificial staple fibres, carded, combed or otherwise processed for spinning
	55.08	**化学纤维短纤纺制的缝纫线，不论是否供零售用:**							**Sewing thread of man-made staple fibres, whether or not put up for retail sale:**
4000	5508.1000	-合成纤维短纤纺制	5	0 4.5	文莱BN,印尼ID,马来西亚MY,缅甸MM,菲律宾PH,新加坡*SG*,泰国TH,越南VT,智利CL,巴基斯坦PK,新西兰NZ,秘鲁PE,哥斯达黎加CR,香港HK,澳门MO 亚太APTA	0	最不发达35国LDC35,最不发达4国LDC4	90	-Of synthetic staple fibres
4001	5508.2000	-人造纤维短纤纺制	5	0	东盟ASEAN,智利CL,巴基斯坦PK,新西兰NZ,秘鲁PE,哥斯达黎加CR	0	最不发达35国LDC35,最不发达4国LDC4	70	-Of artificial staple fibres

序号 No.	税则号列 Tariff Line	货品名称	最惠国税率 MFN(%)	协定税率 Agreement(%)		特惠税率 S.P.(%)		普通税率 Gen.(%)	Article Description
	55.09	**合成纤维短纤纺制的纱线（缝纫线除外），非供零售用:**							**Yarn (other than sewing thread) of synthetic staple fibres, not put up for retail sale:**
		-按重量计尼龙或其他聚酰胺短纤含量在85%及以上:							-Containing 85% or more by weight of staple fibres of nylon or other polyamides:
4002	5509.1100	--单纱	5	0	东盟ASEAN,智利CL,巴基斯坦PK,新西兰NZ,秘鲁PE,哥斯达黎加CR,香港HK,澳门MO	0	最不发达35国LDC35,最不发达4国LDC4	90	--Single yarn
4003	5509.1200	--多股纱线或缆线	5	0	东盟ASEAN,智利CL,巴基斯坦PK,新西兰NZ,秘鲁PE,哥斯达黎加CR,香港HK,澳门MO	0	最不发达35国LDC35,最不发达4国LDC4	90	--Multiple(folded)or cabled yarn
		-按重量计聚酯短纤含量在85%及以上:							-Containing 85% or more by weight of polyester staple fibres:
4004	5509.2100	--单纱	5	0	文莱BN,印尼ID,马来西亚MY,缅甸MM,菲律宾PH,新加坡*SG*,泰国TH,越南VT,智利CL,巴基斯坦PK,新西兰NZ,秘鲁PE,哥斯达黎加CR,香港HK,澳门MO	0	最不发达35国LDC35,最不发达4国LDC4	90	--Single yarn
4005	5509.2200	--多股纱线或缆线	5	0	文莱BN,印尼ID,马来西亚MY,缅甸MM,菲律宾PH,新加坡*SG*,泰国TH,越南VT,智利CL,巴基斯坦PK,新西兰NZ,秘鲁PE,哥斯达黎加CR,香港HK,澳门MO	0	最不发达35国LDC35,最不发达4国LDC4	90	--Multiple(folded)or cabled yarn
		-按重量计聚丙烯腈或变性聚丙烯腈短纤含量在85%及以上:							-Containing 85% or more by weight of acrylic or modacrylic staple fibres:
4006	5509.3100	--单纱	5	0	文莱BN,印尼ID,马来西亚MY,缅甸MM,菲律宾PH,新加坡*SG*,泰国TH,越南VT,智利CL,巴基斯坦PK,新西兰NZ,秘鲁PE,哥斯达黎加CR,香港HK,澳门MO	0	最不发达35国LDC35,最不发达4国LDC4	90	--Single yarn
4007	5509.3200	--多股纱线或缆线	5	0	文莱BN,印尼ID,马来西亚MY,缅甸MM,菲律宾PH,新加坡*SG*,泰国TH,越南VT,智利CL,巴基斯坦PK,新西兰NZ,秘鲁PE,哥斯达黎加CR,香港HK,澳门MO,台湾TW	0	最不发达35国LDC35,最不发达4国LDC4	90	--Multiple(folded)or cabled yarn
				4.8	亚太APTA				

序号 No.	税则号列 Tariff Line	货品名称	最惠国税率 MFN(%)	协定税率 Agreement(%)		特惠税率 S.P.(%)		普通税率 Gen.(%)	Article Description
		-其他纱线，按重量计合成纤维短纤含量在85%及以上:							-Other yarn, containing 85% or more by weight of synthetic staple fibres:
4008	5509.4100	--单纱	5	0	文莱BN,印尼ID,马来西亚MY,缅甸MM,菲律宾PH,新加坡*SG*,泰国TH,越南VT,智利CL,巴基斯坦PK,新西兰NZ,秘鲁PE,哥斯达黎加CR,香港HK,澳门MO	0	最不发达35国LDC35,最不发达4国LDC4	90	--Single yarn
4009	5509.4200	--多股纱线或缆线	5	0	文莱BN,印尼ID,马来西亚MY,缅甸MM,菲律宾PH,新加坡*SG*,泰国TH,越南VT,智利CL,巴基斯坦PK,新西兰NZ,秘鲁PE,哥斯达黎加CR,香港HK,澳门MO	0	最不发达35国LDC35,最不发达4国LDC4	90	--Multiple (folded) or cabled yarn
		-其他聚酯短纤纺制的纱线:							-Other yarn, of polyester staple fibres:
4010	5509.5100	--主要或仅与人造纤维短纤混纺	5	0	文莱BN,印尼ID,马来西亚MY,缅甸MM,菲律宾PH,新加坡*SG*,泰国TH,越南VT,智利CL,巴基斯坦PK,新西兰NZ,秘鲁PE,哥斯达黎加CR,香港HK,澳门MO	0	最不发达35国LDC35,最不发达4国LDC4	90	--Mixed mainly or solely with artificial staple fibres
4011	5509.5200	--主要或仅与羊毛或动物细毛混纺	5	0	文莱BN,印尼ID,马来西亚MY,缅甸MM,菲律宾PH,新加坡*SG*,泰国TH,越南VT,智利CL,巴基斯坦PK,新西兰NZ,秘鲁PE,哥斯达黎加CR,香港HK,澳门MO	0	最不发达35国LDC35,最不发达4国LDC4	90	--Mixed mainly or solely with wool or fine animal hair
4012	5509.5300	--主要或仅与棉混纺	5	0	文莱BN,印尼ID,马来西亚MY,缅甸MM,菲律宾PH,新加坡*SG*,泰国TH,越南VT,智利CL,巴基斯坦PK,新西兰NZ,秘鲁PE,哥斯达黎加CR,香港HK,澳门MO,台湾TW	0	最不发达35国LDC35,最不发达4国LDC4	90	--Mixed maninly or solely with cotton
				3.5	亚太APTA				
4013	5509.5900	--其他	5	0	文莱BN,印尼ID,马来西亚MY,缅甸MM,菲律宾PH,新加坡*SG*,泰国TH,越南VT,智利CL,巴基斯坦PK,新西兰NZ,秘鲁PE,哥斯达黎加CR,香港HK,澳门MO	0	最不发达35国LDC35,最不发达4国LDC4	90	--Other
		-其他聚丙烯腈或变性聚丙烯腈短纤纺制的纱线:							-Other yarn, of acrylic or modacrylic staple fibres:

序号 No.	税则号列 Tariff Line	货品名称	最惠国税率 MFN(%)	协定税率 Agreement(%)		特惠税率 S.P.(%)		普通税率 Gen.(%)	Article Description
4014	5509.6100	--主要或仅与羊毛或动物细毛混纺	5	0	文莱BN,印尼ID,马来西亚MY,缅甸MM,菲律宾PH,新加坡*SG*,泰国TH,越南VT,智利CL,巴基斯坦PK,新西兰NZ,秘鲁PE,哥斯达黎加CR,香港HK,澳门MO	0	最不发达35国LDC35,最不发达4国LDC4	90	--Mixed mainly or solely with wool or fine animal hair
4015	5509.6200	--主要或仅与棉混纺	5	0	文莱BN,印尼ID,马来西亚MY,缅甸MM,菲律宾PH,新加坡*SG*,泰国TH,越南VT,智利CL,巴基斯坦PK,新西兰NZ,秘鲁PE,哥斯达黎加CR,香港HK,澳门MO	0	最不发达35国LDC35,最不发达4国LDC4	90	--Mixed mainly or solely with cotton
				4.8	亚太APTA				
4016	5509.6900	--其他	5	0	文莱BN,印尼ID,马来西亚MY,缅甸MM,菲律宾PH,新加坡*SG*,泰国TH,越南VT,智利CL,巴基斯坦PK,新西兰NZ,秘鲁PE,哥斯达黎加CR,香港HK,澳门MO	0	最不发达35国LDC35,最不发达4国LDC4	90	--Other
		-其他纱线:							-Other yarn:
4017	5509.9100	--主要或仅与羊毛或动物细毛混纺	5	0	文莱BN,印尼ID,马来西亚MY,缅甸MM,菲律宾PH,新加坡*SG*,泰国TH,越南VT,智利CL,巴基斯坦PK,新西兰NZ,秘鲁PE,哥斯达黎加CR,香港HK,澳门MO	0	最不发达35国LDC35,最不发达4国LDC4	90	--Mixed nainly or solely with wool or fine animal hair
4018	5509.9200	--主要或仅与棉混纺	5	0	文莱BN,印尼ID,马来西亚MY,缅甸MM,菲律宾PH,新加坡*SG*,泰国TH,越南VT,智利CL,巴基斯坦PK,新西兰NZ,秘鲁PE,哥斯达黎加CR,香港HK,澳门MO,台湾TW	0	最不发达35国LDC35,最不发达4国LDC4	90	--Mixed mainly or solely with cotton
4019	5509.9900	--其他	5	0	文莱BN,印尼ID,马来西亚MY,缅甸MM,菲律宾PH,新加坡*SG*,泰国TH,越南VT,智利CL,巴基斯坦PK,新西兰NZ,秘鲁PE,哥斯达黎加CR,香港HK,澳门MO	0	最不发达35国LDC35,最不发达4国LDC4	90	--Other
	55.10	**人造纤维短纤纺制的纱线（缝纫线除外），非供零售用:**							**Yarn (other than sewing thread) of artificial staple fibres, not put up for retail sale:**
		-按重量计人造纤维短纤含量在85%及以上:							-Containing 85% or more by weight of artificial staple fibres:

序号 No.	税则号列 Tariff Line	货品名称	最惠国税率 MFN(%)	协定税率 Agreement(%)		特惠税率 S.P.(%)		普通税率 Gen.(%)	Article Description
4020	5510.1100	--单纱	5	0 4.5	东盟ASEAN,智利CL,巴基斯坦PK,新西兰NZ,秘鲁PE,哥斯达黎加CR,香港HK,澳门MO,台湾TW 亚太APTA	0	最不发达35国LDC35,最不发达4国LDC4	70	--Single yarn
4021	5510.1200	--多股纱线或缆线	5	0	东盟ASEAN,智利CL,巴基斯坦PK,新西兰NZ,秘鲁PE,哥斯达黎加CR,香港HK,澳门MO,台湾TW	0	最不发达35国LDC35,最不发达4国LDC4	70	--Multiple (folded) or cabled yarn
4022	5510.2000	-其他纱线,主要或仅与羊毛或动物细毛混纺	5	0	东盟ASEAN,智利CL,巴基斯坦PK,新西兰NZ,秘鲁PE,哥斯达黎加CR,香港HK,澳门MO	0	最不发达35国LDC35,最不发达4国LDC4	70	-Other yarn, mixed mainly or solely with wool or fine animal hair
4023	5510.3000	-其他纱线,主要或仅与棉混纺	5	0 3.5	东盟ASEAN,智利CL,巴基斯坦PK,新西兰NZ,秘鲁PE,哥斯达黎加CR,香港HK,澳门MO,台湾TW 亚太APTA	0	最不发达35国LDC35,最不发达4国LDC4	70	-Other yarn, mixed mainly or solely with cotton
4024	5510.9000	-其他	5	0 4.5	东盟ASEAN,智利CL,巴基斯坦PK,新西兰NZ,秘鲁PE,哥斯达黎加CR,香港HK,澳门MO 亚太APTA	0	最不发达35国LDC35,最不发达4国LDC4	70	-Other yarn
	55.11	**化学纤维短纤纺制的纱线（缝纫线除外），供零售用:**							**Yarn (other than sewing thread) of man-made staple fibres, put up for retail sale:**
4025	5511.1000	-按重量计合成纤维短纤含量在85%及以上	5	0	文莱BN,印尼ID,马来西亚MY,缅甸MM,菲律宾PH,新加坡*SG*,泰国TH,越南VT,智利CL,巴基斯坦PK,新西兰NZ,秘鲁PE,哥斯达黎加CR	0	最不发达35国LDC35,最不发达4国LDC4	90	-Of synthetic staple fibres, containing 85% or more by weight of such fibres
4026	5511.2000	-按重量计合成纤维短纤含量在85%以下	5	0	文莱BN,印尼ID,马来西亚MY,缅甸MM,菲律宾PH,新加坡*SG*,泰国TH,越南VT,智利CL,巴基斯坦PK,新西兰NZ,秘鲁PE,哥斯达黎加CR	0	最不发达35国LDC35,最不发达4国LDC4	90	-Of synthetic staple fibres, containing less than 85% by weight of such fibres
4027	5511.3000	-人造纤维短纤纺制	5	0	东盟ASEAN,智利CL,巴基斯坦PK,新西兰NZ,秘鲁PE,哥斯达黎加CR	0	最不发达35国LDC35,最不发达4国LDC4	90	-Of artificial staple fibres

序号 No.	税则号列 Tariff Line	货品名称	最惠国税率 MFN(%)	协定税率 Agreement(%)		特惠税率 S.P.(%)		普通税率 Gen.(%)	Article Description
	55.12	**合成纤维短纤纺制的机织物，按重量计合成纤维短纤含量在85%及以上:**							**Woven fabrics of synthetic staple fibres, containing 85% or more by weight of synthetic staple fibres:**
		-按重量计聚酯短纤含量在85%及以上:							-Containing 85% or more by weight of polyester staple fibres:
4028	5512.1100	--未漂白或漂白	15	0 3 7.5 10.5	东盟ASEAN,智利CL,巴基斯坦PK,新加坡SG,新西兰NZ,台湾TW 哥斯达黎加CR 秘鲁PE 亚太APTA	0	最不发达35国LDC35,最不发达4国LDC4	130	--Unbleached or bleached
4029	5512.1900	--其他	10	0 5	东盟ASEAN,智利CL,巴基斯坦PK,新加坡SG,新西兰NZ,哥斯达黎加CR,香港HK,台湾TW 秘鲁PE	0	最不发达35国LDC35,最不发达4国LDC4	130	--Other
		-按重量计聚丙烯腈或变性聚丙烯腈短纤含量在85%及以上:							-Containing 85% or more by weight of acrylic or modacrylic staple fibres:
4030	5512.2100	--未漂白或漂白	13	0 2.6	东盟ASEAN,智利CL,巴基斯坦PK,新加坡SG,新西兰NZ,秘鲁PE 哥斯达黎加CR	0	最不发达35国LDC35,最不发达4国LDC4	130	--Unbleached or bleached
4031	5512.2900	--其他	10	0 9.3	东盟ASEAN,智利CL,巴基斯坦PK,新加坡SG,新西兰NZ,秘鲁PE,哥斯达黎加CR 亚太APTA	0	最不发达35国LDC35	130	--Other
		-其他:							-Other:
4032	5512.9100	--未漂白或漂白	18	0 3.6 9	东盟ASEAN,智利CL,巴基斯坦PK,新加坡SG,新西兰NZ 哥斯达黎加CR 秘鲁PE	0	最不发达35国LDC35	130	--Unbleached or bleached
4033	5512.9900	--其他	10	0	东盟ASEAN,智利CL,巴基斯坦PK,新加坡SG,新西兰NZ,秘鲁PE,哥斯达黎加CR,香港HK,澳门MO,台湾TW	0	最不发达35国LDC35,最不发达4国LDC4,缅甸MM,老挝LA,柬埔寨KH	130	--Other

序号 No.	税则号列 Tariff Line	货品名称	最惠国 税 率 MFN(%)	协定税率 Agreement(%)		特惠税率 S.P.(%)		普通 税率 Gen.(%)	Article Description
	55.13	**合成纤维短纤纺制的机织物，按重量计合成纤维短纤含量在85%以下，主要或仅与棉混纺，每平方米重量不超过170克：**							**Woven fabrics of synthetic staple fibres, containing less than 85% by weight of such fibres, mixed mainly or solely with cotton, of a weight not exceeding 170g/m²:**
		-未漂白或漂白:							-Unbleached or bleached:
		--聚酯短纤纺制的平纹机织物:							--Of polyester staple fibres, plain weave:
4034	5513.1110	---未漂白	16	0 3.2 8	东盟ASEAN,智利CL,巴基斯坦PK,新加坡SG,新西兰NZ,香港HK 哥斯达黎加CR 秘鲁PE	0	最不发达35国LDC35	130	---Unbleached
4035	5513.1120	---漂白	15	0 3 7.5	东盟ASEAN,智利CL,巴基斯坦PK,新加坡SG,新西兰NZ,香港HK 哥斯达黎加CR 秘鲁PE	0	最不发达35国LDC35	130	---Bleached
		--聚酯短纤纺制的三线或四线斜纹机织物，包括双面斜纹机织物:							--3-thread or 4-thread twill, including cross twill, of polyester staple fibres:
4036	5513.1210	---未漂白	16	0 3.2 8	东盟ASEAN,智利CL,巴基斯坦PK,新加坡SG,新西兰NZ,香港HK 哥斯达黎加CR 秘鲁PE	0	最不发达35国LDC35	130	---Unbleached
4037	5513.1220	---漂白	18	0 3.6 9	东盟ASEAN,智利CL,巴基斯坦PK,新加坡SG,新西兰NZ,香港HK 哥斯达黎加CR 秘鲁PE	0	最不发达35国LDC35	130	---Bleached
		--其他聚酯短纤纺制的机织物:							--Other woven fabrics of polyester staple fibres:
4038	5513.1310	---未漂白	16	0 3.2 8	东盟ASEAN,智利CL,巴基斯坦PK,新加坡SG,新西兰NZ 哥斯达黎加CR 秘鲁PE	0	最不发达35国LDC35	130	---Unbleached
4039	5513.1320	---漂白	18	0 3.6 9	东盟ASEAN,智利CL,巴基斯坦PK,新加坡SG,新西兰NZ 哥斯达黎加CR 秘鲁PE	0	最不发达35国LDC35	130	---Bleached
4040	5513.1900	--其他机织物	18	0 3.6 9	东盟ASEAN,智利CL,巴基斯坦PK,新加坡SG,新西兰NZ 哥斯达黎加CR 秘鲁PE	0	最不发达35国LDC35	130	--Other woven fabrics
		-染色:							-Dyed:

序号 No.	税则号列 Tariff Line	货品名称	最惠国税率 MFN(%)	协定税率 Agreement(%)		特惠税率 S.P.(%)		普通税率 Gen.(%)	Article Description
4041	5513.2100	--聚酯短纤纺制的平纹机织物	10	0 9.1	东盟ASEAN,智利CL,巴基斯坦PK,新加坡SG,新西兰NZ,秘鲁PE,哥斯达黎加CR,香港HK,澳门MO,台湾TW 亚太APTA	0	最不发达35国LDC35	130	--Of polyester staple fibres, plain weave
		--其他聚酯短纤纺制的机织物:							--Other woven fabrics of polyester staple fibres:
4042	5513.2310	---聚酯短纤纺制的三线或四线斜纹机织物，包括双面斜纹机织物	10	0	东盟ASEAN,智利CL,巴基斯坦PK,新加坡SG,新西兰NZ,秘鲁PE,哥斯达黎加CR,香港HK	0	最不发达35国LDC35	130	---3-thread or 4-thread twil, including crosst-will, of polyester staple fibres
4043	5513.2390	---其他	10	0	东盟ASEAN,智利CL,巴基斯坦PK,新加坡SG,新西兰NZ,秘鲁PE,哥斯达黎加CR	0	最不发达35国LDC35	130	---Other
4044	5513.2900	--其他机织物	10	0	东盟ASEAN,智利CL,巴基斯坦PK,新加坡SG,新西兰NZ,秘鲁PE,哥斯达黎加CR	0	最不发达35国LDC35,最不发达4国LDC4	130	--Other woven fabrics
		-色织:							-Of yarns of different colours:
4045	5513.3100	--聚酯短纤纺制的平纹机织物	10	0	东盟ASEAN,智利CL,巴基斯坦PK,新加坡SG,新西兰NZ,秘鲁PE,哥斯达黎加CR,香港HK	0	最不发达35国LDC35	130	--Of polyester staple fibres, plain weave
		--其他机织物:							--Other:
4046	5513.3910	---聚酯短纤纺制的三线或四线斜纹机织物，包括双面斜纹机织物	10	0 8.8	东盟ASEAN,智利CL,巴基斯坦PK,新加坡SG,新西兰NZ,秘鲁PE,哥斯达黎加CR,香港HK 亚太APTA	0	最不发达35国LDC35	130	---3-thread or 4-thread twill, including cross twill, of polyester staple fibres
4047	5513.3920	---其他聚酯短纤纺制的机织物	10	0	东盟ASEAN,智利CL,巴基斯坦PK,新加坡SG,新西兰NZ,秘鲁PE,哥斯达黎加CR,香港HK	0	最不发达35国LDC35	130	---Other woven fabrics of polyester staple fibres
4048	5513.3990	---其他机织物	10	0	东盟ASEAN,智利CL,巴基斯坦PK,新加坡SG,新西兰NZ,秘鲁PE,哥斯达黎加CR	0	最不发达35国LDC35	130	---Other woven fabrics
		-印花:							-Printed:
4049	5513.4100	--聚酯短纤纺制的平纹机织物	10	0	东盟ASEAN,智利CL,巴基斯坦PK,新加坡SG,新西兰NZ,秘鲁PE,哥斯达黎加CR	0	最不发达35国LDC35,最不发达4国LDC4,缅甸MM,老挝LA,柬埔寨KH	130	--Of polyester staple fibres, plain weave
		--其他机织物:							--Other:

序号 No.	税则号列 Tariff Line	货品名称	最惠国税率 MFN(%)	协定税率 Agreement(%)		特惠税率 S.P.(%)		普通税率 Gen.(%)	Article Description
4050	5513.4910	---聚酯短纤纺制的三线或四线斜纹机织物，包括双面斜纹机织物	10	0	东盟ASEAN,智利CL,巴基斯坦PK,新加坡SG,新西兰NZ,秘鲁PE,哥斯达黎加CR	0	最不发达35国LDC35	130	---3-thread or 4-thread twill, including cross twill, of polyester staple fibres
4051	5513.4920	---其他聚酯短纤纺制的机织物	10	0	东盟ASEAN,智利CL,巴基斯坦PK,新加坡SG,新西兰NZ,秘鲁PE,哥斯达黎加CR	0	最不发达35国LDC35	130	---Other woven fabrics of polyester staple fibres
4052	5513.4990	---其他	10	0	东盟ASEAN,智利CL,巴基斯坦PK,新加坡SG,新西兰NZ,秘鲁PE,哥斯达黎加CR	0	最不发达35国LDC35	130	---Other
	55.14	**合成纤维短纤纺制的机织物，按重量计合成纤维短纤含量在85%以下，主要或仅与棉混纺，每平方米重量超过170克:**							**Woven fabrics of synthetic staple fibres, containing less than 85% by weight of such fibres, mixed mainly or solely with cotton, of a weight exceeding 170g/m^2 :**
		-未漂白或漂白:							-Unbleached or bleached:
		--聚酯短纤纺制的平纹机织物:							--Of polyester staple fibres, plain weave:
4053	5514.1110	---未漂白	16	0 3.2 8 14.4	东盟ASEAN,智利CL,巴基斯坦PK,新加坡SG,新西兰NZ 哥斯达黎加CR 秘鲁PE 亚太APTA	0	最不发达35国LDC35	130	---Unbleached
4054	5514.1120	---漂白	18	0 3.6 9	东盟ASEAN,智利CL,巴基斯坦PK,新加坡SG,新西兰NZ 哥斯达黎加CR 秘鲁PE	0	最不发达35国LDC35	130	---Bleached
		--聚酯短纤纺制的三线或四线斜纹机织物，包括双面斜纹机织物:							--3-thread or 4-thread twill, including cross twill, of polyester staple fibres:
4055	5514.1210	---未漂白	16	0 3.2 8	东盟ASEAN,智利CL,巴基斯坦PK,新加坡SG,新西兰NZ,香港HK 哥斯达黎加CR 秘鲁PE	0	最不发达35国LDC35	130	---Unbleached
4056	5514.1220	---漂白	18	0 3.6 9	东盟ASEAN,智利CL,巴基斯坦PK,新加坡SG,新西兰NZ,香港HK 哥斯达黎加CR 秘鲁PE	0	最不发达35国LDC35	130	---Bleached
		--其他机织物:							--Other woven fabrics:
		---聚酯短纤纺制的机织物:							---Other woven fabrics of polyester staple fibres:

序号 No.	税则号列 Tariff Line	货品名称	最惠国税率 MFN(%)	协定税率 Agreement(%)		特惠税率 S.P.(%)		普通税率 Gen.(%)	Article Description
4057	5514.1911	----未漂白	16	0	东盟ASEAN,智利CL,巴基斯坦PK,新加坡SG,新西兰NZ	0	最不发达35国LDC35	130	----Unbleached
				3.2	哥斯达黎加CR				
				8	秘鲁PE				
4058	5514.1912	----漂白	18	0	东盟ASEAN,智利CL,巴基斯坦PK,新加坡SG,新西兰NZ	0	最不发达35国LDC35	130	----Bleached
				3.6	哥斯达黎加CR				
				9	秘鲁PE				
4059	5514.1990	---其他	16	0	东盟ASEAN,智利CL,巴基斯坦PK,新加坡SG,新西兰NZ	0	最不发达35国LDC35	130	---Other
				3.2	哥斯达黎加CR				
				8	秘鲁PE				
				15.2	亚太APTA				
		-染色:							-Dyed:
4060	5514.2100	--聚酯短纤纺制的平纹机织物	10	0	东盟ASEAN,智利CL,巴基斯坦PK,新加坡SG,新西兰NZ,秘鲁PE,哥斯达黎加CR,香港HK	0	最不发达35国LDC35	130	--Of polyester staple fibres, plain weave
4061	5514.2200	--聚酯短纤纺制的三线或四线斜纹机织物，包括双面斜纹机织物	10	0	东盟ASEAN,智利CL,巴基斯坦PK,新加坡SG,新西兰NZ,秘鲁PE,哥斯达黎加CR,香港HK	0	最不发达35国LDC35	130	--3-thread or 4-thread twill, including cross twill, of polyester staple fibres
4062	5514.2300	--其他聚酯短纤纺制的机织物	10	0	东盟ASEAN,智利CL,巴基斯坦PK,新加坡SG,新西兰NZ,秘鲁PE,哥斯达黎加CR	0	最不发达35国LDC35,最不发达4国LDC4,缅甸MM,老挝LA,柬埔寨KH	130	--Other woven fabrics of polyester staple fibres
4063	5514.2900	--其他机织物	10	0	东盟ASEAN,智利CL,巴基斯坦PK,新加坡SG,新西兰NZ,秘鲁PE,哥斯达黎加CR	0	最不发达35国LDC35,最不发达4国LDC4	130	--Other woven fabrics
		-色织:							-Of yarns of different colours:
4064	5514.3010	---聚酯短纤纺制的平纹机织物	10	0	东盟ASEAN,智利CL,巴基斯坦PK,新加坡SG,新西兰NZ,秘鲁PE,哥斯达黎加CR,香港HK	0	最不发达35国LDC35	130	---Of polyester staple fibres, plain weave
4065	5514.3020	---聚酯短纤纺制的三线或四线斜纹机织物，包括双面斜纹机织物	10	0	东盟ASEAN,智利CL,巴基斯坦PK,新加坡SG,新西兰NZ,秘鲁PE,哥斯达黎加CR,香港HK	0	最不发达35国LDC35	130	---3-thread or 4-thread twill, including cross twill, of polyester staple fibres
4066	5514.3030	---其他聚酯短纤纺制的机织物	10	0	东盟ASEAN,智利CL,巴基斯坦PK,新加坡SG,新西兰NZ,秘鲁PE,哥斯达黎加CR	0	最不发达35国LDC35	130	---Other woven fabrics of polyester staple fibres

序号 No.	税则号列 Tariff Line	货品名称	最惠国税率 MFN(%)	协定税率 Agreement(%)		特惠税率 S.P.(%)		普通税率 Gen.(%)	Article Description
4067	5514.3090	---其他机织物	10	0	东盟ASEAN,智利CL,巴基斯坦PK,新加坡SG,新西兰NZ,秘鲁PE,哥斯达黎加CR	0	最不发达35国LDC35	130	---Other woven fabrics
		-印花:							-Printed:
4068	5514.4100	--聚酯短纤纺制的平纹机织物	10	0	东盟ASEAN,智利CL,巴基斯坦PK,新加坡SG,新西兰NZ,秘鲁PE,哥斯达黎加CR	0	最不发达35国LDC35	130	--Of polyester staple fibres, plain weave
4069	5514.4200	--聚酯短纤纺制的三线或四线斜纹机织物，包括双面斜纹机织物	10	0	东盟ASEAN,智利CL,巴基斯坦PK,新加坡SG,新西兰NZ,秘鲁PE,哥斯达黎加CR	0	最不发达35国LDC35	130	--3-thread or 4-thread twill, including cross twill, of polyester staple fibres
4070	5514.4300	--其他聚酯短纤纺制的机织物	10	0	东盟ASEAN,智利CL,巴基斯坦PK,新加坡SG,新西兰NZ,秘鲁PE,哥斯达黎加CR	0	最不发达35国LDC35	130	--Other woven fabrics of polyester staple fibres
4071	5514.4900	--其他机织物	10	0	东盟ASEAN,智利CL,巴基斯坦PK,新加坡SG,新西兰NZ,秘鲁PE,哥斯达黎加CR	0	最不发达35国LDC35	130	--Other woven fabrics
	55.15	**合成纤维短纤纺制的其他机织物:**							**Other woven fabrics of synthetic staple fibres:**
		-聚酯短纤纺制:							-Of polyester staple fibres:
4072	5515.1100	--主要或仅与粘胶纤维短纤混纺	10	0	东盟ASEAN,智利CL,巴基斯坦PK,新加坡SG,新西兰NZ,秘鲁PE,哥斯达黎加CR,台湾TW	0	最不发达35国LDC35	130	--Mixed mainly or solely with viscose rayon staple fibres
				8.8	亚太APTA				
4073	5515.1200	--主要或仅与化学纤维长丝混纺	10	0	东盟ASEAN,智利CL,巴基斯坦PK,新加坡SG,新西兰NZ,秘鲁PE,哥斯达黎加CR,台湾TW	0	最不发达35国LDC35	130	--Mixed mainly or solely with man-made filaments
				9	亚太APTA				
4074	5515.1300	--主要或仅与羊毛或动物细毛混纺	10	0	东盟ASEAN,智利CL,巴基斯坦PK,新加坡SG,新西兰NZ,秘鲁PE,哥斯达黎加CR	0	最不发达35国LDC35	130	--Mixed mainly or solely with wool or fine animal hair
4075	5515.1900	--其他	10	0	东盟ASEAN,智利CL,巴基斯坦PK,新加坡SG,新西兰NZ,秘鲁PE,哥斯达黎加CR	0	最不发达35国LDC35	130	--Other
				9	亚太APTA				
		-聚丙烯腈或变性聚丙烯腈短纤纺制:							-Of acrylic or modacrylic staple fibres:
4076	5515.2100	--主要或仅与化学纤维长丝混纺	10	0	东盟ASEAN,智利CL,巴基斯坦PK,新加坡SG,新西兰NZ,秘鲁PE,哥斯达黎加CR	0	最不发达35国LDC35	130	--Mixed mainly or solely with man-made filaments
4077	5515.2200	--主要或仅与羊毛或动物细毛混纺	12	0	东盟ASEAN,智利CL,巴基斯坦PK,新加坡SG,新西兰NZ,秘鲁PE	0	最不发达35国LDC35,最不发达4国LDC4	130	--Mixed mainly or solely with wool or fine animal hair
				2.4	哥斯达黎加CR				

序号 No.	税则号列 Tariff Line	货品名称	最惠国税率 MFN(%)	协定税率 Agreement(%)		特惠税率 S.P.(%)		普通税率 Gen.(%)	Article Description
4078	5515.2900	--其他	10	0	东盟ASEAN,智利CL,巴基斯坦PK,新加坡SG,新西兰NZ,秘鲁PE,哥斯达黎加CR	0	最不发达35国LDC35	130	--Other
		-其他机织物:							-Other woven fabrics:
4079	5515.9100	--主要或仅与化学纤维长丝混纺	10	0	东盟ASEAN,智利CL,巴基斯坦PK,新加坡SG,新西兰NZ,秘鲁PE,哥斯达黎加CR	0	最不发达35国LDC35	130	--Mixed mainly or solely with man-made filaments
4080	5515.9900	--其他	10	0	东盟ASEAN,智利CL,巴基斯坦PK,新加坡SG,新西兰NZ,秘鲁PE,哥斯达黎加CR	0	最不发达35国LDC35	130	--Other
				9	亚太APTA				
	55.16	**人造纤维短纤纺制的机织物:**							**Woven fabrics of artificial staple fibres:**
		-按重量计人造纤维短纤含量在85%及以上:							-Containing 85% or more by weight of artificial staple fibres:
4081	5516.1100	--未漂白或漂白	12	0	东盟ASEAN,智利CL,巴基斯坦PK,新加坡SG,新西兰NZ,秘鲁PE,香港HK	0	最不发达35国LDC35,最不发达4国LDC4	130	--Unbleached or bleached
				2.4	哥斯达黎加CR				
4082	5516.1200	--染色	10	0	东盟ASEAN,智利CL,巴基斯坦PK,新加坡SG,新西兰NZ,秘鲁PE,哥斯达黎加CR,香港HK,台湾TW	0	最不发达35国LDC35	130	--Dyed
4083	5516.1300	--色织	10	0	东盟ASEAN,智利CL,巴基斯坦PK,新加坡SG,新西兰NZ,秘鲁PE,哥斯达黎加CR,香港HK	0	最不发达35国LDC35	130	--Of yarns of different colours
4084	5516.1400	--印花	10	0	东盟ASEAN,智利CL,巴基斯坦PK,新加坡SG,新西兰NZ,秘鲁PE,哥斯达黎加CR,香港HK	0	最不发达35国LDC35	130	--Printed
		-按重量计人造纤维短纤含量在85%以下，主要或仅与化学纤维长丝混纺:							-Containing less than 85% by weight of artificial staple fibres, mixed mainly or solely with man-made filaments:
4085	5516.2100	--未漂白或漂白	12	0	东盟ASEAN,智利CL,巴基斯坦PK,新加坡SG,新西兰NZ,秘鲁PE,香港HK	0	最不发达35国LDC35	130	--Unbleached or bleached
				2.4	哥斯达黎加CR				
4086	5516.2200	--染色	10	0	东盟ASEAN,智利CL,巴基斯坦PK,新加坡SG,新西兰NZ,秘鲁PE,哥斯达黎加CR,香港HK,台湾TW	0	最不发达35国LDC35	130	--Dyed
				9.5	亚太APTA				

序号 No.	税则号列 Tariff Line	货品名称	最惠国税率 MFN(%)	协定税率 Agreement(%)		特惠税率 S.P.(%)		普通税率 Gen.(%)	Article Description
4087	5516.2300	--色织	10	0	东盟ASEAN,智利CL,巴基斯坦PK,新加坡SG,新西兰NZ,秘鲁PE,哥斯达黎加CR,香港HK	0	最不发达35国LDC35	130	--Of yarns of different colours
4088	5516.2400	--印花	10	0	东盟ASEAN,智利CL,巴基斯坦PK,新加坡SG,新西兰NZ,秘鲁PE,哥斯达黎加CR,香港HK	0	最不发达35国LDC35	130	--Printed
		-按重量计人造纤维短纤含量在85%以下，主要或仅与羊毛或动物细毛混纺:							-Containing less than 85% by weight of artificial staple fibres, mixed mainly or solely with wool or fine animal hair:
4089	5516.3100	--未漂白或漂白	12	0 2.4	东盟ASEAN,智利CL,巴基斯坦PK,新加坡SG,新西兰NZ,秘鲁PE,香港HK 哥斯达黎加CR	0	最不发达35国LDC35	130	--Unbleached or bleached
4090	5516.3200	--染色	10	0	东盟ASEAN,智利CL,巴基斯坦PK,新加坡SG,新西兰NZ,秘鲁PE,哥斯达黎加CR,香港HK	0	最不发达35国LDC35	130	--Dyed
4091	5516.3300	--色织	10	0	东盟ASEAN,智利CL,巴基斯坦PK,新加坡SG,新西兰NZ,秘鲁PE,哥斯达黎加CR,香港HK	0	最不发达35国LDC35	130	--Of yarns of different colours
4092	5516.3400	--印花	10	0	东盟ASEAN,智利CL,巴基斯坦PK,新加坡SG,新西兰NZ,秘鲁PE,哥斯达黎加CR,香港HK	0	最不发达35国LDC35	130	--Printed
		-按重量计人造纤维短纤含量在85%以下，主要或仅与棉混纺:							-Containing less than 85% by weight of artificial staple fibres, mixed mainly or solely with cotton:
4093	5516.4100	--未漂白或漂白	12	0 2.4	东盟ASEAN,智利CL,巴基斯坦PK,新加坡SG,新西兰NZ,秘鲁PE,香港HK 哥斯达黎加CR	0	最不发达35国LDC35	130	--Unbleached or bleached
4094	5516.4200	--染色	12	0 2.4	东盟ASEAN,智利CL,巴基斯坦PK,新加坡SG,新西兰NZ,秘鲁PE,香港HK 哥斯达黎加CR	0	最不发达35国LDC35	130	--Dyed
4095	5516.4300	--色织	10	0	东盟ASEAN,智利CL,巴基斯坦PK,新加坡SG,新西兰NZ,秘鲁PE,哥斯达黎加CR,香港HK	0	最不发达35国LDC35	130	--Of yarns of different colours
4096	5516.4400	--印花	10	0	东盟ASEAN,智利CL,巴基斯坦PK,新加坡SG,新西兰NZ,秘鲁PE,哥斯达黎加CR,香港HK	0	最不发达35国LDC35	130	--Printed
		-其他:							-Other:

序号 No.	税则号列 Tariff Line	货品名称	最惠国税率 MFN(%)	协定税率 Agreement(%)		特惠税率 S.P.(%)		普通税率 Gen.(%)	Article Description
4097	5516.9100	--未漂白或漂白	12	0	东盟ASEAN,智利CL,巴基斯坦PK,新加坡SG,新西兰NZ,秘鲁PE,香港HK	0	最不发达35国LDC35	130	--Unbleached or bleached
				2.4	哥斯达黎加CR				
4098	5516.9200	--染色	10	0	东盟ASEAN,智利CL,巴基斯坦PK,新加坡SG,新西兰NZ,秘鲁PE,哥斯达黎加CR,香港HK	0	最不发达35国LDC35,最不发达4国LDC4	130	--Dyed
4099	5516.9300	--色织	10	0	东盟ASEAN,智利CL,巴基斯坦PK,新加坡SG,新西兰NZ,秘鲁PE,哥斯达黎加CR,香港HK	0	最不发达35国LDC35	130	--Of yarns of different colours
4100	5516.9400	--印花	10	0	东盟ASEAN,智利CL,巴基斯坦PK,新加坡SG,新西兰NZ,秘鲁PE,哥斯达黎加CR,香港HK	0	最不发达35国LDC35	130	--Printed
				9.4	亚太APTA				

第五十六章
絮胎、毡呢及无纺织物；特种纱线；线、绳、索、缆及其制品

Chapter 56
Wadding, felt and nonwovens; special yarns; twine, cordage, ropes and cables and articles thereof

注释：

一、本章不包括：

（一）用各种物质或制剂（例如，第三十三章的香水或化妆品、税号 34.01 的肥皂或洗涤剂、税号 34.05 的光洁剂及类似制剂、税号 38.09 的织物柔软剂）浸渍、涂布、包覆的絮胎、毡呢或无纺织物，其中的纺织材料仅作为承载介质；

（二）税号 58.11 的纺织产品；

（三）以毡呢或无纺织物为底的砂布及类似品（税号 68.05）；

（四）以毡呢或无纺织物为底的粘聚或复制云母（税号 68.14）；

（五）以毡呢或无纺织物为底的金属箔（通常为第十四类或第十五类）；或

（六）税目 96.19 的卫生巾（护垫）及止血塞、婴儿尿布及尿布衬里和类似品。

二、所称“毡呢”，包括针刺机制毡呢以及纤维本身通过缝编工序增强了抱合力的纺织纤维网状织物。

三、税号 56.02 及 56.03 分别包括用各种性质（紧密结构或泡沫状）的塑料或橡胶浸渍、涂布、包覆或层压的毡呢及无纺织物。

税号 56.03 还包括用塑料或橡胶作粘合材料的无纺织物。

但税号 56.02 及 56.03 不包括：

（一）用塑料或橡胶浸渍、涂布、包覆或层压，按重量计纺织材料含量在 50%及以下的毡呢或者完全嵌入塑料或橡胶之内的毡呢（第三十九章或第四十章）；

（二）完全嵌入塑料或橡胶之内的无纺织物，以及用肉眼可辨别出两面都用塑料或橡胶涂布、包覆的无纺织物，涂布或包覆所引起的颜色变化可不予考虑（第三十九章或第四十章）；

Notes:

1.This Chapter does not cover:

(a) Wadding，felt or nonwovens，impregnated，coated or covered with substances or preparations (for example，pefumes or cosmetics of Chapter 33，soaps or detergents of heading No.34.01，polishes，creams or similar preparations of heading No.34.05，fabric softeners of heading No.38.09) where the textile material is present merely as a carrying medium;

(b) Textile products of heading No.58.11;

(c) Natural or artificial abrasive powder or grain，on a backing of felt or nonwovens (heading No.68.05);

(d) Agglomerated or reconstituted mica，on a backing of felt or nonwovens (heading No.68.14);

(e) Metal foil on a backing of felt or nonwovens (Generelly Section XIV or Section ⅩⅤ); or

(f) Sanitary towels (pads) and tampons, napkins and napkin liners for babies and similar articles of heading 96.19.

2. The term “felt” includes needleloom felt and fabrics consisting of a web of textile fibres the cohesion of which has been enhanced by a stitch-bonding process using fibres from the web itself.

3. Headings Nos.56.02 and 56.03 cover respectively felt and nonwovens，impregnated，coated，covered or laminated with plastics or rubber whatever the nature of these materials (compact or cellular).

Heading No.56.03 also includes nonwovens in which plastics or rubber forms the bonding substance.

Headings Nos.56.02 and 56.03 do not，however，cover:

(a) Felt impregnated，coated，covered or laminated with plastics or rubber，containing 50% or less by weight of textile material or felt completely embedded in plastics or rubber (Chapter 39 or 40);

(b) Nonwovens，either completely embedded in plastics or rubber，or entirely coated or covered on both sides with such materials，provided that such coating or covering can be seen with the naked eye with no ac-

（三）与毡呢或无纺织物混制的泡沫塑料或海绵橡胶板、片或扁条，纺织材料仅在其中起增强作用（第三十九章或第四十章）。

四、税号 56.04 不包括用肉眼无法辨别出是否经过浸渍，涂布或包覆的纺织纱线或税号 54.04 或 54.05 的扁条及类似品（通常归入第五十章至第五十五章）;运用本条规定，可不考虑浸渍、涂布或包覆所引起的颜色变化。

count being taken of any resulting change of colour (Chapter 39 or 40); or

(c) Plates，sheets or strips of cellular plastics or cellular rubber combined with felt or nonwovens，where the textile material is present merely for reinforcing purposes (Chapter 39 or 40).

4. Heading No.56.04 does not cover textile yarn，or strip or the like of heading No.54.04 or 54.05，in which the impregnation，coating or covering cannot be seen with the naked eye (usually Chapters 50 to55); for the purpose of this provision，no account should be taken of any resulting change of colour.

序号 No.	税则号列 Tariff Line	货品名称	最惠国税 率 MFN(%)	协定税率 Agreement(%)		特惠税率 S.P.(%)		普通税率 Gen.(%)	Article Description
	56.01	**纺织材料絮胎及其制品；长度不超过5毫米的纺织纤维（纤维屑）、纤维粉末及球结：**							**Wadding of textile materials and articles thereof; textile fibres, not exceeding 5mm in length (flock), textile dust and mill neps:**
		-絮胎;其他絮胎制品:							-Wadding; other articles of wadding:
4101	5601.2100	--棉制	10	0 5	东盟ASEAN,智利CL,新加坡SG,新西兰NZ,秘鲁PE,哥斯达黎加CR,澳门MO 巴基斯坦PK	0	最不发达35国LDC35	50	--Of cotton
		--化学纤维制:							--Of manmade fibres:
4102	5601.2210	---卷烟滤嘴	12	0 2.4 6	东盟ASEAN,智利CL,新加坡SG,新西兰NZ,秘鲁PE 哥斯达黎加CR 巴基斯坦PK	0	最不发达35国LDC35	100	---Cigarette filter tips
4103	5601.2290	---其他	12	0 2.4	东盟ASEAN,智利CL,新加坡SG,新西兰NZ,秘鲁PE,台湾TW 哥斯达黎加CR	0	最不发达35国LDC35,最不发达4国LDC4	100	---Other
4104	5601.2900	--其他	10	0 5	东盟ASEAN,智利CL,新加坡SG,新西兰NZ,秘鲁PE,哥斯达黎加CR 巴基斯坦PK	0	最不发达35国LDC35,最不发达4国LDC4	90	--Other
4105	5601.3000	-纤维屑、纤维粉末及球结	10	0 5	东盟ASEAN,智利CL,新加坡SG,新西兰NZ,秘鲁PE,哥斯达黎加CR 巴基斯坦PK	0	最不发达35国LDC35	100	-Textile flock and dust and mill neps
	ex56013000	由两种或两种以上有机聚合物纺制的纤维（横截面为皮芯结构或并列结构或海岛结构），长度不超过5毫米	△5						of two or more kinds of polymers (with cross section of skin-core or juxtapose or island structure), length not more than 5mm

序号 No.	税则号列 Tariff Line	货品名称	最惠国税率 MFN(%)	协定税率 Agreement(%)		特惠税率 S.P.(%)		普通税率 Gen.(%)	Article Description
	56.02	**毡呢，不论是否浸渍、涂布、包覆或层压:**							**Felt, whether or not impregnated, coated, covered or laminated:**
4106	5602.1000	-针刺机制毡呢及纤维缝编织物	10	0 5	东盟ASEAN,智利CL,新加坡SG,新西兰NZ,秘鲁PE,哥斯达黎加CR 巴基斯坦PK	0	最不发达35国LDC35	100	-Needleloom felt and stitch-bonded fibre fabrics
		-其他毡呢，未浸渍、涂布、包覆或层压:							-Other felt, not impregnated, coated, covered or laminated:
4107	5602.2100	--羊毛或动物细毛制	10	0 5	东盟ASEAN,智利CL,新加坡SG,新西兰NZ,秘鲁PE,哥斯达黎加CR 巴基斯坦PK	0	最不发达35国LDC35	100	--Of wool or fine animal hair
4108	5602.2900	--其他纺织材料制	10	0 5	东盟ASEAN,智利CL,新加坡SG,新西兰NZ,秘鲁PE,哥斯达黎加CR 巴基斯坦PK	0	最不发达35国LDC35	100	--Of other textile materials
4109	5602.9000	-其他	10	0 5	东盟ASEAN,智利CL,新加坡SG,新西兰NZ,秘鲁PE,哥斯达黎加CR 巴基斯坦PK	0	最不发达35国LDC35,最不发达4国LDC4	100	-Other
	56.03	**无纺织物，不论是否浸渍、涂布、包覆或层压:**							**Nonwovens, whether or not impre-gnated, coated, covered or laminated:**
		-化学纤维长丝制:							-Of manmade filaments:
		--每平方米重量不超过25克:							--Weighing not more than $25g/m^2$:
4110	5603.1110	---经浸渍、涂布、包覆或层压	10	0 8.5	东盟ASEAN,智利CL,巴基斯坦PK,新加坡SG,新西兰NZ,秘鲁PE,哥斯达黎加CR,台湾TW 亚太APTA	0	最不发达35国LDC35,最不发达4国LDC4,缅甸MM,老挝LA,柬埔寨KH	70	---Impregnated, coated, covered or laminated
4111	5603.1190	---其他	10	0 8.5	东盟ASEAN,智利CL,巴基斯坦PK,新加坡SG,新西兰NZ,秘鲁PE,哥斯达黎加CR 亚太APTA	0	最不发达35国LDC35	130	---Other
		--每平方米重量超过25克，但不超过70克:							--Weighing more than $25g/m^2$ but not more than $70g/m^2$:

序号 No.	税则号列 Tariff Line	货品名称	最惠国税 率 MFN(%)	协定税率 Agreement(%)		特惠税率 S.P.(%)		普通税率 Gen.(%)	Article Description
4112	5603.1210	---经浸渍、涂布、包覆或层压	10	0 8.5	东盟ASEAN,智利CL,巴基斯坦PK,新加坡SG,新西兰NZ,秘鲁PE,哥斯达黎加CR,香港HK,澳门MO 亚太APTA	0	最不发达35国LDC35,最不发达4国LDC4,缅甸MM,老挝LA,柬埔寨KH	70	---Impregnated, coated, covered or laminated
4113	5603.1290	---其他	10	0	东盟ASEAN,智利CL,巴基斯坦PK,新加坡SG,新西兰NZ,秘鲁PE,哥斯达黎加CR,香港HK,澳门MO,台湾TW	0	最不发达35国LDC35,最不发达4国LDC4	130	---Other
		--每平方米重量超过70克，但不超过150克:							--Weighing more than 70g/m^2 but not more than 150g/m^2:
4114	5603.1310	---经浸渍、涂布、包覆或层压	10	0 8.5	东盟ASEAN,智利CL,巴基斯坦PK,新加坡SG,新西兰NZ,秘鲁PE,哥斯达黎加CR,澳门MO,台湾TW 亚太APTA	0	最不发达35国LDC35	70	---Impregnated, coated, covered or laminated
4115	5603.1390	---其他	10	0	东盟ASEAN,智利CL,巴基斯坦PK,新加坡SG,新西兰NZ,秘鲁PE,哥斯达黎加CR,澳门MO,台湾TW	0	最不发达35国LDC35,最不发达4国LDC4	130	---Other
		--每平方米重量超过150克:							--Weighing more than 150g/m^2
4116	5603.1410	---经浸渍、涂布、包覆或层压	10	0 8.5	东盟ASEAN,智利CL,巴基斯坦PK,新加坡SG,新西兰NZ,秘鲁PE,哥斯达黎加CR,台湾TW 亚太APTA	0	最不发达35国LDC35	70	---regnated, coated, covered or laminated
4117	5603.1490	---其他	10	0 7	东盟ASEAN,智利CL,巴基斯坦PK,新加坡SG,新西兰NZ,秘鲁PE,哥斯达黎加CR,台湾TW 亚太APTA	0	最不发达35国LDC35,最不发达4国LDC4	130	---Other
		-其他:							-Other:
		--每平方米重量不超过25克:							--Weighing not more than 25g/m^2:
4118	5603.9110	---经浸渍、涂布、包覆或层压	10	0 8.5	东盟ASEAN,智利CL,巴基斯坦PK,新加坡SG,新西兰NZ,秘鲁PE,哥斯达黎加CR 亚太APTA	0	最不发达35国LDC35	70	---Impregnated, coated, covered or laminated

序号 No.	税则号列 Tariff Line	货品名称	最惠国税率 MFN(%)	协定税率 Agreement(%)		特惠税率 S.P.(%)		普通税率 Gen.(%)	Article Description
4119	5603.9190	---其他	10	0 8.5	东盟ASEAN,智利CL,巴基斯坦PK,新加坡SG,新西兰NZ,秘鲁PE,哥斯达黎加CR 亚太APTA	0	最不发达35国LDC35	85	---Other
		--每平方米重量超过25克，但不超过70克:							--Weighing more than $25g/m^2$ but not more than $70g/m^2$:
4120	5603.9210	---经浸渍、涂布、包覆或层压	10	0 8.5	东盟ASEAN,智利CL,巴基斯坦PK,新加坡SG,新西兰NZ,秘鲁PE,哥斯达黎加CR,香港HK,澳门MO 亚太APTA	0	最不发达35国LDC35	70	---Impregnated, coated, covered or laminated
4121	5603.9290	---其他	10	0 9.3	东盟ASEAN,智利CL,巴基斯坦PK,新西兰NZ,秘鲁PE,哥斯达黎加CR,香港HK,澳门MO,台湾TW 亚太APTA	0	最不发达35国LDC35,最不发达4国LDC4,缅甸MM,老挝LA,柬埔寨KH	85	---Other
		--每平方米重量超过70克，但不超过150克:							--Weighing more than $70g/m^2$ but not more than $150g/m^2$:
4122	5603.9310	---经浸渍、涂布、包覆或层压	10	0 8.5	东盟ASEAN,智利CL,巴基斯坦PK,新加坡SG,新西兰NZ,秘鲁PE,哥斯达黎加CR,香港HK,澳门MO 亚太APTA	0	最不发达35国LDC35	70	---Impregnated, coated, covered or laminated
4123	5603.9390	---其他	10	0 9.3	东盟ASEAN,智利CL,巴基斯坦PK,新加坡SG,新西兰NZ,秘鲁PE,哥斯达黎加CR,香港HK,澳门MO,台湾TW 亚太APTA	0	最不发达35国LDC35	85	---Other
		--每平方米重量超过150克:							--Weighing more than $150g/m^2$:
4124	5603.9410	---经浸渍、涂布、包覆或层压	10	0 8.5	东盟ASEAN,智利CL,巴基斯坦PK,新加坡SG,新西兰NZ,秘鲁PE,哥斯达黎加CR,香港HK,台湾TW 亚太APTA	0	最不发达35国LDC35	70	---Impregnated, coated, covered or laminated
4125	5603.9490	---其他	10	0 9.3	东盟ASEAN,智利CL,巴基斯坦PK,新加坡SG,新西兰NZ,秘鲁PE,哥斯达黎加CR,香港HK,台湾TW 亚太APTA	0	最不发达35国LDC35,最不发达4国LDC4,缅甸MM,老挝LA,柬埔寨KH	85	---Other

序号 No.	税则号列 Tariff Line	货品名称	最惠国 税 率 MFN(%)	协定税率 Agreement(%)		特惠税率 S.P.(%)		普通 税率 Gen.(%)	Article Description
	56.04	**用纺织材料包覆的橡胶线及绳;用橡胶或塑料浸渍、涂布、包覆或套裹的纺织纱线及税号 54.04 或 54.05 的扁条及类似品:**							**Rubber thread and cord, textile covered; textile yarn, and strip and the like of heading No.54.04 or 54.05, impregnated, coated, covered or sheathed with rubber or plastics:**
4126	5604.1000	-用纺织材料包覆的橡胶线及绳	5	0	文莱BN,印尼ID,马来西亚MY,缅甸MM,菲律宾PH,新加坡*SG*,泰国TH,越南VT,智利CL,巴基斯坦PK,新西兰NZ,秘鲁PE,哥斯达黎加CR,澳门MO	0	最不发达 35 国 LDC35,最不发达 4 国 LDC4,缅甸MM,老挝LA,柬埔寨KH	80	-Rubber thread and cord, textile covered
4127	5604.9000	-其他	5	0	文莱BN,印尼ID,马来西亚MY,缅甸MM,菲律宾PH,新加坡*SG*,泰国TH,越南VT,智利CL,巴基斯坦PK,新西兰NZ,秘鲁PE,哥斯达黎加CR,澳门MO	0	最不发达 35 国 LDC35,最不发达 4 国 LDC4	80	-Other
	56.05	**含金属纱线，不论是否螺旋花线，由纺织纱线或税号 54.04 或 54.05 的扁条及类似品与金属线、扁条或粉末混合制得或用金属包覆制得:**							**Metallized yarn, whether or not gimped, being textile yarn, or strip or the like of heading No.54.04 or 54.05, combined with metal in the form of thread, strip or powder or covered with metal:**
4128	5605.0000	含金属纱线，不论是否螺旋花线，由纺织纱线或税号 54.04 或 54.05 的扁条及类似品与金属线、扁条或粉末混合制得或用金属包覆制得	5	0	文莱BN,印尼ID,马来西亚MY,缅甸MM,菲律宾PH,新加坡*SG*,泰国TH,越南VT,智利CL,巴基斯坦PK,新西兰NZ,秘鲁PE,哥斯达黎加CR,澳门MO	0	最不发达 35 国 LDC35,最不发达 4 国 LDC4	70	Metallzied yarn, whether or not gimped, being textile yarn, or strip or the like of heading No.54.04 or 54.05, combined with metal in the form of thread, strip or powder or covered with metal
	56.06	**粗松螺旋花线，税号 54.04 或 54.05 的扁条及类似品制的螺旋花线（税号 56.05 的货品及马毛粗松螺旋花线除外）;绳绒线（包括植绒绳绒线）;纵行起圈纱线:**							**Gimped yarn, and strip and the like of heading No.54.04 or 54.05, gimped (other than those of heading No.56.05 and gimped horsehair yarn); chenille yarn (including flock chenille yarn); loop waleyarn:**

序号 No.	税则号列 Tariff Line	货品名称	最惠国税率 MFN(%)	协定税率 Agreement(%)		特惠税率 S.P.(%)		普通税率 Gen.(%)	Article Description
4129	5606.0000	粗松螺旋花线，税号 54.04 或 54.05 的扁条及类似品制的螺旋花线（税号 56.05 的货品及马毛粗松螺旋花线除外）;绳绒线（包括植绒绳绒线）;纵行起圈纱线	5	0	文莱BN,印尼ID,马来西亚MY,缅甸MM,菲律宾PH,新加坡*SG*,泰国TH,越南VT,智利CL,巴基斯坦PK,新西兰NZ,秘鲁PE,哥斯达黎加CR,澳门MO	0	最不发达 35 国 LDC35,最不发达 4 国 LDC4	70	Gimped yarn, and strip and the like of heading No.54.04 or 54.05, gimped (other than those of heading No.56.05 and gimped horsehair yarn); chenille yarn (including flock chenille yarn); loop waleyarn
	56.07	**线、绳、索、缆，不论是否编织或编结而成，也不论是否用橡胶或塑料浸渍，涂布、包覆或套裹:**							**Twine, cordage, ropes and cables, whether or not plaited or braided and whether or not impregnated, coated, covered or sheathed with rubber or plastics:**
		-西沙尔麻或其他纺织用龙舌兰类纤维纺制:							-Of sisal or other textile fibres of the genus Agave:
4130	5607.2100	--包扎用绳	5	0	东盟ASEAN,智利CL,巴基斯坦PK,新西兰NZ,秘鲁PE,哥斯达黎加CR,澳门MO	0	最不发达 35 国 LDC35,最不发达 4 国 LDC4	50	--Binder or baler twine
4131	5607.2900	--其他	5	0	东盟ASEAN,智利CL,巴基斯坦PK,新西兰NZ,秘鲁PE,哥斯达黎加CR,澳门MO	0	最不发达 35 国 LDC35,最不发达 4 国 LDC4	50	--Other
		-聚乙烯或聚丙烯纺制:							-Of polyethylene or polypropylene:
4132	5607.4100	--包扎用绳	5	0	文莱BN,印尼ID,马来西亚MY,缅甸MM,菲律宾PH,新加坡*SG*,泰国TH,越南VT,智利CL,巴基斯坦PK,新西兰NZ,秘鲁PE,哥斯达黎加CR,澳门MO	0	最不发达 35 国 LDC35,最不发达 4 国 LDC4	100	--Binder or baler twine
4133	5607.4900	--其他	5	0	文莱BN,印尼ID,马来西亚MY,缅甸MM,菲律宾PH,新加坡*SG*,泰国TH,越南VT,智利CL,巴基斯坦PK,新西兰NZ,秘鲁PE,哥斯达黎加CR,澳门MO	0	最不发达 35 国 LDC35,最不发达 4 国 LDC4	100	--Other
4134	5607.5000	-其他合成纤维纺制	5	0	文莱BN,印尼ID,马来西亚MY,缅甸MM,菲律宾PH,新加坡*SG*,泰国TH,越南VT,智利CL,巴基斯坦PK,新西兰NZ,秘鲁PE,哥斯达黎加CR,澳门MO,台湾TW	0	最不发达 35 国 LDC35,最不发达 4 国 LDC4	100	-Of other synthetic fibres
		-其他:							-Other:

序号 No.	税则号列 Tariff Line	货品名称	最惠国税率 MFN(%)	协定税率 Agreement(%)		特惠税率 S.P.(%)		普通税率 Gen.(%)	Article Description
4135	5607.9010	---蕉麻（马尼拉麻）或其他硬质（叶）纤维纺制	5	0	东盟ASEAN,智利CL,巴基斯坦PK,新西兰NZ,秘鲁PE,哥斯达黎加CR,澳门MO	0	最不发达35国LDC35,最不发达4国LDC4	50	---Of abaca (Manila hemp or Musa textilis Nee) or other hard (leaf) fibres
4136	5607.9090	---其他	5	0	文莱BN,印尼ID,马来西亚MY,缅甸MM,菲律宾PH,新加坡*SG*,泰国TH,越南VT,智利CL,巴基斯坦PK,新西兰NZ,秘鲁PE,哥斯达黎加CR,澳门MO	0 2.5	最不发达35国LDC35,最不发达4国LDC4,缅甸MM,老挝LA,柬埔寨KH 亚太2国APTA2	100	---Other
	56.08	**线、绳或索结制的网料;纺织材料制成的渔网及其他网:**							**Knotted netting of twine, cordage or rope; made up fishing nets and other made up nets, of textile materials:**
		-化学纤维材料制:							-Of man-made textile materials:
4137	5608.1100	--制成的渔网	10	0 5	东盟ASEAN,智利CL,新西兰NZ,哥斯达黎加CR 巴基斯坦PK,秘鲁PE	0	最不发达35国LDC35,最不发达4国LDC4	50	--Made up fishing nets
4138	5608.1900	--其他	12	0 2.4 6	东盟ASEAN,智利CL,新加坡SG,新西兰NZ,秘鲁PE,台湾TW 哥斯达黎加CR 巴基斯坦PK	0	最不发达35国LDC35	100	--Other
4139	5608.9000	-其他	10	0 5	东盟ASEAN,智利CL,新西兰NZ,秘鲁PE,哥斯达黎加CR,香港HK 巴基斯坦PK	0	最不发达35国LDC35,最不发达4国LDC4	100	-Other
	56.09	**用纱线、税号54.04或54.05的扁条及类似品或线、绳、索、缆制成的其他税号未列名物品:**							**Articles of yarn, strip or the like of heading No.54.04 or 54.05, twine, cordage, rope or cables, not elsewhere specified or included:**
4140	5609.0000	用纱线、税号54.04或54.05的扁条及类似品或线、绳、索、缆制成的其他税号未列名物品	10	0 5	东盟ASEAN,智利CL,新西兰NZ,秘鲁PE,哥斯达黎加CR 巴基斯坦PK	0	最不发达35国LDC35,最不发达4国LDC4,亚太2国APTA2	100	Articles of yarn, strip or the like of heading No.54.04 or 54.05, twine, cordage, rope or cables, not elsewhere specified or included

第五十七章
地毯及纺织材料的其他铺地制品

Chapter 57
Carpets and other textile floor coverings

注释：

一、本章所称“地毯及纺织材料的其他铺地制品”，是指使用时以纺织材料作面的铺地制品，也包括具有纺织材料铺地制品特征但作其他用途的物品。

二、本章不包括铺地制品衬垫。

Notes:

1. For the purposes of this Chapter, the term “carpets and other textile floor coverings” means floor coverings in which textile materials serve as the exposed surface of the article when in use and includes articles having the characteristics of textile floor coverings but intended for use for other purposes.

2.This Chapter does not cover floor covering underlays.

序号 No.	税则号列 Tariff Line	货品名称	最惠国税率 MFN(%)	协定税率 Agreement(%)		特惠税率 S.P.(%)		普通税率 Gen.(%)	Article Description
	57.01	**结织栽绒地毯及纺织材料的其他结织栽绒铺地制品，不论是否制成的:**							**Carpets and other textile floor coverings knotted, whether or not made up:**
4141	5701.1000	-羊毛或动物细毛制	14	0 2.8	东盟ASEAN,智利CL,新加坡SG,新西兰NZ,秘鲁PE 哥斯达黎加CR	0	最不发达35国LDC35,最不发达4国LDC4	130	-Of wool or fine animal hair
		-其他纺织材料制:							-Of other textile materials:
4142	5701.9010	---化学纤维制	16	0 3.2 8 12.8	东盟ASEAN,智利CL,新加坡SG,新西兰NZ 哥斯达黎加CR 秘鲁PE 巴基斯坦PK	0	最不发达35国LDC35,最不发达4国LDC4	130	---Of man-made textile materials
4143	5701.9020	---丝制	14	0 2.8 7	东盟ASEAN,智利CL,新加坡SG,新西兰NZ,秘鲁PE 哥斯达黎加CR 巴基斯坦PK	0	最不发达35国LDC35	100	---Of silk
4144	5701.9090	---其他	14	0 2.8 7	东盟ASEAN,智利CL,新加坡SG,新西兰NZ,秘鲁PE 哥斯达黎加CR 巴基斯坦PK	0	最不发达35国LDC35	100	---Other
	57.02	**机织地毯及纺织材料的其他机织铺地制品，未簇绒或未植绒，不论是否制成的，包括“开来姆”、“苏麦克”、“卡拉马尼”及类似的手织地毯:**							**Carpets and other textile floor cover-ings, woven, not tufted or flocked, whether or not made up, including “Kelem”, “Schumacks”, “Karamanie”and similar handwoven rugs:**

序号 No.	税则号列 Tariff Line	货品名称	最惠国税率 MFN(%)	协定税率 Agreement(%)		特惠税率 S.P.(%)		普通税率 Gen.(%)	Article Description
4145	5702.1000	-“开来姆”、“苏麦克”、“卡拉马尼”及类似的手织地毯	14	0 2.8	东盟ASEAN,智利CL,巴基斯坦PK,新加坡SG,新西兰NZ,秘鲁PE 哥斯达黎加CR	0	最不发达35国LDC35,最不发达4国LDC4,亚太2国APTA2	130	-“Kelem”, “Schumacks”, “Karamanie”and similar hand-woven rugs
4146	5702.2000	-椰壳纤维制的铺地制品	14	0 2.8	东盟ASEAN,智利CL,巴基斯坦PK,新加坡SG,新西兰NZ,秘鲁PE 哥斯达黎加CR	0	最不发达35国LDC35	100	-Floor coverings of coconut fibres(coir)
		-其他起绒结构的铺地制品，未制成的:							-Other, of pile construction, not made up:
4147	5702.3100	--羊毛或动物细毛制	10	0	东盟ASEAN,智利CL,巴基斯坦PK,新加坡SG,新西兰NZ,秘鲁PE,哥斯达黎加CR	0	最不发达35国LDC35,最不发达4国LDC4	130	--Of wool or fine animal hair
4148	5702.3200	--化学纤维制	16	0 3.2 8	东盟ASEAN,智利CL,巴基斯坦PK,新加坡SG,新西兰NZ 哥斯达黎加CR 秘鲁PE	0	最不发达35国LDC35	130	--Of man-made textile materials
4149	5702.3900	--其他纺织材料制	14	0 2.8	东盟ASEAN,智利CL,巴基斯坦PK,新加坡SG,新西兰NZ,秘鲁PE 哥斯达黎加CR	0	最不发达35国LDC35,最不发达4国LDC4,亚太2国APTA2	100	--Of other textile materials
		-其他起绒结构的铺地制品，制成的:							-Ohter, of pile construction, made up:
4150	5702.4100	--羊毛或动物细毛制	10	0	东盟ASEAN,智利CL,巴基斯坦PK,新加坡SG,新西兰NZ,秘鲁PE,哥斯达黎加CR	0	最不发达35国LDC35,最不发达4国LDC4	130	--Of wool or fine animal hair
4151	5702.4200	--化学纤维制	10	0	东盟ASEAN,智利CL,巴基斯坦PK,新加坡SG,新西兰NZ,秘鲁PE,哥斯达黎加CR	0	最不发达35国LDC35,最不发达4国LDC4	130	--Of man-made textile materials
4152	5702.4900	--其他纺织材料制	14	0 2.8 9.3	东盟ASEAN,智利CL,巴基斯坦PK,新加坡SG,新西兰NZ,秘鲁PE 哥斯达黎加CR 亚太APTA	0	最不发达35国LDC35	100	--Of other textile materials

序号 No.	税则号列 Tariff Line	货品名称	最惠国税率 MFN(%)		协定税率 Agreement(%)		特惠税率 S.P.(%)	普通税率 Gen.(%)	Article Description
		-其他非起绒结构的铺地制品，未制成的:							-Ohter, not of pile construction, not made up:
4153	5702.5010	---羊毛或动物细毛制	14	0 2.8	东盟ASEAN,智利CL,巴基斯坦PK,新加坡SG,新西兰NZ,秘鲁PE 哥斯达黎加CR	0	最不发达35国LDC35	130	---Of wool or fine animal hair
4154	5702.5020	---化学纤维制	16	0 3.2 8	东盟ASEAN,智利CL,巴基斯坦PK,新加坡SG,新西兰NZ 哥斯达黎加CR 秘鲁PE	0	最不发达35国LDC35	130	---Of man-made textile materials
4155	5702.5090	---其他纺织材料制	14	0 2.8	东盟ASEAN,智利CL,巴基斯坦PK,新加坡SG,新西兰NZ,秘鲁PE 哥斯达黎加CR	0	最不发达35国LDC35	100	---Of other textile materials
		-其他非起绒结构的铺地制品，制成的:							-Other, not of pile construction, made up:
4156	5702.9100	--羊毛或动物细毛制	14	0 2.8	东盟ASEAN,智利CL,巴基斯坦PK,新加坡SG,新西兰NZ,秘鲁PE 哥斯达黎加CR	0	最不发达35国LDC35	130	--Of wool or fine animal hair
4157	5702.9200	--化学纤维制	16	0 3.2 8	东盟ASEAN,智利CL,巴基斯坦PK,新加坡SG,新西兰NZ 哥斯达黎加CR 秘鲁PE	0	最不发达35国LDC35	130	--Of man-made textile materials
4158	5702.9900	--其他纺织材料制	14	0 2.8	东盟ASEAN,智利CL,巴基斯坦PK,新加坡SG,新西兰NZ,秘鲁PE 哥斯达黎加CR	0	最不发达35国LDC35	100	--Of other textile materials
	57.03	**簇绒地毯及纺织材料的其他簇绒铺地制品，不论是否制成的:**							**Carpets and other textile floor coverings, tufted, whether or not made up:**
4159	5703.1000	-羊毛或动物细毛制	14	0 2.8	东盟ASEAN,智利CL,新加坡SG,新西兰NZ,秘鲁PE 哥斯达黎加CR	0	最不发达35国LDC35,最不发达4国LDC4	130	-Of wool or fine animal hair
4160	5703.2000	-尼龙或其他聚酰胺制	10	0 5	东盟ASEAN,智利CL,新加坡SG,新西兰NZ,秘鲁PE,哥斯达黎加CR 巴基斯坦PK	0	最不发达35国LDC35,最不发达4国LDC4	130	-Of nylon or other polyamides
4161	5703.3000	-其他化学纤维制	10	0	东盟ASEAN,智利CL,新加坡SG,新西兰NZ,秘鲁PE,哥斯达黎加CR	0	最不发达35国LDC35,最不发达4国LDC4	130	-Of other man-made textile materials

序号 No.	税则号列 Tariff Line	货品名称	最惠国税率 MFN(%)	协定税率 Agreement(%)		特惠税率 S.P.(%)		普通税率 Gen.(%)	Article Description
4162	5703.9000	-其他纺织材料制	14	0 2.8 11.2	东盟ASEAN,智利CL,新加坡SG,新西兰NZ,秘鲁PE 哥斯达黎加CR 巴基斯坦PK	0	最不发达35国LDC35,最不发达4国LDC4,亚太2国APTA2	100	-Of other textile materials
	57.04	**毡呢地毯及纺织材料的其他毡呢铺地制品，未簇绒或未植绒，不论是否制成的：**							**Carpets and other textile floor coverings, of felt, not tufted or flocked, whether or not made up:**
4163	5704.1000	-最大表面面积不超过0.3平方米	14	0 2.8 7	东盟ASEAN,智利CL,新加坡SG,新西兰NZ,秘鲁PE 哥斯达黎加CR 巴基斯坦PK	0	最不发达35国LDC35	130	-Tiles, having a maximum surface area of 0.3 ㎡
4164	5704.9000	-其他	10	0 5	东盟ASEAN,智利CL,新加坡SG,新西兰NZ,秘鲁PE,哥斯达黎加CR 巴基斯坦PK	0	最不发达35国LDC35,最不发达4国LDC4	130	-Other
	57.05	**其他地毯及纺织材料的其他铺地制品，不论是否制成的：**							**Other carpets and other textile floor coverings, whether or not made up:**
4165	5705.0010	---羊毛或动物细毛制	14	0 2.8 11.2	东盟ASEAN,智利CL,新加坡SG,新西兰NZ,秘鲁PE 哥斯达黎加CR 巴基斯坦PK	0	最不发达35国LDC35,最不发达4国LDC4,亚太2国APTA2	130	---Of wool or fine animal hair
4166	5705.0020	---化学纤维制	10	0 5	东盟ASEAN,智利CL,新加坡SG,新西兰NZ,秘鲁PE,哥斯达黎加CR 巴基斯坦PK	0	最不发达35国LDC35,最不发达4国LDC4,亚太2国APTA2	130	---Of man-made textile materials
4167	5705.0090	---其他纺织材料制	14	0 2.8 11.2	东盟ASEAN,智利CL,新加坡SG,新西兰NZ,秘鲁PE 哥斯达黎加CR 巴基斯坦PK	0	最不发达35国LDC35,最不发达4国LDC4,亚太2国APTA2	100	---Of other textile materialsr

第五十八章
特种机织物；簇绒织物；花边；装饰毯；装饰带；刺绣品

注释:

一、本章不适用于经浸渍、涂布、包覆或层压的第五十九章注释一所述的纺织物或第五十九章的其他货品。

二、税号58.01也包括因未将浮纱割断而使表面无竖绒的纬起绒织物。

三、税号58.03所称"纱罗"，是指经线全部或部分由地经纱和绞经纱构成的织物，其中绞经纱绕地经纱半圈、一圈或几圈而形成圈状，纬纱从圈中穿过。

四、税号58.04不适用于税号56.08的线、绳、索结制的网状织物。

五、税号58.06所称"狭幅机织物"，是指:

（一）幅宽不超过30厘米的机织物，不论是否织成或从宽幅料剪成，但两侧必须有织成的、胶粘的或用其他方法制成的布边;

（二）压平宽度不超过30厘米的圆筒机织物;

（三）折边的斜裁滚条布，其未折边时的宽度不超过30厘米。

流苏状的狭幅织物归入税号58.08。

六、税号58.10所称"刺绣品"，除了一般纺织材料绣线绣制的刺绣品外，还包括在可见底布上用金属线或玻璃线刺绣的刺绣品，也包括用珠片、饰珠、纺织材料或其他材料制的装饰用花纹图案所缝绣的贴花织物。但不包括手工针绣嵌花装饰毯(税号58.05)。

七、除税号58.09的产品外，本章还包括金属线制 的用于衣着、装饰及类似用途的物品。

Chapter 58
Special woven fabrics; tufted textile fabrics; lace; tapestries; trimmings; embroidery

Notes:

1. This Chapter does not apply to textile fabrics referred to in Note 1 to Chapter 59，impregnated，coated，covered or laminated，or to other goods of Chapter 59.

2. Heading 58.01 also includes woven weft pile fabrics which have not yet had the floats cut，at which stage they have no pile standing up.

3. For the purpose of heading 58.03，"gauze" means a fabric with a warp composed wholly or in part of standing or ground threads and crossing or doup threads which cross the standing or ground threads making a half turn，a complete turn or more to form loops through which weft threads pass.

4. Heading 58.04 does not apply to knotted net fabrics of twine，cordage or rope，of heading 56.08.

5. For the purposes of heading 58.06，the expression "narrow woven fabrics" means:

(a) Woven fabrics of a width not exceeding 30cm，whether woven as such or cut from wider pieces，provided with selvedges (woven，gummed or otherwise made) on both edges;

(b) Tubular woven fabrics of a flattened width not exceeding 30cm; and

(c) Bias binding with folded edges，of a width when unfolded not exceeding 30cm.

Narrow woven fabrics with woven fringes are to be classified in heading No.58.08.

6. In heading No.58.10，the expression "embroidery" means，*inter alia*，embroidery with metal or glass thread on a visible ground of textile fabric，and sewn applique work of sequins，beads or ornamental motifs of textile or other materials. The heading does not apply to needlework tapestry (heading 58.05).

7. In addition to the products of heading 58.09，this Chapter also includes articles made of metal thread and of a kind used in apparel，as furnishing fabrics or for similar purposes.

序号 No.	税则号列 Tariff Line	货品名称	最惠国税率 MFN(%)	协定税率 Agreement(%)		特惠税率 S.P.(%)		普通税率 Gen.(%)	Article Description
	58.01	**起绒机织物及绳绒织物，但税号 58.02 或 58.06 的织物除外:**							**Woven pile fabrics and chenille fabrics, other than fabrics of heading No.58.02 or 58.06:**
4168	5801.1000	-羊毛或动物细毛制	10	0	东盟ASEAN,智利CL,巴基斯坦PK,新加坡SG,新西兰NZ,秘鲁PE,哥斯达黎加CR	0	最不发达 35 国 LDC35,最不发达 4 国 LDC4	130	-Of wool or fine animal hair
		-棉制:							-Of cotton:
4169	5801.2100	--不割绒的纬起绒织物	12	0	东盟ASEAN,智利CL,巴基斯坦PK,新加坡SG,新西兰NZ,秘鲁PE	0	最不发达 35 国 LDC35	70	--Uncut weft pile fabrics
				2.4	哥斯达黎加CR				
4170	5801.2200	--割绒的灯芯绒	10	0	东盟ASEAN,智利CL,巴基斯坦PK,新西兰NZ,秘鲁PE,哥斯达黎加CR,香港HK,台湾TW	0	最不发达 35 国 LDC35,最不发达 4 国 LDC4	70	--Cut corduroy
4171	5801.2300	--其他纬起绒织物	10	0	东盟ASEAN,智利CL,巴基斯坦PK,新西兰NZ,秘鲁PE,哥斯达黎加CR	0	最不发达 35 国 LDC35,最不发达 4 国 LDC4	70	--Other weft pile fabrics
4172	5801.2600	--绳绒织物	10	0	东盟ASEAN,智利CL,巴基斯坦PK,新西兰NZ,秘鲁PE,哥斯达黎加CR	0	最不发达 35 国 LDC35,最不发达 4 国 LDC4	70	--Chenille fabrics
		--经起绒织物:							--Warp pile fabrics:
4173	5801.2710	---不割绒的（棱纹绸）	10	0	东盟ASEAN,智利CL,巴基斯坦PK,新西兰NZ,秘鲁PE,哥斯达黎加CR	0	最不发达 35 国 LDC35,最不发达 4 国 LDC4	70	---èpinglè (uncut)
4174	5801.2720	---割绒的	10	0	东盟ASEAN,智利CL,巴基斯坦PK,新西兰NZ,秘鲁PE,哥斯达黎加CR,香港HK	0	最不发达 35 国 LDC35,最不发达 4 国 LDC4	70	---Cut
		-化学纤维制:							-Of man-made fibres:
4175	5801.3100	--不割绒的纬起绒织物	10	0	东盟ASEAN,智利CL,巴基斯坦PK,新加坡SG,新西兰NZ,秘鲁PE,哥斯达黎加CR	0	最不发达 35 国 LDC35,最不发达 4 国 LDC4	130	--Uncut weft pile fabrics

序号 No.	税则号列 Tariff Line	货品名称	最惠国税率 MFN(%)	协定税率 Agreement(%)		特惠税率 S.P.(%)		普通税率 Gen.(%)	Article Description
4176	5801.3200	--割绒的灯芯绒	10	0	东盟ASEAN,智利CL,巴基斯坦PK,新加坡SG,新西兰NZ,秘鲁PE,哥斯达黎加CR	0	最不发达35国LDC35,最不发达4国LDC4	130	--Cut corduroy
4177	5801.3300	--其他纬起绒织物	10	0	东盟ASEAN,智利CL,巴基斯坦PK,新加坡SG,新西兰NZ,秘鲁PE,哥斯达黎加CR,台湾TW	0	最不发达35国LDC35,最不发达4国LDC4,缅甸MM,老挝LA,柬埔寨KH	130	--Other weft pile fabrics
4178	5801.3600	--绳绒织物	10	0	东盟ASEAN,智利CL,巴基斯坦PK,新加坡SG,新西兰NZ,秘鲁PE,哥斯达黎加CR	0	最不发达35国LDC35,最不发达4国LDC4	130	--Chenille fabrics
		--经起绒织物:							--Warp pile fabrics:
4179	5801.3710	---不割绒的（棱纹绸）	10	0	东盟ASEAN,智利CL,巴基斯坦PK,新加坡SG,新西兰NZ,秘鲁PE,哥斯达黎加CR	0	最不发达35国LDC35,最不发达4国LDC4	130	---èpinglè (uncut)
4180	5801.3720	---割绒的	10	0	东盟ASEAN,智利CL,巴基斯坦PK,新加坡SG,新西兰NZ,秘鲁PE,哥斯达黎加CR	0	最不发达35国LDC35,最不发达4国LDC4	130	---Cut
		-其他纺织材料制:							-Of other textile materials:
4181	5801.9010	---丝及绢丝制	10	0	东盟ASEAN,智利CL,巴基斯坦PK,新加坡SG,新西兰NZ,秘鲁PE,哥斯达黎加CR	0	最不发达35国LDC35,最不发达4国LDC4	130	---Of silk or silk waste
4182	5801.9090	---其他	10	0	东盟ASEAN,智利CL,巴基斯坦PK,新加坡SG,新西兰NZ,秘鲁PE,哥斯达黎加CR	0	最不发达35国LDC35,最不发达4国LDC4	80	---Other
	58.02	**毛巾织物及类似的毛圈机织物，但税号58.06的狭幅织物除外;簇绒织物，但税号57.03的产品除外:**							**Terry towelling and similar woven terry fabrics, other than narrow fabrics of heading No.58.06; tufted textile fabrics, other than products of heading No.57.03:**

序号 No.	税则号列 Tariff Line	货品名称	最惠国税率 MFN(%)	协定税率 Agreement(%)		特惠税率 S.P.(%)		普通税率 Gen.(%)	Article Description
		-棉制毛巾织物及类似毛圈机织物:							-Terry towelling and similar woven terry fabrics, of cotton:
4183	5802.1100	--未漂白	12	0 2.4	东盟ASEAN,智利CL,巴基斯坦PK,新加坡SG,新西兰NZ,秘鲁PE,澳门MO 哥斯达黎加CR	0	最不发达35国LDC35,最不发达4国LDC4,亚太2国APTA2	70	--Unbleached
4184	5802.1900	--其他	10	0	东盟ASEAN,智利CL,巴基斯坦PK,新西兰NZ,秘鲁PE,哥斯达黎加CR,澳门MO	0	最不发达35国LDC35,最不发达4国LDC4	70	--Other
		-其他纺织材料制的毛巾织物及类似的毛圈机织物:							-Terry towelling and similar woven terry fabrics, of other textile materials:
4185	5802.2010	---丝及绢丝制	12	0 2.4	东盟ASEAN,智利CL,巴基斯坦PK,新加坡SG,新西兰NZ,秘鲁PE,澳门MO 哥斯达黎加CR	0	最不发达35国LDC35,最不发达4国LDC4,亚太2国APTA2	130	---Of silk or silk waste
4186	5802.2020	---羊毛或动物细毛制	12	0 2.4	东盟ASEAN,智利CL,巴基斯坦PK,新加坡SG,新西兰NZ,秘鲁PE,澳门MO 哥斯达黎加CR	0	最不发达35国LDC35,最不发达4国LDC4,亚太2国APTA2	130	---Of wool or fine animal hair
4187	5802.2030	---化学纤维制	14	0 2.8	东盟ASEAN,智利CL,巴基斯坦PK,新加坡SG,新西兰NZ,秘鲁PE,澳门MO 哥斯达黎加CR	0	最不发达35国LDC35,最不发达4国LDC4,亚太2国APTA2	130	---Of man-made fibres
4188	5802.2090	---其他	12	0 2.4	东盟ASEAN,智利CL,巴基斯坦PK,新加坡SG,新西兰NZ,秘鲁PE,澳门MO 哥斯达黎加CR	0	最不发达35国LDC35,最不发达4国LDC4,亚太2国APTA2	80	---Other
		-簇绒织物:							-Tufted textile fabrics:

序号 No.	税则号列 Tariff Line	货品名称	最惠国税率 MFN(%)	协定税率 Agreement(%)		特惠税率 S.P.(%)		普通税率 Gen.(%)	Article Description
4189	5802.3010	---丝及绢丝制	10	0	东盟ASEAN,智利CL,巴基斯坦PK,新加坡SG,新西兰NZ,秘鲁PE,哥斯达黎加CR	0	最不发达35国LDC35,最不发达4国LDC4	130	---Of silk or silk waste
4190	5802.3020	---羊毛或动物细毛制	10	0	东盟ASEAN,智利CL,巴基斯坦PK,新加坡SG,新西兰NZ,秘鲁PE,哥斯达黎加CR	0	最不发达35国LDC35,最不发达4国LDC4	130	---Of wool or fine animal hair
4191	5802.3030	---棉或麻制	10	0	东盟ASEAN,智利CL,巴基斯坦PK,新西兰NZ,秘鲁PE,哥斯达黎加CR	0	最不发达35国LDC35,最不发达4国LDC4	70	---Of cotton or bast fibre
4192	5802.3040	---化学纤维制	10	0 5	东盟ASEAN,智利CL,巴基斯坦PK,新加坡SG,新西兰NZ,哥斯达黎加CR 秘鲁PE	0	最不发达35国LDC35,最不发达4国LDC4	130	---Of manmade fibres
4193	5802.3090	---其他纺织材料制	10	0	东盟ASEAN,智利CL,巴基斯坦PK,新加坡SG,新西兰NZ,秘鲁PE,哥斯达黎加CR	0	最不发达35国LDC35,最不发达4国LDC4	80	---Of other textile materials
	58.03	**纱罗，但税号58.06的狭幅织物除外:**							**Gauze, other than narrow fabrics of heading No.58.06:**
4194	5803.0010	---棉制	10	0 5	东盟ASEAN,智利CL,新西兰NZ,秘鲁PE,哥斯达黎加CR 巴基斯坦PK	0	最不发达35国LDC35,最不发达4国LDC4	70	---Of cotton
4195	5803.0020	---丝及绢丝制	10	0 5	东盟ASEAN,智利CL,新加坡SG,新西兰NZ,秘鲁PE,哥斯达黎加CR 巴基斯坦PK	0	最不发达35国LDC35,最不发达4国LDC4	130	---Of silk or silk waste
4196	5803.0030	---化学纤维制	10	0 5	东盟ASEAN,智利CL,新加坡SG,新西兰NZ,秘鲁PE,哥斯达黎加CR 巴基斯坦PK	0	最不发达35国LDC35,最不发达4国LDC4	130	---Of man-made fibres

序号 No.	税则号列 Tariff Line	货品名称	最惠国税率 MFN(%)	协定税率 Agreement(%)		特惠税率 S.P.(%)		普通税率 Gen.(%)	Article Description
4197	5803.0090	---其他纺织材料制	10	0 5	东盟ASEAN,智利CL,新加坡SG,新西兰NZ,秘鲁PE,哥斯达黎加CR 巴基斯坦PK	0	最不发达35国LDC35,最不发达4国LDC4	80	---Of other textile materials
	58.04	**网眼薄纱及其他网眼织物,但不包括机织物、针织物或钩编织物;成卷、成条或成小块图案的花边,但税号60.02的织物除外:**							**Tulles and other net fabrics, not including woven, knitted or crocheted fabrics; lace in the piece, in strips or in motifs, other than fabrics of heading No.60.02:**
		-网眼薄纱及其他网眼织物:							-Tulles and other net fabrics:
4198	5804.1010	---丝及绢丝制	10	0 5 7	东盟ASEAN,智利CL,新加坡SG,新西兰NZ,秘鲁PE,哥斯达黎加CR 巴基斯坦PK 亚太APTA	0	最不发达35国LDC35,最不发达4国LDC4	130	---Of silk or silk waste
4199	5804.1020	---棉制	10	0 5 7	东盟ASEAN,智利CL,新西兰NZ,秘鲁PE,哥斯达黎加CR 巴基斯坦PK 亚太APTA	0	最不发达35国LDC35,最不发达4国LDC4	70	---Of cotton
4200	5804.1030	---化学纤维制	12	0 2.4 5 8.4	东盟ASEAN,智利CL,新加坡SG,新西兰NZ,秘鲁PE,台湾TW 哥斯达黎加CR 巴基斯坦PK 亚太APTA	0	最不发达35国LDC35,最不发达4国LDC4,缅甸MM,老挝LA,柬埔寨KH	130	---Of man-made fibres
4201	5804.1090	---其他纺织材料制	10	0 5 7	东盟ASEAN,智利CL,新加坡SG,新西兰NZ,秘鲁PE,哥斯达黎加CR,台湾TW 巴基斯坦PK 亚太APTA	0	最不发达35国LDC35,最不发达4国LDC4	90	---Of other textile materials
		-机制花边:							-Mechanically made lace:
4202	5804.2100	--化学纤维制	10	0 5	东盟ASEAN,智利CL,新加坡SG,新西兰NZ,秘鲁PE,哥斯达黎加CR,香港HK,澳门MO,台湾TW 巴基斯坦PK	0	最不发达35国LDC35,最不发达4国LDC4	130	--Of man-made fibres
		--其他纺织材料制:							--Of other textile materials:

序号 No.	税则号列 Tariff Line	货品名称	最惠国税率 MFN(%)	协定税率 Agreement(%)		特惠税率 S.P.(%)		普通税率 Gen.(%)	Article Description
4203	5804.2910	---丝及绢丝制	10	0 5	东盟ASEAN,智利CL,新加坡SG,新西兰NZ,秘鲁PE,哥斯达黎加CR 巴基斯坦PK	0	最不发达35国LDC35,最不发达4国LDC4	130	---Of silk or silk waste
4204	5804.2920	---棉制	10	0 5	东盟ASEAN,智利CL,新西兰NZ,秘鲁PE,哥斯达黎加CR 巴基斯坦PK	0	最不发达35国LDC35,最不发达4国LDC4,缅甸MM,老挝LA,柬埔寨KH	70	---Of cotton
4205	5804.2990	---其他	10	0 5	东盟ASEAN,智利CL,新加坡SG,新西兰NZ,秘鲁PE,哥斯达黎加CR 巴基斯坦PK	0	最不发达35国LDC35,最不发达4国LDC4	90	---Other
4206	5804.3000	-手工制花边	10	0 5	东盟ASEAN,智利CL,新加坡SG,新西兰NZ,秘鲁PE,哥斯达黎加CR 巴基斯坦PK	0	最不发达35国LDC35,最不发达4国LDC4	100	-Hand-made lace
	58.05	**"哥白林"、"弗朗德"、"奥步生"、"波威"及类似式样的手织装饰毯，以及手工针绣嵌花装饰毯（例如，小针脚或十字绣），不论是否制成的:**							**Hand-woven tapestries of the type Gobelins, Flanders, Aubusson, Beauvais and the like, and meedle-worked tapestries (for example, petit point, cross stitch), whether or not made up:**
4207	5805.0010	---手工针绣嵌花装饰毯	12	0 2.4 6	东盟ASEAN,智利CL,新加坡SG,新西兰NZ,秘鲁PE 哥斯达黎加CR 巴基斯坦PK	0	最不发达35国LDC35,最不发达4国LDC4	130	---Needleworked tapestries
4208	5805.0090	---其他	12	0 2.4 6	东盟ASEAN,智利CL,新加坡SG,新西兰NZ,秘鲁PE 哥斯达黎加CR 巴基斯坦PK	0	最不发达35国LDC35,最不发达4国LDC4	130	---Other
	58.06	**狭幅机织物，但税号58.07的货品除外;用粘合剂粘合制成的有经纱而无纬纱的狭幅织物（包扎匹头用带）:**							**Narrow woven fabrics, other than goods of heading No.58.07; narrow fabrics consisting of warp without weft assembled by means of an adhesive (bolducs):**

序号 No.	税则号列 Tariff Line	货品名称	最惠国税率 MFN(%)	协定税率 Agreement(%)	特惠税率 S.P.(%)	普通税率 Gen.(%)	Article Description
		-起绒机织物(包括毛巾织物及类似的毛圈织物)及绳绒织物:					-Woven pile fabrics (including terry towelling and similar terry fabris) and chenille fabrics:
4209	5806.1010	---棉或麻制	10	0 东盟ASEAN,智利CL,新西兰NZ,秘鲁PE,哥斯达黎加CR 5 巴基斯坦PK	0 最不发达35国LDC35,最不发达4国LDC4	70	---Of cotton or bast fibres
4210	5806.1090	---其他纺织材料制	10	0 东盟ASEAN,智利CL,新加坡SG,新西兰NZ,秘鲁PE,哥斯达黎加CR,台湾TW 5 巴基斯坦PK 9.1 亚太APTA	0 最不发达35国LDC35,最不发达4国LDC4,缅甸MM,老挝LA,柬埔寨KH	80	---Of other textile materials
4211	5806.2000	-按重量计弹性纱线或橡胶线含量在5%及以上的其他机织物	10	0 东盟ASEAN,智利CL,新加坡SG,新西兰NZ,秘鲁PE,哥斯达黎加CR,香港HK,澳门MO,台湾TW 5 巴基斯坦PK	0 最不发达35国LDC35,最不发达4国LDC4,缅甸MM,老挝LA,柬埔寨KH	100	-Other woven fabrics, containing by weight 5% or more of elastomeric yarn or rubber thread
		-其他机织物:					-Other woven fabrics:
4212	5806.3100	--棉制	10	0 东盟ASEAN,智利CL,新西兰NZ,秘鲁PE,哥斯达黎加CR 5 巴基斯坦PK	0 最不发达35国LDC35,最不发达4国LDC4,缅甸MM,老挝LA,柬埔寨KH	70	--Of cotton
4213	5806.3200	--化学纤维制	10	0 东盟ASEAN,智利CL,新加坡SG,新西兰NZ,秘鲁PE,哥斯达黎加CR,澳门MO,台湾TW 5 巴基斯坦PK 7 亚太APTA	0 最不发达35国LDC35,最不发达4国LDC4,缅甸MM,老挝LA,柬埔寨KH	130	--Of man-made fibres
		--其他纺织材料制:					--Of other textile materials:

序号 No.	税则号列 Tariff Line	货品名称	最惠国税率 MFN(%)	协定税率 Agreement(%)		特惠税率 S.P.(%)		普通税率 Gen.(%)	Article Description
4214	5806.3910	---丝及绢丝制	10	0 5	东盟ASEAN,智利CL,新加坡SG,新西兰NZ,秘鲁PE,哥斯达黎加CR 巴基斯坦PK	0	最不发达35国LDC35,最不发达4国LDC4	130	---Of silk or silk waste
4215	5806.3920	---羊毛或动物细毛制	10	0 5	东盟ASEAN,智利CL,新加坡SG,新西兰NZ,秘鲁PE,哥斯达黎加CR 巴基斯坦PK	0	最不发达35国LDC35,最不发达4国LDC4	130	---Of wool or fine animal hair
4216	5806.3990	---其他	10	0 5	东盟ASEAN,智利CL,新加坡SG,新西兰NZ,秘鲁PE,哥斯达黎加CR 巴基斯坦PK	0	最不发达35国LDC35,最不发达4国LDC4	80	---Other
		-用粘合剂粘合制成的有经纱而无纬纱的织物（包扎匹头用带）:							-Fabrics consisting of warp without weft assembled by means of an adhesive (bolducs):
4217	5806.4010	---棉或麻制	10	0 5	东盟ASEAN,智利CL,新西兰NZ,秘鲁PE,哥斯达黎加CR 巴基斯坦PK	0	最不发达35国LDC35,最不发达4国LDC4	70	---Of cotton or bast fibres
4218	5806.4090	---其他纺织材料制	10	0 5	东盟ASEAN,智利CL,新加坡SG,新西兰NZ,秘鲁PE,哥斯达黎加CR 巴基斯坦PK	0	最不发达35国LDC35,最不发达4国LDC4	80	---Of other textile materials
	58.07	**非绣制的纺织材料制标签、徽章及类似品，成匹、成条或裁成一定形状或尺寸:**							**Labels, badges and similar articles of textile materials, in the piece, in strips or cut to shape or size, not embroidered:**
4219	5807.1000	-机织	10	0 5 8.5	东盟ASEAN,智利CL,新加坡SG,新西兰NZ,哥斯达黎加CR,香港HK,澳门MO,台湾TW 秘鲁PE 亚太APTA,巴基斯坦PK	0	最不发达35国LDC35,最不发达4国LDC4,缅甸MM,老挝LA,柬埔寨KH	100	-Woven
4220	5807.9000	-其他	10	0 5	东盟ASEAN,智利CL,新加坡SG,新西兰NZ,秘鲁PE,哥斯达黎加CR 巴基斯坦PK	0	最不发达35国LDC35,最不发达4国LDC4	100	-Other

序号 No.	税则号列 Tariff Line	货品名称	最惠国税率 MFN(%)	协定税率 Agreement(%)		特惠税率 S.P.(%)		普通税率 Gen.(%)	Article Description
	58.08	**成匹的编带;非绣制的成匹装饰带,但针织或钩编的除外;流苏、绒球及类似品:**							**Braids in the piece; ornamental trimmings in the piece, without embroidery, other than knitted or crocheted; tassels, pompons and similar articles:**
4221	5808.1000	-成匹的编带	10	0	东盟ASEAN,智利CL,新加坡SG,新西兰NZ,秘鲁PE,哥斯达黎加CR,澳门MO	0	最不发达35国LDC35,最不发达4国LDC4	100	-Braids in the piece
4222	5808.9000	-其他	10	0 5	东盟ASEAN,智利CL,新加坡SG,新西兰NZ,秘鲁PE,哥斯达黎加CR,澳门MO 巴基斯坦PK	0	最不发达35国LDC35,最不发达4国LDC4,缅甸MM,老挝LA,柬埔寨KH	100	-Other
	58.09	**其他税号未列名的金属线机织物及税号56.05所列含金属纱线的机织物,用于衣着、装饰及类似用途:**							**Woven fabrics of metal thread and woven fabrics of metallized yarn of heading No.56.05, of a kind used in apparel, as furnishing fabrics or for similar purposes, not elsewhere specified or included:**
4223	5809.0010	---与棉混制	10	0 5	东盟ASEAN,智利CL,新加坡SG,新西兰NZ,秘鲁PE,哥斯达黎加CR 巴基斯坦PK	0	最不发达35国LDC35,最不发达4国LDC4	90	---Combined with cotton
4224	5809.0020	---与化学纤维混制	10	0 5	东盟ASEAN,智利CL,新加坡SG,新西兰NZ,秘鲁PE,哥斯达黎加CR 巴基斯坦PK	0	最不发达35国LDC35,最不发达4国LDC4	130	---Combined with man-made fibres
4225	5809.0090	---其他	10	0 5	东盟ASEAN,智利CL,新加坡SG,新西兰NZ,秘鲁PE,哥斯达黎加CR 巴基斯坦PK	0	最不发达35国LDC35,最不发达4国LDC4	100	---Other
	58.10	**成匹、成条或成小块图案的刺绣品:**							**Embroidery in the piece, in strips or in motifs:**

序号 No.	税则号列 Tariff Line	货品名称	最惠国税率 MFN(%)	协定税率 Agreement(%)		特惠税率 S.P.(%)		普通税率 Gen.(%)	Article Description
4226	5810.1000	-不见底布的刺绣品	10	0 5	东盟ASEAN,智利CL,新加坡SG,新西兰NZ,秘鲁PE,哥斯达黎加CR 巴基斯坦PK	0	最不发达35国LDC35,最不发达4国LDC4	130	-Embroidery without visible ground
		-其他刺绣品:							-Other embroidery:
4227	5810.9100	--棉制	10	0 5	东盟ASEAN,智利CL,新加坡SG,新西兰NZ,哥斯达黎加CR 秘鲁PE	0	最不发达35国LDC35,最不发达4国LDC4	130	--Of cotton
4228	5810.9200	--化学纤维制	10	0 5	东盟ASEAN,智利CL,新加坡SG,新西兰NZ,秘鲁PE,哥斯达黎加CR,台湾TW 巴基斯坦PK	0	最不发达35国LDC35,最不发达4国LDC4	130	--Of man-made fibres
4229	5810.9900	--其他纺织材料制	10	0 5	东盟ASEAN,智利CL,新加坡SG,新西兰NZ,秘鲁PE,哥斯达黎加CR 巴基斯坦PK	0	最不发达35国LDC35,最不发达4国LDC4	130	--Of other textile materials
	58.11	**用一层或几层纺织材料与胎料经绗缝或其他方法组合制成的被褥状纺织品,但税号58.10的刺绣品除外:**							**Quilted textile products in the piece, composed of one or more layers of textile materials assembled with padding by stitching or otherwise, other than embroidery of heading No.58.10:**
4230	5811.0010	---丝及绢丝制	10	0	东盟ASEAN,智利CL,巴基斯坦PK,新加坡SG,新西兰NZ,秘鲁PE,哥斯达黎加CR	0	最不发达35国LDC35,最不发达4国LDC4	130	---Of silk or silk waste
4231	5811.0020	---羊毛或动物细毛制	10	0	东盟ASEAN,智利CL,巴基斯坦PK,新加坡SG,新西兰NZ,秘鲁PE,哥斯达黎加CR	0	最不发达35国LDC35,最不发达4国LDC4	130	---Of wool or fine animal hair
4232	5811.0030	---棉制	10	0	东盟ASEAN,智利CL,巴基斯坦PK,新西兰NZ,秘鲁PE,哥斯达黎加CR	0	最不发达35国LDC35,最不发达4国LDC4	80	---Of cotton

序号 No.	税则号列 Tariff Line	货品名称	最惠国税率 MFN(%)	协定税率 Agreement(%)		特惠税率 S.P.(%)		普通税率 Gen.(%)	Article Description
4233	5811.0040	---化学纤维制	12	0 2.4	东盟ASEAN,智利CL,巴基斯坦PK,新加坡SG,新西兰NZ,秘鲁PE 哥斯达黎加CR	0	最不发达35国LDC35,最不发达4国LDC4	130	---Of man-made fibres
4234	5811.0090	---其他纺织材料制	10	0	东盟ASEAN,智利CL,巴基斯坦PK,新加坡SG,新西兰NZ,秘鲁PE,哥斯达黎加CR	0	最不发达35国LDC35,最不发达4国LDC4	90	---Of other textile materials

第五十九章
浸渍、涂布、包覆或层压的纺织物；工业用纺织制品

注释:

一、除条文另有规定的以外，本章所称“纺织物”，仅适用于第五十章至第五十五章、税号 58.03 及 58.06 的机织物、税号 58.08 的成匹编带和装饰带及税号 60.02 至 60.06 的针织物或钩编织物。

二、税号 59.03 适用于:

（一）用塑料浸渍、涂布、包覆或层压的纺织物，不论每平方米重量多少以及塑料的性质如何（紧密结构或泡沫状的），但下列各项除外:

1. 用肉眼无法辨别出是否经过浸渍、涂布、包覆或层压的织物（通常归入第五十章至第五十五章、第五十八章或第六十章），但由于浸渍、涂布、包覆或层压所引起的颜色变化可不予考虑;
2. 温度在 15℃至 30℃时，用手工将其绕于直径 7 毫米的圆柱体上会发生断裂的产品（通常归入第三十九章）;
3. 纺织物完全嵌入塑料内或在其两面均用塑料完全包覆或涂布，而这种包覆或涂布用肉眼是能够辨别出的产品（但由于包覆或涂布所引起的颜色变化可不予考虑）(第三十九章);
4. 用塑料部分涂布或包覆并由此而形成图案的织物（通常归入第五十章至第五十五章、第五十八章或第六十章）;
5. 与纺织物混制而其中纺织物仅起增强作用的泡沫塑料板、片或带（第三十九章）;
6. 税号 58.11 的纺织品。

（二）由税号 56.04 的用塑料浸渍、涂布、包覆或套裹的纱线、扁条或类似品制成的织物。

Chapter 59
Impregnated, coated, covered or laminated textile fabrics; textile articles of a kind suitable for industrial use

Notes:

1. Except where the context otherwise requires，for the purposes of this Chapter the expression “textile fabrics” applies only to the woven fabrics of Chapters 50 to 55 and headings Nos.58.03and 58.06，the braids and ornamental trimmings in the piece of heading No.58.08 and the knitted or crocheted fabrics of headings No. 60. 02 to 60.06.

2. Heading No.59.03 applies to:

(a) Textile fabrics，impregnated，coated，covered or laminated with plastics，whatever the weight per square metre and whatever the nature of the plastic material (compact or cellular)，other than:

(1) Fabrics in which the impregnation，coating，or covering cannot be seen with the naked eye (usually Chapters 50 to 55，58 or 60); for the purpose of this provision，no account should be taken of any resulting change of colour;

(2) Products which cannot，without fracturing，be bent manually around a cylinder of a diameter of 7mm，at a temperature between15°C and 30°C (usually Chapter 39);

(3) Products in which the textile fabric is either completely embedded in plastics or entirely coated or covered on both sides with such materal，provided that such coating or covering can be seen with the naked eye with no account being taken of any resulting change of colour (Chapter 39);

(4) Fabrics partially coated or partially covered with plastics and bearing designs resulting from these treatments (usually Chapters 50 to 55，58 or 60);

(5) Plates，sheets of strip of cellular plastics，combined with textile fabric，where the textile fabric is present merely for reinforcing purposes (Chapter 39); or

(6) Textile products of heading No.58.11;

(b) Fabrics made from yarn，strip or the like，impregnated，coated，covered or sheathed with plastics，of heading No.56.04.

三、税号 59.05 所称“糊墙织物”，是指以纺织材料作面，固定在一衬背上或在背面进行处理（浸渍或涂布以便于裱糊），适于装饰墙壁或天花板，且宽度不小于 45 厘米的成卷产品。

但本税号不适用于以纺织纤维屑或粉末直接粘于纸上（税号 48.14）或布底上（通常归入税号 59.07）的糊墙物品。

四、税号 59.06 所称“用橡胶处理的纺织物”是指：

（一）用橡胶浸渍、涂布、包覆或层压的纺织物：

1. 每平方米重量不超过 1500 克；
2. 每平方米重量超过 1500 克，按重量计纺织材料含量在 50%以上；

（二）由税号 56.04 的用橡胶浸渍、涂布、包覆或套裹的纱线、扁条或类似品制成的织物；

（三）平行纺织纱线经橡胶粘合的织物，不论每平方米重量多少。

但本税号不包括与纺织物混制而其中纺织物仅起增强作用的海绵橡胶板、片或带（第四十章），也不包括税号 58.11 的纺织品。

五、税号 59.07 不适用于：

（一）用肉眼无法辨别出是否经过浸渍、涂布或包覆的织物（通常归入第五十章至第五十五章、第五十八章或第六十章），但由于浸渍、涂布或包覆所引起的颜色变化可不予考虑；

（二）绘有图画的织物（作为舞台、摄影布景或类似品的已绘制的画布除外）；

（三）用短绒、粉末、软木粉或类似品部分覆面并由此而形成图案的织物，但仿绒织物仍归入本税号；

（四）以淀粉或类似物质为基本成分的普通浆料上浆整理的织物；

（五）以纺织物为底的木饰面板（税号 44.08）；

（六）以纺织物为底的砂布及类似品（税号 68.05）；

3. For the purposes of heading No.59.05, the expression "textile wall coverings" applies to products in rolls, of a width of not less than 45cm, suitable for wall or ceiling decoration, consisting of a textile surface which has beenfixed on a backing or has been treated on the back (impregnated or coated to permit pasting).

This heading does not, however, apply to wall coverings consisting of textile flock or dust fixed directly on backing of paper (heading No.48.14) or on a textile backing (generally heading No.59.07).

4. For the purposes of heading No.59.06, the expression "rubberized textile fabrics" means:

(a) Textile fabrics impregnated, coated, covered or laminated with rubber:

(Ⅰ) Weighing not more than $1500g/m^2$; or

(Ⅱ) Weighing more than $1500g/m^2$ and containing more than 50% by weight of textile material;

(b) Fabrics made from yarn, strip or the like, impregnated, coated, covered or sheathed with rubber, of heading No.56.04; and

(c) Fabrics composed of parallel textile yarns agglomerated with rubber, irrespective of their weight per square metre.

This heading does not, however, apply to plates, sheets or strip of cellular rubber, combined with textile fabric, where the textile fabric is present merely for reinforcing purposes (Chapter 40), or textile products of heading No.58.11.

5. Heading No.59.07 does not apply to:

(a) Fabrics in which the impregnation, coating or covering cannot be seen with the naked eye (usually Chapters 50 to 55, 58 or 60); for the purpose of this provision, no account should be taken of any resulting change of colour;

(b) Fabrics painted with designs (other than painted canvas being theatrical scenery, studio backcloths or the like);

(c) Fabrics partially covered with flock, dust, powdered cork or the like and bearing designs resulting from these treatments; however, imitation pile fabrics remain classified in this heading;

(d) Fabrics finished with normal dressings having a basis of amylaceous or similar substances;

(e) Wood veneered on a backing of textile fabrics (heading No. 44. 08);

(f) Natural or artificial abrasive powder or grain, on a backing of textile fabrics (heading No.68.05);

（七）以纺织物为底的粘聚或复制云母片（税号68.14）；

（八）以纺织物为底的金属箔（通常为第十四类或第十五类）。

(g) Agglomerated or reconstituted mica, on a backing of textile fabrics (heading No.68.14); or

(h) Metal foil on a backing of textile fabrics (Generally Section XIV or Section XV).

六、税号59.10不适用于：

（一）厚度小于3毫米的纺织材料制传动带或输送带；

（二）用橡胶浸渍、涂布、包覆或层压的织物制成的或用橡胶浸渍、涂布、包覆或套裹的纱线或绳制成的传动带及运输带（税号40.10）。

6. Heading No.59.10 does not apply to:

(a) Transmission or conveyor belting, of textile material, of a thickness of less than 3mm; or

(b) Transmission or conveyor belts or belting of textile fabric impregnated, coated, covered or laminated with rubber or made from textile yarn or cord impregnated, coated, covered or sheathed with rubber (heading No.40.10).

七、税号59.11适用于下列不能归入第十一类其他税号的货品：

（一）下列成匹的、裁成一定长度或仅裁成矩形（包括正方形）的纺织产品（具有税号59.08至59.10所列产品特征的产品除外）：

1. 用橡胶、皮革或其他材料涂布、包覆或层压的作针布用的纺织物、毡呢及毡呢衬里机织物，以及其他专门技术用途的类似织物，包括用橡胶浸渍的用于包覆纺锤（织轴）的狭幅丝绒织物；

2. 筛布；

3. 用于榨油机器或类似机器的纺织材料制或人发制滤布；

4. 用多股经纱或纬纱平织而成的纺织物，不论是否毡化、浸渍或涂布，通常用于机械或其他专门技术用途；

5. 专门技术用途的增强纺织物；

6. 工业上作填塞或润滑材料的线绳、编带及类似品，不论是否涂布、浸渍或用金属加强。

（二）专门技术用途的纺织制品（税号59.08至59.10的货品除外），例如，造纸机器或类似机器（如制浆机或制石棉水泥的机器）用的环状或装有联接装置的纺织物或毡呢、密封垫、垫圈、抛光盘及其他机器零件。

7. Heading No.59.11 applies to the following goods, which do not fall in any other heading of Section XI:

(a) Textile products in the piece, cut to length or simply cut to rectangular (including square) shape (other than those having the character of the products of headings No.59.08 to 59.10), the following only:

(1) Textile fabrics, felt and felt lined woven fabrics, coated, covered or laminated with rubber, leather or other material, of a kind used for card clothing, and similar fabrics of a kind used for other technical purposes, including narrow fabrics made of velvet impregnated with rubber, for covering weaving spindles (weaving beams);

(2) Bolting cloth;

(3) Straining cloth of a kind used in oil presses or the like, of textile material or of human hair;

(4) Flat woven textile fabrics with multiple warp or weft, whether or not felted, impregnated or coated, of a kind used in machinery or for other technical purposes;

(5) Textile fabrics reinforced with metal, of a kind used for technical purposes;

(6) Cords, braids and the like, whether or not coated, impregnated or reinforced with metal, of a kind used in industry as packing or lubricating materials.

(b) Textile articles (other than those of headings Nos.59.08 to 59.10) of a kind used for technical purposes, for example, textile fabrics and felts, endless or fitted with linking devicse, of a kind used in paper-making or similar machines (for example, for pulp or asbestos-cement), gaskets, washers, polishing discs and other machinery parts.

序号 No.	税则号列 Tariff Line	货品名称	最惠国税率 MFN(%)	协定税率 Agreement(%)	特惠税率 S.P.(%)	普通税率 Gen.(%)	Article Description
	59.01	**用胶或淀粉物质涂布的纺织物，作书籍封面及类似用途的；描图布；制成的油画布；作帽里的硬衬布及类似硬挺纺织物：**					**Textile fabrics coated with gum or amylaceous substances, of a kind used for the outer covers of books or the like; tracing cloth; prepared painting canvas; buckram and similar stiffened textile fabrics of a kind used for hat foundations:**
		-用胶或淀粉物质涂布的纺织物，作书籍封面及类似用途的:					-Textile fabrics coated with gum or amylaceous substances, of a kind used for the outer covers of books or the like:
4235	5901.1010	---棉或麻制	10	0 东盟ASEAN,智利CL,新加坡SG,新西兰NZ,秘鲁PE,哥斯达黎加CR 5 巴基斯坦PK	0 最不发达35国LDC35,最不发达4国LDC4	80	---Of cotton or bast fibres
4236	5901.1020	---化学纤维制	10	0 东盟ASEAN,智利CL,新加坡SG,新西兰NZ,秘鲁PE,哥斯达黎加CR 5 巴基斯坦PK	0 最不发达35国LDC35,最不发达4国LDC4	130	---Of man-made fibres
4237	5901.1090	---其他	10	0 东盟ASEAN,智利CL,新加坡SG,新西兰NZ,秘鲁PE,哥斯达黎加CR 5 巴基斯坦PK	0 最不发达35国LDC35,最不发达4国LDC4	100	---Other
		-其他:					-Other:
4238	5901.9010	---制成的油画布	10	0 东盟ASEAN,智利CL,新西兰NZ,秘鲁PE,哥斯达黎加CR 5 巴基斯坦PK	0 最不发达35国LDC35,最不发达4国LDC4	50	---Prepared painting canvas
		---其他:					---Other:
4239	5901.9091	----棉或麻制	10	0 东盟ASEAN,智利CL,新西兰NZ,秘鲁PE,哥斯达黎加CR 5 巴基斯坦PK	0 最不发达35国LDC35,最不发达4国LDC4,缅甸MM,老挝LA,柬埔寨KH	80	----Of cotton or bast fibres

序号 No.	税则号列 Tariff Line	货品名称	最惠国税率 MFN(%)	协定税率 Agreement(%)		特惠税率 S.P.(%)		普通税率 Gen.(%)	Article Description
4240	5901.9092	----化学纤维制	10	0 5	东盟ASEAN,智利CL,新西兰NZ,秘鲁PE,哥斯达黎加CR 巴基斯坦PK	0	最不发达35国LDC35,最不发达4国LDC4	130	----Of man-made fibres
4241	5901.9099	----其他	10	0 5	东盟ASEAN,智利CL,新西兰NZ,秘鲁PE,哥斯达黎加CR 巴基斯坦PK	0	最不发达35国LDC35,最不发达4国LDC4	100	----Other
	59.02	**尼龙或其他聚酰胺,聚酯或粘胶纤维高强力纱制的帘子布:**							**Tyre cord fabric of high tenacity yarn of nylon or other polyamides, polyesters or viscose rayon:**
		-尼龙或其他聚酰胺制:							-Of nylon or other polyamides:
4242	5902.1010	---聚酰胺-6（尼龙-6）制	10	0 5 9	东盟ASEAN,智利CL,新加坡SG,新西兰NZ,秘鲁PE,哥斯达黎加CR 巴基斯坦PK 亚太APTA	0	最不发达35国LDC35,最不发达4国LDC4	40	---Of nylon-6
4243	5902.1020	---聚酰胺-6，6（尼龙-6，6）制	10	0 5 9	东盟ASEAN,智利CL,新加坡SG,新西兰NZ,秘鲁PE,哥斯达黎加CR 巴基斯坦PK 亚太APTA	0	最不发达35国LDC35,最不发达4国LDC4	40	---Of nylon-6,6
4244	5902.1090	---其他	10	0 5 9	东盟ASEAN,智利CL,新加坡SG,新西兰NZ,秘鲁PE,哥斯达黎加CR 巴基斯坦PK 亚太APTA	0	最不发达35国LDC35,最不发达4国LDC4	40	---Other
4245	5902.2000	-聚酯制	10	0 5 9	东盟ASEAN,智利CL,新加坡SG,新西兰NZ,秘鲁PE,哥斯达黎加CR 巴基斯坦PK 亚太APTA	0	最不发达35国LDC35,最不发达4国LDC4	40	-Of polyesters
4246	5902.9000	-其他	10	0 5	东盟ASEAN,智利CL,新西兰NZ,秘鲁PE,哥斯达黎加CR 巴基斯坦PK	0	最不发达35国LDC35,最不发达4国LDC4	40	-Other
	59.03	**用塑料浸渍、涂布、包覆或层压的纺织物，但税号59.02的货品除外:**							**Textile fabrics impregnated, coated, covered or laminated with plastics, other than those of heading No.59.02:**

序号 No.	税则号列 Tariff Line	货品名称	最惠国税率 MFN(%)	协定税率 Agreement(%)		特惠税率 S.P.(%)		普通税率 Gen.(%)	Article Description
		-用聚氯乙烯浸渍、涂布、包覆或层压的:							-With poly (vinyl chloride):
4247	5903.1010	---绝缘布或带	10	0 5 8.5	东盟ASEAN,智利CL,新西兰NZ,秘鲁PE,哥斯达黎加CR 巴基斯坦PK 亚太APTA	0	最不发达35国LDC35,最不发达4国LDC4	40	---Insulating cloth or tape
4248	5903.1020	---人造革	10	0 5 8.5	东盟ASEAN,智利CL,新加坡SG,新西兰NZ,秘鲁PE,哥斯达黎加CR,香港HK,台湾TW 巴基斯坦PK 亚太APTA	0	最不发达35国LDC35,最不发达4国LDC4	70	---Imitation leather
4249	5903.1090	---其他	10	0 5 8.5	东盟ASEAN,智利CL,新加坡SG,新西兰NZ,秘鲁PE,哥斯达黎加CR,香港HK,台湾TW 巴基斯坦PK 亚太APTA	0	最不发达35国LDC35,最不发达4国LDC4	90	---Other
		-用聚氨基甲酸酯浸渍、涂布、包覆或层压的:							-With polyurethane:
4250	5903.2010	---绝缘布或带	10	0 5 8.5	东盟ASEAN,智利CL,新西兰NZ,秘鲁PE,哥斯达黎加CR 巴基斯坦PK 亚太APTA	0	最不发达35国LDC35,最不发达4国LDC4	40	---Insulating cloth or tape
4251	5903.2020	---人造革	10	0 5 8.5	东盟ASEAN,智利CL,新加坡SG,新西兰NZ,秘鲁PE,哥斯达黎加CR,台湾TW 巴基斯坦PK 亚太APTA	0	最不发达35国LDC35,最不发达4国LDC4	70	---Imitation leather
4252	5903.2090	---其他	10	0 8.5	东盟ASEAN,智利CL,新加坡SG,新西兰NZ,秘鲁PE,哥斯达黎加CR,香港HK,台湾TW 亚太APTA,巴基斯坦PK	0	最不发达35国LDC35,最不发达4国LDC4	90	---Other
		-其他:							-Other:
4253	5903.9010	---绝缘布或带	10	0 5 8.5	东盟ASEAN,智利CL,新西兰NZ,秘鲁PE,哥斯达黎加CR 巴基斯坦PK 亚太APTA	0	最不发达35国LDC35,最不发达4国LDC4	40	---Insulating cloth or tape
4254	5903.9020	---人造革	10	0 5 8.5	东盟ASEAN,智利CL,新加坡SG,新西兰NZ,秘鲁PE,哥斯达黎加CR,台湾TW 巴基斯坦PK 亚太APTA	0	最不发达35国LDC35,最不发达4国LDC4	70	---Imitation leather

序号 No.	税则号列 Tariff Line	货品名称	最惠国税率 MFN(%)	协定税率 Agreement(%)		特惠税率 S.P.(%)		普通税率 Gen.(%)	Article Description
4255	5903.9090	---其他	10	0	东盟ASEAN,智利CL,新加坡SG,新西兰NZ,秘鲁PE,哥斯达黎加CR,香港HK,台湾TW	0	最不发达35国LDC35,最不发达4国LDC4,缅甸MM,老挝LA,柬埔寨KH	90	---Other
				8.5	亚太APTA,巴基斯坦PK				
	59.04	**列诺伦（亚麻油地毡），不论是否剪切成形;以织物为底布经涂布或覆面的铺地制品，不论是否剪切成形:**							**Linoleum, whether or not cut to shape; floor coverings consisting of a coating or covering applied on a textile backing, whether or not cut to shape:**
4256	5904.1000	-列诺伦（亚麻油地毡）	14	0	东盟ASEAN,智利CL,新加坡SG,新西兰NZ,秘鲁PE	0	最不发达35国LDC35	90	-Linoleum
				2.8	哥斯达黎加CR				
				11.2	巴基斯坦PK				
4257	5904.9000	-其他	14	0	东盟ASEAN,智利CL,新加坡SG,新西兰NZ,秘鲁PE	0	最不发达35国LDC35	90	-Other
				2.8	哥斯达黎加CR				
				7	巴基斯坦PK				
	59.05	**糊墙织物:**							**Textile wall coverings:**
4258	5905.0000	糊墙织物	10	0	东盟ASEAN,智利CL,新加坡SG,新西兰NZ,秘鲁PE,哥斯达黎加CR	0	最不发达35国LDC35,最不发达4国LDC4	80	Textile wall coverings
				5	巴基斯坦PK				
	59.06	**用橡胶处理的纺织物，但税号59.02的货品除外:**							**Rubberized teztile fabrics, other than those of heading No.59.02:**
		-宽度不超过20厘米的胶粘带:							-Adhesive tape of a width not exceeding 20cm:
4259	5906.1010	---绝缘带	10	0	东盟ASEAN,智利CL,新西兰NZ,秘鲁PE,哥斯达黎加CR	0	最不发达35国LDC35,最不发达4国LDC4	40	---Insulating tape
				5	巴基斯坦PK				
4260	5906.1090	---其他	10	0	东盟ASEAN,智利CL,新加坡SG,新西兰NZ,秘鲁PE,哥斯达黎加CR	0	最不发达35国LDC35,最不发达4国LDC4	100	---Other
				5	巴基斯坦PK				
		-其他:							-Other:

序号 No.	税则号列 Tariff Line	货品名称	最惠国税率 MFN(%)	协定税率 Agreement(%)		特惠税率 S.P.(%)		普通税率 Gen.(%)	Article Description
4261	5906.9100	--针织或钩编的	10	0 5	东盟ASEAN,智利CL,新加坡SG,新西兰NZ,秘鲁PE,哥斯达黎加CR,台湾TW 巴基斯坦PK	0	最不发达35国LDC35,最不发达4国LDC4	130	--Knitted or crocheted
		--其他:							--Other:
4262	5906.9910	---绝缘布或带	10	0 5	东盟ASEAN,智利CL,新西兰NZ,秘鲁PE,哥斯达黎加CR 巴基斯坦PK	0	最不发达35国LDC35,最不发达4国LDC4	40	---Insulating cloth or tape
4263	5906.9990	---其他	10	0 5	东盟ASEAN,智利CL,新加坡SG,新西兰NZ,秘鲁PE,哥斯达黎加CR,台湾TW 巴基斯坦PK	0	最不发达35国LDC35,最不发达4国LDC4	100	---Other
	59.07	**用其他材料浸渍、涂布或包覆的纺织物;作舞台、摄影布景或类似用途的已绘制画布:**							**Textile fabrics otherwise impregnated, coated or covered; painted canvas being theatrical scenery, studio back-cloths or the like:**
4264	5907.0010	---绝缘布或带	10	0 5 8.5	东盟ASEAN,智利CL,新西兰NZ,秘鲁PE,哥斯达黎加CR 巴基斯坦PK 亚太APTA	0	最不发达35国LDC35,最不发达4国LDC4	40	---Insulating cloth or tape
4265	5907.0020	---已绘制画布	10	0 5 8.5	东盟ASEAN,智利CL,新西兰NZ,秘鲁PE,哥斯达黎加CR 巴基斯坦PK 亚太APTA	0	最不发达35国LDC35,最不发达4国LDC4	50	---Painted canvas
4266	5907.0090	---其他	10	0 5 8.5	东盟ASEAN,智利CL,新加坡SG,新西兰NZ,秘鲁PE,哥斯达黎加CR 巴基斯坦PK 亚太APTA	0	最不发达35国LDC35,最不发达4国LDC4	100	---Other
	59.08	**用纺织材料机织、编结或针织而成的灯芯、炉芯、打火机芯、烛芯或类似品;煤气灯纱筒及纱罩，不论是否浸渍:**							**Textile wicks, woven, platied or knitted, for lamps, stoves, lighters, candles or the like; incandescent gas mantles and tubular knitted gas mantle fabric therefor, whether or not impregnated:**

序号 No.	税则号列 Tariff Line	货品名称	最惠国税率 MFN(%)	协定税率 Agreement(%)		特惠税率 S.P.(%)		普通税率 Gen.(%)	Article Description
4267	5908.0000	用纺织材料机织、编结或针织而成的灯芯、炉芯、打火机芯、烛芯或类似品;煤气灯纱筒及纱罩，不论是否浸渍	10	0 5	东盟ASEAN,智利CL,新西兰NZ,秘鲁PE,哥斯达黎加CR 巴基斯坦PK	0	最不发达35国LDC35,最不发达4国LDC4	70	Textile wicks, woven, plaited or knitted, for lamps, stoves, lighters, candles or the like; incandescent gas mantles and tubular knitted gas mantle fbric therefor, whether or not impregnated
	59.09	**纺织材料制的水龙软管及类似的管子，不论有无其他材料作衬里、护套或附件:**							**Textile hosepiping and similar textile tubing, with or without lining, armour or accessories of other materials:**
4268	5909.0000	纺织材料制的水龙软管及类似的管子，不论有无其他材料作衬里、护套或附件	8	0 5	东盟ASEAN,智利CL,新西兰NZ,秘鲁PE,哥斯达黎加CR,澳门MO 巴基斯坦PK	0	最不发达35国LDC35,最不发达4国LDC4	35	Textile hosepiping and similar textile tubing, with or without lining, armour or accessories of other materials
	59.10	**纺织材料制的传动带或输送带及带料，不论是否用塑料浸渍、涂布、包覆或压层，也不论是否用金属或其他材料加强:**							**Transmission or conveyor belts or belting, of textile material, whether or not impregnated, coated, covered or laminated with plastics, or reinforced with metal or other material:**
4269	5910.0000	纺织材料制的传动带或输送带及带料，不论是否用塑料浸渍、涂布、包覆或压层，也不论是否用金属或其他材料加强	8	0 5	东盟ASEAN,智利CL,新西兰NZ,秘鲁PE,哥斯达黎加CR,台湾TW 巴基斯坦PK	0	最不发达35国LDC35,最不发达4国LDC4	35	Transmission or conveyor belts or belting, of textile material, whether or not impregnated, coated, covered or laminated with plastics, or reinforced with metal or other material
	59.11	**本章注释七所规定的作专门技术用途的纺织产品及制品:**							**Textile products and articles, for technical uses, specified in Note 7 to this Chapter:**
		-用橡胶、皮革或其他材料涂布、包覆或层压的作针布用的纺织物、毡呢及毡呢衬里机织物，以及作专门技术用途的类似织物，包括用橡胶浸渍的、用于包覆纺锤（织轴）的狭幅丝绒织物:							-Textile fabrics, felt and felt-lined woven fabrics, coated, covered or laminated with rubber, leather or other material, of a kind used for card clothing, and similar fabrics of a kind used for other technical purposes, including narrow fabrics made of velvet impregnated with rubber, for covering weaving spindles (weaving beams):

序号 No.	税则号列 Tariff Line	货品名称	最惠国税率 MFN(%)	协定税率 Agreement(%)		特惠税率 S.P.(%)		普通税率 Gen.(%)	Article Description
4270	5911.1010	---用橡胶浸渍的、用于包覆纺缍（织轴）的狭幅丝绒织物	8	0 5 7.2	东盟ASEAN,智利CL,新西兰NZ,秘鲁PE,哥斯达黎加CR 巴基斯坦PK 亚太APTA	0	最不发达35国LDC35,最不发达4国LDC4	75	---Narrow fabrics made of velvet impregnated with rubber, for covering weaving spindles (weaving beams)
4271	5911.1090	---其他	8	0 5	东盟ASEAN,智利CL,新西兰NZ,秘鲁PE,哥斯达黎加CR 巴基斯坦PK	0	最不发达35国LDC35,最不发达4国LDC4	35	---Other
4272	5911.2000	-筛布，不论是否制成的	8	0 5	东盟ASEAN,智利CL,新西兰NZ,秘鲁PE,哥斯达黎加CR 巴基斯坦PK	0	最不发达35国LDC35,最不发达4国LDC4	35	-Bolting cloth, whether or not made up
		-环状或装有联接装置的纺织物及毡呢，用于造纸机器或类似机器（例如，制浆机或制石棉水泥的机器）：							-Textile fabrics and felts, endless or fitted with linking devices, of a kind used in paper-making or similar machines (for example, for pulp or asbestos-cement):
4273	5911.3100	--每平方米重量在650以下	8	0 5	东盟ASEAN,智利CL,新西兰NZ,秘鲁PE,哥斯达黎加CR 巴基斯坦PK	0	最不发达35国LDC35,最不发达4国LDC4	35	--Weighing less than $650g/m^2$
4274	5911.3200	--每平方米重量在650克及以上	8	0 5	东盟ASEAN,智利CL,新西兰NZ,秘鲁PE,哥斯达黎加CR 巴基斯坦PK	0	最不发达35国LDC35,最不发达4国LDC4	35	--Weighing $650g/m^2$ or more
4275	5911.4000	-用于榨油机器或类似机器的滤布，包括人发制滤布	8	0 5	东盟ASEAN,智利CL,新西兰NZ,秘鲁PE,哥斯达黎加CR 巴基斯坦PK	0	最不发达35国LDC35,最不发达4国LDC4	35	-Straining cloth of a kind used in oil presses or the like, including that of human hair
4276	5911.9000	-其他	8	0 5	东盟ASEAN,智利CL,新西兰NZ,秘鲁PE,哥斯达黎加CR 巴基斯坦PK	0	最不发达35国LDC35,最不发达4国LDC4	35	-Other

第六十章
针织物及钩编织物

Chapter 60
Knitted or crocheted fabrics

注释:

一、本章不包括:

（一）税号 58.04 的钩编花边;

（二）税号 58.07 的针织或钩编的标签、徽章及类似品;

（三）第五十九章的经浸渍、涂布、包覆或层压的针织物及钩编织物。但经浸渍、涂布、包覆或层压的起绒针织物及起绒钩编织物仍归入税号 60.01。

二、本章还包括用金属线制的用于衣着、装饰或类似用途的织物。

三、本目录所称"针织物",包括由纺织纱线用链式针法构成的缝编织物。

Notes:

1. This Chapter does not cover:

(a) Crochet lace of heading No.58.04;

(b) Labels, badges or similar articles, knitted or crocheted, of heading No.58.07; or

(c) Knitted or crocheted fabrics, impregnated, coated, covered or laminated, of Chapter 59. However, knitted or crocheted plie fabrics, impregnated, coated, covered or laminated, remain classified in heading No.60.01.

2. This Chapter also includes fabrics made of metal thread and of a kind used in apparel, as furnishing fabrics or for similar purposes.

3. Throughout the Nomenclature any reference to "knitted" goods includes a reference to stitch-bonded goods in which the chain stitches are formed of textile yarn.

序号 No.	税则号列 Tariff Line	货品名称	最惠国税率 MFN(%)	协定税率 Agreement(%)		特惠税率 S.P.(%)		普通税率 Gen.(%)	Article Description
	60.01	**针织或钩编的起绒织物,包括"长毛绒"织物及毛圈织物:**							**Pile fabrics, including "long pile" fabrics and terry fabrics, knitted or crocheted:**
4277	6001.1000	-"长毛绒"织物	10	0 8.5	东盟ASEAN,智利CL,巴基斯坦PK,新加坡SG,新西兰NZ,秘鲁PE,哥斯达黎加CR 亚太APTA	0	最不发达35国LDC35,最不发达4国LDC4	130	-"Long pile" fabrics
		-毛圈绒头织物:							-Looped pile fabrics:
4278	6001.2100	--棉制	10	0 8.5	东盟ASEAN,智利CL,巴基斯坦PK,新西兰NZ,秘鲁PE,哥斯达黎加CR 亚太APTA	0	最不发达35国LDC35,最不发达4国LDC4	70	--Of cotton
4279	6001.2200	--化学纤维制	10	0 8.5	东盟ASEAN,智利CL,巴基斯坦PK,新加坡SG,新西兰NZ,秘鲁PE,哥斯达黎加CR 亚太APTA	0	最不发达35国LDC35,最不发达4国LDC4	130	--Of man-made fibres
4280	6001.2900	--其他纺织材料制	12	0 2.4	东盟ASEAN,智利CL,巴基斯坦PK,新加坡SG,新西兰NZ,秘鲁PE 哥斯达黎加CR	0	最不发达35国LDC35	130	--Of other textile materials

序号 No.	税则号列 Tariff Line	货品名称	最惠国税率 MFN(%)	协定税率 Agreement(%)		特惠税率 S.P.(%)		普通税率 Gen.(%)	Article Description
		-其他:							-Other:
4281	6001.9100	--棉制	10	0 7	东盟ASEAN,智利CL,巴基斯坦PK,新西兰NZ,秘鲁PE,哥斯达黎加CR 亚太APTA	0	最不发达35国LDC35,最不发达4国LDC4	70	--Of cotton
4282	6001.9200	--化学纤维制	10	0 8.5	东盟ASEAN,智利CL,巴基斯坦PK,新加坡SG,新西兰NZ,秘鲁PE,哥斯达黎加CR,香港HK,澳门MO,台湾TW 亚太APTA	0	最不发达35国LDC35,最不发达4国LDC4	130	--Of man-made fibres
4283	6001.9900	--其他纺织材料制	12	0 2.4	东盟ASEAN,智利CL,巴基斯坦PK,新加坡SG,新西兰NZ,秘鲁PE 哥斯达黎加CR	0	最不发达35国LDC35	130	--Of other textile materials
	60.02	**宽度不超过30厘米，按重量计弹性纱线或橡胶线含量在5%及以上的针织物或钩编织物，但税目60.01的货品除外:**							**Knitted or crocheted fabrics of a width not exceeding 30cm, containing by weight 5%or more of elastomeric yarn or rubber thread, other than those of heading 60.01:**
		-按重量计弹性纱线含量在5%及以上，但不含橡胶线:							-Containing by weight 5% or more of elastomeric yarn but not containing rubber thread:
4284	6002.4010	---棉制	10	0 8.5	东盟ASEAN,智利CL,巴基斯坦PK,新西兰NZ,秘鲁PE,哥斯达黎加CR 亚太APTA	0	最不发达35国LDC35,最不发达4国LDC4	70	---Of cotton
4285	6002.4020	---丝及绢丝制	10	0 8.5	东盟ASEAN,智利CL,巴基斯坦PK,新加坡SG,新西兰NZ,秘鲁PE,哥斯达黎加CR 亚太APTA	0	最不发达35国LDC35,最不发达4国LDC4	130	---Of silk or silk waste
4286	6002.4030	---合成纤维制	10	0	东盟ASEAN,智利CL,巴基斯坦PK,新加坡SG,新西兰NZ,秘鲁PE,哥斯达黎加CR	0	最不发达35国LDC35,最不发达4国LDC4	130	---Of synthetic fibres
4287	6002.4040	---人造纤维制	10	0	东盟ASEAN,智利CL,巴基斯坦PK,新加坡SG,新西兰NZ,秘鲁PE,哥斯达黎加CR	0	最不发达35国LDC35,最不发达4国LDC4	130	---Of artificial fibres

序号 No.	税则号列 Tariff Line	货品名称	最惠国税率 MFN(%)	协定税率 Agreement(%)		特惠税率 S.P.(%)		普通税率 Gen.(%)	Article Description
4288	6002.4090	---其他	10	0 7	东盟ASEAN,智利CL,巴基斯坦PK,新加坡SG,新西兰NZ,秘鲁PE,哥斯达黎加CR 亚太APTA	0	最不发达35国LDC35,最不发达4国LDC4	130	---Other
		-其他:							-Other:
4289	6002.9010	---棉制	10	0 8.5	东盟ASEAN,智利CL,巴基斯坦PK,新西兰NZ,秘鲁PE,哥斯达黎加CR 亚太APTA	0	最不发达35国LDC35,最不发达4国LDC4,缅甸MM,老挝LA,柬埔寨KH	70	---Of cotton
4290	6002.9020	---丝及绢丝制	10	0 8.5	东盟ASEAN,智利CL,巴基斯坦PK,新加坡SG,新西兰NZ,秘鲁PE,哥斯达黎加CR 亚太APTA	0	最不发达35国LDC35,最不发达4国LDC4	130	---Of silk or silk waste
4291	6002.9030	---合成纤维制	10	0 5	东盟ASEAN,智利CL,巴基斯坦PK,新加坡SG,新西兰NZ,秘鲁PE,哥斯达黎加CR 亚太APTA	0	最不发达35国LDC35,最不发达4国LDC4,缅甸MM,老挝LA,柬埔寨KH	130	---Of synthetic fibres
4292	6002.9040	---人造纤维制	10	0 5	东盟ASEAN,智利CL,巴基斯坦PK,新加坡SG,新西兰NZ,秘鲁PE,哥斯达黎加CR 亚太APTA	0	最不发达35国LDC35,最不发达4国LDC4	130	---Of artificial fibres
4293	6002.9090	---其他	10	0 8.5	东盟ASEAN,智利CL,巴基斯坦PK,新加坡SG,新西兰NZ,秘鲁PE,哥斯达黎加CR 亚太APTA	0	最不发达35国LDC35,最不发达4国LDC4	130	---Other
	60.03	**宽度不超过30厘米的针织或钩编织物，但税目60.01或60.02的货品除外:**							**Knitted or crocheted fabrics of a width not exceeding 30cm, other than those of heading 60.01 or 60.02:**

序号 No.	税则号列 Tariff Line	货品名称	最惠国税率 MFN(%)	协定税率 Agreement(%)		特惠税率 S.P.(%)		普通税率 Gen.(%)	Article Description
4294	6003.1000	-羊毛或动物细毛制	10	0	东盟ASEAN,智利CL,巴基斯坦PK,新加坡SG,新西兰NZ,秘鲁PE,哥斯达黎加CR	0	最不发达35国LDC35,最不发达4国LDC4	130	-Of wool or fine animal hair
4295	6003.2000	-棉制	10	0	东盟ASEAN,智利CL,巴基斯坦PK,新西兰NZ,秘鲁PE,哥斯达黎加CR	0	最不发达35国LDC35,最不发达4国LDC4	70	-Of cotton
4296	6003.3000	-合成纤维制	10	0 9.4	东盟ASEAN,智利CL,巴基斯坦PK,新加坡SG,新西兰NZ,秘鲁PE,哥斯达黎加CR 亚太APTA	0	最不发达35国LDC35,最不发达4国LDC4	130	-Of synthetic fibres
4297	6003.4000	-人造纤维制	10	0 9.4	东盟ASEAN,智利CL,巴基斯坦PK,新加坡SG,新西兰NZ,秘鲁PE,哥斯达黎加CR 亚太APTA	0	最不发达35国LDC35,最不发达4国LDC4	130	-Of artificial fibres
4298	6003.9000	-其他	10	0	东盟ASEAN,智利CL,巴基斯坦PK,新加坡SG,新西兰NZ,秘鲁PE,哥斯达黎加CR	0	最不发达35国LDC35,最不发达4国LDC4	130	-Other
	60.04	**宽度超过30厘米，按重量计弹性纱线或橡胶线含量在5%及以上的针织物或钩编织物，但税目60.01的货品除外：**							**Knitted or crocheted fabrics of a width exceeding 30cm, containing by weight 5% or more elastomeric yarn or rubber thread, other than those of heading 60.01:**
		-按重量计弹性纱线含量在5%及以上，但不含橡胶线:							-Containing by weight 5% or more of elastomeric yarn but not containing rubber thread:
4299	6004.1010	---棉制	10	0 7	东盟ASEAN,智利CL,巴基斯坦PK,新加坡SG,新西兰NZ,秘鲁PE,哥斯达黎加CR,香港HK 亚太APTA	0	最不发达35国LDC35,最不发达4国LDC4,缅甸MM,老挝LA,柬埔寨KH	70	---Of cotton

序号 No.	税则号列 Tariff Line	货品名称	最惠国税率 MFN(%)	协定税率 Agreement(%)		特惠税率 S.P.(%)		普通税率 Gen.(%)	Article Description
4300	6004.1020	---丝及绢丝制	10	0 8.5	东盟ASEAN,智利CL,巴基斯坦PK,新加坡SG,新西兰NZ,秘鲁PE,哥斯达黎加CR 亚太APTA	0	最不发达35国LDC35,最不发达4国LDC4	130	---Of silk or silk waste
4301	6004.1030	---合成纤维制	10	0	东盟ASEAN,智利CL,巴基斯坦PK,新加坡SG,新西兰NZ,秘鲁PE,哥斯达黎加CR,香港HK,澳门MO,台湾TW	0	最不发达35国LDC35,最不发达4国LDC4	130	---Of synthetic fibres
4302	6004.1040	---人造纤维制	10	0	东盟ASEAN,智利CL,巴基斯坦PK,新加坡SG,新西兰NZ,秘鲁PE,哥斯达黎加CR,香港HK,澳门MO	0	最不发达35国LDC35,最不发达4国LDC4	130	---Of artificial fibres
4303	6004.1090	---其他	10	0 8.5	东盟ASEAN,智利CL,巴基斯坦PK,新加坡SG,新西兰NZ,秘鲁PE,哥斯达黎加CR,香港HK,澳门MO,台湾TW 亚太APTA	0	最不发达35国LDC35,最不发达4国LDC4	130	---Other
		-其他:							-Other:
4304	6004.9010	---棉制	10	0 8.5	东盟ASEAN,智利CL,巴基斯坦PK,新西兰NZ,秘鲁PE,哥斯达黎加CR,香港HK 亚太APTA	0	最不发达35国LDC35,最不发达4国LDC4	70	---Of cotton
4305	6004.9020	---丝及绢丝制	10	0 8.5	东盟ASEAN,智利CL,巴基斯坦PK,新加坡SG,新西兰NZ,秘鲁PE,哥斯达黎加CR 亚太APTA	0	最不发达35国LDC35,最不发达4国LDC4	130	---Of silk or silk waste
4306	6004.9030	---合成纤维制	10	0	东盟ASEAN,智利CL,巴基斯坦PK,新加坡SG,新西兰NZ,秘鲁PE,哥斯达黎加CR,香港HK,澳门MO,台湾TW	0	最不发达35国LDC35,最不发达4国LDC4	130	---Of synthetic fibres
4307	6004.9040	---人造纤维制	10	0	东盟ASEAN,智利CL,巴基斯坦PK,新加坡SG,新西兰NZ,秘鲁PE,哥斯达黎加CR,香港HK,澳门MO	0	最不发达35国LDC35,最不发达4国LDC4	130	---Of artificial fibres
4308	6004.9090	---其他	10	0 7	东盟ASEAN,智利CL,巴基斯坦PK,新加坡SG,新西兰NZ,秘鲁PE,哥斯达黎加CR,香港HK,澳门MO,台湾TW 亚太APTA	0	最不发达35国LDC35,最不发达4国LDC4	130	---Other

序号 No.	税则号列 Tariff Line	货品名称	最惠国税率 MFN(%)	协定税率 Agreement(%)		特惠税率 S.P.(%)		普通税率 Gen.(%)	Article Description
	60.05	**经编织物（包括由花边针织机织成的），但税目 60.01 至 60.04 的货品除外:**							**Warp knit fabrics (including those made on galloon knitting machines), other than those of headings 60.01 to 60.04:**
		-棉制:							-Of cotton:
4309	6005.2100	--未漂白或漂白	10	0	东盟ASEAN,智利CL,巴基斯坦PK,新西兰NZ,秘鲁PE,哥斯达黎加CR,香港HK	0	最不发达 35 国 LDC35,最不发达 4 国 LDC4	70	--Unbleached or bleached
4310	6005.2200	--染色	10	0	东盟ASEAN,智利CL,巴基斯坦PK,新西兰NZ,秘鲁PE,哥斯达黎加CR,香港HK	0	最不发达 35 国 LDC35,最不发达 4 国 LDC4	70	--Dyed
4311	6005.2300	--色织	10	0	东盟ASEAN,智利CL,巴基斯坦PK,新西兰NZ,秘鲁PE,哥斯达黎加CR,香港HK	0	最不发达 35 国 LDC35,最不发达 4 国 LDC4	70	--Of yarns of different colours
4312	6005.2400	--印花	10	0	东盟ASEAN,智利CL,巴基斯坦PK,新西兰NZ,秘鲁PE,哥斯达黎加CR,香港HK	0	最不发达 35 国 LDC35,最不发达 4 国 LDC4	70	--Printed
		-合成纤维制							-Of synthetic fibres:
4313	6005.3100	--未漂白或漂白	10	0 8.5	东盟ASEAN,智利CL,巴基斯坦PK,新加坡SG,新西兰NZ,秘鲁PE,哥斯达黎加CR,台湾TW 亚太APTA	0	最不发达 35 国 LDC35,最不发达 4 国 LDC4	130	--Unbleached or bleached
4314	6005.3200	--染色	10	0 8.5	东盟ASEAN,智利CL,巴基斯坦PK,新加坡SG,新西兰NZ,秘鲁PE,哥斯达黎加CR,台湾TW 亚太APTA	0	最不发达 35 国 LDC35,最不发达 4 国 LDC4,缅甸MM,老挝LA,柬埔寨KH	130	--Dyed
4315	6005.3300	--色织	10	0 8.5	东盟ASEAN,智利CL,巴基斯坦PK,新加坡SG,新西兰NZ,秘鲁PE,哥斯达黎加CR 亚太APTA	0	最不发达 35 国 LDC35,最不发达 4 国 LDC4	130	--Of yarns of different colours

序号 No.	税则号列 Tariff Line	货品名称	最惠国税率 MFN(%)	协定税率 Agreement(%)		特惠税率 S.P.(%)		普通税率 Gen.(%)	Article Description
4316	6005.3400	--印花	10	0 8.5	东盟ASEAN,智利CL,巴基斯坦PK,新加坡SG,新西兰NZ,秘鲁PE,哥斯达黎加CR 亚太APTA	0	最不发达35国LDC35,最不发达4国LDC4	130	--Printed
		-人造纤维制:							-Of artificial fibres:
4317	6005.4100	--未漂白或漂白	10	0 8.5	东盟ASEAN,智利CL,巴基斯坦PK,新加坡SG,新西兰NZ,秘鲁PE,哥斯达黎加CR 亚太APTA	0	最不发达35国LDC35,最不发达4国LDC4	130	--Unbleached or bleached
4318	6005.4200	--染色	10	0 8.5	东盟ASEAN,智利CL,巴基斯坦PK,新加坡SG,新西兰NZ,秘鲁PE,哥斯达黎加CR 亚太APTA	0	最不发达35国LDC35,最不发达4国LDC4	130	--Dyed
4319	6005.4300	--色织	10	0 8.5	东盟ASEAN,智利CL,巴基斯坦PK,新加坡SG,新西兰NZ,秘鲁PE,哥斯达黎加CR 亚太APTA	0	最不发达35国LDC35,最不发达4国LDC4	130	--Of yarns of different colours
4320	6005.4400	--印花	10	0 8.5	东盟ASEAN,智利CL,巴基斯坦PK,新加坡SG,新西兰NZ,秘鲁PE,哥斯达黎加CR 亚太APTA	0	最不发达35国LDC35,最不发达4国LDC4	130	--Printed
		-其他:							-Other:
4321	6005.9010	---羊毛或动物细毛制	12	0 2.4	东盟ASEAN,智利CL,巴基斯坦PK,新加坡SG,新西兰NZ,秘鲁PE 哥斯达黎加CR	0	最不发达35国LDC35	130	---Of wool or fine animal hair
4322	6005.9090	---其他	12	0 2.4	东盟ASEAN,智利CL,巴基斯坦PK,新加坡SG,新西兰NZ,秘鲁PE 哥斯达黎加CR	0	最不发达35国LDC35	130	---Other
	60.06	**其他针织或钩编织物:**							**Other knitted or crocheted fabrics:**
4323	6006.1000	-羊毛或动物细毛制	12	0 2.4	东盟ASEAN,智利CL,巴基斯坦PK,新加坡SG,新西兰NZ,秘鲁PE 哥斯达黎加CR	0	最不发达35国LDC35	130	-Of wool or fine animal hair
		-棉制:							-Of cotton:
4324	6006.2100	--未漂白或漂白	10	0 7	东盟ASEAN,智利CL,巴基斯坦PK,新西兰NZ,秘鲁PE,哥斯达黎加CR,香港HK,澳门MO 亚太APTA	0	最不发达35国LDC35,最不发达4国LDC4	70	--Unbleached or bleached

序号 No.	税则号列 Tariff Line	货品名称	最惠国税率 MFN(%)	协定税率 Agreement(%)		特惠税率 S.P.(%)		普通税率 Gen.(%)	Article Description
4325	6006.2200	--染色	10	0 8.5	东盟ASEAN,智利CL,巴基斯坦PK,新加坡SG,新西兰NZ,秘鲁PE,哥斯达黎加CR,香港HK,澳门MO 亚太APTA	0	最不发达35国LDC35,最不发达4国LDC4,缅甸MM,老挝LA,柬埔寨KH	70	--Dyed
4326	6006.2300	--色织	10	0 7	东盟ASEAN,智利CL,巴基斯坦PK,新加坡SG,新西兰NZ,秘鲁PE,哥斯达黎加CR,香港HK,澳门MO 亚太APTA	0	最不发达35国LDC35,最不发达4国LDC4,缅甸MM,老挝LA,柬埔寨KH	70	--Of yarns of different colours
4327	6006.2400	--印花	10	0 8.5	东盟ASEAN,智利CL,巴基斯坦PK,新西兰NZ,秘鲁PE,哥斯达黎加CR,香港HK,澳门MO,台湾TW 亚太APTA	0	最不发达35国LDC35,最不发达4国LDC4	70	--Printed
		-合成纤维制:							-Of synthetic fibres:
4328	6006.3100	--未漂白或漂白	10	0 8.5	东盟ASEAN,智利CL,巴基斯坦PK,新加坡SG,新西兰NZ,秘鲁PE,哥斯达黎加CR,香港HK,澳门MO,台湾TW 亚太APTA	0	最不发达35国LDC35,最不发达4国LDC4	130	--Unbleached or bleached
4329	6006.3200	--染色	10	0 8.5	东盟ASEAN,智利CL,巴基斯坦PK,新加坡SG,新西兰NZ,秘鲁PE,哥斯达黎加CR,香港HK,澳门MO,台湾TW 亚太APTA	0	最不发达35国LDC35,最不发达4国LDC4	130	--Dyed
4330	6006.3300	--色织	10	0 8.5	东盟ASEAN,智利CL,巴基斯坦PK,新加坡SG,新西兰NZ,秘鲁PE,哥斯达黎加CR,香港HK,澳门MO,台湾TW 亚太APTA	0	最不发达35国LDC35,最不发达4国LDC4	130	--Of yarns of different colours
4331	6006.3400	--印花	10	0 8.5	东盟ASEAN,智利CL,巴基斯坦PK,新加坡SG,新西兰NZ,秘鲁PE,哥斯达黎加CR,香港HK,澳门MO,台湾TW 亚太APTA	0	最不发达35国LDC35,最不发达4国LDC4	130	--Printed
		-人造纤维制:							-Of artificial fibres:

序号 No.	税则号列 Tariff Line	货品名称	最惠国税率 MFN(%)	协定税率 Agreement(%)		特惠税率 S.P.(%)		普通税率 Gen.(%)	Article Description
4332	6006.4100	--未漂白或漂白	10	0	东盟ASEAN,智利CL,巴基斯坦PK,新加坡SG,新西兰NZ,秘鲁PE,哥斯达黎加CR,香港HK,澳门MO	0	最不发达35国LDC35,最不发达4国LDC4	130	--Unbleached or bleached
				8.5	亚太APTA				
4333	6006.4200	--染色	10	0	东盟ASEAN,智利CL,巴基斯坦PK,新加坡SG,新西兰NZ,秘鲁PE,哥斯达黎加CR,香港HK,澳门MO,台湾TW	0	最不发达35国LDC35,最不发达4国LDC4	130	--Dyed
				8.5	亚太APTA				
4334	6006.4300	--色织	10	0	东盟ASEAN,智利CL,巴基斯坦PK,新加坡SG,新西兰NZ,秘鲁PE,哥斯达黎加CR,香港HK,澳门MO	0	最不发达35国LDC35,最不发达4国LDC4	130	--Of yarns of different colours
				8.5	亚太APTA				
4335	6006.4400	--印花	10	0	东盟ASEAN,智利CL,巴基斯坦PK,新加坡SG,新西兰NZ,秘鲁PE,哥斯达黎加CR,香港HK,澳门MO	0	最不发达35国LDC35,最不发达4国LDC4	130	--Printed
				8.5	亚太APTA				
4336	6006.9000	-其他	12	0	东盟ASEAN,智利CL,巴基斯坦PK,新加坡SG,新西兰NZ,秘鲁PE	0	最不发达35国LDC35	130	-Other
				2.4	哥斯达黎加CR				
				10.2	亚太APTA				

第六十一章
针织或钩编的服装及衣着附件

注释：

一、本章仅适用于制成的针织品或钩编织品。

二、本章不包括：

（一）税号 62.12 的货品；

（二）税号 63.09 的旧衣着或其他旧物品；

（三）矫形器具、外科手术带、疝气带及类似品（税号 90.21）。

三、税号 61.03 及 61.04 所称：

（一）"西服套装"，是指面料用相同的织物制成的两件套或三件套的下列成套服装：

一件人体上半身穿着的外套或短上衣，除袖子外，其面料数为四片或四片以上；也可附带一件西服背心，这件背心的前片面料应与套装其他各件的面料相同，后片面料则应与外套或短上衣的衬里料相同；

以及一件人体下半身穿着的服装，即不带背带或护胸的长裤、马裤、短裤（游泳裤除外）、裙子或裙裤。西服套装各件面料质地、颜色及构成必须相同，其款式也必须相同，尺寸大小还须相互般配，但可以用不同织物滚边（缝口上缝入长条织物）。

如果数件人体下半身穿着的服装同时进口或出口（例如，两条长裤、长裤与短裤、裙子或裙裤与长裤），构成西服套装下装的应是一条长裤，而对于女式西服套装，则应是一条裙子或裙裤，其他服装应分别归类。

所称"西服套装"，包括不论是否完全符合上述条件的下列配套服装：

Chapter 61
Articles of apparel and clothing accessories, knitted or crocheted

Notes:

1.This Chapter applies only to made up knitted or crocheted articles.

2.This Chapter does not cover:

(a) Goods of heading No.62.12;

(b) Worn clothing or other worn articles of heading No.63.09; or

(c) Orthopaedic appliances, surgical belts, trusses or the like (heaing No.90.21).

3. For the purposes of headings Nos.61.03 and 61.04:

(a) The term "suit" means a set of garments composed of two or three pieces made up, in respect of their outer surface, in identical fabric and comprising:

-One suit coat or jacket the outer shell of which, exclusive of sleeves, consists of four or more panels, designed to cover the upper part of the body, possibly with a tailored waistcoat in addition whose front panel is made from the same fabric as the outer shell of the other components of the set and whose rear panel is made from the same fabric as the lining of the suit coat or jacket; and

-One garment designed to cover the lower part of the body and consisting of trousers, breeches or shorts (other than swimwear), a skirt or a divided skirt, having neither braces nor bibs.All of the components of a suit must be of the same fabric construction, colour and composition; they must also be of the same style and of corresponding or compatible size. However, these components may have piping (a strip of fabric sewn into the seam) in a different fabric.

If several separate components to cover the lower part of the body are presented together（for example, two pairs of trousers or trousers and shorts, or a skirt or divided skirt and trousers）, the constituent lower part shall be one pair of trousers or, in the case of women's or girls' suits, the skirt or divided skirt, the other garments being considered separately.

The term "suit" includes the following sets of garments, whether or not they fulfill all the above conditions:

1. 常礼服，由一件后襟下垂并下端开圆弧形叉的素色短上衣和一条条纹长裤组成；

2. 晚礼服（燕尾服），一般用黑色织物制成，上衣前襟较短且不闭合，背后有燕尾；

3. 无燕尾套装夜礼服，其中上衣款式与普通上衣相似（可以更为显露衬衣前胸），但有光滑丝质或仿丝质的翻领。

（二）“便服套装”，是指面料相同并作零售包装的下列成套服装（西服套装及税号 61.07、61.08 或 61.09 的物品除外）：

一件人体上半身穿着的服装，但套衫及背心除外，因为套衫可在两件套服装中作为内衣，背心也可作为内衣；

以及一件或两件不同的人体下半身穿着的服装，即长裤、护胸背带工装裤、马裤、短裤（游泳裤除外）、裙子或裙裤。

便服套装各件面料质地、款式、颜色及构成必须相同；尺寸大小也须相互般配。所称“便服套装”，不包括税号 61.12 的运动服及滑雪服。

四、税号 61.05 及 61.06 不包括在腰围以下有口袋的服装、带有罗纹腰带及以其他方式收紧下摆的服装或其织物至少在 10 厘米 × 10 厘米的面积内沿各方向的直线长度上平均每厘米少于 10 针的服装。税号 61.05 不包括无袖服装。

五、税号 61.09 不包括带有束带、罗纹腰带或其他方式收紧下摆的服装。

六、对于税号 61.11：

（一）所称“婴儿服装及衣着附件”，是指用于身高不超过 86 厘米幼儿的服装；

(1) morning dress, comprising a plain jacket (cutaway) with rounded tails hanging well down at the back and striped trousers;

(2) evening dress (tailcoat), generally made of black fabric, the jacket of which is relatively short at the front, does not close and has narrow skirts cut in at the hips and hanging down behind;

(3)dinner jacket suits, in which the jacket is similar in style to an ordinary jacket (though perhaps revealing more of the shirt front), but has shiny silk or imitation silk lapels.

(b) The term “ensemble” means a set of garments (other than suits and articles of heading No.61.07, 61.08 or 61.09), composed of several pieces made up in identical fabric, put up for retail sale, and comprising:

-One garment designed to cover the upper part of the body, with the exception of pullovers which may form a sceond upper garment in the sole context of twin sets, and of waistcoats which may also form a second upper garment; and

-One or two different garments, designed to cover the lower part of the body and consisting of trousers, bib and brace overalls, breeches, shorts (other than swimwear), a skirt or a divided skirt.

All of the components of an ensemble must be of the same fabric construction, style, colour and composition; they also must be of corresponding or compatible size. The term “ensemble” does not apply to track suits or ski suits, of heading No.61.12.

4. Headings Nos.61.05 and 61.06 do not cover garments with pockets below the waist, with a ribbed waistband or other means of tightening at the bottom of the garment, or garments having an average of less than10 stitches per linear centimetre in each direction counted on an area measuring at least 10cm × 10cm. Heading No.61.05 does not cover sleeveless garments.

5. Heading No.61.09 does not cover garments with a drawstring, a ribbed waistband or other means of tightening at the bottom of the garment.

6. For the purposes of heading No.61.11:

(a) The expression “babies’ garments and clothing accessories” means articles for young children of a body height not exceeding 86cm;

（二）既可归入税号 61.11，也可归入本章其他税号的物品，应归入税号 61.11。

七、税号 61.12 所称“滑雪服”，是指从整个外观和织物质地来看，主要在滑雪（速度滑雪或高山滑雪）时穿着的下列服装或成套服装：

（一）“滑雪连身服”，即上下身连在一起的单件服装；除袖子和领子外，滑雪连身服可有口袋或脚带；或

（二）“滑雪套装”即由两件或三件构成一套并作零售包装的下列服装：

一件用一条拉链扣合的带风帽的厚夹克、防风衣、防风短上衣或类似的服装，可以附带一件背心；

以及一条不论是否过腰的长裤、一条马裤或一条护胸背带工装裤。

“滑雪套装”也可由一件类似以上（一）款所述的连身服和一件可套在连身服外面的有胎料背心组成。

“滑雪套装”各件颜色可以不同，但面料质地、款式及构成必须相同；尺寸大小也须相互般配。

八、既可归入税号 61.13，也可归入本章其他税号的服装，除税号 61.11 所列的仍归入该税号外，其余的应一律归入税号 61.13。

九、本章的服装，凡门襟为左压右的，应视为男式；右压左的，应视为女式。但本规定不适用于其式样已明显为男式或女式的服装。无法区别是男式还是女式的服装，应按女式服装归入有关税号。

十、本章物品可用金属线制成。

(b) Articles which are, *prima facie*, classifiable both in heading No.61.11and in other headings of this Chapter are to be classified in heading No.61.11.

7. For the purposes of heading No.61.12, “ski suits” means garments or sets of garments which, by their general appearance and texture, are identifiable as intended to be worn principally for sking(cross-country or alpine). They consist either of:

(a) a“ski overall”, that is, a one-piece garment designed to cover the upper and the lower parts of the body; in addition to sleeves and a collar the ski overall may have pockets or footstraps; or

(b) a “ski ensemble”, that is, a set of garments composed of two or three pieces, put up for retail sale and comprising:

-one garment such as an anorak, wind cheater, wind-jacket or similar article, closed by a slide fastener (zipper), possibly with a waistcoat in addition; and

-one pair of trousers whether or not extending above waist-level, one pair of breeches or one bib and brace overall.

The “ski ensemble” may also consist of an overall similar to the one mentioned in paragraph (a) above and a type of padded, sleeveless jacket worn over the overall.

All the components of a “ski ensemble” must be made up in a fabric of the same texture, style and composition whether or not of the same colour; they also must be of corresponding or compatible size.

8. Garments which are, *prima facie*, classifiable both in heading No.61.13 and in other headings of this Chapter, excluding heading No.61.11, are to be classified in heading No.61.13.

9. Garments of this Chapter desinged for left over right closure at the front shall be regarded as men's or boys' garments, and those designed for right over left closure at the front as women's or girls' garments. These provisions do not apply where the cut of the garment clearly indicates that it is designed for one or other of the sexes.

Garments which cannot be identified as either men's or boys' garments or as women's or girls' garments are to be classified in the headings covering women or girls garments.

10. Articles of this Chapter may be made of metal thread.

序号 No.	税则号列 Tariff Line	货品名称	最惠国税率 MFN(%)	协定税率 Agreement(%)		特惠税率 S.P.(%)		普通税率 Gen.(%)	Article Description
	61.01	**针织或钩编的男式大衣、短大衣、斗篷、短斗篷、带风帽的防寒短上衣（包括滑雪短上衣）、防风衣、防风短上衣及类似品，但税号61.03的货品除外:**							**Men's or boys'overcoats, car-coats, capes, cloaks, anoraks (including ski-jackets), wind-cheaters, wind-jackets and similar articles, knitted or crocheted, other than those of heading No.61.03:**
4337	6101.2000	-棉制	17.5	0 3.5 8.8 14	东盟ASEAN,智利CL,新加坡SG,新西兰NZ,香港HK,澳门MO 哥斯达黎加CR 秘鲁PE 亚太APTA,巴基斯坦PK	0	最不发达35国LDC35,最不发达4国LDC4	90	-Of cotton
4338	6101.3000	-化学纤维制	17.5	0 3.5 8.8 12.3	东盟ASEAN,智利CL,新加坡SG,新西兰NZ,香港HK,澳门MO 哥斯达黎加CR 巴基斯坦PK,秘鲁PE 亚太APTA	0	最不发达35国LDC35,最不发达4国LDC4	130	-Of man-made fibres
		-其他纺织材料制:							-Of other textile materials:
4339	6101.9010	---羊毛或动物细毛制	25	0 5 12.5 18	东盟ASEAN,智利CL,新加坡SG,新西兰NZ,香港HK,澳门MO 哥斯达黎加CR 秘鲁PE 亚太APTA,巴基斯坦PK	0	最不发达35国LDC35	130	---Of wool or fine animal hair
4340	6101.9090	---其他	17.5	0 3.5 8.8 12.3	东盟ASEAN,智利CL,新加坡SG,新西兰NZ,香港HK,澳门MO 哥斯达黎加CR 巴基斯坦PK,秘鲁PE 亚太APTA	0	最不发达35国LDC35	130	---Other
	61.02	**针织或钩编的女式大衣、短大衣、斗篷、短斗篷、带风帽的防寒短上衣（包括滑雪短上衣）、防风衣、防风短上衣及类似品，但税号61.04的货品除外:**							**Women's or girls overcoats, car-coats, capes, cloaks, anoraks (including ski-jackets), wind-cheaters, wind-jackets and similar articles, knitted or crocheted, other than those of heading No.61.04:**
4341	6102.1000	-羊毛或动物细毛制	25	0 5 12.5 18	东盟ASEAN,智利CL,新加坡SG,新西兰NZ,香港HK,澳门MO 哥斯达黎加CR 秘鲁PE 亚太APTA,巴基斯坦PK	0	最不发达35国LDC35	130	-Of wool or fine animal hair
4342	6102.2000	-棉制	17.5	0 3.5 14	东盟ASEAN,智利CL,新加坡SG,新西兰NZ,香港HK,澳门MO 哥斯达黎加CR 亚太APTA,巴基斯坦PK	0	最不发达35国LDC35,最不发达4国LDC4	90	-Of cotton

序号 No.	税则号列 Tariff Line	货品名称	最惠国税率 MFN(%)	协定税率 Agreement(%)		特惠税率 S.P.(%)		普通税率 Gen.(%)	Article Description
4343	6102.3000	-化学纤维制	17.5	0	东盟ASEAN,智利CL,新加坡SG,新西兰NZ,香港HK,澳门MO	0	最不发达35国LDC35,最不发达4国LDC4	130	-Of man-made fibres
				3.5	哥斯达黎加CR				
				8.8	巴基斯坦PK,秘鲁PE				
				12.3	亚太APTA				
4344	6102.9000	-其他纺织材料制	20	0	东盟ASEAN,智利CL,新加坡SG,新西兰NZ,香港HK,澳门MO	0	最不发达35国LDC35	130	-Of other textile materials
				4	哥斯达黎加CR				
				10	巴基斯坦PK,秘鲁PE				
				13.8	亚太APTA				
	61.03	**针织或钩编的男式西服套装、便服套装、上衣、长裤、护胸背带工装裤、马裤及短裤（游泳裤除外）：**							**Men's or boys' suits, ensembles, jackets, blazers, trousers, bib and brace overalls, breeches and shorts (other than swimwear), knitted or crocheted:**
		-西服套装:							-Suits:
4345	6103.1010	---羊毛或动物细毛制	25	0	东盟ASEAN,智利CL,新加坡SG,新西兰NZ,香港HK,澳门MO	0	最不发达35国LDC35	130	---Of wool or fine animal hair
				5	哥斯达黎加CR				
				12.5	秘鲁PE				
				18	亚太APTA,巴基斯坦PK				
4346	6103.1020	---合成纤维制	25	0	东盟ASEAN,智利CL,新加坡SG,新西兰NZ,香港HK,澳门MO	0	最不发达35国LDC35	130	---Of synthetic fibres
				5	哥斯达黎加CR				
				12.5	秘鲁PE				
				18	亚太APTA,巴基斯坦PK				
4347	6103.1090	---其他纺织材料制	17.5	0	东盟ASEAN,智利CL,新加坡SG,新西兰NZ,香港HK,澳门MO	0	最不发达35国LDC35,最不发达4国LDC4,老挝LA	130	---Of other textile materials
				3.5	哥斯达黎加CR				
				8.8	巴基斯坦PK,秘鲁PE				
				12.3	亚太APTA				
		-便服套装:							-Ensembles:
4348	6103.2200	--棉制	20	0	东盟ASEAN,智利CL,新加坡SG,新西兰NZ,香港HK,澳门MO	0	最不发达35国LDC35,最不发达4国LDC4,老挝LA	90	--Of cotton
				4	哥斯达黎加CR				
				10	秘鲁PE				
				14.8	亚太APTA,巴基斯坦PK				
4349	6103.2300	--合成纤维制	25	0	东盟ASEAN,智利CL,新加坡SG,新西兰NZ,香港HK,澳门MO	0	最不发达35国LDC35	130	--Of synthetic fibres
				5	哥斯达黎加CR				
				12.5	秘鲁PE				
				18	亚太APTA,巴基斯坦PK				

序号 No.	税则号列 Tariff Line	货品名称	最惠国税率 MFN(%)	协定税率 Agreement(%)		特惠税率 S.P.(%)		普通税率 Gen.(%)	Article Description
		--其他纺织材料制:							--Of other textile materials:
4350	6103.2910	---羊毛或动物细毛制	25	0	东盟ASEAN,智利CL,新加坡SG,新西兰NZ,香港HK,澳门MO	0	最不发达35国LDC35	130	---Of wool or fine animal hair
				5	哥斯达黎加CR				
				12.5	秘鲁PE				
				18	亚太APTA,巴基斯坦PK				
4351	6103.2990	---其他	25	0	东盟ASEAN,智利CL,新加坡SG,新西兰NZ,澳门MO	0	最不发达35国LDC35,最不发达4国LDC4,老挝LA	130	---Other
				5	哥斯达黎加CR				
				12.5	秘鲁PE				
				18	亚太APTA,巴基斯坦PK				
		-上衣:							-Jackets and blazers:
4352	6103.3100	--羊毛或动物细毛制	16	0	东盟ASEAN,智利CL,新加坡SG,新西兰NZ,香港HK,澳门MO	0	最不发达35国LDC35	130	--Of wool or fine animal hair
				3.2	哥斯达黎加CR				
				8	巴基斯坦PK,秘鲁PE				
				11.7	亚太APTA				
4353	6103.3200	--棉制	16	0	东盟ASEAN,智利CL,新加坡SG,新西兰NZ,香港HK,澳门MO	0	最不发达35国LDC35,最不发达4国LDC4,缅甸MM,老挝LA,柬埔寨KH	90	--Of cotton
				3.2	哥斯达黎加CR				
				8	巴基斯坦PK,秘鲁PE				
				12	亚太APTA				
4354	6103.3300	--合成纤维制	19	0	东盟ASEAN,智利CL,新加坡SG,新西兰NZ,香港HK,澳门MO	0	最不发达35国LDC35,最不发达4国LDC4,柬埔寨KH	130	--Of synthetic fibres
				3.8	哥斯达黎加CR				
				9.5	巴基斯坦PK,秘鲁PE				
				13.6	亚太APTA				
4355	6103.3900	--其他纺织材料制	16	0	东盟ASEAN,智利CL,新加坡SG,新西兰NZ,香港HK,澳门MO	0	最不发达35国LDC35,最不发达4国LDC4,老挝LA,柬埔寨KH	130	--Of other textile materials
				3.2	哥斯达黎加CR				
				8	巴基斯坦PK,秘鲁PE				
				11.7	亚太APTA				
		-长裤、护胸背带工装裤、马裤及短裤:							-Trousers, bib and brace overalls, breeches and shorts:

序号 No.	税则号列 Tariff Line	货品名称	最惠国税率 MFN(%)	协定税率 Agreement(%)		特惠税率 S.P.(%)		普通税率 Gen.(%)	Article Description
4356	6103.4100	--羊毛或动物细毛制	16	0 3.2 8 11.7	东盟ASEAN,智利CL,新加坡SG,新西兰NZ,香港HK,澳门MO 哥斯达黎加CR 巴基斯坦PK,秘鲁PE 亚太APTA	0	最不发达35国LDC35,最不发达4国LDC4,亚太2国APTA2	130	--Of wool or fine animal hair
4357	6103.4200	--棉制	16	0 3.2 8 13.6	东盟ASEAN,智利CL,新加坡SG,新西兰NZ,香港HK,澳门MO 哥斯达黎加CR 巴基斯坦PK,秘鲁PE 亚太APTA	0 6.4	最不发达35国LDC35,最不发达4国LDC4,缅甸MM,老挝LA,柬埔寨KH 亚太2国APTA2	90	--Of cotton
4358	6103.4300	--合成纤维制	17.5	0 3.5 8.8 12.3	东盟ASEAN,智利CL,新加坡SG,新西兰NZ,香港HK,澳门MO 哥斯达黎加CR 巴基斯坦PK,秘鲁PE 亚太APTA	0	最不发达35国LDC35,最不发达4国LDC4,亚太2国APTA2,柬埔寨KH	130	--Of synthetic fibres
4359	6103.4900	--其他纺织材料制	16	0 3.2 8 11.7	东盟ASEAN,智利CL,新加坡SG,新西兰NZ,香港HK,澳门MO 哥斯达黎加CR 巴基斯坦PK,秘鲁PE 亚太APTA	0	最不发达35国LDC35,最不发达4国LDC4,亚太2国APTA2,老挝LA,柬埔寨KH	130	--Of other textile materials
	61.04	**针织或钩编的女式西服套装、便服套装、上衣、连衣裙、裙子、裙裤、长裤、护胸背带工装裤、马裤及短裤（游泳服除外）：**							**Women's or girls' suits, ensembles, jackets, blazers, dresses, skirts, divided skirts, trousers, bib and brace overalls, breeches and shorts (other than swimwear), knitted or crocheted:**
		-西服套装:							-Suits:

序号 No.	税则号列 Tariff Line	货品名称	最惠国税率 MFN(%)	协定税率 Agreement(%)		特惠税率 S.P.(%)		普通税率 Gen.(%)	Article Description
4360	6104.1300	--合成纤维制	25	0 5 12.5 18	东盟ASEAN,智利CL,新加坡SG,新西兰NZ,香港HK,澳门MO 哥斯达黎加CR 秘鲁PE 亚太APTA,巴基斯坦PK	0	最不发达35国LDC35	130	--Of synthetic fibres
		--其他纺织材料制:							--Of other textile materials:
4361	6104.1910	---羊毛或动物细毛制	17.5	0 3.5 8.8 12.3	东盟ASEAN,智利CL,新加坡SG,新西兰NZ,香港HK,澳门MO 哥斯达黎加CR 巴基斯坦PK,秘鲁PE 亚太APTA	0	最不发达35国LDC35,最不发达4国LDC4	130	---Of wool or fine animal hair
4362	6104.1920	---棉制	17.5	0 3.5 8.8 14	东盟ASEAN,智利CL,新加坡SG,新西兰NZ,香港HK,澳门MO 哥斯达黎加CR 秘鲁PE 亚太APTA,巴基斯坦PK	0	最不发达35国LDC35,最不发达4国LDC4,老挝LA	90	---Of cotton
4363	6104.1990	---其他	17.5	0 3.5 8.8 12.3	东盟ASEAN,智利CL,新加坡SG,新西兰NZ,香港HK,澳门MO 哥斯达黎加CR 巴基斯坦PK,秘鲁PE 亚太APTA	0	最不发达35国LDC35,最不发达4国LDC4,老挝LA	130	---Other
		-便服套装:							-Ensembles:
4364	6104.2200	--棉制	17.5	0 3.5 8.8 14	东盟ASEAN,智利CL,新加坡SG,新西兰NZ,香港HK,澳门MO 哥斯达黎加CR 秘鲁PE 亚太APTA,巴基斯坦PK	0	最不发达35国LDC35,最不发达4国LDC4,老挝LA	90	--Of cotton
4365	6104.2300	--合成纤维制	25	0 5 12.5 18	东盟ASEAN,智利CL,新加坡SG,新西兰NZ,香港HK,澳门MO 哥斯达黎加CR 秘鲁PE 亚太APTA,巴基斯坦PK	0	最不发达35国LDC35	130	--Of synthetic fibres
		--其他纺织材料制:							--Of other textile materials:
4366	6104.2910	---羊毛或动物细毛制	17.5	0 3.5 8.8 12.3	东盟ASEAN,智利CL,新加坡SG,新西兰NZ,香港HK,澳门MO 哥斯达黎加CR 巴基斯坦PK,秘鲁PE 亚太APTA	0	最不发达35国LDC35	130	---Of wool or fine animal hair
4367	6104.2990	---其他纺织材料制	15	0 3 7.5 10.4	东盟ASEAN,智利CL,新加坡SG,新西兰NZ,香港HK,澳门MO 哥斯达黎加CR 巴基斯坦PK,秘鲁PE 亚太APTA	0	最不发达35国LDC35,最不发达4国LDC4	130	---Other

序号 No.	税则号列 Tariff Line	货品名称	最惠国 税 率 MFN(%)		协定税率 Agreement(%)		特惠税率 S.P.(%)	普通 税率 Gen.(%)	Article Description
		-上衣:							-Jackets and blazers:
4368	6104.3100	--羊毛或动物细毛制	16	0	东盟ASEAN,智利CL,新加坡SG,新西兰NZ,香港HK,澳门MO	0	最不发达35国LDC35,最不发达4国LDC4	130	--Of wool or fine animal hair
				3.2	哥斯达黎加CR				
				8	巴基斯坦PK,秘鲁PE				
				11.7	亚太APTA				
4369	6104.3200	--棉制	16	0	东盟ASEAN,智利CL,新加坡SG,新西兰NZ,香港HK,澳门MO	0	最不发达35国LDC35,最不发达4国LDC4,缅甸MM,老挝LA,柬埔寨KH	90	--Of cotton
				3.2	哥斯达黎加CR				
				8	秘鲁PE				
				13.6	亚太APTA,巴基斯坦PK				
4370	6104.3300	--合成纤维制	19	0	东盟ASEAN,智利CL,新加坡SG,新西兰NZ,香港HK,澳门MO	0	最不发达35国LDC35,最不发达4国LDC4,柬埔寨KH	130	--Of synthetic fibres
				3.8	哥斯达黎加CR				
				9.5	巴基斯坦PK,秘鲁PE				
				13.6	亚太APTA				
4371	6104.3900	--其他纺织材料制	16	0	东盟ASEAN,智利CL,新加坡SG,新西兰NZ,香港HK,澳门MO	0	最不发达35国LDC35,最不发达4国LDC4,柬埔寨KH	130	--Of other textile materials
				3.2	哥斯达黎加CR				
				8	巴基斯坦PK,秘鲁PE				
				11.7	亚太APTA				
		-连衣裙:							-Dresses:
4372	6104.4100	--羊毛或动物细毛制	16	0	东盟ASEAN,智利CL,新加坡SG,新西兰NZ,香港HK,澳门MO	0	最不发达35国LDC35	130	--Of wool or fine animal hair
				3.2	哥斯达黎加CR				
				8	巴基斯坦PK,秘鲁PE				
				11.7	亚太APTA				
4373	6104.4200	--棉制	16	0	东盟ASEAN,智利CL,新加坡SG,新西兰NZ,香港HK,澳门MO	0	最不发达35国LDC35,最不发达4国LDC4	90	--Of cotton
				3.2	哥斯达黎加CR				
				8	巴基斯坦PK,秘鲁PE				
				13.6	亚太APTA				
4374	6104.4300	--合成纤维制	17.5	0	东盟ASEAN,智利CL,新加坡SG,新西兰NZ,香港HK,澳门MO	0	最不发达35国LDC35,最不发达4国LDC4,柬埔寨KH	130	--Of synthetic fibres
				3.5	哥斯达黎加CR				
				8.8	巴基斯坦PK,秘鲁PE				
				12.3	亚太APTA				

序号 No.	税则号列 Tariff Line	货品名称	最惠国税率 MFN(%)	协定税率 Agreement(%)		特惠税率 S.P.(%)		普通税率 Gen.(%)	Article Description
4375	6104.4400	--人造纤维制	16	0 3.2 8 11.7	东盟ASEAN,智利CL,新加坡SG,新西兰NZ,香港HK,澳门MO 哥斯达黎加CR 巴基斯坦PK,秘鲁PE 亚太APTA	0	最不发达35国LDC35,最不发达4国LDC4,柬埔寨KH	130	--Of artificial fibres
4376	6104.4900	--其他纺织材料制	16	0 3.2 8 11.7	东盟ASEAN,智利CL,新加坡SG,新西兰NZ,香港HK,澳门MO 哥斯达黎加CR 巴基斯坦PK,秘鲁PE 亚太APTA	0	最不发达35国LDC35,最不发达4国LDC4,柬埔寨KH	130	--Of other textile materials
		-裙子及裙裤:							-Skirts and divided skirts:
4377	6104.5100	--羊毛或动物细毛制	14	0 2.8 7 10.8	东盟ASEAN,智利CL,新加坡SG,新西兰NZ,秘鲁PE,香港HK,澳门MO 哥斯达黎加CR 巴基斯坦PK 亚太APTA	0	最不发达35国LDC35	130	--Of wool or fine animal hair
4378	6104.5200	--棉制	14	0 2.8 7 10.3	东盟ASEAN,智利CL,新加坡SG,新西兰NZ,秘鲁PE,香港HK,澳门MO 哥斯达黎加CR 巴基斯坦PK 亚太APTA	0	最不发达35国LDC35,最不发达4国LDC4	90	--Of cotton
4379	6104.5300	--合成纤维制	16	0 3.2 8 11.7	东盟ASEAN,智利CL,新加坡SG,新西兰NZ,香港HK,澳门MO 哥斯达黎加CR 巴基斯坦PK,秘鲁PE 亚太APTA	0	最不发达35国LDC35,最不发达4国LDC4,柬埔寨KH	130	--Of synthetic fibres
4380	6104.5900	--其他纺织材料制	14	0 2.8 7 10.8	东盟ASEAN,智利CL,新加坡SG,新西兰NZ,秘鲁PE,香港HK,澳门MO 哥斯达黎加CR 巴基斯坦PK 亚太APTA	0	最不发达35国LDC35,最不发达4国LDC4,缅甸MM,老挝LA,柬埔寨KH	130	--Of other textile materials
		-长裤、护胸背带工装裤、马裤及短裤:							-Trousers, bib and brace overalls, breeches and shorts:
4381	6104.6100	--羊毛或动物细毛制	16	0 3.2 8 11.7	东盟ASEAN,智利CL,新加坡SG,新西兰NZ,香港HK,澳门MO 哥斯达黎加CR 巴基斯坦PK,秘鲁PE 亚太APTA	0	最不发达35国LDC35,最不发达4国LDC4	130	--Of wool or fine animal hair

序号 No.	税则号列 Tariff Line	货品名称	最惠国 税　率 MFN(%)	协定税率 Agreement(%)	特惠税率 S.P.(%)	普通 税率 Gen.(%)	Article Description
4382	6104.6200	--棉制	16	0 东盟ASEAN,智利CL,新加坡SG,新西兰NZ,香港HK,澳门MO 3.2 哥斯达黎加CR 8 巴基斯坦PK,秘鲁PE 13.6 亚太APTA	0 最不发达35国LDC35,最不发达4国LDC4 6.4 亚太2国APTA2	90	--Of cotton
4383	6104.6300	--合成纤维制	17.5	0 东盟ASEAN,智利CL,新加坡SG,新西兰NZ,香港HK,澳门MO 3.5 哥斯达黎加CR 8.8 巴基斯坦PK,秘鲁PE 12.3 亚太APTA	0 最不发达35国LDC35,最不发达4国LDC4	130	--Of synthetic fibres
4384	6104.6900	--其他纺织材料制	16	0 东盟ASEAN,智利CL,新加坡SG,新西兰NZ,香港HK,澳门MO 3.2 哥斯达黎加CR 8 巴基斯坦PK,秘鲁PE 12 亚太APTA	0 最不发达35国LDC35,最不发达4国LDC4,亚太2国APTA2	130	--Of other textile materials
	61.05	**针织或钩编的男衬衫:**					**Men's or boys' shirts, knitted or crocheted:**
4385	6105.1000	-棉制	16	0 东盟ASEAN,智利CL,新加坡SG,新西兰NZ,香港HK,澳门MO,台湾TW 3.2 哥斯达黎加CR 13.6 亚太APTA,巴基斯坦PK	0 最不发达35国LDC35,最不发达4国LDC4,缅甸MM,老挝LA,柬埔寨KH 11.2 亚太2国APTA2	90	-Of cotton
4386	6105.2000	-化学纤维制	17.5	0 东盟ASEAN,智利CL,新加坡SG,新西兰NZ,香港HK,澳门MO 3.5 哥斯达黎加CR 8.8 巴基斯坦PK,秘鲁PE 12.3 亚太APTA	0 最不发达35国LDC35,最不发达4国LDC4,亚太2国APTA2	130	-Of man-made fibres
4387	6105.9000	-其他纺织材料制	16	0 东盟ASEAN,智利CL,新加坡SG,新西兰NZ,香港HK,澳门MO 3.2 哥斯达黎加CR 8 巴基斯坦PK,秘鲁PE 11.7 亚太APTA	0 最不发达35国LDC35,最不发达4国LDC4,亚太2国APTA2	130	-Of other textile materials

序号 No.	税则号列 Tariff Line	货品名称	最惠国税率 MFN(%)	协定税率 Agreement(%)		特惠税率 S.P.(%)		普通税率 Gen.(%)	Article Description
	61.06	**针织或钩编的女衬衫:**							**Women's or girls' blouses, shirts and shirtblouses, knitted or crocheted:**
4388	6106.1000	-棉制	16	0	东盟ASEAN,智利CL,新加坡SG,新西兰NZ,香港HK,澳门MO	0	最不发达35国LDC35,最不发达4国LDC4,缅甸MM,老挝LA,柬埔寨KH	90	-Of cotton
				3.2	哥斯达黎加CR	6.4	亚太2国APTA2		
				8	巴基斯坦PK,秘鲁PE				
				13.6	亚太APTA				
4389	6106.2000	-化学纤维制	17.5	0	东盟ASEAN,智利CL,新加坡SG,新西兰NZ,香港HK,澳门MO	0	最不发达35国LDC35,最不发达4国LDC4,亚太2国APTA2	130	-Of man-made fibres
				3.5	哥斯达黎加CR				
				8.8	巴基斯坦PK,秘鲁PE				
				12.3	亚太APTA				
4390	6106.9000	-其他纺织材料制	16	0	东盟ASEAN,智利CL,新加坡SG,新西兰NZ,香港HK,澳门MO,台湾TW	0	最不发达35国LDC35,最不发达4国LDC4,亚太2国APTA2	130	-Of other textile materials
				3.2	哥斯达黎加CR				
				8	巴基斯坦PK,秘鲁PE				
				11.7	亚太APTA				
	61.07	**针织或钩编的男式内裤、三角裤、长睡衣、睡衣裤、浴衣、晨衣及类似品:**							**Men's or boys' underpants, briefe, night-shirts, pyjamas, bathrobes, dressing gowns and similar articles, knitted or crocheted:**
		-内裤及三角裤:							-Underpants and briefs:
4391	6107.1100	--棉制	14	0	东盟ASEAN,智利CL,新加坡SG,新西兰NZ,香港HK,澳门MO	0	最不发达35国LDC35,最不发达4国LDC4,缅甸MM,老挝LA,柬埔寨KH	90	--Of cotton
				2.8	哥斯达黎加CR	5.6	亚太2国APTA2		
				7	秘鲁PE				
				11.2	巴基斯坦PK				

序号 No.	税则号列 Tariff Line	货品名称	最惠国税率 MFN(%)	协定税率 Agreement(%)		特惠税率 S.P.(%)		普通税率 Gen.(%)	Article Description
4392	6107.1200	--化学纤维制	16	0	东盟ASEAN,智利CL,新加坡SG,新西兰NZ,香港HK,澳门MO	0	最不发达35国LDC35	130	--Of man-made fibres
				3.2	哥斯达黎加CR				
				8	巴基斯坦PK,秘鲁PE				
				10.9	亚太APTA				
		--其他纺织材料制:							--Of other textile materials:
4393	6107.1910	---丝及绢丝制	14	0	东盟ASEAN,智利CL,新加坡SG,新西兰NZ,秘鲁PE,香港HK,澳门MO	0	最不发达35国LDC35	130	---Of silk or silk waste
				2.8	哥斯达黎加CR				
				7	巴基斯坦PK				
				9.3	亚太APTA				
4394	6107.1990	---其他	14	0	东盟ASEAN,智利CL,新加坡SG,新西兰NZ,秘鲁PE,香港HK,澳门MO	0	最不发达35国LDC35	130	---Other
				2.8	哥斯达黎加CR				
				7	巴基斯坦PK				
				9.3	亚太APTA				
		-长睡衣及睡衣裤:							-Nightshirts and pyjamas:
4395	6107.2100	--棉制	14	0	东盟ASEAN,智利CL,新加坡SG,新西兰NZ,香港HK,澳门MO	0	最不发达35国LDC35,最不发达4国LDC4,缅甸MM,老挝LA,柬埔寨KH	90	--Of cotton
				2.8	哥斯达黎加CR	5.6	亚太2国APTA2		
				11.2	巴基斯坦PK				
4396	6107.2200	--化学纤维制	16	0	东盟ASEAN,智利CL,新加坡SG,新西兰NZ,香港HK,澳门MO	0	最不发达35国LDC35,最不发达4国LDC4,亚太2国APTA2	130	--Of man-made fibres
				3.2	哥斯达黎加CR				
				8	巴基斯坦PK,秘鲁PE				
				10.9	亚太APTA				
		--其他纺织材料制:							--Of other textile materials:
4397	6107.2910	---丝及绢丝制	14	0	东盟ASEAN,智利CL,新加坡SG,新西兰NZ,秘鲁PE,香港HK	0	最不发达35国LDC35,最不发达4国LDC4,亚太2国APTA2	130	---Of silk or silk waste
				2.8	哥斯达黎加CR				
				7	巴基斯坦PK				
				9.3	亚太APTA				

序号 No.	税则号列 Tariff Line	货品名称	最惠国税率 MFN(%)	协定税率 Agreement(%)		特惠税率 S.P.(%)		普通税率 Gen.(%)	Article Description
4398	6107.2990	---其他	14	0 2.8 7 9.3	东盟ASEAN,智利CL,新加坡SG,新西兰NZ,秘鲁PE,香港HK 哥斯达黎加CR 巴基斯坦PK 亚太APTA	0	最不发达35国LDC35,最不发达4国LDC4,亚太2国APTA2,缅甸MM,老挝LA,柬埔寨KH	130	---Other
		-其他:							-Other:
4399	6107.9100	--棉制	14	0 2.8 7	东盟ASEAN,智利CL,新加坡SG,新西兰NZ,秘鲁PE,香港HK 哥斯达黎加CR 巴基斯坦PK	0	最不发达35国LDC35	90	--Of cotton
		--其他纺织材料制:							--Of other textile materials:
4400	6107.9910	---化学纤维制	16	0 3.2 8 10.9	东盟ASEAN,智利CL,新加坡SG,新西兰NZ,香港HK 哥斯达黎加CR 巴基斯坦PK,秘鲁PE 亚太APTA	0	最不发达35国LDC35	130	---Of man-made fibres
4401	6107.9990	---其他	14	0 2.8 7 9.3	东盟ASEAN,智利CL,新加坡SG,新西兰NZ,秘鲁PE 哥斯达黎加CR 巴基斯坦PK 亚太APTA	0	最不发达35国LDC35	130	---Other
	61.08	**针织或钩编的女式长衬裙、衬裙、三角裤、短衬裤、睡衣、睡衣裤、浴衣、晨衣及类似品:**							**Women's or girls' slips, petticoats, briefs, panties, nightdresses, pyjamas, nègligès, bathrobes, dressing gowns and similar articles, knitted or crocheted:**
		-长衬裙及衬裙:							-Slips and petticoats:
4402	6108.1100	--化学纤维制	16	0 3.2 8 10.9	东盟ASEAN,智利CL,新加坡SG,新西兰NZ,香港HK 哥斯达黎加CR 巴基斯坦PK,秘鲁PE 亚太APTA	0	最不发达35国LDC35	130	--Of man-made fibres
		--其他纺织材料制:							--Of other textile materials:
4403	6108.1910	---棉制	14	0 2.8 7	东盟ASEAN,智利CL,新加坡SG,新西兰NZ,秘鲁PE,香港HK 哥斯达黎加CR 巴基斯坦PK	0	最不发达35国LDC35,最不发达4国LDC4	90	---Of cotton

序号 No.	税则号列 Tariff Line	货品名称	最惠国税率 MFN(%)	协定税率 Agreement(%)	特惠税率 S.P.(%)	普通税率 Gen.(%)	Article Description
4404	6108.1920	---丝及绢丝制	14	0 东盟ASEAN,智利CL,新加坡SG,新西兰NZ,秘鲁PE,香港HK 2.8 哥斯达黎加CR 7 巴基斯坦PK	0 最不发达35国LDC35	130	---Of silk or silk waste
4405	6108.1990	---其他	14	0 东盟ASEAN,智利CL,新加坡SG,新西兰NZ,秘鲁PE,香港HK 2.8 哥斯达黎加CR 7 巴基斯坦PK 9.3 亚太APTA	0 最不发达35国LDC35	130	---Other
		-三角裤及短衬裤:					-Briefs and panties:
4406	6108.2100	--棉制	14	0 东盟ASEAN,智利CL,新加坡SG,新西兰NZ,秘鲁PE,香港HK,澳门MO 2.8 哥斯达黎加CR 11.2 巴基斯坦PK	0 最不发达35国LDC35,最不发达4国LDC4,缅甸MM,老挝LA,柬埔寨KH	90	--Of cotton
4407	6108.2200	--化学纤维制	16	0 东盟ASEAN,智利CL,新加坡SG,新西兰NZ,香港HK,澳门MO 3.2 哥斯达黎加CR 8 巴基斯坦PK,秘鲁PE 10.9 亚太APTA	0 最不发达35国LDC35,最不发达4国LDC4	130	--Of man-made fibres
		--其他纺织材料制:					--Of other textile materials:
4408	6108.2910	---丝及绢丝制	14	0 东盟ASEAN,智利CL,新加坡SG,新西兰NZ,秘鲁PE,香港HK,澳门MO 2.8 哥斯达黎加CR 7 巴基斯坦PK 9.3 亚太APTA	0 最不发达35国LDC35	130	---Of silk or silk waste
4409	6108.2990	---其他	14	0 东盟ASEAN,智利CL,新加坡SG,新西兰NZ,秘鲁PE,香港HK,澳门MO 2.8 哥斯达黎加CR 7 巴基斯坦PK 9.3 亚太APTA	0 最不发达35国LDC35	130	---Other
		-睡衣及睡衣裤:					-Nightdresses and pyjamas:
4410	6108.3100	--棉制	14	0 东盟ASEAN,智利CL,新加坡SG,新西兰NZ,香港HK,澳门MO	0 最不发达35国LDC35,最不发达4国LDC4,缅甸MM,老挝LA,柬埔寨KH	90	--Of cotton

序号 No.	税则号列 Tariff Line	货品名称	最惠国税率 MFN(%)	协定税率 Agreement(%)		特惠税率 S.P.(%)		普通税率 Gen.(%)	Article Description
				2.8 7 11.2	哥斯达黎加CR 秘鲁PE 巴基斯坦PK	5.6	亚太2国APTA2		
4411	6108.3200	--化学纤维制	16	0 3.2 8 10.9	东盟ASEAN,智利CL,新加坡SG,新西兰NZ,香港HK,澳门MO 哥斯达黎加CR 巴基斯坦PK,秘鲁PE 亚太APTA	0	最不发达35国LDC35,最不发达4国LDC4,亚太2国APTA2	130	--Of man-made fibres
		--其他纺织材料制:							--Of other textile materials:
4412	6108.3910	---丝及绢丝制	14	0 2.8 7 9.3	东盟ASEAN,智利CL,新加坡SG,新西兰NZ,秘鲁PE,香港HK 哥斯达黎加CR 巴基斯坦PK 亚太APTA	0	最不发达35国LDC35,最不发达4国LDC4,亚太2国APTA2	130	---Of silk or silk waste
4413	6108.3990	---其他	14	0 2.8 7 9.3	东盟ASEAN,智利CL,新加坡SG,新西兰NZ,秘鲁PE,香港HK 哥斯达黎加CR 巴基斯坦PK 亚太APTA	0	最不发达35国LDC35,最不发达4国LDC4,亚太2国APTA2	130	---Other
		-其他:							-Other:
4414	6108.9100	--棉制	14	0 2.8 7 11.2	东盟ASEAN,智利CL,新加坡SG,新西兰NZ,香港HK,澳门MO 哥斯达黎加CR 秘鲁PE 巴基斯坦PK	0	最不发达35国LDC35,最不发达4国LDC4,缅甸MM,老挝LA,柬埔寨KH	90	--Of cotton
4415	6108.9200	--化学纤维制	16	0 3.2 8 10.9	东盟ASEAN,智利CL,新加坡SG,新西兰NZ,香港HK,澳门MO 哥斯达黎加CR 巴基斯坦PK,秘鲁PE 亚太APTA	0	最不发达35国LDC35,最不发达4国LDC4	130	--Of man-made fibres
4416	6108.9900	--其他纺织材料制	14	0 2.8 7 9.3	东盟ASEAN,智利CL,新加坡SG,新西兰NZ,秘鲁PE,香港HK,澳门MO 哥斯达黎加CR 巴基斯坦PK 亚太APTA	0	最不发达35国LDC35	130	--Of other textile materials

序号 No.	税则号列 Tariff Line	货品名称	最惠国税率 MFN(%)	协定税率 Agreement(%)	特惠税率 S.P.(%)	普通税率 Gen.(%)	Article Description
	61.09	**针织或钩编的T恤衫、汗衫及其他背心:**					**T-shirts, singlets and other vests, knitted or crocheted:**
4417	6109.1000	-棉制	14	0 东盟ASEAN,智利CL,新加坡SG,新西兰NZ,香港HK,澳门MO 2.8 哥斯达黎加CR 7 秘鲁PE 9.4 亚太APTA,巴基斯坦PK	0 最不发达35国LDC35,最不发达4国LDC4,缅甸MM,老挝LA,柬埔寨KH	90	-Of cotton
		-其他纺织材料制:					-Of other textile materials:
4418	6109.9010	---丝及绢丝制	14	0 东盟ASEAN,智利CL,新加坡SG,新西兰NZ,秘鲁PE,香港HK,澳门MO 2.8 哥斯达黎加CR 7 巴基斯坦PK 9.3 亚太APTA	0 最不发达35国LDC35,最不发达4国LDC4,亚太2国APTA2	130	---Of silk or silk waste
4419	6109.9090	---其他	14	0 东盟ASEAN,智利CL,新加坡SG,新西兰NZ,香港HK,澳门MO 2.8 哥斯达黎加CR 7 秘鲁PE 9.3 亚太APTA,巴基斯坦PK	0 最不发达35国LDC35,最不发达4国LDC4,亚太2国APTA2,缅甸MM,老挝LA,柬埔寨KH	130	---Other
	61.10	**针织或钩编的套头衫、开襟衫、背心及类似品:**					**Jerseys, pullovers, cardigans, waistcoats and similar articles, knitted or crocheted:**
		-羊毛或动物细毛制:					-Of wool or fine animal hair:
4420	6110.1100	--羊毛制	14	0 东盟ASEAN,智利CL,巴基斯坦PK,新加坡SG,新西兰NZ,香港HK,澳门MO,台湾TW 2.8 哥斯达黎加CR 7 秘鲁PE 9.3 亚太APTA	0 最不发达35国LDC35,最不发达4国LDC4,亚太2国APTA2,缅甸MM,老挝LA,柬埔寨KH	130	--Of wool

序号 No.	税则号列 Tariff Line	货品名称	最惠国税率 MFN(%)	协定税率 Agreement(%)		特惠税率 S.P.(%)		普通税率 Gen.(%)	Article Description
4421	6110.1200	--喀什米尔山羊细毛制	14	0 2.8 9.3	东盟ASEAN,智利CL,巴基斯坦PK,新加坡SG,新西兰NZ,秘鲁PE,香港HK,澳门MO 哥斯达黎加CR 亚太APTA	0	最不发达35国LDC35,最不发达4国LDC4	130	--Of kashmir (cashmere) goats
		--其他:							--Other:
4422	6110.1910	---其他山羊细毛制	14	0 2.8 9.3	东盟ASEAN,智利CL,巴基斯坦PK,新加坡SG,新西兰NZ,秘鲁PE,香港HK,澳门MO 哥斯达黎加CR 亚太APTA	0	最不发达35国LDC35,最不发达4国LDC4	130	---Of other goats
4423	6110.1920	---兔毛制	14	0 2.8 9.3	东盟ASEAN,智利CL,巴基斯坦PK,新加坡SG,新西兰NZ,秘鲁PE,香港HK,澳门MO 哥斯达黎加CR 亚太APTA	0	最不发达35国LDC35	130	---Of rabbit and hare
4424	6110.1990	---其他	14	0 2.8 7 9.3	东盟ASEAN,智利CL,巴基斯坦PK,新加坡SG,新西兰NZ,香港HK,澳门MO 哥斯达黎加CR 秘鲁PE 亚太APTA	0	最不发达35国LDC35,最不发达4国LDC4	130	---Other
4425	6110.2000	-棉制	14	0 2.8 7 11	东盟ASEAN,智利CL,巴基斯坦PK,新加坡SG,新西兰NZ,香港HK,澳门MO,台湾TW 哥斯达黎加CR 秘鲁PE 亚太APTA	0 5.6	最不发达35国LDC35,最不发达4国LDC4,缅甸MM,老挝LA,柬埔寨KH 亚太2国APTA2	90	-Of cotton
4426	6110.3000	-化学纤维制	16	0 3.2 8 10.9	东盟ASEAN,智利CL,巴基斯坦PK,新加坡SG,新西兰NZ,香港HK,澳门MO,台湾TW 哥斯达黎加CR 秘鲁PE 亚太APTA	0	最不发达35国LDC35,最不发达4国LDC4,亚太2国APTA2	130	-Of man-made fibres
		-其他纺织材料制:							-Of other textile materials:
4427	6110.9010	---丝及绢丝制	14	0 2.8 9.3	东盟ASEAN,智利CL,巴基斯坦PK,新加坡SG,新西兰NZ,秘鲁PE,香港HK,澳门MO 哥斯达黎加CR 亚太APTA	0	最不发达35国LDC35,最不发达4国LDC4,亚太2国APTA2	130	---Of silk or silk waste

序号 No.	税则号列 Tariff Line	货品名称	最惠国税率 MFN(%)	协定税率 Agreement(%)		特惠税率 S.P.(%)		普通税率 Gen.(%)	Article Description
4428	6110.9090	---其他	14	0 2.8 7 9.3	东盟ASEAN,智利CL,巴基斯坦PK,新加坡SG,新西兰NZ,香港HK,澳门MO 哥斯达黎加CR 秘鲁PE 亚太APTA	0	最不发达35国LDC35,最不发达4国LDC4,亚太2国APTA2	130	---Other
	61.11	**针织或钩编的婴儿服装及衣着附件:**							**Babies'garments and clothing accessories, knitted or crocheted:**
4429	6111.2000	-棉制	14	0 2.8 11.2	东盟ASEAN,智利CL,新加坡SG,新西兰NZ,秘鲁PE,香港HK,澳门MO 哥斯达黎加CR 巴基斯坦PK	0	最不发达35国LDC35,最不发达4国LDC4	90	-Of cotton
4430	6111.3000	-合成纤维制	16	0 3.2 8 10.9	东盟ASEAN,智利CL,新加坡SG,新西兰NZ,香港HK,澳门MO 哥斯达黎加CR 巴基斯坦PK,秘鲁PE 亚太APTA	0	最不发达35国LDC35,最不发达4国LDC4	130	-Of synthetic fibres
		-其他纺织材料制:							-Of other textile materials
4431	6111.9010	---羊毛或动物细毛制	14	0 2.8 7 9.3	东盟ASEAN,智利CL,新加坡SG,新西兰NZ,秘鲁PE,香港HK,澳门MO 哥斯达黎加CR 巴基斯坦PK 亚太APTA	0	最不发达35国LDC35,最不发达4国LDC4	130	---Of wool or fine animal hair
4432	6111.9090	---其他	14	0 2.8 7 9.3	东盟ASEAN,智利CL,新加坡SG,新西兰NZ,香港HK,澳门MO 哥斯达黎加CR 巴基斯坦PK,秘鲁PE 亚太APTA	0	最不发达35国LDC35	130	---Other
	61.12	**针织或钩编的运动服、滑雪服及游泳服:**							**Track suits, ski suits and swimwear, knitted or crocheted:**
		-运动服:							-track suits:
4433	6112.1100	--棉制	16	0 3.2 8 13.6	东盟ASEAN,智利CL,新加坡SG,新西兰NZ,香港HK,澳门MO 哥斯达黎加CR 巴基斯坦PK,秘鲁PE 亚太APTA	0	最不发达35国LDC35	90	--Of cotton
4434	6112.1200	--合成纤维制	17.5	0 3.5 8.8 12.3	东盟ASEAN,智利CL,新加坡SG,新西兰NZ,香港HK,澳门MO 哥斯达黎加CR 巴基斯坦PK,秘鲁PE 亚太APTA	0	最不发达35国LDC35,最不发达4国LDC4	130	--Of synthetic fibres

序号 No.	税则号列 Tariff Line	货品名称	最惠国税率 MFN(%)	协定税率 Agreement(%)		特惠税率 S.P.(%)		普通税率 Gen.(%)	Article Description
4435	6112.1900	--其他纺织材料制	16	0 3.2 8 11.7	东盟ASEAN,智利CL,新加坡SG,新西兰NZ,香港HK,澳门MO 哥斯达黎加CR 巴基斯坦PK,秘鲁PE 亚太APTA	0	最不发达35国LDC35	130	--Of other textile materials
		-滑雪服:							-Ski suits:
4436	6112.2010	---棉制	16	0 3.2 8 13.6	东盟ASEAN,智利CL,新加坡SG,新西兰NZ 哥斯达黎加CR 巴基斯坦PK,秘鲁PE 亚太APTA	0	最不发达35国LDC35,最不发达4国LDC4	90	---Of cotton
4437	6112.2090	---其他	19	0 3.8 9.5 13.6	东盟ASEAN,智利CL,新加坡SG,新西兰NZ 哥斯达黎加CR 巴基斯坦PK,秘鲁PE 亚太APTA	0	最不发达35国LDC35	130	---Other
		-男式游泳服:							-Men's or boys' swimwear:
4438	6112.3100	--合成纤维制	17.5	0 3.5 8.8 12.3	东盟ASEAN,智利CL,新加坡SG,新西兰NZ,香港HK 哥斯达黎加CR 巴基斯坦PK,秘鲁PE 亚太APTA	0	最不发达35国LDC35	130	--Of synthetic fibres
4439	6112.3900	--其他纺织材料制	16	0 3.2 8 11.7	东盟ASEAN,智利CL,新加坡SG,新西兰NZ,香港HK 哥斯达黎加CR 巴基斯坦PK,秘鲁PE 亚太APTA	0	最不发达35国LDC35	130	--Of other textile materials
		-女式游泳服:							-Women's or girls' swimwear:
4440	6112.4100	--合成纤维制	17.5	0 3.5 8.8 12.3	东盟ASEAN,智利CL,新加坡SG,新西兰NZ,香港HK,台湾TW 哥斯达黎加CR 巴基斯坦PK,秘鲁PE 亚太APTA	0	最不发达35国LDC35	130	--of synthetic fibres
4441	6112.4900	--其他纺织材料制	16	0 3.2 8 11.7	东盟ASEAN,智利CL,新加坡SG,新西兰NZ,香港HK 哥斯达黎加CR 巴基斯坦PK,秘鲁PE 亚太APTA	0	最不发达35国LDC35	130	--Of other textile materials
	61.13	**用税号59.03、59.06或59.07的针织物或钩编织物制成的服装:**							**Garments, made up of knitted or crocheted fabrics of heading No.59.03, 59.06 or 59.07:**

序号 No.	税则号列 Tariff Line	货品名称	最惠国税 率 MFN(%)	协定税率 Agreement(%)		特惠税率 S.P.(%)		普通税率 Gen.(%)	Article Description
4442	6113.0000	用税号 59.03、59.06 或 59.07 的针织物或钩编织物制成的服装	16	0 3.2 8 11.7	东盟ASEAN,智利CL,新加坡SG,新西兰NZ,香港HK,澳门MO 哥斯达黎加CR 巴基斯坦PK,秘鲁PE 亚太APTA	0	最不发达 35 国 LDC35,最不发达 4 国 LDC4,亚太 2 国 APTA2	130	Garments, made up of knitted or crocheted fabrics of heading No.59.03, 59.06 or 59.07
	61.14	**针织或钩编的其他服装:**							**Other garments, knitted or crocheted:**
4443	6114.2000	-棉制	16	0 3.2 12.8	东盟ASEAN,智利CL,新加坡SG,新西兰NZ,香港HK,澳门MO 哥斯达黎加CR 巴基斯坦PK	0 6.4	最不发达 35 国 LDC35,最不发达 4 国 LDC4 亚太 2 国 APTA2	90	-Of cotton
4444	6114.3000	-化学纤维制	17.5	0 3.5 8.8 14	东盟ASEAN,智利CL,新加坡SG,新西兰NZ,香港HK,澳门MO 哥斯达黎加CR 秘鲁PE 巴基斯坦PK	0	最不发达 35 国 LDC35,最不发达 4 国 LDC4	130	-Of man-made fibres
		-其他纺织材料制:							-Of other textile materials:
4445	6114.9010	---羊毛或动物细毛制	16	0 3.2 8 12.8	东盟ASEAN,智利CL,新加坡SG,新西兰NZ,香港HK 哥斯达黎加CR 秘鲁PE 巴基斯坦PK	0	最不发达 35 国 LDC35	130	---Of wool or fine animal hair
4446	6114.9090	---其他	16	0 3.2 8 12.8	东盟ASEAN,智利CL,新加坡SG,新西兰NZ,香港HK 哥斯达黎加CR 秘鲁PE 巴基斯坦PK	0	最不发达 35 国 LDC35	130	---Other
	61.15	**针织或钩编的连裤袜、紧身裤袜、长统袜、短袜及其他袜类,包括用以治疗静脉曲张的长统袜和无外绱鞋底的鞋类:**							**Panty hose, tights, stockings, socks and other hosiery, including stockings for varicose veins and footwear without applied soles, knitted or crocheted:**
4447	6115.1000	-渐紧压袜类(例如,用以治疗静脉曲张的长统袜)	16	0 3.2 8 9.3	东盟ASEAN,智利CL,新加坡SG,新西兰NZ,香港HK 哥斯达黎加CR 巴基斯坦PK,秘鲁PE 亚太APTA	0	最不发达 35 国 LDC35	130	-Stockings, gradually press tighted (including stockings for varicose veins and footwear without applied soles)
		-其他连裤袜及紧身裤袜:							-Other panty hose and tights:

序号 No.	税则号列 Tariff Line	货品名称	最惠国税率 MFN(%)	协定税率 Agreement(%)		特惠税率 S.P.(%)		普通税率 Gen.(%)	Article Description
4448	6115.2100	--每根单丝细度在67分特以下的合成纤维制	16	0 3.2 8 12.8 14.4	东盟ASEAN,智利CL,新加坡SG,新西兰NZ,香港HK,澳门MO 哥斯达黎加CR 秘鲁PE 巴基斯坦PK 亚太APTA	0	最不发达35国LDC35	130	--Of synthetic fibres, measuring per single yarn less than 67 decitex
4449	6115.2200	--每根单丝细度在67分特及以上的合成纤维制	16	0 3.2 8 10.9	东盟ASEAN,智利CL,新加坡SG,新西兰NZ,澳门MO,台湾TW 哥斯达黎加CR 巴基斯坦PK,秘鲁PE 亚太APTA	0	最不发达35国LDC35	130	--Of synthetic fibres, measuring per single yarn 67 decitex or more
		--其他纺织材料制:							--Of other textile materials:
4450	6115.2910	---棉制	14	0 2.8 11.2	东盟ASEAN,智利CL,新加坡SG,新西兰NZ,秘鲁PE,澳门MO 哥斯达黎加CR 巴基斯坦PK	0	最不发达35国LDC35,最不发达4国LDC4	90	---cotton
4451	6115.2990	---其他	14	0 2.8 7 9.3	东盟ASEAN,智利CL,新加坡SG,新西兰NZ,秘鲁PE,澳门MO,台湾TW 哥斯达黎加CR 巴基斯坦PK 亚太APTA	0	最不发达35国LDC35	130	---Other
4452	6115.3000	-女式长统袜及中统袜，每根单丝细度在67分特以下	14	0 2.8 7 9.3	东盟ASEAN,智利CL,新加坡SG,新西兰NZ,秘鲁PE 哥斯达黎加CR 巴基斯坦PK 亚太APTA	0	最不发达35国LDC35,最不发达4国LDC4,亚太2国APTA2	130	-Women's full-length or knee-length hosiery, measuring per single yarn less than 67 decitex
		-其他:							-Other:
4453	6115.9400	--羊毛或动物细毛制	14	0 2.8 11.2	东盟ASEAN,智利CL,新加坡SG,新西兰NZ,秘鲁PE,香港HK 哥斯达黎加CR 巴基斯坦PK	0	最不发达35国LDC35	130	--Of wool or fine animal hair
4454	6115.9500	--棉制	14	0 2.8 7 11.2	东盟ASEAN,智利CL,新加坡SG,新西兰NZ,香港HK 哥斯达黎加CR 秘鲁PE 巴基斯坦PK	0	最不发达35国LDC35,最不发达4国LDC4	90	--Of cotton
4455	6115.9600	--合成纤维制	16	0 3.2 8 10.9	东盟ASEAN,智利CL,新加坡SG,新西兰NZ,香港HK 哥斯达黎加CR 巴基斯坦PK,秘鲁PE 亚太APTA	0	最不发达35国LDC35,最不发达4国LDC4	130	--Of synthetic fibres

序号 No.	税则号列 Tariff Line	货品名称	最惠国税率 MFN(%)	协定税率 Agreement(%)		特惠税率 S.P.(%)		普通税率 Gen.(%)	Article Description
4456	6115.9900	--其他纺织材料制	14	0 2.8 7 9.3	东盟ASEAN,智利CL,新加坡SG,新西兰NZ,秘鲁PE,香港HK,台湾TW 哥斯达黎加CR 巴基斯坦PK 亚太APTA	0	最不发达35国LDC35	130	--Of other textile materials
	61.16	**针织或钩编的分指手套、连指手套及露指手套:**							**Gloves, mittens and mitts, knitted or crocheted:**
4457	6116.1000	-用塑料或橡胶浸渍、涂布或包覆的	14	0 2.8	东盟ASEAN,智利CL,新加坡SG,新西兰NZ,秘鲁PE,香港HK 哥斯达黎加CR	0	最不发达35国LDC35,最不发达4国LDC4	130	-Gloves impregnated, coated or covered with plastics or rubber
		-其他:							-Other:
4458	6116.9100	--羊毛或动物细毛制	14	0 2.8 7	东盟ASEAN,智利CL,新加坡SG,新西兰NZ,秘鲁PE,香港HK 哥斯达黎加CR 巴基斯坦PK	0	最不发达35国LDC35,最不发达4国LDC4	130	--Of wool of fine animal hair
4459	6116.9200	--棉制	14	0 2.8	东盟ASEAN,智利CL,新加坡SG,新西兰NZ,秘鲁PE,香港HK,澳门MO 哥斯达黎加CR	0	最不发达35国LDC35	90	--Of cotton
4460	6116.9300	--合成纤维制	16	0 3.2 8 10.9	东盟ASEAN,智利CL,新加坡SG,新西兰NZ,香港HK,澳门MO 哥斯达黎加CR 巴基斯坦PK,秘鲁PE 亚太APTA	0	最不发达35国LDC35,最不发达4国LDC4	130	--Of synthetic fibres
4461	6116.9900	--其他纺织材料制	14	0 2.8 7 9.3	东盟ASEAN,智利CL,新加坡SG,新西兰NZ,香港HK 哥斯达黎加CR 秘鲁PE 亚太APTA,巴基斯坦PK	0	最不发达35国LDC35,最不发达4国LDC4	130	--Of other textile materials
	61.17	**其他制成的针织或钩编的衣着附件;服装或衣着附件的针织或钩编的零件:**							**Other made up clothing accessories, knitted or crocheted; knitted or crocheted parts of garments or of clothing accessories:**
		-披巾、头巾、围巾、披纱、面纱及类似品:							-Shawls, scarves, mufflers, mantillas, veils and the like:
		---动物细毛制:							---Of fine animal hair:
4462	6117.1011	----山羊绒制	14	0 2.8 7 9.3	东盟ASEAN,智利CL,巴基斯坦PK,新加坡SG,新西兰NZ,香港HK 哥斯达黎加CR 秘鲁PE 亚太APTA	0	最不发达35国LDC35,最不发达4国LDC4	130	----Of cashmere

序号 No.	税则号列 Tariff Line	货品名称	最惠国税率 MFN(%)	协定税率 Agreement(%)		特惠税率 S.P.(%)		普通税率 Gen.(%)	Article Description
4463	6117.1019	----其他	14	0 2.8 7 9.3	东盟ASEAN,智利CL,巴基斯坦PK,新加坡SG,新西兰NZ,香港HK 哥斯达黎加CR 秘鲁PE 亚太APTA	0	最不发达35国LDC35,最不发达4国LDC4	130	----Other
4464	6117.1020	---羊毛制	14	0 2.8 7 9.3	东盟ASEAN,智利CL,巴基斯坦PK,新加坡SG,新西兰NZ,香港HK 哥斯达黎加CR 秘鲁PE 亚太APTA	0	最不发达35国LDC35,最不发达4国LDC4	130	---Of wool
4465	6117.1090	---其他	14	0 2.8 7 9.3	东盟ASEAN,智利CL,巴基斯坦PK,新加坡SG,新西兰NZ,香港HK 哥斯达黎加CR 秘鲁PE 亚太APTA	0	最不发达35国LDC35,最不发达4国LDC4	130	---Other
		-其他附件:							-Other accessories:
4466	6117.8010	---领带及领结	14	0 2.8 9.3	东盟ASEAN,智利CL,巴基斯坦PK,新加坡SG,新西兰NZ,秘鲁PE,香港HK,台湾TW 哥斯达黎加CR 亚太APTA	0	最不发达35国LDC35,最不发达4国LDC4	130	---Ties, bow ties and cravats
4467	6117.8090	---其他	14	0 2.8 7 9.3	东盟ASEAN,智利CL,巴基斯坦PK,新加坡SG,新西兰NZ,香港HK,台湾TW 哥斯达黎加CR 秘鲁PE 亚太APTA	0	最不发达35国LDC35,最不发达4国LDC4	130	---Other
4468	6117.9000	-零件	14	0 2.8 7	东盟ASEAN,智利CL,巴基斯坦PK,新加坡SG,新西兰NZ,秘鲁PE,香港HK,澳门MO,台湾TW 哥斯达黎加CR 亚太APTA	0	最不发达35国LDC35,最不发达4国LDC4	130	-Parts

第六十二章
非针织或非钩编的服装及衣着附件

Chapter 62
Articles of apparel and clothing accessories，not knitted or crocheted

注释:

一、本章仅适用于除絮胎以外任何纺织物的制成品，但不适用于针织品或钩编织品（税号 62.12 的除外）。

二、本章不包括：

（一）税号 63.09 的旧衣着或其他旧物品；

（二）矫形器具、外科手术带、疝气带及类似品（税号 90.21）。

三、税号 62.03 及 62.04 所称：

（一）“西服套装”，是指面料用相同的织物制成的两件套或三件套的下列成套服装：

一件人体上半身穿着的外套或短上衣，除袖子外，其面料数为四片或四片以上；也可附带一件西服背心，这件背心的前片面料应与套装其他各件的面料相同，后片料则应与外套或短上衣的衬里料相同；

以及一件人体下半身穿着的服装，即不带背带或护胸的长裤、马裤、短裤（游泳裤除外）、裙子或裙裤。

西服套装各件面料质地、颜色及构成必须相同，其款式也必须相同，尺寸大小还须相互般配，但可以用不同织物滚边（缝口上缝入长条织物）。

如果数件人体下半身穿着的服装同时进口或出口（例如，两条长裤、长裤与短裤、裙子或裙裤与长裤），构成西服套装下装的应是一条长裤，而对于女式西服套装，则应是一条裙子或裙裤，其他服装应分别归类。

所称“西服套装”，包括不论是否完全符合上述条件的下列配套服装：

Notes:

1. This Chapter applies only to made up articles of any textile fabric other than wadding，excluding knitted or rocheted articles (other than those of heading No.62.12).

2. This Chapter does not cover:

(a) Worn clothing or other worn articles of heading No.63. 09; or

(b) Orthopaedic appliances，surgical belts，trusses or the like (heading No.90.21).

3. For the purposes of headings Nos.62.03 and 62.04:

(a) The term“suit”means a set of garments composed of two or three pieces made up in respect of their outer surface, in identical fabric and comprising:

-one suit coat or jacket the outer shell of which, exclusive of sleeves，consists of four or more panels，designed to cover the upper part of the body，possibly with a tailored waistcoat in addition whose front panel is made from the same fabric as the lining of the suit coat or jacket; and

-one garment designed to cover the lower part of the body and consisting of trousers，breeches or shorts (other than swimwear)，a skirt or a divided skirt，having neither braces nor bibs.

All of the components of a “suit” must be of the same fabric construction，colour and composition; they must also be of the same style and of corresponding or compatible size. However，these components may have piping (a strip of fabric sewn into the seam) in a different fabric.

If several separate components to cover the lower part of the body are presented together（for example，two pairs of trousers or trousers and shorts，or a skirt or divided skirt and trousers），the constituent lower part shall be the trousers，or，in the case of women’s or girls’suits，the skirt or divided skirt，the other garments being considered separately.

The term “suit” includes the following sets of garments，whether or not they fulfil all the above conditions:

1. 常礼服，由一件后襟下垂并下端开圆弧形叉的素色短上衣和一条条纹长裤组成；

2. 晚礼服（燕尾服），一般用黑色织物制成，上衣前襟较短且不闭合，背后有燕尾；

3. 无燕尾套装夜礼服，其中上衣款式与普通上衣相似（可以更为显露衬衣前胸），但有光滑丝质或仿丝质的翻领。

（二）“便服套装”，是指面料相同并作零售包装的下列成套服装（西服套装及税号 62.07 或 62.08 的物品除外）：

一件人体上半身穿着的服装，但背心除外，因为背心可作为内衣；

以及一件或两件不同的人体下半身穿着的服装，即长裤、护胸背带工装裤、马裤、短裤（泳裤除外）、裙子或裙裤。

便服套装各件面料质地、款式、颜色及构成必须相同；尺寸大小也须相互般配。所称“便服套装”，不包括税号 62.11 的运动服及滑雪服。

四、对于税号 62.09:

（一）所称“婴儿服装及衣着附件”，是指用于身高不超过 86 厘米幼儿的服装；

（二）既可归入税号 62.09，也可归入本章其他税号的物品，应归入税号 62.09；

五、既可归入税号 62.10，也可归入本章其他税号的服装，除税号 62.09 所列的仍归入该税号外，其余的应一律归入税号 62.10。

六、税号 62.11 所称“滑雪服”，是指从整个外观和织物质地来看，主要在滑雪（速度滑雪和高山滑雪）时穿着的下列服装或成套服装：

(1) morning dress，comprising a plain jacket (cutaway) with rounded tails hanging well down at the back and striped trousers;

(2) evening dress（tailcoat），generally made of black cloth，the jacket of which is relatively short at the front，does not close and has narrow skirts cut in at the hips and hanging down behind;

(3) dinner jacket suits，in which the jacket is similar in style to an ordinary jacket（though perhaps revealing more of the shirt front），but has shiny silk or imitation silk lapels.

(b) The term“ensemble”means a set of garments (other than suits and articles of heading No.62.07 or 62.08) composed of several pieces made up in identical fabric，put up for retail sale，and comprising:

-one garment designed to cover the upper part of the body，with the exception of waistcoats which may also form a second upper garment，and

-one or two different garments，designed to cover the lower part of the body and consisting of trousers，bib and brace overalls，breeches，shorts（other than swimwear），a skirt or a divided skirt.

All of the components of an ensemble must be of the same fabric construction，style，colour and composition; they also must be of corresponding or compatible size. The term“ensemble”does not apply to track suits or ski suits，of heading No. 62.11.

4. For the purposes of heading No.62.09:

(a) The expression“babies' garments and clothing accessories”means articles for young children of a body height not exceeding 86cm;

(b) Articles which are，*prima facie*，classifiable both in heading No.62.09 and in other headings of this Chapter are to be classified in heading No.62.09.

5. Garments which are，*prima facie*，classifiable both in heading No.62.10 and in other headings of this Chapter，excluding heading No. 62. 09，are to be classified in heading No.62.10.

6. For the purposes of heading No.62.11，“ski suits”means garments or sets of garments which，by their general appearance and texture，are identifiable as intended to be worn principally for skiing (cross-country or alpine). They consist either of:

（一）“滑雪连身服”，即上下身连在一起的单件服装；除袖子和领子外，滑雪连身服可有口袋或脚带；或

（二）“滑雪套装”，即由两件或三件构成一套并作零售包装的下列服装：

一件用一条拉链扣合的带风帽的厚夹克、防风衣、防风短上衣或类似的服装，可以附带一件背心；

以及一条不论是否过腰的长裤、一条马裤或一条护胸背带工装裤。

“滑雪套装”也可由一件类似以上（一）款所述的连身服和一件可套在连身服外面的有胎料背心组成。

“滑雪套装”各件颜色可以不同，但面料质地、款式及构成必须相同；尺寸大小也须相互般配。

七、正方形或近似正方形的围巾及围巾式样的物品，如果每边均不超过 60 厘米，应作为手帕归类（税号 62.13）。任何一边超过 60 厘米的手帕，应归入税号 62.14。

八、本章的服装，凡门襟为左压右的，应视为男式；右压左的，应视为女式。但本规定不适用于其式样已明显为男式或女式的服装。无法区别是男式还是女式的服装，应按女式服装归入有关税号。

九、本章物品可用金属线制成。

(a) a“ski overall”, that is, a one-piece garment designed to cover the upper and the lower parts of the body; in addition to sleeves and a collar the ski overall may have pockets or footstraps; or

(b) a “ski ensemble”, that is, a set of garments composed of two or three pieces, put up for retail sale and comprising:

-one garment such as an anorak, wind-cheater, wind-jacket or similar article, closed by a slide fastener (zipper), possibly with a waistcoat in addition, and

-one pair of trousers whether or not extending above waist-level, one pair of breeches or one bib and brace overall.

The “ski ensemble” may also consist of an overall similar to the one mentioned in paragraph (a) above and a type of padded, sleeveless jacket worn over the overall.

All the components of a“ski ensemble”must be made up in a fabric of the same texture, style and composition whether or not of the same colour; they also must be of corresponding or compatible size.

7. Scarves and articles of the scarf type, square or approximately square, of which no side exceeds 60cm, are to be classified as handkerchiefs (heading No.62.13). Handkerchiefs of which any side exceeds 60cm are to be classified in heading No.62.14.

8. Garments of this Chapter designed for left over right closure at the front shall be regarded as men's or boys' garments, and those designed for right over left closure at the front as women's or girls' garments. These provisions do not apply where the cut of the garment clearly indicates that it is designed for other of sexes.

Garments which cannot be identified as either men's or boys' garments or as women's or girls' garments are to be classified in the headings concerning women s or girls garments.

9. Articles of this chapter may be made of metal thread.

序号 No.	税则号列 Tariff Line	货品名称	最惠国税率 MFN(%)	协定税率 Agreement(%)	特惠税率 S.P.(%)	普通税率 Gen.(%)	Article Description
	62.01	**男式大衣、短大衣、斗篷、短斗篷、带风帽的防寒短上衣（包括滑雪短上衣）、防风衣、防风短上衣及类似品，但税号62.03的货品除外:**					**Men's or boys' overcoats, car-coats, capes, cloaks, anoraks (including skijackets), wind-cheaters, wind-jackets and similar articles, other than those of heading No.62.03:**
		-大衣、雨衣、短大衣、斗篷、短斗篷及类似品:					-Overcoats, raincoats, car-coats, capes, cloaks and similar articles:
4469	6201.1100	--羊毛或动物细毛制	16	0 东盟ASEAN,智利CL,新加坡SG,新西兰NZ,香港HK,澳门MO 3.2 哥斯达黎加CR 8 巴基斯坦PK,秘鲁PE 11.7 亚太APTA	0 最不发达35国LDC35,最不发达4国LDC4	130	--Of wool or fine animal hair
		--棉制:					--Of cotton:
4470	6201.1210	---羽绒服	16	0 东盟ASEAN,智利CL,新加坡SG,新西兰NZ,香港HK,澳门MO 3.2 哥斯达黎加CR 8 秘鲁PE 12.8 巴基斯坦PK	0 最不发达35国LDC35	90	---Padded with feathers or down
4471	6201.1290	---其他	16	0 东盟ASEAN,智利CL,新加坡SG,新西兰NZ,香港HK,澳门MO 3.2 哥斯达黎加CR 8 秘鲁PE 12.8 巴基斯坦PK	0 最不发达35国LDC35,最不发达4国LDC4	90	---Other
		--化学纤维制:					--Of man-made fibres:
4472	6201.1310	---羽绒服	17.5	0 东盟ASEAN,智利CL,新加坡SG,新西兰NZ,香港HK,澳门MO 3.5 哥斯达黎加CR 8.8 巴基斯坦PK,秘鲁PE 12.3 亚太APTA	0 最不发达35国LDC35,最不发达4国LDC4	130	---Padded with feathers or down
4473	6201.1390	---其他	17.5	0 东盟ASEAN,智利CL,新加坡SG,新西兰NZ,香港HK,澳门MO 3.5 哥斯达黎加CR 8.8 巴基斯坦PK,秘鲁PE 12.3 亚太APTA	0 最不发达35国LDC35,最不发达4国LDC4	130	---Other
4474	6201.1900	--其他纺织材料制	16	0 东盟ASEAN,智利CL,新加坡SG,新西兰NZ,香港HK,澳门MO 3.2 哥斯达黎加CR 8 巴基斯坦PK,秘鲁PE 11.7 亚太APTA	0 最不发达35国LDC35,最不发达4国LDC4	100	--Of other textile materials
		-其他:					-Other:

序号 No.	税则号列 Tariff Line	货品名称	最惠国税率 MFN(%)	协定税率 Agreement(%)		特惠税率 S.P.(%)		普通税率 Gen.(%)	Article Description
4475	6201.9100	--羊毛或动物细毛制	16	0 3.2 8 11.7	东盟ASEAN,智利CL,新加坡SG,新西兰NZ,香港HK,澳门MO 哥斯达黎加CR 巴基斯坦PK,秘鲁PE 亚太APTA	0	最不发达35国LDC35,最不发达4国LDC4	130	--Of wool or fine animal hair
		--棉制:							--Of cotton:
4476	6201.9210	---羽绒服	16	0 3.2 8 12.8	东盟ASEAN,智利CL,新加坡SG,新西兰NZ,香港HK,澳门MO 哥斯达黎加CR 秘鲁PE 巴基斯坦PK	0	最不发达35国LDC35,最不发达4国LDC4	90	---Padded with feathers or down
4477	6201.9290	---其他	16	0 3.2 8 12.8	东盟ASEAN,智利CL,新加坡SG,新西兰NZ,香港HK,澳门MO 哥斯达黎加CR 秘鲁PE 巴基斯坦PK	0	最不发达35国LDC35,最不发达4国LDC4,缅甸MM,老挝LA,柬埔寨KH	90	---Other
		--化学纤维制:							--Of man-made fibres:
4478	6201.9310	---羽绒服	17.5	0 3.5 8.8 12.3	东盟ASEAN,智利CL,新加坡SG,新西兰NZ,香港HK,澳门MO 哥斯达黎加CR 巴基斯坦PK,秘鲁PE 亚太APTA	0	最不发达35国LDC35,最不发达4国LDC4	130	---Padded with feathers or down
4479	6201.9390	---其他	17.5	0 3.5 8.8 12.3	东盟ASEAN,智利CL,新加坡SG,新西兰NZ,香港HK,澳门MO 哥斯达黎加CR 巴基斯坦PK,秘鲁PE 亚太APTA	0	最不发达35国LDC35,最不发达4国LDC4	130	---Other
4480	6201.9900	--其他纺织材料制	16	0 3.2 8 11.7	东盟ASEAN,智利CL,新加坡SG,新西兰NZ,香港HK,澳门MO 哥斯达黎加CR 巴基斯坦PK,秘鲁PE 亚太APTA	0	最不发达35国LDC35,最不发达4国LDC4,缅甸MM	100	--Of other textile materials
	62.02	**女式大衣、短大衣、斗篷、短斗篷、带风帽的防寒短上衣(包括滑雪短上衣)、防风衣、防风短上衣及类似品，但税号62.04的货品除外:**							**Women's or girls' overcoats, car-coats, capes, cloaks, anoraks (including skijackets), wind-cheaters, wind-jackets and similar articles, other than those of heading No.62.04:**
		-大衣、雨衣、短大衣、斗篷、短斗篷及类似品:							-Overcoats, raincoats, car-coats, capes, cloaks and similar articles:

序号 No.	税则号列 Tariff Line	货品名称	最惠国税率 MFN(%)	协定税率 Agreement(%)		特惠税率 S.P.(%)		普通税率 Gen.(%)	Article Description
4481	6202.1100	--羊毛或动物细毛制	16	0 3.2 8 11.7	东盟ASEAN,智利CL,新加坡SG,新西兰NZ,香港HK,澳门MO 哥斯达黎加CR 巴基斯坦PK,秘鲁PE 亚太APTA	0	最不发达35国LDC35,最不发达4国LDC4	130	--Of wool or fine animal hair
		--棉制:							--Of cotton:
4482	6202.1210	---羽绒服	16	0 3.2 8 12.8	东盟ASEAN,智利CL,新加坡SG,新西兰NZ,香港HK,澳门MO 哥斯达黎加CR 秘鲁PE 巴基斯坦PK	0	最不发达35国LDC35	90	---Padded with feathers or down
4483	6202.1290	---其他	16	0 3.2 8 12.8	东盟ASEAN,智利CL,新加坡SG,新西兰NZ,香港HK,澳门MO 哥斯达黎加CR 秘鲁PE 巴基斯坦PK	0	最不发达35国LDC35,最不发达4国LDC4	90	---Other
		--化学纤维制:							--Of man-made fibres:
4484	6202.1310	---羽绒服	19	0 3.8 9.5 13.6	东盟ASEAN,智利CL,新加坡SG,新西兰NZ,香港HK,澳门MO 哥斯达黎加CR 巴基斯坦PK,秘鲁PE 亚太APTA	0	最不发达35国LDC35,最不发达4国LDC4	130	---Padded with feathers or down
4485	6202.1390	---其他	19	0 3.8 9.5 13.6	东盟ASEAN,智利CL,新加坡SG,新西兰NZ,香港HK,澳门MO 哥斯达黎加CR 巴基斯坦PK,秘鲁PE 亚太APTA	0	最不发达35国LDC35,最不发达4国LDC4	130	---Other
4486	6202.1900	--其他纺织材料制	16	0 3.2 8 11.7	东盟ASEAN,智利CL,新加坡SG,新西兰NZ,香港HK,澳门MO 哥斯达黎加CR 巴基斯坦PK,秘鲁PE 亚太APTA	0	最不发达35国LDC35,最不发达4国LDC4	100	--Of other textile materials
		-其他:							-Other:
4487	6202.9100	--羊毛或动物细毛制	16	0 3.2 8 11.7	东盟ASEAN,智利CL,新加坡SG,新西兰NZ,香港HK,澳门MO 哥斯达黎加CR 巴基斯坦PK,秘鲁PE 亚太APTA	0	最不发达35国LDC35	130	--Of wool or fine animal hair
		--棉制:							--Of cotton:
4488	6202.9210	---羽绒服	16	0 3.2 8 12.8	东盟ASEAN,智利CL,新加坡SG,新西兰NZ,香港HK,澳门MO 哥斯达黎加CR 秘鲁PE 巴基斯坦PK	0	最不发达35国LDC35	90	---Padded with feathers or down

序号 No.	税则号列 Tariff Line	货品名称	最惠国税率 MFN(%)	协定税率 Agreement(%)		特惠税率 S.P.(%)		普通税率 Gen.(%)	Article Description
4489	6202.9290	---其他	16	0 3.2 8 12.8	东盟ASEAN,智利CL,新加坡SG,新西兰NZ,香港HK,澳门MO 哥斯达黎加CR 秘鲁PE 巴基斯坦PK	0	最不发达35国LDC35,最不发达4国LDC4	90	---Other
		--化学纤维制:							--Of man-made fibres:
4490	6202.9310	---羽绒服	17.5	0 3.5 8.8 12.3	东盟ASEAN,智利CL,新加坡SG,新西兰NZ,香港HK,澳门MO 哥斯达黎加CR 巴基斯坦PK,秘鲁PE 亚太APTA	0	最不发达35国LDC35,最不发达4国LDC4	130	---Padded with feathers or down
4491	6202.9390	---其他	17.5	0 3.5 8.8 12.3	东盟ASEAN,智利CL,新加坡SG,新西兰NZ,香港HK,澳门MO 哥斯达黎加CR 巴基斯坦PK,秘鲁PE 亚太APTA	0	最不发达35国LDC35,最不发达4国LDC4	130	---Other
4492	6202.9900	--其他纺织材料制	16	0 3.2 8 11.7	东盟ASEAN,智利CL,新加坡SG,新西兰NZ,香港HK,澳门MO 哥斯达黎加CR 巴基斯坦PK,秘鲁PE 亚太APTA	0	最不发达35国LDC35,最不发达4国LDC4	100	--Of other textile materials
	62.03	**男式西服套装、便服套装、上衣、长裤、护胸背带工装裤、马裤及短裤(游泳裤除外):**							**Men's or boys' suits, ensembles, jackets, blazers, trousers, bib and brace overalls, breeches and shorts (other than swim wear):**
		-西服套装:							-Suits:
4493	6203.1100	--羊毛或动物细毛制	17.5	0 3.5 8.8 12.3	东盟ASEAN,智利CL,新加坡SG,新西兰NZ,香港HK,澳门MO 哥斯达黎加CR 巴基斯坦PK,秘鲁PE 亚太APTA	0	最不发达35国LDC35,最不发达4国LDC4	130	--Of wool or fine animal hair
4494	6203.1200	--合成纤维制	17.5	0 3.5 8.8 12.3	东盟ASEAN,智利CL,新加坡SG,新西兰NZ,香港HK,澳门MO 哥斯达黎加CR 巴基斯坦PK,秘鲁PE 亚太APTA	0	最不发达35国LDC35,最不发达4国LDC4	130	--Of synthetic fibres
		--其他纺织材料制:							--Of other textile materials:
4495	6203.1910	---丝及绢丝制	17.5	0 3.5 8.8 12.3	东盟ASEAN,智利CL,新加坡SG,新西兰NZ,香港HK,澳门MO 哥斯达黎加CR 巴基斯坦PK,秘鲁PE 亚太APTA	0	最不发达35国LDC35	100	---Of silk or silk waste

序号 No.	税则号列 Tariff Line	货品名称	最惠国税率 MFN(%)	协定税率 Agreement(%)		特惠税率 S.P.(%)		普通税率 Gen.(%)	Article Description
4496	6203.1990	---其他	17.5	0 3.5 8.8 12.3	东盟ASEAN,智利CL,新加坡SG,新西兰NZ,香港HK,澳门MO 哥斯达黎加CR 巴基斯坦PK,秘鲁PE 亚太APTA	0	最不发达35国LDC35	100	---Other
		-便服套装:							-Ensembles:
4497	6203.2200	--棉制	17.5	0 3.5 8.8 14	东盟ASEAN,智利CL,新加坡SG,新西兰NZ,香港HK,澳门MO 哥斯达黎加CR 秘鲁PE 巴基斯坦PK	0	最不发达35国LDC35,最不发达4国LDC4	90	--Of cotton
4498	6203.2300	--合成纤维制	17.5	0 3.5 8.8 12.3	东盟ASEAN,智利CL,新加坡SG,新西兰NZ,香港HK,澳门MO 哥斯达黎加CR 巴基斯坦PK,秘鲁PE 亚太APTA	0	最不发达35国LDC35,最不发达4国LDC4	130	--Of synthetic fibres
		--其他纺织材料制:							--Of other textile materials:
4499	6203.2910	---丝及绢丝制	17.5	0 3.5 8.8 12.3	东盟ASEAN,智利CL,新加坡SG,新西兰NZ,澳门MO 哥斯达黎加CR 巴基斯坦PK,秘鲁PE 亚太APTA	0	最不发达35国LDC35	130	---Of silk or silk waste
4500	6203.2920	---羊毛或动物细毛制	17.5	0 3.5 8.8 12.3	东盟ASEAN,智利CL,新加坡SG,新西兰NZ,香港HK,澳门MO 哥斯达黎加CR 巴基斯坦PK,秘鲁PE 亚太APTA	0	最不发达35国LDC35	130	---Of wool or fine animal hair
4501	6203.2990	---其他	17.5	0 3.5 8.8 12.3	东盟ASEAN,智利CL,新加坡SG,新西兰NZ,香港HK,澳门MO 哥斯达黎加CR 巴基斯坦PK,秘鲁PE 亚太APTA	0	最不发达35国LDC35	100	---Other
		-上衣:							-Jackets and blazers:
4502	6203.3100	--羊毛或动物细毛制	16	0 3.2 8 11.7	东盟ASEAN,智利CL,新加坡SG,新西兰NZ,香港HK,澳门MO 哥斯达黎加CR 巴基斯坦PK,秘鲁PE 亚太APTA	0 9.6	最不发达35国LDC35,最不发达4国LDC4,缅甸MM,老挝LA,柬埔寨KH 亚太2国APTA2	130	--Of wool or fine animal hair

序号 No.	税则号列 Tariff Line	货品名称	最惠国税率 MFN(%)	协定税率 Agreement(%)		特惠税率 S.P.(%)		普通税率 Gen.(%)	Article Description
4503	6203.3200	--棉制	16	0 3.2 8 12.8 14.4	东盟ASEAN,智利CL,新加坡SG,新西兰NZ,香港HK,澳门MO 哥斯达黎加CR 秘鲁PE 巴基斯坦PK 亚太APTA	0 11.2	最不发达35国LDC35,最不发达4国LDC4,缅甸MM,老挝LA,柬埔寨KH 亚太2国APTA2	90	--Of cotton
4504	6203.3300	--合成纤维制	17.5	0 3.5 8.8 12.3	东盟ASEAN,智利CL,新加坡SG,新西兰NZ,香港HK,澳门MO 哥斯达黎加CR 巴基斯坦PK,秘鲁PE 亚太APTA	0	最不发达35国LDC35,最不发达4国LDC4	130	--Of synthetic fibres
		--其他纺织材料制:							--Of other textile materials:
4505	6203.3910	---丝及绢丝制	16	0 3.2 8 11.7	东盟ASEAN,智利CL,新加坡SG,新西兰NZ,香港HK,澳门MO 哥斯达黎加CR 巴基斯坦PK,秘鲁PE 亚太APTA	0 9.6	最不发达35国LDC35,最不发达4国LDC4 亚太2国APTA2	130	---Of silk or silk waste
4506	6203.3990	---其他	16	0 3.2 8 11.7	东盟ASEAN,智利CL,新加坡SG,新西兰NZ,香港HK,澳门MO 哥斯达黎加CR 巴基斯坦PK,秘鲁PE 亚太APTA	0 9.6	最不发达35国LDC35,最不发达4国LDC4 亚太2国APTA2	100	---Other
		-长裤、护胸背带工装裤、马裤及短裤:							-Trousers, bib and brace overalls, breeches and shorts:
4507	6203.4100	--羊毛或动物细毛制	16	0 3.2 8 11.7	东盟ASEAN,智利CL,新加坡SG,新西兰NZ,香港HK,澳门MO 哥斯达黎加CR 巴基斯坦PK,秘鲁PE 亚太APTA	0	最不发达35国LDC35,最不发达4国LDC4,亚太2国APTA2	130	--Of wool or fine animal hair
		--棉制:							--Of cotton:

序号 No.	税则号列 Tariff Line	货品名称	最惠国税率 MFN(%)	协定税率 Agreement(%)		特惠税率 S.P.(%)		普通税率 Gen.(%)	Article Description
4508	6203.4210	---阿拉伯裤	16	0 3.2 8 12.9	东盟ASEAN,智利CL,新加坡SG,新西兰NZ,香港HK,澳门MO 哥斯达黎加CR 巴基斯坦PK,秘鲁PE 亚太APTA	0 11.2	最不发达35国LDC35 亚太2国APTA2	90	---Arabian trousers
4509	6203.4290	---其他	16	0 3.2 8 12.9	东盟ASEAN,智利CL,新加坡SG,新西兰NZ,香港HK,澳门MO 哥斯达黎加CR 巴基斯坦PK,秘鲁PE 亚太APTA	0 11.2	最不发达35国LDC35,最不发达4国LDC4,缅甸MM,老挝LA,柬埔寨KH 亚太2国APTA2	90	---Other
		--合成纤维制:							--Of synthetic fibres:
4510	6203.4310	---阿拉伯裤	17.5	0 3.5 8.8 13.1	东盟ASEAN,智利CL,新加坡SG,新西兰NZ,香港HK,澳门MO 哥斯达黎加CR 巴基斯坦PK,秘鲁PE 亚太APTA	0	最不发达35国LDC35	130	---Arabian trousers
4511	6203.4390	---其他	17.5	0 3.5 8.8 13.1	东盟ASEAN,智利CL,新加坡SG,新西兰NZ,香港HK,澳门MO 哥斯达黎加CR 巴基斯坦PK,秘鲁PE 亚太APTA	0	最不发达35国LDC35,最不发达4国LDC4	130	---Other
		--其他纺织材料制:							--Of other textile materials:
4512	6203.4910	---阿拉伯裤	16	0 3.2 8 11.7	东盟ASEAN,智利CL,新加坡SG,新西兰NZ,香港HK,澳门MO 哥斯达黎加CR 巴基斯坦PK,秘鲁PE 亚太APTA	0	最不发达35国LDC35,最不发达4国LDC4,亚太2国APTA2	100	---Arabian trousers
4513	6203.4990	---其他	16	0 3.2 8 11.7	东盟ASEAN,智利CL,新加坡SG,新西兰NZ,香港HK,澳门MO 哥斯达黎加CR 巴基斯坦PK,秘鲁PE 亚太APTA	0	最不发达35国LDC35,最不发达4国LDC4,亚太2国APTA2	100	---Other

序号 No.	税则号列 Tariff Line	货品名称	最惠国税率 MFN(%)	协定税率 Agreement(%)		特惠税率 S.P.(%)		普通税率 Gen.(%)	Article Description
	62.04	**女式西服套装、便服套装、上衣、连衣裙、裙子、裙裤、长裤、护胸背带工装裤、马裤及短裤（游泳服除外）：**							**Women's or girls'suits, ensembles, jackets, blazers dresses, skirts, divided skirts, trousers, bib and brace overalls, breeches and shorts (other than swimwear):**
		-西服套装:							-Suits:
4514	6204.1100	--羊毛或动物细毛制	17.5	0 3.5 8.8 12.3	东盟ASEAN,智利CL,新加坡SG,新西兰NZ,香港HK,澳门MO 哥斯达黎加CR 巴基斯坦PK,秘鲁PE 亚太APTA	0	最不发达35国LDC35	130	--Of wool or fine animal hair
4515	6204.1200	--棉制	17.5	0 3.5 8.8 14	东盟ASEAN,智利CL,新加坡SG,新西兰NZ,香港HK,澳门MO 哥斯达黎加CR 秘鲁PE 巴基斯坦PK	0	最不发达35国LDC35	90	--Of cotton
4516	6204.1300	--合成纤维制	17.5	0 3.5 8.8 12.3	东盟ASEAN,智利CL,新加坡SG,新西兰NZ,香港HK,澳门MO 哥斯达黎加CR 巴基斯坦PK,秘鲁PE 亚太APTA	0	最不发达35国LDC35	130	--Of synthetic fibres
		--其他纺织材料制:							--Of other textile materials:
4517	6204.1910	---丝及绢丝制	17.5	0 3.5 8.8 12.3	东盟ASEAN,智利CL,新加坡SG,新西兰NZ,香港HK,澳门MO 哥斯达黎加CR 巴基斯坦PK,秘鲁PE 亚太APTA	0	最不发达35国LDC35	100	---Of silk or silk waste
4518	6204.1990	---其他	17.5	0 3.5 8.8 12.3	东盟ASEAN,智利CL,新加坡SG,新西兰NZ,香港HK,澳门MO 哥斯达黎加CR 巴基斯坦PK,秘鲁PE 亚太APTA	0	最不发达35国LDC35	100	---Other
		-便服套装:							-Ensembles:
4519	6204.2100	--羊毛或动物细毛制	17.5	0 3.5 8.8 12.3	东盟ASEAN,智利CL,新加坡SG,新西兰NZ,香港HK,澳门MO 哥斯达黎加CR 巴基斯坦PK,秘鲁PE 亚太APTA	0	最不发达35国LDC35	130	--Of wool or fine animal hair
4520	6204.2200	--棉制	17.5	0 3.5 8.8 14	东盟ASEAN,智利CL,新加坡SG,新西兰NZ,香港HK,澳门MO 哥斯达黎加CR 秘鲁PE 巴基斯坦PK	0	最不发达35国LDC35	90	--Of cotton

序号 No.	税则号列 Tariff Line	货品名称	最惠国税率 MFN(%)	协定税率 Agreement(%)		特惠税率 S.P.(%)		普通税率 Gen.(%)	Article Description
4521	6204.2300	--合成纤维制	20	0	东盟ASEAN,智利CL,新加坡SG,新西兰NZ,香港HK,澳门MO	0	最不发达35国LDC35	130	--Of synthetic fibres
				4	哥斯达黎加CR				
				10	巴基斯坦PK,秘鲁PE				
				13.8	亚太APTA				
		--其他纺织材料制:							--Of other textile materials:
4522	6204.2910	---丝及绢丝制	20	0	东盟ASEAN,智利CL,新加坡SG,新西兰NZ,澳门MO	0	最不发达35国LDC35	130	---Of silk or silk waste
				4	哥斯达黎加CR				
				10	巴基斯坦PK,秘鲁PE				
				13.8	亚太APTA				
4523	6204.2990	---其他	14	0	东盟ASEAN,智利CL,新加坡SG,新西兰NZ,秘鲁PE,香港HK,澳门MO	0	最不发达35国LDC35	100	---Other
				2.8	哥斯达黎加CR				
				7	巴基斯坦PK				
				9.9	亚太APTA				
		-上衣:							-Jackets and blazers:
4524	6204.3100	--羊毛或动物细毛制	16	0	东盟ASEAN,智利CL,新加坡SG,新西兰NZ,香港HK,澳门MO	0	最不发达35国LDC35,最不发达4国LDC4	130	--Of wool or fine animal hair
				3.2	哥斯达黎加CR				
				8	巴基斯坦PK,秘鲁PE				
				11.7	亚太APTA				
4525	6204.3200	--棉制	16	0	东盟ASEAN,智利CL,新加坡SG,新西兰NZ,香港HK,澳门MO	0	最不发达35国LDC35,最不发达4国LDC4,缅甸MM,老挝LA,柬埔寨KH	90	--Of cotton
				3.2	哥斯达黎加CR	6.4	亚太2国APTA2		
				8	秘鲁PE				
				12.8	巴基斯坦PK				
4526	6204.3300	--合成纤维制	17.5	0	东盟ASEAN,智利CL,新加坡SG,新西兰NZ,香港HK,澳门MO	0	最不发达35国LDC35,最不发达4国LDC4,亚太2国APTA2	130	--Of synthetic fibres
				3.5	哥斯达黎加CR				
				8.8	巴基斯坦PK,秘鲁PE				
				12.3	亚太APTA				
		--其他纺织材料制:							--Of other textile materials:

序号 No.	税则号列 Tariff Line	货品名称	最惠国税率 MFN(%)	协定税率 Agreement(%)		特惠税率 S.P.(%)		普通税率 Gen.(%)	Article Description
4527	6204.3910	---丝及绢丝制	16	0 3.2 8 11.7	东盟ASEAN,智利CL,新加坡SG,新西兰NZ,香港HK,澳门MO 哥斯达黎加CR 巴基斯坦PK,秘鲁PE 亚太APTA	0	最不发达35国LDC35,最不发达4国LDC4,亚太2国APTA2	130	---Of silk or silk waste
4528	6204.3990	---其他	16	0 3.2 8 11.7	东盟ASEAN,智利CL,新加坡SG,新西兰NZ,香港HK,澳门MO 哥斯达黎加CR 巴基斯坦PK,秘鲁PE 亚太APTA	0	最不发达35国LDC35,最不发达4国LDC4,亚太2国APTA2	100	---Other
		-连衣裙:							-Dresses:
4529	6204.4100	--羊毛或动物细毛制	16	0 3.2 8 11.7	东盟ASEAN,智利CL,新加坡SG,新西兰NZ,香港HK,澳门MO 哥斯达黎加CR 巴基斯坦PK,秘鲁PE 亚太APTA	0	最不发达35国LDC35,最不发达4国LDC4	130	--Of wool or fine animal hair
4530	6204.4200	--棉制	16	0 3.2 8 12.8	东盟ASEAN,智利CL,新加坡SG,新西兰NZ,香港HK,澳门MO 哥斯达黎加CR 秘鲁PE 巴基斯坦PK	0	最不发达35国LDC35,最不发达4国LDC4,缅甸MM,老挝LA,柬埔寨KH	90	--Of cotton
4531	6204.4300	--合成纤维制	17.5	0 3.5 8.8 12.3	东盟ASEAN,智利CL,新加坡SG,新西兰NZ,香港HK,澳门MO 哥斯达黎加CR 巴基斯坦PK,秘鲁PE 亚太APTA	0	最不发达35国LDC35,最不发达4国LDC4	130	--Of synthetic fibres
4532	6204.4400	--人造纤维制	16	0 3.2 8 11.7	东盟ASEAN,智利CL,新加坡SG,新西兰NZ,香港HK,澳门MO 哥斯达黎加CR 巴基斯坦PK,秘鲁PE 亚太APTA	0	最不发达35国LDC35,最不发达4国LDC4	130	--Of artificial fibres
		--其他纺织材料制:							--Of other textile materials:
4533	6204.4910	---丝及绢丝制	16	0 3.2 8 11.7	东盟ASEAN,智利CL,新加坡SG,新西兰NZ,香港HK,澳门MO 哥斯达黎加CR 巴基斯坦PK,秘鲁PE 亚太APTA	0	最不发达35国LDC35,最不发达4国LDC4	130	---Of silk or silk waste

序号 No.	税则号列 Tariff Line	货品名称	最惠国税率 MFN(%)	协定税率 Agreement(%)		特惠税率 S.P.(%)		普通税率 Gen.(%)	Article Description
4534	6204.4990	---其他	16	0 3.2 8 11.7	东盟ASEAN,智利CL,新加坡SG,新西兰NZ,香港HK,澳门MO 哥斯达黎加CR 巴基斯坦PK,秘鲁PE 亚太APTA	0	最不发达35国LDC35,最不发达4国LDC4	100	---Other
		-裙子及裙裤:							-Skirts and divided skirts:
4535	6204.5100	--羊毛或动物细毛制	14	0 2.8 7 9.3	东盟ASEAN,智利CL,新加坡SG,新西兰NZ,秘鲁PE,香港HK,澳门MO 哥斯达黎加CR 巴基斯坦PK 亚太APTA	0	最不发达35国LDC35,最不发达4国LDC4	130	--Of wool or fine animal hair
4536	6204.5200	--棉制	14	0 2.8 11.2	东盟ASEAN,智利CL,新加坡SG,新西兰NZ,秘鲁PE,香港HK,澳门MO 哥斯达黎加CR 巴基斯坦PK	0	最不发达35国LDC35,最不发达4国LDC4	90	--Of cotton
4537	6204.5300	--合成纤维制	16	0 3.2 8 11.7	东盟ASEAN,智利CL,新加坡SG,新西兰NZ,香港HK,澳门MO 哥斯达黎加CR 巴基斯坦PK,秘鲁PE 亚太APTA	0	最不发达35国LDC35,最不发达4国LDC4	130	--Of synthetic fibres
		--其他纺织材料制:							--Of other textile materials:
4538	6204.5910	---丝及绢丝制	14	0 2.8 7 9.3	东盟ASEAN,智利CL,新加坡SG,新西兰NZ,秘鲁PE,香港HK,澳门MO 哥斯达黎加CR 巴基斯坦PK 亚太APTA	0	最不发达35国LDC35,最不发达4国LDC4	130	---Of silk or silk waste
4539	6204.5990	---其他	14	0 2.8 7 9.3	东盟ASEAN,智利CL,新加坡SG,新西兰NZ,香港HK,澳门MO 哥斯达黎加CR 巴基斯坦PK,秘鲁PE 亚太APTA	0	最不发达35国LDC35,最不发达4国LDC4	100	---Other
		-长裤、护胸背带工装裤、马裤及短裤:							-Trousers, bib and brace overalls, breeches and shorts:
4540	6204.6100	--羊毛或动物细毛制	16	0 3.2 8 11.7	东盟ASEAN,智利CL,新加坡SG,新西兰NZ,香港HK,澳门MO 哥斯达黎加CR 巴基斯坦PK,秘鲁PE 亚太APTA	0	最不发达35国LDC35,最不发达4国LDC4	130	--Of wool or fine animal hair

序号 No.	税则号列 Tariff Line	货品名称	最惠国税率 MFN(%)	协定税率 Agreement(%)		特惠税率 S.P.(%)		普通税率 Gen.(%)	Article Description
4541	6204.6200	--棉制	16	0	东盟ASEAN,智利CL,新加坡SG,新西兰NZ,香港HK,澳门MO	0	最不发达35国LDC35,最不发达4国LDC4,缅甸MM,老挝LA,柬埔寨KH	90	--Of cotton
				3.2	哥斯达黎加CR	11.2	亚太2国APTA2		
				8	秘鲁PE				
				12.8	巴基斯坦PK				
				14.4	亚太APTA				
4542	6204.6300	--合成纤维制	17.5	0	东盟ASEAN,智利CL,新加坡SG,新西兰NZ,香港HK,澳门MO	0	最不发达35国LDC35,最不发达4国LDC4	130	--Of synthetic fibres
				3.5	哥斯达黎加CR				
				8.8	巴基斯坦PK,秘鲁PE				
				12.3	亚太APTA				
4543	6204.6900	--其他纺织材料制	16	0	东盟ASEAN,智利CL,新加坡SG,新西兰NZ,香港HK,澳门MO	0	最不发达35国LDC35,最不发达4国LDC4	100	--Of other textile materials
				3.2	哥斯达黎加CR				
				8	巴基斯坦PK,秘鲁PE				
				12	亚太APTA				
	62.05	**男衬衫:**							**Men's or boys' shirts:**
4544	6205.2000	-棉制	16	0	东盟ASEAN,智利CL,新加坡SG,新西兰NZ,香港HK,澳门MO	0	最不发达35国LDC35,最不发达4国LDC4,缅甸MM,老挝LA,柬埔寨KH	90	-Of cotton
				3.2	哥斯达黎加CR	6.4	亚太2国APTA2		
				8	亚太APTA,巴基斯坦PK,秘鲁PE				
4545	6205.3000	-化学纤维制	16	0	东盟ASEAN,智利CL,新加坡SG,新西兰NZ,香港HK,澳门MO	0	最不发达35国LDC35,最不发达4国LDC4,亚太2国APTA2	130	-Of man-made fibres
				3.2	哥斯达黎加CR				
				8	巴基斯坦PK,秘鲁PE				
				11.7	亚太APTA				
4546	6205.9010	---丝及绢丝制	16	0	东盟ASEAN,智利CL,新加坡SG,新西兰NZ,香港HK,澳门MO	0	最不发达35国LDC35,最不发达4国LDC4,亚太2国APTA2	130	---Of silk or silk waste
				3.2	哥斯达黎加CR				
				8	巴基斯坦PK,秘鲁PE				
				11.7	亚太APTA				

序号 No.	税则号列 Tariff Line	货品名称	最惠国税率 MFN(%)	协定税率 Agreement(%)		特惠税率 S.P.(%)		普通税率 Gen.(%)	Article Description
4547	6205.9020	---羊毛或动物细毛制	16	0 3.2 8 11.7	东盟ASEAN,智利CL,新加坡SG,新西兰NZ,香港HK,澳门MO 哥斯达黎加CR 巴基斯坦PK,秘鲁PE 亚太APTA	0	最不发达35国LDC35,最不发达4国LDC4,亚太2国APTA2	100	---Of wool or fine animal hair
4548	6205.9090	---其他	16	0 3.2 8 11.7	东盟ASEAN,智利CL,新加坡SG,新西兰NZ,香港HK,澳门MO 哥斯达黎加CR 巴基斯坦PK,秘鲁PE 亚太APTA	0	最不发达35国LDC35,最不发达4国LDC4,亚太2国APTA2	100	---Other
	62.06	**女衬衫:**							**Women's or girls' blouses, shirts and shirtblouses:**
4549	6206.1000	-丝及绢丝制	16	0 3.2 8 11.7	东盟ASEAN,智利CL,新加坡SG,新西兰NZ,香港HK,澳门MO 哥斯达黎加CR 巴基斯坦PK,秘鲁PE 亚太APTA	0	最不发达35国LDC35,最不发达4国LDC4	130	-Of silk or silk waste
4550	6206.2000	-羊毛或动物细毛制	16	0 3.2 8 11.7	东盟ASEAN,智利CL,新加坡SG,新西兰NZ,香港HK,澳门MO 哥斯达黎加CR 巴基斯坦PK,秘鲁PE 亚太APTA	0	最不发达35国LDC35	130	-Of wool or fine animal hair
4551	6206.3000	-棉制	16	0 3.2 8 13.6	东盟ASEAN,智利CL,新加坡SG,新西兰NZ,香港HK,澳门MO 哥斯达黎加CR 巴基斯坦PK,秘鲁PE 亚太APTA	0 6.4	最不发达35国LDC35,最不发达4国LDC4,缅甸MM,老挝LA,柬埔寨KH 亚太2国APTA2	90	-Of cotton
4552	6206.4000	-化学纤维制	17.5	0 3.5 8.8 12.3	东盟ASEAN,智利CL,新加坡SG,新西兰NZ,香港HK,澳门MO 哥斯达黎加CR 巴基斯坦PK,秘鲁PE 亚太APTA	0	最不发达35国LDC35,最不发达4国LDC4	130	-Of man-made fibres

序号 No.	税则号列 Tariff Line	货品名称	最惠国税率 MFN(%)	协定税率 Agreement(%)		特惠税率 S.P.(%)		普通税率 Gen.(%)	Article Description
4553	6206.9000	-其他纺织材料制	16	0 3.2 8 11.7	东盟ASEAN,智利CL,新加坡SG,新西兰NZ,香港HK,澳门MO 哥斯达黎加CR 巴基斯坦PK,秘鲁PE 亚太APTA	0	最不发达35国LDC35,最不发达4国LDC4,亚太2国APTA2	100	-Of other textile materials
	62.07	**男式背心及其他内衣、内裤、三角裤、长睡衣、睡衣裤、浴衣、晨衣及类似品:**							**Men's or boys' singlets and other vests, underpants, briefs, nightshirts, pyjamas, bathrobes, dressing gowns and similar articles:**
		-内裤及三角裤:							-Underpants and briefs:
4554	6207.1100	--棉制	14	0 2.8 7 10.3	东盟ASEAN,智利CL,新加坡SG,新西兰NZ,香港HK,澳门MO 哥斯达黎加CR 巴基斯坦PK,秘鲁PE 亚太APTA	0	最不发达35国LDC35,最不发达4国LDC4	90	--Of cotton
		--其他纺织材料制:							--Of other textile materials:
4555	6207.1910	---丝及绢丝制	14	0 2.8 7	东盟ASEAN,智利CL,新加坡SG,新西兰NZ,秘鲁PE,香港HK,澳门MO 哥斯达黎加CR 巴基斯坦PK	0	最不发达35国LDC35	130	---Of silk or silk waste
4556	6207.1920	---化学纤维制	16	0 3.2 8 12.8	东盟ASEAN,智利CL,新加坡SG,新西兰NZ,香港HK,澳门MO 哥斯达黎加CR 秘鲁PE 巴基斯坦PK	0	最不发达35国LDC35	130	---Of man-made fibres
4557	6207.1990	---其他	14	0 2.8 7	东盟ASEAN,智利CL,新加坡SG,新西兰NZ,秘鲁PE,香港HK,澳门MO 哥斯达黎加CR 巴基斯坦PK	0	最不发达35国LDC35	100	---Other
		-长睡衣及睡衣裤:							-Nightshirts and pyjamas:
4558	6207.2100	--棉制	14	0 2.8 11.2	东盟ASEAN,智利CL,新加坡SG,新西兰NZ,秘鲁PE,香港HK,澳门MO 哥斯达黎加CR 巴基斯坦PK	0	最不发达35国LDC35,最不发达4国LDC4,缅甸MM,老挝LA,柬埔寨KH	90	--Of cotton

序号 No.	税则号列 Tariff Line	货品名称	最惠国税率 MFN(%)	协定税率 Agreement(%)		特惠税率 S.P.(%)		普通税率 Gen.(%)	Article Description
4559	6207.2200	--化学纤维制	16	0 3.2 8 12.8	东盟ASEAN,智利CL,新加坡SG,新西兰NZ,香港HK,澳门MO 哥斯达黎加CR 秘鲁PE 巴基斯坦PK	0	最不发达35国LDC35	130	--Of man-made fibres
		--其他纺织材料制:							--Of other textile materials:
4560	6207.2910	---丝及绢丝制	14	0 2.8 7	东盟ASEAN,智利CL,新加坡SG,新西兰NZ,秘鲁PE 哥斯达黎加CR 巴基斯坦PK	0	最不发达35国LDC35	130	---Of silk or silk waste
4561	6207.2990	---其他	14	0 2.8 7	东盟ASEAN,智利CL,新加坡SG,新西兰NZ,秘鲁PE 哥斯达黎加CR 巴基斯坦PK	0	最不发达35国LDC35,最不发达4国LDC4,缅甸MM,老挝LA,柬埔寨KH	100	---Other
		-其他:							-Other:
4562	6207.9100	--棉制	14	0 2.8 11.2	东盟ASEAN,智利CL,新加坡SG,新西兰NZ,秘鲁PE,香港HK,澳门MO 哥斯达黎加CR 巴基斯坦PK	0	最不发达35国LDC35,最不发达4国LDC4	90	--Of cotton
		-其他纺织材料制:							--Of other textile materials:
4563	6207.9910	---丝及绢丝制	14	0 2.8 7 12.6	东盟ASEAN,智利CL,新加坡SG,新西兰NZ,秘鲁PE,香港HK,澳门MO 哥斯达黎加CR 巴基斯坦PK 亚太APTA	0	最不发达35国LDC35	130	---Of silk or silk waste
4564	6207.9920	---化学纤维制	16	0 3.2 8 12.8	东盟ASEAN,智利CL,新加坡SG,新西兰NZ,香港HK,澳门MO 哥斯达黎加CR 秘鲁PE 巴基斯坦PK	0	最不发达35国LDC35,最不发达4国LDC4	130	---Of man-made fibres
4565	6207.9990	---其他	14	0 2.8 7 12.6	东盟ASEAN,智利CL,新加坡SG,新西兰NZ,秘鲁PE,香港HK,澳门MO 哥斯达黎加CR 巴基斯坦PK 亚太APTA	0	最不发达35国LDC35,最不发达4国LDC4	100	---Other

序号 No.	税则号列 Tariff Line	货品名称	最惠国 税率 MFN(%)	协定税率 Agreement(%)		特惠税率 S.P.(%)		普通 税率 Gen.(%)	Article Description
	62.08	**女式背心及其他内衣、长衬裙、衬裙、三角裤、短衬裤、睡衣、睡衣裤、浴衣、晨衣及类似品:**							**Women's or girls' singlets and other vests, slips, petticoats, briefs, panties, nightdresses, pyjamas, nègligès, bathrobes, dressing gowns and similar articles:**
		-长衬裙及衬裙:							-Slips and petticoats:
4566	6208.1100	--化学纤维制	16	0 3.2 8 12.8	东盟ASEAN,智利CL,新加坡SG,新西兰NZ,香港HK 哥斯达黎加CR 秘鲁PE 巴基斯坦PK	0	最不发达 35 国 LDC35	130	--Of man-made fibresr
		--其他纺织材料制:							--Of other textile materials:
4567	6208.1910	---丝及绢丝制	14	0 2.8 7	东盟ASEAN,智利CL,新加坡SG,新西兰NZ,秘鲁PE,香港HK 哥斯达黎加CR 巴基斯坦PK	0	最不发达 35 国 LDC35	130	---Of silk or silk waste
4568	6208.1920	---棉制	14	0 2.8 7	东盟ASEAN,智利CL,新加坡SG,新西兰NZ,秘鲁PE,香港HK 哥斯达黎加CR 巴基斯坦PK	0	最不发达 35 国 LDC35,最不发达 4 国 LDC4	90	---Of cotton
4569	6208.1990	---其他	14	0 2.8 7	东盟ASEAN,智利CL,新加坡SG,新西兰NZ,秘鲁PE,香港HK 哥斯达黎加CR 巴基斯坦PK	0	最不发达 35 国 LDC35	100	---Other
		-睡衣及睡衣裤:							-Nightdresses and pyjamas:
4570	6208.2100	--棉制	14	0 2.8 7 10.3	东盟ASEAN,智利CL,新加坡SG,新西兰NZ,秘鲁PE,香港HK,澳门MO 哥斯达黎加CR 巴基斯坦PK 亚太APTA	0	最不发达 35 国 LDC35,最不发达 4 国 LDC4,缅甸MM,老挝LA,柬埔寨KH	90	--Of cotton
4571	6208.2200	--化学纤维制	16	0 3.2 8 12.8	东盟ASEAN,智利CL,新加坡SG,新西兰NZ,香港HK,澳门MO 哥斯达黎加CR 秘鲁PE 巴基斯坦PK	0	最不发达 35 国 LDC35,最不发达 4 国 LDC4,缅甸MM,老挝LA,柬埔寨KH	130	--Of man-made fibres

序号 No.	税则号列 Tariff Line	货品名称	最惠国税率 MFN(%)	协定税率 Agreement(%)		特惠税率 S.P.(%)		普通税率 Gen.(%)	Article Description
		--其他纺织材料制:							--Of other textile materials:
4572	6208.2910	---丝及绢丝制	14	0 2.8 7	东盟ASEAN,智利CL,新加坡SG,新西兰NZ,秘鲁PE,香港HK 哥斯达黎加CR 巴基斯坦PK	0	最不发达35国LDC35	130	---Of silk or silk waste
4573	6208.2990	---其他	14	0 2.8 7	东盟ASEAN,智利CL,新加坡SG,新西兰NZ,秘鲁PE,香港HK 哥斯达黎加CR 巴基斯坦PK	0	最不发达35国LDC35	100	---Other
		-其他:							-Other:
4574	6208.9100	--棉制	14	0 2.8 7 11.2	东盟ASEAN,智利CL,新加坡SG,新西兰NZ,香港HK,澳门MO 哥斯达黎加CR 秘鲁PE 巴基斯坦PK	0	最不发达35国LDC35,最不发达4国LDC4,缅甸MM,老挝LA,柬埔寨KH	90	--Of cotton
4575	6208.9200	--化学纤维制	16	0 3.2 8 12.8	东盟ASEAN,智利CL,新加坡SG,新西兰NZ,香港HK,澳门MO,台湾TW 哥斯达黎加CR 秘鲁PE 巴基斯坦PK	0	最不发达35国LDC35,最不发达4国LDC4,缅甸MM,老挝LA,柬埔寨KH	130	--Of man-made fibres
		--其他纺织材料制:							--Of other textile materials:
4576	6208.9910	---丝及绢丝制	14	0 2.8 7 12.6	东盟ASEAN,智利CL,新加坡SG,新西兰NZ,秘鲁PE,香港HK,澳门MO 哥斯达黎加CR 巴基斯坦PK 亚太APTA	0	最不发达35国LDC35	130	---Of silk or silk waste
4577	6208.9990	---其他	14	0 2.8 7 12.6	东盟ASEAN,智利CL,新加坡SG,新西兰NZ,秘鲁PE,香港HK,澳门MO 哥斯达黎加CR 巴基斯坦PK 亚太APTA	0	最不发达35国LDC35,最不发达4国LDC4	100	---Other
	62.09	**婴儿服装及衣着附件:**							**Babies garments and clothing accessories:**
4578	6209.2000	-棉制	14	0 2.8 7	东盟ASEAN,智利CL,新加坡SG,新西兰NZ,秘鲁PE,香港HK,澳门MO 哥斯达黎加CR 巴基斯坦PK	0	最不发达35国LDC35,最不发达4国LDC4	90	-Of cotton

序号 No.	税则号列 Tariff Line	货品名称	最惠国税率 MFN(%)	协定税率 Agreement(%)		特惠税率 S.P.(%)		普通税率 Gen.(%)	Article Description
4579	6209.3000	-合成纤维制	16	0 3.2 8 12.8	东盟ASEAN,智利CL,新加坡SG,新西兰NZ,香港HK,澳门MO 哥斯达黎加CR 秘鲁PE 巴基斯坦PK	0	最不发达35国LDC35,最不发达4国LDC4	130	-Of synthetic fibres
		-其他纺织材料制:							-Of other textile materials:
4580	6209.9010	---羊毛或动物细毛制	14	0 2.8 7	东盟ASEAN,智利CL,新加坡SG,新西兰NZ,秘鲁PE,香港HK,澳门MO 哥斯达黎加CR 巴基斯坦PK	0	最不发达35国LDC35	130	---Of wool or fine animal hair
4581	6209.9090	---其他	14	0 2.8 7	东盟ASEAN,智利CL,新加坡SG,新西兰NZ,秘鲁PE,香港HK,澳门MO 哥斯达黎加CR 巴基斯坦PK	0	最不发达35国LDC35	100	---Other
	62.10	**用税号56.02、56.03、59.03、59.06或59.07的织物制成的服装:**							**Garments, made up of fabrics of heading No.56.02, 56.03, 59.03, 59.06 or 59.07:**
		-用税号56.02或56.03的织物制成的服装:							-Of fabrics of heading No.56.02 or 56.03:
4582	6210.1010	---羊毛或动物细毛制	16	0 3.2 8 11.7	东盟ASEAN,智利CL,新加坡SG,新西兰NZ,香港HK,澳门MO 哥斯达黎加CR 巴基斯坦PK,秘鲁PE 亚太APTA	0	最不发达35国LDC35,最不发达4国LDC4,亚太2国APTA2	130	---Of wool or fine animal hair
4583	6210.1020	---棉或麻制	16	0 3.2 8 12.8	东盟ASEAN,智利CL,新加坡SG,新西兰NZ,香港HK,澳门MO 哥斯达黎加CR 秘鲁PE 巴基斯坦PK	0 6.4	最不发达35国LDC35 亚太2国APTA2	90	---Of cotton or bast fibres
4584	6210.1030	---化学纤维制	17.5	0 3.5 8.8 12.3	东盟ASEAN,智利CL,新加坡SG,新西兰NZ,香港HK,澳门MO 哥斯达黎加CR 巴基斯坦PK,秘鲁PE 亚太APTA	0	最不发达35国LDC35,最不发达4国LDC4,亚太2国APTA2	130	---Of manmade fibres
4585	6210.1090	---其他纺织材料制	16	0 3.2 8 12.8	东盟ASEAN,智利CL,新加坡SG,新西兰NZ,香港HK,澳门MO 哥斯达黎加CR 秘鲁PE 巴基斯坦PK	0	最不发达35国LDC35,最不发达4国LDC4,亚太2国APTA2	100	---Of other textile materials

序号 No.	税则号列 Tariff Line	货品名称	最惠国税率 MFN(%)	协定税率 Agreement(%)		特惠税率 S.P.(%)		普通税率 Gen.(%)	Article Description
4586	6210.2000	-子目号 6201.11 至 6201.19 所列类型的其他服装	16	0 3.2 8 11.7	东盟ASEAN,智利CL,新加坡SG,新西兰NZ,香港HK,澳门MO 哥斯达黎加CR 巴基斯坦PK,秘鲁PE 亚太APTA	0	最不发达35国LDC35,最不发达4国LDC4,亚太2国APTA2	100	-Other garments, of the type described in subheadings 6201.11 to 6201.19
4587	6210.3000	-子目号 6202.11 至 6202.19 所列类型的其他服装	16	0 3.2 8 11.7	东盟ASEAN,智利CL,新加坡SG,新西兰NZ,香港HK,澳门MO 哥斯达黎加CR 巴基斯坦PK,秘鲁PE 亚太APTA	0	最不发达35国LDC35,最不发达4国LDC4	100	-Other garments, of the type described in subheadings 6202.11 to 6202.19
4588	6210.4000	-其他男式服装	16	0 3.2 8 11.7	东盟ASEAN,智利CL,新加坡SG,新西兰NZ,香港HK,澳门MO 哥斯达黎加CR 巴基斯坦PK,秘鲁PE 亚太APTA	0	最不发达35国LDC35,最不发达4国LDC4,亚太2国APTA2	100	-Other men's or boys' garments
4589	6210.5000	-其他女式服装	16	0 3.2 8 11.7	东盟ASEAN,智利CL,新加坡SG,新西兰NZ,香港HK,澳门MO 哥斯达黎加CR 巴基斯坦PK,秘鲁PE 亚太APTA	0	最不发达35国LDC35,最不发达4国LDC4,亚太2国APTA2	100	-Other women's or girls' garments
	62.11	**运动服、滑雪服及游泳服;其他服装:**							**Track suits, ski suits and swimwear; other garments:**
		-游泳服:							-Swimwear:
4590	6211.1100	--男式	16	0 3.2 8 11.7	东盟ASEAN,智利CL,新加坡SG,新西兰NZ,香港HK,澳门MO 哥斯达黎加CR 巴基斯坦PK,秘鲁PE 亚太APTA	0	最不发达35国LDC35	130	--Men's or boys'
4591	6211.1200	--女式	16	0 3.2 8 11.7	东盟ASEAN,智利CL,新加坡SG,新西兰NZ,香港HK 哥斯达黎加CR 巴基斯坦PK,秘鲁PE 亚太APTA	0	最不发达35国LDC35,最不发达4国LDC4	130	--Women's or girls'
		-滑雪服:							-Ski suits:
4592	6211.2010	---棉制	16	0 3.2 8 12.8	东盟ASEAN,智利CL,新加坡SG,新西兰NZ,香港HK 哥斯达黎加CR 秘鲁PE 巴基斯坦PK	0	最不发达35国LDC35,最不发达4国LDC4	90	---Of cotton

序号 No.	税则号列 Tariff Line	货品名称	最惠国税率 MFN(%)	协定税率 Agreement(%)		特惠税率 S.P.(%)		普通税率 Gen.(%)	Article Description
4593	6211.2090	---其他纺织材料制	19	0 3.8 9.5 13.6	东盟ASEAN,智利CL,新加坡SG,新西兰NZ,香港HK 哥斯达黎加CR 巴基斯坦PK,秘鲁PE 亚太APTA	0	最不发达35国LDC35	130	---Of other textile materials
		-其他男式服装:							-Other garments, men's or boys':
		--棉制:							--Of cotton:
4594	6211.3210	---阿拉伯袍	16	0 3.2 8 12.8	东盟ASEAN,智利CL,新加坡SG,新西兰NZ,香港HK 哥斯达黎加CR 秘鲁PE 巴基斯坦PK	0	最不发达35国LDC35	90	---Arabian robes
4595	6211.3220	---运动服	16	0 3.2 8	东盟ASEAN,智利CL,新加坡SG,新西兰NZ,香港HK,澳门MO 哥斯达黎加CR 秘鲁PE	0	最不发达35国LDC35,最不发达4国LDC4	90	---Sports wear
4596	6211.3290	---其他	16	0 3.2 8	东盟ASEAN,智利CL,新加坡SG,新西兰NZ,香港HK,澳门MO 哥斯达黎加CR 秘鲁PE	0	最不发达35国LDC35,最不发达4国LDC4	90	---Other
		--化学纤维制:							--Of man-made fibres:
4597	6211.3310	---阿拉伯袍	17.5	0 3.5 8.8 12.3	东盟ASEAN,智利CL,新加坡SG,新西兰NZ,香港HK 哥斯达黎加CR 巴基斯坦PK,秘鲁PE 亚太APTA	0	最不发达35国LDC35	130	---Arabian robes
4598	6211.3320	---运动服	18	0 3.6 9 12.3	东盟ASEAN,智利CL,新加坡SG,新西兰NZ,香港HK,澳门MO 哥斯达黎加CR 秘鲁PE 亚太APTA,巴基斯坦PK	0	最不发达35国LDC35,最不发达4国LDC4	130	---Sports wear
4599	6211.3390	---其他	17.5	0 3.5 8.8 12.3	东盟ASEAN,智利CL,新加坡SG,新西兰NZ,香港HK,澳门MO 哥斯达黎加CR 秘鲁PE 亚太APTA,巴基斯坦PK	0	最不发达35国LDC35,最不发达4国LDC4	130	---Other
		--其他纺织材料制:							--Of other textile materials:
4600	6211.3910	---丝及绢丝制	16	0 3.2 8 11.7	东盟ASEAN,智利CL,新加坡SG,新西兰NZ,香港HK,澳门MO 哥斯达黎加CR 巴基斯坦PK,秘鲁PE 亚太APTA	0	最不发达35国LDC35	130	---Of silk or silk waste

序号 No.	税则号列 Tariff Line	货品名称	最惠国税率 MFN(%)	协定税率 Agreement(%)		特惠税率 S.P.(%)		普通税率 Gen.(%)	Article Description
4601	6211.3920	---羊毛或动物细毛制	16	0 3.2 8 11.7	东盟ASEAN,智利CL,新加坡SG,新西兰NZ,香港HK,澳门MO 哥斯达黎加CR 巴基斯坦PK,秘鲁PE 亚太APTA	0	最不发达35国LDC35	130	---Of wool or fine animal hair
4602	6211.3990	---其他	16	0 3.2 8 11.7	东盟ASEAN,智利CL,新加坡SG,新西兰NZ,香港HK,澳门MO 哥斯达黎加CR 巴基斯坦PK,秘鲁PE 亚太APTA	0	最不发达35国LDC35	100	---Other
		-其他女式服装:							-Other garments, women's or girls':
		--棉制:							--Of cotton:
4603	6211.4210	---运动服	16	0 3.2 8 12.8	东盟ASEAN,智利CL,新加坡SG,新西兰NZ,香港HK,澳门MO 哥斯达黎加CR 秘鲁PE 巴基斯坦PK	0	最不发达35国LDC35,最不发达4国LDC4	90	---Sports wear
4604	6211.4290	---其他	16	0 3.2 8 12.8	东盟ASEAN,智利CL,新加坡SG,新西兰NZ,香港HK,澳门MO 哥斯达黎加CR 秘鲁PE 巴基斯坦PK	0	最不发达35国LDC35,最不发达4国LDC4	90	---Other
		--化学纤维制:							--Of man-made fibres:
4605	6211.4310	---运动服	17.5	0 3.5 8.8 12.3	东盟ASEAN,智利CL,新加坡SG,新西兰NZ,香港HK,澳门MO 哥斯达黎加CR 巴基斯坦PK,秘鲁PE 亚太APTA	0	最不发达35国LDC35,最不发达4国LDC4	130	---Sports wear
4606	6211.4390	---其他	17.5	0 3.5 8.8 12.3	东盟ASEAN,智利CL,新加坡SG,新西兰NZ,香港HK,澳门MO 哥斯达黎加CR 巴基斯坦PK,秘鲁PE 亚太APTA	0	最不发达35国LDC35,最不发达4国LDC4	130	---Other
		--其他纺织材料制:							--Of other textile materials:
4607	6211.4910	---丝及绢丝制	16	0 3.2 8 11.7	东盟ASEAN,智利CL,新加坡SG,新西兰NZ,香港HK,澳门MO 哥斯达黎加CR 巴基斯坦PK,秘鲁PE 亚太APTA	0	最不发达35国LDC35	130	---Of silk or silk waste
4608	6211.4990	---其他	16	0 3.2 8 11.7	东盟ASEAN,智利CL,新加坡SG,新西兰NZ,香港HK,澳门MO 哥斯达黎加CR 巴基斯坦PK,秘鲁PE 亚太APTA	0	最不发达35国LDC35,最不发达4国LDC4	100	---Other

序号 No.	税则号列 Tariff Line	货品名称	最惠国税率 MFN(%)	协定税率 Agreement(%)	特惠税率 S.P.(%)	普通税率 Gen.(%)	Article Description
	62.12	**胸罩、束腰带、紧身胸衣、吊裤带、吊袜带、束袜带和类似品及其零件，不论是否针织或钩编的:**					**Brassières, girdles, corsets, braces, suspenders, garters and similar articles and parts thereof, whether or not knitted or crocheted:**
		-胸罩:					-Brassières:
4609	6212.1010	---化学纤维制	16	0 东盟ASEAN,智利CL,新加坡SG,新西兰NZ,香港HK,澳门MO,台湾TW 3.2 哥斯达黎加CR 8 秘鲁PE 12.8 巴基斯坦PK 14.4 亚太APTA	0 最不发达35国LDC35,最不发达4国LDC4,缅甸MM,老挝LA,柬埔寨KH	130	---Of man-made fibres
4610	6212.1090	---其他纺织材料制	14	0 东盟ASEAN,智利CL,新加坡SG,新西兰NZ,秘鲁PE,香港HK,澳门MO,台湾TW 2.8 哥斯达黎加CR 7 巴基斯坦PK 12.6 亚太APTA	0 最不发达35国LDC35,最不发达4国LDC4	100	---Of other textile materials
		-束腰带及腹带:					-Girdles and panty-girdles:
4611	6212.2010	---化学纤维制	16	0 东盟ASEAN,智利CL,新加坡SG,新西兰NZ,香港HK,澳门MO,台湾TW 3.2 哥斯达黎加CR 8 秘鲁PE 12.8 巴基斯坦PK	0 最不发达35国LDC35	130	---Of man-made fibres
4612	6212.2090	---其他纺织材料制	14	0 东盟ASEAN,智利CL,新加坡SG,新西兰NZ,秘鲁PE,香港HK,澳门MO,台湾TW 2.8 哥斯达黎加CR 11.2 巴基斯坦PK	0 最不发达35国LDC35,最不发达4国LDC4	100	---Of other textile materials
		-束腰胸衣:					-Corselettes:
4613	6212.3010	---化学纤维制	16	0 东盟ASEAN,智利CL,新加坡SG,新西兰NZ,香港HK,澳门MO 3.2 哥斯达黎加CR 8 秘鲁PE 12.8 巴基斯坦PK	0 最不发达35国LDC35	130	---Of man-made fibres
4614	6212.3090	---其他纺织材料制	14	0 东盟ASEAN,智利CL,新加坡SG,新西兰NZ,秘鲁PE,香港HK,澳门MO 2.8 哥斯达黎加CR 7 巴基斯坦PK	0 最不发达35国LDC35,最不发达4国LDC4	100	---Of other textile materials
		-其他:					-Other:

序号 No.	税则号列 Tariff Line	货品名称	最惠国税率 MFN(%)	协定税率 Agreement(%)		特惠税率 S.P.(%)		普通税率 Gen.(%)	Article Description
4615	6212.9010	---化学纤维制	16	0 3.2 8 12.8 14.4	东盟ASEAN,智利CL,新加坡SG,新西兰NZ,香港HK,澳门MO,台湾TW 哥斯达黎加CR 秘鲁PE 巴基斯坦PK 亚太APTA	0	最不发达35国LDC35	130	---Of man-made fibres
4616	6212.9090	---其他纺织材料制	14	0 2.8 7 12.6	东盟ASEAN,智利CL,新加坡SG,新西兰NZ,秘鲁PE,香港HK,澳门MO,台湾TW 哥斯达黎加CR 巴基斯坦PK 亚太APTA	0	最不发达35国LDC35	100	---Of other textile materials
	62.13	**手帕:**							**Handkerchiefs:**
		-棉制:							-Of cotton:
4617	6213.2010	---刺绣的	14	0 2.8 7	东盟ASEAN,智利CL,新加坡SG,新西兰NZ,秘鲁PE,香港HK 哥斯达黎加CR 巴基斯坦PK	0	最不发达35国LDC35,最不发达4国LDC4,老挝LA	90	---Embroidered
4618	6213.2090	---其他	14	0 2.8 11.2	东盟ASEAN,智利CL,新加坡SG,新西兰NZ,秘鲁PE,香港HK 哥斯达黎加CR 巴基斯坦PK	0	最不发达35国LDC35,最不发达4国LDC4,老挝LA	90	---Other
		-其他纺织材料制:							-Of other textile materials:
4619	6213.9020	---刺绣的	14	0 2.8 7	东盟ASEAN,智利CL,新加坡SG,新西兰NZ,秘鲁PE 哥斯达黎加CR 巴基斯坦PK	0	最不发达35国LDC35,最不发达4国LDC4,老挝LA	100	---Embroidered
4620	6213.9090	---其他	14	0 2.8 7	东盟ASEAN,智利CL,新加坡SG,新西兰NZ,秘鲁PE,香港HK 哥斯达黎加CR 巴基斯坦PK	0	最不发达35国LDC35,最不发达4国LDC4,老挝LA	100	---Other
	62.14	**披巾、领巾、围巾、披纱、面纱及类似品:**							**Shawls, scarves, mufflers, mantillas, veils and the like:**
4621	6214.1000	-丝或绢丝制	14	0 2.8 11.2	东盟ASEAN,智利CL,新加坡SG,新西兰NZ,秘鲁PE,香港HK 哥斯达黎加CR 巴基斯坦PK	0	最不发达35国LDC35,最不发达4国LDC4	130	-Of silk or silk waste

序号 No.	税则号列 Tariff Line	货品名称	最惠国税率 MFN(%)	协定税率 Agreement(%)		特惠税率 S.P.(%)		普通税率 Gen.(%)	Article Description
		-羊毛或动物细毛制:							-Of wool or fine animal hair:
4622	6214.2010	---羊毛制	14	0 2.8 7 11.2	东盟ASEAN,智利CL,新加坡SG,新西兰NZ,香港HK 哥斯达黎加CR 秘鲁PE 巴基斯坦PK	0	最不发达35国LDC35,最不发达4国LDC4	130	---Of wool
4623	6214.2020	---山羊绒制	14	0 2.8 7 11.2	东盟ASEAN,智利CL,新加坡SG,新西兰NZ,香港HK 哥斯达黎加CR 秘鲁PE 巴基斯坦PK	0	最不发达35国LDC35,最不发达4国LDC4	130	---Of cashmere
4624	6214.2090	---其他	14	0 2.8 7 11.2	东盟ASEAN,智利CL,新加坡SG,新西兰NZ,香港HK 哥斯达黎加CR 秘鲁PE 巴基斯坦PK	0	最不发达35国LDC35,最不发达4国LDC4	130	---Other
4625	6214.3000	-合成纤维制	16	0 3.2 8 12.8	东盟ASEAN,智利CL,新加坡SG,新西兰NZ,香港HK 哥斯达黎加CR 秘鲁PE 巴基斯坦PK	0	最不发达35国LDC35,最不发达4国LDC4	130	-Of synthetic fibres
4626	6214.4000	-人造纤维制	14	0 2.8 11.2	东盟ASEAN,智利CL,新加坡SG,新西兰NZ,秘鲁PE,香港HK 哥斯达黎加CR 巴基斯坦PK	0	最不发达35国LDC35,最不发达4国LDC4	130	-Of artificial fibres
4627	6214.9000	-其他纺织材料制	14	0 2.8 11.2	东盟ASEAN,智利CL,新加坡SG,新西兰NZ,秘鲁PE,香港HK 哥斯达黎加CR 巴基斯坦PK	0	最不发达35国LDC35,最不发达4国LDC4	100	-Of other textile materials
	62.15	**领带及领结:**							**Ties, bow ties and cravats:**
4628	6215.1000	-丝或绢丝制	14	0 2.8 11.2	东盟ASEAN,智利CL,新加坡SG,新西兰NZ,秘鲁PE,香港HK 哥斯达黎加CR 巴基斯坦PK	0	最不发达35国LDC35,最不发达4国LDC4	130	-Of silk or silk waste
4629	6215.2000	-化学纤维制	16	0 3.2 8 12.8 14.4	东盟ASEAN,智利CL,新加坡SG,新西兰NZ,香港HK 哥斯达黎加CR 秘鲁PE 巴基斯坦PK 亚太APTA	0	最不发达35国LDC35,最不发达4国LDC4	130	-Of man-made fibres

序号 No.	税则号列 Tariff Line	货品名称	最惠国税率 MFN(%)	协定税率 Agreement(%)		特惠税率 S.P.(%)		普通税率 Gen.(%)	Article Description
4630	6215.9000	-其他纺织材料制	14	0 2.8 7	东盟ASEAN,智利CL,新加坡SG,新西兰NZ,秘鲁PE,香港HK 哥斯达黎加CR 巴基斯坦PK	0	最不发达35国LDC35,最不发达4国LDC4	100	-Of other textile materials
	62.16	**分指手套、连指手套及露指手套:**							**Gloves, mittens and mitts:**
4631	6216.0000	分指手套、连指手套及露指手套	14	0 2.8	东盟ASEAN,智利CL,新加坡SG,新西兰NZ,秘鲁PE,香港HK,澳门MO 哥斯达黎加CR	0	最不发达35国LDC35,最不发达4国LDC4	100	Gloves, mittens and mitts
	62.17	**其他制成的衣着附件;服装或衣着附件的零件,但税号62.12的货品除外:**							**Other made up clothing accessories; parts of garments or of clothing accessories, other than those of heading No.62.12:**
		-附件:							-Accessories:
4632	6217.1010	---袜子及袜套	14	0 2.8 7 12.2	东盟ASEAN,智利CL,新加坡SG,新西兰NZ,秘鲁PE,台湾TW 哥斯达黎加CR 巴基斯坦PK 亚太APTA	0	最不发达35国LDC35	130	---Stocking, socks and sockettes
4633	6217.1020	---和服腰带	14	0 2.8 7 12.2	东盟ASEAN,智利CL,新加坡SG,新西兰NZ,秘鲁PE,香港HK,台湾TW 哥斯达黎加CR 巴基斯坦PK 亚太APTA	0	最不发达35国LDC35,最不发达4国LDC4	100	---Kimono belts
4634	6217.1090	---其他	14	0 2.8 12.2	东盟ASEAN,智利CL,新加坡SG,新西兰NZ,秘鲁PE,香港HK,台湾TW 哥斯达黎加CR 亚太APTA,巴基斯坦PK	0	最不发达35国LDC35,最不发达4国LDC4,缅甸MM,老挝LA,柬埔寨KH	100	---Other
4635	6217.9000	-零件	14	0 2.8 12.6	东盟ASEAN,智利CL,新加坡SG,新西兰NZ,秘鲁PE,香港HK,澳门MO,台湾TW 哥斯达黎加CR 亚太APTA,巴基斯坦PK	0	最不发达35国LDC35,最不发达4国LDC4,缅甸MM,老挝LA,柬埔寨KH	100	-Parts

第六十三章
其他纺织制成品；成套物品；旧衣着及旧纺织品；碎织物

Chapter 63
Other made up textile articles; sets; worn clothing and worn textile articles; rags

注释：

一、第一分章仅适用于各种纺织物制成的物品。

二、第一分章不包括：

（一）第五十六章至第六十二章的货品；

（二）税号 63.09 的旧衣着或其他旧物品。

三、税号 63.09 仅适用于下列货品：

（一）纺织材料制品：

1. 衣着和衣着附件及其零件；

2. 毯子及旅行毯；

3. 床上、餐桌、盥洗及厨房用的织物制品；

4. 装饰用织物制品，但税号 57.01 至 57.05 的地毯及税号 58.05 的装饰毯除外。

（二）用石棉以外其他任何材料制成的鞋帽类。

上述物品只有同时符合下列两个条件才能归入本税号：

1. 必须明显看得出穿用过；

2. 必须以散装、捆装、袋装或类似的大包装形式进口或出口。

Notes:

1. Sub-Chapter 1 applies only to made up articles，of any textile fabric.

2. Sub-Chapter 1 does not cover:

(a) Goods of Chapters 56 to 62; or

(b) Worn clothing or other worn articles of heading No.63.09.

3. Heading No.63.09 applies only to the following goods:

(a) Articles of textile materials:

(1) Clothing and clothing accessories，and parts thereof;

(2) Blankets and travelling rugs;

(3) Bed linen，table linen，toilet lined and kitchen linen;

(4) Furnishing articles，other than carpets of headings Nos. 57.01 to 57.05 and tapestries of heading No.58.05.

(b) Footwear and headgear of any material other than asbestos.

In order to be classified in this heading，the articles mentioned above must comply with both of the following requirements:

(1) they must show signs of appreciable wear; and

(2) they must be presented in bulk or in bales，sacks or similar packings.

序号 No.	税则号列 Tariff Line	货品名称	最惠国税率 MFN(%)	协定税率 Agreement(%)		特惠税率 S.P.(%)		普通税率 Gen.(%)	Article Description
		第一分章 其他纺织制成品							Ⅰ.OTHER MADE UP TEXTILE ARTICLES
	63.01	**毯子及旅行毯:**							**Blankets and travelling rugs:**
4636	6301.1000	-电暖毯	16	0	东盟ASEAN,智利CL,新加坡SG,新西兰NZ	0	最不发达35国LDC35	100	-Electric blankets
				3.2	哥斯达黎加CR				
				8	秘鲁PE				
				12.8	巴基斯坦PK				

序号 No.	税则号列 Tariff Line	货品名称	最惠国税率 MFN(%)	协定税率 Agreement(%)		特惠税率 S.P.(%)		普通税率 Gen.(%)	Article Description
4637	6301.2000	-羊毛或动物细毛制的毯子（电暖毯除外）及旅行毯	16	0 3.2 8 12.8	东盟ASEAN,智利CL,新加坡SG,新西兰NZ,澳门MO 哥斯达黎加CR 秘鲁PE 巴基斯坦PK	0	最不发达35国LDC35,最不发达4国LDC4	130	-Blankets (other than electric blankets) and travelling rugs, of wool or of fine animal hair
4638	6301.3000	-棉制的毯子（电暖毯除外）及旅行毯	16	0 3.2 8 12.8	东盟ASEAN,智利CL,新加坡SG,新西兰NZ,澳门MO 哥斯达黎加CR 秘鲁PE 巴基斯坦PK	0	最不发达35国LDC35,最不发达4国LDC4	90	-Blankets (other than electric blankets) and travelling rugs, of cotton
4639	6301.4000	-合成纤维制的毯子（电暖毯除外）及旅行毯	17.5	0 3.5 8.8 14	东盟ASEAN,智利CL,新加坡SG,新西兰NZ,澳门MO 哥斯达黎加CR 秘鲁PE 巴基斯坦PK	0	最不发达35国LDC35,最不发达4国LDC4	130	-Blankets (other than electric blankets) and travelling rugs, of synthetic fibres
4640	6301.9000	-其他毯子及旅行毯	16	0 3.2 8 12.8	东盟ASEAN,智利CL,新加坡SG,新西兰NZ,澳门MO,台湾TW 哥斯达黎加CR 秘鲁PE 巴基斯坦PK	0	最不发达35国LDC35,最不发达4国LDC4	90	-Other blankets and travelling rugs
	63.02	**床上、餐桌、盥洗及厨房用的织物制品:**							**Bed linen, table linen, toilet linen and kitchen linen:**
		-针织或钩编的床上用织物制品:							-Bed linen, knitted or crocheted:
4641	6302.1010	---棉制	14	0 2.8	东盟ASEAN,智利CL,巴基斯坦PK,新加坡SG,新西兰NZ,秘鲁PE 哥斯达黎加CR	0	最不发达35国LDC35,最不发达4国LDC4	90	---Of cotton
4642	6302.1090	---其他纺织材料制品	14	0 2.8	东盟ASEAN,智利CL,巴基斯坦PK,新加坡SG,新西兰NZ,秘鲁PE 哥斯达黎加CR	0	最不发达35国LDC35	130	---Other
		-其他印花的床上用织物制品:							-Other bed linen, printed:
		--棉制:							--Of cotton:
4643	6302.2110	---床单	14	0 2.8	东盟ASEAN,智利CL,巴基斯坦PK,新加坡SG,新西兰NZ,秘鲁PE 哥斯达黎加CR	0	最不发达35国LDC35,最不发达4国LDC4	90	---Bed sheets
4644	6302.2190	---其他	14	0 2.8	东盟ASEAN,智利CL,巴基斯坦PK,新加坡SG,新西兰NZ,秘鲁PE 哥斯达黎加CR	0	最不发达35国LDC35,最不发达4国LDC4	90	---Other

序号 No.	税则号列 Tariff Line	货品名称	最惠国税率 MFN(%)	协定税率 Agreement(%)		特惠税率 S.P.(%)		普通税率 Gen.(%)	Article Description
		--化学纤维制:							--Of man-made fibres:
4645	6302.2210	---床单	16	0 3.2 8	东盟ASEAN,智利CL,巴基斯坦PK,新加坡SG,新西兰NZ 哥斯达黎加CR 秘鲁PE	0	最不发达35国LDC35,最不发达4国LDC4	130	---Bed sheets
4646	6302.2290	---其他	16	0 3.2 8	东盟ASEAN,智利CL,巴基斯坦PK,新加坡SG,新西兰NZ 哥斯达黎加CR 秘鲁PE	0	最不发达35国LDC35,最不发达4国LDC4	130	---Other
		--其他纺织材料制:							--Of other textile materials:
4647	6302.2910	---丝及绢丝制	14	0 2.8	东盟ASEAN,智利CL,巴基斯坦PK,新加坡SG,新西兰NZ,秘鲁PE 哥斯达黎加CR	0	最不发达35国LDC35	130	---Of silk or silk waste
4648	6302.2920	---麻制	14	0 2.8	东盟ASEAN,智利CL,巴基斯坦PK,新加坡SG,新西兰NZ,秘鲁PE 哥斯达黎加CR	0	最不发达35国LDC35	90	---Of bast fibres
4649	6302.2990	---其他	14	0 2.8	东盟ASEAN,智利CL,巴基斯坦PK,新加坡SG,新西兰NZ,秘鲁PE 哥斯达黎加CR	0	最不发达35国LDC35	100	---Other
		-其他床上用织物制品:							-Other bed linen:
		--棉制:							--Of cotton:
4650	6302.3110	---刺绣的	14	0 2.8	东盟ASEAN,智利CL,巴基斯坦PK,新加坡SG,新西兰NZ,秘鲁PE 哥斯达黎加CR	0	最不发达35国LDC35,最不发达4国LDC4	90	---Embroidered
		---其他:							---Other:
4651	6302.3191	----床单	14	0 2.8	东盟ASEAN,智利CL,巴基斯坦PK,新加坡SG,新西兰NZ,秘鲁PE 哥斯达黎加CR	0	最不发达35国LDC35,最不发达4国LDC4	90	----Bed sheets
4652	6302.3192	----毛巾被	14	0 2.8	东盟ASEAN,智利CL,巴基斯坦PK,新加坡SG,新西兰NZ,秘鲁PE 哥斯达黎加CR	0	最不发达35国LDC35	90	----Towelling coverlets
4653	6302.3199	----其他	14	0 2.8	东盟ASEAN,智利CL,巴基斯坦PK,新加坡SG,新西兰NZ,秘鲁PE 哥斯达黎加CR	0	最不发达35国LDC35,最不发达4国LDC4	90	----Other
		--化学纤维制:							--Of man-made fibres:

序号 No.	税则号列 Tariff Line	货品名称	最惠国税率 MFN(%)	协定税率 Agreement(%)		特惠税率 S.P.(%)		普通税率 Gen.(%)	Article Description
4654	6302.3210	---刺绣的	16	0 3.2 8	东盟ASEAN,智利CL,巴基斯坦PK,新加坡SG,新西兰NZ 哥斯达黎加CR 秘鲁PE	0	最不发达35国LDC35,最不发达4国LDC4	130	---Embroidered
4655	6302.3290	---其他	16	0 3.2 8	东盟ASEAN,智利CL,巴基斯坦PK,新加坡SG,新西兰NZ 哥斯达黎加CR 秘鲁PE	0	最不发达35国LDC35,最不发达4国LDC4	130	---Other
		--其他纺织材料制:							--Of other textile materials:
4656	6302.3910	---丝及绢丝制	14	0 2.8	东盟ASEAN,智利CL,巴基斯坦PK,新加坡SG,新西兰NZ,秘鲁PE 哥斯达黎加CR	0	最不发达35国LDC35	130	---Of silk or silk waste
		---麻制:							---Of bast fibres:
4657	6302.3921	----刺绣的	14	0 2.8	东盟ASEAN,智利CL,巴基斯坦PK,新加坡SG,新西兰NZ,秘鲁PE 哥斯达黎加CR	0	最不发达35国LDC35	90	----Embroidered
4658	6302.3929	----其他	14	0 2.8	东盟ASEAN,智利CL,巴基斯坦PK,新加坡SG,新西兰NZ,秘鲁PE 哥斯达黎加CR	0	最不发达35国LDC35	90	----Other
		---其他:							---Other:
4659	6302.3991	----刺绣的	14	0 2.8	东盟ASEAN,智利CL,巴基斯坦PK,新加坡SG,新西兰NZ,秘鲁PE 哥斯达黎加CR	0	最不发达35国LDC35	100	----Embroidered
4660	6302.3999	----其他	14	0 2.8	东盟ASEAN,智利CL,巴基斯坦PK,新加坡SG,新西兰NZ,秘鲁PE 哥斯达黎加CR	0	最不发达35国LDC35,最不发达4国LDC4	100	----Other
		-针织或钩编的餐桌用织物制品:							-Table linen, knitted or crocheted:
4661	6302.4010	---手工制	14	0 2.8	东盟ASEAN,智利CL,巴基斯坦PK,新加坡SG,新西兰NZ,秘鲁PE 哥斯达黎加CR	0	最不发达35国LDC35	100	---Hand-worked
4662	6302.4090	---其他	14	0 2.8	东盟ASEAN,智利CL,巴基斯坦PK,新加坡SG,新西兰NZ,秘鲁PE 哥斯达黎加CR	0	最不发达35国LDC35,最不发达4国LDC4	100	---Other
		-其他餐桌用织物制品:							-Other table linen:
		--棉制:							--Of cotton:

序号 No.	税则号列 Tariff Line	货品名称	最惠国税率 MFN(%)	协定税率 Agreement(%)		特惠税率 S.P.(%)		普通税率 Gen.(%)	Article Description
4663	6302.5110	---刺绣的	14	0 2.8	东盟ASEAN,智利CL,巴基斯坦PK,新加坡SG,新西兰NZ,秘鲁PE,香港HK 哥斯达黎加CR	0	最不发达35国LDC35	90	---Embroidered
4664	6302.5190	---其他	14	0 2.8	东盟ASEAN,智利CL,巴基斯坦PK,新加坡SG,新西兰NZ,秘鲁PE,香港HK,澳门MO 哥斯达黎加CR	0	最不发达35国LDC35,最不发达4国LDC4	90	---Other
		--化学纤维制:							--Of man-made fibres:
4665	6302.5310	---刺绣的	14	0 2.8	东盟ASEAN,智利CL,巴基斯坦PK,新加坡SG,新西兰NZ,秘鲁PE 哥斯达黎加CR	0	最不发达35国LDC35	130	---Embroidered
4666	6302.5390	---其他	16	0 3.2 8	东盟ASEAN,智利CL,巴基斯坦PK,新加坡SG,新西兰NZ 哥斯达黎加CR 秘鲁PE	0	最不发达35国LDC35,最不发达4国LDC4	130	---Other
		--其他纺织材料制:							--Of other textile materials:
		---亚麻制:							---Of flax:
4667	6302.5911	----刺绣的	14	0 2.8	东盟ASEAN,智利CL,巴基斯坦PK,新加坡SG,新西兰NZ,秘鲁PE 哥斯达黎加CR	0	最不发达35国LDC35	90	----Embroidered
4668	6302.5919	----其他	14	0 2.8	东盟ASEAN,智利CL,巴基斯坦PK,新加坡SG,新西兰NZ,秘鲁PE 哥斯达黎加CR	0	最不发达35国LDC35	90	----Other
4669	6302.5990	---其他	14	0 2.8	东盟ASEAN,智利CL,巴基斯坦PK,新加坡SG,新西兰NZ,秘鲁PE 哥斯达黎加CR	0	最不发达35国LDC35	100	---Other
		-盥洗及厨房用棉制毛巾织物或类似的毛圈织物的制品:							-Toilet linen and kitchen linen, of terry towelling or similar terry fabrics, of cotton:
4670	6302.6010	---浴巾	14	0 2.8	东盟ASEAN,智利CL,巴基斯坦PK,新加坡SG,新西兰NZ,秘鲁PE,台湾TW 哥斯达黎加CR	0	最不发达35国LDC35,最不发达4国LDC4	90	---Bath towels
4671	6302.6090	---其他	14	0 2.8	东盟ASEAN,智利CL,巴基斯坦PK,新加坡SG,新西兰NZ,秘鲁PE,台湾TW 哥斯达黎加CR	0	最不发达35国LDC35,最不发达4国LDC4	90	---Other
		-其他:							-Other:

序号 No.	税则号列 Tariff Line	货品名称	最惠国税率 MFN(%)	协定税率 Agreement(%)		特惠税率 S.P.(%)		普通税率 Gen.(%)	Article Description
4672	6302.9100	--棉制	14	0 2.8	东盟ASEAN,智利CL,巴基斯坦PK,新加坡SG,新西兰NZ,秘鲁PE 哥斯达黎加CR	0	最不发达35国LDC35,最不发达4国LDC4	90	--Of cotton
4673	6302.9300	--化学纤维制	16	0 3.2 8	东盟ASEAN,智利CL,巴基斯坦PK,新加坡SG,新西兰NZ,香港HK 哥斯达黎加CR 秘鲁PE	0	最不发达35国LDC35	130	--Of man-made fibres
		--其他纺织材料制:							--Of other textile materials:
4674	6302.9910	---亚麻制	14	0 2.8	东盟ASEAN,智利CL,巴基斯坦PK,新加坡SG,新西兰NZ,秘鲁PE 哥斯达黎加CR	0	最不发达35国LDC35	90	---Of flax
4675	6302.9990	---其他	14	0 2.8	东盟ASEAN,智利CL,巴基斯坦PK,新加坡SG,新西兰NZ,秘鲁PE 哥斯达黎加CR	0	最不发达35国LDC35	100	---Other
	63.03	**窗帘（包括帷帘）及帐幔;帘帷或床帷:**							**Curtains (including drapes) and interior blinds; curtain or bed valances:**
		-针织或钩编的:							-Knitted or crocheted:
		--合成纤维制:							--Of synthetic fibres:
4676	6303.1210	---针织的	16	0 3.2 8	东盟ASEAN,智利CL,巴基斯坦PK,新加坡SG,新西兰NZ 哥斯达黎加CR 秘鲁PE	0	最不发达35国LDC35	130	---Knitted
4677	6303.1220	---钩编的	16	0 3.2 8	东盟ASEAN,智利CL,巴基斯坦PK,新加坡SG,新西兰NZ 哥斯达黎加CR 秘鲁PE	0	最不发达35国LDC35	130	---Crocheted
		--其他纺织材料制:							--Of other textile materials:
		---棉制:							---Of cotton:
4678	6303.1931	----针织的	14	0 2.8	东盟ASEAN,智利CL,巴基斯坦PK,新加坡SG,新西兰NZ,秘鲁PE 哥斯达黎加CR	0	最不发达35国LDC35,最不发达4国LDC4	90	----Knitted
4679	6303.1932	----钩编的	14	0 2.8	东盟ASEAN,智利CL,巴基斯坦PK,新加坡SG,新西兰NZ,秘鲁PE 哥斯达黎加CR	0	最不发达35国LDC35	90	----Crocheted
		---其他:							---Other:
4680	6303.1991	----针织的	14	0 2.8	东盟ASEAN,智利CL,巴基斯坦PK,新加坡SG,新西兰NZ,秘鲁PE 哥斯达黎加CR	0	最不发达35国LDC35	130	----Knitted

序号 No.	税则号列 Tariff Line	货品名称	最惠国税率 MFN(%)	协定税率 Agreement(%)		特惠税率 S.P.(%)		普通税率 Gen.(%)	Article Description
4681	6303.1992	----钩编的	14	0 2.8	东盟ASEAN,智利CL,巴基斯坦PK,新加坡SG,新西兰NZ,秘鲁PE 哥斯达黎加CR	0	最不发达35国LDC35	130	----Crocheted
		-其他:							-Other:
4682	6303.9100	--棉制	14	0 2.8	东盟ASEAN,智利CL,巴基斯坦PK,新加坡SG,新西兰NZ,秘鲁PE 哥斯达黎加CR	0	最不发达35国LDC35,最不发达4国LDC4	90	--Of cotton
4683	6303.9200	--合成纤维制	16	0 3.2 8	东盟ASEAN,智利CL,巴基斯坦PK,新加坡SG,新西兰NZ,香港HK 哥斯达黎加CR 秘鲁PE	0	最不发达35国LDC35,最不发达4国LDC4	130	--Of synthetic fibres
4684	6303.9900	--其他纺织材料制	14	0 2.8	东盟ASEAN,智利CL,巴基斯坦PK,新加坡SG,新西兰NZ,秘鲁PE 哥斯达黎加CR	0	最不发达35国LDC35,最不发达4国LDC4	100	--Of other textile materials
	63.04	**其他装饰用织物制品，但税号94.04的货品除外:**							**Other furnishing articles, excluding those of heading No.94.04:**
		-床罩:							-Bedspreads:
		--针织或钩编的:							--Knitted or crocheted:
		---针织的:							---Knitted:
4685	6304.1121	----手工制	14	0 2.8 7	东盟ASEAN,智利CL,新加坡SG,新西兰NZ,秘鲁PE,澳门MO 哥斯达黎加CR 巴基斯坦PK	0	最不发达35国LDC35	100	----Hand-worked
4686	6304.1129	----其他	14	0 2.8 7	东盟ASEAN,智利CL,新加坡SG,新西兰NZ,秘鲁PE,澳门MO 哥斯达黎加CR 巴基斯坦PK	0	最不发达35国LDC35	100	----Other
		---钩编的:							Crocheted:
4687	6304.1131	----手工制	14	0 2.8 7	东盟ASEAN,智利CL,新加坡SG,新西兰NZ,秘鲁PE 哥斯达黎加CR 巴基斯坦PK	0	最不发达35国LDC35,最不发达4国LDC4	100	----Hand-worked
4688	6304.1139	----其他	14	0 2.8 7	东盟ASEAN,智利CL,新加坡SG,新西兰NZ,秘鲁PE 哥斯达黎加CR 巴基斯坦PK	0	最不发达35国LDC35,最不发达4国LDC4	100	----Other
		--其他:							--Other:

序号 No.	税则号列 Tariff Line	货品名称	最惠国税率 MFN(%)	协定税率 Agreement(%)		特惠税率 S.P.(%)		普通税率 Gen.(%)	Article Description
4689	6304.1910	---丝及绢丝制	14	0 2.8 7	东盟ASEAN,智利CL,新加坡SG,新西兰NZ,秘鲁PE 哥斯达黎加CR 巴基斯坦PK	0	最不发达35国LDC35	130	---Of silk or silk waste
		---棉或麻制:							---Of cotton or bast fibres:
4690	6304.1921	----刺绣的	14	0 2.8 7	东盟ASEAN,智利CL,新加坡SG,新西兰NZ,秘鲁PE 哥斯达黎加CR 巴基斯坦PK	0	最不发达35国LDC35	90	----Embroidered
4691	6304.1929	----其他	14	0 2.8	东盟ASEAN,智利CL,新加坡SG,新西兰NZ,秘鲁PE 哥斯达黎加CR	0	最不发达35国LDC35,最不发达4国LDC4	90	----Other
		---化学纤维制:							---Of man-made fibres:
4692	6304.1931	----刺绣的	16	0 3.2 8 12.8	东盟ASEAN,智利CL,新加坡SG,新西兰NZ 哥斯达黎加CR 秘鲁PE 巴基斯坦PK	0	最不发达35国LDC35	130	----Embroidered
4693	6304.1939	----其他	16	0 3.2 8 12.8	东盟ASEAN,智利CL,新加坡SG,新西兰NZ 哥斯达黎加CR 秘鲁PE 巴基斯坦PK	0	最不发达35国LDC35	130	----Other
		---其他纺织材料制:							---Of other textile materials:
4694	6304.1991	----刺绣的	14	0 2.8 7	东盟ASEAN,智利CL,新加坡SG,新西兰NZ,秘鲁PE 哥斯达黎加CR 巴基斯坦PK	0	最不发达35国LDC35	100	----Embroidered
4695	6304.1999	----其他	14	0 2.8 7	东盟ASEAN,智利CL,新加坡SG,新西兰NZ,秘鲁PE 哥斯达黎加CR 巴基斯坦PK	0	最不发达35国LDC35	100	----Other
		-其他:							-Other:
		--针织或钩编的:							--Knitted or crocheted:
		---针织的:							---Knitted:
4696	6304.9121	----手工制	14	0 2.8 7	东盟ASEAN,智利CL,新加坡SG,新西兰NZ,秘鲁PE 哥斯达黎加CR 巴基斯坦PK	0	最不发达35国LDC35,最不发达4国LDC4	100	----Hand-worked
4697	6304.9129	----其他	14	0 2.8 7	东盟ASEAN,智利CL,新加坡SG,新西兰NZ,秘鲁PE,澳门MO 哥斯达黎加CR 巴基斯坦PK	0	最不发达35国LDC35,最不发达4国LDC4	100	----Other

序号 No.	税则号列 Tariff Line	货品名称	最惠国税率 MFN(%)	协定税率 Agreement(%)		特惠税率 S.P.(%)		普通税率 Gen.(%)	Article Description
		---钩编的:							---Crocheted:
4698	6304.9131	----手工制	14	0 2.8 11.2	东盟ASEAN,智利CL,新加坡SG,新西兰NZ,秘鲁PE 哥斯达黎加CR 巴基斯坦PK	0	最不发达35国LDC35	100	----Hand-worked
4699	6304.9139	----其他	14	0 2.8 7	东盟ASEAN,智利CL,新加坡SG,新西兰NZ,秘鲁PE 哥斯达黎加CR 巴基斯坦PK	0	最不发达35国LDC35	100	----Other
		--非针织或非钩编的，棉制:							--Not knitted or crocheted, of cotton:
4700	6304.9210	---刺绣的	14	0 2.8 7	东盟ASEAN,智利CL,新加坡SG,新西兰NZ,秘鲁PE 哥斯达黎加CR 巴基斯坦PK	0	最不发达35国LDC35	90	---Embroidered
4701	6304.9290	---其他	14	0 2.8 11.2	东盟ASEAN,智利CL,新加坡SG,新西兰NZ,秘鲁PE 哥斯达黎加CR 巴基斯坦PK	0	最不发达35国LDC35,最不发达4国LDC4	90	---Other
		--非针织或非钩编的，合成纤维制:							--Not knitted or crocheted, of synthetic fibres:
4702	6304.9310	---刺绣的	16	0 3.2 8 12.8	东盟ASEAN,智利CL,新加坡SG,新西兰NZ 哥斯达黎加CR 秘鲁PE 巴基斯坦PK	0	最不发达35国LDC35	130	---Embroidered
4703	6304.9390	---其他	16	0 3.2 8 12.8	东盟ASEAN,智利CL,新加坡SG,新西兰NZ 哥斯达黎加CR 秘鲁PE 巴基斯坦PK	0	最不发达35国LDC35,最不发达4国LDC4	130	---Other
		--非针织或非钩编的，其他纺织材料制:							--Not knitted or crocheted, of other textile materials:
4704	6304.9910	---丝及绢丝制	14	0 2.8 7	东盟ASEAN,智利CL,新加坡SG,新西兰NZ,秘鲁PE 哥斯达黎加CR 巴基斯坦PK	0	最不发达35国LDC35,最不发达4国LDC4	130	---Of silk or silk waste
		---麻制:							---Of bast fibres:
4705	6304.9921	----刺绣的	14	0 2.8 7	东盟ASEAN,智利CL,新加坡SG,新西兰NZ,秘鲁PE 哥斯达黎加CR 巴基斯坦PK	0	最不发达35国LDC35	90	----Embroidered

序号 No.	税则号列 Tariff Line	货品名称	最惠国税率 MFN(%)	协定税率 Agreement(%)		特惠税率 S.P.(%)		普通税率 Gen.(%)	Article Description
4706	6304.9929	----其他	14	0 2.8 7	东盟ASEAN,智利CL,新加坡SG,新西兰NZ,秘鲁PE 哥斯达黎加CR 巴基斯坦PK	0	最不发达35国LDC35	90	----Other
4707	6304.9990	---其他	14	0 2.8 7	东盟ASEAN,智利CL,新加坡SG,新西兰NZ,秘鲁PE 哥斯达黎加CR 巴基斯坦PK	0	最不发达35国LDC35,最不发达4国LDC4	100	---Other
	63.05	**货物包装用袋:**							**Sacks and bags, of a kind used for the packing of goods:**
4708	6305.1000	-黄麻或税号53.03的其他韧皮纺织纤维制	10	0 5	东盟ASEAN,智利CL,新西兰NZ,秘鲁PE,哥斯达黎加CR 巴基斯坦PK	0	最不发达35国LDC35,最不发达4国LDC4,亚太2国APTA2	40	-Of jute or of other textile bast fibres of heading No.53.03
4709	6305.2000	-棉制	16	0 3.2 8 12.8	东盟ASEAN,智利CL,新加坡SG,新西兰NZ 哥斯达黎加CR 秘鲁PE 巴基斯坦PK	0	最不发达35国LDC35,最不发达4国LDC4	90	-Of cotton
		-化学纤维材料制:							-Of man-made textile materials:
4710	6305.3200	--散装货物储运软袋	16	0 3.2 8 12.8	东盟ASEAN,智利CL,新加坡SG,新西兰NZ 哥斯达黎加CR 秘鲁PE 巴基斯坦PK	0	最不发达35国LDC35,最不发达4国LDC4	100	--Flexible intermediate bulk containers
4711	6305.3300	--其他，聚乙烯、聚丙烯扁条或类似材料制	16	0 3.2 8 13.6	东盟ASEAN,智利CL,新加坡SG,新西兰NZ 哥斯达黎加CR 巴基斯坦PK,秘鲁PE 亚太APTA	0	最不发达35国LDC35	100	--Other, of polyethylene or polypropy lene strip or the like
4712	6305.3900	--其他	16	0 3.2 8 12.8	东盟ASEAN,智利CL,新加坡SG,新西兰NZ 哥斯达黎加CR 秘鲁PE 巴基斯坦PK	0	最不发达35国LDC35	100	--Other
4713	6305.9000	-其他纺织材料制	14	0 2.8 11.2	东盟ASEAN,智利CL,新加坡SG,新西兰NZ,秘鲁PE 哥斯达黎加CR 巴基斯坦PK	0	最不发达35国LDC35,最不发达4国LDC4	90	-Of other textile materials

序号 No.	税则号列 Tariff Line	货品名称	最惠国 税 率 MFN(%)	协定税率 Agreement(%)		特惠税率 S.P.(%)		普通 税率 Gen.(%)	Article Description
	63.06	**油苫布、天篷及遮阳篷;帐篷;风帆;野营用品:**							**Tarpaulins, awnings and sunblinds; tents; sails for boats, sailboards or landcraft; camping goods:**
		-油苫布、天篷及遮阳篷:							-Tarpaulins, awnings and sunblinds:
4714	6306.1200	--合成纤维制	16	0 3.2 8	东盟ASEAN,智利CL,巴基斯坦PK,新加坡SG,新西兰NZ 哥斯达黎加CR 秘鲁PE	0	最不发达35国LDC35	130	--Of synthetic fibres
		--其他纺织材料制:							--Of other textile materials:
4715	6306.1910	---麻制	14	0 2.8	东盟ASEAN,智利CL,巴基斯坦PK,新加坡SG,新西兰NZ,秘鲁PE 哥斯达黎加CR	0	最不发达35国LDC35	80	---Of bast fibres
4716	6306.1920	---棉制	14	0 2.8	东盟ASEAN,智利CL,巴基斯坦PK,新加坡SG,新西兰NZ,秘鲁PE 哥斯达黎加CR	0	最不发达35国LDC35	80	---Of cotton
4717	6306.1990	---其他	14	0 2.8	东盟ASEAN,智利CL,巴基斯坦PK,新加坡SG,新西兰NZ,秘鲁PE 哥斯达黎加CR	0	最不发达35国LDC35	100	---Other
		-帐篷:							-Tents:
4718	6306.2200	--合成纤维制	16	0 3.2 8	东盟ASEAN,智利CL,巴基斯坦PK,新加坡SG,新西兰NZ 哥斯达黎加CR 秘鲁PE	0	最不发达35国LDC35,最不发达4国LDC4	130	--Of synthetic fibres
		--其他纺织材料制:							--Of other textile materials:
4719	6306.2910	---棉制	14	0 2.8	东盟ASEAN,智利CL,巴基斯坦PK,新加坡SG,新西兰NZ,秘鲁PE 哥斯达黎加CR	0	最不发达35国LDC35	80	---Of cotton
4720	6306.2990	---其他	14	0 2.8	东盟ASEAN,智利CL,巴基斯坦PK,新加坡SG,新西兰NZ,秘鲁PE 哥斯达黎加CR	0	最不发达35国LDC35,最不发达4国LDC4	100	---Other
		-风帆:							-Sails:
4721	6306.3010	---合成纤维制	16	0 3.2 8	东盟ASEAN,智利CL,巴基斯坦PK,新加坡SG,新西兰NZ,香港HK 哥斯达黎加CR 秘鲁PE	0	最不发达35国LDC35	130	---Of synthetic fibres
4722	6306.3090	---其他纺织材料制	14	0 2.8	东盟ASEAN,智利CL,巴基斯坦PK,新加坡SG,新西兰NZ,秘鲁PE 哥斯达黎加CR	0	最不发达35国LDC35	100	---Of other textile materials

序号 No.	税则号列 Tariff Line	货品名称	最惠国税率 MFN(%)	协定税率 Agreement(%)		特惠税率 S.P.(%)		普通税率 Gen.(%)	Article Description
		-充气褥垫:							-Pneumatic mattresses:
4723	6306.4010	---棉制	14	0	东盟ASEAN,智利CL,巴基斯坦PK,新加坡SG,新西兰NZ,秘鲁PE	0	最不发达35国LDC35	80	---Of cotton
				2.8	哥斯达黎加CR				
4724	6306.4020	---化学纤维制	16	0	东盟ASEAN,智利CL,巴基斯坦PK,新加坡SG,新西兰NZ	0	最不发达35国LDC35,最不发达4国LDC4	130	---Of man-made fibres
				3.2	哥斯达黎加CR				
				8	秘鲁PE				
4725	6306.4090	---其他纺织材料制	14	0	东盟ASEAN,智利CL,巴基斯坦PK,新加坡SG,新西兰NZ,秘鲁PE	0	最不发达35国LDC35	100	---Of other textile materials
				2.8	哥斯达黎加CR				
		-其他:							-Other:
4726	6306.9010	---棉制	14	0	东盟ASEAN,智利CL,巴基斯坦PK,新加坡SG,新西兰NZ,秘鲁PE	0	最不发达35国LDC35,最不发达4国LDC4	80	---Of cotton
				2.8	哥斯达黎加CR				
4727	6306.9020	---麻制	14	0	东盟ASEAN,智利CL,巴基斯坦PK,新加坡SG,新西兰NZ,秘鲁PE	0	最不发达35国LDC35	80	---Of bast fibres
				2.8	哥斯达黎加CR				
4728	6306.9030	---化学纤维制	16	0	东盟ASEAN,智利CL,巴基斯坦PK,新加坡SG,新西兰NZ	0	最不发达35国LDC35	130	---Of man-made fibres
				3.2	哥斯达黎加CR				
				8	秘鲁PE				
4729	6306.9090	---其他	14	0	东盟ASEAN,智利CL,巴基斯坦PK,新加坡SG,新西兰NZ,秘鲁PE	0	最不发达35国LDC35	100	---Other
				2.8	哥斯达黎加CR				
	63.07	**其他制成品，包括服装裁剪样:**							**Other made up articles, including dress patterns:**
4730	6307.1000	-擦地布、擦碗布、抹布及类似擦拭用布	14	0	东盟ASEAN,智利CL,新加坡SG,新西兰NZ,秘鲁PE,台湾TW	0	最不发达35国LDC35	130	-Floor-cloths, dish-cloths, dusters and similar cleaning cloths
				2.8	哥斯达黎加CR				
				7	巴基斯坦PK				
				11.9	亚太APTA				
4731	6307.2000	-救生衣及安全带	14	0	东盟ASEAN,智利CL,新加坡SG,新西兰NZ,秘鲁PE	0	最不发达35国LDC35,最不发达4国LDC4	70	-Life-jackets and life-belts
				2.8	哥斯达黎加CR				
				11.2	巴基斯坦PK				

序号 No.	税则号列 Tariff Line	货品名称	最惠国税率 MFN(%)	协定税率 Agreement(%)		特惠税率 S.P.(%)		普通税率 Gen.(%)	Article Description
4732	6307.9000	-其他	14	0 2.8 11.2	东盟ASEAN,智利CL,新加坡SG,新西兰NZ,秘鲁PE,香港HK,澳门MO 哥斯达黎加CR 巴基斯坦PK	0	最不发达35国LDC35,最不发达4国LDC4,缅甸MM,老挝LA,柬埔寨KH	100	-Other
		第二分章 成套物品							II.SETS
	63.08	**由机织物及纱线构成的零售包装成套物品，不论是否带附件，用以制作小地毯、装饰毯、绣花台布、餐巾或类似的纺织物品:**							**Sets consisting of woven fabric and yarn, whether or not with accessories, for making up into urgs, tapestries, embroidered table cloths or serviettes, or similar textile articles, put up in packings for retail sale:**
4733	6308.0000	由机织物及纱线构成的零售包装成套物品，不论是否带附件，用以制作小地毯、装饰毯、绣花台布、餐巾或类似的纺织物品	14	0 2.8 7	东盟ASEAN,智利CL,新加坡SG,新西兰NZ,秘鲁PE 哥斯达黎加CR 巴基斯坦PK	0	最不发达35国LDC35	130	Sets consisting of woven fabric and yarn, whether or not with accessories, for making up into rugs, tapestries, embroidered table cloths or serviettes, or similar textile articles, put up in packings for retail sale
		第三分章 旧衣着及旧纺织品;碎织物							III. WORN CLOTHING AND WORN TEXTILE ARTICLES; RAGS
	63.09	**旧衣物:**							**Worn clothing and other worn articles:**
4734	6309.0000	旧衣物	14	0 2.8 7	东盟ASEAN,智利CL,新加坡SG,新西兰NZ,秘鲁PE 哥斯达黎加CR 巴基斯坦PK	0	最不发达35国LDC35	130	Worn clothing and other worn articles
	63.10	**纺织材料的新的或旧的碎织物及废线、绳、索、缆及其制品:**							**Used or new rags, scrap twine, cordage, rope and cables and worn out articles of twine, cordage, rope or cables, of textile materials:**
4735	6310.1000	-经分拣的	14	0 2.8 11.2	东盟ASEAN,智利CL,新加坡SG,新西兰NZ,秘鲁PE 哥斯达黎加CR 巴基斯坦PK	0	最不发达35国LDC35,最不发达4国LDC4	50	-Sorted

序号 No.	税则号列 Tariff Line	货品名称	最惠国税率 MFN(%)	协定税率 Agreement(%)		特惠税率 S.P.(%)		普通税率 Gen.(%)	Article Description
4736	6310.9000	-其他	14	0 2.8	东盟ASEAN,智利CL,新加坡SG,新西兰NZ,秘鲁PE 哥斯达黎加CR	0	最不发达35国LDC35,最不发达4国LDC4,缅甸MM,老挝LA,柬埔寨KH	50	-Other

第十二类
鞋、帽、伞、杖、鞭及其零件；已加工的羽毛及其制品；人造花；人发制品

第六十四章
鞋靴、护腿和类似品及其零件

注释：

一、本章不包括：

（一）易损材料（例如，纸、塑料薄膜）制的无外绱鞋底的一次性鞋靴罩或套，这些产品应按其构成材料归类；

（二）纺织材料制的鞋靴，没有用粘、缝或其他方法将外底固定或安装在鞋面上的（第十一类）；

（三）税号 63.09 的旧鞋靴；

（四）石棉制品（税号 68.12）；

（五）矫形鞋靴或其他矫形器具及其零件（税号 90.21）；

（六）玩具鞋及装有冰刀或轮子的滑冰鞋；护胫或类似的运动防护服装（第九十五章）。

二、税号 64.06 所称"零件"，不包括鞋钉、护鞋铁掌、鞋眼、鞋钩、鞋扣、饰物、编带、鞋带、绒球或其他装饰带（应分别归入相应税号）及税号 96.06 的钮扣或其他货品。

三、本章所称：

（一）"橡胶"及"塑料"，包括能用肉眼辨出其外表有一层橡胶或塑料的机织物或其他纺织产品，运用本款时，橡胶或塑料仅引起颜色变化的不计在内。

（二）"皮革"，是指税号 41.07 及 41.12 至 41.14 的货品。

四、除本章注释三另有规定的以外：

（一）鞋面的材料应以占表面面积最大的那种材料为准，计算表面面积可不考虑附件及加

SECTION Ⅻ
FOOTWEAR, HEADGEAR, UMBRELLAS, SUN UMBRELLAS, WALKING-STICKS, SEAT-STICKS, WHIPS, RIDING-CROPS AND PARTS THEREOF; PREPARED FEATHERS AND ARTICLES MADE THEREWITH; ARTIFICIAL FLOWERS; ARTICLES OF HUMAN HAIR

Chapter 64
Footwear, gaiters and the like; parts of such articles

Notes:

1. This Chapter does not cover :

(a) Disposable foot or shoe coverings of flimsy material (for example, paper, sheeting of plastics) without applied soles. These products are classified according to their constituent material;

(b) Footwear of textile material, without an outer sole glued, sewn or otherwise affixed or applied to the upper (Section Ⅺ);

(c) Worn footwear of heading No.63.09;

(d) Articles of asbestos (heading No.68.12);

(e) Orthopaedic footwear or other orthopaedic appliances, or parts thereof (heading No.90.21); or

(f) Toy footwear or skating boots with ice or roller skates attached; shin guards or similar protective sportswear (Chapter 95).

2. For the purposes of heading No.64.06, the term "parts" does not include pegs, protectors, eyelets, hooks, buckles, ornaments, braid, laces, pompons or other trimmings (which are to be classified in their appropriate headings) or buttons or other goods of heading No.96.06.

3. For the purposes of this Chapter:

(a) the terms "rubber" and "plastics" include woven fabrics or other textile products with an external layer of rubber or plastics being visible to the naked eye; for the purpose of this provision, no account should be taken of any resulting change of colour; and

(b) the term "leather" refers to the goods of headings 41.07 and 41.12 to 41.14.

4. Subject to Note 3 to this Chapter:

(a) the material of the upper shall be taken to be the constituent material having the greatest external surface ar-

固件，例如，护踝、裹边、饰物、扣子、拉襻、鞋眼或类似附属件；

（二）外底的主要材料应以与地面接触最广的那种材料为准，计算接触面时可不考虑鞋底钉、铁掌或类似附属件。

ea, no account being taken of accessories or reinforcements such as ankle patches, edging, ornamentation, buckles, tabs, eyelet stays or similar attachments;

(b) the constituent material of the outer sole shall be taken to be the material having the greatest surface area in contact with the ground, no account being taken of accessories or reinforcements such as spikes, bars, nails, protectors or similar attachments.

子目注释：

子目号 6402.12、6402.19、6403.12、6403.19 及 6404.11 所称“运动鞋靴”，仅适用于：

一、带有或可装鞋底钉、止滑柱、夹钳、马蹄掌或类似品的体育专用鞋靴；

二、滑冰靴、滑雪靴及越野滑雪用鞋靴、滑雪板靴、角力靴、拳击靴及赛车鞋。

Subheading Notes:

For the purposes of subheadings Nos.6402.12, 6402.19, 6403.12, 6403.19 and 6404.11, the expression “sports footwear” applies only to:

1. footwear which is designed for a sporting activity and has, or has provision for the attachment of, spikes, sprigs, stops, clips, bars or the like;
2. skating boots, ski-boots and cross-country ski footwear, snowboard boots, wrestling boots, boxing boots and cycling shoes.

序号 No.	税则号列 Tariff Line	货品名称	最惠国税率 MFN(%)	协定税率 Agreement(%)		特惠税率 S.P.(%)		普通税率 Gen.(%)	Article Description
	64.01	**橡胶或塑料制外底及鞋面的防水鞋靴，其鞋面不是用缝、铆、钉、旋、塞或类似方法固定在鞋底上的：**							**Waterproof footwear with outer soles and uppers of rubber or of plastics, the uppers of which are neither fixed to the sole nor assembled by stitching, riveting, nailing, screwing, plugging or similar processes:**
		-装有金属防护鞋头的鞋靴：							-Footwear incorporating a protective metal toe-cap:
4737	6401.1010	---橡胶制鞋面的	24	0 4.8 12	东盟ASEAN,智利CL,新加坡SG,新西兰NZ 哥斯达黎加CR 亚太APTA,巴基斯坦PK,秘鲁PE	0	最不发达35国LDC35	100	---With uppers of rubber
4738	6401.1090	---塑料制鞋面的	24	0 4.8 12	东盟ASEAN,智利CL,新加坡SG,新西兰NZ 哥斯达黎加CR 亚太APTA,巴基斯坦PK,秘鲁PE	0	最不发达35国LDC35	100	---With uppers of plastics
		-其他鞋靴：							-Other footwear:
		--中、短统靴（过踝但未到膝）：							--Covering the ankle but not covering the knee:

序号 No.	税则号列 Tariff Line	货品名称	最惠国税率 MFN(%)	协定税率 Agreement(%)		特惠税率 S.P.(%)		普通税率 Gen.(%)	Article Description
4739	6401.9210	---橡胶制鞋面的	24	0 4.8 12	东盟ASEAN,智利CL,新加坡SG,新西兰NZ 哥斯达黎加CR 亚太APTA,巴基斯坦PK,秘鲁PE	0	最不发达35国LDC35	100	---With uppers of rubber
4740	6401.9290	---塑料制鞋面的	24	0 4.8 12	东盟ASEAN,智利CL,新加坡SG,新西兰NZ 哥斯达黎加CR 亚太APTA,巴基斯坦PK,秘鲁PE	0	最不发达35国LDC35	100	---With uppers of plastics
4741	6401.9900	--其他	24	0 4.8 12	东盟ASEAN,智利CL,新加坡SG,新西兰NZ 哥斯达黎加CR 亚太APTA,巴基斯坦PK,秘鲁PE	0	最不发达35国LDC35	100	--Other
	64.02	**橡胶或塑料制外底及鞋面的其他鞋靴:**							**Other footwear with outer soles and uppers of rubber or plastics:**
		-运动鞋靴:							-Sports footwear:
4742	6402.1200	--滑雪靴、越野滑雪鞋靴及滑雪板靴	10	0 5	东盟ASEAN,智利CL,新西兰NZ,秘鲁PE,哥斯达黎加CR 亚太APTA,巴基斯坦PK	0	最不发达35国LDC35,最不发达4国LDC4	100	--Ski-boots, cross-country ski footwear and snowboard boots
4743	6402.1900	--其他	24	0 4.8 12	东盟ASEAN,智利CL,新加坡SG,新西兰NZ 哥斯达黎加CR 亚太APTA,巴基斯坦PK,秘鲁PE	0	最不发达35国LDC35	100	--Other
4744	6402.2000	-用栓塞方法将鞋面条带装配在鞋底上的鞋	24	0 4.8 12	东盟ASEAN,智利CL,新加坡SG,新西兰NZ 哥斯达黎加CR 亚太APTA,巴基斯坦PK,秘鲁PE	0	最不发达35国LDC35	100	-Footwear with upper straps or thongs assembled to the sole by means of plugs
		-其他鞋靴:							-Other footwear:
4745	6402.9100	--短统靴（过踝）	24	0 4.8 12	东盟ASEAN,智利CL,新加坡SG,新西兰NZ,澳门MO 哥斯达黎加CR 亚太APTA,巴基斯坦PK,秘鲁PE	0	最不发达35国LDC35	100	--Covering the ankle
		--其他:							--Other:
4746	6402.9910	---橡胶制鞋面的	24	0 4.8 12	东盟ASEAN,智利CL,新加坡SG,新西兰NZ,澳门MO 哥斯达黎加CR 亚太APTA,巴基斯坦PK,秘鲁PE	0	最不发达35国LDC35,最不发达4国LDC4	100	---With uppers of rubber
		---塑料制鞋面的:							---With uppers of plastics:

序号 No.	税则号列 Tariff Line	货品名称	最惠国税率 MFN(%)		协定税率 Agreement(%)		特惠税率 S.P.(%)	普通税率 Gen.(%)	Article Description
4747	6402.9921	----以机织物或其他纺织材料作衬底的	24	0 4.8 12	东盟ASEAN,智利CL,新加坡SG,新西兰NZ,澳门MO 哥斯达黎加CR 亚太APTA,巴基斯坦PK,秘鲁PE	0	最不发达35国LDC35,最不发达4国LDC4	100	----Woven fabrics or other textile products as substrate
4748	6402.9929	----其他	24	0 4.8 12	东盟ASEAN,智利CL,新加坡SG,新西兰NZ,澳门MO 哥斯达黎加CR 亚太APTA,巴基斯坦PK,秘鲁PE	0	最不发达35国LDC35,最不发达4国LDC4	100	----Other
	64.03	**橡胶、塑料、皮革或再生皮革制外底，皮革制鞋面的鞋靴：**							**Footwear with outer soles of rubber, plastics, leather or composition leather and upers of leather:**
		-运动鞋靴：							-Sports footwear:
4749	6403.1200	--滑雪靴、越野滑雪鞋靴及滑雪板靴	24	0 4.8 12	东盟ASEAN,智利CL,新加坡SG,新西兰NZ 哥斯达黎加CR 秘鲁PE	0	最不发达35国LDC35,最不发达4国LDC4,柬埔寨KH	100	--Ski-boots, cross-country ski footwear and snow-board boots
4750	6403.1900	--其他	15	0 3 7.5 12	东盟ASEAN,智利CL,新加坡SG,新西兰NZ,澳门MO 哥斯达黎加CR 秘鲁PE 巴基斯坦PK	0	最不发达35国LDC35,最不发达4国LDC4,柬埔寨KH	100	--Other
4751	6403.2000	-皮革制外底，由交叉于脚背并绕大脚趾的皮革条带构成鞋面的鞋	24	0 4.8 12	东盟ASEAN,智利CL,新加坡SG,新西兰NZ,澳门MO 哥斯达黎加CR 秘鲁PE	0	最不发达35国LDC35,最不发达4国LDC4,柬埔寨KH	100	-Footwear with outer soles of leather, and uppers which consist of leather straps across the instep and around the big toe
4752	6403.4000	-装有金属防护鞋头的其他鞋靴	24	0 4.8 12	东盟ASEAN,智利CL,新加坡SG,新西兰NZ 哥斯达黎加CR 秘鲁PE	0	最不发达35国LDC35,最不发达4国LDC4,柬埔寨KH	100	-Other footwear, incorporating a protective metal toe-cap
		-皮革制外底的其他鞋靴：							-Other footwear with outer soles of leather:
		--短统靴（过踝）：							--Covering the ankle:
		---过脚踝但低于小腿的短统靴，按内底长度分类：							---No part of the calf, with insoles of a length:

序号 No.	税则号列 Tariff Line	货品名称	最惠国税率 MFN(%)	协定税率 Agreement(%)		特惠税率 S.P.(%)		普通税率 Gen.(%)	Article Description
4753	6403.5111	----小于 24 厘米的	10	0 5	东盟ASEAN,智利CL,新西兰NZ,秘鲁PE,哥斯达黎加CR,澳门MO 巴基斯坦PK	0	最不发达 35 国 LDC35,最不发达 4 国 LDC4,柬埔寨KH	100	----Of less than 24cm
4754	6403.5119	----其他	10	0 5	东盟ASEAN,智利CL,新西兰NZ,秘鲁PE,哥斯达黎加CR 巴基斯坦PK	0	最不发达 35 国 LDC35,最不发达 4 国 LDC4,柬埔寨KH	100	----Other
		---其他，按内底长度分类:							---Other, with insoles of a length:
4755	6403.5191	----小于 24 厘米的	10	0 5	东盟ASEAN,智利CL,新西兰NZ,秘鲁PE,哥斯达黎加CR 巴基斯坦PK	0	最不发达 35 国 LDC35,最不发达 4 国 LDC4,柬埔寨KH	100	----Of less than 24cm
4756	6403.5199	----其他	10	0 5	东盟ASEAN,智利CL,新西兰NZ,秘鲁PE,哥斯达黎加CR 巴基斯坦PK	0	最不发达 35 国 LDC35,最不发达 4 国 LDC4,柬埔寨KH	100	----Other
4757	6403.5900	--其他	10	0 5	东盟ASEAN,智利CL,新西兰NZ,哥斯达黎加CR,澳门MO 巴基斯坦PK,秘鲁PE	0	最不发达 35 国 LDC35,最不发达 4 国 LDC4,柬埔寨KH	100	--Other
		-其他鞋靴: --短统靴（过踝）: ---过脚踝但低于小腿的短统靴，按内底长度分类:							-Other footwear: --Covering the ankle: ---No part of the calf, with insoles of a length:
4758	6403.9111	----小于 24 厘米的	10	0 5	东盟ASEAN,智利CL,新加坡SG,新西兰NZ,秘鲁PE,哥斯达黎加CR,澳门MO 巴基斯坦PK	0	最不发达 35 国 LDC35,最不发达 4 国 LDC4,柬埔寨KH	100	----Of less than 24cm
4759	6403.9119	----其他	10	0 5	东盟ASEAN,智利CL,新加坡SG,新西兰NZ,秘鲁PE,哥斯达黎加CR,澳门MO 巴基斯坦PK	0	最不发达 35 国 LDC35,最不发达 4 国 LDC4,柬埔寨KH	100	----Other

序号 No.	税则号列 Tariff Line	货品名称	最惠国税率 MFN(%)	协定税率 Agreement(%)		特惠税率 S.P.(%)		普通税率 Gen.(%)	Article Description
		---其他，按内底长度分类:							---Other, with insoles of a length:
4760	6403.9191	----小于 24 厘米的	10	0 5	东盟ASEAN,智利CL,新加坡SG,新西兰NZ,秘鲁PE,哥斯达黎加CR,澳门MO 巴基斯坦PK	0	最不发达 35 国 LDC35,最不发达 4 国 LDC4,柬埔寨KH	100	----Of less than 24cm
4761	6403.9199	----其他	10	0 5	东盟ASEAN,智利CL,新加坡SG,新西兰NZ,秘鲁PE,哥斯达黎加CR,澳门MO 巴基斯坦PK	0	最不发达 35 国 LDC35,最不发达 4 国 LDC4,柬埔寨KH	100	----Other
4762	6403.9900	--其他	10	0 5 8.5	东盟ASEAN,智利CL,新加坡SG,新西兰NZ,秘鲁PE,哥斯达黎加CR,澳门MO 巴基斯坦PK 亚太APTA	0	最不发达 35 国 LDC35,最不发达 4 国 LDC4,柬埔寨KH	100	--Other
	64.04	**橡胶、塑料、皮革或再生皮革制外底，用纺织材料制鞋面的鞋靴:**							**Footwear with outer soles of rubber, plastics, leather or composition leather and uppers of textile materials:**
		-橡胶或塑料制外底的鞋靴:							-Footwear with outer soles of rubber or plastics:
4763	6404.1100	--运动鞋靴;网球鞋、篮球鞋、体操鞋、训练鞋及类似鞋	24	0 4.8 12	东盟ASEAN,智利CL,新加坡SG,新西兰NZ,澳门MO 哥斯达黎加CR 亚太APTA,巴基斯坦PK,秘鲁PE	0	最不发达 35 国 LDC35	100	--Sports footwear, tennis shoes, basketba-ll shoes, gym shoes, training shoes and the like
4764	6404.1900	--其他	24	0 4.8 12	东盟ASEAN,智利CL,新加坡SG,新西兰NZ,澳门MO 哥斯达黎加CR 亚太APTA,巴基斯坦PK,秘鲁PE	0	最不发达 35 国 LDC35	100	--Other
4765	6404.2000	-皮革或再生皮革制外底的鞋靴	24	0 4.8 12	东盟ASEAN,智利CL,新加坡SG,新西兰NZ 哥斯达黎加CR 亚太APTA,巴基斯坦PK,秘鲁PE	0	最不发达 35 国 LDC35	100	-Footwear with outer soles of leather or composition leather
	64.05	**其他鞋靴:**							**Other footwear:**
		-皮革或再生皮革制鞋面的:							-With uppers of leather or composition leather:
4766	6405.1010	---橡胶、塑料、皮革及再生皮革制外底的	24	0 4.8 12	东盟ASEAN,智利CL,新加坡SG,新西兰NZ 哥斯达黎加CR 亚太APTA,巴基斯坦PK,秘鲁PE	0	最不发达 35 国 LDC35	100	---With outer soles of rubber, plastics, leather or composition leather

序号 No.	税则号列 Tariff Line	货品名称	最惠国税率 MFN(%)	协定税率 Agreement(%)		特惠税率 S.P.(%)		普通税率 Gen.(%)	Article Description
4767	6405.1090	---其他材料制外底的	24	0 4.8 12	东盟ASEAN,智利CL,新加坡SG,新西兰NZ 哥斯达黎加CR 亚太APTA,巴基斯坦PK,秘鲁PE	0	最不发达35国LDC35	100	---With outer soles of other materials
4768	6405.2000	-纺织材料制鞋面的	22	0 4.4 11	东盟ASEAN,智利CL,新加坡SG,新西兰NZ 哥斯达黎加CR 亚太APTA,巴基斯坦PK,秘鲁PE	0	最不发达35国LDC35	100	-With uppers of textile material
		-其他:							-Other:
4769	6405.9010	---橡胶、塑料、皮革及再生皮革制外底的	15	0 3 7.5 10.5	东盟ASEAN,智利CL,新加坡SG,新西兰NZ 哥斯达黎加CR 巴基斯坦PK,秘鲁PE 亚太APTA	0	最不发达35国LDC35	100	---With outer soles of rubber, plastics, leather or composition leather
4770	6405.9090	---其他材料制外底的	15	0 3 7.5 10.5	东盟ASEAN,智利CL,新加坡SG,新西兰NZ 哥斯达黎加CR 巴基斯坦PK,秘鲁PE 亚太APTA	0	最不发达35国LDC35	100	---With outer soles of other materials
	64.06	**鞋靴零件（包括鞋面，不论是否带有除外底以外的其他鞋底）;活动式鞋内底、跟垫及类似品;护腿、裹腿和类似品及其零件:**							**Parts of footwear (including uppers whether or not attached to soles other than outer soles); removable in-soles, heel cushions and similar articles; gaiters, leggings and similar articles, and parts thereof:**
4771	6406.1000	-鞋面及其零件,但硬衬除外	15	0 3 7.5 13.2	东盟ASEAN,智利CL,新加坡SG,新西兰NZ,台湾TW 哥斯达黎加CR 巴基斯坦PK,秘鲁PE 亚太APTA	0	最不发达35国LDC35	90	-Uppers and parts thereof, other than stiffeners
		-橡胶或塑料制的外底及鞋跟:							-Other soles and heels, of rubber or plastics:
4772	6406.2010	---橡胶制的	15	0 3 7.5 12	东盟ASEAN,智利CL,新加坡SG,新西兰NZ,台湾TW 哥斯达黎加CR 秘鲁PE 巴基斯坦PK	0	最不发达35国LDC35,最不发达4国LDC4	90	---Of rubber
4773	6406.2020	---塑料制的	15	0 3 7.5 12	东盟ASEAN,智利CL,新加坡SG,新西兰NZ 哥斯达黎加CR 秘鲁PE 巴基斯坦PK	0	最不发达35国LDC35,最不发达4国LDC4	90	---Of plastics
		-其他:							-Other:
4774	6406.9010	---木制	15	0 3 7.5 10.5	东盟ASEAN,智利CL,新加坡SG,新西兰NZ 哥斯达黎加CR 巴基斯坦PK,秘鲁PE 亚太APTA	0	最不发达35国LDC35	90	---Of wood

序号 No.	税则号列 Tariff Line	货品名称	最惠国税率 MFN(%)	协定税率 Agreement(%)		特惠税率 S.P.(%)		普通税率 Gen.(%)	Article Description
		---其他材料制:							---Of other materials:
4775	6406.9091	----活动式鞋内底、跟垫及类似品	15	0	东盟ASEAN,智利CL,新加坡SG,新西兰NZ,香港HK,澳门MO,台湾TW	0	最不发达35国LDC35	90	----Non-wood removable insoles, heel cushions and similar articles
				3	哥斯达黎加CR				
				7.5	巴基斯坦PK,秘鲁PE				
				10.5	亚太APTA				
4776	6406.9092	----护腿、裹腿和类似品及其零件	15	0	东盟ASEAN,智利CL,新加坡SG,新西兰NZ,香港HK,澳门MO,台湾TW	0	最不发达35国LDC35	90	----Non-wood gaiters, leggings and similar articles, and parts thereof
				3	哥斯达黎加CR				
				7.5	巴基斯坦PK,秘鲁PE				
				10.5	亚太APTA				
4777	6406.9099	----其他	15	0	东盟ASEAN,智利CL,新加坡SG,新西兰NZ,香港HK,澳门MO,台湾TW	0	最不发达35国LDC35	90	----Of other materials
				3	哥斯达黎加CR				
				7.5	巴基斯坦PK,秘鲁PE				
				10.5	亚太APTA				

第六十五章 帽类及其零件

Chapter 65 Headgear and parts thereof

注释：

一、本章不包括：

（一）税号 63.09 的旧帽类；

（二）石棉制帽类（税号 68.12）；

（三）第九十五章的玩偶帽、其他玩具帽或狂欢节用品。

二、税号 65.02 不包括缝制的帽坯，但仅将条带缝成螺旋形的除外。

Notes:

1. This Chapter does not cover:

(a) Worn headgear of heading No.63.09;

(b) Asbestos headgear (Heading No.68.12); or

(c) Dolls' hats, other toy hats or carnival articles of Chapter 95.

2. Heading No.65.02 does not cover hat-shapes made by sewing, other than those obtained simply by sewing strips in spirals.

序号 No.	税则号列 Tariff Line	货品名称	最惠国税率 MFN(%)	协定税率 Agreement(%)	特惠税率 S.P.(%)	普通税率 Gen.(%)	Article Description
	65.01	**毡呢制的帽坯、帽身及帽兜，未楦制成形，也未加帽边；毡呢制的圆帽片及制帽用的毡呢筒（包括裁开的毡呢筒）：**					**Hat-forms, hat bodies and hoods of felt, neither blocked to shape nor with made brims; plateaux and manchons (including slit manchons), of felt:**
4778	6501.0000	毡呢制的帽坯、帽身及帽兜，未楦制成形，也未加帽边；毡呢制的圆帽片及制帽用的毡呢筒（包括裁开的毡呢筒）	22	0 东盟ASEAN,智利CL,新加坡SG,新西兰NZ 4.4 哥斯达黎加CR 11 秘鲁PE	0 最不发达35国LDC35	100	Hat-forms, hat bodies and hoods of felt, neither blocked to shape nor with made brims; plateaux and manchons (including slit manchons), of felt
	65.02	**编结的帽坯或用任何材料的条带拼制而成的帽坯，未楦制成形，也未加帽边、衬里或装饰物：**					**Hat-shapes, plaited or made by assembling strips of any material, neither blocked to shape, nor with made brims, nor lined, nor trimmed:**
4779	6502.0000	编结的帽坯或用任何材料的条带拼制而成的帽坯，未楦制成形，也未加帽边、衬里或装饰物	20	0 东盟ASEAN,智利CL,新加坡SG,新西兰NZ 4 哥斯达黎加CR 10 秘鲁PE	0 最不发达35国LDC35	100	Hat-shapes, plaited or made by assembling strips of any material, neither blocked to shape, nor with made brims, nor lined, nor trimmed
	65.04	**编结帽或用任何材料的条带拼制而成的帽类，不论有无衬里或装饰物：**					**Hats and other headgear, plaited or made by assembling strips of any material, whether or not lined or trimmed:**
4780	6504.0000	编结帽或用任何材料的条带拼制而成的帽类，不论有无衬里或装饰物	20	0 东盟ASEAN,智利CL,新加坡SG,新西兰NZ 4 哥斯达黎加CR 10 秘鲁PE	0 最不发达35国LDC35	130	Hats and other headgear, plaited or made by assembling strips of any material, whether or not lined or trimmed

序号 No.	税则号列 Tariff Line	货品名称	最惠国税率 MFN(%)	协定税率 Agreement(%)		特惠税率 S.P.(%)		普通税率 Gen.(%)	Article Description
	65.05	**针织或钩编的帽类，用成匹的花边、毡呢或其他纺织物（条带除外）制成的帽类，不论有无衬里或装饰物;任何材料制的发网，不论有无衬里或装饰物:**							**Hats and other headgear, knitted or crocheted, or made up from lace, felt or other textile fabric, in the piece (but not in strips), whether or not lined or trimmed; hair-nets of any material, whether or not lined or trimmed:**
4781	6505.0010	---发网	10	0 5	东盟ASEAN,智利CL,新西兰NZ,秘鲁PE,哥斯达黎加CR 巴基斯坦PK	0	最不发达35国LDC35,最不发达4国LDC4	130	---Hair-nets
4782	6505.0020	---钩编的帽类	20	0 2 4 10 19	东盟ASEAN,新加坡SG,新西兰NZ 智利CL 哥斯达黎加CR 秘鲁PE 亚太APTA,巴基斯坦PK	0	最不发达35国LDC35,最不发达4国LDC4	130	---Hats and other headgear, knitted or crocheted
		---其他:							---Other :
4783	6505.0091	----用税号65.01的帽身、帽兜或圆帽片制成的毡呢帽类，不论有无衬里或装饰物	22	0 4.4 11	东盟ASEAN,智利CL,新加坡SG,新西兰NZ 哥斯达黎加CR 秘鲁PE	0	最不发达35国LDC35	130	----Felt hats and other felt headgear, made from the hat bodies, hoods or plateaux of heading No.65.01, whether or not lined or trimmed
4784	6505.0099	----其他	20	0 2 4 10 19	东盟ASEAN,新加坡SG,新西兰NZ,澳门MO 智利CL 哥斯达黎加CR 秘鲁PE 亚太APTA,巴基斯坦PK	0	最不发达35国LDC35,最不发达4国LDC4	130	----Other
	65.06	**其他帽类，不论有无衬里或装饰物:**							**Other headgear, whether or not lined or trimmed:**
4785	6506.1000	-安全帽	10	0 5	东盟ASEAN,智利CL,新西兰NZ,秘鲁PE,哥斯达黎加CR 巴基斯坦PK	0	最不发达35国LDC35	100	-Safety headgear
		-其他:							-Other:
4786	6506.9100	--橡胶或塑料制	10	0 1 5	东盟ASEAN,新西兰NZ,秘鲁PE,哥斯达黎加CR 智利CL 巴基斯坦PK	0	最不发达35国LDC35	100	--Of rubber or of plastics
		--其他材料制:							--Of other materials:
4787	6506.9910	---皮革制	10	0 1 5	东盟ASEAN,新西兰NZ,秘鲁PE,哥斯达黎加CR 智利CL 巴基斯坦PK	0	最不发达35国LDC35	130	---Of leather

序号 No.	税则号列 Tariff Line	货品名称	最惠国税率 MFN(%)	协定税率 Agreement(%)		特惠税率 S.P.(%)		普通税率 Gen.(%)	Article Description
4788	6506.9920	---毛皮制	10	0 5	东盟ASEAN,智利CL,新西兰NZ,秘鲁PE,哥斯达黎加CR,香港HK 巴基斯坦PK	0	最不发达35国LDC35,最不发达4国LDC4	130	---Of furskin
4789	6506.9990	---其他	24	0 2.4 4.8 12	东盟ASEAN,新加坡SG,新西兰NZ 智利CL 哥斯达黎加CR 秘鲁PE	0	最不发达35国LDC35,最不发达4国LDC4	100	---Other
	65.07	**帽圈、帽衬、帽套、帽帮、帽骨架、帽舌及帽颏带:**							**Head-bands, linings, covers, hat foundations, hat frames, peaks and chinstraps, for headgear:**
4790	6507.0000	帽圈、帽衬、帽套、帽帮、帽骨架、帽舌及帽颏带	24	0 4.8 12	东盟ASEAN,智利CL,新加坡SG,新西兰NZ,澳门MO 哥斯达黎加CR 秘鲁PE	0	最不发达35国LDC35	100	Head-bands, linings, covers, hat foundations, hat frames, peaks and chinstraps, for headgear

第六十六章
雨伞、阳伞、手杖、鞭子、马鞭及其零件

Chapter 66
Umbrellas，sun umbrellas，walking-sticks，seat-sticks，whips，riding-crops and parts thereof

注释：

一、本章不包括：

（一）丈量用杖及类似品（税号 90.17）；

（二）火器手杖、刀剑手杖、灌铅手杖及类似品（第九十三章）；

（三）第九十五章的货品（例如，玩具雨伞、玩具阳伞）。

二、税号 66.03 不包括纺织材料制的零件、附件及装饰品或者任何材料制的罩套、流苏、鞭梢、伞套及类似品。此类货品即使与税号 66.01 或 66.02 的物品一同进口或出口，只要未装配在一起，则不应视为上述税号所列物品的组成零件，而应分别归入各有关税号。

Notes:

1. This Chapter does not cover:

(a) Measure walking-sticks or the like (heading No.90.17);

(b) Firearm-sticks，sword-sticks，loaded walking-sticks or the like (Chapter 93); or

(c) Goods of Chapter 95 (for example, toy umbrellas, toy sun umbrellas).

2.Heading No.66.03 does not cover parts，trimmings or accessories of textile material，or covers，tassels，thongs，umbrella cases or the like，of any material. Such goods presented with，but not fitted to，articles of heading No.66.01 or 66.02 are to be classified separately and not to be treated as forming part of those articles.

序号 No.	税则号列 Tariff Line	货品名称	最惠国税率 MFN(%)	协定税率 Agreement(%)		特惠税率 S.P.(%)		普通税率 Gen.(%)	Article Description
	66.01	**雨伞及阳伞（包括手杖伞、庭园用伞及类似伞）：**							**Umbrellas and sun umbrellas (including walking-stick umbrellas, garden umbrellas and similar umbrellas):**
4791	6601.1000	-庭园用伞及类似伞	14	0 2.8 7	东盟ASEAN,智利CL,新加坡SG,新西兰NZ,秘鲁PE 哥斯达黎加CR 巴基斯坦PK	0	最不发达35国LDC35	130	-Garden or similar umbrellas
		-其他:							-Other:
4792	6601.9100	--折叠伞	10	0 5	东盟ASEAN,智利CL,新西兰NZ,秘鲁PE,哥斯达黎加CR 巴基斯坦PK	0	最不发达35国LDC35,最不发达4国LDC4	130	--Having a telescopic shaft
4793	6601.9900	--其他	10	0 5	东盟ASEAN,智利CL,新西兰NZ,秘鲁PE,哥斯达黎加CR 巴基斯坦PK	0	最不发达35国LDC35	130	--Other
	66.02	**手杖、带座手杖、鞭子、马鞭及类似品:**							**Walking-sticks, seat-sticks, whips, riding-crops and the like:**
4794	6602.0000	手杖、带座手杖、鞭子、马鞭及类似品	10	0 5	东盟ASEAN,智利CL,新西兰NZ,秘鲁PE,哥斯达黎加CR 巴基斯坦PK	0	最不发达35国LDC35	130	Walking-sticks, seat-sticks, whips, riding-crops and the like

序号 No.	税则号列 Tariff Line	货品名称	最惠国税 率 MFN(%)	协定税率 Agreement(%)		特惠税率 S.P.(%)		普通税率 Gen.(%)	Article Description
	66.03	**税号 66.01 或 66.02 所列物品的零件及装饰品:**							**Parts, trimmings and accessories of articles of heading No.66.01 or 66.02:**
4795	6603.2000	-伞骨,包括装在伞柄上的伞骨	14	0 2.8 11.2	东盟ASEAN,智利CL,新加坡SG,新西兰NZ,秘鲁PE 哥斯达黎加CR 巴基斯坦PK	0	最不发达 35 国 LDC35	130	-Umbrella frames, including frames mounted on shafts (sticks)
4796	6603.9000	-其他	14	0 2.8 11.2	东盟ASEAN,智利CL,新加坡SG,新西兰NZ,秘鲁PE 哥斯达黎加CR 巴基斯坦PK	0	最不发达 35 国 LDC35,最不发达 4 国 LDC4	130	-Other

第六十七章
已加工羽毛、羽绒及其制品；人造花；人发制品

注释：

一、本章不包括：

（一）人发制滤布（税号 59.11）；

（二）花边、刺绣品或其他纺织物制成的花卉图案（第十一类）；

（三）鞋靴（第六十四章）；

（四）帽类及发网（第六十五章）；

（五）玩具、运动用品或狂欢节用品（第九十五章）；

（六）羽毛掸帚、粉扑及人发制的筛子（第九十六章）。

二、税号 67.01 不包括：

（一）羽毛或羽绒仅在其中作为填充料的物品（例如税号 94.04 的寝具）；

（二）羽毛或羽绒仅作为饰物或填充料的衣服或衣着附件；

（三）税号 67.02 的人造花、叶及其部分品，以及它们的制成品。

三、税号 67.02 不包括：

（一）玻璃制品（第七十章）；

（二）用陶器、石料、金属、木料或其他材料经模铸、锻造、雕刻、冲压或其他方法整件制成形的人造花、叶或果实；用捆扎、胶粘及类似方法以外的其他方法将部分品组合而成的上述制品。

Chapter 67
Prepared feathers and down and articles made of feathers or of down; artificial flowers; articles of human hair

Notes:

1. This Chapter does not cover:

(a) Straining cloth of human hair (heading No.59.11);

(b) Floral motifs of lace, of embroidery or other textile fabric (Section XI);

(c) Footwear (Chapter 64);

(d) Headgear or hair-nets (Chapter 65);

(e) Toys, sports requisites or carnival articles (Chapter 95); or

(f) Feather dusters, powder-puffs or hair sieves (Chapter 96).

2. Heading No.67.01 does not cover:

(a) Articles in which feathers or down constitute only filling or padding (for example, bedding of heading No.94.04);

(b) Articles of apparel or clothing accessories in which feathers or down constitute no more than mere trimming or padding; or

(c) Artificial flowers or foliage or parts thereof or made up articles of heading No.67.02.

3. Heading No.67.02 does not cover:

(a) Articles of glass (Chapter 70); or

(b) Artificial flowers, foliage or fruit of pottery, stone, metal, wood or other materials, obtained in one piece by moulding, forging, carving, stamping or other process, or consisting of parts assembled otherwise than by binding, glueing, fitting into one another or similar methods.

序号 No.	税则号列 Tariff Line	货品名称	最惠国税率 MFN(%)	协定税率 Agreement(%)	特惠税率 S.P.(%)	普通税率 Gen.(%)	Article Description
	67.01	**带羽毛或羽绒的鸟皮及鸟体其他部分、羽毛、部分羽毛、羽绒及其制品（税号05.05 的货品和经加工的羽管及羽轴除外）：**					**Skins and other parts of birds with their feathers or down, feathers, parts of feathers, down and articles thereof (other than goods of heading No.05.05 and worked quills and scapes):**

序号 No.	税则号列 Tariff Line	货品名称	最惠国税率 MFN(%)	协定税率 Agreement(%)		特惠税率 S.P.(%)		普通税率 Gen.(%)	Article Description
4797	6701.0000	带羽毛或羽绒的鸟皮及鸟体其他部分、羽毛、部分羽毛、羽绒及其制品（税号05.05的货品和经加工的羽管及羽轴除外）	20	0 4 10	东盟ASEAN,智利CL,新加坡SG,新西兰NZ,澳门MO 哥斯达黎加CR 秘鲁PE	0	最不发达35国LDC35	130	Skins and other parts of birds with their feathers or down, feathers, parts of feathers, down and articles thereof (other than goods of heading No.05.05 and worked quills and scapes)
	67.02	**人造花、叶、果实及其零件;用人造花、叶或果实制成的物品:**							**Artificial flowers, foliage and fruit and parts thereof; articles made of artificial flowers, foliage or fruit:**
4798	6702.1000	-塑料制	20	0 4 10	东盟ASEAN,智利CL,新加坡SG,新西兰NZ 哥斯达黎加CR 秘鲁PE	0	最不发达35国LDC35	130	-Of plastics
		-其他材料制:							-Of other materials:
4799	6702.9010	---羽毛制	20	0 4 10	东盟ASEAN,智利CL,新加坡SG,新西兰NZ 哥斯达黎加CR 秘鲁PE	0	最不发达35国LDC35	130	---Of feathers or down
4800	6702.9020	---丝及绢丝制	24	0 4.8 12	东盟ASEAN,智利CL,新加坡SG,新西兰NZ 哥斯达黎加CR 秘鲁PE	0	最不发达35国LDC35	130	---Of silk or silk waste
4801	6702.9030	---化学纤维制	24	0 4.8 12	东盟ASEAN,智利CL,新加坡SG,新西兰NZ 哥斯达黎加CR 秘鲁PE	0	最不发达35国LDC35	130	---Of man-made fibres
4802	6702.9090	---其他	20	0 4 10	东盟ASEAN,智利CL,新加坡SG,新西兰NZ 哥斯达黎加CR 秘鲁PE	0	最不发达35国LDC35	130	---Other
	67.03	**经梳理、稀疏、脱色或其他方法加工的人发;作假发及类似品用的羊毛、其他动物毛或其他纺织材料:**							**Human hair, dressed, thinned, bleached or otherwise worked; wool or other animal hair or other textile materials, prepared for use in making wigs or the like:**
4803	6703.0000	经梳理、稀疏、脱色或其他方法加工的人发;作假发及类似品用的羊毛、其他动物毛或其他纺织材料	20	0 4 10 18	东盟ASEAN,智利CL,新加坡SG,新西兰NZ 哥斯达黎加CR 秘鲁PE 亚太APTA,巴基斯坦PK	0	最不发达35国LDC35	100	Human hair, dressed, thinned, bleached or otherwise worked; wool or other animal hair or other textile materials, prepared for use in making wigs or the like
	67.04	**人发、动物毛或纺织材料制的假发、假胡须、假眉毛、假睫毛及类似品;其他税号未列名的人发制品:**							**Wigs, false beards, eyebrows and eyelashes, switches and the like, of human or animal hair or of textile materials; articles of human hair not elsewhere specified or included:**

序号 No.	税则号列 Tariff Line	货品名称	最惠国税率 MFN(%)	协定税率 Agreement(%)		特惠税率 S.P.(%)		普通税率 Gen.(%)	Article Description
		-合成纤维纺织材料制:							-Of synthetic textile materials:
4804	6704.1100	--整头假发	25	0	东盟ASEAN,智利CL,新加坡SG,新西兰NZ	0	最不发达35国LDC35,最不发达4国LDC4	130	--Complete wigs
				5	哥斯达黎加CR				
				12.5	秘鲁PE				
4805	6704.1900	--其他	25	0	东盟ASEAN,智利CL,新加坡SG,新西兰NZ,澳门MO	0	最不发达35国LDC35,最不发达4国LDC4	130	--Other
				5	哥斯达黎加CR				
				12.5	秘鲁PE				
4806	6704.2000	-人发制	15	0	东盟ASEAN,智利CL,新加坡SG,新西兰NZ,澳门MO	0	最不发达35国LDC35,最不发达4国LDC4	130	-Of human hair
				3	哥斯达黎加CR				
				7.5	秘鲁PE				
				12	巴基斯坦PK				
4807	6704.9000	-其他材料制	25	0	东盟ASEAN,智利CL,新加坡SG,新西兰NZ,澳门MO	0	最不发达35国LDC35,最不发达4国LDC4	130	-Of other materials
				5	哥斯达黎加CR				
				12.5	秘鲁PE				

第十三类
石料、石膏、水泥、石棉、云母及类似材料的制品；陶瓷产品；玻璃及其制品

SECTION XIII
ARTICLES OF STONE, PLASTER, CEMENT, ASBESTOS, MICA OR SIMILAR MATERIALS; CERAMIC PRODUCTS; GLASS AND GLASSWARE

第六十八章
石料、石膏、水泥、石棉、云母及类似材料的制品

注释：

一、本章不包括：

（一）第二十五章的货品；

（二）税号 48.10 或 48.11 的经涂布、浸渍或覆盖的纸及纸板（例如，用云母粉或石墨涂布的纸及纸板、沥青纸及纸板）；

（三）第五十六章或第五十九章的经涂布、浸渍或包覆的纺织物（例如，用云母粉、沥青涂布或包覆的织物）；

（四）第七十一章的物品；

（五）第八十二章的工具及其零件；

（六）税号 84.42 的印刷用石板；

（七）绝缘子（税号 85.46）或绝缘材料制的零件（税号 85.47）；

（八）牙科用磨锉（税号 90.18）；

（九）第九十一章的物品（例如，钟及钟壳）；

（十）第九十四章的物品（例如，家具、灯具及照明装置、活动房屋）；

（十一）第九十五章的物品（例如，玩具、游戏品及运动用品）；

（十二）用第九十六章注释二（二）所述材料制成的税号 96.02 的物品或税号 96.06 的物品（例如钮扣）、税号 96.09 的物品（例如石笔）或税号 96.10 的物品（例如绘画石板）；

（十三）第九十七章的物品（例如艺术品）。

二、税号 68.02 所称"已加工的碑石或建筑用石"，不仅适用于已加工的税号 25.15、25.16 的各种石料，也适用于所有经类似加工的其他天然石料（例如，石英岩、燧石、白云石及冻石），但不适用于板岩。

Chapter 68
Articles of stone, plaster, cement, asbestos, mica or similar materials

Notes:

1. This Chapter does not cover :

(a) Goods of Chapter 25;

(b) Coated, impregnated or covered paper and paperboard of heading No.48.10 or 48.11 (for example, paper and paperboard coated with mica powder or graphite, bituminised or asphalted paper and paperboard);

(c) Coated, impregnated or covered textile fabric of Chapter 56 or 59 (for example, fabric coated or covered with mica powder, bituminised or asphalted fabric);

(d) Articles of Chapter 71;

(e) Tools or parts of tools, of Chapter 82;

(f) Lithographic stones of heading No.84.42;

(g) Electrical insulators (heading No.85.46) or fittings of insulating material of heading No.85.47;

(h) Dental burrs (heading No.90.18);

(i) Articles of Chapter 91 (for example, clocks and clock cases);

(j) Articles of Chapter 94 (for example, furniture, lamps and lighting fittings, prefabricated buildings);

(k) Articles of Chapter 95 (for example, toys, games and sports requisites);

(l) Articles of heading No.96.02, if made of materials specified in Note 2 (b) to Chapter 96, or of heading No.96.06 (for example, buttons) , No.96.09 (for example, slate pencils) or No.96.10 (for example, drawing slates);or

(m) Articles of Chapter 97 (for example, works of art) .

2. In heading No.68.02, the expression "worked monumental or building stone" applies not only to the varieties of stone referred to in heading No.25.15 or 25.16, but also to all other natural stone (for example, quartzite, flint, dolomite and steatite) similarly worked; it does not, however, apply to slate.

序号 No.	税则号列 Tariff Line	货品名称	最惠国税率 MFN(%)	协定税率 Agreement(%)		特惠税率 S.P.(%)		普通税率 Gen.(%)	Article Description
	68.01	**天然石料（不包括板岩）制的长方砌石、路缘石、扁平石:**							**Setts, curbstones and flagstones, of natural stone (except slate):**
4808	6801.0000	天然石料（不包括板岩）制的长方砌石、路缘石、扁平石	12	0 2.4 6	东盟ASEAN,智利CL,新加坡SG,新西兰NZ,秘鲁PE,澳门MO 哥斯达黎加CR 巴基斯坦PK	0	最不发达35国LDC35	70	Setts, curbstones and flagstones, of natural stone (except slate)
	68.02	**已加工的碑石或建筑用石（不包括板岩）及其制品，但税号68.01的货品除外;天然石料（包括板岩）制的镶嵌石（马赛克）及类似品，不论是否有衬背;天然石料（包括板岩）制的人工染色石粒、石片及石粉:**							**Worked monumental or building stone (except slate) and articles thereof, other than goods of heading No.68.01; mosaic cubes and the like, of natural stone (including slate), whether or not on a backing; artificially coloured granules, chippings and powder, of natural stone (including slate):**
		-砖、瓦、方块及类似品，不论是否为矩形（包括正方形），其最大表面积以可置入边长小于7厘米的方格为限;人工染色的石粒、石片及石粉:							-Tiles, cubes and similar articles, whether or not rectangular (including square), the largest surface area of which is capable of being enclosed in a square the side of which is less than 7cm; artificially coloured granules, chippings and powder:
4809	6802.1010	---大理石	24	0 4.8 19.2	东盟ASEAN,智利CL,巴基斯坦PK,新加坡SG,新西兰NZ,秘鲁PE,香港HK,澳门MO 哥斯达黎加CR 亚太APTA	0	最不发达35国LDC35,最不发达4国LDC4	90	---Marble
4810	6802.1090	---其他	20	0 4 16	东盟ASEAN,智利CL,巴基斯坦PK,新加坡SG,新西兰NZ,秘鲁PE,香港HK,澳门MO 哥斯达黎加CR 亚太APTA	0	最不发达35国LDC35	90	---Other
		-简单切削或锯开并具有一个平面的其他碑石或建筑用石及其制品:							-Other monumental or building stone and articles thereof, simply cut or sawn, with a flat or even surface:
		--大理石、石灰华及蜡石:							--Marble, travertine and alabaster:

序号 No.	税则号列 Tariff Line	货品名称	最惠国税率 MFN(%)	协定税率 Agreement(%)		特惠税率 S.P.(%)		普通税率 Gen.(%)	Article Description
4811	6802.2110	---大理石	10	0	东盟ASEAN,智利CL,巴基斯坦PK,新西兰NZ,秘鲁PE,哥斯达黎加CR,澳门MO	0	最不发达35国LDC35,最不发达4国LDC4	90	---Marble
4812	6802.2120	---石灰华	24	0	东盟ASEAN,智利CL,巴基斯坦PK,新加坡SG,新西兰NZ,秘鲁PE,澳门MO	0	最不发达35国LDC35	90	---Travertine
				4.8	哥斯达黎加CR				
4813	6802.2190	---其他	24	0	东盟ASEAN,智利CL,巴基斯坦PK,新加坡SG,新西兰NZ,秘鲁PE	0	最不发达35国LDC35	90	---Other
				4.8	哥斯达黎加CR				
4814	6802.2300	--花岗岩	10	0	东盟ASEAN,智利CL,巴基斯坦PK,新西兰NZ,秘鲁PE,哥斯达黎加CR,澳门MO	0	最不发达35国LDC35,最不发达4国LDC4	90	--Granite
				9.2	亚太APTA				
		--其他石:							--Other stone:
4815	6802.2910	---其他石灰石	24	0	东盟ASEAN,智利CL,巴基斯坦PK,新加坡SG,新西兰NZ,澳门MO	0	最不发达35国LDC35	90	---Other calcareous stone
				4.8	哥斯达黎加CR				
				12	秘鲁PE				
4816	6802.2990	---其他	15	0	东盟ASEAN,智利CL,巴基斯坦PK,新加坡SG,新西兰NZ,澳门MO	0	最不发达35国LDC35,最不发达4国LDC4	90	---Other
				3	哥斯达黎加CR				
				7.5	秘鲁PE				
		-其他:							-Other:
		--大理石、石灰华及蜡石:							--Marble, travertine and alabaster:
4817	6802.9110	---石刻	24	0	东盟ASEAN,智利CL,巴基斯坦PK,新加坡SG,新西兰NZ,秘鲁PE,澳门MO	0	最不发达35国LDC35	90	---Carvings
				4.8	哥斯达黎加CR				
4818	6802.9190	---其他	10	0	东盟ASEAN,智利CL,巴基斯坦PK,新西兰NZ,秘鲁PE,哥斯达黎加CR,香港HK,澳门MO	0	最不发达35国LDC35,最不发达4国LDC4	90	---Other
		--其他石灰石:							--Other calcareous stone:
4819	6802.9210	---石刻	24	0	东盟ASEAN,智利CL,巴基斯坦PK,新加坡SG,新西兰NZ,澳门MO	0	最不发达35国LDC35	90	---Carvings
				4.8	哥斯达黎加CR				
				12	秘鲁PE				

序号 No.	税则号列 Tariff Line	货品名称	最惠国税率 MFN(%)	协定税率 Agreement(%)		特惠税率 S.P.(%)		普通税率 Gen.(%)	Article Description
4820	6802.9290	---其他	10	0	东盟ASEAN,智利CL,巴基斯坦PK,新西兰NZ,哥斯达黎加CR,香港HK,澳门MO	0	最不发达35国LDC35,最不发达4国LDC4	90	---Other
				5	秘鲁PE				
		--花岗岩:							--Granite:
		---石刻:							---Carvings:
4821	6802.9311	----墓碑石	24	0	东盟ASEAN,智利CL,巴基斯坦PK,新加坡SG,新西兰NZ,澳门MO	0	最不发达35国LDC35	90	----Tombstone
				4.8	哥斯达黎加CR				
				12	秘鲁PE				
4822	6802.9319	----其他	24	0	东盟ASEAN,智利CL,巴基斯坦PK,新加坡SG,新西兰NZ,香港HK,澳门MO	0	最不发达35国LDC35	90	----Other
				4.8	哥斯达黎加CR				
				12	秘鲁PE				
4823	6802.9390	---其他	10	0	东盟ASEAN,智利CL,巴基斯坦PK,新西兰NZ,秘鲁PE,哥斯达黎加CR,澳门MO	0	最不发达35国LDC35,最不发达4国LDC4	90	---Other
				9.2	亚太APTA				
		--其他石:							--Other stone:
4824	6802.9910	---石刻	24	0	东盟ASEAN,巴基斯坦PK,新加坡SG,新西兰NZ,秘鲁PE,澳门MO	0	最不发达35国LDC35	90	---Carvings
				2.4	智利CL				
				4.8	哥斯达黎加CR				
4825	6802.9990	---其他	24	0	东盟ASEAN,巴基斯坦PK,新加坡SG,新西兰NZ,秘鲁PE,香港HK,澳门MO	0	最不发达35国LDC35,最不发达4国LDC4	90	---Other
				2.4	智利CL				
				4.8	哥斯达黎加CR				
	68.03	**已加工的板岩及板岩或粘聚板岩的制品:**							**Worked slate and articles of slate or of agglomerated slate:**
		已加工的板岩及板岩或粘聚板岩的制品:							Worked slate and articles of slate or of agglomerated slate:
4826	6803.0010	---板岩制	20	0	东盟ASEAN,智利CL,新加坡SG,新西兰NZ,澳门MO	0	最不发达35国LDC35	80	---Of slate
				4	哥斯达黎加CR				
				10	秘鲁PE				
4827	6803.0090	---其他	20	0	东盟ASEAN,智利CL,新加坡SG,新西兰NZ	0	最不发达35国LDC35	80	---Other
				4	哥斯达黎加CR				
				10	秘鲁PE				

序号 No.	税则号列 Tariff Line	货品名称	最惠国税率 MFN(%)	协定税率 Agreement(%)		特惠税率 S.P.(%)		普通税率 Gen.(%)	Article Description
	68.04	**未装支架的石磨、石碾、砂轮和类似品及其零件，用于研磨、磨刃、抛光、整形或切割，以及手用磨石、抛光石及其零件，用天然石料、粘聚的天然磨料、人造磨料或陶瓷制成，不论是否装有由其他材料制成的零件：**							**Millstones, grindstones, grinding wheels and the like, without frameworks, for grinding, sharpening, polishing, trueing or cutting, hand sharpening or polishing stones, and parts thereof, of natural stone, of agglomerated natural or artificial abrasives, or of ceramics, with or without parts of other materials:**
4828	6804.1000	-碾磨或磨浆用石磨、石碾	8	0 5	东盟ASEAN,智利CL,新西兰NZ,秘鲁PE,哥斯达黎加CR 巴基斯坦PK	0	最不发达35国LDC35,最不发达4国LDC4	40	-Millstones and grindstones for milling, grinding or pulping
		-其他石磨、石碾、砂轮及类似品:							-Other millstones, grindstones, grinding wheels and the like:
4829	6804.2100	--粘聚合成或天然金刚石制	8	0 5	东盟ASEAN,智利CL,新西兰NZ,秘鲁PE,哥斯达黎加CR,香港HK 巴基斯坦PK	0	最不发达35国LDC35,最不发达4国LDC4	17	--Of agglomerated synthetic or natural diamond
		--其他粘聚磨料制或陶瓷制:							--Of other agglomerated abrasives or of ceramics:
4830	6804.2210	---砂轮	8	0 5	东盟ASEAN,智利CL,新西兰NZ,秘鲁PE,哥斯达黎加CR,香港HK 巴基斯坦PK	0	最不发达35国LDC35,最不发达4国LDC4	17	---Grinding wheels
4831	6804.2290	---其他	8	0 5	东盟ASEAN,智利CL,新西兰NZ,秘鲁PE,哥斯达黎加CR,香港HK 巴基斯坦PK	0	最不发达35国LDC35,最不发达4国LDC4	40	---Other
		--天然石料制:							--Of natural stone:
4832	6804.2310	---砂轮	8	0 5	东盟ASEAN,智利CL,新西兰NZ,秘鲁PE,哥斯达黎加CR 巴基斯坦PK	0	最不发达35国LDC35,最不发达4国LDC4	17	---Grinding wheels

序号 No.	税则号列 Tariff Line	货品名称	最惠国税率 MFN(%)	协定税率 Agreement(%)		特惠税率 S.P.(%)		普通税率 Gen.(%)	Article Description
4833	6804.2390	---其他	8	0 5	东盟ASEAN,智利CL,新西兰NZ,秘鲁PE,哥斯达黎加CR 巴基斯坦PK	0	最不发达35国LDC35,最不发达4国LDC4	40	---Other
		-手用磨石及抛光石:							-Hand sharpening or polishing stones:
4834	6804.3010	---琢磨油石	8	0 5 6.4	东盟ASEAN,智利CL,新西兰NZ,秘鲁PE,哥斯达黎加CR 巴基斯坦PK 亚太APTA	0	最不发达35国LDC35,最不发达4国LDC4	17	---Oilstones
4835	6804.3090	---其他	8	0 5 6.4	东盟ASEAN,智利CL,新西兰NZ,秘鲁PE,哥斯达黎加CR 巴基斯坦PK 亚太APTA	0	最不发达35国LDC35,最不发达4国LDC4	40	---Other
	68.05	**砂布、砂纸及以其他材料为底的类似品,不论是否裁切、缝合或用其他方法加工成形:**							**Natural or artificial abrasive powder or grain, on a base of textile material, of paper, of paperboard or of other materials, whether or not cut to shape or sewn or otherwise made up:**
4836	6805.1000	-砂布	8	0 0.8 5	东盟ASEAN,新西兰NZ,秘鲁PE,哥斯达黎加CR 智利CL 巴基斯坦PK	0	最不发达35国LDC35,最不发达4国LDC4	40	-On a base of woven textile fabric only
4837	6805.2000	-砂纸	8	0 0.8 5	东盟ASEAN,新西兰NZ,秘鲁PE,哥斯达黎加CR 智利CL 巴基斯坦PK	0	最不发达35国LDC35,最不发达4国LDC4	40	-On a base of paper or paperboard only
4838	6805.3000	-其他	8	0 5	东盟ASEAN,智利CL,新西兰NZ,秘鲁PE,哥斯达黎加CR 巴基斯坦PK	0	最不发达35国LDC35,最不发达4国LDC4	40	-On a base of other materials

序号 No.	税则号列 Tariff Line	货品名称	最惠国税率 MFN(%)	协定税率 Agreement(%)		特惠税率 S.P.(%)		普通税率 Gen.(%)	Article Description
	68.06	**矿渣棉、岩石棉及类似的矿质棉;页状蛭石、膨胀粘土、泡沫矿渣及类似的膨胀矿物材料;具有隔热、隔音或吸音性能的矿物材料的混合物及制品，但税号68.11、68.12或第六十九章的货品除外:**							**Slag wool, rock wool and similar mineral wools; exfoliated vermiculite, expanded clays, foamed slag and similar expanded mineral materials; mixtures and articles of heat-insulating, soundinsulating or sound-absorbing mineral materials, other than those of heading No.68.11 or 68.12 or of Chapter 69:**
		-矿渣棉、岩石棉及类似的矿质棉（包括其相互混合物），块状、成片或成卷:							-Slag wool, rock wool and similar mineral wools (including intermixtures thereof), in bulk, sheets or rolls:
4839	6806.1010	---硅酸铝纤维及其制品	10.5	0 2.1 5	东盟ASEAN,智利CL,新加坡SG,新西兰NZ,秘鲁PE 哥斯达黎加CR 巴基斯坦PK	0	最不发达35国LDC35,最不发达4国LDC4	40	---Aluminium silicate fibre and its products
4840	6806.1090	---其他	10.5	0 2.1 5	东盟ASEAN,智利CL,新加坡SG,新西兰NZ,秘鲁PE 哥斯达黎加CR 巴基斯坦PK	0	最不发达35国LDC35,最不发达4国LDC4	40	---Other
	ex68061090	矿物纤维，渣球含量小于5%	△5						Mineral fiber, of a shot content less than 5%
4841	6806.2000	-页状蛭石、膨胀粘土、泡沫矿渣及类似的膨胀矿物材料(包括其相互混合物)	10.5	0 2.1 5	东盟ASEAN,智利CL,新加坡SG,新西兰NZ,秘鲁PE 哥斯达黎加CR 巴基斯坦PK	0	最不发达35国LDC35,最不发达4国LDC4	40	-Exfoliated vermiculite, expanded clays, foamed slag and similar expanded mineral materials (including intermixtures thereof)
4842	6806.9000	-其他	10	0 5	东盟ASEAN,智利CL,新西兰NZ,秘鲁PE,哥斯达黎加CR 巴基斯坦PK	0	最不发达35国LDC35,最不发达4国LDC4	50	-Other
	68.07	**沥青或类似原料（例如，石油沥青或煤焦油沥青）的制品:**							**Articles of asphalt or of similar material (for example, petroleum bitumen or coal tar pitch):**
4843	6807.1000	-成卷	12	0 2.4 6	东盟ASEAN,智利CL,新加坡SG,新西兰NZ,秘鲁PE 哥斯达黎加CR 巴基斯坦PK	0	最不发达35国LDC35	50	-In rolls

序号 No.	税则号列 Tariff Line	货品名称	最惠国税率 MFN(%)	协定税率 Agreement(%)		特惠税率 S.P.(%)		普通税率 Gen.(%)	Article Description
	ex68071000	聚脂—铜复合胎基改性沥青根阻防水卷材	△1						Root resistant and waterproof modified bitumen membrane with composite carrier of copper and polyester
4844	6807.9000	-其他	12	0 2.4 5 9.6	东盟ASEAN,智利CL,新加坡SG,新西兰NZ,秘鲁PE 哥斯达黎加CR 巴基斯坦PK 亚太APTA	0	最不发达35国LDC35	50	-Other
	68.08	**镶板、平板、瓦、砖及类似品，用水泥、石膏及其他矿物粘合材料粘合植物纤维、稻草、刨花、木片屑、木粉、锯末或木废料制成:**							**Panels, boards, tiles, blocks and similar articles of vegetable fibre, of straw or of shavings, chips, particles, sawdust or other waste, of wood, agglomerated with cement, plaster or other mineral binders:**
4845	6808.0000	镶板、平板、瓦、砖及类似品，用水泥、石膏及其他矿物粘合材料粘合植物纤维、稻草、刨花、木片屑、木粉、锯末或木废料制成	10.5	0 2.1 5	东盟ASEAN,智利CL,新加坡SG,新西兰NZ,秘鲁PE 哥斯达黎加CR 巴基斯坦PK	0	最不发达35国LDC35	40	Panels, boards, tiles, blocks and similar articles of vegetable fibre, of straw or of shavings, chips, particles, sawdust or other waste, of wood, agglomerated with cement, plaster or other mineral binders
	68.09	**石膏制品及以石膏为基本成分的混合材料制品:** -未经装饰的板、片、砖、瓦及类似品:							**Articles of plaster or of compositions based on plaster:** -Boards, sheets, panels, tiles and similar articles, not ornamented:
4846	6809.1100	--仅用纸、纸板贴面或加强的	28	0 2.8 5.6 14	东盟ASEAN,新加坡SG,新西兰NZ 智利CL 哥斯达黎加CR 秘鲁PE	0	最不发达35国LDC35	100	--Faced or reinforced with paper or paper board only
4847	6809.1900	--其他	25	0 5 12.5	东盟ASEAN,智利CL,新加坡SG,新西兰NZ,澳门MO 哥斯达黎加CR 秘鲁PE	0	最不发达35国LDC35	100	--Other
4848	6809.9000	-其他制品	25	0 5 12.5	东盟ASEAN,智利CL,新加坡SG,新西兰NZ 哥斯达黎加CR 秘鲁PE	0	最不发达35国LDC35	100	-Other articles
	68.10	**水泥、混凝土或人造石制品，不论是否加强:** -砖、瓦、扁平石及类似品:							**Articles of cement, of concrete or of artificial stone, whether or not reinforced:** -Tiles, flagstones, bricks and similar articles:

序号 No.	税则号列 Tariff Line	货品名称	最惠国税率 MFN(%)	协定税率 Agreement(%)		特惠税率 S.P.(%)		普通税率 Gen.(%)	Article Description
4849	6810.1100	--建筑用砖及石砌块	10.5	0 2.1 5 8.4	东盟ASEAN,智利CL,新加坡SG,新西兰NZ,秘鲁PE,香港HK 哥斯达黎加CR 巴基斯坦PK 亚太APTA	0	最不发达35国LDC35,最不发达4国LDC4	40	--Building blocks and bricks
		--其他:							--Other:
4850	6810.1910	---人造石制	10.5	0 1.1 2.1 5 8.4	东盟ASEAN,新加坡SG,新西兰NZ,秘鲁PE,澳门MO 智利CL 哥斯达黎加CR 巴基斯坦PK 亚太APTA	0	最不发达35国LDC35,最不发达4国LDC4	70	---Of artificial stone
4851	6810.1990	---其他	10.5	0 1.1 2.1 5 8.4	东盟ASEAN,新加坡SG,新西兰NZ,秘鲁PE 智利CL 哥斯达黎加CR 巴基斯坦PK 亚太APTA	0	最不发达35国LDC35,最不发达4国LDC4	70	---Other
		-其他制品: --建筑或土木工程用的预制结构件:							-Other articles: --Prefabricated structural components for building or civil engineering:
4852	6810.9110	---钢筋混凝土和预应力混凝土管、杆、板、桩等	10.5	0 2.1 5	东盟ASEAN,智利CL,新加坡SG,新西兰NZ,秘鲁PE,香港HK 哥斯达黎加CR 巴基斯坦PK	0	最不发达35国LDC35,最不发达4国LDC4	40	---Reinforced concrete and prestressed concrete tubes, pipes, rods, plates, piles and similar articles
4853	6810.9190	---其他	10.5	0 2.1 5	东盟ASEAN,智利CL,新加坡SG,新西兰NZ,秘鲁PE,香港HK,澳门MO 哥斯达黎加CR 巴基斯坦PK	0	最不发达35国LDC35,最不发达4国LDC4	40	---Other
		--其他:							--Other:
4854	6810.9910	---铁道用水泥枕	8	0 5	东盟ASEAN,智利CL,新西兰NZ,秘鲁PE,哥斯达黎加CR 巴基斯坦PK	0	最不发达35国LDC35,最不发达4国LDC4	14	---Railway sleepers of concrete
4855	6810.9990	---其他	10.5	0 2.1 5	东盟ASEAN,智利CL,新加坡SG,新西兰NZ,秘鲁PE 哥斯达黎加CR 巴基斯坦PK	0	最不发达35国LDC35,最不发达4国LDC4	70	---Other
	68.11	**石棉水泥、纤维素水泥或类似材料的制品:** -含石棉的:							**Articles of asbestos-cement, of cellulose fibre-cement or the like:** -Containing asbestos:

序号 No.	税则号列 Tariff Line	货品名称	最惠国税率 MFN(%)	协定税率 Agreement(%)		特惠税率 S.P.(%)		普通税率 Gen.(%)	Article Description
4856	6811.4010	---瓦楞板	5	0	东盟ASEAN,智利CL,巴基斯坦PK,新西兰NZ,秘鲁PE,哥斯达黎加CR	0	最不发达35国LDC35	40	---Corrugated sheets
4857	6811.4020	---其他片、板、砖、瓦及类似制品	10.5	0	东盟ASEAN,新加坡SG,新西兰NZ,秘鲁PE	0	最不发达35国LDC35	40	---Other sheets, panels, tiles and similar articles
				1.1	智利CL				
				2.1	哥斯达黎加CR				
				5	巴基斯坦PK				
4858	6811.4030	---管子及管子附件	8	0	东盟ASEAN,智利CL,新西兰NZ,秘鲁PE,哥斯达黎加CR	0	最不发达35国LDC35	40	---Tubes, pipes and tube or pipe fittings
				5	巴基斯坦PK				
4859	6811.4090	---其他制品	8.4	0	东盟ASEAN,智利CL,新西兰NZ,秘鲁PE,哥斯达黎加CR	0	最不发达35国LDC35	40	---Other articles
				5	巴基斯坦PK				
		-不含石棉的:							-Not containing asbestos:
4860	6811.8100	--瓦楞板	5	0	东盟ASEAN,智利CL,巴基斯坦PK,新西兰NZ,秘鲁PE,哥斯达黎加CR	0	最不发达35国LDC35	40	--Corrugated sheets
4861	6811.8200	--其他片、板、砖、瓦及类似制品	10.5	0	东盟ASEAN,新加坡SG,新西兰NZ,秘鲁PE	0	最不发达35国LDC35	40	--Other sheets, panels, tiles and similar articles
				1.1	智利CL				
				2.1	哥斯达黎加CR				
				5	巴基斯坦PK				
		--其他制品:							--Other articles:
4862	6811.8910	---管子及管子附件	8	0	东盟ASEAN,智利CL,新西兰NZ,秘鲁PE,哥斯达黎加CR	0	最不发达35国LDC35	40	---Tubes, pipes and tube or pipe fittings
				5	巴基斯坦PK				
4863	6811.8990	---其他制品	8.4	0	东盟ASEAN,智利CL,新西兰NZ,秘鲁PE,哥斯达黎加CR	0	最不发达35国LDC35	40	---Other articles
				5	巴基斯坦PK				
	68.12	**已加工的石棉纤维;以石棉为基本成分或以石棉和碳酸镁为基本成分的混合物;上述混合物或石棉的制品(例如,纱线、机织物、服装、帽类、鞋靴、衬垫),不论是否加强,但税号68.11或68.13的货品除外:**							**Fabricated asbestos fibres;mixtures with a basis of asbestos or with a basis of asbestos and magnesium carbonate; articles of such mixtures or of asbestos (for example, thread, woven fabric, clothing, headgear, footwear, gaskets), whether or not reinforced, other than goods of heading No.68.11 or 68.13:**
4864	6812.8000	-青石棉的	10.5	0	东盟ASEAN,智利CL,新加坡SG,新西兰NZ,秘鲁PE	0	最不发达35国LDC35,最不发达4国LDC4	40	-Of crocidolite
				2.1	哥斯达黎加CR				
				5	巴基斯坦PK				

序号 No.	税则号列 Tariff Line	货品名称	最惠国税率 MFN(%)	协定税率 Agreement(%)		特惠税率 S.P.(%)		普通税率 Gen.(%)	Article Description
		-其他:							-Other:
4865	6812.9100	--服装、衣着附件、帽类及鞋靴	10.5	0 2.1 5	东盟ASEAN,智利CL,新加坡SG,新西兰NZ,秘鲁PE 哥斯达黎加CR 巴基斯坦PK	0	最不发达35国LDC35,最不发达4国LDC4	40	--Clothing, clothing accessories, footwear and headgear
4866	6812.9200	--纸、麻丝板及毡子	10.5	0 2.1 5	东盟ASEAN,智利CL,新加坡SG,新西兰NZ,秘鲁PE 哥斯达黎加CR 巴基斯坦PK	0	最不发达35国LDC35,最不发达4国LDC4	40	--Paper, millboard and felt
4867	6812.9300	--成片或成卷的压缩石棉纤维接合材料	10.5	0 2.1 5	东盟ASEAN,智利CL,新加坡SG,新西兰NZ,秘鲁PE 哥斯达黎加CR 巴基斯坦PK	0	最不发达35国LDC35,最不发达4国LDC4	40	--Compressed asbestos fibre jointing, in sheets or rolls
4868	6812.9900	--其他	10	0 5	东盟ASEAN,智利CL,新西兰NZ,秘鲁PE,哥斯达黎加CR 巴基斯坦PK	0	最不发达35国LDC35,最不发达4国LDC4	40	--Other
	68.13	**以石棉、其他矿物质或纤维素为基本成分的未装配摩擦材料及其制品（例如，片、卷、带、盘、圈、垫及扇形），适于作制动器、离合器及类似品，不论是否与织物或其他材料结合而成:**							**Friction material and articles thereof (for example, sheets, rolls, strips, segments, discs, washers, pads), not mounted, for brakes, for clutches or the like, with a basis of asbestos, of other mineral substances or of cellulose, whether or not combined with textile or other materials:**
		-含石棉的:							-Containing asbestos:
4869	6813.2010	---闸衬、闸垫	10	0 1 5	东盟ASEAN,新西兰NZ,秘鲁PE,哥斯达黎加CR 智利CL 巴基斯坦PK	0	最不发达35国LDC35,最不发达4国LDC4	40	---Brake linings and pads
4870	6813.2090	---其他	12	0 1.2 2.4 6	东盟ASEAN,新加坡SG,新西兰NZ,秘鲁PE 智利CL 哥斯达黎加CR 巴基斯坦PK	0	最不发达35国LDC35	40	---Other
		-不含石棉的:							-Not containing asbestos:

序号 No.	税则号列 Tariff Line	货品名称	最惠国税率 MFN(%)	协定税率 Agreement(%)		特惠税率 S.P.(%)		普通税率 Gen.(%)	Article Description
4871	6813.8100	--闸衬、闸垫	10	0 1 5	东盟ASEAN,新西兰NZ,秘鲁PE,哥斯达黎加CR 智利CL 巴基斯坦PK	0	最不发达35国LDC35,最不发达4国LDC4	40	--Brake linings and pads
4872	6813.8900	--其他	12	0 1.2 2.4 6	东盟ASEAN,新加坡SG,新西兰NZ,秘鲁PE 智利CL 哥斯达黎加CR 巴基斯坦PK	0	最不发达35国LDC35	40	--Other
	68.14	**已加工的云母及其制品,包括粘聚或复制的云母,不论是否附于纸、纸板或其他材料上:**							**Worked mica and articles of mica, including agglomerated or reconstituted mica, whether or not on a support of paper, paperboard or other materials:**
4873	6814.1000	-粘聚或复制云母制的板、片、带,不论是否附于其他材料上	10.5	0 2.1 5	东盟ASEAN,智利CL,新加坡SG,新西兰NZ,秘鲁PE 哥斯达黎加CR 巴基斯坦PK	0	最不发达35国LDC35,最不发达4国LDC4	35	-Plates, sheets and strips of agglomerated or reconstituted mica, whether or not on a support
4874	6814.9000	-其他	10.5	0 2.1 5	东盟ASEAN,智利CL,新加坡SG,新西兰NZ,秘鲁PE 哥斯达黎加CR 巴基斯坦PK	0	最不发达35国LDC35,最不发达4国LDC4	35	-Other
	68.15	**其他税号未列名的石制品及其他矿物制品(包括碳纤维及其制品和泥煤制品):**							**Articles of stone or of other mineral substances (including carbon fibres, articles of carbon fibres and articles of peat), not elsewhere specified or included:**
4875	6815.1000	-非电器用的石墨或其他碳精制品	15	0 3 7.5 12	东盟ASEAN,智利CL,新加坡SG,新西兰NZ 哥斯达黎加CR 秘鲁PE 巴基斯坦PK	0	最不发达35国LDC35,最不发达4国LDC4	70	-Non-electrical articles of graphite or other carbon
4876	6815.2000	-泥煤制品	15	0 3 7.5 12	东盟ASEAN,智利CL,新加坡SG,新西兰NZ 哥斯达黎加CR 秘鲁PE 巴基斯坦PK	0	最不发达35国LDC35	70	-Articles of peat
		-其他制品:							-Other articles:
4877	6815.9100	--含有菱镁矿、白云石或铬铁矿的	15	0 3 7.5 12	东盟ASEAN,智利CL,新加坡SG,新西兰NZ 哥斯达黎加CR 秘鲁PE 巴基斯坦PK	0	最不发达35国LDC35	70	--Containing magnesite, dolomite or chromite
		--其他:							--Other:

序号 No.	税则号列 Tariff Line	货品名称	最惠国税率 MFN(%)	协定税率 Agreement(%)		特惠税率 S.P.(%)		普通税率 Gen.(%)	Article Description
4878	6815.9920	---碳纤维	17.5	0 1.8 3.5 8.8	东盟ASEAN,新加坡SG,新西兰NZ 智利CL 哥斯达黎加CR 秘鲁PE	0	最不发达35国LDC35,最不发达4国LDC4	70	---Carbon fibres
		---碳纤维制品：							---Articles of carbon fibres:
4879	6815.9931	----碳布	17.5	0 1.8 3.5 8.8	东盟ASEAN,新加坡SG,新西兰NZ 智利CL 哥斯达黎加CR 秘鲁PE	0	最不发达35国LDC35,最不发达4国LDC4	70	----Carbon fibre fabric
4880	6815.9932	----碳纤维预浸料	17.5	0 1.8 3.5 8.8	东盟ASEAN,新加坡SG,新西兰NZ 智利CL 哥斯达黎加CR 秘鲁PE	0	最不发达35国LDC35,最不发达4国LDC4	70	----Carbon fibre prepreg
4881	6815.9939	----其他	17.5	0 1.8 3.5 8.8	东盟ASEAN,新加坡SG,新西兰NZ 智利CL 哥斯达黎加CR 秘鲁PE	0	最不发达35国LDC35,最不发达4国LDC4	70	----Other
	ex68159939	碳纤维纱线（碳元素含量大于90%）	△15						Carbon fibre yarn (containg more than 90% Carbon)
4882	6815.9940	---玄武岩纤维及其制品	17.5	0 1.8 3.5 8.8	东盟ASEAN,新加坡SG,新西兰NZ 智利CL 哥斯达黎加CR 秘鲁PE	0	最不发达35国LDC35,最不发达4国LDC4	70	---Basalt fiber and its product
4883	6815.9990	---其他	17.5	0 1.8 3.5 8.8	东盟ASEAN,新加坡SG,新西兰NZ 智利CL 哥斯达黎加CR 秘鲁PE	0	最不发达35国LDC35,最不发达4国LDC4	70	---Other

第六十九章 陶瓷产品

Chapter 69 Ceramic products

注释：

一、本章仅适用于成形后经过烧制的陶瓷产品。税号69.04至69.14仅适用于不能归入税号69.01至69.03的产品。

二、本章不包括：

（一）税号28.44的产品；

（二）税号68.04的物品；

（三）第七十一章的物品（例如，仿首饰）；

（四）税号81.13的金属陶瓷；

（五）第八十二章的物品；

（六）绝缘子（税号85.46）或绝缘材料制的零件（税号85.47）；

（七）假牙（税号90.21）；

（八）第九十一章的物品（例如，钟及钟壳）；

（九）第九十四章的物品（例如，家具、灯具及照明装置、活动房屋）；

（十）第九十五章的物品（例如，玩具、游戏品及运动用品）；

（十一）税号96.06的物品（例如，钮扣）或税号96.14的物品（例如，烟斗）；

（十二）第九十七章的物品（例如，艺术品）。

Notes:

1. This Chapter applies only to ceramic products which have been fired after shaping. Headings Nos.69.04 to 69.14 apply only to such products other than those classifiable in headings Nos.69.01 to 69.03.

2. This Chapter does not cover:

(a) Products of heading No.28.44;

(b) Articles of heading No.68.04;

(c) Articles of Chapter 71 (for example, imitation jewellery);

(d) Cermets of heading No.81.13;

(e) Articles of Chapter 82;

(f) Electrical insulators (heading No.85.46) or fittings of insulating material of heading No.85.47;

(g) Artificial teeth (heading No.90.21);

(h) Articles of Chapter 91 (for example, clocks and clock cases);

(i) Articles of Chapter 94 (for example, furniture, lamps and lighting fittings, prefabricated buildings);

(j) Articles of Chapter 95 (for example, toys, games and sports requisites);

(k) Articles of heading No.96.06 (for example, buttons) or of heading No.96.14 (for example, smoking pipes); or

(l) Articles of Chapter 97 (for example, works of art).

序号 No.	税则号列 Tariff Line	货品名称	最惠国税率 MFN(%)	协定税率 Agreement(%)	特惠税率 S.P.(%)	普通税率 Gen.(%)	Article Description
		第一分章 硅化石粉或类似硅土及耐火材料制品					Ⅰ.GOODS OF SILICEOUS FOSSIL MEALS OR OF SIMILAR SILICEOUS EARTHS, AND REFRACTORY GOODS
	69.01	**硅质化石粉（例如各种硅藻土）或类似硅土制的砖、块、瓦及其他陶瓷制品：**					**Bricks, blocks, tiles and other ceramic goods of siliceous fossil meals (for example, kieselguhr, tripolite or diatomite) or of similar siliceous earths:**

序号 No.	税则号列 Tariff Line	货品名称	最惠国税率 MFN(%)	协定税率 Agreement(%)		特惠税率 S.P.(%)		普通税率 Gen.(%)	Article Description
4884	6901.0000	硅质化石粉（例如各种硅藻土）或类似硅土制的砖、块、瓦及其他陶瓷制品	8	0 5 6.4	东盟ASEAN,智利CL,新西兰NZ,秘鲁PE,哥斯达黎加CR 巴基斯坦PK 亚太APTA	0	最不发达35国LDC35	50	Bricks, blocks, tiles and other ceramic goods of siliceous fossil meals (for example, kieselguhr, tripolite or diatomite) or of similar siliceous earths
	69.02	**耐火砖、块、瓦及类似耐火陶瓷建材制品，但硅质化石粉及类似硅土制的除外：**							**Refractory bricks, blocks, tiles and similar refractory ceramic constructional goods, other than those of siliceous fossil meals or similar siliceous earths:**
4885	6902.1000	-单独或同时含有按重量计超过50%的镁、钙或铬（分别以氧化镁、氧化钙及三氧化二铬的含量计）	8	0 0.8 5	东盟ASEAN,新西兰NZ,秘鲁PE,哥斯达黎加CR 智利CL 巴基斯坦PK	0	最不发达35国LDC35,最不发达4国LDC4	30	-Containing by weight, singly or together, more than 50% of the elements Mg, Ca or Cr, expressed as MgO, CaO or Cr_2O_3
4886	6902.2000	-含有按重量计超过50%的三氧化二铝、二氧化硅或其混合物或化合物	8	0 0.8 5	东盟ASEAN,新西兰NZ,秘鲁PE,哥斯达黎加CR 智利CL 巴基斯坦PK	0	最不发达35国LDC35,最不发达4国LDC4	30	-Containing by weight more than 50% of alumina (Al_2O_3), of silica (SiO_2) or of a mixture or compound of these products
4887	6902.9000	-其他	8	0 5	东盟ASEAN,智利CL,新西兰NZ,秘鲁PE,哥斯达黎加CR 巴基斯坦PK	0	最不发达35国LDC35,最不发达4国LDC4	30	-Other
	69.03	**其他耐火陶瓷制品（例如，甑、坩埚、马弗罩、喷管、栓塞、支架、烤钵、管子、护套及棒条），但硅质化石粉及类似硅土制的除外：**							**Other refractory ceramic goods (for example, retorts, crucibles, muffles, nozzles, plugs, supports, cupels, tubes, pipes, sheaths and rods), other than those of siliceous fossil meals or of similar siliceous earths:**
4888	6903.1000	-含有按重量计超过50%的石墨、其他碳或其混合物	8	0 5	东盟ASEAN,智利CL,新西兰NZ,秘鲁PE,哥斯达黎加CR 巴基斯坦PK	0	最不发达35国LDC35,最不发达4国LDC4,老挝LA	20	-Containing by weight more than 50% of graphite or other carbon or of a mixture of these products
4889	6903.2000	-含有按重量计超过50%的三氧化二铝或三氧化二铝和二氧化硅的混合物或化合物	8	0 0.8 5	东盟ASEAN,新西兰NZ,秘鲁PE,哥斯达黎加CR 智利CL 巴基斯坦PK	0	最不发达35国LDC35,最不发达4国LDC4,老挝LA	20	-Containing by weight more than 50% of alumina (Al_2O_3) or of a mixture of compound of alumina and of silica (SiO_2)

序号 No.	税则号列 Tariff Line	货品名称	最惠国税率 MFN(%)	协定税率 Agreement(%)	特惠税率 S.P.(%)	普通税率 Gen.(%)	Article Description
4890	6903.9000	-其他	8	0 东盟ASEAN,新西兰NZ,秘鲁PE,哥斯达黎加CR 0.8 智利CL 5 巴基斯坦PK	0 最不发达35国LDC35,最不发达4国LDC4,老挝LA	20	-Other
		第二分章 其他陶瓷产品					II.OTHER CERAMIC PRODUCTS
	69.04	**陶瓷制建筑用砖、铺地砖、支撑或填充用砖及类似品:**					**Ceramic building bricks, flooring blocks, support or filler tiles and the like:**
4891	6904.1000	-建筑用砖	15	0 东盟ASEAN,智利CL,新加坡SG,新西兰NZ 3 哥斯达黎加CR 7.5 秘鲁PE 12 巴基斯坦PK	0 最不发达35国LDC35,最不发达4国LDC4	90	-Building bricks
4892	6904.9000	-其他	24.5 △15	0 东盟ASEAN,智利CL,新加坡SG,新西兰NZ 4.9 哥斯达黎加CR 12.3 秘鲁PE	0 最不发达35国LDC35	90	-Other
	69.05	**屋顶瓦、烟囱罩、通风帽、烟囱衬壁、建筑装饰物及其他建筑用陶瓷制品:**					**Roofing tiles, chimney-pots, cowls, chimney liners, architectural ornaments and other ceramic constructional goods:**
4893	6905.1000	-屋顶瓦	24.5 △15	0 东盟ASEAN,智利CL,新加坡SG,新西兰NZ 4.9 哥斯达黎加CR 12.3 秘鲁PE	0 最不发达35国LDC35	90	-Roofing tiles
4894	6905.9000	-其他	24.5 △15	0 东盟ASEAN,智利CL,新加坡SG,新西兰NZ 4.9 哥斯达黎加CR 12.3 秘鲁PE	0 最不发达35国LDC35	90	-Other
	69.06	**陶瓷套管、导管、槽管及管子附件:**					**Ceramic pipes, conduits, guttering and pipe fittings:**
4895	6906.0000	陶瓷套管、导管、槽管及管子附件	15 △10	0 东盟ASEAN,智利CL,新加坡SG,新西兰NZ 3 哥斯达黎加CR 7.5 秘鲁PE 12 巴基斯坦PK	0 最不发达35国LDC35	90	Ceramic pipes, conduits, guttering and pipe fittings
	69.07	**未上釉的陶瓷贴面砖、铺面砖,包括炉面砖及墙面砖;未上釉的陶瓷镶嵌砖(马赛克)及类似品,不论是否有衬背:**					**Unglazed ceramic flags and paving, hearth or wall tiles; unglazed ceramic mosaic cubes and the like, whether or not on a backing:**

序号 No.	税则号列 Tariff Line	货品名称	最惠国税率 MFN(%)	协定税率 Agreement(%)		特惠税率 S.P.(%)		普通税率 Gen.(%)	Article Description
4896	6907.1000	-砖、瓦、块及类似品，不论是否矩形，其最大表面积以可置入边长小于7厘米的方格为限	24.5 △12	0 4.9 12.3	东盟ASEAN,智利CL,新加坡SG,新西兰NZ 哥斯达黎加CR 秘鲁PE	0	最不发达35国LDC35	90	-Tiles, cubes and similar articles, whether or not rectangular, the largest surface area of which is capable of being enclosed in a square the side of which is less than 7cm
4897	6907.9000	-其他	12 △8	0 2.4 6	东盟ASEAN,智利CL,新加坡SG,新西兰NZ,秘鲁PE 哥斯达黎加CR 巴基斯坦PK	0	最不发达35国LDC35	90	-Other
	69.08	**上釉的陶瓷贴面砖、铺面砖，包括炉面砖及墙面砖;上釉的陶瓷镶嵌砖（马赛克）及类似品，不论是否有衬背:**							**Glazed ceramic flags and paving, hearth or wall tiles; glazed ceramic mosaic cubes and the like, whether or not on a backing:**
4898	6908.1000	-砖、瓦、块及类似品，不论是否矩形，其最大表面积以可置入边长小于7厘米的方格为限	12	0 2.4 5 10.4	东盟ASEAN,智利CL,新加坡SG,新西兰NZ,秘鲁PE 哥斯达黎加CR 巴基斯坦PK 亚太APTA	0	最不发达35国LDC35	100	-Tiles, cubes and similar articles, whether or not rectangular, the largest surface area of which is capable of being enclosed in a square the side of which is less than 7cm
4899	6908.9000	-其他	12	0 2.4 6	东盟ASEAN,智利CL,新加坡SG,新西兰NZ,秘鲁PE 哥斯达黎加CR 巴基斯坦PK	0	最不发达35国LDC35	100	-Other
	69.09	**实验室、化学或其他专门技术用途的陶瓷器;农业用陶瓷槽、缸及类似容器;通常供运输及盛装货物用的陶瓷罐、坛及类似品:**							**Ceramic wares for laboratory, chemical or other technical uses; ceramic troughs, tubs and similar receptacles of a kind used in agriculture; ceramic pots, jars and similar articles of a kind used for the conveyance or packing of goods:**
		-实验室、化学或其他专门技术用途的陶瓷器:							-Ceramic wares for laboratory, chemical or other technical uses:
4900	6909.1100	--瓷制	8	0 5	东盟ASEAN,智利CL,新西兰NZ,秘鲁PE,哥斯达黎加CR 巴基斯坦PK	0	最不发达35国LDC35,最不发达4国LDC4	30	--Of porcelain or china

序号 No.	税则号列 Tariff Line	货品名称	最惠国税率 MFN(%)	协定税率 Agreement(%)		特惠税率 S.P.(%)		普通税率 Gen.(%)	Article Description
4901	6909.1200	--莫氏硬度为9或以上的物品	8	0 5	东盟ASEAN,智利CL,新西兰NZ,秘鲁PE,哥斯达黎加CR 巴基斯坦PK	0	最不发达35国LDC35,最不发达4国LDC4	30	--Articles having a hardness equivalent to 9 or more on the Mohs scale
4902	6909.1900	--其他	8	0 0.8 5	东盟ASEAN,新西兰NZ,秘鲁PE,哥斯达黎加CR 智利CL 巴基斯坦PK	0	最不发达35国LDC35,最不发达4国LDC4	30	--Other
4903	6909.9000	-其他	21 △15	0 4.2 10.5	东盟ASEAN,智利CL,新加坡SG,新西兰NZ 哥斯达黎加CR 秘鲁PE	0	最不发达35国LDC35	90	-Other
	69.10	**陶瓷洗涤槽、脸盆、脸盆座、浴缸、坐浴盆、抽水马桶、水箱、小便池及类似的固定卫生设备:**							**Ceramic sinks, wash basins, wash basin pedestals, baths, bidets, water closet pans, flushing cisterns, urinals and similar sanitary fixtures:**
4904	6910.1000	-瓷制	10	0 5 9	东盟ASEAN,智利CL,新加坡SG,新西兰NZ,秘鲁PE,哥斯达黎加CR 巴基斯坦PK 亚太APTA	0	最不发达35国LDC35,最不发达4国LDC4	100	-Of porcelain or china
4905	6910.9000	-其他	10	0 1 5	东盟ASEAN,新加坡SG,新西兰NZ,秘鲁PE,哥斯达黎加CR 智利CL 巴基斯坦PK	0	最不发达35国LDC35,最不发达4国LDC4	100	-Other
	69.11	**瓷餐具、厨房器具及其他家用或盥洗用瓷器:**							**Tableware, kitchenware, other household articles and toilet articles, of porcelain or china:**
		-餐具及厨房器具:							-Tableware and kitchenware:
		---餐具:							---Tableware:
4906	6911.1011	----骨瓷	12 △8	0 1.2 2.4 5 10	东盟ASEAN,新加坡SG,新西兰NZ,秘鲁PE 智利CL 哥斯达黎加CR 巴基斯坦PK 亚太APTA	0	最不发达35国LDC35,最不发达4国LDC4	100	----Bone porcelain
4907	6911.1019	----其他	12 △8	0 1.2 2.4 5 10	东盟ASEAN,新加坡SG,新西兰NZ,秘鲁PE 智利CL 哥斯达黎加CR 巴基斯坦PK 亚太APTA	0	最不发达35国LDC35,最不发达4国LDC4	100	----Other

序号 No.	税则号列 Tariff Line	货品名称	最惠国税率 MFN(%)	协定税率 Agreement(%)		特惠税率 S.P.(%)		普通税率 Gen.(%)	Article Description
		---厨房器具:							---Kitchenware:
4908	6911.1021	----刀具	15 △10	0 1.5 3 7.5 12.5	东盟ASEAN,新加坡SG, 新西兰NZ 智利CL 哥斯达黎加CR 巴基斯坦PK,秘鲁PE 亚太APTA	0	最不发达35国LDC35	100	----Knife
4909	6911.1029	----其他	15 △10	0 1.5 3 7.5 12.5	东盟ASEAN,新加坡SG, 新西兰NZ 智利CL 哥斯达黎加CR 巴基斯坦PK,秘鲁PE 亚太APTA	0	最不发达35国LDC35	100	----Other
4910	6911.9000	-其他	24.5	0 4.9 12.3 20	东盟ASEAN,智利CL, 新加坡SG,新西兰NZ 哥斯达黎加CR 秘鲁PE 亚太APTA,巴基斯坦PK	0	最不发达35国LDC35	100	-Other
	69.12	**陶餐具、厨房器具及其他家用或盥洗用陶器:**							**Ceramic tableware, kitchenware, other household articles and toilet articles, other than of porcelain or china:**
4911	6912.0010	---餐具	15 △10	0 1.5 3 7.5 12	东盟ASEAN,新加坡SG, 新西兰NZ 智利CL 哥斯达黎加CR 秘鲁PE 巴基斯坦PK	0	最不发达35国LDC35,最不发达4国LDC4	100	---Tableware
4912	6912.0090	---其他	15 △10	0 1.5 3 7.5 12	东盟ASEAN,新加坡SG, 新西兰NZ 智利CL 哥斯达黎加CR 秘鲁PE 巴基斯坦PK	0	最不发达35国LDC35	100	---Other
	69.13	**塑像及其他装饰用陶瓷制品:**							**Statuettes and other ornamental ceramic articles:**
4913	6913.1000	-瓷制	15	0 3 7.5 12	东盟ASEAN,智利CL, 新加坡SG,新西兰NZ 哥斯达黎加CR 秘鲁PE 巴基斯坦PK	0	最不发达35国LDC35,最不发达4国LDC4	100	-Of porcelain or china
4914	6913.9000	-其他	15	0 1.5 3 7.5 12	东盟ASEAN,新加坡SG, 新西兰NZ 智利CL 哥斯达黎加CR 秘鲁PE 巴基斯坦PK	0	最不发达35国LDC35,最不发达4国LDC4	100	-Other

序号 No.	税则号列 Tariff Line	货品名称	最惠国税率 MFN(%)	协定税率 Agreement(%)		特惠税率 S.P.(%)		普通税率 Gen.(%)	Article Description
	69.14	**其他陶瓷制品:**							**Other ceramic articles:**
4915	6914.1000	-瓷制	24.5	0 4.9 12.3	东盟ASEAN,智利CL,新加坡SG,新西兰NZ 哥斯达黎加CR 秘鲁PE	0	最不发达35国LDC35	100	-Of porcelain or china
4916	6914.9000	-其他	10	0 5	东盟ASEAN,智利CL,新加坡SG,新西兰NZ,秘鲁PE,哥斯达黎加CR 巴基斯坦PK	0	最不发达35国LDC35,最不发达4国LDC4	100	-Other

第七十章
玻璃及其制品

Chapter 70
Glass and glassware

注释:

一、本章不包括:

（一）税号 32.07 的货品（例如，珐琅和釉料、搪瓷玻璃料及其他玻璃粉、粒或粉片）;

（二）第七十一章的物品（例如，仿首饰）;

（三）税号 85.44 的光缆、税号 85.46 的绝缘子或税号 85.47 所列绝缘材料制的零件;

（四）光导纤维、经光学加工的光学元件、注射用针管、假眼、温度计、气压计、液体比重计或第九十章的其他物品;

（五）有永久固定电光源的灯具及照明装置、灯箱标志或名牌和类似品及其零件(税号 94.05);

（六）玩具、游戏品、运动用品、圣诞树装饰品及第九十五章的其他物品（供玩偶或第九十五章其他物品用的无机械装置的玻璃假眼除外）;

（七）钮扣、保温瓶、香水喷雾器和类似的喷雾器及第九十六章的其他物品。

二、对于税号 70.03、70.04 及 70.05:

（一）玻璃在退火前的各种处理都不视为“已加工”;

（二）玻璃切割成一定形状并不影响其作为板片归类;

（三）所称“吸收、反射或非反射层”，是指极薄的金属或化合物（例如，金属氧化物）镀层，该镀层可以吸收红外线等光线或可以提高玻璃的反射性能，同时仍然使玻璃具有一定程度的透明性或半透明性；或者该镀层可以防止光线在玻璃表面的反射。

三、税号 70.06 所述产品，不论是否具有制成品的特性仍归入该税号。

Notes:

1. This Chapter does not cover:

(a) Goods of heading No.32.07 (for example, vitrifiable enamels and glazes, glass frit, other glass in the form of powder, granules or flakes);

(b) Articles of Chapter 71 (for example, imitation jewellery);

(c) Optical fibre cables (heading No.85.44), electrical insulators (heading No.85.46) or fitting of insulating material of heading No.85.47;

(d) Optical fibres, optically worked optical elements, hypodermic syringes, artificial eyes, thermometers, barometers, hydrometers or other articles of Chapter 90;

(e) Lamps or lighting fittings, illuminated signs, illuminated nameplates or the like, having a permanently fixed light source, or parts thereof of heading No. 94.05;

(f) Toys, games, sports requisites, Christmas tree ornaments or other articles of Chapter 95 (excluding glass eyes without mechanisms for dolls or for other articles of Chapter 95); or

(g) Buttons, fitted vacuum flasks, scent or similar sprays or other articles of Chapter 96.

2. For the purposes of headings Nos.70.03, 70.04 and 70.05:

(a) glass is not regarded as “worked” by reason of any process it has undergone before annealing;

(b) cutting to shape does not affect the classification of glass in sheets;

(c) the expression “absorbent, reflecting or nonreflecting layer” means a microscopically thin coating of metal or of a chemical compound (for example, metal oxide) which absorbs, for example, infrared light or improves the reflecting qualities of the glass while still allowing it to retain a degree of transparency or translucency; or which prevents light from being reflected on the surface of the glass.

3. The products referred to in heading No.70.06 remain classified in that heading whether or not they have the character of articles.

四、税号 70.19 所称“玻璃棉”，是指：

（一）按重量计二氧化硅的含量在 60%及以上的矿质棉；

（二）按重量计二氧化硅的含量在 60%以下，但碱性氧化物（氧化钾或氧化钠）的含量在 5%以上或氧化硼的含量在 2%以上的矿质棉。

不符合上述规定的矿质棉归入税号 68.06。

五、本目录所称“玻璃”，包括熔融石英及其他熔融硅石。

4. For the purposes of heading No.70.19, the expression “glass wool” means:

(a) Mineral wools with a silica (SiO_2) content not less than 60% by weight;

(b) Mineral wools with a silica (SiO_2) content less than60%but with an alkaline oxide (K_2O or Na_2O) content exceeding 5% by weight or a boric oxide (B_2O_3) content exceeding 2% by weight.

Mineral wools which do not comply with the above specifications fall in heading No.68.06.

5. Throughout the Nomenclature, the expression “glass” includes fused quartz and other fused silica.

子目注释：

子目号 7013.22、7013.33、7013.41 及 7013.91 所称“铅晶质玻璃”，仅指按重量计氧化铅含量不低于 24%的玻璃。

Subheading Note:

For the purposes of subheadings Nos.7013.22, 7013.33, 7013.41 and 7013.91, the expression “lead crystal” means only glass having a minimum lead monoxide (PbO) content by weight of 24%.

序号 No.	税则号列 Tariff Line	货品名称	最惠国税率 MFN(%)	协定税率 Agreement(%)		特惠税率 S.P.(%)		普通税率 Gen.(%)	Article Description
	70.01	**碎玻璃及废玻璃;玻璃块料:**							**Cullet and other waste and scrap of glass; glass in the mass:**
4917	7001.0000	碎玻璃及废玻璃;玻璃块料	12	0 2.4 6	东盟ASEAN,智利CL,新加坡SG,新西兰NZ,秘鲁PE 哥斯达黎加CR 巴基斯坦PK	0	最不发达 35 国 LDC35	50	Cullet and other waste and scrap of glass; glass in the mass
	70.02	**未加工的玻璃球、棒及管（税号 70.18 的微型玻璃球除外）:**							**Glass in balls (other than microspheres of heading No.70.18), roads or tubes, unworked:**
4918	7002.1000	-玻璃球	12	0 2.4 6	东盟ASEAN,智利CL,新加坡SG,新西兰NZ,秘鲁PE 哥斯达黎加CR 巴基斯坦PK	0	最不发达 35 国 LDC35	50	-Balls
		-玻璃棒:							-Rods:
4919	7002.2010	---光导纤维预制棒	6	0 5	东盟ASEAN,智利CL,新西兰NZ,秘鲁PE,哥斯达黎加CR 巴基斯坦PK	0	最不发达 35 国 LDC35	50	---Preformed bars for drawing optical fibre
4920	7002.2090	---其他	12	0 2.4 6	东盟ASEAN,智利CL,新加坡SG,新西兰NZ,秘鲁PE 哥斯达黎加CR 巴基斯坦PK	0	最不发达 35 国 LDC35	50	---Other
		-玻璃管: --熔融石英或其他熔融硅石制:							-Tubes: --Of fused quartz or other fused silica:

序号 No.	税则号列 Tariff Line	货品名称	最惠国税率 MFN(%)	协定税率 Agreement(%)		特惠税率 S.P.(%)		普通税率 Gen.(%)	Article Description
4921	7002.3110	---光导纤维用波导级石英玻璃管	5 △1	0	东盟ASEAN,智利CL,巴基斯坦PK,新西兰NZ,秘鲁PE,哥斯达黎加CR	0	最不发达35国LDC35	17	---Waveguide quartz tubes for optical fibres use
4922	7002.3190	---其他	14	0 2.8 11.2	东盟ASEAN,智利CL,新加坡SG,新西兰NZ,秘鲁PE 哥斯达黎加CR 巴基斯坦PK	0	最不发达35国LDC35	50	---Other
4923	7002.3200	--温度在0℃至300℃时线膨胀系数不超过5×10^{-6}/开尔文的其他玻璃制	12	0 2.4 6	东盟ASEAN,智利CL,新加坡SG,新西兰NZ,秘鲁PE 哥斯达黎加CR 巴基斯坦PK	0	最不发达35国LDC35	50	--Of other glass having a linear coefficient of expansion not exceeding 5×10^{-6} per Kelvin within a tempera-ture range of 0°C to 300°C
4924	7002.3900	--其他	12	0 2.4 6	东盟ASEAN,智利CL,新加坡SG,新西兰NZ,秘鲁PE 哥斯达黎加CR 巴基斯坦PK	0	最不发达35国LDC35	50	--Other
	ex70023900	光通信用微光组件的玻璃毛细管、定位管（外径小于3mm）	△3						Micro capillary and galass tube for optical communication (out diameter < 3 mm)
	70.03	**铸制或轧制玻璃板、片或型材及异型材，不论是否有吸收、反射或非反射层，但未经其他加工:**							**Cast glass and rolled glass, in sheets or profiles, whether or not having an absorbent, reflecting or nonreflecting layer, but not otherwise worked:**
		-非夹丝玻璃板、片:							-Non-wired sheets:
4925	7003.1200	--整块着色、不透明、镶色或具有吸收、反射或非反射层的	15	0 3 7.5 12	东盟ASEAN,智利CL,新加坡SG,新西兰NZ 哥斯达黎加CR 秘鲁PE 巴基斯坦PK	0	最不发达35国LDC35	50	--Coloured throughout the mass (body tinted), opacified, flashed or having an absorbent, or nonreflecting reflecting layer, but not otherwise worked
4926	7003.1900	--其他	17.5	0 3.5 8.8 14	东盟ASEAN,智利CL,新加坡SG,新西兰NZ,台湾TW 哥斯达黎加CR 秘鲁PE 巴基斯坦PK	0	最不发达35国LDC35	50	--Other
	ex70031900	液晶或有机发光二极管（OLED）显示屏用原板玻璃，包括保护屏用含碱玻璃	△3						Bare glass for liquid crystal or organic light emitting diode display,inculding the protective glass containing alkali
4927	7003.2000	-夹丝玻璃板、片	15	0 3 7.5 12	东盟ASEAN,智利CL,新加坡SG,新西兰NZ 哥斯达黎加CR 秘鲁PE 巴基斯坦PK	0	最不发达35国LDC35	50	-Wired sheets

序号 No.	税则号列 Tariff Line	货品名称	最惠国税率 MFN(%)	协定税率 Agreement(%)		特惠税率 S.P.(%)		普通税率 Gen.(%)	Article Description
4928	7003.3000	-型材及异型材	15	0 3 7.5 12	东盟ASEAN,智利CL,新加坡SG,新西兰NZ 哥斯达黎加CR 秘鲁PE 巴基斯坦PK	0	最不发达35国LDC35	50	-Profiles
	70.04	**拉制或吹制玻璃板、片，不论是否有吸收、反射或非反射层，但未经其他加工：**							**Drawn glass and blown glass, in sheets, whether or not having an absorbent, reflecting or nonreflecting layer, but not otherwise worked:**
4929	7004.2000	-整块着色、不透明、镶色或具有吸收、反射或非反射层的	17.5	0 3.5 8.8 14	东盟ASEAN,智利CL,新加坡SG,新西兰NZ 哥斯达黎加CR 秘鲁PE 巴基斯坦PK	0	最不发达35国LDC35,最不发达4国LDC4	50	-Glass, coloured throughout the mass (body tinted), opacified, flashed or having an absorbent, reflecting or nonreflecting layer
4930	7004.9000	-其他玻璃	17.5	0 3.5 8.8 14	东盟ASEAN,智利CL,新加坡SG,新西兰NZ 哥斯达黎加CR 秘鲁PE 巴基斯坦PK	0	最不发达35国LDC35	50	-Other glass
	ex70049000	光学平板玻璃，厚度0.7毫米以下	△9						Optical flat glass, of a thickness less than 0.7mm
	70.05	**浮法玻璃板、片及表面研磨或抛光玻璃板、片，不论是否有吸收、反射或非反射层，但未经其他加工：**							**Float glass and surface ground or polished glass, in sheets, whether or not having an absorbent, reflecting or nonreflecting layer, but not otherwise worked:**
4931	7005.1000	-具有吸收、反射或非反射层的非夹丝玻璃	15	0 3 7.5 12	东盟ASEAN,智利CL,新加坡SG,新西兰NZ 哥斯达黎加CR 秘鲁PE 巴基斯坦PK	0	最不发达35国LDC35	50	-Non-wired glass, having an absorbent, reflecting or noon-reflecting layer
		-其他非夹丝玻璃:							-Other non-wired glass:
4932	7005.2100	--整块着色、不透明、镶色或仅表面研磨的	15	0 1.5 3 7.5 12	东盟ASEAN,新加坡SG,新西兰NZ 智利CL 哥斯达黎加CR 秘鲁PE 巴基斯坦PK	0	最不发达35国LDC35	50	--Coloured throughout the mass (body tinted), opacified, flashed or merely surface ground
4933	7005.2900	--其他	15	0 1.5 3 7.5 12	东盟ASEAN,新加坡SG,新西兰NZ 智利CL 哥斯达黎加CR 秘鲁PE 巴基斯坦PK	0	最不发达35国LDC35	50	--Other

序号 No.	税则号列 Tariff Line	货品名称	最惠国税率 MFN(%)	协定税率 Agreement(%)		特惠税率 S.P.(%)		普通税率 Gen.(%)	Article Description
	ex70052900	液晶或有机发光二极管（OLED）显示屏用原板玻璃，包括保护屏用含碱玻璃	△3						Float glass, for liquid crystal or organic light emitting diode display, inculding the protective glass containing alkali
4934	7005.3000	-夹丝玻璃	17.5	0 3.5 8.8 14	东盟ASEAN,智利CL,新加坡SG,新西兰NZ 哥斯达黎加CR 秘鲁PE 巴基斯坦PK	0	最不发达35国LDC35	50	-Wired glass
	70.06	**经弯曲、磨边、镂刻、钻孔、涂珐琅或其他加工的税号70.03、70.04或70.05的玻璃，但未用其他材料镶框或装配:**							**Glass of heading No.70.03, 70.04 or 70.05, bent, edge-worked, engraved, drilled, enamelled or otherwise worked, but not framed or fitted with other materials:**
4935	7006.0000	经弯曲、磨边、镂刻、钻孔、涂珐琅或其他加工的税号70.03、70.04或70.05的玻璃，但未用其他材料镶框或装配	15	0 3 7.5 12	东盟ASEAN,智利CL,新加坡SG,新西兰NZ,台湾TW 哥斯达黎加CR 秘鲁PE 巴基斯坦PK	0	最不发达35国LDC35	50	Glass of heading No.70.03, 70.04 or 70.05, bent, edge-worked, engraved, drilled, enamelled or otherwise worked, but not framed or fitted with other materials
	ex70060000	液晶玻璃基板,6代(1850mm*1500mm)以上，不含6代	△4						Glass parts for liquid crystal display,above the 6 generation (1850mm*1500mm)
	ex70060000	液晶玻璃基板,6代(1850mm*1500mm)及以下	△6						Glass parts for liquid crystal display, the 6 generation (1850mm*1500mm) and below
	70.07	**钢化或层压玻璃制的安全玻璃:**							**Safety glass, consisting of toughened (tempered) or laminated glass:**
		-钢化安全玻璃:							-Toughened (tempered) safety glass:
		--规格及形状适于安装在车辆、航空器、航天器及船舶上:							--Of size and shape suitable for incorporation in vehicles, aircraft, spacecraft or vessels:
4936	7007.1110	---航空器、航天器及船舶用	2	0	东盟ASEAN,智利CL,巴基斯坦PK,新西兰NZ,秘鲁PE,哥斯达黎加CR,香港HK	0	最不发达35国LDC35,最不发达4国LDC4	11	---For aircraft, spacecraft or vessels
	ex70071110	空载重量25吨及以上飞机的挡风玻璃	△1						Windshield for airplane unloaden weight≥25t
4937	7007.1190	---其他	10	0 5	东盟ASEAN,智利CL,新西兰NZ,秘鲁PE,哥斯达黎加CR,香港HK 巴基斯坦PK	0	最不发达35国LDC35,最不发达4国LDC4	50	---Other

序号 No.	税则号列 Tariff Line	货品名称	最惠国税率 MFN(%)	协定税率 Agreement(%)		特惠税率 S.P.(%)		普通税率 Gen.(%)	Article Description
4938	7007.1900	--其他	14	0 1.4 2.8 11.2	东盟ASEAN,新加坡SG,新西兰NZ,秘鲁PE 智利CL 哥斯达黎加CR 巴基斯坦PK	0	最不发达35国LDC35	50	--Other
	ex70071900	低铁钢化太阳能电池组件封装专用玻璃（最大含铁量0.02% Fe_2O_3，玻璃厚度2.5mm~3.5mm）	△12						Ferrless toughen glass for solar energy battery rncapsulation (Max Fe 0.02% Fe_2O_3, thinkness of glass: 2.5~3.5mm)
		-层压安全玻璃:							-Laminated safety glass:
		--规格及形状适于安装在车辆、航空器、航天器及船舶上:							--Of size and shape suitable for incorporation in vehicles, aircraft, spacecraft or vessels:
4939	7007.2110	---航空器、航天器及船舶用	2	0	东盟ASEAN,智利CL,巴基斯坦PK,新西兰NZ,秘鲁PE,哥斯达黎加CR	0	最不发达35国LDC35,最不发达4国LDC4	11	---for aircraft, spacecraft or vessels
4940	7007.2190	---其他	20	0 2 4 10	东盟ASEAN,新加坡SG,新西兰NZ 智利CL 哥斯达黎加CR 秘鲁PE	0	最不发达35国LDC35,最不发达4国LDC4	50	---Other
4941	7007.2900	--其他	14	0 1.4 2.8 11.2	东盟ASEAN,新加坡SG,新西兰NZ,秘鲁PE 智利CL 哥斯达黎加CR 巴基斯坦PK	0	最不发达35国LDC35	50	--Other
	70.08	**多层隔温、隔音玻璃组件:**							**Multiple-walled insulating units of glass:**
		多层隔温、隔音玻璃组件:							Multiple-walled insulating units of glass:
4942	7008.0010	---中空或真空隔温、隔音玻璃	14	0 2.8 11.2	东盟ASEAN,智利CL,新加坡SG,新西兰NZ,秘鲁PE 哥斯达黎加CR 巴基斯坦PK	0	最不发达35国LDC35	50	---Sealed or vacuum insulating glass
4943	7008.0090	---其他	14	0 2.8 11.2	东盟ASEAN,智利CL,新加坡SG,新西兰NZ,秘鲁PE,澳门MO 哥斯达黎加CR 巴基斯坦PK	0	最不发达35国LDC35	50	---Other
	70.09	**玻璃镜（包括后视镜），不论是否镶框:**							**Glass mirrors, whether or not framed, including rear-view mirrors:**
4944	7009.1000	-车辆后视镜	10	0 1 5	东盟ASEAN,新加坡SG,新西兰NZ,秘鲁PE,哥斯达黎加CR,台湾TW 智利CL 巴基斯坦PK	0	最不发达35国LDC35,最不发达4国LDC4	100	-Rear-view mirrors for vehicles

序号 No.	税则号列 Tariff Line	货品名称	最惠国税率 MFN(%)	协定税率 Agreement(%)		特惠税率 S.P.(%)		普通税率 Gen.(%)	Article Description
		-其他:							-Other:
4945	7009.9100	--未镶框	21	0 2.1 4.2 10.5	东盟ASEAN,新加坡SG,新西兰NZ 智利CL 哥斯达黎加CR 秘鲁PE	0	最不发达35国LDC35	70	--Unframed
	ex70099100	槽式太阳能抛物面反射镜	△10						Parabolic trough in Solar Energy Generating Systems (SEGS)
4946	7009.9200	--已镶框	12	0 1.2 2.4 5 10.8	东盟ASEAN,新加坡SG,新西兰NZ,秘鲁PE 智利CL 哥斯达黎加CR 巴基斯坦PK 亚太APTA	0	最不发达35国LDC35,最不发达4国LDC4	100	--Framed
	70.10	**玻璃制的坛、瓶、缸、罐、安瓿及其他容器,用于运输或盛装货物;玻璃制保藏罐;玻璃塞、盖及类似的封口器:**							**Carboys, bottles, flasks, jars, pots, phials, ampoules and other containers, of glass, of a kind used for the conveyance or packing of goods; preserving jars of glass; stoppers, lids and other closures, of glass:**
4947	7010.1000	-安瓿	14	0 1.4 2.8 11.2	东盟ASEAN,新加坡SG,新西兰NZ,秘鲁PE 智利CL 哥斯达黎加CR 巴基斯坦PK	0	最不发达35国LDC35	50	-Ampoules
4948	7010.2000	-塞、盖及类似的封口器	14	0 2.8 11.2	东盟ASEAN,智利CL,新加坡SG,新西兰NZ,秘鲁PE 哥斯达黎加CR 巴基斯坦PK	0	最不发达35国LDC35	50	-Stoppers, lids and other closures
		-其他:							-Other, of a capacity:
4949	7010.9010	---超过1升	14	0 1.4 2.8 11.2	东盟ASEAN,新加坡SG,新西兰NZ,秘鲁PE 智利CL 哥斯达黎加CR 巴基斯坦PK	0	最不发达35国LDC35	50	---Exceeding 1L
4950	7010.9020	---超过0.33升,但不超过1升	14	0 1.4 2.8 11.2	东盟ASEAN,新加坡SG,新西兰NZ,秘鲁PE 智利CL 哥斯达黎加CR 巴基斯坦PK	0	最不发达35国LDC35	50	---Exceeding 0.33L but not exceeding 1L
4951	7010.9030	---超过0.15升,但不超过0.33升	14	0 1.4 2.8 11.2	东盟ASEAN,新加坡SG,新西兰NZ,秘鲁PE 智利CL 哥斯达黎加CR 巴基斯坦PK	0	最不发达35国LDC35	50	---Exceeding 0.15L but not exceeding 0.33L

序号 No.	税则号列 Tariff Line	货品名称	最惠国 税率 MFN(%)	协定税率 Agreement(%)		特惠税率 S.P.(%)		普通税率 Gen.(%)	Article Description
4952	7010.9090	---不超过 0.15 升	14	0 1.4 2.8 11.2	东盟ASEAN,新加坡SG,新西兰NZ,秘鲁PE 智利CL 哥斯达黎加CR 巴基斯坦PK	0	最不发达 35 国 LDC35,最不发达 4 国 LDC4	50	---Not exceeding 0.15L
	70.11	**制灯泡、阴极射线管及类似品用的未封口玻璃外壳（包括玻璃泡及管）及其玻璃零件，但未装有配件:**							**Glass envelopes (including bulbs and tubes), open, and glass parts thereof, without fittings, for electric lamps, cathode-ray tubes or the like:**
4953	7011.1000	-电灯用	21	0 4.2 10.5	东盟ASEAN,智利CL,新加坡SG,新西兰NZ 哥斯达黎加CR 秘鲁PE	0	最不发达 35 国 LDC35	80	-For electric lighting
		-阴极射线管用:							-For cathode-ray tubes:
4954	7011.2010	---显像管玻壳及其零件	10	0 5 7	东盟ASEAN,智利CL,新西兰NZ,秘鲁PE,哥斯达黎加CR 巴基斯坦PK 亚太APTA	0	最不发达 35 国 LDC35	35	---Glass envelopes for kinescope and glass parts there of
4955	7011.2090	---其他	10	0 5 7	东盟ASEAN,智利CL,新西兰NZ,秘鲁PE,哥斯达黎加CR 巴基斯坦PK 亚太APTA	0	最不发达 35 国 LDC35	35	---Other
	ex70112090	显示管玻壳及其零件	△6						Glass envelopes and parts thereof for display tubes
		-其他:							-Other:
4956	7011.9010	---电子管用（阴极射线管用的除外）	8	0 5	东盟ASEAN,智利CL,新西兰NZ,秘鲁PE,哥斯达黎加CR 巴基斯坦PK	0	最不发达 35 国 LDC35	35	---For electronic tubes and valves (other than cathode-ray tubes)
4957	7011.9090	---其他	21	0 4.2 10.5	东盟ASEAN,智利CL,新加坡SG,新西兰NZ 哥斯达黎加CR 秘鲁PE	0	最不发达 35 国 LDC35	80	---Other
	70.13	**玻璃器，供餐桌、厨房、盥洗室、办公室、室内装饰或类似用途（税号 70.10 或 70.18 的货品除外）:**							**Glassware of a kind used for table, kitchen, toilet, office, indoor decoration or similar purposes (other than that of heading No.70.10 or 70.18):**
4958	7013.1000	-玻璃陶瓷制	24.5	0 4.9 12.3	东盟ASEAN,智利CL,新加坡SG,新西兰NZ 哥斯达黎加CR 秘鲁PE	0	最不发达 35 国 LDC35,最不发达 4 国 LDC4	100	-Of glass-ceramics

序号 No.	税则号列 Tariff Line	货品名称	最惠国税率 MFN(%)	协定税率 Agreement(%)		特惠税率 S.P.(%)		普通税率 Gen.(%)	Article Description
		-高脚杯，但玻璃陶瓷制的除外:							-Stemware drinking glasses, other than of glass-ceramics:
4959	7013.2200	--铅晶质玻璃制	24.5 △15	0 4.9 12.3	东盟ASEAN,智利CL,新加坡SG,新西兰NZ 哥斯达黎加CR 秘鲁PE	0	最不发达35国LDC35	100	--Of lead crystal
4960	7013.2800	--其他	8	0 5	东盟ASEAN,智利CL,新加坡SG,新西兰NZ,秘鲁PE,哥斯达黎加CR 巴基斯坦PK	0	最不发达35国LDC35,最不发达4国LDC4	100	--Other
		-其他杯子，但玻璃陶瓷制的除外:							-Other drinking glasses, other than of glass-ceramics:
4961	7013.3300	--铅晶质玻璃制	24.5 △15	0 4.9 12.3	东盟ASEAN,智利CL,新加坡SG,新西兰NZ 哥斯达黎加CR 秘鲁PE	0	最不发达35国LDC35	100	--Of lead crystal
4962	7013.3700	--其他	8	0 5	东盟ASEAN,智利CL,新加坡SG,新西兰NZ,秘鲁PE,哥斯达黎加CR 巴基斯坦PK	0	最不发达35国LDC35,最不发达4国LDC4	100	--Other
		-餐桌或厨房用玻璃器皿（不包括杯子），但玻璃陶瓷制的除外:							-Glassware of a kind used for table (other than drinking glasses) or kitchen purposes other than of glass-ceramics:
4963	7013.4100	--铅晶质玻璃制	24.5 △15	0 4.9 12.3	东盟ASEAN,智利CL,新加坡SG,新西兰NZ 哥斯达黎加CR 秘鲁PE	0	最不发达35国LDC35	100	--Of lead crystal
4964	7013.4200	--温度在0℃至300℃时线膨胀系数不超过5×10^{-6}/开尔文的其他玻璃制	10	0 5	东盟ASEAN,智利CL,新加坡SG,新西兰NZ,秘鲁PE,哥斯达黎加CR 巴基斯坦PK	0	最不发达35国LDC35,最不发达4国LDC4	100	--Of glass having a linear coefficient of expansion not exceeding 5×10^{-6} per Kelvin within a temperature range of 0°C to 300°C
4965	7013.4900	--其他	10	0 5	东盟ASEAN,智利CL,新加坡SG,新西兰NZ,秘鲁PE,哥斯达黎加CR 巴基斯坦PK	0	最不发达35国LDC35,最不发达4国LDC4	100	--Other
		-其他玻璃器:							-Other glassware:
4966	7013.9100	--铅晶质玻璃制	10	0 5	东盟ASEAN,智利CL,新加坡SG,新西兰NZ,秘鲁PE,哥斯达黎加CR 巴基斯坦PK	0	最不发达35国LDC35,最不发达4国LDC4	100	--Of lead crystal

序号 No.	税则号列 Tariff Line	货品名称	最惠国税率 MFN(%)	协定税率 Agreement(%)		特惠税率 S.P.(%)		普通税率 Gen.(%)	Article Description
4967	7013.9900	--其他	10	0 1 5	东盟ASEAN,新加坡SG,新西兰NZ,秘鲁PE,哥斯达黎加CR 智利CL 巴基斯坦PK	0	最不发达35国LDC35,最不发达4国LDC4	100	--Other
	70.14	**未经光学加工的信号玻璃器及玻璃制光学元件（税号70.15的货品除外）:**							**Signalling glassware and optical elements of glass (other than those of heading No.70.15), not optically worked:**
4968	7014.0010	---光学仪器用光学元件毛坯	10	0 5	东盟ASEAN,智利CL,新加坡SG,新西兰NZ,秘鲁PE,哥斯达黎加CR,澳门MO 巴基斯坦PK	0	最不发达35国LDC35,最不发达4国LDC4	40	---Blanks of optical elements, for optical instruments
4969	7014.0090	---其他	17.5	0 3.5 8.8 14	东盟ASEAN,智利CL,新加坡SG,新西兰NZ 哥斯达黎加CR 秘鲁PE 巴基斯坦PK	0	最不发达35国LDC35	80	---Other
	ex70140090	带有抗红外和防反射薄膜的滤波玻璃	△9						Wave-filter galss with anti-IR and anti-reflection film
	70.15	**钟表玻璃及类似玻璃、视力矫正或非视力矫正眼镜用玻璃，呈弧面、弯曲、凹形或类似形状但未经光学加工的;制造上述玻璃用的凹面圆形及扇形玻璃:**							**Clock or watch glasses and similar glasses, glasses for non-corrective or corrective spectacles, curved, bent, hollowed or the like, not optically worked; hollow glass spheres and their segments, for the manufacture of such glasses:**
		-视力矫正眼镜用玻璃:							-Glasses for corrective spectacles:
4970	7015.1010	---变色镜片坯件	21 △15	0 4.2 10.5	东盟ASEAN,智利CL,新加坡SG,新西兰NZ 哥斯达黎加CR 秘鲁PE	0	最不发达35国LDC35	80	---Blanks for photochromic spectacles
4971	7015.1090	---其他	17.5 △10	0 3.5 8.8 14	东盟ASEAN,智利CL,新加坡SG,新西兰NZ 哥斯达黎加CR 秘鲁PE 巴基斯坦PK	0	最不发达35国LDC35	70	---Other
		-其他:							-Other:
4972	7015.9010	---钟表玻璃	17.5	0 3.5 8.8 14	东盟ASEAN,智利CL,新加坡SG,新西兰NZ 哥斯达黎加CR 秘鲁PE 巴基斯坦PK	0	最不发达35国LDC35	70	---Clock and watch glasses

序号 No.	税则号列 Tariff Line	货品名称	最惠国 税　率 MFN(%)	协定税率 Agreement(%)		特惠税率 S.P.(%)		普通 税率 Gen.(%)	Article Description
4973	7015.9020	---平光变色镜片坯件	18 △10	0 3.6 9 14.4	东盟ASEAN,智利CL, 新加坡SG,新西兰NZ 哥斯达黎加CR 秘鲁PE 巴基斯坦PK	0	最不发达35国LDC35	80	---Blanks for plane photochromic spectacles
4974	7015.9090	---其他	12	0 2.4 6	东盟ASEAN,智利CL, 新加坡SG,新西兰NZ,秘鲁PE 哥斯达黎加CR 巴基斯坦PK	0	最不发达35国LDC35,最不发达4国LDC4	80	---Other
	70.16	**建筑用压制或模制的铺面用玻璃块、砖、片、瓦及其他制品，不论是否夹丝；供镶嵌或类似装饰用的玻璃马赛克及其他小件玻璃品，不论是否有衬背;花饰铅条窗玻璃及类似品;多孔或泡沫玻璃块、板、片及类似品:**							**Paving blocks, slabs, bricks, squares, tiles and other articles of pressed or moulded glass, whether or not wired, of a kind used for building or construction purposes; glass cubes and other glass smallwares, whether or not on a backing, for mosaics or similar decorative purposes; leaded lights and the like; multicellular or foam glass in blocks, panels, plates, shells or similar forms:**
4975	7016.1000	-供镶嵌或类似装饰用的玻璃马赛克及其他小件玻璃品，不论是否有衬背	22	0 4.4 11	东盟ASEAN,智利CL, 新加坡SG,新西兰NZ 哥斯达黎加CR 秘鲁PE	0	最不发达35国LDC35	100	-Glass cubes and other glass smallwares, whether or not on a backing, for mosaics or similar decorative purposes
		-其他:							-Other:
4976	7016.9010	---花饰铅条窗玻璃及类似品	24	0 4.8 12	东盟ASEAN,智利CL, 新加坡SG,新西兰NZ 哥斯达黎加CR 秘鲁PE	0	最不发达35国LDC35	90	---Leaded lights and the like
4977	7016.9090	---其他	18	0 3.6 9	东盟ASEAN,智利CL, 新加坡SG,新西兰NZ 哥斯达黎加CR 秘鲁PE	0	最不发达35国LDC35	90	---Other
	70.17	**实验室、卫生及配药用的玻璃器，不论有无刻度或标量:**							**Laboratory, hygienic or pharmaceutical glassware, whether or not graduated or calibrated:**
4978	7017.1000	-熔融石英或其他熔融硅石制	0			0	最不发达35国LDC35,最不发达4国LDC4	30	-Of fused quartz or other fused silica

序号 No.	税则号列 Tariff Line	货品名称	最惠国 税 率 MFN(%)	协定税率 Agreement(%)	特惠税率 S.P.(%)	普通 税率 Gen.(%)	Article Description
4979	7017.2000	-温度在0℃至300℃时线膨胀系数不超过5×10^{-6}/开尔文的其他玻璃制	8	0 东盟ASEAN,智利CL,新西兰NZ,秘鲁PE,哥斯达黎加CR 5 巴基斯坦PK	0 最不发达35国LDC35,最不发达4国LDC4	30	-Of other glass having a linear coefficient of expansion not exceeding 5×10^{-6} per Kelvin within a temperature range of 0°C to 300°C
4980	7017.9000	-其他	8	0 东盟ASEAN,智利CL,新西兰NZ,秘鲁PE,哥斯达黎加CR 5 巴基斯坦PK	0 最不发达35国LDC35,最不发达4国LDC4	30	-Other
	70.18	**玻璃珠、仿珍珠、仿宝石或仿半宝石和类似小件玻璃品及其制品，但仿首饰除外;玻璃假眼，但医用假眼除外;灯工方法制作的玻璃塑像及其他玻璃装饰品，但仿首饰除外;直径不超过1毫米的微型玻璃球:**					**Glass beads, imitation pearls, imitation precious or semi-precious stones and similar glass smallwares, and articles thereof other than imitation jewellery; glass eyes other than prosthetic articles; statuettes and other ornaments of lamp-worked glass, other than imitation jewellery; glass microspheres not exceeding 1mm in diameter:**
4981	7018.1000	-玻璃珠、仿珍珠、仿宝石或仿半宝石及类似小件玻璃品	10	0 东盟ASEAN,智利CL,新加坡SG,新西兰NZ,秘鲁PE,哥斯达黎加CR 5 巴基斯坦PK	0 最不发达35国LDC35,最不发达4国LDC4	100	-Glass beads, imitation pearls, imitation precious or semiprecious stones and similar glass smallwares
4982	7018.2000	-直径不超过1毫米的微型玻璃球	20	0 东盟ASEAN,智利CL,新加坡SG,新西兰NZ 4 哥斯达黎加CR 10 秘鲁PE	0 最不发达35国LDC35	100	-Glass microspheres not exceeding1mm in diameter
	ex70182000	熔融球形二氧化硅微粉，直径小于等于100μm	△5.5				Fused spherical SiO_2, diameter not exceeding 100 micron
4983	7018.9000	-其他	20 △10	0 东盟ASEAN,智利CL,新加坡SG,新西兰NZ 4 哥斯达黎加CR 10 秘鲁PE	0 最不发达35国LDC35	100	-Other
	70.19	**玻璃纤维（包括玻璃棉）及其制品（例如，玻璃纤维纱线及其织物）:**					**Glass fibres (including glass wool) and articles thereof (for example, yarn, woven fabrics):**
		-梳条、粗纱、纱线及短切纤维:					-Slivers, rovings, yarn and chopped strands:
4984	7019.1100	--长度不超过50毫米的短切纤维	12	0 东盟ASEAN,智利CL,新加坡SG,新西兰NZ,秘鲁PE,台湾TW 2.4 哥斯达黎加CR 6 巴基斯坦PK	0 最不发达35国LDC35,最不发达4国LDC4	50	--Chopped strands, of a length of not more than 50mm

序号 No.	税则号列 Tariff Line	货品名称	最惠国税率 MFN(%)	协定税率 Agreement(%)		特惠税率 S.P.(%)		普通税率 Gen.(%)	Article Description
4985	7019.1200	--粗纱	12	0 2.4 6	东盟ASEAN,智利CL,新加坡SG,新西兰NZ,秘鲁PE 哥斯达黎加CR 巴基斯坦PK	0	最不发达35国LDC35,最不发达4国LDC4	50	--Rovings
4986	7019.1900	--其他	10	0 5	东盟ASEAN,智利CL,新西兰NZ,秘鲁PE,哥斯达黎加CR,澳门MO,台湾TW 巴基斯坦PK	0	最不发达35国LDC35,最不发达4国LDC4	50	--Other
		-薄片（巴厘纱）、纤维网、席、垫、板及类似无纺产品:							-Thin sheets (voiles), webs, mats, mattresses, boards and similar nonwoven products:
4987	7019.3100	--席	5	0	东盟ASEAN,智利CL,巴基斯坦PK,新西兰NZ,秘鲁PE,哥斯达黎加CR	0	最不发达35国LDC35,最不发达4国LDC4	40	--Mats
4988	7019.3200	--薄片（巴厘纱）	14	0 2.8 11.2	东盟ASEAN,智利CL,新加坡SG,新西兰NZ,秘鲁PE 哥斯达黎加CR 巴基斯坦PK	0	最不发达35国LDC35	40	--Thin sheets (voiles)
		--其他:							--Other:
4989	7019.3910	---垫	10.5	0 1.1 2.1 5	东盟ASEAN,新加坡SG,新西兰NZ,秘鲁PE,台湾TW 智利CL 哥斯达黎加CR 巴基斯坦PK	0	最不发达35国LDC35,最不发达4国LDC4	40	---Mattresses
4990	7019.3990	---其他	10.5	0 1.1 2.1 5	东盟ASEAN,新加坡SG,新西兰NZ,秘鲁PE,台湾TW 智利CL 哥斯达黎加CR 巴基斯坦PK	0	最不发达35国LDC35,最不发达4国LDC4	40	---Other
4991	7019.4000	-粗纱机织物	12	0 2.4 6	东盟ASEAN,智利CL,新加坡SG,新西兰NZ,秘鲁PE 哥斯达黎加CR 巴基斯坦PK	0	最不发达35国LDC35,最不发达4国LDC4	40	-Woven fabrics of rovings
		-其他机织物:							-Other woven fabrics:
4992	7019.5100	--宽度不超过30厘米的	12	0 2.4 6	东盟ASEAN,智利CL,新加坡SG,新西兰NZ,秘鲁PE,香港HK 哥斯达黎加CR 巴基斯坦PK	0	最不发达35国LDC35,最不发达4国LDC4	40	--Of a width not exceeding 30cm

序号 No.	税则号列 Tariff Line	货品名称	最惠国税率 MFN(%)	协定税率 Agreement(%)		特惠税率 S.P.(%)		普通税率 Gen.(%)	Article Description
4993	7019.5200	--宽度超过30厘米的长丝平纹织物，每平方米重量不超过250克，单根纱线细度不超过136特克斯	12	0 2.4 6	东盟ASEAN,智利CL,新加坡SG,新西兰NZ,秘鲁PE,香港HK,澳门MO 哥斯达黎加CR 巴基斯坦PK	0	最不发达35国LDC35,最不发达4国LDC4	40	--Of a width exceeding 30cm, plain weave, weighing less than 250g/m^2, of filaments measuring per single yarn not more than 136tex
	ex70195200	覆铜板用玻璃纤维长丝平纹布，开纤或每平方米重不超过180克	△10						Glass fiber colth, covered with copper foil, open filament fabric or weighting less than or equal to 180g/m^2
4994	7019.5900	--其他	12	0 2.4 5 8.4	东盟ASEAN,智利CL,新加坡SG,新西兰NZ,秘鲁PE,香港HK,澳门MO 哥斯达黎加CR 巴基斯坦PK 亚太APTA	0	最不发达35国LDC35,最不发达4国LDC4	40	--Other
		-其他:							-Other:
4995	7019.9010	---玻璃棉及其制品	7	0 0.7 5	东盟ASEAN,新西兰NZ,秘鲁PE,哥斯达黎加CR,澳门MO 智利CL 巴基斯坦PK	0	最不发达35国LDC35,最不发达4国LDC4	40	---Glass wool and their product
		---玻璃纤维布浸胶制品:							---Glass fiber cloth dipped product:
4996	7019.9021	----每平方米重量小于450克	7	0 0.7 5	东盟ASEAN,新西兰NZ,秘鲁PE,哥斯达黎加CR,澳门MO 智利CL 巴基斯坦PK	0	最不发达35国LDC35,最不发达4国LDC4	40	----Weighting less than 450g/m^2
4997	7019.9029	----其他	7	0 0.7 5	东盟ASEAN,新西兰NZ,秘鲁PE,哥斯达黎加CR,澳门MO 智利CL 巴基斯坦PK	0	最不发达35国LDC35,最不发达4国LDC4	40	----Other
4998	7019.9090	---其他	7	0 0.7 5	东盟ASEAN,新西兰NZ,秘鲁PE,哥斯达黎加CR,澳门MO 智利CL 巴基斯坦PK	0	最不发达35国LDC35,最不发达4国LDC4	40	---Other
	70.20	**其他玻璃制品:**							**Other articles of glass:**
		---工业用:							---For technical use:
4999	7020.0011	----导电玻璃	10.5 △7	0 1.1 2.1 5	东盟ASEAN,新加坡SG,新西兰NZ,秘鲁PE,香港HK 智利CL 哥斯达黎加CR 巴基斯坦PK	0	最不发达35国LDC35,最不发达4国LDC4	40	----Conductivity glass

序号 No.	税则号列 Tariff Line	货品名称	最惠国税率 MFN(%)	协定税率 Agreement(%)		特惠税率 S.P.(%)		普通税率 Gen.(%)	Article Description
5000	7020.0012	----绝缘子用玻璃伞盘	10.5	0 1.1 2.1 5 9.5	东盟ASEAN,新加坡SG,新西兰NZ,秘鲁PE 智利CL 哥斯达黎加CR 巴基斯坦PK 亚太APTA	0	最不发达35国LDC35,最不发达4国LDC4	40	----Glass umbrella for insulator
5001	7020.0013	----熔融石英或其他熔融硅石制	10.5	0 1.1 2.1 5 8.9	东盟ASEAN,新加坡SG,新西兰NZ,秘鲁PE 智利CL 哥斯达黎加CR 巴基斯坦PK 亚太APTA	0	最不发达35国LDC35,最不发达4国LDC4	40	----Of fused quartz or other fused silica
	ex70200013	用于插入熔化和氧化炉内以制备半导体晶片的石英反应管及夹持器	0						Quartz reactor tubes and holders designed for insertion into diffusion and oxidation furnaces for production of semiconductor wafers
5002	7020.0019	----其他	10.5	0 1.1 2.1 5 8.9	东盟ASEAN,新加坡SG,新西兰NZ,秘鲁PE 智利CL 哥斯达黎加CR 巴基斯坦PK 亚太APTA	0	最不发达35国LDC35,最不发达4国LDC4	40	----Other
	ex70200019	用于插入熔化和氧化炉内以制备半导体晶片的石英反应管及夹持器	0						Quartz reactor tubes and holders designed for insertion into diffusion and oxidation furnaces for production of semiconductor wafers
	ex70200019	等离子模块生产用高应变点玻璃（应变点在550摄氏度及以上）	△5						High strain point glass used for PDP model production（strain point ≥550°C）
		---其他:							---Other:
5003	7020.0091	----保温瓶或其他保温容器用的玻璃胆	21	0 4.2 10.5	东盟ASEAN,智利CL,新加坡SG,新西兰NZ,香港HK 哥斯达黎加CR 秘鲁PE	0	最不发达35国LDC35	100	----Glass inners for vacuum flasks or for other vacuum vessels
5004	7020.0099	----其他	15	0 1.5 3 7.5 12.8	东盟ASEAN,新加坡SG,新西兰NZ,香港HK 智利CL 哥斯达黎加CR 巴基斯坦PK,秘鲁PE 亚太APTA	0	最不发达35国LDC35,最不发达4国LDC4	100	----Other
	ex70200099	石英玻璃，平整度小于等于1微米	△4						Quartz glass, of a flatness less than or equal to 1μm

第十四类
天然或养殖珍珠、宝石或半宝石、贵金属、包贵金属及其制品；仿首饰；硬币

SECTION XIV
NATURAL OR CULTURED PEARLS, PRECIOUS OR SEMI-PRECIOUS STONES, PRECIOUS METALS, METALS CLAD WITH PRECIOUS METAL, AND ARTICLES THEREOF; IMITATION JEWELLERY; COIN

第七十一章
天然或养殖珍珠、宝石或半宝石、贵金属、包贵金属及其制品；仿首饰；硬币

Chapter 71
Natural or cultured pearls, precious or semi-precious stones, precious metals, metals clad with precious metal, and articles thereof; imitation jewellery; coin

注释：

一、除第六类注释一（一）及下列各款另有规定的以外，凡制品的全部或部分由下列物品构成，均应归入本章：

（一）天然或养殖珍珠、宝石或半宝石（天然、合成或再造）；

（二）贵金属或包贵金属。

二、（一）税号 71.13、71.14 及 71.15 不包括带有贵金属或包贵金属制的小零件或小装饰品（例如，交织字母、套、圈、套环）的制品，上述注释一（二）也不适用于这类制品；

（二）税号 71.16 不包括含有贵金属或包贵金属（仅作为小零件或小装饰品的除外）的制品。

三、本章不包括：

（一）贵金属汞齐及胶态贵金属（税号 28.43）；

（二）第三十章的外科用无菌缝合材料、牙科填料或其他货品；

（三）第三十二章的货品（例如光瓷釉）；

（四）载体催化剂（税号 38.15）；

（五）第四十二章注释三（二）所述的税号 42.02 或 42.03 的物品；

Notes:

1. Subject to Note1 (a) to SectionⅥand except as provided below, all articles consisting wholly or partly:

(a) Of natural or cultured pearls or of precious or semi-precious stones (natural, synthetic or reconstructed); or

(b) Of precious metal or of metal clad with precious metal, are to be classified in this Chapter.

2. (a) Headings Nos.71.13, 71.14 and 71.15 do not cover articles in which precious metal or metal clad with precious metal is present as minor constituents only, such as minor fittings or minor ornamentation (for example, monograms, ferrules and rims), and paragraph (b) of the foregoing Note does not apply to such articles;

(b) Heading No.71.16 does not cover articles containing precious metal or metal clad with precious metal (other than as minor constituents) .

3. This Chapter does not cover:

(a) Amalgams of precious metal, or colloidal precious metal (heading No.28.43);

(b) Sterile surgical suture materials, dental fillings or other goods of Chapter 30;

(c) Goods of Chapter 32 (for example, lustres);

(d) Supported catalysts (heading No.38.15);

(e) Articles of heading No.42.02 or 42.03 referred to in Note 3 (B) to Chapter 42;

（六）税号 43.03 或 43.04 的物品；

（七）第十一类的货品（纺织原料及纺织制品）；

（八）第六十四章或第六十五章的鞋靴、帽类及其他物品；

（九）第六十六章的伞、手杖及其他物品；

（十）税号 68.04 或 68.05 及第八十二章含有宝石或半宝石（天然或合成）粉末的研磨材料制品；第八十二章装有宝石或半宝石（天然、合成或再造）工作部件的器具；第十六类的机器、机械器具、电气设备及其零件。然而，完全以宝石或半宝石（天然、合成或再造）制成的物品及其零件，除未安装的唱针用已加工蓝宝石或钻石外（税号 85.22），其余仍应归入本章；

（十一）第九十章、第九十一章或第九十二章的物品（科学仪器、钟表及乐器）；

（十二）武器及其零件（第九十三章）；

（十三）第九十五章注释二所述物品；

（十四）根据第九十六章注释四应归入该章的物品；

（十五）雕塑品原件（税号 98.03）、收藏品（税号 98.05）或超过一百年的古物（税号 98.06）、但天然或养殖珍珠、宝石及半宝石除外。

(f) Articles of heading No.43.03 or 43.04;

(g) Goods of SectionXI (textiles and textile articles);

(h) Footwear, headgear or other articles of Chapter 64 or 65;

(i) Umbrellas, walking-sticks or other articles of Chapter 66;

(j) Abrasive goods of heading No.68.04 or 68.05 or Chapter 82, containing dust or powder of precious or semiprecious stones (natural or synthetic); articles of Chapter 82with a working part of precious or semi-precious stones (natural, synthetic or reconsturcted); machinery, mechanical appliances or electrical goods, or parts thereof, of Section X VI.However, articles and parts thereof, wholly of precious or semiprecious stones (natural, synthetic or reconstructed) remain classified in this Chapter, except unmounted worked sapphires and diamonds for styli (heading No.85.22);

(k) Articles of Chapter90, 91 or 92 (scientific instruments, clocks and watches, musical instruments);

(l) Arms or parts thereof (Chapter 93);

(m) Articles covered by Note 2 to Chapter 95;

(n) Articles classified in Chapter 96 by virtue of Note 4 to that Chapter;

(o) Original sculptures or statuary (heading No.97.03) , collectors pieces (heading No.97.05) or antiques of an age exceeding one hundred years (heading No.97.06), other than natural or cultured pearls or precious or semi-precious stones.

四、

（一）所称“贵金属”，是指银、金及铂。

（二）所称“铂”，是指铂、铱、锇、钯、铑及钌。

（三）所称“宝石或半宝石”，不包括第九十六章注释二（二）所述任何物质。

4.

(a) The expression “precious metal” means silver, gold and platinum;

(b) The expression “platinum” means platinum, iridium, osmium, palladium, rhodium and ruthenium;

(c) The expression “precious or semi-precious stones” does not include any of the substances specified in Note 2 (b) to Chapter 96.

五、含有贵金属的合金（包括烧结及化合的），只要其中任何一种贵金属的含量达到合金重量的 2%，即应视为本章的贵金属合金。贵金属合金应按下列规则归类：

（一）按重量计含铂量在 2%及以上的合金，应视为铂合金；

（二）按重量计含金量在 2%及以上，但不含铂或

5. For the purposes of this Chapter, any alloy (including a sintered mixture and an inter-metallic compound) containing precious metal is to be treated as an alloy of precious metal if any one precious metal constitutes as much as 2%, by weight, of the alloy. Alloys of precious metal are to be classified according to the following rules:

(a) An alloy containing 2% or more, by weight, of platinum is to be treated as an alloy of platinum;

(b) An alloy containing 2% or more, by weight, of gold

按重量计含铂量在2%以下的合金，应视为金合金；

（三）按重量计含银量在2%及以上的其他合金，应视为银合金。

六、除条文另有规定的以外，本目录所称贵金属应包括上述注释五所规定的贵金属合金，但不包括包贵金属或表面镀以贵金属的贱金属及非金属。

七、本目录所称“包贵金属”，是指以贱金属为底料，在其一面或多面用焊接、熔接、热轧或类似机械方法覆盖一层贵金属的材料。除条文另有规定的以外，也包括镶嵌贵金属的贱金属。

八、除第六类注释一（一）另有规定的以外，凡符合税号71.12规定的货品，应归入该税号而不归入本目录的其他税号。

九、税号71.13所称“首饰”，是指：

（一）个人用小饰物（不论是否镶嵌宝石）（例如，戒指、手镯、项圈、饰针、耳环、表链、表链饰物、垂饰、领带别针、袖扣、饰扣、宗教性或其他勋章及徽章）；

（二）通常放置在衣袋、手提包或佩戴在身上的个人用品（例如，烟盒、鼻烟盒、口香丸和药丸盒、粉盒、链袋或念珠）。

这些物品可以和下列物品组合或镶嵌下列物品：例如，天然或养殖珍珠、宝石或半宝石、合成或再造的宝石或半宝石、玳瑁壳、珍珠母、兽牙、天然或再生琥珀、黑玉或珊瑚。

十、税号71.14所称“金银器”，包括装饰品、餐具、梳妆用具、吸烟用具及类似的家庭、办公室或宗教用的其他物品。

but no platinum, or less than 2%, by weight, of platinum, is to be treated as an alloy of gold;

(c) Other alloys containing 2% or more, by weight, of silver are to be treated as alloys of silver.

6. Except where the context otherwise requires, any reference in the Nomenclature to precious metal or to any particular precious metal includes a reference to alloys treated as alloys of precious metal or of the particular metal in accordance with the rules in Note5above, but not to metal clad with precious metal or to base metal or nonmetals plated with precious metal.

7. Throughout the Nomenclature the expression “metal clad with precious metal” means material made with a base of metal upon one or more surfaces of which there is affixed by soldering, brazing, welding, hot-rolling or similar mechanical means a covering of precious metal. Except where the context otherwise requires, the expression also covers base metal inlaid with precious metal.

8. Subject to Note1 (a) to SectionⅥ, goods answering to a description in heading No.71.12 are to be classified in that heading and in no other heading of the Nomenclature.

9. For the purposes of heading No.71.13, the expression “articles of jewellery” means:

(a) Any small objects of personal adornment (gem-set or not) (for example, rings, bracelets, necklaces, brooches, earrings, watch-chains, fobs, pendants, tie-pins, cufflinks, dress-studs, religious or other medals and insignia); and

(b) Articles of personal use of a kind normally carried in the pocket, in the handbag or on the person (for example, cigar or cigarette cases, snuff boxes, cachou or pill boxes, cachou powder boxes, chain purses or prayer beads) .

These articles may be combined or set, for example, with natural or cultured pearls, precious or semi-precious stones, synthetic or reconstructed precious or semi-precious stones, tortoise shell, mother-of pearl, ivory, natural or reconstituted amber, jet or coral.

10. For the purposes of heading No.71.14, the expression “articles of goldsmiths or silversmiths wares” includes such articles as ornaments, tableware, toilet-ware, smokers requisites and other articles of household, office or religious use.

十一、税号 71.17 所称"仿首饰"，是指不含天然或养殖珍珠、宝石或半宝石（天然、合成或再造）及贵金属或包贵金属（仅作为镀层或小零件、小装饰品的除外）的上述注释九（一）所述的首饰（不包括税号 96.06 的钮扣及其他物品或税号 96.15 的梳子、发夹及类似品）。

11. For the purposes of heading No.71.17, the expression "imitation jewellery" means articles of jewellery within the meaning of paragraph (a) of Note 9 above (but not including buttons or other articles of heading No.96.06, or dress-combs, hair-slides or the like, or hairpins, of heading No.96.15), not incorporating natural or cultured pearls, precious or semiprecious stones (natural, synthetic or reconstructed) nor (except as plating or as minor constituents) precious metal or metal clad with precious metal.

子目注释:

一、子目号 7106.10、7108.11、7110.11、7110.21、7110.31 及 7110.41 所称"粉末"，是指按重量计 90%及以上可从网眼孔径为 0.5 毫米的筛子通过的产品。

二、子目号 7110.11 及 7110.19 所称"铂"，可不受本章注释四（二）的规定约束，不包括铱、锇、钯、铑及钌。

三、对于税号 71.10 项下的子目所列合金的归类，按其所含铂、钯、铑、铱、锇或钌中重量最大的一种金属归类。

Subheading Notes:

1. For the purposes of subheadings Nos.7106.10, 7108.11, 7110.11, 7110.21, 7110.31 and 7110.41, the expressions "powder" and "in powder form" mean products of which90%or more by weight passes through a sieve having a mesh aperture of 0.5mm.
2. Notwithstanding the provisions of Chapter Note4 (b) , for the purposes of subheadings Nos.7110.11 and 7110.19, the expression "platinum" does not include indium, osmium, palladium, rhodium or ruthenium.
3. For the classification of alloys in the subheadings of heading No.71.10, each alloy is to be classified with that metal, platinum, palladium, rhodium, iridium, osmium or ruthenium which predominates by weight over each other of these metals.

序号 No.	税则号列 Tariff Line	货品名称	最惠国税率 MFN(%)	协定税率 Agreement(%)	特惠税率 S.P.(%)	普通税率 Gen.(%)	Article Description
		第一分章 天然或养殖珍珠、宝石或半宝石					Ⅰ.NATURAL OR CULTURED PEARLS AND PRECIOUS OR SEMI-PRECIOUS STONES
	71.01	**天然或养殖珍珠，不论是否加工或分级，但未成串或镶嵌;天然或养殖珍珠，为便于运输而暂穿成串:**					**Pearls, natural or cultured, whether or not worked or graded but not strung, mounted or set; ungraded pearls, natural or cultured, temporarily strung for convenience of transport:**
		-天然珍珠:					-Natural pearls:
		---未分级:					---Ungraded:
5005	7101.1011	----黑珍珠	21 △0	0 东盟ASEAN,智利CL,新加坡SG,新西兰NZ 4.2 哥斯达黎加CR 10.5 秘鲁PE	0 最不发达35国LDC35	100	----Tahitian pearls

序号 No.	税则号列 Tariff Line	货品名称	最惠国税率 MFN(%)	协定税率 Agreement(%)	特惠税率 S.P.(%)	普通税率 Gen.(%)	Article Description
5006	7101.1019	----其他	21	0 东盟ASEAN,智利CL,新加坡SG,新西兰NZ 4.2 哥斯达黎加CR 10.5 秘鲁PE	0 最不发达35国LDC35	100	----Other
		---其他:					---Other:
5007	7101.1091	----黑珍珠	21 △0	0 东盟ASEAN,智利CL,新加坡SG,新西兰NZ 4.2 哥斯达黎加CR 10.5 秘鲁PE	0 最不发达35国LDC35	130	----Tahitian pearls
5008	7101.1099	----其他	21	0 东盟ASEAN,智利CL,新加坡SG,新西兰NZ 4.2 哥斯达黎加CR 10.5 秘鲁PE	0 最不发达35国LDC35	130	----Other
		-养殖珍珠:					-Cultured pearls:
		--未加工:					--Unworked:
5009	7101.2110	---未分级	21	0 东盟ASEAN,智利CL,新加坡SG,新西兰NZ 4.2 哥斯达黎加CR 10.5 秘鲁PE	0 最不发达35国LDC35	100	---Ungraded
	ex71012110	养殖黑珍珠	△0				Cultured tahitian pearls
5010	7101.2190	---其他	21	0 东盟ASEAN,智利CL,新加坡SG,新西兰NZ 4.2 哥斯达黎加CR 10.5 秘鲁PE	0 最不发达35国LDC35	130	---Other
	ex71012190	养殖黑珍珠	△0				Cultured tahitian pearls
		--已加工:					--Worked:
5011	7101.2210	---未分级	21	0 东盟ASEAN,智利CL,新加坡SG,新西兰NZ 4.2 哥斯达黎加CR 10.5 秘鲁PE	0 最不发达35国LDC35	100	---Ungraded
	ex71012210	养殖黑珍珠	△0				Cultured tahitian pearls
5012	7101.2290	---其他	21	0 东盟ASEAN,智利CL,新加坡SG,新西兰NZ 4.2 哥斯达黎加CR 10.5 秘鲁PE	0 最不发达35国LDC35	130	---Other
	ex71012290	养殖黑珍珠	△0				Cultured tahitian pearls
	71.02	**钻石，不论是否加工，但未镶嵌:**					**Diamonds, whether or not worked, but not mounted or set:**
5013	7102.1000	-未分级	3	0 东盟ASEAN,智利CL,巴基斯坦PK,新西兰NZ,秘鲁PE,哥斯达黎加CR	0 最不发达35国LDC35,最不发达4国LDC4	14	-Unsorted
		-工业用:					-Industrial:
5014	7102.2100	--未加工或经简单锯开、劈开或粗磨	0		0 最不发达35国LDC35,最不发达4国LDC4	14	--Unworked or simply sawn, cleaved or bruted

序号 No.	税则号列 Tariff Line	货品名称	最惠国税率 MFN(%)	协定税率 Agreement(%)		特惠税率 S.P.(%)		普通税率 Gen.(%)	Article Description
5015	7102.2900	--其他	0			0	最不发达35国LDC35,最不发达4国LDC4	14	--Other
		-非工业用:							-Non-industrial:
5016	7102.3100	--未加工或经简单锯开、劈开或粗磨	3	0	东盟ASEAN,智利CL,巴基斯坦PK,新西兰NZ,秘鲁PE,哥斯达黎加CR,香港HK	0	最不发达35国LDC35,最不发达4国LDC4	14	--Unworked or simply sawn, cleaved or bruted
5017	7102.3900	--其他	8	0	东盟ASEAN,亚太APTA,智利CL,巴基斯坦PK,新西兰NZ,秘鲁PE,哥斯达黎加CR	0	最不发达35国LDC35,最不发达4国LDC4	35	--Other
	71.03	**宝石（钻石除外）或半宝石，不论是否加工或分级，但未成串或镶嵌;未分级的宝石（钻石除外）或半宝石，为便于运输而暂穿成串:**							**Precious stones (other than diamonds) and semiprecious stones, whether or not worked or graded but not strung, mounted or set; ungraded precious stones (other than diamonds) and semiprecious stones, temporarily strung for convenience of transport:**
5018	7103.1000	-未加工或经简单锯开或粗制成形	3	0 2.8	东盟ASEAN,智利CL,巴基斯坦PK,新西兰NZ,秘鲁PE,哥斯达黎加CR 亚太APTA	0	最不发达35国LDC35,最不发达4国LDC4,老挝LA	14	-Unworked or simply sawn or roughly shaped
		-经其他加工:							-Otherwise worked:
5019	7103.9100	--红宝石、蓝宝石、祖母绿	8	0 4	东盟ASEAN,智利CL,巴基斯坦PK,新西兰NZ,秘鲁PE,哥斯达黎加CR 亚太APTA	0	最不发达35国LDC35,最不发达4国LDC4,老挝LA	35	--Rubies, sapphires and emeralds
		--其他:							--Other:
5020	7103.9910	---翡翠	8	0 4	东盟ASEAN,智利CL,巴基斯坦PK,新西兰NZ,秘鲁PE,哥斯达黎加CR 亚太APTA	0	最不发达35国LDC35,最不发达4国LDC4	35	---Jadeite

序号 No.	税则号列 Tariff Line	货品名称	最惠国税率 MFN(%)	协定税率 Agreement(%)		特惠税率 S.P.(%)		普通税率 Gen.(%)	Article Description
5021	7103.9920	---水晶	8	0 4	东盟ASEAN,智利CL,巴基斯坦PK,新西兰NZ,秘鲁PE,哥斯达黎加CR 亚太APTA	0	最不发达35国LDC35,最不发达4国LDC4	35	---Crystal
5022	7103.9930	---碧玺	8	0 4	东盟ASEAN,智利CL,巴基斯坦PK,新西兰NZ,秘鲁PE,哥斯达黎加CR 亚太APTA	0	最不发达35国LDC35,最不发达4国LDC4	35	---Tourmaline
5023	7103.9940	---软玉	8	0 4	东盟ASEAN,智利CL,巴基斯坦PK,新西兰NZ,秘鲁PE,哥斯达黎加CR 亚太APTA	0	最不发达35国LDC35,最不发达4国LDC4	35	---Nephrite
5024	7103.9990	---其他	8	0 4	东盟ASEAN,智利CL,巴基斯坦PK,新西兰NZ,秘鲁PE,哥斯达黎加CR 亚太APTA	0	最不发达35国LDC35,最不发达4国LDC4	35	---Other
	71.04	**合成或再造的宝石或半宝石，不论是否加工或分级，但未成串或镶嵌的;未分级的合成或再造的宝石或半宝石，为便于运输而暂穿成串:**							**Synthetic or reconstructed precious or semiprecious stones, whether or not worked or graded but not strung, mounted or set; ungraded synthetic or reconstructed precious or semiprecious stones, temporarily strung for convenience of transport:**
5025	7104.1000	-压电石英	6	0 5	东盟ASEAN,智利CL,新西兰NZ,秘鲁PE,哥斯达黎加CR 巴基斯坦PK	0	最不发达35国LDC35,最不发达4国LDC4	14	-Piezo-electric quartz
		-其他，未加工或经简单锯开或粗制成形:							-Other, unworked or simply sawn or roughly shaped:
5026	7104.2010	---钻石	0			0	最不发达35国LDC35,最不发达4国LDC4	14	---diamonds

序号 No.	税则号列 Tariff Line	货品名称	最惠国税率 MFN(%)	协定税率 Agreement(%)		特惠税率 S.P.(%)		普通税率 Gen.(%)	Article Description
5027	7104.2090	---其他	0	0	香港HK	0	最不发达35国LDC35,最不发达4国LDC4	14	---other
		-其他: ---工业用:							-Other: ---For technical use:
5028	7104.9011	----钻石	6	0 5	东盟ASEAN,智利CL,新西兰NZ,秘鲁PE,哥斯达黎加CR 巴基斯坦PK	0	最不发达35国LDC35,最不发达4国LDC4	14	----Diamonds
5029	7104.9012	----蓝宝石	6	0 5	东盟ASEAN,智利CL,新西兰NZ,秘鲁PE,哥斯达黎加CR,香港HK 巴基斯坦PK	0	最不发达35国LDC35,最不发达4国LDC4	14	----Sapphires
	ex71049012	蓝宝石衬底（由人造刚玉加工而成，厚度小于0.5毫米）	△1						Sapphire substrate (made of synthetic corundum, with thickness less than 0.5mm)
5030	7104.9019	----其他	6	0 5	东盟ASEAN,智利CL,新西兰NZ,秘鲁PE,哥斯达黎加CR 巴基斯坦PK	0	最不发达35国LDC35,最不发达4国LDC4	14	----Other
		---其他:							---Other:
5031	7104.9091	----钻石	8	0 5	东盟ASEAN,智利CL,新西兰NZ,秘鲁PE,哥斯达黎加CR 巴基斯坦PK	0	最不发达35国LDC35,最不发达4国LDC4	35	----Diamonds
5032	7104.9099	----其他	8	0 5	东盟ASEAN,智利CL,新西兰NZ,秘鲁PE,哥斯达黎加CR 巴基斯坦PK	0	最不发达35国LDC35,最不发达4国LDC4	35	----Other
	71.05	**天然或合成的宝石或半宝石的粉末:**							**Dust and powder of natural or synthetic precious or semiprecious stones:**
		-钻石的:							-Of diamonds:
5033	7105.1010	---天然的	0			0	最不发达35国LDC35,最不发达4国LDC4	17	---Natural

序号 No.	税则号列 Tariff Line	货品名称	最惠国税率 MFN(%)	协定税率 Agreement(%)	特惠税率 S.P.(%)	普通税率 Gen.(%)	Article Description
5034	7105.1020	---人工合成的	0		0 最不发达35国LDC35, 最不发达4国LDC4	17	---Synthetic
5035	7105.9000	-其他	0		0 最不发达35国LDC35, 最不发达4国LDC4	17	-Other
		第二分章 贵金属及包贵金属					Ⅱ.PRECIOUS METALS AND METALS CLAD WITH PRECIOUS METAL
	71.06	**银（包括镀金、镀铂的银），未锻造、半制成或粉末状:**					**Silver (including silver plated with gold or platinum), unwrought or in semi-manufactured forms, or in powder form:**
		-银粉: ---非片状粉末:					-Powder: ---Not Flake:
5036	7106.1011	----平均粒径小于3微米	0		0 最不发达35国LDC35, 最不发达4国LDC4	0	----Average diameter less than 3micron
5037	7106.1019	----其他	0		0 最不发达35国LDC35, 最不发达4国LDC4	0	----Other
		---片状粉末:					----Flake:
5038	7106.1021	----平均粒径小于10微米	0		0 最不发达35国LDC35, 最不发达4国LDC4	0	----Average diameter less than 10micron
5039	7106.1029	----其他	0		0 最不发达35国LDC35, 最不发达4国LDC4	0	----Other
		-其他: --未锻造:					-Other: --Unwrought:

序号 No.	税则号列 Tariff Line	货品名称	最惠国税率 MFN(%)	协定税率 Agreement(%)		特惠税率 S.P.(%)		普通税率 Gen.(%)	Article Description
5040	7106.9110	---纯度达 99.99%及以上	0			0	最不发达35国LDC35,最不发达4国LDC4	0	---Of a purity of 99.99 percent or more
5041	7106.9190	---其他	0			0	最不发达35国LDC35,最不发达4国LDC4	0	---Other
		--半制成:							--Semi-manufactured:
5042	7106.9210	---纯度达 99.99%及以上	0			0	最不发达35国LDC35,最不发达4国LDC4	50	---Of a purity of 99.99 percent or more
5043	7106.9290	---其他	0			0	最不发达35国LDC35,最不发达4国LDC4	50	---Other
	71.07	**以贱金属为底的包银材料:**							**Base metals clad with silver, not further worked than semi-manufactured:**
5044	7107.0000	以贱金属为底的包银材料	10.5	0 2.1 5	东盟ASEAN,智利CL,新加坡SG,新西兰NZ,秘鲁PE 哥斯达黎加CR 巴基斯坦PK	0	最不发达35国LDC35,最不发达4国LDC4,老挝LA	50	Base metals clad with silver, not further worked than semi-manufactured
	71.08	**金(包括镀铂的金),未锻造、半制成或粉末状:**							**Gold (including gold plated with platinum) unwrought or in semi-manufactured forms, or in powder form:**
		-非货币用:							-Non-monetary:
5045	7108.1100	--金粉	0			0	最不发达35国LDC35,最不发达4国LDC4	0	--Powder
5046	7108.1200	--其他未锻造形状	0			0	最不发达35国LDC35,最不发达4国LDC4	0	--Other unwrought forms

序号 No.	税则号列 Tariff Line	货品名称	最惠国税率 MFN(%)	协定税率 Agreement(%)		特惠税率 S.P.(%)		普通税率 Gen.(%)	Article Description
5047	7108.1300	--其他半制成形状	0			0	最不发达35国LDC35,最不发达4国LDC4	50	--Other semi-manufactured forms
5048	7108.2000	-货币用	0			0	最不发达35国LDC35,最不发达4国LDC4	0	-Monetary
	71.09	**以贱金属或银为底的包金材料:**							**Base metals or silver, clad with gold, not further worked than semi-manuf-actured:**
5049	7109.0000	以贱金属或银为底的包金材料	10.5	0 2.1 5	东盟ASEAN,智利CL,新加坡SG,新西兰NZ,秘鲁PE 哥斯达黎加CR 巴基斯坦PK	0	最不发达35国LDC35,最不发达4国LDC4	50	Base metals or silver, clad with gold, not further worked than semi-manufactured
	71.10	**铂，未锻造、半制成或粉末状:**							**Platinum, unwrought or in semi-manufactured forms, or in powder form:**
		-铂:							-Platinum:
5050	7110.1100	--未锻造或粉末状	0			0	最不发达35国LDC35,最不发达4国LDC4	0	--Unwrought or in powder form
		--其他:							--Other:
5051	7110.1910	---板、片	0			0	最不发达35国LDC35,最不发达4国LDC4	0	---Plates and sheets
5052	7110.1990	---其他	3	0	东盟ASEAN,智利CL,巴基斯坦PK,新西兰NZ,秘鲁PE,哥斯达黎加CR,香港HK	0	最不发达35国LDC35,最不发达4国LDC4	11	---Other
		-钯:							-Palladium:
5053	7110.2100	--未锻造或粉末状	0			0	最不发达35国LDC35,最不发达4国LDC4	10	--Unwrought or in powder form
		--其他:							--Other:

序号 No.	税则号列 Tariff Line	货品名称	最惠国税率 MFN(%)	协定税率 Agreement(%)		特惠税率 S.P.(%)		普通税率 Gen.(%)	Article Description
5054	7110.2910	---板、片	0			0	最不发达35国LDC35,最不发达4国LDC4	0	---Plates and sheets
5055	7110.2990	---其他	3	0	东盟ASEAN,智利CL,巴基斯坦PK,新西兰NZ,秘鲁PE,哥斯达黎加CR,香港HK	0	最不发达35国LDC35,最不发达4国LDC4	11	---Other
		-铑:							-Rhodium:
5056	7110.3100	--未锻造或粉末状	0			0	最不发达35国LDC35,最不发达4国LDC4	0	--Unwrought or in powder form
		--其他:							--Other:
5057	7110.3910	---板、片	0			0	最不发达35国LDC35,最不发达4国LDC4	0	---Plates and sheets
5058	7110.3990	---其他	3	0	东盟ASEAN,智利CL,巴基斯坦PK,新西兰NZ,秘鲁PE,哥斯达黎加CR	0	最不发达35国LDC35,最不发达4国LDC4	11	---Other
		-铱、锇及钌:							-Iridium, osmium and ruthenium:
5059	7110.4100	--未锻造或粉末状	0			0	最不发达35国LDC35,最不发达4国LDC4	0	--Unwrought or in powder form
		--其他:							--Other:
5060	7110.4910	---板、片	0			0	最不发达35国LDC35,最不发达4国LDC4	0	---Plates and sheets
5061	7110.4990	---其他	3	0	东盟ASEAN,智利CL,巴基斯坦PK,新西兰NZ,秘鲁PE,哥斯达黎加CR	0	最不发达35国LDC35,最不发达4国LDC4	11	---Other

序号 No.	税则号列 Tariff Line	货品名称	最惠国税率 MFN(%)	协定税率 Agreement(%)		特惠税率 S.P.(%)		普通税率 Gen.(%)	Article Description
	71.11	**以贱金属、银或金为底的包铂材料:**							**Base metals, silver or gold, clad with platinum, not further worked than semi-manufactured:**
5062	7111.0000	以贱金属、银或金为底的包铂材料:	3	0	东盟ASEAN,智利CL,巴基斯坦PK,新西兰NZ,秘鲁PE,哥斯达黎加CR	0	最不发达35国LDC35	11	Base metals, silver or gold, clad with platinum, not further worked than semi-manufactured
	71.12	**贵金属或包贵金属的废碎料;含有贵金属或贵金属化合物的其他废碎料,主要用于回收贵金属:**							**Waste and scrap of precious metal or of metal clad with precious metal; other waste and scrap containing precious metal or precious metal compounds, of a kind used principally for the recovery of precious metal:**
		-含有贵金属或金属化合物的灰:							-Ash containing precious metal or precious metal compounds:
5063	7112.3010	---含有银或银化合物的	8	0 5	东盟ASEAN,智利CL,新西兰NZ,秘鲁PE,哥斯达黎加CR 巴基斯坦PK	0	最不发达35国LDC35,最不发达4国LDC4	50	---Of silver or silver compounds
5064	7112.3090	---其他	6	0 5	东盟ASEAN,智利CL,新西兰NZ,秘鲁PE,哥斯达黎加CR 巴基斯坦PK	0	最不发达35国LDC35,最不发达4国LDC4	50	---Other
		-其他:							-Other:
		--金及包金的废碎料,但含有其他贵金属的除外:							--Of gold, including metal clad with gold but excluding sweepings containing other precious metals:
5065	7112.9110	---金及包金的废碎料	0			0	最不发达35国LDC35,最不发达4国LDC4	0	---Of gold or gold compounds
5066	7112.9120	---含有金或金化合物的废碎料	6	0 5	东盟ASEAN,智利CL,新西兰NZ,秘鲁PE,哥斯达黎加CR 巴基斯坦PK	0	最不发达35国LDC35,最不发达4国LDC4	35	---Waste and scrap with gold or gold compounds

序号 No.	税则号列 Tariff Line	货品名称	最惠国税率 MFN(%)	协定税率 Agreement(%)		特惠税率 S.P.(%)		普通税率 Gen.(%)	Article Description
		--铂及包铂的废碎料，但含有其他贵金属的除外:							--Of platinum, including metal clad with platinum but excluding sweepings containing other precious metals:
5067	7112.9210	---铂及包铂的废碎料	0			0	最不发达35国LDC35,最不发达4国LDC4	0	---Of platinum
5068	7112.9220	---含有铂或铂化合物的废碎料	6	0 0.6 5	东盟ASEAN,新西兰NZ,秘鲁PE,哥斯达黎加CR 智利CL 巴基斯坦PK	0	最不发达35国LDC35,最不发达4国LDC4	35	---Wasted and scrap with plutinum
	ex71129220	铂含量在3%以上的其他含铂或铂化合物的废碎料	△0						Waste and scrap with plutinum containing by weight more than 3% plutinum
		--其他:							--Other:
5069	7112.9910	---含有银或银化合物的废碎料	8	0 0.8 5	东盟ASEAN,新西兰NZ,秘鲁PE,哥斯达黎加CR 智利CL 巴基斯坦PK	0	最不发达35国LDC35,最不发达4国LDC4	35	---Waste and scrap with silver or silver compounds
5070	7112.9920	---含有其他贵金属或贵金属化合物的废碎料	6	0 0.6 5	东盟ASEAN,新西兰NZ,秘鲁PE,哥斯达黎加CR 智利CL 巴基斯坦PK	0	最不发达35国LDC35,最不发达4国LDC4	35	---Waste and scrap with other precious metals
5071	7112.9990	---其他	0			0	最不发达35国LDC35,最不发达4国LDC4	50	---Other
		第三分章 珠宝首饰、金银器及其他制品							III.JEWELLERY, GOLDSMITHS’AND SILVERSMITHS’WARES AND OTHER ARTICLES
	71.13	**贵金属或包贵金属制的首饰及其零件:**							**Articles of jewellery and parts thereof, of precious metal or of metal clad with precious metal:**
		-贵金属制,不论是否包、镀贵金属:							-Of precious metal whether or not plated or clad with precious metal:

序号 No.	税则号列 Tariff Line	货品名称	最惠国税率 MFN(%)	协定税率 Agreement(%)		特惠税率 S.P.(%)		普通税率 Gen.(%)	Article Description
		--银制，不论是否包、镀其他贵金属：							--Of silver, whether or not plated or clad with other precious metal:
5072	7113.1110	---镶嵌钻石的	20	0	东盟ASEAN,新加坡SG,新西兰NZ,香港HK,澳门MO	0	最不发达35国LDC35	130	---Diamond mounted or set
				2	智利CL				
				4	哥斯达黎加CR				
				10	秘鲁PE				
				16	巴基斯坦PK				
				16.5	亚太APTA				
5073	7113.1190	---其他	20	0	东盟ASEAN,新加坡SG,新西兰NZ,香港HK,澳门MO	0	最不发达35国LDC35,最不发达4国LDC4	130	---Other
				2	智利CL				
				4	哥斯达黎加CR				
				10	秘鲁PE				
				16	巴基斯坦PK				
				16.5	亚太APTA				
		--其他贵金属制，不论是否包、镀贵金属：							--Of other precious metal, whether or not plated or clad with precious metal:
		---黄金制:							---Of gold:
5074	7113.1911	----镶嵌钻石的	20	0	东盟ASEAN,新加坡SG,新西兰NZ,香港HK,澳门MO	0	最不发达35国LDC35	130	----Diamond mounted
				2	智利CL				
				4	哥斯达黎加CR				
				10	秘鲁PE				
				14	亚太APTA,巴基斯坦PK				
5075	7113.1919	----其他	20	0	东盟ASEAN,新加坡SG,新西兰NZ,香港HK,澳门MO	0	最不发达35国LDC35	130	----Other
				2	智利CL				
				4	哥斯达黎加CR				
				10	秘鲁PE				
				16	亚太APTA,巴基斯坦PK				
		---铂制:							---Of platinum:
5076	7113.1921	----镶嵌钻石的	35	0	东盟ASEAN,新加坡SG,新西兰NZ,香港HK,澳门MO	0	最不发达35国LDC35	130	----Diamond mounted
				3.5	智利CL				
				7	哥斯达黎加CR				
				17.5	秘鲁PE				
				28	亚太APTA,巴基斯坦PK				
5077	7113.1929	----其他	35	0	东盟ASEAN,新加坡SG,新西兰NZ,香港HK,澳门MO	0	最不发达35国LDC35,最不发达4国LDC4	130	----Other
				3.5	智利CL				
				7	哥斯达黎加CR				
				17.5	秘鲁PE				
				28	亚太APTA,巴基斯坦PK				
		---其他:							---Other:

序号 No.	税则号列 Tariff Line	货品名称	最惠国税率 MFN(%)	协定税率 Agreement(%)		特惠税率 S.P.(%)		普通税率 Gen.(%)	Article Description
5078	7113.1991	----镶嵌钻石的	35	0 3.5 7 17.5 28	东盟ASEAN,新加坡SG,新西兰NZ,香港HK,澳门MO 智利CL 哥斯达黎加CR 秘鲁PE 亚太APTA,巴基斯坦PK	0	最不发达35国LDC35	130	----Diamond mounted or set
5079	7113.1999	----其他	35	0 3.5 7 17.5 28	东盟ASEAN,新加坡SG,新西兰NZ,香港HK,澳门MO 智利CL 哥斯达黎加CR 秘鲁PE 亚太APTA,巴基斯坦PK	0	最不发达35国LDC35,最不发达4国LDC4	130	----Other
		-以贱金属为底的包贵金属制:							-Of base metal clad with precious metal:
5080	7113.2010	---镶嵌钻石的	35	0 7 17.5 30	东盟ASEAN,智利CL,新加坡SG,新西兰NZ,香港HK,澳门MO 哥斯达黎加CR 秘鲁PE 亚太APTA,巴基斯坦PK	0	最不发达35国LDC35	130	---Diamond mounted or set
5081	7113.2090	---其他	35	0 7 17.5 30	东盟ASEAN,智利CL,新加坡SG,新西兰NZ,香港HK,澳门MO 哥斯达黎加CR 秘鲁PE 亚太APTA,巴基斯坦PK	0	最不发达35国LDC35	130	---Other
	71.14	**贵金属或包贵金属制的金银器及其零件:**							**Articles of goldsmiths' or silversmiths' wares and parts thereof, of precious metal or of metal clad with precious metal:**
		-贵金属制,不论是否包、镀贵金属:							-Of precious metal whether or not plated or clad with precious metal:
5082	7114.1100	--银制,不论是否包、镀其他贵金属	35	0 7	东盟ASEAN,智利CL,新加坡SG,新西兰NZ,秘鲁PE,香港HK,澳门MO 哥斯达黎加CR	0	最不发达35国LDC35,最不发达4国LDC4	100	--Of silver, whether or not plated or clad with other precious metal
5083	7114.1900	--其他贵金属制,不论是否包、镀贵金属	35	0 7 17.5	东盟ASEAN,智利CL,新加坡SG,新西兰NZ,香港HK,澳门MO 哥斯达黎加CR 秘鲁PE	0	最不发达35国LDC35	100	--Of other precious metal, whether or not plated or clad with precious metal
5084	7114.2000	-以贱金属为底的包贵金属制	35	0 7 17.5	东盟ASEAN,智利CL,新加坡SG,新西兰NZ,香港HK,澳门MO 哥斯达黎加CR 秘鲁PE	0	最不发达35国LDC35,最不发达4国LDC4	100	-Of base metal clad with precious metal

序号 No.	税则号列 Tariff Line	货品名称	最惠国税率 MFN(%)	协定税率 Agreement(%)		特惠税率 S.P.(%)		普通税率 Gen.(%)	Article Description
	71.15	**贵金属或包贵金属的其他制品:**							**Other articles of precious metal or of metal clad with precious metal:**
5085	7115.1000	-金属丝布或格栅形状的铂催化剂	3	0	东盟ASEAN,智利CL,巴基斯坦PK,新西兰NZ,秘鲁PE,哥斯达黎加CR,香港HK	0	最不发达35国LDC35,最不发达4国LDC4	11	-Catalysts in the form of wire cloth or grill, of platinum
		-其他:							-Other:
5086	7115.9010	---工业或实验室用	3 △0	0	东盟ASEAN,智利CL,巴基斯坦PK,新西兰NZ,秘鲁PE,哥斯达黎加CR,香港HK,澳门MO	0	最不发达35国LDC35,最不发达4国LDC4	11	---For technical or laboratory use
5087	7115.9090	---其他	35	0 7 17.5	东盟ASEAN,智利CL,新加坡SG,新西兰NZ,香港HK,澳门MO 哥斯达黎加CR 秘鲁PE	0	最不发达35国LDC35	100	---Other
	71.16	**用天然或养殖珍珠、宝石或半宝石(天然、合成或再造)制成的物品:**							**Articles of natural or cultured pearls, precious or semi-precious stones (natural, synthetic or reconstructed):**
5088	7116.1000	-天然或养殖珍珠制	35	0 7 17.5	东盟ASEAN,智利CL,新加坡SG,新西兰NZ,香港HK,澳门MO 哥斯达黎加CR 秘鲁PE	0	最不发达35国LDC35	130	-Of natural or cultured pearls
5089	7116.2000	-宝石或半宝石(天然、合成或再造)制	35	0 3.5 7 17.5	东盟ASEAN,新加坡SG,新西兰NZ,香港HK,澳门MO 智利CL 哥斯达黎加CR 秘鲁PE	0	最不发达35国LDC35,最不发达4国LDC4	130	-Of precious or semi-precious stones (natural, synthetic or reconstructed)
	71.17	**仿首饰:**							**Imitation jewellery:**
		-贱金属制,不论是否镀贵金属:							-Of base metal, whether or not plated with precious metal:
5090	7117.1100	--袖扣、饰扣	35	0 7 17.5	东盟ASEAN,智利CL,新加坡SG,新西兰NZ,香港HK,澳门MO 哥斯达黎加CR 秘鲁PE	0	最不发达35国LDC35	130	--Cuff-links and studs
5091	7117.1900	--其他	17	0 1.7 3.4 8.5 13.6 15.3	东盟ASEAN,新加坡SG,新西兰NZ,香港HK,澳门MO 智利CL 哥斯达黎加CR 秘鲁PE 巴基斯坦PK 亚太APTA	0	最不发达35国LDC35,最不发达4国LDC4	130	--Other

序号 No.	税则号列 Tariff Line	货品名称	最惠国税率 MFN(%)	协定税率 Agreement(%)		特惠税率 S.P.(%)		普通税率 Gen.(%)	Article Description
5092	7117.9000	-其他	35	0 3.5 7 17.5 30	东盟ASEAN,新加坡SG,新西兰NZ,香港HK,澳门MO 智利CL 哥斯达黎加CR 秘鲁PE 亚太APTA,巴基斯坦PK	0	最不发达35国LDC35,最不发达4国LDC4	130	-Other
	71.18	**硬币:**							**Coin:**
5093	7118.1000	-非法定货币的硬币（金币除外）	0			0	最不发达35国LDC35,最不发达4国LDC4	0	-Coin (other than gold coin), not being legal tender
5094	7118.9000	-其他	0			0	最不发达35国LDC35,最不发达4国LDC4	0	-Other

第十五类
贱金属及其制品

注释：

一、本类不包括：

（一）以金属粉末为基本成分的调制油漆、油墨或其他产品（税号32.07至32.10、32.12、32.13或32.15）；

（二）铈铁或其他引火合金（税号36.06）；

（三）税号65.06或65.07的帽类及其零件；

（四）税号66.03的伞骨及其他物品；

（五）第七十一章的货品（例如，贵金属合金、以贱金属为底的包贵金属、仿首饰）；

（六）第十六类的物品（机器、机械器具及电气设备）；

（七）已装配的铁路或电车轨道（税号86.08）或第十七类的其他物品（车辆、船舶、航空器）；

（八）第十八类的仪器及器具，包括钟表发条；

（九）做弹药用的铅弹（税号93.06）或第十九类的其他物品（武器、弹药）；

（十）第九十四章的物品（例如，家具、弹簧床垫、灯具及照明装置、发光标志、活动房屋）；

（十一）第九十五章的物品（例如，玩具、游戏品及运动用品）；

（十二）手用筛子、钮扣、钢笔、铅笔套、钢笔尖或第九十六章的其他物品（杂项制品）；

（十三）第九十七章的物品（例如，艺术品）。

二、本目录所称"通用零件"，是指：

（一）税号73.07、73.12、73.15、73.17或73.18的物品及其他贱金属制的类似品；

（二）贱金属制的弹簧及弹簧片，但钟表发条（税号91.14）除外；

（三）税号83.01、83.02、83.08、83.10的物品及税号83.06的贱金属制的框架及镜子。

第七十三章至第七十六章（税号73.15除外）及第七十八章至第八十二章所列货品的零件，不包括上述的通用零件。

SECTION XV
BASE METALS AND ARTICLES OF BASE METAL

Notes:

1.This Section does not cover:

(a) Prepared paints, inks or other products with a basis of metallic flakes or powder (headings Nos.32.07 to 32.10, 32.12, 32.13 or 32.15);

(b) Ferro-cerium or other pyrophoric alloys (heading No.36.06);

(c) Headgear or parts thereof of heading No.65.06 or 65.07;

(d) Umbrella frames or other articles of heading No.66.03;

(e) Goods of Chapter 71 (for example, precious metal alloys, base metal clad with precious metal, imitation jewellery);

(f) Articles of Section XVI (machinery, mechanical appliances and electrical goods);

(g) Assembled railway or tramway track (heading No.86.08) or other articles of Section XVII (vehicles, ships and boats, aircraft);

(h) Instruments or apparatus of Section XVIII, including clock or watch springs;

(ij) Lead shot prepared for anmmunition (heading No.93.06) or other articles of Section XIX (arms and ammunition);

(k) Articles of Chapter 94 (for example, furniture, mattress supports, lamps and lighting fittings, illuminated signs, prefabricated buildings);

(l) Articles of Chapter 95 (for example, toys, games, sports requisites);

(m) Hand sieves, buttons, pens, pencil-holders, pen nibs or other articles of Chapter 96 (miscellaneous manufactured articles); or

(n) Articles of Chapter 97 (for example, works of art).

2.Throughout the Nomenclature, the expression "parts of general use" means:

(a) Articles of heading No.73.07, 73.12, 73.15, 73.17 or 73.18 and similar articles of other base metal;

(b) Springs and leaves for springs, of base metal, other than clock or watch springs (heading No.91.14); and

(c) Articles of headings Nos.83.01, 83.02, 83.08, 83.10 and frames and mirrors, of base metal, of heading No.83.06.

In Chapters 73 to76 and 78 to 82 (but not in heading No.73.15) references to parts of goods do not include references to parts of general use as defined above.

除上段及第八十三章注释一另有规定的以外，第七十二章至第七十六章及第七十八章至第八十一章不包括第八十二章、第八十三章的物品。

三、本目录所称"贱金属"是指：铁及钢、铜、镍、铝、铅、锌、锡、钨、钼、钽、镁、钴、铋、镉、钛、锆、锑、锰、铍、铬、锗、钒、镓、铪、铟、铌(钶)、铼及铊。

四、本目录所称"金属陶瓷"是指金属与陶瓷成分以极细微粒不均匀结合而成的产品。"金属陶瓷"包括硬质合金(金属碳化物与金属烧结而成)。

五、合金的归类规则(第七十二章、第七十四章所规定的铁合金及母合金除外)：

(一) 贱金属的合金按其所含重量最大的金属归类；

(二) 由本类的贱金属和非本类的元素构成的合金，如果所含贱金属的总重量等于或超过所含其他元素的总重量，应作为本类贱金属合金归类；

(三) 本类所称"合金"，包括金属粉末的烧结混合物、熔化而得的不均匀紧密混合物(金属陶瓷除外)及金属间化合物。

六、除条文另有规定的以外，本目录所称的贱金属包括贱金属合金，这类合金应按上述注释五的规则进行归类。

七、复合材料制品的归类规则：

除各税号另有规定的以外，贱金属制品(包括根据"归类总规则"作为贱金属制品的混合材料制品)如果含有两种或两种以上贱金属的，按其所含重量最大的贱金属的制品归类。为此：

(一) 钢、铁或不同种类的钢铁，均视为一种金属；

(二) 按照注释五的规定作为某一种金属归类的合金，应视为一种金属；

(三) 税号81.13的金属陶瓷，应视为一种贱金属。

subject to the preceding paragraph and to Note1to Chapter 83, the articles of Chapter 82 or 83 are excluded from Chapters 72 to 76 and 78 to 81.

3.Throughout the Nomenclature, the expression "base metals" means:iron and steel, copper, nickel, aluminium, lead, zinc, tin, tungsten (wolfram), molybdenum, tantalum, magnesium, cobalt, bismuth, cadmium, titanium, zirconium, antimony, manganese, beryllium, chromium, germanium, vanadium, gallium, hafnium, indium, niobium (columbium), rhenium and thallium.

4.Throughout the Nomenclature, the term "cermets" means products containing a microscopic heterogeneous combination of a metallic component and a ceramic component. The term "cermets" includes sintered metal carbides (metal carbides sintered with a metal).

5.Classification of alloys (other than ferro-alloys and master alloys as defined in Chapters 72 and 74):

(a) An alloy of base metals is to be classified as an alloy of the metal which predominates by weight over each of the other metals;

(b) An alloy composed of base metals of this Section and of elements not falling within this Section is to be treated as an alloy of base metals of this Section if the total weight of such metals equals or exceeds the total weight of the other elements present;

(c) In this Section the term "alloys" includes sintered mixtures of metal powders, heterogeneous intimate mixtures obtained by melting (other than cermets) and intermetallic compounds.

6.Unless the context otherwise requires, any reference in the Nomenclature to base metal includes a reference to alloys which, by virtue of Note5above, are to be classified as alloys of that metal.

7.Classification of composite articles:

Except where the headings otherwise require, articles of base metal (including articles of mixed materials treated as articles of base metal under the Interpretative Rules) containing two or more base metals are to be treated as articles of the base metal predominating by weight over each of the other metals.For this purpose:

(a) Iron and steel, or different kinds of iron or steel, are regarded as one and the same metal;

(b)An alloy is regarded as being entirely composed of that metal as an alloy of which, by virtue of Note5, it is classified; and

(c)A cermet of heading No.81.13is regarded as a single base metal.

八、本类所用有关名词解释如下:

（一）废碎料

在金属生产或机械加工中产生的废料及碎屑以及因破裂、切断、磨损及其他原因而明显不能作为原物使用的金属货品。

（二）粉末

按重量计90%及以上可从网眼孔径为1毫米的筛子通过的产品。

8.In this Section, the following expressions have the meanings hereby assigned to them:

(a) Waste and scrap

Metal waste and scrap from the manufacture of mechanical working of metals, and metal goods definitely not usable as such because of breakage, cuttingup, wear or other reasons.

(b)Powders

Products of which 90% or more by weight passes through a sieve having a mesh aperture of 1mm.

第七十二章
钢 铁

Chapter 72
Iron and steel

注释:

一、本章所述有关名词解释如下(本条注释(四)、(五)、(六)适用于本目录其他各章):

（一）生铁:

无实用可锻性的铁碳合金，按重量计含碳量在2%以上并可含有一种或几种下列含量范围的其他元素:

铬不超过10%;

锰不超过6%;

磷不超过3%;

硅不超过8%;

其他元素合计不超过10%。

（二）镜铁:

按重量计含锰量在6%以上，但不超过30%的铁碳合金，其他方面符合上述（一）款所列标准。

（三）铁合金:

锭、块、团或类似初级形状、连续铸造而形成的各种形状及颗粒、粉末状的合金，不论是否烧结，通常用于其他合金生产过程中的添加剂或在黑色金属冶炼中作除氧剂、脱硫剂及类似用途，一般无实用可锻性，按重量计铁元素含量在4%及以上并含有下列一种或几种元素:

铬超过10%;

锰超过30%;

磷超过3%;

硅超过8%;

除碳以外的其他元素，合计超过10%，但最

Notes:

1.In this Chapter and, in the case of Notes (d), (e) and (f) throughout the Nomenclature, the following expressions have the meanings hereby assigned to them:

(a)Pig iron:

Iron-carbon alloys not usefully malleable, containing more than 2% by weight of carbon and which may contain by weight one or more other elements within the following limits:

-not more than 10% of chromium;

-not more than 6% of manganese;

-not more than 3% of phosphorus;

-not more than 8% of silicon;

-a total of not more than 10% of other elements.

(b)Spiegeleisen:

Iron-carbon alloys containing by weight more than 6% but not more than 30% of manganese and otherwise conforming to the specification at (a) above.

(c)Ferro-alloys:

Alloys in pigs, blocks, lumps or similar primary forms, in forms obtained by continuous casting and also in granular or powder forms, whether or not agglomerated, commonly used as an additive in the manufacture of other alloys or as de-oxidants, de-sulphurizing agents or for similar uses in ferrous metal-lurgy and generally not usefully malleable, containing by weight 4% or more of the element iron and one or more of the following:

-more than 10% of chromium;

-more than 30% of manganese;

-more than 3% of phosphorus;

-more than 8% of silicon;

-a total of more than10%of other elements, excluding

高含铜量不得超过10%。

（四）钢：

除税号72.03以外的黑色金属材料（某些铸造而成的种类除外），具有实用可锻性，按重量计含碳量在2%及以下，但铬钢可具有较高的含碳量。

（五）不锈钢：

按重量计含碳量在1.2%及以下，含铬量在10.5%及以上的合金钢，不论是否含有其他元素。

（六）其他合金钢：

不符合以上不锈钢定义的钢，含有一种或几种按重量计符合下列含量比例的元素：

铝0.3%及以上；
硼0.0008%及以上；
铬0.3%及以上；
钴0.3%及以上；
铜0.4%及以上；
铅0.4%及以上；
锰1.65%及以上；
钼0.08%及以上；
镍0.3%及以上；
铌0.06%及以上；
硅0.6%及以上；
钛0.05%及以上；
钨0.3%及以上；
钒0.1%及以上；
锆0.05%及以上；
其他元素（硫、磷、碳及氮除外）单项含量在0.1%及以上。

（七）供再熔的碎料钢铁锭：

粗铸成形无缩孔或冒口的锭块产品，表面有明显瑕疵，化学成分不同于生铁、镜铁及铁合金。

（八）颗粒：

按重量计不到90%可从网眼孔径为1毫米的筛子通过，而90%及以上可从网眼孔径为5毫米的筛子通过的产品。

carbon, subject to a maximum content of 10% in the case of copper.

(d)Steel:

Ferrous materials other than those of heading No.72.03 which (with the exception of certain types produced in the form of castings) are usefully malleable and which contain by weight 2% or less of carbon. However, chromium steels may contain higher proportions of carbon.

(e)Stainless steel:

Alloy steels containing, by weight, 1.2% or less of carbon and 10.5% or more of chromium, with or without other elements.

(f)Other alloy steel:

Steels not complying with the definition of stainless steel and containing by weight one or more of the following elements in the proportion shown:

-0.3% or more of aluminium;
-0.0008% or more of boron;
-0.3% or more of chromium;
-0.3% or more of cobalt;
-0.4% or more of copper;
-0.4% or more of lead;
-1.65% or more of manganese;
-0.08% or more of molybdenum;
-0.3% or more of nickel;
-0.06% or more of niobium;
-0.6% or more of silicon;
-0.05% or more of titanium;
-0.3% or more of tungsten(wolfram);
-0.1% or more of vanadium;
-0.05% or more of zirconium;
-0.1% or more of other elements (except sulphur, phosphorus, carbon and nitrogen), taken separately.

(g)Remelting scrap ingots of iron or steel:

Products roughly cast in the form of ingots without feeder-heads or hot tops, or of pigs, having obvious surface faults and not complying with the chemical composition of pig iron, spiegeleisen or ferro-alloys.

(h)Granules:

Products of which less than 90% by weight passes through a sieve with a mesh aperture of 1mm and of which 90% or more by weight passes through a sieve with a mesh aperture of 5mm.

（九）半制成品：

连续铸造的实心产品，不论是否初步热轧；其他实心产品，除经初步热轧或锻造粗制成形以外未经进一步加工，包括角材、型材及异型材的坯件。

本类产品不包括成卷的产品。

（十）平板轧材：

截面为矩形（正方形除外）并且不符合以上第（九）款所述定义的下列形状实心轧制产品：

1. 层叠的卷材；
2. 平直形状，其厚度如果在4.75毫米以下，则宽度至少是厚度的十倍；其厚度如果在4.75毫米及以上，其宽度应超过150毫米，并且至少应为厚度的两倍。

平板轧材包括直接轧制而成并有凸起式样（例如，凹槽、肋条形、格槽、珠粒、菱形）的产品以及穿孔、抛光或制成瓦楞形的产品，但不具有其他税号所列制品或产品的特征。

各种规格的平板轧材（矩形或正方形除外），但不具有其他税号所列制品或产品的特征，都应作为宽度为600毫米及以上的产品归类。

（十一）不规则盘绕的热轧条、杆：

经热轧不规则盘绕的实心产品，其截面为圆形、扇形、椭圆形、矩形（包括正方形）、三角形或其他外凸多边形（包括"扁圆形"及"变形矩形"，即相对两边为弧拱形，另外两边为等长平行直线形）。这类产品可带有在轧制过程中产生的凹痕、凸缘、槽沟或其他变形（钢筋）。

（十二）其他条、杆：

不符合上述（九）、（十）、（十一）款或"丝"定义的实心产品，其全长截面均为圆形、扇形、椭圆形、矩形（包括正方形）、

(i)Semi-finished products:

Continuous cast products of solid section, whether or not subjected to primary hot-rolling; and Other products of solid section, which have not been further worked than subjected to primary hot-rolling or roughly shaped by forging, including blanks for angles, shapes or sections.

These products are not presented in coils.

(j)Flat-rolled products:

Rolled products of solid rectangular (other than square) cross-section, which do not conform to the definition at (ij) above in the form of:

(1)coils of successively superimposed layers; or

(2)straight lenghths, which if of a thickness less than 4.75mm are of a width measuring at least ten times the thickness or if of a thickness of 4.75mm or more are of a width which exceeds 150mm and measures at least twice the thickness.

Flat-rolled products include those with patterns in relief derived directly from rolling (for example, grooves, ribs, chequers, tears, buttons, lozenges) and those which have been perforated, corrugated or polished, provided that they do not thereby assume the character of articles or products of other headings.

Flat-rolled products of a shape other than rectangular or square, of any size, are to be classified as products of a width of 600mm or more, provided that they do not assume the character of articles or products of other headings.

(k)Bars and rods, hot-rolled, in irregularly wound coils:

Hot-rolled products in irregularly wound coils, which have a solid cross-section in the shape of circles, segments of circles, ovals, rectangles (including squares), triangles or other convex polygons (including "flattened circles" and modified rectangles of which two opposite sides are convex arcs, the other two sides being straight, of equal length and paralled). These products may have indentations, ribs, grooves or other deformations produced during the rolling process (reinforcing bars and rods).

(l)Other bars and rods:

Products which do not conform to any of the definitions at (ij), (k) or (l) above or to the definition of wire, which have a uniform solid cross-section along their

三角形或其他外凸多边形（包括“扁圆形”及“变形矩形”，即相对两边为弧拱形，另两边为等长平行直线形）。这些产品可以：

1. 带有在轧制过程中产生的凹痕、凸缘、槽沟或其他变形（钢筋）；

2. 轧制后扭曲的。

（十三）角材、型材及异型材：

不符合上述（九）、（十）、（十一）、（十二）款或“丝”定义，但其全长截面均为同样形状的实心产品。

第七十二章不包括税号73.01或73.02的产品。

（十四）丝：

不符合平板轧材定义但全长截面均为同样形状的盘卷冷成形实心产品。

（十五）空心钻钢：

适合钻探用的各种截面的空心条、杆，其最大外形尺寸超过15毫米但不超过52毫米，最大内孔尺寸不超过最大外形尺寸的二分之一。不符合本定义的钢铁空心条、杆应归入税号73.04。

二、用一种黑色金属包覆不同种类的黑色金属，应按其中重量最大的材料归类。

三、用电解沉积法、压铸法或烧结法所得的钢铁产品，应按其形状、成分及外观归入本章类似热轧产品的相应税号。

子目注释：

一、本章所用有关名词解释如下：

（一）合金生铁：

按重量计含有一种或几种下列比例的元素的生铁：

whole length in the shape of circles, segments of circles, ovals, rectangles (including squares), triangles or other convex polygons (including “flattened circles” and “modified rectangles”, of which two opposite sides are convex arcs, the other two sides being straight, of equal length and parallel). These products may:

-have indentations, ribs, grooves or other deforma-tions produced during the rolling process (reinforcing bars and rods);

-be twisted after rolling.

(m) Angles, shapes and sections:

Products having a uniform solid cross-section along their whole length which do not conform to any of the definitions at (ij), (k), (l) or (m) above or to the definition of wire.

Chapter 72 does not include products of heading No.73.01 or 73.02.

(n)Wire:

Cold-formed products in coils, of any uniform solid cross-section along their whole length, which do not conform to the definition of flat-rolled products.

(o)Hollow drill bars and rods:

Hollow bars and rods of any cross-section, suitable for drills, of which the greatest external dimension of the cross-section exceeds 15mm but does not exceed 52mm, and of which the greatest internal dimension does not exceed one half of the greatest external dimension. Hollow bars and rods of iron or steel not conforming to this definition are to be classified in heading No.73.04.

2. Ferrous metals clad with another ferrous metal are to be classified as products of the ferrous metal predominating by weight.

3. Iron or steel products obtained by electrolytic deposition, by pressure casting or by sintering are to be classified, according to their form, their composition and their appearance, in the headings of this Chapter appropriate to similar hot-rolled products.

Subheading Notes:

1. In this Chapter the following expressions have the meanings hereby assigned to them:

(a)Alloy pig iron:

Pig iron containing, by weight, one or more of the following elements in the specified proportions:

铬0.2%以上;
铜0.3%以上;
镍0.3%以上;
0.1%以上的任何下列元素:
铝、钼、钛、钨、钒。

(二)非合金易切削钢:
按重量计含有一种或几种下列比例的元素的非合金钢:
硫0.08%及以上;
铅0.1%及以上;
硒0.05%以上;
碲0.01%以上;
铋0.05%以上。

(三)硅电钢:
按重量计含硅量至少为0.6%但不超过6%,含碳量不超过0.08%的合金钢。这类钢还可含有按重量计不超过1%的铝,但所含其他元素的比例并不使其具有其他合金钢的特性。

(四)高速钢:
不论是否含有其他元素,但至少含有按重量计合计含量在7%及以上的钼、钨、钒中两种元素的合金钢,按重量计其含碳量在0.6%及以上,含铬量在3%~6%。

(五)硅锰钢:
按重量计同时含有下列元素的合金钢:
碳不超过0.7%;
锰0.5%及以上,但不超过1.9%;
硅0.6%及以上,但不超过2.3%;
所含其他元素的比例并不使其具有其他合金钢的特性。

二、税号72.02项下的子目所列铁合金,应按照下列规则归类:
对于只有一种元素超出本章注释一(三)规定的最低百分比的铁合金,应作为二元合金归入相应的子目号。以此类推,如果有两种或三种合金元素超出了最低百分比的,则可分别作为三元或四元合金。

在运用本规定时,本章注释一(三)所述的未列名的"其他元素",按重量计单项含量必须超过10%。

-more than 0.2% of chromiumi;
-more than 0.3% of copper;
-more than 0.3% of nickel;
-more than 0.1% of any of the following elements: aluminium, molybdenum, titanium, tungsten (wolfram), vanadium.

(b)Non-alloy free-cutting steel:
Non-alloy steel containing, by weight, one or more of the following elements in the specified proportions:
-0.08% or more of sulphur
-0.1% or more of lead;
-more than 0.05% of selenium;
-more than 0.01% of tellurium;
-more than 0.05% of bismuth.

(c)Silicon-electrical steel:
Alloy steels containing by weight at least 0.6% but notmore than 6% of silicon and not more than 0.08% of carbon. They may also contain by weight not more than 1% of aluminium but no other element in a proportion that would give the steel the characteristics of another alloy steel.

(d)High speed steel:
Alloy steels containing, with or without other elements, at least two of the three elements molybdenum, tungsten and vanadium with a combined content by weight of 7% or more, 0.6% or more of carbon and 3% to 6% of chromium.

(e)Silico-manganese steel:
Alloy steels containing by weight:
-not more than 0.7% of carbon;
-0.5% or more but not more than 1.9% of man-ganese; and
-0.6% or more but not more than 2.3% of silicon; but no other element in a proportion that would give the steel the characteristics of another alloy steel.

2. For the classification of ferroalloys in the subheadings of heading No.72.02 the following rule should be observed:
A ferro-alloy is considered as binary and classified under the relevant subheading (if it exists) if only one of the alloy elements exceeds the minimum percentage laid down in Chapter Note1(c); by analogy, it is considered respectively as ternary or quaternary if two or three alloy elements exceed the minimum percentage.

For the application of this rule the unspecified "other elements" referred to in Chapter Note1(c) must each exceed 10% by weight.

序号 No.	税则号列 Tariff Line	货品名称	最惠国税 率 MFN(%)	协定税率 Agreement(%)		特惠税率 S.P.(%)		普通税率 Gen.(%)	Article Description
		第一分章 原料;粒状及粉状产品							I.PRIMARY ATERIALS; PRODUCTS IN GRANULAR OR POWDER FORM
	72.01	**生铁及镜铁，锭、块或其他初级形状:**							**Pig iron and spiegeleisen in pigs, blocks or other primary forms:**
5095	7201.1000	-非合金生铁，按重量计含磷量在0.5%及以下	1	0	东盟ASEAN,智利CL,巴基斯坦PK,新西兰NZ,秘鲁PE,哥斯达黎加CR	0	最不发达35国LDC35,最不发达4国LDC4	8	-Non-alloy pig iron containing by weight 0.5% or less of phosphorus
5096	7201.2000	-非合金生铁，按重量计含磷量在0.5%以上	1	0	东盟ASEAN,智利CL,巴基斯坦PK,新西兰NZ,秘鲁PE,哥斯达黎加CR	0	最不发达35国LDC35,最不发达4国LDC4	8	-Non-alloy pig iron containing by weight more than 0.5% of phosphorus
5097	7201.5000	-合金生铁;镜铁	1	0	东盟ASEAN,智利CL,巴基斯坦PK,新西兰NZ,秘鲁PE,哥斯达黎加CR	0	最不发达35国LDC35,最不发达4国LDC4	8	-Alloy pig iron; spiegeleisen
	72.02	**铁合金:**							**Ferro-alloys:**
		-锰铁:							-Ferro-manganese:
5098	7202.1100	--按重量计含碳量在2%以上	2	0	东盟ASEAN,智利CL,巴基斯坦PK,新西兰NZ,秘鲁PE,哥斯达黎加CR	0	最不发达35国LDC35,最不发达4国LDC4	11	--Containing by weight more than 2% of carbon
5099	7202.1900	--其他	2	0	东盟ASEAN,智利CL,巴基斯坦PK,新西兰NZ,秘鲁PE,哥斯达黎加CR	0	最不发达35国LDC35,最不发达4国LDC4	11	--Other
		-硅铁:							-Ferro-silicon:
5100	7202.2100	--按重量计含硅量55%以上	2	0	东盟ASEAN,智利CL,巴基斯坦PK,新西兰NZ,秘鲁PE,哥斯达黎加CR	0	最不发达35国LDC35,最不发达4国LDC4	11	--Containing by weight more than 55% of silicon
5101	7202.2900	--其他	2	0	东盟ASEAN,智利CL,巴基斯坦PK,新西兰NZ,秘鲁PE,哥斯达黎加CR	0	最不发达35国LDC35,最不发达4国LDC4	11	--Other

序号 No.	税则号列 Tariff Line	货品名称	最惠国税率 MFN(%)	协定税率 Agreement(%)		特惠税率 S.P.(%)		普通税率 Gen.(%)	Article Description
5102	7202.3000	-硅锰铁	2	0	东盟ASEAN,智利CL,巴基斯坦PK,新西兰NZ,秘鲁PE,哥斯达黎加CR	0	最不发达35国LDC35,最不发达4国LDC4	11	-Ferro-silico-manganese
		-铬铁:							-Ferro-chromium:
5103	7202.4100	--按重量计含碳量在4%以上	2 △1	0	东盟ASEAN,智利CL,巴基斯坦PK,新西兰NZ,秘鲁PE,哥斯达黎加CR	0	最不发达35国LDC35,最不发达4国LDC4	8	--Containing by weight more than 4% of carbon
5104	7202.4900	--其他	2 △1	0	东盟ASEAN,智利CL,巴基斯坦PK,新西兰NZ,秘鲁PE,哥斯达黎加CR	0	最不发达35国LDC35,最不发达4国LDC4	8	--Other
5105	7202.5000	-硅铬铁	2	0	东盟ASEAN,智利CL,巴基斯坦PK,新西兰NZ,秘鲁PE,哥斯达黎加CR	0	最不发达35国LDC35,最不发达4国LDC4	11	-Ferro-silico-chromium
5106	7202.6000	-镍铁	2 △1	0	东盟ASEAN,智利CL,巴基斯坦PK,新西兰NZ,秘鲁PE,哥斯达黎加CR	0	最不发达35国LDC35,最不发达4国LDC4	11	-Ferro-nickel
5107	7202.7000	-钼铁	2 △1	0	东盟ASEAN,智利CL,巴基斯坦PK,新西兰NZ,秘鲁PE,哥斯达黎加CR	0	最不发达35国LDC35,最不发达4国LDC4	11	-Ferro-molybdenum
		-钨铁及硅钨铁:							-Ferro-tungstenand ferro-silico-tungsten:
5108	7202.8010	---钨铁	2 △1	0	东盟ASEAN,智利CL,巴基斯坦PK,新西兰NZ,秘鲁PE,哥斯达黎加CR	0	最不发达35国LDC35,最不发达4国LDC4	11	---Ferro-tungsten
5109	7202.8020	---硅钨铁	2	0	东盟ASEAN,智利CL,巴基斯坦PK,新西兰NZ,秘鲁PE,哥斯达黎加CR	0	最不发达35国LDC35,最不发达4国LDC4	11	---Ferro-silico-tungsten
		-其他:							-Other:

序号 No.	税则号列 Tariff Line	货品名称	最惠国税率 MFN(%)	协定税率 Agreement(%)		特惠税率 S.P.(%)		普通税率 Gen.(%)	Article Description
5110	7202.9100	--钛铁及硅钛铁	2 △1	0	东盟ASEAN,智利CL,巴基斯坦PK,新西兰NZ,秘鲁PE,哥斯达黎加CR	0	最不发达35国LDC35,最不发达4国LDC4	11	--Ferro-titanium and ferrosilicotitanium
		--钒铁:							--Ferro-vanadium:
5111	7202.9210	---按重量计含钒量在75%及以上	9	0 5	东盟ASEAN,智利CL,新西兰NZ,秘鲁PE,哥斯达黎加CR 巴基斯坦PK	0	最不发达35国LDC35,最不发达4国LDC4	30	---Containing by weight more than 75% of ranadium
5112	7202.9290	---其他	9	0 5	东盟ASEAN,智利CL,新西兰NZ,秘鲁PE,哥斯达黎加CR 巴基斯坦PK	0	最不发达35国LDC35,最不发达4国LDC4	30	---Other
5113	7202.9300	--铌铁	2 △1	0	东盟ASEAN,智利CL,巴基斯坦PK,新西兰NZ,秘鲁PE,哥斯达黎加CR	0	最不发达35国LDC35,最不发达4国LDC4	11	--Ferro-niobium
		--其他: ---钕铁硼合金:							--Other: ---Neodynium-ferro-boron:
5114	7202.9911	----速凝永磁片	2	0	东盟ASEAN,智利CL,巴基斯坦PK,新西兰NZ,秘鲁PE,哥斯达黎加CR	0	最不发达35国LDC35,最不发达4国LDC4	11	----permanent magnetic strip-casting flakes
5115	7202.9912	----磁粉	2	0	东盟ASEAN,智利CL,巴基斯坦PK,新西兰NZ,秘鲁PE,哥斯达黎加CR	0	最不发达35国LDC35,最不发达4国LDC4	11	----magnetic powders
5116	7202.9919	----其他	2	0	东盟ASEAN,智利CL,巴基斯坦PK,新西兰NZ,秘鲁PE,哥斯达黎加CR	0	最不发达35国LDC35,最不发达4国LDC4	11	----Other
		---其他:							---Other:
5117	7202.9991	----按重量计稀土元素总含量在10%以上的	2	0	东盟ASEAN,智利CL,巴基斯坦PK,新西兰NZ,秘鲁PE,哥斯达黎加CR	0	最不发达35国LDC35,最不发达4国LDC4	11	----Containing by weight more than 10% of rare-earth elements

序号 No.	税则号列 Tariff Line	货品名称	最惠国税率 MFN(%)	协定税率 Agreement(%)		特惠税率 S.P.(%)		普通税率 Gen.(%)	Article Description
5118	7202.9999	----其他	2	0	东盟ASEAN,智利CL,巴基斯坦PK,新西兰NZ,秘鲁PE,哥斯达黎加CR	0	最不发达35国LDC35,最不发达4国LDC4	11	----Other
	72.03	**直接从铁矿还原所得的铁产品及其他海绵铁产品,块、团、团粒及类似形状;按重量计纯度在99.94%及以上的铁,块、团、团粒及类似形状:**							**Ferrous products obtained by direct reduction of iron ore and other spongy ferrous products, in lumps, pellets or similar forms; iron having a minimum purity by weight of 99.94%, in lumps, pellets or similar forms:**
5119	7203.1000	-直接从铁矿还原所得的铁产品	2	0	东盟ASEAN,智利CL,巴基斯坦PK,新西兰NZ,秘鲁PE,哥斯达黎加CR	0	最不发达35国LDC35	8	-Ferrous products obtained by direct reduction of iron ore
	ex72031000	热压铁块	△0						Hot Briguetted Iron (HBI)
5120	7203.9000	-其他	2	0	东盟ASEAN,智利CL,巴基斯坦PK,新西兰NZ,秘鲁PE,哥斯达黎加CR	0	最不发达35国LDC35	8	-Other
	72.04	**钢铁废碎料;供再熔的碎料钢铁锭:**							**Ferrous waste and scrap; remelting scrap ingots of iron steel:**
5121	7204.1000	-铸铁废碎料	2 △0	0	东盟ASEAN,智利CL,巴基斯坦PK,新西兰NZ,秘鲁PE,哥斯达黎加CR	0	最不发达35国LDC35,最不发达4国LDC4	8	-Waste and scrap of cast iron
		-合金钢废碎料:							-Waste and scrap of alloy steel:
5122	7204.2100	--不锈钢废碎料	0			0	最不发达35国LDC35,最不发达4国LDC4	8	--Of stainless steel
5123	7204.2900	--其他	0			0	最不发达35国LDC35,最不发达4国LDC4	8	--Other
5124	7204.3000	-镀锡钢铁废碎料	2 △0	0	东盟ASEAN,智利CL,巴基斯坦PK,新西兰NZ,秘鲁PE,哥斯达黎加CR	0	最不发达35国LDC35,最不发达4国LDC4	8	-Waste and scrap of tinned iron or steel

序号 No.	税则号列 Tariff Line	货品名称	最惠国税率 MFN(%)	协定税率 Agreement(%)		特惠税率 S.P.(%)		普通税率 Gen.(%)	Article Description
		-其他废碎料:							-Other waste and scrap:
5125	7204.4100	--车、刨、铣、磨、锯、锉、剪、冲加工过程中产生的废料，不论是否成捆	2 △0	0	东盟ASEAN,智利CL,巴基斯坦PK,新西兰NZ,秘鲁PE,哥斯达黎加CR	0	最不发达35国LDC35,最不发达4国LDC4	8	--Turnings, shavings, chips, milling waste, sawdust, filings, trimmings and stampings, whether or not in bundles
5126	7204.4900	--其他	0			0	最不发达35国LDC35,最不发达4国LDC4	8	--Other
5127	7204.5000	-供再熔的碎料钢铁锭	0			0	最不发达35国LDC35,最不发达4国LDC4	8	-Remelting scrap ingots
	72.05	**生铁、镜铁及钢铁的颗粒和粉末:**							**Granules and powders, of pig iron, spiegeleisen, iron or steel:**
5128	7205.1000	-颗粒	2	0	东盟ASEAN,智利CL,巴基斯坦PK,新西兰NZ,秘鲁PE,哥斯达黎加CR	0	最不发达35国LDC35,最不发达4国LDC4	30	-Granules
		-粉末:							-Powders:
5129	7205.2100	--合金钢的	2	0	东盟ASEAN,智利CL,巴基斯坦PK,新西兰NZ,秘鲁PE,哥斯达黎加CR	0	最不发达35国LDC35,最不发达4国LDC4	17	--Of alloy steel
5130	7205.2900	--其他	2	0	东盟ASEAN,智利CL,巴基斯坦PK,新西兰NZ,秘鲁PE,哥斯达黎加CR	0	最不发达35国LDC35,最不发达4国LDC4	17	--Other
		第二分章 铁及非合金钢							Ⅱ.IRON AND NON-ALLOY STEEL
	72.06	**铁及非合金钢，锭状或其他初级形状（税号72.03的铁除外）:**							**Iron and non-alloy steel in ingots or other primary forms (excluding iron of heading No.72.03):**
5131	7206.1000	-锭状	2	0	东盟ASEAN,智利CL,巴基斯坦PK,新西兰NZ,秘鲁PE,哥斯达黎加CR	0	最不发达35国LDC35	11	-Ingots

序号 No.	税则号列 Tariff Line	货品名称	最惠国税率 MFN(%)	协定税率 Agreement(%)		特惠税率 S.P.(%)		普通税率 Gen.(%)	Article Description
5132	7206.9000	-其他	2	0	东盟ASEAN,智利CL,巴基斯坦PK,新西兰NZ,秘鲁PE,哥斯达黎加CR	0	最不发达35国LDC35	11	-Other
	72.07	**铁及非合金钢的半制成品:**							**Semi-finished products of iron or non-alloy steel:**
		-按重量计含碳量在0.25%以下:							-Containing by weight less than 0.25% of carbon:
5133	7207.1100	--矩形（包括正方形）截面，宽度小于厚度的两倍	2	0	东盟ASEAN,智利CL,巴基斯坦PK,新西兰NZ,秘鲁PE,哥斯达黎加CR	0	最不发达35国LDC35	11	--Of rectangular (including square) crosssection, the width measuring less than twice the thickness
5134	7207.1200	--其他矩形（正方形除外）截面的	2	0	东盟ASEAN,智利CL,巴基斯坦PK,新西兰NZ,秘鲁PE,哥斯达黎加CR	0	最不发达35国LDC35	11	--Other, of rectangular (other than square) cross-section
5135	7207.1900	--其他	2	0	东盟ASEAN,智利CL,巴基斯坦PK,新西兰NZ,秘鲁PE,哥斯达黎加CR	0	最不发达35国LDC35	11	--Other
5136	7207.2000	-按重量计含碳量在0.25%及以上	2	0	东盟ASEAN,智利CL,巴基斯坦PK,新西兰NZ,秘鲁PE,哥斯达黎加CR	0	最不发达35国LDC35	11	-Containing by weight 0.25% or more of carbon
	72.08	**宽度在600毫米及以上的铁或非合金钢平板轧材，经热轧，但未经包覆、镀层或涂层:**							**Flat-rolled products of iron or nonalloy steel of a width of 600mm or more, hotrolled, not clad, plated or coated:**
5137	7208.1000	-除热轧外未经进一步加工的卷材，已轧压花纹	5	0	东盟ASEAN,智利CL,巴基斯坦PK,新西兰NZ,秘鲁PE,哥斯达黎加CR	0	最不发达35国LDC35,最不发达4国LDC4	14	-In coils, not further worked than hotrolled, with patterns in relief
		-其他经酸洗的卷材，除热轧外未经进一步加工:							-Other, in coils, not further worked than hot-rolled, pickled:
5138	7208.2500	--厚度在4.75毫米及以上	5	0	东盟ASEAN,智利CL,巴基斯坦PK,新西兰NZ,秘鲁PE,哥斯达黎加CR	0	最不发达35国LDC35,最不发达4国LDC4	14	--Of a thickness of 4.75mm or more
		--厚度在3毫米及以上，但小于4.75毫米:							--Of a thickness of 3mm or more but less than 4.75mm:
5139	7208.2610	---屈服强度大于355牛顿/平方毫米	5	0	东盟ASEAN,智利CL,巴基斯坦PK,新西兰NZ,秘鲁PE,哥斯达黎加CR	0	最不发达35国LDC35,最不发达4国LDC4	14	---Of a yield strength exceeding 355N/mm^2

序号 No.	税则号列 Tariff Line	货品名称	最惠国税率 MFN(%)	协定税率 Agreement(%)		特惠税率 S.P.(%)		普通税率 Gen.(%)	Article Description
5140	7208.2690	---其他	5	0	东盟ASEAN,智利CL,巴基斯坦PK,新西兰NZ,秘鲁PE,哥斯达黎加CR	0	最不发达35国LDC35,最不发达4国LDC4	14	---Other
		--厚度小于3毫米:							--Of a thickness of less than 3mm:
5141	7208.2710	---厚度小于1.5毫米	5	0	东盟ASEAN,智利CL,巴基斯坦PK,新西兰NZ,秘鲁PE,哥斯达黎加CR	0	最不发达35国LDC35,最不发达4国LDC4	14	---Of a thickness of less than1.5mm
5142	7208.2790	---其他	5	0	东盟ASEAN,智利CL,巴基斯坦PK,新西兰NZ,秘鲁PE,哥斯达黎加CR,台湾TW	0	最不发达35国LDC35,最不发达4国LDC4	14	---Other
		-其他卷材,除热轧外未经进一步加工:							-Other, in coils, not further worked than hot-rolled:
5143	7208.3600	--厚度超过10毫米	6	0 5	东盟ASEAN,智利CL,新西兰NZ,秘鲁PE,哥斯达黎加CR 巴基斯坦PK	0	最不发达35国LDC35,最不发达4国LDC4	14	--Of a thickness exceeding 10mm
5144	7208.3700	--厚度在4.75毫米及以上，但不超过10毫米	5	0	东盟ASEAN,智利CL,巴基斯坦PK,新西兰NZ,秘鲁PE,哥斯达黎加CR	0	最不发达35国LDC35,最不发达4国LDC4	14	--Of a thickness of 4.75mm or more but not exceeding 10mm
		--厚度在3毫米及以上，但小于4.75毫米:							--Of a thickness of 3mm or more but less than 4.75mm:
5145	7208.3810	---屈服强度大于355牛顿/平方毫米	5	0	东盟ASEAN,智利CL,巴基斯坦PK,新西兰NZ,秘鲁PE,哥斯达黎加CR	0	最不发达35国LDC35,最不发达4国LDC4	14	---Of a yield strength exceeding 355N/mm^2
5146	7208.3890	---其他	5	0	东盟ASEAN,智利CL,巴基斯坦PK,新西兰NZ,秘鲁PE,哥斯达黎加CR,台湾TW	0	最不发达35国LDC35,最不发达4国LDC4	14	---Other
		--厚度小于3毫米:							--Of a thickness of less than 3mm:

序号 No.	税则号列 Tariff Line	货品名称	最惠国税率 MFN(%)	协定税率 Agreement(%)		特惠税率 S.P.(%)		普通税率 Gen.(%)	Article Description
5147	7208.3910	---厚度小于 1.5 毫米	3	0	东盟ASEAN,智利CL,巴基斯坦PK,新西兰NZ,秘鲁PE,哥斯达黎加CR	0	最不发达 35 国 LDC35,最不发达 4 国 LDC4	14	---Of a thickness of less than 1.5mm
5148	7208.3990	---其他	3	0	东盟ASEAN,智利CL,巴基斯坦PK,新西兰NZ,秘鲁PE,哥斯达黎加CR,台湾TW	0	最不发达 35 国 LDC35,最不发达 4 国 LDC4	14	---Other
5149	7208.4000	-已轧压花纹的非卷材，除热轧外未经进一步加工	6	0 5	东盟ASEAN,智利CL,新西兰NZ,秘鲁PE,哥斯达黎加CR 巴基斯坦PK	0	最不发达 35 国 LDC35,最不发达 4 国 LDC4	17	-Not in coils, not further worked than hotrolled, with patterns in relief
		-其他非卷材，除热轧外未经进一步加工:							-Other, not in coils, not further worked than hot-rolled:
		--厚度超过 10 毫米:							--Of a thickness exceeding 10mm:
5150	7208.5110	---厚度超过 50 毫米	6	0 0.6 5	东盟ASEAN,新西兰NZ,秘鲁PE,哥斯达黎加CR 智利CL 巴基斯坦PK	0	最不发达 35 国 LDC35,最不发达 4 国 LDC4	17	---Of a thickness exceeding 50mm
5151	7208.5120	---厚度在 20 毫米以上，但不超过 50 毫米	6	0 0.6 5	东盟ASEAN,新西兰NZ,秘鲁PE,哥斯达黎加CR 智利CL 巴基斯坦PK	0	最不发达 35 国 LDC35,最不发达 4 国 LDC4	17	---Of a thickness exceeding 20mm but not exceeding 50mm
5152	7208.5190	---其他	6	0 0.6 5	东盟ASEAN,新西兰NZ,秘鲁PE,哥斯达黎加CR 智利CL 巴基斯坦PK	0	最不发达 35 国 LDC35,最不发达 4 国 LDC4	17	---Other
5153	7208.5200	--厚度在 4.75 毫米及以上，但不超过 10 毫米	6	0 5	东盟ASEAN,智利CL,新西兰NZ,秘鲁PE,哥斯达黎加CR 巴基斯坦PK	0	最不发达 35 国 LDC35,最不发达 4 国 LDC4	17	--Of a thickness of 4.75mm or more but not exceeding 10mm
		--厚度在 3 毫米及以上，但小于 4.75 毫米:							--Of a thickness of 3mm or more but less than 4.75mm:
5154	7208.5310	---屈服强度大于 355 牛顿/平方毫米	6	0 5.1	东盟ASEAN,智利CL,巴基斯坦PK,新西兰NZ,秘鲁PE,哥斯达黎加CR 亚太APTA	0	最不发达 35 国 LDC35,最不发达 4 国 LDC4	17	---Of a yield strength exceeding 355N/mm^2

序号 No.	税则号列 Tariff Line	货品名称	最惠国税率 MFN(%)	协定税率 Agreement(%)		特惠税率 S.P.(%)		普通税率 Gen.(%)	Article Description
5155	7208.5390	---其他	6	0 5.1	东盟ASEAN,智利CL,巴基斯坦PK,新西兰NZ,秘鲁PE,哥斯达黎加CR 亚太APTA	0	最不发达35国LDC35,最不发达4国LDC4	17	---Other
		--厚度小于3毫米:							--Of a thickness of less than 3mm:
5156	7208.5410	---厚度小于1.5毫米	6	0 5.1	东盟ASEAN,智利CL,巴基斯坦PK,新西兰NZ,秘鲁PE,哥斯达黎加CR 亚太APTA	0	最不发达35国LDC35,最不发达4国LDC4	17	---Of a thickness of less than 1.5mm
5157	7208.5490	---其他	6	0 5.1	东盟ASEAN,智利CL,巴基斯坦PK,新西兰NZ,秘鲁PE,哥斯达黎加CR 亚太APTA	0	最不发达35国LDC35,最不发达4国LDC4	17	---Other
5158	7208.9000	-其他	6	0 5	东盟ASEAN,智利CL,新西兰NZ,秘鲁PE,哥斯达黎加CR 巴基斯坦PK	0	最不发达35国LDC35,最不发达4国LDC4	17	-Other
	72.09	**宽度在600毫米及以上的铁或非合金钢平板轧材，经冷轧，但未经包覆、镀层或涂层:**							**Flat-rolled products of iron or non-alloy steel, of a width of 600mm or more, coldrolled (cold-reduced), not clad, plated or coated:**
		-卷材，除冷轧外未经进一步加工:							-In coils, not further worked than cold-rolled (cold-reduced):
		--厚度在3毫米及以上:							--Of a thickness of 3mm or more:
5159	7209.1510	---屈服强度大于355牛顿/平方毫米	6	0 5	东盟ASEAN,智利CL,新西兰NZ,秘鲁PE,哥斯达黎加CR 巴基斯坦PK	0	最不发达35国LDC35,最不发达4国LDC4	17	---Of a yield strength exceeding 355N/mm^2
5160	7209.1590	---其他	6	0 5	东盟ASEAN,智利CL,新西兰NZ,秘鲁PE,哥斯达黎加CR 巴基斯坦PK	0	最不发达35国LDC35,最不发达4国LDC4	17	---Other
		--厚度超过1毫米，但小于3毫米:							--Of a thickness exceeding 1mm but less than 3mm:

序号 No.	税则号列 Tariff Line	货品名称	最惠国税率 MFN(%)	协定税率 Agreement(%)		特惠税率 S.P.(%)		普通税率 Gen.(%)	Article Description
5161	7209.1610	---屈服强度大于 275 牛顿/平方毫米	6	0 0.6 4.2	东盟ASEAN,巴基斯坦PK,新西兰NZ,秘鲁PE,哥斯达黎加CR 智利CL 亚太APTA	0	最不发达 35 国 LDC35,最不发达 4 国 LDC4	17	---Of a yield strength exceeding 275N/mm^2
5162	7209.1690	---其他	6	0 0.6 4.2	东盟ASEAN,巴基斯坦PK,新西兰NZ,秘鲁PE,哥斯达黎加CR,台湾TW 智利CL 亚太APTA	0	最不发达 35 国 LDC35,最不发达 4 国 LDC4	17	---Other
		--厚度在 0.5 毫米及以上，但不超过 1 毫米:							--Of a thickness of 0.5mm or more but not exceeding 1mm:
5163	7209.1710	---屈服强度大于 275 牛顿/平方毫米	3	0 2.1	东盟ASEAN,智利CL,巴基斯坦PK,新西兰NZ,秘鲁PE,哥斯达黎加CR 亚太APTA	0	最不发达 35 国 LDC35,最不发达 4 国 LDC4	17	---Of a yield strength exceeding 275N/mm^2
5164	7209.1790	---其他	3	0 2.1	东盟ASEAN,智利CL,巴基斯坦PK,新西兰NZ,秘鲁PE,哥斯达黎加CR,台湾TW 亚太APTA	0	最不发达 35 国 LDC35,最不发达 4 国 LDC4	17	---Other
		--厚度小于 0.5 毫米:							--Of a thickness of less than 0.5mm:
5165	7209.1810	---厚度小于 0.3 毫米	6	0 0.6 4.2	东盟ASEAN,巴基斯坦PK,新西兰NZ,秘鲁PE,哥斯达黎加CR 智利CL 亚太APTA	0	最不发达 35 国 LDC35,最不发达 4 国 LDC4	17	---Of a thickness less than 0.3mm
5166	7209.1890	---其他	6	0 0.6 4.2	东盟ASEAN,巴基斯坦PK,新西兰NZ,秘鲁PE,哥斯达黎加CR,台湾TW 智利CL 亚太APTA	0	最不发达 35 国 LDC35,最不发达 4 国 LDC4	17	---Other
		-非卷材,除冷轧外未经进一步加工:							-Not in coils, not further worked than cold-rolled (cold-reduced):
5167	7209.2500	--厚度在 3 毫米及以上	6	0 5	东盟ASEAN,智利CL,新西兰NZ,秘鲁PE,哥斯达黎加CR 巴基斯坦PK	0	最不发达 35 国 LDC35,最不发达 4 国 LDC4	17	--Of a thickness of 3mm or more
5168	7209.2600	--厚度超过 1 毫米，但小于 3 毫米	6	0 5	东盟ASEAN,智利CL,新西兰NZ,秘鲁PE,哥斯达黎加CR 巴基斯坦PK	0	最不发达 35 国 LDC35,最不发达 4 国 LDC4	17	--Of a thickness exceeding 1mm but less than 3mm

序号 No.	税则号列 Tariff Line	货品名称	最惠国税率 MFN(%)	协定税率 Agreement(%)		特惠税率 S.P.(%)		普通税率 Gen.(%)	Article Description
5169	7209.2700	--厚度在 0.5 毫米及以上，但不超过 1 毫米	6	0 4.2	东盟ASEAN,智利CL,巴基斯坦PK,新西兰NZ,秘鲁PE,哥斯达黎加CR 亚太APTA	0	最不发达 35 国 LDC35,最不发达 4 国 LDC4	17	--Of a thickness of 0.5mm or more but not exceeding 1mm
5170	7209.2800	--厚度小于 0.5 毫米	6	0 5	东盟ASEAN,智利CL,新西兰NZ,秘鲁PE,哥斯达黎加CR 巴基斯坦PK	0	最不发达 35 国 LDC35,最不发达 4 国 LDC4	17	--Of a thickness of less than 0.5mm
5171	7209.9000	-其他	6	0 4.2	东盟ASEAN,智利CL,巴基斯坦PK,新西兰NZ,秘鲁PE,哥斯达黎加CR 亚太APTA	0	最不发达 35 国 LDC35,最不发达 4 国 LDC4	17	-Other
	72.10	**宽度在 600 毫米及以上的铁或非合金钢平板轧材，经包覆、镀层或涂层:**							**Flat-rolled products of iron or non-alloy steel, of a width of 600mm of more, clad, plated or coated:**
		-镀或涂锡的:							-Plated or coated with tin:
5172	7210.1100	--厚度在 0.5 毫米及以上	10	0 5	东盟ASEAN,智利CL,新加坡SG,新西兰NZ,秘鲁PE,哥斯达黎加CR 巴基斯坦PK	0	最不发达 35 国 LDC35,最不发达 4 国 LDC4	20	--Of a thickness of 0.5mm or more
5173	7210.1200	--厚度小于 0.5 毫米	5	0 0.5	东盟ASEAN,巴基斯坦PK,新西兰NZ,秘鲁PE,哥斯达黎加CR 智利CL	0	最不发达 35 国 LDC35,最不发达 4 国 LDC4	20	--Of a thickness of less than 0.5mm
5174	7210.2000	-镀或涂铅的，包括镀铅锡钢板	4	0	东盟ASEAN,智利CL,巴基斯坦PK,新西兰NZ,秘鲁PE,哥斯达黎加CR	0	最不发达 35 国 LDC35,最不发达 4 国 LDC4	20	-Plated or coated with lead, including terne-plate
5175	7210.3000	-电镀锌的	8	0 5	东盟ASEAN,智利CL,新西兰NZ,秘鲁PE,哥斯达黎加CR,台湾TW 巴基斯坦PK	0	最不发达 35 国 LDC35,最不发达 4 国 LDC4	20	-Electrolytically plated or coated with zinc
		-用其他方法镀或涂锌的:							-Otherwise plated or coated with zinc:
5176	7210.4100	--瓦楞形	8	0 5	东盟ASEAN,智利CL,新西兰NZ,秘鲁PE,哥斯达黎加CR 巴基斯坦PK	0	最不发达 35 国 LDC35,最不发达 4 国 LDC4	20	--Corrugated

序号 No.	税则号列 Tariff Line	货品名称	最惠国税率 MFN(%)	协定税率 Agreement(%)		特惠税率 S.P.(%)		普通税率 Gen.(%)	Article Description
5177	7210.4900	--其他	4	0	东盟ASEAN,智利CL,巴基斯坦PK,新西兰NZ,秘鲁PE,哥斯达黎加CR,台湾TW	0	最不发达35国LDC35,最不发达4国LDC4	20	--Other
5178	7210.5000	-镀或涂氧化铬或铬及氧化铬的	8	0 5	东盟ASEAN,智利CL,新西兰NZ,秘鲁PE,哥斯达黎加CR 巴基斯坦PK	0	最不发达35国LDC35,最不发达4国LDC4	20	-Plated or coated with chromium oxides or with chromium and chromium oxides
		-镀或涂铝的:							-Plated or coated with aluminium:
5179	7210.6100	--镀或涂铝锌合金的	8	0 0.8 5	东盟ASEAN,新西兰NZ,秘鲁PE,哥斯达黎加CR 智利CL 巴基斯坦PK	0	最不发达35国LDC35,最不发达4国LDC4	20	--Plated or coated with aluminium-zinc alloys
5180	7210.6900	--其他	8	0 5	东盟ASEAN,智利CL,新西兰NZ,秘鲁PE,哥斯达黎加CR 巴基斯坦PK	0	最不发达35国LDC35,最不发达4国LDC4	20	--Other
		-涂漆或涂塑的:							-Painted, varnished or coated with plastics:
5181	7210.7010	---厚度小于1.5毫米	4	0 0.4	东盟ASEAN,巴基斯坦PK,新西兰NZ,秘鲁PE,哥斯达黎加CR,香港HK 智利CL	0	最不发达35国LDC35,最不发达4国LDC4	20	---Of a thickness less than 1.5mm
5182	7210.7090	---其他	4	0 0.4	东盟ASEAN,巴基斯坦PK,新西兰NZ,秘鲁PE,哥斯达黎加CR,香港HK 智利CL	0	最不发达35国LDC35,最不发达4国LDC4	20	---Other
5183	7210.9000	-其他	8	0 5	东盟ASEAN,智利CL,新西兰NZ,秘鲁PE,哥斯达黎加CR 巴基斯坦PK	0	最不发达35国LDC35,最不发达4国LDC4	20	-Other
	72.11	**宽度小于600毫米的铁或非合金钢平板轧材，但未经包覆、镀层或涂层:**							**Flat-rolled products of iron or non-alloy steel, of a width of less than 600mm, not clad, plated or coated:**
		-除热轧外未经进一步加工:							-Not further worked than hot-rolled:

序号 No.	税则号列 Tariff Line	货品名称	最惠国税率 MFN(%)	协定税率 Agreement(%)		特惠税率 S.P.(%)		普通税率 Gen.(%)	Article Description
5184	7211.1300	--经四面轧制或在闭合匣内轧制的非卷材，宽度超过150毫米，厚度不小于4毫米，未轧压花纹	6	0 5	东盟ASEAN,智利CL,新西兰NZ,秘鲁PE,哥斯达黎加CR 巴基斯坦PK	0	最不发达35国LDC35,最不发达4国LDC4	30	--Rolled on four faces or in a closed box pass, of a width exceeding 150mm and a thickness of not less than 4mm, not in coils and without patterns in relief
5185	7211.1400	--其他，厚度在4.75毫米及以上	6	0 5	东盟ASEAN,智利CL,新西兰NZ,秘鲁PE,哥斯达黎加CR 巴基斯坦PK	0	最不发达35国LDC35,最不发达4国LDC4	30	--Other, of a thickness of 4.75mm or more
5186	7211.1900	--其他	6	0 5	东盟ASEAN,智利CL,新西兰NZ,秘鲁PE,哥斯达黎加CR 巴基斯坦PK	0	最不发达35国LDC35,最不发达4国LDC4	30	--Other
		-除冷轧外未经进一步加工:							-Not further worked than cold-rolled (cold-reduced):
5187	7211.2300	--按重量计含碳量低于0.25%	6	0 5	东盟ASEAN,智利CL,新西兰NZ,秘鲁PE,哥斯达黎加CR 巴基斯坦PK	0	最不发达35国LDC35,最不发达4国LDC4	30	--Containing by weight less than 0.25% of carbon
5188	7211.2900	--其他	6	0 5	东盟ASEAN,智利CL,新西兰NZ,秘鲁PE,哥斯达黎加CR 巴基斯坦PK	0	最不发达35国LDC35,最不发达4国LDC4	30	--Other
5189	7211.9000	-其他	6	0 0.6 5	东盟ASEAN,新西兰NZ,秘鲁PE,哥斯达黎加CR 智利CL 巴基斯坦PK	0	最不发达35国LDC35,最不发达4国LDC4	30	-Other
	72.12	**宽度小于600毫米的铁或非合金钢平板轧材，经包覆、镀层或涂层:**							**Flat-rolled products of iron or non-alloy steel, of a width of less than 600mm, clad, plated or coated:**
5190	7212.1000	-镀或涂锡的	5	0	东盟ASEAN,智利CL,巴基斯坦PK,新西兰NZ,秘鲁PE,哥斯达黎加CR	0	最不发达35国LDC35,最不发达4国LDC4	20	-Plated or coated with tin
5191	7212.2000	-电镀锌的	8	0 5	东盟ASEAN,智利CL,新西兰NZ,秘鲁PE,哥斯达黎加CR 巴基斯坦PK	0	最不发达35国LDC35,最不发达4国LDC4	20	-Electrolytically plated or coated with zinc

序号 No.	税则号列 Tariff Line	货品名称	最惠国 税率 MFN(%)	协定税率 Agreement(%)		特惠税率 S.P.(%)		普通 税率 Gen.(%)	Article Description
5192	7212.3000	-用其他方法镀或涂锌的	8	0 0.8 5	东盟ASEAN,新西兰NZ,秘鲁PE,哥斯达黎加CR 智利CL 巴基斯坦PK	0	最不发达35国LDC35,最不发达4国LDC4	20	-Otherwise plated or coated with zinc
5193	7212.4000	-涂漆或涂塑的	4	0 0.4	东盟ASEAN,巴基斯坦PK,新西兰NZ,秘鲁PE,哥斯达黎加CR,香港HK 智利CL	0	最不发达35国LDC35,最不发达4国LDC4	20	-Painted, varnished or coated with plastics
5194	7212.5000	-镀或涂其他材料的	8	0 5	东盟ASEAN,智利CL,新西兰NZ,秘鲁PE,哥斯达黎加CR 巴基斯坦PK	0	最不发达35国LDC35,最不发达4国LDC4	20	-Otherwise plated or coated
5195	7212.6000	-经包覆的	8	0 5	东盟ASEAN,智利CL,新西兰NZ,秘鲁PE,哥斯达黎加CR 巴基斯坦PK	0	最不发达35国LDC35,最不发达4国LDC4	20	-Clad
	72.13	**不规则盘卷的铁及非合金钢的热轧条、杆:**							**Bars and rods, hot-rolled, in irregularly wound coils, of iron or non-alloy steel:**
5196	7213.1000	-带有轧制过程中产生的凹痕、凸缘、槽沟及其他变形的	3	0	东盟ASEAN,智利CL,巴基斯坦PK,新西兰NZ,秘鲁PE,哥斯达黎加CR	0	最不发达35国LDC35,最不发达4国LDC4	20	-Containing indentations, ribs, grooves or other deformations produced during the rolling process
5197	7213.2000	-其他，易切削钢制	3	0	东盟ASEAN,智利CL,巴基斯坦PK,新西兰NZ,秘鲁PE,哥斯达黎加CR	0	最不发达35国LDC35,最不发达4国LDC4	20	-Other, of free-cutting steel
		-其他:							-Other:
5198	7213.9100	--直径小于14毫米圆形截面的	5	0 0.5 4.3	东盟ASEAN,巴基斯坦PK,新西兰NZ,秘鲁PE,哥斯达黎加CR 智利CL 亚太APTA	0	最不发达35国LDC35,最不发达4国LDC4	20	--Of circular cross-section measuring less than 14mm in diameter
5199	7213.9900	--其他	5	0	东盟ASEAN,智利CL,巴基斯坦PK,新西兰NZ,秘鲁PE,哥斯达黎加CR	0	最不发达35国LDC35,最不发达4国LDC4	20	--Other

序号 No.	税则号列 Tariff Line	货品名称	最惠国税率 MFN(%)	协定税率 Agreement(%)		特惠税率 S.P.(%)		普通税率 Gen.(%)	Article Description
	72.14	**铁或非合金钢的其他条、杆，除锻造、热轧、热拉拔或热挤压外未经进一步加工，包括轧制后扭曲的:**							**Other bars and rods of iron or non-alloy steel, not further worked than forged, hot rolled, hot-drawn or hotextruded, but including those twisted after rolling:**
5200	7214.1000	-锻造的	7	0 0.7 5	东盟ASEAN,新西兰NZ,秘鲁PE,哥斯达黎加CR 智利CL 巴基斯坦PK	0	最不发达35国LDC35,最不发达4国LDC4	10	-Forged
5201	7214.2000	-带有轧制过程中产生的凹痕、凸缘、槽沟或其他变形以及轧制后扭曲的	3	0	东盟ASEAN,亚太APTA,智利CL,巴基斯坦PK,新西兰NZ,秘鲁PE,哥斯达黎加CR,香港HK	0	最不发达35国LDC35,最不发达4国LDC4	20	-Containing indentations, ribs, grooves or other deformations produced during the rolling process or twisted after rolling
5202	7214.3000	-其他，易切削钢制	7	0 5	东盟ASEAN,智利CL,新西兰NZ,秘鲁PE,哥斯达黎加CR 巴基斯坦PK	0	最不发达35国LDC35,最不发达4国LDC4	20	-Other, of free-cutting steel
		-其他:							-Other:
5203	7214.9100	--矩形（正方形除外）截面的	3	0	东盟ASEAN,智利CL,巴基斯坦PK,新西兰NZ,秘鲁PE,哥斯达黎加CR	0	最不发达35国LDC35,最不发达4国LDC4	20	--Of rectangular cross section (other than square)
5204	7214.9900	--其他	3	0	东盟ASEAN,智利CL,巴基斯坦PK,新西兰NZ,秘鲁PE,哥斯达黎加CR	0	最不发达35国LDC35,最不发达4国LDC4	20	--Other
	72.15	**铁及非合金钢的其他条、杆:**							**Other bars and rods of iron or non-alloy steel:**
5205	7215.1000	-易切削钢制，除冷成形或冷加工外未经进一步加工	7	0 5	东盟ASEAN,智利CL,新西兰NZ,秘鲁PE,哥斯达黎加CR 巴基斯坦PK	0	最不发达35国LDC35,最不发达4国LDC4	20	-Of free-cutting steel, not further worked than cold-formed or cold-finished
5206	7215.5000	-其他，除冷成形或冷加工外未经进一步加工	7	0 5	东盟ASEAN,智利CL,新西兰NZ,秘鲁PE,哥斯达黎加CR 巴基斯坦PK	0	最不发达35国LDC35,最不发达4国LDC4	20	-Other, not further worked than cold-formed or cold-finished

序号 No.	税则号列 Tariff Line	货品名称	最惠国税率 MFN(%)	协定税率 Agreement(%)		特惠税率 S.P.(%)		普通税率 Gen.(%)	Article Description
5207	7215.9000	-其他	3	0	东盟ASEAN,智利CL,巴基斯坦PK,新西兰NZ,秘鲁PE,哥斯达黎加CR	0	最不发达35国LDC35,最不发达4国LDC4	20	-Other
	72.16	**铁或非合金钢的角材、型材及异型材:**							**Angles, shapes and sections of iron or non-alloy steel:**
		-槽钢、工字钢及H型钢，除热轧、热拉拔或热挤压外未经进一步加工，截面高度低于80毫米:							-U, I or H sections, not further worked than hot-rolled, hot-drawn or extruded, of a height of less than 80mm:
5208	7216.1010	---H型钢	3	0	东盟ASEAN,智利CL,巴基斯坦PK,新西兰NZ,秘鲁PE,哥斯达黎加CR	0	最不发达35国LDC35,最不发达4国LDC4	14	---H sections
5209	7216.1020	---工字钢	3	0	东盟ASEAN,智利CL,巴基斯坦PK,新西兰NZ,秘鲁PE,哥斯达黎加CR	0	最不发达35国LDC35,最不发达4国LDC4	14	---I sections
5210	7216.1090	---其他	3	0	东盟ASEAN,智利CL,巴基斯坦PK,新西兰NZ,秘鲁PE,哥斯达黎加CR	0	最不发达35国LDC35,最不发达4国LDC4	14	---Other
		-角钢及丁字钢,除热轧、热拉拔或热挤压外未经进一步加工，截面高度低于80毫米:							-L or T sections, not further worked than hot-rolled, hot-drawn or extruded, of a height of less than 80mm:
5211	7216.2100	--角钢	6	0 0.6 5	东盟ASEAN,新西兰NZ,秘鲁PE,哥斯达黎加CR 智利CL 巴基斯坦PK	0	最不发达35国LDC35,最不发达4国LDC4	17	--L sections
5212	7216.2200	--丁字钢	6	0 5	东盟ASEAN,智利CL,新西兰NZ,秘鲁PE,哥斯达黎加CR 巴基斯坦PK	0	最不发达35国LDC35,最不发达4国LDC4	14	--T sections
		-槽钢、工字钢及H型钢，除热轧、热拉拔或热挤压外未经进一步加工，截面高度在80毫米及以上:							-U, I or H sections, not further worked than hot-rolled, hot-drawn or extruded of a height of 80mm or more:

序号 No.	税则号列 Tariff Line	货品名称	最惠国税率 MFN(%)	协定税率 Agreement(%)		特惠税率 S.P.(%)		普通税率 Gen.(%)	Article Description
5213	7216.3100	--槽钢	6	0 0.6 5	东盟ASEAN,新西兰NZ,秘鲁PE,哥斯达黎加CR 智利CL 巴基斯坦PK	0	最不发达35国LDC35,最不发达4国LDC4	14	--U sections
		--工字钢:							--I sections:
5214	7216.3210	---截面高度在200毫米以上	6	0 5	东盟ASEAN,智利CL,新西兰NZ,秘鲁PE,哥斯达黎加CR 巴基斯坦PK	0	最不发达35国LDC35,最不发达4国LDC4	14	---Of a height exceeding 200mm
5215	7216.3290	---其他	6	0 5	东盟ASEAN,智利CL,新西兰NZ,秘鲁PE,哥斯达黎加CR 巴基斯坦PK	0	最不发达35国LDC35,最不发达4国LDC4	14	---Other
		--H型钢:							--H sections:
		---截面高度在200毫米以上:							---Of a height exceeding 200mm:
5216	7216.3311	----截面高度在800毫米以上	6	0 5	东盟ASEAN,智利CL,新西兰NZ,秘鲁PE,哥斯达黎加CR 巴基斯坦PK	0	最不发达35国LDC35,最不发达4国LDC4	14	----Of a height exceeding 800mm
5217	7216.3319	----其他	6	0 5	东盟ASEAN,智利CL,新西兰NZ,秘鲁PE,哥斯达黎加CR 巴基斯坦PK	0	最不发达35国LDC35,最不发达4国LDC4	14	----Other
5218	7216.3390	---其他	6	0 5	东盟ASEAN,智利CL,新西兰NZ,秘鲁PE,哥斯达黎加CR 巴基斯坦PK	0	最不发达35国LDC35,最不发达4国LDC4	14	---Other
		-角钢及丁字钢，除热轧、热拉拔或热挤压外未经进一步加工，截面高度在80毫米及以上:							-L or T sections, not further worked than hot-rolled, hot-drawn or extruded, of a height of 80mm or more:
5219	7216.4010	---角钢	3	0	东盟ASEAN,智利CL,巴基斯坦PK,新西兰NZ,秘鲁PE,哥斯达黎加CR	0	最不发达35国LDC35,最不发达4国LDC4	17	---L sections

序号 No.	税则号列 Tariff Line	货品名称	最惠国税率 MFN(%)	协定税率 Agreement(%)		特惠税率 S.P.(%)		普通税率 Gen.(%)	Article Description
5220	7216.4020	---丁字钢	3	0	东盟ASEAN,智利CL,巴基斯坦PK,新西兰NZ,秘鲁PE,哥斯达黎加CR	0	最不发达35国LDC35,最不发达4国LDC4	14	---T sections
		-其他角材、型材及异型材，除热轧、热拉拔或热挤压外未经进一步加工:							-Other angles, shapes and sections, not further worked than hot-rolled, hotdrawn or extruded:
5221	7216.5010	---乙字钢	6	0 5	东盟ASEAN,智利CL,新西兰NZ,秘鲁PE,哥斯达黎加CR 巴基斯坦PK	0	最不发达35国LDC35,最不发达4国LDC4	14	---Z sections
5222	7216.5020	---球扁钢	3	0	东盟ASEAN,智利CL,巴基斯坦PK,新西兰NZ,秘鲁PE,哥斯达黎加CR	0	最不发达35国LDC35,最不发达4国LDC4	20	---Bulb flat steel
5223	7216.5090	---其他	3	0	东盟ASEAN,智利CL,巴基斯坦PK,新西兰NZ,秘鲁PE,哥斯达黎加CR	0	最不发达35国LDC35,最不发达4国LDC4	20	---Other
		-角材、型材及异型材，除冷成形或冷加工外未经进一步加工:							-Angles, shapes and sections, not fur-ther worked than cold-formed or cold-finished:
5224	7216.6100	--平板轧材制的	3	0	东盟ASEAN,智利CL,巴基斯坦PK,新西兰NZ,秘鲁PE,哥斯达黎加CR	0	最不发达35国LDC35,最不发达4国LDC4	20	--Obtained from flat-rolled products
5225	7216.6900	--其他	3	0	东盟ASEAN,智利CL,巴基斯坦PK,新西兰NZ,秘鲁PE,哥斯达黎加CR	0	最不发达35国LDC35,最不发达4国LDC4	20	--Other
		-其他:							-Other:
5226	7216.9100	--平板轧材经冷成形或冷加工制的	3	0	东盟ASEAN,智利CL,巴基斯坦PK,新西兰NZ,秘鲁PE,哥斯达黎加CR	0	最不发达35国LDC35,最不发达4国LDC4	20	--Cold-formed or cold-finished from flatrolled products

序号 No.	税则号列 Tariff Line	货品名称	最惠国税率 MFN(%)	协定税率 Agreement(%)		特惠税率 S.P.(%)		普通税率 Gen.(%)	Article Description
5227	7216.9900	--其他	3	0	东盟ASEAN,智利CL,巴基斯坦PK,新西兰NZ,秘鲁PE,哥斯达黎加CR	0	最不发达35国LDC35,最不发达4国LDC4	20	--Other
	72.17	**铁丝或非合金钢丝:**							**Wire of iron or non-alloy steel:**
5228	7217.1000	-未经镀或涂层,不论是否抛光	8	0 0.8 5	东盟ASEAN,新西兰NZ,秘鲁PE,哥斯达黎加CR,台湾TW 智利CL 巴基斯坦PK	0	最不发达35国LDC35,最不发达4国LDC4	40	-Not plated or coated, whether or not polished
5229	7217.2000	-镀或涂锌的	8	0 0.8 5	东盟ASEAN,新西兰NZ,秘鲁PE,哥斯达黎加CR 智利CL 巴基斯坦PK	0	最不发达35国LDC35,最不发达4国LDC4	40	-Plated or coated with zinc
		-镀或涂其他贱金属的:							-Plated or coated with other base metals:
5230	7217.3010	---镀或涂铜的	8	0 0.8 5 6.4	东盟ASEAN,新西兰NZ,秘鲁PE,哥斯达黎加CR 智利CL 巴基斯坦PK 亚太APTA	0	最不发达35国LDC35,最不发达4国LDC4	40	---Plated or coated with copper
5231	7217.3090	---其他	8	0 0.8 5 6.4	东盟ASEAN,新西兰NZ,秘鲁PE,哥斯达黎加CR 智利CL 巴基斯坦PK 亚太APTA	0	最不发达35国LDC35,最不发达4国LDC4	40	---Other
5232	7217.9000	-其他	8	0 5	东盟ASEAN,智利CL,新西兰NZ,秘鲁PE,哥斯达黎加CR,香港HK 巴基斯坦PK	0	最不发达35国LDC35,最不发达4国LDC4	40	-Other
		第三分章 不锈钢							III.STAINLESS STEEL
	72.18	**不锈钢,锭状或其他初级形状;不锈钢半制成品:**							**Stainless steel in ingots or other primary forms; semi-finished products of stainless steel:**
5233	7218.1000	-锭状及其他初级形状	2	0	东盟ASEAN,智利CL,巴基斯坦PK,新西兰NZ,秘鲁PE,哥斯达黎加CR	0	最不发达35国LDC35,最不发达4国LDC4	11	-Ingots and other primary forms
		-其他:							-Other:

序号 No.	税则号列 Tariff Line	货品名称	最惠国税率 MFN(%)	协定税率 Agreement(%)		特惠税率 S.P.(%)		普通税率 Gen.(%)	Article Description
5234	7218.9100	--矩形（正方形除外）截面的	2	0	东盟ASEAN,智利CL,巴基斯坦PK,新西兰NZ,秘鲁PE,哥斯达黎加CR	0	最不发达35国LDC35,最不发达4国LDC4	11	--Of rectangular (other than quare) crosssection
5235	7218.9900	--其他	2	0	东盟ASEAN,智利CL,巴基斯坦PK,新西兰NZ,秘鲁PE,哥斯达黎加CR	0	最不发达35国LDC35,最不发达4国LDC4	11	--Other
	72.19	**不锈钢平板轧材，宽度在600毫米及以上:**							**Flat-rolled products of stainless steel, of a width of 600mm or more:**
		-除热轧外未经进一步加工的卷材:							-Not further worked than hot-rolled, in coils:
5236	7219.1100	--厚度超过10毫米	4	0	东盟ASEAN,智利CL,巴基斯坦PK,新西兰NZ,秘鲁PE,哥斯达黎加CR	0	最不发达35国LDC35,最不发达4国LDC4	14	--Of a thickness exceeding 10mm
5237	7219.1200	--厚度在4.75毫米及以上，但不超过10毫米	4	0	东盟ASEAN,智利CL,巴基斯坦PK,新西兰NZ,秘鲁PE,哥斯达黎加CR,台湾TW	0	最不发达35国LDC35,最不发达4国LDC4	14	--Of a thickness of 4.75mm or more but not exceeding 10mm
		--厚度在3毫米及以上，但小于4.75毫米:							--Of a thickness of 3mm or more but less than 4.75mm:
		---未经酸洗的:							---Not acid Pickled:
5238	7219.1312	----按重量计含锰量在5.5%及以上的铬锰系不锈钢	4	0	东盟ASEAN,智利CL,巴基斯坦PK,新西兰NZ,秘鲁PE,哥斯达黎加CR	0	最不发达35国LDC35,最不发达4国LDC4	14	----Containing by weight no less than 5.5% of manganese of Ferro-chromium-manganese steel
5239	7219.1319	----其他	4	0	东盟ASEAN,智利CL,巴基斯坦PK,新西兰NZ,秘鲁PE,哥斯达黎加CR,台湾TW	0	最不发达35国LDC35,最不发达4国LDC4	14	----Other
		---经酸洗的:							---Acid pickled:
5240	7219.1322	----按重量计含锰量在5.5%及以上的铬锰系不锈钢	4	0	东盟ASEAN,智利CL,巴基斯坦PK,新西兰NZ,秘鲁PE,哥斯达黎加CR	0	最不发达35国LDC35,最不发达4国LDC4	14	----Containing by weight no less than 5.5% of manganese of Ferro-chromium-manganese steel

序号 No.	税则号列 Tariff Line	货品名称	最惠国 税　率 MFN(%)	协定税率 Agreement(%)		特惠税率 S.P.(%)		普通 税率 Gen.(%)	Article Description
5241	7219.1329	----其他	4	0	东盟ASEAN,智利CL,巴基斯坦PK,新西兰NZ,秘鲁PE,哥斯达黎加CR,台湾TW	0	最不发达35国LDC35,最不发达4国LDC4	14	----Other
		--厚度小于3毫米:							--Of a thickness of less than 3mm:
		---未经酸洗的:							---Not acid Pickled:
5242	7219.1412	----按重量计含锰量在5.5%及以上的铬锰系不锈钢	4	0	东盟ASEAN,智利CL,巴基斯坦PK,新西兰NZ,秘鲁PE,哥斯达黎加CR	0	最不发达35国LDC35,最不发达4国LDC4	14	----Containing by weight no less than 5.5% of manganese of Fer-ro-chromium-manganese steel
5243	7219.1419	----其他	4	0	东盟ASEAN,智利CL,巴基斯坦PK,新西兰NZ,秘鲁PE,哥斯达黎加CR	0	最不发达35国LDC35,最不发达4国LDC4	14	----Other
		---经酸洗的:							---Acid pickled:
5244	7219.1422	----按重量计含锰量在5.5%及以上的铬锰系不锈钢	4	0	东盟ASEAN,智利CL,巴基斯坦PK,新西兰NZ,秘鲁PE,哥斯达黎加CR	0	最不发达35国LDC35,最不发达4国LDC4	14	----Containing by weight no less than 5.5% of manganese of Fer-ro-chromium-manganese steel
5245	7219.1429	----其他	4	0	东盟ASEAN,智利CL,巴基斯坦PK,新西兰NZ,秘鲁PE,哥斯达黎加CR	0	最不发达35国LDC35,最不发达4国LDC4	14	----Other
		-除热轧外未经进一步加工的非卷材:							-Not further worked than hot-rolled, not in coils:
5246	7219.2100	--厚度超过10毫米	10	0 5 9.3	东盟ASEAN,智利CL,新加坡SG,新西兰NZ,秘鲁PE,哥斯达黎加CR,香港HK 巴基斯坦PK 亚太APTA	0	最不发达35国LDC35	40	--Of a thickness exceeding10mm
5247	7219.2200	--厚度在4.75毫米及以上，但不超过10毫米	10	0 1 5 9.3	东盟ASEAN,新加坡SG,新西兰NZ,哥斯达黎加CR,香港HK 智利CL 巴基斯坦PK,秘鲁PE 亚太APTA	0	最不发达35国LDC35	40	--Of a thickness of 4.75mm or more but not exceeding 10mm
5248	7219.2300	--厚度在3毫米及以上，但小于4.75毫米	10	0 5 9.3	东盟ASEAN,智利CL,新加坡SG,新西兰NZ,秘鲁PE,哥斯达黎加CR,台湾TW 巴基斯坦PK 亚太APTA	0	最不发达35国LDC35	40	--Of a thickness of 3mm or more but less than 4.75mm

序号 No.	税则号列 Tariff Line	货品名称	最惠国税率 MFN(%)	协定税率 Agreement(%)		特惠税率 S.P.(%)		普通税率 Gen.(%)	Article Description
		--厚度小于3毫米:							--Of a thickness of less than 3mm:
5249	7219.2410	---厚度超过1毫米但小于3毫米	10	0	东盟ASEAN,智利CL,新加坡SG,新西兰NZ,秘鲁PE,哥斯达黎加CR,台湾TW	0	最不发达35国LDC35	40	---Of a thickness exceeding1mm but less than 3mm
				5	巴基斯坦PK				
				9.3	亚太APTA				
5250	7219.2420	---厚度在0.5毫米及以上，但不超过1毫米	10	0	东盟ASEAN,智利CL,新加坡SG,新西兰NZ,秘鲁PE,哥斯达黎加CR	0	最不发达35国LDC35	40	---Of a thickness of 0.5mm or more but not exceeding1mm
				5	巴基斯坦PK				
				9.3	亚太APTA				
5251	7219.2430	---厚度小于0.5毫米	10	0	东盟ASEAN,智利CL,新加坡SG,新西兰NZ,秘鲁PE,哥斯达黎加CR	0	最不发达35国LDC35	40	---Of a thickness of less than 0.5mm
				5	巴基斯坦PK				
				9.3	亚太APTA				
		-除冷轧外未经进一步加工:							-Not further worked than cold-rolled (cold-reduced):
5252	7219.3100	--厚度在4.75毫米及以上	10	0	东盟ASEAN,新加坡SG,新西兰NZ,哥斯达黎加CR,台湾TW	0	最不发达35国LDC35	40	--Of a thickness of 4.75mm or more
				1	智利CL				
				5	巴基斯坦PK,秘鲁PE				
5253	7219.3200	--厚度在3毫米及以上，但小于4.75毫米	10	0	东盟ASEAN,新加坡SG,新西兰NZ,哥斯达黎加CR,台湾TW	0	最不发达35国LDC35	40	--Of a thickness of 3mm or more but less than 4.75mm
				1	智利CL				
				5	巴基斯坦PK,秘鲁PE				
		--厚度超过1毫米，但小于3毫米:							--Of a thickness exceeding 1mm but less than 3mm:
5254	7219.3310	---按重量计含锰量在5.5%及以上的铬锰系不锈钢	10	0	东盟ASEAN,新加坡SG,新西兰NZ,哥斯达黎加CR,香港HK,台湾TW	0	最不发达35国LDC35	40	---Containing by weight no less than 5.5% of manganese of Terrochromium manganese steel
				1	智利CL				
				5	巴基斯坦PK,秘鲁PE				
5255	7219.3390	---其他	10	0	东盟ASEAN,新加坡SG,新西兰NZ,哥斯达黎加CR,香港HK,台湾TW	0	最不发达35国LDC35	40	---Other
				1	智利CL				
				5	巴基斯坦PK,秘鲁PE				
5256	7219.3400	--厚度在0.5毫米及以上，但不超过1毫米	10	0	东盟ASEAN,新加坡SG,新西兰NZ,哥斯达黎加CR,香港HK,台湾TW	0	最不发达35国LDC35	40	--Of a thickness of 0.5mm or more but not exceeding 1mm
				1	智利CL				
				5	巴基斯坦PK,秘鲁PE				
5257	7219.3500	--厚度小于0.5毫米	10	0	东盟ASEAN,新加坡SG,新西兰NZ,哥斯达黎加CR,香港HK,台湾TW	0	最不发达35国LDC35	40	--Of a thickness of less than 0.5mm
				1	智利CL				
				5	巴基斯坦PK,秘鲁PE				

序号 No.	税则号列 Tariff Line	货品名称	最惠国税率 MFN(%)	协定税率 Agreement(%)		特惠税率 S.P.(%)		普通税率 Gen.(%)	Article Description
5258	7219.9000	-其他	10	0 5	东盟ASEAN,智利CL,新加坡SG,新西兰NZ,秘鲁PE,哥斯达黎加CR,台湾TW 巴基斯坦PK	0	最不发达35国LDC35	40	-Other
	72.20	**不锈钢平板轧材，宽度小于600毫米:**							**Flat-rolled products stainless steel, of a width of less than 600mm:**
		-除热轧外未经进一步加工:							-Not further worked than hot-rolled:
5259	7220.1100	--厚度在4.75毫米及以上	10	0 5	东盟ASEAN,智利CL,新加坡SG,新西兰NZ,秘鲁PE,哥斯达黎加CR,香港HK 巴基斯坦PK	0	最不发达35国LDC35	20	--Of a thickness of 4.75mm or more
5260	7220.1200	--厚度小于4.75毫米	10	0 5	东盟ASEAN,智利CL,新加坡SG,新西兰NZ,秘鲁PE,哥斯达黎加CR 巴基斯坦PK	0	最不发达35国LDC35	20	--Of a thickness of less than 4.75mm
		-除冷轧外未经进一步加工:							-Not further worked than cold-rolled (cold-reduced):
5261	7220.2020	---厚度在0.35毫米及以下	10	0 5	东盟ASEAN,智利CL,新加坡SG,新西兰NZ,秘鲁PE,哥斯达黎加CR 巴基斯坦PK	0	最不发达35国LDC35	20	---Of a thickness of 0.35mm or less
5262	7220.2030	---厚度在0.35毫米以上但小于3毫米	10	0 5	东盟ASEAN,智利CL,新加坡SG,新西兰NZ,秘鲁PE,哥斯达黎加CR 巴基斯坦PK	0	最不发达35国LDC35	20	---Of a thickness of more than 0.35mm but not exceeding 3mm
5263	7220.2040	---厚度在3毫米及以上	10	0 5	东盟ASEAN,智利CL,新加坡SG,新西兰NZ,秘鲁PE,哥斯达黎加CR 巴基斯坦PK	0	最不发达35国LDC35	20	---Of a thickness of 3mm or more
5264	7220.9000	-其他	10	0 5	东盟ASEAN,智利CL,新加坡SG,新西兰NZ,秘鲁PE,哥斯达黎加CR,台湾TW 巴基斯坦PK	0	最不发达35国LDC35	20	-Other
	72.21	**不规则盘卷的不锈钢热轧条、杆:**							**Bars and rods, hot-rolled, in irregularly wound coils, of stainless steel:**
5265	7221.0000	不规则盘卷的不锈钢热轧条、杆	10	0 5 8	东盟ASEAN,智利CL,新加坡SG,新西兰NZ,秘鲁PE,哥斯达黎加CR 巴基斯坦PK 亚太APTA	0	最不发达35国LDC35	20	Bars and rods, hot-rolled, in irregularly wound coils, of stainless steel
	72.22	**不锈钢其他条、杆；不锈钢角材、型材及异型材:**							**Other bars and rods of stainless steel:angles, shapes and sections of stainless steel:**
		-条、杆，除热轧、热拉拔或热挤压外未经进一步加工:							-Bars and rods, not further worked than hot-rolled, hot-drawn or extruded:

序号 No.	税则号列 Tariff Line	货品名称	最惠国税率 MFN(%)	协定税率 Agreement(%)		特惠税率 S.P.(%)		普通税率 Gen.(%)	Article Description
5266	7222.1100	--圆形截面的	10	0	东盟ASEAN,智利CL,新加坡SG,新西兰NZ,秘鲁PE,哥斯达黎加CR	0	最不发达35国LDC35	40	--Of circular cross-section
				5	巴基斯坦PK				
				9	亚太APTA				
5267	7222.1900	--其他	10	0	东盟ASEAN,智利CL,新加坡SG,新西兰NZ,秘鲁PE,哥斯达黎加CR	0	最不发达35国LDC35	40	--Other
				5	巴基斯坦PK				
				9	亚太APTA				
5268	7222.2000	-条、杆，除冷成形或冷加工外未经进一步加工	10	0	东盟ASEAN,智利CL,新加坡SG,新西兰NZ,秘鲁PE,哥斯达黎加CR	0	最不发达35国LDC35	40	-Bars and rods, not further worked than cold-formed or cold-finished
				5	巴基斯坦PK				
5269	7222.3000	-其他条、杆	10	0	东盟ASEAN,智利CL,新加坡SG,新西兰NZ,秘鲁PE,哥斯达黎加CR	0	最不发达35国LDC35	40	-Other bars and rods
				5	巴基斯坦PK				
				8.9	亚太APTA				
5270	7222.4000	-角材、型材及异型材	10	0	东盟ASEAN,智利CL,新加坡SG,新西兰NZ,秘鲁PE,哥斯达黎加CR	0	最不发达35国LDC35	17	-Angles, shapes and sections
				5	巴基斯坦PK				
	72.23	**不锈钢丝:**							**Wire of stainless steel:**
5271	7223.0000	不锈钢丝	10	0	东盟ASEAN,新加坡SG,新西兰NZ,秘鲁PE,哥斯达黎加CR,香港HK	0	最不发达35国LDC35,最不发达4国LDC4	20	Wire of stainless steel
				1	智利CL				
				5	巴基斯坦PK				
		第四分章 其他合金钢;合金钢或非合金钢制的空心钻钢							Ⅳ.OTHER ALLOY STEEL; HOLLOW DRILL BARS AND RODS, OF ALLOY OR NON-ALLOY STEEL
	72.24	**其他合金钢，锭状或其他初级形状;其他合金钢制的半制成品:**							**Other alloy steel in ingots or other primary forms;semi-finished products of other alloy steel:**
5272	7224.1000	-锭状及其他初级形状	2	0	东盟ASEAN,智利CL,巴基斯坦PK,新西兰NZ,秘鲁PE,哥斯达黎加CR	0	最不发达35国LDC35,最不发达4国LDC4	11	-Ingots and other primary forms
		-其他:							-Other:
5273	7224.9010	---单件重量在10吨及以上的粗铸锻件坯	2	0	东盟ASEAN,智利CL,巴基斯坦PK,新西兰NZ,秘鲁PE,哥斯达黎加CR	0	最不发达35国LDC35,最不发达4国LDC4	11	---Raw casting forging stocks, individ-ual piece weight of 10T or more

序号 No.	税则号列 Tariff Line	货品名称	最惠国税率 MFN(%)	协定税率 Agreement(%)		特惠税率 S.P.(%)		普通税率 Gen.(%)	Article Description
5274	7224.9090	---其他	2	0	东盟ASEAN,智利CL,巴基斯坦PK,新西兰NZ,秘鲁PE,哥斯达黎加CR	0	最不发达35国LDC35,最不发达4国LDC4	11	---Other
	72.25	**其他合金钢平板轧材，宽度在600毫米及以上:**							**Flat-rolled products of other alloy steel, of a width of 600mm or more:**
		-硅电钢制:							-Of silicon-electrical steel:
5275	7225.1100	--取向性硅电钢:	3	0 2.1	东盟ASEAN,智利CL,巴基斯坦PK,新西兰NZ,秘鲁PE,哥斯达黎加CR 亚太APTA	0	最不发达35国LDC35,最不发达4国LDC4	20	--Grain-oriented
5276	7225.1900	--其他	6	0 5	东盟ASEAN,智利CL,新西兰NZ,秘鲁PE,哥斯达黎加CR,台湾TW 巴基斯坦PK	0	最不发达35国LDC35,最不发达4国LDC4	20	--Other
5277	7225.3000	-其他卷材,除热轧外未经进一步加工	3	0	东盟ASEAN,智利CL,巴基斯坦PK,新西兰NZ,秘鲁PE,哥斯达黎加CR	0	最不发达35国LDC35,最不发达4国LDC4	14	-Other, not further worked than hot-rolled, in coils
		-其他非卷材,除热轧外未经进一步加工:							-Other, not further worked than hot-rolled, not in coils:
5278	7225.4010	---工具钢	3	0	东盟ASEAN,智利CL,巴基斯坦PK,新西兰NZ,秘鲁PE,哥斯达黎加CR	0	最不发达35国LDC35,最不发达4国LDC4	17	---Tool steel
		---其他:							---Other:
5279	7225.4091	----含硼合金钢	3	0	东盟ASEAN,智利CL,巴基斯坦PK,新西兰NZ,秘鲁PE,哥斯达黎加CR	0	最不发达35国LDC35,最不发达4国LDC4	17	----Boron steel
5280	7225.4099	----其他	3	0	东盟ASEAN,智利CL,巴基斯坦PK,新西兰NZ,秘鲁PE,哥斯达黎加CR	0	最不发达35国LDC35,最不发达4国LDC4	17	----Other

序号 No.	税则号列 Tariff Line	货品名称	最惠国税率 MFN(%)	协定税率 Agreement(%)		特惠税率 S.P.(%)		普通税率 Gen.(%)	Article Description
5281	7225.5000	-其他，除冷轧外未经进一步加工	3	0	东盟ASEAN,智利CL,巴基斯坦PK,新西兰NZ,秘鲁PE,哥斯达黎加CR	0	最不发达35国LDC35,最不发达4国LDC4	17	-Other, not further worked than cold-rolled (cold-reduced)
		-其他:							-Other:
5282	7225.9100	--电镀或涂锌的	7	0	东盟ASEAN,智利CL,新西兰NZ,秘鲁PE,哥斯达黎加CR	0	最不发达35国LDC35,最不发达4国LDC4	17	--Electrolytically plated or coated with zinc
				5	巴基斯坦PK				
5283	7225.9200	--用其他方法镀或涂锌的	7	0	东盟ASEAN,智利CL,新西兰NZ,秘鲁PE,哥斯达黎加CR	0	最不发达35国LDC35,最不发达4国LDC4	17	--Otherwise plated or coated with zinc
				5	巴基斯坦PK				
		--其他:							--Other:
5284	7225.9910	---高速钢制	3	0	东盟ASEAN,智利CL,巴基斯坦PK,新西兰NZ,秘鲁PE,哥斯达黎加CR	0	最不发达35国LDC35,最不发达4国LDC4	17	---Of high speed steel
5285	7225.9990	---其他	7	0	东盟ASEAN,智利CL,新西兰NZ,秘鲁PE,哥斯达黎加CR	0	最不发达35国LDC35,最不发达4国LDC4	17	---Other
				5	巴基斯坦PK				
	72.26	**其他合金钢平板轧材，宽度小于600毫米:**							**Flat-rolled products of other alloy steel, of a width of less than 600mm:**
		-硅电钢制:							-Of silicon-electrical steel:
5286	7226.1100	--取向性硅电钢:	3	0	东盟ASEAN,智利CL,巴基斯坦PK,新西兰NZ,秘鲁PE,哥斯达黎加CR	0	最不发达35国LDC35,最不发达4国LDC4	20	--Grain-oriented
5287	7226.1900	--其他:	3	0	东盟ASEAN,智利CL,巴基斯坦PK,新西兰NZ,秘鲁PE,哥斯达黎加CR	0	最不发达35国LDC35,最不发达4国LDC4	20	--Other
5288	7226.2000	-高速钢制	3	0	东盟ASEAN,智利CL,巴基斯坦PK,新西兰NZ,秘鲁PE,哥斯达黎加CR	0	最不发达35国LDC35,最不发达4国LDC4	20	-Of high speed steel
		-其他:							-Other:

序号 No.	税则号列 Tariff Line	货品名称	最惠国税率 MFN(%)	协定税率 Agreement(%)		特惠税率 S.P.(%)		普通税率 Gen.(%)	Article Description
		--除热轧外未经进一步加工:							--Not further worked than hot-rolled:
5289	7226.9110	---工具钢	3	0	东盟ASEAN,智利CL,巴基斯坦PK,新西兰NZ,秘鲁PE,哥斯达黎加CR	0	最不发达35国LDC35,最不发达4国LDC4	20	---Tool steel
		---其他:							---Other:
5290	7226.9191	----含硼合金钢	3	0	东盟ASEAN,智利CL,巴基斯坦PK,新西兰NZ,秘鲁PE,哥斯达黎加CR	0	最不发达35国LDC35,最不发达4国LDC4	20	----Boron steel
5291	7226.9199	----其他	3	0	东盟ASEAN,智利CL,巴基斯坦PK,新西兰NZ,秘鲁PE,哥斯达黎加CR	0	最不发达35国LDC35,最不发达4国LDC4	20	----Other
5292	7226.9200	--除冷轧外未经进一步加工	3	0	东盟ASEAN,智利CL,巴基斯坦PK,新西兰NZ,秘鲁PE,哥斯达黎加CR	0	最不发达35国LDC35,最不发达4国LDC4	20	--Not further worked than cold-rolled (cold-reduced)
		--其他:							--Other:
5293	7226.9910	---电镀或涂锌的	7	0 5	东盟ASEAN,智利CL,新西兰NZ,秘鲁PE,哥斯达黎加CR 巴基斯坦PK	0	最不发达35国LDC35,最不发达4国LDC4	20	---Electrolytically plated or coated with zinc
5294	7226.9920	---用其他方法镀或涂锌的	7	0 5	东盟ASEAN,智利CL,新西兰NZ,秘鲁PE,哥斯达黎加CR 巴基斯坦PK	0	最不发达35国LDC35,最不发达4国LDC4	20	---Otherwise plated or coated with zinc
5295	7226.9990	---其他	7	0 5	东盟ASEAN,智利CL,新西兰NZ,秘鲁PE,哥斯达黎加CR 巴基斯坦PK	0	最不发达35国LDC35,最不发达4国LDC4	20	---Other
	ex72269990	铁镍合金带材（生产集成电路框架用），宽度小于600毫米	△4						Fe-Ni alloy strip (production of the frame for electronic integrated circuits), of a width less than 600mm

序号 No.	税则号列 Tariff Line	货品名称	最惠国 税 率 MFN(%)	协定税率 Agreement(%)		特惠税率 S.P.(%)		普通 税率 Gen.(%)	Article Description
	72.27	**不规则盘卷的其他合金钢热轧条、杆:**							**Bars and rods, hot-rolled, in irregularly wound coils, of other alloy steel:**
5296	7227.1000	-高速钢制	3	0	东盟ASEAN,智利CL,巴基斯坦PK,新西兰NZ,秘鲁PE,哥斯达黎加CR	0	最不发达35国LDC35,最不发达4国LDC4	20	-Of high speed steel
5297	7227.2000	-硅锰钢制	6	0 5	东盟ASEAN,智利CL,新西兰NZ,秘鲁PE,哥斯达黎加CR 巴基斯坦PK	0	最不发达35国LDC35,最不发达4国LDC4	20	-Of silico-manganese steel
		-其他:							-Other:
5298	7227.9010	---含硼合金钢制	3	0	东盟ASEAN,智利CL,巴基斯坦PK,新西兰NZ,秘鲁PE,哥斯达黎加CR	0	最不发达35国LDC35,最不发达4国LDC4	20	---Of boron steel
5299	7227.9090	---其他	3	0	东盟ASEAN,智利CL,巴基斯坦PK,新西兰NZ,秘鲁PE,哥斯达黎加CR	0	最不发达35国LDC35,最不发达4国LDC4	20	---Other
	72.28	**其他合金钢条、杆;其他合金钢角材、型材及异型材;合金钢或非合金钢制的空心钻钢:**							**Other bars and rods of other alloy steel; angles, shapes and sections, of other alloy steel; hollow drill bars and rods, of alloy or non-alloy steel:**
5300	7228.1000	-高速钢条、杆	3	0	东盟ASEAN,智利CL,巴基斯坦PK,新西兰NZ,秘鲁PE,哥斯达黎加CR	0	最不发达35国LDC35,最不发达4国LDC4	20	-Bars and rods, of high speed steel
5301	7228.2000	-硅锰钢条、杆	6	0 5	东盟ASEAN,智利CL,新西兰NZ,秘鲁PE,哥斯达黎加CR 巴基斯坦PK	0	最不发达35国LDC35,最不发达4国LDC4	20	-Bars and rods, of silico-manganese steel
		-其他条、杆,除热轧、热拉拔或热挤压外未经进一步加工:							-Other bars and rods, not further worked than hot-crolled, hot-drawn or extruded:

序号 No.	税则号列 Tariff Line	货品名称	最惠国税 率 MFN(%)	协定税率 Agreement(%)		特惠税率 S.P.(%)		普通税率 Gen.(%)	Article Description
5302	7228.3010	---含硼合金钢制	3	0	东盟ASEAN,智利CL,巴基斯坦PK,新西兰NZ,秘鲁PE,哥斯达黎加CR	0	最不发达35国LDC35,最不发达4国LDC4	20	---Of boron steel
5303	7228.3090	---其他	3	0	东盟ASEAN,智利CL,巴基斯坦PK,新西兰NZ,秘鲁PE,哥斯达黎加CR	0	最不发达35国LDC35,最不发达4国LDC4	20	---Other
5304	7228.4000	-其他条、杆,除锻造外未经进一步加工	3	0	东盟ASEAN,智利CL,巴基斯坦PK,新西兰NZ,秘鲁PE,哥斯达黎加CR	0	最不发达35国LDC35,最不发达4国LDC4	20	-Other bars and rods, not further worked than forged
5305	7228.5000	-其他条、杆,除冷成形或冷加工外未经进一步加工	3	0	东盟ASEAN,智利CL,巴基斯坦PK,新西兰NZ,秘鲁PE,哥斯达黎加CR	0	最不发达35国LDC35,最不发达4国LDC4	20	-other bars and rods, not further worked than cold-formed Of cold-finished
5306	7228.6000	-其他条、杆	3	0	东盟ASEAN,智利CL,巴基斯坦PK,新西兰NZ,秘鲁PE,哥斯达黎加CR	0	最不发达35国LDC35,最不发达4国LDC4	20	-Other bars and rods
		-角材、型材及异型材:							-Angles, shapes and sections:
5307	7228.7010	---履带板型钢	6	0 0.65	东盟ASEAN,新西兰NZ,秘鲁PE,哥斯达黎加CR 智利CL 巴基斯坦PK	0	最不发达35国LDC35,最不发达4国LDC4	17	---Shapes of crawler tread
5308	7228.7090	---其他	6	0 0.65	东盟ASEAN,新西兰NZ,秘鲁PE,哥斯达黎加CR 智利CL 巴基斯坦PK	0	最不发达35国LDC35,最不发达4国LDC4	17	---Other
5309	7228.8000	-空心钻钢	7	0 0.75	东盟ASEAN,新西兰NZ,秘鲁PE,哥斯达黎加CR 智利CL 巴基斯坦PK	0	最不发达35国LDC35,最不发达4国LDC4	35	-Hollow drill bars and rods

序号 No.	税则号列 Tariff Line	货品名称	最惠国税率 MFN(%)	协定税率 Agreement(%)		特惠税率 S.P.(%)		普通税率 Gen.(%)	Article Description
	72.29	**其他合金钢丝:**							**Wire of other alloy steel:**
5310	7229.2000	-硅锰钢制	7	0	东盟ASEAN,智利CL,新西兰NZ,秘鲁PE,哥斯达黎加CR	0	最不发达35国LDC35	20	-Of silico-manganese steel
				5	巴基斯坦PK				
		-其他:							-Other:
5311	7229.9010	---高速钢制	3	0	东盟ASEAN,智利CL,巴基斯坦PK,新西兰NZ,秘鲁PE,哥斯达黎加CR	0	最不发达35国LDC35	20	---Of high speed steel
5312	7229.9090	---其他	7	0	东盟ASEAN,新西兰NZ,秘鲁PE,哥斯达黎加CR	0	最不发达35国LDC35	20	---Other
				0.7	智利CL				
				5	巴基斯坦PK				

第七十三章
钢铁制品

Chapter 73
Articles of iron or steel

注释:

一、称"铸铁",适用于经铸造而得的产品,按重量计其铁元素含量超过其他元素单项含量并与第七十二章注释一(四)所述的钢的化学成分不同。

二、本章所称"丝",是指热或冷成形的任何截面形状的产品,但其截面尺寸均不超过16毫米。

Notes:

1. In this Chapter the expression "cast iron" applies to products obtained by casting in which iron predominates by weight over each of the other elements and which do not comply with the chemical composition of steel as defined in Note1 (d) to Chapter 72.
2. In this Chapter the word "wire"means hot or cold-formed products of any cross-sectional shape, of which no cross-sectional dimension exceeds 16mm.

序号 No.	税则号列 Tariff Line	货品名称	最惠国税率 MFN(%)	协定税率 Agreement(%)		特惠税率 S.P.(%)		普通税率 Gen.(%)	Article Description
	73.01	**钢铁板桩,不论是否钻孔、打眼或组装;焊接的钢铁角材、型材及异型材:**							**Sheet piling of iron or steel, whether or not drilled, punched or made from assembled elements;welded angles, shapes and sections, of iron or steel:**
5313	7301.1000	-钢铁板桩	7	0 5 6.3	东盟ASEAN,智利CL,新西兰NZ,秘鲁PE,哥斯达黎加CR 巴基斯坦PK 亚太APTA	0	最不发达35国LDC35,最不发达4国LDC4	20	-Sheet piling
5314	7301.2000	-角材、型材及异型材	7	0 5	东盟ASEAN,智利CL,新西兰NZ,秘鲁PE,哥斯达黎加CR 巴基斯坦PK	0	最不发达35国LDC35,最不发达4国LDC4	30	-Angles, shapes and sections
	73.02	**铁道及电车道铺轨用钢铁材料(钢轨、护轨、齿轨、道岔尖轨、辙叉、尖轨拉杆及其他叉道段体、轨枕、鱼尾板、轨座、轨座楔、钢轨垫板、钢轨夹、底板、固定板及其他专门用于连接或加固路轨的材料):**							**Railway or tramway track construction material of iron or steel, the following: rails, check-rails and rack rails, switch blades, crossing frogs, point rods and other crossing pieces, sleepers (cross-ties), fishplates, chairs, chair wedges, sole plates (base plates), rail clips, bedplates, ties and other material specialized for jointing or fixing rails:**

序号 No.	税则号列 Tariff Line	货品名称	最惠国税率 MFN(%)	协定税率 Agreement(%)		特惠税率 S.P.(%)		普通税率 Gen.(%)	Article Description
5315	7302.1000	-钢轨	6	0 5	东盟ASEAN,智利CL,新西兰NZ,秘鲁PE,哥斯达黎加CR 巴基斯坦PK	0	最不发达35国LDC35,最不发达4国LDC4	14	-Rails
5316	7302.3000	-道岔尖轨、辙叉、尖轨拉杆及其他叉道段体	8	0 5	东盟ASEAN,智利CL,新西兰NZ,秘鲁PE,哥斯达黎加CR 巴基斯坦PK	0	最不发达35国LDC35,最不发达4国LDC4	17	-Switch blades, crossing frogs, point rods and other crossing pieces
5317	7302.4000	-鱼尾板及钢轨垫板	7	0 5	东盟ASEAN,智利CL,新西兰NZ,秘鲁PE,哥斯达黎加CR 巴基斯坦PK	0	最不发达35国LDC35,最不发达4国LDC4	17	-Fish-plates and sole plates
		-其他:							-Other:
5318	7302.9010	---轨枕	6	0 5.1	东盟ASEAN,智利CL,巴基斯坦PK,新西兰NZ,秘鲁PE,哥斯达黎加CR 亚太APTA	0	最不发达35国LDC35,最不发达4国LDC4	14	---Sleepers (cross-ties)
5319	7302.9090	---其他	7	0 5 6	东盟ASEAN,智利CL,新西兰NZ,秘鲁PE,哥斯达黎加CR 巴基斯坦PK 亚太APTA	0	最不发达35国LDC35,最不发达4国LDC4	17	---Other
	73.03	**铸铁管及空心异型材:**							**Tubes, pipes and hollow profiles, of cast iron:**
5320	7303.0010	---内径在500毫米及以上的圆形截面管	4	0	东盟ASEAN,智利CL,巴基斯坦PK,新西兰NZ,秘鲁PE,哥斯达黎加CR	0	最不发达35国LDC35,最不发达4国LDC4	40	---Tubes and pipes of circular crosssection, of the internal diameter of 500mm or more
5321	7303.0090	---其他	4	0	东盟ASEAN,智利CL,巴基斯坦PK,新西兰NZ,秘鲁PE,哥斯达黎加CR	0	最不发达35国LDC35,最不发达4国LDC4	40	---Other
	73.04	**无缝钢铁管及空心异型材(铸铁的除外):**							**Tubes, pipes and hollow profiles, seamless, of iron (other than cast iron) or steel:**
		-石油或天然气管道管:							-Line pipe of a kind used for oil or gas pipelines:
		--不锈钢制:							--Of stainless steel:

序号 No.	税则号列 Tariff Line	货品名称	最惠国税率 MFN(%)	协定税率 Agreement(%)		特惠税率 S.P.(%)		普通税率 Gen.(%)	Article Description
5322	7304.1110	---外径大于等于215.9毫米，但不超过406.4毫米	5	0	东盟ASEAN,智利CL,巴基斯坦PK,新西兰NZ,秘鲁PE,哥斯达黎加CR	0	最不发达35国LDC35,最不发达4国LDC4	17	---Having an outside diameter of 215.9mm or more but not exceeding 406.4 mm
5323	7304.1120	---外径超过114.3毫米，但小于215.9毫米	5	0	东盟ASEAN,智利CL,巴基斯坦PK,新西兰NZ,秘鲁PE,哥斯达黎加CR	0	最不发达35国LDC35,最不发达4国LDC4	17	---Having an outside diameter exceeding 114.3mm but less than 215.9mm
5324	7304.1130	---外径不超过114.3毫米	5	0	东盟ASEAN,智利CL,巴基斯坦PK,新西兰NZ,秘鲁PE,哥斯达黎加CR	0	最不发达35国LDC35,最不发达4国LDC4	17	---Having an outside diameter not exceeding 114.3mm
5325	7304.1190	---其他	5	0	东盟ASEAN,智利CL,巴基斯坦PK,新西兰NZ,秘鲁PE,哥斯达黎加CR	0	最不发达35国LDC35,最不发达4国LDC4	17	---Other
		--其他:							--Other:
5326	7304.1910	---外径大于等于215.9毫米，但不超过406.4毫米	5	0	东盟ASEAN,智利CL,巴基斯坦PK,新西兰NZ,秘鲁PE,哥斯达黎加CR	0	最不发达35国LDC35,最不发达4国LDC4	17	---Having an outside diameter of 215.9mm or more but not exceeding 406.4 mm
5327	7304.1920	---外径超过114.3毫米，但小于215.9毫米	5	0	东盟ASEAN,智利CL,巴基斯坦PK,新西兰NZ,秘鲁PE,哥斯达黎加CR	0	最不发达35国LDC35,最不发达4国LDC4	17	---Having an outside diameter exceeding 114.3mm but less than 215.9mm
5328	7304.1930	---外径不超过114.3毫米	5	0	东盟ASEAN,智利CL,巴基斯坦PK,新西兰NZ,秘鲁PE,哥斯达黎加CR	0	最不发达35国LDC35,最不发达4国LDC4	17	---Having an outside diameter not exceeding 114.3mm
5329	7304.1990	---其他	5	0	东盟ASEAN,智利CL,巴基斯坦PK,新西兰NZ,秘鲁PE,哥斯达黎加CR	0	最不发达35国LDC35,最不发达4国LDC4	17	---Other
		-钻探石油及天然气用的套管、导管及钻管:							-Casing, tubing and drill pipe, of a kind used in drilling for oil or gas:
		--不锈钢制钻管:							--Drill pipe, of stainless steel:

序号 No.	税则号列 Tariff Line	货品名称	最惠国税率 MFN(%)	协定税率 Agreement(%)		特惠税率 S.P.(%)		普通税率 Gen.(%)	Article Description
5330	7304.2210	---外径不超过 168.3 毫米	4	0 0.4	东盟ASEAN,巴基斯坦PK,新西兰NZ,秘鲁PE,哥斯达黎加CR 智利CL	0	最不发达 35 国 LDC35,最不发达 4 国 LDC4	17	---Having an outside diameter not exceeding 168.3mm
5331	7304.2290	---其他	4	0 0.4	东盟ASEAN,巴基斯坦PK,新西兰NZ,秘鲁PE,哥斯达黎加CR 智利CL	0	最不发达 35 国 LDC35,最不发达 4 国 LDC4	17	---Other
		--其他钻管:							--Other orill pipe:
5332	7304.2310	---外径不超过 168.3 毫米	4	0 0.4	东盟ASEAN,巴基斯坦PK,新西兰NZ,秘鲁PE,哥斯达黎加CR 智利CL	0	最不发达 35 国 LDC35,最不发达 4 国 LDC4	17	---Having an outside diameter not exceeding 168.3mm
5333	7304.2390	---其他	4	0 0.4	东盟ASEAN,巴基斯坦PK,新西兰NZ,秘鲁PE,哥斯达黎加CR 智利CL	0	最不发达 35 国 LDC35,最不发达 4 国 LDC4	17	---Other
5334	7304.2400	--其他不锈钢管	4	0 2	东盟ASEAN,智利CL,巴基斯坦PK,新西兰NZ,秘鲁PE,哥斯达黎加CR 亚太APTA	0	最不发达 35 国 LDC35,最不发达 4 国 LDC4	17	--Other pipe, of stainless steel
		--其他:							--Other:
5335	7304.2910	---屈服强度小于 552 兆帕的	4	0 2	东盟ASEAN,智利CL,巴基斯坦PK,新西兰NZ,秘鲁PE,哥斯达黎加CR 亚太APTA	0	最不发达 35 国 LDC35,最不发达 4 国 LDC4	17	---Of a yield strength less than 552MPa
5336	7304.2920	---屈服强度大于等于 552 兆帕，但小于 758 兆帕的	4	0 2	东盟ASEAN,智利CL,巴基斯坦PK,新西兰NZ,秘鲁PE,哥斯达黎加CR 亚太APTA	0	最不发达 35 国 LDC35,最不发达 4 国 LDC4	17	---Of a yield strength of 552MPa or more but less than 758MPa
5337	7304.2930	---屈服强度大于等于 758 兆帕的	4	0 2	东盟ASEAN,智利CL,巴基斯坦PK,新西兰NZ,秘鲁PE,哥斯达黎加CR 亚太APTA	0	最不发达 35 国 LDC35,最不发达 4 国 LDC4	17	---Of a yield strength of 758MPa or more
		-铁或非合金钢的其他圆形截面管:							-Other, of circular cross-section, of iron or non-alloysteel:
		--冷拔或冷轧的:							--Cold-drawn or cold-rolled (cold-reduced):

序号 No.	税则号列 Tariff Line	货品名称	最惠国税率 MFN(%)	协定税率 Agreement(%)		特惠税率 S.P.(%)		普通税率 Gen.(%)	Article Description
5338	7304.3110	---锅炉管	4	0 0.4	东盟ASEAN,巴基斯坦PK,新西兰NZ,秘鲁PE,哥斯达黎加CR 智利CL	0	最不发达35国LDC35,最不发达4国LDC4	17	---Boiler tubes and pipes
5339	7304.3120	---地质钻管、套管	8	0 0.8 5	东盟ASEAN,新西兰NZ,秘鲁PE,哥斯达黎加CR 智利CL 巴基斯坦PK	0	最不发达35国LDC35,最不发达4国LDC4	17	---Geological casing and drill pipes
5340	7304.3190	---其他	4	0 0.4	东盟ASEAN,巴基斯坦PK,新西兰NZ,秘鲁PE,哥斯达黎加CR 智利CL	0	最不发达35国LDC35,最不发达4国LDC4	17	---Other
		--其他:							--Other:
5341	7304.3910	---锅炉管	4	0	东盟ASEAN,智利CL,巴基斯坦PK,新西兰NZ,秘鲁PE,哥斯达黎加CR,香港HK	0	最不发达35国LDC35,最不发达4国LDC4	17	---Boiler tubes and pipes
5342	7304.3920	---地质钻管、套管	5	0	东盟ASEAN,智利CL,巴基斯坦PK,新西兰NZ,秘鲁PE,哥斯达黎加CR,香港HK	0	最不发达35国LDC35,最不发达4国LDC4	17	---Geological casing and drill pipes
5343	7304.3990	---其他	4	0	东盟ASEAN,智利CL,巴基斯坦PK,新西兰NZ,秘鲁PE,哥斯达黎加CR,香港HK	0	最不发达35国LDC35,最不发达4国LDC4	17	---Other
		-不锈钢的其他圆形截面管:							-Other, of circular cross-section, of stainless steel:
		--冷拔或冷轧的:							--Cold-drawn or cold-rolled (cold-reduced):
5344	7304.4110	---锅炉管	10	0 5	东盟ASEAN,智利CL,新加坡SG,新西兰NZ,秘鲁PE,哥斯达黎加CR 巴基斯坦PK	0	最不发达35国LDC35	17	---Boiler tubes and pipes
5345	7304.4190	---其他	10	0 5	东盟ASEAN,智利CL,新加坡SG,新西兰NZ,秘鲁PE,哥斯达黎加CR 巴基斯坦PK	0	最不发达35国LDC35	40	---Other
		--其他:							--Other:
5346	7304.4910	---锅炉管	10	0 5	东盟ASEAN,智利CL,新加坡SG,新西兰NZ,秘鲁PE,哥斯达黎加CR 巴基斯坦PK	0	最不发达35国LDC35	17	---Boiler tubes and pipes

序号 No.	税则号列 Tariff Line	货品名称	最惠国 税率 MFN(%)	协定税率 Agreement(%)		特惠税率 S.P.(%)		普通 税率 Gen.(%)	Article Description
5347	7304.4990	---其他	10	0 5	东盟ASEAN,智利CL,新加坡SG,新西兰NZ,秘鲁PE,哥斯达黎加CR 巴基斯坦PK	0	最不发达35国LDC35	40	---Other
		-其他合金钢的其他圆形截面管:							-Other, of circular cross-section, of other alloy steel:
		--冷拔或冷轧的:							--Cold-drawn or cold-rolled (cold-reduced):
5348	7304.5110	---锅炉管	4	0	东盟ASEAN,智利CL,巴基斯坦PK,新西兰NZ,秘鲁PE,哥斯达黎加CR	0	最不发达35国LDC35,最不发达4国LDC4	17	---Boiler tubes and pipes
5349	7304.5120	---地质钻管、套管	4	0	东盟ASEAN,智利CL,巴基斯坦PK,新西兰NZ,秘鲁PE,哥斯达黎加CR	0	最不发达35国LDC35,最不发达4国LDC4	17	---Geological casing and drill pipes
5350	7304.5190	---其他	4	0	东盟ASEAN,智利CL,巴基斯坦PK,新西兰NZ,秘鲁PE,哥斯达黎加CR	0	最不发达35国LDC35,最不发达4国LDC4	17	---Other
		--其他:							--Other:
5351	7304.5910	---锅炉管	4	0 0.4	东盟ASEAN,巴基斯坦PK,新西兰NZ,秘鲁PE,哥斯达黎加CR 智利CL	0	最不发达35国LDC35,最不发达4国LDC4	17	---Boiler tubes and pipes
5352	7304.5920	---地质钻管、套管	4	0 0.4	东盟ASEAN,巴基斯坦PK,新西兰NZ,秘鲁PE,哥斯达黎加CR 智利CL	0	最不发达35国LDC35,最不发达4国LDC4	17	---Geological casing and drill pipes
5353	7304.5990	---其他	4	0 0.4	东盟ASEAN,巴基斯坦PK,新西兰NZ,秘鲁PE,哥斯达黎加CR 智利CL	0	最不发达35国LDC35,最不发达4国LDC4	17	---Other
5354	7304.9000	-其他	4	0	东盟ASEAN,智利CL,巴基斯坦PK,新西兰NZ,秘鲁PE,哥斯达黎加CR	0	最不发达35国LDC35,最不发达4国LDC4	17	-Other

序号 No.	税则号列 Tariff Line	货品名称	最惠国税率 MFN(%)	协定税率 Agreement(%)		特惠税率 S.P.(%)		普通税率 Gen.(%)	Article Description
	73.05	**其他圆形截面钢铁管（例如，焊、铆及用类似方法接合的管），外径超过406.4毫米:**							**Other tubes and pipes (for example, welded, riveted or similarly closed), having circular cross-sections, the external diameter of which exceeds 406.4mm, of iron or steel:**
		-石油或天然气管道管:							-Line pipe of a kind used for oil or gas pipelines:
5355	7305.1100	--纵向埋弧焊接的	7	0 0.7 5	东盟ASEAN,新西兰NZ,秘鲁PE,哥斯达黎加CR 智利CL 巴基斯坦PK	0	最不发达35国LDC35,最不发达4国LDC4	17	--Longitudinally submerged arc welded
5356	7305.1200	--其他纵向焊接的	3	0	东盟ASEAN,智利CL,巴基斯坦PK,新西兰NZ,秘鲁PE,哥斯达黎加CR	0	最不发达35国LDC35,最不发达4国LDC4	17	--Other, longitudinally welded
5357	7305.1900	--其他	7	0 5	东盟ASEAN,智利CL,新西兰NZ,秘鲁PE,哥斯达黎加CR 巴基斯坦PK	0	最不发达35国LDC35,最不发达4国LDC4	17	--Other
5358	7305.2000	-钻探石油或天然气用套管	7	0 5	东盟ASEAN,智利CL,新西兰NZ,秘鲁PE,哥斯达黎加CR 巴基斯坦PK	0	最不发达35国LDC35,最不发达4国LDC4	17	-Casing of a kind used in drilling for oil or gas
		-其他焊接的:							-Other, welded:
5359	7305.3100	--纵向焊接的	6	0 0.6 5	东盟ASEAN,新西兰NZ,秘鲁PE,哥斯达黎加CR 智利CL 巴基斯坦PK	0	最不发达35国LDC35,最不发达4国LDC4	30	--Longitudinally welded
5360	7305.3900	--其他	6	0 0.6 5	东盟ASEAN,新西兰NZ,秘鲁PE,哥斯达黎加CR 智利CL 巴基斯坦PK	0	最不发达35国LDC35,最不发达4国LDC4	30	--Other
5361	7305.9000	-其他	6	0 5	东盟ASEAN,智利CL,新西兰NZ,秘鲁PE,哥斯达黎加CR 巴基斯坦PK	0	最不发达35国LDC35,最不发达4国LDC4	30	-Other

序号 No.	税则号列 Tariff Line	货品名称	最惠国税率 MFN(%)	协定税率 Agreement(%)		特惠税率 S.P.(%)		普通税率 Gen.(%)	Article Description
	73.06	**其他钢铁管及空心异型材（例如，辊缝、焊、铆及类似方法接合的）：**							**Other tubes, pipes and hollow profiles (for example, open seam or welded, riveted or similarly closed), of iron or steel:**
		-石油及天然气管道管：							-Line pipe of a kind used for oil or gas pipelines:
5362	7306.1100	--不锈钢焊缝管	7	0 5	东盟ASEAN,智利CL,新西兰NZ,秘鲁PE,哥斯达黎加CR 巴基斯坦PK	0	最不发达35国LDC35,最不发达4国LDC4	17	--Welded, of stainless steel
5363	7306.1900	--其他	7	0 5	东盟ASEAN,智利CL,新西兰NZ,秘鲁PE,哥斯达黎加CR 巴基斯坦PK	0	最不发达35国LDC35,最不发达4国LDC4	17	--Welded, other
		-钻探石油及天然气用的套管及导管：							-Casing and tubing of a kind used in drilling for oil or gas:
5364	7306.2100	--不锈钢焊缝管	3	0	东盟ASEAN,智利CL,巴基斯坦PK,新西兰NZ,秘鲁PE,哥斯达黎加CR	0	最不发达35国LDC35,最不发达4国LDC4	17	--Welded, of stainless steel
5365	7306.2900	--其他	3	0	东盟ASEAN,智利CL,巴基斯坦PK,新西兰NZ,秘鲁PE,哥斯达黎加CR	0	最不发达35国LDC35,最不发达4国LDC4	17	--Welded, other
		-铁或非合金钢的其他圆形截面焊缝管：							-Other, welded, of circular cross-section, of iron or non-alloy steel:
		---外径不超过10毫米的：							---Having an outside diameter not exceeding 10mm:
5366	7306.3011	----壁厚在0.7毫米及以下	3	0	东盟ASEAN,智利CL,巴基斯坦PK,新西兰NZ,秘鲁PE,哥斯达黎加CR	0	最不发达35国LDC35,最不发达4国LDC4	30	----Of a wall thickness of 0.7mm or less
5367	7306.3019	----其他	3	0	东盟ASEAN,智利CL,巴基斯坦PK,新西兰NZ,秘鲁PE,哥斯达黎加CR	0	最不发达35国LDC35,最不发达4国LDC4	30	----Other

序号 No.	税则号列 Tariff Line	货品名称	最惠国税率 MFN(%)	协定税率 Agreement(%)		特惠税率 S.P.(%)		普通税率 Gen.(%)	Article Description
5368	7306.3090	---其他	3	0	东盟ASEAN,智利CL,巴基斯坦PK,新西兰NZ,秘鲁PE,哥斯达黎加CR	0	最不发达35国LDC35,最不发达4国LDC4	30	---Other
5369	7306.4000	-不锈钢的其他圆形截面焊缝管	6	0 5	东盟ASEAN,智利CL,新西兰NZ,秘鲁PE,哥斯达黎加CR 巴基斯坦PK	0	最不发达35国LDC35,最不发达4国LDC4	30	-Other, welded, of circular cross-section, of stainless steel
5370	7306.5000	-其他合金钢的圆形截面焊缝管	3	0	东盟ASEAN,智利CL,巴基斯坦PK,新西兰NZ,秘鲁PE,哥斯达黎加CR	0	最不发达35国LDC35,最不发达4国LDC4	30	-Other, welded, of circular cross-section, of other alloy steel
		-非圆形截面的其他焊缝管:							-Other, welded, of non-circular cross-section:
5371	7306.6100	--矩形或正方形截面	3	0	东盟ASEAN,智利CL,巴基斯坦PK,新西兰NZ,秘鲁PE,哥斯达黎加CR	0	最不发达35国LDC35,最不发达4国LDC4	30	--Of square or rectangular cross-section
5372	7306.6900	--其他非圆形截面	3	0	东盟ASEAN,智利CL,巴基斯坦PK,新西兰NZ,秘鲁PE,哥斯达黎加CR	0	最不发达35国LDC35,最不发达4国LDC4	30	--Of other non-circular cross-section
5373	7306.9000	-其他	6	0 0.6 5	东盟ASEAN,新西兰NZ,秘鲁PE,哥斯达黎加CR 智利CL 巴基斯坦PK	0	最不发达35国LDC35,最不发达4国LDC4	30	-Other
	73.07	**钢铁管子附件（例如，接头、肘管、管套）：**							**Tube or pipe fittings (for example, couplings, elbows, sleeves), of iron or steel:**
		-铸件:							-Cast fittings:
5374	7307.1100	--无可锻性铸铁制	5	0	东盟ASEAN,智利CL,巴基斯坦PK,新西兰NZ,秘鲁PE,哥斯达黎加CR	0	最不发达35国LDC35,最不发达4国LDC4	20	--Of non-malleable cast iron
5375	7307.1900	--其他	8	0 0.8 5	东盟ASEAN,新西兰NZ,秘鲁PE,哥斯达黎加CR 智利CL 巴基斯坦PK	0	最不发达35国LDC35,最不发达4国LDC4	20	--Other

序号 No.	税则号列 Tariff Line	货品名称	最惠国税率 MFN(%)	协定税率 Agreement(%)		特惠税率 S.P.(%)		普通税率 Gen.(%)	Article Description
		-其他，不锈钢制:							-Other, of stainless steel:
5376	7307.2100	--法兰	8.4	0 5 6.7	东盟ASEAN,智利CL,新西兰NZ,秘鲁PE,哥斯达黎加CR 巴基斯坦PK 亚太APTA	0	最不发达35国LDC35,最不发达4国LDC4	20	--Flanges
5377	7307.2200	--螺纹肘管、弯管及管套	8.4	0 5	东盟ASEAN,智利CL,新西兰NZ,秘鲁PE,哥斯达黎加CR,香港HK 巴基斯坦PK	0	最不发达35国LDC35,最不发达4国LDC4	20	--Threaded elbows, bends and sleeves
5378	7307.2300	--对焊件	8.4	0 5	东盟ASEAN,智利CL,新西兰NZ,秘鲁PE,哥斯达黎加CR 巴基斯坦PK	0	最不发达35国LDC35,最不发达4国LDC4	20	--Butt welding fittings
5379	7307.2900	--其他	8.4	0 0.8 5	东盟ASEAN,新西兰NZ,秘鲁PE,哥斯达黎加CR,香港HK 智利CL 巴基斯坦PK	0	最不发达35国LDC35,最不发达4国LDC4	20	--Other
		-其他:							-Other:
5380	7307.9100	--法兰	7	0 5	东盟ASEAN,智利CL,新西兰NZ,秘鲁PE,哥斯达黎加CR 巴基斯坦PK	0	最不发达35国LDC35,最不发达4国LDC4	20	--Flanges
5381	7307.9200	--螺纹肘管、弯管及管套	4	0	东盟ASEAN,智利CL,巴基斯坦PK,新西兰NZ,秘鲁PE,哥斯达黎加CR	0	最不发达35国LDC35,最不发达4国LDC4	20	--Threaded elbows, bends and sleeves
5382	7307.9300	--对焊件	7	0 5	东盟ASEAN,智利CL,新西兰NZ,秘鲁PE,哥斯达黎加CR 巴基斯坦PK	0	最不发达35国LDC35,最不发达4国LDC4	20	--Butt welding fittings
5383	7307.9900	--其他	4	0 0.4	东盟ASEAN,巴基斯坦PK,新西兰NZ,秘鲁PE,哥斯达黎加CR 智利CL	0	最不发达35国LDC35,最不发达4国LDC4	20	--Other

序号 No.	税则号列 Tariff Line	货品名称	最惠国税率 MFN(%)	协定税率 Agreement(%)		特惠税率 S.P.(%)		普通税率 Gen.(%)	Article Description
	73.08	**钢铁结构体（税号94.06的活动房屋除外）及其部件（例如，桥梁及桥梁体段、闸门、塔楼、格构杆、屋顶、屋顶框架、门窗及其框架、门槛、百叶窗、栏杆、支柱及立柱）；上述结构体用的已加工钢铁板、杆、角材、型材、异型材、管子及类似品:**							**Structures (excluding prefabricated buildings of heading No.94.06) and parts of structures (for example, bridges and bridge-sections, lockgates, towers, lattice masts, roofs, roofing frameworks, doors and windows and their frames and thresholds for doors, shutters, balustrades, pillars and columns), of iron or steel; plates, rods, angles, shapes, sections, tubes and the like, prepared for use in structures, of iron or steel:**
5384	7308.1000	-桥梁及桥梁体段	8	0 0.8	东盟ASEAN,巴基斯坦PK,新西兰NZ,秘鲁PE,哥斯达黎加CR 智利CL	0	最不发达35国LDC35,最不发达4国LDC4	30	-Bridges and bridge-sections
5385	7308.2000	-塔楼及格构杆	8.4	0 0.8	东盟ASEAN,巴基斯坦PK,新西兰NZ,秘鲁PE,哥斯达黎加CR 智利CL	0	最不发达35国LDC35,最不发达4国LDC4	30	-Towers and lattice masts
5386	7308.3000	-门窗及其框架、门槛	10	0	东盟ASEAN,智利CL,巴基斯坦PK,新加坡SG,新西兰NZ,秘鲁PE,哥斯达黎加CR,香港HK,澳门MO	0	最不发达35国LDC35,最不发达4国LDC4	50	-Doors, windows and their frames and thresholds for doors
5387	7308.4000	-脚手架、模板或坑道支撑用的支柱及类似设备	8.4	0 0.8	东盟ASEAN,巴基斯坦PK,新西兰NZ,秘鲁PE,哥斯达黎加CR 智利CL	0	最不发达35国LDC35,最不发达4国LDC4	30	-Equipment for scaffolding, shuttering, propping or pit-propping
5388	7308.9000	-其他	4	0 0.4	东盟ASEAN,巴基斯坦PK,新西兰NZ,秘鲁PE,哥斯达黎加CR,香港HK 智利CL	0	最不发达35国LDC35,最不发达4国LDC4	30	-Other

序号 No.	税则号列 Tariff Line	货品名称	最惠国税率 MFN(%)	协定税率 Agreement(%)		特惠税率 S.P.(%)		普通税率 Gen.(%)	Article Description
	73.09	**盛装物料用的钢铁囤、柜、罐、桶及类似容器（装压缩气体或液化气体的除外），容积超过300升，不论是否衬里或隔热，但无机械或热力装置:**							**Reservoirs, tanks, vats and similar containers for any material (other than compressed or liquefied gas), of iron or steel, of a capacity exceeding 300L, whether or not lined or heat-in-sulated, but not fitted with mechanical or thermal equipment:**
5389	7309.0000	盛装物料用的钢铁囤、柜、罐、桶及类似容器（装压缩气体或液化气体的除外），容积超过300升，不论是否衬里或隔热，但无机械或热力装置	10.5	0 1.1 2.1 5 5.3	东盟ASEAN,新加坡SG,新西兰NZ 智利CL 哥斯达黎加CR 巴基斯坦PK 秘鲁PE	0	最不发达35国LDC35,最不发达4国LDC4	35	Reservoirs, tanks, vats and similar containers for any material (other than compressed or liquefied gas), of iron or steel, of a capacity exceeding 300L, whether or not lined or heat-insulated, but not fitted with mechanical or thermal equipment
	73.10	**盛装物料用的钢铁柜、桶、罐、听、盒及类似容器（装压缩气体或液化气体的除外），容积不超过300升，不论是否衬里或隔热，但无机械或热力装置:**							**Tanks, casks, drums, cans, boxes and similar containers, for any material (other than compressed or liquefied gas), of iron or steel, of a capacity not exceeding 300L, whether or not lined or heat-insulated, but not fitted with mechanical or thermal equipment:**
5390	7310.1000	-容积在50升及以上	10.5	0 1.1 2.1 5 5.3	东盟ASEAN,新加坡SG,新西兰NZ,香港HK 智利CL 哥斯达黎加CR 巴基斯坦PK 秘鲁PE	0	最不发达35国LDC35,最不发达4国LDC4	40	-Of a capacity of 50L or more
		-容积在50升以下:							-Of a capacity of less than 50L:
		--焊边或卷边接合的罐:							--Cans which are to be closed by soldering or crimping:
5391	7310.2110	---易拉罐及罐体	17.5	0 1.8 3.5 8.8 14	东盟ASEAN,新加坡SG,新西兰NZ,香港HK 智利CL 哥斯达黎加CR 秘鲁PE 巴基斯坦PK	0	最不发达35国LDC35	70	---Steel tear tab ends and bodies thereof
5392	7310.2190	---其他	17.5	0 1.8 3.5 8.8 14	东盟ASEAN,新加坡SG,新西兰NZ,香港HK 智利CL 哥斯达黎加CR 秘鲁PE 巴基斯坦PK	0	最不发达35国LDC35	70	---Other

序号 No.	税则号列 Tariff Line	货品名称	最惠国税率 MFN(%)	协定税率 Agreement(%)	特惠税率 S.P.(%)	普通税率 Gen.(%)	Article Description
		--其他:					--Other:
5393	7310.2910	---易拉罐及罐体	17.5	0 东盟ASEAN,新加坡SG,新西兰NZ,香港HK 1.8 智利CL 3.5 哥斯达黎加CR 8.8 秘鲁PE 14 巴基斯坦PK	0 最不发达35国LDC35,最不发达4国LDC4	70	---Steel tear tab ends and bodies thereof
5394	7310.2990	---其他	17.5	0 东盟ASEAN,新加坡SG,新西兰NZ,香港HK 1.8 智利CL 3.5 哥斯达黎加CR 8.8 秘鲁PE 14 巴基斯坦PK	0 最不发达35国LDC35,最不发达4国LDC4	70	---Other
	73.11	**装压缩气体或液化气体用的钢铁容器:**					**Containers for compressed orliquefied gas, of iron or steel:**
5395	7311.0010	---零售包装用	17.5	0 东盟ASEAN,新加坡SG,新西兰NZ,香港HK 1.8 智利CL 3.5 哥斯达黎加CR 8.8 秘鲁PE 14 巴基斯坦PK	0 最不发达35国LDC35	70	---For retail packing
5396	7311.0090	---其他	8	0 东盟ASEAN,新西兰NZ,秘鲁PE,哥斯达黎加CR,香港HK 0.8 智利CL 5 巴基斯坦PK	0 最不发达35国LDC35	17	---Other
	73.12	**非绝缘的钢铁绞股线、绳、缆、编带、吊索及类似品:**					**Stranded wire, ropes, cables, plaited bands, slings and the like, of iron or steel, not electrically insulated:**
5397	7312.1000	-绞股线、绳、缆	4	0 东盟ASEAN,巴基斯坦PK,新西兰NZ,秘鲁PE,哥斯达黎加CR 0.4 智利CL	0 最不发达35国LDC35	20	-Stranded wire, ropes and cables
5398	7312.9000	-其他	4	0 东盟ASEAN,智利CL,巴基斯坦PK,新西兰NZ,秘鲁PE,哥斯达黎加CR	0 最不发达35国LDC35,最不发达4国LDC4	20	-Other
	73.13	**带刺钢铁丝;围篱用的钢铁绞带或单股扁丝(不论是否带刺)及松绞的双股丝:**					**Barbed wire of iron or steel; twisted hoop or single flat wire, barbed or not, and loosely twisted double wire, of a kind used for fencing, of iron or steel:**
5399	7313.0000	带刺钢铁丝;围篱用的钢铁绞带或单股扁丝(不论是否带刺)及松绞的双股丝	7	0 东盟ASEAN,新西兰NZ,秘鲁PE,哥斯达黎加CR 0.7 智利CL 5 巴基斯坦PK 6.3 亚太APTA	0 最不发达35国LDC35,最不发达4国LDC4	70	Barbed wire of iron or steel;twisted hoop or single flat wire, barbed or not, and loosely twisted double wire, of a kind used for fencing, of iron or steel

序号 No.	税则号列 Tariff Line	货品名称	最惠国税率 MFN(%)	协定税率 Agreement(%)		特惠税率 S.P.(%)		普通税率 Gen.(%)	Article Description
	73.14	**钢铁丝制的布(包括环形带)、网、篱、格栅;网眼钢铁板:**							**Cloth (including endless bands), grill, netting and fencing, of iron or steel wire;expanded metal of iron or steel:**
		-机织品:							-Woven cloth:
5400	7314.1200	--不锈钢制的机器用环形带	12	0 2.4 6	东盟ASEAN,智利CL,新加坡SG,新西兰NZ,秘鲁PE 哥斯达黎加CR 巴基斯坦PK	0	最不发达35国LDC35,最不发达4国LDC4	20	--Endless bands for machinery, of stainless steel
5401	7314.1400	--不锈钢制的其他机织品	12	0 2.4 6	东盟ASEAN,智利CL,新加坡SG,新西兰NZ,秘鲁PE 哥斯达黎加CR 巴基斯坦PK	0	最不发达35国LDC35,最不发达4国LDC4	20	--Other woven cloth, of stainless steel
5402	7314.1900	--其他	7	0 3.5	东盟ASEAN,智利CL,新西兰NZ,秘鲁PE,哥斯达黎加CR 巴基斯坦PK	0	最不发达35国LDC35,最不发达4国LDC4	20	--Other
5403	7314.2000	-交点焊接的网、篱及格栅,其丝的最大截面尺寸在3毫米及以上,网眼尺寸在100平方厘米及以上	7	0 5	东盟ASEAN,智利CL,新西兰NZ,秘鲁PE,哥斯达黎加CR,香港HK 巴基斯坦PK	0	最不发达35国LDC35,最不发达4国LDC4	70	-Grill, netting and fencing, welded at the intersection, of wire with a maximum cross-sectional dimension of 3mm or more and having a mesh size of $100cm^2$ or more
		-其他交点焊接的网、篱及格栅:							-Other grill, netting and fencing, welded at the intersection:
5404	7314.3100	--镀或涂锌的	7	0 5	东盟ASEAN,智利CL,新西兰NZ,秘鲁PE,哥斯达黎加CR,香港HK 巴基斯坦PK	0	最不发达35国LDC35,最不发达4国LDC4	70	--Plated or coated with zinc
5405	7314.3900	--其他	7	0 5	东盟ASEAN,智利CL,新西兰NZ,秘鲁PE,哥斯达黎加CR,香港HK 巴基斯坦PK	0	最不发达35国LDC35,最不发达4国LDC4	70	--Other
		-其他网、篱及格栅:							-Other grill, netting and fencing:
5406	7314.4100	--镀或涂锌的	8	0 0.8 5 6	东盟ASEAN,新西兰NZ,秘鲁PE,哥斯达黎加CR 智利CL 巴基斯坦PK 亚太APTA	0	最不发达35国LDC35,最不发达4国LDC4	20	--Plated or coated with zinc

序号 No.	税则号列 Tariff Line	货品名称	最惠国税率 MFN(%)	协定税率 Agreement(%)		特惠税率 S.P.(%)		普通税率 Gen.(%)	Article Description
5407	7314.4200	--涂塑的	8	0 5	东盟ASEAN,智利CL,新西兰NZ,秘鲁PE,哥斯达黎加CR 巴基斯坦PK	0	最不发达35国LDC35,最不发达4国LDC4	20	--Coated whith plastics
5408	7314.4900	--其他	8	0 0.8 5	东盟ASEAN,新西兰NZ,秘鲁PE,哥斯达黎加CR 智利CL 巴基斯坦PK	0	最不发达35国LDC35,最不发达4国LDC4	20	--Other
5409	7314.5000	-网眼钢铁板	8	0 5	东盟ASEAN,智利CL,新西兰NZ,秘鲁PE,哥斯达黎加CR,香港HK 巴基斯坦PK	0	最不发达35国LDC35,最不发达4国LDC4	70	-Expanded metal
	73.15	**钢铁链及其零件:**							**Chain and parts thereof, of iron or steel:**
		-铰接链及其零件:							-Articulated link chain and parts thereof:
		--滚子链:							--Roller chain:
5410	7315.1110	---自行车用	12	0 2.4 6	东盟ASEAN,智利CL,新加坡SG,新西兰NZ,秘鲁PE,香港HK 哥斯达黎加CR 巴基斯坦PK	0	最不发达35国LDC35	80	---For bicycles
5411	7315.1120	---摩托车用	12	0 2.4 6	东盟ASEAN,智利CL,新加坡SG,新西兰NZ,秘鲁PE,香港HK 哥斯达黎加CR 巴基斯坦PK	0	最不发达35国LDC35	80	---For motorcycles
5412	7315.1190	---其他	12	0 2.4 6	东盟ASEAN,智利CL,新加坡SG,新西兰NZ,秘鲁PE,香港HK 哥斯达黎加CR 巴基斯坦PK	0	最不发达35国LDC35	80	---Other
5413	7315.1200	--其他链	12	0 2.4 6	东盟ASEAN,智利CL,新加坡SG,新西兰NZ,秘鲁PE 哥斯达黎加CR 巴基斯坦PK	0	最不发达35国LDC35	80	--Other chain
5414	7315.1900	--零件	12	0 2.4 6	东盟ASEAN,智利CL,新加坡SG,新西兰NZ,秘鲁PE 哥斯达黎加CR 巴基斯坦PK	0	最不发达35国LDC35	80	--Parts
5415	7315.2000	-防滑链	12	0 2.4 6	东盟ASEAN,智利CL,新加坡SG,新西兰NZ,秘鲁PE 哥斯达黎加CR 巴基斯坦PK	0	最不发达35国LDC35	80	-Skid chain
		-其他链:							-Other chain:

序号 No.	税则号列 Tariff Line	货品名称	最惠国税率 MFN(%)	协定税率 Agreement(%)		特惠税率 S.P.(%)		普通税率 Gen.(%)	Article Description
5416	7315.8100	--日字环节链	12	0 2.4 6	东盟ASEAN,智利CL,新加坡SG,新西兰NZ,秘鲁PE 哥斯达黎加CR 巴基斯坦PK	0	最不发达35国LDC35	80	--Stud-link
5417	7315.8200	--其他焊接链	12	0 2.4 6	东盟ASEAN,智利CL,新加坡SG,新西兰NZ,秘鲁PE 哥斯达黎加CR 巴基斯坦PK	0	最不发达35国LDC35,最不发达4国LDC4	80	--Other, welded link
5418	7315.8900	--其他	12	0 1.2 2.4 6	东盟ASEAN,新加坡SG,新西兰NZ 智利CL 哥斯达黎加CR 巴基斯坦PK,秘鲁PE	0	最不发达35国LDC35	80	--Other
5419	7315.9000	-其他零件	10	0 5	东盟ASEAN,智利CL,新西兰NZ,秘鲁PE,哥斯达黎加CR 巴基斯坦PK	0	最不发达35国LDC35	80	-Other parts
	73.16	**钢铁锚、多爪锚及其零件:**							**Anchors, grapnels and parts thereof, of iron or steel:**
5420	7316.0000	钢铁锚、多爪锚及其零件	10	0 5	东盟ASEAN,智利CL,新西兰NZ,秘鲁PE,哥斯达黎加CR 巴基斯坦PK	0	最不发达35国LDC35	40	Anchors, grapnels and parts thereof, of iron or steel
	73.17	**钢铁制的钉、平头钉、图钉、波纹钉、U形钉(税号83.05的货品除外)及类似品,不论钉头是否用其他材料制成,但不包括铜头钉:**							**Nails, tacks, drawing pins, corrugated nails, staples (other than those of heading No.83.05) and similar articles, of iron or steel, whether or not with heads of other material, but excluding such articles with heads of copper:**
5421	7317.0000	钢铁制的钉、平头钉、图钉、波纹钉、U形钉(税号83.05的货品除外)及类似品,不论钉头是否用其他材料制成,但不包括铜头钉	10	0 1 5	东盟ASEAN,新西兰NZ,哥斯达黎加CR 智利CL 巴基斯坦PK,秘鲁PE	0	最不发达35国LDC35	80	Nails, tacks, drawing pins, corrugated nails, staples (other than those of heading No.83.05) and similar articles, of iron or steel, whether or not with heads of other material, but excluding such articles with heads of copper
	73.18	**钢铁制的螺钉、螺栓、螺母、方头螺钉、钩头螺钉、铆钉、销、开尾销、垫圈(包括弹簧垫圈)及类似品:**							**Screws, bolts, nuts, coach screws, screw hooks, rivets, cotters, cotterpins, washers (including spring washers) and similar articles, of iron of steel:**
		-螺纹制品:							-Threaded articles:

序号 No.	税则号列 Tariff Line	货品名称	最惠国税率 MFN(%)	协定税率 Agreement(%)		特惠税率 S.P.(%)		普通税率 Gen.(%)	Article Description
5422	7318.1100	--方头螺钉	10	0 1 5	东盟ASEAN,新西兰NZ,哥斯达黎加CR 智利CL 巴基斯坦PK,秘鲁PE	0	最不发达35国LDC35	80	--Coach screws
5423	7318.1200	--其他木螺钉	10	0 1 5	东盟ASEAN,新西兰NZ,哥斯达黎加CR 智利CL 巴基斯坦PK,秘鲁PE	0	最不发达35国LDC35	80	--Other wood screws
5424	7318.1300	--钩头螺钉及环头螺钉	10	0 5	东盟ASEAN,智利CL,新西兰NZ,秘鲁PE,哥斯达黎加CR 巴基斯坦PK	0	最不发达35国LDC35	80	--Screw hooks and screw rings
5425	7318.1400	--自攻螺钉	10	0 1 5	东盟ASEAN,新加坡SG,新西兰NZ,哥斯达黎加CR 智利CL 巴基斯坦PK,秘鲁PE	0	最不发达35国LDC35	80	--Self-tapping screws
		--其他螺钉及螺栓,不论是否带有螺母或垫圈:							--Other screws and bolts, whether or not with their nuts or washers:
5426	7318.1510	---抗拉强度在800兆帕及以上的	8	0 0.8 4	东盟ASEAN,巴基斯坦PK,新西兰NZ,秘鲁PE,哥斯达黎加CR,香港HK 智利CL 亚太APTA	0	最不发达35国LDC35,最不发达4国LDC4	80	---Of tensile strength of 800Mpa or more
5427	7318.1590	---其他	8	0 0.8 4	东盟ASEAN,巴基斯坦PK,新西兰NZ,秘鲁PE,哥斯达黎加CR,香港HK 智利CL 亚太APTA	0	最不发达35国LDC35,最不发达4国LDC4	80	---Other
5428	7318.1600	--螺母	8	0 0.8 5	东盟ASEAN,新西兰NZ,秘鲁PE,哥斯达黎加CR 智利CL 巴基斯坦PK	0	最不发达35国LDC35,最不发达4国LDC4	80	--Nuts
5429	7318.1900	--其他	5	0	东盟ASEAN,智利CL,巴基斯坦PK,新西兰NZ,秘鲁PE,哥斯达黎加CR	0	最不发达35国LDC35,最不发达4国LDC4	80	--Other
		-无螺纹制品:							-Non-threaded articles:
5430	7318.2100	--弹簧垫圈及其他防松垫圈	10	0 5	东盟ASEAN,智利CL,新加坡SG,新西兰NZ,秘鲁PE,哥斯达黎加CR,香港HK 巴基斯坦PK	0	最不发达35国LDC35,最不发达4国LDC4	80	--Spring washers and other lock washers
5431	7318.2200	--其他垫圈	10	0 5	东盟ASEAN,智利CL,新加坡SG,新西兰NZ,哥斯达黎加CR 巴基斯坦PK,秘鲁PE	0	最不发达35国LDC35,最不发达4国LDC4	80	--Other washers

序号 No.	税则号列 Tariff Line	货品名称	最惠国税率 MFN(%)	协定税率 Agreement(%)		特惠税率 S.P.(%)		普通税率 Gen.(%)	Article Description
5432	7318.2300	--铆钉	10	0 5	东盟ASEAN,智利CL,新加坡SG,新西兰NZ,秘鲁PE,哥斯达黎加CR,香港HK 巴基斯坦PK	0	最不发达35国LDC35,最不发达4国LDC4	80	--Rivets
5433	7318.2400	--销及开尾销	10	0 5	东盟ASEAN,智利CL,新加坡SG,新西兰NZ,秘鲁PE,哥斯达黎加CR 巴基斯坦PK	0	最不发达35国LDC35,最不发达4国LDC4	80	--Cotters and cotter-pins
5434	7318.2900	--其他	10	0 1 5	东盟ASEAN,新加坡SG,新西兰NZ,秘鲁PE,哥斯达黎加CR 智利CL 巴基斯坦PK	0	最不发达35国LDC35,最不发达4国LDC4	80	--Other
	73.19	**钢铁制的手工缝针、编织针、引针、钩针、刺绣穿孔锥及类似制品;其他税号未列名的钢铁制安全别针及其他别针:**							**Sewing needles, knitting needles, bodkins, crochet hooks, embroidery stilettos and similar articles, for use in the hand, of iron or steel; safety pins and other pins of iron or steel, not elsewhere specified or included:**
		-安全别针及其他别针:							-Safety pins and other pins:
5435	7319.4010	---安全别针	10	0 5	东盟ASEAN,智利CL,新西兰NZ,秘鲁PE,哥斯达黎加CR,澳门MO 巴基斯坦PK	0	最不发达35国LDC35,最不发达4国LDC4	90	---Safety pins
5436	7319.4090	---其他别针	10	0 5	东盟ASEAN,智利CL,新西兰NZ,秘鲁PE,哥斯达黎加CR 巴基斯坦PK	0	最不发达35国LDC35	90	---Other pins
5437	7319.9000	-其他	10	0 5	东盟ASEAN,智利CL,新西兰NZ,哥斯达黎加CR 巴基斯坦PK,秘鲁PE	0	最不发达35国LDC35,最不发达4国LDC4	80	-Other
	73.20	**钢铁制弹簧及弹簧片:**							**Springs and leaves for springs, of iron or steel:**
		-片簧及簧片:							-Leaf-springs and leaves thereof:
5438	7320.1010	---铁道车辆用	6	0 5	东盟ASEAN,智利CL,新西兰NZ,秘鲁PE,哥斯达黎加CR 巴基斯坦PK	0	最不发达35国LDC35,最不发达4国LDC4	14	---For railway locomotives and rollingstock

序号 No.	税则号列 Tariff Line	货品名称	最惠国税率 MFN(%)	协定税率 Agreement(%)		特惠税率 S.P.(%)		普通税率 Gen.(%)	Article Description
5439	7320.1020	---汽车用	10	0 5	东盟ASEAN,智利CL,新西兰NZ,秘鲁PE,哥斯达黎加CR 巴基斯坦PK	0	最不发达35国LDC35,最不发达4国LDC4	14	---For motor vehicles
5440	7320.1090	---其他	10	0 5	东盟ASEAN,智利CL,新加坡SG,新西兰NZ,秘鲁PE,哥斯达黎加CR 巴基斯坦PK	0	最不发达35国LDC35,最不发达4国LDC4	50	---Other
		-螺旋弹簧:							-Helical springs:
5441	7320.2010	---铁道车辆用	6	0 0.6 5	东盟ASEAN,新西兰NZ,秘鲁PE,哥斯达黎加CR 智利CL 巴基斯坦PK	0	最不发达35国LDC35,最不发达4国LDC4	14	---For railway locomotives and rollingstock
5442	7320.2090	---其他	10	0 1 5 8.5	东盟ASEAN,新加坡SG,新西兰NZ,秘鲁PE,哥斯达黎加CR 智利CL 巴基斯坦PK 亚太APTA	0	最不发达35国LDC35,最不发达4国LDC4	50	---Other
		-其他:							-Other:
5443	7320.9010	---铁道车辆用	6	0 5	东盟ASEAN,智利CL,新西兰NZ,秘鲁PE,哥斯达黎加CR 巴基斯坦PK	0	最不发达35国LDC35,最不发达4国LDC4	14	---For railway locomotives and rolling-stock
5444	7320.9090	---其他	12	0 2.4 6	东盟ASEAN,智利CL,新加坡SG,新西兰NZ,秘鲁PE 哥斯达黎加CR 巴基斯坦PK	0	最不发达35国LDC35,最不发达4国LDC4	50	---Other
	73.21	**非电热的钢铁制家用炉、灶（包括附有集中供暖用的热水锅的炉）、烤肉架、烤炉、煤气灶、加热板和类似非电热的家用器具及其零件:**							**Stoves, ranges, grates, cookers (including those with subsidiary boilers for central heating), barbecues, braziers, gas-rings, plate warmers and similar non-electric domestic appliances, and parts thereof, of iron or steel:**
		-炊事器具及加热板:							-Cooking appliances and plate warmers:
5445	7321.1100	--使用气体燃料或可使用气体燃料及其他燃料的	15	0 1.5 3 7.5 12	东盟ASEAN,新加坡SG,新西兰NZ 智利CL 哥斯达黎加CR 秘鲁PE 巴基斯坦PK	0	最不发达35国LDC35	80	--For gas fuel or for both gas and other fuels

序号 No.	税则号列 Tariff Line	货品名称	最惠国税率 MFN(%)	协定税率 Agreement(%)		特惠税率 S.P.(%)		普通税率 Gen.(%)	Article Description
		--使用液体燃料的:							--For liquid fuel:
5446	7321.1210	---煤油炉	21	0 4.2 10.5	东盟ASEAN,智利CL,新加坡SG,新西兰NZ 哥斯达黎加CR 秘鲁PE	0	最不发达35国LDC35	80	---Kerosene cooking stoves
5447	7321.1290	---其他	21	0 4.2 10.5	东盟ASEAN,智利CL,新加坡SG,新西兰NZ 哥斯达黎加CR 秘鲁PE	0	最不发达35国LDC35	80	---Other
5448	7321.1900	--其他，包括使用固体燃料的	21	0 4.2 10.5	东盟ASEAN,智利CL,新加坡SG,新西兰NZ 哥斯达黎加CR 秘鲁PE	0	最不发达35国LDC35	80	--Other, including for solid fuel
		-其他器具:							-Other appliances:
5449	7321.8100	--使用气体燃料或可使用气体燃料及其他燃料的	23	0 4.6 11.5 13.8	东盟ASEAN,智利CL,新加坡SG,新西兰NZ 哥斯达黎加CR 巴基斯坦PK,秘鲁PE 亚太APTA	0	最不发达35国LDC35	80	--For gas fuel or for both gas and other fuels
5450	7321.8200	--使用液体燃料的	21	0 2.1 4.2 10.5	东盟ASEAN,新加坡SG,新西兰NZ 智利CL 哥斯达黎加CR 秘鲁PE	0	最不发达35国LDC35	80	--For liquid fuel
5451	7321.8900	--其他，包括使用固体燃料的	21	0 2.1 4.2 10.5	东盟ASEAN,新加坡SG,新西兰NZ 智利CL 哥斯达黎加CR 秘鲁PE	0	最不发达35国LDC35	80	--Other, including for solid fuel
5452	7321.9000	-零件	12	0 1.2 2.4 5 6 9.6	东盟ASEAN,新加坡SG,新西兰NZ 智利CL 哥斯达黎加CR 巴基斯坦PK 秘鲁PE 亚太APTA	0	最不发达35国LDC35,最不发达4国LDC4	80	-Parts
	73.22	**非电热的钢铁制集中供暖用散热器及其零件;非电热的钢铁制空气加热器、暖气分布器（包括可分布新鲜空气或调节空气的）及其零件，装有电动风扇或鼓风机:**							**Radiators for central heating, not electrically heated, and parts thereof, of iron or steel; air heaters and hot air distributors (including distributors which can also distribute fresh or conditioned air), not electrically heated, incorporating a motor-dirven fan or blower, and parts thereof, of iron or steel:**
		-散热器及其零件:							-Radiators and parts thereof:
5453	7322.1100	--铸铁制	21	0 4.2 10.5	东盟ASEAN,智利CL,新加坡SG,新西兰NZ 哥斯达黎加CR 秘鲁PE	0	最不发达35国LDC35	80	--Of cast iron

序号 No.	税则号列 Tariff Line	货品名称	最惠国税率 MFN(%)	协定税率 Agreement(%)		特惠税率 S.P.(%)		普通税率 Gen.(%)	Article Description
5454	7322.1900	--其他	21	0 4.2 10.5	东盟ASEAN,智利CL,新加坡SG,新西兰NZ 哥斯达黎加CR 秘鲁PE	0	最不发达35国LDC35	80	--Other
5455	7322.9000	-其他	20	0 2 4 10	东盟ASEAN,新加坡SG,新西兰NZ 智利CL 哥斯达黎加CR 秘鲁PE	0	最不发达35国LDC35,最不发达4国LDC4	80	-Other
	73.23	**餐桌、厨房或其他家用钢铁器具及其零件;钢铁丝绒;钢铁制擦锅器、洗刷擦光用的块垫、手套及类似品:**							**Table, kitchen or other household articles and parts thereof, of iron or steel; iron or steel wool; pot scourers and scouring or polishing pads, gloves and the like, of iron or steel:**
5456	7323.1000	-钢铁丝绒;擦锅器及洗刷擦光用的块垫、手套及类似品	14	0 1.4 2.8 7 11.2	东盟ASEAN,新加坡SG,新西兰NZ 智利CL 哥斯达黎加CR 秘鲁PE 巴基斯坦PK	0	最不发达35国LDC35	80	-Iron or steel wool; pot scourers and scouring or polishing pads, gloves and the like
		-其他:							-Other:
5457	7323.9100	--铸铁制，未搪瓷	20 △10	0 4 10	东盟ASEAN,智利CL,新加坡SG,新西兰NZ 哥斯达黎加CR 秘鲁PE	0	最不发达35国LDC35	80	--Of cast iron, not enamelled
5458	7323.9200	--铸铁制，已搪瓷	20 △10	0 4 10	东盟ASEAN,智利CL,新加坡SG,新西兰NZ 哥斯达黎加CR 秘鲁PE	0	最不发达35国LDC35	100	--Of cast iron, enamelled
5459	7323.9300	--不锈钢制	12	0 1.2 2.4 5 8.4	东盟ASEAN,新加坡SG,新西兰NZ,秘鲁PE,香港HK,澳门MO 智利CL 哥斯达黎加CR 巴基斯坦PK 亚太APTA	0	最不发达35国LDC35,最不发达4国LDC4	80	--Of stainless steel
		--钢铁（铸铁除外）制，已搪瓷:							--Of iron (other than cast iron) or steel, enamelled:
5460	7323.9410	---面盆	20 △10	0 2 4 10	东盟ASEAN,新加坡SG,新西兰NZ 智利CL 哥斯达黎加CR 秘鲁PE	0	最不发达35国LDC35	100	---Basin
5461	7323.9420	---烧锅	20 △10	0 2 4 10	东盟ASEAN,新加坡SG,新西兰NZ 智利CL 哥斯达黎加CR 秘鲁PE	0	最不发达35国LDC35	100	---Casserole

序号 No.	税则号列 Tariff Line	货品名称	最惠国税率 MFN(%)	协定税率 Agreement(%)		特惠税率 S.P.(%)		普通税率 Gen.(%)	Article Description
5462	7323.9490	---其他	20	0 2 4 10	东盟ASEAN,新加坡SG,新西兰NZ 智利CL 哥斯达黎加CR 秘鲁PE	0	最不发达35国LDC35	100	---Other
5463	7323.9900	--其他	20	0 2 4 10	东盟ASEAN,新加坡SG,新西兰NZ 智利CL 哥斯达黎加CR 秘鲁PE	0	最不发达35国LDC35	80	--Other
	73.24	**钢铁制卫生器具及其零件:**							**Sanitary ware and parts thereof, of iron or steel:**
5464	7324.1000	-不锈钢制洗涤槽及脸盆	18 △10	0 3.6 9	东盟ASEAN,智利CL,新加坡SG,新西兰NZ,香港HK 哥斯达黎加CR 秘鲁PE	0	最不发达35国LDC35,最不发达4国LDC4	80	-Sinks and wash basins, of stainless steel
		-浴缸:							-Baths:
5465	7324.2100	--铸铁制，不论是否搪瓷	10	0 1 5	东盟ASEAN,新加坡SG,新西兰NZ,哥斯达黎加CR 智利CL 巴基斯坦PK,秘鲁PE	0	最不发达35国LDC35	100	--Of cast iron, whether or not enam-elled
5466	7324.2900	--其他	30 △15	0 6 15	东盟ASEAN,智利CL,新加坡SG,新西兰NZ 哥斯达黎加CR 秘鲁PE	0	最不发达35国LDC35	100	--Other
5467	7324.9000	-其他，包括零件	25 △15	0 2.5 5 12.5	东盟ASEAN,新加坡SG,新西兰NZ 智利CL 哥斯达黎加CR 秘鲁PE	0	最不发达35国LDC35	100	-Other, including parts
	73.25	**其他钢铁铸造制品:**							**Other cast articles of iron or steel:**
		-无可锻性铸铁制:							-Of non-malleable cast iron:
5468	7325.1010	---工业用	7	0 5	东盟ASEAN,智利CL,新西兰NZ,秘鲁PE,哥斯达黎加CR 巴基斯坦PK	0	最不发达35国LDC35,最不发达4国LDC4	40	---For technical use
5469	7325.1090	---其他	20	0 4 10	东盟ASEAN,智利CL,新加坡SG,新西兰NZ 哥斯达黎加CR 秘鲁PE	0	最不发达35国LDC35	90	---Other
		-其他:							-Other:
5470	7325.9100	--研磨机用的研磨球及类似品	10.5	0 1.1 2.1 5 5.2	东盟ASEAN,新加坡SG,新西兰NZ 智利CL 哥斯达黎加CR 巴基斯坦PK 秘鲁PE	0	最不发达35国LDC35	40	--Grinding balls and similar articles for mills

序号 No.	税则号列 Tariff Line	货品名称	最惠国税率 MFN(%)	协定税率 Agreement(%)	特惠税率 S.P.(%)	普通税率 Gen.(%)	Article Description
		--其他:					--Other:
5471	7325.9910	---工业用	10.5	0 东盟ASEAN,新加坡SG,新西兰NZ 1.1 智利CL 2.1 哥斯达黎加CR 5 巴基斯坦PK 5.2 秘鲁PE 8.9 亚太APTA	0 最不发达35国LDC35	40	---For technical use
5472	7325.9990	---其他	20	0 东盟ASEAN,新加坡SG,新西兰NZ 2 智利CL 4 哥斯达黎加CR 10 巴基斯坦PK,秘鲁PE 12 亚太APTA	0 最不发达35国LDC35	90	---Other
	73.26	**其他钢铁制品:**					**Other articles of iron or steel:**
		-经锻造或冲压,但未经进一步加工:					-Forged or stamped, but not further worked:
5473	7326.1100	--研磨机用的研磨球及类似品	10.5	0 东盟ASEAN,新加坡SG,新西兰NZ 1.1 智利CL 2.1 哥斯达黎加CR 5 巴基斯坦PK 5.2 秘鲁PE	0 最不发达35国LDC35	40	--Grinding balls and similar articles for mills
		--其他:					--Other:
5474	7326.1910	---工业用	10.5	0 东盟ASEAN,新加坡SG,新西兰NZ 1.1 智利CL 2.1 哥斯达黎加CR 5 巴基斯坦PK 5.2 秘鲁PE	0 最不发达35国LDC35	40	---For technical use
5475	7326.1990	---其他	20	0 东盟ASEAN,新加坡SG,新西兰NZ 2 智利CL 4 哥斯达黎加CR 10 秘鲁PE	0 最不发达35国LDC35	90	---Other
		-钢铁丝制品:					-Articles of iron or steel wire:
5476	7326.2010	---工业用	10	0 东盟ASEAN,智利CL,新西兰NZ,秘鲁PE,哥斯达黎加CR 5 亚太APTA,巴基斯坦PK	0 最不发达35国LDC35	40	---For technical use
5477	7326.2090	---其他	18	0 东盟ASEAN,智利CL,新加坡SG,新西兰NZ 3.6 哥斯达黎加CR 9 巴基斯坦PK,秘鲁PE 12.6 亚太APTA	0 最不发达35国LDC35	90	---Other
		-其他:					-Other:
		---工业用:					---For technical use:

序号 No.	税则号列 Tariff Line	货品名称	最惠国税率 MFN(%)	协定税率 Agreement(%)		特惠税率 S.P.(%)		普通税率 Gen.(%)	Article Description
5478	7326.9011	----钢铁纤维及其制品	10.5	0	东盟ASEAN,新加坡SG,新西兰NZ,香港HK	0	最不发达35国LDC35,最不发达4国LDC4	40	----Iron or steel fibres and articles thereof
				1.1	智利CL				
				2.1	哥斯达黎加CR				
				5	巴基斯坦PK				
				5.2	秘鲁PE				
				8.9	亚太APTA				
5479	7326.9019	----其他	10.5	0	东盟ASEAN,新加坡SG,新西兰NZ,香港HK	0	最不发达35国LDC35,最不发达4国LDC4	40	----Other
				1.1	智利CL				
				2.1	哥斯达黎加CR				
				5	巴基斯坦PK				
				5.2	秘鲁PE				
				8.9	亚太APTA				
5480	7326.9090	---其他	8	0	东盟ASEAN,新加坡SG,新西兰NZ,秘鲁PE,哥斯达黎加CR,香港HK	0	最不发达35国LDC35,最不发达4国LDC4	90	---Other
				0.8	智利CL				
				5	巴基斯坦PK				
				6.8	亚太APTA				

第七十四章
铜及其制品

注释：

本章所用有关名词解释如下：

一、精炼铜

按重量计含铜量至少为99.85%的金属；或按重量计含铜量至少为97.5%，但其他各种元素的含量不超过下表中规定的限量的金属：

其他元素表

元素		所含重量百分比
Ag	银	0.25
As	砷	0.5
Cd	镉	1.3
Cr	铬	1.4
Mg	镁	0.8
Pb	铅	1.5
S	硫	0.7
Sn	锡	0.8
Te	碲	0.8
Zn	锌	1
Zr	锆	0.3
其他元素*，每种		0.3

*其他元素，例如，铝、铍、钴、铁、锰、镍、硅。

二、铜合金

除未精炼铜以外的金属物质，按重量计含铜量大于其他元素单项含量，但：

1. 按重量计至少有一种其他元素的含量超过上表中规定的限量；

2. 按重量计其他元素的总含量超过2.5%。

三、铜母合金

含有其他元素，但按重量计含铜量超过10%的合金，该合金无实用可锻性，通常用作生产其他合金的添加剂或用作冶炼有色金属的脱氧剂、脱硫剂及类似用途。但按重量计含磷量超过15%的磷化铜归入税号28.48。

Chapter 74
Copper and articles thereof

Notes:

In this Chapter the following expressions have the meanings hereby assigned to them:

1. Refined copper

Metal containing at least 99.85% by weight of copper; or metal containing at least 97.5% by weight of copper, provided that the content by weight of any other element does not exceed the limit specified in the following table:

TABLE-Other elements

Element		Limiting content % by weight
Ag	Silver	0.25
As	Arsenic	0.5
Cd	Cadmium	1.3
Cr	Chromium	1.4
Mg	Magnesium	0.8
Pb	Lead	1.5
S	Sulphur	0.7
Sn	Tin	0.8
Te	Tellurium	0.8
Zn	Zinc	1
Zr	Zirconium	0.3
Other elements*, each		0.3

*Other elements are, for example, Al, Be, Co, Fe, Mn, Ni, Si.

2. Copper alloys

Metallic substances other than unrefined copper in which copper predominates by weight over each of the other elements, provided that:

(1) the content by weight of at least one of the other elements is greater than the limit specified in the foregoing table; or

(2) the total content by weight of such other elements exceeds 2.5%.

3. Master alloys Alloys containing with other elements more than 10% by weight of copper, not usefully malleable and commonly used as an additive in the manufacture of other alloys or as de-oxidants, de-sulphurizing agents or for similar uses in the metallurgy of non-ferrous metals. However, copper phosphide (phosphor copper) containing more than 15% by weight of phosphorus falls in heading No.28.48.

四、条、杆

轧、挤、拔或锻制的实心产品，非成卷的，其全长截面均为圆形、椭圆形、矩形（包括正方形）、等边三角形或规则外凸多边形(包括相对两边为弧拱形，另外两边为等长平行直线的“扁圆形”及“变形矩形”）。对于矩形（包括正方形）、三角形或多边形截面的产品,其全长边角可经磨圆。矩形（包括“变形矩形”）截面的产品，其厚度应大于宽度的十分之一。所述条、杆也包括同样形状及尺寸的铸造或烧结产品。该产品在铸造或烧结后再经加工(简单剪修或去氧化皮的除外),但不具有其他税号所列制品或产品的特征。

线锭及坯段，已具锥形尾端或经其他简单加工以便送入机器制成盘条或管子等的，仍应作为未锻轧铜归入税号74.03。

4. Bars and rods

Rolled, extruded, drawn or forged products, not in coils, which have a uniform solid cross-section along their whole length in the shape of circles, ovals, rectangles (including squares), equilateral triangles or regular convex polygons (including“flattened circles”and“modified rectangles”, of which two opposite sides are convex arcs, the other two sides being straight, of equal length and parallel). Products, with a rectangular (including square), triangular or polygonal cross-section may have corners rounded along their whole length. The thickness of such products which have a rectangular (including“modified rectangular”) cross-section exceeds one-tenth of the width.The expression also covers cast or sintered products, of the same forms and dimensions, which have been subsequently worked after production (otherwise than by simple trimming or de-scaling), provided that they have not thereby assumed the character of articles or products of other headings.

Wire-bars and billets with their ends tapered or otherwise worked simply tofacilitate their entry into machines for converting them into, for example, drawing stock (wire-rod) or tubes, are however to be taken to be unwrought copper of heading No.74.03.

五、型材及异型材

轧、挤、拔、锻制的产品或其他成型产品，不论是否成卷，其全长截面相同，但与条、杆、丝、板、片、带、箔、管的定义不相符合。同时也包括同样形状的铸造或烧结产品。该产品在铸造或烧结后再经加工(简单剪修或去氧化皮的除外),但不具有其他税号所列制品或产品的特征。

5. Profiles

Rolled, extruded, drawn, forged or formed pruducts, coiled or not, of a uniform cross-section along their whole length, which do not conform to any of the definitions of bars, rods, wire, plates, sheets, strip, foil, tubes or pipes.The expression also covers cast or sintered products, of the same forms, which have been subsequently worked after production (otherwise than by simple trimming or descaling), provided that they have not thereby assumed the character of articles or products of other headings.

六、丝

盘卷的轧、挤或拔制实心产品，其全长截面均为圆形、椭圆形、矩形（包括正方形）、等边三角形或规则外凸多边形（包括相对两边为弧拱形，另外两边为等长平行直线的“扁圆形”及“变形矩形”）。对于矩形（包括正方形）、三角形或多边形截面的产品，其全长边角可经磨圆。矩形（包括“变形矩形”）截面的产品，其厚度应大于宽度的十分之一。

6. Wire

Rolled, extruded or drawn products, in coils, which have a uniform solid cross-section along their whole length in the shape of circles, ovals, rectangles (including squares), e-quilateral triangles or regular convex polygons (including “flattened circles”and“modified rectangles”, of which two opposite sides are convex arcs, the other two sides being straight, of equal length and parallel). Products with a rectangular (including square), triangular or polygonal cross-section may have corners rounded along their whole length.The thickness of such products which have a rectangular (including “modified rectangular”) cross-section exceeds one-tenth of the width.

七、板、片、带、箔

成卷或非成卷的平面产品(税号74.03的未锻轧产品除外)，截面均为厚度相同的实心矩形(不包括正方形)，不论边角是否磨圆(包括相对两边为弧拱形，另外两边为等长平行直线的“变形矩形”)，并且符合以下规格:

1. 矩形(包括正方形)的，厚度不超过宽度的十分之一;

2. 矩形或正方形以外形状的，任何尺寸，但不具有其他税号所列制品或产品的特征。

税号74.09及74.10还适用于具有花样(例如，凹槽、肋条形、格槽、珠粒及菱形)的板、片、带、箔以及穿孔、抛光、涂层或制成瓦楞形的这类产品，但不具有其他税号所列制品或产品的特征。

八、管

全长截面及管壁厚度相同并只有一个闭合空间的空心产品，成卷或非成卷的，其截面为圆形、椭圆形、矩形(包括正方形)、等边三角形或规则外凸多边形。对于截面为矩形(包括正方形)、等边三角形或规则外凸多边形的产品，不论全长边角是否磨圆，只要其内外截面为同一圆心并为同样形状及同一轴向，也可视为管子。上述截面的管子可经抛光、涂层、弯曲、攻丝、钻孔、缩腰、胀口、成锥形或装法　兰、颈圈或套环。

7. Plates, sheets, strip and foil

Flat-surfaced products (other than the unwrought products of heading No.74.03), coiled or not, of soild rectangular (other than square) cross-section with or without rounded corners (including “modified rectangles” of which two opposite sides are convex arcs, the other two sides being straight, of equal length and parallel) of a uniform thickness, which are:

-of rectanglular (including square) shape with a thickness not exceeding one-tenth of the width.

-of a shape other than rectangular or square, of any size, provided that they do not assume the character of articles or products of other headings.

Headings Nos.74.09 and 74.10 apply, *inter alia*, to plates, sheets, strip and foil with patterns (for example, grooves, ribs, chequers, tears, buttons, lozenges) and to such products which have been perforated, corrugated, polished or coated, provided that they do not thereby assume the character of articles or products of other headings.

8.Tubes and pipes

Hollow products, coiled or not, which have a uniform cross-section with only one enclosed void along their whole length in the shape of circles, ovals, rectangles (including squares), equilateral triangles or regular convex polygons, and which have a uniform wall thickness. Products with a rectangular (including square), equilateral triangular or regular convex polygonal cross-section, which may have corners rounded along their whole length, are also to be taken to be tubes and pipes provided the inner and outer cross-sections are concentric and have the same form and orientation.Tubes and pipes of the foregoing cross-sections may be polished, coated, bent, threaded, drilled, waisted, expanded, cone_shaped or fitted with flanges, collars or rings.

子目注释:

本章所用有关名词解释如下:

一、铜锌合金(黄铜)铜与锌的合金，不论是否含有其他元素。含有其他元素时:

按重量计含锌量应大于其他各种元素的单项含量;

按重量计含镍量应低于5%[参见铜镍锌合金(德银)];

按重量计含锡量应低于 3%[参见铜锡合金(青铜)]。

二、铜锡合金(青铜)

铜与锡的合金，不论是否含有其他元素。含有其

Subheading Notes:

In this Chapter the following expressions have the meanings hereby assigned to them:

1. opper-zinc base alloys (brasses)

Alloys of copper and zinc, with or without other elements.When other elments are present:

-zinc predominates by weight over each of such other elements;

-any nickel content by weight is less than 5% (seecopper-nickel- zinc alloys (nickel silvers)); and-any tin content by weight is less than 3% (see copper-tinalloys (bronzes)).

2. Copper-tin base alloys (bronzes)

Alloys of copper and tin, with or without other ele-

他元素时，按重量计含锡量应大于其他各种元素的单项含量。当按重量计含锡量在3%及以上时，锌的含量可大于锡的含量，但必须小于10%。

三、铜镍锌合金（德银）

铜、镍、锌的合金，不论是否含有其他元素，按重量计含镍量在5%及以上[参见铜锌合金(黄铜)]。

四、铜镍合金

铜与镍的合金，不论是否含有其他元素，但按重量计含锌量不得大于1%。含有其他元素时，按重量计含镍量应大于其他各种元素的单项含量。

ments.When other elements are present, tin predominates by weight over each of such other elements, except that when the tin content is 3% or more the zinc content by weight may exceed that of tin but must be less than 10%.

3. Copper-nickel-zinc base alloys (nickel silvers)

Alloys of copper, nickel and zinc, with or without other elements. The nickel content is 5% or more by weight (see copper- zinc alloys(brasses)).

4. Copper-nickel base alloys

Alloys of copper and nickel, with or without other elements but in any case containing by weight not more than 1% of zinc.When other elements are present, nickel predominates by weight over each of such other elements.

序号 No.	税则号列 Tariff Line	货品名称	最惠国税率 MFN(%)	协定税率 Agreement(%)		特惠税率 S.P.(%)		普通税率 Gen.(%)	Article Description
	74.01	**铜锍;沉积铜(泥铜):**							**Copper mattes; cement copper (precipitated copper):**
5481	7401.0000	-铜锍,沉积铜(泥铜)	2	0	东盟ASEAN,智利CL,巴基斯坦PK,新西兰NZ,秘鲁PE,哥斯达黎加CR	0	最不发达35国LDC35,最不发达4国LDC4,老挝LA	11	-Copper mattes, cement copper (precipitated copped)
	ex74010000	铜锍	△0						Copper mattes
	74.02	**未精炼铜;电解精炼用的铜阳极:**							**Unrefined copper; copper anodes for electrolytic refining:**
5482	7402.0000	未精炼铜;电解精炼用的铜阳极	2 △0	0	东盟ASEAN,智利CL,巴基斯坦PK,新西兰NZ,哥斯达黎加CR	0	最不发达35国LDC35,最不发达4国LDC4	11	Unrefined copper; copper anodes for electrolytic refining
	74.03	**未锻轧的精炼铜及铜合金:**							**Refined copper and copper alloys, un-wrought:**
		-精炼铜:							-Refined copper:
		--阴极及阴极型材:							--Cathodes and sections of cathodes:
		---阴极:							---Cathodes:
5483	7403.1111	----按重量计铜含量超过99.9935%的	2 △0	0	东盟ASEAN,智利CL,巴基斯坦PK,新西兰NZ,秘鲁PE,哥斯达黎加CR	0	最不发达35国LDC35,最不发达4国LDC4	11	----Containing by weight more than 99.9935% of copper

序号 No.	税则号列 Tariff Line	货品名称	最惠国 税　率 MFN(%)		协定税率 Agreement(%)		特惠税率 S.P.(%)	普通 税率 Gen.(%)	Article Description
5484	7403.1119	----其他	2 △0	0	东盟ASEAN,智利CL,巴基斯坦PK,新西兰NZ,秘鲁PE,哥斯达黎加CR	0	最不发达35国LDC35,最不发达4国LDC4	11	----Other
5485	7403.1190	---阴极型材	2 △0	0	东盟ASEAN,智利CL,巴基斯坦PK,新西兰NZ,秘鲁PE,哥斯达黎加CR	0	最不发达35国LDC35,最不发达4国LDC4	11	---Sections of cathodes
5486	7403.1200	--线锭	2 △0	0	东盟ASEAN,智利CL,巴基斯坦PK,新西兰NZ,秘鲁PE,哥斯达黎加CR	0	最不发达35国LDC35,最不发达4国LDC4	11	--Wire-bars
5487	7403.1300	--坯段	2 △0	0	东盟ASEAN,智利CL,巴基斯坦PK,新西兰NZ,秘鲁PE,哥斯达黎加CR	0	最不发达35国LDC35,最不发达4国LDC4	11	--Billets
5488	7403.1900	--其他	2 △0	0	东盟ASEAN,智利CL,巴基斯坦PK,新西兰NZ,秘鲁PE,哥斯达黎加CR	0	最不发达35国LDC35,最不发达4国LDC4	11	--Other
		-铜合金:							-Copper alloys:
5489	7403.2100	--铜锌合金（黄铜）	1	0	东盟ASEAN,智利CL,巴基斯坦PK,新西兰NZ,秘鲁PE,哥斯达黎加CR,澳门MO	0	最不发达35国LDC35,最不发达4国LDC4	14	--Copper-zinc base alloys (brass)
5490	7403.2200	--铜锡合金（青铜）	1	0	东盟ASEAN,智利CL,巴基斯坦PK,新西兰NZ,秘鲁PE,哥斯达黎加CR	0	最不发达35国LDC35,最不发达4国LDC4	17	--Copper-tin base alloys (bronze)
5491	7403.2900	--其他铜合金（税号74.05的铜母合金除外）	1	0	东盟ASEAN,智利CL,巴基斯坦PK,新西兰NZ,秘鲁PE,哥斯达黎加CR	0	最不发达35国LDC35,最不发达4国LDC4	17	--Other copper alloys (other than master alloys of heading No.74.05)
	74.04	**铜废碎料:**							**Copper waste and scrap:**

序号 No.	税则号列 Tariff Line	货品名称	最惠国税率 MFN(%)	协定税率 Agreement(%)		特惠税率 S.P.(%)		普通税率 Gen.(%)	Article Description
5492	7404.0000	铜废碎料	1.5 △0	0	东盟ASEAN,智利CL,巴基斯坦PK,新西兰NZ,哥斯达黎加CR,香港HK	0	最不发达35国LDC35,最不发达4国LDC4,老挝LA	11	Copper waste and scrap
	74.05	**铜母合金:**							**Master alloys of copper:**
5493	7405.0000	铜母合金	4	0	东盟ASEAN,巴基斯坦PK,新西兰NZ,秘鲁PE,哥斯达黎加CR,香港HK	0	最不发达35国LDC35	17	Master alloys of copper
				0.4	智利CL				
	74.06	**铜粉及片状粉末:**							**Copper powders and flakes:**
		-非片状粉末:							-Powders of non-lamellar structure:
5494	7406.1010	---精炼铜制	3	0	东盟ASEAN,智利CL,巴基斯坦PK,新西兰NZ,秘鲁PE,哥斯达黎加CR	0	最不发达35国LDC35,最不发达4国LDC4	14	---Of refined copper
5495	7406.1020	---铜镍合金（白铜）或铜镍锌合金（德银）制	6	0	东盟ASEAN,新西兰NZ,秘鲁PE,哥斯达黎加CR	0	最不发达35国LDC35,最不发达4国LDC4	40	---Of copper-nickel base alloys (cupronickel) or copper-nickel-zinc base alloys (nickel silver)
				0.6	智利CL				
				5	巴基斯坦PK				
5496	7406.1030	---铜锌合金（黄铜）制	6	0	东盟ASEAN,新西兰NZ,秘鲁PE,哥斯达黎加CR	0	最不发达35国LDC35,最不发达4国LDC4	30	---Of copper-zinc base alloys (brass)
				0.6	智利CL				
				5	巴基斯坦PK				
5497	7406.1040	---铜锡合金（青铜）制	6	0	东盟ASEAN,新西兰NZ,秘鲁PE,哥斯达黎加CR	0	最不发达35国LDC35,最不发达4国LDC4	30	---Of copper-tin base alloys (bronze)
				0.6	智利CL				
				5	巴基斯坦PK				
5498	7406.1090	---其他铜合金制	6	0	东盟ASEAN,新西兰NZ,秘鲁PE,哥斯达黎加CR	0	最不发达35国LDC35,最不发达4国LDC4	30	---Other
				0.6	智利CL				
				5	巴基斯坦PK				
		-片状粉末:							-Powders of lamellar structure; flakes:
5499	7406.2010	---精炼铜制	4	0	东盟ASEAN,巴基斯坦PK,新西兰NZ,秘鲁PE,哥斯达黎加CR	0	最不发达35国LDC35,最不发达4国LDC4	14	---Of refined copper
				0.4	智利CL				

序号 No.	税则号列 Tariff Line	货品名称	最惠国税率 MFN(%)	协定税率 Agreement(%)		特惠税率 S.P.(%)		普通税率 Gen.(%)	Article Description
5500	7406.2020	---铜镍合金（白铜）或铜镍锌合金（德银）制	6	0 0.6 5	东盟ASEAN,新西兰NZ,秘鲁PE,哥斯达黎加CR 智利CL 巴基斯坦PK	0	最不发达35国LDC35,最不发达4国LDC4	40	---Of copper-nickel base alloys (cupronickel) or copper-nickel-zinc base alloys (nickel silver)
5501	7406.2090	---其他铜合金制	6	0 0.6 5	东盟ASEAN,新西兰NZ,秘鲁PE,哥斯达黎加CR 智利CL 巴基斯坦PK	0	最不发达35国LDC35,最不发达4国LDC4	30	---Other
	74.07	**铜条、杆、型材及异型材:**							**Copper bars, rods and profiles:**
		-精炼铜制:							-Of refined copper:
5502	7407.1010	---铬锆铜制	4	0 0.4	东盟ASEAN,巴基斯坦PK,新西兰NZ,秘鲁PE,哥斯达黎加CR,台湾TW 智利CL	0	最不发达35国LDC35,最不发达4国LDC4	14	---Of chrominm and zirconium copper
5503	7407.1090	---其他	4	0 0.4	东盟ASEAN,巴基斯坦PK,新西兰NZ,秘鲁PE,哥斯达黎加CR,台湾TW 智利CL	0	最不发达35国LDC35,最不发达4国LDC4	14	---Other
		-铜合金制: --铜锌合金（黄铜）:							-Of copper alloys: --Of copper-zinc base alloys (brass):
		---铜条、杆:							---Copper bars and rods:
5504	7407.2111	----直线度不大于0.5毫米/米	7	0 0.7 5	东盟ASEAN,新西兰NZ,秘鲁PE,哥斯达黎加CR,澳门MO,台湾TW 智利CL 巴基斯坦PK	0	最不发达35国LDC35,最不发达4国LDC4	20	----Of a straightness not exceeding 0.5mm/m
5505	7407.2119	----其他	7	0 0.7 5	东盟ASEAN,新西兰NZ,秘鲁PE,哥斯达黎加CR,澳门MO,台湾TW 智利CL 巴基斯坦PK	0	最不发达35国LDC35,最不发达4国LDC4	20	----Other
5506	7407.2190	---其他	7	0 0.7 5	东盟ASEAN,新西兰NZ,秘鲁PE,哥斯达黎加CR,澳门MO,台湾TW 智利CL 巴基斯坦PK	0	最不发达35国LDC35,最不发达4国LDC4	20	---Other
5507	7407.2900	--其他	7	0 5	东盟ASEAN,智利CL,新西兰NZ,秘鲁PE,哥斯达黎加CR,台湾TW 巴基斯坦PK	0	最不发达35国LDC35,最不发达4国LDC4	20	--Other

序号 No.	税则号列 Tariff Line	货品名称	最惠国税率 MFN(%)	协定税率 Agreement(%)		特惠税率 S.P.(%)		普通税率 Gen.(%)	Article Description
	74.08	**铜丝:**							**Copper wire:**
		-精炼铜制:							-Of refined copper:
5508	7408.1100	--最大截面尺寸超过6毫米	4	0 0.4 2 2.8	东盟ASEAN,巴基斯坦PK,新西兰NZ,哥斯达黎加CR,台湾TW 智利CL 秘鲁PE 亚太APTA	0	最不发达35国LDC35,最不发达4国LDC4	14	--Of which the maximum cross-sectional dimension exceeds 6mm
5509	7408.1900	--其他	4	0 0.4 3.4	东盟ASEAN,巴基斯坦PK,新西兰NZ,秘鲁PE,哥斯达黎加CR,香港HK,台湾TW 智利CL 亚太APTA	0	最不发达35国LDC35,最不发达4国LDC4	14	--Other
	ex74081900	其他含氧量小于5PPM的精炼铜丝	△2						Other refined copper wire, containing oxygen not more than 5PPM
		-铜合金制:							-Of copper alloys:
5510	7408.2100	--铜锌合金（黄铜）	7	0 0.7 5	东盟ASEAN,新西兰NZ,秘鲁PE,哥斯达黎加CR,台湾TW 智利CL 巴基斯坦PK	0	最不发达35国LDC35,最不发达4国LDC4	20	--Of copper-zinc base alloys (brass)
		--铜镍合金（白铜）或铜镍锌合金（德银）:							--Of copper-nickel base alloys (cupronickel) or copper-nickel-zinc base alloys (nickel silver):
5511	7408.2210	---铜镍锌铅合金(加铅德银)	8	0 5	东盟ASEAN,智利CL,新西兰NZ,秘鲁PE,哥斯达黎加CR 巴基斯坦PK	0	最不发达35国LDC35,最不发达4国LDC4	40	---Of copper-nickel-zinc-lead base alloys (leaded nickel silver)
5512	7408.2290	---其他	8	0 5	东盟ASEAN,智利CL,新西兰NZ,秘鲁PE,哥斯达黎加CR 巴基斯坦PK	0	最不发达35国LDC35,最不发达4国LDC4	40	---Other
5513	7408.2900	--其他	7	0 5	东盟ASEAN,智利CL,新西兰NZ,秘鲁PE,哥斯达黎加CR 巴基斯坦PK	0	最不发达35国LDC35,最不发达4国LDC4	20	--Other
	74.09	**铜板、片及带，厚度超过0.15毫米:**							**Copper plates, sheets and strip, of a thickness exceeding 0.15mm:**
		-精炼铜制:							-Of refined copper:
		--盘卷的:							--In coils:
5514	7409.1110	---氧含量不超过10PPM	4	0 0.4	东盟ASEAN,巴基斯坦PK,新西兰NZ,秘鲁PE,哥斯达黎加CR 智利CL	0	最不发达35国LDC35,最不发达4国LDC4	14	---Containing oxygen not more than 10PPM

序号 No.	税则号列 Tariff Line	货品名称	最惠国税率 MFN(%)	协定税率 Agreement(%)		特惠税率 S.P.(%)		普通税率 Gen.(%)	Article Description
5515	7409.1190	---其他	4	0 0.4	东盟ASEAN,巴基斯坦PK,新西兰NZ,秘鲁PE,哥斯达黎加CR 智利CL	0	最不发达35国LDC35,最不发达4国LDC4	14	---Other
5516	7409.1900	--其他	4	0 0.4	东盟ASEAN,巴基斯坦PK,新西兰NZ,秘鲁PE,哥斯达黎加CR,台湾TW 智利CL	0	最不发达35国LDC35,最不发达4国LDC4	14	--Other
		-铜锌合金(黄铜)制:							-Of copper-zinc base alloys (brass):
5517	7409.2100	--盘卷的	7	0 0.7 5	东盟ASEAN,新西兰NZ,秘鲁PE,哥斯达黎加CR,香港HK,台湾TW 智利CL 巴基斯坦PK	0	最不发达35国LDC35,最不发达4国LDC4	20	--In coils
5518	7409.2900	--其他	7	0 0.7 5	东盟ASEAN,新西兰NZ,秘鲁PE,哥斯达黎加CR,香港HK,台湾TW 智利CL 巴基斯坦PK	0	最不发达35国LDC35,最不发达4国LDC4	20	--Other
		-铜锡合金(青铜)制:							-Of copper-tin base alloys (bronze):
5519	7409.3100	--盘卷的	7	0 5	东盟ASEAN,智利CL,新西兰NZ,秘鲁PE,哥斯达黎加CR,台湾TW 巴基斯坦PK	0	最不发达35国LDC35,最不发达4国LDC4	20	--In coils
5520	7409.3900	--其他	7	0 5	东盟ASEAN,智利CL,新西兰NZ,秘鲁PE,哥斯达黎加CR,台湾TW 巴基斯坦PK	0	最不发达35国LDC35,最不发达4国LDC4	20	--Other
5521	7409.4000	-铜镍合金(白铜)或铜镍锌合金(德银)制	7	0 0.7 5	东盟ASEAN,新西兰NZ,秘鲁PE,哥斯达黎加CR,台湾TW 智利CL 巴基斯坦PK	0	最不发达35国LDC35,最不发达4国LDC4	40	-Of copper-nickel base alloys (cupronickel) or copper-nickel-zinc base alloys (nickel silver)
5522	7409.9000	-其他铜合金制	7	0 5	东盟ASEAN,智利CL,新西兰NZ,秘鲁PE,哥斯达黎加CR,香港HK,台湾TW 巴基斯坦PK	0	最不发达35国LDC35,最不发达4国LDC4	20	-Of other copper alloys

序号 No.	税则号列 Tariff Line	货品名称	最惠国税率 MFN(%)	协定税率 Agreement(%)		特惠税率 S.P.(%)		普通税率 Gen.(%)	Article Description
	74.10	**铜箔（不论是否印花或用纸、纸板、塑料或类似材料衬背），厚度（衬背除外）不超过 0.15 毫米:**							**Copper foil (whether or not printed or backed with paper, paperboard, plastics or similar backing materials) of a thickness (excluding any backing) not exceeding 0.15mm:**
		-无衬背:							-Not backed:
5523	7410.1100	--精炼铜制	4	0	东盟ASEAN,巴基斯坦PK,新西兰NZ,秘鲁PE,哥斯达黎加CR,香港HK,台湾TW	0	最不发达 35 国 LDC35	14	--Of refined copper
				0.4	智利CL				
				2.8	亚太APTA				
	ex74101100	覆铜板及印刷线路板用铜箔，厚度≤0.15 毫米	△3						Foil of refined Cu, not backed, for printed circuits
		--铜合金制:							--Of copper alloys:
5524	7410.1210	---铜镍合金（白铜）或铜镍锌合金（德银）	7	0	东盟ASEAN,智利CL,新西兰NZ,秘鲁PE,哥斯达黎加CR,台湾TW	0	最不发达 35 国 LDC35	40	---Of copper-nickel base alloys (cupronickel) or copper-nickel-zinc base alloys (nickel silver)
				5	巴基斯坦PK				
5525	7410.1290	---其他	7	0	东盟ASEAN,智利CL,新西兰NZ,秘鲁PE,哥斯达黎加CR,台湾TW	0	最不发达 35 国 LDC35	20	---Other
				5	巴基斯坦PK				
		-有衬背:							-Backed:
		--精炼铜制:							--Of refined copper:
5526	7410.2110	---印制电路用覆铜板	4	0	东盟ASEAN,智利CL,巴基斯坦PK,新西兰NZ,秘鲁PE,哥斯达黎加CR,香港HK,澳门MO,台湾TW	0	最不发达 35 国 LDC35	14	---Suitable for manufacturing printed circuit board
				3.4	亚太APTA				
5527	7410.2190	---其他	4	0	东盟ASEAN,智利CL,巴基斯坦PK,新西兰NZ,秘鲁PE,哥斯达黎加CR,香港HK,澳门MO,台湾TW	0	最不发达 35 国 LDC35	14	---Other
				3.4	亚太APTA				
		--铜合金制:							--Of copper alloys:
5528	7410.2210	---铜镍合金（白铜）或铜镍锌合金（德银）	7	0	东盟ASEAN,智利CL,新西兰NZ,秘鲁PE,哥斯达黎加CR	0	最不发达 35 国 LDC35	40	---Of copper-nickel base alloys (cupronickel) or copper-nickel-zinc base alloys (nickel silver)
				5	巴基斯坦PK				
5529	7410.2290	---其他	7	0	东盟ASEAN,智利CL,新西兰NZ,秘鲁PE,哥斯达黎加CR	0	最不发达 35 国 LDC35	20	---Other
				5	巴基斯坦PK				
	74.11	**铜管:**							**Copper tubes and pipes:**

序号 No.	税则号列 Tariff Line	货品名称	最惠国税率 MFN(%)	协定税率 Agreement(%)		特惠税率 S.P.(%)		普通税率 Gen.(%)	Article Description
		-精炼铜制 ---外径不超过25毫米的:							-Of refined copper ---The external diameter not exceeds 25mm:
5530	7411.1011	----带有螺纹或翅片的	4	0 0.4 2.8	东盟ASEAN,巴基斯坦PK,新西兰NZ,秘鲁PE,哥斯达黎加CR 智利CL 亚太APTA	0	最不发达35国LDC35,最不发达4国LDC4	14	----With screw thread or wing
5531	7411.1019	----其他	4	0 0.4 2.8	东盟ASEAN,巴基斯坦PK,新西兰NZ,秘鲁PE,哥斯达黎加CR 智利CL 亚太APTA	0	最不发达35国LDC35,最不发达4国LDC4	14	----Other
	ex74111019	其他含氧量小于5PPM，外径不超过25毫米的精炼铜管	△2						Other refined copper tubes and pipes with the external diameter not exceeding 25mm, containing oxygen not more than 5PPM
5532	7411.1020	---外径超过70毫米的	4	0 0.4 2.8	东盟ASEAN,巴基斯坦PK,新西兰NZ,秘鲁PE,哥斯达黎加CR 智利CL 亚太APTA	0	最不发达35国LDC35,最不发达4国LDC4	14	---The external diameter exceeds 70mm
5533	7411.1090	---其他	4	0 0.4 2.8	东盟ASEAN,巴基斯坦PK,新西兰NZ,秘鲁PE,哥斯达黎加CR 智利CL 亚太APTA	0	最不发达35国LDC35,最不发达4国LDC4	14	---Other
		-铜合金制: --铜锌合金（黄铜）							-Of copper alloys: --Of copper-zinc base alloys (brass)
5534	7411.2110	---盘卷的	7	0 0.7 5	东盟ASEAN,新西兰NZ,秘鲁PE,哥斯达黎加CR,香港HK 智利CL 巴基斯坦PK	0	最不发达35国LDC35,最不发达4国LDC4	20	---Circumvolution
5535	7411.2190	---其他	7	0 0.7 5	东盟ASEAN,新西兰NZ,秘鲁PE,哥斯达黎加CR,香港HK 智利CL 巴基斯坦PK	0	最不发达35国LDC35,最不发达4国LDC4	20	---Other
5536	7411.2200	--铜镍合金（白铜）或铜镍锌合金（德银）	7	0 5	东盟ASEAN,智利CL,新西兰NZ,秘鲁PE,哥斯达黎加CR 巴基斯坦PK	0	最不发达35国LDC35,最不发达4国LDC4	40	--Of copper-nickel base alloys (cupronickel) or copper-nickel-zinc base alloys (nickel silver)

序号 No.	税则号列 Tariff Line	货品名称	最惠国税率 MFN(%)	协定税率 Agreement(%)		特惠税率 S.P.(%)		普通税率 Gen.(%)	Article Description
5537	7411.2900	--其他	7	0 5	东盟ASEAN,智利CL,新西兰NZ,秘鲁PE,哥斯达黎加CR 巴基斯坦PK	0	最不发达35国LDC35,最不发达4国LDC4	20	--Other
	74.12	**铜制管子附件（例如，接头、肘管、管套）：**							**Copper tube or pipe fittings (for example, couplings, elbows, sleeves):**
5538	7412.1000	-精炼铜制	4	0	东盟ASEAN,智利CL,巴基斯坦PK,新西兰NZ,秘鲁PE,哥斯达黎加CR	0	最不发达35国LDC35,最不发达4国LDC4	14	-Of refined copper
		-铜合金制:							-Of copper alloys:
5539	7412.2010	---铜镍合金（白铜）或铜镍锌合金（德银）	7	0 0.7 5 6	东盟ASEAN,新西兰NZ,秘鲁PE,哥斯达黎加CR 智利CL 巴基斯坦PK 亚太APTA	0	最不发达35国LDC35,最不发达4国LDC4	40	---Of coppernickel base alloys (cupronickel) or copper-nickel-zinc base alloys (nickel silver)
5540	7412.2090	---其他	7	0 0.7 5 6	东盟ASEAN,新西兰NZ,秘鲁PE,哥斯达黎加CR 智利CL 巴基斯坦PK 亚太APTA	0	最不发达35国LDC35,最不发达4国LDC4	20	---Other
	74.13	**非绝缘的铜丝绞股线、缆、编带及类似品:**							**Stranded wire, cables, plaited bands and the like, of copper, not electrically insulated:**
5541	7413.0000	非绝缘的铜丝绞股线、缆、编带及类似品	5	0 0.5	东盟ASEAN,巴基斯坦PK,新西兰NZ,秘鲁PE,哥斯达黎加CR 智利CL	0	最不发达35国LDC35,最不发达4国LDC4	14	Stranded wire, cables plaited bands and the like, of copper, not electrically insulated
	74.15	**铜制或钢铁制带铜头的钉、平头钉、图钉、U形钉（税号83.05的货品除外）及类似品;铜制螺钉、螺栓、螺母、钩头螺钉、铆钉、销、开尾销、垫圈（包括弹簧垫圈）及类似品:**							**Nails, tacks, drawing pins, staples (other than those of heading No.83.05) and similar articles, of copper or of iron or steel with heads of copper;screws, bolts, nuts, screw hooks, rivets, cotters, cotter-pins, washers (including spring washers) and similar articles:**
5542	7415.1000	-钉、平头钉、图钉、U形钉及类似品	8	0 5	东盟ASEAN,智利CL,新西兰NZ,秘鲁PE,哥斯达黎加CR 巴基斯坦PK	0	最不发达35国LDC35,最不发达4国LDC4	80	-Nails and tacks, drawing pins, staples and similar articles

序号 No.	税则号列 Tariff Line	货品名称	最惠国税率 MFN(%)	协定税率 Agreement(%)		特惠税率 S.P.(%)		普通税率 Gen.(%)	Article Description
		-其他无螺纹制品:							-Other articles, not threaded:
5543	7415.2100	--垫圈（包括弹簧垫圈）	10	0 5	东盟ASEAN,智利CL,新加坡SG,新西兰NZ,秘鲁PE,哥斯达黎加CR,香港HK 巴基斯坦PK	0	最不发达35国LDC35,最不发达4国LDC4	80	--Washers (including spring washers)
5544	7415.2900	--其他	10	0 5	东盟ASEAN,智利CL,新加坡SG,新西兰NZ,秘鲁PE,哥斯达黎加CR,香港HK 巴基斯坦PK	0	最不发达35国LDC35,最不发达4国LDC4	80	--Other
		-其他螺纹制品:							-Other threaded articles:
		--螺钉;螺栓及螺母:							--Screws;bolts and nuts:
5545	7415.3310	---木螺钉	8	0 0.8 5	东盟ASEAN,新西兰NZ,秘鲁PE,哥斯达黎加CR,香港HK 智利CL 巴基斯坦PK	0	最不发达35国LDC35,最不发达4国LDC4	80	---Screws for wood
5546	7415.3390	---其他	8	0 0.8 5	东盟ASEAN,新西兰NZ,秘鲁PE,哥斯达黎加CR,香港HK 智利CL 巴基斯坦PK	0	最不发达35国LDC35,最不发达4国LDC4	80	---Other
5547	7415.3900	--其他	10	0 5	东盟ASEAN,智利CL,新西兰NZ,秘鲁PE,哥斯达黎加CR,香港HK 巴基斯坦PK	0	最不发达35国LDC35,最不发达4国LDC4	80	--Other
	74.18	**餐桌、厨房或其他家用铜制器具及其零件;铜制擦锅器、洗刷擦光用的块垫、手套及类似品;铜制卫生器具及其零件:**							**Table, kitchen or other household articles and parts thereof, of copper; pot scourers and scouring or polishing pads, gloves and the like, of copper; sanitary ware and parts thereof, of copper:**
		-餐桌、厨房或其他家用器具及其零件;擦锅器及洗刷擦光用的块垫、手套及类似品:							-Table, kitchen or other household articles and parts thereof; pot scourers and scouring or polishing pads, gloves and the like:
5548	7418.1010	---擦锅器及洗刷、擦光用的块垫、手套及类似品	18	0 1.8 3.6 9 14.4	东盟ASEAN,新加坡SG,新西兰NZ 智利CL 哥斯达黎加CR 秘鲁PE 巴基斯坦PK	0	最不发达35国LDC35,最不发达4国LDC4	80	---Pot scourers and scouring or polishing pads, gloves and the like

序号 No.	税则号列 Tariff Line	货品名称	最惠国 税　率 MFN(%)	协定税率 Agreement(%)	特惠税率 S.P.(%)	普通 税率 Gen.(%)	Article Description
5549	7418.1020	---非电热的铜制家用烹饪器具及其零件	20	0 东盟ASEAN,新加坡SG,新西兰NZ 2 智利CL 4 哥斯达黎加CR 10 秘鲁PE	0 最不发达35国LDC35	80	---Cooking or heating apparatus of a kind used for domestic purposes, non-electric, and parts thereof, of copper
5550	7418.1090	---其他	18 △10	0 东盟ASEAN,智利CL,新加坡SG,新西兰NZ 3.6 哥斯达黎加CR 9 秘鲁PE 14.4 巴基斯坦PK	0 最不发达35国LDC35,最不发达4国LDC4	80	---Other
5551	7418.2000	-卫生器具及其零件	18 △10	0 东盟ASEAN,智利CL,新加坡SG,新西兰NZ 3.6 哥斯达黎加CR 9 秘鲁PE	0 最不发达35国LDC35,最不发达4国LDC4	80	-Sanitary ware and parts thereof
	74.19	**其他铜制品:**					**Other articles of copper:**
5552	7419.1000	-链条及其零件	14	0 东盟ASEAN,智利CL,新加坡SG,新西兰NZ,秘鲁PE,香港HK 2.8 哥斯达黎加CR 11.2 巴基斯坦PK	0 最不发达35国LDC35	80	-Chain and parts thereof
		-其他: --铸造、模压、冲压或锻造,但未经进一步加工的:					-Other: --Cast, moulded, stamped or forged, but not further worked:
5553	7419.9110	---工业用	10	0 东盟ASEAN,智利CL,新加坡SG,新西兰NZ,秘鲁PE,哥斯达黎加CR 5 巴基斯坦PK	0 最不发达35国LDC35,最不发达4国LDC4	40	---For technical use
5554	7419.9190	---其他	20	0 东盟ASEAN,智利CL,新加坡SG,新西兰NZ 4 哥斯达黎加CR 10 秘鲁PE	0 最不发达35国LDC35	80	---Other
		--其他:					--Other:
5555	7419.9920	---铜弹簧	10	0 东盟ASEAN,智利CL,新西兰NZ,秘鲁PE,哥斯达黎加CR 5 巴基斯坦PK	0 最不发达35国LDC35	40	---Copper springs
5556	7419.9930	---铜丝制的布(包括环形带)	7	0 东盟ASEAN,智利CL,新西兰NZ,秘鲁PE,哥斯达黎加CR 5.6 巴基斯坦PK	0 最不发达35国LDC35,最不发达4国LDC4	20	---Cloth (including endless bands), of copper wire

序号 No.	税则号列 Tariff Line	货品名称	最惠国税率 MFN(%)	协定税率 Agreement(%)		特惠税率 S.P.(%)		普通税率 Gen.(%)	Article Description
5557	7419.9940	---铜丝制的网、格栅、网眼铜板	8	0 6.4	东盟ASEAN,智利CL,新西兰NZ,秘鲁PE,哥斯达黎加CR 巴基斯坦PK	0	最不发达35国LDC35,最不发达4国LDC4	20	---Grill and netting, of copper wire; expanded meta of copper
5558	7419.9950	---非电热的铜制家用供暖器具及其零件	20	0 2 4 10	东盟ASEAN,新加坡SG,新西兰NZ 智利CL 哥斯达黎加CR 秘鲁PE	0	最不发达35国LDC35	80	---Cooking or heating apparatus of a kind used for domestic purposes, non-electric, and parts thereof, of copper
		---其他:							---Other:
5559	7419.9991	----工业用	10	0 1 5 8.5	东盟ASEAN,新加坡SG,新西兰NZ,秘鲁PE,哥斯达黎加CR 智利CL 巴基斯坦PK 亚太APTA	0	最不发达35国LDC35,最不发达4国LDC4	40	----For technical use
5560	7419.9999	----其他	20	0 2 4 10 16 17	东盟ASEAN,新加坡SG,新西兰NZ 智利CL 哥斯达黎加CR 秘鲁PE 巴基斯坦PK 亚太APTA	0	最不发达35国LDC35,最不发达4国LDC4	80	----Other

第七十五章
镍及其制品

注释:

本章所用有关名词解释如下:

一、条、杆

轧、挤、拔或锻制的实心产品，非成卷的，其全长截面均为圆形、椭圆形、矩形（包括正方形）、等边三角形或规则外凸多边形（包括相对两边为弧拱形，另外两边为等长平行直线的“扁圆形”及“变形矩形”）。对于矩形（包括正方形）、三角形或多边形截面的产品，其全长边角可经磨圆。矩形（包括“变形矩形”）截面的产品，其厚度应大于宽度的十分之一。所述条、杆也包括同样形状及尺寸的铸造或烧结产品。该产品在铸造或烧结后再经加工（简单剪修或去氧化皮的除外），但不具有其他税号所列制品或产品的特征。

二、型材及异型材

轧、挤、拔、锻制的产品或其他成型产品，不论是否成卷，其全长截面相同，但与条、杆、丝、板、片、带、箔、管的定义不相符合。同时也包括同样形状的铸造或烧结产品。该产品在铸造或烧结后再经加工（简单剪修或去氧化皮的除外），但不具有其他税号所列制品或产品的特征。

三、丝

盘卷的轧、挤或拔制实心产品，其全长截面均为圆形、椭圆形、矩形（包括正方形）、等边三角形或规则外凸多边形（包括相对两边为弧拱形，另外两边为等长平行直线的“扁圆形”及“变形矩形”）。对于矩形（包括正方形）、三角形或多边形截面的产品，其全长边角可经磨圆。矩形（包括“变形矩形”）截面的产品，其厚度应大于宽度的十分之一。

Chapter 75
Nickel and articles thereof

Notes:

In this Chapter the following expressions have the meanings hereby assigned to them:

1. Bars and rods

Rolled, extruded, drawn or forged products, not in coils, which have a uniform soild cross-section along their whole length in the shape of circles, ovals, rectangles (including squares), equilateral triangles or regular con-vex polygons (including "flattened circles" and "modified rectangles", of which two opposite sides are convex arcs, the other two sides being straight, of equal length and parallel). Products with a rectangular (including square), triangular or polygonal cross-section may have corners rounded along their whole length. The thickness of such products which have a rectangular (including "modified rectangular") cross-section exceeds one-tenth of the width. The expression also covers cast or sintered products, of the same forms and dimensions, which have been subsequently worked after production (otherwise than by simple trimming or de-scaling), provided that they have not thereby assumed the character of articles or products of other headings.

2. Profiles

Rolled, extruded, drawn, forged or formed products, coiled or not, of a uniform cross-section along their whole length, which do not conform to any of the definitions of bars, rods, wire, plates, sheets, strip, foil, tubes or pipes. The expression also covers cast or sintered products, of the same forms, which have been subsequently worked after production (otherwise than by simple trim-ming or descaling), provided that they have not thereby assumed the character of articles or products of other headings.

3. Wire

Rolled, extruded or drawn products, in coils, which have a uniform soild cross-section along their whole length in the shape of circles, ovals, rectangles (including squares), equilateral triangles or regular convex polygons (including "flattened circles" and "modified rectangles", of which two opposite sides are convex arcs, the other two sides being straight, of equal length and parallel).Products with a rectangular (including square), triangular or polygonal cross-section may have corners rounded along their whole length. The thickness of such products which have a rectangular (including "modified rectangular") cross-section exceeds one-tenth of the width.

四、板、片、带、箔

成卷或非成卷的平面产品（税号75.02的未锻轧产品除外），截面均为厚度相同的实心矩形（不包括正方形），不论边角是否磨圆（包括相对两边为弧拱形，另外两边为等长平行直线的"变形矩形"），并且符合以下规格:

矩形（包括正方形）的，厚度不超过宽度的十分之一;

矩形或正方形以外形状的，任何尺寸，但不具有其他税号所列制品或产品的特征。

税号75.06还适用于具有花样（例如，凹槽、肋条形、格槽、珠粒及菱形）的板、片、带、箔以及穿孔、抛光、涂层或制成瓦楞形的这类产品，但不具有其他税号所列制品或产品的特征。

五、管

全长截面及管壁厚度相同并只有一个闭合空间的空心产品，成卷或非成卷的，其截面为圆形、椭圆形、矩形（包括正方形）、等边三角形或规则外凸多边形。对于截面为矩形（包括正方形）、等边三角形或规则外凸多边形的产品，不论全长边角是否磨圆，只要其内外截面为同一圆心并为同样形状及同一轴向，也可视为管子。上述截面的管子可经抛光、涂层、弯曲、攻丝、钻孔、缩腰、胀口、成锥形或装法兰、颈圈或套环。

4. Plates, sheets, strip and foil

Flat-surfaced products (other than the unwrought products of heading No.75.02), coiled or not, of soild rectangular (other than square) cross-section with or without rounded corners (including "modified rectangles" of which two opposite sides are convex arcs, the other two sides being straight, of equal length and parallel) of a uniform thickness, which are:

-of rectanglular (including square) shape with a thickness not exceeding one-tenth of the width.

-of a shape other than rectangular or square, of any size, provided that they do not assume the character of articles or products of other headings.

Heading No.75.06 applies, *inter alia*, to plates, sheets, strip and foil with patterns (for example, grooves, ribs, chequers, tears, buttons, lozenges) and to such products which have been perforated, corrugated, polished or coated, provided that they do not thereby assume the character of articles or products of other headings.

5. Tubes and pipes

Hollow products, coiled or not, which have a uniform crosssection with only one enclosed void along their whole length in the shape of circles, ovals, rectangles (including squares), equilateral triangles of regular convex polygons, and which have a uniform wall thickness. Products with a rectangular (including square), equilateral triangular, or regular convex polygonal cross-section, which may have corners rounded along their whole length, are also to be considered as tubes and pipes provided the inner and outer cross-sections are concentric and have the same form and orientation.Tubes and pipes of the foregoing cross-sections may be polished, coated, bent, threaded, drilled, waisted, expanded, cone-shaped or fitted with flanges, collars or rings.

子目注释:

一、本章所用有关名词解释如下:

（一）非合金镍

按重量计镍及钴的含量至少为99%的金属，但:

1.按重量计含钴量不超过1.5%;

2.按重量计其他各种元素的含量不超过下表中规定的限量:

Subheading Notes:

1. In this Chapter the following expressions have the meanings hereby assigned to them:

(a) Nickel, not alloyed

Metal containing by weight at least 99% of nickel plus cobalt, provided that:

(1) the cobalt by weight does not exceed 1.5%; and

(2) the content by weight of any other element does not exceed the limit specified in the following table:

其他元素表

元素		所含重量百分比
Fe	铁	0.5
O	氧	0.4
其他元素，每种		0.3

（二）镍合金

按重量计含镍量大于其他元素单项含量的金属物质，但:

1. 按重量计含钴量超过1.5%;
2. 按重量计至少有一种其他元素的含量超过上表中规定的限量;
3. 除镍及钴以外，按重量计其他元素的总含量超过1%。

二、子目号7508.10所称"丝"，不受本章注释三的限制，仅适用于截面尺寸不超过6毫米的任何截面形状的产品，不论是否盘卷。

TABLE-Other elements

Element		Limiting content % by weight
Fe	Iron	0.5
O	Oxygen	0.4
Other elements, each		0.3

(b) Nickel alloys

Metallic substances in which nickel predominates by weight over each of the other elements provided that:

(1) the content by weight of cobalt exceeds 1.5%;

(2) the content by weight of at least one of the other elements is greater than the limit specified in the foregoing table;or

(3) the total content by weight of elements other than nickel plus cobalt exceeds 1%.

2. Notwithstanding the provisions of Chapter Note1 (c), for the purposes of subheading No.7508.10 the term "wire" applies only to products, whether or not in coils, of any cross-sectional shape, of which no cross-sectional dimension exceeds 6mm.

序号 No.	税则号列 Tariff Line	货品名称	最惠国税率 MFN(%)	协定税率 Agreement(%)		特惠税率 S.P.(%)		普通税率 Gen.(%)	Article Description
	75.01	**镍锍、氧化镍烧结物及镍冶炼的其他中间产品:**							**Nickel mattes, nickel oxide sinters and other intermediate products of nickel metallurgy:**
5561	7501.1000	-镍锍	3 △0	0	东盟ASEAN,智利CL,巴基斯坦PK,新西兰NZ,秘鲁PE,哥斯达黎加CR	0	最不发达35国LDC35,最不发达4国LDC4	11	-Nickel mattes
		-氧化镍烧结物及镍冶炼的其他中间产品:							-Nickel oxide sinters and other intermediate products of nickel metallurgy:
5562	7501.2010	---镍湿法冶炼中间品	3 △0	0	东盟ASEAN,智利CL,巴基斯坦PK,新西兰NZ,秘鲁PE,哥斯达黎加CR	0	最不发达35国LDC35,最不发达4国LDC4	11	---Nickelintermediate products obtained by hydrometallurgical processing

序号 No.	税则号列 Tariff Line	货品名称	最惠国税率 MFN(%)	协定税率 Agreement(%)		特惠税率 S.P.(%)		普通税率 Gen.(%)	Article Description
5563	7501.2090	---其他	3 △0	0	东盟ASEAN,智利CL,巴基斯坦PK,新西兰NZ,秘鲁PE,哥斯达黎加CR	0	最不发达35国LDC35,最不发达4国LDC4	11	---Other
	75.02	**未锻轧镍:**							**Unwrought nickel:**
		-非合金镍:							-Nickel, not alloyed:
5564	7502.1010	---按重量计镍、钴总量在99.99%及以上的，但钴含量不超过0.005%	3 △1	0	东盟ASEAN,智利CL,巴基斯坦PK,新西兰NZ,秘鲁PE,哥斯达黎加CR	0	最不发达35国LDC35,最不发达4国LDC4	11	---Containing by weight no less than 99.99% of copper and cobalt, but no more than 0.005% of cobalt
5565	7502.1090	---其他	3 △1	0	东盟ASEAN,智利CL,巴基斯坦PK,新西兰NZ,秘鲁PE,哥斯达黎加CR	0	最不发达35国LDC35,最不发达4国LDC4	11	---Other
5566	7502.2000	-镍合金	3	0	东盟ASEAN,智利CL,巴基斯坦PK,新西兰NZ,秘鲁PE,哥斯达黎加CR	0	最不发达35国LDC35,最不发达4国LDC4	11	-Nickel, alloys
	75.03	**镍废碎料:**							**Nickel waste and scrap:**
5567	7503.0000	镍废碎料	1.5 △1	0	东盟ASEAN,智利CL,巴基斯坦PK,新西兰NZ,秘鲁PE,哥斯达黎加CR	0	最不发达35国LDC35,最不发达4国LDC4	11	Nickel waste and scrap
	75.04	**镍粉及片状粉末:**							**Nickel powders and flakes:**
5568	7504.0010	---非合金镍粉及片状粉末	4	0	东盟ASEAN,智利CL,巴基斯坦PK,新西兰NZ,秘鲁PE,哥斯达黎加CR	0	最不发达35国LDC35	17	---Nickel powders and flakes, not alloyed
5569	7504.0020	---合金镍粉及片状粉末	4	0	东盟ASEAN,智利CL,巴基斯坦PK,新西兰NZ,秘鲁PE,哥斯达黎加CR	0	最不发达35国LDC35	17	---Nickel powders and flakes, alloys
	75.05	**镍条、杆、型材及异型材或丝:**							**Nickel bars, rods, profiles and wire:**
		-条、杆、型材及异型材:							-Bars, rods and profiles:
5570	7505.1100	--非合金镍制	6	0 5	东盟ASEAN,智利CL,新西兰NZ,秘鲁PE,哥斯达黎加CR 巴基斯坦PK	0	最不发达35国LDC35,最不发达4国LDC4	14	--Of nickel, not alloyed

序号 No.	税则号列 Tariff Line	货品名称	最惠国税率 MFN(%)	协定税率 Agreement(%)		特惠税率 S.P.(%)		普通税率 Gen.(%)	Article Description
5571	7505.1200	--镍合金制	6	0 5	东盟ASEAN,智利CL,新西兰NZ,秘鲁PE,哥斯达黎加CR 巴基斯坦PK	0	最不发达35国LDC35,最不发达4国LDC4	14	--Of nickel alloys
		-丝:							-Wire:
5572	7505.2100	--非合金镍制	6	0 5	东盟ASEAN,智利CL,新西兰NZ,秘鲁PE,哥斯达黎加CR 巴基斯坦PK	0	最不发达35国LDC35,最不发达4国LDC4	17	--Of nickel, not alloyed
5573	7505.2200	--镍合金制	6	0 5	东盟ASEAN,智利CL,新西兰NZ,秘鲁PE,哥斯达黎加CR 巴基斯坦PK	0	最不发达35国LDC35,最不发达4国LDC4	17	--Of nickel alloys
	75.06	**镍板、片、带、箔:**							**Nickel plates, sheets, strip and foil:**
5574	7506.1000	-非合金镍制	6	0 5	东盟ASEAN,智利CL,新西兰NZ,秘鲁PE,哥斯达黎加CR 巴基斯坦PK	0	最不发达35国LDC35	14	-Of nickel, not alloyed
5575	7506.2000	-镍合金制	6	0 5	东盟ASEAN,智利CL,新西兰NZ,秘鲁PE,哥斯达黎加CR,香港HK 巴基斯坦PK	0	最不发达35国LDC35	14	-Of nickel alloys
	75.07	**镍管及管子附件(例如,接头、肘管、管套):**							**Nickel tubes, pipes and tube or pipe fittings (for example, couplings, elbows, sleeves):**
		-镍管:							-Tubes and pipes:
5576	7507.1100	--非合金镍制	6	0 5	东盟ASEAN,智利CL,新西兰NZ,秘鲁PE,哥斯达黎加CR 巴基斯坦PK	0	最不发达35国LDC35	17	--Of nickel, not alloyed
5577	7507.1200	--镍合金制	6	0 5	东盟ASEAN,智利CL,新西兰NZ,秘鲁PE,哥斯达黎加CR 巴基斯坦PK	0	最不发达35国LDC35	17	--Of nickel alloys
5578	7507.2000	-管子附件	6	0 5	东盟ASEAN,智利CL,新西兰NZ,秘鲁PE,哥斯达黎加CR 巴基斯坦PK	0	最不发达35国LDC35	17	-Tube or pipe fittings
	75.08	**其他镍制品:**							**Other articles of nickel:**
		-镍丝布、网及格栅:							-Cloth, grill and netting, of nickel wire:
5579	7508.1010	---镍丝布	6	0 5	东盟ASEAN,智利CL,新西兰NZ,秘鲁PE,哥斯达黎加CR 巴基斯坦PK	0	最不发达35国LDC35	20	---Wire cloth

序号 No.	税则号列 Tariff Line	货品名称	最惠国税率 MFN(%)	协定税率 Agreement(%)		特惠税率 S.P.(%)		普通税率 Gen.(%)	Article Description
5580	7508.1080	---其他工业用镍制品	6	0 5	东盟ASEAN,智利CL,新西兰NZ,秘鲁PE,哥斯达黎加CR 巴基斯坦PK	0	最不发达35国LDC35	40	---Other articles of nickel, for technical use
5581	7508.1090	---其他	6	0 5	东盟ASEAN,智利CL,新西兰NZ,秘鲁PE,哥斯达黎加CR 巴基斯坦PK	0	最不发达35国LDC35	70	---Other
		-其他:							-Other:
5582	7508.9010	---电镀用镍阳极	4	0	东盟ASEAN,智利CL,巴基斯坦PK,新西兰NZ,秘鲁PE,哥斯达黎加CR	0	最不发达35国LDC35	14	---Electroplating anodes
5583	7508.9080	---其他工业用镍制品	6	0 5	东盟ASEAN,智利CL,新西兰NZ,秘鲁PE,哥斯达黎加CR 巴基斯坦PK	0	最不发达35国LDC35	40	---Other articles of nickel, for technical use
5584	7508.9090	---其他	6	0 5	东盟ASEAN,智利CL,新西兰NZ,秘鲁PE,哥斯达黎加CR 巴基斯坦PK	0	最不发达35国LDC35	70	---Other

第七十六章
铝及其制品

注释:

本章所用有关名词解释如下:

一、条、杆

轧、挤、拔或锻制的实心产品，非成卷的，其全长截面均为圆形、椭圆形、矩形（包括正方形）、等边三角形或规则外凸多边形（包括相对两边为弧拱形，另外两边为等长平行直线的“扁圆形”及“变形矩形”）。对于矩形（包括正方形）、三角形或多边形截面的产品，其全长边角可经磨圆。矩形（包括“变形矩形”）截面的产品其厚度应大于宽度的十分之一。所述条、杆也包括同样形状及尺寸的铸造或烧结产品。该产品在铸造或烧结后再经加工（简单剪修或去氧化皮的除外），但不具有其他税号所列制品或产品的特征。

二、型材及异型材

轧、挤、拔、锻制的产品或其他成型产品，不论是否成卷，其全长截面相同，但与条、杆、丝、板、片、带、箔、管的定义不相符合。同时也包括同样形状的铸造或烧结产品。该产品在铸造或烧结后再经加工（简单剪修或去氧化皮的除外），但不具有其他税号所列制品或产品的特征。

三、丝

盘卷的轧、挤或拔制实心产品，其全长截面均为圆形、椭圆形、矩形（包括正方形）等边三角形或规则外凸多边形（包括相对两边为弧拱形，另外两边为等长平行直线的“扁圆形”及“变形矩形”）。对于矩形（包括正方形）、三角形或多边形截面的产品，其全长边角可经磨圆。矩形（包括“变形矩形”）截面的产品，其厚度应大于宽度的十分之一。

Chapter 76
Aluminium and articles thereof

Notes:

In this Chapter the following expressions have the meanings hereby assigned to them:

1. Bars and rods

Rolled, extruded, drawn or forged products, not in coils, which have a uniform solid cross-section along their whole length in the shape of circles, ovals, rectangles (including squares), equilateral triangles or regular convex polygons (including "flattened circles" and "modified rectangles", of which two opposite sides are convex arcs, the other two sides being straight, of equal length and parallel). Products with a rectangular (including square), triangular or polygonal cross-section may have corners rounded along their whole length. The thickness of such products which have a rectangular (including "modified rectangular") cross-section exceeds one-tenth of the width. The expression also covers cast or sintered products, of the same forms and dimensions, which have been subsequently worked after production (otherwise than by simple trimming or de-scaling), provided that they have not thereby assumed the character of articles or products of other headings.

2. Profiles

Rolled, extruded, drawn, forged or formed products, coiled or not, of a uniform cross-section along their whole length, which do not conform to any of the definitions of bars, rods, wire, plates, sheets, strip, foil, tubes or pipes. The expression also covers cast or sintered products, of the same forms, which have been subsequently worked after production (otherwise than by simple trimming or descaling), provided that they have not thereby assumed the character of articles or products of other headings.

3. Wire

Rolled, extruded or drawn products, in coils, which have a uniform soild cross-section along their whole length in the shape of circles, ovals, rectangles (including squares), equilateral triangles or regular convex polygons(including "flattened circles" and "modified rectangles", of which two opposite sides are convex arcs, the other two sides being straight, of equal length and parallel). Products with a rectangular (including square), triangular or polygonal cross-section may have corners rounded along their whole length. The thickness of such products which have a rectangular (including "modified rectangular") cross-section exceeds one-tenth of the width.

四、板、片、带、箔

成卷或非成卷的平面产品（税号 76.01 的未锻轧产品除外），截面均为厚度相同的实心矩形（不包括正方形），不论边角是否磨圆（包括相对两边为弧拱形，另外两边为等长平行直线的“变形矩形”），并且符合以下规格：

1. 矩形（包括正方形）的，厚度不超过宽度的十分之一；
2. 矩形或正方形以外形状的，任何尺寸，但不具有其他税号所列制品或产品的特征。税号 76.06 和 76.07 还适用于具有花样（例如，凹槽、肋条形、格槽、珠粒及菱形）的板、片、带、箔以及穿孔、抛光、涂层或制成瓦楞形的这类产品，但不具有其他税号所列制品或产品的特征。

4. Plates, sheets, strip and foil

Flat-surfaced products (other than the unwrought products of heading No.76.01), coiled or not, of solid rectangular (other than square) cross-section with or without rounded corners (including "modified rectangles" of which two opposite sides are convex arcs, the other two sides being straight, of equal length and parallel) of a uniform thick-ness, which are:

-of rectangular (including square) shape with a thickness not exceed- ing one-tenth of the width;

-of a shape other than rectangular or square, of any size, provided that they do not assume the character of articles or products of other headings. Headings No. 76.06 and 76.07 apply, *inter alia*, to plates, sheets, strip and foil with patterns (for example, grooves, ribs, chequers, tears, buttons, lozenges) and to such products which have been perforated, corrugated, polished or coated, provided that they do not thereby assume the character of articles or products of other headings.

五、管

全长截面及管壁厚度相同并只有一个闭合空间的空心产品，成卷或非成卷的，其截面为圆形、椭圆形、矩形（包括正方形）、等边三角形或规则外凸多边形。对于截面为矩形（包括正方形）、等边三角形或规则外凸多边形的产品，不论全长边角是否磨圆，只要其内外截面为同一圆心并为同样形状及同一轴向，也可视为管子。上述截面的管子可经抛光、涂层、弯曲、攻丝、钻孔、缩腰、胀口、成锥形或装法兰、颈圈或套环。

5. Tubes and pipes

Hollow products, coiled or not, which have a uniform cross-section with only one enclosed void along their whole length in the shape of circles, ovals, rectangles (including squares), equilateral triangles or regular convex polygons, and which have a uniform wall thickness. Products with a rectangular (including square), equilateral triangular or regular convex polygonal cross-section, which may have corners rounded along their whole length, are also to be considered as tubes and pipes provided the inner and outer cross-sections are concentric and have the same form and orientation. Tubes and pipes of the foregoing cross-sections may be polished, coated, bent, threaded, drilled, waisted, expanded, cone-shaped or fitted with flanges, collars or rings.

子目注释：

一、本章所用有关名词解释如下：

（一）非合金铝

按重量计含铝量至少为 99%的金属，但其他各种元素的含量不超过下表中规定的限量：

Subheading Notes:

1. In this Chapter the following expressions have the meanings hereby assigned to them:

(a) Aluminium, not alloyed

Metal containing by weight at least 99% of aluminium, provided that the content by weight of any other element does not exceed the limit specified in he following table:

其他元素表

元　素	所含重量百分比
Fe+Si（铁+硅）	1
其他元素（1），每种	0.1(2)

（1）其他元素，例如，铬、铜、镁、锰、镍、锌。

（2）含铜成分可大于0.1%，但不得大于0.2%，且铬和锰的含量均不得超过0.05%。

（二）铝合金

按重量计含铝量大于其他元素单项含量的金属物质，但：

1. 按重量计至少有一种其他元素或铁加硅的含量大于上表中规定的限量；

2. 按重量计其他元素的总含量超过1%。

二、子目号7616.91所称“丝”，不受本章注释三的限制，仅适用于截面尺寸不超过6毫米的任何截面形状的产品，不论是否盘卷。

TABLE-Other elements

Element	Limiting content % by weight
Fe+Si（iron plus silicon）	1
Other elements（1），each	0.1（2）

(1) Other elements are, for example, Cr, Cu, Mg, Mn, Ni, Zn.

(2) Copper is permitted in a proportion greater than 0.1% but not more than 0.2%, provided that neither the chromium nor manganese content exceeds 0.05%.

(b) Aluminium alloys

Metallic substances in which aluminium predominates by weight over each of the other elements, provided that:

(1) the content by weight of at least one of the other elements or of iron plus silicon taken together is greater than the limit specified in the foregoing table; or

(2) the total content by weight of such other elements exceeds 1%.

2. Notwithstanding the provisions of Chapter Note1 (c), for the purposes of subheading No.7616.91 the term “wire” applies only to products, whether or not in coils, of any crosssectional shape, of which no cross-sectional dimension exceeds 6mm.

序号 No.	税则号列 Tariff Line	货品名称	最惠国税率 MFN(%)	协定税率 Agreement(%)		特惠税率 S.P.(%)		普通税率 Gen.(%)	Article Description
	76.01	**未锻轧铝:**							**Unwrought aluminium:**
		-非合金铝:							-Aluminium, not alloyed
5585	7601.1010	---按重量计含铝量在99.95%及以上	5	0	东盟ASEAN,智利CL,巴基斯坦PK,新西兰NZ,秘鲁PE,哥斯达黎加CR,香港HK	0	最不发达35国LDC35,最不发达4国LDC4	14	---Containing by weight 99.95% or more of aluminium
5586	7601.1090	---其他	5 △0	0	东盟ASEAN,智利CL,巴基斯坦PK,新西兰NZ,秘鲁PE,哥斯达黎加CR,香港HK	0	最不发达35国LDC35,最不发达4国LDC4	14	---Other
5587	7601.2000	-铝合金	7	0 5 6	东盟ASEAN,智利CL,新西兰NZ,秘鲁PE,哥斯达黎加CR,澳门MO 巴基斯坦PK 亚太APTA	0	最不发达35国LDC35,最不发达4国LDC4	14	-Aluminium alloys

序号 No.	税则号列 Tariff Line	货品名称	最惠国税率 MFN(%)	协定税率 Agreement(%)		特惠税率 S.P.(%)		普通税率 Gen.(%)	Article Description
	76.02	**铝废碎料:**							**Aluminium waste and scrap:**
5588	7602.0000	铝废碎料	1.5 △0	0	东盟ASEAN,智利CL,巴基斯坦PK,新西兰NZ,哥斯达黎加CR,香港HK	0	最不发达35国LDC35,最不发达4国LDC4	14	Aluminium waste and scrap
	76.03	**铝粉及片状粉末:**							**Aluminium powders and flakes:**
5589	7603.1000	-非片状粉末	6	0 0.6 5	东盟ASEAN,新西兰NZ,秘鲁PE,哥斯达黎加CR 智利CL 巴基斯坦PK	0	最不发达35国LDC35,最不发达4国LDC4	30	-Powders of non-lamellar structure
5590	7603.2000	-片状粉末	7	0 5	东盟ASEAN,智利CL,新西兰NZ,秘鲁PE,哥斯达黎加CR 巴基斯坦PK	0	最不发达35国LDC35,最不发达4国LDC4	30	-Powders of lamellar structure; flakes
	76.04	**铝条、杆、型材及异型材:**							**Aluminium bars, rods and profiles:**
		-非合金铝制:							-Of aluminium, not alloyed:
5591	7604.1010	---铝条、杆	5	0 0.5	东盟ASEAN,巴基斯坦PK,新西兰NZ,秘鲁PE,哥斯达黎加CR 智利CL	0	最不发达35国LDC35,最不发达4国LDC4	30	---Aluminium bars, rods
5592	7604.1090	---其他	5	0 0.5	东盟ASEAN,巴基斯坦PK,新西兰NZ,秘鲁PE,哥斯达黎加CR 智利CL	0	最不发达35国LDC35,最不发达4国LDC4	30	---Other
		-铝合金制:							-Of aluminium alloys:
5593	7604.2100	--空心异型材	5	0	东盟ASEAN,智利CL,巴基斯坦PK,新西兰NZ,秘鲁PE,哥斯达黎加CR	0	最不发达35国LDC35,最不发达4国LDC4	30	--Hollow profiles
		--其他:							--Other:
5594	7604.2910	---铝合金条、杆	5	0 3.5	东盟ASEAN,智利CL,巴基斯坦PK,新西兰NZ,秘鲁PE,哥斯达黎加CR 亚太APTA	0	最不发达35国LDC35,最不发达4国LDC4	30	---Aluminium alloys bars, rods

序号 No.	税则号列 Tariff Line	货品名称	最惠国税率 MFN(%)	协定税率 Agreement(%)		特惠税率 S.P.(%)		普通税率 Gen.(%)	Article Description
5595	7604.2990	---其他	5	0	东盟ASEAN,智利CL,巴基斯坦PK,新西兰NZ,秘鲁PE,哥斯达黎加CR	0	最不发达35国LDC35,最不发达4国LDC4	30	---Other
				3.5	亚太APTA				
	76.05	**铝丝:**							**Aluminium wire:**
		-非合金铝制:							-Of aluminium, not alloyed:
5596	7605.1100	--最大截面尺寸超过7毫米	8	0	东盟ASEAN,新西兰NZ,秘鲁PE,哥斯达黎加CR	0	最不发达35国LDC35	17	--Of which the maximum cross-sectional dimension exceeding 7mm
				0.8	智利CL				
				5	巴基斯坦PK				
5597	7605.1900	--其他	8	0	东盟ASEAN,智利CL,新西兰NZ,秘鲁PE,哥斯达黎加CR,香港HK	0	最不发达35国LDC35	17	--Other
				5	巴基斯坦PK				
				6.8	亚太APTA				
		-铝合金制:							-Of aluminium alloys:
5598	7605.2100	--最大截面尺寸超过7毫米	8	0	东盟ASEAN,智利CL,新西兰NZ,秘鲁PE,哥斯达黎加CR	0	最不发达35国LDC35	17	--Of which the maximum cross-sectional dimension exceeding 7mm
				5	巴基斯坦PK				
5599	7605.2900	--其他	8	0	东盟ASEAN,智利CL,新西兰NZ,秘鲁PE,哥斯达黎加CR	0	最不发达35国LDC35	17	--Other
				5	巴基斯坦PK				
	76.06	**铝板、片及带，厚度超过0.2毫米:**							**Aluminium plates, sheets and strip, of a thickness exceeding 0.2mm:**
		-矩形(包括正方形):							-Rectangular (including square):
		--非合金铝制:							--Of aluminium, not alloyed:
		---厚度在0.30毫米及以上，但不超过0.36毫米:							---Of a thickness of 0.30mm or more but not exceeding 0.36mm:
5600	7606.1121	----铝塑复合的	6	0	东盟ASEAN,智利CL,巴基斯坦PK,新西兰NZ,秘鲁PE,哥斯达黎加CR	0	最不发达35国LDC35,最不发达4国LDC4	50	----Of aluminium-plastic composite
				4.2	亚太APTA				
5601	7606.1129	----其他	6 △4	0	东盟ASEAN,智利CL,巴基斯坦PK,新西兰NZ,秘鲁PE,哥斯达黎加CR	0	最不发达35国LDC35,最不发达4国LDC4	50	----Other
				4.2	亚太APTA				
		---其他:							---Other:

序号 No.	税则号列 Tariff Line	货品名称	最惠国税率 MFN(%)	协定税率 Agreement(%)		特惠税率 S.P.(%)		普通税率 Gen.(%)	Article Description
5602	7606.1191	----铝塑复合的	6	0 4.2	东盟ASEAN,智利CL,巴基斯坦PK,新西兰NZ,秘鲁PE,哥斯达黎加CR,香港HK,台湾TW 亚太APTA	0	最不发达35国LDC35,最不发达4国LDC4	30	----Of aluminium-plastic composite
5603	7606.1199	----其他	6	0 4.2	东盟ASEAN,智利CL,巴基斯坦PK,新西兰NZ,秘鲁PE,哥斯达黎加CR,香港HK,台湾TW 亚太APTA	0	最不发达35国LDC35,最不发达4国LDC4	30	----Other
		--铝合金制:							--Of aluminium alloys:
5604	7606.1220	---厚度小于0.28毫米	6	0 4.2	东盟ASEAN,智利CL,巴基斯坦PK,新西兰NZ,秘鲁PE,哥斯达黎加CR,香港HK,台湾TW 亚太APTA	0	最不发达35国LDC35,最不发达4国LDC4	30	---Of a thickness less than 0.28mm
5605	7606.1230	---厚度在0.28毫米及以上，但不超过0.35毫米	6	0 4.2	东盟ASEAN,智利CL,巴基斯坦PK,新西兰NZ,秘鲁PE,哥斯达黎加CR,香港HK,台湾TW 亚太APTA	0	最不发达35国LDC35,最不发达4国LDC4	30	---Of a thickness of 0.28mm or more but not exceeding 0.35mm
		---厚度在0.35毫米以上,但不超过4毫米:							---Of a thickness of 0.35mm or more but not exceeding 4mm:
5606	7606.1251	----铝塑复合的	6	0 4.2	东盟ASEAN,智利CL,巴基斯坦PK,新西兰NZ,秘鲁PE,哥斯达黎加CR,香港HK 亚太APTA	0	最不发达35国LDC35,最不发达4国LDC4	50	----Of aluminium-plastic composite
5607	7606.1259	----其他	6	0 4.2	东盟ASEAN,智利CL,巴基斯坦PK,新西兰NZ,秘鲁PE,哥斯达黎加CR,香港HK 亚太APTA	0	最不发达35国LDC35,最不发达4国LDC4	50	----Other
5608	7606.1290	---其他	6	0 4.2	东盟ASEAN,智利CL,巴基斯坦PK,新西兰NZ,秘鲁PE,哥斯达黎加CR,香港HK 亚太APTA	0	最不发达35国LDC35,最不发达4国LDC4	50	---Other
		-其他:							-Other:
5609	7606.9100	--非合金铝制	6	0 5	东盟ASEAN,智利CL,新西兰NZ,秘鲁PE,哥斯达黎加CR,香港HK,台湾TW 巴基斯坦PK	0	最不发达35国LDC35,最不发达4国LDC4	30	--Of aluminium, not alloyed

序号 No.	税则号列 Tariff Line	货品名称	最惠国税率 MFN(%)	协定税率 Agreement(%)		特惠税率 S.P.(%)		普通税率 Gen.(%)	Article Description
5610	7606.9200	--铝合金制	10	0 5	东盟ASEAN,智利CL,新加坡SG,新西兰NZ,秘鲁PE,哥斯达黎加CR,香港HK,台湾TW 巴基斯坦PK	0	最不发达35国LDC35,最不发达4国LDC4	30	--Of aluminium alloys
	76.07	**铝箔（不论是否印花或用纸、纸板、塑料或类似材料衬背），厚度（衬背除外）不超过0.2毫米:**							**Aluminium foil (whether or not printed or backed with paper, paper-board, plastics or similar backing materlals) of a thickness (excluding any backing) not exceeding 0.2mm:**
		-无衬背:							-Not backed:
		--轧制后未经进一步加工的:							--Rolled but not further worked:
5611	7607.1110	---厚度不超过0.007毫米	6	0 0.6 5 5.7	东盟ASEAN,新西兰NZ,秘鲁PE,哥斯达黎加CR 智利CL 巴基斯坦PK 亚太APTA	0	最不发达35国LDC35	35	---Of a thickness not exceeding 0.007mm
5612	7607.1120	---厚度大于0.007毫米，但不超过0.01毫米	6	0 0.6 5 5.7	东盟ASEAN,新西兰NZ,秘鲁PE,哥斯达黎加CR 智利CL 巴基斯坦PK 亚太APTA	0	最不发达35国LDC35	35	---Of a thickness exceeding 0.007mm, but not exceeding 0.01mm
5613	7607.1190	---其他	6	0 0.6 5 5.7	东盟ASEAN,新西兰NZ,秘鲁PE,哥斯达黎加CR,台湾TW 智利CL 巴基斯坦PK 亚太APTA	0	最不发达35国LDC35	35	---Other
5614	7607.1900	--其他	6	0 0.6 5 5.1	东盟ASEAN,新西兰NZ,秘鲁PE,哥斯达黎加CR,台湾TW 智利CL 巴基斯坦PK 亚太APTA	0	最不发达35国LDC35	35	--Other
	ex76071900	化成箔	△3						Formed Al foil
5615	7607.2000	-有衬背	6	0 0.6 5	东盟ASEAN,新西兰NZ,秘鲁PE,哥斯达黎加CR,香港HK,台湾TW 智利CL 巴基斯坦PK	0	最不发达35国LDC35	35	-Backed
	76.08	**铝管:**							**Aluminium tubes and pipes:**
5616	7608.1000	-非合金铝制	8	0 0.8 5	东盟ASEAN,新西兰NZ,秘鲁PE,哥斯达黎加CR 智利CL 巴基斯坦PK	0	最不发达35国LDC35,最不发达4国LDC4	30	-Of aluminium, not alloyed

序号 No.	税则号列 Tariff Line	货品名称	最惠国税率 MFN(%)	协定税率 Agreement(%)	特惠税率 S.P.(%)	普通税率 Gen.(%)	Article Description
		-铝合金制:					-Of aluminium alloys:
5617	7608.2010	---外径不超过 10 厘米的	8	0 东盟ASEAN,新西兰NZ,秘鲁PE,哥斯达黎加CR 0.8 智利CL 5 巴基斯坦PK	0 最不发达 35 国 LDC35,最不发达 4 国 LDC4	30	---Having an outside diameter not exceeding 10cm
		---其他:					---Other:
5618	7608.2091	----壁厚不超过 25 毫米	8	0 东盟ASEAN,新西兰NZ,秘鲁PE,哥斯达黎加CR 0.8 智利CL 5 巴基斯坦PK	0 最不发达 35 国 LDC35,最不发达 4 国 LDC4	30	----Having a wall thickness not exceeding 25mm
5619	7608.2099	----其他	8	0 东盟ASEAN,新西兰NZ,秘鲁PE,哥斯达黎加CR 0.8 智利CL 5 巴基斯坦PK	0 最不发达 35 国 LDC35,最不发达 4 国 LDC4	30	----Other
	76.09	**铝制管子附件(例如,接头、肘管、管套):**					**Aluminium tube or pipe fittings (for example, couplings, elbows, sleeves):**
5620	7609.0000	铝制管子附件(例如,接头、肘管、管套)	8	0 东盟ASEAN,智利CL,新西兰NZ,秘鲁PE,哥斯达黎加CR 5 巴基斯坦PK	0 最不发达 35 国 LDC35,最不发达 4 国 LDC4	35	Aluminium tube or pipe fittings (for example, couplings, elbows, sleeves)
	76.10	**铝制结构体(税号 94.06 的活动房屋除外)及其部件(例如,桥梁及桥梁体段、塔、格构杆、屋顶、屋顶框架、门窗及其框架、门槛、栏杆、支柱及立柱);上述结构体用的已加工铝板、杆、型材、异型材、管子及类似品:**					**Aluminium structures (excluding prefabricated buildings of heading No.94.06) and parts of structures (for example, bridges and bridgesections, towers, lattice masts, roofs, roofing frameworks, doors and windows and their frames and thresholds for doors, pillars, balustrades, pillars and columns); aluminium plates, rods, profiles, tubes and the like, prepared for use in structures:**
5621	7610.1000	-门窗及其框架、门槛	25	0 东盟ASEAN,智利CL,新加坡SG,新西兰NZ,澳门MO 5 哥斯达黎加CR 12.5 秘鲁PE	0 最不发达 35 国 LDC35	80	-Doors, windows and their frames and thresholds for doors

序号 No.	税则号列 Tariff Line	货品名称	最惠国税率 MFN(%)	协定税率 Agreement(%)		特惠税率 S.P.(%)		普通税率 Gen.(%)	Article Description
5622	7610.9000	-其他	6	0 0.6 5	东盟ASEAN,新西兰NZ,秘鲁PE,哥斯达黎加CR 智利CL 巴基斯坦PK	0	最不发达35国LDC35,最不发达4国LDC4	50	-Other
	76.11	**盛装物料用的铝制囤、柜、罐、桶及类似容器(装压缩气体或液化气体的除外),容积超过300升,不论是否衬里或隔热,但无机械或热力装置:**							**Aluminium reservoirs, tanks, vats and similar containers, for any material (other than compressed or liquefied gas), of a capacity exceeding 300L, whether or not lined or heat-insulated, but not fitted with mechanical or thermal equipment:**
5623	7611.0000	盛装物料用的铝制囤、柜、罐、桶及类似容器(装压缩气体或液化气体的除外),容积超过300升,不论是否衬里或隔热,但无机械或热力装置	12	0 2.4 6	东盟ASEAN,智利CL,新加坡SG,新西兰NZ,秘鲁PE 哥斯达黎加CR 巴基斯坦PK	0	最不发达35国LDC35	35	Aluminium reservoirs, tanks, vats and similar containers, for any material (other than compressed or liquefied gas), of a capacity exceedIng 300L, whether or not lined or heat-insulated, but not fitted with mechanical or thermal equipment
	76.12	**盛装物料用的铝制桶、罐、听、盒及类似容器,包括软管容器及硬管容器(装压缩气体或液化气体的除外),容积不超过300升,不论是否衬里或隔热,但无机械或热力装置:**							**Aluminium casks, drums, cans, boxes and similar containers (including rigid or collapsible tubular containers), for any material (other than compressed or liquefied gas), of a capacity not exceeding 300L, whether or not lined or heat-insulated, but not fitted with mechanical or thermal equipment:**
5624	7612.1000	-软管容器	12	0 1.2 2.4 6	东盟ASEAN,新加坡SG,新西兰NZ 智利CL 哥斯达黎加CR 巴基斯坦PK,秘鲁PE	0	最不发达35国LDC35,最不发达4国LDC4	50	-Collapsible tubular containers
		-其他:							-Other:
5625	7612.9010	---易拉罐及罐体	30	0 3 6 15	东盟ASEAN,新加坡SG,新西兰NZ 智利CL 哥斯达黎加CR 秘鲁PE	0	最不发达35国LDC35	100	---Tear tab ends and bodies thereof

序号 No.	税则号列 Tariff Line	货品名称	最惠国税率 MFN(%)	协定税率 Agreement(%)		特惠税率 S.P.(%)		普通税率 Gen.(%)	Article Description
5626	7612.9090	---其他	12	0 1.2 2.4 6	东盟ASEAN,新加坡SG,新西兰NZ 智利CL 哥斯达黎加CR 巴基斯坦PK,秘鲁PE	0	最不发达35国LDC35,最不发达4国LDC4	70	---Other
	76.13	**装压缩气体或液化气体用的铝制容器:**							**Aluminium containers for compressed or liquefied gas:**
5627	7613.0010	---零售包装用	12	0 2.4 6	东盟ASEAN,智利CL,新加坡SG,新西兰NZ,秘鲁PE 哥斯达黎加CR 巴基斯坦PK	0	最不发达35国LDC35	70	---For retail packing
5628	7613.0090	---其他	6	0 5	东盟ASEAN,智利CL,新西兰NZ,秘鲁PE,哥斯达黎加CR 巴基斯坦PK	0	最不发达35国LDC35	17	---Other
	76.14	**非绝缘的铝制绞股线、缆、编带及类似品:**							**Stranded wire, cables, plaited bands and the like, of aluminium, not electrically insulated:**
5629	7614.1000	-带钢芯的	6	0 5	东盟ASEAN,智利CL,新西兰NZ,秘鲁PE,哥斯达黎加CR 巴基斯坦PK	0	最不发达35国LDC35,最不发达4国LDC4	20	-With steel core
5630	7614.9000	-其他	6	0 5	东盟ASEAN,智利CL,新西兰NZ,秘鲁PE,哥斯达黎加CR 巴基斯坦PK	0	最不发达35国LDC35,最不发达4国LDC4	20	-Other
	76.15	**餐桌、厨房或其他家用铝制器具及其零件;铝制擦锅器、洗刷擦光用的块垫、手套及类似品;铝制卫生器具及其零件:**							**Table, kitchen or other household articles and parts thereof, of aluminium;pot scourers and scouring or polishing pads, gloves and the like, of aluminium; sanitary ware and parts thereof, of aluminium:**
		-餐桌、厨房或其他家用器具及其零件;擦锅器及洗刷擦光用的块垫、手套及类似品:							-Table, kitchen or other household articles and parts thereof; pot scourers and scouring or polishing pads, gloves and the like:
5631	7615.1010	---擦锅器、洗刷、擦光用的块垫、手套及类似品	18	0 3.6 9 14.4	东盟ASEAN,智利CL,新加坡SG,新西兰NZ 哥斯达黎加CR 秘鲁PE 巴基斯坦PK	0	最不发达35国LDC35,最不发达4国LDC4	90	---Pot scourers and scouring or polishing pads, gloves and the like

序号 No.	税则号列 Tariff Line	货品名称	最惠国税率 MFN(%)	协定税率 Agreement(%)		特惠税率 S.P.(%)		普通税率 Gen.(%)	Article Description
5632	7615.1090	---其他	15 △10	0 1.5 3 7.5 12	东盟ASEAN,新加坡SG,新西兰NZ 智利CL 哥斯达黎加CR 秘鲁PE 巴基斯坦PK	0	最不发达35国LDC35,最不发达4国LDC4	90	---Other
5633	7615.2000	-卫生器具及其零件	18	0 1.8 3.6 9 14.4	东盟ASEAN,新加坡SG,新西兰NZ 智利CL 哥斯达黎加CR 秘鲁PE 巴基斯坦PK	0	最不发达35国LDC35	90	-Sanitary ware and parts thereof
	76.16	**其他铝制品:**							**Other articles of aluminium:**
5634	7616.1000	-钉、平头钉、U形钉(税号83.05的货品除外)、螺钉、螺栓、螺母、钩头螺钉、铆钉、销、开尾销、垫圈及类似品其他:	10	0 5 8.5	东盟ASEAN,智利CL,新加坡SG,新西兰NZ,秘鲁PE,哥斯达黎加CR,香港HK 巴基斯坦PK 亚太APTA	0	最不发达35国LDC35,最不发达4国LDC4	40	-Nails, tacks, staples (other than those of heading No.83.05), screws, bolts, nuts, screw hooks, rivets, cotters, cotter-pins, washers and similar articles-other:
5635	7616.9100	--铝丝制的布、网、篱及格栅	10	0	东盟ASEAN,智利CL,新加坡SG,新西兰NZ,秘鲁PE,哥斯达黎加CR	0	最不发达35国LDC35,最不发达4国LDC4	40	--Cloth, grill, netting and fencing, of aluminium wire
		--其他:							--Other:
5636	7616.9910	---工业用	10	0 1 5 8.5	东盟ASEAN,新加坡SG,新西兰NZ,哥斯达黎加CR 智利CL 巴基斯坦PK,秘鲁PE 亚太APTA	0	最不发达35国LDC35,最不发达4国LDC4	40	---For technical use
5637	7616.9990	---其他	15	0 1.5 3 7.5 12.8	东盟ASEAN,新加坡SG,新西兰NZ 智利CL 哥斯达黎加CR 巴基斯坦PK,秘鲁PE 亚太APTA	0	最不发达35国LDC35,最不发达4国LDC4	80	---Other

第七十八章
铅及其制品

注释:

本章所用有关名词解释如下:

一、条、杆

轧、挤、拔或锻制的实心产品，非成卷的，其全长截面均为圆形、椭圆形、矩形（包括正方形）、等边三角形或规则外凸多边形（包括相对两边为弧拱形，另外两边为等长平行直线的“扁圆形”及“变形矩形”）。对于矩形（包括正方形）、三角形或多边形截面的产品，其全长边角可经磨圆。矩形（包括“变形矩形”）截面的产品，其厚度应大于宽度的十分之一。所述条、杆也包括同样形状及尺寸的铸造或烧结产品。该产品在铸造或烧结后再经加工（简单剪修或去氧化皮的除外），但不具有其他税号所列制品或产品的特征。

二、型材及异型材

轧、挤、拔、锻制的产品或其他成型产品，不论是否成卷，其全长截面相同，但与条、杆、丝、板、片、带、箔、管的定义不相符合。同时也包括同样形状的铸造或烧结产品。该产品在铸造或烧结后再经加工（简单剪修或去氧化皮的除外），但不具有其他税号所列制品或产品的特征。

三、丝

盘卷的轧、挤或拔制实心产品，其全长截面均为圆形、椭圆形、矩形（包括正方形）、等边三角形或规则外凸多边形（包括相对两边为弧拱形，另外两边为等长平行直线的“扁圆形”及“变形矩形”）。对于矩形（包括正方形）、三角形或多边形截面的产品，其全长边角可经磨圆。矩形（包括“变形矩形”）截面的产品，其厚度应大于宽度的十分之一。

Chapter 78
Lead and articles therof

Notes:

In this Chapter the following expressions have the meanings hereby assigned to them:

1. Bars and rods

Rolled, extruded, drawn or forged products, not in coils, which have a uniform solid cross-section along their whole length in the shape of circles, ovals, rectangles (including squares), equilateral triangles or regular convex polygons (including “flattened circles” and “modified rectangles”, of which two opposite sides are convex arcs, the other two sides being straight, of equal length and parallel). Products with a rectangular (including square), triangular or polygonal cross-section may have corners rounded along their whole length. The thickness of such products which have a rectangular (including “modified rectangular”) cross-section exceeds one-tenth of the width. The expression also covers cast or sintered products, of the same forms and dimensions, which have been subsequently worked after production (otherwise than by simple trimming or de-scaling), provided that they have not thereby assumed the character of articles or products of other headings.

2. Profiles

Rolled, extruded, drawn, forged or formed products, coiled or not, of a uniform cross-section along their whole length, which do not conform to any of the definitions of bars, rods, wire, plates, sheets, strip, foil, tubes or pipes. The expression also covers cast or sintered products, of the same forms, which have been subsequently worked after production (otherwise than by simple trimming of descaling), provided that they have not thereby assumed the character of articles or products of other headings.

3. Wire

Rolled, extruded or drawn products, in coils, which have a uniform soild cross-section along their whole length in the shape of circles, ovals, rectangles (including squares), equilateral triangles or regular convex polygons (including “flattened circles” and “modified rectangles”, of which two opposite sides are convex arcs, the other two sides being straight, of equal length and parallel).Products with a rectangular (including square), triangular or polygonal cross-section may have corners rounded along their whole length. The thickness of such products which have a rectangular (including "modified rectangular") cross-section exceeds one-tenth of the width.

四、板、片、带、箔

成卷或非成卷的平面产品（税号 78.01 的未锻轧产品除外），截面均为厚度相同的实心矩形（不包括正方形），不论边角是否磨圆（包括相对两边为弧拱形，另外两边为等长平行直线的“变形矩形”），并且符合以下规格：

1. 矩形（包括正方形）的，厚度不超过宽度的十分之一；
2. 矩形或正方形以外形状的，任何尺寸，但不具有其他税号所列制品或产品的特征。

税号 78.04 还适用于具有花样（例如，凹槽、肋条形、格槽、珠粒及菱形）的板、片、带、箔以及穿孔、抛光、涂层或制成瓦楞形的这类产品，但不具有其他税号所列制品或产品的特征。

4. Plates, sheets, strip and foil

Flat-surfaced products (other than the unwrought products of heading No.78.01), coiled or not, of solid rectangular (other than square) cross-section with or without rounded corners (including "modified rectanges" of which two opposite sides are convex arcs, the other two sides being straight, of equal length and parallel) of a uniform thickness, which are:

(1) of rectangular (including square) shape with a thickness not exceeding, one-tenth of the width,

(2) of a shape other than rectangular or square, of any size, proviede that they do not assume the character of articles or products of other headings.

Heading No. 78.04 applies, *inter alia*, to plates, sheets, strip and foil with patterns (for example, grooves, ribs, chequers, tears, buttons, lozenges) and to such products which have been perforated, corrugated, polished or coated, provided that they do not thereby assume the character of articles or products of other headings.

五、管

全长截面及管壁厚度相同并只有一个闭合空间的实心产品，成卷或非成卷的，其截面为圆形、椭圆形、矩形（包括正方形）、等边三角形或规则外凸多边形。对于截面为矩形（包括正方形）、等边三角形或规则外凸多边形的产品，不论全长边角是否磨圆，只要其内外截面为同一圆心并为同样形状及同一轴向，也可视为管子。上述截面的管子可经抛光、涂层、弯曲、攻丝、钻孔、缩腰、胀口、成锥形或装法兰、颈圈或套环。

5. Tubes and pipes

Hollow products, coiled or not, which have a uniform cross-section with only one enclosed void along their whole langth in the shape of circles, ovals, rectangles (including squares), equilateral triangles or regular convex polygons, and which have a uniform wall thickness. Products with a rectangular (including square), equilateral triangular or regular convex polygonal cross-section, which may have corners rounded along their whole length, are also to be considered as tubes and pipes provided the inner and outer cross-sections are concentric and have the same form and orientation. Tubes and pipes of the foregoing cross-sections may be polished, coated, bent, threaded, drilled, waisted, expanded, cone-shaped or fitted with flanges, collars or rings.

子目注释：

本章所称“精炼铅”，是指：

按重量计含铅量至少为 99.9%的金属，但其他各种元素的含量不超过下表中规定的限量：

Subheading Note:

In this Chapter the expression "refined lead" means:

Metal containing by weight at least 99.9% of lead, provided that the content by weight of any other element does not exceed the limit specified in the following table:

其他元素表

元　　素	所含重量百比
Ag 银	0.02
As 砷	0.005
Bi 铋	0.05
Ca 钙	0.002
Cd 镉	0.002
Cu 铜	0.08
Fe 铁	0.002
S 硫	0.002
Sb 锑	0.005
Sn 锡	0.005
Zn 锌	0.002
其他（例如碲），每种	0.001

TABLE—Other elements

Element	Limiting conten % by weight
Ag Silver	0.02
As Arsenic	0.005
Bi Bismuth	0.05
Ca Calcium	0.002
Cd Cadmium	0.002
Cu Copper	0.08
Fe Iron	0.002
S Sulphur	0.002
Sb Antimony	0.005
Sn Tin	0.005
Zn Zinc	0.002
Other(for example Te), each	0.001

序号 No.	税则号列 Tariff Line	货品名称	最惠国税率 MFN(%)	协定税率 Agreement(%)	特惠税率 S.P.(%)	普通税率 Gen.(%)	Article Description
	78.01	**未锻轧铅:**					**Unwrought lead:**
5638	7801.1000	-精炼铅	3	0 东盟ASEAN,智利CL,巴基斯坦PK,新西兰NZ,秘鲁PE,哥斯达黎加CR	0 最不发达35国LDC35,最不发达4国LDC4	20	-Refined lead
		-其他:					-Other:
5639	7801.9100	--按重量计所含其他元素是以锑为主的	3	0 东盟ASEAN,智利CL,巴基斯坦PK,新西兰NZ,秘鲁PE,哥斯达黎加CR	0 最不发达35国LDC35,最不发达4国LDC4	20	--Containing by weight antimony as the principal other element
5640	7801.9900	--其他	3	0 东盟ASEAN,智利CL,巴基斯坦PK,新西兰NZ,秘鲁PE,哥斯达黎加CR	0 最不发达35国LDC35,最不发达4国LDC4	20	--Other
	78.02	**铅废碎料:**					**Lead waste and scrap:**
5641	7802.0000	铅废碎料	1.5	0 东盟ASEAN,智利CL,巴基斯坦PK,新西兰NZ,秘鲁PE,哥斯达黎加CR	0 最不发达35国LDC35	10	Lead waste and scrap
	78.04	**铅板、片、带、箔;铅粉及片状粉末:**					**Lead plates sheets, strip and foil; lead powders and flakes:**
		-板、片、带、箔:					-Plates, sheets, strip and foil:

序号 No.	税则号列 Tariff Line	货品名称	最惠国税率 MFN(%)	协定税率 Agreement(%)		特惠税率 S.P.(%)		普通税率 Gen.(%)	Article Description
5642	7804.1100	--片、带及厚度（衬背除外）不超过0.2毫米的箔	6	0 5	东盟ASEAN,智利CL,新西兰NZ,秘鲁PE,哥斯达黎加CR 巴基斯坦PK	0	最不发达35国LDC35,最不发达4国LDC4	30	--Sheets, strip and foil of a thickness (excluding any backing) not exceeding 0.2mm
5643	7804.1900	--其他	6	0 5	东盟ASEAN,智利CL,新西兰NZ,秘鲁PE,哥斯达黎加CR 巴基斯坦PK	0	最不发达35国LDC35,最不发达4国LDC4	30	--Other
5644	7804.2000	-粉末及片状粉末	6	0 5	东盟ASEAN,智利CL,新西兰NZ,秘鲁PE,哥斯达黎加CR 巴基斯坦PK	0	最不发达35国LDC35,最不发达4国LDC4	35	-Powders and flakes
	78.06	**其他铅制品:**							**Other articles of lead:**
5645	7806.0010	---铅条、杆、型材及异型材或丝	6	0 5	东盟ASEAN,智利CL,新西兰NZ,秘鲁PE,哥斯达黎加CR 巴基斯坦PK	0	最不发达35国LDC35,最不发达4国LDC4	30	---Lead bars, rods, profiles and wire
5646	7806.0090	--其他	6	0 5	东盟ASEAN,智利CL,新西兰NZ,秘鲁PE,哥斯达黎加CR 巴基斯坦PK	0	最不发达35国LDC35,最不发达4国LDC4	40	--Other

第七十九章
锌及其制品

注释：

本章所用名词解释如下：

一、条、杆

轧、挤、拔或锻制的实心产品，非成卷的，其全长截面均为圆形、椭圆形、矩形（包括正方形）、等边三角形或规则外凸多边形（包括相对两边为弧拱形，另外两边为等长平行直线的“扁圆形”及“变形矩形”）。对于矩形（包括正方形）、三角形或多边形截面的产品，其全长边角可经磨圆。矩形（包括“变形矩形”）截面的产品，其厚度应大于宽度的十分之一。所述条、杆也包括同样形状及尺寸的铸造或烧结产品。该产品在铸造或烧结后再经加工（简单剪修或去氧化皮的除外），但不具有其他税号所列制品或产品的特征。

二、型材及异型材

轧、挤、拔、锻制的产品或其他成型产品，不论是否成卷，其全长截面相同，但与条、杆、丝、板、片、带、箔、管的定义不相符合。同时也包括同样形状的铸造或烧结产品。该产品在铸造或烧结后再经加工（简单剪修或去氧化皮的除外），但不具有其他税号所列制品或产品的特征。

三、丝

盘卷的轧、挤或拔制实心产品，其全长截面均为圆形、椭圆形、矩形（包括正方形）、等边三角形或规则外凸多边形（包括相对两边为弧拱形，另外两边为等长平行直线的“扁圆形”及“变形矩形”）。对于矩形（包括正方形）、三角形或多边形截面的产品，其全长边角可经磨圆。矩形（包括“变形矩形”）截面的产品，其厚度应大于宽度的十分之一。

Chapter 79
Zinc and articles therof

Notes:

In this Chapter the following expressions have the meanings hereby assigned to them:

1. Bars and rods

Rolled, extruded, drawn or forged products, not in coils, which have a uniform solid cross-section along their whole length in the shape of circles, ovals, rectangle (including squares), equilateral triangles or regular convex polygons (including "flattened circles" and "modified rectangles", of which two opposite sides are convex arcs, the other two sides being straight, of equal length and parallel). Products with a rectangular (including square), triangular or polygonal cross-section may have corners rounded alongtheir whole length. The thickness of such products which have a rectangular (including "modified rectangular") cross-section exceeds one-tenth of the width. The expression also covers cast or sintered products, of the same forms and dimensions, which have been subsequently worked after production (otherwise than by simple trimming or de-scaling), provided that they have not thereby assumed the character of articles or products of other headings.

2. Profiles

Rolled, extruded, drawn, forged or formed products, coiled or not, of a uniform cross-section along their whole length, which do not conform to any of the definitions of bars, rods, wire, plates, sheets, strip, foil, tubes or pipes. The expression also covers cast or sintered products, of the same forms, which have been subsequently worked after production (otherwise than by simple trimming or descaling), provided that they have not thereby assumed the character of articles or products of other headings.

3. Wire

Rolled, extruded or drawn products, in coils, which have a uniform soild cross-section along their whole length in the shape of circles, ovals, rectangles (including squares), equilateral triangles or regular convex polygons (including "flattened circles" and "modified rectangles", of which two opposite sides are convex arcs, the other two sides being straight, of equal length and parallel). Products with a rectangular (including square), triangular or polygonal cross-section may have corners rounded along their whole length. The thickness of such products which have a rectangular (including "modified rectangular") cross-section exceeds one-tenth of the width.

四、板、片、带、箔

成卷或非成卷的平面产品（税号 79.01 的未锻轧产品除外），截面均为厚度相同的实心矩形（不包括正方形），不论边角是否磨圆（包括相对两边为弧拱形，另外两边为等长平行直线的“变形矩形”），并且符合以下规格：

1. 矩形（包括正方形）的，厚度不超过宽度的十分之一；
2. 矩形或正方形以外形状的，任何尺寸，但不具有其他税号所列制品或产品的特征。

税号 79.05 还适用于具有花样（例如，凹槽、肋条形，格槽、珠粒及菱形）的板、片、带、箔以及穿孔、抛光、涂层或制成瓦楞形的这类产品，但不具有其他税号所列制品或产品的特征。

4. Plates, sheets, strip and foil

Flat-surfaced products (other than the unwrought products of heading No.79.01), coiled or not, of solid rectangular (other than square) cross-section with or without rounded corners (including "modified rectangles" of which two opposite sides are convex arcs, the other two sides being straight, of equal length and parallel) of a uniform thickness, which are:

(1) of rectangular (including square) shape with a thickness not exceeding, one-tenth of the width,
(2) of a shape other than rectangular or square, of any size, provided that they do not assume the character of articles or products of other headings.

Heading No.79.05 applies, *inter alia*, to plates, sheets, strip and foil with patterns (for example, grooves, ribs chequers, tears, buttons, lozenges) and to such products which have been perforated, corrugated, polished or coated, provided that they do not thereby assume the character of articles or products of other headings.

五、管

全长截面及管壁厚度相同并只有一个闭合空间的实心产品，成卷或非成卷的，其截面为圆形、椭圆形、矩形（包括正方形）、等边三角形或规则外凸多边形。对于截面为矩形（包括正方形）、等边三角形或规则外凸多边形的产品，不论全长边角是否磨圆，只要其内外截面为同一圆心并为同样形状及同一轴向，也可视为管子。上述截面的管子可经抛光、涂层、弯曲、攻丝、钻孔、缩腰、胀口、成锥形或装法兰、颈圈或套环。

5. Tubes and pipes

Hollow products, coiled or not, which have a uniform cross-section with only one enclosed void along their whole length in the shape of circles, ovals, rectangles (including squares), equilateral triangles or regular convex polygons, and which have a uniform wall thickness. Products with a rectangular (including square), equilateral triangular or regular convex polygonal cross-section, which may have corners rounded along their whole length, are also to be considered as tubes and pipes provided the inner and outer cross-sections are concentric and have the same form and orientation. Tubes and pipes of the foregoing cross-sections may be polished, coated, bent, threaded, drilled, waisted, expanded, cone-shaped or fitted with flanges, collars or rings.

子目注释：

本章所用有关名词解释如下：

一、非合金锌

按重量计含锌量至少为 97.5%的金属。

Subheading Notes:

In this Chapter the following expressions have the meanings hereby assigned to them:

1. Zinc, not alloyed

Metal containing by weight at least 97.5% of zinc.

二、锌合金

按重量计含锌量大于其他元素单项含量的金属物质，但按重量计其他元素的总含量超过 2.5%。

三、锌末

冷凝锌雾所得的锌末。该产品由球形微粒组成，比锌粉更为精细，按重量计至少 80%的微粒可以通过孔径为 63 微米的筛子，而且必须含有按重量计至少为 85%的金属锌。

2. Zinc alloys

Metallic substances in which zinc predominates by weight over each of the other elements, provided that the total content by weight of such other elements exceeds 2.5%.

3. Zinc dust

Dust obtained by condensation of zinc vapour, consisting of spherical particles which are finer than zinc powders. At least 80% by weight of the particles pass through a sieve with 63 micrometres (microns) mesh. It must contain at least 85% by weight of metallic zinc.

序号 No.	税则号列 Tariff Line	货品名称	最惠国税率 MFN(%)	协定税率 Agreement(%)		特惠税率 S.P.(%)		普通税率 Gen.(%)	Article Description
	79.01	**未锻轧锌:**							**Unwrought zinc:**
		-非合金锌:							-Zinc, not alloyed:
		--按重量计含锌量在 99.99%及以上:							--Containing by weight 99.99% or more of zinc:
5647	7901.1110	---按重量计含锌量在 99.995%及以上	3 △1	0	东盟ASEAN,智利CL,巴基斯坦PK,新西兰NZ,秘鲁PE,哥斯达黎加CR	0	最不发达 35 国 LDC35,最不发达 4 国 LDC4	20	---Containing by weight 99.995% or more of zinc
5648	7901.1190	---其他	3 △1	0	东盟ASEAN,智利CL,巴基斯坦PK,新西兰NZ,秘鲁PE,哥斯达黎加CR	0	最不发达 35 国 LDC35,最不发达 4 国 LDC4	20	---Other
5649	7901.1200	--按重量计含锌量低于 99.99%	3 △1	0	东盟ASEAN,智利CL,巴基斯坦PK,新西兰NZ,秘鲁PE,哥斯达黎加CR	0	最不发达 35 国 LDC35,最不发达 4 国 LDC4	20	--Containing by weight less than 99.99% of zinc
5650	7901.2000	-锌合金	3 △1	0	东盟ASEAN,智利CL,巴基斯坦PK,新西兰NZ,秘鲁PE,哥斯达黎加CR,香港HK	0	最不发达 35 国 LDC35,最不发达 4 国 LDC4	20	-Zinc alloys
	79.02	**锌废碎料:**							**Zinc waste and scrap:**
5651	7902.0000	锌废碎料	1.5 △1	0	东盟ASEAN,智利CL,巴基斯坦PK,新西兰NZ,秘鲁PE,哥斯达黎加CR	0	最不发达 35 国 LDC35,最不发达 4 国 LDC4	20	Zinc waste and scrap

序号 No.	税则号列 Tariff Line	货品名称	最惠国税率 MFN(%)	协定税率 Agreement(%)		特惠税率 S.P.(%)		普通税率 Gen.(%)	Article Description
	79.03	**锌末、锌粉及片状粉末:**							**Zinc dust, powders and flakes:**
5652	7903.1000	-锌末	6	0 5	东盟ASEAN,智利CL,新西兰NZ,秘鲁PE,哥斯达黎加CR 巴基斯坦PK	0	最不发达35国LDC35,最不发达4国LDC4	20	-Zinc dust
5653	7903.9000	-其他	6	0 5	东盟ASEAN,智利CL,新西兰NZ,秘鲁PE,哥斯达黎加CR 巴基斯坦PK	0	最不发达35国LDC35,最不发达4国LDC4	20	-Other
	79.04	**锌条、杆、型材及异型材或丝:**							**Zinc bars, rods, profiles and wire:**
5654	7904.0000	锌条、杆、型材及异型材或丝	6	0 5	东盟ASEAN,智利CL,新西兰NZ,秘鲁PE,哥斯达黎加CR 巴基斯坦PK	0	最不发达35国LDC35	30	Zinc bars, rods, profiles and wire
	79.05	**锌板、片、带、箔:**							**Zinc plates, sheets, strip and foil:**
5655	7905.0000	锌板、片、带、箔	6	0 0.6 5	东盟ASEAN,新西兰NZ,秘鲁PE,哥斯达黎加CR 智利CL 巴基斯坦PK	0	最不发达35国LDC35,最不发达4国LDC4	30	Zinc plates, sheets, strip and foil
	79.07	**其他锌制品:**							**Other articles of zinc:**
5656	7907.0020	---锌管及锌制管子附件(例如,接头、肘管、管套)	6	0 5	东盟ASEAN,智利CL,新西兰NZ,秘鲁PE,哥斯达黎加CR 巴基斯坦PK	0	最不发达35国LDC35,最不发达4国LDC4	30	---Zinc tubes or pipes and zinc tube or pipe fittings (for example, couplings, elbows, sleeves)
5657	7907.0030	---电池壳体坯料(锌饼)	6	0 4.5 5	东盟ASEAN,智利CL,新西兰NZ,哥斯达黎加CR 秘鲁PE 巴基斯坦PK	0	最不发达35国LDC35,最不发达4国LDC4	40	---Cellpacking blanks (zinc biscuits)
5658	7907.0090	---其他	6	0 5	东盟ASEAN,智利CL,新西兰NZ,秘鲁PE,哥斯达黎加CR 巴基斯坦PK	0	最不发达35国LDC35,最不发达4国LDC4	40	---Other

第八十章
锡及其制品

注释:

本章所用有关名词解释如下:

一、条、杆

轧、挤、拔或锻制的实心产品，非成卷的，其全长截面均为圆形、椭圆形、矩形（包括正方形）、等边三角形或规则外凸多边形(包括相对两边为弧拱形，另外两边为等长平行直线的“扁圆形”及“变形矩形”）。对于矩形（包括正方形）、三角形或多边形截面的产品,其全长边角可经磨圆。矩形(包括“变形矩形”）截面的产品，其厚度应大于宽度的十分之一。所述条、杆也包括同样形状及尺寸的铸造或烧结产品。该产品在铸造或烧结后再经加工（简单剪修或去氧化皮的除外），但不具有其他税号所列制品或产品的特征。

二、型材及异型材

轧、挤、拔、锻制的产品或其他成型产品，不论是否成卷，其全长截面相同，但与条、杆、丝、板、片、带、箔、管的定义不相符合。同时也包括同样形状的铸造或烧结产品。该产品在铸造或烧结后再经加工（简单剪修或去氧化皮的除外），但不具有其他税号所列制品或产品的特征。

三、丝

盘卷的轧、挤或拔制实心产品，其全长截面均为圆形、椭圆形、矩形（包括正方形）、等边三角形或规则外凸多边形（包括相对两边为弧拱形，另外两边为等长平行直线的“扁圆形”及“变形矩形”）。对于矩形（包括正方形）、三角形或多边形截面的产品，其全长边角可经磨圆。矩形（包括“变形矩形”)截面的产品，其厚度应大于宽度的十分之一。

Chapter 80
Tin and articles therof

Notes:

In this Chapter the following expressions have the meanings hereby assigned to them:

1. Bars and rods

Rolled, extruded, drawn or forged products, not in coils, which have a uniform solid cross-section along their whole length in the shape of circles, ovals, rectangle (including squares), equilateral triangles or regular convex polygons (including "flattened circles" and "modified rectangles", of which two opposite sides are convex arcs, the other two sides being straight, of equal length and parallel). Products with a rectangular (including square), triangular or polygonal cross-section may have corners rounded alongtheir whole length.The thickness of such products which have a rectangular (including "modified rectangular") cross-section exceeds one-tenth of the width. The expression also covers cast or sintered products, of the same forms and dimensions, which have been subsequently worked after production (otherwise than by simple trimming or de-scaling), provided that they have not thereby assumed the character of articles or products of other headings.

2. Profiles

Rolled, extruded, drawn, forged or formed products, coiled or not, of a uniform cross-section along their whole length, which do not conform to any of the definitions of bars, rods, wire, plates, sheets, strip, foil, tubes or pipes. The expression also covers cast or sintered products, of the same forms, which have been subsequently worked after production (otherwise than by simple trimming or descaling), provided that they have not thereby assumed the character of articles or products of other headings.

3. Wire

Rolled, extruded or drawn products, in coils, which have a uniform solid cross-section along their whole length in the shape of circles, ovals, rectanges (including squares), equilateral triangles or regular convex polygons (including "flattened circles" and "modified rectangles", of which two opposite sides are convex arcs, the other two sides being straight, of equal length and parallel). Products with a rectangular (including square), triangular or polygonal cross-section may have corners rounded along their whole length. The thickness of such products which have a rectangular (including "modified rectangular") cross-section exceeds one-tenth of the width;

四、板、片、带、箔

成卷或非成卷的平面产品(税号 80.01 的未锻轧产品除外)，截面均为厚度相同的实心矩形（不包括正方形），不论边角是否磨圆（包括相对两边为弧拱形，另外两边为等长平行直线的“变形矩形”），并且符合以下规格:

1. 矩形（包括正方形）的，厚度不超过宽度的十分之一;
2. 矩形或正方形以外形状的，任何尺寸，但不具有其他税号所列制品或产品的特征。

4. Plates, sheets, strip and foil

Flat-surfaced products (other than the unwrought products of heading No.80.01), coiled or not, of solid rectangular (other than square) cross-section with or without rounded corners (including "modified rectanges" of which two opposite sides are convex arcs, the other two sides being straight, of equal length and parallel) of a uniform thickness, which are:

-of rectangular (including square) shape with a thickness not exceeding one-tenth of the width;

-of a shape other than rectangular or square, of any size, provided that they do not assume the character of articles or products of other headings.

五、管

全长截面及管壁厚度相同并只有一个闭合空间的实心产品，成卷或非成卷的，其截面为圆形、椭圆形、矩形（包括正方形）、等边三角形或规则外凸多边形。对于截面为矩形（包括正方形）、等边三角形或规则外凸多边形的产品，不论全长边角是否磨圆，只要其内外截面为同一圆心并为同样形状及同一轴向，也可视为管子。上述截面的管子可经抛光、涂层、弯曲、攻丝、钻孔、缩腰、胀口、成锥形或装法兰、颈圈或套环。

5. Tubes and pipes

Hollow products, coiled or not, which have a uniform cross-section with only one enclosed void along their whole langth in the shape of circles, ovals, rectangles (including squares), equilateral triangles or regular convex polygons, and which have a uniform wall thickness. Products with a rectangular (including square), equilateral triangular or regular convex polygonal cross-section, which may have corners rounded along their whole length, are also to be considered as tubes and pipes provided the inner and outer cross-sections are concentric and have the same form and orientation. Tubes and pipes of the foregoing cross-sections may be polished, coated, bent, threaded, drilled, waisted, expanded, cone-shaped or fitted with flanges, collars or rings.

子目注释:

本章所用有关名词解释如下:

一、非合金锡

按重量计含锡量至少为 99%的金属，但含铋量或含铜量不超过下表中规定的限量:

Subheading Notes:

In this Chapter the following expressions have the meanings hereby assigned to them:

1. Tin, not alloyed.

Metal containing by weight at least 99% of tin, provided that the content by weight of any bismuth or copper is less than the limit specified in the following table:

其他元素表

元 素	所含重量百分比
Bi 铋	0.1
Cu 铜	0.4

TABLE Other elements

Element	Limiting content % by weight
Bi Bismuth	0.1
Cu Copper	0.4

二、锡合金

按重量计含锡量大于其他元素单项含量的金属物质，但:

2. Tin alloys

Metallic substances in which tin predominates by weight over each of the other elements, provided that:

（一）按重量计其他元素的总含量超过1%;或

（二）按重量计含铋量或含铜量应等于或大于上表中规定的限量。

(a) the total content by weight of such other elements exceeds 1%; or

(b) the content by weight of either bismuth or copper is equal to or greater than the limit specified in the foregoing table.

序号 No.	税则号列 Tariff Line	货品名称	最惠国税率 MFN(%)	协定税率 Agreement(%)		特惠税率 S.P.(%)		普通税率 Gen.(%)	Article Description
	80.01	**未锻轧锡:**							**Unwrought tin:**
5659	8001.1000	-非合金锡	3	0	东盟ASEAN,智利CL,巴基斯坦PK,新西兰NZ,秘鲁PE,哥斯达黎加CR,香港HK	0	最不发达35国LDC35,最不发达4国LDC4	20	-Tin, not alloyed
		-锡合金:							-Tin alloys:
5660	8001.2010	---锡基巴毕脱合金	3	0	东盟ASEAN,智利CL,巴基斯坦PK,新西兰NZ,秘鲁PE,哥斯达黎加CR,香港HK	0	最不发达35国LDC35,最不发达4国LDC4	20	---Babbitt metal
		---焊锡:							---Solder:
5661	8001.2021	----按重量计含铅量在0.1%以下的	3	0	东盟ASEAN,智利CL,巴基斯坦PK,新西兰NZ,秘鲁PE,哥斯达黎加CR,香港HK,澳门MO	0	最不发达35国LDC35,最不发达4国LDC4	30	----Containing by weight less than 0.1% of lead
5662	8001.2029	----其他	3	0	东盟ASEAN,智利CL,巴基斯坦PK,新西兰NZ,秘鲁PE,哥斯达黎加CR,香港HK,澳门MO	0	最不发达35国LDC35,最不发达4国LDC4	30	----Other
5663	8001.2090	---其他	3	0	东盟ASEAN,智利CL,巴基斯坦PK,新西兰NZ,秘鲁PE,哥斯达黎加CR,香港HK	0	最不发达35国LDC35,最不发达4国LDC4	30	---Other
	80.02	**锡废碎料:**							**Tin waste and scrap:**
5664	8002.0000	锡废碎料	1.5	0	东盟ASEAN,智利CL,巴基斯坦PK,新西兰NZ,秘鲁PE,哥斯达黎加CR,香港HK	0	最不发达35国LDC35	30	Tin waste and scrap
	80.03	**锡条、杆、型材及异型材或丝:**							**Tin bars, rods, profiles and wire:**
5665	8003.0000	锡条、杆、型材及异型材或丝	8	0 5	东盟ASEAN,智利CL,新西兰NZ,秘鲁PE,哥斯达黎加CR,香港HK 巴基斯坦PK	0	最不发达35国LDC35,最不发达4国LDC4	40	Tin bars, rods, profiles and wire

序号 No.	税则号列 Tariff Line	货品名称	最惠国税率 MFN(%)	协定税率 Agreement(%)		特惠税率 S.P.(%)		普通税率 Gen.(%)	Article Description
	80.07	**其他锡制品:**							**Other articles of tin:**
5666	8007.0020	---锡板、片及带，厚度超过 0.2 毫米	8	0 5	东盟ASEAN,智利CL,新西兰NZ,秘鲁PE,哥斯达黎加CR 巴基斯坦PK	0	最不发达 35 国 LDC35	40	---Tin plates, sheets and strip, of a thick-ness exceeding 0.2mm
5667	8007.0030	---锡箔（不论是否印花或用纸、纸板、塑料或类似材料衬背），厚度（衬背除外）不超过 0.2 毫米;锡粉及片状粉末	8	0 5	东盟ASEAN,智利CL,新西兰NZ,秘鲁PE,哥斯达黎加CR 巴基斯坦PK	0	最不发达 35 国 LDC35	40	---Tin foil (whether or not printed or backed with paper, paper-board, plastics or similar backing mate-rials), of a thickness (excluding any back-ing) not exceeding 0.2mm; tin powders and flakes
5668	8007.0040	---锡管及管子附件（例如，接头、肘管、管套）	8	0 5	东盟ASEAN,智利CL,新西兰NZ,秘鲁PE,哥斯达黎加CR 巴基斯坦PK	0	最不发达 35 国 LDC35	45	---Tin tubes, pipes and tube or pipe fittings (for example, cou-plings, elbows, sleeves)
5669	8007.0090	---其他	8	0 6.4	东盟ASEAN,智利CL,新西兰NZ,秘鲁PE,哥斯达黎加CR,香港HK 巴基斯坦PK	0	最不发达 35 国 LDC35	80	---Other

第八十一章
其他贱金属、金属陶瓷及其制品

Chapter 81
Other base metals; cermets; artiles thereof

子目注释:

第七十四章注释中有关“条、杆”、“型材及异型材”、“丝”及“板、片、带、箔”的规定也适用于本章。

Subheading Note:

Note 1 to Chapter 74, defining “bars and rods”, “profiles”, “wire” and “plates, sheets, strip and foil” applies, *mutatis mutandis*, to this Chapter.

序号 No.	税则号列 Tariff Line	货品名称	最惠国税率 MFN(%)	协定税率 Agreement(%)		特惠税率 S.P.(%)		普通税率 Gen.(%)	Article Description
	81.01	**钨及其制品，包括废碎料:**							**Tungsten (wolfram) and articles thereof, including waste and scrap:**
5670	8101.1000	-粉末	6	0 5	东盟ASEAN,智利CL,新西兰NZ,秘鲁PE,哥斯达黎加CR 巴基斯坦PK	0	最不发达35国LDC35	20	-Powders
		-其他:							-Other:
5671	8101.9400	--未锻轧钨，包括简单烧结而成的条、杆	3	0	东盟ASEAN,智利CL,巴基斯坦PK,新西兰NZ,秘鲁PE,哥斯达黎加CR	0	最不发达35国LDC35	20	--Unwrought tungsten, including bars and rods obtained simply by sintering
5672	8101.9600	--丝	8	0 5	东盟ASEAN,智利CL,新西兰NZ,秘鲁PE,哥斯达黎加CR 巴基斯坦PK	0	最不发达35国LDC35	20	--Wire
5673	8101.9700	--废碎料	3 △1	0	东盟ASEAN,智利CL,巴基斯坦PK,新西兰NZ,秘鲁PE,哥斯达黎加CR	0	最不发达35国LDC35	20	--Waste and scrap
		--其他:							--Other:
5674	8101.9910	---条、杆，但简单烧结而成的除外;型材及异型材、板、片、带、箔	5	0	东盟ASEAN,智利CL,巴基斯坦PK,新西兰NZ,秘鲁PE,哥斯达黎加CR	0	最不发达35国LDC35	30	---Bars and rods, other than those obtained simply by sintering, pro-files, plates, sheets, strip and foil
5675	8101.9990	---其他	8	0 5	东盟ASEAN,智利CL,新西兰NZ,秘鲁PE,哥斯达黎加CR 巴基斯坦PK	0	最不发达35国LDC35	70	---Other
	81.02	**钼及其制品，包括废碎料:**							**Molybdenum and articles thereof, including waste and scrap:**
5676	8102.1000	-粉末	6	0 5	东盟ASEAN,智利CL,新西兰NZ,秘鲁PE,哥斯达黎加CR 巴基斯坦PK	0	最不发达35国LDC35	20	-Powders
		-其他:							-Other:
5677	8102.9400	--未锻轧钼，包括简单烧结而成的条、杆	3	0	东盟ASEAN,智利CL,巴基斯坦PK,新西兰NZ,秘鲁PE,哥斯达黎加CR	0	最不发达35国LDC35	20	--Unwrought molybdenum, including bars and rods obtained simply by sintering

序号 No.	税则号列 Tariff Line	货品名称	最惠国税率 MFN(%)	协定税率 Agreement(%)		特惠税率 S.P.(%)		普通税率 Gen.(%)	Article Description
5678	8102.9500	--条、杆，但简单烧结而成的除外;型材及异型材、板、片、带、箔	8	0 5	东盟ASEAN,智利CL,新西兰NZ,秘鲁PE,哥斯达黎加CR 巴基斯坦PK	0	最不发达35国LDC35	30	--Bars and rods, other than those obtained simply by sintering, pro-files, plates, sheets, strip and foil
5679	8102.9600	--丝	8	0 5	东盟ASEAN,智利CL,新西兰NZ,秘鲁PE,哥斯达黎加CR 巴基斯坦PK	0	最不发达35国LDC35	20	--Wire
5680	8102.9700	--废碎料	3	0	东盟ASEAN,智利CL,巴基斯坦PK,新西兰NZ,秘鲁PE,哥斯达黎加CR	0	最不发达35国LDC35	20	--Waste and scrap
5681	8102.9900	--其他	8	0 5	东盟ASEAN,智利CL,新西兰NZ,秘鲁PE,哥斯达黎加CR 巴基斯坦PK	0	最不发达35国LDC35	70	--Other
	81.03	**钽及其制品，包括废碎料:**							**Tantalum and articles thereof, including waste and scrap:**
		-未锻轧钽，包括简单烧结而成的条、杆;粉末							-Unwrought tantalum, including bars and rods obtained simply by sin-tering; powders
		---钽粉:							---Powder:
5682	8103.2011	----松装密度小于 2.2g/cm³	6	0 5	东盟ASEAN,智利CL,新西兰NZ,秘鲁PE,哥斯达黎加CR 巴基斯坦PK	0	最不发达35国LDC35	14	----Loose density less than 2.2g/cm³
5683	8103.2019	----其他	6	0 5	东盟ASEAN,智利CL,新西兰NZ,秘鲁PE,哥斯达黎加CR 巴基斯坦PK	0	最不发达35国LDC35	14	----Other
5684	8103.2090	---其他	6	0 5	东盟ASEAN,智利CL,新西兰NZ,秘鲁PE,哥斯达黎加CR 巴基斯坦PK	0	最不发达35国LDC35	14	---Other
5685	8103.3000	-废碎料	6 △0	0 5	东盟ASEAN,智利CL,新西兰NZ,秘鲁PE,哥斯达黎加CR 巴基斯坦PK	0	最不发达35国LDC35	14	-Waste and scrap
		-其他:							-Other:
		---钽丝:							---Wire:
5686	8103.9011	----直径小于 0.5mm	8	0 5	东盟ASEAN,智利CL,新西兰NZ,秘鲁PE,哥斯达黎加CR 巴基斯坦PK	0	最不发达35国LDC35	30	----Smaller than 0.5mm in diameter
5687	8103.9019	----其他	8	0 5	东盟ASEAN,智利CL,新西兰NZ,秘鲁PE,哥斯达黎加CR 巴基斯坦PK	0	最不发达35国LDC35	30	----Other
5688	8103.9090	---其他	8	0 5	东盟ASEAN,智利CL,新西兰NZ,秘鲁PE,哥斯达黎加CR 巴基斯坦PK	0	最不发达35国LDC35	30	---Other

序号 No.	税则号列 Tariff Line	货品名称	最惠国税率 MFN(%)	协定税率 Agreement(%)		特惠税率 S.P.(%)		普通税率 Gen.(%)	Article Description
	81.04	**镁及其制品，包括废碎料:**							**Magnesium and articles thereof, including waste and scrap:**
		-未锻轧镁:							-Unwrought magnesium:
5689	8104.1100	--按重量计含镁量至少为 99.8%	6	0	东盟ASEAN,智利CL,巴基斯坦PK,新西兰NZ,秘鲁PE,哥斯达黎加CR	0	最不发达 35 国 LDC35	20	--Containing at least 99.8% by weight of magnesium
				4.2	亚太APTA				
5690	8104.1900	--其他	6	0	东盟ASEAN,智利CL,新西兰NZ,秘鲁PE,哥斯达黎加CR	0	最不发达 35 国 LDC35	20	--Other
				5	巴基斯坦PK				
5691	8104.2000	-废碎料	1.5	0	东盟ASEAN,智利CL,巴基斯坦PK,新西兰NZ,秘鲁PE,哥斯达黎加CR	0	最不发达 35 国 LDC35	20	-Waste and scrap
5692	8104.3000	-锉屑、车屑及颗粒，已按规格分级的;粉末	8	0	东盟ASEAN,智利CL,新西兰NZ,秘鲁PE,哥斯达黎加CR	0	最不发达 35 国 LDC35	30	-Raspings, turnings and granules, graded according to size; powders
				5	巴基斯坦PK				
		-其他:							-Other:
5693	8104.9010	---锻轧镁	8	0	东盟ASEAN,智利CL,新西兰NZ,秘鲁PE,哥斯达黎加CR	0	最不发达 35 国 LDC35	30	---Wrought magnesium
				5	巴基斯坦PK				
5694	8104.9020	---镁制品	8.4	0	东盟ASEAN,智利CL,新西兰NZ,秘鲁PE,哥斯达黎加CR	0	最不发达 35 国 LDC35	70	---Magnesium articles
				5	巴基斯坦PK				
	81.05	**钴锍及其他冶炼钴时所得的中间产品;钴及其制品，包括废碎料:**							**Cobalt mattes and other intermediate products of cobalt metallurgy; cobalt and articles thereof, including waste and scrap:**
		-钴锍及其他冶炼钴时所得的中间产品;未锻轧钴;粉末:							-Cobalt mattes and other intermediate products of cobalt metallurgy; unwrought cobalt; powders
5695	8105.2010	---钴湿法冶炼中间品	4 △0	0	东盟ASEAN,智利CL,巴基斯坦PK,新西兰NZ,秘鲁PE,哥斯达黎加CR	0	最不发达 35 国 LDC35,最不发达 4 国 LDC4	14	---Intermediate products of cobalt wet processing metallurgy
5696	8105.2020	---未锻轧钴	4	0	东盟ASEAN,智利CL,巴基斯坦PK,新西兰NZ,秘鲁PE,哥斯达黎加CR	0	最不发达 35 国 LDC35,最不发达 4 国 LDC4	14	---Unwrought cobalt

序号 No.	税则号列 Tariff Line	货品名称	最惠国税率 MFN(%)	协定税率 Agreement(%)		特惠税率 S.P.(%)		普通税率 Gen.(%)	Article Description
5697	8105.2090	---其他	4	0	东盟ASEAN,智利CL,巴基斯坦PK,新西兰NZ,秘鲁PE,哥斯达黎加CR	0	最不发达35国LDC35,最不发达4国LDC4	14	---Other
	ex81052090	钴锍及其他冶炼钴时所得的中间产品	△0						Cobalt mattes and other inter-mediate products of cobalt metallurgy
5698	8105.3000	-废碎料	4	0	东盟ASEAN,智利CL,巴基斯坦PK,新西兰NZ,秘鲁PE,哥斯达黎加CR	0	最不发达35国LDC35,最不发达4国LDC4	14	-waste and scrap
5699	8105.9000	-其他	8	0 0.8 5	东盟ASEAN,新西兰NZ,秘鲁PE,哥斯达黎加CR 智利CL 巴基斯坦PK	0	最不发达35国LDC35,最不发达4国LDC4	30	-Other
	81.06	**铋及其制品，包括废碎料:**							**Bismuth and articles thereof, including waste and scrap:**
5700	8106.0010	---未锻轧铋;废碎料;粉末	3	0	东盟ASEAN,智利CL,巴基斯坦PK,新西兰NZ,秘鲁PE,哥斯达黎加CR	0	最不发达35国LDC35	20	---Unwroght bismuth; waste and scrap; powders
	ex81060010	未锻轧铋	△1						Unwrought bismuth
5701	8106.0090	---其他	8	0 5	东盟ASEAN,智利CL,新西兰NZ,秘鲁PE,哥斯达黎加CR 巴基斯坦PK	0	最不发达35国LDC35	30	---Other
	81.07	**镉及其制品，包括废碎料:**							**Cadmium and articles thereof, including waste and scrap:**
5702	8107.2000	-未锻轧镉;粉末	3	0	东盟ASEAN,智利CL,巴基斯坦PK,新西兰NZ,哥斯达黎加CR	0	最不发达35国LDC35	14	-Unwrought cadmium; powders
5703	8107.3000	-废碎料	3	0	东盟ASEAN,智利CL,巴基斯坦PK,新西兰NZ,秘鲁PE,哥斯达黎加CR	0	最不发达35国LDC35	14	-waste and scrap
5704	8107.9000	-其他	8	0 5	东盟ASEAN,智利CL,新西兰NZ,秘鲁PE,哥斯达黎加CR 巴基斯坦PK	0	最不发达35国LDC35	30	-Other
	81.08	**钛及其制品，包括废碎料:**							**Titanium and articles thereof, including waste and scrap:**
		-未锻轧钛;粉末:							-Unwrought titanium; powders:
		---未锻轧钛:							---Unwrought tatanium:

序号 No.	税则号列 Tariff Line	货品名称	最惠国税率 MFN(%)	协定税率 Agreement(%)		特惠税率 S.P.(%)		普通税率 Gen.(%)	Article Description
5705	8108.2021	----海绵钛	3	0	东盟ASEAN,智利CL,巴基斯坦PK,新西兰NZ,秘鲁PE,哥斯达黎加CR	0	最不发达35国LDC35	14	----Titanium sponge
5706	8108.2029	----其他	3	0	东盟ASEAN,智利CL,巴基斯坦PK,新西兰NZ,秘鲁PE,哥斯达黎加CR	0	最不发达35国LDC35	14	----Other
5707	8108.2030	---粉末	3	0	东盟ASEAN,智利CL,巴基斯坦PK,新西兰NZ,秘鲁PE,哥斯达黎加CR	0	最不发达35国LDC35	14	---Powders
5708	8108.3000	-废碎料	3	0	东盟ASEAN,智利CL,巴基斯坦PK,新西兰NZ,秘鲁PE,哥斯达黎加CR	0	最不发达35国LDC35	14	-Waste and scrap
		-其他:							-Other:
5709	8108.9010	---条、杆、型材及异型材	8	0 5	东盟ASEAN,智利CL,新西兰NZ,秘鲁PE,哥斯达黎加CR 巴基斯坦PK	0	最不发达35国LDC35	30	---Bars、rods、shapes and sections
5710	8108.9020	---丝	8	0 5	东盟ASEAN,智利CL,新西兰NZ,秘鲁PE,哥斯达黎加CR 巴基斯坦PK	0	最不发达35国LDC35	30	---Wire
		---板、片、带、箔:							---Plates, sheets, strap, foil:
5711	8108.9031	----厚度不超过0.8毫米	8 △4	0 5	东盟ASEAN,智利CL,新西兰NZ,秘鲁PE,哥斯达黎加CR 巴基斯坦PK	0	最不发达35国LDC35	30	----Of a thickness not more than 0.8mm
5712	8108.9032	----厚度超过0.8毫米	8 △4	0 5	东盟ASEAN,智利CL,新西兰NZ,秘鲁PE,哥斯达黎加CR 巴基斯坦PK	0	最不发达35国LDC35	30	----Of a thickness more than 0.8mm
5713	8108.9040	---管	8	0 5	东盟ASEAN,智利CL,新西兰NZ,秘鲁PE,哥斯达黎加CR 巴基斯坦PK	0	最不发达35国LDC35	30	---Tubes or pipes
5714	8108.9090	---其他	8	0 5	东盟ASEAN,智利CL,新西兰NZ,秘鲁PE,哥斯达黎加CR 巴基斯坦PK	0	最不发达35国LDC35	30	---Other
	81.09	**锆及其制品，包括废碎料:**							**Zirconium and articles thereof, including waste and scrap:**
5715	8109.2000	-未锻轧锆;粉末	3	0	东盟ASEAN,智利CL,巴基斯坦PK,新西兰NZ,秘鲁PE,哥斯达黎加CR	0	最不发达35国LDC35	20	-Unwrought zirconium; powders
5716	8109.3000	-废碎料	3	0	东盟ASEAN,智利CL,巴基斯坦PK,新西兰NZ,秘鲁PE,哥斯达黎加CR	0	最不发达35国LDC35	20	-waste and scrap

序号 No.	税则号列 Tariff Line	货品名称	最惠国税率 MFN(%)	协定税率 Agreement(%)		特惠税率 S.P.(%)		普通税率 Gen.(%)	Article Description
5717	8109.9000	-其他	8	0 5	东盟ASEAN,智利CL,新西兰NZ,秘鲁PE,哥斯达黎加CR 巴基斯坦PK	0	最不发达35国LDC35	30	-Other
	81.10	**锑及其制品，包括废碎料:**							**Antimony and articles thereof, including waste and scrap:**
		-未锻轧锑;粉末:							-Unwrought antimony; powders:
5718	8110.1010	---未锻轧锑	3 △1	0	东盟ASEAN,智利CL,巴基斯坦PK,新西兰NZ,秘鲁PE,哥斯达黎加CR	0	最不发达35国LDC35	30	---Unwrought antimony
5719	8110.1020	---粉末	3	0	东盟ASEAN,智利CL,巴基斯坦PK,新西兰NZ,秘鲁PE,哥斯达黎加CR	0	最不发达35国LDC35	30	---powders
5720	8110.2000	-废碎料	3	0	东盟ASEAN,智利CL,巴基斯坦PK,新西兰NZ,秘鲁PE,哥斯达黎加CR	0	最不发达35国LDC35	30	-Antimony waste and scrap
5721	8110.9000	-其他	8	0 5	东盟ASEAN,智利CL,新西兰NZ,秘鲁PE,哥斯达黎加CR 巴基斯坦PK	0	最不发达35国LDC35	40	-Other
	81.11	**锰及其制品，包括废碎料:**							**Manganese and articles thereof, including waste and scrap:**
5722	8111.0010	---未锻轧锰;废碎料;粉末	3	0	东盟ASEAN,智利CL,巴基斯坦PK,新西兰NZ,秘鲁PE,哥斯达黎加CR	0	最不发达35国LDC35,最不发达4国LDC4	20	---Unwrought manganese; waste and scrap; powders
5723	8111.0090	---其他	8	0 5	东盟ASEAN,智利CL,新西兰NZ,秘鲁PE,哥斯达黎加CR 巴基斯坦PK	0	最不发达35国LDC35,最不发达4国LDC4	30	---Other
	81.12	**铍、铬、锗、钒、镓、铪、铟、铼、铌、铊及其制品，包括废碎料:**							**Beryllium, chromium, germanium, vanadium, gallium, hafnium, indium, niobium (columbium), rhenium and thallium, and articles of these metals, including waste and scrap:**
		-铍:							-Beryllium:
5724	8112.1200	--未锻轧铍;粉末	3	0	东盟ASEAN,智利CL,巴基斯坦PK,新西兰NZ,秘鲁PE,哥斯达黎加CR	0	最不发达35国LDC35,最不发达4国LDC4	30	--Unwrought;powders

序号 No.	税则号列 Tariff Line	货品名称	最惠国 税　率 MFN(%)	协定税率 Agreement(%)		特惠税率 S.P.(%)		普通 税率 Gen.(%)	Article Description
5725	8112.1300	--废碎料	3	0	东盟ASEAN,智利CL,巴基斯坦PK,新西兰NZ,秘鲁PE,哥斯达黎加CR	0	最不发达35国LDC35,最不发达4国LDC4	30	--waste and scrap
5726	8112.1900	--其他	8	0 5	东盟ASEAN,智利CL,新西兰NZ,秘鲁PE,哥斯达黎加CR 巴基斯坦PK	0	最不发达35国LDC35,最不发达4国LDC4	30	--Other
		-铬:							-Chromium:
5727	8112.2100	--未锻轧铬;粉末	3	0	东盟ASEAN,智利CL,巴基斯坦PK,新西兰NZ,秘鲁PE,哥斯达黎加CR	0	最不发达35国LDC35,最不发达4国LDC4	20	--Unwrought; powders
5728	8112.2200	--废碎料	3	0	东盟ASEAN,智利CL,巴基斯坦PK,新西兰NZ,秘鲁PE,哥斯达黎加CR	0	最不发达35国LDC35,最不发达4国LDC4	20	--Waste and Scrap
5729	8112.2900	--其他	3	0	东盟ASEAN,智利CL,巴基斯坦PK,新西兰NZ,秘鲁PE,哥斯达黎加CR	0	最不发达35国LDC35,最不发达4国LDC4	20	--Other
		-铊:							-Thallium:
5730	8112.5100	--未锻轧铊;粉末	3	0	东盟ASEAN,智利CL,巴基斯坦PK,新西兰NZ,秘鲁PE,哥斯达黎加CR	0	最不发达35国LDC35,最不发达4国LDC4	20	--Unwrought; powders
5731	8112.5200	--废碎料	3	0	东盟ASEAN,智利CL,巴基斯坦PK,新西兰NZ,秘鲁PE,哥斯达黎加CR	0	最不发达35国LDC35,最不发达4国LDC4	20	--Waste and Scrap
5732	8112.5900	--其他	8	0 5	东盟ASEAN,智利CL,新西兰NZ,秘鲁PE,哥斯达黎加CR 巴基斯坦PK	0	最不发达35国LDC35,最不发达4国LDC4	30	--Other
		-其他:							-Other:
		--未锻轧;废碎料;粉末:							--Unwrought; waste and scrap; powders:

序号 No.	税则号列 Tariff Line	货品名称	最惠国税率 MFN(%)	协定税率 Agreement(%)		特惠税率 S.P.(%)		普通税率 Gen.(%)	Article Description
5733	8112.9210	---锗	3	0	东盟ASEAN,智利CL,巴基斯坦PK,新西兰NZ,秘鲁PE,哥斯达黎加CR	0	最不发达35国LDC35,最不发达4国LDC4	20	---Germanium
5734	8112.9220	---钒	3 △0	0	东盟ASEAN,智利CL,巴基斯坦PK,新西兰NZ,秘鲁PE,哥斯达黎加CR	0	最不发达35国LDC35,最不发达4国LDC4	20	---Vanadium
5735	8112.9230	---铟	3	0	东盟ASEAN,智利CL,巴基斯坦PK,新西兰NZ,秘鲁PE,哥斯达黎加CR	0	最不发达35国LDC35,最不发达4国LDC4	20	---Indium
5736	8112.9240	---铌	3 △1	0	东盟ASEAN,智利CL,巴基斯坦PK,新西兰NZ,秘鲁PE,哥斯达黎加CR	0	最不发达35国LDC35,最不发达4国LDC4	20	---Niobium
5737	8112.9290	---其他	3	0	东盟ASEAN,智利CL,巴基斯坦PK,新西兰NZ,秘鲁PE,哥斯达黎加CR	0	最不发达35国LDC35,最不发达4国LDC4	20	---Other
		--其他:							--Other:
5738	8112.9910	---锗	3	0	东盟ASEAN,智利CL,巴基斯坦PK,新西兰NZ,秘鲁PE,哥斯达黎加CR	0	最不发达35国LDC35,最不发达4国LDC4	20	---Germanium
5739	8112.9920	---钒	3	0	东盟ASEAN,智利CL,巴基斯坦PK,新西兰NZ,秘鲁PE,哥斯达黎加CR	0	最不发达35国LDC35,最不发达4国LDC4	20	---Vanadium
	ex81129920	其他钒氮合金	△0						Other vanadic-nitrogen
5740	8112.9930	---铟	8	0 0.8 5	东盟ASEAN,新西兰NZ,秘鲁PE,哥斯达黎加CR 智利CL 巴基斯坦PK	0	最不发达35国LDC35,最不发达4国LDC4	20	---Indium
5741	8112.9940	---铌	8	0 0.8 5	东盟ASEAN,新西兰NZ,秘鲁PE,哥斯达黎加CR 智利CL 巴基斯坦PK	0	最不发达35国LDC35,最不发达4国LDC4	20	---Niobium

序号 No.	税则号列 Tariff Line	货品名称	最惠国税率 MFN(%)	协定税率 Agreement(%)		特惠税率 S.P.(%)		普通税率 Gen.(%)	Article Description
5742	8112.9990	---其他	8	0 0.8	东盟ASEAN,巴基斯坦PK,新西兰NZ,秘鲁PE,哥斯达黎加CR 智利CL	0	最不发达35国LDC35,最不发达4国LDC4	30	---Other
	81.13	**金属陶瓷及其制品，包括废碎料:**							**Cermets and articles thereof, including waste and scrap:**
		金属陶瓷及其制品，包括废碎料:							Cermets and articles thereof, including waste and scrap:
5743	8113.0010	---颗粒;粉末	8.4	0 5	东盟ASEAN,智利CL,新西兰NZ,秘鲁PE,哥斯达黎加CR,台湾TW 巴基斯坦PK	0	最不发达35国LDC35	30	---Granules and powders
5744	8113.0090	---其他	8.4	0 5	东盟ASEAN,智利CL,新西兰NZ,秘鲁PE,哥斯达黎加CR,台湾TW 巴基斯坦PK	0	最不发达35国LDC35	30	---Other

第八十二章
贱金属工具、器具、利口器、餐匙、餐叉及其零件

注释:

一、除喷灯、轻便锻炉、带支架的砂轮、修指甲和修脚用器具及税号 82.09 的货品外，本章仅包括带有用下列材料制成的刀片、工作刃、工作面或其他工作部件的物品:

（一）贱金属;

（二）硬质合金或金属陶瓷;

（三）装于贱金属、硬质合金或金属陶瓷底座上的宝石或半宝石（天然、合成或再造）;

（四）附于贱金属底座上的磨料，当附上磨料后，所具有的切齿、沟、槽或类似结构仍保持其特性及功能。

二、本章所列物品的贱金属零件，应与该制品归入同一税号，但具体列名的零件及手工工具的工具夹具（税号 84.66）除外。第十五类注释二所述的通用零件，均不归入本章。电动剃须刀及电动毛发推剪的刀头、刀片应归入税号 85.10。

三、由税号 82.11 的一把或多把刀具与税号 82.15 至少数量相同的物品构成的成套货品应归入税号 82.15。

Chapter 82
Tools, implements, cutlery, spoons and forks, of base metal

Notes:

1. Apart from blow lamps, portable forges, grinding wheels with frameworks, manicure or pedicure sets, and goods of heading No.82.09, this Chapter covers only articles with a blade, working edge, working surface or other working part of:

(a) Base metal;

(b) Metal carbides or cermets;

(c) Precious or semi-precious stones (natural, synthetic or reconstructed) on a support of base metal, metal carbide or cermet; or

(d) Abrasive materials on a support of base metal, provided that the articles have cutting teeth, flutes, grooves, or the like, of base metal, which retain their identity and function after the application of the abrasive.

2. Parts of base metal of the articles of this Chapter are to be classified with the articles of which they are parts, except parts separately specified as such and tool-holders for hand tools (heading No.84.66) . However, parts of general use as defined in Note 2 to Section XV are in all cases excluded from this Chapter. Heads, blades and cutting plates for electric shavers or electric hair clippers are to be classified in heading No.85.10.

3. Sets consisting of one or more knives of heading No.82.11 and at least an equal number of articles of heading No.82.15 are to be classified in heading No.82.15.

序号 No.	税则号列 Tariff Line	货品名称	最惠国税率 MFN(%)	协定税率 Agreement(%)	特惠税率 S.P.(%)	普通税率 Gen.(%)	Article Description
	82.01	锹、铲、镐、锄、叉及耙;斧子、钩刀及类似砍伐工具;各种修枝用剪刀;镰刀、秣刀、树篱剪、伐木楔子及其他农业、园艺或林业用手工工具:					Hand tools, the following: spades, shovels, mattocks, picks, hoes, forks and rakes; axes, bill hooks and similar hewing tools; secateurs and prundrs of any kind; scythes, hay knives, hedge shears, timber wedges and other tools of a kind used in agriculture, horticulture or forestry:

序号 No.	税则号列 Tariff Line	货品名称	最惠国税率 MFN(%)	协定税率 Agreement(%)		特惠税率 S.P.(%)		普通税率 Gen.(%)	Article Description
5745	8201.1000	-锹及铲	8	0 5	东盟ASEAN,智利CL,新西兰NZ,秘鲁PE,哥斯达黎加CR 巴基斯坦PK	0	最不发达35国LDC35,最不发达4国LDC4	50	-Spades and shovels
5746	8201.3000	-镐、锄及耙	8	0 5	东盟ASEAN,智利CL,新西兰NZ,秘鲁PE,哥斯达黎加CR 巴基斯坦PK	0	最不发达35国LDC35,最不发达4国LDC4	50	-Mattocks, picks, hoes and rakes
5747	8201.4000	-斧子、钩刀及类似砍伐工具	8	0 5	东盟ASEAN,智利CL,新西兰NZ,秘鲁PE,哥斯达黎加CR 巴基斯坦PK	0	最不发达35国LDC35,最不发达4国LDC4	50	-Axes, bill hooks and similar hewing tools
5748	8201.5000	-修枝剪及类似的单手操作剪刀（包括家禽剪）	8	0 5	东盟ASEAN,智利CL,新西兰NZ,秘鲁PE,哥斯达黎加CR 巴基斯坦PK	0	最不发达35国LDC35,最不发达4国LDC4	50	-Secateurs and similar one-handed pruners and shears (including poultry shears)
5749	8201.6000	-树篱剪、双手修枝剪及类似的双手操作剪刀	8	0 5	东盟ASEAN,智利CL,新西兰NZ,秘鲁PE,哥斯达黎加CR 巴基斯坦PK	0	最不发达35国LDC35,最不发达4国LDC4	50	-Hedge shears, two-handed pruning shears and similar two-handed shears
		-用于农业、园艺或林业的其他手工工具：							-Other hand tools of a kind used in agriculture, horticulture or forestry:
5750	8201.9010	---叉	8	0 5	东盟ASEAN,智利CL,新西兰NZ,秘鲁PE,哥斯达黎加CR 巴基斯坦PK	0	最不发达35国LDC35,最不发达4国LDC4	50	---Forks
5751	8201.9090	---其他	8	0 5	东盟ASEAN,智利CL,新西兰NZ,秘鲁PE,哥斯达黎加CR 巴基斯坦PK	0	最不发达35国LDC35,最不发达4国LDC4	50	---Other
	82.02	**手工锯;各种锯的锯片（包括切条、切槽或无齿锯片）：**							**Hand saws;blades for saws of all kinds (including slitting, slotting or toothless saw blades):**
5752	8202.1000	-手工锯	8.4	0 5	东盟ASEAN,智利CL,新西兰NZ,秘鲁PE,哥斯达黎加CR 巴基斯坦PK	0	最不发达35国LDC35,最不发达4国LDC4	50	-Hand saws

序号 No.	税则号列 Tariff Line	货品名称	最惠国税率 MFN(%)	协定税率 Agreement(%)		特惠税率 S.P.(%)		普通税率 Gen.(%)	Article Description
		-带锯片:							-Band saw blades:
5753	8202.2010	---双金属带锯条	8	0 5	东盟ASEAN,智利CL,新西兰NZ,秘鲁PE,哥斯达黎加CR 巴基斯坦PK	0	最不发达35国LDC35,最不发达4国LDC4	20	---Bi-metal band saw blades
5754	8202.2090	---其他	8	0 5	东盟ASEAN,智利CL,新西兰NZ,秘鲁PE,哥斯达黎加CR 巴基斯坦PK	0	最不发达35国LDC35,最不发达4国LDC4	20	---Other
		-圆锯片(包括切条或切槽锯片):							-Circular saw blades (including slitting or slotting saw blades):
5755	8202.3100	--带有钢制工作部件	8	0 5	东盟ASEAN,智利CL,新西兰NZ,秘鲁PE,哥斯达黎加CR 巴基斯坦PK	0	最不发达35国LDC35,最不发达4国LDC4	20	--With working part of steel
		--其他，包括部件:							--Other, including parts:
5756	8202.3910	---带有天然或合成金刚石、立方氮化硼制的工作部件	8	0 5	东盟ASEAN,智利CL,新西兰NZ,秘鲁PE,哥斯达黎加CR,香港HK 巴基斯坦PK	0	最不发达35国LDC35,最不发达4国LDC4	20	---With working part of natural or synthetic diamonds or cubic boron nitride
5757	8202.3990	---其他	8	0 5	东盟ASEAN,智利CL,新西兰NZ,秘鲁PE,哥斯达黎加CR,香港HK 巴基斯坦PK	0	最不发达35国LDC35,最不发达4国LDC4	20	---Other
5758	8202.4000	-链锯片	8	0 5	东盟ASEAN,智利CL,新西兰NZ,秘鲁PE,哥斯达黎加CR 巴基斯坦PK	0	最不发达35国LDC35,最不发达4国LDC4	20	-Chain saw blades
		-其他锯片:							-Other saw blades:
		--直锯片，加工金属用:							--Straight saw blades, for working metal:
5759	8202.9110	---机械锯用	8	0 5 7	东盟ASEAN,智利CL,新西兰NZ,秘鲁PE,哥斯达黎加CR 巴基斯坦PK 亚太APTA	0	最不发达35国LDC35,最不发达4国LDC4	20	---For sawing machines
5760	8202.9190	---其他	8	0 5	东盟ASEAN,智利CL,新西兰NZ,秘鲁PE,哥斯达黎加CR 巴基斯坦PK	0	最不发达35国LDC35,最不发达4国LDC4	50	---Other

序号 No.	税则号列 Tariff Line	货品名称	最惠国税率 MFN(%)	协定税率 Agreement(%)		特惠税率 S.P.(%)		普通税率 Gen.(%)	Article Description
		--其他:							--Other:
5761	8202.9910	---机械锯用	8.4	0 5	东盟ASEAN,智利CL,新西兰NZ,秘鲁PE,哥斯达黎加CR 巴基斯坦PK	0	最不发达35国LDC35,最不发达4国LDC4	20	---For sawing machines
5762	8202.9990	---其他	10.5	0 2.1 5	东盟ASEAN,智利CL,新加坡SG,新西兰NZ,秘鲁PE 哥斯达黎加CR 巴基斯坦PK	0	最不发达35国LDC35	50	---Other
	82.03	**钢锉、木锉、钳子(包括剪钳)、镊子、白铁剪、切管器、螺栓切头器、打孔冲子及类似手工工具:**							**Files, rasps, pliers (including cutting pliers), pincers, tweezers, metal cutting shears, pipe-cutters, bolt croppers, perforating punches and similar hand tools:**
5763	8203.1000	-钢锉、木锉及类似工具	10.5	0 2.1 5	东盟ASEAN,智利CL,新加坡SG,新西兰NZ,秘鲁PE 哥斯达黎加CR 巴基斯坦PK	0	最不发达35国LDC35,最不发达4国LDC4	50	-Files, rasps and similar tools
5764	8203.2000	-钳子(包括剪钳)、镊子及类似工具	10.5	0 2.1	东盟ASEAN,智利CL,新加坡SG,新西兰NZ,秘鲁PE,澳门MO,台湾TW 哥斯达黎加CR	0	最不发达35国LDC35	50	-Pliers (including cutting pliers), pincers, tweezers and similar tools
5765	8203.3000	-白铁剪及类似工具	10.5	0 2.1 5	东盟ASEAN,智利CL,新加坡SG,新西兰NZ,秘鲁PE 哥斯达黎加CR 巴基斯坦PK	0	最不发达35国LDC35	50	-Metal cutting shears and similar tools
5766	8203.4000	-切管器、螺栓切头器、打孔冲子及类似工具	10.5	0 2.1 5	东盟ASEAN,智利CL,新加坡SG,新西兰NZ,秘鲁PE 哥斯达黎加CR 巴基斯坦PK	0	最不发达35国LDC35	50	-Pipe-cutters, bolt croppers, perforating punches and similar tools
	82.04	**手动扳手及扳钳(包括转矩扳手,但不包括丝锥扳手);可互换的扳手套筒,不论是否带手柄:**							**Hand-operated spanners and wrenches (including torque meter wrenches but not including tap wrenches); interchangeable spaner sockets, with or without handles:**
		-手动扳手及扳钳:							-Hand-operated spanners and wrenches:
5767	8204.1100	--固定的	10.5	0 2.1 5	东盟ASEAN,智利CL,新加坡SG,新西兰NZ,秘鲁PE 哥斯达黎加CR 巴基斯坦PK	0	最不发达35国LDC35,最不发达4国LDC4	50	--Non-adjustable

序号 No.	税则号列 Tariff Line	货品名称	最惠国税率 MFN(%)	协定税率 Agreement(%)		特惠税率 S.P.(%)		普通税率 Gen.(%)	Article Description
5768	8204.1200	--可调的	10	0 5	东盟ASEAN,智利CL,新西兰NZ,秘鲁PE,哥斯达黎加CR,台湾TW 巴基斯坦PK	0	最不发达35国LDC35,最不发达4国LDC4	50	--Adjustable
5769	8204.2000	-可互换的扳手套筒，不论是否带手柄	10	0 5	东盟ASEAN,智利CL,新西兰NZ,秘鲁PE,哥斯达黎加CR 巴基斯坦PK	0	最不发达35国LDC35	50	-Interchangeable spanner sockets, with or without handles
	82.05	**其他税号未列名的手工工具(包括玻璃刀);喷灯;台钳、夹钳及类似品，但作为机床附件或零件的除外;砧;轻便锻炉;带支架的手摇或脚踏砂轮:**							**Hand tools (including glaziers' diamonds), not elsewhere specified or included; blow lamps; vices, clamps and the like, other than accessories for and parts of, machine tools; anvils; portable forges; hand or pedal operated grinding wheels with frame works:**
5770	8205.1000	-钻孔或攻丝工具	10	0 5	东盟ASEAN,智利CL,新西兰NZ,秘鲁PE,哥斯达黎加CR 巴基斯坦PK	0	最不发达35国LDC35	50	-Drilling, threading or tapping tools
5771	8205.2000	-锤子	10	0 5	东盟ASEAN,智利CL,新西兰NZ,秘鲁PE,哥斯达黎加CR,台湾TW 巴基斯坦PK	0	最不发达35国LDC35,最不发达4国LDC4	50	-Hammers and sledge hammers
5772	8205.3000	-木工用刨子、凿子及类似切削工具	10.5	0 2.1 5	东盟ASEAN,智利CL,新加坡SG,新西兰NZ,秘鲁PE 哥斯达黎加CR 巴基斯坦PK	0	最不发达35国LDC35	50	-Planes, chisels, gouges and similar cutting tools for working wood
5773	8205.4000	-螺丝刀	10.5	0 2.1 5	东盟ASEAN,智利CL,新加坡SG,新西兰NZ,秘鲁PE,台湾TW 哥斯达黎加CR 巴基斯坦PK	0	最不发达35国LDC35,最不发达4国LDC4	50	-Screwdrivers
		-其他手工工具(包括玻璃刀):							-Other hand tools (including glaziers' diamonds):
5774	8205.5100	--家用工具	10.5	0 1.1 2.1 5	东盟ASEAN,新加坡SG,新西兰NZ,秘鲁PE 智利CL 哥斯达黎加CR 巴基斯坦PK	0	最不发达35国LDC35	50	--Household tools
5775	8205.5900	--其他	10	0 5 8.5	东盟ASEAN,智利CL,新西兰NZ,秘鲁PE,哥斯达黎加CR,台湾TW 巴基斯坦PK 亚太APTA	0	最不发达35国LDC35	50	--Other

序号 No.	税则号列 Tariff Line	货品名称	最惠国税率 MFN(%)	协定税率 Agreement(%)		特惠税率 S.P.(%)		普通税率 Gen.(%)	Article Description
5776	8205.6000	-喷灯	10	0 5	东盟ASEAN,智利CL,新西兰NZ,秘鲁PE,哥斯达黎加CR 巴基斯坦PK	0	最不发达35国LDC35	50	-Blow lamps
5777	8205.7000	-台钳、夹钳及类似品	10.5	0 2.1 5	东盟ASEAN,智利CL,新加坡SG,新西兰NZ,秘鲁PE 哥斯达黎加CR 巴基斯坦PK	0	最不发达35国LDC35	50	-Vices, clamps and the like
5778	8205.9000	-其他，包括由本税目项下两个或多个子目所列物品组成的成套货品	10.5	0 2.1 5	东盟ASEAN,智利CL,新加坡SG,新西兰NZ,秘鲁PE 哥斯达黎加CR 巴基斯坦PK	0	最不发达35国LDC35	50	-Other, inculding sets of articles of two or more of subheadings of this heading
	82.06	**由税号82.02至82.05中两个或多个税目所列工具组成的零售包装成套货品:**							**Tools of two or more of the headings Nos.82.02 to 82.05, put up in sets for retail sale:**
5779	8206.0000	由税号82.02至82.05中两个或多个税目所列工具组成的零售包装成套货品	10.5	0 1.1 2.1 5	东盟ASEAN,新加坡SG,新西兰NZ,秘鲁PE 智利CL 哥斯达黎加CR 巴基斯坦PK	0	最不发达35国LDC35	50	Tools of two or more of the headings Nos.82.02 to 82.05, put up in sets for retail sale
	82.07	**手工工具（不论是否有动力装置）及机床（例如，锻压、冲压、攻丝、钻孔、镗孔、铰孔及铣削、车削或上螺丝用的机器）的可互换工具，包括金属拉拔或挤压用模以及凿岩或钻探工具:**							**Interchangeable tools for hand tools, whether or not power-operated, or for machine-tools (for example, for pressing, stamping, punching, tapping, threading, drilling, boring, broaching, milling, turning or screw driving), including dies for drawing or extruding metal, and rock drilling or earth boring tools:**
		-凿岩或钻探工具:							-Rock drilling or earth boring tools:
5780	8207.1300	--带有金属陶瓷制的工作部件	8	0 0.8 5	东盟ASEAN,新西兰NZ,秘鲁PE,哥斯达黎加CR 智利CL 巴基斯坦PK	0	最不发达35国LDC35,最不发达4国LDC4	20	--With working part of cermets
		--其他，包括部件:							--Other, including parts:
5781	8207.1910	---带有天然或合成金刚石、立方氮化硼制的工作部件	8	0 0.8 5	东盟ASEAN,新西兰NZ,秘鲁PE,哥斯达黎加CR 智利CL 巴基斯坦PK	0	最不发达35国LDC35,最不发达4国LDC4	20	---With working part of natural or synthetic diamonds or cubic boron nitride

序号 No.	税则号列 Tariff Line	货品名称	最惠国税率 MFN(%)	协定税率 Agreement(%)		特惠税率 S.P.(%)		普通税率 Gen.(%)	Article Description
5782	8207.1990	---其他	8	0 0.8 5	东盟ASEAN,新西兰NZ,秘鲁PE,哥斯达黎加CR 智利CL 巴基斯坦PK	0	最不发达35国LDC35,最不发达4国LDC4	20	---Other
		-金属拉拔或挤压用模:							-Dies for drawing or extruding metal:
5783	8207.2010	---带有天然或合成金刚石、立方氮化硼制的工作部件	8	0 5	东盟ASEAN,智利CL,新西兰NZ,秘鲁PE,哥斯达黎加CR,台湾TW 巴基斯坦PK	0	最不发达35国LDC35,最不发达4国LDC4	20	---With working part of natural or synthetic diamonds or cubic boron nitride
5784	8207.2090	---其他	8	0 5	东盟ASEAN,智利CL,新西兰NZ,秘鲁PE,哥斯达黎加CR,台湾TW 巴基斯坦PK	0	最不发达35国LDC35,最不发达4国LDC4	20	---Other
5785	8207.3000	-锻压或冲压工具	8	0 0.8 5 6.8	东盟ASEAN,新西兰NZ,秘鲁PE,哥斯达黎加CR,香港HK,台湾TW 智利CL 巴基斯坦PK 亚太APTA	0	最不发达35国LDC35,最不发达4国LDC4	20	-Tools for pressing, stamping or punching
	ex82073000	加工小轿车车身冲压件用的4种关键模具（侧围外板模具、翼子板模具、拼接整体侧围内板模具、拼焊整体侧围加强板模具）	△4						Four key dies, used for processing stamping parts of car body (side outer panels dies , fender dies, dies for joining the whole side inner panels, dies for joining and welding the whole side-panel reinforcement)
	ex82073000	加工小轿车车身冲压件用的4种特种模具（σb≥980N/mm^2,的冷冲压模具、热成型模具、内高压成型模具和铝板模具）	△4						Four special dies, used for processing stamping parts of car body (cold stamping dies with σb≥980N/mm^2, hot forming dies, inside high pressure forming dies and aluminium panel dies)
5786	8207.4000	-攻丝工具	8	0 5	东盟ASEAN,智利CL,新西兰NZ,秘鲁PE,哥斯达黎加CR,台湾TW 巴基斯坦PK	0	最不发达35国LDC35,最不发达4国LDC4	20	-Tools for tapping or threading
		-钻孔工具,但凿岩及钻探用的除外:							-Tools for drilling, other than for rock drilling:

序号 No.	税则号列 Tariff Line	货品名称	最惠国税率 MFN(%)	协定税率 Agreement(%)		特惠税率 S.P.(%)		普通税率 Gen.(%)	Article Description
5787	8207.5010	---带有天然或合成金刚石、立方氮化硼制的工作部件	8	0 0.8 5	东盟ASEAN,新西兰NZ,秘鲁PE,哥斯达黎加CR,香港HK,台湾TW 智利CL 巴基斯坦PK	0	最不发达35国LDC35,最不发达4国LDC4	20	---With working part of natural or synthetic diamonds or cubic boron nitride
5788	8207.5090	---其他	8	0 0.8 5	东盟ASEAN,新西兰NZ,秘鲁PE,哥斯达黎加CR,香港HK,台湾TW 智利CL 巴基斯坦PK	0	最不发达35国LDC35,最不发达4国LDC4	20	---Other
		-镗孔或铰孔工具:							-Tools for boring or broaching:
5789	8207.6010	---带有天然或合成金刚石、立方氮化硼制的工作部件	8	0 5	东盟ASEAN,智利CL,新西兰NZ,秘鲁PE,哥斯达黎加CR,台湾TW 巴基斯坦PK	0	最不发达35国LDC35,最不发达4国LDC4	20	---With working part of natural or synthetic diamonds or cubic boron nitride
5790	8207.6090	---其他	8	0 5	东盟ASEAN,智利CL,新西兰NZ,秘鲁PE,哥斯达黎加CR 巴基斯坦PK	0	最不发达35国LDC35,最不发达4国LDC4	20	---Other
		-铣削工具:							-Tools for milling:
5791	8207.7010	---带有天然或合成金刚石、立方氮化硼制的工作部件	8	0 0.8 5	东盟ASEAN,新西兰NZ,秘鲁PE,哥斯达黎加CR,香港HK,台湾TW 智利CL 巴基斯坦PK	0	最不发达35国LDC35,最不发达4国LDC4	20	---With working part of natural or synthetic diamonds or cubic boron nitride
5792	8207.7090	---其他	8	0 0.8 5	东盟ASEAN,新西兰NZ,秘鲁PE,哥斯达黎加CR,香港HK,台湾TW 智利CL 巴基斯坦PK	0	最不发达35国LDC35,最不发达4国LDC4	20	---Other
		-车削工具:							-Tools for turning:
5793	8207.8010	---带有天然或合成金刚石、立方氮化硼制的工作部件	8	0 5 6.8	东盟ASEAN,智利CL,新西兰NZ,秘鲁PE,哥斯达黎加CR,台湾TW 巴基斯坦PK 亚太APTA	0	最不发达35国LDC35,最不发达4国LDC4	20	---With working part of natural or synthetic diamonds or cubic boron nitride
5794	8207.8090	---其他	8	0 5 6.8	东盟ASEAN,智利CL,新西兰NZ,秘鲁PE,哥斯达黎加CR,台湾TW 巴基斯坦PK 亚太APTA	0	最不发达35国LDC35,最不发达4国LDC4	20	---Other
		-其他可互换工具:							-Other interchangeable tools:

序号 No.	税则号列 Tariff Line	货品名称	最惠国税率 MFN(%)	协定税率 Agreement(%)		特惠税率 S.P.(%)		普通税率 Gen.(%)	Article Description
5795	8207.9010	---带有天然或合成金刚石、立方氮化硼制的工作部件	8	0 5 6.8	东盟ASEAN,智利CL,新西兰NZ,秘鲁PE,哥斯达黎加CR,香港HK,台湾TW 巴基斯坦PK 亚太APTA	0	最不发达35国LDC35,最不发达4国LDC4	20	---with working part of natural or synthetic diamonds or cubic boron nitride
5796	8207.9090	---其他	8	0 5 6.8	东盟ASEAN,智利CL,新西兰NZ,秘鲁PE,哥斯达黎加CR,香港HK,台湾TW 巴基斯坦PK 亚太APTA	0	最不发达35国LDC35,最不发达4国LDC4	20	---Other
	82.08	**机器或机械器具的刀及刀片:**							**Knives and cutting blades, for machines or for mechanical appliances:**
		-金属加工用: ---硬质合金制的:							-For metal working: ---Of cemented carbide:
5797	8208.1011	----经镀或涂层的	8	0 5	东盟ASEAN,智利CL,新西兰NZ,秘鲁PE,哥斯达黎加CR,香港HK 巴基斯坦PK	0	最不发达35国LDC35	20	----Plated or coated
5798	8208.1019	----其他	8	0 5	东盟ASEAN,智利CL,新西兰NZ,秘鲁PE,哥斯达黎加CR,香港HK 巴基斯坦PK	0	最不发达35国LDC35	20	----Other
5799	8208.1090	---其他	8	0 5	东盟ASEAN,智利CL,新西兰NZ,秘鲁PE,哥斯达黎加CR,香港HK 巴基斯坦PK	0	最不发达35国LDC35	20	---Other
5800	8208.2000	-木器加工用	8	0 5	东盟ASEAN,智利CL,新西兰NZ,秘鲁PE,哥斯达黎加CR,台湾TW 巴基斯坦PK	0	最不发达35国LDC35,最不发达4国LDC4	20	-For wood working
5801	8208.3000	-厨房器具或食品工业机器用	8	0 5	东盟ASEAN,智利CL,新西兰NZ,秘鲁PE,哥斯达黎加CR 巴基斯坦PK	0	最不发达35国LDC35,最不发达4国LDC4	20	-For kitchen appliances or for machines used by the food industry
5802	8208.4000	-农业、园艺或林业机器用	8	0 5	东盟ASEAN,智利CL,新西兰NZ,秘鲁PE,哥斯达黎加CR,台湾TW 巴基斯坦PK	0	最不发达35国LDC35	20	-For agricultural, horticultural or forestry machines
5803	8208.9000	-其他	8	0 5 7.2	东盟ASEAN,智利CL,新西兰NZ,秘鲁PE,哥斯达黎加CR,台湾TW 巴基斯坦PK 亚太APTA	0	最不发达35国LDC35	20	-Other
	82.09	**未装配的工具用金属陶瓷板、杆、刀头及类似品:**							**Plates, sticks, tips and the like for tools, unmounted, of cermets:**

序号 No.	税则号列 Tariff Line	货品名称	最惠国税率 MFN(%)	协定税率 Agreement(%)		特惠税率 S.P.(%)		普通税率 Gen.(%)	Article Description
		未装配的工具用金属陶瓷板、杆、刀头及类似品:							Plates, sticks, tips and the like for tools, unmounted, of cermets:
5804	8209.0010	---板	8	0 5 7.2	东盟ASEAN,智利CL,新西兰NZ,秘鲁PE,哥斯达黎加CR 巴基斯坦PK 亚太APTA	0	最不发达35国LDC35,最不发达4国LDC4	20	---Plates
		---条、杆:							---Sticks:
5805	8209.0021	----晶粒度小于0.8微米的	8	0 5 7.2	东盟ASEAN,智利CL,新西兰NZ,秘鲁PE,哥斯达黎加CR 巴基斯坦PK 亚太APTA	0	最不发达35国LDC35,最不发达4国LDC4	20	----Of a grain size of less than 0.8 microns
5806	8209.0029	----其他	8	0 5 7.2	东盟ASEAN,智利CL,新西兰NZ,秘鲁PE,哥斯达黎加CR 巴基斯坦PK 亚太APTA	0	最不发达35国LDC35,最不发达4国LDC4	20	----Other
5807	8209.0030	---刀头	8	0 5 7.2	东盟ASEAN,智利CL,新西兰NZ,秘鲁PE,哥斯达黎加CR 巴基斯坦PK 亚太APTA	0	最不发达35国LDC35,最不发达4国LDC4	20	---Tips
5808	8209.0090	---其他	8	0 5 7.2	东盟ASEAN,智利CL,新西兰NZ,秘鲁PE,哥斯达黎加CR 巴基斯坦PK 亚太APTA	0	最不发达35国LDC35,最不发达4国LDC4	20	---Other
	82.10	**用于加工或调制食品或饮料的手动机械器具,重量不超过10公斤:**							**Hand-operated mechanical appliances, weighing 10kg or less, used in the preparation, conditioning or serving of food or drink:**
5809	8210.0000	用于加工或调制食品或饮料的手动机械器具,重量不超过10公斤	18	0 1.8 3.6 9 14.4 16.2	东盟ASEAN,新加坡SG,新西兰NZ,澳门MO 智利CL 哥斯达黎加CR 秘鲁PE 巴基斯坦PK 亚太APTA	0	最不发达35国LDC35	80	Hand-operated mechanical appliances, weighing 10kg or less, used in the preparation, conditioning or serving of food or drink
	82.11	**有刃口的刀及其刀片,不论是否有锯齿(包括整枝刀),但税号82.08的刀除外:**							**Knives with cutting blades, serrated or not (including pruning knives), other than knives of heading No.82.08, and blades therefor:**

序号 No.	税则号列 Tariff Line	货品名称	最惠国税率 MFN(%)	协定税率 Agreement(%)		特惠税率 S.P.(%)		普通税率 Gen.(%)	Article Description
5810	8211.1000	-成套货品	18 △10	0 3.6 9	东盟ASEAN,智利CL,巴基斯坦PK,新加坡SG,新西兰NZ 哥斯达黎加CR 秘鲁PE	0	最不发达35国LDC35	80	-Sets of assorted articles
		-其他:							-Other:
5811	8211.9100	--刃面固定的餐刀	18 △10	0 3.6 9	东盟ASEAN,智利CL,巴基斯坦PK,新加坡SG,新西兰NZ 哥斯达黎加CR 秘鲁PE	0	最不发达35国LDC35	80	--Table knives having fixed blades
5812	8211.9200	--刃面固定的其他刀	12	0 2.4	东盟ASEAN,智利CL,巴基斯坦PK,新加坡SG,新西兰NZ,秘鲁PE 哥斯达黎加CR	0	最不发达35国LDC35,最不发达4国LDC4	80	--Other knives having fixed blades
5813	8211.9300	--刃面不固定的刀	18 △10	0 3.6 9	东盟ASEAN,智利CL,巴基斯坦PK,新加坡SG,新西兰NZ 哥斯达黎加CR 秘鲁PE	0	最不发达35国LDC35	80	--Knives having other than fixed blades
5814	8211.9400	--刀片	14	0 2.8	东盟ASEAN,智利CL,巴基斯坦PK,新加坡SG,新西兰NZ,秘鲁PE 哥斯达黎加CR	0	最不发达35国LDC35	80	--Blades
5815	8211.9500	--贱金属制的刀柄	12	0 2.4	东盟ASEAN,智利CL,巴基斯坦PK,新加坡SG,新西兰NZ,秘鲁PE 哥斯达黎加CR	0	最不发达35国LDC35,最不发达4国LDC4	80	--Handles of base metal
	82.12	**剃刀及其刀片(包括未分开的刀片条):**							**Razors and razor blades (including razor blade blanks in strips):**
5816	8212.1000	-剃刀	12	0 2.4	东盟ASEAN,智利CL,巴基斯坦PK,新加坡SG,新西兰NZ,秘鲁PE 哥斯达黎加CR	0	最不发达35国LDC35,最不发达4国LDC4	80	-Razors
5817	8212.2000	-安全刀片,包括未分开的刀片条	14	0 1.4 2.8	东盟ASEAN,巴基斯坦PK,新加坡SG,新西兰NZ,秘鲁PE 智利CL 哥斯达黎加CR	0	最不发达35国LDC35	80	-Safety razor blades, including razor blade blanks in strips
5818	8212.9000	-其他零件	12	0 2.4	东盟ASEAN,智利CL,巴基斯坦PK,新加坡SG,新西兰NZ,秘鲁PE 哥斯达黎加CR	0	最不发达35国LDC35,最不发达4国LDC4	80	-Other parts

序号 No.	税则号列 Tariff Line	货品名称	最惠国税率 MFN(%)	协定税率 Agreement(%)		特惠税率 S.P.(%)		普通税率 Gen.(%)	Article Description
	82.13	**剪刀、裁缝剪刀及类似品、剪刀片:**							**Scissors, tailors'shears and similar shears, and blades therefor:**
5819	8213.0000	剪刀、裁缝剪刀及类似品、剪刀片	12	0 2.4 10.8	东盟ASEAN,智利CL,巴基斯坦PK,新加坡SG,新西兰NZ,秘鲁PE 哥斯达黎加CR 亚太APTA	0	最不发达35国LDC35,最不发达4国LDC4	80	Scissors, tailors'shears and similar shears, and blades therefor
	82.14	**其他利口器(例如,理发推剪、屠刀、砍骨刀、切肉刀、切菜刀、裁纸刀);修指甲及修脚用具(包括指甲锉):**							**Other articles of cutlery (for example, hair clippers, butchers' or kitchen cleavers, choppers and mincing knives, paper knives); manicure or pedicure sets and instruments (including nail files):**
5820	8214.1000	-裁纸刀、开信刀、改错刀、铅笔刀及其刀片	12	0 2.4 5 10.8	东盟ASEAN,智利CL,新加坡SG,新西兰NZ,秘鲁PE 哥斯达黎加CR 巴基斯坦PK 亚太APTA	0	最不发达35国LDC35,最不发达4国LDC4	80	-Paper knives, letter openers, erasing knives, pencil sharpeners and blades therefor
5821	8214.2000	-修指甲及修脚用具(包括指甲锉)	18	0 1.8 3.6 9 16.2	东盟ASEAN,新加坡SG,新西兰NZ 智利CL 哥斯达黎加CR 秘鲁PE 亚太APTA,巴基斯坦PK	0	最不发达35国LDC35,最不发达4国LDC4	90	-Manicure or pedicure sets and instruments (including nail files)
5822	8214.9000	-其他	18	0 3.6 9	东盟ASEAN,智利CL,新加坡SG,新西兰NZ 哥斯达黎加CR 秘鲁PE	0	最不发达35国LDC35	80	-Other
	82.15	**餐匙、餐叉、长柄勺、漏勺、糕点夹、鱼刀、黄油刀、糖块夹及类似的厨房或餐桌用具:**							**Spoons, forks, ladles, skimmers, cakeservers, fish-knives, butter-knives, sugar tongs and similar kitchen or tableware:**
5823	8215.1000	-成套货品,至少其中一件物品是镀贵金属的	18	0 1.8 3.6 9	东盟ASEAN,巴基斯坦PK,新加坡SG,新西兰NZ 智利CL 哥斯达黎加CR 秘鲁PE	0	最不发达35国LDC35	80	-Sets of assorted articles containing at least one article plated with precious metal
5824	8215.2000	-其他成套货品	18	0 3.6 9	东盟ASEAN,智利CL,巴基斯坦PK,新加坡SG,新西兰NZ 哥斯达黎加CR 秘鲁PE	0	最不发达35国LDC35	80	-Other sets of assorted articles
		-其他:							-Other:

序号 No.	税则号列 Tariff Line	货品名称	最惠国税率 MFN(%)	协定税率 Agreement(%)		特惠税率 S.P.(%)		普通税率 Gen.(%)	Article Description
5825	8215.9100	--镀贵金属的	18	0 3.6 9	东盟ASEAN,智利CL,巴基斯坦PK,新加坡SG,新西兰NZ 哥斯达黎加CR 秘鲁PE	0	最不发达35国LDC35	80	--Plated with precious metal
5826	8215.9900	--其他	18 △10	0 1.8 3.6 9	东盟ASEAN,巴基斯坦PK,新加坡SG,新西兰NZ,香港HK 智利CL 哥斯达黎加CR 秘鲁PE	0	最不发达35国LDC35,最不发达4国LDC4	80	--Other

第八十三章
贱金属杂项制品

Chapter 83
Miscellaneous articles of base metal

注释:

一、在本章，贱金属零件应与制品一同归类。但税号73.12、73.15、73.17、73.18及73.20的钢铁制品或其他贱金属（第七十四章至第七十六章及第七十八章至第八十一章）制的类似物品不应视为本章制品的零件。

二、税号83.02所称“脚轮”，是指直径（对于有胎的，连胎计算在内，下同）不超过75毫米的或直径虽超过75毫米，但所装轮或胎的宽度必须小于30毫米的脚轮。

Notes:

1. For the purposes of this Chapter, parts of base metal are to be classified with their parent artcles. However, articles of iron or steel of heading No.73.12, 73.15, 73.17, 73.18 or 73.20, or similar articles of other base metal (Chapters 74 to 76 and 78 to 81) are not to be taken as parts of articles of this Chapter.
2. For the purposes of heading No.83.02, the word “castors” means those having a diameter (including, where appropriate, tyres) not exceeding 75mm, or those having a diameter (including, where appropriatetyres) exceeding 75mm pro-vided that the width of the wheel or tyre fitted thereto is less than 30mm.

序号 No.	税则号列 Tariff Line	货品名称	最惠国税率 MFN(%)	协定税率 Agreement(%)		特惠税率 S.P.(%)		普通税率 Gen.(%)	Article Description
	83.01	**贱金属制的锁（钥匙锁、数码锁及电动锁）;贱金属制带锁的扣环及扣环框架;上述锁的贱金属制钥匙:**							**Padlocks and locks (key, combination or electrically operated), of base metal; clasps and frames with clasps, incorporating locks, of base metal; keys for any of the foregoing articles, of base metal:**
5827	8301.1000	-挂锁	14	0 2.8 11.2	东盟ASEAN,智利CL,新加坡SG,新西兰NZ,秘鲁PE 哥斯达黎加CR 巴基斯坦PK	0	最不发达35国LDC35	80	-Padlocks
		-机动车用锁:							-Locks of a kind used for motor vehicles:
5828	8301.2010	---中央控制门锁	10	0	智利CL,新西兰NZ,秘鲁PE,哥斯达黎加CR	0	最不发达35国LDC35,最不发达4国LDC4	80	---Central control door lock
5829	8301.2090	---其他	10	0	智利CL,新西兰NZ,秘鲁PE,哥斯达黎加CR	0	最不发达35国LDC35,最不发达4国LDC4	80	---Other

序号 No.	税则号列 Tariff Line	货品名称	最惠国税率 MFN(%)	协定税率 Agreement(%)		特惠税率 S.P.(%)		普通税率 Gen.(%)	Article Description
5830	8301.3000	-家具用锁	14	0 2.8 11.2	东盟ASEAN,智利CL,新加坡SG,新西兰NZ,秘鲁PE 哥斯达黎加CR 巴基斯坦PK	0	最不发达35国LDC35,最不发达4国LDC4	80	-Locks of a kind used for furniture
5831	8301.4000	-其他锁	14	0 1.4 2.8 11.2	东盟ASEAN,新加坡SG,新西兰NZ,秘鲁PE 智利CL 哥斯达黎加CR 巴基斯坦PK	0	最不发达35国LDC35,最不发达4国LDC4	80	-Other locks
5832	8301.5000	-带锁的扣环及扣环框架	14	0 2.8 11.2	东盟ASEAN,智利CL,新加坡SG,新西兰NZ,秘鲁PE,香港HK 哥斯达黎加CR 巴基斯坦PK	0	最不发达35国LDC35	80	-Clasps and frames with clasps, incorporating locks
5833	8301.6000	-零件	12	0 2.4 6	东盟ASEAN,智利CL,新加坡SG,新西兰NZ,秘鲁PE 哥斯达黎加CR 巴基斯坦PK	0	最不发达35国LDC35,最不发达4国LDC4	80	-Parts
5834	8301.7000	-钥匙	10	0 5	东盟ASEAN,智利CL,新西兰NZ,秘鲁PE,哥斯达黎加CR 巴基斯坦PK	0	最不发达35国LDC35,最不发达4国LDC4	80	-Keys presented separately
	83.02	**用于家具、门窗、楼梯、百叶窗、车厢、鞍具、衣箱、盒子及类似品的贱金属附件及架座;贱金属制帽架、帽钩、托架及类似品;用贱金属做支架的小脚轮;贱金属制的自动闭门器:**							**Base metal mountings, fittings and similar articles suitable for furniture, doors, staircases, windows, blinds, coachwork, saddlery, trunks, chests, caskets, or the like; base metal hatracks, hat-pegs, brackets and similar fixtures; castors with mountings of base metal; automatic door closers of base metal:**
5835	8302.1000	-铰链(折叶)	10	0 1 5	东盟ASEAN,新西兰NZ,秘鲁PE,哥斯达黎加CR,香港HK 智利CL 巴基斯坦PK	0	最不发达35国LDC35,最不发达4国LDC4	80	-Hinges
5836	8302.2000	-小脚轮	12	0 1.2 2.4 6	东盟ASEAN,新加坡SG,新西兰NZ,秘鲁PE 智利CL 哥斯达黎加CR 巴基斯坦PK	0	最不发达35国LDC35,最不发达4国LDC4	80	-Castors

序号 No.	税则号列 Tariff Line	货品名称	最惠国税率 MFN(%)	协定税率 Agreement(%)		特惠税率 S.P.(%)		普通税率 Gen.(%)	Article Description
5837	8302.3000	-机动车辆用的其他附件及架座	10	0 5	东盟ASEAN,智利CL,新西兰NZ,秘鲁PE,哥斯达黎加CR 巴基斯坦PK	0	最不发达35国LDC35,最不发达4国LDC4	80	-Other mountings, fittings and similar articles suitable for motor vehicles
		-其他附件及架座:							-Other mountings, fittings and similar articles:
5838	8302.4100	--建筑用	14	0 2.8 11.2	东盟ASEAN,智利CL,新加坡SG,新西兰NZ,秘鲁PE 哥斯达黎加CR 巴基斯坦PK	0	最不发达35国LDC35	80	--Suitable for buildings
5839	8302.4200	--其他，家具用	12	0 1.2 2.4 6	东盟ASEAN,新加坡SG,新西兰NZ,秘鲁PE 智利CL 哥斯达黎加CR 巴基斯坦PK	0	最不发达35国LDC35,最不发达4国LDC4	80	--Other, suitable for furniture
5840	8302.4900	--其他	12	0 2.4 6	东盟ASEAN,智利CL,新加坡SG,新西兰NZ,秘鲁PE 哥斯达黎加CR 巴基斯坦PK	0	最不发达35国LDC35,最不发达4国LDC4	80	--Other
5841	8302.5000	-帽架、帽钩、托架及类似品	14	0 1.4 2.8 11.2	东盟ASEAN,新加坡SG,新西兰NZ,秘鲁PE 智利CL 哥斯达黎加CR 巴基斯坦PK	0	最不发达35国LDC35	80	-Hat-racks, hat-pegs, brackets and similar fixtures
5842	8302.6000	-自动闭门器	12	0 2.4 6	东盟ASEAN,智利CL,新加坡SG,新西兰NZ,秘鲁PE 哥斯达黎加CR 巴基斯坦PK	0	最不发达35国LDC35,最不发达4国LDC4	80	-Automatic door closers
	83.03	**装甲或加强的贱金属制保险箱、保险柜及保险库的门和带锁保险储存橱、钱箱、契约箱及类似品:**							**Armoured or reinforced safes, strong-boxes and doors and safe deposit lockers for strong-rooms, cash or deed boxes and the like, of base metal:**
5843	8303.0000	装甲或加强的贱金属制保险箱、保险柜及保险库的门和带锁保险储存橱、钱箱、契约箱及类似品	14	0 1.4 2.8 11.2	东盟ASEAN,新加坡SG,新西兰NZ,秘鲁PE 智利CL 哥斯达黎加CR 巴基斯坦PK	0	最不发达35国LDC35	50	Armoured or reinforced safes, strong-boxes and doors and safe deposit lockers for strong-rooms, cash or deed boxes and the like, of base metal

序号 No.	税则号列 Tariff Line	货品名称	最惠国税率 MFN(%)	协定税率 Agreement(%)		特惠税率 S.P.(%)		普通税率 Gen.(%)	Article Description
	83.04	**贱金属制的档案柜、卡片索引柜、文件盘、文件篮、笔盘、公章架及类似的办公用具，但税号94.03的办公室家具除外:**							**Filing cabinets, card-index cabinets, paper trays, paper rests, pen trays, office-stamp stands and similar office or desk equipment, of base metal, other than office furniture of heading No.94.03:**
5844	8304.0000	贱金属制的档案柜、卡片索引柜、文件盘、文件篮、笔盘、公章架及类似的办公用具，但税号94.03的办公室家具除外	10.5	0 2.1 5	东盟ASEAN,智利CL,新加坡SG,新西兰NZ,秘鲁PE,香港HK 哥斯达黎加CR 巴基斯坦PK	0	最不发达35国LDC35,最不发达4国LDC4	80	Filing cabinets, card-index cabinets, paper trays, paper rests, pen trays, office-stamp stands and similar office or desk equipment, of base metal, other than office furniture of heading No.94.03
	83.05	**活页夹、卷宗夹的贱金属附件，贱金属制的信夹、信角、文件夹、索引标签及类似的办公用品;贱金属制的成条钉书钉（例如，供办公室、室内装饰或包装用）:**							**Fittings for loose-leaf binders or files, letter clips, letter corners, paper clips, indexing tags and similar office articles, of base metal; staples in strips (for example, for offices, upholstery, packaging), of base metal:**
5845	8305.1000	-活页夹或卷宗夹的附件	10.5	0 1.1 2.1 5	东盟ASEAN,新加坡SG,新西兰NZ,秘鲁PE 智利CL 哥斯达黎加CR 巴基斯坦PK	0	最不发达35国LDC35,最不发达4国LDC4	80	-Fittings for loose-leaf binders of files
5846	8305.2000	-成条钉书钉	10.5	0 2.1 5	东盟ASEAN,智利CL,新加坡SG,新西兰NZ,秘鲁PE 哥斯达黎加CR 巴基斯坦PK	0	最不发达35国LDC35,最不发达4国LDC4	80	-Staples in strips
5847	8305.9000	-其他，包括零件	10.5	0 2.1 5	东盟ASEAN,智利CL,新加坡SG,新西兰NZ,秘鲁PE,香港HK 哥斯达黎加CR 巴基斯坦PK	0	最不发达35国LDC35,最不发达4国LDC4	80	-Other, including parts
	83.06	**非电动的贱金属铃、钟、锣及类似品;贱金属雕塑像及其他装饰品;贱金属相框或画框及类似框架;贱金属镜子:**							**Bells, gongs and the like, non-electric, of base metal; statuettes and other ornaments, of base metal; photograph, picture or similar frames, of base metal; mirrors of base metal:**

序号 No.	税则号列 Tariff Line	货品名称	最惠国税率 MFN(%)	协定税率 Agreement(%)		特惠税率 S.P.(%)		普通税率 Gen.(%)	Article Description
5848	8306.1000	-铃、钟、锣及类似品	8	0	东盟ASEAN,智利CL,新西兰NZ,秘鲁PE,哥斯达黎加CR	0	最不发达35国LDC35,最不发达4国LDC4	80	-Bells, gongs and the like
				5	巴基斯坦PK				
		-雕塑像及其他装饰品:							-Statuettes and other ornaments:
5849	8306.2100	--镀贵金属的	8	0	东盟ASEAN,智利CL,新西兰NZ,秘鲁PE,哥斯达黎加CR	0	最不发达35国LDC35,最不发达4国LDC4	100	--Plated with precious metal
				5	巴基斯坦PK				
		--其他:							--Other:
5850	8306.2910	---景泰蓝的	8	0	东盟ASEAN,新西兰NZ,秘鲁PE,哥斯达黎加CR	0	最不发达35国LDC35,最不发达4国LDC4	100	---Cloisonne
				0.8	智利CL				
				5	巴基斯坦PK				
5851	8306.2990	---其他	8	0	东盟ASEAN,新加坡SG,新西兰NZ,秘鲁PE,哥斯达黎加CR	0	最不发达35国LDC35,最不发达4国LDC4	100	---Other
				0.8	智利CL				
				5	巴基斯坦PK				
5852	8306.3000	-相框、画框及类似框架;镜子	8	0	东盟ASEAN,智利CL,新西兰NZ,秘鲁PE,哥斯达黎加CR	0	最不发达35国LDC35,最不发达4国LDC4	100	-Photograph, picture or similar frames; mirrors
				5	巴基斯坦PK				
	83.07	**贱金属软管，不论是否有附件:**							**Flexible tubing of base metal, with or without fittings:**
5853	8307.1000	-钢铁制	8.4	0	东盟ASEAN,智利CL,新西兰NZ,秘鲁PE,哥斯达黎加CR	0	最不发达35国LDC35,最不发达4国LDC4	35	-Of iron or steel
				5	巴基斯坦PK				
5854	8307.9000	-其他贱金属制	8.4	0	东盟ASEAN,智利CL,新西兰NZ,秘鲁PE,哥斯达黎加CR,香港HK	0	最不发达35国LDC35,最不发达4国LDC4	35	-Of other base metal
				5	巴基斯坦PK				

序号 No.	税则号列 Tariff Line	货品名称	最惠国税率 MFN(%)	协定税率 Agreement(%)		特惠税率 S.P.(%)		普通税率 Gen.(%)	Article Description
	83.08	**贱金属制的扣、钩、环、眼及类似品，用于衣着、鞋靴、天篷、提包、旅行用品或其他制成品;贱金属制的管形铆钉及开口铆钉;贱金属制的珠子及亮晶片:**							**Clasps, frames with clasps, buckles, buckle-clasps, hooks, eyes, eyelets and the like, of base metal, of a kind used for clothing, footwear, awnings, handbags, travel goods or other made up articles; tubular or bifurcated rivets, of base metal; beads and spangles, of base metal:**
5855	8308.1000	-钩、环及眼	10.5	0 2.1 5	东盟ASEAN,智利CL,新加坡SG,新西兰NZ,秘鲁PE,香港HK 哥斯达黎加CR 巴基斯坦PK	0	最不发达35国LDC35,最不发达4国LDC4	80	-Hooks, eyes and eyelets
5856	8308.2000	-管形铆钉及开口铆钉	10.5	0 2.1 5	东盟ASEAN,智利CL,新加坡SG,新西兰NZ,秘鲁PE,香港HK 哥斯达黎加CR 巴基斯坦PK	0	最不发达35国LDC35,最不发达4国LDC4	80	-Tubular or bifurcated rivets
5857	8308.9000	-其他，包括零件	10.5	0 2.1 5	东盟ASEAN,智利CL,新加坡SG,新西兰NZ,秘鲁PE,香港HK 哥斯达黎加CR 巴基斯坦PK	0	最不发达35国LDC35,最不发达4国LDC4	80	-Other, including parts
	83.09	**贱金属制的塞子、盖子（包括冠形瓶塞、螺口盖及倒水塞）、瓶帽、螺口塞、塞子帽、封志及其他包装用附件:**							**Stoppers, caps and lids (including crown corks, screw caps and pouring stoppers), capsules for bottles, threaded bungs, bung covers, seals and other packing accessories, of base metal:**
5858	8309.1000	-冠形瓶塞	18	0 3.6 14.4	东盟ASEAN,智利CL,新加坡SG,新西兰NZ,秘鲁PE,香港HK 哥斯达黎加CR 巴基斯坦PK	0	最不发达35国LDC35	90	-Crown corks
5859	8309.9000	-其他	12	0 1.2 2.4 6	东盟ASEAN,新加坡SG,新西兰NZ,秘鲁PE,香港HK 智利CL 哥斯达黎加CR 巴基斯坦PK	0	最不发达35国LDC35,最不发达4国LDC4	80	-Other

序号 No.	税则号列 Tariff Line	货品名称	最惠国税率 MFN(%)	协定税率 Agreement(%)		特惠税率 S.P.(%)		普通税率 Gen.(%)	Article Description
	83.10	**贱金属制的标志牌、铭牌、地名牌及类似品、号码、字母及类似标志，但税号94.05的货品除外:**							**Sign-plates, name-plates, addressplates and similar plates, numbers, letters and other symbols, of base metal, excluding those of heading No.94.05:**
5860	8310.0000	贱金属制的标志牌、铭牌、地名牌及类似品、号码、字母及类似标志，但税号94.05的货品除外	18	0 3.6 9	东盟ASEAN,智利CL,新加坡SG,新西兰NZ 哥斯达黎加CR 秘鲁PE	0	最不发达35国LDC35	80	Sign-plates, name-plates, address-plates and similar plates, numbers, letters and other sym-bols, of base metal, excluding those of heading No.94.05
	83.11	**贱金属或硬质合金制的丝、条、管、板、电极及类似品，以焊剂涂面或以焊剂为芯，用于焊接或沉积金属、硬质合金;贱金属粉粘聚而成的丝或条，供金属喷镀用:**							**Wire, rods, tubes, plates, electrodes and similar products, of base metal or of metal carbides, coated or cored with flux material, of a kind used for soldering, brazing, welding or deposition of metal or of metal carbides; wire and rods, of agglomerated base metal powder, used for metal spraying:**
5861	8311.1000	-以焊剂涂面的贱金属制电极，电弧焊用	8	0 0.8 5	东盟ASEAN,新西兰NZ,秘鲁PE,哥斯达黎加CR,香港HK 智利CL 巴基斯坦PK	0	最不发达35国LDC35,最不发达4国LDC4	30	-Coated electrodes of base metal, for electric arc-welding
5862	8311.2000	-以焊剂为芯的贱金属制焊丝，电弧焊用	8	0 5	东盟ASEAN,智利CL,新西兰NZ,秘鲁PE,哥斯达黎加CR,香港HK 巴基斯坦PK	0	最不发达35国LDC35,最不发达4国LDC4	30	-Cored wire of base metal, for electric arcwelding
5863	8311.3000	-以焊剂涂面或以焊剂为芯的贱金属条或丝，钎焊或气焊用	8	0 0.8 5	东盟ASEAN,新西兰NZ,秘鲁PE,哥斯达黎加CR,香港HK 智利CL 巴基斯坦PK	0	最不发达35国LDC35,最不发达4国LDC4	30	Coated rods and cored wire, of base metal, for soldering, brazing or welding by flame
5864	8311.9000	-其他	8	0 0.8 5 5.6	东盟ASEAN,新西兰NZ,秘鲁PE,哥斯达黎加CR,香港HK 智利CL 巴基斯坦PK 亚太APTA	0	最不发达35国LDC35,最不发达4国LDC4	30	-Other

第十六类

机器、机械器具、电气设备及其零件；录音机及放声机、电视图像、声音的录制和重放设备及其零件、附件

注释：

一、本类不包括：

(一)第三十九章的塑料或税号 40.10 的硫化橡胶制的传动带、输送带，除硬质橡胶以外的硫化橡胶制的机器、机械器具、电气器具或其他专门技术用途的物品(税号 40.16)；

(二)机器、机械器具或其他专门技术用途的皮革、再生皮革(税号 42.05)或毛皮(税号 43.03)的制品；

(三)各种材料(例如，第三十九章、第四十章、第四十四章、第四十八章及第十五类的材料)制的筒管、卷轴、纡子、锥形筒管、芯子、线轴及类似品；

(四)提花机及类似机器用的穿孔卡片(例如，归入第三十九章、第四十八章或第十五类的)；

(五)纺织材料制的传动带、输送带或带料(税号 59.10)或专门技术用途的其他纺织材料制品(税号 59.11)；

(六)税号 71.02 至 71.04 的宝石或半宝石(天然、合成或再造)或税号 71.16 的完全以宝石或半宝石制成的物品，但已加工未装配的唱针用蓝宝石和钻石除外(税号 85.22)；

(七)第十五类注释二所规定的贱金属制通用零件(第十五类)及塑料制的类似品(第三十九章)；

(八)钻管(税号 73.04)；

(九)金属丝、带制的环形带(第十五类)；

(十)第八十二章或第八十三章的物品；

(十一)第十七类的物品；

(十二)第九十章的物品；

(十三)第九十一章的钟、表及其他物品；

(十四)税号 82.07 的可互换工具及作为机器零件的刷子(税号 96.03)；类似的可互换工具应按其构成工作部件的材料归类(例如，归入第四十章、第四十二章、第四十三章、第四十五章、第五十九章或税号 68.04、69.09)；

SECTION XVI

MACHINERY AND MECHANICAL APPLIANCES; ELECTRICAL EQUIPMENT; PARTS THEREOF; SOUND RECORDERS AND REPRODUCERS, TELEVISION IMAGE AND SOUND RECORDERS AND REPRODUCERS, AND PARTS AND ACCESSORIES OF SUCH ARTICLES

Notes:

1. This Section does not cover:

(a) Transmission or conveyor belts or belting, of plastics of Chapter 39, or of vulcanized rubber (heading No. 40.10), or other articles of a kind used in machinery or mechanical or electrical appliances or for other technical uses, of vulcanized rubber other than hard rubber (heading No. 40.16);

(b) Articles of leather or of composition leather (heading No. 42.05) or of furskin (heading No. 43.03), of a kind used in machinery or mechanical appliances or for other technical uses;

(c) Bobbins, spools, cops, cones, cores, reels or similar supports of any material (for example, Chapter 39, 40, 44 or 48 or Section XV);

(d) Perforated cards for Jacquard or similar machines (for example, Chapter 39 or 48 Section XV);

(e) Transmission or conveyor belts or belting of textile material (heading No. 59.10) or other articles of textile material for technical uses (heading No. 59.11);

(f) Precious or semi-precious stones (natural, synthetic or reconstructed) of headings Nos. 71.02 to 71.04, or articles wholly of such stones of heading No. 71.16, except unmounted worked sapphires and diamonds for styli (heading No. 85.22);

(g) Parts of general use, as defined in Note 2 to Section XV, of base metal (Section XV), or similar goods of plastics (Chapter 39);

(h) Drill pipe (heading No. 73.04);

(i) Endless belts of metal wire or strip (Section XV);

(j) Articles of Chapter 82 or 83;

(k) Articles of Section XVII;

(l) Articles of Chapter 90;

(m) Clocks, watches or other articles of Chapter 91;

(n) Interchangeable tools of heading No. 82.07 brushes of a kind used as parts of machines (heading No. 96.03), similar interchangable tools are to be classified according to the material of working parts (for example, Chapter 40, 42, 43, 45, 59 or heading No. 68.04 or 69.09);

(十五)第九十五章的物品;

(十六)打字机色带或类似色带，不论是否装轴或装盒(按其材料属性归类;如已上油或经其他方法处理能着色的，应归入税号 96.12)。

二、除本类注释一、第八十四章注释一及第八十五章注释一另有规定的以外，机器零件(不属于税号 84.84、85.44、85.45、85.46 或 85.47 所列物品的零件)应按下列规定归类:

(一)凡在第八十四章、第八十五章的税号(税号 84.09、84.31、84.48、84.66、84.73、84.87、85.03、85.22、85.29、85.38 及 85.48 除外)列名的货品，均应归入该两章的相应税号;

(二)专用于或主要用于某一种机器或同一税号的多种机器(包括税号 84.79 或 85.43 的机器)的零件，应与该种机器一并归类，或酌情归入税号 84.09、84.31、84.48、84.66、84.73、85.03、85.22、85.29 或 85.38。但能同时主要用于税号 85.17 和 85.25 至 85.28 所列机器的零件，应归入税号 85.17;

(三)所有其他零件应酌情归入税号 84.09、84.31、84.48、84.66、84.73、85.03、85.22、85.29 或 85.38，如不能归入上述税号，则应归入税号 84.87 或 85.48。

三、由两部及两部以上机器装配在一起形成的组合式机器，或具有两种及两种以上互补或交替功能的机器，除条文另有规定的以外，应按具有主要功能的机器归类。

四、由不同独立部件(不论是否分开或由管道、传动装置、电缆或其他装置连接)组成的机器(包括机组)，如果组合后明显具有一种第八十四章或第八十五章某个税号所列功能，则全部机器应按其功能归入有关税号。

五、上述各注释所称“机器”，是指第八十四章或第八十五章各税号所列的各种机器、设备、装置及器具。

(o)Articles of Chapter 95;

(p)Typewriter or similar ribbons, whether or not on spools or in cartridges (classified according to their constituent material, or in heading 96.12 if inked or otherwise prepared for giving impressions).

2. Subject to Note1to this Section, Note1to Chapter 84 and Note 1 to Chapter 85, parts of machines (not being parts of the articles of heading No. 84.84, 85.44, 85.45, 85.46 or 85.47) are to be classified according to the following rules:

(a) Parts which are goods included in any of the headings of Chapter 84 or 85 (other than headings Nos. 84.09, 84.31, 84.48, 84.66, 84.73, 84.87, 85.03, 85.22, 85.29, 85.38, and 85.48) are in all cases to be classified in their respective headings;

(b) Other parts, if suitable for use solely or principally with a particular kind of machine, or with a number of machines of the same heading (including machines of heading No. 84.79 or 85.43) are to be classified with the machines of that kind or in heading No. 84.09, 84.31, 84.48, 84.66, 84.73, 85.03, 85.22, 85.29 or 85.38 as appropriate.However, parts which are equally suitable for use principally with the goods of headings Nos. 85.17 and 85.25 to 85.28 are to be classified inheading No. 85.17;

(c) All other parts are to be classified in heading No. 84.09, 84.31, 84.48, 84.66, 84.73, 85.03, 85.22, 85.29 or 85.38 as appropriate or, failing that, in heading No.84.87or 85.48.

3. Unless the context otherwise requires, composite machines consisting of two or more machines fitted together to form a whole and other machines adapted for the purpose of performing two or more complementary or alternative functions are to be classified as if consisting only of that component or as being thatmachine which performs the principal function.

4. Where a machine (including a combination of machines) consists of individual components (whether separate or interconnected by piping, by transmission devices, by electric cables or by other devices) intended to contribute together to a clearly defined function covered by one of the headings in Chapter 84 or Chapter 85, then the whole falls to be classified in the heading appropriate to that function.

5. For the purposes of these Notes, the expression “machine” means any machine, machinery, plant, equipment, apparatus or appliance cited in the headings of Chapter 84 or 85.

第八十四章 核反应堆、锅炉、机器、机械器具及其零件

Chapter 84 Nuclear reactors, boilers, machinery and mechanical appliances;parts thereof

注释:

一、本章不包括:

(一)第六十八章的石磨、石碾及其他物品;

(二)陶瓷材料制的机器或器具(例如，泵)及供任

Notes:

1. This Chapter does not cover:

(a) Millstones, grindstones or other articles of Chapter 68;

(b) Machinery or appliances (for example, pumps) of ce-

何材料制的机器或器具用的陶瓷零件(第六十九章);

(三)实验室用玻璃器(税号 70.17);玻璃制的机器、器具或其他专门技术用途的物品及其零件(税号 70.19 或 70.20);

(四)税号 73.21 或 73.22 的物品或其他贱金属制的类似物品(第七十四章至第七十六章或第七十八章至第八十一章);

(五)税号 85.08 的真空吸尘器;

(六)税号 85.09 的家用电动器具;或税号 85.25 的数字照相机;

(七)非机动的手工操作地板清扫器(税号 96.03)。

二、除第十六类注释三及本章注释九另有规定的以外，如果某种机器或器具既符合税号 84.01 至 84.24 或税目 84.86 中一个或几个税号的规定，又符合税号 84.25 至 84.80 中一个或几个税号的规定，则应归入税号 84.01 至 84.24 或税目 84.86 中的相应税号，而不归入税号 84.25 至 84.80 中的有关税号。

但税号 84.19 不包括:

(一)催芽装置、孵卵器或育雏器(税号 84.36);

(二)谷物调湿机(税号 84.37);

(三)萃取糖汁的浸提装置(税号 84.38);

(四)纱线、织物及纺织制品的热处理机器(税号 84.51);

(五)温度变化(即使必不可少)仅作为辅助功能的机器设备。

税号 84.22 不包括:

(一)缝合袋子或类似品用的缝纫机(税号 84.52);

(二)税号 84.72 的办公室用机器。

税号 84.24 不包括:

（一）喷墨印刷(打印)机器(税号 84.43);

（二）水射流切割机（税号 84.56）。

三、如果用于加工各种材料的某种机床既符合税号 84.56 的规定，又符合税号 84.57、84.58、84.59、84.60、84.61、84.64 或 84.65 的规定，则应归入税号 84.56。

四、税号 84.57 仅适用于可以完成下列不同形式机械操作的金属加工机床，但车床(包括车削中心)除外:

(一)按照机械加工程序从刀具库中自动更换刀具(加工中心);

ramic material and ceramic parts of machinery or appliances of any material (Chapter 69);

(c) Laboratory glassware(heading No. 70.17); machinery, appliances or otherarticles for technical uses or parts thereof, of glass (heading No. 70.19 or 70.20);

(d) Articles of heading No. 73.21 or 73.22 or similar articles of other base metals (Chapters 74 to 76 or 78 to 81);

(e) Vacuum cleaners of heading 85.08;

(f) Electro-mechanical domestic appliances of heading No. 85.09; or digital cameras of heading 85.25;

(g) Hand-operated mechanical floor sweepers, not motorized (heading No. 96.03).

2. Subject to the operation of Note 3 to Section XVI and subject to Note 9 to this Chapter, a machine or appliance which answers to a description in one or more of the headings 84.01 to 84.24, or heading 84.86 and at the same time to a description in one or other of the headings Nos. 84.25 to 84.80 is to be classified under the appropriate heading of the former group or under heading 84.86, as the case may be, and not the latter.

Heading No. 84.19 does not, however, cover:

(a) Germination plant, incubators or brooders (heading No. 84.36);

(b) Grain dampening machines (heading No. 84.37);

(c) Diffusing apparatus for sugar juice extraction (heading No. 84.38);

(d) Machinery for the heat-treatment of textile yarns, fabrics or made up textile articles (heading No. 84.51); or

(e) Machinery or plant, designed for mechanical operation, in which a change of temperature, even if necessary, is subsidiary.

Heading No. 84.22 does not cover:

(a) Sewing machines for closing bags or similar containers (heading No. 84.52); or

(b) Office machinery of heading No. 84.72.

Heading No. 84.24 does not cover:

(a) Ink-jet printing machines (heading No. 84.43);or

(b) Water-jet cutting machines(heading No.84.56).

3. A machine-tool for working any material which answers to a description in heading No. 84.56 and at the same time to a description in heading No. 84.57, 84.58, 84.59, 84.60, 84.61, 84.64 or 84.65 is to be classified in heading No. 84.56.

4. Heading No. 84.57 applies only to machine-tools for working metal other than lathes (including turning centres), which can carry out different types of machining operations either:

(a) by automatic tool change from a magazine or the like in conformity with a machining programme (machining centres);

(二)同时或顺序地自动使用不同的动力头对固定不动的工件进行加工(单工位组合机床);

(b) by the automatic use, simultaneously or sequentially, of different unit heads working on a fixed position workpiece (unit construction machines, single station), or

(三)自动将工件送向不同的动力头(多工位组合机床)。

(c) by the automatic transfer of the workpiece to different unit heads (multi-station transfer machines).

五、

5.

(一)税号 84.71 所称“自动数据处理设备”,是指具有如下功能的机器:

(a) For the purposes of heading No. 84.71, theexpression “automatic data processing machines” means machines capable of:

1.存储处理程序和执行程序直接需要的起码的数据;

(1) storing the processing program or programs and at least the data immediately necessary for the execution of the program;

2.按照用户的要求随意编辑程序;

(2) being freely programmed in accordance with the requirements of the user;

3.按照用户指令进行算术计算;以及

(3) performing arthmetical computations specified by the user; and

4.在运行过程中,可不需人为干预而通过逻辑判断,执行一个处理程序,这个处理程序可改变计算机指令的执行。

(4) executing, without human intervention, a processing program which requires them to modify their execution, by logical decision during the processing run.

(二)自动数据处理设备可以是一套由若干单独部件所组成的系统。

(b) Automatic data processing machines may be in theform of systems consisting of a variable number of separate units.

(三)除本条注释(四)、(五)另有规定的以外,一个部件如果符合下列所有规定,即可视为自动数据处理系统的一部分:

(c) Subject to paragraph (d) and (e) below, a unit is to be regarded as being a part of a complete system if it meets all of the following conditions:

1. 专用于或主要用于自动数据处理系统;

(1) It is of a kind solely or principally used in an automatic data processing system;

2. 可以直接或通过一个或几个其他部件同中央处理器相联接;

(2) It is connectable to the central processing unit either directly or through one or more other units; and

3. 能够以本系统所使用的方式(代码或信号)接收或传送数据。

(3) It is able to accept or deliver data in a form (codes or signals) which can be used by the system.

自动数据处理设备的部件如果单独报验,应归入税号 84.71。

Separately presented units of an automatic data processing machine are to be classified in heading 84.71.

但是,键盘、X—Y 座标输入装置及盘(片)式存储部件,只要符合上述注释(三)2、3 所列的规定,应一律作为税号 84.71 的部件归类。

However, keyboards, X-Y co-ordinate input devices and disk storage units which satisfy the conditions of paragraphs (c) (2) and (c) (3) above, are in all cases to be classified as units of heading No. 84.71.

(四)税目 84.71 不包括单独报验的下述设备,即使该设备符合本条注释五(三)的所有规定:

(d)Heading 84.71does not cover the following when presented separately, even if they meet all of the conditions set forth in Note 5(c) above:

1. 打印机、复印机及传真机,不论是否组合在一起;

(1) Printers, copyingmachines, facsimile machines, whether or not combined;

2. 发送或接收声音、图像或其他数据的设备,包括无线或有线网络的通信设备(如局域网或广播网);

(2) Apparatus for the transmission or reception of voice, images or other data,including apparatus for communication in a wired or wireless network (such as a local or wide area network);

3. 扬声器和传声器(麦克风);

(3) Loudspeakers and microphones;

4. 电视摄像机、数字照相机、视频摄录一体机;

(4) Television cameras, digital cameras and video camera recorders;

5. 监视器和投影机，未装有电视接收装置.

(五)装有自动数据处理装置或与自动数据处理设备连接使用，但却从事数据处理以外的某项专门功能的机器，应按其功能归入相应的税号，对于无法按功能归类的，应归入未列名税号。

六、税号 84.82 还包括最大直径及最小直径与标称直径相差均不超过 1%或 0.05 毫米(以相差数值较小的为准)的抛光钢珠，其他钢珠归入税号 73.26。

七、具有一种以上用途的机器在归类时，其主要用途可作为唯一的用途对待。除本章注释二、第十六类注释三另有规定的以外，凡任何税号都未列明其主要用途的机器，以及没有哪一种用途是主要用途的机器，均应归入税号 84.79。税号 84.79 还包括将金属丝、纺织纱线或其他各种材料以及它们的混合材料制成绳、缆的机器(例如，捻股机、绞扭机、制缆机)。

八、税号 84.70 所称“袖珍式”，仅适用于外形尺寸不超过 170 毫米×100 毫米×45 毫米的机器。

九、

(一)第八十五章注释八(一)、(二)中对“半导体器件”和“集成电路”的相关描述同样适用于本条注释和税目 84.86。本条注释和税目 84.86 的描述中所称“半导体器件”也包括光敏半导体器件和发光二极管。

(二)本条注释和税目 84.86 所称“平板显示器的制造设备”包括将各层基片制造成平板的设备。但不包括玻璃的制造设备、将印刷电路板或其他电子元件装配在平板上的设备。“平板显示 ”不包括阴极射线管技术。

(三)税目 84.86 也包括下列机器及装置，其专用或主要用于：

1.制造或修补掩膜版及投影掩膜版；

2.组装半导体器件或集成电路；

3.升降、搬运、装卸单晶柱、晶圆、半导体器件、集成电路和平板显示器；

(四)除十六类注释一和第八十四章注释一另有规定的以外，符合税目 84.86 规定的机器及装置应归入该税目而不归入本目录的其他税目。

(5) Monitors and projectors, not incorporating television reception apparatus.

(e) Machines performing a specific function other than data processing and incorporating or working in conjunction with an automatic data processing machine are to be classified in the headings appropriate to their respective functions or, failing that, in residual headings.

6. Heading No. 84.82 applies, *inter alia*, to polished steel balls, the maximum and minimum diameters of which do not differ from the nominal diameter by more than 1% or by more than 0.05mm, whichever is less. Other steel balls are to be classified in heading No. 73.26.

7. A machine which is used for more than one purpose is, for the purposes of classification, to be treated as if its principal purpose were its sole purpose. Subject to Note 2 to this Chapter and Note 3 to Section XVI, a machine, the principal purpose of which is not described in any heading or for which no one purpose is the principal purpose, unless the context otherwise requires, is to be classified in heading No. 84.79. Heading No. 84.79 also covers machines for making rope or cable (for example, stranding, twisting or cabling machines) from metal wire, textile yarn or any other material or from a combination of such materials.

8. For the purposes of heading No. 84.70, the term “pocket-size” applies only to machines the dimensions of which do not exceed 170mm×100mm×45mm.

9.

(a) Notes 8(a) and 8(b) to Chapter 85 also apply with respect to the expressions “semiconductor devices” and “electronic integrated circuits”. However, for the purposes of this Note and of heading No. 84.86, the expression “semiconductor devices” also covers photosensitive semiconductor devices and light emitting diodes.

(b) For the purposes of this Note and of heading No. 84.86, the expression “manufacture of flat panel displays” covers the fabrication of substrates into a flat panel. It does not cover the or other electronic components onto the flat panel. The expression “flat panel display” does not cover cathode-ray tube technology.

(c) Heading No. 84.86 also includes machines and apparatus solely or principally of a kind used for:

(1) the manufacture or repair of masks and reticles;

(2) assembling semiconductor devices or electronic integrated circuits;

(3) lifting, handling, loading or unlading of boules, wafers, semiconductor devices, electronic integrated circuits and flat panel displays.

(d) Subject to Note 1 to Section XVI and Note 1 to Chapter 84, machines and apparatus answering to the description in heading No. 84.86 are to be classified in that heading and in no other heading of the Nomenclature.

子目注释：

一、子目号 8471.49 所称"系统"，是指各部件符合第八十四章注释五（三）所列条件，并且至少由一个中央处理部件、一个输入部件（例如，键盘或扫描器）及一个输出部件（例如，视频显示器或打印机）组成的自动数据处理设备。

二、子目号 8482.40 仅包括滚柱直径相同，最大不超过 5 毫米，且长度至少是直径三倍的圆滚柱轴承，滚柱的两端可以磨圆。

Subheading Notes:

1. For the purposes of subheading No.8471.49, the term "systems" means automatic data processing machines whose units satisfy the conditions laid down in Note 5(c) to Chapter 84 and which comprise at least a central processing unit, one input unit (e.g. a keyboard or a scanner), and one output unit (e.g. a visual display unit or a printer).

2. Subheading No. 8482.40 applies only to bearings with cylindrical rollers of a uniform diameter not exceeding 5mm and having a length which is at least three times the diameter. The ends of the rollers may be rounded.

序号 No.	税则号列 Tariff Line	货品名称	最惠国税率 MFN(%)	协定税率 Agreement(%)		特惠税率 S.P.(%)		普通税率 Gen.(%)	Article Description
	84.01	**核反应堆;核反应堆的未辐照燃料元件（释热元件）;同位素分离机器及装置:**							**Nuclear reactors; fuel elements (cartridges), non-irradiated, for nuclear reactors; machinery and apparatus for isotopic separation:**
5865	8401.1000	-核反应堆	2	0	东盟ASEAN,智利CL,巴基斯坦PK,新西兰NZ,秘鲁PE,哥斯达黎加CR	0	最不发达35国LDC35	8	-Nuclear reactors
5866	8401.2000	-同位素分离机器、装置及其零件	1	0	东盟ASEAN,智利CL,巴基斯坦PK,新西兰NZ,秘鲁PE,哥斯达黎加CR	0	最不发达35国LDC35	8	-Machinery and apparatus for isotopic separation, and parts thereof
		-未辐照燃料元件（释热元件）:							-Fuel elements (cartridges), non-irradiated:
5867	8401.3010	---未辐照燃料元件	2	0	东盟ASEAN,智利CL,巴基斯坦PK,新西兰NZ,秘鲁PE,哥斯达黎加CR	0	最不发达35国LDC35	8	---Fuel elements, non-irrdadiated
5868	8401.3090	---未辐照燃料元件的零件	1	0	东盟ASEAN,智利CL,巴基斯坦PK,新西兰NZ,秘鲁PE,哥斯达黎加CR	0	最不发达35国LDC35	8	---Parts for fuel elements non-irradiated
		-核反应堆零件:							-Parts of nuclear reactors:
5869	8401.4010	---未辐照相关组件	1	0	东盟ASEAN,智利CL,巴基斯坦PK,新西兰NZ,秘鲁PE,哥斯达黎加CR	0	最不发达35国LDC35	8	---Non-irradiated Associated Assembly
5870	8401.4020	---堆内构件	1	0	东盟ASEAN,智利CL,巴基斯坦PK,新西兰NZ,秘鲁PE,哥斯达黎加CR	0	最不发达35国LDC35	8	---Reactor internals
5871	8401.4090	---其他	1	0	东盟ASEAN,智利CL,巴基斯坦PK,新西兰NZ,秘鲁PE,哥斯达黎加CR	0	最不发达35国LDC35	8	---Other

序号 No.	税则号列 Tariff Line	货品名称	最惠国税率 MFN(%)	协定税率 Agreement(%)		特惠税率 S.P.(%)		普通税率 Gen.(%)	Article Description
	84.02	**蒸汽锅炉（能产生低压水蒸汽的集中供暖用的热水锅炉除外）;过热水锅炉:**							**Steam or other vapour generating boilers (other than central heating hot water boilers capable also of producing low pressure steam); super-heated water boilers:**
		-蒸汽锅炉:							-Steam or other vapour generating boilers:
		--蒸发量超过45吨/时的水管锅炉:							--Watertube boilers with a steam production exceeding 45t per hour:
5872	8402.1110	---蒸发量在900吨/时及以上的发电用锅炉	3	0 2.5	东盟ASEAN,智利CL,巴基斯坦PK,新西兰NZ,秘鲁PE,哥斯达黎加CR 亚太APTA	0	最不发达35国LDC35	11	---Boilers for generating electricity with a steam production 900t or more per hour
5873	8402.1190	---其他	14	0 1.4 2.8 7 13.3	东盟ASEAN,新加坡SG,新西兰NZ,秘鲁PE 智利CL 哥斯达黎加CR 巴基斯坦PK 亚太APTA	0	最不发达35国LDC35	35	---Other
5874	8402.1200	--蒸发量不超过45吨/时的水管锅炉	5	0 3.9	东盟ASEAN,智利CL,巴基斯坦PK,新西兰NZ,秘鲁PE,哥斯达黎加CR 亚太APTA	0	最不发达35国LDC35	35	--Watertube boilers with a steam production not exceeding 45t per hour
5875	8402.1900	--其他蒸汽锅炉,包括混合式锅炉	5	0	东盟ASEAN,智利CL,巴基斯坦PK,新西兰NZ,秘鲁PE,哥斯达黎加CR	0	最不发达35国LDC35	35	--Other vapour generating boilers, including hybrid boilers
5876	8402.2000	-过热水锅炉	16	0 3.2 8 12.8	东盟ASEAN,智利CL,新加坡SG,新西兰NZ 哥斯达黎加CR 秘鲁PE 巴基斯坦PK	0	最不发达35国LDC35	35	-Super-heated water boilers
5877	8402.9000	-零件	2	0	东盟ASEAN,智利CL,巴基斯坦PK,新西兰NZ,秘鲁PE,哥斯达黎加CR	0	最不发达35国LDC35	11	-Parts
	84.03	**集中供暖用的热水锅炉,但税号84.02的货品除外:**							**Central heating boilers other than those of heading No.84.02:**
5878	8403.1010	-家用型	10	0 5 9.5	东盟ASEAN,智利CL,新西兰NZ,秘鲁PE,哥斯达黎加CR 巴基斯坦PK 亚太APTA	0	最不发达35国LDC35	80	-Household type
5879	8403.1090	-其他	10	0 5 9.5	东盟ASEAN,智利CL,新西兰NZ,秘鲁PE,哥斯达黎加CR 巴基斯坦PK 亚太APTA	0	最不发达35国LDC35	80	-Other

序号 No.	税则号列 Tariff Line	货品名称	最惠国税率 MFN(%)	协定税率 Agreement(%)		特惠税率 S.P.(%)		普通税率 Gen.(%)	Article Description
5880	8403.9000	-零件	6	0 5	东盟ASEAN,智利CL,新西兰NZ,秘鲁PE,哥斯达黎加CR 巴基斯坦PK	0	最不发达35国LDC35	80	-Parts
	84.04	**税号84.02或84.03所列锅炉的辅助设备(例如,节热器、过热器、除灰器、气体回收器);水蒸汽或其他蒸汽动力装置的冷凝器:**							**Auxiliary plant for use with boilers of heading No. 84.02 or 84.03 (for example, economizers, super-heaters, soot removers, gas recoverers); condensers for steam or other vapour power units:**
		-税号84.02或84.03所列锅炉的辅助设备:							-Auxiliary plant for use with boilers of heading No. 84.02 or 84.03:
5881	8404.1010	---税号84.02所列锅炉的辅助设备	7	0 3.5	东盟ASEAN,智利CL,巴基斯坦PK,新西兰NZ,秘鲁PE,哥斯达黎加CR 亚太APTA	0	最不发达35国LDC35	35	---For use with boilers of heading No. 84.02
5882	8404.1020	---税号84.03所列锅炉的辅助设备	10	0 5	东盟ASEAN,智利CL,新西兰NZ,秘鲁PE,哥斯达黎加CR 亚太APTA,巴基斯坦PK	0	最不发达35国LDC35	80	---For use with boilers of heading No. 84.03
5883	8404.2000	-水蒸汽或其他蒸汽动力装置的冷凝器	14	0 2.8 11.2	东盟ASEAN,智利CL,新加坡SG,新西兰NZ,秘鲁PE 哥斯达黎加CR 巴基斯坦PK	0	最不发达35国LDC35	35	-Condensers for steam or other vapour power units
		-零件:							-Parts:
5884	8404.9010	---子目号8404.1020所列设备的零件	10	0	东盟ASEAN,亚太APTA,智利CL,巴基斯坦PK,新西兰NZ,秘鲁PE,哥斯达黎加CR	0	最不发达35国LDC35	80	---Of the auxiliary plant of subheading No. 8404.1020
5885	8404.9090	---其他	7	0	东盟ASEAN,亚太APTA,智利CL,巴基斯坦PK,新西兰NZ,秘鲁PE,哥斯达黎加CR	0	最不发达35国LDC35	35	---Other
	84.05	**煤气发生器,不论有无净化器;乙炔发生器及类似的水解气体发生器,不论有无净化器:**							**Producer gas or water gas generators, with or without their purifiers; acetylene gas generators and similar water process gas generators, with or without their purifiers:**
5886	8405.1000	-煤气发生器,不论有无净化器;乙炔发生器及类似的水解气体发生器,不论有无净化器	14	0 1.4 2.8 11.2	东盟ASEAN,新加坡SG,新西兰NZ,秘鲁PE 智利CL 哥斯达黎加CR 巴基斯坦PK	0	最不发达35国LDC35	30	-Producer gas or water gas generators, with or without their purifiers; acetylene gas generators and similar water process gas generators, with or without their purifiers

序号 No.	税则号列 Tariff Line	货品名称	最惠国税 率 MFN(%)	协定税率 Agreement(%)		特惠税率 S.P.(%)		普通税率 Gen.(%)	Article Description
5887	8405.9000	-零件	8	0 5	东盟ASEAN,智利CL,新西兰NZ,秘鲁PE,哥斯达黎加CR 巴基斯坦PK	0	最不发达35国LDC35	30	-Parts
	84.06	**汽轮机:**							**Steam turbines and other vapour turbines:**
5888	8406.1000	-船舶动力用汽轮机	5	0	东盟ASEAN,智利CL,巴基斯坦PK,新西兰NZ,秘鲁PE,哥斯达黎加CR	0	最不发达35国LDC35,最不发达4国LDC4	35	-Turbines for marine propulsion
		-其他汽轮机:							-Other turbines:
		--输出功率超过40兆瓦的:							--Of an output exceeding 40MW:
5889	8406.8110	---输出功率不超过100兆瓦的	5	0	东盟ASEAN,智利CL,巴基斯坦PK,新西兰NZ,秘鲁PE,哥斯达黎加CR	0	最不发达35国LDC35,最不发达4国LDC4	35	---Of an output not exceeding 100MW
5890	8406.8120	---输出功率超过100兆瓦,但不超过350兆瓦的	5	0	东盟ASEAN,智利CL,巴基斯坦PK,新西兰NZ,秘鲁PE,哥斯达黎加CR	0	最不发达35国LDC35,最不发达4国LDC4	35	---Of an output exceeding 100MW but not exceeding 350MW
5891	8406.8130	---输出功率超过350兆瓦的	6	0 5	东盟ASEAN,智利CL,新西兰NZ,秘鲁PE,哥斯达黎加CR 巴基斯坦PK	0	最不发达35国LDC35,最不发达4国LDC4	11	---Of an output exceeding 350MW
5892	8406.8200	--输出功率不超过40兆瓦的	5	0	东盟ASEAN,智利CL,巴基斯坦PK,新西兰NZ,秘鲁PE,哥斯达黎加CR	0	最不发达35国LDC35,最不发达4国LDC4	35	--Of an output not exceeding 40MW
5893	8406.9000	-零件	2	0	东盟ASEAN,智利CL,巴基斯坦PK,新西兰NZ,秘鲁PE,哥斯达黎加CR	0	最不发达35国LDC35,最不发达4国LDC4	11	-Parts
	84.07	**点燃往复式或旋转式活塞内燃发动机:**							**Spark-ignition reciprocating or rotary internal combustion piston engines:**
		-航空器发动机:							-Aircraft engines:
5894	8407.1010	---输出功率不超过298千瓦	2 △1	0	东盟ASEAN,智利CL,巴基斯坦PK,新西兰NZ,秘鲁PE,哥斯达黎加CR	0	最不发达35国LDC35	11	---Of an output not exceeding 298kW

序号 No.	税则号列 Tariff Line	货品名称	最惠国税率 MFN(%)	协定税率 Agreement(%)		特惠税率 S.P.(%)		普通税率 Gen.(%)	Article Description
5895	8407.1020	---输出功率超过298千瓦	2 △1	0	东盟ASEAN,智利CL,巴基斯坦PK,新西兰NZ,秘鲁PE,哥斯达黎加CR	0	最不发达35国LDC35	11	---Of an output exceeding 298kW
		-船舶发动机:							-Marine propulsion engines:
5896	8407.2100	--舷外发动机	8	0 5	东盟ASEAN,智利CL,新西兰NZ,秘鲁PE,哥斯达黎加CR 巴基斯坦PK	0	最不发达35国LDC35	35	--Outboard motors
5897	8407.2900	--其他	8	0 5	东盟ASEAN,智利CL,新西兰NZ,秘鲁PE,哥斯达黎加CR 巴基斯坦PK	0	最不发达35国LDC35	20	--Other
		-用于第八十七章所列车辆的往复式活塞发动机:							-Reciprocating piston engines of a kind used for the propulsion of vehicles of Chapter87:
5898	8407.3100	--气缸容量(排气量)不超过50毫升	10	0 5	东盟ASEAN,智利CL,新西兰NZ,秘鲁PE,哥斯达黎加CR 巴基斯坦PK	0	最不发达35国LDC35	35	--Of a cylinder capacity not exceeding 50cc
5899	8407.3200	--气缸容量(排气量)超过50毫升,但不超过250毫升	10	0 5	东盟ASEAN,智利CL,新西兰NZ,秘鲁PE,哥斯达黎加CR 巴基斯坦PK	0	最不发达35国LDC35	35	--Of a cylinder capacity exceeding 50cc but not exceeding 250cc
5900	8407.3300	--气缸容量(排气量)超过250毫升,但不超过1000毫升	10	0 8	东盟ASEAN,智利CL,新加坡SG,新西兰NZ,秘鲁PE,哥斯达黎加CR,香港HK 巴基斯坦PK	0	最不发达35国LDC35	70	--Of a cylinder capacity exceeding 250cc but not exceeding 1000cc
		--气缸容量(排气量)超过1000毫升:							--Of a cylinder capacity exceeding 1000 cc:
5901	8407.3410	---气缸容量(排气量)超过1000毫升,但不超过3000毫升	10	0 7	智利CL,新西兰NZ,哥斯达黎加CR,香港HK 亚太APTA,巴基斯坦PK			70	---Of a cylinder capacity exceeding 1000cc but not exceeding 3000cc
5902	8407.3420	---气缸容量(排气量)超过3000毫升	10	0 7	智利CL,新西兰NZ,哥斯达黎加CR,香港HK 亚太APTA,巴基斯坦PK			35	---Of a cylinder capacity exceeding 3000cc
		-其他发动机:							-Other engines:
5903	8407.9010	---沼气发动机	12	0 2.4 6	东盟ASEAN,智利CL,新加坡SG,新西兰NZ,秘鲁PE 哥斯达黎加CR 巴基斯坦PK	0	最不发达35国LDC35	35	---Firedamp engines
5904	8407.9090	---其他	18	0 3.6 9	东盟ASEAN,智利CL,新加坡SG,新西兰NZ 哥斯达黎加CR 秘鲁PE	0	最不发达35国LDC35	35	---Other
	ex84079090	立式输出轴汽油发动机	△9						Petrol engines with a vertical crankshaft

序号 No.	税则号列 Tariff Line	货品名称	最惠国税率 MFN(%)	协定税率 Agreement(%)		特惠税率 S.P.(%)		普通税率 Gen.(%)	Article Description
	84.08	**压燃式活塞内燃发动机（柴油或半柴油发动机）:**							**Compression-ignition internal combustion piston engines (diesel or semidiesel engines):**
5905	8408.1000	-船舶发动机	5	0 0.5 2.5	东盟ASEAN,巴基斯坦PK,新加坡SG,新西兰NZ,秘鲁PE,哥斯达黎加CR 智利CL 亚太APTA	0	最不发达35国LDC35	11	-Marine propulsion engines
		-用于第八十七章所列车辆的发动机:							-Engines of a kind used for the propulsion of vehicles of Chapter 87:
5906	8408.2010	---输出功率在132.39千瓦（180马力）及以上	9	0 0.9 6.3	新西兰NZ,秘鲁PE,哥斯达黎加CR,香港HK 智利CL 亚太APTA,巴基斯坦PK	0	最不发达35国LDC35	14	---Of an output power of 132.39kW (180PS) or more
	ex84082010	输出功率在441千瓦（600马力）及以上的柴油发动机	△4						Diesel engines with an output power of 441kW (600HP) or more
5907	8408.2090	---其他	25	0 2.5 5 17.5 20	新西兰NZ 智利CL 哥斯达黎加CR 亚太APTA,巴基斯坦PK 东盟ASEAN			35	---Other
	ex84082090	升功率≥40千瓦的轿车用柴油发动机	△10						Diesel engines for cars, power density ≥ 40kW
		-其他发动机:							-Other engines:
5908	8408.9010	---机车发动机	6	0 0.6 5.4	东盟ASEAN,巴基斯坦PK,新西兰NZ,秘鲁PE,哥斯达黎加CR 智利CL 亚太APTA	0	最不发达35国LDC35	11	---Locomotive engines
		---其他:							---Other:
5909	8408.9091	----输出功率不超过14千瓦	5	0 0.5 4.5	东盟ASEAN,巴基斯坦PK,新西兰NZ,秘鲁PE,哥斯达黎加CR 智利CL 亚太APTA	0	最不发达35国LDC35	35	----Of an output not exceeding 14kW
5910	8408.9092	----输出功率超过14千瓦, 但小于132.39千瓦（180马力）	8.4	0 0.8 5 7.6	东盟ASEAN,新西兰NZ,秘鲁PE,哥斯达黎加CR 智利CL 巴基斯坦PK 亚太APTA	0	最不发达35国LDC35	35	----Of an output exceeding14kW but not exceeding 132.39kW (180PS)
5911	8408.9093	----输出功率在132.39千瓦（180马力）及以上	5	0 0.5 4.5	东盟ASEAN,巴基斯坦PK,新西兰NZ,秘鲁PE,哥斯达黎加CR 智利CL 亚太APTA	0	最不发达35国LDC35	14	----Of an output of 132.39kW (180PS) or more
	84.09	**专用于或主要用于税号84.07或84.08所列发动机的零件:**							**Parts suitable for use solely or principally with the engines of heading No. 84.07 or 84.08:**

序号 No.	税则号列 Tariff Line	货品名称	最惠国税率 MFN(%)	协定税率 Agreement(%)		特惠税率 S.P.(%)		普通税率 Gen.(%)	Article Description
5912	8409.1000	-航空器发动机用	2	0	东盟ASEAN,智利CL,巴基斯坦PK,新西兰NZ,秘鲁PE,哥斯达黎加CR	0	最不发达35国LDC35,最不发达4国LDC4	11	-For aircraft engines
		-其他:							-Other:
		--专用于或主要用于点燃式活塞内燃发动机的:							--Suitable for use solely or principally with spark-ignition internal combustion piston engines:
5913	8409.9110	---船舶发动机用	6	0 4.2	东盟ASEAN,智利CL,巴基斯坦PK,新西兰NZ,秘鲁PE,哥斯达黎加CR 亚太APTA	0	最不发达35国LDC35,最不发达4国LDC4	17	---For marine propulsion engines
		---其他:							---Other:
5914	8409.9191	----电控燃油喷射装置	5	0 3.5	东盟ASEAN,智利CL,巴基斯坦PK,新加坡SG,新西兰NZ,秘鲁PE,哥斯达黎加CR 亚太APTA	0	最不发达35国LDC35,最不发达4国LDC4	35	----Electronic fuel injection devices
5915	8409.9199	----其他	5	0 3.5	东盟ASEAN,智利CL,巴基斯坦PK,新加坡SG,新西兰NZ,秘鲁PE,哥斯达黎加CR 亚太APTA	0	最不发达35国LDC35,最不发达4国LDC4	35	----Other
		--其他:							--Other:
5916	8409.9910	---船舶发动机用	5	0 0.5 4.5	东盟ASEAN,巴基斯坦PK,新加坡SG,新西兰NZ,秘鲁PE,哥斯达黎加CR 智利CL 亚太APTA	0	最不发达35国LDC35,最不发达4国LDC4	11	---For marine propulsion engines
5917	8409.9920	---机车发动机用	2	0 1.5	东盟ASEAN,智利CL,巴基斯坦PK,新西兰NZ,秘鲁PE,哥斯达黎加CR 亚太APTA	0	最不发达35国LDC35,最不发达4国LDC4	11	---For locomotive engines
		---其他:							---Other:
5918	8409.9991	----输出功率在132.39千瓦（180马力）及以上的发动机用	2	0 1.5	东盟ASEAN,智利CL,巴基斯坦PK,新西兰NZ,秘鲁PE,哥斯达黎加CR 亚太APTA	0	最不发达35国LDC35,最不发达4国LDC4	11	----For engines with an output of 132.39kW (180PS) or more
5919	8409.9999	----其他	8.4	0 0.8 5 8	东盟ASEAN,新加坡SG,新西兰NZ,秘鲁PE,哥斯达黎加CR 智利CL 巴基斯坦PK 亚太APTA	0	最不发达35国LDC35,最不发达4国LDC4	35	----Other

序号 No.	税则号列 Tariff Line	货品名称	最惠国税率 MFN(%)	协定税率 Agreement(%)		特惠税率 S.P.(%)		普通税率 Gen.(%)	Article Description
	ex84099999	电控柴油喷射装置	△5						Electronic diesel oil injection devices
	84.10	**水轮机、水轮及其调节器:**							**Hydraulic turbines, water wheels, and regulators therefor:**
		-水轮机及水轮:							-Hydraulic turbines and water wheels:
5920	8410.1100	--功率不超过1000千瓦	10	0 5	东盟ASEAN,智利CL,新西兰NZ,秘鲁PE,哥斯达黎加CR 巴基斯坦PK	0	最不发达35国LDC35	35	--Of a power not exceeding 1000kW
5921	8410.1200	--功率超过1000千瓦,但不超过10000千瓦	10	0 5	东盟ASEAN,智利CL,新加坡SG,新西兰NZ,秘鲁PE,哥斯达黎加CR 巴基斯坦PK	0	最不发达35国LDC35	35	--Of a power exceeding 1000kW but not exceeding 10000kW
		--功率超过10000千瓦:							--Of a power exceeding 10000kW:
5922	8410.1310	---功率超过30000千瓦的击式水轮机及水轮	10	0 5	东盟ASEAN,智利CL,新加坡SG,新西兰NZ,秘鲁PE,哥斯达黎加CR 巴基斯坦PK	0	最不发达35国LDC35	35	---Impulse hydraulic turbines and water wheels of a power＞30000kW
5923	8410.1320	---功率超过35000千瓦的贯流式水轮机及水轮	10	0 5	东盟ASEAN,智利CL,新加坡SG,新西兰NZ,秘鲁PE,哥斯达黎加CR 巴基斯坦PK	0	最不发达35国LDC35	35	---Radial hydraulic turbines and water wheels of a power＞35000kW
5924	8410.1330	---功率超过200000千瓦的水泵水轮机及水轮	10	0 5	东盟ASEAN,智利CL,新西兰NZ,秘鲁PE,哥斯达黎加CR 巴基斯坦PK	0	最不发达35国LDC35	35	---Pumping hydraulic turbines and water wheels of a power ＞200000kW
5925	8410.1390	---其他	10	0 5	东盟ASEAN,智利CL,新西兰NZ,秘鲁PE,哥斯达黎加CR 巴基斯坦PK	0	最不发达35国LDC35	35	---Other
		-零件,包括调节器:							-Parts, including regulators:
5926	8410.9010	---调节器	6	0 5	东盟ASEAN,智利CL,新西兰NZ,秘鲁PE,哥斯达黎加CR 巴基斯坦PK	0	最不发达35国LDC35	35	---Regulators
5927	8410.9090	---其他	6	0 5	东盟ASEAN,智利CL,新西兰NZ,秘鲁PE,哥斯达黎加CR 巴基斯坦PK	0	最不发达35国LDC35	35	---Other
	84.11	**涡轮喷气发动机,涡轮螺桨发动机及其他燃气轮机:**							**Turbo-jets, turbo-propellers and other gas turbines:**
		-涡轮喷气发动机:							-Turbo-jets:
		--推力不超过25千牛顿:							--Of a thrust not exceeding 25kN:

序号 No.	税则号列 Tariff Line	货品名称	最惠国税率 MFN(%)	协定税率 Agreement(%)		特惠税率 S.P.(%)		普通税率 Gen.(%)	Article Description
5928	8411.1110	---涡轮风扇发动机	1	0	东盟ASEAN,智利CL,巴基斯坦PK,新西兰NZ,秘鲁PE,哥斯达黎加CR	0	最不发达35国LDC35,最不发达4国LDC4	11	---Turbofan engines
5929	8411.1190	---其他	1	0	东盟ASEAN,智利CL,巴基斯坦PK,新西兰NZ,秘鲁PE,哥斯达黎加CR	0	最不发达35国LDC35,最不发达4国LDC4	11	---Other
		--推力超过25千牛顿:							--Of a thrust exceeding 25kN:
5930	8411.1210	---涡轮风扇发动机	1	0	东盟ASEAN,亚太APTA,智利CL,巴基斯坦PK,新西兰NZ,秘鲁PE,哥斯达黎加CR	0	最不发达35国LDC35,最不发达4国LDC4	11	---Turbofan engines
5931	8411.1290	---其他	1	0 0.5	东盟ASEAN,智利CL,巴基斯坦PK,新西兰NZ,秘鲁PE,哥斯达黎加CR 亚太APTA	0	最不发达35国LDC35,最不发达4国LDC4	11	---Other
		-涡轮螺桨发动机:							-Turbo-propellers:
5932	8411.2100	--功率不超过1100千瓦	2	0	东盟ASEAN,智利CL,巴基斯坦PK,新西兰NZ,秘鲁PE,哥斯达黎加CR	0	最不发达35国LDC35,最不发达4国LDC4	11	--Of a power not exceeding 1100kW
		--功率超过1100千瓦:							--Of a power exceeding 1100kW:
5933	8411.2210	---功率超过1100千瓦,但不超过2238千瓦	2	0	东盟ASEAN,智利CL,巴基斯坦PK,新西兰NZ,秘鲁PE,哥斯达黎加CR	0	最不发达35国LDC35,最不发达4国LDC4	11	---Of a power exceeding 1100kW but not exceeding 2238kW
5934	8411.2220	---功率超过2238千瓦,但不超过3730千瓦	2	0	东盟ASEAN,智利CL,巴基斯坦PK,新西兰NZ,秘鲁PE,哥斯达黎加CR	0	最不发达35国LDC35,最不发达4国LDC4	11	---Of a power exceeding 2238kW but not exceeding 3730kW
5935	8411.2230	---功率超过3730千瓦	2	0	东盟ASEAN,智利CL,巴基斯坦PK,新西兰NZ,秘鲁PE,哥斯达黎加CR	0	最不发达35国LDC35,最不发达4国LDC4	11	---Of a power exceeding 3730kW
		-其他燃气轮机:							-Other gas turbines:

序号 No.	税则号列 Tariff Line	货品名称	最惠国税率 MFN(%)	协定税率 Agreement(%)		特惠税率 S.P.(%)		普通税率 Gen.(%)	Article Description
5936	8411.8100	--功率不超过 5000 千瓦	15	0 1.5 3 7.5 12	东盟ASEAN,新加坡SG,新西兰NZ 智利CL 哥斯达黎加CR 秘鲁PE 巴基斯坦PK	0	最不发达 35 国 LDC35	35	--Of a power not exceeding 5000kW
	ex84118100	涡轮轴航空发动机	△1						Turbo shaft engines for aircraft
5937	8411.8200	--功率超过 5000 千瓦	3	0	东盟ASEAN,智利CL,巴基斯坦PK,新西兰NZ,秘鲁PE,哥斯达黎加CR	0	最不发达 35 国 LDC35,最不发达 4 国 LDC4	35	--Of a power exceeding 5000kW
		-零件:							-Parts:
5938	8411.9100	--涡轮喷气发动机或涡轮螺桨发动机用	1	0	东盟ASEAN,智利CL,巴基斯坦PK,新西兰NZ,秘鲁PE,哥斯达黎加CR	0	最不发达 35 国 LDC35,最不发达 4 国 LDC4	11	--Of turbo-jets or turbo-propellers
		--其他:							--Other:
5939	8411.9910	---涡轮轴发动机用	5	0 0.5	东盟ASEAN,巴基斯坦PK,新西兰NZ,秘鲁PE,哥斯达黎加CR 智利CL	0	最不发达 35 国 LDC35,最不发达 4 国 LDC4	35	---Of turboshaft engines
	ex84119910	涡轮轴航空发动机用零件	△0						Parts of turbo shaft engines for aircraft
5940	8411.9990	---其他	5	0 0.5	东盟ASEAN,巴基斯坦PK,新西兰NZ,秘鲁PE,哥斯达黎加CR 智利CL	0	最不发达 35 国 LDC35,最不发达 4 国 LDC4	35	---Other
	84.12	**其他发动机及动力装置:**							**Other engines and motors:**
		-喷气发动机,但涡轮喷气发动机除外:							-Jet engines other than turbo-jets:
5941	8412.1010	---航空器及航天器用	3	0	东盟ASEAN,智利CL,巴基斯坦PK,新西兰NZ,秘鲁PE,哥斯达黎加CR	0	最不发达 35 国 LDC35,最不发达 4 国 LDC4	11	---For aircraft or spacecraft
5942	8412.1090	---其他	10	0 5	东盟ASEAN,智利CL,新西兰NZ,秘鲁PE,哥斯达黎加CR 巴基斯坦PK	0	最不发达 35 国 LDC35	35	---Other
		-液压动力装置:							-Hydraulic power engines and motors:

序号 No.	税则号列 Tariff Line	货品名称	最惠国税率 MFN(%)	协定税率 Agreement(%)		特惠税率 S.P.(%)		普通税率 Gen.(%)	Article Description
5943	8412.2100	--直线作用(液压缸)的	12	0	东盟ASEAN,新加坡SG,新西兰NZ,香港HK,台湾TW	0	最不发达35国LDC35	35	--Linear acting (cylinders)
				1.2	智利CL				
				2.4	哥斯达黎加CR				
				6	巴基斯坦PK,秘鲁PE				
		--其他:							--Other:
5944	8412.2910	---液压马达	10	0	东盟ASEAN,新加坡SG,新西兰NZ,秘鲁PE,哥斯达黎加CR	0	最不发达35国LDC35	35	---Hydraulic motors
				1	智利CL				
				5	巴基斯坦PK				
5945	8412.2990	---其他	14	0	东盟ASEAN,新加坡SG,新西兰NZ,秘鲁PE	0	最不发达35国LDC35	35	---Other
				1.4	智利CL				
				2.8	哥斯达黎加CR				
				11.2	巴基斯坦PK				
	ex84122990	抓桩器(抱桩器)	△7						Skirt Pile Grippers Assembly
		-气压动力装置:							-Pneumatic power engines and motors:
5946	8412.3100	--直线作用(气压缸)的	14	0	东盟ASEAN,智利CL,新加坡SG,新西兰NZ,秘鲁PE,台湾TW	0	最不发达35国LDC35	35	--Linear acting (cylinders)
				2.8	哥斯达黎加CR				
				7	巴基斯坦PK				
				13.3	亚太APTA				
	ex84123100	三坐标测量机用平衡气缸	△7						Cylinder balance for coordinate measuring machine of three dimensions
5947	8412.3900	--其他	14	0	东盟ASEAN,智利CL,新加坡SG,新西兰NZ,秘鲁PE	0	最不发达35国LDC35	35	--Other
				2.8	哥斯达黎加CR				
				11.2	巴基斯坦PK				
5948	8412.8000	-其他	10	0	东盟ASEAN,智利CL,新西兰NZ,秘鲁PE,哥斯达黎加CR	0	最不发达35国LDC35	35	-Other
				5	巴基斯坦PK				
		-零件:							-Parts:
5949	8412.9010	---子目号8412.1010所列机器的零件	2	0	东盟ASEAN,智利CL,巴基斯坦PK,新西兰NZ,秘鲁PE,哥斯达黎加CR	0	最不发达35国LDC35,最不发达4国LDC4	11	---For machines of subheading No. 8412.1010
5950	8412.9090	---其他	8	0	东盟ASEAN,智利CL,新西兰NZ,秘鲁PE,哥斯达黎加CR	0	最不发达35国LDC35,最不发达4国LDC4	35	---Other
				5	巴基斯坦PK				

序号 No.	税则号列 Tariff Line	货品名称	最惠国税率 MFN(%)	协定税率 Agreement(%)		特惠税率 S.P.(%)		普通税率 Gen.(%)	Article Description
	84.13	**液体泵,不论是否装有计量装置;液体提升机:**							**Pumps for liquids, whether or not fitted with a measuring device; liquid elevators:**
		-装有或可装计量装置的泵:							-Pumps fitted or designed to be fitted with a measuring device:
5951	8413.1100	--分装燃料或润滑油的泵,用于加油站或车库	10 △6	0 5	东盟ASEAN,智利CL,新加坡SG,新西兰NZ,秘鲁PE,哥斯达黎加CR 巴基斯坦PK	0	最不发达35国LDC35,最不发达4国LDC4	30	--Pumps for dispensing fuel or lubricants, of the type used in filling-stations or in garages
5952	8413.1900	--其他	10 △6	0 5	东盟ASEAN,智利CL,新加坡SG,新西兰NZ,秘鲁PE,哥斯达黎加CR 巴基斯坦PK	0	最不发达35国LDC35,最不发达4国LDC4	30	--Other
5953	8413.2000	-手泵,但子目号8413.11或8413.19的货品除外	10	0 5	东盟ASEAN,智利CL,新加坡SG,新西兰NZ,秘鲁PE,哥斯达黎加CR 巴基斯坦PK	0	最不发达35国LDC35,最不发达4国LDC4	30	-Hand pumps, other than those of subheading No. 8413.11 or 8413.19
		-活塞式内燃发动机用的燃油泵、润滑油泵或冷却剂泵:							-Fuel, lubricating or cooling medium pumps for internal combustion piston engines:
		---燃油泵:							---Fuel pumps:
5954	8413.3021	----输出功率在132.39千瓦(180马力)及以上的发动机用燃油泵	3	0 2.5	东盟ASEAN,智利CL,巴基斯坦PK,新西兰NZ,秘鲁PE,哥斯达黎加CR 亚太APTA	0	最不发达35国LDC35,最不发达4国LDC4	30	----Fuel pumps for engines of an output of 132.39kW(180PS) or more
5955	8413.3029	----其他	3	0	东盟ASEAN,智利CL,巴基斯坦PK,新西兰NZ,秘鲁PE,哥斯达黎加CR	0	最不发达35国LDC35,最不发达4国LDC4	30	----Other
5956	8413.3030	---润滑油泵	3	0	东盟ASEAN,智利CL,巴基斯坦PK,新西兰NZ,秘鲁PE,哥斯达黎加CR	0	最不发达35国LDC35,最不发达4国LDC4	30	---Lubricating oil pumps
5957	8413.3090	---其他	3	0 2.5	东盟ASEAN,智利CL,巴基斯坦PK,新西兰NZ,秘鲁PE,哥斯达黎加CR 亚太APTA	0	最不发达35国LDC35,最不发达4国LDC4	30	---Other

序号 No.	税则号列 Tariff Line	货品名称	最惠国税率 MFN(%)	协定税率 Agreement(%)		特惠税率 S.P.(%)		普通税率 Gen.(%)	Article Description
5958	8413.4000	-混凝土泵	8	0 0.8 5	东盟ASEAN,新西兰NZ,秘鲁PE,哥斯达黎加CR,香港HK 智利CL 巴基斯坦PK	0	最不发达35国LDC35,最不发达4国LDC4	30	-Concrete pumps
		-其他往复式排液泵:							-Other reciprocating positive displacement pumps:
5959	8413.5010	---气动式	10 △6	0 5	东盟ASEAN,智利CL,新加坡SG,新西兰NZ,秘鲁PE,哥斯达黎加CR 巴基斯坦PK	0	最不发达35国LDC35,最不发达4国LDC4	40	---Pneumatic
5960	8413.5020	---电动式	10 △6	0 5	东盟ASEAN,智利CL,新加坡SG,新西兰NZ,秘鲁PE,哥斯达黎加CR,香港HK 巴基斯坦PK	0	最不发达35国LDC35,最不发达4国LDC4	40	---Electric
		---液压式:							---Hydraulic:
5961	8413.5031	----柱塞泵	10 △6	0 1 5	东盟ASEAN,新加坡SG,新西兰NZ,秘鲁PE,哥斯达黎加CR 智利CL 巴基斯坦PK	0	最不发达35国LDC35,最不发达4国LDC4	40	----Plunger pump
5962	8413.5039	----其他	10 △6	0 1 5	东盟ASEAN,新加坡SG,新西兰NZ,秘鲁PE,哥斯达黎加CR 智利CL 巴基斯坦PK	0	最不发达35国LDC35,最不发达4国LDC4	40	----Other
5963	8413.5090	---其他	10 △6	0 1 5	东盟ASEAN,新加坡SG,新西兰NZ,哥斯达黎加CR 智利CL 巴基斯坦PK,秘鲁PE	0	最不发达35国LDC35,最不发达4国LDC4	40	---Other
		-其他回转式排液泵:							-Other rotary positive displacement pumps:
		---齿轮泵:							---gear pump:
5964	8413.6021	----电动式	10 △6	0 5	东盟ASEAN,智利CL,新加坡SG,新西兰NZ,秘鲁PE,哥斯达黎加CR 巴基斯坦PK	0	最不发达35国LDC35,最不发达4国LDC4	40	----Electric
5965	8413.6022	----液压式	10	0 5	东盟ASEAN,智利CL,新西兰NZ,秘鲁PE,哥斯达黎加CR 巴基斯坦PK	0	最不发达35国LDC35,最不发达4国LDC4	40	----Hydraulic

序号 No.	税则号列 Tariff Line	货品名称	最惠国税率 MFN(%)	协定税率 Agreement(%)		特惠税率 S.P.(%)		普通税率 Gen.(%)	Article Description
	ex84136022	回转式液压油泵,输入转速＞2000r/min,输入功率＞190kW,最大流量＞2*280 L/min	△3						Rotating hydraulic oil pump,input rotating speed ＞2000r/min, input power ＞190kW, maximum flow ＞2*280 L/min
	ex84136022	其他液压式齿轮回转泵	△6						Other hydraulic gear rotating pump
5966	8413.6029	----其他	10 △6	0 5	东盟ASEAN,智利CL,新西兰NZ,秘鲁PE,哥斯达黎加CR 巴基斯坦PK	0	最不发达35国LDC35,最不发达4国LDC4	40	----Other
		---叶片泵:							---Vane pump:
5967	8413.6031	----电动式	10 △6	0 5	东盟ASEAN,智利CL,新西兰NZ,秘鲁PE,哥斯达黎加CR 巴基斯坦PK	0	最不发达35国LDC35,最不发达4国LDC4	40	----Electric
5968	8413.6032	----液压式	10 △6	0 5	东盟ASEAN,智利CL,新西兰NZ,秘鲁PE,哥斯达黎加CR 巴基斯坦PK	0	最不发达35国LDC35,最不发达4国LDC4	40	----Hydraulic
5969	8413.6039	----其他	10 △6	0 5	东盟ASEAN,智利CL,新西兰NZ,秘鲁PE,哥斯达黎加CR 巴基斯坦PK	0	最不发达35国LDC35,最不发达4国LDC4	40	----Other
5970	8413.6040	---螺杆泵	10 △6	0 5	东盟ASEAN,智利CL,新西兰NZ,秘鲁PE,哥斯达黎加CR 巴基斯坦PK	0	最不发达35国LDC35,最不发达4国LDC4	40	---Screw pump
5971	8413.6050	---径向柱塞泵	10 △6	0 5	东盟ASEAN,智利CL,新西兰NZ,秘鲁PE,哥斯达黎加CR 巴基斯坦PK	0	最不发达35国LDC35,最不发达4国LDC4	40	---Radial plunger pump
5972	8413.6060	---轴向柱塞泵	10 △6	0 5	东盟ASEAN,智利CL,新西兰NZ,秘鲁PE,哥斯达黎加CR 巴基斯坦PK	0	最不发达35国LDC35,最不发达4国LDC4	40	---Axial plunger pump
5973	8413.6090	---其他	10 △6	0 5	东盟ASEAN,智利CL,新加坡SG,新西兰NZ,秘鲁PE,哥斯达黎加CR 巴基斯坦PK	0	最不发达35国LDC35,最不发达4国LDC4	40	---Other

序号 No.	税则号列 Tariff Line	货品名称	最惠国 税 率 MFN(%)	协定税率 Agreement(%)		特惠税率 S.P.(%)		普通 税率 Gen.(%)	Article Description
		-其他离心泵:							-Other centrifugal pumps:
5974	8413.7010	---转速在10000转/分及以上	8	0 5 7.6	东盟ASEAN,智利CL,新西兰NZ,秘鲁PE,哥斯达黎加CR 巴基斯坦PK 亚太APTA	0	最不发达35国LDC35,最不发达4国LDC4	40	---Rotational speed no less than10000r/min
		---其他:							---Other:
5975	8413.7091	----电动潜油泵及潜水电泵	10 △8	0 5	东盟ASEAN,智利CL,新加坡SG,新西兰NZ,秘鲁PE,哥斯达黎加CR 巴基斯坦PK	0	最不发达35国LDC35,最不发达4国LDC4	40	----Electric submersible oil pumps and electric submersible pumps
5976	8413.7099	----其他	8	0 5 7.6	东盟ASEAN,智利CL,新西兰NZ,秘鲁PE,哥斯达黎加CR,香港HK 巴基斯坦PK 亚太APTA	0	最不发达35国LDC35,最不发达4国LDC4	40	----Other
		-其他泵;液体提升机:							-Other pumps; liquid elevators:
5977	8413.8100	--泵	8	0 4	东盟ASEAN,智利CL,巴基斯坦PK,新西兰NZ,秘鲁PE,哥斯达黎加CR,台湾TW 亚太APTA	0	最不发达35国LDC35,最不发达4国LDC4	40	--Pumps
5978	8413.8200	--液体提升机	8	0 5	东盟ASEAN,智利CL,新西兰NZ,秘鲁PE,哥斯达黎加CR 巴基斯坦PK	0	最不发达35国LDC35,最不发达4国LDC4	30	--Liquid elevators
		-零件:							-Parts:
5979	8413.9100	--泵用	5	0 2.5	东盟ASEAN,智利CL,巴基斯坦PK,新西兰NZ,秘鲁PE,哥斯达黎加CR,香港HK,台湾TW 亚太APTA	0	最不发达35国LDC35,最不发达4国LDC4	30	--Of pumps
5980	8413.9200	--液体提升机用	6 △4	0 5	东盟ASEAN,智利CL,新西兰NZ,秘鲁PE,哥斯达黎加CR 巴基斯坦PK	0	最不发达35国LDC35,最不发达4国LDC4	30	--Of liquid elevators
	84.14	**空气泵或真空泵、空气及其他气体压缩机、风机、风扇;装有风扇的通风罩或循环气罩,不论是否装有过滤器:**							**Air or vacuum pumps, air or other gas compressors and fans; ventilating or recycling hoods incorporating a fan, whether or not fitted with filters:**

序号 No.	税则号列 Tariff Line	货品名称	最惠国税率 MFN(%)	协定税率 Agreement(%)		特惠税率 S.P.(%)		普通税率 Gen.(%)	Article Description
5981	8414.1000	-真空泵	8 △5	0 5	东盟ASEAN,智利CL,新西兰NZ,秘鲁PE,哥斯达黎加CR,台湾TW 巴基斯坦PK	0	最不发达35国LDC35	30	-Vacuum pumps
5982	8414.2000	-手动或脚踏式空气泵	8	0 5	东盟ASEAN,智利CL,新西兰NZ,秘鲁PE,哥斯达黎加CR 巴基斯坦PK	0	最不发达35国LDC35	30	-Hand-or foot-operated pumps
		-用于制冷设备的压缩机:							-Compressors of a kind used in refrigerating equipment:
		---电动机驱动的压缩机:							---Driven by a motor:
5983	8414.3011	----冷藏箱或冷冻箱用,电动机额定功率不超过0.4千瓦	8	0 0.8 5 5.9	东盟ASEAN,新加坡SG,新西兰NZ,秘鲁PE,哥斯达黎加CR,香港HK 智利CL 巴基斯坦PK 亚太APTA	0	最不发达35国LDC35,最不发达4国LDC4	80	----For refrigerators or freezers, of a motor power not exceeding 0.4kW
	ex84143011	功率≤0.4kW的冷藏、冷冻箱用无级变速压缩机	△3						Stepless speed regulation compressors for refrige/freezer, motor power ≤0.4kW
5984	8414.3012	----冷藏箱或冷冻箱用,电动机额定功率超过0.4千瓦,但不超过5千瓦	10	0 1 5 8.5	东盟ASEAN,新加坡SG,新西兰NZ,哥斯达黎加CR,香港HK 智利CL 巴基斯坦PK,秘鲁PE 亚太APTA	0	最不发达35国LDC35,最不发达4国LDC4	80	----For refrigerators or freezers, of a motor power exceeding 0.4kW but not exceeding 5kW
5985	8414.3013	----空气调节器用,电动机额定功率超过0.4千瓦,但不超过5千瓦	10	0 1 5 8.5	东盟ASEAN,新加坡SG,新西兰NZ,哥斯达黎加CR,香港HK,台湾TW 智利CL 巴基斯坦PK,秘鲁PE 亚太APTA	0	最不发达35国LDC35,最不发达4国LDC4	80	----For air conditioning machines, of a motor power exceeding 0.4kW but not exceeding 5kW
	ex84143013	0.4kW＜功率≤5kW的空气调节器用无级变速压缩机	△3						Stepless speed regulation compressors for aircon-ditioner, 0.4kW＜motor power≤5kW
	ex84143013	0.4kW＜功率≤5kW的空气调节器用定速压缩机	△6						Fixed speed compressors for airconditioner, 0.4kW ＜motor power ≤5kW
5986	8414.3014	----空气调节器用,电动机额定功率超过5千瓦	10	0 1 5 8.5	东盟ASEAN,新加坡SG,新西兰NZ,哥斯达黎加CR,香港HK,台湾TW 智利CL 巴基斯坦PK,秘鲁PE 亚太APTA	0	最不发达35国LDC35,最不发达4国LDC4	80	----For air conditioning machines, of a motor power exceeding 5kW
	ex84143014	功率＞5kW的空气调节器用无级变速压缩机	△3						Stepless speed regulation compressors for aircon-ditioner, motor power ＞5kW

序号 No.	税则号列 Tariff Line	货品名称	最惠国税率 MFN(%)	协定税率 Agreement(%)		特惠税率 S.P.(%)		普通税率 Gen.(%)	Article Description
	ex84143014	功率＞5kW的空气调节器用定速压缩机	△6						Fixed speed compressors for airconditioner, motor power＞5kW
5987	8414.3015	----冷冻或冷藏设备用,电动机额定功率超过5千瓦	10	0 1 5 9.2	东盟ASEAN,新西兰NZ,哥斯达黎加CR,香港HK 智利CL 巴基斯坦PK,秘鲁PE 亚太APTA	0	最不发达35国LDC35,最不发达4国LDC4	30	----For refrigerators or freezers, of a motor power exceeding 5kW
	ex84143015	冷冻或冷藏设备用，电动机额定功率＞5kW的电动机驱动的无级变速压缩机	△4						Stepless speed regulation compressors driven by a motor, for refrigerators or freezes, of a motor power exceeding 5kW
	ex84143015	冷冻或冷藏设备用，电动机额定功率＞5kW的电动机驱动定速压缩机	△6						Fixed speed compressors driven by a motor, for refrigerators or freezes, of a motor power exceeding 5kW
5988	8414.3019	----其他	10	0 1 5 9	东盟ASEAN,新加坡SG,新西兰NZ,哥斯达黎加CR,香港HK 智利CL 巴基斯坦PK,秘鲁PE 亚太APTA	0	最不发达35国LDC35,最不发达4国LDC4	30	----Other
	ex84143019	其他制冷设备用无级变速压缩机	△4						Other stepless speed regulation compressors driven by a motor
	ex84143019	其他制冷设备用定速压缩机	△6						Other fixed speed compressors driven by a motor
5989	8414.3090	---非电动机驱动的压缩机	9	0 0.9 5 8.1	东盟ASEAN,新加坡SG,新西兰NZ,秘鲁PE,哥斯达黎加CR,香港HK 智利CL 巴基斯坦PK 亚太APTA	0	最不发达35国LDC35,最不发达4国LDC4	80	---Driven by a non-motor
5990	8414.4000	-装在拖车底盘上的空气压缩机	8	0 0.8 5	东盟ASEAN,新西兰NZ,秘鲁PE,哥斯达黎加CR,香港HK 智利CL 巴基斯坦PK	0	最不发达35国LDC35	30	-Air compressors mounted on a wheeled chassis for towing
		-风机、风扇: --台扇、落地扇、壁扇、换气扇或吊扇,包括风机,本身装有一个输出功率不超过125瓦的电动机:							-Fans: --Table, floor, wall, window, ceiling or roof fans, with a self-contained electric motor of an output not exceeding 125W:

序号 No.	税则号列 Tariff Line	货品名称	最惠国税率 MFN(%)	协定税率 Agreement(%)		特惠税率 S.P.(%)		普通税率 Gen.(%)	Article Description
5991	8414.5110	---吊扇	20	0 4 10	东盟ASEAN,智利CL,新加坡SG,新西兰NZ 哥斯达黎加CR 秘鲁PE	0	最不发达35国LDC35,最不发达4国LDC4,老挝LA	130	---Ceiling or roof fans
5992	8414.5120	---换气扇	20	0 4 10	东盟ASEAN,智利CL,新加坡SG,新西兰NZ,台湾TW 哥斯达黎加CR 秘鲁PE	0	最不发达35国LDC35,最不发达4国LDC4,老挝LA	130	---Window fans
5993	8414.5130	---具有旋转导风轮的风扇	12	0 2.4 6	东盟ASEAN,智利CL,新加坡SG,新西兰NZ,秘鲁PE 哥斯达黎加CR 巴基斯坦PK	0	最不发达35国LDC35,最不发达4国LDC4,老挝LA	130	---Repeating front louver fan
		---其他:							---Other:
5994	8414.5191	----台扇	10	0 5	东盟ASEAN,智利CL,新西兰NZ,秘鲁PE,哥斯达黎加CR 巴基斯坦PK	0	最不发达35国LDC35,最不发达4国LDC4,老挝LA	130	----Table fans
5995	8414.5192	----落地扇	10	0 5	东盟ASEAN,智利CL,新西兰NZ,秘鲁PE,哥斯达黎加CR 巴基斯坦PK	0	最不发达35国LDC35,最不发达4国LDC4,老挝LA	130	----Floor fans
5996	8414.5193	----壁扇	10	0 5	东盟ASEAN,智利CL,新西兰NZ,秘鲁PE,哥斯达黎加CR 巴基斯坦PK	0	最不发达35国LDC35,最不发达4国LDC4,老挝LA	130	----Wall fans
5997	8414.5199	----其他	10	0 5	东盟ASEAN,智利CL,新加坡SG,新西兰NZ,秘鲁PE,哥斯达黎加CR,台湾TW 巴基斯坦PK	0	最不发达35国LDC35,最不发达4国LDC4,老挝LA	130	----Other
		--其他:							--Other:

序号 No.	税则号列 Tariff Line	货品名称	最惠国 税率 MFN(%)	协定税率 Agreement(%)		特惠税率 S.P.(%)		普通 税率 Gen.(%)	Article Description
5998	8414.5910	---吊扇	8	0	东盟ASEAN,新西兰NZ,秘鲁PE,哥斯达黎加CR	0	最不发达35国LDC35	30	--- Ceiling or roof fans
				0.8	智利CL				
				5	巴基斯坦PK				
				7.2	亚太APTA				
5999	8414.5920	---换气扇	8	0	东盟ASEAN,新西兰NZ,秘鲁PE,哥斯达黎加CR	0	最不发达35国LDC35	30	---Window fans
				0.8	智利CL				
				5	巴基斯坦PK				
				7.2	亚太APTA				
6000	8414.5930	---离心通风机	10	0	东盟ASEAN,新加坡SG,新西兰NZ,哥斯达黎加CR	0	最不发达35国LDC35	30	---Centrifugal ventilation fans
				1	智利CL				
				5	巴基斯坦PK,秘鲁PE				
				9.5	亚太APTA				
6001	8414.5990	---其他	8	0	东盟ASEAN,新西兰NZ,秘鲁PE,哥斯达黎加CR,台湾TW	0	最不发达35国LDC35,最不发达4国LDC4	30	---Other
				0.8	智利CL				
				5	巴基斯坦PK				
				7.2	亚太APTA				
		-罩的平面最大边长不超过120厘米的通风罩或循环气罩:							-Hoods having a maximum horizontal side not exceeding 120cm:
6002	8414.6010	---抽油烟机	10 △6	0	东盟ASEAN,智利CL,新西兰NZ,秘鲁PE,哥斯达黎加CR	0	最不发达35国LDC35,最不发达4国LDC4,老挝LA	130	---Range hoods
				5	巴基斯坦PK				
6003	8414.6090	---其他	10	0	东盟ASEAN,智利CL,新加坡SG,新西兰NZ,秘鲁PE,哥斯达黎加CR	0	最不发达35国LDC35,最不发达4国LDC4,老挝LA	130	---Other
				5	巴基斯坦PK				
		-其他:							-Other:
6004	8414.8010	---燃气轮机用的自由活塞式发生器	8	0	东盟ASEAN,新西兰NZ,秘鲁PE,哥斯达黎加CR	0	最不发达35国LDC35	50	---Free piston generators for gas turbines
				0.8	智利CL				
				5	巴基斯坦PK				
				5.6	亚太APTA				
6005	8414.8020	---二氧化碳压缩机	7	0	东盟ASEAN,巴基斯坦PK,新西兰NZ,秘鲁PE,哥斯达黎加CR	0	最不发达35国LDC35	30	---CO_2 compressors
				0.7	智利CL				
				4.9	亚太APTA				

序号 No.	税则号列 Tariff Line	货品名称	最惠国税率 MFN(%)	协定税率 Agreement(%)		特惠税率 S.P.(%)		普通税率 Gen.(%)	Article Description
6006	8414.8030	---发动机用增压器	7	0 4.9	东盟ASEAN,智利CL,巴基斯坦PK,新西兰NZ,哥斯达黎加CR 亚太APTA			30	---Superchargers for engines
	ex84148030	乘用车机械增压器	△5						Mechanical superchargers for Passenger cars
6007	8414.8090	---其他	7	0 4.9	东盟ASEAN,智利CL,巴基斯坦PK,新西兰NZ,秘鲁PE,哥斯达黎加CR,香港HK,台湾TW 亚太APTA	0	最不发达35国LDC35	30	---Other
		-零件:							-Parts:
		---子目号8414.3011至8414.3014及8414.3090所列机器的零件:							---Of the machines of subheadings Nos.8414.3011 to 8414.3014 and 8414. 3090:
6008	8414.9011	----压缩机进、排气阀片	8 △5	0 0.8 5 7.2	东盟ASEAN,新西兰NZ,秘鲁PE,哥斯达黎加CR 智利CL 巴基斯坦PK 亚太APTA	0	最不发达35国LDC35,最不发达4国LDC4,老挝LA	80	----In take valve leaf or discharge valve leaf
6009	8414.9019	----其他	8 △5	0 0.8 5 7.2	东盟ASEAN,新西兰NZ,秘鲁PE,哥斯达黎加CR,台湾TW 智利CL 巴基斯坦PK 亚太APTA	0	最不发达35国LDC35	80	----Other
6010	8414.9020	---子目号8414.5110至8414.5199及8414.6000所列机器的零件	12 △6	0 1.2 2.4 6 11.4	东盟ASEAN,新加坡SG,新西兰NZ,台湾TW 智利CL 哥斯达黎加CR 巴基斯坦PK,秘鲁PE 亚太APTA	0	最不发达35国LDC35	130	---Of the machines of subheadings Nos.8414.5110 to 8414.5199 or 8414.6000
6011	8414.9090	---其他	7 △4	0 0.7 5 6.5	东盟ASEAN,新西兰NZ,秘鲁PE,哥斯达黎加CR,香港HK,台湾TW 智利CL 巴基斯坦PK 亚太APTA	0	最不发达35国LDC35	30	---Other
	84.15	**空气调节器,装有电扇及调温、调湿装置,包括不能单独调湿的空调器:**							**Air conditioning machines, comprising a motor-driven fan and elements for changing the temperature and humidity, including those machines in which the humidity cannot be separately regulated:**
		-窗式或壁式,独立的或分体的:							-Window or wall types, self-contained or split-system:

序号 No.	税则号列 Tariff Line	货品名称	最惠国税率 MFN(%)	协定税率 Agreement(%)		特惠税率 S.P.(%)		普通税率 Gen.(%)	Article Description
6012	8415.1010	---独立式	15	0 3 7.5 13.5	东盟ASEAN,智利CL,新加坡SG,新西兰NZ 哥斯达黎加CR 巴基斯坦PK,秘鲁PE 亚太APTA	0	最不发达35国LDC35	130	---Self-contained
		---分体式:							---Split-system:
6013	8415.1021	----制冷量不超过4000大卡/时	15	0 3 7.5 13.5	东盟ASEAN,智利CL,新加坡SG,新西兰NZ 哥斯达黎加CR 巴基斯坦PK,秘鲁PE 亚太APTA	0	最不发达35国LDC35	130	----Of a refrigerating effect not exceeding 4000Cal per hour
6014	8415.1022	----制冷量超过4000大卡/时	15	0 3 7.5 13.5	东盟ASEAN,智利CL,新加坡SG,新西兰NZ 哥斯达黎加CR 巴基斯坦PK,秘鲁PE 亚太APTA	0	最不发达35国LDC35	90	----Of a refrigerating effect exceeding 4000 Cal per hour
6015	8415.2000	-机动车辆上供人使用的	20 △10	0 2 4	新西兰NZ,香港HK 智利CL 哥斯达黎加CR			110	-Of a kind used for persons, in motor vehicles
		-其他:							-Other:
		--装有制冷装置及一个冷热循环换向阀的（可逆式热泵）:							--Incorporating a refrigerating unit and a valve for reversal of the cooling/heat cycle (reversible heat pumps):
6016	8415.8110	---制冷量不超过4000大卡/时	15	0 3 7.5 12	东盟ASEAN,智利CL,新加坡SG,新西兰NZ 哥斯达黎加CR 秘鲁PE 巴基斯坦PK	0	最不发达35国LDC35	130	---Of a refrigerating effect not exceeding 4000 Cal per hour
6017	8415.8120	---制冷量超过4000大卡/时	20 △12	0 4 10	东盟ASEAN,智利CL,新加坡SG,新西兰NZ 哥斯达黎加CR 秘鲁PE	0	最不发达35国LDC35	90	---Of a refrigerating effect exceeding 4000 Cal per hour
		--其他,装有制冷装置的:							--Other, incorporating a refrigerating unit:
6018	8415.8210	---制冷量不超过4000大卡/时	15	0 3 7.5 12	东盟ASEAN,智利CL,新加坡SG,新西兰NZ 哥斯达黎加CR 秘鲁PE 巴基斯坦PK	0	最不发达35国LDC35	130	---Of a refrigerating effect not exceeding 4000 Cal per hour
6019	8415.8220	---制冷量超过4000大卡/时	20 △12	0 4 10	东盟ASEAN,智利CL,新加坡SG,新西兰NZ 哥斯达黎加CR 秘鲁PE	0	最不发达35国LDC35	90	---Of a refrigerating effect exceeding 4000 Cal per hour
6020	8415.8300	--未装有制冷装置的	10	0 5	东盟ASEAN,智利CL,新加坡SG,新西兰NZ,秘鲁PE,哥斯达黎加CR 巴基斯坦PK	0	最不发达35国LDC35,最不发达4国LDC4	90	--Not incorporating a refrigerating unit
		-零件:							-Parts:

序号 No.	税则号列 Tariff Line	货品名称	最惠国 税 率 MFN(%)	协定税率 Agreement(%)	特惠税率 S.P.(%)	普通 税率 Gen.(%)	Article Description
6021	8415.9010	---子目号8415.1010、8415.1021、8415.8110及8415.8210所列设备的零件	10 △6	0 东盟ASEAN,智利CL,新加坡SG,新西兰NZ,秘鲁PE,哥斯达黎加CR,香港HK 5 巴基斯坦PK 8 亚太APTA	0 最不发达35国LDC35,最不发达4国LDC4	130	---Of the machines of subheading No.8415.1010, 8415.1021, 8415.8110 or 8415.8210
6022	8415.9090	---其他	10 △6	0 东盟ASEAN,智利CL,新加坡SG,新西兰NZ,秘鲁PE,哥斯达黎加CR,香港HK,台湾TW 5 巴基斯坦PK 8 亚太APTA	0 最不发达35国LDC35,最不发达4国LDC4	90	---Other
	84.16	**使用液体燃料、粉状固体燃料或气体燃料的炉用燃烧器;机械加煤机,包括其机械炉篦、机械出灰器及类似装置:**					**Furnace burners for liquid fuel, for pulverized solid fuel or for gas; mechanical stokers, including their mechanical grates, mechanical ash dischargers and similar appliances:**
6023	8416.1000	-使用液体燃料的炉用燃烧器	10	0 东盟ASEAN,新加坡SG,新西兰NZ,秘鲁PE,哥斯达黎加CR 1 智利CL 5 巴基斯坦PK 9.5 亚太APTA	0 最不发达35国LDC35	35	-Furnace burners for liquid fuel
		-其他炉用燃烧器,包括复式燃烧器:					-Other furnace burners, including combination burners:
		---气体的:					---For gas:
6024	8416.2011	----使用天然气的	10.5	0 东盟ASEAN,智利CL,新加坡SG,新西兰NZ,秘鲁PE 2.1 哥斯达黎加CR 5 巴基斯坦PK	0 最不发达35国LDC35	35	----Of using natural gas
	ex84162011	溴化锂空调用天然气燃烧机	△5				Natural gas burners for lithium bromide air conditioners
6025	8416.2019	----其他	10.5	0 东盟ASEAN,智利CL,新加坡SG,新西兰NZ,秘鲁PE 2.1 哥斯达黎加CR 5 巴基斯坦PK	0 最不发达35国LDC35	35	----Other
6026	8416.2090	---其他	10.5	0 东盟ASEAN,智利CL,新加坡SG,新西兰NZ,秘鲁PE 2.1 哥斯达黎加CR 5 巴基斯坦PK	0 最不发达35国LDC35	35	---Other
	ex84162090	溴化锂空调用复式燃烧机	△5				Combination burners for lithium bromide air conditioners

序号 No.	税则号列 Tariff Line	货品名称	最惠国税率 MFN(%)	协定税率 Agreement(%)		特惠税率 S.P.(%)		普通税率 Gen.(%)	Article Description
6027	8416.3000	-机械加煤机,包括其机械炉篦、机械出灰器及类似装置	8.4	0 5	东盟ASEAN,智利CL,新西兰NZ,秘鲁PE,哥斯达黎加CR 巴基斯坦PK	0	最不发达35国LDC35	35	-Mechanical stokers, including their mechanical grates, mechanical ash dis-chargers and similar appliances
6028	8416.9000	-零件	6	0 5	东盟ASEAN,智利CL,新西兰NZ,秘鲁PE,哥斯达黎加CR 巴基斯坦PK	0	最不发达35国LDC35	35	-Parts
	84.17	**非电热的工业或实验室用炉及烘箱,包括焚烧炉:**							**Industrial or laboratory furnaces and ovens, including incinerators, non-electric:**
6029	8417.1000	-矿砂、黄铁矿或金属的焙烧、熔化或其他热处理用炉及烘箱	10	0 5	东盟ASEAN,智利CL,新加坡SG,新西兰NZ,秘鲁PE,哥斯达黎加CR 巴基斯坦PK	0	最不发达35国LDC35	35	-Furnaces and ovens for the roasting, melting or other heat-treatment of ores, pyrites or of metals
6030	8417.2000	-面包房用烤炉及烘箱,包括做饼干用的	10	0 5	东盟ASEAN,智利CL,新西兰NZ,秘鲁PE,哥斯达黎加CR 巴基斯坦PK	0	最不发达35国LDC35	35	-Bakery ovens, including biscuit ovens
		-其他:							-Other:
6031	8417.8010	---炼焦炉	10	0 5	东盟ASEAN,智利CL,新西兰NZ,秘鲁PE,哥斯达黎加CR 巴基斯坦PK	0	最不发达35国LDC35	35	---Coke ovens
6032	8417.8020	---放射性废物焚烧炉	5	0	东盟ASEAN,智利CL,巴基斯坦PK,新西兰NZ,秘鲁PE,哥斯达黎加CR	0	最不发达35国LDC35	35	---Burn furnaces for radioactive waste
6033	8417.8030	---水泥回转窑	10	0 5	东盟ASEAN,智利CL,新加坡SG,新西兰NZ,秘鲁PE,哥斯达黎加CR 巴基斯坦PK	0	最不发达35国LDC35	35	---Cement rotary kilns
6034	8417.8040	---石灰石分解炉	10	0 5	东盟ASEAN,智利CL,新西兰NZ,秘鲁PE,哥斯达黎加CR 巴基斯坦PK	0	最不发达35国LDC35	35	---Limestone decomposition furnace
6035	8417.8050	---垃圾焚烧炉	10	0 5	东盟ASEAN,智利CL,新加坡SG,新西兰NZ,秘鲁PE,哥斯达黎加CR,台湾TW 巴基斯坦PK	0	最不发达35国LDC35	35	---Refuse incinerator
6036	8417.8090	---其他	10	0 5	东盟ASEAN,智利CL,新加坡SG,新西兰NZ,秘鲁PE,哥斯达黎加CR,台湾TW 巴基斯坦PK	0	最不发达35国LDC35	35	---Other
		-零件:							-Parts:
6037	8417.9010	---海绵铁回转窑用	7	0 5	东盟ASEAN,智利CL,新西兰NZ,秘鲁PE,哥斯达黎加CR 巴基斯坦PK	0	最不发达35国LDC35	35	---For sponge iron rotary kiln

序号 No.	税则号列 Tariff Line	货品名称	最惠国税率 MFN(%)	协定税率 Agreement(%)		特惠税率 S.P.(%)		普通税率 Gen.(%)	Article Description
6038	8417.9020	---炼焦炉用	7	0 5	东盟ASEAN,智利CL,新西兰NZ,秘鲁PE,哥斯达黎加CR 巴基斯坦PK	0	最不发达35国LDC35	35	---For coke ovens
6039	8417.9090	---其他	7	0 5	东盟ASEAN,智利CL,新西兰NZ,秘鲁PE,哥斯达黎加CR 巴基斯坦PK	0	最不发达35国LDC35	35	---Other
	84.18	**电气或非电气的冷藏箱、冷冻箱及其他制冷设备;热泵,但税号84.15的空气调节器除外:**							**Refrigerators, freezers and other refrigerating or freezing equipment, electric or other; heat pumps other than air conditioning machines of heading No.84.15:**
		-冷藏—冷冻组合机,各自装有单独外门的:							-Combined refrigerator-freezers, fitted with separate external doors:
6040	8418.1010	---容积超过500升	10	0 1 5	东盟ASEAN,新加坡SG,新西兰NZ,哥斯达黎加CR 智利CL 巴基斯坦PK,秘鲁PE	0	最不发达35国LDC35,最不发达4国LDC4	100	---Of a capacity exceeding 500L
6041	8418.1020	---容积超过200升,但不超过500升	15	0 1.5 3 7.5 12	东盟ASEAN,新加坡SG,新西兰NZ 智利CL 哥斯达黎加CR 秘鲁PE 巴基斯坦PK	0	最不发达35国LDC35	130	---Of a capacity exceeding 200L, not exceeding 500L
6042	8418.1030	---容积不超过200升	15	0 1.5 3 7.5 12	东盟ASEAN,新加坡SG,新西兰NZ 智利CL 哥斯达黎加CR 秘鲁PE 巴基斯坦PK	0	最不发达35国LDC35	130	---Of a capacity not exceeding 200L
		-家用型冷藏箱:							-Refrigerators, household type:
		--压缩式:							--Compression-type:
6043	8418.2110	---容积超过150升	10	0 1 5	东盟ASEAN,新加坡SG,新西兰NZ,秘鲁PE,哥斯达黎加CR 智利CL 巴基斯坦PK	0	最不发达35国LDC35,最不发达4国LDC4	130	---Of a capacity exceeding 150L
6044	8418.2120	---容积超过50升,但不超过150升	10	0 1 5 9	东盟ASEAN,新加坡SG,新西兰NZ,秘鲁PE,哥斯达黎加CR 智利CL 巴基斯坦PK 亚太APTA	0	最不发达35国LDC35,最不发达4国LDC4	130	---Of a capacity exceeding 50L, not exceeding 150L
6045	8418.2130	---容积不超过50升	10	0 1 5 9	东盟ASEAN,新加坡SG,新西兰NZ,秘鲁PE,哥斯达黎加CR 智利CL 巴基斯坦PK 亚太APTA	0	最不发达35国LDC35,最不发达4国LDC4	130	---Of a capacity not exceeding 50L

序号 No.	税则号列 Tariff Line	货品名称	最惠国税率 MFN(%)	协定税率 Agreement(%)		特惠税率 S.P.(%)		普通税率 Gen.(%)	Article Description
		--其他:							--Other:
6046	8418.2910	---半导体制冷式	30	0 6 15	东盟ASEAN,智利CL,新加坡SG,新西兰NZ 哥斯达黎加CR 秘鲁PE	0	最不发达35国LDC35	130	---Semiconductor-type
6047	8418.2920	---电气吸收式	15	0 3 7.5 12	东盟ASEAN,智利CL,新加坡SG,新西兰NZ 哥斯达黎加CR 秘鲁PE 巴基斯坦PK	0	最不发达35国LDC35	130	--Absorption-type, electrical
6048	8418.2990	---其他	30	0 6 15	东盟ASEAN,智利CL,新加坡SG,新西兰NZ 哥斯达黎加CR 秘鲁PE	0	最不发达35国LDC35	130	---Other
		-柜式冷冻箱,容积不超过800升:							-Freezers of the chest type, not exceeding 800L capacity:
6049	8418.3010	---制冷温度在-40℃及以下	9	0 5	东盟ASEAN,智利CL,新西兰NZ,秘鲁PE,哥斯达黎加CR,澳门MO 巴基斯坦PK	0	最不发达35国LDC35,最不发达4国LDC4	50	---Of a refrigerating temperature of -40°Cor lower
		---制冷温度在-40℃以上:							---Of a refrigerating temperature higher than -40°C:
6050	8418.3021	----容积超过500升	23	0 4.6 11.5	东盟ASEAN,智利CL,新加坡SG,新西兰NZ,澳门MO 哥斯达黎加CR 秘鲁PE	0	最不发达35国LDC35	100	----Of a capacity exceeding 500L
6051	8418.3029	----其他	30	0 6 15	东盟ASEAN,智利CL,新加坡SG,新西兰NZ,澳门MO 哥斯达黎加CR 秘鲁PE	0	最不发达35国LDC35	130	----Other
		-立式冷冻箱,容积不超过900升:							-Freezers of the upright type, not exceeding 900L capacity:
6052	8418.4010	---制冷温度在-40℃及以下	9	0 5	东盟ASEAN,智利CL,新西兰NZ,秘鲁PE,哥斯达黎加CR,澳门MO 巴基斯坦PK	0	最不发达35国LDC35,最不发达4国LDC4	50	---Of a refrigerating temperature of -40°C or lower
		---制冷温度在-40℃以上:							---Of a refrigerating temperature higher than -40℃:
6053	8418.4021	----容积超过500升	15	0 3 7.5 12	东盟ASEAN,智利CL,新加坡SG,新西兰NZ,澳门MO 哥斯达黎加CR 秘鲁PE 巴基斯坦PK	0	最不发达35国LDC35	100	----Of a capacity exceeding 500L

序号 No.	税则号列 Tariff Line	货品名称	最惠国税率 MFN(%)	协定税率 Agreement(%)		特惠税率 S.P.(%)		普通税率 Gen.(%)	Article Description
6054	8418.4029	----其他	30	0 6 15	东盟ASEAN,智利CL,新加坡SG,新西兰NZ,澳门MO 哥斯达黎加CR 秘鲁PE	0	最不发达35国LDC35	130	----Other
6055	8418.5000	-装有冷藏或冷冻装置的其他设备(柜、箱、展示台、陈列箱及类似品),用于存储及展示	10	0 1 5	东盟ASEAN,新加坡SG,新西兰NZ,哥斯达黎加CR,香港HK,澳门MO 智利CL 巴基斯坦PK,秘鲁PE	0	最不发达35国LDC35,最不发达4国LDC4	100	-Other furniture (chests, cabinets, display counters, show-cases and the like) for storage and display, incorporating refrigerating or freezing equipment
		-其他制冷设备;热泵:							-Other refrigerating or freezing equipment; heat pumps:
		--热泵,税目8415的空气调节器除外:							-- Heat pumps other than air conditioning machines of heading 84.15:
6056	8418.6120	---压缩式	10	0 5 7	东盟ASEAN,智利CL,新加坡SG,新西兰NZ,秘鲁PE,哥斯达黎加CR 巴基斯坦PK 亚太APTA	0	最不发达35国LDC35,最不发达4国LDC4	90	---Compression type units
6057	8418.6190	---其他	15	0 1.5 3 7 7.5	东盟ASEAN,新加坡SG,新西兰NZ,澳门MO 智利CL 哥斯达黎加CR 亚太APTA,巴基斯坦PK 秘鲁PE	0	最不发达35国LDC35	130	---Other
		--其他:							--Other:
6058	8418.6920	---制冷机组	10	0 5 7	东盟ASEAN,智利CL,新加坡SG,新西兰NZ,秘鲁PE,哥斯达黎加CR,澳门MO 巴基斯坦PK 亚太APTA	0	最不发达35国LDC35,最不发达4国LDC4	90	---Refrigerating units
6059	8418.6990	---其他	10	0 5 7	东盟ASEAN,智利CL,新加坡SG,新西兰NZ,哥斯达黎加CR,澳门MO 巴基斯坦PK,秘鲁PE 亚太APTA	0	最不发达35国LDC35,最不发达4国LDC4	130	---Other
		-零件:							-Parts:
6060	8418.9100	--冷藏或冷冻设备专用的特制家具	18	0 3.6 9 14.4 17.1	东盟ASEAN,智利CL,新加坡SG,新西兰NZ 哥斯达黎加CR 秘鲁PE 巴基斯坦PK 亚太APTA	0	最不发达35国LDC35	130	--Furniture designed to receive refrigerating or freezing equipment
		--其他:							--Other:
6061	8418.9910	---制冷机组及热泵用	10 △6	0 1 5	东盟ASEAN,新加坡SG,新西兰NZ,哥斯达黎加CR 智利CL 巴基斯坦PK,秘鲁PE	0	最不发达35国LDC35,最不发达4国LDC4	90	---Of refrigerating units and heat pumps

序号 No.	税则号列 Tariff Line	货品名称	最惠国 税 率 MFN(%)	协定税率 Agreement(%)	特惠税率 S.P.(%)	普通 税率 Gen.(%)	Article Description
		---其他:					---Other:
6062	8418.9991	----制冷温度在-40℃及以下的冷冻设备用	9.5 △6	0 东盟ASEAN,新西兰NZ,秘鲁PE,哥斯达黎加CR,澳门MO 1 智利CL 5 巴基斯坦PK	0 最不发达35国LDC35,最不发达4国LDC4	50	----Of freezing equipment of a refrigerating temperature of -40°C or lower
6063	8418.9992	----制冷温度在-40℃以上,但容积超过500升的冷藏或冷冻设备用	10 △6	0 东盟ASEAN,新西兰NZ,哥斯达黎加CR,澳门MO 1 智利CL 5 巴基斯坦PK,秘鲁PE	0 最不发达35国LDC35,最不发达4国LDC4	100	----Of refrigerating or freezing equipment of a refrigerating temperature higher than -40°C and a capacity exceeding 500L
6064	8418.9999	----其他	10 △6	0 东盟ASEAN,新加坡SG,新西兰NZ,哥斯达黎加CR,澳门MO 1 智利CL 5 巴基斯坦PK,秘鲁PE	0 最不发达35国LDC35,最不发达4国LDC4	130	----Other
	84.19	**利用温度变化处理材料的机器、装置及类似的实验室设备,例如,加热、烹煮、烘炒、蒸馏、精馏、消毒、灭菌、汽蒸、干燥、蒸发、气化、冷凝、冷却的机器设备,不论是否电热的(不包括税目8514的炉、烘箱及其他设备),但家用的除外;非电热的快速热水器或贮备式热水器:**					**Machinery, plant or laboratory equipment, whether or not electrically heated (excluding furnaces, ovens and other equipment of heading 85.14), for the treatment of materials by a process involving a change of temperature such as heating, cooking, roasting, distilling, rectifying, sterilizing, pasteurizing, steaming, drying, evaporating, vaporizing, condensing or cooling, other than machinery or plant of a kind used for domestic purposes; instantaneous or storage water heaters, non-electric:**
		-非电热的快速热水器或贮备式热水器:					-Instantaneous or storage water heaters, non-electric:
6065	8419.1100	--燃气快速热水器	35	0 东盟ASEAN,新加坡SG,新西兰NZ 3.5 智利CL 7 哥斯达黎加CR 17.5 秘鲁PE	0 最不发达35国LDC35	100	--Instantaneous gas water heaters
		--其他:					--Other:
6066	8419.1910	---太阳能热水器	35	0 东盟ASEAN,智利CL,新加坡SG,新西兰NZ,台湾TW 7 哥斯达黎加CR 17.5 秘鲁PE	0 最不发达35国LDC35	100	---Solar water heaters

序号 No.	税则号列 Tariff Line	货品名称	最惠国税率 MFN(%)	协定税率 Agreement(%)		特惠税率 S.P.(%)		普通税率 Gen.(%)	Article Description
6067	8419.1990	---其他	35	0 7 17.5	东盟ASEAN,智利CL,新加坡SG,新西兰NZ,台湾TW 哥斯达黎加CR 秘鲁PE	0	最不发达35国LDC35	100	---Other
6068	8419.2000	-医用或实验室用消毒器具	4	0 0.4	东盟ASEAN,巴基斯坦PK,新西兰NZ,秘鲁PE,哥斯达黎加CR 智利CL	0	最不发达35国LDC35	30	-Medical, surgical or laboratory sterilizers
		-干燥器:							-Dryers:
6069	8419.3100	--农产品干燥用	8	0 5	东盟ASEAN,智利CL,新西兰NZ,秘鲁PE,哥斯达黎加CR 巴基斯坦PK	0	最不发达35国LDC35,最不发达4国LDC4,老挝LA	30	--For agricultural products
6070	8419.3200	--木材、纸浆、纸或纸板干燥用	9	0 0.9 5	东盟ASEAN,新西兰NZ,秘鲁PE,哥斯达黎加CR,台湾TW 智利CL 巴基斯坦PK	0	最不发达35国LDC35,最不发达4国LDC4,老挝LA	30	--For wood, paper pulp, paper or pa-perboard
		--其他:							--Other:
6071	8419.3910	---微空气流动陶瓷坯件干燥器	9	0 0.9 4.5	东盟ASEAN,新西兰NZ,秘鲁PE,哥斯达黎加CR 智利CL 亚太APTA,巴基斯坦PK	0	最不发达35国LDC35	30	---Breeze pottery blanks dryers
6072	8419.3990	---其他	9	0 0.9 4.5	东盟ASEAN,新西兰NZ,秘鲁PE,哥斯达黎加CR,台湾TW 智利CL 亚太APTA,巴基斯坦PK	0	最不发达35国LDC35	30	---Other
	ex84193990	生产奶粉用干燥器	△4						Dryers for producing powdered milk
	ex84193990	污泥涡轮干燥机	△4						Sludge turbo dryer
		-蒸馏或精馏设备:							-Distilling or rectifying plant:
6073	8419.4010	---提净塔	10	0 5	东盟ASEAN,智利CL,新加坡SG,新西兰NZ,秘鲁PE,哥斯达黎加CR 巴基斯坦PK	0	最不发达35国LDC35	30	---Stripping towers
6074	8419.4020	---精馏塔	10	0 5	东盟ASEAN,智利CL,新加坡SG,新西兰NZ,秘鲁PE,哥斯达黎加CR 巴基斯坦PK	0	最不发达35国LDC35	30	---Rectifying towers
6075	8419.4090	---其他	10	0 5	东盟ASEAN,智利CL,新加坡SG,新西兰NZ,秘鲁PE,哥斯达黎加CR 巴基斯坦PK	0	最不发达35国LDC35	30	---Other

序号 No.	税则号列 Tariff Line	货品名称	最惠国税率 MFN(%)	协定税率 Agreement(%)	特惠税率 S.P.(%)	普通税率 Gen.(%)	Article Description
6076	8419.5000	-热交换装置	10	0 东盟ASEAN,新加坡SG,新西兰NZ,哥斯达黎加CR,香港HK,台湾TW 1 智利CL 5 巴基斯坦PK,秘鲁PE 9.5 亚太APTA	0 最不发达35国LDC35,最不发达4国LDC4,老挝LA	30	-Heat exchange units
		-液化空气或其他气体的机器:					-Machinery for liquefying air or other gases:
		---制氧机:					---Oxygen producers:
6077	8419.6011	----制氧量在15000立方米/小时及以上	12	0 东盟ASEAN,智利CL,新加坡SG,新西兰NZ,秘鲁PE,香港HK 2.4 哥斯达黎加CR 6 巴基斯坦PK	0 最不发达35国LDC35	30	----Oxygen preparation volume no less than 15000m^3/h
6078	8419.6019	----其他	13	0 东盟ASEAN,智利CL,新加坡SG,新西兰NZ,秘鲁PE,香港HK 2.6 哥斯达黎加CR 6.5 巴基斯坦PK	0 最不发达35国LDC35	30	----Other
6079	8419.6090	---其他	10	0 东盟ASEAN,智利CL,新加坡SG,新西兰NZ,秘鲁PE,哥斯达黎加CR,香港HK 5 巴基斯坦PK	0 最不发达35国LDC35	30	---Other
		-其他机器设备:					-Other machinery, plant and equipment:
6080	8419.8100	--加工热饮料或烹调、加热食品用	10 △6	0 东盟ASEAN,新加坡SG,新西兰NZ,哥斯达黎加CR 1 智利CL 5 巴基斯坦PK,秘鲁PE	0 最不发达35国LDC35,最不发达4国LDC4,老挝LA	30	--For making hot drinks of for cooking or heating food
		--其他:					--Other:
6081	8419.8910	---加氢反应器	0		0 最不发达35国LDC35,最不发达4国LDC4	30	---Hydroformer vessels
6082	8419.8990	---其他	0		0 最不发达35国LDC35,最不发达4国LDC4	30	---Other
		-零件:					-Parts:
6083	8419.9010	---热水器用	0		0 最不发达35国LDC35,最不发达4国LDC4	100	---Of water heaters

序号 No.	税则号列 Tariff Line	货品名称	最惠国税率 MFN(%)	协定税率 Agreement(%)		特惠税率 S.P.(%)		普通税率 Gen.(%)	Article Description
6084	8419.9090	---其他	4	0 0.4	东盟ASEAN,巴基斯坦PK,新西兰NZ,秘鲁PE,哥斯达黎加CR,香港HK,台湾TW 智利CL	0	最不发达35国LDC35	30	---Other
	84.20	**研光机或其他滚压机器及其滚筒,但加工金属或玻璃用的除外:**							**Calendering or other rolling machines, other than for metals or glass, and cylinders therefor:**
6085	8420.1000	-研光机或其他滚压机器	8.4	0 0.8 5	东盟ASEAN,新西兰NZ,秘鲁PE,哥斯达黎加CR,台湾TW 智利CL 巴基斯坦PK	0	最不发达35国LDC35,最不发达4国LDC4	30	-Calendering or other rolling machines
	ex84201000	织物轧光机	△6						Woven fabrics calender
		-零件:							-Parts:
6086	8420.9100	--滚筒	8	0 5	东盟ASEAN,智利CL,新西兰NZ,秘鲁PE,哥斯达黎加CR 巴基斯坦PK	0	最不发达35国LDC35,最不发达4国LDC4	30	--Cylinders
6087	8420.9900	--其他	8	0 5	东盟ASEAN,智利CL,新西兰NZ,秘鲁PE,哥斯达黎加CR 巴基斯坦PK	0	最不发达35国LDC35,最不发达4国LDC4	30	--Other
	84.21	**离心机,包括离心干燥机;液体或气体的过滤、净化机器及装置:**							**Centrifuges, including centrifugal dryers; filtering or purifying machinery and apparatus, for liquids or gases:**
		-离心机,包括离心干燥机:							-Centrifuges, including centrifugal dryers:
6088	8421.1100	--奶油分离器	8.4	0 5	东盟ASEAN,智利CL,新西兰NZ,秘鲁PE,哥斯达黎加CR 巴基斯坦PK	0	最不发达35国LDC35	30	--Cream separators
		--干衣机:							--Clothes-dryers:
6089	8421.1210	---干衣量不超过10公斤	17.5	0 1.8 3.5 8.8 14	东盟ASEAN,新加坡SG,新西兰NZ 智利CL 哥斯达黎加CR 秘鲁PE 巴基斯坦PK	0	最不发达35国LDC35	70	---Of a dry linen capacity not exceeding 10kg
6090	8421.1290	---其他	8	0 0.8 5	东盟ASEAN,新西兰NZ,秘鲁PE,哥斯达黎加CR 智利CL 巴基斯坦PK	0	最不发达35国LDC35	30	---Other
		--其他:							--Other:

序号 No.	税则号列 Tariff Line	货品名称	最惠国税率 MFN(%)	协定税率 Agreement(%)		特惠税率 S.P.(%)		普通税率 Gen.(%)	Article Description
6091	8421.1910	---脱水机	10 △6	0 1 5	东盟ASEAN,新西兰NZ,秘鲁PE,哥斯达黎加CR 智利CL 巴基斯坦PK	0	最不发达35国LDC35	30	---Dewaterers
6092	8421.1920	---固液分离机	10	0 1 5	东盟ASEAN,新加坡SG,新西兰NZ,秘鲁PE,哥斯达黎加CR 智利CL 巴基斯坦PK	0	最不发达35国LDC35	30	---Solid-liquor separators
6093	8421.1990	---其他	10	0 1 5	东盟ASEAN,新加坡SG,新西兰NZ,秘鲁PE,哥斯达黎加CR 智利CL 巴基斯坦PK	0	最不发达35国LDC35	30	---Other
		-液体的过滤、净化机器及装置:							-Filtering or purifying machinery and apparatus for liquids:
		--过滤或净化水用:							--For filtering or purifying water:
6094	8421.2110	---家用型	25 △12	0 2.5 5 12.5 17.5	东盟ASEAN,新加坡SG,新西兰NZ,香港HK,澳门MO 智利CL 哥斯达黎加CR 秘鲁PE 亚太APTA,巴基斯坦PK	0	最不发达35国LDC35	63	---Of the household type
		---其他:							---Other:
6095	8421.2191	----船舶压载水处理设备	5	0 0.5 3.5	东盟ASEAN,巴基斯坦PK,新西兰NZ,秘鲁PE,哥斯达黎加CR,香港HK,澳门MO,台湾TW 智利CL 亚太APTA	0	最不发达35国LDC35	50	----Ship ballast water teatment apparatus
6096	8421.2199	----其他	5	0 0.5 3.5	东盟ASEAN,巴基斯坦PK,新西兰NZ,秘鲁PE,哥斯达黎加CR,香港HK,澳门MO,台湾TW 智利CL 亚太APTA	0	最不发达35国LDC35	50	----Other
	ex84212199	船舶压载水处理设备用过滤器	△2						Filters for ship ballast water treatment apparatus
	ex84212199	喷灌设备用叠式净水过滤器	△0						Stackable, filtering or purifying machines for irrigation equipment
6097	8421.2200	--过滤或净化饮料（水除外）用	12	0 2.4 6	东盟ASEAN,智利CL,新加坡SG,新西兰NZ,秘鲁PE,澳门MO 哥斯达黎加CR 巴基斯坦PK	0	最不发达35国LDC35	40	--For filtering or purifying beverages other than water

序号 No.	税则号列 Tariff Line	货品名称	最惠国税率 MFN(%)	协定税率 Agreement(%)		特惠税率 S.P.(%)		普通税率 Gen.(%)	Article Description
6098	8421.2300	--内燃发动机的滤油器	10	0 1 5	东盟ASEAN,新加坡SG,新西兰NZ,哥斯达黎加CR,香港HK 智利CL 巴基斯坦PK,秘鲁PE	0	最不发达35国LDC35	40	--Oil or petrol-filters for internal combustion engines
		--其他:							--Other:
6099	8421.2910	---压滤机	5	0 0.5 3.5	东盟ASEAN,巴基斯坦PK,新西兰NZ,秘鲁PE,哥斯达黎加CR,香港HK 智利CL 亚太APTA	0	最不发达35国LDC35	40	---Press filters
6100	8421.2990	---其他	5	0 0.5 3.5	东盟ASEAN,巴基斯坦PK,新西兰NZ,秘鲁PE,哥斯达黎加CR,香港HK,台湾TW 智利CL 亚太APTA	0	最不发达35国LDC35,最不发达4国LDC4	40	---Other
		-气体的过滤、净化机器及装置:							-Filtering or purifying machinery and apparatus for gases:
6101	8421.3100	--内燃发动机的进气过滤器	10	0 1 5	东盟ASEAN,新西兰NZ,哥斯达黎加CR,香港HK 智利CL 巴基斯坦PK,秘鲁PE	0	最不发达35国LDC35	40	--Intake air filters for internal combustion engines
		--其他:							--Other:
6102	8421.3910	---家用型	15 △8	0 1.5 3 7.5 10.5	东盟ASEAN,新加坡SG,新西兰NZ,香港HK,台湾TW 智利CL 哥斯达黎加CR 巴基斯坦PK,秘鲁PE 亚太APTA	0	最不发达35国LDC35	100	---Of the household type
		---工业用除尘器:							---Dust collectors for industry uses:
6103	8421.3921	----静电除尘器	5	0 0.5 3.5	东盟ASEAN,巴基斯坦PK,新西兰NZ,秘鲁PE,哥斯达黎加CR,香港HK,台湾TW 智利CL 亚太APTA	0	最不发达35国LDC35	40	----Electrostatic
6104	8421.3922	----袋式除尘器	5	0 0.5 3.5	东盟ASEAN,巴基斯坦PK,新西兰NZ,秘鲁PE,哥斯达黎加CR,香港HK 智利CL 亚太APTA	0	最不发达35国LDC35	40	----Baghoused
6105	8421.3923	----旋风式除尘器	5	0 0.5 3.5	东盟ASEAN,巴基斯坦PK,新西兰NZ,秘鲁PE,哥斯达黎加CR,香港HK,台湾TW 智利CL 亚太APTA	0	最不发达35国LDC35	40	----Cyclone

序号 No.	税则号列 Tariff Line	货品名称	最惠国税率 MFN(%)	协定税率 Agreement(%)		特惠税率 S.P.(%)		普通税率 Gen.(%)	Article Description
6106	8421.3924	----电袋复合除尘器	5	0 0.5 3.5	东盟ASEAN,巴基斯坦PK,新西兰NZ,秘鲁PE,哥斯达黎加CR,香港HK,台湾TW 智利CL 亚太APTA	0	最不发达35国LDC35	40	----Electrostatic fabric filter
6107	8421.3929	----其他	5	0 0.5 3.5	东盟ASEAN,巴基斯坦PK,新西兰NZ,秘鲁PE,哥斯达黎加CR,香港HK,台湾TW 智利CL 亚太APTA	0	最不发达35国LDC35	40	----Other
6108	8421.3930	---内燃发动机排气过滤及净化装置	5	0 0.5 3.5	东盟ASEAN,巴基斯坦PK,新西兰NZ,秘鲁PE,哥斯达黎加CR,香港HK 智利CL 亚太APTA	0	最不发达35国LDC35,最不发达4国LDC4	40	---Exhaust-gas filters or purifiers for internal combustion engines
	ex84213930	摩托车发动机排气过滤及净化装置	△3						Filtering or purifying machines for motorcycle engine
6109	8421.3940	---烟气脱硫装置	5	0 0.5 3.5	东盟ASEAN,巴基斯坦PK,新西兰NZ,秘鲁PE,哥斯达黎加CR,香港HK,台湾TW 智利CL 亚太APTA	0	最不发达35国LDC35,最不发达4国LDC4	40	---Flue gas desulfurization units
6110	8421.3950	---烟气脱硝装置	5	0 0.5 3.5	东盟ASEAN,巴基斯坦PK,新西兰NZ,秘鲁PE,哥斯达黎加CR,香港HK,台湾TW 智利CL 亚太APTA	0	最不发达35国LDC35,最不发达4国LDC4	40	---Flue gas denitrification units
6111	8421.3990	---其他	5	0 0.5 3.5	东盟ASEAN,巴基斯坦PK,新西兰NZ,秘鲁PE,哥斯达黎加CR,香港HK,台湾TW 智利CL 亚太APTA	0	最不发达35国LDC35,最不发达4国LDC4	40	---Other
		-零件: --离心机用,包括离心干燥机用:							-Parts: --Of centrifuges, including centrifugal dryers:
6112	8421.9110	---干衣量不超过10公斤的干衣机用	0			0	最不发达35国LDC35,最不发达4国LDC4	70	---Of clothes-dryers of a dry linen capacity not exceeding 10kg
6113	8421.9190	---其他	0			0	最不发达35国LDC35,最不发达4国LDC4	30	---Other

序号 No.	税则号列 Tariff Line	货品名称	最惠国税率 MFN(%)	协定税率 Agreement(%)		特惠税率 S.P.(%)	普通税率 Gen.(%)	Article Description
		--其他:						--Other:
6114	8421.9910	---家用型过滤、净化装置用	10 △6	0 1 5 9	东盟ASEAN,新加坡SG,新西兰NZ,哥斯达黎加CR,香港HK 智利CL 巴基斯坦PK,秘鲁PE 亚太APTA	0 最不发达35国LDC35	100	---Of household-type filtering or purifying machines
6115	8421.9990	---其他	5	0 0.5 4.5	东盟ASEAN,巴基斯坦PK,新西兰NZ,秘鲁PE,哥斯达黎加CR,香港HK,台湾TW 智利CL 亚太APTA	0 最不发达35国LDC35,最不发达4国LDC4	40	---Other
	84.22	**洗碟机;瓶子及其他容器的洗涤或干燥机器;瓶、罐、箱、袋或其他容器装填、封口、密封、贴标签的机器;瓶、罐、管、筒或类似容器的包封机器;其他包装或打包机器(包括热缩包装机器);饮料充气机:**						**Dish washing machines; machinery for cleaning or drying bottles or other containers; machinery for filling, closing, sealing or labeling bottles, cans, boxes, bags or other containers; machinery for capsuling bootles, jars, tubes and similar containers other packing or wrapping machinery (including heat-shrink wrapping machinery); machinery for aerating beverages:**
		-洗碟机:						-Dish washing machines:
6116	8422.1100	--家用型	10 △6	0 5	东盟ASEAN,智利CL,新西兰NZ,秘鲁PE,哥斯达黎加CR 巴基斯坦PK	0 最不发达35国LDC35,最不发达4国LDC4	90	--Of the household type
6117	8422.1900	--其他	14	0 2.8 11.2	东盟ASEAN,智利CL,新加坡SG,新西兰NZ,秘鲁PE 哥斯达黎加CR 巴基斯坦PK	0 最不发达35国LDC35	90	--Other
6118	8422.2000	-瓶子或其他容器的洗涤或干燥机器	10	0 1 5	东盟ASEAN,新加坡SG,新西兰NZ,哥斯达黎加CR,澳门MO 智利CL 巴基斯坦PK,秘鲁PE	0 最不发达35国LDC35,最不发达4国LDC4	35	-Machinery for cleaning or drying bottles or other containers
		-瓶、罐、箱、袋或其他容器的装填、封口、密封、贴标签的机器;瓶、罐、管、筒或类似容器的包封机器;饮料充气机:						-Machinery for filling, closing, sealing, or labelling bottles, cans, boxes, bags or other containers; machinery for capsuling bottles, jars, tubes and similar containers; machinery for aerating beverages:

序号 No.	税则号列 Tariff Line	货品名称	最惠国税率 MFN(%)	协定税率 Agreement(%)	特惠税率 S.P.(%)	普通税率 Gen.(%)	Article Description
6119	8422.3010	---饮料及液体食品灌装设备	12	0 东盟ASEAN,新加坡SG,新西兰NZ,秘鲁PE,香港HK 1.2 智利CL 2.4 哥斯达黎加CR 5 巴基斯坦PK 8.4 亚太APTA	0 最不发达35国LDC35,最不发达4国LDC4	45	---Bottling or canning machinery for beverages or liquid food:
	ex84223010	乳品加工用自动化灌装设备	△6				Automatic bottling or canning equipment for producing dairy
		---水泥包装机:					---Machinery for packing cement:
6120	8422.3021	----全自动灌包机	12	0 东盟ASEAN,新加坡SG,新西兰NZ,香港HK 1.2 智利CL 2.4 哥斯达黎加CR 5 巴基斯坦PK 6 秘鲁PE 8.4 亚太APTA	0 最不发达35国LDC35,最不发达4国LDC4	45	----Automatic filling and sacking machines
6121	8422.3029	----其他	12	0 东盟ASEAN,新加坡SG,新西兰NZ,香港HK 1.2 智利CL 2.4 哥斯达黎加CR 5 巴基斯坦PK 6 秘鲁PE 8.4 亚太APTA	0 最不发达35国LDC35,最不发达4国LDC4	45	----Other
6122	8422.3030	---其他包装机	10	0 东盟ASEAN,新加坡SG,新西兰NZ,哥斯达黎加CR,香港HK 1 智利CL 5 巴基斯坦PK,秘鲁PE 7 亚太APTA	0 最不发达35国LDC35,最不发达4国LDC4	35	---Other packing machines
	ex84223030	全自动无菌灌装生产线用包装机,加工速度≥20000只/小时	△6				Packing machines of automatic aseptic filling producion line, processing output≥20000 package/hour
6123	8422.3090	---其他	10	0 东盟ASEAN,新加坡SG,新西兰NZ,哥斯达黎加CR,香港HK 1 智利CL 5 巴基斯坦PK,秘鲁PE 7 亚太APTA	0 最不发达35国LDC35,最不发达4国LDC4	35	---Other
	ex84223090	全自动无菌灌装生产线用贴吸管机,加工速度≥22000只/小时	△6				Straw applicators of automatic aseptic filling prodution line, processing output≥22000 package/hour
6124	8422.4000	-其他包装或打包机器（包括热缩包装机器）	10	0 东盟ASEAN,新加坡SG,新西兰NZ,哥斯达黎加CR,香港HK 1 智利CL 5 巴基斯坦PK,秘鲁PE 9.5 亚太APTA	0 最不发达35国LDC35,最不发达4国LDC4	35	-Other packing or wrapping machinery (including heat-shrink wrapping machinery)

序号 No.	税则号列 Tariff Line	货品名称	最惠国税率 MFN(%)	协定税率 Agreement(%)		特惠税率 S.P.(%)		普通税率 Gen.(%)	Article Description
		-零件:							-Parts:
6125	8422.9010	---洗碟机用	10.5 △6	0 1.1 2.1 5 5.2	东盟ASEAN,新加坡SG,新西兰NZ 智利CL 哥斯达黎加CR 巴基斯坦PK 秘鲁PE	0	最不发达35国LDC35,最不发达4国LDC4	90	---Of dish washing machines
6126	8422.9020	---饮料及液体食品灌装设备用	8.5	0 0.9 5	东盟ASEAN,新西兰NZ,秘鲁PE,哥斯达黎加CR 智利CL 巴基斯坦PK	0	最不发达35国LDC35,最不发达4国LDC4	45	---Of bottling or canning machinery for beverages or liquid food
6127	8422.9090	---其他	8.5	0 0.9 5	东盟ASEAN,新西兰NZ,秘鲁PE,哥斯达黎加CR,香港HK 智利CL 巴基斯坦PK	0	最不发达35国LDC35,最不发达4国LDC4	35	---Other
	84.23	**衡器(感量为50毫克或更精密的天平除外),包括计数或检验用的衡器;衡器用的各种砝码、秤砣:**							**Weighing machinery (excluding balances of a sensitivity of 50mg or better), including weight operated counting or checking machines; weighing machine weights of all kinds:**
6128	8423.1000	-体重计,包括婴儿秤;家用秤	10.5	0 2.1 5	东盟ASEAN,智利CL,新加坡SG,新西兰NZ,秘鲁PE,澳门MO 哥斯达黎加CR 巴基斯坦PK	0	最不发达35国LDC35,最不发达4国LDC4	80	-Personal weighing machines, including baby scales; household scales
		-输送带上连续称货的秤:							-Scales for continuous weighing of goods on conveyors:
6129	8423.2010	---电子皮带秤	10	0 5	东盟ASEAN,智利CL,新西兰NZ,秘鲁PE,哥斯达黎加CR 巴基斯坦PK	0	最不发达35国LDC35,最不发达4国LDC4	80	---Electronic belt weighing machines
6130	8423.2090	---其他	10	0 5	东盟ASEAN,智利CL,新西兰NZ,秘鲁PE,哥斯达黎加CR 巴基斯坦PK	0	最不发达35国LDC35,最不发达4国LDC4	80	---Other
		-恒定秤、物料定量装袋或装容器用的秤,包括库秤:							-Constant weight scales and scales for discharging a predetermined weight of material into a bag or container, including hopper scales:

序号 No.	税则号列 Tariff Line	货品名称	最惠国税率 MFN(%)	协定税率 Agreement(%)	特惠税率 S.P.(%)	普通税率 Gen.(%)	Article Description
6131	8423.3010	---定量包装秤	10.5	0 东盟ASEAN,智利CL,新加坡SG,新西兰NZ,秘鲁PE 2.1 哥斯达黎加CR 5 巴基斯坦PK	0 最不发达35国LDC35,最不发达4国LDC4	80	---Rationed packing scales
6132	8423.3020	---定量分选秤	10.5	0 东盟ASEAN,智利CL,新加坡SG,新西兰NZ,秘鲁PE 2.1 哥斯达黎加CR 5 巴基斯坦PK	0 最不发达35国LDC35,最不发达4国LDC4	80	---Rationed sorting scales
6133	8423.3030	---配料秤	10.5	0 东盟ASEAN,智利CL,新加坡SG,新西兰NZ,秘鲁PE 2.1 哥斯达黎加CR 5 巴基斯坦PK	0 最不发达35国LDC35,最不发达4国LDC4	80	---Proporating scales
6134	8423.3090	---其他	10.5	0 东盟ASEAN,智利CL,新加坡SG,新西兰NZ,秘鲁PE 2.1 哥斯达黎加CR 5 巴基斯坦PK	0 最不发达35国LDC35,最不发达4国LDC4	80	---Other
		-其他衡器:					-Other weighing machinery:
		--最大称量不超过30公斤:					--Having a maximum weighing capacity not exceeding 30kg:
6135	8423.8110	---计价秤	10.5	0 东盟ASEAN,智利CL,新加坡SG,新西兰NZ,秘鲁PE 2.1 哥斯达黎加CR 5 巴基斯坦PK	0 最不发达35国LDC35,最不发达4国LDC4	80	---Account balances
6136	8423.8120	---弹簧秤	10.5	0 东盟ASEAN,智利CL,新加坡SG,新西兰NZ,秘鲁PE 2.1 哥斯达黎加CR 5 巴基斯坦PK	0 最不发达35国LDC35,最不发达4国LDC4	80	---Spring balances
6137	8423.8190	---其他	10.5	0 东盟ASEAN,智利CL,新加坡SG,新西兰NZ,秘鲁PE 2.1 哥斯达黎加CR 5 巴基斯坦PK	0 最不发达35国LDC35,最不发达4国LDC4	80	---Other
		--最大称量超过30公斤,但不超过5000公斤:					--Having a maximum weighing capacity exceeding 30kg but not exceeding 5000kg:

序号 No.	税则号列 Tariff Line	货品名称	最惠国税率 MFN(%)	协定税率 Agreement(%)	特惠税率 S.P.(%)	普通税率 Gen.(%)	Article Description
6138	8423.8210	---地中衡	10.5	0 东盟ASEAN,智利CL,新加坡SG,新西兰NZ,秘鲁PE 2.1 哥斯达黎加CR 5 巴基斯坦PK	0 最不发达35国LDC35,最不发达4国LDC4	80	---Weighbridges
6139	8423.8290	---其他	10.5	0 东盟ASEAN,智利CL,新加坡SG,新西兰NZ,秘鲁PE 2.1 哥斯达黎加CR 5 巴基斯坦PK	0 最不发达35国LDC35,最不发达4国LDC4	80	---Other
		--其他:					--Other:
6140	8423.8910	---地中衡	10	0 东盟ASEAN,新西兰NZ,哥斯达黎加CR 1 智利CL 5 巴基斯坦PK,秘鲁PE	0 最不发达35国LDC35,最不发达4国LDC4	80	---Weighbridges
6141	8423.8920	---轨道衡	10	0 东盟ASEAN,新西兰NZ,哥斯达黎加CR 1 智利CL 5 巴基斯坦PK,秘鲁PE	0 最不发达35国LDC35,最不发达4国LDC4	80	---Track scales
6142	8423.8930	---吊秤	10	0 东盟ASEAN,新西兰NZ,哥斯达黎加CR 1 智利CL 5 巴基斯坦PK,秘鲁PE	0 最不发达35国LDC35,最不发达4国LDC4	80	---Hanging scales
6143	8423.8990	---其他	10	0 东盟ASEAN,新西兰NZ,哥斯达黎加CR 1 智利CL 5 巴基斯坦PK,秘鲁PE	0 最不发达35国LDC35,最不发达4国LDC4	80	---Other
6144	8423.9000	-衡器用的各种砝码、秤砣;衡器的零件	10	0 东盟ASEAN,智利CL,新加坡SG,新西兰NZ,秘鲁PE,哥斯达黎加CR 5 巴基斯坦PK	0 最不发达35国LDC35,最不发达4国LDC4	80	-Weighing machine weights of all kinds; parts of weighing machinery
	84.24	**液体或粉末的喷射、散布或喷雾的机械器具(不论是否手工操作);灭火器,不论是否装药;喷枪及类似器具;喷汽机、喷砂机及类似的喷射机器:**					**Mechanical appliances (whether or not hand-operated) for projecting, dispersing or spraying liquids or powders; fire extinguishers, whether or not charged; spray guns and similar appliances; steam or sand blasting machines and similar jet projecting machines:**

序号 No.	税则号列 Tariff Line	货品名称	最惠国税率 MFN(%)	协定税率 Agreement(%)		特惠税率 S.P.(%)		普通税率 Gen.(%)	Article Description
6145	8424.1000	-灭火器,不论是否装药	8.4	0	东盟ASEAN,智利CL,新西兰NZ,秘鲁PE,哥斯达黎加CR	0	最不发达35国LDC35	70	-Fire extinguishers, whether or not charged
				5	巴基斯坦PK				
6146	8424.2000	-喷枪及类似器具	8.4	0	东盟ASEAN,智利CL,新西兰NZ,秘鲁PE,哥斯达黎加CR	0	最不发达35国LDC35	40	-Spray guns and similar appliances
				5	巴基斯坦PK				
				8	亚太APTA				
6147	8424.3000	-喷汽机、喷砂机及类似的喷射机器	8.4	0	东盟ASEAN,智利CL,新西兰NZ,秘鲁PE,哥斯达黎加CR,台湾TW	0	最不发达35国LDC35	40	-Steam or sand blasting machines and similar jet projecting machines
				5	巴基斯坦PK				
		-其他器具:							-Other appliances:
6148	8424.8100	--农业或园艺用	8	0	东盟ASEAN,新西兰NZ,秘鲁PE,哥斯达黎加CR,香港HK	0	最不发达35国LDC35	30	--Agricultural or horticultural
				0.8	智利CL				
				5	巴基斯坦PK				
				7.6	亚太APTA				
		--其他:							--Other:
6149	8424.8910	---家用型	0			0	最不发达35国LDC35,最不发达4国LDC4	80	---Of the household type
6150	8424.8920	---喷涂机器人	0			0	最不发达35国LDC35,最不发达4国LDC4	30	---Spray painting robots
		---其他:							---Other:
6151	8424.8991	----船用洗舱机	0			0	最不发达35国LDC35,最不发达4国LDC4	30	----Marine cabinet washer
6152	8424.8999	----其他	0			0	最不发达35国LDC35,最不发达4国LDC4	30	----Other
		-零件:							-Parts:
6153	8424.9010	---子目号8424.1000所列器具的零件	0			0	最不发达35国LDC35,最不发达4国LDC4	70	---Of the apparatus of subheading No.8424.1000

序号 No.	税则号列 Tariff Line	货品名称	最惠国税率 MFN(%)	协定税率 Agreement(%)	特惠税率 S.P.(%)	普通税率 Gen.(%)	Article Description
6154	8424.9020	---子目号 8424.8910 所列器具的零件	0		0 最不发达 35 国 LDC35, 最不发达 4 国 LDC4	80	---Of the apparatus of subheading No.8424.8910
6155	8424.9090	---其他	0		0 最不发达 35 国 LDC35, 最不发达 4 国 LDC4	30	---Other
	84.25	**滑车及提升机,但倒卸式提升机除外;卷扬机及绞盘;千斤顶:**					**Pulley tackle and hoists other than skip hoists; winches and capstans; jacks:**
		-滑车及提升机,但倒卸式提升机及提升车辆用的提升机除外:					-Pulley tackle and hoists other than skip hoists or hoists of a kind used for raising vehicles:
6156	8425.1100	--电动的	6	0 东盟ASEAN,智利CL,新西兰NZ,秘鲁PE,哥斯达黎加CR 5 巴基斯坦PK	0 最不发达 35 国 LDC35, 最不发达 4 国 LDC4	30	--Powered by electric motor
6157	8425.1900	--其他	5	0 东盟ASEAN,巴基斯坦PK,新西兰NZ,秘鲁PE,哥斯达黎加CR 0.5 智利CL	0 最不发达 35 国 LDC35, 最不发达 4 国 LDC4	30	--Other
		-卷扬机;绞盘:					-Winches; capstans:
		--电动的:					--Powered by electric motor:
6158	8425.3110	---矿井口卷扬装置;专为井下使用设计的卷扬机	10	0 东盟ASEAN,智利CL,新西兰NZ,秘鲁PE,哥斯达黎加CR 5 巴基斯坦PK	0 最不发达 35 国 LDC35, 最不发达 4 国 LDC4	30	---Pit-head winding gear; winches specially designed for use underground
6159	8425.3190	---其他	5	0 东盟ASEAN,巴基斯坦PK,新西兰NZ,秘鲁PE,哥斯达黎加CR 0.5 智利CL	0 最不发达 35 国 LDC35, 最不发达 4 国 LDC4	30	---Other
		--其他:					--Other:
6160	8425.3910	---矿井口卷扬装置;专为井下使用设计的卷扬机	10	0 东盟ASEAN,智利CL,新西兰NZ,秘鲁PE,哥斯达黎加CR 5 巴基斯坦PK	0 最不发达 35 国 LDC35, 最不发达 4 国 LDC4	30	---Pit-head winding gear; winches specially designed for use underground

序号 No.	税则号列 Tariff Line	货品名称	最惠国税率 MFN(%)	协定税率 Agreement(%)		特惠税率 S.P.(%)		普通税率 Gen.(%)	Article Description
6161	8425.3990	---其他	5	0 0.5	东盟ASEAN,巴基斯坦PK,新西兰NZ,秘鲁PE,哥斯达黎加CR,香港HK 智利CL	0	最不发达35国LDC35,最不发达4国LDC4	30	---Other
		-千斤顶;提升车辆用的提升机:							-Jacks; hoists of a kind used for raising vehicles:
6162	8425.4100	--车库中使用的固定千斤顶系统	3	0 2.5	东盟ASEAN,智利CL,巴基斯坦PK,新西兰NZ,秘鲁PE,哥斯达黎加CR 亚太APTA	0	最不发达35国LDC35,最不发达4国LDC4	30	--Built-in jacking systems of a type used in garages
		--其他液压千斤顶及提升机:							--Other jacks and hoists, hydraulic:
6163	8425.4210	---液压千斤顶	3	0	东盟ASEAN,智利CL,巴基斯坦PK,新西兰NZ,秘鲁PE,哥斯达黎加CR	0	最不发达35国LDC35,最不发达4国LDC4	30	---Hydraulic jacks
6164	8425.4290	---其他	5	0 0.5	东盟ASEAN,巴基斯坦PK,新西兰NZ,秘鲁PE,哥斯达黎加CR 智利CL	0	最不发达35国LDC35,最不发达4国LDC4	30	---Other
		--其他:							--Other:
6165	8425.4910	---其他千斤顶	5	0 0.5	东盟ASEAN,巴基斯坦PK,新西兰NZ,秘鲁PE,哥斯达黎加CR 智利CL	0	最不发达35国LDC35,最不发达4国LDC4	30	---Other jacks
6166	8425.4990	---其他	10	0 1 5	东盟ASEAN,新西兰NZ,哥斯达黎加CR 智利CL 巴基斯坦PK,秘鲁PE	0	最不发达35国LDC35,最不发达4国LDC4	30	---Other
	84.26	**船用桅杆式起重机;起重机,包括缆式起重机;移动式吊运架、跨运车及装有起重机的工作车:**							**Ships derricks; cranes, including cable cranes; mobile lifting frames, straddle carriers and works trucks fitted with a crane:**
		-高架移动式起重机、桁架桥式起重机、龙门起重机、桥式起重机、移动式吊运架及跨运车:							-Overhead traveling cranes, transporter cranes, gantry cranes, bridge cranes, mobile lifting frames and straddle carriers:

序号 No.	税则号列 Tariff Line	货品名称	最惠国税率 MFN(%)	协定税率 Agreement(%)		特惠税率 S.P.(%)		普通税率 Gen.(%)	Article Description
		--固定支架的高架移动式起重机:							--Overhead traveling cranes on fixed support:
6167	8426.1120	---通用桥式起重机	8	0 0.8 5	东盟ASEAN,新西兰NZ,秘鲁PE,哥斯达黎加CR 智利CL 巴基斯坦PK	0	最不发达35国LDC35,最不发达4国LDC4	30	---Bridge cranes, all-purpose
6168	8426.1190	---其他	8	0 0.8 5	东盟ASEAN,新西兰NZ,秘鲁PE,哥斯达黎加CR 智利CL 巴基斯坦PK	0	最不发达35国LDC35,最不发达4国LDC4	30	---Other
6169	8426.1200	--带胶轮的移动式吊运架及跨运车	6	0 5	东盟ASEAN,智利CL,新西兰NZ,秘鲁PE,哥斯达黎加CR 巴基斯坦PK	0	最不发达35国LDC35,最不发达4国LDC4	30	--Mobile lifting frames on tyres and straddle carriers
		--其他:							--Other:
6170	8426.1910	---装船机	5	0 2.5	东盟ASEAN,智利CL,巴基斯坦PK,新西兰NZ,秘鲁PE,哥斯达黎加CR 亚太APTA	0	最不发达35国LDC35,最不发达4国LDC4	30	---Ship loading cranes
		---卸船机:							---Ship unloading cranes:
6171	8426.1921	----抓斗式	5	0 3.5	东盟ASEAN,智利CL,巴基斯坦PK,新西兰NZ,秘鲁PE,哥斯达黎加CR 亚太APTA	0	最不发达35国LDC35,最不发达4国LDC4	30	----Grab ship unloading cranes
6172	8426.1929	----其他	5	0 3.5	东盟ASEAN,智利CL,巴基斯坦PK,新西兰NZ,秘鲁PE,哥斯达黎加CR 亚太APTA	0	最不发达35国LDC35,最不发达4国LDC4	30	----Other
6173	8426.1930	---龙门式起重机	10	0 5 7	东盟ASEAN,智利CL,新西兰NZ,秘鲁PE,哥斯达黎加CR 巴基斯坦PK 亚太APTA	0	最不发达35国LDC35,最不发达4国LDC4	30	---Gantry cranes
		---装卸桥:							---Loading and unlcading bridges:
6174	8426.1941	----门式装卸桥	10	0 5 7	东盟ASEAN,智利CL,新西兰NZ,秘鲁PE,哥斯达黎加CR 巴基斯坦PK 亚太APTA	0	最不发达35国LDC35,最不发达4国LDC4	30	----Frame loading and unloading bridges

序号 No.	税则号列 Tariff Line	货品名称	最惠国税率 MFN(%)	协定税率 Agreement(%)		特惠税率 S.P.(%)		普通税率 Gen.(%)	Article Description
6175	8426.1942	----集装箱装卸桥	10	0 5 7	东盟ASEAN,智利CL,新西兰NZ,秘鲁PE,哥斯达黎加CR 巴基斯坦PK 亚太APTA	0	最不发达35国LDC35,最不发达4国LDC4	30	----Container loading and unloading bridges
6176	8426.1943	----其他动臂式装卸桥	10	0 5 7	东盟ASEAN,智利CL,新西兰NZ,秘鲁PE,哥斯达黎加CR 巴基斯坦PK 亚太APTA	0	最不发达35国LDC35,最不发达4国LDC4	30	----Derrick loading and unloading bridges
6177	8426.1949	----其他	10	0 5 7	东盟ASEAN,智利CL,新西兰NZ,秘鲁PE,哥斯达黎加CR 巴基斯坦PK 亚太APTA	0	最不发达35国LDC35,最不发达4国LDC4	30	----Other
6178	8426.1990	---其他	10	0 5 7	东盟ASEAN,智利CL,新加坡SG,新西兰NZ,秘鲁PE,哥斯达黎加CR 巴基斯坦PK 亚太APTA	0	最不发达35国LDC35,最不发达4国LDC4	30	---Other
6179	8426.2000	-塔式起重机	10	0 5	东盟ASEAN,智利CL,新西兰NZ,秘鲁PE,哥斯达黎加CR 巴基斯坦PK	0	最不发达35国LDC35,最不发达4国LDC4	30	-Tower cranes
6180	8426.3000	-门座式起重机及座式旋臂起重机	6	0 5	东盟ASEAN,智利CL,新西兰NZ,秘鲁PE,哥斯达黎加CR 巴基斯坦PK	0	最不发达35国LDC35,最不发达4国LDC4	30	-Portal or pedestal jib cranes
		-其他自推进机械:							-Other machinery, self-propelled:
		--带胶轮的:							--On tyres:
6181	8426.4110	---轮胎式起重机	5	0 0.5	东盟ASEAN,巴基斯坦PK,新西兰NZ,秘鲁PE,哥斯达黎加CR 智利CL	0	最不发达35国LDC35,最不发达4国LDC4	30	---Wheel-mounted cranes
6182	8426.4190	---其他	5	0 0.5	东盟ASEAN,巴基斯坦PK,新西兰NZ,秘鲁PE,哥斯达黎加CR 智利CL	0	最不发达35国LDC35,最不发达4国LDC4	30	---Other
		--其他:							--Other:

序号 No.	税则号列 Tariff Line	货品名称	最惠国税率 MFN(%)	协定税率 Agreement(%)		特惠税率 S.P.(%)		普通税率 Gen.(%)	Article Description
6183	8426.4910	---履带式起重机	8	0 0.8 5	东盟ASEAN,新西兰NZ,秘鲁PE,哥斯达黎加CR,香港HK 智利CL 巴基斯坦PK	0	最不发达35国LDC35,最不发达4国LDC4	30	---Crawler cranes
6184	8426.4990	---其他	13	0 1.3 2.6 6.5	东盟ASEAN,新加坡SG,新西兰NZ,香港HK 智利CL 哥斯达黎加CR 巴基斯坦PK,秘鲁PE	0	最不发达35国LDC35	30	---Other
		-其他机械:							-Other machinery:
6185	8426.9100	--供装于公路车辆的	10	0 5	东盟ASEAN,智利CL,新西兰NZ,秘鲁PE,哥斯达黎加CR 巴基斯坦PK	0	最不发达35国LDC35,最不发达4国LDC4	30	--Designed for mounting on road vehicles
6186	8426.9900	--其他	6	0 0.6 5	东盟ASEAN,新西兰NZ,秘鲁PE,哥斯达黎加CR 智利CL 巴基斯坦PK	0	最不发达35国LDC35,最不发达4国LDC4	30	--Other
	84.27	**叉车;其他装有升降或搬运装置的工作车:**							**Fork-lift trucks; other works trucks fitted with lifting or handling equipment:**
		-电动机推进的机动车:							-Self-propelled trucks powered by an electric motor:
6187	8427.1010	---有轨巷道堆垛机	9	0 0.9 5	东盟ASEAN,新西兰NZ,秘鲁PE,哥斯达黎加CR 智利CL 巴基斯坦PK	0	最不发达35国LDC35,最不发达4国LDC4	30	---Track alleyway stackers
6188	8427.1020	---无轨巷道堆垛机	9	0 0.9 5	东盟ASEAN,新西兰NZ,秘鲁PE,哥斯达黎加CR 智利CL 巴基斯坦PK	0	最不发达35国LDC35,最不发达4国LDC4	30	---Trackless alleyway stackers
6189	8427.1090	---其他	9	0 0.9 5	东盟ASEAN,新西兰NZ,秘鲁PE,哥斯达黎加CR 智利CL 巴基斯坦PK	0	最不发达35国LDC35,最不发达4国LDC4	30	---Other
		-其他机动车:							-Other self-propelled trucks:

序号 No.	税则号列 Tariff Line	货品名称	最惠国税率 MFN(%)	协定税率 Agreement(%)		特惠税率 S.P.(%)		普通税率 Gen.(%)	Article Description
6190	8427.2010	---集装箱叉车	9	0 5 8.6	东盟ASEAN,智利CL,新西兰NZ,秘鲁PE,哥斯达黎加CR 巴基斯坦PK 亚太APTA	0	最不发达35国LDC35,最不发达4国LDC4	30	---Fork-lift trucks cranes
6191	8427.2090	---其他	9	0 5 8.6	东盟ASEAN,智利CL,新西兰NZ,秘鲁PE,哥斯达黎加CR 巴基斯坦PK 亚太APTA	0	最不发达35国LDC35,最不发达4国LDC4	30	---Other
6192	8427.9000	-其他车	9	0 5	东盟ASEAN,智利CL,新西兰NZ,秘鲁PE,哥斯达黎加CR 巴基斯坦PK	0	最不发达35国LDC35,最不发达4国LDC4	30	-Other trucks
	84.28	**其他升降、搬运、装卸机械（例如,升降机、自动梯、输送机、缆车）：**							**Other lifting, handling, loading or unloading machinery (for example, lifts, escalators, conveyors, teleferics):**
		-升降机及倒卸式起重机:							-Lifts and skip hoists:
6193	8428.1010	---载客电梯	8	0 5 5.6	东盟ASEAN,智利CL,新加坡SG,新西兰NZ,秘鲁PE,哥斯达黎加CR,香港HK,澳门MO 巴基斯坦PK 亚太APTA	0	最不发达35国LDC35,最不发达4国LDC4	30	---Designed for the transport of persons
	ex84281010	无障碍升降机	△4						Lift facilities for the disabled
6194	8428.1090	---其他	6	0 4.2	东盟ASEAN,智利CL,巴基斯坦PK,新西兰NZ,秘鲁PE,哥斯达黎加CR,香港HK,澳门MO,台湾TW 亚太APTA	0	最不发达35国LDC35,最不发达4国LDC4	30	---Other
6195	8428.2000	-气压升降机及输送机	5	0 0.5	东盟ASEAN,巴基斯坦PK,新西兰NZ,秘鲁PE,哥斯达黎加CR 智利CL	0	最不发达35国LDC35,最不发达4国LDC4	30	-Pneumatic elevators and conveyors
		-其他用于连续运送货物或材料的升降机及输送机:							-Other continuous-action elevators and conveyors, for goods or materials:
6196	8428.3100	--地下专用的	5	0	东盟ASEAN,智利CL,巴基斯坦PK,新西兰NZ,秘鲁PE,哥斯达黎加CR	0	最不发达35国LDC35,最不发达4国LDC4	30	--Specially designed for underground use

序号 No.	税则号列 Tariff Line	货品名称	最惠国税率 MFN(%)	协定税率 Agreement(%)		特惠税率 S.P.(%)		普通税率 Gen.(%)	Article Description
6197	8428.3200	--其他,斗式	5	0	东盟ASEAN,智利CL,巴基斯坦PK,新西兰NZ,秘鲁PE,哥斯达黎加CR,香港HK	0	最不发达35国LDC35,最不发达4国LDC4	30	--Other, bucket type
6198	8428.3300	--其他,带式	5	0	东盟ASEAN,巴基斯坦PK,新西兰NZ,秘鲁PE,哥斯达黎加CR,香港HK,台湾TW	0	最不发达35国LDC35,最不发达4国LDC4	30	--Other, belt type
				0.5	智利CL				
				4.3	亚太APTA				
		--其他:							--Other:
6199	8428.3910	---链式	5	0	东盟ASEAN,巴基斯坦PK,新西兰NZ,秘鲁PE,哥斯达黎加CR,香港HK,台湾TW	0	最不发达35国LDC35,最不发达4国LDC4	30	---Chain type
				0.5	智利CL				
				3.5	亚太APTA				
6200	8428.3920	---辊式	5	0	东盟ASEAN,巴基斯坦PK,新西兰NZ,秘鲁PE,哥斯达黎加CR,香港HK,台湾TW	0	最不发达35国LDC35,最不发达4国LDC4	30	---Roller type
				0.5	智利CL				
				3.5	亚太APTA				
6201	8428.3990	---其他	5	0	东盟ASEAN,巴基斯坦PK,新西兰NZ,秘鲁PE,哥斯达黎加CR,香港HK,台湾TW	0	最不发达35国LDC35,最不发达4国LDC4	30	---Other
				0.5	智利CL				
				3.5	亚太APTA				
6202	8428.4000	-自动梯及自动人行道	5	0	东盟ASEAN,智利CL,巴基斯坦PK,新西兰NZ,秘鲁PE,哥斯达黎加CR	0	最不发达35国LDC35,最不发达4国LDC4	30	-Escalators and moving walkWays
		-缆车、座式升降机、滑雪拉索、索道用牵引装置:							-Teleferics, chair-lifts, skidraglines; traction mechanisms for funiculars:
6203	8428.6010	---货运架空索道	8	0	东盟ASEAN,智利CL,新西兰NZ,秘鲁PE,哥斯达黎加CR	0	最不发达35国LDC35,最不发达4国LDC4	30	---Cargo aerial cableways
				5	巴基斯坦PK				
		---客运架空索道:							---Passanger aerial cableways:
6204	8428.6021	----单线循环式	8	0	东盟ASEAN,智利CL,新西兰NZ,秘鲁PE,哥斯达黎加CR	0	最不发达35国LDC35,最不发达4国LDC4	30	----Monocable endless
				5	巴基斯坦PK				

序号 No.	税则号列 Tariff Line	货品名称	最惠国税率 MFN(%)	协定税率 Agreement(%)		特惠税率 S.P.(%)		普通税率 Gen.(%)	Article Description
6205	8428.6029	----其他	8	0 5	东盟ASEAN,智利CL,新西兰NZ,秘鲁PE,哥斯达黎加CR 巴基斯坦PK	0	最不发达35国LDC35,最不发达4国LDC4	30	----Other
6206	8428.6090	---其他	8	0 5	东盟ASEAN,智利CL,新西兰NZ,秘鲁PE,哥斯达黎加CR 巴基斯坦PK	0	最不发达35国LDC35,最不发达4国LDC4	30	---Other
		-其他机械:							-Other machinery:
6207	8428.9010	---矿车推动机、铁道机车或货车的转车台、货车倾卸装置及类似的铁道货车搬运装置	10	0 5	东盟ASEAN,智利CL,新西兰NZ,秘鲁PE,哥斯达黎加CR 巴基斯坦PK	0	最不发达35国LDC35,最不发达4国LDC4	30	---Mine wagon pushers, locmotive or wagon traversers, wagon tippers and similar railway wagon handling equipment
6208	8428.9020	---机械式停车设备	5	0 0.5	东盟ASEAN,巴基斯坦PK,新西兰NZ,秘鲁PE,哥斯达黎加CR,香港HK 智利CL	0	最不发达35国LDC35,最不发达4国LDC4	30	---Mechanical parking equipments
		---其他装卸机械:							---Other loading and unloading machinery:
6209	8428.9031	----堆取料机械	5	0 0.5	东盟ASEAN,巴基斯坦PK,新西兰NZ,秘鲁PE,哥斯达黎加CR,香港HK,台湾TW 智利CL	0	最不发达35国LDC35,最不发达4国LDC4	30	----Stacking and reclaiming machines
6210	8428.9039	----其他	5	0 0.5	东盟ASEAN,巴基斯坦PK,新西兰NZ,秘鲁PE,哥斯达黎加CR,香港HK,台湾TW 智利CL	0	最不发达35国LDC35,最不发达4国LDC4	30	----Other
6211	8428.9040	---搬运机器人	5	0 0.5	东盟ASEAN,巴基斯坦PK,新西兰NZ,秘鲁PE,哥斯达黎加CR,香港HK,台湾TW 智利CL	0	最不发达35国LDC35,最不发达4国LDC4	30	---Transfering robots
6212	8428.9090	---其他	5	0 0.5	东盟ASEAN,巴基斯坦PK,新西兰NZ,秘鲁PE,哥斯达黎加CR,香港HK,台湾TW 智利CL	0	最不发达35国LDC35,最不发达4国LDC4	30	---Other

序号 No.	税则号列 Tariff Line	货品名称	最惠国税率 MFN(%)	协定税率 Agreement(%)		特惠税率 S.P.(%)		普通税率 Gen.(%)	Article Description
	84.29	**机动推土机、侧铲推土机、筑路机、平地机、铲运机、机械铲、挖掘机、机铲装载机、捣固机械及压路机:**							**Self-propelled bulldozers, angledozers, graders, levellers, scrapers, mechanical shovels, excavators, shovel loaders, tamping machines and road rollers:**
		-推土机及侧铲推土机:							-Bulldozers and angledozers:
		--履带式:							--Track laying:
6213	8429.1110	---发动机输出功率超过235.36千瓦（320马力）的	7	0 0.7 5	东盟ASEAN,新西兰NZ,秘鲁PE,哥斯达黎加CR 智利CL 巴基斯坦PK	0	最不发达35国LDC35,最不发达4国LDC4	17	---With an engine of an output exceeding 235.36kW(320PS)
6214	8429.1190	---其他	7	0 0.7 5	东盟ASEAN,新西兰NZ,秘鲁PE,哥斯达黎加CR 智利CL 巴基斯坦PK	0	最不发达35国LDC35,最不发达4国LDC4	30	---Other
		--其他:							--Other:
6215	8429.1910	---发动机输出功率超过235.36千瓦（320马力）的	7	0 5	东盟ASEAN,智利CL,新西兰NZ,秘鲁PE,哥斯达黎加CR 巴基斯坦PK	0	最不发达35国LDC35,最不发达4国LDC4	17	---With an engine of an output exceeding 235.36kW(320PS)
6216	8429.1990	---其他	7	0 5	东盟ASEAN,智利CL,新西兰NZ,秘鲁PE,哥斯达黎加CR 巴基斯坦PK	0	最不发达35国LDC35,最不发达4国LDC4	30	---Other
		-筑路机及平地机:							-Graders and levellers:
6217	8429.2010	---发动机输出功率超过235.36千瓦（320马力）的	5	0 0.5	东盟ASEAN,巴基斯坦PK,新西兰NZ,秘鲁PE,哥斯达黎加CR 智利CL	0	最不发达35国LDC35,最不发达4国LDC4	17	---With an engine of an output exceeding 235.36kW(320PS)
6218	8429.2090	---其他	5	0 0.5	东盟ASEAN,巴基斯坦PK,新西兰NZ,秘鲁PE,哥斯达黎加CR 智利CL	0	最不发达35国LDC35,最不发达4国LDC4	30	---Other
		-铲运机:							-Scrapers:
6219	8429.3010	---斗容量超过10立方米的	3	0	东盟ASEAN,智利CL,巴基斯坦PK,新西兰NZ,秘鲁PE,哥斯达黎加CR	0	最不发达35国LDC35,最不发达4国LDC4	17	---Having a capacity of shovel exceeding $10m^3$

序号 No.	税则号列 Tariff Line	货品名称	最惠国税率 MFN(%)	协定税率 Agreement(%)		特惠税率 S.P.(%)		普通税率 Gen.(%)	Article Description
6220	8429.3090	---其他	5	0	东盟ASEAN,智利CL,巴基斯坦PK,新西兰NZ,秘鲁PE,哥斯达黎加CR	0	最不发达35国LDC35,最不发达4国LDC4	30	---Other
		-捣固机械及压路机:							-Tamping machines and road rollers:
		---机动压路机:							---Self-propelled road rollers:
6221	8429.4011	----机重18吨及以上的振动压路机	7	0 0.7 5	东盟ASEAN,新西兰NZ,秘鲁PE,哥斯达黎加CR 智利CL 巴基斯坦PK	0	最不发达35国LDC35,最不发达4国LDC4	20	----Vibration type, of a deadweight of 18t or more
6222	8429.4019	----其他	8	0 0.8 5	东盟ASEAN,新西兰NZ,秘鲁PE,哥斯达黎加CR 智利CL 巴基斯坦PK	0	最不发达35国LDC35,最不发达4国LDC4	40	----Other
6223	8429.4090	---其他	6	0 0.6 5	东盟ASEAN,新西兰NZ,秘鲁PE,哥斯达黎加CR 智利CL 巴基斯坦PK	0	最不发达35国LDC35,最不发达4国LDC4	30	---Other
		-机械铲、挖掘机及机铲装载机:							-Mechanical shovels, excavators and shovel loaders:
6224	8429.5100	--前铲装载机	5	0 0.5	东盟ASEAN,巴基斯坦PK,新西兰NZ,秘鲁PE,哥斯达黎加CR 智利CL	0	最不发达35国LDC35,最不发达4国LDC4	30	--Front-end shovel loaders
		--上部结构可旋转360度的机械:							--Machinery with a 360° revolving superstructure:
		---挖掘机:							---Excavators:
6225	8429.5211	----轮胎式	8	0 0.8 5 7.2	东盟ASEAN,新西兰NZ,秘鲁PE,哥斯达黎加CR 智利CL 巴基斯坦PK 亚太APTA	0	最不发达35国LDC35,最不发达4国LDC4	30	----Tyre-mounted
6226	8429.5212	----履带式	8	0 0.8 5	东盟ASEAN,新西兰NZ,秘鲁PE,哥斯达黎加CR,香港HK 智利CL 巴基斯坦PK	0	最不发达35国LDC35,最不发达4国LDC4	30	----Track-mounted

序号 No.	税则号列 Tariff Line	货品名称	最惠国税率 MFN(%)	协定税率 Agreement(%)		特惠税率 S.P.(%)		普通税率 Gen.(%)	Article Description
6227	8429.5219	----其他	8	0 0.8 5 7.2	东盟ASEAN,新西兰NZ,秘鲁PE,哥斯达黎加CR 智利CL 巴基斯坦PK 亚太APTA	0	最不发达35国LDC35,最不发达4国LDC4	30	----Other
6228	8429.5290	---其他	8	0 0.8 5 7.2	东盟ASEAN,新西兰NZ,秘鲁PE,哥斯达黎加CR 智利CL 巴基斯坦PK 亚太APTA	0	最不发达35国LDC35,最不发达4国LDC4	30	---Other
6229	8429.5900	--其他	8	0 0.8 5	东盟ASEAN,新西兰NZ,秘鲁PE,哥斯达黎加CR 智利CL 巴基斯坦PK	0	最不发达35国LDC35,最不发达4国LDC4	30	--Other
	84.30	**泥土、矿物或矿石的运送、平整、铲运、挖掘、捣固、压实、开采或钻探机械;打桩机及拔桩机;扫雪机及吹雪机:**							**Other moving, grading, levelling, scraping, excavating, tamping, compacting, extracting or boring machinery, for earth, minerals or ores; piledrivers and pile-extractors; snowploughs and snow-blowers:**
6230	8430.1000	-打桩机及拔桩机	10	0 5	东盟ASEAN,智利CL,新西兰NZ,秘鲁PE,哥斯达黎加CR 巴基斯坦PK	0	最不发达35国LDC35,最不发达4国LDC4	30	-Pile-drivers and pile-extranctors
6231	8430.2000	-扫雪机及吹雪机	10	0 5	东盟ASEAN,智利CL,新西兰NZ,秘鲁PE,哥斯达黎加CR 巴基斯坦PK	0	最不发达35国LDC35,最不发达4国LDC4	30	-Snow-ploughs and snow-blowers
		-采(截)煤机、凿岩机及隧道掘进机:							-Coal winning, rock drill and tunnel boring machine:
		--自推进的:							--Self-propelle:
6232	8430.3110	---采(截)煤机	10	0 1 5	东盟ASEAN,新加坡SG,新西兰NZ,哥斯达黎加CR 智利CL 巴基斯坦PK,秘鲁PE	0	最不发达35国LDC35,最不发达4国LDC4	30	---Coal winning machine
6233	8430.3120	---凿岩机	10	0 1 5	东盟ASEAN,新加坡SG,新西兰NZ,哥斯达黎加CR 智利CL 巴基斯坦PK,秘鲁PE	0	最不发达35国LDC35,最不发达4国LDC4	30	---Rock drill machine

序号 No.	税则号列 Tariff Line	货品名称	最惠国税率 MFN(%)	协定税率 Agreement(%)		特惠税率 S.P.(%)		普通税率 Gen.(%)	Article Description
6234	8430.3130	---隧道掘进机	10	0 1 5	东盟ASEAN,新加坡SG,新西兰NZ,哥斯达黎加CR 智利CL 巴基斯坦PK,秘鲁PE	0	最不发达35国LDC35,最不发达4国LDC4	30	---Tunnel boring machine
6235	8430.3900	--其他	6	0 5	东盟ASEAN,智利CL,新西兰NZ,秘鲁PE,哥斯达黎加CR 巴基斯坦PK	0	最不发达35国LDC35,最不发达4国LDC4	30	--Other
		-其他钻探或凿井机械:							-Other boring or sinking machinery:
		--自推进的:							--self-propelled:
		---石油及天然气钻探机:							---Oil and natural gas drilling machinery:
6236	8430.4111	----钻探深度在6000米及以上的	5	0 0.5	东盟ASEAN,巴基斯坦PK,新西兰NZ,秘鲁PE,哥斯达黎加CR,香港HK 智利CL	0	最不发达35国LDC35,最不发达4国LDC4	11	----Of drilling depth of 6000m or more
6237	8430.4119	----其他	5	0 0.5	东盟ASEAN,巴基斯坦PK,新西兰NZ,秘鲁PE,哥斯达黎加CR,香港HK 智利CL	0	最不发达35国LDC35,最不发达4国LDC4	17	----Other
		---其他钻探机:							---Other drilling machinery:
6238	8430.4121	----钻探深度在6000米及以上的	5	0 0.5	东盟ASEAN,巴基斯坦PK,新西兰NZ,秘鲁PE,哥斯达黎加CR,香港HK 智利CL	0	最不发达35国LDC35,最不发达4国LDC4	11	----Of drilling depth of 6000m or more
6239	8430.4122	----钻探深度在6000米以下的履带式自推进钻机	5	0 0.5	东盟ASEAN,巴基斯坦PK,新西兰NZ,秘鲁PE,哥斯达黎加CR,香港HK 智利CL	0	最不发达35国LDC35,最不发达4国LDC4	17	----Crawler boring machinery of drilling depth＜6000m
6240	8430.4129	----钻探深度在6000米以下的其他钻探机	5	0 0.5	东盟ASEAN,巴基斯坦PK,新西兰NZ,秘鲁PE,哥斯达黎加CR,香港HK 智利CL	0	最不发达35国LDC35,最不发达4国LDC4	17	----Other boring machinery of drilling depth ＜6000m
6241	8430.4190	---其他	5	0 0.5	东盟ASEAN,巴基斯坦PK,新西兰NZ,秘鲁PE,哥斯达黎加CR,香港HK 智利CL	0	最不发达35国LDC35,最不发达4国LDC4	30	---Other

序号 No.	税则号列 Tariff Line	货品名称	最惠国税率 MFN(%)	协定税率 Agreement(%)		特惠税率 S.P.(%)		普通税率 Gen.(%)	Article Description
6242	8430.4900	--其他	5	0 0.5	东盟ASEAN,巴基斯坦PK,新西兰NZ,秘鲁PE,哥斯达黎加CR 智利CL	0	最不发达35国LDC35,最不发达4国LDC4	30	--Other
		-其他自推进机械:							-Other machinery, self-propelled:
6243	8430.5010	---其他采油机械	3	0	东盟ASEAN,智利CL,巴基斯坦PK,新西兰NZ,秘鲁PE,哥斯达黎加CR	0	最不发达35国LDC35,最不发达4国LDC4	17	---For oil production
6244	8430.5020	---矿用电铲	7	0 0.7 5	东盟ASEAN,新西兰NZ,秘鲁PE,哥斯达黎加CR 智利CL 巴基斯坦PK	0	最不发达35国LDC35,最不发达4国LDC4	30	---Mining power shovels
		---采矿钻机:							---Mining drills:
6245	8430.5031	----牙轮直径380毫米及以上	5	0 0.5	东盟ASEAN,巴基斯坦PK,新西兰NZ,秘鲁PE,哥斯达黎加CR 智利CL	0	最不发达35国LDC35,最不发达4国LDC4	30	----Gear wheel diameter more than 380mm
6246	8430.5039	----其他	5	0 0.5	东盟ASEAN,巴基斯坦PK,新西兰NZ,秘鲁PE,哥斯达黎加CR 智利CL	0	最不发达35国LDC35,最不发达4国LDC4	30	----Other
6247	8430.5090	---其他	5	0 0.5	东盟ASEAN,巴基斯坦PK,新西兰NZ,秘鲁PE,哥斯达黎加CR 智利CL	0	最不发达35国LDC35,最不发达4国LDC4	30	---Other
		-其他非自推进机械:							-Other machinery, not self-propelled:
6248	8430.6100	--捣固或压实机械	6	0 5	东盟ASEAN,智利CL,新西兰NZ,秘鲁PE,哥斯达黎加CR 巴基斯坦PK	0	最不发达35国LDC35,最不发达4国LDC4	30	--Tamping or compacting machinery
		--其他:							--Other:
		---工程钻机:							---Engineering drills:
6249	8430.6911	----钻筒直径3米及以上	6	0 5	东盟ASEAN,智利CL,新西兰NZ,秘鲁PE,哥斯达黎加CR 巴基斯坦PK	0	最不发达35国LDC35,最不发达4国LDC4	30	----Boring casing diameter more than 3m

序号 No.	税则号列 Tariff Line	货品名称	最惠国税率 MFN(%)	协定税率 Agreement(%)		特惠税率 S.P.(%)		普通税率 Gen.(%)	Article Description
6250	8430.6919	----其他	6	0 5	东盟ASEAN,智利CL,新西兰NZ,秘鲁PE,哥斯达黎加CR 巴基斯坦PK	0	最不发达35国LDC35,最不发达4国LDC4	30	----Other
6251	8430.6920	---铲运机	6	0 5	东盟ASEAN,智利CL,新西兰NZ,秘鲁PE,哥斯达黎加CR 巴基斯坦PK	0	最不发达35国LDC35,最不发达4国LDC4	30	---Scrapers
6252	8430.6990	---其他	6	0 5	东盟ASEAN,智利CL,新西兰NZ,秘鲁PE,哥斯达黎加CR 巴基斯坦PK	0	最不发达35国LDC35,最不发达4国LDC4	30	---Other
	84.31	**专用于或主要用于税号84.25至84.30所列机械的零件:**							**Parts suitable for use solely or principally with the machinery of headings Nos.84.25 to 84.30:**
6253	8431.1000	-税号84.25所列机械的零件	3	0	东盟ASEAN,智利CL,巴基斯坦PK,新西兰NZ,秘鲁PE,哥斯达黎加CR	0	最不发达35国LDC35,最不发达4国LDC4	30	-Of machinery of heading No.84.25
		-税号84.27所列机械的零件:							-Of machinery of heading No.84.27:
6254	8431.2010	---装有差速器的驱动桥及其零件,不论是否装有其他传动部件	6	0 5.4	东盟ASEAN,智利CL,巴基斯坦PK,新西兰NZ,秘鲁PE,哥斯达黎加CR 亚太APTA	0	最不发达35国LDC35,最不发达4国LDC4	30	---Drive-axles with differential, whether or not provided with other transmission components, parts thereof
6255	8431.2090	---其他	6 △3	0 5.4	东盟ASEAN,智利CL,巴基斯坦PK,新西兰NZ,秘鲁PE,哥斯达黎加CR 亚太APTA	0	最不发达35国LDC35,最不发达4国LDC4	30	---Other
		-税号84.28所列机械的零件:							-Of machinery of heading No.84.28:
6256	8431.3100	--升降机、倒卸式起重机或自动梯的零件	3	0	东盟ASEAN,智利CL,巴基斯坦PK,新西兰NZ,秘鲁PE,哥斯达黎加CR	0	最不发达35国LDC35,最不发达4国LDC4	30	--Of lifts, skip hoists or escalators
	ex84313100	无障碍升降机的零件	△1						Parts, for Lift facilities for the disabled

序号 No.	税则号列 Tariff Line	货品名称	最惠国税率 MFN(%)	协定税率 Agreement(%)		特惠税率 S.P.(%)		普通税率 Gen.(%)	Article Description
6257	8431.3900	--其他	5	0 0.5 2.5	东盟ASEAN,巴基斯坦PK,新西兰NZ,秘鲁PE,哥斯达黎加CR,香港HK 智利CL 亚太APTA	0	最不发达35国LDC35,最不发达4国LDC4	30	--Other
		-税号84.26、84.29、或84.30所列机械的零件:							-Of machinery of heading No.84.26, 84.29 or 84.30:
6258	8431.4100	--戽斗、铲斗、抓斗及夹斗	6	0 0.6 5.4	东盟ASEAN,巴基斯坦PK,新西兰NZ,秘鲁PE,哥斯达黎加CR 智利CL 亚太APTA	0	最不发达35国LDC35,最不发达4国LDC4	17	--Buckets, shovels, grabs and grips
6259	8431.4200	--推土机或侧铲推土机用铲	6	0 5	东盟ASEAN,智利CL,新西兰NZ,秘鲁PE,哥斯达黎加CR 巴基斯坦PK	0	最不发达35国LDC35,最不发达4国LDC4	17	--Bulldozer or angle-dozer blades
		--子目号8430.41或8430.49所列钻探或凿井机械的零件:							--Parts of boring or sinking machinery of sub-heading No.8430.41 or 8430.49:
6260	8431.4310	---石油或天然气钻探机用	4	0 0.4 2.8	东盟ASEAN,巴基斯坦PK,新西兰NZ,秘鲁PE,哥斯达黎加CR,香港HK 智利CL 亚太APTA	0	最不发达35国LDC35,最不发达4国LDC4	11	---Of oil and natural gas drilling machinery
6261	8431.4320	---其他钻探机用	4	0 0.4 2.8	东盟ASEAN,巴基斯坦PK,新西兰NZ,秘鲁PE,哥斯达黎加CR,香港HK 智利CL 亚太APTA	0	最不发达35国LDC35,最不发达4国LDC4	11	---Of other drilling machinery
6262	8431.4390	---其他	5	0 0.5 3.5	东盟ASEAN,巴基斯坦PK,新西兰NZ,秘鲁PE,哥斯达黎加CR,香港HK 智利CL 亚太APTA	0	最不发达35国LDC35,最不发达4国LDC4	17	---Other
		--其他:							--Other:
6263	8431.4920	---装有差速器的驱动桥及其零件,不论是否装有其他传动部件	5	0 0.5 4.5	东盟ASEAN,巴基斯坦PK,新西兰NZ,秘鲁PE,哥斯达黎加CR,香港HK 智利CL 亚太APTA	0	最不发达35国LDC35,最不发达4国LDC4	17	---Drive-axles with differential, whether or not provided with other transmission components, parts thereof
		---其他:							---Other:

序号 No.	税则号列 Tariff Line	货品名称	最惠国税率 MFN(%)	协定税率 Agreement(%)	特惠税率 S.P.(%)	普通税率 Gen.(%)	Article Description
6264	8431.4991	----矿用电铲用	5	0 东盟ASEAN,巴基斯坦PK,新西兰NZ,秘鲁PE,哥斯达黎加CR,香港HK 0.5 智利CL 4.5 亚太APTA	0 最不发达35国LDC35,最不发达4国LDC4	17	----For mining power shovels
6265	8431.4999	----其他	5	0 东盟ASEAN,巴基斯坦PK,新西兰NZ,秘鲁PE,哥斯达黎加CR,香港HK 0.5 智利CL 4.5 亚太APTA	0 最不发达35国LDC35,最不发达4国LDC4	17	---Other
	84.32	**农业、园艺及林业用整地或耕作机械;草坪及运动场地滚压机:**					**Agricultural, horticultural or forestry machinery for soil preparation or cultivation; lawn or sports-ground rollers:**
6266	8432.1000	-犁	5	0 东盟ASEAN,智利CL,巴基斯坦PK,新西兰NZ,秘鲁PE,哥斯达黎加CR	0 最不发达35国LDC35,最不发达4国LDC4	30	-Ploughs
		-耙、松土机、中耕机、除草机及耕耘机:					-Harrows, scarifiers, cultivators, weeders and hoes:
6267	8432.2100	--圆盘耙	5	0 东盟ASEAN,智利CL,巴基斯坦PK,新西兰NZ,秘鲁PE,哥斯达黎加CR	0 最不发达35国LDC35,最不发达4国LDC4	30	--Disc harrows
6268	8432.2900	--其他	4	0 东盟ASEAN,智利CL,巴基斯坦PK,新西兰NZ,秘鲁PE,哥斯达黎加CR	0 最不发达35国LDC35	30	--Other
		-播种机、种植机及移植机:					-Seeders, planters and transplanters:
		---播种机:					---Seeders:
6269	8432.3011	----谷物播种机	4	0 东盟ASEAN,智利CL,巴基斯坦PK,新西兰NZ,秘鲁PE,哥斯达黎加CR 3.5 亚太APTA	0 最不发达35国LDC35	30	----Grain seeders
6270	8432.3019	----其他	4	0 东盟ASEAN,智利CL,巴基斯坦PK,新西兰NZ,秘鲁PE,哥斯达黎加CR 3.5 亚太APTA	0 最不发达35国LDC35	30	----Other
		---种植机:					---Planters:

序号 No.	税则号列 Tariff Line	货品名称	最惠国税率 MFN(%)	协定税率 Agreement(%)		特惠税率 S.P.(%)		普通税率 Gen.(%)	Article Description
6271	8432.3021	----马铃薯种植机	4	0	东盟ASEAN,智利CL,巴基斯坦PK,新西兰NZ,秘鲁PE,哥斯达黎加CR	0	最不发达35国LDC35	30	----Tuber planters
				3.5	亚太APTA				
6272	8432.3029	----其他	4	0	东盟ASEAN,智利CL,巴基斯坦PK,新西兰NZ,秘鲁PE,哥斯达黎加CR	0	最不发达35国LDC35	30	----Other
				3.5	亚太APTA				
		---移植机(栽植机):							---Transplanters:
6273	8432.3031	----水稻插秧机	4	0	东盟ASEAN,智利CL,巴基斯坦PK,新西兰NZ,秘鲁PE,哥斯达黎加CR	0	最不发达35国LDC35	30	----Rice transplanters
				3.5	亚太APTA				
6274	8432.3039	----其他	4	0	东盟ASEAN,智利CL,巴基斯坦PK,新西兰NZ,秘鲁PE,哥斯达黎加CR	0	最不发达35国LDC35	30	----Other
				3.5	亚太APTA				
6275	8432.4000	-施肥机	4	0	东盟ASEAN,智利CL,巴基斯坦PK,新西兰NZ,秘鲁PE,哥斯达黎加CR	0	最不发达35国LDC35	30	-Manure spreaders and fertilizer distributors
		-其他机械:							-Other machinery:
6276	8432.8010	---草坪及运动场地滚压机	7	0	东盟ASEAN,智利CL,新西兰NZ,秘鲁PE,哥斯达黎加CR	0	最不发达35国LDC35	40	---Lawn or sports-ground rollers
				5	巴基斯坦PK				
6277	8432.8090	---其他	4	0	东盟ASEAN,智利CL,巴基斯坦PK,新西兰NZ,秘鲁PE,哥斯达黎加CR	0	最不发达35国LDC35	30	---Other
6278	8432.9000	-零件	4	0	东盟ASEAN,巴基斯坦PK,新西兰NZ,秘鲁PE,哥斯达黎加CR	0	最不发达35国LDC35	17	-Parts
				0.4	智利CL				
	84.33	**收割机、脱粒机,包括草料打包机;割草机;蛋类、水果或其他农产品的清洁、分选、分级机器,但税号84.37的机器除外:**							**Harvesting or threshing machinery, including straw or fodder balers; grass or hay mowers; machines for cleaning, sorting or grading eggs, fruit or other agricultural produce, other than machinery of heading No.84.37:**
		-草坪、公园或运动场地用的割草机:							-Mowers for lawns, parks or sports grounds:
6279	8433.1100	--机动的,切割装置在同一水平面上旋转的	6	0	东盟ASEAN,智利CL,新西兰NZ,秘鲁PE,哥斯达黎加CR	0	最不发达35国LDC35	30	--Powered, with the cutting device rotating in a horizontal plane
				5	巴基斯坦PK				

序号 No.	税则号列 Tariff Line	货品名称	最惠国税率 MFN(%)	协定税率 Agreement(%)		特惠税率 S.P.(%)		普通税率 Gen.(%)	Article Description
6280	8433.1900	--其他	6	0 5	东盟ASEAN,智利CL,新西兰NZ,秘鲁PE,哥斯达黎加CR 巴基斯坦PK	0	最不发达35国LDC35	30	--Other
6281	8433.2000	-其他割草机,包括牵引装置用的刀具杆	4	0	东盟ASEAN,智利CL,巴基斯坦PK,新西兰NZ,秘鲁PE,哥斯达黎加CR	0	最不发达35国LDC35	30	-Other mowers, including cutter bars for tractor mounting
6282	8433.3000	-其他干草切割、翻晒机器	5	0	东盟ASEAN,智利CL,巴基斯坦PK,新西兰NZ,秘鲁PE,哥斯达黎加CR	0	最不发达35国LDC35	30	-Other haymaking machinery
6283	8433.4000	-草料打包机,包括收集打包机	5	0	东盟ASEAN,智利CL,巴基斯坦PK,新西兰NZ,秘鲁PE,哥斯达黎加CR	0	最不发达35国LDC35	30	-Straw or fodder balers, including pickup balers
		-其他收割机;脱粒机:							-Other harvesting machinery; threshing machinery:
6284	8433.5100	--联合收割机	8	0 5 7.6	东盟ASEAN,智利CL,新西兰NZ,秘鲁PE,哥斯达黎加CR 巴基斯坦PK 亚太APTA	0	最不发达35国LDC35	17	--Combine harvester-threshers
	ex84335100	功率≥160马力的联合收割机	△5						Combine harvester-threshers, power not less than 160H.P
6285	8433.5200	--其他脱粒机	8	0 5	东盟ASEAN,智利CL,新西兰NZ,秘鲁PE,哥斯达黎加CR 巴基斯坦PK	0	最不发达35国LDC35	30	--Other threshing machinery
6286	8433.5300	--根茎或块茎收获机	8	0 5	东盟ASEAN,智利CL,新西兰NZ,秘鲁PE,哥斯达黎加CR 巴基斯坦PK	0	最不发达35国LDC35	30	--Root or tuber harvesting machines
	ex84335300	功率≥160马力的土豆、甜菜收获机	△4						Potato or sugar beet harvestors, power no less than 160 HP
		--其他:							--Other:
6287	8433.5910	---甘蔗收获机	8	0 0.8 5	东盟ASEAN,新西兰NZ,秘鲁PE,哥斯达黎加CR 智利CL 巴基斯坦PK	0	最不发达35国LDC35	30	---Sugarcane harvesters
	ex84335910	功率≥160马力的甘蔗收获机	△4						Sugarcane harvestors, power no less than 160 HP
6288	8433.5920	---棉花采摘机	8 △5	0 0.8 5	东盟ASEAN,新西兰NZ,秘鲁PE,哥斯达黎加CR 智利CL 巴基斯坦PK	0	最不发达35国LDC35	30	---Cotton picker

序号 No.	税则号列 Tariff Line	货品名称	最惠国税率 MFN(%)	协定税率 Agreement(%)		特惠税率 S.P.(%)		普通税率 Gen.(%)	Article Description
6289	8433.5990	---其他	8	0 0.8 5	东盟ASEAN,新西兰NZ,秘鲁PE,哥斯达黎加CR 智利CL 巴基斯坦PK	0	最不发达35国LDC35	30	---Other
	ex84335990	茶叶采摘机	△4						Tea pickers
	ex84335990	自走式青储饲料收获机	△5						Mobile silage harvesters
6290	8433.6000	-蛋类、水果或其他农产品的清洁、分选、分级机器	5	0 0.5	东盟ASEAN,巴基斯坦PK,新西兰NZ,秘鲁PE,哥斯达黎加CR 智利CL	0	最不发达35国LDC35	30	-Machines for cleaning, sorting or grading eggs, fruit or other agricultural product
		-零件:							-Parts:
6291	8433.9010	---联合收割机用	5	0	东盟ASEAN,智利CL,巴基斯坦PK,新西兰NZ,秘鲁PE,哥斯达黎加CR	0	最不发达35国LDC35	11	---Of combined harvester-thrashers
6292	8433.9090	---其他	3	0	东盟ASEAN,智利CL,巴基斯坦PK,新西兰NZ,秘鲁PE,哥斯达黎加CR	0	最不发达35国LDC35,最不发达4国LDC4	17	---Other
	84.34	**挤奶机及乳品加工机器:**							**Milking machines and dairy machinery:**
6293	8434.1000	-挤奶机	10	0 2.2 5	东盟ASEAN,智利CL,哥斯达黎加CR 新西兰NZ 巴基斯坦PK	0	最不发达35国LDC35	20	-Milking machines
6294	8434.2000	-乳品加工机器	6 △2	0 0.6 5	东盟ASEAN,新西兰NZ,秘鲁PE,哥斯达黎加CR 智利CL 巴基斯坦PK	0	最不发达35国LDC35	30	-Dairy machinery
6295	8434.9000	-零件	5	0 0.5	东盟ASEAN,巴基斯坦PK,新西兰NZ,秘鲁PE,哥斯达黎加CR 智利CL	0	最不发达35国LDC35	17	-Parts
	84.35	**制酒、制果汁或制类似饮料用的压榨机、轧碎机及类似机器:**							**Presses, crushers and similar machinery used in the manufacture of wine, cider, fruit juices or similar beverages:**
6296	8435.1000	-机器	10	0 1 5	东盟ASEAN,新西兰NZ,秘鲁PE,哥斯达黎加CR,澳门MO 智利CL 巴基斯坦PK	0	最不发达35国LDC35	30	-Machinery
6297	8435.9000	-零件	6	0 5	东盟ASEAN,智利CL,新西兰NZ,秘鲁PE,哥斯达黎加CR 巴基斯坦PK	0	最不发达35国LDC35	30	-Part

序号 No.	税则号列 Tariff Line	货品名称	最惠国税率 MFN(%)	协定税率 Agreement(%)		特惠税率 S.P.(%)		普通税率 Gen.(%)	Article Description
	84.36	**农业、园艺、林业、家禽饲养业或养蜂业用的其他机器,包括装有机械或热力装置的催芽设备;家禽孵卵器及育雏器:**							**Other agricultural, horticultural, forestry, poultry-keeping or bee-keeping machinery, including germination plant fitted with mechanical or thermal equipment; poultry incubators and brooders:**
6298	8436.1000	-动物饲料配制机	7	0 5	东盟ASEAN,智利CL,新西兰NZ,秘鲁PE,哥斯达黎加CR 巴基斯坦PK	0	最不发达35国LDC35	30	-Machinery for preparing animal feeding stuffs
		-家禽饲养用的机器;家禽孵卵器及育雏器:							-Poultry-keeping machinery; poultry incubators and brooders:
6299	8436.2100	--家禽孵卵器及育雏器	5	0	东盟ASEAN,智利CL,巴基斯坦PK,新西兰NZ,秘鲁PE,哥斯达黎加CR	0	最不发达35国LDC35	30	--Poultry incubators and brooders
6300	8436.2900	--其他	10	0 1 5	东盟ASEAN,新西兰NZ,秘鲁PE,哥斯达黎加CR 智利CL 巴基斯坦PK	0	最不发达35国LDC35	30	--Other
6301	8436.8000	-其他机器	10	0 5	东盟ASEAN,智利CL,新西兰NZ,秘鲁PE,哥斯达黎加CR 巴基斯坦PK	0	最不发达35国LDC35	30	-Other machinery
	ex84368000	自走式饲料搅拌投喂车	△5						Self waking type feed mixing and feeding vehicles
	ex84368000	青储饲料切割上料机	△3						Feeder of silage harvesters
		-零件:							-Parts:
6302	8436.9100	--家禽饲养用机器的零件或家禽孵卵器及育雏器的零件	6	0 5	东盟ASEAN,智利CL,新西兰NZ,秘鲁PE,哥斯达黎加CR 巴基斯坦PK	0	最不发达35国LDC35	17	--Of poultry-keeping machinery or poultry incubators and brooders
6303	8436.9900	--其他	6	0 5	东盟ASEAN,智利CL,新西兰NZ,秘鲁PE,哥斯达黎加CR 巴基斯坦PK	0	最不发达35国LDC35	17	--Other
	84.37	**种子、谷物或干豆的清洁、分选或分级机器;谷物磨粉业加工机器或谷物、干豆加工机器,但农业用机器除外:**							**Machines for cleaning, sorting or grading seed, grain or dried leguminous vegetables; machinery used in the milling industry or for the working of cereals or dried leguminous vegetables, other than farm-type machinery:**

序号 No.	税则号列 Tariff Line	货品名称	最惠国 税 率 MFN(%)	协定税率 Agreement(%)		特惠税率 S.P.(%)		普通 税率 Gen.(%)	Article Description
		-种子、谷物或干豆的清洁、分选或分级机器:							-Machines for cleaning, sorting or grading seed, grain or dried leguminous vegetables:
6304	8437.1010	---光学色差颗粒选别机（色选机）	10	0 5	东盟ASEAN,智利CL,新西兰NZ,秘鲁PE,哥斯达黎加CR 巴基斯坦PK	0	最不发达35国LDC35	30	---Optical color sorting machines for grains (color sorters)
6305	8437.1090	---其他	10	0 5	东盟ASEAN,智利CL,新西兰NZ,秘鲁PE,哥斯达黎加CR 巴基斯坦PK	0	最不发达35国LDC35	30	---Other
6306	8437.8000	-其他机器	10	0 5 8.5	东盟ASEAN,智利CL,新西兰NZ,秘鲁PE,哥斯达黎加CR 巴基斯坦PK 亚太APTA	0	最不发达35国LDC35	30	-Other machinery
6307	8437.9000	-零件	6	0 5	东盟ASEAN,智利CL,新西兰NZ,秘鲁PE,哥斯达黎加CR 巴基斯坦PK	0	最不发达35国LDC35	30	-Parts
	84.38	**本章其他税号未列名的食品、饮料工业用的生产或加工机器,但提取、加工动物油脂或植物固定油脂的机器除外:**							**Machinery, not specified or included elsewhere in this chapter, for the industrial preparation or manufacture of food or drink, other than machinery for the extraction or preparation of animal or fixed vegetable fats or oils:**
6308	8438.1000	-糕点加工机器及生产通心粉、面条或类似产品的机器	7	0 0.7 5	东盟ASEAN,新西兰NZ,秘鲁PE,哥斯达黎加CR 智利CL 巴基斯坦PK	0	最不发达35国LDC35,最不发达4国LDC4	30	-Bakery machinery and machinery for the manufacture of macaroni, spaghetti or similar products
6309	8438.2000	-生产糖果、可可粉、巧克力的机器	8	0 0.8 5	东盟ASEAN,新西兰NZ,秘鲁PE,哥斯达黎加CR 智利CL 巴基斯坦PK	0	最不发达35国LDC35,最不发达4国LDC4	30	-Machinery for the manufacture of confectionery, cocoa or chocolate
6310	8438.3000	-制糖机器	10	0 5	东盟ASEAN,智利CL,新西兰NZ,秘鲁PE,哥斯达黎加CR 巴基斯坦PK	0	最不发达35国LDC35,最不发达4国LDC4	30	-Machinery for sugar manufacture
6311	8438.4000	-酿酒机器	7	0 5	东盟ASEAN,智利CL,新西兰NZ,秘鲁PE,哥斯达黎加CR 巴基斯坦PK	0	最不发达35国LDC35,最不发达4国LDC4	30	-Brewery machinery

序号 No.	税则号列 Tariff Line	货品名称	最惠国税率 MFN(%)	协定税率 Agreement(%)	特惠税率 S.P.(%)	普通税率 Gen.(%)	Article Description
6312	8438.5000	-肉类或家禽加工机器	7	0 东盟ASEAN,新西兰NZ,秘鲁PE,哥斯达黎加CR 0.7 智利CL 5 巴基斯坦PK	0 最不发达35国LDC35,最不发达4国LDC4	30	-Machinery for the preparation of meat or poultry
6313	8438.6000	-水果、坚果或蔬菜加工机器	10	0 东盟ASEAN,新加坡SG,新西兰NZ,哥斯达黎加CR 1 智利CL 5 巴基斯坦PK,秘鲁PE	0 最不发达35国LDC35,最不发达4国LDC4	30	-Machinery for the preparation of fruits, nuts or vegetables
6314	8438.8000	-其他机器	8.5	0 东盟ASEAN,新西兰NZ,秘鲁PE,哥斯达黎加CR,台湾TW 0.9 智利CL 5 巴基斯坦PK 8.1 亚太APTA	0 最不发达35国LDC35,最不发达4国LDC4	30	-Other machinery
6315	8438.9000	-零件	5	0 东盟ASEAN,巴基斯坦PK,新西兰NZ,秘鲁PE,哥斯达黎加CR 0.5 智利CL	0 最不发达35国LDC35,最不发达4国LDC4	30	-Parts
	84.39	**纤维素纸浆、纸及纸板的制造或整理机器:**					**Machinery for making pulp of fibrous cellulosic material or for making or finishing paper or paperboard:**
6316	8439.1000	-制造纤维素纸浆的机器	8.4	0 东盟ASEAN,新西兰NZ,秘鲁PE,哥斯达黎加CR 0.8 智利CL 5 巴基斯坦PK	0 最不发达35国LDC35,最不发达4国LDC4	30	-Machinery for making pulp of fibrous cellulosic material
6317	8439.2000	-纸或纸板的抄造机器	8.4	0 东盟ASEAN,智利CL,新西兰NZ,秘鲁PE,哥斯达黎加CR,台湾TW 5 巴基斯坦PK	0 最不发达35国LDC35,最不发达4国LDC4	30	-Machinery for making paper or paper board
6318	8439.3000	-纸或纸板的整理机器	8.4	0 东盟ASEAN,智利CL,新西兰NZ,秘鲁PE,哥斯达黎加CR,台湾TW 5 巴基斯坦PK	0 最不发达35国LDC35,最不发达4国LDC4	30	-Machinery for finishing paper or paper board
		-零件:					-Parts:
6319	8439.9100	--制造纤维素纸浆的机器用	6	0 东盟ASEAN,新西兰NZ,秘鲁PE,哥斯达黎加CR 0.6 智利CL 5 巴基斯坦PK	0 最不发达35国LDC35,最不发达4国LDC4	30	--Of machinery for making pulp of fibrous cellulosic material

序号 No.	税则号列 Tariff Line	货品名称	最惠国税率 MFN(%)	协定税率 Agreement(%)		特惠税率 S.P.(%)		普通税率 Gen.(%)	Article Description
6320	8439.9900	--其他	6	0 0.6 3	东盟ASEAN,巴基斯坦PK,新西兰NZ,秘鲁PE,哥斯达黎加CR 智利CL 亚太APTA	0	最不发达35国LDC35,最不发达4国LDC4	30	--Other
	84.40	**书本装订机器,包括锁线订书机:**							**Book-binding machinery, including book-sewing machines:**
		-机器:							-Machinery:
6321	8440.1010	---锁线装订机	10	0 5	东盟ASEAN,智利CL,新西兰NZ,秘鲁PE,哥斯达黎加CR 巴基斯坦PK	0	最不发达35国LDC35	35	---Sewing bookbinders
6322	8440.1020	---胶订机	12	0 2.4 6	东盟ASEAN,智利CL,新加坡SG,新西兰NZ,秘鲁PE 哥斯达黎加CR 巴基斯坦PK	0	最不发达35国LDC35	35	---Glueing bookbinders
6323	8440.1090	---其他	12	0 2.4 6	东盟ASEAN,智利CL,新加坡SG,新西兰NZ,秘鲁PE 哥斯达黎加CR 巴基斯坦PK	0	最不发达35国LDC35	35	---Other
6324	8440.9000	-零件	8	0 5	东盟ASEAN,智利CL,新西兰NZ,秘鲁PE,哥斯达黎加CR 巴基斯坦PK	0	最不发达35国LDC35	35	-Parts
	84.41	**其他制造纸浆制品、纸制品或纸板制品的机器,包括各种切纸机:**							**Other machinery for making up paper pulp, paper or paperboard, including cutting machines of all kinds:**
6325	8441.1000	-切纸机	12	0 1.2 2.4 6	东盟ASEAN,新加坡SG,新西兰NZ,秘鲁PE,台湾TW 智利CL 哥斯达黎加CR 巴基斯坦PK	0	最不发达35国LDC35,最不发达4国LDC4	50	-Cutting machines
6326	8441.2000	-制造包、袋或信封的机器	12	0 1.2 2.4 6 11.4	东盟ASEAN,新加坡SG,新西兰NZ 智利CL 哥斯达黎加CR 巴基斯坦PK,秘鲁PE 亚太APTA	0	最不发达35国LDC35,最不发达4国LDC4	30	-Machines for making bags, sacks or envelopes
		-制造箱、盒、管、桶或类似容器的机器,但模制成型机器除外:							-Machines for making cartons, boxes, cases, tubes, drums or similar containers, other than by moulding:
6327	8441.3010	---制造纸塑铝复合罐的生产设备	13.5	0 1.4 2.7 6.8 12.8	东盟ASEAN,新加坡SG,新西兰NZ 智利CL 哥斯达黎加CR 巴基斯坦PK,秘鲁PE 亚太APTA	0	最不发达35国LDC35	30	---Machines for paper, plastic and aluminium composite can manufacture

序号 No.	税则号列 Tariff Line	货品名称	最惠国税率 MFN(%)	协定税率 Agreement(%)	特惠税率 S.P.(%)	普通税率 Gen.(%)	Article Description
6328	8441.3090	---其他	13.5	0 东盟ASEAN,新加坡SG,新西兰NZ 1.4 智利CL 2.7 哥斯达黎加CR 6.8 巴基斯坦PK,秘鲁PE 12.8 亚太APTA	0 最不发达35国LDC35	30	---Other
6329	8441.4000	-纸浆、纸或纸板制品模制成型机器	12	0 东盟ASEAN,智利CL,新加坡SG,新西兰NZ,秘鲁PE 2.4 哥斯达黎加CR 6 巴基斯坦PK	0 最不发达35国LDC35,最不发达4国LDC4	30	-Machines for moulding articles in paper pulp, paper or paperboard
		-其他机器:					-Other machinery:
6330	8441.8010	---制造纸塑铝软包装的生产设备	12	0 东盟ASEAN,新加坡SG,新西兰NZ,秘鲁PE 1.2 智利CL 2.4 哥斯达黎加CR 6 巴基斯坦PK 11.4 亚太APTA	0 最不发达35国LDC35,最不发达4国LDC4	30	---Machines for paper plastic and aluminium flexible packaging manufacture
6331	8441.8090	---其他	12	0 东盟ASEAN,新加坡SG,新西兰NZ,秘鲁PE,台湾TW 1.2 智利CL 2.4 哥斯达黎加CR 6 巴基斯坦PK 11.4 亚太APTA	0 最不发达35国LDC35,最不发达4国LDC4	30	---Other
		-零件:					-Parts:
6332	8441.9010	---切纸机用	8	0 东盟ASEAN,新西兰NZ,秘鲁PE,哥斯达黎加CR 0.8 智利CL 5 巴基斯坦PK	0 最不发达35国LDC35,最不发达4国LDC4	50	---Of cutting machines
	ex84419010	切纸机用弧形辊	△4				Curved metal spreader roll of cutting machines
	ex84419010	切纸机用横切刀单元	△3				Crosscut knife units of cutting machines
6333	8441.9090	---其他	8.4	0 东盟ASEAN,新西兰NZ,秘鲁PE,哥斯达黎加CR 0.8 智利CL 5 巴基斯坦PK	0 最不发达35国LDC35,最不发达4国LDC4	30	---Other
	84.42	**制版用的机器、器具及设备（税号84.56至84.65的机床除外）;印刷用版（片）、滚筒及其他部件;制成供印刷用（例如，刨平、压纹或抛光）的版（片）、滚筒及石板:**					**Machinery, apparatus and equipment (other than the machine-tools of headings Nos.84.56 to 84.65), for preparing or making plates, cylinders or other printing components; plates, cylinders and other printing components; plates, cylinders and lithographic stones, prepared for printing purposes (for example, planed, grained or polished):**

序号 No.	税则号列 Tariff Line	货品名称	最惠国税率 MFN(%)	协定税率 Agreement(%)		特惠税率 S.P.(%)	普通税率 Gen.(%)	Article Description
		-机器、器具及设备:						-Machinery, apparatus and equipment:
6334	8442.3010	---铸字机	9	0 5	东盟ASEAN,智利CL,新西兰NZ,秘鲁PE,哥斯达黎加CR 巴基斯坦PK	0 最不发达35国LDC35,最不发达4国LDC4	35	---Type casters
		---制版机器、器具及设备:						---Other machinery, apparatus and equipment for typesetting:
6335	8442.3021	----计算机直接制版设备	9 △5	0 5	东盟ASEAN,智利CL,新西兰NZ,秘鲁PE,哥斯达黎加CR 巴基斯坦PK	0 最不发达35国LDC35,最不发达4国LDC4	35	----Computer-to-plate equipments
6336	8442.3029	----其他	9	0 5	东盟ASEAN,智利CL,新西兰NZ,秘鲁PE,哥斯达黎加CR 巴基斯坦PK	0 最不发达35国LDC35,最不发达4国LDC4	35	----Other
6337	8442.3090	---其他	9	0 5	东盟ASEAN,智利CL,新西兰NZ,秘鲁PE,哥斯达黎加CR 巴基斯坦PK	0 最不发达35国LDC35,最不发达4国LDC4	35	---Other
6338	8442.4000	-上述机器、器具及设备的零件	7	0 5	东盟ASEAN,智利CL,新西兰NZ,秘鲁PE,哥斯达黎加CR 巴基斯坦PK	0 最不发达35国LDC35,最不发达4国LDC4	20	-Parts of the foregoing machinery, apparatus or equipment
	ex84424000	计算机直接制版机器用零件	△0					Parts of computer-to-plate equipments
6339	8442.5000	-印刷用版、滚筒及其他印刷部件;制成供印刷用(例如,刨平、压纹或抛光)的版、滚筒及石板	7	0 5	东盟ASEAN,智利CL,新西兰NZ,秘鲁PE,哥斯达黎加CR,香港HK 巴基斯坦PK	0 最不发达35国LDC35,最不发达4国LDC4	35	-Plates, cylinders and other printing components; plates, cylinders and lithographic stones, prepared for printing purposes (for example, planed, grained or polished)
	84.43	**用于税目84.42的印刷用版(片)、滚筒及其他印刷部件进行印刷的机器;其他打印机、复印机及传真机,不论是否组合式;上述机器的零件及附件:**						**Printing machinery used for printing by means of plates, cylinders and other printing components of heading 84.42; other printers, copying machines and facsimile machines, whether or not combined; parts and accessories thereof:**

序号 No.	税则号列 Tariff Line	货品名称	最惠国税率 MFN(%)	协定税率 Agreement(%)	特惠税率 S.P.(%)	普通税率 Gen.(%)	Article Description
		-用税目84.42的印刷用版（片）、滚筒及其他印刷部件进行印刷的机器：					-Printing machinery used for printing by means of plates, cylinders and other printing components of heading 84.42:
6340	8443.1100	--卷取进料式胶印机	10	0 东盟ASEAN,新西兰NZ,哥斯达黎加CR 1 智利CL 5 巴基斯坦PK,秘鲁PE 7 亚太APTA	0 最不发达35国LDC35,最不发达4国LDC4	35	--Offset printing machinery, reel-fed
6341	8443.1200	--办公室用片取进料式胶印机（展开片尺寸一边长不超过22厘米,另一边长不超过36厘米）	12	0 东盟ASEAN,智利CL,新加坡SG,新西兰NZ,秘鲁PE 2.4 哥斯达黎加CR 6 巴基斯坦PK	0 最不发达35国LDC35,最不发达4国LDC4	35	--Offset printing machinery, sheet-fed, office type (using sheets with one side not exceeding 22cm and the other side not exceeding 36cm in the unfolded state)
		--其他胶印机:					--Other offset printing machinery:
		---平张纸进料式:					---Sheet fed:
6342	8443.1311	----单色机	10	0 东盟ASEAN,新西兰NZ,秘鲁PE,哥斯达黎加CR 1 智利CL 5 巴基斯坦PK 7 亚太APTA	0 最不发达35国LDC35,最不发达4国LDC4	35	----Single-color printing press
6343	8443.1312	----双色机	10	0 东盟ASEAN,新西兰NZ,秘鲁PE,哥斯达黎加CR 1 智利CL 5 巴基斯坦PK 7 亚太APTA	0 最不发达35国LDC35,最不发达4国LDC4	35	----Double-color printing press
6344	8443.1313	----四色机	10	0 东盟ASEAN,新西兰NZ,秘鲁PE,哥斯达黎加CR 1 智利CL 5 巴基斯坦PK 7 亚太APTA	0 最不发达35国LDC35,最不发达4国LDC4	35	----Quadruple-color printing press
	ex84431313	四色平张纸胶印机，对开单张纸单面印刷速度≥17000张/小时；对开单张纸双面印刷速度≥13000张/小时；全张或超全张单张纸单面印刷速度≥13000张/小时	△7				Four-color sheet-fed offset press, Folio size, maximum out-put of single-sided printing ≥17000iph; Folio size, maximum out-put of perfect (double-sided) printing≥13000iph; Full size or super large format, maximum out-put of single-sided printing≥13000 iph

序号 No.	税则号列 Tariff Line	货品名称	最惠国税率 MFN(%)	协定税率 Agreement(%)		特惠税率 S.P.(%)		普通税率 Gen.(%)	Article Description
6345	8443.1319	----其他	10	0 1 5 7	东盟ASEAN,新西兰NZ,秘鲁PE,哥斯达黎加CR 智利CL 巴基斯坦PK 亚太APTA	0	最不发达35国LDC35,最不发达4国LDC4	35	----Other
	ex84431319	五色及以上平张纸胶印机，对开单张纸单面印刷速度≥17000张/小时；对开单张纸双面印刷速度≥13000张/小时；全张或超全张单张纸单面印刷速度≥13000张/小时	△7						Five-color and more sheet-fed offset printing machines, Folio size, maximum out-put of single-sided printing ≥17000iph; Folio size, maximum out-put of perfect (double-sided) printing ≥13000iph; Full size or super large format, maximum out-put of single-sided printing≥ 13000iph
6346	8443.1390	---其他	10	0 1 5 7	东盟ASEAN,新西兰NZ,秘鲁PE,哥斯达黎加CR 智利CL 巴基斯坦PK 亚太APTA	0	最不发达35国LDC35,最不发达4国LDC4	35	---Other
6347	8443.1400	--卷取进料式凸版印刷机,但不包括苯胺印刷机	12	0 2.4 6	东盟ASEAN,智利CL,新加坡SG,新西兰NZ,秘鲁PE,香港HK 哥斯达黎加CR 巴基斯坦PK	0	最不发达35国LDC35,最不发达4国LDC4	35	--Letterpress printing machinery, reel fed, excluding flexographic printing
6348	8443.1500	--其他凸版印刷机,但不包括苯胺印刷机	12	0 1.2 2.4 6	东盟ASEAN,新加坡SG,新西兰NZ,秘鲁PE 智利CL 哥斯达黎加CR 巴基斯坦PK	0	最不发达35国LDC35,最不发达4国LDC4	35	--Letterpress printing machinery, other than reel fed, excluding flexographic printing
6349	8443.1600	--苯胺印刷机	10	0 1 5	东盟ASEAN,新西兰NZ,秘鲁PE,哥斯达黎加CR 智利CL 巴基斯坦PK	0	最不发达35国LDC35,最不发达4国LDC4	35	--Flexographic printing machinery
	ex84431600	苯胺印刷机（柔性版印刷机），线速度≥350米/分钟，幅宽≥800毫米	△3						Flexographic printing machines, press line speed≥350m/min, web width≥800mm
	ex84431600	具有烫印或全息或丝网印刷功能单元的机组式柔性版印刷机,线速度≥160米/分钟，250毫米≤幅宽＜800毫米	△5						Multi-functional narrow-web flexographic printing machine with module of stamping or holographic or screen printing, line speed ≥ 160m/min, 250mm≤web width＜800mm

序号 No.	税则号列 Tariff Line	货品名称	最惠国税率 MFN(%)	协定税率 Agreement(%)	特惠税率 S.P.(%)	普通税率 Gen.(%)	Article Description
6350	8443.1700	--凹版印刷机	18	0 东盟ASEAN,智利CL,新加坡SG,新西兰NZ 3.6 哥斯达黎加CR 9 秘鲁PE 14.4 巴基斯坦PK 16.2 亚太APTA	0 最不发达35国LDC35	35	--Gravure printing machinery
	ex84431700	凹版印刷机,印刷速度≥350米/分钟	△9				Gravure printing machinery, printing speed≥350m/min
		--其他:					--Other:
		---网式印刷机:					---Screen printing machinery:
6351	8443.1921	----圆网印刷机	10	0 东盟ASEAN,智利CL,新西兰NZ,秘鲁PE,哥斯达黎加CR 5 巴基斯坦PK 9 亚太APTA	0 最不发达35国LDC35,最不发达4国LDC4	35	----Cylinder screen press
	ex84431921	纺织用圆网印花机	△6				Cylinder screen woven fabric printing range
6352	8443.1922	----平网印刷机	10	0 东盟ASEAN,智利CL,新西兰NZ,秘鲁PE,哥斯达黎加CR,台湾TW 5 巴基斯坦PK 9 亚太APTA	0 最不发达35国LDC35,最不发达4国LDC4	35	----Platen screen press
	ex84431922	纺织用平网印花机	△6				Flate screen woven fabric printing range
6353	8443.1929	----其他	10	0 东盟ASEAN,智利CL,新加坡SG,新西兰NZ,秘鲁PE,哥斯达黎加CR,台湾TW 5 巴基斯坦PK 9 亚太APTA	0 最不发达35国LDC35,最不发达4国LDC4	35	----Other
6354	8443.1980	---其他	8	0 东盟ASEAN,智利CL,新西兰NZ,秘鲁PE,哥斯达黎加CR,香港HK,台湾TW 5 巴基斯坦PK 7.2 亚太APTA	0 最不发达35国LDC35,最不发达4国LDC4	35	---Other
		-其他印刷(打印)机、复印机及传真机,不论是否组合式:					-Other printers, copying machines and facsimile machines, whether or not combined:
		--具有打印、复印或传真中两种及以上功能的机器,可与自动数据处理设备或网络连接:					--Machines which perform two or more of the functions of printing, copying or facsimile transmission, capable of connecting to an automatic data processing machine or to a network:

序号 No.	税则号列 Tariff Line	货品名称	最惠国税率 MFN(%)	协定税率 Agreement(%)		特惠税率 S.P.(%)		普通税率 Gen.(%)	Article Description
6355	8443.3110	---静电感光式	10 △3	0 1 5	东盟ASEAN,新加坡SG,新西兰NZ,秘鲁PE,哥斯达黎加CR 智利CL 巴基斯坦PK	0	最不发达35国LDC35,最不发达4国LDC4	70	---Electrostatic photo type
6356	8443.3190	---其他	0			0	最不发达35国LDC35,最不发达4国LDC4	17	---Other
		--其他,可与自动数据处理设备或网络连接:							--Other, capable of connecting to an automatic data processing machine or to a network:
		---专用于税目8471所列设备的打印机:							---Printer suitable for use solely with the machines of heading No.8471:
6357	8443.3211	----针式打印机	0			0	最不发达35国LDC35,最不发达4国LDC4	14	----Stylus printers
6358	8443.3212	----激光打印机	0			0	最不发达35国LDC35,最不发达4国LDC4	14	----Laser printers
6359	8443.3213	----喷墨打印机	0			0	最不发达35国LDC35,最不发达4国LDC4	14	----Ink-jet printers
6360	8443.3214	----热敏打印机	0			0	最不发达35国LDC35,最不发达4国LDC4	14	----Thermal printers
6361	8443.3219	----其他	0			0	最不发达35国LDC35,最不发达4国LDC4	14	----Other
		---数字式印刷设备:							---Digital printing machines:

序号 No.	税则号列 Tariff Line	货品名称	最惠国税率 MFN(%)	协定税率 Agreement(%)	特惠税率 S.P.(%)	普通税率 Gen.(%)	Article Description
6362	8443.3221	----喷墨印刷机	8	0 东盟ASEAN,智利CL,新加坡SG,新西兰NZ,秘鲁PE,哥斯达黎加CR 5 巴基斯坦PK	0 最不发达35国LDC35,最不发达4国LDC4	30	----Ink-jet printing machines
	ex84433221	幅宽＞60cm的喷墨印刷设备,可与网络或自动数据处理设备连接	△3				Ink-jet printing machines, with breadth of printing＞60cm, capable of connecting to an automatic data processing machine or to a network
	ex84433221	297mm＜幅宽≤360mm的喷墨印刷设备,可与网络或自动数据处理设备连接	△5				Ink-jet printing machines, 297mm ＜ breadth of printing ≤360mm, capable of connecting to an automatic data processing machine or to a network
6363	8443.3222	----静电照相印刷机(激光印刷机)	8	0 东盟ASEAN,智利CL,新西兰NZ,秘鲁PE,哥斯达黎加CR 5 巴基斯坦PK 7.2 亚太APTA	0 最不发达35国LDC35,最不发达4国LDC4	35	----Electrostatic photographic printing machines (laser printing machines)
	ex84433222	幅宽≥32.9cm的静电照相印刷设备（激光印刷机）,可与网络或自动数据处理设备连接	△3				Electrostatic photographic printing machines (laser printing machines), with breadth of printing≥32.9cm, capable of connecting to an automatic data processing machine or to a network
6364	8443.3229	----其他	8	0 东盟ASEAN,智利CL,新西兰NZ,秘鲁PE,哥斯达黎加CR 5 巴基斯坦PK 7.2 亚太APTA	0 最不发达35国LDC35,最不发达4国LDC4	30	----Other
6365	8443.3290	---其他	0		0 最不发达35国LDC35,最不发达4国LDC4	17	---Other
		--其他:					--Other:
		---静电感光复印设备:					---Electrostatic photocopying apparatus:

序号 No.	税则号列 Tariff Line	货品名称	最惠国税率 MFN(%)	协定税率 Agreement(%)		特惠税率 S.P.(%)		普通税率 Gen.(%)	Article Description
6366	8443.3911	----将原件直接复印的（直接法）	0			0	最不发达35国LDC35,最不发达4国LDC4	70	----Operating by reproducing the original image directly onto the copy (direct process)
6367	8443.3912	----将原件通过中间体转印的（间接法）	10	0 1 5	东盟ASEAN,新加坡SG,新西兰NZ,秘鲁PE,哥斯达黎加CR 智利CL 巴基斯坦PK	0	最不发达35国LDC35,最不发达4国LDC4	70	----Operating by reproducing the original image via an intermediate onto the copy (indirect process)
		---其他感光复印设备：							---Other photocopying apparatus:
6368	8443.3921	----带有光学系统的	0			0	最不发达35国LDC35,最不发达4国LDC4	70	----Incorporating an optical system
6369	8443.3922	----接触式的	20	0 4 10	东盟ASEAN,智利CL,新加坡SG,新西兰NZ 哥斯达黎加CR 秘鲁PE	0	最不发达35国LDC35	70	----Of the contact type
6370	8443.3923	----热敏复印设备	20	0 4 10	东盟ASEAN,智利CL,新加坡SG,新西兰NZ 哥斯达黎加CR 秘鲁PE	0	最不发达35国LDC35	70	----Heat-sensitive copying apparatus
6371	8443.3924	----热升华复印设备	20	0 4 10	东盟ASEAN,智利CL,新加坡SG,新西兰NZ 哥斯达黎加CR 秘鲁PE	0	最不发达35国LDC35	70	----Heat-sublimated copying apparatus
		---数字式印刷设备：							---Digital printing machines:
6372	8443.3931	----喷墨印刷机	8	0 5	东盟ASEAN,智利CL,新加坡SG,新西兰NZ,秘鲁PE,哥斯达黎加CR 巴基斯坦PK	0	最不发达35国LDC35,最不发达4国LDC4	30	----Ink-jet printing machines
6373	8443.3932	----静电照相印刷机(激光印刷机)	8	0 5 7.2	东盟ASEAN,智利CL,新西兰NZ,秘鲁PE,哥斯达黎加CR 巴基斯坦PK 亚太APTA	0	最不发达35国LDC35,最不发达4国LDC4	35	----Electrostatic photographic printing machines (laser printing machines)
6374	8443.3939	----其他	8	0 5 7.2	东盟ASEAN,智利CL,新加坡SG,新西兰NZ,秘鲁PE,哥斯达黎加CR 巴基斯坦PK 亚太APTA	0	最不发达35国LDC35,最不发达4国LDC4	30	----Other

序号 No.	税则号列 Tariff Line	货品名称	最惠国税 率 MFN(%)	协定税率 Agreement(%)	特惠税率 S.P.(%)	普通税率 Gen.(%)	Article Description
6375	8443.3990	---其他	0		0 最不发达35国LDC35, 最不发达4国LDC4	30	---Other
		-零件及附件:					-Parts and accessories:
		--用于税目84.42的印刷用版、滚筒及其他印刷部件进行印刷的机器零件及附件:					--Parts and accessories of printing machinery used for printing by means of plates, cylinders and other printing components of heading 84.42:
		---印刷用辅助机器:					---Machines for uses ancillary to printing:
6376	8443.9111	----卷筒料给料机	12	0 东盟ASEAN,新加坡SG,新西兰NZ,秘鲁PE 1.2 智利CL 2.4 哥斯达黎加CR 6 巴基斯坦PK	0 最不发达35国LDC35, 最不发达4国LDC4	35	----Splicers of web press
	ex84439111	卷筒料自动给料机,给料线速度≥12米/秒	△4				Automatic splicer of web offset press, splicing speed ≥12m/s
6377	8443.9119	----其他	12 △6	0 东盟ASEAN,新加坡SG,新西兰NZ,秘鲁PE 1.2 智利CL 2.4 哥斯达黎加CR 6 巴基斯坦PK	0 最不发达35国LDC35, 最不发达4国LDC4	35	----Other
6378	8443.9190	---其他	6	0 东盟ASEAN,智利CL,新西兰NZ,秘鲁PE,哥斯达黎加CR 5 巴基斯坦PK	0 最不发达35国LDC35, 最不发达4国LDC4	20	---Other
	ex84439190	胶印机用墨量遥控装置(包括墨色控制装置、墨量调节装置、墨斗体等组成部分)	△0				Ink remote control unit for offset printing machinery (including ink coclor control unit and ink adjust device and inking pot)
	ex84439190	传统印刷机用零件及附件(胶印机用墨量遥控装置除外)	△3				Parts and accessories of printing machinery (with the exception of ink remote control unit)
		--其他:					--Other:
6379	8443.9910	---数字印刷设备用辅助机器	12	0 东盟ASEAN,新加坡SG,新西兰NZ,秘鲁PE 1.2 智利CL 2.4 哥斯达黎加CR 6 巴基斯坦PK	0 最不发达35国LDC35, 最不发达4国LDC4	35	---Machines for uses ancillary to digital printing

序号 No.	税则号列 Tariff Line	货品名称	最惠国税率 MFN(%)	协定税率 Agreement(%)		特惠税率 S.P.(%)		普通税率 Gen.(%)	Article Description
		---数字印刷设备的零件:							---Parts of digital printing machinery:
6380	8443.9921	----热敏打印头	6	0 5	东盟ASEAN,智利CL,新西兰NZ,秘鲁PE,哥斯达黎加CR 巴基斯坦PK	0	最不发达35国LDC35,最不发达4国LDC4	20	----Thermal printer heads
6381	8443.9929	----其他	6	0 5	东盟ASEAN,智利CL,新西兰NZ,秘鲁PE,哥斯达黎加CR 巴基斯坦PK	0	最不发达35国LDC35,最不发达4国LDC4	20	----Other
	ex84439929	压电式喷墨头	△3						Piezoelectric inkjet print head
6382	8443.9990	---其他	0			0	最不发达35国LDC35,最不发达4国LDC4	35	---Other
	84.44	**化学纺织纤维挤压、拉伸、变形或切割机器:**							**Machines for extruding, drawing, texturing or cutting man-made textile materials:**
6383	8444.0010	---合成纤维长丝纺丝机	10	0 5 7	东盟ASEAN,智利CL,新西兰NZ,秘鲁PE,哥斯达黎加CR,台湾TW 巴基斯坦PK 亚太APTA	0	最不发达35国LDC35	30	---Synthetic filaments spinning jets
6384	8444.0020	---合成纤维短纤纺丝机	10	0 5 7	东盟ASEAN,智利CL,新西兰NZ,秘鲁PE,哥斯达黎加CR 巴基斯坦PK 亚太APTA	0	最不发达35国LDC35	30	---Synthetic staple fibres spinning jets
6385	8444.0030	---人造纤维纺丝机	10	0 5 7	东盟ASEAN,智利CL,新西兰NZ,秘鲁PE,哥斯达黎加CR 巴基斯坦PK 亚太APTA	0	最不发达35国LDC35	30	---Artificial fibres spinning jets
6386	8444.0040	---化学纤维变形机	10	0 5 7	东盟ASEAN,智利CL,新西兰NZ,秘鲁PE,哥斯达黎加CR 巴基斯坦PK 亚太APTA	0	最不发达35国LDC35	30	---Man-made filaments crimping machinery
6387	8444.0050	---化学纤维切断机	10	0 5 7	东盟ASEAN,智利CL,新西兰NZ,秘鲁PE,哥斯达黎加CR 巴基斯坦PK 亚太APTA	0	最不发达35国LDC35	30	---Manmade filaments cutting machinery
6388	8444.0090	---其他	10	0 5 7	东盟ASEAN,智利CL,新西兰NZ,秘鲁PE,哥斯达黎加CR 巴基斯坦PK 亚太APTA	0	最不发达35国LDC35	30	---Other

序号 No.	税则号列 Tariff Line	货品名称	最惠国税 率 MFN(%)	协定税率 Agreement(%)		特惠税率 S.P.(%)		普通税率 Gen.(%)	Article Description
	84.45	**纺织纤维的预处理机器;纺纱机、并线机、加捻机及其他生产纺织纱线的机器;摇纱机、络纱机(包括卷纬机)及处理税号 84.46 或 84.47 所列机器用的纺织纱线的机器:**							**Machines for preparing textile fibres; spinning, doubling or twisting machines and other-machinery for producing textile yarns; textile reeling or winding (including weft-winding) machines and machines for preparing textile yarns for use on the machines of heading No.84.46 or 84.47:**
		-纺织纤维的预处理机器:							-Machines for preparing textile fibres:
		--梳理机:							--Carding machines:
		---棉纤维型:							---For cotton type fibres:
6389	8445.1111	----清梳联合机	10	0 5 9	东盟ASEAN,智利CL,新西兰NZ,秘鲁PE,哥斯达黎加CR 巴基斯坦PK 亚太APTA	0	最不发达 35 国 LDC35,最不发达 4 国 LDC4	30	----Blowing-carding Machinery
6390	8445.1112	----自动抓棉机	10	0 5 9	东盟ASEAN,智利CL,新西兰NZ,秘鲁PE,哥斯达黎加CR 巴基斯坦PK 亚太APTA	0	最不发达 35 国 LDC35,最不发达 4 国 LDC4	30	----Bale Plucker
6391	8445.1113	----梳棉机	10	0 5 9	东盟ASEAN,智利CL,新西兰NZ,秘鲁PE,哥斯达黎加CR 巴基斯坦PK 亚太APTA	0	最不发达 35 国 LDC35,最不发达 4 国 LDC4	30	----Card or Carding Mackine
6392	8445.1119	----其他	10	0 5 9	东盟ASEAN,智利CL,新西兰NZ,秘鲁PE,哥斯达黎加CR 巴基斯坦PK 亚太APTA	0	最不发达 35 国 LDC35,最不发达 4 国 LDC4	30	----Other
6393	8445.1120	---毛纤维型	10	0 5 9	东盟ASEAN,智利CL,新西兰NZ,秘鲁PE,哥斯达黎加CR 巴基斯坦PK 亚太APTA	0	最不发达 35 国 LDC35,最不发达 4 国 LDC4	30	---For wool type fibres
6394	8445.1190	---其他	10	0 5 9	东盟ASEAN,智利CL,新西兰NZ,秘鲁PE,哥斯达黎加CR 巴基斯坦PK 亚太APTA	0	最不发达 35 国 LDC35,最不发达 4 国 LDC4	30	---Other

序号 No.	税则号列 Tariff Line	货品名称	最惠国 税率 MFN(%)	协定税率 Agreement(%)	特惠税率 S.P.(%)	普通 税率 Gen.(%)	Article Description
	ex84451190	宽幅非织造布梳理机，工作幅宽＞3.5米，工作速度＞120米/分钟	△6				Nonwoven carding machines,working width＞3.5m, working speed＞120m/min
		--精梳机:					--Combing machines:
6395	8445.1210	---棉精梳机	10	0 东盟ASEAN,智利CL,新西兰NZ,秘鲁PE,哥斯达黎加CR 5 巴基斯坦PK	0 最不发达35国LDC35,最不发达4国LDC4	30	---Cotton Comber
6396	8445.1220	---毛精梳机	10	0 东盟ASEAN,智利CL,新西兰NZ,秘鲁PE,哥斯达黎加CR 5 巴基斯坦PK	0 最不发达35国LDC35,最不发达4国LDC4	30	---Worsted Comber
6397	8445.1290	---其他	10	0 东盟ASEAN,智利CL,新西兰NZ,秘鲁PE,哥斯达黎加CR 5 巴基斯坦PK	0 最不发达35国LDC35,最不发达4国LDC4	30	---Other
		--拉伸机或粗纱机:					--Drawing or roving machines:
6398	8445.1310	---拉伸机	10	0 东盟ASEAN,智利CL,新西兰NZ,秘鲁PE,哥斯达黎加CR 5 巴基斯坦PK	0 最不发达35国LDC35,最不发达4国LDC4	30	---Drawing machines
		---粗纱机:					---Roving machines:
6399	8445.1321	----棉纺粗纱机	10	0 东盟ASEAN,智利CL,新西兰NZ,秘鲁PE,哥斯达黎加CR 5 巴基斯坦PK	0 最不发达35国LDC35,最不发达4国LDC4	30	----Cotton Roving Frames
6400	8445.1322	----毛纺粗纱机	10	0 东盟ASEAN,智利CL,新西兰NZ,秘鲁PE,哥斯达黎加CR 5 巴基斯坦PK	0 最不发达35国LDC35,最不发达4国LDC4	30	----Worsted Roving Machines
6401	8445.1329	----其他	10	0 东盟ASEAN,智利CL,新西兰NZ,秘鲁PE,哥斯达黎加CR 5 巴基斯坦PK	0 最不发达35国LDC35,最不发达4国LDC4	30	----Other
6402	8445.1900	--其他	10	0 东盟ASEAN,新西兰NZ,哥斯达黎加CR 1 智利CL 5 巴基斯坦PK,秘鲁PE 9 亚太APTA	0 最不发达35国LDC35,最不发达4国LDC4	30	--Other

序号 No.	税则号列 Tariff Line	货品名称	最惠国税率 MFN(%)	协定税率 Agreement(%)	特惠税率 S.P.(%)	普通税率 Gen.(%)	Article Description
		-纺纱机:					-Textile spinning machines:
		---自由端纺纱机:					---Open-end spinner:
6403	8445.2031	----转杯纺纱机	10	0 东盟ASEAN,智利CL,新西兰NZ,秘鲁PE,哥斯达黎加CR 5 巴基斯坦PK 9 亚太APTA	0 最不发达35国LDC35,最不发达4国LDC4	30	----Rotor spinning machine
	ex84452031	全自动转杯纺纱机	△5				Automatic rotor spinning machines
6404	8445.2032	----喷气纺纱机	10	0 东盟ASEAN,智利CL,新西兰NZ,秘鲁PE,哥斯达黎加CR 5 巴基斯坦PK	0 最不发达35国LDC35,最不发达4国LDC4	30	----Jet spinner
6405	8445.2039	----其他	10	0 东盟ASEAN,智利CL,新西兰NZ,秘鲁PE,哥斯达黎加CR 5 巴基斯坦PK	0 最不发达35国LDC35,最不发达4国LDC4	30	----Other
		---环锭细纱机:					---Ring spinning frames:
6406	8445.2041	----棉细纱机	10.5	0 东盟ASEAN,智利CL,新加坡SG,新西兰NZ,秘鲁PE 2.1 哥斯达黎加CR 5 巴基斯坦PK 9.5 亚太APTA	0 最不发达35国LDC35,最不发达4国LDC4	40	----Cotton Ring Spinning Frame
6407	8445.2042	----毛细纱机	10	0 东盟ASEAN,智利CL,新西兰NZ,秘鲁PE,哥斯达黎加CR 5 巴基斯坦PK	0 最不发达35国LDC35,最不发达4国LDC4	40	----Worsted Ring Spinning Frame
6408	8445.2049	----其他	10	0 东盟ASEAN,智利CL,新西兰NZ,秘鲁PE,哥斯达黎加CR 5 巴基斯坦PK	0 最不发达35国LDC35,最不发达4国LDC4	40	----Other
6409	8445.2090	---其他	10	0 东盟ASEAN,智利CL,新西兰NZ,秘鲁PE,哥斯达黎加CR 5 巴基斯坦PK 9 亚太APTA	0 最不发达35国LDC35,最不发达4国LDC4	30	---Other
6410	8445.3000	-并线机或加捻机	10	0 东盟ASEAN,智利CL,新西兰NZ,秘鲁PE,哥斯达黎加CR 5 巴基斯坦PK 9 亚太APTA	0 最不发达35国LDC35,最不发达4国LDC4	30	-Textile doubling or twisting machines

序号 No.	税则号列 Tariff Line	货品名称	最惠国税率 MFN(%)	协定税率 Agreement(%)		特惠税率 S.P.(%)		普通税率 Gen.(%)	Article Description
		-络纱机（包括卷纬机）或摇纱机:							-Textile winding (including weft-winding) or reeling machines:
6411	8445.4010	---自动络筒机	10 △6	0 1 5 9	东盟ASEAN,新西兰NZ,哥斯达黎加CR 智利CL 巴基斯坦PK,秘鲁PE 亚太APTA	0	最不发达35国LDC35,最不发达4国LDC4	30	---Automatic bobbin winders
6412	8445.4090	---其他	10	0 1 5 9	东盟ASEAN,新西兰NZ,哥斯达黎加CR 智利CL 巴基斯坦PK,秘鲁PE 亚太APTA	0	最不发达35国LDC35,最不发达4国LDC4	30	---Other
		-其他:							-Other:
6413	8445.9010	---整经机	10	0 1 5 9	东盟ASEAN,新西兰NZ,秘鲁PE,哥斯达黎加CR 智利CL 巴基斯坦PK 亚太APTA	0	最不发达35国LDC35,最不发达4国LDC4	30	---Warping machines
6414	8445.9020	---浆纱机	10	0 1 5 9	东盟ASEAN,新西兰NZ,秘鲁PE,哥斯达黎加CR 智利CL 巴基斯坦PK 亚太APTA	0	最不发达35国LDC35,最不发达4国LDC4	30	---Sizing machines
6415	8445.9090	---其他	10	0 1 5 9	东盟ASEAN,新西兰NZ,秘鲁PE,哥斯达黎加CR 智利CL 巴基斯坦PK 亚太APTA	0	最不发达35国LDC35,最不发达4国LDC4	30	---Other
	84.46	**织机:**							**Weaving machines (looms):**
6416	8446.1000	-所织织物宽度不超过30厘米的织机	8	0 5 7.2	东盟ASEAN,智利CL,新西兰NZ,秘鲁PE,哥斯达黎加CR 巴基斯坦PK 亚太APTA	0	最不发达35国LDC35	30	-For weaving fabrics of a width not exceeding 30cm
		-所织织物宽度超过30厘米的梭织机:							-For weaving fabrics of width exceeding 30cm, shuttle type:
		--动力织机:							--Power looms:
6417	8446.2110	---地毯织机	12	0 1.2 2.4 5 6 10.8	东盟ASEAN,新加坡SG,新西兰NZ 智利CL 哥斯达黎加CR 巴基斯坦PK 秘鲁PE 亚太APTA	0	最不发达35国LDC35	35	---For making carpets or rugs

序号 No.	税则号列 Tariff Line	货品名称	最惠国税率 MFN(%)	协定税率 Agreement(%)		特惠税率 S.P.(%)		普通税率 Gen.(%)	Article Description
6418	8446.2190	---其他	10	0 1 5 9	东盟ASEAN,新加坡SG,新西兰NZ,哥斯达黎加CR 智利CL 巴基斯坦PK,秘鲁PE 亚太APTA	0	最不发达35国LDC35	30	---Other
6419	8446.2900	--其他	10	0 1 5	东盟ASEAN,新西兰NZ,哥斯达黎加CR 智利CL 巴基斯坦PK,秘鲁PE	0	最不发达35国LDC35	30	--Other
		-所织织物宽度超过30厘米的无梭织机:							-For weaving fabrics of a width exceeding 30cm, shuttleless type:
6420	8446.3020	---剑杆织机	8	0 0.8 5 6.8	东盟ASEAN,新西兰NZ,秘鲁PE,哥斯达黎加CR 智利CL 巴基斯坦PK 亚太APTA	0	最不发达35国LDC35	30	---Rapier looms
6421	8446.3030	---片梭织机	8	0 0.8 5 5.6	东盟ASEAN,新西兰NZ,秘鲁PE,哥斯达黎加CR 智利CL 巴基斯坦PK 亚太APTA	0	最不发达35国LDC35	30	---Carrier looms
6422	8446.3040	---喷水织机	8	0 0.8 5 6.8	东盟ASEAN,新西兰NZ,秘鲁PE,哥斯达黎加CR,台湾TW 智利CL 巴基斯坦PK 亚太APTA	0	最不发达35国LDC35	30	---Water jet looms
6423	8446.3050	---喷气织机	8 △0	0 0.8 5 6.8	东盟ASEAN,新西兰NZ,秘鲁PE,哥斯达黎加CR 智利CL 巴基斯坦PK 亚太APTA	0	最不发达35国LDC35	30	---Air jet looms
6424	8446.3090	---其他	8	0 0.8 5 6.8	东盟ASEAN,新西兰NZ,秘鲁PE,哥斯达黎加CR 智利CL 巴基斯坦PK 亚太APTA	0	最不发达35国LDC35	30	---Other
	84.47	**针织机、缝编机及制粗松螺旋花线、网眼薄纱、花边、刺绣品、装饰带、编织带或网的机器及簇绒机:**							**Knitting machines, stitch-bonding machines and machines for making gimped yarn, tulle lace, embroidery, trimmings, braid or net and machines for tufting:**
		-圆型针织机:							-Circular knitting machines:

序号 No.	税则号列 Tariff Line	货品名称	最惠国税率 MFN(%)	协定税率 Agreement(%)		特惠税率 S.P.(%)		普通税率 Gen.(%)	Article Description
6425	8447.1100	--圆筒直径不超过165毫米	8	0 5 7	东盟ASEAN,智利CL,新西兰NZ,秘鲁PE,哥斯达黎加CR,台湾TW 巴基斯坦PK 亚太APTA	0	最不发达35国LDC35,最不发达4国LDC4	30	--With cylinder diameter not exceeding 165mm
6426	8447.1200	--圆筒直径超过165毫米	8	0 5	东盟ASEAN,智利CL,新西兰NZ,秘鲁PE,哥斯达黎加CR,台湾TW 巴基斯坦PK	0	最不发达35国LDC35,最不发达4国LDC4	30	--With cylinder diameter exceeding 165mm
		-平型针织机;缝编机:							-Flat knitting machines; stitch-bonding machines:
		---经编机:							---Warp knitting machines:
6427	8447.2011	----特里科经编机	8	0 5 6.8	东盟ASEAN,智利CL,新西兰NZ,秘鲁PE,哥斯达黎加CR 巴基斯坦PK 亚太APTA	0	最不发达35国LDC35,最不发达4国LDC4	30	----Tricot warp knitting machines
6428	8447.2012	----拉舍尔经编机	8	0 5 6.8	东盟ASEAN,智利CL,新西兰NZ,秘鲁PE,哥斯达黎加CR 巴基斯坦PK 亚太APTA	0	最不发达35国LDC35,最不发达4国LDC4	30	----Raschel warp knitting machine
6429	8447.2019	----其他	8	0 5 6.8	东盟ASEAN,智利CL,新西兰NZ,秘鲁PE,哥斯达黎加CR 巴基斯坦PK 亚太APTA	0	最不发达35国LDC35,最不发达4国LDC4	30	----Other
6430	8447.2020	---平型纬编机	8	0 5 6.8	东盟ASEAN,智利CL,新西兰NZ,秘鲁PE,哥斯达黎加CR,台湾TW 巴基斯坦PK 亚太APTA	0	最不发达35国LDC35,最不发达4国LDC4	30	---Flat weft knitting machines
6431	8447.2030	---缝编机	8	0 5 6.8	东盟ASEAN,智利CL,新西兰NZ,秘鲁PE,哥斯达黎加CR 巴基斯坦PK 亚太APTA	0	最不发达35国LDC35,最不发达4国LDC4	30	---Stitch-bonding machines
		-其他:							-Other:
		---簇绒机:							---Tufting machines:
6432	8447.9011	----地毯织机	7	0 4.9	东盟ASEAN,智利CL,巴基斯坦PK,新西兰NZ,秘鲁PE,哥斯达黎加CR 亚太APTA	0	最不发达35国LDC35,最不发达4国LDC4	35	----For making carpets or rugs

序号 No.	税则号列 Tariff Line	货品名称	最惠国税率 MFN(%)	协定税率 Agreement(%)	特惠税率 S.P.(%)	普通税率 Gen.(%)	Article Description
6433	8447.9019	----其他	8	0 东盟ASEAN,智利CL,新西兰NZ,秘鲁PE,哥斯达黎加CR 5 巴基斯坦PK 5.6 亚太APTA	0 最不发达35国LDC35,最不发达4国LDC4	30	----Other
6434	8447.9020	---绣花机	8	0 东盟ASEAN,智利CL,新西兰NZ,秘鲁PE,哥斯达黎加CR 5 巴基斯坦PK 6.8 亚太APTA	0 最不发达35国LDC35,最不发达4国LDC4	30	---Embroidery machines
6435	8447.9090	---其他	10	0 东盟ASEAN,智利CL,新西兰NZ,秘鲁PE,哥斯达黎加CR 5 亚太APTA,巴基斯坦PK	0 最不发达35国LDC35,最不发达4国LDC4	30	---Other
	84.48	**税号84.44、84.45、84.46或84.47所列机器的辅助机器（例如,多臂机、提花机、自停装置及换梭装置）;专用于或主要用于税号84.44、84.45、84.46或84.47所列机器的零件、附件(例如,锭子、锭壳、钢丝针布、梳、喷丝头、梭子、综丝、综框、针织机用针）:**					**Auxiliary machinery for use with machines of heading No.84.44, 84.45, 84.46 or 84.47 (for example, dobbies, Jacquards, automatic stop motions, shuttle changing mechanisms); parts and accessories suitable for use solely or principally with the machines of this heading or of heading No.84.44, 84.45, 84.46 or 84.47 (for example, spindles and spindle flyers, card clothing, combs, extruding nipples, shuttles, healds and heald-frames, hosiery needles):**
		-税号84.44、84.45、84.46或84.47所列机器的辅助机器:					-Auxiliary machinery for machines of heading No.84.44, 84.45, 84.46 or 84.47:
6436	8448.1100	--多臂机或提花机及其所用的卡片缩小、复制、穿孔或汇编机器	8	0 东盟ASEAN,智利CL,新西兰NZ,秘鲁PE,哥斯达黎加CR 5 巴基斯坦PK	0 最不发达35国LDC35,最不发达4国LDC4	20	--Dobbies and Jacquards; card reducing, copying, punching or assembling machines for use therewith
	ex84481100	多臂机或提花机，转速指标：500转/分以上	△4				Dobbies or Jacquards, rotational speed ＞ 500 r/min

序号 No.	税则号列 Tariff Line	货品名称	最惠国税率 MFN(%)	协定税率 Agreement(%)		特惠税率 S.P.(%)		普通税率 Gen.(%)	Article Description
6437	8448.1900	--其他	8	0 5	东盟ASEAN,智利CL,新西兰NZ,秘鲁PE,哥斯达黎加CR 巴基斯坦PK	0	最不发达35国LDC35,最不发达4国LDC4	20	--Other
		-税号84.44所列机器及其辅助机器的零件、附件:							-Parts and accessories of machines of heading No.84.44 or of their auxiliary machinery:
6438	8448.2020	---喷丝头或喷丝板	6	0 5	东盟ASEAN,智利CL,新西兰NZ,秘鲁PE,哥斯达黎加CR 巴基斯坦PK	0	最不发达35国LDC35,最不发达4国LDC4	14	---Extruding nipples or spinnerets
6439	8448.2090	---其他	6	0 5	东盟ASEAN,智利CL,新西兰NZ,秘鲁PE,哥斯达黎加CR 巴基斯坦PK	0	最不发达35国LDC35,最不发达4国LDC4	17	---Other
		-税号84.45所列机器及其辅助机器的零件、附件:							-Parts and accessories of machines of heading No.84.45 or of their auxiliary machinery:
6440	8448.3100	--钢丝针布	6	0 5	东盟ASEAN,智利CL,新西兰NZ,秘鲁PE,哥斯达黎加CR 巴基斯坦PK	0	最不发达35国LDC35,最不发达4国LDC4	17	--Card clothing
6441	8448.3200	--纺织纤维预处理机器的零件、附件,但钢丝针布除外	6	0 5	东盟ASEAN,智利CL,新西兰NZ,秘鲁PE,哥斯达黎加CR 巴基斯坦PK	0	最不发达35国LDC35,最不发达4国LDC4	17	--Of machines for preparing textile fibres, other than card clothing
		--锭子、锭壳、纺丝环、钢丝圈:							--Spindles, spindle flyers, spinning rings and ring travellers:
6442	8448.3310	---络筒锭	6	0 5	东盟ASEAN,智利CL,新西兰NZ,秘鲁PE,哥斯达黎加CR 巴基斯坦PK	0	最不发达35国LDC35,最不发达4国LDC4	17	---Winding spindle
6443	8448.3390	---其他	6	0 5	东盟ASEAN,智利CL,新西兰NZ,秘鲁PE,哥斯达黎加CR 巴基斯坦PK	0	最不发达35国LDC35,最不发达4国LDC4	17	---Other
		--其他:							--Other:

序号 No.	税则号列 Tariff Line	货品名称	最惠国税率 MFN(%)	协定税率 Agreement(%)		特惠税率 S.P.(%)		普通税率 Gen.(%)	Article Description
6444	8448.3910	---气流杯	6	0 5	东盟ASEAN,智利CL,新西兰NZ,秘鲁PE,哥斯达黎加CR 巴基斯坦PK	0	最不发达35国LDC35,最不发达4国LDC4	14	---Open-end rotors
6445	8448.3920	---电子清纱器	6 △3	0 5	东盟ASEAN,智利CL,新西兰NZ,秘鲁PE,哥斯达黎加CR 巴基斯坦PK	0	最不发达35国LDC35,最不发达4国LDC4	17	---Electronic yarn clearers
6446	8448.3930	---空气捻接器	6 △3	0 5	东盟ASEAN,智利CL,新西兰NZ,秘鲁PE,哥斯达黎加CR 巴基斯坦PK	0	最不发达35国LDC35,最不发达4国LDC4	17	---Air twisting devices
6447	8448.3940	---环锭细纱机紧密纺装置	6 △0	0 5	东盟ASEAN,智利CL,新西兰NZ,秘鲁PE,哥斯达黎加CR 巴基斯坦PK	0	最不发达35国LDC35,最不发达4国LDC4	17	---Compact set of ring spinning frames
6448	8448.3990	---其他	6 △3	0 5	东盟ASEAN,智利CL,新西兰NZ,秘鲁PE,哥斯达黎加CR 巴基斯坦PK	0	最不发达35国LDC35,最不发达4国LDC4	17	---Other
		-织机及其辅助机器的零件、附件:							-Parts and accessories of weaving machines (looms) or of their auxiliary machinery:
6449	8448.4200	--织机用筘、综丝及综框	6	0 5	东盟ASEAN,智利CL,新西兰NZ,秘鲁PE,哥斯达黎加CR 巴基斯坦PK	0	最不发达35国LDC35,最不发达4国LDC4	50	--Reeds for looms, healds and heald frames
		--其他:							--Other:
6450	8448.4910	---接、投梭箱	6	0 5	东盟ASEAN,智利CL,新西兰NZ,秘鲁PE,哥斯达黎加CR 巴基斯坦PK	0	最不发达35国LDC35,最不发达4国LDC4	17	---Catching and throwing shuttle boxes
6451	8448.4920	---引纬、送经装置	6 △3	0 5	东盟ASEAN,智利CL,新西兰NZ,秘鲁PE,哥斯达黎加CR 巴基斯坦PK	0	最不发达35国LDC35,最不发达4国LDC4	17	---Weft insertion and let-off motions

序号 No.	税则号列 Tariff Line	货品名称	最惠国税 率 MFN(%)	协定税率 Agreement(%)	特惠税率 S.P.(%)	普通税率 Gen.(%)	Article Description
6452	8448.4930	---梭子	6	0 东盟ASEAN,智利CL,新西兰NZ,秘鲁PE,哥斯达黎加CR 5 巴基斯坦PK	0 最不发达35国LDC35,最不发达4国LDC4	50	---Shuttles
6453	8448.4990	---其他	6 △3	0 东盟ASEAN,智利CL,新西兰NZ,秘鲁PE,哥斯达黎加CR 5 巴基斯坦PK	0 最不发达35国LDC35,最不发达4国LDC4	17	---Other
		-税号84.47所列机器及其辅助机器的零件、附件:					-Parts and accessories of machines of heading No.84.47 or of their auxiliary machinery:
		--沉降片、织针及其他成圈机件:					--Sinkers, needles and other articles used in forming stitches:
6454	8448.5120	---针织机用28号以下的弹簧针、钩针及复合针	6	0 东盟ASEAN,智利CL,新西兰NZ,秘鲁PE,哥斯达黎加CR 5 巴基斯坦PK	0 最不发达35国LDC35,最不发达4国LDC4	50	---Barbered needles, crotchet hooks and complex needles for knitting machines, smaler than gauge No.28
6455	8448.5190	---其他	6	0 东盟ASEAN,智利CL,新西兰NZ,秘鲁PE,哥斯达黎加CR 5 巴基斯坦PK	0 最不发达35国LDC35,最不发达4国LDC4	17	---Other
6456	8448.5900	--其他	6 △3	0 东盟ASEAN,智利CL,新西兰NZ,秘鲁PE,哥斯达黎加CR,香港HK,台湾TW 5 巴基斯坦PK	0 最不发达35国LDC35,最不发达4国LDC4	17	--Other
	84.49	**成匹、成形的毡呢或无纺织物制造或整理机器,包括制毡呢帽机器;帽模:**					**Machinery for the manufacture or finishing of felt or nonwovens in the piece or in shapes, including machinery for making felt hats; blocks for making hats:**
		成匹、成形的毡呢或无纺织物制造或整理机器,包括制毡呢帽机器;帽模					Machinery for the manufacture or finishing of felt or nonwovens in the piece or in shapes, including machinery for making felt hats; blocks for making hats

序号 No.	税则号列 Tariff Line	货品名称	最惠国税率 MFN(%)	协定税率 Agreement(%)		特惠税率 S.P.(%)		普通税率 Gen.(%)	Article Description
6457	8449.0010	---针刺机	8	0 5	东盟ASEAN,智利CL,新西兰NZ,秘鲁PE,哥斯达黎加CR 巴基斯坦PK	0	最不发达35国LDC35	30	---Needle punching machine
	ex84490010	高速针刺机，针刺频率＞2000次/分钟	△6						High speed needle punching machine, punching frequecny ＞ 2000bis/min
6458	8449.0020	---水刺设备	8	0 5	东盟ASEAN,智利CL,新西兰NZ,秘鲁PE,哥斯达黎加CR 巴基斯坦PK	0	最不发达35国LDC35	30	---Spunlace equipment
	ex84490020	高速宽幅水刺设备，工作幅宽＞3.5米，工作速度＞250米/分钟，水刺压力≥400帕	△6						High speed width spunlace equipment, working width＞3.5m, workding speed＞250m/min, spunlace pressure≥400Pa
6459	8449.0090	---其他	8	0 5	东盟ASEAN,智利CL,新西兰NZ,秘鲁PE,哥斯达黎加CR 巴基斯坦PK	0	最不发达35国LDC35	30	---Other
	84.50	**家用型或洗衣房用洗衣机,包括洗涤干燥两用机:**							**Household or laundry-type washing machines, including machines which both wash and dry:**
		-干衣量不超过10公斤的洗衣机:							-Machines, each of a dry linen capacity not exceeding 10kg:
		--全自动的:							--Fully-automatic machines:
6460	8450.1110	---波轮式	10	0 1 5 8.7	东盟ASEAN,新加坡SG,新西兰NZ,秘鲁PE,哥斯达黎加CR 智利CL 巴基斯坦PK 亚太APTA	0	最不发达35国LDC35,最不发达4国LDC4	130	---Of the continuously rotating impeller
6461	8450.1120	---滚筒式	10	0 1 5 8.7	东盟ASEAN,新加坡SG,新西兰NZ,秘鲁PE,哥斯达黎加CR 智利CL 巴基斯坦PK 亚太APTA	0	最不发达35国LDC35,最不发达4国LDC4	130	---Of the drum type
6462	8450.1190	---其他	10	0 1 5 8.7	东盟ASEAN,新加坡SG,新西兰NZ,秘鲁PE,哥斯达黎加CR 智利CL 巴基斯坦PK 亚太APTA	0	最不发达35国LDC35,最不发达4国LDC4	130	---Other

序号 No.	税则号列 Tariff Line	货品名称	最惠国税率 MFN(%)	协定税率 Agreement(%)		特惠税率 S.P.(%)		普通税率 Gen.(%)	Article Description
6463	8450.1200	--其他机器,装有离心甩干机	30	0 6 15 24.9	东盟ASEAN,智利CL,新加坡SG,新西兰NZ 哥斯达黎加CR 秘鲁PE 亚太APTA,巴基斯坦PK	0	最不发达35国LDC35	130	--Other machines, with built-in centrifugal drier
6464	8450.1900	--其他	30	0 6 15	东盟ASEAN,智利CL,新加坡SG,新西兰NZ 哥斯达黎加CR 秘鲁PE	0	最不发达35国LDC35	130	--Other
		-干衣量超过10公斤的洗衣机:							-Machines, each of a dry linen capacity exceeding 10kg:
		---全自动的:							---Fully-automatic machines:
6465	8450.2011	----波轮式	10	0 5	东盟ASEAN,智利CL,新西兰NZ,秘鲁PE,哥斯达黎加CR 巴基斯坦PK	0	最不发达35国LDC35,最不发达4国LDC4	80	----Of the continuously rotating impeller
6466	8450.2012	----滚筒式	10	0 5	东盟ASEAN,智利CL,新西兰NZ,秘鲁PE,哥斯达黎加CR 巴基斯坦PK	0	最不发达35国LDC35,最不发达4国LDC4	80	----Of the drum type
6467	8450.2019	----其他	10	0 5	东盟ASEAN,智利CL,新西兰NZ,秘鲁PE,哥斯达黎加CR 巴基斯坦PK	0	最不发达35国LDC35,最不发达4国LDC4	80	----Other
6468	8450.2090	---其他	10	0 5	东盟ASEAN,智利CL,新西兰NZ,秘鲁PE,哥斯达黎加CR 巴基斯坦PK	0	最不发达35国LDC35,最不发达4国LDC4	80	---Other
		-零件:							-Parts:
6469	8450.9010	---干衣量不超过10公斤的洗衣机用	5	0 4.2	东盟ASEAN,智利CL,巴基斯坦PK,新西兰NZ,秘鲁PE,哥斯达黎加CR 亚太APTA	0	最不发达35国LDC35,最不发达4国LDC4	130	---Of the machines of subheadings Nos. 8450.1110 to 8450.1900
6470	8450.9090	---其他	16 △5	0 3.2 8 12.8 14.4	东盟ASEAN,智利CL,新加坡SG,新西兰NZ 哥斯达黎加CR 秘鲁PE 巴基斯坦PK 亚太APTA	0	最不发达35国LDC35	80	---Other

序号 No.	税则号列 Tariff Line	货品名称	最惠国税率 MFN(%)	协定税率 Agreement(%)		特惠税率 S.P.(%)		普通税率 Gen.(%)	Article Description
	84.51	**纱线、织物及纺织制品的洗涤、清洁、绞拧、干燥、熨烫、挤压（包括熔压）、漂白、染色、上浆、整理、涂布或浸渍机器（税号 84.50 的机器除外）；列诺伦（亚麻油地毡）及类似铺地制品的布基或其他底布的浆料涂布机器；纺织物的卷绕、退绕、折叠、剪切或剪齿边机器：**							**Machinery (other than machines of heading No.84.50) for washing, cleaning, wringing, drying, ironing, pressing (including fusing presses), bleaching, dyeing, dressing, finishing, coating or impregnating textile yarns, fabrics or made up textile articles and machines for applying the paste to the base fabric or other support used in the manufacture of floor coverings such as linoleum; machines for reeling, unreeling, folding, cutting or pinking textile fabrics:**
6471	8451.1000	-干洗机	21	0 4.2 10.5 16	东盟ASEAN,智利CL,新加坡SG,新西兰NZ 哥斯达黎加CR 秘鲁PE 亚太APTA,巴基斯坦PK	0	最不发达 35 国 LDC35	80	-Dry-cleaning machines
		-干燥机:							-Drying machines:
6472	8451.2100	--干衣量不超过 10 公斤	15	0 1.5 3 7.5 13.5	东盟ASEAN,新加坡SG,新西兰NZ 智利CL 哥斯达黎加CR 巴基斯坦PK,秘鲁PE 亚太APTA	0	最不发达 35 国 LDC35	80	--Each of a dry linen capacity not exceeding 10kg
6473	8451.2900	--其他	8	0 5 7.2	东盟ASEAN,智利CL,新西兰NZ,秘鲁PE,哥斯达黎加CR 巴基斯坦PK 亚太APTA	0	最不发达 35 国 LDC35,最不发达 4 国 LDC4	30	--Other
6474	8451.3000	-熨烫机及挤压机（包括熔压机）	8	0 5 7.2	东盟ASEAN,智利CL,新加坡SG,新西兰NZ,秘鲁PE,哥斯达黎加CR 巴基斯坦PK 亚太APTA	0	最不发达 35 国 LDC35,最不发达 4 国 LDC4	30	-Ironing machines and presses (including fusing presses)
6475	8451.4000	-洗涤、漂白或染色机器	8.4	0 5 7	东盟ASEAN,智利CL,新西兰NZ,秘鲁PE,哥斯达黎加CR,香港HK,澳门MO,台湾TW 巴基斯坦PK 亚太APTA	0	最不发达 35 国 LDC35,最不发达 4 国 LDC4	20	-Washing, bleaching or dyeing machines
6476	8451.5000	-纺织物的卷绕、退绕、折叠、剪切或剪齿边机器	8	0 0.8 5 7.2	东盟ASEAN,新西兰NZ,秘鲁PE,哥斯达黎加CR,台湾TW 智利CL 巴基斯坦PK 亚太APTA	0	最不发达 35 国 LDC35,最不发达 4 国 LDC4	20	-Machines for reeling, unreeling, folding, cutting or pinking textile fabrics

序号 No.	税则号列 Tariff Line	货品名称	最惠国税率 MFN(%)	协定税率 Agreement(%)		特惠税率 S.P.(%)		普通税率 Gen.(%)	Article Description
6477	8451.8000	-其他机器	12	0 1.2 2.4 5 6 10.8	东盟ASEAN,新加坡SG,新西兰NZ,香港HK,台湾TW 智利CL 哥斯达黎加CR 巴基斯坦PK 秘鲁PE 亚太APTA	0	最不发达35国LDC35,最不发达4国LDC4	30	-Other machinery
	ex84518000	柔软整理机	△10						Supple finishing machine
	ex84518000	磨毛机、丝光机	△10						Napping grinder, mercerizing range
	ex84518000	定型机	△10						Boarding machine
	ex84518000	涂层机	△8						Coating machine
	ex84518000	罐蒸机、精炼机	△10						Potting steamer, refining machine
	ex84518000	剪绒、洗缩联合机	△10						Pile shearing and shrinking combine
	ex84518000	预缩机	△10						Sanforizer
	ex84518000	服装液氨整理机	△10						Dress aqua ammoniae finishing range
	ex84518000	服装定型焙烘炉	△10						Dress shaping cabinet
	ex84518000	剪毛联合机	△10						Sheepshearing combination machine
6478	8451.9000	-零件	8	0 5 7.2	东盟ASEAN,智利CL,新西兰NZ,秘鲁PE,哥斯达黎加CR 巴基斯坦PK 亚太APTA	0	最不发达35国LDC35,最不发达4国LDC4	20	-Parts
	84.52	**缝纫机,但税号84.40的锁线订书机除外;缝纫机专用的特制家具、底座及罩盖;缝纫机针:**							**Sewing machines, other than book- sewing machines of heading No.84.40; furniture, bases and covers specially designed for sewing machines; sewing machine needles:**
		-家用型缝纫机:							-Sewing machines of household type:
6479	8452.1010	---多功能型	21	0 2.1 4.2 10.5 16.8 17	东盟ASEAN,新加坡SG,新西兰NZ 智利CL 哥斯达黎加CR 秘鲁PE 巴基斯坦PK 亚太APTA	0	最不发达35国LDC35	80	---Multifunctional
		---其他:							---Other:
6480	8452.1091	----手动式	21	0 2.1 4.2 10.5 16.8 17	东盟ASEAN,新加坡SG,新西兰NZ 智利CL 哥斯达黎加CR 秘鲁PE 巴基斯坦PK 亚太APTA	0	最不发达35国LDC35	80	----Hand-operated

序号 No.	税则号列 Tariff Line	货品名称	最惠国税率 MFN(%)	协定税率 Agreement(%)	特惠税率 S.P.(%)	普通税率 Gen.(%)	Article Description
6481	8452.1099	----其他	21	0 东盟ASEAN,新加坡SG,新西兰NZ 2.1 智利CL 4.2 哥斯达黎加CR 10.5 秘鲁PE 16.8 巴基斯坦PK 17 亚太APTA	0 最不发达35国LDC35	80	----Other
		-其他缝纫机:					-Other sewing machines:
		--自动的:					--Automatic units:
6482	8452.2110	---平缝机	12	0 东盟ASEAN,新加坡SG,新西兰NZ,秘鲁PE 1.2 智利CL 2.4 哥斯达黎加CR 5 巴基斯坦PK 10.7 亚太APTA	0 最不发达35国LDC35,最不发达4国LDC4	40	---Flatseam
6483	8452.2120	---包缝机	12	0 东盟ASEAN,新加坡SG,新西兰NZ,秘鲁PE,台湾TW 1.2 智利CL 2.4 哥斯达黎加CR 5 巴基斯坦PK 10.7 亚太APTA	0 最不发达35国LDC35,最不发达4国LDC4	40	---Overlock stitch
6484	8452.2130	---绷缝机	12	0 东盟ASEAN,新加坡SG,新西兰NZ,秘鲁PE,台湾TW 1.2 智利CL 2.4 哥斯达黎加CR 5 巴基斯坦PK 10.7 亚太APTA	0 最不发达35国LDC35,最不发达4国LDC4	40	---Covering stitch
6485	8452.2190	---其他	12	0 东盟ASEAN,新加坡SG,新西兰NZ,秘鲁PE,台湾TW 1.2 智利CL 2.4 哥斯达黎加CR 5 巴基斯坦PK 10.7 亚太APTA	0 最不发达35国LDC35,最不发达4国LDC4	40	---Other
6486	8452.2900	--其他	12	0 东盟ASEAN,新加坡SG,新西兰NZ,秘鲁PE,香港HK 1.2 智利CL 2.4 哥斯达黎加CR 5 巴基斯坦PK 10.8 亚太APTA	0 最不发达35国LDC35,最不发达4国LDC4	40	--Other
6487	8452.3000	-缝纫机针	14	0 东盟ASEAN,智利CL,新加坡SG,新西兰NZ,秘鲁PE 2.8 哥斯达黎加CR 7 巴基斯坦PK 12.6 亚太APTA	0 最不发达35国LDC35	100	-Sewing machine needles
		-缝纫机专用的特制家具、底座和罩盖及其零件；缝纫机的其他零件:					-Furniture, bases and covers for sewing machines and parts thereof; other parts of sewing machines:

序号 No.	税则号列 Tariff Line	货品名称	最惠国税率 MFN(%)	协定税率 Agreement(%)		特惠税率 S.P.(%)		普通税率 Gen.(%)	Article Description
		---家用型缝纫机用:							---Of sewing machines of the household type:
6488	8452.9011	----旋梭	14	0 1.4 2.8 7 9.8	东盟ASEAN,新加坡SG,新西兰NZ,秘鲁PE 智利CL 哥斯达黎加CR 巴基斯坦PK 亚太APTA	0	最不发达35国LDC35	80	----Rotating shuttles
6489	8452.9019	----其他	14	0 1.4 2.8 7 9.8	东盟ASEAN,新加坡SG,新西兰NZ,秘鲁PE 智利CL 哥斯达黎加CR 巴基斯坦PK 亚太APTA	0	最不发达35国LDC35	80	----Other
		---其他:							---Other:
6490	8452.9091	----旋梭	14	0 1.4 2.8 7 9.8	东盟ASEAN,新加坡SG,新西兰NZ,秘鲁PE 智利CL 哥斯达黎加CR 巴基斯坦PK 亚太APTA	0	最不发达35国LDC35,最不发达4国LDC4	80	----Rotating shuttles
6491	8452.9092	----缝纫机专用的特制家具、底座和罩盖及其零件	14	0 2.8 11.2	东盟ASEAN,智利CL,新加坡SG,新西兰NZ,秘鲁PE 哥斯达黎加CR 巴基斯坦PK	0	最不发达35国LDC35	100	----Furniture, bases and covers for sewing machines and parts thereof
6492	8452.9099	----其他	14	0 1.4 2.8 7 9.8	东盟ASEAN,新加坡SG,新西兰NZ,秘鲁PE,台湾TW 智利CL 哥斯达黎加CR 巴基斯坦PK 亚太APTA	0	最不发达35国LDC35,最不发达4国LDC4	80	----Other
	84.53	**生皮、皮革的处理、鞣制或加工机器,鞋靴、毛皮及其他皮革制品的制作或修理机器,但缝纫机除外:**							**Machinery for preparing, tanning or working hides, skins or leather or for making or repairing footwear or other articles of hides, skins or leather, other than sewing machines:**
6493	8453.1000	-生皮、皮革的处理、鞣制或加工机器	8.4	0 0.8 5 8	东盟ASEAN,新西兰NZ,秘鲁PE,哥斯达黎加CR 智利CL 巴基斯坦PK 亚太APTA	0	最不发达35国LDC35	30	-Machinery for preparing, tanning or working hides, skins or leather
6494	8453.2000	-鞋靴制作或修理机器	8.4	0 5 8	东盟ASEAN,智利CL,新西兰NZ,秘鲁PE,哥斯达黎加CR 巴基斯坦PK 亚太APTA	0	最不发达35国LDC35	30	-Machinery for making or repairing footwear

序号 No.	税则号列 Tariff Line	货品名称	最惠国税率 MFN(%)	协定税率 Agreement(%)		特惠税率 S.P.(%)		普通税率 Gen.(%)	Article Description
6495	8453.8000	-其他机器	8.4	0 5	东盟ASEAN,智利CL,新西兰NZ,秘鲁PE,哥斯达黎加CR 巴基斯坦PK	0	最不发达35国LDC35	30	-Other machinery
6496	8453.9000	-零件	8	0 5	东盟ASEAN,智利CL,新西兰NZ,秘鲁PE,哥斯达黎加CR 巴基斯坦PK	0	最不发达35国LDC35	30	-Parts
	84.54	**金属冶炼及铸造用的转炉、浇包、锭模及铸造机:**							**Converters, ladles, ingot moulds and casting machines, of a kind used in metallurgy or in metal foundries:**
6497	8454.1000	-转炉	8.4	0 5	东盟ASEAN,智利CL,新西兰NZ,秘鲁PE,哥斯达黎加CR 巴基斯坦PK	0	最不发达35国LDC35,最不发达4国LDC4	35	-Converters
		-锭模及浇包:							-Ingot moulds and ladles:
6498	8454.2010	---炉外精炼设备	8.4	0 5	东盟ASEAN,智利CL,新西兰NZ,秘鲁PE,哥斯达黎加CR 巴基斯坦PK	0	最不发达35国LDC35,最不发达4国LDC4	35	---Fining equipments, outside of converters
6499	8454.2090	---其他	8.4	0 5	东盟ASEAN,智利CL,新西兰NZ,秘鲁PE,哥斯达黎加CR 巴基斯坦PK	0	最不发达35国LDC35,最不发达4国LDC4	35	---Other
		-铸造机:							-Casting machines:
6500	8454.3010	---冷室压铸机	12	0 2.4 6 11.4	东盟ASEAN,智利CL,新加坡SG,新西兰NZ,秘鲁PE 哥斯达黎加CR 巴基斯坦PK 亚太APTA	0	最不发达35国LDC35,最不发达4国LDC4	35	---Cold chamber die-casting machines
		---钢坯连铸机:							---Ingot continuous casting machines:
6501	8454.3021	----方坯连铸机	10	0 5 9.5	东盟ASEAN,智利CL,新西兰NZ,秘鲁PE,哥斯达黎加CR 巴基斯坦PK 亚太APTA	0	最不发达35国LDC35,最不发达4国LDC4	35	----Ingot block
6502	8454.3022	----板坯连铸机	12	0 2.4 6 11.4	东盟ASEAN,智利CL,新加坡SG,新西兰NZ,秘鲁PE 哥斯达黎加CR 巴基斯坦PK 亚太APTA	0	最不发达35国LDC35,最不发达4国LDC4	35	----Ingot slab

序号 No.	税则号列 Tariff Line	货品名称	最惠国税率 MFN(%)	协定税率 Agreement(%)		特惠税率 S.P.(%)		普通税率 Gen.(%)	Article Description
6503	8454.3029	----其他	12	0 2.4 6 11.4	东盟ASEAN,智利CL,新加坡SG,新西兰NZ,秘鲁PE 哥斯达黎加CR 巴基斯坦PK 亚太APTA	0	最不发达35国LDC35,最不发达4国LDC4	35	----Other
6504	8454.3090	---其他	12	0 2.4 6 11.4	东盟ASEAN,智利CL,新加坡SG,新西兰NZ,秘鲁PE 哥斯达黎加CR 巴基斯坦PK 亚太APTA	0	最不发达35国LDC35,最不发达4国LDC4	35	---Other
		-零件:							-Parts:
6505	8454.9010	---炉外精炼设备用	8	0 0.8 5	东盟ASEAN,新西兰NZ,秘鲁PE,哥斯达黎加CR 智利CL 巴基斯坦PK	0	最不发达35国LDC35,最不发达4国LDC4	20	---For the fining equipments outside of converters
		---钢坯连铸机用:							---For ingot continuous casting machines:
6506	8454.9021	----结晶器	8	0 0.8 5	东盟ASEAN,新西兰NZ,秘鲁PE,哥斯达黎加CR 智利CL 巴基斯坦PK	0	最不发达35国LDC35,最不发达4国LDC4	20	----Crystallizers
6507	8454.9022	----振动装置	8	0 0.8 5	东盟ASEAN,新西兰NZ,秘鲁PE,哥斯达黎加CR 智利CL 巴基斯坦PK	0	最不发达35国LDC35,最不发达4国LDC4	20	----Vibrating devices
6508	8454.9029	----其他	8	0 0.8 5	东盟ASEAN,新西兰NZ,秘鲁PE,哥斯达黎加CR 智利CL 巴基斯坦PK	0	最不发达35国LDC35,最不发达4国LDC4	20	----Other
6509	8454.9090	---其他	8	0 0.8 5	东盟ASEAN,新西兰NZ,秘鲁PE,哥斯达黎加CR 智利CL 巴基斯坦PK	0	最不发达35国LDC35,最不发达4国LDC4	20	---Other
	84.55	**金属轧机及其轧辊:**							**Metal-rolling mills and rolls thereof:**
		-轧管机:							-Tube mills:
6510	8455.1010	---热轧管机	12	0 2.4 5 8.4	东盟ASEAN,智利CL,新加坡SG,新西兰NZ,秘鲁PE 哥斯达黎加CR 巴基斯坦PK 亚太APTA	0	最不发达35国LDC35,最不发达4国LDC4	35	---Tube mills, for hot-rolled

序号 No.	税则号列 Tariff Line	货品名称	最惠国税率 MFN(%)	协定税率 Agreement(%)		特惠税率 S.P.(%)		普通税率 Gen.(%)	Article Description
6511	8455.1020	---冷轧管机	12	0 2.4 5 8.4	东盟ASEAN,智利CL,新加坡SG,新西兰NZ,秘鲁PE 哥斯达黎加CR 巴基斯坦PK 亚太APTA	0	最不发达35国LDC35,最不发达4国LDC4	35	---Tube mills for cold-rolled
6512	8455.1030	---定减径轧管机	12	0 2.4 5 8.4	东盟ASEAN,智利CL,新加坡SG,新西兰NZ,秘鲁PE 哥斯达黎加CR 巴基斯坦PK 亚太APTA	0	最不发达35国LDC35,最不发达4国LDC4	35	---Fixed and reduced tube mills
6513	8455.1090	---其他	12	0 2.4 5 8.4	东盟ASEAN,智利CL,新加坡SG,新西兰NZ,秘鲁PE 哥斯达黎加CR 巴基斯坦PK 亚太APTA	0	最不发达35国LDC35,最不发达4国LDC4	35	---Other
		-其他轧机: --热轧机或冷热联合轧机:							-Other rolling mills: --Hot or combination hot and cold:
6514	8455.2110	---板材热轧机	15	0 1.5 3 7.5 10.5	东盟ASEAN,新加坡SG,新西兰NZ 智利CL 哥斯达黎加CR 巴基斯坦PK,秘鲁PE 亚太APTA	0	最不发达35国LDC35	35	---Sheet mills, hot-rolled
6515	8455.2120	---型钢轧机	15	0 1.5 3 7.5 10.5	东盟ASEAN,新加坡SG,新西兰NZ 智利CL 哥斯达黎加CR 巴基斯坦PK,秘鲁PE 亚太APTA	0	最不发达35国LDC35	35	---Rolled-steel section mills
6516	8455.2130	---线材轧机	15	0 1.5 3 7.5 10.5	东盟ASEAN,新加坡SG,新西兰NZ 智利CL 哥斯达黎加CR 巴基斯坦PK,秘鲁PE 亚太APTA	0	最不发达35国LDC35	35	---Wire mills
6517	8455.2190	---其他	15	0 1.5 3 7.5 10.5	东盟ASEAN,新加坡SG,新西兰NZ 智利CL 哥斯达黎加CR 巴基斯坦PK,秘鲁PE 亚太APTA	0	最不发达35国LDC35	35	---Other
		--冷轧机:							--Cold mills:
6518	8455.2210	---板材冷轧机	10	0 5	东盟ASEAN,智利CL,新西兰NZ,秘鲁PE,哥斯达黎加CR 巴基斯坦PK	0	最不发达35国LDC35	35	---Sheet mills
6519	8455.2290	---其他	15	0 3 7.5 12	东盟ASEAN,智利CL,新加坡SG,新西兰NZ 哥斯达黎加CR 秘鲁PE 巴基斯坦PK	0	最不发达35国LDC35	35	---Other

序号 No.	税则号列 Tariff Line	货品名称	最惠国 税 率 MFN(%)	协定税率 Agreement(%)	特惠税率 S.P.(%)	普通 税率 Gen.(%)	Article Description
6520	8455.3000	-轧机用轧辊	8.4	0 东盟ASEAN,智利CL,新西兰NZ,秘鲁PE,哥斯达黎加CR 5 巴基斯坦PK	0 最不发达35国LDC35,最不发达4国LDC4	20	-Rolls for rolling mills
6521	8455.9000	-其他零件	8	0 东盟ASEAN,智利CL,巴基斯坦PK,新西兰NZ,秘鲁PE,哥斯达黎加CR 4 亚太APTA	0 最不发达35国LDC35,最不发达4国LDC4	20	-Other parts
	84.56	**用激光、其他光、光子束、超声波、放电、电化学法、电子束、离子束或等离子弧处理各种材料的加工机床；水射流切割机：**					**Machine-tools for working any material by removal of material, by laser or other light or photon beam, ultrasonic, electro-discharge, electro-chemical, electron beam, ionic-beam or plasma arc processes; water-jet cutting machines:**
6522	8456.1000	-用激光、其他光或光子束处理的	0		0 最不发达35国LDC35,最不发达4国LDC4	30	-Operated by laser or other light or photon beam processes
6523	8456.2000	-用超声波处理的	10	0 东盟ASEAN,智利CL,新加坡SG,新西兰NZ,秘鲁PE,哥斯达黎加CR 5 巴基斯坦PK	0 最不发达35国LDC35	30	-Operated by ultrasonic processes
		-用放电处理的:					-Operated by electro-discharge processes:
6524	8456.3010	---数控的	9.7	0 东盟ASEAN,智利CL,新西兰NZ,秘鲁PE,哥斯达黎加CR 5 巴基斯坦PK	0 最不发达35国LDC35	30	---Numerically controlled
6525	8456.3090	---其他	10	0 东盟ASEAN,智利CL,新加坡SG,新西兰NZ,秘鲁PE,哥斯达黎加CR 5 巴基斯坦PK	0 最不发达35国LDC35	30	---Other
		-其他:					-Other:
6526	8456.9010	---等离子切割机	0		0 最不发达35国LDC35,最不发达4国LDC4	30	---Cutting machines of plasma arc

序号 No.	税则号列 Tariff Line	货品名称	最惠国税率 MFN(%)	协定税率 Agreement(%)		特惠税率 S.P.(%)		普通税率 Gen.(%)	Article Description
6527	8456.9020	---水射流切割机	0			0	最不发达35国LDC35,最不发达4国LDC4	30	---Water-jet cutting machines
6528	8456.9090	---其他	0			0	最不发达35国LDC35,最不发达4国LDC4	30	---Other
	84.57	**加工金属的加工中心、单工位组合机床及多工位组合机床:**							**Machining centres, unit construction machines (single station) and multistation transfer machines, for working metal:**
		-加工中心:							-Machining centres:
6529	8457.1010	---立式	9.7	0 5 6.8	东盟ASEAN,智利CL,新西兰NZ,秘鲁PE,哥斯达黎加CR 巴基斯坦PK 亚太APTA	0	最不发达35国LDC35	20	---Vertical
6530	8457.1020	---卧式	9.7	0 5 8.8	东盟ASEAN,智利CL,新西兰NZ,秘鲁PE,哥斯达黎加CR 巴基斯坦PK 亚太APTA	0	最不发达35国LDC35	20	---Horizontal
6531	8457.1030	---龙门式	9.7	0 5 6.8	东盟ASEAN,智利CL,新西兰NZ,秘鲁PE,哥斯达黎加CR 巴基斯坦PK 亚太APTA	0	最不发达35国LDC35	20	---Plano
		---其他:							---Other:
6532	8457.1091	----铣车复合	9.7	0 5 6.8	东盟ASEAN,智利CL,新西兰NZ,秘鲁PE,哥斯达黎加CR 巴基斯坦PK 亚太APTA	0	最不发达35国LDC35	20	----Turning with milling
6533	8457.1099	----其他	9.7	0 5 6.8	东盟ASEAN,智利CL,新西兰NZ,秘鲁PE,哥斯达黎加CR 巴基斯坦PK 亚太APTA	0	最不发达35国LDC35	20	----Other
6534	8457.2000	-单工位组合机床	8	0 5	东盟ASEAN,智利CL,新西兰NZ,秘鲁PE,哥斯达黎加CR 巴基斯坦PK	0	最不发达35国LDC35	20	-Unit construction machines (single station)
6535	8457.3000	-多工位组合机床	5	0 0.5	东盟ASEAN,巴基斯坦PK,新西兰NZ,秘鲁PE,哥斯达黎加CR 智利CL	0	最不发达35国LDC35	20	-Multi-station transfer machines

序号 No.	税则号列 Tariff Line	货品名称	最惠国税率 MFN(%)	协定税率 Agreement(%)		特惠税率 S.P.(%)		普通税率 Gen.(%)	Article Description
	84.58	**切削金属的车床（包括车削中心）：**							**Lathes (including turning centres) for removing metal:**
		-卧式车床:							-Horizontal lathes:
6536	8458.1100	--数控的	9.7	0 5	东盟ASEAN,智利CL,新西兰NZ,秘鲁PE,哥斯达黎加CR,香港HK,台湾TW 巴基斯坦PK	0	最不发达35国LDC35,最不发达4国LDC4	20	--Numerically controlled
6537	8458.1900	--其他	12	0 2.4 6	东盟ASEAN,智利CL,新加坡SG,新西兰NZ,秘鲁PE,香港HK 哥斯达黎加CR 巴基斯坦PK	0	最不发达35国LDC35,最不发达4国LDC4	50	--Other
		-其他车床:							-Other lathes:
		--数控的:							--Numerically controlled:
6538	8458.9110	---立式	5	0	东盟ASEAN,智利CL,巴基斯坦PK,新西兰NZ,秘鲁PE,哥斯达黎加CR,台湾TW	0	最不发达35国LDC35,最不发达4国LDC4	20	---Vertical
6539	8458.9120	---其他	5	0	东盟ASEAN,智利CL,巴基斯坦PK,新西兰NZ,秘鲁PE,哥斯达黎加CR,台湾TW	0	最不发达35国LDC35,最不发达4国LDC4	20	---Other
6540	8458.9900	--其他	12	0 2.4 6	东盟ASEAN,智利CL,新加坡SG,新西兰NZ,秘鲁PE 哥斯达黎加CR 巴基斯坦PK	0	最不发达35国LDC35,最不发达4国LDC4	50	--Other
	84.59	**切削金属的钻床、镗床、铣床、攻丝机床（包括直线移动式动力头钻床),但税号84.58的车床（包括车削中心）除外:**							**Machine-tools (including waytype unit head machines) for drilling, boring, milling, threading or tapping by removing metal, other than lathes (including turning centres) of heading No.84.58:**
6541	8459.1000	-直线移动式动力头钻床	15	0 3 7.5 12	东盟ASEAN,智利CL,新加坡SG,新西兰NZ 哥斯达黎加CR 秘鲁PE 巴基斯坦PK	0	最不发达35国LDC35	50	-Way-type unit head machines
		-其他钻床:							-Other drilling machines:
6542	8459.2100	--数控的	9.7	0 5	东盟ASEAN,智利CL,新西兰NZ,秘鲁PE,哥斯达黎加CR,台湾TW 巴基斯坦PK	0	最不发达35国LDC35,最不发达4国LDC4	20	--Numerically controlled

序号 No.	税则号列 Tariff Line	货品名称	最惠国税率 MFN(%)	协定税率 Agreement(%)	特惠税率 S.P.(%)	普通税率 Gen.(%)	Article Description
6543	8459.2900	--其他	15	0 东盟ASEAN,智利CL,新加坡SG,新西兰NZ 3 哥斯达黎加CR 7.5 秘鲁PE 12 巴基斯坦PK	0 最不发达35国LDC35	50	--Other
		-其他镗铣机床:					-Other boring-milling machines:
6544	8459.3100	--数控的	9.7	0 东盟ASEAN,智利CL,新西兰NZ,秘鲁PE,哥斯达黎加CR 5 巴基斯坦PK	0 最不发达35国LDC35,最不发达4国LDC4	20	--Numerically controlled
6545	8459.3900	--其他	10	0 东盟ASEAN,智利CL,新西兰NZ,秘鲁PE,哥斯达黎加CR 5 巴基斯坦PK	0 最不发达35国LDC35,最不发达4国LDC4	50	--Other
		-其他镗床:					-Other boring machines:
6546	8459.4010	---数控的	9.7	0 东盟ASEAN,智利CL,新西兰NZ,秘鲁PE,哥斯达黎加CR 5 巴基斯坦PK	0 最不发达35国LDC35,最不发达4国LDC4	20	---Numerically controlled
6547	8459.4090	---其他	15	0 东盟ASEAN,智利CL,新加坡SG,新西兰NZ 3 哥斯达黎加CR 7.5 秘鲁PE 12 巴基斯坦PK	0 最不发达35国LDC35	50	---Other
		-升降台式铣床:					-Milling machines, knee-type:
6548	8459.5100	--数控的	9.7	0 东盟ASEAN,智利CL,新西兰NZ,秘鲁PE,哥斯达黎加CR 5 巴基斯坦PK	0 最不发达35国LDC35,最不发达4国LDC4	20	--Numerically controlled
6549	8459.5900	--其他	15	0 东盟ASEAN,智利CL,新加坡SG,新西兰NZ 3 哥斯达黎加CR 7.5 秘鲁PE 12 巴基斯坦PK	0 最不发达35国LDC35	50	--Other
		-其他铣床:					-Other milling machines:
		--数控的:					--Numerically controlled:
6550	8459.6110	---龙门铣床	5	0 东盟ASEAN,智利CL,巴基斯坦PK,新西兰NZ,秘鲁PE,哥斯达黎加CR	0 最不发达35国LDC35,最不发达4国LDC4	20	---Planomilling machines

序号 No.	税则号列 Tariff Line	货品名称	最惠国 税　率 MFN(%)	协定税率 Agreement(%)		特惠税率 S.P.(%)		普通 税率 Gen.(%)	Article Description
6551	8459.6190	---其他	5	0	东盟ASEAN,智利CL,巴基斯坦PK,新西兰NZ,秘鲁PE,哥斯达黎加CR	0	最不发达35国LDC35,最不发达4国LDC4	20	---Other
		--其他:							--Other:
6552	8459.6910	---龙门铣床	12	0 2.4 5 10	东盟ASEAN,智利CL,新加坡SG,新西兰NZ,秘鲁PE 哥斯达黎加CR 巴基斯坦PK 亚太APTA	0	最不发达35国LDC35,最不发达4国LDC4	50	---Planomilling machines
6553	8459.6990	---其他	12	0 2.4 6 11	东盟ASEAN,智利CL,新加坡SG,新西兰NZ,秘鲁PE 哥斯达黎加CR 巴基斯坦PK 亚太APTA	0	最不发达35国LDC35,最不发达4国LDC4	50	---Other
6554	8459.7000	-其他攻丝机床	12	0 2.4 6	东盟ASEAN,智利CL,新加坡SG,新西兰NZ,秘鲁PE 哥斯达黎加CR 巴基斯坦PK	0	最不发达35国LDC35,最不发达4国LDC4	50	-Other threading or tapping machines
	84.60	**用磨石、磨料或抛光材料对金属或金属陶瓷进行去毛刺、刃磨、磨削、珩磨、研磨、抛光或其他精加工的机床,但税号84.61的切齿机、齿轮磨床或齿轮精加工机床除外:**							**Machine-tools for deburring, sharpening, grinding, honing, lapping, polishing or otherwise finishing metal or cermets by means of grinding stones, abrasives or polishing products, other than gear cutting, gear grinding or gear finishing machines of heading 84.61:**
		-平面磨床,在任一坐标的定位精度至少是0.01毫米:							-Flat-surface grinding machines, in which the positioning in any one axis can be set up to an accuracy of at least 0.01mm:
6555	8460.1100	--数控的	9.7	0 5	东盟ASEAN,智利CL,新西兰NZ,秘鲁PE,哥斯达黎加CR,台湾TW 巴基斯坦PK	0	最不发达35国LDC35,最不发达4国LDC4	20	--Numerically controlled
6556	8460.1900	--其他	15	0 3 7.5 12	东盟ASEAN,智利CL,新加坡SG,新西兰NZ 哥斯达黎加CR 秘鲁PE 巴基斯坦PK	0	最不发达35国LDC35	50	--Other

序号 No.	税则号列 Tariff Line	货品名称	最惠国税率 MFN(%)	协定税率 Agreement(%)		特惠税率 S.P.(%)		普通税率 Gen.(%)	Article Description
		-其他磨床,在任一坐标的定位精度至少是 0.01 毫米:							-Other grinding machines, in which the positioning in any one axis can be set up to an accuracy of at least 0.01mm:
		--数控的:							--Numerically controlled:
		---外圆磨床:							---Cylindrical grinding machines:
6557	8460.2111	----曲轴磨床	9.7	0 5	东盟ASEAN,智利CL,新西兰NZ,秘鲁PE,哥斯达黎加CR 巴基斯坦PK	0	最不发达 35 国 LDC35,最不发达 4 国 LDC4	20	----Crankshaft grinding
6558	8460.2119	----其他	9.7	0 5	东盟ASEAN,智利CL,新西兰NZ,秘鲁PE,哥斯达黎加CR 巴基斯坦PK	0	最不发达 35 国 LDC35,最不发达 4 国 LDC4	20	----Other
6559	8460.2120	---内圆磨床	9.7	0 5	东盟ASEAN,智利CL,新西兰NZ,秘鲁PE,哥斯达黎加CR 巴基斯坦PK	0	最不发达 35 国 LDC35,最不发达 4 国 LDC4	20	---Internal grinding machines
6560	8460.2190	---其他	9.7	0 5	东盟ASEAN,智利CL,新西兰NZ,秘鲁PE,哥斯达黎加CR 巴基斯坦PK	0	最不发达 35 国 LDC35,最不发达 4 国 LDC4	20	---Other
		--其他:							--Other:
6561	8460.2910	---外圆磨床	15	0 3 7.5 12	东盟ASEAN,智利CL,新加坡SG,新西兰NZ 哥斯达黎加CR 秘鲁PE 巴基斯坦PK	0	最不发达 35 国 LDC35	50	---Cylindrical grinding machines
6562	8460.2920	---内圆磨床	15	0 3 7.5 12	东盟ASEAN,智利CL,新加坡SG,新西兰NZ 哥斯达黎加CR 秘鲁PE 巴基斯坦PK	0	最不发达 35 国 LDC35	50	---Internal grinding machines
6563	8460.2930	---轧辊磨床	13	0 2.6 6.5	东盟ASEAN,智利CL,新加坡SG,新西兰NZ,秘鲁PE 哥斯达黎加CR 巴基斯坦PK	0	最不发达 35 国 LDC35	50	---Grinding machines of roll
6564	8460.2990	---其他	13	0 2.6 6.5	东盟ASEAN,智利CL,新加坡SG,新西兰NZ,秘鲁PE 哥斯达黎加CR 巴基斯坦PK	0	最不发达 35 国 LDC35	50	---Other

序号 No.	税则号列 Tariff Line	货品名称	最惠国 税率 MFN(%)	协定税率 Agreement(%)		特惠税率 S.P.(%)		普通 税率 Gen.(%)	Article Description
		-刃磨（工具或刀具）机床:							-Sharpening (tool or cutter grinding) machines:
6565	8460.3100	--数控的	9.7	0 5	东盟ASEAN,智利CL,新西兰NZ,秘鲁PE,哥斯达黎加CR 巴基斯坦PK	0	最不发达35国LDC35,最不发达4国LDC4	20	--Numerically controlled
6566	8460.3900	--其他	15	0 3 7.5 12	东盟ASEAN,智利CL,新加坡SG,新西兰NZ,香港HK 哥斯达黎加CR 秘鲁PE 巴基斯坦PK	0	最不发达35国LDC35	50	--Other
		-珩磨或研磨机床:							-Honing or lapping machines:
6567	8460.4010	---珩磨	13	0 2.6 6.5	东盟ASEAN,智利CL,新加坡SG,新西兰NZ,秘鲁PE 哥斯达黎加CR 巴基斯坦PK	0	最不发达35国LDC35	50	---Honing
6568	8460.4020	---研磨	13	0 2.6 6.5	东盟ASEAN,智利CL,新加坡SG,新西兰NZ,秘鲁PE,台湾TW 哥斯达黎加CR 巴基斯坦PK	0	最不发达35国LDC35	50	---Lapping
		-其他:							-Other:
6569	8460.9010	---砂轮机	15	0 1.5 3 7.5 12	东盟ASEAN,新加坡SG,新西兰NZ,台湾TW 智利CL 哥斯达黎加CR 秘鲁PE 巴基斯坦PK	0	最不发达35国LDC35	50	---Grinding wheel machines
6570	8460.9020	---抛光机床	15	0 1.5 3 7.5 12	东盟ASEAN,新加坡SG,新西兰NZ,台湾TW 智利CL 哥斯达黎加CR 秘鲁PE 巴基斯坦PK	0	最不发达35国LDC35	50	---Polishing machines
6571	8460.9090	---其他	15	0 1.5 3 7.5 12	东盟ASEAN,新加坡SG,新西兰NZ 智利CL 哥斯达黎加CR 秘鲁PE 巴基斯坦PK	0	最不发达35国LDC35	50	---Other
	84.61	**切削金属或金属陶瓷的刨床、牛头刨床、插床、拉床、切齿机、齿轮磨床或齿轮精加工机床、锯床、切断机及其他税号未列名的切削机床:**							**Machine-tools for planing, shaping, slotting, broaching, gear cutting, gear grinding or gear finishing, sawing, cutting-off and other machine-tools working by removing metal or cermets, not elsewhere specified or included:**

序号 No.	税则号列 Tariff Line	货品名称	最惠国 税 率 MFN(%)	协定税率 Agreement(%)		特惠税率 S.P.(%)		普通 税率 Gen.(%)	Article Description
		-牛头刨床或插床:							-Shaping or slotting machines:
6572	8461.2010	---牛头刨床	15	0 3 7.5 12	东盟ASEAN,智利CL,新加坡SG,新西兰NZ 哥斯达黎加CR 秘鲁PE 巴基斯坦PK	0	最不发达35国LDC35	50	---Shaping machines
6573	8461.2020	---插床	15	0 3 7.5 12	东盟ASEAN,智利CL,新加坡SG,新西兰NZ,台湾TW 哥斯达黎加CR 秘鲁PE 巴基斯坦PK	0	最不发达35国LDC35	50	---Slotting machines
6574	8461.3000	-拉床	12	0 2.4 6	东盟ASEAN,智利CL,新加坡SG,新西兰NZ,秘鲁PE,台湾TW 哥斯达黎加CR 巴基斯坦PK	0	最不发达35国LDC35	50	-Broaching machines
		-切齿机、齿轮磨床或齿轮精加工机床:							-Gear cutting, gear grinding or gear finishing machines:
		---数控的:							---Numerically controlled:
6575	8461.4011	----齿轮磨床	9.7	0 5	东盟ASEAN,智利CL,新西兰NZ,秘鲁PE,哥斯达黎加CR 巴基斯坦PK	0	最不发达35国LDC35,最不发达4国LDC4	20	----Gear grinding
6576	8461.4019	----其他	9.7	0 5	东盟ASEAN,智利CL,新西兰NZ,秘鲁PE,哥斯达黎加CR 巴基斯坦PK	0	最不发达35国LDC35,最不发达4国LDC4	20	----Other
6577	8461.4090	---其他	15	0 3 7.5 12	东盟ASEAN,智利CL,新加坡SG,新西兰NZ 哥斯达黎加CR 秘鲁PE 巴基斯坦PK	0	最不发达35国LDC35	50	---Other
6578	8461.5000	-锯床或切断机	12	0 2.4 6	东盟ASEAN,智利CL,新加坡SG,新西兰NZ,秘鲁PE,台湾TW 哥斯达黎加CR 巴基斯坦PK	0	最不发达35国LDC35	50	-Sawing or cutting-off machines
		-其他:							-Other:
		---刨床:							---Planing machines:
6579	8461.9011	----龙门刨床	15	0 3 7.5 12	东盟ASEAN,智利CL,新加坡SG,新西兰NZ,台湾TW 哥斯达黎加CR 秘鲁PE 巴基斯坦PK	0	最不发达35国LDC35	50	----Double-column (open-side) planing machines

序号 No.	税则号列 Tariff Line	货品名称	最惠国税率 MFN(%)	协定税率 Agreement(%)	特惠税率 S.P.(%)	普通税率 Gen.(%)	Article Description
6580	8461.9019	----其他	15	0 东盟ASEAN,智利CL,新加坡SG,新西兰NZ,台湾TW 3 哥斯达黎加CR 7.5 秘鲁PE 12 巴基斯坦PK	0 最不发达35国LDC35	50	----Other
6581	8461.9090	---其他	12	0 东盟ASEAN,智利CL,新加坡SG,新西兰NZ,秘鲁PE 2.4 哥斯达黎加CR 6 巴基斯坦PK	0 最不发达35国LDC35	50	---Other
	84.62	**加工金属的锻造（包括模锻）或冲压机床;加工金属的弯曲、折叠、矫直、矫平、剪切、冲孔或开槽机床;其他加工金属或硬质合金的压力机:**					**Machine-tools (including presses) for working metal by forging, hammering or die-stamping; machine-tools (including presses) for working metal by bending, folding, straightening, flattening, shearing, punching or notching; presses for working metal or metal carbides, not specified above:**
		-锻造（包括模锻）或冲压机床及锻锤:					-Forging or die-stamping machines (including presses) and hammers:
6582	8462.1010	---数控的	9.7	0 东盟ASEAN,新西兰NZ,秘鲁PE,哥斯达黎加CR,台湾TW 1 智利CL 5 巴基斯坦PK 6.8 亚太APTA	0 最不发达35国LDC35,最不发达4国LDC4	20	---Numerically controlled
6583	8462.1090	---其他	12	0 东盟ASEAN,新加坡SG,新西兰NZ,台湾TW 1.2 智利CL 2.4 哥斯达黎加CR 5 巴基斯坦PK 6 秘鲁PE 8.4 亚太APTA	0 最不发达35国LDC35,最不发达4国LDC4	50	---Other
		-弯曲、折叠、矫直或矫平机床:					-Bending, folding, straightening or flattening machines (including presses):
		--数控的:					--Numerically controlled:
6584	8462.2110	---矫直机	9.7	0 东盟ASEAN,智利CL,新西兰NZ,秘鲁PE,哥斯达黎加CR 5 巴基斯坦PK	0 最不发达35国LDC35,最不发达4国LDC4	20	---Straightening machines
6585	8462.2190	---其他	9.7	0 东盟ASEAN,智利CL,新西兰NZ,秘鲁PE,哥斯达黎加CR 5 巴基斯坦PK	0 最不发达35国LDC35,最不发达4国LDC4	20	---Other

序号 No.	税则号列 Tariff Line	货品名称	最惠国税率 MFN(%)	协定税率 Agreement(%)	特惠税率 S.P.(%)	普通税率 Gen.(%)	Article Description
		--其他:					--Other:
6586	8462.2910	---矫直机	10	0 东盟ASEAN,新西兰NZ,哥斯达黎加CR 1 智利CL 5 巴基斯坦PK,秘鲁PE	0 最不发达35国LDC35,最不发达4国LDC4	50	---Straightening machines
6587	8462.2990	---其他	10	0 东盟ASEAN,新加坡SG,新西兰NZ,哥斯达黎加CR 1 智利CL 5 巴基斯坦PK,秘鲁PE	0 最不发达35国LDC35,最不发达4国LDC4	50	---Other
		-剪切机床,但冲剪两用机除外:					-Shearing machines (including presses), other than combined punching and shearing machines:
		--数控的:					--Numerically controlled:
6588	8462.3110	---板带纵剪机	7	0 东盟ASEAN,智利CL,新西兰NZ,秘鲁PE,哥斯达黎加CR 5 巴基斯坦PK	0 最不发达35国LDC35,最不发达4国LDC4	20	---Shearing lengthwise
6589	8462.3120	---板带横剪机	7	0 东盟ASEAN,智利CL,新西兰NZ,秘鲁PE,哥斯达黎加CR 5 巴基斯坦PK	0 最不发达35国LDC35,最不发达4国LDC4	20	---Shearing transverse
6590	8462.3190	---其他	7	0 东盟ASEAN,智利CL,新西兰NZ,秘鲁PE,哥斯达黎加CR 5 巴基斯坦PK	0 最不发达35国LDC35,最不发达4国LDC4	20	---Other
		--其他:					--Other:
6591	8462.3910	---板带纵剪机	10	0 东盟ASEAN,智利CL,新西兰NZ,秘鲁PE,哥斯达黎加CR 5 巴基斯坦PK 9.5 亚太APTA	0 最不发达35国LDC35,最不发达4国LDC4	50	---Shearing lengthwise
6592	8462.3920	---板带横剪机	10	0 东盟ASEAN,智利CL,新西兰NZ,秘鲁PE,哥斯达黎加CR 5 巴基斯坦PK 9.5 亚太APTA	0 最不发达35国LDC35,最不发达4国LDC4	50	---Shearing transverse
6593	8462.3990	---其他	10	0 东盟ASEAN,智利CL,新西兰NZ,秘鲁PE,哥斯达黎加CR 5 巴基斯坦PK 9.5 亚太APTA	0 最不发达35国LDC35,最不发达4国LDC4	50	---Other

序号 No.	税则号列 Tariff Line	货品名称	最惠国税率 MFN(%)	协定税率 Agreement(%)	特惠税率 S.P.(%)	普通税率 Gen.(%)	Article Description
		-冲孔或开槽机床,包括冲剪两用机:					-Punching or notching machines (including presses), including combined punching and shearing machines:
		--数控的:					--Numerically controlled:
		---冲床:					---Punch press:
6594	8462.4111	----自动模式数控步冲压力机	9.7	0 东盟ASEAN,智利CL,新西兰NZ,秘鲁PE,哥斯达黎加CR 5 巴基斯坦PK	0 最不发达35国LDC35,最不发达4国LDC4	20	----CNC automatic tool change punch press
6595	8462.4119	----其他	9.7	0 东盟ASEAN,智利CL,新西兰NZ,秘鲁PE,哥斯达黎加CR 5 巴基斯坦PK	0 最不发达35国LDC35,最不发达4国LDC4	20	----Other
6596	8462.4190	---其他	9.7	0 东盟ASEAN,智利CL,新西兰NZ,秘鲁PE,哥斯达黎加CR 5 巴基斯坦PK	0 最不发达35国LDC35,最不发达4国LDC4	20	---Other
6597	8462.4900	--其他	10	0 东盟ASEAN,智利CL,新加坡SG,新西兰NZ,秘鲁PE,哥斯达黎加CR,台湾TW 5 巴基斯坦PK	0 最不发达35国LDC35,最不发达4国LDC4	50	--Other
		-其他:					-Other:
		--液压压力机:					--Hydraulic presses:
6598	8462.9110	---金属型材挤压机	10	0 东盟ASEAN,新西兰NZ,秘鲁PE,哥斯达黎加CR 1 智利CL 5 巴基斯坦PK 9.2 亚太APTA	0 最不发达35国LDC35,最不发达4国LDC4	50	---Metal section squeezing machine
6599	8462.9190	---其他	10	0 东盟ASEAN,新加坡SG,新西兰NZ,秘鲁PE,哥斯达黎加CR 1 智利CL 5 巴基斯坦PK 9.2 亚太APTA	0 最不发达35国LDC35,最不发达4国LDC4	50	---Other
		--其他:					--Other:
6600	8462.9910	---机械压力机	10	0 东盟ASEAN,新加坡SG,新西兰NZ,秘鲁PE,哥斯达黎加CR,台湾TW 1 智利CL 5 巴基斯坦PK 9.5 亚太APTA	0 最不发达35国LDC35,最不发达4国LDC4	50	---Mechanical presses

序号 No.	税则号列 Tariff Line	货品名称	最惠国 税 率 MFN(%)	协定税率 Agreement(%)		特惠税率 S.P.(%)		普通 税率 Gen.(%)	Article Description
6601	8462.9990	---其他	10	0 1 5 9.5	东盟ASEAN,新加坡SG,新西兰NZ,秘鲁PE,哥斯达黎加CR 智利CL 巴基斯坦PK 亚太APTA	0	最不发达35国LDC35,最不发达4国LDC4	50	---Other
	84.63	**金属或金属陶瓷的其他非切削加工机床:**							**Other machine-tools for working metal or cermets, without removing material:**
		-杆、管、型材、异型材、丝及类似品的拉拔机:							-Draw-benches for bars, tubes, profiles, wire or the like:
		---冷拔管机:							---Cold-drawing tube benches:
6602	8463.1011	----拉拔力为300吨及以下	10	0 5	东盟ASEAN,智利CL,新西兰NZ,秘鲁PE,哥斯达黎加CR 巴基斯坦PK	0	最不发达35国LDC35	50	----Drawing power ≤300t
6603	8463.1019	----其他	10	0 5	东盟ASEAN,智利CL,新加坡SG,新西兰NZ,秘鲁PE,哥斯达黎加CR,台湾TW 巴基斯坦PK	0	最不发达35国LDC35	50	----Other
6604	8463.1020	---拔丝机	10	0 5	东盟ASEAN,智利CL,新西兰NZ,秘鲁PE,哥斯达黎加CR 巴基斯坦PK	0	最不发达35国LDC35	50	---Wiredrawing machines
6605	8463.1090	---其他	10	0 5	东盟ASEAN,智利CL,新西兰NZ,秘鲁PE,哥斯达黎加CR 巴基斯坦PK	0	最不发达35国LDC35	50	---Other
6606	8463.2000	-螺纹滚轧机	15	0 3 7.5 12	东盟ASEAN,智利CL,新加坡SG,新西兰NZ 哥斯达黎加CR 秘鲁PE 巴基斯坦PK	0	最不发达35国LDC35	50	-Thread rolling machines
6607	8463.3000	-金属丝加工机	10	0 5	东盟ASEAN,智利CL,新西兰NZ,秘鲁PE,哥斯达黎加CR 巴基斯坦PK	0	最不发达35国LDC35	50	-Machines for working wire
6608	8463.9000	-其他	10	0 1 5	东盟ASEAN,新西兰NZ,哥斯达黎加CR 智利CL 巴基斯坦PK,秘鲁PE	0	最不发达35国LDC35	50	-Other
	84.64	**石料、陶瓷、混凝土、石棉水泥或类似矿物材料的加工机床、玻璃冷加工机床:**							**Machine-tools for working stone, ceramics, concrete, asbestos-cement or like mineral materials or for cold working glass:**
		-锯床:							-Sawing machines:

序号 No.	税则号列 Tariff Line	货品名称	最惠国税率 MFN(%)	协定税率 Agreement(%)	特惠税率 S.P.(%)	普通税率 Gen.(%)	Article Description
6609	8464.1010	---圆盘锯	0		0 最不发达35国LDC35, 最不发达4国LDC4	30	---Of disk saw
6610	8464.1020	---钢丝锯	0		0 最不发达35国LDC35, 最不发达4国LDC4	30	---Of scroll saw
6611	8464.1090	---其他	0		0 最不发达35国LDC35, 最不发达4国LDC4	30	---Other
		-研磨或抛光机床:					-Grinding or polishing machines:
6612	8464.2010	---玻璃研磨或抛光机床	0		0 最不发达35国LDC35, 最不发达4国LDC4	30	---Machines for grinding or polishing glass or glassware
6613	8464.2090	---其他	0		0 最不发达35国LDC35, 最不发达4国LDC4	30	---Other
		-其他:					-Other:
		---玻璃的其他冷加工机床:					---Other machines for cold-working glass or glassware:
6614	8464.9011	----切割机	0		0 最不发达35国LDC35, 最不发达4国LDC4	30	----Cutting-off machines
6615	8464.9012	----刻花机	0		0 最不发达35国LDC35, 最不发达4国LDC4	30	----Carving machines
6616	8464.9019	----其他	0		0 最不发达35国LDC35, 最不发达4国LDC4	30	----Other

序号 No.	税则号列 Tariff Line	货品名称	最惠国 税　率 MFN(%)	协定税率 Agreement(%)	特惠税率 S.P.(%)	普通 税率 Gen.(%)	Article Description
6617	8464.9090	---其他	0		0 最不发达35国LDC35,最不发达4国LDC4	30	---Other
	84.65	**木材、软木、骨、硬质橡胶、硬质塑料或类似硬质材料的加工机床（包括用打钉或打U形钉、胶粘或其他方法组合前述材料的机器）：**					**Machine-tools (including machines for nailing, stapling, glueing or otherwise assembling) for working wood, cork, bone, hard rubber, hard plastics or similar hard materials:**
6618	8465.1000	-不需更换工具即可进行不同机械加工的机器	10	0 东盟ASEAN,新加坡SG,新西兰NZ,哥斯达黎加CR,香港HK 1 智利CL 5 巴基斯坦PK,秘鲁PE	0 最不发达35国LDC35	30	-Machines which can carry out different types of machining operations without tool change between such operations
		-其他:					-Other:
6619	8465.9100	--锯床	10	0 东盟ASEAN,新西兰NZ,哥斯达黎加CR,香港HK 1 智利CL 5 巴基斯坦PK,秘鲁PE	0 最不发达35国LDC35	30	--Sawing machines
6620	8465.9200	--刨、铣或切削成形机器	10	0 东盟ASEAN,智利CL,新加坡SG,新西兰NZ,秘鲁PE,哥斯达黎加CR,香港HK 5 巴基斯坦PK	0 最不发达35国LDC35	30	--Planing, milling or moulding (by cut-ting) machines
6621	8465.9300	--研磨、砂磨或抛光机器	10	0 东盟ASEAN,智利CL,新西兰NZ,秘鲁PE,哥斯达黎加CR,香港HK 5 巴基斯坦PK	0 最不发达35国LDC35	30	--Grinding, sanding or polishing machines
6622	8465.9400	--弯曲或装配机器	10	0 东盟ASEAN,智利CL,新加坡SG,新西兰NZ,秘鲁PE,哥斯达黎加CR 5 巴基斯坦PK	0 最不发达35国LDC35	30	--Bending or assembling machines
6623	8465.9500	--钻孔或凿榫机器	10	0 东盟ASEAN,智利CL,新加坡SG,新西兰NZ,秘鲁PE,哥斯达黎加CR,香港HK 5 巴基斯坦PK	0 最不发达35国LDC35	30	--Drilling or mortising machines
6624	8465.9600	--剖开、切片或刮削机器	10	0 东盟ASEAN,智利CL,新加坡SG,新西兰NZ,秘鲁PE,哥斯达黎加CR 5 巴基斯坦PK	0 最不发达35国LDC35	30	--Splitting, slicing or paring machines
6625	8465.9900	--其他	10	0 东盟ASEAN,新加坡SG,新西兰NZ,哥斯达黎加CR,香港HK 1 智利CL 5 巴基斯坦PK,秘鲁PE	0 最不发达35国LDC35	30	--Other

序号 No.	税则号列 Tariff Line	货品名称	最惠国税率 MFN(%)	协定税率 Agreement(%)		特惠税率 S.P.(%)		普通税率 Gen.(%)	Article Description
	84.66	**专用于或主要用于税号 84.56 至 84.65 所列机器的零件、附件,包括工件或工具的夹具、自启板牙切头、分度头及其他专用于机床的附件;各种手提工具的工具夹具:**							**Parts and accessories suitable for use solely or principally with the machines of headings Nos.84.56 to 84.65, including work or tool holders, self-opening dieheads, dividing heads and other special attachments for machine-tools; tool holders for any type of tool for working in the hand:**
6626	8466.1000	-工具夹具及自启板牙切头	7	0 5	东盟ASEAN,智利CL,新西兰NZ,秘鲁PE,哥斯达黎加CR 巴基斯坦PK	0	最不发达 35 国 LDC35,最不发达 4 国 LDC4	17	-Tool holders and self-opening dieheads
6627	8466.2000	-工件夹具	7	0 4.9	东盟ASEAN,智利CL,巴基斯坦PK,新西兰NZ,秘鲁PE,哥斯达黎加CR,台湾TW 亚太APTA	0	最不发达 35 国 LDC35,最不发达 4 国 LDC4	17	-Work holders
6628	8466.3000	-分度头及其他专用于机床的附件	7	0 5	东盟ASEAN,智利CL,新西兰NZ,秘鲁PE,哥斯达黎加CR 巴基斯坦PK	0	最不发达 35 国 LDC35,最不发达 4 国 LDC4	17	-Dividing heads and other special attachments for machine-tools
		-其他:							-Other:
6629	8466.9100	--税号 84.64 所列机器用	0			0	最不发达 35 国 LDC35,最不发达 4 国 LDC4	17	--For machines of heading No.84.64
6630	8466.9200	--税号 84.65 所列机器用	6	0 5	东盟ASEAN,智利CL,新西兰NZ,秘鲁PE,哥斯达黎加CR,香港HK 巴基斯坦PK	0	最不发达 35 国 LDC35,最不发达 4 国 LDC4	17	--For machines of heading No.84.65
		--税号 84.56 至 84.61 所列机器用:							--For machines of headings Nos.84.56 to 84.61:
6631	8466.9310	---刀库及自动换刀装置	0			0	最不发达 35 国 LDC35,最不发达 4 国 LDC4	17	---Tool magazine & ATC (Automatic Tool Changer)

序号 No.	税则号列 Tariff Line	货品名称	最惠国税率 MFN(%)	协定税率 Agreement(%)	特惠税率 S.P.(%)	普通税率 Gen.(%)	Article Description
6632	8466.9390	---其他	0		0 最不发达35国LDC35,最不发达4国LDC4	17	---Other
6633	8466.9400	--税号84.62或84.63所列机器用	6	0 东盟ASEAN,新西兰NZ,秘鲁PE,哥斯达黎加CR,台湾TW 0.6 智利CL 5 巴基斯坦PK	0 最不发达35国LDC35,最不发达4国LDC4	17	--For machines of heading No.84.62 or 84.63
	84.67	**手提式风动或液压工具及本身装有电动或非电动动力装置的手提式工具:**					**Tools for working in the hand, pneumatic hydraulic or with self-contained electric or non-electric motor: contained electric or non-electric motor:**
		-风动的:					-Pneumatlic:
6634	8467.1100	--旋转式（包括旋转冲击式的）	8	0 东盟ASEAN,智利CL,新西兰NZ,秘鲁PE,哥斯达黎加CR 5 巴基斯坦PK	0 最不发达35国LDC35,最不发达4国LDC4	30	--Rotary type (including combined rotarypercussion)
6635	8467.1900	--其他	8	0 东盟ASEAN,智利CL,新西兰NZ,秘鲁PE,哥斯达黎加CR 5 巴基斯坦PK	0 最不发达35国LDC35,最不发达4国LDC4	30	--Other
		-本身装有电动动力装置的:					-With self-contained electric motor:
6636	8467.2100	--各种钻	10	0 东盟ASEAN,新加坡SG,新西兰NZ,哥斯达黎加CR,香港HK 1 智利CL 5 巴基斯坦PK,秘鲁PE 9 亚太APTA	0 最不发达35国LDC35,最不发达4国LDC4	30	--Drills of all kinds
		--锯:					--Saws:
6637	8467.2210	---链锯	10	0 东盟ASEAN,新西兰NZ,哥斯达黎加CR,香港HK 1 智利CL 5 巴基斯坦PK,秘鲁PE 9 亚太APTA	0 最不发达35国LDC35,最不发达4国LDC4	30	---Chain saws
6638	8467.2290	---其他	10	0 东盟ASEAN,新加坡SG,新西兰NZ,哥斯达黎加CR,香港HK 1 智利CL 5 巴基斯坦PK,秘鲁PE 9 亚太APTA	0 最不发达35国LDC35,最不发达4国LDC4	30	---Other
		--其他:					--Other tools:

序号 No.	税则号列 Tariff Line	货品名称	最惠国税率 MFN(%)	协定税率 Agreement(%)		特惠税率 S.P.(%)		普通税率 Gen.(%)	Article Description
6639	8467.2910	---砂磨工具（包括磨光机、砂光机、砂轮机等）	10	0 1 5 8	东盟ASEAN,新加坡SG,新西兰NZ,哥斯达黎加CR,香港HK 智利CL 巴基斯坦PK,秘鲁PE 亚太APTA	0	最不发达35国LDC35,最不发达4国LDC4	30	---Grinding tools (induding burnisher, belt sander, wheel-sander)
6640	8467.2920	---电刨	10	0 1 5 8	东盟ASEAN,新西兰NZ,哥斯达黎加CR,香港HK 智利CL 巴基斯坦PK,秘鲁PE 亚太APTA	0	最不发达35国LDC35,最不发达4国LDC4	30	---Planings
6641	8467.2990	---其他	10	0 1 5 8	东盟ASEAN,新加坡SG,新西兰NZ,哥斯达黎加CR,香港HK 智利CL 巴基斯坦PK,秘鲁PE 亚太APTA	0	最不发达35国LDC35,最不发达4国LDC4	30	---Other
		-其他工具:							-Other tools:
6642	8467.8100	--链锯	8	0 5	东盟ASEAN,智利CL,新西兰NZ,秘鲁PE,哥斯达黎加CR 巴基斯坦PK	0	最不发达35国LDC35,最不发达4国LDC4	30	--Chain saws
6643	8467.8900	--其他	8	0 5	东盟ASEAN,智利CL,新西兰NZ,秘鲁PE,哥斯达黎加CR 巴基斯坦PK	0	最不发达35国LDC35,最不发达4国LDC4	30	--Other
		-零件:							-Parts:
		--链锯用:							--Of chain saws:
6644	8467.9110	---电动的	6	0 4.8	东盟ASEAN,智利CL,巴基斯坦PK,新西兰NZ,秘鲁PE,哥斯达黎加CR,香港HK 亚太APTA	0	最不发达35国LDC35,最不发达4国LDC4	30	---With self-contained electric motor
6645	8467.9190	---其他	6	0 5	东盟ASEAN,智利CL,新西兰NZ,秘鲁PE,哥斯达黎加CR 巴基斯坦PK	0	最不发达35国LDC35,最不发达4国LDC4	30	---Other
6646	8467.9200	--风动工具用	6	0 5	东盟ASEAN,智利CL,新西兰NZ,秘鲁PE,哥斯达黎加CR 巴基斯坦PK	0	最不发达35国LDC35,最不发达4国LDC4	30	--Of pneumatic tools
		--其他:							--Other:

序号 No.	税则号列 Tariff Line	货品名称	最惠国税率 MFN(%)	协定税率 Agreement(%)		特惠税率 S.P.(%)		普通税率 Gen.(%)	Article Description
6647	8467.9910	---电动工具用	10	0 5 9	东盟ASEAN,智利CL,新加坡SG,新西兰NZ,秘鲁PE,哥斯达黎加CR,香港HK 巴基斯坦PK 亚太APTA	0	最不发达35国LDC35,最不发达4国LDC4	30	---With self-contained electric motor
6648	8467.9990	---其他	6	0 5	东盟ASEAN,智利CL,新西兰NZ,秘鲁PE,哥斯达黎加CR 巴基斯坦PK	0	最不发达35国LDC35,最不发达4国LDC4	30	---Other
	84.68	**焊接机器及装置,不论是否兼有切割功能,但税号85.15的货品除外;气体加温表面回火机器及装置:**							**Machinery and apparatus for soldering, brazing or welding, whether or not capable of cutting, other than those of heading No.85.15; gas-operated surface tempering machines and appliances:**
6649	8468.1000	-手提喷焊器	12	0 2.4 6	东盟ASEAN,智利CL,新加坡SG,新西兰NZ,秘鲁PE 哥斯达黎加CR 巴基斯坦PK	0	最不发达35国LDC35,最不发达4国LDC4	30	-Hand-held blow pipes
6650	8468.2000	-其他气体焊接或表面回火机器及装置	12	0 2.4 6	东盟ASEAN,智利CL,新加坡SG,新西兰NZ,秘鲁PE 哥斯达黎加CR 巴基斯坦PK	0	最不发达35国LDC35,最不发达4国LDC4	30	-Other gas-operated machinery and apparatus
6651	8468.8000	-其他机器及装置	12	0 2.4 6	东盟ASEAN,智利CL,新加坡SG,新西兰NZ,秘鲁PE 哥斯达黎加CR 巴基斯坦PK	0	最不发达35国LDC35,最不发达4国LDC4	30	-Other machinery and apparatus
6652	8468.9000	-零件	7 △3	0 5	东盟ASEAN,智利CL,新西兰NZ,秘鲁PE,哥斯达黎加CR 巴基斯坦PK	0	最不发达35国LDC35,最不发达4国LDC4	30	-Parts
	84.69	**打字机,但税号84.43的打印机除外;文字处理机:**							**Typewriters other than printers of heading No.84.43; word-processing machines:**
		---自动打字机及文字处理机:							---Automatic typewriters and word-processing machines:

序号 No.	税则号列 Tariff Line	货品名称	最惠国税率 MFN(%)	协定税率 Agreement(%)		特惠税率 S.P.(%)		普通税率 Gen.(%)	Article Description
6653	8469.0011	----文字处理机	0			0	最不发达35国LDC35,最不发达4国LDC4	40	----Word-processing machines
6654	8469.0012	----自动打字机	12	0	东盟ASEAN,智利CL,新加坡SG,新西兰NZ,秘鲁PE	0	最不发达35国LDC35	40	----Automatic typewriters
				2.4	哥斯达黎加CR				
				6	巴基斯坦PK				
6655	8469.0020	---其他电动打字机	12	0	东盟ASEAN,智利CL,新加坡SG,新西兰NZ,秘鲁PE	0	最不发达35国LDC35	40	---Other typewriters, electric
				2.4	哥斯达黎加CR				
				5	巴基斯坦PK				
				10.8	亚太APTA				
6656	8469.0030	---其他非电动打字机	12	0	东盟ASEAN,智利CL,新加坡SG,新西兰NZ,秘鲁PE	0	最不发达35国LDC35	40	---Other typewriters, non-electric
				2.4	哥斯达黎加CR				
				6	巴基斯坦PK				
	84.70	**计算机器及具有计算功能的袖珍式数据记录、重现及显示机器;装有计算装置的会计计算机、邮资盖戳机、售票机及类似机器;现金出纳机:**							**Calculating machines and pocket-size data recording, reproducing and displaying machines with calculating functions; accounting machines, postage-franking machines, ticket-issuing machines and similar machines, incorporating a calculating device; cash registers:**
6657	8470.1000	-不需外接电源的电子计算器及具有计算功能的袖珍式数据记录、重现及显示机器	0			0	最不发达35国LDC35,最不发达4国LDC4	80	-Electronic calculators capable of operation without an external source of electric power and pocket-size data recording, reproducing and displaying machines with calculating functions
		-其他电子计算器:							-Other electronic calculating machines:
6658	8470.2100	--装有打印装置的	0			0	最不发达35国LDC35,最不发达4国LDC4	80	--Incorporating a printing device

序号 No.	税则号列 Tariff Line	货品名称	最惠国税率 MFN(%)	协定税率 Agreement(%)	特惠税率 S.P.(%)	普通税率 Gen.(%)	Article Description
6659	8470.2900	--其他	0		0 最不发达35国LDC35,最不发达4国LDC4	80	--Other
6660	8470.3000	-其他计算机器	0		0 最不发达35国LDC35,最不发达4国LDC4	40	-Other calculating machines
		-现金出纳机:					-Cash registers:
6661	8470.5010	---销售点终端出纳机	0		0 最不发达35国LDC35,最不发达4国LDC4	40	---Terminal registers for market
6662	8470.5090	---其他	0		0 最不发达35国LDC35,最不发达4国LDC4	40	---Other
6663	8470.9000	-其他	0		0 最不发达35国LDC35,最不发达4国LDC4	40	-Other
	84.71	**自动数据处理设备及其部件;其他税号未列名的磁性或光学阅读机、将数据以代码形式转录到数据记录媒体的机器及处理这些数据的机器:**					**Automatic data processing machines and units thereof; magnetic or optical readers, machines for transcribing data onto data media in coded form and machines for processing such data, not elsewhere specified or included:**
		-重量不超过10公斤的便携自动数据处理设备,至少由一个中央处理部件、一个键盘及一个显示器组成:					-Portable automatic data processing machines, weighing not more than 10kg, consisting of at least a central processing unit, a keyboard and a display:
6664	8471.3010	---平板电脑	0		0 最不发达35国LDC35,最不发达4国LDC4	70	---Tablet computer

序号 No.	税则号列 Tariff Line	货品名称	最惠国税率 MFN(%)	协定税率 Agreement(%)	特惠税率 S.P.(%)	普通税率 Gen.(%)	Article Description
6665	8471.3090	---其他	0		0 最不发达35国 LDC35, 最不发达4国 LDC4	70	---Other
		-其他自动数据处理设备:					-Other automatic data processing machines:
		--同一机壳内至少有一个中央处理部件及一个输入和输出部件,不论是否组合式:					--Comprising in the same housing at least a central processing unit and an input and output unit, whether or not combined:
6666	8471.4110	---巨型机、大型机及中型机	0		0 最不发达35国 LDC35, 最不发达4国 LDC4	14	---Mainframes
6667	8471.4120	---小型机	0		0 最不发达35国 LDC35, 最不发达4国 LDC4	14	---Mini-computers
6668	8471.4140	---微型机	0		0 最不发达35国 LDC35, 最不发达4国 LDC4	70	---Microprocessings
6669	8471.4190	---其他	0		0 最不发达35国 LDC35, 最不发达4国 LDC4	70	---Other
		--其他,以系统形式进口或出口的:					--Other, presented in the form of systems:
6670	8471.4910	---巨型机、大型机及中型机	0		0 最不发达35国 LDC35, 最不发达4国 LDC4	29	---Mainframes
6671	8471.4920	---小型机	0		0 最不发达35国 LDC35, 最不发达4国 LDC4	29	---Mini-computers

序号 No.	税则号列 Tariff Line	货品名称	最惠国税率 MFN(%)	协定税率 Agreement(%)	特惠税率 S.P.(%)	普通税率 Gen.(%)	Article Description
6672	8471.4940	---微型机	0		0 最不发达35国LDC35,最不发达4国LDC4	70	---Microprocessings
		---其他:					---Other:
6673	8471.4991	----分散型工业过程控制设备	0		0 最不发达35国LDC35,最不发达4国LDC4	70	----Processing machines for the dis-tributed control system
6674	8471.4999	----其他	0		0 最不发达35国LDC35,最不发达4国LDC4	70	----Other
		-子目号8471.41或8471.49所列以外的处理部件,不论是否在同一机壳内有一个或两个下列部件:存储部件、输入部件、输出部件:					-Processing units other than those of subheading 8471.41 or 8471.49, whether or not containing in the same housing one or two of the following types of unit: storage units, input units, output units:
6675	8471.5010	---巨型机、大型机及中型机的	0		0 最不发达35国LDC35,最不发达4国LDC4	14	---Of mainframes
6676	8471.5020	---小型机的	0		0 最不发达35国LDC35,最不发达4国LDC4	14	---Of mini-computers
6677	8471.5040	---微型机的	0		0 最不发达35国LDC35,最不发达4国LDC4	70	---Of microprocessings
6678	8471.5090	---其他	0		0 最不发达35国LDC35,最不发达4国LDC4	70	---Other

序号 No.	税则号列 Tariff Line	货品名称	最惠国税率 MFN(%)	协定税率 Agreement(%)	特惠税率 S.P.(%)	普通税率 Gen.(%)	Article Description
		-输入或输出部件,不论是否在同一机壳内有存储部件:					-Input or output units, whether or not containing storage units in the same housing:
6679	8471.6040	---巨型机、大型机、中型机及小型机用终端	0		0 最不发达 35 国 LDC35, 最不发达 4 国 LDC4	14	---Terminating machines for the huge computers, mainframes and mini-computers
6680	8471.6050	---扫描仪	0		0 最不发达 35 国 LDC35, 最不发达 4 国 LDC4	14	---Scanner
6681	8471.6060	---数字化仪	0		0 最不发达 35 国 LDC35, 最不发达 4 国 LDC4	14	---Digitizer
		---键盘、鼠标器:					---Keyboards, mouses:
6682	8471.6071	----键盘	0		0 最不发达 35 国 LDC35, 最不发达 4 国 LDC4	40	----Keyboards
6683	8471.6072	----鼠标器	0		0 最不发达 35 国 LDC35, 最不发达 4 国 LDC4	40	----Mouses
6684	8471.6090	---其他	0		0 最不发达 35 国 LDC35, 最不发达 4 国 LDC4	14	---Other
		-存储部件:					-Storage units:
6685	8471.7010	---硬盘驱动器	0		0 最不发达 35 国 LDC35, 最不发达 4 国 LDC4	14	---Rigid disk drivers
6686	8471.7020	---软盘驱动器	0		0 最不发达 35 国 LDC35, 最不发达 4 国 LDC4	14	---Floppy disk drivers

序号 No.	税则号列 Tariff Line	货品名称	最惠国税率 MFN(%)	协定税率 Agreement(%)		特惠税率 S.P.(%)		普通税率 Gen.(%)	Article Description
6687	8471.7030	---光盘驱动器	0			0	最不发达35国LDC35,最不发达4国LDC4	14	---CD drivers
6688	8471.7090	---其他	0			0	最不发达35国LDC35,最不发达4国LDC4	14	---Other
6689	8471.8000	-自动数据处理设备的其他部件	0			0	最不发达35国LDC35,最不发达4国LDC4	40	-Other units automatic data processing machines
6690	8471.9000	-其他	0			0	最不发达35国LDC35,最不发达4国LDC4	40	-Other
	84.72	**其他办公室用机器（例如,胶版复印机、油印机、地址印写机、自动付钞机、硬币分类、计数及包装机、削铅笔机、打洞机或订书机）：**							**Other office machines (for example, hectograph or stencil duplicating machines, addressing machines, automatic banknote dispensers, coin-sorting machines, coin counting or wrapping machines, pencil-sharpening machines, perforating or stapling machines):**
6691	8472.1000	-胶版复印机、油印机	14	0 2.8 11.2	东盟ASEAN,智利CL,新加坡SG,新西兰NZ,秘鲁PE 哥斯达黎加CR 巴基斯坦PK	0	最不发达35国LDC35	40	-Duplicating machines
		-信件分类或折叠机或信件装封机、信件开封或闭封机、粘贴或盖销邮票机:							-Machines for sorting or folding mail or for inserting mail in envelopes or bands, machines for opening, closing or sealing mail and machines for affixing or cancelling postage stamps:
6692	8472.3010	---邮政信件分拣及封装设备	10	0 5	东盟ASEAN,智利CL,新西兰NZ,秘鲁PE,哥斯达黎加CR 巴基斯坦PK	0	最不发达35国LDC35,最不发达4国LDC4	40	---Machines for sorting or banding mail

序号 No.	税则号列 Tariff Line	货品名称	最惠国税率 MFN(%)	协定税率 Agreement(%)		特惠税率 S.P.(%)		普通税率 Gen.(%)	Article Description
6693	8472.3090	---其他	14	0 2.8 7	东盟ASEAN,智利CL,新加坡SG,新西兰NZ,秘鲁PE 哥斯达黎加CR 巴基斯坦PK	0	最不发达35国LDC35	40	---Other
		-其他:							-Other:
6694	8472.9010	---自动柜员机	0			0	最不发达35国LDC35,最不发达4国LDC4	40	---Automated teller
		---装订用机器:							---Stapling machines:
6695	8472.9021	----打洞机	0			0	最不发达35国LDC35,最不发达4国LDC4	40	----Perforator
6696	8472.9022	----订书机	0			0	最不发达35国LDC35,最不发达4国LDC4	40	----Stapler
6697	8472.9029	----其他	0			0	最不发达35国LDC35,最不发达4国LDC4	40	----Other
6698	8472.9030	---碎纸机	0			0	最不发达35国LDC35,最不发达4国LDC4	40	---Paper shrudders
6699	8472.9040	---地址印写机及地址铭牌压印机	14	0 2.8 11.2	东盟ASEAN,智利CL,新加坡SG,新西兰NZ,秘鲁PE 哥斯达黎加CR 巴基斯坦PK	0	最不发达35国LDC35	40	---Addressing machines and address plate embossing machines
6700	8472.9090	---其他	0			0	最不发达35国LDC35,最不发达4国LDC4	40	---Other
	84.73	**专用于或主要用于税号84.69至84.72所列机器的零件、附件（罩套、提箱及类似品除外）:**							**Parts and accessories (other than covers, carrying cases and the like) suit-able for use solely or principally with machines of headings Nos.84.69 to 84.72:**

序号 No.	税则号列 Tariff Line	货品名称	最惠国税率 MFN(%)	协定税率 Agreement(%)		特惠税率 S.P.(%)		普通税率 Gen.(%)	Article Description
6701	8473.1000	-税号84.69所列机器的零件、附件	8	0 5	东盟ASEAN,智利CL,新西兰NZ,秘鲁PE,哥斯达黎加CR 巴基斯坦PK	0	最不发达35国LDC35,最不发达4国LDC4	35	-Parts and accessories of the machines of heading No.84.69
		-税号84.70所列机器的零件、附件:							-Parts and accessories of the machines of heading No.84.70:
6702	8473.2100	--子目号8470.10、8470.21或8470.29所列电子计算器的零件、附件	0			0	最不发达35国LDC35,最不发达4国LDC4	50	--Of the electronic calculating ma-chines of subheading No.8470.10, 8470.21 or 8470.29
6703	8473.2900	--其他	0			0	最不发达35国LDC35,最不发达4国LDC4	35	--Other
		-税号84.71所列机器的零件、附件:							-Parts and accessories of the machines of heading No.84.71:
6704	8473.3010	---子目号8471.4110、8471.4120、8471.4910、8471.4920、8471.5010、8471.5020、8471.6090、8471.7010、8471.7020、8471.7030及8471.7090所列机器及装置的零件、附件	0			0	最不发达35国LDC35,最不发达4国LDC4	14	---Of the machines of subheading 8471.4110, 8471.4120, 8471.4910, 8471.4920, 8471.5010, 8471.5020, 8471.6090, 8471.7019, 8471.7020, 8471.7030 or 8471.7090
6705	8473.3090	---其他	0			0	最不发达35国LDC35,最不发达4国LDC4	40	---Other
		-税号84.72所列机器的零件、附件:							-Parts and accessories of the machines of heading No.84.72:
6706	8473.4010	---自动柜员机用出钞器	10.5 △1	0 2.1 5	东盟ASEAN,智利CL,新加坡SG,新西兰NZ,秘鲁PE 哥斯达黎加CR 巴基斯坦PK	0	最不发达35国LDC35,最不发达4国LDC4	35	---Banknote dispenser of automated teller

序号 No.	税则号列 Tariff Line	货品名称	最惠国税率 MFN(%)	协定税率 Agreement(%)		特惠税率 S.P.(%)		普通税率 Gen.(%)	Article Description
6707	8473.4090	---其他	10.5	0 2.1 5	东盟ASEAN,智利CL,新加坡SG,新西兰NZ,秘鲁PE 哥斯达黎加CR 巴基斯坦PK	0	最不发达35国LDC35,最不发达4国LDC4	35	---Other
	ex84734090	钞票清分机零附件	△3						Parts of banknote processing system
6708	8473.5000	-同样适用于税号84.69至84.72中两个或两个以上税号所列机器的零件、附件	0			0	最不发达35国LDC35,最不发达4国LDC4	35	-Parts and accessories equally suitable for use with machines of two or more of the headings No.84.69 to 84.72
	84.74	**泥土、石料、矿石或其他固体（包括粉状、浆状）矿物质的分类、筛选、分离、洗涤、破碎、磨粉、混合或搅拌机器;固体矿物燃料、陶瓷坯泥、未硬化水泥、石膏材料或其他粉状、浆状矿产品的粘聚或成形机器;铸造用砂模的成形机器:**							**Machinery for sorting, screening, separating, washing, crushing, grinding, mixing or kneading earth, stone, ores or other mineral substances, in solid (including powder or paste) form; machinery for agglomerating, shaping or moulding solid mineral fuels, ceramic past:**
6709	8474.1000	-分类、筛选、分离或洗涤机器	5	0 0.5	东盟ASEAN,巴基斯坦PK,新西兰NZ,秘鲁PE,哥斯达黎加CR 智利CL	0	最不发达35国LDC35,最不发达4国LDC4	30	-Sorting, screening, separating or washing machines
		-破碎或磨粉机器:							-Crushing or grinding machines:
6710	8474.2010	---齿辊式	5	0 0.5	东盟ASEAN,巴基斯坦PK,新西兰NZ,秘鲁PE,哥斯达黎加CR 智利CL	0	最不发达35国LDC35,最不发达4国LDC4	30	---Toothing roller type
6711	8474.2020	---球磨式	5	0 0.5	东盟ASEAN,巴基斯坦PK,新西兰NZ,秘鲁PE,哥斯达黎加CR 智利CL	0	最不发达35国LDC35,最不发达4国LDC4	30	---Em-Peters type
6712	8474.2090	---其他	5	0 0.5	东盟ASEAN,巴基斯坦PK,新西兰NZ,秘鲁PE,哥斯达黎加CR 智利CL	0	最不发达35国LDC35,最不发达4国LDC4	30	---Other
		-混合或搅拌机器:							-Mixing or kneading machines:

序号 No.	税则号列 Tariff Line	货品名称	最惠国税率 MFN(%)	协定税率 Agreement(%)		特惠税率 S.P.(%)		普通税率 Gen.(%)	Article Description
6713	8474.3100	--混凝土或砂浆混合机器	7	0 5	东盟ASEAN,智利CL,新西兰NZ,秘鲁PE,哥斯达黎加CR 巴基斯坦PK	0	最不发达35国LDC35,最不发达4国LDC4	30	--Concrete or mortar mixers
6714	8474.3200	--矿物与沥青的混合机器	7	0 0.7 5	东盟ASEAN,新西兰NZ,秘鲁PE,哥斯达黎加CR 智利CL 巴基斯坦PK	0	最不发达35国LDC35,最不发达4国LDC4	30	--Machines for mixing mineral substances with bitumen
6715	8474.3900	--其他	5	0 0.5	东盟ASEAN,巴基斯坦PK,新西兰NZ,秘鲁PE,哥斯达黎加CR 智利CL	0	最不发达35国LDC35,最不发达4国LDC4	30	--Other
		-其他机器:							-Other machinery:
6716	8474.8010	---辊压成型机	5	0 0.5 4.5	东盟ASEAN,巴基斯坦PK,新西兰NZ,秘鲁PE,哥斯达黎加CR 智利CL 亚太APTA	0	最不发达35国LDC35,最不发达4国LDC4	30	---Rolling forming machines
6717	8474.8020	---模压成型机	5	0 0.5 4.5	东盟ASEAN,巴基斯坦PK,新西兰NZ,秘鲁PE,哥斯达黎加CR 智利CL 亚太APTA	0	最不发达35国LDC35,最不发达4国LDC4	30	---Mould pressing machines
6718	8474.8090	---其他	5	0 0.5 4.5	东盟ASEAN,巴基斯坦PK,新西兰NZ,秘鲁PE,哥斯达黎加CR 智利CL 亚太APTA	0	最不发达35国LDC35,最不发达4国LDC4	30	---Other
6719	8474.9000	-零件	5	0 0.5	东盟ASEAN,巴基斯坦PK,新西兰NZ,秘鲁PE,哥斯达黎加CR 智利CL	0	最不发达35国LDC35,最不发达4国LDC4	30	-Parts
	84.75	**白炽灯泡、灯管、放电灯管、电子管、闪光灯泡及类似品的封装机器;玻璃或玻璃制品的制造或热加工机器:**							**Machines for assembling electric or electronic lamps, tubes or valves or flashbulbs, in glass envelopes; machines for manufacturing or hot working glass or glassware:**
6720	8475.1000	-白炽灯泡、灯管、放电灯管、电子管、闪光灯泡及类似品的封装机器	8	0 0.8 5	东盟ASEAN,新西兰NZ,秘鲁PE,哥斯达黎加CR 智利CL 巴基斯坦PK	0	最不发达35国LDC35,最不发达4国LDC4	30	-Machines for assembling electric or electronic lamps, tubes or valves or flashbulbs, in glass envelopes

序号 No.	税则号列 Tariff Line	货品名称	最惠国税率 MFN(%)	协定税率 Agreement(%)		特惠税率 S.P.(%)		普通税率 Gen.(%)	Article Description
		-玻璃或玻璃制品的制造或热加工机器:							-Machines for manufacturing or hot working glass or glassware:
6721	8475.2100	--制造光导纤维及其预制棒的机器	10	0 5	东盟ASEAN,智利CL,新加坡SG,新西兰NZ,秘鲁PE,哥斯达黎加CR 巴基斯坦PK	0	最不发达35国LDC35,最不发达4国LDC4	30	--Machines for making optical fibres and preforms thereof
		--其他:							--Other:
		---玻璃的热加工设备:							---Equipments for hot working glass or glasswares:
6722	8475.2911	----连续式玻璃热弯炉	10	0 5	东盟ASEAN,智利CL,新西兰NZ,秘鲁PE,哥斯达黎加CR 巴基斯坦PK	0	最不发达35国LDC35,最不发达4国LDC4	30	----Continuous hot bending furnaces
6723	8475.2912	----玻璃纤维拉丝机（光纤拉丝机除外）	10	0 5	东盟ASEAN,智利CL,新西兰NZ,秘鲁PE,哥斯达黎加CR 巴基斯坦PK	0	最不发达35国LDC35,最不发达4国LDC4	30	----Fiber glass winder (excluding Opticaefiber winder)
6724	8475.2919	----其他	10	0 5	东盟ASEAN,智利CL,新加坡SG,新西兰NZ,秘鲁PE,哥斯达黎加CR 巴基斯坦PK	0	最不发达35国LDC35,最不发达4国LDC4	30	----Other
6725	8475.2990	---其他	10	0 5	东盟ASEAN,智利CL,新西兰NZ,秘鲁PE,哥斯达黎加CR 巴基斯坦PK	0	最不发达35国LDC35,最不发达4国LDC4	30	---Other
6726	8475.9000	-零件	8	0 0.8 5	东盟ASEAN,新西兰NZ,秘鲁PE,哥斯达黎加CR 智利CL 巴基斯坦PK	0	最不发达35国LDC35,最不发达4国LDC4	30	-Parts
	84.76	**自动售货机（例如，出售邮票、香烟、食品或饮料的机器），包括钱币兑换机:**							**Automatic goods-vending machines (for example, postage stamp, cigarette, food or beverage machines), including money-changing machines:**
		-饮料自动销售机:							-Automatic beveragevending machines:

序号 No.	税则号列 Tariff Line	货品名称	最惠国税率 MFN(%)	协定税率 Agreement(%)		特惠税率 S.P.(%)		普通税率 Gen.(%)	Article Description
6727	8476.2100	--装有加热或制冷装置的	14	0 1.4 2.8 11.2	东盟ASEAN,新加坡SG,新西兰NZ,秘鲁PE 智利CL 哥斯达黎加CR 巴基斯坦PK	0	最不发达35国LDC35	50	--Incorporating heating or refrigerating devices
6728	8476.2900	--其他	15	0 3 7.5 12	东盟ASEAN,智利CL,新加坡SG,新西兰NZ 哥斯达黎加CR 秘鲁PE 巴基斯坦PK	0	最不发达35国LDC35	50	--Other
		-其他机器:							-Other machines:
6729	8476.8100	--装有加热或制冷装置的	14	0 2.8 7	东盟ASEAN,智利CL,新加坡SG,新西兰NZ,秘鲁PE 哥斯达黎加CR 巴基斯坦PK	0	最不发达35国LDC35	50	--Incorporating heating or refrigerating devices
6730	8476.8900	--其他	15	0 1.5 3 7.5 12	东盟ASEAN,新加坡SG,新西兰NZ 智利CL 哥斯达黎加CR 秘鲁PE 巴基斯坦PK	0	最不发达35国LDC35	50	--Other
6731	8476.9000	-零件	10	0 5	东盟ASEAN,智利CL,新西兰NZ,秘鲁PE,哥斯达黎加CR 巴基斯坦PK	0	最不发达35国LDC35,最不发达4国LDC4	50	-Parts
	84.77	**本章其他税号未列名的橡胶或塑料及其产品的加工机器:**							**Machinery for working rubber or plastics or for the manufacture of products from these materials, not specified or included elsewhere in this Chapter:**
		-注射机:							-Injection-moulding machines:
6732	8477.1010	---注塑机	0			0	最不发达35国LDC35,最不发达4国LDC4	45	---For working plastics
6733	8477.1090	---其他	0			0	最不发达35国LDC35,最不发达4国LDC4	30	---Other
		-挤出机:							-Extruders:
6734	8477.2010	---塑料造粒机	5	0 4.5	东盟ASEAN,智利CL,巴基斯坦PK,新西兰NZ,秘鲁PE,哥斯达黎加CR,香港HK,台湾TW 亚太APTA	0	最不发达35国LDC35,最不发达4国LDC4	30	---Plastic pelletizers

序号 No.	税则号列 Tariff Line	货品名称	最惠国税率 MFN(%)	协定税率 Agreement(%)		特惠税率 S.P.(%)		普通税率 Gen.(%)	Article Description
6735	8477.2090	---其他	5	0 4.5	东盟ASEAN,智利CL,巴基斯坦PK,新西兰NZ,秘鲁PE,哥斯达黎加CR,香港HK,台湾TW 亚太APTA	0	最不发达35国LDC35,最不发达4国LDC4	30	---Other
		-吹塑机:							-Blow moulding machines:
6736	8477.3010	---挤出吹塑机	5	0 0.5	东盟ASEAN,巴基斯坦PK,新西兰NZ,秘鲁PE,哥斯达黎加CR,香港HK 智利CL	0	最不发达35国LDC35,最不发达4国LDC4	30	---Extruding blow molding machines
6737	8477.3020	---注射吹塑机	5	0 0.5	东盟ASEAN,巴基斯坦PK,新西兰NZ,秘鲁PE,哥斯达黎加CR,香港HK 智利CL	0	最不发达35国LDC35,最不发达4国LDC4	30	---Injecting blow molding machines
6738	8477.3090	---其他	5	0 0.5	东盟ASEAN,巴基斯坦PK,新西兰NZ,秘鲁PE,哥斯达黎加CR,香港HK 智利CL	0	最不发达35国LDC35,最不发达4国LDC4	30	---Other
		-真空模塑机器及其他热成型机器:							-Vacuum moulding machines and other thermoforming machines:
6739	8477.4010	---塑料中空成型机	5	0 4.5	东盟ASEAN,智利CL,巴基斯坦PK,新西兰NZ,秘鲁PE,哥斯达黎加CR,台湾TW 亚太APTA	0	最不发达35国LDC35,最不发达4国LDC4	30	---Plastics brideg-die-forming machines
6740	8477.4020	---塑料压延成型机	5	0 4.5	东盟ASEAN,智利CL,巴基斯坦PK,新西兰NZ,秘鲁PE,哥斯达黎加CR,台湾TW 亚太APTA	0	最不发达35国LDC35,最不发达4国LDC4	30	---Plastics calender-forming machines
6741	8477.4090	---其他	5	0 4.5	东盟ASEAN,智利CL,巴基斯坦PK,新西兰NZ,秘鲁PE,哥斯达黎加CR,台湾TW 亚太APTA	0	最不发达35国LDC35,最不发达4国LDC4	30	---Other
		-其他模塑或成型机器:							-Other machinery for moulding or otherwise forming:
6742	8477.5100	--用于充气轮胎模塑或翻新的机器及内胎模塑或用其他方法成型的机器	5	0 0.5	东盟ASEAN,巴基斯坦PK,新西兰NZ,秘鲁PE,哥斯达黎加CR 智利CL	0	最不发达35国LDC35,最不发达4国LDC4	30	--For moulding or retreading pneumat-ic tyres or for moulding or otherwise forming inner tubes

序号 No.	税则号列 Tariff Line	货品名称	最惠国税率 MFN(%)	协定税率 Agreement(%)	特惠税率 S.P.(%)	普通税率 Gen.(%)	Article Description
		--其他:					--Other:
6743	8477.5910	---三维打印机（3D打印机）	5	0 东盟ASEAN,智利CL,巴基斯坦PK,新西兰NZ,秘鲁PE,哥斯达黎加CR,香港HK,台湾TW 3.5 亚太APTA	0 最不发达35国LDC35,最不发达4国LDC4	30	---3D printers
6744	8477.5990	---其他	5	0 东盟ASEAN,智利CL,巴基斯坦PK,新西兰NZ,秘鲁PE,哥斯达黎加CR,香港HK,台湾TW 3.5 亚太APTA	0 最不发达35国LDC35,最不发达4国LDC4	30	---Other
6745	8477.8000	-其他机器	5	0 东盟ASEAN,智利CL,巴基斯坦PK,新西兰NZ,秘鲁PE,哥斯达黎加CR,香港HK,台湾TW 4.5 亚太APTA	0 最不发达35国LDC35,最不发达4国LDC4	30	-Other machinery
6746	8477.9000	-零件	0		0 最不发达35国LDC35,最不发达4国LDC4	30	-Parts
	84.78	**本章其他税号未列名的烟草加工及制作机器:**					**Machinery for preparing or making up tobacco, not specified or included elsewhere in this Chapter:**
6747	8478.1000	-机器	5	0 东盟ASEAN,智利CL,巴基斯坦PK,新西兰NZ,秘鲁PE,哥斯达黎加CR 2.5 亚太APTA	0 最不发达35国LDC35	30	-Machinery
6748	8478.9000	-零件	10 △5	0 东盟ASEAN,智利CL,新西兰NZ,秘鲁PE,哥斯达黎加CR 5 巴基斯坦PK	0 最不发达35国LDC35	30	-Parts
	84.79	**本章其他税号未列名的具有独立功能的机器及机械器具:**					**Machines and mechanical appliances having individual functions, not specified or included elsewhere in this Chapter:**
		-公共工程用机器:					-Machinery for public works, building or the like:
		---摊铺机:					---Spreading machines:
6749	8479.1021	----沥青混凝土摊铺机	8	0 东盟ASEAN,新西兰NZ,秘鲁PE,哥斯达黎加CR 0.8 智利CL 5 巴基斯坦PK 5.6 亚太APTA	0 最不发达35国LDC35,最不发达4国LDC4	30	----Machines for spreading bituminous concrete

序号 No.	税则号列 Tariff Line	货品名称	最惠国税率 MFN(%)	协定税率 Agreement(%)		特惠税率 S.P.(%)		普通税率 Gen.(%)	Article Description
6750	8479.1022	----稳定土摊铺机	8	0 0.8 5 5.6	东盟ASEAN,新西兰NZ,秘鲁PE,哥斯达黎加CR 智利CL 巴基斯坦PK 亚太APTA	0	最不发达35国LDC35,最不发达4国LDC4	30	----Stabilizer spreading machines
6751	8479.1029	----其他	8	0 0.8 5 5.6	东盟ASEAN,新西兰NZ,秘鲁PE,哥斯达黎加CR 智利CL 巴基斯坦PK 亚太APTA	0	最不发达35国LDC35,最不发达4国LDC4	30	----Other
6752	8479.1090	---其他	8	0 0.8 5 5.6	东盟ASEAN,新西兰NZ,秘鲁PE,哥斯达黎加CR 智利CL 巴基斯坦PK 亚太APTA	0	最不发达35国LDC35,最不发达4国LDC4	30	---Other
6753	8479.2000	-提取、加工动物油脂或植物固定油脂的机器	10	0 1 5	东盟ASEAN,新加坡SG,新西兰NZ,秘鲁PE,哥斯达黎加CR 智利CL 巴基斯坦PK	0	最不发达35国LDC35,最不发达4国LDC4	30	-Machinery for the extraction or preparation of animal or fixed vegetable fats or oils
6754	8479.3000	-木碎料板或木纤维板的挤压机及其他木材或软木处理机	10	0 5	东盟ASEAN,智利CL,新西兰NZ,秘鲁PE,哥斯达黎加CR 巴基斯坦PK	0	最不发达35国LDC35,最不发达4国LDC4	30	-Presses for the manufacture of particle board or fibre building board or wood or other ligneous materials and other machinery for treating wood or cork
6755	8479.4000	-绳或缆的制造机器	7 △5	0 5	东盟ASEAN,智利CL,新西兰NZ,秘鲁PE,哥斯达黎加CR 巴基斯坦PK	0	最不发达35国LDC35,最不发达4国LDC4	30	-Rope or cable-making machines
		-未列名工业机器人:							-Industrial robots, not elsewhere specified or included:
6756	8479.5010	---多功能工业机器人	0			0	最不发达35国LDC35,最不发达4国LDC4	20	---Industrial robots for multiple functions
6757	8479.5090	---其他	0			0	最不发达35国LDC35,最不发达4国LDC4	30	---Other

序号 No.	税则号列 Tariff Line	货品名称	最惠国税率 MFN(%)	协定税率 Agreement(%)	特惠税率 S.P.(%)	普通税率 Gen.(%)	Article Description
6758	8479.6000	-蒸发式空气冷却器	10	0 东盟ASEAN,智利CL,新西兰NZ,秘鲁PE,哥斯达黎加CR 5 巴基斯坦PK 9 亚太APTA	0 最不发达35国LDC35,最不发达4国LDC4	30	-Evaporative air coolers
		-旅客登机船(桥):					-Passenger boarding bridges:
6759	8479.7100	--用于机场的	0		0 最不发达35国LDC35,最不发达4国LDC4	30	--Used in airports
6760	8479.7900	--其他	0		0 最不发达35国LDC35,最不发达4国LDC4	30	--Other
		-其他机器及机械器具: --处理金属的机械,包括线圈绕线机:					-Other machines and mechanical appliances: --For treating metal, including electric wire coil-winders:
6761	8479.8110	---绕线机	9.5	0 东盟ASEAN,新西兰NZ,秘鲁PE,哥斯达黎加CR,香港HK,台湾TW 1 智利CL 5 巴基斯坦PK 9 亚太APTA	0 最不发达35国LDC35,最不发达4国LDC4	30	---Filament winding machines
6762	8479.8190	---其他	9.5	0 东盟ASEAN,新西兰NZ,秘鲁PE,哥斯达黎加CR,香港HK,台湾TW 1 智利CL 5 巴基斯坦PK 9 亚太APTA	0 最不发达35国LDC35,最不发达4国LDC4	30	---Other
6763	8479.8200	--混合、搅拌、轧碎、研磨、筛选、均化或乳化机器	7	0 东盟ASEAN,智利CL,巴基斯坦PK,新西兰NZ,秘鲁PE,哥斯达黎加CR,台湾TW 4.9 亚太APTA	0 最不发达35国LDC35,最不发达4国LDC4	30	--Mixing, kneading, crushing, grinding, screening, sifting, homogenizing, emulsifying or stirring machines
		--其他:					--Other:
6764	8479.8910	---船舶用舵机及陀螺稳定器	0		0 最不发达35国LDC35,最不发达4国LDC4	14	---Steering and rudder equipment or gyroscopic stabilizers for ships
6765	8479.8920	---空气增湿器及减湿器	0		0 最不发达35国LDC35,最不发达4国LDC4	70	---Air humidifiers or dehumidifiers

序号 No.	税则号列 Tariff Line	货品名称	最惠国税率 MFN(%)	协定税率 Agreement(%)	特惠税率 S.P.(%)	普通税率 Gen.(%)	Article Description
6766	8479.8940	---邮政用包裹、印刷品分拣设备	0		0 最不发达35国 LDC35, 最不发达4国 LDC4	30	---Bundle and printed matter sorting machines used in post offices
6767	8479.8950	---放射性废物压实机	0		0 最不发达35国 LDC35, 最不发达4国 LDC4	30	---Presses for radioactive waste material
		---在印刷电路电路板上装配元器件的机器:					---Machines for assemblying elements on printed circuit boards:
6768	8479.8961	----自动插件机	0		0 最不发达35国 LDC35, 最不发达4国 LDC4	30	----Automatic plugin machines
6769	8479.8962	----自动贴片机	0		0 最不发达35国 LDC35, 最不发达4国 LDC4	30	----Automatic coreslice adhering machines
6770	8479.8969	----其他	0		0 最不发达35国 LDC35, 最不发达4国 LDC4	30	----Other
		---其他:					---Other:
6771	8479.8992	----自动化立体仓储设备	0		0 最不发达35国 LDC35, 最不发达4国 LDC4	30	----Automated high-rise warehouse
6772	8479.8999	----其他	0		0 最不发达35国 LDC35, 最不发达4国 LDC4	30	----Other
		-零件:					-Parts:
6773	8479.9010	---船舶用舵机及陀螺稳定器用	0		0 最不发达35国 LDC35, 最不发达4国 LDC4	14	---Of the machines of subheading No.8479.8910

序号 No.	税则号列 Tariff Line	货品名称	最惠国税率 MFN(%)	协定税率 Agreement(%)	特惠税率 S.P.(%)	普通税率 Gen.(%)	Article Description
6774	8479.9020	---空气增湿器及减湿器用	0		0 最不发达35国LDC35,最不发达4国LDC4	70	---Of the machines of subheading No.8479.8920
6775	8479.9090	---其他	0		0 最不发达35国LDC35,最不发达4国LDC4	20	---Other
	84.80	**金属铸造用型箱;型模底板;阳模;金属用型模(锭模除外)、硬质合金、玻璃、矿物材料、橡胶或塑料用型模:**					**Moulding boxes for metal foundry; mould bases; moulding patterns; moulds for metal (other than ingot moulds), metal carbides, glass, mineral materials, rubber or plastics:**
6776	8480.1000	-金属铸造用型箱	10	0 东盟ASEAN,智利CL,新西兰NZ,秘鲁PE,哥斯达黎加CR 5 巴基斯坦PK	0 最不发达35国LDC35,最不发达4国LDC4	20	-Moulding boxes for metal foundry
6777	8480.2000	-型模底板	8	0 东盟ASEAN,智利CL,新西兰NZ,秘鲁PE,哥斯达黎加CR 5 巴基斯坦PK	0 最不发达35国LDC35,最不发达4国LDC4	20	-Mould bases
6778	8480.3000	-阳模	10	0 东盟ASEAN,智利CL,新加坡SG,新西兰NZ,秘鲁PE,哥斯达黎加CR 5 巴基斯坦PK	0 最不发达35国LDC35,最不发达4国LDC4	20	-Moulding patterns
		-金属、硬质合金用型模: --注模或压模:					-Moulds for metal or metal carbides: --Injection or compression types:
6779	8480.4110	---压铸模	8	0 东盟ASEAN,智利CL,新西兰NZ,秘鲁PE,哥斯达黎加CR,香港HK,台湾TW 5 巴基斯坦PK 5.6 亚太APTA	0 最不发达35国LDC35,最不发达4国LDC4	20	---Die casting moulds
6780	8480.4120	---粉末冶金用压模	8	0 东盟ASEAN,智利CL,新西兰NZ,秘鲁PE,哥斯达黎加CR,香港HK,台湾TW 5 巴基斯坦PK 5.6 亚太APTA	0 最不发达35国LDC35,最不发达4国LDC4	20	---Compression moulds for power metallurgy

序号 No.	税则号列 Tariff Line	货品名称	最惠国税率 MFN(%)	协定税率 Agreement(%)		特惠税率 S.P.(%)		普通税率 Gen.(%)	Article Description
6781	8480.4190	---其他	8	0 5 5.6	东盟ASEAN,智利CL,新西兰NZ,秘鲁PE,哥斯达黎加CR,香港HK,台湾TW 巴基斯坦PK 亚太APTA	0	最不发达35国LDC35,最不发达4国LDC4	20	---Other
6782	8480.4900	---其他	8	0 5 5.6	东盟ASEAN,智利CL,新西兰NZ,秘鲁PE,哥斯达黎加CR 巴基斯坦PK 亚太APTA	0	最不发达35国LDC35,最不发达4国LDC4	20	--Other
6783	8480.5000	-玻璃用型模	8.4	0 5	东盟ASEAN,智利CL,新西兰NZ,秘鲁PE,哥斯达黎加CR 巴基斯坦PK	0	最不发达35国LDC35,最不发达4国LDC4	20	-Moulds for glass
6784	8480.6000	-矿物材料用型模	8.4	0 0.8 5	东盟ASEAN,新西兰NZ,秘鲁PE,哥斯达黎加CR 智利CL 巴基斯坦PK	0	最不发达35国LDC35,最不发达4国LDC4	20	-Moulds for mineral materials
		-塑料或橡胶用型模:							-Moulds for rubber or plastics:
		--注模或压模:							--Injection or compression types:
6785	8480.7110	---硫化轮胎用囊式型模	0			0	最不发达35国LDC35,最不发达4国LDC4	20	---"Bladder" moulds for vulcanising tyres
6786	8480.7190	---其他	0			0	最不发达35国LDC35,最不发达4国LDC4	20	---Other
6787	8480.7900	--其他	5	0 3.5	东盟ASEAN,智利CL,巴基斯坦PK,新西兰NZ,秘鲁PE,哥斯达黎加CR,香港HK,台湾TW 亚太APTA	0	最不发达35国LDC35,最不发达4国LDC4	20	--Other
	84.81	**用于管道、锅炉、罐、桶或类似品的龙头、旋塞、阀门及类似装置,包括减压阀及恒温控制阀:**							**Taps, cocks, valves and similar appliances for pipes, boiler shells, tanks, vats or the like, including pressure-reducing valves and thermostatically controlled valves:**

序号 No.	税则号列 Tariff Line	货品名称	最惠国税率 MFN(%)	协定税率 Agreement(%)		特惠税率 S.P.(%)		普通税率 Gen.(%)	Article Description
6788	8481.1000	-减压阀	5	0 0.5	东盟ASEAN,巴基斯坦PK,新西兰NZ,秘鲁PE,哥斯达黎加CR 智利CL	0	最不发达35国LDC35,最不发达4国LDC4	30	-Pressure-reducing valves
	ex84811000	喷灌设备用减压阀	△2						Pressure reducing valves for sprinkler equipment
		-油压或气压传动阀:							-Valves for oleohydraulic or pneumatic transmissions:
6789	8481.2010	---油压的	5	0 0.5	东盟ASEAN,巴基斯坦PK,新西兰NZ,秘鲁PE,哥斯达黎加CR,台湾TW 智利CL	0	最不发达35国LDC35,最不发达4国LDC4	30	---For oleohydraulic transmissions
6790	8481.2020	---气压的	5	0 0.5	东盟ASEAN,巴基斯坦PK,新西兰NZ,秘鲁PE,哥斯达黎加CR 智利CL	0	最不发达35国LDC35,最不发达4国LDC4	30	---For pneumatic transmissions
6791	8481.3000	-止回阀	5 △3	0 0.5	东盟ASEAN,巴基斯坦PK,新西兰NZ,秘鲁PE,哥斯达黎加CR,台湾TW 智利CL	0	最不发达35国LDC35,最不发达4国LDC4	30	-Check (nonreturn) valves
6792	8481.4000	-安全阀或溢流阀	5	0 0.5	东盟ASEAN,巴基斯坦PK,新西兰NZ,秘鲁PE,哥斯达黎加CR,台湾TW 智利CL	0	最不发达35国LDC35,最不发达4国LDC4	30	-Safety or relief valves
		-其他器具:							-Other appliances:
		---换向阀:							---Directional control valves:
6793	8481.8021	----电磁式	7	0 0.7 4.9	东盟ASEAN,巴基斯坦PK,新西兰NZ,秘鲁PE,哥斯达黎加CR,香港HK,台湾TW 智利CL 亚太APTA	0	最不发达35国LDC35,最不发达4国LDC4	30	----Electromagnetical operated
6794	8481.8029	----其他	7	0 0.7 4.9	东盟ASEAN,巴基斯坦PK,新西兰NZ,秘鲁PE,哥斯达黎加CR,香港HK,台湾TW 智利CL 亚太APTA	0	最不发达35国LDC35,最不发达4国LDC4	30	----Other
		---流量阀:							---Flow valves:

序号 No.	税则号列 Tariff Line	货品名称	最惠国税率 MFN(%)	协定税率 Agreement(%)		特惠税率 S.P.(%)		普通税率 Gen.(%)	Article Description
6795	8481.8031	----电子膨胀阀	7	0	东盟ASEAN,巴基斯坦PK,新西兰NZ,秘鲁PE,哥斯达黎加CR,香港HK,台湾TW	0	最不发达35国LDC35,最不发达4国LDC4	30	----Electronic expansion valves
				0.7	智利CL				
				4.9	亚太APTA				
6796	8481.8039	----其他	7	0	东盟ASEAN,巴基斯坦PK,新西兰NZ,秘鲁PE,哥斯达黎加CR,香港HK,台湾TW	0	最不发达35国LDC35,最不发达4国LDC4	30	----Other
				0.7	智利CL				
				4.9	亚太APTA				
6797	8481.8040	---其他阀门	7 △3	0	东盟ASEAN,巴基斯坦PK,新西兰NZ,秘鲁PE,哥斯达黎加CR,香港HK,台湾TW	0	最不发达35国LDC35,最不发达4国LDC4	30	---Other valves
				0.7	智利CL				
				4.9	亚太APTA				
6798	8481.8090	---其他	5	0	东盟ASEAN,巴基斯坦PK,新西兰NZ,秘鲁PE,哥斯达黎加CR,香港HK	0	最不发达35国LDC35,最不发达4国LDC4	50	---Other
				0.5	智利CL				
		-零件:							-Parts:
6799	8481.9010	---阀门用	8 △4	0	东盟ASEAN,新西兰NZ,秘鲁PE,哥斯达黎加CR,台湾TW	0	最不发达35国LDC35,最不发达4国LDC4	30	---Of valves
				0.8	智利CL				
				5	巴基斯坦PK				
6800	8481.9090	---其他	8	0	东盟ASEAN,新西兰NZ,秘鲁PE,哥斯达黎加CR,台湾TW	0	最不发达35国LDC35,最不发达4国LDC4	50	---Other
				0.8	智利CL				
				5	巴基斯坦PK				
	84.82	**滚动轴承:**							**Ball or roller bearings:**
		-滚珠轴承:							-Ball bearings:
6801	8482.1010	---调心球轴承	8	0	东盟ASEAN,新加坡SG,新西兰NZ,秘鲁PE,哥斯达黎加CR,香港HK	0	最不发达35国LDC35,最不发达4国LDC4	20	---Self-aligning ball bearing
				0.8	智利CL				
				5	巴基斯坦PK				
				7.6	亚太APTA				
6802	8482.1020	---深沟球轴承	8	0	东盟ASEAN,新加坡SG,新西兰NZ,秘鲁PE,哥斯达黎加CR,香港HK	0	最不发达35国LDC35,最不发达4国LDC4	20	---Deep groove ball bearing
				0.8	智利CL				
				5	巴基斯坦PK				
				7.6	亚太APTA				

序号 No.	税则号列 Tariff Line	货品名称	最惠国税率 MFN(%)	协定税率 Agreement(%)		特惠税率 S.P.(%)		普通税率 Gen.(%)	Article Description
6803	8482.1030	---角接触轴承	8	0 0.8 5 7.6	东盟ASEAN,新加坡SG,新西兰NZ,秘鲁PE,哥斯达黎加CR,香港HK 智利CL 巴基斯坦PK 亚太APTA	0	最不发达35国LDC35,最不发达4国LDC4	20	---Angular contact ball bearing
6804	8482.1040	---推力球轴承	8	0 0.8 5 7.6	东盟ASEAN,新加坡SG,新西兰NZ,秘鲁PE,哥斯达黎加CR,香港HK 智利CL 巴基斯坦PK 亚太APTA	0	最不发达35国LDC35,最不发达4国LDC4	20	---Thrust ball bearing
6805	8482.1090	---其他	8	0 0.8 5 7.6	东盟ASEAN,新加坡SG,新西兰NZ,秘鲁PE,哥斯达黎加CR,香港HK 智利CL 巴基斯坦PK 亚太APTA	0	最不发达35国LDC35,最不发达4国LDC4	20	---Other
6806	8482.2000	-锥形滚子轴承,包括锥形滚子组件	8	0 5	东盟ASEAN,智利CL,新西兰NZ,秘鲁PE,哥斯达黎加CR 巴基斯坦PK	0	最不发达35国LDC35,最不发达4国LDC4	20	-Tapered roller bearings, including cone and tapered roller assemblies
6807	8482.3000	-鼓形滚子轴承	8 △6	0 5	东盟ASEAN,智利CL,新西兰NZ,秘鲁PE,哥斯达黎加CR 巴基斯坦PK	0	最不发达35国LDC35,最不发达4国LDC4	20	-Spherical roller bearings
6808	8482.4000	-滚针轴承	8 △6	0 5	东盟ASEAN,智利CL,新西兰NZ,秘鲁PE,哥斯达黎加CR,台湾TW 巴基斯坦PK	0	最不发达35国LDC35,最不发达4国LDC4	20	-Needle roller bearings
6809	8482.5000	-其他圆柱形滚子轴承	8	0 5	东盟ASEAN,智利CL,新加坡SG,新西兰NZ,秘鲁PE,哥斯达黎加CR 巴基斯坦PK	0	最不发达35国LDC35,最不发达4国LDC4	20	-Other cylindrical roller bearings
	ex84825000	三环偏心滚动轴承	△4						Eccentric 3-ring roller bearing
6810	8482.8000	-其他,包括球、柱混合轴承	8	0 0.8 5 5.6	东盟ASEAN,新西兰NZ,秘鲁PE,哥斯达黎加CR 智利CL 巴基斯坦PK 亚太APTA	0	最不发达35国LDC35,最不发达4国LDC4	20	-Other, including combined ball/roller bearings
		-零件:							-Parts:

序号 No.	税则号列 Tariff Line	货品名称	最惠国税率 MFN(%)	协定税率 Agreement(%)	特惠税率 S.P.(%)	普通税率 Gen.(%)	Article Description
6811	8482.9100	--滚珠、滚针及滚柱	8 △6	0 东盟ASEAN,智利CL,新西兰NZ,秘鲁PE,哥斯达黎加CR 5 巴基斯坦PK	0 最不发达35国LDC35,最不发达4国LDC4	20	--Balls, needles and rollers
6812	8482.9900	--其他	6 △3	0 东盟ASEAN,智利CL,新西兰NZ,秘鲁PE,哥斯达黎加CR,台湾TW 5 巴基斯坦PK	0 最不发达35国LDC35,最不发达4国LDC4	20	--Other
	84.83	**传动轴（包括凸轮轴及曲柄轴）及曲柄;轴承座及滑动轴承;齿轮及齿轮传动装置;滚珠或滚子螺杆传动装置;齿轮箱及其他变速装置,包括扭矩变换器;飞轮及滑轮,包括滑轮组;离合器及联轴器（包括万向节）:**					**Transmission shafts (including cam shafts and crank shafts) and cranks; bearing housings and plain shaft bearings; gears and gearing ball or roller screws; gear boxes and other speed changers, including torque converters; flywheels and pulleys, including pulley blocks; clutches and shaft couplings (including universal joints):**
		-传动轴(包括凸轮轴及曲柄轴）及曲柄:					-Transmission shafts (including cam shafts and crank shafts) and cranks:
		---船舶用传动轴:					---Transmission shafts for ships:
6813	8483.1011	----柴油机曲轴	6	0 东盟ASEAN,新西兰NZ,秘鲁PE,哥斯达黎加CR,香港HK,澳门MO 0.6 智利CL 5 巴基斯坦PK 5.1 亚太APTA	0 最不发达35国LDC35,最不发达4国LDC4	14	----Diesel engine crankshaft
6814	8483.1019	----其他	6	0 东盟ASEAN,新西兰NZ,秘鲁PE,哥斯达黎加CR,香港HK,澳门MO 0.6 智利CL 5 巴基斯坦PK 5.1 亚太APTA	0 最不发达35国LDC35,最不发达4国LDC4	14	----Other
6815	8483.1090	---其他	6	0 东盟ASEAN,新西兰NZ,秘鲁PE,哥斯达黎加CR,香港HK,澳门MO 0.6 智利CL 5 巴基斯坦PK 5.4 亚太APTA	0 最不发达35国LDC35,最不发达4国LDC4	30	---Other

序号 No.	税则号列 Tariff Line	货品名称	最惠国税率 MFN(%)	协定税率 Agreement(%)		特惠税率 S.P.(%)		普通税率 Gen.(%)	Article Description
6816	8483.2000	-装有滚珠或滚子轴承的轴承座	6	0 5	东盟ASEAN,智利CL,新西兰NZ,秘鲁PE,哥斯达黎加CR,澳门MO 巴基斯坦PK	0	最不发达35国LDC35,最不发达4国LDC4	30	-Bearing housings, incorporating ball or roller bearings
6817	8483.3000	-未装有滚珠或滚子轴承的轴承座;滑动轴承	6 △3	0 0.6 5	东盟ASEAN,新西兰NZ,秘鲁PE,哥斯达黎加CR,澳门MO 智利CL 巴基斯坦PK	0	最不发达35国LDC35,最不发达4国LDC4	30	-Bearing housings, not incorporating ball or roller bearings; plain shaft bearings
		-齿轮及齿轮传动装置,但单独进口或出口的带齿的轮、链轮及其他传动元件除外;滚珠或滚子螺杆传动装置;齿轮箱及其他变速装置,包括扭矩变换器:							-Gears and gearing, other than toothed wheels, chain sprockets and other transmission elements presented separately; ball or roller screws;gear boxes and other speed changers, including torque converters:
6818	8483.4010	---滚子螺杆传动装置	8	0 0.8 5 5.6	东盟ASEAN,新西兰NZ,秘鲁PE,哥斯达黎加CR,香港HK,澳门MO,台湾TW 智利CL 巴基斯坦PK 亚太APTA	0	最不发达35国LDC35,最不发达4国LDC4	30	---Roller Screws
6819	8483.4020	---行星齿轮减速器	8	0 0.8 5 5.6	东盟ASEAN,新西兰NZ,秘鲁PE,哥斯达黎加CR,香港HK,澳门MO 智利CL 巴基斯坦PK 亚太APTA	0	最不发达35国LDC35,最不发达4国LDC4	30	---Planet decelerators
	ex84834020	磨煤机用行星齿轮减速器 (由螺旋伞齿轮加行星齿轮二级立式减速机构组成, 转盘外圆直径为: 1300~2400毫米)	△2						Planetary decelerators for use with coal mill, (composed of helical bevel gear and planetary gear two-stage vertical reducing mechanism, rotary table outline diameter: 1300~2400mm)
6820	8483.4090	---其他	8	0 0.8 5 5.6	东盟ASEAN,新西兰NZ,秘鲁PE,哥斯达黎加CR,香港HK,澳门MO,台湾TW 智利CL 巴基斯坦PK 亚太APTA	0	最不发达35国LDC35,最不发达4国LDC4	30	---Other

序号 No.	税则号列 Tariff Line	货品名称	最惠国税率 MFN(%)	协定税率 Agreement(%)		特惠税率 S.P.(%)		普通税率 Gen.(%)	Article Description
6821	8483.5000	-飞轮及滑轮,包括滑轮组	8	0 5	东盟ASEAN,智利CL,新西兰NZ,秘鲁PE,哥斯达黎加CR,澳门MO 巴基斯坦PK	0	最不发达35国LDC35,最不发达4国LDC4	30	-Flywheels and pulleys, including pulley blocks
6822	8483.6000	-离合器及联轴器(包括万向节)	8	0 5	东盟ASEAN,智利CL,新西兰NZ,秘鲁PE,哥斯达黎加CR,澳门MO 巴基斯坦PK	0	最不发达35国LDC35,最不发达4国LDC4	30	-Clutches and shaft couplings (including universal joints)
	ex84836000	压力机用组合式湿式离合/制动器,离合扭距为60KNM~300KNM,制动扭距为30KNM~100KNM	△4						Hydraulic actuated clutch/brake, for press machinery, 60KNM≤clutch torque ≤300KNM, 30KNM≤braking torque≤100KNM
6823	8483.9000	-单独报验的带齿的轮、链轮及其他传动元件;零件	8	0 0.8 5	东盟ASEAN,新西兰NZ,秘鲁PE,哥斯达黎加CR,香港HK,澳门MO,台湾TW 智利CL 巴基斯坦PK	0	最不发达35国LDC35,最不发达4国LDC4	30	-Toothed wheels, chain sprockets and other transmission elements presented separately; parts
	84.84	**密封垫或类似接合衬垫,用金属片与其他材料制成或用双层或多层金属片制成;成套或各种不同材料的密封垫或类似接合衬垫,装于袋、套或类似包装内;机械密封件:**							**Gaskets and similar joints of metal sheeting combined with other material or of two or more layers of metal; sets or assortments of gaskets and similar joints, dissimilar in composition, put up in pouches, envelopes or similar packings mechanical seals:**
6824	8484.1000	-密封垫或类似接合衬垫,用金属片与其他材料制成或用双层或多层金属片制成	8 △5	0 5	东盟ASEAN,智利CL,新西兰NZ,秘鲁PE,哥斯达黎加CR,台湾TW 巴基斯坦PK	0	最不发达35国LDC35,最不发达4国LDC4	30	-Gaskets and similar joints of metal sheeting combined with other material or of two or more layers of metal
6825	8484.2000	-机械密封件	8 △5	0 5	东盟ASEAN,智利CL,新西兰NZ,秘鲁PE,哥斯达黎加CR 巴基斯坦PK	0	最不发达35国LDC35,最不发达4国LDC4	30	-Mechanical seals
6826	8484.9000	-其他	8 △5	0 5	东盟ASEAN,智利CL,新西兰NZ,秘鲁PE,哥斯达黎加CR 巴基斯坦PK	0	最不发达35国LDC35,最不发达4国LDC4	30	-Other

序号 No.	税则号列 Tariff Line	货品名称	最惠国税率 MFN(%)	协定税率 Agreement(%)	特惠税率 S.P.(%)	普通税率 Gen.(%)	Article Description
	84.86	**专用于或主要用于制造半导体单晶柱或晶圆、半导体器件、集成电路或平板显示器的机器及装置；本章注释九（三）规定的机器及装置；零件及附件：**					**Machines and apparatus of a kind used solely or principally for the manufacture of semiconductor boules or wafers, semiconductor devices, electronic integrated circuits or flat panel displays; machines and apparatus specified in Note 9 (C) to this Chapter**
		-制造单晶柱或晶圆用的机器及装置：					-Machines and apparatus for the manufacture of boules or wafers:
6827	8486.1010	---利用温度变化处理单晶硅的机器及装置	0		0 最不发达35国 LDC35，最不发达4国 LDC4	30	---Machines and apparatus for the manufacture of boules by aprocess involving a change of temperature
6828	8486.1020	---研磨设备	0		0 最不发达35国 LDC35，最不发达4国 LDC4	30	---Grinding machines
6829	8486.1030	---切割设备	0		0 最不发达35国 LDC35，最不发达4国 LDC4	30	---Sawing or cutting-off machines
6830	8486.1040	---化学机械抛光设备（CMP）	0		0 最不发达35国 LDC35，最不发达4国 LDC4	30	---Chemical mechanical polishers (CMP)
6831	8486.1090	---其他	0		0 最不发达35国 LDC35，最不发达4国 LDC4	30	---Other
		-制造半导体器件或集成电路用的机器及装置：					-Machines and apparatus for the manufacture of semiconductor devices or of electronic integrated circuits:
6832	8486.2010	---氧化、扩散、退火及其他热处理设备	0		0 最不发达35国 LDC35，最不发达4国 LDC4	30	---Diffusion, oxidation or annealing furnaces, ovens and other heating equipments

序号 No.	税则号列 Tariff Line	货品名称	最惠国税率 MFN(%)	协定税率 Agreement(%)	特惠税率 S.P.(%)	普通税率 Gen.(%)	Article Description
		---薄膜沉积设备:					---Film deposition equipments:
6833	8486.2021	----化学气相沉积装置（CVD）	0		0 最不发达35国LDC35，最不发达4国LDC4	30	----Chemical Vapour Deposition (CVD) equipment
6834	8486.2022	----物理气相沉积装置（PVD）	0		0 最不发达35国LDC35，最不发达4国LDC4	30	----Physical Vapour Deposition (PVD) equipment
6835	8486.2029	----其他	0		0 最不发达35国LDC35，最不发达4国LDC4	30	----Other
		---将电路图投影或绘制到感光半导体材料上的装置:					---Apparatus for the projection or drawing of circuit patterns on sensitized semiconductor materials:
6836	8486.2031	----分步重复光刻机（步进光刻机）	0		0 最不发达35国LDC35，最不发达4国LDC4	100	----Step and repeat aligners
6837	8486.2039	----其他	0		0 最不发达35国LDC35，最不发达4国LDC4	100	----Other
		---刻蚀及剥离设备:					---Etching and stripping equipments:
6838	8486.2041	----等离子体干法刻蚀机	0		0 最不发达35国LDC35，最不发达4国LDC4	30	----Dry plasma etching
6839	8486.2049	----其他	0		0 最不发达35国LDC35，最不发达4国LDC4	30	----Other

序号 No.	税则号列 Tariff Line	货品名称	最惠国税 率 MFN(%)	协定税率 Agreement(%)	特惠税率 S.P.(%)	普通税率 Gen.(%)	Article Description
6840	8486.2050	---离子注入机	0		0 最不发达35国LDC35,最不发达4国LDC4	11	---Ion Implanters for doping
6841	8486.2090	---其他	0		0 最不发达35国LDC35,最不发达4国LDC4	30	---Other
		-制造平板显示器用的机器及装置：					-Machines and apparatus for the manufacture of flat panel displays:
6842	8486.3010	---扩散、氧化、退火及其他热处理设备	0		0 最不发达35国LDC35,最不发达4国LDC4	30	---Diffusion, oxidation or annealing furnaces, ovens and other heating equipments
		---薄膜沉积设备：					---Film deposition equipments:
6843	8486.3021	----化学气相沉积设备（CVD）	0		0 最不发达35国LDC35,最不发达4国LDC4	30	----Chemical Vapour Deposition (CVD) equipment
6844	8486.3022	----物理气相沉积设备(PVD)	0		0 最不发达35国LDC35,最不发达4国LDC4	30	----Physical Vapour Deposition (PVD) equipment
6845	8486.3029	----其他	0		0 最不发达35国LDC35,最不发达4国LDC4	30	----Other
		---将电路图投影或绘制到感光半导体材料上的装置：					---Apparatus for the projection or drawing of circuit patterns on sensitized semiconductor materials:
6846	8486.3031	----分布重复光刻机	0		0 最不发达35国LDC35,最不发达4国LDC4	100	----Step and repeat aligners

序号 No.	税则号列 Tariff Line	货品名称	最惠国税率 MFN(%)	协定税率 Agreement(%)		特惠税率 S.P.(%)		普通税率 Gen.(%)	Article Description
6847	8486.3039	----其他	0			0	最不发达35国LDC35,最不发达4国LDC4	100	----Other
		---湿法蚀刻、显影、剥离、清洗装置:							---Apparatus for wet-etching, developing, stripping or cleaning:
6848	8486.3041	----超声波清洗装置	10 △5	0 5	东盟ASEAN,智利CL,新加坡SG,新西兰NZ,秘鲁PE,哥斯达黎加CR 巴基斯坦PK	0	最不发达35国LDC35,最不发达4国LDC4	30	----Cleaning apparatus operated by ultrasonic processes
6849	8486.3049	----其他	0			0	最不发达35国LDC35,最不发达4国LDC4	30	----Other
6850	8486.3090	---其他	0			0	最不发达35国LDC35,最不发达4国LDC4	30	---Other
		-本章注释九(三)规定的机器及装置:							-Machines and apparatus specified in Note 9 (C) to this Chapter:
6851	8486.4010	---主要用于或专用于制作和修复掩膜版或投影掩膜版的装置	0			0	最不发达35国LDC35,最不发达4国LDC4	70	---Machines and apparatus solely or principally of a kind used for the manufacture or repair of masks and reticles
		---主要用于或专用于装配与封装半导体器件或集成电路的设备:							---Machines and apparatus solely or principally of a kind used for assembling semiconductor devices or electronic integrated circuits:
6852	8486.4021	----塑封机	5	0 4.5	东盟ASEAN,智利CL,巴基斯坦PK,新西兰NZ,秘鲁PE,哥斯达黎加CR 亚太APTA	0	最不发达35国LDC35,最不发达4国LDC4	30	----Encapsulation equipment for making the plastic casings
6853	8486.4022	----引线键合装置	8	0 5 7.6	东盟ASEAN,智利CL,新西兰NZ,秘鲁PE,哥斯达黎加CR,香港HK 巴基斯坦PK 亚太APTA	0	最不发达35国LDC35,最不发达4国LDC4	30	----Wire bonders

序号 No.	税则号列 Tariff Line	货品名称	最惠国税率 MFN(%)	协定税率 Agreement(%)	特惠税率 S.P.(%)	普通税率 Gen.(%)	Article Description
	ex84864022	全自动铝丝焊接机	△6				Automatic aluminum wire bonders
6854	8486.4029	----其他	0		0 最不发达35国LDC35,最不发达4国LDC4	17	----Other
		---主要用于或专用于升降、装卸、搬运单晶柱、晶圆、半导体器件、集成电路或平板显示器的装置:					---Machines and apparatus solely or principally of a kind used for lifting, handling, loading or unloading of boules, wafers, semiconductor devices, electronic integrated circuits and flat panel displays:
6855	8486.4031	----集成电路工厂专用的自动搬运机器人	0		0 最不发达35国LDC35,最不发达4国LDC4	20	----Automated material handling robots solely of a kind used for transport in electronic integrated circuits industry
6856	8486.4039	----其他	5	0 东盟ASEAN,巴基斯坦PK,新西兰NZ,秘鲁PE,哥斯达黎加CR 0.5 智利CL 3.5 亚太APTA	0 最不发达35国LDC35,最不发达4国LDC4	30	----Other
		-零件及附件:					- Parts and accessories:
6857	8486.9010	---升降、搬运、装卸机器用（自动搬运设备用除外）	5	0 东盟ASEAN,巴基斯坦PK,新西兰NZ,秘鲁PE,哥斯达黎加CR 0.5 智利CL 2.5 亚太APTA	0 最不发达35国LDC35,最不发达4国LDC4	30	---Of machines and apparatus for lifting, handling, loading or unloading (excluding automated material handling machines)
6858	8486.9020	---引线键合装置用	6	0 东盟ASEAN,智利CL,新西兰NZ,秘鲁PE,哥斯达黎加CR 5 巴基斯坦PK 5.7 亚太APTA	0 最不发达35国LDC35,最不发达4国LDC4	30	---Of wire bonders
		---其他:					---Other:
6859	8486.9091	----带背板的溅射靶材组件	0		0 最不发达35国LDC35,最不发达4国LDC4	17	----Sputtering targets modules with backing plate
6860	8486.9099	----其他	0		0 最不发达35国LDC35,最不发达4国LDC4	17	----Other

序号 No.	税则号列 Tariff Line	货品名称	最惠国 税 率 MFN(%)	协定税率 Agreement(%)		特惠税率 S.P.(%)		普通 税率 Gen.(%)	Article Description
	84.87	**本章其他税号未列名的机器零件,不具有电气接插件、绝缘体、线圈、触点或其他电气器材特征的:**							**Machinery parts, not containing elec-trical connectors, insulators, coils, contacts or other electrical features, not specified or included elsewhere in this Chap-ter:**
6861	8487.1000	-船用推进器及桨叶	6	0 5	东盟ASEAN,智利CL,新西兰NZ,秘鲁PE,哥斯达黎加CR 巴基斯坦PK	0	最不发达35国LDC35,最不发达4国LDC4	14	-Ships' or boats' propel-lers and blades
6862	8487.9000	-其他	8	0 0.8 5	东盟ASEAN,新西兰NZ,秘鲁PE,哥斯达黎加CR,香港HK,台湾TW 智利CL 巴基斯坦PK	0	最不发达35国LDC35,最不发达4国LDC4	30	-Other

第八十五章
电机、电气设备及其零件；录音机及放声机、电视图像、声音的录制和重放设备及其零件、附件

注释：

一、本章不包括：

（一）电暖的毯子、褥子、足套及类似品，电暖的衣服、靴、鞋、耳套或其他供人穿戴的电暖物品；

（二）税号 70.11 的玻璃制品；

（三）税号 84.86 的机器及装置；

（四）用于医疗、外科、牙科或兽医的真空设备（税号 90.18）；

（五）第九十四章的电热家具。

二、税号 85.01 至 85.04 不适用于税号 85.11、85.12、85.40、85.41 或 85.42 的货品，但金属槽汞弧整流器仍归入税号 85.04。

三、税号 85.09 仅包括通常供家用的下列电动器具：

（一）任何重量的地板打蜡机、食品研磨机及食品搅拌器，水果或蔬菜的榨汁器；

（二）重量不超过 20 公斤的其他机器。

但该税号不适用于风机、风扇或装有风扇的通风罩及循环气罩（不论是否装有过滤器）（税号 84.14）、离心干衣机（税号 84.21）、洗碟机（税号 84.22）、家用洗衣机（税号 84.50）、滚筒式或其他形式的熨烫机器（税号 84.20 或 84.51）、缝纫机（税号 84.52）、电剪子（税号 84.67）或电热器具（税号 85.16）。

四、税号 85.23 所称：

（一）“固态、非易失性存储器件”（例如，“闪存卡”或“电子闪存卡”）是指带有接口的存储器件，其在同一壳体内包含一块或多块闪存（FLASH E^2PROM），以集成电路的形式装配在一块印刷电路板上。它们可以包括一个集成电路形式的控制器及分立无源元件，例如，电容器及电阻器；

Chapter 85
Electrical machinery and equipment and parts thereof; sound recorders and reproducers, television image and sound recorders and reproducers, and parts and accessories of such articles

Notes:

1. This Chapter does not cover:

(a) Electrically warmed blankets, bed pads, foot-muffs or the like; electrically warmed clothing, footwear or ear pads or other electrically warmed articles worn on or about the person;

(b) Articles of glass of heading No.70.11;

(c) Machines and apparatus of heading 84.86;

(d) Vacuum apparatus of a kind used in medical, surgical, dental or veterinary sciences (heading 90.18); or

(e) Electrically heated furniture of Chapter 94.

2. Headings No.85.01 to 85.04 do not apply to goods described in heading No.85.11, 85.12, 85.40, 85.41 or 85.42.However, metal tank mercury arc rectifiers remain classified in heading No.85.04.

3. Heading No.85.09 covers only the following electro mechanical machines of the kind commonly used for domestic purposes:

(a) Floor polishers, food grinders and mixers, and fruit or vegetable juice extractors, of any weight;

(b) Other machines provided the weight of such machines does not exceed 20kg.

The heading does not, however, apply to fans or ventilating or recycling hoods incorporating a fan, whether or not fitted with filters (heading No.84.14), centrifugal clothes-dryers (heading No.84.21), dish washing machines (heading No.84.22), household washing machines (heading No.84.50) , roller or other ironing machines (heading No.84.20 or 84.51), sewing machines (heading No.84.52), electric scissors (heading No.84.67) or to electrochemical appliances (heading No.85.16) .

4. For the purposes of heading 85.23 :

(a) "Solid-state non-volatile storage devices" (for example, "flash memory cards" or "flash electronic storage cards") are storage devices with a connecting socket, comprising in the same housing one or more flash memories (for example, "FLASH E^2PROM") in the form of integrated circuits mounted on a printed circuit board. They may include a controller in the form of an integrated circuit and discrete passive components, such as capacitors and resistors;

（二）所称"智能卡"，是指装有一块或多块集成电路(微处理器、随机存取存储器（RAM）或只读存储器（ROM）)芯片的卡。这些卡可带有触点、磁条或嵌入式天线，但不包含任何其他有源或无源电路元件。

(b) The term "smart cards" means cards which have embedded in them one or more electronic integrated circuits (a microprocessor, random access memory (RAM) or read-only memory (ROM)) in the form of chips. These cards may contain contacts, a magnetic stripe or an embedded antenna but do not contain any other active or passive circuit elements.

五、税号 85.34 所称"印刷电路"，是指采用各种印制方法（例如，压印、覆镀、腐蚀）或采用"膜电路"工艺，将导线、接点或其他印制元件（例如，电感器、电阻器、电容器）按预定的图形单独或互相连接地印制在绝缘基片上的电路，但能够产生、整流、调制或放大电信号的元件（例如，半导体元件）除外。

5. For the purposes of heading No.85.34 "printed circuits" are circuits obtained by forming on an insulating base, by any printing process (for example, embossing, plating up, etching) or by the "film circuit" technique, conductor elements, contacts or other printed components (for example, inductances, resistors, capacitors) alone or interconnected according to a preestablished pattern, other than elements which can produce, rectify, modulate or amplify an electrical signal (for example, semiconductor elements).

所称"印刷电路"，不包括装有非印制元件的电路，也不包括单个的分立式电阻器、电容器及电感器。但印刷电路可配有非经印刷的连接元件。

The expression "printed circuits" does not cover circuits combined with elements other than those obtained during the printing process, nor does it cover individual, discrete resistors, capacitors or inductances.

用同样工艺制得的无源元件及有源元件组成的薄膜电路或厚膜电路应归入税号 85.42。

Thinor thick-film circuits comprising passive and active elements obtained during the same technological process are to be classified in heading No.85.42.

六、税号 85.36 所称"光导纤维、光导纤维束或光缆用连接器"，是指在有线数字通讯设备中，简单机械地把光纤端部相连成一线的连接器。它们不具备诸如对信号进行放大、再生或修正等其他功能。

6. For the purpose of heading 85.36, "connectors for optical fibres, optical fibre bundles or cables" means connectors that simply mechanically align optical fibres end to end in a digital line system. They perform no other function, such as the amplification, regeneration or modification of a signal.

七、税号 85.37 不包括电视接收机或其他电气设备用的无绳红外遥控器（税号 85.43）。

7. Heading 85.37 does not include cordless infrared devices for the remote control of television receivers or other electrical equipment (heading 85.43).

八、税号 85.41 及 85.42 所称:

8. For the purposes of headings No.85.41 and 85.42:

（一）"二极管、晶体管及类似的半导体器件"，是指那些依靠外加电场引起电阻率的变化而进行工作的半导体器件。

(a) "Diodes, transistors and similar semiconductor devices" are semiconductor devices the operation of which depends on variations in resistivity on the application of an electric field;

（二）"集成电路"，是指:

(b) "Electronic integrated circuits" are:

1. 单片集成电路，即电路元件（二极管、晶体管、

(1) Monolithic integrated circuits in which the circuit

电阻器、电容器、电感器等）主要整体制作在一片半导体材料或化合物半导体材料（例如掺杂硅、砷化镓、硅锗或磷化铟）基片的表面，并不可分割地连接在一起的电路；

2. 混合集成电路，即通过薄膜或厚膜工艺制得的无源元件（电阻器、电容器、电感器等）和通过半导体工艺制得的有源元件（二极管、晶体管、单片集成电路等）用互连或连接线不可分割地组合在同一绝缘基片（玻璃、陶瓷等）上的电路。这种电路也可包括分立元件；

3. 多芯片集成电路是由两个或多个单片集成电路不可分割地组合在一片或多片绝缘基片上构成的电路，不论是否带有引线框架，但不带有其他有源或无源的电路元件。

本注释所述物品在归类时，即使本目录其他税号涉及上述的物品，尤其是物品的功能，仍应优先考虑归入税号 85.41 及 85.42。

九、税号 85.48 所称“废原电池、废原电池组及废蓄电池”，是指因破损、拆解、耗尽或其他原因而不能再使用，也不能再充电的电池。

子目注释：

子目号 8527.12 仅包括有内置放大器但无内置扬声器的盒式磁带放声机，不需外接电源即能工作，且外形尺寸不超过 170 毫米×100 毫米×45 毫米。

elements, (diodes, transistors, resistors, capacitors, inductances, etc.) are created in the mass (essentially) and on the surface of a semiconductor or compound semiconductor material (for example, doped silicon, gallium arsenide, silicon germanium, indium phosphide) and are inseparably associated;

(2) Hybrid integrated circuits in which passive elements (resistors, capacitors, inductances, etc.), obtained by thin-or thick-film technology, and active elements (diodes, transistors, monolithic integrated circuits, etc.), obtained by semiconductor technology, are combined to all intents and purposes indivisibly, by interconnections or interconnecting cables, on a single insulating substrate (glass, ceramic, etc.). These circuits may also include discrete components;

(3) Multichip integrated circuits consisting of two or more interconnected monolithic integrated circuits combined to all intents and purposes indivisibly, whether or not on one or more insulating substrates, with or without leadframes, but with no other active or passive circuit elements.

For the classification of the articles defined in this Note, headings 85.41 and 85.42 shall take precedence over any other heading in the Nomenclature which might cover them by reference to, in particular, their function.

9. For the purposes of heading No.85.48, spent primary cells, "spent primary batteries and spent electric accumulators" are those which are neither usable as such because of breakage, cutting-up, wear or other reasons, nor capable of being recharged.

Subheading Note:

1. Subheadings 8527.12 covers only cassetteplayers with built-in amplifier, without built-in loudspeaker, capable of operating without an external source of electric power and the dimensions of which do not exceed 170mm×100mm×45mm.

序号 No.	税则号列 Tariff Line	货品名称	最惠国税率 MFN(%)	协定税率 Agreement(%)		特惠税率 S.P.(%)		普通税率 Gen.(%)	Article Description
	85.01	**电动机及发电机（不包括发电机组）：**							**Electric motors and generators (excluding generating sets):**
		-输出功率不超过37.5瓦的电动机:							-Motors of an output not exceeding 37.5W:
6863	8501.1010	---玩具用	24.5	0 4.9 12.3 23.3	东盟ASEAN,智利CL,新加坡SG,新西兰NZ,香港HK,台湾TW 哥斯达黎加CR 秘鲁PE 亚太APTA,巴基斯坦PK	0	最不发达35国LDC35	80	---For use in toys
		---其他:							---Other:
6864	8501.1091	----微电机，机座尺寸在20毫米及以上，但不超过39毫米	9	0 5 8.6	东盟ASEAN,智利CL,新加坡SG,新西兰NZ,秘鲁PE,哥斯达黎加CR,香港HK 巴基斯坦PK 亚太APTA	0	最不发达35国LDC35,最不发达4国LDC4	70	----Micromotors with a housing size of 20mm or more but not exceeding 39mm
	ex85011091	激光视盘机机芯精密微型电机（1瓦≤功率≤18瓦，20mm≤直径≤30mm）	△5						Minitype precise motor for mechanism of laser disc player (1W≤power ≤18W, 20mm≤diameter ≤30mm)
	ex85011091	摄像机、摄录一体机用精密微型电机(0.5瓦≤功率≤10瓦，20mm≤直径≤39mm）	△5						Minitype precise motor for mechanism of video cameras or camera recorders (0.5W≤power≤10W, 20mm≤diameter ≤39mm)
6865	8501.1099	----其他	9	0 5 8.6	东盟ASEAN,智利CL,新加坡SG,新西兰NZ,秘鲁PE,哥斯达黎加CR,香港HK,台湾TW 巴基斯坦PK 亚太APTA	0	最不发达35国LDC35,最不发达4国LDC4	35	----Other
	ex85011099	功率不大于0.5瓦(圆柱型:直径不大于6毫米,高不大于25毫米;扁圆型:直径不大于15毫米,厚不大于5毫米)非用于激光视盘机机芯的微型电机	△5						Micromotors with a cylindrical housing diameter not exceeding 6mm and height not exceeding 25mm or a oblate-cylindrical housing diameter not exceeding 15mm and thickness not exceeding 5mm, (Not including minitype motor for mechanism of laser disc player)
	ex85011099	激光视盘机机芯用精密微型电机(0.5瓦≤功率≤2瓦，5mm≤直径<20mm）	△5						Minitype precise motor for mechanism of laser disc player (0.5W≤power≤2W, 5mm≤diameter<20mm)
	ex85011099	摄像机、摄录一体机用精密微型电机(0.5瓦≤功率≤10瓦，5mm≤直径<20mm或39mm<直径≤40mm）	△5						Minitype precise motor for mechanism of video cameras or camera recorders(0.5W≤power≤10W, 5mm≤diameter<20mm or 9mm<diameter ≤40mm)

序号 No.	税则号列 Tariff Line	货品名称	最惠国税率 MFN(%)	协定税率 Agreement(%)		特惠税率 S.P.(%)		普通税率 Gen.(%)	Article Description
6866	8501.2000	-交直流两用电动机，输出功率超过 37.5 瓦	12	0 1.2 2.4 6	东盟ASEAN,新加坡SG,新西兰NZ 智利CL 哥斯达黎加CR 巴基斯坦PK,秘鲁PE	0	最不发达 35 国 LDC35,最不发达 4 国 LDC4	35	-Universal AC/DC motors of an output exceeding 37.5W
		-其他直流电动机;直流发电机:							-Other DC motors; DC generators:
6867	8501.3100	--输出功率不超过 750 瓦	12	0 2.4 6 11	东盟ASEAN,智利CL,新加坡SG,新西兰NZ,秘鲁PE,香港HK,澳门MO,台湾TW 哥斯达黎加CR 巴基斯坦PK 亚太APTA	0	最不发达 35 国 LDC35,最不发达 4 国 LDC4	35	--Of an output not exceeding 750W
6868	8501.3200	--输出功率超过 750 瓦，但不超过 75 千瓦	10	0 5	东盟ASEAN,智利CL,新加坡SG,新西兰NZ,秘鲁PE,哥斯达黎加CR 巴基斯坦PK	0	最不发达 35 国 LDC35,最不发达 4 国 LDC4	35	--Of an output exceeding 750W but not exceeding 75kW
6869	8501.3300	--输出功率超过 75 千瓦，但不超过 375 千瓦	5	0 0.5	东盟ASEAN,巴基斯坦PK,新西兰NZ,秘鲁PE,哥斯达黎加CR 智利CL	0	最不发达 35 国 LDC35,最不发达 4 国 LDC4	35	--Of an output exceeding 75kW but not exceeding 375kW
6870	8501.3400	--输出功率超过 375 千瓦	12	0 1.2 2.4 6	东盟ASEAN,新加坡SG,新西兰NZ,秘鲁PE 智利CL 哥斯达黎加CR 巴基斯坦PK	0	最不发达 35 国 LDC35,最不发达 4 国 LDC4	35	--Of an output exceeding 375kW
6871	8501.4000	-其他单相交流电动机	12	0 1.2 2.4 6	东盟ASEAN,新加坡SG,新西兰NZ 智利CL 哥斯达黎加CR 巴基斯坦PK,秘鲁PE	0	最不发达 35 国 LDC35,最不发达 4 国 LDC4	35	-Other AC motors, single-phase
		-其他多相交流电动机:							-Other AC motors, multi-phase:
6872	8501.5100	--输出功率不超过 750 瓦	5	0	东盟ASEAN,智利CL,巴基斯坦PK,新西兰NZ,秘鲁PE,哥斯达黎加CR	0	最不发达 35 国 LDC35,最不发达 4 国 LDC4	35	--Of an output not exceeding 750W
6873	8501.5200	--输出功率超过 750 瓦，但不超过 75 千瓦	10	0 5	东盟ASEAN,智利CL,新加坡SG,新西兰NZ,秘鲁PE,哥斯达黎加CR 巴基斯坦PK	0	最不发达 35 国 LDC35,最不发达 4 国 LDC4	35	--Of an output exceeding 750W but not exceeding 75kW

序号 No.	税则号列 Tariff Line	货品名称	最惠国税率 MFN(%)	协定税率 Agreement(%)		特惠税率 S.P.(%)		普通税率 Gen.(%)	Article Description
6874	8501.5300	--输出功率超过 75 千瓦	12	0 2.4 6 11.4	东盟ASEAN,智利CL,新加坡SG,新西兰NZ,秘鲁PE 哥斯达黎加CR 巴基斯坦PK 亚太APTA	0	最不发达 35 国 LDC35,最不发达 4 国 LDC4	35	--Of an output exceeding 75kW
	ex85015300	高速(200km/h)电力机车的交流异步牵引电动机	△3						AC asyncronous traction motor for high speed electric locomotive (200km/h)
		-交流发电机:							-AC generators (alternators):
6875	8501.6100	--输出功率不超过 75 千伏安	5	0 0.5	东盟ASEAN,巴基斯坦PK,新西兰NZ,秘鲁PE,哥斯达黎加CR 智利CL	0	最不发达 35 国 LDC35,最不发达 4 国 LDC4	30	--Of an output not exceeding 75kVA
6876	8501.6200	--输出功率超过 75 千伏安，但不超过 375 千伏安	12	0 1.2 2.4 6	东盟ASEAN,新加坡SG,新西兰NZ 智利CL 哥斯达黎加CR 巴基斯坦PK,秘鲁PE	0	最不发达 35 国 LDC35,最不发达 4 国 LDC4	30	--Of an output exceeding 75kVA but not exceeding 375kVA
6877	8501.6300	--输出功率超过 375 千伏安，但不超过 750 千伏安	12	0 1.2 2.4 6	东盟ASEAN,新加坡SG,新西兰NZ 智利CL 哥斯达黎加CR 巴基斯坦PK,秘鲁PE	0	最不发达 35 国 LDC35,最不发达 4 国 LDC4	30	--Of an output exceeding 375kVA but not exceeding 750kVA
		--输出功率超过 750 千伏安:							--Of an output exceeding 750kVA:
6878	8501.6410	---输出功率超过 750 千伏安，但不超过 350 兆伏安	10	0 1 5	东盟ASEAN,新加坡SG,新西兰NZ,哥斯达黎加CR 智利CL 巴基斯坦PK,秘鲁PE	0	最不发达 35 国 LDC35,最不发达 4 国 LDC4	30	---Of an output exceeding 750kVA but not exceeding 350MVA
6879	8501.6420	---输出功率超过 350 兆伏安，但不超过 665 兆伏安	5.8	0 0.6 5	东盟ASEAN,新西兰NZ,秘鲁PE,哥斯达黎加CR 智利CL 巴基斯坦PK	0	最不发达 35 国 LDC35,最不发达 4 国 LDC4	14	---Of an output exceeding 350MVA but not exceeding 665MVA
6880	8501.6430	---输出功率超过 665 兆伏安	6	0 0.6 5	东盟ASEAN,新西兰NZ,秘鲁PE,哥斯达黎加CR 智利CL 巴基斯坦PK	0	最不发达 35 国 LDC35,最不发达 4 国 LDC4	11	---Of an output exceeding 665MVA
	85.02	**发电机组及旋转式变流机:**							**Electric generating sets and rotary converters:**

序号 No.	税则号列 Tariff Line	货品名称	最惠国税率 MFN(%)	协定税率 Agreement(%)	特惠税率 S.P.(%)	普通税率 Gen.(%)	Article Description
		-装有压燃式活塞内燃发动机（柴油或半柴油发动机）的发电机组:					-Generating sets with compression-ignition internal combustion piston engines (diesel or semi-diesel engines):
6881	8502.1100	--输出功率不超过 75 千伏安	10	0 东盟ASEAN,智利CL,新加坡SG,新西兰NZ,秘鲁PE,哥斯达黎加CR,香港HK 5 巴基斯坦PK	0 最不发达 35 国 LDC35,最不发达 4 国 LDC4	45	--Of an output not exceeding 75kVA
6882	8502.1200	--输出功率超过 75 千伏安，但不超过 375 千伏安	10	0 东盟ASEAN,新加坡SG,新西兰NZ,哥斯达黎加CR,香港HK 1 智利CL 5 巴基斯坦PK,秘鲁PE	0 最不发达 35 国 LDC35,最不发达 4 国 LDC4	45	--Of an output exceeding 75kVA but not exceeding 375kVA
		--输出功率超过 375 千伏安:					--Of an output exceeding 375kVA:
6883	8502.1310	---输出功率超过 375 千伏安，但不超过 2 兆伏安	10	0 东盟ASEAN,智利CL,新加坡SG,新西兰NZ,秘鲁PE,哥斯达黎加CR,香港HK 5 巴基斯坦PK 7 亚太APTA	0 最不发达 35 国 LDC35,最不发达 4 国 LDC4	45	---Of an output exceeding 375kVA but not exceeding 2MVA
6884	8502.1320	---输出功率超过 2 兆伏安	10	0 东盟ASEAN,智利CL,新加坡SG,新西兰NZ,秘鲁PE,哥斯达黎加CR,香港HK 5 巴基斯坦PK 7 亚太APTA	0 最不发达 35 国 LDC35,最不发达 4 国 LDC4	30	---Of an output exceeding 2MVA
6885	8502.2000	-装有点燃式活塞内燃发动机的发电机组	10	0 东盟ASEAN,智利CL,新加坡SG,新西兰NZ,秘鲁PE,哥斯达黎加CR 5 巴基斯坦PK	0 最不发达 35 国 LDC35,最不发达 4 国 LDC4	45	-Generating sets with spark-ignition internal combustion piston engines
		-其他发电机组:					-Other generating sets:
6886	8502.3100	--风力驱动的	8	0 东盟ASEAN,智利CL,新西兰NZ,秘鲁PE,哥斯达黎加CR 5 巴基斯坦PK	0 最不发达 35 国 LDC35,最不发达 4 国 LDC4	30	--Wind-powered
6887	8502.3900	--其他	10	0 东盟ASEAN,智利CL,新西兰NZ,秘鲁PE,哥斯达黎加CR 5 巴基斯坦PK	0 最不发达 35 国 LDC35,最不发达 4 国 LDC4	30	--Other
6888	8502.4000	-旋转式变流机	10	0 东盟ASEAN,智利CL,新西兰NZ,秘鲁PE,哥斯达黎加CR 5 巴基斯坦PK	0 最不发达 35 国 LDC35,最不发达 4 国 LDC4	30	-Electric rotary converters

序号 No.	税则号列 Tariff Line	货品名称	最惠国税率 MFN(%)	协定税率 Agreement(%)		特惠税率 S.P.(%)		普通税率 Gen.(%)	Article Description
	85.03	**专用于或主要用于税号 85.01 或 85.02 所列机器的零件:**							**Parts suitable for use solely or principally with the machines of heading No.85.01 or 85.02:**
6889	8503.0010	---子目号 8501.1010 及 8501.1091 所列电动机用	12	0 1.2 2.4 6 11.4	东盟ASEAN,新加坡SG,新西兰NZ,香港HK,台湾TW 智利CL 哥斯达黎加CR 巴基斯坦PK,秘鲁PE 亚太APTA	0	最不发达 35 国 LDC35,最不发达 4 国 LDC4	70	---Of the motors of subheading No.8501.1010 or 8501.1091
6890	8503.0020	---子目号 8501.6420 及 8501.6430 所列发电机用	3	0 2.5	东盟ASEAN,智利CL,巴基斯坦PK,新西兰NZ,秘鲁PE,哥斯达黎加CR,香港HK 亚太APTA	0	最不发达 35 国 LDC35,最不发达 4 国 LDC4	11	---Of the generators of subheading No.8501.6420 or 8501.6430
6891	8503.0030	---子目号 8502.3100 所列发电机组用	3 △1	0 2.5	东盟ASEAN,智利CL,巴基斯坦PK,新西兰NZ,秘鲁PE,哥斯达黎加CR,香港HK 亚太APTA	0	最不发达 35 国 LDC35,最不发达 4 国 LDC4	30	---Of the generating sets of subheading No.8502.3100
6892	8503.0090	---其他	8	0 0.8 5 7.6	东盟ASEAN,新西兰NZ,秘鲁PE,哥斯达黎加CR,香港HK,台湾TW 智利CL 巴基斯坦PK 亚太APTA	0	最不发达 35 国 LDC35,最不发达 4 国 LDC4	30	---Other
	85.04	**变压器、静止式变流器（例如整流器）及电感器:**							**Electrical transformers, static converters (for example, rectifiers) and inductors:**
		-放电灯或放电管用镇流器:							-Ballasts for discharge lamps or tubes:
6893	8504.1010	---电子镇流器	10	0 1 5	东盟ASEAN,新加坡SG,新西兰NZ,哥斯达黎加CR,澳门MO 智利CL 巴基斯坦PK,秘鲁PE	0	最不发达 35 国 LDC35,最不发达 4 国 LDC4	35	---Electronic ballats
6894	8504.1090	---其他	10	0 1 5	东盟ASEAN,新西兰NZ,哥斯达黎加CR,澳门MO 智利CL 巴基斯坦PK,秘鲁PE	0	最不发达 35 国 LDC35,最不发达 4 国 LDC4	35	---Other
		-液体介质变压器:							-Liquid dielectric transformers:
6895	8504.2100	--额定容量不超过 650 千伏安	10.5	0 1.1 2.1 5 5.3	东盟ASEAN,新加坡SG,新西兰NZ 智利CL 哥斯达黎加CR 巴基斯坦PK 秘鲁PE	0	最不发达 35 国 LDC35,最不发达 4 国 LDC4	50	--Having a power handling capacity not exceeding 650kVA

序号 No.	税则号列 Tariff Line	货品名称	最惠国税率 MFN(%)	协定税率 Agreement(%)		特惠税率 S.P.(%)		普通税率 Gen.(%)	Article Description
6896	8504.2200	--额定容量超过650千伏安，但不超过10兆伏安	12.6	0 1.3 2.5 6.3	东盟ASEAN,新加坡SG,新西兰NZ 智利CL 哥斯达黎加CR 巴基斯坦PK,秘鲁PE	0	最不发达35国LDC35,最不发达4国LDC4	50	--Having a power handling capacity exceeding 650kVA but not exceeding 10MVA
		--额定容量超过10兆伏安:							--Having a power handling capacity exceeding 10MVA:
		---额定容量超过10兆伏安，但小于400兆伏安:							---Having a power handling capacity exceeding 10MVA but less than 400MVA:
6897	8504.2311	----额定容量超过10兆伏安，但小于220兆伏安	10	0 5 7	东盟ASEAN,智利CL,新西兰NZ,秘鲁PE,哥斯达黎加CR 巴基斯坦PK 亚太APTA	0	最不发达35国LDC35,最不发达4国LDC4	50	----Having a power handling capacity exceeding 10MVA but less than 220MVA
6898	8504.2312	----额定容量在220兆伏安及以上，但小于330兆伏安	10	0 5 7	东盟ASEAN,智利CL,新西兰NZ,秘鲁PE,哥斯达黎加CR 巴基斯坦PK 亚太APTA	0	最不发达35国LDC35,最不发达4国LDC4	50	----Having a power handling capacity exceeding 220MVA but less than 330MVA
6899	8504.2313	----额定容量在330兆伏安及以上，但小于400兆伏安	10	0 5 7	东盟ASEAN,智利CL,新西兰NZ,秘鲁PE,哥斯达黎加CR 巴基斯坦PK 亚太APTA	0	最不发达35国LDC35,最不发达4国LDC4	50	----Having a power handling capacity exceeding 330MVA but less than 400MVA
		---额定容量在400兆伏安及以上:							---Having a power handling capacity of 400MVA or more:
6900	8504.2321	----额定容量在400兆伏安及以上，但小于500兆伏安	6	0 4.2	东盟ASEAN,智利CL,巴基斯坦PK,新西兰NZ,秘鲁PE,哥斯达黎加CR 亚太APTA	0	最不发达35国LDC35,最不发达4国LDC4	11	----Having a power handling capacity exceeding 400MVA but less than 500MVA
6901	8504.2329	----其他	6	0 4.2	东盟ASEAN,智利CL,巴基斯坦PK,新西兰NZ,秘鲁PE,哥斯达黎加CR 亚太APTA	0	最不发达35国LDC35,最不发达4国LDC4	11	----Other
		-其他变压器:							-Other transformers:
		--额定容量不超过1千伏安:							--Having a power handling capacity not exceeding 1kVA:
6902	8504.3110	---互感器	5	0 4.3	东盟ASEAN,智利CL,巴基斯坦PK,新西兰NZ,秘鲁PE,哥斯达黎加CR,澳门MO,台湾TW 亚太APTA	0	最不发达35国LDC35,最不发达4国LDC4	50	---Mutual inductor

序号 No.	税则号列 Tariff Line	货品名称	最惠国 税 率 MFN(%)	协定税率 Agreement(%)		特惠税率 S.P.(%)		普通 税率 Gen.(%)	Article Description
6903	8504.3190	---其他	5	0 4.3	东盟ASEAN,智利CL,巴基斯坦PK,新加坡SG,新西兰NZ,秘鲁PE,哥斯达黎加CR,香港HK,澳门MO,台湾TW 亚太APTA	0	最不发达35国LDC35,最不发达4国LDC4	50	---Other
		--额定容量超过1千伏安，但不超过16千伏安:							--Having a power handling capacity exceeding 1kVA but not exceeding 16kVA:
6904	8504.3210	---互感器	5	0	东盟ASEAN,智利CL,巴基斯坦PK,新西兰NZ,秘鲁PE,哥斯达黎加CR,澳门MO	0	最不发达35国LDC35,最不发达4国LDC4	50	---Mutual inductor
6905	8504.3290	---其他	5	0	东盟ASEAN,智利CL,巴基斯坦PK,新西兰NZ,秘鲁PE,哥斯达黎加CR,澳门MO	0	最不发达35国LDC35,最不发达4国LDC4	50	---Other
		--额定容量超过16千伏安，但不超过500千伏安:							--Having a power handling capacity exceeding 16kVA but not exceeding 500kVA:
6906	8504.3310	---互感器	5	0 0.5	东盟ASEAN,巴基斯坦PK,新西兰NZ,秘鲁PE,哥斯达黎加CR,澳门MO 智利CL	0	最不发达35国LDC35,最不发达4国LDC4	50	---Mutual inductor
6907	8504.3390	---其他	5	0 0.5	东盟ASEAN,巴基斯坦PK,新西兰NZ,秘鲁PE,哥斯达黎加CR,澳门MO 智利CL	0	最不发达35国LDC35,最不发达4国LDC4	50	---Other
		--额定容量超过500千伏安:							--Having a power handling capacity exceeding 500kVA:
6908	8504.3410	---互感器	14	0 2.8 11.2	东盟ASEAN,智利CL,新加坡SG,新西兰NZ,秘鲁PE,澳门MO 哥斯达黎加CR 巴基斯坦PK	0	最不发达35国LDC35	50	---Mutual inductor
6909	8504.3490	---其他	14	0 2.8 11.2	东盟ASEAN,智利CL,新加坡SG,新西兰NZ,秘鲁PE,澳门MO 哥斯达黎加CR 巴基斯坦PK	0	最不发达35国LDC35	50	---Other
		-静止式变流器:							-Static converters:
		---稳压电源:							---Voltage-stabilized suppliers:

序号 No.	税则号列 Tariff Line	货品名称	最惠国税率 MFN(%)	协定税率 Agreement(%)		特惠税率 S.P.(%)		普通税率 Gen.(%)	Article Description
6910	8504.4013	----税号84.71所列机器用	0			0	最不发达35国LDC35,最不发达4国LDC4	40	----Of the machines of heading No.84.71
6911	8504.4014	----其他直流稳压电源，功率小于1千瓦，精度低于万分之一	7 △3	0 0.7 5 5.6	东盟ASEAN,新西兰NZ,秘鲁PE,哥斯达黎加CR 智利CL 巴基斯坦PK 亚太APTA	0	最不发达35国LDC35,最不发达4国LDC4	80	----Other DC Voltage-stabilized suppliers, of a power of less than 1kW and an accuracy of not better than 0.0001
6912	8504.4015	----其他交流稳压电源，功率小于10千瓦，精度低于千分之一	0			0	最不发达35国LDC35,最不发达4国LDC4	80	----Other AC voltage-stabilized suppliers, of a power of less than 10kW and an accuracy of not better than 0.001
6913	8504.4019	----其他	0			0	最不发达35国LDC35,最不发达4国LDC4	50	----Other
6914	8504.4020	---不间断供电电源	10	0 5 8.5	东盟ASEAN,智利CL,新加坡SG,新西兰NZ,秘鲁PE,哥斯达黎加CR,香港HK 巴基斯坦PK 亚太APTA	0	最不发达35国LDC35,最不发达4国LDC4	50	---Uninterrupted power suppliers
6915	8504.4030	---逆变器	10	0 1 5	东盟ASEAN,新加坡SG,新西兰NZ,哥斯达黎加CR,香港HK,澳门MO 智利CL 巴基斯坦PK,秘鲁PE	0	最不发达35国LDC35,最不发达4国LDC4	30	---Inverters
	ex85044030	电动汽车用逆变器模块，功率密度≥8千瓦/升	△6						Inverter module for electric vehicles, power density≥8000W/L
		---其他:							---Other:
6916	8504.4091	----具有变流功能的半导体模块	10 △3	0 1 5	东盟ASEAN,新加坡SG,新西兰NZ,哥斯达黎加CR,香港HK,澳门MO 智利CL 巴基斯坦PK,秘鲁PE	0	最不发达35国LDC35,最不发达4国LDC4	30	----Semiconductor modules with converting function
	ex85044091	自动数据处理设备机器及组件、电讯设备用的具有变流动能的半导体模块	△0						Semicondutor modules with converting function for automatic data processing machines and units thereof, and telecommunication apparatus

序号 No.	税则号列 Tariff Line	货品名称	最惠国税率 MFN(%)	协定税率 Agreement(%)		特惠税率 S.P.(%)		普通税率 Gen.(%)	Article Description
6917	8504.4099	----其他	10	0 1 5	东盟ASEAN,新加坡SG,新西兰NZ,哥斯达黎加CR,香港HK,澳门MO 智利CL 巴基斯坦PK,秘鲁PE	0	最不发达35国LDC35,最不发达4国LDC4	30	----Other
	ex85044099	自动数据处理设备机器及组件、电讯设备用的其他静止变流器;ITA产品用的印刷电路组件，包括外接组件，如符合PCMCIA标准的卡	△0						Other stastic converters for automatic data processing machines and units thereof, and telecommunication apparatus; Printed Circuit Assemblies for products falling within the ITA, including such assemblies for external connections such as cards that conform to the PCMCIA standard
	ex85044099	高速(200km/h)电力机车的牵引变流器	△3						Traction converter for high speed electric locomotive (≥200km/h)
	ex85044099	汽车冲压线用压力机变频调速装置	△5						Frequency conversion speed regulation set for punch press machine for manufacture automobiles
	ex85044099	电动汽车用电机控制器	△6						Motor controller for electric vehicles
6918	8504.5000	-其他电感器	0			0	最不发达35国LDC35,最不发达4国LDC4	35	-Other inductors
		-零件: ---变压器用:							-Parts: ---Of transformers:
6919	8504.9011	----子目号8504.2321，8504.2329所列变压器用	5	0 4.5	东盟ASEAN,智利CL,巴基斯坦PK,新西兰NZ,秘鲁PE,哥斯达黎加CR,香港HK 亚太APTA	0	最不发达35国LDC35,最不发达4国LDC4	11	----Of the transformers of subheading No. 8504.2321, 8504.2329
6920	8504.9019	----其他	8	0 4.5	东盟ASEAN,智利CL,新西兰NZ,秘鲁PE,哥斯达黎加CR,香港HK,台湾TW 亚太APTA,巴基斯坦PK	0	最不发达35国LDC35,最不发达4国LDC4	50	----Other
6921	8504.9020	---稳压电源及不间断供电电源用	8	0 5 5.6	东盟ASEAN,智利CL,新西兰NZ,秘鲁PE,哥斯达黎加CR,香港HK,澳门MO,台湾TW 巴基斯坦PK 亚太APTA	0	最不发达35国LDC35,最不发达4国LDC4	50	---Of voltage-stabilized suppliers and uninterrupted power suppliers

序号 No.	税则号列 Tariff Line	货品名称	最惠国 税 率 MFN(%)	协定税率 Agreement(%)		特惠税率 S.P.(%)		普通 税率 Gen.(%)	Article Description
6922	8504.9090	---其他	8	0 5 5.6	东盟ASEAN,智利CL,新西兰NZ,秘鲁PE,哥斯达黎加CR,香港HK,澳门MO,台湾TW 巴基斯坦PK 亚太APTA	0	最不发达35国LDC35,最不发达4国LDC4	30	---Other
	85.05	**电磁铁;永磁铁及磁化后准备制永磁铁的物品;电磁铁或永磁铁卡盘、夹具及类似的工件夹具;电磁联轴节、离合器及制动器;电磁起重吸盘:**							**Electro-magnets; permanent magnets and articles intended to become permanent magnets after magnetization; electromagnetic or permanent magnet chucks, clamps and similar holding devices; electromagnetic couplings, clutches and brakes; electromagnetic lifting heads:**
		-永磁铁及磁化后准备制永磁铁的物品:							-Permanent magnets and articles intended to become permanent magnets after magnetization:
		--金属的:							--Of metal:
6923	8505.1110	---稀土的	7	0 5	东盟ASEAN,智利CL,新西兰NZ,秘鲁PE,哥斯达黎加CR,台湾TW 巴基斯坦PK	0	最不发达35国LDC35,最不发达4国LDC4	20	---Of rare-earth metals
6924	8505.1190	---其他	7	0 5	东盟ASEAN,智利CL,新西兰NZ,秘鲁PE,哥斯达黎加CR,香港HK,台湾TW 巴基斯坦PK	0	最不发达35国LDC35,最不发达4国LDC4	20	---Other
6925	8505.1900	--其他	7	0 5 6.7	东盟ASEAN,智利CL,新西兰NZ,秘鲁PE,哥斯达黎加CR,香港HK 巴基斯坦PK 亚太APTA	0	最不发达35国LDC35,最不发达4国LDC4	20	--Other
6926	8505.2000	-电磁联轴节、离合器及制动器	8	0 5 7.6	东盟ASEAN,智利CL,新西兰NZ,秘鲁PE,哥斯达黎加CR 巴基斯坦PK 亚太APTA	0	最不发达35国LDC35,最不发达4国LDC4	20	-Electromagnetic couplings, clutches and brakes
		-其他，包括零件:							-Other, including parts:
6927	8505.9010	---电磁起重吸盘	8	0 5	东盟ASEAN,智利CL,新西兰NZ,秘鲁PE,哥斯达黎加CR 巴基斯坦PK	0	最不发达35国LDC35,最不发达4国LDC4	20	---Electromagnetic lifting heads

序号 No.	税则号列 Tariff Line	货品名称	最惠国税率 MFN(%)	协定税率 Agreement(%)		特惠税率 S.P.(%)		普通税率 Gen.(%)	Article Description
6928	8505.9090	---其他	8	0	东盟ASEAN,智利CL,新西兰NZ,秘鲁PE,哥斯达黎加CR	0	最不发达35国LDC35,最不发达4国LDC4	20	---Other
				5	巴基斯坦PK				
				7.6	亚太APTA				
	85.06	**原电池及原电池组:**							**Primary cells and primary batteries:**
		-二氧化锰的:							-Manganese dioxide:
		---碱性锌锰的:							---Alkaline zinc-manganese dioxide:
6929	8506.1011	----扣式	20	0	东盟ASEAN,智利CL,新加坡SG,新西兰NZ,香港HK	0	最不发达35国LDC35	80	----Button type
				4	哥斯达黎加CR				
				10	秘鲁PE				
6930	8506.1012	----圆柱式	20	0	东盟ASEAN,智利CL,新加坡SG,新西兰NZ,香港HK	0	最不发达35国LDC35	80	----Cylinder type
				4	哥斯达黎加CR				
				10	秘鲁PE				
6931	8506.1019	----其他	20	0	东盟ASEAN,智利CL,新加坡SG,新西兰NZ,香港HK	0	最不发达35国LDC35	80	----Other
				4	哥斯达黎加CR				
				10	秘鲁PE				
6932	8506.1090	---其他	20	0	东盟ASEAN,智利CL,新加坡SG,新西兰NZ,香港HK	0	最不发达35国LDC35	80	---Other
				4	哥斯达黎加CR				
				10	秘鲁PE				
6933	8506.3000	-氧化汞的	14	0	东盟ASEAN,智利CL,新加坡SG,新西兰NZ,秘鲁PE	0	最不发达35国LDC35	40	-Mercuric oxide
				2.8	哥斯达黎加CR				
				11.2	巴基斯坦PK				
6934	8506.4000	-氧化银的	14	0	东盟ASEAN,智利CL,新加坡SG,新西兰NZ,秘鲁PE	0	最不发达35国LDC35	40	-Silver oxide
				2.8	哥斯达黎加CR				
				11.2	巴基斯坦PK				
6935	8506.5000	-锂的	14	0	东盟ASEAN,智利CL,新加坡SG,新西兰NZ,秘鲁PE	0	最不发达35国LDC35	40	-Lithium
				2.8	哥斯达黎加CR				
				11.2	巴基斯坦PK				
6936	8506.6000	-锌空气的	14	0	东盟ASEAN,智利CL,新加坡SG,新西兰NZ,秘鲁PE	0	最不发达35国LDC35	40	-Air-zinc
				2.8	哥斯达黎加CR				
				11.2	巴基斯坦PK				

序号 No.	税则号列 Tariff Line	货品名称	最惠国税率 MFN(%)	协定税率 Agreement(%)		特惠税率 S.P.(%)		普通税率 Gen.(%)	Article Description
6937	8506.8000	-其他原电池及原电池组	14	0 2.8 11.2	东盟ASEAN,智利CL,新加坡SG,新西兰NZ,秘鲁PE,香港HK 哥斯达黎加CR 巴基斯坦PK	0	最不发达35国LDC35,最不发达4国LDC4	40	-Other primary cells and primary batteries
		-零件:							-Parts:
6938	8506.9010	---子目号8506.1000所列电池用	14	0 2.8 11.2	东盟ASEAN,智利CL,新加坡SG,新西兰NZ,秘鲁PE 哥斯达黎加CR 巴基斯坦PK	0	最不发达35国LDC35	80	---Of the cells of sub-heading No.8506.1000
6939	8506.9090	---其他	10	0 5	东盟ASEAN,智利CL,新加坡SG,新西兰NZ,秘鲁PE,哥斯达黎加CR 巴基斯坦PK	0	最不发达35国LDC35	40	---Other
	85.07	**蓄电池，包括隔板，不论是否矩形（包括正方形）：**							**Electric accumulators, including separators therefor, whether or not rectangular (including square):**
6940	8507.1000	-铅酸蓄电池,用于起动活塞式发动机	10	0 1 5 6.9	东盟ASEAN,新加坡SG,新西兰NZ,哥斯达黎加CR,澳门MO 智利CL 巴基斯坦PK,秘鲁PE 亚太APTA	0	最不发达35国LDC35	90	-Lead-acid, of a kind used for starting piston engines
6941	8507.2000	-其他铅酸蓄电池	10	0 5 6.9	东盟ASEAN,智利CL,新加坡SG,新西兰NZ,秘鲁PE,哥斯达黎加CR,澳门MO 巴基斯坦PK 亚太APTA	0	最不发达35国LDC35	90	-Other lead-acid accumulators
6942	8507.3000	-镍镉蓄电池	10	0 5 8	东盟ASEAN,智利CL,新加坡SG,新西兰NZ,秘鲁PE,哥斯达黎加CR,香港HK 巴基斯坦PK 亚太APTA	0	最不发达35国LDC35	40	-Nickel-cadmium
6943	8507.4000	-镍铁蓄电池	12	0 2.4 5 9.6	东盟ASEAN,智利CL,新加坡SG,新西兰NZ,秘鲁PE 哥斯达黎加CR 巴基斯坦PK 亚太APTA	0	最不发达35国LDC35	40	–Nickel-iron
6944	8507.5000	-镍氢蓄电池	12	0 2.4 5 9.6	东盟ASEAN,智利CL,新加坡SG,新西兰NZ,秘鲁PE,香港HK 哥斯达黎加CR 巴基斯坦PK 亚太APTA	0	最不发达35国LDC35	40	–Nickel-metal hydride

序号 No.	税则号列 Tariff Line	货品名称	最惠国税率 MFN(%)	协定税率 Agreement(%)		特惠税率 S.P.(%)		普通税率 Gen.(%)	Article Description
	ex85075000	电动汽车用镍氢蓄电池单体，容量≥6Ah，比功率≥1000W/kg	△8						Nickel-metal hydride accumulators cell for electric vehicles, capacity≥6Ah and power density≥1000W/kg
	ex85075000	电动汽车用镍氢蓄电池系统（包含蓄电池模块、容器、盖、冷却系统、管理系统等），比功率≥700W/kg	△10						Nickel-metal hydride accumulators system for electric vehicles, power density≥700W/kg
6945	8507.6000	-锂离子蓄电池	12	0 2.4 5 9.6	东盟ASEAN,智利CL,新加坡SG,新西兰NZ,秘鲁PE,香港HK,台湾TW 哥斯达黎加CR 巴基斯坦PK 亚太APTA	0	最不发达35国LDC35	40	-Lithium ion
	ex85076000	电动汽车或插电式混合动力汽车用锂离子蓄电池单体，容量≥10Ah，比能量≥110Wh/kg	△6						Lithium ion accumulators cell for electric vehicles or plug-in hybrid elctric vehicles, capacity≥10Ah and energy density≥110Wh/kg
	ex85076000	电动汽车或插电式混合动力汽车用锂离子蓄电池系统（包含蓄电池模块、容器、盖、冷却系统、管理系统等），比能量≥80Wh/kg	△8						Lithium ion accumulators system for electric vehicles or plug-in hybrid elctric vehicles, energy density≥80Wh/kg
		-其他蓄电池:							-Other accumulators:
6946	8507.8030	---全钒液流电池	12	0 2.4 5 9	东盟ASEAN,智利CL,新加坡SG,新西兰NZ,秘鲁PE,香港HK 哥斯达黎加CR 巴基斯坦PK 亚太APTA	0	最不发达35国LDC35	40	---All-vanadium redox flow batteries
6947	8507.8090	---其他	12	0 2.4 5 9	东盟ASEAN,智利CL,新加坡SG,新西兰NZ,秘鲁PE,香港HK 哥斯达黎加CR 巴基斯坦PK 亚太APTA	0	最不发达35国LDC35	40	---Other
		-零件:							-Parts:
6948	8507.9010	---铅酸蓄电池用	10	0 5	东盟ASEAN,智利CL,新西兰NZ,秘鲁PE,哥斯达黎加CR,香港HK 巴基斯坦PK	0 5	最不发达35国LDC35 亚太2国APTA2	90	---Of lead-acid accumulators
	ex85079010	铅酸蓄电池电极（仅保留电极）	△5						Electrodes of lead-acid accumulators (only including Electrodes)

序号 No.	税则号列 Tariff Line	货品名称	最惠国税率 MFN(%)	协定税率 Agreement(%)		特惠税率 S.P.(%)		普通税率 Gen.(%)	Article Description
6949	8507.9090	---其他	8 △5	0 5	东盟ASEAN,智利CL,新西兰NZ,秘鲁PE,哥斯达黎加CR,香港HK 巴基斯坦PK	0 4	最不发达35国LDC35,最不发达4国LDC4 亚太2国APTA2	40	---Other
	85.08	**真空吸尘器:** -电动的:							**Vacuum cleaners:** -With self-contained electric motor :
6950	8508.1100	--功率不超过1500瓦，且带有容积不超过20升的集尘袋或其他集尘容器	10	0 5 8.2	东盟ASEAN,智利CL,新加坡SG,新西兰NZ,秘鲁PE,哥斯达黎加CR,香港HK,台湾TW 巴基斯坦PK 亚太APTA	0	最不发达35国LDC35,最不发达4国LDC4	130	--Of a power not exceeding 1500W and having a dust bag or other receptacle capacity not exceeding 20L
6951	8508.1900	--其他	0			0	最不发达35国LDC35,最不发达4国LDC4	30	--Other
6952	8508.6000	-其他真空吸尘器	0			0	最不发达35国LDC35,最不发达4国LDC4	30	-Other vacuum cleaners
		-零件:							-Parts:
6953	8508.7010	---子目8508.1100所列吸尘器用	12	0 2.4 6	东盟ASEAN,智利CL,新加坡SG,新西兰NZ,秘鲁PE,香港HK 哥斯达黎加CR 巴基斯坦PK	0	最不发达35国LDC35	100	---For the goods of heading No.8508.1100
6954	8508.7090	---其他	0			0	最不发达35国LDC35,最不发达4国LDC4	20	---Other
	85.09	**家用电动器具，税目85.08的真空吸尘器除外:**							**Electro-mechanical domestic appliances, with self-contained electric motor, other than vacuum cleaners of heading 85.08:**
		-食品研磨机及搅拌器;水果或蔬菜的榨汁机:							-Food grinders and mixers; fruit or vegetable juice extractors:

序号 No.	税则号列 Tariff Line	货品名称	最惠国税率 MFN(%)	协定税率 Agreement(%)		特惠税率 S.P.(%)		普通税率 Gen.(%)	Article Description
6955	8509.4010	---水果或蔬菜的榨汁机	10 △6	0	东盟ASEAN,智利CL,新加坡SG,新西兰NZ,秘鲁PE,哥斯达黎加CR,澳门MO	0	最不发达35国LDC35	100	---Fruit or vegetable juice extractors
				5	巴基斯坦PK				
6956	8509.4090	---其他	10 △6	0	东盟ASEAN,智利CL,新加坡SG,新西兰NZ,秘鲁PE,哥斯达黎加CR,台湾TW	0	最不发达35国LDC35	100	---Other
				5	巴基斯坦PK				
		-其他器具:							-Other appliances:
6957	8509.8010	---地板打蜡机	30	0	东盟ASEAN,新加坡SG,新西兰NZ	0	最不发达35国LDC35	100	---Floor polishers
				3	智利CL				
				6	哥斯达黎加CR				
				15	秘鲁PE				
6958	8509.8020	---厨房废物处理器	20	0	东盟ASEAN,智利CL,新加坡SG,新西兰NZ	0	最不发达35国LDC35	100	---Kitchen waste disposers
				4	哥斯达黎加CR				
				10	秘鲁PE				
6959	8509.8090	---其他	30 △15	0	东盟ASEAN,新加坡SG,新西兰NZ	0	最不发达35国LDC35	100	---Other
				3	智利CL				
				6	哥斯达黎加CR				
				15	秘鲁PE				
6960	8509.9000	-零件	12 △6	0	东盟ASEAN,智利CL,新加坡SG,新西兰NZ,秘鲁PE,香港HK	0	最不发达35国LDC35	100	-Parts
				2.4	哥斯达黎加CR				
				6	巴基斯坦PK				
	85.10	**电动剃须刀、电动毛发推剪及电动脱毛器:**							**Shavers, hair clippers and hair-removing appliances, with self-contained electric motor:**
6961	8510.1000	-剃须刀	30 △15	0	东盟ASEAN,智利CL,新加坡SG,新西兰NZ	0	最不发达35国LDC35	100	-Shavers
				6	哥斯达黎加CR				
				15	秘鲁PE				
6962	8510.2000	-毛发推剪	30	0	东盟ASEAN,智利CL,新加坡SG,新西兰NZ,香港HK	0	最不发达35国LDC35	100	-Hair clippers
				6	哥斯达黎加CR				
				15	秘鲁PE				
6963	8510.3000	-脱毛器	20	0	东盟ASEAN,智利CL,新加坡SG,新西兰NZ,澳门MO	0	最不发达35国LDC35	100	-Hair-removing appliances
				4	哥斯达黎加CR				
				10	秘鲁PE				
6964	8510.9000	-零件	24.5 △12	0	东盟ASEAN,智利CL,新加坡SG,新西兰NZ	0	最不发达35国LDC35	100	-Parts
				4.9	哥斯达黎加CR				
				12.2	秘鲁PE				

序号 No.	税则号列 Tariff Line	货品名称	最惠国税率 MFN(%)	协定税率 Agreement(%)		特惠税率 S.P.(%)		普通税率 Gen.(%)	Article Description
	85.11	**点燃式或压燃式内燃发动机用的电点火及电起动装置（例如，点火磁电机、永磁直流发电机、点火线圈、火花塞、电热塞及起动电机）;附属于上述内燃发动机的发电机（例如，直流发电机、交流发电机）及断流器:**							**Electrical ignition or starting equipment of a kind used for spark-ignition or compression-ignition internal combustion engines (for example, ignition magnetos, magnetodynamos, ignition coils, sparking plugs and glow plugs, starter motors); generators (for example, dynamos, alternators) and cutouts of a kind used in conjunction with such engines:**
6965	8511.1000	-火花塞	10	0 5	东盟ASEAN,智利CL,新加坡SG,新西兰NZ,哥斯达黎加CR 巴基斯坦PK,秘鲁PE	0	最不发达35国LDC35	30	-Sparking plugs
		-点火磁电机;永磁直流发电机;磁飞轮:							-Ignition magnetos; magneto-dynamos; magnetic flywheels:
6966	8511.2010	---机车、航空器及船舶用	5	0	东盟ASEAN,智利CL,巴基斯坦PK,新西兰NZ,秘鲁PE,哥斯达黎加CR	0	最不发达35国LDC35,最不发达4国LDC4	11	---For locomotives, aircraft or ships
6967	8511.2090	---其他	10	0 5	东盟ASEAN,智利CL,新西兰NZ,秘鲁PE,哥斯达黎加CR 巴基斯坦PK	0	最不发达35国LDC35,最不发达4国LDC4	30	---Other
		--分电器;点火线圈:							--Distributors; Ignition coils:
6968	8511.3010	---机车、航空器及船舶用	5	0	东盟ASEAN,智利CL,巴基斯坦PK,新西兰NZ,秘鲁PE,哥斯达黎加CR	0	最不发达35国LDC35,最不发达4国LDC4	11	---For locomotives, aircraft or ships
6969	8511.3090	---其他	8.4	0 5	东盟ASEAN,智利CL,新西兰NZ,秘鲁PE,哥斯达黎加CR 巴基斯坦PK	0	最不发达35国LDC35,最不发达4国LDC4	30	---Other
		-起动电机及两用启动发电机:							-Starter motors and dual purpose starter-generators:

序号 No.	税则号列 Tariff Line	货品名称	最惠国税率 MFN(%)	协定税率 Agreement(%)		特惠税率 S.P.(%)		普通税率 Gen.(%)	Article Description
6970	8511.4010	---机车、航空器及船舶用	5	0	东盟ASEAN,智利CL,巴基斯坦PK,新西兰NZ,秘鲁PE,哥斯达黎加CR	0	最不发达35国LDC35,最不发达4国LDC4	11	---For locomotives, aircraft or ships
		---其他:							---Other:
6971	8511.4091	----输出功率在132.39千瓦（180马力）及以上的发动机用启动电机	8.4	0 5	东盟ASEAN,智利CL,新西兰NZ,秘鲁PE,哥斯达黎加CR 巴基斯坦PK	0	最不发达35国LDC35,最不发达4国LDC4	30	----Starter motors for engines of an output of 132.39kW (180HP) or more
6972	8511.4099	----其他	8.4	0 5	东盟ASEAN,智利CL,新西兰NZ,秘鲁PE,哥斯达黎加CR 巴基斯坦PK	0	最不发达35国LDC35,最不发达4国LDC4	30	----Other
		-其他发电机:							-Other generators:
6973	8511.5010	---机车、航空器及船舶用	5	0 0.5	东盟ASEAN,巴基斯坦PK,新西兰NZ,秘鲁PE,哥斯达黎加CR 智利CL	0	最不发达35国LDC35,最不发达4国LDC4	11	---For locomotives, aircraft or ships
6974	8511.5090	---其他	8.4	0 0.8 5	东盟ASEAN,新西兰NZ,秘鲁PE,哥斯达黎加CR 智利CL 巴基斯坦PK	0	最不发达35国LDC35,最不发达4国LDC4	30	---Other
6975	8511.8000	-其他装置	8.4	0 0.8 5	东盟ASEAN,新西兰NZ,秘鲁PE,哥斯达黎加CR 智利CL 巴基斯坦PK	0	最不发达35国LDC35,最不发达4国LDC4	30	-Other equipment
		-零件:							-Parts:
6976	8511.9010	---本税号所列供机车、航空器及船舶用的各种装置的零件	4.5	0	东盟ASEAN,智利CL,巴基斯坦PK,新西兰NZ,秘鲁PE,哥斯达黎加CR	0	最不发达35国LDC35,最不发达4国LDC4	11	---Of the equipment of heading No.85.11 used for locomotives, aircraft or ships
6977	8511.9090	---其他	5	0	东盟ASEAN,智利CL,巴基斯坦PK,新西兰NZ,秘鲁PE,哥斯达黎加CR	0	最不发达35国LDC35,最不发达4国LDC4	30	---Other

序号 No.	税则号列 Tariff Line	货品名称	最惠国税率 MFN(%)	协定税率 Agreement(%)		特惠税率 S.P.(%)		普通税率 Gen.(%)	Article Description
	85.12	**自行车或机动车辆用的电气照明或信号装置(税号85.39的物品除外)、风挡刮水器、除霜器及去雾器:**							**Electrical lighting or signalling equipment (excluding articles of heading No.85.39), wind-screen wipers, defrosters and demisters, of a kind used for cycles or motor vehicles:**
6978	8512.1000	-自行车用照明或视觉信号装置	10.5	0 2.1 5	东盟ASEAN,智利CL,新加坡SG,新西兰NZ,秘鲁PE 哥斯达黎加CR 巴基斯坦PK	0	最不发达35国LDC35,最不发达4国LDC4	45	-Lighting or visual signalling equipment of a kind used on bicycles
		-其他照明或视觉信号装置:							-Other lighting or visual signalling equipment:
6979	8512.2010	---机动车辆用照明装置	10	0	智利CL,新西兰NZ,秘鲁PE,哥斯达黎加CR,台湾TW	0	最不发达35国LDC35,最不发达4国LDC4	45	---Lighting equipment of a kind used for motor vehicles
6980	8512.2090	---其他	10	0	智利CL,新西兰NZ,秘鲁PE,哥斯达黎加CR	0	最不发达35国LDC35,最不发达4国LDC4	45	---Other
		-音响信号装置:							-Sound signalling equipment:
		---机动车辆用:							---For motor Vehicles:
6981	8512.3011	----喇叭、蜂鸣器	10	0 8.5	智利CL,新西兰NZ,秘鲁PE,哥斯达黎加CR 亚太APTA,巴基斯坦PK	0	最不发达35国LDC35,最不发达4国LDC4	45	----Loudspeaker, buzzers
6982	8512.3012	----防盗报警器	10	0 1 5 9	东盟ASEAN,新西兰NZ,秘鲁PE,哥斯达黎加CR 智利CL 巴基斯坦PK 亚太APTA	0	最不发达35国LDC35,最不发达4国LDC4	40	----Burglar alarms
6983	8512.3019	----其他	10	0 8.5	智利CL,新西兰NZ,秘鲁PE,哥斯达黎加CR 亚太APTA,巴基斯坦PK	0	最不发达35国LDC35,最不发达4国LDC4	45	----other

序号 No.	税则号列 Tariff Line	货品名称	最惠国税率 MFN(%)	协定税率 Agreement(%)		特惠税率 S.P.(%)		普通税率 Gen.(%)	Article Description
6984	8512.3090	---其他	10	0 8.5	智利CL,新西兰NZ,秘鲁PE,哥斯达黎加CR 亚太APTA,巴基斯坦PK	0	最不发达35国LDC35,最不发达4国LDC4	45	---other
6985	8512.4000	-风挡刮水器、除霜器及去雾器	10	0	智利CL,新西兰NZ,秘鲁PE,哥斯达黎加CR	0	最不发达35国LDC35,最不发达4国LDC4	45	-Windscreen wipers, defrosters and demisters
6986	8512.9000	-零件	8	0 5	东盟ASEAN,智利CL,新西兰NZ,秘鲁PE,哥斯达黎加CR,台湾TW 巴基斯坦PK	0	最不发达35国LDC35,最不发达4国LDC4	45	-Parts
	85.13	**自供能源（例如，使用干电池、蓄电池、永磁发电机）的手提式电灯，但税号85.12的照明装置除外:**							**Portable electric lamps designed to function by their own source of energy (for example, dry batteries, accumulators, magnetos), other than lighting equipment of heading No.85.12:**
		-灯:							-Lamps:
6987	8513.1010	---手电筒	15	0 1.5 3 7.5 13.2	东盟ASEAN,新加坡SG,新西兰NZ,澳门MO 智利CL 哥斯达黎加CR 巴基斯坦PK,秘鲁PE 亚太APTA	0	最不发达35国LDC35,最不发达4国LDC4	100	---Portable electric torches designed to function by dry batteries
6988	8513.1090	---其他	17.5	0 1.8 3.5 8.8 14	东盟ASEAN,新加坡SG,新西兰NZ,澳门MO 智利CL 哥斯达黎加CR 秘鲁PE 巴基斯坦PK	0	最不发达35国LDC35	70	---Other
		-零件:							-Parts:
6989	8513.9010	---手电筒用	14	0 2.8 11.2	东盟ASEAN,智利CL,新加坡SG,新西兰NZ,秘鲁PE,香港HK,澳门MO 哥斯达黎加CR 巴基斯坦PK	0	最不发达35国LDC35,最不发达4国LDC4	100	---Of the torches of subheading No.8513.1010
6990	8513.9090	---其他	14	0 2.8 11.2	东盟ASEAN,智利CL,新加坡SG,新西兰NZ,秘鲁PE,香港HK,澳门MO 哥斯达黎加CR 巴基斯坦PK	0	最不发达35国LDC35	70	---Other

序号 No.	税则号列 Tariff Line	货品名称	最惠国税率 MFN(%)	协定税率 Agreement(%)		特惠税率 S.P.(%)		普通税率 Gen.(%)	Article Description
	85.14	**工业或实验室用电炉及电烘箱(包括通过感应或介质损耗工作的)；工业或实验室用其他通过感应或介质损耗对材料进行热处理的设备:**							**Industrial or laboratory electric furnaces and ovens (including those functioning by induction or dielectric loss); other industrial or laboratory equipment for the heat treatment of materials by induction or dielectric loss:**
		-电阻加热的炉及烘箱:							-Resistance heated furnaces and ovens:
6991	8514.1010	---可控气氛热处理炉	0			0	最不发达35国LDC35,最不发达4国LDC4	30	---Furnaces for heat treatment, atmosphere controllable
6992	8514.1090	---其他	0			0	最不发达35国LDC35,最不发达4国LDC4	30	---Other
6993	8514.2000	-通过感应或介质损耗工作的炉及烘箱	0			0	最不发达35国LDC35,最不发达4国LDC4	30	-Furnaces and ovens functioning by induction or dielectric loss
6994	8514.3000	-其他炉及烘箱	0			0	最不发达35国LDC35,最不发达4国LDC4	30	-Other furnaces and ovens
6995	8514.4000	-其他通过感应或介质损耗对材料进行热处理的设备	10	0 5	东盟ASEAN,智利CL,新加坡SG,新西兰NZ,秘鲁PE,哥斯达黎加CR 巴基斯坦PK	0	最不发达35国LDC35,最不发达4国LDC4	30	-Other equipment for the heat treatment of materials by induction or dielectric loss
	ex85144000	焊缝中频退火装置	△7						Intermediate frequency annealing device for weld
		-零件:							-Parts:
6996	8514.9010	---炼钢电炉用	8	0 5	东盟ASEAN,智利CL,新西兰NZ,秘鲁PE,哥斯达黎加CR 巴基斯坦PK	0	最不发达35国LDC35,最不发达4国LDC4	30	---Of steel making electric furnaces

序号 No.	税则号列 Tariff Line	货品名称	最惠国 税率 MFN(%)	协定税率 Agreement(%)		特惠税率 S.P.(%)		普通 税率 Gen.(%)	Article Description
6997	8514.9090	---其他	0			0	最不发达35国LDC35,最不发达4国LDC4	30	---Other
	85.15	**电气（包括电热气体）、激光、其他光、光子束、超声波、电子束、磁脉冲或等离子弧焊接机器及装置，不论是否兼有切割功能;用于热喷金属或金属陶瓷的电气机器及装置:**							**Electric (including electrically heated gas), laser or other light or photon beam, ultrasonic, electron beam, mag-netic pulse or plasma are soldering, brazing or welding machines and app-aratus, whether or not capable of cut-ting; electric machines and apparatus for hot spraying of metals or cermets:**
		-钎焊机器及装置:							-Brazing or soldering machines and apparatus:
6998	8515.1100	--烙铁及焊枪	10	0 5	东盟ASEAN,智利CL,新加坡SG,新西兰NZ,秘鲁PE,哥斯达黎加CR 巴基斯坦PK	0	最不发达35国LDC35,最不发达4国LDC4	30	--Soldering irons and guns
6999	8515.1900	--其他	10	0 5	东盟ASEAN,智利CL,新加坡SG,新西兰NZ,秘鲁PE,哥斯达黎加CR 巴基斯坦PK	0	最不发达35国LDC35,最不发达4国LDC4	30	--Other
		-电阻焊接机器及装置:							-Machines and apparatus for resistance welding of metals:
		--全自动或半自动的:							--Fully or partly automatic:
7000	8515.2120	---机器人	10	0 1 5	东盟ASEAN,新加坡SG,新西兰NZ,秘鲁PE,哥斯达黎加CR,香港HK 智利CL 巴基斯坦PK	0	最不发达35国LDC35,最不发达4国LDC4	30	---Robots
	ex85152120	汽车生产线电阻焊接机器人	△5						Resistance welding robots, used for automobile production line
		---其他:							---Other:
7001	8515.2191	----直缝焊管机	10	0 1 5	东盟ASEAN,新西兰NZ,秘鲁PE,哥斯达黎加CR,香港HK 智利CL 巴基斯坦PK	0	最不发达35国LDC35,最不发达4国LDC4	30	----Aligning tube welding machines

序号 No.	税则号列 Tariff Line	货品名称	最惠国税率 MFN(%)	协定税率 Agreement(%)		特惠税率 S.P.(%)		普通税率 Gen.(%)	Article Description
7002	8515.2199	----其他	10	0 1 5	东盟ASEAN,新加坡SG,新西兰NZ,秘鲁PE,哥斯达黎加CR,香港HK 智利CL 巴基斯坦PK	0	最不发达35国LDC35,最不发达4国LDC4	30	----Other
7003	8515.2900	--其他	10	0 5 9.5	东盟ASEAN,智利CL,新加坡SG,新西兰NZ,秘鲁PE,哥斯达黎加CR 巴基斯坦PK 亚太APTA	0	最不发达35国LDC35,最不发达4国LDC4	30	--Other
		-电弧（包括等离子弧）焊接机器及装置:							-Machines and apparatus for arc (including plasma arc) welding of metals:
		--全自动或半自动的:							--Fully or partly automatic:
7004	8515.3120	---机器人	10	0 1	新西兰NZ,秘鲁PE,哥斯达黎加CR 智利CL	0	最不发达35国LDC35,最不发达4国LDC4	30	---Robots
		---其他:							---Other:
7005	8515.3191	----螺旋焊管机	10	0 1 5	东盟ASEAN,新西兰NZ,秘鲁PE,哥斯达黎加CR 智利CL 巴基斯坦PK	0	最不发达35国LDC35,最不发达4国LDC4	30	----Spiralling tube welding machines
7006	8515.3199	----其他	10	0 1	新西兰NZ,秘鲁PE,哥斯达黎加CR 智利CL	0	最不发达35国LDC35,最不发达4国LDC4	30	----Other
7007	8515.3900	--其他	10	0 1 5	东盟ASEAN,新西兰NZ,秘鲁PE,哥斯达黎加CR 智利CL 巴基斯坦PK	0	最不发达35国LDC35,最不发达4国LDC4	30	--Other
		-其他机器及装置:							-Other machines and apparatus:
7008	8515.8010	---激光焊接机器人	8	0 5 7.6	东盟ASEAN,智利CL,新西兰NZ,秘鲁PE,哥斯达黎加CR,香港HK,台湾TW 巴基斯坦PK 亚太APTA	0	最不发达35国LDC35,最不发达4国LDC4	30	---Laserwelding robots
	ex85158010	汽车生产线激光焊接机器人	△5						Laser welding robots, used for automobile production line

序号 No.	税则号列 Tariff Line	货品名称	最惠国税率 MFN(%)	协定税率 Agreement(%)		特惠税率 S.P.(%)		普通税率 Gen.(%)	Article Description
7009	8515.8090	---其他	8	0 5 7.6	东盟ASEAN,智利CL,新西兰NZ,秘鲁PE,哥斯达黎加CR,香港HK,台湾TW 巴基斯坦PK 亚太APTA	0	最不发达35国LDC35,最不发达4国LDC4	30	---Other
7010	8515.9000	-零件	6 △3	0 5 5.7	东盟ASEAN,智利CL,新西兰NZ,秘鲁PE,哥斯达黎加CR,香港HK 巴基斯坦PK 亚太APTA	0	最不发达35国LDC35,最不发达4国LDC4	30	-Parts
	85.16	**电热的快速热水器、储存式热水器、浸入式液体加热器;电气空间加热器及土壤加热器;电热的理发器具（例如，电吹风机、电卷发器、电热发钳）及干手器;电熨斗;其他家用电热器具;加热电阻器，但税号85.45的货品除外:**							**Electric instantaneous or storage water heaters and immersion heaters; electric space heating apparatus and soil heating apparatus; electro-thermic hair-dressing apparatus (for example, hair dryers, hair curlers, curling tong heaters) and hand dryers; electric smoothing irons; other electro-thermic appliances of a kind used for domestic purposes; electric heating resistors, other than those of heading No.85.45:**
		-电热的快速热水器、储存式热水器、浸入式液体加热器:							-Electric instantaneous or storage waterheaters and immersion heaters:
7011	8516.1010	---储存式电热水器	10	0 1 5	东盟ASEAN,新加坡SG,新西兰NZ,秘鲁PE,哥斯达黎加CR 智利CL 巴基斯坦PK	0	最不发达35国LDC35,最不发达4国LDC4	100	---Electrical storage water heaters
7012	8516.1020	---即热式电热水器	10	0 1 5	东盟ASEAN,新加坡SG,新西兰NZ,秘鲁PE,哥斯达黎加CR 智利CL 巴基斯坦PK	0	最不发达35国LDC35,最不发达4国LDC4	100	---Electrical geysers
7013	8516.1090	---其他	10	0 1 5	东盟ASEAN,新加坡SG,新西兰NZ,秘鲁PE,哥斯达黎加CR 智利CL 巴基斯坦PK	0	最不发达35国LDC35,最不发达4国LDC4	100	---Other
		-电气空间加热器及土壤加热器:							-Electric space heating apparatus and electric soil heating apparatus:

序号 No.	税则号列 Tariff Line	货品名称	最惠国税率 MFN(%)	协定税率 Agreement(%)		特惠税率 S.P.(%)		普通税率 Gen.(%)	Article Description
7014	8516.2100	--储存式散热器	35	0 7 17.5	东盟ASEAN,智利CL,新加坡SG,新西兰NZ,澳门MO,台湾TW 哥斯达黎加CR 秘鲁PE	0	最不发达35国LDC35	100	--Storage heating radiators
		--其他:							--Other:
7015	8516.2910	---土壤加热器	10	0 1 5	东盟ASEAN,新西兰NZ,秘鲁PE,哥斯达黎加CR,香港HK,澳门MO 智利CL 巴基斯坦PK	0	最不发达35国LDC35,最不发达4国LDC4	40	---Electric soil heating apparatus
7016	8516.2920	---辐射式空间加热器	10	0 1 5	东盟ASEAN,新加坡SG,新西兰NZ,秘鲁PE,哥斯达黎加CR,香港HK,澳门MO 智利CL 巴基斯坦PK	0	最不发达35国LDC35,最不发达4国LDC4	100	---Radiation space heaters
		---对流式空间加热器:							---Convection space heaters:
7017	8516.2931	----风扇式	10	0 1 5	东盟ASEAN,新加坡SG,新西兰NZ,秘鲁PE,哥斯达黎加CR,香港HK,澳门MO 智利CL 巴基斯坦PK	0	最不发达35国LDC35,最不发达4国LDC4	100	----Fan heaters
7018	8516.2932	----充液式	10	0 1 5	东盟ASEAN,新加坡SG,新西兰NZ,秘鲁PE,哥斯达黎加CR,香港HK,澳门MO 智利CL 巴基斯坦PK	0	最不发达35国LDC35,最不发达4国LDC4	100	----Liquid filled heaters
7019	8516.2939	----其他	10	0 1 5	东盟ASEAN,新加坡SG,新西兰NZ,秘鲁PE,哥斯达黎加CR,香港HK,澳门MO 智利CL 巴基斯坦PK	0	最不发达35国LDC35,最不发达4国LDC4	100	----Others
7020	8516.2990	---其他	10	0 1 5	东盟ASEAN,新加坡SG,新西兰NZ,秘鲁PE,哥斯达黎加CR,香港HK,澳门MO 智利CL 巴基斯坦PK	0	最不发达35国LDC35,最不发达4国LDC4	100	---Other
		-电热的理发器具及干手器:							-Electro-thermic hair-dressing or hand-drying apparatus:
7021	8516.3100	--吹风机	10	0 5	东盟ASEAN,智利CL,新加坡SG,新西兰NZ,秘鲁PE,哥斯达黎加CR,澳门MO 巴基斯坦PK	0	最不发达35国LDC35,最不发达4国LDC4	100	--Hair dryers

序号 No.	税则号列 Tariff Line	货品名称	最惠国税率 MFN(%)	协定税率 Agreement(%)		特惠税率 S.P.(%)		普通税率 Gen.(%)	Article Description
7022	8516.3200	--其他理发器具	35	0 7 17.5	东盟ASEAN,智利CL,新加坡SG,新西兰NZ,澳门MO 哥斯达黎加CR 秘鲁PE	0	最不发达35国LDC35	100	--Other hair-dressing apparatus
7023	8516.3300	--干手器	35	0 7 17.5	东盟ASEAN,智利CL,新加坡SG,新西兰NZ,澳门MO 哥斯达黎加CR 秘鲁PE	0	最不发达35国LDC35	100	--Hand-drying apparatus
7024	8516.4000	-电熨斗	35 △17	0 7 17.5	东盟ASEAN,智利CL,新加坡SG,新西兰NZ,澳门MO,台湾TW 哥斯达黎加CR 秘鲁PE	0	最不发达35国LDC35	100	-Electric smoothing irons
7025	8516.5000	-微波炉	15 △8	0 3 7.5 13.5	东盟ASEAN,智利CL,新加坡SG,新西兰NZ 哥斯达黎加CR 巴基斯坦PK,秘鲁PE 亚太APTA	0	最不发达35国LDC35	130	-Microwave ovens
		-其他炉;电锅、电热板、加热环、烧烤炉及烘烤器:							-Other ovens; cookers, cooking plates, boiling rings, grillers and roasters:
7026	8516.6010	---电磁炉	15	0 3 7.5 12	东盟ASEAN,智利CL,新加坡SG,新西兰NZ,澳门MO 哥斯达黎加CR 秘鲁PE 巴基斯坦PK	0	最不发达35国LDC35	130	---Electromagnetic ovens
7027	8516.6030	---电饭锅	15 △8	0 3 7.5 12	东盟ASEAN,智利CL,新加坡SG,新西兰NZ,澳门MO,台湾TW 哥斯达黎加CR 秘鲁PE 巴基斯坦PK	0	最不发达35国LDC35	130	---Electric rice cookers
7028	8516.6040	---电炒锅	15	0 3 7.5 12	东盟ASEAN,智利CL,新加坡SG,新西兰NZ,澳门MO 哥斯达黎加CR 秘鲁PE 巴基斯坦PK	0	最不发达35国LDC35	130	---Electric frying pans
7029	8516.6050	---电烤箱	15 △8	0 3 7.5 12	东盟ASEAN,智利CL,新西兰NZ,澳门MO,台湾TW 哥斯达黎加CR 秘鲁PE 巴基斯坦PK	0	最不发达35国LDC35	130	---Electric roasters
7030	8516.6090	---其他	15 △8	0 3 7.5 12	东盟ASEAN,智利CL,新加坡SG,新西兰NZ,澳门MO 哥斯达黎加CR 秘鲁PE 巴基斯坦PK	0	最不发达35国LDC35	130	---Other

序号 No.	税则号列 Tariff Line	货品名称	最惠国税率 MFN(%)	协定税率 Agreement(%)		特惠税率 S.P.(%)		普通税率 Gen.(%)	Article Description
		-其他电热器具:							-Other electro-thermic appliances:
		--咖啡壶或茶壶:							--Coffee or tea makers:
7031	8516.7110	---滴液式咖啡机	32 △16	0 6.4 16	东盟ASEAN,智利CL,新加坡SG,新西兰NZ,澳门MO 哥斯达黎加CR 秘鲁PE	0	最不发达35国LDC35	130	---Drip coffee makers
7032	8516.7120	---蒸馏渗滤式咖啡机	32 △16	0 6.4 16	东盟ASEAN,智利CL,新加坡SG,新西兰NZ,澳门MO 哥斯达黎加CR 秘鲁PE	0	最不发达35国LDC35	130	---Steam espresso makers
7033	8516.7130	---泵压式咖啡机	32 △16	0 6.4 16	东盟ASEAN,智利CL,新加坡SG,新西兰NZ,澳门MO 哥斯达黎加CR 秘鲁PE	0	最不发达35国LDC35	130	---Pump espresso makers
7034	8516.7190	---其他	32 △16	0 6.4 16	东盟ASEAN,智利CL,新加坡SG,新西兰NZ,澳门MO 哥斯达黎加CR 秘鲁PE	0	最不发达35国LDC35	130	---Other
		--烤面包器:							--Toasters:
7035	8516.7210	---家用自动面包机	32	0 6.4 16	东盟ASEAN,智利CL,新加坡SG,新西兰NZ,澳门MO,台湾TW 哥斯达黎加CR 秘鲁PE	0	最不发达35国LDC35	130	---Automatic bread makers
7036	8516.7220	---片式烤面包机(多士炉)	32	0 6.4 16	东盟ASEAN,智利CL,新加坡SG,新西兰NZ,澳门MO 哥斯达黎加CR 秘鲁PE	0	最不发达35国LDC35	130	---Slice pop-up toasters
7037	8516.7290	---其他	32	0 6.4 16	东盟ASEAN,智利CL,新加坡SG,新西兰NZ,澳门MO 哥斯达黎加CR 秘鲁PE	0	最不发达35国LDC35	130	---Other
		--其他:							--Other:
7038	8516.7910	---电热饮水机	32	0 6.4 16	东盟ASEAN,智利CL,新加坡SG,新西兰NZ,澳门MO 哥斯达黎加CR 秘鲁PE	0	最不发达35国LDC35	100	---Electro-thermic water dispensers
7039	8516.7990	---其他	32 △16	0 6.4 16	东盟ASEAN,智利CL,新加坡SG,新西兰NZ,香港HK,澳门MO 哥斯达黎加CR 秘鲁PE	0	最不发达35国LDC35	100	---Other
7040	8516.8000	-加热电阻器	10	0 5	东盟ASEAN,智利CL,新加坡SG,新西兰NZ,秘鲁PE,哥斯达黎加CR 巴基斯坦PK	0	最不发达35国LDC35,最不发达4国LDC4	40	-Electric heating resistors

序号 No.	税则号列 Tariff Line	货品名称	最惠国税率 MFN(%)	协定税率 Agreement(%)		特惠税率 S.P.(%)		普通税率 Gen.(%)	Article Description
		-零件:							-Parts:
7041	8516.9010	---土壤加热器及加热电阻器用	8	0 5	东盟ASEAN,智利CL,新西兰NZ,秘鲁PE,哥斯达黎加CR,香港HK 巴基斯坦PK	0	最不发达35国LDC35,最不发达4国LDC4	40	---Of apparatus of subheading No.8516.2910 or 8516.8000
7042	8516.9090	---其他	12 △8	0 2.4 6	东盟ASEAN,智利CL,新加坡SG,新西兰NZ,秘鲁PE,香港HK 哥斯达黎加CR 巴基斯坦PK	0	最不发达35国LDC35,最不发达4国LDC4	100	---Other
	85.17	**电话机，包括用于蜂窝网络或其他无线网络的电话机；其他发送或接收声音、图像或其他数据用的设备，包括有线或无线网络（例如，局域网或广域网）的通信设备，税目84.43、85.25、85.27或85.28的发送或接收设备除外：**							**Telephone sets, including telephones for cellular networks or for other wireless networks; other apparatus for the transmission or reception of voice, images or other data, including apparatus for communication in a wired or wireless network (such as a local or wide area network), other than transmission or reception apparatus of heading 84.43, 85.25, 85.27 or 85.28 :**
		-电话机，包括蜂窝网络或其他无线网络用电话机:							-Telephone sets, including telephones for cellular networks or for other wireless networks:
7043	8517.1100	--无绳电话机	0			0	最不发达35国LDC35,最不发达4国LDC4	30	--Line telephone sets with cordless handsets
		--用于蜂窝网络或其他无线网络的电话机:							--Telephones for cellular networks or for other wireless networks:
7044	8517.1210	---手持（包括车载）式无线电话机	0			0	最不发达35国LDC35,最不发达4国LDC4	20	---Radio telephone handsets (including vehicle installed)
7045	8517.1220	---对讲机	0			0	最不发达35国LDC35,最不发达4国LDC4	17	---Walkie-talkie

序号 No.	税则号列 Tariff Line	货品名称	最惠国税率 MFN(%)	协定税率 Agreement(%)	特惠税率 S.P.(%)	普通税率 Gen.(%)	Article Description
7046	8517.1290	---其他	0		0 最不发达35国LDC35,最不发达4国LDC4	14	---Other
7047	8517.1800	--其他	0		0 最不发达35国LDC35,最不发达4国LDC4	30	--Other
		-其他发送或接收声音、图像或其他数据用的设备，包括有线或无线网络（例如，局域网或广域网）的通信设备:					-Other apparatus for transmission or reception of voice, images or other data, including apparatus for communication in a wired or wireless network (such as a local or wide area network) :
		--基站:					--Base stations:
7048	8517.6110	---移动通信基站	0		0 最不发达35国LDC35,最不发达4国LDC4	14	---Mobile communication base station
7049	8517.6190	---其他	0		0 最不发达35国LDC35,最不发达4国LDC4	14	---Other
		--接收、转换并且发送或再生声音、图像或其他数据用的设备，包括交换及路由设备:					--Machines for the reception, conversion and transmission or regeneration of voice, images or other data, including switching and routing apparatus:
		---数字式程控电话或电报交换机:					---Digital program-controlled switching systems:
7050	8517.6211	----局用电话交换机；长途电话交换机；电报交换机	0		0 最不发达35国LDC35,最不发达4国LDC4	17	----Public telephonic switching systems, toll telephonic or telegraphic switching systems
7051	8517.6212	----移动通信交换机	0		0 最不发达35国LDC35,最不发达4国LDC4	40	----Mobile communication switching systems

序号 No.	税则号列 Tariff Line	货品名称	最惠国税率 MFN(%)	协定税率 Agreement(%)	特惠税率 S.P.(%)	普通税率 Gen.(%)	Article Description
7052	8517.6219	----其他电话交换机	0		0 最不发达35国LDC35, 最不发达4国LDC4	40	----Other telephonic switching system
		---光通讯设备:					---Optical communication equipments:
7053	8517.6221	----光端机及脉冲编码调制设备(PCM)	0		0 最不发达35国LDC35, 最不发达4国LDC4	17	----Optical line terminal equipments and pulse code modulation mutilexers
7054	8517.6222	----波分复用光传输设备	0		0 最不发达35国LDC35, 最不发达4国LDC4	30	----Optical transmission equipments for wave-division multiplexing
7055	8517.6229	----其他	0		0 最不发达35国LDC35, 最不发达4国LDC4	30	----Other
		---其他有线数字通信设备:					---Other telecommunication apparatus for digit line system:
7056	8517.6231	----通信网络时钟同步设备	0		0 最不发达35国LDC35, 最不发达4国LDC4	30	----Communication network synchronizing equipments
7057	8517.6232	----以太网络交换机	0		0 最不发达35国LDC35, 最不发达4国LDC4	30	----Ethernet exchangers
7058	8517.6233	----IP电话信号转换设备	0		0 最不发达35国LDC35, 最不发达4国LDC4	30	----IP telephone signal converters
7059	8517.6234	----调制解调器	0		0 最不发达35国LDC35, 最不发达4国LDC4	30	----Modem

序号 No.	税则号列 Tariff Line	货品名称	最惠国税率 MFN(%)	协定税率 Agreement(%)		特惠税率 S.P.(%)		普通税率 Gen.(%)	Article Description
7060	8517.6235	----集线器	0			0	最不发达35国LDC35,最不发达4国LDC4	40	----Network concentrators
7061	8517.6236	----路由器	0			0	最不发达35国LDC35,最不发达4国LDC4	40	----Network path-control devices
7062	8517.6237	----有线网络接口卡	0			0	最不发达35国LDC35,最不发达4国LDC4	30	----Wired network interface card
7063	8517.6239	----其他	0			0	最不发达35国LDC35,最不发达4国LDC4	30	----Thermograph recording heads
		---其他:							---Other:
7064	8517.6292	----无线网络接口卡	0			0	最不发达35国LDC35,最不发达4国LDC4	14	----Wireless network interface card
7065	8517.6293	----无线接入固定台	0			0	最不发达35国LDC35,最不发达4国LDC4	14	----Fixed wireless communicating terminal
7066	8517.6294	----无线耳机	0			0	最不发达35国LDC35,最不发达4国LDC4	14	----Wireless headset
7067	8517.6299	----其他	0			0	最不发达35国LDC35,最不发达4国LDC4	14	----Other
		--其他:							--Other:
7068	8517.6910	---其他无线设备	9	0	东盟ASEAN,智利CL,巴基斯坦PK,新西兰NZ,秘鲁PE,哥斯达黎加CR	0	最不发达35国LDC35,最不发达4国LDC4	14	---Other apparatus for communication in a wireless network

序号 No.	税则号列 Tariff Line	货品名称	最惠国税率 MFN(%)	协定税率 Agreement(%)		特惠税率 S.P.(%)		普通税率 Gen.(%)	Article Description
	ex85176910	用于呼叫、提示和寻呼的便携式接收器	△0						Portable receivers for calling, alerting or paging
7069	8517.6990	---其他有线设备	0			0	最不发达35国LDC35,最不发达4国LDC4	30	---Other apparatus for communication in a wired network
		-零件:							-Parts:
7070	8517.7010	---数字式程控电话或电报交换机用	0			0	最不发达35国LDC35,最不发达4国LDC4	14	---Of digital program-controlled switching apparatus
7071	8517.7020	---光端机及脉冲编码调制设备（PCM）用	0			0	最不发达35国LDC35,最不发达4国LDC4	14	---Of the equipment of subheading No.8517.6221
7072	8517.7030	---手持式无线电话机用(天线除外)	0			0	最不发达35国LDC35,最不发达4国LDC4	17	---Of radio telephone handsets (other than aerials)
7073	8517.7040	---对讲机用(天线除外)	8	0 0.8 5 5.6	东盟ASEAN,新西兰NZ,秘鲁PE,哥斯达黎加CR,香港HK 智利CL 巴基斯坦PK 亚太APTA	0	最不发达35国LDC35,最不发达4国LDC4	20	---Of walkie-talkie (other than aerials)
7074	8517.7060	---光通信设备的激光收发模块	0			0	最不发达35国LDC35,最不发达4国LDC4	30	---Laser transmitting and receiving unit of laser communication equipment
7075	8517.7070	---税号8517所列设备用天线及其零件	2	0	东盟ASEAN,智利CL,巴基斯坦PK,新西兰NZ,秘鲁PE,哥斯达黎加CR	0	最不发达35国LDC35,最不发达4国LDC4	20	---Aerials or parts thereof for use with the apparatus of No.8517
	ex85177070	无线电话电报装置的天线	△0						Aerials or antennae of a kind used with apparatus for radio-telephony and radio-telegraphy

序号 No.	税则号列 Tariff Line	货品名称	最惠国税率 MFN(%)	协定税率 Agreement(%)		特惠税率 S.P.(%)		普通税率 Gen.(%)	Article Description
7076	8517.7090	---其他	0			0	最不发达35国LDC35,最不发达4国LDC4	20	---Other
	85.18	**传声器（麦克风）及其座架;扬声器，不论是否装成音箱;耳机、耳塞机，不论是否装有传声器，由传声器及一个或多个扬声器组成的组合机;音频扩大器;电气扩音机组:**							**Microphones and stands therefor; loudspeakers, whether or not mounted in their enclosures; headphones, earphones, whether or not combined with a microphone, and sets consisting of a microphone and one or more loudspeakers; audio frequency electric amplifiers; electric sound amplifier sets:**
7077	8518.1000	-传声器（麦克风）及其座架	10	0 5	东盟ASEAN,智利CL,新加坡SG,新西兰NZ,秘鲁PE,哥斯达黎加CR,香港HK,台湾TW 巴基斯坦PK	0	最不发达35国LDC35,最不发达4国LDC4	40	-Microphones and stands therefor
	ex85181000	电讯用麦克风，频率范围在300赫兹到3.4千赫之间，直径不超过10毫米，高度不超过3毫米	△0						Microphones having a frequency range of 300Hz to 3.4kHz with a diameter of not exceeding 10mm and a height not exceeding 3mm，for telecommunication use
	ex85181000	传声器(麦克风)及其座架(列入ITA的电讯用麦克风除外)	△6						Microphones and stands therefor (not inculding microphones for tele-com-communicaiton use within ITA)
		-扬声器，不论是否装成音箱:							-Loudspeakers, whether or not mounted in their enclosures:
7078	8518.2100	--单喇叭音箱	10 △6	0 1 5	东盟ASEAN,新加坡SG,新西兰NZ,秘鲁PE,哥斯达黎加CR,香港HK 智利CL 巴基斯坦PK	0	最不发达35国LDC35,最不发达4国LDC4	40	--Single loudspeakers, mounted in their enclosures
7079	8518.2200	--多喇叭音箱	10 △6	0 1 5	东盟ASEAN,新加坡SG,新西兰NZ,哥斯达黎加CR,香港HK 智利CL 巴基斯坦PK,秘鲁PE	0	最不发达35国LDC35,最不发达4国LDC4	40	--Multiple loudspeakers, mounted in the same enclosure

序号 No.	税则号列 Tariff Line	货品名称	最惠国税率 MFN(%)	协定税率 Agreement(%)		特惠税率 S.P.(%)		普通税率 Gen.(%)	Article Description
7080	8518.2900	--其他	0			0	最不发达35国LDC35,最不发达4国LDC4	40	--Other
7081	8518.3000	-耳机、耳塞机，不论是否装有传声器，由传声器及一个或多个扬声器组成的组合机	0			0	最不发达35国LDC35,最不发达4国LDC4	40	-Headphones and earphones, whether or not combined with a microphone, and sets consisting of a microphone and one or more loudspeakers
7082	8518.4000	-音频扩大器	12	0 1.2 2.4 6	东盟ASEAN,新加坡SG,新西兰NZ,香港HK,台湾TW 智利CL 哥斯达黎加CR 巴基斯坦PK,秘鲁PE	0	最不发达35国LDC35,最不发达4国LDC4	40	-Audio-frequency electric amplifiers
	ex85184000	列入ITA的有线电话重复器用的电器扩音器	△0						Electric amplifiers when used as repeaters in line telephony products falling within the ITA
7083	8518.5000	-电气扩音机组	10	0 5	东盟ASEAN,智利CL,新加坡SG,新西兰NZ,秘鲁PE,哥斯达黎加CR 巴基斯坦PK	0	最不发达35国LDC35,最不发达4国LDC4	40	-Electric sound amplifier sets
7084	8518.9000	-零件	10.5	0 2.1 5	东盟ASEAN,智利CL,新加坡SG,新西兰NZ,秘鲁PE,香港HK,台湾TW 哥斯达黎加CR 巴基斯坦PK	0	最不发达35国LDC35,最不发达4国LDC4	40	-Parts
	ex85189000	列入ITA的有线电话重复器用的电器扩音器的零件	△0						Parts of electric amplifiers when used as repeaters in line telephony products falling within the ITA
	85.19	**声音录制或重放设备:**							**Sound recording or reproducing apparatus:**
7085	8519.2000	-用硬币、钞票、银行卡、代币或其他支付方式使其工作的设备	20	0 4 10 16.4	东盟ASEAN,智利CL,新加坡SG,新西兰NZ 哥斯达黎加CR 秘鲁PE 亚太APTA,巴基斯坦PK	0	最不发达35国LDC35	80	-Apparatus operated by coins, banknotes, bank cards, tokens or by other means of payment
7086	8519.3000	-转盘（唱机唱盘）	30	0 6 15	东盟ASEAN,智利CL,新加坡SG,新西兰NZ 哥斯达黎加CR 秘鲁PE	0	最不发达35国LDC35	130	-Turntables (record-decks)

序号 No.	税则号列 Tariff Line	货品名称	最惠国税率 MFN(%)	协定税率 Agreement(%)	特惠税率 S.P.(%)	普通税率 Gen.(%)	Article Description
7087	8519.5000	-电话应答机	0		0 最不发达35国LDC35,最不发达4国LDC4	80	-Telephone answering machines
		-其他设备: --使用磁性、光学或半导体媒体的: ---使用磁性媒体的:					-Other apparatus : --Using magnetic, optical or semiconductor media: ---Using magnetic media:
7088	8519.8111	----未装有声音录制装置的盒式磁带型声音重放装置，编辑节目用放声机除外	17	0 东盟ASEAN,智利CL,新加坡SG,新西兰NZ 3.4 哥斯达黎加CR 8.5 秘鲁PE 13.6 巴基斯坦PK	0 最不发达35国LDC35	130	----Cassette-players, not incorporating a sound recording device, not including transcribing machines
7089	8519.8112	----装有声音重放装置的盒式磁带型录音机	30	0 东盟ASEAN,智利CL,新加坡SG,新西兰NZ 6 哥斯达黎加CR 15 秘鲁PE	0 最不发达35国LDC35	130	----Cassette-type magnetic tape recorders incorporating sound reproducing apparatus
7090	8519.8119	----其他	20	0 东盟ASEAN,智利CL,新加坡SG,新西兰NZ 4 哥斯达黎加CR 10 秘鲁PE 16.4 亚太APTA,巴基斯坦PK	0 最不发达35国LDC35	80	----Other
		---使用光学媒体的:					---Using optical media:
7091	8519.8121	----激光唱机，未装有声音录制装置	30	0 东盟ASEAN,智利CL,新加坡SG,新西兰NZ 6 哥斯达黎加CR 15 秘鲁PE 26 亚太APTA,巴基斯坦PK	0 最不发达35国LDC35	80	----Compact disc players, not incorporating a sound recording devices
7092	8519.8129	----其他	20	0 东盟ASEAN,智利CL,新加坡SG,新西兰NZ 4 哥斯达黎加CR 10 秘鲁PE 16 巴基斯坦PK 16.4 亚太APTA	0 最不发达35国LDC35	80	----Other
		---使用半导体媒体的:					---Using semiconductor media:
7093	8519.8131	----装有声音重放装置的闪速存储器型声音录制设备	20 △12	0 东盟ASEAN,新加坡SG,新西兰NZ 2 智利CL 4 哥斯达黎加CR 10 秘鲁PE	0 最不发达35国LDC35	80	----Flash memory recorders incorporating sound reproducing apparatus
7094	8519.8139	----其他	20 △12	0 东盟ASEAN,智利CL,新加坡SG,新西兰NZ 4 哥斯达黎加CR 10 秘鲁PE 16.4 亚太APTA,巴基斯坦PK	0 最不发达35国LDC35	80	----Other
		--其他:					--Other:
7095	8519.8910	---不带录制装置的其他唱机，不论是否带有扬声器	30	0 东盟ASEAN,智利CL,新加坡SG,新西兰NZ 6 哥斯达黎加CR 15 秘鲁PE	0 最不发达35国LDC35	130	---record-players, not incorporating a sound recording device

序号 No.	税则号列 Tariff Line	货品名称	最惠国税率 MFN(%)	协定税率 Agreement(%)	特惠税率 S.P.(%)	普通税率 Gen.(%)	Article Description
7096	8519.8990	---其他声音录制或重放设备	20 △12	0 东盟ASEAN,智利CL,新加坡SG,新西兰NZ 4 哥斯达黎加CR 10 秘鲁PE 16 巴基斯坦PK 16.4 亚太APTA	0 最不发达35国LDC35	80	---Other
	85.21	**视频信号录制或重放设备，不论是否装有高频调谐器:**					**Video recording or reproducing apparatus, whether or not incorporating a video tuner:**
		-磁带型:					-Magnetic tape type:
		---录像机:					---Video tape recorders:
7097	8521.1011	----广播级	① △③	0 东盟ASEAN,智利CL,新加坡SG,新西兰NZ 6 哥斯达黎加CR 15 秘鲁PE ④ 亚太APTA,巴基斯坦PK	0 最不发达35国LDC35	②	----Broadcast quality
7098	8521.1019	----其他	①	0 东盟ASEAN,智利CL,新加坡SG,新西兰NZ 6 哥斯达黎加CR 15 秘鲁PE ⑤ 亚太APTA,巴基斯坦PK	0 最不发达35国LDC35	②	----Other
7099	8521.1020	---放像机	①	0 东盟ASEAN,智利CL,新加坡SG,新西兰NZ 6 哥斯达黎加CR 15 秘鲁PE ⑥ 亚太APTA,巴基斯坦PK	0 最不发达35国LDC35	②	---Video tape reproducers
		-其他:					-Other:
		---激光视盘机:					---Laser video compact disk player:
7100	8521.9011	----视频高密光盘(VCD)播放机	20	0 东盟ASEAN,智利CL,新加坡SG,新西兰NZ 4 哥斯达黎加CR 10 秘鲁PE 16 亚太APTA,巴基斯坦PK	0 最不发达35国LDC35	130	----Video Compact Disc player
7101	8521.9012	----数字化视频光盘(DVD)播放机	20	0 东盟ASEAN,智利CL,新加坡SG,新西兰NZ 4 哥斯达黎加CR 10 秘鲁PE 16 亚太APTA,巴基斯坦PK	0 最不发达35国LDC35	130	----Digital Video Disc player

① 完税价格不高于 2000 美元/台：30%；完税价格高于 2000 美元/台：3%，加 3283 元。
② 完税价格不高于 2000 美元/台：130%；完税价格高于 2000 美元/台：6%，加 20600 元。
③ 完税价格不高于 5000 美元/台：15%；完税价格高于 5000 美元/台：3%，加 3648 元。
④ 完税价格不高于 2000 美元/台：16%；完税价格高于 2000 美元/台：3%，加 1581 元。
⑤ 完税价格不高于 2000 美元/台：24.5%；完税价格高于 2000 美元/台：3%，加 2614 元。
⑥ 完税价格不高于 2000 美元/台：18%；完税价格高于 2000 美元/台：3%，加 1824 元。

序号 No.	税则号列 Tariff Line	货品名称	最惠国税率 MFN(%)	协定税率 Agreement(%)		特惠税率 S.P.(%)		普通税率 Gen.(%)	Article Description
7102	8521.9019	----其他	20	0	东盟ASEAN,智利CL,新加坡SG,新西兰NZ	0	最不发达35国LDC35	130	----Other
				4	哥斯达黎加CR				
				10	秘鲁PE				
				16	亚太APTA,巴基斯坦PK				
7103	8521.9090	---其他	20	0	东盟ASEAN,新加坡SG,新西兰NZ,香港HK	0	最不发达35国LDC35	130	---Other
				2	智利CL				
				4	哥斯达黎加CR				
				10	秘鲁PE				
				16	亚太APTA,巴基斯坦PK				
	ex85219090	光盘型广播级录像机	△⑦						CD-type video recorder, broadcast quality
	85.22	**专用于或主要用于税号85.19或85.21所列设备的零件、附件:**							**Parts and accessories suitable for use solely or principally with the apparatus of headings Nos.85.19 or 85.21:**
7104	8522.1000	-拾音头	35	0	东盟ASEAN,智利CL,新加坡SG,新西兰NZ,香港HK	0	最不发达35国LDC35	130	-Pick up cartridges
				7	哥斯达黎加CR				
				17.5	秘鲁PE				
		-其他:							-Other:
7105	8522.9010	---转盘或唱机用	25	0	东盟ASEAN,智利CL,新加坡SG,新西兰NZ,香港HK	0	最不发达35国LDC35	130	---Of turntables (record decks) or recordplayers
				5	哥斯达黎加CR				
				12.5	秘鲁PE				
				20	亚太APTA,巴基斯坦PK				
		---盒式磁带录音机或放声机用:							---Of cassette magnetic tape recorders or reproducers:
7106	8522.9021	----走带机构(机芯),不论是否装有磁头	25	0	东盟ASEAN,智利CL,新加坡SG,新西兰NZ,香港HK	0	最不发达35国LDC35	100	----Transport mechanisms, whether or not incorporating a magnetic head
				5	哥斯达黎加CR				
				12.5	秘鲁PE				
				22.5	亚太APTA,巴基斯坦PK				
7107	8522.9022	----磁头	25	0	东盟ASEAN,智利CL,新加坡SG,新西兰NZ,香港HK	0	最不发达35国LDC35	100	----Magnetic heads
				5	哥斯达黎加CR				
				12.5	秘鲁PE				
				22.5	亚太APTA,巴基斯坦PK				

⑦ 完税价格不高于7000美元/台：15%；完税价格高于7000美元/台：5%，加4256元。

序号 No.	税则号列 Tariff Line	货品名称	最惠国税率 MFN(%)	协定税率 Agreement(%)		特惠税率 S.P.(%)		普通税率 Gen.(%)	Article Description
7108	8522.9023	----磁头零件	20	0 4 10 18	东盟ASEAN,智利CL,新加坡SG,新西兰NZ,香港HK 哥斯达黎加CR 秘鲁PE 亚太APTA,巴基斯坦PK	0	最不发达35国LDC35	100	----Parts of magnetic heads
7109	8522.9029	----其他	30 △15	0 6 15 27	东盟ASEAN,智利CL,新加坡SG,新西兰NZ,香港HK 哥斯达黎加CR 秘鲁PE 亚太APTA,巴基斯坦PK	0	最不发达35国LDC35	100	----Other
		---视频信号录制或重放设备用:							---Of video recording or reproducing apparatus:
7110	8522.9031	----激光视盘机的机芯	30	0 6 15 21	东盟ASEAN,智利CL,新加坡SG,新西兰NZ,香港HK 哥斯达黎加CR 秘鲁PE 亚太APTA,巴基斯坦PK	0	最不发达35国LDC35	100	----Movements for Laser video compact disk player
	ex85229031	车载导航仪视频播放机机芯	△17						Movements for video players in the navigation system in vehicle
7111	8522.9039	----其他	30	0 6 15 21	东盟ASEAN,智利CL,新加坡SG,新西兰NZ,香港HK 哥斯达黎加CR 秘鲁PE 亚太APTA,巴基斯坦PK	0	最不发达35国LDC35	100	----Other
	ex85229039	其他视频信号录制或重放设备的零件	△15						Other parts/accessories of video recording or reproducing apparatus
	ex85229039	激光视盘机激光收发装置用的零件	△8						Parts of Laser transmitting and receiving device of laser disc player
		---其他:							---Other:
7112	8522.9091	----车载音频转播器或发射器	20 △10	0 4 10 16	东盟ASEAN,智利CL,新加坡SG,新西兰NZ,香港HK 哥斯达黎加CR 秘鲁PE 亚太APTA,巴基斯坦PK	0	最不发达35国LDC35,最不发达4国LDC4	80	----Car audio frequency relays ware or FM car transmitter
7113	8522.9099	----其他	20 △10	0 4 10 16	东盟ASEAN,智利CL,新加坡SG,新西兰NZ,香港HK 哥斯达黎加CR 秘鲁PE 亚太APTA,巴基斯坦PK	0	最不发达35国LDC35,最不发达4国LDC4	80	----Other

序号 No.	税则号列 Tariff Line	货品名称	最惠国税率 MFN(%)	协定税率 Agreement(%)	特惠税率 S.P.(%)	普通税率 Gen.(%)	Article Description
	85.23	**录制声音或其他信息用的圆盘、磁带、固态非易失性数据存储器件、“智能卡”及其他媒体，不论是否已录制，包括供复制圆盘用的母片及母带，但不包括第三十七章的产品:**					**Discs, tapes, solid-state non-volatile storage devices, “smart cards” and other media for the recording of sound or of other phenomena, whether or not recorded, including matrices and masters for the production of discs, but excluding products of Chapter 37:**
		-磁性媒体:					-Magnetic media:
		--磁条卡:					--Cards incorporating a magnetic stripe:
7114	8523.2110	---未录制	17.5	0 东盟ASEAN,智利CL,新加坡SG,新西兰NZ,香港HK,澳门MO 3.5 哥斯达黎加CR 8.8 秘鲁PE 14 巴基斯坦PK	0 最不发达35国LDC35	70	---Prepared unrecorded
7115	8523.2120	---已录制	15	0 东盟ASEAN,智利CL,新加坡SG,新西兰NZ,香港HK,澳门MO 3 哥斯达黎加CR 7.5 秘鲁PE 12 巴基斯坦PK	0 最不发达35国LDC35	130	---Recorded
		--其他:					--Other:
		---磁盘:					---Magnetic discs:
7116	8523.2911	----未录制	0		0 最不发达35国LDC35,最不发达4国LDC4	14	----Prepared unrecorded
7117	8523.2919	----其他	0		0 最不发达35国LDC35,最不发达4国LDC4	14	----Other
		---磁带:					---Magnetic tapes:
7118	8523.2921	----未录制的宽度不超过4毫米磁带	0		0 最不发达35国LDC35,最不发达4国LDC4	130	----Prepared unrecorded, of a width not exceeding 4mm
7119	8523.2922	----未录制的宽度超过4毫米，但不超过6.5毫米的磁带	0		0 最不发达35国LDC35,最不发达4国LDC4	130	----Prepared unrecorded, of a width exceeding 4mm but not exceeding 6.5mm

序号 No.	税则号列 Tariff Line	货品名称	最惠国税 率 MFN(%)	协定税率 Agreement(%)		特惠税率 S.P.(%)		普通税率 Gen.(%)	Article Description
7120	8523.2923	----未录制的宽度超过6.5毫米的磁带	0			0	最不发达35国LDC35,最不发达4国LDC4	20	----Prepared unrecorded, of a width exceeding 6.5mm
7121	8523.2928	----重放声音或图像信息的磁带	10 △6	0 1 5	东盟ASEAN,新加坡SG,新西兰NZ,秘鲁PE,哥斯达黎加CR,香港HK 智利CL 巴基斯坦PK	0	最不发达35国LDC35,最不发达4国LDC4	130	----For reproducing sound or image
7122	8523.2929	----已录制的其他磁带	0			0	最不发达35国LDC35,最不发达4国LDC4	14	----Other, recorded
7123	8523.2990	---其他	0			0	最不发达35国LDC35,最不发达4国LDC4	14	---Other
		-光学媒体:							-Optical media:
7124	8523.4100	--未录制	0			0	最不发达35国LDC35,最不发达4国LDC4	14	--Unrecorded
		--其他:							--Other:
7125	8523.4910	---仅用于重放声音信息的	10 △6	0 1 5	东盟ASEAN,新西兰NZ,秘鲁PE,哥斯达黎加CR,香港HK,澳门MO 智利CL 巴基斯坦PK	0	最不发达35国LDC35	130	---For reproducing sound only, recorded
7126	8523.4920	---用于重放声音、图像以外信息的，税号84.71所列机器用	0			0	最不发达35国LDC35,最不发达4国LDC4	14	---For the machines of heading No.84.71 reproducing phenomena other than sound or image, recorded
7127	8523.4990	---其他	0			0	最不发达35国LDC35,最不发达4国LDC4	14	---Other
		-半导体媒体:							-Semiconductor media :
		--固态非易失性存储器件（闪速存储器）:							--Solid-state non-volatile storage devices (flash memorizer):

序号 No.	税则号列 Tariff Line	货品名称	最惠国 税 率 MFN(%)	协定税率 Agreement(%)	特惠税率 S.P.(%)	普通 税率 Gen.(%)	Article Description
7128	8523.5110	---未录制	0		0 最不发达35国LDC35,最不发达4国LDC4	70	---Prepared unrecorded
7129	8523.5120	---已录制	0		0 最不发达35国LDC35,最不发达4国LDC4	14	---Recorded
		--“智能卡”:					--“Smart cards”:
7130	8523.5210	---未录制	0		0 最不发达35国LDC35,最不发达4国LDC4	21	---Prepared unrecorded
7131	8523.5290	---其他	0		0 最不发达35国LDC35,最不发达4国LDC4	21	---Other
		--其他:					--Other:
7132	8523.5910	---未录制	0		0 最不发达35国LDC35,最不发达4国LDC4	70	---Prepared unrecorded
7133	8523.5920	---已录制	0		0 最不发达35国LDC35,最不发达4国LDC4	14	---Recorded
		-其他:					-Other:
		---唱片:					---Gramophone records:
7134	8523.8011	----已录制唱片	15	0 东盟ASEAN,智利CL,新加坡SG,新西兰NZ,澳门MO 3 哥斯达黎加CR 7.5 秘鲁PE 12 巴基斯坦PK	0 最不发达35国LDC35	130	----Prepared recorded
7135	8523.8019	----其他	0		0 最不发达35国LDC35,最不发达4国LDC4	70	----Other
		---税号84.71所列机器用:					---For the machines of heading No.84.71:

序号 No.	税则号列 Tariff Line	货品名称	最惠国税率 MFN(%)	协定税率 Agreement(%)	特惠税率 S.P.(%)	普通税率 Gen.(%)	Article Description
7136	8523.8021	----未录制	0		0 最不发达35国LDC35,最不发达4国LDC4	14	----Prepared unrecorded
7137	8523.8029	----其他	0		0 最不发达35国LDC35,最不发达4国LDC4	14	----Other
		---其他:					---Other:
7138	8523.8091	----未录制	0		0 最不发达35国LDC35,最不发达4国LDC4	14	----Prepared unrecorded
7139	8523.8099	----其他	0		0 最不发达35国LDC35,最不发达4国LDC4	14	----Other
	85.25	**无线电广播、电视发送设备，不论是否装有接收装置或声音的录制、重放装置；电视摄像机、数字照相机及视频摄录一体机:**					**Transmission apparatus for radio-broadcasting or television, whether or not incorporating reception apparatus or sound recording or reproducing apparatus; television cameras, digital cameras and video camera recorders:**
7140	8525.5000	-发送设备	0		0 最不发达35国LDC35,最不发达4国LDC4	30	-Transmission apparatus
		-装有接收装置的发送设备:					-Transmission apparatus incorporating reception apparatus:
7141	8525.6010	---卫星地面站设备	0		0 最不发达35国LDC35,最不发达4国LDC4	14	---Satellite earth station
7142	8525.6090	---其他	0		0 最不发达35国LDC35,最不发达4国LDC4	30	---Other

序号 No.	税则号列 Tariff Line	货品名称	最惠国税率 MFN(%)	协定税率 Agreement(%)		特惠税率 S.P.(%)		普通税率 Gen.(%)	Article Description
		-电视摄像机、数字照相机及视频摄录一体机:							-Television cameras, digital cameras and video camera recorders:
		---电视摄像机:							---Television cameras:
7143	8525.8011	----特种用途的	10	0 5 9	东盟ASEAN,智利CL,新加坡SG,新西兰NZ,秘鲁PE,哥斯达黎加CR 巴基斯坦PK 亚太APTA	0	最不发达35国LDC35	17	----For special purposes
7144	8525.8012	----非特种用途的,广播级	⑧	0 7 17.5 ⑩	东盟ASEAN,智利CL,新加坡SG,新西兰NZ 哥斯达黎加CR 秘鲁PE 亚太APTA,巴基斯坦PK	0	最不发达35国LDC35	⑨	----Other, broadcast quality
7145	8525.8013	----非特种用途的,其他类型	⑧	0 7 17.5 ⑩	东盟ASEAN,智利CL,新加坡SG,新西兰NZ,香港HK,澳门MO,台湾TW 哥斯达黎加CR 秘鲁PE 亚太APTA,巴基斯坦PK	0	最不发达35国LDC35	⑨	----Other
	ex85258013	手机用摄像组件(由镜头+CCD/CMOS+数字信号处理电路三部分构成)	△4						Camera subassembly used for mobile telephone made up of lens, CCD/CMOS sensor and digital signal processing circuit, not broadcast quality
	ex85258013	高清摄像头(必须满足以下三个条件:1.镜头元件必须使用5层及以上玻璃镜头;2.使用USB2.0及以上高速接口;3.硬件传感器像素达到130万及以上)	△10						High definition video cameras (must satisfy the 3 points below: (1) lens unit must use 5 and more lenses; (2) using connectors not less than USB2.0; (3) the pixels of imager must be over 1.3 million)
		---数字照相机:							---Digital cameras:
7146	8525.8021	----特种用途的	0			0	最不发达35国LDC35,最不发达4国LDC4	17	----For special purposes
7147	8525.8022	----非特种用途的,单镜头反光型	0			0	最不发达35国LDC35,最不发达4国LDC4	⑨	----Other, single lens reflex

⑧ 完税价格不高于5000美元/台:35%;完税价格高于5000美元/台:3%,加9728元。
⑨ 完税价格不高于5000美元/台:130%;完税价格高于5000美元/台:6%,加51500元。
⑩ 完税价格不高于5000美元/台:29.8%;完税价格高于5000美元/台:3%,加8147元。

序号 No.	税则号列 Tariff Line	货品名称	最惠国税率 MFN(%)	协定税率 Agreement(%)	特惠税率 S.P.(%)	普通税率 Gen.(%)	Article Description
7148	8525.8025	----非特种用途的,其他可换镜头的	0		0 最不发达35国LDC35,最不发达4国LDC4	⑪	----Other, lens interchangeable
7149	8525.8029	----非特种用途的,其他类型	0		0 最不发达35国LDC35,最不发达4国LDC4	⑪	----Other
		---视频摄录一体机:					---Video camera recorders:
7150	8525.8031	----特种用途的	0		0 最不发达35国LDC35,最不发达4国LDC4	17	----For special purposes
7151	8525.8032	----非特种用途的,广播极	0		0 最不发达35国LDC35,最不发达4国LDC4	⑪	----Other, broadcast quality
7152	8525.8033	----非特种用途的,家用型	0		0 最不发达35国LDC35,最不发达4国LDC4	130	----Other, household
7153	8525.8039	----非特种用途的,其他类型	0		0 最不发达35国LDC35,最不发达4国LDC4	⑪	----Other
	85.26	**雷达设备、无线电导航设备及无线电遥控设备:**					**Radar apparatus, radio navigational aid apparatus and radio remote control apparatus:**
		-雷达设备:					-Radar apparatus:
7154	8526.1010	---导航用	2	0 东盟ASEAN,智利CL,巴基斯坦PK,新西兰NZ,秘鲁PE,哥斯达黎加CR	0 最不发达35国LDC35	8	---For navigational aid
7155	8526.1090	---其他	5	0 东盟ASEAN,智利CL,巴基斯坦PK,新西兰NZ,秘鲁PE,哥斯达黎加CR	0 最不发达35国LDC35	14	---Other

⑪ 完税价格不高于5000美元/台：130%；完税价格高于5000美元/台：6%，加51500元。

序号 No.	税则号列 Tariff Line	货品名称	最惠国税率 MFN(%)	协定税率 Agreement(%)		特惠税率 S.P.(%)		普通税率 Gen.(%)	Article Description
	ex85261090	飞机机载雷达（包括气象雷达、地形雷达和空中交通管制应答系统）	△1						Airborne radars (including aeroradars, terrain-following radars and air-traffic-control-interrogator-responder systems)
	ex85261090	雷达生命探测仪	△2						Radar life detectors
		-其他:							-Other:
		--无线电导航设备:							--Radio navigational aid apparatus:
7156	8526.9110	---机动车辆用	2	0	东盟ASEAN,智利CL,巴基斯坦PK,新西兰NZ,秘鲁PE,哥斯达黎加CR	0	最不发达35国LDC35	8	---For motor vehicles
7157	8526.9190	---其他	2	0	东盟ASEAN,智利CL,巴基斯坦PK,新西兰NZ,秘鲁PE,哥斯达黎加CR	0	最不发达35国LDC35	8	---Other
7158	8526.9200	--无线电遥控设备	5	0	东盟ASEAN,智利CL,巴基斯坦PK,新西兰NZ,秘鲁PE,哥斯达黎加CR	0	最不发达35国LDC35	14	--Radio remote control apparatus
	85.27	**无线电广播接收设备，不论是否与声音的录制、重放装置或时钟组合在同一机壳内:**							**Reception apparatus for radio-broadcasting, whether or not combined, in the same housing, with sound recording or reproducing apparatus or a clock:**
		-不需外接电源的无线电收音机:							-Radio-broadcast receivers capable of operating without an external source of power:
7159	8527.1200	--袖珍盒式磁带收放机	20	0 4 10	东盟ASEAN,智利CL,新加坡SG,新西兰NZ 哥斯达黎加CR 秘鲁PE	0	最不发达35国LDC35	130	--Pocket-size radio cassette-players
7160	8527.1300	--其他收录（放）音组合机	15	0 3 7.5 12	东盟ASEAN,智利CL,新加坡SG,新西兰NZ 哥斯达黎加CR 秘鲁PE 巴基斯坦PK	0	最不发达35国LDC35	130	--Other apparatus combined with sound recording or reproducing apparatus
7161	8527.1900	--其他	15	0 3 7.5 12	东盟ASEAN,智利CL,新加坡SG,新西兰NZ 哥斯达黎加CR 秘鲁PE 巴基斯坦PK	0	最不发达35国LDC35	130	--Other

序号 No.	税则号列 Tariff Line	货品名称	最惠国税率 MFN(%)	协定税率 Agreement(%)		特惠税率 S.P.(%)		普通税率 Gen.(%)	Article Description
		-需外接电源的汽车用无线电收音机:							-Radio-broadcast receivers not capable of operating without an external source of power, of a kind used in motor vehicles:
7162	8527.2100	--收录（放）音组合机	15 △8	0 3 7.5 12	东盟ASEAN,智利CL,新加坡SG,新西兰NZ 哥斯达黎加CR 秘鲁PE 巴基斯坦PK	0	最不发达35国LDC35	130	--Combined with sound recording or reproducing apparatus
7163	8527.2900	--其他	15 △8	0 3 7.5 12	东盟ASEAN,智利CL,新加坡SG,新西兰NZ 哥斯达黎加CR 秘鲁PE 巴基斯坦PK	0	最不发达35国LDC35	130	--Other
		-其他:							-Other:
7164	8527.9100	--收录（放）音组合机	15 △8	0 3 7.5 12	东盟ASEAN,智利CL,新加坡SG,新西兰NZ 哥斯达黎加CR 秘鲁PE 巴基斯坦PK	0	最不发达35国LDC35	130	--Combined with sound recording or reproducing apparatus
7165	8527.9200	--带时钟的收音机	15	0 3 7.5 12	东盟ASEAN,智利CL,新加坡SG,新西兰NZ 哥斯达黎加CR 秘鲁PE 巴基斯坦PK	0	最不发达35国LDC35	130	--Not combined with sound recording or reproducing apparatus but combined with a clock
7166	8527.9900	--其他	27 △8	0 5.4 13.5	东盟ASEAN,智利CL,新加坡SG,新西兰NZ 哥斯达黎加CR 秘鲁PE	0	最不发达35国LDC35	130	--Other
	85.28	**监视器及投影机，未装电视接收装置；电视接收装置，不论是否装有无线电收音装置或声音、图像的录制或重放装置:**							**Monitors and projectors, not incorporating television reception apparatus; reception apparatus for television, whether or not incorporating radio-broadcast receivers or sound or video recording or reproducing apparatus:**
		-阴极射线管监视器:							-Cathode-ray tube monitors:
7167	8528.4100	--专用于或主要用于税目84.71的自动数据处理系统的	0			0	最不发达35国LDC35,最不发达4国LDC4	40	--Of a kind solely or principally used in an automatic data processing system of heading 84.71
		--其他:							--Other:
7168	8528.4910	---彩色的	30	0 3 6 15 26	东盟ASEAN,新加坡SG,新西兰NZ,澳门MO 智利CL 哥斯达黎加CR 秘鲁PE 亚太APTA,巴基斯坦PK	0	最不发达35国LDC35	130	---Colour

序号 No.	税则号列 Tariff Line	货品名称	最惠国税率 MFN(%)	协定税率 Agreement(%)		特惠税率 S.P.(%)	普通税率 Gen.(%)	Article Description
7169	8528.4990	---单色的	19	0 1.9 3.8 9.5 15.2	东盟ASEAN,新加坡SG,新西兰NZ,澳门MO 智利CL 哥斯达黎加CR 秘鲁PE 亚太APTA,巴基斯坦PK	0 最不发达35国LDC35	100	---Monochrome
		-其他监视器: --专用于或主要用于税目84.71的自动数据处理系统的:						-Other monitors: --Of a kind solely or principally used in an automatic data processing system of heading 84.71:
7170	8528.5110	---液晶显示器的	0			0 最不发达35国LDC35,最不发达4国LDC4	40	---With liquid crystal display
7171	8528.5190	---其他	0			0 最不发达35国LDC35,最不发达4国LDC4	40	---Other
		--其他:						--Other:
7172	8528.5910	---彩色的	30	0 3 15 26	东盟ASEAN,新加坡SG,新西兰NZ,澳门MO 智利CL 秘鲁PE 亚太APTA,巴基斯坦PK	0 最不发达35国LDC35	130	---Colour
	ex85285910	专用于车载导航仪的液晶监视器	△15					Liquid crystal display monitors for use solely with car navigation instruments
7173	8528.5990	---单色的	19	0 1.9 3.8 9.5 15.2	东盟ASEAN,新加坡SG,新西兰NZ,香港HK,澳门MO 智利CL 哥斯达黎加CR 秘鲁PE 亚太APTA,巴基斯坦PK	0 最不发达35国LDC35	100	--- Monochrome
		-投影机:						Projectors:
7174	8528.6100	--专用于或主要用于税目84.71的自动数据处理系统的	0			0 最不发达35国LDC35,最不发达4国LDC4	14	--Of a kind solely or principally used in an automatic data processing system of heading 84.71
		--其他:						--Other:
7175	8528.6910	---彩色的	30	0 3 6 15 25.5	东盟ASEAN,新加坡SG,新西兰NZ,香港HK,澳门MO 智利CL 哥斯达黎加CR 秘鲁PE 亚太APTA,巴基斯坦PK	0 最不发达35国LDC35	130	---Colour

序号 No.	税则号列 Tariff Line	货品名称	最惠国税率 MFN(%)	协定税率 Agreement(%)		特惠税率 S.P.(%)		普通税率 Gen.(%)	Article Description
7176	8528.6990	---单色的	15	0 1.5 3 7.5 12	东盟ASEAN,新加坡SG,新西兰NZ,澳门MO 智利CL 哥斯达黎加CR 秘鲁PE 巴基斯坦PK	0	最不发达35国LDC35	100	---Monochrome
		-电视接收装置,不论是否装有无线电收音装置或声音、图像的录制或重放装置:							-Reception apparatus for television, whether or not incorporating radio-broadcast receivers or sound or video recording or reproducing apparatus:
		--在设计上不带有视频显示器或屏幕的:							--Not designed to incorporate a video display or screen:
7177	8528.7110	---彩色卫星电视接收机	30	0 3 6 24	新西兰NZ 智利CL 哥斯达黎加CR 亚太APTA,巴基斯坦PK			130	---Satellite television receivers
7178	8528.7180	---其他彩色的	30	0 3 6 21	东盟ASEAN,新加坡SG,新西兰NZ 智利CL 哥斯达黎加CR 亚太APTA,巴基斯坦PK			130	---Other, colour
7179	8528.7190	---单色的	15	0 1.5 3 7.5 12	东盟ASEAN,新加坡SG,新西兰NZ,澳门MO 智利CL 哥斯达黎加CR 秘鲁PE 巴基斯坦PK	0	最不发达35国LDC35	100	---Monochrome
		--其他，彩色的:							--Other, colour:
		---阴极射线显像管的:							---Cathode-ray tube monitors:
7180	8528.7211	----模拟电视接收机	30	0 3 6 21	新西兰NZ 智利CL 哥斯达黎加CR 亚太APTA,巴基斯坦PK			130	----Analog television
7181	8528.7212	----数字电视接收机	30	0 3 6 21	新西兰NZ 智利CL 哥斯达黎加CR 亚太APTA,巴基斯坦PK			130	----Digital television
7182	8528.7219	----其他	30	0 3 6 21	新西兰NZ 智利CL 哥斯达黎加CR 亚太APTA,巴基斯坦PK			130	----Other
		---液晶显示器的:							---With liquid crystal display:
7183	8528.7221	----模拟电视接收机	30	0 3 20 21	新西兰NZ,澳门MO 智利CL 东盟ASEAN 亚太APTA,巴基斯坦PK			130	----Analog television
7184	8528.7222	----数字电视接收机	30	0 3 20 21	新西兰NZ 智利CL 东盟ASEAN 亚太APTA,巴基斯坦PK			130	----Digital television

序号 No.	税则号列 Tariff Line	货品名称	最惠国税率 MFN(%)	协定税率 Agreement(%)		特惠税率 S.P.(%)		普通税率 Gen.(%)	Article Description
7185	8528.7229	----其他	30	0	新西兰NZ,澳门MO			130	----Other
				3	智利CL				
				20	东盟ASEAN				
				21	亚太APTA,巴基斯坦PK				
		---等离子显示器的:							---With plasma display Panels:
7186	8528.7231	----模拟电视接收机	30	0	新西兰NZ,澳门MO			130	----Analog television
				3	智利CL				
				20	东盟ASEAN				
				21	亚太APTA,巴基斯坦PK				
7187	8528.7232	----数字电视接收机	30	0	新西兰NZ			130	----Digital television
				3	智利CL				
				20	东盟ASEAN				
				21	亚太APTA,巴基斯坦PK				
7188	8528.7239	----其他	30	0	新西兰NZ,澳门MO			130	----Other
				3	智利CL				
				20	东盟ASEAN				
				21	亚太APTA,巴基斯坦PK				
		---其他:							---Other:
7189	8528.7291	----模拟电视接收机	30	0	新西兰NZ	0	最不发达35国LDC35	130	----Analog television
				3	智利CL				
				6	哥斯达黎加CR				
				12	文莱BN,菲律宾PH,新加坡*SG*				
				15	秘鲁PE				
				20	柬埔寨KH,印尼ID,老挝LA,马来西亚MY,缅甸MM,泰国TH,越南VT				
				21	亚太APTA,巴基斯坦PK				
7190	8528.7292	----数字电视接收机	30	0	新西兰NZ			130	----Digital television
				3	智利CL				
				12	文莱BN,菲律宾PH,新加坡*SG*				
				20	柬埔寨KH,印尼ID,老挝LA,马来西亚MY,缅甸MM,泰国TH,越南VT				
				21	亚太APTA,巴基斯坦PK				
7191	8528.7299	----其他	30	0	新西兰NZ			130	----Other
				3	智利CL				
				6	哥斯达黎加CR				
				12	文莱BN,菲律宾PH,新加坡*SG*				
				20	柬埔寨KH,印尼ID,老挝LA,马来西亚MY,缅甸MM,泰国TH,越南VT				
				21	亚太APTA,巴基斯坦PK				
7192	8528.7300	--其他,单色的	15	0	东盟ASEAN,新加坡SG,新西兰NZ,澳门MO	0	最不发达35国LDC35	100	--Other, monochrome
				1.5	智利CL				
				3	哥斯达黎加CR				
				7.5	秘鲁PE				
				12	巴基斯坦PK				

序号 No.	税则号列 Tariff Line	货品名称	最惠国税率 MFN(%)	协定税率 Agreement(%)		特惠税率 S.P.(%)		普通税率 Gen.(%)	Article Description
	85.29	**专用于或主要用于税号 85.25 至 85.28 所列装置或设备的零件:**							**Parts suitable for use solely or principally with the apparatus of headings No.85.25 to 85.28:**
		-各种天线或天线反射器及其零件:							-Aerials and aerial reflectors of all kinds; parts suitable for use therewith:
7193	8529.1010	---雷达设备及无线电导航设备用	1.5	0	东盟ASEAN,智利CL,巴基斯坦PK,新西兰NZ,秘鲁PE,哥斯达黎加CR,香港HK	0	最不发达 35 国 LDC35	8	---For radar apparatus and radio navigational aid apparatus
7194	8529.1020	---无线电收音机及其组合机、电视接收机用	0			0	最不发达 35 国 LDC35, 最不发达 4 国 LDC4	90	---For radio-broadcast receivers and their combinations, television receivers
7195	8529.1090	---其他	2	0	东盟ASEAN,智利CL,巴基斯坦PK,新西兰NZ,秘鲁PE,哥斯达黎加CR	0	最不发达 35 国 LDC35	20	---Other
		-其他:							-Other:
7196	8529.9010	---电视发送、差转设备及卫星电视地面接收转播设备用	0			0	最不发达 35 国 LDC35, 最不发达 4 国 LDC4	30	---Of television transmission or translation apparatus, satellite television ground receiving and relaying apparatus
		---电视摄像机、视频摄录一体机、数字照相机用:							---Of television cameras, video camera recorders and digital cameras:
7197	8529.9041	----特种用途的	8	0 0.8 5 6.8	东盟ASEAN,新西兰NZ,秘鲁PE,哥斯达黎加CR,香港HK 智利CL 巴基斯坦PK 亚太APTA	0	最不发达 35 国 LDC35	17	----Of special purpose
7198	8529.9042	----非特种用途的取像模块	12	0 1.2 2.4 5 6 10.8	东盟ASEAN,新加坡SG,新西兰NZ,香港HK,台湾TW 智利CL 哥斯达黎加CR 巴基斯坦PK 秘鲁PE 亚太APTA	0	最不发达 35 国 LDC35	100	----Camera modules without special purpose
	ex85299042	摄录一体机、数码相机用取像模块	△2						Camera modules for video camera recorders, digital cameras
	ex85299042	手机、平板电脑用取像模块	△4						Camera modules for mobile telephones and tablet computers

序号 No.	税则号列 Tariff Line	货品名称	最惠国税率 MFN(%)	协定税率 Agreement(%)		特惠税率 S.P.(%)		普通税率 Gen.(%)	Article Description
7199	8529.9049	----其他	12 △2	0 1.2 2.4 5 10.8	东盟ASEAN,新加坡SG,新西兰NZ,秘鲁PE,香港HK,台湾TW 智利CL 哥斯达黎加CR 巴基斯坦PK 亚太APTA	0	最不发达35国LDC35	100	----Other
7200	8529.9050	---雷达设备及无线电导航设备用	1.5	0 1.4	东盟ASEAN,智利CL,巴基斯坦PK,新西兰NZ,秘鲁PE,哥斯达黎加CR 亚太APTA	0	最不发达35国LDC35	8	---Of radar apparatus and radio navigational aid apparatus
7201	8529.9060	---无线电收音机及其组合机用	15 △7	0 1.5 3 7.5 12	东盟ASEAN,新加坡SG,新西兰NZ,香港HK 智利CL 哥斯达黎加CR 巴基斯坦PK,秘鲁PE 亚太APTA	0	最不发达35国LDC35,最不发达4国LDC4	130	---Of radio-broadcast receivers and their combinations
		---电视接收机用（高频调谐器除外）:							---Of television receivers (Other than H.F. turners):
7202	8529.9081	----彩色电视接收机用（等离子显像组件及其零件除外）	15 △6	0 7.5 12	东盟ASEAN,智利CL,新加坡SG,新西兰NZ 巴基斯坦PK,秘鲁PE 亚太APTA	0	最不发达35国LDC35	80	----Of colour television receivers (Other than plasma display modules or parts thereof)
7203	8529.9082	----等离子显像组件及其零件	15 △5	0 7.5 12	东盟ASEAN,智利CL,新西兰NZ 巴基斯坦PK 亚太APTA			80	----Plasma display modules and part thereof
7204	8529.9083	----有机发光二极管显示屏	15 △5	0 7.5 12	东盟ASEAN,智利CL,新加坡SG,新西兰NZ 巴基斯坦PK,秘鲁PE 亚太APTA	0	最不发达35国LDC35	80	----Of colour television receiver (Other than plasma display modules of parts thereof, oled panel)
7205	8529.9089	----其他	0			0	最不发达35国LDC35,最不发达4国LDC4	50	----Other
7206	8529.9090	---其他	0			0	最不发达35国LDC35,最不发达4国LDC4	57	---Other
	85.30	**铁道、电车道、道路或内河航道、停车场、港口或机场用的电气信号、安全或交通管理设备（税号86.08的货品除外）：**							**Electrical signaling, safety or traffic control equipment for railways, tram-ways, roads, inland waterways, parking facilities, port installations or airfields (other than those of heading No. 86.08):**

序号 No.	税则号列 Tariff Line	货品名称	最惠国税率 MFN(%)	协定税率 Agreement(%)		特惠税率 S.P.(%)		普通税率 Gen.(%)	Article Description
7207	8530.1000	-铁道或电车道用的设备	10	0 5	东盟ASEAN,智利CL,新西兰NZ,秘鲁PE,哥斯达黎加CR 巴基斯坦PK	0	最不发达35国LDC35	20	-Equipment for railways or tramways
7208	8530.8000	-其他设备	8	0 0.8 5	东盟ASEAN,新西兰NZ,秘鲁PE,哥斯达黎加CR 智利CL 巴基斯坦PK	0	最不发达35国LDC35,最不发达4国LDC4	20	-Other equipment
7209	8530.9000	-零件	8	0 5	东盟ASEAN,智利CL,新西兰NZ,秘鲁PE,哥斯达黎加CR 巴基斯坦PK	0	最不发达35国LDC35,最不发达4国LDC4	20	-Parts
	85.31	**电气音响或视觉信号装置(例如,电铃、电笛、显示板、防盗或防火报警器),但税号85.12或85.30的货品除外:**							**Electric sound or visual signaling apparatus (for example, bells, sirens, indicator panels, burglar or fire alarms), other than those of heading No.85.12 or 85.30:**
7210	8531.1000	-防盗或防火报警器及类似装置	10	0 5	东盟ASEAN,智利CL,新加坡SG,新西兰NZ,秘鲁PE,哥斯达黎加CR,香港HK 巴基斯坦PK	0	最不发达35国LDC35,最不发达4国LDC4	40	-Burglar or fire alarms and similar apparatus
7211	8531.2000	-装有液晶装置(LCD)或发光二极管(LED)的显示板	0			0	最不发达35国LDC35,最不发达4国LDC4	70	-Indicator panels incorporating liquid crystal devices (LCD) or light emitting diodes (LED)
		-其他装置:							-Other apparatus:
7212	8531.8010	---蜂鸣器	15	0 3 7.5 12	东盟ASEAN,智利CL,新加坡SG,新西兰NZ,香港HK 哥斯达黎加CR 秘鲁PE 巴基斯坦PK	0	最不发达35国LDC35	70	---Buzzers
	ex85318010	音量不超过110dB的小型蜂鸣器	△7.5						Minitype electric buzzers, maximum volume not exceeding 110dB
7213	8531.8090	---其他	10	0 5	东盟ASEAN,智利CL,新加坡SG,新西兰NZ,秘鲁PE,哥斯达黎加CR,香港HK 巴基斯坦PK	0	最不发达35国LDC35	70	---Other
		-零件:							-Parts:

序号 No.	税则号列 Tariff Line	货品名称	最惠国税率 MFN(%)	协定税率 Agreement(%)	特惠税率 S.P.(%)	普通税率 Gen.(%)	Article Description
7214	8531.9010	---防盗或防火报警器及类似装置用	0		0 最不发达35国LDC35,最不发达4国LDC4	40	---Of burglar or fire alarms and similar apparatus
7215	8531.9090	---其他	0		0 最不发达35国LDC35,最不发达4国LDC4	70	---Other
	85.32	**固定、可变或可调(微调)电容器:**					**Electrical capacitors, fixed, variable or adjustable (pre-set):**
7216	8532.1000	-固定电容器，用于50/60赫兹电路，其额定无功功率不低于0.5千乏(电力电容器)	0		0 最不发达35国LDC35,最不发达4国LDC4	20	-Fixed capacitors designed for use in 50/60 Hz circuits and having a reactive power handling capacity of not less than 0.5kVar (power capacitors)
		-其他固定电容器:					-Other fixed capacitors:
		--钽电容器:					--Tantalum:
7217	8532.2110	---片式	0		0 最不发达35国LDC35,最不发达4国LDC4	35	---Laminate
7218	8532.2190	---其他	0		0 最不发达35国LDC35,最不发达4国LDC4	35	---Other
		--铝电解电容器:					--Aluminium electrolytic:
7219	8532.2210	---片式	0		0 最不发达35国LDC35,最不发达4国LDC4	35	---Laminate
7220	8532.2290	---其他	0		0 最不发达35国LDC35,最不发达4国LDC4	35	---Other
7221	8532.2300	--单层瓷介电容器	0		0 最不发达35国LDC35,最不发达4国LDC4	35	--Ceramic dielectric, single layer

序号 No.	税则号列 Tariff Line	货品名称	最惠国税率 MFN(%)	协定税率 Agreement(%)	特惠税率 S.P.(%)		普通税率 Gen.(%)	Article Description
		--多层瓷介电容器:						--Ceramic dielectric, multilayer:
7222	8532.2410	---片式	0		0	最不发达35国LDC35,最不发达4国LDC4	35	---Laminate
7223	8532.2490	---其他	0		0	最不发达35国LDC35,最不发达4国LDC4	35	---Other
		--纸介质或塑料介质电容器:						--Dielectric of paper or plastics:
7224	8532.2510	---片式	0		0	最不发达35国LDC35,最不发达4国LDC4	35	---Laminate
7225	8532.2590	---其他	0		0	最不发达35国LDC35,最不发达4国LDC4	35	---Other
7226	8532.2900	--其他	0		0	最不发达35国LDC35,最不发达4国LDC4	35	--Other
7227	8532.3000	-可变或可调（微调）电容器	0		0	最不发达35国LDC35,最不发达4国LDC4	35	-Variable or adjustable (pre-set) capacitors
		-零件:						-Parts:
7228	8532.9010	---子目号8532.1000所列电容器用	0		0	最不发达35国LDC35,最不发达4国LDC4	20	---Of the capacitors of subheading No. 8532.1000
7229	8532.9090	---其他	0		0	最不发达35国LDC35,最不发达4国LDC4	35	---Other

序号 No.	税则号列 Tariff Line	货品名称	最惠国税率 MFN(%)	协定税率 Agreement(%)	特惠税率 S.P.(%)	普通税率 Gen.(%)	Article Description
	85.33	**电阻器（包括变阻器及电位器），但加热电阻器除外：**					**Electrical resistors (including rheostats and potentiometers), other than heating resistors:**
7230	8533.1000	-固定碳质电阻器，合成或薄膜式	0		0 最不发达35国LDC35，最不发达4国LDC4	50	-Fixed carbon resistors, composition or film types
		-其他固定电阻器:					-Other fixed resistors:
		--额定功率不超过20瓦:					--For a power handling capacity not exceeding 20W:
7231	8533.2110	---片式	0		0 最不发达35国LDC35，最不发达4国LDC4	50	---Laminate
7232	8533.2190	---其他	0		0 最不发达35国LDC35，最不发达4国LDC4	50	---Other
7233	8533.2900	--其他	0		0 最不发达35国LDC35，最不发达4国LDC4	50	--Other
		-线绕可变电阻器，包括变阻器及电位器:					-Wirewound variable resistors, including rheostats and potentiometers:
7234	8533.3100	--额定功率不超过20瓦	0		0 最不发达35国LDC35，最不发达4国LDC4	50	--For a power handling capacity not exceeding 20W
7235	8533.3900	--其他	0		0 最不发达35国LDC35，最不发达4国LDC4	50	--Other
7236	8533.4000	-其他可变电阻器，包括变阻器及电位器	0		0 最不发达35国LDC35，最不发达4国LDC4	50	-Other variable resistors, including rheostats and potentiometers

序号 No.	税则号列 Tariff Line	货品名称	最惠国税率 MFN(%)	协定税率 Agreement(%)		特惠税率 S.P.(%)		普通税率 Gen.(%)	Article Description
7237	8533.9000	-零件	0			0	最不发达35国LDC35,最不发达4国LDC4	50	-Parts
	85.34	**印刷电路:**							**Printed circuits:**
7238	8534.0010	---4层以上的	0			0	最不发达35国LDC35,最不发达4国LDC4	35	---Of more than 4 layers
7239	8534.0090	---其他	0			0	最不发达35国LDC35,最不发达4国LDC4	50	---Other
	85.35	**电路的开关、保护或连接用的电气装置(例如，开关、熔断器、避雷器、电压限幅器、电涌抑制器、插头及其他连接器、接线盒)，用于电压超过1000伏的线路:**							**Electrical apparatus for switching or protecting electrical circuits, or for making connections to or in electrical circuits (for example, switches, fuses, lightning arresters, voltage limiters, surge suppressors, plugs and other connectors, junction boxes), for a voltage exceeding 1000 volts:**
7240	8535.1000	-熔断器	14	0 2.8 11.2	东盟ASEAN,智利CL,新加坡SG,新西兰NZ,秘鲁PE 哥斯达黎加CR 巴基斯坦PK	0	最不发达35国LDC35	50	-Fuses
		-自动断路器:							-Automatic circuit breakers:
7241	8535.2100	--用于电压低于72.5千伏的线路	14	0 2.8 11.2	东盟ASEAN,智利CL,新加坡SG,新西兰NZ,秘鲁PE 哥斯达黎加CR 巴基斯坦PK	0	最不发达35国LDC35	50	--For a voltage of less than 72.5kV
		--其他:							--Other:
7242	8535.2910	---用于电压在72.5千伏及以上，但不高于220千伏的线路	10	0 5	东盟ASEAN,智利CL,新西兰NZ,秘鲁PE,哥斯达黎加CR 巴基斯坦PK	0	最不发达35国LDC35,最不发达4国LDC4	50	---For a voltage of 72.5kV or more, but not exceeding 220kV
7243	8535.2920	---用于电压高于220千伏，但不高于750千伏的线路	10	0 5	东盟ASEAN,智利CL,新西兰NZ,秘鲁PE,哥斯达黎加CR 巴基斯坦PK	0	最不发达35国LDC35,最不发达4国LDC4	50	---For a voltage exceeding 220kV, but not exceeding 750kV

序号 No.	税则号列 Tariff Line	货品名称	最惠国税率 MFN(%)	协定税率 Agreement(%)		特惠税率 S.P.(%)		普通税率 Gen.(%)	Article Description
7244	8535.2990	---其他	10	0 5	东盟ASEAN,智利CL,新西兰NZ,秘鲁PE,哥斯达黎加CR 巴基斯坦PK	0	最不发达35国LDC35,最不发达4国LDC4	50	---Other
		-隔离开关及断续开关:							-Isolating switches and make-and-break switches:
7245	8535.3010	---用于电压在72.5千伏及以上，但不高于220千伏的线路	10	0 5	东盟ASEAN,智利CL,新西兰NZ,秘鲁PE,哥斯达黎加CR 巴基斯坦PK	0	最不发达35国LDC35,最不发达4国LDC4	50	---For a voltage of 72.5kV or more, but not exceeding 220kV
7246	8535.3020	---用于电压高于220千伏，但不高于750千伏的线路	10	0 5	东盟ASEAN,智利CL,新西兰NZ,秘鲁PE,哥斯达黎加CR 巴基斯坦PK	0	最不发达35国LDC35,最不发达4国LDC4	50	---For a voltage exceeding 220kV, but not exceeding 750kV
7247	8535.3090	---其他	10	0 5	东盟ASEAN,智利CL,新西兰NZ,秘鲁PE,哥斯达黎加CR 巴基斯坦PK	0	最不发达35国LDC35,最不发达4国LDC4	50	---Other
7248	8535.4000	-避雷器、电压限幅器及电涌抑制器	18	0 3.6 9	东盟ASEAN,智利CL,新加坡SG,新西兰NZ,香港HK 哥斯达黎加CR 秘鲁PE	0	最不发达35国LDC35	50	-Lightning arresters, voltage limiters and surge suppressors
7249	8535.9000	-其他	10	0 1 5 9.5	东盟ASEAN,新加坡SG,新西兰NZ,哥斯达黎加CR,香港HK 智利CL 巴基斯坦PK,秘鲁PE 亚太APTA	0	最不发达35国LDC35,最不发达4国LDC4	50	-Other
	85.36	**电路的开关、保护或连接用的电器装置（例如，开关、继电器、熔断器、电涌抑制器、插头、插座、灯座及其他连接器、接线盒），用于电压不超过1000伏的线路；光导纤维、光导纤维束或光缆用连接器:**							**Electrical apparatus for switching or protecting electrical circuits, or for making connections to or in electrical circuits (for example, switches, relays, fuses, surge suppressors, plugs, sockets, lamp-holders and other connectors, junction boxes), for a voltage not exceeding 1,000 volts; connectors for optical fibres, optical fibre bundles or cables:**

序号 No.	税则号列 Tariff Line	货品名称	最惠国税率 MFN(%)	协定税率 Agreement(%)		特惠税率 S.P.(%)		普通税率 Gen.(%)	Article Description
7250	8536.1000	-熔断器	10	0 5	东盟ASEAN,智利CL,新加坡SG,新西兰NZ,秘鲁PE,哥斯达黎加CR,香港HK,台湾TW 巴基斯坦PK	0	最不发达35国LDC35,最不发达4国LDC4	50	-Fuses
7251	8536.2000	-自动断路器	9	0 5	东盟ASEAN,智利CL,新西兰NZ,秘鲁PE,哥斯达黎加CR,香港HK 巴基斯坦PK	0	最不发达35国LDC35,最不发达4国LDC4	50	-Automatic circuit breakers
7252	8536.3000	-其他电路保护装置	9	0 5	东盟ASEAN,智利CL,新西兰NZ,秘鲁PE,哥斯达黎加CR,香港HK 巴基斯坦PK	0	最不发达35国LDC35,最不发达4国LDC4	50	-Other apparatus for protecting electrical circuits
		-继电器: --用于电压不超过60伏的线路:							-Relays: --For a voltage not exceeding 60V:
7253	8536.4110	---用于电压不超过36伏的线路	10	0 5	东盟ASEAN,智利CL,新加坡SG,新西兰NZ,秘鲁PE,哥斯达黎加CR 巴基斯坦PK	0	最不发达35国LDC35,最不发达4国LDC4	50	---For a voltage not exceeding 36V
7254	8536.4190	---其他	10	0 5	东盟ASEAN,智利CL,新加坡SG,新西兰NZ,秘鲁PE,哥斯达黎加CR 巴基斯坦PK	0	最不发达35国LDC35,最不发达4国LDC4	50	---Other
7255	8536.4900	--其他	10	0 1 5	东盟ASEAN,新加坡SG,新西兰NZ,哥斯达黎加CR,香港HK 智利CL 巴基斯坦PK,秘鲁PE	0	最不发达35国LDC35,最不发达4国LDC4	50	--Other
7256	8536.5000	-其他开关	0			0	最不发达35国LDC35,最不发达4国LDC4	50	-Other switches
		-灯座、插头及插座:							-Lamp-holders, plugs and sockets:
7257	8536.6100	--灯座	10	0 5	东盟ASEAN,智利CL,新加坡SG,新西兰NZ,秘鲁PE,哥斯达黎加CR 巴基斯坦PK	0	最不发达35国LDC35,最不发达4国LDC4	50	--Lamp-holders

序号 No.	税则号列 Tariff Line	货品名称	最惠国税 率 MFN(%)	协定税率 Agreement(%)		特惠税率 S.P.(%)		普通税率 Gen.(%)	Article Description
7258	8536.6900	--其他	0			0	最不发达35国LDC35,最不发达4国LDC4	50	--Other
7259	8536.7000	-光导纤维、光导纤维束或光缆用连接器	8	0 0.8 5	东盟ASEAN,新西兰NZ,秘鲁PE,哥斯达黎加CR,香港HK,澳门MO 智利CL 巴基斯坦PK	0	最不发达35国LDC35,最不发达4国LDC4	30	-Connectors for optical fibres, optical fibre bundles or cables
		-其他装置:							-Other apparatus:
		---接插件:							---Connector:
7260	8536.9011	----工作电压不超过36伏的	0			0	最不发达35国LDC35,最不发达4国LDC4	50	----For a voltage not exceeding 36V
7261	8536.9019	----其他	0			0	最不发达35国LDC35,最不发达4国LDC4	50	----Other
7262	8536.9090	---其他	0			0	最不发达35国LDC35,最不发达4国LDC4	50	---Other
	85.37	**用于电气控制或电力分配的盘、板、台、柜及其他基座，装有两个或多个税号85.35或85.36所列的装置，包括装有第九十章所列的仪器或装置，以及数控装置，但税号85.17的交换机除外:**							**Boards, panels, consoles, desks, cabinets and other bases, equipped with two or more apparatus of heading No.85.35 or 85.36, for electric control or the distribution of electricity, including those incorporating instruments or apparatus of Chapter 90, and numerical control apparatus, other than switching apparatus of heading No.85.17:**
		-用于电压不超过1000伏的线路:							-For a voltage not exceeding 1000V:
		---数控装置:							---Numerical control panels:

序号 No.	税则号列 Tariff Line	货品名称	最惠国税率 MFN(%)	协定税率 Agreement(%)		特惠税率 S.P.(%)		普通税率 Gen.(%)	Article Description
7263	8537.1011	----可编程序控制器	5	0 0.5 2.5	东盟ASEAN,巴基斯坦PK,新西兰NZ,秘鲁PE,哥斯达黎加CR,香港HK,台湾TW 智利CL 亚太APTA	0	最不发达35国LDC35,最不发达4国LDC4	14	----Programmable controuers
	ex85371011	机床用可编程序控制器（PLC）	△3						Programmable logic controllers (PLC) for machine tools
7264	8537.1019	----其他	5	0 0.5 2.5	东盟ASEAN,巴基斯坦PK,新西兰NZ,秘鲁PE,哥斯达黎加CR,香港HK,台湾TW 智利CL 亚太APTA	0	最不发达35国LDC35,最不发达4国LDC4	14	----Other
	ex85371019	机床用数控单元（包括单独进口的CNC操作单元）	△3						Numerical control equipment for machine tools (including CNC unit imported separately)
7265	8537.1090	---其他	8.4	0 0.8 4.2	东盟ASEAN,巴基斯坦PK,新西兰NZ,秘鲁PE,哥斯达黎加CR,香港HK,澳门MO 智利CL 亚太APTA	0	最不发达35国LDC35,最不发达4国LDC4	50	---Other
	ex85371090	电梯用控制柜及控制柜专用印刷电路板	△4						Control cabinets for elevator and printed circuits solely used for control cabinets
		-用于电压超过1000伏的线路:							-For a voltage exceeding 1000V:
7266	8537.2010	---全封闭组合式高压开关装置，用于电压在500千伏及以上的线路	8.4	0 0.8 4.2	东盟ASEAN,巴基斯坦PK,新西兰NZ,秘鲁PE,哥斯达黎加CR 智利CL 亚太APTA	0	最不发达35国LDC35,最不发达4国LDC4	30	---Gas insulated switchgear, for a voltage of 500kV or more
7267	8537.2090	---其他	8.4	0 0.8 4.2	东盟ASEAN,巴基斯坦PK,新西兰NZ,秘鲁PE,哥斯达黎加CR,香港HK 智利CL 亚太APTA	0	最不发达35国LDC35,最不发达4国LDC4	50	---Other
	85.38	**专用于或主要用于税号85.35、85.36或85.37所列装置的零件:**							**Parts suitable for use solely or principally with the apparatus of heading No.85.35, 85.36 or 85.37:**
		-税号85.37所列货品用的盘、板、台、柜及其他基座，但未装有关装置:							-Boards, panels, consoles, desks, cabinets and other bases for the goods of heading No.85.37, not equipped with their apparatus:

序号 No.	税则号列 Tariff Line	货品名称	最惠国税率 MFN(%)	协定税率 Agreement(%)		特惠税率 S.P.(%)		普通税率 Gen.(%)	Article Description
7268	8538.1010	---税号 8537.2010 所列货品用	8.4	0 0.8 4.2	东盟ASEAN,巴基斯坦PK,新西兰NZ,秘鲁PE,哥斯达黎加CR 智利CL 亚太APTA	0	最不发达35国LDC35,最不发达4国LDC4	50	---For the goods of heading No.8537.2010
7269	8538.1090	---其他	7	0 0.7 3.5	东盟ASEAN,巴基斯坦PK,新西兰NZ,秘鲁PE,哥斯达黎加CR 智利CL 亚太APTA	0	最不发达35国LDC35,最不发达4国LDC4	50	---Other
7270	8538.9000	-其他	7	0 0.7 5	东盟ASEAN,新西兰NZ,秘鲁PE,哥斯达黎加CR,香港HK,台湾TW 智利CL 巴基斯坦PK	0	最不发达35国LDC35,最不发达4国LDC4	50	-Other
	85.39	**白炽灯泡、放电灯管,包括封闭式聚光灯及紫外线灯管或红外线灯泡;弧光灯:**							**Electric filament or discharge lamps, including sealed beam lamp units and ultraviolet or infrared lamps; arclamps:**
7271	8539.1000	-封闭式聚光灯	10	0 5	东盟ASEAN,智利CL,新西兰NZ,秘鲁PE,哥斯达黎加CR 巴基斯坦PK	0	最不发达35国LDC35,最不发达4国LDC4	45	-Sealed beam lamp units
		-其他白炽灯泡,但不包括紫外线灯管或红外线灯泡:							-Other filament lamps, excluding ultraviolet or infrared lamps:
		--卤钨灯:							--Tungsten halogen:
7272	8539.2110	---科研、医疗专用	8	0 0.8 5	东盟ASEAN,新西兰NZ,秘鲁PE,哥斯达黎加CR 智利CL 巴基斯坦PK	0	最不发达35国LDC35,最不发达4国LDC4	20	---For scientific or medical uses only
7273	8539.2120	---火车、航空器及船舶用	8	0 0.8 5	东盟ASEAN,新西兰NZ,秘鲁PE,哥斯达黎加CR 智利CL 巴基斯坦PK	0	最不发达35国LDC35,最不发达4国LDC4	20	---For locomotives and rolling-stock, aircraft or ships
7274	8539.2130	---机动车辆用	10	0 1 5	东盟ASEAN,新西兰NZ,秘鲁PE,哥斯达黎加CR 智利CL 巴基斯坦PK	0	最不发达35国LDC35,最不发达4国LDC4	45	---For motor vehicles

序号 No.	税则号列 Tariff Line	货品名称	最惠国税率 MFN(%)	协定税率 Agreement(%)		特惠税率 S.P.(%)		普通税率 Gen.(%)	Article Description
7275	8539.2190	---其他	10.5	0 1.1 2.1	东盟ASEAN,新加坡SG,新西兰NZ,秘鲁PE 智利CL 哥斯达黎加CR	0	最不发达35国LDC35,最不发达4国LDC4	70	---Other
		--其他灯，功率不超过200瓦，但额定电压超过100伏:							--Other, of a power not exceeding 200W and for a voltage exceeding 100V:
7276	8539.2210	---科研、医疗专用	10.5	0 1.1 2.1 5	东盟ASEAN,新加坡SG,新西兰NZ,秘鲁PE 智利CL 哥斯达黎加CR 巴基斯坦PK	0	最不发达35国LDC35,最不发达4国LDC4	20	---For scientific or medical uses only
7277	8539.2290	---其他	5	0 0.5	东盟ASEAN,巴基斯坦PK,新西兰NZ,秘鲁PE,哥斯达黎加CR 智利CL	0	最不发达35国LDC35,最不发达4国LDC4	70	---Other
		--其他:							--Other:
7278	8539.2910	---科研、医疗专用	5	0 0.5	东盟ASEAN,巴基斯坦PK,新西兰NZ,秘鲁PE,哥斯达黎加CR 智利CL	0	最不发达35国LDC35,最不发达4国LDC4	20	---For scientific or medical uses only
7279	8539.2920	---火车、航空器及船舶用	10.5	0 1.1 2.1 5	东盟ASEAN,新加坡SG,新西兰NZ,秘鲁PE 智利CL 哥斯达黎加CR 巴基斯坦PK	0	最不发达35国LDC35,最不发达4国LDC4	20	---For locomotives and rolling-stock, aircraft or ships
7280	8539.2930	---机动车辆用	5	0 0.5	东盟ASEAN,巴基斯坦PK,新西兰NZ,秘鲁PE,哥斯达黎加CR 智利CL	0	最不发达35国LDC35,最不发达4国LDC4	45	---For motor vehicles
		---其他:							---Other:
7281	8539.2991	----12伏及以下的	12	0 1.2 2.4 6	东盟ASEAN,新加坡SG,新西兰NZ,秘鲁PE,香港HK 智利CL 哥斯达黎加CR 巴基斯坦PK	0	最不发达35国LDC35,最不发达4国LDC4	70	----Of a voltage 12V or less
7282	8539.2999	----其他	12	0 1.2 2.4 6	东盟ASEAN,新加坡SG,新西兰NZ,秘鲁PE 智利CL 哥斯达黎加CR 巴基斯坦PK	0	最不发达35国LDC35,最不发达4国LDC4	70	----Other

序号 No.	税则号列 Tariff Line	货品名称	最惠国税率 MFN(%)	协定税率 Agreement(%)		特惠税率 S.P.(%)		普通税率 Gen.(%)	Article Description
		-放电灯管，但紫外线灯管除外:							-Discharge lamps, other than ultraviolet lamps:
		--热阴极荧光灯:							--Fluorescent, hot cathode:
7283	8539.3110	---科研、医疗专用	8	0 0.8 5	东盟ASEAN,新西兰NZ,秘鲁PE,哥斯达黎加CR 智利CL 巴基斯坦PK	0	最不发达35国LDC35,最不发达4国LDC4	20	---For scientific or medical uses only
7284	8539.3120	---火车、航空器及船舶用	8	0 0.8 5	东盟ASEAN,新西兰NZ,秘鲁PE,哥斯达黎加CR 智利CL 巴基斯坦PK	0	最不发达35国LDC35,最不发达4国LDC4	20	---For locomotives and rolling-stock, aircraft or ships
		---其他:							---Other:
7285	8539.3191	----紧凑型	8	0 0.8 5	东盟ASEAN,新西兰NZ,秘鲁PE,哥斯达黎加CR 智利CL 巴基斯坦PK	0	最不发达35国LDC35,最不发达4国LDC4	70	----Compact fluorescent lamp
7286	8539.3199	----其他	8	0 0.8 5	东盟ASEAN,新西兰NZ,秘鲁PE,哥斯达黎加CR 智利CL 巴基斯坦PK	0	最不发达35国LDC35,最不发达4国LDC4	70	----Other
		--汞或钠蒸汽灯;金属卤化物灯:							--Mercury or sodium vapour lamps; metal halide lamps:
7287	8539.3230	---钠蒸气灯	8	0 5	东盟ASEAN,智利CL,新西兰NZ,秘鲁PE,哥斯达黎加CR 巴基斯坦PK	0	最不发达35国LDC35,最不发达4国LDC4	20	---Sodium-vapour lamps
7288	8539.3240	---汞蒸气灯	8	0 5	东盟ASEAN,智利CL,新西兰NZ,秘鲁PE,哥斯达黎加CR 巴基斯坦PK	0	最不发达35国LDC35,最不发达4国LDC4	20	---Mercury-vapour lamps
	ex85393240	彩色投影机的照明光源	△3						Illumiation light source of colour projectors
7289	8539.3290	---其他	8	0 5	东盟ASEAN,智利CL,新西兰NZ,秘鲁PE,哥斯达黎加CR 巴基斯坦PK	0	最不发达35国LDC35,最不发达4国LDC4	70	---Other
		--其他:							--Other:

序号 No.	税则号列 Tariff Line	货品名称	最惠国税率 MFN(%)	协定税率 Agreement(%)		特惠税率 S.P.(%)		普通税率 Gen.(%)	Article Description
7290	8539.3910	---科研、医疗专用	8	0 5	东盟ASEAN,智利CL,新西兰NZ,秘鲁PE,哥斯达黎加CR 巴基斯坦PK	0	最不发达35国LDC35,最不发达4国LDC4	20	---For scientific or medical uses only
7291	8539.3920	---火车、航空器及船舶用	8	0 5	东盟ASEAN,智利CL,新西兰NZ,秘鲁PE,哥斯达黎加CR 巴基斯坦PK	0	最不发达35国LDC35,最不发达4国LDC4	20	---For locomotives and rolling-stock, aircraft or ships
7292	8539.3990	---其他	8	0 5	东盟ASEAN,智利CL,新西兰NZ,秘鲁PE,哥斯达黎加CR,澳门MO,台湾TW 巴基斯坦PK	0	最不发达35国LDC35,最不发达4国LDC4	70	---Other
	ex85393990	液晶显示器背光模组用冷阴极灯管	△3						Cold cathode fluorescent lamp for backlight module of liquid crystal display
		-紫外线灯管或红外线灯泡;弧光灯:							-Ultraviolet or infrared lamps; arclamps:
7293	8539.4100	--弧光灯	8	0 5	东盟ASEAN,智利CL,新西兰NZ,秘鲁PE,哥斯达黎加CR 巴基斯坦PK	0	最不发达35国LDC35,最不发达4国LDC4	20	--Arclamps
7294	8539.4900	--其他	8	0 5	东盟ASEAN,智利CL,新西兰NZ,秘鲁PE,哥斯达黎加CR 巴基斯坦PK	0	最不发达35国LDC35,最不发达4国LDC4	20	--Other
7295	8539.9000	-零件	8	0 5	东盟ASEAN,智利CL,新西兰NZ,秘鲁PE,哥斯达黎加CR,台湾TW 巴基斯坦PK	0	最不发达35国LDC35,最不发达4国LDC4	20	-Parts
	85.40	**热电子管、冷阴极管或光阴极管（例如，真空管或充气管、汞弧整流管、阴极射线管、电视摄像管）：**							**Thermionic, cold cathode or photocathode valves and tubes (for example, vacuum or vapour or gas filled valves and tubes, mercury arc rectifying valves and tubes, cathoderay tubes, television camera tubes):**

序号 No.	税则号列 Tariff Line	货品名称	最惠国税率 MFN(%)	协定税率 Agreement(%)		特惠税率 S.P.(%)		普通税率 Gen.(%)	Article Description
		-阴极射线电视显像管，包括视频监视器用阴极射线管:							-Cathode-ray television picture tubes, including video monitor cathode-ray tubes:
7296	8540.1100	--彩色的	12	0 2.4 6	东盟ASEAN,智利CL,新加坡SG,新西兰NZ,秘鲁PE 哥斯达黎加CR 巴基斯坦PK	0	最不发达35国LDC35	40	--Colour
7297	8540.1200	--单色的	15	0 3 7.5 12	东盟ASEAN,智利CL,新加坡SG,新西兰NZ 哥斯达黎加CR 秘鲁PE 巴基斯坦PK	0	最不发达35国LDC35	40	--Monochrome
		-电视摄像管;变像管及图像增强管;其他光阴极管:							-Television camera tubes; image converters and intensifiers; other photo-cathode tubes:
7298	8540.2010	---电视摄像管	12	0 2.4 6	东盟ASEAN,智利CL,新加坡SG,新西兰NZ,秘鲁PE 哥斯达黎加CR 巴基斯坦PK	0	最不发达35国LDC35	35	---Television camera tubes
7299	8540.2090	---其他	8	0 5	东盟ASEAN,智利CL,新西兰NZ,秘鲁PE,哥斯达黎加CR 巴基斯坦PK	0	最不发达35国LDC35,最不发达4国LDC4	17	---Other
		-单色的数据/图形显示管；彩色的数据/图形显示管，屏幕荧光点间距小于0.4毫米:							-Data/graphic display tubes, black and white or other monochrome; data/graphic display tubes, colour, with a phosphor dot screen pitch less than 0.4mm:
7300	8540.4010	---彩色的数据/图形显示管，屏幕荧光点间距小于0.4毫米	8	0 5	东盟ASEAN,智利CL,新西兰NZ,秘鲁PE,哥斯达黎加CR,香港HK 巴基斯坦PK	0	最不发达35国LDC35,最不发达4国LDC4	17	---Data/graphic display tubes, colour, with a phosphor dot screen pitch less than 0.4mm
7301	8540.4020	---单色的数据/图形显示管	8	0 5	东盟ASEAN,智利CL,新西兰NZ,秘鲁PE,哥斯达黎加CR 巴基斯坦PK	0	最不发达35国LDC35,最不发达4国LDC4	17	---Data/graphic display tubes, black and white or other monochrome
		-其他阴极射线管:							-Other cathode-ray tubes:
7302	8540.6010	---雷达显示管	6	0 5	东盟ASEAN,智利CL,新西兰NZ,秘鲁PE,哥斯达黎加CR 巴基斯坦PK	0	最不发达35国LDC35,最不发达4国LDC4	14	---Radar display tubes

序号 No.	税则号列 Tariff Line	货品名称	最惠国税率 MFN(%)	协定税率 Agreement(%)		特惠税率 S.P.(%)		普通税率 Gen.(%)	Article Description
7303	8540.6090	---其他	8	0 5	东盟ASEAN,智利CL,新西兰NZ,秘鲁PE,哥斯达黎加CR 巴基斯坦PK	0	最不发达35国LDC35,最不发达4国LDC4	17	---Other
		-微波管（例如，磁控管、速调管、行波管、返波管），但不包括栅控管:							-Microwave tubes (for example, magnetrons, klystrons, travelling wave tubes, carcinotrons), excluding gridcontrolled tubes:
7304	8540.7100	--磁控管	8	0 5	东盟ASEAN,智利CL,新西兰NZ,秘鲁PE,哥斯达黎加CR 巴基斯坦PK	0	最不发达35国LDC35,最不发达4国LDC4	17	--Magnetrons
		--其他:							--Other:
7305	8540.7910	---速调管	8	0 5	东盟ASEAN,智利CL,新西兰NZ,秘鲁PE,哥斯达黎加CR 巴基斯坦PK	0	最不发达35国LDC35,最不发达4国LDC4	17	---Klystrons
7306	8540.7990	---其他	8	0 5	东盟ASEAN,智利CL,新西兰NZ,秘鲁PE,哥斯达黎加CR 巴基斯坦PK	0	最不发达35国LDC35,最不发达4国LDC4	17	---Other
		-其他管:							-Other valves and tubes:
7307	8540.8100	--接收管或放大管	8	0 5	东盟ASEAN,智利CL,新西兰NZ,秘鲁PE,哥斯达黎加CR 巴基斯坦PK	0	最不发达35国LDC35,最不发达4国LDC4	17	--Receiver or amplifier valves and tubes
7308	8540.8900	--其他	8	0 5	东盟ASEAN,智利CL,新西兰NZ,秘鲁PE,哥斯达黎加CR,台湾TW 巴基斯坦PK	0	最不发达35国LDC35,最不发达4国LDC4	17	--Other
		-零件:							-Parts:
		--阴极射线管用:							--Of cathode-ray tubes:
7309	8540.9110	---电视显像管用	6 △3	0 5	东盟ASEAN,智利CL,新西兰NZ,秘鲁PE,哥斯达黎加CR 巴基斯坦PK	0	最不发达35国LDC35,最不发达4国LDC4	40	---Of television picture tubes

序号 No.	税则号列 Tariff Line	货品名称	最惠国税率 MFN(%)	协定税率 Agreement(%)		特惠税率 S.P.(%)		普通税率 Gen.(%)	Article Description
7310	8540.9120	---雷达显示管用	5	0	东盟ASEAN,智利CL,巴基斯坦PK,新西兰NZ,秘鲁PE,哥斯达黎加CR	0	最不发达35国LDC35,最不发达4国LDC4	14	---Of radar display tubes
7311	8540.9190	---其他	8 △4	0 5	东盟ASEAN,智利CL,新西兰NZ,秘鲁PE,哥斯达黎加CR 巴基斯坦PK	0	最不发达35国LDC35,最不发达4国LDC4	17	---Other
		--其他:							--Other:
7312	8540.9910	---电视摄像管用	8	0 5	东盟ASEAN,智利CL,新西兰NZ,秘鲁PE,哥斯达黎加CR 巴基斯坦PK	0	最不发达35国LDC35,最不发达4国LDC4	35	---Of television camera tubes
7313	8540.9990	---其他	8	0 5	东盟ASEAN,智利CL,新西兰NZ,秘鲁PE,哥斯达黎加CR 巴基斯坦PK	0	最不发达35国LDC35,最不发达4国LDC4	17	---Other
	85.41	**二极管、晶体管及类似的半导体器件;光敏半导体器件,包括不论是否装在组件内或组装成块的光电池;发光二极管;已装配的压电晶体:**							**Diodes, transistors and similar semiconductor devices; photosensitive semi-conductor devices, including photo-voltaic cells whether or not assembled in modules or made up into panels; light emitting diodes; mounted piezoelectric crystals:**
7314	8541.1000	-二极管,但光敏二极管或发光二极管除外	0			0	最不发达35国LDC35,最不发达4国LDC4	30	-Diodes, other than photosensitive or light emitting diodes
		-晶体管,但光敏晶体管除外:							-Transistors, other than photosensitive transistors:
7315	8541.2100	--耗散功率小于1瓦的	0			0	最不发达35国LDC35,最不发达4国LDC4	30	--With a dissipation rate of less than 1W

序号 No.	税则号列 Tariff Line	货品名称	最惠国 税　率 MFN(%)	协定税率 Agreement(%)	特惠税率 S.P.(%)	普通 税率 Gen.(%)	Article Description
7316	8541.2900	--其他	0		0 最不发达35国LDC35,最不发达4国LDC4	30	--Other
7317	8541.3000	-半导体开关元件、两端交流开关元件及三端双向可控硅开关元件，但光敏器件除外	0		0 最不发达35国LDC35,最不发达4国LDC4	30	-Thyristors, diacs and triacs, other than photo-sensitive devices
		-光敏半导体器件，包括不论是否装在组件内或组装成块的光电池;发光二极管:					-Photosensitive semi-conductor devices, including photovoltaic cells whether or not assembled in modules or made up into panels; light emitting diodes:
7318	8541.4010	---发光二极管	0		0 最不发达35国LDC35,最不发达4国LDC4	30	---Light emitting diodes
7319	8541.4020	---太阳能电池	0		0 最不发达35国LDC35,最不发达4国LDC4	30	---Solar cells
7320	8541.4090	---其他	0		0 最不发达35国LDC35,最不发达4国LDC4	30	---Other
7321	8541.5000	-其他半导体器件	0		0 最不发达35国LDC35,最不发达4国LDC4	30	-Other semiconductor devices
7322	8541.6000	-已装配的压电晶体	0		0 最不发达35国LDC35,最不发达4国LDC4	30	-Mounted piezoelectric crystals
7323	8541.9000	-零件	0		0 最不发达35国LDC35,最不发达4国LDC4	30	-Parts

序号 No.	税则号列 Tariff Line	货品名称	最惠国税率 MFN(%)	协定税率 Agreement(%)		特惠税率 S.P.(%)		普通税率 Gen.(%)	Article Description
	85.42	**集成电路:**							**Electronic integrated circuits:**
		-集成电路:							-Electronic integrated circuits :
7324	8542.3100	--处理器及控制器，不论是否带有存储器、转换器、逻辑电路、放大器、时钟及时序电路或其他电路	0			0	最不发达35国LDC35,最不发达4国LDC4	24	--Processors and controllers, whether or not combined with memories, converters, logic circuits, amplifiers, clock and timing circuits, or other circuits
7325	8542.3200	--存储器	0			0	最不发达35国LDC35,最不发达4国LDC4	24	--Memories
7326	8542.3300	--放大器	0			0	最不发达35国LDC35,最不发达4国LDC4	24	--Amplifiers
7327	8542.3900	--其他	0			0	最不发达35国LDC35,最不发达4国LDC4	24	--Other
7328	8542.9000	-零件	0			0	最不发达35国LDC35,最不发达4国LDC4	30	-Parts
	85.43	**本章其他税号未列名的具有独立功能的电气设备及装置:**							**Electrical machines and apparatus, having individual functions, not specified or included elsewhere in this Chapter:**
7329	8543.1000	-粒子加速器	5	0	东盟ASEAN,智利CL,巴基斯坦PK,新西兰NZ,秘鲁PE,哥斯达黎加CR	0	最不发达35国LDC35,最不发达4国LDC4	11	-Particle accelerators
		-信号发生器:							-Signal generators:
7330	8543.2010	---输出信号频率在1500兆赫兹以下的通用信号发生器	15	0	东盟ASEAN,新加坡SG,新西兰NZ,台湾TW	0	最不发达35国LDC35	80	---Universal signal generators, with a frequency range of less than 1500MHz
				1.5	智利CL				
				3	哥斯达黎加CR				
				7.5	秘鲁PE				
				12	巴基斯坦PK				

序号 No.	税则号列 Tariff Line	货品名称	最惠国税率 MFN(%)	协定税率 Agreement(%)	特惠税率 S.P.(%)	普通税率 Gen.(%)	Article Description
7331	8543.2090	---其他	8	0 东盟ASEAN,新西兰NZ,秘鲁PE,哥斯达黎加CR,台湾TW 0.8 智利CL 5 巴基斯坦PK	0 最不发达35国LDC35,最不发达4国LDC4	20	---Other
7332	8543.3000	-电镀、电解或电泳设备及装置	0		0 最不发达35国LDC35,最不发达4国LDC4	35	-Machines and apparatus for electro-plating, electrolysis or electrophoresis
		-其他设备及装置:					-Other machines and apparatus:
7333	8543.7091	----金属、矿藏探测器	0		0 最不发达35国LDC35,最不发达4国LDC4	17	----Metal or mine detectors
7334	8543.7092	----高、中频放大器	0		0 最不发达35国LDC35,最不发达4国LDC4	17	----High or intermediate frequency amplifiers
7335	8543.7093	----电篱网激发器	10	0 东盟ASEAN,智利CL,新加坡SG,新西兰NZ,秘鲁PE,哥斯达黎加CR 5 巴基斯坦PK	0 最不发达35国LDC35,最不发达4国LDC4	35	----Electric fence energizers
7336	8543.7099	----其他	0		0 最不发达35国LDC35,最不发达4国LDC4	35	----Other
		-零件:					-Parts:
7337	8543.9010	---粒子加速器用	0		0 最不发达35国LDC35,最不发达4国LDC4	11	---Of particle accelerators
		---信号发生器用:					---Of signal generators:
7338	8543.9021	----输出信号频率在1500兆赫兹以下的通用信号发生器用	0		0 最不发达35国LDC35,最不发达4国LDC4	80	----Of the generators of subheading No.8543.2010

序号 No.	税则号列 Tariff Line	货品名称	最惠国税率 MFN(%)	协定税率 Agreement(%)		特惠税率 S.P.(%)		普通税率 Gen.(%)	Article Description
7339	8543.9029	----其他	0			0	最不发达35国LDC35,最不发达4国LDC4	20	----Other
7340	8543.9030	---金属、矿藏探测器用	0			0	最不发达35国LDC35,最不发达4国LDC4	17	---Of metal or mine detectors
7341	8543.9040	---高、中频放大器用	0			0	最不发达35国LDC35,最不发达4国LDC4	17	---Of high or intermediate frequency amplifiers
7342	8543.9090	---其他	0			0	最不发达35国LDC35,最不发达4国LDC4	35	---Other
	85.44	**绝缘（包括漆包或阳极化处理）电线、电缆（包括同轴电缆）及其他绝缘电导体，不论是否有接头;由每根被覆光纤组成的光缆，不论是否与电导体装配或装有接头:**							**Insulated (including enamelled or anodized) wire, cable (including co-axial cable) and other insulated electric conductors, whether or not ritted with connectors; optical fibre cables, made up of individually sheathed fibres, whether or not assembled with electric conductors or fitted with connectors:**
		-绕组电线:							-Winding wire:
7343	8544.1100	--铜制	10 △6	0 5 7	东盟ASEAN,智利CL,新加坡SG,新西兰NZ,秘鲁PE,哥斯达黎加CR,香港HK,澳门MO,台湾TW 巴基斯坦PK 亚太APTA	0	最不发达35国LDC35,最不发达4国LDC4	70	--Of copper
7344	8544.1900	--其他	20	0 4 10	东盟ASEAN,智利CL,新加坡SG,新西兰NZ 哥斯达黎加CR 秘鲁PE	0	最不发达35国LDC35	70	--Other

序号 No.	税则号列 Tariff Line	货品名称	最惠国税率 MFN(%)	协定税率 Agreement(%)		特惠税率 S.P.(%)		普通税率 Gen.(%)	Article Description
7345	8544.2000	-同轴电缆及其他同轴电导体	10	0 1 5 9	东盟ASEAN,新加坡SG,新西兰NZ,哥斯达黎加CR,台湾TW 智利CL 巴基斯坦PK,秘鲁PE 亚太APTA	0	最不发达35国LDC35,最不发达4国LDC4	20	-Co-axial cable and other co-axial electric conductors
		-车辆、航空器、船舶用点火布线组及其他布线组:							-Ignition wiring sets and other wiring sets of a kind used in vehicles, aircraft or ships:
7346	8544.3020	---机动车辆用	10	0	智利CL,新西兰NZ,秘鲁PE,哥斯达黎加CR	0	最不发达35国LDC35,最不发达4国LDC4	20	---For motor vehicles
	ex85443020	车辆用电控柴油机的线束	△5						Wiring harness of electric diesel engines used for vehicles
7347	8544.3090	---其他	5	0	智利CL,新西兰NZ,秘鲁PE,哥斯达黎加CR	0	最不发达35国LDC35,最不发达4国LDC4	70	---Other
		-其他电导体,额定电压不超过1000伏:							-Other electric conductors, for a voltage not exceeding 1000V:
		--有接头:							--Fitted with connectors:
		---额定电压不超过80伏:							---for a voltage not exceeding 80V:
7348	8544.4211	----电缆	0			0	最不发达35国LDC35,最不发达4国LDC4	20	----Electric cable
7349	8544.4219	----其他	0			0	最不发达35国LDC35,最不发达4国LDC4	70	----Other
		---额定电压超过80伏,但不超过1000伏:							---Other electric conductors, for a voltage exceeding 80V but not exceeding 1000V:
7350	8544.4221	----电缆	0			0	最不发达35国LDC35,最不发达4国LDC4	20	----Electric cable

序号 No.	税则号列 Tariff Line	货品名称	最惠国税率 MFN(%)	协定税率 Agreement(%)		特惠税率 S.P.(%)		普通税率 Gen.(%)	Article Description
7351	8544.4229	----其他	0			0	最不发达35国LDC35,最不发达4国LDC4	70	----Other
		--其他:							--Other:
		---额定电压不超过80伏:							---For a voltage not exceeding 80V:
7352	8544.4911	----电缆	0			0	最不发达35国LDC35,最不发达4国LDC4	20	----Electric cable
7353	8544.4919	----其他	0			0	最不发达35国LDC35,最不发达4国LDC4	70	----Other
		---额定电压超过80伏，但不超过1000伏:							---Other electric conductors, for a voltage exceeding 80V but not exceeding 1000V:
7354	8544.4921	----电缆	6	0 0.6 4.2	东盟ASEAN,巴基斯坦PK,新西兰NZ,秘鲁PE,哥斯达黎加CR,香港HK 智利CL 亚太APTA	0	最不发达35国LDC35,最不发达4国LDC4	20	----Electric cable
7355	8544.4929	----其他	12	0 1.2 2.4 5 8.4	东盟ASEAN,新加坡SG,新西兰NZ,秘鲁PE,香港HK,澳门MO,台湾TW 智利CL 哥斯达黎加CR 巴基斯坦PK 亚太APTA	0	最不发达35国LDC35,最不发达4国LDC4	70	----Other
		-其他电导体，额定电压超过1000伏:							-Other electric conductors, for a voltage exceeding 1000V:
		---电缆:							---Electric cable:
7356	8544.6012	----额定电压不超过35千伏	10	0 1 5 8.9	东盟ASEAN,新加坡SG,新西兰NZ,秘鲁PE,哥斯达黎加CR,香港HK 智利CL 巴基斯坦PK 亚太APTA	0	最不发达35国LDC35,最不发达4国LDC4	50	----For a voltage not exceeding 35kV
7357	8544.6013	----额定电压超过35千伏，但不超过110千伏	8.4	0 0.8 5 8	东盟ASEAN,新西兰NZ,秘鲁PE,哥斯达黎加CR,香港HK 智利CL 巴基斯坦PK 亚太APTA	0	最不发达35国LDC35,最不发达4国LDC4	20	----For a voltage exceeding 35kV but not exceeding 110kV

序号 No.	税则号列 Tariff Line	货品名称	最惠国税率 MFN(%)	协定税率 Agreement(%)		特惠税率 S.P.(%)		普通税率 Gen.(%)	Article Description
7358	8544.6014	----额定电压超过110千伏，但不超过220千伏	8.4	0 0.8 5 8	东盟ASEAN,新西兰NZ,秘鲁PE,哥斯达黎加CR,香港HK 智利CL 巴基斯坦PK 亚太APTA	0	最不发达35国LDC35,最不发达4国LDC4	20	----For a voltage exceeding 110kV but not exceeding 220kV
7359	8544.6019	----其他	8.4	0 0.8 5 8	东盟ASEAN,新西兰NZ,秘鲁PE,哥斯达黎加CR,香港HK 智利CL 巴基斯坦PK 亚太APTA	0	最不发达35国LDC35,最不发达4国LDC4	20	----Other
7360	8544.6090	---其他	21	0 2.1 4.2 10.5 20	东盟ASEAN,新加坡SG,新西兰NZ,香港HK 智利CL 哥斯达黎加CR 秘鲁PE 亚太APTA,巴基斯坦PK	0	最不发达35国LDC35	70	---Other
	ex85446090	额定电压为500千伏及以上的气体绝缘金属封闭输电线	△10						Gas insulated metal enclosed transmission line, for a voltage of 500kV or more
7361	8544.7000	-光缆	0			0	最不发达35国LDC35,最不发达4国LDC4	20	-Optical fibre cables
	85.45	**碳电极、碳刷、灯碳棒、电池碳棒及电气设备用的其他石墨或碳精制品，不论是否带金属:**							**Carbon electrodes, carbon brushes, lamp carbons, battery carbons and other articles of graphite or other carbon, with or without metal, of a kind used for electrical purposes:**
		-碳电极:							-Carbon electrodes:
7362	8545.1100	--炉用	8	0 5	东盟ASEAN,智利CL,新西兰NZ,秘鲁PE,哥斯达黎加CR 巴基斯坦PK	0	最不发达35国LDC35,最不发达4国LDC4	35	--Of a kind used for furnaces
7363	8545.1900	--其他	10.5	0 2.1 5	东盟ASEAN,智利CL,新加坡SG,新西兰NZ,秘鲁PE 哥斯达黎加CR 巴基斯坦PK	0	最不发达35国LDC35,最不发达4国LDC4	35	--Other
7364	8545.2000	-碳刷	10.5	0 1.1 2.1 5	东盟ASEAN,新加坡SG,新西兰NZ,秘鲁PE 智利CL 哥斯达黎加CR 巴基斯坦PK	0	最不发达35国LDC35,最不发达4国LDC4	35	-Brushes

序号 No.	税则号列 Tariff Line	货品名称	最惠国税率 MFN(%)	协定税率 Agreement(%)		特惠税率 S.P.(%)		普通税率 Gen.(%)	Article Description
7365	8545.9000	-其他	10.5	0 2.1 5	东盟ASEAN,智利CL,新加坡SG,新西兰NZ,秘鲁PE 哥斯达黎加CR 巴基斯坦PK	0	最不发达35国LDC35,最不发达4国LDC4	35	-Other
	85.46	**各种材料制的绝缘子:**							**Electrical insulators of any material:**
7366	8546.1000	-玻璃制	10.5	0 2.1 5	东盟ASEAN,智利CL,新加坡SG,新西兰NZ,秘鲁PE 哥斯达黎加CR 巴基斯坦PK	0	最不发达35国LDC35,最不发达4国LDC4	35	-Of glass
		-陶瓷制:							-Of ceramics:
7367	8546.2010	---输变电线路绝缘瓷套管	6	0 0.6 5	东盟ASEAN,新西兰NZ,秘鲁PE,哥斯达黎加CR 智利CL 巴基斯坦PK	0	最不发达35国LDC35,最不发达4国LDC4	35	---Power transmission and converting ceramic bushings
7368	8546.2090	---其他	12	0 1.2 2.4 6	东盟ASEAN,新加坡SG,新西兰NZ 智利CL 哥斯达黎加CR 巴基斯坦PK,秘鲁PE	0	最不发达35国LDC35,最不发达4国LDC4	35	---Other
	ex85462090	输变电架空线路用长棒形瓷绝缘子瓷件(单支长度为1~2米,实芯)	△3						Long solid rod ceramic insulator body for power overhead transmission and converting lines (each rod is 1~2 meters in length)
7369	8546.9000	-其他	10	0 5	东盟ASEAN,智利CL,新加坡SG,新西兰NZ,秘鲁PE,哥斯达黎加CR 巴基斯坦PK	0	最不发达35国LDC35,最不发达4国LDC4	35	-Other
	85.47	**电气机器、器具或设备用的绝缘零件,除了为装配需要而在模制时装入的小金属零件(例如螺纹孔)以外,全部用绝缘材料制成,但税号85.46的绝缘子除外;内衬绝缘材料的贱金属制线路导管及其接头:**							**Insulating fittings for electrical machines, appliances or equipment, being fittings wholly of insulating material apart from any minor components of metal (for example, threaded sockets) incorporated during moulding solely for purposes of assembly, other than insulators of heading No.85.46; electrical conduit tubing and joints therefor, of base metal lined with insulating material:**

序号 No.	税则号列 Tariff Line	货品名称	最惠国税率 MFN(%)	协定税率 Agreement(%)		特惠税率 S.P.(%)		普通税率 Gen.(%)	Article Description
7370	8547.1000	-陶瓷制绝缘零件	8	0 5	东盟ASEAN,智利CL,新西兰NZ,秘鲁PE,哥斯达黎加CR 巴基斯坦PK	0	最不发达35国LDC35,最不发达4国LDC4	35	-Insulating fittings of ceramics
7371	8547.2000	-塑料制绝缘零件	8	0 5	东盟ASEAN,智利CL,新西兰NZ,秘鲁PE,哥斯达黎加CR,香港HK 巴基斯坦PK	0	最不发达35国LDC35,最不发达4国LDC4	35	-Insulating fittings of plastics
		-其他:							-Other:
7372	8547.9010	---内衬绝缘材料的贱金属制线路导管及其接头	10	0 5	东盟ASEAN,智利CL,新加坡SG,新西兰NZ,秘鲁PE,哥斯达黎加CR 巴基斯坦PK	0	最不发达35国LDC35,最不发达4国LDC4	50	---Electrical conduit tubing and joints therefor, of base metal lined with insulating material
7373	8547.9090	---其他	8	0 5	东盟ASEAN,智利CL,新西兰NZ,秘鲁PE,哥斯达黎加CR 巴基斯坦PK	0	最不发达35国LDC35,最不发达4国LDC4	35	---Other
	85.48	**原电池、原电池组及蓄电池的废碎料;废原电池、废原电池组及废蓄电池;机器或设备的本章其他税号未列名的电气零件:**							**Waste and scrap of primary cells, primary batteries and electric accumulators; spent primary cells, spent primary batteries and spent electric accumulators; electrical parts of machinery or apparatus, not specified or included elsewhere in this Chapter:**
7374	8548.1000	-原电池、原电池组及蓄电池的废碎料;废原电池、废原电池组及废蓄电池	8	0 0.8 5	东盟ASEAN,新西兰NZ,秘鲁PE,哥斯达黎加CR 智利CL 巴基斯坦PK	0 4	最不发达35国LDC35 亚太2国APTA2	36	-Waste and scrap of primary cells, primary batteries and electric accumulators; spent primary cells, spent primary batteries and spent electric accumulators
7375	8548.9000	-其他	12	0 2.4 6	东盟ASEAN,智利CL,新加坡SG,新西兰NZ,秘鲁PE 哥斯达黎加CR 巴基斯坦PK	0	最不发达35国LDC35	40	-Other
	ex85489000	电磁干扰滤波器	△3						Electromagnetic interference filters
	ex85489000	非电磁干扰滤波器	△6						Non electromagnetic interference filters

第十七类

车辆、航空器、船舶及有关运输设备

注释：

一、本类不包括税号 95.03 或 95.08 的物品以及税号 95.06 的长雪橇、平底雪橇及类似品。

二、本类所称“零件”及“零件、附件”，不适用于下列货品，不论其是否确定为供本类货品使用：

（一）各种材料制的接头、垫圈或类似品（按其构成材料归类或归入税号 84.84）或硫化橡胶（硬质橡胶除外）的其他制品（税号 40.16）；

（二）第十五类注释二所规定的贱金属制通用零件（第十五类）或塑料制的类似品（第三十九章）；

（三）第八十二章的物品（工具）；

（四）税号 83.06 的物品；

（五）税号 84.01 至 84.79 的机器或装置及其零件；税号 84.81 或 84.82 的物品及税号 84.83 的物品（这些物品是构成发动机或其他动力装置所必需的）；

（六）电机或电气设备（第八十五章）；

（七）第九十章的物品；

（八）第九十一章的物品；

（九）武器（第九十三章）；

（十）税号 94.05 的灯具或照明装置；

（十一）作为车辆零件的刷子（税号 96.03）。

三、第八十六章至第八十八章所称“零件”或“附件”，不适用于那些非专用于或非主要用于这几章所列物品的零件、附件。同时符合这几章内两个或两个以上税号规定的零件、附件，应按其主要用途归入相应的税号。

四、在本类中：

（一）既可在道路上又可在轨道上行驶的特殊构造的车辆，应归入第八十七章的相应税号；

（二）水陆两用的机动车辆，应归入第八十七章的相应税号；

SECTION XVII

VEHICLES，AIRCRAFT，VESSELS AND ASSOCIATED TRANSPORT EQUIPMENT

Notes:

1. This Section does not cover articles of heading No.95.03 or 95.08，or bobsleighs，toboggans or the like of heading No.95.06.

2. The expressions “parts” and “parts and accessories” do not apply to the following articles，whether or not they are identifiable as for the goods of this Section:

(a) Joints，washers or the like of any material (classified according to their constituent material or in heading No.84.84) or other articles of vulcanized rubber other than hard rubber (heading No.40.16);

(b) Parts of general use，as defined in Note 2 to Section XV，of base metal (Section XV)，or similar goods of plastics (Chapter 39);

(c) Articles of Chapter 82 (tools);

(d) Articles of heading No. 83.06;

(e) Machines or apparatus of headings Nos.84.01 to 84.79，or parts thereof; articles of heading No.84.81 or 84.82 or，provided they constitute integral parts of engines or motors，articles of heading No.84.83;

(f) Electrical machinery or equipment (Chapter 85);

(g) Articles of Chapter 90;

(h) Articles of Chapter 91;

(i) Arms(Chapter 93);

(j) Lamps or lighting fittings of heading No. 94.05; or

(k) Brushes of a kind used as parts of vehicles (heading No. 96.03).

3. References in Chapters 86 to 88 to “parts” or “accessories” do not apply to parts or accessories which are not suitable for use solely or principally with the articles of those Chapters. A part or accessory which answers to a description in two or more of the headings of those Chapters is to be classified under that heading which corresponds to the principal use of that part or accessory.

4. For the purposes of this Section:

(a) Vehicles specially constructed to travel on both road and rail are classified under the appropriate heading of Chapter 87;

(b) Amphibious motor vehicles are classified under the appropriate heading of Chapter 87;

（三）可兼作地面车辆使用的特殊构造的航空器，应归入第八十八章的相应税号。

(c) Aircraft specially constructed so that they can also be used as road vehicles are classified under the appropriate heading of Chapter 88.

五、气垫运输工具应按本类最相似的运输工具归类，其规定如下：

5. Air cushion vehicles are to be classified within this Section with the vehicles to which they are most akin as follows:

（一）在导轨上运行的（气垫火车），归入第八十六章；

(a) In Chapter 86 if designed to travel on a guide-track (hovertrains)；

（二）在陆地行驶或水陆两用的，归入第八十七章；

(b) In Chapter 87 if designed to travel over land or over both land and water;

（三）在水上航行的，不论能否在海滩或浮码头登陆及能否在冰上行驶，一律归入第八十九章。

(c) In Chapter 89 if designed to travel over water，whether or not able to land on beaches or landingstages or also able to travel over ice.

气垫运输工具的零件、附件，应按照上述规定，与最相类似的运输工具的零件、附件一并归类。

Parts and accessories of air-cushion vehicles are to be classified in the same way as those of vehicles of the heading in which the air-cushion vehicles are classified under the above provisions.

气垫火车的导轨固定装置及附件应与铁道轨道固定装置及附件一并归类。气垫火车运行系统的信号、安全或交通管理设备应与铁路的信号、安全或交通管理设备一并归类。

Hovertrain track fixtures and fittings are to be classified as railway track fixtures and fittings，and signalling，safety or traffic control equipment for hovertrain transport systems as signalling，safety or traffic control equipment for railways.

第八十六章
铁道及电车道机车、车辆及其零件；铁道及电车道轨道固定装置及其零件、附件；各种机械（包括电动机械）交通信号设备

Chapter 86
Railway or tramway locomotives，rolling-stock and parts thereof; railway or tramway track fixtures and fittings and parts thereof; mechanical (including electro-mechanical)traffic signaling equipment of all kinds

注释：

Notes:

一、本章不包括：

1. This Chapter does not cover:

（一）木制或混凝土制的铁道或电车道轨枕及气垫火车用的混凝土导轨（税号44.06或68.10）；

(a) Railway or tramway sleepers of wood or of concrete，or concrete guide-track sections for hovertrain (heading No. 44.06 or 68.10);

（二）税号73.02的铁道及电车道铺轨用钢铁材料；

(b) Railway or tramway track construction material of iron or steel of heading No. 73.02; or

（三）税号85.30的电气信号、安全或交通管理设备。

(c) Electrical signalling，safety of traffic control equipment of heading No.85.30.

二、税号86.07主要适用于：

2. Heading No.86.07applies，*inter alia*，to:

（一）轴、轮、行走机构、金属轮箍、轮圈、毂及轮子的其他零件；

(a) Axles，wheels，wheel sets (running gear)，metal tyres，hoops and hubs and other parts of wheels;

（二）车架、底架、转向架；

(b) Frames，underframes，bogies and bissel-bogies;

（三）轴箱；制动装置；

(c) Axle boxes; brake gear;

（四）车辆缓冲器；钩或其他联结器及车厢走廊联结装置；

（五）车身。

三、除上述注释一另有规定的以外，税号86.08包括：

（一）已装配的轨道、转车台、站台缓冲器、量载规；

（二）铁道及电车道、道路、内河航道、停车场、港口或机场用的臂板信号机、机械信号盘、平交道口控制器、信号及道岔控制器及其他机械（包括电动机械）信号、安全或交通管理设备，不论是否装有电力照明装置。

(d) Buffers for rolling-stock ; hooks and other coupling gear and corridor connections;

(e) Coachwork.

3. Subject to the provisions of Note 1 above, heading No. 86.08 applies, *inter alia*, to:

(a) Assembled track, turntables, platform buffers, loading gauges;

(b) Semaphores, mechanical signal discs, level crossing control gear, signal and point controls, and other mechanical (including electro-mechanical) signalling, safety or traffic control equipment, whether or not fitted with electric lighting, for railways, tramways, roads, inland waterways, parking facilities, port installations or airfields.

序号 No.	税则号列 Tariff Line	货品名称	最惠国税率 MFN(%)	协定税率 Agreement(%)		特惠税率 S.P.(%)		普通税率 Gen.(%)	Article Description
	86.01	**铁道电力机车，由外部电力或蓄电池驱动：**							**Rail locomotives powered from an external source of electricity or by electric accumulators:**
		-由外部电力驱动:							-Powered from an external source of electricity:
		---直流电机驱动的:							---Drived by DC motors:
7376	8601.1011	----微型机控制的	3	0	东盟ASEAN,智利CL,巴基斯坦PK,新西兰NZ,秘鲁PE,哥斯达黎加CR	0	最不发达35国LDC35,最不发达4国LDC4	11	----Controlled by micro-processings
7377	8601.1019	----其他	3	0	东盟ASEAN,智利CL,巴基斯坦PK,新西兰NZ,秘鲁PE,哥斯达黎加CR	0	最不发达35国LDC35,最不发达4国LDC4	11	----Other
7378	8601.1020	---交流电机驱动的	3	0	东盟ASEAN,智利CL,巴基斯坦PK,新西兰NZ,秘鲁PE,哥斯达黎加CR	0	最不发达35国LDC35,最不发达4国LDC4	11	---Drived by AC motors
7379	8601.1090	---其他	3	0	东盟ASEAN,智利CL,巴基斯坦PK,新西兰NZ,秘鲁PE,哥斯达黎加CR	0	最不发达35国LDC35,最不发达4国LDC4	11	---Other

序号 No.	税则号列 Tariff Line	货品名称	最惠国税率 MFN(%)	协定税率 Agreement(%)		特惠税率 S.P.(%)		普通税率 Gen.(%)	Article Description
7380	8601.2000	-由蓄电池驱动	3	0	东盟ASEAN,智利CL,巴基斯坦PK,新西兰NZ,秘鲁PE,哥斯达黎加CR	0	最不发达35国LDC35,最不发达4国LDC4	11	-Powered by electric accumulators
	86.02	**其他铁道机车;机车煤水车:**							**Other rail locomotives; locomotive tenders:**
		-柴油电力机车:							-Diesel-electric locomotives:
7381	8602.1010	---微型机控制的	3	0	东盟ASEAN,智利CL,巴基斯坦PK,新西兰NZ,秘鲁PE,哥斯达黎加CR	0	最不发达35国LDC35,最不发达4国LDC4	11	---Controled by micro-processings
7382	8602.1090	---其他	3	0	东盟ASEAN,智利CL,巴基斯坦PK,新西兰NZ,秘鲁PE,哥斯达黎加CR	0	最不发达35国LDC35,最不发达4国LDC4	11	---Other
7383	8602.9000	---其他	3	0	东盟ASEAN,智利CL,巴基斯坦PK,新西兰NZ,秘鲁PE,哥斯达黎加CR	0	最不发达35国LDC35,最不发达4国LDC4	11	-Other
	86.03	**铁道及电车道用的机动客车、货车、敞车，但税号86.04的货品除外:**							**Self-propelled railway or tramway coaches, vans and trucks, other than those of heading No.86.04:**
7384	8603.1000	-由外部电力驱动	3	0	东盟ASEAN,智利CL,巴基斯坦PK,新西兰NZ,秘鲁PE,哥斯达黎加CR	0	最不发达35国LDC35,最不发达4国LDC4	11	-Powered from an external source of electricity:
7385	8603.9000	-其他	3	0	东盟ASEAN,智利CL,巴基斯坦PK,新西兰NZ,秘鲁PE,哥斯达黎加CR	0	最不发达35国LDC35,最不发达4国LDC4	11	-Other
	86.04	**铁道及电车道用的维修或服务车，不论是否机动（例如，工场车、起重机车、道碴捣固车、轨道校正车、检验车及查道车）:**							**Railway or tramway maintenance or service vehicles, whether or not self-propelled (for example, workshops, cranes, ballast tampers, trackliners, testing coaches and track inspection vehicles):**

序号 No.	税则号列 Tariff Line	货品名称	最惠国税率 MFN(%)	协定税率 Agreement(%)		特惠税率 S.P.(%)		普通税率 Gen.(%)	Article Description
		---检验车及查道车:							---Testing coaches and track inspection vehicles
7386	8604.0011	----隧道限界检查车	3	0	东盟ASEAN,智利CL,巴基斯坦PK,新西兰NZ,秘鲁PE,哥斯达黎加CR	0	最不发达35国LDC35,最不发达4国LDC4	14	----Inspection vehicles for tunnel learance
7387	8604.0012	----钢轨在线打磨列车	3	0	东盟ASEAN,智利CL,巴基斯坦PK,新西兰NZ,秘鲁PE,哥斯达黎加CR	0	最不发达35国LDC35,最不发达4国LDC4	14	----Sanding vehicles for on-line rails
7388	8604.0019	----其他	5	0 0.5	东盟ASEAN,巴基斯坦PK,新西兰NZ,秘鲁PE,哥斯达黎加CR 智利CL	0	最不发达35国LDC35,最不发达4国LDC4	14	----Other
		---其他:							---Other:
7389	8604.0091	----电气化接触网架线机（轨行式）	5	0 0.5	东盟ASEAN,巴基斯坦PK,新西兰NZ,秘鲁PE,哥斯达黎加CR 智利CL	0	最不发达35国LDC35,最不发达4国LDC4	20	----Installing vehicles for suspension of contact wire (running on rails)
7390	8604.0099	----其他	7	0 0.7 5	东盟ASEAN,新西兰NZ,秘鲁PE,哥斯达黎加CR 智利CL 巴基斯坦PK	0	最不发达35国LDC35,最不发达4国LDC4	20	----Other
	86.05	**铁道及电车道用的非机动客车;行李车、邮政车和其他铁道及电车道用的非机动特殊用途车辆(税号86.04的货品除外):**							**Railway or tramway passenger coaches, not self-propelled; luggage vans, post office coaches and other special purpose railway or tramway coaches, not self-propelled (excluding those of heading No.86.04):**
7391	8605.0010	---铁道客车	5	0	东盟ASEAN,智利CL,巴基斯坦PK,新西兰NZ,秘鲁PE,哥斯达黎加CR	0	最不发达35国LDC35,最不发达4国LDC4	14	---Railway passenger coaches
7392	8605.0090	---其他	5	0	东盟ASEAN,智利CL,巴基斯坦PK,新西兰NZ,秘鲁PE,哥斯达黎加CR	0	最不发达35国LDC35,最不发达4国LDC4	14	---Other

序号 No.	税则号列 Tariff Line	货品名称	最惠国 税　率 MFN(%)	协定税率 Agreement(%)		特惠税率 S.P.(%)		普通 税率 Gen.(%)	Article Description
	86.06	**铁道及电车道用的非机动有篷及无篷货车:**							**Railway or tramway goods vans and wagons, not self-propelled:**
7393	8606.1000	-油罐货车及类似车	5	0	东盟ASEAN,智利CL,巴基斯坦PK,新西兰NZ,秘鲁PE,哥斯达黎加CR	0	最不发达35国LDC35,最不发达4国LDC4	14	-Tank wagons and the like
7394	8606.3000	-自卸货车，但子目号8606.1000或8606.2000的货品除外	5	0	东盟ASEAN,智利CL,巴基斯坦PK,新西兰NZ,秘鲁PE,哥斯达黎加CR	0	最不发达35国LDC35,最不发达4国LDC4	14	-Self-discharging vans and wagons, other than those of subheading No. 8606.1000 or 8606.2000
		-其他:							-Other:
7395	8606.9100	--带篷及封闭的	5	0	东盟ASEAN,智利CL,巴基斯坦PK,新西兰NZ,秘鲁PE,哥斯达黎加CR	0	最不发达35国LDC35,最不发达4国LDC4	14	--Covered and closed
7396	8606.9200	--敞篷的，厢壁固定且高度超过60厘米	5	0	东盟ASEAN,智利CL,巴基斯坦PK,新西兰NZ,秘鲁PE,哥斯达黎加CR	0	最不发达35国LDC35,最不发达4国LDC4	14	--Open, with non-removable sides of a height exceeding 60cm
7397	8606.9900	--其他	5	0	东盟ASEAN,智利CL,巴基斯坦PK,新西兰NZ,秘鲁PE,哥斯达黎加CR	0	最不发达35国LDC35,最不发达4国LDC4	14	--Other
	86.07	**铁道及电车道机车或其他车辆的零件:**							**Parts of railway or tramway locomotives or rolling-stock:**
		-转向架、轴、轮及其零件:							-Bogies, bissel-bogies, axles and wheels, and parts thereof:
7398	8607.1100	--驾驶转向架	3	0	东盟ASEAN,智利CL,巴基斯坦PK,新西兰NZ,秘鲁PE,哥斯达黎加CR	0	最不发达35国LDC35,最不发达4国LDC4	11	--Driving bogies and bissel-bogies
7399	8607.1200	--其他转向架	3	0	东盟ASEAN,智利CL,巴基斯坦PK,新西兰NZ,秘鲁PE,哥斯达黎加CR	0	最不发达35国LDC35,最不发达4国LDC4	11	--Other bogies and bissel-bogies
		--其他，包括零件:							--Other, including parts:

序号 No.	税则号列 Tariff Line	货品名称	最惠国税率 MFN(%)	协定税率 Agreement(%)		特惠税率 S.P.(%)		普通税率 Gen.(%)	Article Description
7400	8607.1910	---轴	3	0	东盟ASEAN,智利CL,巴基斯坦PK,新西兰NZ,秘鲁PE,哥斯达黎加CR	0	最不发达35国LDC35,最不发达4国LDC4	11	---Axles
7401	8607.1990	---其他	3	0	东盟ASEAN,智利CL,巴基斯坦PK,新西兰NZ,秘鲁PE,哥斯达黎加CR	0	最不发达35国LDC35,最不发达4国LDC4	11	---Other
		-制动装置及其零件:							-Brakes and parts thereof:
7402	8607.2100	--空气制动器及其零件	3	0	东盟ASEAN,智利CL,巴基斯坦PK,新西兰NZ,秘鲁PE,哥斯达黎加CR	0	最不发达35国LDC35,最不发达4国LDC4	11	--Air brakes and parts thereof
7403	8607.2900	--其他	3	0	东盟ASEAN,智利CL,巴基斯坦PK,新西兰NZ,秘鲁PE,哥斯达黎加CR	0	最不发达35国LDC35,最不发达4国LDC4	11	--Other
7404	8607.3000	-钩、其他联结器、缓冲器及其零件	3	0	东盟ASEAN,智利CL,巴基斯坦PK,新西兰NZ,秘鲁PE,哥斯达黎加CR	0	最不发达35国LDC35,最不发达4国LDC4	11	-Hooks and other coupling devices, buffers, and parts thereof
		-其他:							-Other:
7405	8607.9100	--机车用	3	0	东盟ASEAN,智利CL,巴基斯坦PK,新西兰NZ,秘鲁PE,哥斯达黎加CR	0	最不发达35国LDC35,最不发达4国LDC4	11	--Of locomotives
7406	8607.9900	--其他	3	0	东盟ASEAN,智利CL,巴基斯坦PK,新西兰NZ,秘鲁PE,哥斯达黎加CR	0	最不发达35国LDC35,最不发达4国LDC4	11	--Other
	86.08	**铁道及电车道轨道固定装置及附件;供铁道、电车道、道路、内河航道、停车场、港口或机场用的机械（包括电动机械）信号、安全或交通管理设备;上述货品的零件:**							**Railway or tramway track fixtures and fittings; mechanical (including electro-mechanical) signalling, safety or traffic control equipment for railways, tramways, roads, inland waterways, parking facilities, port installations or airfields; parts of the foregoing:**

序号 No.	税则号列 Tariff Line	货品名称	最惠国税率 MFN(%)	协定税率 Agreement(%)		特惠税率 S.P.(%)		普通税率 Gen.(%)	Article Description
7407	8608.0010	---轨道自动计轴设备	3	0	东盟ASEAN,智利CL,巴基斯坦PK,新西兰NZ,秘鲁PE,哥斯达黎加CR	0	最不发达35国LDC35,最不发达4国LDC4	20	---Rail automatic axle counting equipments
7408	8608.0090	---其他	4	0	东盟ASEAN,智利CL,巴基斯坦PK,新西兰NZ,秘鲁PE,哥斯达黎加CR	0	最不发达35国LDC35,最不发达4国LDC4	20	---Other
	86.09	**集装箱（包括运输液体的集装箱），经特殊设计、装备适用于各种运输方式:**							**Containers (including containers for the transport of fluids) specially designed and equipped for carriage by one or more modes of transport:**
		---20 英尺的:							---Of 20 feet:
7409	8609.0011	----保温式	10.5	0 1.1 2.1 5	东盟ASEAN,新加坡SG,新西兰NZ,秘鲁PE 智利CL 哥斯达黎加CR 巴基斯坦PK	0	最不发达35国LDC35,最不发达4国LDC4	35	----Thermal
7410	8609.0012	----罐式	10.5	0 1.1 2.1 5	东盟ASEAN,新加坡SG,新西兰NZ,秘鲁PE 智利CL 哥斯达黎加CR 巴基斯坦PK	0	最不发达35国LDC35,最不发达4国LDC4	35	----Tank
7411	8609.0019	----其他	10.5	0 1.1 2.1 5	东盟ASEAN,新加坡SG,新西兰NZ,秘鲁PE 智利CL 哥斯达黎加CR 巴基斯坦PK	0	最不发达35国LDC35,最不发达4国LDC4	35	----Other
		---40 英尺的:							---Of 40 feet:
7412	8609.0021	----保温式	10.5	0 1.1 2.1 5	东盟ASEAN,新加坡SG,新西兰NZ,秘鲁PE 智利CL 哥斯达黎加CR 巴基斯坦PK	0	最不发达35国LDC35,最不发达4国LDC4	35	----Thermal
7413	8609.0022	----罐式	10.5	0 1.1 2.1 5	东盟ASEAN,新加坡SG,新西兰NZ,秘鲁PE 智利CL 哥斯达黎加CR 巴基斯坦PK	0	最不发达35国LDC35,最不发达4国LDC4	35	----Tank

序号 No.	税则号列 Tariff Line	货品名称	最惠国税率 MFN(%)	协定税率 Agreement(%)		特惠税率 S.P.(%)		普通税率 Gen.(%)	Article Description
7414	8609.0029	----其他	10.5	0 1.1 2.1 5	东盟ASEAN,新加坡SG,新西兰NZ,秘鲁PE 智利CL 哥斯达黎加CR 巴基斯坦PK	0	最不发达35国LDC35,最不发达4国LDC4	35	----Other
7415	8609.0030	---45、48、53英尺的	10.5	0 1.1 2.1 5	东盟ASEAN,新加坡SG,新西兰NZ,秘鲁PE 智利CL 哥斯达黎加CR 巴基斯坦PK	0	最不发达35国LDC35,最不发达4国LDC4	35	---Of 45, 48, 53 feet
7416	8609.0090	---其他	10.5	0 1.1 2.1 5	东盟ASEAN,新加坡SG,新西兰NZ,秘鲁PE 智利CL 哥斯达黎加CR 巴基斯坦PK	0	最不发达35国LDC35,最不发达4国LDC4	35	---Other

第八十七章 车辆及其零件、附件，但铁道及电车道车辆除外

Chapter 87 Vehicles other than railway or tramway rolling-stock，and parts and accessories thereof

注释:

一、本章不包括仅可在钢轨上运行的铁道及电车道车辆。

二、本章所称“牵引车、拖拉机”，是指主要为牵引或推动其他车辆、器具或重物的车辆。除了上述主要用途以外，不论其是否还具有装运工具、种子、肥料或其他货品的辅助装置。

用于安装在税号 87.01 的牵引车或拖拉机上，作为可替换设备的机器或作业工具，即使与牵引车或拖拉机一同进口或出口，不论其是否已安装在车（机）上，仍应归入其各自相应的税号。

三、装有驾驶室的机动车辆底盘，应归入税号 87.02 至 87.04，而不归入税号 87.06。

四、税号 87.12 包括所有儿童两轮车，其他儿童脚踏车归入税号 95.03。

Notes:

1. This Chapter does not cover railway or tramway rolling-stock designed solely for running on rails.

2. For the purposes of this Chapter，“tractors” means vehicles constructed essentially for hauling or pushing another vehicle，appliance or load，whether or not they contain subsidiary provision for the transport，in connection with the main use of the tractor，of tools，seeds，fertilizers or other goods.

Machines and working tools designed for fitting to tractors of heading No.87.01as interchangeable equipment remain classified in their respective headings even if presented with the tractor，and whether or not mounted on it.

3. Motor chassis fitted with cabs fall in headings Nos.87.02 to 87.04，and not in heading No.87.06.

4. Heading No.87.12 includes all children’s bicycles. Other children’s cycles fall in heading No.95.03.

序号 No.	税则号列 Tariff Line	货品名称	最惠国税率 MFN(%)	协定税率 Agreement(%)		特惠税率 S.P.(%)		普通税率 Gen.(%)	Article Description
	87.01	**牵引车、拖拉机（税号 87.09 的牵引车除外）：**							**Tractors (other than tractors of heading No.87.09):**
7417	8701.1000	-手扶拖拉机	9	0	东盟ASEAN,智利CL,新西兰NZ,秘鲁PE,哥斯达黎加CR	0	最不发达35国 LDC35	20	-Pedestrian controlled tractors
				5	巴基斯坦PK				
7418	8701.2000	-半挂车用的公路牵引车	6	0	智利CL,新西兰NZ,哥斯达黎加CR			20	-Road tractors for semi-trailers
7419	8701.3000	-履带式牵引车、拖拉机	6	0	东盟ASEAN,智利CL,新西兰NZ,秘鲁PE,哥斯达黎加CR	0	最不发达35国 LDC35	20	-Track-laying tractors
				5	巴基斯坦PK				
		-其他:							-Other:
		---拖拉机:							---Tractors:
7420	8701.9011	----轮式	8	0	东盟ASEAN,智利CL,新西兰NZ,秘鲁PE,哥斯达黎加CR	0	最不发达35国 LDC35	20	----Wheeled
				5	巴基斯坦PK				

序号 No.	税则号列 Tariff Line	货品名称	最惠国税率 MFN(%)	协定税率 Agreement(%)		特惠税率 S.P.(%)		普通税率 Gen.(%)	Article Description
	ex87019011	功率大于150马力的轮式拖拉机	△5						Wheeled tractors with power more than 150H.P.
7421	8701.9019	----其他	8	0	东盟ASEAN,智利CL,新西兰NZ,秘鲁PE,哥斯达黎加CR	0	最不发达35国LDC35	20	----Other
				5	巴基斯坦PK				
	ex87019019	功率大于150马力的其他拖拉机	△5						Other tractors with power more than 150H.P.
7422	8701.9090	---其他	8	0	东盟ASEAN,智利CL,新西兰NZ,秘鲁PE,哥斯达黎加CR	0	最不发达35国LDC35	20	---Other
				5	巴基斯坦PK				
	87.02	**客运机动车辆，10座及以上（包括驾驶座）：**							**Motor vehicles for the transport of ten or more persons, including the driver:**
		-装有压燃式活塞内燃发动机（柴油或半柴油发动机）的车辆:							-With compression-ignition internal combustion piston engine (diesel or semi-diesel):
7423	8702.1020	---机坪客车	4	0	东盟ASEAN,智利CL,巴基斯坦PK,新西兰NZ,秘鲁PE,哥斯达黎加CR	0	最不发达35国LDC35	90	---Buses for transport passengers at airport
		---其他:							---Other:
7424	8702.1091	----30座及以上（大型客车）	25	0	智利CL,新西兰NZ			90	----With 30 seats or more
				5	哥斯达黎加CR				
7425	8702.1092	----20座及以上，但不超过29座	25	0	智利CL,新西兰NZ			230	----With 20 seats or more, but not exceeding 29 seats
				5	哥斯达黎加CR				
7426	8702.1093	----10座及以上，但不超过19座	25	0	智利CL,新西兰NZ			230	----With 10 seats or more, but not exceeding 19 seats
				5	哥斯达黎加CR				
		-其他:							-Other:
7427	8702.9010	---30座及以上（大型客车）	25	0	智利CL,新西兰NZ			90	---With 30 seats or more
				5	哥斯达黎加CR				
				20	东盟ASEAN				
7428	8702.9020	---20座及以上，但不超过29座	25	0	智利CL,新西兰NZ			230	---With 20 seats or more, but not exceeding 29 seats
				5	哥斯达黎加CR				
				20	东盟ASEAN				
7429	8702.9030	---10座及以上，但不超过19座	25	0	智利CL,新西兰NZ	0	最不发达35国LDC35	230	---With 10 seats or more, but not exceeding 19 seats
				5	哥斯达黎加CR				
				12.5	秘鲁PE				
				20	东盟ASEAN				
	87.03	**主要用于载人的机动车辆（税号87.02的货品除外），包括旅行小客车及赛车:**							**Motor cars and other motor vehicles principally designed for the transport of persons (other than those of heading No.87.02), including station wagons and racing cars:**

序号 No.	税则号列 Tariff Line	货品名称	最惠国税率 MFN(%)	协定税率 Agreement(%)		特惠税率 S.P.(%)		普通税率 Gen.(%)	Article Description
		-雪地行走专用车;高尔夫球车及类似车辆:							-Vehicles specially designed for travelling on snow; golf cars and similar vehicles:
		---高尔夫球车及类似车辆:							---Golf cars and similar vehicles:
7430	8703.1011	----全地形车	25	0 5 12.5	东盟ASEAN,智利CL,新加坡SG,新西兰NZ 哥斯达黎加CR 秘鲁PE	0	最不发达 35 国 LDC35	150	----All Terrain Vehicles
7431	8703.1019	----其他	25	0 5 12.5	东盟ASEAN,智利CL,新加坡SG,新西兰NZ 哥斯达黎加CR 秘鲁PE	0	最不发达 35 国 LDC35	150	----Other
7432	8703.1090	---其他	25	0 5 12.5	东盟ASEAN,智利CL,新加坡SG,新西兰NZ 哥斯达黎加CR 秘鲁PE	0	最不发达 35 国 LDC35	150	---Other
		-装有点燃往复式活塞内燃发动机的其他车辆:							-Other vehicles, with spark-ignition internal combustion reciprocating piston engine:
		--气缸容量(排气量)不超过 1000 毫升:							--Of a cylinder capacity not exceeding 1000 cc:
7433	8703.2130	---小轿车	25	0 5 22.5	智利CL,新西兰NZ 哥斯达黎加CR 亚太APTA,巴基斯坦PK			230	---Saloon cars
7434	8703.2140	---越野车(4 轮驱动)	25	0 5 22.5	智利CL,新西兰NZ 哥斯达黎加CR 亚太APTA,巴基斯坦PK			230	---Cross-country Cars (4WD)
7435	8703.2150	---9 座及以下的小客车	25	0 5 22.5	智利CL,新西兰NZ 哥斯达黎加CR 亚太APTA,巴基斯坦PK			230	---Station Wagons (with 9 seats or less)
7436	8703.2190	---其他	25	0 5 22.5	智利CL,新西兰NZ 哥斯达黎加CR 亚太APTA,巴基斯坦PK			230	---Other
		--气缸容量(排气量)超过 1000 毫升,但不超过 1500 毫升:							--Of a cylinder capacity exceeding 1000cc but not exceeding 1500 cc:
7437	8703.2230	---小轿车	25	0 5 22.5	智利CL,新西兰NZ 哥斯达黎加CR 亚太APTA,巴基斯坦PK			230	---Saloon cars
7438	8703.2240	---越野车(4 轮驱动)	25	0 5 22.5	智利CL,新西兰NZ 哥斯达黎加CR 亚太APTA,巴基斯坦PK			230	---Cross-country cars (4WD)
7439	8703.2250	---9 座及以下的小客车	25	0 5 22.5	智利CL,新西兰NZ 哥斯达黎加CR 亚太APTA,巴基斯坦PK			230	---Station wagons (with 9 seats or less)
7440	8703.2290	---其他	25	0 5 22.5	智利CL,新西兰NZ 哥斯达黎加CR 亚太APTA,巴基斯坦PK			230	---Other

序号 No.	税则号列 Tariff Line	货品名称	最惠国税率 MFN(%)	协定税率 Agreement(%)		特惠税率 S.P.(%)	普通税率 Gen.(%)	Article Description
		---气缸容量（排气量）超过1500毫升，但不超过2000毫升:						---Of a cylinder capacity exceeding 1500cc but not exceeding 2000cc:
7441	8703.2341	----小轿车	25	0 5 22.5	智利CL,新西兰NZ 哥斯达黎加CR 亚太APTA,巴基斯坦PK		230	----Saloon Cars
7442	8703.2342	----越野车（4轮驱动）	25	0 5 22.5	智利CL,新西兰NZ 哥斯达黎加CR 亚太APTA,巴基斯坦PK		230	----Cross-country Cars (4WD)
7443	8703.2343	----9座及以下的小客车	25	0 5 22.5	智利CL,新西兰NZ 哥斯达黎加CR 亚太APTA,巴基斯坦PK		230	----Station Wagons (with 9 seats or less)
7444	8703.2349	----其他	25	0 5 22.5	智利CL,新西兰NZ 哥斯达黎加CR 亚太APTA,巴基斯坦PK		230	----Other
		---气缸容量（排气量）超过2000毫升，但不超过2500毫升:						---Of a cylinder capacity exceeding 2000cc but not exceeding 2500cc:
7445	8703.2351	----小轿车	25	0 5 22.5	智利CL,新西兰NZ 哥斯达黎加CR 亚太APTA,巴基斯坦PK		230	----Saloon Cars
7446	8703.2352	----越野车（4轮驱动）	25	0 5 22.5	智利CL,新西兰NZ 哥斯达黎加CR 亚太APTA,巴基斯坦PK		230	----Cross-country Cars (4WD)
7447	8703.2353	----9座及以下的小客车	25	0 5 22.5	智利CL,新西兰NZ 哥斯达黎加CR 亚太APTA,巴基斯坦PK		230	----Station Wagons (with 9 seats or less)
7448	8703.2359	----其他	25	0 5 22.5	智利CL,新西兰NZ 哥斯达黎加CR 亚太APTA,巴基斯坦PK		230	----Other
		---气缸容量（排气量）超过2500毫升，但不超过3000毫升:						---Of a cylinder capacity exceeding 2500cc but not exceeding 3000cc:
7449	8703.2361	----小轿车	25	0 5 22.5	智利CL,新西兰NZ 哥斯达黎加CR 亚太APTA,巴基斯坦PK		270	----Saloon Cars
7450	8703.2362	----越野车（4轮驱动）	25	0 5 22.5	东盟ASEAN,智利CL, 新加坡SG,新西兰NZ 哥斯达黎加CR 亚太APTA,巴基斯坦PK		270	----Cross-country Cars (4WD)
7451	8703.2363	----9座及以下的小客车	25	0 5 22.5	东盟ASEAN,智利CL, 新加坡SG,新西兰NZ 哥斯达黎加CR 亚太APTA,巴基斯坦PK		270	----Station Wagons (with 9 seats or less)
7452	8703.2369	----其他	25	0 5 22.5	东盟ASEAN,智利CL, 新加坡SG,新西兰NZ 哥斯达黎加CR 亚太APTA,巴基斯坦PK		270	----Other

序号 No.	税则号列 Tariff Line	货品名称	最惠国税率 MFN(%)	协定税率 Agreement(%)		特惠税率 S.P.(%)		普通税率 Gen.(%)	Article Description
		---气缸容量（排气量）超过3000毫升，但不超过4000毫升:							---Of a cylinder capacity exceeding 3000cc but not exceeding 4000cc:
7453	8703.2411	----小轿车	25	0 5 22.5	智利CL,新西兰NZ 哥斯达黎加CR 亚太APTA,巴基斯坦PK			270	----Saloon cars
7454	8703.2412	----越野车（4轮驱动）	25	0 5 22.5	智利CL,新西兰NZ 哥斯达黎加CR 亚太APTA,巴基斯坦PK			270	----Cross-country cars (4WD)
7455	8703.2413	----9座及以下的小客车	25	0 5 22.5	智利CL,新西兰NZ 哥斯达黎加CR 亚太APTA,巴基斯坦PK			270	----Station wagons (with 9 seats or less)
7456	8703.2419	----其他	25	0 5 22.5	智利CL,新西兰NZ 哥斯达黎加CR 亚太APTA,巴基斯坦PK			270	----Other
		---气缸容量（排气量）超过4000毫升:							---Of a cylinder capacity exceeding 4000cc:
7457	8703.2421	----小轿车	25	0 5 22.5	智利CL,新西兰NZ 哥斯达黎加CR 亚太APTA,巴基斯坦PK			270	----Saloon Cars
7458	8703.2422	----越野车（4轮驱动）	25	0 5 22.5	智利CL,新西兰NZ 哥斯达黎加CR 亚太APTA,巴基斯坦PK			270	----Cross-country Cars(4WD)
7459	8703.2423	----9座及以下的小客车	25	0 5 22.5	智利CL,新西兰NZ 哥斯达黎加CR 亚太APTA,巴基斯坦PK			270	----Station Wagons (with 9 seats or less)
7460	8703.2429	----其他	25	0 5 22.5	智利CL,新西兰NZ 哥斯达黎加CR 亚太APTA,巴基斯坦PK			270	----Other
		-装有压燃式活塞内燃发动机（柴油或半柴油发动机）的其他车辆:							-Other vehicles, with compression-ignition internal combustion piston engine (diesel or semi-diesel):
		---气缸容量（排气量）不超过1000毫升:							---Of a cylinder capacity not exceeding 1000cc:
7461	8703.3111	----小轿车	25	0 5	智利CL,新西兰NZ 哥斯达黎加CR			230	----Saloon cars
7462	8703.3119	----其他	25	0 5 12.5	东盟ASEAN,智利CL,新加坡SG,新西兰NZ 哥斯达黎加CR 秘鲁PE	0	最不发达35国LDC35	230	----Cross-country cars (4WD)
		---气缸容量（排气量）超过1000毫升，但不超过1500毫升:							---Of a cylinder capacity exceeding 1000cc but not exceeding 1500cc:
7463	8703.3121	----小轿车	25	0 5	智利CL,新西兰NZ 哥斯达黎加CR			230	----Saloon cars
7464	8703.3122	----越野车（4轮驱动）	25	0 5	智利CL,新西兰NZ 哥斯达黎加CR			230	----Cross-country cars (4WD)

序号 No.	税则号列 Tariff Line	货品名称	最惠国税率 MFN(%)	协定税率 Agreement(%)	特惠税率 S.P.(%)	普通税率 Gen.(%)	Article Description
7465	8703.3123	----9座及以下的小客车	25	0 智利CL,新西兰NZ 5 哥斯达黎加CR		230	----Station wagons (with 9 seats or less)
7466	8703.3129	----其他	25	0 东盟ASEAN,智利CL,新加坡SG,新西兰NZ 5 哥斯达黎加CR 12.5 秘鲁PE	0 最不发达35国LDC35	230	----Other
		---气缸容量（排气量）超过1500毫升，但不超过2000毫升:					---Of a cylinder capacity exceeding 1500cc but not exceeding 2000cc:
7467	8703.3211	----小轿车	25	0 智利CL,新西兰NZ 5 哥斯达黎加CR 22.5 亚太APTA,巴基斯坦PK		230	----Saloon Cars
7468	8703.3212	----越野车（4轮驱动）	25	0 智利CL,新西兰NZ 5 哥斯达黎加CR 22.5 亚太APTA,巴基斯坦PK		230	----Cross-country Cars (4WD)
7469	8703.3213	----9座及以下的小客车	25	0 智利CL,新西兰NZ 5 哥斯达黎加CR 22.5 亚太APTA,巴基斯坦PK		230	----Station Wagons (with 9 seats or less)
7470	8703.3219	----其他	25	0 智利CL,新西兰NZ 5 哥斯达黎加CR 22.5 亚太APTA,巴基斯坦PK		230	----Other
		---气缸容量（排气量）超过2000毫升，但不超过2500毫升:					---Of a cylinder capacity exceeding 2000cc but not exceeding 2500cc:
7471	8703.3221	----小轿车	25	0 智利CL,新西兰NZ 5 哥斯达黎加CR 22.5 亚太APTA,巴基斯坦PK		230	----Saloon Cars
7472	8703.3222	----越野车（4轮驱动）	25	0 智利CL,新西兰NZ 5 哥斯达黎加CR 22.5 亚太APTA,巴基斯坦PK		230	----Cross-country Cars (4WD)
7473	8703.3223	----9座及以下的小客车	25	0 智利CL,新西兰NZ 5 哥斯达黎加CR 22.5 亚太APTA,巴基斯坦PK		230	----Station Wagons (with 9 seats or less)
7474	8703.3229	----其他	25	0 智利CL,新西兰NZ 5 哥斯达黎加CR 22.5 亚太APTA,巴基斯坦PK		230	----Other
		---气缸容量（排气量）超过2500毫升，但不超过3000毫升:					---Of a cylinder capacity exceeding 2500cc but not exceeding 3000cc:
7475	8703.3311	----小轿车	25	0 东盟ASEAN,智利CL,新加坡SG,新西兰NZ 5 哥斯达黎加CR 22.5 亚太APTA,巴基斯坦PK		270	----Saloon Cars
7476	8703.3312	----越野车（4轮驱动）	25	0 东盟ASEAN,智利CL,新加坡SG,新西兰NZ 5 哥斯达黎加CR 22.5 亚太APTA,巴基斯坦PK		270	----Cross-country Cars (4WD)
7477	8703.3313	----9座及以下的小客车	25	0 东盟ASEAN,智利CL,新加坡SG,新西兰NZ		270	----Station Wagons (with 9 seats or less)

序号 No.	税则号列 Tariff Line	货品名称	最惠国税率 MFN(%)	协定税率 Agreement(%)		特惠税率 S.P.(%)		普通税率 Gen.(%)	Article Description
				5	哥斯达黎加CR				
				22.5	亚太APTA,巴基斯坦PK				
7478	8703.3319	----其他	25	0	东盟ASEAN,智利CL,新加坡SG,新西兰NZ			270	----Other
				5	哥斯达黎加CR				
				22.5	亚太APTA,巴基斯坦PK				
		---气缸容量（排气量）超过3000毫升，但不超过4000毫升:							---Of a cylinder capacity exceeding 3000cc but not exceeding 4000cc:
7479	8703.3321	----小轿车	25	0	东盟ASEAN,智利CL,新加坡SG,新西兰NZ			270	----Saloon Cars
				5	哥斯达黎加CR				
				22.5	亚太APTA,巴基斯坦PK				
7480	8703.3322	----越野车（4轮驱动）	25	0	东盟ASEAN,智利CL,新加坡SG,新西兰NZ			270	----Cross-country Cars (4WD)
				5	哥斯达黎加CR				
				22.5	亚太APTA,巴基斯坦PK				
7481	8703.3323	----9座及以下的小客车	25	0	东盟ASEAN,智利CL,新加坡SG,新西兰NZ			270	----Station Wagons (with 9 seats or less)
				5	哥斯达黎加CR				
				22.5	亚太APTA,巴基斯坦PK				
7482	8703.3329	----其他	25	0	东盟ASEAN,智利CL,新加坡SG,新西兰NZ			270	----Other
				5	哥斯达黎加CR				
				22.5	亚太APTA,巴基斯坦PK				
		---气缸容量（排气量）超过4000毫升:							---Of a cylinder capacity exceeding 4000cc:
7483	8703.3361	----小轿车	25	0	东盟ASEAN,智利CL,新加坡SG,新西兰NZ			270	----Saloon Cars
				5	哥斯达黎加CR				
				22.5	亚太APTA,巴基斯坦PK				
7484	8703.3362	----越野车（4轮驱动）	25	0	东盟ASEAN,智利CL,新加坡SG,新西兰NZ			270	----Cross-country Cars (4WD)
				5	哥斯达黎加CR				
				22.5	亚太APTA,巴基斯坦PK				
7485	8703.3363	----9座及以下的小客车	25	0	东盟ASEAN,智利CL,新加坡SG,新西兰NZ			270	----Station Wagons (with 9 seats or less)
				5	哥斯达黎加CR				
				22.5	亚太APTA,巴基斯坦PK				
7486	8703.3369	----其他	25	0	东盟ASEAN,智利CL,新加坡SG,新西兰NZ			270	----Other
				5	哥斯达黎加CR				
				22.5	亚太APTA,巴基斯坦PK				
7487	8703.9000	-其他	25	0	东盟ASEAN,智利CL,新加坡SG,新西兰NZ	0	最不发达35国LDC35	270	-Other
				5	哥斯达黎加CR				
				12.5	秘鲁PE				
				22.5	亚太APTA,巴基斯坦PK				
	87.04	**货运机动车辆:**							**Motor vehicles for the transport of goods:**
		-非公路用自卸车:							-Dumpers designed for off-highway use:

序号 No.	税则号列 Tariff Line	货品名称	最惠国税率 MFN(%)	协定税率 Agreement(%)		特惠税率 S.P.(%)		普通税率 Gen.(%)	Article Description
7488	8704.1030	---电动轮货运自卸车	6	0 5	东盟ASEAN,智利CL,新西兰NZ,秘鲁PE,哥斯达黎加CR 巴基斯坦PK	0	最不发达35国LDC35,最不发达4国LDC4	20	---Electric-wheel dumpers for the transport of goods
7489	8704.1090	---其他	6	0 5	东盟ASEAN,智利CL,新西兰NZ,秘鲁PE,哥斯达黎加CR 巴基斯坦PK	0	最不发达35国LDC35,最不发达4国LDC4	20	---Other
		-装有压燃式活塞内燃发动机（柴油或半柴油发动机）的其他货车:							-Other, with compression-ignition internal combustion piston engine (diesel or semi-diesel):
7490	8704.2100	--车辆总重量不超过5吨	25	0 5	智利CL,新西兰NZ 哥斯达黎加CR			70	--G.V.W. not exceeding 5 tons
		--车辆总重量超过5吨,但不超过20吨:							--G.V.W. exceeding 5 tons but not exceeding 20 tons:
7491	8704.2230	---车辆总重量超过5吨，但小于14吨	20	0 4 10 18	智利CL,新西兰NZ 哥斯达黎加CR 秘鲁PE 亚太APTA,巴基斯坦PK	0	最不发达35国LDC35	70	---G.V.W. exceeding 5 tons but not exceeding 14 tons
7492	8704.2240	---车辆总重量在14吨及以上，但不超过20吨	20	0 4 10 18	智利CL,新西兰NZ 哥斯达黎加CR 秘鲁PE 亚太APTA,巴基斯坦PK	0	最不发达35国LDC35	40	---G.V.W. of 14 tons or more but not exceeding 20 tons
7493	8704.2300	--车辆总重量超过20吨	15	0 3	智利CL,新西兰NZ 哥斯达黎加CR			40	--G.V.W. exceeding 20 tons
	ex87042300	装有驾驶室的固井水泥车、压裂车、混砂车用底盘 （车辆总重量超过35吨）	△10						Chassis (incoraporating cabs) of cementing unit trucks, fractruring unit trucks and mixing sand trucks (G.V.W exceeding 35t)
	ex87042300	起重55吨及以上的汽车起重机用底盘	△8						Chassis (incoraporating cabs) of crane lorries, eifting capacity≥55t
	ex87042300	车辆总重量≥31吨清障车专用底盘	△10						Special chassis for the wrecker of G.V.W≥31t
		-装有点燃式活塞内燃发动机的其他货车:							-Other, with spark-ignition internal combustion piston engine:
7494	8704.3100	--车辆总重量不超过5吨	25	0 2.5 5 20	新西兰NZ 智利CL 哥斯达黎加CR 东盟ASEAN			70	--G.V.W. not exceeding 5 tons
		--车辆总重量超过5吨:							--G.V.W. exceeding 5 tons:

序号 No.	税则号列 Tariff Line	货品名称	最惠国税率 MFN(%)	协定税率 Agreement(%)		特惠税率 S.P.(%)		普通税率 Gen.(%)	Article Description
7495	8704.3230	---车辆总重量超过5吨，但不超过8吨	20	0 4 10	智利CL,新西兰NZ 哥斯达黎加CR 秘鲁PE	0	最不发达35国LDC35	70	---G.V.W. exceeding 5 tons, but not exceeding 8 tons.
7496	8704.3240	---车辆总重量超过8吨	20	0 4 10	智利CL,新西兰NZ 哥斯达黎加CR 秘鲁PE	0	最不发达35国LDC35	70	---G.V.W. exceeding 8 tons
7497	8704.9000	-其他	25	0 5 12.5	东盟ASEAN,智利CL,新加坡SG,新西兰NZ 哥斯达黎加CR 秘鲁PE	0	最不发达35国LDC35	70	-Other
	87.05	**特殊用途的机动车辆（例如，抢修车、起重车、救火车、混凝土搅拌车、道路清洁车、喷洒车、流动工场车及流动放射线检查车），但主要用于载人或运货的车辆除外：**							**Special purpose motor vehicles, other than those principally designed for the transport of persons or goods(for example, breakdown lorries, crane lorries, fire fighting vehicles, concrete-mixer lorries, road sweeper lorries, spraying lorries, mobile workshops, mobile radiological units):**
		-起重车:							-Crane lorries:
		---全路面起重车:							---All-road crane lorries:
7498	8705.1021	----最大起重重量不超过50吨	15	0 3 7.5 12	东盟ASEAN,智利CL,新加坡SG,新西兰NZ 哥斯达黎加CR 秘鲁PE 巴基斯坦PK	0	最不发达35国LDC35	30	----Of maximum hoisting capacity not more than 50 tons
7499	8705.1022	----最大起重重量超过50吨，但不超过100吨	10	0 5	东盟ASEAN,智利CL,新加坡SG,新西兰NZ,秘鲁PE,哥斯达黎加CR 巴基斯坦PK	0	最不发达35国LDC35,最不发达4国LDC4	30	----Of a maximum hoisting capacity exceeding 50 tons but not exceeding 100 tons
7500	8705.1023	----最大起重重量超过100吨	10	0 5	东盟ASEAN,智利CL,新加坡SG,新西兰NZ,秘鲁PE,哥斯达黎加CR 巴基斯坦PK	0	最不发达35国LDC35,最不发达4国LDC4	30	----Of a maximum hoisting capacity exceeding 100 tons
		---其他:							---Other:
7501	8705.1091	----最大起重重量不超过50吨	15	0 3 7.5 12	东盟ASEAN,智利CL,新加坡SG,新西兰NZ 哥斯达黎加CR 秘鲁PE 巴基斯坦PK	0	最不发达35国LDC35	30	----Of maximum hoisting capacity not more than 50 tons
7502	8705.1092	----最大起重重量超过50吨，但不超过100吨	10	0 5	东盟ASEAN,智利CL,新加坡SG,新西兰NZ,秘鲁PE,哥斯达黎加CR 巴基斯坦PK	0	最不发达35国LDC35,最不发达4国LDC4	30	----Of a maximum hoisting capacity exceeding 50 tons but not exceeding 100 tons

序号 No.	税则号列 Tariff Line	货品名称	最惠国税率 MFN(%)	协定税率 Agreement(%)		特惠税率 S.P.(%)		普通税率 Gen.(%)	Article Description
7503	8705.1093	----最大起重重量超过100吨	10	0 5	东盟ASEAN,智利CL,新加坡SG,新西兰NZ,秘鲁PE,哥斯达黎加CR 巴基斯坦PK	0	最不发达35国LDC35,最不发达4国LDC4	30	----Of a maximum hoisting capacity exceeding 100 tons
7504	8705.2000	-钻探车	12	0 2.4 6	东盟ASEAN,智利CL,新加坡SG,新西兰NZ,秘鲁PE 哥斯达黎加CR 巴基斯坦PK	0	最不发达35国LDC35,最不发达4国LDC4	17	-Mobile drilling derricks
		-救火车:							-Fire fighting vehicles:
7505	8705.3010	---装有云梯的救火车	3	0	东盟ASEAN,智利CL,巴基斯坦PK,新西兰NZ,秘鲁PE,哥斯达黎加CR	0	最不发达35国LDC35,最不发达4国LDC4	8	---Mounted with scaling ladder
7506	8705.3090	---其他	3	0	东盟ASEAN,智利CL,巴基斯坦PK,新西兰NZ,秘鲁PE,哥斯达黎加CR	0	最不发达35国LDC35,最不发达4国LDC4	8	---Other
7507	8705.4000	-混凝土搅拌车	15	0 3 7.5 13.5	东盟ASEAN,智利CL,新加坡SG,新西兰NZ 哥斯达黎加CR 巴基斯坦PK,秘鲁PE 亚太APTA	0	最不发达35国LDC35	35	-Concrete-mixer lorries
		-其他:							-Other:
7508	8705.9010	---无线电通信车	9	0 5 8.1	东盟ASEAN,智利CL,新加坡SG,新西兰NZ,秘鲁PE,哥斯达黎加CR 巴基斯坦PK 亚太APTA	0	最不发达35国LDC35,最不发达4国LDC4	35	---Radio communication vans
7509	8705.9020	---放射线检查车	9	0 5 8.1	东盟ASEAN,智利CL,新西兰NZ,秘鲁PE,哥斯达黎加CR 巴基斯坦PK 亚太APTA	0	最不发达35国LDC35,最不发达4国LDC4	14	---Mobile radiological units
7510	8705.9030	---环境监测车	12	0 2.4 5 10.8	东盟ASEAN,智利CL,新加坡SG,新西兰NZ,秘鲁PE 哥斯达黎加CR 巴基斯坦PK 亚太APTA	0	最不发达35国LDC35	20	---Mobile environmental monitoring units
7511	8705.9040	---医疗车	12	0 2.4 5 10.8	东盟ASEAN,智利CL,新加坡SG,新西兰NZ,秘鲁PE 哥斯达黎加CR 巴基斯坦PK 亚太APTA	0	最不发达35国LDC35	30	---Mobile clinics

序号 No.	税则号列 Tariff Line	货品名称	最惠国税率 MFN(%)	协定税率 Agreement(%)		特惠税率 S.P.(%)		普通税率 Gen.(%)	Article Description
		---电源车:							---Mobile electric generator sets:
7512	8705.9051	----航空电源车（频率为 400 赫兹）	12	0 2.4 5 10.8	东盟ASEAN,智利CL,新加坡SG,新西兰NZ,秘鲁PE 哥斯达黎加CR 巴基斯坦PK 亚太APTA	0	最不发达 35 国 LDC35	30	----Airplane charging vehicles (frequency 400 Hz)
7513	8705.9059	----其他	12	0 2.4 5 10.8	东盟ASEAN,智利CL,新加坡SG,新西兰NZ,秘鲁PE 哥斯达黎加CR 巴基斯坦PK 亚太APTA	0	最不发达 35 国 LDC35	30	----Other
7514	8705.9060	---飞机加油车、调温车、除冰车	12	0 2.4 5 10.8	东盟ASEAN,智利CL,新加坡SG,新西兰NZ,秘鲁PE 哥斯达黎加CR 巴基斯坦PK 亚太APTA	0	最不发达 35 国 LDC35	35	---Mobile vehicles for aircraft refuelling, air-conditioning or de-icing
7515	8705.9070	---道路（包括跑道）扫雪车	12	0 2.4 5 10.8	东盟ASEAN,智利CL,新加坡SG,新西兰NZ,秘鲁PE 哥斯达黎加CR 巴基斯坦PK 亚太APTA	0	最不发达 35 国 LDC35	35	---Snow sweepers vehicles for cleansing streets or airfield runways
7516	8705.9080	---石油测井车、压裂车、混沙车	12	0 2.4 5 10.8	东盟ASEAN,智利CL,新加坡SG,新西兰NZ,秘鲁PE 哥斯达黎加CR 巴基斯坦PK 亚太APTA	0	最不发达 35 国 LDC35	35	---Petroleum well logging trucks, fracturing unit trucks and mixing sand trucks
		---其他:							---Other:
7517	8705.9091	----混凝土泵车	12	0 2.4 5 10.8	东盟ASEAN,智利CL,新加坡SG,新西兰NZ,秘鲁PE 哥斯达黎加CR 巴基斯坦PK 亚太APTA	0	最不发达 35 国 LDC35	35	----Concrete pump truck
7518	8705.9099	----其他	12	0 2.4 5 10.8	东盟ASEAN,智利CL,新加坡SG,新西兰NZ,秘鲁PE 哥斯达黎加CR 巴基斯坦PK 亚太APTA	0	最不发达 35 国 LDC35	35	----Other
	ex87059099	跑道除冰车	△10						Runway deicing trucks
	87.06	**装有发动机的机动车辆底盘，税号 87.01 至 87.05 所列车辆用:**							**Chassis fitted with engines, for the motor vehicles of headings Nos. 87.01 to 87.05:**
7519	8706.0010	---非公路用自卸车底盘	8	0 5	东盟ASEAN,智利CL,新西兰NZ,秘鲁PE,哥斯达黎加CR 巴基斯坦PK	0	最不发达 35 国 LDC35	14	---For the vehicles of subheading No. 8704.1030 or 8704.1090

序号 No.	税则号列 Tariff Line	货品名称	最惠国税率 MFN(%)	协定税率 Agreement(%)	特惠税率 S.P.(%)	普通税率 Gen.(%)	Article Description
		---货车底盘:					---For the vehicles of subheading Nos. 8704.2100 to 8704.9000:
7520	8706.0021	----车辆总重量在14吨及以上的	10	0 智利CL,新西兰NZ,哥斯达黎加CR		30	----For vehicles G.V.W of 14 tons or more
7521	8706.0022	----车辆总重量在14吨以下的	10	0 智利CL,新西兰NZ,秘鲁PE,哥斯达黎加CR	0 最不发达35国LDC35	45	----For vehicles G.V.W less than 14 tons
7522	8706.0030	---大型客车底盘	20	0 东盟ASEAN,智利CL,新加坡SG,新西兰NZ 4 哥斯达黎加CR		70	---For passenger motor vehicles with 30 seats or more
7523	8706.0040	---汽车起重机底盘	20	0 东盟ASEAN,智利CL,新加坡SG,新西兰NZ 4 哥斯达黎加CR 10 秘鲁PE	0 最不发达35国LDC35	100	---For crane trucks
7524	8706.0090	---其他	10	0 东盟ASEAN,智利CL,新加坡SG,新西兰NZ,秘鲁PE,哥斯达黎加CR	0 最不发达35国LDC35	100	---Other
	87.07	**机动车辆的车身（包括驾驶室），税号87.01至87.05所列车辆用:**					**Bodies (including cabs), for the motor vehicles of headings Nos.87.01 to 87.05:**
7525	8707.1000	-税号87.03所列车辆用	10	0 东盟ASEAN,智利CL,新加坡SG,新西兰NZ,秘鲁PE,哥斯达黎加CR	0 最不发达35国LDC35	100	-For the vehicles of heading No.87.03
		-其他:					-Other:
7526	8707.9010	---税号8702.1092、8702.1093、8702.9020及8702.9030所列车辆用	10	0 东盟ASEAN,智利CL,新加坡SG,新西兰NZ,秘鲁PE,哥斯达黎加CR 5 巴基斯坦PK 9 亚太APTA	0 最不发达35国LDC35	70	---For the vehicles of subheading No.8702.1092、8702.1093、8702.9020 or 8702.9030
7527	8707.9090	---其他	10	0 东盟ASEAN,智利CL,新加坡SG,新西兰NZ,秘鲁PE,哥斯达黎加CR 5 巴基斯坦PK 9 亚太APTA	0 最不发达35国LDC35	70	---Other
	87.08	**机动车辆的零件、附件，税号87.01至87.05所列车辆用:**					**Parts and accessories of the motor vehicles of headings Nos. 87.01 to 87.05:**
7528	8708.1000	-缓冲器（保险杠）及其零件	10	0 东盟ASEAN,智利CL,新加坡SG,新西兰NZ,秘鲁PE,哥斯达黎加CR,台湾TW 5 巴基斯坦PK 9.6 亚太APTA	0 最不发达35国LDC35,最不发达4国LDC4	100	-Bumpers and parts thereof
		-车身（包括驾驶室）的其他零件、附件:					-Other parts and accessories of bodies (including cabs):
7529	8708.2100	--座椅安全带	10	0 东盟ASEAN,智利CL,新加坡SG,新西兰NZ,秘鲁PE,哥斯达黎加CR,澳门MO 5 巴基斯坦PK	0 最不发达35国LDC35,最不发达4国LDC4	100	--Safety seat belts

序号 No.	税则号列 Tariff Line	货品名称	最惠国税率 MFN(%)	协定税率 Agreement(%)		特惠税率 S.P.(%)		普通税率 Gen.(%)	Article Description
		--其他:							--Other:
7530	8708.2930	---车窗玻璃升降器	10	0 9	智利CL,新西兰NZ,秘鲁PE,哥斯达黎加CR,香港HK,台湾TW 亚太APTA,巴基斯坦PK	0	最不发达35国LDC35,最不发达4国LDC4	100	---Windowpane raiser
		---天窗:							---Sunroofs:
7531	8708.2941	----电动的	10	0 5 9	东盟ASEAN,智利CL,新加坡SG,新西兰NZ,秘鲁PE,哥斯达黎加CR,香港HK,台湾TW 巴基斯坦PK 亚太APTA	0	最不发达35国LDC35,最不发达4国LDC4	100	----Electric
7532	8708.2942	----手动的	10	0 5 9	东盟ASEAN,智利CL,新加坡SG,新西兰NZ,秘鲁PE,哥斯达黎加CR,香港HK,台湾TW 巴基斯坦PK 亚太APTA	0	最不发达35国LDC35,最不发达4国LDC4	100	----Manual
		---其他车身覆盖件:							---Other body Coverings:
7533	8708.2951	----侧围	10	0 5 9	东盟ASEAN,智利CL,新加坡SG,新西兰NZ,秘鲁PE,哥斯达黎加CR,台湾TW 巴基斯坦PK 亚太APTA	0	最不发达35国LDC35,最不发达4国LDC4	100	----Side panels
7534	8708.2952	----车门	10	0 5 9	东盟ASEAN,智利CL,新加坡SG,新西兰NZ,秘鲁PE,哥斯达黎加CR,台湾TW 巴基斯坦PK 亚太APTA	0	最不发达35国LDC35,最不发达4国LDC4	100	----Car doors
7535	8708.2953	----发动机罩盖	10	0 5 9	东盟ASEAN,智利CL,新加坡SG,新西兰NZ,秘鲁PE,哥斯达黎加CR,台湾TW 巴基斯坦PK 亚太APTA	0	最不发达35国LDC35,最不发达4国LDC4	100	----Engine hood
7536	8708.2954	----前围	10	0 5 9	东盟ASEAN,智利CL,新加坡SG,新西兰NZ,秘鲁PE,哥斯达黎加CR,台湾TW 巴基斯坦PK 亚太APTA	0	最不发达35国LDC35,最不发达4国LDC4	100	----Front wall
7537	8708.2955	----行李箱盖（或背门）	10	0 5 9	东盟ASEAN,智利CL,新加坡SG,新西兰NZ,秘鲁PE,哥斯达黎加CR,台湾TW 巴基斯坦PK 亚太APTA	0	最不发达35国LDC35,最不发达4国LDC4	100	----Baggage compartment lids (or back door)

序号 No.	税则号列 Tariff Line	货品名称	最惠国税率 MFN(%)	协定税率 Agreement(%)		特惠税率 S.P.(%)		普通税率 Gen.(%)	Article Description
7538	8708.2956	----后围	10	0 5 9	东盟ASEAN,智利CL,新加坡SG,新西兰NZ,秘鲁PE,哥斯达黎加CR,台湾TW 巴基斯坦PK 亚太APTA	0	最不发达35国LDC35,最不发达4国LDC4	100	----Rear wall
7539	8708.2957	----翼子板（或叶子板）	10	0 5 9	东盟ASEAN,智利CL,新加坡SG,新西兰NZ,秘鲁PE,哥斯达黎加CR,台湾TW 巴基斯坦PK 亚太APTA	0	最不发达35国LDC35,最不发达4国LDC4	100	----Fender
7540	8708.2959	----其他	10	0 5 9	东盟ASEAN,智利CL,新加坡SG,新西兰NZ,秘鲁PE,哥斯达黎加CR,台湾TW 巴基斯坦PK 亚太APTA	0	最不发达35国LDC35,最不发达4国LDC4	100	----Other
7541	8708.2990	---其他	10	0 5 9	东盟ASEAN,智利CL,新加坡SG,新西兰NZ,秘鲁PE,哥斯达黎加CR,台湾TW 巴基斯坦PK 亚太APTA	0	最不发达35国LDC35,最不发达4国LDC4	100	---Other
		-制动器、助力制动器及其零件:							-Brakes and servo-brakes and parts thereof:
7542	8708.3010	---装在蹄片上的制动摩擦片	10	0 5	东盟ASEAN,智利CL,新加坡SG,新西兰NZ,哥斯达黎加CR 巴基斯坦PK,秘鲁PE	0	最不发达35国LDC35,最不发达4国LDC4	100	---Mounted brake linings
		---防抱死制动系统:							---Anti-skid brake system:
7543	8708.3021	----子目号87.01、8704.1030及8704.1090所列车辆用	6	0 5.4	东盟ASEAN,智利CL,巴基斯坦PK,新西兰NZ,秘鲁PE,哥斯达黎加CR 亚太APTA	0	最不发达35国LDC35,最不发达4国LDC4	11	----Of the vehicles of subheading No.87.01, 8704.1030 or 8704.1090
7544	8708.3029	----其他	10	0 9	智利CL,新西兰NZ,秘鲁PE,哥斯达黎加CR 亚太APTA,巴基斯坦PK	0	最不发达35国LDC35,最不发达4国LDC4	100	----Other
		---其他:							---Other:
7545	8708.3091	----税号87.01所列车辆用	6	0 5.4	东盟ASEAN,智利CL,巴基斯坦PK,新西兰NZ,秘鲁PE,哥斯达黎加CR 亚太APTA	0	最不发达35国LDC35,最不发达4国LDC4	14	----Of the vehicles of heading No.87.01

序号 No.	税则号列 Tariff Line	货品名称	最惠国税率 MFN(%)	协定税率 Agreement(%)		特惠税率 S.P.(%)		普通税率 Gen.(%)	Article Description
7546	8708.3092	----子目号 8702.1091 及 8702.9010 所列车辆用	10	0 9	智利CL,新西兰NZ,秘鲁PE,哥斯达黎加CR 亚太APTA,巴基斯坦PK	0	最不发达 35 国 LDC35,最不发达 4 国 LDC4	70	----Of the vehicles of sub-heading No.8702.1091 or 8702.9010
7547	8708.3093	----子目号 8704.1030 及 8704.1090 所列车辆用	6	0 5.4	东盟ASEAN,智利CL,巴基斯坦PK,新西兰NZ,秘鲁PE,哥斯达黎加CR 亚太APTA	0	最不发达 35 国 LDC35,最不发达 4 国 LDC4	11	----Of the vehicles of sub-heading No.8704.1030 or 8704.1090
7548	8708.3094	----子目号 8704.2100、8704.2230、8704.3100 及 8704.3230 所列车辆用	10	0 9	智利CL,新西兰NZ,秘鲁PE,哥斯达黎加CR 亚太APTA,巴基斯坦PK	0	最不发达 35 国 LDC35,最不发达 4 国 LDC4	45	----Of the vehicles of sub-heading No.8704.2100, 8704.2230, 8704.3100 or 8704.3230
7549	8708.3095	----子目号 8704.2240、8704.2300 及 8704.3240 所列车辆用	10	0 5 9	东盟ASEAN,智利CL,新加坡SG,新西兰NZ,秘鲁PE,哥斯达黎加CR 巴基斯坦PK 亚太APTA	0	最不发达 35 国 LDC35,最不发达 4 国 LDC4	30	----Of the vehicles of sub-heading No.8704.2240, 8704.2300 or 8704.3240
7550	8708.3096	----税号 87.05 所列车辆用	10	0 5 9	东盟ASEAN,智利CL,新加坡SG,新西兰NZ,秘鲁PE,哥斯达黎加CR 巴基斯坦PK 亚太APTA	0	最不发达 35 国 LDC35,最不发达 4 国 LDC4	100	----Of the vehicles of heading No.87.05
7551	8708.3099	----其他:	10	0 9	智利CL,新西兰NZ,秘鲁PE,哥斯达黎加CR 亚太APTA,巴基斯坦PK	0	最不发达 35 国 LDC35,最不发达 4 国 LDC4	100	----Other:
		-变速箱及其零件:							-Gear boxes and parts thereof:
7552	8708.4010	---税号 87.01 所列车辆用	6	0 5	东盟ASEAN,智利CL,新西兰NZ,秘鲁PE,哥斯达黎加CR,台湾TW 巴基斯坦PK	0	最不发达 35 国 LDC35,最不发达 4 国 LDC4	14	---Of the vehicles of heading No.87.01
7553	8708.4020	---子目号 8702.1091 及 8702.9010 所列车辆用	10	0	智利CL,新西兰NZ,哥斯达黎加CR,台湾TW			70	---Of the vehicles of sub-heading No.8702.1091 or 8702.9010
7554	8708.4030	---子目号 8704.1030 及 8704.1090 所列车辆用	6	0 5	东盟ASEAN,智利CL,新西兰NZ,哥斯达黎加CR,台湾TW 巴基斯坦PK			11	---Of the vehicles of sub-heading No. 8704.1030 or 8704.1090
	ex87084030	扭矩>1500Nm非公路自卸车用变速箱	△3						Gear boxes of dumpers designed for off-highway use, torque＞1500Nm

序号 No.	税则号列 Tariff Line	货品名称	最惠国 税 率 MFN(%)	协定税率 Agreement(%)		特惠税率 S.P.(%)	普通 税率 Gen.(%)	Article Description
7555	8708.4040	---子目号8704.2100、8704.2230、8704.3100及8704.3230所列车辆用	10	0	智利CL,新西兰NZ,哥斯达黎加CR,台湾TW		45	---Of the vehicles of subheading No. 8704.2100, 8704.2230, 8704.3100 or 8704.3230
7556	8708.4050	---子目号8704.2240、8704.2300及8704.3240所列车辆用	10	0	智利CL,新西兰NZ,哥斯达黎加CR,台湾TW		30	---Of the vehicles of subheading No. 8704.2240, 8704.2300 or 8704.3240
7557	8708.4060	---税号87.05所列车辆用	10	0 5	东盟ASEAN,智利CL,新加坡SG,新西兰NZ,秘鲁PE,哥斯达黎加CR,台湾TW 巴基斯坦PK	0 最不发达35国LDC35,最不发达4国LDC4	100	---Of the vehicles of heading No.87.05
		---其他:						---Other:
7558	8708.4091	----小轿车用自动换档变速箱及其零件	10	0	智利CL,新西兰NZ,哥斯达黎加CR		100	----Automatic transmission for saloon cars and parts thereof
	ex87084091	小轿车用自动换档变速箱及其零件(6档及6档以上)	△6.5					Automatic transmission and parts thereof for saloon cars (6-speed and above)
7559	8708.4099	----其他	10	0	东盟ASEAN,智利CL,新加坡SG,新西兰NZ,哥斯达黎加CR,台湾TW		100	----Other
		-装有差速器的驱动桥及其零件,不论是否装有其他传动部件;非驱动桥及其零件:						-Drive-axles with differential, whether or not provided with other transmission components, and non-driving axles; parts thereof:
		---装有差速器的驱动桥及其零件,不论是否装有其他传动部件:						---Drive-axles with differential, whether or not provided with other transmission components, parts thereof:
7560	8708.5071	----税号87.01所列车辆用	6	0 5.4	东盟ASEAN,智利CL,巴基斯坦PK,新西兰NZ,秘鲁PE,哥斯达黎加CR 亚太APTA	0 最不发达35国LDC35,最不发达4国LDC4	14	----Of the vehicles of heading No.87.01
7561	8708.5072	----子目号8702.1091及8702.9010所列车辆用	10	0 9	智利CL,新西兰NZ,秘鲁PE,哥斯达黎加CR 亚太APTA,巴基斯坦PK	0 最不发达35国LDC35,最不发达4国LDC4	70	----Of the vehicles of subheading No. 8702.1091 or 8702.9010
	ex87085072	轴荷≥10t的中后驱动桥的零件	△8					Parts of middle and rear drive-axles, axle capacity≥10t

序号 No.	税则号列 Tariff Line	货品名称	最惠国税率 MFN(%)	协定税率 Agreement(%)		特惠税率 S.P.(%)		普通税率 Gen.(%)	Article Description
7562	8708.5073	----子目号 8704.1030 及 8704.1090 所列车辆用	6	0 5.4	东盟ASEAN,智利CL,巴基斯坦PK,新西兰NZ,秘鲁PE,哥斯达黎加CR 亚太APTA	0	最不发达35国LDC35,最不发达4国LDC4	11	----Of the vehicles of subheading No. 8704.1030 or 8704.1090
7563	8708.5074	----子目号 8704.2100、8704.2230、8704.3100 及 8704.3230 所列车辆用	10	0 9	智利CL,新西兰NZ,秘鲁PE,哥斯达黎加CR 亚太APTA,巴基斯坦PK	0	最不发达35国LDC35,最不发达4国LDC4	45	----Of the vehicles of subheading No. 8704.2100, 8704.2230, 8704.3100 or 8704.3230
7564	8708.5075	----子目号 8704.2240、8704.2300 及 8704.3240 所列车辆用	10	0 9	智利CL,新西兰NZ,秘鲁PE,哥斯达黎加CR 亚太APTA,巴基斯坦PK	0	最不发达35国LDC35,最不发达4国LDC4	30	----Of the vehicles of subheading No. 8704.2240, 8704.2300 or 8704.3240
7565	8708.5076	----税号 87.05 所列车辆用	10	0 5 9	东盟ASEAN,智利CL,新加坡SG,新西兰NZ,秘鲁PE,哥斯达黎加CR 巴基斯坦PK 亚太APTA	0	最不发达35国LDC35,最不发达4国LDC4	100	----Of the vehicles of heading No.87.05
7566	8708.5079	----其他	10	0 9	智利CL,新西兰NZ,秘鲁PE,哥斯达黎加CR 亚太APTA,巴基斯坦PK	0	最不发达35国LDC35,最不发达4国LDC4	100	----Other
		---非驱动的桥及其零件:							---Non-driving axles and parts thereof:
7567	8708.5081	----税号 87.01 所列车辆用	6	0 5	东盟ASEAN,智利CL,新西兰NZ,秘鲁PE,哥斯达黎加CR 巴基斯坦PK	0	最不发达35国LDC35,最不发达4国LDC4	14	----Of the vehicles of heading No.87.01
7568	8708.5082	----子目号 8702.1091 及 8702.9010 所列车辆用	15	0 3 7.5 9.7	东盟ASEAN,智利CL,新加坡SG,新西兰NZ 哥斯达黎加CR 秘鲁PE 巴基斯坦PK	0	最不发达35国LDC35	70	----Of the vehicles of subheading No. 8702.1091 or 8702.9010
7569	8708.5083	----子目号 8704.1030 及 8704.1090 所列车辆用	6	0 5	东盟ASEAN,智利CL,新西兰NZ,秘鲁PE,哥斯达黎加CR 巴基斯坦PK	0	最不发达35国LDC35,最不发达4国LDC4	11	----Of the vehicles of subheading No. 8704.1030 or 8704.1090
7570	8708.5084	----子目号 8704.2100、8704.2230、8704.3100 及 8704.3230 所列车辆用	10	0 5	东盟ASEAN,智利CL,新加坡SG,新西兰NZ,秘鲁PE,哥斯达黎加CR 巴基斯坦PK	0	最不发达35国LDC35,最不发达4国LDC4	45	----Of the vehicles of subheading No. 8704.2100, 8704.2230, 8704.3100 or 8704.3230

序号 No.	税则号列 Tariff Line	货品名称	最惠国税率 MFN(%)	协定税率 Agreement(%)		特惠税率 S.P.(%)		普通税率 Gen.(%)	Article Description
7571	8708.5085	----子目号8704.2240、8704.2300及8704.3240所列车辆用	10	0 5	东盟ASEAN,智利CL,新加坡SG,新西兰NZ,秘鲁PE,哥斯达黎加CR 巴基斯坦PK	0	最不发达35国LDC35,最不发达4国LDC4	30	----Of the vehicles of subheading No.8704.2240, 8704.2300 or 8704.3240
7572	8708.5086	----税号87.05所列车辆用	10	0 5	东盟ASEAN,智利CL,新加坡SG,新西兰NZ,秘鲁PE,哥斯达黎加CR 巴基斯坦PK	0	最不发达35国LDC35,最不发达4国LDC4	100	----Of the vehicles of heading No.87.05
7573	8708.5089	----其他	10	0 5	东盟ASEAN,智利CL,新加坡SG,新西兰NZ,秘鲁PE,哥斯达黎加CR 巴基斯坦PK	0	最不发达35国LDC35,最不发达4国LDC4	100	----Other
		-车轮及其零件、附件:							-Road wheels and parts and accessories thereof:
7574	8708.7010	---子目号87.01所列车辆用	6	0 5	东盟ASEAN,智利CL,新西兰NZ,秘鲁PE,哥斯达黎加CR,台湾TW 巴基斯坦PK	0	最不发达35国LDC35,最不发达4国LDC4	14	---Of the vehicles of heading No.87.01
7575	8708.7020	---子目号8702.1091及8702.9010所列车辆用	10	0 5	东盟ASEAN,智利CL,新加坡SG,新西兰NZ,秘鲁PE,哥斯达黎加CR,台湾TW 巴基斯坦PK	0	最不发达35国LDC35,最不发达4国LDC4	70	---Of the vehicles of subheading No.8702.1091 or 8702.9010
7576	8708.7030	---子目号8704.1030及8704.1090所列车辆用	6	0 5	东盟ASEAN,智利CL,新西兰NZ,秘鲁PE,哥斯达黎加CR,台湾TW 巴基斯坦PK	0	最不发达35国LDC35,最不发达4国LDC4	11	---Of the vehicles of subheading No.8704.1030 or 8704.1090
7577	8708.7040	---子目号8704.2100、8704.2230、8704.3100及8704.3230所列车辆用	10	0 5	东盟ASEAN,智利CL,新加坡SG,新西兰NZ,秘鲁PE,哥斯达黎加CR,台湾TW 巴基斯坦PK	0	最不发达35国LDC35,最不发达4国LDC4	45	---Of the vehicles of subheading No.8704.2100, 8704.2230, 8704.3100 or 8704.3230
7578	8708.7050	---子目号8704.2240、8704.2300及8704.3240所列车辆用	10	0 5	东盟ASEAN,智利CL,新加坡SG,新西兰NZ,秘鲁PE,哥斯达黎加CR,台湾TW 巴基斯坦PK	0	最不发达35国LDC35,最不发达4国LDC4	30	---Of the vehicles of subheading No.8704.2240, 8704.2300 or 8704.3240
7579	8708.7060	---税号87.05所列车辆用	10	0 5	东盟ASEAN,智利CL,新加坡SG,新西兰NZ,秘鲁PE,哥斯达黎加CR,台湾TW 巴基斯坦PK	0	最不发达35国LDC35,最不发达4国LDC4	100	---Of the vehicles of heading No.87.05

序号 No.	税则号列 Tariff Line	货品名称	最惠国 税 率 MFN(%)	协定税率 Agreement(%)		特惠税率 S.P.(%)		普通 税率 Gen.(%)	Article Description
		---其他:							---Other:
7580	8708.7091	----铝合金制的	10	0 5	东盟ASEAN,智利CL,新加坡SG,新西兰NZ,秘鲁PE,哥斯达黎加CR,台湾TW 巴基斯坦PK	0	最不发达35国LDC35,最不发达4国LDC4	100	----of Aluminium alloy
7581	8708.7099	----其他	10	0 5	东盟ASEAN,智利CL,新加坡SG,新西兰NZ,秘鲁PE,哥斯达黎加CR,台湾TW 巴基斯坦PK	0	最不发达35国LDC35,最不发达4国LDC4	100	----Other
		-悬挂系统及其零件（包括减震器）:							-Suspension systems and parts thereof (including shock-absorbers):
7582	8708.8010	---税号87.03所列车辆用	10	0 5 9	东盟ASEAN,智利CL,新加坡SG,新西兰NZ,秘鲁PE,哥斯达黎加CR 巴基斯坦PK 亚太APTA	0	最不发达35国LDC35,最不发达4国LDC4	100	---Of the vehicles of heading No.87.03
7583	8708.8090	---其他	10	0 5 9	东盟ASEAN,智利CL,新加坡SG,新西兰NZ,秘鲁PE,哥斯达黎加CR 巴基斯坦PK 亚太APTA	0	最不发达35国LDC35,最不发达4国LDC4	100	---Other
		-其他零件、附件:							-Other parts and accessories:
		--散热器及其零件:							--Radiators and parts thereof:
7584	8708.9110	---水箱散热器	10	0 5	东盟ASEAN,智利CL,新加坡SG,新西兰NZ,秘鲁PE,哥斯达黎加CR 巴基斯坦PK	0	最不发达35国LDC35,最不发达4国LDC4	100	---Radiator
7585	8708.9120	---机油冷却器	10	0 5	东盟ASEAN,智利CL,新加坡SG,新西兰NZ,秘鲁PE,哥斯达黎加CR 巴基斯坦PK	0	最不发达35国LDC35,最不发达4国LDC4	100	---Oil Coolor
7586	8708.9190	---其他	10	0 5	东盟ASEAN,智利CL,新加坡SG,新西兰NZ,秘鲁PE,哥斯达黎加CR 巴基斯坦PK	0	最不发达35国LDC35,最不发达4国LDC4	100	---Other
7587	8708.9200	--消声器（消音器）、排气管及其零件	10	0 5	东盟ASEAN,智利CL,新加坡SG,新西兰NZ,秘鲁PE,哥斯达黎加CR 巴基斯坦PK	0	最不发达35国LDC35,最不发达4国LDC4	100	--Silencers (mufflers) and exhaust pipes; parts thereof

序号 No.	税则号列 Tariff Line	货品名称	最惠国税率 MFN(%)	协定税率 Agreement(%)		特惠税率 S.P.(%)		普通税率 Gen.(%)	Article Description
		--离合器及其零件:							--Clutches and parts thereof:
7588	8708.9310	---税号 87.01 所列车辆用	6	0 5	东盟ASEAN,智利CL,新西兰NZ,秘鲁PE,哥斯达黎加CR 巴基斯坦PK	0	最不发达35国LDC35,最不发达4国LDC4	14	---Of the vehicles of heading No.87.01
7589	8708.9320	---子目号 8702.1091 及 8702.9010 所列车辆用	10	0 5	东盟ASEAN,智利CL,新加坡SG,新西兰NZ,秘鲁PE,哥斯达黎加CR 巴基斯坦PK	0	最不发达35国LDC35,最不发达4国LDC4	70	---Of the vehicles of sub-heading No. 8702.1091 or 8702.9010
7590	8708.9330	---子目号 8704.1030 及 8704.1090 所列车辆用	6	0 5	东盟ASEAN,智利CL,新西兰NZ,秘鲁PE,哥斯达黎加CR 巴基斯坦PK	0	最不发达35国LDC35,最不发达4国LDC4	11	---Of the vehicles of sub-heading No.8704.1030 or 8704.1090
7591	8708.9340	---子目号8704.2100、8704.2230、8704.3100 及 8704.3230 所列车辆用	10	0 5	东盟ASEAN,智利CL,新加坡SG,新西兰NZ,秘鲁PE,哥斯达黎加CR 巴基斯坦PK	0	最不发达35国LDC35,最不发达4国LDC4	45	---Of the vehicles of sub-heading No.8704.2100, 8704.2230, 8704.3100 or 8704.3230
7592	8708.9350	---子目号8704.2240、8704.2300 及 8704.3240 所列车辆用	10	0 5	东盟ASEAN,智利CL,新加坡SG,新西兰NZ,秘鲁PE,哥斯达黎加CR 巴基斯坦PK	0	最不发达35国LDC35,最不发达4国LDC4	30	---Of the vehicles of sub-heading No.8704.2240, 8704.2300 or 8704.3240
7593	8708.9360	---税号 87.05 所列车辆用	10	0 5	东盟ASEAN,智利CL,新加坡SG,新西兰NZ,秘鲁PE,哥斯达黎加CR 巴基斯坦PK	0	最不发达35国LDC35,最不发达4国LDC4	100	---Of the vehicles of heading No.87.05
7594	8708.9390	---其他	10	0 5	东盟ASEAN,智利CL,新加坡SG,新西兰NZ,秘鲁PE,哥斯达黎加CR 巴基斯坦PK	0	最不发达35国LDC35,最不发达4国LDC4	100	---Other
		--转向盘、转向柱及转向器及其零件:							--Steering wheels, steering columns and steering boxes; parts thereof:
7595	8708.9410	---税号 87.01 所列车辆用	6	0 5	东盟ASEAN,智利CL,新西兰NZ,秘鲁PE,哥斯达黎加CR 巴基斯坦PK	0	最不发达35国LDC35,最不发达4国LDC4	14	---Of the vehicles of heading No.87.01

序号 No.	税则号列 Tariff Line	货品名称	最惠国税率 MFN(%)	协定税率 Agreement(%)		特惠税率 S.P.(%)		普通税率 Gen.(%)	Article Description
7596	8708.9420	---子目号 8702.1091 及 8702.9010 所列车辆用	10	0 5	东盟ASEAN,智利CL,新加坡SG,新西兰NZ,秘鲁PE,哥斯达黎加CR 巴基斯坦PK	0	最不发达 35 国 LDC35,最不发达 4 国 LDC4	70	---Of the vehicles of sub-heading No.8702.1091 or 8702.9010
	ex87089420	30 座及以上客车用转向器的零件	△8						Parts of steering boxes of buses with 30 seats of more
7597	8708.9430	---子目号 8704.1030 及 8704.1090 所列车辆用	6	0 5	东盟ASEAN,智利CL,新西兰NZ,秘鲁PE,哥斯达黎加CR 巴基斯坦PK	0	最不发达 35 国 LDC35,最不发达 4 国 LDC4	11	---Of the vehicles of sub-heading No.8704.1030 or 8704.1090
7598	8708.9440	---子目号 8704.2100、8704.2230、8704.3100 及 8704.3230 所列车辆用	10	0 5	东盟ASEAN,智利CL,新加坡SG,新西兰NZ,秘鲁PE,哥斯达黎加CR 巴基斯坦PK	0	最不发达 35 国 LDC35,最不发达 4 国 LDC4	45	---Of the vehicles of sub-heading No.8704.2100, 8704.2230, 8704.3100 or 8704.3230
7599	8708.9450	---子目号 8704.2240、8704.2300 及 8704.3240 所列车辆用	10	0 5	东盟ASEAN,智利CL,新加坡SG,新西兰NZ,秘鲁PE,哥斯达黎加CR 巴基斯坦PK	0	最不发达 35 国 LDC35,最不发达 4 国 LDC4	30	---Of the vehicles of sub-heading No.8704.2240, 8704.2300 or 8704.3240
	ex87089450	总重≥14 吨柴油型货车转向器的零件	△8						Parts of steering boxes for diesel trucks of G.V.W≥14t
7600	8708.9460	---税号 87.05 所列车辆用	10	0 5	东盟ASEAN,智利CL,新加坡SG,新西兰NZ,秘鲁PE,哥斯达黎加CR 巴基斯坦PK	0	最不发达 35 国 LDC35,最不发达 4 国 LDC4	100	---Of the vehicles of heading No.87.05
7601	8708.9490	---其他	10	0 5	东盟ASEAN,智利CL,新加坡SG,新西兰NZ,秘鲁PE,哥斯达黎加CR 巴基斯坦PK	0	最不发达 35 国 LDC35,最不发达 4 国 LDC4	100	---Other
	ex87089490	采用电动转向系统的转向盘、转向柱及转向器及其零件	△8						Steering wheels, steering columns, steering gears with electric powder steering and their parts
7602	8708.9500	--带充气系统的安全气囊及其零件	10	0 9	智利CL,新西兰NZ,哥斯达黎加CR,香港HK 亚太APTA,巴基斯坦PK			100	---Safety airbags with inflater system; parts thereof
		--其他:							--Other:
7603	8708.9910	---税号 87.01 所列车辆用	6	0 5	东盟ASEAN,智利CL,新西兰NZ,秘鲁PE,哥斯达黎加CR 巴基斯坦PK	0	最不发达 35 国 LDC35,最不发达 4 国 LDC4	14	---Of the vehicles of heading No.87.01

序号 No.	税则号列 Tariff Line	货品名称	最惠国税率 MFN(%)	协定税率 Agreement(%)		特惠税率 S.P.(%)		普通税率 Gen.(%)	Article Description
		---子目号 8702.1091 及 8702.9010 所列车辆用:							---Of the vehicles of sub-heading No.8702.1091 or 8702.9010:
7604	8708.9921	----车架	25	0 5 12.5	东盟ASEAN,智利CL,新加坡SG,新西兰NZ 哥斯达黎加CR 秘鲁PE	0	最不发达 35 国 LDC35	70	----Frames
7605	8708.9929	----其他	25	0 5 12.5	东盟ASEAN,智利CL,新加坡SG,新西兰NZ 哥斯达黎加CR 秘鲁PE	0	最不发达 35 国 LDC35	70	----Other
		---子目号 8704.1030 及 8704.1090 所列车辆用:							---Of the vehicles of sub-heading No.8704.1030 or 8704.1090:
7606	8708.9931	----车架	6	0 5	东盟ASEAN,智利CL,新西兰NZ,秘鲁PE,哥斯达黎加CR 巴基斯坦PK	0	最不发达 35 国 LDC35,最不发达 4 国 LDC4	11	----Frames
7607	8708.9939	----其他	6 △3	0 5	东盟ASEAN,智利CL,新西兰NZ,秘鲁PE,哥斯达黎加CR 巴基斯坦PK	0	最不发达 35 国 LDC35,最不发达 4 国 LDC4	11	----Other
		---子目号 8704.2100、8704.2230、8704.3100 及 8704.3230 所列车辆用:							---Of the vehicles of sub-heading No.8704.2100, 8704.2230, 8704.3100 or 8704.3230:
7608	8708.9941	----车架	25	0 5 12.5	东盟ASEAN,智利CL,新加坡SG,新西兰NZ 哥斯达黎加CR 秘鲁PE	0	最不发达 35 国 LDC35	45	----Frames
7609	8708.9949	----其他	25	0 5 12.5	东盟ASEAN,智利CL,新加坡SG,新西兰NZ 哥斯达黎加CR 秘鲁PE	0	最不发达 35 国 LDC35	45	----Other
		---子目号 8704.2240、8704.2300 及 8704.3240 所列车辆用:							---Of the vehicles of sub-heading No. 8704.2240, 8704.2300 or 8704.3240:
7610	8708.9951	----车架	10	0 5	东盟ASEAN,智利CL,新加坡SG,新西兰NZ,秘鲁PE,哥斯达黎加CR 巴基斯坦PK	0	最不发达 35 国 LDC35,最不发达 4 国 LDC4	30	----Frames
7611	8708.9959	----其他	10	0 5	东盟ASEAN,智利CL,新加坡SG,新西兰NZ,秘鲁PE,哥斯达黎加CR 巴基斯坦PK	0	最不发达 35 国 LDC35,最不发达 4 国 LDC4	30	----Other

序号 No.	税则号列 Tariff Line	货品名称	最惠国税率 MFN(%)	协定税率 Agreement(%)		特惠税率 S.P.(%)		普通税率 Gen.(%)	Article Description
7612	8708.9960	---税号 87.05 所列车辆用	15	0 3 7.5 12	东盟ASEAN,智利CL,新加坡SG,新西兰NZ 哥斯达黎加CR 秘鲁PE 巴基斯坦PK	0	最不发达 35 国 LDC35	100	---Of the vehicles of heading No.87.05
		---其他:							---Other:
7613	8708.9991	----车架	10	0 5	东盟ASEAN,智利CL,新加坡SG,新西兰NZ,秘鲁PE,哥斯达黎加CR,台湾TW 巴基斯坦PK	0	最不发达 35 国 LDC35,最不发达 4 国 LDC4	100	----Frames
7614	8708.9992	----传动轴	10	0 5	东盟ASEAN,智利CL,新加坡SG,新西兰NZ,秘鲁PE,哥斯达黎加CR,台湾TW 巴基斯坦PK	0	最不发达 35 国 LDC35,最不发达 4 国 LDC4	100	---- driving shafts
7615	8708.9999	----其他	10	0 5	东盟ASEAN,智利CL,新加坡SG,新西兰NZ,秘鲁PE,哥斯达黎加CR,台湾TW 巴基斯坦PK	0	最不发达 35 国 LDC35,最不发达 4 国 LDC4	100	---Other
	ex87089999	混合动力汽车动力传动装置，由发电机、电动机和动力分配装置组成	△6						Hybird vehicle transimission unit, composed of generator, motor, power delivery unit
	87.09	**短距离运输货物的机动车辆，未装有提升或搬运设备，用于工厂、仓库、码头或机场;火车站台上用的牵引车;上述车辆的零件:**							**Works trucks, self-propelled, not fitted with lifting or handling equipment, of the type used in factories, warehouses, dock areas or airports for short istance transport of goods; tractors of the type used on railway station platforms; parts of the foregoing vehicles:**
		-车辆:							-Vehicles:
		--电动的:							--Electrical:
7616	8709.1110	---牵引车	10	0 5	东盟ASEAN,智利CL,新加坡SG,新西兰NZ,秘鲁PE,哥斯达黎加CR 巴基斯坦PK	0	最不发达 35 国 LDC35,最不发达 4 国 LDC4	30	---Tractors
7617	8709.1190	---其他	10	0 5	东盟ASEAN,智利CL,新加坡SG,新西兰NZ,秘鲁PE,哥斯达黎加CR 巴基斯坦PK	0	最不发达 35 国 LDC35,最不发达 4 国 LDC4	30	---Other

序号 No.	税则号列 Tariff Line	货品名称	最惠国税率 MFN(%)	协定税率 Agreement(%)		特惠税率 S.P.(%)		普通税率 Gen.(%)	Article Description
		--其他:							--Other:
7618	8709.1910	---牵引车	10.5	0 2.1 5	东盟ASEAN,智利CL,新加坡SG,新西兰NZ,秘鲁PE 哥斯达黎加CR 巴基斯坦PK	0	最不发达35国LDC35,最不发达4国LDC4	30	---Tractors
7619	8709.1990	---其他	10.5	0 2.1 5	东盟ASEAN,智利CL,新加坡SG,新西兰NZ,秘鲁PE 哥斯达黎加CR 巴基斯坦PK	0	最不发达35国LDC35,最不发达4国LDC4	30	---Other
7620	8709.9000	-零件	8.4	0 5	东盟ASEAN,智利CL,新西兰NZ,秘鲁PE,哥斯达黎加CR 巴基斯坦PK	0	最不发达35国LDC35,最不发达4国LDC4	17	-Parts
	87.10	**坦克及其他机动装甲战斗车辆,不论是否装有武器;上述车辆的零件:**							**Tanks and other armoured fighting vehicles, motorized, whether or not fitted with weapons, and parts of such vehicles:**
7621	8710.0010	---整车	15	0 3 7.5 12	东盟ASEAN,智利CL,新加坡SG,新西兰NZ 哥斯达黎加CR 秘鲁PE 巴基斯坦PK	0	最不发达35国LDC35	100	---Assembled
7622	8710.0090	---零件	15	0 3 7.5 12	东盟ASEAN,智利CL,新加坡SG,新西兰NZ 哥斯达黎加CR 秘鲁PE 巴基斯坦PK	0	最不发达35国LDC35	100	---Parts and accessories
	87.11	**摩托车(包括机器脚踏两用车)及装有辅助发动机的脚踏车,不论有无边车;边车:**							**Motorcycles (including mopeds) and cycles fitted with an auxiliary motor, with or without side-cars; side-cars:**
7623	8711.1000	-装有往复式活塞内燃发动机,气缸容量(排气量)不超过50毫升	45	0 9 22.5	东盟ASEAN,智利CL,新加坡SG,新西兰NZ 哥斯达黎加CR 秘鲁PE	0	最不发达35国LDC35	150	-With reciprocating internal combustion piston engine of a cylinder capacity not exceeding 50cc
		-装有往复式活塞内燃发动机,气缸容量(排气量)超过50毫升,但不超过250毫升:							-With reciprocating internal combustion piston engine of a cylinder capacity exceeding50cc but not exceeding 250cc:
7624	8711.2010	---气缸容量超过50毫升,但不超过100毫升	45	0 9 22.5	东盟ASEAN,智利CL,新加坡SG,新西兰NZ 哥斯达黎加CR 秘鲁PE	0	最不发达35国LDC35	150	---Of a cylinder capacity exceeding50cc but not exceeding 100cc

序号 No.	税则号列 Tariff Line	货品名称	最惠国税率 MFN(%)	协定税率 Agreement(%)		特惠税率 S.P.(%)		普通税率 Gen.(%)	Article Description
7625	8711.2020	---气缸容量超过 100 毫升，但不超过 125 毫升	45	0 9 22.5	东盟ASEAN,智利CL,新加坡SG,新西兰NZ 哥斯达黎加CR 秘鲁PE	0	最不发达 35 国 LDC35	150	---Of a cylinder capacity exceeding 100cc but not exceeding 125cc
7626	8711.2030	---气缸容量超过 125 毫升，但不超过 150 毫升	45	0 9 22.5	东盟ASEAN,智利CL,新加坡SG,新西兰NZ 哥斯达黎加CR 秘鲁PE	0	最不发达 35 国 LDC35	150	---Of a cylinder capacity exceeding 125cc but not exceeding 150cc
7627	8711.2040	---气缸容量超过 150 毫升，但不超过 200 毫升	45	0 9	东盟ASEAN,智利CL,新加坡SG,新西兰NZ 哥斯达黎加CR			150	---Of a cylinder capacity exceeding 150cc but not exceeding 200cc
7628	8711.2050	---气缸容量超过 200 毫升，但不超过 250 毫升	45	0 9	东盟ASEAN,智利CL,新加坡SG,新西兰NZ 哥斯达黎加CR			150	---Of a cylinder capacity exceeding 200cc but not exceeding 250cc
		-装有往复式活塞内燃发动机，气缸容量（排气量）超过 250 毫升，但不超过 500 毫升:							-With reciprocating internal combustion piston engine of a cylinder capacity exceeding 250cc but not exceeding 500cc:
7629	8711.3010	---气缸容量超过 250 毫升，但不超过 400 毫升	45	0 9 32.8	东盟ASEAN,智利CL,新加坡SG,新西兰NZ 哥斯达黎加CR 亚太APTA,巴基斯坦PK			150	---Of a cylinder capacity exceeding 250cc but not exceeding 400cc
7630	8711.3020	---气缸容量超过 400 毫升，但不超过 500 毫升	45	0 9 32.8	东盟ASEAN,智利CL,新加坡SG,新西兰NZ 哥斯达黎加CR 亚太APTA,巴基斯坦PK			150	---Of a cylinder capacity exceeding 400cc but not exceeding 500cc
7631	8711.4000	-装有往复式活塞内燃发动机，气缸容量（排气量）超过 500 毫升，但不超过 800 毫升	40	0 8	东盟ASEAN,智利CL,新加坡SG,新西兰NZ 哥斯达黎加CR			150	-With reciprocating internal combustion piston engine of a cylinder capacity exceeding 500cc but not exceeding 800cc
7632	8711.5000	-装有往复式活塞内燃发动机，气缸容量（排气量）超过 800 毫升	30	0 6	东盟ASEAN,智利CL,新加坡SG,新西兰NZ 哥斯达黎加CR			150	-With reciprocating internal combustion piston engine of a cylinder capacity exceeding 800cc
		-其他:							-Other:
7633	8711.9010	---电动及电动助力的	45	0 9	东盟ASEAN,智利CL,新加坡SG,新西兰NZ 哥斯达黎加CR			150	---Electric and electric auxiliary
7634	8711.9090	---其他	45	0 9	东盟ASEAN,智利CL,新加坡SG,新西兰NZ 哥斯达黎加CR			150	---Other
	87.12	**自行车及其他非机动脚踏车（包括运货三轮脚踏车）：**							**Bicycles and other cycles (including delivery tricycles), not motorized:**
7635	8712.0020	---竞赛型自行车	13	0 2.6 5 9.1	东盟ASEAN,智利CL,新加坡SG,新西兰NZ,秘鲁PE,台湾TW 哥斯达黎加CR 巴基斯坦PK 亚太APTA	0	最不发达 35 国 LDC35	130	---Racing bicycle

序号 No.	税则号列 Tariff Line	货品名称	最惠国税率 MFN(%)	协定税率 Agreement(%)		特惠税率 S.P.(%)		普通税率 Gen.(%)	Article Description
7636	8712.0030	---山地自行车	13	0 2.6 5 9.1	东盟ASEAN,智利CL,新加坡SG,新西兰NZ,秘鲁PE,台湾TW 哥斯达黎加CR 巴基斯坦PK 亚太APTA	0	最不发达35国LDC35	130	---Mountain bicycle
		---越野自行车:							---Cross-country bicycles:
7637	8712.0041	----16、18及20英寸	13	0 2.6 5 9.1	东盟ASEAN,智利CL,新加坡SG,新西兰NZ,秘鲁PE,台湾TW 哥斯达黎加CR 巴基斯坦PK 亚太APTA	0	最不发达35国LDC35,最不发达4国LDC4	130	----16″, 18″or 20″
7638	8712.0049	----其他	13	0 2.6 5 9.1	东盟ASEAN,智利CL,新加坡SG,新西兰NZ,秘鲁PE,台湾TW 哥斯达黎加CR 巴基斯坦PK 亚太APTA	0	最不发达35国LDC35	130	----Other
		---其他自行车:							---Other cycles:
7639	8712.0081	----16英寸及以下	13	0 2.6 5 9.1	东盟ASEAN,智利CL,新加坡SG,新西兰NZ,秘鲁PE,澳门MO,台湾TW 哥斯达黎加CR 巴基斯坦PK 亚太APTA	0	最不发达35国LDC35	130	----Not larger than16″
7640	8712.0089	----其他	13	0 2.6 5 9.1	东盟ASEAN,智利CL,新加坡SG,新西兰NZ,秘鲁PE,澳门MO,台湾TW 哥斯达黎加CR 巴基斯坦PK 亚太APTA	0	最不发达35国LDC35	130	----Other
7641	8712.0090	---其他	23	0 4.6 11.5 16.1	东盟ASEAN,智利CL,新加坡SG,新西兰NZ,澳门MO,台湾TW 哥斯达黎加CR 秘鲁PE 亚太APTA,巴基斯坦PK	0	最不发达35国LDC35	130	---Other
	87.13	**残疾人用车，不论是否机动或其他机械驱动:**							**Carriages for disabled persons, whether or not motorized or otherwise mechanically propelled:**
7642	8713.1000	-非机械驱动	6	0 5	东盟ASEAN,智利CL,新西兰NZ,秘鲁PE,哥斯达黎加CR 巴基斯坦PK	0	最不发达35国LDC35	20	-Not mechanically propelled
7643	8713.9000	-其他	4	0	东盟ASEAN,智利CL,巴基斯坦PK,新西兰NZ,秘鲁PE,哥斯达黎加CR	0	最不发达35国LDC35	20	-Other
	87.14	**零件、附件、税号87.11至87.13所列车辆用:**							**Parts and accessories of vehicles of headings Nos. 87.11 to 87.13:**

序号 No.	税则号列 Tariff Line	货品名称	最惠国税率 MFN(%)	协定税率 Agreement(%)		特惠税率 S.P.(%)		普通税率 Gen.(%)	Article Description
7644	8714.1000	-摩托车（包括机器脚踏两用车）用	30	0 6 15	东盟ASEAN,智利CL,新加坡SG,新西兰NZ 哥斯达黎加CR 秘鲁PE	0	最不发达35国LDC35	100	-Of motorcycles (including mopeds)
	ex87141000	星型轮及碟刹件	△10						Planetary gears and Plate brake
7645	8714.2000	-残疾人车辆用	5	0	东盟ASEAN,智利CL,巴基斯坦PK,新西兰NZ,秘鲁PE,哥斯达黎加CR	0	最不发达35国LDC35,最不发达4国LDC4	17	-Of carriages for disabled persons
		-其他:							-Other:
7646	8714.9100	--车架、轮叉及其零件	12	0 2.4 6	东盟ASEAN,智利CL,新加坡SG,新西兰NZ,秘鲁PE,台湾TW 哥斯达黎加CR 巴基斯坦PK	0	最不发达35国LDC35	80	--Frames and forks, and parts thereof
		--轮圈及辐条:							--Wheel rims and spokes:
7647	8714.9210	---轮圈	12	0 2.4 6	东盟ASEAN,智利CL,新加坡SG,新西兰NZ,秘鲁PE,台湾TW 哥斯达黎加CR 巴基斯坦PK	0	最不发达35国LDC35	80	---Wheel rims
7648	8714.9290	---辐条	12	0 2.4 6	东盟ASEAN,智利CL,新加坡SG,新西兰NZ,秘鲁PE,台湾TW 哥斯达黎加CR 巴基斯坦PK	0	最不发达35国LDC35	80	---Spokes
		--轮毂（倒轮制动毂及毂闸除外）;飞轮、链轮:							--Hubs, other than coaster braking hubs and hub brakes; and free-wheel, sprocket wheels
7649	8714.9310	---轮毂	12	0 2.4 6	东盟ASEAN,智利CL,新加坡SG,新西兰NZ,秘鲁PE,台湾TW 哥斯达黎加CR 巴基斯坦PK	0	最不发达35国LDC35	80	---Hubs
7650	8714.9320	---飞轮	12	0 2.4 6	东盟ASEAN,智利CL,新加坡SG,新西兰NZ,秘鲁PE,台湾TW 哥斯达黎加CR 巴基斯坦PK	0	最不发达35国LDC35	80	---Free wheel
7651	8714.9390	---其他	12	0 2.4 6	东盟ASEAN,智利CL,新加坡SG,新西兰NZ,秘鲁PE,台湾TW 哥斯达黎加CR 巴基斯坦PK	0	最不发达35国LDC35	80	---Other
7652	8714.9400	--制动器（包括倒轮制动毂及毂闸）及其零件	12	0 2.4 6	东盟ASEAN,智利CL,新加坡SG,新西兰NZ,秘鲁PE,台湾TW 哥斯达黎加CR 巴基斯坦PK	0	最不发达35国LDC35	80	--Brakes, including coaster braking hubs and hub brakes, and parts thereof

序号 No.	税则号列 Tariff Line	货品名称	最惠国 税　率 MFN(%)	协定税率 Agreement(%)		特惠税率 S.P.(%)		普通 税率 Gen.(%)	Article Description
7653	8714.9500	--鞍座	12	0 2.4 6	东盟ASEAN,智利CL,新加坡SG,新西兰NZ,秘鲁PE,台湾TW 哥斯达黎加CR 巴基斯坦PK	0	最不发达35国LDC35	80	--Saddles
		--脚蹬、曲柄链轮及其零件:							--Pedals and crank-gear, and parts thereof:
7654	8714.9610	---脚蹬及其零件	12	0 2.4 6	东盟ASEAN,智利CL,新加坡SG,新西兰NZ,秘鲁PE,台湾TW 哥斯达黎加CR 巴基斯坦PK	0	最不发达35国LDC35	80	---Pedals and parts thereof
7655	8714.9620	---曲柄链轮及其零件	12	0 2.4 6	东盟ASEAN,智利CL,新加坡SG,新西兰NZ,秘鲁PE,台湾TW 哥斯达黎加CR 巴基斯坦PK	0	最不发达35国LDC35	80	---Crank-gear and parts thereof
7656	8714.9900	--其他	12	0 2.4 5 8.4	东盟ASEAN,智利CL,新加坡SG,新西兰NZ,秘鲁PE,台湾TW 哥斯达黎加CR 巴基斯坦PK 亚太APTA	0	最不发达35国LDC35	80	--Other
	87.15	**婴孩车及其零件:**							**Baby carriages and parts thereof:**
7657	8715.0000	婴孩车及其零件	20	0 4 10	东盟ASEAN,智利CL,新加坡SG,新西兰NZ,澳门MO 哥斯达黎加CR 秘鲁PE	0	最不发达35国LDC35	80	Baby carriages and parts thereof
	87.16	**挂车及半挂车或其他非机械驱动车辆及其零件:**							**Trailers and semi-trailers; Other vehicles, not mechanically propelled; parts thereof:**
7658	8716.1000	-供居住或野营用厢式挂车及半挂车	10	0 5	东盟ASEAN,智利CL,新加坡SG,新西兰NZ,秘鲁PE,哥斯达黎加CR 巴基斯坦PK	0	最不发达35国LDC35	35	-Trailers and semi-trailers of the caravan type, for housing or camping
7659	8716.2000	-农用自装或自卸式挂车及半挂车	10	0 5	东盟ASEAN,智利CL,新西兰NZ,秘鲁PE,哥斯达黎加CR 巴基斯坦PK	0	最不发达35国LDC35	35	-Self-loading or self-unloading trailers and semi-trailers for agricultural purposes
		-其他货运挂车及半挂车:							-Other trailers and semi-trailers for the transport of goods:
		--罐式挂车及半挂车:							--Tanker trailers and tanker semi-trailers:
7660	8716.3110	---油罐挂车及半挂车	10	0 5	东盟ASEAN,智利CL,新加坡SG,新西兰NZ,秘鲁PE,哥斯达黎加CR 巴基斯坦PK	0	最不发达35国LDC35	20	---Oil tanker trailers and semi-trailers
7661	8716.3190	---其他	10	0 5	东盟ASEAN,智利CL,新西兰NZ,秘鲁PE,哥斯达黎加CR 巴基斯坦PK	0	最不发达35国LDC35	35	---Other

序号 No.	税则号列 Tariff Line	货品名称	最惠国税 率 MFN(%)	协定税率 Agreement(%)		特惠税率 S.P.(%)		普通税率 Gen.(%)	Article Description
		--其他:							--Other:
7662	8716.3910	---货柜挂车及半挂车	10	0 5	东盟ASEAN,智利CL,新西兰NZ,秘鲁PE,哥斯达黎加CR 巴基斯坦PK	0	最不发达35国LDC35	20	---Van trailers and semi-trailers
7663	8716.3990	---其他	10	0 5	东盟ASEAN,智利CL,新西兰NZ,秘鲁PE,哥斯达黎加CR 巴基斯坦PK	0	最不发达35国LDC35	35	---Other
7664	8716.4000	-其他挂车及半挂车	10	0 5	东盟ASEAN,智利CL,新西兰NZ,秘鲁PE,哥斯达黎加CR 巴基斯坦PK	0	最不发达35国LDC35	35	-Other trailers and semi-trailers
7665	8716.8000	-其他车辆	10	0 5	东盟ASEAN,智利CL,新加坡SG,新西兰NZ,秘鲁PE,哥斯达黎加CR,澳门MO 巴基斯坦PK	0	最不发达35国LDC35	80	-Other vehicles
7666	8716.9000	-零件	10	0 5	东盟ASEAN,智利CL,新加坡SG,新西兰NZ,秘鲁PE,哥斯达黎加CR 巴基斯坦PK	0	最不发达35国LDC35,最不发达4国LDC4	35	-Parts

第八十八章
航空器、航天器及其零件

Chapter 88
Aircraft，spacecraft and parts thereof

子目注释:

子目号 8802.11 至 8802.40 所称“空载重量”，是指航空器在正常飞行状态下，除去机组人员、燃料及非永久性安装设备后的重量。

Note:

For the purposes of subheadings Nos. 8802.11 to 8802.40, the expression “unladen weight” means the weight of the machine in normal flying order, excluding the weight of the crew and of fuel and equipment other than permanently fitted items of equipment.

序号 No.	税则号列 Tariff Line	货品名称	最惠国税率 MFN(%)	协定税率 Agreement(%)		特惠税率 S.P.(%)		普通税率 Gen.(%)	Article Description
	88.01	**气球及飞艇;滑翔机、悬挂滑翔机及其他无动力航空器:**							**Balloons and dirigibles; gliders, hang gliders and other non-powered aircraft:**
7667	8801.0010	---滑翔机及悬挂滑翔机	3	0	东盟ASEAN,智利CL,巴基斯坦PK,新西兰NZ,秘鲁PE,哥斯达黎加CR	0	最不发达35国LDC35,最不发达4国LDC4	11	---Gliders and hang gliders
7668	8801.0090	---其他	3	0	东盟ASEAN,智利CL,巴基斯坦PK,新西兰NZ,秘鲁PE,哥斯达黎加CR	0	最不发达35国LDC35,最不发达4国LDC4	11	---Other
	88.02	**其他航空器（例如，直升机、飞机）;航天器（包括卫星）及其运载工具、亚轨道运载工具:**							**Other aircraft (for example, helicopters, aeroplanes); spacecraft (including satellites) and suborbital and spacecraft launch vehicles:**
		-直升机:							-Helicopters:
7669	8802.1100	--空载重量不超过2000公斤	2	0	东盟ASEAN,智利CL,巴基斯坦PK,新西兰NZ,秘鲁PE,哥斯达黎加CR	0	最不发达35国LDC35,最不发达4国LDC4	11	--Of an unladen weight not exceeding 2000kg
		--空载重量超过2000公斤:							--Of an unladen weight exceeding 2000kg:
7670	8802.1210	---空载重量超过2000公斤，但不超过7000公斤	2	0	东盟ASEAN,智利CL,巴基斯坦PK,新西兰NZ,秘鲁PE,哥斯达黎加CR	0	最不发达35国LDC35,最不发达4国LDC4	11	---Of an unladen weight exceeding 2000kg but not exceeding 7000kg

序号 No.	税则号列 Tariff Line	货品名称	最惠国税率 MFN(%)	协定税率 Agreement(%)		特惠税率 S.P.(%)		普通税率 Gen.(%)	Article Description
7671	8802.1220	---空载重量超过7000公斤	2	0	东盟ASEAN,智利CL,巴基斯坦PK,新西兰NZ,秘鲁PE,哥斯达黎加CR	0	最不发达35国LDC35,最不发达4国LDC4	11	---Of an unladen weight exceeding 7000kg
7672	8802.2000	-飞机及其他航空器，空载重量不超过2000公斤	5	0	东盟ASEAN,巴基斯坦PK,新西兰NZ,秘鲁PE,哥斯达黎加CR	0	最不发达35国LDC35,最不发达4国LDC4	11	-Aeroplanes and other aircraft, of an unladen weight not exceeding 2000kg
				0.5	智利CL				
7673	8802.3000	-飞机及其他航空器，空载重量超过2000公斤，但不超过15000公斤	4	0	东盟ASEAN,巴基斯坦PK,新西兰NZ,秘鲁PE,哥斯达黎加CR	0	最不发达35国LDC35,最不发达4国LDC4	11	-Aeroplanes and other aircraft, of an unladen weight exceeding 2000kg but not exceeding 15000kg
				0.4	智利CL				
		-飞机及其他航空器，空载重量超过15000公斤:							-Aeroplanes and other aircraft, of an unladen weight exceeding 15000kg:
7674	8802.4010	---空载重量超过15000公斤，但不超过45000公斤	5	0	东盟ASEAN,智利CL,巴基斯坦PK,新西兰NZ,秘鲁PE,哥斯达黎加CR	0	最不发达35国LDC35,最不发达4国LDC4	11	---Of an unladen weight exceeding 15000kg but not exceeding 45000kg
				3.5	亚太APTA				
7675	8802.4020	---空载重量超过45000公斤	1	0	东盟ASEAN,智利CL,巴基斯坦PK,新西兰NZ,秘鲁PE,哥斯达黎加CR	0	最不发达35国LDC35,最不发达4国LDC4	11	---Of an unladen weight exceeding 45000kg
				0.7	亚太APTA				
7676	8802.6000	-航天器（包括卫星）及其运载工具、亚轨道运载工具	2	0	东盟ASEAN,智利CL,巴基斯坦PK,新西兰NZ,秘鲁PE,哥斯达黎加CR	0	最不发达35国LDC35,最不发达4国LDC4	11	-Spacecraft (including satellites) and suborbital and spacecraft launch vehicles
	88.03	**税号88.01或88.02所列货品的零件:**							**Parts of goods of heading No.88.01 or 88.02:**
7677	8803.1000	-推进器、水平旋翼及其零件	1	0	东盟ASEAN,智利CL,巴基斯坦PK,新西兰NZ,秘鲁PE,哥斯达黎加CR	0	最不发达35国LDC35,最不发达4国LDC4	11	-Propellers and rotors and parts thereof
7678	8803.2000	-起落架及其零件	1	0	东盟ASEAN,智利CL,巴基斯坦PK,新西兰NZ,秘鲁PE,哥斯达黎加CR	0	最不发达35国LDC35,最不发达4国LDC4	11	-Under-carriages and parts thereof

序号 No.	税则号列 Tariff Line	货品名称	最惠国税 率 MFN(%)	协定税率 Agreement(%)		特惠税率 S.P.(%)		普通税率 Gen.(%)	Article Description
7679	8803.3000	-飞机及直升机的其他零件	1	0	东盟ASEAN,智利CL,巴基斯坦PK,新西兰NZ,秘鲁PE,哥斯达黎加CR	0	最不发达35国LDC35	11	-Other parts of aeroplanes or helicopters
7680	8803.9000	-其他	0			0	最不发达35国LDC35,最不发达4国LDC4	11	-Other
	88.04	**降落伞（包括可操纵降落伞及滑翔伞）、旋翼降落伞及其零件、附件:**							**Parachutes (including dirigible parachutes and paragliders) and rotochutes; parts thereof and accessories thereto:**
7681	8804.0000	降落伞（包括可操纵降落伞及滑翔伞）、旋翼降落伞及其零件、附件	2	0	东盟ASEAN,智利CL,巴基斯坦PK,新西兰NZ,秘鲁PE,哥斯达黎加CR	0	最不发达35国LDC35,最不发达4国LDC4	11	Parachutes (including dirigible parachutes and paragliders) and rotochutes; parts thereof and accessories thereto
	88.05	**航空器的发射装置、甲板停机装置或类似装置和地面飞行训练器及其零件:**							**Aircraft launching gear; deck-arrestor or similar gear; ground flying trainers; parts of the foregoing articles:**
7682	8805.1000	-航空器的发射装置及其零件;甲板停机装置或类似装置及其零件	1.5	0	东盟ASEAN,智利CL,巴基斯坦PK,新西兰NZ,秘鲁PE,哥斯达黎加CR	0	最不发达35国LDC35,最不发达4国LDC4	11	-Aircraft launching gear and parts thereof; deck-arrestor or similar gear and parts thereof
		-地面飞行训练器及其零件:							-Ground flying trainers and parts thereof:
7683	8805.2100	--空战模拟器及其零件	1.5	0	东盟ASEAN,智利CL,巴基斯坦PK,新西兰NZ,秘鲁PE,哥斯达黎加CR	0	最不发达35国LDC35	11	--Air combat simulators and parts thereof
7684	8805.2900	--其他	1.5	0	东盟ASEAN,智利CL,巴基斯坦PK,新西兰NZ,秘鲁PE,哥斯达黎加CR	0	最不发达35国LDC35,最不发达4国LDC4	11	--Other

第八十九章 船舶及浮动结构体

Chapter89 Ships, boats and floating structures

注释:

已装配、未装配或已拆卸的船体、未完工或不完整的船舶以及未装配或已拆卸的完整船舶，如果不具有某种船舶的基本特征，应归入税号 89.06。

Notes:

A hull, an unfinished or incomplete vessel, assembled, unassembled or disassembled, or a complete vessel unassembled or disassembled, is to be classified in heading No.89.06 if it does not have the essential character of a vessel of a particular kind.

序号 No.	税则号列 Tariff Line	货品名称	最惠国税率 MFN(%)	协定税率 Agreement(%)		特惠税率 S.P.(%)		普通税率 Gen.(%)	Article Description
	89.01	**巡航船、游览船、渡船、货船、驳船及类似的客运或货运船舶:**							**Cruise ships, excursion boats, ferryboats, cargo ships, barges and similar vessels for the transport of persons or goods:**
		-巡航船、游览船及主要用于客运的类似船舶;各式渡船:							-Cruise ships, excursion boats and similar vessels principally designed for the transport of persons; ferry-boats of all kinds:
7685	8901.1010	---机动船舶	5	0 0.5	东盟ASEAN,巴基斯坦PK,新加坡SG,新西兰NZ,秘鲁PE,哥斯达黎加CR,香港HK 智利CL	0	最不发达35国LDC35	14	---Motor vessels
7686	8901.1090	---非机动船舶	8	0 0.8 5	东盟ASEAN,新西兰NZ,秘鲁PE,哥斯达黎加CR 智利CL 巴基斯坦PK	0	最不发达35国LDC35	30	---Other
		-液货船:							-Tankers:
		---成品油船:							---Finished oil tankers:
7687	8901.2011	----载重量不超过10万吨	9	0	智利CL,新西兰NZ,秘鲁PE,哥斯达黎加CR	0	最不发达35国LDC35	14	----Loading not exceeding 100000t
7688	8901.2012	----载重量超过10万吨，但不超过30万吨	9	0	智利CL,新西兰NZ,秘鲁PE,哥斯达黎加CR	0	最不发达35国LDC35	14	----Loading exceeding 100000t, but not exceeding 300000t
7689	8901.2013	----载重量超过30万吨	6	0	智利CL,新西兰NZ,秘鲁PE,哥斯达黎加CR	0	最不发达35国LDC35	14	----Loading exceeding 300000t
		---原油船:							---Crude oil tankers:
7690	8901.2021	----载重量不超过15万吨	9	0	智利CL,新西兰NZ,秘鲁PE,哥斯达黎加CR	0	最不发达35国LDC35	14	----Loading not exceeding 150000t
7691	8901.2022	----载重量超过15万吨，但不超过30万吨	9	0	智利CL,新西兰NZ,秘鲁PE,哥斯达黎加CR	0	最不发达35国LDC35	14	----Loading exceeding 150000t, but not exceeding 300000t

序号 No.	税则号列 Tariff Line	货品名称	最惠国税率 MFN(%)	协定税率 Agreement(%)		特惠税率 S.P.(%)		普通税率 Gen.(%)	Article Description
7692	8901.2023	----载重量超过30万吨	6	0	智利CL,新西兰NZ,秘鲁PE,哥斯达黎加CR	0	最不发达35国LDC35	14	----Loading exceeding 300000t
		---液化石油气船:							---Liquified petroleum gas carriers:
7693	8901.2031	----容积在20000立方米及以下	9	0	智利CL,新西兰NZ,秘鲁PE,哥斯达黎加CR	0	最不发达35国LDC35	14	----Volume with 20000m^3 or less
7694	8901.2032	----容积在20000立方米以上	6	0	智利CL,新西兰NZ,秘鲁PE,哥斯达黎加CR	0	最不发达35国LDC35	14	----Volume more than 20000m^3
		---液化天然气船:							---Liquified natural gas carriers:
7695	8901.2041	----容积在20000立方米及以下	9	0	智利CL,新西兰NZ,秘鲁PE,哥斯达黎加CR	0	最不发达35国LDC35	14	----Volume with 20000m^3 or less
7696	8901.2042	----容积在20000立方米以上	6	0	智利CL,新西兰NZ,秘鲁PE,哥斯达黎加CR	0	最不发达35国LDC35	14	----Volume more than 20000m3
7697	8901.2090	---其他	9	0	智利CL,新西兰NZ,秘鲁PE,哥斯达黎加CR	0	最不发达35国LDC35	14	---Other
7698	8901.3000	-冷藏船，但子目号8901.20的船舶除外	9	0 5	东盟ASEAN,智利CL,新加坡SG,新西兰NZ,秘鲁PE,哥斯达黎加CR 巴基斯坦PK	0	最不发达35国LDC35	14	-Refrigerated vessels, other than those of subheading No.8901.20
		-其他货运船舶及其他客货兼运船舶:							-Other vessels for the transport of goods and other vessels for the transport of both persons and goods:
		---机动集装箱船:							---Motor container vessels:
7699	8901.9021	----可载标准集装箱在6000箱及以下	9	0 0.9	新西兰NZ,秘鲁PE,哥斯达黎加CR 智利CL	0	最不发达35国LDC35	14	----Capable loading standard containers with 6000 or less
7700	8901.9022	----可载标准集装箱在6000箱以上	6	0 0.6	新西兰NZ,秘鲁PE,哥斯达黎加CR 智利CL	0	最不发达35国LDC35	14	----Capable loading standard containers more than 6000
		---机动滚装船:							---Motor Ro-Ro carriers:
7701	8901.9031	----载重量在2万吨及以下	9	0 0.9	新西兰NZ,秘鲁PE,哥斯达黎加CR 智利CL	0	最不发达35国LDC35	14	----Loading with 20000t or less
7702	8901.9032	----载重量在2万吨以上	6	0 0.6	新西兰NZ,秘鲁PE,哥斯达黎加CR 智利CL	0	最不发达35国LDC35	14	----Loading more than 20000t
		---机动散货船:							---Motor bulk carriers:
7703	8901.9041	----载重量不超过15万吨	9	0 0.9	新西兰NZ,秘鲁PE,哥斯达黎加CR 智利CL	0	最不发达35国LDC35	14	----Loading not exceeding 150000t
7704	8901.9042	----载重量超过15万吨，但不超过30万吨	9	0 0.9	新西兰NZ,秘鲁PE,哥斯达黎加CR 智利CL	0	最不发达35国LDC35	14	----Loading exceeding 150000t, not exceeding 300000t

序号 No.	税则号列 Tariff Line	货品名称	最惠国税率 MFN(%)	协定税率 Agreement(%)		特惠税率 S.P.(%)		普通税率 Gen.(%)	Article Description
7705	8901.9043	----载重量超过 30 万吨	9	0 0.9	新西兰NZ,秘鲁PE,哥斯达黎加CR 智利CL	0	最不发达 35 国 LDC35	14	----Loading exceeding 300000t
7706	8901.9050	---机动多用途船	9	0 0.9	新西兰NZ,秘鲁PE,哥斯达黎加CR 智利CL	0	最不发达 35 国 LDC35	14	---Multi-purposes motor vessels
7707	8901.9080	---其他，机动的	9	0 0.9 5	东盟ASEAN,新加坡SG,新西兰NZ,秘鲁PE,哥斯达黎加CR 智利CL 巴基斯坦PK	0	最不发达 35 国 LDC35	14	---Other motor vessels
7708	8901.9090	---非机动的	8	0 0.8 5	东盟ASEAN,新加坡SG,新西兰NZ,秘鲁PE,哥斯达黎加CR 智利CL 巴基斯坦PK	0	最不发达 35 国 LDC35	30	---Other non-motor vessels
	89.02	**捕鱼船;加工船及其他加工保藏鱼类产品的船舶:**							**Fishing vessels; factory ships and other vessels for processing or preserving fishery products:**
7709	8902.0010	---机动船舶	7	0 0.7 5	东盟ASEAN,新加坡SG,新西兰NZ,秘鲁PE,哥斯达黎加CR 智利CL 巴基斯坦PK	0	最不发达 35 国 LDC35	14	---Motor vessels
7710	8902.0090	---非机动船舶	8	0 0.8 5	东盟ASEAN,新西兰NZ,秘鲁PE,哥斯达黎加CR 智利CL 巴基斯坦PK	0	最不发达 35 国 LDC35	30	---Other
	89.03	**娱乐或运动用快艇及其他船舶;划艇及轻舟:**							**Yachts and other vessels for pleasure or sports; rowing boats and canoes:**
7711	8903.1000	-充气的	10	0 5	东盟ASEAN,智利CL,新西兰NZ,秘鲁PE,哥斯达黎加CR 巴基斯坦PK	0	最不发达 35 国 LDC35,最不发达 4 国 LDC4	30	-Inflatable
		-其他:							-Other:
7712	8903.9100	--帆船，不论是否装有辅助发动机	8	0 0.8 5	东盟ASEAN,新西兰NZ,秘鲁PE,哥斯达黎加CR 智利CL 巴基斯坦PK	0	最不发达 35 国 LDC35,最不发达 4 国 LDC4	30	--Sailboats, with or without auxiliary motor
7713	8903.9200	--汽艇，但装有舷外发动机的除外	10.5	0 1.1 2.1 5 5.2	东盟ASEAN,新加坡SG,新西兰NZ,香港HK 智利CL 哥斯达黎加CR 巴基斯坦PK 秘鲁PE	0	最不发达 35 国 LDC35,最不发达 4 国 LDC4	30	--Motorboats, other than outboard motorboats

序号 No.	税则号列 Tariff Line	货品名称	最惠国税率 MFN(%)	协定税率 Agreement(%)		特惠税率 S.P.(%)		普通税率 Gen.(%)	Article Description
7714	8903.9900	--其他	10	0 1 5	东盟ASEAN,新西兰NZ,秘鲁PE,哥斯达黎加CR 智利CL 巴基斯坦PK	0	最不发达35国LDC35,最不发达4国LDC4	30	--Other
	89.04	**拖轮及顶推船:**							**Tugs and pusher craft:**
7715	8904.0000	拖轮及顶推船	9	0 0.9 5	东盟ASEAN,新加坡SG,新西兰NZ,秘鲁PE,哥斯达黎加CR 智利CL 巴基斯坦PK	0	最不发达35国LDC35,最不发达4国LDC4	14	Tugs and pusher craft
	89.05	**灯船、消防船、挖泥船、起重船及其他不以航行为主要功能的船舶;浮船坞;浮动或潜水式钻探或生产平台:**							**Light-vessels, fire-floats, dredgers, floating cranes, and other vessels the navigability of which is subsidiary their main function; floating docks; floating or submersible drilling or roduction platforms:**
7716	8905.1000	-挖泥船	3	0	东盟ASEAN,智利CL,巴基斯坦PK,新西兰NZ,秘鲁PE,哥斯达黎加CR	0	最不发达35国LDC35,最不发达4国LDC4	11	-Dredgers
7717	8905.2000	-浮动或潜水式钻探或生产平台	6	0 5	东盟ASEAN,智利CL,新西兰NZ,秘鲁PE,哥斯达黎加CR 巴基斯坦PK	0	最不发达35国LDC35,最不发达4国LDC4	11	-Floating or submersible drilling or production platforms
		-其他:							-Other:
7718	8905.9010	---浮船坞	8	0 0.8	新西兰NZ,秘鲁PE,哥斯达黎加CR 智利CL	0	最不发达35国LDC35,最不发达4国LDC4	30	---Floating docks
7719	8905.9090	---其他	3	0	东盟ASEAN,智利CL,巴基斯坦PK,新西兰NZ,秘鲁PE,哥斯达黎加CR	0	最不发达35国LDC35,最不发达4国LDC4	11	---Other
	89.06	**其他船舶，包括军舰及救生船，但划艇除外:**							**Other vessels, including warships and lifeboats other than rowing boats:**
7720	8906.1000	-军舰	5	0	东盟ASEAN,智利CL,巴基斯坦PK,新西兰NZ,秘鲁PE,哥斯达黎加CR	0	最不发达35国LDC35	14	-Warships

序号 No.	税则号列 Tariff Line	货品名称	最惠国税率 MFN(%)	协定税率 Agreement(%)		特惠税率 S.P.(%)		普通税率 Gen.(%)	Article Description
		-其他:							-Other:
7721	8906.9010	---机动船舶	5	0 0.5	东盟ASEAN,巴基斯坦PK,新西兰NZ,秘鲁PE,哥斯达黎加CR 智利CL	0	最不发达35国LDC35,最不发达4国LDC4	14	---Motor vessels
7722	8906.9020	---非机动船舶	8	0 0.8 5	东盟ASEAN,新西兰NZ,秘鲁PE,哥斯达黎加CR 智利CL 巴基斯坦PK	0	最不发达35国LDC35,最不发达4国LDC4	30	---Non-motor vessels
7723	8906.9030	---未制成或不完整的船舶,包括船舶分段	8	0 0.8 5	东盟ASEAN,新西兰NZ,秘鲁PE,哥斯达黎加CR 智利CL 巴基斯坦PK	0	最不发达35国LDC35,最不发达4国LDC4	30	---Incomplete or unfinished vessels, including subsections of vessels
	89.07	**其他浮动结构体（例如，筏、柜、潜水箱、浮码头、浮筒及航标）:**							**Other floating structures (for example, rafts, tanks, coffer-dams, landing-stages, buoys and beacons):**
7724	8907.1000	-充气筏	8	0 5	东盟ASEAN,智利CL,新西兰NZ,秘鲁PE,哥斯达黎加CR 巴基斯坦PK	0	最不发达35国LDC35,最不发达4国LDC4	30	-Inflatable rafts
7725	8907.9000	-其他	8	0 0.8 5	东盟ASEAN,新西兰NZ,秘鲁PE,哥斯达黎加CR 智利CL 巴基斯坦PK	0	最不发达35国LDC35,最不发达4国LDC4	30	-Other
	89.08	**供拆卸的船舶及其他浮动结构体:**							**Vessels and other floating structures for breaking up:**
7726	8908.0000	供拆卸的船舶及其他浮动结构体	3	0	东盟ASEAN,智利CL,巴基斯坦PK,新西兰NZ,秘鲁PE,哥斯达黎加CR	0	最不发达35国LDC35,最不发达4国LDC4	11	Vessels and other floating structures for breaking up

第十八类

光学、照相、电影、计量、检验、医疗或外科用仪器及设备、精密仪器及设备；钟表；乐器；上述物品的零件、附件

第九十章

光学、照相、电影、计量、检验、医疗或外科用仪器及设备、精密仪器及设备；上述物品的零件、附件

注释：

一、本章不包括：

（一）机器、设备或其他专门技术用途的硫化橡胶（硬质橡胶除外）制品（税号40.16）、皮革或再生皮革制品（税号42.04）或纺织材料制品（税号59.11）；

（二）纺织材料制的承托带及其他承托物品，其承托器官的作用仅依靠自身的弹性（例如，孕妇用的承托带，用于胸部、腹部、关节或肌肉的承托绷带）（第十一类）；

（三）税号69.03的耐火材料制品；税号69.09的实验室、化学或其他专门技术用途的陶瓷器；

（四）税号70.09的未经光学加工的玻璃镜及税号83.06或第七十一章的非光学元件的贱金属或贵金属制的镜子；

（五）税号70.07、70.08、70.11、70.14、70.15或70.17的货品；

（六）第十五类注释二所规定的贱金属制通用零件（第十五类）或塑料制的类似品（第三十九章）；

SECTION XVIII

OPTICAL, PHOTOGRAPHIC, CINEMATOGRAPHIC, MEASURING, CHECKING, PRECISION, MEDICAL OR SURGICAL INSTRUMENTS AND APPARATUS; CLOCKS AND WATCHES; MUSICAL INSTRUMENTS; PARTS AND ACCESSORIES THEREOF

Chapter 90

Optical, photographic, cinematographic, measuring, checking, precision, medical or surgical instruments and apparatus; parts and accessories thereof

Notes:

1. This Chapter does not cover:

(a) Articles of a kind used in machines, appliances or for other technical uses, of vulcanized rubber other than hard rubber (heading No.40.16), of leather or of composition leather (heading No. 42.04) or of textile material (heading No.59.11);

(b) Supporting belts or other support articles of textile material, whose intended effect on the organ to be supported or held derives solely from their elasticity (for example, maternity belts, thoracic support bandages, abdominal support bandages, supports for joints or muscles) (Section XI);

(c) Refractory goods of heading No.69.03; ceramic wares for laboratory, chemical or other technical uses, of heading No.69.09;

(d) Glass mirrors, not optically worked, of heading No.70.09, or mirrors of base metal or of precious metal, not being optical elements (heading No.83.06 or Chapter 71);

(e) Goods of heading No.70.07, 70.08, 70.11, 70.14, 70.15 or 70.17;

(f) Parts of general use, as defined in Note 2 to Section XV, of base metal (Section XV) or similar goods of plastics (Chapter 39);

（七）税号 84.13 的装有计量装置的泵；计数和检验用的衡器或单独进口或出口的天平砝码（税号 84.23）；升降、起重及搬运机械（税号 84.25 至 84.28）；纸张或纸板的各种切割机器（税号 84.41）；税号 84.66 的用于机床上调整工件或工具的附件，包括具有读度用的光学装置的附件（例如，“光学”分度头），但其本身主要是光学仪器的除外（例如校直望远镜）；计算机器（税号 84.70）；税号 84.81 的阀门及其他装置；税目 84.86 的机器及装置（包括将电路图投影或绘制到感光半导体材料上的装置）；

(g) Pumps incorporating measuring devices, of heading No.84.13; weight-operated counting or checking machinery, or separately presented weights for balances (heading No.84.23); lifting or handling machinery (headings Nos.84.25to84.28); paper or paperboard cutting machines of all kinds (heading No.84.41); fittings for adjusting work or tools on machine-tools, of heading No.84.66, including fittings with optical devices for reading the scale (for example, "optical" dividing heads) but not those which are in themselves essentially optical instruments (for example, alignment telescopes); calculating machines (heading No.84.70); valves or other appliances of heading No.84.81; machines and apparatus (including apparatus for the projection or drawing of circuit pattern on sensitized semicon- ductor materials) of heading 84.86;

（八）自行车或机动车辆用探照灯或聚光灯（税号 85.12）；税号 85.13 的手提式电灯；电影录音机、还音机及转录机（税号 85.19）；拾音头或录音头（税号 85.22）；电视摄像机、数字照相机及视频摄录一体机(税目 85.25)；雷达设备、无线电导航设备或无线电遥控设备（税目 85.26)；光导纤维、光导纤维束或光缆用连接器（税目 85.36)；税目 85.37 的数控装置；税号 85.39 的封闭式聚光灯；税号 85.44 的光缆；

(h) Searchlights or spotlights of a kind used for cycles or motor vehicles (heading 85.12); portable electric lamps of heading 85.13; cinematographic sound recording, reproducing or re-recording apparatus (heading 85.19); sound-heads (heading 85.22); television cameras, digital cameras and video camera recorders (heading 85.25); and radar apparatus, radio navigational aid apparatus or radio remote control apparatus (heading 85.26); connectors for optical fibres, optical fibre bundles or cables (heading 85.36); numerical control apparatus of heading 85.37; sealed beam lamp units of heading 85.39; optical fibre cables of heading 85.44;

（九）税号 94.05 的探照灯及聚光灯；

(i) Searchlights or spotlights of heading No.94.05;

（十）第九十五章的物品；

(j) Articles of Chapter 95;

（十一）容量的计量器具（按其构成的材料归类）；

(k) Capacity measures, which are to be classified according to their constituent material; or

（十二）卷轴、线轴及类似芯子（按其构成材料归类，例如，归入税号 39.23 或第十五类）。

(l) Spools, reels or similar supports (which are to be classified according to their constituent material, for example, in heading No.39.23 or Section XV).

二、除上述注释一另有规定的以外，本章各税号所列机器、设备、仪器或器具的零件、附件，应按下列规定归类：

2. Subject to Note1above, parts and accessories for machines, apparatus, instruments or articles of this Chapter are to be classified according to the following rules:

（一）凡零件、附件本身已构成本章或第八十四章、第八十五章或第九十一章各税号（税号 84.87、

(a) Parts and accessories which are goods included in

84.85、85.48 或 90.33 除外）所包括的货品，应一律归入其相应的税号；

any of the headings of this Chapter or of Chapter84, 85 or 91 (other than heading 84.87, 84.85, 85.48 or 90.33) are in all cases to be classified in their respective headings;

（二）其他零件、附件，如果专用于或主要用于某种或同一税号项下的多种机器、仪器或器具（包括税号 90.10、90.13 或 90.31 的机器、仪器或器具），应归入相应机器、仪器或器具的税号；

(b) Other parts and accessories, if suitable for use solely or principally with a particular kind of machine, instrument or apparatus, or with a number of machines, instruments or apparatus of the same heading (including a machine, instrument or apparatus of heading No.90.10, 90.13 or 90.31)are to be classified with the machines, instruments or apparatus of that kind;

（三）所有其他零件、附件均应归入税号 90.33。

(c) All other parts and accessories are to be classified in heading No.90.33.

三、第十六类的注释三、四也适用于本章。

3. The provisions of Note 3 and 4 to Section XVI apply also to this Chapter.

四、税号 90.05 不包括武器用望远镜瞄准具、潜艇或坦克上的潜望镜式望远镜及本章或第十六类的机器、设备、仪器或器具用的望远镜;这类望远镜瞄准具及望远镜应归入税号 90.13。

4. Heading No.90.05does not apply to telescopic sights for fitting to arms, periscopic telescopes for fitting to submarines or tanks, or to telescopes for machines, appliances, instruments or apparatus of this Chapter of Section XVI; such telescopic sights and elescopes are to be classified in heading No.90.13.

五、计量或检验用的光学仪器、器具或机器，如果既可归入税号90.13，又可归入税号90.31，则应归入税号90.31。

5. Measuring or checking optical instruments, appliances or machines which, but for this Note, could be classified both in heading No. 90.13 and in heading No. 90.31 are to be classified in heading No. 90.31.

六、税目 90.21 所称“矫形器具”，是指下列用途的器具：

6. For the purposes of heading 90.21, the expression "orthopaedic appliances" means appliances for:

预防或矫正人体畸变；

生病、手术或受伤后人体部位支撑或固定；

-Preventing or correcting bodily deformities; or

-Supporting or holding parts of the body following an illness, operation or injury.

矫形器具包括用于矫正畸形的鞋及特种鞋垫，但需符合下列任一条件：

Orthopaedic appliances include footwear and special insoles designed to correct orthopaedic conditions, provided that they are either:

（一）定制的；

（二）成批生产的、单独报验、且不成双的、设计为左右两脚同样适用。

(1) made to measure; or

(2) mass-produced, presented singly.

七、税号 90.32 仅适用于：

7. Heading 90.32 applies only to:

（一）液体或气体的流量、液位、压力或其他变化量的自动控制仪器及装置或温度自动控制装置，不论其是否依靠要被自控的因素所发生的电现象来进行工作，这些仪器或装置将被自控因

(a) Instruments and apparatus for automatically controlling the flow, level, pressure or other variables of liquids or gases, or for automatically controlling temperature, whether or not their operation depends on an electrical

素调到并保持在一设定值上，通过持续或定期测量实际值来保持稳定，修正偏差；

（二）电量自动调节器及自动控制非电量的仪器或装置，依靠要被控制的因素所发生的电现象来进行工作，这些仪器或装置将被控制的因素调到并保持在一设定值上，通过持续或定期测量实际来保持稳定，修正偏差。

phenomenon which varies according to the factor to be automatically controlled, which are designed to bring this factor to, and maintain it at, a desired value, stabilised against disturbances, by constantly or periodically measuring its actual value; and

(b) Automatic regulators of electrical quantities, and instruments or apparatus for automatically controlling non-electrical quantities the operation of which depends on an electrical phenomenon varying according to the factor to be controlled, which are designed to bring this factor to, and maintain it at, a desired value, stabilised against disturbances, by constantly or periodically measuring its actual value.

序号 No.	税则号列 Tariff Line	货品名称	最惠国税率 MFN(%)	协定税率 Agreement(%)		特惠税率 S.P.(%)		普通税率 Gen.(%)	Article Description
	90.01	**光导纤维及光导纤维束；光缆，但税号85.44的货品除外；偏振材料制的片及板；未装配的各种材料制透镜（包括隐形眼镜片）、棱镜、反射镜及其他光学元件，但未经光学加工的玻璃制上述元件除外：**							**Optical fibres and optical fibre bundles; optical fibre cables, other than those of heading No. 85.44; sheets and plates of polarizing material; lenses (including contact lenses), prisms, mirrors and other optical elements, of any material, unmounted, other than such elements of glass not optically worked:**
7727	9001.1000	-光导纤维、光导纤维束及光缆	5	0 4.5	东盟ASEAN,智利CL,巴基斯坦PK,新西兰NZ,秘鲁PE,哥斯达黎加CR,香港HK 亚太APTA	0	最不发达35国LDC35,最不发达4国LDC4	20	-Optical fibres, optical fibre bundles and cables
7728	9001.2000	-偏振材料制的片及板	8	0 5 7.6	东盟ASEAN,智利CL,新西兰NZ,秘鲁PE,哥斯达黎加CR,香港HK 巴基斯坦PK 亚太APTA	0	最不发达35国LDC35,最不发达4国LDC4	20	-Sheets and plates of polarizing material
	ex90012000	液晶投影仪用偏光板	△6						Polarizing Plate or sheet for liquid-crystal projectors
	ex90012000	数字电影放映机用偏光板	△6						Polarizing plates or sheets for digital cinema projector
7729	9001.3000	-隐形眼镜片	10 △6	0 5	东盟ASEAN,智利CL,新加坡SG,新西兰NZ,秘鲁PE,哥斯达黎加CR,香港HK 巴基斯坦PK	0	最不发达35国LDC35,最不发达4国LDC4	70	-Contact lenses

序号 No.	税则号列 Tariff Line	货品名称	最惠国 税　率 MFN(%)	协定税率 Agreement(%)	特惠税率 S.P.(%)	普通 税率 Gen.(%)	Article Description
		-玻璃制眼镜片:					-Spectacle lenses of glass:
7730	9001.4010	---变色镜片	20 △15	0　东盟ASEAN,智利CL,新加坡SG,新西兰NZ,香港HK 4　哥斯达黎加CR 10　秘鲁PE	0　最不发达35国LDC35	90	---Photochromic
		---其他:					---Other:
7731	9001.4091	----太阳镜片	20	0　东盟ASEAN,智利CL,新加坡SG,新西兰NZ,香港HK 4　哥斯达黎加CR 10　秘鲁PE	0　最不发达35国LDC35	90	----For sunglasses
7732	9001.4099	----其他	20	0　东盟ASEAN,智利CL,新加坡SG,新西兰NZ,香港HK 4　哥斯达黎加CR 10　秘鲁PE	0　最不发达35国LDC35	70	----Other
		-其他材料制眼镜片:					-Spectacle lenses of other materials:
7733	9001.5010	---变色镜片	20 △15	0　东盟ASEAN,智利CL,新加坡SG,新西兰NZ,香港HK 4　哥斯达黎加CR 10　秘鲁PE	0　最不发达35国LDC35	90	---Photochromic
		---其他:					---Other:
7734	9001.5091	----太阳镜片	20	0　东盟ASEAN,智利CL,新加坡SG,新西兰NZ,香港HK 4　哥斯达黎加CR 10　秘鲁PE	0　最不发达35国LDC35	90	----For sunglasses
7735	9001.5099	----其他	20 △12	0　东盟ASEAN,智利CL,新加坡SG,新西兰NZ,香港HK 4　哥斯达黎加CR 10　秘鲁PE	0　最不发达35国LDC35	70	----Other
		-其他:					-Other:
7736	9001.9010	---彩色滤光片	8	0　东盟ASEAN,智利CL,新西兰NZ,秘鲁PE,哥斯达黎加CR,香港HK 5　巴基斯坦PK 7.6　亚太APTA	0　最不发达35国LDC35,最不发达4国LDC4	20	---Color filter
7737	9001.9090	---其他	8	0　东盟ASEAN,智利CL,新西兰NZ,秘鲁PE,哥斯达黎加CR,香港HK 5　巴基斯坦PK 7.6　亚太APTA	0　最不发达35国LDC35,最不发达4国LDC4	20	---Other
	ex90019090	非涅耳透镜投影屏（屏幕对角线≥80英寸，投射比≤0.26，增益比≥0.8，镜头间距≤100微米）	△6				Fresnel lens porojection screen (the length of diagoncal screen≥80 inch, Projection ratio≤0.26, ratio of gains ≥0.8, lens spacing≤100 microns)

序号 No.	税则号列 Tariff Line	货品名称	最惠国税率 MFN(%)	协定税率 Agreement(%)		特惠税率 S.P.(%)		普通税率 Gen.(%)	Article Description
	ex90019090	光通信用微光组件的光学元件（包括工作波长为800nm～1700nm的薄膜滤光片、自聚焦透镜、法拉第旋转片）	△0						Micro-optic component for optical communication (including thin film filter, gradient index lens and faraday Rotator, with working wavelength between 800nm and 1700nm)
	ex90019090	激光视盘机激光收发装置用的微型镜片	△3						Mini lens use for with laser transmitting and receving device of laser disc player
	ex90019090	液晶显示屏背光模组的光学元件(包括导光板、反射板、扩散片、增亮片)	△2						Optical elements for backlight module of liquid crystal display (including light guide, reflect sheet, diffuser,prism sheet to enhance brightness)
	ex90019090	液晶投影仪用偏光元件	△6						Polarizer for liquid-crystal projectors
	ex90019090	数字电影放映机用偏光元件	△6						Polarizer for digital cinema projector
	90.02	**已装配的各种材料制透镜、棱镜、反射镜及其他光学元件，作为仪器或装置的零件、配件，但未经光学加工的玻璃制上述元件除外：**							**Lenses, prisms, mirrors and other optical elements, of any material, mounted, being parts of or fittings for instruments or apparatus, other than such elements of glass not optically worked:**
		-物镜:							-Objective lenses:
		--照相机、投影仪、照片放大机及缩片机用:							--For cameras, projectors or photographic enlargers or reducers:
7738	9002.1110	---子目号9006.1010至9006.3000所列照相机用	8	0 5	东盟ASEAN,智利CL,新西兰NZ,秘鲁PE,哥斯达黎加CR 巴基斯坦PK	0	最不发达35国LDC35,最不发达4国LDC4	14	---For the photographic cameras of subheadings Nos. 9006.1010 to 9006.3000
7739	9002.1120	---缩微阅读机用	8	0 5	东盟ASEAN,智利CL,新西兰NZ,秘鲁PE,哥斯达黎加CR 巴基斯坦PK	0	最不发达35国LDC35,最不发达4国LDC4	14	---For microfilm, microfiche or other microform readers
		---其他照相机用:							---For other photographic cameras:
7740	9002.1131	----单反相机镜头	15 △4	0 3 7.5 12	东盟ASEAN,智利CL,新加坡SG,新西兰NZ 哥斯达黎加CR 秘鲁PE 巴基斯坦PK	0	最不发达35国LDC35	80	----For single lens reflex cameras

序号 No.	税则号列 Tariff Line	货品名称	最惠国税率 MFN(%)	协定税率 Agreement(%)		特惠税率 S.P.(%)		普通税率 Gen.(%)	Article Description
7741	9002.1139	----其他	15 △4	0 3 7.5 12	东盟ASEAN,智利CL,新加坡SG,新西兰NZ 哥斯达黎加CR 秘鲁PE 巴基斯坦PK	0	最不发达35国LDC35,最不发达4国LDC4	80	----Other
7742	9002.1190	---其他	15	0 3 7.5 12	东盟ASEAN,智利CL,新加坡SG,新西兰NZ,台湾TW 哥斯达黎加CR 秘鲁PE 巴基斯坦PK	0	最不发达35国LDC35,最不发达4国LDC4	80	---Other
	ex90021190	彩色投影机和数字光处理器的镜头及镜头组件	△4						Lens and lens assembly of colour projectors or digital light proceesors
		--其他:							--Other:
7743	9002.1910	---摄影机或放映机用	15	0 3 7.5 12	东盟ASEAN,智利CL,新加坡SG,新西兰NZ 哥斯达黎加CR 秘鲁PE 巴基斯坦PK	0	最不发达35国LDC35	40	---For cinematographic cameras or projectors
7744	9002.1990	---其他	15	0 3 7.5 12	东盟ASEAN,智利CL,新加坡SG,新西兰NZ,香港HK,台湾TW 哥斯达黎加CR 秘鲁PE 巴基斯坦PK	0	最不发达35国LDC35,最不发达4国LDC4	50	---Other
	ex90021990	摄像机、摄录一体机的镜头	△4						Lens for video cameras or camcorders
	ex90021990	手机、平板电脑用物镜（800万像素及以上）	△10						Objective lens for mobile telephones and tablet computers (pixels≥8million)
		-滤色镜:							-Filters:
7745	9002.2010	---照相机用	15	0 3 7.5 12 14.3	东盟ASEAN,智利CL,新加坡SG,新西兰NZ 哥斯达黎加CR 秘鲁PE 巴基斯坦PK 亚太APTA	0	最不发达35国LDC35	80	---For cameras
7746	9002.2090	---其他	15	0 3 7.5 12 14.3	东盟ASEAN,智利CL,新加坡SG,新西兰NZ 哥斯达黎加CR 秘鲁PE 巴基斯坦PK 亚太APTA	0	最不发达35国LDC35	40	---Other
		-其他:							-Other:
7747	9002.9010	---照相机用	15	0 1.5 3 7.5 12	东盟ASEAN,新加坡SG,新西兰NZ,香港HK,台湾TW 智利CL 哥斯达黎加CR 秘鲁PE 巴基斯坦PK	0	最不发达35国LDC35	80	---For cameras

序号 No.	税则号列 Tariff Line	货品名称	最惠国 税 率 MFN(%)	协定税率 Agreement(%)		特惠税率 S.P.(%)		普通 税率 Gen.(%)	Article Description
	ex90029010	照相机用带屈光度调节装置的目镜	△10						Eyepieces with diopter adjustment devices for cameras
7748	9002.9090	---其他	15	0 1.5 3 7.5 12	东盟ASEAN,新加坡SG,新西兰NZ,香港HK,台湾TW 智利CL 哥斯达黎加CR 秘鲁PE 巴基斯坦PK	0	最不发达35国LDC35,最不发达4国LDC4	40	---Other
	ex90029090	其他带屈光度调节装置的目镜	△10						Other eyepieces with diopter adjustment devices
	ex90029090	掩膜版	△10						Photo masks
	90.03	**眼镜架及其零件:**							**Frames and mountings for spectacles, goggles or the like, and parts thereof:**
		-眼镜架:							-Frames and mountings:
7749	9003.1100	--塑料制	18 △12	0 3.6 9	东盟ASEAN,智利CL,新加坡SG,新西兰NZ,香港HK,澳门MO 哥斯达黎加CR 秘鲁PE	0	最不发达35国LDC35	70	--Of plastics
		--其他材料制:							--Of other materials:
7750	9003.1910	---金属材料制	10 △6	0 1 5	东盟ASEAN,新西兰NZ,秘鲁PE,哥斯达黎加CR,香港HK,澳门MO 智利CL 巴基斯坦PK	0	最不发达35国LDC35	70	---Of metal materials
7751	9003.1920	---天然材料制	10	0 1 5	东盟ASEAN,新西兰NZ,秘鲁PE,哥斯达黎加CR,香港HK,澳门MO 智利CL 巴基斯坦PK	0	最不发达35国LDC35	70	---Of narural materials
7752	9003.1990	---其他	10	0 1 5	东盟ASEAN,新西兰NZ,秘鲁PE,哥斯达黎加CR,香港HK,澳门MO 智利CL 巴基斯坦PK	0	最不发达35国LDC35	70	---Other
7753	9003.9000	-零件	10 △6	0 5	东盟ASEAN,智利CL,新西兰NZ,秘鲁PE,哥斯达黎加CR,香港HK 巴基斯坦PK	0	最不发达35国LDC35	70	-Parts
	90.04	**矫正视力、保护眼睛或其他用途的眼镜、挡风镜及类似品:**							**Spectacles, goggles and the like, corrective, protective or other:**
7754	9004.1000	-太阳镜	20 △12	0 2 4 10	东盟ASEAN,新加坡SG,新西兰NZ,香港HK,澳门MO 智利CL 哥斯达黎加CR 秘鲁PE	0	最不发达35国LDC35	100	-Sunglasses
		-其他:							-Other:

序号 No.	税则号列 Tariff Line	货品名称	最惠国税率 MFN(%)	协定税率 Agreement(%)		特惠税率 S.P.(%)		普通税率 Gen.(%)	Article Description
7755	9004.9010	---变色镜	16 △10	0 3.2 8 12.8	东盟ASEAN,智利CL,新加坡SG,新西兰NZ,香港HK,澳门MO 哥斯达黎加CR 秘鲁PE 巴基斯坦PK	0	最不发达35国LDC35	100	---Photochromic spectacles
7756	9004.9090	---其他	20 △12	0 4 10	东盟ASEAN,智利CL,新加坡SG,新西兰NZ,香港HK,澳门MO 哥斯达黎加CR 秘鲁PE	0	最不发达35国LDC35	90	---Other
	90.05	**双筒望远镜、单筒望远镜、其他光学望远镜及其座架;其他天文仪器及其座架，但不包括射电天文仪器:**							**Binoculars, monoculars, other optical telescopes, and mountings thereof; other astronomical instruments and mountings thereof, but not including instruments for radio-astronomy:**
7757	9005.1000	-双筒望远镜	15	0 3 7.5 12	东盟ASEAN,智利CL,新加坡SG,新西兰NZ 哥斯达黎加CR 秘鲁PE 巴基斯坦PK	0	最不发达35国LDC35	50	-Binoculars
		-其他仪器:							-Other instruments:
7758	9005.8010	---天文望远镜及其他天文仪器	3	0	东盟ASEAN,智利CL,巴基斯坦PK,新西兰NZ,秘鲁PE,哥斯达黎加CR	0	最不发达35国LDC35,最不发达4国LDC4	8	---Astronomical telescopes and other astronomical instruments
7759	9005.8090	---其他	12	0 2.4 6	东盟ASEAN,智利CL,新加坡SG,新西兰NZ,秘鲁PE 哥斯达黎加CR 巴基斯坦PK	0	最不发达35国LDC35,最不发达4国LDC4	50	---Other
		-零件、附件(包括座架):							-Parts and accessories (including mountings):
7760	9005.9010	---天文望远镜及其他天文仪器用	2	0	东盟ASEAN,智利CL,巴基斯坦PK,新西兰NZ,秘鲁PE,哥斯达黎加CR	0	最不发达35国LDC35,最不发达4国LDC4	8	---Of instruments of subheading No.9005.8010
7761	9005.9090	---其他	8	0 5	东盟ASEAN,智利CL,新西兰NZ,秘鲁PE,哥斯达黎加CR 巴基斯坦PK	0	最不发达35国LDC35,最不发达4国LDC4	30	---Other

序号 No.	税则号列 Tariff Line	货品名称	最惠国税率 MFN(%)	协定税率 Agreement(%)		特惠税率 S.P.(%)		普通税率 Gen.(%)	Article Description
	90.06	**照相机（电影摄影机除外）;照相闪光灯装置及闪光灯泡，但税号 85.39 的放电灯泡除外:**							**Photographic (other than cinematographic) cameras; photographic flashlight apparatus and flashbulbs, other than discharge lamps of heading No.85.39:**
		-制版照相机:							-Cameras of a kind used for preparing printing plates or cylinders:
7762	9006.1010	---电子分色机	12	0 2.4 6	东盟ASEAN,智利CL,新加坡SG,新西兰NZ,秘鲁PE 哥斯达黎加CR 巴基斯坦PK	0	最不发达 35 国 LDC35,最不发达 4 国 LDC4	20	---Electronic colour scanners
7763	9006.1090	---其他	10	0 5	东盟ASEAN,智利CL,新西兰NZ,秘鲁PE,哥斯达黎加CR 巴基斯坦PK	0	最不发达 35 国 LDC35,最不发达 4 国 LDC4	20	---Other
7764	9006.3000	-水下、航空测量或体内器官检查用的特种照相机;法庭或犯罪学用的比较照相机	9	0 5	东盟ASEAN,智利CL,新西兰NZ,秘鲁PE,哥斯达黎加CR 巴基斯坦PK	0	最不发达 35 国 LDC35,最不发达 4 国 LDC4	17	-Cameras specially designed for underwater use, for aerial survey or for medical or surgical examination of internal organs; comparison cameras for forensic or criminological purposes
7765	9006.4000	-一次成像照相机	5	0	东盟ASEAN,智利CL,巴基斯坦PK,新西兰NZ,秘鲁PE,哥斯达黎加CR	0	最不发达 35 国 LDC35,最不发达 4 国 LDC4	70	-Instant print cameras
		-其他照相机:							-Other cameras:
7766	9006.5100	--通过镜头取景（单镜头反光式（SLR)），使用胶片宽度不超过 35 毫米	25	0 5	东盟ASEAN,智利CL,新加坡SG,新西兰NZ 哥斯达黎加CR			100	--With a through-the-lens viewfinder (single lens reflex (SLR)), for roll film of a width not exceeding 35mm
		--其他，使用胶片宽度小于 35 毫米:							--Other, for roll film of a width less than 35mm:
7767	9006.5210	---缩微照相机，使用缩微胶卷、胶片或其他缩微品的	9	0 5	东盟ASEAN,智利CL,新西兰NZ,秘鲁PE,哥斯达黎加CR 巴基斯坦PK	0	最不发达 35 国 LDC35,最不发达 4 国 LDC4	17	---Cameras of a kind used for recording documents on microfilm, microfiche or other microforms
7768	9006.5290	---其他	25	0 5	东盟ASEAN,智利CL,新加坡SG,新西兰NZ 哥斯达黎加CR			100	---Other

序号 No.	税则号列 Tariff Line	货品名称	最惠国税率 MFN(%)	协定税率 Agreement(%)	特惠税率 S.P.(%)	普通税率 Gen.(%)	Article Description
7769	9006.5300	--其他，使用胶片宽度为 35 毫米	20	0 东盟ASEAN,新加坡SG,新西兰NZ 2 智利CL 4 哥斯达黎加CR 10 秘鲁PE	0 最不发达 35 国 LDC35	100	--Other, for roll film of a width of 35mm
		--其他:					--Other
7770	9006.5910	---激光照相排版设备	9	0 东盟ASEAN,智利CL,新加坡SG,新西兰NZ,秘鲁PE,哥斯达黎加CR 5 巴基斯坦PK	0 最不发达 35 国 LDC35,最不发达 4 国 LDC4	35	---Laser photo typesetting equipments
7771	9006.5990	---其他	25	0 东盟ASEAN,智利CL,新加坡SG,新西兰NZ 5 哥斯达黎加CR		100	---Other
		-照相闪光灯装置及闪光灯泡:					-photographic flashlight apparatus and flashbulbs:
7772	9006.6100	--放电式（电子式）闪光灯装置	18	0 东盟ASEAN,智利CL,新加坡SG,新西兰NZ 3.6 哥斯达黎加CR 9 秘鲁PE	0 最不发达 35 国 LDC35	80	--Discharge lamp (“electronic”) flashlight apparatus
	ex90066100	照相手机用闪光灯组件	△4				Flashlight modules for mobile telephones with camera function
	ex90066100	照相机外置式电子闪光灯(闪光指数GN≥30,具有无线闪光功能,支持自动变焦)	△15				External flashlights for cameras (Flash guide number≥30, with wireless flash and automatic focusing function)
		--其他:					--Other:
7773	9006.6910	---闪光灯泡	18	0 东盟ASEAN,智利CL,新加坡SG,新西兰NZ 3.6 哥斯达黎加CR 9 秘鲁PE 14.4 巴基斯坦PK	0 最不发达 35 国 LDC35	80	---Flashbulbs
7774	9006.6990	---其他	18	0 东盟ASEAN,智利CL,新加坡SG,新西兰NZ 3.6 哥斯达黎加CR 9 秘鲁PE 14.4 巴基斯坦PK	0 最不发达 35 国 LDC35	80	---Other
		-零件、附件:					-Parts and accessories:
		--照相机用:					--For cameras:
7775	9006.9110	---子目号 9006.1010 至 9006.3000 所列相机用	8	0 东盟ASEAN,智利CL,新西兰NZ,秘鲁PE,哥斯达黎加CR,香港HK 5 巴基斯坦PK 5.6 亚太APTA	0 最不发达 35 国 LDC35,最不发达 4 国 LDC4,亚太 2 国 APTA2	17	---For cameras of subheadings No.9006.1010 to 9006.3000

序号 No.	税则号列 Tariff Line	货品名称	最惠国税率 MFN(%)	协定税率 Agreement(%)		特惠税率 S.P.(%)		普通税率 Gen.(%)	Article Description
7776	9006.9120	---一次成像照相机用	5	0 3.5	东盟ASEAN,智利CL,巴基斯坦PK,新西兰NZ,秘鲁PE,哥斯达黎加CR,香港HK 亚太APTA	0	最不发达35国LDC35,最不发达4国LDC4,亚太2国APTA2	100	---For instant print cameras
		---其他:							---Other:
7777	9006.9191	----自动调焦组件	10 △6	0 5 7	东盟ASEAN,智利CL,新加坡SG,新西兰NZ,秘鲁PE,哥斯达黎加CR,香港HK 巴基斯坦PK 亚太APTA	0	最不发达35国LDC35,最不发达4国LDC4,亚太2国APTA2	100	----Automatic focal setting units
7778	9006.9192	----快门组件	10 △6	0 5 7	东盟ASEAN,智利CL,新加坡SG,新西兰NZ,秘鲁PE,哥斯达黎加CR,香港HK 巴基斯坦PK 亚太APTA	0	最不发达35国LDC35,最不发达4国LDC4,亚太2国APTA2	100	----Shutter units
7779	9006.9199	----其他	10 △6	0 5 7	东盟ASEAN,智利CL,新加坡SG,新西兰NZ,秘鲁PE,哥斯达黎加CR,香港HK 巴基斯坦PK 亚太APTA	0	最不发达35国LDC35,最不发达4国LDC4,亚太2国APTA2	100	----Other
7780	9006.9900	--其他	12	0 2.4 6	东盟ASEAN,智利CL,新加坡SG,新西兰NZ,秘鲁PE 哥斯达黎加CR 巴基斯坦PK	0	最不发达35国LDC35,最不发达4国LDC4	80	--Other
	90.07	**电影摄影机、放映机,不论是否带有声音的录制或重放装置:**							**Cinematographic cameras and projectors, whether or not incorporating sound recording or reproducing apparatus:**
		-摄影机:							-Cameras:
7781	9007.1010	---高速摄影机	14	0 1.4 2.8 7	东盟ASEAN,新加坡SG,新西兰NZ,秘鲁PE 智利CL 哥斯达黎加CR 巴基斯坦PK	0	最不发达35国LDC35	40	---High speed cameras
7782	9007.1090	---其他	14	0 2.8 11.2	东盟ASEAN,智利CL,新加坡SG,新西兰NZ,秘鲁PE 哥斯达黎加CR 巴基斯坦PK	0	最不发达35国LDC35	40	---Other

序号 No.	税则号列 Tariff Line	货品名称	最惠国税率 MFN(%)	协定税率 Agreement(%)		特惠税率 S.P.(%)		普通税率 Gen.(%)	Article Description
		-放映机:							-Projectors:
7783	9007.2010	---数字式	14	0	东盟ASEAN,智利CL,新加坡SG,新西兰NZ,秘鲁PE,香港HK	0	最不发达35国LDC35	40	---Digital
				2.8	哥斯达黎加CR				
				11.2	巴基斯坦PK				
	ex90072010	2K及以上分辨率的硬盘式数字电影放映机	△8						Digital cinematographs with magnetic discs, resolving power ≥2k
7784	9007.2090	---其他	14	0	东盟ASEAN,智利CL,新加坡SG,新西兰NZ,秘鲁PE	0	最不发达35国LDC35	40	---Other
				2.8	哥斯达黎加CR				
				11.2	巴基斯坦PK				
		-零件、附件:							-Parts and accessories:
7785	9007.9100	--摄影机用	8.4 △5	0	东盟ASEAN,智利CL,新西兰NZ,秘鲁PE,哥斯达黎加CR	0	最不发达35国LDC35	40	--For cameras
				5	巴基斯坦PK				
7786	9007.9200	--放映机用	8.4 △5	0	东盟ASEAN,智利CL,新西兰NZ,秘鲁PE,哥斯达黎加CR	0	最不发达35国LDC35	40	--For projectors
				5	巴基斯坦PK				
	90.08	**影像投影仪，但电影用除外;照片（电影片除外）放大机及缩片机:**							**Image projectors, other than cinematographic; photographic (other than cinematographic) enlargers and reducers:**
		-投影仪、放大机及缩片机:							-Projector,enlargers and reducers:
7787	9008.5010	---幻灯机	14	0	东盟ASEAN,智利CL,新加坡SG,新西兰NZ,秘鲁PE	0	最不发达35国LDC35	40	---Slide projectors
				2.8	哥斯达黎加CR				
				7	巴基斯坦PK				
7788	9008.5020	---缩微胶卷、缩微胶片或其他缩微品的阅读机，不论是否可以进行复制	10	0	东盟ASEAN,智利CL,新西兰NZ,秘鲁PE,哥斯达黎加CR	0	最不发达35国LDC35	40	---Microfilm, microfiche or other microform readers, whether or not capable of producing copies
				5	巴基斯坦PK				
		---其他影像投影仪:							---Other image projectors:
7789	9008.5031	----正射投影仪	18	0	东盟ASEAN,智利CL,新加坡SG,新西兰NZ	0	最不发达35国LDC35	40	----Orthographical projectors
				3.6	哥斯达黎加CR				
				9	秘鲁PE				
7790	9008.5039	----其他	18	0	东盟ASEAN,新加坡SG,新西兰NZ	0	最不发达35国LDC35	40	----Other
				1.8	智利CL				
				3.6	哥斯达黎加CR				
				9	秘鲁PE				
7791	9008.5040	---照片（电影片除外）放大机及缩片机	20	0	东盟ASEAN,智利CL,新加坡SG,新西兰NZ	0	最不发达35国LDC35	80	---Photographic (other than cinematographic) enlargers and reducers
				4	哥斯达黎加CR				
				10	秘鲁PE				

序号 No.	税则号列 Tariff Line	货品名称	最惠国税率 MFN(%)	协定税率 Agreement(%)		特惠税率 S.P.(%)		普通税率 Gen.(%)	Article Description
		-零件、附件:							-Parts and accessories:
7792	9008.9010	---缩微阅读机用	8	0 5	东盟ASEAN,智利CL,新西兰NZ,秘鲁PE,哥斯达黎加CR 巴基斯坦PK	0	最不发达35国LDC35	17	---Of microfilm, microfiche or other microform readers
7793	9008.9020	---照片放大机及缩片机用	14	0 2.8 7	东盟ASEAN,智利CL,新加坡SG,新西兰NZ,秘鲁PE 哥斯达黎加CR 巴基斯坦PK	0	最不发达35国LDC35	80	---Of photographic enlargers and reducers
7794	9008.9090	---其他	14	0 2.8 11.2	东盟ASEAN,智利CL,新加坡SG,新西兰NZ,秘鲁PE 哥斯达黎加CR 巴基斯坦PK	0	最不发达35国LDC35	40	---Other
	90.10	**本章其他税号未列名的照相（包括电影）洗印用装置及设备;负片显示器;银幕及其他投影屏幕:**							**Apparatus and equipment for photographic (including cinematographic) laboratories, not specified or included elsewhere in this Chapter; negatoscopes; projection screens:**
		-照相（包括电影）胶卷或成卷感光纸的自动显影装置及设备或将已冲洗胶卷自动曝光到成卷感光纸上的装置及设备:							-Apparatus and equipment for automatically developing photographic (including cinematographic) film or paper in rolls or for automatically exposing developed film to rolls of photographic paper:
7795	9010.1010	---电影用	14	0 1.4 2.8 7	东盟ASEAN,新加坡SG,新西兰NZ,秘鲁PE,香港HK 智利CL 哥斯达黎加CR 巴基斯坦PK	0	最不发达35国LDC35	40	---Of a kind used in cinematographic film
7796	9010.1020	---特种照相用	8.4	0 0.8 5	东盟ASEAN,新西兰NZ,秘鲁PE,哥斯达黎加CR,香港HK 智利CL 巴基斯坦PK	0	最不发达35国LDC35,最不发达4国LDC4	20	---Of a kind used in special photographic film or paper
		---其他:							---Other:
7797	9010.1091	----彩色胶卷用	25	0 2.5 5 12.5	东盟ASEAN,新加坡SG,新西兰NZ,香港HK 智利CL 哥斯达黎加CR 秘鲁PE	0	最不发达35国LDC35	100	----For the colour photographic film in rolls
7798	9010.1099	----其他	15	0 1.5 3 7.5 12	东盟ASEAN,新加坡SG,新西兰NZ,香港HK 智利CL 哥斯达黎加CR 秘鲁PE 巴基斯坦PK	0	最不发达35国LDC35	100	----Other

序号 No.	税则号列 Tariff Line	货品名称	最惠国税率 MFN(%)	协定税率 Agreement(%)		特惠税率 S.P.(%)		普通税率 Gen.(%)	Article Description
		-照相（包括电影）洗印用其他装置及设备;负片显示器:							-Other apparatus and equipment for photo-graphic (including cine-matographic) laborato-ries; negatoscope:
7799	9010.5010	---负片显示器	14	0 2.8 7	东盟ASEAN,智利CL,新加坡SG,新西兰NZ,秘鲁PE 哥斯达黎加CR 巴基斯坦PK	0	最不发达35国LDC35	50	---Negatoscopes
		---其他:							---Other:
7800	9010.5021	----电影用	14	0 2.8 11.2	东盟ASEAN,智利CL,新加坡SG,新西兰NZ,秘鲁PE 哥斯达黎加CR 巴基斯坦PK	0	最不发达35国LDC35	40	----Of a kind used in cinematographic film
7801	9010.5022	----特种照相用	8.4	0 5	东盟ASEAN,智利CL,新西兰NZ,秘鲁PE,哥斯达黎加CR 巴基斯坦PK	0	最不发达35国LDC35,最不发达4国LDC4	20	----Of a kind used in special photo-graphic film or paper
7802	9010.5029	----其他	17	0 3.4 8.5 13.6	东盟ASEAN,智利CL,新加坡SG,新西兰NZ 哥斯达黎加CR 秘鲁PE 巴基斯坦PK	0	最不发达35国LDC35	100	----Other
7803	9010.6000	-银幕及其他投影屏幕	14	0 2.8 11.2	东盟ASEAN,智利CL,新加坡SG,新西兰NZ,秘鲁PE 哥斯达黎加CR 巴基斯坦PK	0	最不发达35国LDC35	50	-Projection screens
		-零件、附件:							-Parts and accessories:
7804	9010.9010	---电影用	0			0	最不发达35国LDC35,最不发达4国LDC4	40	---Of a kind used in cinematographic film
7805	9010.9020	---特种照相用	0			0	最不发达35国LDC35,最不发达4国LDC4	20	---Of a kind used in spe-cial photographic film or paper
7806	9010.9090	---其他	0			0	最不发达35国LDC35,最不发达4国LDC4	100	---Other
	90.11	**复式光学显微镜，包括用于缩微照相、显微电影摄影及显微投影的:**							**Compound optical mi-croscopes, including those for photomicrog-raphy, cinephotomi-crography or micro-projection:**

序号 No.	税则号列 Tariff Line	货品名称	最惠国税率 MFN(%)	协定税率 Agreement(%)		特惠税率 S.P.(%)		普通税率 Gen.(%)	Article Description
7807	9011.1000	-立体显微镜	0			0	最不发达35国LDC35,最不发达4国LDC4	14	-Stereoscopic microscopes
7808	9011.2000	-缩微照相、显微电影摄影及显微投影用的其他显微镜	0			0	最不发达35国LDC35,最不发达4国LDC4	14	-Other microscopes, for photomicrography, cinephotomi-crography or microprojection
7809	9011.8000	-其他显微镜	7	0	东盟ASEAN,智利CL,新西兰NZ,秘鲁PE,哥斯达黎加CR	0	最不发达35国LDC35	14	-Other microscopes
				5	巴基斯坦PK				
	ex90118000	高倍测量显微镜，放大倍数≥1000倍，分辨率≤0.08微米	△3						high power microscope , enlargment ratio≥1000, resolution ration≤0.08μm
7810	9011.9000	-零件、附件	0			0	最不发达35国LDC35,最不发达4国LDC4	14	-Parts and accessories
	90.12	**显微镜，但光学显微镜除外;衍射设备:**							**Microscopes other than optical microscopes; diffraction apparatus:**
7811	9012.1000	-显微镜,但光学显微镜除外;衍射设备	0			0	最不发达35国LDC35,最不发达4国LDC4	14	-Microscopes other than optical microscopes; and diffraction apparatus
7812	9012.9000	-零件、附件	0			0	最不发达35国LDC35,最不发达4国LDC4	14	-Parts and accessories
	90.13	**其他税号未列名的液晶装置;激光器，但激光二极管除外;本章其他税号未列名的光学仪器及器具:**							**Liquid crystal devices not constituting articles provided for more specifically in other headings; lasers, other than laser diodes; other optical appliances and instruments, not specified or included elsewhere in this Chapter:**

序号 No.	税则号列 Tariff Line	货品名称	最惠国税率 MFN(%)	协定税率 Agreement(%)		特惠税率 S.P.(%)		普通税率 Gen.(%)	Article Description
7813	9013.1000	-武器用望远镜瞄准具;潜望镜式望远镜;作为本章或第十六类的机器、设备、仪器或器具部件的望远镜	8	0 5	东盟ASEAN,智利CL,新西兰NZ,秘鲁PE,哥斯达黎加CR 巴基斯坦PK	0	最不发达35国LDC35	14	-Telescopic sights for fitting to arms; periscopes; telescopes designed to formparts of machines, appliances, instruments or apparatus of this Chapter or Section XVI
7814	9013.2000	-激光器,但激光二极管除外	6	0 5	东盟ASEAN,智利CL,新西兰NZ,秘鲁PE,哥斯达黎加CR,澳门MO 巴基斯坦PK	0	最不发达35国LDC35	11	-Lasers, other than laser diodes
	ex90132000	2.5G b/s及以上SDH、波分复用光传输设备的980纳米、1480纳米的泵浦激光器	△3						980nm and1480nm pump laster of SDH≥2.5GB/S, optical transmission equipment for wave-divison multiplexing
	ex90132000	激光切割机用气体激光发生器,切割功率≥2千瓦	△3						Gas laser oscillators for laser cutting machines, cutting powr≥2kW
		-其他装置、仪器及器具:							-Other devices, appliances and instruments:
7815	9013.8010	---放大镜	12	0 2.4 5 8.4	东盟ASEAN,智利CL,新加坡SG,新西兰NZ,秘鲁PE,香港HK,澳门MO 哥斯达黎加CR 巴基斯坦PK 亚太APTA	0	最不发达35国LDC35	50	---Hand magnifying glasses
7816	9013.8020	---光学门眼	12	0 2.4 5 8.4	东盟ASEAN,智利CL,新加坡SG,新西兰NZ,秘鲁PE 哥斯达黎加CR 巴基斯坦PK 亚太APTA	0	最不发达35国LDC35	50	---Door eyes
7817	9013.8030	---液晶显示板	5	0	东盟ASEAN,智利CL,巴基斯坦PK,新西兰NZ,香港HK,澳门MO			50	---Liquid crystal display panel
7818	9013.8090	---其他	5	0	东盟ASEAN,智利CL,巴基斯坦PK,新西兰NZ,秘鲁PE,哥斯达黎加CR,香港HK,澳门MO	0	最不发达35国LDC35	17	---Other
		-零件、附件:							-Parts and accessories:
7819	9013.9010	---子目录9013.1000及9013.2000所列货品用	6	0 5	东盟ASEAN,智利CL,新西兰NZ,秘鲁PE,哥斯达黎加CR,香港HK,澳门MO 巴基斯坦PK	0	最不发达35国LDC35	11	---For goods of subheading No. 9013.1000 or 9013.2000
7820	9013.9020	---子目录9013.8030所列货品用	8	0 5	东盟ASEAN,智利CL,新西兰NZ,秘鲁PE,哥斯达黎加CR,香港HK,澳门MO 巴基斯坦PK	0	最不发达35国LDC35	17	---For goods of subheading No.9013.8030

序号 No.	税则号列 Tariff Line	货品名称	最惠国税率 MFN(%)	协定税率 Agreement(%)		特惠税率 S.P.(%)		普通税率 Gen.(%)	Article Description
7821	9013.9090	---其他	8	0 5	东盟ASEAN,智利CL,新西兰NZ,秘鲁PE,哥斯达黎加CR,香港HK,澳门MO 巴基斯坦PK	0	最不发达35国LDC35	17	---Other
	90.14	**定向罗盘;其他导航仪器及装置:**							**Direction finding compasses; other navigational instruments and appliances:**
7822	9014.1000	-定向罗盘	2	0	东盟ASEAN,智利CL,巴基斯坦PK,新西兰NZ,秘鲁PE,哥斯达黎加CR	0	最不发达35国LDC35,最不发达4国LDC4	8	-Direction finding compasses
		-航空或航天导航仪器及装置（罗盘除外）:							-Instruments and appliances for aeronautical or space navigation (other than compasses):
7823	9014.2010	---自动驾驶仪	2 △1	0	东盟ASEAN,智利CL,巴基斯坦PK,新西兰NZ,秘鲁PE,哥斯达黎加CR	0	最不发达35国LDC35,最不发达4国LDC4	8	---Automatic pilot
7824	9014.2090	---其他	2	0	东盟ASEAN,智利CL,巴基斯坦PK,新西兰NZ,秘鲁PE,哥斯达黎加CR	0	最不发达35国LDC35,最不发达4国LDC4	8	---Other
	ex90142090	航空惯性导航仪	△1						Aviation inetial navigator
7825	9014.8000	-其他仪器及装置	2	0	东盟ASEAN,智利CL,巴基斯坦PK,新西兰NZ,秘鲁PE,哥斯达黎加CR	0	最不发达35国LDC35,最不发达4国LDC4	8	-Other instruments and appliances
		-零件、附件:							-Parts and accessories:
7826	9014.9010	---自动驾驶仪用	1.5 △1	0	东盟ASEAN,智利CL,巴基斯坦PK,新西兰NZ,秘鲁PE,哥斯达黎加CR	0	最不发达35国LDC35,最不发达4国LDC4	8	---For automatic pilot
7827	9014.9090	---其他	1.5	0	东盟ASEAN,智利CL,巴基斯坦PK,新西兰NZ,秘鲁PE,哥斯达黎加CR	0	最不发达35国LDC35	8	---Other

序号 No.	税则号列 Tariff Line	货品名称	最惠国税率 MFN(%)	协定税率 Agreement(%)		特惠税率 S.P.(%)		普通税率 Gen.(%)	Article Description
	90.15	**大地测量（包括摄影测量）、水道测量、海洋、水文、气象或地球物理用仪器及装置，不包括罗盘；测距仪：**							**Surveying (including photogrammetrical surveying), hydrographic, oceanographic, hydrological, meteorological or geophysical instruments and appliances, excluding compasses; rangefinders:**
7828	9015.1000	-测距仪	9	0 5	东盟ASEAN,智利CL,新西兰NZ,秘鲁PE,哥斯达黎加CR 巴基斯坦PK	0	最不发达35国LDC35,最不发达4国LDC4	14	-Rangefinders
7829	9015.2000	-经纬仪及视距仪	9	0 5	东盟ASEAN,智利CL,新西兰NZ,秘鲁PE,哥斯达黎加CR 巴基斯坦PK	0	最不发达35国LDC35,最不发达4国LDC4	14	-Theodolites and tachymeters(tacheometers)
7830	9015.3000	-水平仪	9	0 5	东盟ASEAN,智利CL,新西兰NZ,秘鲁PE,哥斯达黎加CR 巴基斯坦PK	0	最不发达35国LDC35,最不发达4国LDC4	14	-Levels
7831	9015.4000	-摄影测量用仪器及装置	9	0 5	东盟ASEAN,智利CL,新西兰NZ,秘鲁PE,哥斯达黎加CR 巴基斯坦PK	0	最不发达35国LDC35,最不发达4国LDC4	14	-Photogrammetrical surveying instruments and appliances
7832	9015.8000	-其他仪器及装置	5	0 0.5 3.5	东盟ASEAN,巴基斯坦PK,新西兰NZ,秘鲁PE,哥斯达黎加CR 智利CL 亚太APTA	0	最不发达35国LDC35,最不发达4国LDC4	14	-Other instruments and appliances
7833	9015.9000	-零件、附件	5	0	东盟ASEAN,智利CL,巴基斯坦PK,新西兰NZ,秘鲁PE,哥斯达黎加CR	0	最不发达35国LDC35,最不发达4国LDC4	14	-Parts and accessories
	90.16	**感量为50毫克或更精密的天平，不论是否带有砝码：**							**Balances of a sensitivity of 50mg or better, with or without weights:**
7834	9016.0010	---感量为0.1毫克或更精密的天平	9	0 5	东盟ASEAN,智利CL,新西兰NZ,秘鲁PE,哥斯达黎加CR 巴基斯坦PK	0	最不发达35国LDC35,最不发达4国LDC4	14	---Of a sensitivity of 0.1mg or better

序号 No.	税则号列 Tariff Line	货品名称	最惠国税率 MFN(%)	协定税率 Agreement(%)		特惠税率 S.P.(%)		普通税率 Gen.(%)	Article Description
7835	9016.0090	---其他	10.5	0 2.1 5	东盟ASEAN,智利CL,新加坡SG,新西兰NZ,秘鲁PE 哥斯达黎加CR 巴基斯坦PK	0	最不发达35国LDC35,最不发达4国LDC4	30	---Other
	90.17	**绘图、划线或数学计算仪器及器具（例如，绘图机、比例缩放仪、分度规、绘图工具、计算尺及盘式计算器）;本章其他税号未列名的手用测量长度的器具（例如，量尺、量带、千分尺及卡尺）：**							**Drawing, marking-out or mathematicalcalculating instruments (for example, drafting machines, pantographs, protractors, drawing sets, slide rules, disc calculators); instruments for measuring length, for use in the hand (for example, measuring rods and tapes, micrometers, callipers), not specified or included else-where in this in this Chapter:**
7836	9017.1000	-绘图台及绘图机，不论是否自动	8	0 5	东盟ASEAN,智利CL,新西兰NZ,秘鲁PE,哥斯达黎加CR 巴基斯坦PK	0	最不发达35国LDC35,最不发达4国LDC4	20	-Drafting tables and machines, whether or not automatic
7837	9017.2000	-其他绘图、划线或数学计算器具	0			0	最不发达35国LDC35,最不发达4国LDC4	70	-Other drawing, marking-out or mathematical calculating instruments
7838	9017.3000	-千分尺、卡尺及量规	8	0 5	东盟ASEAN,智利CL,新西兰NZ,秘鲁PE,哥斯达黎加CR 巴基斯坦PK	0	最不发达35国LDC35,最不发达4国LDC4	20	-Micrometers, callipers and gauges
7839	9017.8000	-其他仪器及器具	8	0 5	东盟ASEAN,智利CL,新西兰NZ,秘鲁PE,哥斯达黎加CR 巴基斯坦PK	0	最不发达35国LDC35,最不发达4国LDC4	20	-Other instruments
7840	9017.9000	-零件、附件	0			0	最不发达35国LDC35,最不发达4国LDC4	20	-Parts and accessories

序号 No.	税则号列 Tariff Line	货品名称	最惠国税率 MFN(%)	协定税率 Agreement(%)		特惠税率 S.P.(%)		普通税率 Gen.(%)	Article Description
	90.18	**医疗、外科、牙科或兽医用仪器及器具，包括闪烁扫描装置、其他电气医疗装置及视力检查仪器:**							**Instruments and appliances used in medical, surgical, dental or veterinary sciences, including scintigraphic apparatus, other electro-medical apparatus and sight-testing instruments:**
		-电气诊断装置(包括功能检查或生理参数检查用装置）:							-Electro-diagnostic apparatus (including apparatus for functional exploratory examination or for checking physiological parameters):
7841	9018.1100	--心电图记录仪	5	0	东盟ASEAN,智利CL,巴基斯坦PK,新西兰NZ,秘鲁PE,哥斯达黎加CR	0	最不发达35国LDC35,最不发达4国LDC4	17	--Electro-cardiographs
		--超声波扫描装置:							--Ultrasonic scanning apparatus:
7842	9018.1210	---B型超声波诊断仪	7	0 6	东盟ASEAN,智利CL,巴基斯坦PK,新西兰NZ,秘鲁PE,哥斯达黎加CR 亚太APTA	0	最不发达35国LDC35,最不发达4国LDC4	35	---B-ultrasonic diagnostic equipment
		---其他:							---Other:
7843	9018.1291	----彩色超声波诊断仪	5	0 4.5	东盟ASEAN,智利CL,巴基斯坦PK,新西兰NZ,秘鲁PE,哥斯达黎加CR 亚太APTA	0	最不发达35国LDC35,最不发达4国LDC4	17	----Chromoscope ultrasonic diagnostic equipment
7844	9018.1299	----其他	5	0 4.5	东盟ASEAN,智利CL,巴基斯坦PK,新西兰NZ,秘鲁PE,哥斯达黎加CR 亚太APTA	0	最不发达35国LDC35,最不发达4国LDC4	17	----Other
		--核磁共振成像装置:							--Magnetic resonance imaging apparatus:
7845	9018.1310	---成套装置	4	0	东盟ASEAN,智利CL,巴基斯坦PK,新西兰NZ,秘鲁PE,哥斯达黎加CR,香港HK	0	最不发达35国LDC35,最不发达4国LDC4	17	---Complete set of appartus
7846	9018.1390	---零件	4	0	东盟ASEAN,智利CL,巴基斯坦PK,新西兰NZ,秘鲁PE,哥斯达黎加CR,香港HK	0	最不发达35国LDC35,最不发达4国LDC4	17	---Parts

序号 No.	税则号列 Tariff Line	货品名称	最惠国税率 MFN(%)	协定税率 Agreement(%)		特惠税率 S.P.(%)		普通税率 Gen.(%)	Article Description
7847	9018.1400	--闪烁摄影装置	5	0	东盟ASEAN,智利CL,巴基斯坦PK,新西兰NZ,秘鲁PE,哥斯达黎加CR	0	最不发达35国LDC35,最不发达4国LDC4	17	--Scintigraphic apparatus
		--其他:							--Other:
7848	9018.1930	---病员监护仪	4	0	东盟ASEAN,智利CL,巴基斯坦PK,新西兰NZ,秘鲁PE,哥斯达黎加CR	0	最不发达35国LDC35,最不发达4国LDC4	17	---Patient monitors:
				3.5	亚太APTA				
		---听力诊断装置:							---Audio-diagnostic apparatus:
7849	9018.1941	----听力计	4	0	东盟ASEAN,智利CL,巴基斯坦PK,新西兰NZ,秘鲁PE,哥斯达黎加CR	0	最不发达35国LDC35,最不发达4国LDC4	17	----Audiometer
				3.5	亚太APTA				
7850	9018.1949	----其他	4	0	东盟ASEAN,智利CL,巴基斯坦PK,新西兰NZ,秘鲁PE,哥斯达黎加CR	0	最不发达35国LDC35,最不发达4国LDC4	17	----Other
				3.5	亚太APTA				
7851	9018.1990	---其他	4	0	东盟ASEAN,智利CL,巴基斯坦PK,新西兰NZ,秘鲁PE,哥斯达黎加CR	0	最不发达35国LDC35,最不发达4国LDC4	17	---Other
				3.5	亚太APTA				
7852	9018.2000	-紫外线及红外线装置	4	0	东盟ASEAN,智利CL,巴基斯坦PK,新西兰NZ,秘鲁PE,哥斯达黎加CR	0	最不发达35国LDC35,最不发达4国LDC4	17	-Ultra-violet or infra-red ray apparatus
		-注射器、针、导管、插管及类似品:							-Syringes, needles, catheters, cannulae and the like:
7853	9018.3100	--注射器，不论是否装有针头	8	0	东盟ASEAN,巴基斯坦PK,新西兰NZ,秘鲁PE,哥斯达黎加CR	0	最不发达35国LDC35,最不发达4国LDC4	50	--Syringes, with or without needles
				0.8	智利CL				
				7.6	亚太APTA				
		--管状金属针头及缝合用针:							--Tubular metal needles and needles for sutures:
7854	9018.3210	---管状金属针头	8	0	东盟ASEAN,智利CL,巴基斯坦PK,新西兰NZ,秘鲁PE,哥斯达黎加CR	0	最不发达35国LDC35,最不发达4国LDC4	50	---Tubular metal needles
				7	亚太APTA				

序号 No.	税则号列 Tariff Line	货品名称	最惠国税率 MFN(%)	协定税率 Agreement(%)		特惠税率 S.P.(%)		普通税率 Gen.(%)	Article Description
7855	9018.3220	---缝合用针	4	0 3.5	东盟ASEAN,智利CL,巴基斯坦PK,新西兰NZ,秘鲁PE,哥斯达黎加CR 亚太APTA	0	最不发达35国LDC35,最不发达4国LDC4	17	---Needles for sutures
7856	9018.3900	--其他	4	0 0.4	东盟ASEAN,巴基斯坦PK,新西兰NZ,秘鲁PE,哥斯达黎加CR 智利CL	0	最不发达35国LDC35,最不发达4国LDC4	17	--Other
		-牙科用其他仪器及器具:							-Other instruments and appliances, used in dental sciences:
7857	9018.4100	--牙钻机，不论是否与其他牙科设备组装在同一底座上	4	0	东盟ASEAN,智利CL,巴基斯坦PK,新西兰NZ,秘鲁PE,哥斯达黎加CR	0	最不发达35国LDC35,最不发达4国LDC4	17	--Dental drill engines, whether or not combined on a single base with other dental equipment
		--其他:							--Other:
7858	9018.4910	---装有牙科设备的牙科用椅	4	0 0.4	东盟ASEAN,巴基斯坦PK,新西兰NZ,秘鲁PE,哥斯达黎加CR 智利CL	0	最不发达35国LDC35,最不发达4国LDC4	17	---Dentists chairs incorporating dental equipment
7859	9018.4990	---其他	4	0 0.4	东盟ASEAN,巴基斯坦PK,新西兰NZ,秘鲁PE,哥斯达黎加CR 智利CL	0	最不发达35国LDC35,最不发达4国LDC4	17	---Other
7860	9018.5000	-眼科用其他仪器及器具	4	0 0.4 3.5	东盟ASEAN,巴基斯坦PK,新西兰NZ,秘鲁PE,哥斯达黎加CR 智利CL 亚太APTA	0	最不发达35国LDC35,最不发达4国LDC4	17	-Other ophthalmic instruments and appliances
		-其他仪器及器具:							-Other instruments and appliances:
7861	9018.9010	---听诊器	4	0 0.4 3.5	东盟ASEAN,巴基斯坦PK,新西兰NZ,秘鲁PE,哥斯达黎加CR,香港HK 智利CL 亚太APTA	0	最不发达35国LDC35,最不发达4国LDC4	17	---Stethoscopes
7862	9018.9020	---血压测量仪器及器具	4	0 0.4 3.5	东盟ASEAN,巴基斯坦PK,新西兰NZ,秘鲁PE,哥斯达黎加CR,香港HK 智利CL 亚太APTA	0	最不发达35国LDC35,最不发达4国LDC4	17	---Sphygmomanometers

序号 No.	税则号列 Tariff Line	货品名称	最惠国税率 MFN(%)	协定税率 Agreement(%)		特惠税率 S.P.(%)		普通税率 Gen.(%)	Article Description
7863	9018.9030	---内窥镜	4	0 0.4 3.5	东盟ASEAN,巴基斯坦PK,新西兰NZ,秘鲁PE,哥斯达黎加CR,香港HK 智利CL 亚太APTA	0	最不发达35国LDC35,最不发达4国LDC4	17	---Endoscopes
7864	9018.9040	---肾脏透析设备（人工肾）	4	0 0.4 3.5	东盟ASEAN,巴基斯坦PK,新西兰NZ,秘鲁PE,哥斯达黎加CR,香港HK 智利CL 亚太APTA	0	最不发达35国LDC35,最不发达4国LDC4	17	---Artificial kidney (dialysis) apparatus
7865	9018.9050	---透热疗法设备	4	0 0.4 3.5	东盟ASEAN,巴基斯坦PK,新西兰NZ,秘鲁PE,哥斯达黎加CR,香港HK 智利CL 亚太APTA	0	最不发达35国LDC35,最不发达4国LDC4	17	---Diathermy apparatus
7866	9018.9060	---输血设备	4	0 0.4 3.5	东盟ASEAN,巴基斯坦PK,新西兰NZ,秘鲁PE,哥斯达黎加CR,香港HK 智利CL 亚太APTA	0	最不发达35国LDC35,最不发达4国LDC4	17	---Blood transfusion apparatus
7867	9018.9070	---麻醉设备	4	0 0.4 3.5	东盟ASEAN,巴基斯坦PK,新西兰NZ,秘鲁PE,哥斯达黎加CR,香港HK 智利CL 亚太APTA	0	最不发达35国LDC35,最不发达4国LDC4	17	---Anaesthetic apparatus and instruments
7868	9018.9080	---宫内节育器	4 △0	0 0.4 2	东盟ASEAN,巴基斯坦PK,新西兰NZ,秘鲁PE,哥斯达黎加CR,香港HK 智利CL 亚太APTA	0	最不发达35国LDC35,最不发达4国LDC4	17	---Intrauterine contraceptive device
7869	9018.9090	---其他	4	0 0.4 3.5	东盟ASEAN,巴基斯坦PK,新西兰NZ,秘鲁PE,哥斯达黎加CR,香港HK,澳门MO 智利CL 亚太APTA	0	最不发达35国LDC35,最不发达4国LDC4	17	---Other
	90.19	**机械疗法器具;按摩器具;心理功能测验装置;臭氧治疗器;氧气治疗器、喷雾治疗器、人工呼吸器及其他治疗用呼吸器具:**							**Mechano-therapy appliances; massage apparatus; psychological aptitudetesting apparatus; ozone therapy, oxygen therapy, aerosol therapy, artificial respiration or other therapeutic respiration apparatus:**

序号 No.	税则号列 Tariff Line	货品名称	最惠国税率 MFN(%)	协定税率 Agreement(%)		特惠税率 S.P.(%)		普通税率 Gen.(%)	Article Description
		-机械疗法器具;按摩器具;心理功能测验装置:							-Mechano-therapy appliances; massage apparatus; psychological aptitudetesting apparatus:
7870	9019.1010	---按摩器具	15	0 1.5 3 7.5 12	东盟ASEAN,新加坡SG,新西兰NZ,香港HK 智利CL 哥斯达黎加CR 秘鲁PE 巴基斯坦PK	0	最不发达35国LDC35	40	---Massage apparatus
7871	9019.1090	---其他	4	0 0.4	东盟ASEAN,巴基斯坦PK,新西兰NZ,秘鲁PE,哥斯达黎加CR,香港HK 智利CL	0	最不发达35国LDC35,最不发达4国LDC4	30	---Other
7872	9019.2000	-臭氧治疗器、氧气治疗器、喷雾治疗器、人工呼吸器及其他治疗用呼吸器具	4	0	东盟ASEAN,智利CL,巴基斯坦PK,新西兰NZ,秘鲁PE,哥斯达黎加CR,澳门MO	0	最不发达35国LDC35,最不发达4国LDC4	17	-Ozone therapy, oxygen therapy, aerosol therapy, artificial respiration or other therapeutic respiration apparatus
	90.20	**其他呼吸器具及防毒面具，但不包括既无机械零件又无可互换过滤器的防护面具:**							**Other breathing appliances and gas masks, excluding protective masks having neither mechanical parts nor replaceable filters:**
7873	9020.0000	其他呼吸器具及防毒面具，但不包括既无机械零件又无可互换过滤器的防护面具	8 △4	0 0.8 5	东盟ASEAN,新西兰NZ,秘鲁PE,哥斯达黎加CR,香港HK,澳门MO 智利CL 巴基斯坦PK	0	最不发达35国LDC35,最不发达4国LDC4	30	Other breathing appliances and gas masks, excluding protective masks having neither mechanical parts nor replaceable filters
	90.21	**矫形器具，包括支具、外科手术带、疝气带;夹板及其他骨折用具;人造的人体部分;助听器及为弥补生理缺陷或残疾而穿戴、携带或植入人体内的其他器具:**							**Orthopaedic appliances, including crutches, surgical belts and trusses; splints and other fracture appliances; artificial parts of the body; hearing aids and other appliances which are worn or carried, or implanted in the body, to compensate for a defect or disability:**
7874	9021.1000	-矫形或骨折用器具:	4	0 0.4	东盟ASEAN,巴基斯坦PK,新西兰NZ,秘鲁PE,哥斯达黎加CR 智利CL	0	最不发达35国LDC35,最不发达4国LDC4	17	-Orthopaedic or fracture appliances
		-假牙及牙齿固定件:							-Artificial teeth and dental fittings:

序号 No.	税则号列 Tariff Line	货品名称	最惠国税率 MFN(%)	协定税率 Agreement(%)		特惠税率 S.P.(%)		普通税率 Gen.(%)	Article Description
7875	9021.2100	--假牙	4	0	东盟ASEAN,智利CL,巴基斯坦PK,新西兰NZ,秘鲁PE,哥斯达黎加CR,香港HK	0	最不发达35国LDC35,最不发达4国LDC4	17	--Artificial teeth
7876	9021.2900	--其他	4	0	东盟ASEAN,智利CL,巴基斯坦PK,新西兰NZ,秘鲁PE,哥斯达黎加CR	0	最不发达35国LDC35,最不发达4国LDC4	17	--Other
		-其他人造的人体部分:							-Other artificial parts of the body:
7877	9021.3100	--人造关节	4	0	东盟ASEAN,智利CL,巴基斯坦PK,新西兰NZ,秘鲁PE,哥斯达黎加CR,台湾TW	0	最不发达35国LDC35,最不发达4国LDC4	17	--Artificial joints
7878	9021.3900	--其他	4	0 0.4	东盟ASEAN,巴基斯坦PK,新西兰NZ,秘鲁PE,哥斯达黎加CR 智利CL	0	最不发达35国LDC35,最不发达4国LDC4	17	--Other
7879	9021.4000	-助听器，不包括零件、附件	4	0	东盟ASEAN,智利CL,巴基斯坦PK,新西兰NZ,秘鲁PE,哥斯达黎加CR	0	最不发达35国LDC35,最不发达4国LDC4	17	-Hearing aids, excluding parts and accessories
7880	9021.5000	-心脏起搏器,不包括零件、附件	4 △2	0	东盟ASEAN,智利CL,巴基斯坦PK,新西兰NZ,秘鲁PE,哥斯达黎加CR	0	最不发达35国LDC35,最不发达4国LDC4	17	-Pacemakers for stimulating heart muscles, excluding parts and accessories
		-其他:							-Other:
		---支架:							---Stents:
7881	9021.9011	----血管支架	4 △2	0 0.4	东盟ASEAN,巴基斯坦PK,新西兰NZ,秘鲁PE,哥斯达黎加CR 智利CL	0	最不发达35国LDC35,最不发达4国LDC4	17	----Intravascular stents
7882	9021.9019	----其他	4 △2	0 0.4	东盟ASEAN,巴基斯坦PK,新西兰NZ,秘鲁PE,哥斯达黎加CR 智利CL	0	最不发达35国LDC35,最不发达4国LDC4	17	----Other

序号 No.	税则号列 Tariff Line	货品名称	最惠国税率 MFN(%)	协定税率 Agreement(%)	特惠税率 S.P.(%)	普通税率 Gen.(%)	Article Description
7883	9021.9090	---其他	4	0 东盟ASEAN,巴基斯坦PK,新西兰NZ,秘鲁PE,哥斯达黎加CR 0.4 智利CL	0 最不发达35国LDC35,最不发达4国LDC4	17	---Other
	ex90219090	人工耳蜗植入装置	△0				Artificial cochlear implant appliances
	90.22	**X射线或α射线、β射线、γ射线的应用设备，不论是否用于医疗、外科、牙科或兽医，包括射线照相及射线治疗设备，X射线管及其他X射线发生器、高压发生器、控制板及控制台、荧光屏、检查或治疗用的桌、椅及类似品:**					**Apparatus based on the use of X-rays or of alpha, beta or gamma radiations, whether or not for medical, surgical, dental or veterinary uses, including radiography or radiotherapy apparatus, X-ray tubes and other X-ray generators, high tension generators, control panels and desks, screens, examination or treatment tables, chairs and the like:**
		-X射线的应用设备，不论是否用于医疗、外科、牙科或兽医，包括射线照相或射线治疗设备:					-Apparatus based on the use of X-rays, whether or not for medical, surgical, dental or veterinary uses, including radiography or radiotherapy apparatus:
7884	9022.1200	--X射线断层检查仪	4	0 东盟ASEAN,智利CL,巴基斯坦PK,新西兰NZ,秘鲁PE,哥斯达黎加CR 2.8 亚太APTA	0 最不发达35国LDC35,最不发达4国LDC4	11	--Computed tomography apparatus
7885	9022.1300	--其他，牙科用	4	0 东盟ASEAN,智利CL,巴基斯坦PK,新西兰NZ,秘鲁PE,哥斯达黎加CR	0 最不发达35国LDC35,最不发达4国LDC4	11	--Other, for dental uses
7886	9022.1400	--其他，医疗、外科或兽医用	4	0 东盟ASEAN,智利CL,巴基斯坦PK,新西兰NZ,秘鲁PE,哥斯达黎加CR	0 最不发达35国LDC35,最不发达4国LDC4	11	--Other, for medical, surgical or veterinary uses
		--其他:					--For other uses:
7887	9022.1910	---低剂量X射线安全检查设备	4	0 东盟ASEAN,智利CL,巴基斯坦PK,新西兰NZ,秘鲁PE,哥斯达黎加CR	0 最不发达35国LDC35,最不发达4国LDC4	11	---Low dosage X-ray security inspecting equipment

序号 No.	税则号列 Tariff Line	货品名称	最惠国税率 MFN(%)	协定税率 Agreement(%)		特惠税率 S.P.(%)		普通税率 Gen.(%)	Article Description
7888	9022.1920	---X射线无损探伤检测仪	4	0	东盟ASEAN,智利CL,巴基斯坦PK,新西兰NZ,秘鲁PE,哥斯达黎加CR,香港HK	0	最不发达35国LDC35,最不发达4国LDC4	11	---X-ray Non-destructive testing instruments
7889	9022.1990	---其他	4	0	东盟ASEAN,智利CL,巴基斯坦PK,新西兰NZ,秘鲁PE,哥斯达黎加CR,香港HK	0	最不发达35国LDC35,最不发达4国LDC4	11	---Other
		-α射线、β射线、γ射线的应用设备，不论是否用于医疗、外科、牙科或兽医，包括射线照相或射线治疗设备:							-Apparatus based on the use of alpha, beta or gamma radiations, whether or not for medical, surgical, dental or veterinary uses, including radiography or radiotherapy apparatus:
7890	9022.2100	--医疗、外科、牙科或兽医用	4	0	东盟ASEAN,智利CL,巴基斯坦PK,新西兰NZ,秘鲁PE,哥斯达黎加CR	0	最不发达35国LDC35,最不发达4国LDC4	11	--For medical, surgical, dental or veterinary uses
		--其他:							--For other uses:
7891	9022.2910	---γ射线无损探伤检测仪	6	0 5	东盟ASEAN,智利CL,新西兰NZ,秘鲁PE,哥斯达黎加CR 巴基斯坦PK	0	最不发达35国LDC35,最不发达4国LDC4	11	---γ-ray Non-destructive testing instruments
7892	9022.2990	---其他	6	0 5	东盟ASEAN,智利CL,新西兰NZ,秘鲁PE,哥斯达黎加CR 巴基斯坦PK	0	最不发达35国LDC35,最不发达4国LDC4	11	---Other
7893	9022.3000	-X射线管	2	0	东盟ASEAN,智利CL,巴基斯坦PK,新西兰NZ,秘鲁PE,哥斯达黎加CR	0	最不发达35国LDC35,最不发达4国LDC4	11	-X-ray tubes
		-其他，包括零件、附件:							-Other, including parts and accessories:
7894	9022.9010	---X射线影像增强器	6	0 0.6 5	东盟ASEAN,新西兰NZ,秘鲁PE,哥斯达黎加CR 智利CL 巴基斯坦PK	0	最不发达35国LDC35,最不发达4国LDC4	11	---X-ray intensifiers

序号 No.	税则号列 Tariff Line	货品名称	最惠国税率 MFN(%)	协定税率 Agreement(%)	特惠税率 S.P.(%)	普通税率 Gen.(%)	Article Description
7895	9022.9090	---其他	6	0 东盟ASEAN,新西兰NZ,秘鲁PE,哥斯达黎加CR 0.6 智利CL 5 巴基斯坦PK	0 最不发达35国LDC35,最不发达4国LDC4	11	---Other
	ex90229090	射线发生器的零部件	△1				Parts of ray generators
	90.23	**专供示范（例如，教学或展览）而无其他用途的仪器、装置及模型:**					**Instruments, apparatus and models, designed for demonstrational purposes (for example, in education or exhibitions), unsuitable for other uses:**
7896	9023.0000	专供示范（例如，教学或展览）而无其他用途的仪器、装置及模型	7	0 东盟ASEAN,智利CL,新西兰NZ,秘鲁PE,哥斯达黎加CR 5 巴基斯坦PK	0 最不发达35国LDC35,最不发达4国LDC4	20	Instruments, apparatus and models, designed for demonstrational purposes (for example, in education or exhibitions), unsuitable for other uses
	90.24	**各种材料（例如，金属、木材、纺织材料、纸张、塑料）的硬度、强度、压缩性、弹性或其他机械性能的试验机器及器具:**					**Machines and appliances for testing the hardness, strength, compressibility, elasticity or other mechanical properties of materials (for example, metals, wood, textiles, paper, plastics):**
		-金属材料的试验用机器及器具:					-Machines and appliances for testing metals:
7897	9024.1010	---电子万能试验机	7	0 东盟ASEAN,智利CL,新西兰NZ,秘鲁PE,哥斯达黎加CR 5 巴基斯坦PK 6.5 亚太APTA	0 最不发达35国LDC35,最不发达4国LDC4	20	---Electronic universal testing machine
7898	9024.1020	---硬度计	7	0 东盟ASEAN,智利CL,新西兰NZ,秘鲁PE,哥斯达黎加CR 5 巴基斯坦PK 6.5 亚太APTA	0 最不发达35国LDC35,最不发达4国LDC4	20	---Sclerometer
7899	9024.1090	---其他	7	0 东盟ASEAN,智利CL,新西兰NZ,秘鲁PE,哥斯达黎加CR 5 巴基斯坦PK 6.5 亚太APTA	0 最不发达35国LDC35,最不发达4国LDC4	20	---Other
7900	9024.8000	-其他机器及器具	5	0 东盟ASEAN,智利CL,巴基斯坦PK,新西兰NZ,秘鲁PE,哥斯达黎加CR	0 最不发达35国LDC35,最不发达4国LDC4	20	-Other machines and appliances

序号 No.	税则号列 Tariff Line	货品名称	最惠国税率 MFN(%)	协定税率 Agreement(%)		特惠税率 S.P.(%)		普通税率 Gen.(%)	Article Description
7901	9024.9000	-零件、附件	6	0 5	东盟ASEAN,智利CL,新西兰NZ,秘鲁PE,哥斯达黎加CR 巴基斯坦PK	0	最不发达35国LDC35,最不发达4国LDC4	20	-Parts and accessories
	90.25	**记录式或非记录式的液体比重计及类似的浮子式仪器、温度计、高温计、气压计、温度计、干湿球温度计及其组合装置:**							**Hydrometers and similar floating instruments, thermometers and pyrometers, barometers, hygrometers and psychrometers, recording or not, and any combination of these instruments:**
		-温度计及高温计,未与其他仪器组合:							-Thermometers and pyrometers, not combined with other instruments:
7902	9025.1100	--液体温度计,可直接读数	4	0	东盟ASEAN,智利CL,巴基斯坦PK,新西兰NZ,秘鲁PE,哥斯达黎加CR,澳门MO	0	最不发达35国LDC35,最不发达4国LDC4	40	--Liquid-filled, for direct reading
		--其他:							--Other:
7903	9025.1910	---工业用	8.4	0 0.8 5 8	东盟ASEAN,新西兰NZ,秘鲁PE,哥斯达黎加CR 智利CL 巴基斯坦PK 亚太APTA	0	最不发达35国LDC35,最不发达4国LDC4	20	---For technical use
7904	9025.1990	---其他	8.4	0 0.8 5 8	东盟ASEAN,新西兰NZ,秘鲁PE,哥斯达黎加CR,澳门MO 智利CL 巴基斯坦PK 亚太APTA	0	最不发达35国LDC35,最不发达4国LDC4	80	---Other
	ex90251990	红外线人体测温仪	△4						Body temperature measuring apparatus by infrared ray
7905	9025.8000	-其他仪器	11	0 1.1 2.2 5 5.5	东盟ASEAN,新加坡SG,新西兰NZ 智利CL 哥斯达黎加CR 巴基斯坦PK 秘鲁PE	0	最不发达35国LDC35	30	-Other instruments
7906	9025.9000	-零件、附件	8	0 0.8 5 7.6	东盟ASEAN,新西兰NZ,秘鲁PE,哥斯达黎加CR 智利CL 巴基斯坦PK 亚太APTA	0	最不发达35国LDC35,最不发达4国LDC4	20	-Parts and accessories

序号 No.	税则号列 Tariff Line	货品名称	最惠国税率 MFN(%)	协定税率 Agreement(%)	特惠税率 S.P.(%)	普通税率 Gen.(%)	Article Description
	ex90259000	红外线测温仪传感器元件	△3				Sensors of infrared temperature measuring apparatus
	90.26	**液体或气体的流量、液位、压力或其他变化量的测量或检验仪器及装置（例如，流量计、液位计、压力表、热量计），但不包括税号 90.14、90.15、90.28 或 90.32 的仪器及装置:**					**Instruments and apparatus for measuring or checking the flow, level, pressure or other variables of liquids or gases (for example, flow meters, level gauges, manometers, heat meters), excluding instruments and apparatus of heading No.90.14, 90.15, 90.28 or 90.32:**
7907	9026.1000	-测量、检验液体流量或液位的仪器及装置	0		0 最不发达 35 国 LDC35, 最不发达 4 国 LDC4	17	-For measuring or checking the flow or level of liquids
		-测量、检验压力的仪器及装置:					-For measuring or checking pressure:
7908	9026.2010	---压力/差压变送器	0		0 最不发达 35 国 LDC35, 最不发达 4 国 LDC4	17	---Pressure/differential pressure transmitters
7909	9026.2090	---其他	0		0 最不发达 35 国 LDC35, 最不发达 4 国 LDC4	17	---Other
		-其他仪器及装置:					-Other instruments or apparatus:
7910	9026.8010	---测量气体流量的仪器及装置	0		0 最不发达 35 国 LDC35, 最不发达 4 国 LDC4	17	---Instruments and apparatus for measuring the flow of gas
7911	9026.8090	---其他	0		0 最不发达 35 国 LDC35, 最不发达 4 国 LDC4	17	---Other
7912	9026.9000	-零件、附件	0		0 最不发达 35 国 LDC35, 最不发达 4 国 LDC4	17	-Parts and accessories

序号 No.	税则号列 Tariff Line	货品名称	最惠国税率 MFN(%)	协定税率 Agreement(%)		特惠税率 S.P.(%)		普通税率 Gen.(%)	Article Description
	90.27	**理化分析仪器及装置（例如，偏振仪、折光仪、分光仪、气体或烟雾分析仪）；测量或检验粘性、多孔性、膨胀性、表面张力及类似性能的仪器及装置;测量或检验热量、声量或光量的仪器及装置（包括曝光表）;检镜切片机:**							**Instruments and apparatus for physical or chemical analysis (for example, polarimeters, refractometers, spectrometers, gas or smoke analysis apparatus); instruments and apparatus for measuring or checking viscosity, porosity, expansion, surface tension or the like; instruments and apparatus for measuring or checking quantities of heat, sound or light (including exposure meters); microtomes:**
7913	9027.1000	-气体或烟雾分析仪	7	0 0.75	东盟ASEAN,新西兰NZ,秘鲁PE,哥斯达黎加CR,香港HK 智利CL 巴基斯坦PK	0	最不发达35国LDC35,最不发达4国LDC4	17	-Gas or smoke analysis apparatus
		-色谱仪及电泳仪:							-Chromatographs and electrophoresis instruments:
		---色谱仪:							---Chromatographs instruments:
7914	9027.2011	----气相色谱仪	0			0	最不发达35国LDC35,最不发达4国LDC4	17	----Gas-chromatrographs instruments
7915	9027.2012	----液相色谱仪	0			0	最不发达35国LDC35,最不发达4国LDC4	17	----Liquid-chromatrographs instruments
7916	9027.2019	----其他	0			0	最不发达35国LDC35,最不发达4国LDC4	17	----Other
7917	9027.2020	---电泳仪	0			0	最不发达35国LDC35,最不发达4国LDC4	17	---Electrophoresis instruments

序号 No.	税则号列 Tariff Line	货品名称	最惠国税率 MFN(%)	协定税率 Agreement(%)		特惠税率 S.P.(%)		普通税率 Gen.(%)	Article Description
7918	9027.3000	-使用光学射线(紫外线、可见光、红外线)的分光仪、分光光度计及摄谱仪	0			0	最不发达35国LDC35,最不发达4国LDC4	17	-Spectrometers, spectrophotometers and spectrographs using optical radiations (UV, visible, IR)
7919	9027.5000	-使用光学射线(紫外线、可见光、红外线)的其他仪器及装置	0			0	最不发达35国LDC35,最不发达4国LDC4	17	-Other instruments and apparatus using optical radiations (UV, visible, IR)
		-其他仪器及装置:							-Other instruments and apparatus:
		---质谱仪:							---Mass spectrograph:
7920	9027.8011	----集成电路生产用氦质谱检漏台	0			0	最不发达35国LDC35,最不发达4国LDC4	17	----Integrated circuit belium spectra leak detectors
7921	9027.8012	----质谱联用仪	0			0	最不发达35国LDC35,最不发达4国LDC4	17	----Combined instruments or apparatus utilized mass spectrograph
7922	9027.8019	----其他	0			0	最不发达35国LDC35,最不发达4国LDC4	17	----Other
		---其他:							---Other:
7923	9027.8091	----曝光表	14	0 2.8 11.2	东盟ASEAN,智利CL,新加坡SG,新西兰NZ,秘鲁PE 哥斯达黎加CR 巴基斯坦PK	0	最不发达35国LDC35	70	----Exposure meters
7924	9027.8099	----其他	0			0	最不发达35国LDC35,最不发达4国LDC4	17	----Other
7925	9027.9000	-检镜切片机;零件、附件	0			0	最不发达35国LDC35,最不发达4国LDC4	17	-Microtomes; parts and accessories

序号 No.	税则号列 Tariff Line	货品名称	最惠国税率 MFN(%)	协定税率 Agreement(%)		特惠税率 S.P.(%)		普通税率 Gen.(%)	Article Description
	90.28	**生产或供应气体、液体及电力用的计量仪表，包括它们的校准仪表:**							**Gas, liquid or electricity supply or production meters, including calibrating meters therefor:**
		-气量计:							-Gas meters:
7926	9028.1010	---煤气表	10	0	东盟ASEAN,智利CL,新西兰NZ,秘鲁PE,哥斯达黎加CR	0	最不发达35国LDC35	30	---Coal gas meters
				5	巴基斯坦PK				
7927	9028.1090	---其他	10	0	东盟ASEAN,智利CL,新加坡SG,新西兰NZ,秘鲁PE,哥斯达黎加CR	0	最不发达35国LDC35	30	---Other
				5	巴基斯坦PK				
		-液量计:							-Liquid meters:
7928	9028.2010	---水表	10	0	东盟ASEAN,新加坡SG,新西兰NZ,秘鲁PE,哥斯达黎加CR	0	最不发达35国LDC35	30	---Water meters
				1	智利CL				
				5	巴基斯坦PK				
7929	9028.2090	---其他	10	0	东盟ASEAN,新加坡SG,新西兰NZ,哥斯达黎加CR	0	最不发达35国LDC35	30	---Other
				1	智利CL				
				5	巴基斯坦PK,秘鲁PE				
		-电量计:							-Electricity meters:
		---电度表:							---Watt-hour meter:
7930	9028.3011	----单相感应式	10	0	东盟ASEAN,新西兰NZ,秘鲁PE,哥斯达黎加CR,香港HK	0	最不发达35国LDC35	30	----Single-phase induction
				1	智利CL				
				5	巴基斯坦PK				
7931	9028.3012	----三相感应式	10	0	东盟ASEAN,新西兰NZ,秘鲁PE,哥斯达黎加CR,香港HK	0	最不发达35国LDC35	30	----Triple-phase induction
				1	智利CL				
				5	巴基斯坦PK				
7932	9028.3013	----单相电子式(静止式)	10	0	东盟ASEAN,新西兰NZ,秘鲁PE,哥斯达黎加CR,香港HK	0	最不发达35国LDC35	30	----Single-phase static
				1	智利CL				
				5	巴基斯坦PK				
7933	9028.3014	----三相电子式(静止式)	10	0	东盟ASEAN,新西兰NZ,秘鲁PE,哥斯达黎加CR,香港HK	0	最不发达35国LDC35	30	----Triple-phase static
				1	智利CL				
				5	巴基斯坦PK				
7934	9028.3019	----其他	10	0	东盟ASEAN,新西兰NZ,秘鲁PE,哥斯达黎加CR,香港HK	0	最不发达35国LDC35	30	----Other
				1	智利CL				
				5	巴基斯坦PK				
7935	9028.3090	---其他	10	0	东盟ASEAN,新加坡SG,新西兰NZ,秘鲁PE,哥斯达黎加CR,香港HK	0	最不发达35国LDC35	30	---Other
				1	智利CL				
				5	巴基斯坦PK				

序号 No.	税则号列 Tariff Line	货品名称	最惠国税率 MFN(%)	协定税率 Agreement(%)		特惠税率 S.P.(%)		普通税率 Gen.(%)	Article Description
		-零件、附件:							-Parts and accessories:
7936	9028.9010	---工业用	8.4	0 0.8 5	东盟ASEAN,新西兰NZ,秘鲁PE,哥斯达黎加CR 智利CL 巴基斯坦PK	0	最不发达35国LDC35,最不发达4国LDC4	30	---For technical use
7937	9028.9090	---其他	8.4	0 0.8 5	东盟ASEAN,新西兰NZ,秘鲁PE,哥斯达黎加CR 智利CL 巴基斯坦PK	0	最不发达35国LDC35,最不发达4国LDC4	50	---Other
	90.29	**转数计、产量计数器、车费计、里程计、步数计及类似仪表;速度计及转速表,税号90.14及90.15的仪表除外;频闪观测仪:**							**Revolution counters, production counters, taximeters, mileometers, pedometers and the like; speed indicators and tachometers, other than those of heading No.90.14 or 90.15; stroboscopes:**
		-转数计、产量计数器、车费计、里程计、步数计及类似仪表:							-Revolution counters, production counters, taximeters, mileometers, pedometers and the like:
7938	9029.1010	---转数计	15	0 3 7.5 12	东盟ASEAN,智利CL,新加坡SG,新西兰NZ 哥斯达黎加CR 秘鲁PE 巴基斯坦PK	0	最不发达35国LDC35	50	---Revolution counters
7939	9029.1020	---车费计、里程计	15	0 3 7.5 12	东盟ASEAN,智利CL,新加坡SG,新西兰NZ 哥斯达黎加CR 秘鲁PE 巴基斯坦PK	0	最不发达35国LDC35	35	---Taximeters and mileometers
7940	9029.1090	---其他	15	0 3 7.5 12	东盟ASEAN,智利CL,新加坡SG,新西兰NZ 哥斯达黎加CR 秘鲁PE 巴基斯坦PK	0	最不发达35国LDC35	35	---Other
		-速度计及转速表,频闪观测仪:							-Speed indicators and tachometers; stroboscopes:
7941	9029.2010	---车辆用速度计	10	0 5	东盟ASEAN,智利CL,新西兰NZ,秘鲁PE,哥斯达黎加CR 巴基斯坦PK	0	最不发达35国LDC35	35	---Speed indicators for motor vehicles
7942	9029.2090	---其他	10	0 5	东盟ASEAN,智利CL,新西兰NZ,秘鲁PE,哥斯达黎加CR 巴基斯坦PK	0	最不发达35国LDC35	35	---Other

序号 No.	税则号列 Tariff Line	货品名称	最惠国税率 MFN(%)	协定税率 Agreement(%)		特惠税率 S.P.(%)		普通税率 Gen.(%)	Article Description
7943	9029.9000	-零件、附件	6	0 5	东盟ASEAN,智利CL,新西兰NZ,秘鲁PE,哥斯达黎加CR 巴基斯坦PK	0	最不发达35国LDC35,最不发达4国LDC4	35	-Parts and accessories
	90.30	**示波器、频谱分析仪及其他用于电量测量或检验的仪器和装置，但不包括税号90.28的各种仪表;α射线、β射线、γ射线、X射线、宇宙射线或其他离子射线的测量或检验仪器及装置:**							**Oscilloscopes, spectrum analysers and other instruments and apparatus for measuring or checking eclectrical quantities, excluding meters of heading No.90.28; instruments and apparatus for measuring or detecting alpha, beta, gamma, X-ray, cosmic or other ionizing radiations:**
7944	9030.1000	-离子射线的测量或检验仪器及装置	5	0	东盟ASEAN,智利CL,巴基斯坦PK,新西兰NZ,秘鲁PE,哥斯达黎加CR	0	最不发达35国LDC35,最不发达4国LDC4	20	-Instruments and apparatus for measuring or detecting ionizing radiations
		-示波器:							-Oscilloscopes and oscillographs:
7945	9030.2010	---测试频率在300兆赫兹以下的通用示波器	8	0 5	东盟ASEAN,智利CL,新加坡SG,新西兰NZ,秘鲁PE,哥斯达黎加CR 巴基斯坦PK	0	最不发达35国LDC35,最不发达4国LDC4	80	---For general use, of test frequency less than 300MHz
7946	9030.2090	---其他	5	0	东盟ASEAN,智利CL,巴基斯坦PK,新西兰NZ,秘鲁PE,哥斯达黎加CR	0	最不发达35国LDC35,最不发达4国LDC4	20	---Other
		-检测电压、电流、电阻或功率的其他仪器及装置:							-Other instruments and apparatus, for measuring or checking voltage, current, resistance or power:
		--万用表，不带记录装置:							--Multimeters without a recording device:
7947	9030.3110	---量程在五位半及以下的数字万用表	15	0 3 7.5 12	东盟ASEAN,智利CL,新加坡SG,新西兰NZ,澳门MO 哥斯达黎加CR 秘鲁PE 巴基斯坦PK	0	最不发达35国LDC35	130	---Digital, of measuring range of 5 1/2 or less

序号 No.	税则号列 Tariff Line	货品名称	最惠国税率 MFN(%)	协定税率 Agreement(%)		特惠税率 S.P.(%)		普通税率 Gen.(%)	Article Description
7948	9030.3190	---其他	5	0	东盟ASEAN,智利CL,巴基斯坦PK,新西兰NZ,秘鲁PE,哥斯达黎加CR	0	最不发达35国LDC35,最不发达4国LDC4	20	---Other
7949	9030.3200	--万用表，带记录装置	8	0	东盟ASEAN,智利CL,新西兰NZ,秘鲁PE,哥斯达黎加CR	0	最不发达35国LDC35,最不发达4国LDC4	20	--Multimeters with a recording device
				5	巴基斯坦PK				
		--其他，不带记录装置:							--Other, without a recording device:
7950	9030.3310	---量程在五位半及以下的数字电流表、电压表	15	0	东盟ASEAN,新加坡SG,新西兰NZ,香港HK	0	最不发达35国LDC35	130	---Digital ammeters or voltmeters, of measuring rang of 5 1/2 or less
				1.5	智利CL				
				3	哥斯达黎加CR				
				7.5	秘鲁PE				
				12	巴基斯坦PK				
7951	9030.3320	---电阻测试仪	14	0	东盟ASEAN,新加坡SG,新西兰NZ,秘鲁PE,香港HK	0	最不发达35国LDC35	80	---Resistance measuring instruments
				1.4	智利CL				
				2.8	哥斯达黎加CR				
				11.2	巴基斯坦PK				
7952	9030.3390	---其他	9	0	东盟ASEAN,新西兰NZ,秘鲁PE,哥斯达黎加CR,香港HK	0	最不发达35国LDC35,最不发达4国LDC4	20	---Other
				0.9	智利CL				
				5	巴基斯坦PK				
7953	9030.3900	--其他,带记录装置	8	0	东盟ASEAN,智利CL,新西兰NZ,秘鲁PE,哥斯达黎加CR	0	最不发达35国LDC35,最不发达4国LDC4	20	--Other, with a recording device
				5	巴基斯坦PK				
		-通信专用的其他仪器及装置（例如，串音测试器、增益测量仪、失真度表、噪声计）:							-Other instruments and apparatus, specially designed for telecommunications (for example, cross-talk meters, gain measuring instruments, distortion factor meters, psophometers):
7954	9030.4010	---测试频率在12.4千兆赫兹以下的数字式频率计	0			0	最不发达35国LDC35,最不发达4国LDC4	80	---Digital frequency meters, of test frequency less than 12.4GHz

序号 No.	税则号列 Tariff Line	货品名称	最惠国税率 MFN(%)	协定税率 Agreement(%)		特惠税率 S.P.(%)		普通税率 Gen.(%)	Article Description
7955	9030.4090	---其他	0			0	最不发达 35 国 LDC35,最不发达 4 国 LDC4	20	---Other
		-其他仪器及装置:							-Other instruments and apparatus:
7956	9030.8200	--测试或检验半导体晶片或器件用	0			0	最不发达 35 国 LDC35,最不发达 4 国 LDC4	20	--For measuring or checking semiconductor wafers or devices
		--其他，带记录装置的:							--Other, with a recording device:
7957	9030.8410	---电感及电容测试仪	10	0 5	东盟ASEAN,智利CL,新加坡SG,新西兰NZ,秘鲁PE,哥斯达黎加CR 巴基斯坦PK	0	最不发达 35 国 LDC35	80	---For measuring inductances or capacitances
7958	9030.8490	---其他	8	0 5	东盟ASEAN,智利CL,新西兰NZ,秘鲁PE,哥斯达黎加CR 巴基斯坦PK	0	最不发达 35 国 LDC35,最不发达 4 国 LDC4	20	---Other
		--其他:							--Other:
7959	9030.8910	---电感及电容测试仪	14	0 1.4 2.8 11.2	东盟ASEAN,新加坡SG,新西兰NZ,秘鲁PE 智利CL 哥斯达黎加CR 巴基斯坦PK	0	最不发达 35 国 LDC35	80	---For measuring inductances or capacitances
7960	9030.8990	---其他	8	0 0.8 5	东盟ASEAN,新西兰NZ,秘鲁PE,哥斯达黎加CR 智利CL 巴基斯坦PK	0	最不发达 35 国 LDC35,最不发达 4 国 LDC4	20	---Other
7961	9030.9000	-零件、附件	7	0 5	东盟ASEAN,智利CL,新西兰NZ,秘鲁PE,哥斯达黎加CR,香港HK 巴基斯坦PK	0	最不发达 35 国 LDC35,最不发达 4 国 LDC4	17	-Parts and accessories
	ex90309000	用于检测半导体晶片及器件的仪器的零件和附件;ITA产品用的印刷电路组件，包括外接组件，如符合PCMCIA标准的卡	△0						Parts and accessories of instruments and apparatus for measuring or checking semiconductor wafers or devices; Printed Circuit Assemblies for products falling within the ITA, including such assemblies for external connections such as cards that conform to the PCMCIA standard

序号 No.	税则号列 Tariff Line	货品名称	最惠国税率 MFN(%)	协定税率 Agreement(%)		特惠税率 S.P.(%)		普通税率 Gen.(%)	Article Description
	90.31	**本章其他税号未列名的测量或检验仪器、器具及机器;轮廓投影仪:**							**Measuring or checking instruments, appliances and machines, not specified or included elsewhere in this Chapter; profile projectors:**
7962	9031.1000	-机械零件平衡试验机	7	0 5 6.5	东盟ASEAN,智利CL,新西兰NZ,秘鲁PE,哥斯达黎加CR 巴基斯坦PK 亚太APTA	0	最不发达35国LDC35,最不发达4国LDC4	17	-Machines for balancing mechanical parts
7963	9031.2000	-试验台	7	0 5	东盟ASEAN,智利CL,新西兰NZ,秘鲁PE,哥斯达黎加CR 巴基斯坦PK	0	最不发达35国LDC35,最不发达4国LDC4	17	-Test benches
		-其他光学仪器及器具:							-Other optical instruments and appliances:
7964	9031.4100	--制造半导体器件时检验半导体晶片、器件或检测光掩模或光栅用	0			0	最不发达35国LDC35,最不发达4国LDC4	17	--For inspecting semiconductor wafers or devices or for inspecting photomasks or reticles used in manufacturing semiconductor devices
		--其他:							--Other:
7965	9031.4910	---轮廓投影仪	10	0 5	东盟ASEAN,智利CL,新西兰NZ,秘鲁PE,哥斯达黎加CR 巴基斯坦PK	0	最不发达35国LDC35,最不发达4国LDC4	20	---Profile projectors
7966	9031.4920	---光栅测量装置	0			0	最不发达35国LDC35,最不发达4国LDC4	17	---Grating measuring instrument
7967	9031.4990	---其他	0			0	最不发达35国LDC35,最不发达4国LDC4	17	---Other
		-其他仪器、器具及机器:							-Other instruments, appliances and machines:
7968	9031.8010	---光纤通信及光纤性能测试仪	5	0 0.5 4	东盟ASEAN,巴基斯坦PK,新西兰NZ,秘鲁PE,哥斯达黎加CR,香港HK 智利CL 亚太APTA	0	最不发达35国LDC35,最不发达4国LDC4	17	---Optical telecommunication and optical fibre performance testing instruments

序号 No.	税则号列 Tariff Line	货品名称	最惠国税率 MFN(%)	协定税率 Agreement(%)		特惠税率 S.P.(%)		普通税率 Gen.(%)	Article Description
7969	9031.8020	---坐标测量仪	5	0 0.5	东盟ASEAN,巴基斯坦PK,新西兰NZ,秘鲁PE,哥斯达黎加CR,香港HK 智利CL	0	最不发达35国LDC35,最不发达4国LDC4	17	---Coordinate measuring machine
		---无损探伤检测仪器（射线探伤仪除外）:							---Instrument for nondestructive testing (other than instruments using radiations):
7970	9031.8031	----超声波探伤检测仪	5	0 0.5 4	东盟ASEAN,巴基斯坦PK,新西兰NZ,秘鲁PE,哥斯达黎加CR,香港HK 智利CL 亚太APTA	0	最不发达35国LDC35,最不发达4国LDC4	17	----Ultrasonic inspection instrument
7971	9031.8032	----磁粉探伤检测仪	5	0 0.5 4	东盟ASEAN,巴基斯坦PK,新西兰NZ,秘鲁PE,哥斯达黎加CR,香港HK 智利CL 亚太APTA	0	最不发达35国LDC35,最不发达4国LDC4	17	----Inspection instrument for magnetic particle testing
7972	9031.8033	----涡流探伤检测仪	5 △3	0 0.5 4	东盟ASEAN,巴基斯坦PK,新西兰NZ,秘鲁PE,哥斯达黎加CR,香港HK 智利CL 亚太APTA	0	最不发达35国LDC35,最不发达4国LDC4	17	----Inspection instrument for eddy current testing
7973	9031.8039	----其他	5	0 0.5 4	东盟ASEAN,巴基斯坦PK,新西兰NZ,秘鲁PE,哥斯达黎加CR,香港HK 智利CL 亚太APTA	0	最不发达35国LDC35,最不发达4国LDC4	17	----Other
7974	9031.8090	---其他	5	0 0.5 4	东盟ASEAN,巴基斯坦PK,新西兰NZ,秘鲁PE,哥斯达黎加CR,香港HK,台湾TW 智利CL 亚太APTA	0	最不发达35国LDC35,最不发达4国LDC4	17	---other
	ex90318090	音频生命探测仪	△2						Audio life detectors
	ex90318090	音视频生命探测仪	△2						Audio and video life detectors
	ex90318090	跑道摩擦系数测试仪	△3						Runway friction coefficient tester
7975	9031.9000	-零件、附件	0			0	最不发达35国LDC35,最不发达4国LDC4	17	-Parts and accessories
	90.32	**自动调节或控制仪器及装置:**							**Automatic regulating or controlling instruments and apparatus:**

序号 No.	税则号列 Tariff Line	货品名称	最惠国税率 MFN(%)	协定税率 Agreement(%)		特惠税率 S.P.(%)		普通税率 Gen.(%)	Article Description
7976	9032.1000	-恒温器	7	0 5	东盟ASEAN,智利CL,新西兰NZ,秘鲁PE,哥斯达黎加CR,香港HK 巴基斯坦PK	0	最不发达35国LDC35,最不发达4国LDC4	17	-Thermostats
7977	9032.2000	-恒压器	7	0 5	东盟ASEAN,智利CL,新西兰NZ,秘鲁PE,哥斯达黎加CR,香港HK 巴基斯坦PK	0	最不发达35国LDC35,最不发达4国LDC4	17	-Manostats
		-其他仪器及装置:							-Other instruments and apparatus:
7978	9032.8100	--液压或气压的	7	0 5 6.5	东盟ASEAN,智利CL,新西兰NZ,秘鲁PE,哥斯达黎加CR,香港HK 巴基斯坦PK 亚太APTA	0	最不发达35国LDC35,最不发达4国LDC4	17	--Hydraulic or pneumatic
		--其他:							--Other:
		---列车自动控制系统（ATC）车载设备:							---On-board equipments of automatic train Control system:
7979	9032.8911	----列车自动防护系统(ATP)车载设备	7	0 0.7 5	东盟ASEAN,新西兰NZ,秘鲁PE,哥斯达黎加CR,香港HK 智利CL 巴基斯坦PK	0	最不发达35国LDC35,最不发达4国LDC4	17	----On-board equipments of automatic train Protection
7980	9032.8912	----列车自动运行系统(ATO)车载设备	7	0 0.7 5	东盟ASEAN,新西兰NZ,秘鲁PE,哥斯达黎加CR,香港HK 智利CL 巴基斯坦PK	0	最不发达35国LDC35,最不发达4国LDC4	17	----On-board equipments of automatic train Operation
7981	9032.8919	----其他	7	0 0.7 5	东盟ASEAN,新西兰NZ,秘鲁PE,哥斯达黎加CR,香港HK 智利CL 巴基斯坦PK	0	最不发达35国LDC35,最不发达4国LDC4	17	----Other
7982	9032.8990	---其他	7	0 0.7 5	东盟ASEAN,新西兰NZ,秘鲁PE,哥斯达黎加CR,香港HK 智利CL 巴基斯坦PK	0	最不发达35国LDC35,最不发达4国LDC4	17	---Other
	ex90328990	电喷点火程序控制单元	△3						Program controlling units for electric ignition
	ex90328990	机床用成套数控伺服装置（包括CNC操作单元，带有配套的伺服放大器和伺服电机）	△3						Numerical control servomechanism for machine tools (including CNC unit, with servo amplifier and servomotor)

序号 No.	税则号列 Tariff Line	货品名称	最惠国税率 MFN(%)	协定税率 Agreement(%)		特惠税率 S.P.(%)		普通税率 Gen.(%)	Article Description
	ex90328990	印刷机用成套数控伺服传动装置（包括运动控制器或可编程序自动控制器、人机界面单元，带有配套的伺服驱动器和伺服电机）	△3						Complete set of CNC servo devices used for printers (including PAC and HMI units, servo drivers and sero motoers)
	ex90328990	三坐标测量机用自动控制柜	△3						Automatic controller for coordinate measuring machine of three dimensions
	ex90328990	风力发电设备用控制器	△4						Controller for windmill generating electricity equipment
	ex90328990	飞机自动驾驶系统（包括自动驾驶、电子控制飞行、自动故障分析、警告系统配平系统及推力监控设备及其相关仪表）	△1						Parts of automatic piloting systems for aircraft (including automatic pilotting, electronic flight contral, automatic failure analysis, warning systems, trimming systems, thrust monitoring equipments and the meters thereof)
7983	9032.9000	-零件、附件	5	0	东盟ASEAN,智利CL,巴基斯坦PK,新西兰NZ,秘鲁PE,哥斯达黎加CR	0	最不发达35国LDC35,最不发达4国LDC4	17	-Parts and accessories
	ex90329000	飞机自动驾驶系统（包括自动驾驶、电子控制飞行、自动故障分析、警告系统配平系统及推力监控设备及其相关仪表）的零件	△1						Parts of automatic piloting systems for aircraft (including automatic pilotting, electronic flight contral, automatic failure analysis, warning systems, trimming systems, thrust monitoring equipments and the meters therof)
	90.33	**第九十章所列机器、器具、仪器或装置用的本章其他税号未列名的零件、附件:**							**Parts and accessories (not specified or included elsewhere in this Chapter) for machines, appliances, instruments or apparatus of Chapter 90:**
7984	9033.0000	第九十章所列机器、器具、仪器或装置用的本章其他税号未列名的零件、附件	6	0 5	东盟ASEAN,智利CL,新西兰NZ,秘鲁PE,哥斯达黎加CR 巴基斯坦PK	0	最不发达35国LDC35,最不发达4国LDC4	17	Parts and accessories(not specified or in cluded elsewhere in this Chapter)for machines, appliances, instruments or apparatus of Chapter 90

第九十一章
钟表及其零件

注释:

一、本章不包括:

（一）钟表玻璃及钟锤（按其构成材料归类）；

（二）表链（根据不同情况，归入税号71.13 或71.17）；

（三）第十五类注释二所规定的贱金属制通用零件（第十五类）、塑料制的类似品（第三十九章）及贵金属或包贵金属制的类似品（一般归入税号71.15）；但钟、表发条则应作为钟、表的零件归类（税号91.14）；

（四）轴承滚珠（根据不同情况，归入税号73.26或84.82）；

（五）税号84.12的物品，不需擒纵器可以工作的;

（六）滚珠轴承（税号84.82）；

（七）第八十五章的物品，本身未组装在或未与其他零件组装在钟、表机芯内，也未组装成专用于或主要用于钟、表机芯零件的（第八十五章）。

二、税号 91.01 仅包括表壳完全以贵金属或包贵金属制的表，以及用贵金属或包贵金属与税号 71.01 至 71.04 的天然、养殖珍珠或宝石、半宝石（天然、合成或再造）合制的表。用贱金属上镶嵌贵金属制成表壳的表应归入税号 91.02。

三、本章所称"表芯"，是指由摆轮及游丝、石英晶体或其他能确定时间间隔的装置来进行调节的机构，并带有显示器或可装机械指示器的系统。表芯的厚度不超过12 毫米，长、宽或直径不超过 50 毫米。

四、除注释一另有规定的以外，钟、表的机芯及其他零件，既适用于钟或表，又适用于其他物品(例如精密仪器）的，均应归入本章。

Chapter 91
Clocks and watches and parts thereof

Notes:

1. This Chapter does not cover:

(a) Clock or watch glasses or weights (classified according to their constituent material) ;

(b) Watch chains (heading No.71.13 or 71.17， as the case may be);

(c) Parts of general use defined in Note 2 to Section XV，of base metal (Section XV)，or similar goods of plastics (Chapter 39) or of precious metal or metal clad with precious metal (generally heading No. 71.15); clock or watch springs are, however, to be classified as clock or watch parts (heading No.91.14);

(d) Bearing balls (heading No. 73.26 or 84.82， as the case may be) ;

(e) Articles of heading No. 84.12 constructed to work without an escapement;

(f) Ball bearings (heading No.84.82); or

(g) Articles of Chapter 85，not yet assembled together or with other components into watch or clock movements or into articles suitable for use solely or principally as parts of such movements (Chapter 85) .

2. Heading No. 91.01 covers only watches with case wholly of precious metal or of metal clad with precious metal, or of the same materials combined with natural or cultured pearls, or precious or semiprecious stones (natural, synthetic or reconstructed) of headings No.71.01 to 71.04. Watches with case of base metal inlaid with precious metal fall in heading No. 91.02.

3. For the purposes of this Chapter, the expression "watch move ments" means devices regulated by a balance-wheel and hairspring, quartz crystal or any other system capable of determining intevals of time, with a display or a system to which a mechanical display can be incorporated. Such watch movements shall not exceed 12mm in thickness and 50mm in width，length or diameter.

4. Except as provided in Note 1，movements and other parts suitable for use both in clocks or watches and in other articles (for example, precision instruments) are to be classified in this Chapter.

序号 No.	税则号列 Tariff Line	货品名称	最惠国税率 MFN(%)	协定税率 Agreement(%)		特惠税率 S.P.(%)		普通税率 Gen.(%)	Article Description
	91.01	**手表、怀表及其他表，包括秒表，表壳用贵金属或包贵金属制成的:**							**Wrist-watches, pocket-watches and other watches, including stop-watches, with case of precious metal or of metal clad with pre-cious metal:**
		-电力驱动的手表,不论是否附有秒表装置:							-Wrist-watches, electrically operated whether or not incorporating a stop-watch facility:
7985	9101.1100	--仅有机械指示器的	11	0	东盟ASEAN,智利CL,新加坡SG,新西兰NZ,秘鲁PE	0	最不发达35国LDC35	100	--With mechanical dis-play only
				2.2	哥斯达黎加CR				
				5	巴基斯坦PK				
				9.9	亚太APTA				
		--其他:							--Other:
7986	9101.1910	---仅有光电显示器的	16	0	东盟ASEAN,智利CL,新加坡SG,新西兰NZ	0	最不发达35国LDC35	100	---With opto-electronic display only
				3.2	哥斯达黎加CR				
				8	秘鲁PE				
				12.8	巴基斯坦PK				
7987	9101.1990	---其他	15	0	东盟ASEAN,智利CL,新加坡SG,新西兰NZ	0	最不发达35国LDC35	100	---Other
				3	哥斯达黎加CR				
				7.5	秘鲁PE				
				12	巴基斯坦PK				
		-其他手表,不论是否附有秒表装置:							-Other wrist-watches, whether or not incorpo-rating a stop-watch fa-cility:
7988	9101.2100	--自动上弦的	11	0	东盟ASEAN,智利CL,新加坡SG,新西兰NZ,秘鲁PE	0	最不发达35国LDC35	80	--Automatic winding
				2.2	哥斯达黎加CR				
				5	巴基斯坦PK				
7989	9101.2900	--其他	15	0	东盟ASEAN,智利CL,新加坡SG,新西兰NZ	0	最不发达35国LDC35	80	--Other
				3	哥斯达黎加CR				
				7.5	秘鲁PE				
				12	巴基斯坦PK				
		-其他:							-Other:
7990	9101.9100	--电力驱动的	15	0	东盟ASEAN,智利CL,新加坡SG,新西兰NZ	0	最不发达35国LDC35	100	--Electrically operated
				3	哥斯达黎加CR				
				7.5	秘鲁PE				
				12	巴基斯坦PK				
7991	9101.9900	--其他	20	0	东盟ASEAN,智利CL,新加坡SG,新西兰NZ	0	最不发达35国LDC35	80	--Other
				4	哥斯达黎加CR				
				10	秘鲁PE				

序号 No.	税则号列 Tariff Line	货品名称	最惠国税率 MFN(%)	协定税率 Agreement(%)		特惠税率 S.P.(%)		普通税率 Gen.(%)	Article Description
	91.02	**手表、怀表及其他表，包括秒表，但税号 91.01 的货品除外:**							**Wrist-watches, pocket-watches and other watches, including stop-watches, other than those of heading No.91.01:**
		-电力驱动的手表，不论是否附有秒表装置:							-Wrist-watches, electrically operated, whether or not incorporating a stop-watch facility:
7992	9102.1100	--仅有机械指示器的	12.5	0	东盟ASEAN,新加坡SG,新西兰NZ,秘鲁PE,香港HK,澳门MO	0	最不发达 35 国 LDC35	100	--With mechanical display only
				1.3	智利CL				
				2.5	哥斯达黎加CR				
				6.2	巴基斯坦PK				
				11.1	亚太APTA				
7993	9102.1200	--仅有光电显示器的	23	0	东盟ASEAN,智利CL,新加坡SG,新西兰NZ,香港HK,澳门MO	0	最不发达 35 国 LDC35	100	--With opto-electronic display only
				4.6	哥斯达黎加CR				
				11.5	秘鲁PE				
7994	9102.1900	--其他	15	0	东盟ASEAN,智利CL,新加坡SG,新西兰NZ	0	最不发达 35 国 LDC35	100	--Other
				3	哥斯达黎加CR				
				7.5	秘鲁PE				
				12	巴基斯坦PK				
		-其他手表，不论是否装有秒表装置:							-Other wrist-watches, whether or not incorporating a stop-watch facility:
7995	9102.2100	--自动上弦的	11	0	东盟ASEAN,新加坡SG,新西兰NZ,秘鲁PE,香港HK	0	最不发达 35 国 LDC35	80	--Automatic winding
				1.1	智利CL				
				2.2	哥斯达黎加CR				
				5	巴基斯坦PK				
7996	9102.2900	--其他	15	0	东盟ASEAN,智利CL,新加坡SG,新西兰NZ,香港HK	0	最不发达 35 国 LDC35	80	--Other
				3	哥斯达黎加CR				
				7.5	秘鲁PE				
				12	巴基斯坦PK				
		-其他:							-Other:
7997	9102.9100	--电力驱动的	15	0	东盟ASEAN,智利CL,新加坡SG,新西兰NZ	0	最不发达 35 国 LDC35	100	--Electrically operated
				3	哥斯达黎加CR				
				7.5	秘鲁PE				
				12	巴基斯坦PK				
7998	9102.9900	--其他	20	0	东盟ASEAN,智利CL,新加坡SG,新西兰NZ	0	最不发达 35 国 LDC35	80	--Other
				4	哥斯达黎加CR				
				10	秘鲁PE				

序号 No.	税则号列 Tariff Line	货品名称	最惠国税率 MFN(%)	协定税率 Agreement(%)		特惠税率 S.P.(%)		普通税率 Gen.(%)	Article Description
	91.03	**以表芯装成的钟，但不包括税号 91.04 的钟:**							**Clocks with watch movements, excluding clocks of heading No.91.04:**
7999	9103.1000	-电力驱动的	23	0 4.6 11.5	东盟ASEAN,智利CL,新加坡SG,新西兰NZ,香港HK,澳门MO 哥斯达黎加CR 秘鲁PE	0	最不发达 35 国 LDC35	100	-Electrically operated
8000	9103.9000	-其他	20	0 4 10	东盟ASEAN,智利CL,新加坡SG,新西兰NZ 哥斯达黎加CR 秘鲁PE	0	最不发达 35 国 LDC35	100	-Other
	91.04	**仪表板钟及车辆、航空器、航天器或船舶用的类似钟:**							**Instrument panel clocks and clocks of a similar type for vehicles, aircraft, spacecraft or vessels:**
8001	9104.0000	仪表板钟及车辆、航空器、航天器或船舶用的类似钟	10	0 5	东盟ASEAN,智利CL,新西兰NZ,秘鲁PE,哥斯达黎加CR 巴基斯坦PK	0	最不发达 35 国 LDC35	100	Instrument panel clocks and clocks of a similar type for vehicles, aircraft, sp-ace-craft or vessels
	91.05	**其他钟:**							**Other clocks:**
		-闹钟:							-Alarm clocks:
8002	9105.1100	--电力驱动的	23	0 4.6 11.5	东盟ASEAN,智利CL,新加坡SG,新西兰NZ,香港HK,澳门MO 哥斯达黎加CR 秘鲁PE	0	最不发达 35 国 LDC35,最不发达 4 国 LDC4	100	--Electrically operated
8003	9105.1900	--其他	20	0 4 10	东盟ASEAN,智利CL,新加坡SG,新西兰NZ 哥斯达黎加CR 秘鲁PE	0	最不发达 35 国 LDC35	100	--Other
		-挂钟:							-Wall clocks:
8004	9105.2100	--电力驱动的	23	0 2.3 4.6 11.5	东盟ASEAN,新加坡SG,新西兰NZ 智利CL 哥斯达黎加CR 秘鲁PE	0	最不发达 35 国 LDC35	100	--Electrically operated
8005	9105.2900	--其他	20	0 4 10	东盟ASEAN,智利CL,新加坡SG,新西兰NZ 哥斯达黎加CR 秘鲁PE	0	最不发达 35 国 LDC35	100	--Other
		-其他:							-Other:
		--电力驱动的:							--Electrically operated:
8006	9105.9110	---天文钟	3	0	东盟ASEAN,智利CL,巴基斯坦PK,新西兰NZ,秘鲁PE,哥斯达黎加CR	0	最不发达 35 国 LDC35,最不发达 4 国 LDC4	8	---Astronomical chronometer
8007	9105.9190	---其他	23	0 4.6 11.5	东盟ASEAN,智利CL,新加坡SG,新西兰NZ 哥斯达黎加CR 秘鲁PE	0	最不发达 35 国 LDC35	100	---Other

序号 No.	税则号列 Tariff Line	货品名称	最惠国税率 MFN(%)	协定税率 Agreement(%)		特惠税率 S.P.(%)		普通税率 Gen.(%)	Article Description
8008	9105.9900	--其他	16	0 3.2 8 12.8	东盟ASEAN,智利CL,新加坡SG,新西兰NZ 哥斯达黎加CR 秘鲁PE 巴基斯坦PK	0	最不发达35国LDC35	100	--Other
	91.06	**时间记录器以及测量、记录或指示时间间隔的装置，装有钟、表机芯或同步电动机的（例如，考勤钟、时刻记录器）：**							**Time of day recording apparatus and apparatus for measuring, recording or otherwise indicating intervals of time, with clock or watch movement or with synchronous motor (for exam-ple, time-regis-ters, time-recorders):**
8009	9106.1000	-考勤钟、时刻记录器	16	0 3.2 8 12.8	东盟ASEAN,智利CL,新加坡SG,新西兰NZ 哥斯达黎加CR 秘鲁PE 巴基斯坦PK	0	最不发达35国LDC35	50	-Time-registers; time-recorders
8010	9106.9000	-其他	16	0 1.6 3.2 8 12.8	东盟ASEAN,新加坡SG,新西兰NZ 智利CL 哥斯达黎加CR 秘鲁PE 巴基斯坦PK	0	最不发达35国LDC35	50	-Other
	91.07	**装有钟、表机芯或同步电动机的定时开关：**							**Time switches with clock or watch movement or with synchronous motor:**
8011	9107.0000	装有钟、表机芯或同步电动机的定时开关	12	0 2.4 6	东盟ASEAN,智利CL,新加坡SG,新西兰NZ,秘鲁PE 哥斯达黎加CR 巴基斯坦PK	0	最不发达35国LDC35	50	Time switches with clock or watch movement or with synchronous motor
	91.08	**已组装的完整表芯：**							**Watch movements, com-plete and asse-mbled:**
		-电力驱动的:							-Electrically operated:
8012	9108.1100	--仅有机械指示器或有可装机械指示器的装置的	16 △10	0 3.2 8 12.8	东盟ASEAN,智利CL,新加坡SG,新西兰NZ,香港HK,澳门MO 哥斯达黎加CR 秘鲁PE 巴基斯坦PK	0	最不发达35国LDC35	80	--With mechanical dis-play only or with a de-vice to which a me-chanical display can be incorporated
8013	9108.1200	--仅有光电显示器的	16	0 3.2 8 12.8	东盟ASEAN,智利CL,新加坡SG,新西兰NZ,香港HK,澳门MO 哥斯达黎加CR 秘鲁PE 巴基斯坦PK	0	最不发达35国LDC35	80	--With opto-electronic display only
8014	9108.1900	--其他	16	0 3.2 8 12	东盟ASEAN,智利CL,新加坡SG,新西兰NZ,香港HK,澳门MO 哥斯达黎加CR 巴基斯坦PK,秘鲁PE 亚太APTA	0	最不发达35国LDC35	80	--Other

序号 No.	税则号列 Tariff Line	货品名称	最惠国税率 MFN(%)	协定税率 Agreement(%)		特惠税率 S.P.(%)		普通税率 Gen.(%)	Article Description
8015	9108.2000	-自动上弦的	16	0 3.2 8 12.8	东盟ASEAN,智利CL,新加坡SG,新西兰NZ 哥斯达黎加CR 秘鲁PE 巴基斯坦PK	0	最不发达35国LDC35	80	-Automatic winding
		-其他:							-Other:
8016	9108.9010	---表面尺寸在33.8毫米及以下	16	0 3.2 8 12.8	东盟ASEAN,智利CL,新加坡SG,新西兰NZ 哥斯达黎加CR 秘鲁PE 巴基斯坦PK	0	最不发达35国LDC35	80	---Measuring 33.8mm or less
8017	9108.9090	---其他	16	0 3.2 8 12.8	东盟ASEAN,智利CL,新加坡SG,新西兰NZ,香港HK,澳门MO 哥斯达黎加CR 秘鲁PE 巴基斯坦PK	0	最不发达35国LDC35	80	---Other
	91.09	**已组装的完整钟芯:**							**Clock movements, complete and assembled:**
8018	9109.1000	-电力驱动的	16	0 3.2 8 12.8	东盟ASEAN,智利CL,新加坡SG,新西兰NZ 哥斯达黎加CR 秘鲁PE 巴基斯坦PK	0	最不发达35国LDC35	100	-Eletrically operated
8019	9109.9000	-其他	16	0 3.2 8 12.8	东盟ASEAN,智利CL,新加坡SG,新西兰NZ 哥斯达黎加CR 秘鲁PE 巴基斯坦PK	0	最不发达35国LDC35	100	-Other
	91.10	**未组装或部分组装的完整钟、表机芯(机芯套装件);已组装的不完整钟、表机芯;未组装的不完整钟、表机芯:**							**Complete watch or clock movements, unassembled or partly assembled (movement sets); incomplete watch or clock movements, assembled; rough watch or clock movements:**
		-表的:							-Of watches:
8020	9110.1100	--未组装或部分组装的完整机芯(机芯套装件)	16	0 3.2 8 12.8	东盟ASEAN,智利CL,新加坡SG,新西兰NZ 哥斯达黎加CR 秘鲁PE 巴基斯坦PK	0	最不发达35国LDC35	80	--Complete movements, unassembled or partly assembled (movement sets)
8021	9110.1200	--已组装的不完整机芯	16	0 3.2 8 12.8	东盟ASEAN,智利CL,新加坡SG,新西兰NZ 哥斯达黎加CR 秘鲁PE 巴基斯坦PK	0	最不发达35国LDC35	70	--Incomplete movements, assembled
8022	9110.1900	--未组装的不完整机芯	16	0 3.2 8 12.8	东盟ASEAN,智利CL,新加坡SG,新西兰NZ 哥斯达黎加CR 秘鲁PE 巴基斯坦PK	0	最不发达35国LDC35	70	--Rough movements
		-其他:							-Other:

序号 No.	税则号列 Tariff Line	货品名称	最惠国税率 MFN(%)	协定税率 Agreement(%)		特惠税率 S.P.(%)		普通税率 Gen.(%)	Article Description
8023	9110.9010	---未组装或部分组装的完整机芯	16	0 3.2 8 12.8	东盟ASEAN,智利CL,新加坡SG,新西兰NZ 哥斯达黎加CR 秘鲁PE 巴基斯坦PK	0	最不发达35国LDC35	100	---Complete movements, unassembled or partly assembled
8024	9110.9090	---其他	16	0 3.2 8 12.8	东盟ASEAN,智利CL,新加坡SG,新西兰NZ 哥斯达黎加CR 秘鲁PE 巴基斯坦PK	0	最不发达35国LDC35	80	---Other
	91.11	**表壳及其零件:**							**Watch cases and parts thereof:**
8025	9111.1000	-贵金属表壳或包贵金属表壳	14	0 2.8 11.2	东盟ASEAN,智利CL,新加坡SG,新西兰NZ,秘鲁PE 哥斯达黎加CR 巴基斯坦PK	0	最不发达35国LDC35	80	-Cases of precious metal or of metal clad with precious metal
8026	9111.2000	-贱金属表壳,不论是否镀金或镀银	14	0 2.8 7 10	东盟ASEAN,智利CL,新加坡SG,新西兰NZ,秘鲁PE,香港HK,澳门MO 哥斯达黎加CR 巴基斯坦PK 亚太APTA	0	最不发达35国LDC35	80	-Cases of base metal, whether or not gold or silver-plated
8027	9111.8000	-其他表壳	14	0 2.8 11.2	东盟ASEAN,智利CL,新加坡SG,新西兰NZ,秘鲁PE 哥斯达黎加CR 巴基斯坦PK	0	最不发达35国LDC35	80	-Other cases
8028	9111.9000	-零件	14	0 2.8 11.2	东盟ASEAN,智利CL,新加坡SG,新西兰NZ,秘鲁PE 哥斯达黎加CR 巴基斯坦PK	0	最不发达35国LDC35	80	-Parts
	91.12	**钟壳和本章所列其他货品的类似外壳及其零件:**							**Clock cases and cases of a similar type for other goods of this Chapter, and parts thereof:**
8029	9112.2000	-壳	14	0 2.8 11.2	东盟ASEAN,智利CL,新加坡SG,新西兰NZ,秘鲁PE 哥斯达黎加CR 巴基斯坦PK	0	最不发达35国LDC35	80	-Cases
8030	9112.9000	-零件	12	0 2.4 6	东盟ASEAN,智利CL,新加坡SG,新西兰NZ,秘鲁PE 哥斯达黎加CR 巴基斯坦PK	0	最不发达35国LDC35	80	-Parts
	91.13	**表带及其零件:**							**Watch straps, watch bands and watch bracelets, and parts thereof:**
8031	9113.1000	-贵金属或包贵金属制	20	0 4 10	东盟ASEAN,智利CL,新加坡SG,新西兰NZ 哥斯达黎加CR 秘鲁PE	0	最不发达35国LDC35	130	-Of precious metal or of metal clad with precious metal

序号 No.	税则号列 Tariff Line	货品名称	最惠国税率 MFN(%)	协定税率 Agreement(%)		特惠税率 S.P.(%)		普通税率 Gen.(%)	Article Description
8032	9113.2000	-贱金属制，不论是否镀金或镀银	14	0 2.8 11.2	东盟ASEAN,智利CL,新加坡SG,新西兰NZ,秘鲁PE,香港HK,澳门MO 哥斯达黎加CR 巴基斯坦PK	0	最不发达35国LDC35	100	-Of base metal, whether or not gold or silver-plated
8033	9113.9000	-其他	14	0 2.8 11.2	东盟ASEAN,智利CL,新加坡SG,新西兰NZ,秘鲁PE,香港HK 哥斯达黎加CR 巴基斯坦PK	0	最不发达35国LDC35,最不发达4国LDC4	100	-Other
	91.14	**钟、表的其他零件:**							**Other clock or watch parts:**
8034	9114.1000	-发条，包括游丝	14	0 2.8 7	东盟ASEAN,智利CL,新加坡SG,新西兰NZ,秘鲁PE 哥斯达黎加CR 巴基斯坦PK	0	最不发达35国LDC35	50	-Springs, including hair-springs
8035	9114.3000	-钟面或表面	14	0 2.8 11.2	东盟ASEAN,智利CL,新加坡SG,新西兰NZ,秘鲁PE 哥斯达黎加CR 巴基斯坦PK	0	最不发达35国LDC35	50	-Dials
8036	9114.4000	-夹板及横担（过桥）	14	0 2.8 11.2	东盟ASEAN,智利CL,新加坡SG,新西兰NZ,秘鲁PE 哥斯达黎加CR 巴基斯坦PK	0	最不发达35国LDC35	50	-Plates and bridges
		-其他:							-Other:
8037	9114.9010	---宝石轴承	14	0 2.8 7	东盟ASEAN,智利CL,新加坡SG,新西兰NZ,秘鲁PE 哥斯达黎加CR 巴基斯坦PK	0	最不发达35国LDC35	50	---Jewel bearings
8038	9114.9090	---其他	14	0 2.8 11.2	东盟ASEAN,智利CL,新加坡SG,新西兰NZ,秘鲁PE,香港HK,澳门MO 哥斯达黎加CR 巴基斯坦PK	0	最不发达35国LDC35	70	---Other

第九十二章
乐器及其零件、附件

Chapter 92
Musical instruments; parts and accessories of such articles

注释:

一、本章不包括:

（一）第十五类注释二所规定的贱金属制通用零件（第十五类）或塑料制的类似品（第三十九章）;

（二）第八十五章或第九十章的传声器、扩大器、扬声器、耳机、开关、频闪观测仪及其他附属仪器、器具或设备，虽用于本章物品但未与该物品组成一体或安装在同一机壳内;

（三）玩具乐器或器具（税号95.03）;

（四）清洁乐器用的刷子（税号96.03）;

（五）收藏品或古物（税号97.05或97.06）。

二、用于演奏税号92.02、92.06所列乐器的弓、槌及类似品，如果与该乐器一同进口或出口，数量合理，用途明确，应归入有关乐器的相应税号。

税号92.09的卡片、盘或卷，即使与乐器一同进口或出口，也不视为该乐器的组成部分，而应作为单独进口或出口的物品对待。

Notes:

1. This Chapter does not cover:

(a) Parts of general use，as defined in Note 2 to Section XV , of base metal (Section XV), or similar goods of plastics (Chapter 39);

(b) Microphones，amplifiers，loudspeakers，headphones，switches, stroboscopes or other accessory instruments, apparatus or equipment of Chapter 85 or 90, for use with but not incorporated in or housed in the same cabinet as instruments of this Chapter;

(c) Toy instruments or apparatus (heading No. 95.03);

(d) Brushes for cleaning musical instruments (heading No. 96.03); or

(e) Collectors' pieces or antiques (heading No.97.05 or 97.06).

2. Bows and sticks and similar devices used in playing the musical instruments of heading No. 92.02 or 92.06 presented with such instruments in numbers normal thereto and clearly intended for use therewith, are to be classified in the same heading as the relative instruments.

Cards, discs and rolls of heading No. 92.09 presented with an instrument are to be treated as separate articles and not as forming a part of such instrument.

序号 No.	税则号列 Tariff Line	货品名称	最惠国税 率 MFN(%)	协定税率 Agreement(%)		特惠税率 S.P.(%)		普通税率 Gen.(%)	Article Description
	92.01	**钢琴，包括自动钢琴、拨弦古钢琴及其他键盘弦乐器:**							**Pianos, including automatic pianos; harpsichords and other keyboard stringed instruments:**
8039	9201.1000	-竖式钢琴	17.5	0 3.5 8.8 14	东盟ASEAN,智利CL,新加坡SG,新西兰NZ,澳门MO 哥斯达黎加CR 秘鲁PE 巴基斯坦PK	0	最不发达35国LDC35	70	-Upright pianos
8040	9201.2000	-大钢琴	17.5	0 3.5 8.8 14	东盟ASEAN,智利CL,新加坡SG,新西兰NZ 哥斯达黎加CR 秘鲁PE 巴基斯坦PK	0	最不发达35国LDC35	70	-Grand pianos

序号 No.	税则号列 Tariff Line	货品名称	最惠国税 率 MFN(%)	协定税率 Agreement(%)		特惠税率 S.P.(%)		普通税率 Gen.(%)	Article Description
	ex92012000	完税价格50000美元及以上的大钢琴	△1						Grand pianos, the duty-paying value ≥50000USD
8041	9201.9000	-其他	17.5	0 3.5 8.8 14	东盟ASEAN,智利CL,新加坡SG,新西兰NZ 哥斯达黎加CR 秘鲁PE 巴基斯坦PK	0	最不发达35国LDC35	70	-Other
	92.02	**其他弦乐器（例如，吉他、小提琴、竖琴）：**							**Other string musical instruments (for example, guitars, violins, har-ps):**
8042	9202.1000	-弓弦乐器	17.5	0 3.5 8.8 14	东盟ASEAN,智利CL,新加坡SG,新西兰NZ 哥斯达黎加CR 秘鲁PE 巴基斯坦PK	0	最不发达35国LDC35,最不发达4国LDC4	70	-Played with a bow
	ex92021000	完税价格15000美元及以上的弓弦乐器	△1						Played with a bow, the duty-paying value≥15000USD
8043	9202.9000	-其他	17.5	0 3.5 8.8 14	东盟ASEAN,智利CL,新加坡SG,新西兰NZ 哥斯达黎加CR 秘鲁PE 巴基斯坦PK	0	最不发达35国LDC35,最不发达4国LDC4	70	-Other
	92.05	**管乐器（例如，键盘管风琴、手风琴、单簧管、小号、风笛），但游艺场风琴及手摇风琴除外:**							**Wind musical instruments (for example, keyboard pipe organs, accordions, clarinets, trumpets, bagpipes), other than fairground organs and mechanical street organs:**
8044	9205.1000	-铜管乐器	17.5	0 3.5 8.8 14	东盟ASEAN,智利CL,新加坡SG,新西兰NZ 哥斯达黎加CR 秘鲁PE 巴基斯坦PK	0	最不发达35国LDC35,最不发达4国LDC4	70	-Brass-wind instruments
	ex92051000	完税价格2000美元及以上的铜管乐器	△1						Brass-wind instruments, the duty-paying value ≥2000USD
		-其他:							-Other:
8045	9205.9010	---键盘管风琴;簧风琴及类似的游离金属簧片键盘乐器	20	0 4 10	东盟ASEAN,智利CL,新加坡SG,新西兰NZ 哥斯达黎加CR 秘鲁PE	0	最不发达35国LDC35	80	---Keyboard pipe organs; harmoniums and similar keyboard instruments with free metal reeds
8046	9205.9020	---手风琴及类似乐器	21	0 4.2 10.5	东盟ASEAN,智利CL,新加坡SG,新西兰NZ 哥斯达黎加CR 秘鲁PE	0	最不发达35国LDC35	80	---Accordions and similar instruments
8047	9205.9030	---口琴	21	0 4.2 10.5	东盟ASEAN,智利CL,新加坡SG,新西兰NZ 哥斯达黎加CR 秘鲁PE	0	最不发达35国LDC35	80	---Mouth organs

序号 No.	税则号列 Tariff Line	货品名称	最惠国税率 MFN(%)	协定税率 Agreement(%)		特惠税率 S.P.(%)		普通税率 Gen.(%)	Article Description
8048	9205.9090	---其他	17.5	0 1.8 3.5 8.8 14	东盟ASEAN,新加坡SG,新西兰NZ 智利CL 哥斯达黎加CR 秘鲁PE 巴基斯坦PK	0	最不发达35国LDC35	70	---Other
	ex92059090	完税价格10000美元及以上的其他管乐器	△1						Other wind musical instruments, the duty-paying value≥10000USD
	92.06	**打击乐器(例如,鼓、木琴、铙、钹、响板、响葫芦):**							**Percussion musical instruments (for example, drums, xylophones, cymbals, castanets, maracas):**
8049	9206.0000	打击乐器(例如,鼓、木琴、铙、钹、响板、响葫芦)	17.5	0 3.5 14	东盟ASEAN,智利CL,新加坡SG,新西兰NZ,秘鲁PE 哥斯达黎加CR 巴基斯坦PK	0	最不发达35国LDC35,最不发达4国LDC4	70	Percussion musical instruments (for example, drums, xylophones, cymbals, castanets, maracas)
	92.07	**通过电产生或扩大声音的乐器(例如,电风琴、电吉他、电手风琴):**							**Musical instruments, the sound of which is produced or must be amplifi-ed electrically (for example, organs, guitars, accordions):**
8050	9207.1000	-键盘乐器,但手风琴除外	30 △15	0 6 15	东盟ASEAN,智利CL,新加坡SG,新西兰NZ 哥斯达黎加CR 秘鲁PE	0	最不发达35国LDC35	100	-Keyboard instruments, other than accordions
8051	9207.9000	-其他	30	0 6 15	东盟ASEAN,智利CL,新加坡SG,新西兰NZ 哥斯达黎加CR 秘鲁PE	0	最不发达35国LDC35	100	-Other
	92.08	**百音盒、游艺场风琴、手摇风琴、机械鸣禽、乐锯及本章其他税号未列名的其他乐器;各种媒诱音响器、哨子、号角、口吹音响信号器:**							**Musical boxes, fairground organs, mechanical street organs, mechanical singing birds, musical saws and other musical instruments not falling within any other heading of this Chapter; decoy calls of all kinds; whistles, call horns and other mouth-blown sound signalling instruments:**
8052	9208.1000	-百音盒	22	0 4.4 11	东盟ASEAN,智利CL,新加坡SG,新西兰NZ 哥斯达黎加CR 秘鲁PE	0	最不发达35国LDC35	80	-Musical boxes
8053	9208.9000	-其他	22	0 4.4 11	东盟ASEAN,智利CL,新加坡SG,新西兰NZ 哥斯达黎加CR 秘鲁PE	0	最不发达35国LDC35	80	-Other

序号 No.	税则号列 Tariff Line	货品名称	最惠国税率 MFN(%)	协定税率 Agreement(%)		特惠税率 S.P.(%)		普通税率 Gen.(%)	Article Description
	92.09	**乐器的零件（例如百音盒的机械装置）、附件（例如，机械乐器用的卡片、盘及带卷），节拍器、音叉及各种定音管：**							**Parts (for example, mechanisms for musical boxes) and accessories (for example, cards, discs and rolls for mechanical instruments) of musical instruments; metronomes, tuning forks and pitch pipes of all kinds:**
8054	9209.3000	-乐器用的弦	17.5	0 3.5 8.8 14	东盟ASEAN,智利CL,新加坡SG,新西兰NZ 哥斯达黎加CR 秘鲁PE 巴基斯坦PK	0	最不发达35国LDC35	70	-Musical instrument strings
		-其他:							-Other:
8055	9209.9100	--钢琴的零件、附件	17.5	0 3.5 8.8 14	东盟ASEAN,智利CL,新加坡SG,新西兰NZ 哥斯达黎加CR 秘鲁PE 巴基斯坦PK	0	最不发达35国LDC35	70	--Parts and accessories for pianos
8056	9209.9200	--税号92.02所列乐器的零件、附件	17.5	0 3.5 8.8 14	东盟ASEAN,智利CL,新加坡SG,新西兰NZ 哥斯达黎加CR 秘鲁PE 巴基斯坦PK	0	最不发达35国LDC35,最不发达4国LDC4	70	--Parts and accessories for the musical instruments of heading No.92.02
8057	9209.9400	--税号92.07所列乐器的零件、附件	17.5 △10	0 3.5 8.8 14	东盟ASEAN,智利CL,新加坡SG,新西兰NZ 哥斯达黎加CR 秘鲁PE 巴基斯坦PK	0	最不发达35国LDC35	70	--Parts and accessories for the musical instruments of heading No.92.07
		--其他:							--Other:
8058	9209.9910	---节拍器、音叉及定音管	17.5	0 3.5 8.8 14	东盟ASEAN,智利CL,新加坡SG,新西兰NZ 哥斯达黎加CR 秘鲁PE 巴基斯坦PK	0	最不发达35国LDC35	70	---Metronomes, tuning forks and pitch pipes
8059	9209.9920	---百音盒的机械装置	17.5	0 3.5 8.8 14	东盟ASEAN,智利CL,新加坡SG,新西兰NZ 哥斯达黎加CR 秘鲁PE 巴基斯坦PK	0	最不发达35国LDC35	70	---Mechanisms for musical boxes
8060	9209.9990	---其他	17.5	0 3.5 8.8 14	东盟ASEAN,智利CL,新加坡SG,新西兰NZ 哥斯达黎加CR 秘鲁PE 巴基斯坦PK	0	最不发达35国LDC35,最不发达4国LDC4	70	---Other

第十九类

武器、弹药及其零件、附件

SECTION XIX

ARMS AND AMMUNITION; PARTS AND ACCESSORIES THEREOF

第九十三章
武器、弹药及其零件、附件

Chapter 93
Arms and ammunition; parts and accessories thereof

注释:

一、本章不包括:

（一）第三十六章的货品（例如，火帽、雷管、信号弹）;

（二）第十五类注释二所规定的贱金属制通用零件（第十五类）或塑料制的类似品(第三十九章）;

（三）装甲战斗车辆（税号87.10）;

（四）武器用的望远镜瞄准具及其他光学装置（第九十章），但安装在武器上或与武器一同进口或出口以备安装在该武器上的除外;

（五）弓、箭、钝头击剑或玩具（第九十五章）;

（六）收藏品及古物（税号97.05或97.06）。

二、税号93.06所称"零件"，不包括税号85.26的无线电设备及雷达设备。

Notes:

1. This Chapter does not cover:

(a) Goods of Chapter 36 (for example, percussion caps, detonators, signalling flares);

(b) Parts of general use, as defined in Note 2 to Section XV, of base metal (Section XV), or similar goods of plastics (Chapter 39);

(c) Armoured fighting vehicles (heading No.87.10);

(d) Telescopic sights or other optical devices suitable for use with arms, unless mounted on a firearm or presented with the firearm on which they are designed to be mounted (Chapter 90);

(e) Bows, arrows, fencing foils or toys (Chapter 95); or

(f) Collectors' pieces or antiques (heading No.97.05 or 97.06).

2.In heading No. 93.06, the reference to "parts thereof" does not include radio or radar apparatus of heading No. 85.26.

序号 No.	税则号列 Tariff Line	货品名称	最惠国税率 MFN(%)	协定税率 Agreement(%)		特惠税率 S.P.(%)		普通税率 Gen.(%)	Article Description
	93.01	**军用武器，但左轮手枪、其他手枪及税目93.07的兵器除外:**							**Military weapons, other than revolvers, pistols and the arms of heading 93.07.**
		-火炮武器（例如，榴弹炮及迫击炮）:							-Artillery weapons (for example, guns, howitzers and mortars):
8061	9301.1010	---自推进的	13	0	东盟ASEAN,智利CL,新加坡SG,新西兰NZ,秘鲁PE	0	最不发达35国LDC35	80	---Self-propelled
				2.6	哥斯达黎加CR				
				6.5	巴基斯坦PK				
8062	9301.1090	---其他	13	0	东盟ASEAN,新加坡SG,新西兰NZ,秘鲁PE	0	最不发达35国LDC35	80	---Other
				1.3	智利CL				
				2.6	哥斯达黎加CR				
				6.5	巴基斯坦PK				
8063	9301.2000	-火箭发射装置;火焰喷射器;手榴弹发射器;鱼雷发射管及类似发射装置自推进的	13	0	东盟ASEAN,智利CL,新加坡SG,新西兰NZ,秘鲁PE	0	最不发达35国LDC35	80	-Rocket launchers; flame-throwers; grenade launchers; torpedo tubes and similar projectors
				2.6	哥斯达黎加CR				
				6.5	巴基斯坦PK				

序号 No.	税则号列 Tariff Line	货品名称	最惠国税率 MFN(%)	协定税率 Agreement(%)		特惠税率 S.P.(%)		普通税率 Gen.(%)	Article Description
8064	9301.9000	-其他	13	0 1.3 2.6 6.5	东盟ASEAN,新加坡SG,新西兰NZ,秘鲁PE 智利CL 哥斯达黎加CR 巴基斯坦PK	0	最不发达35国LDC35	80	-Other
	93.02	**左轮手枪及其他手枪，但税号 93.03 或 93.04 的货品除外：**							**Revolvers and pistols, other than those of heading No.93.03 or 93.04:**
8065	9302.0000	左轮手枪及其他手枪，但税号 93.03 或 93.04 的货品除外	13	0 2.6 6.5	东盟ASEAN,智利CL,新加坡SG,新西兰NZ,秘鲁PE 哥斯达黎加CR 巴基斯坦PK	0	最不发达35国LDC35	80	Revolvers and pistols, other than those of heading No.93.03 or 93.04
	93.03	**靠爆炸药发射的其他火器及类似装置（例如，运动用猎枪及步枪、前装枪、维利式信号枪及其他专为发射信号弹的装置、发射空包弹的左轮手枪和其他手枪、弩枪式无痛捕杀器、抛缆枪）：**							**Other firearms and similar devices which operate by the firing of an explosive charge (for example, sporting shotguns and rifles, muzzleloading firearms, Very pistols and other devices designed to project only signal flares, pistols and revolvers for firing blank ammunition, captive-bolt humane killers, linethrowing guns):**
8066	9303.1000	-前装枪	13	0 2.6 6.5	东盟ASEAN,智利CL,新加坡SG,新西兰NZ,秘鲁PE 哥斯达黎加CR 巴基斯坦PK	0	最不发达35国LDC35	80	-Muzzle-loading firearms
8067	9303.2000	-其他运动、狩猎或打靶用猎枪，包括组合式滑膛来复枪	13	0 2.6 6.5	东盟ASEAN,智利CL,新加坡SG,新西兰NZ,秘鲁PE 哥斯达黎加CR 巴基斯坦PK	0	最不发达35国LDC35	80	-Other sporting, hunting or target shooting shotguns, including combination shotgunrifles
8068	9303.3000	-其他运动、狩猎或打靶用步枪	13	0 2.6 6.5	东盟ASEAN,智利CL,新加坡SG,新西兰NZ,秘鲁PE 哥斯达黎加CR 巴基斯坦PK	0	最不发达35国LDC35	80	-Other sporting, hunting or target shooting rifles
8069	9303.9000	-其他	13	0 2.6 6.5	东盟ASEAN,智利CL,新加坡SG,新西兰NZ,秘鲁PE 哥斯达黎加CR 巴基斯坦PK	0	最不发达35国LDC35	80	-Other
	93.04	**其他武器（例如，弹簧枪、气枪、气手枪、警棍），但不包括税号 93.07 的货品：**							**Other arms (for example, spring, air or gas guns and pistols, truncheons), excluding those of heading No. 93.07:**

序号 No.	税则号列 Tariff Line	货品名称	最惠国税率 MFN(%)	协定税率 Agreement(%)		特惠税率 S.P.(%)		普通税率 Gen.(%)	Article Description
8070	9304.0000	其他武器（例如，弹簧枪、气枪、气手枪、警棍），但不包括税号 93.07 的货品	13	0 2.6 6.5	东盟ASEAN,智利CL,新加坡SG,新西兰NZ,秘鲁PE 哥斯达黎加CR 巴基斯坦PK	0	最不发达 35 国 LDC35	80	Other arms (for example, spring, air or gas guns and pistols, truncheons) excluding those of heading No.93.07
	93.05	**税号 93.01 至 93.04 所列物品的零件、附件:**							**Parts and accessories of articles of headings No. 93.01 to 93.04:**
8071	9305.1000	-左轮手枪或其他手枪用	13	0 2.6 6.5	东盟ASEAN,智利CL,新加坡SG,新西兰NZ,秘鲁PE 哥斯达黎加CR 巴基斯坦PK	0	最不发达 35 国 LDC35	80	-Of revolvers or pistols
8072	9305.2000	-税号 93.03 的猎枪或步枪用	13	0 2.6 6.5	东盟ASEAN,智利CL,新加坡SG,新西兰NZ,秘鲁PE 哥斯达黎加CR 巴基斯坦PK	0	最不发达 35 国 LDC35	80	-Of shotguns or rifles of heading No.93.03
		-其他:							-Other:
8073	9305.9100	--税目 93.01 的军用武器用	13	0 2.6 6.5	东盟ASEAN,智利CL,新加坡SG,新西兰NZ,秘鲁PE 哥斯达黎加CR 巴基斯坦PK	0	最不发达 35 国 LDC35	80	--Of military weapons of heading 93.01
8074	9305.9900	--其他	13	0 2.6 6.5	东盟ASEAN,智利CL,新加坡SG,新西兰NZ,秘鲁PE 哥斯达黎加CR 巴基斯坦PK	0	最不发达 35 国 LDC35	80	--Other
	93.06	**炸弹、手榴弹、鱼雷、地雷、水雷、导弹及类似武器及其零件；子弹、其他弹药和射弹及其零件，包括弹丸及弹垫:**							**Bombs, grenades, torpedoes, mines, missiles, and similar munitions of war and parts thereof; cartridges and other ammunition and projectiles and parts thereof, including shot and cartridge wads:**
		-猎枪子弹及其零件；气枪弹丸:							-Shotgun cartridges and parts thereof; air gun pellets:
8075	9306.2100	--猎枪子弹	13	0 2.6 6.5	东盟ASEAN,智利CL,新加坡SG,新西兰NZ,秘鲁PE 哥斯达黎加CR 巴基斯坦PK	0	最不发达 35 国 LDC35	80	--Cartridges
8076	9306.2900	--其他	13	0 2.6 6.5	东盟ASEAN,智利CL,新加坡SG,新西兰NZ,秘鲁PE 哥斯达黎加CR 巴基斯坦PK	0	最不发达 35 国 LDC35	80	--Other
		-其他子弹及其零件:							-Other cartridges and parts thereof:

序号 No.	税则号列 Tariff Line	货品名称	最惠国税 率 MFN(%)	协定税率 Agreement(%)		特惠税率 S.P.(%)		普通税率 Gen.(%)	Article Description
8077	9306.3080	---铆接机或类似工具用及弩枪式无痛捕杀器用子弹及其零件	13	0 2.6 6.5	东盟ASEAN,智利CL,新加坡SG,新西兰NZ,秘鲁PE 哥斯达黎加CR 巴基斯坦PK	0	最不发达35国LDC35	80	---Cartridges for riveting or similar tools or for captivebolt humane killers and parts thereof
8078	9306.3090	---其他子弹及其零件	13	0 2.6 6.5	东盟ASEAN,智利CL,新加坡SG,新西兰NZ,秘鲁PE 哥斯达黎加CR 巴基斯坦PK	0	最不发达35国LDC35	80	---Other cartridges and parts thereof
8079	9306.9000	-其他	13	0 1.3 2.6 6.5	东盟ASEAN,新加坡SG,新西兰NZ,秘鲁PE 智利CL 哥斯达黎加CR 巴基斯坦PK	0	最不发达35国LDC35	80	-Other
	93.07	**剑、短弯刀、刺刀、长矛和类似的武器及其零件;刀鞘、剑鞘:**							**Swords, cutlasses, bayonets, lances and similar arms and parts thereof and scabbards and sheaths therefor:**
		剑、短弯刀、刺刀、长矛和类似的武器及其零件;刀鞘、剑鞘:							Swords, cutlasses, bayonets, lances and similar arms and parts thereof and scabbards and sheaths therefor:
8080	9307.0010	---军用	13	0 2.6 6.5	东盟ASEAN,智利CL,新加坡SG,新西兰NZ,秘鲁PE 哥斯达黎加CR 巴基斯坦PK	0	最不发达35国LDC35,最不发达4国LDC4	80	---Military
8081	9307.0090	---其他	13	0 2.6 6.5	东盟ASEAN,智利CL,新加坡SG,新西兰NZ,秘鲁PE 哥斯达黎加CR 巴基斯坦PK	0	最不发达35国LDC35,最不发达4国LDC4	80	---Other

第二十类

杂项制品

第九十四章

家具；寝具、褥垫、弹簧床垫、软座垫及类似的填充制品；未列名灯具及照明装置；发光标志、发光铭牌及类似品；活动房屋

注释:

一、本章不包括:

（一）第三十九章、第四十章或第六十三章的充气或充水的褥垫、枕头及座垫;

（二）落地镜〔例如税号 70.09 的试衣镜（旋转镜）〕;

（三）第七十一章的物品;

（四）第十五类注释二所规定的贱金属制通用零件（第十五类）、塑料制的类似品（第三十九章）或税号 83.03 的保险箱;

（五）冷藏或冷冻设备专用的特制家具（税号 84.18）；缝纫机专用的特制家具（税号 84.52）;

（六）第八十五章的灯具及照明装置;

（七）税目 85.18、85.19、85.21 或税目 85.25 至 85.28 所列装置专用的特制家具（应分别归入税目 85.18、85.22 或 85.29）;

（八）税号 87.14 的物品;

（九）装有税号 90.18 所列牙科用器具或漱口盂的牙科用椅（税号 90.18）;

（十）第九十一章的物品（例如，钟及钟壳）;

（十一）玩具家具、玩具灯或玩具照明装置（税号 95.03）、台球桌或其他供游戏用的特制家具（税号 95.04）、魔术用的特制家具或中国灯笼及类似的装饰品（电气彩灯串除外）（税号 95.05）。

SECTION XX

MISCELLANEOUS MANUFACTURED ARTICLES

Chapter 94

Furniture; bedding, mattresses, mattress supports, cushions and similar stuffed furnishings; lamps and lighting fittings, not elsewhere specified or included; illuminated signs, illuminated name-plates and the like; prefabricated buildings

Notes:

1. This Chapter does not cover:

(a) Pneumatic or water mattresses, pillows or cushions, of Chapter 39, 40 or 63;

(b) Mirrors designed for placing on the floor or ground (for example, cheval-glasses (swing-mirrors) of heading No. 70.09);

(c) Articles of Chapter 71;

(d) Parts of general use as defined in Note 2 to Section XV, of base metal(Section XV), or similar goods of plastics (Chapter 39), or safes of heading No.83.03;

(e) Furniture specially designed as parts of refrigerating or freezing equipment of heading No.84.18; furniture specially designed for sewing machines (heading No.84.52);

(f) Lamps or lighting fittings of Chapter 85;

(g) Furniture specially designed as parts of apparatus of heading No.85.18 (heading No.85.18), of headings No.85.19 or 85.21 (heading No.85.22) or of headings No.85.25 to 85.28 (heading No.85.29);

(h) Articles of heading No.87.14;

(ij) Dentists' chairs incorporating dental appliances of heading No.90.18 or dentists' spittoons (heading No.90.18);

(k) Articles of Chapter 91(for example, clocks and clock cases); or

(l) Toy furniture or toy lamps or lighting fittings (heading No.95.03), billiard tables or other furniture specially constructed for games (heading No.95.04), furniture for conjuring tricks or decorations (other than electric garlands) such as Chinese lanterns (heading No.95.05).

二、税号 94.01 至 94.03 的物品（零件除外），只适用于落地式的物品。

对下列物品，即使是悬挂的、固定在墙壁上的或叠摞的，仍归入上述各税号：

（一）碗橱、书柜、架式家具及组合家具；

（二）座具及床。

三、

（一）税号 94.01 至 94.03 所列货品的零件，不包括玻璃（包括镜子）、大理石或其他石料以及第六十八章及第六十九章所列任何其他材料的片、块（不论是否切割成形，但未与其他零件组装）。

（二）税号 94.04 的货品，如果单独进口或出口，不能作为税号 94.01、94.02 或 94.03 所列货品的零件归类。

四、税号 94.06 所称"活动房屋"，是指在工厂制成成品或制成部件并一同进口或出口，供以后在有关地点上组装的房屋，例如，工地用房、办公室、学校、店铺、工作棚、车房或类似的建筑物。

2. The articles (other than parts) referred to in headings No.94.01 to 94.03 are to be classified in those headings only if they are designed for placing on the floor or ground.

The following are, however, to be classified in the abovementioned headings even if they are designed to be hung, to be fixed to the wall or to stand one on the other:

(a) Cupboards, bookcases, other shelved furniture and unit furniture;

(b) Seats and beds.

3.

(a) In headings No.94.01 to 94.03references to parts of goods do not include references to sheets or slabs (whether or not cut to shape but not combined with other parts) of glass (including mirrors), marble or other stone or of any other material referred to in Chapter 68 or 69.

(b) Goods described in heading No. 94.04, presented separately, are not to be classified in heading No.94.01, 94.02 or 94.03 as parts of goods.

4. For the purposes of heading No.94.06, the expression "prefabricated buildings" means buildings which are finished in the factory or put up as elements, presented together, to be assembled on site, such as housing or worksite accommodation, offices, schools, shops, sheds, garages or similar buildings.

序号 No.	税则号列 Tariff Line	货品名称	最惠国税率 MFN(%)	协定税率 Agreement(%)		特惠税率 S.P.(%)		普通税率 Gen.(%)	Article Description
	94.01	**座具（包括能作床用的两用椅，但税号94.02的货品除外）及其零件:**							**Seats (other than those of heading No. 94.02), whether or not convertible into beds, and parts thereof:**
8082	9401.1000	-飞机用座具	0			0	最不发达35国LDC35,最不发达4国LDC4	100	-Seats of a kind used for aircraft
		-机动车辆用座具:							Seats of a kind used for motor vehicles:
8083	9401.2010	---皮革或再生皮革面的	10	0	智利CL,新西兰NZ,秘鲁PE,哥斯达黎加CR,澳门MO	0	最不发达35国LDC35	100	---With outer surface of leather or composition leather

序号 No.	税则号列 Tariff Line	货品名称	最惠国税率 MFN(%)	协定税率 Agreement(%)		特惠税率 S.P.(%)		普通税率 Gen.(%)	Article Description
8084	9401.2090	---其他	10	0	智利CL,新西兰NZ,秘鲁PE,哥斯达黎加CR,澳门MO	0	最不发达35国LDC35	100	---Other
8085	9401.3000	-可调高度的转动座具	0			0	最不发达35国LDC35,最不发达4国LDC4	100	-Swivel seats with variable height adjustment
		-能作床用的两用椅,但庭园座具或野营设备除外:							-Seats other than garden seats or camping equipment, convertible into beds:
8086	9401.4010	---皮革或再生皮革面的	0			0	最不发达35国LDC35,最不发达4国LDC4	100	---With outer surface of leather or composition leather
8087	9401.4090	---其他	0			0	最不发达35国LDC35,最不发达4国LDC4	100	---Other
		-藤、柳条、竹及类似材料制的座具:							-Seats of cane, osier, bamboo or similar materials:
8088	9401.5100	--竹制或藤制的	0			0	最不发达35国LDC35,最不发达4国LDC4	100	--Of bamboo or rattan
8089	9401.5900	--其他	0			0	最不发达35国LDC35,最不发达4国LDC4	100	--Other
		-木框架的其他座具:							-Other seats, with wooden frames:
		--装软垫的:							--upholstered:
8090	9401.6110	---皮革或再生皮革面的	0			0	最不发达35国LDC35,最不发达4国LDC4	100	---With outer surface of leather or composition leather
8091	9401.6190	---其他	0			0	最不发达35国LDC35,最不发达4国LDC4	100	---Other

序号 No.	税则号列 Tariff Line	货品名称	最惠国税率 MFN(%)	协定税率 Agreement(%)		特惠税率 S.P.(%)		普通税率 Gen.(%)	Article Description
8092	9401.6900	--其他	0			0	最不发达35国LDC35,最不发达4国LDC4	100	--Other
		-金属框架的其他座具:							-Other seats, with metal frames:
		-装软垫的:							--Upholstered:
8093	9401.7110	---皮革或再生皮革面的	0			0	最不发达35国LDC35,最不发达4国LDC4	100	---With outer surface of leather or composition leather
8094	9401.7190	---其他	0			0	最不发达35国LDC35,最不发达4国LDC4	100	---Other
8095	9401.7900	--其他	0			0	最不发达35国LDC35,最不发达4国LDC4	100	--Other
		-其他座具:							-Other seats:
8096	9401.8010	---石制的	0			0	最不发达35国LDC35,最不发达4国LDC4	100	---Of stone
8097	9401.8090	---其他	0			0	最不发达35国LDC35,最不发达4国LDC4	100	---Other
		-零件:							-Parts:
		---机动车辆用:							---Of the motor Vehicles:
8098	9401.9011	----座椅调角器	10	0 1 5	新西兰NZ,哥斯达黎加CR,香港HK 智利CL 秘鲁PE	0	最不发达35国LDC35,最不发达4国LDC4	100	----Seat angle regulating devices
8099	9401.9019	----其他	0			0	最不发达35国LDC35,最不发达4国LDC4	100	----Other

序号 No.	税则号列 Tariff Line	货品名称	最惠国税率 MFN(%)	协定税率 Agreement(%)	特惠税率 S.P.(%)	普通税率 Gen.(%)	Article Description
8100	9401.9090	---其他	0		0 最不发达35国LDC35,最不发达4国LDC4	100	---Other
	94.02	**医疗、外科、牙科或兽医用家具（例如，手术台、检查台、带机械装置的病床、牙科用椅）;有旋转、倾斜、升降装置的理发用椅及类似椅;上述物品的零件:**					**Medical, surgical, dental or veterinary furniture (for example, operating tables, examination tables, hospital beds with mechanical fittings, dentists'chairs); barbers'chairs and similar chairs, having rotating as well as both reclining and elevating movements; parts of the foregoing articles:**
		-牙科、理发及类似用途的椅及其零件:					-Dentists', barbers'or similar chairs and parts thereof:
8101	9402.1010	---理发用椅及其零件	0		0 最不发达35国LDC35,最不发达4国LDC4	100	---Barbers chair and parts thereof
8102	9402.1090	---其他	0		0 最不发达35国LDC35,最不发达4国LDC4	30	---Other
8103	9402.9000	-其他	0		0 最不发达35国LDC35,最不发达4国LDC4	30	-Other
	94.03	**其他家具及其零件:**					**Other furniture and parts thereof:**
8104	9403.1000	-办公室用金属家具	0		0 最不发达35国LDC35,最不发达4国LDC4	100	-Metal furniture of a kind used in offices
8105	9403.2000	-其他金属家具	0		0 最不发达35国LDC35,最不发达4国LDC4	100	-Other metal furniture

序号 No.	税则号列 Tariff Line	货品名称	最惠国税率 MFN(%)	协定税率 Agreement(%)	特惠税率 S.P.(%)		普通税率 Gen.(%)	Article Description
8106	9403.3000	-办公室用木家具	0		0	最不发达35国LDC35,最不发达4国LDC4	100	-Wooden furniture of a kind used in offices
8107	9403.4000	-厨房用木家具	0		0	最不发达35国LDC35,最不发达4国LDC4	100	-Wooden furniture of a kind used in the kitchen
		-卧室用木家具:						-Wooden furniture of a kind used in the bedroom:
8108	9403.5010	---红木制	0		0	最不发达35国LDC35,最不发达4国LDC4	100	---Of rose wood
		---其他:						---Other:
8109	9403.5091	----天然漆（大漆）漆木家具	0		0	最不发达35国LDC35,最不发达4国LDC4	100	----Wooden furniture of nature binders
8110	9403.5099	----其他	0		0	最不发达35国LDC35,最不发达4国LDC4	100	----Other
		-其他木家具:						-Other wooden furniture:
8111	9403.6010	---红木制	0		0	最不发达35国LDC35,最不发达4国LDC4	100	---Of rose wood
		---其他:						---Other:
8112	9403.6091	----天然漆（大漆）漆木家具	0		0	最不发达35国LDC35,最不发达4国LDC4	100	----Wooden furniture of nature binders
8113	9403.6099	----其他	0		0	最不发达35国LDC35,最不发达4国LDC4	100	----Other

序号 No.	税则号列 Tariff Line	货品名称	最惠国税率 MFN(%)	协定税率 Agreement(%)	特惠税率 S.P.(%)	普通税率 Gen.(%)	Article Description
8114	9403.7000	-塑料家具	0		0 最不发达35国LDC35, 最不发达4国LDC4	100	-Furniture of plastics
		-其他材料制的家具，包括藤、柳条、竹或类似材料制的:					-Furniture of other materials, including cane, osier, bamboo or similar materials:
8115	9403.8100	--竹制或藤制的	0		0 最不发达35国LDC35, 最不发达4国LDC4	100	--Of bamboo or rattan
		--其他:					--Other:
8116	9403.8910	---柳条及类似材料制	0		0 最不发达35国LDC35, 最不发达4国LDC4	100	---Of osier, or similar materials
8117	9403.8920	---石制的	0		0 最不发达35国LDC35, 最不发达4国LDC4	100	---Of stone
8118	9403.8990	---其他	0		0 最不发达35国LDC35, 最不发达4国LDC4	100	---Other
8119	9403.9000	-零件	0		0 最不发达35国LDC35, 最不发达4国LDC4	100	-Parts
	94.04	**弹簧床垫;寝具及类似用品，装有弹簧、内部用任何材料填充、衬垫或用海绵橡胶、泡沫塑料制成，不论是否包面（例如，褥垫、棉被、羽绒被、靠垫、座垫及枕头）:**					**Mattress supports; articles of bedding and similar furnishing (for example, mattresses, quilts, eiderdowns, cush-ions, pouffes and pillows) fitted with springs or stuffed or internally fitted with any material or of cellular rubber or plastics, whether or not covered:**

序号 No.	税则号列 Tariff Line	货品名称	最惠国税率 MFN(%)	协定税率 Agreement(%)		特惠税率 S.P.(%)		普通税率 Gen.(%)	Article Description
8120	9404.1000	-弹簧床垫	20 △10	0 2 4 10	东盟ASEAN,新加坡SG,新西兰NZ 智利CL 哥斯达黎加CR 秘鲁PE	0	最不发达35国LDC35	100	-Mattress supports
		-褥垫:							-Mattresses:
8121	9404.2100	--海绵橡胶或泡沫塑料制，不论是否包面	20 △10	0 4 10	东盟ASEAN,智利CL,新加坡SG,新西兰NZ,香港HK,澳门MO 哥斯达黎加CR 秘鲁PE	0	最不发达35国LDC35,最不发达4国LDC4	100	--Of cellular rubber or plastics, whether or not covered
8122	9404.2900	--其他材料制	20 △10	0 2 4 10 14	东盟ASEAN,新加坡SG,新西兰NZ,香港HK,澳门MO 智利CL 哥斯达黎加CR 秘鲁PE 亚太APTA,巴基斯坦PK	0	最不发达35国LDC35,最不发达4国LDC4	100	--Of other materials
		-睡袋:							-Sleeping bags:
8123	9404.3010	---羽毛或羽绒填充的	20 △10	0 4 10	东盟ASEAN,智利CL,新加坡SG,新西兰NZ,澳门MO 哥斯达黎加CR 秘鲁PE	0	最不发达35国LDC35,最不发达4国LDC4	130	---Stuffed with feathers or down
8124	9404.3090	---其他	20 △10	0 4 10	东盟ASEAN,智利CL,新加坡SG,新西兰NZ,澳门MO 哥斯达黎加CR 秘鲁PE	0	最不发达35国LDC35,最不发达4国LDC4	100	---Other
		-其他:							-Other:
8125	9404.9010	---羽毛或羽绒填充的	20 △10	0 2 4 10	东盟ASEAN,新加坡SG,新西兰NZ,香港HK,澳门MO 智利CL 哥斯达黎加CR 秘鲁PE	0	最不发达35国LDC35,最不发达4国LDC4	130	---Stuffed with feathers or down
8126	9404.9020	---兽毛填充的	20 △10	0 2 4 10	东盟ASEAN,新加坡SG,新西兰NZ,香港HK,澳门MO 智利CL 哥斯达黎加CR 秘鲁PE	0	最不发达35国LDC35,最不发达4国LDC4	130	---Stuffed with animal hair
8127	9404.9030	---丝棉填充的	20 △10	0 2 4 10	东盟ASEAN,新加坡SG,新西兰NZ,香港HK,澳门MO 智利CL 哥斯达黎加CR 秘鲁PE	0	最不发达35国LDC35,最不发达4国LDC4	130	---Stuffed with silk wadding

序号 No.	税则号列 Tariff Line	货品名称	最惠国税率 MFN(%)	协定税率 Agreement(%)		特惠税率 S.P.(%)		普通税率 Gen.(%)	Article Description
8128	9404.9040	---化纤棉填充的	20 △10	0 2 4 10	东盟ASEAN,新加坡SG,新西兰NZ,香港HK,澳门MO 智利CL 哥斯达黎加CR 秘鲁PE	0	最不发达35国LDC35,最不发达4国LDC4	130	---Stuffed with man-made fibres
8129	9404.9090	---其他	20 △10	0 2 4 10	东盟ASEAN,新加坡SG,新西兰NZ,香港HK,澳门MO 智利CL 哥斯达黎加CR 秘鲁PE	0	最不发达35国LDC35,最不发达4国LDC4	130	---Other
	94.05	**其他税号未列名的灯具及照明装置，包括探照灯、聚光灯及其零件;装有固定光源的发光标志、发光铭牌及类似品，以及其他税号未列名的这些货品的零件:**							**Lamps and lighting fittings including searchlights and spotlights and parts thereof, not elsewhere specified or included; illuminated signs, illu-minated name-plates and the like, ha-ving a permanently fixed light source, and parts thereof not elsewhere specified or included:**
8130	9405.1000	-枝形吊灯及天花板或墙壁上的其他电气照明装置，但不包括公共露天场所或街道上的电气照明装置	10	0 1 5	东盟ASEAN,新西兰NZ,秘鲁PE,哥斯达黎加CR 智利CL 巴基斯坦PK	0	最不发达35国LDC35,最不发达4国LDC4	80	-Chandeliers and other electric ceiling or wall lighting fittings, excluding those of a kind used for lighting public open spaces or thorough-fares
8131	9405.2000	-电气的台灯、床头灯或落地灯	20	0 2 4 10	东盟ASEAN,新加坡SG,新西兰NZ 智利CL 哥斯达黎加CR 秘鲁PE	0	最不发达35国LDC35,最不发达4国LDC4	80	-Electric table, desk, bedside or floor-standing lamps
8132	9405.3000	-圣诞树用的成套灯具	16	0 3.2 8 12.8	东盟ASEAN,智利CL,新加坡SG,新西兰NZ 哥斯达黎加CR 秘鲁PE 巴基斯坦PK	0	最不发达35国LDC35,最不发达4国LDC4	100	-Lighting sets of a kind used for Christmas trees
		-其他电灯及照明装置:							-Other electric lamps and lighting fittings:
8133	9405.4010	---探照灯	17.5	0 1.8 3.5 8.8 14	东盟ASEAN,新加坡SG,新西兰NZ,澳门MO 智利CL 哥斯达黎加CR 秘鲁PE 巴基斯坦PK	0	最不发达35国LDC35,最不发达4国LDC4	70	---Searchlights
8134	9405.4020	---聚光灯	17.5	0 1.8 3.5	东盟ASEAN,新加坡SG,新西兰NZ,澳门MO 智利CL 哥斯达黎加CR	0	最不发达35国LDC35,最不发	70	---Spotlights

序号 No.	税则号列 Tariff Line	货品名称	最惠国税率 MFN(%)	协定税率 Agreement(%)		特惠税率 S.P.(%)		普通税率 Gen.(%)	Article Description
				8.8 14	秘鲁PE 巴基斯坦PK		达4国LDC4		
8135	9405.4090	---其他	10	0 1 5	东盟ASEAN,新加坡SG,新西兰NZ,秘鲁PE,哥斯达黎加CR,香港HK,澳门MO 智利CL 巴基斯坦PK	0	最不发达35国LDC35,最不发达4国LDC4	80	---Other
8136	9405.5000	-非电气的灯具及照明装置	20	0 4 10	东盟ASEAN,智利CL,新加坡SG,新西兰NZ 哥斯达黎加CR 秘鲁PE	0	最不发达35国LDC35	80	-Non-electrical lamps and lighting fittings
8137	9405.6000	-发光标志、发光铭牌及类似品	20	0 4 10	东盟ASEAN,智利CL,新加坡SG,新西兰NZ,香港HK 哥斯达黎加CR 秘鲁PE	0	最不发达35国LDC35	80	-Illuminated signs, illuminated name plates and the like
		-零件:							-Parts:
8138	9405.9100	--玻璃制	20	0 4 10	东盟ASEAN,智利CL,新加坡SG,新西兰NZ 哥斯达黎加CR 秘鲁PE	0	最不发达35国LDC35	70	--Of glass
8139	9405.9200	--塑料制	20	0 4 10	东盟ASEAN,智利CL,新加坡SG,新西兰NZ,澳门MO 哥斯达黎加CR 秘鲁PE	0	最不发达35国LDC35	70	--Of plastics
8140	9405.9900	--其他	20	0 2 4 10	东盟ASEAN,新加坡SG,新西兰NZ,澳门MO 智利CL 哥斯达黎加CR 秘鲁PE	0	最不发达35国LDC35,最不发达4国LDC4	70	--Other
	94.06	**活动房屋:**							**Prefabricated buildings:**
8141	9406.0000	活动房屋	10	0 1 5 7	东盟ASEAN,新加坡SG,新西兰NZ,哥斯达黎加CR,澳门MO 智利CL 巴基斯坦PK,秘鲁PE 亚太APTA	0	最不发达35国LDC35,最不发达4国LDC4	70	Prefabricated buildings

第九十五章
玩具、游戏品、运动用品及其零件、附件

注释:

一、本章不包括:

（一）蜡烛（税号 34.06）；

（二）税号 36.04 的烟花、爆竹或其他烟火制品;

（三）已切成一定长度但未制成钓鱼线的纱线、单丝、绳、肠线及类似品（第三十九章、税号 42.06 或第十一类）；

（四）税号 42.02、43.03 或 43.04 的运动用袋或其他容器;

（五）第六十一章或第六十二章的纺织品制的运动服或化妆舞会服装;

（六）第六十三章的纺织品制的旗帜及帆板或滑行车用帆;

（七）第六十四章的运动鞋靴（装有冰刀或滑轮的溜冰鞋除外）或第六十五章的运动用帽;

（八）手杖、鞭子、马鞭或类似品（税号 66.02）及其零件（税号 66.03）；

（九）税号 70.18 的未装配的玩偶或其他玩具用的玻璃假眼;

（十）第十五类注释二所规定的贱金属制通用零件（第十五类）或塑料制的类似货品（第三十九章）；

（十一）税号 83.06 的铃、钟、锣及类似品;

（十二）液体泵（税号 84.13）、液体或气体的过滤、净化机器及装置（税号 84.21）、电动机（税号 85.01）、变压器（税号 85.04）或无线电遥控设备（税号 85.26）；

（十三）第十七类的运动用车辆（长雪橇、平底雪橇及类似品除外）；

（十四）儿童两轮车（税号 87.12）；

（十五）运动用船艇，例如，轻舟、赛艇（第八十九章）及其桨、橹和类似品（木制的归入第四十四章）；

（十六）运动及户外游戏用的眼镜、护目镜及类似品（税号 90.04）；

（十七）媒诱音响器及哨子（税号 92.08）；

Chapter 95
Toys，games and sports requisites; parts and accessories thereof

Notes:

1. This Chapter does not cover:

(a) Candles (heading No.34.06);

(b) Fireworks or other pyrotechnic articles of heading No.36.04;

(c) Yarns，monofilament，cords or gut or the like for fishing，cut to length but not made up into fishing lines，of Chapter 39，heading No.42.46 or Section XI;

(d) Sports bags or other containers of heading No.42.02，43.03 or 43.04;

(e) Sports clothing or fancy dress，of textiles，of Chapter 61 or 62;

(f) Textile flags or bunting，or sails for boats，sailboards or land craft，of Chapter 63;

(g) Sports footwear (other than skating boots with ice or roller skates attached) of Chapter 64, or sports head-gear of Chapter 65;

(h) Walking-sticks, whips, riding-crops or the like (heading No.66.02), or parts thereof (heading No.66.03);

(i) Unmounted glass eyes for dolls or other toys，of heading No.70.18;

(j) Parts of general use，as defined in Note 2 to Section XV，of base metal (Section XV)，or similar goods of plastics (Chapter 39);

(k) Bells，gongs or the like of heading No.83.06;

(l) Pumps for liquids (heading No.84.13)，filtering or purifying machinery and apparatus for liquids or gases (heading No.84.21)，electric motors (heading No.85.01)，electric transformers (heading No.85.04) or radio remote control apparatus (heading No.85.26);

(m) Sports vehicles(other than bobsleighs，toboggans and the like)of Section XVII;

(n) Children' s bicycles(heading No.87.12);

(o) Sports craft such as canoes and skiffs (Chapter 89)，or their means of propulsion (Chapter 44 for such articles made of wood);

(p) Spectacles，goggles or the like，for sports or outdoor games (heading No.90.04);

(q) Decoy calls or whistles (heading No.92.08);

（十八）第九十三章的武器及其他物品；

（十九）各种电气彩灯串（税号 94.05）；

（二十）球拍线、帐篷或类似的野营用品、手套、棒球手套和露指手套（按其构成材料归类）；或

（二十一）餐具、厨房用具、盥洗用品、地毯及纺织材料制的其他铺地制品、服装、床上及餐桌用织物制品、盥洗及厨房用织物制品及具有实用功能的类似货品（按其构成材料归类）。

二、本章包括天然或养殖珍珠、宝石或半宝石（天然、合成或再造）、贵金属或包贵金属只作为小零件的物品。

三、除上述注释一另有规定的以外，凡专用于或主要用于本章各税号所列物品的零件、附件，应与有关物品一并归类。

四、除上述注释一另有规定的以外，税目 95.03 特别适用于该税目物品与一项或多项其他货品组合而成的物品，只要这些物品为零售包装，且组合后具有玩具的基本特征。这些组合物品不能视为归类总规则三（二）所指的成套货品，如果单独报验，应归入其他税目。

五、税目 95.03 不包括因其设计、形状或构成材料可确认为专供动物使用的物品，例如“宠物玩具”归入其相应的税目。

六、子目 9504.50 包括：

（一）在电视机、监视器或其他外部屏幕或表面上重放图像的视频游戏控制器；或

（二）自带显示屏的视频游戏设备，不论是否便携式。

本子目不包括用硬币、钞票、银行卡、代币或任何其他支付方式使其工作的视频游戏控制器或设备（子目 9504.30）。

(r) Arms or other articles of Chapter 93;

(s) Electric garlands of all kinds (heading No.94.05);

(t) Racket strings, tents or other camping goods, or gloves, mittens and mitts (classified according to their constituent material); or

(u) Tableware, kitchenware, toilet articles, carpets and other textile floor coverings, apparel, bed linen, table linen, toilet linen, kitchen linen and similar articles having a utilitarian function (classified according to their constituent material).

2. This Chapter includes articles in which natural or cultured pearls, precious or semi-precious stones (natural, synthetic or recons tructed), precious metal or metal clad with precious metal constitute only minor consistuents.

3. Subject to Note 1 above, parts and accessories which are suitable for use solely or principally with articles of this Chapter are to be classified with those articles.

4. Subject to the provisions of Note 1 above, heading 95.03 applies, *inter alia*, to articles of this heading combined with one or more items, which cannot be considered as sets under the terms of General Interpretative Rule 3(b), and which, if presented separately, would be classified in other headings, provided the articles are put up together for retail sale and the combinations have the essential character of toys.

5. Heading No.95.03 does not cover articles which, on account of their design, shape or constituent material, are identifiable as intended exclusively for animals, for example, “pet toys” (classification in their own appropriate heading).

6. Subheading 9504.50 covers :

(a) Video game consoles from which the image is reproduced on atelevision receiver, a monitor or other external screen or surface; or

(b) Video game machines having a self-contained video screen, whetheror not portable.

This subheading does not cover video game consoles or machines operated by coins, banknotes, bank cards, tokens or by any other means of payment(subheading 9504.30).”

序号 No.	税则号列 Tariff Line	货品名称	最惠国税率 MFN(%)	协定税率 Agreement(%)	特惠税率 S.P.(%)		普通税率 Gen.(%)	Article Description
	95.03	**三轮车、踏板车、踏板汽车和类似的带轮玩具；玩偶车；玩偶；其他玩具；缩小（按比例缩小）的模型及类似的娱乐用模型，不论是否活动；各种智力玩具：**						**Tricycles, scooters, pedal cars and similar wheeled toys; dolls' carriages; dolls; other toys; reduced-size ("scale") models and similar recreational models, working or not; puzzles of all kinds:**
8142	9503.0010	---供儿童乘骑的带轮玩具（例如，三轮车、踏板车、踏板汽车）；玩偶车	0		0	最不发达35国LDC35，最不发达4国LDC4	80	---Wheeled toys designed to be ridden by children (for example, tricycles, scooters, pedal cars); doll's carriages
		---玩偶，不论是否着装；玩具动物:						---Dolls, whether or not dressed; Toys representing animals or non-human creatures:
8143	9503.0021	----动物	0		0	最不发达35国LDC35，最不发达4国LDC4	80	----Toys representing animals or non-human creatures
8144	9503.0029	----其他	0		0	最不发达35国LDC35，最不发达4国LDC4	80	----Other
		---缩小（按比例缩小）的全套模型组件，不论是否活动:						---Reduced-size ("scale") model assembly kits, whether or not working:
8145	9503.0031	----电动火车	0		0	最不发达35国LDC35，最不发达4国LDC4	80	----Electric trains
8146	9503.0039	----其他	0		0	最不发达35国LDC35，最不发达4国LDC4	80	----Other
8147	9503.0040	---其他建筑套件及建筑玩具	0		0	最不发达35国LDC35，最不发达4国LDC4	80	---Other construction sets and constructional toys

序号 No.	税则号列 Tariff Line	货品名称	最惠国税率 MFN(%)	协定税率 Agreement(%)	特惠税率 S.P.(%)	普通税率 Gen.(%)	Article Description
8148	9503.0050	---玩具乐器	0		0 最不发达35国LDC35, 最不发达4国LDC4	80	---Toy musical instruments and apparatus
8149	9503.0060	---智力玩具	0		0 最不发达35国LDC35, 最不发达4国LDC4	80	---Puzzles
		---其他玩具:					---Other toys:
8150	9503.0081	----组装成套或全套的	0		0 最不发达35国LDC35, 最不发达4国LDC4	80	----Put up in sets or outfits
8151	9503.0082	----其他带动力装置的玩具及模型	0		0 最不发达35国LDC35, 最不发达4国LDC4	80	----Other, incorporating a motor
8152	9503.0089	----其他	0		0 最不发达35国LDC35, 最不发达4国LDC4	80	----Other
8153	9503.0090	---零件、附件	0		0 最不发达35国LDC35, 最不发达4国LDC4	80	---Parts and accessories
	95.04	**视频游戏控制器及设备、游艺场所、桌上或室内游戏用品，包括弹球机、台球、娱乐专用桌及保龄球自动球道设备:**					**Video games consoles and machines, articles for funfair, table or parlour games, including pintables, billiards, special tables for casino games and automatic bowling alley equipment:**
8154	9504.2000	-台球用品及附件	0		0 最不发达35国LDC35, 最不发达4国LDC4	80	-Articles and accessories for billiards of all kinds

序号 No.	税则号列 Tariff Line	货品名称	最惠国税率 MFN(%)	协定税率 Agreement(%)	特惠税率 S.P.(%)	普通税率 Gen.(%)	Article Description
		-使用硬币、钞票、银行卡、代币或任何其他支付方式使其工作的其他游戏用品，但保龄球自动球道设备除外:					-Other games, operated by coins, banknotes, bank cards, tokens or by anyother means of payment, other than automatic bowling alley equipment:
8155	9504.3010	---电子游戏机	0		0 最不发达35国 LDC35, 最不发达4国 LDC4	130	---Video games
8156	9504.3090	---其他	0		0 最不发达35国 LDC35, 最不发达4国 LDC4	80	---Other
8157	9504.4000	-扑克牌	0		0 最不发达35国 LDC35, 最不发达4国 LDC4	80	-Playing cards
		-视频游戏控制器及设备，但子目9504.30的货品除外:					-Video games consoles and machines, other than those of heading No.9504.30:
		---与电视接收机配套使用的:					---Used with a television receiver:
8158	9504.5011	----零件	0		0 最不发达35国 LDC35, 最不发达4国 LDC4	130	----Parts
8159	9504.5019	----其他	0		0 最不发达35国 LDC35, 最不发达4国 LDC4	130	----Other
		---其他:					---Other:
8160	9504.5091	----零件	0		0 最不发达35国 LDC35, 最不发达4国 LDC4	130	----Parts
8161	9504.5099	----其他	0		0 最不发达35国 LDC35, 最不发达4国 LDC4	130	----Other

序号 No.	税则号列 Tariff Line	货品名称	最惠国税率 MFN(%)	协定税率 Agreement(%)	特惠税率 S.P.(%)	普通税率 Gen.(%)	Article Description
		-其他:					-Other:
8162	9504.9010	---其他电子游戏机	0		0 最不发达35国LDC35,最不发达4国LDC4	130	---Other video games
		---保龄球自动球道设备及器具:					---Automatic bowling alley equipments and appliances:
8163	9504.9021	----保龄球自动分瓶机	0		0 最不发达35国LDC35,最不发达4国LDC4	80	----Automatic bowling pin distributing machines
8164	9504.9022	----保龄球	0		0 最不发达35国LDC35,最不发达4国LDC4	80	----Bowling balls
8165	9504.9023	----保龄球瓶	0		0 最不发达35国LDC35,最不发达4国LDC4	80	----Bowling pins
8166	9504.9029	----其他	0		0 最不发达35国LDC35,最不发达4国LDC4	80	----Other
8167	9504.9030	---中国象棋、国际象棋、跳棋等棋类用品	0		0 最不发达35国LDC35,最不发达4国LDC4	80	---Chess and other board games, including Chinese chess, international chess, Chinese cherkers and draughts
8168	9504.9040	---麻将及类似桌上游戏用品	0		0 最不发达35国LDC35,最不发达4国LDC4	80	---Mahjong and similar table games
8169	9504.9090	---其他	0		0 最不发达35国LDC35,最不发达4国LDC4	80	---Other

序号 No.	税则号列 Tariff Line	货品名称	最惠国税率 MFN(%)	协定税率 Agreement(%)		特惠税率 S.P.(%)		普通税率 Gen.(%)	Article Description
	95.05	**节日（包括狂欢节）用品或其他娱乐用品，包括魔术道具及嬉戏品:**							**Festive, carnival or other entertainm-ent articles, including conjuring tricks and novelty jokes:**
8170	9505.1000	-圣诞节用品	0			0	最不发达35国LDC35,最不发达4国LDC4	100	-Articles for Christmas festivities
8171	9505.9000	-其他	0			0	最不发达35国LDC35,最不发达4国LDC4	100	-Other
	95.06	**一般的体育活动、体操、竞技及其他运动（包括乒乓球运动）或户外游戏用的本章其他税号未列名用品及设备;游泳池或戏水池:**							**Articles and equipment for general physical exercise, gymnastics, athleti-cs, other sports (including table-tennis) or out door games, not specified or included elsewhere in this Chapter; swimming pools and paddling pools:**
		-滑雪屐及其他滑雪用具:							-Snow-skis and other snow-ski equipment:
8172	9506.1100	--滑雪屐	14	0 2.8	东盟ASEAN,智利CL,巴基斯坦PK,新加坡SG,新西兰NZ,秘鲁PE 哥斯达黎加CR	0	最不发达35国LDC35	50	--Skis
8173	9506.1200	--滑雪屐扣件（滑雪屐带）	14	0 2.8	东盟ASEAN,智利CL,巴基斯坦PK,新加坡SG,新西兰NZ,秘鲁PE 哥斯达黎加CR	0	最不发达35国LDC35	50	--Ski-fastenings (ski-bindings)
8174	9506.1900	--其他	14	0 2.8	东盟ASEAN,智利CL,巴基斯坦PK,新加坡SG,新西兰NZ,秘鲁PE 哥斯达黎加CR	0	最不发达35国LDC35	50	--Other
		-滑水板、冲浪板、帆板及其他水上运动用具:							-Water-skis, surf-boards, sailboards and other water-sport equipment:
8175	9506.2100	--帆板	12	0 2.4	东盟ASEAN,智利CL,巴基斯坦PK,新加坡SG,新西兰NZ,秘鲁PE 哥斯达黎加CR	0	最不发达35国LDC35	50	--Sailboards
8176	9506.2900	--其他	14	0 2.8	东盟ASEAN,智利CL,巴基斯坦PK,新加坡SG,新西兰NZ,秘鲁PE,香港HK 哥斯达黎加CR	0	最不发达35国LDC35	50	--Other
		-高尔夫球棍及其他高尔夫球用具:							-Golf clubs and other golf equipment:

序号 No.	税则号列 Tariff Line	货品名称	最惠国税率 MFN(%)	协定税率 Agreement(%)		特惠税率 S.P.(%)		普通税率 Gen.(%)	Article Description
8177	9506.3100	--棍，全套	14	0 2.8	东盟ASEAN,智利CL,巴基斯坦PK,新加坡SG,新西兰NZ,秘鲁PE 哥斯达黎加CR	0	最不发达35国LDC35,最不发达4国LDC4	50	--Clubs, complete
8178	9506.3200	--球	12	0 2.4	东盟ASEAN,智利CL,巴基斯坦PK,新加坡SG,新西兰NZ,秘鲁PE 哥斯达黎加CR	0	最不发达35国LDC35	50	--Balls
8179	9506.3900	--其他	14	0 2.8	东盟ASEAN,智利CL,巴基斯坦PK,新加坡SG,新西兰NZ,秘鲁PE,台湾TW 哥斯达黎加CR	0	最不发达35国LDC35,最不发达4国LDC4	50	--Other
		-乒乓球运动用品及器械:							-Articles and equipment for table-tennis:
8180	9506.4010	---乒乓球	12	0 1.2 2.4	东盟ASEAN,巴基斯坦PK,新加坡SG,新西兰NZ,秘鲁PE 智利CL 哥斯达黎加CR	0	最不发达35国LDC35	50	---Table-tennis balls
8181	9506.4090	---其他	14 △7	0 1.4 2.8	东盟ASEAN,巴基斯坦PK,新加坡SG,新西兰NZ,秘鲁PE 智利CL 哥斯达黎加CR	0	最不发达35国LDC35	50	---Other
		-网球拍、羽毛球拍或类似的球拍，不论是否装弦:							-Tennis, badminton or similar rackets, whether or not strung:
8182	9506.5100	--草地网球拍，不论是否装弦	14	0 2.8	东盟ASEAN,智利CL,巴基斯坦PK,新加坡SG,新西兰NZ,秘鲁PE 哥斯达黎加CR	0	最不发达35国LDC35	50	--Lawn-tennis rackets, whether or not strung
8183	9506.5900	--其他	14	0 2.8	东盟ASEAN,智利CL,巴基斯坦PK,新加坡SG,新西兰NZ,秘鲁PE 哥斯达黎加CR	0	最不发达35国LDC35	50	--Other
		-球，但高尔夫球及乒乓球除外:							-Balls, other than golf balls and table-tennis balls:
8184	9506.6100	--草地网球	12	0 2.4	东盟ASEAN,智利CL,巴基斯坦PK,新加坡SG,新西兰NZ,秘鲁PE 哥斯达黎加CR	0	最不发达35国LDC35	50	--Lawn-tennis balls
		--可充气的球:							--Inflatable:
8185	9506.6210	---篮球、足球、排球	12 △6	0 1.2 2.4	东盟ASEAN,巴基斯坦PK,新加坡SG,新西兰NZ,秘鲁PE 智利CL 哥斯达黎加CR	0	最不发达35国LDC35	50	---Basketballs, footballs or volley balls
8186	9506.6290	---其他	12	0 1.2 2.4	东盟ASEAN,巴基斯坦PK,新加坡SG,新西兰NZ,秘鲁PE 智利CL 哥斯达黎加CR	0	最不发达35国LDC35	50	---Other

序号 No.	税则号列 Tariff Line	货品名称	最惠国税率 MFN(%)	协定税率 Agreement(%)		特惠税率 S.P.(%)		普通税率 Gen.(%)	Article Description
8187	9506.6900	--其他	12	0	东盟ASEAN,智利CL,巴基斯坦PK,新加坡SG,新西兰NZ,秘鲁PE	0	最不发达35国LDC35	50	--Other
				2.4	哥斯达黎加CR				
		-溜冰鞋及旱冰鞋,包括装有冰刀的溜冰靴:							-Ice skates and roller skates, including skating boots with skates attached:
8188	9506.7010	---溜冰鞋	14	0	东盟ASEAN,智利CL,巴基斯坦PK,新加坡SG,新西兰NZ,秘鲁PE	0	最不发达35国LDC35	50	---Ice skates
				2.8	哥斯达黎加CR				
				12	亚太APTA				
8189	9506.7020	---旱冰鞋	14	0	东盟ASEAN,智利CL,巴基斯坦PK,新加坡SG,新西兰NZ,秘鲁PE	0	最不发达35国LDC35	50	---Roller skates
				2.8	哥斯达黎加CR				
				12	亚太APTA				
		-其他:							-Other:
		--一般的体育活动、体操或竞技用品及设备:							--Articles and equipment for general physical exercise, gymnastics or athletics:
		---健身及康复器械:							---Equipment for exercise and recovery:
8190	9506.9111	----跑步机	12 △6	0	东盟ASEAN,巴基斯坦PK,新加坡SG,新西兰NZ,秘鲁PE,香港HK,台湾TW	0	最不发达35国LDC35	50	----Treadmill
				1.2	智利CL				
				2.4	哥斯达黎加CR				
8191	9506.9119	----其他	12 △6	0	东盟ASEAN,巴基斯坦PK,新加坡SG,新西兰NZ,秘鲁PE,香港HK,台湾TW	0	最不发达35国LDC35	50	----Other
				1.2	智利CL				
				2.4	哥斯达黎加CR				
8192	9506.9120	---滑板	12 △6	0	东盟ASEAN,巴基斯坦PK,新加坡SG,新西兰NZ,秘鲁PE,香港HK	0	最不发达35国LDC35	50	---Skateboards
				1.2	智利CL				
				2.4	哥斯达黎加CR				
8193	9506.9190	---其他	12 △6	0	东盟ASEAN,巴基斯坦PK,新加坡SG,新西兰NZ,秘鲁PE,香港HK,澳门MO	0	最不发达35国LDC35,最不发达4国LDC4	50	---Other
				1.2	智利CL				
				2.4	哥斯达黎加CR				
8194	9506.9900	--其他	12	0	东盟ASEAN,巴基斯坦PK,新加坡SG,新西兰NZ,秘鲁PE,香港HK,澳门MO	0	最不发达35国LDC35	50	--Other
				1.2	智利CL				
				2.4	哥斯达黎加CR				

序号 No.	税则号列 Tariff Line	货品名称	最惠国税率 MFN(%)	协定税率 Agreement(%)		特惠税率 S.P.(%)		普通税率 Gen.(%)	Article Description
	95.07	**钓鱼竿、钓鱼钩及其他钓鱼用品;捞鱼网、捕蝶网及类似网;化子“鸟”(税号92.08或97.05的货品除外)以及类似的狩猎用品:**							**Fishing rods, fish-hooks and other line fishing tackle; fish landing nets, butterfly nets and similar nets; decoy “birds” (other than those of heading No.92.08 or 97.05) and similar hunting or shooting requisites:**
8195	9507.1000	-钓鱼竿	21	0 4.2 10.5	东盟ASEAN,智利CL,新加坡SG,新西兰NZ 哥斯达黎加CR 秘鲁PE	0	最不发达35国LDC35	80	-Fishing rods
8196	9507.2000	-钓鱼钩,不论有无系钩丝	21	0 2.1 4.2 10.5	东盟ASEAN,新加坡SG,新西兰NZ 智利CL 哥斯达黎加CR 秘鲁PE	0	最不发达35国LDC35,最不发达4国LDC4	80	-Fish-hooks, whether or not snelled
8197	9507.3000	-钓线轮	21	0 4.2 10.5	东盟ASEAN,智利CL,新加坡SG,新西兰NZ 哥斯达黎加CR 秘鲁PE	0	最不发达35国LDC35	80	-Fishing reels
8198	9507.9000	-其他	21	0 4.2 10.5 18.9	东盟ASEAN,智利CL,新加坡SG,新西兰NZ 哥斯达黎加CR 秘鲁PE 亚太APTA,巴基斯坦PK	0	最不发达35国LDC35	80	-Other
	95.08	**旋转木马、秋千、射击用靶及其他游乐场的娱乐设备;流动马戏团及流动动物园;流动剧团:**							**Roundabouts, swings, shooting galleries and other fairground amusements; traveling circuses and travelling ména-geries; travelling theatres:**
8199	9508.1000	-流动马戏团及流动动物园	15	0 3 7.5 12	东盟ASEAN,智利CL,新加坡SG,新西兰NZ 哥斯达黎加CR 秘鲁PE 巴基斯坦PK	0	最不发达35国LDC35	100	-Travelling circuses and travelling menageries
8200	9508.9000	-其他	15	0 1.5 3 7.5 12	东盟ASEAN,新加坡SG,新西兰NZ 智利CL 哥斯达黎加CR 秘鲁PE 巴基斯坦PK	0	最不发达35国LDC35	100	-Other

第九十六章
杂项制品

注释:

一、本章不包括:

（一）化妆盥洗用笔（第三十三章）;

（二）第六十六章的制品（例如，伞或手杖的零件）;

（三）仿首饰（税号 71.17）;

（四）第十五类注释二所规定的贱金属制通用零件（第十五类）或塑料制的类似品（第三十九章）;

（五）第八十二章的利口器及其他物品，其柄或其他零件是雕刻或模塑材料制的;但税号 96.01 或 96.02 适用于单独进口或出口的上述物品的柄或其他零件;

（六）第九十章的物品，例如，眼镜架（税号 90.03）、数学绘图笔（税号 90.17）、各种牙科、医疗、外科或兽医专用刷子（税号 90.18）;

（七）第九十一章的物品（例如，钟壳或表壳）;

（八）乐器及其零件、附件（第九十二章）;

（九）第九十三章的物品（武器及其零件）;

（十）第九十四章的物品（例如，家具、灯具及照明装置）;

（十一）第九十五章的物品（玩具、游戏品、运动用品）;

（十二）艺术品、收藏品及古物（第九十七章）。

二、税号 96.02 所称“植物质或矿物质雕刻材料”，是指:

（一）用于雕刻的硬种子、硬果核、硬果壳、坚果及类似植物材料（例如，象牙果及棕榈子）;

Chapter 96
Miscellaneous manufactured articles

Notes:

1.This Chapter does not cover:

(a) Pencils for cosmetic or toilet uses (Chapter 33);

(b) Articles of Chapter 66 (for example, parts of umbrellas or walking-sticks);

(c)Imitation jewellery (heading No.71.17);

(d) Parts of general use, as defined in Note 2 to Section XV, of base metal (Section XV), or similar goods of plastics (Chapter 39);

(e) Cutlery or other articles of Chapter 82 with handles or other parts of carving or moulding materials; heading No. 96.01 or 96.02 applies, however, to separately presented handles or other parts of such articles;

(f) Articles of Chapter 90, for example, spectacle frames (heading No.90.03), mathematical drawing pens (heading No.90.17), brushes of a kind specialized for use in dentistry or for medical, surgical or veterinary purposes (heading No.90.18);

(g) Articles of Chapter 91 (for example, clock or watch cases);

(h) Musical instruments or parts or accessories thereof (Chapter 92);

(i) Articles of Chapter 93 (arms and parts thereof);

(j) Articles of Chapter 94 (for example, furniture, lamps and lighting fittings);

(k) Articles of Chapter 95 (toys, games, sports requisites); or

(l) Works of art, collectors' pieces or antiques (Chapter 97).

2.In heading No.96.02 the expression "vegetable or mineral carving material" means:

(a) Hard seeds, pips, hulls and nuts and similar vegetable materials of a kind used for carving (for example, corozo and dom);

（二）琥珀、海泡石、粘聚琥珀、粘聚海泡石、黑玉及其矿物代用品。

(b) Amber, meerschaum, agglomerated amber and agglomerated meerschaum, jet and mineral substitutes for jet.

三、税号96.03所称"制帚、制刷用成束、成簇的材料"，仅指未装配的成束、成簇的兽毛、植物纤维或其他材料。这些成束、成簇的材料无需分开即可安装在帚、刷之上，或只需经过简单加工（例如将顶端修剪成形）即可安装的。

3. In heading No. 96.03 the expression "prepared knots and tufts for broom or brush making" applies only to unmounted knots and tufts of animal hair, vegetable fibre or other material, which are ready for incorporation without division in brooms or brushes, or which require only such further minor processes as trimming to shape at the top, to render them ready for such incorporation.

四、除税号96.01至96.06或96.15的货品以外，本章的物品还包括全部或部分用贵金属、包贵金属、天然或养殖珍珠、宝石或半宝石（天然、合成或再造）制成的物品。而且，税号96.01至96.06及96.15包括天然或养殖珍珠、宝石或半宝石（天然、合成或再造）、贵金属或包贵金属只作为小零件的物品。

4. Articles of this Chapter, other than those of headings No.96.01 to 96.06 or 96.15, remain classified in the Chapter whether or not composed wholly or partly of precious metal or metal clad with precious metal, of natural or cultured pearls, or precious or semi-precious stones (natural, synthetic or reconstructed). However, headings No.96.01 to 96.06 and 96.15 include articles in which natural or cultured pearls, precious or semi-precious stones (natural, synthetic or reconstructed), precious metal or metal clad with precious metal constitute only minor constituents.

序号 No.	税则号列 Tariff Line	货品名称	最惠国税率 MFN(%)	协定税率 Agreement(%)		特惠税率 S.P.(%)		普通税率 Gen.(%)	Article Description
	96.01	**已加工的兽牙、骨、玳瑁壳、角、鹿角、珊瑚、珍珠母及其他动物质雕刻材料及其制品（包括模塑制品）：**							**Worked ivory, bone, tortoise-shell, horn, antlers, coral, mother-of-pearl and other animal carving material and articles of these materials (including articles obtained by moulding):**
8201	9601.1000	-已加工的兽牙及其制品	20	0 4 10	东盟ASEAN,智利CL,新加坡SG,新西兰NZ 哥斯达黎加CR 秘鲁PE	0	最不发达35国LDC35	100	-Worked ivory and articles of ivory
8202	9601.9000	-其他	20	0 4 10	东盟ASEAN,智利CL,新加坡SG,新西兰NZ 哥斯达黎加CR 秘鲁PE	0	最不发达35国LDC35,最不发达4国LDC4	100	-Other

序号 No.	税则号列 Tariff Line	货品名称	最惠国税率 MFN(%)	协定税率 Agreement(%)		特惠税率 S.P.(%)		普通税率 Gen.(%)	Article Description
	96.02	**已加工的植物质或矿物质雕刻材料及其制品;蜡、硬脂、天然树胶、天然树脂或塑型膏制成的模塑或雕刻制品以及其他税号未列名的模塑或雕刻制品;已加工的未硬化明胶(税号35.03的明胶除外)及未硬化明胶制品:**							**Worked vegetable or mineral carving material and articles of these materials; moulded or carved articles of wax, of stearin, of natural gums or natural resins or of modelling pastes, and other moulded or carved articles, not elsewhere specified or included; worked, unhardened gelatin (except gelatin of heading No. 35.03) and articles of unhardened gelatin:**
8203	9602.0010	---装药用胶囊	10.5	0 2.1 5	东盟ASEAN,智利CL,新加坡SG,新西兰NZ,秘鲁PE 哥斯达黎加CR 巴基斯坦PK	0	最不发达35国LDC35	40	---Pharmaceutical capsules
8204	9602.0090	---其他	25	0 5 12.5	东盟ASEAN,智利CL,新加坡SG,新西兰NZ 哥斯达黎加CR 秘鲁PE	0	最不发达35国LDC35,最不发达4国LDC4	100	---Other
	96.03	**帚、刷(包括作为机器、器具、车辆零件的刷)、非机动的手工操作地板清扫器、拖把及毛掸;供制帚、刷用的成束或成簇的材料;油漆块垫及滚筒;橡皮扫帚(橡皮辊除外):**							**Brooms, brushes (including brushes constituting parts of machines, appli-ances or vehicles), hand-operated mechanical floor sweepers, not motori-zed, mops and feather dusters; prepar-ed knots and tufts for broom or brush making; paint pads and rollers; squee-gees (other than roller squeegees):**
8205	9603.1000	-用枝条或其他植物材料捆扎而成的帚及刷,不论是否有把	25	0 5 12.5	东盟ASEAN,智利CL,新加坡SG,新西兰NZ,澳门MO 哥斯达黎加CR 秘鲁PE	0	最不发达35国LDC35	100	-Brooms and brushes, consisting of twigs or other vegetable materi-als bound together, with or without handles
		-牙刷、剃须刷、发刷、指甲刷、睫毛刷及其他人体化妆用刷,包括作为器具零件的上述刷:							-Tooth brushes, shaving brushes, hair brushes, nail brushes, eyelash brushes and other toilet brushes for use on the person, including such brushes constitu-ting parts of appliances:

序号 No.	税则号列 Tariff Line	货品名称	最惠国税率 MFN(%)	协定税率 Agreement(%)		特惠税率 S.P.(%)		普通税率 Gen.(%)	Article Description
8206	9603.2100	--牙刷，包括齿板刷	25 △10	0	东盟ASEAN,智利CL,新加坡SG,新西兰NZ,香港HK,澳门MO	0	最不发达35国LDC35	100	--Tooth brushes, including dental-plate brushes
				5	哥斯达黎加CR				
				12.5	秘鲁PE				
8207	9603.2900	--其他	15	0	东盟ASEAN,新加坡SG,新西兰NZ,澳门MO	0	最不发达35国LDC35,最不发达4国LDC4	100	--Other
				1.5	智利CL				
				3	哥斯达黎加CR				
				7.5	巴基斯坦PK,秘鲁PE				
				13.5	亚太APTA				
		-画笔、毛笔及化妆用的类似笔:							-Artists'brushes, writing brushes and similar brushes for the application of cosmetics:
8208	9603.3010	---画笔	25	0	东盟ASEAN,新加坡SG,新西兰NZ	0	最不发达35国LDC35	100	---Artists'brushes
				2.5	智利CL				
				5	哥斯达黎加CR				
				12.5	秘鲁PE				
				15	亚太APTA,巴基斯坦PK				
8209	9603.3020	---毛笔	20	0	东盟ASEAN,新加坡SG,新西兰NZ	0	最不发达35国LDC35	100	---Writing brushes
				2	智利CL				
				4	哥斯达黎加CR				
				10	秘鲁PE				
				18	亚太APTA,巴基斯坦PK				
8210	9603.3090	---其他	25	0	东盟ASEAN,新加坡SG,新西兰NZ	0	最不发达35国LDC35	100	---Other
				2.5	智利CL				
				5	哥斯达黎加CR				
				12.5	秘鲁PE				
				22.5	亚太APTA,巴基斯坦PK				
		-油漆刷、涂料刷、清漆刷及类似的刷（子目号9603.30的货品除外）;油漆块垫及滚筒:							-Paint, distemper, varnish or similar brushes (other than brushes of subheading No. 9603.30); paint pads and rollers:
		---漆刷及类似刷:							---Paint, distemper, varnish or similar brushes:
8211	9603.4011	----猪鬃制	20	0	东盟ASEAN,智利CL,新加坡SG,新西兰NZ	0	最不发达35国LDC35	100	----Of pigs', hogs' or boars' bristle
				4	哥斯达黎加CR				
				10	秘鲁PE				
8212	9603.4019	----其他	23	0	东盟ASEAN,智利CL,新加坡SG,新西兰NZ	0	最不发达35国LDC35	100	----Other
				4.6	哥斯达黎加CR				
				11.5	秘鲁PE				
8213	9603.4020	---油漆块垫及滚筒	23	0	东盟ASEAN,智利CL,新加坡SG,新西兰NZ	0	最不发达35国LDC35	100	---Paint pads and rollers
				4.6	哥斯达黎加CR				
				11.5	秘鲁PE				

序号 No.	税则号列 Tariff Line	货品名称	最惠国税率 MFN(%)	协定税率 Agreement(%)	特惠税率 S.P.(%)	普通税率 Gen.(%)	Article Description
		-作为机器、器具、车辆零件的刷:					-Other brushes constituting parts of ma-chines, appliances or vehicles:
		---金属丝刷:					---Brushes of metal wire:
8214	9603.5011	----作为机器、器具零件的刷	14	0 东盟ASEAN,新加坡SG,新西兰NZ,秘鲁PE 1.4 智利CL 2.8 哥斯达黎加CR 11.2 巴基斯坦PK	0 最不发达35国LDC35	50	----Constituting parts of machines or ap-pliances
8215	9603.5019	----其他	14	0 东盟ASEAN,新加坡SG,新西兰NZ,秘鲁PE 1.4 智利CL 2.8 哥斯达黎加CR 7 巴基斯坦PK	0 最不发达35国LDC35	100	----Other
		---其他:					---Other:
8216	9603.5091	----作为机器、器具零件的刷	14	0 东盟ASEAN,新加坡SG,新西兰NZ,秘鲁PE 1.4 智利CL 2.8 哥斯达黎加CR 11.2 巴基斯坦PK	0 最不发达35国LDC35	50	----Constituting parts of machines or appli-ances
8217	9603.5099	----其他	14	0 东盟ASEAN,新加坡SG,新西兰NZ,秘鲁PE 1.4 智利CL 2.8 哥斯达黎加CR 7 巴基斯坦PK	0 最不发达35国LDC35	100	----Other
		-其他:					-Other:
8218	9603.9010	---羽毛掸	21	0 东盟ASEAN,新加坡SG,新西兰NZ 2.1 智利CL 4.2 哥斯达黎加CR 10.5 秘鲁PE 18.9 亚太APTA,巴基斯坦PK	0 最不发达35国LDC35	130	---Feather dusters
8219	9603.9090	---其他	15	0 东盟ASEAN,新加坡SG,新西兰NZ 1.5 智利CL 3 哥斯达黎加CR 7.5 秘鲁PE	0 最不发达35国LDC35	100	---Other
	96.04	**手用粗筛、细筛:**					**Hand sieves and hand riddles:**
8220	9604.0000	手用粗筛、细筛	21	0 东盟ASEAN,智利CL,新加坡SG,新西兰NZ 4.2 哥斯达黎加CR 10.5 秘鲁PE	0 最不发达35国LDC35	100	Hand sieves and hand riddles
	96.05	**个人梳妆、缝纫或清洁鞋靴、衣服用的成套旅行用具:**					**Travel sets for personal toilet, sewing or shoe or clothes cleaning:**
8221	9605.0000	个人梳妆、缝纫或清洁鞋靴、衣服用的成套旅行用具	15	0 东盟ASEAN,智利CL,新加坡SG,新西兰NZ 3 哥斯达黎加CR 7.5 秘鲁PE 12 巴基斯坦PK	0 最不发达35国LDC35	100	Travel sets for personal toilet, sewing or shoe or clothes cleaning

序号 No.	税则号列 Tariff Line	货品名称	最惠国税率 MFN(%)	协定税率 Agreement(%)		特惠税率 S.P.(%)		普通税率 Gen.(%)	Article Description
	96.06	**钮扣、揿扣、钮扣芯及钮扣和揿扣的其他零件;钮扣坯:**							**Buttons, press-fasteners, snap-fasteners and press-studs, button moulds and other parts of these articles; button blanks:**
8222	9606.1000	-揿扣及其零件	21	0 4.2 10.5	东盟ASEAN,智利CL,新加坡SG,新西兰NZ 哥斯达黎加CR 秘鲁PE	0	最不发达35国LDC35	100	-Press-fasteners, snap-fasteners and pre ss-studs and parts therefor
		-钮扣:							-Buttons:
8223	9606.2100	--塑料制，未用纺织材料包裹	21	0 4.2 10.5	东盟ASEAN,智利CL,新加坡SG,新西兰NZ,台湾TW 哥斯达黎加CR 秘鲁PE	0	最不发达35国LDC35,最不发达4国LDC4	100	--Of plastics, not covered with textile material
8224	9606.2200	--贱金属制,未用纺织材料包裹	15	0 3 7.5 12	东盟ASEAN,智利CL,新加坡SG,新西兰NZ,香港HK,澳门MO,台湾TW 哥斯达黎加CR 秘鲁PE 巴基斯坦PK	0	最不发达35国LDC35,最不发达4国LDC4	100	--Of base mental, not covered with textile material
8225	9606.2900	--其他	15	0 3 7.5 12	东盟ASEAN,智利CL,新加坡SG,新西兰NZ,香港HK 哥斯达黎加CR 秘鲁PE 巴基斯坦PK	0	最不发达35国LDC35,最不发达4国LDC4	100	--Other
8226	9606.3000	-钮扣芯及钮扣的其他零件;钮扣坯	15	0 3 7.5 12	东盟ASEAN,智利CL,新加坡SG,新西兰NZ,香港HK 哥斯达黎加CR 秘鲁PE 巴基斯坦PK	0	最不发达35国LDC35,最不发达4国LDC4	100	-Button moulds and other parts of buttons; button blanks
	96.07	**拉链及其零件:**							**Slide fasteners and parts thereof:**
		-拉链:							-Slide fasteners:
8227	9607.1100	--装有贱金属制咪牙齿的	21	0 4.2 10.5	东盟ASEAN,智利CL,新加坡SG,新西兰NZ,香港HK,澳门MO 哥斯达黎加CR 秘鲁PE	0	最不发达35国LDC35,最不发达4国LDC4	130	--Fitted with chain scoops of base metal
8228	9607.1900	--其他	21	0 4.2 10.5 14.7	东盟ASEAN,智利CL,新加坡SG,新西兰NZ,香港HK,澳门MO 哥斯达黎加CR 秘鲁PE 亚太APTA,巴基斯坦PK	0	最不发达35国LDC35	130	--Other
8229	9607.2000	-零件	21	0 4.2 10.5	东盟ASEAN,智利CL,新加坡SG,新西兰NZ 哥斯达黎加CR 秘鲁PE	0	最不发达35国LDC35	130	-Parts

序号 No.	税则号列 Tariff Line	货品名称	最惠国税率 MFN(%)	协定税率 Agreement(%)		特惠税率 S.P.(%)		普通税率 Gen.(%)	Article Description
	96.08	**圆珠笔;毡尖和其他渗水式笔尖笔及唛头笔;自来水笔、铁笔型自来水笔及其他钢笔;蜡纸铁笔;活动铅笔;钢笔杆、铅笔套及类似的笔套;上述物品的零件（包括帽、夹），但税号96.09的货品除外:**							**Ball point pens; felt tipped and other poroustipped pens and markers; fountain pens, stylograph pens and other pens; duplicating stylos; propelling or sliding pencils; pen-holders, pencil-holders and similar holders; parts (including caps and clips) of the foregoing articles, other than those of heading No. 96.09:**
8230	9608.1000	-圆珠笔	15	0 1.5 3 7.5 13.5	东盟ASEAN,新加坡SG,新西兰NZ 智利CL 哥斯达黎加CR 巴基斯坦PK,秘鲁PE 亚太APTA	0	最不发达35国LDC35,最不发达4国LDC4	80	-Ball point pens
8231	9608.2000	-毡尖和其他渗水式笔尖笔及唛头笔	21	0 4.2 10.5	东盟ASEAN,智利CL,新加坡SG,新西兰NZ 哥斯达黎加CR 秘鲁PE	0	最不发达35国LDC35	80	-Felt tipped and other porous tipped pens and markers
		-自来水笔、铁笔型自来水笔及其他钢笔:							-Fountain pens, stylograph pens and other pens:
8232	9608.3010	---墨汁画笔	21	0 4.2 10.5	东盟ASEAN,智利CL,新加坡SG,新西兰NZ 哥斯达黎加CR 秘鲁PE	0	最不发达35国LDC35	80	---Indian ink drawing pens
8233	9608.3020	---自来水笔	21	0 4.2 10.5	东盟ASEAN,智利CL,新加坡SG,新西兰NZ 哥斯达黎加CR 秘鲁PE	0	最不发达35国LDC35,最不发达4国LDC4	80	---Fountain pens
8234	9608.3090	---其他	21	0 4.2 10.5	东盟ASEAN,智利CL,新加坡SG,新西兰NZ 哥斯达黎加CR 秘鲁PE	0	最不发达35国LDC35,最不发达4国LDC4	80	---Other
8235	9608.4000	-活动铅笔	21	0 4.2 10.5	东盟ASEAN,智利CL,新加坡SG,新西兰NZ 哥斯达黎加CR 秘鲁PE	0	最不发达35国LDC35	80	-Propelling or sliding pencils
8236	9608.5000	-由上述两个或多个子目所列物品组成的成套货品	21	0 4.2 10.5	东盟ASEAN,智利CL,新加坡SG,新西兰NZ 哥斯达黎加CR 秘鲁PE	0	最不发达35国LDC35	80	-Sets of articles from two or more of the foregoing subheadings
8237	9608.6000	-圆珠笔芯,由圆珠笔头和墨芯构成	21	0 4.2 10.5	东盟ASEAN,智利CL,新加坡SG,新西兰NZ,香港HK,澳门MO 哥斯达黎加CR 秘鲁PE	0	最不发达35国LDC35	80	-Refills for ball point pens, comprising the ball point and ink-reservoir

序号 No.	税则号列 Tariff Line	货品名称	最惠国税率 MFN(%)	协定税率 Agreement(%)		特惠税率 S.P.(%)		普通税率 Gen.(%)	Article Description
		-其他:							-Other:
8238	9608.9100	--钢笔头及笔尖粒	12	0	东盟ASEAN,智利CL,新加坡SG,新西兰NZ,秘鲁PE,香港HK,澳门MO	0	最不发达35国LDC35	70	--Pen nibs and nib points
				2.4	哥斯达黎加CR				
				6	巴基斯坦PK				
		--其他:							--Other:
8239	9608.9910	---机器、仪器用笔	17.5	0	东盟ASEAN,智利CL,新加坡SG,新西兰NZ,香港HK	0	最不发达35国LDC35	40	---Of a kind used on machines or instruments
				3.5	哥斯达黎加CR				
				8.8	秘鲁PE				
				14	巴基斯坦PK				
8240	9608.9920	---蜡纸铁笔;钢笔杆、铅笔杆及类似的笔杆	21	0	东盟ASEAN,智利CL,新加坡SG,新西兰NZ,香港HK,澳门MO	0	最不发达35国LDC35	80	---Duplicating stylos; pen-holders, pencil-holders and similar holders
				4.2	哥斯达黎加CR				
				10.5	秘鲁PE				
8241	9608.9990	---其他	21	0	东盟ASEAN,智利CL,新加坡SG,新西兰NZ,香港HK,澳门MO	0	最不发达35国LDC35	80	---Other
				4.2	哥斯达黎加CR				
				10.5	秘鲁PE				
	96.09	**铅笔(税号96.08的铅笔除外)、颜色铅笔、铅笔芯、蜡笔、图画碳笔、书写或绘画用粉笔及裁缝划粉:**							**Pencils (other than pencils of heading No.96.08), crayons, pencil leads, pastels, drawing charcoals, writing or drawing chalks and tailors' chalks:**
		-铅笔及颜色铅笔:							-Pencils and crayons, with leads encased in a rigid sheath:
8242	9609.1010	---铅笔	21	0	东盟ASEAN,新加坡SG,新西兰NZ	0	最不发达35国LDC35,最不发达4国LDC4	80	---Pencils
				2.1	智利CL				
				4.2	哥斯达黎加CR				
				10.5	秘鲁PE				
8243	9609.1020	---颜色铅笔	21	0	东盟ASEAN,新加坡SG,新西兰NZ	0	最不发达35国LDC35	80	---Crayons
				2.1	智利CL				
				4.2	哥斯达黎加CR				
				10.5	秘鲁PE				
8244	9609.2000	-铅笔芯,黑的或其他颜色的	21	0	东盟ASEAN,新加坡SG,新西兰NZ	0	最不发达35国LDC35	80	-Pencil leads, black or coloured
				2.1	智利CL				
				4.2	哥斯达黎加CR				
				10.5	秘鲁PE				
8245	9609.9000	-其他	15	0	东盟ASEAN,新加坡SG,新西兰NZ	0	最不发达35国LDC35	80	-Other
				1.5	智利CL				
				3	哥斯达黎加CR				
				7.5	秘鲁PE				
				12	巴基斯坦PK				

序号 No.	税则号列 Tariff Line	货品名称	最惠国税率 MFN(%)	协定税率 Agreement(%)		特惠税率 S.P.(%)	普通税率 Gen.(%)	Article Description
	96.10	**具有书写或绘画面的石板、黑板及类似板，不论是否镶框:**						**Slates and boards, with writing or drawing surfaces, whether or not framed:**
8246	9610.0000	具有书写或绘画面的石板、黑板及类似板，不论是否镶框	15	0 3 7.5 12	东盟ASEAN,智利CL,新加坡SG,新西兰NZ 哥斯达黎加CR 秘鲁PE 巴基斯坦PK	0 最不发达35国LDC35	80	Slates and boards, with writing or drawing surfaces, whether or not framed
	96.11	**手用日期戳、封缄戳、编号戳及类似印戳（包括标签压印器）;手工操作的排字盘及带有排字盘的手印器:**						**Date, sealing or numbering stamps, and the like (including devices for printing or embossing labels), designed for operating in the hand; hand-operated composing sticks and hand printing sets incorporating such composing sticks:**
8247	9611.0000	手用日期戳、封缄戳、编号戳及类似印戳（包括标签压印器);手工操作的排字盘及带有排字盘的手印器	21	0 2.1 4.2 10.5	东盟ASEAN,新加坡SG,新西兰NZ 智利CL 哥斯达黎加CR 秘鲁PE	0 最不发达35国LDC35	80	Date, sealing or numbering stamps, and the like (including devices for printing or embossing labels), designed for operating in the hand; and operated composing sticks and hand printing sets incorporating such composing sticks
	96.12	**打字机色带或类似色带，已上油或经其他方法处理能着色的，不论是否装轴或装盒;印台，不论是否已加印油或带盒子:**						**Typewriter or similar ribbons, inked or otherwise prepared for giving impressions, whether or not on spools or in cartridges; ink-pads, whether or not inked, with or without boxes:**
8248	9612.1000	-色带	10.5	0 2.1 5	东盟ASEAN,智利CL,新加坡SG,新西兰NZ,秘鲁PE,澳门MO 哥斯达黎加CR 巴基斯坦PK	0 最不发达35国LDC35,最不发达4国LDC4	35	-Inked ribbons
8249	9612.2000	-印台	25	0 5 12.5	东盟ASEAN,智利CL,新加坡SG,新西兰NZ 哥斯达黎加CR 秘鲁PE	0 最不发达35国LDC35	100	-Ink-pads
	96.13	**香烟打火机和其他打火器（不论是机械的，还是电气的）及其零件，但打火石及打火机芯除外:**						**Cigarette lighters and other lighters, whether or not mechanical or electri-cal, and parts thereof other than flints and wicks:**

序号 No.	税则号列 Tariff Line	货品名称	最惠国税率 MFN(%)	协定税率 Agreement(%)		特惠税率 S.P.(%)		普通税率 Gen.(%)	Article Description
8250	9613.1000	-袖珍气体打火机，一次性的	25	0 2.5 5 12.5	东盟ASEAN,新加坡SG,新西兰NZ 智利CL 哥斯达黎加CR 秘鲁PE	0	最不发达35国LDC35	130	-Pocket lighters, gas fuelled, non refillable
8251	9613.2000	-袖珍气体打火机，可充气的	25	0 5 12.5	东盟ASEAN,智利CL,新加坡SG,新西兰NZ 哥斯达黎加CR 秘鲁PE	0	最不发达35国LDC35	130	-Pocket lighters, gas fuelled, refillable
8252	9613.8000	-其他打火器	25	0 5 12.5	东盟ASEAN,智利CL,新加坡SG,新西兰NZ 哥斯达黎加CR 秘鲁PE	0	最不发达35国LDC35	130	-Other lighters
8253	9613.9000	-零件	25	0 5 12.5	东盟ASEAN,智利CL,新加坡SG,新西兰NZ 哥斯达黎加CR 秘鲁PE	0	最不发达35国LDC35	130	-Parts
	96.14	**烟斗（包括烟斗头）和烟嘴及其零件:**							**Smoking pipes (including pipe bowls) and cigar or cigarette holders, and parts thereof:**
8254	9614.0010	---烟斗及烟斗头	25	0 5 12.5	东盟ASEAN,智利CL,新加坡SG,新西兰NZ 哥斯达黎加CR 秘鲁PE	0	最不发达35国LDC35	130	---Pipes and pipe bowls
8255	9614.0090	---其他	25	0 5 12.5	东盟ASEAN,智利CL,新加坡SG,新西兰NZ 哥斯达黎加CR 秘鲁PE	0	最不发达35国LDC35	130	---Other
	96.15	**梳子、发夹及类似品；发卡、卷发夹、卷发器或类似品及其零件，但税号 85.16 的货品除外:**							**Combs, hair-slides and the like; hair-pins, curling pins, curling grips, hair-curlers and the like, other than those of heading No.85.16, and parts thereof:**
		-梳子、发夹及类似品:							-Combs, hair-slides and the like:
8256	9615.1100	--硬质橡胶或塑料制	18	0 1.8 3.6 9 14.4 16.2	东盟ASEAN,新加坡SG,新西兰NZ 智利CL 哥斯达黎加CR 秘鲁PE 巴基斯坦PK 亚太APTA	0	最不发达35国LDC35,最不发达4国LDC4	130	--Of hard rubber or plastics
8257	9615.1900	--其他	18	0 3.6 9	东盟ASEAN,智利CL,新加坡SG,新西兰NZ 哥斯达黎加CR 秘鲁PE	0	最不发达35国LDC35,最不发达4国LDC4	130	--Other

序号 No.	税则号列 Tariff Line	货品名称	最惠国税率 MFN(%)	协定税率 Agreement(%)	特惠税率 S.P.(%)	普通税率 Gen.(%)	Article Description
8258	9615.9000	-其他	18	0 东盟ASEAN,智利CL,新加坡SG,新西兰NZ 3.6 哥斯达黎加CR 9 秘鲁PE 14.4 巴基斯坦PK 16.2 亚太APTA	0 最不发达35国LDC35,最不发达4国LDC4	130	-Other
	96.16	**香水喷雾器或类似的化妆用喷雾器及其座架、喷头;粉扑及粉拍，施敷脂粉或化妆品用:**					**Scent sprays and similar toilet sprays, and mounts and heads therefor; powderpuffs and pads for the application of cosmetics or toilet preparations:**
8259	9616.1000	-香水喷雾器或类似的化妆用喷雾器及其座架、喷头	18	0 东盟ASEAN,新加坡SG,新西兰NZ 1.8 智利CL 3.6 哥斯达黎加CR 9 秘鲁PE 14.4 巴基斯坦PK 16.2 亚太APTA	0 最不发达35国LDC35	130	-Scent sprays and similar toilet sprays, and mounts and heads therefor
8260	9616.2000	-粉扑及粉拍，施敷脂粉或化妆品用	18	0 东盟ASEAN,智利CL,新加坡SG,新西兰NZ 3.6 哥斯达黎加CR 9 秘鲁PE 14.4 巴基斯坦PK 16.2 亚太APTA	0 最不发达35国LDC35	130	-Powder-puffs and pads for the applic-ation of cosmetics or toilet preparations
	96.17	**带壳的保温瓶和其他真空容器及其零件，但玻璃瓶胆除外:**					**Vacuum flasks and other vacuum vessels, complete with cases; parts therof other than glass inners:**
		---保温瓶:					---Vacuum flasks:
8261	9617.0011	----玻璃内胆制	24	0 东盟ASEAN,智利CL,新加坡SG,新西兰NZ,香港HK 4.8 哥斯达黎加CR 12 秘鲁PE	0 最不发达35国LDC35	130	----Of glass inners
8262	9617.0019	----其他	24	0 东盟ASEAN,智利CL,新加坡SG,新西兰NZ,香港HK 4.8 哥斯达黎加CR 12 秘鲁PE	0 最不发达35国LDC35	130	----Other
8263	9617.0090	---其他	18	0 东盟ASEAN,智利CL,新加坡SG,新西兰NZ,香港HK 3.6 哥斯达黎加CR 9 秘鲁PE	0 最不发达35国LDC35	130	---Other
	96.18	**裁缝用人体模型及其他人体活动模型;橱窗装饰用的自动模型及其他活动陈列品:**					**Tailors dummies and other lay figures; automata and other animated displays used for shop window dressing:**

序号 No.	税则号列 Tariff Line	货品名称	最惠国税率 MFN(%)	协定税率 Agreement(%)		特惠税率 S.P.(%)		普通税率 Gen.(%)	Article Description
8264	9618.0000	裁缝用人体模型及其他人体活动模型;橱窗装饰用的自动模型及其他活动陈列品	21	0 4.2 10.5	东盟ASEAN,智利CL,新加坡SG,新西兰NZ 哥斯达黎加CR 秘鲁PE	0	最不发达35国LDC35	80	Tailors' dummies and other lay figures; automata and other animated displays used for shop window dressing
	96.19	**任何材料制的卫生巾(护垫)及止血塞、婴儿尿布及尿布衬里和类似品:**							**Sanitary towels (pads) and tampons, napkins and napkin liners for babies and similar articles, of any material:**
		任何材料制的卫生巾(护垫)及止血塞、婴儿尿布及尿布衬里和类似品:							Sanitary towels (pads) and tampons, napkins and napkin liners for babies and similar articles, of any material:
8265	9619.0010	---尿裤及尿布	7.5	0 1.5	东盟ASEAN,智利CL,新西兰NZ,秘鲁PE,香港HK,澳门MO,台湾TW 哥斯达黎加CR	0	最不发达35国LDC35,最不发达4国LDC4	80	---Diapers and napkins
8266	9619.0020	---卫生巾(护垫)及止血塞	10	0 7.5	东盟ASEAN,智利CL,新西兰NZ,秘鲁PE,哥斯达黎加CR,香港HK,澳门MO,台湾TW 巴基斯坦PK	0	最不发达35国LDC35,最不发达4国LDC4	80	---Sanitary towels (pads) and tampons
8267	9619.0090	---其他	14	0 2.8 7 7.5 9.3	东盟ASEAN,智利CL,新加坡SG,新西兰NZ,香港HK,澳门MO,台湾TW 哥斯达黎加CR 秘鲁PE 巴基斯坦PK 亚太APTA	0	最不发达35国LDC35,最不发达4国LDC4	80	---Other

第二十一类

艺术品、收藏品及古物

第九十七章
艺术品、收藏品及古物

注释:

一、本章不包括:

（一）在指运国流通或新发行的未经使用的邮票、印花税票、邮政信笺（印有邮票的纸品）及类似的票证（第四十九章）；

（二）作舞台、摄影的布景及类似用途的已绘制画布（税号 59.07），但可归入税号 97.06 的除外;

（三）天然或养殖珍珠、宝石或半宝石（税号 71.01 至 71.03）。

二、税号 97.02 所称“雕版画、印制画、石印画的原本”，是指以艺术家完全手工制作的单块或数块印版直接印制出来的黑白或彩色原本，不论艺术家使用何种方法或材料，但不包括使用机器或照相制版方法制作的。

三、税号 97.03 不适用于成批生产的复制品及具有商业性质的传统手工艺品，即使这些物品是艺术家设计或创造的。

四、

（一）除上述注释一至三另有规定的以外，可归入本章各税号的物品，均应归入本章的相应税号而不归入本目录的其他税号;

（二）税号 97.06 不适用于可以归入本章其他各税号的物品。

五、已装框的油画、粉画及其他绘画、版画、拼贴画及类似装饰板，如果框架的种类及价值与作品相称，应与作品一并归类。如果框架的种类及价值与作品不相称，应分别归类。

SECTION XXI

WORKS OF ART, COLLECTORS' PIECES AND ANTIQUES

Chapter 97
Works of art, collectors' pieces and antiques

Notes:

1.This Chapter does not cover:

(a)Unused postage or revenue stamps, postal stationery (stamped paper) or the like, of heading 49.07;

(b)Theatrical scenery, studio back-cloths or the like, of painted canvas (heading No.59.07) except if they may be classified in heading No.97.06; or

(c)Pearls, natural or cultured, or precious or semi-precious stones (headings No.71.01 to 71.03).

2. For the purposes of heading No.97.02, the expression "original engravings, prints and lithographs" means impressions produced directly, in black and white or in colour, of one or of several plates wholly executed by hand by the artist, irrespective of the process or of the material employed by him, but not including any mechanical or photomechanical process.

3.Heading No.97.03 does not apply to mass-produced reproductions or works of conventional craftsmanship of a commercial character, even if these articles are designed or created by artists.

4.

(a) Subject to Notes 1 to 3 above, articles of this Chapter are to be classified in this Chapter and not in any other Chapter of the Nomenclature;

(b) Heading No.97.06 does not apply to articles of the preceding headings of this Chapter.

5.Frames around paintings, drawings, pastels, collages or similar decorative plaques, engravings, prints or lithographs are to be classified with those articles, provided they are of a kind and of a value normal to those articles. Frames which are not of a kind or of a value normal to the articles referred to in this Note are to be classified separately.

序号 No.	税则号列 Tariff Line	货品名称	最惠国税率 MFN(%)	协定税率 Agreement(%)		特惠税率 S.P.(%)		普通税率 Gen.(%)	Article Description
	97.01	**油画、粉画及其他手绘画，但带有手工绘制及手工描饰的制品或税号 49.06 的图纸除外;拼贴画及类似装饰板:**							**Paintings, drawings and pastels, executed entirely by hand, other than drawings of heading No.49.06 and other than hand-painted or hand-decorated manufactured articles; collages and si-milar decorative plaques:**
		-油画、粉画及其他手绘画: ---原件:							-Paintings, drawings and pastels: ---The originals:
8268	9701.1011	----唐卡	12	0 1.2 2.4 6	东盟ASEAN,新加坡SG,新西兰NZ 智利CL 哥斯达黎加CR 巴基斯坦PK,秘鲁PE	0	最不发达35国LDC35,最不发达4国LDC4	50	----Tangka
8269	9701.1019	----其他	12	0 1.2 2.4 6	东盟ASEAN,新加坡SG,新西兰NZ 智利CL 哥斯达黎加CR 巴基斯坦PK,秘鲁PE	0	最不发达35国LDC35,最不发达4国LDC4	50	----Other
8270	9701.1020	---复制品	14	0 1.4 2.8 11.2	东盟ASEAN,新加坡SG,新西兰NZ,秘鲁PE 智利CL 哥斯达黎加CR 巴基斯坦PK	0	最不发达35国LDC35,最不发达4国LDC4	50	---Reproductions
8271	9701.9000	-其他	14	0 2.8 11.2	东盟ASEAN,智利CL,新加坡SG,新西兰NZ,秘鲁PE 哥斯达黎加CR 巴基斯坦PK	0	最不发达35国LDC35,最不发达4国LDC4	50	-Other
	97.02	**雕版画、印制画、石印画的原本:**							**Original engravings, prints and lithographs:**
8272	9702.0000	雕版画、印制画、石印画的原本	12 △6	0 2.4 6	东盟ASEAN,智利CL,新加坡SG,新西兰NZ 哥斯达黎加CR 巴基斯坦PK,秘鲁PE	0	最不发达35国LDC35	50	Original engravings, prints and lithographs
	97.03	**各种材料制的雕塑品原件:**							**Original sculptures and statuary, in any material:**
8273	9703.0000	各种材料制的雕塑品原件	12 △6	0 2.4 6	东盟ASEAN,智利CL,新加坡SG,新西兰NZ,秘鲁PE 哥斯达黎加CR 巴基斯坦PK	0	最不发达35国LDC35,最不发达4国LDC4	50	Original sculptures and statuary, in any material

序号 No.	税则号列 Tariff Line	货品名称	最惠国税率 MFN(%)	协定税率 Agreement(%)		特惠税率 S.P.(%)		普通税率 Gen.(%)	Article Description
	97.04	**使用过或未使用过的邮票、印花税票、邮戳印记、首日封、邮政信笺（印有邮票的纸品）及类似品，但税目 49.07 的货品除外:**							**Used or unused postage or revenue stamps, stamp-postmarks, first-day covers, postal stationery (stamped paper), and the like, other than those of heading No.49.07:**
8274	9704.0010	---邮票	8	0 5	东盟ASEAN,智利CL,新西兰NZ,秘鲁PE,哥斯达黎加CR,香港HK,澳门MO 巴基斯坦PK	0	最不发达 35 国 LDC35,最不发达 4 国 LDC4	50	---Postage
8275	9704.0090	---其他	14	0 2.8 7	东盟ASEAN,智利CL,新加坡SG,新西兰NZ,秘鲁PE,香港HK,澳门MO 哥斯达黎加CR 巴基斯坦PK	0	最不发达 35 国 LDC35	50	---Other
	97.05	**具有动物学、植物学、矿物学、解剖学、历史学、考古学、古生物学、人种学或钱币学意义的收集品及珍藏品:**							**Collections and collectors pieces of zoological, botanical, mineralogical, anatomical, historical, archaeological, palaeontological, ethnographic**
									or numismatic interest:
8276	9705.0000	具有动物学、植物学、矿物学、解剖学、历史学、考古学、古生物学、人种学或钱币学意义的收集品及珍藏品	0			0	最不发达 35 国 LDC35,最不发达 4 国 LDC4	0	Collections and collectors pieces of zoological, botanical, mineralogical, anatomical, historical, archaeological, palaeontological, ethnographic or numismatic interest
	97.06	**超过一百年的古物:**							**Antiques of an age exceeding one hundred years:**
8277	9706.0000	超过一百年的古物	0			0	最不发达 35 国 LDC35,最不发达 4 国 LDC4	0	Antiques of an age exceeding one hundred years

中华人民共和国出口税则

（2014 年 1 月 1 日起实施）

Customs Tariff of Export of the

People's Republic of China

（Enforced from January 1，2014）

序号 No.	税则号列 Tariff Item	货品名称	出口税率(%) Export Duty Rate	Article Description
	03.01			
1	03019210	鳗鱼苗	20	Live eels fry
	05.06			
2	05061000	经酸处理的骨胶原及骨	40	Ossein and bones treated with acid
3	05069011	含牛羊成分的骨粉及骨废料	40	Power and waste bones, containing bovine composition or sheep and goat's thereof
4	05069019	其他骨粉及骨废料	40	Other powder and waste of bones
5	05069090	其他骨及角柱	40	Bones and horn-cores, unworked, defatted, simply prepared, not cut to shape, nes
	26.07			
6	26070000	铅矿砂及其精矿	30	Lead ores & concentrates
	26.08			
7	26080000	锌矿砂及其精矿	30	Zinc ores & concentrates
	26.09			
8	26090000	锡矿砂及其精矿	50	Tin ores & concentrates
	26.11			
9	26110000	钨矿砂及其精矿	20	Tungsten ores & concentrates
	26.15			
10	26159010	水合钽铌原料（钽铌富集物）	30	Hydrated Tantalum/Niobium materials or enriched materials from Tantalum/Niobium ore
11	26159090	其他铌钽矿砂及其精矿	30	Niobium, tantalum & vanadium ores & concentrates, others
	26.17			
12	26171010	生锑（锑精矿，选矿产品）	20	Crude antimony (Antimony concentrates which are mineral products)
	28.04			
13	28047010	黄磷(白磷)	20	Yellow phosphorus (white phosphorus)
14	28047090	其他磷	20	Phosphorus, nes
	28.26			
15	ex28269090	氟钽酸钾	30	Potassium fluotantalate
	29.02			
16	29022000	苯	40	Benzene
	41.03			
17	41039011	经退鞣处理的山羊板皮	20	Raw hides and skins of goats，have undergone a reversible tanning process
18	41039019	山羊板皮，经退鞣处理的除外	20	Raw hides and skins of goats，nes
	72.01			
19	72011000	非合金生铁，含磷量小于或等于 0.5%	20	Non-alloy pig iron, by wt.≤0.5% of phosphorus in primary forms
20	72012000	非合金生铁，含磷量大于 0.5%	20	Non-alloy pig iron, by wt.＞0.5% of phosphorus in primary forms

序号 No.	税则号列 Tariff Item	货品名称	出口税率(%) Export Duty Rate	Article Description
21	72015000	合金生铁	20	Alloy pig iron; spiegeleisen
	72.02			
22	72021100	锰铁，含碳量>2%	20	Ferro-manganese, containing by weight more than 2% of carbon
23	72021900	锰铁，含碳量≤2%	20	Ferro-manganese, nes
24	72022100	硅铁，含硅量>55%	25	Ferro-silicon, containing by weight more than 55% of silicon
25	72022900	硅铁，含硅量≤55%	25	Ferro-silicon, nes
26	72023000	硅锰铁	20	Ferro-silico-manganese
27	72024100	铬铁，含碳量>4%	40	Ferro-chromium containing by weight more than 4% of carbon
28	72024900	铬铁，含碳量≤4%	40	Ferro-chromium, nes
	72.04			
29	72041000	铸铁废碎料	40	Waste & scrap, cast iron
30	72042100	不锈钢废碎料	40	Waste & scrap, stainless steel
31	72042900	其他合金钢废碎料	40	Waste & scrap, of alloy steel, other than stainless
32	72043000	镀锡钢铁废碎料	40	Waste & scrap, of tinned iron or steel
33	72044100	机械加工中产生的废料	40	Ferrous waste & scrap, i/s, from the mechanical working of mtl, nes
34	72044900	其他钢铁废碎料	40	Ferrous waste & scrap, iron or steel, nes
35	72045000	供再熔的碎料钢铁锭	40	Remelting scrap ingots, of iron or steel
	74.02			
36	74020000	未精炼铜，电解精炼用的铜阳极	30	Cu unrefined, Cu anodes for electrolytic refining
	74.03			
37	74031111	按重量计铜含量超过 99.9935%的精炼铜阴极	30	Cu cathodes containing more than 99.9935% Cu by weight, unwrought
38	74031119	其他精炼铜阴极	30	Cu cathodes, unwrought, nes
39	74031190	精炼铜阴极型材	30	sections of Cu cathodes unwrought
40	74031200	精炼铜的线锭	30	Wire bars, Cu, unwrought
41	74031300	精炼铜的坯段	30	Billets, Cu, unwrought
42	74031900	其他未锻轧的精炼铜	30	Refined Cu products, unwrought, nes
43	74032100	未锻轧的铜锌合金(黄铜)	30	Cu-zinc base alloys, unwrought
44	74032200	未锻轧的铜锡合金(青铜)	30	Cu-tin base alloys, unwrought
45	74032900	未锻轧的其他铜合金	30	Cu alloys, unwrought (other than master alloys of heading No 74.05)
	74.04			
46	74040000	铜废碎料	30	Waste & scrap, Copper
	74.07			
47	74071010	铬锆铜制条、杆及型材及异型材	30	Bars, rods & profiles of chromium and zirconium copper
48	74071090	其他精炼铜条、杆及型材及异型材	30	Other bars, rods & profiles of other refined Cu

序号 No.	税则号列 Tariff Item	货 品 名 称	出口税率(%) Export Duty Rate	Article Description
49	74072111	直线度不大于 0.5 毫米/米铜锌合金条、杆	30	Copper-zinc base alloys (brass) bars and rods, of a straightness not exceeding 0.5mm/m
50	74072119	其他铜锌合金条、杆	30	Other bars, rods of copper-zinc base alloys(brass)
51	74072190	其他铜锌合金型材及异型材	30	Profiles of Cu-Zn base alloys
52	74072900	其他铜合金条杆、型材及异型材	30	Bars, rods & profiles, Cu alloy nes
	74.08			
53	74081100	最大截面尺寸＞6 毫米的精炼铜丝	30	Wire of refined Cu of which the max cross sectional dimension＞6mm
54	74081900	其他精炼铜丝	30	Wire of refined Cu of which the max cross sectional dimension≤6mm
55	74082100	铜锌合金丝	30	Wire, Cu-zinc base alloy
56	74082210	铜镍锌铅合金（加铅德银）丝	30	Wire, of copper-nickel-zinc-lead base alloys(leaded nickel silver)
57	74082290	其他白铜或德银丝	30	Other wire, of Copper-Ni base alloy or Copper-Ni-zinc base alloy
58	74082900	其他铜合金丝	30	Wire, Cu alloy, nes
	74.09			
59	74091110	含氧量不超过 10PPM 盘卷的精炼铜板、片、带	30	Plate, sheet & strip of refined Cu, in coil, containing Oxygen no more than 10PPM
60	74091190	其他成卷精炼铜板、片、带	30	Plate, sheet & strip of refined Cu, in coil, nes
61	74091900	其他精炼铜板、片、带	30	Plate, sheet & strip of refined Cu, not in coil
62	74092100	成卷的铜锌合金板、片、带	30	Plate, sheet & strip of Cu-Zn base alloys, in coil
63	74092900	其他铜锌合金板、片、带	30	Plate, sheet & strip of Cu-Zn base alloys, not in coil
64	74093100	成卷的铜锡合金板、片、带	30	Plate, sheet & strip of Cu-tin base alloys, in coil
65	74093900	其他铜锡合金板、片、带	30	Plate, sheet & strip of Cu-tin base alloys, not in coil
66	74094000	铜镍合金或铜镍锌合金板、片、带	30	Plate, sheet & strip of Cu-Ni′ Cu-Ni-Zn base alloy
67	74099000	其他铜合金板、片、带	30	Plate, sheet & strip of Cu alloy, nes
	75.02			
68	75021010	按重量计镍、钴总量在 99.99%及以上的，但含钴量不超过 0.005%的未锻轧非合金镍	40	Ni contain more than 99.99% Ni and Co, and Co less then 0.005% by weight, unwrought, not alloyed
69	75021090	其他未锻轧非合金镍	40	Ni unwrought, not alloyed, nes
70	75022000	未锻轧镍合金	40	Ni unwrought, alloyed
	75.08			
71	75089010	电镀用镍阳极	40	Electroplating anodes of Ni
	76.01			
72	76011010	按重量计含铝量在 99.95%及以上的非合金铝	30	Containing by weight 99.95% or more of aluminium unwrought aluminium, not alloyed
73	76011090	按重量计含铝量在 99.95%以下的非合金铝	30	Al unwrought, not alloyed, nes
74	76012000	未锻轧铝合金	30	Al unwrought, alloyed

序号 No.	税则号列 Tariff Item	货品名称	出口税率(%) Export Duty Rate	Article Description
	76.02			
75	76020000	铝废碎料	30	Waste & scrap, Al
	76.04			
76	76041010	非合金铝条、杆	20	Bars, rods, Al, not alloyed
77	76041090	非合金型材及异型材	20	Profiles, Al, not alloyed
78	76042100	铝合金制空心异型材	20	Profiles, hollow, Al, alloyed
79	76042910	铝合金制条、杆	20	Bars, rods, Al alloyed
80	76042990	铝合金制其他型材及异型材	20	Other profiles, Al alloyed
	76.05			
81	76051100	最大截面尺寸超过 7 毫米的非合金铝丝	20	Wire, Al, not alloyed, with a max cross sectional dimension exceeding 7mm
82	76051900	其他非合金铝丝	20	Wire, Al, not alloyed, with a max cross sectional dimension not exceeding 7mm
83	76052100	最大截面尺寸超过 7 毫米的铝合金丝	20	Wire, Al alloy, with a max cross sectional dimension exceeding 7mm
84	76052900	其他铝合金丝	20	Wire, Al alloy, with a max cross sectional dimension not exceeding 7mm
	76.06			
85	76061121	0.3 毫米≤厚度＜0.36 毫米的非合金铝与塑料复合的矩形板、片及带	20	Rectangular plates, sheets and strip, of not alloyed aluminium-plastic composite, 0.3mm ≤ thickness ＜ 0.36mm
86	76061129	其他 0.3 毫米≤厚度＜0.36 毫米的非合金铝制矩形铝板、片及带	20	Other rectangular plates, sheets and strip, of not alloyed aluminium-plastic composite, 0.3mm ≤ thickness＜0.36mm
87	76061191	其他非合金铝与塑料复合的矩形板、片及带	20	Rectangular plates, sheets and strip, of not alloyed aluminium-plastic composite, nes
88	76061199	纯铝制矩形的其他板、片及带	20	Other rectangular plates, sheets and strip, of not alloyed aluminium-plastic composite, nes
89	76061220	厚度＜0.28 毫米的铝合金制矩形铝板、片及带	20	Plate, sheet & strip, Al alloy, rectangular (including square), of a thickness exceeding 0.2mm, but less than 0.28mm
90	76061230	0.28 毫米≤厚度≤0.35 毫米的铝合金制矩形铝板、片及带	20	Plate, sheet & strip, Al alloy, rectangular (including square), of a thickness 0.28mm or more but not exceeding 0.35mm
91	76061251	0.35 毫米＜厚度≤0.4 毫米的铝合金与塑料复合的矩形板、片及带	20	Rectangular plates, sheets and strip of aluminium alloys-plastic composite, of a thickness of 0.35mm or more but not exceeding 4mm
92	76061259	其他 0.35 毫米＜厚度≤0.4 毫米的铝合金制矩形铝板、片及带	20	Other rectangular plates, sheets and strip of aluminium alloys, of a thickness of 0.35mm or more but not exceeding 4mm
93	76061290	厚度＞0.4 毫米的铝合金制矩形铝板、片及带	20	Rectangular plates, sheets and strip of aluminium alloys, of a thickness exceeding 0.4mm
94	76069100	非合金铝制非矩形的板、片及带	20	Plate, sheet & strip, Al, not alloyed, of a thickness exceeding 0.2mm, nes

序号 No.	税则号列 Tariff Item	货品名称	出口税率(%) Export Duty Rate	Article Description
95	76069200	铝合金制非矩形的板、片及带	20	Plate, sheet & strip, Al alloy, of a thickness exceeding 0.2mm, nes
	79.01			
96	79011110	含锌量≥99.995%的未锻轧锌	20	Unwrought zinc, not alloyed, containing by weight 99.995% or more of zinc
97	79011190	99.99%≤含锌量<99.995%的未锻轧锌	20	Unwrought zinc, not alloyed, containing by weight 99.99% or more, but less than 99.995% of zinc
98	79011200	含锌量<99.99%的未锻轧锌	20	Unwrought zinc, not alloyed, containing by weight less than 99.99% of zinc
99	79012000	未锻轧锌合金	20	Zinc alloys unwrought
	81.10			
100	81101010	未锻轧锑	20	Antimony unwrought
101	81101020	锑粉末	20	Antimony powders
102	81102000	锑废碎料	20	Antimony waste & scrap

出口商品暂定税率表

Interim Duty Rate on Exported Goods

序号 No	EX	税则号列 Tariff Item	货 品 名 称	出口税率 (%) Export Duty Rate	暂定税率 (%) Interim Duty Rate	Article Description
1		03019210	鳗鱼苗	20		Live eels fry
2		05061000	经酸处理的骨胶原及骨	40		Ossein and bones treated with acid
3		05069011	含牛羊成分的骨粉及骨废料	40		Power and waste bones, containing bovine composition or sheep and goat's thereof
4		05069019	其他骨粉及骨废料	40		Other powder and waste of bones
5	ex	05069090	其他骨及角柱(已脱胶骨、角柱除外)	40		Bones and horn-cores, unworked, defatted, simply prepared, not cut to shape, nes
6	ex	05069090	已脱胶骨、角柱	40	0	Degelantinized bones
7		25041010	鳞片状天然石墨		20	Natural graphite in flakes
8		25041099	其它粉末状天然石墨		20	Other natural graphite in powder
9		25049000	其他天然石墨		20	Other natural graphite (excl. in powder or in flakes)
10		25085000	红柱石,蓝晶石及硅线石，不论是否煅烧		10	Andalusite, kyanite & sillimanite, whether or not calcined
11		25086000	富铝红柱石		10	Mullite
12		25101010	未碾磨磷灰石		35	Unground apatites
13		25101090	未碾磨天然磷酸钙、天然磷酸铝钙及磷酸盐白垩，磷灰石除外		35	Unground natural calcium phosphates, natural aluminium calcium phosphates and phosphatic chalk, excl. apatites
14		25102010	已碾磨磷灰石		35	Ground apatites
15		25102090	已碾磨天然磷酸钙、天然磷酸铝钙及磷酸盐白垩，磷灰石除外		35	Ground natural calcium phosphates, natural aluminium calcium phosphates and phosphatic chalk, excl. apatites
16		25111000	天然硫酸钡（重晶石）		10	Natural barium sulphate (barytes)
17		25112000	天然碳酸钡（毒重石），不论是否煅烧		10	Natural barium carbonate (whitherite), whether or not calcined
18		25191000	天然碳酸镁（菱镁矿）		5	Natural magnesium carbonate (magnesite)
19		25199010	熔凝镁氧矿		10	Fused magnesia
20		25199020	烧结镁氧矿（重烧镁）		10	Dead-burned (sintered) magnesia
21		25199030	碱烧镁（轻烧镁）		5	Light-burned magnesia
22		25199099	非纯氧化镁		5	Magnesium oxide, excl. chemically pure
23		25261020	未破碎及未研粉的滑石,不论是否粗加修整或切割成矩形板块		10	Talc, not crushed, not powdered, whether or not roughly trimmed or merely cut into blocks or slabs of a rectangular (incl. square) shape
24	ex	25262020	已破碎或已研粉的天然滑石（体积百分比 90%及以上的产品粒度小于等于 18 微米的滑石粉除外）		10	Talc, crushed or powdered,except for talc powder containing at least 90% by volume with granulatity size ≤18μm
25	ex	25262020	体积百分比 90%及以上的产品粒度小于等于 18 微米的滑石粉		5	Talc powder containing at least 90% by volume with granulatity size ≤18μm
26		25301010	未膨胀的绿泥石		10	Chlorites, unexpanded
27		25309020	稀土金属矿		15	Ores of rare-earth metals
28	ex	25309099	其他氧化镁含量在 70%(含 70%)以上的矿产品		5	Other mineral substances containing by weight not less than 70% of magnesium oxide

序号 No	EX	税则号列 Tariff Item	货 品 名 称	出口税率 (%) Export Duty Rate	暂定税率 (%) Interim Duty Rate	Article Description
29		26011110	平均粒径小于 0.8 毫米的未煅烧铁矿砂及其精矿；但焙烧黄铁矿除外		10	Of a granularity less than 0.8mm, non-agglomerated iron ores and concentrates, other than roasted iron pyrites
30		26011120	平均粒径不小于 0.8 毫米，但不大于 6.3 毫米的未煅烧铁矿砂及其精矿；但焙烧黄铁矿除外		10	Of a granularity of 0.8mm or more, but not exceeding 6.3mm, non-agglomerated iron ores and concentrates, other than roasted iron pyrites
31		26011190	平均粒径大于 6.3 毫米的未烧结铁矿砂及其精矿，但焙烧黄铁矿除外		10	Of a granularity exceeding 6.3mm, non-agglomerated iron ores and concentrates, other than roasted iron pyrites
32		26011200	已烧结铁矿砂及其精矿		10	Agglomerated iron ores & concentrates, other than roasted iron pyrites
33		26012000	焙烧黄铁矿		10	Roasted iron pyrites
34		26030000	铜矿砂及其精矿		10	Copper ores & concentrates
35		26040000	镍矿砂及其精矿		15	Nickel ores & concentrates
36		26050000	钴矿砂及其精矿		15	Cobalt ores & concentrates
37		26070000	铅矿砂及其精矿	30		Lead ores & concentrates
38	ex	26080000	锌矿砂及其精矿（氧化锌含量大于 80%的灰色饲料氧化锌除外）	30		Zinc ores & concentrates, except for Gray feed grade zinc oxide (containing by weight more than 80% of ZnO)
39	ex	26080000	灰色饲料氧化锌（氧化锌 ZnO 含量大于 80%）	30	0	Gray feed grade zinc oxide (containing by weight more than 80% of ZnO)
40		26090000	锡矿砂及其精矿	50	20	Tin ores & concentrates
41		26100000	铬矿砂及其精矿		15	Chromium ores & concentrates
42		26110000	钨矿砂及其精矿	20		Tungsten ores & concentrates
43		26121000	铀矿砂及其精矿		10	Uranium ores & concentrates
44		26122000	钍矿砂及其精矿		10	Thorium ores & concentrates
45		26131000	已焙烧钼矿砂及其精矿		15	Roasted molybdenum ores & concentrates
46		26139000	其他钼矿砂及其精矿		15	Molybdenum ores & concentrates (excl. roasted)
47		26140000	钛矿砂及其精矿		10	Titanium ores & concentrates
48		26151000	锆矿砂及其精矿		10	Zirconium ores & concentrates
49		26159010	水合钽铌原料（钽铌富集物）	30		Hydrated Tantalum/Niobium materials or enriched materials from Tantalum/Niobium ore
50		26159090	其他铌钽矿砂及其精矿	30		Niobium, tantalum & vanadium ores & concentrates ,others
51		26161000	银矿砂及其精矿		10	Silver ores & concentrates
52		26169000	其他贵金属矿砂及其精矿		10	Precious metal (excl. silver) ores & concentrates
53		26171010	生锑（锑精矿，选矿产品）	20		Crude antimony(Antimony concentrates which are mineral products)
54		26171090	其他锑矿砂及其精矿		10	Antimony ores & concentrates (excl.crude)
55		26179010	朱砂(辰砂)		10	Cinnabar
56		26179090	其他矿砂及其精矿		10	Ores & concentrates, nes
57		26180010	冶炼钢铁产生的锰渣		10	Granulated slag mainly containing manganese (slag sand) from the manufacture of iron or steel
58		26180090	冶炼钢铁产生的其他粒状熔渣(熔渣砂)		10	Granulated slag (slag sand) from the manufacture of iron or steel
59		26190000	冶炼钢铁产生的熔渣、浮渣、氧化皮及其他废料		10	Slag, dross (other than granulated slag & slag sand), scaling and other from manufacture of iron or steel

序号 No	EX	税则号列 Tariff Item	货品名称	出口税率 (%) Export Duty Rate	暂定税率 (%) Interim Duty Rate	Article Description
60		26202100	含铅汽油的淤渣及含铅抗震化合物的淤渣		10	Leaded gasoline sludge and leaded anti-knock compound sludge
61		26202900	其他主要含铅的矿灰及残渣		10	Ash & residues containing mainly lead & compound thereof, nes
62		26203000	主要含铜的矿灰及残渣		10	Ash & residues containing mainly copper & compound thereof
63		26206000	含砷、汞、铊及其混合物，用于提取或生产砷、汞、铊及其化合物的矿灰及残渣		10	Ash & residues containing arsenic, mercopperry, thallium or their mixtures, of a kind used for the extraction of arsenic or those metals or for the manufacture of their chemical compound
64		26209100	含锑、铍、镉、铬及其混合物的矿灰及残渣		10	Ash & residues containing antimony, beryllium, cadmium, chromium or their mixture
65		26209910	主要含钨的矿灰及残渣		10	Ash & residues containing mainly tungsten & compound thereof
66		26209990	含其他金属及化合物的矿灰及残渣		10	Ash & residues containing metals & compound thereof, nes
67		27011100	未制成型的无烟煤，不论是否粉化		10	Anthracite, not agglomerated, whether or not pulverized
68		27011210	未制成型的炼焦烟煤，不论是否粉化		10	Bituminous coking coal, not agglomerated, whether or not pulverized
69		27011290	未制成型的其他烟煤，不论是否粉化		10	Other bituminous coal, other than coking coal, not agglomerated, whether or not pulverized
70		27011900	未制成型的其他煤，不论是否粉化		10	Coal nes, not agglomerated, whether or not pulverized
71		27012000	煤砖、煤球及类似用煤制固体燃料		10	Briquettes, ovoids & similar solid fuels manufactured from coal
72		27021000	褐煤		10	Lignite, not agglomerated, whether or not pulverized
73		27022000	制成型的褐煤		10	Agglomerated lignite
74		27030000	泥煤(包括肥料用泥煤) 不论是否成型		10	Peat (incl. peat litter), whether or not agglomerated
75	ex	27060000	从煤、褐煤、或泥煤蒸馏所得的焦油及矿物焦油，不论是否脱水或部分蒸馏，包括再造焦油（含蒽油≥50%及沥青≥40%的“炭黑油”除外）		15	Tar distilled from coal, lignite or peat & other mineral tars, whether or not dehydrated or partially distilled, incl. reconstituted tars
76		27071000	粗苯		10	Benzole
77		27090000	石油原油及从沥青矿物提取的原油		5	Petroleum oils & oils obtained from bituminous minerals, crude
78		28047010	黄磷(白磷)	20		Yellow phosphorus (white phosphorus)
79		28047090	其他磷	20	10	Phosphorus, nes
80		28053011	钕		25	Neodymium
81		28053012	镝		25	Dysprosium
82		28053013	铽		25	Terbium
83		28053014	镧		25	Lanthanum
84		28053015	铈		25	Cerium
85		28053016	镨		25	Praseodymium

序号 No	EX	税则号列 Tariff Item	货 品 名 称	出口税率 (%) Export Duty Rate	暂定税率 (%) Interim Duty Rate	Article Description
86		28053017	钇		25	Yttrium
87		28053019	其他未相互混合或熔合的稀土金属、钪及钇		25	Rare-earth metals nes, scandium and yttrium, not intermixed or interalloyed
88		28053021	已相互混合或熔合的稀土金属、钪及钇，电池级		25	Rare-earth metals, scandium and yttrium, intermixed or interalloyed, battery quality
89		28053029	其他已相互混合或熔合的稀土金属、钪及钇		25	Rare-earth metals, scandium and yttrium, intermixed or interalloyed, other than battery quality
90		28092019	磷酸		300 元/吨	Phosphoric acid, metaphosphoric and pyrophosphoric acid
91		28111100	氢氟酸（氟化氢）		10	Hydrogen fluoride (hydrofluoric acid)
92		28141000	氨		180 元/吨	Anhydrous ammonia
93		28142000	氨水		60 元/吨	Ammonia in aqueous solution
94		28220090	其他钴的氧化物及氢氧化物；商品氧化钴		10	Cobalt oxides and hydroxides; commercial cobalt oxides,others
95		28253010	五氧化二钒		5	Divanadium pentaoxide
96	ex	28256000	锗的氧化物		5	Germanium oxides and zirconium dioxides
97		28257000	钼的氧化物及氢氧化物		5	Molybdenum oxides and hydroxides
98		28259011	钨酸		5	Tungstic acid
99		28259012	三氧化钨		5	Tungsten trioxides
100		28259019	其他钨的氧化物和氢氧化物		5	Tungsten oxides and hydroxides, nes
101		28261290	其他氟化铝		5	Other fluorides of aluminium
102		28261920	钠的氟化物		5	Fluorides of sodium
103		28261990	其他氟化物		5	Other fluorides
104	ex	28269090	氟钽酸钾	30		Potassium fluotantalate
105		28271010	肥料用氯化铵		5	Ammonium chloride, use as fertilizer
106		28331100	硫酸钠		5	Disodium sulphate
107		28342110	肥料用硝酸钾		5	Nitrates of potassium, use as fertilizer
108		28417010	钼酸铵		5	Ammonium molybdates
109		28417090	其他钼酸盐		5	Molybdates other than of ammonium
110		28418010	仲钨酸铵		5	Ammonium paratungstate
111		28418020	钨酸钠		5	Sodium tungstate
112		28418030	钨酸钙		5	Calcium tungstate
113		28418040	偏钨酸铵		5	Ammonium metatungstates
114		28418090	其他钨酸盐		5	Tungstates, nes
115		28461010	氧化铈		15	Cerium oxide
116		28461020	氢氧化铈		15	Cerium hydroxide
117		28461030	碳酸铈		15	Cerium carbonate
118		28461090	铈的其他化合物		15	Cerium compounds, nes
119		28469011	氧化钇		25	Yttrium oxide
120		28469012	氧化镧		15	Lanthanum oxide
121		28469013	氧化钕		15	Neodymium oxide
122		28469014	氧化铕		25	Europium oxide
123		28469015	氧化镝		25	Dysprosium oxide
124		28469016	氧化铽		25	Terbium oxide
125		28469017	氧化镨		25	Praseodymium oxide
126	ex	28469019	其他氧化稀土（灯用红粉除外）		15	Rare-earth oxides, nes (except for lamp fluorescent powder)
127		28469021	氯化铽		25	Terbium chlorinates

序号 No	EX	税则号列 Tariff Item	货 品 名 称	出口税率 (%) Export Duty Rate	暂定税率 (%) Interim Duty Rate	Article Description
128		28469022	氯化镝		25	Dysprosium chlorinates
129		28469023	氯化镧		25	Lanthanum chlorinates
130		28469024	氯化钕		15	Neodymium chlorinates
131		28469025	氯化镨		15	Praseodymium chlorinates
132		28469026	氯化钇		15	Yttrium chlorinates
133		28469028	混合氯化稀土		15	Other rare-earth chlorinates,mixed
134		28469029	未混合氯化稀土		15	Other rare-earth chlorinates ,unmixed
135		28469031	氟化铽		15	Terbium fluorides
136		28469032	氟化镝		15	Dysprosium fluorides
137		28469033	氟化镧		15	Lanthanum fluorides
138		28469034	氟化钕		15	Neodymium fluorides
139		28469035	氟化镨		15	Praseodymium fluorides
140		28469036	氟化钇		15	Yttrium fluorides
141		28469039	其他氟化稀土		15	Other rare-earth fluorides
142		28469041	碳酸镧		15	Lanthanum carbonates
143		28469042	碳酸铽		25	Terbium carbonates
144		28469043	碳酸镝		25	Dysprosium carbonates
145		28469044	碳酸钕		15	Neodymium carbonates
146		28469045	碳酸镨		15	Praseodymium carbonates
147		28469046	碳酸钇		15	Yttrium carbonates
148		28469048	混合碳酸稀土		15	Other rare-earth carbonates, mixed
149		28469049	未混合碳酸稀土		15	Other rare-earth carbonates, unmixed
150		28469091	镧的其他化合物		25	Compounds of Lanthanum
151		28469092	钕的其他化合物		25	Compounds of Neodymium
152		28469093	铽的其他化合物		25	Compounds of Terbium
153		28469094	镝的其他化合物		25	Compounds of Dysprosium
154		28469095	镨的其他化合物		25	Compounds of Praseodymium
155		28469096	钇的其他化合物（LED 用荧光粉除外）		25	Conpounds of Yttrium(Other than LED phosphors)
156		28469099	稀土金属、钇、钪的其他化合物（LED 用荧光粉除外）		25	Other compounds of rare-earth,Yttrium or Scandium (Other than LED phosphors)
157		28499020	碳化钨		5	Carbides of tungsten, whether or not chemically defined
158		29022000	苯	40	0	Benzene
159		31021000	尿素		淡季（7~10 月）：40 元/吨 旺季（1~6 月，11、12 月）：15%，加上 40 元/吨	Urea，whether or not in aqueous solution
160		31029090	其他矿物氮肥及化学氮肥，包括上述子目未列名的混合物		淡季（7~10 月）：40 元/吨 旺季（1~6 月，11、12 月）：15%，加上 40 元/吨	Other mineral or chemical fertilizers, nitrogenous, including mixtures not specified in the foregoing subheadings
161		31031010	重过磷酸钙		5	Triple superphosphates
162		31031090	其他过磷酸钙		5	Other superphosphates
163		31039000	其他矿物磷肥或化学磷肥		5	Mineral or chemical fertilizers, phosphatic, nes
164		31042090	其他氯化钾		600 元/吨	Potassium chloride, nes
165		31043000	硫酸钾		600 元/吨	Potassium sulphate

序号 No	EX	税则号列 Tariff Item	货 品 名 称	出口税率 (%) Export Duty Rate	暂定税率 (%) Interim Duty Rate	Article Description
166		31049010	光卤石、钾盐及其他天然粗钾盐		30	Carnallite, sylvite and other crude natural potassium salts
167		31049090	其他矿物钾肥及化学钾肥		30	Mineral or chemical fertilizers, potassic, other than potassium chloride and potassium sulphate and other crude natural potassium salts
168		31051000	制成片状及类似形状或每包毛重不超过10公斤的31章各货品		淡季（5月16日~10月15日）：50元/吨；旺季（1月1日~5月15日，10月16日~12月31日）：15%，加上50元/吨；	Goods of chapter 31 in tables or similar forms or in packages of a gross weight ≤10kg
169		31052000	三元复合肥		30	Mineral or chemical fertilizers containing the three fertilizing elements nitrogen, phosphorus & potassium
170		31053000	磷酸氢二铵		淡季（5月16日~10月15日）：50元/吨；旺季（1月1日~5月15日，10月16日~12月31日）：15%，加上50元/吨	Diammonium hydrogenorthophosphate (diammonium phosphate)
171		31054000	磷酸二氢铵及磷酸二氢铵与磷酸氢二铵的混合物		淡季（5月16日~10月15日）：50元/吨；旺季（1月1日~5月15日，10月16日~12月31日）：15%，加上50元/吨	Ammonium dihydrogenorthophosphate (monoammonium phosphate) and mixtures thereof with diammonium hydrogenorthophosphate (diammonium phosphate)
172		31055100	含有硝酸盐及磷酸盐的肥料		5	Mineral or chemical fertilizers containing nitrates & phosphates
173		31055900	其他含氮磷两种肥效元素的矿物肥料或化学肥料		淡季（5月16日~10月15日）：50元/吨；旺季（1月1日~5月15日，10月16日~12月31日）：15%，加上50元/吨	Mineral or chemical fertilizers containing the two fertilizing elements nitrogen & phosphorus, nes
174		31056000	含磷钾两种元素的肥料		5	Mineral or chemical fertilizers with phosphorus & potassium, nes
175		31059000	其他肥料		淡季（5月16日~10月15日）：50元/吨；旺季（1月1日~5月15日，10月16日~12月31日）：15%，加上50元/吨	Mineral or chemical fertilizers, nes

序号 No	EX	税则号列 Tariff Item	货 品 名 称	出口税率 (%) Export Duty Rate	暂定税率 (%) Interim Duty Rate	Article Description
176		38249091	含滑石 50%以上的混合物		10	Mixture containing more than 50% talc by weight
177		41039011	经退鞣处理的山羊板皮	20		Dried hides and skins of goats, have undergone a reversible tanning process
178		41039019	山羊板皮，经退鞣处理的除外	20		Dried hides and skins of goats other than those have undergone a reversible tanning process
179		44012100	针叶木木片或木粒		15	Coniferous wood in chips or particles
180		44012200	非针叶木木片或木粒		15	Non-coniferous wood in chips or articles
181		44091010	针叶木地板条（块）		10	Floor board strips of Coniferous
182		44092910	其他非针叶木地板条		10	Floor board strips of non-coniferous other than those of bamboo
183		44190031	木制一次性筷子		10	One-time chopsticks, of wood
184		44219021	木制圆签、圆棒、冰果棒、压舌片及类似一次性制品		10	Round picks and sticks, sticks for icesucker, spatulas and similar one-time articles, of wood
185		47010000	机械木浆		10	Mechanical wood pulp
186		47020000	化学木浆，溶解级		10	Chemical wood pulp, dissolving grades
187		47031100	未漂白针叶木碱木浆或硫酸盐木浆		10	Unbleached coniferous chemical wood pulp, soda or sulphite, other than dissolving grades
188		47031900	未漂白非针叶木碱木浆或硫酸盐木浆		10	Unbleached non-coniferous chemical wood pulp, soda or sulphite, other than dissolving grades
189		47032100	漂白针叶木碱木浆或硫酸盐木浆		10	Semi-bleached or bleached coniferous chemical wood pulp, soda or sulphite, other than dissolving grades
190		47032900	漂白非针叶木碱木浆或硫酸盐木浆		10	Semi-bleached or bleached non-coniferous chemical wood pulp, soda or sulphite, other than dissolving grades
191		47041100	未漂白的针叶木亚硫酸盐木浆		10	Unbleached coniferous chemical wood pulp, sulphite, other than dissolving grades
192		47041900	未漂白的非针叶木亚硫酸盐木浆		10	Unbleached non-coniferous chemical wood pulp, sulphite, other than dissolving grades
193		47042100	漂白的针叶木亚硫酸盐木浆		10	Semi-bleached or bleached coniferous chemical wood pulp, sulphite, other than dissolving grades
194		47042900	漂白的非针叶木亚硫酸盐木浆		10	Semi-bleached or bleached non-coniferous chemical wood pulp, sulphite, other than dissolving grades
195		47050000	半化学木浆		10	Semi-chemical wood pulp
196		47062000	从回收纸或纸板提取的纤维浆		10	Pulp of fibres derived from recovered (waste and scrap) paper or paperboard
197		47063000	竹浆		10	Pulps of bamboo
198		47069100	其他纤维状纤维素机械浆		10	Mechanical pulp of fibrous cellulosic material, nes
199		47069200	其他纤维状纤维素化学浆		10	Chemical pulp of fibrous cellulosic material, nes
200		47069300	其他纤维状纤维素半化学浆		10	Semi-chemical pulp of fibrous cellulosic material, nes

序号 No	EX	税则号列 Tariff Item	货 品 名 称	出口税率 (%) Export Duty Rate	暂定税率 (%) Interim Duty Rate	Article Description
201		72011000	非合金生铁，含磷量小于或等于 0.5%	20	25	Non-alloy pig iron, containing by weight 0.5% or less of phosphorus in primary forms
202		72012000	非合金生铁，含磷量大于 0.5%	20	25	Non-alloy pig iron, containing by weight more than 0.5% of phosphorus in primary forms
203		72015000	合金生铁	20	25	Alloy pig iron; spiegeleisen
204		72021100	锰铁,含碳量>2%	20		Ferro-manganese, containing by weight more than 2% of carbon
205		72021900	锰铁,含碳量≤2%	20		Ferro-manganese,containing by weight 2% or less of carbon
206		72022100	硅铁,含硅量>55%	25		Ferro-silicon, containing by weight more than 55% of silicon
207		72022900	硅铁,含硅量≤55%	25		Ferro-silicon, nes
208		72023000	硅锰铁	20		Ferro-silico-manganese
209		72024100	铬铁,含碳量>4%	40	20	Ferro-chromium containing by weight more than 4% of carbon
210		72024900	铬铁,含碳量≤4%	40	20	Ferro-chromium containing by weight no more than 4% of carbon
211		72025000	硅铬铁		20	Ferro-silico-chromium
212		72026000	镍铁		20	Ferro-nickel
213		72027000	钼铁		20	Ferro-molybdenum
214		72028010	钨铁		20	Ferro-tungsten
215		72028020	硅钨铁		20	Ferro-silico-tungsten
216		72029100	钛铁及硅钛铁		20	Ferro-titanium & ferro-silico-titanium
217		72029290	其他钒铁		20	Ferro-vanadium containing by weight no more than 75% of vanadium
218		72029300	铌铁		20	Ferro-niobium
219		72029911	钕铁硼速凝永磁片		20	Neodynium-ferro-boron permanent magnetic strip-casting flakes
220		72029919	其他钕铁硼合金		20	Neodynium-ferro-boron alloys, nes
221		72029991	按重量计含稀土元素 10%以上的铁合金		25	Other ferro-alloys, containing by weight more than 10% of rare-earth elements
222		72029999	其他铁合金		20	Ferro-alloys, nes
223		72031000	直接从铁矿还原的铁产品		25	Ferrous products obtained by direct reduction of iron ore
224		72039000	其他铁，海绵铁,产品纯度>99.94%		25	Spongy ferrous products / iron having a minimum purity by weight of 99.94%
225		72041000	铸铁废碎料	40		Waste & scrap, cast iron
226		72042100	不锈钢废碎料	40		Waste & scrap, stainless steel
227		72042900	其他合金钢废碎料	40		Waste & scrap, of alloy steel, other than stainless
228		72043000	镀锡钢铁废碎料	40		Waste & scrap, of tinned iron or steel
229		72044100	机械加工中产生的废料	40		Ferrous waste & scrap,i/s,from the mechanical working of mtl,nes
230		72044900	其他钢铁废碎料	40		Ferrous waste & scrap, iron or steel, nes
231		72045000	供再熔的碎料钢铁锭	40		Remelting scrap ingots, of iron or steel
232	ex	72051000	生铁、镜铁及钢铁颗粒(不带球弧面的棱角形颗粒数量大于 80%的棱角钢砂、筛网孔径在 0.3~2.8mm 的铸钢丸和铸钢砂除外)		25	Granules of pig iron,spiegeleisen iron or steel,other than steel grit in which number of angular granules without cambered surface more than 80%,other than cast steel shot and cast steel grit with the mesh size 0.3mm to 2.8mm

序号 No	EX	税则号列 Tariff Item	货 品 名 称	出口税率 (%) Export Duty Rate	暂定税率 (%) Interim Duty Rate	Article Description
233	ex	72052900	生铁、镜铁及其他钢铁粉末(平均粒径小于10μm的超细铁粉除外)		25	Powders of pig iron, spiegeleisen, iron or non-alloy steel, other than superfine iron powders in which a mean diameter ＜10μm
234		72061000	铁及非合金钢锭		25	Iron and non-alloy steel in ingots
235		72069000	其他初级形状的铁及非合金钢		25	Iron and non-alloy steel in other primary forms
236		72071100	宽度＜厚度两倍的矩形截面钢坯,C<0.25%		25	Semi-finished product, of iron or non-alloy steel, of rectangular (including square) cross-section, containing by weight less than 0.25% of carbon, the width measuring less than twice the thickness
237		72071200	其他矩形截面钢坯,C<0.25%		25	Semi-finished product, of iron or non-alloy steel, of rectangular (other than square) cross-section, containing by weight less than 0.25% of carbon
238		72071900	其他含碳量＜0.25%的钢坯		25	Other semi-finished product, of iron or non-alloy steel, containing by weight less than 0.25% of carbon
239		72072000	含碳量≥0.25%的钢坯		25	Semi-finished product, of iron or non-alloy steel, containing by weight 0.25% or more of carbon
240		72131000	带有轧制花纹的热轧盘条		15	Bars & rods, of iron or non-alloy steel, hot-rolled, in irregularly wound coils, containing indent, ribs, etc produced during process
241		72132000	其他易切削钢制热轧盘条		15	Bars & rods, of iron or non-alloy steel, hot-rolled, in irregularly wound coils, of free coppertting steel
242		72139100	直径＜14mm 圆截面的其他热轧盘条		15	Bars & rods, of iron or non-alloy steel, hot-rolled, in irregularly wound coils, of circopperlar cross-section, measuring less than 14mm in diameter
243		72139900	其他热轧盘条		15	Bars & rods, of iron or non-alloy steel, hot-rolled, in irregularly wound coils, of circopperlar cross-section, nes
244		72142000	热加工带有轧制花纹的条、杆		15	Bars & rods, of iron or non-alloy steel, forged, hot-rolled, hot-drawn or hot-extended, containing indentations, ribs, etc, produced during the process
245		72143000	热加工易切削钢的条、杆		15	Bars & rods, of iron or non-alloy steel, forged, hot-rolled, hot-drawn or hot-extended, of free coppertting steel, nes
246		72149100	热加工其他矩形截面的条杆		15	Bars & rods, of iron or non-alloy steel, forged, hot-rolled, hot-drawn or hot-extended, of rectangular cross section
247		72149900	热加工其他条、杆		15	Bars & rods, of iron or non-alloy steel, forged, hot-rolled, hot-drawn or hot-extended, nes
248		72151000	冷加工其他易切削钢制条、杆		15	Bars & rods, of iron or non-alloy steel, not further worked than cold formed or finished, of free coppertting steel

序号 No	EX	税则号列 Tariff Item	货品名称	出口税率 (%) Export Duty Rate	暂定税率 (%) Interim Duty Rate	Article Description
249		72155000	冷加工或冷成形的其他条、杆		15	Bars & rods, of iron or non-alloy steel, not further worked than cold formed or finished
250		72159000	铁及非合金钢的其他条、杆		15	Bars & rods, of iron or non-alloy steel, nes
251		72181000	不锈钢锭及其他初级形状产品		15	Ingots & other primary forms of stainless steel
252		72189100	矩形截面的不锈钢半制成品		15	Semi-finished products of stainless steel, rectangular cross-section
253		72189900	其他不锈钢半制成品		15	Other semi-finished products of stainless steel
254		72191312	厚度在 3 毫米及以上，但小于 4.75 毫米的未经酸洗的按重量计含锰量在 5.5%及以上的铬锰系不锈钢卷板		10	Ferro-chromiam-manganese stainless steel, in coil, not acid pickled，of a thickness of 3mm or more but less than 4.75mm, containing by weight more than 5.5% of manganese
255		72191322	厚度在 3 毫米及以上，但小于 4.75 毫米的经酸洗的按重量计含锰量在 5.5%及以上的铬锰系不锈钢卷板		10	Ferro-chromiam-manganese stainless steel, in coil, acid pickled，of a thickness of 3mm or more but less than 4.75mm, containing by weight more than 5.5% of manganese
256		72191412	厚度小于 3 毫米的未经酸洗的按重量计含锰量在5.5%及以上的铬锰系不锈钢卷板		10	Ferro-chromiam-manganese stainless steel, in coil, not acid pickled, of a thickness less than 3mm , containing by weight more than 5.5% of manganese
257		72191422	厚度小于 3 毫米的经酸洗的按重量计含锰量在 5.5%及以上的铬锰系不锈钢卷板		10	Ferro-chromiam-manganese stainless steel, in coil, acid pickled, of a thickness less than 3mm, containing by weight more than 5.5% of manganese
258		72241000	合金钢锭及其他初级形状合金钢		15	Ingots & other primary forms of alloy steel, other than stainless
259		72249010	单重≥10 吨的粗铸锻件坯		15	Raw casting forging stocks, of alloy steel other than stainless, individual piece weight of 10T or more
260		72249090	其他合金钢坯		15	Semi-finished products of alloy steel other than stainless, nes
261		74010000	铜锍、沉积铜（泥铜）		15	Copper mattes; cement copper (precipitated copper)
262		74020000	未精炼铜，电解精炼用的铜阳极	30	15	Copper unrefined, Copper anodes for electrolytic refining
263	ex	74031111	高纯阴极铜（铜含量不低于 99.9999%）	30	0	Copper cathodes containing by weight no less than 99.9999% of copper, unwrought
264	ex	74031111	高纯阴极铜（铜含量高于 99.9935%，但低于 99.9999%）	30	5	Copper cathodes containing by weight more than 99.9935% but less than 99.9999% of copper , unwrought
265		74031119	其他阴极精炼铜	30	10	Other Copper cathodes, unwrought
266		74031190	其他精炼铜的阴极型材	30	10	Copper sections of cathodes, unwrought
267		74031200	精炼铜的线锭	30	10	Wire bars, Copper, unwrought
268		74031300	精炼铜的坯段	30	10	Billets, Copper, unwrought
269		74031900	其他未锻轧的精炼铜	30	10	Refined Copper products, unwrought, nes
270		74032100	未锻轧的铜锌合金(黄铜)	30	5	Copper-zinc base alloys, unwrought
271		74032200	未锻轧的铜锡合金(青铜)	30	5	Copper-tin base alloys, unwrought

序号 No	EX	税则号列 Tariff Item	货 品 名 称	出口税率 (%) Export Duty Rate	暂定税率 (%) Interim Duty Rate	Article Description
272		74032900	未锻轧的其他铜合金	30	5	Copper alloys, unwrought (other than master alloys of heading No 74.05)
273		74040000	铜废碎料	30	15	Waste & scrap, Copper
274		74050000	铜母合金	30	10	Master alloys of Copper
275		74071010	铬锆铜制条、杆及型材及异型材	30	0	Bars, rods & profiles of chrominm and zirconium copper
276		74071090	其他精炼铜制条、杆及型材及异型材	30	0	Other bars, rods & profiles of other refined Cu
277		74072111	直线度不大于 0.5 毫米/米铜锌合金条、杆	30	0	Copper-zinc base alloys(brass) bars and rods, of a straightness not exceeding 0.5mm/m
278		74072119	其他铜锌合金条、杆	30	0	Other bars, rods of copper-zinc base alloys (brass)
279		74072190	其他铜锌合金型材及异型材	30	0	Profiles of Cu-Zn base alloys
280		74072900	其他铜合金条杆、型材及异型材	30	0	Bars, rods & profiles, of Copper alloy, nes
281		74081100	最大截面尺寸＞6mm 的精炼铜丝	30	0	Wire of refined Copper of which the max cross-sectional dimension exceeds 6mm
282		74081900	其它精炼铜丝	30	0	Wire of refined Copper of which the max cross-sectional dimension not exceeds 6mm
283		74082100	铜锌合金丝	30	0	Wire, of Copper-zinc base alloy
284		74082210	铜镍锌铅合金（加铅德银）丝	30	0	Wire, of copper-nickel-zinc-lead base alloys (leaded nickel silver)
285		74082290	其他白铜或德银丝	30	0	Other wire, of Copper-Ni base alloy or Copper- Ni-zinc base alloy
286		74082900	其他铜合金丝	30	0	Wire, of Copper alloy, nes
287		74091110	含氧量不超过 10PPM 的成卷的精炼铜板、片、带	30	0	Plate, sheet & strip of refined Copper, in coil, of a thickness exceeding 0.15mm，containing Oxygen no more than 10PPM
288		74091190	其他成卷的精炼铜板、片、带	30	0	Plate, sheet & strip of refined Copper, in coil, of a thickness exceeding 0.15mm, nes
289		74091900	其他精炼铜板、片、带	30	0	Plate, sheet & strip of refined Copper, not in coil, of a thickness exceeding 0.15mm
290		74092100	成卷的铜锌合金板、片、带	30	0	Plate, sheet & strip of Copper-Zn base alloys, in coil, of a thickness exceeding 0.15mm
291		74092900	其他铜锌合金板、片、带	30	0	Plate, sheet & strip of Copper-Zn base alloys, not in coil, of a thickness exceeding 0.15mm
292		74093100	成卷的铜锡合金板、片、带	30	0	Plate, sheet & strip of Copper-tin base alloys, in coil, of a thickness exceeding 0.15mm
293		74093900	其他铜锡合金板、片、带	30	0	Plate, sheet & strip of Copper-tin base alloys, not in coil, of a thickness exceeding 0.15mm
294		74094000	铜镍合金或铜镍锌合金板、片、带	30	0	Plate, sheet & strip of Copper-Ni or Copper-Ni-Zn base alloy, of a thickness exceeding 0.15mm

序号 No	EX	税则号列 Tariff Item	货品名称	出口税率 (%) Export Duty Rate	暂定税率 (%) Interim Duty Rate	Article Description
295		74099000	其他铜合金板、片、带	30	0	Plate, sheet & strip of Copper alloy, of a thickness exceeding 0.15mm, nes
296		75021010	高纯镍（镍含量大于99.99%，钴含量不大于0.005%)	40	5	Ni, containing Ni more than 99.99%, and Co less then 0.005% by weight, unwrought, not alloyed
297		75021090	未锻轧的非合金镍	40	15	Ni unwrought, not alloyed
298		75022000	未锻轧镍合金	40	15	Ni unwrought, alloyed
299		75030000	镍废碎料		10	Waste & scrap, Ni
300		75089010	电镀用镍阳极	40	15	Electroplating anodes of Ni
301		76011010	按重量计含铝量在 99.95%及以上的非合金铝	30	0	Containing by weight 99.95% or more of aluminium unwrought aluminium, not alloyed
302		76011090	按重量计含铝量在 99.95%以下的非合金铝	30	15	Al unwrought, not alloyed, nes
303		76012000	未锻轧铝合金	30	15	Al unwrought, alloyed
304		76020000	铝废碎料	30	15	Waste & scrap of Al
305		76041010	非合金铝条、杆	20	15	Bars, rods, of Al, not alloyed
306		76041090	非合金铝型材及异型材	20	0	Bars, rods & profiles, of Al, not alloyed
307		76042100	铝合金制空心异型材	20	0	Profiles, hollow, of Al, alloyed
308	ex	76042910	截面周长大于等于 210 毫米的铝合金制条、杆	20	15	Al alloyed bars and rods of perimeter of cross-section of 210mm or more
309	ex	76042910	截面周长小于 210 毫米的铝合金条杆	20	5	Al alloyed bars and rods of perimeter of cross-section less than 210mm
310		76042990	铝合金制其他型材及异型材	20	0	Bars, rods & other profiles, Al alloyed
311		76051100	最大截面尺寸超过 7mm 的非合金铝丝	20	0	Wire, Al, not alloyed, with a max cross sectional dimension exceeding 7mm
312		76051900	其他非合金铝丝	20	0	Wire, Al, not alloyed, with a max cross sectional dimension not exceeding 7mm
313		76052100	最大截面尺寸超过 7mm 的铝合金丝	20	0	Wire, Al alloy, with a max cross sectional dimension exceeding 7mm
314		76052900	其他铝合金丝	20	0	Wire, Al alloy, with a max cross sectional dimension not exceeding 7mm
315		76061121	厚度在 0.3mm 及以上，但不超过 0.36mm 的非合金铝与塑料复合的矩形铝板片带	20	0	Rectangular plates, sheets and strip, of not alloyed aluminium-plastic composite, 0.3mm≤thickness<0.36mm
316		76061129	厚度在 0.3mm 及以上，但不超过 0.36mm 的其他非合金铝制矩形铝板片带	20	0	Other rectangular plates, sheets and strip, of not alloyed aluminium-plastic composite, 0.3mm≤thickness<0.36mm
317		76061191	非合金铝与塑料复合的矩形的其他板、片及带	20	0	Rectangular plates, sheets and strip, of not alloyed aluminium-plastic composite, nes
318		76061199	非合金铝制矩形的其他板、片及带	20	0	Other rectangular plates, sheets and strip, of not alloyed aluminium-plastic composite, nes
319		76061220	厚度小于 0.28mm 的铝合金制矩形铝板片带	20	0	Plate, sheet & strip, Al alloy, rectangular (including square), of a thickness exceeding 0.2mm, but less than 0.28mm
320		76061230	厚度在 0.28mm 及以上，但不超过 0.35mm 的铝合金制矩形铝板片带	20	0	Plate, sheet & strip, Al alloy, rectangular (including square), of a thickness 0.28mm or more but not exceeding 0.35mm

序号 No	EX	税则号列 Tariff Item	货品名称	出口税率 (%) Export Duty Rate	暂定税率 (%) Interim Duty Rate	Article Description
321		76061251	厚度在 0.35mm 以上,但不超过 4mm 的铝合金与塑料复合的矩形铝板片带	20	0	Rectangular plates, sheets and strip of aluminium alloys-plastic composite, of a thickness of 0.35mm or more but not exceeding 4mm
322		76061259	厚度在 0.35mm 以上,但不超过 4mm 的其他铝合金制矩形铝板片带	20	0	Other rectangular plates, sheets and strip of aluminium alloys, of a thickness of 0.35mm or more but not exceeding 4mm
323		76061290	厚度>4mm 的铝合金制矩形铝板片带	20	0	Rectangular plates, sheets and strip of aluminium alloys, of a thickness exceeding 0.4mm
324		76069100	非合金铝制非矩形的板、片及带	20	0	Plate, sheet & strip, Al, not alloyed, of a thickness exceeding 0.2mm, nes
325		76069200	铝合金制非矩形的板、片及带	20	0	Plate, sheet & strip, Al alloy, of a thickness exceeding 0.2mm, nes
326		78011000	未锻轧精炼铅		10	Lead refined unwrought
327		78020000	铅废碎料		10	Lead waste & scrap
328		79011110	按重量计含锌量在 99.995%及以上的未锻轧锌	20	0	Unwrought zinc, not alloyed, containing by weight 99.995% or more of zinc
329		79011190	99.99≤含锌量<99.995%的未锻轧锌	20	5	Unwrought zinc, not alloyed, containing by weight 99.99% or more, but less than 99.995% of zinc
330		79011200	含锌量＜99.99%的未锻轧锌	20	15	Unwrought zinc, not alloyed, containing by weight less than 99.99% of zinc
331		79012000	未锻轧锌合金	20	0	Zinc alloys unwrought
332		80011000	非合金锡		10	Tin not alloyed unwrought
333		80020000	锡废碎料		10	Tin waste, scrap
334		81011000	钨粉		5	Tungsten powders
335		81019400	未锻轧钨		5	Tungsten unwrought, including bars/rods simply sintered
336		81019700	钨废碎料		15	Tungsten waste and scrap
337		81021000	钼粉		5	Molybdenum powders
338		81029400	未锻轧钼		5	Molybdenum unwrought, including bars/rods simply /sintered
339		81029700	钼废碎料		15	Molybdenum waste and scrap
340		81033000	钽废碎料		10	Tantalum waste and scrap
341		81101010	未锻轧锑	20	5	Antimony unwrought
342		81101020	锑粉末	20		Antimony powders
343		81102000	锑废碎料	20		Antimony waste, scrap
344		81122100	未锻轧铬、铬粉末		15	Chromium unwrought; powders
345		81122200	铬废碎料		15	Chromium waste, scrap
346		81129230	未锻轧铟；铟废碎料；铟粉末		2	Indium; unwrought, waste and scrap，powders

部分本国子目注释

Domestic Heading Explanation Notes

子目 0304.6211	斑点叉尾鮰鱼亦称沟鲶，属于鲇形目、鮰科、叉尾鮰属。体形较长，体前部宽于后部，头较小，吻稍尖，口亚端位，体表光滑无鳞，粘液丰富，侧线完全，皮肤上有明显的侧线孔。体两侧背部淡灰色，腹部乳白色。头部上下颌具有深灰色触须 4 对，其中鼻须 1 对，颌须 1 对，颐须 2 对，长短各异，以颌须为最长，末端超过胸鳍基部，鼻须最短。鳃孔较大，鳃膜不连于峡部，颐部有较明显而不规则的斑点，成年鱼斑点逐步消失。具有脂鳍一个，尾鳍分叉较深，各鳍均为深灰色。冻鱼片呈乳白色，色泽自然，肉质细嫩，冰衣均匀。
子目 0603.1500	百合花是百合科百合属多年生草本球根植物，花着生于茎杆顶端，单生、簇生或呈总状花序，花色因品种不同而色彩多样，也有一朵花具多种色彩的。
子目 0704.9010	学名结球甘蓝，又名圆白菜、洋白菜，属十字花科芸苔属甘蓝变种。外观近圆形，结球紧实个头大，层层包裹成球状体，重量 1~2 公斤，颜色绿，芯白或淡黄色。其嫩叶可供食用。
子目 0704.9020	西兰花，又称青花菜、绿菜花，属十字花科芸苔属甘蓝变种。花球紧实鲜嫩，无现蕾现象，色泽浓绿，成熟度适中。其食用部分为绿色幼嫩花茎和花蕾。
子目 0714.4000	芋头又称芋艿，为天南星科芋属植物。块茎粗大，常为卵形或长椭圆形，褐色，有纤毛。其地下肉质球茎（母芋）和侧生子芋可供食用。按其需水量的不同，分为旱芋和水芋两种。
子目 1517.9010	起酥油是指动、植物油脂的食用氢化油、高级精制油或上述油脂的混合物，经过速冷捏和制造的固状油脂，或不经速冷捏和制造的固状、半固体状或流动状的具有良好起酥性能的油脂制品。
子目 1604.1931	斑点叉尾鮰鱼亦称沟鲶，属于鲇形目、鮰科、叉尾鮰属。体形较长，体前部宽于后部，头较小，吻稍尖，口亚端位，体表光滑无鳞，粘液丰富，侧线完全，皮肤上有明显的侧线孔。体两侧背部淡灰色，腹部乳白色。头部上下颌具有深灰色触须 4 对，其中鼻须 1 对，颌须 1 对，颐须 2 对，长短各异，以颌须为最长，末端超过胸鳍基部，鼻须最短。鳃孔较大，鳃膜不连于峡部，颐部有较明显而不规则的斑点，成年鱼斑点逐步消失。具有脂鳍一个，尾鳍分叉较深，各鳍均为深灰色。
子目 2206.0010	黄酒是指以稻米、黍米、玉米、小米、小麦等为主要原料，经蒸煮、加曲、糖化、发酵、压榨、过滤、煎酒、贮存、勾兑而成的酿造酒。
子目 2208.9020	白酒是指以高粱等谷物为主要原料，以大曲、小曲或麸曲及酒母等为糖化发酵剂，经蒸煮、糖化、发酵、蒸馏、陈酿、勾兑而制成的蒸馏酒。
子目 2504.1091	球化石墨是天然石墨经过球化加工，将微观结构从原来的鳞片状变为球形或半球形后，分级得到的产品，直径在 120 微米以下。
子目 2809.2011	食品级磷酸的具体技术指标参考 GB3149-2004。
子目 2811.2210	本子目所指硅胶，包括全部或部分着色产品。

子目 2826.1210	无水氟化铝是无水氟化氢气体与氢氧化铝经气固反应生产的氟化铝产品,其主要技术指标为:氟质量分数≥61%,铝质量分数≥31.5%,烧减量≤0.5%,松装密度≥1.5 克/立方厘米。
子目 2917.3611	白色针状结晶或粉末，密度 1.510，约在 300°C 升华。能溶于碱溶液，稍溶于热乙醇，不溶于乙醚、冰醋酸和氯仿。用于制造合成树脂、合成纤维和增塑剂等。主要技术指标为 4-羧基苯甲醛（4-CBA）≤25PPM。
子目 3104.2020	本税目所指“纯氯化钾”，按重量计氯化钾含量不小于 99.5%
子目 3802.1010	木质活性炭以锯末、树皮、木屑、竹子等为原料生产，广泛用于医药、果汁、饮料等领域，其干品填充密度小于 0.5 克/立方厘米（粉状，200 目晒余物 20%以内）。
子目 3808.9112	生物杀虫剂是指以多杀霉素、除虫菊素、苦参碱、鱼藤酮、乙蒜素、诱虫烯中的一种或多种为有效成分的杀虫剂。
子目 3824.9093	该产品主要用于电池正极，通常由镍盐与碱反应制备，并按需要掺杂一定比例的碳，以及进行表面覆钴加工。
子目 4802.1010	宣纸是采用产自安徽省泾县境内及周边地区的青檀皮和沙田稻草，不掺杂其他原材料，并利用泾县独有的山泉水，按照传统工艺经过特殊的传统工艺配方，在严密的技术监控下，在安徽省泾县内以传统工 艺生产的，具有润墨和耐久等独特性能，供书画、裱拓、水印等用途的高级艺术用纸。
子目 5003.0011	下茧、茧衣、长吐、滞头是指不适合缫丝的下茧、茧衣、长吐、滞头等缫丝副产品按一定的比例混合后的产品，该产品是重要的绢纺原料。该产品需符合中华人民共和国纺织行业标准——桑蚕绢纺原料（FZ/T41001-94）。
子目 5003.0012	回收纤维是指将碎绸布或其他丝绸织物及制品的废碎料拉松成纤维状的废丝。
子目 5003.0091	绵球是指不能缫丝的下茧、茧衣、长吐、滞头等缫丝副产品经精练、脱胶、干燥处理后既成为白色的精干绵，再经梳理后制成无杂质的绵球（包括绵条、绵片）等。
子目 5402.1110、5503.1110、5506.1011	聚间苯二甲酰间苯二胺纤维，属芳香族聚酰胺，因其高分子链上的酰胺键位于苯环的 1、3 位，所以又称之为芳纶 1313，或间位芳纶。
子目 5402.1120、5503.1120、5506.1012	聚对苯二甲酰对苯二胺纤维，属芳香族聚酰胺纤维，因其高分子链上的酰胺键位于苯环的 1、4 位，又称之为芳纶 1414，或对位芳纶。
子目 5402.4910、5402.5920	这种纱线是由分子量在 100 万及以上，500 万以下的线形聚乙烯制得的长丝纱线，断裂强度大于等于 22cN/dtex,且初始模量大于等于 750cN/dtex。
子目 5504.1021	阻燃粘胶纤维是通过添加无机阻燃剂制成的,氧指数应在 28%以上,回潮率应在 13%及以下。

子目 6802.9311	墓碑石用天然石材加工成的立在坟墓前面或后面的石碑套件，一般由墓碑和外栅组成，上面刻有相关文字图案和造型。
子目 6815.9932	碳纤维预浸料是碳纤维在环氧树脂等基体树脂中浸渍而成的材料。
子目 6815.9940	玄武岩纤维是以玄武岩为原料经高温熔融后拉制而成的无机纤维（国标 GB/T25045-2010）。
子目 7020.0013	该产品是以天然水晶、优质硅石或四氯化硅为主要原料经过电熔、气熔等不同工艺生产的由二氧化硅单一组分构成的特种工业玻璃。
子目 7103.9920	根据中华人民共和国国家标准 GB/T 16552-2010《珠宝玉石 名称》，水晶的矿物名称为石英，品种包括紫晶、黄晶、烟晶、绿水晶、芙蓉石、发晶。
子目 7103.9930	根据中华人民共和国国家标准 GB/T 16552-2010《珠宝玉石 名称》，碧玺的矿物名称为电气石。
子目 7103.9940	根据中华人民共和国国家标准 GB/T 16552-2010《珠宝玉石 名称》，软玉的主要组成矿物为透闪石、阳起石，品种包括和田玉、白玉、青白玉、青玉、碧玉、墨玉、糖玉。
子目 7202.9911	以稀土金属（主要为钕）、纯铁、硼铁等初级产品为原料，经真空高温熔融、速凝成晶、破碎、热处理制成的薄片状合金。其组成成分为稀土（钕、镨、镝、铽）25%～39%，硼 0.8%～1.3%，其他为铁及少量铜、钴、铝、锆、镓等添加元素。形状为不规则薄片，厚度 0.1%～0.8 毫米。经加工后，充磁制成永磁体，应用于计算机、通讯产品、电子设备等高科技领域。
子目 7202.9912	钕铁硼磁粉是以铁合金、钕和其他金属等初级产品为原料，经高温二次重熔、快淬、破碎、退火制成的粉末，其组成成分为钕 20%~32%，钴 0%~16%，硼 0.8%~1.3%，铌 0%~2.5%,其他为铁。钕铁硼磁粉主要应用于计算机、通讯产品电子设备等高科技领域。
子目 7225.4010	除不锈钢、高速钢以外的合金钢，按重量计，成份含量范围符合下列任一条款，不论是否含有其他元素：碳含量大于 1.2%，同时铬含量大于 10.5%的；或者碳含量大于等于 0.3%，同时铬含量大于等于 1.25%，且小于 10.5%的；或者铬含量大于等于 0.9%，且小于等于 1.2%，同时钼含量大于等于 0.9%，且小于等于 1.4%的；或者含碳量大于等于 0.5%，同时钼含量大于等于 3.5%的；或者碳含量大于等于 0.5%，同时钨含量大于等于 5.5%的。
子目 7326.9011	本税目所指的钢铁纤维，是单根直径为 40 纳米至 40 微米的多功能合金纤维，主要材质为不锈钢、铁铬铝合金等。钢铁纤维主要通过表面处理（在原料不锈钢或铁铬铝合金表面电化学涂覆金属或物理涂覆非金属隔离层，制得复合丝）、封装集束复合材料（采用封装材料封装被嵌入基体的不锈钢或铁铬铝合金复合丝，形成一种复合材料）、细晶强化（压实封装之后的复合材料，然后经过多次减径拉拔和退火成为成品复合线）、选择性分离（将成品复合线采用电化学分离的方式，除去封装及基体材料，最终获得钢铁纤维）等工艺流程制备。钢铁纤维及其制品的主要用途包括汽车尾气颗粒捕集、高温气体、熔体过滤，化纤行业过滤，汽车玻璃膜布，电磁屏蔽材料、防静电导电材料等。
子目 7407.1010	铬锆铜的主要成分为铜、铬、锆，按重量计铬含量 0.6%~1.4%，锆含量 0.05%~0.3%。

子目 7408.2210	铜、镍、锌、铅的合金，是在锌白铜的基础上添加微量的易切削元素铅,形成的易切削的白铜。按重量计含铜量 40%~65%，含镍量 9%~16%，含铅量 1.0%~2.5%，含锰量 0.05%~6.5%。锌为余量，且铁、磷、硫、锡等杂质元素总和不大于 0.9%。
子目 7411.1011	一般用作空调、冰箱及其他系统的热交换管材，整根管的内或外表面具有一定数量、一定规则螺纹或翅片。
子目 8103.2011	主要用于电容器生产，松装密度可用“振动漏斗法”（GB/T5061-1998）测定。
子目 8202.2010	双金属带锯条主要用于金属切割，其齿部材料为高速钢或高性能高速钢或硬质合金，锯条体的材料是低合金弹簧钢。齿部硬度不低于 62HRC（766HV），锯条体经过热处理后硬度不低于 436HV（45HRC）。
子目 8413.5031	柱塞泵的工作原理与活塞泵相同，由泵缸、柱塞、吸入阀、排出阀和驱动机构，区别在于柱塞是穿过装在泵缸上的固定填料密封件在缸体内运动，其密封性较活塞的好。
子目 8413.6040	螺杆泵由相互啮合的螺杆和泵体内包括螺杆的泵套组成。螺杆泵按螺杆根数分为单螺杆泵、双螺杆泵、三螺杆泵和五螺杆泵。
子目 8413.6050	径向柱塞泵由壳体、油缸主体、配液轴、若干个柱塞和弹簧等组成。配液轴偏心固定在壳体上，当它转动时，柱塞在缸筒内做径向往返运动，进行吸液和注液。
子目 8413.6060	轴向柱塞泵按其结构特征可分为直轴式（斜盘式）和斜轴式（摆缸式）两大类。斜盘式柱塞泵由壳体、转子（驱动轴、缸筒、柱塞）和斜盘组成。壳体端面配有配液盘；缸筒体内安装着若干个柱塞，沿圆周方向均布在缸筒体内，并能在其中滑动。斜盘固定在壳体上，并与转动轴线的垂线成一定的夹角，斜盘不随转子转动。但转子转动时，驱动轴带动缸筒体转动，柱塞也随之转动，同时柱塞在缸筒内作轴向的往返运动，进行吸液和注液，柱塞端部始终紧靠在斜盘上。摆缸式轴向柱塞泵的特点是：转子轴线与传动轴轴线之间成一个角度；转子及其各钢筒体内的柱塞分别用带万向接头的连杆与传动轴相连。转子转动时，传动轴带动缸筒体和柱塞一起旋转，同时柱塞在缸筒内作轴向的往返运动，进行吸液和注液。
子目 8417.8050	垃圾焚烧炉由垃圾前处理系统、焚烧系统、烟气净化系统及煤气发生炉等组成，具有自动送料、分筛、烘干、焚烧、除尘、控制等功能。可用于处理城市生活垃圾、危险废弃物(含医用垃圾)、一般工业垃圾，分为机械炉排焚烧炉、流化床焚烧炉、回转式焚烧炉、CAO 焚烧炉等类型。
子目 8419.1910	太阳能热水器是利用太阳能将水从低温加热到高温的装置，由全玻璃真空集热管、储水箱、支架及相关附件组成，主要依靠玻璃真空集热管把太阳能转换成热能，使水产生微循环而达到所需热水。
子目 8421.2191	船舶压载水处理设备主要是为了有效控制和防止船舶压载水传播有害水生物和病原体。该设备通常采用电解海水制氯技术对压载水进行杀菌，并采用中和技术除去压载水中的余氯，从而达到压载水排放标准。
子目 8421.3924	电袋复合除尘器由前级电场除尘、后级布袋除尘、检测系统、保护系统、电气控制系统等组成。烟气从进口喇叭进入前级电除尘区，烟尘在电场电晕电流作用下荷电，大部分被电场收集下来，少量未被捕集粉尘随烟气进入后级布袋除尘区，经滤袋过滤后达到烟气净化目的。

子目 8421.3940	烟气脱硫设备主要用于火电厂烟气脱硫和重要工业领域（如烧结机脱硫），主导的烟气脱硫工艺为石灰石/石灰—石膏脱硫（设备）与烟气循环硫化床法脱硫（设备）。脱硫设备一般包括烟气脱硫反应器、循环浆液泵、水力旋流分离器、脱硫增压风机、除雾器、烟气挡板门、搅拌器等部分。
子目 8421.3950	烟气脱硝装置主要用于火电站、有色金属冶炼等工业领域，主要利用还原剂与氮氧化物（NOX）发生化学反应生成氮气和气态水，降低烟气中氮氧化物排放量。主流装置为选择催化还原法（SCR）脱硝技术，该装置主要包括 SCR 反应器、氨存储与供应系统、测试与控制系统等组成。
子目 8424.8920	本税目所指喷涂机器人是指专用于自动喷漆或喷涂其他涂料的工业机器人，由机器人本体、减速器、控制系统、伺服系统、喷具和涂料输供系统等部分组成。主要应用于汽车、船舶、仪表、电器、搪瓷等工艺生产部门。
子目 8428.9020	机械式停车设备是通过机械方式搬运、停放车辆的机械设备。此类设备大多采用自动控制、计算机管理等手段，综合应用机、电、声、光、自动化等技术，达到存取储放车辆的高效率、高可靠性和高安全性。此类设备分为升降横移类、垂直循环类、水平循环类、多层循环类、平面移动类、巷道堆垛类、垂直升降类和简易升降类等多种型式。主要由钢结构件、传动系统、控制系统等部分组成。
子目 8428.9031	堆取料机械是大型料场专用设备，一般分为臂式斗轮堆取料机、桥门式斗轮堆取料机和刮板式取料机三类。臂式一般由取料机构（堆料机无取料机构）、输送机构、回转、俯仰、行走机构、金属结构、电气控制设备等组成。桥门式和刮板式结构形式不同，但工作原理基本类似。
子目 8428.9040	本税目所指搬运机器人是指专用于自动化搬运作业的工业机器人，由机器人本体、减速器、控制系统和伺服系统等部分组成。主要应用于机械、电子、食品、医疗等行业的搬运、传输。
子目 8430.3110	采煤机（含截煤机、割煤机），由装有风镐的棒条或圆盘组成，按装在自推进的轮式或履带式底盘上，以旋转工作机劈开或击碎煤层，并将其装入输送机或其他运输设备。
子目 8430.3120	凿岩机是用来直接开采石料的工具，由一环形切割链环绕一金属臂运作，切割平面和角度均可调节，一般与工程车、液压挖掘机等配套使用。
子目 8430.3130	隧道掘进机是用机械破碎岩石、出碴和支护实行连续作业的一种综合设备，利用回转刀具开挖，破碎洞内围岩及掘进，形成整个隧道断面。一般由刀盘、主驱动、盾体、推进系统、输送机、注浆系统、液压系统、控制系统、导向测量系统、管片拼装系统、润滑系统等组成。
子目 8431.2010	税号 84.27 所列机械用驱动桥是传动系统组成部分，由主减速器、差速器、半轴、轮边减速器、桥壳等构成，主要功能是增大由传动轴或变速器产生的转矩，并将动力合理分配给左右驱动轮。
子目 8431.4920	税号 84.26、84.29 或 84.30 所列机械用驱动桥是传动系统组成部分，由主减速器、差速器、半轴、轮边减速器、桥壳等构成，主要功能是增大由传动轴或变速器产生的转矩，并将动力合理分配给左右驱动轮。
子目 8432.3011	按规定播量和行距在田间播种谷物种子的农业机具，主要完成开沟、排种、覆土和镇压等作业，按排种方式的不同，排种器分为槽轮式、磨盘式等，我国生产的谷物播种机大都有播种时同时施肥的功能。

子目 8432.3021	按一定行距、种薯间距和栽种深度栽植马铃薯的机具。能一次完成开沟、施肥、栽种薯块和覆土等作业。
子目 8432.3031	按一定的行距、株距、秧苗数和栽植深度将水稻秧苗栽植于水田的机具。由秧箱、送秧机构、分插秧机构、动力驱动、行走装置等部件组成。
子目 8433.5920	棉花采摘机的基本机构：除驾驶室、发动机、行走机构外，主要工作部件还有采棉滚筒、气流输送装置、集棉箱等。在棉花采摘机前进时，扶导器压缩棉株，并把棉株引入由采棉滚筒及固定护板组成的工作室（采棉区），棉株宽度被积压成 8~9 厘米，旋转着的采棉滚筒有规律地把摘锭送入采棉区，旋转的摘锭伸出栅板，插入被挤压的棉株，同开裂棉铃相遇，其钩齿抓住籽棉，把棉絮从开裂的棉铃中拉出，缠绕在摘锭上。然后摘锭进入脱棉区，高速旋转的橡胶圆盘式脱棉器将摘锭上的籽棉脱下，落入集棉室，有气流管道送入集棉箱。摘锭从湿润器下边通过时，表面涂上一层水，清除掉绿色汁液和泥土垢（以利于采棉和脱棉）重新进入采棉区。
子目 8437.1010	光学色差颗粒选别机（色选机）是运用特定的光学方法，凸显被选物料与正常物料的颜色或形状差异，这些差异被电子视觉系统检测，经控制系统处理产生输出信号，控制执行机构剔除被选物料，得到品质一致的物料。该设备广泛应用于粮食及食品的精深加工领域，同时还适用于工业领域（塑料、矿石等）的分选。
子目 8443.3214	热敏打印机采用加热显色技术实现打印输出。该产品的结构相对比较简单，仅包括热敏打印头、进纸胶辊及进纸电机等，不需要各种复杂的辅助机构。热敏打印机可作为模块嵌入到各种终端设备中使用。热敏打印机广泛应用于条码、标签、收据、日志等专业打印领域。
子目 8443.9111	卷筒料给料机按更换料卷方式分为高速接料和零速接料两类。高速自动给料机是指机器在全速或略微降速的运行过程中，在料卷运行状态下完成粘结料卷、更换料卷的自动接料装置。零速接料是指料卷在静止状态下完成粘接，而印刷机仍在正常高速运行，在此期间是由给料机的料卷储存装置——储料器向印刷机供给输送料带。
子目 8443.9921	热敏头组件由小型电加热器和逻辑电路组成，小型加热器排成方阵，由逻辑电路控制加热器工作。同时也控制进纸，当加热器被驱动时在介质上就会产生一个与加热元素相对应的图形，从而完成输出图像的任务。热敏打印的介质是热敏纸，热敏纸上覆有一层透明膜，将膜加热一段时间以后纸会变成深色（蓝或黑），热敏打印就是利用热敏纸的这种特性，通过热敏打印头将打印介质上的热敏材料加热、熔化、变色，生成所需要的文字和图形。
子目 8447.2011	特里科经编机织物相对于织针平面近似成直角状牵拉，织物张力由织针承担。在成圈配置以及编织方面的特点如下：(1) 沉降片上纱线接触点为 2 个。(2) 经轴一般放在机器后面或者放在机器的上面。(3) 织针可以从机前更换。(4) 老式特里科经编机导纱梳栉编号从机后到机前(从 2001 年 1 月开始，编号从机前到机后)。 (5) 目前最多使用 5 把梳栉。(6) 使用复合针。(7) 没有牵拉就可以起头编织。(8) 光编链组织不能编织(编链衬纬可以编织)。(9) 纱线与坯布牵拉成 90°，织针受力较大。
子目 8447.2012	拉舍尔经编机织物相对于织针平面近似成平行状牵拉，织物张力对织针不大起作用。在成圈配置以及编织方面的特点如下：(1) 沉降片纱线接触点为 3 个。(2) 经轴一般放在机器的顶部。(3) 织针必须从机后更换。(4) 导纱梳栉的编号从机前到机后。(5) 最多使用 78 把梳栉。(6) 使用复合针和舌针。(7) 没有牵拉不能起头编织。(8) 光编链线圈也能编织。(9) 纱线与坯布牵拉成 170°，织针受力较小。

子目 8448.3940	紧密纺装置是在环锭细纱机设备的基础上,突破传统纺纱工艺,在牵引部分增加集聚、吸风和气流导向装置，通过对加捻点的纺纱三角区中纤维的控制，纺出了高质量的紧密纱线。该纱具有纺纱强力高、毛羽少、条干好等特点，可适应纺多种纤维。
子目 8449.0010	针刺法是一种机械加固方法,其基本原理是用截面为三角形（或其他形状）且棱边带有钩刺的针，对蓬松的纤网进行反复针刺，将纤网加工成具有一定厚度和强度的针刺法非织造布。针刺机按加工纤网的状态可分为预针刺机和主针刺机；按结构可分为单针梁式和双针梁式；按传动形式可分为上传动式和下传动式。针刺机的机构由以下几部分组成：送网机构、针刺机构、牵拉机构、花纹机构（仅花纹针刺机由此机构）、传动机构、附属机构、机架等。
子目 8449.0020	水刺法又称射流喷射网法、力缠结法、喷水成布法，采用高速高压的水流促使纤维相互缠结抱合，达到加固纤网，制成水刺非织造布。水刺设备主要由水刺装置（水刺头）、输送网帘和水循环装置组成。水刺装置是由内部带有通水孔的集流腔体与水针板组成，采用耐腐蚀和耐高压材料制成。水针板是一个长条薄型不锈钢板，根据工艺要求，在针板上开有单排孔、双排孔或三排孔。一般水刺装置的配置为四上四下，可以水平排列，也可以圆周排列。水刺设备一般是将两组或多组水刺装置串联使用。
子目 8450.2011	波轮式全自动洗衣机主要结构由箱体、洗涤桶、外桶（盛水桶）、电机、传动部件以及全自动程序控制器、传感器等电控系统组成，电机等洗涤系统轴向垂直设置。其工作原理为：通过各种器件组成的控制电路来控制电机、进水阀、排水阀，使洗衣机实现程序运转；依靠装在洗衣桶底部的波轮正、反旋转形成水流，带动衣物上、下、左、右翻转，使衣物在洗涤液中进行柔和地摩擦，在洗涤剂的作用下实现去污清洗，洗涤过程全自动控制。
子目 8450.2012	滚筒式全自动洗衣机主要结构由箱体、洗涤桶、外桶（盛水桶）、电机、传动部件、平衡块以及全自动程序控制器、传感器等电控系统组成，电机等洗涤系统轴向水平设置。其工作原理为：通过各种器件组成的控制电路来控制电机、进水阀、排水阀，使洗衣机实现程序运转；模仿棒锤击打衣物原理设计，利用电动机的机械做功使滚筒旋转，带动衣物在滚筒中不断地被提升摔下，再提升再摔下，做重复运动，加上洗涤剂与水的共同作用使衣物洗涤干净，洗涤过程全自动控制。
子目 8452.1091	手动式小缝纫机又称为缝纫器，产品体积通常小于 15*10*15 厘米，重量轻于 2 公斤，可随身携带，手握按压式动力，作单线链式线迹缝纫，能够轻松自如地缝纫悬挂着的窗帘、壁挂、手帕、围裙、枕套等，也可缝制小衣物等。
子目 8452.2120	包缝机是由针线和弯针线，通过机器的运动循环穿套在缝料边缘形成包缝链式线迹（500 类包缝链式线迹），将缝料包边并缝合的工业缝纫机。自动包缝机采用微型计算机控制，具有自动剪线、定针位、抬压脚等自动功能。机器由机壳、传动机构、针杆机构、勾线机构、送料机构、压脚机构、切刀机构以及机架、台板、控制系统、驱动电机等机构与部件组成，产品主要用于服装的包边、包缝、镶边等，能有效防止缝料边缘脱散，广泛应用于印染、服装、地毯等行业。
子目 8452.2130	绷缝机是利用针、梭两种缝线自连、互连、交织，在缝料底面形成单面覆盖链式线迹，或在缝料正面再增加覆盖线形成双面覆盖链式线迹（400 类多线链式线迹），将两层或多层缝料缝合的工业用缝纫机。自动绷缝机采用微型计算机控制，具有自动剪线、拔线、倒缝、定针位及抬压脚等自动功能，产品主要由机壳、刺料机构、主轴传动机构、上轴传动及挑线机构、勾线机构、绷针机构、送料机构、输回油机构以及机架、台板、控制系统、驱动电机等组成，主要应用于针织服装厂缝制棉毛衫、汗衫及类似的化纤织物的搭缝连接、针织服装的滚领、滚边、折边、拼接缝等作业。

子目 8457.1091	数控铣车复合加工中心是在车床基础上复合了铣车功能,利用刀具移动或旋转和工件旋转的合成运动实现对工件表面的切削加工的设备。工件主轴为水平或垂直状态，并配有自动换刀装置（刀库机械手），主要用于工序多、形状复杂的回转体零件的加工。与车削中心相比,增加了一个旋转轴和自动换刀装置(刀库机械手)。
子目 8458.9110	数控立式车床主要由床身、立柱、刀架、卡盘（或工作盘）、X/Z 轴进给等组成，其主轴处于垂直位置，主要有两种结构形式：(1)主轴和工作台位于下方的床身上，刀架在立柱上，适于加工大型和重型零件，通常称为数控立式(正置)车床；(2)主轴和卡盘位于立柱上，刀架则位于下方床身上，适于加工中小型盘、盖类零件，自动化程度高，通常称为数控立式倒置车床。
子目 8460.2111	数控曲轴磨床是曲轴精加工设备,一般由基础部分（床身、工作台）、支承部分（头架、尾架、卡盘、中心架等）、砂轮架、进给机构、数控系统、液压系统、对刀测量装置等组成的。主要用于磨削汽车、拖拉机、机车内燃机、柴油机及船用发动机用曲轴。
子目 8461.4011	数控齿轮磨床是利用磨具对齿轮表面进行磨削加工的精加工设备，一般由主轴部件、床具、进给单元、辅助单元等组成。按齿轮型式分为渐开线圆柱齿轮磨床和锥齿轮磨床。
子目 8466.9310	刀库是存放待换工具的装置，自动换刀装置则是能自动更换加工中所用工具的装置。刀库系统是提供自动化加工过程中所需储刀及换刀需求的一种装置，由自动换刀机构及可以储放多把刀具的刀库构成。该装置由电脑程序控制，可完成各种不同的加工需求，如铣削、钻孔、镗孔、攻牙等，大幅缩短加工时程，降低生产成本。刀库可分为斗笠式、圆盘式、链条式，自动换刀装置则可分为油压机构、气压机构、电气凸轮机构三类。目前电气凸轮机构因设计简单使用操作可靠被广泛采用。
子目 8471.3010	平板电脑是指输入输出部件集成在一起、以触摸屏为基本输入设备的便携式电脑。（通常屏幕大于等于 7 英寸）。
子目 8477.3010	挤出吹塑机是挤出机和合模机构的组合体,由挤出机及型坯模头、吹胀装置、合模机构、型坯厚度控制系统和传动机构组成。
子目 8477.3020	注射吹塑机是注塑机与吹塑机构的组合体，包括塑化机构、液压系统、控制电器及其他机械部件。注射吹塑机生产的塑料容器尺寸精确，无需二次加工，但模具费用较高。
子目 8477.3090	其他吹塑机包括特殊结构的吹塑机，这些吹塑机是用片材、熔融材和冷坯为型坯吹塑具有特殊形状和用途的空心体的吹塑机。
子目 8477.5910	本税目所指三维打印机（3D 打印机）是以数字模型文件为基础，加工材质以塑料或橡胶及其制品为主，通过逐层打印的方式实现固态物体成型，属于增材技术的重要应用。一般由打印头、控制组件、机械组件、耗材和介质等组成，主要应用于模具制造、工业设计等领域。
子目 8479.8991	机场用旅客登机桥是供旅客上、下飞机通行的、联接飞机与机场航站楼之间的活动封闭式通道。按结构可分为轮式登机桥、柱座式登机桥和其他形式登机桥，其中轮式又分为旋转式和旋转伸缩式。按传动方式可分为液压式、机电式和液压机电混合式。外观侧壁材料可由波纹板、钢板或玻璃板构成。旅客登机桥整桥由旋转平台、活动通道、升降机构、接机平台、接机口、行走机构、服务梯、立柱及固定通道等组成。旅客登机桥采用 PLC 可编程序控制，具有终端控制、自动预靠、自动退桥等功能。

子目 8480.4110	压铸模一般是由两个互补冷硬铸模组成，其型腔与所需铸件两面的形状形同，合模后将融熔状态的金属液体注入模腔，经加压、保压、冷却、开模，生产出各种压铸件。
子目 8480.4120	粉末冶金用压模用于压制各种粉末冶金件。将模具组装到压力机上，调试，在开模状态下装入金属粉末（钢粉、铜粉、不锈钢及各种合金粉等）压力机动作，加压、模具压紧，经过烧结的金属粉末在高压下成型为零件。
子目 8480.7110	硫化轮胎用囊式型模由两个可调节的金属冷硬铸模组成，用蒸汽或电加热，内有环状的充气袋或热水袋，以将胎坯牢牢地压向型模的内壁。
子目 8481.8021	电磁换向阀是利用电磁铁的推力来驱动阀芯运动以变换流体流动方向的控制阀，简称电磁阀。电磁换向阀有滑阀和球阀两种结构。通常所说的电磁换向阀为滑阀结构，球状或锥状阀芯的电磁换向阀被称为电磁换向座阀，也称电磁球阀。电磁换向阀的品种繁多，按其工作位置数和通路数可分为二位二通、二位三通、二位四通、三位四通等；按其复位和定位形式可分为弹簧复位式、钢球定位式、无复位弹簧式；按其阀体与电磁铁的连接形式可分为法兰连接和螺纹连接；按其配电磁铁的结构形式可分为干式和湿式。
子目 8481.8031	电子膨胀阀主要用于变频制冷系统中，实现对系统制冷流量的自动调节，使系统始终保持在最佳的工况下运行。电子膨胀阀由阀体和线圈两部分组成，阀体由阀座部件、转子部件和止动器三个部件组成，线圈由缠绕在骨架上的上下绕组、导磁体和引出电缆等组成。线圈与阀体内永磁转子组成永磁步进电机，通过控制线圈的脉冲输入信号可以实现阀体内转子部件的正反向旋转。转子的转动通过丝杆和螺母的螺纹传动，将转子部件的旋转运动转化为阀针轴向移动，从而调节阀口通流面积的大小，实现系统制冷流量大小的自动调节。电子膨胀阀是采用步进电机驱动的电力驱动阀门。
子目 8482.1010	调心轴承的滚道是球面形的,能够适应两滚道轴心线间的角偏差及角运动的轴承。
子目 8482.1020	深沟球轴承属于径向接触的向心轴承，主要用于承受径向载荷，其公称接触角为 0°。
子目 8482.1030	角接触轴承是指角接触向心轴承，也是主要用于承受径向载荷，0°＜其公称接触角≤45°。该税目不包括角接触推力球轴承。
子目 8482.1040	推力球轴承是指主要用于承受轴向载荷的球轴承，45°＜其公称接触角≤90°。按公称接触角的不同，又分为：轴向接触轴承——公称接触角为 90°的推力球轴承；角接触推力轴承——公称接触角为 45°但小于 90°的推力球轴承。
子目 8483.1011	曲轴是船用柴油机的重要组成部分，主要作用是与连杆配合将活塞上的气体压力转变为传动轴（包括曲轴）的旋转动力，曲轴一般由主轴颈、连杆轴颈、曲柄、平衡块、前端和后段等组成。大功率低速船用曲轴的结构比较复杂，在工作过程中受到各种冲击力、扭距、磨损、应力等作用，因此对曲轴的材质和加工工艺要求比较高。
子目 8486.9091	溅射靶材组件由裸靶和支撑背板两部分组成，背板与裸靶通过焊接连接为一体。裸靶原材料通常为高纯金属或金属合金，通过特殊的热机械处理和精密机械加工制造而成，背板通常带有与溅射机配合的连接孔、定位突起或卡环、卡口等结构。单金属裸靶无背板结构按原材料归类。

子目 8504.4030	逆变器是一种将直流电变成交流电的装置，它由逆变桥、控制逻辑和滤波电路组成。逆变器根据发电源的不同，分为煤电逆变器、太阳能发电逆变器、风能发电逆变器、水能发电逆变器以及柴油机发电逆变器等；根据用途不同，分为独立控制逆变器和并网逆变器；按照输出波形，分为正弦波逆变器和方波逆变器。
子目 8507.8030	全钒液流电池是一种高效电化学储能设备。由电堆单元、能量存储部分及控制部分组成。钒电解质溶液在循环泵的推动下流经电堆，实现电能的存储与释放。全钒液流电池系统因其突出的寿命长、可深度充放电、安全环保等优势，是解决太阳能、风能等可再生能源发电并网瓶颈，构建智能电网的首选储能技术之一。
子目 8512.3012	该品目包括所有机动车辆用防盗报警器,无论其是否带有视觉信号报警装置。
子目 8515.2120	本税目所指机器人是指利用电阻热进行自动焊接的工业机器人，由机器人本体、控制系统、传感器、焊钳、电阻焊机及控制器等部分组成。主要应用于汽车制造、电工电子等领域。
子目 8515.3120	本税目所指机器人是指专门用于电弧（包括等离子弧）焊接的工业机器人，由机器人本体、控制系统、传感器、焊枪、焊机、自动送丝装置等部分组成。主要应用于汽车、工程机械、摩托车、船舶、运动器材、航空、航天、锅炉等领域。
子目 8515.8010	本税目所指激光焊接机器人是指以激光器为焊接源的焊接机器人，由机器人本体、控制系统、传感器、激光头、激光系统等部分组成。主要应用于汽车、电子、冶金等行业。
子目 8516.1010	储存式电热水器是将水加热的固定式容器，它可以长期临时储存非饮用热水，并装有控制或限制水温的装置。这种热水器为配有浸入式加热元件的保温水箱，水可在其中逐渐得到加热。
子目 8516.1020	即热式电热水器又称快速热水器，指没有储存容器，可用电即时加热非饮用水的固定式容器。水流过此类热水器时即可加热。
子目 8516.2920	产品结构以发热管、辐射板、控制部分等构成。其中辐射板通常是抛物柱面的反射镜。发热管通常是卤素管或石英管等。
子目 8516.2931	风扇式加热器又称强制对流式加热器，利用风扇鼓动空气流经电热元件，再将暖风送出。通常分为离心式、轴流式、贯流式、涡轮式等型式，基本结构包括电热元件、风扇、温度控制器和外壳构成。
子目 8516.2932	充液式加热器又称充液式散热器、电热油汀，封闭的装置中充有导热油或导热液作为传热媒介，电气元件将传热媒介加热，然后把热量散发到周围的空气中。根据不同的功率大小，充液式加热器分为板式和多片式等结构。
子目 8516.6050	电烤箱(Roaster Oven)是用于烘烤鸡、肉、汉堡包等食物的厨房炊事器具（家用烤面包机除外），其结构由箱体、门、发热器（单个或上下双势）、烤盘、控制系统等组成，靠热风加热或靠电热管加热事物，根据不同容积分别设有一层或两层烤盘，按容积分为 9 升、12 升、16 升、22 升不等，功率为 600W~1200W。电烤箱与多士炉、三明治炉最大的不同是，前者是将生鲜食材经加热制成熟食，内部结构更为复杂。

子目 8516.7110	滴液式咖啡机占据了咖啡机市场的主要销售份额,主要结构由水箱、加热器、过滤器、保温盘、咖啡壶、微电脑控制部件和附件等七部分构成。其工作原理为：将咖啡粉放入过滤器内，水箱内加满水，开启咖啡机。加热器将对进入加热器内的水进行加热，并将热水从过滤器上部洒下。对过滤器内的咖啡粉进行充分浸泡，利用水的自重将咖啡粉内的咖啡精华通过过滤网滤出。滤出的咖啡液流到下部的咖啡壶内，即完成咖啡的制作。
子目 8516.7120	蒸馏渗滤式咖啡机：主要结构由水罐（含加热功能）、漏斗、微电脑控制部件和附件等四部分构成。其工作原理为：制作咖啡的水放入水罐内，加热后产生高温高压的水蒸气，利用虹吸原理将高温高压的水蒸汽通过水罐中心的水管引流到装有咖啡粉的漏斗内。让水蒸气瞬间穿过咖啡粉的细胞壁，将咖啡的内在精华萃取出来制作咖啡。
子目 8516.7130	泵压式咖啡机主要结构由水箱、水泵、加热器、漏斗、微电脑控制部件和附件等六大部分组成。水箱与水泵连接，通过微电脑控制部件控制水泵从水箱抽水至加热器，水通过加热器加热后，由于水泵提供的压力使热水流至加热器下部的压力过滤漏斗内，热水从而将压力过滤漏斗内的咖啡粉的精华过滤出来。同时通过过滤网内的小孔作用产生丰富的泡沫。
子目 8516.7210	家用自动面包机是通过微电脑控制搅面、发酵、醒面和焙烤来制作各种特色面包蛋糕的家电产品，只要将面粉，水，糖，酵母等所有配料放入面包桶后, 启动机器就能自动完成面包制作的全过程。
子目 8516.7220	多士炉主要功能是烘烤面包片、面包圈、法式面包、华夫饼、酥皮馅饼，可烤制出不同焦硬度，口感和烧色图案。有 2 片、3 片和 4 片多士炉。多士炉由炉身组件、炉胆组件、发热板组件、滑动机构组件、电子板控制组件、电磁铁组件和炉底组件构成。使用时将面包放入面包槽腔内，压下提手，滑动组件向下运动，网架将整片面包夹持归中，并沉入烘烤腔内，电子板工作，发热板开始发热，进行烘烤；电子板组件控制线圈的通断电时间，从而控制磁吸片的吸合时间，到达设定的时间后，电子板组件控制线圈断电，磁铁吸力消失，滑动组件弹起，同时发热板断电不再加热；托架将烤好的面包托至炉胆上端，方便用户取出，完成烘烤过程。
子目 8517.6237	网卡是物理上连接自动数据处理设备或其他网络设备终端与网络的一种数字式适配器。有线网卡是指网卡连接网络设备和终端设备的两个端口都是以有线形式实现的。其设备端接口常见的有 PCI 接口和 USB 接口；其网络端接口常见的有 PJ-45 接口、BNC 接口和光纤接口。
子目 8517.6292	无线网卡，通常其设备端接口以有线方式实现，常见的有 PCMCIA 接口和 USB 接口，而其网络端接口以无线方式通过天线和基站连接，常见的无线局域网使用的接入标准包括 IEEE802.11a、IEEE802.11b、IEEE802.11g 三种。无线网络接入卡的结构主要由主板（基带+射频+电源管理+外围器件+PCB 板）、射频天线、MD 结构件等组成。
子目 8517.6293	无线接入固定台是一种采用无线通信技术体制的无线终端接入设备，这种产品具备语音通信功能，有的还可具备收发短信、手机模式上网等功能。能在无线网络覆盖的范围内,将无线网络信号转化为普通固定电话模拟信号,适用于固定电话不易布线地区,可直接代替固定电话。该设备可以是一部无线固定电话机，也可以是一部无线接入系统多用户固定台。可以为多个用户提供服务并具有内部交换功能，多个用户共用若干个无线信道。该设备一般包括天馈线、电源模块、接口单元、主控单元和模块化的射频单元。对于带传真功能的产品还会有传真模块。
子目 8522.9091	车载音频转播器或发射器通常包括三个部分：一个液晶显示屏，一个控制器，一个输入输出终端。多数产品可以通过 FM 发射和汽车的收音模块相接，通过汽车或者家中的 FM 立体声接收机来收听（iPod、MP3、MP4、CD 唱机）中的音乐。有些产品还可以用音频线与汽车音箱直接相连。
子目 8529.9083	有机发光二极管显示屏是利用有机半导体发光材料将电能直接转换成光能的显示器件。电视用 OLED 显示屏还包括背板、驱动电路相关部件。

子目 8536.9011	接插件是指连接两个器件的连接器，用于传输电流或信号(光缆用连接器除外),工作电压不超过 36 伏。
子目 8539.3191	紧凑型荧光灯(又称节能灯,国外简称 CFL 灯)，具有体积小、省电、发光效率高、光线柔和等特点。紧凑型荧光灯与普通荧光灯相比，最主要的特点在于灯管的结构是紧凑型的，通常被弯成 H 形、U 形、双 n 形、螺旋形等；多数紧凑型荧光灯的灯管、电子镇流器部件和灯头部件通常是有机地结合成一体的，在不损坏其中部件的情况下一般是可拆卸的。紧凑型节能灯节能主要是通过节能灯管的节能和电子镇流器低功耗的体现。
子目 8539.3230	钠灯是利用钠蒸气放电产生可见光的电光源。钠灯又分低压钠灯和高压钠灯。低压钠灯的工作蒸气压不超过几个帕。低压钠灯的放电辐射集中在 589.0 纳米和 589.6 纳米的两条双 D 谱线上，其发光效率极高，目前已达到 200 流每瓦（lm / W），成为各种电光源中发光效率最高的节能型光源。高压钠灯的工作蒸气压大于 0.01 兆帕。高压钠灯是由半透明的多晶氧化铝（PCA）陶瓷电弧管，外泡壳，金属支架，消气剂和灯头组成。电弧管为核心元件，内充汞，钠和惰性气体。放电时，内部的钠蒸气压力为 10~100kPa。高压钠灯具有发光效率高，耗电少，寿命长，透雾强和不诱虫等特点。主要有普通型，高显色型，高光效型，低汞型，农用型等。
子目 8539.3240	汞灯是利用汞放电时产生汞蒸气获得可见光的电光源。汞灯可分为低压汞灯、高压汞灯和超高压汞灯三种。低压汞灯点燃时汞蒸气压小于一个大气压，此时汞原子主要辐射波长为 253.7nm 的紫外线。这类灯又称灭菌灯、冷阴极和热阴极灯。低压汞灯光强低，光固化速度慢，但发热量小，不需冷却就可使用，在印刷制版上用得较多。也可用作杀菌灯。高压汞灯的工作汞蒸气压为 0.2~1 兆帕。其发光效率可达 35~50 流 / 瓦(lm / W)，广泛用于环境温度为-20~40℃的街道、广场、高大建筑物、交通运输场所作为室内外照明光源。超高压汞灯的工作汞蒸气压为 1 兆帕以上。该灯从长波紫外到可见光都有很强的辐射，电弧亮度极高。超高压汞灯有短弧超高压汞灯和毛细管超高压汞灯两种。短弧超高压汞灯是辐射极强的长波紫外光和可见光的点光源。广泛用于荧光显微镜、紫外分光仪、全息照相等光学仪器，也用于集成电路光刻制版工艺。毛细管超高压汞灯主要用于照相制版和彩色显像管涂荧光屏制版工艺。
子目 8541.4010	发光二极管或电发光二极管是一种可把电能变成可见光线、红外线或紫外线的半导体器件。本品目包括有机发光二极管（OLED）和聚合物发光二极管（PLED）。有机发光二极管（OLED）的基本结构是由一层薄而透明具半导体特征的铟锡氧化物（ITO）与电力的正极相连，再加上另一个金属阴极，包成如三明治的结构。整个结构由阴极、电子输运层、发光层、空穴输运层和阳极组成。当电力供应到适当电压时，电子从阴极注入到电子输运层，同时，空穴由阳极注入到空穴输运层，它们在发光层重新结合而发光。
子目 8541.4020	太阳能电池是一种硅阻挡层光电池，可直接把太阳光变成电能。太阳能电池通常成组作为电源使用。例如，用于探索太空的火箭及人造卫星；山区呼救送话器。本税号也包括不论是否装在组件内或组装成块的太阳电池。但本税号不包括配有元件，直接为电动机、电解槽等供电的电池板及电池组件，不论所配元件如何简单（例如，用于控制电流方向的二极管）（税号 85.01）。
子目 8609.0011	保温集装箱是指安装有制冷设备，用于运输易腐食物或者货物的集装箱。
子目 8609.0012	罐式集装箱是指圆筒型罐式结构，配有支撑架使其可固定于车辆或船舶，用于运输液体、气体或其他特种货物的集装箱。
子目 9001.9010	彩色滤光片通常是作为液晶显示器的关键部件使用,液晶显示器依靠彩色滤光片实现图像的彩色。彩色滤光片是镀有 BM、R、G、B、ITO 镀层的有色玻璃。彩色滤光片的制备方法有四种,包括颜料分散法、染色法、印刷法和电沉积法（该税目不包括等离子显示器用滤光片,等离子显示器用滤光片带有电磁屏蔽夹层,不属于纯粹的光学元件,应按专用零件归类，不在该税目项下）。

子目 9003.1910	用于眼镜架的金属材料有铜合金、镍合金和贵金属三大类，要求具有一定的硬度、柔软性、弹性、耐磨性、耐腐蚀性、重量轻、有光泽和色泽好等。因此，用于制作眼镜架的金属材料几乎都是合金或在金属表面加工处理后使用。
子目 9003.1920	用于制作眼镜架的天然材料有玳瑁、特殊木材和动物头角等。一般木质眼镜架和牛角架很少见，常见的是玳瑁眼镜架。
子目 9014.2010	自动驾驶仪用于暂时替代驾驶员,保持稳定飞机以及使飞机按给定参数(高度、航向等)飞行的装置，主要由直接操作或伺服马达控制机构（通常为替代驾驶员动作的液压马达）以及调整仪表读数和伺服机构动作的自动感应装置（高速陀螺仪）构成。
子目 9018.1310	核磁共振成像成套装置由电磁体、梯度系统、频射发生器以及用于进行数据分析的自动数据处理主机、接口控制器、外部控制器、外部设备、软件等部分组成。其中外部设备包括外部存储设备、成像仪、图像处理器、测量控制系统、操作台等设备，这些设备由应用软件提供数据。软件部分包括操作系统和应用软件。该税目不包括单独进口的零部件。
子目 9021.9011	血管支架由支架和导管输送系统组成。通过导管输送器将支架输送至病变部位，植入支架以达到支撑狭窄闭塞段血管，保持管壁血流通畅的目的。血管支架主要分为冠脉支架、脑血管支架、肾动脉支架、大动脉支架等。支架通常由金属材料、覆膜材料或生物材料制成，部分支架表面涂覆治疗药物。支架按照在血管内展开的方式可分为自展式和球囊扩张式两种。
子目 9022.1920	利用 X 射线的电磁辐射检测物体内部缺陷的装置。X 射线能够使胶片感光或激发某些材料发出荧光，射线在穿透物体过程中按一定的规律衰减，利用衰减程度与射线感光或激发荧光的关系可检查物体内部的缺陷。X 射线是由 X 射线管加高压电激发而成，可以通过所加电压、电流来调节 X 射线的强度。射线穿过材料到达底片，会使底片感光；如果遇到裂缝、洞孔以及气泡和夹渣等缺陷，将会在底片上显示出暗影区来。这种方法能检测出缺陷的大小和形状，还能测定材料的厚度。
子目 9022.2910	利用 γ 射线的电磁辐射检测物体内部缺陷的装置。γ 射线是由放射性元素激发，强度不能调节，只随时间呈指数倍减少。不同厚度的物体需要用不同能量的射线来穿透。
子目 9024.1010	电子万能试验机适用于各种金属、非金属、复合材料的拉伸（δ_{su}，δ_{sl}，$\delta_{0.2}$，δ_b，E）压缩、弯曲、剪切、剥离撕裂及金属簿板塑性应变比 r 值，拉伸硬化指数 n 值等多项试验,但其主要功能是测金属材料的性能。
子目 9024.1020	硬度是衡量金属材料软硬程度的一项重要的性能指标，是材料弹性、塑性、强度和韧性等力学性能的综合指标。硬度试验根据其测试方法的不同可分为静压法（如布氏硬度、洛氏硬度、维氏硬度等）、划痕法（如莫氏硬度）、回跳法（如肖氏硬度）及里氏硬度（电磁原理，硬度值是冲击回跳速度与冲击速度之比表示）显微硬度、高温硬度等多种方法。利用上述方法测量金属材料硬度的仪器分别称为布氏硬度计、洛氏硬度计、维氏硬度计、里氏硬度计等。
子目 9026.8010	用不同原理和方法测量管道中气体的瞬时流量和累计流量的仪器及装置。
子目 9027.8012	质谱联用仪主要包括色谱质谱联用仪、光谱质谱联用仪、磁质谱联用仪等，质谱联用仪将色谱、光谱、磁场等对混合物出色的分离技术和质谱对单一物质精准的检测分析能力相结合，可以使样品的分离、定性及定量一次完成，其中质谱仪起到主要作用。
子目 9028.3011	单相感应式电度表主要用于居民用电的计量、计费。感应式电度表采用电磁感应的原理把电压、电流、相位转变为磁力矩，推动铝制圆盘转动，圆盘的轴（蜗杆）带动齿轮驱动计度器的鼓轮转动，转动的过程即是时间量累积的过程。感应式电度表有很多种类，它们的基本结构一般都由驱动元件、转动元件、制动元件、机架、轴承、计度器、铭牌、端钮盒、表盖等构成。

子目 9028.3012	三相感应式电度表是主要用于工商业等大用户的用电计量、计费。结构基本原理同上。
子目 9028.3013	电子式（静止式）电能表是采用固态（电子）器件测量电能及相关被测量的电度表。一般由锰铜分流器或电流互感器、电阻分压网络或电压互感器、电能测量芯片、机电计度器或液晶显示器、接口及电源电路等构成。由于运用数字技术，分时记费电度表、预付费电度表、多用户电度表、多功能电度表等。载波电度表利用电力载波技术，用于远程自动集中抄表，属于电子式电度表。
子目 9028.3014	三相电子式(静止式)电度表主要用于电厂、变电站、大用户及电网间的关口计量，是电力系统计量管理的关键设备，结构基本原理同上。
子目 9031.4920	光栅测量装置是利用光栅的光学原理工作的测量装置,主要由标尺光栅、光电读数头和数显表组成,通常标尺光栅固定在机床活动部件上,光栅读数头固定在机床固定部件上,指示光栅装在光栅读数头中。光栅测量装置经常应用于机床和加工中心等方面，可用作直线位移和角位移的检测。
子目 9031.8031	运用超声检测的方法来检测的仪器称之为超声波探伤仪。它的原理是：超声波在被检测材料中传播时,材料的声学特性和内部组织的变化对超声波的传播产生一定的影响，通过对超声波受影响程度和状况的探测了解材料性能和结构变化的技术称为超声检测。超声检测方法通常有穿透法、脉冲反射法、串列法等。
子目 9031.8032	磁粉探伤是检测铁磁性材料表面及近表面缺陷的一种无损检测方法，运用该方法来检测的仪器称之为磁粉探伤仪。磁粉探伤原理是:有表面和近表面缺陷的工件磁化后，当缺陷方向和磁场方向成一定角度时，由于缺陷处的磁导率的变化使磁力线逸出工件表面，产生漏磁场，可以吸附磁粉而产生磁痕显示。
子目 9031.8033	涡流检测法利用的是电磁感应原理,运用该方法来检测的仪器称之为涡流探伤仪。涡流检测法适用于检测导电材料。检测线圈通以交变电流，线圈子内交变电流的流动将在线圈子周围产生一个交变磁场，这种磁场称为“原磁场”。把一导体置于原磁场中时，在导体内将产生感应电流，这种电流叫做涡流。导体中的电特性（如电阻、磁导率等）变化时，将引起涡流的变化。利用涡流的变化检测工件中的不连续性的方法称为涡流检测原理。
子目 9032.8911	主要功能：防止列车相撞，保证列车运行的安全。工作原理：自动检测列车实际运行位置，自动确定列车最大安全运行速度，连续不断地实行速度监督，实现超速防护，自动监测列车运行间隔，以保证实现规定地行车间隔。ATP 是整个 ATC 系统的基础，ATO 和 ATS 子系统都依托于 ATP 子系统的工作。
子目 9032.8912	主要功能保证列车正常的运行和行车调整的优化。作用：代替司机来自动驾驶，包括平滑加速、调速和车站程序定点停车。ATO 辅助 ATP 工作，接受 ATP 的信息，其中有 ATP 速度指令、列车实际速度和列车走行距离。此外还从 ATS 子系统和地面标志线圈接受列车运行等级等信息。根据以上信息，ATO 通过牵引/制动线控制列车，使其维持在一个参考速度上运行，并在设有屏蔽门的站台准确停车。
子目 9307.0010	军用刀是指刺刀、多用途刀具、伞兵刀、飞行员刀等纳入军品出口管理清单的军用刀具。
子目 9506.9111	跑步机是具有单方向运动表面,在该运动面上可进行漫步或跑步,脚可以自由地离开运动表面的训练器械。一般由跑步表面、跑步板、防滑面、紧急停止装置、前把手、侧扶手、前护罩、后滚筒及护罩、脚踏平台以及显示器等组成。

附　　录

Appendix

附录一

关税配额商品税目税率表
Tariff Quota Rate on Imported Goods

序号 No.	货 品 类 别 Article Description	税则号列 Tariff Item	普通税率 General(%)	最惠国税率 M.F.N.(%)	关税配额税率 In Quota Duty Rate(%)	国别关税配额税率（中国—新西兰自贸区）Country-Specific Quota Duty Rate (China-New Zealand FTA) (%)
1	小麦 Wheat	10011100	180	65	1	
		10011900	180	65	1	
		10019100	180	65	1	
		10019900	180	65	1	
		11010000	130	65	6	
		11031100	130	65	9	
		11032010	180	65	10	
2	玉米 Corn	10051000	180	20	1	
		10059000	180	65	1	
		11022000	130	40	9	
		11031300	130	65	9	
		11042300	180	65	10	
3	稻谷和大米 Rice, whether or not husked	10061011	180	65	1	
		10061019	180	65	1	
		10061091	180	65	1	
		10061099	180	65	1	
		10062010	180	65	1	
		10062090	180	65	1	
		10063010	180	65	1	
		10063090	180	65	1	
		10064010	180	65	1	
		10064090	180	65	1	
		11029011	130	40	9	
		11029019	130	40	9	
		11031921	70	10	9	
		11031929	70	10	9	
4	糖 Sugar	17011200	125	50	15	
		17011300	125	50	15	
		17011400	125	50	15	
		17019100	125	50	15	
		17019910	125	50	15	
		17019920	125	50	15	
		17019990	125	50	15	
5	羊毛 Wool	51011100	50	38	1	0
		51011900	50	38	1	0
		51012100	50	38	1	0
		51012900	50	38	1	0
		51013000	50	38	1	0
		51031010	50	38	1	0

序号 No.	货 品 类 别 Article Description	税则号列 Tariff Item	普通税率 General(%)	最惠国税率 M.F.N.(%)	关税配额税率 In Quota Duty Rate(%)	国别关税配额税率（中国—新西兰自贸区）Country-Specific Quota Duty Rate (China-New Zealand FTA) (%)
6	毛条 Wool tops	51051000	50	38	3	0
		51052100	50	38	3	0
		51052900	50	38	3	0
7	棉花 Cotton	52010000	125	40[①]	1	
		52030000	125	40	1	
8	化肥 Chemical fertilizer	31021000	150	50	4[②]	
		31052000	150	50	4[②]	
		31053000	150	50	4[②]	

[①]对配额外进口的一定数量棉花，适用滑准税形式暂定关税，具体方式如下：

(1) 当进口棉花完税价格高于或等于 15.000 元/千克时，按 0.570 元/千克计征从量税；

(2) 当进口棉花完税价格低于 15.000 元/千克时，暂定从价税率按下式计算：

$$Ri=9.337/Pi+2.77\%\times Pi-1$$

对上式计算结果四舍五入保留 3 位小数。其中 Ri 为暂定从价税率，当按上式计算值高于 40%时，Ri 取值 40%；Pi 为关税完税价格，单位为元/千克。

[②]暂定税率为 1%。

进口商品暂定税率表
Interim Duty Rate on Imported Goods

序号 No	EX	税则号列 Tariff Item	货品名称	最惠国税率(%) M.F.N.	暂定税率(%) Interim Duty Rate	Article Description
1		01061211	改良种用鲸、海豚和鼠海豚；改良种用海牛及儒艮	10	0	Whales, dolphins and porpoises, for pure-bred breading manatees and dugongs, for pure-bred breeding
2	ex	01064190	赤眼蜂	10	0	Live trichogramma
3	ex	01064990	捕食螨	10	0	Live predatory mite
4		03033110	冻格陵兰庸鲽鱼	10	5	Frozen Greenland halibut
5		03033200	冻鲽鱼，但鱼肝及鱼卵除外	12	2	Frozen plaice, excluding livers and roes
6		03035100	冻鲱鱼，但鱼肝及鱼卵除外	10	2	Frozen herrings, excluding livers and roes
7		03036300	冻鳕鱼，但鱼肝及鱼卵除外	10	2	Frozen cod, excluding livers and roes
8		04041000	乳清及改性乳清	6	2	Whey and modified whey
9		05051000	填充用羽毛;羽绒	10	5	Raw feathers for stuffing; down
10		05119111	受精鱼卵	12	0	Fertilized fish eggs
11		08013100	鲜或干的未去壳腰果	20	10	Walnuts in shell
12		08021100	鲜或干的未去壳巴旦杏	24	10	Almonds in shell, fresh or dried
13		08024190	鲜或干的未去壳栗子(板栗除外)	25	20	Other chestnuts in shell, fresh or dried
14		08024290	鲜或干的去壳栗子(板栗除外)	25	20	Other chestnuts, shelled, fresh or dried
15		08025100	鲜或干的未去壳阿月浑子果(开心果)	10	5	Pistachios in shell, fresh or dried
16		08025200	鲜或干的去壳阿月浑子果(开心果)	10	5	Pistachios, shelled, fresh or dried
17		08029020	鲜或干的白果	25	20	Gingko nuts, fresh or dried
18		12119036	甘草	6	0	Liquorice roots
19		12122190	其他适合供人食用的海草及藻类	15	2	Other edible seaweeds and algae
20		12122900	其他海草及藻类	15	2	Other seaweeds and algae
21	ex	12149000	其他紫苜蓿（粗粉及团粒除外）	9	7	Other lucerne (alfalfa), excluding meal and pcllcts
22	ex	12149000	以除紫苜蓿外的禾本科和豆科为主的多种混合天然饲草	9	4	Mixed non-artificial forage grass majorly composed of poaceae and fabaceae other than lucerne
23		13021200	甘草汁液及浸膏	6	0	Saps and extracts of liquorice
24	ex	13021990	苦参碱	20	3	Matrine
25		15021000	牛羊油脂	8	4	Tallow
26		15029000	其他牛羊脂肪	8	4	Other fats of bovine animals, sheep or goats
27	ex	15119020	固态棕榈硬脂（50 度≤熔点≤56 度）	8	2	Solid palm stearin (melting point no less than 50 centigrade and no more than 56 centigrade)

序号 No	EX	税则号列 Tariff Item	货品名称	最惠国税率(%) M.F.N.	暂定税率(%) Interim Duty Rate	Article Description
28		15200000	粗甘油；甘油水及甘油碱液	20	6	Glycerol, crude; glycerol waters and glycerol lyes
29		18010000	整颗或破碎的可可豆，生的或焙炒的	8	2	Cocoa beans, whole or broken, raw or roasted
30		19011010	供婴幼儿食用的零售包装配方奶粉	15	5	Formula milk powder for infant use, put up for retail sale
31		19011090	其他供婴幼儿食用的零售包装食品	15	5	Other preparations for infant use, put up for retail sale
32		19019000	麦精以及细粉、粗粉、粗粒、淀粉或麦精制的其他未列名食品	10	5	Other food preparations of flour, etc.
33		21031000	酱油	28	15	Soya sauce
34	ex	21069090	乳蛋白部分水解配方、乳蛋白深度水解配方、氨基酸配方、无乳糖配方特殊婴幼儿奶粉	20	5	Partial hydrolyzed,extensively hydrolyzed milk protein, amino acid based, and lactose-free inftant formula milk powder
35		22072000	任何浓度的改性乙醇及其他酒精	30	5	Ethyl alcohol & other denatured spirits of any strength
36		22090000	醋及醋酸制得的醋代用品	20	15	Vinegar and substitutes for vinegar obtained from acetic acid
37		23099090	其他配制的动物饲料	6.5	4	Other preparations of a kind used in animal feeding
38	ex	24039100	再造烟草	57	40	Reconstituted tobacco
39		25020000	未焙烧的黄铁矿	3	1	Unroasted iron pyrites
40		25030000	硫磺	3	1	Sulphur
41		25041010	鳞片石墨	3	1	Natural graphite in flakes
42		25051000	硅砂及石英砂，不论是否着色	3	1	Silica sands & quartz sands, whether or not coloured
43		25059000	其他天然砂，不论是否着色	3	1	Natural sands, whether or not coloured
44		25061000	石英	3	1	Quartz
45		25062000	石英岩，不论是否切割成矩形板、块	3	1	Quartzite, wether or not by sawing into blocks or slabs of a rectangular shape
46		25070010	高岭土	3	1	Kaolin
47		25070090	高岭土的类似土	3	1	Other kaolinic clays
48		25083000	耐火粘土,不论是否煅烧	3	1	Fire-clay, whether or not calcined
49		25101010	未碾磨的磷灰石	3	0	Unground apatites
50		25102010	已碾磨的磷灰石	3	0	Ground apatites
51		25111000	天然硫酸钡（重晶石）	3	1	Natural barium sulphate (barytes)
52		25151100	原状或粗加修正的大理石	4	0	Marble & travertine crude or roughly trimmed
53		25151200	矩形大理石及石灰华	4	0	Marble & travertine merely cut into a square or rectangular shape
54		25152000	其他石灰质碑用或建筑用石；蜡石，不论是否粗加修整或切割成矩形板块	3	0	Ecaussine and other calcarcous monumental or building stone; alabaster, whether or not roughly trimmed or cut into blocks or slabs of a rectangular (incl. square) shape
55		25161100	原状或粗加修正的花岗石	4	0	Granite, crude or roughly trimmed
56		25161200	矩形或正方形的花岗岩	4	0	Granite, merely cut into blocks or slabs of a rectangular (incl. square) shape
57		25162000	原状或粗加修正的砂岩	3	0	Sandstone, crude or roughly trimmed

序号 No	EX	税则号列 Tariff Item	货品名称	最惠国税率(%) M.F.N.	暂定税率(%) Interim Duty Rate	Article Description
58		25169000	其他碑用或建筑用石	3	0	Other monumental or building stones
59		25181000	未煅烧或烧结的白云石	3	1	Dolomite, not calcined or sintered
60		25182000	已煅烧或烧结的白云石	3	1	Dolomite, calcined or sintered
61		25183000	夯混白云石	3	1	Dolomite ramming mix
62		25191000	天然碳酸镁（菱镁矿）	3	1	Natural magnesium carbonate (magnesite)
63		25199010	熔凝镁氧矿（电熔镁，包括喷补料）	3	1	Fused magnesia
64		25199020	烧结镁氧矿（重烧镁，包括喷补料）	3	1	Dead-burned (sintered) magnesia
65		25199030	碱烧镁（轻烧镁）	3	1	Light-burned magnesia
66	ex	25199099	其他氧化镁含量在70%（含70%）以上的矿产品	3	1	Other mineral substances,containing MgO 70% or more
67		25251000	原状云母或破开的云母片	5	1	Crude mica and mica rifted into sheets or splittings
68		25261020	未破碎及未研粉的滑石	3	1	Talc, not crushed, not powdered
69		25262020	已破碎或已研粉的其他天然滑石	3	1	Talc, powdered
70		25280010	天然硼砂及其精矿	3	0	Natural sodium borates and concentrates thereof (calcined or not)
71		25280090	天然粗硼酸,含硼酸干重不超过85%	5	0	Natural sodium borates and concentrates thereof (calcined or not)
72		25291000	长石	3	1	Felspar
73	ex	25309099	天青石	3	1	Celesite
74	ex	25309099	锂辉石矿	3	0	Spodumene
75	ex	25309099	废镁砖	3	1	Waste magnesia brick
76	ex	25309099	未煅烧的水镁石	3	1	Brucite
77	ex	26180010	冶炼钢铁产生的锰渣，含锰量大于25%	4	1	Granulated slag from the manufacture of iron or steel,containing manganese more than 25%
78	ex	26190000	冶炼钢铁产生的熔渣、浮渣、氧化皮及其他废料，五氧化二钒含量大于20%	4	1	Slag, dross scalings and other from manufacture of iron or steel, containing V_2O_5>20%
79	ex	26209990	含其他金属及化合物的矿灰及残渣，五氧化二钒含量大于20%	4	1	Ash and residues containing V_2O_5>20%
80		27011100	未制成型的无烟煤，不论是否粉化	3	0	Anthracite, not agglomerated, whether or not pulverized
81		27011210	炼焦煤	3	0	Bituminous coking coal, not agglomerated, whether or not pulverized
82		27011290	其他烟煤	6	0	Other bituminous coal,other than coking coal,not agglomerated,whether or not pulverized
83		27011900	未制成型的其他煤，不论是否粉化	5	0	Coal nes, not agglomerated, whether or not pulverized
84		27012000	煤砖、煤球及类似用煤制固体燃料	5	0	Briquettes, ovoids & similar solid fuels manufactured from coal
85		27040010	煤制焦炭及半焦炭不论是否成型	5	0	Lignite
86		27040090	甑炭	5	0	Agglomerated lignite
87		27050000	煤气、水煤气、炉煤气及类似气体，石油气及其他烃类气除外	5	1	Coke & semi-coke, whether or not agglomerated

序号 No	EX	税则号列 Tariff Item	货 品 名 称	最惠国税率 (%) M.F.N.	暂定税率(%) Interim Duty Rate	Article Description
88		27060000	从煤、褐煤、或泥煤蒸馏所得的焦油及矿物焦油，不论是否脱水或部分蒸馏，包括再造焦油	6	1	Retort carbon
89		27073000	粗二甲苯	6	2	Coal, water, producer gas & similar gases, other than petroleum gases & gaseous hydrocarbons
90		27075000	其他芳烃混合物	7	3	Tar distilled from coal, lignite or peat & other mineral tars, whether or not dehydrated or partially distilled, incl. reconstituted tars
91	ex	27082000	针状沥青焦	6	3	Xylole
92		27101210	车用汽油及航空汽油	5	1	Other aromatic hydrocarbon mixtures
93		27101220	石脑油	6	0	Needle Pitch coke
94	ex	27101291	壬烯(碳九混合异构体含量高于90%)	9	4	Motor gasoline & aviation gasoline
95	ex	27101299	异戊烯同分异构体混合物	9	5	ISOpentene
96		27101911	航空煤油	9	0	Aviation kerosene
97	ex	27101919	正构烷烃(C9～C13)	6	2	n-Alkanes (C9～C13)
98		27101922	5～7 号燃料油	6	1	Fuel oil No.5 to No.7 (National Code)
99		27101923	柴油	6	1	Diesel oil
100	ex	27101929	350 度以下馏出物体积百分比小于 20%，550 度以下馏出物体积百分比大于 80%的蜡油	6	0	Paraffin oils: 350°C distillage<20%, 550°C distillage>80%
101		27111200	液化丙烷	5	1	Propane, liquefied
102		27111390	其他液化丁烷	5	1	Liquefied butanes, nes
103		27149010	天然沥青	8	4	Natural bitumen and asphalt
104		28013020	溴	5.5	1	Bromine
105		28020000	升华硫磺、沉淀硫磺、胶态硫磺	5.5	1	Sulphur, sublimed or precipitated; colloidal sulphur
106	ex	28045000	碲	5.5	0	Polysilicon
107	ex	28046190	多晶硅(纯度高于 99.9999999%)	4	1	Polycrystalline silicon (containing Si >99.9999999%)
108		28049090	其他硒	5.5	0	Selenium nes
109		28051100	钠	5.5	1	Sodium
110		28051200	钙	5.5	1	Calcium
111		28051900	其他碱金属及碱土金属	5.5	1	Alkali or alkaline-earth metals (excl. sodium and calcium)
112		28053011	钕	5.5	0	Neodymium
113		28053012	镝	5.5	0	Dysprosium
114		28053013	铽	5.5	0	Terbium
115		28053014	镧	5.5	0	Lanthanum
116		28053015	铈	5.5	0	Cerium
117		28053016	镨	5.5	0	Praseodymium
118		28053017	钇	5.5	0	Yttrium
119		28053019	其他未相互混合或熔合的稀土金属、钪及钇	5.5	0	Rare-earth metals nes, scandium and yttrium, not intermixed or interalloyed
120		28053021	已相互混合或熔合的稀土金属、钪及钇，电池级	5.5	0	Rare-earth metals, scandium and yttrium, intermixed or interalloyed, battery quality

序号 No	EX	税则号列 Tariff Item	货品名称	最惠国税率 (%) M.F.N.	暂定税率(%) Interim Duty Rate	Article Description
121		28053029	其他已相互混合或熔合的稀土金属、钪及钇	5.5	0	Rare-earth metals, scandium and yttrium, intermixed or interalloyed, other than battery quality
122		28070000	硫酸、发烟硫酸	5.5	1	Sulphuric acid; oleum
123		28121010	氯化亚砜	5.5	2	Sulphoxide chloride
124		28141000	氨	5.5	0	Anhydrous ammonia
125		28142000	氨水	5.5	0	Ammonia in aqueous solution
126		28164000	锶或钡的氧化物、氢氧化物及过氧化物	5.5	2	Oxide, hydroxide and peroxide of strontium or of barium
127		28182000	氧化铝，但人造刚玉除外	8	0	Aluminium oxide, other than artificial corundum
128		28220010	四氧化三钴	5.5	2	Cobalt tetroxide
129		28220090	其他钴的氧化物和氢氧化物	5.5	2	Other Cobalt oxides and hydroxides
130		28254000	镍的氧化物和氢氧化物	5.5	2	Nickel oxides and hydroxides
131		28342110	肥料用硝酸钾	4	1	Nitrates of potassium, use as fertilizer
132	ex	28342990	硝酸钡	5.5	2	Barium nitrate
133		28366000	碳酸钡	5.5	1	Barium carbonate
134		28369100	锂的碳酸盐	5.5	2	Lithium curbonates
135		28369200	锶的碳酸盐	5.5	2	Strontium carbonate
136		28369930	碳酸钴	5.5	2	Cobaltous carbonate
137	ex	28399000	锆的硅酸盐	5.5	2	Ziconium silicate
138		28401100	无水四硼酸钠	5.5	2	Anhydrous disodium tetraborate
139		28401900	其他四硼酸钠	5.5	2	Disodium tetraborate,other than anhydrous
140	ex	28419000	钴酸锂	5.5	2	Lithium cobaltate
141		28461010	氧化铈	5.5	0	Cerium oxide
142		28461020	氢氧化铈	5.5	0	Cerium hydroxide
143		28461030	碳酸铈	5.5	0	Cerium carbonate
144		28461090	铈的其他化合物	5.5	0	Cerium compounds, nes
145		28469011	氧化钇	5.5	0	Yttrium oxide
146		28469012	氧化镧	5.5	0	Lanthanum oxide
147		28469013	氧化钕	5.5	0	Neodymium oxide
148		28469014	氧化铕	5.5	0	Europium oxide
149		28469015	氧化镝	5.5	0	Dysprosium oxide
150		28469016	氧化铽	5.5	0	Terbium oxide
151		28469017	氧化镨	5.5	0	Praseodymium oxide
152		28469019	其他氧化稀土	5.5	0	Other Rare-earth oxides
153		28469021	氯化铽	5.5	0	Other Rare-earth chlorinates,mixed
154		28469022	氯化镝	5.5	0	Terbium chlorinates
155		28469023	氯化镧	5.5	0	Dysprosium chlorinates
156		28469024	氯化钕	5.5	0	Neodymium chlorinates
157		28469025	氯化镨	5.5	0	Praseodymium chlorinates
158		28469026	氯化钇	5.5	0	Yttrium chlorinates
159		28469028	混合氯化稀土	5.5	0	Rare-earth chlorinates other than of cerium, mixed
160		28469029	未混合氯化稀土	5.5	0	Other Rare-earth chlorinates, unmixed
161		28469031	氟化铽	5.5	0	Other Rare-earth fluorides
162		28469032	氟化镝	5.5	0	Dysprosium fluorides
163		28469033	氟化镧	5.5	0	Lanthanum fluorides
164		28469034	氟化钕	5.5	0	Neodymium fluorides

序号 No	EX	税则号列 Tariff Item	货 品 名 称	最惠国税率 (%) M.F.N.	暂定税率(%) Interim Duty Rate	Article Description
165		28469035	氟化镨	5.5	0	Praseodymium fluorides
166		28469036	氟化钇	5.5	0	Yttrium fluorides
167		28469039	其他氟化稀土	5.5	0	Rare-earth fluorides,nes
168		28469041	碳酸镧	5.5	0	Lanthanum carbonates
169		28469042	碳酸铽	5.5	0	Terbium carbonates
170		28469043	碳酸镝	5.5	0	Dysprosium carbonates
171		28469044	碳酸钕	5.5	0	Neodymium carbonates
172		28469045	碳酸镨	5.5	0	Praseodymium carbonates
173		28469046	碳酸钇	5.5	0	Yttrium carbonates
174		28469048	混合碳酸稀土	5.5	0	Rare-earth carbonates other than of cerium, mixed
175		28469049	未混合碳酸稀土	5.5	0	Rare-earth carbonates other than of cerium, unmixed
176		28469091	镧的其他化合物	5.5	0	Compounds of Lanthanum
177		28469092	钕的其他化合物	5.5	0	Compounds of Neodymium
178		28469093	铽的其他化合物	5.5	0	Compounds of Terbium
179		28469094	镝的其他化合物	5.5	0	Compounds of Dysprosium
180		28469095	镨的其他化合物	5.5	0	Compounds of Praseodymium
181		28469096	钇的其他化合物	5.5	0	Compounds of Yttrium
182		28469099	稀土金属、钇、钪的其他化合物	5.5	0	Other compounds of rare-earth, yttrium or scandium
183		29012200	丙烯	2	1	Propene (propylene)
184		29031500	1,2-二氯乙烷(ISO)	5.5	1	1,2-Dichloroethane (ISO) (ethylene dichloride)
185		29032100	氯乙烯	5.5	1	chloroethylene
186		29051210	正丙醇	5.5	3	Propan-l-ol(propyl alcohol)
187		29053200	1，2－丙二醇	5.5	3	1,2-dihydroxypropare
188	ex	29053990	1，3－丙二醇	5.5	3	1,3-dihydroxypropare
189		29054500	丙三醇（甘油）	14	3	Glycerol
190		29061310	固醇	5.5	3	Sterols, and their halogenated, sulphonated, nitrated or nitrosated derivatives
191		29071211	间甲酚	5.5	3	m-Cresols
192		29071212	邻甲酚	5.5	3	o-Cresols
193		29071910	邻仲丁基酚、邻异丙基酚	4	2	o-Sec-butyl phenol,o-Isopropyl phenol
194		29094100	二甘醇	5.5	3	2,2-Oxydiethanol (diethylene glycol,digol)
195	ex	29121900	乙二醛	5.5	3	Glyoxal(Ethanedial)
196		29155010	丙酸	5.5	3	Propionic acid
197	ex	29209090	碳酸二苯酯	6.5	2	Diphenyl carbonate
198		29211920	异丙胺	6.5	2	Isopropyl amine
199		29224210	谷氨酸	10	5	Glutamic acid
200		29261000	丙烯腈	6.5	3	Acrylonitrile
201	ex	29269090	己二腈	6.5	1	Hexanedinitrile
202	ex	29309090	DL－羟基蛋氨酸	6.5	5	DL-hydroxy-methionine
203		30021000	抗血清、其他血份及修饰免疫制品(不论是否通过生物工艺加工制得)	3	0	Antisera & other blood fractions & modified immunological products, whether or not obtained by means of biotechnological processes
204		30022000	人用疫苗	3	0	Vaccines for human medicine

序号 No	EX	税则号列 Tariff Item	货 品 名 称	最惠国税率 (%) M.F.N.	暂定税率(%) Interim Duty Rate	Article Description
205		30029040	遗传物质和基因修饰生物体	3	0	Genetics material and Gene modified organism
206		30029090	人血；治病、防病或诊断用动物血制品；其他毒素、培养微生物（不包括酵母）及类似产品	3	0	Human blood; animal blood prepared for therapeutic, prophylactic or diagnostic uses; other toxins, cultures of micro-organisms (excl. yeasts) and similar products, nes
207		31031010	重过磷酸钙	4	1	Triple superphosphates
208		31031090	其他过磷酸钙	4	1	Other superphosphates
209		31039000	其他矿物磷肥或化学磷肥	4	1	Mineral or chemical fertilizers, phosphatic, nes
210		31042090	其他氯化钾	3	1	Potassium chloride, nes
211		31043000	硫酸钾	3	1	Potassium sulphate
212		31049010	光卤石、钾盐及其他天然粗钾盐	3	1	Carnallite, sylvite & other crude natural potassium salts
213		31049090	其他矿物钾肥及化学钾肥	3	1	Mineral or chemical fertilizers, potassic, nes
214		31051000	制成片状及类似形状或每包毛重不超过 10 公斤的 31 章各货品	4	1	Goods of chapter 31 in tables or similar forms or in packages of a gross weight≤10kg
215		31054000	磷酸二氢铵及磷酸二氢铵与磷酸氢二铵的混合物	4	1	Ammonium dihydrogenorthophosphate (monoammonium phosphate) and mixtures thereof with diammonium hydrogenorthophosphate (diammonium phosphate)
216		31055100	含有硝酸盐及磷酸盐的肥料	4	1	Mineral or chemical fertilizers containing nitrates & phosphates
217		31055900	其他含氮、磷两种肥效元素的矿物肥料或化学肥料	4	1	Mineral or chemical fertilizers containing the two fertilizing elements nitrogen & phosphorus, nes
218		31056000	含磷、钾两种元素的肥料	4	1	Mineral or chemical fertilizers with phosphorus & potassium, nes
219		31059000	其他肥料	4	1	Mineral or chemical fertilizers, nes
220	ex	32082010	分散于或溶于非水介质的光导纤维用涂料（主要成分为聚胺酯丙烯酸酯类化合物）	10	6	Paint for optial fibers (based on polyaminate acrylate resin polymers), dispersed or dissolved in a nonaqueous medium
221	ex	32089010	光导纤维用涂料（主要成分为聚胺酯丙烯酸酯类化合物）	10	6	Paint for optial fibers (based on polyaminate acrylate resin polymers)
222	ex	32100000	光导纤维用涂料	10	6	Paint for optial fibers
223		33012500	其他薄荷油	15	5	Other oils of mints (incl. concretes & absolutes), nes
224	ex	33012999	黄樟油	15	7	Sassafras oil
225		33013010	鸢尾凝脂（香膏类）	20	10	Balsam of irises
226		33043000	指(趾)甲化妆品	15	10	Manicure or pedicure preparations
227	ex	33049900	护肤品	6.5	5	Skin care products
228		33052000	烫发剂	15	10	Preparations for permanent waving or straightening
229		33053000	定型剂	15	10	Hair lacquers

序号 No	EX	税则号列 Tariff Item	货 品 名 称	最惠国税率 (%) M.F.N.	暂定税率(%) Interim Duty Rate	Article Description
230		34011990	其他用肥皂及有机表面活性产品，条、块状或模制形状的，以及用肥皂或洗涤剂浸渍、涂面或包覆的纸、絮胎、毡呢及无纺织物	15	10	Other soap and organic surface-active products & preparations for use as soap,in bars, cakes , moulded pieces or shapes; paper, wadding , felt & nonwovens, impregnated ,coated or covered with soap or detergent
231		34012000	其他形状的肥皂	15	10	Soap in other forms
232	ex	34029000	十二烷基苯磺酸钙甲醇溶液(十二烷基苯磺酸钙含量应高于70%)	9	7	Calcium dodecyl benzosulfonate methanol solution (Calcium dodecyl benzosulfonate content>70%)
233		34031100	用于纺织、皮革、毛皮或其他材料油脂处理的制剂	10	8	Preparations for the oil or grease treatment of textile, materials , leathers , furskins or other materials
234		34031900	其他含有石油或从沥青矿物提取的油类	10	8	Lubricating preparations, containing petroleum oils or oils obtained from bituminous minerals
235		34039100	处理纺织材料、皮革、毛皮或其他材料的制剂	10	8	Preparations for the oil or grease treatment of textiles, materials, leathers, furskins or other materials
236	ex	35030010	明胶	12	5	Gelatin
237		35051000	糊精及其他改性淀粉	12	6	Dextrins & other modified starches
238		37011000	X 光片	20	10	Photographic plates & film for X-ray, in the flat, sensitized, unexposed, of any material other than paper, paperboard or textiles
239	ex	37019920	石英玻璃基质的未曝光感光硬片	10	5	Photographic plates and film, unexposed, quartz based
240	ex	37024292	红色或红外激光胶片，宽度>80cm，长度大于 1000m	16	1.05 元/平方米	Red or infra-red laser film width>80cm, length>1000m
241		37025520	未曝光的窄长彩色电影胶卷(正片)	26	6 元/平方米	Unexposed polychrome cinematographicture film in rolls
242	ex	37071000	感光乳剂（不含银的）	8	4	Sensitizing emulsions(without silver component)
243		37079020	复印机用化学制剂	10	8	Chemical preparations, unmixed products for photographic uses , for photo-copying machines
244		38011000	人造石墨	6.5	3	Artificial graphite
245		38151200	以贵金属及其化合物为活性物的载体催化剂	6.5	4	Supported catalysts with precious metal or its compounds as the active substances
246		38231200	油酸	16	8	Industrial oleic acid
247	ex	38231900	植物酸性油	16	5	Botanic acid oil
248		38237000	工业用脂肪醇	13	9	Aliphatic alcohols for Industrial uses
249	ex	38249099	高钛渣（二氧化钛质量百分含量大于 70%的）	6.5	0	The Ag electrode paste, dieletric paste, barrier ribs paste phosphor paste used for the plasma display panel production
250	ex	38249099	按重量计氧化锌含量在 50%及以上的混合物	6.5	3	Mixture containing ZnO 50% or more
251	ex	39011000	比重小于 0.94 的聚乙烯（进口 CIF 价高于 3800 美元/吨）	6.5	3	Polyethylene, gravity<0.94, (import CIF≥3800usd/t)

序号 No	EX	税则号列 Tariff Item	货 品 名 称	最惠国税率 (%) M.F.N.	暂定税率(%) Interim Duty Rate	Article Description
252	ex	39012000	比重在 0.94 及以上的聚乙烯(进口 CIF 价高于 3800 美元/吨)	6.5	3	Polyethylene, gravity≥0.94, (import CIF ≥3800usd/t)
253	ex	39021000	电工级初级形状聚丙烯树脂(灰分含量不大于 30ppm)	6.5	3	Electrotechonical polypropylene resin in primary forms (Ash content not more than 30ppm)
254	ex	39069090	聚丙烯酸钠	6.5	3	Sodium polyacrylate
255		39072010	聚四亚甲基醚二醇	6.5	3	Polvtetramethylene Ether Glycol
256	ex	39073000	溴的质量百分含量在 18%及以上或进口 CIF 价格高于 3800 美元/吨的环氧树脂（如溶于溶剂，以纯环氧树脂折算溴的百分含量）	6.5	4	Epoxyresins containing by weight more than 18% Bromine or import CIF>3800usd/t (base on pure epoxyresins if dissolved in solvent)
257		39074000	初级形状的聚碳酸酯	6.5	3	Polycarbonates, in primary forms
258		39077000	初级形状的聚乳酸	6.5	3	Poly (lactic acid)
259	ex	39119000	偏苯三酸酐和异氰酸预缩聚物	6.5	3	Precondensed polymer of modified trihydroxy acetate
260	ex	39119000	芳基酸与芳基胺预缩聚物	6.5	3	Precondensed polymer of modified trihydroxy acetate
261	ex	39119000	改性三羟乙基脲酸酯类预缩聚物	6.5	3	Precondensed polymer of modified trihydroxy acetate
262		39201010	乙烯聚合物制电池隔膜	6.5	3	Battery separator, of polymers of ethylene
263	ex	39209100	聚乙烯醇缩丁醛膜（厚度不超过 3 毫米）	6.5	3	Polyvinyl butyral membrane (Thickness≤3mm)
264	ex	39209990	聚酰亚胺膜（厚度不超过 0.03 毫米）	6.5	3	Membrane of polyimide(thickness ≤ 0.03mm)
265	ex	39219090	离子交换膜	6.5	5	Ion exchange membrane
266		40011000	天然胶乳	20	10%或 720 元/吨，两者从低	Natural rubber latex
267		40012100	烟胶片	20	20%或 1200 元/吨，两者从低	Smoked sheets of natural rubber
268		40012200	技术分类天然橡胶	20	20%或 1200 元/吨，两者从低	Technically specified natural rubber, in primary forms or in plates, sheets or strip
269	ex	40112000	断面宽度 30 英寸及以上的轮胎	10	3	Tyres, having a fracture surface of a width of 30 inches or more
270	ex	40116100	断面宽度 24 英寸及以上的轮胎	17.5	6	Tyres,having a fracture surface of a width of 24 inches or more
271	ex	40116300	断面宽度 24 英寸及以上的轮胎	17.5	8	Tyres,having a fracture surface of a width of 24 inches or more
272	ex	40116900	断面宽度 30 英寸及以上的轮胎	17.5	6	Tyres, having a fracture surface of a width of 30 inches or more
273	ex	40119200	断面宽度 24 英寸及以上的轮胎	25	6	Tyres,having a fracture surface of a width of 24 inches or more
274	ex	40119400	断面宽度 24 英寸及以上的轮胎	25	8	Tyres,having a fracture surface of a width of 24 inches or more
275	ex	40119900	断面宽度 30 英寸及以上的轮胎	25	5	Tyres, having a fracture surface of a width of 30 inches or more
276		40121300	航空器用翻新轮胎	20	8	Retreaded tyres of rubber, of a kind used on aircraft

序号 No	EX	税则号列 Tariff Item	货 品 名 称	最惠国税率 (%) M.F.N.	暂定税率(%) Interim Duty Rate	Article Description
277		40129010	航空用实心或半实心橡胶轮胎	3	1	Aircraft solid or cushion rubber tyres
278		40139010	航空用橡胶内胎	3	1	Aircraft rubber inner tubes
279	ex	40169500	液压隔离式蓄能器用胶囊	18	9	Hydraulic pressure-insulation type accumulator bladder
280	ex	40169910	奶衬	8	4	Liner
281	ex	40169990	动车组用胶囊、外风挡板	10	5	Locomotive fording intercar barrier, gangway bellows
282		41041111	全粒面未剖层或粒面剖层蓝湿牛皮	7	3	Chrome-tanned bovine leather (wet blue skin leather), full grain, unsplit, or grain splits, not further prepared
283		41041911	其他蓝湿牛皮	6	3	Wet blue bovine leather, not further prepared, nes
284		41041920	其他湿马皮	7	5	Equine leather, wet state, not further prepared, nes
285		41044100	全粒面未剖层革 粒面剖层革的牛干革（坯革）	5	3	Bovine or equine leather, without hair on, dry state (crust), full grains, unsplit, or grain splits, not further prepared
286		41051010	蓝湿绵羊、羔羊皮	14	10	Wet-blue sheep or lamb skin leather, without wool on, but not further prepared, whether or not split
287	ex	41062100	蓝湿山羊皮	14	10	Goat skin leather, in the wet-blue state, without hair on, but not further prepared, whether or not split
288		41063110	蓝湿猪皮	14	10	Wet-blue swine leather, without hair on, but not further prepared, whether or not split
289		41071210	已鞣粒面剖层整张牛皮革	8	6	Leather further prepared after tanning or crusting, including parchment-dressed leather, of bovine (including buffalo) animals, without hair on, other than leather of heading 41.14, whole hides and skins, grain splits
290		43011000	整张水貂皮，不论是否带头、尾、爪	15	10	Raw furskins of mink, whole, with or without head, tail or paws
291		43016000	整张狐皮，不论是否带头、尾、爪	20	15	Raw furskins of fox, whole, with or without head, tail or paws
292		44089012	温带非针叶木制饰面用单板	3	1	Wood nes veneer sheets, whether or not planed, sanded or finger-jointed, of a thickness not exceeding 6mm, of temperate non-coniferous wood
293	ex	44089019	家具饰面单板	3	1	Veneer sheets for furniture
294	ex	44089029	胶合板用旋切单板	3	1	Peeled sheets for plywood
295		45011000	未经加工或简单加工的天然软木	6	1	Natural cork, raw or simply prepared
296		48022010	照相原纸	7.5	5	Photo paper base
297		48064000	高光泽透明或半透明纸	7.5	5	Glassine and other glazed transparent or translucent papers

序号 No	EX	税则号列 Tariff Item	货 品 名 称	最惠国税率 (%) M.F.N.	暂定税率(%) Interim Duty Rate	Article Description
298		48070000	成卷或成张的复合纸及纸板，未经表面涂布或未浸渍	7.5	5	Composite paper and paperboard (made by sticking flat layers of paper or paperboard together with an adhesive), not surface-coated or impregnated, whether or not internally reinforced, in rolls or sheets
299		48115110	彩色相纸用双面涂塑纸，每平方米重量超过 150 克	7.5	1	Paper coated on both sides with plastics (excl. adhesives) for color photography, bleached, weighing＞150g/m^2, in rolls or sheets
300	ex	49070090	特许权使用凭证（包括软件升级许可证、软件用户许可证等。但游戏软件升级许可证、游戏软件用户许可证除外。）	7.5	0	Certificate of Franchise license inculding software upgrade license、software user license, etc.excl.game software upgrade license、software user license
301	ex	49119910	印有自动数据处理设备用程序的纸张	7.5	0	Paper printed with process for automatic data handling devices
302		52101100	与化纤混纺未漂白轻质平纹棉布	12	6	Unbleached plain cotton weave, mixed mainly or solely with man-made fibres, with less than 85% by weight of cotton, weighting ≤200g/m^2
303		52101910	化纤混纺未漂白轻质 3、4 线斜纹棉布	12	6	Unbleached woven fabrics, 3-thread or 4-thread twill, including cross twill, mixed mainly or solely with man-made fibres, with less than 85% by weight of cotton, weighting ≤200g/m^2
304		52101990	与化纤混纺未漂白轻质其他棉布	12	6	Other unbleached fabrics of cotton, mixed mainly or solely with man-made fibres, with less than 85% by weight of cotton, weighting ≤200g/m^2
305		52111100	与化纤混纺未漂白重质平纹棉布	12	6	Unbleached plain cotton weave, mixed mainly or solely with man-made fibres, with less than 85% by weight of cotton, weighting ＞200g/m^2
306		52111200	化纤混纺未漂白重质三线或四线斜纹棉布	12	6	Unbleached woven fabrics, 3-thread or 4-thread twill, including cross twill, mixed mainly or solely with man-made fibres, with less than 85% by weight of cotton, weighting ＞200g/m^2
307		52111900	与化纤混纺未漂白重质其他棉布	12	6	Other unbleached fabrics of cotton, mixed mainly or solely with man-made fibres, with less than 85% by weight of cotton, weighting ＞200g/m^2
308		52121100	未漂白的其他混纺轻质棉布	12	6	Other unbleached woven fabrics of cotton, weighting ≤200g/m^2
309		52122100	未漂白的其他混纺重质棉布	12	6	Other unbleached woven fabrics of cotton, weighting ＞200g/m^2
310		53012100	破开的麻或打成的麻	6	1	Broken or scutched flax
311		53013000	亚麻短纤及废麻	6	1	Flax tow and waste (incl. yarn waste & garnetted stock)

序号 No	EX	税则号列 Tariff Item	货 品 名 称	最惠国税率 (%) M.F.N.	暂定税率(%) Interim Duty Rate	Article Description
312		53062000	亚麻多股纱线或缆线	10	5	Multiple (folded) or cabled flax yarn
313	ex	55041029	高湿模量粘胶纤维（湿强≥2.0cn/dtex,干强≥3.0cn/dtex,干伸＞14%，湿伸＞18%，纤度0.89~2.67dtex。）	5	2	High wet modulus rayon fiber (wet strength ≥2.0cn/dtex,dry strength≥3.0cn/dtex,dry elongation ＞ 14% , wet elongation ＞ 18%,titre :0.89~2.67dtex.)
314	ex	56013000	由两种或两种以上有机聚合物纺制的纤维（横截面为皮芯结构或并列结构或海岛结构），长度不超过 5 毫米	10	5	of two or more kinds of polymers(with cross section of skin-core or juxtapose or island structure), length not more than 5mm
315	ex	68061090	矿物纤维，渣球含量小于 5%	10.5	5	Mineral fiber, of a shot content less than5%
316	ex	68071000	聚脂-铜复合胎基改性沥青根阻防水卷材	12	1	Root resistant and waterproof modified bitumen membrane with composite carrier of copper and polyester
317	ex	68159939	碳纤维纱线（碳元素含量大于 90%）	17.5	15	Carbon fibre yarn (containg more than 90% Carbon)
318		69049000	陶瓷制铺地砖、支撑或填充用砖	24.5	15	Ceramic flooring blocks, support or filler tiles & the like
319		69051000	陶瓷制屋顶瓦	24.5	15	Roofing tiles, ceramic
320		69059000	其他建筑用陶瓷制品	24.5	15	Chimney-pots, cowls, chimney liners etc & oth ceramic constructnl goods
321		69060000	陶瓷套管、导管、槽管及管子配件	15	10	Ceramic pipes, conduits, guttering & pipe fittings
322		69071000	未上釉的小陶瓷砖、瓦、块及类似品	24.5	12	Tiles, cubes & sim<7 cm rect or not etc, unglazed ceramics
323		69079000	未上釉的大陶瓷砖、瓦、块及类似品	12	8	Tiles, cubes & sim nes, unglazed ceramics
324		69099000	农业用、运输或盛装货物用陶瓷容器	21	15	Ceramic troughs, tubes etc used in agriculture, ceramic pots etc
325		69111011	骨瓷餐具	12	8	Bone porcelain tableware
326		69111019	其他瓷餐具	12	8	Other tableware of porcelain or china
327		69111021	陶瓷刀具	15	10	Knife of porcelain or china
328		69111029	其他瓷厨房器具	15	10	Other kitchenware of porcelain or china
329		69120010	陶餐具	15	10	Ceramic tableware
330		69120090	陶制厨房器具	15	10	Ceramic kitchenware and other household or toilet articles nes
331		70023110	光导纤维用波导级石英玻璃管	5	1	Tubes of fused quartz, of waveguide-level, for optical fibre use
332	ex	70023900	光通信用微光组件的玻璃毛细管、定位管（外径小于 3mm）	12	3	Micro capillary and galass tube for optical communication (out diameter < 3 mm)
333	ex	70031900	液晶或有机发光二极管（OLED）显示屏用原板玻璃，包括保护屏用含碱玻璃	17.5	3	Bare glass for liquid crystal or organic light emitting diode display,inculding the protective glass containing alkali
334	ex	70049000	光学平板玻璃，厚度 0.7 毫米以下	17.5	9	Optical flat glass, of a thickness less than 0.7mm
335	ex	70052900	液晶或有机发光二极管（OLED）显示屏用原板玻璃，包括保护屏用含碱玻璃	15	3	Float glass, for liquid crystal or organic light emitting diode display,inculding the protective glass containing alkali

序号 No	EX	税则号列 Tariff Item	货品名称	最惠国税率(%) M.F.N.	暂定税率(%) Interim Duty Rate	Article Description
336	ex	70060000	液晶玻璃基板, 6 代（1850mm×1500mm）以上, 不含 6 代	15	4	Glass parts for liquid crystal display, above the 6 generation (1850mm×1500mm)
337	ex	70060000	液晶玻璃基板, 6 代（1850mm×1500mm）及以下	15	6	Glass parts for liquid crystal display,the 6 generation (1850mm×1500mm) and below
338	ex	70071110	空载重量 25 吨及以上飞机的挡风玻璃	2	1	Windshield for airplane unloaden weight ≥25t
339	ex	70071900	低铁钢化太阳能电池组件封装专用玻璃（最大含铁量 0.02% Fe_2O_3，玻璃厚度 2.5mm~3.5mm）	14	12	Ferrless toughen glass for solar energy battery rncapsulation (Max Fe 0.02% Fe_2O_3, thinkness of glass:2.5～3.5mm)
340	ex	70099100	槽式太阳能抛物面反射镜	21	10	Parabolic trough in Solar Energy Generating Systems (SEGS)
341	ex	70112090	显示管玻壳及其零件	10	6	Glass envelopes and parts thereof for display tubes
342		70132200	铅晶质高脚杯	24.5	15	Stemware drinking glasses of lead crystal
343		70133300	其他铅晶质玻璃杯	24.5	15	Other drinking glasses, of lead crystal, other than of glass-ceramics
344		70134100	铅晶质玻璃制餐桌、厨房用器皿	24.5	15	Glassware of a kind used for table kitchen, etc, of lead crystal
345	ex	70140090	带有抗红外和防反射薄膜的滤波玻璃	17.5	9	Wave-filter galss with anti-IR and anti-reflection film
346		70151010	视力矫正眼镜用变色镜片坯件	21	15	Glasses for corrective photochromic spectacles, not optically worked
347		70151090	其他视力矫正眼镜用镜片坯件	17.5	10	Other glasses for corrective spectacles, not optically worked
348		70159020	平光变色镜片坯件	18	10	Glasses for non-corrective photochromic spectacles, not opticll worked
349	ex	70182000	熔融球形二氧化硅微粉，直径小于等于 100um	20	5.5	Fused spherical SiO_2, diameter not exceeding 100 micron
350		70189000	玻璃假眼；灯工方法制的玻璃塑像及玻璃饰品	20	10	Glass eyes, statuetts and oth ornaments of lamp-workd glass
351	ex	70195200	覆铜板用玻璃纤维长丝平纹布，开纤或每平方米重不超过 180 克	12	10	Glass fiber colth, covered with copper foil, open filament fabric or weighting less than or equal to 180g/m^2
352		70200011	导电玻璃	10.5	7	Conductive glass
353	ex	70200019	等离子模块生产用高应变点玻璃(应变点在 550 摄氏度及以上)	10.5	5	High strain point glass used for PDP model production (strain point≥550℃)
354	ex	70200099	石英玻璃，平整度小于等于 1 微米	15	4	Quartz glass, of a flatness less than or equal to 1 μ m
355		71011011	天然黑珍珠	21	0	Tahitian pearls
356		71011091	天然黑珍珠	21	0	Tahitian pearls
357	ex	71012110	养殖黑珍珠	21	0	Cultured tahitian pearls
358	ex	71012190	养殖黑珍珠	21	0	Cultured tahitian pearls
359	ex	71012210	养殖黑珍珠	21	0	Cultured tahitian pearls
360	ex	71012290	养殖黑珍珠	21	0	Cultured tahitian pearls
361	ex	71049012	蓝宝石衬底（由人造刚玉加工而成，厚度小于 0.5 毫米）	6	1	Sapphire substrate (made of synthetic corundum, with thickness less than 0.5mm)
362	ex	71129220	铂含量在 3%以上的其他含铂或铂化合物的废碎料	6	0	Waste and scrap with plutinum containing by weight more than 3% plutinum

序号 No	EX	税则号列 Tariff Item	货 品 名 称	最惠国税率 (%) M.F.N.	暂定税率(%) Interim Duty Rate	Article Description
363		71159010	工业或试验室用贵或包金属制品	3	0	Other articles of precious metal, for technical or lab use
364		72024100	铬铁，含碳量>4%	2	1	Ferro-chromium containing by weight more than 4% of carbon
365		72024900	铬铁，含碳量≤4%	2	1	Ferro-chromium, nes
366		72026000	镍铁	2	1	Ferro-nickel
367		72027000	钼铁	2	1	Ferro-molybdenum
368		72028010	钨铁	2	1	Ferro-tungsten
369		72029100	钛铁及硅钛铁	2	1	Ferro-titanium and Ferro-silico-titanium
370		72029300	铌铁	2	1	Ferro-niobium
371	ex	72031000	热压铁块	2	0	Hot Briguetted Iron (HBI)
372		72041000	铸铁废碎料	2	0	Waste and scrap, cast iron
373		72043000	镀锡钢铁废碎料	2	0	Waste and scrap, of tinned iron or steel
374		72044100	机械加工中产生的钢铁废料	2	0	Ferrous waste and scrap, of iron or steel, from the mechanical working of metal, nes
375	ex	72269990	铁镍合金带材（生产集成电路框架用），宽度小于 600 毫米	7	4	Fe-Ni alloy strip (production of the frame for electronic integrated circuits), of a width less than 600mm
376		73239100	餐桌、厨房等家用铸铁制器具	20	10	Table, kitchen and other household articles and parts thereof, of cast iron, not enamelled
377		73239200	餐桌、厨房等家用铸铁制搪瓷器	20	10	Table, kitchen and other household articles and parts, of cast iron, enamelled
378		73239410	钢铁制搪瓷面盆	20	10	Basin of iron or steel, enamelled
379		73239420	钢铁制搪瓷烧锅	20	10	Casserole of iron or steel, enamelled
380		73241000	不锈钢制洗涤槽及脸盆	18	10	Sinks and wash basins, stainless steel
381		73242900	其他钢铁制浴缸	30	15	Other iron baths
382		73249000	其他钢铁制卫生器具及零件	25	15	Sanitary ware & parts thereof, of iron or steel nes, for example bedpans, douche cans
383	ex	74010000	铜锍	2	0	Copper mattes
384		74020000	未精炼铜、电解精炼用铜阳极	2	0	Unrefined copper, copper anodes for electrolytic refining
385		74031111	精炼铜阴极，按重量计铜含量超过 99.9935%的	2	0	Unrefined copper cathodes containing by weight more than 99.9935% of copper
386		74031119	其他精炼铜阴极	2	0	Other unrefined copper cathodes
387		74031190	精炼铜阴极型材	2	0	Unrefined copper sections of cathodes
388		74031200	精炼铜线锭	2	0	Unrefined copper wire-bars
389		74031300	精炼铜坯段	2	0	Unrefined copper billets
390		74031900	其他未锻轧精炼铜	2	0	Other unrefined copper
391		74040000	铜废碎料	1.5	0	Copper waste and scrap
392	ex	74081900	其他含氧量小于 5PPM 的精炼铜丝	4	2	Other refined copper wire, containing oxygen not more than 5PPM
393	ex	74101100	覆铜板及印刷线路板用铜箔，厚度≤0.15 毫米	4	3	Foil of refined Cu, not backed, for printed circuits
394	ex	74111019	其他含氧量小于 5PPM，外径不超过 25 毫米的精炼铜管	4	2	Other refined copper tubes and pipes with the external diameter not exceeding 25mm, containing oxygen not more than 5PPM
395		74181090	餐桌厨房等家用铜制器具及其零件	18	10	Table kitchen or other household articles and parts thereof, of copper

序号 No	EX	税则号列 Tariff Item	货 品 名 称	最惠国税率 (%) M.F.N.	暂定税率(%) Interim Duty Rate	Article Description
396		74182000	铜制卫生器具及其零件	18	10	Sanitary ware & parts thereof of Cu
397		75011000	镍锍	3	0	Nickel matte
398		75012010	镍湿法冶炼中间品	3	0	Nickel intermediate products obtained by hydrometallurgical processing
399		75012090	其他冶炼镍时所得的中间品	3	0	Ni oxide sinters & other intermediate products of Ni metallurgy
400		75021010	按重量计镍、钴总量在 99.99%及以上的，但钴含量不超过0.005%的非合金镍	3	1	Nickel, contain more than 99.99% Nickel and Cobalt, and Cobalt less than 0.005% by weight
401		75021090	其他非合金镍	3	1	Other unwrought nickel
402		75030000	镍废碎料	1.5	1	Nickel waste and scrap
403		76011090	电解铝	5	0	Al unwrought, not alloyed, nes
404		76020000	铝废碎料	1.5	0	Aluminium waste and scrap
405		76061129	厚度在0.3毫米及以上,但不超过0.36 毫米的其他非合金铝制矩形板、片、带	6	4	Aluminium plates, of a thickness of 0.3mm or more but not exceeding 0.36mm
406	ex	76071900	化成箔	6	3	Formed Al foil
407		76151090	餐桌厨房等家用铝制器具及其零件	15	10	Table kitchen or other household articles and parts thereof, of aluminium
408		79011110	按重量计含锌量在99.995%及以上的未锻轧锌	3	1	Unerought zinc, not alloyed, containing by weight 99.995% or more of zinc
409		79011190	含锌量不小于 99.99%，并小于99.995%的未锻轧锌	3	1	Unerought zinc, not alloyed, containing by weight 99.99% or more and less than 99.995% of zinc
410		79011200	含锌量＜99.99%的未锻轧锌	3	1	Unerought zinc, not alloyed, containing by weight less than 99.99% of zinc
411		79012000	未锻轧锌合金	3	1	Unwrought zinc alloys
412		79020000	锌废碎料	1.5	1	Zinc waste and scrap
413		81019700	钨废碎料	3	1	Tungsten waste and scrap
414		81033000	钽废碎料	6	0	Tantalum waste and scrap
415		81052010	钴湿法冶炼中间品	4	0	Cobalt intermediate products obtained by hydrometallurgical processing
416	ex	81052090	钴锍及其他冶炼钴时所得的中间产品	4	0	Cobalt mattes and other inter-mediate products of cobalt metallurgy
417	ex	81060010	未锻轧铋	3	1	Unwrought bismuth
418		81089031	厚度≤0.8 毫米钛板、片、带、箔	8	4	Titanium plates, sheets, strip, foil, of a thickness not more than 0.8mm
419		81089032	厚度＞0.8 毫米钛板、片、带、箔	8	4	Titanium plates, sheets, strip, foil, of a thickness more than 0.8mm
420		81101010	未锻轧锑	3	1	Unwrought antimony
421	ex	81129220	未锻轧、废碎料或粉末状的钒氮合金	3	0	Vanadic-nitrogen; unwroght, waste and scrape, powder
422		81129240	未锻轧铌；铌废碎料；铌粉末	3	1	Niobium; unwrought, waste and scrap, powders
423	ex	81129920	其他钒氮合金	3	0	Other vanadic-nitrogen
424	ex	82073000	加工小轿车车身冲压件用的4种关键模具（侧围外板模具、翼子板模具、拼接整体侧围内板模具、拼焊整体侧围加强板模具）	8	4	Four key dies, used for processing stamping parts of car body (side outer panels dies , fender dies, dies for joining the whole side inner panels, dies for joining and welding the whole side-panel reinforcement)

序号 No	EX	税则号列 Tariff Item	货品名称	最惠国税率(%) M.F.N.	暂定税率(%) Interim Duty Rate	Article Description
425	ex	82073000	加工小轿车车身冲压件用的4种特种模具（σb≥980N/mm^{2}的冷冲压模具、热成型模具、内高压成型模具和铝板模具）	8	4	Four special dies, used for processing stamping parts of car body (cold stamping dies with σb≥980N/mm^2, hot forming dies, inside high pressure forming dies and aluminium panel dies)
426		82111000	以刀为主的成套货品	18	10	Sets of assorted knives
427		82119100	刃面固定的餐刀	18	10	Table knives having fixed blades
428		82119300	可换刃面刀	18	10	Knives having other than fixed blades
429		82159900	其他非成套的厨房或餐桌用具	18	10	Other kitchen or tableware articles not in sets (not plated with precious metal)
430		84071010	输出功率不超过298千瓦的点燃往复式或旋转式活塞内燃发动机（航空器发动机）	2	1	Spark-ignition reci-procating or rotary internal combustion piston engines for Aircraft,of an output not exceeding 298kW
431		84071020	输出功率超过298千瓦的点燃往复式或旋转式活塞内燃发动机（航空器发动机）	2	1	Spark-ignition reci-procating or rotary internal combustion piston engines for Aircraft,of an output exceeding 298kW
432	ex	84079090	立式输出轴汽油发动机	18	9	Petrol engines with a vertical crankshaft
433	ex	84082010	输出功率在441千瓦(600马力)及以上的柴油发动机	9	4	Diesel engines with an output power of 441 kW (600HP) or more
434	ex	84082090	升功率≥40千瓦的轿车用柴油发动机	25	10	Diesel engines for cars, power density ≥ 40 kW
435	ex	84099999	电控柴油喷射装置	8.4	5	Electronic diesel oil injection devices
436	ex	84118100	涡轮轴航空发动机	15	1	Turbo shaft engines for aircraft
437	ex	84119910	涡轮轴航空发动机用零件	5	0	Parts of turbo shaft engines for aircraft
438	ex	84122990	抓桩器（抱桩器）	14	7	Skirt Pile Grippers Assembly
439	ex	84123100	三坐标测量机用平衡气缸	14	7	Cylinder balance for coordinate measuring machine of three dimensions
440		84131100	分装燃料或润滑油的泵	10	6	Pumps for dispersing fuel or lubricants used in fillng-stations or in garage
441		84131900	其他装有或可装计量装置的泵	10	6	Pumps fitted or designed to be fitted with a measuring device
442		84135010	气动式往复式排液泵	10	6	Pneumatic reciprocating positive displacement pumps
443		84135020	电动式往复式排液泵	10	6	Electric reciprocating positive displacement pumps
444		84135031	液压式往复式柱塞泵	10	6	Plunger pump
445		84135039	液压式往复式排液泵	10	6	Hydraulic reciprocating positive displacement pumps
446		84135090	其他往复式排液泵	10	6	Other reciprocating positive displacement pumps
447		84136021	电动式齿轮回转泵	10	6	Electric gear rotary pump
448	ex	84136022	回转式液压油泵,输入转速＞2000r/min,输入功率＞190kw,最大流量＞2×280 L/min	10	3	Rotating hydraulic oil pump,input rotating speed＞2000r/min, input power＞190kw, maximum flow＞2×280 L/min
449	ex	84136022	其他液压式齿轮回转泵	10	6	Other hydraulic gear rotating pump
450		84136029	其他齿轮回转泵	10	6	Other gear rotary pump
451		84136031	电动式叶片回转泵	10	6	Electric vane rotary pump
452		84136032	液压式叶片回转泵	10	6	Hydraulic vane rotary pump
453		84136039	其他叶片回转泵	10	6	Other vane rotary pump

序号 No	EX	税则号列 Tariff Item	货 品 名 称	最惠国税率 (%) M.F.N.	暂定税率(%) Interim Duty Rate	Article Description
454		84136040	螺杆回转泵	10	6	Screw rotary pump
455		84136050	径向柱塞泵	10	6	Radial plunger pump
456		84136060	轴向柱塞泵	10	6	Axial plunger pump
457		84136090	其他回转式排液泵	10	6	Other rotary positive displacement pumps
458		84137091	电动潜油泵及潜水电泵	10	8	Submersible oil pump and submersible pump
459		84139200	液体提升机用零件	6	4	Parts of liquid elevators
460		84141000	真空泵	8	5	Vacuum pumps
461	ex	84143011	功率≤0.4kW 的冷藏、冷冻箱用无级变速压缩机	8	3	Stepless speed regulation compressors for refrige/freezer,motor power≤0.4kW
462	ex	84143013	0.4kW＜功率≤5kW 的空气调节器用无级变速压缩机	10	3	Stepless speed regulation compressors for airconditioner, 0.4kW <motor power≤5kW
463	ex	84143013	0.4kW＜功率≤5kW 的空气调节器用定速压缩机	10	6	Fixed speed compressors for airconditioner, 0.4kW <motor power≤5kW
464	ex	84143014	功率＞5kW 的空气调节器用无级变速压缩机	10	3	Stepless speed regulation compressors for airconditioner, motor power>5 kW
465	ex	84143014	功率＞5kW 的空气调节器用定速压缩机	10	6	Fixed speed compressors for airconditioner, motor power>5 kW
466	ex	84143015	冷冻或冷藏设备用，电动机额定功率＞5kW 的电动机驱动的无级变速压缩机	10	4	Stepless speed regulation compressors driven by a motor, for refrigerators or freezes, of a motor power exceeding 5kW
467	ex	84143015	冷冻或冷藏设备用，电动机额定功率＞5kW 的电动机驱动定速压缩机	10	6	Fixed speed compressors driven by a motor, for refrigerators or freezes, of a motor power exceeding 5kW
468	ex	84143019	其他制冷设备用无级变速压缩机	10	4	Other stepless speed regulation compressors driven by a motor
469	ex	84143019	其他制冷设备用定速压缩机	10	6	Other fixed speed compressors driven by a motor
470		84146010	抽油烟机	10	6	Range hoods
471	ex	84148030	乘用车机械增压器	7	5	Mechanical superchargers for Passenger cars
472		84149011	用于制冷设备的压缩机进、排气阀片	8	5	Air inlet on discharge valve plates for compressoors for refrigerating equipment
473		84149019	其他用于制冷设备的压缩机零件	8	5	Other parts of compressors for refrigerating equipment
474		84149020	风机、风扇、通风罩及循环气罩零件	12	6	Parts of machines of ventilators, fan,ventilating or recycling hoods
475		84149090	税号 84.14 其他所列机器零件	7	4	Parts of of machines of other subheadings of 84.14
476		84152000	机动车辆上供人使用的空气调节器	20	10	Air conditioning machines used for persons in motor vehicles
477		84158120	制冷量＞4 千大卡/时热泵式空调器	20	12	Air-conditioner, with refrigerating unit of a refrigerating effect>4000 Kcal/h and a valve for reversal of cooling/heat cycle
478		84158220	制冷量＞4 千大卡/时的其他空调器	20	12	Other air-conditioner, with refrigerating unit of a refrigerating effect>4000 Kcal/h
479		84159010	制冷量≤4 千大卡/时等空调的零件	10	6	Parts of air conditners with rerefrigerating unit of a refrigerating effect≤4000 Kcal/h

序号 No	EX	税则号列 Tariff Item	货品名称	最惠国税率 (%) M.F.N.	暂定税率(%) Interim Duty Rate	Article Description
480		84159090	制冷量＞4 千大卡/时等空调的零件	10	6	Parts of air conditioners with refrigerating unit of a refrigerating effect>4000 Kcal/h
481	ex	84162011	溴化锂空调用天然气燃烧机	10.5	5	Natural gas burners for lithium bromide air conditioners
482	ex	84162090	溴化锂空调用复式燃烧机	10.5	5	Combination burners for lithium bromide air conditioners
483		84189910	制冷机组及热泵用零件	10	6	Parts of refrigerating units and heat pumps
484		84189991	制冷温度≤-40℃冷冻设备零件	9.5	6	Parts of freezing equipment of refrigeration temperature≤-40℃
485		84189992	制冷温度＞-40℃，容积＞500L 冷藏设备零件	10	6	Parts of refrigerating or freezing equip of refrigeration temperature > -40℃, capacity >500L
486		84189999	税号 84.18 其他制冷设备用零件	10	6	Parts of other refrigerating or freezing equipment of subheading 84.18
487	ex	84193990	生产奶粉用干燥器	9	4	Dryers for producing powdered milk
488	ex	84193990	污泥涡轮干燥机	9	4	Sludge turbo dryer
489		84198100	加工热饮料、烹调、加热食品的机器	10	6	Machinery for making hot drinks of for cooking or heating food, non domestic
490	ex	84201000	织物轧光机	8.4	6	Woven fabrics calender
491		84211910	脱水机	10	6	Dehydrators
492		84212110	家用型过滤或净化水的机器及装置	25	12	Filtering or purifying machines for water, household type
493	ex	84212199	船舶压载水处理设备用过滤器	5	2	Filters for ship ballast water treatment apparatus
494	ex	84212199	喷灌设备用叠式净水过滤器	5	0	Stackable, filtering or purifying machines for irrigation equipment
495		84213910	家用型气体过滤、净化机器及装置	15	8	Filtering or purifying machines for gases , household type
496	ex	84213930	摩托车发动机排气过滤及净化装置	5	3	Filtering or purifying machines for motorcycle engine
497		84219910	家用型过滤、净化装置用零件	10	6	Filtering or purifying machines for water, household type
498		84221100	家用型洗碟机	10	6	Dish washing machines of the home type
499	ex	84223010	乳品加工用自动化灌装设备	12	6	Automatic bottling or canning equipment for producing dairy
500	ex	84223030	全自动无菌灌装生产线用包装机,加工速度≥20000 只/小时	10	6	Packing machines of automatic aseptic filling producion line, processing output ≥20000 package/hour
501	ex	84223090	全自动无菌灌装生产线用贴吸管机,加工速度≥22000 只/小时	10	6	Straw applicators of automatic aseptic filling prodution line, processing output ≥22000 package/hour
502		84229010	洗碟机用零件	10.5	6	Parts of dish washing machines
503	ex	84281010	无障碍升降机	8	4	Lift facilities for the disabled
504		84312090	叉车及装有升降或搬运装置的工作车用其他零件	6	3	Parts suitable for Fork-lift trucks; other works trucks fitted with lifting or handling equip-ment.
505	ex	84313100	无障碍升降机的零件	3	1	Parts, for Lift facilities for the disabled
506	ex	84335100	功率≥160 马力的联合收割机	8	5	Combine harvester-threshers, power not less than 160H.P

序号 No	EX	税则号列 Tariff Item	货品名称	最惠国税率(%) M.F.N.	暂定税率(%) Interim Duty Rate	Article Description
507	ex	84335300	功率≥160 马力的土豆、甜菜收获机	8	4	Potato or sugar beet harvestors , power no less than 160 HP
508	ex	84335910	功率≥160 马力的甘蔗收获机	8	4	Sugarcane harvestors, power no less than 160 HP
509		84335920	棉花采摘机	8	5	Cotton pickers
510	ex	84335990	茶叶采摘机	8	4	Tea pickers
511	ex	84335990	自走式青储饲料收获机	8	5	Mobile silage harvesters
512		84342000	乳品加工机器	6	2	Dairy machinery
513	ex	84368000	自走式饲料搅拌投喂车	10	5	Self waking type feed mixing and feeding vehicles
514	ex	84368000	青储饲料切割上料机	10	3	Feeder of silage harvesters
515	ex	84419010	切纸机用弧形辊	8	4	Curved metal spreader roll of cutting machines
516	ex	84419010	切纸机用横切刀单元	8	3	Crosscut knife units of cutting machines
517		84423021	计算机直接制版设备(CTP)	9	5	Computer-to-plate equipments (CTP)
518	ex	84424000	计算机直接制版机器用零件	7	0	Parts of computer-to-plate equipments
519	ex	84431313	四色平张纸胶印机，对开单张纸单面印刷速度≥17000 张/小时；对开单张纸双面印刷速度≥13000 张/小时；全张或超全张单张纸单面印刷速度≥13000 张/小时	10	7	Four-color sheet-fed offset press,Folio size,maximum out-put of single-sided printing≥17000 iph；Folio size,maximum out-put of perfect(double-sided) printing ≥13000 iph；Full size or super large format, maximum out-put of single-sided printing≥13000 iph
520	ex	84431319	五色及以上平张纸胶印机，对开单张纸单面印刷速度≥17000 张/小时；对开单张纸双面印刷速度≥13000 张/小时；全张或超全张单张纸单面印刷速度≥13000 张/小时	10	7	Five-color and more sheet-fed offset printing machines,Folio size,maximum out-put of single-sided printing≥17000 iph；Folio size,maximum out-put of perfect (double-sided) printing≥13000 iph；Full size or super large format, maximum out-put of single-sided printing≥13000 iph
521	ex	84431600	苯胺印刷机（柔性版印刷机），线速度≥350 米/分钟，幅宽≥800 毫米	10	3	Flexographic printing machines,press line speed≥350m/min, web width≥800mm
522	ex	84431600	具有烫印或全息或丝网印刷功能单元的机组式柔性版印刷机，线速度≥160 米/分钟，250 毫米≤幅宽<800 毫米	10	5	Multi-functional narrow-wcb flcxographic printing machine with module of stamping or holographic or screen printing，line speed≥160m/min,250mm≤web width<800mm
523	ex	84431700	凹版印刷机,印刷速度≥350 米/分钟	18	9	Gravure printing machinery, printing speed ≥350m/min
524	ex	84431921	纺织用圆网印花机	10	6	Cylinder screen woven fabric printing range
525	ex	84431922	纺织用平网印花机	10	6	Flate screen woven fabric printing range
526		84433110	静电感光式多功能一体机	10	3	Electrostatic photo type multifunctional machines

序号 No	EX	税则号列 Tariff Item	货 品 名 称	最惠国税率(%) M.F.N.	暂定税率(%) Interim Duty Rate	Article Description
527	ex	84433221	幅宽>60cm 的喷墨印刷设备,可与网络或自动数据处理设备连接	8	3	Ink-jet printing machines, with breadth of printing>60cm, capable of connecting to an automatic data processing machine or to a network
528	ex	84433221	297mm<幅宽≤360mm 的喷墨印刷设备,可与网络或自动数据处理设备连接	8	5	Ink-jet printing machines, 297mm< breadth of printing≤360mm, capable of connecting to an automatic data processing machine or to a network
529	ex	84433222	幅宽≥32.9cm 的静电照相印刷设备（激光印刷机）,可与网络或自动数据处理设备连接	8	3	Electrostatic photographic printing machines (laser printing machines), with breadth of printing≥32.9cm, capable of connecting to an automatic data processing machine or to a network
530	ex	84439111	卷筒料自动给料机，给料线速度≥12 米/秒	12	4	Automatic splicer of web offset press, splicing speed ≥12m/s
531		84439119	其他传统印刷机用辅助机器	12	6	Other general accessory machines
532	ex	84439190	胶印机用墨量遥控装置（包括墨色控制装置、墨量调节装置、墨斗体等组成部分）	6	0	Ink remote control unit for offset printing machinery (including ink coclor control unit and ink adjust device and inking pot)
533	ex	84439190	传统印刷机用零件及附件(胶印机用墨量遥控装置除外)	6	3	Parts and accessories of printing machinery (with the exception of ink remote control unit)
534	ex	84439929	压电式喷墨头	6	3	Piezoelectric inkjet print head
535	ex	84451190	宽幅非织造布梳理机,工作幅宽＞3.5 米，工作速度＞120 米/分钟	10	6	Nonwoven carding machines,working width＞3.5m, working speed＞120m/min
536	ex	84452031	全自动转杯纺纱机	10	5	Automatic rotor spinning machines
537		84454010	自动络筒机	10	6	Automatic bobbin winders
538		84463050	喷气织机	8	0	Air jet looms
539	ex	84481100	多臂机或提花机转速指标：500 转/分以上	8	4	Dobbies or Jacquards, rotational speed >500r/min
540		84483920	电子清纱器	6	3	Electronic yarn cleaner
541		84483930	空气捻接器	6	3	Air twisting devices
542		84483940	环锭细纱机紧密纺装置	6	0	Compact set of ring spinning frames
543		84483990	税号 84.45 所列机器用的其他零附件	6	3	Other parts or accessories of machines of 84.45 or of their auxiliary machinery
544		84484920	引纬、送经装置	6	3	Catching and throwing shuttle boxes
545		84484990	织机及其辅助机器用其他零附件	6	3	Other parts and accessories of weaving mches or of their auxiliary machinery
546		84485900	税号 84.47 机器用的其他零附件	6	3	Other parts and accessories of machns of 84.47 or of their auxiliary machinery
547	ex	84490010	高速针刺机，针刺频率＞2000 次/分钟	8	6	High speed needle punching machine, punching frequecny＞2000bis/min
548	ex	84490020	高速宽幅水刺设备，工作幅宽＞3.5 米，工作速度＞250 米/分钟，水刺压力≥400 帕	8	6	High speed width spunlace equipment, working width＞3.5m, workding speed＞250m/min,spunlace pressure≥400Pa
549		84509090	干衣量＞10kg 的洗衣机零件	16	5	Parts of washing machines, dry linen capacity>10kg
550	ex	84518000	柔软整理机	12	10	Supple finishing machine

序号 No	EX	税则号列 Tariff Item	货品名称	最惠国税率 (%) M.F.N.	暂定税率(%) Interim Duty Rate	Article Description
551	ex	84518000	磨毛机、丝光机	12	10	Napping grinder, mercerizing range
552	ex	84518000	定型机	12	10	Boarding machine
553	ex	84518000	涂层机	12	8	Coating machine
554	ex	84518000	罐蒸机、精炼机	12	10	Potting steamer, refining machine
555	ex	84518000	剪绒、洗缩联合机	12	10	Pile shearing and shrinking combine
556	ex	84518000	预缩机	12	10	Sanforizer
557	ex	84518000	服装液氨整理机	12	10	Dress aqua ammoniae finishing range
558	ex	84518000	服装定型焙烘炉	12	10	Dress shaping cabinet
559	ex	84518000	剪毛联合机	12	10	Sheepshearing combination machine
560		84689000	焊接机器用零件	7	3	Welding machinery parts
561		84734010	自动柜员机出钞器	10.5	1	Banknote dispenser of automated teller
562	ex	84734090	钞票清分机零附件	10.5	3	Parts of banknote processing system
563		84789000	烟草加工及制作机器的零件	10	5	Parts of machinery for preparing or making up tobacco
564		84794000	绳或缆的制造机器	7	5	Rope or cable-making machines
565	ex	84811000	喷灌设备用减压阀	5	2	Pressure reducing valves for sprinkler equipment
566		84813000	止回阀	5	3	Valves, check
567		84818040	其他阀门	7	3	Other valves
568		84819010	阀门用零件	8	4	Parts of valves
569		84823000	鼓形滚子轴承	8	6	Bearings, spherical roller
570		84824000	滚针轴承	8	6	Bearings, needle roller
571	ex	84825000	三环偏心滚动轴承	8	4	Eccentric 3-ring roller bearing
572		84829100	滚珠、滚针及滚柱	8	6	Balls, needles and rollers for bearings
573		84829900	滚动轴承的其他零件	6	3	Other parts of bearings
574		84833000	未装滚珠或滚子轴承的轴承座；滑动轴承	6	3	Bearing housings,not incorporating ball or roller bearing;plain shaft bearing
575	ex	84834020	磨煤机用行星齿轮减速器(由螺旋伞齿轮加行星齿轮二级立式减速机构组成，转盘外圆直径为：1300~2400毫米)	8	2	Planetary decelerators for use with coal mill,（composed of helical bevel gear and planetary gear two-stage vertical reducing mechanism, rotary table outline diameter: 1300mm～2400mm）
576	ex	84836000	压力机用组合式湿式离合/制动器,离合扭距为60KNM~300KNM,制动扭距为30KNM~100KNM	8	4	Hydraulic actuated clutch/brake, for press machinery, 60KNM ≤ clutch torque ≤ 300KNM, 30KNM ≤ braking torque ≤ 100KNM
577		84841000	金属片密封垫或类似接合衬垫	8	5	Gaskets of metal sheeting combined with other material
578		84842000	机械密封件	8	5	Mechnical seals
579		84849000	其他材料制密封垫及类似接合衬垫	8	5	Gasket sets consisting of gaskets of different materials
580		84863041	制造平板显示器用超声波清洗装置	10	5	Cleaning apparatus opparatus operated by ultrasonic process, for the manufacture of flat panel displays
581	ex	84864022	全自动铝丝焊接机	8	6	Automatic aluminum wire bonders
582	ex	85011091	激光视盘机机芯精密微型电机（1瓦≤功率≤18瓦，20mm≤直径≤30mm）	9	5	Minitype precise motor for mechanism of laser disc player(1W ≤ power ≤ 18W, 20mm≤diameter≤30mm)

序号 No	EX	税则号列 Tariff Item	货品名称	最惠国税率(%) M.F.N.	暂定税率(%) Interim Duty Rate	Article Description
583	ex	85011091	摄像机、摄录一体机用精密微型电机(0.5 瓦≤功率≤10 瓦，20mm≤直径≤39mm)	9	5	Minitype precise motor for mechanism of video cameras or camera recorders(0.5W≤power≤10W, 20mm≤diameter≤39mm)
584	ex	85011099	功率不大于 0.5 瓦(圆柱型:直径不大于6毫米,高不大于25毫米;扁圆型:直径不大于15毫米,厚不大于 5 毫米)非用于激光视盘机机芯的微型电机	9	5	Micromotors with a cylindrical housing diameter not exceeding 6mm and height not exceeding 25mm or a oblatecylindrical housing diameter not exceeding 15mm and thickness not exceeding 5mm, (Not including minitype motor for mechanism of laser disc player)
585	ex	85011099	激光视盘机机芯用精密微型电机(0.5 瓦≤功率≤2 瓦，5mm≤直径＜20mm)	9	5	Minitype precise motor for mechanism of laser disc player(0.5W≤power≤2W, 5mm≤diameter<20mm)
586	ex	85011099	摄像机、摄录一体机用精密微型电机(0.5 瓦≤功率≤10 瓦，5mm≤直径＜20mm 或 39mm＜直径≤40mm)	9	5	Minitype precise motor for mechanism of video cameras or camera recorders(0.5W≤power≤10W, 5mm≤diameter<20mm or 39mm<diameter≤40mm)
587	ex	85015300	高速(200km/h)电力机车的交流异步牵引电动机	12	3	AC asyncronous traction motor for high speed electric locomotive（200KM/h）
588		85030030	风力发电设备的零件	3	1	Parts of windmill generating sets
589		85044014	功率小于 1 千瓦,稳压系数低于万分之一的直流稳压电源(税号8471 所列机器用除外)	7	3	DC voltage-stabilized suppliers of a power of less than 1kW and an accuracy of not better than0.0001（excluding those used for the machines of heading No.84.71）
590	ex	85044030	电动汽车用逆变器模块，功率密度≥8 千瓦/升	10	6	Inverter module for electric vehicles,power density≥8000W/L
591		85044091	具有变流功能的半导体模块	10	3	Semiconductor modules with converting function
592	ex	85044099	高速(200km/h)电力机车的牵引变流器	10	3	Traction converter for high speed electric locomotive（≥200KM/h）
593	ex	85044099	汽车冲压线用压力机变频调速装置	10	5	Frequency conversion speed regulation set for punch press machine for manufacture automobiles
594	ex	85044099	电动汽车用电机控制器	10	6	Motor controller for electric vehicles
595	ex	85075000	电动汽车用镍氢蓄电池单体，容量≥6Ah，比功率≥1000W/kg	12	8	Nickel-metal hydride accumulators cell for electric vehicles,capacity≥6Ah and power density≥1000W/kg
596	ex	85075000	电动汽车用镍氢蓄电池系统（包含蓄电池模块、容器、盖、冷却系统、管理系统等），比功率≥700W/kg	12	10	Nickel-metal hydride accumulators system for electric vehicles,power density ≥700W/kg
597	ex	85076000	电动汽车或插电式混合动力汽车用锂离子蓄电池单体，容量≥10Ah，比能量≥110Wh/kg	12	6	Lithium ion accumulators cell for electric vehicles or plug-in hybrid elctric vehicles,capacity ≥ 10Ah and energy density≥110Wh/kg
598	ex	85076000	电动汽车或插电式混合动力汽车用锂离子蓄电池系统（包含蓄电池模块、容器、盖、冷却系统、管理系统等），比能量≥80Wh/kg	12	8	Lithium ion accumulators system for electric vehicles or plug-in hybrid elctric vehicles,energy density≥80Wh/kg

序号 No	EX	税则号列 Tariff Item	货品名称	最惠国税率(%) M.F.N.	暂定税率(%) Interim Duty Rate	Article Description
599	ex	85079010	铅酸蓄电池电极（仅保留电极）	10	5	Electrodes of lead-acid accumulators (only including Electrodes)
600		85079090	其他蓄电池(铅酸蓄电池除外)用零件	8	5	Parts of other electric accumulators, nes
601		85094010	水果或蔬菜榨汁机	10	6	Fruit or vegetable juice extractors
602		85094090	食品研磨机及搅拌器	10	6	Other domestic food grinders and mixers; fruit or veg juice extractors
603		85098090	其他家用电动器具	30	15	Other electro-mechanical domestic appliances
604		85099000	家用电动器具用零件	12	6	Parts of electro-mechanical domestic appliances with electric motor
605		85101000	电动剃须刀	30	15	Shavers, with self-contained electric motor
606		85109000	税号 85.10 所列货品的零件	24.5	12	Parts of headings No. 85.10
607	ex	85144000	焊缝中频退火装置	10	7	Intermediate frequency annealing device for weld
608	ex	85152120	汽车生产线电阻焊接机器人	10	5	Resistance welding robots, used for automobile production line
609	ex	85158010	汽车生产线激光焊接机器人	8	5	Laser welding robots, used for automobile production line
610		85159000	电气等焊接机器及装置零件	6	3	Parts of electric machine for weld/cut metal
611		85164000	电熨斗	35	17	Electric smoothing irons
612		85165000	微波炉	15	8	Microwave ovens
613		85166030	电饭锅	15	8	Electric cookers
614		85166050	电烤箱	15	8	Electric oven
615		85166090	其他电热炉	15	8	Other electric ovens
616		85167110	滴液式咖啡机	32	16	Drip coffee makers
617		85167120	蒸馏渗滤式咖啡机	32	16	Steam espresso makers
618		85167130	泵压式咖啡机	32	16	Pump espresso makers
619		85167190	其他电热咖啡壶或茶壶	32	16	Other electric-thermic coffee or tea makers
620		85167990	其他电热器具	32	16	Other electro-thermic appliances
621		85169090	税号 85.16 所列货品的其他零件	12	8	Parts of ofther apparatus of heading No. 85.16
622	ex	85181000	传声器(麦克风)及其座架(列入ITA 的电讯用麦克风除外)	10	6	Microphones and stands therefor (not inculding microphones for telecom-communicaiton use within ITA)
623		85182100	单喇叭音箱	10	6	Single loudspeakers, mounted in the same enclosure
624		85182200	多喇叭音箱	10	6	Multiple loudspeakers, mounted in the same enclosure
625		85198131	闪速存储器型声音录放机	20	12	Flash memory recorders incorporating sound reproducing apparatus
626		85198139	使用半导体媒体的其他声音录放装置	20	12	Other sound recording or reproducing apparatus, using semiconductor media
627		85198990	其他声音录制或重放设备	20	12	Other sound recording or reproducing apparatus
628		85211011	磁带型广播级录像机	完税价格不高于 2000 美元/台：30%；完税价格高于 2000 美元/台：3%，加 3283 元	完税价格不超过 5000 美元/台：15%；完税价格高于 5000 美元/台：3%，加 3648 元	Magnetic video tape recorders,broadcast quality

序号 No	EX	税则号列 Tariff Item	货品名称	最惠国税率(%) M.F.N.	暂定税率(%) Interim Duty Rate	Article Description
629	ex	85219090	光盘型广播级录像机	20	完税价格不超过7000美元/台：15%；完税价格高于7000美元/台：5%，加4256元	CD-type video recorder,broadcast quality
630		85229029	盒式磁带录音机或放声机其他零件	30	15	Other parts/accessories of magnetic tape sound recorder/reprducer
631	ex	85229031	车载导航仪视频播放机机芯	30	17	Movements for video players in the navigation system in vehicle
632	ex	85229039	其他视频信号录制或重放设备的零件	30	15	Other parts/accessories of video recording or reproducing apparatus
633	ex	85229039	激光视盘机激光收发装置用的零件	30	8	Parts of Laser transmitting and receiving device of laser disc player
634		85229091	车载音频转播器或发射器	20	10	Car audio frequency relays ware or FM car transmitter
635		85229099	声音录制或重放设备用其他零件	20	10	Other parts/accessories for sound recorder or playback equipment
636		85232928	重放声音或图像信息的磁带	10	6	Tapes for reproducing sound or image
637		85234910	仅用于重放声音信息的已录制光盘	10	6	Recorded optical media, for reproducing sound only
638	ex	85258013	手机用摄像组件（由镜头+CCD/CMOS+数字信号处理电路三部分构成）	完税价格不高于5000美元/台：35%；完税价格高于5000美元/台：3%，加9728元	4	Camera subassembly used for mobile telephone made up of lens, CCD/CMOS sensor and digital signal processing circuit, not broadcast quality
639	ex	85258013	高清摄像头（必须满足以下三个条件：1.镜头元件必须使用5层及以上玻璃镜头；2.使用USB2.0及以上高速接口；3.硬件传感器像素达到130万及以上）	完税价格不高于5000美元/台：35%；完税价格高于5000美元/台：3%，加9728元	10	High definition video cameras (must satisfy the 3 points below: 1.lens unit must use 5 and more lenses; 2.using connectors not less than USB2.0; 3.the pixels of imager must be over 1.3 million)
640	ex	85261090	飞机机载雷达（包括气象雷达、地形雷达和空中交通管制应答系统）	5	1	Airborne radars（including aero- radars, terrain-following radars and air-traffic-control-interrogator-responder systems）
641	ex	85261090	雷达生命探测仪	5	2	Radar life detectors
642		85272100	需外接电源汽车收录(放)音组合机	15	8	Combined radio/sound recorder-player, need external power for motor vehicle
643		85272900	需外接电源汽车用无线电收音机	15	8	Other radio broad receiver need external power for motor vehicles
644		85279100	其他收录(放)音组合机	15	8	Other reception apparatus for radio-broadcasting, combined with sound recording or reproducing apparatus
645		85279900	其他收音机	27	8	Other reception apparatus for radio- broadcasting
646	ex	85285910	专用于车载导航仪的液晶监视器	30	15	Liquid crystal display monitors for use solely with car navigation instruments
647	ex	85299042	摄录一体机、数码相机用取像模块	12	2	Camera modules for video camera recorders, digital cameras

序号 No	EX	税则号列 Tariff Item	货品名称	最惠国税率(%) M.F.N.	暂定税率(%) Interim Duty Rate	Article Description
648	ex	85299042	手机、平板电脑用取像模块	12	4	Camera modules for mobile telephones and tablet computers
649		85299049	摄像机、摄录一体机、数码相机的其他零件	12	2	Parts for video cameras or camera recorders or digital cameras
650		85299060	无线电收音机及其组合机用零件	15	7	Parts for radio broacast receivers and their combinations
651		85299081	彩色电视机零件(等离子组件及其零件、有机发光二极管显示屏除外)	15	6	Parts for colour TV receivers (with the exception of Plasma display modules and parts)
652		85299082	等离子显像组件及其零件（含滤光片）	15	5	Plasma display modules and parts thereof （including filter glass）
653		85299083	彩色电视机的有机发光二极管显示屏	15	5	Oled panel for colour television receivers
654	ex	85318010	音量不超过 110dB 的小型蜂鸣器	15	7.5	Minitype electric buzzers, maximum volume not exceeding110dB
655	ex	85371011	机床用可编程序控制器（PLC）	5	3	Programmable logic controllers (PLC) for machine tools
656	ex	85371019	机床用数控单元(包括单独进口的 CNC 操作单元)	5	3	Numerical control equipment for machine tools (including CNC unit imported separately)
657	ex	85371090	电梯用控制柜及控制柜专用印刷电路板	8.4	4	Control cabinets for elevator and printed circuits solely used for control cabinets
658	ex	85393240	彩色投影机的照明光源	8	3	Illumiation light source of colour projectors
659	ex	85393990	液晶显示器背光模组用冷阴极灯管	8	3	Cold cathode fluorescent lamp for backlight module of liquid crystal display
660		85409110	电视显像管零件	6	3	Parts of TV picture tubes
661		85409190	其他阴极射线管零件	8	4	Other parts of cathode-ray tubes
662		85441100	铜制绕组电线	10	6	Insulated winding wire of copper
663	ex	85443020	车辆用电控柴油机的线束	10	5	Wiring harness of electric diesel engines used for vehicles
664	ex	85446090	额定电压为 500 千伏及以上的气体绝缘金属封闭输电线	21	10	Gas insulated metal enclosed transmission line,for a voltage of 500KV or more
665	ex	85462090	输变电架空线路用长棒形瓷绝缘子瓷件(单支长度为 1~2 米,实芯)	12	3	Long solid rod ceramic insulator body for power overhead transmission and converting lines (each rod is 1~2 meters in length)
666	ex	85489000	电磁干扰滤波器	12	3	Electromagnetic interference filters
667	ex	85489000	非电磁干扰滤波器	12	6	Non electromagnetic interference filters
668	ex	87019011	功率大于 150 马力的轮式拖拉机	8	5	Wheeled tractors with power more than 150H.P.
669	ex	87019019	功率大于 150 马力的其他拖拉机	8	5	Other tractors with power more than 150H.P.
670	ex	87042300	装有驾驶室的固井水泥车、压裂车、混砂车用底盘 （车辆总重量超过 35 吨）	15	10	Chassis (incoraporating cabs) of cementing unit trucks, fractruring unit trucks and mixing sand trucks (G.V.W exceeding 35t)
671	ex	87042300	起重 55 吨及以上的汽车起重机用底盘	15	8	Chassis (incoraporating cabs) of crane lorries, eifting capacity≥55t
672	ex	87042300	车辆总重量≥31 吨清障车专用底盘	15	10	Special chassis for the wrecker of G.V.W ≥31t

序号 No	EX	税则号列 Tariff Item	货品名称	最惠国税率(%) M.F.N.	暂定税率(%) Interim Duty Rate	Article Description
673	ex	87059099	跑道除冰车	12	10	Runway deicing trucks
674	ex	87084030	扭矩>1500Nm 非公路自卸车用变速箱	6	3	Gear boxes of dumpers designed for off-highway use, torque＞1500Nm
675	ex	87084091	小轿车用自动换档变速箱及其零件（6档及6档以上）	10	6.5	Automatic transmission and parts thereof for saloon cars (6-speed and above)
676	ex	87085072	轴荷≥10t 的中后驱动桥的零件	10	8	Parts of middle and rear drive-axles, axle capacity≥10t
677	ex	87089420	30 座及以上客车用转向器的零件	10	8	Parts of steering boxes of buses with 30 seats of more
678	ex	87089450	总重≥14 吨柴油型货车转向器的零件	10	8	Parts of steering boxes for diesel trucks of G.V.W≥14t
679	ex	87089490	采用电动转向系统的转向盘、转向柱及转向器及其零件	10	8	Steering wheels, steering columns, steering gears with electric powder steering and their parts
680		87089939	非公路用自卸车未列名零部件	6	3	Not specified parts of dumpers designed for off-highway use
681	ex	87089999	混合动力汽车动力传动装置，由发电机、电动机和动力分配装置组成	10	6	Hybird vehicle transimission unit, composed of generator, motor, power delivery unit
682	ex	87141000	星型轮及碟刹件	30	10	Planetary gears and Plate brake
683	ex	90012000	液晶投影仪用偏光板	8	6	Polarizing Plate or sheet for liquid-crystal projectors
684	ex	90012000	数字电影放映机用偏光板	8	6	Polarizing plates or sheets for digital cinema projector
685		90013000	隐形眼镜片	10	6	Contact lenses
686		90014010	玻璃制变色镜片	20	15	Photochromic spectacle lenses of glass
687		90015010	非玻璃制变色镜片	20	15	Photochromic spectacle lenses of other materials
688		90015099	非玻璃材料制其他眼镜片	20	12	Spectacle lenses of other materials, not photochromic
689	ex	90019090	非涅耳透镜投影屏（屏幕对角线≥80 英寸，投射比≤0.26，增益比≥0.8，镜头间距≤100 微米）	8	6	Fresnel lens porojection screen (the length of diagoncal screen≥80 inch,Projection ratio≤0.26,ratio of gains≥0.8,lens spacing ≤100 microns)
690	ex	90019090	光通信用微光组件的光学元件（包括工作波长为 800nm～1700nm 的薄膜滤光片、自聚焦透镜、法拉第旋转片）	8	0	Micro-optic component for optical communication (including thin film filter, gradient index lens and faraday Rotator, with working wavelength between 800nm and 1700nm)
691	ex	90019090	激光视盘机激光收发装置用的微型镜片	8	3	Mini lens use for with laser transmitting and receving device of laser disc player
692	ex	90019090	液晶显示屏背光模组的光学元件(包括导光板、反射板、扩散片、增亮片)	8	2	Optical elements for backlight module of liquid crystal display (including light guide, reflect sheet, diffuser,prism sheet to enhance brightness)
693	ex	90019090	液晶投影仪用偏光元件	8	6	Polarizer for liquid-crystal projectors
694	ex	90019090	数字电影放映机用偏光元件	8	6	Polarizer for digital cinema projector

序号 No	EX	税则号列 Tariff Item	货品名称	最惠国税率(%) M.F.N.	暂定税率(%) Interim Duty Rate	Article Description
695		90021131	单反相机的镜头	15	4	Lens of digital single lens reflex camera
696		90021139	普通相机(单反相机除外)的镜头	15	4	Lens of digital camera (exception to digital single lens reflex camera)
697	ex	90021190	彩色投影机和数字光处理器的镜头及镜头组件	15	4	Lens and lens assembly of colour projectors or digital light proceesors
698	ex	90021990	摄像机、摄录一体机的镜头	15	4	Lens for video cameras or camcorders
699	ex	90021990	手机、平板电脑用物镜（800 万像素及以上）	15	10	Objective lens for mobile telephones and tablet computers (pixels≥8 million)
700	ex	90029010	照相机用带屈光度调节装置的目镜	15	10	Eyepieces with diopter adjustment devices for cameras
701	ex	90029090	其他带屈光度调节装置的目镜	15	10	Other eyepieces with diopter adjustment devices
702	ex	90029090	掩膜版	15	10	Photo masks
703		90031100	塑料制眼镜架	18	12	Frames and mountings for spectacles, goggles or the like, of plastic
704		90031910	金属材料制眼镜架	10	6	Frames and mountings of metal materials
705		90039000	眼镜架零件	10	6	Parts for frames and mountings for spectacles, goggles or the like
706		90041000	太阳镜	20	12	Sunglasses
707		90049010	变色镜	16	10	Photochromic spectacles
708		90049090	其他眼镜	20	12	Other spectacles, goggles
709	ex	90066100	照相手机用闪光灯组件	18	4	Flashlight modules for mobile telephones with camera function
710	ex	90066100	照相机外置式电子闪光灯(闪光指数 GN≥30,具有无线闪光功能,支持自动变焦)	18	15	External flashlights for cameras (Flash guide number≥30, with wireless flash and automatic focusing function)
711		90069191	照相机自动调焦组件	10	6	Automatic focal setting units of photo cameras
712		90069192	其他照相机的快门组件	10	6	Shutter units of photo cameras
713		90069199	其他照相机的其他零附件	10	6	Parts and accessories nes of other photo cameras
714	ex	90072010	2K 及以上分辨率的硬盘式数字电影放映机	14	8	Digital cinematographs with magnetic discs, resolving power≥2k
715		90079100	电影摄影机用零附件	8.4	5	Parts and accessories for cinematographic cameras
716		90079200	电影放映机用零附件	8.4	5	Parts and accessories for cinematographic projectors
717	ex	90118000	高倍测量显微镜，放大倍数≥1000 倍，分辨率≤0.08 微米	7	3	high power microscope , enlargment ratio ≥1000, resolution ration≤0.08μm
718	ex	90132000	2.5G b/s 及以上 SDH、波分复用光传输设备的 980 纳米、1480 纳米的泵浦激光器	6	3	980nm and1480nm pump laster of SDH≥2.5GB/S, optical transmission equipment for wave divison multiplexing
719	ex	90132000	激光切割机用气体激光发生器,切割功率≥2 千瓦	6	3	Gas laser oscillators for laser cutting machines, cutting powr≥2kW
720		90142010	自动驾驶仪	2	1	Automatic pilot
721	ex	90142090	航空惯性导航仪	2	1	Aviation inetial navigator
722		90149010	自动驾驶仪的零件、附件	1.5	1	Parts/accessories for automatic pilot
723		90189080	宫内节育器	4	0	Intrauterine device (IUD)
724		90200000	其他呼吸器具及防毒面具	8	4	Other breathing applicances and gas masks

序号 No	EX	税则号列 Tariff Item	货 品 名 称	最惠国税率 (%) M.F.N.	暂定税率(%) Interim Duty Rate	Article Description
725		90215000	心脏起搏器，不包括零件、附件	4	2	Pacemakers for stimulating heart muscles, excluding parts and accessories
726		90219011	血管支架	4	2	Intravascular stents
727		90219019	其他支架	4	2	Other stents
728	ex	90219090	人工耳蜗植入装置	4	0	Artificial cochlear implant appliances
729	ex	90229090	射线发生器的零部件	6	1	Parts of ray generators
730	ex	90251990	红外线人体测温仪	8.4	4	Body temperature measuring apparatus by infrared ray
731	ex	90259000	红外线测温仪传感器元件	8	3	Sensors of infrared temperature measuring apparatus
732		90318033	涡流探伤仪	5	3	Inspection instrument for eddy current testing
733	ex	90318090	音频生命探测仪	5	2	Audio life detectors
734	ex	90318090	音视频生命探测仪	5	2	Audio and video life detectors
735	ex	90318090	跑道摩擦系数测试仪	5	3	Runway friction coefficient tester
736	ex	90328990	电喷点火程序控制单元	7	3	Program controlling units for electric ignition
737	ex	90328990	机床用成套数控伺服装置（包括CNC 操作单元，带有配套的伺服放大器和伺服电机）	7	3	Numerical control servomechanism for machine tools (including CNC unit, with servo amplifier and servomotor)
738	ex	90328990	印刷机用成套数控伺服传动装置（包括运动控制器或可编程序自动控制器、人机界面单元，带有配套的伺服驱动器和伺服电机）	7	3	Complete set of CNC servo devices used for printers (including PAC and HMI units, servo drivers and sero motoers)
739	ex	90328990	三坐标测量机用自动控制柜	7	3	Automatic controller for coordinate measuring machine of three dimensions
740	ex	90328990	风力发电设备用控制器	7	4	Controller for windmill generating electricity equipment
741	ex	90328990	飞机自动驾驶系统（包括自动驾驶、电子控制飞行、自动故障分析、警告系统配平系统及推力监控设备及其相关仪表）	7	1	Parts of automatic pilotting systems for aircraft (including automatic pilotting, electronic flight contral, automatic failure analysis, warning systems, trimming systems, thrust monitoring equipments and the meters thereof)
742	ex	90329000	飞机自动驾驶系统（包括自动驾驶、电子控制飞行、自动故障分析、警告系统配平系统及推力监控设备及其相关仪表）的零件	5	1	Parts of automatic pilotting systems for aircraft (including automatic pilotting, electronic flight contral, automatic failure analysis, warning systems, trimming systems, thrust monitoring equipments and the meters therof)
743		91081100	已组装的机械指示式完整电子表芯	16	10	Electric atch movements, assembled, with mechnical display
744	ex	92012000	完税价格 50000 美元及以上的大钢琴	17.5	1	Grand pianos, the duty-paying value ≥ 50000USD
745	ex	92021000	完税价格 15000 美元及以上的弓弦乐器	17.5	1	Played with a bow, the duty-paying value ≥15000USD
746	ex	92051000	完税价格 2000 美元及以上的铜管乐器	17.5	1	Brass-wind instruments, the duty- paying value≥2000USD

序号 No	EX	税则号列 Tariff Item	货品名称	最惠国税率 (%) M.F.N.	暂定税率(%) Interim Duty Rate	Article Description
747	ex	92059090	完税价格10000美元及以上的其他管乐器	17.5	1	Other wind musical instruments, the duty-paying value≥10000USD
748		92071000	通过电产生或扩大声音的键盘乐器	30	15	Electric keyboard instruments other than accordions
749		92099400	税号9207所列乐器的零附件	17.5	10	Parts & accessories for musical instruments of heading No 92.07
750		94041000	弹簧床垫	20	10	Mattress supports
751		94042100	海绵橡胶或泡沫塑料制褥垫	20	10	Mattresses of cellular rubber or plastics
752		94042900	其他材料制褥垫	20	10	Mattresses fitted with springs or stuffed with any material
753		94043010	羽毛或羽绒填充的睡袋	20	10	Sleeping bags, feather or down stuffed
754		94043090	其他睡袋	20	10	Other sleeping bags, nes
755		94049010	羽绒或羽毛填充的寝具及类似品	20	10	Articles of bedding/furnishing nes, feather or down stuffed
756		94049020	兽毛填充的寝具及类似品	20	10	Articles of bedding/furnishing nes, animal hair stuffed
757		94049030	丝棉填充的寝具及类似品	20	10	Articles of bedding/furnishing nes, silk wadding stuffed
758		94049040	化纤棉填充的寝具及类似品	20	10	Articles of bedding/furnishing nes, man-made fibre stuffed
759		94049090	其他材料制的寝具及类似品	20	10	Articles of bedding/furnishing nes, stuffed, nes
760		95064090	其他乒乓球运动用品及器械	14	7	Articles & equipment for table-tennis, excl balls
761		95066210	篮球、足球、排球	12	6	Basketballs, footballs and volleyballs
762		95069111	跑步机	12	6	Treadmill
763		95069119	其他健身及康复器械	12	6	Gymnasium or recovered equipment
764		95069120	滑板	12	6	Skateboards
765		95069190	一般的体育活动、体操或竞技用品	12	6	General physica exercise / gymnastics/ athletics articl/equipment
766		96032100	牙刷，包括齿板刷	25	10	Tooth brushes, including dental-plate brushes
767		97011010	油画、粉画及其他手绘画原件		6	Original paintings, drawings and pastels
768		97020000	雕版画、印制画、石印画的原本	12	6	Original engravings, prints and lithographs
769		97030000	各种材料制的雕塑品原件	12	6	Original sculptures and statuary, in any material

附录三

进口商品从量税、复合税税目税率表

Specific and Compound Duty Rate on Imported Goods

序号 No.	税则号列 Tariff Item	货品名称	普通税率 Gen.	最惠国税率 M.F.N.	Article Description
1	02071200	冻的整只鸡	5.6元/千克	1.3元/千克	Frozen whole chickens, not cut in pieces
2	02071411	冻的带骨鸡块（包括鸡胸脯、鸡大腿等）	4.2元/千克	0.6元/千克	Frozen chicken cuts, breasts, legs, with bone in
3	02071419	冻的不带骨鸡块（包括鸡胸脯、鸡大腿等）	9.5元/千克	0.7元/千克	Frozen boneless chicken cuts, breasts, legs
4	02071421	冻的鸡翼（不包括翼尖）	8.1元/千克	0.8元/千克	Frozen wing of chicken (other than wingtips)
5	02071422	冻的鸡爪	3.2元/千克	1元/千克	Frozen claw of chicken
6	02071429	冻的其他鸡杂碎（包括鸡翼尖、鸡肝等）	3.2元/千克	0.5元/千克	Frozen offal of chicken, nes
7	05040021	冷、冻的鸡肫（即鸡胃）	7.7元/千克	1.3元/千克	Cold, frozen broiler gizzard
8	22030000	麦芽酿造的啤酒	7.5元/升	0	Beer made from malt
9	27090000	石油原油（包括从沥青矿物提取的原油）	85元/吨	0	Petroleum oils & oils obtained from bituminous minerals, crude
10	37023190	其他未曝光无齿孔彩色窄胶卷（窄胶卷指宽度≤105毫米，彩色摄影用）	433元/平方米	56元/平方米	Other photographic film rolls, unexposed, without perforations, for colour photography, of any material other than paper, paperboard or textiles, width≤105mm
11	37023220	照相制版涂卤化银液无齿孔窄胶卷（成卷未曝光感光胶片，窄胶卷指宽度≤105毫米）	104元/平方米	4.5元/平方米	Photographic film rolls, unexposed, without perforations, with silver halide emulsion, for preparing printing plates or cylinders, of any material other than paper, paper-board or textiles, width≤105mm
12	37023290	其他涂卤化银乳液无齿孔窄胶卷（成卷未曝光感光胶片，窄胶卷指宽度≤105毫米）	202元/平方米	21元/平方米	Photographic film rolls, unexposed, without perforations, with silver halide emulsion, of any material other than paper, paperboard or textiles, width≤105mm, nes
13	37023920	照相制版用其他无齿孔窄感光胶卷（成卷未曝光感光胶片，窄胶卷指宽度≤105毫米）	104元/平方米	12元/平方米	Photographic film rolls, unexposed, without perforations and silver halide emulsion, of any material other than paper, paperboard or textiles, width ≤ 105mm, for preparing printing plates or cylinders
14	37023990	其他用无齿孔窄感光胶卷（成卷未曝光感光胶片，窄胶卷指宽度≤105毫米）	202元/平方米	24元/平方米	Photographic film rolls, unexposed, without perforations and silver halide emulsion, of any material other than paper, paperboard or textiles, width≤105mm, nes

序号 No.	税则号列 Tariff Item	货品名称	普通税率 Gen.	最惠国税率 M.F.N.	Article Description
15	37024100	未曝光无齿孔宽长彩色胶卷（宽长胶卷指宽度>610毫米， 长度>200米）	202元/平方米	7.1元/平方米	Film rolls, for colour photography, unexposed, without perforations, of any material other than paper, paperboard or textiles, width >610mm, length>200m
16	37024221	印刷电路板制造用光致抗蚀干膜（指宽度>610毫米， 长度>200米）	110元/平方米	0.6元/平方米	Wide anticorrosive photographic plate for printed circuit processing, unexposed, without perforations, of any material other than paper, paperboard or textiles, width >610mm, length>200m
17	37024229	照相制版其他未曝光无齿宽长胶卷（宽长指宽度>610毫米， 长度>200米）	110元/平方米	1.6元/平方米	Film rolls for preparing printing plates or cylinders, unexposed, without perforations, of any material other than paper, paperboard or textiles, width >610mm, length >200m, excl. wide anticorrosive photographic plate for printed circuit processing
18	37024292	红色或红外激光胶片	213元/平方米	2.4元/平方米	Infra-red or red laser film,unexposed, without perforations, of any material other than paper, paperboard or textiles, width > 610mm, length>200m, excl. wide anticorrosive photographic plate for printed circuit processing
19	37024299	黑白其他未曝光无齿孔宽长胶卷（宽长胶卷指宽度>610毫米,长度>200米）	213元/平方米	7元/平方米	Unexposed monochrome phtotgraphic film in rolls, without perforations, width >610mm, length>200m
20	37024321	照相制版用激光照排片（宽度>610毫米， 长度≤200米）	104元/平方米	10元/平方米	Laser phototypesetting film, unexposed, without perforations, width>610mm, length≤200m, of any material other than paper, paperboard or textiles
21	37024329	其他照相制版用未曝光无齿孔胶卷（指宽度>610毫米， 长度≤200米）	104元/平方米	3.7元/平方米	Film rolls for preparing printing plates or cylinders, unexposed, without perforations, width >610mm, length≤200m, of any material other than paper, paperboard or textile, excl. laser phototypesetting film
22	37024390	彩色或黑白其他用未曝光无齿孔中长胶卷（中长胶卷指宽度>610毫米， 长度≤200米）	202元/平方米	17元/平方米	Film rolls, unexposed, without perforations, width>610mm, length ≤ 200m, of any material other than paper, paperboard or textiles, nes
23	37024421	照相制版用未曝光激光照排片（宽度>105毫米，≤610毫米）	115元/平方米	2元/平方米	Laser phototypesetting film, unexposed, without perforations, 105mm<width≤610mm, of any material other than paper, paperboard or textiles

序号 No.	税则号列 Tariff Item	货品名称	普通税率 Gen.	最惠国税率 M.F.N.	Article Description
24	37024422	印刷电路板制造用光致抗蚀干膜（宽度>105 毫米，≤610 毫米）	115 元/平方米	5 元/平方米	Narrow anticorrosive photographic plate for printed circuit processing, unexposed, without perforations, 105mm <width≤610mm, of any material other than paper, paperboard or textiles
25	37024429	其他照相制版用无齿孔未曝光胶卷（宽度>105 毫米，≤610 毫米）	115 元/平方米	2.9 元/平方米	Film rolls for preparing printing plates or cylinders, unexposed, without perforations, 105mm <width ≤610mm, of any material other than paper, paperboard or textiles
26	37024490	彩色或黑白其他用无齿孔未曝光中宽胶卷（中宽胶卷指宽度>105 毫米，但≤610 毫米）	202 元/平方米	27 元/平方米	Film rolls, unexposed, without perforations, 105mm<width ≤ 610mm, of any material other than paper, paperboard or textiles, nes
27	37025200	彩色摄影用未曝光彩色胶卷，宽度小于 16 毫米	433 元/平方米	95 元/平方米	Film for colour photography (polychrome), of a width not exceeding 16mm
28	37025300	幻灯片用未曝光彩色摄影胶卷（宽度>16 毫米，但≤35 毫米，长度≤30 米）	433 元/平方米	128 元/平方米	Slide film rolls for colour photography, unexposed, 16mm <width≤ 35mm, length<30m, of any material other than paper, paperboard or textiles
29	37025410	非幻灯片用彩色摄影胶卷（宽度=35 毫米，长度≤2 米）	433 元/平方米	18 元/平方米	Film rolls for colour photography other than for slides, unexposed, width=35mm and length≤2m, of any material other than paper, paperboard or textiles
30	37025490	其他非幻灯片用彩色摄影胶卷（宽度>16 毫米，但≤35 毫米，长度≤30 米）	433 元/平方米	24 元/平方米	Film rolls for colour photography other than for slides, unexposed, 16mm < width < 35mm, 2m < length≤30m, of any material other than paper, paperboard or textiles
31	37025520	未曝光的窄长彩色电影胶卷（窄长胶卷指宽度>16 毫米，但≤35 毫米，长度>30 米）	232 元/平方米	9 元/平方米	Colour cinematographic film rolls, unexposed, 16mm < width ≤ 35mm, length > 30m, of any material other than paper, paperboard or textiles
32	37025590	其他未曝光窄长彩色胶卷（窄长胶卷指宽度>16 毫米，但≤35 毫米，长度>30 米）	433 元/平方米	27 元/平方米	Colour film rolls for colour photography, unexposed, 16mm <width ≤ 35mm, length >30m, excl. cinematographic film
33	37025620	未曝光的中宽彩色电影胶卷（中宽胶卷指宽度>35 毫米）	232 元/平方米	13 元/平方米	Colour cinematographic film rolls, unexposed, width >35mm, of any material other than paper, paperboard or textiles
34	37025690	其他未曝光的中宽彩色胶卷（中宽胶卷指宽度>35 毫米）	433 元/平方米	74 元/平方米	Film in rolls for colour photography, unexposed, width >35mm, of any material other than paper, paperboard or textiles, excl. cinematographic film

序号 No.	税则号列 Tariff Item	货品名称	普通税率 Gen.	最惠国税率 M.F.N.	Article Description
35	37029600	未曝光非彩色胶卷（宽度≤35 毫米，长度≤30 米）	210 元/平方米	21 元/平方米	Film rolls of neutral colour, unexposed, of any material other than paper, paperboard or textiles, of a width not exceeding 35mm and of a length not exceeding 30m
36	37029700	未曝光非彩色胶卷（宽度≤35 毫米， 长度＞30 米）	210 元/平方米	9 元/平方米	Film rolls of neutral colour, unexposed, of any material other than paper, paperboard or textiles, of a width not exceeding 35mm and of a length exceeding 30m
37	37029800	未曝光非彩色胶卷，宽度＞35 毫米	210 元/平方米	10 元/平方米	Film rolls of neutral colour, unexposed, of any material other than paper, paperboard or textiles, of a width exceeding 35mm
38	85211011	广播级磁带录像机	完税价格小于 2000 美元： 130%；完税价格大于 2000 美元： 6%加 20600 元/台	完税价格小于 2000 美元： 30%；完税价格大于 2000 美元： 3%加 3283 元/台	Broadcast quality, magnetic video tape recorders
39	85211019	其他磁带录像机	完税价格不高于 2000 美元：130%；完税价格高于 2000 美元：6%加 20600 元/台	完税价格不高于 2000 美元：30%；完税价格高于 2000 美元： 3%加 3283 元/台	Other magnetic video tape recorders
40	85211020	磁带放像机	完税价格不高于 2000 美元：130%；完税价格高于 2000 美元：6%加 20600 元/台	完税价格不高于 2000 美元：30%；完税价格高于 2000 美元： 3%加 3283 元/台	Magnetic video tape reproducers
41	85258012	非特种用途的广播级电视摄像机	完税价格不高于 5000 美元：130%；完税价格高于 5000 美元：6%加 51500 元/台	完税价格不高于 5000 美元：35%；完税价格高于 5000 美元： 3%加 9728 元/台	Other broadcast quality, television cameras, not for special purposes
42	85258013	非特种用途的其他电视摄像机	完税价格不高于 5000 美元：130%；完税价格高于 5000 美元：6%加 51500 元/台	完税价格不高于 5000 美元：35%；完税价格高于 5000 美元： 3%加 9728 元/台	Other television cameras, not for special purposes
43	85258022	非特种用途的单镜头反光型数字照相机	完税价格不高于 5000 美元：130%；完税价格高于 5000 美元：6%加 51500 元/台	0	Other single lens reflex digital cameras, not for special purposes
44	85258025	非特种用途的其他可换镜头的数字照相机	完税价格不高于 5000 美元/台：130%；完税价格高于 5000 美元/台：6%加 51500 元	0	Other lens interchangeable digital cameras, not for special purposes
45	85258029	非特种用途的其他数字照相机	每台完税价格不高于 5000 美元：130%；每台完税价格高于5000美元：6%加 51500 元/台	0	Other digital cameras
46	85258032	非特种用途的广播级视频摄录一体机	每台完税价格不高于 5000 美元：130%；每台完税价格高于 5000 美元：6%加 51500 元/台	0	Other broadcast quality, video camera recorders
47	85258039	非特种用途的其他视频摄录一体机（家用型摄录一体机除外）	每台完税价格不高于 5000 美元：130%；每台完税价格高于 5000 美元：6%加 51500 元/台	0	Other video camera recorders, other than household video camera recorders

附录四

中华人民共和国进境物品进口税率表

Duty Rate on Inward Articles of the People's Republic of China

序号 No.	物品名称	税率(%) Duty	Article Description
1	书报、刊物、教育专用电影片、幻灯片、原版录音带、录相带； 金、银及其制品； 计算机、视频摄录一体机、数字照相机等信息技术产品、照相机； 食品、饮料； 本表2、3、4税号及备注中所不包含的其他商品	10	Book，newspaper，journal，movie copy for education，slide，cassette，video cassette，gold，silver or article，computer，video camera recorder，digital camera and other IT products，photographic camera，food，beverage，articles other than item 2, 3, 4
2	纺织品及其制成品； 电视摄像机及其他电器用具、自行车、手表、钟表（含配件、附件）	20	Textile product，television camera and other electric products，bicycles，watch，clock
3	高尔夫球及球具、高档手表	30	Golf ball and other golf equipment, luxury watch
4	烟、酒、化妆品	50	Tobacco product，spirits，wine，beer，cosmetic

注：避孕用具和避孕药品，超过海关规定的自用合理数量部分按有关规定予以退运或按货物进口程序办理报关及验放手续。

Note: About contraceptive instruments and contraceptive medicines，the extra amount of which exceeding the reasonable self-using level set by customs regulations should be backtrack，or apply for customs registration and examination as required by goods－importing procedures.

中华人民共和国进出口关税条例

（国务院总理温家宝2003年11月23日签署第392号国务院令，发布《中华人民共和国进出口关税条例》，自2004年1月1日起施行。）

第一章 总 则

第一条 为了贯彻对外开放政策，促进对外经济贸易和国民经济的发展，根据《中华人民共和国海关法》（以下简称《海关法》）的有关规定，制定本条例。

第二条 中华人民共和国准许进出口的货物、进境物品，除法律、行政法规另有规定外，海关依照本条例规定征收进出口关税。

第三条 国务院制定《中华人民共和国进出口税则》（以下简称《税则》）、《中华人民共和国进境物品进口税税率表》（以下简称《进境物品进口税税率表》），规定关税的税目、税则号列和税率，作为本条例的组成部分。

第四条 国务院设立关税税则委员会，负责《税则》和《进境物品进口税税率表》的税目、税则号列和税率的调整和解释，报国务院批准后执行；决定实行暂定税率的货物、税率和期限；决定关税配额税率；决定征收反倾销税、反补贴税、保障措施关税、报复性关税以及决定实施其他关税措施；决定特殊情况下税率的适用，以及履行国务院规定的其他职责。

第五条 进口货物的收货人、出口货物的发货人、进境物品的所有人，是关税的纳税义务人。

第六条 海关及其工作人员应当依照法定职权和法定程序履行关税征管职责，维护国家利益，保护纳税人合法权益，依法接受监督。

第七条 纳税义务人有权要求海关对其商业秘密予以保密，海关应当依法为纳税义务人保密。

Regulations of the People's Republic of China on Import and Export Duties

(Adopted at the 26th Executive Meeting of the State Council on 29 October 2003, promulgated by Decree No. 392 of the State Council of the People's Republic of China on 23 November 2003, and effective as of 1 January 2004.)

Chapter I General Provisions

Article 1 These Regulations are formulated in accordance with the relevant provisions of the Customs Law of the People's Republic of China (hereinafter referred to as the Customs Law) for the purposes of implementing the policy of opening to the outside world and promoting the development of foreign economic relations and foreign trade and the national economy.

Article 2 Unless otherwise provided for by laws or administrative regulations, the Customs shall, in accordance with these Regulations, collect import or export duties on all goods permitted by the People's Republic of China to be imported into or exported out of the Customs territory and all inward articles.

Article 3 The State Council shall formulate the Customs Import and Export Tariff of the People's Republic of China (hereinafter referred to as the Tariff) and the Flat Duty Rates on Inward Articles of the People's Republic of China (hereinafter referred to as the Flat Duty Rates on Inward Articles), providing for tariff items, tariff headings and duty rates, which constitute component parts of these Regulations.

Article 4 The State Council shall establish the Tariff Commission, which is responsible for making adjustment to and interpretation of tariff items, tariff headings and duty rates in the Tariff and the Flat Duty Rates on Inward Articles and implementing such adjustment and interpretation after they are submitted to and approved by the State Council; determining the goods subject to temporary duty rates and the rates and duration thereof; determining tariff quota rates; determining the imposition of anti-dumping duty, countervailing duty, safeguard duty, retaliatory duty or other tariff measures; determining the application of duty rates under special circumstances; and performing other functions and responsibilities prescribed by the State Council.

Article 5 The consignee of import goods, the consignor of export goods and the owner of inward articles are duty payers.

Article 6 The Customs and staff members thereof shall fulfil the responsibility of duty collection in accordance with the statutory authority and procedure, safeguard State interests, protect lawful rights and interests of duty payers, and receive supervision according to law.

Article 7 A duty payer has the right to request the Customs to keep confidential its commercial secrets, and the Customs shall keep confidential such secrets for the duty payer according to law.

第八条 海关对检举或者协助查获违反本条例行为的单位和个人，应当按照规定给予奖励，并负责保密。

Article 8 The Customs shall, in accordance with the relevant provisions, reward units and individuals that inform against violations of these Regulations or provide assistance in investigating such violations, and be responsible for keeping secrets concerned.

第二章 进出口货物关税税率的设置和适用

Chapter II Composition and Application of Duty Rates on Import and Export Goods

第九条 进口关税设置最惠国税率、协定税率、特惠税率、普通税率、关税配额税率等税率。对进口货物在一定期限内可以实行暂定税率。

Article 9 Duty rates on import goods are composed of most-favoured-nation duty rates, conventional duty rates, special preferential duty rates, general duty rates, tariff quota duty rates, etc. Temporary duty rates may apply to import goods within a specific time limit.

出口关税设置出口税率。对出口货物在一定期限内可以实行暂定税率。

Duty rates on export goods are designed to collect export duty. Temporary duty rates may apply to export goods within a specific time limit.

第十条 原产于共同适用最惠国待遇条款的世界贸易组织成员的进口货物，原产于与中华人民共和国签订含有相互给予最惠国待遇条款的双边贸易协定的国家或者地区的进口货物，以及原产于中华人民共和国境内的进口货物，适用最惠国税率。

Article 10 The most-favoured-nation duty rates shall apply to import goods originated from members of the World Trade Organization that are subject to the common application of the most-favoured-nation clause, import goods originated from countries or regions with which the People's Republic of China has concluded a bilateral trade agreement for reciprocally granting of most-favoured-nation treatment, and import goods originated from the Customs territory of the People's Republic of China.

原产于与中华人民共和国签订含有关税优惠条款的区域性贸易协定的国家或者地区的进口货物，适用协定税率。

The conventional duty rates shall apply to import goods originated from countries or regions with which the People's Republic of China has concluded a regional trade agreement that comprises preferential duty clauses.

原产于与中华人民共和国签订含有特殊关税优惠条款的贸易协定的国家或者地区的进口货物，适用特惠税率。

The special preferential duty rates shall apply to import goods originated from countries or regions with which the People's Republic of China has concluded a trade agreement that comprises special preferential duty clauses.

原产于本条第一款、第二款和第三款所列以外国家或者地区的进口货物，以及原产地不明的进口货物，适用普通税率。

The general duty rates shall apply to import goods originated from countries or regions other than those specified in Paragraphs 1, 2 and 3 of this Article or to the import goods of undetermined origins.

第十一条 适用最惠国税率的进口货物有暂定税率的，应当适用暂定税率；适用协定税率、特惠税率的进口货物有暂定税率的，应当从低适用税率；适用普通税率的进口货物，不适用暂定税率。

Article 11 Where there are temporary duty rates on import goods to which the most-favoured-nation duty rates are applicable, such temporary duty rates shall apply; where there are temporary duty rates on import goods to which the conventional duty rates or preferential duty rates are applicable, the lower duty rates shall apply; temporary duty rates shall not apply to import goods to which the general duty rates are applicable.

适用出口税率的出口货物有暂定税率的，应当适用暂定税率。

Where there are temporary duty rates on export goods to which the export duty rates are applicable, such temporary duty rates shall apply.

第十二条 按照国家规定实行关税配额管理的进口货物，关税配额内的，适用关税配额税率；关税配额外的，其税率的适用按照本条例第十条、第十一条的规定执行。

Article 12 Where the quantity of import goods that are subject to tariff quota administration in accordance with the provisions of the State is within the tariff quota, the tariff quota duty rates shall apply; if such quantity exceeds the tariff quota, the application of the duty rates shall be governed by the provisions of Article 10 or 11 of these Regulations.

第十三条 按照有关法律、行政法规的规定对进口货物采取反倾销、反补贴、保障措施的，其税率的适用按照《中华人民共和国反倾销条例》、《中华人民共和国反补贴条例》和《中华人民共和国保障措施条例》的有关规定执行。

Article 13 Where anti-dumping, countervailing or safeguard measures are adopted on import goods in accordance with the provisions of the relevant laws or administrative regulations, the application of duty rates of such import goods shall be governed by the relevant provisions of the Regulations of the People's Republic of China on Anti-Dumping, the Regulations of the People's Republic of China on Countervailing Measures, and the Regulations of the People's Republic of China on Safeguards.

第十四条 任何国家或者地区违反与中华人民共和国签订或者共同参加的贸易协定及相关协定，对中华人民共和国在贸易方面采取禁止、限制、加征关税或者其他影响正常贸易的措施的，对原产于该国家或者地区的进口货物可以征收报复性关税，适用报复性关税税率。

Article 14 Where any country or region, in violation of the trade agreements or other relevant agreements that it concludes or accedes to with the People's Republic of China, unilaterally adopts measures affecting normal trade such as imposition of prohibition or restriction or surcharge of duties in the trade with the People's Republic of China, retaliatory duty may be imposed on import goods originated from such country or region and retaliatory duty rates may apply.

征收报复性关税的货物、适用国别、税率、期限和征收办法，由国务院关税税则委员会决定并公布。

The goods and countries subject to retaliatory duty, as well as the rates, duration and collection measures of retaliatory duty shall be determined and published by the Tariff Commission of the State Council.

第十五条 进出口货物，应当适用海关接受该货物申报进口或者出口之日实施的税率。

Article 15 For any import or export goods, the duty rates implemented on the date when the Customs accepts the declaration for import or export of such goods shall apply.

进口货物到达前，经海关核准先行申报的，应当适用装载该货物的运输工具申报进境之日实施的税率。

Where, upon verification and approval of the Customs, the declaration is made prior to entry of import goods, the duty rates implemented on the date of declaration of the means of transport carrying such goods for entry shall apply.

转关运输货物税率的适用日期，由海关总署另行规定。

The date for application of the duty rates on goods for the transport under Customs transit shall be separately provided for by the General Administration of Customs.

第十六条 有下列情形之一，需缴纳税款的，应当适用海关接受申报办理纳税手续之日实施的税率：

Article 16 Where duty needs to be paid under any of the following circumstances, the duty rates implemented on the date when the Customs accepts the declaration for duty payment shall apply:

（一）保税货物经批准不复运出境的；

(1)where bonded goods are, with approval, not to be re-transported out of the Customs territory;

（二）减免税货物经批准转让或者移作他用的；

(2)where goods subject to duty reduction or exemption are, with approval, to be transferred or diverted to other purposes;

（三）暂准进境货物经批准不复运出境，以及暂准出境货物经批准不复运进境的；

(3)where goods permitted to temporarily enter or leave the Customs territory are, with approval, not to be re transported out of or into the Customs territory;

（四）租赁进口货物，分期缴纳税款的。

(4)where the duty on import goods on lease is to be paid by instalments.

第十七条 补征和退还进出口货物关税，应当按照本条例第十五条或者第十六条的规定确定适用的税率。

Article 17 In the recovery or refund of duties on import or export goods, the duty rates to apply shall be determined in accordance with the provisions of Article 15 or 16 of these Regulations.

因纳税义务人违反规定需要追征税款的，应当适用该行为发生之日实施的税率；行为发生之日不能确定的，适用海关发现该行为之日实施的税率。

Where there is a need to pursue the payment of duties unpaid due to the duty payer's violation of relevant provisions, the duty rates implemented on the date when such violation occurs shall apply; if it is impossible to ascertain the date when such violation occurs, the duty rates implemented on the date when the Customs finds such violation shall apply.

第三章 进出口货物完税价格的确定

Chapter III Determination of Customs Value of Import and Export Goods

第十八条 进口货物的完税价格由海关以符合本条第三款所列条件的成交价格以及该货物运抵中华人民共和国境内输入地点起卸前的运输及其相关费用、保险费为基础审查确定。

Article 18 The customs value of import goods shall be determined by the Customs on the basis of the transaction value which complies with the conditions specified in Paragraph 3 of this Article, as well as the costs of transport, charges associated with transport, and the cost of insurance incurred prior to unloading of such goods at the port or place of entry within the Customs territory of the People's Republic of China.

进口货物的成交价格，是指卖方向中华人民共和国境内销售该货物时买方为进口该货物向卖方实付、应付的，并按照本条例第十九条、第二十条规定调整后的价款总额，包括直接支付的价款和间接支付的价款。

The transaction value of import goods is the price actually paid or payable for the import goods by the buyer when sold by the seller for export to the Customs territory of the People's Republic of China, adjusted in accordance with the provisions of Articles 19 and 20 of these Regulations, including the price paid directly and indirectly.

进口货物的成交价格应当符合下列条件：

The transaction value of import goods shall comply with the following conditions:

（一）对买方处置或者使用该货物不予限制，但法律、行政法规规定实施的限制、对货物转售地域的限制和对货物价格无实质性影响的限制除外；

(1)there are no restrictions as to the disposition or use of the goods by the buyer other than restrictions which are imposed by laws or administrative regulations, restrictions which limit the geographical area in which the goods may be resold, or restrictions which do not substantially affect the value of the goods;

（二）该货物的成交价格没有因搭售或者其他因素的影响而无法确定；

(2)the transaction value of such goods is not subject to some condition or consideration such as tie-in sale for which a value cannot be determined with respect to the goods being valued;

（三）卖方不得从买方直接或者间接获得因该货物进口后转售、处置或者使用而产生的任何收益，或者虽有收益但能够按照本条例第十九条、第二十条的规定进行调整；

(3)no part of the proceeds of any subsequent resale, disposal or use of the import goods by the buyer will accrue directly or indirectly to the seller, or appropriate adjustment can be made to the proceeds, if any, in accordance with the provisions of Articles 19 and 20 of these Regulations;

（四）买卖双方没有特殊关系，或者虽有特殊关系但未对成交价格产生影响。

(4)the buyer and seller are not related or, although the buyer and seller are related, such relationship does not affect the transaction value.

第十九条 进口货物的下列费用应当计入完税价格：

Article 19 The following costs shall be added to the customs value of import goods:

（一）由买方负担的购货佣金以外的佣金和经纪费；

(1)commissions and brokerage incurred by the buyer, except buying commissions;

（二）由买方负担的在审查确定完税价格时与该货物视为一体的容器的费用；

(2)the cost of containers treated as being one for customs purposes with the goods in question, which is incurred by the buyer;

（三）由买方负担的包装材料费用和包装劳务费用；

(3)the cost of packing incurred by the buyer, whether for labour or materials;

（四）与该货物的生产和向中华人民共和国境内销售有关的，由买方以免费或者以低于成本的方式提供并可以按适当比例分摊的料件、工具、模具、消耗材料及类似货物的价款，以及在境外开发、设计等相关服务的费用；

(4)the value, apportioned as appropriate, of such goods as materials, components, parts, tools, dies, moulds, consumed materials and similar items, and such services as development, design and associated services undertaken elsewhere than in the Customs territory of the People's Republic of China where supplied by the buyer free of charge or at reduced cost for use in connection with the production and sale for export of the import goods to the Customs territory of the People's Republic of China;

（五）作为该货物向中华人民共和国境内销售的条件，买方必须支付的、与该货物有关的特许权使用费；

(5)royalties and license fees related to the import goods that the buyer must pay, as a condition for sale of such goods to the Customs territory of the People's Republic of China;

（六）卖方直接或者间接从买方获得的该货物进口后转售、处置或者使用的收益。

(6)the value of any part of the proceeds of any subsequent resale, disposal or use of the goods that accrues directly or indirectly to the seller.

第二十条 进口时在货物的价款中列明的下列税收、费用，不计入该货物的完税价格：

Article 20 The customs value of import goods shall not include the following taxes and charges that are specified in the price of such import goods at the time of importation:

（一）厂房、机械、设备等货物进口后进行建设、安装、装配、维修和技术服务的费用；

(1)charges for construction, erection, assembly, maintenance, or technical assistance, undertaken after importation on import goods such as industrial plant, machinery or equipment;

（二）进口货物运抵境内输入地点起卸后的运输及其相关费用、保险费；

(2)the costs of transport, charges associated with transport, and the cost of insurance incurred after unloading of import goods at the port or place of entry within the Customs territory;

（三）进口关税及国内税收。

(3)import duty and other internal taxes.

第二十一条 进口货物的成交价格不符合本条例第十八条第三款规定条件的，或者成交价格不能确定的，海关经了解有关情况，并与纳税义务人进行价格磋商后，依次以下列价格估定该货物的完税价格：

Article 21 Where the transaction value of import goods does not comply with the conditions prescribed in Paragraph 3 of Article 18 of these Regulations, or it is impossible to determine the transaction value, the Customs shall, after acquainting itself with the relevant information and consulting over price with the duty payer, determine the customs value of the import goods in accordance with the following values in their given order:

（一）与该货物同时或者大约同时向中华人民共和国境内销售的相同货物的成交价格；

(1)the transaction value of identical goods sold for export to the Customs territory of the People's Republic of China and exported at or about the same time as the goods being valued;

（二）与该货物同时或者大约同时向中华人民共和国境内销售的类似货物的成交价格；

(2)the transaction value of similar goods sold for export to the Customs territory of the People's Republic of China and exported at or about the same time as the goods being valued;.

（三）与该货物进口的同时或者大约同时，将该进口货物、相同或者类似进口货物在第一级销售环节销售给无特殊关系买方最大销售总量的单位价格，但应当扣除本条例第二十二条规定的项目；

(3)the unit price at which the import goods or identical or similar import goods are sold in the greatest aggregate quantity, at or about the time of importation of the goods being valued, to an unrelated buyer in the first sale, with all items specified in Article 22 of these Regulations deducted;

（四）按照下列各项总和计算的价格：生产该货物所使用的料件成本和加工费用，向中华人民共和国境内销售同等级或者同种类货物通常的利润和一般费用，该货物运抵境内输入地点起卸前的运输及其相关费用、保险费；

(4)the computed value which consists of the total sum of the following items: the cost or value of materials, components and parts, and fabrication or other processing employed in producing the import goods; an amount for profit and general expenses equal to that usually reflected in sales of goods of the same class or kind as the import goods being valued to the Customs territory of the People's Republic of China; the costs of transport, charges associated with transport, and the cost of insurance incurred prior to unloading of import goods at the port or place of entry within the Customs territory;

（五）以合理方法估定的价格。

(5)the value determined on a reasonable basis.

纳税义务人向海关提供有关资料后，可以提出申请，颠倒前款第（三）项和第（四）项的适用次序。

The duty payer may, after providing relevant information or data to the Customs, make a request to reverse the order of the application of items (3) and (4) of the preceding paragraph.

第二十二条 按照本条例第二十一条第一款第（三）项规定估定完税价格，应当扣除的项目是指：

Article 22 In determining the customs value of import goods in accordance with item (3) of Paragraph 1 of Article 21 of these Regulations, the items that shall be deducted are as follows:

（一）同等级或者同种类货物在中华人民共和国境内第一级销售环节销售时通常的利润和一般费用以及通常支付的佣金；

(1)either profit and general expenses or commissions usually paid in the first sale of import goods of the same class or kind within the Customs territory of the People's Republic of China;

（二）进口货物运抵境内输入地点起卸后的运输及其相关费用、保险费；

(2)the costs of transport, charges associated with transport, and the cost of insurance incurred after unloading of import goods at the port or place of entry within the Customs territory;

（三）进口关税及国内税收。

(3)import duty and internal taxes.

第二十三条 以租赁方式进口的货物，以海关审查确定的该货物的租金作为完税价格。

Article 23 The customs value of import goods on lease shall be the rental determined by the Customs.

纳税义务人要求一次性缴纳税款的，纳税义务人可以选择按照本条例第二十一条的规定估定完税价格，或者按照海关审查确定的租金总额作为完税价格。

Where the duty payer requests to pay the duties in a lump sum, it may choose to have the customs value determined in accordance with the provisions of Article 21 of these Regulations or take total rental determined by the Customs as the customs value.

第二十四条 运往境外加工的货物，出境时已向海关报明并在海关规定的期限内复运进境的，应当以境外加工费和料件费以及复运进境的运输及其相关费用和保险费审查确定完税价格。

Article 24 The customs value of goods which are transported out of the Customs territory for processing with the declaration thereof made to the Customs at the time of departure and re-transported into the Customs territory within the time limit set by the Customs shall be determined on the basis of the charges on overseas processing, the cost of materials, components and parts, the costs of the re-transport, charges associated with re-transport, and the cost of insurance for the re-transport.

第二十五条 运往境外修理的机械器具、运输工具或者其他货物，出境时已向海关报明并在海关规定的期限内复运进境的，应当以境外修理费和料件费审查确定完税价格。

Article 25 The customs value for mechanic appliances, means of transport or any other goods which are transported out of the Customs territory for repairs with the declaration thereof made to the Customs at the time of departure and re-transported into the Customs territory within the time limit set by the Customs shall be determined on the basis of the charges on the repairs and the cost of materials, components and parts used for the repairs.

第二十六条 出口货物的完税价格由海关以该货物的成交价格以及该货物运至中华人民共和国境内输出地点装载前的运输及其相关费用、保险费为基础审查确定。

Article 26 The customs value of export goods shall be determined by the Customs on the basis of the transaction value thereof and the costs of transport, charges associated with transport, and the cost of insurance incurred prior to loading of such goods at the port or place of departure within the Customs territory of the People's Republic of China.

出口货物的成交价格，是指该货物出口时卖方为出口该货物应当向买方直接收取和间接收取的价款总额。

The transaction value of export goods is the total amount of the price that shall be charged by the seller, directly or indirectly, from the buyer for the goods sold for export.

出口关税不计入完税价格。

The export duty shall not be added to the customs value of export goods.

第二十七条 出口货物的成交价格不能确定的，海关经了解有关情况，并与纳税义务人进行价格磋商后，依次以下列价格估定该货物的完税价格：

Article 27 Where it is impossible to determine the transaction value of export goods, the Customs shall, after acquainting itself with the relevant information and consulting over price with the duty payer, determine the customs value of export goods in accordance with the following values in their given order:

（一）与该货物同时或者大约同时向同一国家或者地区出口的相同货物的成交价格；

(1)the transaction value of identical goods sold for export to the same country or region of importation and exported at or about the same time as the goods being valued;

（二）与该货物同时或者大约同时向同一国家或者地区出口的类似货物的成交价格；

(2)the transaction value of similar goods sold for export to the same country or region of importation and exported at or about the same time as the goods being valued;

（三）按照下列各项总和计算的价格：境内生产相同或者类似货物的料件成本、加工费用，通常的利润和一般费用，境内发生的运输及其相关费用、保险费；

(3)the computed value which consists of the total sum of the following items: the cost or value of materials, components and parts and fabrication or other processing employed in producing the identical or similar goods within the Customs territory; normal profit and general expenses; the costs of transport, charges associated with transport, and the cost of insurance incurred within the Customs territory;

（四）以合理方法估定的价格。

(4)the value determined on a reasonable basis.

第二十八条 按照本条例规定计入或者不计入完税价格的成本、费用、税收，应当以客观、可量化的数据为依据。

Article 28 The additions or deductions of costs, charges or taxes to or from the customs value in accordance with the provisions of these Regulations shall be made on the basis of objective and quantifiable data.

第四章 进出口货物关税的征收

Chapter IV Duty Collection on Import and Export Goods

第二十九条 进口货物的纳税义务人应当自运输工具申报进境之日起 14 日内，出口货物的纳税义务人除海关特准的外，应当在货物运抵海关监管区后、装货的 24 小时以前，向货物的进出境地海关申报。进出口货物转关运输的，按照海关总署的规定执行。

Article 29 Declaration of import goods shall be made to the Customs at the port or place of entry by the duty payer within 14 days from the date of declaration of entry of the means of transport; declaration of export goods shall, unless otherwise specially approved by the Customs, be made to the Customs at the port or place of departure by the duty payer after the arrival of the goods at the Customs Surveillance Zone and 24 hours prior to loading thereof. Import or export goods in transit shall be dealt with in accordance with the provisions of the General Administration of Customs.

进口货物到达前，纳税义务人经海关核准可以先行申报。具体办法由海关总署另行规定。

An advance declaration may be made by the duty payer with the approval of the Customs before the arrival of import goods. The specific measures therefore shall be separately formulated by the General Administration of Customs.

第三十条 纳税义务人应当依法如实向海关申报，并按照海关的规定提供有关确定完税价格、进行商品归类、确定原产地以及采取反倾销、反补贴或者保障措施等所需的资料；必要时，海关可以要求纳税义务人补充申报。

Article 30 The duty payer shall make a truthful declaration to the Customs in accordance with the law and provide, as required by the Customs, the relevant information or data needed for determination of customs value, classification of goods, determination of origin, or adoption of antidumping, countervailing, or safeguard measures. When necessary, the Customs may require the duty payer to make a supplementary declaration.

第三十一条 纳税义务人应当按照《税则》规定的目录条文和归类总规则、类注、章注、子目注释以及其他归类注释，对其申报的进出口货物进行商品归类，并归入相应的税则号列；海关应当依法审核确定该货物的商品归类。

Article 31 The duty payer shall classify the declared import or export goods into the corresponding tariff headings in accordance with the terms of the headings, the general rules for the classification, and the notes to sections, chapters or sub-headings as well as other explanatory notes to classification, which are prescribed in the Tariff. The Customs shall verify and determine the goods classification according to law.

第三十二条 海关可以要求纳税义务人提供确定商品归类所需的有关资料；必要时，海关可以组织化验、检验，并将海关认定的化验、检验结果作为商品归类的依据。

Article 32 The Customs may require the duty payer to provide the information or data needed for goods classification and, when necessary, organize laboratory analysis or inspection. The results of the analysis or inspection shall, after being confirmed by the Customs, be taken as the grounds for goods classification.

第三十三条 海关为审查申报价格的真实性和准确性，可以查阅、复制与进出口货物有关的合同、发票、账册、结付汇凭证、单据、业务函电、录音录像制品和其他反映买卖双方关系及交易活动的资料。

Article 33 The Customs may, in order to verify the truth and accuracy of the declared value, examine or copy the contracts, invoices, accounts, certificates for foreign exchange payment and settlement, bills, records, documents, business correspondences, audio and visual products related to import and export goods and other materials reflecting the relationship and transaction between the buyer and the seller.

海关对纳税义务人申报的价格有怀疑并且所涉关税数额较大的，经直属海关关长或者其授权的隶属海关关长批准，凭海关总署统一格式的协助查询账户通知书及有关工作人员的工作证件，可以查询纳税义务人在银行或者其他金融机构开立的单位账户的资金往来情况，并向银行业监督管理机构通报有关情况。

Where the Customs has doubts about the value declared by the duty payer and the duties involved are of a large amount, the Customs may, upon the approval of the director of the Customs office directly under the General Administration of Customs or the director of a Customs office subordinate to and authorized by the former and on the strength of the Notice for Assistance in Account Inquiry with the format unified by the General Administration of Customs and credentials of relevant staff members, inquire about the fund transactions through the unit accounts opened at banks or other financial institutions by the duty payer, and inform the banking regulatory agency of relevant information.

第三十四条 海关对纳税义务人申报的价格有怀疑的，应当将怀疑的理由书面告知纳税义务人，要求其在规定的期限内书面作出说明、提供有关资料。

Article 34 Where the Customs has doubts about the value declared by the duty payer, the Customs shall inform the duty payer in writing of the grounds for such doubts and require the duty payer to provide a written explanation and the relevant information and data within a specified time limit.

纳税义务人在规定的期限内未作说明、未提供有关资料的，或者海关仍有理由怀疑申报价格的真实性和准确性的，海关可以不接受纳税义务人申报的价格，并按照本条例第三章的规定估定完税价格。

If the duty payer fails to provide explanation and relevant information and data within the specified time limit or the Customs still has reasonable doubts about the truth or accuracy of the declared value, the Customs may refuse to accept the declared value and determine the customs value in accordance with the provisions of Chapter III of these Regulations.

第三十五条 海关审查确定进出口货物的完税价格后，纳税义务人可以以书面形式要求海关就如何确定其进出口货物的完税价格作出书面说明，海关应当向纳税义务人作出书面说明。

Article 35 Upon determination of the customs value of import or export goods by the Customs, the duty payer may request the Customs in writing to provide a written explanation as to how the customs value of import or export goods is determined. The Customs shall provide the written explanation to the duty payer accordingly.

第三十六条 进出口货物关税，以从价计征、从量计征或者国家规定的其他方式征收。

Article 36 The duty on import or export goods shall be collected in the form of *ad valorem* duty, specific duty, or other forms prescribed by the State.

从价计征的计算公式为：

应纳税额=完税价格×关税税率

The calculation formula for *ad valorem* duty is:

Duty Payable=Customs Value × Duty Rate

从量计征的计算公式为：

应纳税额=货物数量×单位税额

The calculation formula for specific duty is:

Duty Payable = Quantity of Goods × Unit Duty

第三十七条 纳税义务人应当自海关填发税款缴款书之日起 15 日内向指定银行缴纳税款。纳税义务人未按期缴纳税款的，从滞纳税款之日起，按日加收滞纳税款万分之五的滞纳金。

Article 37 The duty payer shall pay the duties at a designated bank within 15 days after the date of issuance of the memorandum of duty payment by the Customs. In case of any payment in arrears, 0.05% of the total amount of the overdue duties shall be charged as a fine for late payment per day from the date when the delayed payment occurs.

海关可以对纳税义务人欠缴税款的情况予以公告。

The Customs may publish the information about the arrearages on duties by duty payers.

海关征收关税、滞纳金等，应当制发缴款凭证，缴款凭证格式由海关总署规定。

The Customs shall issue a duty-memo for duties collected or receipt for fines for late payment. The format of the duty-memo or receipt shall be prescribed by the General Administration of Customs.

第三十八条 海关征收关税、滞纳金等，应当按人民币计征。

Article 38 The Customs shall collect duties and fines for late payment in terms of RMB.

进出口货物的成交价格以及有关费用以外币计价的，以中国人民银行公布的基准汇率折合为人民币计算完税价

Where the transaction value of import or export goods and associated costs are computed in a foreign currency, such

格；以基准汇率币种以外的外币计价的，按照国家有关规定套算为人民币计算完税价格。适用汇率的日期由海关总署规定。

foreign currency shall be converted into RMB at the basic exchange rate published by the People's Bank of China for the calculation of customs value. Where such basic exchange rate is not available for the foreign currency in question, the customs value shall be converted into RMB in accordance with the relevant provisions of the State. The date when the exchange rate applies shall be prescribed by the General Administration of Customs.

第三十九条 纳税义务人因不可抗力或者在国家税收政策调整的情形下，不能按期缴纳税款的，经海关总署批准，可以延期缴纳税款，但是最长不得超过6个月。

Article 39 Where the duty payer cannot pay duties within the time limit due to force majeure or adjustments to the State's taxation policy, such time limit may be extended upon the approval of the General Administration of Customs, but in any case the extension shall not exceed six months.

第四十条 进出口货物的纳税义务人在规定的纳税期限内有明显的转移、藏匿其应税货物以及其他财产迹象的，海关可以责令纳税义务人提供担保；纳税义务人不能提供担保的，海关可以按照《海关法》第六十一条的规定采取税收保全措施。

Article 40 Where there is an obvious indication that the duty payer of import or export goods is transferring or concealing the dutiable goods or other property in the specified time limit for duty payment, the Customs may order the duty payer to provide a bond; if the duty payer fails to do so, the Customs may take protective measures for duty collection in accordance with the provisions of Article 61 of the Customs Law.

纳税义务人、担保人自缴纳税款期限届满之日起超过3个月仍未缴纳税款的，海关可以按照《海关法》第六十条的规定采取强制措施。

Where the duty payer or the guarantor thereof fails to pay the duties within three months from the date of expiration of the time limit for duty payment, the Customs may take compulsory measures in accordance with the provisions of Article 60 of the Customs Law.

第四十一条 加工贸易的进口料件按照国家规定保税进口的，其制成品或者进口料件未在规定的期限内出口的，海关按照规定征收进口关税。

Article 41 Where the materials, components and parts for processing trade are imported in bond in accordance with the provisions of the State, but such import materials, components and parts or the finished products made thereof are not exported within the specified time limit, the Customs shall collect import duties in accordance with the relevant provisions.

加工贸易的进口料件进境时按照国家规定征收进口关税的，其制成品或者进口料件在规定的期限内出口的，海关按照有关规定退还进境时已征收的关税税款。

Where the import duty has been collected on materials, components and parts for processing trade upon entry in accordance with the provisions of the State and such materials, components and parts or the finished products made thereof are exported within the specified time limit, the Customs shall refund the duties previously collected in accordance with the relevant provisions.

第四十二条 经海关批准暂时进境或者暂时出境的下列货物，在进境或者出境时纳税义务人向海关缴纳相当于应纳税款的保证金或者提供其他担保的，可以暂不缴纳关税，并应当自进境或者出境之日起6个月内复运出境或者复运进境；经纳税义务人申请，海关可以根据海关总署的规定延长复运出境或者复运进境的期限：

Article 42 Where the following goods are permitted by the Customs to temporarily enter or leave the Customs territory and a cash deposit of an amount equivalent to that of the duties payable or a bond in another form has been provided to the Customs by the duty payer upon entry or departure, the duties of such goods may be temporarily exempted, on the condition that such goods shall be re-transported out of or into the Customs territory within six months from the date of entry or departure. Upon the request of the duty payer, the Customs may extend the time limit for re-transportation out of or into the Customs territory in accordance with the provisions of the General Administration of Customs:

（一）在展览会、交易会、会议及类似活动中展示或者使用的货物；

(1)goods for display or use at exhibitions, fairs, meetings or similar events;

（二）文化、体育交流活动中使用的表演、比赛用品；

(2)items for performance or contest in cultural or sports exchange;

（三）进行新闻报道或者摄制电影、电视节目使用的仪器、设备及用品；

(3)apparatus, equipment or items for press, cinematography or television programs;

（四）开展科研、教学、医疗活动使用的仪器、设备及用品；

(4)apparatus, equipment or items for scientific research, pedagogical or medical activities;

（五）在本款第（一）项至第（四）项所列活动中使用的交通工具及特种车辆；

(5)means of transport and special purpose motor vehicles for functions specified in Items (1) through (4) of this Paragraph;

（六）货样；

(6)samples;

（七）供安装、调试、检测设备时使用的仪器、工具；

(7)apparatus and tools for installation, adjustment or test of equipment;

（八）盛装货物的容器；

(8)containers of goods;

（九）其他用于非商业目的的货物。

(9)other goods intended for non-commercial purposes.

第一款所列暂准进境货物在规定的期限内未复运出境的，或者暂准出境货物在规定的期限内未复运进境的，海关应当依法征收关税。

Where the goods permitted to temporarily enter or leave the Customs territory in Paragraph 1 are not re-transported out of or into the Customs territory within the specified time limit, the Customs shall collect duties according to law.

第一款所列可以暂时免征关税范围以外的其他暂准进境货物，应当按照该货物的完税价格和其在境内滞留时间与折旧时间的比例计算征收进口关税。具体办法由海关总署规定。

Import duty on the goods permitted to temporarily enter the Customs territory other than those that are temporarily exempted from duties as prescribed by Paragraph 1 shall be computed on the basis of the customs value of such goods and the proportion of the time when such goods remain inside the Customs territory to the time of depreciation. The specific measures therefore shall be provided for by the General Administration of Customs.

第四十三条 因品质或者规格原因，出口货物自出口之日起 1 年内原状复运进境的，不征收进口关税。

Article 43 No import duty shall be collected on export goods re-transported into the Customs territory in the same state within one year from the date of exportation due to problems with quality or specifications.

因品质或者规格原因，进口货物自进口之日起 1 年内原状复运出境的，不征收出口关税。

No export duty shall be collected on import goods re-transported out of the Customs territory in the same state within one year from the date of importation due to problems with quality or specifications.

第四十四条 因残损、短少、品质不良或者规格不符原因，由进出口货物的发货人、承运人或者保险公司免费补偿或者更换的相同货物，进出口时不征收关税。被免费更换的原进口货物不退运出境或者原出口货物不退运进境的，海关应当对原进出口货物重新按照规定征收关税。

Article 44 Where, due to damage, shortage, poor quality or unconformity to specifications of import or export goods, the consignor or carrier of such goods or the insurance company provides, free of charge, identical import or export goods as compensation or replacement, no duties shall be collected on such identical goods. Where the original import or export goods that are replaced free of charge are not re-transported out of or into the Customs territory, the Customs shall re-collect duties thereon in accordance with the relevant provisions.

第四十五条 下列进出口货物，免征关税：

Article 45 The following import and export goods shall be exempted from duties:

（一）关税税额在人民币 50 元以下的一票货物；

(1)goods of a single consignment on which the duties are estimated to be not more than RMB 50 yuan;

（二）无商业价值的广告品和货样；

(2)advertising matter and samples, which are of no commercial value;

（三）外国政府、国际组织无偿赠送的物资；

(3)goods and materials, which are rendered gratis by international organizations or foreign governments;

（四）在海关放行前损失的货物；

（五）进出境运输工具装载的途中必需的燃料、物料和饮食用品。

在海关放行前遭受损坏的货物，可以根据海关认定的受损程度减征关税。

法律规定的其他免征或者减征关税的货物，海关根据规定予以免征或者减征。

第四十六条 特定地区、特定企业或者有特定用途的进出口货物减征或者免征关税，以及临时减征或者免征关税，按照国务院的有关规定执行。

第四十七条 进口货物减征或者免征进口环节海关代征税，按照有关法律、行政法规的规定执行。

第四十八条 纳税义务人进出口减免税货物的，除另有规定外，应当在进出口该货物之前，按照规定持有关文件向海关办理减免税审批手续。经海关审查符合规定的，予以减征或者免征关税。

第四十九条 需由海关监管使用的减免税进口货物，在监管年限内转让或者移作他用需要补税的，海关应当根据该货物进口时间折旧估价，补征进口关税。

特定减免税进口货物的监管年限由海关总署规定。

第五十条 有下列情形之一的，纳税义务人自缴纳税款之日起 1 年内，可以申请退还关税，并应当以书面形式向海关说明理由，提供原缴款凭证及相关资料：

（一）已征进口关税的货物，因品质或者规格原因，原状退货复运出境的；

（二）已征出口关税的货物，因品质或者规划原因，原状退货复运进境，并已重新缴纳因出口而退还的国内环节有关税收的；

（三）已征出口关税的货物，因故未装运出口，申报退关的。

(4)goods lost prior to Customs release;

(5)fuels, stores, beverages and provisions for use en route loaded on any means of transport, which is in transit across the frontier.

The duties on goods damaged prior to Customs release may be deducted in accordance with the degree of damage confirmed by the Customs.

The Customs shall, in accordance with the relevant provisions, grant duty reduction or exemption to other goods that are subject to duty reduction or exemption prescribed by law.

Article 46 Duty reduction or exemption granted to import and export goods of special areas or special enterprises or for special uses, as well as temporary duty reduction or exemption, shall be governed by the relevant provisions of the State Council.

Article 47 Any reduction or exemption of taxes collected on import goods by the Customs on behalf of other government departments shall be governed by the provisions of relevant laws and administrative regulations.

Article 48 Where the duty payer is to import or export goods granted duty reduction or exemption, the duty payer shall, unless otherwise prescribed, go through the formalities with the Customs for approval of duty reduction or exemption by presenting relevant documents as required before such goods are imported or exported. The duty reduction or exemption shall be granted if the Customs confirms such goods as qualified through examination.

Article 49 Where the import goods which are granted duty reduction or exemption and the use of which are under the Customs control are diverted to other purposes within the duration of Customs control and therefore the recovery of duties is needed, the import duty shall be recovered by the Customs on the basis of the value of import goods depreciated according to the time after importation.

The duration of the Customs control over import goods granted special duty reduction or exemption shall be prescribed by the General Administration of Customs.

Article 50 Under any of the following circumstances, the duty payer may, within one year from the date of duty payment, apply for a refund of duties by stating the reasons therefore in writing to the Customs and providing the original duty-memo and the relevant information and data:

(1)where any goods, on which the import duty has been collected, are re-transported out of the Customs territory in the original state due to problems with quality or specifications;

(2)where any goods, on which the export duty has been collected, are re-transported into the Customs territory in the original state due to problems with quality or specifications and all internal taxes refunded for export have been repaid;

(3)Where any goods, on which the export duty has been paid, are re-declared to the Customs as shut-out cargo because they are not loaded for export due to certain reasons.

海关应当自受理退税申请之日起 30 日内查实并通知纳税义务人办理退还手续。纳税义务人应当自收到通知之日起 3 个月内办理有关退税手续。

The Customs shall, within 30 days from the date of accepting an application for duty refund, ascertain the relevant facts and notify the duty payer to go through the refund formalities. The duty payer shall go through the refund formalities within three months from the date of receipt of the notification.

按照其他有关法律、行政法规规定应当退还关税的，海关应当按照有关法律、行政法规的规定退税。

Where duties shall be refunded in accordance with the provisions of other relevant laws and administrative regulations, the Customs shall refund duties accordingly.

第五十一条 进出口货物放行后，海关发现少征或者漏征税款的，应当自缴纳税款或者货物放行之日起 1 年内，向纳税义务人补征税款。但因纳税义务人违反规定造成少征或者漏征税款的，海关可以自缴纳税款或者货物放行之日起 3 年内追征税款，并从缴纳税款或者货物放行之日起按日加收少征或者漏征税款万分之五的滞纳金。

Article 51 Where the Customs finds that duties are short-collected or not collected on a consignment of import or export goods after the release, the Customs shall recover the duties payable from the duty payer within one year from the date of the duty payment or the release. If the short-collected or non-collected duties are attributable to the duty payer's violation of the provisions, the Customs may pursue the payment of the unpaid duties within three years from the date of the duty payment or the release, and impose a fine for late payment of 0.05% of the short-collected or non-collected duties per day from the date of the duty payment or the release.

海关发现海关监管货物因纳税义务人违反规定造成少征或者漏征税款的，应当自纳税义务人应缴纳税款之日起 3 年内追征税款，并从应缴纳税款之日起按日加收少征或者漏征税款万分之五的滞纳金。

Where the Customs finds that the short-collection or non-collection of duties on goods under Customs control is attributable to the duty payer's violation of the provisions, the Customs shall pursue the payment of the unpaid duties within three years from the date of the duty payment or the release, and impose a fine for late payment of 0.05% of the short-collected or non-collected duties per day from the date of the duty payment or the release.

第五十二条 海关发现多征税款的，应当立即通知纳税义务人办理退还手续。

Article 52 Upon finding any over-collection of duties, the Customs shall immediately notify the duty payer to go through the refund formalities.

纳税义务人发现多缴税款的，自缴纳税款之日起 1 年内，可以以书面形式要求海关退还多缴的税款并加算银行同期活期存款利息；海关应当自受理退税申请之日起 30 日内查实并通知纳税义务人办理退还手续。

Upon finding any over-collection of duties, the duty payer may, within one year from the date of duty payment, request in writing the Customs to refund the over-collected duties together with the interest for the corresponding period computed at the current deposit interest rate of the bank. The Customs shall, within 30 days from the date of accepting the application for duty refund, ascertain the relevant facts and notify the duty payer to go through the refund formalities.

纳税义务人应当自收到通知之日起 3 个月内办理有关退税手续。

The duty payer shall go through the refund formalities within three months from the date of receipt of the notification.

第五十三条 按照本条例第五十条、第五十二条的规定退还税款、利息涉及从国库中退库的，按照法律、行政法规有关国库管理的规定执行。

Article 53 Where the refund of duties or interest incurred therefrom under Articles 50 and 52 of these Regulations involves refund from the State treasury, such refund shall be governed by the provisions of the laws and administrative regulations on administration of the State treasury.

第五十四条 报关企业接受纳税义务人的委托，以纳税义务人的名义办理报关纳税手续，因报关企业违反规定而造成海关少征、漏征税款的，报关企业对少征或者漏征的税款、滞纳金与纳税义务人承担纳税的连带责任。

Article 54 Where a Customs broker that is commissioned by a duty payer to go through the formalities for declaration and duty payment in the name of the duty payer violates the relevant provisions and thus causes the short-collection or non-collection of duties, the Customs broker shall bear the joint and several liability with the duty payer for payment of the short-collected or non-collected duties and fines for late payment.

报关企业接受纳税义务人的委托，以报关企业的名义办理报关纳税手续的，报关企业与纳税义务人承担纳税的连带责任。

Where a Customs broker is commissioned by a duty payer to go through the formalities for declaration and duty payment in the name of the Customs broker, the Customs broker shall bear the joint and several liability with the duty payer for duty payment.

除不可抗力外，在保管海关监管货物期间，海关监管货物损毁或者灭失的，对海关监管货物负有保管义务的人应当承担相应的纳税责任。

Where, except due to force majeure, goods under Customs control are damaged, destroyed or irrecoverably lost during the period of Customs control, the person who is obliged to keep such goods shall bear the corresponding liability for duty payment.

第五十五条 欠税的纳税义务人，有合并、分立情形的，在合并、分立前，应当向海关报告，依法缴清税款。纳税义务人合并时未缴清税款的，由合并后的法人或者其他组织继续履行未履行的纳税义务；纳税义务人分立时未缴清税款的，分立后的法人或者其他组织对未履行的纳税义务承担连带责任。

Article 55 Where a duty payer that is in arrears with duty payment comes under circumstances such as merger or division, the duty payer shall, prior to the merger or division, notify the Customs and pay off the duties. If the duty payer fails to pay off the duties when it is merged, the legal person or other organization that results from the merger shall continue to fulfil the duty payment obligation that has not been fulfilled. If the duty payer fails to pay off the duties when it is divided, the legal person or other organization that results from the division shall bear the joint and several liability for fulfilling the duty payment obligation that has not been fulfilled.

纳税义务人在减免税货物、保税货物监管期间，有合并、分立或者其他资产重组情形的，应当向海关报告。按照规定需要缴税的，应当依法缴清税款；按照规定可以继续享受减免税、保税待遇的，应当到海关办理变更纳税义务人的手续。

Where a duty payer, during the period of Customs control over goods granted duty reduction or exemption or bonded goods, comes under circumstances such as merger, division or any other form of asset restructuring, the duty payer shall make a report thereon to the Customs. Those that need to pay duties in accordance with the relevant provisions shall pay off the duties according to law. Those that may continue to enjoy duty reduction or exemption or bond treatment in accordance with the relevant provisions shall go through the formalities for change of the duty payer with the Customs.

纳税义务人欠税或者在减免税货物、保税货物监管期间，有撤销、解散、破产或者其他依法终止经营情形的，应当在清算前向海关报告。海关应当依法对纳税义务人的应缴税款予以清缴。

Where a duty payer is in arrears with the payment of duties or, during the period of Customs control over goods granted duty reduction or exemption or bonded goods, comes under circumstances such as dissolution, disbandment, bankruptcy or any other statutory form of termination, the duty payer shall make a report thereon to the Customs prior to the liquidation. The Customs shall collect all the duties payable from the duty payer according to law.

第五章 进境物品进口税的征收

Chapter V Collection of Flat Duty on Inward Articles

第五十六条 进境物品的关税以及进口环节海关代征税合并为进口税，由海关依法征收。

Article 56 The import duty on inward articles and taxes collected by the Customs on behalf of other government departments for importation of such articles are amalgamated into the flat duty, which shall be collected by the Customs according to law.

第五十七条 海关总署规定数额以内的个人自用进境物品，免征进口税。

Article 57 Inward articles for personal use the aggregate value or quantity of which is within the quota prescribed by the General Administration of Customs shall be exempted from flat duty.

超过海关总署规定数额但仍在合理数量以内的个人自用进境物品，由进境物品的纳税义务人在进境物品放行前按照规定缴纳进口税。

The flat duty on inward articles for personal use that exceed the quota prescribed by the General Administration of Customs but are still within a reasonable quantity shall be paid by the duty payer of such inward articles in accordance with the relevant provisions prior to the release.

超过合理、自用数量的进境物品应当按照进口货物依法办理相关手续。

Where inward articles exceed the reasonable quantity for personal use, the relevant formalities shall be gone through in accordance with that of import goods.

国务院关税税则委员会规定按货物征税的进境物品，按照本条例第二章至第四章的规定征收关税。

The duty on inward articles that are deemed as import goods by the Tariff Commission of the State Council for duty collection shall be collected in accordance with the provisions of the Chapters II through IV of these Regulations.

第五十八条 进境物品的纳税义务人是指，携带物品进境的入境人员、进境邮递物品的收件人以及以其他方式进口物品的收件人。

Article 58 The duty payer of inward articles refers to the person who carries articles into the Customs territory, the addressee of inward postal items, or the recipient of articles imported in any other ways.

第五十九条 进境物品的纳税义务人可以自行办理纳税手续，也可以委托他人办理纳税手续。接受委托的人应当遵守本章对纳税义务人的各项规定。

Article 59 The duty payer of inward articles may go through the formalities for duty payment on its own or commission an agent to go through such formalities. The agent commissioned shall abide by all the provisions of this Chapter on the duty payer.

第六十条 进口税从价计征。

Article 60 Flat duty shall be collected in terms of *ad valorem* duty.

进口税的计算公式为：

进口税税额=完税价格×进口税税率

The calculation formula of flat duty is:

Flat Duty Payable= Customs Value ×Flat Duty Rate

第六十一条 海关应当按照《进境物品进口税税率表》及海关总署制定的《中华人民共和国进境物品归类表》、《中华人民共和国进境物品完税价格表》对进境物品进行归类、确定完税价格和确定适用税率。

Article 61 The Customs shall determine the classification, customs value and applicable duty rate of inward articles in accordance with the Flat Duty Rates on Inward Articles, and the Classification Table of Inward Articles of the People's Republic of China and Customs Value Table of Inward Articles of the People's Republic of China that are formulated by the General Administration of Customs.

第六十二条 进境物品，适用海关填发税款缴款书之日实施的税率和完税价格。

Article 62 The flat duty rate and customs value implemented on the date when the Customs issues the memorandum of duty payment shall apply to inward articles.

第六十三条 进口税的减征、免征、补征、追征、退还以及对暂准进境物品征收进口税参照本条例对货物征收进口关税的有关规定执行。

Article 63 The reduction, exemption, recovery, pursuit and refund of flat duty and the collection of flat duty on inward articles permitted to be temporarily transported into the Customs territory shall be governed by the relevant provisions of these Regulations on collection of import duty on goods.

第六章 附 则

Chapter VI Supplementary Provisions

第六十四条 纳税义务人、担保人对海关确定纳税义务人、确定完税价格、商品归类、确定原产地、适用税率或者汇率、减征或者免征税款、补税、退税、征收滞纳金、确定计征方式以及确定纳税地点有异议的，应当缴纳税款，并可以依法向上一级海关申请复议。对复议决定不服的，可以依法向人民法院提起诉讼。

Article 64 Where the duty payer or guarantor has objections to the Customs' determination of the duty payer or customs value; goods classification; determination of origin, applicable duty rates or exchange rates; duty reduction, exemption, recovery or refund; collection of fines for late payment; or determination of the manner and place of duty collection; it shall pay the duties and may apply to the Customs at the next higher level for administrative reconsideration according to law; if the duty payer or guarantor refuses to accept the decision of administrative reconsideration, it may lodge a lawsuit to the people's court according to law.

第六十五条 进口环节海关代征税的征收管理，适用关税征收管理的规定。

Article 65 Tax collection by the Customs on behalf of other government departments for importation shall be governed in accordance with the provisions on administration of duty collection.

第六十六条 有违反本条例规定行为的，按照《海关

Article 66 The penalty for violation of the provisions of these

法》、《中华人民共和国海关法行政处罚实施细则》和其他有关法律、行政法规的规定处罚。

Regulations shall be imposed in accordance with the provisions of the Customs Law, the Rules for the Implementation of Administrative Penalty under the Customs Law of the People's Republic of China and other relevant laws and administrative regulations.

第六十七条 本条例自 2004 年 1 月 1 日起施行。1992 年 3 月 18 日国务院修订发布的《中华人民共和国进出口关税条例》同时废止。

Article 67 These Regulations shall be effective as of 1 January 2004. The Regulations of the People's Republic of China on Import and Export Duties revised and promulgated by the State Council on March 18, 1992 shall be simultaneously repealed.